New

WITHDRAWN

Ephraim George Squier and Edwin Hamilton Davis in 1846. Finding in 1882 that the site's original configuration had been greatly compromised by erosion and apparent vandalism, Putnam immediately took steps to ensure its preservation. He negotiated the purchase of the site by Harvard in 1887, conducted an excavation there, and restored it to its original configuration. Harvard then donated Serpent Mound to the state of Ohio as a state park, and the following year the Ohio legislature passed an anti-vandalism law aimed at protecting the site. Putnam regarded the preservation of Serpent Mound to be one of the most important achievements of his career. As he noted, the Peabody Museum had been "the means of bringing about the first law enacted for the protection of the ancient monuments of this country" (Brew, *Early Days of the Peabody Museum*, p. 18). He died in Cambridge, Massachusetts.

Putnam's legacy is that of a true pioneer in archaeological fieldwork and museum work, a fact reflected in the ongoing significance of his personal papers and the mass of cultural materials he either directly or indirectly brought into anthropological museums. He made more than 400 known contributions to scientific journals and popular magazines, and was a cofounder of the *American Naturalist* in 1867–1868 and one of its first editors.

Putnam further promoted the development of anthropology through his roles as permanent secretary of the American Association for the Advancement of Science from 1873 to 1898 and president in 1898; and as president of the American Anthropological Association in 1905–1906, the American Folk-Lore Society in 1891, and the Boston Society of Natural History from 1887 to 1889. Putnam was also active in the National Academy of Sciences, the Archaeological Institute of America, the American Philosophical Society, American Academy of Arts and Sciences, and the American Antiquarian Society.

Putnam's reputation as an originator of archaeological investigations and museum anthropology earned him honory memberships in the anthropological societies of London, Brussels, and Florence, the Geographical Society of Lima, and the Royal Society of Edinburgh; and a chevalier in the French Legion of Honor in 1906. Many of Putnam's students went on to distinguished anthropological careers of their own, adding further testimony to the influence of his remarkable career. Alfred Tozzer, for example, trained an entire generation of students in Middle American archaeology. Putnam's presence is found in virtually all aspects of academic and museum anthropology in the United States in the late nineteenth and early twentieth centuries.

• Putnam's papers are at Harvard University and the Peabody Museum Archives at Harvard. A bibliography of Putnam's writings up to 1909 by F. H. Mead, appears in *Putnam Anniversary Volume: Anthropological Essays Presented to Frederic Ward Putnam in Honor of His Seventieth Birthday*, ed. Franz Boas (1909), pp. 601–27. John Otis Brew, *People and*

Projects of the Peabody Museum (1966) and *Early Days of the Peabody Museum at Harvard University* (1966), provide an overview of the history of the institution and the aims of the expeditions and research projects conducted during Putnam's tenure. The corresponding volumes of the Peabody Museum's *Annual Reports*, *Paper*, and *Memoirs* also contain important information on Putnam's activities.

Biographical sketches are Alfred M. Tozzer, "Frederic Ward Putnam, 1839–1915," National Academy of Sciences, *Biographical Memoirs* 16 (1935): 125–52; and Tozzer, "Memoir of Frederic Ward Putnam," *Proceedings of the Massachusetts Historical Society* 49 (June 1916): 482–87. Assessments of his contributions to anthropology appear in several accounts by Ralf W. Dexter: "Contributions of Frederic Ward Putnam to Ohio Archaeology," *Ohio Journal of Science* 65, no. 3 (1965): 110–17, "Putnam's Problems Popularizing Anthropology," *American Scientist* 54, no. 3 (Sept. 1966): 315–32, and "Frederic Ward Putnam and the Development of Museums of Natural History and Anthropology in the United States," *Curator* 9, no. 2 (1966): 151–55. Context for his work in Ohio is provided in Edward Hoagland Brown, "Harvard and the Ohio Mounds," *New England Quarterly* 22, no. 2 (June 1949): 205–28. Obituaries are by Charles Peabody in *Journal of American Folklore* 28 (July–Sept. 1915): 302–6; A. L. Kroeber in *American Anthropologist* 17 (Oct.–Dec. 1915): 713–18; E. S. Morse in *Essex Institute Historical Collections* 52 (July 1916): 193–96; and in the *Boston Transcript*, 16 Aug. 1915, and *Science* 42 (10 Sept. 1915): 330–32.

TERRY A. BARNHART

PUTNAM, George Haven (2 Apr. 1844–27 Feb. 1930), publisher and author, was born in London, England, the son of George Palmer Putnam, the founder of a publishing house, and Victorine Haven. After the Putnam family returned in 1848 to the United States from London, where George Palmer Putnam had set up a branch of his firm, Wiley & Putnam, they settled in New York City. George Haven attended John MacMullen's School, in which he was both a student and tutor. He also attended the Columbia Grammar School in preparation for Columbia College. Although Putnam passed his entrance examinations for Columbia in 1860, an eye illness prevented his beginning college work. Putnam never was able to pursue a college degree. However, in 1912, after he had attained international success as a publisher and author, he was awarded an honorary doctor of letters from Columbia.

Following doctor's orders, the young Putnam set off on travels to improve his eye condition. From 1860 to 1862 he visited London, Paris, Berlin, and Göttingen, consulting European oculists and completing a treatment of open-air exercise. He also attended lectures at the Sorbonne and took courses in natural science at the University of Göttingen.

While in Europe, Putnam heard news of the Civil War. In the autumn of 1862 he returned home and enlisted in the 176th New York Volunteers. In the course of his service, he held several positions in his regiment—acting chaplain, quartermaster, adjutant—rising in the ranks from private to brevet major. In June 1863 Putnam was taken prisoner in a skirmish at Brashear City, Louisiana, but he escaped and returned to his regiment. He was taken prisoner a second time in

October 1864 at the battle of Cedar Creek during Philip Sheridan's campaign in the Shenandoah Valley of Virginia. Putnam spent about five months in Libby and Danville prisons and was eventually released in a prisoner exchange.

In 1866 Putnam's father made him a partner in the family publishing business. When the elder Putnam died in 1872, George Haven became head of the firm and with his younger brothers, John Bishop Putnam and Irving Putnam, established G. P. Putnam's Sons in New York City. In 1874 the brothers initiated a manufacturing department to handle printing and binding. This department came to be known as the Knickerbocker Press.

Putnam took up his father's fight to establish an international copyright law that would protect literary property. In 1886 he reorganized the American Publishers' Copyright League and served as its secretary until 1889. Largely through his promotional efforts, the League secured the passage of an international copyright law for the United States in 1891; this law was further developed and amended in 1909. The government of France awarded Putnam the Cross of the Legion of Honor for his service to world literature in securing the copyright statute. He wrote about the campaign for international copyright and the development of the concept of literary property in *The Question of Copyright* (1891). He also wrote a detailed scholarly history of the book from the fall of the Roman Empire to the close of the seventeenth century, *Books and Their Makers in the Middle Ages* (1896).

Putnam had a strong interest in public affairs. Believing that free trade among nations was helpful in maintaining world peace, Putnam became a member of the American Free Trade League in 1874 and served as its president from 1916 until his death. In 1879 he served on the executive committee of the National Civil Service Reform Association, promoting independent political stands against party bosses. He served on the New York Grand Jury from 1879 to 1914, frequently coming into conflict with officials in the Tammany Democratic Club. In 1912 Putnam worked for the U.S. presidential nomination of Woodrow Wilson, and he supported the idea of the League of Nations. When the *Lusitania* was sunk in 1915, he helped organize the American Rights League, which promoted American participation with the allies to check international aggression. He also cofounded the National Security League in 1914 to prepare for America's entry into the First World War. Putnam made frequent business trips to England, where he especially enjoyed the scholarly society of Oxford University. In 1918 he became the secretary treasurer of the American division of the English-Speaking Union, founded to promote good relations between the United States and Great Britain. For forty years, beginning with his return from service in the Civil War, Putnam participated in the social and intellectual community of New York's Century Club.

Putnam married twice. In 1869 he married Rebecca Kettell Shepard, with whom he had four daughters.

She died in 1895. In 1899 he married Emily James Smith, with whom he had one son. Emily Putnam became the first dean of Barnard College.

Putnam was respected not only as a publisher and author but also as a social leader. He became an international celebrity by championing the copyright law and promoting international amity. Putnam died at his home in New York City.

• The largest collections of Putnam's letters are at the Library of Congress and Columbia University. Putnam published two autobiographical works, *Memories of My Youth: 1814–1865* (1914) and *Memories of a Publisher: 1865–1915* (1915). Putnam wrote a biography of his father, *George Palmer Putnam* (1912). An ardent supporter of the Union, he wrote about the Civil War and his personal war experiences in *Abraham Lincoln* (1909), *A Prisoner of War in Virginia: 1864–5* (1912), and *Some Memories of the Civil War* (1924). In addition to the works on copyright and book history already cited, Putnam wrote *Authors and Publishers* (1883), *Authors and Their Public in Ancient Times* (1893), and *The Censorship of the Church of Rome* (1907). Putnam also published two fictional works, *The Artificial Mother* (1894) and *The Little Gingerbread Man* (1909). An obituary is in the *New York Times*, 28 Feb. 1930.

CHARLES ZAROBILA

PUTNAM, George Palmer (7 Feb. 1814–20 Dec. 1872), publisher, was born in Brunswick, Maine, the son of Henry Putnam, a Harvard graduate and lawyer, and Catherine Hunt Palmer, a preparatory school proprietor. Because of the father's ill health, the mother's successful school supported the family. George was one of few boys who attended his mother's school, before he began his apprenticeship (c. 1825) with a Boston carpet dealer.

Four years later Putnam left for New York, where he became a clerk in George W. Bleecker's book and stationery store. As one of his many duties Putnam canvassed for subscriptions to his employer's musical periodical, the *Euterpiad*. Over the next few years, he became chief clerk of the Park Place House and then, around 1832, worked for the orthodox Congregationalist bookman Jonathan Leavitt, senior partner to Daniel Appleton. That firm published Putnam's compendium of his reading of 150 standard historical works, *Chronology: An Introduction and Index to Universal History* (1833). The edition sold well and had a long afterlife under the title *The World's Progress*.

Emboldened by this early venture, Putnam began to organize various areas of the book trade. He persuaded West & Trow to issue in 1834 one of the earliest book-trade journals, the *Booksellers' Advertiser*, which continued until 1 March 1836. He arranged with George B. Collins and John Keese the first New York Booksellers' Dinner for Authors on 30 March 1837. The same year he became the secretary for the first international copyright association in the United States.

Putnam's interest in the international book trade led to a long association with English writers and publishers, under the auspices of the firm of Wiley & Long, which he had joined in 1833 with little else but experi-

AMERICAN NATIONAL BIOGRAPHY

AMERICAN
NATIONAL BIOGRAPHY

Published under the auspices of the
AMERICAN COUNCIL OF LEARNED SOCIETIES

General Editors

John A. Garraty
Mark C. Carnes

VOLUME 18

OXFORD UNIVERSITY PRESS
New York   1999   Oxford

OXFORD UNIVERSITY PRESS

Oxford   New York
Athens Auckland Bangkok Bogotá
Buenos Aires Calcutta Cape Town Chennai
Dar es Salaam Delhi Florence Hong Kong Istanbul
Karachi Kuala Lumpur Madrid Melbourne Mexico City
Mumbai Nairobi Paris São Paulo Singapore
Taipei Tokyo Toronto Warsaw
and associated companies in
Berlin Ibadan

Published by Oxford University Press, Inc.,
198 Madison Avenue, New York, New York 10016
http://www.oup-usa.org

Oxford is a registered trademark of Oxford University Press

Funding for this publication was provided in part by
the Andrew W. Mellon Foundation, the Rockefeller Foundation,
and the National Endowment for the Humanities,
a federal agency.

Library of Congress Cataloging-in-Publication Data

American national biography / general editors, John A. Garraty, Mark C. Carnes
p.   cm.
"Published under the auspices of the American Council of Learned Societies."
Includes bibliographical references and index.
1. United States—Biography—Dictionaries. I. Garraty, John Arthur,
1920– . II. Carnes, Mark C. (Mark Christopher), 1950– .
III. American Council of Learned Societies.
CT213.A68   1998   98-20826   920.073—dc21   CIP
ISBN 0-19-520635-5 (set)
ISBN 0-19-512797-8 (vol. 18)

Printing (last digit): 9 8 7 6 5 4 3 2 1

Printed in the United States of America
on acid-free paper

PUTNAM, Alice Harvey Whiting (18 Jan. 1841–19 Jan. 1919), leader in the kindergarten movement, was born in Chicago, Illinois, the daughter of William Loring Whiting, a commission merchant and a founder of the Chicago Board of Trade, and Mary Starr. Alice was educated at home and then at the Dearborn Seminary. In 1868 she married Joseph Robie Putnam, a businessman specializing in real estate; they had four children.

Her interest in her children's education led Putnam to involvement in the beginnings of the kindergarten movement. In 1874 she initiated a mothers' group to study the works of Friedrich Froebel, the German educator who inspired many American proponents of early childhood education. After studying at a training school run by Anna J. Ogden in Columbus, Ohio, Putnam started a kindergarten, one of the first in the city of Chicago. She continued her study of teaching by attending Susan Blow's classes in St. Louis, Maria Kraus-Boelté's school in New York, Francis Parker's summer institute on Martha's Vineyard, and G. Stanley Hall's summer institute at Clark University. Her study with Parker opened her eyes to the possibilities of extending the application of Froebel's ideas on activity as the basis for learning and the unity of mind and body beyond the kindergarten to the elementary school. Her work with Hall confirmed her practical understanding of how important it was for teachers to observe and learn from children.

Putnam was instrumental in the organization in 1880 of the Chicago Froebel Kindergarten Association, which both promoted free kindergartens in the city and trained teachers for them. She continued as the moving spirit of the association and also served as the director of the Froebel Association Training School, which trained eight hundred kindergarten teachers before her retirement in 1910.

Influential in the selection of Parker as principal of the Cook County Normal School in 1882, Putnam supervised a kindergarten class located in the demonstration school and taught a biweekly class to normal school students, in spite of the fact that Parker was unable to persuade the county to support either the kindergarten or the normal school classes. The classes of the Chicago Froebel Kindergarten Association were housed on East Van Buren Street until 1894, when Jane Addams asked Putnam to move her school to the new Children's House at Hull-House, where it remained for seven years, a separate entity but one with many ties to the settlement house.

Putnam was committed to the incorporation of kindergartens into the public schools of Chicago, and in 1886 the Froebel Association supported the first kindergarten in a public school. Following that entering wedge, the Froebel Association assisted a growing number of privately funded kindergartens in public schools, until in 1892 the school system took on ten established kindergartens and in 1899 undertook to include kindergartens in all schools. Putnam's influence on the school system through the normal school graduates who had attended her classes as well as her presence as a respected intellectual and social leader contributed substantially to this outcome.

Putnam was part of a group of influential kindergarten leaders who were active in the intellectual ferment surrounding education in the early years of the University of Chicago, and John Dewey was a guest lecturer at her training program at Hull-House. When Hall initiated a scientific study of children, Putnam was one of the two kindergarten leaders he asked to compose a questionnaire for teachers about children. Her consciousness of the trends in psychology is evident in the many addresses she made to the International Kindergarten Union (IKU) and the National Education Association (NEA), where she used (for example) the stage theory of child development to justify not teaching kindergarten children to read and write.

Putnam was active in local and national organizations that promoted kindergartens. With her student, Elizabeth Harrison, Putnam founded the Chicago Kindergarten Club in 1883. She continued as a leader in the club for many years, serving as its president in 1901. She served on committees and programs in both the IKU and the kindergarten section of the NEA. When the IKU was torn by struggle between devoted followers of Froebel, who clung to the details of his prescribed activities for kindergartens, and teachers who were turning to the systematic study of children to inform decisions about the kindergarten curriculum, Putnam was clearly on the side of the latter; but she never abandoned the belief in the spiritual nature of children that was the source of her affinity to Froebel.

In 1906 Putnam was asked to teach two courses in the correspondence department of the University of Chicago, "The Training of Children (A Course for Mothers)" and "An Introduction to Kindergarten Theory and Practice." She continued to teach these courses until 1917.

Putnam was initially inspired by Froebel but, unlike some of his followers, was open to other viewpoints on early childhood education. She was confident in her own capacities to implement the spirit of his philosophy based on her observations of children. According to one of her former students, she stated, "I could have a kindergarten in a meadow with a group of children and only the flowers, grasses, earth, and my two hands. Let the children lead you, and you will not go far astray. Study them, and let their actions serve as your guide."

Putnam combined an independent mind and a strong ability to organize and inspire co-workers in the kindergarten cause with a never-failing sympathy and respect for children. She died in Chicago.

• Articles by Putnam include "The Use of Kindergarten Material in Primary Schools," in Putnam, Angeline Brooks, Anne L. Page, and Mary H. Peabody, *The Kindergarten and the School, by Four Active Workers* (1886) and "Shall Reading and Writing be Taught in the Kindergarten?" *Proceedings of the International Congress of Education of the World's Columbian Exposition* (1893): 327–28. Her addresses to the International Kindergarten Union were published in *Kindergarten Review*; these include "Work and Play in the Kindergarten," 12 (1902): 37–40, and "Froebel's Suggestions on Fostering Language," 13 (1903): 38–42. Her addresses to the Annual Meetings of the National Education Association were published in the *Journal of Proceedings and Addresses*. These include (among others) "Froebel's Message to Parents," 28 (1884): 473–78, and "Drawing in the Kindergarten," 46 (1902): 523–26. The most complete biographical essay is in Bertha Payne Newell, *Pioneers of the Kindergarten in America* (1924). Other information appears in an anonymously published article, "Evolution of the Kindergarten Idea in Chicago," *Kindergarten Magazine* 5 (1892): 729–33; Elizabeth Dale Ross, *The Kindergarten Crusade: The Establishment of Preschool Education in the United States* (1976); and Michael S. Shapiro, *Child's Garden: The Kindergarten Movement from Froebel to Dewey* (1983).

NANCY S. GREEN

PUTNAM, Caroline F. (29 July 1826–14 Jan. 1917), abolitionist and educator, was born in Massachusetts, the daughter of a Dr. Putnam, a physician, and Eliza Carpenter. Of her father's first name, her middle name, or the town of her birth, nothing is known. Her father died in her early childhood; her mother was remarried in 1840 to Levi Peet, a farmer of modest means from the village of Farmersville, New York.

Putnam enrolled at Oberlin College in 1848, where she met Sallie Holley. Like Holley, who was to become her lifelong companion, Putnam was out of step with Oberlin on evangelical doctrine, eventually embracing Unitarianism. Also at odds with the college's conservative evangelical abolitionism, she followed Holley into the more radical Garrisonian wing of the abolitionist movement. Both women spent their lives in greater female activism and more radical social reform than was endorsed by Oberlin faculty.

When Holley graduated in 1851, Putnam left Oberlin without completing her studies. For the next decade she worked for the abolition of slavery, largely in the shadow of Holley, who became a noted abolitionist lecturer. Putnam traveled with Holley, wrote to newspapers about Holley's speaking engagements, and called door-to-door in villages across the North to explain the tenets of Garrisonianism, though she disliked the rootlessness of constant travel and felt that she lacked the tenacity and emotional resilience required by the work.

In the early 1860s the two women shifted their attention from abolition to aid for the freed slaves. In 1868, however, Putnam stepped from Holley's shadow, establishing new careers for both of them. Putnam moved to Lottsburg, Virginia, to open a school for freed slaves. Although she named it the Holley School in honor of her friend, the school was Putnam's. She taught, looked after administrative tasks, pioneered innovative means of gaining financial support, and earned southern white acceptance without yielding on racial issues. Holley taught alongside Putnam after 1870 but was never reconciled to the isolation of rural Virginia, so she spent months at a time traveling in the North.

Putnam was an innovative, attentive teacher who adapted well to the conditions of southern rural black life. She held classes year-round in order to accommodate the labor demands on black children of different ages; she did not impose strict punctuality on a community without clocks; she and her assistants integrated a wide variety of print sources, objects, and the surrounding fields into the classroom. She remained at her post for forty-five years, teaching the children and grandchildren of the freedmen she had taught when she first ventured into the South. Though she retired in 1903, she remained at the school until her death in Lottsburg, Virginia. Holley had died in 1893.

Putnam maintained her larger reform and abolition commitments throughout her decades in the South. She was a strident activist in the struggle to assure the freedmen access to the ballot box in the 1870s, and she served as their advocate and adviser throughout the rise of the Jim Crow laws. She was uncompromising in her demand for racial equality during a time when most Americans turned their backs on African Americans. After Putnam's retirement she encouraged the emergence of the NAACP and also worked for temperance, world peace, and the protection of animals.

• Many of Putnam's letters were published in the *National Anti-Slavery Standard* (1855–1861). Unpublished letters are scattered across many collections; the more important include the Samuel May Papers, Massachusetts Historical Society, and the Emily Howland Papers, Cornell University. Virtually the only secondary source dealing with Putnam in any detail is Katherine Lydigsen Herbig, "Friends for Freedom: The Lives and Careers of Sallie Holley and Caroline Putnam" (Ph.D. diss., Claremont Graduate School, 1977), though Herbig's focus is on Holley. An obituary is in the *New York Evening Post*, 27 Jan. 1917.

RONALD E. BUTCHART

PUTNAM, Elizabeth Lowell (2 Feb. 1862–5 June 1935), pioneer in prenatal care, antisuffragist, and conservative political activist, was born in Brookline, Massachusetts, the daughter of Augustus Lowell and Katharine Lawrence. From early childhood until age five she lived with her family in France. In 1888 she married a noted Boston lawyer and a distant cousin, William Lowell Putnam. The Putnams had five children. Their daughter Harriet died of impure milk at age two, and her death was probably the catalyst for Putnam's long commitment to infant and maternal health and welfare.

Putnam began her political career in the pure milk movement in 1908 when she formed and led the Committee on Milk within the Women's Municipal League of Boston. In 1910 Putnam helped to establish the Massachusetts Milk Consumers' Association (MMCA) and served as the chair of its executive committee. Infant welfare reformers hoped that improving the milk supply would greatly reduce the infant mortality rate. The MMCA's aim was to "unite consumers in obtaining efficient inspection and a pure milk supply." The emphasis on consumers' rights underscored an important and consistent element in Putnam's reform career. Although committed to infant welfare, she never advocated or involved herself in establishing milk stations for poor people, as did many other social reformers. Her reform strategies revealed a middle-class orientation that would continue throughout her political life and eventually alienate her from the larger, more progressive infant and maternal welfare reform movement.

In 1909 Putnam branched out from her primary focus on milk to begin an innovative prenatal care experiment. Through the Women's Municipal League (WML), she established a small-scale prenatal care clinic for middle-class women in Boston to discern the efficacy of this type of care in lowering both infant and maternal mortality rates. At the end of her five-year experiment, more than 1,500 babies had been delivered with mortality rates considerably below national averages. As in the pure milk movement, the aims of the WML were not philanthropic, but intentionally aimed at the middle class. In an article for *Modern Hospital* (2 Nov. 1917), Putnam argued that "the rich can afford the best care and to the poor . . . it is given free in the clinics of the best hospitals" but that the middle class was "the class in the community always least well cared for." By 1915 the Women's Municipal League had three clinics, and Putnam had gained an international reputation as a lay expert in prenatal care. In 1918 Putnam was elected president of the American Association for the Study and Prevention of Infant Mortality (renamed the American Child Hygiene Association in 1919).

Putnam's activities naturally brought her into contact with the U.S. Children's Bureau (founded in 1912), which she helped in its early days to get congressional funding and advised on infant welfare activities related to infant mortality. Although she would later deny any connection with the Bureau, or sympathy for its agenda, her initial response to its activities revealed a great admiration. Reacting to the bureau's first bulletin, *Prenatal Care*, Putnam wrote, "I like to think what an era it will make—it makes me so proud of your Bureau!" (17 Mar. 1913, box 30, ELP Papers). However, Putnam's support for the bureau extended only to its efforts to gather and disseminate information. Once the bureau attempted to obtain federal funds to coordinate infant and maternal welfare programs on a national scale through the Sheppard-Towner Maternity and Infancy Act, Putnam turned against it and helped to defeat the act in a battle that continued throughout the 1920s. Putnam's opposition to the federal maternity act stemmed from both political and personal reasons. She had had cordial relations with the first bureau chief, Julia Lathrop, but disliked and distrusted Lathrop's successor, Grace Abbott. In addition, Putnam believed that if the federal government should be involved at all in coordinating infant and maternal welfare programs, the job belonged to the Department of Public Health, not the Children's Bureau. She also objected to what she regarded as Sheppard-Towner's emphasis on education at the expense of medical treatment. "It is ignorance that causes deaths in maternity and early infancy, but it is not education that the mother needs to prevent it," she argued. "Prenatal care can never be given by education" (Address, n.d., box 3, ELP Papers).

Except for her commitment to infant and maternal welfare, Putnam had little in common with the vast majority of women reformers with whom she cooperated for a short time. Even during her early days as an activist, Putnam was an outspoken antisuffragist, and she helped lead the antisuffrage movement in Massachusetts. Later she opposed most of the causes associated with social feminism in the interwar years, including the Equal Rights Amendment (ERA), the regulation of midwifery, the Child Labor amendment, Prohibition, and eventually the Children's Bureau itself. Also, throughout the 1920s she gained prominence in the Republican Party. Putnam was the first woman to be elected president of the Massachusetts Electoral College. She also served as vice president of the Republican Club of Massachusetts and in 1923 was elected president of the Coolidge Women's Clubs of America. In the mid-1920s Putnam joined the arch conservative Sentinels of the Republic, a group dedicated to stopping the spread of communism, the expansion of bureaucracy, and encroachments on state and individual rights. Her increasing involvement in conservative causes further fostered a rift between Putnam and social welfare reformers in the Children's Bureau as well as in the liberal-minded General Federation of Women's Clubs. In 1930 Putnam formed the Women's National League to Protect Our Homes and Children to combat what she viewed as federal paternalism and the "nationalization of children." In March of that year she met with President Herbert Hoover to discuss her opposition to the Children Bureau, which she claimed was "being run by a bunch of Communists." Eventually, Putnam accused Grace Abbott of being "directly under the Soviet government" and described the bureau as "the first subversive achievement over American Government and Institutions, and the earliest Communist foothold in the Federal Government" (n.d., box 17). Ill during the last few years of her life, she died at her summer home in Manchester, Massachusetts.

Putnam's reform efforts illustrate the complexities of postsuffrage politics. Although she shared the reform-minded desire to improve the welfare of mothers and infants, she increasingly opposed the mainstream movement's broad social agenda. Unlike Putnam, who feared the intrusion of the federal government, most female reformers wanted a more activist liberal state. Although she was an innovator in the field of prenatal care, Putnam held traditional views about the role of the federal government and the role of women, and she did not connect the vulnerability of mothers and infants to the vulnerability of other members of society, as did female reformers with a feminist and progressive orientation. Indeed, the plight of mothers and children increasingly receded to the background of Putnam's political agenda as her prewar tendencies toward conservatism blossomed into a classically conservative agenda that was diametrically opposed to the one held by the majority of maternalist reformers.

• Putnam's extensive papers are collected at the Schlesinger Library, Radcliffe College, Cambridge, Mass. There is no full-length biographical treatment of Putnam. For a fuller account of her reform career and interpretation of her contributions, see Sonya Michel and Robyn L. Rosen, "The Paradox of Maternalism," *Gender & History* (Autumn 1992): 364–86. Obituaries are in the *Boston Globe* and the *New York Times*, 6 June 1935.

ROBYN L. ROSEN

PUTNAM, Frederic Ward (16 Apr. 1839–14 Aug. 1915), anthropologist, naturalist, and museologist, was born in Salem, Massachusetts, the son of Ebenezer Putnam and Elizabeth Appleton. His early years were devoted to the study of natural history on his own, beginning with a serious interest in the study of birds. Remarkably, he became a curator of ornithology at the Essex Institute in Salem in 1856 at age seventeen. That same year Putnam entered the Lawrence Scientific Schools at Harvard University. There he was a pupil and an assistant of the eminent naturalist Louis Agassiz until completing his studies in 1864. Agassiz's interest in promoting science through the systematic collection and classification of natural specimens made a lasting impression on his young assistant, who would later advance the development of archaeological science by gathering and classifying cultural materials for anthropological museums. Putnam did not formally graduate from Harvard, but his years studying with Agassiz were formative ones. In recognition of that fact, Harvard awarded him an S.B. ("as of" the class of 1862) in 1898.

After concluding his studies at Harvard, Putnam became associated with numerous museums and scientific field surveys. He was curator of vertebrata at the Essex Institute from 1864 to 1866 and superintendent of the museum there from 1866 to 1871, superintendent of the museum of the East India Marine Society at Salem from 1867 to 1869, curator of ichthyology at the Boston Society of Natural History from 1859 to 1868, and director of the museum at the Peabody Academy of Science in Salem from 1869 to 1873. After serving as a field assistant in the Geological Survey of Kentucky in 1874, he next became an assistant for the

U.S. Engineer Corps, directing archaeological surveys west of the 100th meridian from 1876 to 1879, and from 1876 to 1878 was in charge of ichthyology at the Harvard Museum of Comparative Zoology. He had married Adelaide Martha Edmands in 1864; they had three children.

Putnam made what was then a short step from natural history to anthropology when he became curator of Harvard's Peabody Museum in 1875. His simultaneous appointment as Peabody Professor of American Archaeology and Ethnology from 1887 to 1909 enabled him to exert significant influence on the development of those fields as academic and museum-based disciplines. Not all of Putnam's anthropological activities, however, were restricted to Harvard. His web of influence included appointment as curator of anthropology at the American Museum of Natural History at New York from 1894 to 1903 and as professor of anthropology and director of the anthropological museum at the University of California from 1903 to 1909. After the death of his wife in 1879, he had married Esther Orne Clarke in 1882; they had no children.

Putnam's activities as a field investigator, professor, and museum administrator at Harvard and elsewhere in large measure defined the emergence of American anthropology as an organized scientific discipline. Throughout his career he either organized or sponsored what were among the first systematic scientific investigations in the Atlantic coast region, the Ohio Valley, the Southwest, on the Pacific coast, in Central America, Mexico, South America, the West Indies, northeast Asia, and Africa. As director of the anthropological section of the 1893 World's Columbian Exposition in Chicago, Putnam directed field studies expressly for the anthropological exhibits at the exposition, which greatly promoted popular and scientific interest in the subject. Those materials became the nucleus of the Field Museum of Natural History in Chicago.

As the influence of the Peabody Museum's archaeological investigations spread, Putnam observed in 1888, that "our methods of thorough exploration have set an example which others are following, so that American archaeology can no longer be regarded as consisting of an indiscriminate collection of relics of the past." He took great interest in the excavations being conducted at Mariemont, Ohio, in 1878 by physician and avocational archaeologist Charles Lewis Metz, under the sponsorship of the Literary and Scientific Society of Madisonville, Ohio. Putnam recruited Metz as a field agent of the Peabody Museum, making arrangements by 1881 to partially fund the society's fieldwork at what had become known as the Madisonville site. The Peabody Museum acquired a portion of the excavated materials in exchange for its funding, with Putnam himself directing excavations at the Madisonville site in 1883.

Putnam's archaeological activities in Ohio also included the excavation, restoration, and preservation of Serpent Mound on Brush Creek in Adams County, a prehistoric earthwork first surveyed and mapped by

ence and $150 in capital. In 1840, shortly after the departure of Long and the renaming of the firm to Wiley & Putnam, Putnam left for London to scout importation opportunities. He returned the following year to set up a literary agency on behalf of the firm. He brought with him his new bride, the orphaned sixteen-year-old Victorine Haven, a former pupil in his mother's school. The young family, which soon included three children (and eventually eleven), lived in England for the next seven years. During this period Putnam promoted American literature and lifestyle (even, in 1845, writing for the British a book of *American Facts*); acted as foreign correspondent for the *New World*, *Commercial Advertiser*, and other New York papers; and, in general, entertained a wide variety of English literati, continental exiles, and American sojourners.

The appearance in 1845 of one such traveler, Washington Irving, then minister to Madrid, led eventually, after the Putnams' return to the United States in 1847, to Putnam's first important independent publishing venture: a uniform edition of Irving's works. With the amicable dissolution of their partnership in 1847, Wiley had left Putnam scant capital but many slow-selling books; Irving's edition gave Putnam a much-needed standard seller and also revived the author's reputation.

Putnam went on to publish one of the most remarkable lists of American belles lettres of the 1850s. He did so with an attitude of gentility that he consciously poised against the cheap, sometimes sensationalistic pamphlet literature of the 1840s. William Cullen Bryant, James Fenimore Cooper, Andrew Jackson Downing, Nathaniel Hawthorne, John Pendleton Kennedy, James Russell Lowell, William Starbuck Mayo, Francis Parkman, Edgar Allan Poe, Catharine Sedgwick, Bayard Taylor, Henry T. Tuckerman, and Susan Warner and her sister Anna are only a few of the prominent American writers whose work appeared under the Putnam imprint. To these Putnam added important European reprints like Layard's *Nineveh and Its Remains*, Alexander Kinglake's *Eothen*, Eliot Warburton's *Crescent and the Cross*, and Thomas Hood's *Poems*.

In January 1853 Putnam furthered the cause of American literature with his *Putnam's Monthly*, which, according to him, would "combine the popular character of a Magazine, with the higher and graver aims of a Quarterly Review" (*Memoir*, vol. 1, p. 286). Featuring mostly original American contributions and having a circulation of up to twenty thousand, the magazine drew the genteel authors of New England into the vibrant newspaper-oriented New York publishing scene. *Putnam's* and its editor, Charles Frederick Briggs, thus contributed to New York's dominance of national literary culture. The magazine, particularly its pieces by Parke Godwin, also helped articulate the cultural outlook of the emerging Republican party.

Putnam soon encountered a series of mishaps. In 1855 he lost nearly all of his $30,000 investment in a lavishly illustrated guide to the ill-fated New York Crystal Palace Exhibition. The defalcations of his trusted financial manager, John M. Leslie (discovered after the man's death by drowning), caused the firm's insolvency in the summer of 1857, which was exacerbated by financial panic of that fall. To satisfy creditors, Putnam auctioned off most of his property and sold his magazine.

Putnam struggled on until 1862, when, on the recommendation of Bryant, Peter Cooper, and other luminaries, he was appointed collector of internal revenue for the Eighth District. Temporarily assigning his remaining publications to Hurd & Houghton, Putnam remained in this remunerative position until 1866, when the Johnson administration removed him for refusing to pay an unfairly inflated Republican party assessment on officeholders.

Putnam resumed his publishing career with the aid of his sons George Haven Putnam and (eventually) John Bishop Putnam and Irving Putnam; but, hampered by continuing capital shortages, the firm, now named G. P. Putnam & Son, never regained its former lustre. The revival in 1868 of *Putnam's Magazine* lasted only until 1870, when competition forced its merger with *Scribner's Monthly*. As insolvency once more loomed at the end of 1872, Putnam died suddenly in his New York office. His life insurance benefit allowed the firm to keep afloat through the ensuing depression of 1873. The firm, renamed G. P. Putnam's Sons in 1919, continued well into the twentieth century.

Despite his chronic financial difficulties, Putnam's publication of classic American authors, both in book form and in his magazine, and his tireless efforts on behalf of book industry communications earned him a lasting regard. "For a sanguine disposition and one interested in books," he self-consciously reflected in his "Rough Notes on Thirty Years in the Trade," "the most obvious danger in the trade is that of doing too much; and one of the most essential virtues is the courage to say 'no.'" Luckily for American literature if not for him, he did not stifle his affirmative tendency.

• Though most of Putnam's early papers were lost in a fire in 1857, some of his surviving correspondence (1843–1869) can be found at Princeton University. He wrote two travelogues, *The Tourist in Europe* (1838) and *A Pocket Memorandum Book during a Ten Weeks' Trip to Italy and Germany in 1847* (1848). His autobiographical "Rough Notes" first appeared in *American Publishers' Circular* in 1863; it was reprinted in part in George Haven Putnam's often unreliable and self-contradictory *A Memoir of George Palmer Putnam* (2 vols., 1903). In the same source may be found passages from Putnam's "Recollections of Irving" from the *Atlantic Monthly* (Nov. 1860) as well as some of the pieces that were published in his "Leaves from a Publisher's Letter-Book," *Putnam's Magazine* (1869). For a handy biographical sketch see John Tebbel, *A History of Book Publishing in the United States*, vol. 1 (1972). The best assessment of Putnam, his magazine, and his milieu remains Perry Miller, *The Raven and the Whale* (1956), but see also Miriam Naomi Kotzin, "Putnam's Monthly and Its Place in American Literature" (Ph.D. diss., New York Univ., 1969). Heyward Ehrlich challenges Putnam's early role as a copyright advocate in his "The Putnams: The Father, the Son, and a Ghost," *Publications of the Bibliographical Society of*

America 63 (1969): 15–22. A brief look at Putnam's later relations with England can be found in Joel Myerson, "George Palmer Putnam: Literary London in 1869," *Manuscripts* 387 (1968): 155–60.

RONALD J. ZBORAY

PUTNAM, Gideon (17 Apr. 1763–1 Dec. 1812), entrepreneur and developer, was born in Sutton, Massachusetts, the son of Stephen Putnam and Mary Gibbs (occupations unknown). He was a cousin of revolutionary war general Israel Putnam. Gideon Putnam married Doana Risley of Hartford, Connecticut (c. 1783), and moved to Vermont, where they established a farm at the present site of Middlebury College. Dissatisfied with the region, they moved to Rutland, Vermont, and then to Bemis Heights in New York. A major flood caused them to move once again, this time to Saratoga Springs, in 1789. Putnam leased 300 acres in the Kayaderosseras Patent from Derick Lefferts. Starting a farm, he also began to cut lumber and manufacture shingles and staves, which he shipped to New York City. By 1791 he had accumulated enough wealth to purchase the leased land and build a sawmill. A year later the mineral water source, subsequently named Congress Spring, was discovered by John Taylor Gilman. Although the spring was not on his land, Putnam, in 1802, tubed Congress Spring and began his career as a hotel builder and city planner.

That same year he bought one acre of land from Henry Walton in the lower village of Saratoga Springs opposite Congress Spring and began constructing Putnam's Tavern, or Union Hall, as it was later called by Putnam's sons. Union Hall was subsequently expanded and renamed the Grand Union Hotel, which was to become one of the world's largest hotels. In 1805 Putnam bought another tract of land from Henry Walton and he developed a plan to lay out the village of Saratoga Springs on the west side of this property. Several other mineral water springs were located and tubed by Putnam between 1802 and 1809, including Hamilton Spring and Columbian Spring. He erected a bathhouse, first near Congress Spring, and then moved it to Hamilton Spring. His plan for the village included wide streets with the mineral water springs situated in the middle of the streets and publicly owned. He set aside part of his land for a cemetery, which he later gave to the village, and he also provided land for a church of whichever denomination was established first.

In the fall of 1812 a scaffolding on which Putnam and several workers had been standing gave way. Two workmen were killed, and Putnam suffered severe injuries from which he did not recover. In December 1812 he developed pneumonia and died in Saratoga Springs. He was survived by his wife and their nine children. Subsequently, Putnam's plans for the village of Saratoga Springs were not achieved. The completed streets were narrower than Putnam envisioned and not wide enough to accommodate the mineral springs. The springs, which had been public property, were sold to private owners. In his *Handbook of Saratoga*

(1859), Dr. Richard Allen stated that "It was to Putnam that we are indebted . . . for improvements at the Springs. . . . that his name must be co-existent with the history of the village, which his energy did so much to develop" (pp. 25–26).

Putnam recognized the commercial potential of the mineral water springs to the little village of Saratoga Springs and he sought to build upon those possibilities. His untimely death did not permit him to see his plan to fruition, but he laid the groundwork for a thriving and exciting city that has attracted millions of visitors through nearly two centuries.

• No personal papers of Gideon Putnam are available, but the Saratoga Springs Public Library has miscellaneous news articles and a map of Saratoga Springs. Richard L. Allen, *Handbook of Saratoga and Strangers' Guide* (1859), is the earliest description of Saratoga Springs and contains statements of contemporary inhabitants. See also George Baker Anderson, *Descriptive and Biographical Record of Saratoga County, New York* (1890); John Henry Brandow, *Story of Old Saratoga and History of Schuylerville* (1906); and William L. Stone, *Reminiscences of Saratoga and Ballston* (1875). For a modern description, see Grace M. Swanner, *Saratoga: Queen of Spas* (1988).

R. BETH KLOPOTT

PUTNAM, Helen Cordelia (14 Sept. 1857–3 Feb. 1951), physician and public health reformer, was born in Stockton, Minnesota, the daughter of Herbert Asa Putnam, a general store owner, and Celintha T. Gates. She received her A.B. from Vassar College in 1878 and then enrolled in Harvard University's Sargent School of Physical Training. In 1883, having completed that school's course of study, she returned to Vassar as director of physical education. Shortly thereafter she became active in the affairs of the American Association for the Advancement of Physical Education and served as its vice president from 1885 to 1888. She also enrolled in the Woman's Medical College of Pennsylvania, where she specialized in obstetrics and the diseases of women and received her M.D. in 1889. In 1890 she left Vassar to become an intern at the New England Hospital for Women and Children in Boston. Two years later she moved to Providence, Rhode Island, where she practiced gynecology for the next forty-three years.

Putnam never married but chose instead to devote her energy to affecting reforms in a number of areas of particular concern to women and children. She was an enthusiastic advocate of providing prenatal care to expectant mothers of limited means via visiting nurses. Concerned that many non-nursing infants were being fed milk processed in unsanitary circumstances, she was one of the first to advocate government inspection of dairies and milk-bottling plants. In 1907 she attended an international conference on school hygiene in London, England, where she resolved to make it possible for more babies to survive their first year. She used her position as president of the American Academy of Medicine in 1908 to initiate planning for a conference on the prevention of infant mortality to be held the following year, and she chaired that conference's executive committee. This gathering resulted in the founding of the American Association for the Study and Prevention of Infant Mortality, which focused on improving infant feeding and encouraging expectant mothers to seek prenatal care for their babies. It also crusaded against childhood diseases, promoting preventive measures and treatments. In 1923 the association merged with the Child Health Organization and eventually became known as the American Academy of Pediatrics.

Between 1909 and 1912 Putnam wrote a series of articles for *Child-Welfare Magazine*, the journal of the National Congress of Mothers and Parent-Teacher Associations, which was intended to motivate parents to take more notice of the physical environment in which their children were being educated; revised versions of these articles are reprinted in her book *School Janitors, Mothers and Health* (1913). Because she believed that "the surest prevention on the largest scale is to develop thru public schools potential fathers and mothers with wholesome bodies, minds and ideals" (*School Janitors*, dedication page), she promoted physical education and exercise as the bedrock for a child's well-being and insisted that schools provide children with a clean and healthful atmosphere.

Putnam was concerned particularly with the quality of air in the typical schoolhouse. Charging that in most schools it was too hot, dry, dirty, and stale to promote either good health or learning, she insisted that maintenance engineers devise methods for filling every school with plenty of fresh air. She also expressed considerable dismay over the acceptable standards of cleanliness set by school officials, most of whom were men, and urged middle-class mothers to organize clubs to demand the same level of cleanliness in the school that they provided for their own families. To this end, she believed that school janitors should be specially trained to sweep floors, wash walls, and clean chalkboards so that dirt and dust are actually removed from the premises instead of being suspended briefly in midair before resettling in essentially the same spot. She also cofounded the American Child Health Association, which worked to promote clean schools, better health care for children, and the teaching of health education in schools via the involvement of middle-class parents; chaired the executive committee of the National Education Association's committee on racial well-being; and served on the board of directors or its equivalent of the Playground Association of America, the International Union for the Protection of Infants, and the American School Hygiene Association.

In addition to her work to improve the health of children, Putnam contributed much energy to causes related to the welfare of women. For a number of years she served on the board of managers of the Rhode Island Women's Suffrage Association. She also served as secretary of a conference to promote reforms in women's prisons in Rhode Island and was active in the movement to involve the mentally ill in gardening as a means of therapy. She was elected a fellow of the American Academy of Medicine, and she was a member of the American Public Health Association, the American Medical Association, and the American Association for the Advancement of Science.

In 1935 Putnam retired to her home in Providence. Four years later she received a sizable inheritance, most of which she donated to Providence's Butler Hospital and the Rhode Island School of Design and used to establish research fellowships at Radcliffe College and Western Reserve University. She died in Providence.

Putnam contributed to the advance of public health in the United States by serving as a leader of the movement to improve the health and living conditions of children.

• Putnam's papers have not been located. Her contributions are discussed in John Duffy, *The Sanitarians: A History of American Public Health* (1990). Obituaries are in the *New York Times*, 5 Feb. 1951, *American Medical Association Journal* 145 (21 Apr. 1951), and *Recreation* 45 (June 1951).

CHARLES W. CAREY, JR.

PUTNAM, Herbert (20 Sept. 1861–14 Aug. 1955), eighth librarian of Congress, was born George Herbert Putnam in New York City, the son of George Palmer Putnam, founder of the Putnam publishing house, and Victorine Haven. Herbert Putnam attended private schools in New York City. He received his B.A. from Harvard in 1883, graduating magna cum laude. The next year he attended Columbia University Law School, but soon a Minneapolis attorney and former Harvard classmate enticed him to Minneapolis and librarianship. He became librarian of the Minneapolis Athenaeum in 1884 and continued his legal studies independently; he was admitted to the Minnesota bar in 1885. In 1886 he married Charlotte Elizabeth Munroe of Cambridge, Massachusetts; they had two children.

Putnam successfully worked toward the establishment of a public library in Minneapolis, and in 1887 the Athenaeum and the new public library were merged. Two years later he became the city librarian of the newly opened Minneapolis Public Library.

In late 1891 the serious illness of Putnam's mother-in-law forced the Putnams to leave Minnesota and return to Massachusetts, where Putnam was admitted to the bar in 1892. He practiced law in Boston for three years until he was persuaded by local officials to return to librarianship as director of the Boston Public Library, the nation's largest public library. He assumed his duties in 1895, shortly after the library had moved into its new building on Copley Square. At the end of his first year, the library trustees noted that the new librarian "has proved to be most competent and faithful in the discharge of his duties, which have been unusually difficult and trying."

Putnam's leadership abilities and his new position intensified his involvement in the American Library Association (ALA). With Melvil Dewey from the New York State Library, he was a principal ALA witness in late 1896 at congressional hearings about the future of the Library of Congress. Representing the new profession of librarianship, both men emphasized that the Library of Congress now had the opportunity to act as a true national library, in the words of Dewey, "a center to which the libraries of the whole country can turn for inspiration, guidance, and practical help."

In 1897 President William McKinley appointed journalist John Russell Young to the post of librarian of Congress, and Young presided over the library's move from the Capitol into its new building. Young's sudden death in 1899 gave the ALA an opportunity to promote an experienced librarian and professional administrator as the next librarian of Congress. It chose Putnam, who was confirmed by the Senate on 12 December 1899. Putnam held the job for the next forty years, the longest period anyone has served as librarian of Congress.

Putnam moved quickly and skillfully to develop a national leadership role for the Library of Congress. Of particular importance was his creation of a working partnership between the library and American libraries and librarianship.

In 1901 the library published the first volume of its new classification scheme, which had been developed after the librarian and his cataloging experts decided that the Dewey decimal system was inadequate for the library's needs. (By the end of 1901, the Library of Congress, with more than one million volumes, had become America's largest library.) An interlibrary loan system extended access to the library to qualified individuals outside of Washington, and Putnam inaugurated an important bibliographic service: the sale and distribution of three-by-five-inch printed catalog cards to libraries throughout the world. In a 200-page appendix to his 1901 annual report, the librarian presented a comprehensive description of the library's organization, collections, buildings, and services; it soon became a model and a standard for all libraries.

Putnam used his reputation as a library expert to gain support from members of Congress and President Theodore Roosevelt. At Putnam's urging, Roosevelt asked Congress for, and received, additional support for the Library of Congress. In 1903 Roosevelt issued an executive order that transferred the records and papers of the Continental Congress and the personal papers of the Founding Fathers from the State Department to the library.

The development of the library's collections into a nationally useful resource took many forms during Putnam's administration. In 1904 the library began publishing important historical texts from its collections. Putnam was especially farsighted in acquiring significant research materials about other countries and cultures. In 1904 he purchased a unique 4,000-volume collection of Indica. Two years later he obtained the famous 80,000-volume private library of Russian literature owned by G. V. Yudin of Siberia. Large and important collections of Hebraica as well as Chinese and Japanese collections also were acquired. In 1914 Putnam strengthened the library's foremost function, research support for the national legislature,

when he established the Legislative Reference Service as a separate administrative unit.

The Library of Congress Trust Fund Board, which enabled the library to accept, hold, and invest gifts and bequests, was another Putnam innovation. Founded on 3 March 1925, it immediately became an important avenue for acquiring new collections, attracting scholars and consultants, and developing a new cultural role for the institution, particularly as a performance center for chamber music.

Through Putnam's efforts, the Library of Congress also became a repository for documents of democracy and culture. The Declaration of Independence and the Constitution were transferred from the State Department and went on public display in 1921. With congressional approval of $1.5 million for the purchase, the librarian went to Europe in 1930 and returned with one of the three perfect vellum copies of the Gutenberg Bible.

Putnam's last decade in office was not as fruitful or successful as those preceding it. As the library grew, he insisted on maintaining personal control over all its diverse units; administrative stagnation developed, as well as the practical problems of backlogs in cataloging and low staff salaries and morale. A thorough administrative reorganization was a principal accomplishment of Archibald MacLeish, Putnam's successor, who described the Library of Congress in 1939 when he took office as "not so much an organization in its own right as the lengthened shadow of a man—a man of great force, extraordinary abilities, and a personality which left its fortunate impress upon everything he touched" ("The Reorganization of the Library of Congress," *Library Quarterly* 14 [Oct. 1944]: 277–315).

When he retired on 1 October 1939, Putnam received praise from the American Council of Learned Societies for making the Library of Congress the peer of the British Museum and France's Bibliothèque Nationale and from the American Library Association for turning the library into "the world's largest bibliographical institution." He became the first Librarian of Congress Emeritus, and maintained an active interest in the library's affairs until his death in Woods Hole, Massachusetts.

Putnam permanently established the reputation of the Library of Congress as a cultural institution that was "universal in scope, national in service," to use his phrase. He also created the patterns of service to the library's diverse constituencies that exist today, particularly services to libraries, scholarly institutions, and the public. Finally, his success in sharing the library's bibliographic services and standards with other institutions stimulated cooperative efforts that greatly benefited American librarianship and scholarship.

• Putnam's personal papers are in the Manuscript Division, Library of Congress, and his official correspondence is in Library of Congress Archives, also in the Manuscript Division. A detailed description of his career and personality is found in David C. Mearns, "Herbert Putnam: Librarian of the United States," in *An American Library History Reader,* comp. John David Marshall (1961). Putnam's contributions to the Library of Congress are discussed in John Y. Cole, "Herbert Putnam and the National Library," in *Milestones to the Present*, ed. Harold Goldstein (1978), and Cole, "The Library of Congress and American Scholarship, 1865–1939," in *Libraries and Scholarly Communication in the United States*, ed. Phyllis Dain and John Y. Cole (1990). Also see Wayne A. Wiegand, "Herbert Putnam's Appointment as Librarian of Congress," *Library Quarterly* 49 (1979): 255–82. *Herbert Putnam, 1861–1955: A Memorial Tribute* (1956) contains a biographical essay by David C. Mearns, a bibliography of Putnam's writings, addresses and articles about him, and a chronology of his life. An obituary is in the *New York Times*, 16 Aug. 1955.

JOHN Y. COLE

PUTNAM, Israel (7 Jan. 1718–29 May 1790), American Revolution general, was born in Salem Village (now Danvers), Massachusetts, the son of Joseph Putnam, a farmer, and Elizabeth Porter. Born to a prosperous farming family, as a youth Putnam showed scant interest in books and things of the mind. His formal education extended to only a few years of primary school. Instead, a love of physical activity and a fierce competitiveness gave him a local reputation for courage, tenacity, and strength by the time he reached adolescence. These characteristics, along with a hearty sociability and a rural-honed contempt for pretense and artificial distinctions, later became hallmarks of his extraordinary career and proved to be both his making and unmaking as a general.

Putnam married Hannah Pope in 1739, and in 1740 they moved from densely populated Salem Village to a frontier area in northeastern Connecticut where prospects for acquiring land were better. Putnam brought with him enough capital from an inheritance and his wife's dowry to buy over 500 acres of uncleared land in Pomfret, a town near both the Massachusetts and Rhode Island borders. He farmed his land successfully for the remainder of his life. He and Hannah had ten children. After Hannah's death in 1765, he married Deborah Lothrop Gardner. Had it not been for the drama of war and revolution, Putnam would undoubtedly have lived the life of a prosperous farmer, contented husband and father, and local leader and died in relative obscurity. An unusual blend of personal attributes, opportunity, and accident, however, thrust him into a historical limelight that has dimmed little with the passage of time.

In 1755, Putnam marched with the Connecticut militia to Albany, New York, to be part of an intercolonial force mounting an assault on the French garrison at Crown Point during the French and Indian Wars. A 37-year-old second lieutenant, Putnam became battle-hardened in a series of skirmishes around Lake George and then joined a guerrilla unit named Roger's Rangers under the command of Robert Rogers. The expedition's purpose was to "distress the French and their allies by sacking, burning, and destroying their houses, barns, and barracks." This the Rangers did, and Putnam quickly became known as a man of unusual bravery, vigor, and resourcefulness. A superb guerrilla fighter, he was rapidly promoted to captain in 1755 and major in 1758. Captured by Native American allies of the French in the summer of 1758, Putnam endured torture, forced marches, and near starvation before being ransomed that fall. In 1759, he received his first major command as lieutenant colonel of a regiment attacking Fort Ticonderoga and was part of several more expeditions during the war, including one that captured Havana, Cuba, in the spring of 1762.

After the war ended, Putnam returned to his life as a farmer. He also remained active in military and public affairs. In 1764, during Pontiac's Rebellion, the Connecticut General Assembly named Putnam the commander of five militia battalions to fight under the command of Colonel John Bradstreet in the area stretching from Lake Ontario to Fort Detroit. Putnam was recommissioned with the rank of major and then almost immediately promoted to his former militia rank of lieutenant colonel. The Connecticut troops saw little military action during the time they were away between May and December. In 1766 Putnam was elected a deputy from Pomfret to the Connecticut General Assembly and was one of the organizers of the Sons of Liberty in eastern Connecticut. At the first colonywide meeting of the Sons of Liberty, held in Hartford in April 1766, he was elected chairman of its committee of correspondence. He remained active in the Sons of Liberty but served only one more term in the General Assembly, in 1767. Between December 1772 and August 1773 Putnam again went west, this time as the civilian commander of a private expedition to explore the Mississippi River on behalf of a group of land speculators.

Shortly after the battle of Lexington in April 1775, the Connecticut General Assembly appointed him as brigadier general and the third-ranking officer in the colony's militia. Although probably untrue, a legend developed during the American Revolution that upon hearing of the news of Lexington, Putnam, who was plowing for spring planting, rushed to the defense of his country without bothering to unhitch his team of horses. Putnam led the Connecticut militia to Boston, where he sufficiently distinguished himself in a number of minor incidents to induce the Continental Congress to appoint him a major general of the Continental army. As field commander of the troops at Bunker Hill, Putnam gave one of the most famous orders in American military history: "Men, you are marksmen—don't one of you fire until you see the white[s] of their eyes."

Second in rank only to George Washington, Putnam played an important role in planning for the battle of Long Island in August 1776, which ended in a disastrous rout. Historians have often assigned Putnam the lion's share of blame for the debacle. He commanded the left flank of the advancing Continental army and allowed his troops to become entrapped between British assaults from the front and rear; the Americans suffered about 2,000 casualties, the British only about 300. Putnam was more successful in the defense of Philadelphia in the winter of 1776–1777. Enlisted men and junior officers serving under Putnam revered him. He put on no airs, walked among the troops in bivouac and battle, and often shared rum and swapped war stories with them. Washington, a tall, reserved, cautious, dignified patrician, and Putnam, a stocky, garrulous, impetuous man of the people, seem to have had opposite personality types and personal bearing. They liked and respected each other, however, and Washington continued to entrust Putnam with important assignments, even though other high-ranking officers began to complain to the commander in chief that Putnam lacked the military and organizational skills to command a large force of men. Eventually, Washington came to share this opinion based on his observations of Putnam's tactical skills, and when Putnam requested a leave in March 1778 to attend to family business, Washington replaced him with Major General Alexander McDougall (1732–1786). When Putnam returned to duty and applied for reassignment, Washington reluctantly appointed him to replace Major General Charles Lee (1731–1782), who had been removed from his command of Continental troops at White Plains, New York. Little of consequence happened to the troops under Putnam's command in 1779, and he suffered a stroke in December of that year, thus ending his military career. Putnam recovered sufficiently from his stroke to operate a tavern in Pomfret, where he became a famed storyteller. He died at his home in Pomfret.

Israel Putnam's fame rests neither on his efforts as a military strategist nor on his accomplishments as a general but instead on his personal virtues. With the exception of Washington, Putnam was the most celebrated hero of the revolutionary war. Variously called "Old Put," "Old Wolf Put," and "the Plowman of the Revolution," he somehow unified in his person the virtues that average farmers and soldiers wanted to see in themselves and their leaders. Putnam's character and life defined the ideal citizen for the fledgling republic. A self-made man, unlettered but wise, brave yet compassionate, a product of the American forest and field and not of the European salon, a democrat among the aristocrats—Putnam struck a vibrant chord in the emotions of the revolutionary generation, whose children would respond to the same virtues.

• No one primary collection of Putnam's papers exists. Copies of materials relating to him are scattered among the papers of his military colleagues, and the Connecticut Historical Society, Connecticut State Library, Library of Congress, New-York Historical Society, New Hampshire Historical Society, and New York Public Library all have significant numbers of documents. Some of these and others have been published in Albert Bates, ed., *The Two Putnams* (1931), which also contains documents from Israel's cousin, Rufus Putnam, who served with him in both the American Revolution and the French and Indian Wars. Putnam was the subject of the first biography of an American written by an American: David Humphreys, *An Essay on the Life of the Honorable Major General Israel Putnam* (1788), which contains a wonderful store of firsthand anecdotes about him. Several other biographies have been written. The most complete is William Farrand Livingston, *Israel Putnam: Pioneer, Ranger, and Major General, 1718–1790* (1905), and the most recent and interpretive is John Niven, *Connecticut Hero, Israel Putnam* (1977). For a genealogy of the Putnam family, see Eben Putnam, *History of the Putnam Family in England and America* (1891). Ellen Larned, *History of Windham County, Connecticut* (2 vols., 1880), contains much on the local career of Putnam, Pomfret, and eastern Connecticut. See also Rufus Putnam's useful diary, Rowena Buell, comp., *The Memoirs of Rufus Putnam* (1930).

BRUCE C. DANIELS

PUTNAM, James Jackson (3 Oct. 1846–4 Nov. 1918), neurologist, was born in Boston, Massachusetts, the son of Charles Gideon Putnam, a physician, and Elizabeth Cabot Jackson. He graduated from Harvard College in 1866 and from Harvard Medical School in 1870. After an internship at Massachusetts General Hospital, he studied neurology in Leipzig, Vienna, and London; he was influenced by Carl Rokitansky, Theodor Meynert, and, especially, John Hughlings Jackson.

Putnam was one of the pioneers of neurology in the United States. After returning from Europe in 1872, he founded one of the first U.S. neurological clinics, at Massachusetts General Hospital. Because of a lack of hospital facilities at that time, he established a neuropathological laboratory in his own home. In 1873 the Harvard Medical School appointed him lecturer on the application of electricity in nervous diseases, a title that reflects the infant status of the field of neurology at the time. In 1875 Putnam was one of the seven charter members of the American Neurological Association; he served as its president in 1888. He was also a founder of the Boston Society of Psychiatry and Neurology. By 1893 he had risen to the rank of professor of diseases of the nervous system at Harvard, a position he held until 1912, when he was made professor emeritus.

Putnam married Marian Cabot in 1886; they had five children.

During a career that spanned nearly fifty years, Putnam published more than 100 papers on clinical and pathological neurology. His collaboration in the early 1870s with Henry P. Bowditch, a professor of physiology at Harvard, resulted in his publication of "Contribution to the Physiology of the Cortex Cerebri" in the *Boston Medical and Surgical Journal* in 1874. Most of his neurologic work focused on disorders of the spinal cord and peripheral nerves. His first significant publication, in 1881, was the earliest adequate description of paresthesias in the hands. He wrote important papers on neuritis, particularly neuritis caused by lead and arsenic poisoning. He also spoke out on social issues, notably, in 1879, defending the place of women in medicine.

Although Putnam was severely critical of functional or psychological explanations of nervous symptoms during the first decade of his career, his views changed radically over the years. This change appears to have been influenced by his extensive experience giving legal evidence in cases of traumatic neuroses. Between

1890 and 1909 Putnam cooperated informally with psychologists, philosophers, and psychiatrists—including William James, Josiah Royce, and Hugo Munsterberg—to develop a sophisticated, scientific psychotherapy. Although this Boston "school" was aware of Freud's work, their own original work was influenced chiefly by the discoveries of French psychopathologists, primarily Jean Martin Charcot, Hippolyte Bernheim, and Pierre Janet. The first published evidence of Putnam's changing views was an 1895 paper, "Remarks on the Psychical Treatment of Neurasthenia." In 1906 Putnam published the first series of cases in an English-speaking country that attempted to apply the psychoanalytic method to hospitalized patients. From these cases he concluded that Freud's method was not useless, but that it was "difficult of application and often less necessary than one might think" ("Recent Experiences in the Study and Treatment of Hysteria at the Massachusetts General Hospital; with Remarks on Freud's Method of Treatment by 'Psycho-Analysis'," *Journal of Abnormal Psychology* 1 [1906]: 35–36).

In more recent years, Putnam's pioneering work in establishing neurology as a medical specialty in the United States has been overshadowed by interest in his role as a pioneer of the psychoanalytic movement in this country. His serious involvement in psychoanalysis began during Freud's visit to Clark University in 1909, during which the two men had a chance to talk at length. In the last decade of his life Putnam wrote about twenty-two papers on psychoanalysis. Of particular importance was his "Personal Experience with Freud's Psychoanalytic Method," which he read to the American Neurological Association and published in the *Journal of Nervous and Mental Disease* in 1910. Putnam's stature among neurologists secured a hearing for Freud's views within the profession, and his reputation for sound scientific judgment and unimpeachable integrity played a crucial role in the American acceptance of psychoanalysis. Putnam died in Boston.

• The bulk of Putnam's remaining papers are available at the Francis A. Countway Library of Medicine in Boston. His *Addresses on Psychoanalysis* (1921) contains his psychoanalytic writings and an obituary by Ernest Jones. For articles on Putnam see E. W. Taylor, *Archives of Neurology and Psychiatry* 3 (1920): 307–14, and Nathan G. Hale's introduction to *James Jackson Putnam and Psychoanalysis*, ed. Hale (1971). Also see Stephen Young Wilkerson, "Mind Over Body: James Jackson Putnam and the Impact of Neurology on Psychotherapy in Late Nineteenth-Century America" (Ph.D. diss., Duke Univ., 1978), which contains a bibliography of Putnam's prepsychoanalytic works. An obituary is in the *Boston Transcript*, 4 and 7 Nov. 1918.

EDWARD M. BROWN

PUTNAM, Nina Wilcox (28 Nov. 1888–8 Mar. 1962), novelist and humorist, was born in New Haven, Connecticut, the daughter of Marrion Wilcox, an editor and author, and Eleanor Patricia Sanchez, an art dealer. Putnam's early childhood was spent in England.

When she was six years of age, the family returned to Connecticut. Except for a few months spent in a private school that she detested, she was educated at home and was mostly self-taught. She learned to read and write using Stevenson's *Child's Garden of Verse*, which she had heard so often that she knew all the words. "Once I had discovered reading, nothing could stop me," she said. "I was seldom lonely and hardly ever at a loss for amusement, for I had books."

When Putnam was fifteen her father was in South America, her mother was ill, and they were in need of money. Dressed to look older and wearing a hat she had made herself, Putnam got a job as a milliner. She even established her own millinery business for a time and supported the family until her father returned. In 1907 she married Robert Faulkner Putnam; they had one child. After Robert Putnam's death during the flu epidemic of 1918, she married Robert J. Sanderson in 1919. They were subsequently divorced. She married Arthur James Ogle in 1931, but they were divorced in 1932. She married Christian Eliot in 1933, and they remained married until his death.

While growing up, Putnam had met many of her father's literary friends. She spent a day with Lewis Carroll, who gave her a signed copy of *Alice in Wonderland* that later, during a time of desperation, she sold to an unscrupulous bookdealer. This incident became the basis of a short story with a happier ending, "Secondhand Book" (*Woman's Day*, Apr. 1962). Among the guests who came to her mother's Sunday Teas were Mark Twain, Rudyard Kipling, Theodore Roosevelt, and William Howard Taft. William Dean Howells came often and became Putnam's literary godfather, encouraging her to write. At eleven she wrote what she called her first "coherent short story" and sold it for five dollars. It was published on the children's page of the *New York Herald*. When she was eighteen, *Ainslee's* magazine published one of her short stories, and her writing career had begun.

For eleven years Putnam wrote indexes for books and was a first reader for Putnam's Publishing Company, "weeding," as she said, "the worthless from the possible." During that time she began writing short stories regularly for *Ainslee's* and *Everybody's Magazine*.

When Putnam contracted tuberculosis, her doctor treated her at home rather than send her to a sanitarium. During her illness she wrote her first novel, *In Search of Arcady* (1912), while lying in a steamer chair on the roof of the apartment building, writing in longhand, in pencil. When she sold the book rights to Doubleday and the novelette rights to *Munsey Magazine*, she received enough money to follow her doctor's advice to leave the city for a time. She leased a tiny cottage at Cape Ann, Massachusetts, for the summer, away from the dust and heat of New York, where she recovered her health. Her second novel, *The Impossible Boy* (1913), was written that summer.

It was then, too, that Putnam began her revolt against conventional women's clothing, which she considered uncomfortable and unhygienic. She designed a one-piece dress of washable fabric, v-necked, without fastenings of any kind, which she wore over a single, one-piece undergarment, replacing the usual eleven or twelve. Of her new clothes she said, "I had abandoned all the nonsensical clap-trap of dress with which women unconsciously symbolized their bondage." She wrote several articles expressing her opinions on women's fashion. Much ridiculed in the press, she persisted in wearing her unconventional clothes and became active in the woman suffrage movement. When women started wearing simpler clothing, she spoke of the success of her crusade: "I won't say I did it all, but I do know that my early effort helped a lot."

During World War I, Putnam joined the Women's Peace Party and then enlisted in the Motor Corps of America, signing up for and undergoing the rigorous training for the Ambulance Service. During this period her writing was greatly influenced by the war.

In "Ladies Enlist," her first story to be published in the *Saturday Evening Post*, Putnam introduced Marie La Tour, a character who became very popular and led to Putnam's acceptance as a humorist. She wrote in the vernacular, saying, "English was all very well in its place, but it was no good to me when I wanted to say something which was purely American." "Price of Applause," a serial story inspired by the death of Allan Seeger, a young poet killed in the war, became a movie and resulted in a move to Hollywood, where she wrote patriotic propaganda films at the request of the government.

In her next books, *It Pays to Smile* (1920), *Tomorrow We Diet* (1922), and *Laughter Limited* (1922), Putnam continued her move to humor. *Say It with Bricks: a Few Remarks about Husbands* (1923) was printed as a back-to-back book with *Say It with Oil: a Few Remarks about Wives*, by Ring Lardner. After remarking on several bad things about husbands, Putnam tried to show a more positive side:

Other good things about husbands is that they are certainly useful for closing trunks and opening bottles. Also they are good practice for ladies intending to enter the diplomatic service which some of us undoubtedly will, now that we've got the vote, and any woman who has put in a few years managing an average husband will be able to take a foreign diplomat's job.

Putnam wrote more than twenty novels and humorous books, over a thousand short stories and articles, several plays and filmscripts, and four children's books. She spent her later years in Florida and Mexico, where she continued to write almost to the end of her life, her work appearing regularly in *Reader's Digest*, *Colliers*, and other magazines. She died in Cuernavaca, Mexico.

• Putnam's *Laughing Through: Being the Autobiographical Story of a Girl Who Made Her Way* (1930) contains much information on her life and work through 1919. See also *The Making of an American Humorist* (1929) and "Girl of the Nineties: Autobiography," *Saturday Evening Post*, 16 Nov. through 7 Dec. 1929. For information on her later life, see Putnam's "My Land of Flowers" *Forum*, Jan. 1937, pp. 44–47, and "Exodus to Mexico" *American Mercury*, Mar. 1952, pp. 47–55. For discussions on her revolt against women's fashions, see "Woman Who Has Unset the Tyranny of Feminine Fashion," *American Magazine*, May 1913, pp. 34–36; "Fashion and Feminism," *FORUM*, Oct. 1914, pp. 580–84, and "Ventures and Adventures in Dress Reform," *Saturday Evening Post*, 7 Oct. 1922, p. 15, all by Putnam. An obituary is in the *New York Times*, 9 Mar. 1962.

BLANCHE COX CLEGG

PUTNAM, Rufus (9 Apr. 1738–4 May 1824), soldier and pioneer, was born in Sutton, Massachusetts, the son of Elisha Putnam and Susanna Fuller, occupations unknown. Putnam's father died when he was seven years old. When his mother remarried, he lived with a succession of relatives until he was apprenticed to a millwright in 1754.

Ambitious and self-educated, Putnam made a name for himself in military service. As a provincial soldier during the French and Indian War, he won promotion to sergeant in 1759 and learned the rudiments of military engineering. Two decades later, during the American Revolution, Putnam put these skills to good use; he supervised the construction of defensive works around Boston in the winter of 1775–1776 and around New York in 1776 and oversaw the reconstruction of West Point. Congress rewarded him with the rank of colonel in August 1776 and brigadier general in January 1783. While Putnam fought bravely on several occasions, his reputation rested on his engineering achievements.

Despite the opportunities offered by military service, Putnam was ambivalent about it. He loved the camaraderie and the discipline and thrived on executing specific orders, but resented commands that he thought belittled him. In 1759 he agreed to build the army a sawmill only after Brigadier General Timothy Ruggles intervened. Putnam later wrote that he did not want "to offend an officer whom I so highly respected" (Buell, p. 27). Although Putnam did what was expected of him out of a desire to excel, his belief that dutifulness would earn him respect and greater responsibility frequently led to his frustration at not receiving adequate promotions.

Of Putnam's patrons, the most significant was George Washington. Putnam proudly pointed to his various appointments as territorial judge and surveyor as "indubitable evidence of the esteam, frindship, and patronage of so great and good a man" (Buell, p. 99). He tended, however, to be prickly when dealing with institutions. He resigned his commission in a huff in 1776 when Congress refused to create an engineering corps. More important, he became a spokesman for officers and soldiers angered by the lack of compensation and respect extended to them by Congress. Putnam was largely responsible for the Newburgh Petition of June 1783, in which continental officers asked for reserves of bounty land in the Ohio Country.

In the 1760s and 1770s Putnam concentrated on assuring his family's financial independence. His brief first marriage ended in the death of his wife, Elizabeth

Ayres, in November 1761, apparently in childbirth. In January 1765 he married Persis Rice; they had nine children. Between periods of military service, Putnam labored as a farmer and miller in south-central Massachusetts. He learned the valuable skills of a land surveyor and was involved in a 1773 scheme by veterans of the French and Indian War to survey bounty lands in the lower Mississippi Valley.

In 1785 Congress appointed Putnam a surveyor of the national lands northwest of the Ohio River. Together with Benjamin Tupper, another revolutionary war veteran from Massachusetts, Putnam established the Ohio Company of Associates, a joint-stock organization, in a March 1786 meeting in Boston. The bulk of investors in the Ohio Company were military veterans like Putnam who were interested in settling west of the Appalachians. In 1787 Congress sold the group 1.5 million acres in what is now southeastern Ohio.

As superintendent of the Ohio Company, Putnam led a group of men to the mouth of the Muskingum River, where they founded the town of Marietta in April 1788. Putnam supervised the construction of a fort, laid out a plan for a city of 15,000 people, and helped to organize local government under the provisions of the Northwest Ordinance of 1787. He was also instrumental in negotiating a settlement with Congress when the Ohio Company was unable to complete its purchase in the early 1790s. Becoming an important agent of the territorial and national governments, he corresponded with members of the Washington administration, to whom he offered information and advice. In March 1790 President Washington appointed him a territorial judge, and in May 1792 he was commissioned a brigadier general in the regular army. In the latter capacity, he concluded a treaty with some of the Indians of the Wabash region at Vincennes in September 1792. On 1 October 1796, Washington named Putnam surveyor-general of the United States, a job that he performed earnestly but somewhat incompetently.

Putnam was a delegate to the Ohio constitutional convention in 1802. Not an enthusiastic supporter of statehood, he preferred that the territorial government continue to direct the development of the region. As his career was based on patronage, Putnam did not adjust well to the democraticization of politics and society in Ohio. He and his allies lost political power in Marietta, and in 1803 President Thomas Jefferson replaced him as surveyor-general. Putnam was left bereft of the influence over federal patronage and policy that had been the chief source of his power.

Accepting political defeat, Putnam devoted more time to his family, wrote his memoirs, and became a devout Congregationalist. He helped found Ohio University in Athens in 1804 and remained active in organizations designed to develop Marietta and improve the character of its citizens. He died in Marietta, having capitalized on modest talents and considerable determination to reach the position of regional patriarch.

• Most of Putnam's papers are in the Dawes Memorial Library, Marietta College. The basic published source is Rowena Buell, ed., *The Memoirs of Rufus Putnam* (1903). An interesting sketch of his life is in Samuel Prescott Hildreth, *Biographical and Historical Memoirs of the Early Pioneer Settlers of Ohio* (1852). See also Ephraim Cutler Dawes, ed., *Journal of General Rufus Putnam Kept . . . 1757–1760* (1886); Archer Butler Hulbert, ed., *The Records of the Original Proceedings of the Ohio Company* (1917); and Hulbert, ed., *Ohio in the Time of the Confederation* (1918). Relevant secondary works are Fred Anderson, *A People's Army: Massachusetts Soldiers and Society in the Seven Years' War* (1984), and Andrew R. L. Cayton, *The Frontier Republic: Ideology and Politics in the Ohio Country, 1780–1825* (1986).

ANDREW CAYTON

PUTNAM, William LeBaron (26 May 1835–5 Feb. 1918), lawyer and judge, was born in Bath, Maine, the son of Israel Putnam, a physician and politician, and Sarah Emery Frost. After graduating from Bowdoin College in 1855, Putnam studied law in the office of Bronson & Sewall in Bath. At the same time, he edited the *Bath Daily Times* and served briefly as assistant clerk of the Maine House of Representatives during the administration of Democratic governor Samuel Wells. Upon his admission to the bar in 1858, Putnam moved to Portland and formed a partnership with George Evans (1797–1867), an older lawyer who had served in the state legislature and both houses of Congress and was well connected in the Maine business world. Putnam married Octavia B. Robinson of Augusta, Maine, in 1862. The couple had no children.

Evans's influence and Putnam's own intelligence, industriousness, and attention to detail produced for Putnam a large and important clientele. After Evans's death in 1867, Putnam practiced alone until his appointment to the federal bench in 1892. Putnam became one of Maine's leading authorities on business and corporation law. He often represented railroads and was president of the Rumsford & Buckfield Railroad from 1884 until 1892. Putnam also maintained an active interest in politics. A conservative Democrat with a reputation for integrity, he served as mayor of Portland in 1869 and ran unsuccessfully for governor in 1888. At the time of his nomination for the latter office, the *New York Times*, noting his advocacy of tariff and civil service reform, lauded Putnam as "the exponent of all that is best and wisest in the policy of the present Administration" and a "leader of the best tendency of the Democratic Party."

Putnam held a conservative and somewhat elitist view of the legal profession. An organizer of the state bar association and chairman of its committee on law reform, he lamented the prevalence in the United States of the notion that everyone was capable of practicing law. He favored a broad, liberal arts education for aspiring lawyers but thought that the best legal training came through traditional law office apprenticeships rather than law schools. Putnam expected the leaders of the bar to maintain the profession's sense of duty and honor. He doubted the efficacy of legislative attempts to reform the legal system. Long-lasting and beneficial change, he believed, could only be achieved slowly and under the leadership of lawyers devoted, as he was, to established traditions and institutions.

Although Putnam was known in Washington through his appearances before the Supreme Court, he gained national prominence by representing the owners of a Maine fishing vessel seized by the Canadian government in a dispute over the rights of Americans fishing in Canadian waters. The North Atlantic fisheries feud was one of several serious diplomatic controversies involving the United States on one side and Canada and Great Britain on the other. Another stemmed from the seizure of Canadian vessels by American revenue cutters in an effort to prevent pelagic seal hunting by Canadians in the Bering Sea.

In 1887, Secretary of State Thomas F. Bayard, impressed by Putnam's handling of the Maine case, appointed him to a commission to negotiate an Atlantic fisheries agreement. The Senate rejected the resulting treaty; its unpopularity among American fishermen contributed to Putnam's defeat in Maine's 1888 gubernatorial election. In 1896–1897 Putnam served on the Bering Sea Claims Commission that determined the award granted to Canada and Great Britain in the seal-hunting conflict.

As a well-known and highly regarded Democratic lawyer and supporter of President Grover Cleveland, Putnam was mentioned by some as a possible successor to United States Chief Justice Morrison R. Waite after his death in 1888. (Putnam previously had declined offers to become chief justice of Maine.) In 1892 Republican President Benjamin Harrison named Putnam to the newly created First Circuit Court of Appeals. An admirer of English legal principles and practice, Putnam often wrote opinions with an eye to English precedents. A practical man, Putnam wrote without elegance and showed little inclination to innovate or theorize. His strengths as a judge were legal acumen, acquired through long and systematic study, and a sometimes brusque willingness to cut through the technicalities of a case to get at the larger issues.

Of his more than 700 judicial opinions, Putnam took the greatest pride in *Reece Button-Hole Machine Company v. Globe Button-Hole Machine Company* (1894), one of many patent-infringement cases to come before his court. Reece had patented an industrial sewing machine with a movable frame and fixed plate; the defendant employed a machine with a movable plate and fixed frame. Putnam found for Reece; he would not allow a "literal construction of specifications" to destroy "the entire value of this most important, useful, and hitherto profitable invention." The opinion became an important authority on the doctrine of equivalents, which protects patentees from competitors whose inventions differ only in nonessential features.

Putnam's dedication to work and his insistence on dignity and decorum in the courtroom gave him an air of aloofness and sometimes severity, but he was kindly and charitable. He was especially devoted to Bowdoin College, which he served for many years as an overse-

er, trustee, and finance committee chairman. He resigned from the bench in 1917 and died in Portland the following year.

• The Maine Historical Society and the Bowdoin College Library have small collections of Putnam's correspondence. His judicial opinions may be found in vol. 50 through 238 of the *Federal Reports*. Putnam published "Unfair Competition by the Deceptive Use of One's Own Name" in the *Harvard Law Review* 12 (1898): 243–61; addresses on legal and diplomatic matters that he delivered on various occasions were printed for limited circulation. There are no major studies of Putnam, but information on his life and career can be found in *In Memory of the Honorable William LeBaron Putnam: Proceedings of the Cumberland Bar, Maine and of the United States Circuit Court of Appeals for the First Circuit* (1919) and in Parker McCobb Reed, *History of Bath and Environs* (1894).

DAVID M. GOLD

PYLE, Charles C. (25 Mar. 1882–3 Feb. 1939), sports promoter and agent, was born in Van Wert, Ohio, the son of William Pile, a farmer and Methodist minister, and Sidney McMillan. Charles grew up in Delaware, Ohio, where he was active competitively as an amateur bicycle racer, boxer, and basketball player. In 1896 Pyle promoted and staged a bicycle race between Barney Oldfield, a professional rider, and a local young man from Delaware, Ohio, his first of many money-making promotions. He attended Ohio State University for a year in 1897–1898 before beginning an itinerant life of business and entertainment promotion. For a time after his year at Ohio State Pyle traveled by rail in the Far West, attempting unsuccessfully to sell Western Union time-service clocks on commission. From 1902 to 1907 Pyle worked with traveling drama companies as an advance man, publicity agent, business manager, and occasional actor. He later organized his own traveling company and toured the Pacific Coast performing popular melodramas and pseudo-historical plays with himself as the leading man.

In 1908 Pyle bought a film projector and silent films and traveled as an exhibitor in Idaho and Montana. After going bankrupt, Pyle was involved in building a movie palace in Boise and then an amusement park and resident vaudeville theater and troupe. Selling out his interests profitably in each venture, Pyle went to Chicago in 1910. There he settled down, married, and acquired a chain of six movie houses in central Illinois during the next sixteen years.

Pyle's career as a big-time sports promoter began when he saw the opportunity for marketing and showcasing the greatest collegiate football player of the 1920s. In 1925, in the office of one of his two movie theaters in Champaign, Illinois, Pyle approached the University of Illinois All-American football star Harold "Red" Grange and asked him if he would like to make $100,000. On a handshake agreement, Pyle became Grange's exclusive manager and press agent, arranging for him to sign a contract with the Chicago Bears and play professional football after his undergraduate football playing days were concluded. Pyle arranged a tour that took the Bears from Chicago to sixteen cities in the East, South, and Far West. From Thanksgiving Day 1925 through 31 January 1926 they played 18 games in 66 days against National Football League teams and all-star teams. This highly successful barnstorming tour stirred public interest in professional football and made over $100,000 each for Pyle and Grange. Under the terms of the contract Grange received 50 percent of all gate receipts with Pyle getting 40 percent of Grange's earnings. Before Grange's successful tour professional football attracted little publicity or following and was financially unprofitable as well as unstable.

In 1926 Pyle negotiated a film contract for Grange with Joseph P. Kennedy's studio, but the arrangement produced only two films and a serial, none of which were successful. Pyle also arranged for Grange's endorsement of a variety of commercial products and managed all of Grange's personal appearances. After Pyle failed in his effort to negotiate for himself and Grange a one-third ownership of the Chicago Bears franchise, in February 1926 Pyle challenged the National Football League by organizing and holding controlling interest in the American Professional Football League. The league operated with nine teams in the 1926 season, with Red Grange as the star attraction of the New York Yankees franchise. Plagued by financial instability and bad weather, the league lasted only one season. Pyle negotiated further with the owners and officials of the National Football League, and the New York Yankees were accepted into the league as a traveling team for the 1927 season. However, Grange's serious knee injury in the third game of the season dampened fan interest in the team. After the 1927 season the Pyle-Grange franchise was dropped from the National Football League. According to Grange's 1953 autobiography, in the period from November 1925 through 1927 Pyle and Grange attracted an estimated $1 million in professional football revenues. Each of them earned over $250,000, as well as additional income from product endorsements, program sales, and other promotions. In May 1928 Grange decided not to renew the three-year contract he had signed with Pyle, whom Grange in his autobiography called "perhaps the greatest sports impresario the world has ever known."

Pyle organized a professional tennis tour that opened at Madison Square Garden on 9 October 1926 and after stops in forty American and Canadian cities concluded on 14 February 1927. As the star performer and attraction of the tour Pyle signed French tennis star Suzanne Lenglen, winner of six Wimbledon titles. Pyle signed Mary K. Browne, an American tennis star, to play Lenglen in the tour matches. Four male players filled out the tour roster. By 16 February 1927, when Pyle announced he was withdrawing from the promotion of professional tennis, he had made over $100,000 personally from the tour, paid Lenglen $100,000, and paid close to $100,000 to the other five players. The tour ended mainly because of problems Pyle encountered in handling the temperamental Lenglen and the discontent of the secondary performers,

who were underpaid and sometimes unpaid. Pyle also innovatively marketed a Lenglen tennis racket, perfume, dolls, and fashion clothing. He perceptively saw that fans would not only pay to see stars on tour but would buy objects or products connected to or endorsed by the star athlete.

Pyle's risky but financially successful ventures as a sports promoter caused Irving Vaughan, sportswriter for the *Chicago Daily Tribune*, to give him the nickname of "Cash-and-Carry." Pyle knew how to stir up local interest through publicity and how to produce box office profits. He then moved quickly on to another location with profits in hand. However, the Pyle magic touch and method faltered in 1928 when he staged a transcontinental marathon run from Los Angeles to New York City. Pyle planned to make money by collecting entry and lodging fees from the contestants, assessing an advertising fee on the cities and towns through which the run passed, and by selling programs and advertising for the events as well as tickets to a circus side show accompanying the caravan. However, the traveling show and competition failed to capture the public's interest even though Red Grange served as the event's master of ceremonies from Los Angeles through its stop in Chicago. Pyle lost over $150,000 in this cross-country "bunion derby" as it came to be called. However, that did not deter him from staging another in 1929 from New York to Los Angeles. These two failures resulted in a number of lawsuits against Pyle, who moved to Los Angeles in 1930.

After the failures of the cross-country marathons and with the diminished promotional opportunities of the Great Depression, Pyle became president of the Radio Transcription Corporation of America. However, he never completely retired from the promotion business. During the 1933–1934 Century of Progress Exposition in Chicago, Pyle operated a "Believe It or Not" sideshow of freaks and human curiosities, which he subsequently took on tour to other cities. He also managed sports shows at fairs in Chicago, Cleveland, and Dallas. With the financial success from these ventures Pyle was able to pay off his many creditors and settle the lawsuits. In 1936 Effie R. Pyle divorced Charles, and he married Elvia Allman, a radio comedienne, in 1937. He died suddenly of cerebral thrombosis in Los Angeles.

C. C. Pyle was the most successful and notorious promoter of sports during its "Golden Age" of the 1920s. He created a successful promotional team that included his own front and advance men, William Hickman Pickens and Ira D. Pyle, Charles's older brother. Pyle understood how to promote sports stars as popular personalities, fed the public appetite for gossip and news by carefully managed press releases, staged big events and tours that generated publicity and attendance, and used the lure of quick money to persuade amateurs like Grange and Lenglen to turn professional. Many reviled Pyle for corrupting amateur sports with money. They saw him as a fast-talking, dishonest con artist who cared little about the sport he exploited. Grange, however, regarded Pyle as an honest man, a trusted friend, and a promotional genius. Lenglen, though she made substantial money in her professional tennis tour in America, later regretted her association with Pyle and her decision to turn professional in 1926. Pyle's exploits as a big-time sports promoter revealed the possibilities of football and tennis as major professional sports. His association with these sports was relatively brief, and he did not become a permanent part of the professional sports establishment. However, he certainly was an agent of change, as sports became more commercialized, more popular, and more lucrative in the 1920s.

• No collection of Charles C. Pyle's papers exists. Information on Pyle has to be gleaned from sources such as Red Grange and Ira Morton, *The Red Grange Story: An Autobiography* (1953), and George Halas, *Halas by Halas* (1979). Information on the Grange-Pyle relationship can be found in John Underwood, "Was He the Greatest of All Time?" *Sports Illustrated*, 4 Sept. 1985, pp. 115–35. Information on Pyle's 1926 professional tennis tour can be found in Larry Engelmann, *The Goddess and the American Girl: The Story of Suzanne Lenglen and Helen Wills* (1988), and Pyle's cross-country marathon derbies in 1928 and 1929 are covered in "Bunion Derby" *Sports Illustrated*, 2 May 1955, pp. 58–59, and in George Gipe, *The Great American Sports Book* (1978), pp. 274–76. An article on Pyle's contribution to the elevation of professional sports salaries appears in Prescott Sullivan, "Cash and Carry Colorful Figure," *San Francisco Examiner*, 5 Feb. 1939. Alva Johnston, "Cash and Carry," *New Yorker*, 8 Dec. 1928, pp. 31–34 is essential. The most informative obituary is in the *Chicago Daily Tribune*, 4 Feb. 1939.

DOUGLAS A. NOVERR

PYLE, Ernie (3 Aug. 1900–18 Apr. 1945), newspaper reporter, was born Ernest Taylor Pyle near Dana, Indiana, the son of Will Pyle and Maria Taylor, farmers. Pyle graduated from high school and then studied journalism at Indiana University. He quit just short of obtaining his degree to become a reporter for the *La Porte Herald* in La Porte, Indiana, in 1923. After a few months, he was hired as a copy editor for the *Washington Daily News*, owned by the Scripps-Howard newspaper chain.

In 1925 Pyle married Geraldine "Jerry" Siebolds, a civil service worker with a bohemian lifestyle to match his own; they had no children. They quit their jobs the next year and took a 9,000-mile summer drive around the country, ending in New York City, where Pyle worked at the copy desk for the *Evening World* and then the *Evening Post*. He returned to his Washington paper as telegraph editor, started the first daily aviation column in the United States, and became aviation editor for the Scripps-Howard chain. He was named managing editor of the *Daily News* in 1932. Three years later he happily gave up his desk job to become a roving reporter for Scripps-Howard. He crisscrossed the United States, went to Alaska and Hawaii, toured Central and South America, and filed six syndicated columns a week.

The public enthusiastically received his generally lighthearted columns, which included human interest pieces, descriptions of scenery, escapist humor, and self-deprecating anecdotes as well as a few poignant accounts of the downtrodden. His work ultimately appeared in nearly 200 newspapers. His wife, Jerry, who sometimes stayed behind, unfortunately began to treat severe depression with alcohol, sedatives, and amphetamines.

Then came World War II. Leaving Jerry in Albuquerque, Pyle, though in poor health from the effects of influenza, too many cigarettes, chronic head colds, and perhaps incipient anemia, went to England in December 1940 to report on what the German bombardment of London and elsewhere was doing to ordinary citizens. His columns soon began to run in *Stars and Stripes*, the daily U.S. newspaper for service personnel. He returned home in March 1941 and helped his wife recover from an attempt at suicide. He sought treatment for impotence, obtained a divorce in April 1942, had Jerry placed in a Colorado sanatorium briefly, and returned to England. He filed brilliant dispatches on the bulldog courage of the British, on the boredom and dreams of ordinary American GIs training in England and Ireland for the invasion, and on their humorous bouts of culture shock. He shipped to North Africa that fall and reported from the vast front there until the summer of 1943. For the first time he covered sickening carnage and discussed the amorality of wartime killing. He admired combat pilots but positively revered long-suffering infantrymen; they were cold, dirty, apprehensive, lonely, understanding, funny—and routinely brave.

The year 1943 was memorable for Pyle. By proxy on 10 March he remarried Jerry, who was by then clerking for the Air Force in Albuquerque; he also published *Here Is Your War: The Story of G.I. Joe*, written from what he called his "worm's-eye view." After advancing with the troops into Sicily, he returned home to make publicity appearances. He was reunited with his wife but soon had to hospitalize her again. At the end of the year, he compulsively plunged back into war—on the Italian front. He received a Pulitzer Prize for his 1943 reporting. Here is a representative example of Pyle's low-key but gripping prose:

The commanding officer told us to find good places among the rocks . . . and dig in. . . . He didn't have to do any urging. Machine guns were crashing a few hundred yards off. . . . Now and then a bullet would ricochet down among us. We talked only in low voices. The white rocks were like ghosts and gave the illusion of moving. . . . At dawn the artillery . . . increased to a frenzy that seemed to consume the sky (*Ernie's War*, p. 118).

Pyle went to England in the spring of 1944 and landed in Normandy one day after D day. He accompanied French troops into Paris and soon returned home to public adulation. His wife again attempted suicide. She was hospitalized and given shock treatments. Pyle headed for the Pacific theater of operations at the beginning of 1945, eventually getting to Okinawa with U.S. marines. While covering the Okinawa and Iwo

Jima invasions, Pyle was on Ie Shima, a nearby island, when a bullet from a Japanese sniper pierced his left temple, killing him instantly.

In addition to Pyle's war reports comprising *Here Is Your War*, other dispatches had been collected and published as *Ernie Pyle in England* (1941) and *Brave Men* (1944). His *G.I. Joe*, a 1944 overseas-edition compilation, was remarkably popular with troops. The Scripps-Howard *Indianapolis Times* auctioned Pyle's last manuscript and paid into the war-bond drive the incredible winning bid of $10,525,000 (25 June 1945). The movie *The Story of G.I. Joe* premiered in Washington, D.C., on 4 July 1945, starring Burgess Meredith as Pyle and Robert Mitchum as Captain Bill Walker, an infantry officer based on Captain Henry T. Waskow, whose death in combat in Italy Pyle had reported. Seven months after Pyle's death, Jerry suffered kidney failure and died of uremic poisoning.

Ordinary soldiers, in addition to a reading public estimated to number 13 million at the peak of his success, revered Pyle because of his humor, sensitivity, warmth, sense of camaraderie, and eagerness to share their mud-and-blood dangers. His unique style combines detail and terseness, objective evaluation, humor, and poignancy. Many World War II correspondents concentrated on politics, the "big picture," and strategies and tactics. Others analyzed postwar implications of wartime decisions. Still others clung to high and mighty persons and sketched their personalities. Among Pyle's near-peers, Ernest Hemingway, Edward R. Murrow, and William L. Shirer may be named. Pyle almost exclusively sought to interpret the ordinary enlisted man's thoughts and behavior.

• The Weil Journalism Library and the Lilly Library, both of Indiana University, Bloomington, contain much material by and relating to Pyle. *Last Chapter*, a final collection of Pyle's war dispatches, appeared posthumously (1946). Later publications capitalizing on his status as a national hero include a book of pictures, *An Ernie Pyle Album: Indiana to Ie Shima*, with text by Lee G. Miller (1946); *Home Country* (1947), a compilation from *Here Is Your War* and *Brave Men*; *Ernie's War: The Best of Ernie Pyle's World War II Dispatches*, ed. David Nichols (1986); and *Ernie's America: The Best of Ernie Pyle's 1930s Travel Dispatches*, ed. Nichols (1989). Lee G. Miller, who was Pyle's friend, longtime editor, and informal business agent, wrote the standard biography, *The Story of Ernie Pyle* (1950). Paul Lancaster, "Ernie Pyle: Chronicler of 'The Men Who Do the Dying,'" *American Heritage* 32 (Feb.–Mar. 1981): 30–41, is a splendid essay. Frederick S. Voss, *Reporting the War: The Journalistic Coverage of World War II* (1994), places Pyle among his fellow journalists and incidentally pairs him with Bill Mauldin because of their common worm's-eye view. Useful comments about the movie *The Story of G.I. Joe* are contained in Jerry Roberts, *Robert Mitchum: A Bio-Biography* (1992), and Burgess Meredith, *So Far, So Good: A Memoir* (1993). An extensive front-page obituary, "Ernie Pyle Is Killed on Ie Island; Foe Fired When All Seemed Safe," is in the *New York Times*, 19 Apr. 1945.

ROBERT L. GALE

PYLE, Howard (5 Mar. 1853–9 Nov. 1911), artist, writer, and teacher, was born in Wilmington, Delaware, the son of William Pyle, a leather manufacturer, and Margaret Churchman, an amateur writer. His Quaker ancestors came from England in the eighteenth century. Nurtured by his mother's love of books, as a child Pyle read German folk tales, Robin Hood and King Arthur legends, and novels by Charles Dickens and William Makepeace Thackeray. He perused drawings in the illustrated periodicals *Punch* and *Illustrated London News*. In 1869 Pyle began his study at Adolph van der Wielen's art school in Philadelphia, where he received an academic training.

In the fall of 1876 Pyle moved to New York City to pursue a career as a writer and illustrator for the thriving periodicals trade. He submitted fairy tales to *St. Nicholas*, a children's magazine, and drawings to various Scribner's and Harper's publications. He enrolled in life drawing, sketch, and composition classes at the Art Students' League. Among his friends were Harper's staff artists Charles Stanley Reinhart, Edwin Austin Abbey, and Arthur Burdett Frost.

In 1879, after arranging for Harper's to send him articles to illustrate, Pyle returned to Wilmington and established a studio to work as a freelance artist and writer. In 1881 he married Anne Poole, the daughter of a manufacturer of milling machinery, in a Quaker ceremony with Frost serving as best man. The Pyles had seven children.

During his 35-year career Pyle became one of America's most prominent illustrators, completing more than 3,000 illustrations for books and magazines, as well as twenty books and numerous articles. He launched his career as a children's book illustrator in 1883 with the publication of *Robin Hood*; he retold the legend and embellished the pages with his pictures, hand-lettered captions, and decorative borders. The design set a new standard in American book production, and William Morris, leader of the English arts and crafts movement, was among its admirers. Other children's books followed: *Pepper and Salt* (1886), *The Wonder Clock* (1888), *Otto of the Silver Hand* (1888), *The Garden behind the Moon* (1895), and *Twilight Land* (1895).

In 1903 Scribner's published Pyle's *The Story of King Arthur and His Knights* (1903), first serialized in the children's magazine *St. Nicholas*. Because of the popularity of this book, Pyle produced three additional volumes: *Champions of the Round Table* (1905), *Sir Launcelot and His Companions* (1907), and *The Grail and the Passing of Arthur* (1910). In *A History of American Art* (1901), art critic Sadakichi Hartmann referred to Pyle as "one of the few great masters of linear composition of the day" (p. 102).

Pyle did not limit his production to children's publications but also submitted work to magazines for adult readers. He specialized in painting America's past for books such as Henry Cabot Lodge's *The Story of the Revolution* (1898) and two works by Woodrow Wilson—*George Washington* (1897) and *A History of the American People* (1902). "Colonial life appeals so strongly to me," Pyle reported to his students, "that to come across things that have been handed down from that time fills me with a feeling akin to homesickness" (*Howard Pyle* [1973], p. 19).

Pyle created riveting illustrations about pirates, chivalry, adventure and intrigue, and mysticism. The pirate theme attracted him early in articles such as "Buccaneers and Marooners of the Spanish Main" (*Harper's Monthly*, 1887) and culminated in a large painting, *Marooned* (1909, Delaware Art Museum), done near the end of his career. Pyle illustrated books by Robert Louis Stevenson, James Branch Cabell, Oliver Wendell Holmes, S. Weir Mitchell, and William Dean Howells (with whom he corresponded about Swedenborgian theology). Pyle also illustrated his own writings; for example, an allegorical tale, "Travels of the Soul" (1902), and a historical piece, "The Fate of a Treasure Town" (1905), both for *Harper's Monthly*.

In addition to having his illustrations published in leading periodicals of the time, Pyle exhibited his work in major exhibitions—the World's Columbian Exposition (1893) in Chicago, the Society of Arts and Crafts (1899) in Boston, the Exposition Universelle (1900) in Paris, the Pan-American Exposition (1901) in Buffalo, and the Universal Exposition (1904) in St. Louis. He had one-person shows in Philadelphia and Boston (1897); in an Art Institute of Chicago exhibition (1903) that traveled to museums in Toledo, Cincinnati, Detroit, and Indianapolis; and at the Macbeth Gallery (1908) in New York. He was a member of the Grolier Club, the Players Club, and the Salmagundi Club in New York, the Bibliophile Society in Boston, and the Franklin Inn Club in Philadelphia.

Pyle taught illustration at Drexel Institute of Art, Science, and Technology in Philadelphia from 1894 until 1900, when he opened a small private art school in Wilmington. He held summer classes in a grist mill converted into a studio at Chadds Ford, Pennsylvania, from 1898 to 1899 and from 1901 to 1903. On occasion he lectured at the Art Students' League in New York and at the Art Institute of Chicago. Young professional illustrators from Philadelphia and New York frequently attended his Saturday afternoon lecture at his Wilmington studio. Pyle was generous with his time and eager to help students and other illustrators alike. He taught more than 100 students at Drexel and in Wilmington; among them were N. C. Wyeth, Jessie Willcox Smith, Frank Schoonover, Violet Oakley, Elizabeth Shippen Green, and Harvey Dunn. Through his contacts with New York publishing companies, he secured commissions for his students that helped establish their careers. In 1906 Pyle served briefly as art director of *McClure's Magazine*.

In 1905 Pyle turned to mural painting, which was enjoying a renaissance in the United States. The architect Cass Gilbert commissioned two historical subjects from Pyle—*The Battle of Nashville* (1906) for the Minnesota State Capitol (St. Paul) and *The Landing of Carteret* (1907) for the Essex County Court House (Newark, N.J.). In 1910 he completed several murals on the Dutch and English settlements on Manhattan Island for the Hudson County Court House (Jersey City, N.J.).

Though eager for more mural commissions, Pyle recognized his shortcomings as a mural painter and decided to make his first trip to Europe to study the old masters firsthand. With his family he sailed to Italy in November 1910, and he died there from Bright's Disease the next year.

During his lifetime, Pyle raised American book and magazine illustration to new heights and developed new audiences for illustrative art. As a teacher he inspired a generation of illustrators who in turn passed on the Pyle tradition to their students. Pyle's short stories entertained magazine readers of his day, and his children's books were popular. Following his death, Pyle's friends and students founded the Wilmington Society of the Fine Arts (now called the Delaware Art Museum) to purchase a collection of his paintings and drawings.

• Pyle's papers are at the Delaware Art Museum and the Historical Society of Delaware, Wilmington, Del.; the Free Library of Philadelphia; the J. Pierpont Morgan Library, New York City; and the libraries of Harvard University, Princeton University, and the University of Virginia. A valuable biography, Charles D. Abbott, *Howard Pyle: A Chronicle* (1925), quotes at length from Pyle correspondence that is now lost. See also Henry C. Pitz, *Howard Pyle, Writer, Illustrator, Founder of the Brandywine School* (1975), on his career as illustrator and teacher; Willard S. Morse and Gertrude Brincklé, *Howard Pyle: A Record of His Illustrations and Writings* (1921), for a bibliography of his published work; and Elizabeth H. Hawkes, "Drawn in Ink: Book Illustrations by Howard Pyle," *The American Illustrated Book in the Nineteenth Century* (1987), for a study of his book illustrations. The Delaware Art Museum has published exhibition catalogs: *Howard Pyle: Diversity in Depth* (1973), *Artists in Wilmington* (1980), and *Howard Pyle: The Artist and His Legacy* (1987).

ELIZABETH H. HAWKES

PYNCHON, John (c. 1626–17 Jan. 1703), entrepreneur and politician, was born in Springfield, Essex, England, to William Pynchon and Anna Andrew. He sailed with his parents in 1630 to Massachusetts, living with them first in Dorchester and then Roxbury, near Boston. In 1636 the family moved to the Connecticut River, where William Pynchon founded the town of Springfield, which he governed and used to dominate New England's fur trade. In 1645 John Pynchon married Amy Wyllys, daughter of George Wyllys of Hartford, Connecticut. His future trading partners, Samuel Wyllys and John Allyn, were his wife's cousins. The Pynchons had five children, three of whom survived infancy.

Springfield considered joining the government of the three river towns of Connecticut but eventually stayed within Massachusetts's jurisdiction after William Pynchon had a falling out with some of Connecticut's magistrates in the early 1640s. In 1652 he also quarreled with the Massachusetts establishment and abruptly left the colony following the publication of a religious tract, "The Meritorious Price of Our Redemption," which brought the wrath of the colony's orthodox ministry on him. John Pynchon was left at age twenty-six in control of the family businesses, which included managing a near monopoly of the New England fur trade, a variety of mills, and farming or renting a good deal of land in western Massachusetts. Pynchon built on his father's considerable accomplishments. In partnership with William Hathorne of Boston, he established a branch office in Albany, New York, to compete with New York for the trade of the Hudson and Mohawk valleys. He invested his profits from the fur trade in land and saw and grist mills in the new towns of Brookfield and Deerfield, Massachusetts, and Groton, Connecticut. Every town established in western Massachusetts for the half century before Pynchon's death, including Northampton (1653) and Hadley (1659), was laid out and its land initially distributed at Pynchon's direction.

As the fur trade began to deplete the available game in western New England and central New York, Pynchon diversified his operations. He raised sheep, cattle, and hogs, trading these and grain for West India sugar and rum. By the early 1680s he owned the "Cabbage Tree Plantation" on the island of Antigua, plus the ships he had built in Boston to trade there and elsewhere. At the height of his success, in the early 1680s, Pynchon's estate of more than 8,000 in Springfield alone amounted to one-third of the town's assessed wealth. His economic power was unrivaled in New England. More than 40 people worked for him full time, and he rented land to 140 others. The Pynchon-dominated company town of Springfield differed greatly from the typical New England farming community with its dispersed wealth and landholdings.

Political power accompanied Pynchon's economic might. Chosen Springfield selectman in 1650 at the age of twenty-four, he became town clerk in 1652, magistrate in 1653, deputy to the General Court in 1662, and assistant or councillor for most of the last forty years of his life. He was appointed sergeant major for western Massachusetts in 1669 and directed its defenses most of the time until 1695. Aside from building what was later known as the "Old Fort" in 1662, this duty was not particularly onerous until the region's heretofore pacified Indians joined in King Philip's War in 1675. That October Pynchon and forty-five militia were at the town of Hadley, about twenty miles from Springfield, when a surprise attack destroyed all but thirteen houses in the town. Warned by a friendly Indian, Toto, Pynchon hastened back to Springfield and relieved the inhabitants who were crowded into the Old Fort; only four were killed. Although Springfield and Pynchon's economic empire was quickly rebuilt following the war's successful conclusion, the town's destruction demonstrated the folly of sending out militia in the hopes of engaging the native people while leaving towns undefended.

The next challenge to Pynchon's dominance came in the mid-1680s. Unlike most of the leaders in eastern Massachusetts, Pynchon cooperated wholeheartedly with the Dominion of New England established in 1685. He had met Governor Sir Edmund Andros at Albany in 1680, when he had successfully negotiated a truce between the Mohawks and Massachusetts, and was continued on the council. However, when the dominion was overthrown in 1689 and war declared against the French and the Indians, the Connecticut Valley militia refused to follow Pynchon's lead. Headed by a Sergeant King of Northampton, who did "not give three skips of a louse" for Colonel Pynchon's authority, the valley's inhabitants insisted on choosing their own officers. And although the newly constituted government relied on his services in mediating with Indians with whom he had long worked, the General Court repeatedly rebuffed Pynchon's pleas that Massachusetts reimburse his expenses, finally awarding him the insulting sum of £10 in 1697 to shut him up.

Although Pynchon left an estate of more than £8,000 when he died in Springfield, his political influence was severely eroded. His surviving son inherited none of the prestige Pynchon's father had passed on to him fifty years previously.

• *The Pynchon Papers*, ed. Carl Bridenbaugh, have been published by the Colonial Society of Massachusetts (2 vols., 1982, 1985). Stephen Innes, *Labor in a New Land: Economy and Society in Seventeenth-Century Springfield* (1983), deals mostly with Pynchon's career. For Indian relations, see Richard J. Pinkos, "A Lamentable and Woeful Sight: The Indian Attack on Springfield," *Historical Journal of Western Massachusetts* 4 (1975): 1–11; for Pynchon as judge, see Joseph H. Smith, ed., *Colonial Justice in Western Massachusetts: The Pynchon Court Record* (1961).

WILLIAM PENCAK

PYNCHON, William (26 Dec. 1590–29 Oct. 1662), fur trader, magistrate, and founder of Springfield, Massachusetts, was born at Springfield, in Essex, England, the son of John Pynchon and Frances Brett, wealthy gentry. William was educated to read and write Latin, Greek, and Hebrew and served as a warden of Christ Church from 1620 to 1624. Like many members of his class, he supported the Puritans. In 1629 Pynchon invested £25 in the Massachusetts Bay Company and the following year accompanied Governor John Winthrop on the great colonizing expedition. His wife, Anna Andrew, whom he had married in 1624, died shortly after their arrival in Massachusetts. The Pynchons had four children. Pynchon remarried, to the widow Frances Sanford (date unknown).

Pynchon moved immediately into the highest circles of Massachusetts government. He served as an assistant (councillor and magistrate) of the colony from 1630 to 1636 and as treasurer from 1632 to 1634. His principal activity, however, was directing the colony's fur trade, which was operated by a consortium including Governor John Winthrop. At first he made his headquarters in Roxbury, a town bordering on Boston, but then decided to move the business nearer to the source of the pelts. On 3 March 1636 he received permission from the General Court to settle on the "Great," or Connecticut, River. Four months later, he purchased a piece of land five miles long and a mile wide for eighteen of each of the following: pieces of clothing, hoes, hatchets, knives, and fathoms of wampum. The land was on the east side of the river, "the best ground [being so] incumbered with Indians . . . that [I] am compelled to plant on the opposite side to avoid trespassing of them."

Pynchon enjoyed friendly relations with the Agawams from whom he bought his land, although he changed the name of the town from Agawam to Springfield. He kept the Indians' good will for several reasons. First, the Agawams had in 1631 requested help from Massachusetts to resist incursions by the more powerful Mohawks. Second, Pynchon insisted that the Indians "must be esteemed as an independent and free people" until they voluntarily submitted to Massachusetts authority and sold their land. Finally, in cases he judged as magistrate involving disputes between Indians and whites, Pynchon dispensed justice without regard to race. Peace with the Native Americans was maintained in the Massachusetts portion of the Connecticut Valley until King Philip's War in 1675.

Pynchon had far more trouble with the downriver colony of Connecticut and its leader, the Reverend Thomas Hooker. Easily accessible to Hartford by the river and separated from eastern Massachusetts by more than a hundred miles of wilderness, Springfield was originally intended to be part of Connecticut. But at a time of famine in 1638, Pynchon was either unwilling or unable to buy corn requested by the Connecticut government from the Nonotuck Indians; he protested that the price was too high and was waiting for a better deal. Connecticut, however, fined him forty bushels of corn, and Hooker thought with some reason that Pynchon wanted "all the trade to himself, and have all the corn in his own hands . . . and so rack the country at his pleasure." Yet in these early years of settlement, Pynchon's reach exceeded his grasp at times, his own "wants were often so great, that diverse times he had not himself half a bushel of corn in his house for his family."

Pynchon as a result began negotiating with Massachusetts Bay to return Springfield and its environs to its mother colony, a transfer accomplished in June 1641. For this service, Pynchon received "full power and authority to govern the inhabitants at Springfield." For the next several decades he and his son, John Pynchon, ruled what in effect was America's first company town. Pynchon, his son, and two of his sons-in-law, Elizur Holyoke and Henry Smith, among them owned a quarter of Springfield's two thousand acres; sixty-seven acres was the next largest lot. Pynchon presided over the court and the town meeting and outdistanced his nearest competitor in the fur trade by ten to one. To him the settlers owed their lands, supplies, and livelihood through employment in the commerce in deer and beaver pelts. Pynchon's rule seems to have been beyond challenge, for dissent only broke out well into the regime of his son and successor.

Yet surprisingly, and suddenly, in 1651 Pynchon left the community he had founded and guided. The previous year, he had published a religious tract, "The Meritorious Price of Our Redemption," which the Massachusetts General Court branded as heretical: "We utterly dislike it and detest it as erroneous and dangerous." It was burned in the marketplace of Boston, and after consulting with Boston's clergy, Pynchon was made to recant: "It hath pleased God to let me see that I have not spoken in my book so fully of the prize and merit of Christ's sufferings as I should have done, for in my book I call them but trials of his obedience . . . as the only meritorious price of man's redemption. But now at present I am inclined to think that His sufferings were appointed by God for a farther end, namely as the due punishment for our sins by way of satisfaction to divine justice for man's redemption." The worldly public servant and entrepreneur had created an opening, which the Puritan divines were quick to spot, for man's own efforts to aid in his salvation, although the harsh reception Pynchon's tract received may also have reflected Bostonian fears of his high-handed wielding of economic and political power.

Pynchon, however, chose not to continue the contest. He retired to England, at the time governed by a Puritan Parliament, to enjoy his wealth and continue writing theological tracts, in company with the Reverend George Moxon, Springfield's minister and a third son-in-law. Leaving the Connecticut Valley in the capable hands of his son, Pynchon lived quietly at Wraysbury, near Windsor, where he died.

Pynchon was British North America's first great entrepreneur. He established a virtual monopoly of New England's fur trade, with connections as far as New York, Canada, and Nova Scotia. Springfield was a company town dominated by one family rather than the communal enterprise typical of Puritan New England. Yet mammon was not enough for Pynchon. Paradoxically, it was his desire to edify men's souls, rather than his lucrative commerce, that undid him.

• Pynchon's letters are published in the Massachusetts Historical Society, *Proceedings* 48 (1915), and 58 (1925), and *Collections*, 2d ser., 8 (1819), and 4th ser., 6 (1863). The original records of Pynchon's court are at the Harvard Law Library; they have also been published: Joseph H. Smith, ed., *Colonial Justice in Western Massachusetts: The Pynchon Court Record* (1961). Ruth A. McIntyre, *William Pynchon: Merchant and Colonizer* (1961), is the only biography. See also Stephen Innes, *Labor in a New Land: Economy and Society in Seventeenth-Century Springfield* (1983); Samuel Eliot Morison, "William Pynchon," Massachusetts Historical Society, *Proceedings* 64 (1931): 67–107; Philip F. Gura, "The Contagion of Corrupt Opinions in Puritan Massachusetts: The Case of William Pynchon," *William and Mary Quarterly*, 3d ser., 39 (1982): 469–91; Richard J. Pinkos, "A Lamentable and Woeful Sight: The Indian Attack on Springfield," *Historical Journal of Western Massachusetts* 4 (1975): 1–11; and Stephen J. Cote, "The Real William Pynchon: Merchant and Politician," *Historical Journal of Western Massachusetts* 4 (1975): 12–20. A bibliography of Pynchon's writings appears in Joseph Sabin, *Bibliotheca Americana*, vol. 16 (1886), pp. 151–54.

WILLIAM PENCAK

Q

QUANAH. *See* Parker, Quanah.

QUANTRILL, William Clarke (31 July 1837–6 June 1865), pro-Confederate guerrilla leader, was born in Canal Dover (now Dover), Ohio, the son of Thomas H. Quantrill, a tinsmith and teacher, and Caroline Clarke. After acquiring a better-than-average education for the time and place, and following his father's death in 1854, Quantrill taught school in Canal Dover and various other towns in the Midwest before moving to Kansas in 1857. During the next three years he engaged in various occupations—farming, teamstering with an army expedition to Utah, gold prospecting in Colorado—before again teaching school, this time in Stanton, Kansas. In 1860 he moved to Lawrence, Kansas, where under the alias of Charley Hart he became a jayhawker (best defined as a bandit with professed abolitionist sympathies). In December 1860, facing arrest in Lawrence for his criminal activities, he betrayed a group of jayhawkers into an ambush at the farm of Morgan Walker in Jackson County, Missouri, thereby gaining the confidence of the people of that locality, to whom he represented himself as being a native of Maryland and proslavery. After the outbreak of the Civil War he served with Confederate forces in Missouri. Late in 1861 he returned to Jackson County, where he soon became the leader of a guerrilla band, which he led in a series of raids into Kansas and against pro-Union Missourians. Having helped regular Confederate forces capture Independence, Missouri (11 Aug. 1862), he received a captain's commission as a partisan ranger. By this time he was the most notorious of the many "bushwhackers" operating in western Missouri.

The climax of his career came on 21 August 1863 when he led more than 400 guerrillas in a raid on Lawrence, Kansas, that resulted in the destruction of the business district and the massacre of 150 men and boys. This was the most atrocious event of its kind during the Civil War, making Quantrill the most famous, and infamous, guerrilla chieftain of that conflict. On 6 October 1863 his band massacred nearly 100 Union troops at Baxter Springs, Kansas, while on its way to spend the winter in Texas. Thereafter, however, he had a downturn of fortune. First, Confederate military authorities in Texas, outraged by depredations being committed by the Missouri bushwhackers, tried in vain to arrest him and suppress his band. Then, after returning to Missouri in the spring of 1864, he quarreled with his chief lieutenant, George Todd, with the result that Todd supplanted him as leader.

During most of the remainder of 1864 he hid out in Howard County, Missouri, with his teenage mistress,

Kate King. Late in 1864, following the death of Todd and the defeat of a Confederate invasion of Missouri, he resumed command of some of the surviving bushwhackers, whom he led into Kentucky in January 1865. On 10 May 1865 a party of "Federal guerrillas" that had been assigned to hunt him down surprised his band at a farm near Louisville, mortally wounding and capturing him. Nearly a month later he died at a military prison hospital in Louisville. Both a product and producer of the turmoil that reigned along the Kansas-Missouri border during the Civil War era, Quantrill was an exceptionally able and daring, but also unscrupulous and opportunistic, bandit who left behind a well-deserved reputation as "the bloodiest man in American history."

• John N. Edwards, *Noted Guerrillas; or, The War on the Border* (1877), describes Quantrill's career from a pro-Confederate standpoint and contains many exaggerations and falsehoods. William E. Connelley, *Quantrill and the Border Wars* (1910), is the most detailed biography of Quantrill and contains many primary source materials not available elsewhere but is strongly biased from a Union standpoint. Albert Castel, *William Clarke Quantrill: His Life and Times* (1962), seeks to present an objective view of Quantrill and his career.

ALBERT CASTEL

QUARTER, William James (21 Jan. 1806–10 Apr. 1848), first Roman Catholic bishop of Chicago, was born in Killurine, King's County (Offaly), Ireland, the son of Michael Quarter and Ann Bennet. William Quarter was the third of four sons, all but one of whom studied for the priesthood, though the youngest brother died before ordination. His mother tutored him at home until age eight, when he entered a private boarding academy at Tullamore. In 1822, at age sixteen, he left for North America to complete his studies and become a Catholic missionary. Landing in Quebec, he applied to the bishops of Quebec and Montreal but was refused due to his young age. John Dubois, rector of Mount St. Mary's Seminary in Emmitsburg, Maryland, however, accepted him as a seminarian and he was ordained to the priesthood on 19 September 1829. He joined Dubois in New York City, where the latter had been named bishop.

Quarter served as a curate in St. Peter's parish of New York and then in 1833 was named pastor of St. Mary's parish in that city. When a number of new Catholic dioceses were established west of the Atlantic seaboard in 1843, Quarter was chosen as first bishop of the diocese of Chicago. Bishop John Hughes, who had succeeded Dubois in New York, consecrated Quarter on 10 March 1844. He then set out for Chicago with his brother, the Reverend Walter Quarter, arriving in that city on 5 May 1844 after a three-week journey by boat, rail, and stagecoach.

The city of Chicago was a frontier boomtown, only a decade old, when Quarter arrived. He found only one Catholic church, St. Mary's, in the city. By his own account, "the building was not plastered; a temporary altar was stuck up against the western wall. There was no vestry; the sanctuary was enclosed with rough boards. . . . And worse than all, even that much of a church was burdened with about three thousand dollars of debt." Quarter divided the city into districts and assigned parishioners to go from door to door collecting funds. By November 1844 Chicago Catholics had retired St. Mary's debt and raised the first steeple in the city over their church.

The new bishop made two decisions that profoundly affected the subsequent history of Chicago Catholicism. First of all, even before leaving New York he had decided to emphasize education during his ministry. He had written to the Sisters of Mercy in Europe asking them to send nuns to his new diocese, and he met their boat when they landed in New York. On 23 September 1846 six sisters, led by Sister Agatha O'Brien, R.S.M., arrived in Chicago; the following year they established St. Francis Xavier Academy, next door to St. Mary's Church. The Society for the Propagation of the Faith, a European organization that supported mission work throughout the world, provided $3,000 to finance the building. In 1850 the Sisters of Mercy founded Mercy Hospital, the first medical facility in the city. Because government institutions of education and social service were rudimentary or nonexistent, the academy and the hospital provided services to Catholic and non-Catholic alike.

Bishop Quarter also laid the foundations for the education of men, particularly men studying for the priesthood. Although he was a foreign-born missionary, Quarter realized the importance of developing a native-born clergy in the United States and therefore obtained from the state legislature on 19 December 1844 a charter for the University and Seminary of St. Mary of the Lake. Construction of a three-story colonial building began at a site on the north side of the city (where Holy Name Cathedral stands today), and the school opened its doors on 4 July 1846. These early establishments eventually developed into a complete network of elementary, secondary, and postsecondary schools, the nation's largest Catholic school system; at its peak in the 1960s, it was the third largest school system of any kind in the United States.

The first bishop of Chicago set another significant precedent when he organized separate, foreign-language parishes for German Catholics. In 1846 he opened St. Peter's for Germans living on the South Side and St. Joseph's for those living on the North Side. The Leopoldine Association in Germany provided $1,000 to assist in the erection of these parishes. At the same time, he established a second Irish parish, St. Patrick's, with his brother Walter as pastor. This practical solution to the problem of ethnic diversity in the church, the organization of parishes according to language and nationality as well as territory, set the pattern for the future. Eventually the American Catholic church became a conglomerate of "ethnic leagues" in Chicago and other big U.S. cities. This ensured that immigrants could worship in churches that respected their traditions, with priests who spoke their languages. These so-called national parishes therefore served as way stations on the journey between one country and another as well as between this world and the next.

Besides his precedent-setting foundations in Chicago, Bishop Quarter also assisted the growth of the Catholic church throughout Illinois, for his diocese embraced the entire state. He made several lengthy journeys through the rural areas, building a total of thirty churches and ordaining twenty-nine priests. He wore himself out on these missionary journeys, and in the early morning of 10 April 1848 he suffered a heart attack in his rectory in Chicago and died immediately. He was only forty-two years of age and had served in his new diocese for just four years.

Quarter's career as a priest and bishop typified the life of a Catholic missionary in the early United States. Born in Ireland, where so many American Catholics came from, he served in two important cities of the new nation, relying heavily on missionary societies in Europe, such as the German Leopoldine Association and the French Society for the Propagation of the Faith, to finance his endeavors. He wore himself out and died an early death, but his actions set a pattern for big-city, ethnic, brick-and-mortar Catholicism that persisted well into the twentieth century.

• A colleague of Quarter's, the Reverend John E. McGirr, set out the basic facts of the bishop's career in *Life of the Rt. Rev. Wm. Quarter, D.D.: First Catholic Bishop of Chicago* (1850). James J. McGovern, *Souvenir of the Silver Jubilee in the Episcopacy of His Grace the Most Rev. Patrick Augustine Feehan, Archbishop of Chicago* (privately printed, 1891), reprinted McGirr's memoir of Quarter verbatim as well as printed a complete text of the diary that Quarter kept from 1843, when he was named bishop of Chicago, until his death in 1848. Both of these rare volumes are available at the Chicago Historical Society and the archives of the Archdiocese of Chicago. More accessible works that contain information about Quarter are Gilbert J. Garraghan, *The Catholic Church in Chicago, 1673–1871: An Historical Sketch* (1921), and Ellen Skerrett et al., *Catholicism, Chicago Style* (1993).

EDWARD R. KANTOWICZ

QUAY, Matthew Stanley (30 Sept. 1833–28 May 1904), politician, was born in Dillsburg, Pennsylvania, the son of Anderson Beaton Quay, a Presbyterian minister, and Catherine McCain. Matthew Quay experienced poverty throughout his youth but nevertheless received a college education. He matriculated at Jefferson (now a part of Washington and Jefferson) College in Canonsburg, Pennsylvania, where his emphasis was on classical studies. Graduating at age seventeen, he drifted briefly, read law in Pittsburgh for several years, and was admitted to the Beaver

County bar in 1854. That same year he married Agnes Barclay; they had five children.

The following year Quay was appointed to complete an unexpired term as the Beaver County prothonotary (chief clerk of the court). Entering politics at the precise time that the Republican party was taking form in Pennsylvania, he promptly identified with it. He rose rapidly in party ranks and made politics his lifelong career except for two brief periods: service in the military during the Civil War and publication of a weekly newspaper, the *Beaver Radical*, from 1869 to 1872.

Quay's active military service was brief. Commissioned in the summer of 1862, he rose to the rank of colonel and commanded the 134th Regiment of Pennsylvania Volunteers, but typhoid fever forced his resignation before the end of the year. Although relieved of his command, he insisted on remaining with his unit to participate in the battle at Fredericksburg (13 Dec.) before returning home, and for heroic service in that battle, he was awarded the Congressional Medal of Honor. After regaining his health, he rejoined the staff of Pennsylvania governor Andrew G. Curtin, whom he had served in 1861 and early 1862. Quay's primary responsibility was to answer the hundreds of enlistment-related inquiries from Pennsylvania soldiers who had been mustered into federal service. He handled the assignment so adroitly that soldiers throughout the state recognized and respected his name. In the postwar years he converted that recognition to political power and relied heavily on the ex-soldier vote to dominate Pennsylvania politics for the last quarter of the nineteenth century.

Service in Curtin's office provided Quay a springboard to state and national office. As Curtin's power waned, Quay attached himself to the Republican machine of Simon Cameron, who gradually turned the reins of party power over to him. Elected to the state legislature in 1864, 1865, and 1866, Quay was appointed secretary of the Commonwealth, serving in 1873 and again in 1879. Elected state treasurer in 1885, he detected loopholes in the laws governing the state treasurer and converted them to political advantage. With a henchman occupying the treasurer's office for most of the succeeding twenty years, Quay exploited the opportunities it presented. Among other practices, he used his leverage to coerce banks with state deposits to lend him money without either assessing interest charges or requiring collateral. He once quipped, "I don't mind losing a governorship or a legislature now and then, but I always need the state treasuryship."

Under Quay's leadership, Pennsylvania became the most Republican and boss-dominated state in the final decades of the century. His success required considerable manipulation, because he was not able to control the state's burgeoning cities, Philadelphia and Pittsburgh. With his strength residing in the countryside, he kept the cities stirred up by pushing through the legislature charter reforms to limit the power of emerging city leaders or to pit the two cities against each other, but they nevertheless retained their Republican character. Thus, under his direction, the state delivered a Republican-dominated congressional delegation every two years and provided Republican electors every quadrennium. Quay attributed this unbroken success to an application of his definition of politics: "the art of taking money from the few and votes from the many under the pretext of protecting the one from the other."

When Cameron withdrew from the limelight and resigned from the U.S. Senate in 1877, Quay became the foremost Republican spokesman in Pennsylvania. In 1887 the legislature sent him to the U.S. Senate, where he remained until his death. Quay first gained national prominence in 1888, when he served as the Republican national chairman and successfully oversaw Benjamin Harrison's election to the presidency. Although Grover Cleveland received a greater popular vote than Harrison, Quay concentrated his strategy on winning the electoral college, in the process raising the cost of presidential campaigns to a new level. The price appeared to be justified, because victory gave the Republicans simultaneous control of the presidency, the House, and the Senate for the first time since 1881–1883. Quay targeted the allocation of national party funds to certain districts in certain southern states and deployed Pennsylvania henchmen and Pinkerton detectives as organizers and supervisors. These tactics captured nineteen Republican House seats in former Confederate states—enough to give the Republicans control of the House for only the second time in sixteen years.

Quay was more interested in being able to control the flow of legislation than in the substance of legislation, thus he expressed little interest in major committee chairmanships. Although he served on prominent committees such as Commerce, Territories, Indian Affairs, and Manufactures, the only chairmanship he held was that of Public Buildings and Grounds. At one time or another, every congressman and senator was interested in federal buildings within his state, particularly new post offices. The chairman of Public Buildings and Grounds could expedite or delay such projects; to a quid pro quo boss such as Quay, that translated into control over his colleagues on a wide variety of issues.

Using this leverage, Quay proved an effective bargainer in committee rooms and over dinner. He was so efficient as a power broker that Thomas C. Platt, his counterpart in New York, declared that Quay was "the ablest politician this country ever produced." For seventeen years Quay conducted his brand of state and national politics from his U.S. Senate position. Throughout much of that period, he suffered chronically from consumption and typhoid fever, which, along with his penchant for Florida vacations, produced the highest absentee record among his Senate contemporaries.

By 1900 the newly emerged progressive reformers considered Quay a prime target in their campaign to eliminate party bosses. They undertook a concerted effort to defeat him when he stood for reelection to a third term in 1899. When they succeeded in deadlocking the state legislature and preventing his election, the governor appointed Quay to office, but his right to serve was challenged. By a single vote he was denied his seat until endorsed by a new legislature in 1901. Physically exhausted from this bitter ordeal, Quay never fully recovered, and in early 1904 he returned home to Beaver, where he died.

• Quay's papers are in the Manuscript Division, Library of Congress. For further information see William A. Blair, "Practical Politician: The Boss Tactics of Matthew Stanley Quay," *Pennsylvania History* 56 (1989): 77–92; Robert G. Crist, ed., *Pennsylvania Kingmakers* (1985); and James A. Kehl, *Boss Rule in the Gilded Age: Matt Quay of Pennsylvania* (1981). See also *Matthew Stanley Quay: Memorial Addresses Delivered in the Senate and House of Representatives* (1905).

JAMES A. KEHL

QUEBEC, Ike Abrams (17 Aug. 1918–16 Jan. 1963), musician, was born in Newark, New Jersey; little is known of his mother and father. Nothing is known about Quebec's musical background prior to 1940. As a teen in the late 1930s, Quebec worked as a dancer with a traveling show titled "Harlem on Parade." The point at which he entered the musical establishment would prove to be a pivotal time in the history of jazz. Big band swing, with its regular phrasing and predictable dance beat, along with the lively piano blues affectionately known as "boogie-woogie" for its rapidly oscillating bass ostinato, were the reigning popular forms of jazz during the 1930s. They were challenged in the early 1940s by musicians who promoted a new genre featuring greater harmonic and rhythmic complexity. Bebop, a name derived from the syllabic vocal improvisation of a jazz melody more commonly known as scat singing, altered and extended the harmonic vocabulary inherent in swing and combined it with a conceptually different form of rhythmic activity designed to highlight harmonic progressions often found in blues. Within this context, Quebec's career would serve as a transition between bebop and its immediate precursors.

During the early 1940s, Quebec distinguished himself as a worthy jazz musician, performing right away with many of swing's and bebop's legendary performers. Pianist with the Barons of Rhythm from 1940 to 1941, he switched to tenor saxophone in 1942, playing at many Harlem jam sites where he met Thelonious Monk, Bud Powell, and other developing bebop musicians. Quebec worked briefly with scat legend Ella Fitzgerald's Orchestra in 1942 and toured regularly with the swing bands of Roy Eldridge and Frankie Newton in 1943. Quebec worked with Benny Carter from 1942 to 1944 and performed alongside bop forerunner Coleman Hawkins during the same period. Other musicians Quebec performed and recorded with during 1944 include Sammy Price's Texas Blusicians, Orin "Hot Lips" Page—a leading figure in the Kansas City jazz style who started in Texas blues—and swing trombonist Trummy Young. One notable club performance by Quebec took place at the Yacht Club on Fifty-second Street in New York City. The triple bill included the swing-oriented Trummy Young Sextet and Billy Eckstine Orchestra along with Coleman Hawkins' Sextet, which included bop musicians Don Byas and Thelonious Monk.

Early in his musical career Quebec had been exposed to traditional jazz, blues, and swing, which, in turn, influenced his unique musical approach. He counted trumpeter Louis Armstrong and pianist Earl Hines, who were both traditionalists, among the major influences on his musical life, with Coleman Hawkins and Ben Webster, both swing musicians who anticipated the newer bop style, as particular models for his tenor saxophone playing. Other models included pianist and bop precursor Clyde Hart and tenor saxophonist Stan Getz—who was known for his innovations in cool jazz, a subsequent movement following bop's inception—as well as blues-oriented arranger Buster Harding. Steeped in the styles of blues and swing, Quebec's maturing style mirrored a change in orientation toward bebop in jazz. A hard-swinging tenorman, he often contrasted a smooth legato melody with a strong sense of rhythmic intensity. He possessed a very full, round tone with big, fast vibrato that was very clear and powerful. Quebec had a special propensity for the blues, especially slow blues, that emphasized his musical and emotional directness most often in ballads. His uptempo blues and standards reflected his influences from southwestern blues, particularly those of Texas and Kansas City, with their frenetic driving energy.

In the summer of 1944 Quebec joined the Cab Calloway Orchestra, where he found employment in touring, radio broadcasts, and Columbia recording sessions. While with Calloway, Quebec recorded with a smaller spin-off group known as the Cab Jivers. He left Calloway in 1947 or 1948 to form his own band, but he rejoined Calloway occasionally for tours and record dates until 1951.

He made an association with Blue Note records during the mid-to-late 1940s that would effectively transform the label and mark his recording heyday as a tenor saxophonist. Quebec's recording debut as a leader with the label in July 1944 produced the hit "Blue Harlem." Quebec experimented with large combos, generally septets of three horns and four rhythm pieces, in his sessions of the 1940s, which framed the period that Blue Note recorded "swingtets." The flexible instrumentation that allowed swing groups to incorporate newer stylistic developments instigated a transition phase for the label from traditional jazz and boogie-woogie to modern swing and provided an instrumental basis for many bebop combos. In the late 1940s Quebec worked as an Artists and Repertoire (A&R) man for the label and was directly responsible for recruiting bebop musicians such as Thelonious Monk, Bud Powell, Tadd Dameron, and other bop talent that allowed Blue Note to emerge as a leading jazz label. Quebec even contributed two tunes for Monk's first session with Blue Note.

The slowdown in jazz that followed the postwar economic boom created tough economic times for Quebec. He continued to lead a band during the 1950s, but recording and club dates diminished. Quebec recorded as a sideman with Lucky Millinder and Bob Merrill in 1949. He led a quartet with Mal Waldron from 1950 to 1952. With the exception of a session for Hi-Lo in 1952 and a brief record date for Secco in 1953, he gradually faded from public view, partially because of his acknowledged battle with heroin. From 1954 to 1959, Quebec performed most often as a solo act, even playing in Canadian cabaret shows. Ira Gitler, noted jazz critic, spotted him briefly at the Cafe Bohemia in 1955. He was able to get through this tough time by maintaining his contacts from Calloway's band. He traveled somewhat during this period, performing at small venues in Canada, Manhattan, and the British West Indies when he wasn't serving short sentences at Riker's Island prison.

The remaining years of Quebec's life saw a renewed level of musical and business activity. He returned to the jazz scene from July 1959 to late 1962 as both leader and sideman, recording with Jimmy Smith, Duke Pearson, Sonny Clark, Grant Green, and Dodo Greene. Eight tunes recorded by Blue Note in July 1959 were released as singles. These tunes, in addition to the output from several other sessions in September 1960 and September 1962 are included in a 1984 release by Mosaic records. In 1961 Quebec recorded *Heavy Soul* and *Blue and Sentimental* and played on Sonny Clark's *Leapin' and Lopin'*. He recorded prolifically in 1962, including five albums as leader—*It Might as Well Be Spring, Soul Samba, With a Song in My Heart, Congo Lament, Easy Living*—and Grant Green's *Born to Be Blue*. He also returned to Blue Note as a businessman, serving as an A&R man and coproducer. He was responsible for signing new talent such as Freddie Roach as well as older artists like Dexter Gordon and Leo Parker. It is believed that Quebec never married or had any children. Quebec became seriously ill late in 1962 and died of lung cancer in New York City.

Quebec's distinctive playing style, firmly grounded in southwestern blues and modern swing coupled with constant contact with the leading figures of swing and bebop, created his unique niche within the jazz community of the middle twentieth century. His affiliation with Blue Note both as a player and a businessman directly influenced the label's rise to eminence as a jazz icon.

• Michael Cuscuna's biography in the liner notes of *The Complete Blue Note 45 Sessions of Ike Quebec* (Mosaic MD2-121, 1987) is the most comprehensive and includes a detailed listing of Quebec's recording sessions at Blue Note. Additional information regarding his Blue Note sessions is included in *The Complete Blue Note Recordings of Ike Quebec* (Mosaic 107, 1984). See also Douglas K. Ramsey, *Jazz Matters: Reflections on the Music & Some of Its Makers* (1989), and Gunther Schuller, *The Swing Era: The Development of Jazz, 1930–1945* (1989), for contextual information. An obituary is in *Down Beat*, 28 Feb. 1963.

DAVID E. SPIES

QUEEN, Ellery. *See* Dannay, Frederic.

QUENTIN, Patrick. *See* Wheeler, Hugh Callingham.

QUERVELLE, Anthony (1789–31 July 1856), cabinetmaker, was born Antoine Gabriel Quervelle in Paris, France, but virtually nothing is known about his early life. His biographer, art historian Robert C. Smith, has speculated that Quervelle was one of the many Frenchmen who trained during the Napoleonic era and then, disaffected, left the country after the emperor's downfall. Whatever the case, Quervelle had arrived in Philadelphia by 1817. That year he married Louise Geneviève Monet, herself a Parisian living in Philadelphia; they had two children. After the death of his first wife in November 1847, Quervelle married a woman named Caroline; they had one daughter.

Quervelle must have been apprenticed as a cabinetmaker in Paris; he may have been related to Jean-Claude Quervelle, a cabinetmaker at Versailles, although there appears to be no documentation for any relationship. Beginning in 1820 and continuing until his death, he was listed as a cabinetmaker in Philadelphia city directories. He became a U.S. citizen on 23 September 1823. One of the character witnesses at his naturalization was Charles Nolan, who operated a furniture warehouse at 153 South Second Street. Quervelle may have worked for him initially upon his arrival in the United States. In 1823 his shop was at Eleventh and Lombard streets; two years later he opened the United States Fashionable Cabinet Ware House or Cabinet and Sofa Manufactory at 126 South Second Street. He would remain there until 1849, when he moved to 71 Lombard Street.

In the 1820s Quervelle, along with the other major furniture makers of Philadelphia, displayed examples of his work at the annual exhibitions of mechanical arts sponsored by the Franklin Institute. In 1825 he received honorable mention for two pier tables, and the next year he won a bronze medal for a sideboard. In 1827 he achieved a silver medal for his "cabinet bookcase and secretary" (now in the Philadelphia Museum of Art); he also exhibited a sofa in 1828 and a lady's worktable in 1831. By 1830 his shop employed at least seven craftsmen, and Quervelle achieved both artistic and financial success, garnering commissions from wealthy private citizens and from President Andrew Jackson, who ordered several pier tables for the East Room of the White House in 1827. By the 1840s, Quervelle's number of assistants (as recorded in the census records) had dropped to three, and he may have begun to use his success in cabinetmaking as a springboard for conducting real estate and other business activities.

In its heyday in the 1820s and 1830s, Quervelle's shop produced some of the finest and most distinctive examples of American mahogany Empire furniture. Early designs made in his shop were closely allied with French taste, reflecting Quervelle's background and immigrant status, but he soon adapted to the British mode that was more popular with his customers. Quervelle drew upon George Smith's *Collection of De-*

signs for Household Furniture (1808) and *Cabinet-Maker and Upholsterer's Guide* (1826), Rudolph Ackermann's periodical *Repository of Arts*, and other printed works for many of his designs and motifs, utilizing these sources in combinations to create an individual style. His more ambitious pieces feature such details as large fan-like panels of well-chosen veneers, a favorite ornament; beautifully carved dolphins, pedestals, vases, urns, and lion's-paw feet; distinctive gadroon moldings; gilt stencil decoration; marble mosaics; marquetry; and other ornamental features. Tables of various sorts—especially pier tables with scrolled or columnar supports, but also card, center, work, and dining tables—were Quervelle's forte, but his shop produced outstanding architectonic case pieces and a variety of seating furniture and beds as well. Many of his patrons were Philadelphians, but Quervelle advertised in 1830 that "orders from any part of the Union will be promptly executed."

Wealthy at the time of his death in Philadelphia, Quervelle owned several houses, was a partner in the Bristol Iron Works, and held significant investments in securities. He was a member of the French Benevolent and French Beneficial societies and held stock in the Philadelphia Academy of Music. He is buried in the Old St. Mary's Roman Catholic cemetery in Philadelphia.

• Quervelle's work is in many collections, including the Philadelphia Museum of Art, the Baltimore Museum of Art, and the White House. Robert C. Smith, "Philadelphia Empire Furniture by Antoine Gabriel Quervelle," *Antiques* 86, no. 3 (Sept. 1964): 304–9, has a biographical focus. An informative five-part series is Smith, "The Furniture of Anthony G. Quervelle," part 1: "The Pier Tables," *Antiques* 103, no. 5 (May 1973): 984–94; part 2: "The Pedestal Tables," *Antiques* 104, no. 1 (July 1973): 90–99; part 3: "The Worktables," *Antiques* 104, no. 2 (Aug. 1973): 260–68; part 4: "Some Case Pieces," *Antiques* 105, no. 1 (Jan. 1974): 180–93; and part 5: "Sofas, Chairs, and Beds," *Antiques* 105, no. 3 (Mar. 1974): 512–21. See also Philadelphia Museum of Art, *Philadelphia: Three Centuries of American Art* (1976), and Wendy A. Cooper, *Classical Taste in America, 1800–1840* (1993).

GERALD W. R. WARD

QUEZON, Manuel Luis (19 Aug. 1878–1 Aug. 1944), first president of the Philippine Islands, was born in Baler, a small village on the island of Luzon, Philippines, the son of a Filipino father, Lucio Quezon, and a Filipino-Spanish mother, Maria Molina, both schoolteachers. He completed his studies at San Juan de Letrán junior college and was appointed as a lecturer at the University of Santo Tomas, for which he received free room, board, and tuition while studying law. His parents supported the Spanish during the rebellion in 1898, and insurgents killed his father and brother. Although in 1899 he joined the rebels to fight against both the Spanish and later the Americans, he never forgot the attack against his family. Years later, when he became provincial prosecutor, he avenged their deaths by imprisoning the killers as bandits.

Quezon demonstrated courage and initiative in his brief military career, rising to the rank of major before being captured in 1901. The U.S. authorities imprisoned him for six months on suspicion of participating in the killing of American prisoners, but he was finally released owing to lack of evidence. His imprisonment was harsh and possibly was responsible for his contracting tuberculosis.

Quezon ingratiated himself with the Americans and in 1906 narrowly won the governorship of Tayabas Province with their overt assistance. U.S. Army trucks were even used to transport his supporters to the capital to influence voters. After his victory, he formed in 1907 an alliance with Sergio Osmeña to form the *Partido Nacionalista*, a political party that dominated politics in the Philippines until World War II.

At the outset the *Nacionalistas* stressed independence from the United States. After gaining power, Quezon guided a shift in the party's platform to emphasize economic advantage. The Philippines had become dependent on American markets, and Quezon recognized that industrialization would lag without U.S. support. Yet a discernible tie to the Americans was a domestic political liability, so Quezon, like many of his contemporaries, began to play a double role. The consensus is that he was more skillful at this than the others.

In the Philippine Assembly (1907–1909) Quezon was elected floor leader, and in 1909 he maneuvered to have himself appointed as one of two resident commissioners to represent the Philippines in the U.S. House. There the Philippine representatives were allowed to speak, but they could not vote. Quezon stayed in Washington in that capacity until 1916, acquiring sufficient influence to become the virtual author of a bill introduced by Congressman William Atkinson Jones that provided for universal adult male suffrage in the Philippines, legislative autonomy (subject to veto by the American governor general), and independence as soon as a stable government could be established. The bill established no time frame for independence, nor did it define stability.

On his return to Manila in 1916, Quezon was elected the first president of the senate. In 1918 he married his cousin Aurora Aragon; they had three children. His speeches became increasingly nationalistic, and his popularity soared when he returned to Washington in 1925 and 1927 to lobby for independence and to lobby against bills before Congress that he deemed unsatisfactory for the Philippines. In 1934 he was finally satisfied with the Tydings-McDuffie Bill, which created the Philippine Commonwealth, promised full independence in 1946, and provided for duty-free import of most important Philippine products into the United States.

In 1935, shortly before the first presidential election in the Philippines, Quezon attempted to co-opt the other political parties into a new Coalition party and advocated a form of populism he called the "distributive state." Some have suggested that his call for elimination of political parties was to enable him to achieve a dictatorship. This seem incompatible with Quezon's character. It is more likely that he wanted to emasculate his opponents by bringing them all within one party, with himself as nominal head. He won the election in a landslide and promptly set about trying to fight poverty and instill "social justice" for the masses. His strident speeches did not result in the revolutionary reform that might have been expected, possibly because he would have alienated some of his wealthy supporters had he done so. Legislation was vaguely worded and weakly enforced, giving Quezon the dualism of both appearing to help the masses and also protecting the status quo.

Quezon also began a program to enhance the islands' security, primarily through the efforts of General Douglas MacArthur, whom he persuaded to retire as U.S. Army chief of staff and assume responsibilities for defending the commonwealth. By 1938 the plans previously submitted by MacArthur were far behind schedule, and Quezon was convinced that Japanese domination could only be avoided with American help. In essence, he was advocating a reversal of his policy of decolonization. By 1939 Japanese aggression in China caused Quezon to remain decidedly proindependence before home audiences but increasingly pro-American to U.S. listeners. To the Japanese, he professed neutrality, although the agent sent by Japan to secure friends in the Philippines described Quezon as "thoroughly ambiguous." After the attack on the Philippines by Japan in late 1941, ten hours after they bombed Pearl Harbor on 7 December, Quezon apparently vacillated about making an accommodation with the invaders. He finally rejected this, possibly at MacArthur's urging, and in March 1942 left on a submarine for Australia.

Quezon arrived in Washington a sick exile, dying of tuberculosis. He spent his last months writing his memoirs at Saranac Lake, New York, where he died. Despite occasional harsh words for his American mentors over the years of his public life, he ended his days attesting to friendship and affection for the United States.

Quezon was a political conservative and opportunist who exhibited an uncanny sense of timing in his actions and pronouncements. He undertook dramatic actions because he knew it was expected of him as the leader of his party, yet as the Filipino historian Reynaldo Ileto has put it, "Quezon was playing the game in order to contain it." Above all he sought the best for the Philippines, and when security, prosperity, and independence were not mutually compatible, he still managed to pursue all three simultaneously.

• Quezon's private papers are in the Bureau of Public Libraries in Manila, although they were in poor condition and largely uncataloged when reviewed by Theodore Friend in 1958. Quezon's autobiography, *The Good Fight* (1946), is not helpful, although some insights are found in his relationships with political rivals and American administrators. Friend's study, *Between Two Empires: The Ordeal of the Philippines 1929–1946* (1965), is an important contribution. Stephen Rosskamm Shalom, *The United States and the Philippines* (1981), draws interesting comparisons with the era of Ferdinand Marcos. Peter W. Stanley has made valuable research available in his study, *A Nation in the Making: The Philippines and the United States 1899–1921* (1974), and his editing of *Reappraising an Empire* (1984). Daniel Schirmer and Shalom, eds., *The Philippines Reader: A History of Colonialism, Neocolonialism, Dictatorship and Resistance* (1987), offers a brief overview. John Gunther, *Inside Asia* (1939), has remained an insightful look at Asia and the area during the years 1937–1938, and many of the author's observations proved to be prophetic. Stanley Karnow, *In Our Image: America's Empire in the Philippines* (1989), is an excellent source. An obituary is in the *New York Times*, 2 Aug. 1944.

ROGER SOISET

QUICK, Herbert (31 Oct. 1861–10 May 1925), lawyer, politician, and man of letters, was born John Herbert Quick on a farm near Steamboat Rock, Grundy County, Iowa, the son of Martin Quick, a frontier lumberman and farmer, and Margaret Coleman. The couple had migrated by ox-drawn wagon from Wisconsin in 1857. When only twenty months old, Quick contracted infantile paralysis, which left him with deformed feet and ankles. He attended country schools, worked as diligently as he could on the farm, and enrolled in a teachers' institute at Grundy Center, from which he received a certificate of competence. He taught school in several Iowa towns from 1877 to 1890, during which time he rose to the rank of a ward-school principal in Mason City. He read and was greatly influenced by Henry George's *Progress and Poverty*. Studying law in his free time, Quick was admitted to the Iowa bar in 1889. He married Ella Corey in 1890; they had two children. From 1890 to 1908 Quick practiced law in Sioux City. He gained a name for himself by successfully prosecuting corrupt town leaders, became involved in Democratic party politics, and served as mayor in the period 1898–1900. While remaining a Democrat, Quick sympathized with many Populist and Progressive demands, especially loans on nonperishable agricultural commodities, curbing the spoliation of the environment by big business and industry, and reform of outmoded political administrative structures.

Meanwhile, Quick was nurturing a hope for literary fame. In 1901 he published *In the Fairyland of America: A Tale of the Pukwudjies*, a volume of Native-American folklore for juvenile readers. In February 1902 his poem "A Whiff of Smoke" appeared in the *Century*. He published short stories in *Cosmopolitan*, the *Saturday Evening Post*, and the *Century* beginning in 1905. *Double Trouble; or, Every Hero His Own Villain*, his first novel, appeared in 1906. It is a Jekyll-and-Hyde yarn in which hypnotic power triggers a personality change in a formerly decent young banker. Its popularity encouraged Quick to continue mixing literature and law work, with the former gradually dominating. His novel *The Broken Lance* (1907) features a minister in Chicago who quits a comfortable post and, aided by a single-tax philosopher and a sincere young woman, crusades for the benefit of the downtrodden. Discontinuing his law practice, Quick served as associate editor of *La Follette's Weekly Magazine* during 1908–1909 and as editor of *Farm and Fireside* from 1909 to 1916. Meanwhile, he continued writing a curious variety of books—melodramatic fiction long and short, serious novels, and propagandistic works. For example, in *American Inland Waterways* (1909) he advocates better use of dock, harbor, levee, and harbor facilities to complement rail and highway transportation, while his *On Board the Good Ship Earth* (1913) is a series of essays urging better use of natural resources and on the dangers of racism, patriotism, and militarism. In 1916 President Woodrow Wilson appointed Quick to membership in the Federal Farm Loan Bureau, on which he conscientiously served until 1919. In that year he published *From War to Peace: A Plea for a Definite Policy of Reconstruction*, which advises the victorious Allies to exercise patience as they inculcate democracy wherever they can; he also predicts that it will take at least two decades to reestablish personal, religious, and economic liberty widely. Quick chaired a nongovernmental commission, with the civilian rank of "colonel," to superintend final functions of the American Red Cross at Vladivostok, 1919–1920. Work there under harsh Siberian conditions permanently impaired his health.

Then followed the three novels by which Quick is likely to be best remembered: *Vandemark's Folly* (1921), *The Hawkeye* (1923), and *The Invisible Woman* (1924). In 1924 he also published a pamphlet titled *The Real Trouble with the Farmers*, inveighing against unscrupulous land speculators, high tariffs, and exorbitant railroad freight rates, and *There Came Two Women*, an unsuccessful naturalistic blank-verse drama. He also planned autobiographical volumes, of which he completed only *One Man's Life: An Autobiography* (1925), which is of limited value because it takes him only to age twenty-eight or so. Quick had other literary work in mind. He began *Mississippi Steamboatin': A History of Steamboating on the Mississippi and Its Tributaries*. And he collaborated with Elena Stepanoff MacMahon, a Russian emigrée, on a novel about an aristocratic Russian family dramatically aided by a Bolshevik commissar. Quick's son Edward completed *Mississippi Steamboatin'* and published it in 1926. The Russian novel appeared as *We Have Changed All That*, by Quick and MacMahon, in 1928. Although Quick and his wife lived for many years in a farm home near Berkeley Springs, West Virginia, he suffered a fatal heart attack in Columbia, Missouri, after addressing students during journalism week at the University of Missouri.

Quick's trilogy of Iowa novels begins with *Vandemark's Folly*. It was previewed by *The Fairview Idea* (1919), a fictionalized tract in which Quick's narrator describes a communal effort by fellow farmers to preserve their identity and their rural culture, to make their schools offer more practical training, and thus to prevent or at least delay the flight of their children to the cities. The hero of *Vandemark's Folly* is Jacobus Teunis Vandemark, who leaves upper New York State for Iowa to take up a grant of land reluctantly given him by a villainous stepfather and matures with his rural Monterey County neighbors. Melodramatic relationships with two women are untangled at the end. Critics agree that Quick is at his best when rapturously describing the presettlement Iowa prairie along the Old Ridge Road west of Dubuque. The life of the hero of *The Hawkeye*, Fremont McConkey, closely parallels that of Quick himself—teacher, politician, journalist, and opponent of corrupt county politicians. Quick skillfully weaves strands of Iowa history into the plot. Christina Thorkelson, the heroine of *The Invisible Woman*, leaves the family farm to become a law-firm secretary and then a court reporter. Somewhat tedious is Quick's excessive dramatization of courtroom theatrics. Christina is "invisible" because, though powerful and competent, she takes a back seat to the man she loves. Quick merits comparison to Willa Cather for brilliantly dramatizing the degeneration of pioneers from brave to bickering to litigious, and to William Faulkner for developing generations of reappearing characters, including many minor ones with startling names. Quick is surely the finest novelist ever to concern himself with the era of Iowa pioneering.

• Several of Quick's manuscripts are in the Iowa State Department of History and Archives. Other papers are in the Historical Society of Pennsylvania and in libraries at Indiana University, the University of Iowa, Knox College, Temple University, and Wagner College. Herbert Quick, "I Picked My Goal at Ten—Reached It at Sixty," *American Magazine* 94 (Oct. 1922): 50–51, 161–64, is a brief but informative autobiographical sketch. Frank Paluka, *Iowa Authors: A Bio-Bibliography of Sixty Native Writers* (1967), provides details of Quick's twenty book publications. The best discussion of Quick's fiction is in Roy W. Meyer, *The Middle Western Farm Novel in the Twentieth Century* (1965). An obituary is in the *New York Times*, 11 May 1925.

ROBERT L. GALE

QUIDOR, John (26 Dec. 1801–13 Dec. 1881), painter, was born in Tappan, New York, the son of Peter Quidor, a teacher, and Maria Smith. In 1810 Quidor's family moved to New York City. In May 1818 John was apprenticed to the established portraitist John Wesley Jarvis. The arrangement, however, did not progress smoothly. In an early indication of his oppositional attitude toward the establishment, Quidor filed charges against his teacher in August 1822, alleging that Jarvis had neglected his duties and failed to instruct him in the trade of portrait painting. The jury found for Quidor in May 1823 and awarded him $251.35 in damages. Quidor probably received other, more informal artistic training prior to and following the Jarvis incident from sign and fire engine panel painters in the city. This instruction, emphasizing visual clarity, influenced the style and character of Quidor's paintings throughout his career.

Quidor is generally categorized as a literary painter, and his career is known primarily through fewer than forty extant paintings, although forty-six are recorded. In 1994 a Quidor painting emerged when the National Museum of American Art in Washington, D.C., acquired the signed painting *The Headless Horseman Pursuing Ichabod Crane* (1858). Especially in his early work, Quidor looked to popular prints for compositional and character development. These paintings reflected his interest in bright colors, detail, and theatrical lighting. His earliest recorded painting is *Dorothea* (1823, Brooklyn Museum), based on a scene from the first book of Cervantes' *Don Quixote*. Quidor received his first public acclaim as one of the painters of a processional banner carried by New York Fire Company No. 3 in a parade to commemorate the opening of the Erie Canal on 25 October 1825. Although the artist continued to work in this vein off and on, his primary interest (and the dominant sources of inspiration for his paintings) was Washington Irving's tales of old Dutch New York. Although there is no evidence that the two men ever met, Quidor devoted most of his work to personal interpretations of his contemporary's writings. The first painting to attract the attention of New York critics was Quidor's *Ichabod Crane Flying from the Headless Horseman* (c. 1828, Yale University Art Gallery), which he exhibited with *A Landscape Composition* (c. 1828, Newark Museum) and *The Young Artist* (1828, Newark Museum) at the National Academy of Design in the spring of 1828. *Ichabod*, the artist's first depiction of an Irving story, met with criticism for its inappropriate scenery, departure from nature, and heavy emphasis on the artist's imagination. These remarks describe the very nature of Quidor's paintings of Irving subjects: they were not illustrations in the strict sense—visual translations of written text—but rather Quidor's subjective interpretations of pivotal moments in the narrative. His intensely personal vision of fictional text distinguishes his paintings from those of his contemporaries.

The years between 1828 and 1835 were productive for Quidor, and he earned a reputation as a romantic figure painter. Quidor completed several works, mostly based on Irving's tales but also on James Fenimore Cooper's *The Pioneers* (1823). These paintings, *Leatherstocking Meets the Law* (1832, New York State Historical Association, Cooperstown) and two versions of *Leatherstocking's Rescue* (1832, R. H. Love Galleries, Chicago), represent Quidor's only known interpretations of Cooper's work and focus on the fundamental conflict between natural and man-made law. Quidor occasionally taught art lessons and continued to earn recognition in different circles for his work on fire engine panels. One work that attracted much attention and mixed reviews was *The Money Diggers* (1832, Brooklyn Museum), a uniquely theatrical depiction of the nocturnal climax of Irving's *Wolfert Webber; or, Golden Dreams* (1824). Quidor exhibited paintings at the National Academy of Design, the American Institute of the City of New York, the Boston Athenaeum, and the American Academy of Fine Arts (of which he was an associate member). Although little is known of Quidor's personal life, his purported unorderly lifestyle and the company he kept were contrary to the lofty standards set for members of the National Academy.

On 16 December 1835 a devastating fire in New York City destroyed much of the central business district on which Quidor's studio bordered. This disaster, in combination with city-wide economic problems and cholera epidemics, probably compelled Quidor to abandon New York in 1836 and move his family to Quincy, Illinois. In 1823 Quidor had purchased 320 acres in that area for a total of $100, but at the height of the great western migration he took advantage of land boom prices and sold the property for a healthy profit. On 20 April 1837 Quidor and his wife, Eliza Jane Harkins, whom he had married by the mid-1830s and with whom he had at least two children, signed a land deed confirming their residency in Quincy. The artist set up a studio there and sent two paintings, *Battle Scene from Knickerbocker's History* (1838, Museum of Fine Arts, Boston) and *Antony Van Corlear Brought into the Presence of Peter Stuyvesant* (1839, Munson-Williams-Proctor Institute, Utica, N.Y.), to New York for the National Academy of Design exhibitions in 1838 and 1839. In 1844 he entered into an agreement to paint seven large religious paintings in exchange for ownership of a 520-acre farm. Although Quidor did complete the seven paintings (now lost), the plan fell through, and by the summer of 1849 Quidor had moved his family back to New York.

Quidor's return to New York City marked the beginning of his mature period consisting of at least twenty known paintings. During this time, he returned to Irving's literary characters for artistic inspiration and produced some of his most interesting work. Quidor seemed to display a new affinity for the protagonist confronting dramatic situations. In particular, the large painting *Rip Van Winkle as He Appeared in the Village after an Absence of Twenty Years* (c. 1849, National Gallery of Art, Washington, D.C.) perhaps echoes Quidor's own feelings of dislocation on his return to a city now doubled in size. Irving's *Knickerbocker's History of New York* (1809) furnished subject matter for many of Quidor's later paintings, which reflect an interest in landscape as well as figure painting. Quidor continued to paint in New York until 1868, when he and his wife moved to Jersey City, New Jersey, to live with their daughter. He died in Jersey City.

While at odds with contemporary expectations of artists as learned gentility, Quidor created paintings that went far beyond simple illustrations of text to visual interpretations of sophisticated complexity. His paintings embodied and asserted a personal romanticism inspired by written words but formulated with an impressive knowledge of historical imagery and compelling portrayals of the repeated experiences of the human condition.

• Quidor's paintings are in the National Gallery of Art, the National Museum of American Art, the Metropolitan Museum, the Brooklyn Museum, the Yale University Art Gallery, and the Museum of Fine Arts, Boston. The first retrospective exhibition of Quidor's work was curated by John I. H. Baur at the Brooklyn Museum in 1942. Baur also authored the first important catalog of Quidor's work, *John Quidor: 1801–1881* (1942). Baur curated and authored the catalog for the Munson-Williams-Proctor Institute exhibition, *John Quidor* (1965). Ernest Rohdenburg, "The Misreported Quidor Court Case," *American Art Journal* 2 (Spring 1970): 74–80, gives a detailed account of Quidor's legal proceedings against Jarvis. David M. Sokol made significant contributions to the knowledge of Quidor in several publications: "John Quidor: Literary Painter," *American Art Journal* 2 (Spring 1970): 60–73; "John Quidor: His Life and Work" (Ph.D. diss., New York Univ., 1971); "John Quidor and the Literary Sources for His Painting," *Antiques* 102 (Oct. 1972): 675–79; and *John Quidor: Painter of American Legend* (1973), the catalog for the exhibition at the Wichita Museum of Art. For more recent articles, see Christopher Kent Wilson, "Engraved Sources for Quidor's Early Work," *American Art Journal* 8 (Nov. 1976): 17–25, and his Ph.D. dissertation, "The Life and Work of John Quidor" (Yale Univ., 1982), which includes a bibliography and catalog of the artist's work. Bryan Jay Wolf's chapter on "Irving, Quidor, and the Catastrophe of Imaginative Vision" in his *Romantic Re-Vision: Culture and Consciousness in Nineteenth-century American Painting and Literature* (1982) provides an interesting psychological analysis of the two artists' works. The American Paintings catalog of the Metropolitan Museum of Art (1994) also contains updated information on Quidor paintings.

A. J. RHODES

QUIGLEY, James Edward (15 Oct. 1854–10 July 1915), Roman Catholic archbishop, was born in Oshawa, Ontario, Canada, the son of James Quigley, a building contractor, and Mary Lacey. While an infant he moved with his parents to Lima, New York, and in 1857 to Rochester, where he developed a close relationship with his paternal uncle, who was a Catholic priest. After graduating from St. Joseph's College in Buffalo in 1872, Quigley briefly studied for the priesthood at the Seminary of Our Lady of Angels (later a part of Niagara University in Buffalo) before transferring to the University of Innsbrück, Austria. In 1874 he enrolled in the Urban College of the Propaganda in Rome, Italy, and five years later he received his doctorate in sacred theology and was ordained.

Later in 1879 Quigley returned to the diocese of Buffalo and was appointed pastor of St. Vincent's Parish in Attica, New York. In 1884 he was made rector of St. Joseph's Church, the diocesan cathedral, and in 1886 he became pastor of St. Bridget's Parish, a working-class neighborhood in Buffalo where a great number of dockworkers lived. In 1897 he was consecrated bishop of Buffalo. His most noteworthy accomplishment in this capacity came in 1899, when he played a crucial role in settling a major strike by the local longshoremen's union over working conditions. After the State Board of Mediation and Arbitration failed to bring the two parties to terms and the dispute threatened to drag on interminably, Quigley began attending the meetings of the strikers, many of whom he knew personally from St. Bridget's. He vowed to support their cause until their employers promised to make suitable concessions regarding hours, safety, and pay. His involvement marked the first time that a U.S. bishop took a prominent prolabor stand and resulted in the amicable settlement of the strike ten days later.

In 1903 Quigley was appointed archbishop of Chicago, Illinois, at the time a hotbed of labor unrest and social upheaval. Chicago was a center for the newly founded Socialist party, which was attracting the attention if not loyalty of a growing number of working people. Although he continued to support the efforts of trade unionists to secure a better standard of living for themselves and their families, he vigorously opposed any alliance between the labor movement and the party because he believed that socialism denied both the existence of God and the right of private ownership. Many of these working people had arrived during the previous decade when half a million immigrants from Eastern and Southern Europe, many of whom were fervent Catholics, had settled in Chicago. As a result many of the archdiocese's parishes were beset by ethnic rivalries, sometimes between segments of a congregation and sometimes between the pastor and his parishioners. Quigley subdivided the existing parishes into smaller ones that catered to a particular nationality with a pastor who spoke the appropriate language. While his predecessor had begun the process on a small scale, Quigley created 113 parishes in twelve years, more than eighty of which were established within the city limits of Chicago. He also implemented a building program, whereby each new parish received a new church, and he encouraged the development of social clubs, lay societies and organizations, and parochial and Sunday schools. These initiatives provided spiritual and social anchors for many of the city's ethnic neighborhoods.

Quigley increased the role of lay people in the administration of the archdiocese by creating lay trustees to oversee the finances of each parish. He played an instrumental role in advancing the cause of Catholic-supported higher education by establishing Loyola and De Paul Universities in Chicago. Demonstrating his interest in the particular needs of orphans and other unfortunate children, he founded and supported St. Mary's Training School, an orphanage where the conditions came as close as possible to those of a normal home, and the Chicago Industrial School for Girls.

In 1905 Quigley furthered the cause of global Catholic evangelization by helping establish the Catholic Church Extension Society. He served for the next ten years as the society's chancellor. Although it was originally founded to contribute financial support for the efforts of Catholic missionaries in rural and small-town America, the society under his guidance became involved in missionary efforts around the world and sponsored Catholic missionary congresses in Chicago in 1908 and Boston, Massachusetts, five years later. Following the outbreak of the Mexican Revolution in 1910, such a hostile environment existed for Mexican prelates in their own country that a number of them and their followers fled to the United States. Quigley committed himself and the society's resources to aiding these refugees and convinced the U.S. State Department to insist that the Mexican government guarantee the safety of its citizens who supported the church.

Quigley never recovered from a stroke he suffered in 1915 in Washington, D.C. He died in Rochester while visiting his brother. In 1961 a seminary in Chicago was named in his honor. A leader of the American Catholic hierarchy, he championed the causes of laborers and "hyphenated" Americans and earned the sobriquet "the bishop of the immigrants."

• Quigley's papers have not been located. His contributions are discussed in Francis Clement Kelley, *Archbishop Quigley: A Tribute* (1915), and Jay P. Dolan, *The American Catholic Experience* (1985). An obituary is in the *New York Times*, 11 July 1915.

CHARLES W. CAREY, JR.

QUILL, Michael Joseph (18 Sept. 1905–28 Jan. 1966), labor leader, was born near the village of Kilgarvan, County Kerry, Ireland, the son of John Daniel Quill, a farmer, and Margaret Lynch. Quill attended National School until he was eleven. Quill's family backed the Irish Republican Army (IRA) during the struggle for Irish independence and the subsequent Civil War. Quill himself belonged to Fianna Eireann, the Republican Boy Scouts, and served with the IRA between 1920 and 1923.

In 1926 Quill moved to New York, where after holding a series of brief jobs he was hired by the Interborough Rapid Transit Company. During the early 1930s layoffs and pay cuts caused growing dissatisfaction among New York's ill-paid, overworked transit workers. Many groups of workers, including one from the Clan na Gael, a semiclandestine organization of IRA supporters in which Quill was active, began agitating for a union. Most quickly joined forces with an organizing drive initiated by the Communist party, resulting in the April 1934 formation of the Transport Workers Union (TWU). Quill was among the union's earliest and most effective organizers. With a knack for speaking and a large number of acquaintances among the heavily Irish work force—the fruit of years of running dances for Irish groups—Quill emerged as one of the union's key leaders. In December 1935 he was elected its president.

In May 1937 the TWU joined the Committee for Industrial Organization (later, Council of Industrial Organizations) with jurisdiction over all nonsteam passenger transportation. It quickly won recognition elections on almost all the New York transit lines. With 30,000 members, the TWU became a major force in the New York labor movement and Quill one of the city's most important labor leaders. With backing from the left-liberal American Labor party (ALP), in November 1937 Quill was elected to the New York City Council, representing the Bronx. That same year he married Maria Theresa O'Neill; they had one child.

In labor and political matters Quill worked closely with the Communist party. After witnesses at a 1938 congressional committee hearing claimed that Quill and other TWU leaders were Communists—a charge Quill repeatedly denied—Quill retorted that he "would rather be called a Red by the rats than a rat by the Reds." Quill's refusal to condemn the 1939 Non-Aggression Treaty between Germany and the Soviet Union cost him ALP endorsement in his bid for reelection to the city council, and he lost his seat. He returned to the council in 1943, running as an independent, and retained his post until 1949, when the city abandoned proportional representation, making it all but impossible for independent or minor party candidates to be elected.

Under Quill's leadership initial TWU efforts to expand beyond the New York transit industry were unsuccessful. However, during World War II the union signed up transit workers in Philadelphia and Chicago, utility workers in Brooklyn, and airline workers in Miami. After the war the union continued to grow in the transit and airline industries and in 1954 absorbed the United Railroad Workers Union (CIO). By the time of Quill's death, the union had 135,000 members.

In 1948, as the Cold War intensified, Quill broke with the Communist party, resigning from the presidency of the Communist-dominated Greater New York Industrial Council (CIO), a post he had assumed the previous year. Taking advantage of support from CIO President Philip Murray and New York mayor William O'Dwyer, Quill was able to defeat the TWU officials who wanted the union to remain allied with the Communists. In 1949 he was elected president of a reorganized New York City CIO council, and in 1950 a CIO national vice president. In New York Quill used an alliance with the Democratic party to win back, without striking, the collective bargaining rights the TWU had lost when the city took over the private subway and elevated lines in 1940. In other situations he resorted to more militant tactics, helping to lead strikes against the Philadelphia transit system, New York bus companies, and the Pennsylvania Railroad.

Quill's intense anticommunist period was brief. In the 1950s he was a vocal critic of McCarthyism and the national Democratic party, calling for the creation of a labor party. He also was the main opponent within the CIO of its 1955 merger with the American Federation of Labor, which he accused of tolerating "the three R's": racial discrimination, raiding, and racketeering. In the 1960s Quill advocated free mass transit, supported the civil rights movement, and expressed sympathy for the National Liberation Front in Vietnam. Despite declining health, he traveled widely. He was a delegate to the International Confederation of Free Trade Unions and returned often to Ireland. In 1961, after the death of his first wife, he married his administrative assistant, Shirley Garry.

In 1965 the election of Republican John V. Lindsay as New York mayor undermined Quill's political influence just as the contract covering the city's transit workers was expiring. Under pressure from dissatisfied union members, on 1 January 1966 Quill defied state antistrike legislation and led municipal transit workers off their jobs, bringing the nation's largest city to a virtual halt. On the fourth day of the strike Quill and other union leaders were jailed. Quill collapsed almost immediately. After twelve days the strike was settled on terms advantageous to the union. Quill died two weeks later in his New York home.

Mike Quill was a prominent member of the generation of activists who during the 1930s and 1940s organized new industrial unions, vastly expanded the size of the labor movement, and dramatically increased its political influence. Quill's expansive personality, razor-sharp wit, and New York base brought him far greater national attention than the modest size of his union alone would dictate. During the 1950s and 1960s, when labor leaders were increasingly bland, the colorful Quill was a favorite guest on television and radio shows. A vocal champion of the redistribution of economic and political power (though his actions rarely were as bold as his words), Quill was for many the living embodiment of the labor movement during its years of peak strength.

• Quill's papers, along with many films in which he appears, are part of the Transport Workers Union Collection at the Robert Wagner Labor Archives, New York University. His views can be followed in the column he wrote for the *Transport Workers Bulletin* and the *TWU Express* and in the *Report of Proceedings: Transport Workers Union of America* (1937–1965). There are two biographies of Quill: L. H. Whittemore, *The Man Who Ran the Subways: The Story of Mike Quill* (1968), and Shirley Quill, *Mike Quill—Himself: A Memoir* (1985). See also Joshua B. Freeman, *In Transit: The Transport Workers Union in New York City, 1933–1966* (1989), Michael Marmo, *More Profile than Courage: The New York City Transit Strike of 1966* (1990), and A. H. Raskin, "Presenting the Phenomenon Called Quill," *New York Times Magazine*, 5 Mar. 1950, pp. 11, 64–68. An obituary is in the *New York Times*, 29 Jan. 1966.

JOSHUA B. FREEMAN

QUIMBY, Edith Hinkley (10 July 1891–11 Oct. 1982), physicist, was born in Rockford, Illinois, the daughter of Arthur S. Hinkley, an architect and farmer, and Harriet Hinkley, whose maiden name and married name were the same. As a child, Edith Hinkley moved with her family from Illinois to Alabama and then to Boise, Idaho, where she attended high school. At Whitman College in Walla Walla, Washington, she studied physics and mathematics and received a B.S. in 1912. She then taught high school science in Nyssa, Oregon, for two years and in 1914 enrolled in the graduate physics program at the University of California at Berkeley. In 1915 she married fellow student Shirley L. Quimby, with whom she had no children, and in 1916 received an M.A. in physics.

After graduating Quimby taught high school science in Antioch, California, for three years, then moved with her husband to New York City when he accepted a position as an instructor of physics at Columbia University. In 1919 she joined the staff of the New York City Memorial Hospital for Cancer and Allied Diseases as an assistant physicist, thus becoming for the moment the only female physicist engaged in medical research in the United States. In collaboration with Gioacchino Failla, the hospital's chief physicist,

she began investigating X rays, which had at the beginning of the twentieth century been adopted as a treatment for tumors. Because doctors knew little about either the proper amount of radiation to apply during therapy or the side effects of such therapy on patients and medical personnel, her first major task was to learn more about radium and X rays. Her experiments, conducted between 1920 and 1940, yielded much information about the characteristics of X rays. The most important result of these experiments was the development of a method for measuring the amount of radiation absorbed by the skin and body during therapy, thus making it much simpler to calculate safe dosages that maximized the retardation of the growth of the tumor while minimizing the risk of harmful side effects. Her findings from these experiments were published in about fifty scholarly articles in scientific journals, the most important being "The Specification of Dosage in Radium Therapy" (*American Journal of Roentgenology* 45, no. 1 [1941]: 1–17). These contributions earned her a promotion to associate physicist in 1932, the Janeway Medal of the American Radium Society (the first time a woman had won this award) in 1940, and the Gold Medal of the Radiological Society of North America in 1941.

Quimby taught radiology at Cornell University Medical College as an assistant professor in 1941–1942, then in 1943 joined the faculty of Columbia University's College of Physicians and Surgeons as an associate professor of radiology. In the latter capacity, she investigated the possibility of using radioactive sodium in medical research after it was synthesized at the university. She and Failla cofounded Columbia's Radiological Research Laboratory, where she experimented with radioactive isotopes to determine their usefulness not only as tracers in studying the circulatory system and diagnosing brain tumors but also for treating cancer and thyroid disorders. During World War II she participated in the development of the first atomic bomb by working on the Manhattan Project and later served as a consultant to the Atomic Energy Commission. After the war she became interested in developing and promoting practices for the safe handling of radioactive isotopes. She advised the U.S. Veterans Administration on the use of radiation therapy, served as an examiner for the American Board of Radiology, and chaired a committee for the National Council on Radiation Protection and Measurements. In 1944 she co-authored, with Otto Glasser, J. L. Weatherwax, and L. S. Taylor, *Physical Foundations of Radiology*, a guide to radiation physics intended primarily for use by radiologists.

All this work did not go unrewarded. In 1947 Quimby won a medal for scientific research at the Exposition of Women's Arts and Industries, and in 1949 she received the Lord and Taylor American Design Award for her work with radioactive isotopes as a new medical tool. In 1954 she was promoted to full professor and elected president of the American Radium Society. She published summations of much of her career research in *Radioactive Isotopes in Clinical Prac-*

tices (1958) and *Safe Handling of Radioactive Isotopes in Medical Practice* (1960) before retiring in 1960 as a professor emeritus. In 1963 she was presented the Gold Medal of the American College of Radiologists. She spent her retirement experimenting, consulting, lecturing, and writing about radiology. She died in New York City.

Quimby's work with X rays and radioactive isotopes made her a pioneer in the fields of radiation physics, radiotherapy, and nuclear medicine. She disseminated the results of her work in more than seventy-five articles and books as well as several book chapters and encyclopedia entries. As the Gold Medal citation of the Radiological Society of North America phrased it, her work with dosages and safety "placed every radiologist in her debt."

• Quimby's papers have not been located. Biographical sketches are in Martha J. Bailey, *American Women in Science: A Biographical Dictionary* (1994), and Emily J. McMurray, ed., *Notable Twentieth-century Scientists*, vol. 3 (1995). An obituary is in the *New York Times*, 13 Oct. 1982.

CHARLES W. CAREY, JR.

QUIMBY, Phineas Parkhurst (16 Feb. 1802–16 Jan. 1866), mental healer, was born in Lebanon, New Hampshire, the son of Jonathan Quimby a blacksmith, and Susannah White. At the age of two, his family moved to Belfast, Maine. He received a common school education and then was apprenticed to the local clockmaker. He proved fairly adept at mechanical work and invented several mechanical devices such as a steering apparatus for boats, an improved chain saw, and a clock movement. In 1827 he married Susannah Haraden, with whom he had four children.

Quimby's life changed significantly in 1838 when Robert Collyer, an itinerant mesmerist, stopped in Belfast. Quimby sat in amazement while Collyer demonstrated his ability to induce a peculiar trancelike condition that apparently gave individuals the power to perform parapsychological feats and made them receptive to a healing energy Collyer called animal magnetism. After the demonstration, Quimby questioned Collyer about animal magnetism, and Collyer encouraged him to take up the art of mesmerist healing himself. Quimby promptly set aside his other duties and followed Collyer from town to town until he had mastered the theory and practice of mesmerism. Thus began what was to be a 28-year career in mental healing.

Quimby soon made the acquaintance of Lucius Burkmar, a young man who proved to be adept at entering into the state of consciousness brought on by mesmerism. Quimby employed Burkmar to assist him in his lecture-demonstrations. He would place Burkmar into a hypnotic trance, and Burkmar would then display mesmeric phenomena such as clairvoyance, telepathy, and the ability to diagnose illnesses. Quimby often directed the entranced Burkmar to prescribe appropriate remedies for ailments suffered by audience members. On other occasions, Quimby claimed to transmit magnetic healing energies from his mind directly into the bodies of his patients. Quimby believed that these healing methods were "the result of animal magnetism, and that electricity had more or less to do with it" (Dresser, p. 30). Whatever the reason, cures abounded. Newspapers began to describe the former clockmaker from Belfast as the world's leading mesmerist healer.

With the passage of time, Quimby began to doubt that animal magnetism alone was responsible for his therapeutic successes. Most of the remedies that Burkmar prescribed were innocuous substances that seemed equally effective for any number of ailments. On one occasion Quimby substituted a less expensive medicine for the costly one Burkmar had recommended, and the patient recovered just the same. Quimby deduced from this that his patients' beliefs and expectations not only helped bring about their recoveries but also caused their illnesses in the first place. He reasoned that if a person is "deceived into a belief that he has, or is liable to have a disease, the belief is catching and the effects follow from it" (Dresser, p. 30).

Quimby was not the first American to suggest the psychological origin of physical illnesses, but he was far less materialistic than his predecessors in his conceptualization of psychosomatic interaction. By identifying "faulty" thinking patterns as the specific cause of psychosomatic distress, he moved the psychology of his day one step closer to modern psychiatry. In Quimby's words, "All sickness is in the mind of belief. . . . To cure the disease is to correct the error, destroy the cause, and the effect will cease" (Dresser, p. 180).

By 1865 nearly 12,000 patients had come to Quimby hoping to be cured. Most had found little help from the "regular" physicians of the day. Quimby's records show that many had been previously diagnosed as suffering from consumption, diphtheria, smallpox, cancer, chronic indigestion, respiratory ailments, and general nervousness. Quimby ignored physiological considerations and instead treated patients according to his conviction that all disease has a mental origin. As he put it, "Disease is what follows an opinion, it is made up of mind diverted by error" (Dresser, p. 180); wrong attitudes or ways of thinking misdirect the mind's energies. He considered it his therapeutic responsibility "to come in contact with your enemy, and restore you to health and happiness. This I do partly [by mesmerism] and partly by talking till I correct the wrong impression and establish the Truth, and the Truth is the cure" (Dresser, p. 194). Quimby's healings thus went beyond mesmerism in that he took seriously the therapeutic importance of substituting his patients' damaging beliefs about themselves with new ones based upon his practice of mind cure.

Quimby developed his method with almost no reliance upon the ideas or published works of others. He gradually reasoned out a therapeutic system that emphasized a patient's need to be educated, or more precisely reeducated, about his or her true nature. His science of health and happiness taught that one's ideas and beliefs are like valves. When individuals become pessimistic or allow the opinions of others to dominate their thinking, they close their unconscious minds to the inflow of animal magnetic energy that, Quimby believed, is responsible for health and vital living. On the other hand, positive or progressive ideas about oneself and the world cause a person to be receptive to this energy, which Quimby described as God's "invisible wisdom which fills all space, and whose attributes are all light, all wisdom, all guidance and love" (Dresser, p. 227).

Believing that most of Christian doctrine was superstition, he nonetheless maintained that all persons are capable of reconciling themselves with God's emanative spirit by employing the principles of mental science. The science of mind cure showed that no other mediator is needed and prompted Quimby to reinterpret Christ as "the God in us all. . . . The Christ or God in us is the same that was in Jesus, only in greater degree in Him" (Dresser, p. 303). Quimby's healing philosophy therefore articulated a distinctive religious and metaphysical outlook borrowed not only from mesmerism, but from other spiritual currents of the day, notably Swedenborgianism.

Quimby was an intense individual; his piercing eyes and focused concentration, combined with a pleasant expression, gave patients confidence in his ability to understand and cure their illnesses. Ironically, he devoted so much of his time and energy to his healing practice that eventually it led to his own poor health. Because he concentrated almost exclusively on healing patients, when he died in Belfast he left behind only loosely organized unpublished manuscripts. His lack of personal ambition and concern with establishing an enduring institution meant that his only legacy was through his patient-disciples. Three of them, Annetta Seabury Dresser, Julius Dresser, and especially Warren Felt Evans, developed Quimby's teachings into the New Thought or Mind Cure philosophy that was popular in the United States in the late nineteenth century. A fourth, Mary Baker Eddy, gradually transformed her interpretation of the as-yet-unpublished Quimby manuscripts into the doctrinal basis of the Church of Christ, Scientist. To be sure, Eddy developed Quimby's ideas in new and original ways, but her debt to him, both personally and intellectually, was profound. His practice of mind cure, in some sense, made Quimby the first secular psychotherapist to practice in the United States as well as the most influential individual in the tradition of mental and metaphysical healing that has continued in American popular culture.

• Quimby's writings are available in Horatio Dresser, ed., *The Quimby Manuscripts* (1921), and Ervin Seale, ed., *Complete Writings of Phineas P. Quimby* (3 vols., 1988). Early overviews of Quimby's thought are Julius A. Dresser, *The True History of Mental Science* (1887), and Annetta Dresser, *The Philosophy of P. P. Quimby* (1895). Charles Braden, *Spirits in Rebellion* (1963), and Robert C. Fuller, *Mesmerism and the American Cure of Souls* (1982), offer more-balanced interpretations of his influence.

ROBERT C. FULLER

QUINCY, Josiah (23 Feb. 1744–26 Apr. 1775), lawyer and political leader, known as Josiah Quincy, Jr., was born in Boston, Massachusetts, the son of Josiah Quincy, a merchant, and Hannah Sturgis. Quincy was educated at Harvard College, graduating with the class of 1763. Delivering the very first English oration at the 1766 commencement, when he was awarded the master's degree, Quincy chose to speak on "Patriotism" in the aftermath of the Stamp Act crisis, using a rhetoric influenced by William Shakespeare, and drawing on his favorite political writers, Algernon Sidney, John Locke, and Cato (John Trenchard and Thomas Gordon). Soon thereafter Samuel Adams drew him into Boston's inner circle of patriot spokesmen; from 1767 onward he was a frequent, though anonymous, contributor of brief newspaper essays and other political statements in opposition to British measures and on behalf of his country's liberty. In October 1769 he married Abigail Phillips, the daughter of merchant William Phillips. The couple would have two children; their son Josiah Quincy (1772–1864) would become a member of Congress, president of Harvard University, and mayor of Boston.

Quincy's temperament and talents were magnetic. When Quincy was nineteen years old, Oxenbridge Thacher, one of Boston's most eminent attorneys, took him on as an apprentice. After Thacher died two years later, Quincy successfully assumed his mentor's practice. Quincy also made himself Massachusetts's first court reporter by compiling reports of cases in the Superior Court of Judicature from 1761 through 1772. The fact that he came from a long line of prosperous, Harvard-educated landowners, merchants and magistrates, and that his older brother Samuel Quincy was a leading barrister, meant that Quincy united prominent connections with his extraordinary natural gifts and his industriousness.

Perhaps this was the reason Quincy was chosen by the patriot leadership of Boston to assist John Adams in defending the British soldiers charged with murder in the Boston Massacre of March 1770. Many contemporaries believed it was paradoxical, or even treasonous, for leading patriot lawyers to defend the "British butchers." Quincy explained that he accepted the assignment at the urging of three Boston representatives to the legislature, the Speaker of the House, Thomas Cushing, as well as Samuel Adams and John Hancock, in addition to his father-in-law of a year's standing, the great merchant William Phillips, and other key leaders. These patriot partisans all recognized that Boston's civic reputation was at stake, and that a kangaroo court would validate charges that mob rule and vigilante justice, not English law, governed Boston.

According to the evidence available and the terms of the law, there was no question that at least some of the soldiers had fired the fatal shots; but as Adams and Quincy argued, the crime was manslaughter at most, not murder. In summarizing the defense argument Quincy invoked the patriot writer John Dickinson, and John Locke's *Second Treatise on Government*. As Quincy put the case to the jury, all true friends of liberty and of the rights of their fellow citizens would vote to acquit the soldiers. After Adams closed the defense, the jury acquitted six of the soldiers and returned verdicts of manslaughter against the other two. Quincy had triumphed in an unpopular cause, establishing his mettle as a public patriot.

Quincy was among the leaders of the Boston Committee of Correspondence, elected in 1772 in opposition to crown control of the colony's judiciary. In this capacity he shared with James Otis and Samuel Adams the task of preparing a radical Whig political pamphlet for the countryside. Soon afterwards, however, Quincy suffered from tuberculosis, and on the advice of physicians in early 1773 he took a voyage to South Carolina and from there undertook a gradual overland journey back to Boston. Thus began the last phase of Quincy's political career, that of agent and emissary for Massachusetts' patriot movement. Here Quincy's personal skills including "the extreme sensibility of his temperament," as his son later put it, the confidence he enjoyed among leading patriots, as well as his learning and independent means, were all put to use. By the time he returned to Boston in May 1773, he had cultivated acquaintances with political and commercial leaders in the Carolinas, the Chesapeake, and Pennsylvania, and brought their perspectives back to his Massachusetts colleagues.

During the ensuing year Quincy resumed his activities as a Whig publicist, writing more newspaper essays over the name of the seventeenth-century English revolutionary journalist "Marchmont Nedham." In response to the Coercive Acts of 1774, he declared: "If to appear for my country is treason, and to arm for her defense is rebellion,—like my fathers, I will glory in the name of rebel and traitor,—as they did in that of puritan and enthusiast." He also published his only sustained criticism of British policy, a long pamphlet, *Observations on the Act of Parliament Commonly Called the Boston Port-Bill; with Thoughts on Civil Society and Standing Armies* (1774). In it Quincy excoriated Parliament for its extra-judicial punishment of a whole community in response to the acts of private persons, and he attacked standing armies as "armed monsters," "fatal to religion, morals, and social happiness," as well as liberty.

Quincy's Massachusetts colleagues sent him to London in September 1774, just as the Continental Congress was meeting, in order to obtain inside political intelligence. In this he appears to have been successful, meeting with many notables (including Lords North, Dartmouth, and Shelburne) and reporting back in numerous letters to correspondents from South Carolina to Boston. But because his most critical intelligence was too sensitive to commit to writing, he sailed for Boston on 16 March 1775. Forty-one days later, with his ship approaching Cape Ann, Massachusetts, Quincy succumbed to tuberculosis, so his urgent political information died with him. The battles of Lexington and Concord one week earlier may well have rendered that information obsolete. Twenty-five years later his second cousin John Quincy Adams, noted Quincy's distinguishing characteristics as "brilliant talents, uncommon eloquence, and indefatigable application" as well as an "early, enlightened, inflexible attachment to his country."

• Quincy's manuscripts, including his diaries of his journeys to South Carolina and England, his commonplace books, some letters, the inventory of his library, his court reports and legal commonplace books are part of the Quincy family collection at the Massachusetts Historical Society. Parts of this are reprinted in *Memoir of the Life of Josiah Quincy, Jun. of Massachusetts: By his Son, Josiah Quincy.* (1825), which also includes extracts from some of his newspaper pieces and the entirety of his 1774 pamphlet. References to Quincy are in the papers of John Adams and of Benjamin Franklin, as well as of many of his correspondents. Quincy's compilations as a court reporter were published as *Reports of Cases . . . in the Superior Court of Judicature of Province of Massachusetts Bay between 1761 and 1772*, ed. Susan M. Quincy (1865).

RICHARD D. BROWN

QUINCY, Josiah (4 Feb. 1772–1 July 1864), Federalist congressman, Boston mayor, and president of Harvard, was born in Boston, Massachusetts, the son of Josiah Quincy (1744–1775), a lawyer and revolutionary pamphleteer, and Abigail Phillips. Quincy's father died in 1775, leaving him to be raised by his mother and grandfather, Colonel Josiah Quincy. At age six he was sent off to Phillips Academy, where he submitted to a regimen of Calvinist doctrine and corporal punishment. In 1786 he enrolled at Harvard, where eleven Phillipses and ten Quincys had preceded him. There he became a Unitarian and class orator.

After graduating from Harvard in 1790, Quincy entered upon a legal apprenticeship. He was admitted to the Massachusetts bar in 1793, but he displayed little passion for the law. He wished to enter public life, a choice eased by an early knack for profitable investments in real estate. Elected to the Boston Town Committee in 1795, he seemed destined for a bright future as a Federalist, even as the national prospects of the party dimmed. In 1797 Quincy married Eliza Susan Morton, the daughter of a New York merchant. They had seven children and were together until her death in 1850.

Quincy ran as a Federalist for Boston's congressional seat in 1800, losing narrowly in the Jeffersonian sweep. In 1802 he made way for John Quincy Adams, but in 1804 he handily won election to the Ninth Congress. In 1805 he moved to Washington, D.C., where he was to spend the next eight years, mostly in lonely boarding-house bachelordom.

After an initial period during which he imagined a crumbling within the Jeffersonian ranks—a view encouraged by his unlikely friendship with the Capitol's most outspoken Jefferson-baiter, the Virginian John Randolph—Quincy accepted that his was a "morbid and unnerving state to which I am doomed." To relieve his boredom as much as to make a political statement, Quincy proposed bills in Congress that had no chance of passage. One, in the closing days of Jefferson's second term, calling for the president's impeachment, failed 117 to 1. During President James Madison's first term, Quincy repeatedly dared the Republicans to match their anti-British verbal ferocity with military action. In 1809 he declared that the majority, for all its talk of war with Great Britain, "could not be kicked into such a declaration."

Although Quincy was correct in 1809, when the Republicans backed away from war and from the Embargo, he was disastrously wrong in 1812 when he taunted newly elected "War Hawks" like John C. Calhoun and Henry Clay to declare war. When his support of naval preparedness measures worried some Federalists, he dismissed their "absurd and palsying fear of a war with Great Britain." Rather than mobilize antiwar contingent in Congress, he dared the pro-war forces to act. When they did so on 12 June 1812, upon Madison's call to declare war on Great Britain, the fact that Quincy voted against the war did little to overcome the judgment that his actions had made the war more likely. Thus ended his miscast turn on the national political stage.

After Quincy left Congress in 1813, several years passed before he again secured a prominent public position. Throughout the War of 1812 he opposed its prosecution as a state senator, declaring the national celebration of occasional naval victories as "not becoming a moral and religious people." He was not, however, a secessionist and stayed away from the Hartford Convention. Agricultural reforms took up some time and energy, but not enough to keep him fully occupied. In 1820, reduced to the junior Boston seat in the General Court, Quincy turned his excess energies to the problem of poor relief. The following year he became a judge on the Municipal Court of Boston, where surprised friends described his situation: "[H]e will try his hand by showing himself a good [man] among whores and rogues."

In 1821 Boston abandoned its town-meeting government in favor of incorporation. The resultant race for mayor pitted Quincy, favored by the city's "middling interests," against the Federalist-backed Harrison Gray Otis, with the result that both lost to the compromise candidate John Phillips. When illness made Phillips unavailable for reelection in 1823, Quincy easily won election as Boston's second mayor.

In his five years as mayor, Quincy left no aspect of Boston's public domain untouched or unimproved. Street cleaning was an early priority, producing a regularization of garbage removal; fire safety was another, which resulted in the creation of a professional fire department. Urban renewal led to the opening of the New Faneuil Hall Market, later renamed the Quincy Market. The mayor's concern with urban poverty led to the construction of the House of Industry, Correction and Juvenile Reform to replace out-of-door relief. Public safety was similarly addressed as was the elimination of prostitution from the city's streets. Such activism was well received by Boston's voters, who enthusiastically reelected him three times. Only in 1828, when Quincy tried to cut expenditures by closing the new and popular High School for Girls, did political opposition form to his administration's "aggression and expense." After two ballotings in December 1828, in which he fell just short of a majority, Quincy withdrew in favor of Harrison Gray Otis. He left Boston the cleanest, most orderly and best governed city in the United States.

Quincy's next job came quickly. Early in 1829, he was asked by friends to succeed John Thornton Kirkland as president of Harvard University. Kirkland had quit in 1828 after a twelve-year presidency marked in its later stages by student rebellions and faculty grumbling. On 15 June 1829 Quincy became the fifteenth president of Harvard University. He promptly took up the problem of student rebelliousness by standardizing the college's grading system and by informing students that the campus would no longer provide a haven for lawbreakers. In 1834, after an open rebellion among freshmen spread upwards, Quincy suspended the entire sophomore class. Only the support of Corporation Fellows Nathaniel Bowditch and ex-President John Quincy Adams sustained him in the face of a threatened boycott of the June commencement by the entire senior class. When the appointed day arrived, most seniors took their degrees, but it was a near thing.

Quincy thereafter directed his attention to curricular reform and the improvement of his faculty. Progress was achieved in both areas, with the classics-dominated fixed curriculum he inherited expanded to make room for science and advanced, elective instruction in history and English literature. Appointments of the botanist Asa Gray and the mathematician Benjamin Peirce gave Harvard standing in the nation's emergent scientific community, while those of Henry Wadsworth Longfellow and Edward T. Channing went well in Boston. Quincy also found time to write a two-volume *History of Harvard University* to mark the university's bicentennial in 1836. Nonetheless, his retirement in 1845, at age seventy-three, came none too soon. As an admiring undergraduate put it: "he was loved and respected but it was the respect due to an old man."

Two decades of active life remained, however. The activities of Quincy's older son, Josiah Quincy, Jr., a Whig and mayor of Boston, kept him attentive to local politics, while the abolitionist convictions of his younger son, Edmund Quincy, drew him into antislavery politics. In 1860 he was a firm supporter of Abraham Lincoln, and the assault on Fort Sumter in 1861 confirmed his old Federalist suspicions of a slaveholders' conspiracy and made him one of Boston's most redoubtable Unionists. He died in Quincy, Massachusetts, confident that his long life had been one of useful public endeavor. Few Americans have had as many reasons to believe as much.

• The bulk of Quincy's papers are divided between the Massachusetts Historical Society and the Harvard University Archives. Papers on his mayoralty are in the Boston Public Library and in the City Clerk's Office, Boston City Hall. The Adams Family Papers at the Massachusetts Historical Society contain much material on several generations of Quincys, who were South Shore neighbors and interrelated. Edmund Quincy's *Life of Josiah Quincy* (1867) is an important source, particularly for his father's congressional years. For a full-length biography, see Robert A. McCaughey, *Josiah Quincy 1772–1864: The Last Federalist* (1974). See also L. H. Butterfield, *A Pride of Quincys* (1969), and Samuel E. Morison, *Three Centuries of Harvard* (1936). Quincy's own writings, including *Memoir of Josiah Quincy, Jr.* (1825), *The History of the Boston Athenaeum* (1851), *A Municipal History of Boston* (1852), and *Memoir of the Life of John Quincy Adams* (1858), are all readable, informative and reliable. A front-page obituary is in the *New York Daily Tribune*, 4 July 1864.

ROBERT A. McCAUGHEY

QUINCY, Josiah (15 Oct. 1859–8 Sept. 1919), mayor of Boston, was born in Quincy, Massachusetts, the son of Josiah Phillips Quincy, an attorney, and Helen Huntington. He was the grandson of Josiah Quincy, Jr., mayor of Boston from 1845 to 1849, and the great-grandson of Josiah Quincy, Boston's second mayor, 1823–1828. Josiah Quincy grew up in Quincy, and following college preparatory training at Adams Academy, he enrolled at Harvard College, from which he graduated in 1880. A fine student, he won a major academic prize each year, was elected to Phi Beta Kappa and to the presidency of the *Crimson*, and was class orator at graduation. After teaching for one year at Adams Academy, he entered Harvard Law School. Upon graduation and after passing the Massachusetts bar in 1884, he set up a private law practice in Boston.

Unlike his father, who had broken the family tradition of public service, Quincy became active in the political arena. By tradition a member of the Republican party, he was involved in the Mugwump revolt in the mid-1880s. In the presidential election of 1884, Quincy and other young Republican idealists campaigned against the party's nominee, James G. Blaine. The young guard of the party, of which Quincy was a member, felt they would never make any headway in the ultraconservative Republican party. By leaving the party they rid themselves of the stain of party corruption and made a break with a history of personal disappointment.

Elected to the Massachusetts General Court in 1885, Quincy's record demonstrated his split with Republican principles and his adoption of Democratic party ideals. In the General Court he was an active advocate of laws to protect the rights of laborers. He supported reforms to improve working conditions and reduce hours, to recognize the rights of labor unions, and to protect workers involved with unions from intimidation by their employers. Quincy also became involved in civil service reform, presenting a bill that incorporated the merit system into the distribution of political appointments. Defeated in his attempt to win a seat in the U.S. House of Representatives as a Democratic candidate in 1888, Quincy continued in the General Court. His support of antitariff issues and other re-

form measures further aligned him with the Cleveland Democrats. He was chairman of the Democratic State Committee in 1891–1892 and was publicity director for the party's national committee during Grover Cleveland's 1892 presidential campaign. For his service, Cleveland appointed Quincy assistant secretary of state, a position he held for less than a year.

Quincy's performance as a state legislator and party manager enhanced his reputation and helped him garner the Democratic mayoral nomination in 1895. Winning the election, he was the first mayor to take office under the provisions of the 1885 municipal charter reform, which increased the mayoral term from one to two years. As mayor, Quincy continued to promote urban reform, beginning with the problem of urban slums. Boston had been overwhelmed by immigrants throughout the mid to late nineteenth century. The tenements, cramped, inadequate housing with primitive sanitary facilities, were a breeding ground for disease and, Quincy believed, crime. He immediately set about establishing a system of public baths, sanitation facilities, and playgrounds that would improve the mental and physical well-being of Boston's inhabitants. Many of Quincy's ideas in this area came from his study during the 1880s of European governmental policy, most notably Germany, which had experimented with public gymnasiums and playgrounds. To further this cause, Quincy also helped initiate effective slum regulation, which enabled the Board of Health to buy substandard tenement buildings and demolish them.

Quincy was a firm believer in the use of appointed, unpaid, nonpartisan boards to advise public officials on key issues. In 1896 he created the Merchant's Municipal Committee, which combined business leaders from Boston's six leading commercial organizations. This group could submit recommendations to the mayor or draft legislation for submission to the state legislature while remaining above partisan politics. Members of the board were committed to creating business support to further Quincy's municipal policies. The Merchant's Municipal Committee represented, in Quincy's words, his desire "to bring the average public-spirited citizen, sincerely desirous of promoting the best interests of the whole community, into some relation with the work the city is doing, and with those who are actually engaged in its performance." He was reelected in 1897.

Though the mayor's position had been considerably strengthened by the 1885 charter reforms, Quincy was still forced to deal with an often fractious city council, whose members were strongly influenced by Boston's powerful ward bosses, such as Martin Lomasney. Equally frustrating were Quincy's efforts to control the Boston School Committee. He had hoped to replace the elected but ineffective and financially wasteful Board of Education with one of his appointed, nonpartisan panels. However, his efforts were stymied by men like Lomasney, who sought to control the board by fielding candidates of their choosing.

Quincy did not seek reelection in 1899. In the years following his mayoralty he unsuccessfully ran for governor in 1901, was a member of the Boston Transit Commission, and served as a director of the Quincy and Boston Street Railway Company. In 1900 he married Ellen Curtis Tyler. They had one child before Ellen died in 1904. A year later he married Mary Honey; they had no children.

Quincy died of heart failure in Boston. His mayoral policies and programs were designed to improve the workings of municipal government and the welfare of the citizenry. He held office during a time of great transition as the country passed from the Gilded Age to the Progressive Era. His progressive approaches to urban problems, such as overcrowding and public health, and his strong support of prolabor legislation mark him as one of the leading big-city mayors of the late nineteenth century.

• The personal papers of the Quincy family are maintained by the Massachusetts Historical Society. Many public papers are in *Boston City Documents*. Quincy's *Inaugural Addresses of 1896 and 1898* and *Valedictory Message to the City Council, 1900* provide insight into his plans and programs. Additional sources are Geoffrey Blodgett, *The Gentle Reformers: Massachusetts Democrats in the Cleveland Era* (1966), and Michele Hilden, "The Mayors Josiah Quincy of Boston" (Ph.D. diss., Clark Univ., 1970). Jon Teaford, *Unheralded Triumph: City Government in America, 1870–1900* (1984), outlines Quincy's Boston and also provides detailed background information on urban government in the era. Obituaries are in the *Boston Globe* and the *Boston Post*, both 9 Sept. 1919.

K. M. GRANFIELD

QUINCY, Samuel (13 Apr. 1734–9 Aug. 1789), lawyer, was born in Braintree (in what is now Quincy), Massachusetts, the son of Josiah Quincy, a Suffolk County militia colonel and justice of the peace, and Hannah Sturgis. Samuel's brother, Josiah, Jr., also a lawyer, was a leading Boston revolutionary.

Quincy graduated from Harvard in 1754. The following year he began the study of law under Benjamin Prat, a leading Boston lawyer who later became chief justice of New York. In November 1758 Quincy, with his Braintree neighbor and Harvard contemporary John Adams, was admitted as an attorney of the Suffolk County Inferior Court of Common Pleas at Boston. He was admitted to the superior court as an attorney in November 1761 and was among those called as a barrister when that rank was established in August 1762.

Quincy married Hannah Hill, daughter of Thomas Hill of Boston, a distiller, on 16 June 1761. The couple settled in Boston and had two sons and a daughter. Quincy quickly became established at the bar. Though his practice was centered in Boston, like other Boston lawyers he traveled with the superior court on circuit throughout the province. A member of Boston's West Church and a Mason, he was a philanthropic supporter of Harvard College and was involved in a variety of town committees. John Singleton Copley, a client, painted him in the late 1760s, wearing the barrister's formal wig and gown. As the Revolution approached, Quincy at least nominally supported the patriot cause, in which his brother Josiah, Jr., was a leader.

Quincy is best known for his role in the episode known to history as the Boston Massacre. In February 1770 Ebenezer Richardson, a British customs informer, fatally shot an eleven-year-old boy during a demonstration. Two weeks later, on 5 March, British soldiers guarding the Customs House fired on a mob of citizens, killing five of them. In the tense and volatile atmosphere produced by these events, Quincy joined Robert Treat Paine as prosecutor both in Richardson's trial and in the separate trials of the officer and eight enlisted men indicted for the Massacre shootings. The two lawyers were specially appointed for these prosecutions because the provincial attorney general, Jonathan Sewall, had absented himself at the time of the proceedings.

Richardson was found guilty, despite the four sitting judges' charges to the jury emphasizing justifiable homicide. In the Massacre trials, Quincy's efforts as prosecutor have been obscured by the legendary performances of Adams and Josiah Quincy, Jr., in vigorously defending the hated British despite the lawyers' strong attachment to and involvement in the revolutionary cause. Whether through the skill of defense counsel or a political instinct to calm the situation, the officer and six of the soldiers were acquitted. Two soldiers were convicted of manslaughter. The transcript and other surviving materials from these unusually well-documented trials show that Quincy demonstrated solid professional skill in his argument and presentation of the evidence, though he did not match the passion and intensity displayed by his opponents.

Subsequently, Quincy, with other leaders of the bar, became objects of royal patronage. In March 1771 he was appointed a justice of the peace for Suffolk County and solicitor general of the province. In the latter position, filled for the first time since 1767, he drew a significant salary from Crown revenues. On the eve of the Revolution, he joined those lawyers and others who manifested loyalty to royal government, signing the farewell address to Governor Thomas Hutchinson and welcoming his successor, General Thomas Gage. Yet, in the confused state of politics at that time, he remained critical of British policy toward the colonies, causing Adams to fume that in his political discourse, Quincy impressed only those "who do not know that he is ignorant of every Rope in the Ship" (letter to Abigail Adams, 7 July 1774). After the battles of Lexington and Concord, Quincy joined other Loyalists in sailing to England, leaving his wife and children in Massachusetts. Although he never sought political preferment or other support from the British government and maintained a steady and affectionate correspondence with his wife and relations in Massachusetts, he incurred the wrath of Boston's patriots. His house was plundered by the Boston mob, and he was among the Loyalists proscribed by Massachusetts legislation of 1778, under which his real estate was confiscated and sold.

Despairing of the possibility of a return to Massachusetts, in 1780 Quincy moved from England to the West Indian colony of Antigua, where he had obtained the position of comptroller of the customs and where he again undertook the practice of law. In the latter pursuit, he evidently made a substantial success and his wife and two younger children soon joined him. When his wife died in 1782, he moved to St. Kitts and ultimately, in 1785, to St. Croix, where his law practice continued to flourish. There, in 1787, he married M. A. Chadwell, widow of Abraham Chadwell. They had no children. In 1789, with his new wife, he embarked for England but became ill on the voyage and died at sea.

Quincy was a solid and successful lawyer who maintained his affection and devotion to family and friends throughout the upheavals incident upon the Revolution and its aftermath. Politically engaged on neither side, he was castigated by those who had made the commitment to the revolutionary movement. In 1776, upon learning of the damage to Quincy's Boston house, John Adams wrote, "I wish I could be clear that it is no moral Evil to pity [Quincy] and his Lady. . . . Whenever Vanity and Gaiety, a Love of Pomp and Dress, Furniture, Equipage, Buildings, great Company, expensive Diversions, and elegant Entertainments get the better of the Principles and Judgments of Men or Women there is no knowing where they will stop, nor into what Evils, natural, moral, or political, they will lead us" (letter to Abigail Adams, 14 Apr. 1776). Yet, in the reflective mood of his later years, Adams recalled Quincy as an "easy, social and benevolent Companion, not without Genius, Elegance and Taste" (Adams, *Autobiography*, 30 Nov. 1804).

• Quincy's papers are among the Quincy papers in the Massachusetts Historical Society, and the Copley portrait is in the Boston Museum of Fine Arts. Quincy's legal career is documented in the Massachusetts Superior Court records and files, 1761–1774, Massachusetts State Archives. A diary of Quincy's life in London, 1776–1777, is printed in the Massachusetts Historical Society, *Proceedings*, 1st ser. 19 (1882): 214–23, and extracts from his correspondence, 1785–1879, appear in James H. Stark, *The Loyalists of Massachusetts* (1910), pp. 367–76. A thorough account of Quincy's life is found in Clifford K. Shipton, *Sibley's Harvard Graduates*, vol. 13 (1965), pp. 478–88. John Adams's contemporary and later comments on Quincy are found in Lyman H. Butterfield et al., eds., *Diary and Autobiography of John Adams*, vols. 1–3 (1961), and *Adams Family Correspondence*, vol. 1 (1963). Quincy's legal career is also documented in L. Kinvin Wroth and Hiller B. Zobel, eds., *Legal Papers of John Adams*, vols. 1–3 (1965), which includes the full transcript and Quincy's notes of the Boston Massacre trials in volume 3. The trials are thoroughly discussed in Hiller B. Zobel, *The Boston Massacre* (1970).

L. KINVIN WROTH

QUINICHETTE, Paul (17 May 1916–25 May 1983), jazz tenor saxophonist, was born in Denver, Colorado, the son of a French surgeon and an African-American businesswoman whose names are unknown. His father, whose surname was originally "Quinichet," died in 1929; in spite of adopting the altered spelling, the family retained the French pronunciation ("Quinishay"). His mother worked her way from head of the stenographic department to the chair of the board of American Woodman, a prosperous African-American insurance company.

With his parents' encouragement to excel in music, Quinichette was given his first clarinet around the age of seven. Under the supervision of a local German teacher, he acquired a strong foundation in the classical tradition. Later he studied the alto saxophone. He studied music briefly at the University of Denver in 1942 and at Tennesse State University in Nashville, where he was a scholarship student for two years. His claim to have graduated from the University of Denver with a music major cannot be documented by institutional records. His involvement with jazz came early—he played along with recordings on his family's manual Victrola and credited the "oldtimers" with helping him learn to improvise (Dance, p. 299). His first professional opportunities, taken without his mother's blessing, occurred in local night spots in his native Denver. Around 1938 he began to devote his summer vacations to on-the-job training as a sideman in the so-called "territory bands" of Lloyd Hunter and Nat Towles (out of Omaha) and Ernie Fields (out of Tulsa) and played a relentless series of one-night stands throughout the upper Midwest. For a time, with the Fields ensemble, he backed up the stage shows of dancer Bill "Bojangles" Robinson, but he grew dissatisfied with the nature of the production as well as the star's personal antics. He worked briefly with Shorty Sherock's quintet in Chicago and played in a band led by Lucky Millinder. During this period he stopped playing the clarinet because of its waning popularity in jazz circles.

In 1941 his dissatisfaction with Robinson's show led to his joining Jay McShann's band in Kansas City as a tenor saxophonist and the opportunity to work alongside a young Charlie Parker. He stayed with McShann for less than a year but identified with the blues-based repertory of that ensemble. Later he characterized himself as "a Kansas City type, a 4-Beat swinger" (Rusch, p. 33). He followed this association with memberships in the bands of rhythm-and-blues drummer Johnny Otis and jazz saxophonist Benny Carter and in the quartet of Sid Catlett. A move to New York City in the late 1940s enabled him to play and record with a variety of ensembles, including those led by Louis Jordan, Millinder, Joe Thomas, Eddie Wilcox, J. C. Heard, Henry "Red" Allen, Dinah Washington, and "Hot Lips" Page. His maturity as an improviser and his prominence as an artist occurred after the heyday of big-band jazz when, between 1951 and 1953, he worked in the smaller ensembles (with five, seven, or nine players) constituted by Count Basie in response to evolving economic conditions and tastes.

During the Basie years Quinichette acquired the nickname "Vice Pres" because of affinities between his personal style and that of jazz immortal Lester Young, known to his intimates as "Pres." Significantly, the two saxophonists were longtime acquaintances. They had known each other and had practiced together before Young left Denver to join Fletcher Henderson's band. As a fledgling performer, Quinichette had the benefit of Young's counsel and advocacy on numerous occasions. Yet Quinichette resisted his reputation as an illustrious disciple or follower of Young or, in the view of harsher critics, as an outright copycat, contending that he did not emulate Young as others did. Much admired for his sense of swing, Quinichette believed that his own sound and concept developed "parallel" to that of Young and that stylistic similarities had been present from the very beginning. He proudly acknowledged his debt to Young and to pioneering jazz saxophonist Frankie Trumbauer, who had likewise profoundly influenced Young and others of their generation. Young, moreover, held Quinichette in high personal and professional esteem.

In the course of his career, Quinichette's talents as an improviser became even more apparent and his solos demonstrated greater originality, while still echoing his southwestern roots. Critic Whitney Balliett, in response to a live performance in New York in January 1974, contrasted Quinichette's seasoned playing with that of Young: "the special quality that infuses the playing of so many Southwestern musicians presses steadily to the fore. The skin is Young but the stuffing is Herschel Evans and Buddy Tate. . . . His tone was somber, and there were blue notes, low-register booms, and abrupt high exclamations. It was the sort of naked lyrical performance that Young could never have lowered his cool for" (Balliett, p. 130).

In early 1953 Quinichette left Basie's band to lead his own combo; he had made five recordings for Mercury as a combo leader in 1952. These endeavors, however, occurred under Basie's guidance; Basie himself participated as pianist in one recording session. Quinichette also performed with the Benny Goodman octet (1955), the Nat Pierce big band (1955), collaborated with John Coltrane (1957), and toured with Billie Holiday for almost a year.

Reduced opportunities for freelance jazz musicians caused by the emerging popularity of rock and roll forced Quinichette to seek an alternate trade. He studied electronics in a three-year course at an RCA-sponsored school in the 1960s and worked as a technician in New York City. After some experiences gigging on weekends, he resurfaced in the New York jazz scene as a regular player in clubs beginning in early 1973. In 1974 he was featured in a Saturday and Sunday series at the West End Cafe in a group called Two Tenor Boogie, which involved pianist Sammy Price and at different times tenor players Buddy Tate, George Kelly, and Harold Ashby. He was also reunited briefly with McShann. Among his last performances was a tribute to Count Basie in January 1975. He died in New York City.

While Quinichette did not succeed in earning a place in the highest tier of jazz artists, the length of his career, the variety of performance contexts, the stature of his associates, and the quality of his improvisations all suggest the quality and durability of his contributions. His recorded legacy is found on both 78-rpm recordings and long-playing records: the former includes as sideman four titles with Johnny Otis and five titles with Count Basie and as leader fourteen titles; the latter include, as sideman, *Kansas City Memories* with Jay McShann, *The Herd Rides Again . . . in Stereo* with Woody Herman, *Borderline* with Mel Powell, *The Big Sound*, with Gene Ammons, *Big Band at the Savoy Ballroom* with Nat Pierce, and *Basie Jazz* and *Wheelin' and Dealin'* with Basie; as leader, *The Vice Pres*, *Moods*, and *The Kid from Denver*; and as coleader, *Cattin' with Coltrane and Quinichette*. He performed in three films: an all-black musical featuring Louis Jordan's ensemble, *Look Out Sister* (1948); and two retrospective documentaries, *The Subject Is Jazz* (segment 5, 1958) and a celebration of Kansas City jazz called *The Last of the Blue Devils* (1979). He was the composer of at least three jazz tunes: "Prevue," "Crossfire," and "Sandstone."

• The most important accounts of Quinichette's life and career appear in published interviews in Robert D. Rusch, *Jazztalk: The Cadence Interviews* (1984) and in studies of the Basie band, notably Raymond Horricks, *Count Basie and His Orchestra: Its Music and Its Musicians* (1957; repr. 1971); and Stanley Dance, *The World of Count Basie* (1980). A brief characterization of his mature playing may be found in Whitney Balliett, *New York Notes: A Journal of Jazz in the Seventies* (1976; repr. 1977). Discographies are included in Roger D. Kinkle, *The Complete Encyclopedia of Popular Music and Jazz, 1900–1950* (1974), and Jorgen Grunnet Jepsen, *Jazz Records, 1942–1962* (1963).

MICHAEL J. BUDDS

QUINLAN, Karen Ann (29 Mar. 1954–11 June 1985), subject of a legal battle concerning the right to terminate hospital life support, was born Mary Ann Monahan in Scranton, Pennsylvania; her birth mother immediately gave her up for adoption by Joseph Quinlan, an accountant, and Julia Duane, a church secretary. Julia Quinlan had previously suffered three miscarriages and one stillbirth on account of an undetected Rh-negative condition, and the Quinlans had given up on the prospect of conceiving children on their own. The Quinlans adopted Karen through Catholic Charities. Karen grew up in the small town of Landing, New Jersey. She graduated from Morris Catholic High School in 1972; her graduation portrait was later used to illustrate many of the news stories about her case. She worked at a series of service and manufacturing jobs while considering earning a living through music. In 1975 she moved out of her parents' house for the first time. A few months later, she rented a room from two acquaintances; eight days later, she lost consciousness.

On the night of 14 April 1975, just sixteen days after she turned twenty-one, Quinlan was at a bar when she appeared to lose consciousness. She had taken a variety of medications (both prescription and over-the-counter) in an attempt to relieve menstrual cramps. After she lost consciousness, her friends brought

Quinlan to her rented room nearby. There she stopped breathing, and a housemate administered cardiopulmonary resuscitation and brought Karen to Newton Memorial Hospital in Newton, New Jersey. She was admitted at 1:23 A.M. on 15 April 1975.

Much has been written about the cause of Quinlan's descent into coma, but the actual etiology remains somewhat uncertain. Her blood tests revealed evidence of quinine (presumably from gin-and-tonics), as well as aspirin, diazepam (Valium), and other substances, but none was present in abnormally high levels. However, this combination of painkillers, tranquilizers, and alcohol sent Quinlan into cardiac arrest, which in turn cut off the supply of blood and oxygen to the brain. The specific damage occurred in the region of the thalamus, and this eventually led to a persistent vegetative state.

After stabilizing the unconscious Quinlan and placing her on a respirator to aid her breathing, physicians at Newton Memorial called in a neurologist, Robert Morse, to examine her. Morse, an osteopath, first saw Quinlan on 18 April. Quinlan, in a "decorticate state," was transferred to St. Clare's Hospital in Denville, New Jersey, on 24 April. By June 1975 she had dropped in weight from 115 to 80 pounds, and Morse's initially hopeful assessment had changed to a more pessimistic prognosis. On 31 July the Quinlans signed a release form directing Morse to discontinue "all extraordinary measures" prolonging the life of their daughter.

Morse expressed doubts about the "moral issues" involved in disconnecting the respirator, and eventually the attorney for St. Clare's informed the Quinlans that the hospital would not remove the machine. Because Karen was an adult living outside her parental home, the hospital did not believe that the Quinlans had the legal right to discontinue treatment. The original legal action in the case, therefore, was a motion to name the Quinlans as legal guardian of their daughter. This was filed 12 September 1975 by Paul Armstrong, a former legal aid attorney who had resigned from that service to take on the Quinlans' case.

The media reaction was immediate and dramatic. This was the first example of a medical-ethics decision being argued in a civil court. The hospital's position was simple: by the norms of the day regarding what constituted death, Quinlan was still alive; therefore, they could not withdraw treatment already commenced. Judge Robert Muir, Jr., an elder of the Presbyterian church who was clear in his decision that he did not wish to "exercise Divine Powers," denied the Quinlans' petition on 10 November 1975. (The Quinlans' own Roman Catholic church also supported their decision.) The New Jersey State Supreme Court accepted the case on appeal and ruled in favor of the Quinlans on 31 March 1976. Chief Justice Richard J. Hughes issued the decision, stating, "There comes a point at which the individual's rights overcome the state's interests." The decision has been characterized by legal experts as especially activist in nature, involving a change to New Jersey's laws rather than an interpretation of existing statutes.

The New Jersey Supreme Court decision had far-reaching implications for medical ethics in the United States. In the medical profession, the Quinlan case opened the door for participation by persons other than physicians in ethical decisions. Furthermore, research into the etiology of Quinlan's condition led to new theories on the role of the thalamus in consciousness. On a legislative level, several states (most notably California) enacted statutes regarding patients' rights, including provisions for a form of "living will." Karen Ann Quinlan herself, however, never saw these developments occur. She survived for approximately nine years after the respirator was removed, finally succumbing to pneumonia at the Morris View Nursing Home in Morris Plains, New Jersey, without ever having regained consciousness.

• The court documents relating to the Karen Ann Quinlan case were collected and published as *In the Matter of Karen Ann Quinlan* (2 vols., 1976), providing a detailed portrait of the medical situation and the stated objectives of all parties in the case. The status of the law at the time of the *Quinlan* decision is illustrated by Karen Teel, "The Physician's Dilemma: A Doctor's View: What the Law Should Be," *Baylor Law Review* 27 (1975): 6–9. An editorial in the *Journal of the American Medical Association* 234 (1975): 1057 argues that the Quinlan case represented a dangerous infringement on doctors' right to practice as they saw fit. Ernan McMullin, ed., *Death and Decision* (1978), collects papers from a symposium on the case; see especially Leslie S. Rothenberg, "The Judicial Dilemma." Popular press works on the case include B. D. Colen, *Karen Ann Quinlan: Dying in the Age of Eternal Life* (1976). Henry R. Glick, *The Right to Die* (1992), covers both popular movements and legal decisions. David J. Rothman's excellent history of bioethics, *Strangers at the Bedside* (1991), sets the case in the context of changing standards of medical responsibility. Personal information on Quinlan is also in the *New York Times* obituary, 12 June 1985; the best source, however, is Joseph Quinlan and Julia Quinlan, with Phyllis Battelle, *Karen Ann: The Quinlans Tell Their Story* (1977).

KEITH L. LOSTAGLIO

QUINN, John (24 Apr. 1870–28 July 1924), lawyer, collector of art and manuscripts, and patron of the arts, was born in Tiffin, Ohio, the son of James Quinn, a prosperous baker, and Mary Quinlan. Quinn's success as a lawyer came early. He took a law degree from Georgetown University in 1893 and a second law degree from Harvard in 1895. Practicing in New York City, he established himself as one of the city's leading financial lawyers in 1905 by dealing with the legal complications of J. B. Ryan's takeover of Equitable Life Assurance Association of the United States, a firm that controlled $400 million in assets. Hard-driving and demanding, Quinn once fired five junior partners in one year. Yet in spite of his preoccupation with his work, he performed inestimable services for the arts.

In 1902 Quinn traveled to Ireland and met several members of the Yeats family, including John Butler Yeats and his two sons, William Butler Yeats and Jack

Butler Yeats. From John Butler Yeats he bought one painting and from Jack Butler Yeats several. From William Butler Yeats he was to buy many manuscripts over a period of years. He began a lifelong correspondence with all three and with George Russell. Back in the United States he helped arrange a lecture tour for William Butler Yeats, a service he later performed for actress Florence Farr and for many other visiting celebrities.

Quinn helped many foreign writers, including John Millington Synge, with copyright problems in the United States, and in 1911 he defended the Abbey Theater Group, which was touring with *The Playboy of the Western World*. It was primarily Quinn's influence that kept the play from being suppressed in Chicago; in Philadelphia he found it necessary to free the troupe on habeas corpus before defending the play itself.

Although the reaction of American Irish to the Irish theater turned Quinn away from the Irish movement somewhat, he maintained his correspondence with Irish literati and continued to collect their manuscripts. Increasingly, however, he concentrated on collecting paintings and sculpture. He made large collections of work by Augustus John, Wyndham Lewis, and Jacob Epstein, but he came to concentrate primarily on contemporary French work. He was one of the moving forces behind the Armory Show, a major introduction of European art to the United States that opened in February 1913. Besides urging John and Epstein to participate, he lent seventy-seven works that he owned, including those of Mary Cassatt, Paul Cézanne, Vincent Van Gogh, Jacob Epstein, and Gwen John.

In the midst of his other enterprises, Quinn provided steady encouragement to John Butler Yeats, who had come to the United States at the age of seventy in 1908 and remained until his death in 1922. Quinn entertained him, bought pictures from him, and helped arrange for portrait commissions. Another major friendship was with Joseph Conrad, from whom Quinn began buying manuscripts in 1911. Soon they corresponded regularly about art, politics, and personal matters, and Quinn came to have an option on Conrad manuscripts. The relationship cooled after 1919, when Quinn discovered Conrad had sold some of his typescript to T. J. Wise, and ended when Conrad avoided meeting him on a trip to the United States in 1923.

Quinn occasionally found himself supporting works toward which he had ambivalent or even hostile feelings, and he had a mixed record of victories and defeats. In 1917 he provided partial financial support for the *Little Review* in spite of his disagreement with its pacifist tendencies and his conviction that blatantly sexual work, whatever its quality, belonged in books for those who wished to read it, not in widely circulating magazines. He unsuccessfully defended the editors, Margaret Anderson and Jane Heap, when they were prosecuted for serializing James Joyce's *Ulysses*, although they had continued to do so against his ad-

vice. The *Little Review* was not excluded from the mails, as Quinn feared it might be, but the women were fined $50 each and forbidden to publish further excerpts. He was unable to find a publisher for *Ulysses*, but in 1922 he arranged T. S. Eliot's contract for *The Waste Land* with Liveright and helped to coordinate the poem's appearance in the *Dial*. Eliot rewarded him by presenting him with a manuscript copy with Ezra Pound's comments, a document that has proved invaluable to scholars since it was rediscovered among Quinn's papers in 1971.

In 1918 Quinn began to suffer from cancer, which eventually proved fatal. He died in New York City. A lifelong bachelor, he had no immediate family and left the bulk of his estate to a sister, Julia Anderson. Bequests were made to two former mistresses, one of whom, Dorothy Coates, tried unsuccessfully to claim status as a wife. The sorting and selection of his literary papers was left to Jeanne Robert Foster, a companion of his last years, who was instructed to deposit the papers finally with the New York Public Library.

Although Quinn was a fascinating and colorful figure, he is most likely to be remembered for his associations with others—as someone who appears at crucial points in many biographies rather than as one remembered for himself. Quinn was a successful lawyer and was active in politics, but he is remembered for the unexampled services he performed for the arts during the first two decades of the twentieth century. As a buyer of manuscripts and works of art, as a patron for individuals and for struggling new periodicals, as a provider of legal service and liaison service with publishers, Quinn advanced the careers of a prodigious number of writers and artists. B. L. Reid sums Quinn up: "Quinn had taste but above all he had nerve and susceptibility, bravery ready for the bravery around him while it was still brave" (p. 662).

• The bulk of Quinn's manuscript collection and letters is in the John Quinn Memorial Collection at the New York Public Library. This collection is indexed and inventoried in *Bulletin of the New York Public Library* 78, no. 2 (1975). Another collection at the Lilly Library, Indiana University, includes letters and the final draft, including holograph corrections, of *The Playboy of the Western World*.

B. L. Reid, *The Man from New York: John Quinn and His Friends* (1968), is the principal biography and includes an admirable bibliography. Timothy Materer has edited *The Selected Letters of Ezra Pound to John Quinn, 1915–1925* (1991). Janis Londraville and Richard Londraville have published several selections of Quinn's correspondence, including "Two Men at War with Time: The Unpublished Correspondence of Wyndham Lewis and John Quinn," *Journal of the English Association* 39, no. 164 (1990): 97–145; "Two Men at War with Time: The Unpublished Correspondence of Wyndham Lewis and John Quinn, Concluded," *Journal of the English Association* 39, no. 165 (1990): 229–51; "The Stage Irishman and Pseudo-Celtic Drama: Selections from the Correspondence of Frank Hugh O'Donnell and John Quinn," *Yeats: An Annual of Critical and Textual Studies* (1991); and "'A First Class Fighting Man': Frank Hugh O'Donnell's Correspondence with John Quinn," *Eire-Ireland: A Journal of Irish Studies* 26, no. 3 (1991): 60–81. Janis Londraville has published Quinn's correspondence with May Morris as "The Private Voice of May Morris," *Journal of Pre-Raphaelite Studies* 2, no. 2 (1993): 28–37. An obituary is in the *New York Times*, 30 July 1924.

DALTON GROSS
MARY JEAN GROSS

QUINNEY, John Waun-Nau-Con (1797–21 July 1855), Stockbridge (Mohican) tribal leader, was born on New Stockbridge reservation near Oneida, New York, the son of Stockbridge parents of whom nothing is known. The Stockbridge had become an impoverished remnant of their former selves, reduced to the small refuge given them by the Oneida tribe. Belonging to the Algonkian linguistic group, the tribe who in their now extinct language called themselves the Muh-he-con-new, "like our waters, which are never still," had formerly owned the Hudson River valley from Manhattan Island to Lake Champlain, from Albany to the Berkshires. Their tragic fate at the hands of corrupt land speculators, fickle white policies, and grinding poverty, coupled with their heavy loss of life fighting for the United States during the Revolution, informed the life of John Quinney. To rescue them from extinction, preserve their culture, and enhance their well-being principled his actions.

Quinney had a distinguished brother, Austin, a tribal leader, and a renowned sister, Electa, the first public school teacher in Wisconsin and a missionary to the Cherokee. When Quinney was a youth, the elders of the tribe took particular interest in him. When the U.S. government offered to pay for the schooling of three Stockbridge, the tribe selected him as one to attend the common English school of Caleb Underhill at Yorktown, New York, from the autumn of 1810 until 1 May 1813. He showed a talent for statesmanship, demonstrated an ability to express himself in English and Mohican, possessed a keen mind, and slowly gained the confidence of the tribe. By the time he entered manhood, the entire business of the tribe had fallen on him.

In his youth Quinney joined the Presbyterian church and eventually became, we assume from secondary references, a preacher in the faith. In 1818 he and Captain Hendrick Aupaumut, a Stockbridge officer in the Revolution, translated the Westminster Assembly (1643–1649) shorter catechism into Mohican, an unusual step for tribes who typically relied on missionaries for this work. The fragments of his manuscripts that have survived, his several speeches, and his official statements, memorials, and legal arguments consistently display a deep knowledge of the tribe's history and culture.

Before the War of 1812 the Stockbridge had decided to migrate to the West. Land speculators, pioneer pressures on their reserve, and the settlement of immoral whites on their border compelled them to depart. In southern Indiana their ancient friends the Miami had sold them sufficient land to start anew, but when the first migrating group arrived in 1818, they found the government alerted by speculators had moved quickly to take it away by a treaty, secured a few days before. The tribal protests, superbly argued and clearly stated by Quinney, made no impression on a callous Congress. In 1821, and again in 1822 to enlarge it, the tribe directed him and two others to obtain land in Wisconsin, near Green Bay. Together with two other New York tribes ready to migrate, the Brothertown and the Oneida, they purchased 7 million acres from the Menominee in a right in common. In 1825, through lengthy negotiation with the New York legislature, Quinney obtained a law that gave the tribe full and fair value for its remaining lands in that state.

Quinney organized and directed the tribe's removal from New York. For several years he proceeded gradually with annual groups to a reservation along the upper Fox River, near present-day South Kaukauna. He escorted the bands, some of which were aged, without loss of life. While in transit the Menominee, with the aid of local French traders and the federal government, questioned the validity of the Stockbridge purchases and broke the contract, leaving the tribe without title in Wisconsin. The controversy consumed much time and considerable energy of the tribal leaders and led to major federal investigations and additional treaties. As part of the process Quinney traveled to Washington, D.C., where he secured a new reservation, two townships in size, on the east side of Lake Winnebago, a day's journey from the original.

In 1833 Quinney framed a constitution for the tribe that led to the abandonment of hereditary powers and implemented republicanism. The federal government delayed payment of tribal funds for years, plunging the members into private debts that meant the sale of the reservation. At the same time some members wanted to migrate west. By Quinney's clever device they sold half of the reservation, paid their debts, funded the disaffected to leave, and saved the rest. Financial reverses coupled with aggressive pressures by whites kept the tribe in turmoil for years.

In 1843 Congress imposed citizenship on the Stockbridge and allotted their lands to the members in fee simple absolute. Quinney resisted the act and formed a tribal faction known as the Indian Party to work for tribal ownership of the land, fearing that white speculators would soon acquire the allotted lands and the tribe would perish. The Citizen Party Stockbridge, assisted by speculators, rose in opposition to resist his every move, sending delegates to Washington to counteract his efforts. Dire poverty dogged his steps. In the midst of the struggle to restore the land the contradictory government made the treaty of 1848 with the tribe to move it west of the Mississippi River to a new home. Quinney then worked with untiring zeal for removal, hoping it would preserve the old culture and finally permit the Stockbridge to have a permanent home. When fear of the Sioux and love of their rich soil in Wisconsin dampened the desire of members to remove, he again turned to Congress, lobbying it to restore to the tribe its own land, customs, and government in Wisconsin. Opposition forces blocked a home in the rich farm land until 1856, when, after Quinney died, federal officials by the crude use of whiskey, bribery, and deception located the tribe on its present poor sandy reserve near Bowler.

In 1852 Quinney again pressed his claim against the government for his expenditures on behalf of the poor tribe made over a period of thirty years. While dispute arose over his claim, he had kept exact records that his then opponents and later commentators never referred to in discussing the issue. Altogether Quinney had made nine visits to Washington for the tribe, giving up six years of his life, neglecting personal business, and sacrificing his private life. Little is known of his wife and children. He was the subject of oil paintings by Amos Hamlin, Charles B. King, and George Catlin.

At Quinney's death in Stockbridge, Wisconsin, an anonymous tribal member eulogized him, lamenting the tribe had sustained "an irreparable loss."

• A few of Quinney's papers are in the State Historical Society of Wisconsin. In the same archive the papers of his nephew John C. Adams (1842–1895), an attorney and famous Stockbridge leader, contain many of his manuscripts; the papers of Cutting Marsh, a missionary to the tribe (1830–1848), are also important. The Museum of the American Indian Library has the Quinney-Miller Family Papers that have some material on John W. as well as his traditional deerskin jacket. The Stockbridge tribe's important historical archives near Bowler contain copies of numerous materials on him. His publications are mostly confined to official documents most often published in the congressional serial set. His 4 July 1854 speech at Reidsville, New York, is in Wisconsin Historical Collections 4 (1859): 313–20, as "Speech of John Quinney." The same volume contains a "historical notice" of him by a tribesman, Levi Konkapot, Jr., titled "The Last of the Mohicans," pp. 303–7; an anonymous Stockbridge obituary, "Death of John W. Quinney," pp. 309–11; and Quinney's "Memorial of John W. Quinney," pp. 321–33, to Congress dated 1852, which includes biographical information. The Assembly's Shorter Catechism (1818) is his only published work. The secondary literature mentioning him includes J. N. Davidson, Muh-he-ka-ne-ok: A History of the Stockbridge Nation (1893), and a portion of Joseph M. Schafer, The Winnebago-Horicon Basin (1937), both outdated. Herman J. Viola, Diplomats in Buckskins: A History of Indian Delegations in Washington City (1981), discusses Quinney but confuses Stockbridge politics. The Amos Hamlin portrait (1849) hangs in the State Historical Society of Wisconsin. The Gilcrease Institute of Tulsa owns the Charles B. King oil (1842), while the George Catlin portrait (1830) is in the Smithsonian.

DAVID R. WRONE

QUINTARD, Charles Todd (22 Dec. 1824–15 Feb. 1898), physician and Protestant Episcopal bishop, was born in Stamford, Connecticut, the son of Isaac Quintard and Clarissa Hoyt Shaw. He attended Columbia College (N.Y.) and the medical college of the University of the City of New York, where he received the M.D. in 1847.

After a year as attending physician at the New York Dispensary, Quintard moved to Athens, Georgia, where he combined a private practice with scholarship on topics such as typhoid fever, the history of medicine, and the fraudulent nature of certain popular medical treatments of the day. He entered a partnership with Dr. William King in Roswell, Georgia, in 1848 and married his partner's cousin Eliza Catherine King Hand. They had three children. In 1851 he joined the faculty of Memphis Medical College to teach physiology and pathological anatomy. There, his writing career continued as the new editor of the Memphis Medical Recorder, and his work evaluating the health of the city prompted local officials to begin keeping public health records.

Quintard began study for ordination in the Protestant Episcopal church in 1854 under the tutelage of James H. Otey, the first bishop of Tennessee. His reasons for changing careers are shrouded in silence; perhaps he had been influenced in that direction by his father, who, he later noted, "delighted in the Church's holy ways." Ordained a priest in 1856, he served as rector of Calvary Church in Memphis in 1857 and of Church of the Advent in Nashville from 1858 until the outbreak of the Civil War.

In 1861 Quintard became chaplain and medical surgeon for the First Tennessee Regiment. He participated in battles in Virginia, Kentucky, and Tennessee; served briefly as an aide to General W. W. Loring; and wrote two books on the meaning of suffering for the men he served: Confederate Soldier's Pocket Manual of Devotions (1863) and Balm for the Weary and Wounded (1864). He also served local congregations in Atlanta and Columbus, Georgia, while stationed in those cities. Recalling these years, a contemporary wrote, "Quick in movement, in apprehension, in sympathy; affectionate, generous; a skilled physician and surgeon, as well as a devout and ardent Christian Priest, he made for himself a place in the hearts and minds of the soldiers of Tennessee" (B. Cheshire, The Church in the Confederate States [1912], p. 84).

Soon after the war, Quintard returned to Nashville and was elected the second Protestant Episcopal bishop of Tennessee in 1865. He was consecrated the same year at the general convention in Philadelphia that reunited the northern and southern churches into a single denomination.

Quintard's 33-year episcopate was characterized by efforts to rebuild war-ravaged churches, educate the southern clergy and youth, and restructure the diocese into smaller administrative units. He was anxious to see his denomination expand, yet he recognized that in the eyes of many, the Episcopal church seemed only the domain of the privileged, or as he once put it, a "first class car on a celestial railroad." In order to make his church "a refuge for all—the lame, halt and blind as well as the rich and the fashionable in clothes of fine linen," he opposed the custom of pew rents, which turned away the poor from the sanctuary, and he instead sought out the "barefoot saints and ragged saints who live down in cellars."

The bishop's urban ministry, prompted by concerns about the distressing social effects of industrialization, anticipated the later work of the Social Gospel movement. After establishing in 1869 a successful "refuge" for the destitute in Memphis, he developed in 1873 a comprehensive plan of social action for his diocese, offering food, shelter, education, and evangelism for the poor. He later founded missions to the laborers at the new foundries in South Pittsburg (1876) and Chattanooga, Tennessee (1880).

Concerned as well to expand into the African-American community, which traditionally had maintained few ties with the Episcopal church, Quintard opposed those in his denomination who sought to segregate blacks into separate churches. He lent valuable support to the Colored Orphan Asylum in Memphis and was instrumental in founding Hoffman Hall, a seminary for African Americans on the campus of Fisk University (Nashville), which opened in 1890 with Quintard as president.

The bishop's theological sympathies lay with the Oxford movement; he emphasized apostolic succession, the sacraments, ritual dignity and beauty, and the liturgical calendar. But he combined these concerns with a personal evangelical piety and a fervent popular preaching style that drew comparisons to early Methodist preachers and placed him in high demand as a speaker. His sermons were celebrated for their vivid imagery, well-turned sentences, careful construction, and demands for ethical reform.

Quintard spoke in pulpits throughout the South, his native Northeast, and England. He was one of the first Americans to preach in the royal chapel at Windsor and was made a chaplain of the Knights of Saint John of Jerusalem. He attended every pan-Anglican conference from 1867 to 1897, calling for a closer communion between the Anglican and American churches.

Perhaps the bishop's most lasting achievement was his reestablishment of the University of the South at Sewanee, Tennessee. Just before the war, Bishops Stephen Elliott of Georgia, Leonidas Polk of Louisiana, and Quintard's predecessor in Tennessee, James Otey, had secured a site, raised an endowment and laid a cornerstone for a new classical school and seminary; but the terrible conflict had swept away all their preparations. In 1866 Quintard organized the trustees and began gathering new funds. He was elected vice chancellor and opened the school in 1868.

Quintard made the new campus his home. In 1872 he retired from the university's direct oversight, but he continued to work on its behalf for the rest of his life. He died in Meridian, Georgia, while visiting there to improve his health.

• Quintard's papers are in the University of the South Archives, the Duke University Archives, and the Diocese of Tennessee Archives. His memoirs of the war years are found in Arthur Howard Noll, ed., *Doctor Quintard, Chaplain C.S.A. and Second Bishop of Tennessee, Being His Story of the War (1861–1865)* (1905). The most complete modern assessment, with a bibliography of his works, is Richard N. Greatwood, "Charles Todd Quintard (1824–1898): His Role and Significance in the Development of the Protestant Episcopal Church in the Diocese of Tennessee and in the South" (Ph.D. diss., Vanderbilt Univ., 1977). See also Episcopal Church, Diocese of Tennessee, *In Memoriam: Charles Todd Quintard, D.D., LL.D., M.D., Bishop of Tennessee, 1865–1898* (1898); Noll, *History of the Church in the Diocese of Tennessee* (1900); G. R. Fairbanks, *History of the University of the South* (1905); Moultrie Guerry, "Charles Todd Quintard," in *Men Who Made Sewanee* (1905); and "Professor Quintard," *Memphis Medical Recorder* 3 (Mar. 1855): 214–18. Obituaries are in the *Nashville American* and the *Knoxville Journal*, 16 Feb. 1898.

THOMAS PAUL THIGPEN

QUINTON, Amelia Stone (31 July 1833–23 June 1926), advocate for Native-American rights and temperance leader, was born in Jamesville, New York, the daughter of Jacob Thompson Stone and Mary Bennett. She was raised in Homer, New York, educated at Cortland Academy, and after graduation taught for several years at various institutions throughout the country. While teaching at a seminary near Madison, Georgia, she met and married the Reverend James Franklin Swanson, a Georgia native. He died within a few years of their marriage. They had no children. She then moved to Philadelphia, taught at Chestnut Street Female Seminary, and formed a lifelong relationship with Mary L. Bonney, a social reformer.

While in Philadelphia, Quinton developed her commitment to religious and moral reform work. During those years she also worked as a volunteer at various correctional institutes in New York. In 1874 she joined the Woman's Christian Temperance Union and quickly began setting up new chapters, serving as the statewide organizer. During her years with the WCTU she developed a network of influence and important organizational skills that aided her in later work with Native Americans.

In 1877 Quinton's tireless work compromised her health, and she traveled to Europe to recuperate. While crossing the ocean, she met Richard L. Quinton, a professor of history and astronomy. They married the following year. The Quintons lived in London for a time, then returned to Philadelphia in the fall of 1878. Upon her return to the United States, and through the influence of Mary Bonney, Quinton became an advocate for Native-American rights.

Quinton's particular concern was the proposed opening of the Oklahoma District to white settlers. In the early 1880s, in response to this concern, Quinton, Bonney, and others founded an organization that was named the Women's National Indian Association (WNIA) in 1883. The women in the organization advocated an end to reservation life and supported the individual ownership of land, as they believed this was the only way to ensure Native-American survival. This philosophy was not without controversy, as it undermined the notion of communal land ownership by tribes.

Quinton advocated Christian education for Native Americans, particularly young women, and was active in establishing libraries, schools, and missions and in raising funds for Native-American home-building projects. She was also a vocal critic of the U.S. government's violation of treaties. In 1880 she presented a petition with 13,000 signatures to President Rutherford B. Hayes, calling for respect of land treaties. Throughout the decade Quinton served as a leader of the WNIA, writing numerous articles and giving speeches throughout New England and the mid-Atlantic states. By 1881 the WNIA had branches in twenty states, as well as the attention of prominent politicians. Quinton was a visible and strong officer of the organization, first serving as secretary, then president. She was a savvy petitioner; her ability to organize petition drives and her wise attention to group endorsements resulted in several major petitions to Congress. One of these was an 1882 petition, with 100,000 signatures, that pressed for individual land allotment, granting of U.S. citizenship, and guaranteed school education.

In 1884 Quinton began her first journey west, touring Indian reservations and speaking at length with the Indian women. While there, she organized women in Kansas, Nebraska, and Dakota as auxiliary units of her organization and encouraged the men to support WNIA. After her western trip she began a head-on campaign to "secure" federal allotment legislation. With members of a Mohonk committee, she pleaded on behalf of Native Americans for money, land, education, and citizenship. By the end of 1886 her women's association had eighty-three branches in twenty-eight states and territories.

During 1885 the headquarters and branches wrote articles for more than 800 periodicals, submitted sixty-five petitions to Congress, held public meetings, and circulated 49,000 copies of fifteen new publications. Quinton wrote five of these publications, delivered over fifty speeches, and still managed to oversee the rest of her administration. Some of her speeches included "Abolition of Unnecessary Agencies" (1897), "Care of the Indian" (1891), "The Indian: First Paper" (1893), "The Woman's National Indian Association" (1893), and "Women's Work for Indians" (1893).

In 1887 Congress passed the Dawes Severalty Act providing the Indians with allotment and citizenship. The act remained in effect until the 1930s, when social and economic decline led to its revision. Elected president of the WNIA in 1887, Quinton served in this capacity for the next eighteen years. During these years she attended Lake Mohonk conferences, traveled continuously in Indian country, and sought reforms, including but not limited to Prohibition, education, and civil service for Native Americans.

Realizing that the South would be a powerful ally, Quinton organized auxiliaries in seven states. By 1891 she had organized ten more branches in the South and twenty-four additional branches in the West. Successful in lobbying for education, protected lands, and a Prohibition bill, Quinton also oversaw the founding of some fifty missions for the Indians. Later the WNIA was responsible for providing teachers, libraries, and education subsidies and marketing Indian goods. In 1901 the WNIA became the National Indian Association, inviting men to become members. Quinton spent the years between 1907 and 1910 establishing chapters in Southern California and eventually settled in Ridgefield Park, New York, where she died.

Amelia Quinton, a humanitarian with a deep religious commitment, believed that all people, regardless of race, deserved to have rights. She spent nearly her entire life working to preserve these rights for the Native-American community. She left a tremendous legacy. Though her name is not widely recognized, with a national organization to her credit and numerous petitions passed through Congress, her work remains an integral part of Native-American rights today.

• Quinton's papers can be found in the Papers of the Indian Rights Association, housed at the Historical Society of Pennsylvania in Philadelphia. Correspondence by Quinton can be found in the records of the Bureau of Indian Affairs, located at the Department of the Interior and the National Archives in Washington, D.C. Concise but valuable biographical sketches on Quinton can be found in Frances E. Willard and Mary A. Livermore, eds., *American Women* (1897); and Nancy Hewitt and Suzanne Lebsock, eds., *Visible Women: New Essays on American Activism* (1993). Several doctoral theses have been written about Quinton and the Native-American movement, including Helen Marie Bannan, "Reformers and the 'Indian Problem,' 1878–1887 and 1922–1934" (Ph.D. diss., Syracuse Univ., 1976); Gregory Coyne Thompson, "The Origin and Implementation of the American Indian Reform Movement, 1867–1912" (Ph.D. diss., Univ. of Utah, 1981); and Helen M. Wanken, "'Women's Sphere' and Indian Reform: The Women's National Indian Association, 1879–1901" (Ph.D. diss., Marquette Univ., 1981). Quinton's own books, such as *The Fourth Mohonk Indian Conference* (1886), *One War Lesson* (1898), and *Suggestions for the Friends of the Women's National Indian Association* (1886), provide valuable insight into her resolutions for Indian rights.

SARA ROMEYN
MICHELLE E. OSBORN

QUITMAN, John Anthony (1 Sept. 1799–17 July 1858), Mexican War general and southern secessionist, was born in Rhinebeck, New York, the son of Frederick Henry Quitman, a Lutheran minister, and Anna Elizabeth Hueck. His father achieved considerable prominence as a minister, and John, in turn, was educated privately for the ministry. From the fall of 1816 until the summer of 1818, he taught and pursued theological studies at Hartwick Seminary in Hartwick, New York. He then became adjunct professor of English at Mount Airy College, a Catholic academy near Philadelphia, before moving to Ohio in the fall of 1819 to pursue a career in law. Though he passed Ohio's bar examination in July 1821, he became discouraged by the state's depressed economy due to the panic of 1819 and traveled, almost penniless, to Natchez, Mississippi, where he arrived in December 1821. The next month, however, he passed Mississippi's bar requirements and soon established a lucrative legal practice, becoming a leading figure in the Mississippi State Bar Association. Marriage in 1824 to Eliza Turner, the niece of the influential Edward Turner, provided John with social respectability. They had ten children. The transplanted northerner relished southern institutions, and through his marriage and subsequent purchases he acquired a Natchez mansion, four plantations in Mississippi and Louisiana, and several hundred slaves.

Quitman, a southern rather than a party partisan, switched political party affiliations several times. He was a member of the Mississippi House of Representatives (1828), chancellor of Mississippi (1828–1834), delegate to the Mississippi Constitutional Convention of 1832, member of the Mississippi Senate (1835–1836), de facto governor (1835–1836), governor (1850–1851), and U.S. representative (1855–1858). He achieved the Masonic rank of Grand Master, the highest in Mississippi. He served as trustee of Jefferson College (near Natchez) and the University of Mississippi, director of the Natchez branch of the Planters' Bank, president of the Mississippi Railroad Company, and delegate to the Memphis Commercial Convention of 1853.

Quitman also played a significant role in state and national military affairs. He helped found, and then captained, a volunteer militia company (the Natchez Fencibles). He served as brigade inspector and major general in the Mississippi militia. During the Texas Revolution, he led Mississippi volunteers into Texas but arrived too late to see action. During the Mexican War, as a volunteer brigadier general in the American army, he won a congressional sword and a promotion to major general for his role at the battle of Monterrey (21–23 Sept. 1846). A year later, General Winfield Scott appointed him civil and military governor of Mexico City in recognition of his heroism at Chapultepec and the Garita de Belén (13–14 Sept. 1847) during the American conquest of the Mexican capital. Later, in Congress, Quitman chaired the Committee on Military Affairs.

A champion of slavery and John C. Calhoun's states' rights theories, Quitman played a central role in Mississippi's nullification movement in the 1830s. While governor in 1850–1851, he opposed the Compromise of 1850 and unsuccessfully urged Mississippians to secede from the Union. In 1852, he ran for vice president of the United States on the Southern Rights party ticket. From 1850 to 1855, he plotted to add one or more slave states to the Union by conquering the Spanish island of Cuba with a privately armed, filibustering expedition. In 1850–1851 and 1854, U.S. authorities prosecuted him for these illegal schemes. The first prosecution caused his resignation as governor of Mississippi. While in Congress, Quitman urged the reopening of the African slave trade and the admission of Kansas as a slave state.

Quitman died at his Natchez mansion, apparently of lingering effects from the "National Hotel disease," a notorious epidemic in Washington, D.C., that broke out in early 1857. Though his death antedated the secession of the South by more than two years, the Yankee-born Quitman is rightly remembered as one of the earliest, most important southern disunionists.

• Significant collections of letters from and to Quitman are in the John Quitman Papers and the J. F. H. Claiborne Papers in the Mississippi Department of Archives and History, the Quitman Family Papers in the Southern Historical Collection at the University of North Carolina, the John Quitman Papers in the Historical Society of Pennsylvania, the John Quitman Papers in the Hill Memorial Library at Louisiana State University, Baton Rouge, the John Quitman Papers in the Houghton Library at Harvard University, the John Quitman Papers in the Alderman Library at the University of Virginia, the Lovell Family Papers in the University of the South Library, and the John Quitman Papers at Monmouth Plantation, Natchez, Mississippi (a private collection). The only published modern biography of Quitman is Robert E. May, *John A. Quitman: Old South Crusader* (1985). J. F. H. Claiborne, *Life and Correspondence of John A. Quitman* (2 vols., 1860), should be consulted for several notable letters and diary fragments. An obituary is in the *New York Times*, 19 July 1858.

ROBERT E. MAY

R

RABI, I. I. (29 July 1898–11 Jan. 1988), physicist, was born Israel Isaac Rabi in Rymanov, Galicia, then in the Austro-Hungarian empire, the son of David Rabi, and Sheindel (maiden name unknown). Rabi's first name was later changed to Isidor. Shortly after he was born, the family left for the United States, making their home at first on the Lower East Side of Manhattan and then moving to Brownsville in Brooklyn. Rabi became fascinated with science, especially astronomy, and rebelled against his traditional Jewish upbringing. He refused to be bar mitzvahed (there was a ceremony at home, however) or to study at the local yeshiva. He instead attended the Manual Training High School in Brooklyn; while there he built radio equipment, some of it by his own design. In 1916 Rabi enrolled at Cornell University. He initially focused on electrical engineering but majored in chemistry. He received his degree in chemistry one year early.

Rabi had difficulty finding suitable work. For a time he worked as a chemical analyst in Brooklyn and then as a bookkeeper. But neither of these jobs was satisfactory, and for several years he remained at home, where he mostly read. He decided to return to Cornell to acquire further training in physics but failed to get the requisite fellowship. In 1923 Rabi enrolled in the graduate program in physics at Columbia University. It was a fortunate choice: Columbia had one of the strongest programs in the nation. During his first year of graduate study, he lived with his parents but had barely enough to eat. He gained needed income by teaching at the City College of New York. In 1926 he received his doctorate for experimental work on the paramagnetic susceptibility of Tutton salts.

At the time, the most exciting advances in physics were taking place in western Europe. Rabi once described the excitement with which each issue of the *Zeitschrift für die Physik* was received in America; he maintained that Columbia had an advantage over Princeton because the journal arrived in New York a day or two earlier. Rabi and Ralph Kronig, a fellow instructor at CCNY, resolved to do something original in their burgeoning field. While pouring over works on differential equations, Rabi came across a form of the confluent hypergeometric equation that he recognized as applicable to the determination of the wave functions and energy level of the symmetric rotator. His and Kronig's paper outlining this result was published in the *Zeitschrift*.

In July 1926 Rabi married Helen Newmark; they were to have two daughters. Like other young American physicists, Rabi knew that the most important developments were unfolding in Europe. Study abroad was imperative for keeping up, if not getting ahead. He was awarded a Barnard fellowship, which would support him while he studied in Europe, but CCNY refused to grant him a leave of absence. Though academic jobs were scarce, Rabi decided to resign from CCNY to take advantage of the fellowship. In the fall of 1927 he left for Europe. During the next two years he met most of the great physicists of the day, including Niels Bohr, Wolfgang Pauli, Werner Heisenberg, and Otto Stern, as well as future American colleagues such as Linus Pauling, Edward Condon, H. P. Robertson, John Slater, and J. Robert Oppenheimer. Rabi owed much to Stern, whose laboratory was exploring molecular beam technology, especially in relation to the nucleus. Always in search of the simplest research systems possible, Rabi was attracted to the molecular beam, which isolated molecular or atomic systems from the complication of interactions with neighboring atoms or the walls of a container. At Stern's suggestion, Rabi successfully performed an atomic beam experiment that used a novel inhomogeneous magnetic field configuration. During his stay in Germany, Rabi wrote an interesting paper on the wave functions of the free Dirac electron in a uniform magnetic field. His solutions provided exact values and were later used in an elegant calculation by Joachim Luttinger and Wolfgang Pauli on the anomalous magnetic moment of the electron. (The same result was obtained by Julian Schwinger, using the new renormalization techniques that earned him the Nobel Prize.)

Rabi's studies in Europe were coming to a close when George B. Pegram, chairman of the physics department at Columbia University, on Heisenberg's recommendation, offered him a teaching position at what seemed to Rabi a munificent salary. In 1929 Rabi accepted the position and thereafter remained closely associated with Columbia. (He was the first Jewish faculty member of the department.) Although chosen to teach the new physics, Rabi increasingly focused on molecular beam technology and space quantization. When several other theoreticians joined the faculty, including Enrico Fermi, Rabi gravitated to the teaching of statistical mechanics. Awkward in the classroom, he was often ill prepared and fumbled at the chalkboard endlessly in trying to regain his elusive thoughts. Yet while meeting students in his office, he was accessible and even inspirational. (His classroom has since been preserved at Pupin Hall as a kind of shrine to the great physicist and Columbia enthusiast.)

Rabi's productive career now took off. His first important work was to study space quantization via the zero moment technique. With Gregory Breit he published a paper graphically depicting the decoupling of the atomic nucleus from the electron angular momentum as a function of an applied magnetic field. This decoupling, still known as the "Breit Rabi" diagram, was used by Rabi in a brilliant explanation of an unexplained result of an experiment by Otto Frisch and Emilio Segrè. With his first doctoral student, Victor William Cohen, Rabi developed the zero moment method for the measurement of nuclear spins in alkali atoms.

During World War II, Rabi became an important statesman of American physics. He was the associate director of the MIT Radiation Laboratory, which became famous for the development of radar. When J. Robert Oppenheimer, director of the atom bomb design project, invited him to come to Los Alamos, New Mexico, to serve as associate director, Rabi declined. Radar, he told Oppenheimer, was of more critical importance in winning the war; moreover, he opposed seeing centuries of research in physics culminate in weapons of mass destruction. Rabi nevertheless advised on different aspects of the Manhattan Project and was present when the first atomic bomb was detonated in Alamogordo, New Mexico, in 1945. At first "jubilant" over the success of the project, he quickly had misgivings: "We turned to one another and offered congratulations for the first few minutes. Then, there was a chill, which was not the morning cold; it was a chill that came to one when one thought . . . of my wooden house in Cambridge, and my laboratory in New York, and of the millions of people living around there."

While he was involved in weighty matters of technological development, Rabi continued to pursue his own research, which was focused on the use of radio frequency resonance magnetic fields to induce transitions in the hyperfine states of atoms. These are the energy states caused by the magnetic interaction between the atomic nucleus and the surrounding electrons. The success of Rabi's work in radio frequency spectroscopy brought about a major revolution in experimental physics, as resonance techniques resulted in a host of applications: paramagnetic resonance, the maser, the laser, and the atomic clock. His research team also succeeded in measuring the quadrupole moment of the deuteron—that is, its deviation from sphericity—an important contribution to the understanding of nuclear forces. In 1944 Rabi earned the Nobel Prize in Physics for his achievements in the field of magnetic resonance.

After World War II Rabi pursued an idea that had been discussed in theoretical terms by Oppenheimer and H. A. Kramers, among others, before the war: namely, the effect of electromagnetic fluctuations of the vacuum on atomic systems. Rabi stimulated students of his, such as Edward Nelson and John Nafe, and fellow Columbia professors Polykarp Kusch and Henry Foley, among others, to devise various methods of measuring shifts in the fine structure of atomic hydrogen and small changes in the magnetic moment of the electron. Their work proved crucial to the development of quantum electrodynamics.

In 1945 Rabi was named chair of the Columbia physics department. He became very close to Dwight D. Eisenhower, who succeeded Nicholas Murray Butler as president of Columbia University in 1948. When Eisenhower became president of the United States, Rabi became his informal science adviser and served on the President's Science Advisory Committee from its inception to the end of its existence under President Richard Nixon.

While conducting research, Rabi found time to contribute to the advancement of physics in the nation more generally. Dismayed that Ernest Lawrence had established the world's most advanced high energy physics laboratory on the West Coast at Berkeley, Rabi, with the assistance of Columbia dean George B. Pegram, proposed a comparable facility on the East Coast. They realized that it was politically impossible for Columbia to lay claim to such a national facility on its own, so in 1947 they helped found the Brookhaven National Laboratory at Yaphank, Long Island, formerly a World War I army base. The Brookhaven laboratory advanced teaching and research in physics for many eastern universities.

Rabi also worked closely with the military, especially the U.S. Navy. He convoked Project Michael, a weeklong meeting at Columbia of the nation's top physicists, to develop academic research support to explore the remote propagation of low frequency sound. This secret project, meant to promote radio communications with submarines, was assigned the code name LOFAR. Although the project involved Bell Laboratories and many navy laboratories, a separate academic facility, called the Hudson Laboratory, was formed in Dobbs Ferry, New York, to work on the project. In addition to his work as a science adviser within the United States, Rabi contributed to the development of physics abroad. Working with James Killian, president of the Massachusetts Institute of Technology, and Detlev Bronk, president of the National Academy of Sciences, Rabi proposed creating CERN (Conseil Européen pour la Recherche Nucléaire). He recognized, even before the Europeans did, that they needed such a facility to keep pace with fast-breaking developments in high energy physics in the United States. He instinctively perceived a need for competition to keep the U.S. effort at its peak, much as he had proposed Brookhaven to match Lawrence's Berkeley lab.

In 1957 Rabi, again in concert with Bronk and Killian, drafted a proposal to form a new division of the North Atlantic Treaty Organization (NATO) for the promotion of science and technology in the member countries. Eisenhower successfully persuaded the European heads of state to accept the recommendation, and Rabi was the first American delegate to the NATO Science Committee, on which he had a lengthy tenure. Embedded within a military alliance, the science committee's activities were well funded. It established a fellowship exchange program that was of special benefit to less developed member nations such as Portugal, Greece, and Turkey. More important still were the NATO "summer schools," which extended the scope of such exchanges.

Rabi continued having students until about 1953, by which time his responsibilities as an administrator and scientific adviser had come to occupy most of his attention. There was an additional reason for Rabi's diversion from active research. He had preferred clean, spare problems that did not rely on expensive testing apparatus. Yet research in physics was shifting from his kind of "small" physics to a new emphasis on solid state physics, a complex system whose functionings were exemplified by the transistor, and high energy physics, which required elaborate and expensive machinery. In yet another way, Rabi differed from academic thinking as it had evolved after World War II. For many years the Columbia physics department had held stringent written examinations for Ph.D. candidates that commonly stretched over two weekends. Some years after the war, a colleague proposed that the written exams be eliminated. The debate grew heated; and when the motion passed, Rabi stormed out of the room. He never again took an active role in the department. Rabi died in New York City.

Rabi was at the leading edge of the greatest generation in the history of the United States. It had survived a massive depression without revolution and had emerged from economic and political disaster to lead in the victory over the fascist threat to the world. The marvelous rebound of western Europe was aided by extraordinary effort of the United States to implement the Marshall Plan. In the post–World War II period the country developed the most sophisticated scientific and innovative infrastructure that the world had ever seen. I. I. Rabi was one of the very few who had the brilliance, the imagination, and the foresight to see that this happened. He was a model of the doers of his generation.

Within his own discipline, Rabi was responsible for one of the most important breakthroughs of the twentieth century. His development of the resonance technique for the analysis of matter took physics from the one-dimensional real axis to the richer two-dimensional complex plane. He was the prime stimulator in the immediate postwar experiments that led to the revolutionary effects of the fluctuations of the vacuum on atomic and nuclear systems; the individual experiments were so far-reaching that he perhaps should have received another Nobel Prize.

• Documents concerning Rabi are in the archives of the American Institute of Physics, College Park, Md., and in the archives of the Department of Physics, Columbia University; an interview, "Reminiscences of Isidor Isaac Rabi," 32 pp., is in the Oral History Collection of Columbia University. An account of his life appears in John S. Rigden, *Rabi, Scientist and Citizen* (1987).

WILLIAM A. NIERENBERG

RABINOWITCH, Eugene (26 Aug. 1901–15 May 1973), chemist and scientific activist and popularizer, was born in St. Petersburg, Russia; information about his parents is not available. He was a student at the University of St. Petersburg, specializing in chemistry. In 1926 he completed a doctorate in chemistry at the University of Berlin. During this period of his life, he married Anya (surname not known); they had two sons. In 1933 the family left Germany for Copenhagen, where Rabinowitch worked with Niels Bohr at the Institute of Theoretical Physics. He later studied at University College, London. He brought his family to the United States in 1938 so that he could take part in a solar energy research project at the Massachusetts Institute of Technology. In 1942 Rabinowitch joined the Metallurgical Project of the Manhattan Engineer District at the University of Chicago, known as the "Met Lab," where he was a senior chemist and a section chief on the Manhattan Project. The main task of the Met Lab was to develop procedures for the large-scale production of plutonium. Work on "weapons theory"—that is, on theoretical aspects of bomb construction—was transferred to Los Alamos in early 1943; thus Met Lab scientists played a relatively minor part in the final stages of the Manhattan Project (which would result in the successful production of the atomic bombs used against Japan in 1945).

Yet even after their role in the project was completed, those who had worked on the Manhattan Project in Chicago remained concerned about the future implications of the atomic bomb, in terms of both international politics and the effects of such weaponry on human lives. In June 1945 a group at the Met Lab, including Rabinowitch, the Nobel Prize–winning chemist James Franck, Leo Szilard, and Glenn T. Seaborg, issued the Franck Report, one of the more notable documents in the debate over the appropriate use of atomic energy. Knowing that the Los Alamos scientists and engineers were close to completing an atomic bomb, the Met Lab committee, chaired by Franck, pleaded eloquently that atomic weapons should not be used on Japan's cities; they argued instead for a demonstration of its destructive potential in an unpopulated area. The sixth section of the Franck Report, entitled "The Impact of Nucleonics on International Relations and the Social Order," was drafted primarily by Rabinowitch. He argued that unannounced use of the bomb against Japan would lead inexorably to a deadly international arms race. Since the basic principles of nuclear technology were known to scientists the world over, the United States could not prevent attempts by other countries to either produce uranium and plutonium or manufacture weapons made from them. Rabinowitch urged that, before any deployment of a Los Alamos bomb, efforts should be made to put the control of atomic and nuclear weapons, from the outset, under international authority. Although prescient in many of its conclusions, the Franck Report had little immediate impact, and certainly none on the decision, by President Harry Truman and his Secretary of War Henry Stimson, to drop the first atomic bombs. But the ideals to which Rabinowitch had committed himself in coauthoring the report were to guide the remainder of his life. As his Chicago colleague Seaborg noted, "Perhaps no other person has played so important and so central a role as he in alerting the world to both the dangers and the more beneficent potentials of atomic energy" (*Bulletin of the Atomic Scientists* 29:11).

In December 1945, Rabinowitch and the physicist Hyman H. Goldsmith started the journal *Bulletin of the Atomic Scientists* as a means of calling public attention to the perils of atomic energy and the urgent need for its control by a civilian—and international—agency. This effort, supported by a group called the Atomic Scientists of Chicago, was instrumental in the Congressional creation of the Atomic Energy Commission as a civilian executive agency in the United States. With an initial board of sponsors that included Albert Einstein, J. Robert Oppenheimer, Linus Pauling, and many other leading scientists, the *Bulletin* quickly became known as a forum and conscience of the international scientific community on a broad array of scientific, environmental, and sociopolitical issues. The journal's "doomsday clock" cover logo, its minute hand ranging over the years from two to seventeen minutes to midnight, according to the editors' judgment of the current international situation, served as a striking visual reminder of the ever-present threat of nuclear war.

Rabinowitch's chief scientific interests after the war centered on the process of photosynthesis. He became a professor of botany and biophysics at the University of Illinois at Urbana in 1947. Yet he remained committed to furthering awareness and discussion of the international nuclear situation in the scientific community. He was among the organizers of the first Pugwash Conference in 1957. This organization meets annually to provide an opportunity for leading international scientists interested in the impact of science on public affairs to explore ideas for "dealing with" as Rabinowitch put it, "the dangerous realities and the exciting potentialities of the scientific age" (*The Atomic Age*, p. 551). Through the conference, Rabinowitch became a key agent in provoking a useful dialogue in the 1950s among Russian, British, and American scientists on questions concerning nuclear weapons policies, including arms control and test bans. His fluency both in his native Russian and in English made him an indispensable arbiter in many critical debates in the Cold War years.

In 1963 Rabinowitch coedited with Morton Grodzins *The Atomic Age: Scientists in National and World Affairs*, an anthology of articles from the first eighteen years of the *Bulletin*; the book still serves as an excellent text for comprehending the cultural impact of nuclear weaponry in the two decades after Hiroshima and Nagasaki. In 1966 he won the Kalinga Prize, awarded annually by the United Nations Educational and Cultural Organization (UNESCO) to honor an outstanding science journalist and popularizer.

Rabinowitch left Urbana in 1968 to join the faculty of the State University of New York at Albany as a professor of chemistry and as director of the Center for Science and the Future of Human Affairs. After the release of the Pentagon Papers (top-secret documents about the Vietnam War) in 1971, he wrote a letter to the *New York Times* expressing his regret that he did not attempt to warn the American people of the government's intention to use the atomic bomb in 1945. In 1972 he took a sabbatical from SUNY to work on a new book as a Woodrow Wilson fellow at the Smithsonian Institution, but never returned to his post, dying of a stroke in Washington, D.C.

Rabinowitch combined the attributes of both scientist and humanist in a career that spanned more than three decades of scientific, military, sociopolitical, and diplomatic changes of great magnitude. The depth and breadth of his intellectual versatility coupled with his modesty and selflessness elicited admiration from most of his colleagues, who included many of the world's leading scientific and political thinkers.

• Rabinowitch's papers are in the Joseph Regenstein Library Special Collections at the University of Chicago. In addition to *The Atomic Age*, his major published works include *Photosynthesis and Related Processes* (1945); *The Dawn of a New Age: Reflections on Science and Human Affairs* (1963); *Man on the Moon: The Impact on Science, Technology and International Cooperation* (1969); *Photosynthesis and Related Processes* (3 vols., 1969); and *Views of Science, Technology, and Development* (1975). Alice Kimball Smith, *A Peril and a Hope: The Scientists' Movement in America, 1945–1947* (1965), is excellent on Rabinowitch's central role in these years; her study benefits from numerous interviews with him and other major participants and access to certain of his personal files. Matt Price, "Roots of Dissent: The Chicago Met Lab and the Origins of the Franck Report," *Isis* 86 (1995): 222–44, effectively places Rabinowitch's contributions in the broader context of the complex institutional and political cultures at the Chicago Met Lab. *Bulletin of the Atomic Scientists* 29 (June 1973): 3–12 includes a tribute to Rabinowitch's life and work by a number of leading scientists. An obituary is in the *New York Times*, 16 May 1973.

MARTIN FICHMAN

RACHMANINOFF, Sergei (2 Apr. 1873–28 Mar. 1943), composer, pianist, and conductor, was born Sergei Vasil'evich Rakhmaninov on his parents' estate at Oneg, near Novgorod, Russia, the son of Vasily Arkad'evich Rakhmaninov, a wealthy but dissolute army officer, and Liubov Petrovna Butokova. As a result of Vasily Rakhmaninov's extravagant ways, the family was forced to liquidate its assets, which included a number of country estates, and in 1882 they moved to a small flat in Saint Petersburg.

From an early age, Sergei Rakhmaninov demonstrated musical talent, a gift evident on both sides of the family. (Notably, his paternal grandfather had been a pupil of the Irish pianist John Field.) Encouraged by his parents, Sergei attended the Saint Petersburg Conservatory between 1882 and 1885 as a pupil of Vladimir Demiansky. Despite excellent progress in piano and music, mainly owing to his sense of absolute pitch and his remarkable memory, the young Rakhmaninov risked dismissal for lackadaisical attitudes toward general subjects. On the advice of his cousin Aleksandr Ziloti, who had studied with Franz Liszt and who was recognized as one of the foremost piano virtuosos in eastern Europe, Rakhmaninov transferred to the Moscow Conservatory expressly to study with Ziloti and with Ziloti's former teacher Nikolai Zverev, a notorious martinet.

In 1886, Rakhmaninov's courses at the Moscow Conservatory included harmony with Anton Arensky and, later, composition with Sergei Taneev. During his student years Rakhmaninov composed his first works, most notably the First Piano Concerto (1891), which he later designated as his opus 1. This composition amply demonstrates that the eighteen-year-old Rakhmaninov already possessed not only a superior understanding of most aspects of composition but also a precocious awareness of orchestral timbres and sonorities.

His interest in composition so angered Zverev that in 1889 Rakhmaninov was forced to complete his piano studies with Ziloti, who had been teaching at the conservatory since 1888. But in 1891, one year before Rakhmaninov was to graduate, internal politics at the conservatory compelled Ziloti to resign his position. Unwilling to change teachers again, Rakhmaninov petitioned to take his final piano examination a year early and finished the piano curriculum in 1891. In 1892 he completed the composition course. Upon graduation he received the Great Gold Medal, an award for expertise in piano and composition that had previously been awarded only twice before: to Taneev in 1875 and to Arseny Koreschenko in 1891.

The years following graduation, 1892–1900, were of mixed success. Although his principal interest was in composition (the famous Prelude in C-sharp Minor dates from this time), he earned his living primarily as a piano teacher, an occupation he particularly disliked. The disastrous premiere of the First Symphony (28 Mar. 1897), a work Rakhmaninov at that time thought a worthy composition, left the composer doubtful of his talent. Later, Rakhmaninov recalled that after the First Symphony he composed nothing for about three years, that he "was like a man who had suffered a stroke, and had lost the use of his head and hands." An appointment as a conductor with Mamontov's Opera Company lasted only one year (1897–1898).

By January 1900 Rakhmaninov's mental condition became so acute that his future in-laws suggested in desperation that he take daily therapy with the Moscow-based psychotherapist Nikolai Dahl. After only three months of treatment, which not only bolstered Rakhmaninov's self-esteem but also his conviction of his own musical talent, he began the famous Second Piano Concerto, probably the most popular work in its genre composed in the twentieth century. The instantaneous success of the concerto rekindled Rakhmaninov's enthusiasm for composition. With the financial help of Ziloti, he resumed work, and this, coupled with his marriage to his first cousin Natalia Satina in May 1902 and the birth of their first daughter, Irina—later the Princess Wolkonsky—the following year initiated a period of great fruitfulness.

Rakhmaninov's influence spread quickly throughout musical circles in Russia. For the 1904–1906 seasons at the Bolshoi Theater he supervised performances of Russian operas in the repertoire. With his Bolshoi conducting debut on 3 September 1904 in Dargomizhsky's *Rusalka*, he singlehandedly revolutionized performance practice at the Russian imperial opera houses, positioning the conductor's podium not in front of the stage, but, in the contemporary European manner, in front of the orchestra. However, the administrative responsibilities at the Bolshoi did not allow him enough time to compose.

Between autumn 1906 and spring 1909 the composer and his family lived in Dresden; outside Russia, he adopted the French spelling of his surname, Rachmaninoff. Only during the summers did the family return to Russia, where, at their estate, "Ivanovka," a second daughter was born. Despite occasional appearances as a conductor or a soloist, Rachmaninoff devoted himself thoroughly to composition while in Dresden, a city he had chosen for the vibrancy of its musical life and proximity to other important music centers. At that time Arthur Nikisch directed the Gewandhaus orchestra in Leipzig, and Ernst von Schuch directed the Dresden Hofoper. Rachmaninoff extolled the Hofoper's performances; he was "enthralled" by their interpretation of Wagner's *Die Meistersinger* and was "absolutely delighted" with their presentation of Richard Strauss's *Salome*.

The Dresden years proved a watershed in Rachmaninoff's maturation as a composer. Careful analysis of the works from this time reveals his evolving control of the post-Wagnerian musical syntax and his ability to fashion this musical rhetoric into extended and yet unified tonal structures. The tone poem *Isle of the Dead* (1909), inspired by the Böcklin painting of the same name, attests to a staggering development in Rachmaninoff's compositional technique. Rachmaninoff based the work on a three-note motive, the presence of which can be traced in small-dimensional melodic detail, through to large-dimensional formal construction.

Although the American media had speculated about an American concert tour as early as the 1907–1908 season, arrangements became definite only in the summer of 1909. During his first American tour in 1909–1910, Rachmaninoff premiered his newly composed Third Piano Concerto with the New York Symphony Orchestra, conducted by Walter Damrosch. Rachmaninoff's recollections of the careful attention with which Gustav Mahler prepared the New York Philharmonic for the second performance of the concerto (16 Jan. 1910) remains one of the most vivid and insightful descriptions of Mahler's rehearsal procedures.

Between 1911 and 1914 Rachmaninoff conducted the Moscow Philharmonic Society, performing repertoire ranging from Bach through Debussy and Richard Strauss. However, composition remained his primary musical focus, and two choral works from this time deserve special mention. While in Rome during the early months of 1913, Rachmaninoff composed what he considered his finest work, his choral symphony based on Konstantine Balmont's superlative Russian translation of Edgar Allan Poe's poem "The

Bells." "This composition," Rachmaninoff recounted to Riesemann, "on which I worked with feverish ardor, is still the one I like best of all my works; after that comes my *Vesper Mass*—then there is a long gap between it and the rest." The *Vespers*, op. 37, composed in January–February 1915, is arguably the most profound musical statement in the Russian Orthodox liturgical repertoire from any period.

In December 1917 the increasing political turmoil in Russia forced Rachmaninoff and his family into exile. Their precipitous departure obliged them to leave their personal effects behind in the safekeeping of relatives. As early as 12 January 1918 Rachmaninoff wrote that he had lost everything, that his estate had been destroyed and all his money and securities confiscated, and that he did not believe the Bolshevik promise that one day it would all be returned.

In order to support his family Rachmaninoff spent ten months giving concerts in Scandinavia. He declined several invitations to replace Karl Muck as resident conductor of the Boston Symphony, concerned that it would take too long to prepare the series of 110 concerts planned for thirty weeks. He declined a similar proposition from the Cincinnati Symphony. Yet, encouraged by these offers, Rachmaninoff obtained an American entry visa on 24 October 1918 and arrived in New York with his family on 10 November 1918. Balancing his options as pianist, composer, and conductor, at the advanced age of forty-five, Rachmaninoff took up the freelance career as a traveling virtuoso.

During each season from 1919 until his death, Rachmaninoff undertook extensive concert tours, using New York as a home base. Concerts in Europe usually preceded vacations there. His appearances left an indelible impression on his audiences. He played with a spellbinding rhythmic drive and an infinite variety of tonal shading. He phrased and shaped melodies with exquisite finesse. His very appearance was awe-inspiring: approaching an almost gaunt six feet, six inches tall, he dressed impeccably and dispatched his exhaustive programs in an effortless and unaffected manner. His repertoire, although taken predominantly from the nineteenth century, ran the gamut from Daquin and Bach to Ravel and Poulenc.

His hectic concert schedules limited his time for composition. However, when one considers the numerous piano transcriptions that Rachmaninoff produced throughout the 1920s, an unbroken chain of creativity becomes apparent. Only after building a permanent holiday home, "Villa Senar" (on the Küssnachtersee, near Hertenstein, Switzerland), in 1933 was Rachmaninoff able to realize the conditions he found conducive for original composition. He composed his last three masterpieces, the *Rhapsody on a Theme of Paganini*, the Third Symphony, and the *Symphonic Dances*, between 1934 and 1940.

The renewed focus on composition coupled with the Soviet ban on his music (1931–1934) forced Rachmaninoff to resign himself to his exile. Both he and his wife became naturalized American citizens on 1 February 1943. The next day the *Washington Evening Star* reported Rachmaninoff as saying, "I am very happy to become a United States Citizen in this land of opportunity and equality."

In 1942 Rachmaninoff and his wife relocated to the then emigré mecca of Beverly Hills. Growing weakness due to malignant carcinomatosis cut short his 1942–1943 season. Rachmaninoff returned to his home on North Elm Drive, where he died. His death certificate listed his "usual occupation" simply as "composer." Sir Henry Wood's personal tribute to Rachmaninoff appeared beneath his *New York Times* obituary on 29 March 1943: "As a pianist I never have heard any one to equal him except Liszt, and as a composer he was a man of enormous talent. His works were a unanimous success throughout the world. He was a unique genius."

Despite the respect accorded him by most of his professional colleagues, Rachmaninoff continually suffered from self-doubt, particularly as a composer. As early as 1912 he wrote to the Russian symbolist poet Marietta Shaginian, "If there was ever a time when I had faith in myself it was long ago—long ago— in my youth! . . . I fear, with the passing years, [this insecurity] digs in ever more deeply. Little wonder that if, after a while, I make up my mind to give up composition entirely and become instead a professional pianist, or conductor, or a farmer, or even a chauffeur."

In the early 1930s Rachmaninoff spoke of the "continuous conflict" he felt between his "musical activities" and his "artistic conscience," saying that he was unable to make up his mind as to which was his true calling—composer, pianist, or conductor. He was constantly troubled that in venturing into too many fields he may have failed to make the "best use" of his life. Using the old Russian phrase, Rachmaninoff mused, "I have 'hunted three hares.' Can I be sure that I have killed one of them?"

But time has shown that Rachmaninoff's personal insecurities were ill founded. As one of the most sought-after piano virtuosos of his day, his extensive concert tours and wealth of recordings set standards for twentieth-century piano excellence. His astounding orchestral control is witnessed in the few recordings he made as conductor of the Philadelphia Orchestra: many consider Rachmaninoff's direction of the *Vocalise*, the *Isle of the Dead* (1929 reading), and the Third Symphony definitive. With respect to composing, most still associate his name with works for the piano—either solo or with orchestra—but in almost every genre Rachmaninoff's original compositions and transcriptions represent the culmination of the Russian post-Wagnerian tradition.

• Rachmaninoff's papers are divided between repositories in Russia and the United States. For the catalog listing of the Rachmaninoff materials at the most important repository in the former Soviet Union, see Rytsareva, *Rachmaninoff Autographs in the Archives of the State Central Glinka Museum of Musical Culture* (1980). The Music Division of the Library of Congress, Washington, D.C., houses virtually all surviving manuscript materials dating from 1918 to the composer's death in 1943. The Music Division published an index for the collection in the Library of Congress, *Music and Books on Music* (1978, pp. 81–82), but it is outdated. A "Finder's Aid" by David Butler Cannata is on file at the Music Division.

Without question, the most indispensable tool for Rachmaninoff research is Robert Threlfall and Geoffrey Norris, *A Catalogue of the Compositions of Sergei Rachmaninoff* (1982). The most comprehensive biography in English remains Sergei Bertensson and Jay Leyda, *Sergei Rachmaninoff: A Lifetime in Music* (1956). See also Fritz Butzbach, *Studien zum "Klavierkonzert N. 1 fis-moll," Op. 1 von S. V. Rachmaninov* (1979); Cannata, "Rachmaninoff's Changing View of Symphonic Structure" (Ph.D. diss., New York Univ., 1992); John Culshaw, *Rachmaninov* (1950); Barrie Martyn, *Rachmaninoff: Composer, Pianist, Conductor* (1990); Geoffrey Norris, *Rachmaninoff* (1993); Oskar von Riesemann, *Rachmaninoff's Recollections Told to Oskar von Riesemann* (1934); Victor Seroff, *Rachmaninoff* (1951); and Robert Threlfall, *Rachmaninoff* (1973). Robert Palmieri, *Sergei Vasil'evich Rachmaninoff: A Guide to Research* (1985), an annotated bibliography, gathers a good amount of the secondary literature in all languages.

Much of the literature published under the aegis of the Soviet State Press was heavily censored. This, unfortunately, diminishes the otherwise careful work of Zarui Apetian—S. *Rachmaninoff Literary Heritage* (1978–1980) and *Reminiscences of Rachmaninoff* (1988)—and Vera Briantseva's *S. V. Rachmaninoff* (1976), the most comprehensive biography in Russian. Yuri Keldysh, *Rachmaninoff and His Time* (1973), stops abruptly at 1917, with no indication that this was to be the first in a series.

The winter 1951–1952 issue of *Tempo* was devoted to articles about Rachmaninoff, as was the April 1973 issue of *Sovetskaia Muzika*, which commemorated the centenary of the composer's birth. BMG Classics issued all the Rachmaninoff RCA Victor recordings in the 10-compact disc set *Sergei Rachmaninoff: The Complete Recordings* (1993).

DAVID BUTLER CANNATA

RADCLIFF, Jacob (20 Apr. 1764–6 May 1844), politician, lawyer, and judge, was born in Rhinebeck, New York, the son of William Radcliff, a lawyer and revolutionary war officer, and Sarah Kip. He graduated from the College of New Jersey (now Princeton University) in 1783 and read law for three years in the Poughkeepsie, New York, office of Egbert Benson, the state attorney general. James Kent was also an apprentice with Benson at the time. In 1786 Radcliff was admitted to the bar and married Juliana Smith, with whom he would have two children.

Radcliff reportedly practiced briefly in Red Hook, New York, outside of Poughkeepsie, before settling in Poughkeepsie itself. An early case, which he lost to fellow legal novice Kent, had Radcliff defending a man who tried to keep a neighbor's three horses after they broke down his fence and trampled a field. The majority of the town's legal work involved debt collection, and Radcliff and Kent both soon grew tired of the monotony. Kent moved to New York City in 1793, and Radcliff followed in either 1796 or 1797. Before leaving Radcliff had gotten involved in politics as a Federalist, serving two terms in the state assembly (1794–1795). He subsequently became assistant attorney general for the state from 1796 to 1798.

Benson had been appointed to the state supreme court in 1794, and in 1798 Governor John Jay selected two of Benson's Federalist protégés, Radcliff and Kent, to join him on the five-member panel. Kent remembered their relationship as "intimate," and wrote that Radcliff "stood very high as a Judge" (Roper, ed., p. 236). When the state legislature mandated in 1801 that state laws be revised and codified, Radcliff and Kent worked together on the project, producing the two-volume *Laws of the State of New York* (1802). Their revisions remained in use for eleven years.

The production of the laws volumes was Radcliff's best-remembered contribution as a judge, as his decisions were unremarkable and his stay on the bench was brief. He had moved back to New York City from Albany in 1802, and in January 1804 he resigned from the court and resumed his law practice. The primary reason was probably monetary, as the supreme court salary was less than what could be made in private practice. It is also possible that with the Federalists on the court reduced since 1801 to himself and Kent, Radcliff had grown weary of bucking the majority. Yet another cause could have been his jealousy of Kent's ascendency, as Kent later declared that Radcliff's departure from the bench was an "Act of folly [that] brought on his ruin. He was ambitious & restless friendless [*sic*] & tormented by a malignant Jealousy" (Roper, ed., p. 236).

Radcliff soon became involved in a major New Jersey land speculation. On 9 April 1804 John Stevens made available 800 small lots in Hoboken, with promises to improve the wharves, build warehouses, and increase ferry service. Sensing the possibilities of a boom, Radcliff and two other prominent attorneys, Anthony Dey and Richard Varick, arranged just eleven days after the Stevens sale to lease the piece of land known as Paulus Hook, across the Hudson River from the tip of Manhattan and due south of Hoboken, for $6,000 a year. With the mapping help of noted engineer Joseph F. Mangin they made plans for what became Jersey City. Kent noted in May 1804 that Radcliff "seems to be absorbed in his Speculations, & it is very uncertain . . . whether it will not turn out a bubble & he make nothing. He appears to me to have sunk down to nothing since he parted with his office!" (Roper, ed., p. 237). Indeed, there was little building or investment in the Paulus Hook area for three decades, so while Radcliff was technically one of the founders of Jersey City, he lost money on the deal.

Radcliff remained active in Federalist politics, serving as a member of their Committees of Correspondence for the 1808 and 1812 presidential elections. When his party gained control of the state legislature in the 1809 elections, the Council of Appointments ousted De Witt Clinton as mayor of New York City and named Radcliff to replace him. His tenure was brief, however, as the 1810 election resulted in a shift that allowed Clinton to be returned to office. Radcliff's most important decision as mayor involved allocating land for the Brooklyn Navy Yard.

The War of 1812 and its aftermath brought political realignment in state politics, with Radcliff breaking with the traditional New York Federalists in 1813 after refusing to back Clinton in the 1812 presidental campaign. As the war came to a successful conclusion, those like Radcliff who had supported it gained the upper hand in New York. Their number was not great enough in 1814 to help Radcliff regain the New York City mayor's office, but by 1815 it was, and Radcliff once again replaced Clinton, serving until 1818.

The political group with which Radcliff was associated became known as the Bucktails and included Martin Van Buren, Daniel D. Tompkins, and Erastus Root. This coalition exerted considerable power in the 1821 state constitutional convention, with Radcliff serving as a delegate from New York City. Radcliff favored universal white manhood suffrage and restructuring of the state judiciary system, two issues that placed him in opposition to his old colleague Kent, who by that time considered Radcliff "hateful to his Former Friends & associates" (Roper, ed., p. 236). Radcliff also supported abolition of the Council of Appointments, the very instrument by which he had gained the position of mayor. Reforms in all of these areas were passed.

The constitutional convention was Radcliff's last public service, and little is known of his final two decades. He apparently was a successful attorney, but Kent recorded that after the convention Radcliff had "sunk into Poverty & Contempt & became at last miserably Destitute . . . a sad Example of bad Temper, & perverted ambition, & want of Steadiness in Business" (Roper, ed., pp. 236–37). Kent, who dated the end of their friendship at the 1813 political realignment, admittedly found Radcliff "bitter & malignant" by the time he wrote, so it is possible that he overstated his former friend's embarrassment. Suffering from cancer of the throat and mouth in 1844, Radcliff left New York City to live with his daughter's family in Troy, New York, but he died only days after arriving.

Although he did not realize gain from the endeavor, Radcliff remains important for the role he played in the development of the Jersey City area, and also is remembered for his terms as mayor of New York City in an era otherwise dominated by Clinton.

• Radcliff's and Kent's correspondence with the legislature concerning statute revision is in the New York Public Library. Radcliff's term on the supreme court can be traced in William Johnson, *Reports of Cases Adjudged in the Supreme Court of Judicature of the State of New York, January, 1799–January, 1803* (3 vols., 1895). The record of his involvement in the constitutional convention is found in Nathaniel H. Carter and William L. Stone, reporters, *Reports of the Proceedings and Debates of the Convention of 1821* (1821). Contemporary accounts of his political activities are Jabez D. Hammond, *The History of Political Parties in the State of New-York From the Ratification of the Federal Constitution to December, 1840* (2 vols., 1842), and Donald M. Roper, ed., "James Kent's Necrologies," *New-York Historical Society Quarterly* 56 (July 1972): 212–37. Works on Kent include John T. Horton,

James Kent: A Study in Conservatism 1763–1847, and William Kent, ed., *Memoirs and Letters of James Kent, LL.D.* An obituary is in the *New York Tribune*, 8 May 1844.

DONALD M. ROPER
KENNETH H. WILLIAMS

RADEMACHER, Hans (3 Apr. 1892–7 Feb. 1969), mathematician, was born in Wandsbeck (near Hamburg), Germany, the son of A. Henry Rademacher, the owner of a local store, and Emma Weinhöver. By the time Rademacher entered the University of Göttingen in 1911, he had developed strong interests in mathematics, the natural sciences, foreign languages, and philosophy. Through the lectures and influence of Erich Hecke, Hermann Weyl, and Richard Courant, Rademacher eventually turned to mathematics. His doctoral dissertation in real analysis was written under the direction of Constantin Carathéodory in 1916; he received his Ph.D. in 1917.

Rademacher's first position was as a teacher in private secondary schools in Bischofstein and Wickersdorf. From 1919 to 1922 he served as a Privatdozent, or unsalaried lecturer, in Berlin. In 1922 he accepted the salaried position of Ausserordentlicher professor at the University of Hamburg, a position he held until being named professor at Breslau in 1925. While in Berlin, he married Suzanne Gaspary, and their daughter was born in 1925. The marriage ended in divorce in 1929.

Throughout his life, Rademacher maintained an active interest in human rights. Not surprisingly, in 1934, not long after Hitler's assumption of power, Rademacher was removed from his position. In that same year, Rademacher accepted a visiting position at the University of Pennsylvania. Also in 1934 Rademacher married Olga Frey; their son was born in 1935.

In 1935 Rademacher was offered an assistant professorship at the University of Pennsylvania, despite the fact that in Germany he had held a full professorship. Nonetheless, Rademacher was grateful to have escaped the horror that was engulfing his native country, and he faithfully served his university until his retirement in 1962. Rademacher's second marriage ended in divorce in 1947, and two years later he married Irma Wolpe, a successful concert pianist and sister of his longtime friend, mathematician I. J. Schoenberg. In 1943 Rademacher became a naturalized citizen of the United States.

In Germany and while at Pennsylvania, Rademacher supervised the doctoral dissertations of twenty-one students. Many of them became well-known, influential mathematicians who, in turn, trained numerous members of the profession.

Rademacher made significant contributions to several areas of mathematics, including real analysis and measure theory, complex analysis, and number theory. Most of the first fourteen papers published by Rademacher concern real analysis and measure theory. In one of these papers, Rademacher introduced an orthogonal system of functions, now known as Rademacher functions. Since its discovery, Rademacher's orthonormal system has been utilized in many instances in several areas of analysis. However, Rademacher is known to most mathematicians as a number theorist. Two of his earliest papers on number theory offered improvements to Brun's sieve, named after the Norwegian number theorist Viggo Brun. Sieves constitute a very important tool in the theory of prime numbers, with many of the most significant theorems in the subject dependent on the deep theory of sieves.

Rademacher's primary contributions to number theory are in modular forms and related areas. Very briefly, if $f(z)$ denotes a modular form, then there is a relation between $f(z)$ and $f(az + b)/(cz + d)$, where a, b, c, and d are integers such that $ad - bc = 1$. In particular, Rademacher's research focused on a certain modular form called the Dedekind eta-function, which is named after the nineteenth-century German mathematician Richard Dedekind. This function is intimately connected with the partition function $p(n)$, the number of ways of expressing the positive integer n as a sum of positive integers. For example, $p(4)=5$, since 4, $3 + 1, 2 + 2, 2 + 1 + 1$, and $1 + 1 + 1 + 1$ are the five ways 4 can be expressed as a sum of positive integers. As n becomes large, $p(n)$ increases very rapidly. For example, $p(200)=3,972,999,029,388$.

In 1917 the English mathematician G. H. Hardy and the Indian mathematician Srinivasa Ramanujan astounded the mathematical world by establishing an asymptotic series for $p(n)$, which can be used to calculate $p(n)$ comparatively rapidly. No one had previously conjectured that such a formula might exist. In 1936 Rademacher made perhaps his most famous discovery by significantly modifying the approach of Hardy and Ramanujan and establishing an exact series representation for $p(n)$. Rademacher's formula was subsequently generalized in several directions by himself and other mathematicians.

Certain values of $p(n)$ were proved or conjectured by Ramanujan to be divisible by powers of 5, 7, and 11. In particular, for every nonnegative integer n, Ramanujan proved that $p(5n + 4)$ is divisible by 5; for example, $p(4)=5$ and $p(9)=30$. Rademacher used the theory of modular forms to give a new proof of this result and to point the way to later work of Rademacher and Joseph Lehner about divisibility by the first, second, and third powers of 11 and eventually to A. O. L. Atkin's complete proof, using modular forms, of all of Ramanujan's conjectures about the divisibility of $p(n)$.

In the formula relating the eta-function at z and $(az + b)/(cz + d)$, there appear certain sums $s(c, d)$ of rational numbers called Dedekind sums. These sums have many beautiful properties, the most elegant of which is a reciprocity law relating $s(c, d)$ and $s(d, c)$. Rademacher found five new proofs of this reciprocity law and devoted several papers to the study of these sums and certain generalizations.

At his death in Bryn Mawr, Pennsylvania, Rademacher was one of the most influential number theorists of the twentieth century. He influenced the course of mathematics not only through his original re-

search but through his teaching, doctoral students, and books. With a colleague at the University of Pennsylvania, he organized a problems seminar that became a requirement for students seeking an advanced degree in mathematics. Rademacher's books have continued to be widely read by students and researchers and are models of clarity.

• Rademacher published seventy-six papers, and in 1974 the MIT Press published his collected papers in two volumes. In addition, Rademacher wrote ten books and sets of lecture notes. His first book, *The Enjoyment of Mathematics* (1957), coauthored with O. Toeplitz, was first published in German in 1930 and was subsequently translated into English by H. S. Zuckerman; the book became very popular. His two most influential books were published after his death. The first, *Dedekind Sums* (1972), was prepared and coauthored by Emil Grosswald. Three of Rademacher's students, Grosswald, Lehner, and Morris Newman, prepared the second, *Topics in Analytic Number Theory* (1973), from a manuscript left by Rademacher. For a more complete, technical survey of Rademacher's work, together with a complete list of Rademacher's papers, books, and published problems, see Bruce C. Berndt's paper in *Acta Arithmetica* 61 (1992): 209–31.

BRUCE C. BERNDT

RADER, Melvin (8 Nov. 1903–14 June 1981), philosopher, was born Melvin Miller Rader in Walla Walla, Washington, the son of Cary Melvin, a lawyer, and Harriet Miller, a schoolteacher. He grew up in the town of Walla Walla and spent much of his childhood with his brother, Ralph, and sister, Martha, fishing, camping, and hiking in the mountains near the town. As a teenager he grew fond of politics and witnessed the "red scare" that followed World War I when his father defended a man accused of being a Communist. His father, a lawyer, believed that everyone had a right to a fair trial and stood firm against town pressure to drop the case. This event and his father's steadfast loyalty to due process and democratic liberalism had a profound effect on Rader's life.

Rader attended the University of Washington in Seattle. He joined the debate club and studied the writings of John Stuart Mill, William Morris, Karl Marx, and Peter Kropotkin. During this time he developed glandular tuberculosis and spent a number of years struggling to regain his health. In the autumn of 1926 he married Katherine Ellis; they had a son. After their divorce, he married Virginia Baker, an artist and schoolteacher, in March 1935; they had four children. After completing his A.B. in 1925, he began doctoral studies at the university, receiving the A.M. in 1927 and Ph.D. in 1929. In the meantime he taught English at the University of Idaho from 1927 to 1928.

Upon completion of his doctorate, Rader became an assistant professor of English at Western Reserve University (now Case Western Reserve University) in Cleveland, Ohio. In 1930 he returned to the University of Washington, where he taught until his death. He was an assistant professor of philosophy from 1930 to 1944, an associate professor from 1944 to 1948, a full professor from 1948–1971, and professor emeritus from 1971 to 1981. He was also Solomon Katz Lecturer, visiting professor at the University of Chicago (1944–1945), recipient of a Rockefeller Foundation research grant (1948–1949), and visiting professor at the University of South Florida (spring 1972).

Along with a number of important articles published in the *Journal of Aesthetics*, the *Antioch Review*, the *Journal of Philosophy*, the *Kenyon Review*, and other philosophical journals, Rader wrote the following books: *Presiding Ideas in Wordsworth's Poetry* (1931); *A Modern Book of Esthetics* (1979); *No Compromise: The Conflict Between Two Worlds* (1939); *Ethics and Society* (1950, repr. 1968); *The Enduring Questions* (1956; 4th ed., 1980); *Ethics and the Human Community* (1964); *Wordsworth: A Philosophical Approach* (1967); *False Witness* (1969); *Art and Human Values* (1976), with Bertram Jessup; *Marx's Interpretation of History* (1979); and *The Right to Hope* (1981).

Rader was a member of the American Philosophical Association, serving as president of the Pacific Division in 1953. He also had a lengthy association with the American Society for Aesthetics, serving as trustee (1955–1957), vice president (1971–1972), and president (1973–1974). He was also president of the Washington State American Civil Liberties Union (1957, 1961–62) and delegate to the American Council of Learned Societies beginning in 1975.

Rader was a defender of Western democratic liberalism. He argued that "welfare consists in the cultivation and fulfillment of positive interests expressive of the whole nature of man, and that the worth of any social order is its efficacy in promoting such welfare" (*Ethics and Society*, p. 354). Real freedom, he claimed, was more than just the absence of impediments. "You cannot really be free when you are badly clad, underfed, wretchedly housed, without education, without money for medicine, living at a miserable wage, or haunted by the fear of war, unemployment, or a penniless old age" (*Ethics and Society*, p. 358). Thus he championed social programs that provided for basic human needs as well as the Bill of Rights, which secured each individual's legal standing. "We need to unite respect for individuality with a realization of the social interdependence; to combine devotion to freedom and individual rights with loyalty to community plans and purposes; to link the democratic spirit of sharing with an aristocratic devotion to excellence; and to supplement economic and technological efficiency with a human appreciation of moral, artistic, and cultural values" (*Ethics and Society*, p. 368).

In 1948 Rader, along with several other professors, was charged with subversive activities by the Canwell Committee, Washington State's equivalent of the U.S. Congress's Un-American Activities Committee. The committee produced a witness who accused Rader of attending a Communist strategy seminar in Kingston, New York, during the summer of 1938. The unsubstantiated accusations of this witness put Rader's career in jeopardy and caused him to spend a number of years trying to clear his name. Later he wrote of the hearing that "the freedoms of the First and Fifth

Amendments were violated . . . There was no judge or jury, no right of cross examination of hostile witnesses, no right to subpoena evidence or introduce witnesses in one's own defense" (*False Witness*). Rader contended that the Canwell Committee had suppressed evidence and that his accuser had lied, proving that he was in fact in Washington that entire summer. Frank Donner, writing for the *Nation*, said that Rader "triumphed over his ordeals because he was able and willing to fight back: he was supported by the powerful tradition of northwestern liberalism and his own strong faith in the democratic process." Nevertheless, the Canwell Committee did not end its investigations. Other witnesses claimed that Rader was a Communist or fellow traveler, and he spent a good part of his life defending himself. He died in Seattle, Washington.

Rader was intellectually honest, and he never abandoned his principles or the democratic cause. In his day he was a fairly significant philosopher, making contributions to political theory, ethics, aesthetics, and social policy.

• For biographical information dealing with Rader, see I. F. Stone, "Dr. Rader's Vindication," *Nation*, 12 Nov. 1949; and Frank J. Donner, *Nation*, 27 Oct. 1969.

ADAM D. MOORE

RADER, Paul (24 Aug. 1879–19 July 1938), fundamentalist evangelist and radio pioneer, was born Daniel Paul Rader in Denver, Colorado, the son of Daniel Leaper Rader, a minister and official in the Methodist Episcopal church, and Eugenia Shackleford. After spending time as a ranchhand in Wyoming and Colorado as a youth, he became a gifted college football player and boxer who spent time as a sparring partner of heavyweight champions Bob Fitzsimmons and James Jeffries; his athletic experiences and time as a cowboy would later color his sermons and add to his popularity with audiences. He never earned an academic degree but spent several years as a student athlete; between 1898 and 1901 Rader attended and played football for the University of Denver, the University of Colorado, and Central Methodist College in Fayette, Missouri. From 1901 to 1903 he played football and served as athletic director (1901–1902) at Hamline University—another Methodist school—in St. Paul where his father was serving as a pastor. After his father accepted a pastorate in Tacoma, Washington, Rader moved west and spent the 1903–1904 academic year as an instructor at the University of Puget Sound.

Enamored of the scholarly image of liberal theology and the reform efforts of the Social Gospel movement during his college days, Rader was ordained into the Congregational ministry in 1904. He served as pastor at the Maverick Congregational Church in East Boston, Massachusetts (1904–1906), and the Holladay Avenue Congregational Church in Portland, Oregon (1907–1908), where he became involved with the efforts of the Anti-Saloon League. In 1906 he married

Mary Caughran, the daughter of a prominent Tacoma family who had attended his father's church; they had three children. In 1909, experiencing growing doubt about the truth of Christianity and disillusioned with the progress of reform, Rader left the ministry for involvement in a series of speculative business ventures.

By 1912 Rader was in New York City, where he came into contact with the dispensational, Holiness-influenced theology of the Christian and Missionary Alliance and, eventually, its founder Albert B. Simpson. Undergoing a dramatic reconversion to the evangelical faith of his youth, Rader reentered the ministry. After two years based in Pittsburgh as an assistant pastor, he became a traveling Alliance evangelist in 1914. Late that year, while conducting a revival in Chicago, he came to the attention of the leadership at the nondenominational Moody Church. After an extremely successful revival there in early 1915, they offered him their church's pastorate. Under Rader, Moody Church flourished as never before, with over 1,200 joining the congregation in his first two years. An aggressive year-round revivalistic effort increased the congregation to the point that the church outgrew its facilities and moved to a 5,000-seat wooden tabernacle at the corner of LaSalle and North avenues.

Rader's appeal, like that of his contemporary Billy Sunday, lay in his masculine image and use of humor. He differed from Sunday and many other fundamentalist evangelists, however, in that his messages consistently emphasized the love of God rather than themes of hellfire and damnation. As a result of his success, Rader became an increasingly important figure on the revival circuit and within the Alliance. He was elected vice president of the denomination in 1919, and when Simpson died later that year, Rader was chosen as his successor. He accepted the office, but his decision to stay on in Chicago as the pastor of Moody Church instead of moving to Alliance headquarters in Nyack, New York, caused friction with both constituencies. Rader's six-month worldwide tour of Alliance missions in 1921 further antagonized Moody Church's leadership, and after vainly attempting to persuade the church to join the Alliance, Rader resigned his pastorate later that year.

In the summer of 1922, however, he was invited back to Chicago by former parishioners for an evangelistic campaign in a newly erected steel-framed tabernacle on the city's North Side. It proved such a success that Rader decided to make the new Chicago Gospel Tabernacle a full-time base for his evangelistic activities. Rader's "Tab" quickly became a center for regional fundamentalism, with nightly services, an ever-changing roster of visiting speakers and musical groups, and a panoply of ministries supporting missions and targeting children, teens, and single women. His decision to resettle in Chicago, however, was a catalyst for new problems with the Alliance. His inattention to denominational duties and his insistence that the Alliance adopt the "Tabernacle Strategy" he had developed in his ministry at Moody Church and his new Chicago tabernacle brought on a new crisis of confidence among influential segments of the denomination's leadership and led to his resignation of the presidency in 1924.

Free of denominational worries, Rader turned his full attention to the development of innovative evangelistic techniques and programs. One of his most influential ventures was his enthusiastic use of radio during the 1920s when many fundamentalists were suspicious of the new technology's practicality and orthodoxy. Rader was the first significant example of a fundamentalist broadcaster who purchased air time and relied on listeners' contributions to fund his broadcasts. From his first radio sermon in 1922, Rader's warm, folksy style and salvation appeals on programs like "The Back Home Hour" found a large following among conservative midwestern Protestants. The Chicago Gospel Tabernacle became the largest religious presence on Chicago radio between 1925 and 1930 with all-day Sunday broadcasts over WHT and, later, WBBM/WJBT. In 1930 Rader became the first independent fundamentalist broadcaster on a national network when his "Breakfast Brigade" was aired on twenty-six stations of the Columbia Broadcasting System.

The depression's effect on his constituency strained the tabernacle's finances, as did Rader's many programs, which by the early 1930s had grown to include a tabernacle in Los Angeles and a food pantry for Chicago's unemployed. Rader resigned his position at the tabernacle in the spring of 1933, and his organization, the World-Wide Christian Couriers, subsequently declared bankruptcy. Short on funds and without a high-profile venue, Rader drifted through a series of short-lived evangelistic ventures, the longest being a stint at the Fort Wayne Gospel Tabernacle during 1935 and part of 1936. Hampered by ill health and plagued by debt, he moved his family to Hollywood, California, where he died of cancer two years later.

The bustling energy, pragmatic emphases, and innovative spirit that characterized Paul Rader's years in Chicago had an enormous impact on a rising generation of younger fundamentalists. Youthful converts and protégés, such as radio evangelist Charles E. Fuller, missionary broadcaster Clarence W. Jones, and Youth for Christ founder Torrey Johnson, played a significant role in the post–World War II resurgence of evangelicalism. Rader's particular contribution lay in his imaginative efforts to harness mass media and popular culture in the service of evangelism. His effective reliance on paid-time broadcasting was crucial to the developing ethos of evangelical radio and foreshadowed the strategy by which the "Electronic Church" would become the dominant force in American religious broadcasting in the 1970s and beyond.

• The Archives of the Billy Graham Center at Wheaton College, Ill., contain a significant collection of primary sources, papers of associates, and oral histories connected with Rader's years at Moody Church and the Chicago Gospel Tabernacle. Rader wrote more than 900 articles and at least as many sermon reprints, which were published in his organizations' periodicals, *Good News* (Moody Church) and the *World-Wide Christian Courier* (Chicago Gospel Tabernacle). He was the author of nearly twenty devotional and topical books during his lifetime; *Straight from the Shoulder Messages* (1917) is a good guide to his pulpit style while *'Round the Round World* (1922) and *Life's Greatest Adventure* (1938) give insight into Rader's views on missions and vision for small-group evangelism. His novel *Big Bug* (1932) is an interesting—and rare—example of early twentieth-century fundamentalist attempts to use fiction to further their cause. Biographical assessments include Larry K. Eskridge, "Only Believe: Paul Rader and the Chicago Gospel Tabernacle, 1922–1933" (master's thesis, Univ. of Maryland, 1985), and W. Leon Tucker, *The Redemption of Paul Rader* (1918), a useful but hagiographic biography of Rader's life written during his days at Moody Church. For information on his role in evangelical broadcasting see Ben Armstrong, *The Electric Church* (1979), and Dennis Voskuil, "The Power of the Air: Evangelicals and the Rise of Religious Broadcasting," in *American Evangelicals and the Mass Media*, ed. Quentin J. Schultze (1990). See also John W. Sawin and Samuel J. Stoesz, *All for Jesus* (1986), for information on Rader's role in the Christian and Missionary Alliance.

LARRY K. ESKRIDGE

RADFORD, Arthur William (27 Feb. 1896–17 Aug. 1973), naval officer, was born in Chicago, Illinois, the son of John Arthur Radford, an electrical engineer, and Agnes Eliza Knight. He was raised in Riverside, Illinois, and Grinnell, Iowa, and in 1916 he graduated from the U.S. Naval Academy and was commissioned an ensign. During World War I Radford served on the battleship *South Carolina*, which escorted one transatlantic convoy, and from 1918 to 1920 he successively was on the staffs of the commander of Atlantic Battleship Division One, the commander of Battleship Division One, and the commander of the Pacific Fleet's Train. Radford married Dorothy Hume in 1920; they had no children and later divorced.

In November 1920 Radford, after completing flight school at Pensacola, Florida, was designated a naval aviator with the rank of lieutenant, and during the next two decades he rotated between shore and sea assignments in the navy's air arm. After a tour at the flight school as a gunnery instructor, Radford between 1921 and 1929 served at the Bureau of Aeronautics, in the air detachment of the aircraft tender *Aroostook*, as a member of Observation Squadron One on the battleships *Colorado* and *Pennsylvania*, and with the rank of lieutenant commander, at the Naval Air Station at San Diego, California. During 1929 he commanded the Alaskan Aerial Survey of forest and mineral resources for the U.S. Geological Survey and the U.S. Forest Service. Over the next seven years he was a fighter squadron commander on the aircraft carrier *Saratoga*, on the staff of Admiral Harry E. Yarnell, commander of the Battle Force's carriers, with the Bureau of Aeronautics, and navigator of the seaplane tender *Wright*. With the rank of commander, Radford in 1936 became tactical and operations officer on the staff of Rear Admiral Frederick J. Horne, commander of Aircraft Battle Force, and a year later he assumed command of the Naval Air Station at Seattle, Washington, remain-

ing there until 1940. In 1939 he married Mariam Jeanette McMichael; they had no children. Following his tour at the Seattle air station, Radford was executive officer of the carrier *Yorktown* until May 1941, and after a brief stint with the Office of the Chief of Naval Operations, he established the naval air station at Trinidad, British West Indies, commanding it until November 1941.

During World War II Radford emerged as a brilliant administrator and as a tough-minded and expert carrier force commander while serving in the Pacific theater, which thereafter was a lifelong interest. From December 1941 to April 1943 Radford, who was promoted to captain in January 1942, was in charge of aviation training in the Bureau of Aeronautics, ably coordinating the training of thousands of new pilots for the navy's burgeoning air arm. After this assignment he briefly served as commander of Carrier Division Two, and in July 1943 he was promoted to rear admiral and given command of Carrier Division Eleven. In this post he participated in the raid against Wake Island in October 1943 and the invasion of the Gilbert Islands in November 1943. Also, he pioneered the use of fighter teams to defend carriers at night. Radford served as chief of staff for Admiral John Towers, Pacific Fleet air forces commander, from December 1943 to March 1944 and then was assigned to Washington, D.C., as assistant to the deputy chief of naval operations for air until October 1944. He returned to sea duty in November 1944 as commander of Carrier Division Six, and until the end of the war in August 1945, he took part in the invasions of Iwo Jima and Okinawa and operations against the Japanese homeland.

Immediately after the war, Radford was appointed Fleet Air commander, and in January 1946 he was named deputy chief of naval operations for air with the rank of vice admiral. Radford commanded the Second Task Fleet in the Atlantic in 1947, and from January 1948 to April 1949 he was vice chief of naval operations. He then was appointed commander of the Pacific Fleet and high commissioner of the Trust Territory of the Pacific Islands. In the fall of 1949 Radford was a prominent figure in the "Revolt of the Admirals" against preferential funding for air force bombers over construction of a "supercarrier" for the navy. In controversial testimony before a congressional committee, he raised doubts about the air force's strategic-bombing concept, branded its B-36 intercontinental bomber a "billion dollar blunder," and argued that congress should provide increased funding for naval aviation. His testimony helped persuade Congress to fund modern carriers in order to provide a more flexible strategy. During the Korean War, Radford, as commander of the Pacific Fleet, exercised overall supervision of naval operations.

In 1953 President Dwight D. Eisenhower, impressed with Radford's fervent anti-Communism, experience in the Far East, administrative acumen, and belief that strategic power could substitute for large armies, named him chair of the Joint Chiefs of Staff (JCS). By appointing Radford, Eisenhower also placated conservative Republican party leaders like Senator Robert Taft of Ohio. They had argued that the JCS needed someone who, in contrast to Radford's predecessor, General Omar Bradley, was not so concerned with defending Europe but had experience in Far East matters. As JCS chair, Radford was a strong advocate of Eisenhower's "New Look" defense strategy, which called for reduced spending on army ground troops and an emphasis on the threat of "massive retaliation" with nuclear weapons as a deterrent to aggression by the Soviet Union. Later, however, he refused to support Eisenhower's austere defense budgets on the grounds that they did not provide enough funds for basic military requirements or for the specific strategic programs needed to give credibility to the doctrine of massive retaliation.

In addition, Radford was the principal "hawk" in the Eisenhower administration, strongly urging the president to resist any Chinese Communist advances in Asia. In 1954 he advised Eisenhower to intervene in the Indochina war with U.S. air power, including nuclear weapons if necessary, to save the besieged French garrison at Dien Bien Phu, advice that Eisenhower rejected. The following year Radford told Eisenhower to launch an atomic attack against Communist China during the crisis over the Chinese Nationalist–held offshore islands of Quemoy and Matsu, advice that Eisenhower also rejected. Radford's views on the New Look and the use of atomic weapons often put him at odds with the army chief of staff, Matthew B. Ridgway, contributing to intraservice feuds. Radford retired in 1957 and thereafter served on several boards of directors of major corporations.

Radford was one of the most able naval officers of his generation. Highly intelligent and outspoken, he was a superb administrator and combat leader during World War II, and after the war he was the principal spokesman for naval aviation. He also stands out for his advocacy of the use of nuclear weapons and of a firm military-diplomatic stance against Communism. Radford died in Bethesda, Maryland.

• Radford's papers are in the U.S. Naval Historical Center, Washington, D.C., and in the Hoover Institution of War, Revolution and Peace at Stanford University. An oral history is in the John Foster Dulles Oral History Project at Princeton University Library. Stephen Jurika, Jr., ed., *From Pearl Harbor to Vietnam: The Memoirs of Admiral Arthur W. Radford* (1980), covers the years 1941–1954. References to Radford's service during World War II are in Clark G. Reynolds, *The Fast Carriers* (1968) and *Admiral John H. Towers: The Struggle for Naval Air Supremacy* (1991). Details of Radford's postwar career are in Michael A. Palmer, *Origins of the Maritime Strategy* (1990); Jeffrey G. Barlow, *The Revolt of the Admirals: The Fight for Naval Aviation, 1945–50* (1994); Stephen E. Ambrose, *Eisenhower*, vol. 2, *The President* (1984); David L. Anderson, *Trapped by Success: The Eisenhower Administration and Vietnam, 1953–1961* (1991); and Mark Perry, *Four Stars* (1989). An obituary is in the *New York Times*, 18 Aug. 1973.

JOHN KENNEDY OHL

RADFORD, William (9 Sept. 1809–8 Jan. 1890), naval officer, was born in Fincastle, Virginia, the son of John Radford, a physician, and Harriet Kennerly. Not long after Radford's birth, the family moved to Maysville, Kentucky, where John Radford died in 1816. Four years later Harriet Radford married William Clark, a widower whose first wife was Harriet's cousin. Clark, a brother of George Rogers Clark, was an explorer and former governor and superintendent of American Indian affairs of Missouri Territory. William Radford attended boarding school at Perth Amboy, New Jersey, and in 1825 was appointed a midshipman in the navy. His first cruise was aboard the *Brandywine* with the marquis de Lafayette, who was returning to France following his highly publicized American tour. During the next ten years, Radford served aboard the *Constitution*, the *John Adams*, the *Erie*, and the *Constellation*, cruising the Mediterranean and the Caribbean. He was promoted to passed midshipman in 1831 and lieutenant in 1837. During 1838 he saw active service in the Florida Seminole War.

When the Mexican War began in 1846, Radford was executive officer aboard the sloop of war *Warren* in California waters. Off the Mexican-held fortress of Mazatlán, Radford led a band of volunteers in a daring daylight raid that resulted in the capture of a Mexican warship and all on board while under the guns of the fort. The following year Radford and a party that included his brother-in-law, Stephen Watts Kearny, returned East by the overland route. While on extended leave during 1848, he married Mary Elizabeth Lovell; they had six children. The couple established a residence in Morristown, New Jersey. Except for one tour of sea duty aboard the storeship *Lexington* in 1851–1852, Radford spent the next several years on shore duty. His promotion to commander came in 1855. Following a year as lighthouse inspector in New York, 1858–1859, he was assigned command of the steam sloop *Dacotah*, which became part of the China Squadron.

During the secession crisis, many southern naval officers resigned their commissions, causing Navy Secretary Gideon Welles to be suspicious of all officers from southern and Border States. As a result, Radford, whose loyalty to the United States was unwavering, was relieved of his command of the *Dacotah*. He once again became lighthouse inspector at New York. Welles eventually realized he had misjudged him, and in February 1862 Radford was placed in command of the warship *Cumberland*, part of the Blockade Squadron off Hampton Roads, Virginia. On 8 March 1862, when the Confederate ironclad *Virginia* first made its appearance, Radford was ashore at Old Point on court-martial duty. Immediately upon learning that the *Virginia* had appeared, Radford hastened to join his ship but was too late. He could only watch in frustration as the *Cumberland* sank from damage inflicted by the Confederate ironclad.

In May 1862 Radford became executive officer of the Brooklyn Navy Yard, serving there for the next two years. He was promoted to captain in July 1862 and commodore in April 1863. As commander of the ironclad steamer *New Ironsides*, he brought the Federal monitors into the action against Fort Fisher, North Carolina, in December 1864 and January 1865. Following the Federal victory there, Radford next commanded the James River Flotilla, protecting General Ulysses S. Grant's supply base at City Point, Virginia. From April to October 1865 he commanded the Atlantic Squadron. As a supporter of President Andrew Johnson's lenient Reconstruction policies after the war, Radford accompanied the president, Admiral David G. Farragut, and others on Johnson's unsuccessful whistle-stop tour to gain public support during August 1866.

Radford was promoted to rear admiral in 1866 while serving as commandant of the Washington Navy Yard. His final sea duty, in 1869, was as commander of the European Squadron. Although he officially retired from the navy in 1870, he remained on special duty in Washington until 1872. Afterward, he continued to reside in Washington, D.C., where he died.

Radford was a courageous and dependable officer. In his official report of the engagement of the monitors against Fort Fisher, Admiral David Porter singled out Radford for special recognition. Porter believed that had it not been for Radford, "victory might not have been ours. Under each and every circumstance, Com. Radford has acquired an enviable reputation, and is deserving of the greatest promotion that can be given to him." Secretary Welles was likewise impressed by Radford's "sound judgment" and "nautical experience."

• Radford's letters and other personal papers of the Civil War period are in the Navy Department Library, Miscellaneous Files. Record Group 45 (Naval Records Collection), National Archives, contains Radford's official correspondence while commanding the *Malvern* and the *New Ironsides*, 1864–1865. Additional Civil War correspondence is in *The Official Records of the Union and Confederate Navies in the War of the Rebellion* (30 vols., 1894–1922). See also Sophie Radford De Meissner, *Old Navy Days: Sketches from the Life of Rear Admiral William Radford* (1920), and Lewis R. Hamersly, *The Records of Living Officers of the U.S. Navy and Marine Corps* (1870). An obituary is in the *Washington Post*, 9 Jan. 1890.

NORMAN C. DELANEY

RADIN, Paul (2 Apr. 1883–21 Feb. 1959), anthropologist and ethnographer, was born in Lodz, Poland, the son of Dr. Adolph M. Radin, a rabbi, and Johanna Theodor. Radin's father, a scholar of Hebrew as well as other ancient and modern languages, was a liberal rabbi active in reform movements. Radin inherited his father's aptitude for languages, scholarship, and radical thinking. The family immigrated to New York from Europe in 1884. Radin's undergraduate career at the College of the City of New York began when he was fourteen and ended at age nineteen. He then attended graduate and postgraduate school at Columbia and also studied at universities in Berlin, Munich, Florence, and Paris. Between 1905 and 1907 he often interrupted his formal training to wander about Europe cultivating his ethical, intellectual, and personal growth. He spent time in Germany, Italy, Switzerland, and Czechoslovakia. During his studies at the University of Berlin in 1906, Radin published his first ethnographic paper, "Zur Netztechnik der Südamerikanischen Indianer," in the *Zeitschrift für Ethnologie*.

While Radin was at Columbia, Franz Boas (anthropology and statistics) and James Harvey Robinson (history) served as his mentors, teachers, and examiners. Radin was grateful to these men for teaching him that before he could understand other cultures, he needed to be firmly anchored in his own. In 1910 Radin married Rose Robinson, lost his father, and passed his oral exams. While Radin was a student under Boas, the curriculum for American anthropology was being conceived and developed. Many of the other students who studied under Boas throughout this period went on to become prominent figures in American anthropology: Alfred Kroeber, Clark Wissler, Edward Sapir, Robert Lowie, Ruth Benedict, Laura Benedict, Margaret Mead, and Zora Neale Hurston. Radin received his doctorate in anthropology from Columbia in 1911.

Radin worked for the Bureau of Ethnology from 1911 to 1912 and the next year received a fellowship from Columbia and Harvard to study Zapotec linguistics and mythology (1912–1913). With his friend Edward Sapir, he was asked to conduct a Cultural and Geological Survey of Canada (1913–1917); Radin's commission was to study the Ojibwa in Ontario. Following these experiences, Radin began a teaching career that spanned forty-two years. His first faculty position was at the University of California, Berkeley (1917–1920). While holding a lectureship at Cambridge University (1920–1925), he was drawn to Zurich by the ideas of the Swiss psychologist C. G. Jung, who exerted a sustained influence on Radin's published writings, especially *Primitive Man as Philosopher* (1927) and *The Trickster: A Study in American Indian Mythology* (1956). After three years at Fiske University (1927–1930), Radin returned to Berkeley, remaining on the faculty of the University of California until 1941. During this time he established professional and personal friendships with Kroeber and Lowie, who edited a monograph series in which Radin published much of his work. From 1941 to 1945 he taught at the innovative Black Mountain College in North Carolina, at the time a haven for experimental artists and writers. Foundation grants then enabled him to write and edit without significant teaching responsibilities; he on occasion lectured at Kenyon College during this period. In 1949 he married his second wife, Doris Woodward, and lectured at universities in Sweden. For the next several years he was a lecturer at Oxford, Cambridge, Manchester, and the C. G. Jung Institute in Zurich (1952–1954). Radin's last university position was at Brandeis, where he served as chair of the anthropology department and held the Samuel Rubin professorship (1957–1959).

Radin's fieldwork took him among the Winnebago (1908–1913), the Ottawa (1925), minority groups in the San Francisco Bay area, Italian immigrants, and native cultures in Mexico. From 1930 to 1940 he studied the Patwin language, spoken by a Native American tribe in California. Although Radin's initial motivation for doing fieldwork was the study of languages, mythologies, and social organizations of primitive societies, he was particularly interested in the life stories of representative individuals. While teaching at Fiske, for example, Radin collected life histories and conversion stories from former slaves living in Nashville.

A friend and colleague of his, Cora DuBois, claimed that Radin's "restlessness"—his moving from place to place—grew out of an intense personal integrity and need to have firsthand experiences. He was rational, skeptical, and unconventional throughout his career. DuBois also said that Radin "never coveted wealth or courted approval. He [was] acquisitive only of books." As a teacher, he engaged in lengthy conversations with individual students in order to promote dialogical exchanges (logical conversations between individuals who hold each other in mutual respect even though their cultural backgrounds might differ) about history, theories, and cultures. This kind of pedagogy was an extension of Radin's ethnographic practices in the field.

In a character sketch of Radin, Stanley Diamond observed, "He is not above being disliked; it does not displease him. Yet, liked or disliked, he is usually loved, for love is what he subtly demands in return for the gift of his being, the man and his work inseparable. He has a sorcerer's charm, undimmed by age; he bewitches. In conversation, he can suddenly switch to a trickster's view of the world, obliterating cant and puncturing the ordinary pieties." His ability to puncture "ordinary pieties" runs through all of Radin's published works and earned him the reputation for being a revolutionary and an iconoclast with regard to Western civilization's evolutionary views of human social, political, and spiritual development. From 1906 through 1959 Radin published 192 monographs, books, articles, and reviews. Among his most enduring writings are *El folklore de Oaxaca* (1917), *The Winnebago Tribe* (1923), *The Method and Theory of Ethnology* (1933), *The Italians of San Francisco* (1935), *Primitive Religion: Its Nature and Origin* (1937), *The Road of Life and Death* (1945), and *African Folktales* (1952).

Evident throughout these works is what Ino Rossi and Edward O'Higgins claim is Radin's singular contribution to the history of anthropology: "Only in the work of Paul Radin is sympathetic understanding raised to the level of a methodological principle." Dennis Tedlock says that this methodological principle "is founded upon the possibility of dialogs that reach back and forth across rifts of linguistic, cultural, and social difference." Dialogic anthropology, as developed by Radin, demands that ethnographers (in Tedlock's words) "understand the philosophies of others," not use "unilateral formulations" by outsiders, and "engage in 'philosophical dialog' with contemplative natives." He believed that the primary duty of any ethnographer was to the "specific tribe" and not to general theories or methods of analyzing cultures from a Western bias. Radin strongly opposed contemporary evolutionary assumptions about primitive peoples. His actual research demonstrated that tribal cultures were, in fact, not on the first rungs of evolutionary development in terms of language, culture, religion, and social organization. Radin was adamant in his belief that the changes in primitive cultures did not indicate a movement from "animism to ethical monotheism" in religion; from "totemistic clan and mother-right to individualized monarchies and republics, and father-right" in governments; or from "simple to complex" advancement in economic, social, or psychological development.

Radin's personal conversations with Native Americans assured him that aboriginal peoples were not inferior in mentality, and he was against Lucien Lévy-Bruhl's contention that primitives possessed prelogical minds. His work with various individual Winnebago men, like Sam and Jasper Blowsnake, led Radin to assert that aboriginal peoples included both "thinkers and men of action." To support his views, he published first-person narratives such as *The Autobiography of a Winnebago Indian* (1920) and *Crashing Thunder: The Autobiography of an American Indian* (1926), which he said "allowed" the Indian "to tell the facts in his own way." Although Arnold Krupat has demonstrated the extent of Radin's influence on the construction and content of these texts, Radin can be said to have begun the important tradition of auto-ethnography, an adjunct to dialogic anthropology.

As conceived by Radin, the dialogic process has several protocols. Ethnographers must have a thorough knowledge of the language, history, and status of their informants, and Radin suggested that each informant usually responds to the knowledge, interests, and personalities of ethnographers. Although many ethnographers have used information gathered from individuals to construct a generic representative of a tribe, Radin contended that ethnographers should avoid reductive thinking about the individuals with whom they converse. Outside or external influences on specific cultures should also be scrutinized so that ethnographers can understand the context of the culture under study at any given moment in their history; these influences include missionary efforts, the impositions of colonial government, ideas of Western ideas, and material adaptation processes. Radin cautioned ethnographers not to equate changes in cultures over time with degeneracy, hybridization, or decline. All cultures, he argued, pass through multiple periods of adaptation, and these transitions must be examined in the context of both external and internal causes.

Radin did not approve of the multiple origins theory of culture or the natural science approach to reclaiming the history and languages of primitive societies—a practice Boas initiated. According to Radin, natural science approaches ignore internal evidence for development in favor of objective facts, theories of diffusion, and the idea of diffusion from common cultural centers. In his view, humans are not material objects to be analyzed; humans are dynamic, adaptive, and creative individuals who respond to particular events, other personalities, and more encompassing environmental forces. By suggesting that most scientists have unconscious assumptions that control their measurements of data, Radin also warned against the illusion of objectivity. If one goes looking for folktales among a people, one will find them; if one goes looking for great works of literature, one will find them also.

Radin's name is especially linked to the Winnebago tribe, among whom he labored over a period of thirty years. Indeed his curiosity and genuine regard for individuals among the Winnebago generated numerous publications and radicalized anthropological theories and Western intellectual assumptions for the better part of three decades. John Dewey claimed that if Radin's findings were "even approximately right," the very foundations of Occidental thought concerning the development of civilizations would need revision.

According to Abram Leon Sachar, president of Brandeis at the time Radin was on the faculty there, he "persistently sought the individual behind the tribe, the mind behind the ritual, the hand behind the tool, and the man behind humanity." Radin died in New York City.

• The American Philosophical Society holds Radin's unpublished records on Wintu, Winnebago, Ojibwa, and Huave linguistics. An excellent biographical sketch of Radin, written by Cora DuBois, appears in Stanley Diamond, ed., *Culture in History: Essays in Honor of Paul Radin* (1960), which includes a bibliography of his writings. A sketch of Radin's work among the Winnebago appears in Nancy Lurie, "Two Dollars," in *Crossing Cultural Boundaries*, ed. Solon Kimball and James B. Watson (1972). Discussions of the historical context of Radin's contributions to the field of anthropology can be found in Robert Lowie, *The History of Ethnographical Theory* (1937); H. R. Hays, *From Ape to Angel: An Informal History of Social Anthropology* (1958); and Marvin Harris, *The Rise of Anthropological Theory: A History of Theories of Culture* (1968). Stanley Diamond evaluates Radin's contributions to cultural studies in the 1971 paperback edition of Radin's *The World of Primitive Man*; see also John Dewey's foreword to Radin's *Primitive Man as Philosopher* (1957 ed.). Arnold Krupat assesses Radin's contributions to autoethnography in the foreword to *Crashing Thunder: The Autobiography of an American Indian* (1983 ed.), ed. Paul Radin, and in Krupat, *For Those Who Come After* (1985). Dennis Tedlock supplied information to the author of this entry in a personal communication, 4 Nov. 1995. Obituaries by Harry Hoijer and J. David Sapir appear in, respectively, *American Anthropologist*, Oct. 1959, and the *Journal of American Folklore*, Jan. 1961. The *New York Times* of 22 Feb. 1959 also has an obituary.

M. SUZANNE EVERTSEN LUNDQUIST

RADO, Sandor (1890–1972), psychoanalyst, was born probably in Hungary. The names of his parents and details of his education are unknown. In 1913 he became, with four others, a founding member of the Hungarian Psychoanalytic Society. He first met Sigmund Freud before World War I, thanks to a letter of introduction from Rado's mentor in Budapest, Sandor Ferenczi, who was a special favorite of Freud's. In 1924, when Rado was already a prominent analyst practicing in Berlin, Freud elevated him to replace Otto Rank as editor in chief of the most important international psychoanalytic journal, *Zeitschrift*. Rado was known as an outstanding theoretician of the movement, and in Europe he analyzed figures such as Wilhelm Reich, Heinz Hartmann, and Otto Fenichel. In addition to Rado's intellectual relationship with Freud, Rado corresponded with him on business matters.

When the New York Psychoanalytic Society was establishing its first training institute in 1931, Rado was invited to come to the United States to be the founding director. Rado spent each of the next summers in Europe. He visited Freud every time, until in 1935 difficulties finally arose between him and Freud. Rado thought that the Viennese analysts around Freud constituted a palace guard of advisers and that they had long envied Rado's special position. Freud himself is known to have resented the way Rado had been successfully helping many analysts to leave the European continent for the United States. Freud blamed Rado for what Freud feared was the increasing isolation of analysis in Europe. Rado had opposed Freud's plan to build a new international institute in Vienna after Hitler had come to power in Germany; Freud allowed himself to entertain such an unrealistic project even though others assured him it was politically impractical.

The crisis that took place between Freud and Rado in 1935 was occasioned by a critical review of one of Rado's monographs; it was written by Jeanne Lampl–de Groot, then an analytic patient of Freud's. The problem was that the review appeared to be published with Freud's tacit endorsement, and Rado never saw Freud again. But Rado remained a most prominent leader within American analysis. Then, shortly after Karen Horney had been demoted from instructor to lecturer by the governing Education Committee of the New York Psychoanalytic Society, Rado himself was deposed as educational director in 1942.

In 1944, just as Rado was about to found the Psychoanalytic Clinic at Columbia University's College of Physicians and Surgeons, he was thrown out of the New York Psychoanalytic Society's institute as a training analyst for future candidates. Starting in the late 1930s Rado had been going off on a different ideological tack, critical of Freud, so that even before 1944 he was viewed as a psychoanalytic Benedict Arnold. Unlike earlier so-called dissidents within Freud's movement, who chose to make their appeal to the general reading public, Rado wanted to go deeper into university medicine.

From the outset of his career at the Berlin Psychoanalytic Institute in the 1920s, Rado had been especially concerned with establishing standards of education and training. Some of his papers from then, on melancholia and drug addiction, for example, are still outstanding. Even as he was becoming notorious as a "deviant" in Freud's movement, Rado was simultaneously succeeding in helping to bring analysis within university life and therefore raising the standards of research and practice in the field. Rado's commitment to science seemed to preclude his writing for the lay public.

As time went on, Rado, like other so-called rebels in analysis, worked out new terms for old concepts, as he sought to express an individual point of view. Yet Rado was not some sort of isolated eccentric. For some years he was a member of the New York State Mental Hygiene Council, and Governors Averell Harriman and Nelson Rockefeller supported his work with grants from the New York state budget. Rado retired from Columbia in 1957, after which he helped to create the New York School of Psychiatry at the State University of New York, where he was director for ten years.

Rado was married three times. His first wife was Ilona Krasso; they had one child. It is not know if she died or if they divorced. He then married Elizabeth Révész, who died in 1923; they had no children. His third wife was Emmy Chrisler, with whom he had one child. Dates of these marriages are unavailable. He died in New York City.

It is widely acknowledged that Rado authored many classic papers within analysis, although it is more controversial how, after his falling out with the ranks of orthodox analysis, his independent thinking led him to develop a theoretical system of his own. For example, he became opposed to the idea that the removal of repressions and the emergence of buried memories have good therapeutic effects, and he thought that the deliberate provocation of transferences was a clinical mistake, since it undermined the patient's capacity for autonomy and self-reliance. In addition, Rado was prescient enough to have emphasized the significance of the study of genetics for the future of psychoanalytic psychiatry.

Rado's later writings can be hard to follow. He disdained popularizations and put his faith in medical science. The future, he believed, would redeem him. He also helped see to it that the Association for Psychoanalytic Medicine got started, and he was one of the founders of the eclectic American Academy of Psychoanalysis.

Like Freud himself, Rado was a spellbinder who spoke like a book. Yet Rado underestimated Freud's contribution to the humanities and was too intolerant of the significance of analysis for philosophy and the social sciences. Within psychiatry itself, Rado may well turn out to have been prophetic about the future of biology. Rado was a thoroughly sophisticated European man of letters; at the same time developments within psychiatry have confirmed Rado's convictions about the importance of genetics and biology for psychiatric knowledge.

Rado belonged to the radical left within the history of analysis, but it remained a fragmented tradition of so-called dissenters. Although Rado was for a time allied with New York City's Abram Kardiner and Rado's work on therapy was also similar to the ideas of fellow Hungarian Franz Alexander, these critics of the "mainstream" in analysis rarely hung together. None of them would have dreamt of citing approvingly any of the earlier "heretics" such as Carl Jung, Alfred Adler, or Otto Rank. The nonconformists have been the ones with the original ideas, even though their position has so far won them inadequate recognition. It is hard to become educated in the real story of analysis because of the sectarianism that has afflicted the movement over the years. Some of today's most persuasive critics of Freud are now only reinventing concepts that were first advanced many years ago but whose origins have been forgotten.

Just as too few people among our contemporaries seem able to be open-minded about appreciating both Freud's accomplishments as well as his limitations, so it is hard for practitioners to be sensitive to both the strictly psychological side of the interaction between patients and therapists as well as to the fundamental biochemical nature of the physiology of our being. Different schools of psychotherapeutic thought are apt to live existences independent of one another, and there seems little support for encouraging a tolerant understanding of contrasting points of view. Rival perspectives in this area tend to be held with a religiously intolerant kind of fervor, and catholicity of understanding is rare.

• Rado's writings include *Psychoanalysis of Behavior: The Collected Papers* (2 vols., 1956–1962) and *Adaptational Psychodynamics: Motivation and Control*, ed. Jean Jameson and Henriette Klein (1969). For more information see Paul Roazen and Bluma Swerdloft, *Heresy: Sandor Rado and the Psychoanalytic Movement* (1995).

PAUL ROAZEN

RAEBURN, Boyd (27 Oct. 1913–2 Aug. 1966), jazz and popular bandleader and saxophonist, was born Boyde Albert Raden in Faith, South Dakota. Nothing is known of his parents and upbringing or the reason for the name change from Raden to Raeburn. Raeburn enrolled at the University of Chicago in 1931 to study medicine but found greater enjoyment playing in the college dance band. Entering a local contest, this band won an engagement at the 1933 Chicago World's Fair, at which point Raeburn abandoned medicine for music.

Operating as a member of the saxophone section, rather than standing in front of the group, Raeburn led an undistinguished midwestern dance band through the 1930s. By mid-decade he was married to the band's singer, Lorraine Olson; nothing more is known of their marriage. In 1939 he turned from a polite dance music modeled after Lawrence Welk and other such orchestras to big band swing. His band held residencies at the Chez Paree nightclub in Chicago in the spring of 1940 and at the Arcadia Ballroom in New York City in November 1942, with Earl Hines's arrangers Budd Johnson and Jerry Valentine contributing to Raeburn's library for the latter engagement.

Returning to Chicago in 1943, he brought the group into the Band Box for a nine-month stand and nightly broadcasts. Bandmembers at this point included saxophonist Johnny Bothwell and singers Shirley Luster (later to become famous under a new name, June Christy) and Ginnie Powell. In January 1944 he toured to New York City with a band that included Bothwell, arranger Eddie Finckel, and several men who would rise to prominence as members of Woody Herman's Herds: trumpeter Sonny Berman, trombonist Earl Swope, and drummer Don Lamond. The group began residencies in late February at the Hotel Lincoln and in May at the Hotel Commodore, where pianist and arranger George Handy replaced Finckel.

By the time of this stay in New York, Raeburn had entirely shed his reputation as the leader of what is known in the trade as a "Mickey Mouse band" and instead had acquired a reputation as an experimentalist and musician's musician who attracted the era's leading jazz players, both African American and white. African-American trumpeter Roy Eldridge and trombonist Trummy Young sat in with the group, trumpeter Little Benny Harris and bassist Oscar Pettiford toured with Raeburn until the group ventured too uncomfortably far South, and trumpeter Dizzy Gillespie brought in what would become his most famous composition, "Night in Tunisia," for Raeburn to perform. Raeburn made the first recordings of this piece, for the V-Disc label (a noncommercial studio recording for American servicemen) in May 1944 and again, retitled "Interlude," for the Guild label in January 1945, with Gillespie and Harris, saxophonists Al Cohn and Serge Chaloff, Pettiford, and drummer Shelly Manne subbing for Raeburn's regulars on the latter occasion.

Handy then left the band to spend six months writing for movie soundtracks in Hollywood. During this time Raeburn switched from tenor saxophone to baritone saxophone and then to bass saxophone, and another prominent sideman, singer David Allyn, joined. Raeburn's repertory was not entirely suited to dancing, and consequently the band failed to draw large audiences. After the Palisades Park ballroom in New Jersey burned down in the course of Raeburn's engagement there, he took the group west to the Palace Hotel in San Francisco, California, where Handy rejoined them in the summer of 1945.

Late in August the band toured south to Los Angeles. Raeburn divorced Olson and married Powell in September 1945, shortly after she rejoined the band; they had no children. Between October 1945 and November 1946 Raeburn's group made recordings for Jewell, the label of former bandleader Ben Pollack, including Handy's compositions "Tonsilectomy" (sic; Handy's spelling), "Xerxa," and "Dalvatore Sally," Finckel's "Boyd Meets Stravinsky," Handy's brooding arrangements of "Forgetful" (featuring Allyn) and "Temptation" (featuring Powell), and his eccentric orchestration of "Over the Rainbow."

During this period Raeburn had trouble finding steady work for the band, apart from a two-month stand at the Club Morocco in Hollywood, in the summer of 1946. In addition, he became involved in an ugly fight, when, while trying to sort out what had been written by Finckel and what by Handy, the writers discovered that Raeburn had registered the pieces in his own name. Arranger Johnny Richards replaced Handy, who quit.

Returning to New York, Raeburn opened at the Vanity Fair, a midtown nightclub, with a twenty-piece band plus singers in February 1947. After broadcasting from this venue for six weeks over CBS and NBC radio, he toured colleges and recorded for Atlantic but once again failed to attract enough business to support the band. Raeburn began leading a small group. He made a few big band albums in mid-1950s, but his career was effectively over in 1950.

Raeburn went into the furniture business, eventually settling in Nassau. Powell, his wife, died in 1959. He was badly injured in an automobile accident in 1963, when his car overturned and he was trapped for twenty-four hours. He never fully recovered and died of a heart attack in Lafayette, Louisiana.

In his era Raeburn was admired as a bandleader whose arrangers contributed to a transformation of jazz from dance music to art music and who in particular encouraged musical and titular connections to contemporary Euro-American high culture. It seems clear from Raeburn's involvement in Gillespie's "Night in Tunisia" that informed jazz musicians felt that he was onto something important, but listening to the band's principal output, one can scarcely understand what that something was. In Finckel's "Boyd Meets Stravinsky," the Boyd portion is based on a fervent bop blues, but the soloists are unequipped to play bop, and the effect echoes the swing and bop of Woody Herman's contemporary First Herd in a less tuneful and less talented way; sandwiched between two Boyds is the Stravinsky portion, with its bits of dissonance blaring over a ponderous bass line of a foursquare rhythmic symmetry that Stravinsky himself would never have maintained. Handy's schizophrenic and perhaps unintentionally comical orchestration of "Over the Rainbow" is reminiscent of Spike Jones's joke recordings, as the arranger juxtaposes several flavors of jazz and pop and movie music. On others of the aforementioned titles on Jewell, Handy's pastiche method remains in evidence, but in general the performances are both less eccentric and less distinctive. Perhaps the admiration for Raeburn's musical progressivism is a product of the 1940s that cannot easily be recaptured.

• Surveys and interviews with Raeburn include George Hoefer, "Boyd Raeburn," *Down Beat*, 26 Apr. 1962, pp. 24–25; and Arthur Jackson, "Boyd Raeburn: 'The Successful Failure,'" *Jazz Monthly* 12 (Nov. 1966): 5–8. See also Jack McKinney's liner notes to Raeburn's album *Jewells* (1980); George T. Simon, *The Big Bands*, 4th ed. (1981); and Stan Woolley, "The Forgotten Ones: Boyd Raeburn," *Jazz Journal International* 37 (Feb. 1984): 18–19. Catalogs of his recordings are in George I. Hall, *Boyd Raeburn and His Or-*

chestra: *A Complete Discography* (1972), updated by Charles Garrod and Bill Korst as *Boyd Raeburn and His Orchestra plus Johnny Bothwell and George Handy* (1985). Obituaries are in the *New York Times*, 4 Aug. 1966, and *Down Beat*, 8 Sept. 1966.

BARRY KERNFELD

RAFFERTY, Maxwell Lewis, Jr. (17 May 1917–13 June 1982), educator, was born in New Orleans, Louisiana, the son of Maxwell Lewis Rafferty, an Irish Roman Catholic store owner and auto plant worker, and DeEtta Cox. In 1921 the family moved to Sioux City, Iowa, and then, in 1931, to Los Angeles, California. Young Max skipped several grades and graduated at age sixteen from Beverly Hills School, where he was remembered for being studious, quick witted, and much younger than his classmates.

After entering the University of California, Los Angeles (UCLA), he majored in history, managed the football and rugby teams, was president of Sigma Pi fraternity, joined the UCLA Americans (an anti-Communist athletic group opposed to leftist students), and received a B.A. in 1938. He enrolled in the UCLA School of Education to become a teacher and later claimed to have reluctantly studied John Dewey's educational philosophy in order to become certified. He taught English and history and coached football at Trona High School in Trona, California, from 1940 to 1948, having been classified physically unfit for the World War II draft because of flat feet. He married a schoolmate (name unknown) in 1940, was divorced in 1943, and married Frances Louella Longman in 1944; they had three children. He earned an M.A. from UCLA in 1949 and an Ed.D. from the University of Southern California in 1955.

Asked later why he chose to be a teacher and school administrator for twenty-one years in isolated southern California desert towns, Rafferty replied that "they paid better salaries and advancement was more rapid." From Trona, where he had risen to be vice principal, he became principal of the high school in Big Bear, a resort town in the San Bernardino Mountains, from 1948 to 1951. He then held school superintendencies at Saticoy (1951–1955), Needles (1955–1961), and La Canada, a prosperous northeast Los Angeles suburb (1961–1962).

Rafferty's speeches to education groups and civic clubs as well as his articles (particularly in *Phi Delta Kappan*, the journal of the education honor society) and books written during these years expressed his contempt for progressive education and school approaches that stressed "life adjustment." He described leftist students of the 1950s and 1960s as "booted, side-burned, ducktailed, unwashed, leather-jacketed slobs." His impassioned speeches and writings soon won him admiration from the John Birch Society and other right-wing groups, many of which had growing memberships in California during these years. His 1961 "Passing of the Patriot" speech to the La Canada school board excoriated educators for having been "so busy educating for 'life adjustment' that we forgot that

the first duty of a nation's schools is to preserve that nation." The speech marked a turning point in his career. Wide press coverage made Rafferty a hero not only of political right wingers, but also of those who yearned more generally for a return to simple and manly virtues. In 1962, backed by a coalition of conservative forces, Rafferty won election as state superintendent of public instruction; he was reelected in 1966. He feuded with the liberal state board of education, especially over books that he wanted removed from school libraries and courses. But his conservative philosophy of education had little real impact because of the checks and balances and local control built into the California school system. In fact, the state's schools were never as progressive as Rafferty claimed.

Encouraged by conservative Republicans, he ran for the U.S. Senate in 1968, won the nomination over liberal Republican California Senator Thomas H. Kuchell, but lost to Democrat Alan M. Cranston in the general election. He also lost his third election bid in 1970 as California's superintendent of public instruction to Wilson Riles, a black educator whom he had appointed his deputy. Having been rejected in California, he left in 1971 to become dean of education at Troy State University in Troy, Alabama. He died near Troy after an automobile accident.

Max Rafferty presaged the New Right's ascendancy to political power through the Republican presidencies of Richard Nixon, Gerald Ford, and particularly Ronald Reagan. Many observers believed that Rafferty preached the conservative gospel as a means of self-promotion rather than out of personal conviction. Despite his talent for invective, opponents as well as allies found him likable and articulate.

• Rafferty's papers as California school superintendent are in the California State Library in Sacramento, and his papers as dean of education at Troy State University are located at the university in Troy, Ala. His best-known books are *Suffer, Little Children* (1962), *What They Are Doing to Your Children* (1964), *Max Rafferty on Education* (1968), and *Classroom Countdown: Education at the Crossroads* (1970). For biographies, see Paul F. Cummins, *Max Rafferty: A Study in Simplicity* (1968), and Franklin Parker, "School Critic Max Rafferty (1917–1982) and the New Right," *Review Journal of Philosophy & Social Science* 10, no. 2 (1985): 129–40. Obituaries are in the *New York Times*, *San Diego Union*, *Oakland Tribune*, and *Los Angeles Times*, 14 June 1982; the *San Francisco Examiner*, 15 June 1982; and the *Birmingham News*, 16 June 1982.

FRANKLIN PARKER

RAFINESQUE, Constantine Samuel (22 Oct. 1783–18 Sept. 1840), naturalist, was born in Constantinople suburb, the son of François G. A. Rafinesque, a Marseillais merchant, and Madeleine Schmaltz. Within a year the family returned to Marseilles. The reversal of the family's fortune after Rafinesque's father's death in 1793 ended the boy's hope for a college education in Switzerland. What little education he had was from private tutors as his mother shunted the children between France and Italy during the French Revolution.

At age nineteen he began an apprenticeship with the Clifford Brothers, merchants in Philadelphia; and during two and a half years in the United States he roamed the countryside making botanical collections.

Returning to Europe in 1805, Rafinesque served as secretary to the American consul in Palermo. Within three years he became financially secure enough through such part-time business activities as exporting medicinal squills that he could give up all employment and devote his full time to Sicilian natural history. His first book, *Caratteri di alcuni nuovi generi e nuove specie di animali e piante della Sicilia* (1810), set the pattern for all of his subsequent scientific publications—the classification and description of new species of plants and animals. During 1814 he edited and published *Specchio delle scienze*, a monthly scientific journal said to be the first in Sicily. To make himself better known on the Continent he published *Analyse de la nature* (1815), modeling it on Linnaeus's *Systema naturae* and writing in French in the belief that that language would become the scientific medium of communication. Meanwhile, during his stay in Sicily, he had formed a liaison with Josephine Vaccaro, who bore him two children, though they could not marry because she was a Roman Catholic and he a Protestant.

Rafinesque lost much of his wealth and all of his scientific collections in a shipwreck on Long Island Sound when he returned to the United States in 1815. In New York, where he was one of the founders of the Lyceum of Natural History, he published *Florula Ludoviciana* (1817), a book causing the animosity of many of his colleagues, such as the botanist William Baldwin, who wrote to William Darlington that Rafinesque's book "is a shocking production, to come from one who has placed himself at the head of the botanical profession in our country." They rightly condemned him for classifying and naming plants that he himself had never seen but took from the published account of the French traveler C. C. Robin. Equally disturbing to them was Rafinesque's system of classification. American botanists followed the Linnaean "artificial" system based on the number, union, and length of stamens for classes and the number of styles for the orders of flowering plants. Rafinesque's "natural" system, adapted from French prototypes developed by Michel Adanson and Antoine de Jussieu, grouped plants according to their perceived morphological relationships, a system that prevailed by the middle of the century.

In the spring of 1818 Rafinesque made a collecting trip down the Ohio River that produced *Ichthyologia Ohiensis* (1820), the earliest attempt to describe all the fishes of the Ohio, and a series of papers on the mollusks of the river. In all, the trip was so fruitful in new species that his work was excluded from the *American Journal of Science* because its editor, Benjamin Silliman, feared he would fill its pages all by himself. Having also run afoul of the publications committee of the Academy of Natural Sciences in Philadelphia for submitting to it an article whose substance he had published already elsewhere, he turned increasingly to self-publication and publication in Europe (in the French language)—both actions further isolating him.

Rafinesque's friend John D. Clifford had gone bankrupt in Philadelphia, but was now successfully reestablished as a merchant in Lexington, Kentucky, where he promoted a professorship for Rafinesque at Transylvania University, of which Clifford was a trustee. Rafinesque remained there from the summer of 1819 until the spring of 1826 despite stormy personal relationships with his colleagues. He was awarded Transylvania's honorary M.A. in 1822 and shortly afterward received an honorary Ph.D. from Germany. When he left Lexington he shipped ahead to Philadelphia forty crates of specimens and books, which served his research needs the rest of his life, though he continued to make short collecting trips and to exchange specimens with others.

In Kentucky Rafinesque had taken up the study of the indigenous people, trying to explain such artifacts as the prehistoric earthen mounds in the Ohio Valley by tracing the migrations of Indian nations through a comparative study of their languages. The most important product of this linguistic research was his two-volume *American Nations* (1836), in which appeared for the first time a fragment of the Walam Olum, said to record the origin of the Lenni Lenape (Delawares) in Asia. Among his accomplishments as a philologist were the first steps toward a theory of lexicostatistics and a start toward deciphering the Mayan glyphs. For the remainder of his life such humanistic studies were interspersed with his scientific ones, among them being such works as a book-length poem on mutability, *The World* (1836), and a linguistic analysis of the *Genius and Spirit of the Hebrew Bible* (1838). His most financially successful book was the two-volume *Medical Flora*, issued in Philadelphia (1828–1830) by the publishers of the *Saturday Evening Post*.

In Philadelphia Rafinesque again edited a scientific quarterly, the *Atlantic Journal*; his most notable botanical works were *New Flora and Botany of North America* (1836–1838), *Flora telluriana* (1837–1838), *Sylva telluriana* (1838), and *Autikon botanikon* (1840). All these were published privately, as were a number of pamphlets during the same period. They were financed by a variety of means: the sale of a proprietary nostrum for tuberculosis; occasional lecturing, including at the Franklin Institute; the sale of natural history specimens; and, for a time, the patronage of the manufacturer Charles Wetherill. Rafinesque also organized a small savings bank for workingmen and, with Wetherill, planned a utopian community in Illinois that never achieved reality. He became a naturalized citizen in 1832.

The sentimental assertion of a near contemporary, Thomas Meehan, that Rafinesque ended his life "in a dingy garret, with scarcely a loaf of bread to eat" has been echoed repeatedly since, but is far from the truth. Though never rich, he was comfortably established in Philadelphia at the end of his life, attended by friends, and receiving the best medical care the city afforded when he died there of cancer of the stomach. But his life's work was totally ignored by his contemporaries, most of whom agreed with fellow botanist L. D. von Schweinitz, who wrote in 1832 that "he is doubtless a man of immense knowledge—as badly digested as may be & crack-brained I am sure" (*Memoirs of the Torrey Botanical Club* 16 [1921]: 270–71). His reputation was rehabilitated about the middle of the twentieth century when it was acknowledged by most botanists that most of Rafinesque's 6,700 Latin plant names had been validly published according to rules since adopted by the botanists themselves. Interest also has focused on his early recognition of the impermanence species. "Every species was once a variety," he wrote, "and every variety is the embryo of a new species" (*The World*, p. 222), a view that caused Darwin to cite him in the sixth edition of the *Origin of Species* as one of only three American naturalists who had had the foresight to appreciate that "species undergo modification."

• The largest collection of Rafinesque papers, including scientific manuscripts and letters, is at the American Philosophical Society; the New York Botanical Garden and the University of Kansas also have important collections. His letters have been found in eight countries, written in four languages; the Linnean Society of London, the Archives du Conservatoire Botanique de Genève, and the Muséum National d'Histoire Naturelle in Paris have significant groups of papers. The principal source for all biographical accounts has been Rafinesque's own inadequate autobiography, *A Life of Travels* (1836), translated by himself from his earlier (1833) *Précis ou abrégé des voyages, travaux, et recherches*, which was unknown until published in 1987. Richard Ellsworth Call, *The Life and Writings of Rafinesque* (1895), also began the task of identifying his scattered publications. The bibliography was advanced by T. J. Fitzpatrick in 1911, and again in his book's most recent revision, *Fitzpatrick's Rafinesque: A Sketch of His Life with Bibliography* (1982). Particular aspects of the biography have been developed by Huntley Dupre, *Rafinesque in Lexington* (1945); Francis W. Pennell, "The Life and Work of Rafinesque," *Transylvania College Bulletin* 15 (1942): 10–70; and Charles Boewe, "Who's Buried in Rafinesque's Tomb?" *Pennsylvania Magazine of History and Biography* 111 (1987): 213–35. Elmer D. Merrill, *Index Rafinesquianus* (1949), brought to light the full record of Rafinesque's accomplishments in descriptive botany. Merrill also began the reprinting in facsimile of Rafinesque's books. A controversial literature initiated by Daniel G. Brinton in *The Lenape and Their Legends* (1885) has focused on the question of whether Rafinesque's Walam Olum is an authentic Indian document.

CHARLES BOEWE

RAFT, George (26 Sept. 1895–24 Nov. 1980), film actor, was born George Ranft in New York City, the son of Conrad Ranft, a worker at odd jobs, and Eva Glockner. He quit elementary school after a few years of sporadic education. Following a fight with his father over his inattentive schooling, he left home, not to return, although he maintained close ties with his mother until her death in 1937. He grew up in New York's Hell's Kitchen, associating with underworld figures such as Owney Madden of the notorious Gophers gang.

After 1910 Raft, who changed his name in 1917, tried a number of professions that drew on his physical grace, from boxer to semiprofessional baseball player, before achieving some success as a professional dancer in vaudeville, on Broadway, and in nightclubs, especially Jimmy Durante's Club Durant and Texas Guinan's El Fey Club. In 1923 Raft married Grayce Mulrooney. They separated within a year but were never divorced; she died in 1970. There also have been unsubstantiated rumors of an earlier marriage, from which Raft was said to have had a son. For the remainder of his life he had a number of brief romantic relationships but none of any significant duration.

In 1929 Raft appeared in his first film, a result of his work with Texas Guinan. It was *Queen of the Night Clubs*, starring Guinan. He went on to play a number of small roles in films until his great success as the coin-flipping gangster Guido Rinaldo in Howard Hawks's *Scarface* (1932). This tough, taciturn, outside-the-law image became the mainstay of his Hollywood career, starting as something to be built on, then as something to be gotten away from, and finally as something to be parodied.

Raft was under contract to Paramount Pictures for most of the 1930s, playing leads in such films as *The Bowery* (1933), *Bolero* (1934), *The Glass Key* (1935), *Souls at Sea* (1937), and *Spawn of the North* (1938). In 1939 he signed with Warner Bros. and made films like *Each Dawn I Die* (1939, with James Cagney), *They Drive by Night* (1940, with Humphrey Bogart), and *Manpower* (1941, with Edward G. Robinson). During his studio days he frequently fought with studio heads over creative control of his roles and his image, and he was often suspended because of the bitterness of those battles. In December 1942 he bought out of his Warner Bros. contract and worked freelance from then on. After the 1940s he received fewer and fewer roles, and many of those were cameos; in some he played himself. His most visible role during these years was as the coin-flipping, self-parodying gangster in Billy Wilder's *Some Like It Hot* (1959). In 1961 a fictionalized biographical film, *The George Raft Story*, appeared.

Raft's tough-guy screen image was reinforced by widely publicized associations with real-life gangsters, the most famous of which was with Benjamin "Bugsy" Siegel. Raft had an engagement to meet Siegel the night that Siegel was murdered in Los Angeles in 1947. When acting roles became scarce, Raft in 1958 became a host at the Capri hotel in Havana, a job that ended abruptly with Fidel Castro's takeover. In 1966–1967 he was host at "George Raft's Colony Club" casino in London but was banned from England in 1967 as persona non grata for his alleged underworld connections.

Raft earned a footnote in film history for some ill-advised attempts to change his image. In the late 1930s he fought to develop a more wholesome image for himself; he tried to escape playing shady or underworld figures, and he did not want to die in his films. During his years of success he turned down a number of roles that catapulted Humphrey Bogart to stardom: *Dead End*, *High Sierra*, and *The Maltese Falcon*. He also turned down the lead in *Double Indemnity* because of the film's shady moral tone. Despite such lost opportunities, however, Raft established a distinctive screen image and maintained a substantial career during Hollywood's golden age. He died in Los Angeles.

• There is no cataloged repository of George Raft's papers. The two major biographies are Lewis Yablonsky, *George Raft* (1973), and James Robert Parish and Steven Whitney, *The George Raft File: The Unauthorized Biography* (1974). Obituaries are in the *New York Times*, 25 Nov. 1980, and *Variety*, 26 Nov. 1980.

WILLIAM LUHR

RAGINI DEVI (18 Aug. 1897–23 Jan. 1982), dancer and American exponent of Indian dance, was born Esther Luella Sherman in Petoskey, Michigan, the daughter of Alexander Otto Sherman, the owner of an establishment for men's made-to-order suits in Minneapolis, and Ida Bell Parker. She grew up in Minneapolis, where she studied the piano, vocal music, and ballet from the age of seven. She completed high school and studied art at the Walker Art Center, but from her childhood her passion was for the dance. From her early teens she studied, composed, and performed international dances, developing an intense interest in Indian dance, which in later life she attributed to having been a Hindu in her previous birth. She met Ramlal Balaram Bajpai, a chemistry student from India, in St. Paul; they continued their friendship in New York City, where from 1920 she pursued her dance career, specializing in Indian dance, took the name Ragini Devi, and adopted the sari.

In May 1921 Bajpai and Ragini Devi married; they had one child. A beautiful woman, she wore her brown hair parted in the middle, gathered in a bun. Through her husband's circle of friends she was able to study Indian vocal and instrumental music and dance; with two Indian musicians, she formed the Trio Ragini of Hindu dance. Among the highlights of her career then was a performance at the Booth Theater in 1924 and in Walter Hampden's production of *Light of Asia* in 1928. Both were well received, and she became determined to study and revive the dying art. Ragini Devi did research at the New York Public Library in ancient texts on Indian dance such as the *Natya Shastra* (200 A.D.) and *The Mirror of Gesture*. Her book *Nritanjali*, the first book in English on the subject of Indian dance, was published in 1928 and widely reviewed and read in India and the United States.

Separating from her husband in 1930, Ragini Devi traveled to India that same year to concentrate on her career. Her only child, a daughter, was born on Ragini Devi's arrival in India and was to become her alter ego. As Indrani (Indrani Rahman), her daughter became one of the foremost of Indian classical dancers, performing internationally and teaching on the faculty of the Juilliard School. In India Ragini Devi studied the Bharata Natyam style in Madras with Mylapore Gauri Amma, an eminent dancer of the Mylapore tem-

ple. She was also the first woman to study the Kathakali dance-drama style, then performed entirely by men, at the original Kerala Kalamandalam under the great guru Ravunni Menon, and she studied the feminine Mohini Attam style under Kalyani Kutty Amma, also at the Kalamandalam. Taking a senior student, Gopinath, as a dance partner, and accompanied by musicians of the highest caliber, she presented excerpts from the dance dramas in major cities of Kerala and India as part of her classical and folk dance program.

Indian dance had fallen into neglect during several hundred years of British colonization. Ragini Devi was one of the pioneers in reviving this art. Her company's performances and her own lecture-demonstrations in universities and theaters throughout India were a revelation to Indian audiences. She also gave command performances for the maharajas of many royal houses. A highlight of her tours was a performance for the Nobel laureate poet Rabindranath Tagore at his university, called Shantiniketan, in Bengal. Tagore presented Ragini Devi with a handwritten tribute: "Those of us belonging to Northern India who have lost the memory of the pure Indian classical dance have experienced a thrill of delight at the exhibition of dancing given by Ragini Devi. I feel grateful at the assurance it has brought to us that the ancient art is still a living tradition."

In 1938 Ragini Devi took a company of Indian dancers and musicians, including her daughter, to tour in Europe; this was the first time that the Kathakali style was performed abroad and that its exponents, Kalamandalam Madhavan and Keshavan, performed outside of India. Ragini Devi's company performed at the Musée Guimet during the Paris Exposition. Sadly for her, fears of World War II caused some cancellations; she sent her company back to India and proceeded to London with her daughter. Her performances in London with local Indian musicians were enthusiastically received, and she was invited to give a series of lectures with demonstrations at the University of London, the first of its kind at an English university.

In 1939 Ragini Devi returned to the United States and performed widely in New York and other cities. She established the India Dance Theater on West Fifty-seventh Street in New York, where she gave regular performances and lecture-demonstrations along with her daughter and her students.

In 1948 Ragini Devi returned to India and received a Rockefeller grant for research for her second book, *Dance Dialects of India*, which was published in 1972 (2d ed., 1990). She toured throughout India in her study and also promoted her daughter's dance career. She was invited to write numerous articles for journals and books.

In 1978 Ragini Devi returned to New York, where on 4 April at the Asia Society, her daughter and granddaughter, Sukanya, performed with her. She had received a grant from the Ford Foundation to complete a book on Indian music and hoped to work on it at the

Actors' Fund Residence in Englewood, New Jersey, which received her through the recommendations of Martha Graham and former *New York Times* dance critic John Martin, but she died before completing the manuscript. On 29 September 1979 Ragini Devi gave her last performance, along with Indrani and Sukanya, a tribute to three generations of Indian classical dance. Anna Kisselgoff, dance critic of the *New York Times*, wrote, "At the end of a brief mime passage at New York University, Ragini Devi received an ovation and expressed happiness at seeing 'the pure tradition' handed down through three generations" (30 Sept. 1979). Ragini Devi died, in the presence of her daughter, at the Actors' Fund Residence.

In March 1982 Ragini Devi's daughter accepted a posthumous award for her mother in New Delhi from the Sangeet Natak Akadami, the prestigious official academy for performing arts in India. It was India's final tribute to a great artist, author, and revivalist of Indian dance.

• Microfilm of Ragini Devi's dance, scrapbook, and press clippings is held by the Dance Collection of the New York Public Library for the Performing Arts at Lincoln Center. An obituary is in the *New York Times*, 26 Jan. 1982.

INDRANI RAHMAN

RAHMAN, Fazlur (21 Sept. 1919–26 July 1988), Islamic scholar, was born in Seraisaleh, in what is now Pakistan, the son of Shihab Din Rahman and Wafadar Qazi. Rahman received both his B.A. (1940) and his M.A. (1942) from Punjab University, Lahore. He spent the next three years there as a researcher before entering Oxford University, from which he received his D.Phil. in 1949. In that year the combination of Pakistan's emergence as an independent, self-declared Islamic state and Rahman's liberal Islamic theology led him to leave his homeland. He remained in England as lecturer in Persian studies and Islamic philosophy at the University of Durham until 1958.

While at Durham, Rahman published his first book, a critical edition and translation of the Arabic text of *Avicenna's Psychology* in 1952. This book made Rahman's international reputation and developed a key component of his understanding and interpretation of the world significance of the Islamic tradition. In his book on Avicenna (Ibn Sīnā) (980–1037), Rahman demonstrated that Islamic philosophy, especially as developed by Avicenna, played a significant role in the development of thought in Europe, particularly through Avicenna's influence on Thomas Aquinas. Much of Aquinas's work can be seen as a Christian incorporation of Avicenna's philosophy, while other parts are struggles at refutation. It was just this engagement with Islamic philosophy, which was the heir of classical thought, that set the stage for the intellectual renaissance that marked Europe in the twelfth century.

In 1958 Rahman left England for Canada, where he served as associate professor at McGill University's Institute for Islamic Studies. Invited to return to Pakistan in 1961, Rahman joined the faculty of the Central Institute of Islamic Research. He assumed the directorship of the institute in 1962 and for the next six years played a significant role in the Pakistani intellectual and cultural life. During this time he was the central intellectual figure involved in crafting and developing the idea of an Islamic state and an Islamic society. Central to this for Rahman was the need to bring Islamic law into a critical engagement with the modern world and to construct a reinterpretation of that law in light of contemporary questions, needs, and concerns. His opponents derided him as "the breaker of *hadīths*" because of his position that *hadīth* (the traditions of what the Prophet Muhammad had done and said) had to be judged against the entire spirit and meaning of the Qur'ān. Increasing hostility from those who rejected his views and political conflict in Pakistan led Rahman to return to the West in 1969, as visiting professor at the University of Southern California. In the autumn of that year Rahman joined the faculty of the University of Chicago, where he served until his death.

During his nineteen years at the University of Chicago, the last two as Harold H. Swift Distinguished Service Professor, Rahman fully developed his modernist interpretation of Islam, grounded, as he would claim, in a correct reading both of Islamic history and Islamic theology. These views Rahman articulated most fully in *Islam and Modernity: Transformation of an Intellectual Tradition*, published in 1982. He argued that Islam, since the ninth and tenth centuries, has been based on a set of incomplete interpretations, if not misinterpretations, of the Qur'ān. For Rahman, the Qur'ān should be viewed as a unity, a coherent and unified text designed to illustrate particular universal principles central to a complete and appropriate understanding of God. These are the goals of God's revelation in the Qur'ān, the book that teaches these universal principles. By the tenth century, however, the Qur'ān increasingly became interpreted as a collection of individual pronouncements. The medieval interpreters would construe a passage of verse in legal terms as though it stood by itself. This framework led to the creation of an inflexible and unchanging form of religious thought and an equally inflexible and rigid educational system. The starkness of this position meant that when confronted with modernization both individual Muslims and the Islamic world in general were faced with either rejecting religion for secularization and modern education or rejecting modernity for their traditional interpretation of the faith.

Rahman, however, argued for a third way. For him the only way to construct a meaningful and adequate understanding of Islamic law and institutions required a twofold movement. "First one must move from the concrete case treatments of the Qur'ān—taking the necessary and relevant social conditions of that time into account—to the general principles upon which the entire teaching converges. Second, from this general level there must be a movement back to specific legislation, taking into account the necessary and relevant social conditions now obtaining."

Needless to say, these views placed Rahman at odds with the two main developments within the Islamic world during the postindependence period: the revolutionary secularists and the revolutionary Islamists or fundamentalists. Both of these demonstrated to Rahman the problems inherent in legalistic interpretations of Islam, a rejection of the tradition as irrelevant or a rejection of the intellectual bases of modernity. Despite the overwhelming opposition to his views, Rahman remained convinced not only that both the conservatives with their slavish adherence to precedence and the secularists who rejected Islam's application to the political and economic spheres were wrong but that his interpretation of the tradition eventually would be vindicated.

Despite the hostility directed at Rahman in many quarters of the Islamic world, he remained an important figure in Islamic studies both in the academy and in the wider world of Islamic education. He was an adviser to the U.S. Department of State on Islamic affairs and the 1983 recipient of the prestigious Giorgio Levi Della Vida Medal in Islamic Studies. Rahman also served as a consultant to the Indonesian Ministry of Religious Affairs on the reformation of Islamic studies in the Indonesian university system and on the overall state of Islam in the country, the world's most populous Muslim nation.

Rahman died in Chicago from complications related to heart surgery. His career as teacher, scholar, theologian, and believer was eloquently summed up by his colleague Rashid Kalidi: "He was one of the world's most eminent scholars in [his] field and perhaps one of the most prominent Islamic liberal reformers of the present generation."

• Rahman published numerous articles as well as several books. Beyond those mentioned above, his books include *Avicenna's De Anima* (a critical Arabic text) (1959), *Intikhāb-I maktūbā-I Shaykh Ahmad Sirhindī* (Selected letters of Shaykh Ahmad Sirhindī) (1968), *Philosophy of Mullā Sadrā* (1975), *Islam* (1966, 1979), *Major Themes of the Qur'ān* (1979), *Prophecy in Islam* (1979), and *Health and Medicine in the Islamic Tradition: Change and Identity* (1987). In the absence of a published biography of Rahman, the key to understanding the man rests in his own writings; the best source of basic biographical information can be found in the press release issued by the University of Chicago following Rahman's death. Other interpretive reflections on the life and work of Rahman are Frederick Mathewson Denny, "Fazlur Rahman: Muslim Intellectual," *Muslim World*, Apr. 1989, pp. 91–111, and Tamara Sonn, "Fazlur Rahman's Islamic Methodology," *Muslim World*, July–Oct. 1991, pp. 212–19. See also Sonn's biographical entry on Rahman in the *Oxford Encyclopedia of the Modern Islamic World*, ed. John L. Esposito et al. (1995).

EDWARD L. QUEEN II

RAHV, Philip (10 Mar. 1908–22 Dec. 1973), literary critic and editor, was born Ivan Greenberg in Kupin in Ukraine. The family ran a dry-goods store in a Jewish ghetto, and in 1916 Rahv's father (first name unknown) emigrated to the United States where he be-

came a house-to-house peddler in Rhode Island. In 1922, following a harrowing escape from the civil war-torn Soviet Union with his mother, Aviva Greenberg, Rahv and his family were briefly united for two years in Providence, Rhode Island, before moving to Palestine.

Shortly thereafter, probably after 1925, Rahv traveled by himself to Oregon where he gave private lessons in Hebrew and wrote copy for an advertising agency. In 1930 he gravitated to New York City where he was drawn into left-wing literary activities. He took the pen name Rahv—the Hebrew word for rabbi—when he joined the Communist party in 1933. In 1934 he joined with other Communist writers in founding *Partisan Review* as an organ of the New York chapter of the party-led writers' organization, the John Reed Clubs.

Rahv's early criticism was distinguished by a zealous Marxist orthodoxy combined with a somewhat strained erudition, as can be seen in his early contributions to the *Daily Worker, New Masses,* and other small left-wing publications in the first part of the 1930s. However, along with his close collaborator, William Phillips, he gradually became attracted to the idea of appropriating features of the literary modernism associated with the 1920s for the proletarian cultural movement. Soon *Partisan Review* became known for the most advanced critical thinking on the Marxist left and also for its campaign against the more simplified versions of Marxism that Rahv and Phillips excoriated as "leftism."

Within a year, however, the Communist party began to abandon its promotion of working-class writing in favor of democratic, antifascist literature in harmony with the turn to the Popular Front (1935). Next, news of the Moscow treason trials (1936–1938) began to agitate some of the writers in the *Partisan Review* circle, who were becoming sympathetic to the ideas of the exiled and persecuted Bolshevik Leon Trotsky. After an ill-fated merger with *Anvil*, a proletarian literary magazine edited by Jack Conroy in the Midwest, *Partisan Review* lapsed into silence and then suddenly resurfaced in late 1937 as an independent revolutionary journal.

From the original editorial board, Rahv and Phillips remained at the helm, but they were now joined by F. W. Dupee, who had formerly belonged to the party and worked for the *New Masses*; Dwight Macdonald and Mary McCarthy, who had briefly been party sympathizers; and George L. K. Morris, a wealthy artist friend of Macdonald. Beyond this, Rahv began to assemble a core group of Marxist contributors such as Sidney Hook, Edmund Wilson, Meyer Schapiro, Harold Rosenberg, Clement Greenberg, Lionel Trilling, and others who would come to be known as "the New York Intellectuals." The new *Partisan Review* brought a dissident revolutionary communism, partly influenced by the ideas of Trotsky, into a tensive relation with the literary modernism associated with T. S. Eliot and James Joyce.

Over the next decades the reputation of the journal grew to the point where the *New York Times Book Review* described it as "the best literary magazine in America" (17 Feb. 1974). In addition to writers associated with the editorial board and core group of contributors, *Partisan Review* promoted Elizabeth Bishop, Delmore Schwartz, Randall Jarrell, Karl Shapiro, Robert Lowell, Eleanor Clark, Isaac Rosenfeld, Jean Stafford, and Saul Bellow. The journal was also noteworthy for its many symposia on such topics as "The New Failure of Nerve" (1943), "The Future of Socialism" (1947), "The State of American Writing" (1947), and "Religion and the Intellectuals" (1950).

Brilliantly adept at political and cultural maneuvers, Rahv led *Partisan Review* from its communist origins through several years of quasi-Trotskyism. But pressure during World War II caused a major rift in the editorial board. Two of the editors, Macdonald and Greenberg, argued that opposition to fascism should not mean abandoning the struggle for socialism and should not require endorsing the Allied war aims, which they believed to be "imperialist." Rahv and Hook wrote in favor of giving "critical support" to the U.S. government. In 1943 Macdonald felt forced to resign, and after this rupture the *Partisan Review*'s connections with the Left became even more tenuous. Rahv remained the dominant political as well as literary voice on *Partisan Review* until he broke with Phillips in 1971 and founded *Modern Occasions*, which lasted for only six issues.

Although Rahv was sharply critical of McCarthyism, he was cautious about expressing his views and was by and large politically silent during the 1950s. In fact, the magazine appeared to drop into political quiescence if not outright antiradicalism, although Rahv would later insist that he had never really abandoned his Marxist-Leninist perspective. In the 1960s he turned sharply left again, bitterly denouncing as sellouts and renegades many of those whose careers he had formerly promoted.

In 1939 he repudiated the proletarian literary movement in a brilliant and influential caricature in the *Southern Review*, "Proletarian Literature: A Political Autopsy." This was followed by two of his most influential essays, "Paleface and Redskin" (*Kenyon Review*, 1939) and "The Cult of Experience in American Writing" (*Partisan Review*, 1940). These analyses were likely developed in opposition to what he saw as the naive literary nationalism of the Popular Front. The argument was a blend of Henry James's (1843–1916) observations about the limitations of the culture of the United States in contrast to that of Europe, and Van Wyck Brooks's view of the existence of a cultural bifurcation between refined and vulgar authors ("highbrow" and "lowbrow").

In the years that followed, Rahv produced many brilliant pieces on U.S. classic literature, especially on Nathaniel Hawthorne ("The Dark Lady of Salem," *Partisan Review*, 1941) and Henry James ("The Heiress of All the Ages," *Partisan Review*, 1943). He was also influential in several studies of Franz Kafka, whom he defended as a repository of rationalism, and over the years he produced sections of an unfinished book on Fyodor Dostoyevsky. Most of his work appears in collections of essays and reviews such as *Image and Idea* (1949), *The Myth and the Powerhouse* (1965), *Literature and the Sixth Sense* (1969), and *Essays on Literature and Politics, 1932–1972* (1978). He also edited and introduced *The Great Short Novels of Henry James* (1944), *The Short Novels of Tolstoy* (1946), *Great Russian Short Novels* (1951), *Eight Great American Short Novels* (1963), and *The Bernard Malamud Reader* (1967). With William Phillips he coedited *The Partisan Reader: Ten Years of the Partisan Review, 1934–1944* (1946), *The New Partisan Reader, 1945–1953* (1953), and *The Partisan Review Anthology* (1963).

Although he never graduated from high school or college, Rahv was appointed a professor of English at Brandeis University in 1957. Following a brief marriage in the early 1930s, he was married to Nathalie Swan from 1940 to 1955; to Theo Stillman, who died in a house fire in 1968; and to Betty Thomas, from whom he was separated at the time of his death in Cambridge, Massachusetts. He had no children.

Rahv's influence has been felt mainly in memoirs and general studies about the history of *Partisan Review* and New York intellectual life from the 1930s through the 1960s. His unique contributions to literary analysis, as well as his related and complex political orientation, have been treated with increasing skepticism by the new generation of scholars who have gained influence toward the end of the twentieth century.

• The *Partisan Review* Papers are at Boston University. The most sustained study of Rahv and bibliography of his writings can be found in the dissertation by Andrew James Dvosin, "Literature in a Political World: The Career and Writings of Philip Rahv" (New York Univ., 1977). Additional memoirs and studies are contained in William Barrett, *The Truants: Adventures among the Intellectuals* (1982); Alexander Bloom, *Prodigal Sons: The New York Intellectuals and Their World* (1986); Terry A. Cooney, *The Rise of the New York Intellectuals: Partisan Review and Its Circle* (1986); Arthur Edelstein, ed., *Images and Ideas in American Culture: Essays in Memory of Philip Rahv* (1979); James Burkhart Gilbert, *Writers and Partisans: A History of Literary Radicalism in America* (1968); Neil Jumonville, *Critical Crossings: The New York Intellectuals in Postwar America* (1991); Mary McCarthy, *Intellectual Memoirs: New York 1936–1938* (1992); and Alan M. Wald, *The New York Intellectuals: The Rise and Decline of the Anti-Stalinist Left from the 1930s to the 1980s* (1987). An obituary is in the *New York Times Book Review*, 17 Feb. 1974.

ALAN M. WALD

RAILROAD BILL (?–7 Mar. 1896), thief and folk hero, was the nickname of an African-American man of such obscure origins that his real name is in question. Most writers have believed him to be Morris Slater, but a rival candidate for the honor is an equally obscure man named Bill McCoy. But in song and story, where he has long had a place, the question is of small interest and Railroad Bill is name enough. A ballad regaling his exploits began circulating among field hands, turpentine camp workers, prisoners, and other groups from the black underclass of the Deep South, several years before it first found its way into print in 1911. A version of this blues ballad was first recorded in 1924 by Gil Tanner and Riley Puckett, and Thomas Dorsey, a blues singer from the 1920s took Railroad Bill as his stage name. The ballad got a second wind during the folk music vogue of the 1950s and 1960s, and in 1981 the musical play *Railroad Bill* by C. R. Portz was produced for the Labor Theater in New York City. It subsequently toured thirty-five cities.

The name Railroad Bill, or often simply "Railroad," was given to him by trainmen and derived from his penchant for riding the cars as an anonymous nonpaying passenger of the Louisville and Nashville Railroad (L&N). Thus he might appear to be no more than a common tramp or hobo, as the large floating population of migratory workers who more or less surreptitiously rode the cars of all the nation's railroads were labeled. But Railroad Bill limited his riding to two adjoining South Alabama counties, Escambia and Baldwin. Sometime in the winter of 1895 he began to be noticed by trainmen often enough that he soon acquired some notoriety and a nickname. It did not make him less worthy of remark that he was always armed, with a rifle and one or more pistols. He was, as it turned out, quite prepared to offer resistance to the rough treatment normally meted out to tramps.

An attitude of armed resistance from a black man was bound inevitably to bring him into conflict with the civil authorities, who were in any case inclined to be solicitous of the L&N, the dominant economic power in South Alabama. The conflict began on 6 March 1895, only a month or two after trainmen first became aware of Railroad Bill. L&N employees discovered him asleep on the platform of a water tank in Baldwin County, on the Flomaton to Mobile run, and tried to take him into custody. He drove them off with gunfire and forced them to take shelter in a nearby shack. When a freight train pulled up to take on water he hijacked it and, after firing additional rounds into the shack, forced the engineer to take him further up the road, whereupon he left the train and disappeared into the woods. After that, pursuit of Railroad Bill was relentless. A month to the day later he was cornered at Bay Minette by a posse led by a railroad detective. A deputy, James H. Stewart, was killed in the ensuing gunfight, but once again the fugitive slipped away. The railroad provided a "special" to transport Sheriff E. S. McMillan from Brewton, the county seat of Escambia, to the scene with a pack of bloodhounds, but a heavy rainfall washed away the scent.

In mid-April a reward was posted by the L&N and the state of Alabama totaling $500. The lure of this reward and a rumored sighting of the fugitive led Sheriff McMillan out of his jurisdiction to Bluff Springs, Florida, where he found Railroad Bill and met with death at his hands. The reward climbed to $1,250, and

the manhunt intensified. A small army with packs of dogs picked up his scent near Brewton in August, but he dove into Murder Swamp near Castelberry and disappeared. During this period, from March to August, the legend of Railroad Bill took shape among poor blacks in the region. He was viewed as a "conjure man," one who could change his shape and slip away from pursuers. He was clever and outwitted his enemies; he was a trickster who laid traps for the trapper and a fighter who refused to bend his neck and submit to the oppressor. He demanded respect, and in time some whites grudgingly gave it: Brewton's *Pine Belt News* reported after Railroad Bill's escape into Murder Swamp that he had "outwitted and outgeneraled at least one hundred men armed to the teeth." During this period a Robin Hood–style Railroad Bill emerged, who, it was said, stole canned goods from boxcars and distributed them to poor illiterate blacks like himself. Carl Carmer, a white writer in the 1930s, claimed that Railroad Bill forced poor blacks at gunpoint to buy the goods from him, but Carmer never explained how it was possible to get money out of people who rarely if ever saw any. Railroad Bill staved off death and capture for an entire year, a virtual impossibility had he not had supporters among the poor black population of the region.

Sightings became infrequent after Murder Swamp, and some concluded Railroad Bill had left the area. The "wanted" poster with its reward was more widely circulated. The result was something like open season on vagrant blacks in the lower South. The *Montgomery Advertiser* reported that "several were shot in Florida, Georgia, Mississippi and even in Texas," adding with unconscious grisly humor, "only one was brought here to be identified." That one arrived at Union Station in a pine box in August, escorted by the two men from Chipley, Florida, who had shot him in hopes of collecting the reward. Doubts about whether he remained in the area were answered on 7 March 1896, exactly a year and a day after the affair at the water tower when determined pursuit began. Railroad Bill was shot without warning, from ambush, by a private citizen seeking the reward, which by now included a lifetime pass on the L&N Railroad. Bill had been sitting on a barrell eating cheese and crackers in a small Atmore, Alabama, grocery. Perhaps he was tired as well as hungry.

Railroad Bill's real name probably will never be known. At the time of the water tower incident and up to the killing of Deputy Stewart he had only the nickname, but in mid-April the first "wanted" posters went up in Mobile identifying Railroad Bill as Morris Slater, who, though the notice did not state it, had been a worker in a turpentine camp near Bluff Springs, Florida. These camps were often little more than penal colonies. They employed convict labor and were heavily into debt peonage. People were not supposed to leave, but Slater did, after killing the marshal of Bluff Springs. When railroad detectives stumbled on this story their interest was primarily in Slater's nickname. He had been called "Railroad Time," and

"Railroad" for short, because of his quick efficient work. The detectives quickly concluded, because of the similarities in nicknames, that Slater was their man. The problem, of course, is that the trainmen called their rider Railroad Bill precisely because they had no idea who he was and well before railroad authorities heard about Slater. If the detectives were right, then it follows that the same man independently won strangely similar nicknames in two different settings, once because he was a good worker, and again because he was a freeloader.

No one from the turpentine camp who had known Slater identified the body, but neither the railroad detectives nor the civil authorities involved questioned the identification. The body was taken to Brewton, on its way to Montgomery, where it would go on display for the public's gratification, but it was also displayed for a time in Brewton and recognized. The *Pine Belt News* reported that residents recognized the body as that of Bill McCoy, a man who would have been about forty, the approximate age of the corpse, since he had been brought to the area from Coldwater, Florida, as a young man eighteen years earlier. McCoy was remembered as a town troublemaker who two years earlier had threatened T. R. Miller, the richest man in town, when he worked in Miller's sawmill and lumberyard. He had fled the scene hastily, not to be seen again until his corpse went on display as Railroad Bill. But, apart from the local newspaper stories, no one disputed the Slater identification, and the local Brewton people seem to have concluded that Morris Slater must have been a name used by Bill McCoy after he fled the town. The problem with that conclusion is that when the incident at Miller's sawmill occurred Morris Slater had already earned the nickname "Railroad Time" in a Florida turpentine camp.

• A more or less complete listing of the literature on Railroad Bill is in A. J. Wright, comp., *Criminal Activity in the Deep South, 1700–1933* (1989). For a codification of the folk ballads, see Howard W. Odum, ed., "Folk-Song and Folk-Poetry as Found in the Secular Songs of the Southern Negroes," *Journal of American Folklore* 24 (1911): 289–93. The Brewton newspapers *Pine Belt News* and *Standard Gauge* are the best places to follow the story. For a fuller discussion of the identification question with citations, see James L. Penick, "Railroad Bill," *Gulf Coast Historical Review* 10 (1994): 85–92.

JAMES L. PENICK

RAIMOND, C. E. *See* Robins, Elizabeth.

RAINES, John (6 May 1840–16 Dec. 1909), Republican politician, lawyer, and insurance agent, was born in Canandaigua, Ontario County, New York, the son of John Raines, a Methodist minister, and Mary Remington. After attending local schools, Raines studied law and graduated from the Albany Law School in 1861. Some time after the outbreak of the Civil War that same year, Raines raised a military unit—Company G, Eighty-fifth Regiment, New York Volunteer Infantry—in which he served as captain, seeing service in Virginia and North Carolina, until his discharge in

1863. He married Catherine A. Wheeler in 1862, and they had six children before Catherine's death in 1879. Following his return to civilian life, Raines practiced law in Geneva (in Ontario County) before moving to Canandaigua, the county seat, in 1867. There he was involved in law, an insurance business, and Republican politics.

Raines made his political mark as a state legislator. First elected to the New York State Assembly from Ontario County in 1880, he was reelected the next year. After sitting out the 1882 elections, which were marked by decisive Democratic victories, including the capture of his vacated assembly seat, Raines suffered his only electoral defeat in 1883, failing to unseat the Democrat elected the previous year. In 1884, however, Raines was returned to the assembly and one year later was elected to the state senate from a district that included Ontario County. He served in the senate until 1889, when he entered the U.S. House of Representatives, to which he had been elected in 1888. Reelected in 1890 but not a candidate in 1892, Raines left the House in 1893. The following year he won a special state senatorial election to fill a vacancy. Regularly reelected thereafter, he remained in the state senate until his death.

As a freshman assemblyman, Raines adhered to the faction of the Republican party led by U.S. senator Roscoe Conkling. He subsequently supported Thomas C. Platt, who rose from Conkling's lieutenant to leader of the state party. Implementing Platt's political strategy following the Republicans' achievement of dominance in New York during 1893–1896, Senator Raines introduced legislation in 1896 to regulate the sale of alcoholic beverages, the Raines Excise Law, which gave him his most lasting claim to fame. The measure substituted a State Department of Excise for local excise boards, weakening the connections between saloon-related interests and Democratic urban organizations and creating new state political jobs. License fees on drinking places were set high and scaled according to the size of local populations. New York City and Brooklyn saloons and taverns contributed the bulk of the revenues generated by the law, one-third going to the state (which reduced property taxes), two-thirds to localities. The law not only reduced the number of drinking establishments, it provided for local option to permit their abolition in upstate rural areas, where prohibitionist sentiment was strongest. The statute continued the state ban on Sunday sales of alcoholic beverages, but it exempted hotels with ten or more beds from this prohibition. This exemption provided some relief for German-Americans and others who chafed at restrictions on their "personal liberty," their freedom to celebrate Sundays as they saw fit, but it also opened wide the door for saloons to serve food and to use adjacent rooms to qualify as "hotels" free to dispense alcohol on Sundays. Saloons had long been associated with prostitution; now "Raines Law hotels" figured prominently as houses of prostitution.

In 1903 Raines became president pro tempore and Republican leader of the state senate. The political and physical decline of Platt enhanced Raines's position in the legislature; no state boss now pulled party strings. Raines's final legislative years coincided with the governorship of Charles Evans Hughes (1907–1910), who differed from his predecessors by stressing executive leadership, administrative expertise, his links with the public, and his distance from political party organizations. Raines and the senate twice thwarted the Republican governor's efforts to oust Otto Kelsey, state insurance superintendent. Though Raines also opposed a few of Hughes's regulatory and reform proposals, he at least acquiesced in, and thereby facilitated, passage of key executive initiatives, including the creation of public service commissions to regulate utilities and transportation companies in New York City and in the rest of the state.

To the end of his life, Raines remained involved in local affairs, serving for twenty-two years as president of the Board of Education of the Union School District. He died in Canandaigua, New York.

• For an uncritical but still useful biographical sketch of Raines, see Charles F. Milliken, *A History of Ontario County, New York, and Its People*, vol. 2 (2 vols., 1911). The following works illuminate Raines and the changing political environment in which he operated: De Alva S. Alexander, *Four Famous New Yorkers: The Political Careers of Cleveland, Platt, Hill, and Roosevelt* (1923); Samuel T. McSeveney, *The Politics of Depression: Political Behavior in the Northeast, 1893–1896* (1972); Richard L. McCormick, *From Realignment to Reform: Political Change in New York State, 1893–1910* (1981); and Robert F. Wesser, *Charles Evans Hughes: Politics and Reform in New York, 1905–1910* (1967). On "Raines Law hotels" and vice, see Timothy J. Gilfoyle, *City of Eros: New York City, Prostitution, and the Commercialization of Sex, 1790–1920* (1992). Obituaries are in the *Rochester Democrat and Chronicle*, 16–17 Dec. 1909, and the *New York Times*, 16 Dec. 1909.

SAMUEL T. MCSEVENEY

RAINEY, Henry Thomas (20 Aug. 1860–19 Aug. 1934), Speaker of the U.S. House of Representatives, was born in Carrollton, Illinois, the son of John Rainey, a farmer and city councilman, and Catherine Thomas. Following two years at Knox College in Galesburg, Illinois, Rainey earned a bachelor's degree in 1883 from Amherst College in Massachusetts, where he excelled in athletics and public speaking. He then studied law at Union College of Law (now Northwestern University Law School) in Chicago, receiving a law degree in 1885. Amherst College awarded him a master of arts degree in 1886, a customary practice for graduates who had completed two years of professional training.

Prior to his election to Congress in 1902, Rainey practiced law in Carrollton, representing railroad interests but also championing civic development, especially in the fields of libraries and public education. His acquaintance with William Jennings Bryan, first in Illinois and later in the free-silver movement, reinforced Rainey's interest in populist and progressive politics, as did his marriage to Ellenora "Ella" McBride in 1888. They had no children. An 1880 graduate of Knox College, Ella Rainey was active in several social welfare organizations and, from 1903 to 1934, served as her husband's chief legislative aide. Rainey expressed his own concept of public service late in his career by observing that the politician "establishes his self-respect only as his ambitions and efforts are for the good of others."

Resident in the solidly Democratic Twentieth Congressional District, Rainey tried unsuccessfully for the Democratic nomination three times before winning the party primary in 1902 in the first nominating primary in Illinois to use the secret ballot. He won a convincing victory by a 2 to 1 margin in the general election and was reelected to every Congress until his death, with the exception of the Sixty-seventh (1921–1923).

Rainey vigorously represented the interests of his agrarian district bordering the Mississippi River on the southwest and extending northeast along both banks of the Illinois River. Not surprisingly, he consistently advocated low tariffs for revenue only and a deep waterway from the Great Lakes to the Gulf Coast. Unlike other champions of the lakes-to-gulf waterway who saw only its regional economic advantages, Rainey supported a comprehensive resource management program to promote water and soil conservation as well. In recognition of his roles in water conservation and flood control, the Civilian Conservation Corps facility near Carrollton was named the Henry T. Rainey Camp in 1934. Unlike many rural progressives, however, Rainey was genuinely interested in the welfare of the urban working class, which led him to support liberal prolabor legislation.

First appointed to the Ways and Means Committee in 1911, Rainey became an advocate of the progressive concept of a "scientific" tariff determined through an independent, bipartisan tariff commission. His bill to create a U.S. Tariff Commission was introduced on 1 February 1916 and subsequently passed as Section Seven of the Revenue Act of 1916. During the illness of Chairman Claude Kitchin, Rainey served as acting chairman much of the time between 1917 and 1919, in which capacity he was instrumental in the passage of war revenue bills, including the institution of an income tax. His defeat in the 1920 election prevented Rainey from succeeding Kitchin to the position of ranking Democrat on the Ways and Means Committee, a post that fell to John Nance Garner in the Republican-controlled Sixty-seventh Congress. Rainey was returned to the committee in 1923, but he had lost most of the advantages of seniority.

Rainey became majority leader of the House in 1931, when the Democrats regained control and elected Garner to the Speakership. The new Speaker had supported Rainey's election to the post, even though the conservative Texan distrusted his Illinois colleague's fiery liberalism. During the 1920s as a spokesman for midwestern agrarian progressivism, Rainey had been in the forefront denouncing Republican economic policies as outrages that would reduce American farmers to the status of European peasantry. For his part, Rainey recognized that his new position would require him to act as "a worker of compromises and a healer of wounds." As majority leader of the Seventy-second Congress, he initiated a plan for an international conference to reduce tariffs, but President Herbert Hoover vetoed the measure. He also supported farm relief legislation, introducing an unsuccessful measure with Republican senator Peter Norbeck. Although Rainey had been considered initially opposed to the McNary-Haugen farm bills of 1924–1928, he supported the subsequent efforts designed to provide "parity" to protect farmers from price fluctuations between domestic and international markets. He reluctantly advocated a national sales tax measure, arguing that levying taxes was "the science of getting the most feathers with the least squawking of the goose," but only forty Democrats voted for the measure when it was defeated in 1932.

After Garner was elected to the vice presidency in 1932, Rainey appeared to be in line to succeed him to the Speaker's chair. The Democratic party was split, however, along sectional and ideological lines. Southern conservatives, including Garner, opposed the election of a midwestern liberal and opted to support Democratic whip John McDuffie of Alabama. Other Democratic candidates included Joseph W. Byrns, William B. Bankhead, and Sam Rayburn, all of whom later served as Speaker. Rainey, who pledged to pass President Franklin Roosevelt's legislative program, received the president's support and that of a majority of newly elected Democratic congressmen. In the party caucus of 2 March 1933, Rainey received 166 votes to McDuffie's 112. On 9 March the House confirmed Rainey's election to the Speakership.

As Speaker during the special and regular sessions of the Seventy-third Congress, Rainey helped marshal congressional support for the New Deal. He admired Roosevelt, whom he once said combined "the idealism and the initiative of a [Woodrow] Wilson with the energy of [an Andrew] Jackson and the wide statesmanship of a [Thomas] Jefferson." Rainey almost always gave preference to the president's program and blocked opposing legislation, giving priority to the passage of relief measures such as the National Industrial Recovery Act. Speaker Rainey broke with Roosevelt only on the issue of the remonetization of silver, leading House members in passing the Dies Bill, which compelled the administration to accept the compromise Silver Purchase Act of 1934.

Although praised in 1933 for leading the House with a firm but gentle touch, Rainey was criticized by the media in 1934 as "an easy-going person who is not much of a disciplinarian." Observers feared the Illinois Democrat lacked the strength to manage the House, suggesting that President Roosevelt might offer Rainey an appointment to the Supreme Court. Rainey remained a loyal lieutenant of the New Deal, however, traveling around the country in the summers of 1933 and 1934 to rally popular support. Rainey died unexpectedly in St. Louis, Missouri, one day short of his seventy-fourth birthday. He was buried three days later in Carrollton following a funeral attended by President Roosevelt and twenty-five of the late Speaker's congressional colleagues.

Standing more than six feet tall and weighing 275 pounds with tousled white hair and a characteristic flowing black bow tie, Rainey presented an impressive figure presiding over the House of Representatives. He was neither forceful nor innovative as Speaker of the House, but he was an effective legislative leader for the early New Deal.

• Rainey's papers are in the Library of Congress Manuscript Division. The twenty containers, consisting primarily of constituent correspondence, cover the period of his congressional career, 1904–1934. A complete biographical treatment of his life is Robert A. Waller, *Rainey of Illinois: A Political Biography, 1903–34* (1977). Marvin Block, "Henry T. Rainey of Illinois," *Journal of the Illinois State Historical Society* 65 (Summer 1972): 142–57, provides a good biographical sketch. Two crucial episodes of Rainey's career are covered in Waller, "The Illinois Waterway from Conception to Completion, 1908–1933," *Journal of the Illinois State Historical Society* 65 (Summer 1972): 125–41; and Waller, "The Selection of Henry T. Rainey as Speaker of the House," *Capitol Studies* 2 (Spring 1973): 37–47. An obituary is in the *New York Times*, 21 Aug. 1934.

DONALD R. KENNON

RAINEY, Joseph Hayne (21 June 1832–2 Aug. 1887), politician, was born a slave in Georgetown, South Carolina, the son of Edward L. Rainey and Gracia C. (maiden name unknown). The elder Rainey purchased his family's freedom and moved with them in about 1846 (the exact date is unknown) to Charleston where he was employed as a barber at the exclusive Mills House hotel. He prospered and purchased two male slaves in the 1850s. Joseph Rainey received a modest education and was trained by his father as a barber. In 1859 he traveled to Philadelphia and married Susan E. (maiden name unknown). As a result of the intervention of several friends, the couple managed to circumvent the state prohibition against free people of color entering or returning to South Carolina, and they moved to Charleston. After the Civil War began, Rainey was conscripted to serve as a steward on a Confederate blockade runner. He was later compelled to work in the construction of Confederate fortifications around Charleston. He escaped with his wife to Bermuda on a blockade runner. They settled first in St. George and then in Hamilton. He resumed barbering, and his wife worked as a dressmaker. They returned to Charleston in 1865, shortly after the war ended.

Rainey and his older brother Edward participated in the 1865 Colored Peoples' Convention in Charleston, and Joseph served as a vice president. The convention endorsed legal and political rights for black men and condemned the recently passed black code, which largely restricted black men and women to agricultural and domestic work, defined a master and servant relationship between white employers and black employees, and severely limited the legal and civil rights of black people. In 1867 Congress passed Reconstruction legislation that divided the South into five military districts, authorized the reestablishment of southern state governments, provided for universal manhood suffrage and black office holding, and disfranchised those who had supported the Confederacy.

In 1867 Rainey and his wife relocated to Georgetown, where he was elected to the constitutional convention in 1868. Later that year he was elected as a Republican to represent Georgetown County in the state senate, and in 1870 he was elected to the U.S. House of Representatives. He filled the unexpired term of white Republican Benjamin F. Whittemore whose seat had been declared vacant by the House after allegations were made that Whittemore sold appointments to the U.S. Military Academy and U.S. Naval Academy.

Rainey was the first black man to serve in the U.S. Congress. He was reelected four times, serving from 1870 to 1879. In 1878, as white Democrats regained political power in South Carolina, he lost his bid for a sixth term. He was a cautious, conservative, and conciliatory political leader. In the constitutional convention he supported an unsuccessful measure to permit creditors to collect debts owed for the purchase of slaves before the Civil War. He was among the minority who favored the imposition of a one-dollar poll tax with the stipulation that the proceeds be devoted to public education, though the measure would disfranchise impoverished freedmen.

In Congress Rainey supported the passage in 1872 of the Ku Klux Klan Act, legislation intended to outlaw the intimidation and violent repression of black people through the enforcement of the Fourteenth and Fifteenth amendments. He also favored a general amnesty to remove remaining disabilities on former Confederates if the civil rights bill prohibiting racial discrimination in public facilities proposed by Senator Charles Sumner was passed. Rainey spoke passionately for both measures on the House floor: "It is not the disposition of my constituents that these disabilities should longer be retained. We are desirous of being magnanimous; it may be that we are so to a fault. Nevertheless we have open and frank hearts towards those who were our former oppressors and taskmasters. We foster no enmity now, and we desire to foster none. . . . I implore you, give support to the Civil-rights Bill." Rainey delivered one of the eulogies following Sumner's death in 1874. The amnesty bill passed immediately, but Sumner's civil rights measure was not enacted until 1875.

Though committed to equal treatment in public facilities, Rainey opposed legislation supporting social equality or interracial marriages. As a black man with a fair complexion, he was ridiculed by a black political opponent in an 1868 campaign appearance in Georgetown and accused of having attempted to act white while attending the National Negro Laborers Convention in Washington, D.C., the previous year. Rainey won the election.

Rainey was a director of the Enterprise Railroad Company, a black-owned Charleston business created in 1870 by several prominent politicians to haul freight by horse-drawn streetcars from the city wharves on the Cooper River to the South Carolina Railroad terminal. The Enterprise did not thrive, and it was taken over by white businessmen in 1873. Rainey also owned stock in the Greenville & Columbia Railroad Company.

Rainey served as an Internal Revenue Service agent in South Carolina from 1879 to 1881. In 1881 he unsuccessfully sought appointment as clerk of the U.S. House of Representatives. His attempt to operate a brokerage and banking business in Washington failed. In poor health and with his finances depleted, he returned in 1887 to Georgetown where he died.

Joseph H. Rainey pursued moderation during Reconstruction. He was determined to protect and to enlarge the civil and political rights of his black constituents while not alienating or offending white citizens.

• There are two small collections of Rainey papers and materials in the South Caroliniana Library at the University of South Carolina and in the Duke University Library. There is no full-length biography, but for a brief treatment of his life, see Cyril Outerbridge Packwood, *Detour— Bermuda, Destination— U.S. House of Representatives: The Life of Joseph Hayne Rainey* (1977). Also see Maurine Christopher, *America's Black Congressmen* (1971); Joel Williamson, *After Slavery: The Negro in South Carolina during Reconstruction, 1861–1877* (1965); Thomas Holt, *Black over White: Negro Political Leadership in South Carolina during Reconstruction* (1977); and George C. Rogers, Jr., *The History of Georgetown County, South Carolina* (1970).

WILLIAM C. HINE

RAINEY, Ma (26 Apr. 1886–22 Dec. 1939), vaudeville, blues, and jazz singer and self-proclaimed "Mother of the Blues," was born Gertrude Malissa Nix Pridgett in Columbus, Georgia, the daughter of Thomas Pridgett and Ella Allen, an employee of the Georgia Central Railroad. Gertrude began her musical career at age fourteen in a local talent show and soon was singing at the Springer Opera House in Columbus. Early in her career, she met William "Pa" Rainey, whom she married in 1904. They toured the South, performing in tent shows, honky-tonks, carnivals, and vaudeville houses with F. S. Wolcott's Rabbit Foot Minstrels and later with their own troupe. "Ma" Rainey earned a reputation as a flamboyant performer who wore gaudy costumes and had a "wild" stage persona that manifested itself in her seductive movements to her blues music. At the time the Raineys and many other black entertainers were booked into their engagements by the Theatre Owners Booking Association (TOBA). The wages paid to black entertainers were so low and the working conditions so exploitative that TOBA came to stand for "Tough on Black Artists," or, more colloquially, "Tough on Black Asses."

Ma Rainey sang a combination of vaudeville songs, southern black folk melodies, and the blues, which had its origins in the cries and field hollers of slavery times and the call-and-response storytelling songs of

West Africa that captive Africans brought with them to the Western Hemisphere. Although Rainey claimed to have given the blues its name, it is more likely that the name evolved over time and has no single origin. The country blues that Rainey sang quickly lent themselves to a twelve-bar musical form that allowed the singer to "converse" in call-and-response style with an accompanying trumpeter or other instrumentalist who used the "blue" notes of the vocalist to bend traditional Western musical pitches. The poetic form is actually that of a rhymed couplet in iambic pentameter, and the texts ranged from the most mundane events of waking up and feeling blue (low in spirits) to the story of a prostitute and her abusive lover in "Hustlin' Blues" ("It's rainin' out here, and the tricks ain't walkin' tonight. / I'm goin' home, and I know I've got to fight"). Her lyrics also touched on such wide-ranging subjects as homosexuality ("Sissy Blues"), depression ("Counting the Blues"), and lost love ("Goodbye Daddy Blues"). She sang mainly for black audiences in the South and in Mexico, under the name "Madame" Rainey, and her earthy performances helped to identify the blues as "down and dirty" music that was not appropriate for polite society. Her music was a major influence on the careers of fellow blues artists Ida Cox and Bessie Smith, whom she discovered and encouraged.

Rainey began her recording career in 1923, by which time she was an established artist among southern black audiences. Paramount Records issued all of her recordings and targeted them to blacks in what were then referred to as "race records." She recorded more than one hundred records for Paramount in five years, most of them under very primitive studio conditions that did not capture the expressiveness of her voice. She recorded her own blues pieces with such jazz luminaries as trumpeters Louis Armstrong and Joe Smith, clarinetist Buster Bailey, saxophonist Coleman Hawkins, and pianist Lovie Austin. Her supporting ensembles included members of Fletcher Henderson's band and her own Georgia Jazz Band and Tub Jug Washboard Band. Among Ma Rainey's more famous recordings were "Bo-weevil Blues," "Moonshine Blues" (both 1923), "Yonder Come the Blues" (1926), and "Ma Rainey's Black Bottom" (1927).

After a long performing career, Ma Rainey retired in 1935, returning to Columbus. She owned and managed two theaters in Rome, Georgia. She devoted her last years to working for the local Friendship Baptist Church. Popular with black audiences in its time, Ma Rainey's music is of historical interest as the blues has become a critical element in the history of American jazz and popular music.

• Ma Rainey's contributions to blues and jazz are discussed in the chapter on the blues in Marshall W. Stearns, *The Story of Jazz* (1956). See also François Postif, "Deux Grandes Chanteuses de Blues, Ma Rainey and Bessie Smith" in *Jazz Hot* (Paris, Sept. 1953); Derrick Stewart-Baxter, *Ma Rainey and the Classic Blues Singers* (1970); Brian Rust, *Jazz Records, 1897–1942*, rev. ed. (1978); and Sandra R. Lieb, *Mother of the Blues: A Study of Ma Rainey* (1981). The article, "Gertrude Ma Rainey," in *Blues Who's Who*, ed. Sheldon Harris (1979), summarizes her performances throughout the 1920s and 1930s. Many of Rainey's recordings have been reissued on the Biograph and Riverside (Jazz Archives Series) labels.

BARBARA L. TISCHLER

RAINS, Claude (10 Nov. 1889–30 May 1967), actor, was born William Claude Rains in London, England, the son of Frederick William Rains, an actor and director of silent films, and Emily Cox. Despite Frederick Rains's active involvement in Film, the family was poor. In interviews Rains would describe himself as having grown up on the wrong side of the Thames. He did not enjoy school, and at the age of nine he ran away from home. He quickly made the acquaintance of a boy who sang in a professional choir and shortly thereafter joined the group. Rains made his London stage debut at age eleven as an extra in *Sweet Nell of Old Drury*, an experience that convinced him to pursue a career in the theater. Throughout his teen years Rains worked his way onto the London stage: building sets, doing electrical work—even fetching a doctor for an ailing George Bernard Shaw during a rehearsal.

At age eighteen Rains was hired as a stage manager, but working backstage was not fulfilling. He wanted to act. His cockney accent and a lisp made him feel self-conscious, however, and he took speech lessons to overcome these "speech defects." His adult London stage debut in *Gods of the Mountain* in 1911 was followed by four very busy years. During that time he toured Australia as a stage manager, joined Harley Granville-Barker's repertory group as an actor and crew member, and toured the United States, where, in 1913, he married actress Isabel Jeans and then divorced her in 1915 before returning to England. Jeans was the first of Rains's six wives; he married Marie Hemingway in 1920 (they divorced that same year), Beatrix Thomson in 1924 (they divorced in 1935), Frances Propper in 1935 (they divorced in 1956 and had one daughter), Agi Jambor in 1959 (they divorced later that year), and Rosemary Clark in 1960.

In 1915, after the outbreak of World War I, Rains enlisted in the London Scottish Regiment—reportedly because of the "gorgeous tartan" that the soldiers wore. He served in France, where he was gassed, and was discharged in 1919, having obtained the rank of captain. Rains immediately returned to the stage, impressing critics in 1920 with his performance in the role of Casca in *Julius Caesar* and as the title character in *The Government Inspector*. Also in this period he taught at the Royal Academy of Dramatic Art; one of his students at the academy was John Gielgud, who would remember Rains as a "delightful teacher."

Returning to the United States in 1926, Rains was cast, with Thomson, in *The Constant Nymph*. Because the roles in New York were plentiful, Rains stayed; his wife did not. He appeared in numerous productions, including *Volpone*, as the title character, and in *And So to Bed*, as Samuel Pepys, both in 1928. That same year he joined the Theatre Guild, becoming its leading character actor until 1933, when he was informed that there were no roles for him in the upcoming season.

Rains thought his acting career was over, but he soon found new opportunities in motion pictures. At age forty-four he took his first screen test, for *A Bill of Divorcement*, having appeared in the stage production. Rains later described it as "the worst screen test in the history of movie-making," and he was not given a role. Nonetheless, he auditioned again, this time for *The Invisible Man* (1933). This screen test was equally weak, but on the strength of Rains's voice, director James Whale cast him in the lead role. After the film was shot Rains returned to New York, where he made the film *Crime without Passion* (1934), which fared poorly. *The Invisible Man*, however, became a huge success, launching a film career that would include fifty-four more films. It would be sixteen years before Rains returned to the theater.

Because his character in *The Invisible Man* is driven insane, Rains played mentally deranged individuals in several films produced between 1934 and 1936, yet he was able to avoid being typecast in this one role. In 1936 he signed with Warner Bros. as a character actor. Two-thirds of these roles, most notably in *The Prince and the Pauper* (1937) and *The Adventures of Robin Hood* (1938), were as villains, but he was not entirely typecast as the bad guy either; he played the comical father in *Four Daughters* (1938) and in its two sequels as well as heavenly emissary in *Here Comes Mr. Jordan* (1941).

His portrayal of the corrupt senator in *Mr. Smith Goes to Washington* (1939) earned Rains the first of his four Academy Award nominations. He later received nominations for his work in *Casablanca* (1942), as the womanizing, gambling, but amiable Louis Renault; for *Mr. Skeffington* (1944), as Bette Davis's disdained husband; and for *Notorious* (1946), as a pro-Nazi spy. Rains never won an Oscar for his film performances, but he did receive an Antoinette Perry (Tony) Award in 1951 for his performance in Arthur Koestler's *Darkness at Noon*, the first of his three theater performances in the 1950s; the other roles were in T. S. Eliot's *The Confidential Clerk* (1954) and Arch Oboler's *The Night of the Auk* (1956).

The 1940s were productive for Rains (he made twenty-four films), but in the 1950s he appeared in only a handful of Hollywood productions. Like many other actors and radio personalities, he turned to television, where he appeared in numerous productions, including *Antigone* and *The Pied Piper of Hamelin*. In the 1960s he made only six films, including *Lawrence of Arabia* (1962) and *The Greatest Story Ever Told* (1965), before his death in Sandwich, New Hampshire.

Casablanca is the best-known of Rains's films, and it is his portrayal of Louis Renault that epitomizes his appeal on screen. Even though Renault is a corrupt government official, Rains embodies him with enough charm, sophistication, and savoire faire that the audience is able to appreciate, sympathize with, even root for an otherwise debauched character. It was precisely his ability to combine the noble with the ignoble that enabled Rains to tackle many varied roles, seemingly without effort.

• Boston University has some of Rains's manuscripts, pictures, and correspondence, including publications by and about Rains. Jeanne Stein, "Claude Rains," *Films in Review*, Nov. 1963, pp. 513–28, presents a great deal of bibliographic material on Rains as well as a list of his plays. Two other strong articles on Rains, both by Jeffrey Richards, are in *Films and Filming*, Feb. and Mar. 1982. An obituary is in the *New York Times*, 31 May 1967.

WILLIAM C. BOLES

RAINS, Gabriel James (4 June 1803–6 Aug. 1881), soldier, scientist, and inventor, was born in Craven County, North Carolina, the son of Gabriel M. Rains and Hester Ambrose. Rains graduated thirteenth in his 1827 class of the U.S. Military Academy and was commissioned in the infantry. He married (date unknown) into one of the South's most venerable families when he wedded Mary Jane McClellan, granddaughter of Governor John Sevier of Tennessee. They raised a family of six children. Rains was promoted to captain and brevet major for gallantry in the Seminole War, 1839–1842, during which he suffered serious wounds. In the war with Mexico he saw action at the battle of Resaca de la Palma. Assigned to recruiting duty, he raised a large number of troops for General Winfield Scott's army. He again distinguished himself in fighting against the Seminoles, earning promotion to major in 1851. He reached the rank of brigadier general of volunteers in 1855 while serving in Washington Territory. He was promoted to lieutenant colonel in the regular army on 5 June 1860.

With the outbreak of the Civil War, Rains accepted a commission as brigadier general in the Confederate army. Assigned command of a brigade under General D. H. Hill, Rains commanded at Yorktown in 1861–1862 and led the retreat before General George McClellan's advancing army. Rains had experimented with explosives long before the Civil War, and at Yorktown he mined the adjoining waters. When he retreated from Yorktown he mined the road against pursuing Union cavalry and again mined the roads at Williamsburg. In the resulting outcry from the Union army and newspapers, his corps commander, General James Longstreet, forbade the use of land mines. The Confederate secretary of war accepted their use but reprimanded Rains for questioning the authority of his corps commander. Rains persisted and convinced President Jefferson Davis of both the ethical legitimacy and the military value of mine warfare. One sign of the shift from limited to total war in tactics was the conversion, as the war progressed, of most of his Confederate and Union critics to the ethical legitimacy of this emerging form of warfare. Rains subsequently used land mines to protect the land approaches to Richmond, Mobile, and Charleston.

Rains commanded a flank movement at Seven Pines that Hill credited with saving the battle. Severely wounded at Seven Pines, in December 1862 Rains was appointed head of the Confederate Bureau of Conscription. Before and during his tenure as head of the Conscription Bureau, Rains worked on the technology of mines, or torpedoes, and on a plan of defense for Confederate harbors. Beginning 25 May 1863 Davis assigned Rains full-time to mine or torpedo defenses. Until he took command of the Torpedo Bureau, Rains manufactured his mines independently, supplying them upon requisition to the navy and the Engineer Bureau. In June 1864 Davis made him superintendent of the new Torpedo Bureau, and in this capacity Rains implemented his plan for southern harbor defense.

Rains advanced mine or torpedo warfare by inventing a very sensitive contact fuse for a percussion-type mine. He also developed some ingenious designs to realize the potential of his fuse. His technical developments improved on previous chemical fuses, dating from the Russian introduction of mine or torpedo warfare in the Crimean War. Rains's developments applied to the chemical fuse, which was the type in Confederate use. In a noteworthy convergence of military careers, Rains's brother, George Washington Rains, manufactured his contact fuse in the Confederate Powder Works, which he built and ran in Augusta, Georgia. Percussion-type torpedoes developed by Rains and a competitor named Singer were those most used by the Confederacy. Singer became famous for the use of his torpedoes in so-called "torpedo rams," a development unique to the Civil War in which torpedo boats carried their weapons to their targets at the end of a lengthy spar. The torpedo rams took a considerable toll. Rains restricted his employment to anchored mines for static water defense or free floating mines that were drifted into position. These modes of deployment also met with considerable success. Rains's most dramatic exploit saw two operatives from his Torpedo Bureau blow up two Federal barges and an ammunition warehouse at City Point, Virginia, in August 1864, inflicting heavy casualties and a $4 million loss.

By the end of the war there was considerable consensus from Davis down through field command that extensive early development, particularly of torpedo rams, might have made a significant difference in the course of the war. The failure in part was due to a late start, but there was a subsequent failure to centralize or at least coordinate mine and torpedo warfare. The engineers, though keen, did not take a firm grip, in part because they thought that the navy should be footing more of the bill; nor did the navy seize available opportunities. The Torpedo Bureau was a belated attempt to focus development and deployment. Though ultimately unsuccessful in affecting the course of the war, mine or torpedo warfare achieved sufficient results to indicate its potential for the future of modern warfare.

After the war Rains lived in Atlanta, Georgia. In 1877 he moved to Charleston, South Carolina, where until 1880 he was a clerk in the U.S. Quartermaster Department. He died in Aiken, South Carolina.

Rains's place in military history, like that of his brother and fellow Confederate officer, derives from his place as inventor and organizer of new explosives technology. He also raised a historically significant debate about moral limits in the military use of Industrial Era technology.

• For Confederate mine or torpedo warfare, see Milton Perry, *Infernal Machines: The Story of Confederate Submarine and Mine Warfare* (1965). For the important involvement of the Confederate Engineer Bureau, see James Lynn Nichols's thorough account in *Confederate Engineers* (1957). The latter is a good source on the considerable journal literature as well as manuscript sources for Rains's involvement in harbor and land defenses. Sound technical studies by participating Confederate officers are W. R. King, *Torpedoes: Their Invention and Use, from the First Application to the Art of War to the Present Time* (1886), and Royal B. Bradford, *History of Torpedo Warfare* (1882). For published documentary sources see U.S. War Department, *The War of the Rebellion: A Compilation of the Official Records of the Union and Confederate Armies* (128 vols., 1880–1901), and U.S. Navy Department, *The Official Records of the Union and Confederate Navies in the War of the Rebellion* (30 vols., 1894–1922). Obituaries are in the (Charleston, S.C.) *News and Courier*, 12 Aug. 1881, and the (Raleigh, N.C.) *News and Observer*, 14 Aug. 1881.

EDWARD HAGERMAN

RAINS, George Washington (1817–21 Mar. 1898), soldier, scientist, engineer, and educator, was born in Craven County, North Carolina, the son of Gabriel M. Rains and Hester Ambrose. Rains graduated third in his 1842 class of the U.S. Military Academy. He was commissioned in the Corps of Engineers but transferred to the artillery. In 1844 Rains was detached to West Point as assistant professor of chemistry, geology, and mineralogy. He served with distinction in the war with Mexico and was breveted captain for gallantry at the battles of Contreras and Churubusco and major for gallantry at Chapultepec. Following postings in the South and Northeast, he resigned his commission in 1856, the same year he married Francis Josephine Ramsdell. The number of their children, if any, is unknown. He served as president of the Washington Iron Works and then the Highland Iron Works, both in Newburgh, New York. Rains joined the ranks of soldier-inventors produced by West Point, when in 1860–1861 he patented several inventions relating to steam engines and boilers.

With the outbreak of the Civil War, Rains joined the Confederate army and was commissioned a major in the artillery. He was quickly assigned to ordnance duties, where Jefferson Davis and Josiah Gorgas, head of the new Ordnance Department, placed him in charge of gunpowder production with full authority. Rains, like all managers of large ordnance establishments, was promoted to lieutenant colonel so as to have equal rank with chief ordnance officers of armies in the field.

Gorgas took advantage of his open mandate to organize ordnance supply without the hindrance of organizational precedents. He created and presided over a structure in which the managers of various functions were given near carte blanche. His managers were expected to exercise broad discretion to plan within their domains while he implemented their plans in relation to shifting priorities and the availability of resources. Part of Gorgas's success lay in selecting outstanding managers, and the combination of Rains in charge of gunpowder production and Isaac Munroe St. John in charge of providing the essential ingredient of nitre with his Nitre Corps, later the Nitre and Mining Bureau, was especially successful.

Rains combined his engineering and scientific ability to develop a modern process and facility to prepare nitre for gunpowder. His great achievement was the building of the large, modern Confederate Powder Works in Augusta, Georgia. He adapted the manufacturing processes of the Waltham Abbey Powder Works in England, then the best in the world, patenting improvements in the process. The available English plans described only the process and machinery, leaving Rains to develop working plans and details of buildings and apparatus. Before the Augusta works went into production on 10 April 1862, Rains inherited a limited and primitive capacity for powder production supplemented by facilities that he organized in New Orleans. The Augusta works, supplemented by works at Richmond and Raleigh, by a few small contractors, and by some blockade running, met Confederate needs by the end of its first year of production. Rains's powder works was the first great achievement of Gorgas's Ordnance Bureau and its most successful long-term project.

Rains played an important advisory role to Gorgas on ordnance issues beyond powder production. By interesting coincidence, Rains's career as soldier, inventor, and military administrator in a technological service paralleled that of his older brother, General Gabriel James Rains, a fellow graduate of West Point, an inventor in mine warfare, and superintendent of the Confederate Torpedo Bureau. In a convergence of brotherly contributions, George Rains's Augusta works manufactured for his brother's Torpedo Bureau the variation on the contact fuse for mines that Gabriel Rains invented. With the difficulty of controlling the whole of his domain following William T. Sherman's cutting of Confederate railroads, Gorgas on 15 March 1865 put the Ordnance Department in the deep South under Rains's independent authority.

Following the war Rains pursued a long career in medical science and administration. In 1866 he was appointed professor of chemistry in the Medical College of Georgia. He served as dean of the college from 1877 to 1883 and retired from the faculty in 1894. He died in Newburgh, New York.

• The George Washington Rains Papers are in the Southern Historical Collection at the University of North Carolina at Chapel Hill. The best account of his role in the Civil War is his own *History of the Confederate Powder Works* (1882). The best secondary account of his role is found in Frank E. Vandiver's excellent *Ploughshares into Swords: Josiah Gorgas and Confederate Ordnance* (1952). Vandiver provides a valuable annotated guide to manuscripts on the Ordnance Depart-

ment, of which the most important are the Records of the Confederate Ordnance Bureau, 154 vols., National Archives of the United States, and the accompanying official records of the Confederate Powder Works. See also Vandiver, ed., *The Civil War Diary of General Josiah Gorgas* (1947). Obituaries are in the (Newburgh, N.Y.) *Daily Register*, 22 Mar. 1898, and the *Army and Navy Journal*, 2 Apr. 1898.

EDWARD HAGERMAN

RAINSFORD, William Stephen (30 Oct. 1850–17 Dec. 1933), clergyman and social reformer, was born near Dublin, Ireland, the son of Marcus Rainsford, an Anglican priest, and Louisa Anne Dickson. Rainsford moved to England in 1865 when his father took charge of a parish in London; he received his bachelor's degree from Cambridge University, where he studied between 1870 and 1873. Ordained a deacon of the Church of England in December 1873 and a priest in 1874, he started his ministry as a curate at St. Giles's parish in Norwich. Dissatisfied with English church life, however, he left Norwich in 1876 and spent the next two years working as a traveling preacher in Canada and the United States. Following a mission he led at St. James' Cathedral in Toronto, Rainsford became assistant rector of that parish in 1878. In April of that year he married Emily Alma Green, a widow, with whom he had three children. He later married Harriette Rogers in 1926, three years after Emily died.

Rainsford's most notable professional achievements took place during his tenure as rector at St. George's Episcopal Church in New York City. Although St. George's had once been a well-to-do parish, it had experienced a steady decline in membership and was struggling to survive in a decaying neighborhood at the time of Rainsford's arrival in 1883. Having won the support of wealthy businessman J. P. Morgan, the church's senior warden, he set to work and not only transformed the parish but also significantly altered the ways in which American Protestants viewed church life. An early exponent of the Social Gospel, Rainsford was unhappy with the tendency of Christians to become so concerned with saving souls that they overlooked the material needs of ordinary men and women. He developed the concept of the "institutional church"—the idea that urban churches could offer both worship services and essential social services for people (parishioners and nonparishioners alike) in their neighborhoods. He insisted, for example, that voluntary financial offerings should replace pew rents, which had been a barrier to the participation of the working class in Episcopal churches; he opened up the church building for both secular and religious activities throughout the week; and he was personally active in various aspects of civic and political reform. Rainsford's ambitious program at St. George's included a boys' club and a girls' club, organizations for men and for women, a trade school, a cadet battalion, a gymnasium, and even a shooting range in the basement of the parish house.

Rainsford based his ministry on a modernist theology that emphasized divine immanence and downplayed the importance of many traditional religious doctrines and creeds. Although his liberal theological assumptions were criticized in some quarters, St. George's prospered under his leadership and became a model for other Episcopal parishes. Poor health, however, forced Rainsford to take a leave of absence from his duties in 1904 and then to resign altogether in 1906. He traveled on a lion-hunting expedition in East Africa from 1906 to 1910, and when he came back to the United States he did not return to the parish ministry.

Rainsford's views grew increasingly humanistic over the years, and he eventually developed a religious philosophy entirely devoid of supernatural elements. The titles of his two major theological works are telling: *The Reasonableness of Faith, and Other Addresses* (1902), and *The Reasonableness of the Religion of Jesus* (1913), which contained his Baldwin Lectures at the University of Michigan in 1911. In time Rainsford found that his theological modernism had taken him beyond the boundaries of orthodox Christianity altogether, and he renounced his Episcopal orders in May 1912. He spent the rest of his life in retirement at Ridgefield, Connecticut; he died in New York while being treated at Roosevelt Hospital.

Despite ending his career outside the theological mainstream of Christianity, Rainsford's early thinking had a profound impact on the development of the Social Gospel in the Protestant denominations of the United States. The institutional church movement of which he was a principal progenitor, while novel in the 1880s, attained enormous popularity at the beginning of the twentieth century and provided an essential model for urban parishes. Rainsford was a dynamic figure who was vitally concerned about the failure of Episcopalians and other Protestants to incorporate poor and working-class citizens into their membership, and he demonstrated at St. George's how parish leaders could extend the ministry of their churches into the neighborhoods that surrounded them.

• A few scattered Rainsford manuscripts are located at the Archives of the Episcopal Diocese of New York. The two major sources for his life and ministry are his own *A Preacher's Story of His Work* (1904) and *The Story of a Varied Life: An Autobiography* (1922). See also Henry Anstice, *History of St. George's Church in the City of New York* (1911), and Elizabeth Moulton, *St. George's Church, New York* (1964). For a brief modern assessment of the implications of Rainsford's "institutional church" idea, see Paul T. Phillips, *A Kingdom on Earth: Anglo-American Social Christianity, 1880–1940* (1996). An obituary appears in the *New York Times*, 18 Dec. 1933, and provides a useful discussion of his career.

GARDINER H. SHATTUCK, JR.

RAINWATER, James (9 Dec. 1917–31 May 1986), physicist, was born Leo James Rainwater in Council, Idaho, the son of Leo Jasper Rainwater, a civil engineer, and Edna Eliza Teague, manager of a general store. When his father died in 1918, his family moved to Hanford, California, where he grew up. Having won a chemistry competition in high school that was sponsored by the California Institute of Technology, in 1935 Rainwater matriculated at that school to study chemistry, but he later switched to physics. He received his B.S. in 1939 and then enrolled in the graduate physics program at Columbia University, where he received his M.A. in 1941. In 1942 he married Emma Louise Smith, with whom he had four children.

Rainwater became affiliated with the U.S. Office of Scientific Research and Development in 1942 as a research scientist. In this capacity he took part in the Manhattan Project and helped to build the first uranium bomb, a device that derives its incredible destructive power by exploiting the principle of nuclear fission in an uncontrolled chain reaction. Scientists of the day knew little more about such a reaction than that it is initiated when an atomic nucleus splits apart while being bombarded by subatomic particles and is sustained when the neutrons of that ruptured nucleus are then propelled into adjacent nuclei. Consequently Rainwater, whose graduate work involved measuring the energy levels of neutrons, was assigned to study neutron behavior by using Columbia's particle accelerator, a device that allows scientists to observe the effects of rapidly moving subatomic particles. The results of these experiments, which were declassified shortly after the end of World War II, formed the basis of his doctoral dissertation; he received his Ph.D. in physics from Columbia in 1946.

Later that year Rainwater joined Columbia's faculty as an instructor of physics. He continued his work with the particle accelerator and began building a synchrocyclotron—a device capable of propelling particles to much higher velocities than could be reached with a regular accelerator—for Columbia's new Nevis Cyclotron Laboratory. He was promoted to assistant professor in 1947 and to associate professor in 1949. During the latter year he developed a professional relationship with Aage Niels Bohr, a visiting Danish physicist whose father had won the 1922 Nobel Prize for physics. Rainwater and Bohr were particularly interested in developing a model of the atomic nucleus that would explain the behavior of protons and neutrons, collectively known as nucleons. At the time two competing theories of atomic structure were being circulated. The liquid-drop theory, first advanced in 1935 by the Russian-born American physicist George Gamow and subsequently promoted by the senior Bohr, emphasized the collective motion of nucleons by suggesting that the nucleus resembles a drop of incompressible water in that it reacts to vibration by constantly changing its shape. The spherical-shell theory, developed jointly in 1949 by the American physicist Maria Goeppert Mayer and the German physicist Johannes Hans Daniel Jensen, emphasized the independent motion of nucleons by suggesting that the nucleus resembles an onion in that it consists of several layers of nucleons that move about within symmetrically concentric orbits, in much the same way that electrons move around the nucleus.

For about a year Rainwater and Bohr were engaged

in an ongoing discussion of the relative merits of both models, neither of which offered them an entirely satisfactory explanation for the behavior of nucleons. These conversations contributed to Rainwater's development of a third theory that incorporated features of both the liquid-drop and spherical-shell theories. He posited that centrifugal forces within the concentric orbits of nucleons probably did not allow for a perfectly spherical nucleus but rather dictated a more flexible one of somewhat oval shape. After Rainwater published his new theory in 1950, Bohr and his Danish colleague Ben Roy Mottelson tested and confirmed Rainwater's theory experimentally, and when they published their results in 1952, they further developed his ideas into what is known today as the deformed-shell or unified theory. According to this model, when the outer shell of the nucleus is not full, as is the case with many atoms, then the shape of the nucleus becomes distorted and assumes an oval shape; however, when the outer shell of the nucleus is full, then it assumes a rounded shape. The work of Rainwater, Bohr, and Mottelson contributed to a more complete understanding of nuclear structure and earned for them the 1975 Nobel Prize for physics.

Most of Rainwater's career involved the Nevis synchrocyclotron, which became operational in 1950. He used it primarily to study subatomic particles such as pions (or pi mesons, highly unstable particles that interact with protons and neutrons and thereby bind them to one another) and muons (relatively massive electron-like particles that do not interact with nucleons but instead decay rapidly via radiation into electrons and other subatomic particles). In 1951 he became director of the Nevis Laboratories, a position he held until 1953 and then again from 1956 to 1961; in 1952 he was promoted to full professor. In 1953, by observing the radiation emitted by muons in lead and bismuth nuclei, Rainwater and Val Logsdon Fitch discovered that protons contain far less mass than scientists had previously believed. He continued to experiment with the synchrocyclotron until 1976, contributing much useful knowledge about the muon, particularly in terms of its angular momentum and magnetic moment. He also conducted a number of experiments for the Atomic Energy Commission (AEC) and its successor, the Energy Research and Development Administration, as well as for the National Science Foundation and the Office of Naval Research. In 1983 he was appointed Michael I. Pupin Professor of Physics. He retired from Columbia in 1986 and died in Yonkers, New York.

Rainwater received the AEC's Ernest Orlando Lawrence Award in 1963. He was elected to the Institute of Electrical and Electronics Engineers in 1965, the National Academy of Sciences and the New York Academy of Sciences in 1968, and the Royal Swedish Academy of Sciences in 1982. His major contribution to science consisted of his theory of the structure of the atomic nucleus. Although later discoveries called into question the degree to which the unified theory—a direct outgrowth of Rainwater's seminal thinking—explains every aspect of nuclear structure, this theory remained in the mid-1990s the best model for the construction of an atomic nucleus.

• Many of Rainwater's papers were published in the Nevis Laboratories Reports and are held in the Columbia University Library. Good biographies of Rainwater include Margo Nash, "James Rainwater," in *Notable Twentieth-Century Scientists*, ed. Emily McMurray (1995), and Tyler Wasson, ed., *Nobel Prize Winners* (1987). Obituaries are in the *New York Times*, 3 June 1986, and *Newsweek*, 16 June 1986.

CHARLES W. CAREY, JR.

RAJNEESH, Bhagwan (11 Dec. 1931–19 Jan. 1990), guru, was born Chandra Mohan Jain in Kuchwada village, Madhya Pradesh, India, the son of Babulal Jain, a cloth merchant, and Saraswati Jain. His family were members of the Jain religion, a non-Hindu minority of ancient origin. The name Rajneesh means, roughly, "lord of kings"; it is not known when he took the name. At Jabalpur University, Rajneesh acquired a reputation for being a passionate thinker, but he was also a lazy student and a troublemaker. This, coupled with his erratic physical and mental health, gave him and those around him reason to doubt his sanity. Ultimately, these problems were attributed to spiritual sensitivity. Indeed, on 21 March 1953 Rajneesh experienced "enlightenment." Nevertheless, he continued his studies and received a B.A. in philosophy in 1955 and an M.A. in 1957. Starting in 1960 he taught philosophy at Jabalpur.

In 1960 Rajneesh, a gifted orator, began to travel around India giving public lectures on psychological and spiritual topics. His views had been influenced particularly by the esoteric philosophies of the Russian mystics Gurdjieff and Ouspensky. His scathing criticisms of organized religion appealed especially to wealthy business patrons, some of whom founded the Jeevan Jagruti Kendra (Life Awakening Center) in Bombay in 1965 as a vehicle for Rajneesh to expound his philosophy.

Rajneesh's method consisted of his own synthesis of Indian Tantric techniques, which sought to awaken and channel sexual energy for spiritual illumination, the "bioenergetic" bodywork of the post-Freudian psychologist Wilhelm Reich, and other assorted ecstatic techniques such as Sufi dancing. This mixture evolved into Rajneesh's "dynamic meditation," which he began to teach in intensive sessions in which participants would shout, scream, laugh, and disrobe. His controversial views caused the university administration to ask him to resign in 1966.

By 1968 Rajneesh had begun to gather disciples, mainly Indian at first but also a growing number of Western people. These followers accorded Rajneesh the status of "guru," an enlightened master who is an earthly representative of the divine and who demands of his disciples a total surrender of ego and rational decision making. As a symbol of their self-abasement, the devotees, called sannyasins, were required to wear exclusively red or orange clothing and necklaces bearing Rajneesh's likeness. In 1970 Rajneesh changed his title from Acharya (teacher) to Bhagwan (god) and in 1974 established a world-renowned center in Poona, near Bombay, to which great numbers of Westerners flocked. His self-styled Tantric philosophy of toleration for all paths attracted many highly educated American and European professionals who otherwise would probably not have been drawn to a religious teacher.

Under pressure from the disapproving Indian government, Rajneesh's commune moved to a ranch in eastern Oregon in 1981, leaving a host of unpaid bills and taxes behind in India. The "Rajneeshees" invaded and took over the town of Antelope, building a 64,229-acre compound called "Rajneeshpunam" that included a shopping mall, a manmade lake, a hospital, a bus system, and hundreds of luxuriously appointed mobile homes, and had its own armed peacekeeping force. Rajneesh himself had a fleet of Rolls-Royces, which eventually numbered more than eighty. In 1982 the 5,000 Rajneeshees (supplemented by thousands of homeless people bused in to swell the voting ranks) were able to elect a majority to the Antelope city council; they passed a measure to rename the town Rajneesh. Yet as the group became more powerful, its tight internal organization fell victim to paranoia and mistrust. The guru went into seclusion, communicating with his disciples only through his assistant, Ma Anand Sheela (Sheila Silverman). Legal difficulties mounted, including charges of inappropriate land use and violation of immigration laws by Rajneesh and his international followers. Rajneesh, who was arrested in October 1985 in Charlotte, North Carolina, en route to Bermuda in his private jet, pled guilty to federal immigration charges, was fined $400,000, and was expelled from the United States for five years. Sheela and two of her assistants were later convicted of numerous offenses including wiretapping, arson, and the attempted murder of a member of the commune they regarded as a threat to the guru. Whether or not Rajneesh knew of these activities is unclear. Rajneesh died in Poona of heart failure, surrounded by 10,000 followers.

• Rajneesh wrote and dictated prolifically during his life, and his devotees continue to bring out collections of his recorded ideas. Among his numerous books are *The Mustard Seed* (1975), *Roots and Wings* (1975), *The Book of the Secrets* (1976), *The Grass Grows by Itself* (1976), *The Art of Dying* (1978), *I Say unto You* (1980), his autobiography, *The Sound of Running Water* (1980), *The Goose Is Out* (1982), *The Secret of Secrets* (1982), *Walking in Zen/Sitting in Zen* (1982), *The Book of Wisdom* (1983–1984), *God's Got a Thing about You* (1983), *Hsin Hsin Ming, the Book of Nothing* (1983), *Tantra, Spirituality, and Sex* (1983), *I Am That* (1984), *Yoga: The Science of the Soul* (1984), *And Now and Here* (1985), *Beyond Enlightenment* (1986), *Sermons in Stones* (1986), *Live Zen* (1988), and *No Mind: The Flowers of Eternity* (1989). Several critical treatments of Rajneesh's community have appeared, including James S. Gordon, *The Golden Guru* (1987), Hugh Milne, *Bhagwan: The God That Failed* (1986), and Kate Strelley with Robert D. San Souci, *The Ultimate Game* (1987). Obituaries are in the *Los Angeles Times* and the *New York Times*, both 20 Jan. 1990.

GAIL HINICH SUTHERLAND

RALL, Harris Franklin (23 Feb. 1870–13 Oct. 1964), professor of theology, was born in Council Bluffs, Iowa, the son of Otto Rall, a minister, and Anna Steiner. He studied at the University of Iowa, Yale Divinity School, and the universities of Halle and Wittenberg, receiving the Ph.D. in 1899. In 1897 he married Rose St. John; they had two children. Rose died in 1921, and in 1922 he married her sister Maud. He was president of Iliff School of Theology in Denver from 1910 to 1915 and professor of systematic theology at Garrett Biblical Institute in Evanston, Illinois, from 1915 to 1945. After retirement, Rall stayed in Evanston, where he became official advisor to Ernest Fremont Tittle, senior minister of the city's First Methodist Church.

Rall was a pivotal figure in Methodist theology, reaching the height of his influence in the 1950s. He considered himself an "evangelical liberal," intending that title to indicate his interest in bringing the Christian claim of personal relationship with God into the context of contemporary intellectual thought. From his Methodist commitment he drew a deep regard for Scripture as well as an emphasis on a conscious, personal fellowship with God, God's free grace as mediated by the Holy Spirit, and an ethical life expressed in both personal and social spheres.

In keeping with his German training, Rall promoted historical and critical study of the Bible, and a scientific worldview permeated his thought. Consequently, he stressed evolutionary growth in nature, confidence in empirical methods and human rationality, belief in the goodness and moral ability of human beings, and commitment to bringing the values of the Kingdom of God to the social order. The theological implications of these basic convictions led him to posit the primacy of the immanence of God and the democratic character of all relationships. Throughout his theology, Jesus Christ is the source of personal trust in God and the fulfillment of human hope.

Rall was an effective teacher, a theological interpreter through the popular press, and an organizer of the required course of study for all Methodist ministers. However, his greatest influence came through his published books. His early writing included a popular interpretation of Scripture, *New Testament History*, and an expression of his theological interests, *A Working Faith*, both published in 1914. The publication of both of these works in the same year reflected the persistent interaction in his thought between biblical exegesis and theological exploration. Altogether, he published fourteen books, including *A Faith for Today* (1936), *Christianity: An Inquiry into Its Nature and Truth* (1940), *The Christian Faith and Way* (1947), *Religion as Salvation* (1953), and *The God of Our Faith* (1955). He died in Evanston.

• Harris Franklin Rall's papers are located in the library of Garrett-Evangelical Theological Seminary in Evanston, Illinois. Discussion of Rall's theology can be found in Georgia Harkness, "The Theology of Dr. Rall," *Garrett Tower* 10 (1964): 18–23. See also Thomas A. Langford, *Practical Di-*

vinity (1983); Murray H. Leiffer, "Dr. Rall and Methodist Social Concerns," *Garrett Tower* 10 (1964): 23–26; and William J. McCutcheon, "American Methodist Thought and Theology, 1919–1960, in vol. 3 of *History of American Methodism*, ed. Emory S. Bucke (1964).

THOMAS A. LANGFORD

RALSTON, Thomas Neely (21 Mar. 1806–25 Nov. 1891), Methodist preacher and theologian, was born in rural Bourbon County, Kentucky, the son of John Ralston and Elizabeth Neely. Nothing is known about his parents' livelihood. Ralston graduated from Georgetown College in Kentucky. In 1826 he underwent a religious conversion that led him to seek ordination in the Methodist Episcopal church. Licensed in 1827 by the Kentucky Conference, he completed the requirements for being ordained as an elder in the Illinois Conference in 1834, whereupon he returned to Kentucky as a traveling preacher on the Mount Sterling Circuit. Known for combining bookish inclinations with evangelistic zeal, he served from 1843 to 1847 as president of the Methodist Female High School in Lexington, Kentucky, but he spent most of his career as the pastor of Methodist congregations in Danville, Versailles, Frankfort, Maysville, Shelbyville, and Louisville, Kentucky.

The Louisville Convention of 1845, which formed the Methodist Episcopal Church, South, as a result of tensions over slavery, elected Ralston as its assistant secretary, a sign of his rising prominence in the new denomination. In 1846 the new church's first General Conference elected him as denominational secretary and also named him as the chair of the committee to revise the Methodist *Discipline*, the book of church order and doctrine with which Methodists governed themselves.

In 1847 he confirmed his eminence among southern Methodists when he published his *Elements of Divinity*, the first systematic and comprehensive body of divinity to be issued by an American Methodist theologian. Ralston later revised and enlarged the book, which remained in the course of study for prospective ministers in the denomination throughout the rest of the nineteenth century. It attempted to reconstruct the thought of John Wesley, the founder of Methodism, in opposition to eighteenth- and nineteenth-century developments in Calvinism, especially the "New Divinity" espoused by the followers of Jonathan Edwards (1703–1758) and the "New Haven theology" associated with Nathaniel William Taylor at Yale. Like most other denominational theologians of his day, Ralston presented familiar arguments for the existence of God and outlined standard evidences that the Bible was a divine revelation. As a Wesleyan, he argued that the efficacy of Christ's atonement extended to all human beings and that God's prevenient grace made salvation possible for all who would appropriate, through faith and obedience, Christ's work of reconciliation. As a moral theologian, he tried to synthesize the "moral sense" theory of the eighteenth-century British ethicist Francis Hutcheson and the theory of the rationality of

conscience advocated by the English theologian Samuel Clarke, but he also criticized their positions by contending that only divine grace could undergird the "moral sense" and that only the biblical revelation of God's will could give the moral faculty appropriate guidance. He drew heavily on the Scottish Common Sense philosophy of Thomas Reid of Glasgow University and Dugald Stewart of Edinburgh University, especially on their appeal to "consciousness" as a ground for overcoming skepticism about the ability of the mind to attain accurate knowledge of the external world. The Scottish critique of skepticism appealed to the American clergy because it supported their conviction that rational, scientific study of the natural order could provide evidence for the existence of God.

In 1851 Ralston served as editor of the *Methodist Monthly*, a popular denominational periodical, but eventually he became disillusioned for a time with the Methodist church, and in 1858 he entered the Episcopal church, serving for two years as the rector of the Episcopal congregation in Covington, Kentucky. In 1861, however, he rejoined the Kentucky Conference of the Methodist church, of which he remained a pastor for the rest of his ministry.

The intellectual Ralston represented the growing respect for learning among educated southern Methodists, and his four-volume edition of the *Posthumous Works of the Rev. Henry B. Bascom* (1855–1856), a scholarly and genteel Kentucky Methodist preacher, promoted education and gentility within a denomination that remained largely ambivalent about those values. In 1875 he tried to look beyond his regional and denominational subculture by publishing a plea for Protestant unity entitled *Ecce Unitas*, in which he called for a confederation of all Protestants. He thought such a union could be achieved if each denomination would agree to establish as terms for communion only articles of belief and practice that would not violate the conscience of any faithful Christian. His proposal, earnest but naive, had little influence even in his own religious circles.

Ralston's eulogists remembered him both as an evangelist whose success in Methodist revivals drew hundreds into the church and as "the scholar" of Kentucky Methodism. He flourished during a period when those two roles could still be thought to overlap. He married twice, first to Josephine Thompson, and then, after her death, to Mary Phister. He died at his residence in the Highlands, near Newport, Kentucky.

• Information about Ralston can be found in the Records of the Kentucky Conference in the *Minutes of the Annual Conferences of the Methodist Episcopal Church, South* (1892); T. J. Dodd, "Memoir," *Nashville Christian Advocate* (26 Dec. 1891), p. 9; Walter N. Vernon, "Thomas Neely Ralston," in *Encyclopedia of World Methodism*, ed. Nolan B. Harmon (1974); and Roy Hunter Short, *Methodism in Kentucky* (1979).

E. BROOKS HOLIFIELD

RAMAGE, Adam (1772?–9 July 1850), printing press builder, was born in Scotland. (His parents are not known.) He emigrated to the United States while still in his early twenties, settling in Philadelphia on 29 January 1795 and filing for citizenship on 13 February 1798. His sponsor, John Innes, was a printers' joiner at No. 77 Dock Street, where Ramage had probably been employed since his arrival in the city and where he may have met Mark Fulton, another journeyman joiner who, also with Innes's sponsorship, became a citizen on the same day as Ramage. Ramage and Fulton apparently bought out Innes sometime in 1799, listing his former address as their new place of business in their first surviving advertisement (*United States Gazette*, 24 Jan. 1800). This partnership ended on 24 May 1800, and thereafter Ramage continued on his own. On 9 May 1806 fire destroyed his establishment and forced him to find temporary quarters in Norris's Alley, but despite such setbacks his business flourished as the population and literacy rate in the United States expanded, providing a growing market for printed material. Ramage was married—he fathered at least two daughters—but neither his wife's name nor the date of their marriage is known.

Ramage's career divides into three overlapping periods. During the first period (1800–1817), he concentrated on constructing and improving the wooden two-pull or common press, facing the platen with brass to increase durability, changing the pitch of the screw to provide greater speed and power of impression, replacing stone beds with iron ones, and making similar small innovations to enhance efficiency while maintaining moderate prices. Although Ramage may not have invented these improvements, he made them commercially successful. He seems to have been the first American press builder to combine woodworking and ironmongery in the same shop and to oversee all work on the premises, an arrangement to which he attributed the success of his products. By 1813 he had sold nearly 400 wooden presses, a figure that had increased to about 500 four years later, to almost 600 within another year and a half, and then, somewhat ominously, to only 677 by 1824. Even at this late date, when other builders had turned almost exclusively to cast iron presses modeled after Charles, the third Earl Stanhope's one-pull apparatus, and despite what seems to have been a decline in sales, Ramage was still working to perfect the wooden two-pull press, seeking to sustain its character as a cheap, durable, reliable, and efficient machine. "The finest book-work in America," he boasted with justification, "has been done on these presses" (*National Gazette and Literary Register*, 24 Jan. 1824).

The second phase of Ramage's career began in 1817, the year he introduced into America a press patented by Edinburgh printer John Ruthven in 1813. The exact nature of his arrangement with Ruthven is not known, but an advertisement published in Edinburgh by Ruthven's former partner, John Morison, in 1824 lists as purchasers of the Ruthven press the same American printers whom Ramage also claimed as clients in some of his advertisements. Perhaps, then, he was simply serving as Ruthven's agent, although it is clear that the two men also exchanged ideas for im-

provements. Ramage probably believed that the compact size of the Ruthven press—it stood only 42 inches high with a maximum surface (for newspaper printing) of 52 square inches—and its comparatively light weight made it ideal for use in the United States and South America, where rugged terrain posed transportation problems of a kind not encountered in England or on the Continent. He made the press a full one-third lighter while strengthening it structurally by substituting wrought for cast iron at all points of stress, eventually enabling it to sustain a pressure of twenty tons at the point of impression. Although Ramage continued to make and sell wooden presses after 1817, the Ruthven press appears to have occupied much of his attention until 1837 or so, by which time he had begun to advertise a number of other presses, including the American press, the Philadelphia press, and several different models of improved proof presses. Such specialized machines sustained his business during the third phase of his career (1837–1850), as printers turned more and more to steam-powered presses to meet the rising demand for disposable reading such as leaflets and pamphlets and inexpensive pulp fiction.

The same advertisement in which Ramage announced completion of modifications to the American version of the Ruthven press in 1824 also carried the first notice of the Ramage galley proof press, which he had patented on 19 May 1823. Especially designed for newspaper work, it was, Ramage claimed, "the most convenient and expeditious mode of taking column proofs yet known" (quoted in Hamilton, p. 19). Another small press, patented on 19 November 1834, employed a toggle joint mechanism, which Ramage also used in his Philadelphia press; described in Thomas Adams's *Typographia* in 1837, it was manufactured after Ramage's death by his successor, Jacob Bronstrup, as the Bronstrup press. Little is known about another of Ramage's presses of this period, the American press, which was reported in *Typographia* as a combination of "the toggles of the Washington Press, and the lever or elbow of the Smith" (p. 331), but in 1842 this press and the galley proof press earned Ramage the commendation of the Scott Committee of the Franklin Institute, a fitting tribute to a lifetime spent making hand presses simple, efficient, and reasonable in price. At his manufactory at 20 Library Street in Philadelphia, Ramage continued to build hand presses until his death in Philadelphia in 1850, a date that may also be seen as marking the passing of the hand press period as well. The most prolific builder of printing presses in the early United States, Ramage was a key figure in the great nationalistic period of American publishing and printing.

• An undated letter to an agent (Historical Society of Pennsylvania), another letter, dated 28 Mar. 1842, to the Scott Committee of the Franklin Institute (Records of the Committee on Science and the Arts of the Franklin Institute, 1824–1900), and an undated set of directions in Spanish for assembling what seems to have been a model of the American press

(Bancroft Library, Univ. of California, Berkeley) constitute the literary remains of Adam Ramage. A brief obituary notice is in *Stryker's American Register and Magazine* (1851), pp. 181–82. The standard account of Ramage's career is Milton W. Hamilton, *Adam Ramage and His Presses* (1942), which has been augmented here by information from P. William Philby, *Philadelphia Naturalization Records . . . 1789–1880 . . .* (1982), and by advertisements in various early American newspapers: *Philadelphia Gazette*, 29 Mar. 1796; *United States Gazette*, 10 and 16 May 1806; *Democratic Press*, 17 June 1813; *Poulson's American Daily Advertiser*, 27 May 1817; *Alexandria Gazette*, 16 Dec. 1819; and the *National Gazette and Literary Register*, 24 Jan. 1824. A useful discussion of Ramage and other early American press builders is Marc Edward Sanders, "Wooden Printing Press Building in America: The 1760s to Mid-19th Century" (Ph.D. diss., Univ. of Maryland, 1982). Elizabeth Harris, "Press-builders in Philadelphia, 1776–1850," *Printing History* 11 (1989): 11–24, has much to say about Ramage but occasionally draws incorrect conclusions, particularly with respect to his work on the Ruthven press. General studies of early American printing presses include Ralph Green, *The Iron Hand Press in America* (1948), which briefly discusses Ramage as an important builder of iron presses (pp. 22–25), and Stephen O. Saxe, *American Iron Hand Presses* (1992), which provides brief chapters on both the Ruthven (pp. 17–20) and the Philadelphia (later the Bronstrup) press (pp. 69–72), repeating, however, some of the prevailing misconceptions concerning Ramage's work on the Ruthven. Descriptions of several of Ramage's presses by a contemporary can be found in Thomas Adams, *Typographia* (1837). For the Ruthven press, see John Morison, *Ruthven's Patent Presses* (1824?); John Ruthven, *Specification of John Ruthven. Printing Presses* (1856); Printing Historical Society, *Printing Patents: Abridgements of Patent Specifications Relating to Printing 1617–1857 First Published in 1859 and Now Reprinted* (London, 1969); and Ruthven's patent application (No. 3746) in the British Library.

ROBERT D. ARNER

RAMAGE, John (c. 1748–24 Oct. 1802), miniature painter and goldsmith, was born probably in Dublin, Ireland. Little is known about his early life, including the identities of his parents. It is believed that he entered the Dublin School of Art in 1763. He married Elizabeth Liddel (d. 1784), the daughter of London merchant Henry Liddel, and they had two children, a boy and a girl, before he emigrated to Halifax, Nova Scotia, at least by 1772, leaving his family in London. No miniatures from this period of residence in Halifax have been identified. In both Boston and New York Ramage received abundant patronage from elite sitters who paid as much for an inch-high miniature by him as for a small oil painting by one of his contemporaries. Ramage was regarded as one of the premier miniature artists of his day; in the late 1780s and early 1790s he dominated the New York market for these small, expensive, and private portraits.

Wars, marriages, and debts, rather than the pursuit of patrons, determined many of Ramage's movements. Halifax court records document suits against him for debts in 1772 and 1774. Soon after the latter suit he moved to Boston. Extant miniatures suggest that he had Tory patronage. Although he had not been divorced, in 1776 Ramage married Maria Victoria Ball in Boston. During the American Revolution he enrolled as a second lieutenant in the Royal Irish Volunteers, which was made up of Loyalist Boston merchants; in March 1776 he fled with them to Halifax. There he married a Mrs. Taylor, whereupon his second wife divorced him. Mrs. Taylor may actually have been Elizabeth Ramage, his first wife. The couple left Halifax in 1777 so that he could avoid prosecution for bigamy and debt. Settling in New York City, Ramage shifted political alliances and served as a lieutenant in Company 7 of the City Militia in New York. He married Catherine Collins, the daughter of New York merchant John Collins, in 1787 and with her had three children, a girl and two boys.

Artist and diarist William Dunlap noted that Ramage, while in New York City, painted "all the military heroes or beaux of the garrison, and all the belles of the place." Many of his patrons, including George Washington, Alexander McDougall, Arthur St. Clair, Nicholas Gilman, and Josiah Parker, had served as officers during the Revolution. Washington noted in his diary in 1789, "Sat for Mr. Rammage [*sic*] near two hours today, who was drawing a miniature Picture of me for Mrs. Washington." Facing left in a three-quarters pose, Washington wears a dark blue coat with buff facings and gold buttons and epaulets; the depth and vibrancy of the coloring of his complexion and clothing typify Ramage's work. Like many other Ramage sitters, he chose to be portrayed after the war had ended in the military uniform that symbolized his role in the nation's founding. Yet Washington's diary entry points out that even for the most famous of patrons, Ramage's miniatures served as private, personal images intended for loved ones.

During Ramage's residence in New York City he painted prominent, wealthy men and women, including Alice deLancey Izard, Philip Van Rensselaer, Catherine Clinton Van Cortlandt, and several members of the Ludlow family. The familial, business, and political connections among these sitters suggest that Ramage probably received commissions by word of mouth. Many of his New York patrons represented families that had long ties to the city and state; their miniature portraits by the same artist, which were exchanged and viewed in closed social and familial circles, reinforced their connections to one another. Ramage's membership in the St. John Masonic Lodge, the New York Marine Society, and particularly the militia also may have helped him earn commissions. He supplemented his portrait business by producing memorial scenes, composed of ink and hair, on ivory; like his miniatures, these images were intended to be worn as jewelry and to express personal sentiments.

During this period Dunlap described Ramage as one who "dressed fashionably, and according to his time, beauishly." Dunlap remarked that Ramage "was in reality the only [miniature] artist in New-York, but he was full of employment and declined teaching." Ramage also portrayed sitters from other areas in the eastern United States, such as Benjamin Tallmadge and Jonathan Trumbull of Connecticut. It is uncertain whether these portraits were done during their visits to New York or on the artist's otherwise undocumented travels. Although Ramage received abundant portrait commissions in New York City, he fled to Montreal in 1794 to elude creditors and later died there.

Ramage's relatively small miniatures are known for their delicacy, coloring, and high amount of detail. In his miniature of Colonel Josiah Parker, for example, Ramage employed relatively broad brush strokes that nonetheless precisely delineated the sitter's hair and carefully shaped his face using a wide range of beige and grey tones. The clothing worn by Parker (and others) is presented in rich, vibrant colors with the subtleties of costume rendered in great detail. The distinctive, oval gold cases that Ramage made for his miniatures are characterized by lavish fluting and chasing. He also imported settings from London. His worktable, tools, and samples of allegorical and memorial scenes (the New-York Historical Society) indicate his diverse skills as an artist and a goldsmith. Dunlap remarked that Ramage worked in pastels; none have been firmly attributed to him. Major repositories for the approximately seventy-five images by Ramage that survive include the Yale University Art Gallery, the Museum of the City of New York, and the Metropolitan Museum of Art.

• Dale Johnson, *American Portrait Miniatures in the Manney Collection* (1990), provides a summary of Ramage's life and work. J. H. Morgan, *A Sketch of the Life of John Ramage, Miniature Painter* (1930), contains transcriptions of important manuscript materials. F. F. Sherman, *John Ramage* (1929), is another significant source. Also see W. S. Dunlap, *A History of the Rise and Progress of the Arts of Design in the U.S.* (1834).

ANNE A. VERPLANCK

RAMÉE, Joseph (26 Apr. 1764–18 May 1842), architect and landscape designer, also known as Joseph-Jacques Ramée was born in Charlemont in northern France, the son of Jacques Ramée and Anne Dieudonnée Lambert. Little is known of Ramée's parents, but an uncle, Jean-Louis Lambert, a chaplain at the Cathedral of St. Pierre in Louvain, helped raise the boy and encouraged his artistic talents. About 1780 Ramée became an apprentice to the architect François-Joseph Belanger in Paris. From Belanger, Charles-Nicolas Ledoux, and other innovators, Ramée assimilated the latest styles of neoclassical architecture, interior design, and picturesque landscape planning.

Ramée began his own practice in Paris in the late 1780s, but the Revolution disrupted his career and his life. As an aide to General Charles-François Dumouriez in 1793, Ramée supported his commander's plot against the revolutionary government, had to flee France, and became one of the proscribed émigrés. Thus began Ramée's years as a nomad. He worked successively in Belgium, Saxony, Hamburg, Mecklenburg-Schwerin, Denmark, and the United States, as wars, economic crises, and personal problems kept him on the move. While Ramée's nomadism was detrimental to his career, it is also the main reason for his historical significance, for he transmitted avant-garde ideas from one country to another and fashioned a unique synthesis of the artistic currents of the period.

Ramée's stay in the United States was brief (1812–1816) but productive. The architect was called to America by David Parish, an international financier from Hamburg. Parish had purchased large tracts of land in northern New York State, where he planned to create industrial enterprises and towns to be designed by his French architect. Most of Parish's plans never materialized, but Ramée found other clients in America, mainly in upstate New York and in the area of Baltimore and Philadelphia, where he lived with his wife, Caroline Dreyer of Hamburg, whom he had married in 1805, and their young son.

Ramée's principal work in the United States was the design of the buildings and grounds of Union College in Schenectady (1813)—the most ambitious plan for an American campus up to that time. This neoclassical scheme, much of which was executed and still exists, comprises linked buildings forming a large courtyard with a domed rotunda in the center, the whole surrounded by landscaped parkland. The design probably contributed to Thomas Jefferson's plan, four years later, for the University of Virginia. Ramée's other American works include country houses, gardens, and at least one church, St. Michael's in Antwerp, New York. Aside from the Union College project, however, Ramée was frustrated in his efforts to obtain important public commissions. He was an unsuccessful entrant in two major architectural competitions in Baltimore: those for the Washington Monument (1813) and the Baltimore Exchange (1815). Ramée's Washington Monument design, which survives, combined parkland, housing, and civic architecture in a manner unprecedented in America at that time.

After the fall of Napoleon and the Bourbon Restoration, Ramée returned to Europe and practiced in Belgium, Germany, and France until his death. In the 1820s and 1830s he published three collections of his architectural and landscape designs.

Ramée was probably the most experienced European architect to work in the United States in the early nineteenth century. He no doubt would have achieved more success, and probably would have stayed in America, if the War of 1812 and other events had not slowed building during the time he was in the country. Ramée nevertheless played an important role in American design. His Union College campus and other plans (several of which were exhibited in 1814 at the Academy of Fine Arts in Philadelphia) introduced to America a new level of sophisticated planning, especially in their integration of architecture and landscape.

• Many of Ramée's drawings for Union College are preserved at the college; the architect's design for the Washington Monument of Baltimore is in the Peale Museum in that city. The principal written records of Ramée's stay in America are found in the papers of David Parish at the New-York Historical Society and at St. Lawrence University. A brief biographical article on Ramée was published in Abbot Boulliot, *Biographie ardennaise*, vol. 2 (1830), pp. 494–96. Studies of Ramée's work in America include Harold A. Larrabee, "Joseph Jacques Ramée, Architect," *Légion d'honneur* 8 (Apr. 1938): 216–21; Roy E. Graham, "Joseph Jacques Ramée and the French Emigré Architects in America" (M.A. thesis, Univ. of Virginia, 1968); Paul F. Norton, "The Architect of Calverton," *Maryland Historical Magazine* 76 (Summer 1981): 113–23; Paul V. Turner, *Campus, an American Planning Tradition* (1984), pp. 68–75; Turner, "David Parish's Country House Reconstructed," *St. Lawrence County Historical Association Quarterly* 31 (Oct. 1986): 3–9; and Turner, *Joseph Ramée, International Architect* (1995).

PAUL V. TURNER

RAMÍREZ, Sara Estela (1881–21 Aug. 1910), poet, radical journalist, and political organizer, was born in Villa Progreso, Coahuila, Mexico. Little is known about her parents except that her mother died when Ramírez was two years old, and her father eventually immigrated to Laredo, Texas, to live with her. Ramírez attended public school in Monterrey, Nuevo León, and at seventeen years of age graduated from the teachers' college, Ateneo Fuentes, in her home state of Coahuila. Upon receiving her teaching certificate, she immediately immigrated to Laredo to teach Spanish to Tex-Mex schoolchildren at the Seminario de Laredo. Although Ramírez studied English while in Laredo, she wrote in Spanish, and it was the Mexican proletariat to whom she remained devoted.

Soon after her arrival in Texas, Ramírez became involved in the leadership and alternative press arm of the Partido Liberal Mexicano (PLM), a progressive sociopolitical group that advocated the rights of Mexican laborers. She and Ricardo Flores Magón, the group's charismatic leader, exchanged letters for years, and it was in her home in 1904 that he briefly reestablished the party's headquarters when the group was exiled from Mexico by President Profirio Díaz, the despot against whom they had organized. Ramírez served as a liaison between the group's Texan and Mexican constituencies, but more importantly, as a staunch advocate for the rights of women, she ensured the specific inclusion of women in discussions concerning economic opportunity and oppression within the ideology and agenda of the PLM.

In conjunction with her position as a PLM organizer, Ramírez made her greatest contribution through the alternative press. Her belief in the utility of the press as an apparatus that could excite and unify people is articulated in a personal letter she wrote to Magón: "We need newspapers that awaken the public spirit; the patriotism of the citizens is entangled in a terror with no name. . . . We need to educate the people and awaken their energy" (trans. Tovar, p. 121). Consequently, from the time she arrived in Laredo, she published poems, essays, and articles in support of "mutualism" and workers' rights in the local Spanish-language newspapers *La Crónica* and *El Demócrata*

Fronterizo. Like many of her colleagues, Ramírez supported the liberal party by devoting her energies to the publication of two literary magazines that incorporated and disseminated the writings of Mexicans. Published between 1904 and 1910 as platforms for political solidarity, Ramírez's magazines included *La Corregidora*, which was named after a Mexican heroine and was distributed in Laredo, San Antonio, and Mexico City, and *Aurora*, which was published daily in Laredo. Often contributing to her own periodicals, Ramírez saw poetry as a vehicle for expressing her political ideology. Eulogized as "The Texas Muse," she praised the inherent goodness of humankind in her writing and instilled an uplifting message of hope, unity, and love for laborers: "May you, beloved workers, integral part of human progress, yet celebrate, uncounted anniversaries, and with your example may you show societies how to love each other so that they may be mutualists and to unite so that they may be strong" (speech to Society of Workers on twenty-fourth anniversary of their founding; trans. Tovar, p. 189). Of her extant writings, few are as overtly political; the majority of her poems eloquently celebrate the pleasures of life, love, and friendship: "How sweet it is to live, when the seductive light of fifteen aprils flutters, inundating with reflections the path of life!; You do not know that there are shadows, do you? And if you know, it is only because someone has told you" ("A Happy World"; trans. Tovar, p. 157). Her literary career expanded into drama with the local production and performance of her play, *Noema*, in which she played a leading role. As a poet and activist, she was respected and loved by those in her community, eulogized as the "favorite of the muses," and described by a Mexican writer as "the most illustrious Mexican woman of Texas." In the states along the border, she was considered the "most noble, most sentimental and first woman poet of the region" ("The Texas Muse Is in Mourning"; trans. Tovar, p. 201).

A feminist, teacher, revolutionary, poet, and journalist, Ramírez died in Laredo after a long illness, just three months before the Mexican Revolution, for which she fought. Even though she eventually became disillusioned by the internal strife that she perceived with Magón and the PLM, she always remained true to her agenda to improve conditions for the proletariat and for women. She was part of an oppositional party that decried the position in which Mexican people were living both north and south of the Rio Grande. As a popular political and literary figure of the borderland region between Texas and northern Mexico at the turn of the century, she can be seen as a precursor to contemporary Chicana feminism, activism, and letters. Her literary contributions are important because they help to substantiate the long history of struggle and resistance of Mexicans in the borderland regions even fifty years after the annexation of the Southwest territories with the Treaty of Guadalupe Hidalgo. Her most famous poem, dedicated "to woman," continues to resonate today: "Rise up! Rise up to life, to activity, to the beauty of truly living; but rise up radiant and powerful, beautiful with qualities splendid with virtues, strong with energies" ("Rise Up"; trans. Tovar, p. 194).

• Although there are no extant copies of *La Corregidora* and *Aurora*, many of her newspaper publications can be found in the Barker Texas History Collection, Center for American History, University of Texas, Austin. Her original letters to Ricardo Flores Magón are at the Archivo General, Secretario de Relaciones Exteriores, Asunto Ricardo Flores Magón, Mexico City. The most comprehensive biography and literary analysis on Ramírez in English is Ines Hernandez Tovar, "Sara Estela Ramírez: The Early Twentieth Century Texas-Mexican Poet" (Ph.D. diss., Univ. of Houston, 1984), which includes a chapter with twenty-one recovered and translated works. For additional information on Ramírez's role in the PLM, see Emilio Zamora, "Sara Estela Ramírez: Una Rosa Roja en el Movimiento" in *Mexican Women in the United States: Struggles Past and Present*, ed. Adelaida R. Del Castillo and Magdalena Mora (1980). On the small group of women with whom Ramírez worked in the PLM, see Maria Antonieta Rascon, "La mujer y la lucha social," in *Imagen y realidad de la mujer*, ed. Elena Urrutia (1975) (in Spanish).

SUSIE LAN CASSEL

RAMSAY, Alexander (1754?–24 Nov. 1824), anatomist and physician, was born in Edinburgh, Scotland. While details of his parentage are unknown, his family seems to have been fairly prominent and wealthy. After attending college, probably at Aberdeen University, Ramsay pursued an education in medicine and anatomy. He studied in London, Edinburgh, and Dublin under several distinguished medical teachers, including William Cruikshank, Matthew Baillie, and Alexander Monro. Returning to Edinburgh in 1790, he founded an anatomical society and school, which generated enough interest to compel the University of Edinburgh to establish a chair of anatomy.

In 1802 Ramsay sailed to Boston, convinced that the United States could become the center of medical and scientific learning. After settling in Fryeburg, Maine, he began lecturing and practicing medicine. The 1803 yellow fever epidemic brought him to New York City, where he developed an innovative fever treatment. This treatment, which rejected bloodletting in favor of profuse sweats and a liberal diet, was later expounded in the July 1812 *Edinburgh Medical Journal*. Yet Ramsay spent most of his efforts planning and canvassing for an anatomical institute in Fryeburg. For years, he pursued private and public funding and tried in vain to bring the small school, library, and museum to national prominence. After a trip back to England in 1805 to receive an honorary M.D. from the University of St. Andrew's, he became involved in an unsuccessful plan to establish another medical school in New York. Despite these setbacks, he gained a reputation as an extraordinary lecturer, dissector, and anatomist. Nathan Smith enlisted Ramsay for a series of lectures at Dartmouth Medical School in 1808 and described him as "the greatest anatomist in the world."

Ramsay's abrasive personality, however, constantly hindered his success in the medical world. He was notorious for his arrogance, antagonistic behavior, and vicious temper. He openly criticized other doctors' methods and once proclaimed, "I acknowledge only two superiors as anatomists—God Almighty and [British anatomist] John Hunter." Smith and Lyman Spalding, two distinguished American physicians, were among the few people who could tolerate and befriend him. Possessing a bodily deformity, possibly the result of a childhood fall, Ramsay once became engaged in a bitter press battle with a Savannah editor who had mocked his physique. While he won the professional respect of most of his colleagues, his disfigurement and difficult nature earned him the name of the "Caliban of Science."

Ramsay returned to Europe in 1810 to lecture and solicit funds for his Fryeburg anatomical school. He maintained connections to some important English medical men, including Baillie and Sir Joseph Banks, president of the Royal Society. Ramsay had drawn and engraved anatomical plates while in Maine, and these were published in his *Anatomy of the Heart, Cranium, and Brain*, the first and only publication of a projected five volumes, issued in 1812 in London and in 1813 in Edinburgh. His work was careful and accurate, and the book met with moderate success. He also wrote several articles for English medical journals, including "The Muscular System, Its Contraction from Intellectual Influence" (*London Medical Journal* [1814]).

In 1816 Ramsay came to the United States once again. He traveled through New England, New York, and eastern Canada as an itinerant lecturer on "practical anatomy," dissection, and natural philosophy. He also brought his teaching to Savannah, Georgia, and Charleston, South Carolina, as he "thought it a duty which I owed the country to develope in the South the improvements of which Anatomy is susceptible" (Ramsay, *Address*, p. 5). The foundering Fryeburg anatomical school remained his passion, and he sought out donors in each new town. In 1819 he published the detailed prospectus for a medical institute that would specialize in anatomy and physiology. His plans included extensive demonstrations and exercises; practical experience, he argued, was essential for a complete education. He was known for his skill in preserving specimens and amassed a considerable anatomical museum. Ramsay, who never married, was teaching in Parsonsfield, Maine, when he died. He was buried in Fryeburg.

Ramsay's dedication to anatomical education directed his life and work. His teachings and writings were influential in his time, leading the New Hampshire Medical Society to elect him as an honorary member. Despite his reputation for irascibility and egotism, his contemporaries knew him as a skilled dissector, a dedicated lecturer, and an eminent anatomist.

• Ramsay's papers, including his letters, manuscripts, and drawings, are in the Maine Historical Society. Ramsay's *Prospectus of Fifteen Lectures on the Animal and Intellectual Economy of Man* (1816) and his *Address and Anatomical Prospectus* (1819) demonstrate his views on anatomy and education. Biographical information can be found in *Records of the New*

Hampshire Medical Society, 1791–1854 (1911) and in G. P. Bradley, *Transactions of the Maine Medical Association, 1883–1885*, vol. 8 (1885). James A. Spalding's article on Ramsay in *Dictionary of American Medical Biography* (1928) provides an unusually detailed sketch of his life. See also Spalding, *Dr. Lyman Spalding* (1916), and Emily A. Smith, *The Life and Letters of Nathan Smith* (1913), on his character and relationships, and Francis R. Packard, *History of Medicine in the United States* (1963), on his professional activities.

NANCY NEIMS PARKS

RAMSAY, David (2 Apr. 1749–8 May 1815), historian and politician, was born in Drumore Township, Lancaster County, Pennsylvania, the son of James Ramsay and Jane Montgomery, Protestant Irish immigrant farmers. Ramsay graduated from the College of New Jersey (now Princeton University) in 1765 and received medical training at the College of Philadelphia (1770–1773) under the tutelage of Benjamin Rush. A man of driving professional and intellectual ambition, Ramsay sought a prosperous, urban environment and in 1773 moved to Charleston, South Carolina, where he lived for most of the rest of his life.

Charleston's thriving economy and severe public health problems made an attractive field for an aspiring physician. Ramsay's rise was meteoric. Not the least of his successes were his three marriages: in 1775 to Sabina Ellis, the daughter of a prosperous merchant family (she died in 1776); in 1783 to Frances Witherspoon, the daughter of Princeton's illustrious president (she died in 1784); and, most notably, in 1787 to Martha Laurens, the daughter of Henry Laurens, one of the colony's wealthiest merchants and president of Continental Congress, who secured for him an impeccable social position and a large family. He had one child with his second wife and eleven with his third.

Marriage was only one sign of Ramsay's prominence. Through his flourishing medical practice, political activity (twenty-three years in the state legislature including six as president of the senate [1791–1797], service as a privy councillor, and two terms in the Confederation Congress and as its acting president [1785–1786]), and civic activism (as a prime mover in Charleston's many cultural, medical, and philanthropic organizations and in public-oriented economic enterprises), he found a place in the hierarchical, cosmopolitan society of late eighteenth-century Charleston. By the day of his death there—shot in the back by a deranged former patient—Ramsay was the much-respected grand old man of Charleston's intellectual elite.

From the beginning, Ramsay was a passionate opponent of British policy. His Whig values were nurtured by Princeton's blending of Christian and classical values into a potent version of radical republicanism and were strengthened while he studied medicine with Rush in the 1770s. If medicine was Ramsay's vocation, revolutionary politics was his most ardent passion. In pamphlets and public orations, in the legislature, and in military service at the sieges of Savannah (1779) and Charleston (1780) as a physician to the Charleston Battalion, he supported the movement for independence and the war effort. During the war he was an ally of the Reverend William Tennent's successful campaign to disestablish the Anglican church (1778). A member of the governor's council, Ramsay stayed in Charleston during the British siege in 1780. After the town capitulated, he was arrested by the British and exiled to St. Augustine, Florida, in 1780–1781. Ramsay and the other Charleston exiles were released in July 1781 and sent to Philadelphia.

A strong supporter of the federal Constitution in his writings and as a member of the state ratifying convention, Ramsay ran for election to the U.S. House of Representatives in 1788. Strongly suspected of favoring the abolition of slavery, he was defeated by William Loughton Smith. His connections with northern abolitionists such as Rush were well known, and in 1779, 1780, and 1782 he had been one of the few South Carolina legislators to support John Laurens's unsuccessful plan to enlist blacks in the Whig militia. His 1794 candidacy for the U.S. Senate also failed because of the slavery issue.

Ramsay's fame was less a consequence of political prominence than of his literary reputation. He was a leader in a second tier of founding fathers. Comprised of men such as historian Jeremy Belknap, geographer Jedidiah Morse, Rush, painter Charles Willson Peale, lexicographer Noah Webster, dramatist William Dunlap, and poet Philip Freneau, this group did not shape American political institutions so much as shape the way subsequent generations thought about them. They were guided by the belief that independence demanded a new intellectual agenda: to define an identity, culture, political ideology, and institutions within the framework of an American nation.

It is no exaggeration to say that Ramsay defined an American national history. Among his contemporaries he stands out not only for his productivity—six major and several minor historical works—but also for having been the first to compose histories addressed to the needs of the newly developing phenomenon of revolutionary nationalism. For Ramsay the achievement of political and cultural nationhood took on the flavor of a crusade. In a letter to Nathanael Greene, Ramsay wrote, "To reconcile to unite, or as the chemists say, to amalgamate the people into one homogeneous body would be a divine work" (10 Sept. 1782; South Caroliniana Library, Univ. of S.C., Columbia).

If any one work marked the beginnings of an American national historical consciousness, it was Ramsay's *History of the American Revolution* (1789). From 1789 to 1865 it went through six American editions, including a serialization in the *Columbian Magazine*, as well as two English, two French, and Irish, German, and Dutch editions.

Although Ramsay's deepest ambition for the nation was to "reconcile to unite," the route was filled with unexpected pitfalls. By the 1790s Ramsay and many of his intellectual colleagues were becoming increasingly frustrated with the prospects for a truly national society and a cultural renaissance, despite the ratification of the federal Constitution. Ramsay also feared that the reformation of society he believed inherent in the Revolution and republicanism would not be realized, especially as symbolized by the issue of slavery, the trauma of personal political defeat in 1788, and the deep political divisions in the revolutionary generation in the 1790s. Ramsay's goal remained the same, but the stark nationalism of the *History of the American Revolution* moved to an ethic of particularism within a nationalist framework as expressed in his *History of South Carolina* (1809). These two works stood as prototypes for Ramsay's generation, and he became the nation's most respected historian and one of its premier literary figures. "America has produced a Ramsay," exulted James K. Polk, who read Ramsay's history as a student at the University of North Carolina. He is "the Tacitus of this western hemisphere to transmit to posterity in the unpolished language of truth, the spirit of liberty which actuated the first founders of the republic."

• Any study of David Ramsay should begin with Robert L. Brunhouse's "David Ramsay, 1749–1815: Selections From His Writings," comprising the entire issue of American Philosophical Society, *Transactions*, n.s., 55 (1965), which contains much of Ramsay's correspondence, reprints of four of his shorter published works, and a complete bibliography of his writings. Among Ramsay's most important writings are *An Oration on the Advantages of American Independence* (1778), *History of the Revolution of South Carolina* (1785), *The History of the American Revolution* (1789), *A Dissertation on the Means of Preserving Health, in Charleston and the Adjacent Low Country* (1790), *An Oration in Commemoration of American Independence* (1794), *A Sketch of the Soil, Climate, Weather, and Diseases of South Carolina* (1796), *A Review of the Improvements, Progress and State of Medicine in the XVIIITH Century* (1801), *The History of South Carolina* (1809), *Memoir of the Life of Martha Laurens Ramsay* (1811), and *The History of the United States* (1816–1817).

The most complete assessment is Arthur H. Shaffer, *To Be an American: David Ramsay and the Making of the American Consciousness* (1991). See also Lawrence J. Friedman, *Inventors of the Promised Land* (1975); Eve Kornfeld, "From Republicanism to Liberalism: The Intellectual Journey of David Ramsay," *Journal of the Early Republic* 9 (1989): 289–314; Page Smith, "David Ramsay and the Causes of the American Revolution," *William and Mary Quarterly* 17 (1960): 51–77; Lester H. Cohen, *The Revolutionary Histories: Contemporary Narratives of the American Revolution* (1980); Shaffer, *The Politics of History: Writing the History of the American Revolution, 1783–1815* (1975), on his historical thought and writing; and Friedman and Shaffer, "History, Politics and Health in Early American Thought: The Case of David Ramsay," *Journal of American Studies* 13 (1979): 37–56, on his medical thought and practice. An obituary is Robert Y. Hayne, "Biographical Memoir of David Ramsay, M.D.," *Analectic Magazine* 6 (1815): 204–14.

ARTHUR SHAFFER

RAMSAY, Francis Munroe (5 Apr. 1835–19 July 1914), naval officer, was born in Washington, D.C., the son of George Douglas Ramsay, a brevet major general in the U.S. Army, and Frances Whetcroft Munroe. Francis was appointed a midshipman from Pennsylva-

nia in 1850 and spent one year at the U.S. Naval Academy. He served from 1851 to 1855 with the Pacific Squadron on the practice ship *Preble* and on the *St. Lawrence*. Returning to Annapolis, he graduated in 1856 and was promoted to passed midshipman. He subsequently served in the Brazil Squadron on the *Falmouth*, in the Pacific Squadron on the *Merrimac*, in the African Squadron on the *Saratoga*, and at the Washington Navy Yard. He was raised to lieutenant in 1858 and lieutenant commander in 1862.

During the Civil War Ramsay held a number of commands, the first being the *Choctaw* in the Mississippi Squadron in 1863. In April he performed well for the squadron and was commended for his actions while his ship was under fire. At the end of April he participated in a feigned attack, at Haynes' Bluff on the Yazoo River, that was so well done that the *Choctaw* was hit over fifty times by Confederate fire. Between the 18th and 23d of May the *Choctaw*, along with other vessels, was involved in an attack on Haynes' Bluff and Yazoo City. At Yazoo City the squadron destroyed three Confederate vessels that were under construction. On 7 June the *Choctaw* repulsed another Confederate assault on a Union garrison at Milliken's Bend. Ramsay commanded a battery of three guns on scows in the battle of Vicksburg, where his command was noted by his commander, Acting Rear Admiral David D. Porter, for its actions: "Every gun the enemy could bring to bear on these boats were fired incessantly at them, but without one moment's cessation of fire on the part of our seamen, though the enemy's shot and shell fell like hail around them. This battery completely enfiladed [*sic*] the batteries and rifle-pits in front of General Sherman and made them untenable." He was also commended along with other commanders, by Porter "for their active and energetic attention to all my orders, and their ready cooperation with the army corps commanders at all times, which enabled them to carry out their plans successfully" (U.S. Naval War Records Office, vol. 25, 277–78).

From July 1863 to September 1864 Ramsay was in command of the Third District of the Mississippi River, including the USS *Chillicothe*. He was involved in skirmishes at Trinity and Harrisonburg, Louisiana, and captured a battery of thirty-pounder rifles near Simmesport, Louisiana. Posted next to Washington, from there he was sent to the command of the gunboat *Unadilla* in the North Atlantic Blockading Squadron. He attacked Fort Fisher in December 1864 and January 1865 and later was involved in attacks on Fort Anderson on the Cape Fear River. He led an expedition on the James River that successfully neutralized all of the enemy torpedoes there and was present at the capture of Richmond.

For a year after the war Ramsay served at the Naval Academy as senior instructor in gunnery and assistant to the commandant. In 1866 he was promoted to commander and served at the Washington Navy Yard, as chief of staff in the South Atlantic Squadron, as commander of the *Guerriere*, and in the Bureau of Ordnance. In 1869 he married Anna Josephine McMahon in Buenos Aires. They had three children. From 1872 to 1873 he was naval attaché in London and then commanded the *Ossipee* in 1874. He next commanded the *Lancaster* and served in the Naval Asylum and at the New York Navy Yard. After being promoted to captain in 1877, he commanded the Torpedo Station and then the *Trenton*, the flagship of the European Station.

In 1881 Ramsay was named superintendent of the Naval Academy, the first alumnus to be promoted into this position. While commandant, he tried to improve discipline; however, his attempt resulted in a lowering of morale and a near mutiny. Severe punishment was meted out to those who disobeyed. For example, twenty cadets were disciplined on graduation day in 1883 for the crime of applauding against orders. Ramsay was supported by the secretary of the navy, but discontent against him still persisted in the unit. Ramsay also revised instruction, moving the professional subjects into the fourth year and abolishing electives. In addition, subjects were limited, and those retained were augmented. Teaching was held to a minimum, and memory and recitation were emphasized, with little presentation of differing views. A good number were not sad to see him leave in 1886.

In 1886 Ramsay was assigned to the Naval Examining Board, and from 1887 to 1888 he commanded the *Boston*. In 1888 he headed the New York Navy Yard, and the following year he was promoted to commodore. Later that same year he was appointed chief of the Bureau of Navigation and was named again to that position in 1893. In 1894 he assumed the rank of rear admiral, and he retired upon reaching the age limit in 1897. His last active duties were on the board of awards dealing with the battle of Santiago and as a member of the Winfield Scott Schley court of inquiry, along with Admiral George Dewey and Rear Admiral Arthur E. K. Benham. He was a member of the Metropolitan Club, Loyal Legion, and Foreign Wars. He died in Washington, D.C. Ramsay was a successful naval officer who served his country well but who stumbled somewhat in his leadership of Annapolis.

• Some of Ramsay's letters are in the U.S. Naval War College Collection, 1884–1914, at the Library of Congress and in the William Alexander Kirkland Papers, East Carolina Manuscript Collection, East Carolina University Library. U.S. Naval War Records Office, *The Official Records of the Union and Confederate Navies in the War of the Rebellion*, ser. 1, vols. 24–26 (30 vols., 1894–1922), presents all of the official correspondence from Ramsay's Civil War actions. U.S. Naval History Division, *Civil War Naval Chronology, 1861–1865* (1971), gives abbreviated descriptions of the battles in which Ramsay was involved. See also L. R. Hamersly, *The Records of Living Officers of the U.S. Navy and Marine Corps*, 4th ed. (1890); and Robert U. Johnson and Clarence C. Buel, eds., *Battles and Leaders of the Civil War*, vol. 3, (1884). John E. Jessup, ed. in chief, and Louise B. Ketz, exec. ed., *Encyclopedia of the American Military: Studies of the History, Traditions, Policies, Institutions, and Roles of the Armed Forces in War and Peace*, vol. 3 (1994), discusses Ramsay's leadership at Annapolis. Obituaries are in the *New York Times*, 21 July 1914, and the *Army and Navy Register*, 25 July 1914.

SCOTT A. MERRIMAN

RAMSAY, Martha Laurens (3 Nov. 1759–10 June 1811), diarist, was born in Charleston, South Carolina, the daughter of Henry Laurens, a wealthy merchant, and Eleanor Ball. As a little girl, Martha, the "apple of a father's eye," was tutored with her only surviving older sibling, John. Serious and precocious, reflecting her Huguenot and Protestant Episcopalian heritage, she began to read at age three. In 1770 her mother died after giving birth to an infant girl. Subsequently Martha and her baby sister were reared by their paternal uncle, James, a book importer and merchant, and his wife, Mary, who were childless. Martha was instructed in an expansive range of subjects, including botany ("drawings from Nature"), French, harpsichord, and the new topic of geography. But her father reminded her that, along with "studying the globes," she also had to master the making of "a plumb pudding" and other essentials of household management. Only a few meditations and letters survive from this youthful period. But on her deathbed, in addition to revealing the existence of her diary, Martha commended to her husband a more remarkable document, written when she was fourteen. A "self-dedication and solemn covenant with God," after the model of British pietist Phillip Doddridge, this personal "constitution" had functioned as her lifelong spiritual reference point, a psychic standard against which she secretly, critically, measured herself in the diary.

Martha spent her late adolescence in England and then in France, where her uncle's household had relocated in 1775 because of his deteriorating health and British hostility to Americans during the revolutionary war. She helped nurse her uncle and aunt, endowed a school for children in their French village, tutored her little sister, and—her most direct political action—petitioned the American representatives in Europe, Benjamin Franklin (1706–1790) and John Adams (1735–1826), to obtain her father's release from imprisonment in London after his capture while on a diplomatic mission to Holland. Her brief courtship with a middle-aged French businessman evoked opposition from her father, who after his release had gone to Bath, England, to recover his health. To nurse him back to health, Martha then traveled unaccompanied across France, "very much the modern woman," in her father's admiring description. When Henry Laurens was appointed one of the three U.S. peace negotiators (1782–1784), she enjoyed a public role as his hostess and secretary—the best clerk he ever had, he later said.

Returning from her European sojourn in 1785, Martha assumed educational, spiritual, and managerial responsibility for her own younger sister, now fifteen; for Fanny, aged six, her war-hero brother's orphaned daughter; and for her father, whose health remained frail. During those first months back in Charleston, Martha became acquainted with his attending physician, Dr. David Ramsay. In January 1787 she became his third wife and mother to the infant son he brought from his second marriage. An appropriate spouse for a Laurens heiress, David was a prominent public figure and a member of the new nation's literati. During their 24-year marriage, David published six more histories and, unusual for his time, gave Martha public credit for her research assistance and intellectual companionship. The couple idealized large republican families and produced eleven children, eight of whom were living when Martha died.

Martha's own background, marriage, and the marriages of her sister and brother into leading families (Pinckney and Rutledge) positioned her in the center of Charlestonian public and intellectual life. She kept abreast of modern trends in education, reading, for example, her friend Benjamin Rush's *Thoughts on the Education of Females* (1789) and constructing her own curriculum for her children. She prepared her oldest son in Latin and Greek for college. Her enlightened pedagogy disdained rote learning in favor of "the substance, not the words of what they read," and she developed her own "packets of historic questions" as a "text" for ensuring comprehension. Her own cosmopolitan reading ranged from Plutarch, Rousseau, and Locke, across Mary Wollstonecraft and the novels of Samuel Richardson, to poetry, including Edward Young's *Night Thoughts* (of which she memorized "almost the entirety"), and hymns of Issac Watts. She enjoyed spiritually articulate Englishwomen like her father's friend, the countess of Huntingdon, and the learned Elizabeth Carter, whose memoirs Martha read a few months before she died. She also exchanged copies of British theological writers with pastors from the Independent Congregational Church in Charleston, which she had joined on marrying David.

Martha remembered 1795 as "the worst year" of her life. Contributing to her depression were ever-deepening financial stringencies resulting from unwise investments and ruinous inflation; the elopement at eighteen of her ward and niece, Fanny, with an unsuitable older man; and anxieties about the future of her children, particularly marriageable daughters without dowries. The literary outpouring of those dark days reveals an articulate woman in extremis, regaining her spiritual equilibrium by literally writing herself back to emotional health in the only psychologically analytic language available to her, Protestant Calvinist religion. Martha lived for another fifteen years, her health gradually worsening and their finances continuing to be "straitened." Nevertheless she enjoyed the respect of her community and was the fond kinkeeper in an extensive household that encompassed three more children born after 1795, students who boarded, and visitors to Charleston. Her death in Charleston after three years of an unnamed debilitating illness was noted as far afield as Boston's *Columbian Centinel* (14 Aug. 1811).

Martha's dying commission was that her newly revealed "private papers" be kept as a "common book of the family," suggesting that she assented to a print memorial. David's motives for creating the *Memoirs*, a collection of her diary and writings, blended the historical and the uxorial. Patriot and moralist, he embraced any opportunity to shape the culture of a new nation. Turning her "literary remains" into a published book allowed David to place a female in the emerging pantheon of "great Americans" and to transform his grief into a prescription for women in the new republic. Her literary work, which originated as a spiritual conversation, contrasts with that of her male contemporaries, whose writings were intended to be read without reference to their daily lives. It also differs from that of the exceptional female journalist of the era, Judith Sargent Murray, who explicitly chose a public authorial voice. Understanding the passionate self-examination confided to Ramsay's journal requires a contextual knowledge of her kinship and religious communities, the daily rituals of family life, and the evolving political sensibilities of the times. Her words themselves, typical of the genre of eighteenth-century diary keepers, were more concerned with deciphering God's hand in the crises that evoked them than with depicting the actual events. Martha Laurens Ramsay's record of spiritual struggle and survival was cited as a model throughout the nineteenth century, institutionally in such journals as the *American Sunday School Union* and personally in the private diaries of numerous women readers. The *Memoirs* were reprinted at least ten times up to the 1890s.

• Primary sources for Mary Laurens Ramsay's writings (the original diary itself has apparently long since disappeared) beyond the version in the *Memoirs of the Life of Martha Laurens Ramsay* (1811), are the published collections of her father's and husband's papers: Philip A. Hamer, *The Henry Laurens Papers*, vol. 1 (1968), and Robert L. Brunhouse, ed., *David Ramsay, 1749–1815, Selections from His Writings*, Transactions of the American Philosophical Society, n.s. 55, pt. 4 (1965), pp. 3–250. Other letters from, to, or about her are found in the South Caroliniana Library, Columbia, the South Carolina Historical Society, Charleston, and the Kendall collection, Kendall Whaling Museum, Sharon, Mass. Arthur H. Schaffer, *To Be an American: David Ramsay and the Making of the American Consciousness* (1991), a biography of David Ramsay, incorporates her life and contributions. David D. Wallace, *The Life of Henry Laurens* (1915), is essential background. Other essays include two by J. B. Gillespie, "Many Gracious Providences: The Religious Cosmos of Martha Laurens Ramsay (1759–1811)," *Colby Library Quarterly* 25 (Sept. 1990): 199–212, and "1795: Martha Laurens Ramsay's Dark Night of the Soul," *William and Mary Quarterly*, 3d ser., 48 (Jan. 1991): 68–92.

JOANNA BOWEN GILLESPIE

RAMSEUR, Stephen Dodson (31 May 1837–20 Oct. 1864), Confederate soldier, was born in Lincolnton, North Carolina, the son of Jacob A. Ramseur, a merchant, and Lucy Mayfield Dodson. A member of the slaveholding class, Ramseur received the best local schooling before spending September 1853–April 1855 at Davidson College. He won appointment in 1855 to West Point, where he became a captain in the Battalion of Cadets and graduated fourteen in the 41-member class of 1860. Described later by a classmate as "a respected, honored, and loved" cadet, he was brevetted second lieutenant on 1 July 1860 and assigned to the Third Artillery. Promotion to second lieutenant of the Fourth Artillery came on 19 March 1861 (to date from 1 Feb.).

Ramseur never took up his new assignment. He had predicted in 1856 that "the Union of the States cannot exist harmoniously" because northerners threatened slavery—" the very source of our existence, the *greatest blessing* both for master & slave." Resigning his commission on 6 April 1861, well before North Carolina seceded, he was commissioned first lieutenant in the Confederate artillery on 22 April. Elected captain of the Ellis Light Artillery of Raleigh (later designated Company A, Tenth Regiment, N.C. State Troops), Ramseur briefly commanded that battery before receiving promotion to major of artillery to rank from 16 May. His gunners fired the salvos that marked North Carolina's withdrawal from the Union on 20 May 1861 before transferring to Virginia in late July. Ramseur subsequently commanded a battalion of artillery under John Bankhead Magruder on the Virginia Peninsula and saw initial action in a skirmish at Dam Number 1 near Yorktown on 16 April 1862.

Ambitious for higher rank, Ramseur was commissioned colonel of the Forty-ninth North Carolina Infantry on 28 April 1862 (to rank from 12 Apr.). He drilled the regiment in North Carolina before returning to the peninsula to join Robert Ransom's brigade of Benjamin Huger's division. Ramseur's major action as colonel of the Forty-ninth came on 1 July 1862 at Malvern Hill, where he received a serious wound in his right arm. He convalesced for six months, a period that brought promotion to brigadier general and command of the brigade that had been George Burgwyn Anderson's. Recovered by January 1863, Ramseur took charge of his brigade, which consisted of the Second, Fourth, Fourteenth, and Thirtieth North Carolina Regiments, and served in Robert E. Rodes's division of Thomas "Stonewall" Jackson's Second Corps.

Over the next sixteen months, Ramseur fashioned a record as one of the most aggressive and successful brigade commanders in the Army of Northern Virginia. A deeply religious Presbyterian, he seemed transformed by battle. His fearlessness became "conspicuous throughout the army," observed one of his subordinates. Another officer noted that he "absolutely reveled in the fierce joys of the strife, his whole being seemed to kindle and burn and glow amid the excitement of danger." The brigade fought doggedly and suffered ghastly casualties at Chancellorsville on 3 May 1863, a performance for which Ramseur, who suffered a second wound, received praise from both Robert E. Lee and Jackson. His men helped break the Union line on Seminary Ridge on 1 July at Gettysburg, participated in the Mine Run campaign, and fought again at the Wilderness on 6 May 1864. Ramseur's finest hour as a brigadier came at Spotsylvania on 12 May 1864, when his regiments mounted a memorable counterattack in the "Mule Shoe" salient. Wounded for a third time, Ramseur was summoned to army headquarters to receive Lee's personal thanks.

Superior service as a brigadier brought assignment on 27 May to head the division formerly under Jubal A. Early, who had been elevated to corps command. He fumbled at Bethesda Church on 30 May but acquitted himself well at Cold Harbor several days later. Ramseur was promoted to major general on 1 June 1864, the day after his twenty-seventh birthday, making him the youngest West Pointer to achieve that rank in Confederate service. In mid-June he and his division accompanied Early and the Second Corps to the Shenandoah Valley.

Ramseur exhibited aptitude for division leadership. His soldiers led Early's column that saved Lynchburg from a Union force under David Hunter on 17–18 June and fought at the battle of the Monocacy on 9 July. Sloppy reconnaissance produced a humiliating reverse at Stephenson's Depot on 20 July, a debacle Ramseur ungenerously blamed on subordinates and men in the ranks. At Third Winchester on 19 September, Ramseur's soldiers overcame initial problems to wage a stalwart defense against imposing odds. Three days later at Fisher's Hill, Ramseur commanded the division of Rodes, who had been killed at Third Winchester. Slow to react to a Federal flank attack, he saw the brigades break and flee the field.

Ramseur's growth as a division leader showed at Cedar Creek on 19 October 1864. His brigades contributed to stunning Confederate success in the morning, then anchored Early's defense as Federal pressure mounted in the late afternoon. Married since the previous October to his cousin Ellen Richmond, Ramseur had learned three days before the battle of the birth of their only child (a daughter—though he did not know it). At Cedar Creek he wore a flower in his lapel to honor the child and seemed to be infused with tremendous energy. One brigadier wrote, "His presence and manner was electrical." At about 5:00 P.M., as Ramseur steadied his troops in the face of Federal assaults, a musket ball pierced his side and punctured both lungs. Captured during a chaotic Confederate retreat and taken to Federal headquarters at Belle Grove, he died the next morning. His body was passed through the lines near Richmond on 3 November.

• The bulk of Ramseur's revealing personal correspondence is in the Southern Historical Collection at the University of North Carolina at Chapel Hill. A smaller collection of papers is at the North Carolina Department of Archives and History in Raleigh. A modern biography is Gary W. Gallagher, *Stephen Dodson Ramseur: Lee's Gallant General* (1985). Also useful are William Ruffin Cox, *Address on the Life and Character of Maj. Gen. Stephen D. Ramseur before the Ladies' Memorial Association of Raleigh, N.C., May 10th, 1891* (1891), and, for Ramseur's relations with other members of the high command of Lee's army, Douglas Southall Freeman, *Lee's Lieutenants: A Study in Command* (3 vols., 1942–1944).

GARY W. GALLAGHER

RAMSEY, Paul (10 Dec. 1913–20 Feb. 1988), theologian and ethicist, was born Robert Paul Ramsey in Mendenhall, Mississippi, the son of John William Ramsey, a Methodist minister, and Mamie McCay. After receiving his B.S. from Millsaps College (1935), he enrolled at Yale Divinity School, earning a B.D. (1940) and Ph.D. (1943). In 1937 he married Effie Register; they had three daughters. Ramsey began his teaching career in 1942 at Garrett Theological Seminary in Evanston, Illinois; he left Garrett for Princeton University's new Department of Religion in 1944 and remained there until his retirement in 1982.

Ramsey made significant contributions to the understanding of theological concepts in Christian ethics. Heavily influenced by the neo-orthodox movement in Protestantism, he tried to reconcile critical historical scholarship with appreciation for the insight found in the Bible and in Christian theology.

In *Basic Christian Ethics* (1950) Ramsey argued that a core message could be extracted from the apocalyptic and mythological language of the Bible. He believed that as God has acted to meet our needs associated with guilt and anxiety, so we must act toward others to meet their more mundane needs for assistance, protection, and community. Ramsey thought that Christianity directed people to focus on the needs of others, not the self. The effect was a radically altruistic ethic of love that had little to do with emotions; love was not a feeling but a duty to commit oneself to the protection of the weak and needy.

Ramsey went to Yale Divinity School as a pacifist and conscientious objector to World War II. The justification of killing preoccupied him throughout the 1940s, and it is the central moral issue discussed in *Basic Christian Ethics*: How can love of my neighbor be reconciled with killing him? Ramsey worked out an answer that led him to give up his pacifism: I may be justified in killing my neighbor if that killing is necessary to protect someone else. In effect, Ramsey shifted the focus from the person killed to the person who could be saved by the killing of a threatening other. This argument separated him from Protestant pacifists.

Beginning in the mid-1950s Ramsey disagreed with the exclusive concern of "realists" such as Reinhold Niebuhr and John C. Bennett with the consequences of actions. He insisted that the love commandment not only could require going to war, it could specify conduct that was morally impermissible in war. Horrible as war was, it could be conducted morally. That meant, for Ramsey, that innocent persons should be protected, whether they be the noncombatant citizens of one's own country or the enemy's.

In *War and the Christian Conscience* (1961) and in articles later collected in *The Just War* (1968), Ramsey defended the notion of "noncombatant immunity" from direct attack. Noncombatants were the innocent; direct attack was intentional attack. To explicate these concepts, Ramsey drew on Roman Catholic moral theology, notably the "rule of double effect," which asserts a morally significant difference between the intended objective of an action and its accidental consequences. Ramsey never said that consequences were irrelevant, but his argument directed attention to the questions of agency and means. He insisted that direct attack on civilians could never be justified, no matter what the goodness of the cause. At the same time, he tolerated unintentional "collateral damage" to civilians.

From the late 1960s on Ramsey defended U.S. involvement in Vietnam; in fact, he was more a critic of critics of the war than a true believer. He took his stand at the podium, in the press, and in scholarly writing at considerable cost to the regard in which he was held among some academics. His style in debate was passionate and unyielding; he assumed that he held the high ground. He believed most U.S. actions in Vietnam were legitimate with reference to noncombatant immunity, and he thought he (and his opponents) had no expertise on the justification of the American cause. He could not share in the distrust of political and military authority that characterized so much opposition to the war.

Ramsey's intellectual engagement with issues of the morality of military action led him to make the most extensive and sympathetic Protestant use of concepts from Catholic moral theology in at least a century. Further, as opposition to the war grew among the Protestant clergy, Ramsey was pushed to address the question of the role of a theological moralist—and of churches as institutions—in political controversy. In *Who Speaks for the Church?* (1967) he held that the church should form conscience and teach principles and concepts but not make judgments about specific policies except in rare cases.

During this peak period of activity—from the early 1960s into the 1980s—Ramsey refined his method of work. On the one hand, he established the practice of basing most of his arguments on specific examples or difficult cases, an approach in which he was encouraged by the work of legal scholar Edmund Cahn. On the other hand, he insisted that these analyses could produce some well-nigh exceptionless rules, and he was a vigorous critic of the "situation ethics" associated with Joseph Fletcher and John A. T. Robinson.

Ramsey's writings on war led directly to his work on medical ethics. His prior study of concepts like the principle of the double effect built a natural bridge to discussion of abortion and euthanasia. After spending extensive time at the Georgetown University Medical Center, Ramsey wrote *The Patient as Person* (1970), one of the best books of the second half of his career. He argued that love or care for another is compatible with "allowing to die" but not with active euthanasia. He also defended the necessity for subject consent in all uses of human beings as research subjects, suggesting the morally problematic character of the use of children as research subjects for procedures or medicines that are not intended for their benefit.

Ramsey's public persona was bluff and sometimes brusque. Although he was not himself an ordained minister, his roots in a Mississippi Methodist parsonage were not hard to discern. To colleagues and students he was an indefatigable friend and conversation partner; his personal advice was invariably pragmatic, down-to-earth, and insightful. Ramsey died in Princeton, New Jersey.

Ramsey's interpretation of the love commandment set the terms of discussion in Christian ethics in the United States for two decades. He was a leader in opening Christian ethics to the work of analytical philosophy. Drawing heavily on work in Catholic moral theology, he helped to establish a pattern of Catholic-Protestant discussion in ethics so pervasive that it is difficult to recall a time when it did not exist. His proposed principles for dealing with issues of war and medicine were immediately important and remain so.

• Ramsey's papers are in the Duke University Library. His *Deeds and Rules in Christian Ethics* (1967) was occasioned by the "situation ethics" discussion; his last methodological statement was his introduction to *The Works of Jonathan Edwards: Ethical Writings* (1989). His *Ethics at the Edges of Life* (1978) is primarily concerned with euthanasia and abortion and stresses the more conservative themes of *The Patient as Person*. An excellent selection of Ramsey's writings is William Werpehowski and Stephen D. Crocco, eds., *The Essential Paul Ramsey: A Collection* (1994). A book-length commentary on Ramsey's work is Charles E. Curran, *Politics, Medicine, and Christian Ethics* (1973). Discussion of Ramsey's interpretation of the love commandment appears in Gene Outka, *Agape: An Ethical Analysis* (1972); for a thoughtful assessment by a contemporary see James M. Gustafson, *Ethics from a Theocentric Perspective*, vol. 2 (1984), pp. 84–94. D. Stephen Long, *Tragedy, Tradition, Transformation: The Ethics of Paul Ramsey* (1993), is a full-length study.

DAVID H. SMITH

RAND, Ayn (2 Feb. 1905–6 Mar. 1982), writer and philosopher, was born Alissa Rosenbaum in St. Petersburg, Russia, the daughter of Fronz Rosenbaum, a chemist of Jewish descent, and Anna (maiden name unknown). The Russian Revolution, the beginning of which Rand witnessed when she was twelve years old, changed her life. Her family lost its financial and social position, and the remainder of her education, including the study of history at the University of Leningrad (1921–1924), was conducted according to Bolshevik guidelines. Rejecting communist economic and social ideology but not its opposition to religion—Rand abandoned her religious heritage first for secular agnosticism and later for militant atheism—she left the Soviet Union in 1926. She changed her name to Ayn (rhymes with "mine") Rand (for the Remington-Rand typewriter that she brought with her) when she came to America. After a brief stay with relatives in Chicago, she made her way to California, where she worked as a Hollywood extra and then as a scriptwriter for two years and in wardrobe for another four. She became a naturalized citizen in 1931.

In Hollywood Rand worked hard to improve her English so that she might sell her fiction. Early attempts to find publishers were frustrated by what readers called a style that was too obscure, characters that were too stereotypical, and a philosophy that was too obvious and strident. At last in 1934 she succeeded with a play, *Penthouse Legen*, which was staged in Hollywood as *Woman on Trial* and then in New York as

The Night of January 16th. From 1935, when the play had its run, until 1943 she lived in New York City, working as a secretary for the Ely Jacques Kahn architectural firm. During that time she published two novels, *We the Living* (1936) and *Anthem* (London, 1938). *We the Living* also had a very brief (five-day) run on Broadway as *The Unconquered* in February 1940. Using her experience in the architectural firm as background, she began writing the novel that would make her name, *The Fountainhead* (1943). Reviews of her third novel were generally unfavorable, but it still became a word-of-mouth bestseller. It is the story of Howard Roark, an architect who is such an individualist and so honorable (that is, so true to himself) that when one of his designs is modified (in his view, adulterated) by mediocre minds, he destroys his own work. For the rest of her life Rand expanded on this theme.

Rand returned to Hollywood in 1943 to write the screenplay for *The Fountainhead*, which was finally released in 1949 (starring Gary Cooper and Patricia Neal), and she stayed to write a number of other screenplays for the Hal Wallis Studios. As a fervent anticommunist, she volunteered to testify against other screenwriters before the House Un-American Activities Committee in 1947. From 1943 until its publication in 1957, she worked on the book that many say is her masterpiece, *Atlas Shrugged*. This novel describes how a genius named John Galt grows weary of supporting a society of ungrateful parasites and one day simply shrugs and walks away. He becomes an inspiration to like-minded men and women, all of whom eventually follow his example, until society, in its agony, calls them back to responsibility and respect. Again reviews were unsympathetic, and again people bought the book.

After *Atlas Shrugged* Rand turned to nonfiction in an attempt to answer the moral and philosophical questions that her novels had raised among both her fans and critics. From 1961 until her death more than twenty years later, she published numerous philosophical treatises: *For the New Intellectual* (1961), *The Virtue of Selfishness* (1964), *Capitalism: The Unknown Ideal* (1966), *Introduction to Objectivist Epistemology* (1967), *The Romantic Manifesto* and *The New Left: The Anti-Industrial Revolution* (1971), and *Philosophy: Who Needs It?* (1982). Much that appeared in these books had been published previously in Rand's successful periodicals, the *Objectivist Newsletter* (1962–1965), *The Objectivist* (1966–1971), and the *Ayn Rand Letter* (1971–1976). Her philosophy clarified, defended, and expanded on her fiction. It advocated radical individualism, strongly defended capitalism, and decried religion. It appealed to readers who dreamed of succeeding in a system free of all restraint—as well as to those who had succeeded and sought assurance that they deserved the rewards they were enjoying.

Soon after her arrival in Hollywood in 1926, Rand met and three years later married actor Frank O'Connor. They remained married until his death in 1979. He followed her and her career to New York in

1935, back to California in 1943, and back again permanently to New York in 1951, always finding work that enabled him to concentrate his energies on Rand, especially on bolstering her work. It was her decision that they not have children. It was in deference to her that he abandoned his Roman Catholicism. Even her longtime affair with her young disciple Nathaniel Branden did not lead to separation or even public estrangement.

Rand met Branden in 1950, when as a UCLA student he wrote her a fan letter. He became first her adoring pupil; then in the mid-1950s, despite his own marriage to Barbara Weidman, her lover; and finally manager and spokesman for her philosophical movement. Soon after he entered graduate school at New York University in 1951, Rand followed him and Weidman to New York. Later she insisted that the school for training her followers in objectivism, located in Manhattan, be called the Nathaniel Branden Institute. There, in a series of well-attended—and profitable—lectures, Branden expounded Rand's doctrines to her converts. After eighteen mutually beneficial years their relationship ended when Rand learned that he had another lover. In violent hysteria she severed her relations with both Brandens and ordered her followers to have nothing more to do with either of them.

After 1968, the year of the schism, Rand's literary and philosophical life slowly came to an end. Following major surgery for cancer in 1975, she discontinued her newsletter. The death of Frank O'Connor in 1979, the year of their fiftieth wedding anniversary, left her alone. She died three years later in her East Thirty-fourth Street apartment, attended only by a nurse. She is buried in Kensico Cemetery in Valhalla, New York.

Rand's objectivism, as exemplified in her novels and explained in her philosophical writings, stands in sharp contrast to what she condemned as the socialistic, relativistic, fuzzy-minded dominant philosophies of the twentieth century. It holds that "objective reality exists independently of any perceiver or of the perceiver's emotions, feelings, wishes, hopes, or fears" and that the human mind is capable of perceiving, understanding, interpreting, and applying this objective reality to all of life. Objectivist reasoning and action lead inevitably to an ethic of self-interest, for "the pursuit of his own happiness is a man's highest moral purpose." Self-interest in turn leads to capitalism and atheism. In Rand's words, "I am not primarily an advocate of capitalism, but of egoism; and I am not primarily an advocate of egoism, but of reason." Her fiction and philosophy have no shades of grays. Asked once if she really believed that all issues are black and white, Rand replied without pause, "You're damned right I do."

Assessments of Ayn Rand's fiction are inevitably affected by the reader's reaction to her philosophy. Her novels cannot be separated from her philosophy, which admits no middle ground. It is virtually impossible to be objective about objectivism. Thus Rand is destined to be one of the most controversial writers—and thinkers—of her time.

• Much of Rand's correspondence from 1926 to 1981 has been published in *Letters of Ayn Rand*, ed. Michael S. Berliner, with an introduction by Leonard Peikoff (1955). Barbara Branden and Nathaniel Branden, *Who Is Ayn Rand?* (1962), written six years before their break with Rand, provides the first biography as well as the first careful explanation of Rand's philosophy. It is still valuable. Barbara Branden, *The Passion of Ayn Rand* (1986), is both a biography of Rand and a memoir of Branden's years as one of Rand's disciples. It provides important information about Rand's effect on the Brandens, who divorced, as well as on other devotees (some former) of objectivism. *Judgment Day: My Years with Ayn Rand* (1989) is Nathaniel Branden's version of the objectivist experience. It is not as well written as *The Passion of Ayn Rand*, and it is gratuitous, but despite the self-pitying tone, it does provide an important perspective on the ordeal of Rand's life. For Rand's early years and education in Russia see Chris Matthew Sciabarra, *Ayn Rand: The Russian Radical* (1995). A critical but not wholly unsympathetic profile is Claudia Roth Pierpont, "Twilight of the Goddess," *New Yorker*, 24 July 1995, pp. 70–81. A substantial obituary, beginning with her photo on p. 1, is in the *New York Times*, 7 Mar. 1982.

JAMES T. BAKER

RAND, Edward Kennard (20 Dec. 1871–28 Oct. 1945), educator and scholar, was born in Boston, Massachusetts, the son of Edward Augustus Rand, a Congregational minister who turned Episcopalian in 1880, and Mary Frances Abbot. After graduating with an A.B. summa cum laude from Harvard University in 1894, he was drawn toward two different fields of professional activity, the clergy and college teaching. He divided the next four years between studying at the Harvard Divinity School and at the Episcopal Theological School in Cambridge, Massachusetts, and serving as instructor in Latin at the University of Chicago. He opted in the end for an academic career but never departed from the patterns of thinking that had drawn him toward the church. Rand's lifelong concern was with the relationship between classical Greek and Roman culture and Christianity as it took shape during the Middle Ages, and to his Harvard classmates on the occasion of their fiftieth reunion he described himself as a "student of Christian humanism" and a "teacher at Harvard." He pursued advanced study in the classics at the University of Munich, by which he was granted a Ph.D. in 1900. At a time when scientific attention to the subject was very new, he developed an interest in Latin paleography under the particular influence of Ludwig Traube. In 1901 he married Belle Brent Palmer of Louisville, Kentucky, whom he is said first to have courted on the hillsides around Munich by reading her the poetry of George Santayana. The couple did not have children.

From 1901 until 1942, except for occasional leaves of absence for sabbaticals, visiting lectureships, or visiting professorships, he was a member of the classics faculty at Harvard University, where he became a full professor in 1909 and Pope Professor of Latin in 1931. He served in 1912–1913 as annual professor at the American Academy in Rome, of which he subsequently became a trustee and life member; in 1919–1920 as

Sather Professor of Classical Literature at the University of California, Berkeley; and in 1933–1934 as exchange professor at the Sorbonne. After his retirement in 1942 he served as senior research fellow at the Dumbarton Oaks Research Library and Collection in Washington, D.C., in 1943–1944, and as resident scholar there in 1944–1945. In recognition of his scholarship and his lifelong devotion to France, he was posthumously awarded the degree of Docteur de l'Université by the University of Paris in December 1945. He belonged to numerous professional societies, both in the United States and abroad. He was president of the American Philological Association in 1922–1923. He was one of the principal founders (in 1925) of the Mediaeval Academy of America, of which he became the first president and the editor of the first three volumes of its journal, *Speculum*, for which he suggested the name.

His most substantial contributions to scholarship were his monumental *Studies in the Script of Tours*, which appeared in two parts, the first in 1929 and the second in 1934, and the view he developed of the relationship between the longer and the shorter forms of Servius's commentaries on Virgil, represented in the two volumes of the so-called Harvard edition of Servius that appeared in 1946 and 1964. Rand saw the longer form (Servius Danielis) essentially the lost commentary of Aelius Donatus, earlier than Servius's own and probably one of the principal sources Servius used. Three of his most widely read books were products of lectureships he held: *Founders of the Middle Ages*, (1928) from his Lowell Institute Lectures in 1928; *The Magical Art of Virgil* (1931), adapted from six lectures, "Virgil the Magician," delivered on the Normal Wait Harris Foundation at Northwestern University in the spring of 1930; and *The Building of Eternal Rome* (1943), from his second set of Lowell Institute Lectures in 1942. He also contributed the popular *Ovid and His Influence* (1925) to the Our Debt to Greece and Rome series, and he wrote two delightful handbooks, *In Quest of Virgil's Birthplace* (1930) and *A Walk to Horace's Farm* (1930).

Although a scholar of international renown, with more than two hundred titles to his credit, Rand felt that his primary commitment was to teaching. "The crown of a professor's activities," he wrote, "is his teaching. Whatever his success in administration and scholarly research, these matter little if they are not caught up into character—*abeunt studia in mores*—and insensibly transmitted to his pupils." To Harvard's President James B. Conant he wrote in April 1935:

As for publication, we should cease to regard it as a major criterion of scholarship. It is true that an inquiring and original mind—which is, of course, a prime essential—cannot help making fresh observations and fruitful discoveries, but it matters not whether he disseminates them on paper or in the intellects of his pupils. The latter way is "productive scholarship" combined with art.

He went on to say, "In the Classics I should rate higher that scholar who has made friends with the great authors of Greece and Rome, who steadily deepens his intimacy with them, and who can inspire his pupils with an eagerness to make the same friendship with them."

Rand's views on education were conservative, even reactionary. Writing in the *Atlantic Monthly* of June 1943 under the title "Bring Back the Liberal Arts," he argued for the restoration after World War II of both Greek and Latin to a central place in the school and college curriculum, with mathematics, science, French, German, history, and English in supporting roles. The wave, at least of the immediate future, was not with him, but a critic observed, "You may think, as I do, that some of his notions of education are either outmoded or unhappily impossible. But at the same time you will hope that, somehow or other, education will continue to produce such men as he."

Rand did not dwell in an ivory tower. Witty and urbane, he found one of his greatest satisfactions in his membership in the Saturday Club of Boston, which had been founded by Ralph Waldo Emerson in the mid-nineteenth century as a forum for good conversation. On the occasion of Rand's retirement from Harvard, Supreme Court justice Felix Frankfurter, who had once been a colleague of Rand's on the Harvard faculty, wrote, "Not the least of my cherished Cambridge memories are the all too infrequent encounters with you. For I never left you without being refreshed and fortified." Rand was an ardent Francophile and an outspoken advocate of U.S. intervention on the side of the Allies in World War II. No doubt as an outgrowth of his intense respect for Catholicism as it developed during the Middle Ages, he became a high church Anglican, and he had passed the collection plate at Boston's Church of the Advent on the morning of the Sunday he died. He died at his home in Cambridge.

• Many of Rand's papers are preserved in the Pusey Library at Harvard University. Leslie Webber Jones, ed., in *Studies in Honor of E. K. Rand* (1938), a festschrift commemorating his forty years of teaching, states that "it does not seem fitting . . . to include in this book a bibliography of a man who will undoubtedly write for many years to come." He did, indeed, live and continue his scholarly activity for another seven years. He was working on a critical edition of the *Opuscula Sacra* of Boethius at the time of his death, and the proof of a little book, *Cicero in the Courtroom of St. Thomas Aquinas*, which was the outgrowth of the Aquinas Lecture for the Aristotelian Society of Marquette University that he delivered in the spring of the year he died, had to be read by others after his death. As a result, no complete bibliography of his work has ever been prepared. The most important things he wrote have been mentioned in the foregoing text. The best source of information about his other writings is the annual bibliography of members of the American Philological Association, which was then published each year in the association's *Transactions and Proceedings*. Further information about his professional career is to be found in the memorial minutes for him printed on pp. xxvi–xxvii of the *Proceedings* of the American Philological Association for 1945 and the memoir appearing in *Speculum* 21 (1946): 378–81.

ARTHUR F. STOCKER

RAND, Ellen Emmet (4 Mar. 1875–18 Dec. 1941), artist, was born Ellen Gertrude Emmet in San Francisco, California, the daughter of Christopher Temple Emmet, a lawyer, and Ellen James. Emmet was the great-granddaughter of the noted lawyer Thomas Addis Emmet. Novelist Henry James was a cousin on her mother's side; three cousins on her father's side, all sisters, became well-known artists: Lydia Field Emmet, Rosina Emmet Sherwood, and Jane Emmet de Glehn.

Ellen Emmet, known to her family and friends as "Bay," was proud of her family connections and kept in close contact with her distinguished cousins. She spent her early years in the San Francisco area, but the family returned east, probably in 1884, after her father's death. She early demonstrated a talent for drawing and received some instruction from the Boston artist Dennis Miller Bunker in 1887. From 1889 to 1893 she took classes at the Art Students League in New York City, where one of her fellow students was her cousin Lydia.

Emmet began her professional career as an illustrator for *Vogue* when she was eighteen. She worked for the magazine in 1893 and 1894 and also, in the latter year, did illustrations for *Harper's*. In 1896 she went to England, where she met John Singer Sargent, whose style would greatly influence her own. She then traveled to Paris to become a pupil of the expatriate American artist Frederick MacMonnies. MacMonnies was primarily a sculptor, but he also painted and taught painting. Emmet's fellow students included her sister Leslie and their friend Mary Foote. MacMonnies was impressed by Emmet and told her cousin Jane Emmet that he "had never seen any man in any school do such good studies" (Hoppin, p. 30). She painted two portraits of her teacher while she was a student, one a formal likeness, the other an informal study showing him painting (William Benton Museum of Art, Univ. of Connecticut). Both recall the style of Sargent, with their thick application of paint and fluid brushwork. Among her other works from this period are a bust-length likeness of her cousin Henry James (private collection) and a lively portrait of her friend and fellow student Mary Foote (private collection).

Emmet returned to the United States in 1900 and settled in New York, where she quickly established herself as a fashionable portrait painter with a studio on Washington Square South. Although she painted both sexes throughout her life, she specialized in portraits of men. Her likeness of the newspaper correspondent Richard Harding Davis (1901, William Benton Museum of Art) represents him in his war correspondent's uniform and with a confident expression, the very image of a dashing journalist. She painted a sensitive, bust-length portrait of cellist Pablo Casals (c. 1905, private collection) and depicted sculptor Augustus Saint-Gaudens (c. 1904, Metropolitan Museum of Art) seated, in right profile, and seemingly lost in thought. Her portraits of Secretary of State John Hay and his successor, Elihu Root, were acquired by the Department of State to serve as the official portraits of these statesmen.

Emmet's one-woman show at the Durand-Ruel Galleries in New York in 1902 attracted much attention. Her one-woman exhibition at Copley Hall in Boston in 1906 was evidence of the high regard in which her work was held; the only artists honored with solo exhibitions there before her were Whistler, Sargent, and Monet. One of her best paintings, *In the Studio* (1910, William Benton Museum of Art), shows her niece Eleanor Peabody seated in front of a mirror and holding a black cat in her lap; Emmet herself is seen reflected in the mirror, painting the portrait. The picture reveals the influences of Diego Velázquez and Sargent—loose brushwork, dark tonalities, and unusual poses—without being imitative of either.

Emmet married William Blanchard Rand of Salisbury, Connecticut, on 6 May 1911 and had three sons in quick succession. Thereafter she and her family divided their time between New York City, where she kept her studio, and Salisbury, where her husband managed the Rand family farm and participated in state and local politics. Neither marriage nor raising a family interfered with her career, and she continued to work for many years. She exhibited regularly at the National Academy of Design and the Pennsylvania Academy of the Fine Arts and won awards throughout her career. Among the more important of these were the two prizes she received for *In the Studio*, the first a gold medal at the Panama-Pacific Exposition in 1915 and the second the National Arts Club Prize in 1925. She also received the Beck Gold Medal from the Pennsylvania Academy of the Fine Arts in 1922 for her portrait of Judge Donald T. Warner (private collection). Among her other notable paintings are portraits of Henry A. du Pont (1906), a businessman who won the Medal of Honor during the Civil War, and his son, the noted collector Henry Francis du Pont (1914; both at the Henry Francis du Pont Winterthur Museum, Winterthur, Del.).

Ellen Emmet Rand's style changed somewhat during the 1920s as she moved away from Sargent's bravura application of paint to a less flamboyant manner with more uniform brushwork. She never lost her ability to compose a picture or capture a likeness. Two notable paintings from this period are a portrait of the Reverend Endicott Peabody (1925, private collection) and *The Green Background* (1928, William Benton Museum of Art), in which a young woman dressed in black is seated against a vivid green wall.

Rand was her family's primary financial support throughout her married life, especially after 1929, when her husband lost most of his money in the stock market crash. As a result she accepted many more commissions than she had in the past; most were portraits of leading businessmen. Her best portraits from the 1930s are of Secretary of State Henry L. Stimson (1933, Department of State, Washington, D.C.) and two of Franklin D. Roosevelt, one painted in 1932 (Home of Franklin D. Roosevelt National Historic Site, Hyde Park, N.Y.) and the other in 1934 (Franklin D. Roosevelt Library, Hyde Park). Roosevelt's mother liked the 1932 portrait and placed it in the living room of the Roosevelt residence at Hyde Park, where it can still be seen. Roosevelt himself preferred the 1934 portrait (as did the artist) and designated it as his official likeness. It hung in the White House during his administration, but President Harry Truman, who liked Frank Salisbury's portrait of Roosevelt better, sent Rand's picture to Hyde Park.

Rand was elected an associate of the National Academy of Design in 1926 and became a full academician in 1934. She remained active up until her death from a heart attack in New York City; she had just returned from a painting trip to Virginia.

Ellen Emmet Rand was an artist of the first rank. Her accomplished portraits, particularly of American men in power in the first half of the twentieth century, are a historic legacy of this gifted artist.

• The largest public collection of Ellen Emmet Rand's work is at the William Benton Museum of Art, University of Connecticut. Most of her paintings, however, remain in private hands. A self-portrait of 1927 belongs to the National Academy of Design, New York City. The best account of her life and career is the essay by Martha J. Hoppin and Lydia Sherwood McClean in the catalog *The Emmets: A Family of Women Painters* (1982), produced for the exhibition at the Berkshire Museum, Pittsfield, Mass., and the Danforth Museum, Framingham, Mass. An obituary is in the *New York Times*, 19 Dec. 1941.

DAVID MESCHUTT

RAND, Marie Gertrude (29 Oct. 1886–30 June 1970), experimental psychologist, scientist, was born in Brooklyn, New York, the daughter of Lyman Fiske Rand, a businessman, and Mary Catherine Moench. Following a family tradition, she attended college at Cornell University, earning an A.B. degree in experimental psychology in 1908. In response to a scholarship award Rand took her graduate training at Bryn Mawr College, receiving both the A.M. and the Ph.D. in 1911. Her doctoral dissertation, "The Factors That Influence the Sensitivity of the Retina to Color: A Quantitative Study and Methods of Standardizing," was done under the guidance of Clarence Errol Ferree. This work led to further collaborative studies with Ferree on the effects of general illumination on color perception, as well as to the development of techniques for measuring the light sensitivity and color discrimination of the retina. The Ferree-Rand perimeter, a tool used to map the perceptual abilities of the retina, was a product of this work.

Rand remained at Bryn Mawr after completing her doctorate, initially as a postdoctoral fellow (1911–1912), then as a Sarah Berliner Research Fellow (1912–1913), and finally as a member of the faculty, holding the positions of demonstrator (1913–1914, 1925–1927) and associate in experimental and applied psychology (1914–1925). She spent the summers of 1912 and 1913 at Columbia University, studying physiological optics and mental measurement respectively. Rand and Ferree were married on 28 September 1918,

ensuring the continuance of a highly compatible as well as productive research team. They had no children. LeGrand H. Hardy observed that Ferree's "great talent was to stimulate others, to enliven their thinking, enrich their imaginations and direct their activities; [Rand's] to comprehend the nature and direction of his aggressive drives, to weave them into a co-ordinated pattern and to bring fresh materials and methods to their furtherance" (p. 668). The couple devoted themselves over the years until Ferree's death to the solution of applied as well as basic questions involving vision and lighting.

While still at Bryn Mawr Rand and Ferree served on the National Research Council Committee on Industrial Lighting (1925–1927). In 1928 both Rand and Ferree became affiliated with Johns Hopkins University, operating a vision research laboratory at the Wilmer Ophthalmological Institute. Rand also taught in the Johns Hopkins Medical School, holding an appointment as associate professor of research ophthalmology and of physiological optics (1928–1936). In 1935 she was named associate director of the Research Laboratory of Physiological Optics in Baltimore (1936–1942). During this period Rand and Ferree continued their applied work, serving as consultants for industries and agencies wrestling with various glare-related lighting problems. They invented instruments and devices which successfully dealt with these problems, including variable illumination lamps, glareless examining lamps, desk lamps and bedreading lamps, and glare-controlled hospital ward lights installed in the Johns Hopkins University Hospital. Undoubtedly their most important illumination project involved them as consultants in the design and construction of the Holland Tunnel. Initially Ferree and Rand were asked to select the type and color of tiles used to line the interior walls of the tunnel; later Rand was asked to design modifications in the tunnel's lighting units to achieve glare reduction while preserving brightness.

After the death of her husband in 1942, Rand returned to New York City. In 1943 she became a research associate at the Knapp Foundation of the College of Physicians and Surgeons of Columbia University, where she taught and conducted research until her retirement in 1957. Working at the Eye Institute of Presbyterian Hospital, Rand collaborated with LeGrand H. Hardy and M. Catherine Rittler on research on colorblindness. An outcome of this work was the development of the Hardy-Rand-Rittler color plates, a simple test for the detection, classification, and assessment of defects in color vision.

In 1943 Rand became a member of the Illuminating Engineering Society; she was a regular contributor to its journals, authoring or coauthoring seventeen technical papers for *Illuminating Engineering* and its predecessor, *Transactions*. In 1952 she was elected a fellow of the society, the first woman to be so honored. In 1963 the society awarded her the Illuminating Engineering Society Gold Medal in recognition of the distinctive contributions she made to the field; once again she was the first woman to earn this distinction. True to her character—as well as, perhaps, the facts—Rand accepted the medal in the names of both her husband and herself, observing in her address that "nearly all our work on lighting in relation to the eye was done as a team" (p. 11A). In 1959 she was named the Edgar D. Tillyer Medalist by the Optical Society of America in recognition of her accomplishments and scientific standing in the field of visual physiology; again she was the first woman to be so honored. (In 1971 Louise Sloan, a former student of Rand, became the second woman to receive the Tillyer Medal.)

In 1951 Rand was made an honorary fellow of the American Academy of Ophthalmology and Otolaryngology, one of the few nonophthalmologists and again the first woman to be so recognized. She was also a fellow of the American Association for the Advancement of Science and the American Psychological Association. Bryn Mawr College in 1960 honored Rand at the 75th Anniversary Convocation in honor of Alumnae of Bryn Mawr with a citation for distinguished service. She died in Stony Brook, New York.

As is evident from the honors awarded her, Rand's life's work, devoted to the study of human vision, made substantive contributions to several disciplines. This work, much of it collaborative, resulted in the publication of 250 scientific articles in journals of psychology, optics, illuminating engineering, education, and ophthalmology, and the receipt of a dozen patents for lighting devices and optical and ophthalmological instruments. Throughout her life Rand remained a diligent student, a tireless researcher, and an inspiring teacher; as such she left a living as well as lasting legacy.

• Material on Rand, including alumni informational questionnaires, is in the Bryn Mawr College and Cornell University archives. Her Gold Medal acceptance address appeared in *Lighting News* 11a (Nov. 1963). A biographical sketch is K. N. Ogle, "Gertrude Rand: Edgar D. Tillyer Medalist for 1959," *Journal of the Optical Society of America* 49 (1959): 937–41. See also L. H. Hardy, "Obituary for Clarence Errol Ferree," *Archives of Ophthalmology* 29 (1943): 668–69. An obituary of Rand is in the *New York Times*, 2 July 1970.

CATHERINE S. MURRAY

RAND, Sally (2 Jan. 1904–31 Aug. 1979), fan dancer, was born Helen Gould Beck in Elkton, Missouri. Her father was a retired army colonel who had fought in the Spanish-American War; her mother was a teacher and correspondent for several local newspapers. Her parents' names are unknown, and little is known about her childhood.

Rand (then Helen Beck) began her career in Kansas City, Missouri. Following one semester at Christian College in Columbia, Missouri, she worked as a milliner's model and as a chorus girl in a Kansas City nightclub. The drama critic for the *Kansas City Journal*, Goodman Ace, praised her nightclub performance, which led to an invitation to join Gus Edwards's juvenile vaudeville revue *School Days*. While still in her teens, Rand appeared in *School Days* and worked as an

acrobat in the Ringling Brothers Circus. By the time she was twenty she had moved to Hollywood, where she appeared in several silent films, including *Man Bait* (1926), *The King of Kings* (1927), and *A Girl in Every Port* (1928). Her stage name was apparently given to her by Cecil B. De Mille—after the Rand McNally atlas. Rand's movie career essentially ended with the rise of the "talkies," and by the early 1930s she was in Chicago performing her newly created fan dance in a nightclub.

Determined to get a job dancing in the "Streets of Paris" concession at the 1933 Chicago World's Fair midway, Rand decided to appear at the concession preview as Lady Godiva. She was hired and began dancing on 31 May 1933. Before the fair closed the 29-year-old dancer was being paid $5,000 a week for her six to eight daily shows and was one of the most famous women in America.

The Chicago fair, launched during the depression and perhaps over-optimistically titled "A Century of Progress," originally saw disappointing attendance and seemingly sure financial disaster. But in the Streets of Paris concession Sally Rand drew enormous crowds, twirling two seven-foot ostrich feather fans around her naked body to the strains of Debussy's "Clair de Lune" and Chopin's "Waltz in C Sharp Minor." Celebrated by newspaper correspondents, who found more colorful stories on the fair's midway than in the educational exhibits, she became an object of controversy throughout the nation.

In July 1935 an article in the *American Mercury* claimed that the Chicago exposition had been "saved by the curling navel of a Hollywood blonde" and continued rhapsodically. "Sally Rand . . . is a symbol, an industry, a state of mind. She has passed into American speech. She is this country's one-woman Trip to Paris. . . . She symbolized the national jag. Beer was back; the New Deal was on; and Sally Rand was dancing behind two fans, naked as the day she was born."

In spite—or because—of her public success, Rand faced several legal challenges to her act. She was arrested several times and after repeated criticisms by Chicago city boosters and reformers was brought to trial on 23 September 1933. She was convicted by the jury, fined $200, and sentenced to a year in prison. The jury was shocked at the sentence; Rand appealed, and a higher court quickly overturned the verdict.

Despite Rand's arrests on charges of indecency, controversy arose not only because of disagreements about propriety, sexuality, and gender roles but also because of differing views about the role of "culture" in a democracy. World's fairs were intended to uplift and educate the public. The popularity of lowbrow entertainment such as fan dancing raised troubling questions about the goals of the Chicago fair and the definition and meaning of culture in a mass society. That attendance was sparse in the Hall of Science while thousands jammed the Streets of Paris seemed a very bad sign to many of America's elite.

Rand's act was discussed when Congress debated whether to continue funding for the fair in 1934. The appropriation was made, but the management of the fair emphasized its educational mission and rejected Rand's services. The Chicago World's Fair reopened in the spring; *Variety* labeled it "the show-men's biggest flop," and the concessionaires actually rioted in June. Rand was back at the fair by early July, this time in the "Italian Village" concession, with a new act—a bubble dance, done with a sixty-inch semitransparent rubber balloon instead of fans. The fair management steadfastly refused to advertise her act, so Rand took out ads with her own money. Although her appearance did not revive the fair's fortunes, it was financially successful for Rand.

Following her celebrated act in Chicago, Rand was in great demand as a performer. She danced in one Hollywood movie, *Bolero* (1934), and at other fairs, including the California Pacific International Exposition (1935–1936) and the San Francisco Golden Gate International Exposition (1939–1940). Her frequent nightclub appearances included the Billy Rose revue *Let's Play Fair*. In 1965 she appeared briefly (replacing Ann Corio) as mistress of ceremonies of the Broadway revue *This Was Burlesque*.

Rand continued to perform her fan dance, changed "not a whit, not a step, not a feather" until 1978, when she was hospitalized for congestive heart failure. Said septuagenarian Rand of her continuing career, "It's better than doing needlepoint on the patio."

Rand was married three times: to rodeo star Thurkel Greenough, to Harry Finkelstein, and to Frederick Lalla, with whom she adopted a son. She died in Glendora, California.

• Photographs, a clippings file, and films of Rand are in the Billy Rose Collection at the New York Public Library for the Performing Arts, Lincoln Center. For feature articles on Rand at the height of her popularity, see T. R. Carskadon, "Sally Rand Dances to the Rescue," *American Mercury*, July 1935; "Bubbles Become Big Business," *Review of Reviews*, Apr. 1935; "Sally's Sadie Proves the Fans Concealed an Actress," *Newsweek*, 7 Sept. 1935; and Q. Reynolds, "Business Woman," *Colliers*, 26 Aug. 1939. An obituary is in the *New York Times*, 1 Sept. 1979.

BETH BAILEY

RANDALL, Alexander Williams (31 Oct. 1819–26 July 1872), governor of Wisconsin and U.S. postmaster general, was born in Ames, New York, the son of Phineas Randall, a lawyer from Massachusetts, and Sarah Beach. After completing his formal education at Cherry Valley Academy, Randall read law with his father. He was admitted to the bar in 1838. Motivated by the hard times that followed the panic of 1837, he moved in 1840 to Prairieville (later Waukesha), Wisconsin, where he established a law office with his brother Edwin Randall, a future chief justice of the Florida Supreme Court. He wed Mary Van Vechten in 1842.

Alert to the effects of foreign emigration—at a time when power in Wisconsin was split between Whig merchants from New England who lived by Lake Michigan and Democratic miners from Missouri who worked in Mineral Point—Randall discarded his father's Whiggish credentials in favor of the territory's growing Democratic majority and was appointed postmaster of Waukesha by President James Polk in 1845. He resigned his postmastership the following year, became the first district attorney of Waukesha County, and served as a delegate to Wisconsin's first constitutional convention. Randall argued for a separate referendum on the question of black suffrage at the convention, but voters later repudiated the Constitution of 1846 and Randall's suffrage provision by wide margins. He resumed his legal career before reentering politics in 1848 as a delegate to Wisconsin's Free Soil convention. Randall rejoined the Democrats in 1849. After his return to Madison in 1855 as a newly elected legislator, Republicans appointed him chairman of the assembly's judiciary committee.

An Independent Democrat since 1854, Randall officially became a Republican when the party nominated him for attorney general in 1855. His bid failed, but Republicans found his talents useful in the election's aftermath. Upon finding reason to discount key returns from his race against Democratic incumbent William Barstow, Coles Bashford, the Republican gubernatorial candidate, formed a team that included Randall to challenge the election's results. Bashford's attorneys successfully overturned the gubernatorial election; as a gesture of support, the new governor appointed Randall to the state's second circuit court in 1856. Republicans came to lament Bashford's victory when rumors of official malfeasance percolated across the state that same year. Bashford, thirteen senators, and fifty-nine assemblymen were eventually implicated in a convoluted scandal involving land grants to and bonds from the La Crosse and Milwaukee Railroad. Turning to Randall because of his unvarnished reputation and Democratic antecedents, Republicans nominated the judge in lieu of Bashford in 1857. He went on to defeat Democrat James Cross by 454 votes out of 88,932 cast.

Personal loss and professional turmoil followed. Governor Randall's first wife died in 1858; the couple's young daughter had passed away previously. A year later Randall fought off a challenge from rival Carl Schurz, the unsuccessful Republican candidate for lieutenant governor in 1857. Randall was eventually renominated over Schurz in 1859 before the recriminations of their followers caused irreparable harm. Republican differences "resolved," Randall triumphed over Harrison Hobart, a Democrat, in a campaign that featured Wisconsin's first statewide debates, by 7,460 votes out of 112,538 cast.

Secession and civil war confronted Randall during his second term. After unceremoniously dumping a high-ranking militia officer from the state's only organized regiment for being unenthusiastic about the prospect of confronting Federal authorities in 1860—Wisconsin was challenging the Supreme Court's decision on the state's personal liberty law at the time—Randall became a bulwark of Unionism. In a remarkable reversal, the governor—an ardent supporter of the state's efforts to nullify the Fugitive Slave Law of 1850—declared in his annual legislative message in 1861 that "secession is revolution; revolution is war; [and] war against the Government of the United States is treason" (quoted in Thwaites, p. 44). Randall organized an infantry regiment and made plans for three others immediately after Fort Sumter; he raised fourteen additional regiments, ten artillery batteries, and three cavalry units before leaving office, exceeding Wisconsin's quota by 3,232 men. Randall even sent representatives with his regiments to ensure that Wisconsin's wounded received proper medical attention and free railroad passes home.

While impressive, Randall's efforts as "war governor" were not flawless. Wisconsin's first soldiers were embarrassingly clad in gray, so costly new uniforms had to be procured for them. A second misstep was averted when the legislature ignored the governor's agricultural proposals, which would have encouraged Wisconsin's farmers to grow sugar cane and develop an improbable alternative to cotton based on flax. Sensitive to criticism, worried about continuing party differences, and possessed of ambitions for higher office, Randall chose not to seek reelection in 1861. He left Wisconsin and sought a military appointment in 1862; instead, President Abraham Lincoln sent him to Rome as minister to the Papal States.

Randall returned to the United States in 1863, married Helen M. Thomas, and became assistant postmaster general. He was the first Wisconsinite elevated to a cabinet post in 1866 when President Andrew Johnson made him postmaster general. Randall supervised construction of post offices across the South and implemented conventions with Europe that improved transatlantic service during his tenure. From his patronage-rich position, his appraisal of politics during Reconstruction led him to also become a staunch Johnson supporter. He played a pivotal role in the National Union Convention of 1866, traveled with the president during his "swing around the circle," contributed to the president's legal defense fund, and testified as a defense witness at Johnson's impeachment trial. Loyal to the end, when Johnson left the White House in 1869, Randall literally went with him. Out of office, Randall traveled across Asia before resuming his law practice. He died of cancer in Elmira, New York.

Like many nineteenth-century politicians, Randall took advantage of frontier opportunities and fell victim to Washington quarrels. Between his rise and fall, however, his ambitions combined with his principles to make him an atypical advocate of the rights of minorities—whether they were black voters, western nullifiers, or unrepentant ex-Confederates.

• Randall's official papers are in the State Historical Society of Wisconsin. Various speeches can be found in Reuben G. Thwaites, ed., *Civil War Messages and Proclamations of Wisconsin War Governors* (1912), and Milo M. Quaife, ed., *The Convention of 1846*, vol. 2, Wisconsin Historical Collections Constitutional Series (1919). Correspondence to, from, and about Randall is in Leo F. Stock, ed., *U.S. Ministers to the Papal States* (1933), and *The Papers of Andrew Johnson*, ed. Leroy P. Graf and Ralph W. Haskins (1967–). Contemporaneous accounts include William De Loss Love, *Wisconsin in the War of the Rebellion* (1866), Edwin B. Quiner, *The Military History of Wisconsin* (1866), Charles R. Tuttle, *An Illustrated History of the State of Wisconsin* (1875), H. A. Tenney and David Atwood, *Memorial Record of the Fathers of Wisconsin* (1880), and Alexander M. Thomson, *A Political History of Wisconsin* (1900). Useful theses include Robert H. Jacobi, "Wisconsin Civil War Governors" (M.S. thesis, Univ. of Wisconsin, 1948), and Carolyn Jane Mattern, "Soldiers When They Go: The Story of Camp Randall, 1861–1865" (M.A. thesis, Univ. of Wisconsin, 1968). An obituary is in the *Milwaukee Sentinel*, 27 July 1872.

ROBERT W. BURG

RANDALL, Benjamin (7 Feb. 1749–22 Oct. 1808), clergyman and one of the founders of the American Freewill Baptist sect, was born in New Castle, New Hampshire, the son of William Randall, a sea captain, and Margaret Mordantt. Some scholars spell his surname Randal. Young Randall often accompanied his father to sea and learned the trades of sail making and tailoring, skills he later used to provide income while an itinerant revivalist. His travels and apprenticeship did not allow for formal schooling, though it is reported by an early biographer that he took great interest in the study of religion.

As a young man Randall was tormented by doubts concerning his salvation. He found little comfort or confidence in the Calvinist doctrines of election and predestination. During one intense period of spiritual self-doubt in September 1770 his friends persuaded him to hear the famed revivalist George Whitefield. At first, Randall was skeptical of Whitefield and his methods. His journal records disdain for the "delusion and enthusiasm of revivalism," and he found the "Grand Itinerant" a "worthless, noisy fellow . . . who raised an evil spirit in me."

Nonetheless, Randall returned to hear Whitefield preach on two other occasions. He was attracted to Whitefield's call for a spiritual New Birth that led to a transformed life and an emotional engagement with Christianity. On his fourth trip to hear Whitefield Randall learned of the revivalist's death. He was convinced that "Whitefield is . . . in heaven, while I am on the road to hell." This reflection led Randall to an emotional conversion experience that he described as being "born again." The date on which he recorded his conversion was 15 October 1770 (Buzzell [1827], pp. 16–19).

Randall returned home a changed man. He joined his local church and later began to hold house meetings of "singing, praying, and the reading of a sermon or other good book" with like-minded congregants (Buzzell [1827], pp. 25–31). Randall's zeal and the popularity of these meetings drew the disapproval of the local minister and much of the local congregation. In disgust, Randall withdrew from the Congregational church and volunteered for the Continental army, serving in both New Hampshire and Maine and rising to the rank of orderly sergeant.

The controversy in his local church and the turmoil of the American Revolution launched Randall on an intense period of spiritual reflection that eventually led to his complete rejection of Calvinism and to a life as a frontier New England revivalist. Such spiritual journeys were common in the religious crucible that marked the birth of the United States. According to historian Stephen Marini, the message of the New Birth "created a generation of seekers who followed the dictates of their own spiritual gifts into schismatic dissent from . . . New England Congregationalism" (p. 1).

Randall was just such a restless spiritual seeker. He left the revolutionary army in 1777 a committed Baptist and vowed "to war out my life in God's cause." As an itinerant he patterned his style and message after Whitefield. He met with some initial success in his home town; however, the city's Congregationalist establishment fiercely opposed Randall. Some of his detractors spread the rumor that he was a traitor who preached revivalism over revolution, lessening the village's commitment to the war effort. He was mobbed and stoned by angry crowds and barely avoided a tar and feathering.

Randall's woes followed him to New Durham, New Hampshire. After gathering a small church in this frontier outpost, Baptist elders challenged his theological background. They correctly sensed his rejection of Calvinism. Randall was untrained in theology and suffered badly in debate with other ministers. He withdrew from the New Durham pulpit at the height of the controversy. During this period, Randall reported experiencing a vision that answered his critics and clarified his future ministry. In terms not unlike later charismatic religious leaders such as Charles Finney and Joseph Smith, Randall reported that while praying in a cornfield a large Bible descended and opened before him. He saw that the Scriptures taught "the universal atonement in the work of redemption by Jesus Christ who tasted death for every man—the universal appearance of grace to all men, and with the universal call of the gospel" (Buzzell [1827], p. 89). Randall entered his cornfield a young itinerant buffeted by political and ecclesiastical enemies and left a prophet with a direct calling from the Holy Spirit. He resumed preaching in New Durham and continued his itinerancy among the Baptist congregations of New Hampshire and Maine.

Randall's universalism and his call for a strenuous Christian life slowly won new converts among the settlers of the New England frontier. By the end of 1783 a dozen like-minded ministers and several congregations had joined him. This fellowship continued to grow in part because of Randall's unfailing efforts and a message that stressed universal atonement, free will, adult baptism by immersion, millennial expectation, and a defiance against the established order.

During the last decades of his life Randall was a religious visionary, spreading a radical form of evangelical Protestantism. He successfully synthesized Baptist practice, Arminian doctrine, Whitefieldian revivalism, and Henry Alline's mystical theology into a unique form of sectarianism that appealed to common frontier folk and would eventually become the region's largest indigenous religion.

Yet Randall recognized early that a successful message was not enough to keep his scattered flock together. In 1783 he devised a system of Quarterly Meetings that provided a nascent institutional framework for the young sect. This structure was not enough, however, to protect the Freewill Baptist churches or Randall from schism and discord. The next decade was marked by external attacks, defections to the more radical Shakers and Universalists, and doubts about Randall's leadership. In 1792 Randall set out a minimal system of polity and organization borrowed from Quaker, Baptist, and Congregationalist sources. He set up a Monthly Meeting of clergy and proposed a Yearly Meeting to determine disciplinary and doctrinal questions. The new plan provided stability for the Freewill Baptist sect and allowed it to flourish during the religious spasms of the Second Great Awakening.

Randall died in New Durham, the recognized founder and leader of the Freewill Baptist sect of New England. In death he was survived by his wife of thirty-seven years, Joanna Oram of Kittery, Maine, and eight of their nine children.

• The existing cache of Randall's letters and manuscripts can be found in the William S. Babcock Papers, American Antiquarian Society, Worcester, Mass., and at the American Baptist Historical Society, Rochester, N.Y. Randall did not leave behind many printed sources; two in particular illustrate his efforts to organize his sect on firm theological grounds: *A Summary of the Order and Disciplines of the Church of New Durham* (1793) and an edited volume of Henry Alline's sermons, *Two Mites, Cast into the Offering of God, for the Benefit of Mankind* (1804). Most of what we know about Randall comes from John Buzzell's *The Life of Elder Benjamin Randal: Principally Taken from Documents Written by Himself* (1827) and *A Religious Magazine, Containing a Short History of the Church of Christ Gathered at New Durham in the Year 1780* (1811). Buzzell was an itinerant who accompanied Randall on his journeys. There are few more recent interpretations of Randall's career. The best biographical information can be found in histories of the Freewill Baptist denomination's early years, including Damon C. Dodd, *The Free Will Baptist Story* (1956); Norman Allen Baxter, *History of the Freewill Baptists* (1957); and especially Stephen Marini, *Radical Sects of Revolutionary New England* (1984).

SCOTT FLIPSE

RANDALL, Clarence Belden (5 Mar. 1891–4 Aug. 1967), steel company executive and government consultant, was born in Newark Valley, New York, the son of Oscar Smith Randall, a local merchant, and Esther Clara Belden. Educated at Harvard University, he graduated Phi Beta Kappa with an A.B. in 1912 and tenth in his law school class with an LL.B. in 1915. Randall practiced law in Ishpeming, Michigan, through the mid-1920s, except for a stint in the U.S. Army during World War I. He married Emily Fitch

Phelps in 1917 and had two daughters. In 1925 he joined the Inland Steel Company of Chicago, Illinois, serving as an assistant vice president, vice president, director, and assistant to the president to 1949, then as president in the following four years before rising to chairman of the board in 1953. He followed a professional administrative path in his development from lawyer to executive rather than progressing through plant management. Although Randall had acquired experience in the legal aspects of iron-ore operations on the Great Lakes, in his various capacities at Inland he became a skilled expert in finding, acquiring, and running independent ore sources, mines, and steel mills. A conservative who opposed overbearing union and government intervention in business, Randall vehemently opposed the Little Steel strike of 1937. He was, however, a business statesman who served successive presidents as a critic of government economic regulation and an advocate of free enterprise at home and abroad.

By 1952 Inland was the seventh largest steelmaker in the United States. Expanding the company's mines, raw materials resources, and shipping, Randall understood the importance of skilled industrial management. He initiated executive recruitment and training programs, for instance, that made Inland's leadership more efficient. A supporter of big business freedom, he nonetheless stressed corporate responsibility to society and particularly to labor. He helped draft Michigan workmen's compensation laws and believed that workers had the right to strike, although Randall claimed that unions tried to monopolize industry. A civic leader by World War II, he joined other internationalist businessmen noted for their concern that America assume leadership in world economic affairs. By the early Cold War, Randall was poised to enter government service.

In 1948 Paul Hoffman, head of the Economic Cooperation Administration, which was part of the Marshall Plan, appointed Randall as steel and coal consultant to assess European industrial capabilities. Randall supported the recovery program as a way to instill free-market capitalism in Europe, but like other conservatives, he worried about wasteful spending. Planners welcomed his support for rebuilding the European steel industry. Like them, Randall concluded that European recovery hinged on linking the vast Franco-German industrial area into an integrated coal and steel common market. But he warned that this enterprise, called the Schuman Plan, would fail if European socialists stifled private enterprise.

Continuing at Inland Steel, Randall in 1951 also joined the Commerce Department's Business Advisory Council, a voice for big business, despite his antipathy to President Harry Truman's Fair Deal policies. In 1949 his first run-in with the Truman administration occurred over workers' rights in the steel industry. Randall had criticized the influence of organized labor on planning boards during the war and feared that government-union collusion would hike wages and lower steel prices. When Truman proposed a fact-finding board to prevent a strike over steelmakers' refusal to pay for pensions and welfare benefits, Randall assailed the panel as socialistic. The ensuing strike ended in a settlement, however, with the costs of welfare shared by industrialists, who also accepted the responsibility for paying for pensions. The episode reinforced Randall's belief that the country was edging toward state control.

His career approached its zenith in 1952 when he led America's ninety-two steel companies against Truman's seizure of the steel mills. By nationalizing the industry, Truman sought to preempt a strike that could cut off steel supplies during wartime and denounced management's plans to tie wage increases to production increases. Randall, then president of Inland Steel, resisted raising pay. But he was more appalled, to the point, he said, of being "physically ill," by what he perceived as Truman's dictatorial action. Chosen by the ninety-two steel companies to represent their views, Randall publicly condemned the seizure on national radio on 9 April 1952, calling it prolabor, deceitful, and an exercise in excessive government authority over the private economy. The president, acting like Mussolini and Hitler, "seized the private property of one million people without the slightest shadow of legal right," announced Randall. Backed by conservatives in and out of politics, steel executives eventually triumphed when the Supreme Court declared Truman's action unconstitutional. The National Association of Manufacturers appreciatively named Randall its Man of the Year. Nevertheless, the strike occurred and resulted in a raise of twenty-one cents an hour.

The steel incident reaffirmed Randall's faith in free enterprise but also in business responsibility. In *A Creed for Free Enterprise* (1952), he advocated business interaction in the community, government, and policymaking. Socialism certainly failed society, yet rather than being a "hunting license" for predatory capitalists, the free enterprise system carried a burden of public welfare. Production was but a tool to achieve prosperity for all. In four editions, the popular book stressed that American industrial leadership must exhibit the advantages of market capitalism over socialism by pursuing liberal trade abroad and smaller government at home. Such responsible conservatism, his Marshall Plan experience, and fame in the steel seizure case brought Randall to Dwight D. Eisenhower's attention in 1953.

In that year the new president appointed Randall chairman of the Commission on Foreign Economic Policy to suggest reforms in U.S. foreign economic policy. Comprising ten members of Congress and seven representatives from the private sector, the commission sought remedies to the World's debilitating shortage of dollars by freer trade. Randall believed that European problems could only be solved by competition. Because Inland Steel had been immune to import pressures in earlier years because of its location on the Great Lakes, he was relatively inexperienced in the need for protectionism. Yet Eisenhower was also a free-trader who placed such importance on the commission that he delayed new policy initiatives until Randall made his report. Randall expertly conducted public hearings, but he was compelled to concede a bit to the influence of the protectionists. While the January 1954 report endorsed lower trade barriers and more presidential authority to increase essential imports, it was weaker than free-traders desired.

The report promoted world economic equilibrium mostly by trade liberalization, called for reduced foreign aid and higher rates of overseas investment, and advocated expanded commerce with communist Eastern Europe for the benefit of Western Europe's economy. The report, explained Randall in *A Foreign Economic Policy for the United States* (1954), adhered to Eisenhower's "trade not aid" strategy to replace Marshall Plan assistance with a permanent foreign trade policy. Aid led to state control; Randall preferred private investment and reciprocal, expanding commerce to combat both big government and communism. Economists criticized the report for neglecting large issues such as European integration, the relationship of foreign policy to foreign economic programs, and the special needs of less-developed nations. Eisenhower used Randall's recommendations as the basis of his legislative agenda in 1954, although protectionist pressures and wariness in Congress toward trade with the Communist bloc forced the president to settle only for a renewal of the reciprocal trade agreements program for three years in 1955. Randall's service earned him honors from the National Foreign Trade Council.

He continued consulting for the government after retiring from Inland Steel in April 1956. Three months later Eisenhower appointed him special assistant on foreign economic policy and then chairman of the Council on Foreign Economic Policy, which advised the White House. Randall became preoccupied with the liberal trade agenda and Soviet competition. He particularly railed at American businessmen for allowing the Communist bloc to capture markets in the underdeveloped world, an area that had received his close attention during his service in the U.S. Economic Mission to Turkey in 1953, when the Soviet threat was apparent in the periphery. In 1958, with Eisenhower's approval, Randall recommended liberalizing travel restrictions between the West and the Communist bloc to ease tensions. He later served President John Kennedy in areas of domestic and international affairs. Randall traveled to Ghana as a special emissary in 1961 to study the Volta River Project, headed a presidential panel in 1962–1963, which recommended pay increases for certain federal employees, and chaired the State Department's advisory committee on international business problems in 1963. Surprisingly, he did not publicly denounce Kennedy's confrontation with the steel industry over price hikes in 1962. When Kennedy championed a national export drive to meet the competition of a recovered Western Europe, Randall was named honorary chairman of Illinois's Committee on Export Expansion in 1962–1963. President Lyndon B. Johnson rewarded Randall for his

government service with the highest peacetime honor, the Presidential Medal of Freedom, in 1963. Remaining active in business organizations, industry, and ornithology, this industrial statesman and author of eleven books and numerous articles died in Ishpeming.

Randall epitomized the American business statesman of the mid-twentieth century who believed that corporate executives must preserve the free enterprise system at home and abroad. To this end he pursued economic liberalism in foreign economic policy and conceded that business must provide for the basic welfare of all Americans, although he remained a foe of unions and government intrusion in the domestic economy. Randall articulately voiced the capitalist values of big business, in agreement with official foreign economic programs that were steeped in free-trade ideology but also in opposition to government social welfare policies. His ability to span the worlds of industry and government, applying his enlightened conservatism, made him a significant business architect of public policy in postwar America.

• The Inland Steel Corporation in Chicago, Ill., holds Randall's papers. His service in the Eisenhower administration can be explored at the Dwight D. Eisenhower Presidential Library in Abilene, Kans., in the records of the U.S. Council on Foreign Economic Policy, the Council's Office of the Chairman (Randall file), and Randall's journal. Randall traces his career to the early 1950s in *Over My Shoulder: A Reminiscence* (1956), and his ideas are expressed in the books cited above as well as in *Freedom's Faith* (1953), *The Communist Challenge to American Business* (1958), *The Folklore of Management* (1961), and *Making Good in Management* (1964). Of particular help in revealing his antipathy to big government is "Mining and Taxation in the Lake Superior District," *American Iron and Steel Yearbook* (1932), pp. 40–54. An excellent analysis of the Randall Commission's work is in Burton Kaufman, *Trade and Aid: Eisenhower's Foreign Economic Policy, 1953–1961* (1982). Eleanora W. Schoenebaum, ed., *Political Profiles: The Truman Years* (1978) and *Political Profiles: The Eisenhower Years* (1977), provide information on all aspects of Randall's relations with Truman and Eisenhower. An obituary is in the *New York Times*, 6 Aug. 1967.

THOMAS W. ZEILER

RANDALL, Henry Stephens (3 May 1811–14 Aug. 1876), author and politician, was born in Brookfield, New York, the son of Roswell Randall and Harriet Stephens, farmers. Two years later his family moved to Cortland, New York, where they prospered and became leading citizens as farmers and merchants. Randall graduated at age nineteen from Union College, where he was a particular favorite of President Eliphalet Nott and became active in the antislavery and the Jeffersonian wing of the Democratic party. He read law and gained admission to the bar but never practiced. He married Jane Rebecca Polhemus in 1834 and moved into the house his father had built for him next to his own; they had three children. Randall had been interested in raising and breeding sheep since boyhood, and in the antebellum period he became the nation's most prolific and practical writer on sheep husbandry. In the 1860s he had more than 800 sheep on his 360-acre farm near Cortland.

An exceptionally energetic man with a warm personality, high forehead, and piercing eyes, Randall had wide-ranging interests and was an indefatigable correspondent. He was especially interested in learning as much as possible about raising sheep and improving the breeds. He joined the fledgling New York State Agricultural Society and organized its Cortland County branch. He also bought and edited a local Democratic newspaper in Cortland and in 1835 served as the youngest regular delegate to the Democratic National Convention. By the 1840s, when sheep raising had become a virtual craze in New England, New York, the Upper South, and the Midwest, Randall had earned a national reputation among agricultural reformers for his books and articles on behalf of better crop and livestock husbandry. As corresponding secretary for the New York State Agricultural Society, he had a wide circle of acquaintances. He helped organize the society's first annual fair and in 1844 won prizes for merino sheep, the breed producing the most valuable wool. He wrote a series of columns for the *Virginia Valley Farmer* in 1845, which earned him the enduring friendship of historian and gentleman farmer Hugh Blair Grisby of Charlotte County, Virginia. Randall also authored a report in 1845 on New York agriculture for U.S. secretary of the treasury Robert J. Walker. His letters to planter R. F. W. Allston of South Carolina were published with other pertinent materials on animal breeding in his first major book on crossbreeding and raising merinos and other types of sheep, *Sheep Husbandry in the South* (1848), which went through five more printings. In 1848 he joined the Free Soil party in protest against the impending extension of slavery, though he soon returned to the antislavery wing of the Democratic party.

Randall continued to pursue his many interests in the 1850s, gaining election in 1851 as secretary of state of New York after a defeat in seeking that office two years before. His chief motive in seeking the post was that, through it, he also became the state superintendent of public instruction. In his two years as secretary, he implemented the creation of a separate state department of public instruction. He also devoted much of his energy during the decade to writing a superior three-volume biography of his political hero, Thomas Jefferson. He had the help of Grisby and the Jefferson family in obtaining access to materials he rightly feared would eventually be lost. The resulting *Life of Thomas Jefferson* (1858), though highly partisan, provided the most detailed study of Jefferson available for more than a century.

With the return during the 1860s of congressional interest in tariff protection for various industries, Randall turned to promoting the interests of both the sheep raisers and the wool processors. He proceeded with his research on sheep raising and maintained his writing of a regular column on sheep husbandry for *Moore's Rural New Yorker*, by then the nation's most prestigious farm journal. His 1861 paper on sheep husbandry for the New York State Agricultural Society appeared in 1863 as his best, most original book, *Fine Wool Sheep Husbandry*, with a lengthy appendix on breeds added. In 1863 he also provided an article on sheep husbandry for the *Report of the Commissioner of Agriculture* and published his bestselling book, *The Practical Shepherd*, which went through thirty printings. It was the first of his writings to earn him money because never before had he accepted payment for his work. In researching these works, Randall corresponded with virtually every leading sheep breeder in the nation, visited many of them, and solicited their recollections about the business. He also built a wide network of acquaintances among wool dealers. He spent the rest of his career helping to organize farmers involved in wool production and promoting and presiding over a statewide organization of wool growers. He helped organize and served as president of the National Wool Growers' Association from 1864 to the 1870s. It became one of the most effective interest groups working on behalf of farmers in the nation, winning tariff protection for its members with the Wool and Woolens Act of 1867 and further benefits in 1872.

Randall meanwhile continued his political activities. Elected to the state legislature in 1871, he served as chair of the committee on public education and pressed for more support for schools. He left office shortly afterward to spend his last years simply as a "practical farmer," the title he always preferred. He died in Cortland.

• For information on Randall, see Frank J. Klingberg and Frank W. Klingberg, eds. *The Correspondence between Henry Stephens Randall and Hugh Blair Grigsby* (1952); Harry J. Brown, ed., *Letters from a Texas Sheep Ranch, Written in the Years 1860 and 1867, by George Wilkins Kendall to Henry Stephens Randall* (1959); and Paul W. Gates, *Agriculture and the Civil War* (1965).

MORTON ROTHSTEIN

RANDALL, James Garfield (24 June 1881–20 Feb. 1953), Civil War historian and Lincoln biographer, was born in Indianapolis, Indiana, the son of Horace Randall, a businessman, and Ellen Amanda Kregelo. He attended public schools in Indianapolis and graduated in 1903 from Butler College. Randall received an M.A. in sociology (1904) and a Ph.D. (1911) in history from the University of Chicago. During his graduate studies he also taught at Illinois College and the University of Michigan. He then taught briefly at Syracuse University and Butler before securing a permanent position at Roanoke College in Salem, Virginia, in 1912. In 1916 Randall took leave to serve as Harrison postdoctoral research fellow at the University of Pennsylvania.

In 1911 Randall had married Edith Laura Abbott, his childhood sweetheart and Butler classmate, who died in 1913. In 1917 he married a Roanoke colleague's daughter, Ruth Elaine Painter. There were no children from either marriage. The war took Randall to Washington as historian of the U.S. Shipping Board. After the armistice he taught for a year at Richmond College. In 1920 Randall received the secure position to which he aspired, at a major academic institution, the University of Illinois, with the atmosphere and resources to foster research and the opportunity to teach graduate students. He remained there, except for summers spent teaching at major universities from coast to coast, until his retirement in 1949.

At the University of Illinois, Randall taught courses in constitutional history, southern history, and historical methodology, while increasingly concentrating on the Civil War years. Both he and his wife took great personal interest in his graduate students, entertaining them in their apartment near the campus. Randall gave his students sound scholarly counsel and continuing encouragement and support. In all, he directed fifty-five master's theses and twenty-six doctoral dissertations.

Randall's own dissertation, written under the direction of Claude H. Van Tyne and Andrew C. McLaughlin, concerned "The Confiscation of Property during the Civil War." Chapters from it appeared in the *American Historical Review* before its publication as a book in 1913. Randall extended his research to other wartime powers assumed by Abraham Lincoln, including arbitrary arrests, martial law, expansion of the army, and the emancipation of slaves, and in 1926 he published *Constitutional Problems under Lincoln*. Although the president, as a necessity for waging effective war, seized vast legislative and judicial powers, Randall concluded, Lincoln's character mitigated the harshness of his actions at the time and the threat of their lasting consequence. A reviewer adjudged that Randall had shown "a quality of mastery, which will give his treatment such finality as one may expect from mortal historians" (Carl Russell Fish, *American Historical Review* 33 [1928]: 420).

Randall considered writing a constitutional history of the United States, but instead he broadened the scope of his study of both the Civil War and the wartime president, becoming the first major academic historian to undertake this scholarly task. The decision was strengthened by the invitation in 1929 from editor Allen Johnson to write the Lincoln sketch for the *Dictionary of American Biography*. This was the *DAB*'s longest entry, and Randall wrote eleven other sketches. In 1933 Randall, collaborating with his colleague Theodore C. Pease, edited the *Diary of Orville Hickman Browning*, the memoirs of a Quincy lawyer and friend of Lincoln who succeeded Stephen A. Douglas in the Senate.

At about this time Allan Nevins of Columbia University urged Randall to write a scholarly synthesis, which under the title *The Civil War and Reconstruction* (1937) resulted in a major interpretation of the war. Considering most earlier writing on this theme "superficial, traditionally narrow, and partisan," Randall included hitherto neglected themes: "border problems, . . . intellectual tendencies, anti-war efforts, religious

and educational movements, propaganda methods," and placed greater emphasis on political, administrative, and constitutional issues than on military aspects of the conflict. Rejecting the older political and the newer economic interpretations that held that the war had been irrepressible, Randall believed rather that "the great American tragedy could have been avoided, supposing of course that something more of statesmanship, moderation, and understanding, and something less of professional patrioteering, slogan making, face-saving, political clamoring, and propaganda had existed on both sides." Randall held to this judgment in his 1940 presidential address before the Mississippi Valley Historical Association, "The Blundering Generation" (reprinted in 1947 in his collection of essays, *Lincoln, the Liberal Statesman*) in which he described all modern war as "irrational, unjustifiable, abhorrent." Yet his conviction that the Civil War could have been avoided, as his student David Herbert Donald has made clear in a biographical sketch of Randall, derived neither from disillusionment with Woodrow Wilson's ideals nor from isolationist attitudes preceding World War I (*DAB*, suppl. 5, pp. 556–58). Instead, it depended on Randall's rejection of deterministic interpretations of history. Randall took challenges to his interpretations with equanimity, realizing that revisionists were themselves bound to be revised. "There is no supreme court of history," he wrote.

The Civil War volume proved to be a bestseller among specialized textbooks and was revised by David Donald in 1961. Randall's Fleming Lectures at Louisiana State University were published as *Lincoln and the South* (1946). In 1949 Randall's students published *Living with Lincoln*, another collection of Randall's essays, all of which were inspired by the opening of the Robert Todd Lincoln collection of Lincoln's father's papers.

The first two volumes of *Lincoln the President*, subtitled *From Springfield to Gettysburg*, were published in 1945; volume three, *Midstream*, in 1952; and the final volume, *Last Full Measure*, in 1955. Randall had written half of the last volume at his death, listed tentative topics for the other chapters, and chosen his colleague Richard N. Current to complete the book. The biography received both the Bancroft and Loubat prizes.

Randall's biography was the academic scholar's life of Lincoln, not a narrative chronology smoothly if narrowly focused on the man but a life-and-times account: Lincoln observed within the broadest context of complex events. The events under discussion governed the work's structure, a series of discrete chapters on problems confronted by the emerging candidate and then by the president. The enormous research preceding the writing did not disappear beneath the presentation; the primary documents supporting Randall's interpretations he placed prominently before the reader's eyes. On points of controversy, Randall cited relevant documents as he argued the case. He also expertly used short quotations from primary sources to give the reader a sense of being involved in the ideas and emotions of times past. Randall, who also had talent as an artist and sketched portraits all his life, imparted this visual sense to his words as well as to his careful selection of illustrations for his books.

In his Lincoln biography, Randall held to the main revisionist principles of his Civil War text. The war had come not because sectional differences were irreconcilable. Randall had kind words for the would-be peacemakers, especially Stephen A. Douglas, and sympathized with border-state dilemmas. Extremists on both sides, abolitionists and fire-eaters, he reasoned, had exacerbated issues beyond reconciliation. When war came, the Radical Republican wing posed Lincoln his greatest problems. "Pulled from right and left till he was nearly torn apart, the conservative Lincoln, President of the dis-United States, found among his own Republicans almost a greater vexation than among those of the opposite party, or even among enemies in arms, . . . the Jacobins of Congress." This internecine battle extended through the war and influenced planning of Reconstruction policy. Lincoln emerged in Randall's pages as not without error but nonetheless a distinguished leader. He dominated his cabinet by "strength of personality combined with gentlemanly dealing," traits that made Lincoln a master of foreign affairs and even skilled in guiding military policy. Regarding slavery, Randall stressed Lincoln's caution: while he held a strong moral belief that the institution was wrong, he favored compensated emancipation with foreign colonization of freedmen. According to Randall, the Emancipation Proclamation played only a minor part in Lincoln's plan; it was a "war measure of limited scope, of doubtful legality, and of inadequate effect."

Randall sought to counter a number of prevailing concepts in historiography. With his wife's research help, he denied the Ann Rutledge romance and the view that Lincoln's marriage to Mary Todd was a disaster; instead, in his account, the Lincolns were a loving and devoted couple. Randall also countered the picture of Lincoln as an ignorant frontiersman who delighted in crude jests, presenting him rather as a shrewd and well-traveled lawyer skilled in social discourse, who used tact and humor to ease tensions and was adept at political maneuver but possessed high standards of propriety, that is, "a tough-minded liberal realist." Randall challenged the view that Lincoln had tricked the Confederacy into firing on Fort Sumter, but he concluded that the president might have planned things so as to retain the loyalty of the border states. Randall admired Lincoln's gifts as a writer and speaker but criticized his lack of leadership of Congress. The president who emerged from Randall's volumes, David Potter concluded, was a Lincoln of "mundane greatness" (*Journal of Southern History* 4 [1956]: 533).

Elected president of the American Historical Association, Randall had hoped to sum up, in his presidential address of December 1952, his concept of "Historianship" (*American Historical Review* 58 [1953]:

249–64). His key standards were "clarity, objectivity, tolerance, discrimination, a sense of proportion, insistence upon freedom of thought, authenticity, caution as to conclusions, wariness as to excessive generalizations combined with readiness to state conclusions fairly reached." His heroes, he stated, were leaders who "believed and affirmed," such figures as Jefferson, Lincoln, Wilson, and Jane Addams. He stressed once more his conviction that, had it been possible to prevent the Civil War by compromise, America would have been the better for it. He softened, however, his criticism of abolitionists, welcoming the "better understanding" accorded them by recent historians.

Leukemia prevented Randall from traveling to Washington to deliver this address and caused his death in Urbana two months later. The revisionism of his own interpretations that Randall had foreseen had already begun. Bernard DeVoto in *Harper's Magazine* (192 [1946]: 123–26) had suggested that Randall's perspective minimized the evil of slavery. In 1949 Arthur Schlesinger, Jr., repeated this charge, insisting that some sins were so egregious as to justify the needful war.

• Collections of Randall manuscripts are at the Library of Congress and the University of Illinois Library in Urbana-Champaign. Ruth P. Randall traces a personal story in *I Ruth: Autobiography of a Marriage* (1968). For Randall's scholarship within a broader historiographical setting, see Benjamin P. Thomas, *Portrait for Posterity: Lincoln and His Biographers* (1947); Thomas J. Pressly, *Americans Interpret Their Civil War* (1954); Don Edward Fehrenbacher, *The Changing Image of Lincoln in American Historiography* (1968); Mark E. Neely, Jr., "The Lincoln Theme since Randall's Call," *Papers of the Abraham Lincoln Association* 1 (1979): 10–70; and John David Smith, "James G. Randall," *Dictionary of Literary Biography* 17 (1983): 373–77. See also James Harvey Young, "Professor James G. Randall," included with the inaugural lecture of Robert W. Johannsen as James G. Randall Distinguished Professor of History, University of Illinois, *A New Era for the United States* (1975). Central to the critique of Randall's conclusions was Arthur Schlesinger, Jr., "The Causes of the Civil War: A Note on Historical Sentimentalism," *Partisan Review* 16 (1949): 969–81. Obituary notices are in the *Mississippi Valley Historical Review* 40 (June 1953), by Frederick C. Dietz; *American Historical Review* 58 (July 1953); and *Journal of the Illinois State Historical Society* 46 (Summer 1953), by Harry E. Pratt, with a bibliography of Randall's works compiled by Wayne C. Temple.

JAMES HARVEY YOUNG

RANDALL, James Ryder (1 Jan. 1839–14 Jan. 1908), journalist, was born in Baltimore, Maryland, the son of John K. Randall, a merchant, and Ruth M. Hooper. Randall was tutored by Joseph H. Clarke, Edgar Allan Poe's former teacher, and he attended Baltimore College, which he left without taking a degree because of problems with his health. After traveling abroad, Randall moved to New Orleans and in 1860 became a tutor in English and Latin at Poydras College. Randall's immediately popular and best-known work, "Maryland! My Maryland!" was inspired by reading of an incident in which the Sixth Massachusetts army and a crowd in Baltimore exchanged gunfire. The poem, known for its heated political rhetoric, was first published in the *New Orleans Delta* (26 Apr. 1861) and then was widely reprinted throughout the southern states. Indeed, it became a battle song for the southern cause.

Randall's "My Maryland!" immediately found sympathetic and eager listeners in the Baltimore home of Wilson Miles Cary, a leader of those in the city who supported the Confederate cause. One of Cary's daughters, Jennie, matched the words of the piece to the German tune "Tannenbaum, O Tannenbaum." When the family was driven from Baltimore, Jennie Cary sang the song to Maryland soldiers in General P. G. T. Beauregard's victorious army just after the first battle of Manassas. It was an instant success. Writing an account of his composition of the work for Brander Matthews, Randall stated that "no one was more surprised than I was at the widespread and instantaneous popularity of the lyric." The suggestion by Jay B. Hubbell in *The South in American Literature, 1607–1900* (1954) that Randall's work might be similar to (or a southern version of) Julia Ward Howe's "The Battle Hymn of the Republic" has no merit. Howe's song is essentially a religious work; it certainly contains none of the one-sided propaganda found in "My Maryland!"

It was Randall's fervent desire, expressed in many of his war verses, that Maryland secede from the Union, following Virginia into the Confederacy. (Maryland was a border slave state that remained in the Union.) Randall enlisted and served briefly in the Confederate army; but he could not continue because of his poor health and was discharged. After the war, Randall lived in Augusta, Georgia, where he edited the *Constitutionalist*. For several years, at different times, he was secretary to two Georgia congressmen, W. H. Fleming and Joseph E. Brown. In 1866 Randall married Katherine Hammond, the daughter of a prominent family from South Carolina; the couple had eight children. Randall wrote for several newspapers and periodicals and was for some time the Washington correspondent for the *Augusta Chronicle*. Toward the end of his life Randall was officially recognized by the state of Maryland and honored for his verse. A collection of his poems, *Maryland! My Maryland! and Other Poems*, was published in 1908.

Although Randall's "war songs" were praised for their passion and skill by such contemporaries as Oliver Wendell Holmes, Brander Matthews, and Matthew Page Andrews, these poems have not found an appreciative contemporary audience. Randall's style is popular, heavily derivative, and marked by triteness of thought and expression; it generally displays a serious deficiency of imagination and lacks elementary poetic craftsmanship. Exclamation marks abound in Randall's verse, which is prosaic, overtly sentimental, and emotionally shallow. As in "Maryland! My Maryland!" his verse is an outpouring of clichés seeking to justify the Confederate cause; the weaknesses in this,

his most successful work, are illustrated in the closing stanza:

> I hear the distant thunder-hum,
>   Maryland!
> The Old Line's bugle, fife, and drum,
>   Maryland!
> She is not dead, nor deaf, nor dumb—
> Huzza! she spurns the Northern scum!
> She breathes! she burns! she'll come! she'll come!
>   Maryland! My Maryland!

Randall's other songs of war, including "There's Life in the Old Land Yet," "The Battle Cry of the South," "The Lone Sentry," "Our Confederate Dead," and "At Arlington," suffer from many of the same deficiencies noted above. "My Maryland!" in particular, unlike American battle tunes such as Francis Scott Key's "Star-Spangled Banner" or panegyrics such as Samuel Francis Smith's "America" or Katherine Lee Bates's "America, the Beautiful," for example, lacks a central and definite point of reference for the speaker's strong feelings. The images necessary to vivid writing are thus absent, and the experience presented is out of focus and vague. Interest in Randall's work may well have less to do with artistic considerations than with historical or ideological ones.

• See Matthew Page Andrews's introductions to *The Poems of James Ryder Randall* (1910) and *The Library of Southern Literature* (1909); G. C. Perine, *The Poets and Verse-Writers of Maryland* (1898); Brander Matthews, "The Songs of the Civil War," in *Pen and Ink* (1902); and J. E. Uhler, "James Ryder Randall in Louisiana," *Louisiana Historical Quarterly* 21 (Apr. 1938): 532–46.

RICHARD E. MEZO

RANDALL, John Herman, Jr. (14 Feb. 1899–1 Dec. 1980), philosopher, historian, and educator, was born in Grand Rapids, Michigan, the son of John Herman Randall, a minister, and Minerva I. Ballard. The family moved to New York City to provide a better education for Randall. After enrolling in Columbia College, he received his A.B. in 1918 and membership in Phi Beta Kappa. The following year he received an M.A. and published his first article, "Instrumentalism and Mythology," in the *Journal of Philosophy*.

The philosophy department at Columbia had by this time risen to national prominence under the leadership of John Dewey and Frederick J. E. Woodbridge. Appointed an instructor in philosophy in 1921, while still a graduate student, Randall continued in that rank and received his doctorate in 1921 with the dissertation "The Problem of Group Responsibility to Society: An Interpretation of the History of American Labor." With the collaboration of other instructors and combining Dewey's and Woodbridge's ideas, he wrote several chapters for the cooperative volume *An Introduction to Reflective Thinking* (1923). In 1922 he married Mercedes Irene Moritz, with whom he had two sons. Promoted in 1925 to assistant professor, he served as the leader in constructing the syllabus for the Introduction to Contemporary Civilization course. In the same year he took over from Woodbridge the general history of philosophy course. He was promoted to associate professor in 1931 and professor in 1935; in 1947 Columbia awarded him the coveted Nicholas Murray Butler Silver Medal for distinguished service. In 1951 he was appointed Woodbridge Professor of Philosophy and in 1956 was elected president of the American Philosophical Association.

An outstanding historian of philosophy and a leading interpreter of American thought, Randall brought together Dewey's instrumentalism and Woodbridge's naturalistic metaphysics. In books, articles, and reviews he assessed philosophical movements from Greek philosophy to recent American and European currents, viewing them primarily as intellectual responses to problems generated by social, cultural, and technological changes that challenged the prevailing organization of rational methods.

Randall's first major work, *The Making of the Modern Mind*, published in 1926 (rev. 1940), is a synthetic critical study of the social, political, economic, and philosophical developments of the Western world. It was followed by *Our Changing Civilization* (1929; German trans. 1932), which outlines the major role played by science and technology in shaping modern society. In collaboration with his father, Randall published *Religion and the Modern World* (1929) and, with Justus Buchler as coauthor, *Philosophy: An Introduction* (1942), the latter emphasizing the method, scope, and principles of a naturalistic pragmatism. In 1946 he wrote for a cooperative volume, with W. E. Hocking et al., part 4 of *Preface to Philosophy*, reissued as a separate treatise and with a new introduction as *The Meaning of Religion for Man* (1968). With Ernst Cassirer and P. O. Kristeller he brought out *The Renaissance Philosophy of Man* (1948).

Over the following decade Randall published numerous articles for journals and special volumes; the pertinent essays, selected and slightly revised, formed the bulk of his *Nature and Historical Experience: Essays in Naturalism and in the Theory of History* (1958). That same year the text of his 1955 Mead-Swing Lectures at Oberlin College was published as *The Role of Knowledge in Western Religion*, a theme elaborated further in his Merrick Lectures at Ohio Wesleyan University in 1961. After establishing the Renaissance Society of America in 1954 and serving as its first president, he created, with Carlo Diano, the Columbia-Padua Institute in 1958. His investigations of the development of the scientific method in the School of Padua, which led to new appraisals of the role of Aristotelianism in modern science, came out in 1961 as a single volume, *The School of Padua and the Emergence of Modern Science*.

The decade 1960–1970 was Randall's most productive period. His original treatment of Greek philosophy, stemming from his earlier association with Woodbridge, appeared in three separate volumes: *Aristotle* (1960), *Plato: Dramatist of the Life of Reason* (1970), and *Hellenistic Ways of Deliverance and the Making of the Christian Synthesis* (1970). Special dis-

tinction came to Randall with the projected three-volume work *The Career of Philosophy*; for volume one, *From the Middle Ages to the Enlightenment* (1962), and volume two, *From the German Enlightenment to the Age of Darwin* (1965), he received the Phi Beta Kappa Ralph Waldo Emerson Award in 1966; volume three was not completed. Several independent essays were collected and edited by Beth Singer in *Philosophy after Darwin: Chapters for the Career of Philosophy, Vol. III, and Other Essays* (1977).

The interpretive principles of the *Career* were presented in summary form in Randall's *How Philosophy Uses Its Past* (1963), based on the Matchette Lectures he presented at Wesleyan University. The work emphasized the theses that the study of the past forms the necessary background to view critically the contemporary prevailing philosophies of experience and that philosophy has historical dimensions just as the history of philosophy has a philosophic function. His main theme from the start was the problem of redefining metaphysics via experience and showing how the encounter of conflicts leads to fruitful resolutions when concepts are critically reconstructed to effect reconciliations. He died in New York City.

As Randall expressed it, philosophy is "a clarification and criticism of fundamental beliefs involved in all great enterprises of human culture, science, art, religion, the moral, social and practical activity, when some new idea or some altered experience has impinged upon them and generated intellectual tensions and maladjustments" (*How Philosophy Uses Its Past*, p. 100). At the center of his philosophy was the view that experience is historical and pluralistic and always has a personal locus, that it is cumulative without being linear, and that it can be progressive only when sufficiently critical. Philosophy as metaphysics is fundamentally the critique of assumptions to be found in traditions and intellectual practices.

• Randall's extensive library was acquired after his death by Texas A & M University. His activities and place in the development of the Department of Philosophy at Columbia University are mentioned in chaps. 2 and 3, written by Randall and Horace Friess, respectively, in *A History of the Faculty of Philosophy, Columbia University*, ed. Jacques Barzun (1957). See also John P. Anton, ed., *Naturalism and Historical Understanding: Essays on the Philosophy of John Herman Randall, Jr.* (1967), esp. the editor's preface, the biographical sketch of Randall, the bibliography of his publications, and, in the "Memoirs and Tributes" section, contributions by Harry Elmer Barnes and James Gutmann. For a special treatment of Randall's ideas see Andrew J. Reck, *The New American Philosophers* (1968), pp. 120–63. Also see references to Randall in W. F. Jones, *Nature and Natural Science: The Philosophy of F. J. E. Woodbridge* (1983), and R. D. Boisvert, *Dewey's Metaphysics* (1988). An obituary is in the *New York Times*, 2 Dec. 1980.

JOHN P. ANTON

RANDALL, Robert Richard (1750?–5 June 1801), merchant and philanthropist, was born probably in Chatham, New Jersey, the son of Thomas Randall and Gertrude Cooke. In the 1740s Randall's father, a native of Scotland, immigrated to New York City, where he became a ship owner and amassed the family's fortune. During the French and Indian War Thomas Randall was given permission by the British Crown to capture ships, owning at one time at least three armed vessels. Thomas Randall was a founder of the Marine Society of the City of New York, which helped to relieve indigent and distressed shipmasters and their orphans and widows. He was also instrumental in convening the New York Colonial Congress and became president of the first Board of Aldermen and Common Council of the liberated city. In addition, his name heads a list of citizens who greeted General George Washington upon his entrance to the city on 25 November 1783. On the day of Washington's inauguration in 1789 Thomas Randall served as the coxswain of the ceremonial boat he had designed to convey the newly elected president from Elizabethport, New Jersey, to the ceremonies in New York City.

Robert Randall served as a partner in his father's New York City mercantile company, Randall, Son & Stewart. Beginning in 1790 he resided in retirement on Manhattan Island on a farm his father had recently purchased. Robert inherited the farm in 1797. He never married. So little is recorded about him that it must be assumed he lived quietly in the shadow of his vibrant father.

Robert Randall's most famous deed occurred on 1 June 1801, when he wrote his will and by this act created the benevolent institution known as Sailors' Snug Harbor. He directed that his Manhattan farm be used to create a home for "aged, decrepit and worn-out sailors" and that his estate be managed by a board of trustees of eight distinguished citizens: the chancellor of the state of New York, the mayor and the recorder of the city of New York, the president of the New York City Chamber of Commerce, the president and the vice president of the Marine Society, the rector of Trinity Church, and the minister of the First Presbyterian Church. After Randall's death and several lawsuits, which required many years to resolve, the trustees decided to hold the Manhattan farm (the city was quickly growing up to it) for leasing and to use the income generated by it to purchase another site and endow the institution. (Randall's twenty-one acres border on Washington Square North and are now leased to New York University.)

In 1831 the trustees acquired a farm on Staten Island, and in 1833 Sailors' Snug Harbor was opened to thirty-seven men. By the turn of the century it housed nearly 1,000 men in magnificent classical revival buildings. In 1979 the institution relocated to Sea Level, North Carolina, and the Staten Island site was purchased by New York City for a cultural center. Randall died at his Manhattan farm and was buried in St. Mark's in-the-Bowery. In 1834 his bones were disinterred and placed on Staten Island beneath a large obelisk before the main building at Sailors' Snug Harbor, where they remain. Decades after his death he was given the honorific title "Captain" by the recipients of his benevolence.

In 1839 Robert E. Launitz, the New York sculptor, created for the trustees a marble bust of Randall in the style of a Roman senator for the main hall of the institution. In 1884 Augustus Saint-Gaudens created a life-size bronze statue of Randall. With no known image (painting or sketch), he used a studio model in colonial costume.

Through his benevolence, Randall perpetuated the generosity, civic-mindedness, and love of the sea that had been so much a part of his and his family's lives.

• Except for his will, no original manuscript materials or artifacts from Randall survive. A facsimile of the will printed by the trustees of Sailors' Snug Harbor in the 1960s is available at the institution and at the Staten Island Historical Society. Printed text versions were frequently published over the years. The archives of Sailors' Snug Harbor at the State University of New York Maritime College, Fort Schuyler, Bronx, N.Y., contain several letters written to Randall. Donald C. Seitz, "Sailors' Snug Harbor: A History of Captain Robert Richard Randall's Foundation for the Toilers of the Sea" (unpublished ms., 1958), in the possession of the board of trustees of Sailors' Snug Harbor, Sea Level, N.C., contains information about the Randall family. See also I. N. Phelps Stokes, *The Iconography of Manhattan Island* (6 vols., 1915–1928); and Barnett Shepherd, *Sailors' Snug Harbor: 1801–1976* (1979).

BARNETT SHEPHERD

RANDALL, Samuel Jackson (10 Oct. 1828–13 Apr. 1890), Speaker of the House of Representatives, was born in Philadelphia, Pennsylvania, the son of Josiah Randall, a lawyer and local Whig politician, and Ann Worrell, the daughter of a leading Philadelphia Jeffersonian Republican. Randall attended the University Academy in that city and went to work at the age of seventeen in the counting room of a silk merchant. He then became a partner in a coal business and at twenty-one formed a partnership to deal in odd-lot iron. In 1851 he married Fannie Agnes Ward (whose father had been a Democratic congressman from New York); they had three children.

Born and married into politically active families, Randall quickly entered rough-and-tumble Philadelphia politics, where he used "his fists as well as his head" (Alexander, p. 129). Apparently attracted by xenophobia, Randall ran for the Philadelphia Common Council as an American (anti-foreign) Whig and served from 1852 to 1856. When the Whig party began disintegrating, Randall and his father (who was a friend of James Buchanan) moved into the Democratic party. From 1858 to 1860 he served as a Democrat in the Pennsylvania Senate, where he was on the committee on retrenchment and reform. He made his mark, however, by securing charters for Philadelphia street railway companies and, aware of the high cost of financing such ventures, by attacking banks for their exorbitant rates. When the Civil War broke out, Randall served for ninety days in 1861 and for a short time during the 1863 Gettysburg campaign without seeing any action. In 1862, prior to that campaign, Randall had been elected as a Democrat to Congress. The Republicans, to carry other congressional seats, had gerrymandered his constituents, most of whom labored on the waterfront or in shops and factories, into an overwhelmingly Democratic district. They reelected Randall thirteen times and he served from 1863 until his death.

Believing that the Civil War's objective was to preserve both the Constitution and the Union without disturbing slavery, Randall was among the twenty-two Democrats who on 29 February 1864 were willing to negotiate a status quo antebellum with Confederate leaders. In April 1864 he also refused to join War Democrats and Republicans in censuring or declaring unworthy two Peace Democrats who supported the Confederacy in the House of Representatives.

During the war Randall voted to oppose conscription and emancipation; to uphold the fugitive slave laws of 1793 and 1850; and to prevent blacks from serving in the army, voting in the territory of Montana, and riding on streetcars in the District of Columbia. As the war drew to a close, Randall and his fellow Democrats argued that the Union did not need to be reconstructed because it had not been dissolved and that the suppression of the rebellion in a state automatically restored its rights under the Constitution. He opposed, without success, Republican-backed constitutional amendments and legislation that required the governments of states that had joined the Confederacy to guarantee freedom, civil rights, and the vote to African Americans.

Although neither imposing in figure nor stylish in dress, Randall's attentiveness, "terse, withering sentences," and "scornful invective" (Alexander, p. 240), delivered in a high, shrill voice, made him a formidable debater and a party leader. His mastery of obstruction was so great that it was called "Samrandallism." In January 1875 dilatory motions, requiring time-consuming roll calls, delayed civil rights legislation, keeping the House in continuous session forty-six and a half hours, and in February he led a 72-hour filibuster, preventing passage of a companion enforcement bill that would have renewed the power of the president to suspend the writ of habeas corpus.

When not opposing Reconstruction measures, Randall hampered Republicans by sponsoring amnesty legislation for those who supported the Confederacy, by trying to pare down appropriations bills, by opposing land grants for railroad construction and mail subsidies for steamship companies, by pressing for investigations of Credit Mobilier and Sanborn contract corruption, by emphasizing Ulysses S. Grant's disastrous second term (through the advocacy of a single six-year term for the president), and by trying to identify the Democrats with retrenchment and reform. As an old Philadelphia Whig, Randall was a protectionist and, to keep the nation dependent on the tariff, opposed the income tax and most excise taxes.

Following the Democratic victory in the 1874 election, Randall angled to become Speaker of the incoming House of Representatives. Although he was a hard-money man for whom full payment of the Civil War debt was a sacred obligation, he flirted with the soft-money men by advocating that the $300 million in banknotes issued by national banks be replaced with greenbacks and by opposing the 1875 act that called for the resumption in 1879 of specie payments for greenbacks. In 1875, by coupling antiresumption with pro-reform, he wrested control of the Pennsylvania Democratic party from pliant politicians identified with the Pennsylvania Railroad. He also campaigned in Ohio for the soft-money Democratic gubernatorial candidate and secured the support of the Ohio delegation for the Speakership. But he lost the friendship of the hard-money men, and by championing the retroactive Salary Grab Act (1873), he tarnished his retrenchment and reform image. In December 1875 he lost to Michael Kerr of Indiana, a hard-money man who had refused to collect his back pay. When Kerr died in August 1876, Randall mended fences with eastern hard-money men and cultivated Samuel J. Tilden, the 1876 Democratic presidential nominee.

When Congress reassembled in December during the crisis over the disputed presidential election, the Democratic majority named Randall the Speaker of the House. With Tilden remaining aloof from the struggle, Randall, who commanded the only branch of the federal government controlled by the Democratic party, became its de facto leader. His objective was to elect Tilden, but when that failed he worked to force Republicans to concede home rule (white supremacy Democratic governments) in the South and to hold his party together in the House (assuring his reelection as Speaker in the next Congress). To achieve these ends Randall fluctuated between moderation and extremism, as he and his party first compromised, then threatened to plunge the nation into chaos by delaying the counting of electoral votes, and finally at the last moment accepted the election of the Republican candidate, Rutherford B. Hayes.

Indeed, Randall was the crucial figure in the disputed election crisis. His committee appointments and his support made the compromise Electoral Commission Act (1877) possible. His rulings, after the commission began to award disputed states to Hayes, allowed the House to recess and delay the count but not reject the commission's decisions. His intemperate remarks in the Democratic caucus both frightened Republicans (with the threat of a filibuster that would force a new presidential election) and panicked southern Democrats (with the threat of dire consequences should they desert to the Republicans to secure home rule). And finally his refusal to entertain dilatory motions of filibusterers enabled Hayes to be inaugurated on schedule. "To me," he later explained, the [Electoral Commission] law was higher than the rules [of the House] when the law came in conflict with the rules" (Follett, p. 123).

Although James G. Blaine, a Republican predecessor as Speaker of the House, remarked that Randall never neglected his public duties and never forgot the interests of the Democratic party, Randall's subsequent moves as Speaker united the Republicans and damaged the Democrats. He supported the Clarkson N. Potter investigation into allegations of Republican fraud in the 1876 election, and he backed attempts to repeal the election laws (designed to protect voting rights under the Fourteenth and Fifteenth amendments) by attaching riders to appropriations bills. Both strategies were failures. The Potter committee uncovered nothing damaging to the Republicans, but by confirming that Tilden's nephew had tried to buy the election for his uncle, it destroyed both Tilden's candidacy and the fraud issue for 1880. By vetoing appropriations bills with riders, Hayes prevented Congress from encroaching on the executive's lawmaking power and rallied Republicans with his stirring defense of voting rights. In the 1880 election the Republicans carried the presidency and the House of Representatives, and Randall ceased to be Speaker in 1881.

As Speaker, Randall exercised great power. He disagreed with the low tariff attitudes of most Democrats and was accused of being too intimate with lobbyists as he stacked committees and made rulings that retained protective tariffs on American manufactures. Led by him the House in 1880 condensed 166 rules into 45 that fostered "order, accuracy, uniformity, and economy of time" (Alexander, p. 195). The new rules enhanced the control of the Speaker by converting the House Rules Committee into a powerful standing committee, which the Speaker chaired.

Increasingly out of step with his party on the tariff issue, Randall was not named Speaker when in 1883 the Democrats regained the House. But as the powerful chair of the Appropriations Committee, he reduced expenditures and controlled legislation requiring funding. In 1884 and 1886 Randall was instrumental in defeating tariff reduction bills proposed by his fellow Democrat and archrival William R. Morrison. In 1888, however, President Grover Cleveland deprived Randall of federal patronage in Pennsylvania and with it the control of that state's Democratic party because Randall had opposed the administration-backed Mills tariff bill. Despite these losses and the ravages of colon cancer, Randall remained a parsimonious, partisan leader of House Democrats until he died in Washington. "There may have been better parliamentarians, men of broader intellect and more learning," Republican Speaker of the House Thomas B. Reed remarked, "but there have been few men with a will more like iron or a courage more unfaltering" (House, p. 135).

• The Randall papers are in the Van Pelt Library of the University of Pennsylvania. See Albert Virgil House, Jr., "The Political Career of Samuel Jackson Randall" (Ph.D. diss., Univ. of Wisconsin, 1934), for the most complete study of Randall. See also Mary Parker Follett, *The Speaker of the House of Representatives* (1902); De Alva Stanwood Alexander, *History and Procedure of the House of Representatives* (1916); and George B. Galloway, *History of the House of Representatives* (1961; rev. ed. 1976). An obituary is in the *New York Times*, 14 Apr. 1890.

ARI HOOGENBOOM

RANDOLPH, Asa Philip (15 Apr. 1889–16 May 1979), founder of the Brotherhood of Sleeping Car Porters and civil rights leader, was born in Crescent City, Florida, the son of James William Randolph, an itinerant African Methodist Episcopal preacher, and Elizabeth Robinson. The family placed great stress on education. Thus Randolph, an honor student, was sent to Cookman Institute in Jacksonville, Florida (later Bethune-Cookman College). Although greatly influenced by his father's political and racial attitudes, Randolph resisted pressure to enter the ministry and later became an atheist. Upon graduation from Cookman, in 1907, he found himself barred by racial prejudice from all but manual labor jobs in the South, and so in 1911 he moved to New York City, where he worked at odd jobs during the day and took social science courses at City College at night.

The radical ideologies advocated by the Socialists and the Industrial Workers of the World, then at their peak of influence, helped form his philosophy. He met Chandler Owen, a student at Columbia Law School, and the pair worked out a synthesis based on Marxian economic ideas and the sociological theories of Lester Frank Ward: men could be truly free only if they were not subject to economic deprivation. Randolph and Owen joined the Socialist party and became soapbox orators propagandizing for black unionism. They opened an employment office in Harlem, began a training program for migrants arriving from the South, and tried, unsuccessfully, to organize black workers into unions. In 1913 Randolph married Lucille Campbell Green, a widow six years older than himself whom he had met while acting in Shakespearean plays for a Harlem theater group. (The couple did not have children.) The theater training accounted for Randolph's Oxford accent and helped him hone his public speaking technique, while Lucille Randolph's earnings as a hairdresser and beauty shop owner supported his subsequent undertakings.

In 1917 Randolph and Owen began publishing the *Messenger* magazine with the slogan the "only magazine of scientific radicalism in the world published by Negroes." Although they were pacifists and were briefly jailed for their opposition to the First World War, the partners concluded that only force, economic or physical, could secure full citizenship rights for African Americans. They argued that only through socialism and labor organization could the race be upgraded economically. For expressing such sentiments, the Department of Justice labeled the *Messenger* "the most able and the most dangerous of all the Negro publications." Later, as the *Messenger* began publishing the work of young black poets and authors, a critic called it "one of the most brilliantly edited magazines in the history of Negro journalism."

Hoping to capitalize on the increased African-American vote resulting from the great migration of blacks from the rural South to the urban North, in 1920 Randolph, his wife, and Owen all ran for office on the Socialist ticket. The majority of African Americans remained unimpressed by socialism, however, and none of the three was elected. Nevertheless, Randolph and Owen started a variety of groups, such as the Friends of Negro Freedom, to draw African Americans into the labor movement. None was particularly successful, perhaps because they vacillated between integrating their organizations and making them racially exclusive.

Randolph's intellectual clique became a victim of the postwar fear of radicalism that developed partly in response to the Bolshevik Revolution. Government repression of both black and white radicals ensued. In addition, the editorial staff of the *Messenger* became deeply divided by three major disagreements in the early 1920s. The issues—support for Marcus Garvey and his Back-to-Africa movement, the ever-widening gulf between West Indian and American blacks, and the rupture of the Socialist party over the Bolshevik Revolution—were interrelated. Garvey's advocacy of racial separatism conflicted with Randolph's promotion of working-class solidarity across racial lines. Because Garvey came from Jamaica, this rift degenerated into a West Indian versus African-American controversy, especially when Randolph and Owen mounted a "Garvey Must Go" campaign in an effort to have him deported. In 1919 most West Indian radicals went into the new Communist party, while most American blacks remained with Randolph's socialist faction; but because of the party's factional infighting, socialist financial support for the *Messenger* declined. These ideological wars made Randolph a confirmed anticommunist.

Randolph began writing for more moderate journals like *Opportunity* and in 1925 was invited to organize the Pullman porters. Because they had steady jobs and traveled the country, the porters were considered the elite of black labor. Yet since they were not unionized, they typified the large segment of exploited and underpaid black employees. As the one occupation where African Americans held a near monopoly, the porters offered possibilities for labor organization that Randolph's previous targets had not, and because Randolph was not employed by Pullman, the company could not fire him. The *Messenger* meanwhile became the official organ of the Brotherhood of Sleeping Car Porters (BSCP).

Seizing on their complaints of onerous work rules, Randolph educated the porters about the value of collective bargaining and trade unionism, giving them a keener appreciation of their unstable economic position as workers. Realizing that the strength of the union ultimately depended on its ability to correct grievances and provide job security, Randolph believed nonetheless that the primary issue was color. Pullman had previously dealt with labor unions, but to sit down and bargain with African Americans was a concept the company was not ready to accept. Amazingly, the brotherhood enrolled 51 percent of the porters within a year. Pullman, consequently, attempted to undermine the union with a series of retaliatory measures including frame-ups, beatings, and firings.

The failure of his efforts to obtain mediation under the 1926 Watson-Parker Railway Labor Act and his attack on the tipping system before the Interstate Commerce Commission forced Randolph into calling a strike in 1928; but striking went against the tradition of black labor. African Americans were accustomed to finding jobs as strikebreakers, and they were afraid that other blacks would be eager to take what was considered to be the plush job of a Pullman porter. In response to rumors that Pullman had nearly 5,000 Filipinos ready to take the places of brotherhood members, William Green, head of the American Federation of Labor (AFL), persuaded Randolph to postpone the strike. Membership in the union then dropped by half, publication of the *Messenger* ceased, and the telephone and electricity at the brotherhood's headquarters were disconnected for lack of funds.

Under President Franklin D. Roosevelt's New Deal, Section 7A of the National Industrial Recovery Act of 1933 guaranteed labor the right to organize and select bargaining representatives without interference from the employer. As a result, membership in the BSCP increased. Aided by its new organ, the *Black Worker*, and William Green's conviction that the brotherhood acted as a barrier to Communist penetration into African-American labor, the BSCP received a charter from the AFL in 1935. Finally, on 25 August 1937 the Pullman Company signed a contract with the nation's first black union. A personal triumph for Randolph, the agreement brought an extra $2 million a year to the porters and their families as well as greater job security and the ability to bargain collectively for better working conditions.

The victory over Pullman gave Randolph enormous prestige in both the black and the white communities. In addition, Randolph courted journalists, thereby assuring that the brotherhood received publicity far out of proportion to its size. Over time, as Randolph used the BSCP for the foundation of all his civil rights organizations, the union came to wield influence much greater than its membership warranted.

To Randolph the brotherhood represented more than an instrument of service to the porters and a tool to wage a nationwide struggle to gain equality for African Americans. He also utilized it to stimulate black participation in unions and to fight discrimination in organized labor. Through the *Black Worker*, Randolph inculcated the porters with such middle-class values as abstaining from alcohol, owning their own homes, and sending their children to college as well as the necessity of supporting his civil rights activities.

By organizing and winning recognition for the BSCP, Randolph developed a loyal following. Known among African Americans as "Mr. Black Labor" and "St. Philip of the Pullman Porters," Randolph also achieved recognition in the white press and became a prominent African-American spokesman in the public arena. He was appointed a member of the New York City Commission on Race, for example, and, in 1935, president of the National Negro Congress (NNC), an umbrella organization to help African Americans cope with the economic distress of the depression. The NNC unfortunately was soon rent by factional infighting, and Randolph resigned in 1940, charging the organization with Communist domination.

By the 1940s, defense preparations were pulling the country out of the depression, but blacks, denied defense jobs because of racial discrimination, remained on the relief rolls in inordinate numbers. When the Roosevelt administration proved impervious to their entreaties, Randolph, influenced by the sit-down techniques of the labor movement and Gandhian nonviolent tactics, conceived the idea of a march of African Americans on Washington to demand jobs and an end to segregation in the military. Fearing a black invasion of segregated Washington and realizing that without some tangible concessions he could not persuade Randolph to call off the march, the president issued Executive Order #8802 creating a temporary wartime Fair Employment Practices Committee (FEPC). Although the order did not include military integration, Randolph agreed to call off the march primarily because he was uncertain how many would actually march. Nevertheless, elated at the success of his strategy of mass nonviolent civil disobedience, Randolph decided to keep his organization, the March On Washington Movement (MOWM), intact to continue the fight for civil rights. The MOWM mounted a series of spectacular rallies in major cities in the summer of 1942 demanding racial equality.

Randolph declined a position on the FEPC and, in 1944, also refused to run for Congress. He chose instead to work for permanent fair employment practices legislation and to this end founded the National Council for a Permanent FEPC. Unlike the racially exclusive MOWM, the National Council was an integrated organization. It brought Randolph further notoriety but failed to achieve its legislative objectives.

When the Cold War caused President Harry S. Truman to ask Congress for a peacetime draft law, Randolph refocused his attention on integration of the military. He counseled young African-American men to refuse to register and be drafted into a segregated military establishment. In July 1948 the politically vulnerable Truman, needing the black vote for his close reelection race, capitulated to Randolph's nonviolent civil disobedience campaign and issued Executive Order #9981 integrating the United States military. Under continual pressure from Randolph's Committee Against Jim Crow in Military Service and Training, the military went from the most segregated to the most successfully integrated institution in the nation, demonstrating once again the effectiveness of nonviolent civil disobedience.

Randolph's philosophy had a direct influence on the midcentury civil rights movement. After the 1954 Supreme Court school desegregation decision, *Brown v. Board of Education*, the Montgomery Bus Boycott was organized by porter E. D. Nixon who had been imbued with Randolph's nonviolent egalitarian ideas. It was Nixon who tapped Martin Luther King, Jr., for leadership of the boycott. When southern school districts used delaying tactics to avoid implementing the school desegregation decision, Randolph mounted a Prayer Pilgrimage in 1957 that brought King wider media exposure. He then sponsored a pair of Youth Marches for Integrated Schools in 1958 and 1959 in the nation's capital. Unlike Randolph's proposed march of 1941, these marches were integrated demonstrations supported by black civil rights groups, white liberals, black and white church groups, and some trade unions. For the day-to-day organizing of the marches, Randolph teamed up with Bayard Rustin, who became his protégé.

Still vacillating between integration and separatism, in 1959, the same year he led the second march for integrated schools, Randolph also launched the all-black Negro American Labor Council (NALC) to fight racism within the labor movement. When the AFL merged with the Congress of Industrial Organizations (AFL-CIO) in 1955, Randolph became one of the federation's two African-American vice presidents. Largely through his efforts, the combined federation committed itself to a policy of backing racial integration with financial contributions. Randolph, however, had always been ambivalent about accepting white assistance, arguing that "where you get your money you also get your ideas and control." He soon concluded that financial support alone was insufficient; the AFL-CIO was not doing enough to cleanse itself of racial discrimination. George Meany, then head of the AFL-CIO, remained unsympathetic, however, demanding of Randolph, "Who the hell appointed you as the guardian of all the Negroes in America?" Both because young African-American unionists did not think that the NALC was militant enough and because Meany resented the organization as a separatist movement, it never had the impact on federation racial practices that Randolph had projected for it.

To counter the lack of African-American economic progress, in his capacity as head of the NALC, Randolph proposed a March on Washington for Jobs and Freedom in 1963. The march came after the nonviolent sit-in movement, under the leadership of the Congress of Racial Equality and Martin Luther King, Jr.'s Southern Christian Leadership Conference, had spread across the South. At the same time, some blacks, especially youths outside of the movement, began responding to police brutality with violence, igniting demonstrations across the country and provoking white counterviolence. The older race betterment organizations, the National Association for the Advancement of Colored People and the National Urban League, also found themselves contending for prestige and financial contributions with more activist groups like the Student Nonviolent Coordinating Committee and the Congress of Racial Equality. Nevertheless, all the groups worked together for the March on Washington. The integrated march, coordinated by Bayard Rustin, was far less militant than Randolph's original 1941 conception. Still, the 250,000 marchers, about a third of whom were white, proved the efficacy of Randolph's coalition approach. Although marred for Randolph by the death of his wife three months earlier, the march marked a high point of the civil rights movement. It did not, however, produce any immediate, tangible achievements, and the coalition quickly dissolved amid struggles over Black Power and racial separatism.

Randolph earned the wrath of more militant African-American groups when he signed the Moratorium on Demonstrations, the purpose of which was to ensure the reelection of Lyndon B. Johnson to the presidency in 1964. During the Freedom Summer of 1964, young people risked their lives in Mississippi to register African Americans to vote and, with local black activists, forged the Mississippi Freedom Democratic party as a challenge to the all-white state delegation to the Democratic National Convention. Further antagonism ensued when Randolph, along with Bayard Rustin, supported Johnson's compromise of allowing only two delegates from the Mississippi Freedom Democratic party to be seated at the convention.

Also in 1964 Randolph founded the A. Philip Randolph Institute to carry on his ideas and methods. The objective of the institute was to promote Randolph's unique vision by strengthening ties between the labor movement, civil rights groups, and other progressive organizations. Through the institute Randolph announced his Freedom Budget for All Americans in 1965. A kind of domestic Marshall Plan, the budget called for a national expenditure of $18.5 billion a year over a ten-year period to implement its proposed solution to the economic problems of African Americans. The budget was based on the thesis that the only way to abolish poverty was to create full employment. By then, however, the country was deeply involved in the Vietnam War, and neither Congress nor the administration was interested in the wholesale budgetary and social changes that Randolph's plan would have entailed.

His health failing, in 1968 Randolph retired as president of the BSCP and vice president of the AFL-CIO executive council. In 1978 his beloved union, which had supplied the core constituency for all of his civil rights organizations, was absorbed into the Brotherhood of Railway and Airline Clerks. Though they had softened, Randolph's ideas and his rhetoric had not basically changed over the years. Yet the historical circumstances within which he operated had altered most significantly. The interracial class coalition that he endeavored to put together, along with his support of the Democratic party leadership, and his backing of the teachers' union in the New York City Teachers' Strike in 1968, caused black observers of the 1960s and 1970s to perceive Randolph as favoring the interests of organized labor over those of the African-American community. Although held in disdain by Black Power advocates at the time, within a decade of his death Randolph came to be regarded as a legendary African-American leader. His career demonstrated that blacks were not merely acted upon in an oppressive society; to a large extent they determined their own destiny. "Rather we die standing on our feet fighting for our rights than to exist upon our knees begging for life," Randolph proclaimed. His virulent anticommunism contributed to Randolph's vacillation between integration and racial exclusivity. Always fearful that the inclusion of whites would bring communist subversion, and wary that the tendency of whites to take over the leadership of interracial organizations retarded the development of black self-esteem, Randolph nevertheless believed in black nationalism merely as a short-term tactic to achieve the long-term goal of integration. He never wavered, however, in his belief that economics held the key to African-American equality.

A man of integrity, Randolph inspired great loyalty among his colleagues, black and white. Unique in that he made his reputation as a labor leader rather than by following the more traditional path to African-American leadership through the clergy, education, or organizational bureaucracy, Randolph attempted to establish a symbiotic relationship between the American labor movement and the cause of civil rights. His most enduring legacy, however, was the influence that his movements, ideology, and tactics had on the younger generation of civil rights leaders. They imbibed Randolph's strategy of nonviolent, mass civil disobedience and put it into practice.

• Randolph's "Reminiscences" were recorded by the Columbia Oral History Research Office. The Chicago Historical Society has the papers of the Chicago Division of the Brotherhood of Sleeping Car Porters as well as some material on Randolph's other activities. A smaller collection of brotherhood papers, along with Randolph's private papers, are at the Library of Congress. Much information on his civil rights work can be gleaned from the papers of the National Association for the Advancement of Colored People and the National Urban League, both at the Library of Congress. The best sources for Randolph's own writings are the *Messenger* and the *Black Worker*. He also contributed articles to *Crisis, Opportunity*, and *American Federationist* through the years. Jervis Anderson wrote *A. Philip Randolph: A Biographical Portrait* (1973). Paula F. Pfeffer analyzed his civil rights activity in *A. Philip Randolph: Pioneer of the Civil Rights Movement* (1990). Theodore Kornweibel, Jr., treated the *Messenger* in *No Crystal Stair: Black Life and the Messenger, 1917–1928* (1975). There are several books on the porters' union: Brailsford Reese Brazeal, *The Brotherhood of Sleeping Car Porters: Its Origin and Development* (1946); William H. Harris, *Keeping the Faith: A. Philip Randolph, Milton P. Webster, and the Brotherhood of Sleeping Car Porters, 1925–37* (1977); Jack Santino, *Miles of Smiles, Years of Struggle: Stories of Black Pullman Porters* (1989); and Joseph F. Wilson, *Tearing Down the Color Bar: A Documentary History and Analysis of the Brotherhood of Sleeping Car Porters* (1989). An obituary is in the *New York Times*, 18 May 1979.

PAULA F. PFEFFER

RANDOLPH, Benjamin Franklin (1820?–Oct. 1868), African-American political leader in Reconstruction South Carolina, was born free in Kentucky, the child of mixed-race parents whose names are unknown. As a child, Randolph's family moved to Ohio where he was educated in local schools. In 1854 he entered Oberlin College's preparatory department, before attending the college from 1857 to 1862. At Oberlin, Randolph received instruction both in the liberal arts and at the college's theological seminary. Soon after graduation he was ordained as a Methodist Episcopal minister. During the Civil War Randolph served as a chaplain in the Twenty-sixth Colored Infantry, which was dispatched to Hilton Head, South Carolina, in 1864.

After the war ended in 1865, Randolph applied for a position with the Freedmen's Bureau. He was not initially given an appointment in the Bureau, and instead he was sent to South Carolina by the American Missionary Association, a northern antislavery organization founded in 1846, which was after the war the most influential and best financed northern society in South Carolina. Once in South Carolina, Randolph founded, with Reverend E. J. Adams, the Charleston *Journal* in 1866, before becoming editor of the Charleston *Advocate* in 1867. Randolph also became active in the organization of the Republican party in South Carolina as an organizer for the Union League. In February 1867 Randolph was appointed as an agent of the education division of the Freedmen's Bureau, first as a teacher, then eventually as assistant superintendent of schools for the Bureau in South Carolina. In that position Randolph advocated for integrated public schooling. He argued that with the help of the Bureau "we are laying the foundation of a new structure here, and the time has come when we shall have to meet things squarely, and we must meet them now or never. The day is coming when we must decide whether the two races shall live together or not." Johnson was recognized by his contemporaries as an eloquent and persuasive speaker. In 1865 Randolph attended the Colored Person's Convention held in Zion Church in Charleston; the secretary of the Convention noted that during an evening rally Randolph delivered a speech "abounding in thought and enforced by a serious earnestness which impressed the minds and commanded the attention of the House." Randolph was "a pleasing speaker, calm and deliberate, and took the position that thought, like the ladies, 'when unadorned is adorned the most.'"

Randolph also remained active in the Methodist church and worked with Reverend B. F. Whittmore to spark political activism in the South by the Northern Methodist church. In 1867 Randolph and Whittmore were admitted to the South Carolina Conference of the Methodist Episcopal church (Northern) on a trial basis, although he did not receive a ministerial assignment until 1868. Randolph was one of several black Northern-Methodist minister-politicians, and he went to several congregations throughout the state as a party organizer when the Republican party began formally organizing in South Carolina in the spring of 1867.

In 1867 Randolph was made vice president of the Republican state executive committee, and the following year he was elected chairman of the committee just before the presidential campaign of 1868. Randolph was too radical even for some in his own party, and following his election as party chairman, several conservative Republicans staged a walkout during the party convention. The following year, Randolph was one of 226 African-American delegates to the 1868 South Carolina Constitutional Convention. Randolph was part of the influential faction of ministers at the convention who were natives of the North and who had come south as missionaries or with the Freedmen's Bureau. At the convention, Democrats accused Randolph of making incendiary speeches.

In that same year Randolph was elected to the South Carolina legislature as a state senator, representing Orangeburg County. In the state senate he worked for legal equality for blacks and, on 31 August 1868, during a debate on a bill that would end many types of public discrimination in South Carolina, demanded that no public accommodation be closed to him or to any other African American on the basis of their race. In mid-October 1868, while canvassing for the Republican party in the predominantly white upcountry districts of South Carolina, Randolph was shot and killed by "unknown parties" in Donaldsville. It was commonly believed that the Ku Klux Klan had ordered his death, almost certainly because Randolph was an outspoken black leader. A white man of questionable sanity later confessed to killing Randolph for money, but he killed himself, or perhaps was murdered, before he identified who allegedly had paid him. Randolph was one of at least twenty-six black delegates to the South Carolina Constitutional Convention who were later victims of Klan attacks, and was one of six delegates who were murdered by the Klan. While Randolph's life was cut short, he is remembered as an early radical and influential black leader, and he is an example of the kind of African-American activist elected to office in South Carolina during Reconstruction.

• A primary source is the *Proceedings of the Constitutional Convention of South Carolina* (2 vols., 1868), which includes quotes from Randolph. Numerous studies of Reconstruction South Carolina consider the work of Randolph, the most useful being Thomas C. Holt, *Black over White: Negro Political Leadership in South Carolina during Reconstruction* (1977). Other studies include Howard N. Rabinowitz, ed., *Southern Black Leaders of the Reconstruction Era* (1982); Philip S. Foner and George Walker, eds., *Proceedings of the Black State Conventions, 1840–65* (2 vols., 1980); Joel Williamson, *After Slavery: The Negro in South Carolina During Reconstruction, 1865–1877* (1965); Leon Litwack and August Meier, eds., *Black Leaders of the Nineteenth Century* (1988); Eric Foner, ed., *Freedom's Lawmakers: A Directory of Black Officeholders during Reconstruction* (1993); Robert H. Woody, *Republican Newspapers of South Carolina* (1936); and Francis Simkins and Woody, *South Carolina during Reconstruction* (1932). For a consideration of Oberlin College's role in training nineteenth-century black activists, see Juanita D. Fletcher, "Against the Consensus: Oberlin College and the Education of American Negroes, 1835–1900" (Ph.D. diss., American Univ., 1974).

DANIEL W. HAMILTON

RANDOLPH, Edmund (10 Aug. 1753–12 Sept. 1813), governor of Virginia, U.S. attorney general, and U.S. secretary of state, was born in "Tazewell Hall," the home of his parents, John Randolph and Ariana Jenings, in Williamsburg, Virginia. Descended from a family that traced its prominence in Virginia's public life to a mid-seventeenth-century English immigrant ancestor, Randolph grew to maturity in a home environment that cherished the law as a profession and politics as the responsibility of members of the educated class. His grandfather Sir John Randolph, his father, and his uncle Peyton Randolph all served as the king's attorney in colonial Virginia, and his mother's father, Edmund Jenings, held the same position in Maryland. Not surprisingly, then, after attending the College of William and Mary, Randolph read law in his father's office and entered practice at age twenty-one.

With the coming of the revolutionary crisis in 1775, Randolph's Loyalist father and mother left Virginia for England. Despite his father's stand, Randolph's support of the patriot cause never appears to have been questioned. In August 1775 he joined the Continental army as an aide to George Washington but served only a short time. Peyton Randolph's sudden death in Philadelphia while serving as president of the Continental Congress forced the younger man to leave the army to accompany the body home and to settle his uncle's affairs.

In the spring of 1776 Randolph was elected as Williamsburg's alternate delegate to the May Virginia Convention in place of George Wythe, who was then serving in Congress. Although the youngest delegate in that body, he was assigned to the prestigious committee that drafted the Virginia Declaration of Rights and the state constitution. Later, his fellow delegates selected him as the commonwealth's first attorney general. Shortly thereafter, on 29 August 1776, he married Elizabeth Nicholas, daughter of Robert Carter Nicholas, revolutionary politician and first Virginia state treasurer.

Initially, Randolph's duties as attorney general occupied little of his time, both because judicial activity had slowed during the early years of the revolutionary war and because the function of the office had yet to be clearly defined. He accepted legislative appointment to the Continental Congress in the spring of 1779, but by the end of the year his legal responsibilities required his return to Virginia. During this period he also served as mayor of Williamsburg, a post that combined significant administrative and legal duties at the local level. Randolph was able to return to Congress in 1781 and served for about nine months. At that time he cemented a lifelong friendship with James Madison and also began to develop a strong sense of the importance of nationalism to the survival of the new nation.

After nearly ten years' service as Virginia's attorney general, Randolph was elected governor by the legislature on 7 November 1786. That same year he also attended the Annapolis Convention, precursor to the Philadelphia Constitutional Convention held the following year. As Virginia's governor, Randolph was the natural choice to head Virginia's delegation to Philadelphia. He opened the convention with a lengthy and able speech about the need for a strong government for the young nation, and later he introduced the so-called Virginia Plan for elective representation. As the convention proceeded, he became disillusioned with the path his colleagues were taking, dissatisfied with the creation of a single executive, opposed to the manner of ratification, and convinced that the overall scheme was not sufficiently republican. He joined George Mason of Virginia and Elbridge Gerry of Massachusetts in refusing to sign the final version of the proposed constitution that was sent to Congress.

Upon his return to Virginia, Randolph drafted a *Letter . . . on the Federal Constitution* (1787) for submission to the general assembly, restating his concerns in part to explain his actions in Philadelphia. Although never forwarded to the legislators, the *Letter* was published in Richmond and distributed widely throughout Virginia and beyond. Consequently, Virginia anti-Federalists in the state ratifying convention were stunned and angered when Randolph announced a reversal of his position shortly after the start of that body's deliberations in June 1788. Although a proponent of acquiring amendments to the plan prior to approval, Randolph had come to the conclusion that ratification by eight states already had reduced Virginia's decision simply to that of "Union or no Union." His strong sense of nationalism overcame his fears of the new plan of government, and he joined James Madison, John Marshall, and Edmund Pendleton as an eloquent and passionate advocate of the federal Constitution in Virginia's convention.

While some of his contemporaries credited this and other such changes in Randolph's political stance to vacillation or expediency, in reality he struggled throughout his political life to rise above faction and to support positions and policies that he deemed worthy of his advocacy. Unfortunately, with the establishment of the federal government and the broadening of the new national political arena, his high-minded approach to public service became increasingly untenable.

Following the ratification struggle in Virginia, Randolph resigned the governorship and returned to the general assembly in November 1788. During the next year George Washington offered him the post of attorney general in the first federal administration. Initially, the federal attorney general served primarily as a legal adviser to the president and to the other department heads. Perhaps Randolph's most important official contribution during those first few months in office involved his submission of a report to the House of Representatives on what he perceived to be defects in the Judiciary Act, along with his recommendations for amendments. Within the cabinet, he gradually became Washington's most trusted adviser as he endeavored to steer a middle course between the increasingly factious Thomas Jefferson and Alexander Hamilton. Uncompromisingly loyal to the president, he argued strongly for neutrality in the war between England and France and drafted speeches and state papers for the president at nearly every turn.

When Jefferson resigned as secretary of state in 1793, Washington hesitantly turned to Randolph to fill the post. Both the president and Jefferson worried about the attorney general's ability to handle the demanding job in the climate of increasing factionalism, and Jefferson was troubled as well by Randolph's perennial financial difficulties. Washington finally opted for his trusted adviser, however, and Randolph proved a creditable statesman, although he eventually fell victim to political intrigue. With Jefferson's departure, Hamilton increasingly dominated the cabinet, and even after his resignation, the factionalism of the president's advisers continued to grow. In that setting, Randolph the moderate became the target of his Federalist colleagues.

Initially, Randolph retained his unofficial status as Washington's chief adviser, and he also served anonymously as the president's defender in the press following Washington's 1794 annual message, in which he had attacked the democratic societies for their alleged involvement in fomenting the Whiskey Insurrection. As "Germanicus," Randolph composed thirteen newspaper essays, later gathered into a pamphlet, but the articles were so cautiously written that they did little to quiet criticism of the president's declarations.

When Randolph took up his new duties as secretary of state in January 1794, the people of the United States were deeply divided in their feelings toward England and France. One of Randolph's first tasks was to rid the country of the troublesome Citizen Edmond Charles Genet, France's meddling minister to America; Randolph managed this assignment tactfully but effectively. He then responded sympathetically to France's request for the recall of Gouverneur Morris and skillfully guided the efforts of the new American minister to France, James Monroe. At the same time he resented Great Britain's failure to abide by the terms of the peace treaty of 1783, as well as that nation's infringement on America's neutral rights. Although he favored the Hamiltonian plan for the appointment of a special envoy to discuss these issues with the British government, Randolph resented Hamilton's intrusiveness into foreign affairs, opposed the selection of Supreme Court chief justice John Jay as the emissary, and objected to the broad powers given to Jay to negotiate a new commercial treaty. Jay treated the secretary with a certain courteous formality in his dispatches from England but took advantage of the long delays between communications virtually to ignore Randolph's instructions. The resulting treaty, extremely unpopular in Randolph's native Virginia, revealed that Jay had made many concessions for relatively little in return. In addition, a British order in Council passed in late 1793 remained in place, authorizing the capture of ships laden with provisions and apparently destined for France. Randolph advised Washington against ratification of the Jay Treaty under these circumstances.

Randolph's Federalist colleagues, who favored the treaty, resented his influence with the president. So, too, did the British minister to America, George Hammond, who suddenly found himself with the means of removing this formidable obstacle. Captured communiques from the new French minister to America, Joseph Fauchet, seemed to suggest that Randolph had revealed certain sensitive information in their conversations and that he had secretly solicited French money. Modern scholarship suggests that Fauchet exaggerated his accounts to win favor with his superiors in Paris, but, nonetheless, Hammond quickly placed these documents in the hands of Timothy Pickering and Oliver Wolcott, who in turn brought them to President Washington. When Washington called Randolph into his office and confronted him with the dispatches in the presence of these two secretaries, Randolph responded angrily. Sensing a rupture in Washington's trust, he hastily resigned. He secured a statement from Fauchet absolving him of all wrongdoing and then drafted and published a *Vindication of Mr. Randolph's Resignation* (1795), in which he reviewed his actions as secretary of state, suggested a British plot to have him removed from office, and fired off an intemperate attack against Washington. While the pamphlet did little to restore his reputation, its treatment of Washington gave the president no room to maneuver and thus effectively ended their personal, as well as their political, relationship. A second vindication, *Political Truth*, published in early 1796, proved to be a calmer, more carefully reasoned and articulated summary of events, designed in part to support Republican congressional efforts to deny the administration funds to put the Jay Treaty into effect, but after that pamphlet appeared Randolph never again expressed himself publicly on an issue of national politics.

With his resignation from the office of secretary of state, Randolph returned to Richmond to reestablish his law practice. He concentrated primarily on cases in the Virginia Court of Appeals, although he also helped to represent Aaron Burr in Burr's 1807 treason trial before the U.S. Circuit Court in Richmond.

During this period Randolph prepared an abridgment of Virginia's laws in 1796 but spent most of his free time with his wife and five children and in drafting a "History of Virginia." This project, begun perhaps as early as the mid-1780s, in a sense served as another, less obvious, vindication of Randolph's career in public service. In the "History," he emphasized the character of the public man in Virginia and lauded what he perceived as the generous, disinterested leadership of the elite governing class over the general populace. He also came to terms with his severed relationship with George Washington and gave prominence to that man in his interpretation of the events of the revolutionary crisis. Randolph's "History" was not published in his lifetime but has appeared in a modern edition.

Unfortunately, Randolph was hounded in his last years by incessant indebtedness, for while he was a skillful attorney, he also proved to be a poor manager of his personal finances. His financial problems were compounded by the relentless pursuit by Oliver Wolcott of State Department funds deemed lost or unaccounted for, for which the former secretary was responsible by law. Randolph placed his entire estate in the hands of his brother-in-law Wilson Cary Nicholas in order to pay off an arbitrator's award of more than $53,000 to the government, although through questionable accounting the debt remained on the State Department ledgers until 1889. Randolph's last years were also troubled by increasing bouts with paralysis and by the loss of his wife in 1810. He spent most of his time at the home of his daughter in Charles Town, Jefferson County (now West Virginia). He died at "Carter Hall" near Millwood, Virginia, and was buried in the Old Chapel Cemetery there. In 1940 the Grand Lodge of Freemasons in Virginia, of which he had been grand master, erected a monument there in his honor.

• No large cache of Randolph's personal papers appears to survive, although much of his correspondence with Washington, Jefferson, and Madison may be found in collections of their papers at the Library of Congress. Official records of his federal government service are also available in appropriate record groups at the National Archives. A modern study by John J. Reardon, *Edmund Randolph: A Biography* (1974), is generally adequate; also helpful is Charles F. Hobson, "The Early Career of Edmund Randolph, 1753–1789" (Ph.D. diss., Emory Univ., 1971). The now dated study by Moncure Daniel Conway, *Omitted Chapters of History Disclosed in the Life and Papers of Edmund Randolph* (1889), remains primarily useful for the copies of documents it contains. Three recent articles focus on Randolph's fall from power and all three exonerate the secretary of state of wrongdoing: Irving Brant, "Edmund Randolph, Not Guilty!" *William and Mary Quarterly*, 3d ser., 7 (1950): 179–98; John G. Clifford, "A Muddy Middle of the Road: The Politics of Edmund Randolph, 1790–1795," *Virginia Magazine of History and Biography* 80 (1972): 286–311; and Mary K. Bonsteel Tachau, "George Washington and the Reputation of Edmund Randolph," *Journal of American History* 73 (June 1986): 15–34. See also Dice Robins Anderson, "Edmund Randolph," in *The American Secretaries of State and Their Diplomacy*, vol. 2, ed. Samuel Flagg Bemis (1927; repr. 1963), pp. 95–159. Arthur H. Shaffer edited and provided a valuable introduction to Randolph's *History of Virginia* (1970).

E. LEE SHEPARD

RANDOLPH, Edward (July 1632–April 1703), surveyor general of customs in colonial America, was born in Canterbury, England, the son of Dr. Edmund Randolph and Deborah Master. The family owned extensive lands in southeastern England. Randolph entered Gray's Inn in 1650 and was admitted to Queens' College, Cambridge, in 1651, but neither took a degree nor practiced law. Probably sometime before 1660, he married Jane Gibbon, whose family also owned land in Kent; they had four daughters. After her death in 1679 Randolph married Grace Grenville, who died three years later. Then, in 1684, Randolph married Sarah Platt, with whom he had another daughter.

During the 1660s Randolph sold timber from his own lands to the Royal Navy, was employed for a time as muster master for the Cinque Ports, and engaged in timber purchasing schemes in Scotland. When his fortunes sank, he and his family were forced to sell land to pay debts. Through his first marriage Randolph became connected to Robert Mason, grandson and heir of Captain John Mason, the original proprietor of New Hampshire. This association began Randolph's career in America.

In England Robert Mason sued before the Committee of the Privy Council for Trade and Plantations, or "Lords of Trade," to gain control of his American lands. The committee employed Randolph to go to Boston with orders to respond to Mason's suit. The Lords also instructed Randolph to report back with his observations on a list of topics they supplied. Randolph arrived in Boston in June and returned to England in September 1676. His "Narrative of the State of New England," which emphasized the autonomy of Massachusetts (among other things it coined money, refused appeals to English courts, and administered its own oath of allegiance), persuaded the Lords to regulate trade to Massachusetts more carefully.

In 1678 Randolph was appointed collector of customs in New England under the Plantation Duty Act. He returned to Boston in December 1679. Massachusetts insisted on its right to self-government under the royal charter of 1629, and Randolph was unable to prosecute illegal trade effectively. He urged the Lords of Trade to take legal action against the charter, which was done in 1684, thus ending fifty-four years of independent rule by the Puritan government in Massachusetts.

Randolph had an important part in creating a new, temporary government for Massachusetts under the leadership of Joseph Dudley but seems to have had no hand in designing the grandiose Dominion of New England that followed. He now held numerous offices in Boston: secretary and register, collector of customs, surveyor of woods, and deputy auditor to William Blathwayt, auditor general for the American colonies. But differences with the governor-general of the Dominion of New England, Sir Edmund Andros, who arrived in December 1686, and hostility from Puritans within the colony combined to frustrate Randolph's expectations of substantial income and authority.

The Glorious Revolution placed William of Orange on the throne of England in February 1689. On 18 April a broad coalition of leaders in Boston led a successful rebellion against Governor Andros. The rebel leaders imprisoned Randolph along with Andros, Joseph Dudley, and other members of the Dominion government until February 1690, when the prisoners were sent back to England. After a brief hearing the Lords of Trade exonerated all the prisoners and reassigned many to American colonial offices outside New England. They appointed Randolph surveyor general of customs for all provinces and colonies of America on 14 October 1691.

Randolph arrived at James City, Virginia, in April 1692 and visited Maryland, Pennsylvania, New York, Massachusetts, and New Hampshire. In Maryland he ran afoul of Governor Lionel Copley when he tried to audit Copley's accounts. Randolph then fled to Virginia but returned to Maryland when Francis Nicholson replaced Copley in 1694; Nicholson soon appointed Randolph to the Maryland Council. In the summer of 1695 Randolph sailed for England with evidence of mismanagement and corruption in colonial governments up and down the coast.

On 16 October 1695, Randolph submitted to the commissioners of customs "An Account of . . . illegal Trade . . . in Virginia Maryland and Pennsylvania, togeather [sic] with Methods for prevention thereof." This report became the basis for legislation passed by Parliament in April 1696; "An Act for Preventing Frauds, and Regulating Abuses . . . in the Plantation Trade" was the last of England's seventeenth-century Navigation Acts. Randolph was given the responsibility of organizing the admiralty courts required in all the colonies by the new law, and he also revised the rules governing the collection of customs in America. In November 1697, he went back to the colonies in his capacity as surveyor general. For two and a half years he traveled through the colonies, administering oaths to governors, installing new court officers, and investigating his suspicions of corruption. His encounters with the governors of Pennsylvania and Bermuda led to their dismissal. He returned to London once again in July 1700.

That year the Board of Trade approached Parliament with the Reunification Bill that would have brought all colonial charter governments (New Hampshire, Massachusetts, Rhode Island, Connecticut, New Jersey, Pennsylvania, Maryland, and Carolina) into a uniform relationship to the Crown. Randolph threw himself into this project, making Pennsylvania his prime target. The bill failed when William Penn and proprietors such as Charles Calvert, third Lord Baltimore, and the Earl of Bath opposed it.

Edward Randolph's career in America coincided with twenty-five years of expanding imperial controls. He was himself a principal agent of that expansion, first in New England, and later by drafting and seeing through Parliament the Navigation Act of 1696. He was often arrogant, especially toward colonists, and excessively scrupulous, so that he had few supporters among other appointees to colonial office. In an age of widespread venality among officeholders and despite a substantial salary after 1692, Randolph died a poor man. His opinions were most valued in London by the Committee for Trade and Plantations, the commissioners of customs, the solicitor general, and the attorney general. After 1700 Randolph's influence declined. He lost his few powerful friends in England and earned an almost universal reputation for irascibility. He sailed for America for the last time in 1702 and died at the home of Charles Scarburgh in Virginia.

• Many Randolph papers are printed with biographical sketches in Robert N. Toppan and Alfred T. S. Goodrick, eds., *Edward Randolph; Including His Letters and Official Papers from the New England, Middle, and Southern Colonies in America: with Other Documents Relating Chiefly to the Vacat-*ing of the Royal Charter of the Colony of Massachusetts Bay, 1676–1703, vols. 24–28, 30–31 (1898–1909). Additional papers are printed in W. Noel Sainsbury et al., eds., *Calendar of State Papers, Colonial Series, America and West Indies, 1674–1703* (1889–1913). A modern biography is Michael G. Hall, *Edward Randolph and the American Colonies, 1676–1703* (1960). See also Thomas C. Barrow, *Trade and Empire: The British Customs Service in Colonial America, 1660–1775* (1967); Richard R. Johnson, *Adjustment to Empire: The New England Colonies, 1675–1715* (1981); J. M. Sosin, *English America and the Restoration Monarchy of Charles II* (1980); and I. K. Steele, *Politics of Colonial Policy: The Board of Trade in Colonial Administration, 1696–1720* (1968).

MICHAEL G. HALL

RANDOLPH, George Wythe (10 Mar. 1818–3 Apr. 1867), Confederate secretary of war, was born at "Monticello" in Albemarle County, Virginia, the son of Thomas Mann Randolph, a former congressman and governor of Virginia, and Martha Jefferson, Thomas Jefferson's daughter. In 1826 Randolph went to live with his sister Ellen Coolidge in Boston, where he attended school. He was appointed midshipman in the U.S. Navy in 1831. In the Atlantic, Caribbean, and Mediterranean as well as in David Farragut's naval school at Norfolk, Randolph became an inspiring leader, but he contracted tuberculosis on the USS *Constitution*. After promotion to passed midshipman, he took a leave in 1837 to study civil engineering and natural philosophy at the University of Virginia. He resigned his commission from the navy in 1839 and obtained his law degree in 1841.

After practicing law in Albemarle County, Randolph moved to Richmond in 1851, where he developed a successful civil and criminal practice. Although a Democrat, he favored many principles championed by the southern Whigs, such as sound money and moderate national tariffs. Having seen the political career of his eldest brother, Thomas Jefferson Randolph, ruined by advocacy of gradual slave emancipation, he either ignored or paid lip service to the "peculiar institution," while relying on slaves as domestic servants. In 1852 he married Mary Elizabeth Adams Pope, a young and wealthy widow; they had no children. Randolph was an officer of the Virginia Historical Society, a member of the local literati, and served on the city council.

After the John Brown raid, Randolph founded the Richmond Howitzers to ensure that Brown was fairly tried and put to death by legal means. Appointed a Virginia arms commissioner, he helped buy enough guns and ammunition to declare that the commonwealth was "better prepared for Civil War than any state in the Union." This commission also adopted the U.S. Articles of War for Virginia's militia and later the Confederacy's army.

Richmond elected Randolph to the Virginia Convention of 1861 as a secessionist. He urged that the state withdraw from the Union as soon as practicable in order to capitalize on its military preparedness and to avoid war. During the convention he was named to a three-man commission to go to Washington, D.C., and learn President Lincoln's intentions. On 13 April the president reiterated his inaugural pledges to hold federal installations, to repel force with force, and not to invade any southern states. After hostilities began at Fort Sumter and Lincoln called for troops to suppress rebellion, Randolph told the convention, "You have got to fight" and posed the question, "which side will you fight with?"

Randolph led the Richmond Howitzers to defend the peninsula between the York and James rivers and was appointed chief of artillery under General John Bankhead Magruder. For his part in the victory at Big Bethel on 10 June 1861, Randolph was promoted first to colonel and later to brigadier general. Briefly, he was a candidate for the Confederate House of Representatives. On 17 March 1862 Jefferson Davis nominated him to be Confederate secretary of war, succeeding Judah P. Benjamin.

Secretary Randolph worked well with senior army officers and southern industries, assembling a staff with superior technical skills in agriculture, engineering, foreign trade, mining, and railroads. He was an early advocate of conscription, and he sought to improve the logistical supply of arms and foodstuffs. Instead of blaming southern governors for hoarding troops, he chastised Confederate commanders for overly generous leaves. He ordered construction at Augusta, Georgia, of the largest ammunition factory in the world and tried to import Bessemer steel. Using an act of the Confederate congress authorizing military priority in railroad traffic, he virtually controlled the southern war economy. Unlike President Davis, he believed that in order to feed the Confederate armed forces and civilian population, the government must buy foodstuffs from abroad and even from the enemy. He schemed with Louisianans to liberate New Orleans by relying not only on conventional soldiers but also on fifth columnists and exploiting the greed of the Union occupying forces under Benjamin F. Butler. Demands for troops elsewhere aborted the half-formed plan. Randolph, the Virginian, desired to send more troops to the West; Davis, the Mississippian, desired to keep more troops in Virginia.

Davis's procrastination and indecisiveness grated on Secretary Randolph generally, but especially when the latter's efforts to increase importation were stalled. After Davis overruled Randolph's grant to a general of conditional authority to cross into the territorial command of another, the secretary resigned on 15 November 1862. This was a "factitious" resignation to avoid public discussion. Randolph was too independent to stomach Davis's heavy-handed treatment of the War Department. He was always ready, however, to do his civic duty. In May 1863 Randolph briefly assumed command of volunteers to defend Richmond against the Stoneman raid. He ignored criticism for successfully defending in a public trial a foolish socialite indicted for treason. Just before the Richmond Bread Riots, while a member of the city council, Randolph encouraged Confederate office workers and mechanics to demand a living wage in times of great inflation.

Diagnosed as tubercular, Randolph in the autumn of 1864 took his wife through the blockade to England to consult doctors and purchase arms. After a winter at Pau, France, and brief sojourns in England, Ireland, and Paris, the Randolphs lost almost all their money when their British bank failed before the Confederate surrender. Fortunately, his sister Ellen and her husband, Joseph Coolidge, came to their aid. The Randolphs sailed to New York in September 1866 and went to Albemarle, where Randolph collapsed in October and died of tuberculosis six months later.

Just as Randolph was too independent to be a merely dutiful naval officer or more than a nominal Democrat, he learned from his naval experience and study of the pre-Marxian socialist Robert du Var to appreciate the workers white or black. He accepted slave emancipation as a boon for whites as well as blacks. He demonstrated zeal for the rights of individuals against Confederate authority, insufficient wages, corporal punishment in the army, and imprisonment of conscientious objectors. He was the most cosmopolitan and sophisticated of the Confederate high command, and his organization of the War Office remained in force until Appomattox.

• Most of Randolph's official and personal papers were lost when Richmond burned and the Confederate Archives were moved to Washington, D.C. The Edgehill Randolph and Ellen Randolph Coolidge papers at the University of Virginia are the best manuscript sources for his personal life. *The War of the Rebellion: A Compilation of the Official Records of the Union and Confederate Armies* (128 vols., 1880–1901) is the best source for Randolph's military service and secretaryship. George Green Shackelford, *George Wythe Randolph and the Confederate Elite* (1988), is a book-length biography of Randolph. At the time of his resignation, the Richmond *Examiner*, 3 May 1863, was laudatory of Randolph and condemned President Davis for desiring only "automatons" in the cabinet. Obituaries are in the *Examiner*, 16 Apr. 1867; the Richmond *Whig*, 5 Apr. 1867; and the *Richmond Times*, 9 Apr. 1867. John R. Thompson's "In Memoriam: George Wythe Randolph" is reprinted in his *Poems* (1920), pp. 206–8.

GEORGE GREEN SHACKELFORD

RANDOLPH, Jacob (25 Nov. 1796–29 Feb. 1848), physician and surgeon, was born in Philadelphia, Pennsylvania, the son of Edward Fitz-Randolph, a merchant, and Anna Julianna Slict. His father, a revolutionary war veteran, was descended from an ancestor of the same name who emigrated from England to America in 1630. Fitz was dropped early in Jacob's father's life, and the family name became Randolph.

Upon completing his early education at the Friends' School on Fourth Street, Randolph decided to study medicine and in 1814 apprenticed himself to Dr. Joseph Wollens, a physician in the Northern Liberties district of Philadelphia. When Wollens died, Randolph continued his medical studies under the tutorship of Dr. Isaac Cleaver, a practitioner in the same district. During the apprenticeship Randolph also attended the lectures in the medical department of the

University of Pennsylvania and received his degree in 1817.

Shortly after graduation he signed on as surgeon on a ship bound for China. On the Atlantic crossing, he suffered so from seasickness that he left the ship when it reached England. He remained in Europe for a few months, spending most of his time in France and Scotland.

Upon his return to Philadelphia he began the practice of medicine. Shortly thereafter he became acquainted with Dr. Philip Syng Physick and his family. He married Physick's eldest daughter, Sarah Emlen Physick, in 1822; they had three children.

As time passed, Dr. Randolph found his medical practice "tiresome," and with the encouragement of Dr. Physick, he decided to devote himself to the practice of surgery. In 1830 he was appointed surgeon to the Philadelphia Almshouse Infirmary. That year he also began teaching courses in the Summer Medical School. He was elected one of the surgeons to the Pennsylvania Hospital in 1835 and held this position until his death. In the last year of his life he was appointed professor of clinical surgery in the medical department of the University of Pennsylvania, a position created especially for him.

Randolph revisited Europe in 1840 and spent two years observing the famous surgeons of France operating in the Paris hospitals. While on this visit he was appointed professor of operative surgery in the Jefferson Medical College but declined this invitation, as it would have necessitated the termination of his European visit.

A conservative but competent and skillful surgeon, Randolph took greatest pride in curing diseases without resorting to the knife. He opposed daring operations and emphasized that minor operations were not "trifling procedures." In his clinic he always employed the simplest instruments, appliances, and dressings. Although Randolph was frequently hesitant to recommend operations, once the surgical course was decided upon, no one proceeded with more "decision of purpose" or was more calm and collected when the "unforeseen" occurred.

As a teacher he was a dignified, clear lecturer, preferring to teach his classes the management of the everyday cases that made up the "principal business" of surgery, rather than lecturing on dramatic cases and obscure diseases. Thus wounds and fractures were his favorite subjects.

Randolph's name will always be associated with the procedure of lithotripsy (breaking the stones) for the removal of stones from the bladder. Although he did not introduce this procedure, he became one of the greatest lithotriptors by practicing inserting the instruments and removing the stones on cadavers. His lithotripsy techniques and results of the procedure are described in three articles published in the *American Journal of Medical Sciences*, in 1834 and 1836.

Throughout his surgical career Randolph always considered the comfort and well-being of his patients. Even while demonstrating lithotripsy to visiting surgeons, he would suddenly discontinue the procedure if the patient suffered undue pain or if he encountered difficulty locating and seizing the stone.

Randolph's contributions to medical literature included journal articles describing his surgical techniques for various procedures such as amputation, treating an aneurysm, and extirpating a parotid gland. His famous memorial, "A Memoir of the Life and Character of Dr. Philip Syng Physick," was read before the Philadelphia County Medical Society and was ordered published by the society in the *American Journal of Medical Sciences* (1839).

Randolph was a member of the American Philosophical Society, the College of Physicians of Philadelphia, and the Philadelphia Medical Society. He was also a consultant to the Philadelphia Medical Dispensary. He died in Philadelphia after a short illness, from repeated intestinal hemorrhages.

• Accounts of the life of Jacob Randolph may be found in T. G. Morton and Frank Woodbury, *The History of the Pennsylvania Hospital—1751–1895* (1895), p. 507; G. W. Norris, "Biographical Notice of Jacob Randolph," *Summary of Transactions of the College of Physicians of Philadelphia* 2 (1848): 283–89; J. A. Meigs, "Jacob Randolph, 1796–1848," in *Lives of Eminent American Physicians and Surgeons of the Nineteenth Century*, ed. Samuel Gross (1861), pp. 512–20; and Norris, "Jacob Randolph, M.D., 1796–1848," *Transactions of the American Medical Association* 3 (1850): 457–59.

DAVID Y. COOPER

RANDOLPH, Sir John (1693–2 Mar. 1737), colonial lawyer and legislator, was born at the "Turkey Island" plantation of his father in Henrico County, Virginia, the son of William Randolph, an attorney, and Mary Isham. Randolph grew up in one of the most prestigious families of colonial Virginia. From an early age he showed a marked aptitude for his studies. After first being tutored by a French Huguenot clergyman, he proceeded to the College of William and Mary. He went to London and was admitted to Gray's Inn on 17 May 1715. Again he excelled in his studies and was admitted to the bar in London on 25 November 1717. Randolph was most likely the first colonial American to have achieved this status.

Randolph returned to Virginia and was named clerk of the House of Burgesses on 28 April 1718. This post soon brought him into contact with all of the leading men of Virginia. He thrived in this position and developed a lucrative private practice of law in conjunction with his public duties. By 1721 he had married Susanna Beverley. The couple had two sons and two daughters. Both sons, Peyton Randolph and John Randolph, followed their father into distinguished public service to Virginia.

Randolph sailed to England in 1728 with a mission with three purposes in mind. First, on behalf of the College of William and Mary, he was to seek a more rigorous collection of the penny-per-pound export on tobacco from Virginia. Second, he was to request of the archbishop of Canterbury the use of part of the Boyle fund for the education of Indians in Virginia.

Third, he had been instructed by the Virginia assembly to ask King George I to repeal the act that prohibited the shipment of stripped tobacco. Little is known of how Randolph communicated these requests in England. However, the act of Parliament regarding the stripped tobacco was repealed, and upon his return to the colony Randolph was voted £1,000 sterling by the Virginia assembly as a reward for his endeavors.

On 8 March 1731 Randolph was again appointed an agent of the colony. In this capacity he went to England to ask for a new way in which to collect the excise tax on tobacco. Although Randolph was not successful in this mission, his efforts on behalf of the colony and his general demeanor apparently impressed King George II to the point that the monarch knighted Randolph, probably in 1732. Sir John Randolph was the only colonial Virginian to receive the honor of knighthood.

Randolph returned to Virginia and continued in his post of clerk until he resigned on 22 April 1734. He was soon chosen by the faculty of the College of William and Mary as its representative in the Virginia assembly. Edwin Conway nominated Randolph for Speaker of the House of Burgesses on 5 August 1736, and he was elected by an overwhelming majority. He was reelected in 1736 and continued in that post until his death. He was also named recorder of the house in 1736. Randolph's health failed suddenly, and he died in Williamsburg.

Randolph was the single most distinguished Virginian of his time. Coming from a family that had assumed political leadership in the new colony and that would provide two to three generations of future leaders, he played an important role in the development of Virginia as part of the transatlantic community in the eighteenth century. As a lawyer and legislator he flourished in his home colony, while as a diplomat he was recognized in England as the true spokesperson for Virginia's interests. His career anticipated that of the colonial agents who were essential to negotiations between the American colonies and Great Britain after 1750.

In his own day Randolph was recognized for his legal skills, for his devotion to public service, and for the knighthood that the king had bestowed upon him. Though there was never a hereditary knighthood within the colonies, Randolph stands out as the only Virginian, and perhaps the only southerner, to have been knighted during the colonial epoch. William Phips, John Randolph, William Pepperrell, William Johnson, John Johnson, and William Pepperrell II are the only colonial figures certain to have been knighted. However, Randolph was the only one to have been a lawyer and legislator rather than soldier, businessman, or conquering hero.

• Randolph probably wrote, with William Maxwell, *The Case of the Planters of Tobacco in Virginia, as Represented by Themselves . . .* (1733), repr. in *Virginia Historical Register and Literary Companion* 4 (1851): 137–41. One of the best sources for understanding the importance of Randolph's family is H. J. Eckenrode, *The Randolphs: The Story of a Virginia Family* (1946). Other sources include the *Journal of the House of Burgesses 1727–1740* (1910); and the *Virginia Magazine of History and Biography*, Jan. 1902, pp. 239–41.

SAMUEL WILLARD CROMPTON

RANDOLPH, John (1727–31 Jan. 1784), king's attorney general for Virginia and Loyalist, was born at the Randolph family estate, "Tazewell Hall," in Williamsburg, Virginia, the son of Sir John Randolph and Susanna Beverley. He grew up in fortunate circumstances. His father, the only Virginian to be knighted during the colonial era, was the leading man in the politics of Virginia until his death, serving as king's attorney, Speaker of the House of Burgesses, and representative of Virginia in London. Whether by accident or by design, both John Randolph and his older brother Peyton Randolph were to follow their father's footsteps into public life and to hold some of the same positions that he had occupied.

Randolph graduated from the College of William and Mary and went to London. He entered the Middle Temple in 1745 and was called to the bar at Westminster in 1750. He soon returned to Virginia to practice law and to serve as the clerk for the House of Burgesses (1752–1756). In or around 1752 he married Ariana Jenings, the daughter of the attorney general of the colony of Maryland. The couple had three children. During the early years of his marriage and working life, Randolph became one of the leading members of Virginia society; he was on intimate terms with George Washington and with Thomas Jefferson, who was his first cousin once removed. Both deists and men of the Enlightenment, Randolph and Jefferson enjoyed one another's company and frequently played the violin together. In 1771 they made a rather strange agreement. If Jefferson were to die first, Randolph would receive £100 sterling worth of Jefferson's books; if the reverse were to occur, then Jefferson would receive Randolph's violin, which he had brought from England.

Randolph's career blossomed during the years prior to the American Revolution. He practiced law with considerable success, and in November 1766 he was named as the king's attorney general for Virginia, replacing his brother Peyton Randolph, who became Speaker of the Virginia House of Burgesses.

Randolph became more conservative as the American Revolution approached. In 1774 he wrote "Considerations on the Present State of Virginia," urging his fellow colonists to consider the value of their connection with Great Britain. In March 1775 he boycotted the Virginia Convention that was called to address the relations of the colonies to the mother country and that was led by his older brother. During the summer of 1775, when hostilities commenced between the governor, Lord Dunmore, and the Virginia patriots, Randolph examined both his conscience and his duty. He later recalled his thought process in a letter to Jefferson: "I read with avidity every thing which was published on the Subject. . . . In this situation I had no resource left but to submit myself solely to the Dictates of my Reason" (Mackall, p. 26). Those dictates bid him to support the governor and the Crown, for Randolph embarked for England with his wife and two daughters. His 22-year-old son, Edmund Randolph, refused to go to England; he remained in Virginia and soon joined the ranks of the patriot cause. Prior to his departure, Randolph sold his violin to Jefferson for £13 sterling.

The Randolph family lived for a time on the Scottish estate of Lord Dunmore, where both of the Randolph daughters married other Virginia Loyalists; Susannah Randolph married John Randolph Grymes, a kinsman, and Ariana Randolph married James Wormeley. The Randolphs moved south to Brompton, England, where they subsisted on a pension from the Crown of £100 per year. Active as ever, Randolph drew up a plan for reconciliation between England and the colonies and offered to lead American Loyalists in defense of England if the French invaded.

In October 1779 Randolph wrote a lengthy letter to Jefferson. Randolph congratulated his kinsman on becoming the governor of the state of Virginia and urged him to do all that was within his power to bring about an understanding between England and the states. Casting aspersions on the value of the American alliance with France, he asserted that England was a match for all of her foes, both American and European. He concluded with a call for reconciliation: "Wou'd it not be prudent, to rescind your Declaration of Independence, be happily reunited to your ancient & natural Friend, & enjoy a Peace which I most religiously think w'd pass all Understanding?" (Mackall, p. 30). It is likely that the letter was never sent.

Randolph died in Brompton of natural causes. His last wish was that he be buried in the soil of Virginia. His daughter Ariana and her husband brought his remains across the ocean to be buried under the chapel of the College of William and Mary next to the burial sites of his father and brother. Randolph's *Treatise on Gardening, By a Citizen of Virginia* was posthumously published in 1793. Believed to be the first American book on kitchen gardening, it showed him to be a man of scholarly temperament with keen powers of observation.

Born into the first family of colonial Virginia, Randolph made a choice in 1775 that cast him out of the world of Virginia society and government that he had previously led. His conscientious choice brought him little but grief. Separation from his son was only the most poignant of the losses that resulted from his loyalty to the Crown. Only a handful of other prominent Loyalists, such as Sir John Johnson of New York and Sir William Pepperrell II of Massachusetts, suffered a comparable loss of property and social standing. Son of the only Virginian to be knighted, himself the attorney general for the king, and father of a patriot who would become the first attorney general and the second secretary of state of the United States, Randolph stood at a critical juncture in the history of his family and the colony of Virginia. His close relationships with men such as Washington and Jefferson stand as a vivid reminder of the fact that the "Great Generation" of Virginia revolutionaries were only removed from Loyalist principles by a few degrees of the political compass. A more far-seeing and benevolent king and Parliament might have been able to retain the loyalty of colonial Virginia in 1775.

• Few sources survive for a study of Randolph. Material exists mainly in books and articles that deal with other prominent Virginians with whom he was associated. Willard Sterne Randall, *Thomas Jefferson: A Life* (1993), discusses the Randolph-Jefferson connection, especially the correspondence between the two in the years 1775 and 1779. The primary source for this material is Julian P. Boyd, ed., *The Papers of Thomas Jefferson*, vol. 1 (1950), and Leonard L. Mackall, ed., "A Letter from the Virginia Loyalist John Randolph to Thomas Jefferson Written in London in 1779," American Antiquarian Society, *Proceedings* 30 (1920). Other valuable sources include John J. Reardon, *Peyton Randolph 1721–1775: One Who Presided* (1982), Moncure Daniel Conway, *Omitted Chapters of History Disclosed in the Life and Papers of Edmund Randolph* (1888), H. J. Eckenrode, *The Randolphs: The Story of a Virginia Family* (1946), and Marjorie Fleming Warner, "The Earliest Book on Kitchen Gardening," *Annual Report of the American Historical Association for the Year 1919*, vol. 1 (1923), pp. 431–42. Randolph's possible authorship of letters attributed at the time to George Washington is discussed in *The Spurious Letters Attributed to Washington* (1889).

SAMUEL WILLARD CROMPTON

RANDOLPH, John (2 June 1773–24 May 1833), member of the U.S. House of Representatives, U.S. senator, and orator, known as John Randolph of Roanoke, was born at "Cawsons," in Prince George County, Virginia, the son of John Randolph, a scion of the Virginian landed slaveholding elite, and Frances Bland. Both parents were descendents of the founding father of the Randolphs of Virginia, William Randolph of Turkey Island. The senior John Randolph died in 1775, and in 1778 his widow married St. George Tucker. John Randolph and his elder brothers Richard and Theodorick studied with Walker Maury in Orange and later Williamsburg. Randolph was precocious but undisciplined. His stays at Princeton and Columbia and then his studying law with Edmund Randolph in New York and at William and Mary did not result in a degree. His mother's death in 1787 and the deaths of his brothers Theodorick, in 1792, and Richard, in 1796, left Randolph with responsibility for family lands and Richard's two sons. Randolph took time to settle into his responsibilities. In the meantime, he sowed some wild oats, being noted for his arrogance, his restlessness, and his intrepidity on the race course and the field of honor.

In 1799 Randolph stood for Congress, more because it was expected of him than for any formed political interest. He made an impressive debut debating Patrick Henry, then running for the Virginia State Senate as a Federalist. Entering politics as a champion of the Jeffersonian opposition to the Federalists, he gained immediate notoriety by attacking the regular army soldiers as "mercenaries" and "ragamuffins" and when insulted by some officers demanding redress from President Adams. With Jefferson's election, Randolph became one of the chief congressional lieutenants of Jefferson's first administration. He chaired the Ways and Means Committee and was for a time an effective floor leader, helping to pass the Louisiana Purchase, a compromise with his views of limited federal power he came to regret.

The issues that defined American politics in Randolph's day were essentially those of making the Constitution real. State versus federal sovereignty and the powers and limits of each of the three branches of the government—not to mention the vexed and uncharted relations between the executive, legislative, and judicial—were the stuff of Randolph's political career. Randolph was formed by the English country-party views of late-eighteenth-century American republicanism. He despised commerce and mistrusted any other basis for political participation than the stake of the independent landholder in the regime and the agrarian way of life. For him, the federal Constitution was not a new founding but an imperfect compact: "The states are the breath in the nostrils of the Constitution." He saw politics in terms of virtue and corruption, drawn from English political ideology and the political satires of the Augustan. He very early decided that the democratic, modernizing tone of nineteenth-century America was a death sentence for the Virginian and American pasts he venerated. "I am an aristocrat," he said, "I love liberty, I hate equality."

Beginning with an uncompromising assertion of states rights, founded in a pre-Madisonian view of the character of republics, Randolph came to see democracy and American nationalism—in commerce and sentiment—as an irresistible threat to slavery. Randolph had never acquired the national vision that Jefferson, Washington, Madison, and so many other southern statesmen did during their experiences in the Revolution. John Greenleaf Whittier put it well: "Too honest or too proud to feign a love he never cherished, beyond Virginia's borderline his patriotism perished."

Randolph's faults of temper and his unwillingness to compromise his attachment to what he considered his principles, not his interests or politics, caused him to break with Jefferson and Madison. Partly this was his own fault. Randolph was a quick but not a studious study. In 1805 the Jeffersonians impeached federal judge Samuel Chase, who expressed his Federalist hostility to the Republicans from his Maryland bench. This formed part of the Jeffersonian strategy to dislodge from the federal judiciary Federalist notions of federal power and judicial review as well as particular Federalist judges. Randolph mismanaged the case disastrously and lost; he was no longer seen as an effective or reliable leader. Randolph in turn became convinced that the pragmatic James Madison and Albert Gallatin had corrupted the Jeffersonians. A compromise with speculators in the Georgia Yazoo land case (which began in the 1790s and was not resolved until John Marshall's decision in *Fletcher v. Peck* in 1810), and the

indirection with which the administration tried to buy Florida signaled to Randolph that Jefferson had betrayed republican principles for the temptations of power. He declared his open opposition to the administration in 1806 and later characterized Jefferson as "St. Thomas of Cantingbury."

With a small group of like-minded purist Republicans, the "quids," Randolph commenced his long career of opposition. There was a consistency in his views: relentless opposition to federal power, defense of state sovereignty—"asking a state to give up part of her sovereignty is like asking a lady to give up part of her chastity"—and an alarmist defense of the property rights of slaveholders. But Randolph's distance from the politics of interest and compromise kept his politics and alliances inconsistent and haphazard. Too, Randolph suffered by comparison to such legislators as Henry Clay, John Calhoun, Daniel Webster, and Thomas Hart Benton. He harried rather than influenced his colleagues; amused, terrorized, infuriated, and frustrated rather than recruited them. The Missouri Compromise of 1820 made Randolph's uncompromising views on the slavery issue plausible to many southerners, and his popularity and even influence revived.

Randolph served in the U.S. House of Representatives from 1800 to 1825, except when even his opposition to the War of 1812 alienated his loyal constituents in Virginia's rural Southside. In 1825 he was elected to the U.S. Senate, but was not reselected in 1827, and returned to the House, where he served until 1829. Also in 1829 Randolph played a major role in the Virginia Constitutional Convention, where he led the eastern slaveholding interest, which objected to constitutional change. In 1830 he served unhappily as ambassador to Russia after a brief alliance with Andrew Jackson.

He returned home to join the southern opposition to President Jackson in the nullification controversy, although he dismissed Calhoun's theory with the same contempt he harbored for anything newfangled or theoretical. In a time when slavery was exactly a subject to be avoided except euphemistically, Randolph spoke of it incessantly. He insisted that his fellow southerners take notice that the strengthening of the federal government, the expansion of the territory and the addition of states was inevitably destructive of the survival of the special institution. He was one of the first to insist that the divided house could not stand. Nor did Randolph care to advance the kinds of positive-good arguments for slavery or the mystifications of antebellum southern medievalism. He came to repudiate the Declaration of Independence and the very notion of equality, accepting the late eighteenth century's rationalizations that slavery was a necessary evil. Randolph was a financially successful slaveholder, who freed his slaves in a will that years of litigation finally vindicated over another will, composed when he was in one of his periods of derangement, which ordered them to be sold.

Randolph's literal-minded adherence to the classic republican and English sources of American ideology suggest how quickly these traditions, which had so much to do with the early republic, became outmoded and outdistanced by the rising nation that succeeded it. Randolph's isolation resulted from the superannuation of some of America's founding traditions and also from his foretelling of sectional truths that it would take Americans another generation to come to grips with. He cannot be said to have had great influence, but Randolph may have taught Calhoun and other southerners more than they acknowledged. His impersonation of the eccentric, wayward Virginian captured the imagination of some of those northern writers like James Kirke Paulding, who played a part in the construction of the nation's antebellum sectional stereotypes. Randolph's antics, his savagery in debate, his duels, and above all his cutting-through the restraints of conventional debate in torrents of allusive, pungent remarks enthralled his constituents, some contemporaries, and many distinguished historians. Henry Adams's partisan, retributive biography of Randolph is a link between his nine-volume *History* of the Jefferson and Madison administrations and *The Education of Henry Adams*. There was something about Randolph that has attracted students of American political culture with an eye for what the celebrated progress of the United States left behind.

Randolph's life was, to use the name of one of his homes, "Bizarre." As a young man Randolph suffered a mysterious malady that left him beardless, treble-voiced, and attenuated. He never married; rumors gathered around his apparent lack of masculinity. His response to such taunts is revealing: "You pride yourself on your animal faculty, in which the negro is your equal and the jackass infinitely your superior." Randolph of Roanoke cut a strange and mesmerizing figure, dressed in the old-fashioned way, striding into Congress with hounds nipping at his heel, quick to take offense and to challenge, and yet magnanimous and oddly fine. His most famous crack came after John Quincy Adams struck what partisans saw as either a brilliant compromise or a corrupt bargain with Henry Clay in 1824, so that Adams became president and Clay his secretary of state. Randolph characterized their alliance as one between "Blifil and Black George, the Puritan and the Blackleg," which provoked Clay to challenge him. Clay shot but missed; Randolph, whose aim was deadly, shot in the air. For a long time, Randolph seemed a touch of comic relief, an oasis of the fantastic in the grim story of tariffs, canals, and politics that seemed to be the stuff of history. Later he came to seem a dire example of the degenerate weirdness of the gothic south, proof of what had gone wrong.

In the end, John Randolph was that rare figure whose voice survives to tell a tale of loss and defeat. Randolph was behind the times in his views but ahead in his understanding of what the consequences of what outmoded them would be. His denunciations of corruption, the arrogance of power, the dangers of commerce, and the abandonment of traditions resonate still because, if Randolph's perspective and his own views strike us as well dispensed with, what that perspective permitted him to see, to feel, and to express abides. Embittered and despairing about the future of his patria and its traditions, Randolph died in Philadelphia, where he had planned to embark on a trip to England. He is said to have traced the word "remorse" in his dying moments and was buried at "Roanoke" facing west so he could keep an eye on Henry Clay.

• Sources on Randolph include the following: Hugh A. Garland, *Life of John Randolph of Roanoke* (2 vols., 1850); Henry Adams, *John Randolph* (1882); William Cabell Bruce, *Randolph of Roanoke* (2 vols., 1922); Russell Kirk, *Randolph of Roanoke: A Study in American Politics, with Selected Letters and Speeches* (3d ed., 1978); William R. Taylor, *Cavalier and Yankee: The Old South and American National Character* (1961); and Robert Dawidoff, *The Education of John Randolph* (1979). Dumas Malone wrote the entry on Randolph for the *Dictionary of American Biography*, vol. 15 (1935).

ROBERT DAWIDOFF

RANDOLPH, Martha Jefferson (27 Sept. 1772–10 Oct. 1836), lifelong confidante to her father, was born at "Monticello" in Albemarle County, Virginia, the daughter of Thomas Jefferson and Martha Wayles. After the death of her mother in 1782, Martha Jefferson, known to her father in childhood as "Patsy," became his most trusted and beloved female companion. Throughout her life she moved in a rarified intellectual and social atmosphere. After spending two years in Philadelphia, in 1784 she and her father moved to Paris, where he served as U.S. minister to France. There she continued the formal education she had begun in Philadelphia by attending the elite Abbaye Royale de Panthémont convent school. Her father maintained an avid interest in her education, frequently writing her letters filled with advice and encouragement; "the more you learn the more I love you," one of his missives averred. During her years in France Martha Jefferson was also introduced to fashionable society, counting as her friends Abigail Adams and the marquis de Lafayette.

In the fall of 1789, with France in the grip of revolution, the Jeffersons returned to Virginia, where on 23 February 1790 Martha Jefferson married her second cousin and childhood friend, Thomas Mann Randolph of "Tuckahoe" in Goochland County, Virginia. Like his father-in-law, Randolph was a well-educated gentleman farmer. The couple resided at "Varina," near Richmond, for six years, and then moved to "Edgehill," near Monticello. Thomas Randolph was frequently away from home on business, leaving Martha Randolph to preside over the education of their twelve children, a job that she, like her father, took very seriously. On the plantation she established her own little school, where she instructed her children in mathematics, history, literature, music, and languages.

Even as Randolph tended to domestic matters, she continued to be deeply involved in her father's career as he climbed the political ladder from secretary of state (1789–1793) to vice president (1797–1801) to president (1801–1809). When Jefferson was away in Washington, Randolph received from him long, affectionate letters in which he discussed political as well as personal matters. In addition to being her father's favorite correspondent, Randolph occasionally served as his secretary, helping him to answer the voluminous mail he received. In 1802–1803 and again in 1805–1806 Martha Randolph acted as the "first lady" in the Jefferson White House, earning a reputation as a woman of uncommon intellectual attainment.

After her father's retirement from public life in 1809, Randolph settled with him at Monticello, where she presided as mistress, even while her husband, who had been a U.S. congressman (1803–1807), served in Richmond as governor of Virginia (1819–1822). What should have been pleasant years for Randolph and her father were marred by financial difficulties: Thomas Mann Randolph, never a successful manager of money, fell progressively deeper into debt; his father-in-law's attempts to sustain him only further encumbered Monticello. After Thomas Jefferson died in 1826, Randolph, prostrate with grief, was eventually forced to sell her father's estate to pay the family's debts. In 1828, Randolph's husband, with whom she had reconciled after a period of estrangement, also died. Randolph turned for companionship to her children, living with her daughters in Boston and then in Washington, D.C., and finally with her son at Edgehill.

In her last years Randolph continued to follow political developments closely, especially those relating to the subject of slavery. Randolph shared her father's ambiguous views on the peculiar institution. While she prided herself on being a kind mistress to her slaves, whom she considered part of her extended "family," she also hoped for the gradual demise of what she believed to be a "system of injustice." Her letters attest that she in turn communicated her hatred of slavery to her children. Her son Thomas Jefferson Randolph championed the cause of gradual emancipation in the famous 1831–1832 slavery debate in the Virginia legislature.

Martha Jefferson Randolph, who was once described by John Randolph (1773–1833) of Roanoke, a political enemy of her husband's, as "the noblest woman in Virginia," died at Edgehill and was buried next to her father at Monticello. Randolph is significant in the history of the early Republic not only because she provides insights into the life of a famous man but also because she embodied her era's ideal of female civic virtue. In private she served her country by raising a virtuous and patriotic family; in public she, along with Dolley Madison and a handful of others, was an international symbol of the refinement and cultivation of women in the young Republic.

• Martha Jefferson Randolph's letters are scattered throughout the Jefferson collections in the Manuscript Department of the Alderman Library, University of Virginia; see especially the Thomas Jefferson Papers, the Edgehill-Randolph Papers, and the correspondence of Ellen Wayles Coolidge, Randolph's daughter. Published collections of Randolph's letters include Sarah N. Randolph, comp., *The Domestic Life of Thomas Jefferson* (1871), and Edwin M. Betts and James A. Bear, Jr., eds., *Family Letters of Thomas Jefferson* (1966). The most informative secondary works on Randolph's life are Gordon Langley Hall, *Mr. Jefferson's Ladies* (1966), and Elizabeth Langhorne, *Monticello: A Family Story* (1987).

ELIZABETH R. VARON

RANDOLPH, Mary (9 Aug. 1762–23 Jan. 1828), cookbook author, was born in Virginia, the daughter of Thomas Mann Randolph, a wealthy planter and colonial legislator, and Anne Cary. Her tombstone lists her birthplace as Ampthill, the home of her mother's family near Richmond, but some genealogists believe that she may have been born at "Tuckahoe," her father's plantation in Goochland County. Nicknamed Molly, she was raised with the expectation that she would marry a man whose lineage was as distinguished as her own. After receiving elementary instruction in reading, writing, and arithmetic, she was trained in the household arts and also took lessons in dancing, music, and drawing. In 1780 she wed a cousin, David Meade Randolph, a revolutionary war officer and tobacco planter. Both Molly and her husband were distant cousins of Thomas Jefferson. Molly's father, orphaned as a baby, had been raised by Jefferson's parents, and the Jefferson and Randolph families saw each other often; one of Molly's younger brothers, Thomas Mann Randolph, married Jefferson's daughter Martha in 1790.

Settling at her husband's James River plantation, "Presqu'Ile," in Chesterfield County, Molly Randolph eventually had eight children, of whom four lived to adulthood. Around 1795 President George Washington appointed David Randolph the U.S. marshal of Virginia, necessitating a move to Richmond. There the couple built an elegant residence known as "Moldavia," after the first names of its owners. Randolph quickly became celebrated for her well-set table and the social gatherings that she and her husband hosted.

This idyllic life changed abruptly in 1801, when David Randolph, who had become a political rival of President Jefferson and was openly critical of him, was removed from his post by his cousin. This was a blow to David Randolph, and the family fortunes declined. To support their family, the Randolphs sold off most of their plantation lands; several years later, they were forced to sell Moldavia as well, and they moved into a rented house. The breach with Jefferson was never healed: for the remainder of their lives, Molly and David Randolph were bitterly outspoken in their opposition to their cousin and denounced him at every opportunity. Molly Randolph, in particular, repeatedly championed rumors of Jefferson's liaison with his slave Sally Hemings.

To support his family, David Randolph became a partner in a coal mining operation. He also had some success as an inventor of several machines for the manufacturing of shoes. Their income was still insufficient, however, and in 1807 Randolph opened a boardinghouse. Already known as one of the best cooks in Richmond, she soon had paying customers. At that time boardinghouses were social necessities in Richmond and other capital cities, where large transient populations required meals—restaurants were then virtually nonexistent—and lodging.

Randolph's boardinghouse was named for her husband, but it quickly became known as "the Queen," after the affectionate name that her boarders gave her. In the early years of the nineteenth century it was one of the most popular sites in Richmond, known for its excellent food, good conversation, and hearty fellowship. The aging Randolph and her husband finally closed the boardinghouse in 1820 and moved to Washington, D.C. Four years later, probably in another effort to augment the family income, the 62-year-old Randolph gathered some of her best-known recipes and published them in a cookbook, *The Virginia Housewife*.

Randolph's book quickly became a bestseller, especially in the South. It was the first widely circulated cooking manual addressed specifically to a U.S. audience; until then, American households had relied on English recipe books. Randolph's guide was concise, practical in its use of ingredients, and specific as to their quantity. The first copies of *The Virginia Housewife* were issued anonymously, reflecting the prevailing view that ladies' names were not supposed to appear in print, but its immediate popularity led its author to allow "By Mrs. Mary Randolph" to appear on the title page of subsequent printings.

Soon after the publication of her cookbook, Randolph's youngest son was severely injured in a shipboard accident, becoming a permanent invalid. His mother became his constant nurse, and the strain of his care is presumed to have led to her death in Washington, D.C. She is described on her tombstone as "a victim to maternal love and duty."

A second edition of *The Virginia Housewife* was published in 1825, and the book was frequently reprinted in the mid-nineteenth century. Today it is valued as a historical document, and in recent years several facsimile editions have been issued.

• For biographical information, see Shirley Abbott, "The Universe of Mary Randolph," the introduction to a facsimile edition of *The Virginia Housewife* (1984), which includes numerous illustrations, among them portraits of Randolph and her husband and a photograph of her tombstone. Information on Randolph and her family is also in Samuel Mordecai, *Richmond in By-gone Days* (1856), and Robert I. Randolph, *The Randolphs of Virginia* (1936). For information on *The Virginia Housewife* and other historic cookbooks, see *Virginia Cookery Past and Present*, published by the Olivet Episcopal Church in Franconia, Va. (1957), and Waldo Lincoln, *American Cookery Books, 1742–1860* (1929; rev. ed., 1954, 1972). Obituaries are in the *National Journal* and *National Intelligencer* (both Washington, D.C.), 24 Jan. 1828, and the *Richmond Enquirer*, 29 Jan. 1828.

ANN T. KEENE

RANDOLPH, Paschal Beverly (8 Oct. 1825–29 July 1875), physician, philosopher, and author, was born in New York City, the son of William Beverly Randolph, a plantation owner, and Flora Beverly, a barmaid. At the age of five or seven Randolph lost his mother to smallpox, and with her the only love he had known. Randolph later stated, "I was born *in* love, of a loving mother, and what she felt, that I lived." His father's devotion is questionable. In 1873 Randolph hinted at his own illegitimacy, stating that his parents "did not stop to pay fees to the justice or to the priest."

Randolph's mother possessed a strong temperament, unusual physical beauty, and intense passions, characteristics that Randolph inherited. Later many, especially his enemies, perceived Randolph as being of "Negro descent," which he denied. Sent to live with his half-sister, Randolph was ignored, unloved, and abused and eventually turned to begging on the streets.

Uneducated, receiving only one year of formal education, Randolph attempted to train himself. At the age of fifteen he left home and spent the next five years as a sailor, traveling around the world. This period was a lonely and bitter one. Forced to leave the sea by an accident incurred while chopping wood, he learned the dyer's and barber's trade. During this interval (1845–1850), he also became interested in medicine and arcane science.

In 1850 Randolph married Mary Jane (maiden name unknown); they would have three children. That same year he befriended Colonel Ethen Allen Hitchcock, who had for some time been interested in alchemy and pantheistic philosophy. With Hitchcock's support, Randolph was admitted in 1850 to a meeting at Frankfort on the Main, Germany, of the *Fraternitas Rosæ Crucis*. The *Fraternitas* then, as in its foundation in 1616, was a brotherhood of esoteric enlightenment that brought together alchemists, magi, Hermetists, Phtonists, Paracelsians, and Gnostics in search of soul consciousness.

Returning to the United States in 1851, Randolph for a short time was active in the Reform party. While in the party movement, Randolph met and befriended Abraham Lincoln, a friendship that would continue until Lincoln's death. Randolph's political and educational views also extended to the plight of African Americans. In a letter to educational reformer Horace Mann in 1851, he asked whether the best way for them to achieve full rights as citizens were not "by cultivating their minds . . . fitting them for self-government."

In 1854 Randolph returned to Europe to continue his esoteric works. While in France, he finished studies in skrying (mirror or crystal gazing) and met with several occult magicians, including Eliphas Lévi, Edward Bulwer-Lytton, and Kenneth MacKenzie.

In 1856 Randolph again visited England and France, preparing for induction as Supreme Grand Master of the *Fraternitas*. Two years later, in Paris at a meeting of the Supreme Grand Dome, Randolph became Supreme Grand Master of the *Fraternitas* for the

Western World. Randolph was also inducted as a Knight of L'Ordre du Lis.

Returning from Paris in 1859, Randolph became active in building the *Fraternitas* by researching, lecturing, and writing. In September 1861 he toured California, delivering a ten-week series of lectures in San Francisco in an attempt to establish the *Fraternitas* on the Pacific Coast.

As Supreme Grand Master, Randolph was also a member of the Council of Three, a position he shared with General Hitchcock and President Lincoln. This group was known as "The Peerless Trio" or "Unshakable Triumvirate."

Leaving San Francisco in November 1861, Randolph traveled to London, where he was inducted by Hargrave Jennings as a knight of the Order of the Rose. From there, he traveled to East Asia, returning to America via France in 1863.

In 1864 Randolph, while living in New York, was requested by President Lincoln to educate the recently freed slaves in Louisiana. While in New Orleans, he served as an officer for the Freedmen's Bureau until July 1866, at which time he resigned to write *After Death; or, Disembodied Man.* . . . During his stay, Randolph taught many, black and white, to read and write. For this act, Randolph states "I was obliged to sleep with pistols in my bed, because the assassins were abroad and red-handed Murder skulked and hovered round my door." Randolph also delivered many lectures on black rights and Spiritualism at Economy Hall in New Orleans.

Upon the assassination of Lincoln in 1865, Randolph traveled with the train carrying the president's body back to Springfield, Illinois. Several procession members brought up his alleged Negro heritage, and he was asked to leave the train. This disappointment was to hurt him deeply. Never once, however, did he seek revenge or retribution.

The following year in Philadelphia, Randolph attended the Southern Loyal Convention. As a delegate from Louisiana, he advocated the African-American vote. Later, joining in a pilgrimage to Lincoln's tomb, he endured such cruelty from fellow delegates that upon leaving the convention, he swore never again to engage in politics. He then settled in Boston, where he practiced medicine until early 1873.

During the 1860s and 1870s many of Randolph's writings concerned the occult (secret) aspects of love and sexuality. Randolph, as a physician, also counseled patients on family relations, marital bliss, and the physical, emotional, and spiritual art of love. These acts of concern and kindness were interpreted by many as condoning free love. In February 1872 he was falsely imprisoned for promoting immoral sex. Randolph was acquitted of all charges, as the court determined that the allegations were made by former business partners to obtain book copyrights.

Shortly before his death Randolph had moved to Toledo, Ohio. While there he continued his writing and his speaking engagements. Generally, however, Randolph led a peaceful and at times secluded life,

with his wife Kate Corson and their son Osiris Budh. No official records appear to exist regarding either this marriage or the end of his first marriage; however, Randolph's first wife was still alive during this time.

Many questioned the coroner's finding that Randolph died in Toledo from a self-inflicted wound to the head, for many of his writings express his aversion to suicide, and the evidence was conflicting. R. Swinburne Clymer, a later Supreme Master of the *Fraternitas*, stressed that years later, in a "death-bed confession," a former friend of Randolph conceded, that in a state of jealousy and temporary insanity, he had killed Randolph.

Randolph produced, under his name, anonymously, or under various pseudonyms, more than fifty books and pamphlets on love, health, philosophy and the occult. Some of his works are *Waa-gu-Mah* (1854), *Lara* (1859), *The Grand Secret* (1860), *The Unveiling* (1860), *Human Love* (1861), *Pre-Adamite Man* (pseud. Griffin Lee, 1863), *A Sad Case; A Great Wrong!* (anon., 1866), *Seership! The Magnetic Mirror* (1868), *Love and Its Hidden History* (pseud. Count de St. Leon, 1869), *Love and the Master Passion* (1870), *The Evils of the Tobacco Habit* (1872), *The New Mola! The Secret of Mediumship* (1873), and *The Book of the Triplicate Order* (1875). Randolph also edited the *Leader* (Boston) and the *Messenger of Light* (New York) between 1852 to 1861 and wrote for the *Journal of Progress* and *Spiritual Telegraph*.

Randolph is to be remembered for his philosophical works on love, marriage, and womanhood. He provided new and unique insight into the then taboo world of sexual love. He aided the education, rights, and equality of both women and blacks. He foresaw the evils of tobacco and drug abuse. Finally, Randolph, through his position as the Americas' first Supreme Grand Master of the *Fraternitas Rosæ Crucis*, directly or indirectly touched the lives of more than 200,000 neophytes (students) comprising the *Fraternitas* and other Rosicrucian orders.

• Randolph's works, including some of his manuscripts and documents, are located at Beverly Hall Corp. (*Fraternitas Rosæ Crucis*), in Quakertown, Pa. This arcane collection also houses the "K" manuscript referring to Randolph's personal life, accomplishments, and honors, which was written either by Kate Randolph or by Randolph himself (1873). Randolph's *Wonderful Story of Ravalette* (1863) and *Curious Life of P. B. Randolph* are important autobiographical sources for providing insight into his life and beliefs. Randolph's concerns about slavery and the role of newly freed African Americans are presented in a letter of 5 Mar. 1851 in the Horace Mann Papers at the Massachusetts Historical Society and newspaper clippings from the New Orleans newspapers including the *New Orleans Tribune* (1864–1866), the *Era* (1864–1866), and the *Daily Independent* (1864–1866). Material on his well-publicized trial are in his work, *The Curious Life of P. B. Randolph*. The most complete historical analysis of Randolph's life, works, and personal views, with an extensive chronological bibliography of Randolph's works, is John Patrick Deveney, *Paschal Beverly Randolph: A Nineteenth-Century Black American Spiritualist, Rosicrucian, and Sex Magician* (1997). R. Swinburne Clymer, *Book of Rosicruciæ* II

(1947), also provides a rather extensive biographical sketch. Bibliographical details are in O. F. Adams, *A Dictionary of American Authors* (1897; repr. 1905), and S. A. Allibone, *A Critical Dictionary of English Literature and British and American Authors* (1871). An unflattering obituary is in the *Toledo Blade*, 29 July 1875. Evidence relating to Randolph's possible murder was taken from Clymer's pamphlet *The August Fraternity in America* (c. 1933).

C. E. LINDGREN

RANDOLPH, Peyton (c. 1721–22 Oct. 1775), planter and revolutionary leader, was born in Williamsburg, Virginia, the son of Sir John Randolph, a Speaker of the Virginia House of Burgesses and attorney general, and Susanna Beverley. Young Randolph matriculated at the College of William and Mary about 1733 but did not graduate; he entered the Middle Temple on 13 October 1739 and was called to the bar in London on 10 February 1744. Through the influence of the London merchant John Hanbury, Randolph became attorney general of Virginia on 7 May 1744 against Governor William Gooch's recommendation. In 1746 Randolph married Elizabeth Harrison of "Berkeley" plantation. They had no children. The couple lived in an elegant home on Nicholson Street in Williamsburg. Randolph owned other lots in the city and two plantations in James City County. At his death he owned 109 slaves.

Randolph became recorder of Norfolk in 1748 and the next year justice of the peace for York County and vestryman of Bruton Parish, Williamsburg. That city first elected him burgess in 1748; four years later he shifted to his father's constituency, the College of William and Mary, which he represented for the rest of his career. By the mid-1750s (the date of his appointment is unknown) he had become judge of the vice admiralty court.

Randolph figured prominently in several crises of the 1750s and rose to be the principal lieutenant of, and prospective successor to, Virginia's most powerful leader, John Robinson, who served as both Speaker of the House of Burgesses and treasurer of Virginia. In 1751 Governor Robert Dinwiddie imposed a fee of one pistole (a Spanish coin used in the colony) to process land patents, raising the issue of taxation without consent. Despite Randolph's position as the king's attorney, he agreed to represent the burgesses before the Board of Trade in London in early 1754. Dinwiddie dismissed him from office. The board compromised by upholding the fee and Randolph's dismissal but advising Dinwiddie to limit collections and reappoint Randolph if he apologized. The burgesses' wish to compensate Randolph remained unsettled until the outbreak of the French and Indian War forced Dinwiddie to agree in order to secure funds for the war.

Randolph did well in the western land speculation of mid-century Virginia. He helped found the New River Company, which obtained a grant of 400,000 acres in 1749, and within five years shared in two other allocations totaling 220,000 acres. He responded more personally than most speculators to France's threat in the Ohio Valley by accepting command of a mounted troop of lawyers and other gentlemen. In May 1756 they marched to help George Washington defend Winchester but, having little training, saw no action and returned home by August.

Appointed to the William and Mary board of visitors about the time the college initially elected him burgess, Randolph encountered controversy there as well. When Randolph's cousin, the Reverend William Stith, declared his candidacy for the college presidency in 1752, Dinwiddie predictably endorsed Stith's opponent, Thomas Dawson. After much altercation, the Randolph clan prevailed.

The Two-Penny Acts of 1755 and 1758 sustained the partisan tension. Crop failures in those years drove tobacco prices to four pence a pound, well above the norm. To relieve Virginians bound by contracts requiring payment in tobacco, particularly Anglican parishes, which by law paid ministers 16,000 pounds of tobacco a year, the assembly authorized conversion to cash at two pennies a pound. To answer appeals to the Privy Council, the legislators in 1759 engaged a permanent agent in London and put Randolph's experience to work on a committee of correspondence to give instructions. The council disallowed the acts, raising an issue of imperial interference in local affairs that foreshadowed the constitutional crisis of the American Revolution.

At the college, where most of the faculty were clergymen, resistance to the acts provoked the visitors to investigate campus morality in an attempt to diminish clerical influence. In 1757, the year Randolph began a one-year term as rector, the visitors discharged the entire faculty, although London restored two of the five. The visitors dismissed two of the replacements and endeavored to tighten their grip throughout the 1760s. The Crown's disallowance of the Two-Penny Acts encouraged suits for back pay—known as Parsons' Causes—in which plaintiffs did poorly, a reflection of the anticlerical trend in prerevolutionary years with which Randolph became identified.

Presented with Parliament's announced intention to enact a stamp tax in the colonies, the burgesses in the fall 1764 session adopted a series of petitions in protest. Randolph composed the petition addressed to the House of Lords. All were firm in opposition to the tax but prudent in rhetoric. When news of enactment came in May 1765, Patrick Henry used more rousing words to introduce resolves hinting at armed resistance. In an emotional debate Randolph and the Speaker partly succeeded in suppressing Henry's motions; Randolph once burst from the chamber exclaiming, "By God, I would have given five hundred guineas for a single vote" (Thomas Jefferson to William Wirt, 14 Aug. 1814). The episode capsulized Randolph's policy throughout the constitutional dispute with Great Britain: a staunch defender of Virginia's local autonomy, he carefully avoided introducing unnecessary obstacles to accommodation.

Randolph faced a career crisis in 1766 following the death of the Speaker. Settling Robinson's estate revealed that he had illegally reissued wartime currency as personal loans to associates. Although Randolph was not personally involved, the burgesses, after a highly charged debate, elected him as Speaker but gave the treasurership, which Robinson had concurrently held for twenty-eight years, to Robert Carter Nicholas, feeding deep-seated enmity between the new officeholders.

Despite this inauspicious beginning, Randolph soon acquired an avuncular mystique as Speaker. Always counseling moderation, he nonetheless lent his prestige to the transfer of power from royal to popular institutions. In 1769 and again in 1774, when the governor dissolved the assembly to still opposition, Randolph chaired extralegal sessions to circumvent the dismissals. Loyal to the empire to the end, he espoused economic measures such as embargoes to pressure Britain to relent and championed colonial union toward that goal. In 1773 he sat on another committee of correspondence to coordinate intelligence among the colonies. In 1774–1775 he chaired the first three Virginia Conventions, and the Continental Congress elected him its first president, symbolizing the bond between New England and the South.

Socially and politically an archconservative in modern eyes compared to Patrick Henry and Thomas Jefferson, Randolph was regarded by contemporary Virginians as the leader of their revolution. When he came from Philadelphia in May 1775 to preside over the last session of the colonial assembly, the *Virginia Gazette* reported that a public reception in Williamsburg greeted him as "*The Father of Your Country*" (1 June 1775). Randolph died of apoplexy in Philadelphia that fall before having to confront the issue of independence.

• There is no large collection of Randolph's papers. Some are in the Randolph Family Papers at the Virginia Historical Society. Peyton Randolph Estate Papers are in the Library of Congress, and Randolph's will and the inventory of his estate are in York County, Wills & Inventories, vol. 22, pp. 308–10, Virginia State Library. Many recipients' copies of correspondence are scattered through other mid-eighteenth-century collections. Edmund Randolph, *History of Virginia*, ed. Arthur H. Shaffer (1970), offers contemporary insights. A recent biography with a thorough bibliography is Gerald Steffins Cowden, "The Randolphs of Turkey Island: A Prosopography of the First Three Generations, 1650–1806" (Ph.D. diss., College of William and Mary, 1977), vol. 2, pp. 578–667. Jack P. Greene, ed., "The Case of the Pistole Fee," *Virginia Magazine of History and Biography* 66 (1958): 399–422, discusses that episode. Susan H. Godson et al., *The College of William and Mary: A History*, vol. 1 (1993), pp. 85–108, describe the actions of the board of visitors in which Randolph participated. Rhys Isaac, *The Transformation of Virginia 1721–1803* (1982), treats the ideological and political implications of the enmity between Randolph and Nicholas. David John Mays, *Edmund Pendleton, 1721–1803* (1984), covers the Robinson affair and many of the prerevolutionary events in which Randolph took part from the view of a Robinson defender. See also John E. Selby, *The Revolution in Virginia, 1775–1783* (1988).

JOHN E. SELBY

RANDOLPH, Sarah Nicholas (12 Oct.1839–25 Apr. 1892), historian and educator, was born at Edge Hill, Ablemarle County, Virginia, the daughter of Thomas Jefferson Randolph, a planter, and Jane Hollins Nicholas. The importance of history and family responsibility was deeply ingrained in Sarah Nicholas Randolph. Her father, Thomas Jefferson's favorite grandson, who served as the manager of his affairs during the last ten years of the former president's life and was the executor of his estate, edited the first collection of Jeffersoniana, *Memoir, Correspondence and Miscellanies from the Papers of Thomas Jefferson* (1829). When, as a result of the Civil War, the family found itself in reduced circumstances, Jane Randolph, along with Sarah and her sister Mary, opened the Edge Hill School for Girls, which catered to the daughters of wealthy Virginia families.

History was always Randolph's primary intellectual interest. From the late 1860s to the mid-1870s she corresponded with the eminent historian of Virginia, Hugh Blair Grigsby, about issues such as the accuracy of John Smith's Pocahontas narrative and William C. Rives's *History of the Life and Times of James Madison*. Her uncle, George Wythe Randolph, secretary of war for the Confederacy, encouraged her to write a child's history of Virginia during the Civil War, but she never did. Instead Randolph later began what became *The Domestic Life of Thomas Jefferson* (1871). Evidently, Randolph had difficulty completing this work because of other familial and financial obligations, confessing to Grigsby: "My work progresses slowly owing to the time to be given to imperious duties, which are at times distasteful to me, but doubly so now, as they take me from a task which is to me more & more a labour of love." In the third edition of the history (1958), Dumas Malone, the distinguished historian, declared that "nobody has given a better picture of [Jefferson] as a family man than Sarah N. Randolph." Randolph also wrote *The Life of General Thomas J. Jackson* (1876), which concludes with southern colors flying, forgiving the state of Virginia for "lagging behind amid such progress as this century has witnessed in science, art, and literature," and praising it for having produced George Washington and the "no less loved, no less honored, and no less brilliant . . . [Robert E.] Lee and [Stonewall] Jackson."

In 1879 Randolph left the school at Edge Hill to become the principal of Patapsco Institute, near Ellicott Mills, Maryland. She finally opened her own institution, Miss Randolph's School for Girls, in Baltimore in 1884. According to her niece, Mrs. William Randolph, Randolph helped memorialize both Robert E. Lee and Ulysses S. Grant by working to erect monuments in their honor.

Randolph died in Baltimore and was buried in the family cemetery at "Monticello" in Virginia.

• Ten letters from Randolph are in the Hugh Blair Grigsby Papers in the collections of the Virginia Historical Society in Richmond. A biographical sketch appears in Clayton Torrence, ed., "Letters of Sarah Nicholas Randolph to Hugh

Blair Grigsby," *Virginia Magazine of History and Biography* 59 (July 1951): 315–36. Obituaries are in the *Baltimore Sun*, 26 Apr. 1892, and the *Richmond Dispatch*, 27 Apr. 1892.

CHERYL B. TORSNEY

RANDOLPH, Thomas Mann (1 Oct. 1768–20 June 1828), member of Congress and governor of Virginia, was born at Tuckahoe in Goochland County, Virginia, the son of Thomas Mann Randolph and Anne Cary. He was a great-great-grandson of William Randolph of Turkey Island, who migrated to Virginia from England in 1673 and became the progenitor of a distinguished American family. Randolph was educated privately by a tutor at home until he entered the University of Edinburgh, where he remained for four years. Although he did not graduate from Edinburgh, he demonstrated an aptitude for scientific subjects while at the university.

Returning to Virginia in 1788, Randolph married his cousin Martha, the daughter of Thomas Jefferson, at Monticello in 1790. The two families were not only bound by ties of kinship, but Jefferson's father had acted as guardian for the elder Randolph, and the two families had lived together for several years at Tuckahoe. The Jeffersons and Randolphs also owned adjoining lands in Albemarle County, and there Randolph established his residence at Edgehill. Randolph and his growing family were often invited by Jefferson to stay at Monticello, where the son-in-law assisted in managing the estate while Jefferson was away on public business. The eleven Randolph children, among whom were Thomas Jefferson Randolph and George Wythe Randolph, became greatly attached to their maternal grandfather, and this may have contributed to Randolph's alienation from his family in later years.

Although Randolph eventually became estranged from his kindly and well-meaning father-in-law, who had often aided him, the two men shared many intellectual interests and held similar political views. Encouraged by Jefferson to participate in public affairs, Randolph served locally as a justice of the peace and as a captain in the Virginia militia. Defeated for election to the Virginia House of Delegates in 1797, he was elected to Congress in 1803 and reelected in 1805. While he supported his father-in-law's administration, his congressional career was uneventful except for a near duel with John Randolph of Roanoke, against whom he was alleged to have used insulting language in the House. Retiring from Congress in 1807, Randolph sought reelection in 1809 but was defeated.

Having risen to be a lieutenant colonel in the Virginia militia, Randolph, who had long advocated war with Britain, was eager to serve in the War of 1812. Nominated to command a regiment in the U.S. Army, Randolph was commissioned as a colonel in March 1813 and was ordered to recruit men for the Twentieth Regiment of Infantry. Ordered to Sackett's Harbor, Lake Ontario, to serve under General James Wilkinson, he saw little action and was allowed to return home. Although he had been appointed a federal collector of revenue for his congressional district in 1813

and had resigned his commission in the army, Randolph returned briefly to military duty during the summer of 1814 when he served as a lieutenant colonel in the Virginia militia guarding the approaches to Richmond.

After his military service, Randolph's financial difficulties arising from inherited debt and bad crops were increased by the declining tobacco economy in Virginia. His personal problems were exacerbated by weakening ties with his family, especially those with his eldest son, upon whom Jefferson increasingly leaned. Despite these unhappy circumstances, Randolph continued his scientific interests and won respect as a botanist from the Portuguese savant, the Abbé Corrêa. He also continued his experimentation with horizontal plowing, which he introduced to the Virginia Piedmont as a means of checking the ravages of soil erosion. For this contribution he was honored by the Albemarle Agricultural Society, of which he was a founder and president.

In 1819 Randolph returned to public life with his election to the Virginia House of Delegates from Albemarle. Elected governor of the commonwealth that same year, he was reelected in 1820 and 1821. While staunchly defending states' rights, he evinced liberal views in his support of the University of Virginia, promotion of canals for improving transportation, and proposals for gradually ending slavery in Virginia. As governor he resisted the opposition and interference of the council of state, which, he said, made the role of the executive little more than that of a "signing clerk." Despite his desire to quit the wrangling at Richmond, he gladly returned to the Virginia House of Delegates from Albemarle in 1823 and 1824. While he continued to support projects such as the University of Virginia, he alienated many of his constituents in his advocacy of a constitutional convention that would give the western counties a greater voice. Defeated for reelection to the house of delegates in 1825, his political career was finished. His last public service was rendered as the federal member of a commission in 1826 and 1827 to determine the boundary between the state of Georgia and the territory of Florida. Although the commission failed in its task, Randolph was not responsible for the failure.

Randolph's last years were overshadowed by continuing financial difficulties that led to the forced sale of his property, alienation from his family, and withdrawal from the family circle at Monticello. Although he returned to Monticello a few months before his death there, he still lived apart from his family; but he was finally reconciled with them and was buried near Jefferson in the family graveyard.

Randolph belonged to the natural aristocracy of virtue and talents idealized by Jefferson, but his irascible temper, erratic nature, and lack of judgment in practical matters prevented his becoming an outstanding leader. Contributing also to his unhappy and unfulfilled life was the necessity of living in the shadow of Thomas Jefferson as his father-in-law, well-disposed toward Randolph though Jefferson may have been.

Yet despite his difficulties and flawed temperament, Randolph's interest in constitutional reform and the ending of slavery, his support of education and improved transportation, and his promotion of scientific agriculture merit recognition.

• Randolph's papers consist largely of his correspondence scattered through the papers of his contemporaries. The most important of these collections are the Thomas Jefferson Papers in the Library of Congress; the Massachusetts Historical Society, Boston; and the University of Virginia Library, Charlottesville. The Edgehill-Randolph Papers and the Carr-Cary Papers in the University of Virginia Library and the Nicholas P. Trist Papers in both the Library of Congress and the Southern History Collection of the University of North Carolina, Chapel Hill, are also important sources.

William H. Gaines, Jr., *Thomas Mann Randolph, Jefferson's Son-in-Law* (1966), is a thorough and scholarly biography. Dumas Malone, *Jefferson and His Time* (6 vols., 1948–1981), is indispensable for family background and Randolph's political and social milieu. There is an obituary in the *Richmond Enquirer*, 27 June 1828.

MALCOLM LESTER

RANDOLPH, Vance (23 Feb. 1892–1 Nov. 1980), folklorist, was born in Pittsburg, Kansas, the son of John Randolph, an attorney and Republican politician, and Theresa Gould, a librarian. Randolph was attracted to the exotic life and radical politics of the mining camps near Pittsburg. He dropped out of high school but eventually graduated from the local college (now Pittsburg State University) in 1914 and completed an M.A. in psychology at Clark University in 1915, writing a thesis on dream analysis for G. Stanley Hall. His first publications appeared in leftist periodicals—a poem in *Masses* in 1915 and several articles in 1917 for the *Appeal to Reason*, the then widely distributed socialist newspaper published in nearby Girard, Kansas.

After short stints as a high school biology teacher and U.S. Army draftee, Randolph took up residence as a "converted hillbilly" in 1920 in Pineville, Missouri, in the Ozark Mountains, where he soon began a long career as a writer and folklore collector. In 1930 he married a local woman, Marie Wardlaw Wilbur, who died in 1937. They had no children. Randolph remained in the Ozarks for the rest of his life, first in Pineville and Galena, Missouri, and later in Eureka Springs and Fayetteville, Arkansas.

From the beginning, Randolph collected widely and assiduously, gathering not only dialect notes and ballad texts, but also beliefs, social traditions, work habits, food customs, medical beliefs, tales, and jokes—anything, in short, said, done, or believed by his Ozark neighbors. His first books, *The Ozarks* (1931) and *Ozark Mountain Folks* (1932), though mostly ignored by academic reviewers at the time and resented by some Ozark residents sensitive to the area's reputation for "backwardness," are appreciated today as early examples of what later came to be called folklife studies. Other works of this period include a short story collection, *From an Ozark Holler* (1933); a book for young readers, *The Camp on Wildcat Creek*

(1934); and a novel, *Hedwig* (1935). In 1933, he went briefly to Hollywood, hired by MGM at $200 a week to work on a movie about Ozark life. The job lasted a month, the movie was never made, and Randolph never made $200 a week again. By the end of the decade, despite the failure of academics to recognize his work, Randolph had a well-established reputation as an "Ozark expert."

Randolph first made his scholarly reputation as a student of dialect when his article-length studies in *American Speech* and *Dialect Notes*, published in the 1920s, were singled out for praise in H. L. Mencken's *The American Language* in 1936. His major work in the field, *Down in the Holler: A Gallery of Ozark Folk Speech*, was not published until 1953, however.

From 1941 to 1943 Randolph was engaged by Alan Lomax to record Ozark folk songs for the Library of Congress's Archive of American Folksong. His own folk song collection, *Ozark Folksongs*, first appeared in four volumes from 1946 to 1950, and *Ozark Superstitions*, titled in later printings *Ozark Magic and Folklore*, was published in 1947. These works, unlike the books of the 1930s, were acclaimed by academic reviewers. Randolph's definitions of folk culture and his collecting methods often anticipated the standards of subsequent periods; folklorist W. K. McNeil's introduction to the 1980 reprint of *Ozark Folksongs*, for example, praised Randolph's inclusion of commercially recorded country music songs, adding that "too few later collectors" have followed this practice. Large as it was, with nearly 900 titles and over 800 tunes, *Ozark Folksongs* did not include the nearly 500 bawdy songs from his collection that remained unpublished until after his death (*Roll Me in Your Arms* [1992]).

The 1950s saw the publication of Randolph's great folktale collections, beginning with *We Always Lie to Strangers*, his tall tale study, in 1951. He then published *Who Blowed Up the Church House?* (1952), *The Devil's Pretty Daughter* (1955), *The Talking Turtle* (1957), and *Sticks in the Knapsack* (1958). Two decades later, his collection of bawdy tales was published as *Pissing in the Snow* (1976).

In 1962 Randolph married Mary Celestia Parler, an English professor and folklore researcher at the University of Arkansas. This marriage was childless as well. *Hot Springs and Hell*, a collection of some 460 Ozark jokes and humorous anecdotes, appeared in 1965, praised by one reviewer as the first American "fully annotated jokebook." This volume, like the earlier folk song collection, contains no obscene jokes. Randolph's collections of "vulgar rhymes," obscene riddles, graffiti, bawdy speech, and other "unprintable" materials were not published until 1992, in a companion volume to the bawdy folk songs entitled *Blow the Candle Out*.

In 1972 Randolph's enormous *Ozark Folklore: A Bibliography* was published; a supplementary second volume, updating the bibliography to 1982, appeared in 1987. Randolph was elected a fellow of the American Folklore Society in 1978. He died in Fayetteville, Arkansas. His long labors of collecting and preserving in print the entire range of Ozark traditional life saved the region's heritage. "His most significant accomplishment," according to folklorist McNeil's introduction to the second volume of *Ozark Folklore: A Bibliography*, "is the compilation of the most complete collection from a single region of the United States."

• Important collections of Randolph's papers are located in the Library of Congress and at the University of Arkansas. For a detailed bibliography, see Robert Cochran and Michael Luster, *For Love and for Money* (1979). A full-length biography is Robert Cochran, *Vance Randolph: An Ozark Life* (1985). For an assessment of Randolph's importance in American folklore studies, see Herbert Halpert, "Obituary: Vance Randolph (1892–1980)," *Journal of American Folklore* 94 (1981): 345–50.

ROBERT COCHRAN

RANEY, George Pettus (11 Oct. 1845–8 Jan. 1911), jurist, was born in Apalachicola, Florida, the son of David G. Raney and Frances H. Jordan. Raney attended local schools for his primary education. In 1862 he entered the University of Virginia, where he studied until September 1863, when the eighteen-year-old enlisted as a private in the Confederate army. During the Civil War Raney served in Georgia and Florida. When the conflict ended, the Union army granted parole to his command in Waynesboro, Georgia.

Shortly after this Raney returned to the University of Virginia and enrolled in its law school. In 1867, following his admission to the bar, the young lawyer commenced private practice in Apalachicola. The next spring voters in Franklin County, Florida, elected him to the state legislature, one of a few Democrats elected to office that year. Subsequently, legislators reorganized the house, selected Raney as Speaker, and appointed him chair of the Judiciary Committee. In 1869 he moved to the state capital, Tallahassee, where he would spend the rest of his life. While living there Raney actively practiced law and dutifully served the public in the various offices he occupied. In the disputed presidential election of 1876, he served as a member of the Democratic State Executive Committee and also as a presidential elector on his party ticket. At the time of the Compromise of 1877, which awarded the disputed presidency to the Republican candidate Rutherford B. Hayes, Florida faced a similar controversy in its gubernatorial election. The Republican-dominated Canvassing Board declared the Republican candidate, Marcellus L. Stearns, the victor; however, the Democratic nominee, George F. Drew, contested the results and took his case against the Canvassing Board to the Florida Supreme Court. Drew selected Raney and two other attorneys to handle the case, and they convinced the court that Drew had won the election. The court ordered the Canvassing Board to validate the election of Governor Drew and thereby restored Democratic rule in Florida. In short, Reconstruction had come to an end.

For Raney's role in bringing this about, Drew appointed him the state's attorney general. In 1881 William D. Bloxham, who succeeded Drew as governor,

reappointed Raney to a second term. During his eight years as Florida's chief counsel, Raney was by virtue of his office attorney of the board of trustees of the state's Internal Improvement Fund. In this capacity he conducted important litigation concerning the land fund of Florida and the interest of the railroads in that fund. This experience helped shape Raney's future position regarding state regulation of the railroads.

In 1885 Raney moved from the office of attorney general to the Florida Supreme Court and became an associate justice. In 1888 he retained his place on the court by election to a six-year term. The following year his colleagues on the bench selected Raney as the chief justice. During the nine years he served on the court, he wrote many important decisions. *The Pensacola & Atlantic Railroad Company v. the State of Florida* (1889) was the most influential opinion of his career. In this 31-page opinion, Raney ruled that the state could not compel a railroad to charge unprofitable rates for freight or passengers. Allowing the government to coerce a railroad to operate without profit, he reasoned, would result in the public seizure of private property without just compensation. As he put it, "To earn money is a purpose and legitimate object of a railroad company." With that ruling Raney championed individual property rights and helped check the regulatory power of government over the railroads, which had begun to expand with *Munn v. Illinois* (1877).

In 1894 Raney resigned his position as chief justice to resume private practice in Tallahassee. For the next five years he held no public office, except for presidential elector in 1896. He became a candidate for the U.S. Senate in 1897 but withdrew from the race before the November election. In 1899 the citizens of Leon County elected him to the Florida House of Representatives. He served in the lower house until he advanced to the state senate in 1902, remaining there until 1906. From 1900 to 1904 he was also a member of the Democratic National Committee for Florida. After his retirement from public office, the Seaboard Railway offered Raney a position as its legal counsel; he accepted and continued in this position until his death.

In 1873 Raney married Mary Elizabeth Lamar of Athens, Georgia, with whom he had four children. She died in 1899, and in 1901 the widower married Evelyn Byrd Cameron, who died accidentally eleven months later.

A member of the Episcopal church and a lifelong Democrat, Raney accomplished much in his life. According to his contemporary, Justice James B. Whitfield, Raney's "high character, his knowledge of the law, his dignity, his vigorous intellect, and his patriotic services distinguish him as one of Florida's most accomplished, useful, and honored citizens." Even so, Raney's greatest achievements were as a judge; he was invariably careful, laborious, and conscientious in reaching his decisions. Contemporaries described Raney as a tall, dignified, kind person, who always offered assistance to those less fortunate than himself. It is no surprise, then, that the residents of Florida expressed great sorrow when Raney died of pneumonia in his Tallahassee home.

• The opinions of Raney fill a significant portion of vols. 21–33 of the *Florida Reports* and provide engaging reading for attorneys as well as informed laypersons. The U.S. Supreme Court affirmed his rulings in the *Pintado* and *Osborne* cases, published in vol. 33. For perhaps the best display of Raney's judicial talent, see *Butler v. State*, vol. 25 (1889), pp. 354–58, and *The Pensacola & Atlantic Railroad v. State*, vol. 25 (1889), p. 310. Accounts of Raney include Rowland H. Rerick, *Memoirs of Florida* (1902), and Benjamin A. Meginniss, "George Pettus Raney, 1845–1911," *Apalachee* (1944): 81–89. Obituaries are in the *Florida Times Union* and the *Tampa Morning Tribune*, both 9 Jan. 1911.

JOHN J. GUTHRIE, JR.

RANGER, Joseph (1760?–?), revolutionary war seaman, was born probably in Northumberland County, Virginia, to unknown parents. Ranger was a free African American, or perhaps a runaway slave, who probably worked as a seaman in Northumberland County and Elizabeth City County before the revolutionary war. In the early eighteenth century, Virginia's waters were sailed extensively by free African Americans and slaves who also worked in the colony's two shipyards. Despite long-standing concern among the elite in the South about arming even free African Americans for fear of inciting slave revolt, the maritime experiences of Virginia's African Americans made them prime candidates for enlistment in the state navy (just as many African-American seamen served in the Continental navy).

Joseph Ranger enlisted in the Virginia navy in 1776, one of many African Americans who served on racially mixed naval crews. Ranger served in the Virginia navy for eleven years, the longest recorded term of service of any African-American sailor. The Virginia navy was composed of a motley assortment of forty vessels, from barges to ships, which were designed to support the cobbled-together navy created by the Continental Congress in 1775 and to protect the exposed Virginia coastline from British invasion. Ranger's home county of Northumberland provided at least six African-American seamen to Virginia's navy.

It was usual for sailors to transfer frequently between ships, and Ranger served aboard four naval vessels, the largest recorded total number of any African-American sailor. Ranger first served for three months aboard the ship *Hero*, one of the ships with the largest number of African-American crew members. For the next four years he served aboard the *Dragon* as one of five African Americans in a crew of 104. Aboard the *Dragon*, Ranger and the other African-American crew members were recorded as receiving full rations of pork, flour, and liquor.

After the *Dragon* was converted into a fire ship in 1780, Ranger transferred to the *Jefferson*, where he served for one year, until it was blown up by the British as it sailed on the James River. After the explosion Ranger was assigned to serve aboard the *Patriot* for approximately six months. Shortly before Cornwallis's surrender at Yorktown on 19 October 1781 Ranger was taken prisoner by the British along with the rest of the *Patriot*'s crew. (He was probably released soon after the surrender.)

The British naval threat to Virginia did not end with the formal cessation of revolutionary war hostilities, and the Continental Congress granted Virginia the right to maintain two armed ships, the *Liberty* and the *Patriot*, after the war ended. Ranger served aboard both of these ships until Virginia's navy was finally disbanded in 1787.

Ranger had been paid for his service in the navy. He was recorded in the Virginia State Auditors' records as having received two pounds, ten shillings, for one month's service in 1786 and five pounds, seven shillings, for two months' service in 1787. Not much is known of Ranger's life or how he earned a living after the disassembly of the Virginia navy, but he may have continued to work as a sailor.

Within a few years after the end of the revolutionary war, Ranger received a land grant from the state of Virginia as a reward for his military service. His grant of 100 acres, located in Virginia's western Kentucky and Ohio territories, represented the usual grant received by Virginia's African-American privates. Ranger probably never occupied his land but more likely sold it to one of many land speculators who bought up soldiers' bounties for a fraction of their worth.

In addition to his land grant from the state of Virginia, Ranger also qualified for a federal revolutionary war pension under the congressional acts of 1818, 1820, and 1832. At least twenty-one African Americans in Virginia qualified for veterans' pensions. Joseph Ranger received $96 a year after he swore out a deposition in a local Virginia court attesting to his wartime naval service.

It is unknown when and where Joseph Ranger died. His revolutionary war service in the Virginia navy exemplifies the importance of African Americans to American military forces, even in states such as Virginia with extremely restrictive slave systems. Ranger's long maritime service shows how African Americans were able to capitalize on their seafaring experience to gain economic status and even freedom. Ranger, like other African-American sailors, was rewarded by his state and his country for his patriotic service.

• The most complete information on Joseph Ranger appears in L. P. Jackson, "Virginia Negro Soldiers and Seamen in the American Revolution," *Journal of Negro History* 27 (1942): 247–85. Jackson summarizes the various Virginia state records that contain information about Ranger.

SARAH J. PURCELL

RANK, Otto (22 Apr. 1884–31 Oct. 1939), psychologist and psychoanalyst, was born Otto Rosenfeld in Vienna, Austria, the son of Simon Rosenfeld, an artisan jeweler, and Karoline Fleischner. His older brother studied law while Otto became a locksmith: the family could not afford higher education for both. Close to his mother but alienated from his alcoholic father, Otto adopted "Rank" in adolescence and formalized it a few years later, symbolizing self-creation, a central theme of his life and work.

Of Jewish background, growing up in Catholic Vienna, Rank was a religious skeptic who wrote his own Ten Commandments, among them "Thou shalt not give birth reluctantly." He read deeply in philosophy and literature, loved music, and considered himself an artist, writing poetry and a literary diary. After encountering Sigmund Freud's *Interpretation of Dreams* (1900) and other works, he applied Freudian ideas in an essay on the artist that impressed Freud so much that he hired Rank to be secretary of the fledgling Vienna Psychoanalytic Society in 1906. At twenty-two, the youngest member—Freud was fifty—Rank became the acknowledged expert on philosophy, literature, and myth. With financial support and mentoring from Freud, who did not encourage a medical career, Rank obtained his Ph.D. from the University of Vienna in 1912, the first to do so with a psychoanalytic thesis.

Otto Rank had become, after Freud, the most prolific psychoanalytic writer, with *The Artist* (1907), *The Myth of the Birth of the Hero* (1909), *The Lohengrin Saga* (1911), and *The Incest Theme in Literature and Legend* (1912; 2d ed. 1926), a 700-page survey of world literature. Except for the posthumous *Beyond Psychology* (1941), all of Rank's books were originally published in his native German. Rank was the only member of Freud's inner circle, the Committee of 7, to reside in Vienna with "the Professor": together they edited journals, ran a publishing house, and trained psychoanalytic candidates from around the world. Rank witnessed the vicissitudes and bitter endings of Freud's relationships with Alfred Adler and Carl Jung; his own tenure with Freud lasted much longer—two decades, matched only by that of his friend Sandor Ferenczi and his foe Ernest Jones.

Rank treated patients as the first "lay" (nonphysician) analyst. During World War I he served with the Austrian army in Poland, where he met and married Beata "Tola" Mincer in 1918; she became a noted lay analyst and practiced in Boston after their separation in 1934. The birth of their only child in 1919 enhanced Rank's interest in the pre-Oedipal phase of development (birth to age three) and the mother-child relationship.

In 1924 Rank's *Trauma of Birth* appeared, developing ideas about the importance of separation and individuation, with their attendant and inevitable anxiety. Until then psychoanalysis had been father-centered, with Oedipal conflict (son's desire for mother, rage at father, and castration fear) the central theme. Rank meant only to balance and extend Freud's work; at forty he made his first visit to the United States—as Freud's emissary but presenting his own ideas. After first praising Rank's innovations, Freud withdrew his support under pressure from Jones and Karl Abraham, who sought to bring down their rival, Freud's favorite son. In 1926 the final break occurred; the Ranks moved to Paris.

Rank's Americanization began in 1924 with plaudits, translations, invitations, eager patients. Over the next decade he lectured, taught, wrote, and practiced a briefer form of psychoanalytic therapy. Psychoanalysis had become a lengthy and intensive ritual; Ferenczi and Rank pioneered "active therapy," which emphasized a more egalitarian relationship between therapist and patient (eventually Ferenczi also broke from Freud). Rank modified the open-ended analytic process by using termination as the focus for healthy separation and independent development.

Orthodox Freudians condemned Rank's deviance and vilified him. The American Psychoanalytic Association ousted him and made his former analysands undergo a second analysis in order to remain in the association. Some historians of psychoanalysis have repeated a baseless assertion that Rank's separation from Freud resulted from Rank's mental illness.

Rank's creativity flourished in his post-Freudian period. Between 1926 and 1931 he wrote major works on developmental psychology and therapeutic technique. The former put him in the vanguard of object-relations theory and ego psychology. His work on therapeutic technique, translated as *Will Therapy* (1936), emphasizes conscious experience, the present, choice, responsibility, and action over the (classical Freudian) unconscious, past history, drives, determinism, and intellectual insight. *Psychology and the Soul* appeared in 1930, *Modern Education* and *Art and Artist*, perhaps his greatest work, in 1932. To Rank, soul and will were essential, unanalyzable elements of personality that psychoanalysis either hid, forgot, or destroyed. Neurotics, he taught, were failed artists; in therapy they could discover and exercise the will that had been sidetracked or paralyzed. The result would be self-creation, or psychological rebirth.

In 1935 Rank emigrated from Europe under the cloud of Nazi Germany to the United States. He taught at the School of Social Work of the University of Pennsylvania and lectured around the country. His Americanization was symbolized by his adoption of the nickname "Huck," with which he signed himself in his most personal letters. His favorite book was Mark Twain's *Adventures of Huckleberry Finn* (1884).

Otto Rank's emphasis on will, relationship, and creativity appealed to psychologists Rollo May, Carl Rogers, Esther Menaker, Paul Goodman, and Henry Murray. Noted psychiatrists influenced by Rank include Frederick Allen, Marion Kenworthy, Robert Jay Lifton, Carl Whitaker, and Irvin Yalom; writers and critics include Ernest Becker, Maxwell Geismar, Max Lerner, Ludwig Lewisohn, Anaïs Nin, Carl Rakosi, and Miriam Waddington.

Rank's companion at the end of his life was Estelle Buel, an American of Swiss descent whom he married just three months before his death. He had applied for U.S. citizenship when a kidney infection led to fatal septicemia; he died in New York City.

Freud's closest associate for twenty years, Rank was, among his inner circle, the most involved in the development of psychotherapy in the United States. His influence was both extensive and muted, the latter due both to his early death and to ostracism by powerful associations, university departments, and even reading lists controlled by Freudians from the 1930s to the 1960s. Since the mid-1970s Rank has been reintroduced by some of the writers mentioned: Becker, Lifton, May, Rogers, Menaker, and Nin.

Rank pioneered in areas of psychology that are now widely accepted; often the ideas were not credited to him because he fell out of favor with the establishment. Some ideas that seemed radical in his time are now in the mainstream of psychoanalytic thought: the importance of the early mother-child relationship; the ego, consciousness, the here-and-now, and the actual relationship—as opposed to transference—in therapy. As a psychotherapist who called himself a "philosopher of helping" he paved the way for interpersonal, existential, client-centered, Gestalt, and relationship therapies. As a social psychologist he contributed to our understanding of myth, religion, art, education, ethics, and organizational behavior.

• The Butler Library, Columbia University, holds the Otto Rank Papers in its rare book and manuscript collections. The *Journal of the Otto Rank Association* appeared twice annually from 1966 to 1983, publishing works by Rank and many others who knew him and/or his writings. Robert Kramer edited a collection of Rank's lectures in English, *A Psychology of Difference: The American Lectures* (1996). Biographies include Jessie Taft, *Otto Rank* (1958), and E. James Lieberman, *Acts of Will: The Life and Work of Otto Rank* (1985; repr. 1993). A psychologist's survey of his work is Esther Menaker, *Otto Rank: A Rediscovered Legacy* (1982). Ludwig Lewisohn's introduction to the original edition of Rank's *Art and Artist* (1932) is an important statement by an authority on American literary history. An obituary is in the *New York Times*, 1 Nov. 1939.

E. JAMES LIEBERMAN

RANKIN, Jeannette Pickering (11 June 1880–18 May 1973), first woman in Congress and peace activist, was born near Missoula, Montana, the daughter of John Rankin, a successful developer, and Olive Pickering, a former schoolteacher. The eldest of seven surviving children, Rankin exhibited considerable sangfroid and sense of responsibility from an early age. An indifferent student at Montana State University in Missoula (now the University of Montana), she lacked direction upon her graduation in 1902. Following an eye-opening tour of the slums of Boston in 1904, she enrolled in the New York School of Philanthropy, which later became the Columbia University School of Social Work. After brief and dissatisfying service as a social worker in Spokane, Washington, she enrolled in a wide range of courses at the University of Washington in Seattle, where in 1910 she began her career in woman suffrage. During a visit to her home state in December of that year she stunned the Montana populace when, in an address on behalf of the Equal Franchise Society, she became the first woman to speak to the legislature.

Following a move to New York, Rankin's talent for public speaking and her commitment to woman suffrage brought her into contact with a broad range of women activists and reformers. The never married Rankin began a lifelong intimate relationship with biographer Katherine Anthony and took part in the great suffrage parade in Washington, D.C., on 3 March 1913, the day before Woodrow Wilson's inauguration. Although Rankin was a tireless speaker on the rights of women, her attention gradually shifted to the coming war in Europe. In 1916 she ran for U.S. Congress on the Republican ticket, promoting a platform that included votes for women, child protection legislation, and "preparedness for peace." Despite a near-sweep of Montana elections by the Democrats, she became the first woman to be elected to the U.S. Congress. Her election made her the focus of international attention. Immensely popular, she wrote a weekly newspaper column and shouldered the expectations of a multitude of feminists and woman suffrage activists.

Votes for women, Congresswoman Rankin declared, represented only the first step in the extension of democracy to all phases of American life, and she intended to promote a wide range of reforms. After only four days in office, however, her agenda was hopelessly overshadowed by her vote against U.S. entry into World War I. Not only did she vote with the minority, she violated the precedent of 140 years of roll call when she prefaced her vote with an explanation to publicize her view and ensure its inclusion in the *Congressional Record*: "I want to stand by my country, but I cannot vote for war." Despite her subsequent efforts on behalf of American labor and woman suffrage, she failed to be reelected. Reaction among women's leaders was mixed, but Carrie Chapman Catt of the National American Woman Suffrage Association spoke for the majority when she warned that Rankin's vote on the war had put the suffrage amendment back by years. Alice Paul of the Women's party, however, lauded Rankin for showing the potential power of women to diminish war if given appropriate authority.

Leaving Congress in 1919, Rankin attended the Women's International Conference for Permanent Peace in Zurich, then held a variety of posts in the Women's International League for Peace and Freedom. The following year she accepted Florence Kelley's invitation to serve as field secretary for the National Consumers' League. In Washington, Rankin lobbied successfully for the passage of social welfare legislation, most notably the Sheppard-Towner bill, which she herself had introduced in the Sixty-fifth Congress, aimed at reducing the maternal and infant mortality rate. Her efforts to promote legislation to improve factory conditions met with failure, however, as did her lobbying in 1924 for a constitutional amendment to prohibit child labor. Rankin left the National

Consumers' League in 1924, and although she had purchased a farm in Georgia the previous year, she took a side trip to Montana to campaign on behalf of her brother Wellington Rankin in his unsuccessful bid for the U.S. Senate.

Settling on her Georgia farm in 1925, Rankin worked briefly as field secretary for the Women's International League for Peace and Freedom. In 1928 she established the Georgia Peace Society and lobbied Congress in 1929 on behalf of the Women's Peace Union. In November 1929 she began a nine-year stint as lobbyist and propagandist for peace with the National Council for the Prevention of War, under the chairmanship of former Methodist minister Frederick J. Libby. However, as the United States gradually strayed from its official commitment to strict neutrality, Rankin's marathon of public speeches and radio addresses fell on increasingly deaf ears.

In 1935 Rankin successfully defended herself against charges, reported in the *Macon Evening Journal*, that she was a communist. She was demoralized the following year, however, when her efforts to undermine the reelection of her old adversary, Montana representative Carl Vinson, failed. Her increasingly insistent pleas for back salary pushed her relationship with Libby to the breaking point, and she left the National Council in 1939.

In 1939, adamant about preserving American peace, Rankin returned to Montana and, backed by her wealthy brother Wellington, ran again for Congress. As war raged in much of the world, Rankin did not advocate an entirely defenseless America. Rather, she advocated such a strong peacetime military defense that the United States would be impregnable, ignoring the strategic implications of the American possessions that had resulted from earlier territorial expansion. Proclaiming that the country's real enemies were not foreign nations but rather hunger, poverty, unemployment, and disease, she won with a plurality of 9,264 votes.

Arriving in Washington in 1941, Rankin continued to urge American neutrality. Even in the immediate aftermath of the bombing of Pearl Harbor, she staunchly maintained, "Killing more people won't help matters" (Josephson, p. 162). As she cast the sole vote against the war resolution, she again violated protocol by stating more than just "nay," proclaiming, "As a woman I can't go to war, and I refuse to send anyone else." Following the vote of 388 to 1, Rankin was obliged to take refuge in a telephone booth and call for security guards to protect her from the angry mob surrounding her. The press was nearly universal in their condemnation of Rankin. Famed journalist William Allen White, however, predicted in the *Emporia Gazette* (10 Dec. 1941), "When in one hundred years from now, courage, sheer courage based on moral indignation, is celebrated in this country, the name of Jeannette Rankin, who stood firm in folly for her faith, will be written in monumental bronze not for what she did but for the way she did it." Aware that her reelection was an impossibility, Rankin finished

her term opposing wartime fraud and championing free speech.

Rankin returned to Montana in 1943 to care for her aging mother, then traveled extensively for the next twenty years, primarily in India. Her global travels reinforced her commitment to peace as the solution to the world's troubles. Although her plans to create a woman's commune on her Georgia property failed to attract any applicants, she returned to the public spotlight on 15 January 1968, leading the Jeannette Rankin Brigade of several thousand marchers in a protest in the nation's capital against U.S. involvement in Vietnam. She and a group of fifteen other women, including Coretta Scott King, then presented a petition to Speaker John McCormack on behalf of the Women's Strike for Peace. When asked by a reporter for the *San Francisco Examiner* (5 June 1970) if she advocated surrender in Vietnam, Rankin replied, "Surrender is a military idea. When you're doing something wrong, you stop."

The swelling tide of feminism combined with growing opposition to U.S. involvement in Vietnam made Rankin a noble figure to a new generation of Americans in the late 1960s and early 1970s. Rankin participated in a variety of antiwar protests. She celebrated her ninetieth birthday at a reception and dinner in her honor at the Rayburn House Office Building, where she was feted by friends and associates, including a variety of Congress members and other dignitaries who touted her commitment to peace, child welfare, and civil rights. She continued to promote feminism and peace through print interviews and television appearances until her death, in Carmel, California, a few weeks short of her ninety-third birthday.

In addition to being the first woman to serve in Congress, Rankin was an enormously effective speaker who was instrumental in achieving woman suffrage and challenging common perceptions of war. In her final years Rankin met with consumer advocate Ralph Nader to discuss congressional reform. The relationship between the two seems particularly appropriate. Like Nader, Rankin evoked contradictory reactions among her contemporaries. For many she was impossibly idealistic, while for others she was an inspirational visionary who refused to confuse the realities of the present with the possibilities of the future.

• Rankin, impatient with the rigors of formal writing, is best known for her extemporaneous speeches. Moreover, what papers she did leave are widely dispersed. Papers highlighting her congressional years are housed at the Arthur and Elizabeth Schlesinger Library on the History of Women in America, at Radcliffe College in Cambridge, Mass. This collection also includes a documentary film, *Jeannette Rankin: First Lady of Peace*, produced by Davis Fisher for television station GWTV in Athens, Ga. The papers of Rankin's administrative secretary, Belle Fligelman Winestine, are housed at the Montana Historical Society Library in Helena. Rankin's work in the peace movement is found in the files of the National Council for Prevention of War in the Swarthmore Peace Collection at Swarthmore College and is discussed in Harriet Alonso, "Jeannette Rankin and the Women's Peace

Union," *Montana: The Magazine of Western History* 39 (1989): 34–49. Rankin was a popular subject in the 1970s, meriting three celebratory but not totally uncritical biographies: Hannah Josephson, *Jeannette Rankin: First Lady in Congress* (1974); Kevin S. Gile's unindexed *Flight of the Dove: The Story of Jeannette Rankin* (1980), based in part on Gile's twenty-year friendship with Rankin; and Ted Carlton Harris, *Jeannette Rankin: Suffragist, First Woman Elected to Congress, and Pacifist* (1972). All include bibliographies listing interview tapes and transcripts, unpublished sources, governmental documents, and periodical literature as well as books. Rankin is also a popular subject among children. Judy Rachel Block, *The First Woman in Congress: Jeannette Rankin* (1978), handsomely illustrated by Terry Kovalcik, is appropriate for grades four through six, while Florence Meiman White, *The First Woman in Congress: Jeannette Rankin* (1980), targets a slightly more sophisticated audience. An obituary is in the *New York Times*, 20 May 1973.

NANCY C. UNGER

RANKIN, John Elliott (29 Mar. 1882–26 Nov. 1960), U.S. congressman, was born in Itawamba County, Mississippi, the son of Thomas Braxton Rankin, a schoolteacher, and Venola Modest Rutledge. Educated in the public schools of Itawamba and Lee counties, he attended the University of Mississippi and received his LL.B. in 1910. He then practiced law at West Point, Mississippi, for several months before moving to Tupelo and associating with a partner in a new law firm. In 1912 he secured the post of prosecuting attorney for Lee County and served for four years. In 1915 he lost a race for district attorney, and the following year he waged an unsuccessful campaign for the Democratic nomination to Congress. He failed again in a second attempt for the congressional post in 1918. In World War I, he enlisted as a private in the field artillery but served only a short time in a training camp. Returning to Tupelo, he edited and published a weekly newspaper, the *New Era*. In 1919 he married Annie Laurie Burrous; they had one child.

After a successful campaign in 1920, Rankin entered Congress in March 1921. Over the next three decades he encountered little opposition in seeking reelection to fifteen consecutive terms. When he left office in January 1953, he had served thirty-one years, nine months, and twenty-one days—longer than any congressman before him. Although responsible for some progressive legislation that brought special benefits to his predominantly white rural constituency in northeastern Mississippi, he also gained notoriety for his reactionary views on social and political issues and his rancorous outbursts against American racial minorities. In Congress Rankin focused primarily on issues relating to public power, war veterans, white supremacy, and anticommunism.

The leader of the public power bloc in the House, Rankin felt that his greatest accomplishment was to bring electricity into his rural district. In 1933 he and Senator George W. Norris of Nebraska cosponsored the bill to create the Tennessee Valley Authority (TVA). Although his hometown, Tupelo, lay outside of the Tennessee River basin, Rankin succeeded in getting David E. Lilienthal, the first director of TVA, to include the city and his entire district within the agency's jurisdiction. The first municipality to receive electricity from TVA, Tupelo welcomed President Franklin D. Roosevelt to the city in 1934 to celebrate its acceptance of hydroelectric power. With the slogan "Let's electrify every farm home in America at rates the people can afford to pay," Rankin also worked diligently to secure congressional authorization of the Rural Electrification Administration (REA), which brought inexpensive electric power to farms all across the country. The REA was authorized by an act of Congress in 1936; in 1939 it was reorganized by Congress as a division of the U.S. Department of Agriculture. At the midpoint of Rankin's congressional career, the *New Republic* ranked him among congressmen who had "the reputation of being liberals, friends of the common voter" (18 Aug. 1937, p. 45).

A staunch advocate of bonuses to World War I veterans, Rankin chaired the Committee on Veterans' Legislation from 1931 until he left office. In 1935 he led the fight to override the presidential veto of a bonus bill. He introduced legislation in 1942 to raise the military base pay from $21 a month to $50. Several years later, however, he delayed passage of the GI Bill of Rights because of objections to its unemployment provisions. He also feared that absentee voting by soldiers would break down barriers against black voting in the South. Toward the end of his congressional career, he introduced legislation to provide each veteran $95 a month at the age of sixty-five and to pension widows, children, and dependent parents of all deceased veterans. Even veterans' groups opposed the exorbitant proposals, and the House soundly defeated them.

Vehement and defiant in defense of white supremacy, Rankin considered segregation as the only feasible means for people of different races to coexist. He argued that approval of antilynching bills would encourage rape. He fought anti–poll tax bills and all other measures to advance the status of blacks. Not confining his prejudices to African Americans, he called the war against Japan a race war and favored putting all Japanese Americans in concentration camps. "Once a Jap, always a Jap," he exclaimed to his congressional colleagues (23 Feb. 1942). He also alleged that Japanese agents plotted to create racial turmoil in the northern cities. Following the executive order to desegregate the armed forces in 1948, he accused President Harry S. Truman of trying to ram the platform of the Communist party down the throats of the American people.

As a member of the House Un-American Activities Committee (HUAC) from 1945 to 1950, Rankin gave full rein to his nativist and racist views. In January 1945 he employed a skillful parliamentary maneuver to make HUAC a standing committee and increase its membership. Bullying and threatening witnesses, he ranted about a Jewish-Communist conspiracy to seize control of the country and branded Hollywood as a hotbed of subversive activity. In response to criticism from the newspaper and radio commentator Walter

Winchell, Rankin called Winchell a "slime-mongering kike" (*New York Times*, 13 Feb. 1946). Embarrassed over his intemperate antics and insidious remarks, Mississippi newspapers, including the *Jackson Daily News* and the *Tupelo Journal*, joined others across the nation in rebuking him.

In 1948 Rankin entered the senatorial race in Mississippi to succeed the deceased Theodore G. Bilbo. He polled only 12 percent of the vote and came in fifth among the six candidates. With Mississippi's loss of a representative after the census in 1950, the state legislature combined most of Rankin's district with that of Congressman Thomas G. Abernethy. Defeated by Abernethy in 1952, Rankin returned to Tupelo at the end of his term and resumed his law practice. Quiet and reflective in retirement, Rankin died at his home in Tupelo.

A product of the late nineteenth century, Rankin did much to improve the quality of life for the people of his district and other rural areas of the country, but he refused to accept the social and political changes brought about by American involvement in two world wars. His indefensible manifestations of racial and religious intolerance not only marred his record but tarnished the image of his state and his country.

• The John Rankin Collection, containing more than 485 linear feet of original documents and memorabilia, is in the archives at the University of Mississippi, although access has been restricted. Newspaper clippings and other information about his activities are in the Rankin file at the Lee County Library in Tupelo, Miss. Remarks and speeches by Rankin are in Gerald L. K. Smith, *Congressman John E. Rankin: Patriot, Christian, Statesman* (1948), a pamphlet published in St. Louis by the Christian Nationalist Crusade. See also *Congressional Record*, 67th–82d Congs., on his speeches and the details of his legislative activity. Biographical information is in Dunbar Rowland, *The Official and Statistical Register of the State of Mississippi* (1923). A comprehensive study of his political career is Kenneth Wayne Vickers, "John Rankin: Democrat and Demagogue" (M.A. thesis, Mississippi State Univ., 1993). See Robert K. Carr, *The House Committee on Un-American Activities* (1952); Walter Goodman, *The Committee* (1968); William F. Buckley, Jr., *The Committee and Its Critics* (1962); and Martha Swain, *Pat Harrison, The New Deal Years* (1978), on his political career. For additional comments about Rankin see "Washington Notes," *New Republic*, 18 Aug. 1937, pp. 45–46; Russell Whelan, "Rankin of Mississippi," *American Mercury* 59 (July 1944): 31–37; William Walton, "Rankin Puts It Plainly," *New Republic*, 8 Dec. 1947, p. 10; and Philip A. Grant, Jr., "Ten Mississippians Who Served in Congress, 1931–1937," *Journal of Mississippi History* 39 (Aug. 1977): 209–12. John Egerton, *Speak Now against the Day* (1995), offers a recent although brief assessment of him. An obituary is in the *New York Times*, 27 Nov. 1960.

THOMAS N. BOSCHERT

RANKIN, McKee (6 Feb. 1841–17 Apr. 1914), actor and theatrical manager, was born Arthur McKee Rankin in Sandwich, Ontario, Canada, the son of Colonel Arthur Rankin, a government official. Sources do not give the name of his mother, but one identifies her as a descendant of the Shawnee chief Tecumseh. McKee

Rankin studied for a while at Upper Canada College but left to start acting at the age of seventeen under the pseudonym George Henly in Rochester, New York. He succumbed to parental pressure and took a post with the Canadian Bureau of Agriculture, but he soon returned to the stage. In 1863 Rankin was hired at Wood's Theatre in Cincinnati, where he made his professional debut on 14 March as the Count in *The Stranger*. In the following years he worked at theaters in other midwestern towns, including Indianapolis, Lexington, Louisville, and Pittsburgh. After the Civil War, in 1865–1866, he acted for Mrs. John Drew at Philadelphia's famous Arch Street Theatre, where his handsome, virile appearance fitted him for the leading man roles. The following season he acted with the New York Theatre Company in the Bowery. From there he moved to Selwyn's Theatre Company in Boston. On 11 December 1869 he married Kitty Blanchard (1847–1911), a noted comedienne with Selwyn's company.

For the next few years he and his wife toured, but in 1873 Rankin joined A. M. Palmer's stock company at the Union Square Theatre in New York. There in 1874 he acted in the premiere production of *The Two Orphans*, Hart Jackson's translation of Cormon and D'Ennery's *Les Deux Orphelines*, taking the part of the brutal Jacques Frochard with his wife as the young Henriette, searching desperately for her blind sister, played by Kate Claxton. The Rankins stayed with Palmer's company for two years, then moved to the Chestnut Street Theatre in Philadelphia, where Rankin played leading man roles with swaggering bravado. It was there that Rankin met the poet Joaquin Miller and secured the production rights for *The Danites, or The Heart of the Sierras*, the stage adaptation of Miller's *First Fam'lies of the Sierras* (1876). (Although Miller was credited with the authorship of the play, it was generally conceded that the adaptation was done by an obscure Philadelphia actor and writer, P. A. Fitzgerald.) The tale of Mormon revenge in a gold-mining town was an immediate hit after its premiere at the Broadway Theatre in New York on 22 August 1877. It played for five weeks and immediately transferred to another New York theater for two more weeks before embarking on prosperous national tours.

Rankin's rendition of the stalwart miner Sandy McGee was praised for its "rugged, hardy manhood . . . as well-nigh perfect as may ever be expected" (*New York Dramatic Mirror*, 1 Feb. 1879). Kitty Blanchard played the heroine, Nancy Williams, who disguises herself as Billy Piper, a miner, to avoid the wrath of a band of Mormon avengers. The touring company in its first years was an exceptionally strong unit with Louis Aldrich, Louis Mesteyer, and Charles Parsloe in major roles in addition to the Rankins. Contemporary reviewers frequently compared *The Danites* to *Davy Crockett* as one of the finest American plays on a native subject, but its melodramatic contrivances and particularly its anti-Mormon bias now render it dated. Rankin took *The Danites* to London in the summer of 1880, where one critic called it "the first time we have had a complete American company on a London stage" (*Walter Pelham's Illustrated Journal*, 24 Apr. 1880). *The Danites* played one hundred performances in London at Sadler's Wells Theatre and the Globe Theatre. The production also played in Liverpool, Manchester, Belfast, Edinburgh, and other cities. The play was generally well received in England, which was undergoing a vogue for the American West at the time, but was apparently not as financially rewarding as Rankin had hoped.

In 1881 Rankin tried a new piece in which he played another gold miner in a play entitled '49. Miller and Rankin wrangled in court over the rights to the play, but it hardly mattered, as '49 did not duplicate the success of *The Danites*. In 1883 Rankin became the manager of the Third Avenue Theatre in New York, but by the end of 1884 the venture had failed and Rankin was back on the road playing the hardy roles, such as Macbeth and Sandy McGee, that were his specialty. In 1890 he introduced a rough-hewn Canadian in *The Canuck*, but the play was not a success. By 1893 Rankin had drifted to the West Coast and was managing the Alcazar Theatre in San Francisco when he hired a young actress named Nance O'Neil. Rankin became her manager and her mentor, exercising what some commentators labeled a Svengali-like influence over the emotional actress, whom he guided through several national and worldwide tours. Eventually O'Neil moved on to the tutelage of David Belasco, leaving Rankin to an inglorious old age. As one of his last projects, in 1896 Rankin established the Murray Hill Theatre in New York, billed as a theater school, where students paid to appear in the productions and receive instruction from Rankin.

Toward the end of his career the once-handsome actor grew monstrously large. His vigorous, old-fashioned acting was ridiculed, his marriage had disintegrated years before, and by 1904 he had declared bankruptcy. Rankin had a reputation as a gambler of the theater, a man who won and lost fortunes, who was always involved in a lawsuit or in trouble with a woman. Yet his vitality was such that even people who claimed to have been misused by him turned around and embraced him again. At his death one writer remembered him as "wild, wonderfully fascinating, and unreliable" (*Chicago News*).

Rankin had two daughters with Kitty Blanchard. Phyllis became an actress and married Harry Davenport. Gladys married Sidney Drew, the son of Mrs. John Drew. Rankin had a third daughter, Doris, who was the first wife of Lionel Barrymore. In his last years Rankin occasionally acted with Phyllis and with Doris and Lionel before his passing in San Francisco.

• Levi Damon Phillips provides extensive information on the actor in his unpublished dissertation, "Arthur McKee Rankin's Touring Production of Joaquin Miller's 'The Danites'" (Univ. of California, Davis, 1981). *Green Book Magazine*, July 1914, pp. 39–42, provides a biographical sketch, and the *Chicago News*, 2 May 1914, contains a touching, bittersweet reminiscence by Amy Leslie. A profile and portrait by William C. Young appear in *Famous Actors and Actresses on the American Stage*, vol. 2 (1975), pp. 943–47. Rankin's obituary is in the *New York Dramatic Mirror*, 22 Apr. 1914.

ROGER A. HALL

RANKINE, William Birch (4 Jan. 1858–30 Sept. 1905), attorney, promoter, and company director, was born in Owego, New York, the son of James Rankine, an Episcopal clergyman, and Fanny Meek. His father was a cousin of the Scottish engineer William John Macquorn Rankine.

Rankine enrolled in the Canandaigua Academy in 1868, and at age fifteen he was admitted to Hobart College in Geneva, New York. At the end of his junior year, Rankine entered Union College, where he graduated summa cum laude with an A.B. in 1877. That September he went to Niagara Falls to study law with the prominent local attorney A. Augustus Porter. The Porter family had been promoting the development of water power at Niagara Falls since 1825, and Rankine became interested in the matter. After completing his studies, Rankine passed the state bar examination with high honors and was admitted to the bar on 10 January 1880. Rankine then relocated to New York City and joined the law firm of Vanderpoel, Greene & Cummings. In 1883 he entered into a partnership with Robert W. Hawkesworth. It was around this time that Rankine first submitted the matter of power development at Niagara Falls to Francis Lynde Stetson, an attorney for J. Pierpont Morgan. Stetson expressed interest but let the matter lie.

In 1886 Rankine developed a serious heart ailment and was ordered to give up his legal career. He left New York City to recuperate in Geneva, New York, where he tutored students from Hobart College. After six months he terminated his convalescence, telling a brother, "a man can only die once, and it's just the same no matter where it catches you. How much better to be called while doing something you really enjoy, something worthwhile, than to be caught trying to hide from its relentless grasp." Returning to his law practice in New York City, Rankine redoubled his efforts to find investors who would back the development of power at Niagara.

That same year saw the incorporation of the Niagara River Hydraulic Tunnel, Power and Sewer Company by Niagara Falls businessmen. After three years of failed attempts to secure investors, the company appointed Rankine as incorporator in January 1889. Rather than charge a fee, Rankine agreed to accept an equal share with the other stockholders in lieu of cash payment for his legal services. By this time Stetson had begun to take the project more seriously. He proposed the formation of the Cataract Construction Company, with Stetson and Rankine as two of its three initial directors. This company would investigate and prepare a method for developing power and would act as the Niagara company's financial agent and contractor. After nine months of intense negotiations, proposals, and counterproposals, a formal contract was executed on 1 April 1890 and the Niagara Falls Power

Company was created. Rankine was authorized by the company to buy up property along the Niagara River that would be used for the power station and industrial sites.

On 4 October 1890 excavation of the Niagara Falls Power Company's "power tunnel" began. Four months later Rankine entirely gave up his law practice in order to devote all of his time to coordinating the power development. In 1892 Rankine and Stetson collaborated to form yet another company, the Canadian Niagara Power Company, which was organized to utilize the water on the Canadian shore of the Niagara River. During the next decade Rankine convinced a large number of industrialists to locate their factories in Niagara Falls by offering them abundant, inexpensive electricity. This made possible the development of new industrial processes and products in the electrochemical and electrometallurgical fields. Rankine persevered in spite of his doctors' warnings after another nearly fatal incident of heart trouble in 1895.

The Niagara Falls Power Company made a significant mark upon history when its power station initiated its transmission of electricity to Buffalo, New York, on 16 November 1896. This was the first time in history that large quantities of polyphase alternating current were available for use in distant cities.

Much of Rankine's business was transacted on passenger trains as he traveled to and from the Niagara Falls Power Company's main office in New York City. He often held meetings on the trains and filled every available minute with productive work, acquiring the nickname of the "Minute-Man." Inventor Nikola Tesla described Rankine as a person "who thinks while others sleep, and works while others think and does while others try, who is in many enterprises and in many hearts" (*Memorabelia*, p. 45).

Rankine served as the second vice president, secretary, treasurer, and resident director of the Niagara Falls Power Company. Rankine was also a director or officer of many other companies, among them the Niagara Junction Railway; the Canadian Niagara Power Company; the Cataract Construction Company; the Cataract Power and Conduit Company; the Tonawanda Power Company; the Suburban Power Company; the Tesla Electric Company; the Francis Hook & Eye & Fastener Company; the Natural Food Company; the Bell Telephone Company; Ramapo Iron Works; Niagara Tachometer and Instrument Company; the International Railway Company; and the Niagara Research Laboratories. In the civic sphere, Rankine was instrumental in establishing a public library, a high school, and a YMCA in Niagara Falls, and although saddled with many professional obligations, he found time to serve as president of the local YMCA and an officer of his church.

Rankine married Annette Kittredge Norton in 1905; they had no children. His heart steadily weakened after his illness in 1886, and he died of congestive heart failure while he and his wife were vacationing in Franconia, New Hampshire.

Without Rankine's involvement, the revolutionary electrical and industrial innovations that took place as a result of power development at Niagara Falls probably would have proceeded at a much slower pace, perhaps with a different and less historic outcome.

• Some Niagara Falls Power Company corporate papers are archived in the George Arents Research Library, Syracuse University. DeLancey Rankine, comp., *Memorabelia* [sic] *of William Birch Rankine of Niagara Falls, New York . . .* (1926), includes tributes written by Rankine's contemporaries, among them Stetson and Rankine's assistant Frederick Lovelace. Also of great help is "An Intimate Account of the Career of Wm. B. Rankine," *Niagara Falls Gazette*, 27 April 1925, which covers much of Rankine's personal life. Edward Dean Adams, *Niagara Power: History of the Niagara Falls Power Company, 1886–1918* (1927), written by the president of the Cataract Construction Company, is the definitive history. "Niagara Power Number," *Cassier's Magazine* 8, no. 3, July 1895, is a collection of ten articles that gives excellent technical descriptions of the work done by the Cataract Construction Company, including many diagrams and schematics. Daniel M. Dumych, *The Canadian Niagara Power Company: One Hundred Years, 1892–1992*, provides an overview of Rankine's work with the company. Detailed obituaries are in the *Niagara Falls Gazette* and the *Daily Cataract Journal*, 30 Sept. 1905.

DANIEL MARTIN DUMYCH

RANNEY, Rufus Percival (30 Oct. 1813–6 Dec. 1891), lawyer, judge, and politician, was born in Blandford, Massachusetts, the son of Dolly Blair and Rufus Ranney, farmers. Joining the westward migration from New England, the family settled in Freedom, Portage County, Ohio, in 1824. Despite frontier conditions, Ranney secured enough education to enter Western Reserve College in 1833, although, compelled to support himself through manual labor and teaching, he remained only a year. Following the recommendation of a college friend, he entered the offices of Benjamin F. Wade and Joshua Giddings in Jefferson, Ohio, in 1834 to study law. Admitted to the bar in 1836, he established a practice in nearby Warren, an important business center.

In 1836 Giddings quit his partnership with Wade, and the latter, needing a new partner following the onset of a depression in 1837, turned to the highly competent Ranney. Their firm, which quickly became one of the most successful in Ohio's Western Reserve, lasted until Wade was elected presiding judge of the Third Judicial District in 1847. In 1839 Ranney married Adaline Warner, with whom he had six children. Since many of Ranney's clients lived in Warren, he eventually moved his residence there.

Ranney was an ardent Democrat, and, although Democrats were a minority in his region, he faithfully represented them in unsuccessful races for Congress in 1842, 1846, and 1848. In 1850 he was one of a slate of Democrats elected to the state constitutional convention to represent Trumbull and Geauga counties. He was chair of the Committees on Future Amendments and on Revision and was a member of the Judicial Committee in the Democratically controlled convention. The energetic young lawyer was highly visible in floor debates, where he spoke on almost every subject and vigorously defended popular rule: elected judges, no veto for the governor, limited legislative terms and restricted legislative powers, no limited liability for corporations, and legislative power to repeal or modify corporate charters. He wanted the highest court to continue to travel among the counties to be closer to the people but was overruled. He emphatically opposed capital punishment and poll taxes.

The Democratic leadership was impressed with Ranney's persuasive powers, legal knowledge, and popular stands that articulated the party's highest ideals. The Democratic legislature in March 1851 selected him to fill a vacancy on the state supreme court under the old constitution, and when the post became elective under the new constitution a few months later, Ranney was chosen by the electorate, serving until 1856. The courteous, soft-spoken judge, who avoided legal jargon and stressed fairness over legal technicalities, was notably effective on the bench. He put protagonists at ease, summarized cases concisely and clearly, and based decisions on logical applications of the principles of the common law. He avoided appeals to emotion and rhetorical flourishes, common in the legal profession of the day.

Ranney's most noteworthy decisions concerned issues arising from Ohio's shift toward a dynamic market economy. Like many Democrats, he feared that the law might become the tool of the rich and powerful. In disputed land titles he favored occupiers of land over absentee claimants. He compelled railroads to take responsibility for injuries caused by their agents and insisted that property seized by eminent domain be fully compensated and taken only when absolutely necessary. He argued that public improvements quickly authorized by the legislature in anticipation of the new constitution's limitations on such enterprises were inherently unconstitutional.

Ranney's stature among Democrats rose with his popular decisions. In 1856 he was a delegate to the party's national convention. President James Buchanan appointed him U.S. attorney for northern Ohio in 1857, but Ranney found that the post interfered with his regular law practice and quickly resigned. He was a serious candidate for the gubernatorial nomination in 1857. In 1859 he did obtain the nomination and ran a vigorous but unsuccessful campaign against William Dennison.

Upon leaving the bench in 1856, Ranney formed a partnership with F. T. Backus and C. W. Noble to practice law in Cleveland. The highly successful firm handled patent, railroad, and commercial cases. Unlike most lawyers, Ranney derived his income almost entirely from his practice, avoiding speculative business ventures.

Ranney, who had never been a friend of slavery, had still hoped civil war with the South might be avoided. When it came, he made recruitment speeches at the request of Governor David Tod, a former Democrat, in the more heavily Democratic counties of cen-tral and southern Ohio. In 1862 Ranney and his law partner Backus were nominated as opposing candidates for the state supreme court. Ranney had no desire to serve again on the court and declined the nomination, but party leaders, seeking to balance their slate between prowar and antiwar factions, kept him on the ballot, and he won in a general Democratic sweep. In a dissenting opinion he opposed the law authorizing Ohio's soldiers to vote in the field, arguing that it was a clear violation of the constitutional provisions regarding elections and that constitutional improvisation, no matter how expedient, was improper. In 1864, with the antiwar faction temporarily in check, he resigned from the bench to resume his law practice. That year he was a delegate to the Democratic National Convention that nominated George B. McClellan for the presidency, and in 1880 he served as a Democratic elector.

Always regretting his lack of much formal education, Ranney devoted his free time to self-study, mastering French and reading voraciously in literature, art, and science. He served on the Board of Trustees of the Case School of Applied Science. In 1881 he was unanimously elected the first president of the Ohio State Bar Association and used the post to lobby for higher professional standards for lawyers and better instruction of citizens in the principles of law. He died at his home in Cleveland. Ranney was regarded as one of the outstanding legal minds of his century and a man of unusual integrity and devotion to principles.

• Ranney's decisions are in the *Ohio Reports*, vol. 20, and *Ohio State Reports*, vols. 1–5, 14, 15. The best biographical sketch is Edwin Jay Blandin, "Rufus Percival Ranney," in *Great American Lawyers*, vol. 6 (1909). See also Carrington T. Marshall, *A History of the Courts and Lawyers of Ohio* (1934). On Ohio politics see Eugene H. Roseboom, *The History of the State of Ohio: The Civil War Era, 1850–1873* (1944). An obituary is in the *Cleveland Plain Dealer*, 7 Dec. 1891.

PHYLLIS F. FIELD

RANNEY, William (9 May 1813–18 Nov. 1857), painter, was born in Middletown, Connecticut, the son of William Ranney, a ship's captain, and Clarissa Gaylord. He did not use his middle name, Tylee. By 1826 William Ranney was living in Fayetteville, North Carolina, with William Nott (an uncle who adopted him after Captain Ranney was lost at sea in 1829) and apprenticed to a tinsmith or a blacksmith. It was in Fayetteville that he began to draw.

By 1833 or 1834 Ranney was in Brooklyn, New York, studying painting and drawing. A major turning point in his career came in 1836 when he enlisted with Captain Henry A. Hubbell in New Orleans and went to Texas to help win its independence from Mexico. Ranney served in Captain C. A. W. Fowler's company, First Regimental Volunteers, as paymaster. After nearly nine months in the army and an honorable discharge, he remained in Texas, making sketches not of the war but of the trappers, wild horses, prairies, and pioneers that would serve as the subject matter for his later paintings. By the spring of 1837 he was living in Brooklyn, and in 1838 he exhibited a portrait of a Mr. Thompson—the first public display of his work—at the National Academy of Design, to which he was later elected an associate member (1850). Ranney's whereabouts from 1839 until about 1842 are obscure; he may have been in North Carolina, or he may have returned to Texas to settle some land claims. He is listed as a portrait painter in New York City directories between 1843 and 1845; two years later he moved to Weehawken, New Jersey. In 1848 he married Margaret Agnes O'Sullivan; they had two children. By 1853 the family had settled in West Hoboken, New Jersey, a town that attracted a number of artists, such as Robert W. Weir, Charles Loring Elliott, and William Mason Brown. It was there that Ranney built his home and a large two-story studio that housed many of his western artifacts, causing the studio to look, according to the critic Henry Tuckerman, like a "pioneer's cabin or a border chieftain's hut."

In West Hoboken Ranney created such paintings as *Hunting Wild Horses* (1846, Joslyn Art Museum, Omaha, Nebr.), *Trapper's Last Shot* (1850, private collection), and *Advice on the Prairie* (1853, Buffalo Bill Historical Center, Cody, Wyo.), which were largely responsible for forming the image of western frontier life in the minds of the eastern public at midcentury. Ranney regularly exhibited these paintings as well as his sporting and genre scenes—*On the Wing* (1850, private collection) and *Sleigh Ride* (1852, private collection)—and historical paintings drawn from the American Revolution—*Marion Crossing the Pedee* (1850, Amon Carter Museum, Fort Worth, Tex.), *Veterans of 1776 Returning from the War* (c. 1848, Dallas Museum of Art), and *First News of the Battle of Lexington* (1847, North Carolina Museum of Art, Raleigh)—in New York at the National Academy of Design and the American Art-Union. The latter issued engravings after Ranney's work that received wide public distribution. Ranney's realistically rendered paintings, many of which were large, were popular and sold well. But by 1853 the artist had developed consumption, which curtailed his ability to work and to support his family. During his last days he converted from Protestantism to the Catholic faith. He died in West Hoboken.

Ranney was well liked by his contemporaries, who organized the Ranney Fund exhibition and sale at the National Academy of Design in 1858 to benefit the artist's family. Comprising more than 200 works (108 by Ranney and the rest donated by ninety-five artists, including George Inness, Frederic Church, John Kensett, and Asher Durand), this sale led to the formation of the Artist's Fund Society.

• A chronology of Ranney's life and work can be found in Francis Grubar, *William Ranney: Painter of the Early West* (1962). See Henry T. Tuckerman, *Book of the Artists: American Artist Life* (repr. 1966), for a contemporary description of the artist's work, and Margaret Ranney, "Appleton's Cyclopaedia Questionnaire" (c. 1883), in manuscript form at the New York Public Library, for additional biographical information. See also Linda Ayres, "William Ranney," in *American Frontier Life: Early Western Painting and Prints*, ed. Ron Tyler et al. (1987), and Mark Thistlethwaite, *William Tylee Ranney East of the Mississippi* (1991). Obituaries are in the *New York Times*, 24 Nov. 1857, the *New York Herald*, 20 Nov. 1857, and *Leslie's Illustrated*, 28 Nov. 1857.

LINDA AYRES

RANSDELL, Joseph Eugene (7 Oct. 1858–27 July 1954), U.S. representative and senator, was born on "Elmwood Plantation" (near Alexandria) in Rapides Parish, Louisiana, the son of John Hickman Ransdell, a journalist and farmer, and Amanda Louisa Terrell, who had inherited the plantation. In 1864 Ransdell's family fled to Texas when Union troops occupied the area. After the Civil War, the family returned to Elmwood, where Ransdell's father converted the plantation from cotton to sugar cane. Shortly afterward his father was killed accidentally by a cane grinder, and his older brother took over the management of the plantation.

Ransdell was educated in both public and Catholic private schools. At eighteen, he found employment teaching in a school twenty-five miles from his home. During this same period he began the study of law in the Alexandria office of Judge Michael Ryan. A local alumnus of Union College in Schenectady, New York, recognized the youth's academic potential and secured from his alma mater a scholarship for Ransdell, who received an A.B. in political science from Union College in 1882. Ransdell then moved to Lake Providence in East Carroll Parish, where he had found a job in the law office of Judge J. W. Montgomery, a relative by marriage. In this position he studied the law for a year and in 1883 passed the Louisiana bar examination. Two years later he married Olive Irene Powell of Lake Providence; they had no children.

The practice of law served as Ransdell's entry into politics. In 1883 he was appointed parish surveyor. The following year the ambitious young Democrat defeated two other candidates for the office of district attorney of East Carroll and Madison parishes, a position he held for twelve years (he had no political opponent in the 1888 and 1892 elections). In 1896 Ransdell was appointed to the Louisiana Fifth District Levee Board, the beginning of his lifelong involvement with the nation's waterways. In 1898 he represented East Carroll Parish at the state constitutional convention. Reflecting the view of his white constituents, he was a strong supporter of a single, four-year term for the governor and the imposition of the one-dollar annual poll tax as a prerequisite for voting. This poll tax helped to destroy the Republican party and to institutionalize one-party politics in Louisiana. No blacks were elected again to the state legislature until 1968.

Ransdell entered U.S. congressional politics in 1899 after the death of Democratic congressman Sam T. Baird, who had represented Northeast Louisiana. Ransdell defeated four opponents in the primary for the Fifth District seat. While his opponents waged a vocal, personal campaign against him, Ransdell took the high road, promising service to his constituents. His strategy worked. He received a majority of the votes in the election, thus launching his fourteen-year career in the House of Representatives. Though a probusiness, conservative Democrat, the longer he served in Congress the broader his outlook became. He evolved into a moderate conservative imbued with a strong sense of noblesse oblige.

Because of his experience with the devastating floods of the Red River in central Louisiana and of the Mississippi River in the plantation parish of East Carroll, Ransdell made his first mark in Congress as an advocate of federal flood control legislation. He served on the House River and Harbors Committee and in 1906 was elected president and chairman of the board of directors of the National Rivers and Harbors Congress, a lobbying group for federal appropriations. His fourteen-year tenure in these positions earned him the title "the father of waterways appropriations."

Ransdell's other major contribution while in the House was sponsorship of legislation to combat Texas tick fever, which had wreaked havoc on cattle in the South. As a result of his 1906 bill, appropriations were made annually for compulsory dipping of cattle to rid them of ticks. The federal program was successful in the eradication of tick fever in the South.

In 1911, after thirteen years in the House of Representatives, Ransdell ran for the U.S. Senate against Murphy J. Foster, the white supremacist incumbent and a former two-term governor. Ransdell portrayed the 62-year-old incumbent as lethargic and out-of-date and noted that Foster had kept his lucrative law practice while serving in the Senate. In addition to touting his work on flood control, levees, and waterways, Ransdell argued that North Louisiana deserved one of the two Senate seats. While accusing Ransdell of indifference to a bill that reduced sugar tariffs, Foster accepted credit for defeat of the bill. The electorate responded by giving Ransdell a slight majority. He carried forty-one of sixty-four parishes, including his own.

Partly in response to charges directed against him in the 1911 campaign, Ransdell opposed the Woodrow Wilson administration by waging a vigorous campaign against the Simmons-Underwood Bill for the removal of sugar tariffs during his first term in the Senate. Although he lost the battle, his opposition to the bill delayed its enactment by three years, earning him the appreciation of sugar cane planters in the state. He continued his efforts to secure federal funding for flood-control projects and ultimately achieved passage of the Flood Control Act of 1928. Ransdell broadened his interests to include public health issues. As chairman of the Senate Committee on Public Health, he was primarily responsible for the establishment of a national leprosarium in 1917.

Except in his opposition to the Simmons-Underwood Bill, Ransdell was one of President Woodrow Wilson's loyalists. He supported U.S. entry into World War I and the ratification of the Versailles peace treaty, including the establishment of the League of Nations. Possessing a more flexible and magnanimous personality than Wilson, Ransdell urged the president to appoint Theodore Roosevelt and other Republicans to the American Peace Commission. On domestic issues, Ransdell was at the forefront of progressive thinking, and he supported both woman suffrage and reforestation legislation.

Ransdell was reelected in the Democratic primary on 9 September 1924 as a result of the endorsement by the Old Regulars of New Orleans and the vote from rural Catholic parishes. Although they agreed on virtually nothing, Huey P. Long campaigned for Ransdell in order to ingratiate himself with southern Catholics in the state. Nonetheless, the electoral margin between Ransdell and his opponent, Shreveport mayor L. E. Thomas, who had the support of the Ku Klux Klan, remained close.

Ransdell's major legislative legacy was his establishment in May 1930 of a National Institute of Health (NIH), which later expanded into multiple institutes and has become the largest biomedical research center in the world. For his pioneering efforts on behalf of his vision for a national research center, Ransdell has earned the unofficial title of "the father of the National Institutes of Health."

Ransdell's political career ended with his 1930 reelection defeat to the clever, 37-year-old lawyer-politician Long, who had portrayed the 71-year-old incumbent as too old and out-of-touch, just as Ransdell had done in his first Senate race to unseat a two-term incumbent. As Louisiana governor, Long had built a well-organized political machine, unlike Ransdell who had never developed a personal political organization. Although neither candidate was a traditional demagogue on race, both had been ready to play the race card. Ransdell's patrician campaign demeanor, however, was ultimately overshadowed by Long's charisma and by the swelling tidal wave of populist revolt that had swept Long into the governorship in 1928. Despite losing the metropolitan vote in New Orleans, Shreveport, and Baton Rouge, Long carried all but eleven of the state's sixty-four parishes.

In 1933 Ransdell returned to Lake Providence, where he lived until his death there. He pursued an active retirement that included farming and business interests, attending weekly Rotary meetings, and serving the Catholic church. He had the satisfaction of outliving Long by nearly two decades and of seeing the solid contributions of his congressional initiatives eclipse any of those proposed by Long.

• The Joseph E. Ransdell Papers (1898–1948), are in the Louisiana and Lower Mississippi Valley Collections, Hill Memorial Library, Louisiana State University at Baton Rouge. The Special Collections Departments in the Robert W. Woodruff Library at Emory University in Atlanta, Ga., has correspondence from 1926 to 1936 in the Charles Holmes Herty Papers regarding the establishment of the National Institute of Health. Though lacking footnotes and a bibliography, a useful biography is Adras P. LaBorde, *A National*

Southerner: Ransdell of Louisiana (1951). For Ransdell's work in establishing the NIH, see Victoria A. Harden, *Inventing the NIH: Federal Biomedical Research Policy, 1887–1937* (1986). Important reevaluations of his political career include Vincent J. Marsala, "U.S. Senator Joseph E. Ransdell, Catholic Statesman: A Reappraisal," *Louisiana History* 35 (1994): 1–15; and Sally D. Montgomery, "Joseph Eugene Ransdell," in *Louisiana's Political Leaders: Ratings and Case Studies*, ed. William D. Pederson and Vincent J. Marsala (1995). The role of religion on his political philosophy is discussed in Marsala, "Civic and Professional Leadership: U.S. Senator Joseph E. Ransdell of Lake Providence," in *Cross, Crozier and Crucible*, ed. Glenn R. Conrad (1993). The 1930 campaign is covered in T. Harry Williams, *Huey Long* (1969); William Ivy Hair, *The Kingfish and His Realm* (1991); and Glen Jeansonne, *Messiah of the Masses: Huey P. Long and the Great Depression* (1993). Background information on domestic legislation and judicial matters is found in George Q. Flynn, "A Louisiana Senator and the Underwood Tariff," *Louisiana History* 10 (1969): 5–34; and Norman W. Provizer and William D. Pederson, eds., *Grassroots Constitutionalism: Shreveport, the South, and the Supreme Law of the Land* (1988). Also see Pederson, "Ransdell: Louisiana's Long Forgotten Senator and Father of the NIH," *Shreveport Journal*, 1 Feb. 1988.

WILLIAM D. PEDERSON

RANSIER, Alonzo Jacob (3 Jan. 1834–17 Aug. 1882), politician, was born in Charleston, South Carolina, to free parents. Contemporary accounts described his education as "limited." In the 1850s he secured a position as a shipping clerk with a prominent commercial firm in Charleston. In 1856 he married Louisa Ann Carroll, and they were the parents of 11 children. Carroll died in 1875, and he married Mary Louisa McKinlay in 1876.

Ransier was a leading figure in Reconstruction and Republican politics in South Carolina. He participated in the 1865 Colored Peoples' Convention in Charleston that urged the state's white leaders to enfranchise black men and abolish the black code, a series of measures designed to limit the rights of black people and to confine them to menial and agricultural labor. In 1867 Congress passed a series of Reconstruction laws that provided for the reorganization of the southern states, the enfranchisement of black men, and the disfranchisement of southerners who had supported the Confederacy. Ransier subsequently represented Charleston in the 1868 constitutional convention. He served as vice president of the State Republican Executive Committee and then as president from 1868 to 1872, following the assassination of Benjamin F. Randolph. He was elected to the state house of representatives in 1868 and was Charleston County auditor from 1868 to 1870. In the state house in 1870 he sponsored a measure that, while not explicitly guaranteeing civil rights for blacks, provided blacks with the same legal right to pursue judicial remedies available to whites. He was a director and secretary of the Enterprise Railroad Company, a corporation organized in 1870 by black political leaders to operate a horse-drawn streetcar line to haul freight between the South Carolina Railroad terminal and the Cooper River wharves. It did not survive as a black-owned business, and by 1873 a group of white businessmen led by S. S. Solomon had taken over the railroad. Ransier joined with several other black political leaders, including Benjamin A. Boseman, Robert Smalls, Robert B. Elliott, and Beverly Nash, in forming the South Carolina Phosphate & Phosphatic River & Mining Company.

Described in 1870 by the Charleston *News and Courier* as exercising "considerable influence," Ransier reached the pinnacle of his political power in the early 1870s. In 1870 he was elected South Carolina's first black lieutenant governor on a ticket headed by incumbent Robert K. Scott. In 1872 he was elected to represent South Carolina's second district in the Forty-Third Congress (1873–1875). From 1875 to 1877 he was the collector for the Internal Revenue Service for South Carolina's second district.

Though Ransier was often regarded as timid and reticent, he was frequently willing to take a bold stand on controversial issues. He joined black delegate William Whipper in speaking out strongly in the constitutional convention in opposition to legalizing the collection of debts incurred in the purchase of slaves prior to the Civil War. In doing so, they opposed three formidable black leaders, Francis L. Cardozo, Joseph Rainey, and William McKinlay, who favored payment. Ransier also joined two other Charleston black leaders, Richard H. Cain and Robert C. De Large, in opposing a literacy requirement for voting, which was easily defeated. Ransier consistently supported woman suffrage and attended an 1870 woman suffrage convention in Columbia. He urged rigid safeguards to protect black voting rights, insisting that voting "is our chief means for self-defense." He opposed segregation in public education so strongly that he abstained from voting on the 1875 Civil Rights Bill in Congress because provisions prohibiting discrimination in education had been deleted from the measure.

Ransier was deeply involved in the struggles of the Republican party. In 1872 as a delegate to the Republican National Convention and to a black convention in New Orleans, Ransier supported Ulysses S. Grant for reelection and would not join reformers who backed Horace Greeley. As a member of the "Charleston Ring," one of the factions that thrived in a divided Republican party in Charleston, Ransier attacked fellow Republicans for their inept leadership of the public schools. In 1871 he cited the bitter conflicts over patronage among Republicans as the cause of the Democratic victory in the municipal election. Yet he was willing to embrace patronage in 1876 when his tenure as Internal Revenue Service collector was about to expire. He pleaded with Governor Daniel Chamberlain for help in securing nomination to office: "I have a large family and no means for their support and would be greatly obliged if my friends will take me into consideration in connection with such a position on the state ticket as they may think me qualified for." He was not nominated, and by 1879 he was reduced to working as a night watchman at the Charleston Customs House for $1.50 per day. He was later employed at the Pacific Guano works and as a street laborer. When he died in obscurity in Charleston, the *News and Courier* did not note his passing.

Though he was one of South Carolina's prominent political figures by the early 1870s, Alonzo Ransier's influence and reputation faded quickly. Having served as a party leader, lieutenant governor, and congressman, he was not able to sustain that leadership until Reconstruction's end in 1877 when white South Carolinians regained political power.

• There are a few letters from Ransier in the Governors' Papers of the South Carolina Department of Archives and History. There is no biography. The chief sources of information on his life and career are Maurine Christopher, *America's Black Congressmen* (1971); Joel Williamson, *After Slavery: The Negro in South Carolina during Reconstruction, 1861–1877* (1965); and Thomas Holt, *Black over White: Negro Political Leadership in South Carolina during Reconstruction* (1977).

WILLIAM C. HINE

RANSOM, John Crowe (30 Apr. 1888–3 July 1974), poet and critic, was born in Pulaski, Tennessee, the son of John James Ransom, a Methodist minister, and Ella Crowe. Raised in a strongly religious though also very open-minded household, the precocious Ransom entered Vanderbilt University in Nashville at age fifteen. Following graduation in 1909 and a stint as a high school teacher, he went on to study classics as a Rhodes Scholar at Oxford from 1910 to 1913. Ransom was appointed to an instructorship in Vanderbilt's English department in 1914 and, apart from service as an artillery officer in France during World War I, remained there until his departure for Kenyon College in Ohio in 1937. In 1920, Ransom married Robb Reavill; the couple had three children.

Ransom's original interest lay more in philosophy than in literature; his letters from Oxford to his father express his sympathies with the American pragmatists and with John Dewey in particular. His growing concern with aesthetic issues, however—such as the need to give a satisfactory account of the "unknown quality of poetry," its preference for the imaginative rather than the logical—and his exposure to arguments about free verse (*vers libre*) as a member of the Fugitive literary group, which he joined on returning to Nashville, inspired him to begin writing poetry. The Fugitives—the other notable members of which were Donald Davidson, Allen Tate, and Robert Penn Warren—had also begun as a philosophically oriented discussion group, but they were soon meeting regularly to offer sustained criticism of one another's poems.

Ransom's first book, *Poems about God* (1919), was completed during his military service. He quickly became disillusioned with these early exercises in rustic skepticism, however, and always refused to have any of the poems republished in subsequent volumes, though both Robert Frost and Robert Graves had warmly praised his work. Ransom's mature style is to be found in the poems that compose *Chills and Fever* (1924) and *Two Gentlemen in Bonds* (1927), which appeared originally in the group's magazine, *The Fugi-*tive (1922–1925). Although Ransom continued to "tinker" with poetry throughout his long career, his reputation rests largely on the output of these three years.

Noted for their metaphysical wit and occasional archaisms, Ransom's poems are most frequently short lyrics in which he explores the ironies of human existence as they are manifested in the domestic scenes of daily life. The death of a small child, for example, is for him but a dramatic instance of the fate that awaits all of us, heightened by the incongruity between the energy of new life and the abruptness of its extinction. Thus, in what may be his best-known poem, "Bells for John Whiteside's Daughter" (1924), when we encounter the corpse of the little girl we are "sternly stopped" and "vexed" to see her "lying so primly propped." Ransom typically used regular meters and seemingly sentimental situations to draw attention to the irregularities and unsentimentality of life itself.

While he is often referred to as a "major minor poet," Ransom was fully convinced of the importance of the kind of contribution he had to make: "With a serious poet each minor poem may be a symbol of a major decision. It is as ranging and comprehensive an action as the mind has ever tried." By 1927 Ransom had come to believe that he had exhausted his themes and generally ceased thereafter to compose new poems. Nevertheless, his poetic work continues to be held in high esteem and, on this ground alone, his is an assured place in the history of American letters. In 1951, many years after he had ended his creative activities in this field, Ransom won the Bollingen Prize for Poetry, and in 1964 he received the National Book Award for his *Selected Poems* published the previous year. English Poet Laureate Ted Hughes spoke in 1977 of Ransom's best poems as "very final objects. . . . There is a solid total range of sensation within the pitch of every word."

The Fugitives had begun as a group much engaged with the intellectual and artistic problems of the modern world and with an ardent desire to escape the "moonlight and magnolia" school of southern writing. But attacks on the region by H. L. Mencken and others during the 1920s—many of them provoked by the Scopes "monkey" trial in Dayton, Tennessee, in 1925—caused them to rethink their position and to become enamored for a time of certain forms of southern nationalism. By 1930 they were ready to argue that the South's distinctive characteristic was that it was still an agrarian society and that as such it stood as a bulwark against the industrial materialism and communism of the age. In *I'll Take My Stand: The South and the Agrarian Tradition*, a collection of essays published in 1930 by twelve southerners, Ransom argued that it was only in an agricultural society that humanity had a true perception of its place in the universe: as beings subject to suffering and death; industrialized society tended to dull this sense of human contingency and so falsified the perception of life.

Ransom defended the arguments presented in the book when they were widely ridiculed and attacked, but by 1936 he was less certain that a return to an agricultural economy could save the nation, and by 1945 he had publicly changed his position: "Without consenting to a division of labor, and hence modern society, we should have not only no effective science, invention, and scholarship, but nothing to speak of in art." In fact, even in 1930, Ransom's ambivalence about modern society was reluctantly expressed in his famous defense of religion, *God without Thunder: An Unorthodox Defense of Orthodoxy*. There, with considerable ingenuity and knowledge of contemporary philosophy and science, he argued at length for the need to revive the Old Testament God who would represent the harshness of the universe as it actually is rather than continue exalting a gentle Jesus (or his parallels in liberal society—the social reformers) who merely confirms our complacencies. However, his book is undercut by Ransom's admission that religion is simply a creation of man and that the modern mind cannot accept many of its traditional premises; thus the argument, as Ransom himself recognized, finally collapsed under the weight of its own contradictions.

At Vanderbilt, Ransom was one of the first academics in the United States to legitimize the position of the poet and critic in English departments, which until then had favored scholars engaged in philological and historical studies. His experience in the classroom, and the influence of I. A. Richards's *Practical Criticism* (1929), persuaded him that too little attention was being given to the actual texts of poems as opposed to the biographical and incidental information surrounding their composition. Thus, both his efforts to correct this deficiency and his philosophical desire to show how poetry could offer a knowledge not provided by the sciences led him to produce a number of essays on the nature of poetry, particularly in the years after the demise of his agrarian interests. In what is probably the best known of these, "Wanted: An Ontological Critic" (1941), Ransom argued that "the differentia of poetry as discourse is an ontological one. It treats an order of existence, a grade of objectivity, which cannot be treated in scientific discourse." Much of his subsequent career was spent attempting to clarify such ideas, his basic contention being that a poem consists of both structure (argument) and texture (images) in precarious harmony. Although he always stressed the limitations of science, Ransom was equally aware that the argument of a poem could not fly in the face of scientific knowledge, a position he came to assert more and more insistently in his later essays.

When Ransom moved to Kenyon College in 1937, he was followed by three of his most distinguished pupils: Randall Jarrell, Peter Taylor, and Robert Lowell. The college president was eager to have him begin a new journal, *The Kenyon Review*, which Ransom was to edit from 1939 to 1959. In the *Review*, one of the most successful of the little magazines, Ransom frequently published authors and views that were quite at odds with his own. He also founded the Kenyon School of English, designed to gather distinguished critics and students together to develop a more critical approach to literature along the lines he had already outlined, though by no means confined to them.

Ransom's practice of literary criticism is often termed "New Criticism," and indeed in 1941 he published a book of essays with that title. Earlier, in "Criticism, Inc." (1937), he had argued that "Criticism must become more scientific, or precise and systematic." But Ransom himself was always more the theoretical than practical critic, and it was left to two former students of Ransom—Cleanth Brooks and Robert Penn Warren—to produce the book that is forever associated with the movement: *Understanding Poetry* (1938). Ransom in fact quickly became skeptical about the New Criticism, especially its tendency to over apply the concepts of paradox and irony to literary texts in order to show their "organic unity" rather than allow for their possible disharmonies. He was also for many years ambivalent about the work of the New Criticism's favorite representative poet, T. S. Eliot, on the grounds of the latter's excessive obscurity, philosophically unfounded religiousness, and overall pessimism about the modern world.

While Ransom is usually regarded as a conservative critic, his mind was in constant evolution, always willing to change a view once held but no longer persuasive. A man of quiet disposition and extreme courtesy—but an avid competitor in games and sports of all kinds—Ransom was a revered and influential teacher. Emphasizing early the harshness of human existence, in the end he advocated a rather benign skepticism, believing that "this is the best of all possible worlds" and that we are unlikely to know a better one.

Following his retirement from teaching and from editorship of the *Kenyon Review* in 1959, Ransom remained active in the academic world, writing new essays, constantly (and perhaps unwisely) revising his early poems, lecturing, and collecting those belated honors and recognitions that usually grace the closing years of a distinguished literary career. Toward the end of his life he suffered from a variety of recurring ailments, which gradually led him into long periods of withdrawal and silence. Ransom died in his sleep at his home on the Kenyon campus.

• Letters and papers pertaining to Ransom are to be found in the Firestone Library of Princeton University, the Library of Congress, the Yale University Library, the Tennessee State Library and Archives, the Lily Library of Indiana University, the Chalmers Library of Kenyon College, the Haverford College Library, the Mona Van Duyn Collection and the William Jay Smith Collection of the Washington University Libraries, and the Jesse E. Wills Collection of the Jean and Alexander Heard Library at Vanderbilt University (which also houses part of Ransom's library). Thomas Daniel Young and George Core published *Selected Letters of John Crowe Ransom* in 1985. Other books by Ransom include *Grace After Meat* (1924), *The World's Body* (1938), *Selected Poems* (1945), and *Beating the Bushes: Selected Essays 1941–1970* (1971). In addition, see Thomas Daniel Young and John Hindle, *Selected Essays of John Crowe Ransom* (1984). The standard biography is *Gentleman in a Dustcoat* (1976), by Thomas Daniel Young, who also edited *John Crowe Ransom: An Annotated Bibliogra-*

phy (1982). An excellent memoir is by Ransom's granddaughter, novelist Robb Forman Dew, "Summer's End," *Mississippi Quarterly* 30 (Winter 1976–1977): 137–54. See also Louise Cowan, *The Fugitive Group: A Literary History* (1959); Robert Buffington, *The Equilibrist: A Study of John Crowe Ransom's Poems, 1916–1963* (1967); Marian Janssen, *The Kenyon Review 1939–1970: A Critical History* (1990); and Kieran Quinlan, *John Crowe Ransom's Secular Faith* (1989).

KIERAN QUINLAN

RANSOM, Leon Andrew (6 Aug. 1899–25 Aug. 1954), lawyer and educator, was born in Zanesville, Ohio, the son of Charles Andrew Ransom, a janitor who later ran a stable, and Nora Belle Lee. He attended Ohio State University for a year (1917–1918), joined the army during World War I (1918), and graduated from Wilberforce University (1920). After five years (1920–1925) working as a dining car waiter and in real estate in Chicago, where he served as assistant executive secretary of the Spring Street Branch of the YMCA, he decided to go to law school. His widow later recounted that he became a lawyer as "a form of protest" against the racial discrimination he saw all around him in Chicago. He earned a law degree with honors at Ohio State University (J.D., 1927). In 1924 he married Willa C. Carter; they had two children. In religion he was African Methodist Episcopalian; in politics he was an active Republican and then an Independent. "Andy" Ransom's easygoing demeanor belied his commitment to racial progress.

After practicing law in Columbus, Ohio, from 1927 to 1931, Ransom moved to Washington, D.C. There he taught law at the Howard University Law School as instructor (1931–1933) and then assistant professor (1933–1934). After time away to earn an advanced degree in law at Harvard University (S.J.D., 1935), as his colleague William H. Hastie had two years earlier, he returned to Howard as associate professor (1935–1939) and then professor (1939–1946). During those years he worked with Charles Hamilton Houston and Hastie to make the Howard University Law School a training ground for African-American civil rights lawyers and an arena for formulating successful strategies to win civil rights victories in the courts. A member of the Washington Bar Association, the National Bar Association, and the National Lawyers Guild, Ransom served on the National Legal Committee of the National Association for the Advancement of Colored People (NAACP) beginning in 1936. From 1941 to 1946 he served as assistant editor of the *Journal of Negro Education*, which was published at Howard, and he wrote a regular section called "Negroes and the Law."

Ransom played various roles in a number of civil rights cases. As early as 1933 he went to Leesburg, Virginia, as cocounsel with Houston to mount a defense of a black man, George Crawford, against charges of murdering a wealthy white woman and her white housekeeper. Nobody in the area, black or white, had ever before seen a black attorney, and Ransom and Houston caused a sensation as they demonstrated their mastery of the craft. Jurors might all be white, but not all witnesses were, and the defense insisted on addressing black witnesses as "Mister" and "Mrs." The judge found himself incapable of so addressing the lawyers, but he settled on an alternative and addressed them as "Doctor Houston" and "Doctor Ransom." Though they learned, to their surprise, that Crawford was in fact guilty, upon conviction he was given a life sentence instead of being executed. Just as Ransom's appointment at Howard University reflected Dean Houston's shift in the early 1930s to law faculty who were both full-time and African American, the Crawford trial reflected the NAACP's shift to all-black counsel in many important cases.

Over the years Ransom participated in many cases and argued a number in the courts. Some of those cases, in Maryland and Virginia, challenged racially discriminatory teachers' salary schedules in the "separate-but-equal" era. Others, in Tennessee and Missouri, challenged the exclusion of black students from public institutions of higher education. Ransom argued a case in 1940 before the Supreme Court, *Chambers v. Florida*, which led to a unanimous decision against coerced confessions. In 1942 in Tennessee, where Ransom was arguing a case about exclusion of blacks from juries, he was struck by a deputy sheriff, who took exception to the kinds of litigation he and his colleagues were bringing. In April 1946 Ransom participated in a significant meeting held in Atlanta, Georgia, to plan the course of litigation on segregation in higher education.

During and after World War II, while Hastie, the law school dean, was away on various assignments with the U.S. government, Ransom served as acting dean. When the Senate confirmed President Harry S. Truman's nomination of Hastie as governor of the Virgin Islands in 1946, Ransom aspired to be appointed permanent dean, but he was bypassed when the board of trustees that year appointed George M. Johnson to the post. The decision has been explained in terms of the politics of the post, but some people at the time spoke of Ransom's decline in mental stability.

Bitterly disappointed, Ransom resigned immediately from Howard and returned to private practice. From 1946 to 1949 he served as chair of the Committee for Racial Democracy in the Nation's Capitol. In 1948 the Grand Chapter of Kappa Alpha Psi awarded him the Laurel Wreath for distinguished public service. He continued to live in Washington, D.C., but faded from view in the next few years. He died on vacation in Point Pleasant, New Jersey, of a cerebral vascular hemorrhage.

• Materials to, by, and about Ransom are in the NAACP Papers at the Library of Congress. The Pauli Murray Papers in the Schlesinger Library at Radcliffe College include correspondence with him. He is mentioned in various works on the civil rights movement in the 1930s and 1940s, including Genna Rae McNeil, *Groundwork: Charles Hamilton Houston and the Struggle for Civil Rights* (1983); Gilbert Ware, *William Hastie: Grace under Pressure* (1984); and Mark V. Tushnet, *Making Civil Rights Law: Thurgood Marshall and the Supreme Court, 1936–1961* (1994). Murray writes warmly of him in her autobiography, *Song in a Weary Throat: An American Pilgrimage* (1987). Accounts of Ransom are in the *Baltimore Afro American*, 15 and 22 Nov. 1958. His gravestone memorial at Maryland National Memorial Park in Laurel, Md., highlights his accomplishments. Obituaries are in the *Washington Post*, 27 Aug. 1954, and the *Richmond Afro American*, 4 Sept. 1954.

PETER WALLENSTEIN

RANSOM, Matt Whitaker (8 Oct. 1826–8 Oct. 1904), U.S. senator, soldier, and diplomat, was born in Warren County, North Carolina, the son of Robert Ransom and Priscilla Whitaker, planters. In 1847 Ransom graduated from the University of North Carolina, where he had read law. Admitted to the bar the same year, he established what became a thriving practice in Warrenton, North Carolina. In 1852 the state legislature named him the state's attorney general, a post from which he resigned three years later. In 1853 Ransom married Martha Anne Exum and thereafter resided on a plantation she owned in Northampton County. The couple would have eight children. Prior to emancipation, their holdings included more than eighty slaves.

Ransom entered political life as a Whig and campaigned for Winfield Scott in 1852. With the party's disintegration as a national organization and the Know Nothings' rise to the fore, however, Ransom aligned himself with the Democrats and served as Northampton County's representative in the North Carolina House of Commons between 1858 and 1861. Like many in his state, he remained unenthusiastic about secession until conflict became inevitable. He served as one of the peace commissioners that the legislature appointed to treat with the provisional Confederate government in Montgomery, Alabama; however, when Abraham Lincoln mobilized Union forces to put down the rebellion, Ransom entered the Confederate army. Enlisting as a private, he was quickly commissioned lieutenant colonel and in April 1862 was elected commander of the Thirty-fifth North Carolina Regiment, soon to become part of a brigade led by his brother Robert Ransom. Matt Ransom and his men took part in the defense of Richmond during the Peninsular Campaign, Ransom being wounded at Malvern Hill. Later in 1862 Ransom fought at Antietam. That winter the brigade was transferred to eastern North Carolina, with Ransom, now a brigadier general, succeeding his brother as its commander in June 1863. The unit saw action at Boone's Mill and in the capture of Plymouth before being called in the spring of 1864 to the defense of Petersburg. Wounded at Drewry's Bluff in May, Ransom returned to command in time to participate in the final battles in the east, including Fort Stedman and Five Forks.

Present at Appomattox during the Confederate surrender, Ransom subsequently returned to North Carolina and again planted cotton and practiced law. An opponent of the Reconstruction regime, he reemerged on the political stage in 1870 when he helped secure the release of men imprisoned as a result of Governor William Holden's effort to crush the Ku Klux Klan. Ransom convinced a federal judge to extend to one of the most prominent prisoners the writ of habeas corpus denied them by state authorities. Ransom's role in the episode, which increased the unpopularity and accelerated the collapse of the Holden regime, evidently so endeared him to Carolina conservatives that he only narrowly missed being their choice for the U.S. Senate later that year. The man sent in his stead, wartime governor Zebulon Vance, was still barred from officeholding, however, so in 1872 the legislature elected Ransom to the seat (Vance joined him in the Senate in 1879). Reelected three times, Ransom developed a loyal following among Carolinians who benefited by his influence in patronage matters. His authority was particularly strong in his home region of eastern North Carolina.

Ransom, the erstwhile Whig, has typically been counted as one of the breed of "New South" Democrats who were friendly to the forces promoting the commercial and industrial development of the region. If anything, though, his career as attorney and planter suggests a certain merger of interests among the agrarian and entrepreneurial elite. Josephus Daniels, who as a young editor hobnobbed with Ransom, recalled that the senator "believed that men who had won wealth and position had always ruled the world and always should. And he deliberately stood with them when he was forced to take sides" (Daniels, *Editor in Politics*, p. 46). But, as Daniels also noted, Ransom preferred not to take sides too prominently on certain controversial matters, ducking, for instance, the much-debated tariff, currency, and prohibition questions. Ransom reconciled himself to the sort of federal activism that materially benefited his region. He supported federal aid for southern railroad projects and voted repeatedly—though with some misgivings—for the Blair bill, which would have made federal funds available for public education (appropriations being apportioned by the extent of illiteracy in a state, the South stood especially to benefit by this measure). Ransom, who hailed from a black-majority county, clearly envisioned no new departure in race relations, however. Even on the hustings, he made plain his conviction that African Americans belonged to an inferior race. In the Senate he helped scotch the Lodge "Force" Bill of 1890, intended to strengthen federal monitoring of elections and voter registration.

In the 1890s Ransom proved ill prepared for the changed politics of his state and the nation. He made an enemy of the Farmers' Alliance, expending little effort to come to terms with its growing power among North Carolina Democrats. Moreover, while not consistently hostile to the coinage of silver, Ransom, unlike most southern Democrats, supported Grover Cleveland in the repeal of the Sherman Silver Purchase Act in 1893. Some said that Ransom took this stand in order to restore himself in Cleveland's good graces (and thus renew his patronage powers) after having failed to support Cleveland at the 1892 Democratic convention. Regardless, his seeming stand against silver and for the gold standard did not play well back home. Ransom's stock fell so low that after a coalition of Populists and Republicans took control of the state legislature in 1894, not even the Democratic minority voted to return him to the Senate. Ransom thus became one of a mere handful of southern Democratic senators to be replaced by a member of an opposition party (in his case, Populist Marion Butler) between 1877 and 1960.

In 1895 Cleveland appointed Ransom minister to Mexico. There he was selected to arbitrate claims arising from a longstanding boundary dispute between Mexico and Guatemala. Returning to North Carolina in 1897, Ransom no longer took a conspicuous part in state politics. However, he did make speeches favoring black disfranchisement during the 1900 campaign. Ransom died four years later near Garysburg, North Carolina.

• There is a large collection of Matt Ransom Papers at the Southern Historical Collection, University of North Carolina, Chapel Hill. Some of Ransom's wartime reports and correspondence are published in *The War of the Rebellion: A Compilation of the Official Records of the Union and Confederate Armies* (128 vols., 1880–1901). Josephus Daniels's memoirs, *Tar Heel Editor* (1939) and *Editor in Politics* (1941), include extended recollections of Ransom, not all of them flattering. Useful on various aspects of Ransom's career are Clayton C. Marlow, *Matt W. Ransom, Confederate General from North Carolina* (1996); William Kimball, "Ransom's North Carolina Brigade Served the Confederacy Bravely," *Civil War Times Illustrated,* May 1962, pp. 45–47; Ronnie Faulkner, "North Carolina Democrats and Silver Fusion Politics, 1892–1896," *North Carolina Historical Review* 59 (1982): 230–51; Alan Bromberg, "'Pure Democracy and White Supremacy': The Redeemer Period in North Carolina, 1876–1894" (Ph.D. diss., Univ. of Virginia, 1977); and Terry Seip, *The South Returns to Congress: Men, Economic Measures, and Intersectional Relationships, 1868–1879* (1983).

PATRICK G. WILLIAMS

RANSOM, Reverdy Cassius (4 Jan. 1861–22 Apr. 1959), African Methodist Episcopal (AME) bishop and civil rights leader, was born in Flushing, Ohio, the son of Harriet Johnson, a domestic worker. He never knew the identity of his father. In 1865 his mother married George Ransom, gave her son his surname, and moved to Washington, Ohio. There he began school in the local AME church. At eight, Ransom moved with his family to Cambridge, Ohio, where he attended school with African-American youth. In addition to his formal schooling, Ransom worked in a local bank and was tutored by family members of his mother's white employers. In 1881 Ransom married Leanna Watkins of Cambridge, Ohio, and entered Wilberforce University. He transferred to Oberlin College at the end of his first year, but, when he challenged racial discrimination at the liberal white institution, he lost his scholarship. He returned to Wilberforce in 1883, graduating in 1886. Despite the birth of a son, he and his first wife divorced that same year.

Licensed to preach in the AME church in 1883, Ransom was ordained a deacon in 1886 and an elder in 1888. He married Emma Sarah Conner of Salem, Ohio, in 1886. They became the parents of one son. From 1886 to 1888 Ransom served small AME congregations in Altoona and Hollidaysburg, Pennsylvania, and from 1888 to 1890 he pastored a church in Allegheny City, Pennsylvania. Ransom then moved to Ohio, serving at North Street AME Church in Springfield from 1890 to 1893 and at St. John's AME Church in Cleveland from 1893 to 1896. In 1896 Ransom moved to Chicago, where he served as pastor of Bethel AME Church from 1896 to 1900. At Bethel he organized a men's Sunday club for the discussion of cultural, moral, and social issues. As early as 1899, Ransom ardently disagreed with Booker T. Washington's accommodationist approach to race relations and the Tuskegean's forceful determination to control the Afro-American Council.

As Ransom observed the needs of black migrants from the South, he bristled at the constraints of a traditional congregation. Influenced by the work of Jane Addams at Hull-House, he left Bethel in 1900 to organize the Institutional Church and Social Settlement. The building included a large auditorium, a kitchen, a dining room, a gymnasium, and eight other rooms for a nursery, a kindergarten, and boys' and girls' club meetings. It offered concerts, an employment bureau, lecture series, a print shop, and classes in cooking, music, and sewing. A year later, when Ransom attacked the policy rackets in Chicago, the building was bombed. Yet his social ministry at Institutional Church and Social Settlement survived for another three years.

In 1904 Ransom moved to AME congregations in New Bedford and Boston, Massachusetts. As pastor of Boston's Charles Street AME Church, he paid tribute to the spirit of the abolitionists and joined W. E. B. Du Bois's Niagara Movement to demand social justice for African Americans. In 1906 Ransom addressed the movement's annual meeting at Harpers Ferry, West Virginia, speaking on "The Spirit of John Brown." Ransom moved to New York's Bethel AME Church in 1907. While there, he helped to organize the National Association for the Advancement of Colored People. In 1912 Ransom was elected editor of the *A.M.E. Church Review*, the denomination's literary and theological journal. For twelve years he directed the publication of articles on a wide range of issues. At heart, however, Ransom was a pastor on a social mission, and consequently he established a mission to black Manhattan in 1913: The Church of Simon of Cyrene, which ministered to destitute African Americans in New York's "Black Tenderloin." In 1918 the United Civic League of New York sought to place Ransom's name on the ballot as a candidate for Congress from Manhattan's Twenty-first District. Dropped from the ballot because of a discrepancy in his filing petition, Ransom lost an uphill battle as a write-in candidate.

Ransom had represented the AME church at conferences of world Methodism in London (1901 and 1921) and Toronto (1911), and in 1924, at the age of sixty-three, he was already an elder statesman in the

AME denomination when he was elected one of its bishops. It is unclear what role his early divorce and rumors of his alcoholism, which were circulated by Booker T. Washington's associates and conservatives within his denomination, may have played in delaying Ransom's elevation to the episcopacy. As a bishop, however, he made his home at Wilberforce University and served as president of the board of trustees from 1932 to 1948. Then, in 1934, Ransom helped to organize the Fraternal Council of Negro Churches and was elected its first president. He was the first African American to serve as a commissioner of Ohio's Board of Pardon and Parole, a position he held from 1936 to 1940, and in 1941 President Franklin D. Roosevelt appointed Ransom as a member of the Volunteer Participation Committee in the Office of Civil Defense. After his wife of fifty-five years died in 1941, Ransom married Georgia Myrtle Teal Hayes of Wilberforce in 1943. A graduate of Cheyney Training School (now Cheyney State University) and Cornell University, she was dean of women at Wilberforce from 1934 to 1943 and an officer of the AME missionary society from 1943 to 1956. In 1952 Ransom retired from the active episcopacy. He died at his home, "Tawawa Chimney Corner," at Wilberforce.

Ransom was his era's foremost advocate of the social gospel in the African-American community. He developed institutional church models for urban black communities and was an important radical ally of Du Bois in the struggles with Booker T. Washington that led to the founding of the NAACP. Later, as a bishop and elder statesman in his denomination, he also made advances in African-American ecumenism.

• The papers of Reverdy Cassius Ransom are in collections at Wilberforce University and at Payne Theological Seminary near Xenia, Ohio. Important Ransom documents are also in *The Booker T. Washington Papers*, ed. Louis R. Harlan et al. (1972–1989). Beyond his autobiography, *The Pilgrimage of Harriet Ransom's Son* (1949), Ransom's publications include *School Days at Wilberforce* (1892), *The Spirit of Freedom and Justice: Oration and Speeches* (1926), and *The Negro: The Hope or the Despair of Christianity* (1935). The best secondary sources on Ransom are Richard R. Wright, *The Bishops of the African American Episcopal Church* (1963); David Wills, "Reverdy C. Ransom, The Making of an A.M.E. Bishop," in *Black Apostles: Afro-American Clergy Confront the Twentieth Century*, ed. Randall K. Burkett and Richard Newman (1978); Mary M. Fisher, "Reverdy Cassius Ransom," in *Dictionary of American Negro Biography*, ed. Rayford W. Logan and Michael R. Winston (1982); and Calvin S. Morris, *Reverdy C. Ransom: Black Advocate of the Social Gospel* (1990). On the intellectual and social context of his early career, see Ralph E. Luker, *The Social Gospel in Black and White: American Racial Reform, 1885–1912* (1991).

RALPH E. LUKER

RANSOM, Thomas Edward Greenfield (29 Nov. 1834–29 Oct. 1864), Union general, was born along the banks of the Connecticut River at Norwich, Vermont, the son of Truman Bishop Ransom, an educator and soldier, and Margaret Morrison Greenfield. His father was president of Norwich University, a celebrated military school, later served as colonel of the Ninth U.S. Infantry, and was killed in action during the storming of Chapultepec (13 Sept. 1847) in the Mexican War. In accordance with his father's wishes, Ransom entered Norwich University. While his father served in Mexico, Ransom left school and studied practical engineering on the Rutland and Burlington Railroad. In 1848 he reentered the civil engineering course at Norwich and graduated in 1851. An ambitious and adventuresome young man, Ransom left New England and settled in Vandalia, Illinois, where he worked as an engineer and in the real estate business.

At the outbreak of the Civil War in April 1861, Ransom recruited a company that became part of the Eleventh Illinois Infantry, and he was elected captain. Two months later he was promoted to major, and upon reorganization of the regiment in July, Ransom became lieutenant colonel. Dynamic, energetic, and brave, he soon proved a promising young officer. In an engagement on 19 August 1861 near Charleston, Missouri, he was slightly wounded in hand-to-hand combat with the enemy. His superior, Colonel Henry Dougherty, reported of Ransom, "Too much praise cannot be bestowed upon [him] for the able and efficient manner in which [he] discharged each and every duty assigned to [him]."

On 15 February 1862 Ransom led the regiment into the maelstrom of battle at Fort Donelson. Struck in the shoulder by a Minié ball, he refused to leave the field. Rather, he turned the regiment over to his second in command "till his wound could be temporarily dressed, he [then] resumed command and remained with his regiment throughout the day." His regiment fought "with all the coolness and precision of veterans," and he earned the praise of his brigade commander, General W. H. L. Wallace (*War of the Rebellion*, ser. 1, vol. 7, pp. 196–97). For his actions, Ransom was elevated to colonel.

Two months later the young colonel led his regiment onto the bloody field at Shiloh (6–7 Apr. 1862). Wounded in the head in the opening actions of his unit, Ransom continued to lead his regiment until his horse was killed and loss of blood forced him to relinquish command. He was carried to the rear for medical treatment but returned to command his regiment on the second day of battle. General John McClernand wrote of Ransom, "Although reeling in the saddle and streaming with blood from a previous wound, [he] performed prodigies of valor." His actions once again earned him distinction and recommendation for promotion.

McClernand was so impressed that he appointed Ransom to serve as inspector general on his staff during the operations that centered on Corinth, Mississippi. In June Ransom became McClernand's chief of staff and later served as inspector general of the Army of the Tennessee. In recognition of his ability, Ransom was elevated to brigade command in December 1862 and the following month was assigned brigade command in the XVII Corps. On 15 April 1863 he was promoted to brigadier general of volunteers to rank from 29 November 1862.

Ransom led his brigade throughout the Vicksburg campaign and participated in the failed assaults of 19 and 22 May against the Confederate fortress. His conspicuous actions throughout the siege of Vicksburg won favorable mention by his superiors. Even General Ulysses S. Grant, the army commander, commended the young officer and wrote that Ransom "would have been equal to the command of a corps at least." Following the siege of Vicksburg, Ransom was selected to lead a foraging expedition to Natchez, Mississippi, during which his troops captured 5,000 head of cattle. Grant was impressed by Ransom's energy and skill and wanted him to assume command of the cavalry, stating he was "the best man I ever had to send on expeditions." Ransom was at that time actively involved in the Red River campaign and thus not available to take over the cavalry arm of Grant's army.

In late 1863 Ransom served in operations along the Texas coast from Aransas Pass to the Matagorda Peninsula and commanded the XIII Corps during the Red River campaign in 1864. On 8 April 1864, at Sabine Cross Roads near Mansfield, Louisiana, he was severely wounded in the leg but continued in command until the enemy attack was checked. Four months later, although not fully recovered, he reported for duty and was given command of a division of the XVI Corps in front of Atlanta. During the course of the campaign, on the wounding of Grenville Dodge, Ransom assumed command of the corps. After the fall of Atlanta, he was assigned to the command of the XVII Corps and pursued the retreating Confederates through northern Georgia and into Alabama. On the return march from Alabama, Ransom fell ill. As the rigors of the campaign had also aggravated old wounds, he succumbed to the lethal combination and died near Rome, Georgia. He had never married.

General Ransom led troops at all levels of command from regiment to corps and played a conspicuous role in the many campaigns in which he was engaged. The western campaigns in which he fought were decisive to Union victory as Federal troops first split the Confederacy in two along the line of the Mississippi River, then pierced the southern heartland as they captured Atlanta. The success of Union armies in the West is linked to his record of achievement.

Ransom repeatedly demonstrated on the field of battle his courage and devotion to duty. He led by personal example and earned both the respect of his superiors and the confidence of his men. His zealous support of the Union war effort and youthful energy, coupled with the cumulative impact of numerous battle wounds and inadequate recovery time, were fatal to this promising officer, whose ability earmarked him for higher command. For gallant and meritorious service during the war, he was brevetted a major general of volunteers to rank from 1 September 1864. In further recognition of his service to the country, the federal government erected a bronze bust of Ransom on the grounds of Vicksburg National Military Park, which was dedicated in March 1916.

• For additional information see *The War of the Rebellion: A Compilation of the Official Records of the Union and Confederate Armies*, ser. 1, vols. 3, 7, 10, 32 (128 vols., 1880–1901); Ezra J. Warner, *Generals in Blue* (1964); Stewart Sifakis, *Who Was Who in the Union* (1988); W. C. Ransom, *Historical Outline of the Ransom Family of America* (1903); and J. G. Wilson, *Biographical Sketches of Illinois Officers* (1862).

TERRENCE J. WINSCHEL

RANSOME, Frederick Leslie (2 Dec. 1868–6 Oct. 1935), economic and engineering geologist, was born in Greenwich, England, the son of Ernest L. Ransome, an engineer and inventor, and Mary Jane Dawson. In 1870, when he was two years old, he emigrated with his family from England to the United States. The family's circumstances undoubtedly had an effect on Ransome's choice of a career: his father, the founder of the Ransome Concrete Machinery Company in San Francisco, constructed the first reinforced concrete bridge in the United States.

Ransome was educated in the public schools and at the University of California in Berkeley, where he was influenced by the charismatic Andrew Lawson, a field geologist and the head of the geology department. He graduated in 1893 and continued his studies in graduate school under Lawson's direction, completing his Ph.D. in 1896. In 1896–1897 he was an assistant professor in mineralogy and petrography at Harvard University. He married Amy Córdoba Rock in 1899; they had four children.

In 1900 Ransome joined the U.S. Geological Survey (USGS) in Washington, D.C., serving first as an assistant geologist and then as a geologist under the supervision of eminent mining geologists S. F. Emmons and Waldemar Lindgren. From 1912 to 1917 he was in charge of the USGS section on western areal geology (geological mapping). From 1915 to 1923 he headed the section on metalliferous deposits. In 1923 he was appointed professor of economic geology at the University of Arizona, where he remained until 1927; he also served as the dean of the graduate college in 1926–1927. In 1928 he taught part time as a professor of economic geology at the California Institute of Technology (Caltech) and consulted on mine litigation, irrigation problems, and dam-site location. He mapped the geology of the Hoover (formerly Boulder) Dam area for the U.S. Bureau of Reclamation and approved the construction site. He also worked for the Bureau of Reclamation on the Madden Dam in the Panama Canal Zone, the Owyhee Dam in southeastern Oregon, and other large dams.

From 1928 to 1935 Ransome worked with the Metropolitan Water District of Southern California conducting studies in support of construction of the Colorado River aqueduct. He was a consulting geologist for the Pine Canyon Dam, built by the city of Pasadena, and for various dams proposed by the city of Los Angeles and the Los Angeles County Flood Control District. He was also appointed to the commission created by the governor of California to determine the cause of the St. Francis Dam failure. The dam, built without a preparatory geological study of the site by the Los Angeles Water and Power Board, collapsed in 1928 shortly after the reservoir was filled, leaving 511 people dead or missing in the valley below. The tragedy, one of the world's most notorious engineering failures, became a landmark case study in engineering geology and led to the widespread use of geological as well as engineering consultants in building dams. Along with his consulting projects, Ransome developed a pioneering course on engineering geology at Caltech, an innovation in the civil engineering curriculum. Engineering geology is distinguished from mining geology, which is confined to problems of mineral extraction, rather than planning and Supervision of large-scale construction.

Ransome's professional affiliations included the National Academy of Sciences (treasurer, 1919–1924), the American Philosophical Society, the Geological Society of London, the Society of Economic Geologists, the Washington Academy of Sciences, and the Cosmos Club in Washington, D.C. Ransome published eight professional papers, fifteen bulletins, six atlas sheets, and an article in a USGS annual report in which he described the gold, silver, lead, zinc, and copper deposits in major mining districts or regions, including the Globe, Bisbee, Ray, and Miami districts in Arizona; the Cripple Creek and Silverton districts of Colorado; the Coeur d'Alene district of Idaho; and the Goldfield and Yerington districts of Nevada. He also published a geological folio on the Mother Lode, located in the Sierra Nevada of California. Together these papers, all USGS reports, comprise an unmatched contribution to the technical description of Western United States mineral deposits. Ransome, however, ventured only the briefest interpretation of his observations in two concise reports: "Some Possible Lines of Research on Ore Deposits" (*Economic Geology* 20: 485–90) and "Historical Review of Geology as Related to Western Mining" in *Ore Deposits of the Western States*, ed. Lindgren (1933).

No other geologist contributed more than Ransome in the area of field geology of important metalliferous deposits in the western United States. He ranks as one of the most important figures in the "glory days" of American mining geology. Although Ransome did some mineralogic research (he gave the mineral Lawsonite its name) and published an important paper, "The Direction of Movement and the Nomenclature of Faults" (*Economic Geology* 1 [1906]: 777–87), he is principally known for his work in mining geology and engineering geology. He was a methodical, systematic worker who emphasized the importance of careful observation and practical application of knowledge. He consistently practiced his work ethic: he firmly believed that observations should be entered on field maps and that field notes should be transcribed every evening to avoid revisions and corrections at a later date—when it might be impossible to return to a site to resolve discrepancies and gaps in documentation. During the latter half of his career, Ransome was responsible for many geological investigations related to bringing adequate water supplies to Los Angeles. In that capacity he provided a vital link between the world of the university and that of the businessman and city planner. Ransome died in Pasadena, California.

• Additional sources of information about Ransome include four biographical memoirs: Edson S. Bastin, National Academy of Sciences, *Biographical Memoirs* 32, no. 8 (1943): 155–70; Waldemar Lindgren, "Frederick Leslie Ransome, 1868–1935: A Memorial," *Economic Geology* 30 (1935): 841–42; Lindgren, Geological Society of London, *Proceedings* (1937): xcv–xcvi; and Leonard J. Spencer, *Mineralogical Magazine*, 6th ser. (1936): 299–300. An obituary is in the *New York Times*, 7 Oct. 1935.

RALPH L. LANGENHEIM, JR.

RANSON, Stephen Walter (28 Aug. 1880–30 Aug. 1942), neuroanatomist and neurologist, was born in Dodge Center, Minnesota, the son of Stephen William Ranson, a physician, and Mary Elizabeth Foster. Known as Walter, the serious young man determined very early to follow the medical tradition set by his father and two siblings who had medical training. He attended the University of Minnesota (1898–1901), spent the fourth year at the University of Chicago with the neurologist Henry H. Donaldson, received a B.A. from Minnesota (1902) and an M.A. (1903) and Ph.D. (1905) in anatomy from Chicago. His first research paper, "On the Medullated Nerve Fibers Crossing the Site of Lesions in the Brain of the White Rat," was published in 1903.

After receiving a medical degree from Rush Medical College (1907) followed by an internship at Cook County Hospital, he tried private practice but found it unrewarding in every sense. In 1909 he welcomed the chance to become acting head of the department of anatomy at Northwestern University Medical School. That same year he married Tessie Greer Rowland of Oak Park, Illinois; they had three children. From then there was no break in his successful ascent of the academic ladder, and by 1912 he was appointed full professor and department chair.

Ranson fulfilled his teaching assignment in the medical school responsibly and innovatively. To the required study of gross anatomy he added a course in the microscopic anatomy of the nervous system, for which he prepared the microscopic slides. Believing that the only text available in English at the time (by C. Judson Herrick, 1915) was too psychologically oriented for medical students, he produced his own. Ranson wrote *The Anatomy of the Nervous System* (1920) "from the dynamic rather than the static point of view . . . with emphasis . . . on the developmental and functional significance of the structure" (preface, p. ii). This novel approach, which also characterized his research, was probably predicated on Ranson's earlier exposure to Donaldson and to his study in 1911 in Germany. He had absorbed ideas about integrating anatomy and physiology that were prevailing in European medical thinking, especially regarding neurological concepts. Ranson thus entered the era of disappearing boundaries between strict disciplines brought about by technological developments at the turn of the century.

In 1924 Ranson moved to Washington University, St. Louis, where he had fewer teaching responsibilities, but four years later he returned to Northwestern, lured by the prospect of directing an Institute of Neurology in a new building, where he could devote his time exclusively to research. His increasing fame in central nervous system morphology and function brought a flood of students and fellows to the institute. Equally demanding of himself and his associates, a prolific publication record was achieved by the institute: 136 papers in thirteen years, on all of which Ranson's name appeared. In the estimation of a student and associate, Joseph C. Hinsey, Ranson's was "one of the most productive schools of neurology that ever existed" (p. 459).

Ranson had three sojourns abroad, accompanied by his close-knit family. The first trip, in 1911, included a visit with Sir Victor Horsley, London's foremost neurosurgeon, in whose laboratory Robert H. Clarke had developed a stereotaxic instrument for the precise targeting of structures below the cortex of the living brain for their electrical stimulation, recording, and lesion-making. Most of the trip, however, was spent in Freiburg, where the unsatisfactory laboratory conditions he encountered convinced him that experience in American laboratories was fully comparable to that abroad. The second trip, in 1926, included a summer at National Hospital, Queen Square, London, seeing patients in its famous neurological clinic with two of the leading British neurologists, Gordon Holmes and Kinnier Wilson. The final trip, in 1931, took him to Bern, Switzerland, for the First International Neurological Congress; Ranson's paper was on the nuclei and tracts concerned in postural responses to midbrain stimulation. He seized the opportunity to film selected notables attending the congress with the newly introduced 8mm camera for amateur movies.

Like that of many early twentieth-century investigators, Ranson's extraordinarily productive research career commenced with study of the peripheral nerves, in his case attempting to learn the clinical applications of pain conduction. In the course of this work he developed a pyridine-silver staining method with which he demonstrated the unsuspected presence in the spinal cord of large numbers of small sensory nerve fibers that lack a myelin sheath. Next he used this method to elucidate the organization of the peripheral autonomic nervous system. While at Washington University he investigated the nervous control of the antigravity muscles and locomotion, formulating a concept of reverberating neuronal circuits to maintain posture, a contemporary issue of great interest to physiologists. At the time of his return to Northwestern in 1928, those studies were taking him deeply into the central nervous system.

During the St. Louis period, Ranson and Hinsey had seen in brief use the second model of the stereotaxic instrument that Ranson had been shown in 1911. In Chicago Ranson commissioned construction of a slightly modified instrument from the original drawings (*Brain* 31 [1908]: 45–124). In the words of Horace W. Magoun, an active participant in this work, "[T]here flowed from his institute a profusion of contributions on the role of the hypothalamus and lower brainstem in visceral integration, emotional expression, the regulation of feeding, fighting, mating and other vital functions that contribute to the stability or well-being of one's internal environment" (1975, pp. 521–22). After Ranson's sudden death in Chicago, the institute gradually disintegrated from lack of administrative support, but the experimental use of the Horsley-Clarke stereotaxic instrument had been firmly established in laboratories throughout the world.

The significance of the contributions to brain research generated in the Institute of Neurology under Ranson's leadership was twofold. Not only was a large body of new knowledge of central nervous system mechanisms rapidly added to the emerging field of neuroscience, but on purely technical grounds, revival of the neglected British invention, the stereotaxic apparatus, was essential to further progress in the field. Ranson imparted enthusiasm and high standards to his associates, and he preserved throughout his career the curiosity to pursue an anomalous experimental finding. For example, the chance observation that a cat could still walk after sustaining a brain transection above the hypothalamus led to studies of muscle tonus and the use of the stereotaxic instrument. And again, an unexpected increase in urine output in an animal after damage to the anterior pituitary gland initiated the resolution of the cause of diabetes insipidus.

Ranson's international recognition as an authority on hypothalamic-pituitary structure and function was attested by invitations to deliver the Weir Mitchell Oration (Philadelphia, 1934) and the Harvey (New York, 1936), Edward K. Dunham (Boston, 1940), and Hughlings Jackson (Montreal, 1941) lectures. He was president of the American Association of Anatomists (1938–1940) and elected to the National Academy of Sciences (1940). Ranson's most prolific collaboration was with H. W. Magoun, who characterized his mentor in these words: "An unremitting worker, of keen mind and quiet, unassuming dignity, perhaps a little austere on first acquaintance, his warm, human, friendly spirit was quickly evident on further association" (1942, p. 304).

• Ranson's international collection of offprints is preserved at the University of California at Los Angeles Brain Research Institute. Among Ranson's research publications, the most important that reveal his major directions of research are "Retrograde Degeneration in the Spinal Nerves," *Journal of Comparative Neurology and Psychology* 16 (1906): 265; "New Evidence in Favor of a Chief Vaso-constrictor Center in the Brain; Studies in the Vasomotor Reflex Arcs, IV," *American Journal of Physiology* 42 (1916): 1; "An Introduction to a Series of Studies on the Sympathetic Nervous System," *Journal* of *Comparative Neurology* 29 (1918): 305; *The Anatomy of the Nervous System* (1920); "On the Use of the Horsley-Clarke Stereotaxic Instrument," *Psychiatrie en Neurologie* 38 (1934): 534–43; with Walter R. Ingram et al., "Results of Stimulation of the Tegmentum with the Horsley-Clarke Stereotaxic Apparatus," *Archives of Neurology and Psychiatry* 28 (1932): 513; with W. Kenneth Hare and Horace W. Magoun, "Electrical Stimulation of the Interior of the Cerebellum in the Decerebrate Cat," *American Journal of Physiology* 117 (1936): 261; with Charles Fisher and Ingram, *Diabetes Insipidus and the Neuro-Hormonal Control of Water Balance: A Contribution to the Structure and Function of the Hypothalamico-hypophyseal System* (1938); and with S. W. Ranson, Jr., and M. Ranson, "Fiber Connections of Corpus Striatum as Seen in Marchi Preparations," *Archives of Neurology and Psychiatry* 46 (1941): 230, one of several collaborations with his son and daughter.

The best source of information about Ranson is William F. Windle, ed., *Stephen Walter Ranson, Ground-Breaking Neuroscientist: Memoirs of Students and Colleagues at His Centenary* (1981). Details and background of Ranson's research and a bibliography are found in Florence R. Sabin, "Biographical Memoir of Stephen Walter Ranson 1880–1942," National Academy of Sciences, *Biographical Memoirs* 23 (1945): 365–97. As his student and collaborator, Magoun writes sensitively about him and his institute in "Stephen Walter Ranson 1880–1942," *Northwestern University Medical School Quarterly Bulletin* 16 (1942): 302–4, in "The Role of the Research Institutes in the Advancement of Neuroscience: Ranson's Institute of Neurology, 1928–1942," *The Neurosciences, Paths of Discovery*, ed. Frederick G. Worden et al. (1975), and in "Stephen Ranson (1880–1942)," *The Founders of Neurology*, ed. Webb Haymaker and Francis Schiller, 2d ed. (1970).

LOUISE H. MARSHALL

RAPAPORT, David (30 Sept. 1911–14 Dec. 1960), psychologist, was born Desző Rapaport in Munkacs, Hungary, the son of middle-class parents, Bela Rapaport, a grain merchant, and Helen Balaban. Rapaport graduated from the Gymnasium in Budapest in 1929, with specialization in mathematics and physics, and then attended the university in Budapest. During his student years he was a leader of a Zionist youth organization and was known for his dramatic oratory. He married Elvira Strasser in 1932; they had two children. Following his graduation from the university in 1933, he spent two years as a surveyor on a kibbutz in what was then Palestine. In 1935 he returned to Hungary to pursue graduate studies in philosophy at Royal Hungarian University, and he received his Ph.D. in 1938. His dissertation was on the history of the association concept from Bacon to Kant, marking the beginning of his intense interest in the psychology of thought processes. He was early attracted to psychoanalytic psychology as a broad theory of cognitive development, and while he was a graduate student, he ghostwrote two books for a psychoanalyst named, coincidentally, Samuel Rappaport. One book was on psychoanalysis and one on "nervous stomach and intestinal ailments." This episode stimulated the young psychologist's interest in hoaxes, a large number of which he went on to collect over the years. The collection never came to publication.

Because of the anti-Semitic climate in Hungary and the impending Nazi influence, Rapaport emigrated to the United States in 1938. His parents remained in Hungary and were later imprisoned in concentration camps, his father in Buchenwald and his mother in Bergen-Belsen. They both survived, and following World War II they too emigrated to the United States.

Rapaport took his first position in 1938 as a clinical psychologist at Mt. Sinai Hospital in New York City. In 1939 he moved to a similar position at Osawatomie State Hospital in Kansas. Karl A. Menninger, chief of staff of the Menninger Clinic, a private psychiatric hospital in nearby Topeka, was impressed by the breadth of his knowledge and the clarity of his thinking and hired him in 1940 as a staff psychologist. He quickly was promoted to chief psychologist and then to director of research. His productive writings on diagnostic psychological testing, psychoanalytic theory, and the psychology of thinking took place within a span of about eighteen years, until his death.

In 1942 Rapaport published *Emotions and Memory*, an exhaustive analysis of the psychology of memory as it is influenced by noncognitive processes. In 1945–1946 he published, with Merton M. Gill and Roy Schafer, *Diagnostic Psychological Testing* (rev. and ed. Robert R. Holt, 1968), a landmark two-volume study of how psychological tests can be used for clinical psychiatric diagnoses. Using both empirical and theoretical studies, they showed how forms of thinking can be used validly to distinguish various forms of mental disorders such as schizophrenia, depression, obsessive compulsive disorder, and hysteria. He formulated three justifying principles for such an effort: (1) every sample of behavior bears the style of that person; (2) psychological pathology is considered to be an exacerbation of trends existing in the healthy person; and (3) diagnostic psychological testing examines the processes by which the organizing principles of the healthy person become transformed into pathology. This effort provided the basis for the elevation of the status of the psychological tester from that of a technician who merely reported a patient's IQ to that of an expert who probed patterns of thought functions in personality, both in health and in pathology. *Diagnostic Psychological Testing* and its subsequent one-volume condensation contain extended and highly original treatises on several aspects of cognition, including anticipation, concept formation, visual-motor coordination, attention, and concentration.

In 1948 Rapaport moved to the Austen Riggs Center in Stockbridge, Massachusetts. One of the reasons he gave for this move was a desire to be free of administrative responsibilities and to be able to devote his full attention to scholarly activities. His abiding interest in the development, stability, disintegration, and reconstruction of thinking, none of which had yet been directly addressed by contemporary psychology or psychiatric practice, drew him to examine closely the principles of psychoanalytic psychology, which, in the form sketched by Freud in his papers on metapsychology, had never been presented systematically even by Freud. Rapaport undertook this systematization as his life's work but principally from the starting point of psychoanalysis as a psychology rather than as a treatment or a theory of pathology. He thus undertook as a major project a penetrating scrutiny of psychoanalysis as a general psychology. Psychoanalysis appealed to him because it encompassed both intrinsic forces within a person (conceived as biological factors) and environmental constraints. He rejected both Locke's environmentalism, in which mind is a tabula rasa written on by the environment, as well as Berkeley's radical subjectivism, in which mind solipsistically creates the perception of the world. Motives, he wrote, do not determine behavior in a direct fashion, as radical psychoanalysts would state; nor does the environment shape a person's behavior in a simple, causal way as the behaviorists believed. Rather, the biological drives safeguard the individual's relative autonomy from environmental input, and environmental input safeguards the individual's relative autonomy from biological drives. He developed these principles in a series of papers and book reviews written between 1947 and his death and collected in *Dynamic Psychology and Kantian Epistemology* (1947), *Some Metapsychological Considerations of Activity and Passivity* (1953), and *The Theory of Attention Cathexis* (1959).

As part of his effort to systematize psychoanalytic psychology, Rapaport translated the work of some seminal theorists, such as Otto Fenichel, Paul Schilder, Heinz Hartmann, and Eugen Bleuler. He also translated and published in *The Organization and Pathology of Thought* (1951) twenty-seven papers by authors whose work, as he wrote, were "often quoted but rarely read." Included are papers that discuss the development of thinking (by Piaget, Ach, Buehler, and Claparède) and the pathological forms of thinking (by Silberer, Nachmansohn, Varendonck, and Bleuler). In the style of the Talmud, he annotated the papers with explanatory and exegetical footnotes that far exceed the texts in length. The volume ends with a succinct but complex chapter summarizing the elements necessary for a psychology of thinking.

In 1959 Rapaport published a comprehensive treatise on psychoanalytic theory, "The Structure of Psychoanalytic Theory: A Systematizing Attempt." In this lucid exposition Rapaport showed that psychoanalysis was not a final statement but an evolving system of thought that was more a guide than a plan for precise deductive experimentation.

In 1960 he began a program of experimental work on attentional processes, but it was cut short by his sudden death in Stockbridge, Massachusetts, probably from cardiac arrest.

Rapaport was a forceful influence on his students and colleagues by way of both his vivid personality and the intensity and clarity of his thought. His introduction of a different way to use psychological tests in a clinical setting revolutionized the use of diagnostic instruments in psychology, and in 1960 the American Psychological Association awarded him a medal for distinguished contributions to clinical psychology. His writings and lectures on thought processes antici-

pated by at least a decade the arrival of the discipline of cognitive science, but they contain much material that has yet to be explored.

He was a demanding teacher whose lectures often displayed his virtuosity and encyclopedic mastery of his subject. He had a formal demeanor with his students but at the same time was extraordinarily generous with his time, gifts, and interest. He was an accomplished raconteur with a large collection of jokes from which he could recall just the right one to illustrate a point in a lecture or discussion.

• Rapaport's published papers, notes, and lectures are in the Library of Congress. The most complete collection available in book-form is *The Collected Papers of David Rapaport*, ed. Merton M. Gill (1967), which contains an introductory, appreciative summary of Rapaport's contributions by Gill and George S. Klein. An informative assessment is Gill and Klein, "The Structuring of Drive and Reality: David Rapaport's Contributions to Psycho-Analysis and Psychology," *International Journal of Psycho-Analysis* 45, no. 4 (Oct. 1964): 483–98. An obituary appears in the *New York Times*, 16 Dec. 1960.

PHILIP S. HOLZMAN

RAPEE, Erno (4 June 1891–26 June 1945), composer, conductor, and pianist, was born in Budapest, Hungary. A piano virtuoso, he studied composition and piano at the Budapest Royal Conservatory, graduating at the age of eighteen. A conducting student of Ernst Schuch, the general musical director of the Dresden Royal Opera House, Rapee held conductor and assistant conductor posts with various European theaters. Following a concert tour of South America and Mexico, he came to New York City in 1912. Arriving literally without funds, Rapee found employment as a musician at New York's Cafe Monopole for $25 a week. He also worked briefly as an accompanist for Harry Lauder, the popular Scottish singer and comedian. In 1913 he was engaged as musical director for New York City's Hungarian Opera Company. The following year he made his American vaudeville debut, playing classical numbers and patriotic medleys on the piano.

In 1917 Rapee was hired as an orchestra conductor for the Rialto, an ornate silent movie theater then under the management of Samuel Lionel "Roxy" Rothafel. It was Rothafel's policy to offer his patrons concerts of classical music in addition to the standard film program. As a classically trained musician, Rapee was eminently qualified to select and conduct the type of music that Rothafel wanted performed. During the next several years, Rapee conducted at major New York theaters such as the Rivoli, the Capitol, and the Roxy, while they were under Rothafel's management. His orchestras ranged in size from 25 to 110 players and represented the crème de la crème of New York City's professional musicians. At a time when orchestra concerts were not generally available to the masses, Rothafel and Rapee were introducing their film theater patrons to complete symphonies and concert works by the great masters. In 1922 Rothafel began a series of weekly radio broadcasts from the Capitol Theater.

Prominently featured in these programs were Rapee and his orchestra, who used the opportunity to introduce early radio listeners to many new major works, notably the symphonic compositions of Richard Strauss and Jean Sibelius.

In addition to conducting, Rapee was one of the leading exponents of compiling musical scores for silent films. Most of his scoring was done patchwork, with snippets of existing music used to underscore and emphasize the moods expressed on the screen. Generally speaking, one-third of a Rapee score would underscore action, one-third would depict psychological situations, and the remaining third would create atmosphere. His score for *The Iron Horse* (1924), dealing with the building of the first transcontinental railroad, contains well-known Protestant hymns, ethnic Irish, Italian, and Native American music, and popular songs from the nineteenth century, in addition to the usual hurries, agitatos, and misteriosos. Rapee also did many theater orchestra arrangements of symphonic works and composed hundreds of incidental mood-music compositions. Among his original compositions were such popular songs as "Charmaine" (1926), introduced in the film *What Price Glory?*; and "Diane" (1927), introduced in the film *Seventh Heaven*. Rapee also prepared scores for such films as *If Winter Comes*, *A Connecticut Yankee*, *The Queen of Sheba*, and *Robin Hood*. After a silent film's initial New York appearance, Rapee's score frequently would be performed wherever the picture was shown.

Rapee published two reference works for silent film musicians. *Motion Picture Moods* (1924) was a cross-indexed collection of music adapted to fit fifty-two moods and situations most commonly encountered in silent films. It was intended for use by pianists, organists, and orchestra leaders in those theaters not large enough to maintain their own musical arranger and librarian. *Erno Rapee's Encyclopedia of Music for Pictures* (1925) was an index of orchestra music then available from various publishers. Individual titles were organized so as to represent, musically, almost every situation that could occur on the screen. Its hundreds of classifications included such entries as "Aeroplane," "Agitato," "American Indian," "Battle," "Cannibal," "Comedy," "Desert," "Mysterioso," "Irish," "Oriental," "Sea Music," among others.

In the mid-1920s Rapee returned to Europe to guest-conduct major symphony orchestras and to prepare "American style" musical programs for a nationwide theater chain controlled by the UFA Film Company of Germany. Following his return to the United States, he was appointed musical director of Warner Bros.–First National Pictures in Hollywood, a pioneer in the production of early sound films. Returning to New York City in 1931, Rapee became the general musical director for the National Broadcasting Company. In this capacity he conducted numerous radio symphony orchestras, including the General Motors Symphony. In 1932, at Rothafel's request, he was appointed musical director in chief of the Radio City Music Hall, a position he held until his death. Here he helped to present "digest" versions of popular grand operas by Verdi, Puccini, and Beethoven on the Music Hall stage. In addition, he scored and conducted many of the elaborate stage shows featuring the music hall's famous precision dance team, the Radio City Rockettes. He and the Radio City Orchestra and chorus were also featured in a popular radio series "Music Hall on the Air." The high point of Rapee's classical radio broadcasts came on 12 April 1942, when he conducted Gustav Mahler's Eighth Symphony in a performance that featured 100 musicians and 300 voices from various New York choirs. In recognition of this performance, he was awarded the Mahler Medal of Honor by the Bruckner Society of America.

During World War II Rapee, a member of the U.S. Coast Guard Reserve and a licensed navigator, taught celestial navigation at Hunter College and New York University. Rapee died suddenly of a heart attack in his Central Park West apartment. He was survived by his wife, Mariska, and two children.

A classically trained composer and concert pianist, Rapee is remembered today primarily for his work in composing and compiling music for silent motion pictures. Through his theater conducting and radio work, he was a pioneer in helping to introduce classical music to the general public as mainstream entertainment.

• The single best reference work on the era of Erno Rapee, Samuel Lionel "Roxy" Rothafel, and the deluxe silent movie theater is Ben M. Hall, *The Best Remaining Seats* (1961). Through photographs, old advertisements, interviews, and a well-researched text, the author successfully recaptures much of the ambience of film theaters, film theater music, and the theatergoing experience during the 1910s, 1920s, and early 1930s. Additional information on Rapee can be gleaned from his obituaries in the *New York Times* and the *New York Herald*, 27 June 1945.

ERIC BEHEIM

RAPER, John Robert (3 Oct. 1911–21 May 1974), botanist and university professor, was born in Davidson County, North Carolina, the son of William Franklin Raper and Julia Crouse, farmers. He attended the University of North Carolina and earned an A.B. (botany) in 1933 and an A.M. (botany) in 1936. Raper earned further graduate degrees at Harvard University: an A.M. and a Ph.D., both in biology and both awarded in 1939. After receipt of his doctoral degree, he worked as a postdoctoral fellow of the National Research Council at the California Institute of Technology from 1939 to 1941.

Raper began teaching botany at Indiana University (1941–1943) and then moved to work with the Manhattan Project in Chicago, Illinois, and Oak Ridge, Tennessee (1943–1946). After the Second World War, Raper served as assistant professor of botany (1946–1949), associate professor of botany (1949–1953), and professor of botany (1953–1954) at the University of Chicago. He became professor of botany at Harvard University in 1954 and served as chair of the Department of Biological Sciences from 1970 to 1974. He was married from 1936 to 1948 to Ruth Scholz, with whom he had one son. In 1949 Raper married Carlene Marie Allen, with whom he had one son and one daughter. He died in Boston, Massachusetts.

Raper's work as a research botanist focused on two major subjects in the control of reproduction and sexuality in the fungi. His first work was the identification of the hormonal control of sexual differentiation in the Oomycetes *Achlya ambisexualis* and *Achlya bisexualis*. One of Raper's first papers on this subject (1939) presented evidence that these water molds produced diffusible hormones that controlled the differentiation of their reproductive structures. Later work led him to postulate several hormones that operated in sequence to govern the entire sexual cycle in *Achlya*. Initiation of the chain of events began when female strains produced Hormone A, which caused male strains to produce antheridial branches, which in turn produced Hormone B and began to grow toward the female strain. Hormone B caused the female strain to form the initial stages of female reproductive structures. When the male antheridial branches grew around the female oogonia, genetic exchange occurred between the two strains. Raper postulated that seven hormones were involved in the sexual cycle and was able to isolate a concentrated solution of Hormone A. In the 1960s work in other laboratories demonstrated that Hormones A and B were steroids, called *antheridiol* and *oogoniol*, respectively.

In the 1950s Raper became interested in a second area of sexuality in fungi, the genetic control of mating compatibility and of reproductive development of the Basidiomycetes, especially *Schizophyllum commune*, a wood-rotting fungus. Earlier research indicated that mating in some Basidiomycetes was governed by a set of two factors, now designated A and B. Both the A and B factors occurred in multiple forms. When two strains of such a fungus formed a fruiting body ("mushroom"), the spores could be placed into four classes based on their mating compatibility with each other. This complex phenomenon was called "tetrapolar sexuality." It was as if the fungus had four sexes instead of two, as is the case for most plants and animals.

Raper's entry into this subject was perhaps somewhat of a surprise to him. In 1948 one of his graduate students at the University of Chicago, Haig P. Papazian, wanted to delve into tetrapolar sexuality for his dissertation. As Raper later recalled, he "advised . . . against [the] investigation . . . as . . . tetrapolarity was a worked-out field . . . . Happily, this well-intended advice received the attention that it deserved: it was ignored." Thus with Raper's reluctant tolerance, Papazian proceeded to open up the field of tetrapolar sexuality for a vigorous period of new research. Papazian's most important conclusion was that the A factor was probably the product of two different genes, each of which had several forms. He also clarified what happened when strains that were not fully compatible came together and the process by which an unmated strain could also be mated by an already mated pair.

Over the following two decades Raper and his colleagues proceeded to build on Papazian's work by delving into the genetic and morphological complexities of tetrapolar sexuality and other aspects of reproductive physiology in *Schizophyllum commune*. In 1966 he summarized the many findings in *Genetics of Sexuality in Higher Fungi*, a book that he whimsically wanted to call *Sexes by the Thousands*. This book remained the standard monographic treatment of the subject for nearly three decades. Subsequent work in several laboratories indicated that the genes governing sexuality in *Schizophyllum* produce regulatory molecules similar to those known in other organisms.

Taken by themselves, each of Raper's major research arenas, hormonal control and genetic control of sexuality in fungi, were intricate and complex puzzles, investigated in species that were not well known to the public. A brief article in *Time* magazine in 1939 may have been the only popular rendition of his work. Furthermore, the species that Raper studied were without significant economic impacts, and he was not particularly interested in the implications of his work for fungal species that do have profound economic impacts, such as the "smuts" and "rusts" that damage agriculture.

Instead, Raper was interested in understanding these organisms for their own sake, because they were interesting and had a strategy of life that was quite different from other sexual processes. He provided insights for understanding how these species develop their forms, how they control the flow of genetic information from one generation to the next, and how the control of form and gene flow governed the evolutionary history and future of the species. He was very keen to place the processes in the fungi in a common context with genetic control of protein synthesis in bacteria and mating incompatibility in the higher plants.

Raper's work did not attract attention in the popular sphere, but he was well honored by his colleagues in science. He was elected to membership in the American Academy of Arts and Sciences (1955) and to the National Academy of Sciences (1964). In 1959–1960 he traveled in Europe and did research at the University of Cologne as a Guggenheim fellow and a Fulbright research fellow.

From 1949 to 1974 Raper worked closely with Carlene Allen Raper, his wife. Together they created an intellectual and personal hospitality that was never forgotten by those who were fortunate enough to share their excitement about some of the most complicated of the "lowly organisms." Their work provided an inspiration to many students and postdoctoral fellows.

• Raper's correspondence and papers are held by his family. He published more than ninety research papers in scientific journals and as chapters of books. One notable chapter was, with K. Esser, "The Fungi," in *The Cell* (1964). A complete bibliography of Raper's work is included in the memorial by his brother, Kenneth B. Raper, National Academy of Sciences, *Biographical Memoirs* 57 (1987): 346–70. A popular account of Raper's work on *Achlya* is in *Time*, 19 June 1939, pp. 30–31. This sketch was based on materials supplied by

Carlene A. Raper plus the author's own recollections as one of Raper's graduate students. An obituary is in the *Harvard Gazette*, 29 Apr. 1977.

JOHN PERKINS

RAPHAELSON, Samson (30 Mar. 1896–16 July 1983), playwright, screenwriter, and short-story author, was born in New York City, the son of Ralph Raphaelson, a cap manufacturer of Jewish descent, and Anna Marks. After graduating from high school in Chicago, where he had rejoined his family after living several years with his paternal grandparents on Manhattan's Lower East Side, Raphaelson attended the Lewis Institute and earned a bachelor's degree at the University of Illinois in 1917. In 1918 he married Raina (maiden name unknown), whom he later divorced. In 1927 he married Dorothy Wegman; the couple had two children.

He worked in Chicago until 1921, first as a reporter for City News Service, then as a writer for an advertising agency and as an assistant to a publisher of popular magazines. He was also an instructor of English and rhetoric at the University of Illinois. Raphaelson moved to New York in 1921 to work as a police reporter for the *New York Times*, switching in 1922 to the advertising business. He turned one of his short stories, "The Day of Atonement," published in 1922, into a contemporary drama, *The Jazz Singer*. Skillfully drawing on the cultural and religious clashes between Old World Jewish immigrants and the Americanized new generation, the play became a Broadway hit in 1925. Warner Bros. bought the rights, and *The Jazz Singer* (1927) became the world's first talking feature (actually a silent film with several sound sequences, including songs, ad-libbed dialogue, and the legendary phrase "You ain't heard nothin' yet"), starring popular singer and entertainer Al Jolson.

Like many other well-known writers and dramatists of his time, Raphaelson was courted by the Hollywood studios to write screenplays for a medium that was radically changed by the advent of sound. His initial reluctance to work for this form of popular entertainment was set aside when financial, professional, and family constraints made him accept an offer in 1929 to become a contract writer at the recently founded RKO Pictures. After six months Raphaelson left RKO having written one screenplay, which was not produced. His newly formed friendship with director William Wyler eventually led to a contract with Paramount Pictures. A fruitful association with celebrated German director Ernst Lubitsch resulted in nine screenplays produced between 1931 and 1948: *The Smiling Lieutenant* (1931); *One Hour with You* (1932); *The Man I Killed* (1932), Lubitsch's only drama of the sound era, retitled *Broken Lullaby*; *Trouble in Paradise* (1932); *The Merry Widow* (1934); *Angel* (1937); *The Shop around the Corner* (1940); *Heaven Can Wait* (1943); and *That Lady in Ermine* (1948), completed by Otto Preminger after the sudden death of Lubitsch. In Raphaelson's memoir "Freundschaft," first published in the *New Yorker* in 1981, he recounted how their close creative collaboration unfolded intermittently over seventeen years. Lubitsch and Raphaelson completely reworked a succession of plays (in three instances with the aid of screenwriter Ernest Vajda) to produce stylized comedies set in foreign or mythical locales that satirized sex, money, and social position, the common themes of their collaboration. With his strong sense of structure and skill for polished dialogue the writer enabled the director to explore through wit, innuendo, and minute psychological and social observation the clash of the sexes, an approach that came to be defined as the "Lubitsch touch."

One of Raphaelson's best-known screenplays was an adaptation of Francis Iles's novel *Before the Fact* (1932), which Alfred Hitchcock filmed for RKO as *Suspicion* (1941), with Cary Grant and Joan Fontaine, who received an Academy Award for best actress. Raphaelson alternated his Hollywood work with a successful Broadway career that lasted until the early 1950s, when he retired to study photography. His stage productions include *Young Love* (1928), *The Magnificent Heel* (1929), *Boolie* (1930), *The Wooden Slipper* (1934), *Accent on Youth* (1934), *White Man* (1936), *Skylark* (1939), *Jason* (1942), *The Perfect Marriage* (1944), and *Hilda Crane* (1950). Several of these stage productions were turned into films for which Raphaelson did not write screenplays: *Accent on Youth* (1935); *Skylark* (1941); *The Perfect Marriage* (1946); *Mr. Music* (1950), based on *Accent on Youth*; *Hilda Crane* (1956); *But Not for Me* (1959), also based on *Accent on Youth*; and two remakes of *The Jazz Singer* (1953 and 1980).

A supporter of Israel, Raphaelson spent two years there in the early 1970s, advising the nation's young film industry. In 1976 Raphaelson was appointed adjunct professor at the School of the Arts at Columbia University, where he taught playwriting until his death in New York City. He received the Writers Guild Laurel Award in 1977 and an honorary degree from Columbia University in 1981. Besides writing more than 100 short stories, more than twenty credited and some uncredited screenplays, and about a dozen produced plays, Raphaelson wrote the radio play *General Armchair* in 1944 and published *The Human Nature of Playwriting* (1949). His fiction was published in the *New Yorker*, the *Saturday Evening Post*, *Atlantic Monthly*, and other magazines.

Film critic Andrew Sarris notes in *Film Comment* that Raphaelson has been underrated as a playwright because "his modest, middle-class brand of romantic humanism did not provide the theatrical intelligentsia with the parables of lost purity they demanded." Ironically, Raphaelson always thought that his plays would stand as his best artistic contribution. His screenplays were "wild doodles," "occasional employment in Hollywood, where you were paid while you wrote, week after week," as he pointed out in his "Freundschaft" memoir. Discussing the similarities and contrasts between Raphaelson's theater and film work, Pauline Kael, longtime critic of the *New Yorker* and a friend of the playwright, remarked in the introduction to Raphaelson's *Three Screen Comedies* that his plays created "a chimerical world of streamlined elegance. It's a dream of high life, in which lovers are articulate, slim-hipped, and witty." In his work for Lubitsch, she noted, Raphaelson "could try out the irresponsible thoughts that came to mind. He could trust his impulses, his instinct." In his *Talking Pictures: Screenwriters in the American Cinema*, Richard Corliss included Raphaelson among the "stylists," remarking that his close collaboration with Lubitsch was similar to that of Robert Riskin and Frank Capra or of Dudley Nichols and John Ford.

• Raphaelson's papers, including film scripts and plays, are at the University of Illinois at Champaign-Urbana. *Three Screen Comedies by Samson Raphaelson: "Trouble in Paradise," The Shop around the Corner," and "Heaven Can Wait"* (1983), reprints "Freundschaft" and lists the produced and published plays and other work. The most complete assessment of Raphaelson's Broadway and Hollywood career is Barry Sabath's profile for the *Dictionary of Literary Biography* 44 (1986). It includes an analysis of plays and screenplays, a filmography, and a list of his play productions with opening dates and theaters. Richard Corliss places Raphaelson in the context of the studio era in *The Hollywood Screenwriters* (1972), a collection of essays and interviews, and in *Talking Pictures: Screenwriters in the American Cinema* (1974), a taxonomy inspired by the French auteur approach to film. A filmography is provided as well as insights into the Lubitsch-Raphaelson collaboration through the analysis of *Trouble in Paradise, Angel,* and *The Shop around the Corner.* Andrew Sarris, Richard Corliss, and Raphaelson's nephew Bob Rafelson, a screenwriter, wrote concise and evocative pieces following the death of the screenwriter in *Film Comment,* Sept.–Oct. 1983, pp. 26 and 29. Obituaries are in the *New York Times* and *Los Angeles Times,* both 17 July 1983, and *Variety,* 20 July 1983.

MARÍA ELENA DE LAS CARRERAS-KUNTZ

RAPHALL, Morris Jacob (3 Oct. 1798–23 June 1868), rabbi, was born in Stockholm, Sweden. His parents' names are unknown. Reared in Copenhagen, Denmark, and educated at the universities of Giessen and Erlangen, Raphall settled in England in 1825. An orator and a writer, he emerged as a spokesman for British Jewry, advocating political rights for Jews and defending Judaism in the face of Christian polemic. In publishing essays and public letters defending Jewish rights, Raphall rejected the claims of Christian missionaries and refuted the blood libel accusations that had emerged in 1840 in Damascus, where several Jews were charged with killing a Christian child to use his blood for the baking of Passover matzah. In addition, Raphall wrote numerous books and articles designed primarily for a popular Jewish audience. His two-volume *Post-Biblical History of the Jews* (1855), for example, was an introduction to Jewish history written for the general reader. Raphall also translated sections of biblical and rabbinic literature into English, including a volume of the Pentateuch, excerpts of Mishnah, and selections from the writings of Maimonides and Joseph Albo. His translation of *Moses Maimonides: Eight Chapters of Ethics* (1835) and *Eighteen Treatises from the Mishna* (1843) enabled laymen unfamiliar with Hebrew to study traditional Jewish texts. From 1834 to 1836 he edited *Gila'ad: Hebrew Review and Magazine of Rabbinical Literature,* the first English language periodical of its kind.

Raphall's literary achievements on behalf of Jews and Judaism were only part of a distinguished career of communal service and religious leadership. In 1840 he became a secretary to Solomon Hirschel, the most illustrious rabbi in London at the time, and the following year, though not ordained, Raphall accepted the position as minister of a synagogue in Birmingham, England, where he remained until 1849.

Immigrating to the United States in 1849, Raphall settled in New York City, where he became rabbi of Congregation B'nai Jeshurun. In the United States, with its political security, economic opportunity, and separation of church and state, Raphall encountered a Jewish society that was, in some ways, notably different from that in Great Britain. In addition, Raphall confronted a community in which Orthodox Judaism was not only threatened by the external forces of assimilation but was internally vulnerable as it faced the growing religious Reform movement. Accordingly, Raphall became a leading preacher and spokesman for the Orthodox Jewish tradition. His discourses and published treatises were designed to persuade an increasingly skeptical congregation that traditional Jewish practice and belief could be meaningful in a modern, American culture. His popular lectures gained notoriety among both Jews and Christians. In 1860 Raphall earned the distinction of becoming the first Jewish clergyman to open a session of the U.S. House of Representatives with a prayer invocation.

During Raphall's tenure at Congregation B'nai Jeshurun, the synagogue surpassed the older and more established Sephardic congregation, Shearith Israel, to become the largest Orthodox synagogue in New York City. A compassionate man, Raphall worked hard to support numerous charities. He also maintained a correspondence with the eminent philanthropist Moses Montefiore in raising money on behalf of the Jewish community of Palestine.

Never fearful of expressing his convictions forcefully, Raphall became involved in the knotty debate regarding slavery in the South. During the political crisis of secession in early 1861, Raphall delivered a lecture, later published as *The Bible View of Slavery,* in which he insisted that the Bible acknowledged the right to own slaves. Although he distinguished between slavery as practiced in the South and biblical law regarding the treatment of slaves, Raphall nonetheless criticized abolitionists for contending that the Bible prohibited slavery. In suggesting that the Bible ensured the right to own slaves, Raphall, not surprisingly, received ample praise from supporters of the southern system while incurring the wrath of abolitionists.

In 1865 Raphall agreed to the request of the directors of Congregation B'nai Jeshurun to curtail his responsibilities and appoint a rabbinic successor. Although his career came to an end as Reform Judaism was beginning to attract greater numbers of American Jews, Raphall's achievements on behalf of Orthodox Judaism set the stage for another wave of Orthodox immigration two decades later. It is not known if Raphall ever married. His remaining years were spent in New York City, where he died.

• Papers related to Raphall can be found in the B'nai Jeshurun Letter Books, Trustees Minutes, and Minutes of the General Meetings, located at Congregation B'nai Jeshurun, New York City.

Raphall's other writings include, as translator *Hartwig Wesseley's Yein Levanon: Comments on Ethics of the Fathers* (1835–1836) and *The Sacred Scriptures in Hebrew and English* (1844); *The Festivals of the Lord as Celebrated by the House of Israel in Every Part of the World* (1839); *Judaism Defended against the Attacks of T.J.C. of Oxford: A Reply to Two Letters on the Damascus Question* (1840); *Ruhama: Devotional Exercises for the Use of the Daughters of Israel for Public and Private Worship* (1852); *The Four Seasons in the History of Israel* (1854); and *The Path to Immortality: On Repentance, a Future State and the Resurrection of the Dead* (1859).

A complete description or assessment of Raphall's life has yet to be published, but brief biographical accounts are included in Henry Morais, *Eminent Israelites of the Nineteenth Century* (1880), pp. 287–91, and Moshe Davis, *The Emergence of Conservative Judaism* (1963), pp. 356–58. Important references to Raphall can be found in Israel Goldstein, *A Century of Judaism in New York* (1930); Hyman B. Grinstein, *The Rise of the Jewish Community of New York 1654–1860* (1945); and Bertram Korn, *Eventful Years and Experiences* (1954). Obituaries are in the *Hebrew Leader*, 26 June 1868, and the *Jewish Chronicle* (London), 17 July 1868.

MOSHE SHERMAN

RAPIER, James Thomas (13 Nov. 1837–31 May 1883), congressman from Alabama, was born of free parents in Florence, Alabama, the son of John H. Rapier, a barber, and Susan (maiden name unknown). As a youngster, he was sent to live with his father's mother, Sally Thomas, and his father's half-brother after whom Rapier was named, James Thomas, and to attend school in Nashville, Tennessee. Sally and James Thomas, although legally slaves, hired their own time and lived autonomous lives. Young Rapier thrived under their care and learned to read and write.

At the age of nineteen Rapier was sent by his father to Buxton, Canada West, an all-black settlement, to continue his education. At a school founded by the Presbyterian minister William King, he studied Latin, Greek, mathematics, and the Bible. He also underwent a religious conversion and later taught school in the settlement. "My coming to Canada is worth all the world to me," he wrote in 1862. "I have a tolerable good education and I am at peace with my Savior."

Returning to the South in 1864, he went to Nashville, and later to Maury County, Tennessee. In 1865 he entered the political arena by delivering a keynote address at the Tennessee Negro Suffrage Convention in Nashville. When former Confederates returned to power during Tennessee's first postwar elections in 1865–1866, Rapier returned home to Florence. With

the assistance of his father he rented a farm on Seven Mile Island in the Tennessee River, hired black tenant farmers, and raised a cotton crop.

Following the passage of the Congressional Reconstruction Acts in 1867, which enfranchised freedmen and provided for new state governments in the South, Rapier again turned to politics. He won a seat at Alabama's first Republican convention in Montgomery and helped draft the new party platform calling for free speech, free press, and free schools. But he knew the fragility of the new coalition of blacks and pro-Union whites and asked fellow Republicans to proceed with "calmness, moderation and intelligence." In November 1867 Rapier attended the Alabama Constitutional Convention, supporting a civil rights plank and a moderate franchise clause that would exclude from the vote only those disfranchised by acts of Congress.

Despite his advocacy of moderation, however, during the tumultuous months preceding the 1868 presidential election, Rapier was driven from his home in Lauderdale County by the Ku Klux Klan. Barely escaping with his life (several fellow blacks were hanged from a bridge near Florence), he fled to Montgomery, where he spent almost a year in seclusion. In 1869 he attended the National Negro Labor Union convention in Washington, D.C. (he also attended two subsequent conventions), and in 1871 he founded the Alabama Negro Labor Union in an effort to improve working conditions for laborers and tenant farmers.

In 1870 Rapier became his party's nominee for secretary of state. Despite a vigorous campaign and publishing a newspaper, the *Republican Sentinel*, he went down to defeat largely because of violence and opposition from white Republicans to any black candidate. But at the national level, as a reward for his party loyalty, he was appointed assessor of internal revenue for the Montgomery district in 1871, the first black to attain such a high patronage position in the state.

Using his Montgomery office, in the heart of the Black Belt, he mounted a campaign for the Second District congressional seat, received the nomination, and during a period of calm following the passage of the Enforcement Acts, which provided for federal suppression of the KKK, defeated the popular one-armed Confederate veteran William Oates by a vote of 19,000–16,000. Before taking his seat in Congress, he represented Alabama at the Fifth International Exhibition in Vienna, Austria, reporting on the state's exhibits. During his congressional term (1873–1875), Rapier pushed through a bill to make Montgomery a port of delivery, making federal funds available to assist in dredging the Alabama River as far inland as Montgomery. He also supported legislation to improve education in the South, arguing that federal funds be used to support public schools, and spoke on behalf of Charles Sumner's civil rights bill, which became law in 1875.

Seeking a second term, Rapier launched a campaign in 1874, but renewed violence, intimidation, and voter fraud led to his defeat. Two years later, in the newly gerrymandered Fourth Congressional District, which included Lowndes County where Rapier rented several cotton plantations, he tried again, but fraud and the entry of Jeremiah Haralson, a black man from Selma, into the 1876 race resulted in a second defeat. The differences between himself and Haralson were hard to pinpoint: both advocated civil rights, voter protection, and leadership roles for blacks. In large measure their difference was a matter of style. Haralson was young, brash, outspoken, and rhetorical; Rapier was older, prudent, diplomatic, and his speeches, while forceful (he was an outstanding orator) and well organized, had few rhetorical flourishes.

With the "redemption" of the state by conservatives, Rapier turned his attention to the emigration movement. Appointed collector of internal revenue for the Second Alabama District in 1877, he used the office to urge former slaves to leave Alabama and settle in the West. The black man, he asserted, would never be accorded equal rights or economic opportunity in the South. He traveled several times to Kansas, purchased land for a settlement in Wabaunsee County along the route of the Kansas-Pacific Railway, gave pro-emigration speeches in Alabama, and testified in Washington, D.C., before a Senate committee on emigration.

During the early 1880s, as his health began to decline, Rapier slowed his activity. He had never married, and despite the hectic pace of his career he was a lonely man who admitted he had few real friends.

By the end of his life, Rapier had come full circle. From seeking to work within the system to gain equal rights for blacks in the South, he now advocated that former slaves and their children should abandon the land of their birth. His efforts, however, were cut short. Rapier died in Lowndes County, Alabama, of pulmonary tuberculosis.

• Rapier correspondence can be found in the Rapier-Thomas Papers, Moorland-Spingarn Collection, Howard University, Washington, D.C. See also Loren Schweninger, *James T. Rapier and Reconstruction* (1978); Eric Foner, *Freedom's Law-makers: A Directory of Black Office Holders during Reconstruction* (1993); and Eugene Feldman, *Black Power in Old Alabama: The Life and Stirring Times of James T. Rapier* (1968).

LOREN SCHWENINGER

RAPP, George (1 Nov. 1757–7 Aug. 1847), religious leader, was born Johann Georg Rapp in Iptingen, Württemberg, Germany, the son of Hans Adam Rapp and Rosine Berger, farmers. His religious fervor was apparent from early childhood, when he would preach to other children. As a young adult he withdrew from his local Lutheran church because he found it a formal shell of empty rituals, devoid of real spirit in its cold rigidity. Thus he embodied the essential outlook of the Pietists, whose attempt to restore a warm and vital inner spiritual life to the state religion had been making inroads in Germany since the late seventeenth century. Rapp married Christine Benzinger in 1783; they had two children.

By the 1780s Rapp was meeting regularly with others of like mind. His sense of mission and purpose was strong; as early as 1791 he openly declared himself a prophet of God. From 1785 onward he and his followers were investigated by the civil and ecclesiastical authorities of their district and urged to give up their unauthorized meetings. As the conflicts deepened, his notoriety brought him new followers, and soon he had perhaps 10,000 sympathizers and hundreds of dedicated core members, some of whom would walk for hours to attend Sunday and holiday meetings with Rapp.

Like other religious dissenters who chafed at their treatment at the hands of the state church, Rapp eventually came to see emigration as a plausible alternative to seemingly endless confrontations with the German authorities and restrictions on his movement. In the summer of 1803 he, along with his son Johannes and two other associates, took a scouting trip to the United States to investigate prospects for settlement there. Soon he sent word for others to join them, and in 1804 the first large group of dissenting separatists, 300 strong, left Württemberg for the United States. Hundreds more undertook the journey later that year and in 1805. Their original plan had been to settle in Ohio, but land acquisition there proved problematic, and finally they located a suitable tract near Pittsburgh, Pennsylvania, where at the beginning of 1805 they began to build the communal town they called Harmony (or Harmonie; the German and English spellings were used interchangeably). The group had experienced neither communal living nor pooled finances in Germany, but from its beginning in the United States the movement was fully communal. Those who joined the organization, which soon came to be called the Harmony Society, signed over to the group all their money and possessions.

The first few years at Harmony were a time of struggle, as some 700 settlers tried to support themselves through farming and the operation of a store and hotel. Rapp's visionary leadership sustained the believers, however; the congregation building its utopia on the American frontier was, he taught, the Sun Woman of Revelation 12:1–6:

And a great portent appeared in heaven, a woman clothed with the sun, with the moon under her feet, and on her head a crown of twelve stars. . . . She brought forth a male child, one who is to rule all the nations with a rod of iron, but her child was caught up to God and to his throne, and the woman fled into the wilderness, where she has a place prepared by God, in which to be nourished for one thousand two hundred and sixty days.

Rapp's millennial expectations were not unusual; many in his day believed that world events suggested that the end of history as we know it was approaching rapidly. For Rapp, however, the imminent coming of the great tribulations that would mark the beginning of the end demanded total consecration on the part of the believer. His congregation would survive the disasters that were to precede the millennium and then, soon, would live with Christ in glory for a thousand years. For such a grand reward no sacrifice was too great. Mindful of the great future promised them by their pastor, the Harmonists worked diligently to build their communal town, quickly erecting dozens of homes and buildings for agriculture and industry.

Soon they also, at Rapp's direction, adopted celibacy as a fitting regimen for a congregation whose members had experienced a high calling from God. Like so many other monastics and millennialists before them, they (or at least Rapp) determined that their quest for holiness would be most fruitful if they transcended sexual relations. As millenialists they saw reproduction as mattering little; with the advent of Christ at hand, why were new babies needed? The move of the community into celibacy occurred over time, and the practice was theoretically voluntary, although it soon became normative behavior; the nonconformists who continued to indulge their fleshly desires tended to leave the society.

The Harmonists from the first had some dissatisfaction with the land on which they lived and worked. It lacked access to a navigable river; the farmland was not very fertile; the climate seemed harsh; increasing population threatened the community's isolation. In April 1814 Rapp and others headed west to search for a new location for the community and soon located and purchased a tract on the Wabash River in southwestern Indiana that seemed ideal. Society members immediately began to move to the new location and to build a new utopia from scratch, again in the remote wilderness. By 1815 the original Harmony had been sold and all of its residents relocated in Indiana in a community again called Harmony. The Sun Woman had again fled into the wilderness.

Another migration from Württemberg in 1817 swelled the Harmonist ranks to around 900 souls, and under Rapp's powerful spiritual leadership (augmented by the administrative acumen of his adopted son Frederick Rapp, who ran the community's business side) the Harmony Society, with its dedicated workers who ran a wide variety of thriving industries, prospered in its new home. The log cabins that had housed the first Indiana settlers soon gave way to substantial brick edifices—houses, dormitories, stores, and an imposing church at the center of the village. The community had an active intellectual and cultural life. At George Rapp's direction vegetable and flower gardens were established everywhere, and trellises for grapes climbed the sides of many buildings, providing some of the raw materials for one substantial Harmonist industry, the manufacture and sale of wine, beer, and liquor—always of the highest quality. A five-acre public garden produced fruit, vegetables, and herbs; at its center was a labyrinth of hedge bushes, manifesting Rapp's teaching that the path to salvation was difficult and confusing, and at the center of the labyrinth was a rustic little hut, whose unexpected presence taught the basic theological tenet that God's truth is not always what we expect it to be.

Undergirding all else in Harmony was the profound religious commitment that George Rapp both preached and embodied, the commitment to living a Christlike life in full harmony with one's fellows. The Kingdom of God was understood to be at hand, and the Harmonists intended to be in the kingdom's vanguard. The strict rules that governed Harmonist daily life helped separate the righteous elect from the worldly majority who were hopelessly caught up in vice and sin.

Despite the prosperity of the Indiana Harmony, some problems gnawed at the society, especially in its relations with its neighbors, who widely disapproved of the Harmonists' celibacy, pacifism, and retention of German language and culture. Envy was undoubtedly a component of the neighbors' ill feelings, for the Harmonists were far better educated and more prosperous than their neighbors, frontier settlers and farmers all. For their part the Harmonists found their unsaved neighbors crude and even physically threatening; Rapp himself at one point said that he remained close to his own house out of fear that local hooligans would attack him. The believers were also unhappy with the Harmony site, whose location on the bottom land of a major river seemed unhealthful. Thus the idea of leaving the utopia on the Wabash was not unthinkable.

After a decade at the Indiana Harmony, George Rapp claimed to receive another divine message commanding that the Sun Woman flee yet again, and in 1824 he secured a third communal location—in Pennsylvania, just a few miles from the original Harmony, but this time right on the Ohio River, which provided ideal access for trade with the outside world. Rapp named this final communal village Economy, evoking the "divine economy" the Harmonists intended to embody in their village—a true and perfect city of God. The sale of the Indiana site, with its good-sized town and more than 20,000 acres of land, proved easy. Robert Owen, the enlightened Scottish industrialist sometimes regarded as the father of modern socialism, was just then looking for a place to start a secular utopian society, and he readily purchased the Rappite holdings. He rechristened the town New Harmony, the name by which it has been known since, and invited would-be communitarians to join him, but for a variety of reasons the communal phase of the Owenite New Harmony ended after about two years.

As had been the case twice before, under George Rapp's personal direction the new settlers at Economy cleared land and built their town and farms. Water was brought in from mountain springs through more than a mile of pipe made of hollowed-out tree trunks. By the fall of 1824 the industrious communitarians had built a dozen houses, a store, and agricultural and industrial buildings. Members of the society moved in stages, some lingering at the Indiana Harmony to close down operations there and others moving on to build the new Economy, but by the early summer of 1825 the move was complete. Soon the new communal village was thriving.

Rapp lived more than two decades as leader of the final Harmonist enclave, and those latter years were the most prosperous of all. The community's industries were so productive and profitable that the Harmonists eventually amassed great wealth. Athough Rapp expected an imminent millennium, he also sought to preserve his community's well-being until its arrival, as he feared that Jacksonian economics might prove disastrous. Thus he quietly collected a large hoard of gold and silver in a secret vault under his house; by the time of his death in 1847 the vault contained more than $500,000. The celibate community slowly declined in numbers as members died and were not replaced by many new converts, and the strictness of communal life chafed on some members as the millennium seemed not to draw closer, but several good decades marked the final Pennsylvania sojourn.

Rapp's one great error of judgment took place in these latter years of his life. One Bernhard Müller, who styled himself "Maximilian Comte de Leon," wrote to Rapp in September 1831, announcing that he had arrived to unite and lead all true believers dedicated to living the true Christian life. Amazingly, the aging George Rapp accepted Müller's grand claims, which fortuitously dovetailed with Rapp's millennial speculations, and declared him the future leader of the Harmonists; the colonists prepared for a triumphant visit from their new superior a few weeks later. Müller in the flesh appeared regal indeed, a penetratingly handsome man whose bearing and ability to deal with people were unsurpassed. Rapp, however, was puzzled by the newcomer and agonized for some time over the earlier judgment he had made, eventually withdrawing his endorsement of Müller. However, some discontent quite unrelated to Müller's presence was afoot within the community, largely among persons tired of the austerity and strict discipline they had so long endured. The upshot was that Müller won over a third of the Harmonists to himself and, when he left Economy in March 1832, took his new followers with him. Moreover, after much contention Müller and his new followers managed to receive a financial settlement of $105,000. They purchased land nearby in Phillipsburgh (now Monaca), Pennsylvania, and founded their own short-lived utopian community called the New Philadelphia Congregation.

The Harmonist treasury was not, however, seriously depleted by the settlement with Müller and those who departed with him, and soon life at Economy was essentially back to normal, with Rapp firmly at the helm. In fact a new spirit of dedication infused the colonists, who had managed to repel a false Christ who would have led them astray. Reverses did afflict the colony, as when the woolen factory, the most important community industry, burned in 1833, or when the gifted businessman Frederick Rapp died the following year. George Rapp did take one momentous step at about the time of his son's death: the society's membership was closed, on the grounds that its members had over their many years of dedication achieved such a level of spiritual advancement that no new joiner could ever expect to catch up to them and also because those existing members had built the prosperity of the society with their own hard labors and should not be expected to share their wealth with newcomers, among whom opportunists might lurk, especially in the event of the national economic collapse Rapp thought likely.

Although the Harmony Society was long-lived and quite unified under its strong leader, Rapp did have his detractors. Critics saw him as an absolute dictator who held his ignorant subjects in virtual slavery and, given the Harmonists' prosperity, as avaricious, the latter perception stemming from both the society's prosperity and Rapp's refusal to repay to departing members the assets they donated upon joining, not to mention compensation for their work as members. Overall, however, the society had a low defection rate, and clearly the general consensus was that Rapp was, as he claimed, a prophet of God.

The last decade of the Harmony Society before the death of Rapp was a time of quiet prosperity. The final words of the great communitarian reflect the abiding faith that always permeated his outlook: "If I did not so fully believe that the Lord has designed me to place our society before his presence in the land of Canaan, I would consider this my last." He was buried like all other believers in an unmarked grave in the community cemetery.

The Harmonists had many notable activities after Rapp's death. Their business successes continued as they became early oil-industry pioneers and builders of railroads. The great wealth of the society, however, was dissipated by John Duss, who had lived at Economy as a child and was accepted as a member when he returned in 1890. Duss spent lavish amounts on pet projects, emptying the society's once brimming treasury. In 1905, the society's celibate membership having dwindled to a handful, it and Economy were dissolved. Today Harmony, New Harmony, and Economy are maintained as museum villages.

Rapp founded and led one of the most important intentional communities in American history. His ideas and organization have been studied ever since by those who would build successful communes.

• Harmony Society archival collections are in the Pennsylvania Historical and Museum Commission in Harrisburg and at the library of Pennsylvania State University in State College. The most extensive biography of Rapp is Karl J. R. Arndt, *George Rapp's Harmony Society, 1785–1847*, rev. ed. (1972). Arndt published a lengthy series of volumes on the Harmony Society, most of which are collections of Harmonist documents. All of the volumes covering the period up to 1847 have extensive primary materials concerning Rapp. See, for example, Arndt, *A Documentary History of the Indiana Decade of the Harmony Society, 1814–1824*, 2 vols. (1978). Several monographs and articles on New Harmony, Indiana, contain substantial material on Rapp; see, for example, William E. Wilson, *The Angel and the Serpent: The Story of New Harmony* (1964), and Donald E. Pitzer and Josephine M. Elliott, "New Harmony's First Utopians," *Indiana Magazine of History* 75, no. 3 (Sept. 1979). Hilda Adam Kring, *The Harmonists: A Folk-Cultural Approach* (1973), contains information on Rapp's theological outlook and his role in the Harmony Society.

TIMOTHY MILLER

RAPP, Wilhelm (14 July 1827–1 Mar. 1907), German-American leader and journalist, was born in Leonberg, Württemberg, Germany, the son of Georg Rapp, a Protestant minister, and Augusta (maiden name unknown). He studied theology, first in a seminary at Blaubeuren, then with the theological faculty at Tübingen. While a student at Tübingen, he was swept up in the revolutionary movements of 1848 in the German states. In May 1849 he was elected by the Democratic Society of Tübingen as a delegate to the revolutionary Peoples Assembly at Reutlingen. He also joined a group of students in the uprising in Baden. After this failed he fled to Switzerland, where he taught for a time in a private school in Ilanz in the canton of Graubünden. In the summer of 1850 Rapp secretly visited his family in Württemberg, whereupon he was apprehended and held for a year in the prison of Hohenasperg, near Ludwigsburg. In 1852 he followed other refugees of the 1848 revolutions to the United States.

Upon arriving in Philadelphia in 1852, Rapp worked as a laborer and tutor; in 1853 he accepted editorship of the *Turn-Zeitung*, the organ of the Turnerbund, the newly formed national association of Turner gymnastic and cultural societies. When that publication was moved from Philadelphia to Cincinnati in 1855, Rapp went with it. In 1855–1856 he also served as the president of the North American Turnerbund.

When the Republican party arose in the 1850s to oppose the spread of slavery, Rapp became a supporter and advocate of the party among the Germans. In 1857 he took over the editorship of the *Baltimore Wecker*, a German Republican paper in a state generally hostile to Republicans and free-soil advocates. Despite threats from local prosouthern groups, Rapp aggressively espoused the Republican cause, raising the concern of the publisher of the *Wecker*, Wilhelm Schnauffer. Ignoring Schnauffer's cautions, Rapp campaigned for Abraham Lincoln in 1860, braving one hostile mob that threw eggs at him at a rally. In early 1861, as southern states began to secede and prosouthern forces gained strength in Baltimore, Rapp was the object of additional threats. The firing upon Fort Sumter further provoked southern sympathizers in Baltimore. On the night of 19 April 1861, prosecessionist riots broke out in the city, and a crowd gathered at the *Wecker* offices, shouting, "We want Rapp." Rapp escaped but the rioters broke down the door and wrecked the plant. Rapp was urged by his supporters to flee the city; he shaved off his beard and went in disguise to Washington, D.C.

Rapp received a sympathetic hearing from the Lincoln administration, which offered him a post in the customs house or the post office; he declined, instead accepting an offer to join the editorial staff of the *Illinois Staats-Zeitung*, the strongly Republican Chicago newspaper. In 1866 he accepted an invitation to return to Baltimore, and he once again became editor of the *Wecker*, this time as part owner of the paper. He married Gesine Budelmann in 1869; they had four children.

In 1872 Rapp sold his share of the *Wecker* and returned to Chicago (which was then rebuilding from the Great Fire of 1871) to become associate editor of the *Illinois Staats-Zeitung*, whose publisher was now the prominent Chicago German politician Anton C. Hesing. When editor Hermann Raster died in 1891, Rapp became the chief editor of the paper, and he remained in that office until his death at his home in Chicago. He was among the last of the generation of 1848 immigrants to remain active in German-American journalism.

Throughout his career Rapp held to the ideals of the revolutions of 1848, and he felt that the same ideals had accomplished the preservation of the Union in the American Civil War. When the German states became unified as the German Empire during the Franco-Prussian War in 1870, Rapp, still in Baltimore, celebrated the event in a public speech, and encouraged his fellow "forty-eighters" to accept the fact that unity was achieved under the once-despised rule of Prussia. When the forty-eighters celebrated the twenty-fifth anniversary of their arrival in America at a festival in Chicago in 1874, Rapp told his fellow refugees that the new German unity would become the basis for a new German freedom: "we are the victorious defeated of 1848 and 1849," he said.

As a journalist, Rapp had a talent for understanding and speaking to a mass readership. He was acknowledged as an influential and persuasive orator for the same reason. Although he wrote extensively on politics, he was also a frequent writer on literary and cultural matters and an advocate of the preservation of a strong German culture in America. In 1890 he was a leading force in the German fight against the Illinois legislation known as the Edwards Law, which sought to eliminate the use of German as a language of instruction in the schools. Rapp was among the more influential of German forty-eighters at rallying the support of the German-American populace.

• A letter by Rapp describing his 1861 flight from Baltimore is Alice Finckh, trans., "Baltimore 1861: We Want Rapp," *Society for the History of Germans in Maryland, Annual Report* 28 (1953): 79–82. Rapp published a collections of his speeches and travel accounts about Germany as *Erinnerungen eines Deutsch-Amerikaners an das alte Vaterland* (1890). Memorial pieces are Emil Mannhardt, "Wilhelm Rapp," *Deutsch-Amerikanische Geschichtsblätter* 7 (1907): 58–61; Carl Haerting, "In Memoriam: Wilhelm Rapp, Leben und Kämpfen eines deutschen Idealisten in Amerika," *Die Glocke* 2 (1907): 33–35; and Wilhelm Vocke, "Erinnerungen an Wilhelm Rapp," *Die Glocke* 2 (1907): 115–20. Another account of his journalistic career is in the jubilee issue of the *Illinois Staats-Zeitung*, 21 Apr. 1898. An obituary is in the *Chicago Tribune*, 2 Mar. 1907.

JAMES M. BERGQUIST

RAREY, John Solomon (6 Dec. 1827–4 Oct. 1866), "Great American Horse Tamer," was born in Groveport, Ohio, the son of Adam Rarey, a farmer and tavern keeper, and Mary Catherine Pontius. A Methodist, Rarey attended Ohio Wesleyan University.

Introduced to horse taming as a farm boy, Rarey was seriously injured in early attempts to train horses forcibly. After softening his approach, he attracted clients as early as age twelve. To test and refine his developing theories of gentler training, Rarey consulted other tamers but found their methods unsatisfactory.

Rarey in 1855 visited the Texas plains to observe the breaking practices of westerners and American Indians. Satisfied that his gentle discipline conserved both horses and people, he gave an exhibition in which he tamed five of the most notorious horses in the Southwest.

Returning to Groveport, Rarey trained a pair of bull elk to a surrey to advertise his lectures on kindness. He outlined his methods in *The Modern Art of Taming Wild Horses* (1855). His work attracted R. A. Goodenough, described as a "Toronto general dealer." Goodenough offered to manage Rarey's performances, beginning with one before Ohio governor Salmon P. Chase. Chase's letter of introduction gained Rarey access to General Sir William Eyre, commander in chief of British forces in Canada. Eyre, seeing a military value in Rarey's system, introduced him to Sir Richard Airey, quartermaster general of the Horse Guards in England.

On his arrival in England in November 1857, Rarey's fame brought him an invitation for the first of four performances before Queen Victoria. A second (Jan. 1858) was for international royalty invited, like Rarey, to the wedding of Victoria's oldest daughter. Despite royal backing, however, Rarey attracted students slowly.

In March-April 1858 Rarey was challenged to tame Lord Dorchester's notorious six-year-old stallion, Cruiser. Rarey's taming of the abused thoroughbred, and later of an "untameable" zebra, was followed by numerous endorsements. They included Lord Palmerston, the politician; Richard Tattersall, the horse broker; and Henry Hall "the Druid" Dixon, the sporting journalist. Even though jealous competitors charged him with cruelty and hypnotism, Rarey attracted 2,000 students, who each paid ten guineas to be instructed. His insistence that he came "not as a gladiator but as an educator" attracted women, who comprised half or more of his students.

Rarey at first held students to a vow of secrecy, giving each a copy of his book. Sensing a profit, Routledge & Company pirated a sixpenny edition of the book, selling 110,000 copies. (Pirated, plagiarized, adulterated, and adapted, Rarey's book had at least forty editions published between 1855 and 1904 and was translated into eight foreign languages.) Although he was forced to release his students from their vow and parted with the "boastful Goodenough" in August 1858, Rarey's fame bounded. He was even immortalized in Staffordshire pottery figurines.

Rarey traveled to France, Sweden, Germany, Russia, and Hungary, giving demonstrations before crowned heads and citizens. A three-month tour took him through Italy to Egypt, Palestine, Syria, Iraq, and Turkey. His farewell lecture in England (Oct. 1860) attracted 8,000 people.

Rarey helped Lord Palmerston market his horses and shared his appreciation for illegal bareknuckled fistfights, supporting the last such on British soil, between American John Carmel Heenan and Briton Tom Sayers on 17 April 1860. Rarey's popularity was said to have helped defuse virulent anti-American feeling in Great Britain and Europe.

In November 1860 Rarey returned—with numerous awards and $100,000—to a welcoming parade in New York City. A full schedule of teaching demonstrations, some with Cushing's Circus, took Rarey throughout the eastern and midwestern states and Cuba. Many of his earnings were donated to charity and church.

Officials of the Union army, like those in the British military, recognized that Rarey's methods would save men and horseflesh, so in 1862 they invited him to teach the Union cavalry. His Groveport home was visited by General William T. Sherman in recognition of Rarey's support of the Union army and his charity performances for Union army widows and orphans.

Rarey's plans for a treatise on the horse and for national awards promoting kindness in horse management were never realized. Worn from travel, performances, and social duties, he suffered a stroke in December 1865, which left him palsied. He died during a visit to Cleveland the next year. Cruiser, brought from England and standing at stud at the Rarey farm, died in 1875 at the age of twenty-three.

Rarey's gentling and taming of unbroken, spoiled horses anticipated much of today's applied ethology. The horse, he argued, must be rid of fear before it can learn or be rehabilitated, and then treated with firm kindness to establish confidence and obedience. Rarey's horses were encouraged to use their senses of smell, sight, taste, and touch to evaluate their handlers and gain confidence. The Rarey Strap, to hobble a foreleg and then cast the horse, used the horse's sense of submission when balance was lost and prepared it to rely on its handler. He was careful to stress that his system was "not a license to torment"—though many would use it so. Like I. P. Pavlov fifty years later, Rarey emphasized that a badly handled animal could be expected to revert.

Rarey's insistence on the existence of equine intelligence—influenced by debates with the Reverend John G. Wood, a campaigner for animal protection—predated behavioral theories by almost 100 years. His studies confirmed that a species exhibits the same requirements and behaviors wherever bred and raised, allowing a uniform approach to their welfare; they also confirmed the value of short lessons and latent learning. He recognized displacement behaviors and the voice's effect on a horse and used what today's ethologists refer to as habituation, personal space, and flight distance (how close a perceived threat can approach before the animal flees or fights).

Abolitionist William Lloyd Garrison cited Rarey's work as teaching "a great and everywhere needed lesson of humanity." Rarey gave early humane societies a much-needed boost. His emphasis on kindness also influenced treatment of the insane, who had been isolated and chained. Mid-nineteenth century educationist John S. Hart incorporated Rarey's philosophy in his writings and work with pupils. "Rareyfy" entered the dictionary to mean taming a horse by kindness.

By the twentieth century Rarey's system was approved in many cavalry manuals, and at the end of the century it was still used by East Anglia's secret Brotherhood of Horsemen and by tamers everywhere. In addition to horse training and veterinary texts, animal behavior studies have continued to describe elements of the system. In 1979 the veterinary writer Matthew Mackay-Smith called Rarey "the greatest horseman of all time."

• In a collection at the Ohio Historical Society, Columbus, are twenty-one pieces of Rarey's correspondence, sketches by the British cartoonist John Leech, press clippings relative to Rarey's trip to Europe in 1858–1860, and an item by Sara Lowe Brown, a relative.
The Sporting Library of the Racquet and Tennis Club, New York City, has the largest collection of editions of Rarey's works, including plagiarized ones, as well as papers and clippings relating to Rarey's career. Its former librarian, R. W. Henderson, published a thorough study of these in *Bookmen's Holiday,* ed. D. Fulton (1943). See also Ellen B. Wells, "Mr Punch and Mr Rarey," *Chronicle of the Horse,* 19 Dec. 1979, pp. 28–29. Brown published some details of Rarey's life and work in *Rarey: The Horse's Master and Friend* (1916) and *The Horse Cruiser and the Rarey Method of Training Horses* (1925).
The National Sporting Library, Middleburg, Va., has the *Cruiser Courier* (1975–1977), a newsletter about Rarey's life, times, and works. The University of Guelph, Ontario, holds copies of *Equine Behaviour,* a semiannual journal frequently touching on Rarey's work. A chapter in George Ewart Evans, *Horse Power and Magic* (1979), discusses the impact of Rarey on horse tamers, as does Josephine Haworth, *The Horsemasters* (1983). E. W. Hayter, *The Troubled Farmer* (1968), details the cruelty to horses and other animals that Rarey challenged.
Dennis Magner, a well-known tamer in the generation following Rarey's, questioned Rarey's reputation in *Facts for Horse Owners* (1894). Magner credited Goodenough with all Rarey's successes and attributed many of the adulterated taming books—which frequently added cruel practices—to Rarey. Magner's claims are unsubstantiated. Obituaries are in *Sporting Review* 56 (Nov. 1866): 317–30 and the *Cork Examiner,* no. 5285, 25 Oct. 1866.

SHARON E. CREGIER

RASCH, Albertina (c. 1891–2 Oct. 1967), ballerina and choreographer, was born in Vienna, Austria, to a family of Polish Jews who were traveling players. Her parents' names are not known. Rasch entered the Imperial Ballet School in Vienna at the age of seven and progressed rapidly, performing solo variations by the age of fourteen. American producer R. H. Burnside

saw her perform at the Royal Opera House and convinced her to come to the United States, where she appeared in 1911 at the New York Hippodrome in the musical comedy *The International Cup.* During this period ballet in the United States was usually performed in reviews and vaudeville, and for the next twelve years Rasch performed on Broadway, in vaudeville productions, and as a guest ballerina with opera companies, including the Metropolitan and the Chicago Opera. Her vaudeville engagements on the Keith-Orpheum Circuit included a corps de ballet.

In 1922 Rasch returned to Europe for a concert tour, and in 1923 she studied with Émile Jaques-Dalcroze, a teacher of eurythmics, in Switzerland and with the choreographer Mary Wigman in Germany. These studies strongly influenced her later choreography. When Rasch returned to New York at the end of 1923, she opened her first dance studio; the girls she trained there became the Albertina Rasch Dancers, who appeared in everything from revues to operas. For the New York Hippodrome shows, the group was expanded to fifty dancers; they performed the first staging of George Gershwin's *Rhapsody in Blue* in 1925. In 1929 Rasch choreographed the first ballet ever staged to Gershwin's *An American in Paris* for Harriet Hoctor and the corps de ballet in the musical *Show Girl.* Rasch was encouraged in her experimentations with jazz music and classical ballet by composer-conductor Dimitri Tiomkin, who became her husband in 1927; they had no children. That year her dancers were featured in five Broadway shows, including *The Ziegfeld Follies* and *Rio Rita,* and Rasch toured the United States with her American Ballet. According to newspaper accounts and interviews, Rasch wanted to establish a permanent American Ballet Company that would combine European training with "the innate esthetic rhythm of the American masses" and become a "New World" ballet. Perhaps owing to her many other commitments, including Broadway shows and movie musicals, Rasch was never able to run the company with any regularity, but her dancers continued to perform in concerts into the 1930s, especially at the Hollywood Bowl.

The 1930s marked the peak of Rasch's career; she choreographed shows on Broadway and in London, ran dance studios in New York and Hollywood, produced concert tours, and choreographed movies for Metro-Goldwyn-Mayer (MGM). In a business dominated by male dance directors, this was a unique achievement. Her Broadway shows include *The Band Wagon* (1931) for Adele Astaire and Fred Astaire. The choreography included a jazzy, syncopated duet called "White Heat"; Fred Astaire's only stage "dream ballet," "The Beggar's Waltz," which he performed with ballerina Tilly Losch; and the dramatic "Dancing in the Dark" for Losch and corps de ballet, with a double revolving stage and slanted platforms. After seeing Rasch's choreography for the show, Brooks Atkinson asserted in the *New York Times* that "it will be difficult for the old-time musical show to hold up its head" (4 June 1931). John Martin, the dance critic for the

Times, was so impressed by Rasch's choreography for *The Ziegfeld Follies of 1931* that he devoted a special column to discussing the higher standards she had brought to the Broadway musical. Other important stage musicals choreographed by Rasch include Jerome Kern's *The Cat and the Fiddle* (1931), *The Great Waltz* (1934, New York; 1935, London), and Cole Porter's *Jubilee* (1935), which introduced "Begin the Beguine" with Rasch's sensuous choreography for June Knight and Charles Walters.

During this period Rasch also commuted to Hollywood, where her dancers were featured in many early talking pictures, predominantly at MGM. These include *The Hollywood Revue of 1929*, for which Rasch insisted that her dancers be photographed in an overhead shot (before Busby Berkeley); *Sally* (1929), in which her ballet troupe, on loan-out to Warner Bros., supported the important Ziegfeld star Marilyn Miller in her first motion picture; and *The Rogue Song* (1930), which features Metropolitan Opera star Lawrence Tibbett. Rasch also choreographed a series of short films, frequently using Tiomkin's music; the films were unusual early experiments with dance and camera photography. After 1934 she became the primary choreographer for the Jeanette MacDonald operettas, including *The Merry Widow* (1934), for which Rasch was the very first to receive screen credit as a choreographer, considered a more artistic title than "Dance Director"; *The Firefly* (1937), which includes intricate Spanish dances for MacDonald and chorus; *The Girl of the Golden West* (1938), which features the Rasch dancers in the elaborate "Mariache" [sic] number; and *Sweethearts* (1938), the first three-strip technicolor film at MGM. The last two films feature MacDonald's popular costar Nelson Eddy, who had previously worked with Rasch on *Rosalie* (1937). For *Rosalie*, Rasch used one of the largest group of dancers ever assembled, in the elaborate birthday celebrations for the Princess Rosalie, played by dancing star Eleanor Powell. Two other important films choreographed by Rasch and produced by MGM include the drama *Marie Antoinette*, starring Norma Shearer (1938), for which Rasch staged all the court festivities, and *The Great Waltz* (1938), in which the Rasch dances were a highlight of this fictionalized story of the Strauss family. Rasch supervised the filming of all her dances, frequently without the director of the film being present; she was the only female dance director in Hollywood to be given such authority.

In 1941 Rasch returned to Broadway to choreograph the dances for Kurt Weill's *Lady in the Dark*, starring Gertrude Lawrence. Rasch made each of the heroine's dreams a cohesive dance-story, a precursor to the dream ballet that Agnes de Mille would stage in *Oklahoma!* in 1943. Rasch's last Broadway musical was *Marinka*, which opened in 1945. Owing to failing health, that same year she returned to Hollywood where she lived with her husband until her death at the Motion Picture County Hospital in Woodland Hills, California.

Rasch was successful working in many mediums, and her style is marked by an unusual eclecticism and adaptability. Her Broadway choreography broke the barriers between classical ballet and modern jazz styles. Rasch's Hollywood choreography, especially after 1933, reflected a return to her Austrian roots, since she specialized in character, social, and ballet dances for operettas. Her concert work combined both jazz and ballet but on a very large scale; some dances were choreographed for forty dancers or more and, while impressive, were economically unfeasible. As a teacher and choreographer, Rasch was known to be a strict disciplinarian, decisive and even ruthless. She paved the way for the combination of European ballet with American jazz styles.

• The most extensive survey of Rasch's career is the series of articles by Frank W. D. Ries in *Dance Chronicle*: "Albertina Rasch: The Broadway Career," 6, no. 2 (1983): 95–137; "Albertina Rasch: The Hollywood Career," 6, no. 4 (1983): 281–362; and "Albertina Rasch: The Concert Career and the Concept of the American Ballet," 7, no. 2 (1984): 159–97. Information is also included in Dimitri Tiomkin's autobiography, *Please Don't Hate Me* (1959); Stanley Green, *Ring Bells! Sing Songs! Broadway Musicals of the 1930's* (1971); Eleanor Knowles, *The Films of Jeanette MacDonald and Nelson Eddy* (1975); and Clive Hirschhorn, *The Hollywood Musical* (1981). Most of the films Rasch worked on are available on video and laser disk. An obituary is in *Variety*, 4 Oct. 1967.

FRANK W. D. RIES

RASKIN, Judith (21 June 1928–21 Dec. 1984), operatic soprano, was born in New York City, the daughter of Harry A. Raskin, a high school music teacher, and Lillian Mendelson, a grade school teacher. As a youth she attended public schools and took piano and violin lessons. On 11 July 1948, she married Raymond A. Raskin, a psychiatrist; they had two children.

Raskin majored in music at Smith College, graduating in 1949. Supported by the Harriet Dey Barnum Scholarship, she took voice lessons from Anna Hamlin, daughter of the American tenor George Hamlin, who performed with the Chicago Opera Association (1911–1916). At the same time she also studied acting with Ludwig Donath. Married at twenty, Raskin had a family before her career began, the first major chapter of which was when she won the prestigious Marian Anderson Award in 1952 and 1953. In 1956 she created the title role in the premiere of Douglas Moore's *The Ballad of Baby Doe* with the Central City Opera in Colorado. She repeated that role when the New York City Opera produced the work in 1960. Her debut with the NBC Opera in 1957 was as Susanna in *Le Nozze di Figaro*. During the summer of 1958 she sang with the Santa Fe Opera in *La Bohème*, *Così fan tutte*, *Capriccio*, and *La Cenerentola*; she returned in 1961 and 1968. In Dallas, she also sang in *La Traviata* (a new Zeffirelli production) and *Medea*, with Maria Callas.

Raskin attracted a great deal of favorable attention from the New York critics for her performance in the revival of Rossini's *Le Comte Ory* at the Juilliard

School of Music in March 1959. Between 1959 and 1964 she appeared with the American Opera Society in such works as Handel's *Samson*. Her New York City Opera debut was as Despina in Mozart's *Così fan tutte* (1959). She made her Metropolitan Opera debut as Susanna in *Le Nozze di Figaro* in February 1962, with Giorgio Tozzi as Figaro, and she was praised for her exquisite phrasing and charming good looks. At this point in her career she was compared favorably with the legendary Elisabeth Schumann. She captivated the audience as Nannetta in Franco Zeffirelli's 1964 production of *Falstaff*, conducted by Leonard Bernstein. Her Sophie in Richard Strauss's *Der Rosenkavalier* the following season added to her growing reputation as a delightful young artist. In her eleven seasons with the Met, she sang eighty-eight performances of seven different roles. During that same period she also starred as Pamina in *Die Zauberflöte* at Glyndebourne (1963, 1964), with Ragnar Ulfung as Tamino.

Raskin's major TV roles include Sister Constance in the American premiere of Poulenc's *Les dialogues des Carmélites* (1957), Marzelline in Beethoven's *Fidelio* (1959), and Zerlina in Mozart's *Don Giovanni* (1960), with a cast that included Cesare Siepi and Leontyne Price. In the premiere of Leonard Kastle's opera *Deseret* (1961) she created the role of Ann Brice, a young woman married to the elder Brigham Young. She also appeared in Bach's *St. Matthew Passion* (1963), created the role of the Wife in the premiere of Gian Carlo Menotti's *Labyrinth* (1963), for which she earned critical acclaim, and starred as Pamina in Mozart's *Die Zauberflöte*, which utilized the cast from the Glyndebourne production (1964). Her recording credits include Anne Trulove in the 1964 CBS pressing of Stravinsky's *The Rake's Progress*, with the composer conducting; the 1965 RCA *Orfeo ed Euridice*, with Shirley Verrett and Anna Moffo; and the 1967 RCA *Così fan tutte*, with Leontyne Price, Tatiana Troyanos, George Shirley, and Sherrill Milnes.

Raskin had a natural and unforced appeal, both as a singer and as an actress, and she was especially noted for her refined musicianship and purity of sound. Possessing a lyric soprano voice with the ability to comfortably negotiate florid passages, she aimed at a poetic approach to music rather than a purely vocal approach. Perhaps because of her strong liberal arts education, she worked hard at becoming the complete artist. She was very good at creating the character she was playing, but she felt this ability was purely instinctual, purely emotional. Her vocal technique and stage movements, however, were the result of hard and unremitting work. Never known to exceed her own limitations, she excelled in the roles she chose to master. With an unusual affinity for Baroque music, she was noted for her performances of Monteverdi's *L'Orfeo* and *L'incoronazione di Poppea* as well as the operas of Handel (the 1971 American premiere of *Ariodante* in a concert version in Carnegie Hall) and Rameau (*Les Indes galantes*, 1961). Her career in the Metropolitan Opera included 105 performances from her 1962 de-

but as Susanna in Mozart's *Le Nozze di Figaro* to her farewell performance on 16 March 1972.

One of the few singers who was equally at home on the operatic stage and in the recital hall, Raskin made her New York recital debut in the Grace Rainey Rogers Auditorium of the Metropolitan Museum of Art in October 1964, where she premiered Ezra Laderman's thirty-minute song cycle *Songs of Eve*, with text by Archibald MacLeish. In her concerts she programmed a wide range of material, including the premieres of several song cycles by Miriam Gideon. In later years her performances were curtailed by illness, and she turned to teaching voice at City College, the Manhattan School of Music, and Mannes College of Music. She died of cancer in New York City after a long struggle with the disease. Of her career, Raskin said: "We never really know what history is going to say about our careers. In my case, though the voice was most important to me in the beginning, I think the thing that will be interesting to remember will be the fact that I had so many involvements." Although opportunities were always available outside of New York City, it is clear that the artist's family was her primary consideration, and she preferred not to travel and be away from home. Given her priorities, Raskin's notable career is a tribute to her ability to balance her many involvements.

• Raskin authored two articles for *Opera News*: "American Bel Canto," 15 Jan. 1966, p. 6, and "How Does a Singer Do It?" 22 Feb. 1969, pp. 28–31. Obituaries are in the *New York Times*, 22 Dec. 1984, and *Opera News*, June 1985.

ROBERT H. COWDEN

RASKOB, John Jakob (19 Mar. 1879–15 Oct. 1950), financier, was born in Lockport, New York, the son of John Raskob, a cigar manufacturer, and Anna Frances Moran. After attending Clark's Business College in Lockport, Raskob became secretary to an attorney in 1898 and the following year secured a job as a stenographer with a Lockport manufacturer. Dissatisfied with his pay, in 1899 Raskob followed a friend's advice and moved to Lorain, Ohio, where he worked for Arthur Moxham, a brilliant but little-known businessman who was then managing the steelworks of the Johnson Company, a firm involved in real estate, street railways, and the manufacture of related equipment. When Moxham later that year moved to Nova Scotia to run a mill, Raskob moved there also to continue working for him. However, Raskob soon grew homesick and in 1900 returned to Lorain, where he secured a position as a bookkeeper and subsequently as a personal secretary to Pierre du Pont, the Johnson Company's manager.

Raskob's quick and agile mind and keen insight into financial matters impressed du Pont, who invited Raskob to accompany him when he moved to Wilmington, Delaware, in 1902 to operate the family firm, E. I. du Pont de Nemours and Company. Pierre and the two cousins who shared control with him initiated a series of mergers and stock acquisitions that quickly elevated the once-small business to a preeminent position in the gunpowder and dynamite industry. By now Pierre's friend as well as his assistant, Raskob participated closely in the intricate financial arrangements undertaken by the firm that, in the process of its expansion, instituted sophisticated methods of corporate management that made unprecedented use of statistical analysis. In 1906 Raskob married Helena Springer Green of Galina, Maryland; they had thirteen children. In later years they maintained separate residences but never divorced.

Raskob's increasing influence in the du Pont company was recognized when he was named treasurer in 1914; he had already been carrying out the duties of treasurer unofficially for several years. In the meantime, he also had become interested in the potential of the automobile industry and had begun investing in General Motors and had persuaded Pierre to do the same. William C. Durant, who got on well with Raskob, was then head of GM, and when a dispute developed between Durant and the bankers who had been financing GM's expansion, in 1915 Raskob was appointed a neutral director on the board chaired by Pierre.

During World War I Raskob directed the financial aspects of the du Pont company's enormous wartime expansion. After the war he resigned his office in the firm to become chairman of the finance committee of General Motors. At the same time, acting on Raskob's recommendation, du Pont used some of its wartime profits to purchase a large block of stock in GM. As finance director, Raskob was expected to and did bring to the automaker the type of modern accounting and auditing methods du Pont had been using in its own operations. Through the use of such methods General Motors became a leader in its field. Raskob also initiated the formation of the General Motors Acceptance Corporation (GMAC), which provided credit to auto dealers and to purchasers, thus allowing dealers to expand their inventories and to sell more cars on credit.

GMAC would eventually prove successful, but the recession of 1920 staggered General Motors. In the ensuing reorganization, the du Ponts and J. P. Morgan and Company provided additional financing on the condition that Durant yield management responsibility to Alfred P. Sloan, Jr., who was believed to possess the superior administrative abilities that Raskob and the other senior executives lacked. Although the reorganization cost Raskob some power in GM, he continued to influence dividend policy and other aspects of financial policymaking. For instance, his input led to the organization in 1922 of the Managers Securities Company, set up to allow several dozen General Motors executives the opportunity to profit from GM's successes and any appreciation in its stock. In the business ethos of the twenties this incentive plan was much praised in financial journals. It upheld Raskob's credo "every employee a partner." Raskob strongly favored other similar plans designed to promote company loyalty and thrift among foremen and employees at large.

In the 1920s Raskob, who had become a millionaire many times over (at times through speculation), increasingly turned his attention to other investments such as the Missouri Pacific Railroad and to writing about financial matters in the popular press. An advocate of installment purchasing, the five-day work week, and the three-day holiday weekend, he became one of the business celebrities of the New Era, whose advice on investments and economic matters received wide attention in the media. In his writings he paid deference to the habit of saving but stressed the relationship between consumption and economic growth. A 1929 interview with Raskob, published under the title "Everybody Ought to Be Rich," was representative of his public utterances.

Friendships with New York governor Alfred E. Smith and some of the men around Smith, such as banker James Riordan, drew Raskob into politics. Like Raskob himself, his new friends were Catholic and either the children or grandchildren of immigrants. They were also, like Raskob, "wet" on the prohibition issue, and the eventual result was that even though Raskob had voted for Calvin Coolidge in 1924 and was listed as a Republican in *Who's Who*, Smith named him head of the Democratic National Committee during the governor's 1928 campaign for the presidency. The appointment was controversial, and Raskob resigned from his remaining posts with GM to concentrate on political matters.

In 1928 Smith and Raskob endeavored to make the Democratic party less dependent on its traditional ties with rural America. Although Smith was soundly defeated, the party gained the loyalty of newly registered voters, the children of the millions of immigrants from Southern and Eastern Europe, in America's largest cities.

After the campaign Raskob remained active in politics, in 1929 establishing the Democratic National Committee's first permanent headquarters in Washington, D.C., with Jouett Shouse as its head. Raskob also joined Smith and others in the corporation that built and managed the Empire State Building. Dissatisfied with the presidency of Franklin D. Roosevelt, whose nomination they had opposed in 1932, Raskob, Smith, and a few other conservatives helped found the American Liberty League in 1934. Although he never regained the prominence he had held in business and political matters between 1914 and 1932, Raskob sought new investments, especially in mining, and remained active in civic affairs and Catholic charities. He died at his farm near Centerville, Maryland.

• Raskob's papers are at the Hagley Museum and Library in Wilmington, Del. Articles written by Raskob include "Installment Purchasing," *Industrial Management* 73 (Feb. 1927): 65–69, and "Management, the Major Factor in All Industry," *Industrial Management* 74 (Sept. 1927): 129–35. Information about Raskob's business activities can be found in Gerard Colby, *Du Pont Dynasty* (1984); Laurence H. Seltzer, *A Financial History of the American Automobile Industry*

(1928); Alfred P. Sloan, Jr., *My Years with General Motors*, ed. John McDonald and Catherine P. Stevens (1963); Bernard A. Weisberger, *The Dream Maker: William C. Durant, Founder of General Motors* (1979); Alfred D. Chandler, Jr., and Stephen Salsbury, *Pierre S. du Pont and the Making of the Modern Corporation* (1971); and Robert Burk, *The Corporate State and the Broker State* (1990). Touching on Raskob's political interests are Douglas B. Craig, *After Wilson: The Struggle for the Democratic Party, 1920–1934* (1993); Elisabeth Israels Perry, *Belle Moskowitz: Feminine Politics and the Exercise of Power in the Age of Alfred E. Smith* (1987); and George Wolfskill, *The Revolt of the Conservatives* (1962). See also Roy Haywood Lopata, "John Jakob Raskob: Conservative Businessman in the Age of Roosevelt" (Ph.D. diss., Univ. of Delaware, 1975). Journal articles include Samuel Crowther, "Everybody Ought to Be Rich: An Interview with John J. Raskob," *Ladies Home Journal*, Aug. 1929, pp. 9 and 36; Samuel Crowther, "John J. Raskob and the World's Largest Business," *World's Work*, Oct. 1920, pp. 612–17; James C. Young, "Raskob of General Motors," *World's Work*, Sept. 1928, pp. 486–92; Robert Cruise McManus, "Raskob," *North American Review* 231 (Jan. 1931): 10–15; and Henry F. Pringle, "John J. Raskob," *Outlook*, 22 Aug. 1928, pp. 645–49. An obituary is in the *New York Times*, 16 Oct. 1950.

LLOYD J. GRAYBAR

RATHBONE, Basil (13 June 1892–21 July 1967), actor, was born Philip St. John Basil Rathbone in Johannesburg, South Africa, the son of British parents Edgar Philip Rathbone, a mining engineer, and Anna Barbara George, a concert violinist and descendant of King Henry IV. The family returned to England after Rathbone was born, and he graduated in 1910 from the Repton School.

After graduating Rathbone announced his intention to become an actor. Less than enthusiastic about his son's choice of occupation, his father persuaded him to spend a year as a junior clerk before contacting his cousin Frank Benson, the founder of the Stratford-upon-Avon Shakespeare festival. Rathbone then began to tour with Benson's second company throughout England, Scotland, and Ireland, playing minor roles and learning the craft of acting. He made his professional debut as Hortensio in the *Taming of the Shrew* in April 1911. The next year Rathbone was promoted to Benson's main company, playing juvenile roles, including Paris in *Romeo and Juliet* and Laertes in *Hamlet*.

In 1914 Rathbone married Ethel Marian Forman, an actress in the company. A year later their only child was born, and that same year Rathbone enlisted in the British army. Commissioned as a second lieutenant, he received a military cross in 1918 for service in France. When World War I ended, Rathbone returned to the theater, but he and his wife separated. In 1919 he was engaged by the New Shakespeare Company in major roles, including Cassius, Romeo, and Florizel.

Rathbone was cast in 1920 in the title role of *Peter Ibbetson*, which opened in February at the Savoy Theatre. He next appeared with Mrs. Patrick Campbell in *Madame Sand* (1920). While these productions were not particularly successful, they brought Rathbone to the attention of motion-picture producer Maurice Elvey. Rathbone made two silent films in 1921 for Elvey, *Innocent* and *The Fruitful Vine*; neither film furthered Rathbone's career in any significant way, and he returned to the theater, where he continued his classical work, appearing at the Royal Court Theatre as Prince Hal and Iago. On the opening night of *Othello*, Rathbone was struck with the hiccups, but reviewers raved about his interpretation of a drunken Iago. He also appeared in nonclassical plays in London, including *The Czarina*, *The Edge o' Beyond*, *East of Suez*, and *R. U. R.* In 1923 Rathbone traveled to New York to play in *The Swan* with Eva La Gallienne and Philip Merivale. *The Swan* ran for 255 performances and catapulted Rathbone to Broadway stardom.

During the run of *The Swan* Rathbone met Ouida Bergere, a Hollywood screenwriter. In 1926 he obtained a divorce from his first wife and married Bergere. They remained married until his death and adopted one child. Rathbone continued performing successfully in the theater until 1929, when his emphasis shifted to film. Rathbone appeared that year in his first talking film, *The Last of Mrs. Cheyney*, and its success instantly made him a sought-after Hollywood actor. In 1930 he appeared in seven motion pictures, of these the most important were *The Bishop Murder Case*, *This Mad World*, and *Sin Takes a Holiday*. Over the next few years Rathbone continued to perform both on the stage and the screen in the United States and England. His more important projects of the next few years were a seven-month tour of the United States playing Robert Browning in the *Barretts of Wimpole Street*, with Katherine Cornell, Romeo in *Romeo and Juliet*, and Morrell in *Candida*. The successful tour was followed by the role of Mr. Murdstone in MGM's film *David Copperfield* (1935).

The Murdstone role launched another phase of Rathbone's film career—for the next few years he was typecast as the villain. Rathbone himself said, "Murdstone has haunted me ever since I played him. I am one of the best equipped actors today, because of my experience . . . but it's closed instead of opening doors for me" (*In and Out of Character*, p. 123). Some of these villainous film roles were the Marquis St. Evremonde in *A Tale of Two Cities* (1935); Sir Guy of Gisbourne in *The Adventures of Robin Hood* (1938); Richard III in *Tower of London* (1939); and Pasquale in *The Mark of Zorro* (1940). Biographer Michael Druxman called Rathbone's handling of these roles a "vivid portrayal of evil incarnate." It proved difficult for Rathbone to rise above the role of villain throughout his career.

Rathbone's first swashbuckling film was *Captain Blood* (1935), in which he crossed swords with Errol Flynn; the two would clash again in *Robin Hood*. Rathbone had extensive fencing training and parried again in the movie version of *Romeo and Juliet*, for which he received his first Academy Award nomination for his portrayal of Tybalt; in *The Mark of Zorro* with Tyrone Power; and humorously in *The Court Jester* with Danny Kaye. In playing the "heavy," Rathbone's characters were often on the losing end of a sharp sword. However, his biographer suggests that Rathbone enjoyed the knowledge that "he could have killed any of his opponents with one thrust." His role in *If I Were King* (1938) garnered him a second Academy Award nomination. Finally not playing a villain, Rathbone was praised by *Variety*: "[He] brilliantly handles the difficult assignment of the eccentric, weazened Louis XI, a role that requires delicacy and shading of characterization in every scene" (21 Sept. 1938).

In 1939 Rathbone was cast again in a role whose image would stay with him far longer than he would have preferred, Sherlock Holmes in *The Hound of the Baskervilles*. He would play Holmes in fourteen films, a radio series that lasted seven years, on the stage (in a version written by his wife), and on television. He became so associated with Holmes that producers would not consider him for another role. In an effort to break out of the villain role, Rathbone had unwittingly fallen into yet another limiting character type. In 1946, after growing tired of Holmes and his inability to get other significant roles, Rathbone did not renew his contracts with the radio or motion-picture studios and moved back to New York.

It took a year for Rathbone to find a good role in New York, and meanwhile he made guest appearances on radio and television. On 29 September 1947, however, Rathbone appeared as the villainous Dr. Sloper in *The Heiress* at the Biltmore Theatre. The show ran for more than a year on Broadway, and critic Brooks Atkinson said that Rathbone "has one of his most actable parts. He plays it with irony and arrogance." Rathbone received a Tony Award for this role. While freed from the curse of Sherlock Holmes, *The Heiress* also proved to be the last major success of his long career.

For the next twenty years Rathbone kept busy doing stage productions in New York, films, television, radio, summer stock, and even vaudeville. He toured a one-man show titled *An Evening with Basil Rathbone* and in 1963 was invited to the White House to give a dramatic reading for President John F. Kennedy. The most notable engagement of his later career was the role of Mr. Zuss (he later played Mr. Nickles) in Archibald MacLeish's *J. B.*, directed by Elia Kazan on Broadway in 1959. His last years were spent making low-budget horror films and television shows in addition to his one-man show. Rathbone continued performing until a few days before his death in New York City.

The last decade of Rathbone's career is not indicative of the versatile and talented actor that was seen best in his early films and stage productions. Despite the fact that his career was hampered by typecasting, according to biographer Linda Obalil, "It is a tribute to his acting ability that he is so strongly associated with two quite opposite roles, both the classical screen villain and the ultimate proponent of law and justice, Sherlock Holmes." Contemporary reviews indicate that Rathbone was often considered to be a stiff and formal actor. In reference to his performance of Romeo, Brooks Atkinson said, "Mr. Rathbone is a neat and tidy actor with an immaculate exterior . . . but he lacks the emotional range to play the part all the way through." In an article for *Etude* magazine Rathbone reveals a very studied actor with solid technique, yet he had the versatility to play the romantic lead, the villainous fiend, and a myriad of character parts with aplomb. While he will be forever remembered as the personification of Holmes and for his villain roles, Rathbone should also be remembered as one of the most versatile, disciplined, and talented actors of his day.

• Rathbone's personality is best seen in his autobiography, *In and Out of Character* (1962). The most comprehensive study of his film work is Michael B. Druxman, *Basil Rathbone: His Life and His Films* (1975). Other sources that include Rathbone are Tony Thomas, *Cads and Cavaliers* (1973), and Jeffery Richards, *Swordsmen of the Screen: From Douglas Fairbanks to Michael York* (1977). A complete list of his films can be found in the *International Dictionary of Films and Filmmakers*, vol. 3, *Actors and Actresses*, and a list of his film, stage, radio, and television performances can be found in the *Biographical Encyclopaedia and Who's Who of the American Theatre* (1966). His stage work is evaluated in William C. Young's essay on him in *Famous Actors and Actresses on the American Stage* (1975), and "How Do You Look at Your Audience?" in *Etude*, Mar. 1951. Obituaries are in the *New York Times* and the *Los Angeles Times*, both 22 July 1967.

MELISSA VICKERY-BAREFORD

RATHBUN, Mary Jane (11 June 1860–4 Apr. 1943), invertebrate zoologist, was born in Buffalo, New York, the daughter of Charles Howland Rathbun, a stonemason, and Jane Furey. The youngest of five children, she was raised by an elderly nurse after her mother died when she was a year old. She graduated from Central High School in Buffalo in 1878 with honors in English, but she soon turned her energies and talents to a career less typical of late nineteenth-century women, zoology.

The Rathbun children's interest in zoology was sparked by fossils found in stone from their father's quarry. Rathbun's first active involvement in the study of marine life came during an 1881 summer stay at Woods Hole, Massachusetts, where her brother Richard was an assistant at the U.S. Fish Commission station. Fascinated by this first view of the ocean and its life, she volunteered to sort and classify specimens. In 1884, impressed by her work, Spencer F. Baird, U.S. Fish Commissioner and secretary of the Smithsonian Institution, appointed her a clerk for the Fish Commission. Of the many young women trained at Woods Hole in the 1880s, only Rathbun and Katharine J. Bush, an assistant to Yale professor Addison Emery Verrill, were able to pursue careers as scientists rather than teachers.

In 1881 the Department (later, from 1898 to 1965, Division) of Marine Invertebrates was created in the U.S. National Museum, with Richard Rathbun as curator. In 1886 Rathbun was appointed copyist and clerk to assist her brother in the work of that department. Frequent travel kept Richard away from the museum much of the time, and thus the day-to-day duties of sorting, labeling, cataloging and classifying specimens, and corresponding with other museums fell largely to Rathbun. Mastering the literature of marine biology, she focused on the classification and nomenclature of decapod crustaceans, that is, shrimps, crabs, and their near relatives. Rathbun amassed a worldwide collection of decapod crustacea from her own fieldwork, the work of the U.S. Fish Commission, the exploring expeditions, and exchanges with collectors and museums. Her contributions to the department included a record-keeping system for specimens, a catalog of the collection, and a personal library on marine invertebrates that she later left to the museum.

Rathbun spent her summers collecting at Woods Hole, as well as South Harpswell, Maine, assisted by the artist Violet Dandridge. In 1891 Rathbun published her first scientific paper, "The Genus *Panopeus*" (U.S. National Museum, *Proceedings* 14:355–85), which while coauthored with her superior in the department, James E. Benedict, is largely credited to her. In 1894 she advanced to aide, and in 1898 she was appointed second assistant curator in the Division of Marine Invertebrates. She was one of only four women scientists at the Smithsonian. In 1896, accompanied by her sister, she made the first of several study visits to European museums. Her sojourn in Paris resulted in her first monograph, *Les Crabes d'eau douce (Potamonidae)* (*Nouvelle Archives*, Paris Museum of Natural History, nos. 6, 7, and 8, 1904–1906).

In 1907 Rathbun was promoted to assistant curator in charge of the division. A heavy curatorial workload prevented her from completing a monographic review of the decapod crustacea of America. The museum could not afford to hire assistants, and thus in 1914 Rathbun resigned so her protégé, Waldo LaSalle Schmitt, could be appointed assistant curator. Her willingness to step aside to provide a salary for a younger scientist made Schmitt her devoted assistant. Rathbun continued as honorary curator for twenty-five years, living off her modest inheritance. No longer burdened by curatorial duties, she completed her monumental four-volume series on the crabs of America: *The Grapsoid Crabs of America, The Spider Crabs of America, The Cancroid Crabs of America of the Families Euryalidae, Portunidae, Atelecyclidae, Cancridae, and Xanthidae,* and *The Oxystomatous and Allied Crabs of America* (*Bulletin of the United States National Museum* 97 [1918], 129 [1925], 152 [1930], and 166 [1937]).

Rathbun also worked on the worldwide fauna of recent and fossil crabs. Her most important works on fossils were *The Fossil Stalk-eyed Crustacea of the Pacific Slope of North America* (*Bulletin of the United States National Museum* 138 [1926]) and *Fossil Crustacea of the Atlantic and Gulf Coastal Plains* (U.S. Geological Survey Special Paper No. 2 [1935]). She was frequently consulted by petroleum geologists for identification of fossils linked to oil-bearing formations. In her 166 publications, she described 1,147 species and subspecies, diagnosed 63 new genera, established five higher

categories, and helped stabilize the nomenclature of decapod crustacea by applying the new International Rules of Zoological Nomenclature.

Her only break from museum service came during World War I, when she devoted her time to preparing bandages as a Red Cross "gray lady." In 1916 she was awarded an honorary M.A. by the University of Pittsburgh and in 1917 qualified for the Ph.D. at George Washington University. She was a member of the American Association for the Advancement of Science and the Washington Academy of Sciences, as well as the Wild Flower Preservation Society. She retired from her honorary curatorship in 1938 because of failing health and died at her home in Washington, D.C.

Diminutive in stature, Rathbun was quiet, dignified, and known for her dry sense of humor. A Unitarian, she displayed a warm interest in her colleagues and encouraged the careers of many younger carcinologists. She never married. She devoted her life to science; indeed, she took her lunch to work to minimize the time taken away from each workday. Although her entrance into the scientific profession was initially facilitated by her brother, once inside she soon established herself as an authority in her own right. She accepted minor positions, such as aide and second assistant curator, and even gave up her salary to a younger male. Self-educated and determined, she made the most of the limited opportunities available to women in the late nineteenth century and left a legacy of a major collection of marine invertebrates and descriptions of previously unknown species.

• The Mary Jane Rathbun Papers, located in the Smithsonian Archives, include a brief autobiographical sketch. Additional information about her can be found in the records of the U.S. National Museum, Richard Rathbun Papers, and Waldo LaSalle Schmitt Papers, also in the Smithsonian Archives. A biography file in the Smithsonian Archives contains a collection of popular newspaper articles written on this unusual woman scientist. Waldo LaSalle Schmitt, "Mary J. Rathbun, 1860–1943," *Crustaceana* 24 (1973): 283–97, contains a detailed biography and a complete bibliography of her works. Margaret W. Rossiter, *Women Scientists in America: Struggles and Strategies to 1940* (1982), places Rathbun's career in context. Obituaries include Schmitt, "Obituary: Mary Jane Rathbun," *Journal of the Washington Academy of Sciences* 33 (1943): 351–52, and Lucile McCain, "Obituary: Mary Jane Rathbun," *Science* 97, no. 2524 (1943): 435–36.

PAMELA M. HENSON

RAUCH, Frederick Augustus (27 July 1806–2 Mar. 1841), philosopher and educator, was born in Kirchbracht (near Darmstadt), Prussia, the son of Heinrich Rauch, a minister, and Friederike Haderman. At the age of eighteen he matriculated at the University of Marburg, which in 1827 awarded him the degree of doctor of philosophy. Subsequently he spent one year each at the University of Giessen and the University of Heidelberg. At Heidelberg, he studied with Karl Daub, Hegel's literary executor. Rauch was appointed *privat docent* and then *professor extraordinarius* at Giessen. In 1831, having just received an appointment to a full professorship in the Department of Metaphysics at the University of Heidelberg, Rauch gave public support to the political fraternities that existed among the students. The government, however, was attempting to suppress these organizations, and Rauch, realizing the seriousness of his predicament, fled the country and sailed to the United States of America. He made his way to Easton, Pennsylvania, where he was befriended by Rev. Thomas Pomp, a German Reformed church minister. At this same time in Easton, Lafayette College, having committed itself by its charter to "forever maintain . . . a Professorship of the German language," was preparing for its very first class of students, and Rauch was appointed professor of German. However, compensation was uncertain, so when the synod of the German Reformed church, meeting in Frederick, Maryland, in September 1832, offered him the dual position of professor of biblical literature in their theological seminary at York, Pennsylvania, and principal of the nascent Classical Institute, a preparatory branch of the seminary, he resigned his position at Lafayette College before his appointment was to have commenced and was installed at York on 17 October 1832. In 1833 he married Phebe Bathiah Moore, daughter of Loammi Moore and Huldah Byram. In 1835, when the Classical Institute, whose name by then had been changed to the High School of the Reformed Church, and the seminary moved to Mercersburg, Pennsylvania, Rauch moved with them. In 1836, when the high school was transformed into Marshall College, Rauch was unanimously elected president and professor of Hebrew, Greek, and German, a position he held for five years until his untimely death in Mercersburg at the age of thirty-five of unknown causes.

Rauch was beloved as a teacher, and his expositions of German speculative philosophy were acclaimed to be profound yet comprehensible. His early publications while in Germany had been mainly in the fields of philology and literature, but in the United States his interests shifted to philosophy and theology. In particular, he wanted to construct a complete system of philosophy based on a spiritual interpretation of the universe and in the process introduce German philosophy, particularly that of Kant and Hegel, to American thinkers. In this effort, which was the beginning of the Mercersburg Theology, he was aided by his colleague and successor as president of Marshall College, John W. Nevin. Rauch's first major publication in this scheme was his *Psychology or a View of the Human Soul, including Anthropology* (1841). This work, he believed, was "the first attempt to unite German and American mental philosophy," a term he used interchangeably with "psychology," as was customary at the time. The work was widely acclaimed and became a textbook in a number of American colleges and universities. Some maintain that it was Rauch who introduced psychology as a distinct science in the United States. He was at work on his next two projects, ethics and aesthetics, when he died. A volume of his sermons, edited by E. V. Gerhart, was published posthu-

mously as *The Inner Life of the Christian* (1856). Although Rauch's lasting contributions to philosophy and theology are difficult to gauge today, the college that he nurtured from its birth lives on, having merged in 1853 with Franklin College to become Franklin and Marshall College in Lancaster, Pennsylvania.

• The best source of information about Rauch's life is G. William Welker, *Eulogy on the Life and Character of Frederick A. Rauch, D.P.* (1841). Other sources include Joseph H. Dubbs, *History of Franklin and Marshall College* (1903); R. C. Schiedt, "Dr. Rauch as Man and Philosopher," *Reformed Church Review* (1906), p. 433; David B. Skillman, *The Biography of a College* (1932); Theodore Appel, *Recollections of College Life* (1886) and *The Life and Work of John Williamson Nevin* (1889); and *Weekly Messenger of the German Reformed Church*, 10 Mar. 1841. For a detailed account of his philosophical work, see Howard J. B. Ziegler, *Frederick Augustus Rauch, American Hegelian* (1953). Other fairly recent accounts include Loyd D. Easton, *Hegel's First American Followers* (1966), and Henry Pochmann, *German Culture in America* (1957). Rauch is mentioned briefly in Elizabeth Flower and Murray G. Murphey, *A History of Philosophy in America*, vol. 2 (1977). For an assessment of Rauch's philosophy by one of his contemporaries, see James Murdock, *Sketches of Modern Philosophy, Especially among the Germans* (1843).

RALPH L. SLAGHT

RAUCH, John Henry (4 Sept. 1828–24 Mar. 1894), leader in public health and regulation of medical education and practice, was born in Lebanon, Pennsylvania, the son of Bernhard Rauch, a farmer and wool dyer, and Jane Brown. He obtained his education at the Lebanon Academy and in 1846 began the study of medicine with John W. Gloninger, a local physician. The following year he entered the medical department of the University of Pennsylvania. After writing a thesis on a medicinal plant, *Convallaria polygonatum*, he received his M.D. in 1849.

Early in 1850 Rauch moved from Lebanon to Burlington, Iowa. For the next eight years he practiced general medicine in that town. He helped found the Iowa State Medical and Chirurgical Society (now the Iowa State Medical Society) in 1850. At the first meeting Rauch was appointed, with two others, to report on the medical and economic botany of the state. He probably wrote most of the 42-page report that resulted. In 1858 he served as president of the society.

Because of his belief that cholera could be spread from buried bodies, Rauch led a successful movement in 1852 to have a cemetery in Burlington vacated. This land, at his urging, was then given to Burlington University. While still in Iowa he served on a federal commission seeking medical aid for mariners on the "western waters." This led to two new U.S. Marine hospitals at Burlington and Galena, Illinois, in 1856.

In 1857 Rush Medical College invited Rauch to join its faculty as professor of materia medica. During his first year with Rush, Rauch continued to live in Burlington and commuted to Chicago for his lectures. The growing city soon attracted him, however, and Rauch moved to Chicago in the fall of 1858. Early the following year Rauch had to resign from Rush, along with Hosmer Johnson, because they were not "well able to carry their share of the indebtedness incurred in enlarging the building" (J. Moses and J. Kirkland, *History of Chicago*, vol. 2 [1895], p. 237).

Rauch served in the Union army from 1861 to 1865 as a surgeon, sanitary inspector, and hospital director. He later wrote that "the practical lessons learned in sanitary science . . . as a medical officer of the army during the war, changed my professional course entirely, and caused me to decide to apply the experience gained to Chicago my home" (address delivered before the New Orleans Auxiliary Sanitary Association [1879], pp. 7–8).

His interest in the interment of bodies, demonstrated in Burlington and expanded during the Civil War, caused Rauch to work toward the removal of a Chicago city cemetery from the land that later became Lincoln Park. He then enlarged and published an address on the subject that he had given in 1858 before the Chicago Historical Society. *Intramural Interments in Populous Cities* appeared in 1866 and ranks as one of Rauch's major publications.

Rauch also became interested in establishing public parks in Chicago and in 1869 published his 108-page *Public Parks: Their Effects upon the Moral, Physical, and Sanitary Conditions of the Inhabitants of Large Cities, with Special Reference to the City of Chicago*. His efforts along these lines earned Rauch the title of "Father of Chicago's Parks."

The Chicago Board of Health had come under political control and deteriorated. The cholera epidemic of 1866 stimulated a mass meeting of citizens, which set up a committee to establish a metropolitan board of health in Chicago similar to the one in New York. Rauch, a member of this committee, was active in the ensuing campaign that resulted in the state legislature's creation of a new board of health for the city on 9 March 1867. Elected president of the board in 1867, Rauch's strong social conscience caused him to improve sanitation and sewerage among the poor, not just among the rich. In 1873 he declined reappointment. A founding member of the American Public Health Association in 1872, Rauch expanded his activities beyond Chicago. He served as president of the APHA in 1876–1877.

At this time Rauch also played a major role in the establishment and development of an Illinois state board of health. The Illinois State Medical Society spearheaded the campaign that caused the state legislature to pass an enabling act in 1877. The board's two main objectives were to regulate medical education and practice and to promote and assist sanitation, quarantine, and hygiene, those public health activities beyond the capabilities of individual physicians.

Rauch was elected president at the organizational meeting and in 1879 moved into the position of real power, secretary. His guiding principle on the board was what he called a "concert of action," the developing of cooperative activity by organizations and individuals. Where necessary organizations were not already in operation, he directly or indirectly initiated them.

Believing strongly in the education of the public, Rauch wrote, or had written, a stream of pamphlets and other publications on most of the topics under the board's mandate. Many were translated into the native languages of the state's ethnic groups. Rauch also initiated and directed regional and village sanitary surveys and vaccination programs.

To improve medical education and practice, the board undertook painstaking investigations of physicians' qualifications and diplomas. In Victor C. Vaughan's opinion, Rauch "was the John the Baptist of reform in medical education in this country" (*A Doctor's Memories* [1926], pp. 438–39). The board also instituted state licensing and examinations. Rauch's detailed and lengthy annual reports played an important role in the regulation of medicine in Illinois and placed the state's public health work on a systematic basis.

Rauch's major publications also include *Report of the Board of Health of the City of Chicago for 1867, 1868, and 1869, and a Sanitary History of Chicago from 1833 to 1870* (1871) and *Preliminary Report to the Illinois State Board of Health: Water Supplies of Illinois and the Pollution of Its Streams* (1889).

After his resignation from the state board in 1891, probably caused by vindictive political pressure, Rauch's health rapidly deteriorated. He finally became so enfeebled that he returned to Lebanon and spent his last months living with his youngest brother. Rauch never married.

Public-spirited, aggressive, persistent, and usually tactful, John Henry Rauch contributed substantially in sanitary, educational, licensing, and public health programs and activities in Illinois. He also encouraged and actively supported individuals and groups interested in these subjects both regionally and nationally.

• There are no substantial collections of Rauch's personal papers. Descriptions of Rauch and his work are found in Arthur R. Reynolds, "Three Chicago and Illinois Public Health Officers: John H. Rauch, Oscar C. De Wolf, and Frank W. Reilly," *Bulletin of the Society of Medical History of Chicago* 1, no. 2 (Aug. 1912): 89–108 (for Rauch), and F. Garvin Davenport, "John Henry Rauch and Public Health in Illinois, 1877–1891," *Journal of the Illinois State Historical Society* 50, no. 3 (Autumn 1957): 277–93. Also of interest is William K. Beatty, "John H. Rauch: Public Health, Parks, and Politics," *Proceedings of the Institute of Medicine of Chicago* 44, no. 4 (Oct./Dec. 1991): 97–118, which includes references to many of Rauch's publications. The only published portraits of Rauch appear in each of these three articles. Other than obituary notices (cited in Beatty) the closest to a contemporary account is found in F. M. Sperry, *A Group of Distinguished Physicians and Surgeons of Chicago* (1904), pp. 117–20.

WILLIAM K. BEATTY

RAUM, Green Berry (3 Dec. 1829–18 Dec. 1909), soldier and federal official, was born in Golconda, Illinois, the son of John Raum, a lawyer and politician, and Julia Cogswell Field. He attended public schools.

In 1851 he married Maria Field, with whom he was to have ten children. After clerking in his father's office, he was admitted to the bar in 1853. In 1856 he and his family joined the antislavery migration to Kansas, where Raum was active in supporting the free-state cause. He soon returned to Illinois and served as clerk of the state house of representatives. A supporter of Stephen A. Douglas's quest for the presidency, Raum attended the Democratic convention in 1860.

Like Douglas, Raum became a "war Democrat" at the outbreak of the Civil War. He entered military service as a major of Illinois volunteers, rising to brevet brigadier general in 1865. Raum saw active service during the war, participating in the battles of Corinth, Mississippi (1862), the Vicksburg and Chattanooga campaigns in 1863, and the battle of Missionary Ridge, Tennessee, where he was severely wounded in 1863. He played an important role in the capture of Atlanta and joined General William T. Sherman's march to the sea. After resigning his commission in 1865, Raum was president of the Cairo and Vincennes Railroad in Illinois. He had become a dedicated Republican and was elected to the national House of Representatives in the Fortieth Congress, 1867–1869. Defeated in 1868, Raum remained active in state politics and was a delegate to the Republican National Convention in 1876.

President Ulysses Grant appointed Raum as commissioner of internal revenue in 1876, soon after the notorious "Whiskey Ring" scandal had discredited the bureau and its leadership. Despite his outspoken partisanship, Raum both served his party and maintained high standards of honesty and efficiency. He was revenue commissioner until 1883, the longest single term of any of these officials in the nineteenth century.

The Bureau of Internal Revenue (now the Internal Revenue Service) was created in 1862 to administer excise taxes to help finance the Union war effort. The most important of these taxes, which have survived to the present, were those on liquor and tobacco. The liquor excise, because it significantly increased the price of whiskey and fruit brandy, was widely resisted. Urban distillers who were officially registered and inspected by the government devised various methods of secretly producing untaxed liquor. Small rural distillers, especially in the South, where mountain people had made whiskey for years, resented a tax that made it impossible for local customers to afford their "corn juice," an important part of the regional economy.

Exposure and breakup of "Whiskey Ring" collusion between revenue officials and large distillers had almost eliminated one major problem of collecting the liquor taxes. Raum concentrated on evasion by southern moonshiners. In an effective campaign to publicize his own bureau and convince Congress and the public to support his efforts, Raum argued that small moonshiners collectively cost the government around $2 million in unpaid excises each year. Also, because they sometimes shot at revenue officers seeking out their hidden stills, they were a serious problem of law enforcement and a threat to federal authority.

The commissioner's campaign emphasized persistence and coordination to intimidate moonshiners. Raum organized posses of revenue officers and U.S. marshals to seize stills and make arrests and made revenue raids seasonal events in many parts of southern Appalachia. He effectively worked with the attorney general and other Justice Department officials to secure their cooperation. Raum did not expect raiding to eliminate moonshining but hoped to reduce it to insignificance. He also cultivated support in Appalachia by encouraging moonshiners to become legal distillers and developed a program of selective leniency in prosecuting first offenders. Gradually, aided by social changes in many mountain areas in the early stages of industrialization, Raum overcame violent resistance and local interference with his subordinates. He slowly won support of many newspaper editors and town dwellers, who had their own objections to mountain people's behavior. By 1882 General Raum declared victory, "The supremacy of the laws of the United States . . . has been established in all parts of the country."

Raum's successors carried on his legacy with mixed results, but Raum had helped establish the excise tax as a bipartisan source of federal revenue and had introduced the "revenuer" as a permanent federal representative in the Mountain South.

Raum's resignation in 1883 was an early example of a bureaucrat leaving office to use his expertise for private clients. Large liquor distillers (allies in the war against moonshine) retained him as a lobbyist to work for legislation in their interest.

After several years of practicing law in Washington, Raum was appointed commissioner of pensions by President Benjamin Harrison in 1889. In this position he headed the nation's first federal welfare institution, a vast and complex bureaucracy responsible for verifying and paying out the pension claims of Union veterans and their survivors. The bureau also had a notorious reputation for soliciting Republican votes through its awarding of pensions. Raum came into office with a reputation as a reformer. However, he was accused of using his influence to advance his various business interests and of favoritism toward his son, who held a position in the bureau. One congressional investigation cleared him by a 3 to 2 committee vote, but a second upheld the charges by the same margin. Raum's supporters charged the Democrats on the committee with attempting to manufacture a scandal to discredit the Republicans in the 1892 presidential election. Though cleared of the severest charges, he had engaged in improper conduct and tarnished his reputation for honesty. Raum remained in office until President Grover Cleveland named his replacement in 1893. Raum then returned to Illinois to practice law in Chicago, where he died.

Raum deserves to be remembered as an example of a transitional bureaucratic official. Both of the agencies he headed represented unprecedented extension of the federal government into the lives of ordinary citizens through taxation and welfare measures. Although his agencies were modern in many respects, he never supported bureaucratic independence from party politics. This tie to the older order damaged his reputation.

• No known collection of Raum papers exists, but the records of the Bureau of Internal Revenue and the Bureau of Pensions, in the National Archives, during his terms of office reveal his attitudes and policies. Similarly, his published reports in the annual House Documents suggest his goals and definitions of the duties of his agencies. Raum was the author of *The Existing Conflict between Republican Government and Southern Oligarchy* (1884), a plea for continuation of Reconstruction civil rights enforcement; *History of Illinois Republicanism* (1900), which includes an autobiographical sketch; *History of the War for the Union* (1905); and *History of Illinois* (1906). His retrospective view of the Revenue Bureau after several years of Democratic control is in *The Republican Party: Its History, Principles, and Policies* (1888). He defended Republican operation of the pension system in "Pensions and Patriotism," *North American Review* 42 (Aug. 1891): 205–14. Wilbur R. Miller, *Revenuers & Moonshiners: Enforcing Federal Liquor Law in the Mountain South, 1865–1900* (1991), details his war against moonshiners. William Barlow, "U.S. Commissioner of Pensions Green B. Raum of Illinois," *Journal of the Illinois State Historical Society* 60 (Autumn 1967): 297–313, discusses the Pension Bureau scandals. For the significance of the Pension Bureau, see Theda Skocpol, *Protecting Soldiers and Mothers* (1991). Obituaries are in the *Chicago Tribune* and the *New York Times*, 19 Dec. 1909.

WILBUR MILLER

RAUSCHENBUSCH, Walter (4 Oct. 1861–25 July 1918), Baptist Social Gospel advocate, was born in Rochester, New York, the son of the Reverend Augustus Rauschenbusch, a seminary professor, and Caroline Rhomp. Responding to a call to minister to German immigrants to the United States, the elder Rauschenbusch immigrated to Missouri in 1846, though he retained close associations with Germany the rest of his life. Consequently, in 1879 he sent his son to the Gymnasium in Gütersloh, Westphalia, from which he graduated in 1883. After receiving his B.A. from the University of Rochester in 1884, Rauschenbusch earned a theology degree in 1886 from Rochester Seminary, where his father was professor of New Testament Interpretation in the German division from 1858 until his retirement in 1888.

Rauschenbusch began his career in 1886 as pastor of the Second German Baptist Church, on the edge of New York City's Hell's Kitchen area. Ministering largely to an immigrant, working-class congregation, he became sensitized to the dehumanizing effects of the rapidly industrializing city, which was adding thousands of immigrants to its population each year. Trapped by low wages and poor working and living conditions, Rauschenbusch's congregants seemed helpless victims of the emerging industrial order. Rauschenbusch quickly became a social activist, supporting the 1886 mayoral campaign of Henry George (1839–1897) because George's platform seemed to offer hope of a more equitable distribution of wealth. In 1888, Rauschenbusch became deaf because of complications resulting from his leaving a sick bed to visit ailing parishioners during a blizzard.

During his eleven-year pastorate, Rauschenbusch devoured the works of Leo Tolstoy, Karl Marx, Edward Bellamy, and others who offered critical analyses of contemporary society. In 1891 and 1892, he took sabbatical leave to the University of Berlin, where he studied economics and the liberal theology that then marked German thinking. During a trip to England, Rauschenbusch gained a firsthand acquaintance with the Fabian socialism espoused by Sidney and Beatrice Webb, the work of the Salvation Army in alleviating urban suffering, and the operation of consumers' cooperatives. He returned to New York determined to adapt what he had seen to an American context; in 1892 he joined with like-minded clergy to form the Brotherhood of the Kingdom, a group committed to practical application of the social teachings of Jesus. In 1893, he married Pauline Rother, and together they had three sons and two daughters.

In 1897, Rauschenbusch assumed his father's professorial chair in the German department of Rochester Seminary, which trained clergy for ministry with German-speaking immigrants. Four years later he became professor of church history, remaining in that post until his death. For his first ten years at Rochester, Rauschenbusch watched labor and industrial strife infect American society, and he became convinced that Christianity's teachings offered resources to alleviate the mounting social dilemma. On a local level, he became involved in civic reform, especially as it involved public education. With Paul Moore Strayer, pastor of Rochester's Third Presbyterian Church and a member of the Central Labor Council, he organized a public, Sunday-evening forum at the church, targeted at a working-class audience, where social issues were debated.

Rauschenbusch's fame in religious circles came with the publication of *Christianity and the Social Crisis* (1907) while he was on leave at the universities in Kiel and Marburg in Germany. Here Rauschenbusch outlined a scheme for translating the New Testament ethic of love into programs for public policy, based on the conviction that the gospel not only offered personal salvation, but also had social implications (hence the label "Social Gospel" or "Social Christianity"). While Rauschenbusch occasionally described his views as "socialist" or "communist," he did not ground them in Marxist ideology, but rather in what he believed the New Testament and the Hebrew prophets prescribed for the common good.

For Rauschenbusch, the ethic of Jesus meant acknowledging the worth and dignity of all humans. In turn that meant providing all with sufficient resources to live in conditions that were not dehumanizing. Specifically, Rauschenbusch called for public ownership of utilities and transportation, fair and equitable wages, improved working conditions, and the redistribution of land to provide adequate housing for workers. Claiming that humanity already possessed the knowledge, technological skills, and resources needed to implement his program, Rauschenbusch insisted that only the willful refusal of Christians to live out the social principles of Jesus prohibited western culture from approaching the reality of the Kingdom of God on earth. In retrospect, Rauschenbusch's vision seems wedded to the values of the emerging urban middle class, but for its day it was perceived as radical. Rauschenbusch was criticized in both religious and academic circles for his apparent attack on laissez-faire capitalism, though he received consistent support from the seminary.

Rauschenbusch was regarded as a dynamic and compelling speaker, and, upon his return to the United States, found himself much in demand as a lecturer on campuses and at public forums. In his lectures, Rauschenbusch conveyed his passion for the Social Gospel by combining trenchant social criticism with a sense of humor that held audiences captive. He also continued to promote the Social Gospel in his writing, his most popular work being the devotional classic *For God and the People: Prayers for the Social Awakening* (1910). He reaffirmed his conviction that Christianity provided the resources for social transformation in a series of lectures delivered at the Pacific School of Religion (1910) and Ohio Wesleyan University (1911), published as *Christianizing the Social Order* (1912). Rauschenbusch's most systematic exposition of the liberal theological underpinnings for Social Christianity came in *A Theology for the Social Gospel* (1917), based on his 1917 Taylor lectures at Yale.

Rauschenbusch was not alone in calling for the social application of New Testament ethical teaching. Similar ideas were promoted by Washington Gladden, Josiah Strong, Richard T. Ely, and others, many of whom were Rauschenbusch's friends. American Catholics, many of whom were part of the urban working class, also sought to effect social reform. The (Protestant) Federal Council of Churches, formed in 1908, took up much of the Social Gospel platform. In political circles, the Progressive movement succeeded in influencing much labor legislation that reflected tenets of the Social Gospel. But by the time *A Theology for the Social Gospel* appeared, much of the western world was mired in the First World War, and the devastation of war demolished the optimistic hope that undergirded much of Rauschenbusch's thinking and its liberal theology. He died in Rochester, disillusioned at the prospects for humanity's ability to make the ethical principles of Jesus the basis for social structures. Nonetheless, Rauschenbusch's insistence that Christian belief and practice encompassed a social as well as a personal dimension has continued to undergird much of the writing in Christian ethics in the United States, though the specific applications he advocated were clearly responses to issues of his own time.

• The Walter Rauschenbusch Papers are in the collection of the American Baptist Historical Society, Rochester, New York. Letters from Rauschenbusch are in the Frederick Taylor Gates Papers, Rockefeller Foundation Archives; the Zona Gale Papers, State Historical Society of Wisconsin; the Richard Henry Edwards Papers and the Edwin Alfred Robert Rumball-Petre Papers, both in the Collection of Regional History, Cornell University Archives. Rauschenbusch's other works include *Das Leben Jesu* (1895); the completion of his father's autobiography, *Leben und Wirken von August Rauschenbusch* (1901); *Die Politische Verfassung Unseres Landes* (1902); *The New Evangelism* (1904); the sections on American church history in *Handbuch der Kirchengeschichte* (1909); *Unto Me* (1912); *Dare We Be Christians?* (1914); and *The Social Principles of Jesus* (1916). For many years, the standard biography was Dores R. Sharpe, *Walter Rauschenbusch* (1942); it is superseded by Paul Minus, *Walter Rauschenbusch, American Reformer* (1988). An obituary appears in the Rochester (New York) *Democrat and Chronicle*, 26 July 1918.

CHARLES H. LIPPY

RAUTENSTRAUCH, Walter (7 Sept. 1880–3 Jan. 1951), engineering educator and industrial engineer, was born in Sedalia, Missouri, the son of Julius Rautenstrauch and Anna Nichter. He graduated with a B.S. from the University of Missouri in 1902 and was awarded his M.S. from the University of Maine in 1903. Rautenstrauch also completed a year of advanced study at Cornell University. In 1904 he married Minerva Babb; the couple had two children. From 1904 to 1906 Rautenstrauch was assistant professor at Cornell; in 1906 he moved to the Columbia School of Engineering, where he became a full professor of mechanical engineering in 1907. In 1918 he offered a course in industrial engineering. By 1920 Rautenstrauch's interest in the field and his administrative influence persuaded President Nicholas Murray Butler to establish a separate industrial engineering department. Rautenstrauch served as the head of the new department from its inception until his retirement in 1945; he remained on the Columbia faculty as emeritus professor, teaching a course in managerial control, until his death.

Rautenstrauch embarked on his career as an engineering educator in a period when engineers were losing their traditional status as independent professionals and machine-shop proprietors and were being drawn into staff positions in the new giant corporations and science-based industries. This experience generated heated debate among engineers as to whether they were, in fact, part of management or independent professionals with a distinct identity and social role. Rautenstrauch was exposed to this ferment at Cornell and, after moving to New York, became active in "progressive" engineering organizations linked to the scientific management movement, which argued for an independent, leadership role in industry and society for professional engineers. Its founder, Frederick Winslow Taylor, outlined an engineering vision of productive efficiency through the application of science to industrial organization and called for engineers (not businessmen) to take responsibility for shop management and to play an active role in society as a whole. Taylor's ideas stimulated the formation of a variety of organizations advocating scientific management and an independent role for engineers, including the Taylor Society, of which Rautenstrauch was a member.

After World War I Rautenstrauch became less outspoken, concentrating his energies instead on building up Columbia's pioneering department of industrial engineering and on a variety of business consultancies. He saw Columbia's industrial engineering department as a vehicle for encouraging the kind of research that would bring the engineer's perspective to business's and the public's attention. At Columbia, he developed and taught a course, "Contemporary Industrial Social Problems," which was designed to foster a sense of social responsibility among engineers.

The arrival of the depression in 1929 intensified Rautenstrauch's belief in the importance of the engineer and drew him toward the technocracy movement of the 1930s, which was to make him famous. Together with the pseudoengineer Howard Scott, who emerged as the movement's leader, Rautenstrauch announced in 1932 the formation of the Committee on Technocracy. Under Scott's leadership, the committee soon initiated an energy survey of North America, which was an ambitious attempt to chart the growth of production and employment in terms of energy expended.

Scott and the technocrats claimed that the United States had become a "high energy" society in danger of collapse, unless the "cultural lag" between the productive capacity of the economy and the organization of society was overcome. They blamed high unemployment on the price system, which was no longer compatible with industrial technology, and argued that neither business nor government was capable of resolving the situation. A scientifically planned restructuring of social institutions was necessary in order to harmonize them with advanced technical production.

Rautenstrauch soon grew uneasy about his association with the movement, however, especially when Scott called for an end to elected government. Rautenstrauch also was unwilling to support Scott's advocacy of a transfer of power to technologists; he envisaged engineers in an advisory role, presenting scientific alternatives to help correct what was wrong with industrialized societies. Under criticism from prominent engineers for his association with Scott, Rautenstrauch and several other charter members resigned from the committee in January 1933, signaling the beginning of the end for the movement. Further damage was done six weeks later when Scott was exposed as a fraud, who had neither the engineering training nor the experience he claimed. A vestigial technocracy movement lived on, but the technocracy craze was over.

Rautenstrauch continued to speak publicly on economic and industrial issues throughout the 1930s, although his pronouncements never excited the kind of attention generated by the technocracy craze. Like many engineers, he was openly critical of the Franklin D. Roosevelt administration's National Recovery Act, which he felt did not get to the root of the problem and unfairly tarred all businesses with the same brush. Nevertheless, he remained critical of many business

practices and of national economic policy, advocating national economic planning (although without specifying what the planning agency would be) and cautioning against placing economic affairs in the hands of unregulated business. He also worked on methods to help businesses evaluate various aspects of their activities, including forecasting profits and the so-called break-even chart, graphic portrayal of the economic characteristics in manufacturing.

Rautenstrauch joined with a group of scientists in 1940 to oppose U.S. entry into World War II, urging the application of the scientific method to the solution of domestic problems. He also worked to help antifascist refugees, criticized Columbia president Butler for what he saw as an attempt to restrict academic freedom during World War II, and opposed the House Un-American Activities Committee's attempt to attack Edward U. Condon, director of the National Bureau of Standards. Rautenstrauch died in New York City.

Rautenstrauch's work is an important example of twentieth-century progressive engineering thinking. While his ideas have not had an enduring influence on public and industrial policy, his work in establishing an academic department of industrial engineering represents a lasting and important achievement.

• Rautenstrauch's papers, including his unpublished correspondence, are at the Butler Library, Columbia University. His major works include *The Successful Control of Profits* (1930), *Who Gets the Money?* (1934), *The Economics of Business Enterprise* (1939), *Industrial Surveys and Reports* (1940), and *Principles of Industrial Economics* (1947). He also coauthored, with Raymond Villers, *The Economics of Industrial Management* (1949) and *Budgetary Control* (1950). The best account of Rautenstrauch's ideas, especially his relationship to the technocracy movement, is William Akin, *Technocracy and the American Dream* (1977). Other discussions of his relationship to technocracy include Allen Raymond, *What Is Technocracy?* (1933), and Henry Elsner, *The Technocrats* (1967). Discussions of engineering ideology and the scientific management movement include Edwin T. Layton, Jr., *The Revolt of the Engineers* (1971), and Peter Meiksins, "The Revolt of the Engineers Reconsidered," *Technology and Culture* 29, no. 2 (1988): 219–46. A detailed obituary is in the *New York Times*, 5 Jan. 1951.

PETER MEIKSINS

RAVALLI, Antonio (14 or 16 or 17 May 1812–2 Oct. 1884), Jesuit priest and missionary, was born in Ferrara, Italy, the son of Giovanni Ravalli, a prominent civil engineer, and Teresa Fioravanti. After receiving his early education from private tutors, he entered the Turin Province of the Society of Jesus in 1827. Despite claims to the contrary in popular accounts of his life, documentary evidence is lacking that Ravalli ever formally studied medicine or biology. He completed the regular Jesuit course of studies in the humanities, philosophy, and theology; and he taught Latin, physics, and mathematics in Jesuit boarding schools in Turin and in other cities in the Piedmont region. Ordained a priest (probably in 1839), he went to Rome in 1843, probably to prepare himself for missionary work in the Jesuits' Rocky Mountain Mission in North America.

He sailed for the Oregon country from Antwerp, Belgium, on 9 January 1844, along with Pierre-Jean De Smet, the mission's founder, and four other Jesuit recruits, including Giovanni Nobili and Michele Accolti, and six sisters of Notre Dame de Namur. The party arrived at Fort Vancouver on the Columbia River eight months later. Ravalli spent some months studying English at St. Francis Xavier Mission, Jesuit headquarters on the Willamette River. A skilled medical amateur, he also cared for Indians in the vicinity who were suffering the effects of an epidemic.

In late 1844 or early 1845 Ravalli was assigned to work with Adrian Hoecken among the Kalispels at St. Ignatius Mission in present-day Montana. During the summer he built a log chapel and cabin among the Kettle Falls tribes of the Columbia River, which became known as St. Paul's Mission. Before the year ended he was reassigned to the Jesuits' Flathead mission to take the place of Pietro Zerbinatti, a missionary who had recently drowned. Life was difficult at St. Mary's where the Jesuits hoped to replicate their famous Paraguay Reductions of seventeenth- and eighteenth-century South America. In both Montana and Paraguay the missionaries sought to isolate the natives from contact with white settlers while converting them to Catholicism and persuading them to substitute nomadic hunting-and-gathering with stable agricultural communities. Ravalli and his co-workers, who included Gregorio Mengarini, lived mainly on buffalo meat, berries, and fish. To augment their diet they contrived a water-powered grist mill to process flour from wheat grown at the mission. Sources claim it was the first flour mill in Montana. Ravalli also learned to extract alcohol from camus root for medicinal purposes. Despite the Jesuits' high hopes for the mission, in 1846 tensions began to surface with the Flatheads as the natives came into increasing contact with white miners and as their expectations about the advantages of converting to Christianity began to wane. Four years later the missionaries abandoned St. Mary's Mission. The reasons for closure were many, including declining Jesuit influence over the tribe and raids from Blackfeet and Bannock enemies of the Flatheads that left the Europeans fearing for their lives. Ravalli also blamed founder De Smet for alienating the tribe by making excessive promises to them that could never be fulfilled.

In 1850 Ravalli transferred to the Coeur d'Alenes at Sacred Heart Mission in present-day Idaho. There he had occasion to exercise his skills as architect, builder, and artisan. He constructed a flour mill with stones brought from Italy; improvised a saw mill; and designed and oversaw the construction of a large timber-and-adobe church, which he decorated with statues and other artwork of his own making. That edifice, planted on a hill overlooking the Coeur d'Alene River in Old Mission, Idaho, was later declared a national historic landmark. Although Ravalli was effective in urging the northern tribes to remain at peace during uprisings of the 1850s, he was not proficient at learning Native-American languages. Superiors, fearing

that his inability to communicate effectively with the Coeur d'Alenes compromised the mission's future, replaced him in 1857 with Joseph Joset, a skilled linguist and administrator. Ravalli returned to St. Paul's Mission near Fort Colville, Washington, which he had helped found. There he worked among local natives, whites, and métis. His successful resuscitation through artificial respiration of a woman who had hanged herself earned him a reputation among the Indian people as a medicine man. He won praise from fellow missionaries and others for his role in pacifying tribes residing to the west of St. Paul's during a period of unrest. Nonetheless, his lack of administrative ability, coupled with changes in native attitudes toward missionaries and problems stemming from an influx of gold miners into the region, led superiors to temporarily close the mission in late 1858. Sometime thereafter, perhaps the following year, Ravalli, discouraged and in ill health, moved to California where he served for several years in various minor capacities at the Jesuits' recently founded Santa Clara College.

He left California in 1863 to return to the Pacific Northwest were Jesuit energies were increasingly absorbed by the needs of the region's growing population of white settlers. Although he continued to minister to Native Americans, Ravalli's activity focused more and more on rural white communities, first from his base of operations at St. Ignatius Mission, Montana, and then during 1864 through 1866 at St. Peter's Mission, located near the trading post of Hell Gate at the mouth of the Bitterroot Valley. In 1866 he assisted in reopening St. Mary's Mission at Stevensville, Montana, where he spent the remainder of his life. From there he made frequent trips throughout the region in his double capacity as priest and homeopathic medical practitioner. When the Nez Percé passed through the Bitterroot Valley in 1877, Ravalli used his influence with the local confederated tribes to keep the peace. According to a government official who once dealt with him, Ravalli was "accomplished and kind, and highly regarded by white and Red" (Burns, p. 82). Explaining his popularity, a Jesuit co-worker described him as "simple as a child" and "affectionate" (Palladino, *Memoir*, p. 10). After his death at St. Mary's in Stevensville, a railway station and county in Montana were named for him. His reputation rested on his role in maintaining the peace between whites and Native Americans during periods of conflict and on his pioneering work as missionary priest and settler.

• Some Ravalli letters and manuscripts are in the Oregon Province Archives of the Society of Jesus, Gonzaga University, Spokane, Wash.; and in the "Montium Saxosorum" Collection (Rocky Mountain Mission Collection) of the Archivum Romanum Societatis Iesu, Rome, Italy. No scholarly analysis of his life exists, but a popular biography is Lucylle H. Evans, *Good Samaritan of the Northwest: Anthony Ravalli, S.J., 1812–1884* (1981). Brief chronologies of his life are found in William N. Bischoff, *The Jesuits in Old Oregon, 1840–1940* (1945); L. B. Palladino, *Indian and White in the Northwest* (1894) and *Anthony Ravalli, S.J., Forty Years a Missionary in the Rocky Mountains, Memoir* (1884); and Helen

Addison Howard, "Padre Ravalli: Versatile Missionary," *Historical Bulletin: A Catholic Quarterly for Teachers and Students of History* 18 (1940): 33–35. A photographic study of his artistic and architectural work is found in Harold Allen, *Father Ravalli's Missions* (1972). See also Robert Ignatius Burns, *The Jesuits and the Indian Wars of the Northwest* (1966); Hiram Martin Chittenden and Alfred Talbot Richardson, eds., *Life, Letters, and Travels of Father Pierre-Jean De Smet, S.J., 1801–1873*, 4 vols. (1905); Gilbert J. Garraghan, *The Jesuits of the Middle United States*, 3 vols. (1938); and Wilfred P. Schoenberg, *Jesuits in Montana, 1840–1960* (1960) and *Paths to the Northwest: A Jesuit History of the Oregon Province* (1982).

GERALD MCKEVITT

RAVENEL, Edmund (8 Dec. 1797–27 July 1871), physician and naturalist, was born in Charleston, South Carolina, the son of Daniel Ravenel, a planter, and Catherine Prioleau. The sixth of nine children born to enterprising Huguenot parents, Ravenel received a sizable inheritance upon the death of his father in 1807. Little is known of his education before he entered the medical school of the University of Pennsylvania, from which he graduated first in his class in 1819. Soon thereafter Ravenel settled in Charleston to practice medicine. By 1823 he had also established a summer residence and a practice on nearby Sullivan's Island, where he began to study fishes and to collect mollusk shells. In 1823 he married Charlotte Matilda Ford, who died in 1826, two days after the birth of a daughter. Three years later, Ravenel married Charlotte's half sister Louisa Catherine Ford, with whom he had seven children.

As a member of the Medical Society of South Carolina, Ravenel played a role in establishing the Medical College of South Carolina in 1824, in which he served as the professor of chemistry and pharmacy. In 1833 a rancorous controversy arose between the faculty of the medical college and the Medical Society of South Carolina over the question of control of the college. During the controversy, Ravenel had informed the medical society that it had "no power to control or regulate my conduct . . . [and] no authority otherwise to interfere with me in any manner whatsoever." Along with his colleagues, he helped to establish a new institution, the Medical College of the State of South Carolina, which opened in 1834.

As early as 1826, Ravenel was collecting and exchanging specimens of fishes and mollusk shells. Eventually, however, he devoted most of his time to conchology, and by the early 1830s, he had developed a large network of correspondents in the United States and abroad. Ravenel was the first conchologist to recognize the lettered olive as a distinct species, which he described as *Oliva sayana*. As a member of Charleston's Literary and Philosophical Society, he actively participated in the discussion of scientific subjects, and he assisted in building the collections of the Charleston Museum, then under the aegis of the society. In 1834 Ravenel published a catalog of his cabinet of shells, which contained more than 700 living and several fossil species.

Illness, and probably a desire to have more time for the pursuit of natural history, led Ravenel to resign from the faculty of the medical college in the spring of 1835. In the meantime, he had purchased a plantation called "The Grove," which was located north of Charleston on the Cooper River. The purchase included 3,364 acres and 104 slaves. Ravenel continued to own property in Charleston and on Sullivan's Island, the latter of which remained as his summer retreat until the end of his life. While successfully operating his plantation, he devoted considerable time to building his collection of shells and invertebrate fossils. Ravenel also acquired a great deal of knowledge about the geology of South Carolina, and in 1842 the famous English geologist Charles Lyell called on him to guide him about the region for the study of geological strata and fossils. Likewise, in 1844, when Michael Tuomey conducted a state-sponsored survey of the geology of South Carolina, he secured information from Ravenel. Possessing a broad interest in natural phenomena, Ravenel also collected zoological specimens for various naturalists.

The visits of the renowned Swiss naturalist Louis Agassiz to Charleston between 1848 and 1853 marked a high point in the development of Charleston as the principal center of scientific activity in the antebellum American South. Agassiz encouraged the rejuvenation and enlargement of the Charleston Museum and the formation of a new society devoted exclusively to the study of natural history. When the Elliott Society of Natural History was established in 1853, Ravenel was appointed one of its vice presidents, and he later contributed specimens to its collections and papers to its proceedings. As with other southerners, Ravenel held Agassiz in high esteem also because of his view that blacks were an inferior and separate creation of God. By 1860 Ravenel owned more than 150 slaves, and, maintaining that northerners did not understand the South's "well-regulated system of negro slave labour," he strongly endorsed South Carolina's secession from the Union in 1861.

In the meantime, Ravenel had continued to collect shells and to publish papers on some of them. By that time, his shell collection had grown to nearly 3,300 species. In a brief history of American conchology, published in 1862, the noted authority George W. Tryon referred to Ravenel as "an experienced conchologist . . . who has done much to further the study" of shells, and he noted that Ravenel owned "a valuable cabinet, rich in marine and other species" of mollusk shells. This collection now belongs to the Charleston Museum and serves as an important source of information for malacologists.

The war, advanced age, and loss of eyesight during the 1860s made it impossible for Ravenel to pursue his work further or to assist the Confederacy. In June 1871 Ravenel fell down the stairway of his home on Sullivan's Island. Severely injured, he was confined to his bed for several weeks before he died. His funeral was held before a large crowd in the Huguenot Church in Charleston, a tribute to his standing in the community and to his advancement of conchology and pale-ontology in the United States.

• Ravenel's papers are not extensive, but a number of them can be found in the Library of the Charleston Museum, at the South Carolina Historical Society, and in the Waring Historical Library of the Medical University of South Carolina. Information about Ravenel and the circumstances of his fatal injury are in the John McCrady diaries from 1869 to 1881, in the private collection of the McCrady Family, Sewanee, Tenn. Ravenel's publications include *Catalogue of Recent Shells in the Cabinet of Edmund Ravenel, M.D.* (1834); "Description of Two New Species of Fossil Scutella, from South Carolina," *Journal of the Academy of Natural Sciences of Philadelphia* 8 (1841–1843): 81–82, 333–36; "Description of Some New Species of Fossil Organic Remains, from the Eocene of South Carolina," *Proceedings of the Academy of Natural Sciences of Philadelphia* 2 (1844–1845): 96–98; "Description of a New Recent Species of Scutella," *Proceedings of the Academy of Natural Sciences of Philadelphia* 2 (1844–1845): 253–54; "On the Recent Squalidae of the Coast of South-Carolina and Catalogue of the Recent and Fossil Echinoderms of South-Carolina," *Proceedings of the American Association for the Advancement of Science* 3 (1850): 159–61; "Description of Three New Species of Univalves, Recent and Fossil," *Proceedings of the Elliott Society of Natural History* 1 (1859): 280–82; "Tellinidae of South Carolina," *Proceedings of the Elliott Society of Natural History* 2 (1855): 33–40; and "Description of New Recent Shells from the Coast of South Carolina," *Proceedings of the Academy of Natural Sciences of Philadelphia* 13 (1861): 41–44. A comprehensive list of shells collected by Ravenel was published in 1874 by his son Edmund, *Catalogue of Recent and Fossil Shells in the Cabinet of the Late Edmund Ravenel, M.D.* Harry G. Lee, M.D., "Edmund Ravenel, Eminent Conchologist of Antebellum Charleston," paper presented before the American Malacological Union, Charleston, S.C., 21 June 1988, gives a valuable assessment of Ravenel's contributions to malacology.

LESTER D. STEPHENS

RAVENEL, Harriott Horry Rutledge (12 Aug. 1832–2 July 1912), author, was born in Charleston, South Carolina, the daughter of Edward Cotesworth Rutledge, a plantation proprietor, and Rebecca Motte Lowndes. She was educated by private tutors at home until she attended Madame Talvande's French School for Young Ladies in Charleston. She enjoyed serious study, writing to her family that she "preferred the study of Latin and ancient history to playing with dolls because 'it has life and spirit in it' as no 'pretty smiling doll' ever did" (Pease, pp. 76–77).

On 20 March 1851 nineteen-year-old Harriott married Dr. St. Julien Ravenel, a physician and agricultural chemist who was twelve years her senior. Both husband and wife were from prominent Charleston families and were a part of antebellum Charleston's social and intellectual life.

The early years of Ravenel's marriage were spent in what she later described as the "care of many little children"—the Ravenels had nine children, six of whom were born in the decade between their marriage and the beginning of the Civil War. In this period, Ravenel quietly pursued her literary interests by writing and collecting poetry for her own enjoyment. Half a centu-

ry later, she would write in *Charleston* (1906) of the predicament of literary women like herself in the antebellum South: "In that day and in that class, ladies shunned all public exercise or display of talent or beauty. Their letters were admirable, but they did not write books" (p. 475).

During the Civil War, Ravenel and her children accompanied her husband to Columbia, the state capital, where he served first as chief surgeon in charge of the Confederate hospital and later as head of the Confederate laboratory, where much of the army's medicine was made. He also was the designer of the torpedo boat *Little David* that was involved in a skirmish with a Union boat. Ravenel and the children were alone in Columbia when Sherman invaded the state; their home, like many others, caught fire. She and her servants stayed up all night fighting the fire, ultimately saving the home and some of their possessions. Mary Boykin Chesnut, a friend of the Ravenels, mentioned the couple several times in her journal, including an account of Harriott Ravenel's heroic actions during Sherman's invasion: "Mrs. St. Julien made good her old John Rutledge blood. She actually awed the Yankees into civil behavior. She was so cool, so dignified, so brave! Jeff Davis had better make her a general, if she can awe the Yankees into good behavior" (Chesnut, p. 763). Ravenel's own written account of the ordeal, "When Columbia Burned," was later published in *South Carolina Women in the Confederacy* (1903). After the war, the family returned to Charleston, and Ravenel concentrated on raising and educating their increasing number of children.

In 1879 Ravenel, using the pseudonym "Mrs. H. Hilton Broom," entered the *Charleston News and Courier* contest for the best fiction story. Her entry, "Ashurst," won the $100 gold prize and was serialized in the *Weekly News* during the following six weeks. The subtitle of the novelette, "The Days That Art Not," not only indicated the nostalgic tone of "Ashurst" but also foreshadowed the reminiscent nature of her future nonfiction works. Though Ravenel may have written under a nom de plume because she could not yet cast off antebellum class strictures concerning women and publishing, she had joined a large cadre of respectable nineteenth-century females whose profusion of sentimentalized novels and magazine stories caused Nathaniel Hawthorne to characterize them as a "damned mob of scribbling women." Ravenel's friend Chesnut also began writing in the 1870s; in 1884 the *News and Courier* bought a short story from her for the small sum of $10, the only money she ever received for the only writing she published in her lifetime.

In 1882, when she was forty-nine, Ravenel became a widow. Three years later, because of the poor health of one of her sons, she moved to Acton, near Statesburg. She kept her Charleston home on the Battery, but because it sustained so much damage in the earthquake of 1886 she did not return to the city until 1893.

Three years after resettling in Charleston, 64-year-old Ravenel published her first book, *Eliza Pinckney*

(1896), a biography of an extraordinary colonial woman who was also her great-great-grandmother. Using family reminiscences and personal letters of Pinckney to create a biography that would illuminate the "thought, the occupations, manners, and customs" of a generation of southern women, Ravenel also wished to defend the "bygone civilization and especially . . . the class which [Pinckney] exemplified" (pp. vii, 322). The book was well received, selling approximately 5,000 copies. Ravenel's second book, *The Life and Times of William Lowndes of South Carolina, 1782–1822* (1901), was a biography of her prominent maternal grandfather as well as a selective, reminiscent history of the social and political life of South Carolina in the early years of the new nation.

A year after the Lowndes book was published, Ravenel recorded her own largely genealogical history with a few personal reflections. In this brief unpublished work, "Reminiscences," she wrote that she had "lived in a civilization that is gone and led a life which is completely that of a vanished time as if it had passed four hundred not forty years ago. This life is so little understood and so constantly misrepresented." She felt compelled to write her thoughts so that her children and grandchildren would "know their ancestors as they were, not as books make them." Four years later, Ravenel's story became a published history that she hoped would educate the reading public. One of a series of informal histories of famous American cities, *Charleston: The Place and the People* (1906) utilized personal anecdotes from Ravenel's extensive kin and friendship connections, thus creating an intimate and lively 250-year history of colonial and antebellum Charleston. Though this approach gave readers a limited historical perspective by telling them far more about the social and political life of Charleston's gentry than about its ordinary citizens, Ravenel's story of the loss of the "Old South" touched a responsive chord in many readers who longed, as she did, for a time they believed was more gracious and civil than their own. Ravenel admitted that her Charleston history was selective in order to illustrate the fortunes and character of those whom she believed had "made the town." She apologized for "the reminiscent tone which has crept into the last chapters," but she believed the proper place to close her narrative of Charleston was a half century earlier with the "fall of the city and of the Confederacy," when the "old life of Charleston ended." Ravenel's books were well reviewed, and *The Independent*, in evaluating *Charleston*, noted that though Ravenel's discussion at one point was naive, "she belongs to that lovely faded wreath of elderly gentlewomen. . . . Events lie quiet in her mind, which gives them the right perspective."

Though Ravenel was chiefly occupied with writing after she returned to Charleston in the 1890s, she also was active in the social and civic life of the city as a member of the Daughters of the Confederacy, the Ladies' Memorial Society, and the South Carolina Society of Colonial Dames, which she served as president from 1896 to 1898. She died in Charleston.

• Most of the biographical material on Ravenel is in the Harriott H. Ravenel Papers and related collections at the South Carolina Historical Society in Charleston. These files contain her brief "Reminiscences," private correspondence, manuscripts of her books and other writings, early book reviews, and assorted personal papers. Correspondence files in the Elizabeth C. Agassiz Papers at the Schlesinger Library, Radcliffe College, include letters written by Agassiz from Charleston that mention the Ravenels and their extended family. Some of her correspondence can also be found in the collection named for her aunt, Harriott Horry Rutledge, at Duke University. Useful information is in Jane H. Pease and William H. Pease, *Ladies, Women, and Wenches: Choice and Constraint in Antebellum Charleston and Boston* (1990), and in Mary Boykin Chesnut's journals, edited by C. Vann Woodward and titled *Mary Chesnut's Civil War* (1981). Book reviews of *Charleston* can be found in *The Independent*, 28 Mar. 1907, and the *New York Times*, 27 Dec. 1906. An obituary is in the *Charleston News and Courier*, 3 July 1912.

MARILYNN WOOD HILL

RAVENEL, Henry William (19 May 1814–17 July 1887), planter and botanist, was born in St. John's Parish, South Carolina, the son of Henry Ravenel, a planter and physician, and Catherine Stevens. Upon the death of his mother in 1816, Henry went to live with his grandparents on the family plantation, "Pooshee," in South Carolina. He was educated locally at Pineville Academy and then studied privately in Columbia for a few months before entering South Carolina College in 1830. He married Elizabeth Gaillard Snowden in 1835; they had four children. Henry wanted to study medicine, but his father dissuaded him, emphasizing the rigors of life as a physician. So the elder Ravenel gave to his son a 600-acre plantation, "Northampton," along with slaves and equipment to operate it. By 1839 Ravenel was well established as a South Carolina planter.

During the 1840s Ravenel turned Northampton into a successful plantation, personally supervising much of its operation and experimenting with crop rotation and fertilizers. It is not surprising, therefore, that he was intrigued by the work of a traveling botanist he met around 1842–1843, who taught him the proper manner for collecting and preserving plant specimens so that they could be used for scientific study. Thus began Ravenel's botanical interest; he would eventually become one of America's leading mycologists.

Ravenel educated himself primarily with Stephen Elliott's *Sketch of the Botany of South Carolina and Georgia*, although he gradually expanded his library. An equally significant element in his botanical education was his correspondence with notables such as Harvard's Asa Gray as well as Moses Ashley Curtis and Miles Joseph Berkeley, the latter a British mycologist. These botanists, challenged by the vast array of the world's flora, depended on men like Ravenel to supply them with well-preserved specimens and descriptions of plant locales. In return, they offered scientific knowledge and friendship.

Throughout his life Ravenel made contact with the scientific world primarily through correspondence. As the national scientific community began to coalesce in the mid-nineteenth century, Ravenel's reluctance to participate in formal organizations essentially eliminated him as a member of the professional inner circle, although he did publish a number of articles in local publications such as *Southern Agriculturist, Horticulturist, and Register of Rural Affairs*; *Southern Journal of Medicine and Pharmacy*; *Charleston Medical Journal and Review*; and *A Meteorological Journal*. He knew most of the men then active in the Charleston scientific community but was not a vital force in their founding of the Elliott Society of Natural History (1853). He did present a paper when the American Association for the Advancement of Science met in Charleston in 1850, but his one trip to Boston and Philadelphia was not a rewarding experience, and he never journeyed to Europe. He further distanced himself from professional meetings with his move in 1853 from Northampton, which he sold, to a farm near Aiken, in the South Carolina upcountry, citing health reasons.

Nonetheless, during the 1850s Ravenel rose to prominence among botanists with his five-volume *Fungi Caroliniani Exsiccati* (1852–1860). Curtis originally proposed this project to Ravenel as a joint venture but withdrew prior to completion of the first volume, citing time constraints. Indeed, such publications were labor intensive. *Exsiccati*, collections of known plant specimens accompanied by brief descriptions, required painstaking effort to affix each specimen to a page and prepare the descriptions. Ravenel produced fewer than fifty copies of each volume, distributing most of them to his correspondents. His interest in the project waxed and waned during the decade, for he grew to dislike intense work with a microscope and always maintained an active interest in his farm. Ravenel's wife died in 1855; in 1858 he married Mary Huger Dawson. They had five children.

The Civil War drastically altered Ravenel's life. Although he did not serve in the Confederate army and his farm was spared, his extensive purchase of Confederate war bonds ruined his financial independence. Ravenel was never destitute, but he did have to search for other sources of income, as his efforts to make a profit from his farm met with only limited success. From time to time he was able to generate income by collecting and selling botanical specimens. His need for payment, however, met with some resistance from scientists who preferred exchanges. It also altered Ravenel's relationship with them, frequently in an uncomfortable manner.

Ravenel did have additional offers of employment. In 1869 he spent a few weeks in Texas serving as botanist for a federal effort to determine the cause of Texas fever among cattle. (He was chosen for this assignment because of his relationship, via correspondence, with John Shaw Billings of the surgeon general's office.) Soon thereafter John Torrey inquired about his possible interest in a teaching position at either the University of California or Washington College (Lexington,

Va.). Ravenel declined, citing encroaching deafness. Even though he had become increasingly hard of hearing, other factors, including an unwillingness to make such a major change in his life, no doubt affected his decision.

During the remainder of his life Ravenel received numerous requests for assistance from younger mycologists; he helped those whose requests were not too extensive or who offered payment. He published a number of brief articles and frequently received credit in the publications of others. Mordecai Cooke of England further enhanced Ravenel's reputation by compiling and publishing eight volumes of *Fungi Americani Exsiccati* (1878–1882), primarily specimens that Ravenel had collected. Despite his renown, though, Ravenel no longer considered himself a student of botany. His activity in the field was limited primarily to writing brief articles and collecting for others, rather than studying his specimens for evidence of variety. No doubt he also recognized the great change that had occurred in the definition of a "professional" scientist, which by the 1880s included an advanced degree, membership in at least one professional organization, evidence of research and publication, and employment as a scientist. He died in Aiken, South Carolina.

Ravenel's life had spanned a momentous evolution in scientific inquiry, and his work contributed to that process. His specialization in one area of botany, his vast knowledge, his wide correspondence, his publications, and the respect afforded him by eminent botanists indicate that he was a significant component, if not a leader, in the emergence of professional scientific inquiry as it came to be defined by the early twentieth century.

• Those interested in Ravenel's own account of his life as a planter should examine his "Recollections of Southern Plantation Life," *Yale Review* 25 (Summer 1936): 748–77, and Arney Robinson, ed., *The Private Journal of Henry William Ravenel, 1859–1887* (1947). His life and work have been discussed in a variety of books and articles that address intellectual activity in the American South during the nineteenth century. The antebellum era has received the most scholarly attention; for a broad overview, see Ronald L. Numbers and Todd L. Savitt, eds., *Science and Medicine in the Old South* (1989). However, all secondary works have been superceded by Tamara Miner Haygood, *Henry William Ravenel, 1814–1887: South Carolina Scientist in the Civil War Era* (1987), an excellent monograph that realistically assesses Ravenel's contributions to the scientific world.

NANCY SMITH MIDGETTE

RAVENEL, Mazÿck Porcher (16 June 1861–14 Jan. 1946), bacteriologist and public health leader, was born in Pendleton, South Carolina, the son of Henry Edmund Ravenel and Selina Eliza Porcher. His father was a seventh generation member of a family of prominent merchants, bankers, and civic leaders whose French Huguenot ancestors had settled near Charleston, South Carolina, after the Edict of Nantes was revoked in 1695. Although his father died when Mazÿck was two, and the Ravenel fortunes suffered severely during the Civil War, Mazÿck attended private schools in Charleston. He graduated from the University of the South, Sewanee, Tennessee, in 1881. In 1884 he received an M.D. from the Medical College of South Carolina in Charleston. He helped found the Charleston Medical School and there taught anatomy and diseases of children, while practicing medicine for six years. His career in public health began with his study of hygiene and bacteriology at the University of Pennsylvania, where he was listed with the first students to take classes at its new Laboratory of Hygiene, opened in 1892 under the direction of John Shaw Billings, one of America's foremost sanitarians and hospital architects. Ravenel was the second person to be awarded the Laboratory of Hygiene's Thomas A. Scott fellowship in hygiene in 1893. In 1895 he furthered his studies in Europe, where he gained research experience in bacteriology at the Pasteur Institute in Paris under the guidance of Jules Bordet and Edmund Nocard. He also studied with Carl Fraenkel at the Institute of Hygiene in Halle, Germany.

Ravenel became the first director of the Hygienic Laboratory of the New Jersey State Board of Health in Princeton in 1895. He returned to Philadelphia within a few months to accept a position as an instructor in bacteriology in the medical and veterinary schools of the University of Pennsylvania. He married Jennie Carlile Boyd in 1898; they had no children. In 1904 he became assistant medical director and bacteriologist for the new Phipps Institute for the Study, Treatment, and Prevention of Tuberculosis, which had opened at the University of Pennsylvania in 1903. He also served as the first bacteriologist for the Pennsylvania State Livestock Sanitary Board from 1896 until 1907.

Ravenel's research centered on one of the major public health questions of the day: Could bovine tuberculosis be transmitted to humans through milk? In 1902 he provided conclusive proof of its transmission when he isolated the bovine tubercle bacillus from the lymph nodes of a child who had died of tuberculous meningitis. His finding challenged a claim made in 1901 by the famed German bacteriologist Robert Koch that bovine tuberculosis did not pose a human health threat. Ravenel and other scientists who believed bovine tuberculosis was a health hazard, especially for children, challenged Koch directly in a memorable exchange at the International Congress on Tuberculosis in Washington, D.C., in 1908. Ravenel considered his tuberculosis research his most important contribution to public health. He was a leader in the national effort to control the spread of tuberculosis and became an ardent supporter of milk pasteurization. In 1904 he became a charter member of the National Tuberculosis Association; he served on the Executive Committee of its board of directors and as its president in 1911–1912.

The University of Wisconsin hired Ravenel in 1907 as professor of bacteriology. The following year he also became director of Wisconsin's State Hygienic Laboratory and its Pasteur Institute for the treatment of rabies. He extended his research on tuberculosis to include studies of the bacteria of milk, an important aspect of the control of bovine tuberculosis. His work for the State Hygienic Laboratory engaged him in studies of typhoid fever, diphtheria, and rabies. During his tenure, the laboratory conducted a survey of water sanitation for the state of Wisconsin, and the overall volume of work at the laboratory increased twofold. As hygienist for the university, he became involved in school hygiene, investigating the sanitary quality of student housing, public drinking fountains, and swimming pools. Despite his skills in bacteriology and public health, Ravenel's forthright and often contentious personality caused his resignation at Wisconsin. He engaged in conflicts with local physicians and the State Board of Health that exacerbated existing tensions on the campus between the College of Letters and Sciences and the College of Agriculture over the teaching of bacteriology. In 1914 he left to become professor and head of the department of bacteriology and preventive medicine at the University of Missouri School of Medicine and director of Missouri's public health laboratory. He retired from teaching in 1932 and was named professor emeritus in 1936.

Ravenel wrote more than 100 scientific articles. His influential work on tuberculosis was first published as "The Intercommunicability of Human and Bovine Tuberculosis" (*University of Pennsylvania Medical Bulletin* 15 [1902]: 66–87). He wrote chapters on anthrax, glanders, and rabies in *Modern Medicine: Its Theory and Practice, in Original Contributions by American and Foreign Authors*, ed. William Osler (1907).

Ravenel served in the U.S. Army Medical Corps during World War I. Stationed at Fort Riley and Camp Funston, Kansas, and at Fort Kearney, California, he attained the rank of lieutenant colonel. In 1919 he was appointed assistant surgeon general of the U.S. Public Health Service (Reserve). When World War II depleted faculty ranks at the University of Missouri, he returned from retirement to teach bacteriology and hygiene courses there from 1942 to 1946. In 1910 Ravenel had married Adele Pettigru Vander Horst; they had no children.

Ravenel is most well known for his work with the American Public Health Association (APHA), of which he became a director in 1915 and president in 1920. In 1924 he took over the editorship of the *American Journal of Public Health*, which was nearly insolvent. Over the next seventeen years, he single-handedly transformed it into the leading public health journal in the country. His breadth of knowledge of medicine and public health and his exacting editorial standards made him a stern but helpful critic. C. C. Young, an APHA colleague, dubbed him the "paternal castigator." Ravenel edited the association's jubilee volume, *A Half Century of Public Health* (1921), which remains a standard reference for the history of public health in America. He also served on the committee that produced the second and third editions of *Standard Methods for the Bacteriological Examination of Milk* (1916, 1921). He died in Columbia, Missouri.

Ravenel played an important role in applying the science of bacteriology to the diagnosis and prevention of tuberculosis. As editor of the *American Journal of Public Health* from 1924 to 1941, he used his historical perspective and editorial skills and influenced the shape of public health in the United States to create a respected publication worthy of the public health professionals it served.

• A large collection of Ravenel's personal papers and correspondence is in the Western Historical Manuscript Collection of the University of Missouri. A family genealogy is given in Henry Edmund Ravenel, *Ravenel Records* (2d ed., 1971). "Appreciations of the Editor Emeritus," *American Journal of Public Health* 31 (Jan 1941): 1–9, provides a bibliography of his works. Biographical accounts include an obituary in the *American Journal of Public Health* 36 (Feb. 1946): 174–75, and one by John F. Norton in the *Year Book of the American Philosophical Society* (1947), pp. 292–93. Secondary sources include Paul F. Clark, *Pioneer Microbiologists of America* (1961), pp. 200–201, and Everett B. Miller, "Bibliographic Briefs on Hermann M. Biggs, M.D., and Three Other Physicians—All Honorary Members of the American Veterinary Medical Association," *Veterinary Heritage* 13 (1990): 50–51. Accounts of the meeting with Robert Koch are found in the *Journal of the American Medical Association* 51 (1908): 1257–60, and the *Washington Post*, 1 and 3 Oct. 1908. An obituary is in the *(Charleston, S.C.) News and Courier*, 15 Jan. 1946.

PATRICIA PECK GOSSEL

RAVENSCROFT, John Stark (17 May 1772–5 Mar. 1830), Episcopal bishop, was born in Prince George County, Virginia, the son of John Ravenscroft, a doctor and gentleman farmer, and Lillias Miller, both of prosperous and established Virginia families. Within a year of his birth, the family moved to Great Britain, leaving extensive properties in Virginia. They settled in the south of Scotland. Ravenscroft received the beginnings of a good education while in Scotland but returned to Virginia when he was sixteen to look after his (now deceased) father's estate there and to study law at William and Mary. The Virginia estate had fallen into disrepair, but his efforts paid off handsomely and made him rich throughout his young adulthood. Ravenscroft was less successful at his academic work, preferring good times to legal studies and earning the nickname "Mad Jack." He never obtained a license to practice law. While at school, he became engaged to Anne Spotswood Burwell and decided to settle in Virginia permanently. After a brief trip to Scotland to settle his inheritance, Ravenscroft married Burwell in 1792 and purchased a new estate of 2,500 acres in Lunenburg County, Virginia.

Ravenscroft lived the life of a slaveholding country gentleman, tending his estates and ignoring all religious matters until 1810, when he began to reflect on his two besetting vices, an uncontrollable temper and terrible profanity. He decided to overcome these vices by the strength of his will but found himself unable to do so. After a period of struggle, he recognized the impossibility of conquering his innate depravity and threw himself on God's mercy. Feeling the need to associate himself with a Christian communion, Ravenscroft joined the Republican Methodists based on his friendship with one of their leaders, John Robinson. When he decided to become a minister, however, he began to question the legitimate authority of the Republican Methodists to ordain and even to celebrate the sacraments. Finding the leadership of the Republican Methodists unconcerned with these issues, he left the denomination and ultimately sought ordination in the Protestant Episcopal church. Richard Channing Moore, bishop of Virginia, licensed Ravenscroft as a lay reader in the Episcopal church in 1816 and ordained him as deacon and then priest the following year. He accepted a call to become rector of Saint James Church in Mecklenburg County, Virginia, where he remained until 1823. In that year, the fledgling North Carolina diocese elected him as its first bishop.

The North Carolina diocese was very weak before Ravenscroft's arrival. Despite earlier efforts, the diocese was not organized until 1817. The entire state had not possessed a single Episcopalian minister in 1816, and by 1823 it had only eight. Twenty-three congregations with a total of about four hundred congregants existed. Because the diocese could not afford to pay a full-time bishop, Ravenscroft, much of his fortune dissipated by this time, also became rector of a new parish in Raleigh, Christ Church. At his arrival, Christ Church had about thirty-five congregants who worshipped in rented space. Christ Church did not obtain its own building until 1829.

Ravenscroft had developed his theological position, which focused on the distinctly apostolic character of the Episcopal church, its ministry, and its sacraments, by the time of his arrival in North Carolina. Like evangelicals, he believed in the necessity of religious experience in the salvation process. On the other hand, like John Henry Hobart, an influential "high church" Episcopal bishop, he coupled his evangelical fervor with an equally strong insistence on the importance of the Church deriving its ordained ministry from Christ's apostles. Only ministers ordained by bishops who could trace their episcopal line back to the apostles could perform valid sacraments. Ravenscroft therefore stressed the distinctiveness of the Episcopal church based on its apostolic ministry, and he discouraged excessive cooperation between Episcopalians and Christians of other denominations. His brand of high church Episcopalianism characterized the religious views of most North Carolina Episcopalians for many years after his death and spread from there to other dioceses through the work of his students.

In 1814, before he had left Virginia, Ravenscroft's wife died. Four years later he married again, to a woman named Sarah Buford from Lunenburg County, Virginia. She accompanied him to North Carolina, where she contributed to his ministry through her personal influence on his clergy. The rigors of his job as bishop, with its requirement of constant travel throughout the state on episcopal visitations, aged him prematurely. By 1828 he felt that he could not continue as rector of

Christ Church. Accordingly, he and his wife moved to Williamsborough, where he took over Saint John's Church, a smaller parish. Sarah Ravenscroft died in Williamsborough within a year of their arrival. Her death reduced his expenses, and the North Carolina diocese offered him a slight raise. Together these two events made it possible for Ravenscroft to resign as rector of Saint John's in order to serve as a full-time bishop. Shortly thereafter he left North Carolina to attend the Episcopal General Convention in Philadelphia, stopping along the way in Tennessee to help arrange a diocese there and in Kentucky. He made it to Philadelphia but in a feeble condition. He grew progressively weaker after his return to North Carolina and died without a struggle in Raleigh. He was survived by his mother and five adopted children. No children were born during either marriage.

Ravenscroft left an important legacy for the Episcopal church in North Carolina. Although the diocese was still small, the number of congregants had approximately doubled to around eight hundred. The clergy shared certain basic theological ideas about the uniqueness of the Episcopal church and the importance of emphasizing its distinctive doctrines. By the time of his death the diocese was growing and had a full-time bishop and a distinctively conservative and high church identity. The diocese as a whole mourned his passing, and memorial services were celebrated across the state.

• Ravenscroft's unpublished correspondence from 1821 until his death is in the Frances L. Hoch and General Convention Collection of Early Episcopal Church Manuscripts at the Episcopal Church Historical Society in Austin, Tex. *Journals of the Proceedings of the Protestant Episcopal Church in the United States, 1817–1830* contains some of Ravenscroft's journals. All of Ravenscroft's published works are gathered in *The Works of the Right Reverend J. S. Ravenscroft*, ed. Jonathan Mayhew Wainwright (2 vols., 1830); the first volume includes a memoir on Ravenscroft's life by Walker Anderson. William B. Sprague, in the fifth volume of his *Annals of the American Pulpit*, has a short biography of Ravenscroft, together with a letter from one of Ravenscroft's students about his life. W. M. Green, another of Ravenscroft's students, gives an anecdotal account of his life and ministry in "Bishop Ravenscroft," *American Quarterly Church Review* 22 (1870–1871): 526–53. John N. Norton published a *Life of Bishop Ravenscroft* (1858), and Marshall DeLancey Haywood has a chapter on his life in *Lives of the Bishops of North Carolina* (1910). The *Evergreen* 7 (June 1850): 161–71, printed an anonymous biographical sketch drawn largely from Ravenscroft's autobiographical memoir. E. Clowes Chorley, *Men and Movements in the American Episcopal Church* (1946; repr. 1961), and Lawrence Foushee London and Sarah McCulloh Lemmon, eds., *The Episcopal Church in North Carolina 1701–1959* (1987), have sections on Ravenscroft within the context of the Episcopal church of North Carolina. Frank M. McClain has an article on Ravenscroft's thought, "The Theology of Bishops Ravenscroft, Otey, and Green Concerning the Church, the Ministry, and the Sacraments," in *Historical Magazine of the Protestant Episcopal Church* 33 (1964): 103–36.

HARVEY HILL

RAWALT, Marguerite (16 Oct. 1895–16 Dec. 1989), women's rights leader and lawyer, was born in Prairie City, Illinois, the daughter of Charles Rawalt, a farmer and farm equipment dealer, and Viola Flake. She attended public and private schools in Illinois, Oklahoma, New Mexico, and Texas. She graduated from Bayview Junior College in 1914 and attended but did not graduate from San Antonio Junior College and the University of Texas. Rawalt's ambition to go to law school was postponed for many years by a combination of financial constraints, World War I patriotism, and her marriage in 1918 to her dashing but emotionally immature and unambitious wartime sweetheart, Jack Tyndale. She worked as secretary and assistant to Texas governor Pat M. Neff from 1921 to 1924. But it was not until her marriage ended in divorce in 1927 and she moved to Washington, D.C., to work again for Neff (then a member of the U.S. Board of Mediation) that she found a law school she could attend at night. George Washington University Law School admitted her even though she did not possess an undergraduate degree, and she graduated in 1933.

Rawalt came to maturity in Democratic political circles while in Texas and began her career as a clubwoman and advocate of women's rights during her law school years in Washington. After graduation, she went to work as a lawyer for the Bureau of Internal Revenue and simultaneously accelerated her activism in legal and women's organizations, including the almost all-male Federal Bar Association, the forward-looking National Association of Women Lawyers, and the feminist National Woman's party. In 1942 she was elected president of the National Association of Women Lawyers; the next year she became the first woman to head the male-dominated Federal Bar Association.

Gratifying though were her personal accomplishments, they left her disappointed that even extraordinary achievement did not assure equality of opportunity for women like herself and had no effect at all, as far as she could see, on the economic and legal status of women in general. Though she continued to hold positions of responsibility at Internal Revenue for another twenty years, after 1944 the better part of her substantial energies were devoted to improving the legal, educational, and economic status of women. By then marriage in 1937 to her supportive second husband, retired army air corpsman Harry Secord, had stabilized her personal life. She had no children with either husband.

Working with a small, nationwide coterie of women lawyers and feminists, Rawalt developed a philosophy of women's rights based on the simple notion that all laws ought to be applied and enforced in exactly the same way for women and men. The way to bring this about, she argued, was by forcing the courts to apply the Fourteenth Amendment to the Constitution to women and by working for the passage of an equal rights amendment. Bringing that philosophy to her leadership of the 160,000-member Federation of Business and Professional Women's Clubs, which she headed from 1954 to 1956, she put that organization in place to lead the women's movement she believed was coming. "Get the facts," she said in speeches made all over the country. "We can't just keep going round throwing up our hands and saying 'it isn't fair.' We have to *do* something. If we give the men in Congress the facts, *they* might have to do something."

By the end of the 1950s she was begging the traditional women's clubs to band together and press for women's rights the way black people were pressing for theirs. "It is almost unthinkable," she wrote in 1956, "that women do not have the conviction and determination which is evidenced every day in our newspapers, of the racial groups, who are getting their rights declared in every shape and form." As her belief in aggressive political action for women grew, her definition of "women's issues" expanded to include child care, uniform jury service, equal pay for equal work, job training, and activist support of the Equal Rights Amendment (ERA).

Her thinking was further radicalized during those years as it became evident that she was never going to get the appointment to a judgeship that epitomized her personal ambitions and that the traditional women's organizations were not going to follow her into the future. Because of disillusionment such as hers, the National Organization for Women (NOW), in which she soon became a leader, was organized in Washington, D.C., in 1966. By then Rawalt was already deeply involved in the muted activism of the President's Commission on the Status of Women, created by John F. Kennedy in 1961 and headed by Eleanor Roosevelt, and the subsequently established Citizens Advisory Council on the Status of Women. It was thanks to the women who came together on those two boards that Title VII of the Civil Rights Act of 1964 prohibited employment discrimination against women as well as minorities and that all restrictions on jury service for women were removed.

On 16 October 1965—her seventieth birthday—Rawalt retired after thirty-three years as a lawyer for the Internal Revenue Service and began a second career of full-time activism for women's legal rights. As first general counsel for NOW and creator of its Legal Defense and Education Fund, she masterminded and managed a number of early cases challenging discriminatory prison sentences for women, sex-segregated employment advertisements, protective labor laws, and other discriminatory practices commonly applied to women in the workforce. The most significant of those cases, *Weeks v. Southern Bell*, resulted in a 1969 ruling in which the Fifth Circuit Court of Appeals declared protective labor laws to be "romantic paternalism" and vested "individual women with the power whether or not to take on unromantic tasks. . . . The promise of Title VII being that women are now to be on equal footing."

As a link between three generations of women's rights activists and a vast network of organizations, Rawalt played a crucial role in the campaign that got the ERA through Congress in 1972 and attempted to secure ratification from the states. The argument on which that campaign was based was the one she had propounded for forty years under the influence of the women lawyers connected to the National Woman's party and the suffrage movement: an equal rights amendment was necessary because the courts still refused women the rights accorded "all persons" by the Fourteenth Amendment.

Undaunted by ERA's failure to gain ratification, Rawalt continued to popularize her beliefs in speeches, articles, and interviews. She remained active in national organizations until 1988 when, after sixty years in Washington, she moved back to Texas to be close to her family. She died in Corpus Christi.

• Rawalt's papers are in the Schlesinger Library at Radcliffe College. With Rawalt's cooperation and access to her personal papers and extensive correspondence, Judith Paterson wrote *Be Somebody: A Biography of Marguerite Rawalt* (1986), with forewords by former congresswoman Martha W. Giffiths and Liz Carpenter, a Texas journalist and political activist. Her role in the women's movement is discussed in Flora Davis, *Moving the Mountain: The Women's Movement in America since 1960* (1991). An obituary is in the *Washington Post*, 22 Dec. 1989.

JUDITH PATERSON

RAWIDOWICZ, Simon (11 Oct. 1896–20 July 1957), scholar and philosopher of Jewish history, was born in Grayevo, Poland (then czarist Russia), the son of Haim Isaac Rawidowicz, a merchant, and Hanna Batya Rembelinka. Rawidowicz received a traditional elementary and secondary Jewish education, during the course of which he became attracted to the secular Jewish enlightenment (haskalah) and modern Hebrew literature. This led him to assume a significant role in the Hebrew cultural and educational life of the Jewish community of nearby Bialystok, where his family had moved in 1914 at the outbreak of the First World War.

Following the war, in 1919 Rawidowicz left Eastern Europe to study philosophy, history, and Semitics at the University of Berlin. In 1926 he received his Ph.D. for his dissertation on the nineteenth-century German philosopher Ludwig Feuerbach, which he expanded into the still-definitive book, *Ludwig Feuerbachs Philosophie: Ursprung und Schicksal* (Ludwig Feuerbach's philosophy: Sources and influence) (1931; repr. 1961).

Concomitantly, Rawidowicz continued his Hebrew scholarly and cultural activities. In 1922 he established the Ayanot Publishing Company in Berlin to make available modern editions of classical Hebrew texts. His edition of *Moreh Nevukhei Hazeman* (Guide for the perplexed of the time) by the nineteenth-century Galician Jewish historiographer Nahman Krochmal was published together with a few articles and letters of Krochmal and prefaced by a definitive introduction under the title *Kitvei Ranak* (The Writings of Nahman Krochmal) (1924; repr. 1961). The work quickly established him as one of the leading scholars of his generation and led to his selection as the editor of the Jewish-themed writings of the German-Jewish philosopher Moses Mendelssohn. In 1926 Rawidowicz married Esther Eugenie Klee, the eldest daughter of the Berlin lawyer and Zionist leader Alfred Klee. They had one child.

At the same time, Rawidowicz continued his involvement in contemporary Jewish life. He strongly supported the development of the Jewish community in the land of Israel but became increasingly concerned over the dominant currents of thought in the Zionist movement, which he felt weakened the will of Jewish survival in the Diaspora outside the land of Israel. In numerous Hebrew articles, Rawidowicz criticized the generally accepted idea that the new Jewish settlement in Israel was to serve as the spiritual center for world Jewry, relegating the Diaspora to the secondary role of receiving the culture created by the new center. He also became increasingly disturbed by the related tendency to denigrate the Diaspora by minimizing its past achievements and denying its future. Despite his love of the land of Israel, Rawidowicz believed that a Jewish Diaspora would continue to exist.

Consequently, in the late 1920s, in response to the concept of spiritual center, Rawidowicz pioneered the alternate concept of "partnership," which posited that rather than being relegated to the inferior role of imitating the spiritual center, the Diaspora should be considered an equal partner. To symbolize this relationship Rawidowicz adopted the figure of an ellipse with two foci, the land of Israel and the Diaspora, with the ellipse itself symbolizing the entirety of the Jewish people. As historical precedent for the coexistence of two such creative centers, Rawidowicz cited the experience of the land of Israel and Babylonia during the classical rabbinic period, when Babylonia had produced a Talmud in no way inferior to that of the land of Israel. Similarly, Rawidowicz maintained that the modern Diaspora had to beware lest it yield either to the debilitating effects of the new claims to hegemony or to the threat posed by cultural assimilation. Considering the preservation of the Hebrew language crucial for Jewish creativity and survival in the Diaspora, in 1931 Rawidowicz moved from writing to action as he convened the Brit Ivrit Olamit (World Union for Hebrew Culture) in Berlin and served as its head. Plans were being made for a large conference to foster the study and use of Hebrew, but the organization was disbanded in 1933 as the Nazis assumed control of the government.

Plans to appoint Rawidowicz to the Department of Philosophy at the University of Berlin were also thwarted by the accession of the Nazis to power. At the same time, his wife was dismissed from her position in cancer tissue-culture research at the medical school of the University of Berlin. Consequently, Rawidowicz accepted an invitation to Jews' College in London, which had established a program for rescuing Jewish scholars from Germany.

In London Rawidowicz continued his academic and ideological pursuits. His research in Jewish philosophy centered around Saadia Gaon, Maimonides, Mendelssohn, and Krochmal, while his ideological writings further developed the concept of partnership.

Combined with his deep commitment to the Hebrew language, his research and writings induced him to establish the Ararat Publishing Company. Its major publications included the seven volumes of the Hebrew miscellany, *Metzudah*, which he edited, and which characteristically contained sections devoted to both scholarship and contemporary issues of Jewish life. He also published in 1954 a Hebrew memorial volume to the martyred Jewish historian Simon Dubnow and his own magnum opus, the two-volume Hebrew presentation of his ideological views, *Babylon and Jerusalem* (1957).

In 1941 the British tailoring magnate Montague Burton endowed a position for Rawidowicz in medieval and modern Hebrew at the University of Leeds, where in 1946 Rawidowicz became chair of the Department of Hebrew Language and Literature. In 1948 Rawidowicz left England for the College of Jewish Studies in Chicago, and in 1951 he was invited to Brandeis University in Waltham, Massachusetts, by its first president, Abram L. Sachar. There he became the first Philip W. Lown Professor of Jewish Philosophy and first chair of the Department of Near Eastern and Judaic Studies, a position that he held until his death in Waltham. Rawidowicz was a Fellow of the American Academy of Arts and Sciences, the Medieval Academy of America, and the American Academy for Jewish Research.

Rawidowicz's impact can be gauged from the following anecdote related in the history of Brandeis University, *A Host at Last* (1976), by Sachar:

It was the deep respect in which he [Rawidowicz] was held by the scholarly world and by the highest echelons of the new Israel that bespoke the influence he created for the Department of Judaic Studies. I remember a reception at the White House in honor of the President of Israel, the late Zalman Shazar. When Thelma and I were presented to him, he exclaimed, 'Brandeis—that's where Rawidowicz is,' and he then held up the receiving line to explain to President Johnson what a magnificent scholar Rawidowicz was! Tragically he was lost to the university and the world of scholarship by an early death. (p. 247)

While Rawidowicz's philosophical research remains basic to the field of Jewish thought, he is perhaps at least equally remembered for his ideological insights; although in his lifetime his approach and conclusions were very sharply and widely criticized by those who rejected his concept of partnership and reaffirmed the traditional Zionist ideology of the centrality of the land of Israel and the negation of the Diaspora, gradually they came to be formulated independently and were increasingly accepted by the leadership and the rank and file of both the Zionist movement and the worldwide Jewish communities.

• Rawidowicz's Hebrew scholarly articles were republished, with an extensive biographical introduction and bibliography, in *Iyyunim Bemahashevet Yisrael* (Hebrew studies in Jewish thought) (2 vols., 1969–1971). An updated bibliography of his writings appears in a bilingual Hebrew and English memorial volume titled *Hagut Umaaseh: Thought and Action: Essays in Memory of Simon Rawidowicz on the Twenty-fifth Anniversary of his Death*, ed. Alfred A. Greenbaum and Alfred L. Ivry (1983). Not included in that bibliography are the subsequent *Sihotai im Bialik* (My conversations with Bialik), ed. Benjamin Ravid and Yehuda Friedlander (1983), a transcription of Hebrew notebooks containing Rawidowicz's summary of conversations with the Hebrew poet Bialik in Berlin in the 1920s together with letters and other material. Also not included is an English selection of Rawidowicz's key ideological essays (most translated from Hebrew and Yiddish) dealing with Jewish survival and the relationship between the state of Israel and the Diaspora published, with a lengthy biographical introduction, under the title *Israel: The Ever-Dying People*, ed. Ravid (1986). Also see Rawidowicz's English volume of scholarly articles, *Studies in Jewish Thought*, ed. Nahum N. Glatzer (1974), and a Yiddish volume of scholarly articles, ideological essays, and letters, *Shriften* (1962).

BENJAMIN RAVID

RAWLE, Francis (c. 1662–5 Mar. 1727), merchant and economist, was born probably in Plymouth, England, the son of Francis Rawle and Jane (maiden name unknown). Rawle's father, a devout Quaker, preferred imprisonment to compromise in matters of conscience; on one occasion he was joined in jail by his son. In search of freedom to express their convictions, the family emigrated to Pennsylvania in 1686. They brought with them a deed from William Penn for a tract of land in Plymouth township in what is now Montgomery County.

Settling in Philadelphia, the younger Rawle became a successful merchant and land promoter. In 1689 he married Martha Turner, the daughter of a wealthy Irish merchant. The couple had ten children. Wealth brought Rawle prominence and political power, and he was either appointed or elected to a succession of public offices—from justice of the peace and judge of the county court in January 1689 to alderman of the city of Philadelphia in 1691 and deputy register of wills in 1692. He subsequently served as a member of the assembly from 1704 to 1709 and again from 1719 to 1727. He is chiefly remembered, however, as an economic thinker, whose views were far from those of a colonist subservient to the interests of his mother country and its merchants.

According to Joseph Dorfman, the "pivotal problem within and between the colonies and between the colonies and the mother country remained the problem of the money supply" (*The Economic Mind in American Civilization*, vol. 1, p. 141). Hard money—coined gold and silver—was perennially scarce not only because British law forbade the export of British coin to the colonies, but mainly because the colonies generally imported goods of greater value than that of their exports. Such hard money as they were able to procure, for example from favorable balances of trade with the West Indies, usually found its way out the other end of the funnel to right the unfavorable balance with England. To remedy the resulting scarcity of specie, the colonies sought to attract coin and bullion by competitively raising their value. After 1704, however, when the English Parliament proclaimed a uniform overvaluation of approximately one-third, paper money became the favored panacea, and all the colonies resorted to its issue.

In this context, Rawle's thought assumes its importance. He attacked both the trade and monetary aspects of the colonial economic problem. In his *Ways and Means for the Inhabitants of Delaware to Become Rich* (1725), and in his 1726 reply to a critic, *A Just Rebuke to a Dialogue betwixt Simon and Timothy*, Rawle argued that the riches of a country consisted of a favorable balance of trade. To maintain this favorable balance, he advocated stimulating exports by the payment of bounties and discouraging imports, especially of West Indian rum, by the imposition of high tariffs. Riches were "the mother of luxury and of idleness," and these "daughters" must be prevented from devouring the mother.

Rawle also advocated issuing moderate amounts of paper money, in the form of public loan bills based on the security of land. He was careful to declare, however, in his 1721 treatise, *Some Remedies Proposed for Restoring the Sunk Credit of the Province of Pennsylvania* (Pennsylvania's overvaluation was higher than that of any other colony), that a law provide that the money be made a full legal tender to avoid the depreciation that would ensue from limiting its uses as currency. Although the treatise was published anonymously, Rawle was the most active member of the committee that drafted the Paper Money Act of 1723. He died in Philadelphia.

• Copies of Rawle's three pamphlets, which are extremely rare, are in the Historical Society of Pennsylvania. Biographical sketches appear in E. J. Rawle, *Records of the Rawle Family* (1898), and in *Memoirs of the Historical Society of Pennsylvania*, vol. 4, pt. 1 (1840). Joseph Dorfman briefly discusses Rawle's economic ideas in *The Economic Mind in American Civilization, 1606–1865*, vol. 1 (5 vols., 1946–1959), pp. 169–71.

STUART BRUCHEY

RAWLINGS, Marjorie Kinnan (8 Aug. 1896–14 Dec. 1953), journalist and author, was born in Washington, D.C., the daughter of Arthur Frank Kinnan, an attorney and principal examiner in the U.S. Patent Office, and Ida May Traphagen. Her father's farm in Maryland was a source of pleasure for her. After his death in 1913 and her graduation from high school in 1914, she moved with her mother and her younger brother Arthur to Madison, Wisconsin, where she received a B.A. in English from the University of Wisconsin in 1918. While a student there, she wrote a fantasy, *Into the Nowhere*, for Union Vodvil, which was copyrighted by the Dramatics Club and performed by school and college groups across the United States. After a successful college career, which included acting in amateur productions of the Dramatics Club and high academic achievement, she worked briefly for the national headquarters of the Young Women's Christian

Association in New York City. In 1919 she married her college sweetheart, Charles A. Rawlings, Jr., a veteran of World War I.

Since childhood Marjorie had wanted to be a writer. Though she had been writing since the age of six, her first recognition came five years later when she won a $2 prize for a story she had entered in a contest sponsored by the *Washington Post*. When she was just turning sixteen she won second prize in *McCall's* Child Authorship Contest for her story "The Reincarnation of Miss Hetty," which was published in the August 1912 issue of the magazine. After her marriage, Marjorie Rawlings spent much of the next decade as a journalist, writing feature articles and human-interest stories for newspapers in Louisville, Kentucky, and Rochester, New York. Charles, also journalistically inclined, was obliged to work as a traveling salesman for a shoe manufacturer. Unsuccessful, he quit the job after four years and obtained work as a newspaper reporter. Though their union was strained, in 1928 they purchased a sizable parcel of land with several thousand citrus trees at Cross Creek in northern Florida with the idea of growing oranges. Before very long Charles, a lover of yachting and sailing, began to tire of his wife's idyllic site for living and writing.

Rawlings strongly disliked urban areas, favoring instead rural retreats and the frontier dwellers she encountered in and around Cross Creek. She explained in her 1942 memoir, *Cross Creek*, that temperamentally and through inheritance she was suited to country and farm life. In a 1935 sonnet, "Having Left Cities behind Me," she wrote of how she despised what was so foreign to her, the "huddling of men by stones," the burned, fused mass of "great towns [she] knew." Her early letters to her husband reveal a radiant, outgoing young woman happily anticipating future joys. After the disillusionment that came with the breakup of her marriage, she seemed—along with a number of the female and male protagonists in her fiction, for example, Penny and Ma Baxter in *The Yearling*—to be fueled by bitter resignation and determination to endure. In addition, Rawlings's fiction was strongly influenced by her deep-seated yearning for a little boy of her own: a desire never fulfilled. As a child in Washington, D.C., she had entertained the neighborhood youngsters that she knew (only the boys, however) with tales of her own devising. Her early story, "The Reincarnation of Miss Hetty," reflected a desire for a male child; this simple wish-motif can be found throughout her fiction.

Rawlings's frustrated literary ambitions were a source of unhappiness in the 1920s, as editors seemed to have responded only with rejection slips. However, the years between 1928, when the couple purchased the Cross Creek property, and 1933, when they divorced, were momentous ones. Her stories and sketches began to be accepted by editors at *Scribner's Magazine* and *Harper's*. Two of her earliest stories written during this period, "Jacob's Ladder" (1931) and "Gal Young Un" (1933), achieved distinction. "Jacob's Ladder" won second prize in the 1931 Scribner Prize Contest; "Gal Young Un" won first prize in the 1933 O. Henry Memorial Award contest for short stories. In the latter year her first novel, *South Moon Under*, was published. These and a number of her subsequent works featured Florida "crackers": poor rural whites of Scottish or English stock, with their own archaic vernacular. Deeply empathetic with them and fascinated by their folkways (moonshining, alligator hunting, making do in the wilderness with minimal resources), she lived not only among the crackers but on occasion with them, gathering rich literary material. Years later, known and admired for the regionalism and local color of her fiction, she nevertheless objected to the term "regional writer," fearing it would degrade her as a literary artist.

Despite her artistic scruples Rawlings could write far below her literary standards now and then—an unsophisticated sentimentality was always one of her weaknesses. She could even admit to her Scribner's editor Maxwell Perkins that her second novel, *Golden Apples* (1935), was "interesting trash instead of literature." Having put a great deal of effort into writing that book, even making a trip to England to get the right "feel" for the English protagonist, Tordell, Rawlings hardly needed the unenthusiastic reviews the novel received to tell her that she had missed the mark. Though *Golden Apples* is a complex work, quite revealing of her personal experiences and inner life, Tordell is so lacking in verisimilitude, as is the poor cracker girl he victimizes, that the story loses much of its intended force; it clearly falls below her earlier novel, *South Moon Under*. At a time when definitive portraits of American life were being produced by Scribner's authors such as Ernest Hemingway, F. Scott Fitzgerald, and Thomas Wolfe, as well as the Nobel laureate Sinclair Lewis, Sherwood Anderson, and John Dos Passos, her ambitious novel of an Englishman's misadventures in the Florida backwoods failed to make a significant statement or even—for all its geographical realism—to create a little social world of its own that would remain with its readers. As with a number of her short stories, it seems on the surface to be a mere commercial job, lacking the focus and intensity of purpose that give a narrative its artistic integrity.

The Yearling (1938), winner of the 1939 Pulitzer Prize in fiction, is the most significant of Rawlings's three novels dealing with cracker life and experience in the late nineteenth century. It is set, like *South Moon Under*, in the Big Scrub country, with its clustered oaks, pines, and palmettos, much of which is within what is now the Ocala National Forest. (*Golden Apples* is set in the adjacent hammock country, less formidable than the Big Scrub, which at that time might still harbor a predatory bear or cougar.) Near the *hamaca*, Spanish for hammock, a forest entanglement of live oaks, magnolias, hickories, palms, and sweet gums, is Rawlings's idyllic Cross Creek: a turn in a country road, where Lochloosa Lake flows into Orange Lake.

In *The Yearling* twelve-year-old Jody Baxter is painfully coming of age in the savage Scrub. Though Jody is not unhappy in his rugged environment, his parents contribute to his difficulties in growing up. His angry and embittered mother, whose numerous other offspring died very early, treats him and his beloved father, Penny Baxter, harshly. The psychologically traumatized Penny, who had been hurt too often by people (in ways unspecified), chose for his family's dwelling place that hostile wilderness area where bears, panthers, and wolves roamed freely, outside human contact could be scarce and infrequent, and the threat of starvation persisted. Jody's necessary sacrifice of his adored fawn, which is devouring the family's food crop, is one of two supreme tests he must pass; the other is reconciliation with his father, from whom he has become alienated as a result of the yearling's death. Rawlings's friend Ellen Glasgow wrote in a letter to Perkins that not many books had ever affected her more profoundly than this novel, and she was tempted to use the term "genius" in connection with it. F. Scott Fitzgerald wrote to Perkins that the novel fascinated him. He ranked it above *South Moon Under* and envied Rawlings for her ease in writing action sequences like the enormously complicated hunt scene.

Cross Creek, justifiably compared with Henry David Thoreau's *Walden*, which is referred to in this latter-day pastoral work, is part autobiography, part nature study, part personal philosophy. It deals with Rawlings's "land of heart's desire," the rural area near the narrow neck of water between Lochloosa and Orange lakes, in the North Florida backwoods, a region of lakes, rivers, and hamlets. Here she made her home to 1947, following her purchase of a 72-acre orange grove, before spending much of each year in upstate New York, until her death. In the book she describes in anecdotal fashion her experiences with the local inhabitants (white and black), the passing of the seasons, and the flora and fauna of the region. She reveals also her cosmic philosophy of life, according to which, living at Cross Creek enabled her to feel intimately at one with the universe most of the time. So important to Rawlings was her bond with the land in the Cross Creek area—which she felt was not owned by her but rather belonged to the birds of the vicinity—that she requested to be and was buried there.

Cross Creek Cookery (1942) is Rawlings's chatty handbook of culinary craft, a worthy companion to its literary namesake. A film version of *The Yearling* was produced in 1946, another of *Gal Young Un* in 1979, and a distorted, inaccurate jumble commingling Rawlings's early adult life, *Cross Creek*, and *The Yearling* was made into the 1983 movie *Cross Creek*. Her story collection *When the Whippoorwill* (1940) contains some of her best cracker material, as well as the fact-based 1936 story "A Mother in Mannville," about a little boy from an orphanage and a lonely woman who felt maternal toward him. She expanded it into a six-part *Saturday Evening Post* serial, "Mountain Prelude" (1947).

In 1941 Rawlings married Norton Baskin, a restaurateur and hotel operator, in Saint Augustine, Florida. Like Charles Rawlings, Baskin was unwilling to live in the Cross Creek area, and after Baskin's return at the end of World War II from a tour of duty with the American Field Service they maintained separate residences during part of each year. In 1947 Rawlings spent the summer in Van Hornesville, in upstate New York, where she bought an old farmhouse that would become her regular summer home. Her next writing project also drew her sympathies far away from Cross Creek. *The Sojourner* is an involved agrarian allegory about a farmer yearning for his long-lost brother and married to a woman with whom he has had many children but whom does not love him. The story was to have been set in Michigan, where Rawlings's maternal grandfather had been a farmer, but she changed the locale to upstate New York; the novel was published the year she died in Saint Augustine.

Marjorie Rawlings's contribution to American literature is her memorable evocation of the harsh, colorful, enchanting cracker realm of north Florida's Big Scrub, the *hamaca*, and the Cross Creek region from the late 1800s to the early 1940s. In particular, she is remembered for her novel of a solitary little boy beginning maturation in a lonely land against the background of an unexplainable world. Although she brought the world of the Florida backwoods and its inhabitants to life as no other writer has quite managed to do, and her last novel, *The Sojourner*, is a haunting narrative of a lonely farmer's attempt to cope with his family problems, Rawlings is not likely to go down in literary history either as a major American writer or a major writer of the depression era. Her forte was not social protest but rather an ongoing protest against the failure of individuals to find love or to return love and her personal protest against her own childlessness. While only a few of her shorter fiction works can really be considered top drawer, *South Moon Under*, *Golden Apples*, and *Sojourner* are passionately expressive of an articulate, unhappy literary artist and might have been major works, had she adopted a less naive literary style and concentrated more intensely on her protagonists and unity of plot. Despite the limitations cited here, Marjorie Rawlings will likely continue to be regarded as one of the best American local colorist writers of the first half of the twentieth century.

• The University of Florida Library in Gainesville holds the bulk of available Rawlings papers, including manuscripts, correspondence, and photographs as well as personal documents. From this material Gordon E. Bigelow and Laura V. Monti edited *Selected Letters of Marjorie Kinnan Rawlings* (1983). A small amount of relevant correspondence can also be found in Julia Scribner Bigham, ed., *The Marjorie Rawlings Reader* (1956), and in John Hall Wheelock, ed., *Editor to Author: The Letters of Maxwell E. Perkins* (1950). Biographical works include Bigelow, *Frontier Eden: The Literary Career of Marjorie Kinnan Rawlings* (1966); Samuel Bellman, *Marjorie Kinnan Rawlings* (1974); and Elizabeth Silverthorne, *Marjorie Kinnan Rawlings: Sojourner at Cross Creek* (1988). For previously unpublished stories by Rawlings, see Bigelow, ed., "Marjorie Kinnan Rawlings' 'Lord Bill of the Suwannee River,'" *Southern Folklore Quarterly* 27 (June 1963): 113–30; and Bigelow, ed., "Fish Fry and Fireworks," *Florida Quarterly* 1 (Summer 1967): 1–18. See also Bigelow, "Marjorie Kinnan Rawlings' Wilderness," *Sewanee Review*

73 (1965): 299–310; and Bellman, "Marjorie Kinnan Rawlings: A Solitary Sojourner in the Florida Backwoods," *Kansas Quarterly* 2 (Spring 1970): 78–87. Additional biographical and bibliographical background on Rawlings is provided by Roger L. Tarr's edition, with preface and introduction, of *Short Stories by Marjorie Kinnan Rawlings* (1994). Tarr includes the previously uncollected story "Miss Moffatt Steps Out." An obituary is in the *New York Times*, 16 Dec. 1953.

SAMUEL I. BELLMAN

RAWLINS, John Aaron (13 Feb. 1831–6 Sept. 1869), army officer and secretary of war, was born at East Galena, Illinois, the son of James Dawson Rawlins, a farmer, and Lovisa (or Louisa, or Lucy) Collier, mother of nine children. John Rawlins grew up on a hardscrabble farm and briefly attended Rock River Seminary in Mount Morris, Illinois. He later studied law with Isaac P. Stevens of Galena and became his partner. Elected city attorney in 1857, Rawlins then formed a partnership with David Sheean that was dissolved during the Civil War. Although a Democratic presidential elector in 1860, his impassioned patriotism in 1861 attracted the attention of fellow townsman Ulysses S. Grant, who, when appointed brigadier general in August, offered Rawlins a staff position. His wife, Emily Smith, whom he married in 1856, died in August 1861. Rawlins arranged for the care of their three children, then joined Grant at Cairo.

Rawlins's career intertwined with that of Grant for the rest of his brief life. Appointed adjutant with the rank of captain of volunteers, he was promoted to major (May 1862) after the battles of Fort Donelson and Shiloh. He then served as lieutenant colonel (November 1862–August 1863) during the Vicksburg campaign and was appointed brigadier general after Vicksburg fell. As adjutant he headed Grant's staff throughout the war, a position recognized formally when he was confirmed as brigadier general in the regular army in March 1865 to fill the newly created post of chief of staff to the commanding general. As chief of staff Rawlins organized headquarters paperwork, issued orders in his commander's name, and maintained offices in the field. He wrote clumsily, and Grant sometimes actually drafted orders for him to sign. Grant invariably drafted his own reports; Rawlins merely inserted copies of pertinent correspondence and verified facts and dates.

Rawlins exaggerated his professional importance to Grant. His significance lies in their personal relationship. Grant depended on him for honesty, friendship, and loyalty. Irascible, profane, and voluble, Rawlins was also an ardent foe of liquor, who once stated that he would rather have a friend drink poison than whiskey and had threatened to resign if Grant ever drank. Throughout the war he maintained constant, if unnecessary, vigilance over Grant, which gained him the reputation of watchdog. No reliable evidence indicates that Rawlins maintained Grant's sobriety or needed to; Grant remained sober during Rawlins's lengthy absences. After Vicksburg surrendered, Grant sent Rawlins to Washington to explain to President Abraham Lincoln the removal of Major General John A. McClernand, a mission Rawlins performed satisfactorily.

After the war Rawlins remained as Grant's chief of staff and won recognition as his political spokesman and adviser. At Vicksburg Rawlins had met Mary E. Hurlburt of Connecticut, governess in a Unionist household, whom he married in 1863; they had two children. After one child died in 1867, Rawlins left on a four-month trip in the West, seeking to recover from tuberculosis. His illness was a matter of increasing concern to Grant, who after his election as president in 1868 planned to send Rawlins to Arizona for his health. Rawlins, however, preferred appointment as secretary of war, and Grant acquiesced. While secretary of war, Rawlins's steadily declining health forced him to conduct government business from home. He took a fervent interest in the independence of Cuba, rising from his deathbed to advocate belligerent rights for Cuban rebels. He owned bonds issued by the revolutionary government, but they more likely reflected than caused his commitment to Cuban independence. Only his death permitted Secretary of State Hamilton Fish to pursue conciliation with Spain. General William T. Sherman, whose march to the sea Rawlins had opposed, remembered him as "violent, passionate, enthusiastic, and personal, but always in the right direction."

• The Chicago Historical Society has a small collection of Rawlins papers. Grant served as Rawlins's executor; some Rawlins papers are located in the Grant papers in the Library of Congress. Important material exists in collections of James Harrison Wilson papers at the Library of Congress, University of Wyoming, and Wyoming State Archives and Historical Department. Wilson incorporated private correspondence no longer available in *The Life of John A. Rawlins* (1916). See also John Y. Simon, ed., *The Papers of Ulysses S. Grant* (1967–).

JOHN Y. SIMON

RAWLS, Katherine Louise (14 June 1917–8 Apr. 1982), swimmer and diver, was born in Nashville, Tennessee, the daughter of William Jennings Bryan Rawls and Sadie Rebecca McDonald, farmers. The family moved to Florida and lived in St. Augustine, Tampa, Hollywood, and Coral Gables, eventually settling in Fort Lauderdale in 1932. While still small, "Katy" contracted rheumatism. When swimming was suggested as a remedy, she took to the water readily and quickly developed natural aquatic skills, as did her younger siblings. The children became known locally as "the water babies."

Katy began competing in state meets at age nine. In 1928 she achieved a third-place finish in the Florida junior girls 220-yard freestyle race. She exhibited earlier promise as a diver, however; coached by Willis Cooling, who previously instructed Olympic champion diver Pete Desjardins, she finished second in the 1930 national Amateur Athletic Union (AAU) senior women's indoor 10-foot springboard diving event. The following year Rawls won her first U.S. swimming victories in the outdoor 220-yard breaststroke and the 300-meter individual medley (100 meters each of breaststroke, backstroke, and freestyle, in that order). She further displayed her remarkable versatility in 1932 by capturing four outdoor AAU titles: the 880-yard freestyle, the 220-yard breaststroke, the 300-meter individual medley, and the 10-foot springboard diving contests. Only Helen Wainwright had previously won both swimming and diving events during the same AAU championship meet. That year Rawls failed to make the U.S. Olympic team in the breaststroke but won the springboard diving tryout, ahead of Georgia Coleman, the favorite. In the Olympic Games in Los Angeles, California, Coleman's last, superlative dive relegated Rawls to second place and the silver medal.

Rawls excelled in the 1933 and 1934 AAU championships, seizing eight more crowns—four in diving, three in individual medleys and, most satisfactorily to her, the 1934 outdoor 300-meter medley relay with her sister Dorothy Rawls and June Burr, representing the Miami Beach (Fla.) Club. On 2 and 3 September 1934 Rawls astounded the sports world by totally dominating the water decathlon, a unique, new competition for women. She won it by almost 2,000 points and beat her six opponents (all AAU champions at one time or another) in all 10 events: 50-meter freestyle, 100-meter breaststroke, 50-meter backstroke, 50-meter rescue race, and 200-meter freestyle on the first day; 10-foot springboard diving, 50-meter breaststroke, 100-meter freestyle, 100-meter backstroke, and 150-meter medley on the second day. Paul Gallico called Rawls "Florida's one-woman swimming team." That year she finished seventh in the voting for the prestigious James E. Sullivan Memorial Trophy, honoring the outstanding American amateur athlete of the year. In 1935 she graduated from Fort Lauderdale High School and added five more AAU titles to her impressive total, including two individual medleys, two breaststroke contests, and one freestyle race.

A dogged competitor who expressed her resolve by saying, "I don't count thirds or seconds, just firsts," Rawls uniformly maintained ideal sportsmanship, humble and gracious in victory and defeat. In 1936 she qualified for the U.S. Olympic team by winning the 100-meter freestyle and the three-meter springboard events. Unfortunately for her, the individual medley—her specialty—never became part of the Olympic program. In the Olympics in Berlin, Germany, she came in seventh and last in the 100-meter freestyle. Once more she received a silver medal in the springboard event, again losing the gold on the last, near-perfect dive of a U.S. teammate, this time to 13-year-old Marjorie Gestring. The final point scores were Gestring, 89.37; Rawls, 88.35; and Dorothy Poynton Hill, 82.36. Rawls also earned a bronze medal as lead-off swimmer on the U.S. women's 400-meter freestyle relay team.

In 1937 and 1938 Rawls won the same six AAU events. These included two indoor events—the 100-meter breaststroke and the 300-yard medley—and four outdoor events—the 440-yard, the 880-yard, and the one-mile freestyle races and the individual medley, also known as the aquatic "grand slam." Her only loss in these meets was a second-place finish to Doris Brennan in the 1937 indoor 500-yard freestyle. In the 1937 Sullivan Trophy voting, Rawls was third after tennis great Don Budge and distance runner Don Lash; in 1938 she finished second behind Lash.

Rawls's slight, 5'2", 108-pound physique and soft Florida drawl belied her tough strength and stamina. Generally considered the best female aquatic star of the 1930s, she was also one of the most accomplished women of all time in swimming and diving, with proven excellence in all strokes and all distances up to one mile and in springboard diving. She set no world records but, on more than twenty occasions, raced to new American records in various events and distances. Her record of 33 individual AAU championships stood until the 1980s, when Tracy Caulkins broke it; by that time the number of events per meet had doubled.

During the late 1930s Rawls shifted her interests from the water to the air. Fascinated by airplanes, she learned to fly them and became a licensed pilot. In May 1938 she married Theodore H. Thompson, an aviator who operated a flying school from a hangar in Fort Lauderdale. Her last appearance in a major swimming meet occurred in the 1939 AAU indoor championships, when, in the 300-yard medley, she finished third behind Brennan and Helen Rains. As a commercial pilot, Rawls flew charter and ferry flights for her husband's enterprise. This and growing certainty that the 1940 Olympics would not be held prompted her decision to end her swimming career.

Rawls had accumulated more than 500 certified flying hours by 1943 when she was accepted as one of the initial 25 pilots of the Women's Auxiliary Flying Squadron (WAFS), whose mission was to fly training and liaison aircraft from factories to domestic airfields and, later, to deliver fighters and twin-engine bombers to combat zones until the end of World War II. Rawls and her husband divorced in 1947, and she married Frank Green, also a commercial pilot, in 1949. During their marriage she accompanied him to his various work stations, including a two-year stay in Saudi Arabia. They were divorced in 1975, and Rawls legally resumed her maiden name. She also taught swimming at the Jack Tar Hotel in Marathon, Florida, and, from 1956 until her retirement in 1978, at the Greenbrier Hotel in White Sulphur Springs, West Virginia. She was elected in 1965 to the International Swimming Hall of Fame among its initial inductees. In retirement she lived in Royal Palm Beach, Florida, and died in Belle Glade, Florida.

• Information about Rawls is in Buck Dawson, *Weismuller to Spitz: An Era to Remember: The First 21 Years—The International Swimming Hall of Fame* (1988), p. 230; Ralph Hickok, *A Who's Who of Sports Champions: Their Stories and Records* (1995), p. 649; Pat Besford, *Encyclopaedia of Swimming* (1971), p. 138; and Jerry Nason, "Katherine Rawls: 'Little Miss Minnow,'" in *Famous American Athletes of Today: Sixth Series* (1934), pp. 199–228. Other articles of note are Jack

Lippert, "The 'Minnow' Girl," *Scholastic*, 6 Oct. 1934; the *Miami Herald*, 17 Nov. 1981; and Helen Hulett Searl, "Girl of the Month: Katherine Rawls, Champion Swimmer and All-Round American Girl," *Good Housekeeping*, Apr. 1938, pp. 93, 239. The *New York Times*, 3 and 4 Sept. 1934, reports Rawls's decathlon victory. The annual *Spalding's Official Athletic Almanac* issues from 1931 to 1940 record her AAU championship wins and placings. An obituary is in the *Miami Herald*, 9 and 10 Apr. 1982.

FRANK V. PHELPS

RAY, Charles Bennett (25 Dec. 1807–15 Aug. 1886), African-American journalist, educator, and minister, was born in Falmouth, Massachusetts, the son of Joseph Aspinwall Ray, a postal worker, and Annis Harrington, a well-read and deeply religious woman. He claimed descent from American Indians, as well as English and Africans. After schooling in Falmouth, Ray went to work for five years on his grandfather's farm in Rhode Island and then settled on Martha's Vineyard to learn the bootmaker's trade.

A profound experience of Christian conversion convinced Ray that he should become a Methodist minister. With financial aid from white abolitionist friends, he gained entrance into the Wesleyan Academy in Wilbraham, Massachusetts. Though he was the only black in the school, the atmosphere was friendly. The principal, Willbur Fisk, was a broad-minded and widely respected Methodist minister and educator. Chosen as the first president of Wesleyan University in Middletown, Connecticut, Fisk admitted Ray to the college in the fall of 1832. Student anger at the presence of an African American, however, forced Ray to withdraw after only six weeks.

During a visit to New York City, Ray met Theodore S. Wright, pastor of Manhattan's thriving First Colored Presbyterian Church. A close friendship developed and was a strong force in Ray's life. Now in his late twenties, Ray set up his trade as a bootmaker in the black district of lower Manhattan, only a few blocks from Wright's home and church. Ray lived in the city for over fifty years and became acquainted and influential with all segments of the city's black community.

By the mid-1830s Ray had acquired as partner in his boot and shoe business Samuel Cornish, a black Presbyterian pastor who founded the first black newspaper, *Freedom's Journal*, in 1827. When some of the city's black leaders founded another paper, the *Colored American*, in 1837, Cornish was asked to be chief editor. He, in turn, invited Ray to be the paper's traveling reporter and promoter of subscriptions. Ray had married Henrietta Green Regulus in 1834, but in October 1836 she died in childbirth, as did her baby. Tragically left without dependents, Ray took to the road with little payment beyond expenses. Over a two-year period, he became an effective link between the *Colored American* and individual blacks living in southern New England, upper New York State, New Jersey, Pennsylvania, and Ohio. The paper published his reports regarding black education, business, and church life in various communities. His eloquent endorsement of the *Colored American* in speeches and sermons (he was ordained a Methodist minister in 1837) built up subscriptions and kept the paper afloat. Its circulation probably ranged between 1,500 and 2,500.

When traveling in New York State, Ray was engaged in overtly political activity, securing signatures for three petitions to the state legislature: 1) to recover full voting rights for black men, of which they had been deprived in the 1820s; 2) to end the policy allowing slaveowners to enter the state with a slave, stay for up to nine months, and leave with their ownership unchallenged; and 3) to secure a jury trial for any black falsely accused of being a runaway slave. The accused were customarily taken by the "slave catcher" to a city magistrate and sworn by bribed witnesses to be runaways from a particular southern slaveowner.

By 1839 Ray became owner and editor of the *Colored American* after Cornish had resigned and some of its early financial backers had withdrawn support. Through it, and in spite of the opposition of many white abolitionists and some black leaders fearful of a white backlash, he successfully promoted a convention of New York State blacks, during the summer of 1840, to organize a statewide petition drive and lobbying effort to recover the vote. Ray's faith in black political activism had been strengthened in May 1840 when the New York State legislature passed and Governor William Henry Seward signed a bill requiring a jury trial for blacks charged with being fugitives. Nearly 140 black delegates met for three days in Albany in August 1840. They endorsed public letters to the state's black citizens and to the white population. Ray and his fellow activist, the young Presbyterian minister Henry Highland Garnet, spent the fall collecting thousands of petition signatures. But in spite of these efforts and the governor's public endorsement of a bill providing re-enfranchisement, the measure was defeated in the state assembly in April 1841 by a vote of forty-six to twenty-nine.

After a long battle to prevent financial collapse of the *Colored American*, Ray closed it out at the end of 1841. However, the paper remained the most impressive black-edited and black-financed paper up to the Civil War (Douglass's journals were financed primarily by whites).

Ray remained active after the paper's closing. He was prominent among the black supporters of the antislavery Liberty party in the early 1840s and remained a leader in both the New York City and state vigilance committees devoted to aiding runaway slaves and preventing the kidnapping of black people by slave-catchers.

Ray was also a central figure in the most highly organized pre–Civil War black attempt to improve schooling for blacks in a large city. With two sons and five daughters borne by his second wife, Charlotte Augusta Burroughs, whom he married in 1840, Ray had a personal stake in better education. In 1847 some of Manhattan's black leaders founded the New York Society for the Promotion of Education Among Colored

Children, and from 1851 to 1865, Ray was the organization's president. The society's most significant achievements were the founding and efficient operation of two new elementary schools for black children, and, in 1859, a thorough review of the whole system of city-run black schools which revealed that only one-fortieth as much had been spent per black child for school sites and buildings as per white child. He urged that New York City schools be desegregated as they had been in Boston. If not, the board should at least provide better school buildings for blacks in less dismal locations. Within two years the board mandated substantial improvements.

Shortly after closing out the *Colored American* Ray had returned to the Christian ministry which had been his original calling. In 1844 he began what would be several decades of work as "City Missionary to the Destitute Colored Population." He did street preaching, conducted Sunday services, and held weekly worship meetings for the poor, the handicapped, and the elderly. In 1845 he was installed as minister of a small new Congregational church, Bethesda, whose members were largely drawn from the "lost souls" he had aided on the city streets of lower Manhattan.

In the aftermath of John Brown's 1859 raid, Ray joined other black clergy in awed tributes to the "Old Man" for his commitment and courage. Once the Civil War had begun, Ray strongly supported black enlistments in the Union army. In 1863, in the wake of the New York City draft riots, which had left scores of blacks dead and thousands homeless, Ray and Henry Highland Garnet teamed up once more to visit three thousand families and ascertain the amount of relief needed.

In later years Charles B. Ray delighted in the accomplishments of his three daughters. In the early 1870s, for instance, Charlotte became the first woman to graduate from the Howard University Law Department and was said to have been the first woman admitted to the practice of law in the District of Columbia. Ray served as pastor of Bethesda Church until 1868 and as city missionary until his death in New York in 1886.

• The most enlightening early biographical work on Ray is the one written by his two daughters, Florence and Henrietta Cordelia Ray, *Sketch of the Life of Rev. Charles B. Ray* (1887). The best biographical sketch of Ray is in the *Dictionary of American Negro Biography*, ed. Rayford W. Logan and Michael R. Winston (1982). The major source of Ray's own writings during the years 1837 to 1841 is the files of the *Colored American* at the Schomburg Center for Research in Black Culture, New York Public Library. Microfilm copies of manuscript letters and reports by Ray are provided in the *Black Abolitionist Papers, 1830–1865*, microfilm edition. This material is arranged chronologically. For an index of the material, arranged by author, see George E. Carter and C. Peter Ripley, eds., *Black Abolitionist Papers, 1830–1865: A Guide to the Microfilm Edition* (1981). See also David E. Swift, *Black Prophets of Justice: Activist Clergy before the Civil War* (1989), a collective biography of Ray, Cornish, Wright, Garnet, Amos Beman, and J. W. C. Pennington.

DAVID SWIFT

RAY, Charlotte E. (13 Jan. 1850–4 Jan. 1911), lawyer, was born in New York City, the daughter of Reverend Charles Bennett Ray, the minister of Bethesda Congregational Church, and his second wife, Charlotte Augusta Burroughs, a native of Savannah, Georgia. Charles Bennett Ray, who apparently was born free in Falmouth, Massachusetts, combined Indian with black and white ancestry. Characterized as eloquent and fearless, the well-known abolitionist pastor was a key figure in assisting slaves to escape from the South through the Underground Railroad. He also had been a former editor of the *Colored American*, an African American newspaper in New York City. Thus, although Ray, one of seven children, was born during the time of slavery, her family background clearly gave her a head start.

In early childhood Ray attended the Institution for the Education of Colored Youth in Washington, D.C. Founded in 1851 by educator Myrtilla Miner, the private institution was one of few schools that black females could attend. By 1869 Ray was a teacher at the Howard University Normal and Preparatory Department. In the evenings she studied law at Howard University, where she specialized in commercial law. As a senior, in February 1872, Ray delivered a well-received paper on chancery (a court of equity in the American judicial system). Listed in school records as one of fourteen graduating seniors in the fifteen-member class of 1872, Ray was the first woman to graduate from the Howard University Law Department. (Another woman would not graduate from the department for a decade.) At her graduation—which took place only seven years after slaves had been set free by the Thirteenth Amendment and only twenty-five years after Macon B. Allen, the first black American lawyer, was admitted to an American bar, in Maine—Ray became the first black female lawyer in the United States.

On 23 April 1872 Ray was admitted to the District of Columbia bar, which only recently had been opened to women. A month later it was announced, in the 23 May 1872 issue of the *New National Era*, a Washington, D.C., paper published by African Americans, that Ray "had been admitted to practice before the Supreme Court of the District of Columbia" (quoted in Logan, p. 50). In addition to being the first black female graduate of any law school in the United States, the first female graduate of Howard University's law school, the first female admitted to the District of Columbia bar, and the first female admitted to practice in the Supreme Court of the District, Ray also is sometimes referred to as the first woman to graduate from any non-profit university law school. As historian Rayford Logan has noted, however, the last two "firsts" are "difficult to establish" (p. 50).

Challenging Ray's designation as the first female lawyer admitted to the D.C. bar is the following, which appears in an 1882 publication: "In the District of Columbia MRS. B. A. LOCKWOOD was admitted in 1870, and CHARLOTTE E. RAY in 1872, on graduating from Howard University" (Hanaford, p. 643). It is not clear, however, to which bar the reference is made—the District of Columbia bar or the Supreme Court of the District of Columbia. Complicating the issue is the fact that this same publication also quotes from the 25 May 1872 *Woman's Journal*, which grants to Ray "the honor of being the first lady lawyer in Washington" (Hanaford, p. 649), the latter statement seeming to contradict the preceding assertion that Lockwood was admitted to the bar in 1870 and Ray in 1872. Another source, however, indicates that Lockwood graduated from law school in 1873 and was admitted to the D.C. bar the same year (McHenry, p. 250). Thus, the listing of Ray's traditionally acknowledged "first" seems to be in order.

Not long after she opened her own law office in Washington, D.C. (presumably in 1872), Ray was forced to give up active practice because Constitutional and legal segregation of the races had precluded her ability to attract sufficient business to remain open. By 1879 she had returned to New York City, where she taught in the Brooklyn public school system along with two of her sisters, one of whom, H. Cordelia Ray, was a poet whose poems were published in the *AME Review*. Sometime after 1886 Ray was married to a man named Fraim. (Nothing more is known about him.)

After 1895 Ray seems to have been active in the National Association of Colored Women, and she also apparently supported the cause of voting rights for women because in 1876 she attended the annual convention of the National Woman Suffrage Association in New York. By 1897 she was living in Woodside, Long Island, where she died fourteen years later of acute bronchitis. She was buried in Brooklyn's Cypress Hill Cemetery in the Ray family plot, but her tombstone records her married name as "Fraim." (She is listed as "Traim" on her death report, apparently a typo.)

Despite the fact that her legal practice was short-lived, Ray should be remembered for her trailblazing efforts in law. Although she apparently was free-born, as a black female she started life with two strikes against her: racism and sexism. Described as a dusky mulatto with an intelligent countenance, she overcame racial segregation to earn a law degree and achieve not only many "firsts" as a lawyer but also a reputation for being one of the country's best lawyers on questions involving corporation law. As one contemporary noted, "Her eloquence is commendable for her sex in the court-room, and her legal advice is authoritative" (Majors, p. 184). According to the 1920 census, Ray was, during the previous decade, one of two women among the 950 black lawyers in the United States.

• Material related to Ray's matriculation in the Law Department at Howard University and information about other aspects of her life can be obtained from the Moorland-Spingarn Research Center, Howard University Archives, Washington, D.C. Regarding the issue of her designation as the first woman admitted to the District of Columbia bar, see Phebe A. Hanaford, *Daughters of America* (1882); Robert McHenry, ed., *Liberty's Women* (1980); Leon A. Higginbotham, Jr., *Blacks in the Law* (1983); and Rayford Logan, *Howard University: The First Hundred Years, 1867–1967* (1969). Other informative sources include Monroe A. Majors, *Noted Negro Women, Their Triumphs and Activities* (1893), and Dorothy Thomas, *Women Lawyers in the U.S.* (1957).

LOIS BALDWIN MORELAND

RAY, Gordon Norton (8 Sept. 1915–15 Dec. 1986), educator, foundation executive, and book collector, was born in New York City, the only child of Jesse Gordon Ray, who was then the New York representative of an Indiana limestone company, and Jessie Norton. His father's business soon took the family to Chicago, where Ray spent his childhood. In 1932, when Ray graduated from New Trier High School in Winnetka, his parents moved to Bloomington, Indiana (having started their own limestone company there in 1927 on land owned by his mother's family), and he enrolled in Indiana University. His studies there brought him membership in three honorary societies and both A.B. and A.M. degrees in French literature in 1936. Moving to Harvard University for graduate school, he took another A.M. (1938) and then completed a Ph.D. dissertation, "Thackeray and France," in 1940. During the course of this work, he became famous among graduate students throughout the country when he was selected as editor of William Makepeace Thackeray's letters by the Thackeray heirs. During the next two and a half years (while teaching at Harvard in 1940–1941 and holding two Guggenheim Fellowships from July 1941 through November 1942), he completed his editing of the letters—just before he was called to active duty in the U.S. Navy on 1 December 1942. His forty months of naval service (to 23 March 1946), in which he attained the rank of lieutenant and earned seven battle stars and a presidential unit citation, included two and a half years as radar officer in the Pacific aboard the aircraft carriers *Belleau Wood* and *Boxer*.

With his four volumes of Thackeray's letters published (1945–1946), he was well launched on a scholarly career. In the autumn of 1946 he became professor of English at the University of Illinois, and during his fourteen years in Urbana (to June 1960) he demonstrated—as he did for the rest of his life—his skill in scholarship, administration, and book collecting. He published a series of distinguished works on Thackeray, culminating in a massive two-volume life (*Thackeray* [1955, 1958]), which remains a masterpiece of literary biography (just as his edition of the letters stands as a model of documentary editing). His influence as a literary scholar was further increased when he acted as general editor (1954–1971) of the Houghton Mifflin Company's Riverside Series, which came to be widely used in college classrooms. During much of his Illinois period, he also chaired the English department (1950–1957) and served as vice president and provost of the university (1957–1960). His book and manuscript collecting, which was a vital part of his life from about 1948 onward, benefited his university as well, for on his annual book-buying trips abroad he bought for the university library whole roomsful of books, as well as the papers of H. G. Wells and the archives of the publishers Richard Bentley and Grant Richards. His extensive buying for himself was made possible after 1956 by the income from the limestone company stock inherited from his parents (he was president of the company from 1974 until his death); during his Illinois years he assembled remarkably comprehensive collections of books and manuscripts documenting English and American literature from 1789 to 1914.

Ray's Illinois period ended in the summer of 1960 when he moved to New York to accept the position of associate secretary general of the John Simon Guggenheim Memorial Foundation. Three years later, upon the retirement of Henry Allen Moe, who had been the chief executive officer of the foundation since its founding in 1925, he became its president. In the twenty-two years of his presidency (1963–1985), he continued the foundation's policy of rewarding excellence in individual achievement and oversaw the expenditure of $96 million to 8,100 fellows. His prominence as a scholarly administrator, his knowledge of the world of learning, and his reputation for evenhandedness and careful judgment combined to make him a favorite choice as a speaker on ceremonial occasions and as a member of boards of directors. He spoke at commencement exercises, at conferences, and at dedications of library buildings, commenting (in addresses that became published essays) on the state of higher education and the role of books in humanistic scholarship, and he served on some three dozen boards and committees, including fifteen years as chairman of the board of the Smithsonian Institution (1970–1985).

His active role as spokesman for the scholarly world did not prevent his continued activity as scholar and collector. For eighteen of his foundation years (1962–1980), he was a professor of English at New York University, teaching popular courses in Victorian literature and directing dissertations. His book *H. G. Wells & Rebecca West* (1974) was the climax of a series of his publications growing out of the Wells papers that he had brought to Illinois. But the major publications of his later years reflected his collecting interests, which had become English and French illustrated books and bindings. Two exhibitions of these items at the Pierpont Morgan Library resulted in two landmark books, *The Illustrator and the Book in England from 1790 to 1914* (1976) and *The Art of the French Illustrated Book, 1700 to 1914* (1982), which impressively demonstrate the relationship between scholarship and collecting. His 1985 Lyell Lectures at Oxford University dealt with French Art Deco bindings and thus completed his account of the books he had collected (all of which were bequeathed to the Morgan Library).

His achievements brought him many honors, including thirteen honorary degrees, three medals, and election to the Royal Society of Literature (1948), the American Academy of Arts and Sciences (1962), the American Antiquarian Society (1971), the American Philosophical Society (1977), and the Roxburghe Club (1982). As a scholar he was known not only through his professional attainments but also through his wide range of personal acquaintance. Though formal and reserved by temperament, he was gregarious and brought to his conversation an enormous fund of literary allusion and perceptive anecdote, and his regular dining with Guggenheim fellows caused him to have a kind of paternal influence on the work of hundreds of other scholars. He may well have been unique in the distinction of his simultaneous contribution to three areas of endeavor; he was the author of several classic scholarly works, one of the great twentieth-century book collectors, and a leading force in the learned community of his time. He died in New York City.

• Ray's papers relating to his work at the John Simon Guggenheim Memorial Foundation, including his correspondence (whether on foundation business or not) with persons who held Guggenheim Fellowships, are in the foundation's archives in New York. His other papers, documenting his writing, his editing of the Riverside Editions, and his collecting, are housed at the Pierpont Morgan Library. The most comprehensive account of his life is G. Thomas Tanselle's introduction to the posthumous volume of Ray's collected essays, *Books as a Way of Life* (1988), which includes a full listing of Ray's publications and Ray's own accounts of his collecting. An obituary is in the *New York Times*, 16 Dec. 1986.

G. THOMAS TANSELLE

RAY, Isaac (16 Jan. 1807–31 Mar. 1881), psychiatrist, was born in Beverly, Massachusetts, the son of Captain Isaac Rea and his second wife, the widow Lydia Symonds. The spelling of the family name was changed sometime between 1807 and the death of Captain Ray in 1814.

Graduated from Phillips Academy in Andover, Massachusetts, Ray attended Bowdoin College for two years and then failed to return for the spring semester for unknown reasons. He was apparently a model student while at Bowdoin. Ray's fellow students included Luther V. Bell, who was to become founding member of the American Psychiatric Association, poet Henry Wadsworth Longfellow, and Franklin Pierce, later the fourteenth president of the United States.

Isaac Ray began the study of medicine as an apprentice to Samuel Hart of Beverly. He then enrolled at Harvard Medical School and was an apprentice to George Cheyne Shattuck of Boston. In 1825 Ray left Harvard to attend the Medical School of Maine at Bowdoin College. At that time, instead of taking courses progressively more difficult, medical students attended two years of the same lectures, prepared a dissertation, and, if they satisfied the faculty as to competence, achievement, and moral character, were graduated as physicians. Eleven manuscript pages in length, Ray's "Dissertation on Pathological Anatomy" is a knowledgeable and thoughtful document. He received his medical degree in 1827 at age twenty.

Ray attempted to set up practice in Portland, Maine. He supplemented his meager income by giving public lectures on natural history and published a textbook on comparative animal physiology. As he observed later in a letter to a former professor at Bowdoin

At the tender age of 20, being a member of the medical profession in regular standing, I offered my services as a practitioner of medicine and surgery, to the people of Portland, in 1827. They manifested no vehement desire to avail themselves of this privilege, & thinking my services might be better appreciated somewhere else, I removed in 1829 to Eastport, where I resided till 1841.

In 1831 Isaac Ray married Abigail May Frothingham, the daughter of the deceased Judge John Frothingham of Portland. They lived in Eastport, Maine, while Ray published articles in the medical literature and wrote *A Treatise on the Medical Jurisprudence of Insanity* (1838). Separate editions were published in Edinburgh and London in 1839. In 1841 a scandal at the Maine Insane Hospital in Augusta resulted in the firing of its first superintendent, Cyrus Knapp. Ray was offered the post and accepted it. The Ray family, which now included two children, moved to Augusta.

Ray was the medical superintendent at the Maine Insane Hospital from 1841 to 1845, during which time he wrote several annual reports that clearly laid out the principles of moral (i.e., psychological) management of the insane and also criticized the then current methods of compiling statistics regarding the insane and their asylums. His major criticisms were that they purported to measure subjective factors (including etiology and treatment outcome) and that they were not standardized in a manner that would allow them to mean the same thing at different asylums or even at the same asylum with a different superintendent. Some discreet comments he made later suggest that he was greatly offended by political interference in the running of the hospital. He had almost decided to leave the field of the medical care of the insane when he accepted in 1845 the superintendency of the yet-to-be-built Butler Hospital in Providence, Rhode Island. His Bowdoin College friend, Luther V. Bell, had been offered the post originally but did not want to leave the McLean Asylum, where he was superintendent. It is very likely that it was he who suggested Isaac Ray for the post.

In 1844, along with twelve other medical superintendents of private and state asylums and hospitals for the insane, Isaac Ray was a founder of the Association of Medical Superintendents of American Institutions for the Insane (AMSAII). Its purpose was to help its members deal with common problems and to facilitate professional education. It became the American Medico-Psychological Society in 1892 and the American Psychiatric Association in 1922. It was the first American medical specialty society and, therefore, psychiatry is the oldest medical specialty in the United States. Its journal, the *American Journal of Insanity*, was for many years owned by the New York State Lunatic Hospital at Utica. It became the *American Journal of Psychiatry* in 1922 and is the oldest medical specialty journal published in the United States.

From the start Ray was dedicated to the moral management and treatment of the insane and to publicizing the benefits of such an approach. "Moral management" and "moral treatment," as applied to nineteenth-century American treatment of the insane, were used to signify the moral powers in faculty psychology (i.e., the volitional and affective functions as distinguished from the cognitive or intellectual functions) and *not* moral in the sense of moralistic or good and evil. In late twentieth-century American language, *moral* would have a meaning similar to the one it has in the phrase "moral support."

In *Second Report of the Superintendent of the Maine Insane Hospital, December 1841*, Ray wrote

It is a cardinal principle in our moral treatment to deal with our patients fairly, honestly and candidly, for we believe that no temporary advantage can counterbalance the mischief that inevitably arises from deceit. . . . [A new patient] is requested, in the language of kindness and regard, to conduct himself with propriety, and assured that the number and kind of his privileges will depend upon the manner in which he uses them. Instead of meeting his unreasonable requests . . . by a tissue of petty deceptions, we prefer telling him the plain truth. . . . It may produce a little irritation at first, but it saves us from the infinite trouble and vexation which are sure to arise from pursuing the opposite course. The moment a patient discovers that we have been deceiving him, his respect for us is gone, and our moral influence over him is at an end. . . . In one word, we endeavor always to treat our patients, as every honorable, well bred man treats another in the common intercourse of society. (Pp. 50–51)

In 1845 Ray resigned from the Maine Insane Hospital and moved his family to Portland, Maine, to await the opening of the Butler Hospital in Providence. His daughter died of a consumptive disease in the following year. Between the time he resigned as superintendent of the Maine Insane Hospital and the opening of the Butler Hospital, Ray traveled to Europe's asylums to study their organization, facilities, and administrative policies. The report of that trip was published in the *American Journal of Insanity* in April 1846. Butler Hospital admitted its first patient in December 1847.

In 1855 Isaac Ray was elected president of the AMSAII and remained in that office until 1859. He was a prolific writer and eloquent educator. In 1829 he had published his first book, *Conversations on the Animal Economy*, a small primer on comparative animal physiology cast in the form of a dialogue between a teacher and his young student Emily. His *Treatise on the Medical Jurisprudence of Insanity* went through five editions (1838, 1844, 1853, 1860, and 1871). In 1863 he published *Mental Hygiene*, designed "mainly to expose the mischievous effects of many practices and customs prevalent in modern society, and to present some practical suggestions relative to the attainment of mental soundness and vigor." His "Project of a Law for Determining the Legal Relations of the Insane" (*American Journal of Insanity* 7 [1850–1851]: 92–96, 215–34) served as the major foundation for a recommended model system of laws for the insane promulgated by the association in 1869. It was also the basis of the first statute in Pennsylvania protecting the legal rights of the insane in that same year.

In 1873 Ray published a selection of his papers, *Contributions to Mental Pathology*. From 1848 through 1865 he wrote the superintendent's report of the Butler Hospital, designed to educate the reader about insanity and about the activities and results of the care at the hospital while it also addressed his fellow medical superintendents worldwide. Under Ray's leadership, Butler Hospital attained an international reputation as an outstanding psychiatric hospital.

Ray remained superintendent of Butler Hospital until his retirement in January 1866. His son, Benjamin Lincoln, after receiving his medical degree from Harvard in 1859, had served his father as the assistant physician. At the time of Ray's retirement, Benjamin Lincoln made it known that he did not intend to continue as a "psychiatrist" (the term did not actually come into vogue until the end of the nineteenth century), and the Ray family relocated to Philadelphia where Benjamin Lincoln established a general medical practice. Soon after this move, Ray was appointed to the board of the Philadelphia Almshouse Department of the Insane and was a founding member of the Philadelphia Social Science Association.

In 1868 Ray began a correspondence with Charles Doe, then associate justice of the New Hampshire Supreme Court. The judge, when a young lawyer, had read Ray's *Treatise* and had been greatly impressed by it. Eventually their correspondence resulted in Judge Doe's formulation of the New Hampshire doctrine, which specifies that the product of insanity cannot be a crime, a contract, or a will, and in Ray's classic article, "On Confinement of the Insane," in the *American Law Review* (3 [Jan. 1869]: 193–217). In that article Ray presented the three necessary elements for any law regarding the involuntary hospitalization of the insane.

In the first place the law should put no hindrance in the way of the prompt use of those instrumentalities which are regarded as the most effectual in promoting the comfort and restoration of the patient. Secondly, it should spare all unnecessary exposure of private troubles and all unnecessary conflict with popular prejudices. Thirdly, it should protect individuals from wrongful imprisonment. It would be objection enough to any legal provision, that it failed to secure these objects, in the completest possible manner.

These elements still remain necessary, valid, and often unachieved.

Ray remained active in the professional world of the superintendents, and, while a member of the Committee of the Insane Department of the Philadelphia Almshouse, he fought the other members of the committee regarding the abuses of the patients by the institution and its staff. In 1873 he presented a paper at the Philadelphia Social Science Association titled "What Shall Philadelphia Do with Its Paupers?," which ex-posed and decried the abominable conditions at the almshouse (later the Philadelphia General Hospital). Following this presentation, Ray's appointment to the almshouse committee was not renewed.

In 1879 Benjamin Lincoln Ray died suddenly (probably of a stroke). Isaac Ray reacted to his son's death with an increase in arthritic symptoms, respiratory difficulties, and clinical depression. He died quietly in his sleep at his home in Philadelphia.

Isaac Ray was one of the outstanding intellects among the founders of the American Psychiatric Association and by example, as well as by his prolific and articulate writings, did more than any other American psychiatrist of his time to advance the medical professionalization of the care of the mentally ill. He was one of very few nineteenth-century American physicians to recognize and attempt to meet his obligations to patients, their families, and their communities. His efforts to make scientific the collecting and reporting of statistics about the disease and the asylums, to provide legal protections, to advance the discipline of forensic psychiatry, and to reform the public care of the mentally ill make Isaac Ray worthy of far more historical study than he has received.

• Most of Ray's papers are in the Isaac Ray Library of Butler Hospital in Providence, R.I., although some are in the archives of Bowdoin College or dispersed among other collections. For commentary on his work and influence, see Jacques M. Quen, "Isaac Ray: Have We Learned His Lessons?," *Bulletin of the American Academy of Psychiatry and Law* 2 (1974): 137–47. See also John Sanbourne Bockoven, *Moral Treatment in American Psychiatry* (1963), and Constance M. McGovern, *Masters of Madness: Social Origins of the American Psychiatric Profession* (1985).

JACQUES M. QUEN

RAY, Johnnie (10 Jan. 1927–24 Feb. 1990), popular singer, pianist, and composer, was born John Alvin Ray in Dallas, Oregon, the son of Elmer Ray and Hazel (maiden name unknown). At age twelve Ray became deaf in his right ear and subsequently wore a hearing aid. Influenced by gospel and rhythm and blues, Ray was a self-taught pianist and vocalist. He began singing on Portland radio and performing in bars and clubs in Portland and in Hollywood, California, at the age of fifteen, and by the late 1940s he was performing small dates throughout the country. In 1951 he attained valuable exposure at Detroit's Flame club.

Ray was signed to Columbia Records in 1951 by Danny Kessler and placed with the company's OKeh label. His first single, "Whiskey and Gin," was a minor hit. The second, "Cry," produced by Mitch Miller and backed by the Four Lads, was a major hit. The song succeeded on both pop and R&B charts, and, according to Kessler, many listeners were under the mistaken impression that Ray was black, some also believing that he was a woman. The record sold a million copies within eight weeks of release, and 2 million copies by June 1952. The b-side, "The Little White Cloud That Cried," was also a success in its own right. In

1952 Ray married Marilyn Morrison, but they had no children and were divorced two years later.

By July 1952 Ray was being described in *Billboard* as "the mainstay of an industry," and the magazine ran a four-part series on his career and finances. He was subsequently transferred to the main division of the Columbia label and had hits with "Please Mr. Sun" (1952), "Here I Am—Broken Hearted" (1952), "Walkin' My Baby Back Home" (1952), and "Somebody Stole My Gal" (1953).

Ray continued to acknowledge his debt to gospel and R&B music, notably in an article that appeared in the May 1953 issue of *Ebony* ("Negroes Taught Me to Sing"). In 1954 he appeared in the motion picture *There's No Business Like Show Business*, alongside Ethel Merman, Dan Daley, and Donald O'Connor, singing "If You Believe" and "Alexander's Ragtime Band." He also continued to perform and record songs originally associated with black artists, such as the Drifters' "Such a Night" (1954) and the Prisonaires' "Just Walkin' in the Rain" (1956). Nevertheless, "Cry" was to be his only crossover success. "Such a Night" was banned by several U.S. pop radio stations. The lyrics were sexually suggestive, but it seems likely that the ban had more to do with the feud between rival performing rights organizations ASCAP and BMI than with the song itself. "Such a Night" was handled by BMI, and at that time ASCAP was mounting a general campaign to remove BMI material from the radio.

Throughout the early 1950s Ray had a large and passionate following among teens, but he also succeeded in building a substantial following among adult audiences through appearances at clubs like New York's Copa. He played an important part in mobilizing the white youth market, prefiguring the forces that would fuel the rise of rock and roll. "Cry" was one of the first records to demonstrate the power of the teen consumer, and Ray's performing style was of considerable symbolic importance. Unlike sophisticated crooners, he delivered his songs in a strained, cracking voice, often breaking into tears during the performance, his face contorted into a mask of grief. His nicknames included "The Prince of Wails," "The Nabob of Sob," "The Howling Success," "Mr. Emotion," and "The Cry Guy." While other hysteria-inducing stars maintained a cool professional distance, Ray allowed himself to be carried away by the emotion. In this way, he formed a stylistic bridge between the urbane sensuality of crooners such as Frank Sinatra and the raw abandon of Elvis Presley. Although his music never really contributed to the development of rock and subsequent popular forms, his image and commercial success did so to a considerable degree.

Shortly after his meteoric rise, Ray began to experience legal complications involving the authorship of songs and the status of various contracts. By the late 1950s gossip columnists were speculating widely about Ray's personal life. All of these factors, in addition to the great shifts in popular musical style during the mid-1950s, might have contributed to the gradual waning of his U.S. career, and by the early 1960s Ray was no longer influential as a recording artist. He remained a popular live performer, however, especially in Great Britain, where his initial success had been as great as in the United States. He continued to make headline appearances there well into the 1980s. At home Ray developed a cabaret act and began appearing more frequently in Las Vegas. The precedent for this direction had been established with his movie appearance, his recordings of show tunes such as "Hey There/Hernando's Hideaway" (1954) and "I'll Never Fall In Love Again" (1958), and his revival of the songs "Here I Am—Broken Hearted" (originally 1927) and "Walkin' My Baby Back Home" (originally 1930). He toured Britain and Europe with Judy Garland in 1969.

In retrospect it seems that Ray was, at heart, a conventional cabaret and theatrical singer whose unique style and showmanship made him well suited to dramatic but brief stardom in the transitional years between big band swing and rock and roll. Ray continued to perform up until a few months before his death in Los Angeles, California.

• Useful biographies are Ray Sonin, *The Johnnie Ray Story* (1955); Clifford Roberts, *The Complete Life of Johnnie Ray* (1955); and Jonny Whiteside, *Cry: The Johnnie Ray Story* (1994). For early portraits of Ray and critical reactions, see "Like Mossadegh," *Time*, 21 Jan. 1952, p. 42; "Mr. Emotion," *Newsweek*, 21 Jan. 1952, p. 56; "Johnnie Ray Sings and Sobs His Way to a Quick Fortune," *Life*, 24 Mar. 1952, p. 99; and the *New York Times*, 27 Apr. 1952. Detailed treatments of the business aspects of Ray's rapid rise to fame can be found in these issues of *Billboard*: 28 June 1952, p. 1; 12 July 1952, p. 1; 19 July 1952, p. 19; 26 July 1952, p. 18; and 2 Aug. 1952, p. 16. For reports on Ray's difficulties during the remainder of the 1950s, see "Johnnie Ray Sued for 'Appropriating' Tunes," *Variety*, 12 Nov. 1952, p. 65; "Pretrial Exam for Franklin vs. Johnnie Ray," *Variety*, 23 Dec. 1953, p. 49; "Lang Charged with Assigning 50 percent Ray $," *Billboard*, 10 Oct. 1953, p. 14; "Ray-Lang Face Pre-Trial Exam," *Billboard*, 26 Dec. 1953, p. 14; and Chris Hodenfield, "Johnny [sic] Ray: The Tears Have Dried," *Rolling Stone*, 11 May 1972, p. 10. Further insights on Ray's career are offered in Arnold Shaw, *Honkers and Shouters* (1978), Charlie Gillet, *The Sound of the City* (1994), and George Lipsitz, *Dangerous Crossroads* (1994). An obituary is in *Variety*, 14 Mar. 1990.

WILLIAM ECHARD

RAY, Man. *See* Man Ray.

RAY, Nicholas (7 Aug. 1911–16 June 1979), film director, was born Raymond Nicholas Kienzle, Jr., in Galesville, Wisconsin, the son of Raymond Kienzle, a builder, and Lena Toppen. The family moved to La Crosse, Wisconsin, at the end of the First World War. Ray became interested in the theater at an early age. While attending high school he wrote and produced radio plays for a local station. A radio adaptation of George Bernard Shaw's *Candida* won him a university scholarship. However, he never put this scholarship to much use: he took a few classes at the University of Chicago in the fall of 1931 before dropping out and then briefly attended the University of Wisconsin at La Crosse. He later recalled: "I had a sense that anything that I might learn in university academic education, I would have to unlearn in order to make a living in the theater" (qtd. in Eisenschitz, p. 15).

During his short time at the University of Chicago, Ray had met the writer Thornton Wilder. Wilder recommended Ray to the architect Frank Lloyd Wright, who in 1933 invited Ray to join him as an apprentice at his Taliesin Fellowship, a utopian center for architectural training in Wisconsin. Ray spent only a few months at Taliesin and left after quarreling with Wright, but while there he learned important lessons in formal visual organization. In 1934 he moved to New York City and joined a left-wing acting troupe, the Theater of Action. In 1935, billed as "Nik" Ray, he performed in his first professional production, *The Young Go First*, an agitprop play critical of the "militaristic" tendencies of the Civilian Conservation Corps. The play was directed by Elia Kazan—a connection that would eventually bring Ray to Hollywood.

In 1936 Ray married Jean Evans, a writer; they had one child before divorcing in 1942. The Theater of Action broke up in 1936, and Ray joined the Federal Theatre Project of the Works Progress Administration. He was the stage manager for one of the first "Living Newspaper" productions, *Injunction Granted*, directed by Joseph Losey. In October 1936 Ray became a drama instructor at the socialist-oriented Brookwood Labor College. In January 1937 he relocated to Washington, D.C., where he became theatrical director for the Department of Agriculture's Resettlement Administration. In this capacity he was responsible for a grass-roots campaign to bring the theater to communities throughout the southern and western United States. Ray became interested in folk music during his travels and in 1940 became a producer of a weekly program on CBS Radio, "Back Where I Came From," that regularly featured Woody Guthrie. Ray attempted to join the army following Pearl Harbor but was rejected because of a rheumatic heart condition. In 1941 John Houseman hired him as the folk music director for the Office of War Information's "Voice of America" radio programs; but Congress investigated the office in 1942 for harboring Communist sympathizers, and as a result in January 1944 Ray was forced to resign.

In March of that year Ray was invited to work as an assistant on Kazan's first film, *A Tree Grows in Brooklyn*, for 20th Century–Fox. In 1946 Houseman, now a producer for RKO, hired him to write a screenplay adaptation of the crime novel *Thieves Like Us*. Ray very much wanted to direct his screenplay, and under the auspices of RKO's "new directors" policy he was given his chance during the summer of 1947. *Thieves Like Us*, retitled *They Live by Night*, was a moody, intimate film noir about lovers on the run, played by Farley Granger and Cathy O'Donnell. The film's opening voiceover—"This boy . . . and this girl . . . were never properly introduced to the world we live in"—anticipated what would become one of Ray's central themes: the plight of romantic individualism in a hostile society. Significantly, the film contained none of the overt violence typical of Hollywood thrillers, but relied on a suffocating atmosphere and often jarring editing to engender a sense of threat. Ray's second film, *A Woman's Secret* (1948, released 1949), was minor; however, one of his actors was Gloria Grahame, whom he married in June 1948. (The couple had one child before divorcing in 1952.) Ray established his commercial viability with *Knock on Any Door* (1949), a social issue movie made while he was on loan to Humphrey Bogart's production company, Santana.

In 1948 Howard Hughes bought a controlling interest in RKO; he proved to be both the benefactor and bane of Ray's career at the studio. Anti-Communist hysteria was gripping Hollywood, and with his leftist pedigree Ray was vulnerable. Hughes, a political conservative, nevertheless used his influence in Washington to protect the director. But Ray was forced to "prove" his loyalty by taking on a number of demeaning assignments. In December 1948 he was offered a film called *I Married a Communist*. The film had previously been offered to several other RKO directors, including Joseph Losey, a leftist who turned it down and was subsequently fired. Ray reluctantly signed on to the project, although a month later he was able to back out. In 1950 he found himself directing an equally flag-waving project, the war film *Flying Leathernecks*, starring John Wayne and Robert Ryan. Ryan recalled that Ray seemed to intentionally overdirect some scenes in his disgust. Ray was also brought in to finish films by directors who had been forced out of the studio: John Cromwell's *The Racket* (1951) and Josef von Sternberg's *Macao* (1952).

Not surprisingly, Ray's most significant film during these years was made while he was on loan from RKO. *In a Lonely Place* (1950) was a Santana production starring Bogart and Grahame. The story concerns an eccentric, violence-prone Hollywood screenwriter (played by Bogart) who is suspected of murdering a young woman; he grows increasingly isolated and angry under the burden of suspicion, so that when his name is finally cleared, his relationship with his lover (played by Grahame) has been irreparably damaged. Many film critics have read *In a Lonely Place* as an indictment of the paranoia then infecting the studios. Ray's best films for Hughes were *On Dangerous Ground* (1951), an intense film noir starring Ryan as a predatory big city cop, and *The Lusty Men* (1952), a rodeo drama starring Robert Mitchum and Susan Hayward. The latter film typified the studio conditions under which the director seemed to work best. Hughes threw the production into chaos when, ignoring the script, he announced that Hayward was to be the focus of the story. With no other guidelines, Ray, Mitchum, and screenwriter David Dortort were able to improvise most of the film on a day-by-day basis.

In 1952 widescreen technology was introduced to filmmaking, fortuitously for Ray. CinemaScope emphasized the width of the screen so that it filled the spectator's peripheral vision. Ray, with his strong architectural sense learned from Frank Lloyd Wright, proved to be a master of the 'Scope frame. The film critic Robin Wood has described how Ray used the inherent horizontal "pull" of the frame but simultaneously fought it by emphasizing vertical elements, such as the actors. As a result, the frame seems to constrict the characters. All of his subsequent Hollywood films were shot in widescreen.

In February 1953 Ray was released from his RKO contract. He promptly signed with the powerful agent Lew Wasserman at MCA; for the rest of his Hollywood career, the director worked as an independent. In 1954 he made a western, *Johnny Guitar*, for Republic Pictures. The film's genesis was unpromising: an original script that was a collection of western clichés and a principal star, Joan Crawford, who disrupted the production to insist that she wanted a bigger, "Clark Gable" part. Ray turned these circumstances into the film's strengths. He and screenwriter Philip Yordan reworked the script to draw attention to the clichés. They also made Crawford's character a gunslinging saloonkeeper with masculine traits. *Johnny Guitar* took on a bizarre tone, skewing the tropes of western film mythology. The bold color scheme heightened the sense of stylized unreality. Crawford had earned the enmity of co-star Mercedes McCambridge, and their rivalry produced ferocious performances. The director Martin Scorsese has called the resulting film "one of the cinema's great operatic works, . . . pitched from beginning to end in a tone that is convulsive and passionate."

In 1955 Ray made his most famous film, *Rebel without a Cause*, for Warner Bros. Before shooting began, he spent several weeks improvising and rehearsing with his young cast, which included James Dean and Natalie Wood. In the role of Jim Stark, Dean proved to be the most galvanic of Ray's outsiders, becoming a pop culture icon. *Rebel* spawned a new film genre that featured alienated youths at rock 'n' roll parties and drag strips; more significantly, it gave a voice on the big screen to a generation of American teenagers, to whom the movie's messages about rebellion and conformity were accessible. With *Bigger Than Life*, made in 1956 for 20th Century–Fox, Ray returned to the intense, off-kilter style of *Johnny Guitar*. Ostensibly about the evils of cortisone, the movie stars James Mason as a schoolteacher who has feelings of God-like invincibility and omniscience under the influence of the drug. Critics have suggested that the film investigates the thwarted aspirations of middle-class life, the "furious nihilism" that lurks beneath the necessary dullness of everyday living.

Although *Johnny Guitar* and *Rebel without a Cause* performed well at the box office, most of Ray's other films did not. As a result, the studios regarded him as "brilliant but unreliable" and doubted his instincts as a commercial director. His behavior on the set was often no help to his reputation. Many of his colleagues felt that he was simply too intense: the screenwriter Budd Schulberg remembered the director grilling a bit player about motivation. In addition, he struggled with a drinking problem. Increasingly, Ray had serious run-ins with the studios. 20th Century–Fox forced him to reshoot crucial scenes from *The True Story of Jesse James* (1957). He was banned from the set on *Wind across the Everglades* (1958). In 1958 he married Betty Utey, a dancer; they had two children but separated in 1964. Ray directed *Party Girl* (1958) for MGM, then abandoned Hollywood to resettle in Europe. In 1960 he went to work for the maverick producer Samuel Bronston, who specialized in epics and wanted to establish a new Hollywood in Spain. That year Ray directed *King of Kings*, but Bronston ran into financial troubles during the shoot and had to rely on MGM to finish the film. The studio edited the picture with no input from Ray. The director suffered a heart attack on the set of a second film for Bronston, *55 Days at Peking* (1963). It was his last commercial film.

Ironically, as his career had declined, Ray was discovered by French film critics at the influential journal *Cahiers du Cinéma*. Many of them became preeminent directors of the French New Wave—François Truffaut, Eric Rohmer, Jean-Luc Godard. They cited Ray as a seminal *auteur*, a director of mass entertainments for the Hollywood studios who nevertheless managed to make uniquely personal films. He was never entirely comfortable with his reputation in France: a relentless self-critic, he hated *Johnny Guitar* and was annoyed when, at a screening of *The Lusty Men*, he tried to point out flaws and was interrupted with shouts of "*magnifique*." But he settled into his role as an inspiration for younger filmmakers. He returned to the United States in the late 1960s. In 1969 he worked on a documentary about the Chicago 7 trial (involving antiwar protestors at the 1968 Democratic National Convention) but aborted the project. In 1971 he met Susan Schwartz, whom he later unofficially married; they had no children. That year he was hired as a film instructor at Harpur College in Binghamton, New York. His reputation as an *auteur* established in the United States, Ray became a fixture on the college lecture circuit. He completed an autobiographical film with his students, *We Can't Go Home Again* (1973). Two documentaries were made about him during his last years, *A Stranger Here Myself* (1975) and Wim Wenders's *Lightning over Water* (1980), the latter detailing Ray's attempt to make one last film, to be called *Nick's Movie*, while undergoing treatment for cancer. He died in New York City.

• Correspondence and production data regarding Ray's RKO films are found at the RKO archive at the Theater Arts Library, University of California, Los Angeles. Correspondence and production data concerning *Rebel without a Cause* are found at the Warner Bros. Collection at the Doheny University Library, University of Southern California. Nicholas Ray, *I Was Interrupted: Nicholas Ray on Making Movies* (1993), collects autobiographical sketches, journal entries, and transcriptions from Ray's classes at Harpur College. Interviews are by Charles Bitsch in *Cahiers du Cinéma* 89 (Nov. 1958) and by Michael Godwin and Naomi Wise in *Take One* 5 (Jan. 1977). The definitive biography is Bernard Eisenschitz, *Nicholas Ray: An American Journey* (1993). John

Kreidl, *Nicholas Ray* (1977), is a discussion of Ray's career with a heavy emphasis on *Rebel without a Cause*. Blaine Allen, *Nicholas Ray: A Guide to References and Resources* (1984), is an excellent if somewhat dated annotated bibliography. For the French appraisal of Ray's films see Jim Hillier, ed., *Cahiers du Cinéma, the 1950s* (1985). V. F. Perkins, "The Cinema of Nicholas Ray," *Movie* 9 (May 1963), is a valuable discussion of Ray's thematics. For readings of individual films see Perkins, "*Johnny Guitar*," in *The Book of Westerns* (1996), ed. Ian Cameron and Douglas Pye; Robin Wood, "Film Favorites: Robin Wood on *Bigger Than Life*," *Film Comment* 8 (Sept.–Oct. 1972); Martin Scorsese's introduction to *Johnny Guitar* (1994 video release, "Martin Scorsese Presents *Johnny Guitar*," Republic International, Inc.); and James Palmer, "*In a Lonely Place*: Paranoia in the Dream Factory," *Literature Film Quarterly* 13, no. 3 (1985). An obituary is in the *New York Times*, 18 June 1979.

THOMAS W. COLLINS, JR.

RAYBURN, Sam (6 Jan. 1882–16 Nov. 1961), Speaker of the U.S. House of Representatives, was born Samuel Taliaferro Rayburn in Roane County, Tennessee, the son of William Marion Rayburn and Martha Clementine Waller, farmers. Rayburn's life is a classic American success story. He was the eighth of eleven children of poor farmers who moved from Tennessee to Texas in 1887 in search of a better life. The Rayburn family settled at Flag Springs, near the town of Bonham in northeast Texas. Sam attended country schools and in 1900 enrolled at East Texas Normal College (commonly called Mayo College) in Commerce. He obtained his bachelor's degree in education in 1903 and taught for three years.

In 1906 Rayburn became a candidate for the Texas House of Representatives. Never a great public speaker, his large family and close ties to the farmers in the district nevertheless resulted in his first political victory. Entering the legislature in 1907, he was a supporter and political protégé of Senator Joseph Weldon Bailey, one of the most dynamic and controversial politicians of that era. Rayburn was reelected in 1908. Additionally, after taking courses at the University of Texas Law School, he passed the bar examination in 1908 and became a member of a small law firm in Bonham.

In 1910 Rayburn was elected to a third term as state representative and then was elected Speaker in 1911. During his three terms Rayburn developed a reputation for integrity, which he maintained throughout his long political career. The policies and programs he supported in those days tended to be progressive. He authored a bill guaranteeing deposits in state banks and supported public school improvements, regulation of utilities, limitations on working hours for women, and pure food standards.

While Rayburn was Speaker of the Texas House, the state legislature redrew the congressional district boundaries as a result of the 1910 census; Rayburn was able to influence the drawing of these boundaries. By then his old friend Joseph Bailey had resigned from the U.S. Senate, and the congressman from the district in which Rayburn lived became a candidate for the vacated Senate seat. Rayburn ran for the House seat only after ensuring that a likely opponent's home county would not be included in the newly reapportioned congressional district.

Winning election to the U.S. House of Representatives in 1912, Rayburn began a congressional career that would last until his death nearly forty-nine years later. As a newly elected congressman, he gained the friendship of a fellow Texas congressman, John Nance Garner, who, like Rayburn, had been a political protégé of Bailey. By 1913 Garner was a powerful figure in the House. It was Garner who aided Rayburn in obtaining a seat on the Interstate and Foreign Commerce Committee in 1913 and who functioned as a mentor to Rayburn for the next twenty years.

With the election of Warren G. Harding in 1920, the Democratic party went into a decline in the Congress. The minority party throughout the 1920s, the Democrats did not regain control of the House until 1931, at which time Rayburn became chairman of the Interstate and Foreign Commerce Committee, and John Nance Garner became Speaker. In 1932 Garner ran for the Democratic nomination for the presidency, and Rayburn became his campaign manager. He was Garner's representative in the negotiations that led to Garner's selection as Franklin Roosevelt's running mate.

After the victory of the Roosevelt-Garner ticket in 1932, Rayburn became one of the congressional workhorses of the New Deal. Through his committee passed some of the most important legislation of the New Deal, including the Federal Securities Act of 1933, the Securities Exchange Act of 1934, the Public Utility Holding Company Act of 1935, and the Rural Electrification Act of 1936. With an impressive legislative record as a committee chair, Rayburn was elected majority leader in 1937. The position of majority leader was a stepping stone to the speakership, a position Rayburn had long desired. As majority leader Rayburn was more heavily involved than ever in the leadership councils of the Roosevelt administration. It was no surprise when, after Speaker William Bankhead's death in 1940, Rayburn was elected Speaker.

As Speaker of the House, Rayburn was even more closely tied to the New Deal and was a strong supporter of the war effort. His best known action as Speaker during the 1940s was an astute parliamentary maneuver over legislation extending the draft. His action led to House passage of the draft extension in 1941 by one vote. The result was that when Pearl Harbor was attacked, the United States had an army four times larger than it would have had if the draft had not been extended.

With the death of Franklin Roosevelt in April 1945, Rayburn became a strong supporter and a trusted friend of Roosevelt's successor, Harry Truman. As a Texan, Rayburn did not have the same political need to take racist positions as did Democratic congressmen from the Deep South. He nevertheless was a segregationist, although his racial views moderated significantly over the years. In 1948 Rayburn's political opponents used Truman's civil rights proposals against him, and in response in his district, Rayburn criticized Truman's civil rights proposals. It was not until 1956 that he quietly endorsed legislation that ultimately became the Civil Rights Act of 1957.

As Rayburn aged he seemed to become increasingly concerned with the career of his protégé, Lyndon Johnson. Rayburn had been in contact with Johnson ever since the 1930s, when Johnson worked on the staff of Texas congressman Richard Kleberg, and their relationship grew increasingly close. By the time Johnson became majority leader of the Senate there was almost a father-son relationship between the two men. They tended to adopt a cooperative stance in dealing with President Dwight Eisenhower, to the dismay of the liberal wing of the Democratic party. In Texas politics as well, Johnson and Rayburn worked together to control the state Democratic party, first in battles against the conservative wing of the party and then in battles against the liberals. Rayburn was a strong supporter of Johnson's bid for the presidency in 1960. When that effort failed, he initially preferred that Johnson remain in the Senate rather than accept the vice presidential nomination, but ultimately he became convinced that Johnson's presence on the ticket was necessary for victory. Although Rayburn initially had little respect for John F. Kennedy, whom he had not regarded as a significant figure in Congress, after the election Rayburn was committed to aiding the new president. In 1961 he fought one of the most difficult battles of his career in breaking the logjam for liberal legislation that was caused by conservative domination of the House Committee on Rules.

For a politician of such national stature, Rayburn was remarkably sensitive to his congressional district. He worked to provide numerous federal benefits to the northeastern Texas district. During World War II he arranged for several airbases and prisoner-of-war camps to be located there. A major veterans hospital and a veterans domiciliary were also constructed. Additionally, his district benefited from his support for rural electrification and farm to market roads. Whenever he returned to visit the district, Rayburn dressed like a farmer and kept in close contact with his farmer constituents. Visitors from the district were always welcome at his home and could see him whether or not they had appointments.

A short, stocky man, Rayburn lost most of his hair early and by middle age was completely bald. He could be kindly and gentle, particularly toward powerless individuals. He had a terrible temper, however, and it was said that when he was aroused his entire head turned purple as he heaped profanities upon the target of his rage. He was described as having a permanent scowl on his face, a face that looked like it had been etched in granite. Yet Rayburn also loved children. One reason for his close friendship with Lyndon and Lady Bird Johnson was that he was immensely fond of their children.

Rayburn was interested primarily in politics and the House of Representatives; he had few outside inter-

ests. As a young man he had been a prohibitionist. After going to Congress, however, he began to drink and regularly met with other congressmen at the end of a legislative day to mix drink with a discussion of politics. Having a strong sense of right and wrong, Rayburn found it hard to forgive if another politician misled him. He personally was honest yet had no qualms about accepting and distributing cash contributions from wealthy oil men to Democrats in need of campaign funds.

Outside of his work, Rayburn has been described as a man consumed by loneliness. He was so tied to the House of Representatives that on weekends he would go to his office and hunt for work to occupy his time. He had been briefly married in 1927 to twenty-seven-year-old Metze Jones, the sister of Texas congressman Marvin Jones, one of Rayburn's closest friends. In less than three months, Metze left, and in October 1928 a divorce was granted. Rayburn was deeply hurt by this. Although he later had several affairs, including a lengthy relationship with the widow of Attorney General Alexander Mitchell Palmer, he never remarried and described himself as a bachelor.

Rayburn's eyesight began to deteriorate in the late 1950s. Eventually he was almost blind. Letters and newspapers had to be read to him. Strangely, his vision problems were only known by those people who were close to him. He was adept at recognizing voices, and he began to keep close associates near him to whisper names in his ear and to help him recognize members of Congress on the floor of the House.

In failing health, he suffered from severe back pain by late spring 1961. By summer he was experiencing loss of appetite and significant weight loss. On August 31 he left Washington for the last time to return to Bonham, Texas, where he died.

• Sam Rayburn's papers are in the Barker Texas History Center at the University of Texas in Austin. The major biography of Rayburn is D. B. Hardeman and Donald C. Bacon, *Rayburn: A Biography* (1987). An early biography of Rayburn that is of considerable value is C. Dwight Dorough, *Mr. Sam* (1962). Alfred Steinberg's *Sam Rayburn: A Biography* (1975) is less cluttered than Dorough's biography but provides little new information on Rayburn. Although Robert A. Caro's *The Years of Lyndon Johnson: The Path to Power* (1982) is about Lyndon Johnson, there is substantial material on Sam Rayburn in the book, including a superb description of Rayburn's physical appearance and his character. Anthony Champagne's *Congressman Sam Rayburn* (1984) explores the relationship between Sam Rayburn and his congressional district. He attempts to explain how Rayburn was able to serve in Congress for forty-nine years, many of those years as a leader of a national party with far more liberal policy objectives than those of his rural congressional district. Anthony Champagne's *Sam Rayburn: A Bio-Bibliography* (1988) contains a lengthy essay on Rayburn's life and times as well as an annotated bibliography of major writing by and about Sam Rayburn. Finally, H. G. Dulaney, Edward Hake Phillips, and MacPhelan Reese's excellent compilation of letters to and from Sam Rayburn in *Speak, Mr. Speaker* (1978) is organized chronologically and topically to present Rayburn's attitudes and values.

ANTHONY CHAMPAGNE

RAYMOND, Alexander Gillespie (2 Oct. 1909–6 Sept. 1956), cartoonist, known as Alex, was born in New Rochelle, New York, the son of Alexander Gillespie Raymond, a civil engineer, and Beatrice Wallaz Crossley. Young Raymond attended Iona Preparatory School in New Rochelle on a football scholarship, and at age eighteen he went to work as an order clerk in the Wall Street brokerage firm of Chisholm and Chapman. When he lost this position in the wake of the 1929 stock market crash, he was encouraged to exploit his talent for drawing by his neighbor Russ Westover, whom he assisted briefly on his comic strip "Tillie the Toiler." Westover soon secured additional work for Raymond in the art department of King Features Syndicate. In 1930 Raymond married Helen Frances Williams; they had five children.

At King Features, Raymond graduated beyond bullpen chores to assist Lyman Young on "Tim Tyler's Luck," a boys' adventure strip that had been running since 13 August 1928. For most of 1933 Raymond ghosted the Sunday strip, drawing realistically in a confident outline style with virtually no shading or cross-hatching; it was thoroughly competent but unremarkable linework.

In late 1933 King Features officials began looking for features to compete with two popular Sunday comic strips offered by rival syndicates—"Buck Rogers," space adventures in a science fiction future, and "Tarzan," jungle action in the mold set by Edgar Rice Burroughs. Raymond submitted samples for both and was awarded a Sunday page with "Flash Gordon" on the bottom two-thirds and "Jungle Jim" at the top. At the same time, Raymond entered the syndicate's competition to find an artist for a new daily strip about crime fighting, which, in order to compete with the soaring popularity of Chester Gould's "Dick Tracy" and Norman Marsh's "Dan Dunn—Secret Operative 48," would be written by the master of hard-boiled detective fiction, Dashiell Hammett. Raymond was selected to do this strip, too, and thus he began 1934 as the illustrator of three comic strips, a virtually unprecedented circumstance—two Sunday features and a daily strip. The "Flash Gordon"/"Jungle Jim" page debuted 7 January, and "Secret Agent X-9" appeared two weeks later on 22 January.

Raymond did "Secret Agent X-9" for less than two years. His superb illustrations give the pulp fiction tales an unexpected patina of the haute monde: Dexter, Hammett's tough-guy hero, is rendered as a dapper fashion plate, and the women are elegantly stylish and very attractive. Despite his surpassing talent as an illustrator, Raymond's use of the daily comic strip medium here is ultimately undistinguished. His strips often lack the variety of panel composition, for instance, that lend visual drama to the story. On his Sunday page, however, Raymond had room to indulge his graphic skills, and there he made his reputation as one of the leading practitioners in the art form.

But it was more than format that fired Raymond's imagination. "Jungle Jim" alone was not a particularly notable accomplishment. Featuring the exploits of a hunter named Jim Bradley as he righted wrongs in the jungles of southeastern Asia, the strip is every bit as well drawn as "Secret Agent X-9," but after a couple of years, it is clear that Raymond's heart was not in the work. His facility in figure drawing sustains the strip visually, but the compositions are dashed off: for panel after panel, the figures stand in studio poses by themselves with no atmospheric background. Raymond's creative energy was being poured into "Flash Gordon."

Written by Don Moore, the space adventure saga focuses on a handsome blond American polo player, who, with bearded scientist Hans Zarkov and a beautiful woman named Dale Arden, is stranded on the planet Mongo, where he battles its tyrant ruler. The stories are built archetypally around Flash as godlike redeemer, a savior from another world, who joins (and leads) an assortment of Ruritanian guerrillas in opposition to Ming the Merciless. But the ingenuity of Moore's suspenseful and fast-paced plots did not imbue the characters with any more personality than required by formula fiction. The appeal of the feature derived almost entirely from Raymond's drawings, which improved rapidly during the first year of the strip, finally achieving a technical virtuosity matched on the comics pages only by Harold Foster in "Prince Valiant."

In rendering the futuristic architecture of Mongo, Raymond was influenced by Franklin Booth; in figure drawing, by illustrators Matt Clark and John LaGatta. Like the latter, Raymond drew beautiful women exotically gowned to reveal rather than conceal their contours. And the pictures are luxuriant with telling backgrounds, providing atmospheric surroundings for the heroic posturing of Raymond's parade of glamorous characters. By 1937 Raymond was a master of drybrush technique, his drawings elaborately modeled, the figures given weight and shape by an intricate pattern of brush strokes, the backgrounds enhanced by an extravagant latticework of shading. His style continued to evolve, and by the 1939 strips, his lines are thinner, more continuous and graceful, and less sketchy; his pictures, defined more by linework and less by shading, are exquisite tableaux, delicately rendered in copious detail. Without question, it is Raymond's art, not Moore's stories, that creates an illusion of reality that is more than convincing: it is spectacular. The resplendent visuals seduce the reader into believing in the characters and their adventures.

All three strips were translated into motion pictures and radio; Buster Crabbe portrayed Flash in three serials (the first in 1936) that are arguably better known than the comic strip. During World War II Raymond served in the U.S. Marine Corps as public information officer and combat artist on the aircraft carrier USS *Gilbert Islands*, seeing action in the South Pacific at Okinawa, Balikpapan, and Borneo. After the war, King Features negotiated with him to do another strip. Starting 4 March 1946 "Rip Kirby" was a daily-only strip about the crime-fighting escapades of a debonair detective.

A Marine officer returning to civilian life, Kirby was a startling departure among comic strip heroes: he was an unabashed intellectual (he even wore spectacles), moved in the best circles of society, and employed a British manservant. Illustrating scripts by Fred Dickenson, Raymond developed yet another distinctive style: deploying solid blacks dramatically in contrast to sketchy fine-line penwork, he gave the strip an appearance that set it apart from his earlier work. His command of the medium in daily format was now masterful, and the strip, in consequence, a tour de force. His tenure on the feature concluded tragically when he was killed in an auto accident on South Morningside Drive near Westport, Connecticut.

His place in the history of his profession, however, is secure, established by his brilliance as an illustrator of four successful and influential comic strips. The technical triumph he achieved in the three strips he launched in 1934 helped establish the illustrative mode as the best way of visualizing a serious adventure story. His work and Foster's created the visual standard by which all such comic strips would henceforth be measured.

• Biographical facts about Alex Raymond can be found in several history books about the comics, chiefly Stephan Becker, *Comic Art in America* (1959); Jerry Robinson, *The Comics: An Illustrated History of Comic Strip Art* (1974); Ron Goulart, *The Adventurous Decade* (1975); and Coulton Waugh, *The Comics* (1945), as well as any of the several encyclopedias of comics—Maurice Horn, ed., *The World Encyclopedia of Comics* (1990), somewhat error-ridden, and the more carefully edited Ron Goulart, *Encyclopedia of American Comics* (1990). Most of these sources are combined in a chapter on Raymond in Robert C. Harvey's *The Art of the Funnies* (1994). All of Raymond's "Flash Gordon" has been reprinted in color in a series of six volumes from Kitchen Sink Press (1990–1993). All of Raymond's "Secret Agent X-9" strips have been reissued in a single volume, *Dashiell Hammett's Secret Agent X-9* (1983), with an informative biographical introduction by William F. Nolan. While both "Jungle Jim" and "Rip Kirby" have been sporadically reprinted in fugitive publications, neither has received the sort of archival treatment that the other two strips have. An obituary is in the *New York Times*, 7 Sept. 1956.

ROBERT C. HARVEY

RAYMOND, George Lansing (3 Sept. 1839–11 July 1929), educator and philosopher, was born in Chicago, Illinois, the son of Benjamin Wright Raymond, a wealthy businessman, and Amelia Porter. He received an A.B. from Williams College in 1862 and graduated from Princeton Theological Seminary in 1865. After studying art in Europe for three years, he was ordained as a Presbyterian minister and assumed the pastorate of a small church in Darby, Pennsylvania. He married Elizabeth Blake in 1872; the couple had two children.

Raymond spent four years as a minister before, as he wrote in his Williams College alumni record, being "called" by the faculty at Williams to a professorship in rhetoric and oratory. Between 1874 and 1880 students in his public speaking and composition courses won a number of intercollegiate prizes. His teaching methods included both lectures and one-on-one tutoring; regular private instruction periods gave him the opportunity to observe his students' individual styles of expression. The time he spent at Williams developing this practice of oratorical instruction was crucial to his later work as a theorist of aesthetics. Raymond left Williams in 1880 for a more independent and prestigious position in oratory and aesthetic criticism at Princeton. He split his time between Princeton and Washington, D.C., until 1906, when health problems led him to move permanently to Washington. He was professor of aesthetics at George Washington University from 1906 until his retirement in 1912. He died in Washington, D.C.

Beginning in 1886 Raymond produced several volumes of art criticism, which were republished in 1909 as a series that he called Comparative Aesthetics. In these texts, Raymond portrayed himself (and perhaps also thought of himself) as an outsider to the disciplines of art, art criticism, and philosophy. This status as an outsider enabled him, on the one hand, to respond with equanimity to detractors in each of these fields, while it also freed him to argue for a radically synthetic system of art appreciation. In his Williams College alumni record, completed shortly before his death, he wrote that his years teaching elocution had convinced him that "all the arts are primarily developments of different forms of expression through the tones and movement of the body." He started from a belief that human motions and gestures have symbolic meanings that can be shown, through careful cross-cultural comparison, to be more or less universal.

From this theoretical foundation, he argued that individual artistic techniques like shading (in painting and drawing), relief (in sculpture and architecture), and accent (in poetry and music) were straightforward extensions of physical, nonverbal techniques for emphasizing meaning. Because his aesthetic theories were so firmly grounded in the physicality of human communication, Raymond believed (as he explained in *Painting, Sculpture and Architecture as Representative Arts* [1895]), that they could be integrated with other physical sciences and pseudosciences like biology, neurology, psychology, phrenology, and palmistry. In his literary criticism, he tried to distinguish his own genteel interest in poetic form from the (to him) decadent dismissal of moral content in the works of European writers like Charles-Pierre Baudelaire, Gustave Flaubert, and Oscar Wilde. He expressed concern that his readers might confuse his attempts to categorize artistic structures with a will to ignore the ethical and didactic messages inherent in "true" art. Describing his own works of poetry and drama, he claimed that "a very high purpose is evident" (Williams College alumni record). When it came to the stylized work of well-known visual artists like Aubrey Beardsley, he complained with alarm about "sheer aesthetic wantonness irresponsibly debauching popular taste" (*Painting*, p. 237).

While his academic writings and personal letters suggest a strong desire to advance his own professional reputation and increase his sphere of intellectual influence, Raymond clearly thought of his life's work in oratory and aesthetics primarily as a form of cultural, if not explicitly public, service. Outside of his academic calling, he worked for causes as diverse as child labor reform, orthographic (spelling) reform, and the gold standard. He was nominated in 1911 to replace Supreme Court justice John Marshall Harlan, but he declined the nomination. His convictions about the universality of physical gestures and the primacy of Western art place him squarely in a nineteenth-century Eurocentric tradition of interpreting cultures. However, his interest in analyzing human sign systems makes him (somewhat ironically, considering the distaste he expressed for modernism in all its forms) an unacknowledged forerunner of twentieth-century structuralist and semiotic theorists in the arts and in anthropology.

As his *A Poet's Cabinet: Selected Quotations* (1914) attests, Raymond wrote poems on subjects ranging from abolition to women's clothing to American expansionism. Raymond's poetry and dramatic verse is characterized by sprightly rhythm and bouncing rhyme, a legacy, perhaps, of his years as a teacher of public speaking. His best-known poetic volume is *The Aztec God, and Other Dramas* (1900). The Comparative Aesthetics series includes these titles: *Poetry as a Representative Art* (1886), *Art in Theory* (1894), *Rhythm and Harmony in Poetry and Music, Together with Music as a Representative Art* (1895), *Proportion and Harmony of Line and Color in Painting, Sculpture, and Architecture* (1899), and *The Representative Significance of Form* (1900). His 1879 *Orator's Manual* was long a standard text for college elocution courses.

• The best source of information about Raymond's life and work is the Williams College library archives. Raymond's *The Mountains About Williamstown*, ed. Marion M. Miller (1913) includes a discussion of Raymond's theories by his friend Miller. An obituary is in the *New York Times*, 12 July 1929.

PRISCILLA PERKINS

RAYMOND, Henry Jarvis (24 Jan. 1820–18 June 1869), politician and editor, was born in Lima, New York, the son of Jarvis Raymond and Lavinia Brockway, farmers. He grew up on his parents' eighty-acre farm in western New York. A precocious child, Henry learned to read, according to some accounts, at three years of age. He attended the University of Vermont, where he became a talented orator, a skill that would later help his political career. Henry Clay, visiting the university in 1839, remarked after hearing one of Raymond's speeches, "that young man will make his mark" (Berger, p. 9). Not only his political ambitions but his journalism can be traced to his years at the university. As a student he sent frequent contributions to Horace Greeley's *New Yorker*. In 1840 Raymond graduated from the university with high honors.

After graduating, Raymond traveled to New York City to ask Greeley for a job. The editor gave the young man a desk and, after a short apprenticeship, started him at eight dollars a week. In his autobiography, Greeley recalled Raymond's abilities, writing, "A cleverer, readier, more generally efficient journalist, I never saw" (Greeley, p. 138). When Greeley founded the *Tribune* in 1841, Raymond was his "first assistant," but Raymond grew increasingly uneasy with his editor's already legendary affection for the various "isms" of the day, including socialism. In 1843, after three years with Greeley, Raymond accepted an offer to become the associate editor of James Watson Webb's *Courier and Enquirer*. Raymond was now twenty-three. That year he married Juliette Weaver, the daughter of Vermont farmers. After their marriage, Juliette became active in New York City social causes and, among other accomplishments, helped to found the New York Women's Hospital. They had seven children, of whom only four lived to adulthood.

Raymond set about to remake the staid *Courier and Enquirer*, and the columns soon became more readable and vigorous. In 1846, after the *Tribune* printed an editorial supporting the views of Charles Fourier, a utopian socialist, Raymond engaged Greeley in a debate about socialism in the pages of the *Tribune* and *Courier and Enquirer*. Greeley argued for utopian socialism, and Raymond responded that social equality was undesirable and unattainable; he also argued that Fourierism, with its radical views on love and marriage, was dangerous and un-Christian. This exchange was widely read and later collected in book form.

Without taking a break from journalism, Raymond also became a politician, first as a Whig assemblyman in 1850 and in 1851, when he became Speaker. In 1852 Raymond won renown for his criticism of the expansion of slavery at the Whig National Convention. In 1854, after the Kansas-Nebraska Act, which he opposed, Raymond encouraged the burgeoning Free Soil movement to avoid forming an independent political party and to join the Whigs instead. For his efforts, Thurlow Weed got Raymond nominated for the position of New York lieutenant governor, to which he was elected in 1854. Weed had passed over Greeley, who desperately wanted the position, and earned the antipathy of the powerful editor. In 1860 Greeley attended the Republican National Convention with an aim to nominate anyone who could beat Weed's man, William H. Seward. The nomination went to Abraham Lincoln, strongly supported by Greeley.

During his two terms as an assemblyman, Raymond had cultivated his friendship with a former coworker at the *New Yorker*, George Jones, who had become a banker in Albany. Jones and Raymond developed their longstanding plan to start a New York daily newspaper. They both sensed that James Gordon Bennett's *Herald* was too often salacious and lacked strong party principles and that Greeley's *Tribune* seemed at times too principled, wearing its politics on its shirt sleeves and rarely meeting an "ism" it did not like. After Jones told Raymond that Greeley had cleared

$60,000 in the past year, the two decided to found a conservative, even-tempered daily that would fill the void left by the *Herald* and the *Tribune*.

Raymond, Jones, and their new partner, another Albany banker named Edward Wesley, quickly raised the necessary $70,000, a sum far greater than the $500 that Bennett had needed to found the *Herald* just sixteen years before. In 1835 Bennett had rented a cellar, placed a board over two barrels for a desk, hired a few printers, and did all the rest himself. By 1851 the newspaper business had become more expensive. With circulation booming, the price of the increasingly sophisticated printing and distribution systems and the burgeoning staffs made the raising of capital necessary.

Eighteen September 1851 marks the first issue of the *New York Daily Times*, as it was called until the "daily" was dropped a few years later. It was a four-page folio of six columns per page. Raymond's inaugural editorial revealed a philosophy that would distinguish the *Times* from other papers throughout his tenure. In fact, Raymond's words represent not only his philosophy of journalism but of politics as well: "We do not mean to write as if we were in a passion—unless that shall really be the case; and we shall make it a point to get into a passion as rarely as possible. There are very few things in this world which it is worth while to get angry about; and they are just the things that anger will not improve."

The *Times* was an immediate success, gaining a circulation of 10,000 within two weeks, 26,000 within a year, and 75,000 by the start of the American Civil War. A contemporary observer ascribed the success of the *Times* to three factors: "1, it was conducted with tact, industry, and prudence; 2, it was not the *Herald*; 3, it was not the *Tribune*" (Parton, p. 382). The *Times* printed six days a week until the exigencies of war pushed Raymond into starting a Sunday edition, which he did the week after the Fort Sumter attack. By this time, the *Times* was one of only three (with the *Herald* and *Tribune*) eight-page dailies in the country, a remarkable feat for a paper less than a decade old. The *Times* also was among the leading papers in circulation and news gathering and was widely clipped throughout the era.

Meanwhile, Raymond's political activities continued. Raymond helped to draft the charter of the new Republican party in 1856, and the *Times* was strongly Republican for the rest of Raymond's life and beyond. In a series of open letters to W. L. Yancey of Alabama right after Lincoln was elected president, Raymond attacked secession and the growing southern belligerency. These letters, along with the debate with Greeley on Fourierism, reflect both Raymond's persistence and his cool, analytical bent. The *Times* was strongly pro-Union before and during the war; its view on slavery was antiexpansion before the war but shifted to abolitionist after the fighting began. The paper's support for Lincoln was much more consistent than the *Tribune*'s, and the *Times* became the administration's lead-ing supporter. Raymond's biography of Lincoln, published during the 1864 election year, was widely read.

The influence of the *Times* grew during the Civil War. Raymond dispatched himself to cover the story of the first battle of Manassas but sent in a premature telegraph claiming that the Union forces had taken the day. When he later tried to send another message to the *Times* correcting his mistake, it was censored by the War Department. This was the last time Raymond reported from the field. Later in the war, during the 1863 draft riot, in which Greeley's office was damaged by the mob, Raymond protected the *Times* building by installing Gatling guns, given to the *Times* by Lincoln's administration as a favor for the paper's support, on the roof of the building. In 1864 Raymond was elected to Congress and, as the chief supporter of Andrew Johnson in the House, fought a losing battle against Thaddeus Stevens and the Radical Republicans. Raymond's support of the president wavered, however, after Johnson's political power began to wane. Raymond was criticized for opposing the Civil Rights Bill of 1866, only to support the Fourteenth Amendment, which sought the same goals, a few months later. For his vacillation, Raymond was called a "wiffler" by Gideon Welles.

The burden of wearing the weighty hats of politics and journalism was often too much for Raymond, and he suffered from various ailments, thought by his contemporaries and later his biographers to be the price of too much work. He had developed feverish deliriums while working hard under Greeley. Later he suffered other physical and mental breakdowns and eventually suffered from paralyzing strokes, the final of which killed him before he reached his fiftieth birthday. Raymond's death was the subject of considerable, if muted, controversy. On the night before his death, he told his family that he was going out to a political meeting. They found him the next morning, prostrate in the parlor, dying of a stroke. According to a number of sources, Raymond was having an affair with a popular actress, in whom his paper's reviewers took an active interest, and suffered a stroke in the woman's room. Two unidentified men transported the ailing Raymond to his home and left him there, to be discovered the next morning by his family.

Like Bennett and Greeley, Raymond helped to define American journalism during the antebellum and Civil War eras. The traits that made Raymond a fine journalist—his coolness, analysis, detachment, and ability to see all sides of an issue—ill served him as a politician, and his congressional term was ineffectual. Raymond was not alone among nineteenth-century journalists who sought political office—joining him were the journalistic giants of the day: Charles Anderson Dana, Webb, Greeley, Frederick Douglass, Joseph Pulitzer, and William R. Hearst, to name a few. Raymond's moderation and conservatism distinguished him from most of the above names and made him much better suited for the editor's chair. Unlike the above editors, who mixed their journalism with a fervent political voice, Raymond's politics and journalism had the shared goal of moderation, seeking to get in the middle of the controversies of his day. The editorial tone of the *Times*, set by Raymond during his tenure, has endured throughout its history. The temperate voice of the *Times* was, in some ways, strikingly consistent from Raymond to Adolph Ochs and beyond.

• Raymond's papers are housed in the New York Public Library and in the *New York Times* building. Raymond's newspaper debate with Greeley was collected in book form, *Association Discussed; or, the Socialism of the Tribune Examined: Being a Controversy between the New York Tribune and the Courier and Enquirer* (1847). Raymond's letters to Yancey were also made into a book, *Disunion and Slavery: A Series of Letters to Hon. W. L. Yancey of Alabama, by Henry J. Raymond, of New York* (1861). Raymond's biography of Lincoln, *The Life of Abraham Lincoln* (1864), was a campaign document and was later revised and reprinted after the assassination. It is surprising that the founder of the *New York Times* has not yet become the subject of a scholarly biography. However, Francis Brown, *Raymond of the Times* (1951), while undocumented, is thorough and generally reliable. Another biography, Augustus Maverick, *Henry J. Raymond and the New York Press, for Thirty Years* (1870), was published within months of Raymond's death. Raymond's life is discussed in a number of histories of the *Times*, including Meyer Berger, *The Story of the New York Times, 1851–1951* (1951); and Gay Talese, *The Kingdom and the Power* (1969). Horace Greeley, *Recollections of a Busy Life* (1868); James Parton, *The Life of Horace Greeley, Editor of the New York Tribune* (1855); and James L. Crouthamel, *James Watson Webb, a Biography* (1969), mention Raymond's early journalism. Extended biographical sketches appeared in the obituaries following Raymond's death. The one in the *New York Times*, 19 June 1869, is the most thorough, although most of the major papers printed remembrances and brief sketches.

DAVID T. Z. MINDICH

RAYMOND, John Howard (7 Mar. 1814–14 Aug. 1878), college president and educational innovator, was born in New York City, the son of Eliakim Raymond, a businessman, and Mary Carrington. He attended the Goold Brown grammar school, where he acquired a taste for the classics, and then New York High School. Entering Columbia College at age fourteen, he at first led his class, but overprepared and overconfident, he was "decapitated," as he put it in his unpublished autobiography—that is, he let his work and standing as a student deteriorate and was expelled from Columbia in his junior year. He subsequently graduated from Union College in 1832 and studied law in New York City and New Haven, Connecticut. Attending the church of Leonard Bacon in New Haven, he was arrested by a question about religious faith and in 1834 experienced a religious conversion. In 1835 he dropped the study of law to enroll in the Baptist Theological Seminary at Madison University in Hamilton, New York, from which, planning to become a missionary, he graduated in 1838.

Raymond changed his career path as he became absorbed in the academic and administrative affairs of Madison as a faculty member (1838–1850), teaching philosophy and belles lettres, and after he met Cornelia Morse, only daughter of prosperous upstate New Yorkers. She challenged him with the question of "why Eve sinned," and Raymond's twelve-page response on the subject apparently satisfied her and led to their engagement. They were married in 1840 and had nine children, one of whom died in infancy, another at age ten.

As a result of a proposal to move Madison University from Hamilton to Rochester, New York, which met stiff opposition both in the town and on campus, a group of professors, calling itself the "Removal Party," left Madison in 1850 and was instrumental in organizing Rochester University (now the University of Rochester). Raymond was a moving force in this group and guided university policy before the first president was chosen. After five years at that institution, where he made many friends among such prominent abolitionists as Frederick Douglass, Wendell Phillips, and Elizabeth Peabody, he resigned in 1855 to become the organizer and president of the Brooklyn Collegiate and Polytechnic Institute.

At the Polytechnic Institute, which opened in 1855, Raymond applied his organizational skills to developing a complete system of education embracing collegiate, scientific, and commercial curricula. He successfully led a faculty of 40 in developing a school program for the approximately 500 students, trying to meet their diverse needs. Under his leadership, the often-divided faculty was made responsible for coherent curricular development. Through debate and consensus, in a forward-looking mode, he led the faculty to ban corporal punishment from the school.

During the summer of 1863 Raymond traveled with the abolitionist Henry Ward Beecher, a close friend, to Europe for a much needed vacation. (He was not well and was getting ready to resign from his Polytechnic position.) The two men discovered a tremendous prejudice against the Union antislavery position among England's upper classes. Beecher addressed a meeting of Congregationalists in London on the subject of slavery and also invited Raymond to speak. Raymond's first sentence, according to Beecher, was "like an explosion," "red-hot," and he gave a very impassioned and angry speech. In September the two men had an audience with King Leopold of Belgium to discuss the Civil War.

Somewhat earlier, in 1860, Raymond had been asked by Matthew Vassar, a trustee of Rochester, to become a charter trustee of Vassar Female College, founded in Poughkeepsie, New York, in 1861. It was this connection that led to his nomination to the Vassar presidency in 1864, after the sudden resignation of first president Milo P. Jewett, before the college actually opened its doors in the fall of 1865. Raymond assumed the Vassar presidency reluctantly, largely because of his health. Nevertheless, driving a bargain that improved his salary, he resigned from Brooklyn Polytechnic and assumed the Vassar presidency in April 1864.

In founding Vassar College in 1861, Matthew Vassar had pioneered in undertaking to offer a liberal arts education for women comparable to that available for men. Vassar himself and Raymond's predecessor Jewett had many ideas of their own about women's education, but it fell to Raymond to deal with the practical realities of implementing and interpreting the founder's vision and the college's mission. For the 14 years of his presidency he dealt with Victorian shibboleths about women's role and women's fragility. His educational standards were high, and many of the early students were unprepared by their earlier studies for the rigors of the curriculum established under his leadership by the nine professors (seven men, two women), as signaled by the entrance exams. Faced with this problem from the first day the college opened, he very shortly established a preparatory division and admitted to full college work no unprepared students. The ambience of the residential life of the college, with its concept of *in loco parentis*, and the closely supervised intellectual life of the classroom established under Raymond created an environment where "women studying together" (as Maria Mitchell, one of the professors, put it) could thrive. By the time of Raymond's death in Poughkeepsie, New York, the Vassar model had served as example for two other women's colleges—Smith College and Wellesley College, both founded in 1875—and the idea of rigorously educating women had begun to take hold.

Raymond had a genius for inventing academic organization. He founded, and successfully developed in their beginning stages, three experimental educational institutions: a university, a comprehensive boys' school, and an institution for the higher education of women in a time when little preparatory education for girls was available. He was a cautious man but a determined one. In his leadership of Vassar he had to combat Victorian public opinion, which questioned the advisability of giving such a rigorous education to women. He was relentless in his conviction that women could attain the highest standards of performance, and he defended the college against its critics. He was strongly supported in this enterprise by an engaged faculty to whom he provided encouragement. He was a pacesetter, and his ideas about curriculum and organization were reflected in subsequent developments in higher education for both men and women.

• The Raymond papers in the Vassar College library contain unpublished speeches, essays, correspondence, scrapbooks, and clippings and are the best source of information about Raymond. His youngest daughter, Cornelia Raymond, was for a time the college historian, and she added many valuable notes about him and his times to the file. Maria Mitchell's letters to Raymond and student letters written back home in the period of his presidency, also in the Vassar College library, fill in many details of Raymond's tenure there. *Life and Letters of John Howard Raymond* (1881), edited by his oldest daughter, Harriet Lloyd, is another valuable source about his life and presidency. Elizabeth Hazelton Haight, ed., *The Autobiography and Letters of Matthew Vassar* (1916), and Haight and James Monroe Taylor, *Vassar* (1915), give insight into Raymond's career, as does Taylor, *Before Vassar Opened* (1914).

ELIZABETH ADAMS DANIELS

RAYMOND, John T. (5 Apr. 1836–10 Apr. 1887), comic actor, was born in Buffalo, New York, to a family named O'Brian or O'Brien. Nothing more is known about his parents, his early education, or why and when he chose his stage name. Raymond began his acting career in 1853 at the Rochester Theatre in New York, playing the role of Lopez in a little-known play called *The Honeymoon*. In 1854 he joined Anna Cora Mowatt's company at Niblo's Garden Theatre in New York and toured throughout New England and the South for several years. In 1859 Raymond replaced Joseph Jefferson in the role of Asa Trenchard in E. A. Sothern's production of Tom Taylor's *Our American Cousin*. He took the same role in Laura Keene's revival of the play in 1861 and thereby gained his first national exposure, as his performance was favorably compared to Jefferson's. He remained with Keene's company until 1863, playing Tony Lumpkin in *She Stoops to Conquer*, the Babby in Edmund Falconer's *The Peep o' Day*, as well as other eccentric and low comedy roles. In 1863 Raymond was fired by Keene, a move of some controversy as reported by the New York newspapers of the time.

Raymond made his London debut in 1867, playing Asa Trenchard in Sother's production of *Our American Cousin* at the Haymarket Theatre. Also that year Raymond and Sothern took the play on tour to Paris, where they performed at the Theatre des Italiens, Scotland, and Ireland.

Sometime in the 1860s Raymond married actress Marie Gordon, who had appeared with him in the London production of *Our American Cousin*. They had no children. In 1869 the couple settled in California, where they added popular melodramas such as *Money* and *The Streets of New York* to their repertoire.

In 1873 a journalist named George Dinsmore gave his dramatization of Mark Twain and Charles Dudley Warner's novel, *The Gilded Age*, to Raymond. The actor had an instant West Coast success with his performance as Colonel Mulberry Sellers. Dinsmore's script had not been authorized by Twain or Warner, however, and Twain successfully sued and forced the production to close. Twain then fashioned his own dramatization of the novel, possibly with Raymond's collaboration, and this version opened in New York at the Park Theatre on 16 September 1874, with Raymond again playing Colonel Sellers.

Although the play was generally considered a weak one by critics, Raymond's creation of Sellers, a man of boundless enthusiasm, prodigious hopes, and small accomplishments, was a comic tour de force. The production was a huge success at the Park Theatre, and Raymond toured with it successfully for many years afterward, eventually playing the role in more than a thousand performances.

Twain himself was less pleased than the general public with Raymond's performance. In his *Autobiography* Twain said that "in the hands of a great actor" (Twain suggested Frank Mayo), Sellers should have "dimmed any manly spectator's eyes with tears and racked his ribs apart with laughter at the same time."

But Raymond was "great in humorous portrayal only." This, argued Twain, was because Raymond "was not a manly man, he was not an honorable man nor an honest man, he was empty and selfish and vulgar and ignorant and silly, and there was a vacancy . . . where his heart should have been."

In fairness to Raymond, this assessment may have been influenced by Twain's bitterness over his lawsuit with Dinsmore; it was not borne out in the remembrances of Raymond's colleagues. In theatrical circles Raymond was known as a man of boundless generosity, honesty, and kindness; given to practical jokes and limited in his acting range but a superb comedian in the right roles.

Although the role of Sellers made for Raymond a great deal of money, the actor lost nearly all of it in a series of poor investments and spent the remainder of his career searching in vain for another dramatic vehicle as lucrative as *The Gilded Age*. In 1879 he played Ichabod Crane in *Wolfert's Roost*, George Fawcett Rowe's adaptation of *The Legend of Sleepy Hollow*, whereby he again invited comparisons with Joseph Jefferson's work, this time unfavorably. In roles such as Fresh in A. C. Gunter's *Fresh, the American* (1881), Major Bob Belter in G. H. Jessop and W. H. Gill's *In Paradise* (1883), and General Limber in David D. Lloyd's *For Congress* (1884), Raymond achieved moderate successes playing characters largely based on Sellers. He did commission and appear in two early plays by Arthur Wing Pinero, *The Magistrate* (1884) and *In Chancery* (1885). He also starred as Gottlieb Weigel in Fred Williams's translation of L'Arronge's *Mein Gottlieb*. In addition to his early work with Keene and Mowatt, he appeared in benefits and limited engagements with some of the outstanding actors of his day, including Edwin Booth, Frank Mayo, and Maurice Barrymore.

Raymond married a second time, to actress Rose Courtney Barnes, daughter of Rose Eytinge of the renowned Eytinge acting family. Details of how his first marriage ended and the date of his second marriage are unknown. Courtney Barnes regularly acted with Raymond, especially on tour, as had Gordon. He and Barnes had one child. Raymond died in 1887 while on tour in Evansville, Indiana.

Raymond was regarded in his day as one of the finest comic actors in America. Although his acting range was narrow and most of his success was achieved in a single role, such limitations were not unusual for the period. Raymond must be ranked with Joseph Jefferson and Frank Mayo as one of the most important American comic talents of the late nineteenth century.

• Information on Raymond's life can be found in Brander Matthews and Laurence Hutton, *Actors and Actresses of Great Britain and the United States* (1886), Charles E. L. Wingate and F. E. McKay, *Famous American Actors of Today* (1896), and R. H. Gabriel, *The Pageant of America*, vol. 8 (1927). References to his New York career are in George C. D. Odell, *Annals of the New York Stage*, vols. 7–13 (1927–1949). He is also discussed at some length in *The Autobiography of Mark Twain*, ed. Charles Neider (1959). His obituary in the *New York Times*, 11 Apr. 1887, is a most complete and detailed source.

ERIC SAMUELSEN

RAYMOND, Miner (29 Aug. 1811–25 Nov. 1897), pastor and theologian, was born in New York City, the son of Nobles Raymond, a shoemaker, and Hannah Wood. Shortly after his birth the family moved to Rensselaerville, New York, in the foothills of the Catskills. The eldest of nine children born to a poor family, Raymond was able to attend school only until age twelve before financial necessity forced him to help his father make shoes in his shop. At age seventeen he had a conversion experience and joined the local Methodist church. In 1830 he attended the Wesleyan academy at Wilbraham, Massachusetts, to prepare for the ministry. He graduated the next year, having achieved an excellent academic record and paid many of his expenses by making shoes.

From 1833 to 1840 Raymond taught at the academy, first English, then mathematics. In 1837 he married Elizabeth Henderson; they would have five children. In 1838, while teaching at the academy, Raymond was admitted to the New England Conference of the Methodist Episcopal church. His preaching ability led him to leave the academy in 1840 to become a full-time minister, and over the next eight years he served congregations in Worcester, Boston, and Westfield, Massachusetts. In 1848 Raymond reluctantly left the pastorate to return to the Wesleyan academy in Wilbraham as principal. An able administrator and energetic leader, during his sixteen years as principal he revitalized the academy, increasing its size and enhancing its reputation. In 1864 Raymond accepted a call to succeed John Dempster as professor of systematic theology at Garrett Biblical Institute in Evanston, Illinois. For three years while serving in that position he also postured the First Methodist Church of Evanston. Elizabeth Raymond died in 1877, and two years later he wed Isabella Hill Binney, who survived him. Raymond continued to teach at Garrett until 1895, when ill health forced him to retire. He died two years later in Evanston.

Although his formal education was limited, Raymond was an inspiring teacher and a gifted theologian. Dissatisfied with the texts he was using in his classes at Garrett, in 1877 he issued the first two volumes of his *Systematic Theology*, the first American Methodist systematic theology. Somewhat dependent on the writings of Richard Watson, an English Wesleyan theologian, Raymond's work sought to reinterpret theology in light of the Arminian doctrine of free personal agency. Combining biblical exegesis with substantial analysis of the history of Christian doctrines, it was widely studied and for two decades was considered the most complete and compelling exposition of Arminian theology in the United States. Raymond insisted that Christ's atonement extended to all people, and he strongly emphasized the doctrine of perfect love, the belief that Christians could reach a state in which every action was governed by the motive of compassion. Raymond's goal was to provide a resource for lay people, not simply for scholars, that plainly stated fundamental biblical truths. By presenting arguments, illustrations, and proofs from Scripture he hoped to enable readers to understand the grounds of their faith. A third volume, on ethics and ecclesiology, was published in 1879. From 1880 until 1908 his work was part of the course of study required of candidates for the Methodist ministry.

In addition to his other activities, Raymond also played a leadership role in his denomination. He was a delegate to the Methodist General Conference six times. Deeply concerned about social issues, he condemned war and campaigned against slavery. At the Northern General Conference held in Indianapolis in 1856, Raymond chaired the Committee on Slavery, which recommended the barring of slaveholders from membership in the northern Methodist church, a resolution that the delegates failed to pass.

Milton Terry, Raymond's friend and colleague at Garrett, wrote of Raymond that his "commanding personality combined at once a majesty and a meekness, a nobleness and a simplicity that everywhere won affection and esteem." Terry contended that Raymond's many accomplishments sprang from his "constitutionally well-balanced mind," his careful, rational analysis, his ability to express convictions forcefully, and his practical wisdom, unbending will, and great optimism (Terry, p. 17). Charles Little, president of Garrett Biblical Institute at the time of Raymond's death, added that Raymond "was not erudite, or subtle, or ingenuous, but he know how to think and how to inspire thinking" (Little, p. 86).

• The best sources of information about Raymond's career, convictions, and accomplishments are "Rev. Dr. Miner Raymond," *Northwest Christian Advocate*, 1 Dec. 1897, pp. 4–5; Milton S. Terry, "Address . . . at the Funeral of the Distinguished Theologian," *Northwest Christian Advocate*, 8 Dec. 1897, pp. 17–18, also published as a pamphlet; and Charles Little, "Rev. Miner Raymond," in *Minutes of the Rock River Annual Conference of the Methodist Episcopal Church* (1898), pp. 84–86. Helpful for understanding his theology and his battle against slavery are Leland Scott, "Methodist Theology in America in the Nineteenth Century" (Ph.D. diss., Yale Univ., 1954); Emory S. Bucke, ed., *History of American Methodism*, vol. 2 (1964); and Robert E. Chiles, *Theological Transition in American Methodism, 1790–1935* (1965). See also *Garrett Biblical Institute: Semi-Centennial Celebration* (1906). An obituary is in the *Daily Inter Ocean* (Chicago), 27 Nov. 1897.

GARY SCOTT SMITH

RAYNAL, Guillaume-Thomas-François (12 Apr. 1713–6 Mar. 1796), journalist and radical propagandist, was born into an ancient bourgeois family in Saint-Geniez, France, the son of Guillaume Raynal and Catherine Girels. After studies at the Jesuit college of Rodez, he entered the Company of Jesus and successively taught humanities, eloquence, and theology at Pézenas, Clermont, and Toulouse. In spite of a heavy meridional accent, he was successful as a preacher. John Adams (1735–1826) later described him as "the most eloquent man I ever heard speak in French."

Toward 1747 his journalistic ambitions caused him to leave the priesthood and move to Paris, where he assumed the editorship of the *Mercure de France*. Gifted with a facile pen and an impulse for aggrandizement, he made his way into the elite world of literary salons, cementing friendships with Jean-Jacques Rousseau, Friedrich Melchior von Grimm, and Denis Diderot. Adopting deistical and libertarian attitudes associated with Montesquieu and Voltaire, he published a series of histories of international scope, the most famous of which is his *Histoire philosophique et politique des établissements et du commerce des Européens dans les deux Indes* (1770). The exoticism, anecdotal style, and strident advocacy of social and economic reforms that characterized this survey of colonialism and commerce, strengthened in the third edition of 1780 by copious additions contributed by Diderot, made it one of the bulwarks of the French Enlightenment. But its open anticlericalism and advocacy of the right of insurrection alarmed the French monarchy and led to a decree of Parliament of 1781 ordering Raynal's arrest and the confiscation of his property.

After taking refuge in Prussia, where his religious heterodoxy was welcomed by Frederick the Great, he returned to France in 1784, eventually settling in Marseilles. In May 1791 he read before the National Assembly a discourse reflecting the liberal principles of a constitutional monarchy. Although this plea for moderation negated the revolutionary fervor of his *Histoire* and drew the censure of the assembly as a whole, that body gave him the right to retain his pensions and privileges. After the censure of the assembly, Raynal lived in seclusion in the village of Montlhéry. He died while on a trip to Paris.

According to Raynal, the last section of his *Histoire philosophique*, also published separately as *Révolution de l'Amérique* (1781), helped to bring about American independence; he also maintained that more than 25,000 copies were distributed throughout the colonies. In June 1780 Joseph Reed, on behalf of the Supreme Council of Philadelphia, sent him a letter full of praise. Other Americans, however, objected to his extensive errors and plagiarisms. The third of Philip Mazzei's four-volume *Recherches historiques et politiques sur les États-Unis* (1788) consists of a critique of Raynal, and Mazzei's patron, Thomas Jefferson, corrected misinformation drawn from Raynal in an article on the United States that had appeared in the *Encyclopédie méthodique* (1796). In his *Notes on Virginia* (1782), Jefferson particularly opposed Raynal's extension of the theory of biological degeneration to "the race of whites transplanted from Europe" to the New World. In reply to Raynal's observation that America had not produced a man of genius in a single art or science, he pointed to George Washington in war and to Benjamin Franklin (1706–1790) and David Rittenhouse in science.

At various points in the *Histoire*, Raynal paraphrased Franklin's theories on population, quoted as an actual historical event Franklin's bogus speech of Polly Baker vindicating single motherhood, incorrectly depicted Philadelphia as Franklin's birthplace, and placed him among the greatest actors in the conflict with Britain. When confronted by Silas Deane and Franklin at the latter's residence in Passy with proof that Polly's speech was a hoax, Raynal replied coolly, "I had rather relate your stories than other men's truths."

The most sober and analytical criticism of Raynal's largely favorable portrayal of the American Revolution appeared in Thomas Paine's *Letter to the abbé Raynal* (1782), which refuted Raynal's opinion that the major reason for the colonists' revolt was the grievance of a slight tax. While branding taxation without representation as legal tyranny and the usurpation of precious and sacred rights, Paine interpreted the struggle for independence as a precursor of the extension from the West of "the circle of civilization" to include the entire world.

Raynal's fame in Europe stems from his radical deism, his belief that only magistrates and legislators should govern the state, and his conviction that all people have the right of rebellion. His contribution to the New World did not consist primarily in inspiring revolutionary sentiment, but rather in justifying to the world the legitimacy of the American cause after the conflict had broken out.

• Raynal's major publications not mentioned in the text are *Histoire du Stadhouderat* (1747), *Histoire du Parlement d'Angleterre* (1748), *Anecdotes littéraires* (1750–1756), and *Anecdotes* (some editions *Mémoires*) *historiques, militaires et politiques de l'Europe* (1753–1763). A manuscript showing Diderot's contribution to *Histoire philosophique* is described by Herbert Dieckmann in *Inventaire du Fonds Vandeul et inédits de Diderot* (1951). See also Hans Wolfe, *Raynal et sa Machine de Guerre: "l'Histoire des deux Indes" et ses perfectionnements* (1957), and Michèle Duchet, *Diderot et l'Histoire des deux Indes* (1978). Anatole Feugère is the author of *Bibliographie critique de l'abbé Raynal* (1922; repr. 1970) and *Un Précurseur de la Révolution, l'abbé Raynal* (1922; repr. 1970). Raynal's relations with Jefferson are treated by Gilbert Chinard, "Eighteenth-century Theories on America as a Human Habitat," *Proceedings of the American Philosophical Society* 19 (1947): 27–57; his relations with Franklin by A. O. Aldridge, *Franklin and His French Contemporaries* (1957; repr. 1976); and his relations with Paine Aldridge, *Thomas Paine's American Ideology* (1984).

A. OWEN ALDRIDGE

RAYNER, John Baptis (13 Nov. 1850–14 July 1918), politician and educator, was born in Raleigh, North Carolina, the son of Kenneth Rayner, a planter, and Mary Ricks, a slave. His father had a long public career as a Whig congressman, Know Nothing party leader, and, after the Civil War, a Republican federal officeholder. The elder Rayner acknowledged that John was his son and helped him secure a college education at Raleigh Theological Institute (today Shaw University) and St. Augustine's Normal and Collegiate Institute.

Before he graduated, young Rayner moved in 1872 to Tarboro, North Carolina, where, as a Republican, he held the local offices of constable and magistrate during Radical Reconstruction. He married Susan Staten in 1874; they had two children. In 1880 Rayner became a labor agent for several Texas cotton planters and persuaded a number of black farm workers to move with him to Robertson County, Texas. He settled in Calvert, where he taught school and preached. Later Rayner attracted considerable attention as a prohibition speaker and political strategist in the state's 1887 prohibition referendum campaign. Also in 1887 his wife died, and later that year he married her sister, Clarissa Staten, with whom he had three children.

Rayner joined the People's (or Populist) party in 1892. Founded by members of the Farmers' Alliance, the party sought to inflate the currency, make credit more available for farmers, and reform a political system that Populists viewed as corrupt. In Texas and some other states, the Populists also sought black support, appealing to African Americans on the grounds that they shared a common financial plight with poor white farmers. By 1894 Rayner had become the new third party's leading black spokesman in Texas. At the Populist state convention that year, delegates elected him to the party's state executive committee and to the platform committee, where he used his influence to move the party toward stronger positions on issues of importance to African Americans. These issues included reforming the convict lease system, placing black trustees in charge of black schools, and providing for fair elections.

Rayner continued to be active in the party as a highly effective lecturer and organizer until the demise of Populism near the end of the century. Billed as the "Silver-Tongued Orator of the Colored Race" (Cantrell, p. 209), he earned his living and a deserved reputation as one of the finest public speakers in Texas, often addressing racially mixed audiences. Rayner's sharp tongue and his advocacy of issues such as seating blacks on juries sometimes brought him threats of physical violence, but he worked hard not to antagonize white Populists, insisting that blacks were not seeking "social equality" with whites and reminding his audiences of the friendship between southern whites and blacks. According to white Texas Populist leader H. S. P. "Stump" Ashby, Rayner was doing work that "no white man can do" (Cantrell, p. 226).

With the rising tide of segregation and the success of efforts to disfranchise blacks in the early years of the twentieth century, Rayner became involved in black vocational education. Between 1904 and 1914 he served as chief fundraiser for two schools, Conroe College and the Farmers' Improvement Society School. Leaving behind his assertive political activism of the Populist years, Rayner publicly adopted an accommodationist stance. Later he became a friend of the famed Texas lumber baron John Henry Kirby, who despite his conservative stance on most political issues contributed to Rayner's educational projects. Kirby also occasionally employed Rayner as a labor recruiter for his mill towns. Later some blacks criticized Rayner because of the extreme lengths to which he went to ingratiate himself with whites such as the politically powerful Kirby. In his private papers, however, Rayner wrote bitterly of the white man's "hallucinated idea of race superiority" (Cantrell, p. 289).

Rayner also reentered politics after the turn of the century as a behind-the-scenes operative. Reversing his position of 1887, when he supported prohibition, he began working against prohibition. The Texas Brewers' Association, a beer cartel, employed him between 1905 and 1912 as an organizer to help get out the antiprohibition vote in the black community. He also became a frequent contributor of essays and editorials to Texas newspapers, offering blacks and whites advice on a variety of topics such as politics, education, and religion. Rayner retired from political activity around 1912, although he continued to write for newspapers. After several years of declining health he died at his home in Calvert.

Rayner's primary historical significance lies in his status as perhaps the most important black southern Populist. In that capacity, he was a major figure in the Populists' attempt to build a biracial coalition in the 1890s. His failure, and the failure of the Populist movement in the South, underscores the strength of white supremacy in the era and the risks that were inherent in challenging the racial status quo. His accommodationist stance in public after the turn of the century demonstrates the degree to which even the most committed black activists were forced to compromise their principles if they hoped to survive as public figures.

• Rayner's papers are on deposit at the Barker Texas History Center, University of Texas at Austin, but they contain material only from the post-1900 period. A microfilm version of the papers is in the Schomburg Center for Research in Black Culture, New York City. The John Henry Kirby Papers at the Houston Metropolitan Research Center contain a significant amount of Rayner correspondence. For a book-length study, see Gregg Cantrell, *Kenneth and John B. Rayner and the Limits of Southern Dissent* (1993); for a briefer treatment, see Jack Abramowitz, "John B. Rayner—A Grass-Roots Leader," *Journal of Negro History* 36 (1951): 160–93. Three Texas newspapers are particularly valuable in tracing his career, the *Southern Mercury* (Dallas) and the *Galveston Daily News* for his Populist years and the *Houston Chronicle* for his later life.

GREGG CANTRELL

RAYNER, Kenneth (20 June 1808–6 Mar. 1884), politician and planter, was born in Bertie County, North Carolina, the son of Amos Rayner and Hannah Williams, planters. His father served as a private in the revolutionary war and as a Baptist minister before marrying his mother, whose fortune enabled the elder Rayner to become a slaveholding planter of modest means. Kenneth Rayner attended the Tarboro Academy in Edgecombe County, and his father gave him a plantation in Hertford County near Winton. In 1830–1831 he read law under the direction of North Carolina Supreme Court chief justice Thomas Ruffin and was admitted to the bar.

Rayner entered politics in 1833 as an unsuccessful candidate for the North Carolina House of Commons. Sketchy evidence suggests that in his early career he was a supporter of John C. Calhoun but that he soon broke with Calhoun over the issue of nullification. As the Whig party took shape in the mid-1830s, Rayner became an ardent admirer of Henry Clay. His first elective position was as delegate to North Carolina's 1835 constitutional convention, where he won acclaim for his strong support for the repeal of the state's religious test for officeholders. Later that year he was elected to the first of three one-year terms in the House of Commons, where he became known as one of the best orators in North Carolina and a fierce partisan of Whig policies such as government-funded internal improvements.

In 1839 Rayner was elected to the first of three consecutive terms in the U.S. House of Representatives. There he continued to support the national Whig party agenda and Henry Clay's campaign for the presidency.

In 1842 he married Susan Polk, daughter of Colonel William Polk. Her inheritance from her wealthy father propelled Rayner into the ranks of the wealthy planters and slaveholders. In the 1840s and 1850s he acquired fine new plantations in North Carolina, Tennessee, and Arkansas. By the Civil War he owned more than three hundred slaves and estimated his worth at over half a million dollars.

Rayner announced his retirement from Congress in 1845, claiming to be disillusioned by the defeat of Henry Clay, which he attributed to the corrupt immigrant vote. He was reelected to his old seat in the North Carolina House of Commons, which he held from 1846 to 1852, and he also served one term in the state senate, from 1852 to 1854. During these years he compiled a record as a progressive legislator, supporting internal improvements, public education, and care for the insane. He also became widely known as a leading agricultural reformer, helping to establish the North Carolina Agricultural Society in 1852. Rayner was his party's consensus choice for governor in 1847, but he declined the nomination. He became increasingly disillusioned with the Whig party after the nominations of Zachary Taylor in 1848 and Winfield Scott in 1852.

In 1854 Rayner abandoned the Whig party and helped to found the nativist American (or Know Nothing) party. He became one of Know Nothingism's preeminent spokesmen and authored the party's Third (or Union) Degree, an oath that bound members to uphold the Union. Rayner introduced Know Nothingism into his home state of North Carolina and traveled widely throughout the nation on behalf of the party. Although he championed the American party as a vehicle for Unionism, he also wholeheartedly embraced its anti-Catholicism and nativism. During the 1856 elections, he campaigned in Philadelphia for a fusion agreement between the American and Republican parties, which led to death threats against him in North Carolina. A bolting wing of northern Know Nothings nominated him for vice president on a ticket with Commodore Robert F. Stockton, but Rayner declined in an effort to avoid further division within his party. With the disintegration of Know Nothingism, Rayner retired from politics.

Rayner continued to hold strong Unionist views until after the election of Abraham Lincoln, but following the firing on Fort Sumter he became a secessionist and served in North Carolina's secession convention. Midway through the war he concluded that the South could not win and secretly participated in an abortive peace movement. In 1865 he headed a delegation that officially surrendered the city of Raleigh to William T. Sherman's army.

In 1866 Rayner anonymously authored *The Life and Times of Andrew Johnson*, a laudatory campaign biography. The following year he sold his property in North Carolina and moved to Mississippi, where he went bankrupt in a massive cotton-planting venture. In desperate financial straits, he became a Republican and sought a federal patronage appointment. In 1874 President Ulysses S. Grant named him judge of the Court of Alabama Claims, on which he served with distinction for three years. In 1877 President Rutherford B. Hayes appointed Rayner solicitor of the Treasury, a post he held until his death from a stroke.

Rayner and his wife had three sons and two daughters who survived to adulthood. Rayner also fathered two mulatto children, a son and a daughter, by one or more women who were his slaves in the 1850s. His mulatto son, John B. Rayner, became a renowned orator and organizer for the Populist party in Texas in the 1890s.

Rayner's primary historical significance lies in his leading role in the Know Nothing movement of the 1850s and in his larger role as a voice of dissent in the nineteenth-century South. Rayner played a major part in articulating the ideology of the Know Nothing party, an ideology resting on the pillars of Unionism, nativism, and a superpatriotic "Americanism." In articulating this ideology—and in his lifelong opposition to the Democratic party in the South—he sought to remove sectionalism and issues related to race from the national political dialogue. His failure to do so cost him the political fame he so wanted, a fate shared by others of his day whose refusal to engage in racial demagoguery violated the South's unwritten political rules.

• Rayner's papers are scattered throughout numerous collections, but the largest body of them can be found in the Kenneth Rayner Papers at the Southern Historical Collection, University of North Carolina, Chapel Hill. Other significant manuscript collections in the Southern Historical Collection that illuminate his career include the Polk-Yeatman Papers, David Outlaw Papers, and William D. Valentine Diaries. Numerous Rayner letters are also in *The Papers of Thomas Ruffin*, ed. J. G. de Roulhac Hamilton (4 vols., 1918); and *The Papers of William Alexander Graham*, ed. Max R. Williams (8 vols., 1957–1993). The only existing book-length study of Rayner is Gregg Cantrell, *Kenneth and John B. Rayner and the Limits of Southern Dissent* (1993).

GREGG CANTRELL

RAZAF, Andy (15 Dec. 1895–3 Feb. 1973), song lyricist, was born Andreamentania Paul Razafkeriefo in Washington, D.C., the son of Henry Razafkeriefo, a military officer and nephew of the queen of Madagascar, and Jennie Maria Waller. His grandfather was John Louis Waller, a U.S. consul to Madagascar whose arrest in Tamatave and subsequent imprisonment in Marseilles, France, touched off an 1895 upheaval in Madagascar resulting in his father's death there and his mother's flight home, where she gave birth. From the spring of 1896, when John Waller returned from prison, the child Razafkeriefo followed in the trail of his grandfather's ultimately unsuccessful political and entrepreneurial activities in Baltimore, Kansas City, Cuba (for two years), Manhattan (from 1900), and Yonkers (from 1905). By 1911—after his grandfather's death in 1907 and his mother's short-lived second marriage, which brought the family to Passaic, New Jersey—he and his mother had settled in Manhattan.

Razafkeriefo dropped out of high school at age sixteen to work as an elevator operator, a telephone operator, butler, cleaner, and custodian while endeavoring to break into the world of popular song. He had a few insignificant successes and early on, in 1913, received the pragmatic suggestion that he shorten his name to Andrea Razaf. This in turn became Andy Razaf, although he did not adopt that name systematically until the mid-1920s.

He married Annabelle Miller in 1915, but Razaf was an incorrigible womanizer, and the relationship never blossomed; the couple had no children. Following World War I he developed a reputation in the African-American press as a poet protesting racism, a genre to which he would contribute for many years. Temporarily abandoning his lyric-writing ambition, he pitched in Cleveland's semi-professional baseball league while working as a porter there in 1920, only to move back to New York City the following year with the prospect of participating in the new craze for blues and jazz. There he met Fats Waller (no relation to John Waller). Razaf's biographer Barry Singer argues that Razaf wrote lyrics to Waller's tune "Squeeze Me" in 1923 or 1925, and that somehow Clarence Williams appropriated Razaf's credit, such appropriations being commonplace in American popular song at that time. If true, then "Squeeze Me" is by far the most important product of Razaf's first dozen years of professional songwriting.

In 1924 Razaf initiated a modest complementary career, singing on radio broadcasts under Williams's direction and, as "Anthony," forming a song and dance duo with Doc Straine at the Club Alabam, where Fletcher Henderson's big band was based. He contributed to and toured with the revue *Desires* from October 1926 through early 1927, wrote with Waller late in 1927 for the Broadway revue *Keep Shufflin'*, and collaborated with songwriter J. C. Johnson for the revue *Brown Skin Models*, with which he toured in 1928. Having achieved modest hits with lyrics to Johnson's songs "My Special Friend," "When," and "Louisiana" (1926–1928), Razaf wrote both words and melody for the delightfully clever, humorous, and risqué song "My Handy Man" (1928).

His greatest work began in February 1929 in collaboration with Waller and songwriter Harvey Brooks (whose precise contribution is unknown) for the show *Hot Feet*, which was modified and renamed *Connie's Hot Chocolates* in June. The show ran at both Connie's Inn in Harlem and the Hudson Theater downtown. "Ain't Misbehavin'" displays Razaf's characteristic talent for expressing an innocently suggestive outlook. By contrast, "(What Did I Do to Be So) Black and Blue?," presented separately by singers Edith Wilson and Louis Armstrong in different portions of the show, is unusual and was the first significant African-American protest in American popular song.

Later that same year Razaf wrote "S'posin'" with another regular collaborator, the English-born songwriter Paul Denniker; "Gee, Baby, Ain't I Good to You?" with Don Redman; and "Honeysuckle Rose" with Waller, this last for a new revue at Connie's Inn, *Load of Coal*. In 1930 he wrote "A Porter's Love Song to a Chambermaid" with James P. Johnson for the *Kitchen Mechanic's Revue* at Smalls' Paradise in Harlem, and "Memories of You" and "My Handy Man Ain't Handy No More" with Eubie Blake for Lew Leslie's *Blackbirds of 1930*. The latter starred Minto Cato, with whom Razaf was living, although he was still married to Annabelle. "Keepin' Out of Mischief Now," written with Waller, was a hit in 1932. From that year into the 1940s, Razaf wrote for new musical comedies at Connie's Inn (which closed in 1933), the Grand Terrace in Chicago, the Cotton Club in Cleveland, and the Ubangi Club (on the site of Connie's Inn), but the content of these shows grew excessively predictable and their success diminished accordingly. Nonetheless, he wrote lyrics for "Christopher Columbus," "Big Chief de Sota" (two marvelously silly songs), and "Stompin' at the Savoy," all from 1936, and "The Joint is Jumpin'" (1937). Despite all this, he was in continuous financial difficulty, as unscrupulous managers, producers, and publishers, both white and African-American, took advantage of him, denying him opportunities and appropriating portions of his composing royalties. No doubt racist structures contributed to this situation, particularly in his exclusion from a new and lucrative forum for lyricists, Hollywood movie musicals; however, Razaf himself exacerbated the situation time and again by shortsightedly bartering away future royalties for modest fixed fees.

Finally divorced, he married Jean Blackwell in 1939, and they settled in Englewood, New Jersey. Amid his continuing financial problems and extramarital affairs during the 1940s, and in the absence of new professional success, the relationship ended. On ob-

taining a second divorce, he married Dorothy Carpenter in 1948 and moved to Los Angeles. Neither marriage produced children. Despite all of his naive dealings, he still received enough royalties as a member of ASCAP (American Society of Publishers, Authors, and Composers) to survive. In 1951 a spinal attack of tertiary syphilis made him a paraplegic. Dorothy supervised his care until, at decade's end, her infidelity led to his third divorce. In January 1963 he was reunited with Alice Wilson, whom he had renamed Alicia when at age fourteen she met him in Chicago in 1934. They married the next month, and she cared for him in his final years. He died in North Hollywood, California.

In the decade 1928–1937, Razaf was one of the most important lyricists in American popular song. His ability to create at a moment's notice a polished verse, perfectly matched to a given melody, was legendary. And however brilliantly spontaneous his method may have been, the results epitomize popular song of the swing era, in which sentiments of joy, nostalgia, politeness, and yearning toy with sensuality.

• The single definitive source is Barry Singer, *Black and Blue: The Life and Lyrics of Andy Razaf* (1992), offering an overview of the era, pointed interpretation of Razaf's achievements and contradictory personality, unique documentary material, a list of known compositions, a selective discography of recordings of these songs, and notes for further reading. R. L. Brackney's survey article "The Musical Legacy of Andy Razaf" appears in *Jazz Report* 8, no. 5 (1974). Obituaries are in the *New York Times* and *Los Angeles Times*, 4 Feb. 1973.

BARRY KERNFELD

REA, Samuel (21 Sept. 1855–24 Mar. 1929), civil engineer and railroad president, was born in Hollidaysburg, Pennsylvania, the son of James D. Rea, a judge, and Ruth Moore. Rea was forced by the death of his father to leave school at age thirteen and become a clerk in a local general store. In 1871 he secured a position as chainman on a Pennsylvania Railroad (PRR) survey gang working near his home but lost the position with the onset of the panic of 1873. He soon found work as a clerk for the Hollidaysburg Iron and Nail Company and in 1875 resumed his employment with the PRR as assistant engineer with the railroad's engineering corps at Connellsville, Pennsylvania.

Also in 1875 Rea was appointed assistant engineer in charge of constructing a chain suspension bridge over the Monongahela River at Pittsburgh. In 1877 he accepted the post of assistant engineer in locating the Pittsburgh and Lake Erie (P&LE) Railroad. When the line opened, he stayed on briefly as cashier at the P&LE freight depot and as passenger ticket agent for the line. While in Pittsburgh, he married Mary Black in 1879; they would have two children.

In 1879 he returned to the Pennsylvania Railroad as assistant engineer in charge of extending the Pittsburgh, Virginia and Charleston Railroad, a line leased by the PRR. From 1880 to 1883 he was placed in charge of regrading the Western Pennsylvania Railroad to allow more efficient freight movement west of the Allegheny Mountains. Here Rea's work was noticed by J. N. DuBarry, assistant to the president, and in 1883 he was promoted to assistant to the vice president and principal assistant engineer, moving to the PRR's corporate headquarters in Philadelphia. In his new post he was responsible for assisting DuBarry with construction work and surveys of new lines. He traveled to England in 1887 to study London railways and on his return to the United States published *The Railways Terminating in London* (1888).

The same year he was named assistant to the second vice president, PRR, but left the railroad's employ in 1889 to accept the more lucrative position of vice president of the Maryland Central (MC) Railroad. While serving in this position, he functioned as chief engineer for the Baltimore Belt Railway, a line that he located and put under construction. Due to ill health, however, Rea was forced to resign from the MC in 1891. After recovering, he returned to the PRR in 1892. The day he reported for work, he left for London to make a detailed study of electric-powered subways of the South London Railway. Railroad officials hoped that electrified subways could be used to access New York City for the PRR.

In his new position as assistant to the president, Rea was placed in charge of general construction work, acquisition of rights-of-way, and promotion of all new lines. In 1899 he was elected fourth vice president of the PRR followed by advancements to third vice president in 1905 and second vice president in 1909. As second vice president, his normal duties were expanded to encompass both engineering and financial departments of the railroad.

Rea was made first vice president in 1911 and a year later was given formal charge of the railroad's New York tunnel and terminal improvements. It was in connection with this project that Rea made his greatest engineering contribution. Until 1910 the PRR had no direct access to New York City. Traffic bound for the city used ferries to make the river crossing from New Jersey, while rival New York Central had direct access to the heart of Manhattan. Since the 1880s PRR executives had searched for a way to gain access to New York. Rea's interest in traversing the Hudson went back to the 1880s when he was involved in an unsuccessful plan to bridge the river. In 1901 Rea had urged the construction of tunnels under the Hudson and East rivers to carry PRR tracks into New York. When the project commenced in 1904, Rea oversaw construction of New York's Pennsylvania Station and the tunnels that accessed it via electrified trackage. His work earned him an honorary doctorate of science degree from the University of Pennsylvania in 1910.

With the resignation of PRR president James McCrea in 1913, Rea was named as his successor. He served until 1925 when he reached the mandatory retirement age of seventy. During his tenure as president he continued to improve railroad facilities around New York, constructing the Hell Gate Bridge, which was completed in 1917. The bridge enabled through-train service from New England to New York City and Washington, D.C., and farther south. At the time, the bridge was the longest metal arch span in the world.

Rea's tenure as president of the PRR coincided with the end of railroad expansion in the United States. Rea devoted himself instead to making internal improvements to the system and simplifying the corporate structure, programs that were needed to handle expanding traffic more efficiently. He was challenged in his work by increasing government regulation, antirailroad public sentiment, rising labor demands, and a national trend toward declining railroad revenues. With the onset of World War I the U.S. government seized control of railroad operations for strategic purposes. After the war came a period of difficult readjustment to private control and an economic recession in the early 1920s that threatened profitability. Rea piloted the company through these difficult times using his financial and engineering skills to keep the company prosperous. To cut costs and improve efficiency he regionalized railroad administration, consolidated subsidiary lines, and ended an archaic division of the PRR system into two separate entities east and west of Pittsburgh. He consolidated repair shop facilities and established a general mortgage on company property that allowed for broad-based funding of long-range capital needs. Rea met a long-term escalation in traffic by overseeing the design and production of heavier, more powerful locomotives and larger railcars with greater capacity. He also furloughed workers and cut wages.

In his personal life Rea loved books and was an avid reader. He enjoyed travel and meeting the public and was active in civic affairs. He once commented, "He will be a poor railroad man if he does not learn a great deal about the public he is called to serve." As the epitome of the self-made American business executive of the late nineteenth and early twentieth centuries, Rea observed that "the world gets nowhere with standpatters or indifferent people."

Rea also was active in numerous engineering societies and social clubs; he was a partner in the investment house of Rea Brothers of Pittsburgh and a member of the New York Stock Exchange. He received several honorary degrees for his engineering achievements and was awarded the Franklin Medal for Engineering in 1926. *Railway Age* magazine called him "an outstanding transportation executive." He died at his home in Gladwyne, Pennsylvania.

• Rea's papers are in the Division of Archives, Pennsylvania Historical and Museum Commission, Harrisburg. Rea's early career is well covered in William Bender Wilson, *History of the Pennsylvania Railroad Company* (1899), and Fred Westing, *Penn Station: Its Tunnels and Side Rodders* (1978). His entire career is summarized in George H. Burgess and Miles C. Kennedy, *Centennial History of the Pennsylvania Railroad* (1946). *Railway Age* summarized his career and management philosophies in its 26 Sept. 1925 issue, pp. 563–66. *Railway Age* also published a thorough biography as part of Rea's obituary, 30 Mar. 1929. For a discussion of Rea's work in the

New York terminal improvements see Patricia Davis, *The End of the Line* (1978), and Lorraine B. Diehl, *The Late Great Pennsylvania Station* (1985).

ROBERT L. EMERSON

REACH, Alfred James (25 May 1840–14 Jan. 1928), baseball player, sporting-goods manufacturer, and franchise owner, was born in London, England, the son of Benjamin Reach, a trading agent, and Elizabeth Dyball. His parents immigrated to Brooklyn, New York, when he was a year old. He had little formal education. Brought up with temperate values and a strong work ethic, Reach sold newspapers on Broadway and worked as a ship caulker. He became an iron-molder, "wielding heavy tools" twelve hours a day in a foundry (*Ledger*, 11 July 1915).

Following in his father's cricket-playing tradition, Reach discovered by the age of seventeen that he possessed a talent for the popular "New York–style" game of baseball. On the sandlots of Brooklyn he gained renown as a catcher and captain of the Jackson Juniors of Williamsburg. His move to the famous blue-collar Eckford Baseball Club of Brooklyn brought him to the attention of prominent teams bidding for the services of promising young players.

Impressed with the integrity and business sense of Colonel Thomas Fitzgerald, the president of the Philadelphia Athletics, Reach joined the Philadelphia club in 1865 as a second baseman and became one of the first "professional" baseball players. Although earning only $25 a week and commuting home to Brooklyn between games, Reach considered it the best decision he had ever made. This sentiment was reinforced at the start of the 1866 season, when Fitzgerald set him up in a downtown cigar-and-tobacco store. The site quickly became a popular gathering spot for the city's sportsmen. Before the year was out Reach began brokering tickets and merchandising baseball gear and uniforms. After his marriage on Christmas Day to Louise Betts of Brooklyn, with whom he had four children, the couple moved to Philadelphia.

For most of the next decade the veteran Reach, nicknamed "Pop" because of his maturity and the respect of his peers, became one of the sport's most popular and admired players. Fast and sure-handed, he set a standard for playing second base. He was known as the "scratcher" for his capability of "digging" up hard-hit balls (*Item*, 1 May 1898). According to *Sporting Life*, Reach was the first second baseman to station himself off the bag in shallow right field between first and second bases (12 Dec. 1888, p. 6). The 5'6" 155-pound Reach hit left-handed with skill and power. His feats and gentlemanly behavior were lauded by the sporting press, which closely followed his playing career through the National Association baseball era, from 1871 to 1875. In 1874 Reach became the playing manager of the Athletics and visited England on baseball's first overseas tour. When the National League was formed two years later, Reach retired to devote his attention to his expanding business ventures. His

peers acknowledged him as the best second baseman of his era.

The year of the English tour Reach anticipated an increased demand for baseball and sporting supplies and established a large retail store in Philadelphia. After seven prosperous years he expanded and took Ben Shibe, a local sportsman and leather manufacturer, as a partner. Later, Reach's son married Shibe's daughter. The *New York Clipper* credited Reach's entrepreneurial rise to his "temperate habits, general disposition . . . sterling integrity . . . [and] steady industry" (15 Apr. 1882). This reputation and Reach's background made him a natural candidate for rescuing the failing Worcester, Massachusetts, baseball franchise.

Joined by Colonel John I. Rogers, an attorney on Governor Pattison's staff, in 1883 Reach became the first president of the Philadelphia Phillies. With no players and nothing but the right of franchise, Reach renovated an old ball park and hastily assembled a team. To mark this inaugural season he also began publishing the annual *Reach's Official . . . Baseball Guide*, which contained summaries and statistics from the previous season, as well as previews of the upcoming year. After a dismal 1883 season (last in the eight-team league), Reach, who was accustomed to success, signed baseball's leading manager, Harry Wright. The team improved immediately, and within a few years the little ball park proved inadequate. Reach responded in 1887 by building a spacious state-of-the-art wooden baseball stadium at Broad and Lehigh streets for the unprecedented cost of $80,000.

These successes were accompanied by problems associated with the growth of professional sports. Faced with rising operational costs, Reach and other owners faced disputes over salaries and the players' reserve clause. In 1890 the players' union established its own baseball league. The subsequent litigation and feuding proved disturbing and expensive for Reach. But he had anticipated these problems by selling his retail outlets to his enterprising rival, Albert Spalding, for $100,000. Reach retained the company's name and the production side of the business. By the mid-1890s he met the growing demand for sportsware with larger factories in Philadelphia and in Brantford, Ontario. Reach's enduring manufacturing successes came partly from his development of a machine for winding baseballs. He and his brother Robert actually set up a school to train young men to make baseballs. Reach also prospered by his ability to anticipate physical fitness equipment needs.

Reach's direct interest in baseball diminished after an 1894 fire destroyed his new ball park. His huge insurance losses were compounded by the expense of rebuilding a new kind of baseball stadium that would eliminate the risk of fires, relegate obstructive posts to the rear of the pavilion, and use a new steel cantilever system for hanging decks and roofs. The astute businessman and promoter built a large lighted, banked asphalt bicycle track around the playing field. But by the end of the decade the contentious Colonel Rogers assumed the daily operations of the franchise. This shift did not improve the ailing finances of the luckless Phillies, who fared poorly in the post-1901 salary wars with the upstart American League. When Shibe acquired the Philadelphia American League franchise and signed leading players from the Phillies, such as Napoleon Lajoie, Reach was awarded the contract for the new league's baseballs. In 1904 Reach and Rogers sold their weakened ball club for $170,000 but retained the title to the stadium and its facilities.

Over the next decade Reach's son, George, and the Spalding Company together dominated the sporting-goods business. Reach, meanwhile, retired to Atlantic City, New Jersey, where he died. Until his health failed, he had maintained an active interest in athletics. Reach's esteemed reputation and an estate valued at more than a million dollars testify to his role and success in the new age of American sports.

• Contemporary accounts of Reach's career are in the *Philadelphia Bulletin, Philadelphia Evening Item, Philadelphia Evening Ledger, Philadelphia Inquirer, Philadelphia Sunday Mercury, Philadelphia Press,* and *New York Clipper.* Other sources include articles published in *Sporting Life* and *Sporting News.* See also Albert Spalding, *America's National Game* (1911); Frederick Lieb and Stan Baumgartner, *The Philadelphia Phillies* (1953); Harold Seymour, *Baseball: The Early Years* (1960); David Q. Voigt, *American Baseball,* vol. 1 (1980); George B. Kirsch, *The Creation of American Team Sports* (1989); William Ryczek, *Blackguards and Red Stockings* (1992); and Rich Westcott and Frank Bilovsky, *The New Phillies Encyclopedia* (1993). Obituaries are in the *Philadelphia Bulletin,* 14 Jan. 1928, and the *New York Times,* 15 Jan. 1928.

JERROLD CASWAY

READ, Conyers (25 Apr. 1881–23 Dec. 1959), historian, was born in Philadelphia, Pennsylvania, the son of William Franklin Read, a textile manufacturer, and Victoria Eliza Conyers. His early schooling was focused on preparing him to enter his father's textile business, and for a time he hoped to become a writer of fiction. At Harvard, under the aegis of Roger Merriman, he became interested in history and graduated summa cum laude in 1903. He received his M.A. in 1904 and his Ph.D. in history in 1908. The following year he received a B.Litt. from Balliol College, having spent the years 1903 to 1905 at Oxford; both degrees were based on his researches on the life of the Elizabethan statesman Sir Francis Walsingham. He attended the University of Paris for a semester and during 1908–1909 went to England to carry out archival research in Elizabethan state papers. He returned to the United States to become assistant to historian Charles H. Haskins at Harvard.

In the fall of 1909, Read became instructor in history at Princeton University. In 1910 he married Edith Coulson Kirk, an interior decorator. They had three children, one of whom, Elizabeth Read (Foster), was to become a distinguished historian of English Parliament in the Stuart period. In the fall of 1911, Read joined the history department of the University of Chi-

cago and was promoted to assistant professor in 1912 and associate professor in 1915.

An active pamphleteer for the Allies, Read was determined to serve in the First World War, although his deafness rendered him unfit for active military duty. In 1918 he went with the American Red Cross to France, where he was assigned to a hospital in Brittany. When armistice was signed, Read returned to Chicago and was made professor.

Although well launched on an academic career, Read felt compelled to take an indefinite leave from his professorship in 1920 and return to Philadelphia to help run his father's textile business. His father had died in 1916, and his older brothers proved incapable of managing the firm without his assistance. Appointed treasurer in 1920, Read became vice president and general manager of the firm in 1927, and president in 1930. His efforts were doomed, however, as three years later the Victoria Mill closed its doors. Although Read did not savor his foray into the business world, his experience in managing a large firm with nearly 500 employees was to serve him in good stead in his subsequent government service and academic life. Although working full-time in business, he continued his research during the evenings and published throughout those years.

In 1933 Read became executive secretary of the American Historical Association, a post he held for eight years, and served as president for the year 1949. He reformed that organization's finances and sought to broaden its connections with the international community. His presidential address (*American Historical Review* 55 [1949–1950]: 275–85) set forth his views on the social responsibilities of the historian, that the historian should promote a society based on freedom, rather than religion or totalitarianism, by providing valid information from past human experience.

Read became professor of history at the University of Pennsylvania in 1934, a post he held until his retirement in 1951. His first wife died in 1938. In 1939 he married Evelyn Plummer Braun, a research assistant with whom he collaborated subsequently on several publications.

As an Anglophile and opponent of fascism and Nazism, Read became an ardent letter writer, pamphleteer, and debater against American isolationism and was chairman of the Philadelphia Committee of the Fight for Freedom. In 1939 he began work with the Committee to Defend America by Aiding the Allies. Even before the United States entered the war, it became apparent that a central agency was necessary for gathering and evaluating detailed information on the economic resources, government, and society of the participants. As Read expressed it later, "total war, be it hot or cold, enlists everyone and calls upon everyone to assume his part. The historian is no freer from this obligation than the physicist." Some half dozen prominent scholars cooperated in setting up what later became the Research and Analysis Branch of the Office of Strategic Services under William J. Donovan. Conyers Read was in charge of the British Empire section and serve as well on the planning group that formulated, assigned, and reviewed intelligence projects. When the war was over, Read left the organization and returned to Philadelphia. His interest in foreign affairs was unabated, and he was instrumental in setting up a Philadelphia group of the Council on Foreign Relations, of which he was the first chairman. He served on the State Department's advisory committee on the publication of captured German documents and published several studies on twentieth-century diplomatic history, such as a study of the London Naval Treaty of 1930 (*Proceedings of the American Philosophical Society* 93, no. 4 [1949]: 290–308). He also edited a large volume on the U.S. Constitution, *The Constitution Reconsidered* (1938).

Conyers Read's researches in English history placed him at the top of his profession. His first major work, a biography of Sir Francis Walsingham, was published in three volumes in 1925. This book, which he described as "something more than a biography of Walsingham and something less than a history of Elizabethan policy," was a contribution of outstanding importance to the study of Tudor England because it went beyond the limits of a standard biography to examine all policies in which the statesman was involved, a pattern followed in his later work on Lord Burghley. It was followed by his *Bibliography of British History, Tudor Period, 1485–1603* (1933; rev. ed., 1959) and a masterful brief monograph, *The Tudors, Personalities and Practical Politics in Sixteenth-Century England* (1936). A series of lectures at the Rice Institute appeared as *Social and Political Forces in the English Reformation* (1953). His later monumental work, a biography of Lord Burghley (2 vols., 1955, 1960), received the Folger Library Prize and the Philadelphia Athenaeum Medal. It was based on his reading of thousands of documents by the Tudor queen's closest adviser and served to deepen Read's admiration for her abilities and achievements. Throughout his life Read contributed many articles and reviews to journals and collective works, for some of which he served also as editor.

In Read's own assessment, a major satisfaction of his life was to exercise his own creative impulse and to live in accordance with clearly defined standards (radio broadcast published in *This I Believe*, ed. Raymond Swing [1954]). He held strong principles, among them that superior education and abilities called for service to society, rather than withdrawal to a study. He saw politics and statecraft as fields in which the learned could devote their energies with honor. If his early academic career had the undoubted advantage of a privileged youth, his government and business experience allowed him perspective unusual in a professional historian. His personality and physical presence suggested firmness and strength, which, combined with critical humor, bluntness of approach, and dislike of sham and caprice, made him a challenging and exacting teacher. He committed himself fully to his students, treating them as future colleagues and sparing no pains in their apprenticeship.

Read died at his home in Villanova, Pennsylvania, in the midst of new undertakings.

• Read's professional papers and correspondence are in the archives of the University of Pennsylvania, Philadelphia. A partial bibliography of his publications is in Norton Downs, ed., *Essays in Honor of Conyers Read* (1953). Autobiographical and introspective materials are in the Harvard class books for the class of 1903. Additional family and personal information can be found in Benjamin R. Foster, "Notes on the Read Family," a typescript deposited in the Genealogical Society of Pennsylvania, Philadelphia. Information on his government service is in *Conyers Read, 1881–1959, Scholar, Teacher, Public Servant* (privately printed, 1963), with contributions by William L. Langer, Sir John E. Neale, and Norton Downs. Obituaries are in the *American Philosophical Society Yearbook* (1960), pp. 172–76 (by William L. Langer), and in the *American Historical Review* 65 (1959–1960): 778–80.

BENJAMIN R. FOSTER

READ, Daniel (16 Nov. 1757–4 Dec. 1836), composer, tunebook compiler, and merchant, was born in Rehoboth (now Attleboro), Massachusetts, the son of "Captain" Daniel Read and Mary White, farmers. He received only a rudimentary "country school" education (only one quarter, according to his son G. F. H. Read) and gained his musical education from attendance at singing schools. (His older brothers Peter and Joel were singing masters.) He may also have attended singing schools conducted by Andrew Law and William Billings in nearby Providence, Rhode Island, in the early 1770s. In the mid-1770s he moved to New Stratford, Connecticut, perhaps to learn the comb-making trade, and served several short tours of duty with Connecticut militia during the revolutionary war.

In 1782 Read established a dry goods and grocery business in New Haven, Connecticut, where he also manufactured horn and ivory combs. In 1783 he married Jerusha Sherman, daughter of Nathaniel Sherman, a prosperous Stratford farmer. Nathaniel Sherman opposed the marriage because of, in Read's words, "the unpardonable crime of poverty," and it caused a breach between Read and the Sherman family that was never healed, in spite of Read's later affluence. The couple had four children, three of whom survived infancy.

Read's most active and innovative period as a musician was between 1785 and 1795. During this time, in addition to his business activities, he taught singing schools and published two important tunebooks, *The American Singing Book* (5 eds., 1785–1795) and *The Columbian Harmonist* (4 eds., 1793–1810). With *The American Singing Book*, Read became only the second American composer, after William Billings, to publish a tunebook devoted exclusively to his music. He also collaborated with engraver Amos Doolittle to issue *The American Musical Magazine* (12 issues, 1786–1787), the first periodical musical publication in America. In 1790 he published *An Introduction to Psalmody*, a music instruction manual for children. After about 1800, as his business prospered, Read became less involved in musical activities, although he continued to lead the choir at the United Society church and to sing in civic events in the New Haven area. In 1817 he and fellow New Haven psalmodist Simeon Jocelin were asked by the United Society church to compile a tunebook for the church's use. It was published as *The New Haven Collection of Sacred Music* (1818), although neither Read's nor Jocelin's name appears on it. Late in his life, Read attempted one more tunebook, *Musica Ecclesiae* (1832), which he offered to the American Home Missionary Society to publish to their benefit. The society, however, declined, and the tunebook was never printed.

As a composer, Read specialized in short, strophic pieces of choral music set to sacred texts. His ninety-four published compositions include eighty-four psalm- and fuging-tunes and ten anthems and set pieces. This represents only a fraction of the pieces he is known to have composed, however, for many remained in manuscript. Two manuscripts of his music, dating from 1777 and 1832, survive in the collections of the New Haven Colony Historical Society. Read began composing about 1774 and continued off and on throughout his life. He was a strong advocate of the fuging-tune, a type of polyphonic psalm-tune much in vogue among the rural singers in both England and America during the eighteenth century. At first, Read employed the informal contrapuntal compositional method used by many contemporary psalmodists, such as William Billings, but during the mid-1780s he came under the influence of George Frideric Handel's music. From that time, Read studied to master the principles of "scientific" music, and his late efforts show that he succeeded, although he received little recognition of this accomplishment.

At his death in New Haven, Read was an affluent retired businessman, one of the city's leading citizens, and a man honored locally. As a composer, however, he was largely forgotten. A radical change in taste in American church music after about 1820 caused his eclipse. Some of his tunes, such as "Windham," "Winter," and "Lisbon," found their way into tunebooks of the 1840s, 1850s, and 1860s, but most of the pieces best known in their day, such as his fuging-tunes "Calvary," "Greenwich," "Naples," "Russia," "Sherburne," and "Stafford" and his psalm-tune "Judgment," were laid aside. Little was heard of Read until after World War II, when in 1952 Irving Lowens published an important article on him in the Music Library Association's periodical *Notes*. A Harvard University doctoral dissertation by Vinson Bushnell, "Daniel Read of New Haven (1757–1836): The Man and His Musical Activities" (1978), shed further light on his life and work. Significant recognition of his prominence as an early American composer was accorded Read in the mid-1990s by the inclusion of his critically edited collected works in the Music of the United States of America series, sponsored by the American Musicological Society.

• Two volumes of letter drafts by Read are in the collections of the New Haven Colony Historical Society, along with two manuscripts of his music and portraits of both Read and his wife. The volume devoted to him in the Music of the United States of America series is *The Collected Works of Daniel Read*, ed. Karl Kroeger (1995). Irving Lowens's article is "Daniel Read's World: The Letters of an Early American Composer," *Notes* 9 (Mar. 1952): 233–48; the article was reprinted in Lowens's *Music and Musicians in Early America* (1964). See also the entry on Read in *American Sacred Music Imprints, 1698–1810: A Bibliography*, ed. Allen P. Britton et al. (1990); George Hood, "Sketches of American Musical Biography and History: Daniel Read," *Musical Herald* 3 (Oct. 1882): 260; and Frank J. Metcalf, *American Writers and Compilers of Sacred Music* (1925; repr. 1967).

KARL KROEGER

READ, George (18 Sept. 1733–21 Sept. 1798), signer of the Declaration of Independence and of the Constitution, was born in Cecil County, Maryland, the son of John Read, a planter, and Mary Howell. John Read was an Anglo-Irish immigrant from Dublin; his wife was born in Wales. Their son George received a classical education at the Reverend Francis Alison's academy in New London, Pennsylvania, and then studied law with John Moland in Philadelphia. The lives of two of his classmates in New London, Thomas McKean and Charles Thomson, were subsequently intertwined with his. In Philadelphia he began what turned out to be close lifelong friendships with Samuel Wharton and John Dickinson (1732–1808).

Admitted to the bar in Philadelphia in 1753, Read settled in New Castle, Delaware, a year later, not long after his parents had moved to the nearby village of Christiana Bridge. Rising rapidly to prominence in law and politics, Read became attorney general in 1763 and retained this position until 1774. He was elected to the assembly in 1765 and upon reelection in 1768 began a long service in the legislature lasting, one year excepted, until 1788. He was president and the most influential delegate in the state constitutional convention of 1776, and as Speaker of the upper house in the new government he became acting president of Delaware in 1777–1778 after the British seized John McKinly.

Opposed to the Stamp Act and active in securing compliance with Philadelphia nonimportation agreements in 1768 and later, Read was a leading member of committees of correspondence established by the colonial assembly. As a delegate to the Continental Congress from 1774 to 1777, Read, like his friend Dickinson, voted against the independence resolution on 2 July 1776, thinking Congress was acting too precipitously. However, unlike Dickinson, he signed the Declaration of Independence once the resolution was adopted.

Originally identified with the proprietary interest, Read became the leader of the moderate party in Delaware during the Revolution. He helped keep Delaware in harmony with its sister states while seeking to calm civil strife and, as the war drew to a conclusion, to reintroduce the numerous neutrals and Loyalists into political life. Radical revolutionaries referred to Read as "the arch-politician" and "the tyrant of Delaware," but when Delaware elections were most democratic his views prevailed. There was no important difference between the two parties in Delaware except for the greater hostility felt by the radicals, who included many Scotch-Irish Presbyterians, toward the English government. Under Read's leadership Delaware made an exceptionally smooth transition from colony to state.

Such was Read's influence that he brought about John Dickinson's reintroduction into local politics and was primarily responsible for the election of three non-residents (Samuel Wharton, Thomas McKean, and John Dickinson's brother Philemon) to Congress in 1782. Read joined with Wharton, a land speculator recently returned from England, in seeking to limit what they thought to be the extravagant claims of Virginia and a few other states to western lands.

Chosen by Congress to be a judge of its court of appeals for admiralty cases, Read became an ardent supporter of a strengthened national government in the postwar period. He represented Delaware at both the Annapolis convention of 1786 and the Philadelphia convention of 1787. Before the latter convention he served as a committee of one in preparing instructions that obliged the Delaware delegates to insist on retaining an equal voice for each state in any new government. When the Virginia delegates proposed a proportional representation in the new Congress, Read declared that his delegation had no power to consider such an arrangement, and the subject was postponed. Yet when the great compromise on representation was proposed, Read was entirely satisfied. Having assured Delaware's equality in the Senate, he was willing to see the state governments reduced in power to the position of counties.

Not surprisingly, Read became an ally of Alexander Hamilton (1755–1804) when the new government was established. He was elected to the Senate in 1788 and reelected in 1790, but in 1793 he resigned to become chief justice of the Delaware supreme court.

Read had been married in 1763 to Gertrude Ross, widow of Thomas Till and sister of another signer of the Declaration of Independence, George Ross. Three of their sons and one daughter lived to maturity. Read's death, after a short illness, apparently occurred in New Castle, where he is buried close to the wall of Immanuel Episcopal Church. The family home, on the Strand in New Castle, was destroyed by fire in 1824.

Not distinguished as a speaker, Read was highly regarded for his learning and acumen. He was the compiler of the two-volume collection of *Laws of Delaware* (1797).

• Manuscript Read papers are in the Historical Society of Delaware, Wilmington; the Historical Society of Pennsylvania, Philadelphia; and the Library of Congress. Many Read letters were published in what is still the most complete biography, William T. Read, *Life and Correspondence of George Read, Signer of the Declaration of Independence* (1870). See also Daniel T. Boughner, *George Read and the Founding of the Delaware State, 1781–1798* (1968); [James Tilton], *The Bio-*graphical History of Dionysius, Tyrant of Delaware* (1788; annotated repr., 1958, vol. 31 of *Delaware Notes*); John A. Munroe, *Federalist Delaware, 1775–1815* (1954); John M. Coleman, *Thomas McKean, Forgotten Leader of the Revolution* (1975); and Milton E. Flower, *John Dickinson, Conservative Revolutionary* (1983).

JOHN A. MUNROE

READ, Opie Percival (22 Dec. 1852–2 Nov. 1939), novelist and humorist, was born in Nashville, Tennessee, the son of Guilford Read, a carriage manufacturer, and Elizabeth Wallace. Read enjoyed a peaceful, comfortable childhood, dividing his time between attending school and helping out in the fields. While Read was still quite young, his father moved the family to Gallatin, Tennessee, a small town northeast of Nashville.

Read did not share his father's Calvinist convictions, nor did he embrace the rigorous work ethic that his father promoted. His father also disapproved of—but did not discourage—Read's preferred pastimes: reading, writing, and storytelling, which would lay the groundwork for Read's career as a newspaper editor, novelist, and traveling lecturer. The two writers that Read most admired were William Shakespeare, whom he once referred to as "the most supreme human being, in that he was most creative," and Benjamin Franklin, in whose *Autobiography* Read found his first professional calling, newspaper printing.

One of Read's earliest mentors was Andrew Kelley, a neighbor who had worked as a typesetter and a reporter. Kelley taught Read the rudiments of the printer's trade and encouraged him to submit one of his stories—an anecdote about a local personality—for publication. The story, bearing the pseudonym "Crawfish," became Read's first published article, appearing in the *Franklin (Ky.) Patriot* (date unknown).

In 1871 Read embarked on an itinerant lifestyle that he would maintain for the better part of a decade. Traveling throughout the Midwest and the mid-South, the young man supported himself during this period by editing and setting type for small local newspapers. He also began polishing his skills and building his repertoire as a master storyteller, occasionally even trading his tales for temporary room and board. Throughout his travels, Read was drawn to unusual people, and he developed a lifelong admiration for those who thrived despite the efforts of conventional authority to discourage their independence. This admiration would become a recurring theme in Read's novels and lectures.

During this period Read settled down long enough to attend Neophogen College (now defunct), a small private institution in Gallatin. During his two years at Neophogen (dates unknown), he helped cover his expenses by setting type for the campus newspaper, the *Pen*. His formal education also included studying law in Little Rock, Arkansas; however, he decided to forgo the bar exam, thus rejecting that potential career.

In 1873 he joined Kelley at the *Patriot*, leaving that paper within a year because he felt confident that he knew enough about newspapers to launch one of his own. (Some sources say he was dismissed after a disagreement with the paper's owner.) After a few more years of freelance typesetting and reporting, Read established the *Prairie Flower* (1878) with his friend Harry Warner in Carlisle, Arkansas. The paper was short-lived, as was its successor, the original *Arkansaw Traveler*. Undeterred, Read continued his career as a journalist for various newspapers throughout the mid-South, eventually settling into the post of city editor at the Little Rock *Arkansas Gazette*.

During this period of travels and career shifts, Read met his future wife, Ada Benham, in Conway, Arkansas. They married in Texarkana, Arkansas, in June 1880, after which they resided in Little Rock. They had three sons and three daughters who lived to adulthood. Two other daughters died in infancy.

Two years after his marriage Read embarked on the enterprise that would bring him his first brush with widespread fame, a "humorous and literary journal" (as Ada's brother Philo Benham called it) that Read dubbed the *Arkansaw Traveler*, despite the failure of his earlier venture by that same name. With Benham as his partner and business manager, Read appointed himself editor of this weekly paper, in which, as Read put it, "I sought to exalt the Arkansas gentleman" (Elfer, p. 281). The paper was an immediate success, and within three years reached a circulation of 85,000. In 1887 Read and Benham decided to relocate the paper to Chicago, where Read would reside for the rest of his life. Four years later Read resigned from the *Arkansaw Traveler*, so that he could devote his considerable energy to writing novels.

Read was most prolific as a novelist between 1888 (when his first novel, *Len Gansett*, was published) and 1906, producing in rapid succession texts that emphasized storytelling over conventional literary finesse. He wrote and published more than fifty books during his lifetime, including *A Kentucky Colonel* (1890), *The Wives of the Prophet* (1894), *The Jucklins* (1896), *My Young Master* (1896), *An Arkansas Planter* (1896), and *The Starbucks* (1902). At the time of his death at his home in Chicago, Read was working on a manuscript titled "Satan's Side of It: The Autobiography of the Devil as Dictated to a Sinner."

When he was not writing books or holding forth at the Chicago Press Club, Read spent some thirty years as a highly popular speaker and storyteller on the Chautauqua lecture circuit, filling so many speaking engagements that he once claimed to have visited "nearly every country in America." Read's audiences—of his novels as well as of his lectures—appreciated his homespun humor, down-to-earth philosophy, and ability to collect characters and anecdotes and then relate them in an engaging manner.

Read's most enduring legacy consists of his novels, several of which were dramatized. These books, unsophisticated by classical literary standards, filled an important niche in the pre-radio market, providing thousands of railway passengers with light, pleasant reading material. Although recent critics have labeled Read's works "provincial" (Starrett, p. 153) or "melodrama[tic]" (Baird, Introduction, p. 12), they also commend him for his simple language that does not condescend to its audience, his directness that never becomes unpleasant or confrontational, and his optimism that suffers no illusions as to human vice. Most of all, Read has been hailed for his keen insight into human nature, particularly his compassion for the newly freed slaves. His distrust of dogmatic religion and of social conventions, together with his consuming interest in reconciling tradition and progress, made Read a suitable spokesman for many middle-class Americans of the late nineteenth and early twentieth centuries.

• Many of Read's most significant novels are, if not still in print, at least readily available in public and academic libraries. Read's personal recollections of his life have been compiled in *I Remember* (1930), and at least two biographies provide further insight to his life and works: Maurice Elfer, *Opie Read* (1940), and Robert L. Morris, *Opie Read: American Humorist* (1965). More recently, Reed A. Baird provides a thorough biographical and critical analysis of Read and his writing in two articles: "Opie Read: An American Traveler," *Tennessee Historical Quarterly* 33, no. 2 (Winter 1974): 410–28; and "Opie Read (1852–1939): An Introduction," *Mark Twain Journal* 19, no. 1 (Winter 1977–1978): 11–13. See also Wayne Mixon's introduction to the 1987 reprinting of *My Young Master*, as well as Vincent Starrett's chapter on Read in his *Buried Caesars: Essays in Literary Appreciation* (1968). Obituaries are in the *Chicago Tribune* and the *New York Times*, both 3 Nov. 1939, the *Chicago Daily News*, 2 Nov. 1939, and the *Saturday Review of Literature*, 11 Nov. 1939.

LAINE A. SCOTT

READ, Thomas Buchanan (22 Mar. 1822–11 May 1872), poet, painter, and sculptor, was born in Corner Ketch, Chester County, Pennsylvania. Very little is known about his parents. The death of Read's father in about 1832 propelled the breakup of the family. Thomas was apprenticed to a tailor whose reputedly cruel treatment of the boy prompted him to run away to Philadelphia. He worked for a cigar maker and a grocer before moving, at about age fifteen, to Cincinnati, the home of a married sister. He evidently received little formal education. In Cincinnati he found employment as a sign painter and a cigar maker, and he also worked as an apprentice tombstone carver for the sculptor Shobal Vail Clevenger. In time, Read set up his own painting studio. Cincinnati horticulturist and millionaire Nicholas Longworth supported his early efforts, albeit with occasional reservations about his protégé's lack of diligence in applying himself to his art. Read first gained public notice in 1840 with his portrait of Whig presidential candidate William Henry Harrison. Read's first published verses appeared in Cincinnati's *Chronicle* and *Times*.

In 1841 Read traveled to New York. He intended to return eventually to Philadelphia, but friends advised him to go instead to Boston because it provided better opportunities for a rising artist. After his move he received encouragement from, among others, poet Henry Wadsworth Longfellow and artist Washington Allston. The *Boston Courier* published his poems, and his novel *Paul Redding, a Tale of the Brandywine* (1845), a melodrama set near Pennsylvania's Brandywine River, also appeared during this time. In 1843 he married Mary J. Pratt of Gambier, Ohio. The couple had three children, but only their daughter Alice survived to adulthood.

Read moved to Philadelphia in 1846. In 1850 he made his first trip to Europe, where he was enthusiastically welcomed into the circle of the English Pre-Raphaelites. Three years later, while living in Florence, the number of commissions he was by then receiving prompted him to write to good friend and patron James L. Claghorn, "I think that we may safely conclude that after a long and dark struggle, *success* has at length begun to dawn upon me" (Archives of American Art). Read's commissions took him to London, Liverpool, Düsseldorf, and other European cities, in addition to more frequent stays in Rome and Florence.

In Florence, Read divided his time between two passions, painting and poetry. In 1854 he finished his epic poem, "The New Pastoral." A romantic vision of his homeland infuses the poem:

> Fair Pennsylvania! than thy midland vales,
> Lying 'twixt hills of green, and bound afar
> By billowy mountains rolling in the blue,
> No lovelier landscape meets the traveller's eye.
> There Labor sows and reaps his sure reward,
> And Peace and Plenty walk amid the glow
> And perfume of full garners.

He wrote of the poem, "I am at least conscious of having had a religious desire to do a great and good work—something worthy of my country, a *national* poem which the world will not willingly let die" (Claghorn papers, Archives of American Art). This productive and happy period in Italy ended with the sudden deaths of his wife and younger daughter of cholera in June 1855. Thirteen months later Read married Harriet Denison Butler of Northampton, Massachusetts; the couple had no children.

Despite the many years he spent abroad, Read retained a passionate love for the United States. After the outbreak of the Civil War in 1861, he closed his studio in Rome and returned to the United States. He enlisted in the Union army and served on the staffs of Generals Lew Wallace and William Rosecrans. The verse he penned during the war expressed his fervent pro-Union sentiments. Friend and elocutionist James E. Murdoch popularized "The Wagoner of the Alleghanies," "The Oath," "The Defenders," and others of Read's patriotic poems while on lecture tours during the war. Read's best-known poem is "Sheridan's Ride," which recounts General Philip Henry Sheridan's ride to rally the Union troops at the battle of Cedar Creek in Virginia on 19 October 1864:

> Up from the South at break of day,
> Bringing to Winchester fresh dismay,
> The affrighted air with a shudder bore,
> Like a herald in haste to the chieftain's door,
> The terrible grumble, and rumble, and roar,
> Telling the battle was on once more,
> And Sheridan twenty miles away.

The poem electrified audiences across the North. Read also depicted General Sheridan's ride on canvas a number of times, initially at the behest of the Union League of Philadelphia. His paintings of Sheridan's ride can be found in the collections of the National Portrait Gallery, the Milwaukee Art Museum, the Winchester-Frederick County Historical Society in Winchester, Virginia, the Newark Museum, the Munson-Williams-Proctor Institute, and the U.S. Military Academy at West Point. Read also sculpted at least two portrait busts of General Sheridan, now housed at the National Portrait Gallery and the Veteran Association of the First Corps of Cadets in Boston.

By 1867, Read and his wife had moved to Rome and joined the vibrant society of artistic and literary expatriates who flourished there. In 1871 a carriage in which Read was a passenger overturned. Never in robust health, he did not recover completely from the accident. He and his wife sailed for the United States in the spring of 1872. He died of pneumonia soon after his arrival in New York. He was buried in Laurel Hill Cemetery in Philadelphia.

During Read's lifetime, American and English critics and poets such as Longfellow and Dante Gabriel Rossetti had lavish praise for his verse. His published work, much of it steeped in the themes of nineteenth-century American nationalism, includes *Poems* (1847), *Lays and Ballads* (1849), *Poems* (1852), *The House by the Sea* (1855), *Sylvia; or, The Last Shepherd* (1857), *A Summer Story, Sheridan's Ride, and Other Poems* (1865), and *The Poetical Works of Thomas Buchanan Read* (1866). His paintings and the few portrait busts he sculpted also inspired accolades. Artistic, literary, and political notables of the day who sat for portraits by Read included painter Emanuel Leutze, philanthropist George Peabody, Longfellow, physician and poet Oliver Wendell Holmes, and Robert Browning and Elizabeth Barrett Browning. Read also interpreted literary and allegorical works and characters on canvas, including Hiawatha, the Angel of Bethlehem, and *A Midsummer Night's Dream*.

His obituary in the *New York Times* comments on Read's worldwide fame as a poet, while artists such as Albert Bierstadt noted the "absolute delicacy and refinement" of Read's painting (Townsend, p. 126). Nonetheless, the great respect for and popularity of his work did not survive into the twentieth century. However, although Read hoped his work would stand the test of time, that apparently was a secondary consideration. In a letter to Henry C. Townsend he wrote, "It is to me a source of infinite pleasure that I can look back upon all the poetry I have ever written and find it contains no line breathing a doubt upon the Blessed Trinity and the great redemption of man. When I have written my verses I have been alone with my soul and with God" (Townsend, p. 12).

• Read's correspondence can be found among the papers of James Lawrence Claghorn and of the Read family in the Archives of American Art, Washington, D.C. A collection of papers is contained in George Norman Highley, comp., *T. Buchanan Read: Artist, Poet, Sculptor* (1972). Significant likenesses include a self-portrait (c. 1837), now at the Cincinnati Historical Society, and a plaster bust by John Adams Jackson (1854) in the collection of the Chester County Historical Society, West Chester, Pa. A biography by one of Read's long-time friends is Henry Clay Townsend, *A Memoir of T. Buchanan Read* (1889). See also Harold Holzer and Mark E. Neely, Jr., *Mine Eyes Have Seen the Glory: The Civil War in Art* (1993), which contains additional sources on Read. An obituary is in the *New York Times*, 12 May 1872.

KATHERINE M. KRILE

READY, Michael Joseph (9 Apr. 1893–2 May 1957), Roman Catholic bishop, was born in New Haven, Connecticut, the son of Michael Thomas Ready, an engineer, and Mary Ellis. His family moved to Mansfield, Ohio, near the turn of the century. He attended St. Vincent College, Latrobe, Pennsylvania (A.B., 1913; A.M., 1915), and subsequently attended St. Bernard's Seminary, Rochester, New York, and St. Mary's Seminary, Cleveland, Ohio. He was ordained a priest for the diocese of Cleveland, Ohio, by Bishop John P. Farrelly on 14 September 1918. He served briefly as a curate at St. Mary's Church, Painesville, Ohio (1918–1919), and then taught Latin at Cathedral Latin School in Cleveland (1919–1922), serving there with Father Edward Mooney, who was later, as an archbishop, to become his patron. He was named curate of Holy Name, Cleveland (1922–1927), and diocesan director of the Propagation of the Faith (1927–1931). In 1931 Ready became the assistant general secretary of the National Catholic Welfare Conference (NCWC), the association of U.S. Catholic bishops, in Washington, D.C. In 1936 he became the general secretary of this organization at the time when Mooney was the chairman. Ready was named a monsignor with the rank of papal chamberlain in 1934 and with the rank of domestic prelate in 1937. He was named the fifth bishop of Columbus, Ohio, on 18 November 1944 and was consecrated a bishop at St. Matthew's Cathedral, Washington, D.C., on 14 December 1944, taking the motto "Quae sunt Dei Deo" ("[Render] to God the things that are God's"). He was installed in his diocese on 4 January 1945. He continued to serve as the administrator of the diocese of Steubenville, newly created from the diocese of Columbus, until 16 March 1945, when the Most Reverend John King Musio was named the bishop of Steubenville.

Ready's leadership of the NCWC was not as direct as that of his predecessor, Monsignor John Burke. The chairman of the NCWC, Archbishop Mooney, exercised a tighter control of Ready and the NCWC than had Burke's superior. Nonetheless, Ready's leadership of the standing secretariat in Washington, D.C., placed him at the head of the NCWC's efforts during the Great Depression and World War II. Prior to U.S. entry into the war, Ready's focus was on solidifying the conference itself, sometimes defending its lay and clerical workers from pressure by those few bishops who were not sympathetic to a national organization. He also oversaw the construction of new headquarters for the NCWC in Washington. With the war, however, the manifest needs for united Catholic action provided the opportunity to demonstrate the conference's contribution to Catholic life. Ready initiated the Catholic bishops' statement of support for the U.S. effort in December 1941; guided Catholic opposition to congressional attempts to void exemptions for clerics and seminarians in the draft or in a possible Universal Military Training program; pressured government officials about the loss of Poland to the U.S.S.R., about educational issues (particularly the development of a federal Department of Education and federal aid to education, which he opposed as harbingers of federal control), and about immigration laws and programs (which he felt should be more liberal and should promote immigrants' full integration into American civil and religious life); supervised the study of Communist activity in the United States; defended Catholicism against false press charges; oversaw the large Catholic relief programs; and encouraged the bishops to curb local priests opposed to federal housing for black Americans. During this time, President Franklin D. Roosevelt named Ready a member of the White House Conference on Children in a Democracy; to an advisory committee on refugees, for which he made four trips abroad; and a member of the Board of Visitors of the U.S. Naval Academy. On 19 January 1941 Ready gave the benediction at Roosevelt's third inauguration. A tribute to his stature and knowledge was his appointment as a papal visitor to Japan in July 1946 to assess the needs of that country. Mooney's sermon on the occasion of Ready's episcopal consecration summarized his activities: "When the history of the Church in our generation comes to be written, the role of the National Catholic Welfare Conference in making Catholic unity effective for the welfare of religion and society will loom large in the annals of these years. In that history the name of Bishop Ready will stand out both for the position of high responsibility he has filled and the quality of service he has given" (Archives of the Archdiocese of Detroit).

In the diocese of Columbus, Ready was often referred to as the "Bishop of the Cornerstones" for his building program. He formed eighteen new parishes, established nine elementary and five high schools, remodeled or expanded thirty more schools, and added fifteen new convents. He expanded the number and size of hospitals and homes for the aged and started a family life clinic. Furthering social programs, he was instrumental in establishing the diocesan Catholic Welfare Bureau (1945) and the Ohio Catholic Welfare Conference (1946) in imitation of the NCWC. He also founded the Laymen's Retreat League, the Diocesan

Council of Catholic Women, and the Catholic Students' Center at Ohio State University, and he invited the Pime Missionaries to establish their first U.S. seminary in his diocese.

Ready was a great orator whose favorite topics were the permanence of marriage, the sanctity of the home, and the rights of children to a Christian education. He received the Honeur et Merite award from the Republic of Haiti for his service to the people of that country. He died in Columbus. Archbishop Amleto Cicognani, apostolic delegate of Pius XII to the United States, celebrated his funeral mass at St. Joseph Cathedral, Columbus, on the feast of the St. Michael. Tributes at Ready's death noted his championing of "the sanctity of labor" (*Columbus Dispatch*, 3 May 1957) and support of workers and "[h]is love for children, his affection for man, his hatred of racial barriers and his fight against Communism" (*Columbus Citizen*, 3 May 1957).

• Ready's papers are held by the diocese of Columbus. See the *Catholic Times* (Columbus, Ohio), 3 May 1957, 10 May 1957, 17 May 1957; the *Columbus Dispatch*, 5 May 1957; the *Carolinian* (St. Charles Preparatory School, Columbus), 17 May 1957; and Earl Boyea, "The National Catholic Welfare Conference: An Experience in Episcopal Leadership, 1935–1945" (Ph.D. diss., Catholic Univ. of America, 1987).

EARL BOYEA

REAGAN, John Henninger (8 Oct. 1818–6 Mar. 1905), U.S. congressman, U.S. senator, and postmaster general of the Confederacy, was born in Sevierville, Tennessee, the son of Timothy Richard Reagan and Elizabeth Lusk, farmers. His early life was not unlike that of many young men in early nineteenth-century frontier America, hunting, fishing, and helping with farm chores. However, in 1834, Reagan decided to follow his own ambitions. After a year of "hiring out" to a local planter, he attended Boyd's Creek Academy for fifteen months. When funds ran low, he worked so that in 1837 he could study for a year at Southwestern Seminary in Maryville.

In 1838 Reagan left Tennessee to seek greater monetary gain. For a brief time he managed a plantation near Natchez before being lured to Texas, where a job, supposedly at Nacogdoches, awaited him. The job never materialized, and in the summer of 1839 he volunteered to fight in the short-lived Cherokee War. Then for the next two years Reagan worked as a deputy surveyor and frontier scout before being elected a justice of the peace and captain of a militia company in Nacogdoches. In 1844 he married Martha Music, who died less than a year after the marriage. After studying law for several years, he procured a temporary law license in 1846 and opened an office at Buffalo on the Trinity River.

In April 1846 Reagan, a Democrat, was elected the first county judge of Henderson County. The next year he became a member of the second legislature of Texas. Reagan lost a legislative election in 1849, but in 1852 he won a special election for a district judgeship.

In 1852 he married Edwina Moss Nelms. They had six children before her death in 1863.

After 1855 Reagan achieved even greater prominence. In East Texas he helped the Democratic party defeat the surging Know Nothing party, thereby contributing to his reelection as judge in 1856 as well as to his own personal popularity. Consequently, in the summer of 1857, the Democrats nominated him, and he was elected congressman from the Eastern District of Texas. In Washington he attended to his constituents' needs and dealt with the disruptive forces evolving from "Bleeding Kansas." He soon became fearful for the safety of the Union and in 1859, together with Sam Houston, who was running for governor, campaigned for the principles of Union against southern firebrand opponents. Both men won impressive victories.

On 16 October 1859, after John Brown attacked the federal arsenal at Harpers Ferry, Virginia, all hope of Union vanished, at least as far as Reagan was concerned. With Republicans controlling the House and inexorably opposed to southerners no matter what the issue and with southern rights men equally adamant, any hope of compromise was remote. Then, with the election of Abraham Lincoln in November 1860, the breakup of the Union began. On 15 January 1861 Reagan resigned his congressional seat and returned to Texas.

In Austin on 30 January 1861 Reagan attended the Texas Secession Convention. He met specifically with Governor Houston and persuaded him to "submit to the will of the people" and recognize the convention. As a result, Texas withdrew from the Union on 1 February, and two days later delegates elected Reagan as one of the state's seven representatives to the Provisional Confederate Congress in Montgomery, Alabama. Within a month Reagan was appointed postmaster general of the Confederacy, whereupon he raided the U.S. Post Office of its documents and southern personnel. Upon the transfer of the Confederate capital to Richmond, Virginia, late in the spring of 1861, he sought ways to make his department self-sufficient by 1 March 1863, as prescribed by the Confederate constitution. He abolished the franking privilege and raised postal rates. He also cut expenses to the bare minimum by eliminating costly routes, including competition for mail runs, and employing a smaller but efficient staff. He was even able to persuade railroad executives to cut transportation charges in half and accept Confederate bonds in whole or partial payment. Although such stringent measures were necessary, the public became dissatisfied, harshly and abusively criticizing Reagan, despite the fact that Union armies had disrupted routes, had demolished postal facilities, and had interrupted mail with increasing frequency.

On 2 April 1865 the end of the Confederacy was at hand. When President Jefferson Davis was forced to flee southward from Richmond, Reagan accompanied him. For five weeks the Confederate government eluded Union patrols both in North and South Carolina.

After Secretary of the Treasury George A. Trenholm resigned on 27 April, Reagan was entrusted with the duties of the Treasury Department—but not for long. On 10 May, near Irwinville, Georgia, Davis, former Texas governor Francis R. Lubbock, and Reagan were captured.

The harsh realities of losing awaited the Confederate leaders. On 25 May 1865 Reagan, along with Vice President Alexander H. Stephens of Georgia, was sent to Fort Warren in Boston Harbor. For the next twenty-two weeks Reagan was imprisoned in solitary confinement. After reading northern journals and newspapers, which revealed the depth of animosity and bitterness for the South, he wrote an open communication to the people of Texas on 11 August. In this Fort Warren letter, he appealed to Texans as conquered people to recognize the authority of the United States, renounce immediately both secession and slavery (which had been decided by force of arms), and, if demanded by the federal government, extend the "elective franchise" to former slaves. Otherwise, he predicted, Texas would face the "twin disasters" of military despotism and universal black male suffrage. After obtaining release from Fort Warren and returning to Texas early in December 1865, Reagan discovered that most Texans had politically disinherited him because of the Fort Warren letter. He therefore retired to "Fort Houston," his family home at Palestine, Texas, and farmed its neglected fields. In 1866 he married Molly Ford Taylor; they had five children.

On 2 March 1867, however, when the First Reconstruction Act went into effect and thereby confirmed his prophecies of military rule and black male suffrage, Reagan became known as the "Old Roman," a modern-day Cincinnatus who had sacrificed popularity and political power in behalf of his fellow Texans. Consequently, he once again assumed a position as a state leader. Although Republican E. J. Davis became governor in 1870, Reagan and other Democrats worked to regain power and end Reconstruction. On 19 January 1874 they forced Davis to surrender the governorship. In the meantime, Reagan was granted amnesty by the federal government and had full citizenship restored. In 1874 he received the Democratic nomination for the First Congressional District and was easily elected.

From 1875 to 1887 Reagan served in Congress but also participated in state politics. In 1875 he was a delegate to the Texas Constitutional Convention, which framed the Constitution of 1876. More importantly, he led a twelve-year fight in Congress to regulate railroads. Despite formidable opposition from these powerful corporations, he coauthored and helped enact into law the Interstate Commerce Act of 1887.

As further appreciation for his congressional record, the legislature elevated Reagan to the U.S. Senate in January 1887, but before the end of his term he changed jobs. Because his good friend Governor James Stephen Hogg had run on a platform of state regulation of railroads, Reagan was persuaded to resign his Senate seat and accept the chairmanship of the newly formed Texas Railroad Commission. After an unsuccessful campaign for governor in 1894, Reagan remained chairman of the Railroad Commission until his retirement in January 1903. His tenure provided the leadership and prestige so necessary to the early years of this extremely powerful state regulatory body.

In the latter part of his life Reagan was much concerned about preserving history as well as his heritage. In 1897 he helped found the Texas State Historical Association. On a number of occasions he attended meetings of the Confederate veterans throughout the state. After his retirement in 1903, he worked for two years to complete his *Memoirs*. The Old Roman died at Fort Houston. Reagan, Houston, Stephen F. Austin, and Hogg are universally recognized as the four greatest Texans of the nineteenth century.

• The John H. Reagan Papers are deposited at the Texas State Archives, Austin. John H. Reagan, *Memoirs*, ed. Walter F. McCaleb (1906), is an important source. The definitive biography is Ben H. Procter, *Not without Honor: The Life of John H. Reagan* (1962).

BEN PROCTER

REALF, Richard (14 June 1834–28 Oct. 1878), Abolitionist and poet, was born in Framfield, Sussex County, England, the son of Richard Realf, a policeman, and Martha Highland. He was the fifth of eight children in what he described as a "very poor" family of "honest peasant ancestry," and he "went to work in the fields at a very tender age." His only formal education, a year or two at a village school beginning at the age of nine, was made possible through the assistance of a family friend. He began writing poetry at fifteen and two years later left home for Brighton, where he met Mrs. Parnell Stafford, a woman of considerable literary tastes and connections who "manifested a great liking for me," Realf recalled; she employed him as her secretary, exposed him to Latin, French, and the classics, and introduced him to such luminaries as Lady Byron, the widow of the famous poet, and Harriet Martineau, the abolitionist and social critic.

In 1853 Realf arranged through Lady Byron to settle on one of her estates in Leicestershire, where he was to learn estate management and cultivate his literary ambition. But shortly after beginning his new career, he became the center of a scandalous event that underscored a central tension throughout his adult life: the romantic struggle between the "real" and the "ideal," between the worldly passions of the flesh and those of the mind and spirit. He fell in love with the eldest daughter of the estate, despite what he realized were "great [social] gulfs between us that could never be bridged." The daughter became pregnant, and Realf, being "desirous of finding some other place in which to dwell" and having "instincts" that "were democratic and republican," fled to the United States.

Realf settled in New York City and began working for the evangelical reformer Louis Pease at the House of Industry in an impoverished section known as Five Points. It was 1854, and Congress had just passed the

Kansas-Nebraska Act, which repealed the Missouri Compromise and led to mass emigration and guerrilla warfare over the right to own slaves in the newly organized Kansas territory. Realf became a self-described "radical abolitionist," meaning that he sought the immediate abolition of slavery and was willing to go to great lengths to effect it. In 1856 he joined a group of Kansas settlers to help defend the territory against slavery. The following year he received an invitation to meet John Brown to discuss vague plans "to make an incursion into the Southern States" in order to "liberate the slaves." Realf liked the plan and agreed to join Brown's small band of insurgents. In May 1858 they met with some expatriate African Americans in Chatham, Canada, to recruit new members for their incursion into the slave South and to establish a "provisional constitution" to govern areas that Brown hoped to liberate from slavery. Realf was appointed secretary of state of Brown's new revolutionary government that expressly sought to fulfill the objectives of the founding fathers by upholding "those eternal and self-evident truths set forth in our Declaration of Independence."

Following the Chatham convention, Realf went to New York City to obtain from Hugh Forbes, a recent traitor to Brown's revolution, incriminating documents in which Brown had outlined his plans for an incursion. Upon reaching New York, however, Realf read Francis Wayland's *Limitations of Human Responsibility*, which caused him to abandon his revolutionary plans. The "book taught me," he recalled, that "certain" ideals should not be acted upon. Instead he returned to England, where he lectured on temperance and literature and sought to "procure the consent of [his] father and mother to join the Catholic Church" in order to become a Jesuit priest. He returned to the United States in 1859, was admitted to the Jesuit College at Spring Hill, Alabama, and then went to New Orleans to further his Jesuit training. Some of his poems were published in the *New Orleans Catholic Standard* during this period.

While Realf was in New Orleans, John Brown and his men raided the federal arsenal at Harpers Ferry, Virginia, in October 1859; Brown was executed in December, and Realf testified in January before a U.S. Senate committee inquiry on Brown's raid. From there he went to Ohio, and in March he became a member of a utopian Shaker community of Believers at Union Village, Ohio, a perfectionist and millennialist sect that required from its members, among other things, absolute celibacy and restraint from all carnal pleasures. He remained with them for approximately five months and attracted large audiences as their public speaker.

In July 1862, a year into the Civil War and a few months before President Abraham Lincoln issued his preliminary Emancipation Proclamation, Realf joined the Eighty-eighth Illinois Volunteer Infantry, in order to renew his fight against slavery. During this period he continued to write his highly romantic verse that was fashioned after that of Byron and Shelley, and some of his poems were published in the *Atlantic Monthly* and *Harper's Monthly*. His military service to John Brown and the Union army—both of which he saw as means for ending slavery—represented the only sustained periods in which he was able to act on his spiritual and reform ideals in a tangible effort to reconcile his struggle between the passions of the flesh and those of the mind and spirit.

After being discharged from the army in June 1865, Realf married Sophia Emery Graves, a native of Maine who was living near Chicago. Within months, however, he had abandoned her. He wrote John Humphrey Noyes in July 1865 and expressed his desire to join Noyes's Oneida, a New York utopian community that practiced group marriage and a sacred form of "free love." "I wanted always to live in accord with the Invisible Truth," Realf told Noyes, "and very many times it seems to me that the struggle in my nature between the beast and the seraph, the flesh and the spirit, was greater than I could bear." He wanted to escape the "howl of the beast" in a world "so very atheistic" and to "become alive to all righteousness" at Noyes's sacred community in Oneida.

But Realf never made it to Oneida. He got as far as Rochester, New York, before succumbing to what he later termed as a "prolonged debauch" that included a bigamous marriage with a prostitute named Catherine Cassidy. He tried to abandon his second wife as well, but she followed him to Vicksburg, Mississippi, where he received a commission in a black regiment of freedmen, taught at a freedmen's school, and wrote for the Republican state paper. His new wife's "violent colorphobia," combined with threats from proslavery southerners, compelled him to return to the North. From 1870 to 1876, he received a modest but steady income as an editorial writer for the *Pittsburgh Commercial* in Pennsylvania. After numerous unsuccessful attempts to flee from Cassidy, he applied for and was granted a divorce in 1873, but it was overturned the following year, and he was ordered to pay a stiff alimony. The reversal crushed him. He left for New York in 1876, lived "hand to mouth" as he put it, and received periodic income from the lecture circuit and from the little money his poems brought. By 1877 he had entered into another relationship with a woman (name unknown), who bore him a son and triplets. He was penniless, sick, and "walking the edges of the abysses," as he put it. In 1878 he borrowed money to move to the West Coast, where he hoped "to get far away, far away" from Cassidy. He arrived in San Francisco in July, found a job through former abolitionist friends, and began saving money to send for his children and their mother. But on 26 October 1878 Cassidy arrived at his door. Two days later Realf took a fatal dose of morphine, "as the only final relief from the incessant persecutions of my divorced wife." He is remembered for his abolitionist efforts.

• The only collection of poetry published in Realf's lifetime is *Guesses at the Beautiful* (1852). Richard J. Hinton, a contemporary of Realf's, collected and edited his poems in *Poems by*

Richard Realf: Poet, Soldier, Workman (1898). In the collection Hinton also included a memoir that contains the most extensive biographical information available on him. Realf's testimony in *The Select Committee of the Senate . . .* (1860) gives an excellent description of his relationship with John Brown. For other contemporary accounts, see Rossiter Johnson, "Richard Realf," *Lippincott's Magazine*, Mar. 1879, pp. 293–300, which is helpful but inaccurate in parts. John Ward Stimson, "An Overlooked American Shelley," *The Arena*, July 1903, pp. 15–26, focuses primarily on Realf's poetry. More recent discussions of Realf's role in the Harpers Ferry affair can be found in Stephen B. Oates, *To Purge This Land with Blood: A Biography of John Brown* (1970), and Jules Abels, *Man on Fire: John Brown and the Cause of Liberty* (1971).

JOHN STAUFFER

REAM, Norman Bruce (5 Nov. 1844–9 Nov. 1915), financier, was born in Somerset County, Pennsylvania, the son of Levi Ream and Highly King, farmers. His education was limited to the local common schools, a brief stint in a normal institute, and a commercial college. Early on Ream did what he could to escape the drudgery of farm life. At age fourteen he took a job as a teacher in a primary school. Interested in a business career, he began a photography business in which he took daguerreotype and ambrotype pictures.

When he was not yet seventeen years old, Ream enlisted in a company of Pennsylvania volunteers as a private to fight in the Civil War; later he was promoted to first lieutenant. Serving in the Union army for three years, he fought under General George McClellan in the Peninsula Campaign and subsequently in North Carolina. In 1864 he was severely wounded, but after a three-month hospitalization he returned to his regiment. Wounded again, he resigned from service, unfit for further duty.

After leaving the army, Ream renewed his business career as a clerk in a general store. In the post–Civil War era the West beckoned to ambitious young men, and in line with this call, Ream moved to Princeton, Illinois, where he worked as a clerk in a general store. He soon bought out his employer and became an entrepreneur in his own right. A fire destroyed the business, however, leaving Ream in debt. In January 1868 Ream moved to Osceola, Iowa, where he entered the grain and farm implement business. Poor crops and overextension of credit to farmers caused him to fail again, leaving him with even heavier debt.

In 1871 Ream moved to Chicago, where he found business opportunities that brought monetary rewards as well as personal satisfaction. He became a livestock commission merchant, a job for which his earlier ventures in Illinois and Iowa had given him a wide acquaintance with farmers and livestock raisers. Because these producers trusted him, they sent him large consignments of livestock that paid healthy commissions. As a result, he became established as a man of substance; having paid off all of his earlier indebtedness, his integrity was widely accepted. In 1876 he married Carrie T. Putnam, who came from a socially prominent family in New York; they had seven children.

By 1875 Ream had become a member of the Chicago Board of Trade. By this time he had gained a reputation for good judgment, a cool temperament, and honesty at least by the modest requirements of the financiers of the period. These traits brought the trust and friendship of the close-knit group of financiers and entrepreneurs of Chicago, including Marshall Field, George Pullman, Phillip D. Armour, and Judge Elbert H. Gary, among others. These associations further enhanced Ream's wealth. For example, when Armour undertook to corner the pork market in 1879, Ream served as his broker. They began buying pork at $6 per barrel and eventually owned nearly all of the world supply of pork, at which time Armour sold out at $19 per barrel. It was of little concern to either man that consumers paid exorbitant prices for pork products; Armour was enriched, and Ream earned commissions on all other transactions. Frequent manipulations in other commodities added to Ream's wealth.

When George Pullman, the sleeping car entrepreneur, died, Ream and Robert Todd Lincoln, the only surviving son of Abraham Lincoln, became coexecutors of the Pullman extate. Their fee for settling the estate was $400,000; more importantly, Lincoln became president of the Pullman Company and Ream became a member of the board of directors. In 1898 Frank Lowden, Pullman's son-in-law, organized the National Biscuit Company, and Ream joined the board of directors of the new company. That same year Elbert H. Gary organized the Federal Steel Company, which he then merged with Andrew Carnegie's holdings in the East to form the United States Steel Corporation. Ream participated at every stage of the organization; he also served on the board of directors of the gigantic new company, which had been put together with the blessing of J. P. Morgan.

Ream invested heavily in railroads and served as a director of the Baltimore and Ohio, Erie, Pere Marquette, Illinois Central and Seaboard Airline Railroads. He was also heavily invested in Chicago real estate. For example, he provided financial backing for the construction of the Rookery Building in Chicago, designed by the architectural firm of Burnham and Root and built in 1889. Ream also built the Midland Hotel in Kansas City and controlled the street railway system in Toledo, Ohio.

Ream had organized the Western Fire Insurance Company in 1883 and was involved in various other financial institutions, including the First National Bank of Chicago, New York Security and Trust Company, Metropolitan Trust Company, the Fidelity Phoenix Insurance Company, and the Equitable Life Assurance Society.

Eventually Ream acquired a seat on the New York Stock Exchange. In 1895 he moved his office to New York as well as his residence, which was located at 903 Park Avenue.

• For details of Ream's life, see Alfred T. Andreas, *History of Chicago* (3 vols., 1886); Edwin Lefevre, "Interesting Personalities in the Business World: Norman Bruce Ream," *The*

Cosmopolitan 37 (May–Oct. 1904), pp. 87–90; *The Biographical Dictionary and Portrait Gallery of Representative Men of Chicago and the World's* Columbian Exposition (1892), pp. 22–24; Charles H. Taylor, ed., *History of the Board of Trade of the City of Chicago* (3 vols., 1907); and *Industrial Chicago: The Commercial Interests* (1894).

DONALD F. TINGLEY

REASON, Charles Lewis (21 July 1818–16 Aug. 1893), educator and reformer, was born in New York City, the son of Michel Reason and Elizabeth Melville, from Haiti. Reason attended the African Free School along with his brothers Elmer Reason and Patrick Reason, the illustrator-engraver, future abolitionists Henry Highland Garnet, Alexander Crummell, and James McCune Smith, and future actor Ira Aldridge. An excellent student in mathematics, Reason became an instructor at the school at age fourteen, receiving a salary of $25 a year. He used some of his earnings to hire tutors to improve his knowledge. Later, he decided to enter the ministry but was rejected because of his race by the General Theological Seminary of the Protestant Episcopal church in New York City. Reason rejected such "sham Christianity" and resigned in protest from St. Philip's Church, the congregation sponsoring his application. Undaunted by Episcopal racism, he studied next at McGrawville College in McGraw, New York.

Reason decided to pursue a career in teaching, believing strongly that education was the best means for black advancement. In British abolitionist Julia Griffiths's *Autographs for Freedom* (1854), he wrote that a black industrial college would prepare free blacks, who were shut out of the "workshops of the country," to become "self-providing artizans [*sic*] vindicating their people from the never-ceasing charge of a fitness for servile positions." In 1847 Reason and Charles B. Ray founded the Society for the Promotion of Education among Colored Children, a black organization authorized by the state legislature to oversee black schools in New York City. Reason served as superintendent of P.S. 2 in 1848, and Frederick Douglass wrote in the *North Star* of 11 May 1849 that, under Reason's leadership, the school became a rigorous refutation of the calumnies of John C. Calhoun about the potentials of free blacks.

In 1849 Reason became the first African American to hold a professorship in an American college when he was hired as professor of belles lettres, Greek, Latin, and French and adjunct professor of mathematics at the integrated New York Central College in Cortland County. In 1852 he became the principal of the Institute for Colored Youth in Philadelphia (later Cheyney State University), where he expanded the enrollment from six students in 1852 to 118 students in 1855, improved the library, and made the school a forum for distinguished visiting speakers.

In 1855 Reason returned to New York City permanently to begin thirty-seven continuous years as a teacher and administrator in city schools. In 1873 he headed the successful movement to outlaw segregation in New York schools. In 1882 teachers, superintendents, and principals of the New York City school system honored him for fifty years of service. He was chairman of the Committee on Grammar School Work of the Teacher's Association in 1887. When Reason resigned in 1892, he held the longest tenure in the school system.

Reason was also active politically throughout his life. He was committed to the antislavery cause and worked unceasingly for improvement of black civil rights. In 1837 Reason, Henry Highland Garnet, and George Downing launched a petition drive in support of full black suffrage. He was also secretary of the 1840 New York State Convention for Negro Suffrage. Reason founded and was executive secretary of the New York Political Improvement Association, which won for fugitive slaves the right to a jury trial in the state. In 1841 he lobbied successfully for the abolition of the sojourner law, which permitted slave owners to visit the state briefly with their slaves. He also lectured on behalf of the Fugitive Aid Society. An active reporter on education to the black national convention movement of the 1850s, he was secretary of the 1853 convention in Rochester, New York. He spoke out against the American Colonization Society and Garnet's African Civilization Society. In 1849 Reason, along with J. W. C. Pennington and Frederick Douglass, sponsored a mass demonstration against colonization at Shiloh Presbyterian Church in New York City. At the meeting, Reason quoted a former American Colonization Society agent in Africa, who claimed that the president and secretary of the society's colony of Liberia had business dealings with European slave traders on the African coast. During the Civil War, Reason served on New York City's Citizen's Civil Rights Committee, which lobbied the New York legislature for expanded black civil rights. After the conflict, he was vice president of the New York State Labor Union. At a union meeting in 1870, he delivered a paper in which he gave statistical proof that education helped New York City blacks gain prosperity.

Reason was also a writer. He contributed verse to the *Colored American* in the 1830s and was a leader of New York City's Phoenix Society in the 1840s. He wrote the poem "Freedom," which celebrated abolitionist Thomas Clarkson and was published in Alexander Crummell's 1849 biography of Clarkson.

Reason's personal life is obscure. He was married and widowed three times; only the identity of his third wife, Clorice Esteve, is known. He died in New York City.

• For accounts of Reason's life, see Anthony R. Mayo, "Charles Lewis Reason," *Negro History Bulletin* 5 (June 1942): 212–15; C. Peter Ripley et al., eds., *The Black Abolitionist Papers* (5 vols., 1985–1992); and W. J. Simmons, *Men of Mark: Eminent, Progressive, and Rising* (1887), pp. 1105–13. On his writing, see Joan R. Sherman, *Invisible Poets: Afro-Americans of the Nineteenth Century*, 2d ed. (1989), pp. 27–32, and Blyden Jackson, *A History of Afro-American Literature*, vol. 1, *The Long Beginning, 1746–1895* (1989).

GRAHAM R. HODGES

REASON, Patrick Henry (1816–12 Aug. 1898), print-maker, abolitionist, and fraternal order leader, was born in New York City, the son of Michel Reason (from St. Anne, Guadeloupe) and Elizabeth Melville (from Saint-Dominique). Reason was baptized as Patrick Rison in the Church of St. Peter on 17 April 1816. While it is not known why the spelling of his name changed, it may have been an homage to political leader Patrick Henry. Reason was among the earliest and most successful African-American printmakers. While a student at the African Free School in New York, his first engraving was published, the frontispiece to Charles C. Andrews's *The History of the New York African Free-Schools* (1830). It carried the byline, "Engraved from a drawing by P. Reason, aged thirteen years." Shortly thereafter, Reason became apprenticed to a white printmaker, Stephen Henry Gimber, then maintained his own studio at 148 Church Street in New York, where he offered a wide variety of engraving services.

A skilled orator, Reason delivered a speech, "Philosophy of the Fine Arts," to the Phoenixonian Literary Society in New York on 4 July 1837. (It is unclear whether this association was the same as the Phoenix Society, a benevolent organization founded by Rev. Peter Williams in 1833.) The *Colored American* reported this speech to be "ably written, well delivered, and indicative of talent and research."

In 1838 Reason won first premium (prize) for india ink drawing at the Mechanics Institute Fair and advertised himself in the *Colored American* newspaper as "Historical, Portrait and Landscape Engraver, Draughtsman & Lithographer . . . Address, Visiting and Business Cards, Certificates, Jewelry &c., neatly engraved." He also gave evening instruction in "scientific methods of drawing," worked for Harpers publishers preparing map plates, and did government engraving. Reason appeared as a "col'd" engraver in New York City directories from 1846 to 1866.

While a staunch abolitionist, Reason did not initially support women's rights; he attended the annual meeting of the American Anti-Slavery Society in 1839 and signed a protest against women voting and serving as officers in the society. Perhaps Reason's best-known works are his copper engravings of chained slaves. The first, featuring a female who asks, "Am I not a Woman and a Sister?" (1835), was a common letterhead of abolitionists from the mid-1830s on and was reproduced on both British and American antislavery plaques, publications, coins, and medals. The later version (1839?) depicted a kneeling, young male slave wearing tattered clothing, his wrists bound by long, thick manacles. With his head cocked to the side in a forlorn expression, he clasps his hands in prayer. *Am I Not a Man and a Brother?* embellished membership certificates of Philadelphia's Vigilant Committee, a group of young African-American activists who aided escaped slaves. Committee secretary Jacob C. White, Sr., or committee president Robert Purvis, whose names are on the certificate, may have commissioned the piece. Reason's source for the imagery may derive from Wedgwood relief designs or a seal (1787) bearing the same motto and a chained kneeling slave in a similar position and attitude, used by the English Committee for the Abolition of the Slave Trade.

As a freelance engraver and lithographer, Reason produced portraits and designs for periodicals and frontispieces in slave narratives in the mid-nineteenth century. Typically, his portraits were profile or three-quarters, bust-length images of men with stoic expressions in coats and ties against black backgrounds. Examples appear in Lydia Maria Child's *The Fountain for Every Day in the Year* (1836), *A Memoir of Granville Sharp* (1836, based on an engraving of the British abolitionist and reformer by T. B. Lord), *Narrative of James Williams, an American Slave: Who Was Several Years a Driver on a Cotton Plantation in Alabama* (1838), John Wesley's *Thoughts on Slavery Written in 1774* (repr. 1839), *Liberty Bell* (1839, "The Church Shall Make You Free"), and *Baptist Memorial* (member of the London Emancipation Society Rev. Baptist Noel and Rev. Thomas Baldwin). Three works by Reason appeared in the *U.S. Magazine and Democratic Review*. These were of antislavery Ohio senator Benjamin Tappan, after a painting by Washington Blanchard (June 1840; this also appeared in *Annual Obituary Notices* for 1857, 1858); lawyer and diplomat George Mifflin Dallas (Feb. 1842); and mathematician Robert Adrian, after a painting by Ingraham (June 1844).

Reason also completed two portraits of antislavery lecturer Henry Bibb, a lithograph (1840) and a copper engraving featured in *Narrative of the Life and Adventures of Henry Bibb, an American Slave* (1849). While the lithograph depicts Bibb standing rigidly before a draped window, the engraving portrays him casually holding a book in his right hand, posed against a dark background. Among Reason's other works were an engraving of a mountainous landscape after a drawing by W. H. Bartlett (in the Schomburg Center) and a copper nameplate for Daniel Webster's coffin. Additional subjects included slave James Williams (1838), African-American abolitionist Rev. Peter Williams, Jr. (who also attended the African Free School and was rector of St. Phillips Church in New York), Governor De Witt Clinton (of New York), and African-American physician Dr. James McCune Smith. In 1838 Reason had arranged a public meeting to honor Smith on his return from a European trip. He would work with Smith at the Albany Convention of Colored Citizens in 1840 to write a response to the U.S. Senate about derogatory remarks concerning African-Americans made by Secretary of State John C. Calhoun to the British minister of the United States in April 1844 regarding a slave revolt on board the *Creole*.

In the 1840s and 1850s Reason was active in a number of civic groups and fraternal orders. He served as secretary of the New York Society for the Promotion of Education among Colored Children, organized in 1847. As a member of the New York Philomathean Society, organized in 1830 for literary improvement and social pleasure, he petitioned the International

Order of Odd Fellows to become a lodge of the association. Although the application was refused, the society received a dispensation from Victoria Lodge No. 448 in Liverpool and became Hamilton Lodge No. 710 in 1844. Reason served as grand master and permanent secretary of the group in the 1850s. His speech at the annual meeting in 1856 was declared the finest given up to that time. Reason not only developed the secret ritual of the order, but he also composed the Ruth degree, the first "degree to be conferred under certain conditions on Females," and he was the first person to receive the honor (1858).

Reason also served as grand secretary of the New York Masons from 1859 to 1860 and as grand master from 1862 to 1868, receiving the Thirty-third Degree of Masonry in 1862. Simultaneously, he was grand master of the Supreme Council for the States, Territories, and Dependencies. The printmaker created original certificates of membership for both the Grand United Order of Odd Fellows and the Masonic Fraternity.

Reason may have taught in the New York Schools after 1850; Public School Number One was associated with the American and Foreign Anti-Slavery Society, an organization with which Reason had close ties. In 1852 Martin Delany described Reason in *The Condition, Elevation, Emigration, and Destiny of the Colored People of the United States* as "a gentleman of ability and a fine artist" who "stands high as an engraver in the city of New York. Mr. Reason has been in business for years . . . and has sent out to the world, many beautiful specimens of his skilled hand."

Reason also produced other artistic work. During the New York draft riots of 1863, merchants formed a committee for the relief of African-American victims. The Reverend Henry Highland Garnet wrote an address to the group that was "elaborately engrossed on parchment and tastefully framed by Patrick Reason, one of their own people."

In 1862 Reason had married Esther Cunningham of Leeds, England; the couple had one son. Invited to work as an engraver with several firms in Cleveland, Reason moved to Ohio in 1869, and for the next fifteen years he worked for the Sylvester Hogan jewelry firm. Reason died in Cleveland.

• Works by Reason are in the Gallery of Art and the Moorland-Spingarn Research Center, Howard University; the Schomburg Center for Research in Black Culture and History, New York Public Library; and the Library Company of Philadelphia. Reproductions of the artist's work are in Cedric Dover, *American Negro Art* (1960); Elsa Honig Fine, *The Afro-American Artist: A Search for Identity* (1973); David Driskell, *Two Centuries of Black American Art* (1976); and Samella Lewis, *African American Art and Artists* (1990). Useful sources include "Indenture, Patrick Reason" (1833), in the Moorland-Spingarn Research Center, Howard University, and his baptismal record in the Church of St. Peter (1816) in the Schomburg Center. A detailed account of Reason's life is in *The Dictionary of American Negro Biography* (1982). His career is briefly discussed by Steven Loring Jones, "A Keen Sense of the Artistic: African-American Material Culture in 19th Century Philadelphia," *International Review of African American Art* 12, no. 2 (1995), and James A. Porter, *Modern Negro Art* (1943). Charles Brooks, *The Official History and Manual of the Grand United Order of Odd Fellows in America* (1871); William H. Grimshaw, *Official History of Masonry among the Colored People of America* (1908); *The Colored American* (12 Apr. 1838 and 22 Sept. 1838); *Weekly Advocate* (Feb. and Sept. 1837); *Emancipator* (23 May 1839 and 26 Sept. 1839), and *Odd Fellows Journal* (21 Oct. 1920 and 18 Nov. 1921) are all good sources. An obituary is in the *Cleveland Gazette*, 20 Aug. 1898.

THERESA LEININGER-MILLER

REASONER, Harry (17 Apr. 1923–6 Aug. 1991), broadcast journalist, was born in Dakota City, Iowa, the son of Harry Ray Reasoner, a school superintendent, and Eunice Nicholl, a teacher. His parents traveled extensively, but Reasoner considered Humboldt, Iowa, his hometown because he had lived there as a child and had spent summers there visiting his grandparents and other relatives. In 1935 the Reasoner family moved to Minneapolis, Minnesota, where he graduated from West High School in 1941. Reasoner worked for the *Minneapolis Times* before briefly attending Stanford University. He returned to Minneapolis to work at the *Times* and to study at the University of Minnesota until he was drafted into the U.S. Army in 1943. Not until 1989, at age sixty-six, did he complete the requirements for a journalism degree from Minnesota.

Returning to Minneapolis in 1946, Reasoner worked as a drama critic at the *Times*. His only novel, the autobiographical *Tell Me about Women*, was published that year when he was twenty-three. He married Kathleen Carroll in 1946; they had seven children. After leaving the *Times* in 1948, Reasoner worked in the public relations department of Northwest Airlines for two years, served as a writer for radio station WCCO in Minneapolis for a year, and worked for the U.S. Information Agency in the Philippines for three years.

A former journalism teacher urged Reasoner to gain experience in television. In 1954 he began a stint as news director for Minneapolis station KEYD. He joined the assignment desk of CBS News in July 1956. Reasoner, who was named the network's first full-time television correspondent in 1957, was among the first generation of CBS broadcasters who had not worked in radio or learned broadcasting during World War II.

Field reporting for television news was relatively new. "The challenge for us was to get something from the scene that would illuminate the story for television without corrupting it for journalism," Reasoner later said. He helped set a high standard for broadcast journalism with reports on school desegregation in Little Rock, Arkansas, a visit to the United States by Soviet premier Nikita S. Khrushchev, and President Dwight D. Eisenhower's tour of the Far East. In his memoir he called the desegregation coverage the best work he had done.

Reasoner developed a reputation as a broadcaster who could write as well as deliver the news. "Even with the pictures the writing is still important," he said. In 1960 he began writing and reporting for twice-a-day newscasts for CBS radio, refining a personal style and injecting dry humor in his reports. He concluded his broadcasts with what he called an "end piece," a commentary on a news event that could be poignant, humorous, ridiculous, or merely odd. His reputation rose after the *New York Times* praised his radio work.

From the fall of 1961 to the fall of 1963 Reasoner hosted "Calendar," bringing his affable personality and end pieces to a half-hour live morning show broadcast Monday through Friday on CBS. Meanwhile, he also substituted for anchors Douglas Edwards and Walter Cronkite on the "CBS Evening News." In 1963 he replaced Eric Sevareid as the anchor of the network's Sunday evening news broadcast, which gained a wider audience for his end pieces. By 1963 viewers preferred Reasoner second only to Cronkite among CBS broadcasters.

Reasoner had developed into an all-around newsman who could handle profiles, essays, and interviews. His work included a variety of assignments, including documentaries for "CBS Reports" and news specials on subjects ranging from race relations and Vietnam to light, lyrical essays about automobiles and doors. A posting as White House correspondent lasted only a year because he found the work routine.

Reasoner was perfectly suited for "60 Minutes," the network's news magazine, when it debuted as a biweekly series in September 1968. With cohost Mike Wallace handling the hard-edged stories, Reasoner applied his wry humor and casual urbanity to lighter fare. When his CBS contract expired in 1970, Reasoner turned to rival ABC to fulfill his ambition to be the regular anchor of an evening newscast.

Sharing anchor duties with Howard K. Smith, Reasoner helped third-place ABC raise its share of the evening news audience from 13 percent to 23 percent in three years. After Smith became the program's commentator in 1975, Reasoner anchored the news alone. ABC, concerned about flagging ratings, brought in Barbara Walters as television's first woman news anchor in 1976. As a team, Reasoner and Walters appeared ill at ease on camera, according to critics. Reasoner, unhappy with what he considered a stunt, left the network in 1978 to return to CBS.

Reasoner rejoined "60 Minutes" in December 1978 and spent the remainder of his career as part of its team of correspondents. With his trademark casual and witty style, he appeared in investigative segments as well as whimsical features, such as one segment pondering the lasting appeal of the film *Casablanca.* The series ranked among the top ten in ratings throughout his tenure, and a 1982 poll by *TV Guide* listed Reasoner as the most trusted newsman in the United States.

Among his numerous awards were five Emmys, one as outstanding television news broadcaster in 1973–1974, two for his work on "60 Minutes," and two for his work on "CBS Reports" programs. In 1966 Reasoner won a Peabody Award for outstanding achievement in news. He received the University of Missouri

Journalism Medal in 1970, the Carr Van Anda Award from Ohio University in 1973, and the Overseas Press Club Award in 1974.

Reasoner and his wife divorced in 1981, and he married Lois Parker Weber in 1988. After surgery for lung cancer in 1987 and 1989, he retired from "60 Minutes" in May 1991. He died in Norwalk, Connecticut.

In a career that spanned five decades, Reasoner brought humor as well as substance to broadcast news and helped establish the value of writing in a visual medium. Reasoner's warm, affable personality was a welcome alternative for viewers tired of broadcasters who thrived on conflict and confrontation.

• Reasoner wrote an informal memoir, *Before the Colors Fade* (1981), and produced a collection of broadcast essays, *The Reasoner Report* (1966). His novel, *Tell Me about Women,* was reprinted in 1966. His lecture on the news media presented at Memphis State University (now University of Memphis) was published in Phineas J. Sparer, ed., *The World Today* (1975). For extensive discussions of Reasoner and his work, see Gary Paul Gates, *Air Time: The Inside Story of CBS News* (1978); Barbara Matusow, *The Evening Stars: The Making of the Network News Anchors* (1983); and Axel Madsen, *"60 Minutes": The Power and the Politics of America's Most Popular TV News Show* (1984). An obituary is in the *New York Times,* 7 Aug. 1991.

DOUGLASS K. DANIEL

REBAY, Hilla (31 May 1890–27 Sept. 1967), artist and curator, was born Baroness Hildegard Anna Augusta Elisabeth Rebay von Ehrenwiesen in Strassburg, Alsace, the daughter of Baron Franz Josef Rebay von Ehrenwiesen, a German military officer and Bavarian noble, and Antonie von Eicken. Rebay's artistic talent was apparent early, and she received lessons from private tutors. By age eleven she was painting portraits. The family moved to Cologne, where she attended secondary school and received further artistic training with August Zinkeisen, a member of the Dusseldorf Academy. At this time Rebay developed what would become a lifelong interest in theosophy, a mystical faith based on Eastern religions and occultism. In 1909 she studied at the Académie Julian in Paris; one year later, at the urging of German jugendstil painter Fritz Erler, she moved to Munich to continue her training. Her first exhibit was during the fall of 1912 in the Cologne Kunstverein. The following year she returned briefly to Paris, then in 1913 she moved to Berlin. After World War I broke out Rebay made several trips to Zurich—where she met painter Hans (Jean) Arp and the group of artists known as the dadaists— but despite the fighting she continued to live and paint in Berlin.

During her sojourn in Munich Rebay had begun a slow break with academic tradition, experimenting with different techniques in search of a personal style. Her theosophical beliefs prompted her to pursue a manner of painting that could convey emotional and spiritual ideas. By 1916 she had abandoned representation and was working in an abstract style. Early works, such as *Collage* (1916) and *Receding* (1918), employ a variety of geometric and organic forms. In such works, line, shape, and color are carefully combined to elicit emotional response. Rebay's work was well received by her artistic contemporaries, and she exhibited with avant-garde groups such as the Munich Secession, the Salon des Independents in Paris, and the November Gruppe and the Krater in Berlin. Her friendship with Arp brought her into contact with Herwarth Walden. Walden owned Der Sturm Gallery in Berlin, where Rebay exhibited in 1917 and came in contact with the work of Wassily Kandinsky, Paul Klee, Marc Chagall, and Franz Marc. Also at this time she met and became intimately involved with artist Rudolf Bauer, Walden's assistant. Rebay was convinced that Bauer was a creative genius and supported him financially and emotionally for years despite the fact that Bauer was moody, mean-spirited, and, in truth, only a moderately talented painter. Rebay eventually left him, but her continued devotion to him and his work proved to be her tragic flaw.

In 1927, disheartened by her affair with Bauer, Rebay came to the United States with hopes of finding support for her own art and for the modern painting she cherished. She began immediately to show her work, but, even more significantly, she was commissioned to paint a portrait of mining tycoon Solomon Guggenheim. The two became friends, and she assumed the role of his artistic adviser, convincing him to start collecting avant-garde European painting. She advised him to purchase works by her contemporaries Bauer, Kandinsky, and Klee but also to collect pieces by Seurat, Mondrian, Moholy-Nagy, and Modigliani. In most cases her choices have withstood the test of time and are highly regarded masterpieces of modern art. Bauer, whose works are some of her poorer choices, returned her favors by starting a rumor that she was a German spy. Rebay cleared her name (she even became a U.S. citizen in 1947) but was so deeply hurt that she finally severed their relationship.

Rebay never married, preferring instead to devote her emotional energy to her own painting and to shaping the Guggenheim collection. By 1939 the Solomon R. Guggenheim Museum of Nonobjective Painting was opened on Fifty-fourth Street in Manhattan with Rebay serving as its director. Guggenheim wholeheartedly supported Rebay's efforts and trusted her judgment, but she did have her detractors. Her support for nonobjective, to the exclusion of representational or figural, works was often questioned, and she was frequently accused of being biased toward the work of her German friends. In addition, her mystical beliefs, imperious manner, and quick temper provided easy targets for criticism. To her credit, Rebay supported a variety of American as well as European artists. After the war she sent money, food, and materials to struggling European artists, and she also aided Americans, such as the young Jackson Pollock, by helping them to obtain employment doing odd jobs for the museum and by giving them exhibitions.

In 1948 the museum moved to temporary quarters to await completion of its new home, Frank Lloyd Wright's spectacular spiral construction. In 1949 Guggenheim died, and three years later his family, who had become increasingly critical of Rebay's handling of the collection, seized the opportunity. Citing her poor health, they asked her to resign as director. When the building Rebay, Guggenheim, and Wright had so carefully conceived was brought to completion in 1959, she had been cut off entirely from the museum's affairs. Nonetheless, she remained a great champion of nonobjective painting, a staunch supporter of struggling artists, and a dedicated artist in her own right. Her later works—realized in watercolor, collage, or oil—always stayed true to her nonobjective goals as she continued to expand on her early vocabulary of abstract organic forms and undulating lines. Rebay's last exhibit was in 1962, and five years later she died at her home in Greens Farms, Connecticut.

In the years immediately following her death, Rebay's reputation suffered. She had very few close friends, and many of her loyal supporters were also dead. Her contributions to the Guggenheim collection were downplayed by the family or occasionally reattributed to others by misinformed biographers, while her mistakes and domineering persona took center stage. However, the passing of time and the availability of her personal correspondence have allowed later biographers to assume a more objective stance and to realize more fully the true scope of her contributions. Although she was an artist of some skill, her greatest contribution to American art was in helping to establish the Guggenheim Museum. Criticized for her stormy temper and her personal biases, Rebay nonetheless possessed a deep commitment to modern painting that resulted in one of the most important collections of early modern European art in the United States.

• Rebay's personal papers and letters are held by the Hilla von Rebay Foundation at the Solomon R. Guggenheim Museum. The most thorough biographic work is Joan Lukach, *Hilla Rebay: Search for the Spirit in Art* (1983). See also Dore Ashton, "Naissance d'un grand musée," *XX siècle,* no. 31 (1968): 137–39; Lawrence Campbell, "The Museum of Nonobjective Painting Revisited," *Art News* (1972): 40–41; and Katherine Kuh, "The Vision of Hilla Rebay," *New York Times,* 7 May 1972. An obituary is in the *New York Times,* 29 Sept. 1967.

NORA C. KILBANE

RECTOR, Eddie (25 Dec. late 1890s–1962), dancer, was born in Orange, New Jersey, and moved to Philadelphia about age seven. His parents' names are unknown. He never studied dancing but began performing while still a child behind Mayme Remington, a former French burlesque dancer turned headliner, as one of her "picks" (pickaninnies, or black children who sang and danced to accompany white stars). Rector first acquired a reputation in the stage show *The Darktown Follies* (1915). Though he joined as a chorus boy, he devised his own act in which he did a military-style tap routine, soon to be imitated by many others, which the producers promptly incorporated into the show. After the show closed Rector remained in New York City, partnering with another chorus boy from the *Darktown Follies* named Toots Davis.

For the remainder of the 1910s and into the 1920s, Rector was one of the best of the tap dance acts in revues that traveled on the TOBA circuit, which was for black performers approximately what vaudeville houses were for whites, providing work for a number of black entertainers before dying out during the depression. The acronym stands for Theatre Owners' Booking Association but because of the pitiful pay scale was universally said to stand for "Tough On Black Ass." A typical TOBA show would start rehearsing in April, spend all summer on the road, and return to New York City in the fall. When in New York City, Rector would hang out at the Hoofer's Club, next door to the Lafayette Theatre.

When he was finally able to give up the TOBA circuit, Rector appeared in such shows as *Liza* (1922) and *Dixie to Broadway* (1924). He sometimes performed with his wife Grace or his brother Harry. In 1928 Rector replaced Bill "Bojangles" Robinson in Lew Leslie's *Blackbirds of 1928* when that show went on tour; Robinson, by then a Broadway star, had refused to go along because of the low pay. Leslie asked Rector to copy Robinson's signature stair dance, provoking a short-lived feud between the two dancers when Rector acquiesced.

The tap dancing of just a few years earlier had been done in two-to-a-bar time in a straight-up, flashy style known as buck-and-wing dancing. Rector was one of those who smoothed out this style, adding more complex rhythms and steps even as he made the dancing seem more effortless. He used the entire stage while performing, gliding across it as if he were on skates. He invented several varieties of traveling time steps for that purpose, the most famous of which was the Bambalina. He "helped perfect a new style of tap dancing (perhaps derived from white minstrel star George Primrose) in which he traveled across the stage with superb grace and elegance, a style that transcended the stereotypes of the strutting or shuffling 'darky' and culminated in the suave 'class acts' of the 1930s and later" (Stearns and Stearns, p. 127). Rector was a profound influence on many younger dancers, including Clarence Bradley, Pete Nugent, and Steve Condos.

Rector's signature step was the sand dance, which he claimed to have originated. A sand dancer does not use tap shoes but disperses sand on the floor and produces the rhythmical effect from rubbing and sliding it around with one's feet. Rector also claimed to have originated the practice of tap dancing on a drum while performing with Duke Ellington at the Cotton Club in Harlem.

Unfortunately, Rector never appeared in a good enough musical to make him a real star and was fated to appear in mediocre shows like *Hot Rhythm* (1930). The last big show in which he appeared during his prime was the flop *Yeah Man* (1932), which closed after four performances. Soon thereafter, Rector was confined to a mental institution for several years in circumstances that are not clear. After his recovery and release, he teamed up with Ralph Cooper in the late 1940s and early 1950s. Though he had lost much of his fire as a performer, he stole the show doing the sand dance in a brief attempt to revive the musical *Shuffle Along* in 1952. In October 1954 he performed in an evening of "nostalgia" at the soon-to-be-closed Savoy Ballroom. By 1960 Rector was working as a night watchman at a theater. Though saddled with callouses, fallen arches, and a frail-looking body, he was still looking for a break in the dance world. He died in New York City.

Eddie Rector was one of the greatest of the soft-shoe artists and a key figure in the transformation of tap dancing from its early buck-and-wing style into a graceful and elegant stage craft.

• Clippings, articles, and other materials about Rector are in the Dance Collection at the New York Public Library for the Performing Arts, Lincoln Center. Marshall Stearns and Jean Stearns, *Jazz Dance* (1968; repr. 1994), is a comprehensive book on tap dancing and includes interviews with Rector and many other by-then elderly tap artists. Also valuable are the notes from these interviews, now at the Institute for Jazz Studies at Rutgers University, Newark, N.J.

ROBERT P. CREASE

RECTOR, Henry Massey (1 May 1816–12 Aug. 1899), lawyer and governor of Arkansas, was born at Fountain's Ferry, Kentucky, the son of Elias Rector, a surveyor and land speculator, and Fannie Bardella Thruston. His father was also prominent in politics, serving in the Missouri General Assembly and as postmaster at St. Louis. Henry Rector's father died in 1822, and his mother married Stephen Trigg, owner of a saltworks in northwestern Missouri. Young Rector worked for Trigg and received most of his education at home from his mother, although he attended the school of Francis Goddard at Louisville, Kentucky, from 1833 to 1835.

Rector moved to Arkansas in 1835 to look after lands in the Hot Springs area that he inherited from his father. He settled first in Little Rock, close to politically powerful relatives. In 1835 his cousin Elias N. Conway, who would serve as governor from 1852 to 1860, was the territorial auditor. Another cousin, James S. Conway, was elected the state's first governor the next year, in 1836. In 1838 Rector connected himself more closely to local political power when he married Jane Elizabeth Field, daughter of the clerk of the U.S. circuit court and niece of John Pope (1770–1845), territorial governor from 1829 to 1835. The couple had eight children before her death in 1857. In 1860 Rector married Ernestine Flora Linke, with whom he had one child.

During his early career in Arkansas, Rector held many patronage jobs at the disposal of the territorial, state, and federal governments. His first position was as teller of the Arkansas State Bank in 1839 and 1840. In 1842 President John Tyler (1790–1862) appointed him U.S. marshal for the District of Arkansas. He left that office in 1845. Between 1853 and 1857 Rector held the position of U.S. surveyor general for Arkansas. In addition to holding these appointments, Rector moved his family in 1841 to Collegeville in Saline County, where he cultivated a farm with a small slave force. In the same year he began reading law. He was admitted to the Arkansas bar at an unknown later date.

Rector was active in politics beginning in 1848, when he was elected to the state senate representing Saline and Perry counties. This was the first of two terms in the senate. He clearly had political ambitions, and his position in 1852 as a Democratic elector brought him increasing visibility in state party politics. In 1854 he moved to Little Rock to open a law office and in 1855 was elected as a Democrat to the lower house of the general assembly. In 1859 he was elected as an associate justice on the state supreme court.

In 1860 Rector ran against the regular Democratic nominee for governor as an independent Democrat. His opponent was Richard H. Johnson, who was backed by the Johnson-Conway-Sevier political faction, known as the Family, to which Rector was tied himself. The race was attributed to Rector's frustration at being overlooked for higher office by the leadership of his party. A major supporter was another outsider, Congressman Thomas C. Hindman of Helena. Rector's chief campaign promise was to delay the payment of the state debt from twenty-five to fifty years in order to divert state revenues to the construction of railroads. Rector won the election with 53 percent of the vote.

When he took office as governor in November 1860, Rector proposed an administration that would increase its support for the state blind and deaf schools and the common schools as well as finish construction of the Memphis to Little Rock railroad. The political crisis created by the election of Abraham Lincoln, however, forced the governor to deal with the secession crisis. Although he was not a strident secessionist, Rector believed that Arkansas had to secede if other southern states withdrew from the Union. On 11 December he urged the general assembly to call a convention immediately to respond to Lincoln's election but settled for a special election on 15 February 1861 to name delegates to a state convention. In the meantime, he prepared for war. On 8 February 1861 he used state militia to seize the U.S. arsenal at Little Rock. The convention, however, was dominated by Unionists, and the majority delayed secession until President Lincoln's call for troops after Fort Sumter solidified state politicians into action. After the state seceded, Rector played a prominent role in war mobilization as the head of a three-man military board appointed by the convention.

As wartime governor of the state, Rector became embroiled in numerous political struggles. He tried to maintain civilian and state control over the state's military forces, and he opposed martial law and Confeder-

ate conscription in the state. Rector even threatened secession from the Confederacy over the question of states' rights. In all these matters he faced opposition from the Richmond government, the Family, and even his former ally Hindman, now a Confederate general. His opponents blamed Rector for lagging recruitment, inefficient use of troops, military failures, and even the serious economic crisis, including inflation and war profiteering, that developed within the first year of the conflict. Although elected for a four-year term in 1860, the Constitution of 1861 required all of the state's executive officers to run again in a general election in 1862. The governor's enemies supported Harris Flanagin against him. In the election on 6 October 1862 the governor lost by a two to one margin. Rector applied for but failed to obtain a commission in the Confederate army after his defeat for reelection. He joined the state Reserve Corps, where he served for the rest of the war as a private.

At the war's end Rector returned to Little Rock, where he supervised his land and farming operations and, with his two sons who had survived the war, hauled cotton between the capital city and Hempstead County. He also helped reorganize the state Democratic party, although he never again played a prominent role. In 1874 he attended the state constitutional convention that wrote the Redeemer constitution as a representative from Garland County.

After the constitutional convention, Rector's political activity declined, and he devoted more time to his farms and expanding his landholdings. He ultimately operated farms in Hempstead, Garland, Pulaski, and Saline counties. He had extensive rental properties throughout central Arkansas. Rector also engaged in a long-term fight in support of his claim to the Hot Springs of Arkansas.

Rector died at Little Rock. Never a religious man, he had joined the Methodist church three days before his death.

• The remains of Rector's official papers are in the Kie Oldham Collection at the Arkansas History Commission in Little Rock. The only scholarly biography is Waddy W. Moore, "Henry Massie Rector," in *The Governors of Arkansas*, ed. Timothy P. Donovan and Willard Gatewood, Jr. (1981). Rector's wartime career is treated extensively by Michael B. Dougan, *Confederate Arkansas* (1976), and James M. Wood, *Rebellion and Realignment: Arkansas's Road to Secession* (1987). A lengthy obituary is in the Little Rock *Arkansas Gazette*, 13 Aug. 1899.

CARL H. MONEYHON

RED CLOUD (c. 1822–10 Dec. 1909), Oglala Lakota war leader and chief, whose tribal name was Mahpiya Luta, was born on the Smoky Hill River in Kansas, the son of Lone Man and Walks As She Thinks. Two loose associations of Oglala bands (*tiyospaye*), nominally led by Bull Bear and Smoke, Red Cloud's uncle, frequented the Upper Platte River valley in the 1830s, trading buffalo robes for Euroamerican goods at Fort William (Laramie). Petty rivalries that had been simmering between the two groups came to a boil in November 1841 with the murder of Bull Bear at the hands of Red Cloud. Some accounts contend that Red Cloud plotted Bull Bear's murder in order to assume the older man's status as chieftain; this implication is plausible only if it is true that the Oglalas willingly followed a small governing elite. Documentary evidence indicates that although Bull Bear's constituency was large, his supporters remained with him only as long as he could promote their best interests. At the time of Bull Bear's demise, Red Cloud would have been a young warrior not yet twenty years of age, hardly old enough to have won widespread recognition and respect as an Oglala band chief—a symbolic father whose primary responsibilities included redistributing wealth and providing for the welfare of the poor and sick.

The death of the influential chief Bull Bear generated an unprecedented schism in Oglala society. Oglala bands divided into two major divisions, eventually dominated by the Kiyuksa band (Bull Bear supporters) to the south and the Bad Faces band (Smoke supporters) to the north. Shortly after Bull Bear's death, Red Cloud began to lead his first war parties against the Pawnees, Shoshonis, and Crows, and by 1861 he had become a prominent Oglala war leader (*blotahunka*). The band had not yet acknowledged him as a *tiyospaye* chief, however.

In 1863 Americans constructed the Bozeman Road, linking the old Oregon Trail to the mining settlements of the Montana Territory. This invasion into some of the best Powder River hunting grounds prompted a number of Lakota (also known as the Teton Sioux) bands to advocate armed resistance against the intruders. The U.S. Congress had earlier awarded a construction contract to James A. Sawyer for an additional wagon road north of the Upper Platte River, and in the summer of 1865 Red Cloud attracted the attention of U.S. leaders by strongly warning Sawyer not to enter the Lakotas' northern hunting grounds.

The U.S. government sent the Taylor Commission to settle the matter in June 1866. Assembled at Fort Laramie, these federal emissaries met with representatives of various Lakota bands, hoping to obtain their consent to the construction of roads and posts through their Powder River domains. During the formal treaty proceedings, tribal councilors discovered that Colonel Henry B. Carrington, commanding several hundred troops of the Eighteenth U.S. Infantry, had already been dispatched to the disputed territory. Presuming that Carrington's detail had entered Sioux land to build roads and garrisons without tribal permission, the Lakota war faction, led primarily by Red Cloud, became enraged. Rejecting the proposed peace treaty, Red Cloud and several chiefs withdrew immediately from the council arena and led approximately one thousand warriors to the Powder River country. Six months later, a Lakota war party annihilated eighty soldiers under the command of Carrington's subordinate Lieutenant Colonel W. J. Fetterman.

After the war faction had departed, the Taylor Commission concluded a treaty primarily with southern Oglalas and Brulés, who consented to the erection and occupation of three posts along the Bozeman Road: Fort Philip Kearny, Fort C. F. Smith, and Fort Reno. However, the treaty was never ratified and failed to prevent warfare from resuming on the northern Plains. For almost two years after the Fort Laramie council, several Lakota bands successfully prosecuted what many historians have termed "Red Cloud's War," finally forcing the United States to abandon the Bozeman posts in the summer of 1868. Lakota customs permitted warriors to decide individually when, where, and with whom they wished to fight. Moreover, the warriors often sought the advice and cooperation of tribal elders during periods of protracted warfare. Thus, it is highly unlikely that Red Cloud alone masterminded the entire two-year conflict. Clarence Three Stars, an Oglala interpreter, claimed in the late 1800s that while Red Cloud's reputation as a fearless warrior was unchallenged, his social status at this juncture did not equal that of Man Afraid of His Horse, the most prominent of the northern Oglala chiefs. American leaders, however, singled out Red Cloud as the "head chief" of the Sioux, who they believed wielded considerable decision-making authority over all Sioux bands.

In the wake of "Red Cloud's War," American leaders drafted a new peace treaty, which included a provision for the establishment of the Great Sioux Reservation in South Dakota. At several independent councils convened throughout 1868, a number of Lakota chiefs, headmen, and renowned warriors, including Red Cloud, signed the Treaty of Fort Laramie. Although many Oglala councilors did not consider Red Cloud a *tiyospaye* chief, they accepted his new role as principal Oglala spokesman for the treaty bands during subsequent negotiations with the United States. In these negotiations, Red Cloud frequently expressed his desire for peace but repeatedly explained that his duties as primary council spokesman did not empower him to make unilateral decisions for all the bands or to control Lakota warrior societies. However, since many American citizens viewed Red Cloud as the personification of Sioux leadership, they believed he could compel the Oglalas to accept reservation life and to undergo the process of "Americanization."

While employees of the Office of Indian Affairs endeavored to settle the Oglalas on the reservation during the early 1870s, the discovery of gold in the Black Hills generated waves of Euroamerican migration into Lakota country. In 1875 federal negotiators attempted to persuade the Sioux to sell the Black Hills and failed, and by the following year, tensions between the Lakotas and the United States had erupted into another full-scale war, culminating in Lieutenant Colonel George A. Custer's defeat at the Little Big Horn. Although Red Cloud did not participate in the Sioux War of 1876, military top brass contended that he had turned against the United States. Thus, Brigadier General George Crook ordered Colonel Ranald MacKenzie to disarm and dismount Red Cloud's band along with the followers of Red Leaf, a Brulé chief.

The general also tried, though unsuccessfully, to "depose" Red Cloud by denouncing him as a traitor to the American people and decreeing that the president of the United States would no longer honor him as "head chief" of the Sioux.

The surrender of the young war leader Crazy Horse in the fall of 1877 marked a turning point in the Lakotas' relationship with the United States. With their military might smashed, the Oglala Sioux were confined to the Pine Ridge agency, and in March 1879 they met their new government agent, Valentine T. McGillycuddy, a former army surgeon. Within months, a political struggle had developed between McGillycuddy and Red Cloud, whom McGillycuddy identified as the leader of the "nonprogressives"—a caucus highly critical of the government's program of acculturation. By this time, Red Cloud claimed supporters not only among the Bad Faces but also among several other reservation bands. Between 1879 and 1886, Chief Red Cloud convened numerous councils and initiated several petitions in his persistent attempts to oust McGillycuddy.

Federal policymakers had decided by 1882 that the Great Sioux Reservation contained more land than the Lakota people needed. Thus, they advocated dividing it into six smaller reserves and negotiating for the cession of "surplus" lands to the public domain. Moreover, the six Lakota reservations would be further divided into individual plots of land under the Dawes Act of 1887. During his protracted dispute with agent McGillycuddy, Red Cloud, with the steadfast support of his wife Wetamahecha (Mary), apparently the chief's only spouse, continued to challenge these policies. So fervidly did Red Cloud fight for the preservation of Lakota lands that American officials labeled him an "obstructionist." However, despite opposition from Red Cloud and other prominent Lakota leaders, Congress proceeded in 1889 with its program to break up the Great Sioux Reservation, to force allotments on the Lakotas, and to open up "surplus" lands to homesteaders. Red Cloud and many of his peers resisted allotment for years, but in 1905, frail and virtually blind, the chief finally accepted an individual plot of land.

In April 1897 Red Cloud paid the last of several personal visits to Washington, D.C. Speaking in behalf of his followers, Red Cloud informed the Senate Committee on Indian Affairs that his people opposed the policy of land allotment. Although the U.S. government no longer considered him an influential chief, Red Cloud's kinsfolk, including many of his former detractors, had grown to respect him for his devotion to protecting Oglala land.

On 4 July 1903, Red Cloud ceremoniously bestowed his chieftainship on his son, Jack, the most well known of Red Cloud's five children. Six years later Red Cloud died at Pine Ridge, South Dakota, and was buried at Holy Rosary Mission cemetery with the full rites of the Catholic church, some of whose teachings he had incorporated into traditional Lakota beliefs.

• Manuscript sources on Red Cloud are at the Nebraska State Historical Society in Lincoln and the National Archives. Pertinent secondary works include George E. Hyde, *Red Cloud's Folk: A History of the Oglala Sioux* (1937), and James C. Olson, *Red Cloud and the Sioux Problem* (1965). An obituary is in the *New York Times*, 11 Dec. 1909.

CATHERINE PRICE

REDDING, Dick (1891–1940?), Negro League baseball pitcher, was born in Atlanta, Georgia. His parents are unknown. Apparently he was unschooled and illiterate. Except for the fact that he played semiprofessional ball with the Atlanta Depins, other details of his early life are sketchy. From 1911 through 1921 "Cannonball" Dick Redding and "Smokey" Joe Williams matched fastballs as teammates and opponents for the title of best pitcher in black baseball. The pitcher Jesse Hubbard, among others, insisted that "Redding and Williams were better pitchers than Satchel Paige. . . . Satchel didn't throw as hard as Dick Redding. You should have seen *him* turn the ball loose!"

Redding reportedly pitched against the New York Giants during spring training in 1911, and manager John McGraw brought him north, where he joined the black Philadelphia Giants. Although facts about the 1911 season are hard to verify, legends abound. Some reports say he won 17 straight games that summer, others claim 29, including five no-hitters, probably against semipro opponents.

In 1912 Redding joined the New York Lincoln Giants, along with shortstop-manager John Henry "Pop" Lloyd and catcher Louis Santop. Unconfirmed reports about 1913 credit Redding with a 43–12 won-lost record, including a perfect game against Jersey City of the white Eastern (later International) League. It is known that in one exhibition game he struck out 24 players on a team gathered from the United States League, a better-than-average group.

In 1915 Redding jumped to the rival New York Lincoln Stars, where he reportedly ran up 20 straight victories. Victory number 17 came against a white all-star club and number 19 against former Detroit Tiger pitcher George Mullin. In the black world series that fall, against Rube Foster's Chicago American Giants, Redding won three games, including a shutout, as the two teams tied at five wins apiece.

Redding went west in 1917 to the American Giants, for whom he compiled a record of 7–1 against other black teams. His career was interrupted by World War I, which he spent in the army in France.

He joined the Brooklyn Royal Giants in 1918, winning three and losing three against black clubs. (Black teams played most of their games against white semipro teams, and records for these games have not been compiled.) One of his three losses came against the Lincoln Giants. Redding threw a two-hitter, but "Smokey" Joe Williams topped him with a no-hitter. In September Redding lost in a 14-inning game to Carl Mays of the New York Yankees by a score of 2–1.

In 1920, after a 6–3 season against black teams, Redding faced Williams in the first black game ever played in Ebbets Field, home of the Brooklyn Dodgers. Redding won it 5–0, and the Royals claimed the black championship of the East. Redding also faced Babe Ruth's all-stars at Shibe Park in Philadelphia, and he beat Ruth and pitcher Mays 9–4 despite a home run by Ruth.

Redding next joined the Bacharach Giants of Atlantic City and had a 17–12 record against black teams in 1921. He was 8–8 in 1922. Then it was back to the Royals in 1923 as manager. He pitched less and less, although he and Ruth met often in postseason exhibitions. At one of these, the promoters told Redding that the fans had paid to see Ruth hit, "so no funny business." Ruth then hit several balls over the fence to the cheers of the crowd, and Redding went home with money in his pocket.

According to Hall-of-Famer William "Judy" Johnson, Redding was 6′4″ with hands as big as shovels. Redding turned his back on the batter before delivering the pitch, which left the hitter ready to dive for cover. Pictures usually showed Redding with a broad smile. "He took everything good-natured," said one of the players he managed, Ted Page. "He didn't have a care in the world, yet he never had much money." Hall-of-Famer Buck Leonard called Redding "a nice fellow, easy-going. He never argued, never cursed, never smoked as I recall."

Redding stayed with the Royals until 1938. Statistics for most of his career are incomplete, but in confirmed games against black opponents, he finished with a mark of 69 victories and 54 defeats. He reportedly compiled 12 no-hitters in his career, although most came against semipro opposition.

Details of his death are not clear. "I know he died in a mental hospital," said Page, "down in Long Island, Islip, I think. Nobody's ever told me why, how, what happened to him."

• For further reading see Jim Riley, *Biographical Encyclopedia of the Negro Leagues* (1994), John B. Holway, *Blackball Stars* (1988), and Larry Lester, *The Ballplayers* (1990). Redding's statistical record is found in the Macmillan *Baseball Encyclopedia*, 9th ed. (1992).

JOHN B. HOLWAY

REDDING, J. Saunders (13 Oct. 1906–2 Mar. 1988), African-American educator, historian, and literary critic, was born in Wilmington, Delaware, the son of Lewis Alfred Redding, a schoolteacher, and Mary Ann Holmes. As graduates of Howard University, Redding's parents maintained a modest middle-class environment for their children; his father was secretary of the local Wilmington branch of the NAACP. Redding graduated from high school in 1923 and entered Lincoln University in Pennsylvania that year, with no discernible career ambitions. In 1924 he transferred to Brown University, where he received his bachelor's degree in 1928.

After graduation Redding became an instructor at Morehouse College in Atlanta, where in 1929 he married Esther Elizabeth James. The Reddings had two children. Redding felt that his liberal political beliefs, which his conservative colleagues believed were "too radical," were a major factor in the Morehouse College administration's decision to fire him in 1931. Redding returned to Brown University for graduate study and received a master's degree in 1932. He then went to Columbia University as a graduate fellow for two years, and he was an adjunct English instructor at Louisville Municipal College in Louisville, Kentucky, in 1934. From 1936 to 1938 Redding taught English at Southern University in Baton Rouge and then joined the faculty at Elizabeth City State Teachers' College in North Carolina, where he remained from 1938 until 1943 as chairman of the English department. During this period, Redding completed his first book, *To Make a Poet Black* (1939), one of the earliest works of literary criticism on African-American literature.

The publication of *To Make a Poet Black* enabled him in 1939 to earn a fellowship that was funded by the Rockefeller Foundation. Redding used this fellowship to travel throughout the American South to prepare his partly autobiographical work, *No Day of Triumph*, written in 1942. *No Day of Triumph* chronicled the daily lives and aspirations of working-class African-American southerners and became a critical success. In this book Redding observed that his life affirmed the importance of integrity, courage, freedom, and hope that African Americans traditionally cherished. In *No Day of Triumph* he wrote that "I set out in nearly hopeless desperation to find out, both as a Negro and as an American, certain values and validities that would hold for me as a man . . . to find among my people those validities that proclaimed them and me as men . . . the highest common denominator of mankind."

Redding joined the faculty at Hampton Institute in Hampton, Virginia, as a professor of English and creative writing in 1943; that same year he received a Guggenheim Fellowship. The National Urban League honored Redding in 1945 for outstanding achievement. Moreover, during that same year Redding became the first African American to hold a full professorship at Brown University when the university invited him to be a visiting professor of English. In 1950 Redding published his only novel, *Stranger and Alone*, which reflected his experiences as a professor in historic all-black colleges.

Redding remained best known for his monographs that document African-American contributions to American history, such as *They Came in Chains: Americans from Africa* (1950), *The Lonesome Road: The Story of the Negro's Part in America* (1958), and *The Negro* (1967). These books utilized biographical vignettes and primary sources to document African-American history and investigate the historical context of American race relations. Redding's fifth book, *On Being Negro in America* (1951), examined psychological dilemmas of racism in American society, while his 1954 work, *An American in India*, described his observations on Indian nationalism and anti-imperialism during a U.S. State Department-sponsored trip to India.

In 1959 Redding received another Guggenheim Fellowship, which allowed him to continue his lecture tours, teaching and book reviewing. During a six-month West African lecture tour in 1963, Redding became a close friend of Nigerian writer Wole Soyinka, who later received a Nobel Prize in Literature in 1986.

In 1964 Redding became a fellow in humanities at Duke University. The following year Redding returned to Hampton Institute, and in 1966 he was the director of research and publication at the National Endowment for the Humanities in Washington, D.C. By 1969 Redding had assumed a professorship in American history and civilization at George Washington University while remaining a special consultant for the National Endowment for the Humanities. He edited an anthology of African-American literature from 1760 to 1970 with Arthur P. Davis at Howard University titled *Cavalcade*. In 1970 Redding received the Ernest I. White Professorship of American Studies and Humane Letters at Cornell University. A program of fellowships for students of color at Cornell University was established in his honor in 1986. When he retired in 1975 from Cornell University, Redding continued his writing and scholarly activities.

As a liberal Democrat, Redding worked with other progressive African-American intellectuals to discuss solutions for confronting racism in American society. During the 1970s he became a member of the Haverford Group, an informal gathering of notable African-American scholars who met to investigate methods to dissuade American youth from racial separatism. This group consisted of psychologist Kenneth B. Clark, historian John Hope Franklin, former secretary of Housing and Urban Development Robert Weaver, and federal judge William B. Hastie. Along with fellow colleagues of the Haverford Group, Redding worked with the Joint Center for Political Studies to devise political strategies for interracial cooperation.

After Redding's death at his home in Ithaca, New York, the 4 March 1988 obituary in *The Ithaca Journal* described him as the dean of African-American scholars whose works influenced younger African-American intellectuals, such as literary critic and director of Harvard University's African American Studies Henry Louis Gates. The *New York Times* 5 March 1988 notice of Redding's death recalled that he was regarded as the first African American to teach at an Ivy League institution. And in an obituary in the 10 March 1988 edition of the *Cornell Chronicle*, Cornell University president Frank H. T. Rhodes commented, "J. Saunders Redding represented the essence of human dignity who often stood alone between the two worlds of white and black, contributing to an understanding of the human condition that transcends race and culture."

• Redding's personal manuscripts are in the John Hay Library at Brown University. The Delaware Heritage Press published posthumously Redding's brief autobiographical account of his childhood and youth, *Troubled in the Mind* (1991). For a selected collection of Redding's publications see *A Scholar's Conscience: Selected Writings of J. Saunders Redding, 1942–1977*, ed. Faith Berry (1992). *Dark Symphony: Negro Literature in America*, ed. James Emanuel and Theodore Gross (1968), examines Redding's significance to modern African-American fiction and prose. His valuable contributions to the history of African-American literary criticism are documented in Jean Wagner, *Black Poets of the United States: From Paul Lawrence Dunbar to Langston Hughes* (1973), and Arthur P. Davis, comp., *From the Dark Tower: Afro-American Writers, 1900 to 1960* (1974).

KIMBERLY WELCH

REDDING, Otis (9 Sept. 1941–10 Dec. 1967), singer and songwriter, was born Otis Redding, Jr., in Dawson, Georgia, the son of Otis Redding, Sr., a maintenance worker and minister, and Fanny (maiden name unknown). In 1944, when the younger Redding was three, the family moved into the Tindall Heights Housing Project in Macon, Georgia. Redding began playing drums and piano in elementary school and sang in his church gospel choir. He was forced to drop out of high school in the tenth grade when his father contracted tuberculosis and lost his job at the local air force base. Redding then worked as a well digger and a gas station attendant and also earned money as a musician with the Upsetters, a rhythm-and-blues band led by the singer and piano player Little Richard. Redding gained fame as an R&B singer in the Macon area when he won several local talent show contests. By 1958 he was prominent in the Macon music scene as the singer for a rhythm-and-blues band called the Pinetoppers.

In 1960 Redding moved to Los Angeles to further his career and in that year recorded "She's All Right" and "Tuff Enuff" with the Shooters for the Trans World and Finer Arts labels. In 1961 Redding returned to Macon and recorded "Shout Bamalama" and "Fat Gal" with the Pinetoppers for the Confederate label. His first hit record came in 1962 with the release of "These Arms of Mine," a delicate, plaintive ballad that reached the rhythm-and-blues record sales charts. The single was released on the Volt label, which was a subsidiary of the Memphis-based Stax label, the company Redding continued recording for until the end of his life.

The following year Redding reached the top of the R&B charts and established himself as a leading soul performer with another ballad, "Pain in My Heart," on which Redding's voice alternated from quavering and tentative to a hoarse gospel shout. From there he recorded and released several hit singles for Volt, including "Security" in 1964; "I've Been Loving You Too Long," "Respect," and "I Can't Turn You Loose" in 1965; and "Try a Little Tenderness" in 1966. Redding's simple, earnest ballads and sparse, horn-punctuated dance tracks came to be considered typical of the "Memphis sound" produced by Stax. Redding often built LPs around hit singles, including *Pain in My Heart* in 1964, *The Great Otis Redding Sings Soul Ballads* and *Otis Blue* in 1965, *The Soul Album* and *Com-*

plete and Unbelievable in 1966, and *King and Queen* (with Carla Thomas) and *Live in Europe* in 1967.

Redding's southern, "country" sensibilities and powerful, husky tenor earned him recognition as one of the most authentic, "soulful" singers in an R&B market dominated by polished Motown vocalists. But his fame grew to international proportions because he was able to appeal to white "pop" audiences. His performance tour in England in 1967 was met by huge crowds and rapturous reviews in the popular music press. Later in that year Redding became one of the few black performers to be embraced by the counterculture movement when he thrilled an audience of 55,000 at the Monterey Pop Festival in California, a seminal event in the "hippie" era. Confirming his success as a crossover act, in 1967 Redding replaced Elvis Presley as the top male vocalist in the world in an annual poll conducted by *Melody Maker* magazine, the leading pop music magazine in England.

On 10 December 1967, while on a performance tour in the Midwest, Redding died when his private airplane crashed into Lake Monona, just outside of Madison, Wisconsin. Recorded three days before his death and released one month later, the wistful ballad "(Sittin' on) the Dock of the Bay" rose to the top of the popular music charts and became the bestselling and most famous recording of his career. Several more hit records were released posthumously, including the singles "The Happy Song" (1968), "Hard to Handle" (1968), and "Love Man" (1969) and the albums *The Dock of the Bay* (1968), *The Immortal Otis Redding* (1968), *In Person at the Whisky A Go Go* (1968), *Love Man* (1969), and *Tell The Truth* (1970).

Though his career was cut short at its peak, within a few years Redding composed, performed, and recorded a remarkable number of rhythm-and-blues hits and emerged as one of the most exciting stage performers in the history of American popular music.

• For a biography of Redding, see Jane Schiesel, *The Otis Redding Story* (1973). Arnold Shaw, *The World of Soul: Black America's Contribution to the Pop Music Scene* (1970), includes a brief biography and an analysis of Redding's music. Two informative and comprehensive chapters are devoted to Redding in Peter Guralnick, *Sweet Soul Music: Rhythm and Blues and the Southern Dream of Freedom* (1986). Further biographical information, including a complete discography, can be gleaned from the booklet included in *The Definitive Otis Redding*, an exhaustive compilation of Redding's music released in 1993 by Rhino Records.

THADDEUS RUSSELL

RED EAGLE. *See* Weatherford, William.

REDFIELD, Amasa Angell (19 May 1837–19 Oct. 1902), lawyer and legal author, was born in Clyde, New York, the son of Luther Redfield, a merchant, and Eliza Angell. Redfield was educated at a school in Bloomfield, New Jersey, and at the University of the City of New York (now New York University), from which he graduated in 1860 with an A.B. After graduation he entered the study of the law under the apprenticeship of Austin Abbot and was admitted to the New York bar in 1862. The following year he published *A Handbook of United States Tax Law*. That same year he married Sarah Louise Cooke. They had two children. A successful general practitioner, he was in turn a member of Barrett, Brinsmade & Redfield (1869–1871); Barrett & Redfield (1871–1874); Redfield & Hill (1874–1883); and Redfield, Hill, & Lydecker (1883–1902).

When Redfield began his practice, which he did independently, he found that the decisions of the important surrogates' courts, which had original jurisdiction in all matters of wills and succession, had not been reported separately for some seven years. In 1871 he was appointed to a five-year term as the official reporter of the surrogates' court and of the court of common pleas in New York City. In 1864, with the assistance of Judge Bradford, who had edited the reports of earlier surrogates' decisions, Redfield published the first volume of *Reports of Cases Argued and Determined in the Surrogates' Courts of the State of New York*. Four other volumes followed, the last in 1882, and the whole series covered more than twenty years, "constituting a most valuable collection of decisions upon wills, trust, and administration of estates" (Lydecker, p. 108). His *Law and Practice of Surrogates' Courts* (3d ed., 1875) went through six editions by 1903. Redfield, however, was far more than a treatise writer, for this early specialization in a highly litigious field brought him clients and led to his employment in important cases. One involved the will of Maria Forman, who, while insane, had destroyed two wills that she had executed almost simultaneously. Redfield's handling of the case, which was complicated, greatly enhanced his reputation.

Redfield also studied other areas of law. With Thomas G. Shearman, he prepared and published *A Treatise on the Law of Negligence* (1869), which soon became the leading book on the subject. Like his other treatises, it was quite successful; the work went through five editions under his editorship. Of lasting scholarly importance is Redfield's support of most nineteenth-century courts in rejecting the "Ryan doctrine," according to which a railroad whose negligent spark causes a spreading fire is liable only for the first building destroyed. The reasoning behind the doctrine is that, because their losses are too "remote," the owners of other structures should be denied recoveries. Most courts and Redfield believed that Ryan was wrong because it was based on policy and not on the "true rule" of proximate cause in negligence cases.

From 1885 to 1897 Redfield lectured at New York University on testamentary subjects. He also became interested in legal history. He wrote a chapter entitled "English Colonial Polity and Judicial Administration" in *History of the Bench and Bar of New York* (1897). In 1899 he delivered an address before the New York State Bar Association, "A Case of Laesae Majestatis in New Amsterdam in 1647." He also collected a substantial amount of material for a planned history of New York. In the last decade of the nineteenth century he retired from active practice and took up his residence in Farmington, Connecticut, where he became successively senior burgess, park commissioner, and finally a delegate to the Connecticut constitutional convention in 1902, in which he played an influential part.

• Early in Redfield's career, he devoted much time to literary work. He was a contributor to the *Knickerbocker* magazine and wrote several legal works. C. E. Lydecker wrote a memorial of Redfield in *Association of the Bar of the City of New York, Annual Reports, 1903*. His antecedents are traced in J. H. Redfield, *Genealogical History of the Redfield Family* (1860). An obituary is in the *New York Times*, 20 Oct. 1902.

CHRISTOPHER ANGLIM

REDFIELD, Isaac Fletcher (10 Apr. 1804–3 Mar. 1876), lawyer, judge, and law writer, was born in Weathersfield, Vermont, the son of Peleg Redfield, a physician, and Hannah Parker. By 1808 the family had moved to a farm in Coventry in sparsely settled northern Vermont. With his father often attending to patients far away, Redfield, the oldest of twelve children, took charge of the farm at an early age. Although he had little formal schooling, he gained admission to Dartmouth College and graduated with honors in 1825. After a brief stint as a schoolteacher, Redfield studied law with Baxter and West in Brownington, Vermont, and in 1827 opened his own office in Derby.

Redfield practiced successfully in Derby for eight years, during the last three of which he served as Orleans County prosecutor. He early on revealed the intellectual bent that would characterize his career; at a time when the rules of pleading were highly technical, better-established attorneys often hired Redfield to draft pleadings for them. In 1835 the Vermont legislature elected the 31-year-old Redfield to the state supreme court. Although it would mean a significant loss of income, Redfield accepted the position as one that would allow greater scope for intellectual inquiry than did the daily grind of the lawyer. In 1836 he married Mary Ward Smith, who died, childless, in 1839. In 1842 he married Catharine Blanchard Clark; they had seven children.

Redfield was a Democrat in a heavily Whig and then Republican state, but the legislature renewed his appointment to the bench annually for twenty-five years; he served as chief justice from 1852 until 1860, when he voluntarily stepped down.

Vermont Supreme Court justices in Redfield's time sat individually as trial judges, with both law and equity jurisdiction, and met together several times a year as an appellate court. In hundreds of appellate opinions, Redfield wrote learnedly on the whole gamut of legal issues. However, as befit a Democrat in the age of Andrew Jackson, he believed that the law should be intelligible to all. In an 1851 case involving an arcane question of real estate transfers, Redfield wrote, "It was no doubt the purpose of the framers of our laws upon conveyancing to have them '*understanded*' of the people, without the necessity of resorting to the study of the

subject in other quarters" (*Gorham v. Daniels*, 23 Vt. 600, 610). In the same spirit, Redfield sought the principles underlying the law and disregarded technical accretions when they seemed no longer to serve the ends of justice.

Redfield became the nineteenth century's leading authority on railroad law, and it may be in this area, more than any other, that the Jacksonian roots of his jurisprudence are most evident. The rail system spread rapidly in the 1850s, raising new questions of corporate, tort, and constitutional law. In 1857 Redfield published *A Practical Treatise upon the Law of Railways*. One of the first American treatises on railroad law, it went through five editions and several titles in the nineteen years before his death. As early as 1854, in *Thorpe v. Rutland and Burlington Railroad*, he had confronted the issue of railroad regulation by the state and had written a sweeping vindication of the legislature's right to regulate railroad corporations in the interest of public safety. At the same time he had found very limited authority for judicial brakes on legislative power.

After the Civil War the railroads became enormously influential in legislative chambers, and state and local governments, often with widespread public support, vied with each other to grant subsidies, tax exemptions, and other special privileges to railroad corporations. Appalled by this state of affairs, Redfield sought some constitutional basis on which courts might check these abuses of legislative power. The old Jacksonian Thomas M. Cooley and other state judges came to his aid with their attacks on "class legislation" that favored one business or segment of the population over others. Redfield was no longer on the bench, but in the pages of the *American Law Register* he applauded the opinions of Cooley and other exponents of what historians would later call "laissez-faire constitutionalism."

Like the laissez-faire constitutionalists, Redfield distinguished between subsidization of private railroad corporations, which he opposed, and state regulation of the roads in the public interest. However, Redfield had reservations about laissez-faire economics, and he went so far as to advocate national regulation or even ownership of the railroads. He claimed that, under the commerce clause of the Constitution, Congress had virtually unlimited power of regulation, including the power to set rates.

Redfield retired from the bench in 1860, on the eve of the Civil War. He opposed slavery and believed in the indissolubility of the Union, but his Democratic, states' rights conservatism put him at odds with political sentiment in Vermont. Redfield found the time opportune to accept an attractive offer from Boston to write and edit legal works. He moved to the suburb of Charlestown, Massachusetts, in 1861 to become an associate editor of the *American Law Register*, for which he wrote many articles and case annotations for fifteen years. He prepared new editions of his book on railroad law; published collections of cases on commercial and railroad law and treatises on civil practice, wills, and carriers and bailments; and contributed to law journals and to John Bouvier's *Law Dictionary and Concise Encyclopedia*; and edited several works by Joseph Story and Simon Greenleaf. A devout and active member of the Protestant Episcopal church, Redfield also wrote articles for religious journals. In 1867 and 1868 he served with Caleb Cushing as legal adviser to American diplomats who were pursuing the U.S. government's claims to Confederate property in England and to recompense for losses caused by Confederate ships outfitted there. Redfield died in Charlestown.

• No important collections of his correspondence have been located, but Redfield left a substantial body of published works. These include dozens of articles and case commentaries in the *American Law Register* between 1861 and 1876, as well as contributions to other legal and nonlegal periodicals and newspapers; several legal treatises; and hundreds of judicial opinions published in the *Vermont Reports* 8–33. The most comprehensive biographical essays on Redfield are William Brunswick Curry Stickney, "Isaac Fletcher Redfield," in *Great American Lawyers*, vol. 5 (1908); Wheelock G. Veasey, *Address in Memory of Hon. Isaac Fletcher Redfield, LL.D.* (1881); and E. J. P[helps], "Hon. Isaac F. Redfield," *Vermont Reports* 49 (1877): 519. On an important aspect of Redfield's constitutional jurisprudence, see David M. Gold, "Redfield, Railroads, and the Roots of 'Laissez-Faire Constitutionalism,'" *American Journal of Legal History* 27 (1983): 254–68.

DAVID M. GOLD

REDFIELD, Justus Starr (2 Jan. 1810–24 Mar. 1888), publisher, was born in Wallingford, Connecticut, the son of William Redfield and Sarah Dejean. He had a limited formal education, turning instead to learning the trades of printing and stereotyping. In 1831 he opened his own printing office in New York City. Redfield's early work included stereotyping for editions of Noah Webster's speller and other textbooks. In 1834 he became the publisher of the *Family Magazine*, one of the first journals to use illustrations routinely and in quantity. Redfield included in the magazine many illustrations by the noted engraver Benson J. Lossing (who also served as editor of the magazine) and by one of Redfield's brothers, W. D. Redfield.

In 1841 the magazine's run ended, and Redfield opened a bookstore. During this time he was also joined in a new stereotyping firm by C. C. Savage, a collaboration that lasted from 1842 to 1848. He also began to publish under his own imprint, locating the publishing offices on Nassau Street in New York City. He moved his business in 1852, when his original rooms were taken over by the Nassau Bank, a firm with many clients in the publishing industry; Redfield was a director of the bank. Throughout his publishing career, he maintained good relationships with others in the industry, which contributed to his success.

Redfield's publishing company was extremely active, producing more than 100 books between 1852 and 1854. One survey of American publishers between 1837 and 1857 places Redfield as the sixteenth most prolific publisher of first-edition American fic-

tion. His 1855 catalog contained forty pages of books in various categories. His firm published many illustrated children's books and textbooks, including several editions of J. G. Chapman's *The American Drawing-Book* ("Any one who can learn to write, can learn to draw").

Redfield's choices of what to publish were sometimes influenced by friendships and business relationships and sometimes by his personal taste. His edition of the complete works of William Gilmore Simms was a project that began because Redfield had enjoyed reading Simms's novels even before he entered the business. Six of the books Simms published with Redfield were first editions, and the fifteen-volume, uniform edition of Simms's work that Redfield produced beginning in 1853 was extremely popular. The plates from that edition were sold from publisher to publisher until the end of the nineteenth century. One of Redfield's most important publishing risks was taken in 1849, when he was persuaded by Rufus Griswold, with whom he had had other business relationships, to produce an edition of the works of Edgar Allan Poe. Redfield's decision helped to keep Poe's work in print at a time when his reputation was such that many other publishers had turned down the opportunity. Four volumes were produced between 1850 and 1857, and the edition was a great financial success for Redfield. In 1858 he published an illustrated edition of Poe's work, which was printed in England.

In 1860 Redfield's publishing ventures failed, and he turned over the firm to William J. Widdleton. Redfield then accepted a position as U.S. consul in Otranto, Italy, in 1861. He transferred to Brindisi, Italy, in 1864. At the time consuls were paid either directly by the U.S. government or were allowed to collect various fees and work independently. Redfield's positions were salaried; he was paid the usual $1,500 per year—a figure that many in the diplomatic service found inadequate. While in Italy he continued to be interested in publishing and was involved in projects that included an edition of Jean Macé's *Histoire d'une Bouchée de Pain* (History of a Loaf of Bread) and Henrietta Caracciolo's *The Mysteries of Neapolitan Convents*. He resigned his post in 1866, returning to the United States.

Upon his return, Redfield purchased a farm in Florence, New Jersey, where he lived until 1888. In March of that year he chose to take his own life, leaving instructions for William Potts, who lived with him at the farm, to bury him there. At the time of his death, his second (possibly third) wife, Elizabeth Jones, was reported to be in an asylum in Trenton. Redfield was father to one son by Elizabeth Hall, his first wife (whom he may have married in 1835 and who died in 1842) and three daughters and a son by Jones.

• Letters from Redfield to Lossing can be found in the Syracuse University Library collection of Lossing manuscripts and letters. Little concentrated information on Redfield is available. J. C. Derby profiles him in *Fifty Years among Authors, Readers, and Publishers* (1884). Details on the *Family Magazine* can be found in Frank Luther Mott, *History of*

American Magazines, 1741–1850 (1930). The March 1854 edition of *Norton's Literary Gazette* copied a *New York Tribune* article on publishing that includes information on the firm's early years. Ronald J. Zboray and Mary Saracino Zboray provided details from their statistical work on American fiction publishing from 1837–1857. Obituaries are in the *New York Times*, 26 Mar. 1888, and *Publishers Weekly*, 31 Mar. 1888.

JOANN E. CASTAGNA

REDFIELD, Robert (4 Dec. 1897–16 Oct. 1958), anthropologist, was born in Chicago, Illinois, the son of Robert Redfield, an attorney, and Bertha Dreier. Redfield was brought up on land northwest of Chicago that had been in the family since the 1830s; most of the near neighbors were his cousins. His father, a successful Lasalle Street lawyer who was active in Democratic politics in the city, seems to have been relatively uninvolved with his family. Redfield's mother, Danish by birth, appears never to have quite felt at home in Chicago and found solace in gathering the local Danish community at her house. Young Robert was thought to be frail and was not sent to school until ninth grade; he spent long hours in solitude, reading and studying the local flora and fauna. He hoped to become a naturalist. His mother thought him too delicate to learn to swim or ice-skate—he never learned either—and his hours were passed with her and with his younger sister Louise. To this sheltered, indeed overprotected, childhood and to his emotionally absent father is perhaps to be ascribed the deep strain of sadness and pessimism that characterized Redfield in adult life, a pessimism that he surmounted with stoic discipline.

In high school at the Laboratory School (founded by philosopher John Dewey), Redfield began his long association with the University of Chicago. He began to write, and he and his sister for some years dominated the school literary magazine. All his life Redfield wrote poetry—although in later life it was mostly light verse—and after "Naturalist," "Poet" became his chosen identity. In 1917 Redfield (against the protests of his parents) joined the American Friends Field Service as an ambulance driver on the Western Front. His French experience was brief—essentially he served through one battle—but it was intense and marked his coming of age. He received the Croix de Guerre.

Redfield attempted to pursue his biological interests at Harvard University; later in life he remembered that nothing living was studied there and that the science stank of formaldehyde. Whether for this or for some other reason (his mother and sister evidently missed him terribly) he lasted at Harvard only one semester. He finished college at the University of Chicago, graduating in 1920 in philosophy because it turned out to be the most convenient major for the credits he had acquired. In the same year he married Margaret Park, the daughter of sociologist Robert Park, at this time a Chicago professor; the couple had four children. They lived with Redfield's parents for a while, until one of the old farm houses on the family land could be made over for them. Redfield wrote poetry

and drifted from job to job until his father, despairing of him, sent him to the University of Chicago Law School. He disliked the law, although (with his usual discipline) he did well enough to make the law review; after graduation he clerked for a federal judge and then practiced with his father's firm. Here his father-in-law intervened; convinced that Redfield's career so far was a waste of Redfield's talents, Park offered the couple $1,000 if they would use it for some kind of self-development. They went to Mexico, where they discovered villages.

Margaret Park Redfield was her father's favorite; he had hoped she would be his intellectual heir. Park believed in plain living, high thinking, and vigorous activity; anthropological fieldwork turned out to combine all three. For Redfield fieldwork was always a personal challenge. His wife sustained him and was deeply involved with his work. Always they came home from their travels to the family land and their country house, where they entertained, at one time or another, most of the major anthropologists of their generation—and many others of note.

Redfield's Mexican experience brought him into sociology at Chicago. (Anthropology was not yet a separate department.) Park was obviously an important influence, but largely informally, and to some extent his influence was transmitted through his daughter. Redfield was impressed by Edward Sapir, but looked upon Fay-Cooper Cole as his most important teacher. In 1926–1927 Redfield took his family to Tepoztlán in central Mexico, where he did the fieldwork for his Ph.D. thesis, with which he graduated in 1928. The work was published in 1930 as *Tepoztlán: A Mexican Village*.

This research boldly applied a novel method to the study of contemporary third-world communities in order to investigate the kinds and directions of social change. The distinctive feature of Redfield's method in this first phase of his career, which extended from 1926 to 1948, was comparison. He made more or less simultaneous observations of present events in several communities of different types, ranging from peasant villages to the capital city of Yucatan. He described the range of variation in terms of the "ideal types" of "folk" and "urban" societies and cultures. The ideal type folk society was conceived to be small, homogeneous, embedded in the sacred, and characterized by strong primary personal relations. Urban society, by contrast, was ideally conceived as the polar opposite: large, heterogeneous, secularized, characterized by formal impersonal relations. Redfield and his associates concluded that folk society and culture became more individualistic, secular, and culturally disorganized as they passed from the tribal village to the peasant village, to the small town, to the city. These changes, in Redfield's view, were not determined primarily by the geographical location and ecology of the different communities, but by the modes of communication between city and country, and by "the adaptive necessities of the social situation as it comes to be" (*The Folk Culture of Yucatan*, p. 361).

In 1925 the University of Colorado hired Redfield as an instructor in anthropology. He was then appointed instructor in anthropology at Chicago in 1927, a year before he received his Ph.D. With the completion of his dissertation, he became an assistant professor; with his dissertation's publication in 1930, an associate professor. In 1934, with the publication of *Chan Kom: A Maya Village*, he was appointed full professor and dean of the Division of Social Sciences; he held the latter position for eleven years. From 1930 to 1947 he was a research associate of the Carnegie Institution in Washington. He was appointed Robert Maynard Hutchins Distinguished Service Professor at Chicago in 1953.

From 1934 Redfield had become increasingly close to Hutchins, the charismatic fifth president of the university. This led to Redfield's involvement not only with university administration but with public affairs. Continuing to teach and do fieldwork, he spent some ten months in the highlands of Guatemala over the period from 1937 to 1941, where he worked in association with Sol Tàx, a younger Chicago anthropologist. This work resulted in Tàx's *Penny Capitalism*; Redfield's research was never published in monograph form. In 1946, after his resignation as dean, Redfield returned to Yucatan and wrote *The Village That Chose Progress* (1950).

In 1948, in quest of a new intellectual orientation, Redfield took his wife and youngest child around the world. His plan to teach for a year at Tsinghua (now National) University was frustrated by the Chinese revolution, which forced him to repair to south China, where he fell ill. He found his way to Europe in January 1949, and there, during a six-week period of recuperation in Sicily, he wrote a set of lectures, which he then delivered in Frankfurt, announcing his new anthropology of civilization.

In Yucatan Redfield had determined that it would not be possible to gain direct access to ancient Mayan civilization through a contemporary village study. The "great tradition" of Mayan civilization, he said, had been "decapitated" by the Spanish conquest and could be recovered only through archaeological and historical research. In China, India, and the Middle East, however, enough of the "great traditions" had survived to justify contemporary study of their presence in "little communities." This concept of civilizations as historic structures where learned, reflective traditions combined with the local folk traditions became the most distinctive achievement of his second phase. He did not abandon the theory of the folk-urban continuum developed in his first phase; he rather projected it into the course of human history, where it could guide his interpretation of the processes of social and cultural transformation of folk and primitive societies into peasantry and cities, processes integral to the beginnings of civilization in the old world and the new. Similarly the concept of what he called "world view," the integration of experience in coherent sense of reality, appeared in both the first and second phases of Redfield's career—first as the "villager's view of life," then

linked to civilization as recreated by literati and intelligentsia. The outlines of this interpretation were published as *The Primitive World and Its Transformations*. (1953).

In 1951 Hutchins, now an officer of the newly organized Ford Foundation, arranged funding for "studies of the characterization and comparison of the great traditions of mankind." This funding, originally provided for a single year, eventually extended well beyond Redfield's life span, to 1961.

The Ford grant galvanized Redfield into an intense and productive burst of thinking, teaching, lecturing, and writing. China having proved inaccessible, he turned to India as the object of a study of an oriental civilization "from the bottom up," through a village community. Although illness frustrated this second attempt at a field study of civilization, from 1951 to 1958 Redfield organized and chaired a continuing seminar on "The Comparison of Cultures," which met twice a week at the University of Chicago to hear and discuss progress reports by local staff and occasional visitors; there was also a series of conferences, research projects, and publications in which senior Indian scholars and their students participated along with American specialists on India.

For his discussion of the comparative history of civilizations Redfield drew on the grand theories of influential thinkers, such as those of Oswald Spengler in *The Decline of the West* and of Arnold Toynbee in *A Study of History*, and also on the more cautious scientific criticism of archaeologists, historians, sociologists and anthropologists, particularly of Alfred Kroeber.

Redfield's anthropological colleagues recorded their appreciation of his accomplishments by electing him president of the American Anthropological Association in 1944 and by awarding him many honors; his usual response was to write yet another lecture developing his thinking about civilization and human nature. A memorandum on "The Nature of Man" written for his fellow members on the board of trustees of the *Encyclopedia Britannica* pointed out the fragmentary nature of the encyclopedia's articles on "Man" and successfully proposed that an article be added to guide the reader. A hectographed outline for a seminar on "Human Nature" was found on Redfield's office desk after his death.

Redfield's research was intimately involved with his teaching, not only in the sense that he taught his current research; it was also true that his research had educational aims. These aims were pursued through his active involvement in the struggle for racial equality and through his involvement in the reform of higher education—particularly in the College of the University of Chicago, which during and just after the Second World War had moved to integrate the eleventh and twelfth grades with the college, to provide a uniform integrated curriculum for all, leading to the B.A. two years earlier than elsewhere. These controversial steps were hotly disputed by members of the graduate faculty. In 1946 Redfield was appointed by Hutchins to chair the college's social science staff, with responsibility for incorporating the state-mandated eleventh-grade American history course into a full three-year interdisciplinary program in the social sciences. Redfield's efforts came to focus on the second course in the sequence, Social Sciences Two, which he proposed study human nature and the diversity of cultures. David Riesman, later a prominent sociologist at Chicago and Harvard, then a new member of Social Sciences Two staff, drafted the revised syllabus, concentrating on the then active field of culture and personality studies.

In 1956 when the Carnegie Corporation gave the college a three-year grant for support of three new year-long courses introducing undergraduates to the civilizations of China, Islam, and India, Dean of the College Robert Streeter and Dean of the Social Sciences Division Chauncy Harris saw an opportunity for a closer approximation to the Redfield model for the study of culture in general education. Though not quite Redfield's model (he once proposed that the first fourteen years of schooling be devoted to a single non-western civilization such as China), the Carnegie program offered a serious beginning to the teaching of comparative history and the dialogue of civilizations. Redfield opened the 1957 "Introduction to Indian Civilization" course with the lecture "Thinking about a Civilization" (published in *Introducing India in Liberal Education*, ed. Singer [1957]).

In the first phase of his career Redfield had sometimes adopted a rather positivistic, scientist rhetoric in calling for an objective social science. In his second phase, after 1948, his moral aims and ethical concerns became unequivocal. In his lectures of 1952, published as *The Primitive World and Its Transformations* (1953), Redfield spoke of the change in his own perspective: "In me, man and anthropologist do not separate themselves sharply. I used to think I could bring about that separation in scientific work about humanity. Now I have come to confess that it is not possible to do so. I now think that what I see men do, and understand as something that human beings do, is seen often with a valuing of it."

Redfield thus made his own contribution to what he saw as the moral work of civilization, as he describes it elsewhere in the same work: "In civilization the technical order certainly becomes great. But we cannot truthfully say that in civilization the moral order becomes small. . . . In civilization the old moral orders suffer, but new states of mind are developed by which the moral order is, to some significant degree, taken in charge. The story of the moral order is attainment of some autonomy through much adversity."

Redfield died in Chicago.

• Redfield's personal papers are in part in the possession of his son James Redfield, and in part in Special Collections at the University of Chicago. The correspondence between Redfield and Tax from 1934 to 1941, during the Guatemalan research, has been published as *Fieldwork: The Correspondence of Robert Redfield and Sol Tax*, ed. Robert A. Rubenstein (1991). For Redfield's stimulation of work by Indian scholars and specialists during the second phase of his career,

see the articles by Redfield, Milton Singer, V. Raghavan, and M. N. Srinivas in *Far Eastern Quarterly* 14 (1954), 15 (1955), and 16 (1956). For Redfield's own progress toward a comparative study of civilizations during the second phase of his career, see, in addition to the works already mentioned in the text, his *Human Nature and the Study of Society* (1962), *The Little Community* (1955), and *Peasant Society and Culture* (1956). A comprehensive list of Redfield's publications was included with the obituary written by two former colleagues, Fay-Cooper Cole and Fred Eggan, in the *American Anthropologist* 61, no. 4 (1959): 652–62.

The 1974 meetings of the American Ethnological Society at Clark University included a section on "The Role of Robert Redfield," organized by John V. Murra, a former student of Redfield's at Chicago. Papers presented there, including those by Charles Leslie, another former student; Asael T. Hansen, who together with his wife undertook the ethnographic research on Merida; and Milton Singer, who collaborated with Redfield on the comparative civilizations project, appear in *American Anthropology: The Early Years*, ed. J. V. Murra (1976). Ricardo Godoy, "The Background and Context of Redfield's *Tepoztlán*," *Journal of the Steward Anthropological Society* 10, no. 1 (Fall 1978): 47–79, gives an excellent account based on papers in Special Collections, the University of Chicago, and on interviews with Margaret Redfield and others. Milton Singer, "Robert Redfield, 1897–1958," in *Remembering the University of Chicago*, ed. Edward Shils (1991), describes some personal reminiscences and impressions. George W. Stocking, "Anthropology at Chicago: Tradition, Discipline, Department" (the catalogue of a Chicago Special Collections exhibition, 1979), describes Redfield's activities there and reprints a photocopy of his 1945 letter to his daughter Lisa after Hiroshima (p. 30). Obituaries are in the *Chicago Tribune* and the *New York Times*, 17 Oct. 1958.

MILTON SINGER
JAMES REDFIELD

RED JACKET (c. 1750–20 Jan. 1830), Seneca chief and orator, also known as Sagoyewatha, was born at either Canoga (on Cayuga Lake in western New York) or Kanadesaga (near modern Geneva, N.Y.), the son of Ahweyneyonh of the Seneca Wolf clan. His father was possibly Cayuga. Red Jacket enters the historical record around the time of the American Revolution when he is said to have habitually worn a red coat provided him by the British, who employed him as a messenger, thus the origin of his English name. During the conflict, his war record was undistinguished. He fled from the field at the battle of Oriskany (6 Aug. 1777), and early in the Cherry Valley campaign (November 1778) he left the Indian-loyalist force, complaining it was too late in the year to fight. Once he exhibited a bloody axe as evidence of his prowess as a warrior, but it was discovered that he had used the axe to kill a cow. War leaders such as the Mohawk Joseph Brant (Thayendanegea) later accused him of cowardice.

It was at the council fire instead of on the battlefield that Red Jacket achieved his position of prominence. He was both arrogant and eloquent in his defense of Seneca values. He once upbraided an inattentive U.S. official at a treaty negotiation: "When a Seneca speaks he ought to be listened to with attention from one extremity of this great island [North America] to the other." Later he told missionaries that before proselytizing among the Seneca, they should first refine the morals of the citizens of Buffalo, New York, so that they would no longer cheat Indians. "Let us know the tree by the blossoms, and the blossoms by the fruit."

Red Jacket played a prominent role in negotiations between the Seneca and the new American republic. He personally maintained greatest influence at Buffalo Creek (now part of Buffalo), which remained the most populous Seneca reservation until its sale, after his death, in 1838. To assert Seneca grievances and claims, Red Jacket headed a delegation of fifty to the seat of U.S. government in Philadelphia in 1792. There George Washington, continuing a French and British diplomatic custom, presented him with a large silver peace medal, which Red Jacket invariably wore when posing for portraits later in his life.

Red Jacket's influence was not without challenge. The Seneca who had settled on the Allegheny River were followers of Cornplanter. There, Cornplanter's half brother, Handsome Lake, experienced a vision in 1799, which instructed him to preach religious reform and revitalization among the Seneca and the other Iroquois nations. Handsome Lake's message was accepted with enthusiasm by many, but not by Red Jacket. Matters came to a head in 1801 when Handsome Lake accused Red Jacket of practicing witchcraft, punishable by death under Seneca norms. Red Jacket's eloquent defense of his personal conduct is credited with clearing him of the charge.

When the War of 1812 broke out, Red Jacket, like many Seneca, became an ally of the United States. In his sixties, he fought bravely at the battles of Fort George (17 Aug. 1813) and Chippawa (5 July 1814), thus disproving earlier charges of cowardice. At the latter, heavy casualties suffered by both the New York Seneca and the Iroquois of Upper Canada led both to reconsider their participation in a non-Indian war. Red Jacket played a leading role in the decision of both to withdraw from the Canadian-American conflict.

Red Jacket's first marriage to Aanjedek ended in divorce, after she bore him ten children. None of these children survived their father, although Jacket as a surname was used by at least some of his grandchildren. Red Jacket then married Awaogoh, the widow of Two Guns, a Seneca chief who had been killed at the battle of Chippawa.

The remainder of Red Jacket's life was devoted to defending Seneca culture and religion against white domination. In 1821 he testified in the successful defense of Tommy Jemmy, a Seneca who was on trial for murder after executing a woman who had been declared a witch. Three years later he brought about the brief expulsion of missionaries from Buffalo Creek. When his second wife became a Christian in 1826, he left her and moved to the Tonawanda Reservation, although they were later reconciled and returned to his home in Buffalo Creek. In 1827 Christians on the Buffalo Creek Reservation attempted to depose him, but he managed to reassert his right to be chief. However, Red Jacket described himself at that time as "an aged tree"—"My leaves are fallen, my branches withered,

and I am shaken by every breeze." He died of cholera on the Buffalo Creek Reservation. Despite his opposition to Christianity, he was buried in the mission cemetery there. His remains were later removed to the Forest Lawn cemetery in Buffalo.

• Notable biographies of Red Jacket are William L. Stone, *Life and Times of Sa-go-ye-wat-ha, or Red Jacket* (1866), and J. Niles Hubbard, *An Account of Sa-go-ye-wat-ha or Red Jacket and His People, 1750–1830* (1886), and an account is included in T. L. McKenney and James Hall, *The Indian Tribes of North America*, vol. 1 (1836; repr. 1933–1934). DeWitt Clinton, "Discourse Delivered before the New-York Historical Society, at Their Anniversary Meeting, 6th December, 1811," in *Collections of the New-York Historical Society*, vol. 2 (1812), pp. 37–116, discusses Red Jacket's trial for witchcraft. Seneca history and the culture of Red Jacket's time are described in Anthony F. C. Wallace, *Death and Rebirth of the Seneca* (1970). His portraits are discussed in Jadviga da Costa Nunes, "Red Jacket: The Man and His Portraits," *American Art Journal* 12, no. 3 (Summer 1980): 4–20.

THOMAS S. ABLER

REDMAN, Don (29 July 1900–30 Nov. 1964), composer, arranger, and alto saxophonist, was born Donald Matthew Redman in Piedmont, West Virginia; the names of his parents are unknown. It is known, however, that Redman came from a musical family and was a child prodigy. He learned to play several instruments as a youngster, and he wrote arrangements for a visiting road band while still in his teens; he even backed up the group with his own band on occasion.

Redman graduated from Storer College in Harpers Ferry, West Virginia, at age twenty with a music degree. He worked professionally for about a year around Piedmont, then joined Billy Paige's Broadway Syncopators in Pittsburgh; he played clarinet and saxophones and wrote arrangements for the popular group. The Syncopators were invited to play in New York City in 1923, but the band broke up soon after its arrival. Redman himself, though, got a call for a recording date, and at the session he met Fletcher Henderson, who led the pick-up group hired to back up singer Florence Mills. Henderson immediately recognized Redman's talent and hired him for several more sessions, eventually asking him to join his own new orchestra. Over the next several years Redman played saxes, clarinet, and other instruments with the Henderson group, but his biggest impact lay in his revolutionary approach to arranging.

At first the Henderson band's tunes consisted mostly of unimaginative stock arrangements. Gradually, Redman completely rewrote the group's book. His August 1923 arrangement of "Dicty Blues" shows that he had already begun to employ improvised ensembles and a variety of section combinations; he separated reeds and brass, pitting the sections against each other. One would play the melodic lead, for instance, and the other would answer during pauses or punctuate the playing with brief, rhythmic figures. The band's recording of "Copenhagen" at the end of 1924 marked a significant step forward in this style, as the music moved from one section or soloist to another twenty-four times in three minutes.

Redman was undoubtedly influenced, in part at least, by the brief presence of Louis Armstrong in the band. Armstrong was still close to the New Orleans collective style of improvisation and thus served as a bridge between it and "the newer solo-and-section style" that Redman pioneered. "Copenhagen" also employed unusual instrumental combinations, contrasting, for instance, brass with clarinet trios. By the end of 1926 Redman had also moved beyond the rhythmic stiffness that characterized even such an advanced piece as "Copenhagen," and in compositions like "Stampede," recorded in May of that year, he was writing fuller, better integrated section passages and eliciting a powerful emotional expressiveness and a richer, full-bodied sound from the band.

Redman left Henderson in March 1927 to become music director of McKinney's Cotton Pickers, a rather nondescript group that he elevated to the level of competent jazz playing. He toured and recorded extensively with the band, which became popular enough to pack Sebastian's Cotton Club in Hollywood nightly during a seven-week engagement in 1930. During this time he also played with Louis Armstrong in Chicago and with Carroll Dickerson's band, and he recorded with Armstrong (1928) and Coleman Hawkins (1929).

In 1931 Redman left McKinney to form his own group; that same year he composed and recorded what some regard as his greatest composition, "Chant of the Weed," with its unusual, almost atonal harmonies. Don Redman and His Orchestra broadcast regularly over the radio and recorded often during the early 1930s for Brunswick Victor and other labels. Redman also used two vocalists—Harlan Lattimore and Chick Bullock—and employed the tap dancing and singing of Bill Robinson with particular effectiveness on a piece called "Doin' the New Low Down." However, the band was not particularly successful in musical terms, and Redman gradually decreased his activity.

Redman had two recording dates in 1934, followed by two and a half years of silence. By the time his orchestra reemerged, Benny Goodman and Count Basie had changed the parameters of big band swing forever. Redman's group performed and recorded sporadically during the late 1930s, disbanding permanently in 1940. He did take Jay McShann's band out under his own name a couple of times in 1942 and led another group at the Club Zanzibar on Broadway.

During the 1940s Redman composed and wrote arrangements for radio and other big bands. He opened an office on Broadway and produced arrangements for bandleaders like Fred Waring, Paul Whiteman, Harry James, Jimmy Dorsey, Jimmy Lunceford, and Basie. In 1946 he toured Europe with a group that included Tyree Glenn, Don Byas, and the young pianist Billy Taylor.

In 1951 Redman became musical director for the singer Pearl Bailey, a job he held for over a decade. He made a few disappointing jazz recordings at the end of the decade, including an unsuccessful reunion with Coleman Hawkins. In the early 1960s he did freelance work for CBS and for transcription and record companies while continuing his position with Bailey. He played little during his last years, writing several extended works that have never been publicly performed. Redman had one daughter with his wife, Gladys Henderson. He died in New York City.

Redman was the first master of jazz orchestration. He came up with the idea of dividing jazz bands into sections, and among later bandleaders, only Basie and Duke Ellington surpassed his innovations. A gentle, kindly man whom musicians truly loved, Redman was cursed by an erratic career and self-defeating professional moves. But as unpredictable as his life was, and as uneven as even the greatest of his arrangements could be, he stands alone as the forerunner of modern jazz arranging.

• There are several excellent overviews of Redman's career and music. The best introductions remain those by Gunther Schuller in *Early Jazz: Its Roots and Musical Development* (1968) and *The Swing Era: The Development of Jazz, 1930–1945* (1989). Concise, perceptive summaries can be found in Frank Tirro, *Jazz: A History* (1993), and Lewis Porter and Michael Ullman, with Edward Hazell, *Jazz: From Its Origins to the Present* (1993). An interview with Redman by Frank Driggs, reprinted in *Jazz Panorama*, ed. Martin Williams (1962), is essential reading. Also worth consulting are Max Harrison, *The Essential Jazz Records*, vol. 1: *Ragtime to Swing* (1984); W. C. Allen, *Hendersonia: The Music of Fletcher Henderson and His Musicians, a Bio-Discography* (1973); and John Chilton, *McKinney's Music: A Bio-Discography of McKinney's Cotton Pickers* (1978). An obituary is in the *New York Times*, 2 Dec. 1964.

RONALD P. DUFOUR

REDMAN, John (27 Feb. 1722–19 Mar. 1808), physician, was born in Philadelphia, Pennsylvania, the son of Joseph Redman, a merchant, and Sarah (maiden name unknown). He attended William Tennent's "Log College" at Neshaminy, Bucks County, Pennsylvania, studied medicine with the elder John Kearsley of Philadelphia, and after a brief period of practice in Bermuda enrolled in the medical school of Edinburgh University, receiving an M.D. in 1748 from Leyden University for a dissertation on abortion. He also visited hospitals in Paris and in 1748–1749 enrolled as a student in Guy's Hospital, London, whose physicians certified to his "great application."

With such excellent preparation Redman quickly achieved professional status and reputation. He was appointed one of the first physicians of the Pennsylvania Hospital in 1751 and ten years later was said to enjoy "the most extensive business of any physician in the city." In 1760 he published a statement recommending inoculation for smallpox (*Pennsylvania Gazette*, 3 July 1760). In the yellow fever epidemic of 1762 he practiced a moderate therapy, prescribing mild purges but discouraging emetics and bleeding. He recalled this experience in a paper to the College of Physicians of Philadelphia for the benefit of practitioners in the greater epidemic of 1793. Redman adhered to no single medical system, but cited the writings of the Dutch and English clinicians Hermannus Boerhaave and Thomas Sydenham, trusted his own observation and experience, and reminded students and fellow physicians "not to slight or neglect the practical observations of even antiquated authors, because they do not quadrate with the more enlightened theories of the present day." His apprentices enhanced his reputation; they included John Morgan, Benjamin Rush, Caspar Wistar, and his grandson John Redman Coxe, all of whom became professors in the medical school of the College of Philadelphia or the University of Pennsylvania, and whom he spoke of as his "professional children." He gave up most of his practice before 1790.

Redman was a trustee of the College of New Jersey (now Princeton University), 1761–1778, and of the College of Philadelphia (now the University of Pennsylvania), 1762–1791. He was elected to the Philadelphia Common Council in 1751 and was briefly a surgeon in one of the provincial regiments in 1756. He was elected to the Philadelphia Medical Society in 1766 or 1767 and to the American Philosophical Society in 1768.

Redman took no side in the bitter personal rivalries that troubled the Philadelphia medical profession for thirty years after 1765. For this reason as well as because of his age and reputation, he was an admirable choice to become the first president of the College of Physicians of Philadelphia when that body was founded in 1786–1787. At the college he was thus a symbol of concord but hardly a leader—his entire inaugural address as president was an apology for the infirmities of age (he was sixty-five), without a word about the purposes and opportunities of the college. In 1803 he joined other physicians in publicly recommending vaccination as "a certain preventive of the small pox." He retired from the presidency of the college in 1805.

A devout Christian, Redman served the Presbyterian church in many capacities; much of his reading, especially in his later years, was devotional. It was to moral character and to the loyal care of his patients that Redman owed his reputation and such offices and appointments as he held.

He had married Mary Sober of Philadelphia in 1751. They had four children, of whom two died in infancy. His wife died in 1807, and Redman died in Philadelphia the next year. His grandson, John Redman Coxe, carried the Redman name and professional reputation in Philadelphia and at the University of Pennsylvania until his death in 1864.

• A few of Redman's miscellaneous manuscripts are in the Historical Society of Pennsylvania and the College of Physicians. Benjamin Rush, "Memoir of the Life and Character of John Redman, M.D.," *Philadelphia Medical Museum* 5 (1808): 49–56, is the principal biographical source by one who knew him. Other sketches include William S. Middleton, "John Redman," *Annals of Medical History* 8 (1926): 213–23; W. B. McDaniel II, "'Your Aged Friend and Fellow Servant, John Redman,'" College of Physicians, *Transactions & Studies*, 4th ser., no. 9 (1941): 35–41; and Whitfield J. Bell, Jr., "John Redman (1722–1808), Medical Preceptor of Philadelphia," College of Physicians, *Transactions & Studies* 25 (1957): 103–15. Redman's addresses to the College of Physicians are printed in William S. W. Ruschenberger, *An Account of the Institution and Progress of the College of Physicians of Philadelphia . . . from January 1787* (1887). Redman's *Account of the Yellow Fever as It Prevailed in Philadelphia in the Autumn of 1762*, though read to the College of Physicians in 1793, was not published until 1865. A description of Redman in old age by John F. Watson is in Samuel Hazard's *Register of Pennsylvania*, vol. 2 (1828), pp. 175–76.

WHITFIELD J. BELL, JR.

REDMOND, Sidney Dillon (11 Oct. 1871–11 Feb. 1948), physician, attorney, and political leader, was born in Holmes County, Mississippi, near the town of Ebenezer, the son of Charles Redmond, a former slave and blacksmith, and Esther Redmond, a former slave. In 1871 large numbers of blacks were elected to state and local government positions. Less than two years earlier a new state constitution had been put into effect that promised to make democracy a reality for both black and white Mississippians. Moreover, abolition of slavery in the United States had occurred six years before Redmond's birth. After leaving the farm near Ebenezer along with the rest of his family, Redmond settled in Holly Springs, Mississippi, where he later attended Rust College. Upon graduation from Rust College in 1894, he entered the field of education and served both as a principal at Mississippi State Normal School in Holly Springs and as a mathematics instructor at Rust College.

He attended medical school at Meharry Medical College. He graduated from the Illinois Medical College in 1897 and worked at his own medical practice in Jackson, Mississippi, for more than a dozen years. He did postgraduate study at Harvard, Massachusetts General Hospital, and Mount Sinai Hospital in Boston. He also organized and became the first president of the Mississippi Medical and Surgical Association.

Not content with treating and healing the sick, Redmond entered and completed law school at the Illinois College of Law. For the greater part of his life thereafter, the practice of law, involvement in political affairs, and his own highly successful business activities consumed his attention. Redmond was also president of the American Trust and Savings Bank, one of two black banks established in Jackson by 1904.

Politically, Redmond became an influential voice for black Mississippians. He submitted accounts about racism encountered by black Mississippians, published in *Crisis* magazine, and in 1919 wrote to W. E. B. Du Bois, informing him of several outrages against blacks. After years of involvement in state and national politics, in 1924 he became head of the Republican party in Mississippi, a position he held until his death. One issue that Redmond championed on behalf of blacks was education. For example, in 1924 he spoke before a joint session of the Mississippi legislature that recommended the passage of legislation on behalf of African Americans in Mississippi. His fight for better schools for black youths was continuous. He called for improved reformatory schools for black boys and girls, contributing to an effort that culminated in the legislature's appropriation of $100,000 for such an institution in 1944. In 1919, years before the federal government established night schools as part of Franklin D. Roosevelt's New Deal, Redmond founded a night school at Smith Robertson School, and during the 1930s he served on the board of trustees of Jackson College.

In 1927 Redmond sought help for many Mississippians who were left in ruins after the tragedy that became known as the 1927 Flood. He investigated the situation on his own and, in turn, wrote letters to President Calvin Coolidge and the U.S. Justice Department complaining about the racist treatment to which black flood victims were subjected. After voicing these complaints, Redmond later served on a special committee headed by Dr. R. R. Moten of the Tuskegee Institute in conjunction with Red Cross relief efforts.

Redmond devoted much of his life to helping others through medicine, law, and other public services; yet as a businessman, he acquired a reputation that was not always complimentary. Some of Redmond's activities strongly suggest that he was sometimes less than fully committed to the advancement of the common good. For example, in 1915 Redmond was disbarred from the practice of law in Mississippi upon charges of "deceit, malpractice, and misbehavior," according to *Mississippi Reports*; he also retired from the practice of medicine as a result of a dispute with the State Board of Health. In 1928 Redmond faced two problems with the law: he and his son were fined for attempting to obtain money under false pretense, and Redmond was accused and arrested for participation in the selling of political office.

But Redmond was not a simple one-dimensional character, interested only in making money; he sought power, and he spoke out on black causes. Furthermore, even in some of the instances in which it appeared he was selfish, in the end it became clear that his position was justified. For example, the Mississippi Supreme Court finally ruled in his favor and permitted him to resume the practice of law. And in another case in which he was sued by a black woman who claimed he overcharged her, the court ultimately ruled in his favor.

Having lived most of his life in Mississippi, the poorest state within the United States at that time, Redmond became one of the ten wealthiest blacks in the United States. He initiated Christmas Cheer Clubs in Jackson, an activity that he sponsored to assist indigent families. During World War II, when a critical shortage of doctors developed, Redmond returned to the practice of medicine to help provide much needed health care.

Involved to the very end, Redmond died in a Jackson hospital while talking to friends about a black rally underway in the city. He left to his heirs an estate valued at $604,801.09—the equivalent of perhaps $10 million at the end of the twentieth century.

• There is no established record of writings by Redmond. Charles Wilson's *God! Make Me a Man* (1950) presents the good qualities of Redmond and embellishes his multitalented professional life. The chapter on Redmond in George Sewell's *Mississippi Black History Makers* (1977) comes close to a scholarly treatment of Redmond. A short article by Rose Ragsdale-Bozeman published in *Sunbelt*, Oct. 1979, shows Redmond as a well-trained, successful black Mississippian. A contemporary biographical sketch of Redmond is Green P. Hamilton, *Beacon of Lights of the Race* (1911). Pete Daniels, *The Shadow of Slavery* (1972), discusses briefly Redmond's work on behalf of blacks during the flood of 1927. Ralph Bunche, *The Political Status of the Negro in the Age of FDR* (1973), presents detailed interview comments by Redmond on black life in Mississippi during the 1930s. The *National Encyclopedia of the Colored Race* (1919) lists information on his educational career as a principal and instructor. The *Jackson Clarion-Ledger*, 12 Aug. 1948, reported the estimated amount of Redmond's estate at the time of his death. The Hinds County, Miss., Circuit Court Records and an article in the *United World*, 19 July 1928, indicate the charges of fraud against Redmond. The *Commercial Appeal*, 13 Feb. 1948, includes published information on Redmond's decision to reopen his medical practice.

E. C. FOSTER

REDPATH, James (24 Aug. 1833–10 Feb. 1891), journalist and entertainment impresario, was born in Berwick-on-Tweed, Scotland, the son of Ninian Davidson Redpath, a teacher, and Maria Main. After being educated in his father's academy, Redpath emigrated with his family to the United States in 1849 and soon found work as a reporter for Horace Greeley's *New York Tribune*. In the mid-1850s he made three journeys through the South, secretly interviewing slaves and publishing their accounts of slavery in abolitionist newspapers and in *The Roving Editor: or, Talks with the Slaves* (1859). He reported finding many discontented slaves prepared to revolt if aided by the abolitionists.

In 1855 Redpath moved to Kansas Territory, where he reported on events for the *St. Louis Missouri Democrat*, the *Chicago Tribune*, the *New York Tribune*, and other northern papers. In 1857 he briefly edited his own newspaper, the *Doniphan* (Kans.) *Crusader of Freedom*. During these years, Redpath became a close associate of John Brown in the campaign to make Kansas Territory a free state. In 1858 Brown encouraged Redpath to move to Boston to help rally support for Brown's plan to incite a southern slave insurrection. After the failure of Brown's attack at Harpers Ferry, Virginia, Redpath participated in unsuccessful efforts to rescue captured raiders. Soon after, Redpath wrote the first biography of the executed abolitionist, *The Public Life of Capt. John Brown* (1860). This work was uncompromisingly sympathetic toward its subject and helped secure for Brown a lasting reputation as a martyr for freedom.

Redpath's first wife was Mary Cotton Kidder, a divorced mother of two when she married Redpath in 1857. She assisted him in his abolitionist and Reconstruction activities and attracted many curious visitors to the Redpath home in Malden, Massachusetts, because of her reputation as a spiritualist. The couple did not have children.

In 1860 Redpath toured Haiti as a reporter and returned to the United States as the official Haitian lobbyist for diplomatic recognition, which he secured within two years. He simultaneously served as director of Haiti's campaign to attract free black emigrants from the United States and Canada. Redpath hoped that a selective emigration of skilled blacks to Haiti would elevate conditions on that island nation and thereby dispel racial prejudice in the United States. He abandoned the scheme when he recognized that North American blacks preferred to stay home once the Civil War seemed to promise a new day of freedom for their race. In 1863 and 1864 Redpath began publishing cheap paperbound books principally intended for distribution to Union army soldiers. This series featured religious, historical, and humorous works by such authors as Louisa May Alcott, Wendell Phillips, and Victor Hugo. A particularly noteworthy title was William Wells Brown's *Clotelle: A Tale of the Southern States*, the first novel written by a black American. Another in this series was a short work by Redpath himself, *Shall We Suffocate Ed Green*, an early anti–capital punishment tract, which relied heavily upon quotations from the New Testament.

Later in the Civil War, Redpath served as a front-line war correspondent with the Union army in Georgia, Tennessee, and South Carolina. In February 1865 federal military authorities appointed Redpath to be the first superintendent of public schools in Charleston. He soon had more than one hundred instructors at work teaching 3,500 students of both races. In May 1865 in Charleston, Redpath organized the first Memorial Day service to honor Union soldiers buried there. His tentative steps toward integrating South Carolina schools worried military officials. They replaced Redpath after only seven months to remove a source of irritation to southern-born President Andrew Johnson. For the remaining years of Reconstruction, Redpath publicly advocated more concerted effort by the federal government to protect southern freedmen's rights.

After the Civil War, Redpath organized one of the first professional lecture booking agencies in the United States. His clients, who frequently became his friends, included Charles Sumner, Frederick Douglass, Wendell Phillips, Henry Ward Beecher, and Anna Dickinson. Later he added magicians, musicians, and especially humorists, including Mark Twain, Josh Billings, and David R. Locke ("Petroleum V. Nasby"), to his ensemble. Expanding the forms of entertainment he provided, Redpath organized operatic and dramatic companies and sent them on successful national tours. In the late 1870s Thomas A. Edison hired Redpath as the principal publicist for his new invention, the phonograph. During this period, Redpath and his wife divorced, in part because of Redpath's romantic attachment to novelist Katharine Sherwood Bonner.

In the 1880s Redpath resumed his earlier career as a reform journalist, beginning with tours of Ireland to report on famine conditions in rural areas. He returned to the United States a convert to the Irish nationalist cause. He edited a New York City newspaper, *Redpath's Weekly*, and lectured nationwide to further that cause. In 1886 he actively supported the New York City mayoral campaign of the utopian reformer Henry George. Afterward, Redpath served as a vice president of Father Edward McGlynn's Anti-Poverty Society, which sought solutions for the deteriorating conditions of urban ethnic neighborhoods.

Redpath ended his professional career as the editor of the *North American Review* and as a ghost writer for the former Confederate president Jefferson Davis. From among his many friends in reform circles, Redpath recruited authors for the *Review* to address pressing social issues in the late nineteenth century, such as woman suffrage, immigration, corporate monopoly, and racial discrimination. Redpath's relationship with Jefferson Davis is an anomaly in his long career as a defender of southern blacks. After Redpath persuaded Davis to write articles for the *Review* on Confederate history, feelings of mutual respect developed between the two men. Redpath lived at "Beauvoir," the Davis household at Biloxi, Mississippi, for several months in 1888 and 1889 and assisted the former Confederate president in preparing a new abridged edition of his history of the Confederacy. After Davis's death, Redpath helped his widow write a biography of her husband. Despite suffering a stroke in 1887, Redpath continued to lead an active life. In 1888 he married Carrie Dunlap Chorpenning, the divorced wife of George Chorpenning, one of the pioneers of the transcontinental mail service. They had no children. Redpath died in a trolley car accident in New York City.

• Important collections of Redpath's letters are located in the Haytian Emigration Bureau Letterbook in the Library of Congress, the Haytian Emigration Bureau Letterbook in the Duke University Library, the James Redpath Papers in the Schomburg Branch of the New York Public Library, and the James Redpath Letterbook in the Boston Public Library. Published works by Redpath other than those mentioned in the text include *A Hand-book to Kansas Territory and the Rocky Mountains' Gold Region* (1859), with Richard J. Hinton; *Echoes of Harper's Ferry* (1860); *Southern Notes for National Circulation* (1860); *A Guide to Hayti* (1860); and *Talks about Ireland* (1881). The only published biography of Redpath is Charles F. Horner, *The Life of James Redpath* (1926).

JOHN R. MCKIVIGAN

RED SHOES (?–June 1747), Choctaw warrior, war captain, and chief also known as Shulush Homa, Shulush Homma, or Soulouche Oumastabé, was born in Jasper County, Mississippi. He belonged to the Okla Hunnah (Six People) clan. Red Shoes held no powerful family connections, nor was he descended from the iksa, or clan of chiefs. He rose in power from warrior to war captain of his town of Couechitto to chief by winning favor with the Europeans who bestowed titles on those Indians who proved their loyalty. Following the 1720s he received the name of Soulouche Oumastabé, signifying his rank as warrior following a battle with the Chickasaw. His increasing prowess in battles and the killing of Indian enemies earned him the name of Red Shoes, or Shulush Homa. Red Shoes took pride in having earned his titles and elevated status of war captain, honors normally not given to a man of his common birth.

The Choctaw lived in the lower Mississippi Valley between rival English and French fur traders who constantly vied for the Indians' friendship. During his early years Red Shoes learned that alliances with the French were advantageous, for they had protected the Choctaw from capture and slavery with the English. The French and English presented gifts to the chiefs, creating tensions between the tribes to gain support. The conflicts helped to establish Red Shoes in a powerful role as he wedged himself boldly into playing off the two countries as the competition for more trade goods at lower prices began.

In 1729 Red Shoes recruited 800 Choctaws to support the French in their attack against the Natchez Indians. The Natchez suffered devastating losses, and the Chickasaws entered the battle to aid them. Tribal warfare ensued as all three nations became embroiled in the English and French conflict. Red Shoes saw the conflict as an opportunity to emerge ahead of the chief of Couechitto, who was attempting to win English favor and gifts. Announcing that he would seize any English goods that passed into their territory, Red Shoes enlisted thirty men by promising French bounty to kill Chickasaws. This brazen move of acting on his own alienated him from the Couechitto chief. It also placed him in a favorable position. The French, realizing his power, honored Red Shoes in 1732 by making him chief of the Red Warriors.

In order to keep warriors subordinate and faithful to him, Red Shoes's life was dominated by the quest to find reliable sources for goods, a hard task in a region fraught with ever-increasing tensions and changing balances of power. Red Shoes severed his coalition with the French in the 1730s after a Frenchman raped his favorite wife. Hoping to open other avenues of trade, Red Shoes sent a peace delegation of men to meet with the Chickasaw in 1739 as the French were attempting to destroy the towns. The Chickasaw murdered the delegation, fearing them to be spies. Red Shoes's loyalty fell on the side of his Choctaw heritage, and he had no choice but to seek revenge against the Chickasaw. This action tied Red Shoes once again to the French.

In 1743 the appearance of a new French governor, the marquis de Vaudreuil, at Fort Tombigbee boded ill for Red Shoes. De Vaudreuil sought to diminish the warrior's influence first by belittling Red Shoes's common origins and then by centralizing each medal chief's power by cutting his district down to between eight and ten towns, excluding Red Shoes from the plan. Red Shoes undermined de Vaudreuil by opening peace negotiations with the Chickasaw and establishing trade relations with the English in Charleston.

When the French murdered three Chickasaw peace delegates on their way to the Choctaw, Red Shoes used the opportunity to win favor with the Chickasaw by having his warriors kill three Frenchmen. Outraged, the French plotted against Red Shoes, but retaliatory efforts failed.

Red Shoes began building trade with English merchants such as James Adair of South Carolina. The influx of English goods persuaded most of the important Choctaw chiefs to support Red Shoes. When bickering and rivalry for Choctaw commerce erupted in disputes among the English officials and traders in South Carolina, the Choctaw were cut off from their usual gifts. The Choctaw once again shifted their allegiance back to the French. The Choctaw realized that their tribal warfare had protected the trading interests of the English and French, and they knew that their continued fighting would mean that the Choctaw would be destroyed. Split again into separate camps, the Okla Falaya went to the English, the Okla Tannap went with the French, and the Okla Hunnah divided between the two. The pro-French side blamed Red Shoes for their troubles, and they refused to allow him to be part of any tribal peace agreement. The French decided Red Shoes had become dangerous and much too troublesome. In 1747 a paid assassin killed the war chief as he escorted an English shipment from Charleston to his village.

Civil war broke out among the villages in 1748 and lasted until 1750. Assuming the role of leadership, Red Shoes's brother retained English trade and renewed the war against the French. But English failure to supply the warriors resulted in the death of 800 followers of Red Shoes in the Choctaw revolt. The signing of the Grandpré Treaty in the 1750s brought a weakened Choctaw nation under French control.

Caught between the French and English greed, Red Shoes understood the complexities of forming alliances between Europeans and Indians as well as the importance of trade goods in balancing these delicate relationships. Willing to take risks to enhance both his own power and that of his Choctaw followers, Red Shoes played rival French, English, chiefs, and warriors against one another. Although Red Shoes lost the gamble, he proved his ability to sway allegiances in the directions he wished through independent and quick maneuvers ahead of his enemies.

• No substantial material exists on the life of Red Shoes. Some information can be located in James Adair, *History of the American Indians* (1775); Charles Gayarreé, *History of Louisiana: The Spanish Dominion* (1854); Angie Debo, *The Rise and Fall of the Choctaw Republic* (1934; repr., 1967); Richard White, "Red Shoes: Warrior and Diplomat," in *Struggle and Survival in Colonial America*, ed. David G. Sweet and Gary B. Nash (1981), pp. 49–68; and White, *The Roots of Dependency: Subsistence, Environment, and Social Change among the Choctaws, Pawnees, and Navajos* (1983), pp. 54–63. In the 1750s Edmond Atkin, who became the superintendent of Indian affairs for the Southern Department, wrote a 30,000-word history of the revolt of the Choctaw Indians against the French. His narrative includes details of Red Shoes.

MARILYN ELIZABETH PERRY

RED WING (c. 1750–4 Mar. 1829), Mdewakanton Dakota chief and war shaman, was born in Minnesota of unknown parentage. He was also known as Scarlet Wing (Hupahuduta), Walking Buffalo (Tatankamani), and He Who Paints Himself Red (Sakiya). Red Wing was said to have been descended from a line of "Red Wing" chiefs before him, but this cannot be historically confirmed. He remembered the visit of English explorer Jonathan Carver in 1767 to the upper Mississippi and claimed that his uncles signed the legendary Carver grant, through which the Dakotas allegedly gave Carver land on the eastern side of the river. Red Wing distinguished himself as a warrior and became the leading war shaman of his tribe; it was said that he never lost a fight. He assisted the British in the American Revolution, later telling Lieutenant Zebulon Pike that the British were proud to have the Dakotas as soldiers. In 1787 Red Wing signed, along with the leaders of other tribes, a treaty at Fort Michilimackinac as the "first war chief" of his tribe. He was particularly well known among his people for his ability to prognosticate.

In the late 1700s Red Wing and his followers broke off from Wapahasha's band and established a new village at the mouth of the Cannon River; he later moved down to the landmark, Barn Bluff, at the head of Lake Pepin (present-day Red Wing, Minn.). The latter site gave rise to the band's name, "Hill-water-wood" (Hemnican). Lieutenant Pike visited Red Wing on 13 April 1806 and referred to him as "a man of sense" and a "very celebrated war chief." Red Wing afterward visited General James Wilkinson, the governor of Louisiana Territory, at St. Louis (27 May 1806).

When the War of 1812 was about to break out, Red Wing initially joined his fellow chiefs in supporting the British. However, he also attended a council with the American agent Nicholas Boilvin and commented, "The heavens were obscured when I entered; now the sun shines again upon us. I see that the Master of Life has pity on us since you erase all suspicions which were given us against our great father and his children." He promised to send his son with Boilvin's delegation to Washington, D.C. Still, the chief apparently joined the British-Indian contingent that occupied Fort Mackinac in the summer of 1812.

Red Wing's son met President James Madison and received a certificate of commendation (26 Aug. 1812) from Secretary of War William Eustis addressed to his father. Because of his son's favorable reception, Red Wing backed off completely from supporting the British. In 1813 he planned to go down to St. Louis to make peace, and in 1814 he spread rumors that the Americans were coming to attack British-held Prairie du Chien. When Captain Thomas Anderson asked the chief why he had turned against the English, Red Wing referred to his dreams and predicted that the two

powers would make peace: "I have had another dream. You know all the blood in my heart is English, but I will not now fight the Big Knives." The British made peace later that year, and Red Wing went to St. Louis to sign a peace agreement with the U.S. government on 19 July 1815. The following year he told American officials that he had withstood British attempts to persuade him to make war on the United States and that his son had been taken as a hostage by the British to Fort Mackinac to force him to go there.

After the war Red Wing was visited by almost every government expedition that traveled the upper Mississippi. William Clark's nephew, Benjamin O'Fallon, visited him in 1818 and commented, "[As Red Wing] wastes with time, so wastes his band; it is much reduced within the last twelve months. . . . This old chief . . . is now left almost alone to die." Other visitors included Michigan governor Lewis Cass in 1820 and, in 1823, Italian Count Beltrami, who commented that the chief was "still much respected by his tribe and almost feared."

In his last recorded speech, Red Wing spoke to agent Lawrence Taliaferro of his refusal to join in the Winnebago uprising of 1827: "Among all of my nation there is not one in it who has held on to the Americans like me and my band—in the worst of times Red Wing never deserted you." When the proud old chief died (site unknown, but it is believed that he was buried at his village), he was succeeded by his stepson, or nephew, Wakute (Shooter).

Red Wing was one of the greatest of the Mdewakanton war shamans and a notable example of the dilemma Native-American leaders found themselves in when trying to determine which of the Euro-American powers to back in times of war.

• The most definitive account of Red Wing's life is in Mark Diedrich, *Famous Chiefs of the Eastern Sioux* (1987); this work was based in large part on Diedrich, "Red Wing: War Chief of the Mdewakanton Dakota," *Minnesota Archaeologist* 40 (1981): 65–77. Several of Red Wing's important speeches are in Diedrich, *Dakota Oratory* (1989), and the Nicholas Boilvin Papers, State Historical Society of Wisconsin, Madison. Good early sources on Red Wing are in the writings of Thomas Anderson, "Personal Narrative of Captain Thomas G. Anderson" and "Capt. T. G. Anderson's Journal, 1814," both in *Wisconsin Historical Collections* 9 (1882): 137–206 and 207–61, and in Journals, Lawrence Taliaferro Papers, Minnesota Historical Society, St. Paul. Other War of 1812 information is in Clarence Carter, ed., *Territorial Papers of the United States*, vol. 16 (1948), and P. L. Scanlan, "Nicholas Boilvin, Indian Agent," *Wisconsin Magazine of History* 27 (1943): 145–69.

MARK F. DIEDRICH

REDWOOD, Abraham (15 Apr. 1709–8 Mar. 1788), Rhode Island merchant and Antigua planter, was born in Antigua, the son of Abraham Redwood, an Antigua plantation owner, and Mehitable Langford. Redwood's family moved to Newport, Rhode Island, in 1712, probably for the more healthful living conditions it offered in comparison with Antigua. Although for a time they lived in Salem, Massachusetts, by 1717 they had returned to Newport. Abraham was the third son but inherited his father's estate as his elder brothers died early in life. A likely prospective husband because of inherited wealth in Antigua and Newport, at the age of seventeen Abraham married Martha Coggeshall, who was like him a Quaker. They married outside the care of the Quaker meeting, that is, in a civil marriage contrary to the Quaker discipline. For this defiance of Quaker marriage rules, the young couple and her father, Abraham Coggeshall, were brought under dealing (faced a disciplinary hearing) by the Rhode Island Monthly Meeting and compelled to acknowledge their misdoings, the young couple for marrying out and Coggeshall for encouraging their "disorderly marriage." They had nine children.

Redwood pursued business interests in Newport for the balance of the 1720s and most of the 1730s. He was a merchant in trade with the West Indies, sending New England timber and fish products south and receiving sugar products in return. He retained ownership of an Antiguan plantation, which contributed to his wealth. In 1737 he returned to the family plantation to correct problems with its management and spent three years there, at times indulging in unQuakerlike carousing. Both his wife and father-in-law were upset at his long absence and urged him to return to Newport, which he finally did in 1739. On occasion, he invested in slave trading voyages to Africa. In Rhode Island, he supported the hard money faction in Newport, which opposed the paper money favored by most colony residents and promoted by Newporters John and William Wanton and their allies. While he did not seek political advancement himself at first, he may have been among those Friends who brought charges in the Quaker meeting against Governor Wanton for having violated his pacifism by signing military commissions. Eventually, he was rewarded for his support of the Wanton opponents when he was elected an assistant in the House of Magistrates in 1746 as a member of the victorious hard money faction supporting Governor William Greene. His other interests, including the management of his inherited Antigua plantation, and a disinterest in political activity impeded greater advancement. Despite the New England Quaker prohibition on slave dealing in the 1760s, Redwood continued to purchase slaves for his Antigua plantation. While Newport Friends probably did not know of his West Indian slave trading, they eventually disowned him in 1775 for refusing to free his Rhode Island slaves.

As a man of great wealth with interest in learning and in enjoying the pleasures of his estate, Redwood sought to cultivate the tastes appropriate for a wealthy gentleman. In 1750 he was among the incorporators of the library that bears his name and for which he is usually remembered. He had given £500 sterling toward the purchase of books in 1747 and, with other directors, appointed the distinguished architect Peter Harrison to design and build a neoclassical structure, the kind of building that departed from Quaker plainness as in some ways did Redwood himself. His endowment of the library followed family tradition—an English uncle had helped found the Bristol library. Ironically, the Redwood Library served to support the increasingly sophisticated and Anglican upper class in Newport. Like many other Newport gentry, Redwood kept a country estate north of Newport in Portsmouth. There he employed a gardener from England who grew exotic plants in greenhouses and a hothouse. Among the upper class, he enjoyed a reputation for charitable giving. He seems gradually to have withdrawn from business in the late 1760s, although he continued to correspond about his Antigua property and to invest in slave trading voyages to Africa.

With the outbreak of the War for Independence, Newport entered a period of decline, and Redwood and other wealthy Newport residents faced a loss of economic standing. Like many other Newport residents, Redwood withdrew to the mainland. He purchased a farm in Mendon, Massachusetts, essentially as a refuge from wartime hazards and lived there in retirement for the balance of his days, safe but without the pleasures of life in Newport before independence. He died in Newport.

• Redwood's papers are housed in the Newport Historical Society, as is a file of useful genealogical information. The best of the works on Redwood are Gladys E. Bolhouse, "Abraham Redwood: Reluctant Quaker, Philanthropist, Botanist," in *Redwood Papers: A Bicentennial Collection*, ed. Lorraine Dexter and Alan Pryce-Jones (1976), Elaine Forman Crane, *A Dependent People: Newport, Rhode Island in the Revolutionary Era* (1985), and Sydney V. James, *Colonial Rhode Island: A History* (1975).

ARTHUR J. WORRALL

REECE, Byron Herbert (14 Sept. 1917–3 June 1958), poet and novelist, was born near Blairsville, Georgia, the son of Juan Welborn Reece and Emma Lance, farmers. Reece was born in a one-room log cabin on Wolf Creek at the foot of Blood Mountain in what is now Vogel State Park. For most of his life his home was a poor mountain farm. The farm was so isolated that Reece was about eight years old before he saw his first automobile.

Before entering a local elementary school in 1923, Reece had read *Pilgrim's Progress* and much of the Bible, the basis of much of his later writing. He liked to read and write as a boy. In 1935 he graduated from Blairsville High School and entered nearby Young Harris College, a small Methodist junior college. He soon had to drop out to help on the family farm. At night he read and wrote down lyrical passages that had come to him during his work that day. His mother encouraged his writing but hardly understood what he was doing.

In 1935 Reece burned all the poems he had written, being unsure of their worth. But by the end of 1938 he had published thirty-one poems in poetry journals or national magazines. Reece spent much of the little money he could get on classical works of English and American poetry. As he worked the farm he recited poetry he had learned and sang mountain ballads and hymns. He also began to fill the pulpit when the minister was absent at Salem Methodist Church, where he was a member. His sermons were simple and straightforward in the mountain idiom.

In 1938 Reece returned to Young Harris College on a work fellowship. While there he was influenced by Professor W. L. Dance and the Quill Club, a student literary club whose members had to produce a weekly sample of their creative writing. This was the first time in his life that Reece was able to discuss writing with kindred spirits. He left Young Harris in 1940 without graduating because he refused to take the required courses in mathematics and French.

Reece returned to the family farm, where he spent several years farming during the day and writing mountain ballads and other poetry at night. In 1945 E. P. Dutton, upon the recommendation of Jesse Stuart, published Reece's first volume of poetry, *Ballad of the Bones*, which garnered many favorable reviews. In January 1950 Reece's novel, *Better a Dinner of Herbs*, was published; although it received favorable criticism, the novel did not sell well. In the fall he accepted an appointment as poet-in-residence at the University of California at Los Angeles. Also that year, a second volume of poetry, *Bow Down in Jericho*, was published and received considerable national publicity. A *Newsweek* article published at that time presented a rather romantic but factual brief history of Reece and his life as a farmer, poet, and teacher—and elicited more than 150 marriage proposals through the mail.

In 1952 Reece published his third volume of poetry, *A Song of Joy*. In 1953 he became poet-in-residence at Young Harris College but had to leave early in 1954 to enter Battey Hospital, a state tuberculosis sanitorium, in Rome, Georgia. In 1955 *The Hawk and the Sun*, a highly symbolic novel about a lynching in a southern town, and his last volume of poetry, *The Season of Flesh*, were published.

In January 1956 Reece was recovered physically enough to become poet-in-resident at Emory University in Atlanta for one quarter. He returned to Young Harris in the fall of that year to resume his former post. A Guggenheim award would have allowed Reece to work on a novel at the Huntington-Hartford Foundation in California during the summer of 1957, but he was forced to return to Georgia because of illness. He returned to Young Harris College that fall and was able to complete the academic year. He committed suicide at the college, probably because of his health problems and loneliness.

Reece struggled against poverty and poor health most of his life. He liked both farming and writing poetry but could never make enough money at either for a decent living for himself and his parents, who were increasingly disabled with tuberculosis. He never married. His few stays away from the North Georgia mountains always left him unhappy and unable to do his best work. He needed the area he knew so well; yet he needed the money that stays away could bring.

Reece was largely self-taught out of the ballad tradition still alive in the North Georgia mountains in his youth and from his reading of the Bible and English and American poets. He once said, "I am not a self-cultivated primitive. My work in the ballad is a natural extension of the early influence of the minstrel tradition." He was a private person with mountain reticence who was generally uncomfortable in academic circles. He had a few friends with whom he discussed poetry by mail.

His poetry was in traditional forms and little influenced by modern poets of his day and will undoubtedly outlast his novels. His main themes were the Bible and religion, nature, love, and death. His poetry reflected a direct freshness and earthiness that came from his mountain farming background. Jesse Stuart said his poetry "stood out as true, honest, and sincere," while Raymond Cook observed, "He wrote literary ballads that have been unsurpassed in this country. Nowhere else can we find ballads more intrinsically Biblical in their tone and phrasing. . . . His poetic dialogue with the reader is always characterized by the implication of a third intelligence—the overwhelming and awe-inspiring presence of God" (1968, p. 84).

His poetry will continue to be read and enjoyed by people who look for the basic beauties and truths in life that were important to Reece. It came out of a civilization that has largely disappeared except in the nostalgia of an earlier generation. Yet it has much that is basic to life in any area and time.

• There are collections of Reece's papers in the libraries of the University of Georgia and Young Harris College. The fullest biography is Raymond Cook, *Mountain Singer: The Life and Legacy of Byron Herbert Reece* (1980), which contains a complete bibliography and 167 pages of Reece's poems. Cook also wrote "Byron Herbert Reece: Ten Years After," *Georgia Review* 22 (Spring 1968): 74–89. A brief biography is Bettie Sellers, *The Bitter Berry: The Life of Byron Herbert Reece* (1992), which contains nineteen pages of poems and is accompanied by a documentary video, *The Bitter Berry: The Life and Work of Byron Herbert Reece*, which presents scenes from North Georgia and Reece's life as a farmer and teacher with words from his journal. The best obituary is in the *Atlanta Journal*, 4 June 1958. The *Atlanta Constitution* has a news item on 4 June 1958 and a column by Ralph McGill, the editor and a friend of Reece's, on 7 June 1958.

KENNETH COLEMAN

REED, David Aiken (21 Dec. 1880–10 Feb. 1953), lawyer and U.S. senator, was born in Pittsburgh, Pennsylvania, the son of James Hay Reed and Kate J. Aiken, socially prominent Republicans and members of the city's conservative elite. His father was a law partner of Philander C. Knox and had close personal and business dealings with Andrew Carnegie, Andrew Mellon, and many others of Pittsburgh's newly rich and powerful industrial and financial class. Reed graduated from Pittsburgh's exclusive Shadyside Academy (1896) and was an indifferent scholar at Princeton University (class of 1900). He was, however, a brilliant student at the University of Pittsburgh Law School, graduating at the top of his class in 1903. That year he passed the bar and joined his father's prestigious law firm, where he became Knox's protégé. Reed devoted most of his practice to defending corporations and public utilities, interests dear to the heart of Knox, Mellon, and members of James Reed's firm. In 1902 Reed married Adele Wilcox; they had two children.

From 1912 to 1915 Reed chaired Pennsylvania's Industrial Accidents Commission and investigated workmen's compensation, in 1915 calling for enactment of the state's first workmen's compensation law. In addition, he defended the United States Steel Corporation before the Supreme Court in a long-running federal antitrust suit (1915–1920). Commissioned a major of field artillery during World War I, he served in various battles and was awarded the Distinguished Service Medal from the United States and the Legion of Honor from France. In 1922 Reed challenged the deathly ill Republican incumbent William E. Crow for his Senate seat with the backing of Mellon's powerful Pittsburgh political faction. Crow died before the primary election, whereupon Reed was appointed to the seat. He won easily in the general election.

As a senator, Reed remained faithful to his patrician roots and Pennsylvania friends in high places, including Mellon, who became President Warren G. Harding's treasury secretary. Reed was reelected in 1928, and during his twelve years in the Senate, he served on several key committees, including Military Affairs, which he chaired from 1927 to 1933. He voted for tax reduction; higher tariffs, particularly for Pennsylvania products; additional Prohibition penalties; and increased expenditures for armaments, particularly for ships and the requests of the army command. He consistently voted against veterans' bonuses.

A nativist who shared his era's racism, Reed outspokenly advocated immigration restriction, particularly for the "newcomers" from southeastern Europe, many of whom had flocked to Pennsylvania's industrial towns and cities. Acting on his recommendation, Congress passed the Reed-Johnson Immigration Act of 1924, which established national origins quotas that drastically restricted the immigration of southeastern Europeans. Years later Reed boasted that this "was one of the few wholly original ideas that I have ever had." When President Herbert Hoover maneuvered to thwart the bill's implementation in 1929, Reed successfully blocked the president.

Lean and lanky with slicked-down hair and a long, lined face, Reed never disguised his beliefs. His haughty manner, somber suits, and unsmiling eyes, when combined with his disdain for the niceties of congressional debate, prompted contemporaries to characterize him as "supercilious" and "the most tactless member of both houses of Congress." Even his friends conceded that arrogance was a major character flaw that caused him to be unconcerned about the sting of his words and actions. He once denounced several western congressmen as "worse than Communists" and slandered his state's voters as "dunder-

heads" for electing Philadelphia machine boss William Vare. In May 1932 Reed bluntly announced in the Senate, "If this country ever needed a Mussolini, it needs one now."

Reed loathed Franklin Delano Roosevelt and angrily voted against New Deal measures. His intemperate remarks, his antiunion statements and actions, and his general reputation as a "servant of money kings" led to his defeat in 1934 by Democrat Joseph F. Guffey. Reed retired to a part-time legal practice and made an unsuccessful stab at a political comeback in 1940. He headed Pittsburgh's isolationist America First unit and lived the life of a squire. His first wife died in 1948, and he married Edna M. French in December of that year. They had no children. He died in Sarasota, Florida.

Reed was very much a man of his time, place, race, and class. For that he offered no apologies and would doubtless expect none from historians of any stripe. Never doubting the rightness of his beliefs and decisions, he cared little for the good opinion of anyone, even those his age deemed "men of the better sort." He left few distinct marks on his time, but his actions, when taken in conjunction with others of his class and convictions, left a lasting influence.

• Reed left few letters, most of which are scattered in the Library of Congress and the major historical societies of Pa., particularly the Pennsylvania Historical and Museum Commission in Harrisburg. Other sources include *Time*, 16 Dec. 1929; Ray T. Tucker, "Leader of the Status Quo: A Portrait of David Aiken Reed," *Outlook and Independent*, 25 Dec. 1929, pp. 649–51, 676, 678; and Lawrence L. Murray, "The Mellons, Their Money, and the Mythical Machine: Organizational Politics in the Republican Twenties," *Pennsylvania History*, July 1975. For the context of Reed's life see Philip S. Klein and Ari Hoogenboom, *A History of Pennsylvania* (1973). Obituaries are in the *New York Times* and *Pittsburgh Post-Gazette*, both 11 Feb. 1953.

BRUCE CLAYTON

REED, Esther De Berdt (22 Oct. 1746–18 Sept. 1780), civic leader for soldiers' relief, was born in London, the only daughter of Dennys De Berdt, a prosperous merchant who was engaged in the British–North American colonial trade, and Martha Symons. The De Berdts were descendants of Flemish Huguenot refugees who had fled to England. In 1765–1770 Dennys De Berdt served as an agent to the British government for Massachusetts and Delaware. Esther De Berdt's early life was spent at her parents' home in Artillery Court, near the Houses of Parliament, and at their summer estate in Enfield, nine miles from London. It is not known whether Esther had any formal education outside of home, but certainly the stern Calvinist precepts imparted by her religiously devout father were tempered by an almost constant flow of merchant visitors to the De Berdt household from England and abroad. William B. Reed, Esther's grandson, described her as "slight of frame, with light hair, and fair complexion, and an air of sprightly intelligence and refinement" (*Life of Esther De Berdt*, p. 23). To family and friends during her youth, Esther was known as "Hetta" and "Hettie."

At age seventeen Esther fell in love with Joseph Reed, a young New Jerseyan who was in England to study at the Middle Temple in London and to represent his father's interests with De Berdt's mercantile firm. The couple first met when Reed was a guest in the De Berdt home in December 1763. The elder De Berdt disapproved of their courtship and forbade Esther to either see or correspond with Joseph Reed, it seems because Reed, soon to be a struggling lawyer, would not be in a station of life worthy of his daughter. Esther and Joseph kept in touch anyway, and De Berdt eventually relented but would not allow the two to become engaged. After promising Esther that he would return to England for marriage and perhaps settle there, Reed set sail for America in 1765. The separation lasted five years, during which time Esther and Joseph regularly corresponded.

Back in England in 1770, Reed hoped to be made a partner in the elder De Berdt's firm but found that another young American, Stephen Sayre, had already accepted that position. Actually, De Berdt's business was on the edge of bankruptcy. Reed could not yet practice law in England, having completed only two of the required three years of study. With the future much brighter in New Jersey, where he had already served as an attorney and as the colony's deputy secretary, Reed decided to stay in England only long enough to marry Esther, an event that occurred on 31 May 1770 at St. Luke's Church in London. Dennys De Berdt, Esther's father, had died on 11 April 1770. Joseph and Esther De Berdt Reed were to have six children, five of whom survived infancy.

The Reeds, with Esther's mother in tow, arrived in America in October 1770 and, after residing several months in Trenton, New Jersey, made their home in Philadelphia, Pennsylvania. Reed prospered as a lawyer and became an important political leader in the city. The Reeds lavishly entertained members of the Continental Congress, including George Washington and John Adams, in fall 1774. Congressman Silas Deane wrote his wife at the time that Esther De Berdt Reed had "a most elegant figure and countenance" and was "a Daughter of Liberty, zealously affected in a good Cause" ("Correspondence of Silas Deane," *Connecticut Historical Society Collections* 2: 185).

Esther De Berdt Reed endured long separations from her husband from July 1775 to January 1777, while he was military secretary to George Washington and then adjutant general of the Continental army. Reed served in the Continental Congress in 1777–1778, and during his presidency of the Pennsylvania Supreme Executive Council, Esther was Pennsylvania's "first lady." During the military campaign of 1777 and the subsequent British occupation of Philadelphia, Esther and her family resided in Norriton (now Norristown), Pennsylvania, and Flemington, New Jersey. During Joseph Reed's presidency, the Reeds had the use of "Laurel Hill," a summer home owned by the state on the Schuylkill River near Philadelphia.

Esther won great praise for her role in forming and leading an organization of thirty-nine women to provide aid for Washington's troops. Between June 1780 and that fall the women collected $200,580 in paper money and £625.68 in specie for a total of $300,634. As many as 1,645 contributors were canvassed door-to-door from across the social spectrum of Philadelphia and its suburbs, and gifts ranged from 7s. 6d. given by Phillis, an African American, to 100 guineas donated by General Marquis de Lafayette in the name of his wife. Esther wanted to spend the funds by giving each Continental soldier two dollars. Washington refused to accept this proposal because this hard money would further demonstrate that the soldiers' pay in paper money was almost worthless, and he also feared that the gifts in money would be used for gambling and drinking. Washington asked Esther to turn over the money to a special "bank" established for purchasing supplies for the army. Esther declined to accept Washington's suggestion. Instead she obtained the backing of her organization to use the contributions to purchase linen, from which Esther and her followers would themselves make shirts for the soldiers. By December 1780 2,200 shirts had been produced. Esther, through correspondence, was also instrumental in persuading women in other Pennsylvania communities, in Trenton, New Jersey, and in Maryland to undertake the same charitable actions as did the Philadelphia women. Esther undoubtedly had a role in writing *The Sentiments of an American Woman*, a broadside published in Philadelphia on 10 January 1780, which in appealing for women's war support declared that women were the equals of men in patriotism.

In January 1780 Esther recovered from the smallpox. She gave birth to George Washington Reed in May. General Washington congratulated Esther for naming "the young Christian" after himself. Martha Washington stayed with the Reeds for a week in June, and for the rest of the summer while Joseph Reed was in the field as a militia commander, Esther and her children resided at Laurel Hill. Shortly after her return to Philadelphia, Esther died there, having been ill for a short time with dysentery. Reed's sister came to live with him and help raise the five children. Sarah Franklin Bache, Benjamin Franklin's daughter, assumed the leadership of the women's relief work in Philadelphia.

An obituary praised Esther De Berdt Reed both for promoting a network of women's relief groups and for preparing "with her own hands many of those garments destined for the soldiery . . . imposing on herself too great a part of the task," thus impairing her health. Esther "is received into the paradise of female patriotism with supereminent distinction. . . . She sacrificed her ease, her health, and it may be her life, for her country." Esther De Berdt Reed's leadership of women for soldiers' relief helped to pave the way for future women's aid and reform groups and their greater involvement in public life in general.

• The Joseph Reed Papers at the New-York Historical Society include the Esther De Berdt Reed–Joseph Reed letters and subscription lists of the Philadelphia women's soldiers' relief committee. William B. Reed, ed., *Life and Correspondence of Joseph Reed*, vol. 2 (1847), contains Esther De Berdt's letters to her husband, Washington, Lafayette, and Esther Cox. William B. Reed, *The Life of Esther De Berdt Afterwards Esther Reed of Pennsylvania* (1853), provides a sketch of Reed's life and a large number of her letters. For information on Reed's father but with none of her correspondence, see *Letters of Dennys De Berdt, 1757–1770*, ed. Albert Matthews (1911). A thorough treatment of Reed's life, post 1763, is found in John F. Roche, *Joseph Reed: A Moderate in the American Revolution* (1957). Elizabeth F. Ellet, *The Eminent and Heroic Women of America* (1873; repr. 1974), offers a brief sketch, and Linda K. Kerber, *Women of the Republic: Intellect and Ideology in Revolutionary America* (1980), places Reed's work in the context of revolutionary development relating to women. John R. Alden, *Stephen Sayre: American Revolutionary Adventurer* (1983), notes the triangular social relationship in England of Sayre, Joseph Reed, and Esther De Berdt Reed. An obituary is in the *Pennsylvania Gazette and Weekly Advertiser*, 27 Sept. 1780.

HARRY M. WARD

REED, Henry Hope (11 July 1808–27 Sept. 1854), lawyer, educator, and litterateur, was born in Philadelphia, the son of Joseph Reed and Maria Ellis Watmough. His father was a lawyer, and his brother, William Bradford Reed, was to become a distinguished lawyer, politician, and statesman. In 1823, at age fifteen, Henry Reed entered the sophomore class at the University of Pennsylvania. He graduated with honors in 1825 and was the Latin salutatorian. He studied law with his uncle John Sergeant (1779–1852), a U.S. congressman and famed constitutional lawyer, and was admitted to the Pennsylvania bar in 1829.

Finding the practice of law unpleasant, Reed accepted an assistant professorship in English literature at the University of Pennsylvania in 1831. Shortly thereafter he became a professor of moral philosophy but was greatly disappointed when he was passed over for promotion. In 1834 he married Elizabeth White Bronson. To this union, six children were born, three of whom died in infancy. In 1835 he became a professor of rhetoric and English literature, a position that he held with distinction until his death.

During his tenure as professor, Reed devoted much of his life to literary editing. His passion for the poetry of William Wordsworth, who was not widely appreciated in the United States at the time, led him to edit the *Complete Works of William Wordsworth* (1837; rev. 1851), which became the standard American edition of Wordsworth and underwent many printings. Reed most appreciated Wordsworth's love of the beauty of natural objects, his moral and religious sentiments, and his respect for the established church. Reed's edition led to a correspondence and friendship with Wordsworth until the latter's death in 1850. Chiefly because of the edition's success Reed was elected a member of the American Philosophical Society in 1838. Wordsworth's leading advocate in the United States, Reed kept the poet before the American public when he next edited *Poems from the Poetical Works of William Wordsworth* (1841), a collection of fifty-one of Wordsworth's favorite poems. Taking a respite from Wordsworth, Reed edited the works of several other English writers, including Thomas Gray's *Poetical Works of Thomas Gray* (1851). Between 1841 and 1850 Reed delivered four series of lectures on British literature which his brother, William Bradford, published posthumously as a memorial to him. These lectures became popular in the United States and Great Britain. He returned to his beloved Wordsworth, who was lately deceased, by directing the publication of an annotated, two-volume edition of Christopher Wordsworth's *Memoirs of William Wordsworth, Poet Laureate, D.C.L.* (1851).

When the chair of moral philosophy at the University of Pennsylvania became vacant in 1854, Reed applied for the position, but for some reason never explained to him, he was rejected for the second time. To deal with his disappointment, he requested and was granted a leave of absence to visit Great Britain and the Continent. Reed sailed from New York on 3 May 1854 aboard the *Asia*. His wife being ill, he was accompanied by his sister-in-law, Anne Emily Bronson. On his European tour, Reed wrote his wife almost daily, serial letters recounting his experiences. These letters reveal him to be a man of great erudition, culture, and deep devotion to his family and the Episcopal faith. The party arrived in Liverpool on 14 May and at Rydal Mount on 17 May. Mary Wordsworth, the poet's widow, entertained them graciously and introduced them to other members of the Wordsworth, Samuel Taylor Coleridge, and Robert Southey families, who in turn gave them entrées to other distinguished literati, savants, and clerics. Following a constant flurry of sight-seeing and social activities in England, they toured Scotland and the Continent. They were thrilled by the Old World castles, cathedrals, palaces, gardens, museums, and galleries, but these sights paled in comparison with the stimulating society that they had experienced in England. Upon returning to England, they spent a few more weeks sight-seeing before they sailed from Liverpool for the United States aboard the steamer *Arctic* on 20 September. A week out of Liverpool the *Arctic* was rammed by a French ship in the dense fog, and Reed and Bronson were among the more than three hundred people drowned in the accident.

Reed was highly respected as a university professor and as a lay figure in the Episcopal church, but his principal legacy was in popularizing the poet Wordsworth. No American enhanced Wordsworth's literary reputation on this side of the Atlantic more than Reed. As Wordsworth's American editor, he produced the first authorized and the best edition of the poet's poems, advised him on financial and copyright matters, and from time to time gave the poet advice on the choice and method of treatment of certain subject matter, which he gladly accepted.

• Most of the manuscript letters by and to Reed are in the Wordsworth Collection in the Olin Library at Cornell University; there is a significant number of letters in the Van Pelt Library at the University of Pennsylvania and in the Historical Society of Pennsylvania. The manuscripts of Reed's lectures, which William Bradford Reed edited, are in the Van Pelt Library.

Other books by Reed include *Lectures on English Literature, from Chaucer to Tennyson*, edited with a preface by William Bradford Reed (1855); *Lectures on English History and Tragic Poetry as Illustrated by Shakespeare*, edited with a preface by William Bradford Reed (1855); *Two Lectures on the History of the American Union*, edited with an introductory notice by William Bradford Reed (1856); and *Lectures on the British Poets*, edited with a preface by William Bradford Reed (2 vols., 1857). Three significant articles by Reed are "Life of Joseph Reed," in *The Library of American Biography*, ed. Jared Sparks, 2d ser., vol. 8 (1846); "William Wordsworth," *New York Review* 4 (Jan. 1839): 1–70; and "A Memorial to Wordsworth," *Literary World* 12 (25 June 1853): 512–13.

The best biography of Henry Hope Reed is by Leslie Nathan Broughton in his introduction to *Wordsworth and Reed: The Poet's Correspondence with his American Editor: 1836–1850, and Henry Reed's Account of his Reception at Rydal Mount, London, and Elsewhere in 1854*, ed. Broughton, Cornell Studies in English, vol. 21 (1933). Also useful in filling out Reed's life is Broughton, ed., *Sara Coleridge and Henry Reed* (1937). Useful essays that deal principally with Reed's life are his obituary by John Frazer, *Proceedings of the American Philosophical Society* 6 (Jan.–Apr. 1855): 87–91; and E. D. Mackerness, "Wordsworth and his American Editor," *Queen's Quarterly* 67 (Spring 1960): 93–104.

GUY R. WOODALL

REED, James Alexander (9 Nov. 1861–8 Sept. 1944), U.S. senator and lawyer, was born in Richland County, Ohio, the son of John A. Reed and Nancy Crawford, farmers. The family moved to Iowa when Reed was three, and he grew up on a farm outside of Cedar Rapids in Linn County. After his father died in 1870, Reed had to go to work on the farm full time, attending rural schools during the winter. At age eighteen, he entered politics as head of the Democratic County Committee in heavily Republican Linn County. He attended Coe Collegiate Institute, taking special courses, and read for the law in Cedar Rapids, joining the Iowa bar in 1885. He married Lura M. Olmsted Mansfield in 1887 and took his new bride to Kansas City, Missouri. The couple had no children.

Reed developed a lucrative law practice and became a speaker and organizer for the Pendergast "Goat" Democratic party faction in Kansas City and surrounding Jackson County. In 1897 he accepted a two-year appointment as county counselor, defeating every suit brought against the county. For two years, beginning in 1898, he held his first elected office as prosecuting attorney of Jackson County, winning 285 of the 287 cases that he considered major criminal cases. In 1900, running on a "reform" ticket, he won a two-year term as mayor of Kansas City, the first Pendergast-backed candidate to triumph citywide. He gained a second term in 1902, but his administration accomplished little beyond minor streamlining of the city government. In retrospect, his most important action

was naming 28-year-old Thomas J. Pendergast, the future notorious boss of Kansas City, as street commissioner. Reed spent most of his time as mayor fighting with the cumbersome two-house city council. "I set out to stop some of the graft and the council opposed me," he said. "They wouldn't confirm my appointments. . . . We had two years of hell."

Reed declined to stand for a third term in 1904. He made an aborted run for governor of Missouri, dropping out early after losing a series of county primary conventions to eventual winner Joseph Folk of St. Louis. For the next six years Reed practiced law and kept himself in the public eye. He spoke throughout Missouri for the Democratic party, acquiring a reputation as a colorful, effective, vindictive, and combative orator. He burst on the national scene in 1910, defeating David Francis of St. Louis in the last legislative election in Missouri for the U.S. Senate, serving continuously in that body from 1911 until 1929. He displayed a high degree of independence, frequently breaking party discipline. He became a bitter foe of President Woodrow Wilson after first supporting his New Freedom domestic agenda, his 1914 military intervention in Mexico, and his foreign policy in the complex situation that led to U.S. entry into World War I. Reed voted for the declaration of war against Germany in 1917 but bitterly criticized food controls and the use overseas of conscripted troops.

Reed took an uncompromising stand against postwar involvement in European affairs, opposing the Versailles treaty and helping to block U.S. participation in the League of Nations. He was a leading member in the Senate of the antileague "Irreconcilables," sometimes called the "Battalion of Death." He denounced Wilson for allegedly supporting "British statesmanship," believing the president had committed "high treason." Reed opposed the unsuccessful proleague Democratic presidential nominee James Cox in 1920, favored the early recall of troops from Germany, railed at the World Court as a creature of the league, denounced proposed war debt settlements, and inveighed against the Republican-supported 1921 Washington Conference on arms limitations. It was little wonder that Wilson bitterly called him "a discredit to the party to which he pretends to belong."

Reed survived opposition from Missouri Wilsonian Democrats in 1922 to win a 44,000-vote primary victory over the former president's handpicked candidate, Breckenridge Long. Reed went on to win the general election, helped by a large vote from Republicans supporting his opposition to Prohibition. Continuing his individualistic ways, he attacked Ku Klux Klan members, anti-Semites, advocates of suffrage for women, proposals for a child labor amendment, protective tariff measures, Republican candidates' use of illegal campaign funds, sugar industry transgressions, and members of the Anti-Saloon League. In 1925 he denounced Washington insiders, saying, "Truth to tell, Washington has become the universal mecca of human freaks."

Reed declined to stand for reelection to the Senate in 1928, making an unsuccessful presidential bid. He ran for the office again in 1932 as the favorite son of a Missouri delegation headed by Thomas Joseph Pendergast, who double-crossed him by secretly backing Franklin D. Roosevelt. Reed returned to the practice of law in Kansas City. A year after the 12 August 1932 death of his first wife, on 13 December 1933 he married Nell Quinlan Donnelly, a Kansas City civic leader and garment manufacturer. They adopted one child. Following the marriage, Reed defended his wife against antiunion charges in a bitter dispute with the International Ladies Garment Worker's Union.

Reed opposed Roosevelt's New Deal, which he considered "socialistic." In 1936 he organized the National Jeffersonian Democrats and campaigned for the unsuccessful Republican candidate Alfred M. Landon. Reed backed Republican Wendell L. Willkie in 1940, when Roosevelt ran for a third term. Prior to the 1944 presidential election, he chaired the Committee on Resolutions of an anti-Roosevelt organization, the American Democratic Committee. Reed died at his summer estate near Fairview, Michigan.

Reed, an imposing figure in his prime known as the "Old Roman," thrived on controversy. He is perhaps best remembered as a foe of the covenant of the League of Nations. In 1929 he stated his philosophy of life in an off the record comment: "No man can amount to anything in this world when he is afraid that somebody else will take his bread and butter away from him. Let him think for himself instead of taking temporary and uninformed opinion, let him have convictions of his own and follow them in spite of every man in the country if necessary."

• The James A. Reed Papers are in the Joint Western Manuscript Collection of the University of Missouri and the State Historical Society of Missouri, Kansas City. Reed wrote "The Pestilence of Fanaticism," *American Mercury*, May 1925, pp. 1–7. See Lee Meriwether, *Jim Reed, "Senatorial Immortal"* (1948); Franklin D. Mitchell, *Embattled Democracy: Missouri Democratic Politics, 1919–1932* (1968); Oswald Garrison Villard, *Prophets, True and False* (1928); William M. Redding, *Tom's Town: Kansas City and the Pendergast Legend* (1947); Lyle Dorsett, *The Pendergast Machine* (1968); and Charles G. Ross, "Reed of Missouri," *Scribners*, Feb. 1928, pp. 151–62; Jack M. Bain, "A Rhetorical Criticism of the Speeches of James A. Reed" (Ph.D. diss., Univ. of Missouri, 1953); and Jan E. Hults, "The Senatorial Career of James Alexander Reed" (Ph.D. diss., Univ. of Kansas, 1987). Obituaries are in the *New York Times* and the *Kansas City Times*, 9 Sept. 1944.

LAWRENCE H. LARSEN

REED, Jimmy (6 Sept. 1925–29 Aug. 1976), blues musician, was born Mathis James Reed in Dunleith, Mississippi, the son of Joseph Reed and Virginia Ross, farmers. One of ten children, young Jimmy did his earliest singing in a local Baptist church. At age ten Jimmy and a playmate, Eddie Taylor, began trying to learn guitar, Taylor with greater success.

In 1939 Jimmy dropped out of school and went to live with a brother in Duncan, Mississippi, where he took a job doing farm work. He sang in a Baptist gospel group in Meltonia but by age sixteen was developing an interest in blues, sparked in part by "King Biscuit Time," a daily radio program featuring blues harmonica player Sonny Boy Williamson No. 2.

In 1944, after being sent to live with family members in Chicago for a few years, Reed was drafted and served in the navy—a hitch that was shortened by health problems and alcohol abuse. Discharged in 1945, Reed returned to his parents' home in Dunleith, where he resumed farming. That same year he married Mary Lee Davis of Lambert, Mississippi; they had nine children.

In 1948 Reed returned to Chicago, joining two brothers and a sister. He stayed in Chicago—later joined by his wife—and found employment as a foundry worker in Gary, Indiana. He revived his interest in music, purchasing a secondhand guitar and working informally with Gary-based blues artists Albert King and husband-and-wife team John and Grace Brim. He also played as a street musician—work that took him to Chicago's Maxwell Street market district (home to many formal and informal blues bands and performers), where he happened to run across his childhood partner Eddie Taylor, who by this time had become an accomplished guitarist and blues artist. Renewing their friendship, the two played together and separately in various bands.

By 1953 Reed and Taylor were confident enough to put together a demonstration record, which they brought to Chess Records in Chicago. Though rejected by Chess, Reed came to the attention of two Gary record store owners, Vivian Carter and Jimmy Bracken, who were looking for talent to launch their Vee Jay record label. In Chicago on 29 and 30 December 1953, Reed's band recorded eight songs for Vee Jay, later to become the country's most successful black-owned record company. The first two songs issued, however, came out on the Chance label, having been leased to Chance's owner to raise needed cash for Vee Jay. The Chance single was not a commercial success, and Reed returned to nonmusical work in the Chicago stockyards. Within the next year, however, he heard a radio playing "You Don't Have to Go," another one of his songs from the December 1953 session. The song, issued on Vee Jay, was a hit.

Reed quit the stockyards to work exclusively in music, beginning the most productive decade of his career, both in numbers of records and artistic success. In the care of a manager, Al Smith, who joined him in 1958 at the behest of Vee Jay, Reed toured extensively with his son James, Jr., who began playing bass at age nine, and Taylor, picking up local musicians as needed or working with house bands. Like fellow blues/rock stars Bo Diddley and Chuck Berry, he played more for white than black audiences, and his records sold well in both markets. During twelve years with Vee Jay, Reed averaged between two and five recording sessions per year, producing an impressive string of classic recordings, among them "Ain't That Loving You Baby," "Honest I Do," "Caress Me Baby," "Take Out Some Insurance," "Baby What You Want Me to Do," "Hush Hush," "Big Boss Man," and "Bright Lights, Big City." On most of these, Reed employed a technique long popular with country blues artists, using a special brace to hold a harmonica so he could play both it and a guitar simultaneously.

Having recorded the first Vee Jay record, Reed stayed with the company until it filed for bankruptcy in 1966. Then, following a stint with Chicago's Exodus Records, he signed with Al Smith's ABC Bluesway.

At his peak, Reed was pulling in several thousand dollars a week, but alcoholism kept him from gaining financial security. Taylor recalled, "From 1956 on, it was pretty hard, because you . . . [c]ouldn't get him to lay off the bottle. . . . You couldn't take your eyes off Jimmy. If you take your eyes off him, Jimmy's got a fifth of whiskey."

Starting in 1957 Reed suffered from epilepsy, exacerbated by his continuous drinking. By 1969 his health had failed to the point where he had to be hospitalized. He dropped out of the public eye for more than four years, and many fans thought that he had died. In 1974 and 1975 he attempted a comeback but was hounded by his reputation as a no-show and a drunk. His years of self-destructive behavior caught up with him in 1976, when he died in Chicago from respiratory failure during a seizure.

Although functionally illiterate, Reed had a gift for catchy song compositions. Some of his songs became repertoire staples not just in blues but in rock music and country and western as well, and were recorded by artists such as the Rolling Stones, Bobby Gentry, and Elvis Presley. His wife, an accomplished songwriter in her own right, often sang with him on recordings and road tours. "Mama," as she was called, was very much a part of the distinctive Jimmy Reed sound.

Marked by lazy, insinuating vocals, rudimentary guitar boogies, and high-pitched harmonica counterpoints, Reed's music was pleasantly primal, well suited to popular dances of the day, and remarkably enduring. During Reed's musical tenure, fourteen of his records made the rhythm-and-blues charts and eleven made the pop charts, establishing him as the major crossover artist of his time. He outsold all blues artists save B. B. King.

He was inducted into the Blues Foundation's Hall of Fame in 1980 and into the Rock and Roll Hall of Fame in 1991.

• For discographical information, see Mike Leadbitter and Neil Slaven, *Blues Records 1943–1970*, vol. 2 (1994). For more detailed information and interviews with Reed and people who knew him, see "The Jimmy Reed Story," *Living Blues*, no. 21 (May–June 1975): 14–41. For more on Vee Jay records, see Robert Pruter, *Chicago Soul* (1991). An obituary is in *Living Blues*, no. 29 (Sept.–Oct. 1979).

BILL MCCULLOCH
BARRY LEE PEARSON

REED, John (22 Oct. 1887–17 Oct. 1920), journalist and revolutionary, was born John Silas Reed in Portland, Oregon, the son of Charles Jerome Reed, a supervisor in the sale of farm equipment and later a U.S. marshal, and Margaret Green, the daughter of a wealthy capitalist. Sickened by kidney troubles, young Reed was sheltered by his mother. Having only his brother Harry as a playmate, Reed read fantasy and history books and developed an active imagination. He was healthy enough by age twelve to attend the prestigious Portland Academy, where he was a shy, mediocre student. In 1904 he enrolled in Morristown, a college preparatory school in New Jersey. There, through his pranks and charm, he became a popular rebel, writing short stories, poems, and essays for the school literary magazine.

Entering Harvard in 1906, Reed expected to take the school by storm. But its size and his western origins (in a bastion of rich eastern families) thwarted him. Lonely, he began submitting articles and poems first to the *Harvard Lampoon*, then to the *Harvard Monthly*. Joining any club that would accept him, Reed slowly developed friendships and became a campus leader. Already a prolific writer when he graduated in 1910, Reed aimed to become a journalist but knew he needed to experience more of life.

After a trip to Europe, for which he earned passage by working on a freighter, Reed moved to New York City's Greenwich Village, a magnet to writers, freethinkers, and radicals of the day. The bohemians, as they were called, included birth control activist Margaret Sanger, journalist Lincoln Steffens, and anarchist Emma Goldman. By mid-1911 Steffens, a friend of Reed's father, had found the aspiring writer a low-paying job correcting proof on the muckraking *American Magazine*. To supplement his income, Reed sold satires, factual reporting, and essays to magazines such as *Collier's* and *Trend*. In November two articles by him appeared in the *American*. Over the next year, more of his work was accepted for publication, but an article about the Harvard administration's attempt to squelch an activist mood on campus was rejected by the *American* because of its antiestablishment leanings. The rebuff forever changed Reed's attitude toward journalism; he began to realize how spineless publications could be when faced with publishing anything against the norm.

In July 1912 Reed's father died. While in Portland attending the funeral, he began writing *The Day in Bohemia; or, Life among the Artists*, a long satirical poem about life in Greenwich Village, which Reed published privately in 1913 and sold to friends for $1 a copy. In December 1912 Reed found a journalistic home when he was named an editor at *The Masses*, a radical magazine dedicated to publishing "free and spirited expressions of every kind." Appearing regularly in its pages were poetry, essays, and stories by gifted opponents of conventional thinking such as Bertrand Russell, Upton Sinclair, and William Carlos Williams.

His activist spirit coming alive, Reed went to Paterson, New Jersey, in the spring of 1913 to publicize the plight of silk workers who, having gone on strike for an eight-hour workday, were arrested and beaten by city authorities. Always seeking "life experience," Reed got himself arrested but was released four days later. In June Reed and other Greenwich Villagers staged a pageant at Madison Square Garden that portrayed the striking workers' clash with the police. Reed fell in love with fellow pageant organizer Mabel Dodge, whose gatherings for food, drink, and intellectual discussion attracted most of bohemia.

Late in 1913 Reed set out to cover the raging Mexican Revolution for *Metropolitan Magazine* and the *New York World*. He interviewed rebel leader Pancho Villa at his headquarters in Chihuahua. Eager to get closer to the fighting, Reed traveled south to ride with La Tropa, a group of peasant soldiers loyal to Villa, and witnessed their massacre by the federal troops. The resulting articles Reed wrote were widely read and made the American public, previously distrustful of Villa, more sympathetic to the revolution and its leader. Reed collected his articles in *Insurgent Mexico* (1914), a fast-paced book that was criticized as biased toward Villa and yet sold well, catapulting Reed into celebrity.

With the outbreak of World War I in August 1914 the *Metropolitan* sent Reed, a pacifist, to report from the western front. Revolted by the bloodshed, which he felt was motivated by greed, Reed proclaimed in an article for *The Masses*, "This is not Our War" ("The Traders' War," Sept. 1914, pp. 16–17). His attempts to reach the front in France proved futile, however, and his reportage from this period was, by his own admission, poor. After a brief return to Greenwich Village, Reed accepted another assignment from the *Metropolitan* in March 1915. Accompanied by illustrator Boardman Robinson, he toured Greece and Serbia and traveled through Russia in further attempts to reach the front lines. In Petrograd Reed saw pervasive corruption but was impressed by the friendliness and dignity of the Russian people. In September Reed came back to the United States and drew on his articles to produce *The War in Eastern Europe*, published in April 1916 with illustrations by Robinson. Reviews of his straightforward account were favorable, but sales were lacking.

During a visit to Portland, Reed had met Louise Bryant, an aspiring journalist who became the great love of his life. On New Year's Eve 1915 she left her husband, a dentist, to move into Reed's Washington Square apartment. (His on-again, off-again relationship with Dodge had ended earlier that year.) Reed and Bryant spent the summer of 1916 in Provincetown, Massachusetts, where they and playwrights Eugene O'Neill and George Cram Cook founded the Provincetown Players. As an ensemble creating its own repertoire, the Players presaged much of modern American drama. In November, before undergoing surgery to remove a kidney, Reed, fearing the worst, married Bryant in order to make her his legal heir.

They had no children, and theirs remained an "open" marriage.

In the spring of 1917 the *Metropolitan* dropped Reed because his articles vehemently denounced U.S. entry into World War I. In the national surge of patriotism, journalists opposing the war found it nearly impossible to get work. Reed finally was hired by the *New York Mail*, and he also continued to write for *The Masses*, whose publication was being hampered by charges that it was violating the Espionage Act of 1917. Disheartened by the actions of his own government, Reed focused on the revolution in Russia that had begun in March.

Sailing to Russia in August, Reed and Bryant's timing was fortuitous, and they immediately entered a whirlwind of events. In their interview of the leader of the provisional government, Alexander Kerensky, they found in him "no real fixity of purpose—as the leader of the Russian Revolution should have" (Reed, "Red Russia—Kerensky," *The Liberator*, Apr. 1918, pp. 18–19). They were a regular presence at the Smolny Institute, the headquarters of the Petrograd Soviet and the Central Committee of the All-Russian Congress of Soviets. A few days before the Bolshevik capture of the Winter Palace, they were able to interview Leon Trotsky, the president of the Petrograd Soviet. Reed himself joined the Bureau of International Revolutionary Propaganda, for which he compiled prorevolutionary publications for delivery to German troops. In January 1918 he met Lenin and addressed the Third Congress of Soviets as an example of an American sympathetic to the Bolshevik cause. On his way home in February 1918 Reed was detained in Norway at the request of the U.S. government (Bryant had returned in January). Although he was issued a visa in April, his papers were seized on his return to the United States.

In late 1917 *The Masses* had been forced out of business (but soon resurfaced as the tamer *Liberator*), and its editors were indicted for conspiracy to obstruct the draft. Reed was arraigned the day after his return home. Like the trials of most of the other editors, Reed's ended in a hung jury. Unable to publish, both because of the seizure of his papers and because of his views on the war, Reed turned to the lecture circuit, where he argued for U.S. recognition of the Bolsheviks and predicted all capitalist countries would eventually become socialist. He was arrested in Philadelphia, Detroit, and New York City, variously for inciting to riot and sedition. At the second *Masses* trial, in September 1918, its editors were accused of, among other charges, impeding the armed forces' recruiting efforts. Reed was singled out for an article on soldier insanity with the headline "Knit a Strait-Jacket for Your Soldier Boy." Again the trial ended in a hung jury. In November Reed's papers were released, and he began work on *Ten Days That Shook the World*, a dramatic, carefully documented, but partisan portrayal of the Russian revolution. Published in March 1919, *Ten Days* sold well (5,000 copies in three months) and won praise from both radical and mainstream reviewers. An eyewitness account, the book is written as a narrative that intersperses poetic prose with reproductions of official documents, bulletins and flyers, and meeting announcements. Reed's sympathy for the Bolsheviks is manifest throughout the work. On seeing a mass funeral in Moscow for dead revolutionaries that was devoid of priests, sacraments, and prayers, Reed observes "that the devout Russian people no longer needed priests to pray them into heaven. On earth they were building a kingdom more bright than any heaven had to offer, and for which it was a glory to die" (*Collected Works*, p. 808).

By early 1919 Reed had turned his attention to what he believed to be the coming revolution in the United States. Involved in the left wing of the Socialist party, he began editing the *New York Communist* in April and submitted articles to *Revolutionary Age* that were meant to prepare workers for the second American revolution. In August Reed helped found the Communist Labor party (CLP) and was appointed to be the liaison between the party and the Communist International (Comintern). He also began editing the *Voice of Labor*, the party's journal.

In September the CLP sent Reed to Russia to gain recognition for the party from Comintern. On his arrival, he found a country tortured by famine and disease. He met with Lenin, who agreed to write an introduction for a new edition of *Ten Days*. During his visit he learned of his indictment in the United States for criminal anarchy as a Socialist party activist. In February he departed from Petrograd, apparently carrying jewels and gold worth more than $1 million supplied by Comintern to support the American Communist party, but was detained in Finland. Convicted of smuggling, he was ignored by U.S. diplomats and held until June. In failing health and aware of the dangers of returning to the United States, Reed went back to Russia. Bryant joined him in September, but their reunion was short lived. Reed died of typhus in Moscow and was honored with burial within the grounds of the Kremlin.

Reed was a paradox. Though he was a serious journalist, many of his contemporaries believed that he was unfocused and that the "central passion of his life [was] an inordinate desire to be arrested" (Walter Lippmann, "Legendary John Reed," *New Republic*, 26 Dec. 1914). Raised in privileged circumstances, he spent his life fighting for workers' rights. While thousands of Russians were dying of starvation and disease in the winter of 1918–1919, Reed was transporting a fortune to the United States to fortify the American Communist party. He did not live long enough to comprehend the nature of the revolution he triumphed, and he could not have foretold its course in the age of Stalin. The U.S. government viewed Reed as a traitor, but his untimely death elevated him to hero status among nonconformists and left-wing activists. During the 1920s and 1930s John Reed clubs were formed to promote his beliefs, and more than sixty years after Reed's death the film *Reds* (1981), directed by Hollywood star Warren Beatty, intensely ro-

manticized his life, winning commercial success in the capitalistic America that Reed despised. Whether viewed as turncoat or martyr, he was a powerfully articulate witness to a tumultuous era.

• The John Reed Papers, Houghton Library, Harvard University, is the largest collection of Reed's papers. Information on Reed can also be found in the Granville Hicks Papers, George Arents Research Library, Syracuse University, and in the Lincoln Steffens Papers at Columbia University. Reed's autobiographical essay, "Almost Thirty," written in 1917, was published in condensed form in the *New Republic*, 15 Apr. 1936, pp. 267–70. The Modern Library published *The Collected Works of John Reed* (1995), which includes *Insurgent Mexico*, *The War in Eastern Europe*, and *Ten Days That Shook the World* in their entirety. The earliest biography is Granville Hicks, *John Reed: The Making of a Revolutionary* (1936). A modern biography is Robert Rosenstone, *Romantic Revolutionary* (1975). For information on Reed and Bryant's relationship, see Barbara Gelb, *So Short a Time: A Biography of John Reed and Louise Bryant* (1973), and Mary V. Dearborn, *Queen of Bohemia: The Life of Louise Bryant* (1996). Louise Bryant published "Last Days with John Reed" in *The Liberator*, Feb. 1921, pp. 11–14, and an obituary is in the *New York Times*, 19 Oct. 1920.

STACEY HAMILTON

REED, Joseph (27 Aug. 1741–5 Mar. 1785), lawyer, soldier, and statesman, was born in Trenton, New Jersey, the son of Andrew Reed, a minor officeholder and merchant, and Theodosia Bowes. Following the family's move to Philadelphia, Reed was enrolled in Francis Alison's Academy of Philadelphia in 1751. Two years later, following the death of Reed's mother, the family returned to Trenton, where Reed attended the College of New Jersey (later Princeton University). For three years following his graduation on 28 October 1757, he studied law at Princeton under the direction of Richard Stockton and worked toward an M.A., which was granted in September 1760. He passed the bar in New Jersey in May 1763 but left in October of that year for London. On 16 December he enrolled at the Middle Temple and studied law for fifteen months.

Through Dennys De Berdt, London agent for his father's mercantile firm, Reed met De Berdt's daughter Esther. Despite opposition from Esther's parents, Reed proposed marriage in September 1764. Ordered to end the relationship, the two nevertheless became informally engaged prior to Reed's departure for Philadelphia in March 1765.

Returning to Trenton to find his father bankrupt, Reed began his law practice in Huntingdon County in the spring of 1765 and assumed responsibility for his family's welfare. Though his practice expanded quickly, Reed was torn between caring for his family and returning to London. His dilemma was resolved in 1767 when he was named deputy secretary of New Jersey and clerk of the council. He was also named assistant to De Berdt, who was colonial agent for Massachusetts. Reed's offices gave him the means to support his family and to return to London to marry Esther De Berdt in 1770.

The couple settled in Philadelphia in December 1770. Reed's law practice there succeeded from the beginning, and he was quickly recognized as one of the more talented members of an outstanding bar. His legal notes later contributed to Alexander J. Dallas's *Reports of Cases Ruled and Adjudged in the Courts of Pennsylvania* (1790). By 1780, the father of four children and a member of the Second Presbyterian Church, Reed had acquired two slaves, become a speculator in land, and was elected to the American Philosophical Society.

Drawn into the imperial dispute, between December 1773 and February 1775 Reed exchanged a dozen letters with Lord Dartmouth, secretary of state for the American colonies. Reed sought to persuade British authorities not to employ force against the colonies and asserted that traditional loyalties would produce a favorable colonial response should their grievances be adequately redressed. Characterizing his letters as "disinterested endeavours to serve both the Mother Country and the Colonies," he emphasized that reconciliation should be energetically and creatively pursued by both sides.

Reed was appointed to the Philadelphia Committee of Correspondence in November 1774 and served as president of Pennsylvania's second Provincial Congress (1775). In January 1776 he was elected to the Pennsylvania Assembly and a month later to the committee of inspection and observation. Additionally, he was appointed secretary to George Washington when Washington became commander in chief of the American army. Reed later was named adjutant general of the Continental army with a rank of colonel. He assumed that post in June 1776.

Persuaded that America's Declaration of Independence was precipitous, that reconciliation was still possible, and that allies were needed if reconciliation failed, Reed nonetheless threw himself into military affairs, subsequently serving creditably at the battles of Long Island, Trenton, Princeton, Brandywine, Germantown, and Monmouth. He successfully defused a situation potentially damaging to his reputation when in 1778 he alerted Congress and the public to attempts by the British Parliament's Carlisle peace commission to bribe him into supporting its scheme for reconciliation. His version of these events appeared in his *Remarks on Governor Johnstone's Speech in Parliament* (1779).

On 20 March 1777 Reed was tendered the chief justiceship of Pennsylvania. Believing that he would be named a brigadier general and given command of the American cavalry, he delayed accepting. Piqued when on 12 May Congress promoted him to brigadier general but failed to give him the cavalry assignment, Reed rejected the congressional offer. Still, advised by friends against either lending his name to the new state government or serving under it, he hesitated to take the chief justice post. He procrastinated until 23 July before rejecting the position. Reed did agree to serve in Congress when chosen for that post in September 1777 but remained only until 12 October. During his tenure he signed the Articles of Confederation for Pennsylvania.

Despite continuing reservations regarding the radically democratic state constitution, in August 1778 Reed agreed to assist in prosecuting treason cases. Throughout the summer he had become increasingly troubled by the willingness of the Republicans, the political party dedicated to destroying the state constitution, to welcome to their ranks individuals who had openly collaborated with the British during the occupation of Philadelphia. Reed believed that Republicans were more interested in strengthening their political coalition in order to subvert the state government than in protecting the interests of America. When the constitutionalist majority in the Pennsylvania Assembly voted to employ "able Council" to assist in the prosecution of those who had worked closely with the British, the council offered Reed the position at a salary of £2,000 a year. He accepted on 2 September. With Attorney General Jonathan Dickinson Sergeant ill, Reed directed many of the twenty-three trials during the fall session of the court of oyer and terminer in Philadelphia, including those in which Quakers Abraham Carlisle and John Roberts were convicted.

Reed also was elected to the state supreme executive council on 24 November 1778. Following an understanding with Republicans that he would not actively oppose a plebiscite on the question of a convention to amend the constitution, he was elected president of the supreme executive council on 1 December. He served ably in that capacity until 1781. Though almost congenitally conciliatory he quarreled on occasion with both conservatives and radicals and with his own supreme court over its judicial policies and pronouncements. Reed frequently was unhappy that Republicans appeared to put more energy into bringing down the state government than in defeating the British and that they opposed policies and practices (such as price controls on bread and other necessities) he deemed in the interest of the general population. He fumed against the radicals' strategy of employing mob action. He also was frustrated by the constitutionalist-created supreme court's willingness to grant writs of habeas corpus to suspected Tories and by its policy of holding the state to strict standards of proof in treason cases, a strategy that led to more acquittals than convictions.

Following his presidency, Reed made an unsuccessful effort to gain election to the Pennsylvania Assembly. An attempt in 1782 to name him chief justice of Pennsylvania failed. In that same year, Reed was among those who successfully argued Pennsylvania claims on the Wyoming Valley, against those of Connecticut, before a court empowered by Congress to settle that dispute. Also in 1782 he became embroiled in a bitter public contest with John Cadwalader, a brigadier general in the Pennsylvania militia, over a charge that he had contemplated abandoning the Revolution in 1776. Most of Reed's contemporaries did not find Cadwalader's case persuasive; nor have later historians.

Although Reed was elected to a congressional seat in 1784, he turned down the chance to serve. Throughout that year, his health, which was often poor, deteriorated rapidly. By January 1785 he was seriously ill, suffering from a partial paralysis of his limbs and a loss of speech. He died at his Philadelphia home.

Reed was a steady, valuable, and moderate contributor to the American cause. He distinguished himself as a soldier. As adjutant general of the Continental army he relieved an overworked Washington by ably assuming many of the commander in chief's administrative burdens. As a member of Congress he used his position as chairman of the Committee on the Reorganization of the Army to bring about reforms urged by Washington. Though initially reluctant to join the movement toward independence, as president of the supreme executive council he became "the standard-bearer of the democratic forces in Pennsylvania which effected the most sweeping internal revolution the War for Independence produced" (Roche, p. 220). He worked to curb the more fiery demands of the state's radicals and to moderate the anti-democratic policies of the Republicans. As a result, his actions were interpreted as coolness to the Revolution by some and as too extreme by others.

• The Joseph Reed Papers are located in the New-York Historical Society. Additional Reed papers can be found in the John Cadwalader Papers, especially vol. 2, and in the Etting Collection, both in the Historical Society of Pennsylvania, and in the Bancroft manuscripts, New York Public Library. Relevant published materials appear in the *Pennsylvania Archives* (9 ser., 138 vols., 1852–1949), especially ser. 1, vols. 3–11, and ser. 2, vol. 3; and in *The Minutes of the Provincial Council of Pennsylvania* (16 vols., 1851–1853). His published works also include *My Late Engagement of a Public Nature . . .* (1781), *Remarks on a Late Publication in the Independent Gazetteer . . .* (1783), and "General Joseph Reed's 'Narrative' of the Movements of the American Army in the Neighborhood of Trenton in the Winter of 1776–77," *Pennsylvania Magazine of History and Biography* (1888): 391–402. The best biography is John F. Roche, *Joseph Reed: A Moderate in the American Revolution* (1957), but William B. Reed, *Life and Correspondence of Joseph Reed* (2 vols., 1847), remains essential. Esther De Berdt's life is treated in William B. Reed, *The Life of Esther De Berdt, Afterwards Esther Reed, of Pennsylvania* (1853). Reed's controversy with Cadwalader can be followed in Horace W. Smith, *Nuts for Future Historians to Crack* (1856); George Bancroft, *Joseph Reed: An Historical Essay* (1867); William B. Reed, *President Reed of Pennsylvania: A Reply to Mr. George Bancroft and Others* (1867) and *A Rejoinder to Mr. Bancroft's Historical Essay* (1867); and William S. Stryker, *The Reed Controversy* (1876). For works offering assessments of various facets of Reed's career, see Robert L. Brunhouse, *The Counter-Revolution in Pennsylvania, 1776–1790* (1942; repr. 1971); Richard Alan Ryerson, *The Revolution Is Now Begun: The Radical Committees of Philadelphia, 1765–1776* (1978); G. S. Rowe, *Thomas McKean: The Shaping of an American Republicanism* (1978); and Steven Rosswurm, *Arms, Country, and Class: The Philadelphia Militia and the 'Lower Sort' during the American Revolution, 1775–1783* (1987).

G. S. ROWE

REED, Luman (4 June 1785–7 June 1836), merchant, art collector, and art patron, was born at Green River (now Austerlitz), in Columbia County, New York, the son of Eliakim Reed II and Rebecca Fitch, farmers. The family lived in Connecticut until Reed's father bought a New York farm in 1779. In 1792 they moved to nearby Coxsackie, where Reed attended a district school. There, in partnership with his cousin Roswell Reed, his father opened a store for the sale of agricultural produce and dry goods, in which Luman Reed worked after school; when his father sold the business, Reed worked for the new owner, Ralph Barker. In 1808 Reed married Barker's sister Mary (known as Polly); the couple had two children.

Soon after his marriage Reed established his own business in Coxsackie with a partner, Theron Skeel, buying, selling, and shipping produce. Traveling to New York City as master of the company sloop, he anticipated the city's potential, and in 1815, with about $8,000 capital, he opened his first shop there at 13 Coenties Slip.

Reed prospered in New York, taking advantage of the city's commercial growth following the War of 1812 and the opening of the Erie Canal in 1825. By 1830 he had become one of New York's 500 wealthiest citizens, and in 1834 he was elected to membership in the Chamber of Commerce of New York State. About 1832 Reed began to delegate his business concerns to Jonathan Sturges, who had become his partner in 1830, leaving himself free to participate actively in New York's cultural life. He befriended actor James Henry Hackett and assisted four young artists—Thomas Cole, Asher B. Durand, William Sidney Mount, and George Whiting Flagg—by commissioning and buying their work. The most important commission went to Cole for a series of five paintings called *The Course of Empire* (1833–1836). Reed's commission of seven presidential portraits to Durand encouraged the engraver to pursue a painter's career; and by subsidizing for seven years Flagg's educational expenses, including eight months' study in Europe, he hoped to stimulate the young man to develop his artistic skills. In 1834 Reed was elected an honorary member of the National Academy of Design and a member of the prestigious Sketch Club.

Reed's magnificent home, designed by Isaac Green Pearson (or Pierson) at 13 Greenwich Street in New York City, also housed his art collection. Built facing a group of townhouses called "Millionaire's Row," Reed's neoclassical house (completed in Aug. 1832) boasted technological innovations such as gas lighting, a furnace, and a rudimentary drainpipe system, as well as opulent mahogany doors and Italian marble. It also featured a third-floor gallery specifically designed to exhibit his art collection. Reed had begun to buy artwork around 1830, and by the time of his death he had accumulated more than fifty paintings, about two-thirds of which were by his four protégés. Although he owned some European works, he demonstrated a clear preference for American artists and American themes, not only because of strong nationalistic feelings, but also because he was wary of possibly fraudulent Old Master paintings. His collection did contain, however, more than 200 valuable engravings of European works important for study purposes, along with an extensive library, all of which he made available to the public upon application. Moreover, he opened his gallery one day a week to the public in the belief that he was thereby contributing to the artistic education of Americans and the cultural development of the country.

From 1832 to 1836 Reed's gallery served as a congenial meeting place for artists, writers, and art patrons. Reed died at home after a short illness. After his death his collection continued to be available to the public until 1844, when the house was sold. The paintings were purchased by an association of Reed's friends to serve as the nucleus of the New-York Gallery of the Fine Arts, which was open to the public at a small admission fee until June 1848. The gallery proved too expensive to maintain, and in 1858 its collection was placed "in perpetuity" in the New-York Historical Society, transforming the society from a repository of books, manuscripts, and historical miscellany into a "treasury of art."

• A portrait of Reed by A. B. Durand (1835) and a replica (c. 1850) are at the New-York Historical Society. Reed's papers are also at the New-York Historical Society; the inventory of his estate is in the Joseph Downs Collection in the Henry Francis du Pont Winterthur Museum Library, Winterthur, Del. Other manuscripts are in the Sketch Club Papers, Century Association, N.Y.; John Durand Papers, New York Public Library; Thomas Cole Papers, Albany Institute of History and Art and Albany State Library, N.Y.; Archives of American Art, Washington, D.C.; Asher B. Durand Papers, New York Public Library; William Sidney Mount Papers, Museums at Stony Brook, N.Y.; and the New-York Historical Society.

The most complete study of Reed, with an extensive bibliography, is E. M. Foshay, *Mr. Luman Reed's Picture Gallery: A Pioneer Collection of American Art* (1990). For his collection, see *Catalogue of the Exhibition of the New-York Gallery of the Fine Arts* (1844–1850); and W. Dunlap, *The History of the Rise and Progress of the Arts of Design in the United States* (2 vols., 1834). Also see J. Durand, *The Life and Times of A. B. Durand* (1894); E. Reed-Wright, *Reed-Read Lineage* (1909); L. B. Miller, *Patrons and Patriotism: The Encouragement of the Fine Arts in the United States, 1790–1860* (1966); E. Pessen, "The Wealthiest New Yorkers of the Jacksonian Era: A New List," *New-York Historical Society Quarterly* 54 (Apr. 1970): 155; R. Lynes, "Luman Reed: A New York Patron," *Apollo* 107 (Feb. 1978): 124–29; W. Craven, "Luman Reed, Patron: His Collection and Gallery," *American Art Journal* 12 (Spring 1980): 40–59; A. B. Gerdts, "Newly-Discovered Records of the New-York Gallery of the Fine Arts," *Archives of American Art Journal* 21, no. 4 (1981): 2–9; and E. C. Parry III, *The Art of Thomas Cole: Ambition and Imagination* (1988).

LILLIAN B. MILLER

REED, Myron Winslow (24 July 1836–30 Jan. 1899), Congregational minister and Christian Socialist, was born in Barnard-Windsor County, Vermont, the son of Fry Bailey Reed, a poverty-stricken minister and abolitionist, and Asenath Smith. After a family quarrel, Reed, then a teen-ager, left home. He worked on a

fishing vessel, then tramped, and finally ended up broke in New York City. There he met newspaper editor Horace Greeley, who recommended him for a position as a recruiter for the Republican State Committee, through which Reed discovered his talent for public speaking. In the mid-1850s he reconciled with his family and joined them in Wisconsin, where he became a dedicated defender of the rights of Native Americans. Much later he became president of the Colorado Indian Rights Association (1893).

Poverty limited Reed's formal education, but always an avid reader, he became self-educated. In Wisconsin Reed took up law, but land titles and civil suits quickly dissatisfied him. Friends pushed him toward the ministry, which Reed was drawn to because he thought it offered greater opportunities for social reform than did the law. He entered Chicago Theological Seminary in 1861 but enlisted in the Eighteenth Michigan Volunteers when the Civil War began. Wounded at Chickamauga, Reed was discharged in 1865 with the rank of captain. He then returned to the seminary and graduated in 1868.

Soon after graduation Reed went to New Orleans, where he became pastor of a Congregational church. There he met Louise Lyon, a Connecticut woman who had come to the South to teach African Americans, and the two were married in 1870; they would have three children. From 1873 to 1877 Reed conducted a ministry in Milwaukee and then accepted a call to serve the prestigious First Presbyterian Church in Indianapolis, where he established a reputation as a proponent of the Social Gospel and a political activist. An unconventional minister, Reed befriended newspapermen, gamblers, and laborers, and he strolled about town dressed in a broad-brimmed slouch hat with a cigar clenched between his teeth. His friend Reverend Oscar McCulloch of the Plymouth Church (Congregational), who had founded organized charity in Indianapolis, introduced Reed to the concepts of scientific charity, which attempted to centrally coordinate relief efforts for maximum efficiency, and the institutional church, the objective of which was to organize so that it could minister to the community seven days a week with a variety of services, such as relief for the poor; classes in sewing, music, and language; lectures on literature and science; concerts; and exhibitions.

Immersed in late nineteenth-century optimism and the New Theology, Reed believed in the inevitable progress of the Kingdom of God on earth and the role of the Christian community in hastening its coming. He advocated a biblical exegesis that took into account the factors of language, time, and cultural development and that stressed God's love rather than retribution. Evolutionary theory never troubled Reed because if it were true, God was the creative force behind it. He believed that traditional church dogma alienated ordinary folk and that a simple theology was needed. Toward that end he offered the life and teachings of Jesus as the summation of theology expressed in servanthood, that is, the idea of cooperation rather than competition. Reed's reputation was as an outstanding preacher, however, not as a theologian. Fifty newspapers published his sermons, which brought him nationwide recognition as the "greatest preacher west of Brooklyn." Known for his epigrams that emphasized activism, Reed once quipped, "I am interested in politics because I believe that every political question is a social question, and that every social question is a religious one."

In April 1884 Reed went to Denver to serve the affluent First Congregational Church. A persistent critic of what he saw as indifferent industrial growth, Reed asserted his independence in his very first interview with the *Rocky Mountain News*, declaring that he would not be a special pleader for rich men and that he would tell his congregation what he thought "whether they like it or not." Reed criticized industrialists for paying low wages, requiring long hours, and discarding workers as if they were obsolete raw material. In the popular four-sermon series "The Evolution of the Tramp" (1886), Reed described the unemployed as victims of the machine age, and he argued that society should guarantee them the right to economic opportunity and the benefits of American culture. The *Rocky Mountain News* published these sermons in booklet form, which made Reed even more popular. In Denver Reed applied the ideas he had learned from Oscar McCulloch, establishing the Associated Charities Organization in 1887 and transforming the First Congregational Church into an institutional church in the 1890s.

As a Christian Socialist, Reed saw politics as a means of accelerating the coming of the new community of God and of creating a western community that would teach the Sermon on the Mount as its ethical creed and manage production for the good of all. If enough like-minded politicians were elected to office, then change would happen. The Democrats nominated him for the state's congressional seat in 1886, but he lost in a hotly disputed election. He turned down the same nomination in 1892, choosing instead to campaign throughout the West for the Populists. In 1892 he outlined his views of Christian socialism, calling for government ownership of the telegraph and railroads and asking, "Why not here in Denver try Socialism?" His last political campaign, a run for the presidency of the Denver Board of Supervisors in 1897, also failed.

Not many clergymen dared to speak out in favor of labor agitation in the 1890s, but Reed's strong support for the 1894 Cripple Creek miners' strike propelled him into the national limelight. After key church leaders complained about his endorsement of the strikers, Reed abruptly resigned. That same year, Samuel Gompers invited Reed to speak at the Denver meeting of the American Federation of Labor, and he accepted.

With the assistance of friends, Reed opened the independent Broadway Temple, housed in the Broadway Theater, on 4 February 1895; the creed of the nondenominational church was brief: "The Fatherhood of God and the Brotherhood of Man." Not surprisingly, the Broadway Temple became a forum for Reed's application of Christian socialism to the key social issues of the late 1890s. In 1896 Reed was elected president of the Brotherhood of the Cooperative Commonwealth, with Socialist Eugene Debs as the national organizer. The purpose of the Brotherhood was to establish socialist colonies in the West. Reed planned to create a Colorado colony but was stopped by illness.

At Reed's death in Denver, some 6,000 persons tried to attend his funeral in the 2,000-seat Broadway Temple. Messages of sympathy arrived from around the country; Debs and the poet James Whitcomb Riley eulogized him. The *Miner's Magazine* printed copies of Reed's sermons for years thereafter, and miners visited his grave whenever they met in Denver. Reed never succeeded in gaining political office or in building a cooperative community. His greatest strengths lay in preaching and in relating one-on-one with ordinary folk. Beyond the West, Reed was known as a voice for downtrodden souls; his was indeed "the people's voice," clearly partisan but identified with everyday people.

• Reed left no collection of writings but did publish *Temple Talks* (1898), a collection of fifteen sermons that illustrates the range of his topics, and the Chicago Historical Society has five of his letters from the 1870s. The most valuable sources for his sermons are the newspapers of Indianapolis and Denver. The Western History Department of the Denver Public Library has several scrapbooks that include articles about Reed, but the Edgar A. Burton Files are the most helpful; they feature a *Rocky Mountain News* index of Reed's sermons, related subjects, and significant sociopolitical issues affecting Colorado in the 1880s–1890s. A scrapbook compiled by Indianapolis judge William P. Fishback, Reed's close friend, is in the Indiana State Library and includes interesting personal information. David Brundage mentions Reed's involvement in organized labor and the 1886 election in *The Making of Western Labor Radicalism: Denver's Organized Workers, 1878–1905* (1994). Ferenc Morton Szasz identifies Reed as an advocate of social justice and "one of the Mountain West's most articulate spokesmen for the cause of labor" in his *The Protestant Clergy in the Great Plains and Mountain West, 1865–1915* (1988). For a more complete bibliography see James A. Denton, *Rocky Mountain Radical: Myron W. Reed, Christian Socialist* (1997).

JAMES A. DENTON

REED, Myrtle (27 Sept. 1874–17 Aug. 1911), novelist, poet, and journalist, was born in Norwood Park, Illinois, the daughter of Hiram Von Reed, a preacher and editor, and Elizabeth Armstrong, a theological scholar and author. From early childhood Reed's parents encouraged her to write. Her first story was published in a children's periodical, *The Acorn*, when she was ten. In high school she was editor of the school paper. During that time she began corresponding with James Sydney McCullough, the editor of a high school paper in Toronto, Canada. In 1906 they were married.

After graduating from high school, Reed became a freelance journalist and writer for magazines. Her poetry, stories, and sketches appeared in the magazines *Bookman*, *Munsey's*, *Harper's Bazaar*, *Cosmopolitan*, the *Critic*, and others. For the first six years she published nothing under her own name; she said later that she had used half a dozen pen names. Her first two novels, *Love Letters of a Musician* (1899) and *Later Love Letters of a Musician* (1900), and *The Spinster Book* (1901), a series of essays on courtship and love, were all successful. However, it was her novel *Lavender and Old Lace* (1902) that firmly established her popularity. Issued in a lavender binding and case with a flower and filigree cover designed by Margaret Armstrong, this story of a loving young couple and their attachment to an older woman friend caught the fancy of the reading public. The novel was to go through forty printings in the next nine years and to become the basis of a 1938 play by Rose Warner. Reed's later novels, most of them also appearing in the lavender Margaret Armstrong bindings, are *At the Sign of the Jack o' Lantern* (1905), *A Spinner in the Sun* (1906), *Flower of the Dusk* (1908), and *The Master's Violin* (1904).

Norma Bright Carson described Reed's work in terms of its idealism, the "optimism that overleaps every obstacle," and the "never failing humor." Carson speaks of laughter close to tears, light and shadows, keen flashes of wit, and occasional "touches of satire . . . not too sharply pointed. . . . without a trace of bitterness." *The Book of Clever Beasts* (1904) showcased Reed's humor and brought her a letter of appreciation from President Theodore Roosevelt.

Like the character Ruth in *Lavender and Old Lace*, Reed wanted to know more about the "gentle art of cooking," and so she not only taught herself to cook but wrote a series of ten cookbooks starting with *What to Have for Breakfast* (1905), including *One Thousand Simple Soups* (1907), and ending with *Everyday Desserts* (1911). For the cookbooks Reed used the pen name Olive Green. *The Myrtle Reed Cookbook* (1916), compiled from the Olive Green cookbooks, supplements its recipes with humorous pieces such as "The Philosophy of Breakfast" and "The Kitchen Rubaiyat."

Reed believed in the ideal happy marriage, writing her novels, short stories, cookbooks, and books of advice with that ideal in mind. According to her friend Ethel Colson, that ideal seemed to have been reached in Reed's own home life. Colson describes the happy home, talks of the charming entertainments given there, of the many friends who visited.

Mary B. Powell speaks of Reed's serious interest in philosophy and her study of Thomas Carlyle, especially *Sartor Resartus*, and of her intent to preach her own philosophy through her writing. Powell reports Reed as saying

We take our sermons and philosophy so much more readily through fiction than fact, than through didactic preaching. See what a rare opportunity I should have of influencing young people—especially young women—for I shall always write stories of simple lives and homes—stories that I hope will make women think of their particular duties in the home life, and that will set before young girls a high ideal of life—the highest ideal as exemplified in daily home life, and, perhaps, home-

ly, simple tasks. I do not believe in divorce, and I am going to try to lift my voice against it by my indirect preaching with the pen.

Scattered through Reed's writings are bits of her philosophy. In *Old Rose and Silver* (1909) she says, "Joy, in reality, is immortal, while pain dies in a day." In *Master of the Vineyard* (1910) she says, "The appointed thing comes at the appointed time in the appointed way. There is no terror save my own fear."

A Weaver of Dreams, called by reviewers a somber novel and Reed's most interesting book, was published in 1911. Shortly afterward Reed took her own life by a drug overdose. Published posthumously were *The Myrtle Reed Year Book* (1911); *Happy Women* (1913), a series of short biographies; *Threads of Grey and Gold* (1913), a collection of prose and verse; and *A Woman's Career, the Exactions and the Obstacles* (1914). Reed died in Chicago, Illinois.

• A collection of letters and clippings on Reed's life is at the Ohio State University. Biographical information is in a monograph, *Myrtle Reed* (1911). Two notable contributions to it are Ethel S. Colson, "Myrtle Reed as Her Friends Know Her," and "Why Myrtle Reed's Books Are Popular," both of which had been published earlier in *Book News Monthly*, Jan. 1911. The forewords by M. B. Powell to *The Myrtle Reed Yearbook* (1911) and *Happy Women* (1913) also have biographical information. See also *Publishers Weekly*, 26 Aug. and 23 Sept. 1911, and news accounts in the *Chicago Daily Tribune*, 19 and 21 Aug. 1911, and *Chicago Daily News*, 18, 19, and 20 Aug. 1911.

BLANCHE COX CLEGG

REED, Philip Dunham (16 Nov. 1899–10 Mar. 1989), corporation executive and internationalist, was born in Milwaukee, Wisconsin, the son of William Dennis Reed, an insurance company executive, and Virginia Brandreth Dunham. He received the B.S. in electrical engineering from the University of Wisconsin with his class of 1921 despite an interruption for army training toward the end of World War I.

After graduation and marriage in 1921 to Mabel Mayhew Smith, Reed was lured to New York City by a $2,000 salary and a clerkship with the patent law firm of Pennie, Davis, Marvin, and Edmonds, which was seeking young engineers to train as lawyers. His firm initiated him into patent law while he studied nights at Fordham University School of Law, earning his LL.B. cum laude in 1924 and admission to the bar the next year. Though prepared for both professions, he thereafter considered himself first a lawyer rather than an engineer.

In 1922 his firm's client, John M. Van Heusen, inventor of the soft shirt collar, persuaded Reed to become counsel at his Van Heusen Products, a patent holding and licensing company. There Reed prepared the brief that won Van Heusen's patent infringement suits brought against shirtmaking companies in Troy, New York. Heeding the advice of lawyer friends, in 1926 he left Van Heusen and a salary of $12,000 to begin his long connection with the General Electric Company (GE) by entering its law department at a salary of $4,500. Two years later he transferred to the incandescent lamp division, where he was made general counsel in 1934, and increasingly came under the eye and the direction of GE president Gerard Swope and chairman Owen D. Young.

Reed's widening tasks included representing GE at National Recovery Act code meetings, defending the company's patent rights, and helping Young to reorganize the bankrupt Federation Bank and Trust Company of the American Federation of Labor. Reed became known as an energetic, knowledgeable, and decisive young company man who went to the core of legal issues, stating them lucidly and succinctly. He had a youthful appearance and an engaging personality of empathy, wit, and modesty. By 1938 he was named assistant to the president and a director of GE; in 1939, one day after his fortieth birthday, on Young's recommendation he was elected chairman of GE by its board of directors.

Chairing GE for fifteen years (1940–1942, 1945–1958), Reed was adept at using the law as a connecting theme among the company's large units and at prudently guiding overall finances. Internal operations were in the hands of President Charles E. Wilson. Shortly before the United States entered World War II both Reed and Wilson became vigorously involved in converting a peacetime economy to a wartime footing. On salaried leave from GE as a dollar-a-year public servant in Washington, Reed worked at a series of jobs within the War Production Board. At first he was a consultant on priorities for the Office of Production Management, then he became deputy director of its materials division (July–Dec. 1941), and finally chief of the Bureau of Industry Operations (Jan.–July 1942).

In chaotic wartime Washington, Congress often was baffled and irritated by the surge to power of civilians in semiautonomous, often duplicate agencies with unclear authority—all under the general direction of the executive branch. Senator Harry S. Truman charged that Reed was slow in bringing "the maximum conversion of private industry to war production" and that "a [dollar-a-year] man's heart is where his pocketbook is," namely within the industry he comes from. Reed's testimony to Congress, supported by the head of the War Production Board, Donald Nelson, and by some congressmen, refuted Truman's accusation. In 1947 President Truman would award Reed the Presidential Certificate of Merit for his wartime service.

Reed began his role in international economic affairs in July 1942, when President Franklin D. Roosevelt named him deputy chief of the U.S. Mission for Economic Affairs in London under W. Averell Harriman. After Harriman's posting to Moscow, Reed became chief of the mission with the rank of minister (Oct. 1943–Jan. 1945). He administered what had expanded from a lend-lease office into an organization representing all American agencies engaged in transporting and supplying munitions to the preinvasion armies and foodstuffs, fuel, and industrial equipment to British civilians. He worked with leading civil and military officers from the allied nations. Alternating with his British counterpart, he presided over the meetings of the London Coordinating Committee, the central agency for allocating supplies to the liberated areas of northern Europe, by "dispos[ing] of business speedily with his statesmanlike breadth, swift sense of proportion, tact, and charm" (Wehle, p. 247).

Envisioning a strong postwar economic world, Reed was reelected chairman of GE in early 1945, confident of what his company could do at home and abroad. His international perspective and associations and his maturity as a negotiator sent him clearly along the path of his mentor, Young. Reed also chaired International GE from 1945 until its merger with the parent company in 1952. He took on tasks outside GE that increasingly made him a helmsman for the electrical industry at large and for industrial, financial, and trading efforts to rebuild war-damaged nations. At San Francisco in 1945, his attendance as a legal consultant to the U.S. delegation to the United Nations Conference on International Organization led to his enduring affiliation with the revived International Chamber of Commerce (1945–1975). As chamber president (1949–1951), he spoke for that portion of resurgent Western capitalism that advocated freedom of international trade, the protection of foreign investments against discriminatory governmental actions, and the convertibility of currencies under a relaxation of government controls over trade and finance.

On trading policies Reed was then at odds with some domestic business organizations such as the National Association of Manufacturers and the U.S. Chamber of Commerce. His convictions were reinforced when he headed the U.S. delegation to the Anglo-American Council on Productivity, a Marshall Plan agency (1948–1952). Allied with these activities and underscoring his prominence among international-minded executives were his long directorship of the Council on Foreign Relations (1946–1969) and his trusteeship of both the Eisenhower Exchange Fellowships (1953–1975) and the Winston Churchill Foundation of the United States (1970–1975). France decorated him an officer of the Legion of Honor in 1947 and a commander in 1951.

Reed presided over GE during its phenomenal growth. Sales grew from $396 million in 1939 to $4.3 billion in 1957; company jobs in that time increased from 79,000 to more than a quarter million, and over a billion dollars were invested in expanding plants and facilities for conversion from military to consumer production. He tended principally to financial planning, government and international relations, and long-range company policies that resulted in a limited manufacture of computers, the development of nuclear energy, designs for space exploration, and the manufacture of jet engines. Reed endorsed the dramatic shift to decentralized management under GE president Ralph Cordiner in the 1950s. This reorganization distanced him from the company's troubled labor-management relations. It also left him and all of the directors unguarded against and unaware of the secret price-fixing actions of some divisional managers that came to light and to a notorious trial after his retirement. Reed's continuing challenge was to grasp and articulate for the directors and shareholders the coherent significance of their huge corporation comprising twenty-seven divisions run as separate businesses.

A Republican, Reed only once stepped close to his party's national affairs, joining fourteen other businessmen to endorse Dwight D. Eisenhower's presidential candidacy in 1952. From a friendship developed during their wartime years in London and sustained throughout Eisenhower's life, Reed was occasionally an informal presidential adviser and envoy. He indeed mirrored the position of the Eisenhower administration during those years by championing economic progress through free enterprise, increased productivity, a broadened "people's capitalism," and American responsibility to help shape world affairs pragmatically in the face of Soviet communism. This credo was stressed by his membership on the Business Advisory Council (1940–1961) and the Committee for Economic Development (1946–1975). From his midwestern, small-city background Reed had become a cosmopolitan figure who moved easily among the Western world's industrial leaders and who won wide respect for his international public services, particularly in fostering working relationships among diverse groups of people.

After his long-planned retirement from GE at the age of sixty, Reed's eminence in corporate finance was confirmed by his appointment to the chairmanship of the Federal Reserve Bank of New York (1960–1965). Reducing the number of his directorships after 1970, he kept his long-standing ones of Bankers Trust, American Express, and Metropolitan Life Insurance. He wintered in Antigua and resided in Rye, New York, his home for fifty years, where he died. He established the Philip D. Reed Foundation in 1955, devoted chiefly to educational and environmental gifts, to be expended within ten years of his death. His wife died in 1984; their two children survived them.

• Reed's papers are in the Hagley Library in Wilmington, Del. Though not dealing with the internal affairs of GE, they cover extensively his government service, many directorships, and offices in public-policy organizations and also contain his datebooks, speeches, a few magazine articles, and wide correspondence. Personal letters from Reed to his wife during wartime London vividly describe his life and work there. Biographical sketches are in the *Milwaukee Journal*, 19 Nov. 1939 and 26 Feb. 1940, on his boyhood; *Fortune*, Jan. 1940, pp. 68–69, 101–4, on becoming chairman of GE; *Newsweek*, 27 June 1949, cover story; *Christian Science Monitor*, 29 and 30 Apr., 1 May 1958; and *Fordham International Law Journal* 14 (1990–1991), the first annual memorial issue in his name. His defense of GE patent licenses is reported in the *New York Times*, 5 Jan. 1934. Senate discussion of the Truman Committee on Investigation of the National Defense Program, including excerpts from a House of Representatives report on the matter, is in the *Congressional Record*, 77th Cong., 18 June 1942, pp. 5324–31 (Reed's testimony is in microfiche *Congressional Hearings* [77] S691-1-B). The London Coordinating Committee is described in Louis B. Wehle,

Hidden Threads of History: Wilson through Roosevelt (1953). Absent any scholarly history of GE, two specialized studies reveal some of the company's internal affairs in Reed's time, Ronald G. Greenwood, *Managerial Decentralization: A Study of the General Electric Philosophy* (1974), and Ronald W. Schatz, *The Electrical Workers: A History of Labor at General Electric and Westinghouse, 1923–60* (1983). An obituary is in the *New York Times*, 11 Mar. 1989.

WILSON SMITH

REED, Sampson (10 June 1800–8 July 1880), author and advocate of Swedenborgianism, was born in West Bridgewater, Massachusetts, the son of John Reed, a Unitarian pastor, and Hannah Sampson. Reed graduated with high honors from Harvard College in 1818 and went on to study at the Divinity School. There he was introduced to the mystical writings of Emanuel Swedenborg by his roommate, Thomas Worcester, and shortly thereafter Reed abandoned his intention to become a Unitarian minister and in 1820 joined the Boston New-Church Society. At his graduation from Harvard with an M.A. in 1821, he delivered an oration on "Genius," which rejected the current Lockean notion that at birth the mind is a tabula rasa that registers only impressions received through the senses and experience. His claim that "Locke's mind will not always be the standard of metaphysics" and his advocacy of intuition as a way of knowing appealed to eighteen-year-old Ralph Waldo Emerson, who sat in the audience.

After serving for three years as an apprentice in William B. White's Boston apothecary, Reed opened his own shop in 1825, eventually building one of the largest wholesale drug businesses in New England. In 1832 he married Catherine Clark; they had three sons and a daughter. Active in public affairs, Reed held several municipal and state offices. He retired from the drug business in 1861.

Meanwhile, Reed was preoccupied with the establishment of the Swedenborgian church in the United States. To this end he published a 44-page pamphlet, *Observations on the Growth of the Mind* (1826), which expounded the ideas of Emanuel Swedenborg without mentioning him specifically. Reed was a regular contributor to the first forty-eight volumes of *New Jerusalem Magazine* (1828–1882), edited for twenty years by his brother Caleb. In 1843 he started the *New Church Magazine for Children*, later titled *Children's New-Church Magazine*, and he became one of the editors of *New Jerusalem* in 1854. In addition to essays, Reed published several pamphlets and books advocating his interpretation of Swedenborgianism. These include *Address on Education* (1842), *Swedenborg and His Mission* (1859), *The Correspondence of the Sun, Heat, and Light* (1862), *The Future of the New Church* (1875), and a *Biographical Sketch of Thomas Worcester* (1880). Reed was active in Boston's New Church throughout his business career and, after his retirement in 1861, served as Sunday school superintendent and chairman of the church committee. He went blind several years before his death in Boston.

Although Reed was part of the young, rebellious generation that opposed Lockean sensualism and Unitarianism, he was not, as his 1838 preface to *Growth of the Mind* makes clear, a Transcendentalist. However, it was Reed's influence on Emerson and other Transcendentalists, primarily through two short works—"Genius" and *Growth of the Mind*—that made him important. His discussion in "Genius" of the Swedenborgian notion that each individual has his "peculium," or "use," and that the exercise of this is the best way to develop character; his claim that men are great simply because they have developed to a greater degree the genius that can be found within each person; his rejection of Locke; his hopeful, oracular tone all served as an early inspiration to Emerson. More importantly, *Growth of the Mind* is credited with introducing Emerson to the Swedenborgian notion of correspondence—that the universe is a physical manifestation of the soul and, therefore, that every natural truth corresponds to a spiritual truth. This work also contains an early formulation of Transcendental aesthetic theory. Reed asserted that the artist produces not by imposing an artificial order on nature but by giving spontaneous expression to the forms of nature. Although Reed served as an early inspiration to Emerson and contributed ideas and language to the Transcendental movement, his ultimate and "principal role in the Transcendental circle," according to Elizabeth Meese, "was as a purveyor of Swedenborgianism" ("Sampson Reed," p. 372).

• Selections from Reed's oration on "Genius" and *Observations on the Growth of the Mind* are most readily found in *The Transcendentalists: An Anthology*, ed. Perry Miller (1950), and in *Selected Writings of the American Transcendentalists*, ed. George Hochfield (1966). The most complete modern assessment is Elizabeth A. Meese, "Sampson Reed," in *The Transcendentalists: A Review of Research and Criticism*, ed. Joel Myerson (1984), pp. 372–74. An older but more complete treatment of Reed's life and writings is Carl F. Strauch's introduction to *Observations on the Growth of the Mind* (1838). For research on the influence of Reed's Swedenborgianism on Emerson, see Clarence Paul Hotson, "Sampson Reed: A Teacher of Emerson," *New England Quarterly* 2 (Apr. 1929): 249–77. On the central contributions Reed made to American Transcendentalist theory, see Meese, "Transcendentalism: The Metaphysics of the Theme," *American Literature* 47 (Mar. 1975): 1–20.

PETER HAWKES

REED, Stanley Forman (31 Dec. 1884–2 Apr. 1980), U.S. Supreme Court justice, was born in Minerva, Kentucky, the son of John A. Reed, a physician, and Frances Forman. He attended local private academies, graduated from Kentucky Wesleyan College in 1902, and received a second bachelor's degree from Yale in 1906. Reed studied law at the University of Virginia, Columbia University, and the Sorbonne, but he never obtained a law degree. He married Winifred Elgin in 1908; they had two children. Admitted to the bar in 1910, he practiced law in Maysville and Ashland,

Kentucky. Active in Democratic politics, Reed represented Mason County in the Kentucky General Assembly for two terms, from 1912 to 1916.

After serving in the army in World War I, Reed resumed his law practice in Maysville until 1929. Because he was general counsel for the Farm Cooperative, Alexander Legge appointed him general counsel to the Federal Farm Board in 1929. In 1932 Herbert Hoover appointed Reed to a similar position in the Reconstruction Finance Corporation, and in 1935 Franklin Roosevelt named him U.S. solicitor general. His major responsibility as solicitor general was to argue cases before the U.S. Supreme Court, and in this position Reed urged the regulation of the economy. Prior to his appointment, Reed was appointed special counsel to argue the Gold Cases. Later he won *Holyoke Power Co. v. American Writing Paper Co.*, the second Gold Case before the Supreme Court. During his tenure as solicitor general, Reed won eleven of the thirteen cases he argued before the Supreme Court. His only losses were *United States v. Schechter* and *Butler v. United States*. Because of his concern for national labor relations cases, Reed argued one of them before the Kentucky circuit court. It was one of labor's few local court victories before the U.S. Supreme Court held the National Labor Relations Act constitutional. Reed's arguments convinced the Court that Congress did not exceed its authority in passing the National Labor Relations Act. Because of his strong loyalty to the New Deal and his experience with the Court, Roosevelt appointed him in 1938 to succeed George Sutherland on the Supreme Court.

At the time of his appointment, most people regarded Reed as a liberal, but he was not. He was an economic liberal but was a conservative on civil rights matters. Actually Reed could best be described as a centrist, operating between liberals and conservatives. His views were shaped by his rural background, as was his belief that individuals cannot always have their own way but must yield "something to the reasonable satisfaction of the needs of all." The Court, he said, must be an arbiter between the different branches of the government and the people and should overturn precedents only if absolutely necessary. As a jurist, Reed usually upheld the powers of the executive and Congress. When the Court rejected Truman's seizure of the steel mills during a strike in *Youngstown Sheet & Tube Co. v. Sawyer* (1952), Reed joined in Chief Justice Fred Vinson's dissent, accusing the Court of "adopting the messenger-boy concept of the Presidency." Later, in *Peters v. Hobby* (1955), he dissented when the Court overturned executive authority in a loyalty review board case. Reed argued that "a reasonable interpretation promptly adopted by the President should be respected by the courts." In *United States v. C.I.O.* (1948), he urged that the Court should carefully interpret congressional enactments to avoid the danger of unconstitutionality.

Reed's strong backing for the government position is shown by his support for suppressing subversive groups. Writing for the majority in *Carlson v. Landon*

(1952), he upheld the jailing of an alien Communist without bail until the attorney general's office determined proper deportation action. Earlier he backed Vinson's opinion in *American Communication Association v. Douds* (1950), upholding the non-Communist oath in the Taft-Hartley Act. Reed also supported Vinson in *Dennis v. United States* (1951), sustaining the conviction of Communist leaders under the Smith Act. His view in these cases was influenced by his support of fellow justice Felix Frankfurter's position rather than that of Hugo Black on the role of the Court in judicial matters. Reed and Frankfurter believed in judicial self-restraint, whereby the Court would not formulate policy or judge the wisdom of statutes passed under clear legislative authority. Black, a judicial activist, sought to eliminate executive and legislative statutes that violated individual liberties. For Black, the Bill of Rights outweighed government interests. Although close to both justices, Reed usually backed Frankfurter's position.

Reed also favored Frankfurter's position opposing a broader interpretation of the Bill of Rights, a stance particularly evident in *United Public Workers v. Mitchell* (1947). Writing for the majority, Reed rejected federal employees' arguments that the Hatch Act denied them their First Amendment rights. "It is accepted constitutional doctrine that fundamental human rights are not absolute. This court must balance the extent of the guarantees of freedom against Congressional enactment to protect a democratic society against the supposed evil of political partisanship by employees of the government." In *Adamson v. California* (1947), Reed rejected Black's adoption of the Bill of Rights into the Fourteenth Amendment. He argued that the purpose of the due process clause is to protect the accused not from a proper conviction but from an unfair conviction. Later, in *Breard v. City of Alexandria, Louisiana* (1951), the Court upheld a city statute that prevented solicitation door to door. In this case, Reed clearly expressed his views on justice and the First and Fourteenth amendments. "All declare for liberty and proceed to disagree among themselves for its true meaning," he wrote. The First and the Fourteenth Amendment "have never been treated as absolute. Freedom of speech or press does not mean that one can talk or distribute where, when and how he chooses." Rights of others are involved, and "by adjustment of rights, we can have both full liberty of expression and orderly life." Later, in *Poulos v. State of New Hampshire* (1953), Reed reiterated his view about the First Amendment when he upheld the conviction of Poulos for not obtaining a license to conduct a religious service in a park in Portsmouth, New Hampshire. He stated that the Court had never held that First Amendment rights cannot be regulated. "It has indicated approval of reasonable nondiscriminatory regulations by governmental authority that preserve peace, order and tranquility without deprivation of the First Amendment guarantees of free speech, press and the exercise of religion."

On matters of censorship, Reed clearly supported Black's position on the Bill of Rights but maintained a narrower focus. In *Winters v. People of New York* (1948), Reed opposed a state statute prohibiting the distribution of printed material that featured violent crime on the grounds that the statute was so vague that a conviction under it could not be sustained. However, he warned that "neither the state nor Congress are prevented by the requirements of specificity from carrying out their duty of eliminating evils to which, in their judgement, such publications give rise." Later he concurred in Justice Tom C. Clark's opinion in *Joseph Burstyn, Inc. v. Wilson et al.* (1952), bringing motion pictures under the protection of the First Amendment, which invalidated a New York censorship law on the grounds that it was too vague. However, Reed pointed out that a state could establish a system of licensing for motion pictures, but the Court must examine each refusal of a license to determine if the First Amendment had been honored.

While the former solicitor general advocated judicial restraint, he was regarded as liberal on economic matters. His most important contribution was in support of the legitimacy of the welfare state and big government's power to impose commercial, financial, and social regulations. Writing for the Court in *United States v. Rock Royal Cooperative* (1939), he upheld the Agricultural Marketing Act and broadened the use of the commerce clause, which he further expanded in later decisions. He supported the decision in *United States v. Appalachian Electric Power Co.* (1940). Writing for the majority, Reed expanded federal authority over the nation's inland waterways and its control over the generation of hydroelectric power. Furthermore, he declared that the government's power over navigable waters was not restricted to promoting navigation but included flood protection, watershed development, and recovery of the cost of improvements through the generation of power.

Judicial restraint was also the watchword of Reed's views on civil rights. In cases involving the First Amendment, Reed narrowly interpreted the establishment of religion clause and supported the separation of church and state. Reed agreed with Black's opinion in *Everson v. Board of Education of the Township of Ewing* (1947) that the county's reimbursement of parents for bus transportation to and from parochial schools did not breach the wall of separation. However, Reed dissented in *McCollum v. Board of Education* (1948), which denied the right of schools to grant release time for religious instruction. He argued that release time does not violate the First Amendment because "the prohibition of enactments respecting the establishment of religion does not bar every friendly gesture between church and state."

Reluctantly, he supported the Court in discrimination cases. Writing for the majority in *Smith v. Allwright* (1944), he invalidated white-only primaries, through which, he argued, a state endorses, adopts, and enforces discrimination against blacks. Later he supported Vinson's opinion in *Sweatt v. Painter*

(1950), which ended segregation in graduate and law schools. Because he lived in a residence that had a restrictive covenant forbidding its sale or rental to blacks, Reed abstained in *Shelley v. Kraemer* (1948), which made such covenants unenforceable in the courts. Under pressure from Chief Justice Earl Warren, Reed joined the Court's decision in *Brown v. Board of Education* (1954), which ended segregation in public schools.

Reed's only nonjudicial assignment while serving on the Court occurred when President Dwight D. Eisenhower appointed him as chairman of the Committee on Civil Service Improvement. Following his retirement in 1957, he accepted numerous assignments to hear cases on the Court of Claims and the Court of Appeals for the District of Columbia. In 1957 Eisenhower appointed him chairman of the U.S. Civil Rights Commission, but he resigned shortly thereafter because he was still subject to call as a federal judge and felt it was inappropriate for a retired justice to serve in such a capacity. Because of ill health, he ended all activities in 1967 and spent the remainder of his life in Huntington, New York, where he died.

Reed served under four chief justices: Charles Evans Hughes, Harlan Fiske Stone, Fred Vinson, and Earl Warren. He wrote 328 opinions: 228 for the Court, 21 concurrences, and 79 dissents. Throughout his career, Reed's views remained consistent, rooted in his rural background, in his years in government service, and in the belief that in every case "everyone must get something." Reed was a moderate in the struggle between judicial activism and judicial self-restraint. Only in economic matters did he demonstrate judicial activism with any regularity. The composition of the Court changed significantly during his justiceship, especially in his last five years, and he frequently found himself in the minority and saw some of his opinions overturned.

• Reed's papers are located in the Margaret I. King Library, University of Kentucky, Lexington. For information on Reed, see F. William O'Brien, *Justice Reed and the First Amendment: The Religious Clause* (1958); C. Herman Pritchett, *The Roosevelt Court: A Study in Judicial Politics and Values* (1948) and *Civil Liberties and the Vinson Court* (1954); and Wesley McCune, "Stanley Reed," in *The Nine Young Men* (1947).

RICHARD P. HEDLUND

REED, Thomas Brackett (18 Oct. 1839–7 Dec. 1902), lawyer and Speaker of the U.S. House of Representatives, was born in Portland, Maine, the son of Thomas Brackett Reed, Sr., a fisherman and watchman, and Mathilda Prince Mitchell. Young Thomas's heritage was rooted in Yankee New England and its seafaring history. His father and grandfather had been mariners in Maine, and Reed's seacoast birthplace remained his principal residence throughout his career, which took him to Washington, D.C., during the congressional season for twenty-two years. In 1860 Reed graduated from Bowdoin College, where he rowed on the crew team, edited the college newspaper, excelled in debating, and taught school to help cover expenses.

Following a year of teaching, Reed set off for California, where he taught school and read law. He returned to Portland in 1863 and signed on with the navy for a comparatively uneventful eighteen months as an acting assistant paymaster aboard ships patrolling the Tennessee and Mississippi rivers. Shortly after his discharge, he was admitted to the bar and began private practice in Portland. In 1870 he married Susan Merrill Jones, a widow, with whom he had two children, one of whom survived infancy.

Reed began his political career as a Republican in 1867 with election to the state legislature. After two terms in the lower house, he served a third in the state senate in 1869 and then won election as Maine's attorney general in 1870. Defeated for renomination in 1873, Reed returned to Portland to serve as the city's attorney, a position he retained until he departed for Washington, D.C., in 1877 to assume the congressional seat vacated by James Blaine, who had moved to the Senate.

Reed was appointed to the House committee investigating the charges of corruption in the disputed presidential election of 1876. Distinguishing himself in this assignment, Reed survived challenges from Greenbackers and Democrats to retain his seat in 1878 and again in 1880, when he narrowly beat back "Fusionist" opponents. His esteem among his House colleagues and his ability to maintain political control of his southern Maine district, which became more safely Republican after 1880, eventually produced twelve consecutive congressional victories. At 6'3" tall and nearly 300 pounds at his heaviest, Reed's physical presence was as formidable as his ability to pillory his opponents oratorically on the stump and on the floor of Congress. Despite a high-pitched, nasal voice and a cherub-like countenance, he was without a peer when it came to defending the Republican party or issues that he supported.

Reed's political skills propelled his rise up the leadership ladder in the House. He won appointment to the Judiciary Committee in the Forty-sixth Congress and became its chair in the next, when he also gained a place on the influential Rules Committee. He received a seat on Ways and Means, the powerful tax committee of the House, in the Forty-eighth Congress. In 1885, when the Congress and the White House were in Democratic hands, Reed was the GOP's nominee for Speaker.

During his first decade of service Reed demonstrated his loyalty to his party and to positions typical of a northeastern Republican. He steadfastly supported the gold standard when advocates of silver coinage sought to put the nation's currency on a bimetallic standard, and he sided with President Grover Cleveland in favoring repeal of the Silver Purchase Act that Congress had passed in 1890. He opposed Democratic efforts to trim expenditures to the bone and to thwart the suffrage of African Americans in the South. He voted for immigration restriction and civil service but had little sympathy for national regulation of business, including railroads, or for intervention in disputes between workers and employers. However, in his unwavering belief in protective tariffs, Reed exhibited his willingness to use governmental power to promote economic development. High tariff rates, he argued, promoted the growth of American industry and increases in workers' wages, which fueled higher consumption. His faith in this centerpiece of Republicanism and his intellectual agility made Reed a logical choice to spearhead the attack on Democratic efforts to reduce custom duties. The nation must act as a unit, not as atomized individuals, he said in the debate over the Mills Tariff Bill in 1888, in order to satisfy the "ever-growing desire of mankind for new worlds of comfort and luxury."

His partisan combativeness, parliamentary skills, and commanding persona boosted Reed's stock among Republicans. These qualities, along with his barbed wit, which could harry Democrats, and his staunch convictions, especially concerning House procedures, won him the Speakership in 1889, when Republicans returned to power. He had prepared for this role since his arrival in the House. Caught between the imperatives of Republican ideology, which emphasized the rights of the minority, and rampant partisanship during the postwar years, the House operated under rules that facilitated both deliberate obstruction of business and unintentional delay. The conventional techniques of frustrating majority rule were the "disappearing quorum," whereby members who remained silent during roll calls were not counted toward a quorum, and the use of dilatory proposals, such as repeated motions to adjourn. Republicans as well as Democrats used these tactics, but during the 1880s Reed displayed increasing impatience with them. "Rules should not be barriers; they should be guides," he wrote ("Obstructions in the National House," p. 425).

The Speakership handed Reed the opportunity to implement these views. At the onset of the Fifty-first Congress, Reed overruled a Democratic challenge of no-quorum following a vote to take up a contested election case. Ignoring precedent, he directed the clerk to record as present any member who was physically in the chamber but who had remained silent during the vote. Reed then proceeded to announce the names of mute members, all of whom were Democrats. Outraged at this breach of tradition, minority members denounced the Speaker's conduct as "revolutionary" but to no avail, for Reed remained steely calm as bedlam erupted on the House floor. When Democrat James B. McCreary objected to Reed counting him present, Reed replied, "The Chair is making a statement of the fact that the gentleman from Kentucky is present. Does he deny it?" (Peters, p. 64). Democratic fury at "Czar" Reed raged for days, as the minority first turned to customary dilatory tactics, then took to hiding under desks and behind screens, and finally boycotted the chamber altogether.

Throughout this drama Reed remained serene, a demeanor he later said was based on his resolution to resign from Congress if he lost the struggle. In the end, on straight party votes, the House adopted rules that based quorums on the physical presence of members, allowed the Speaker to ignore dilatory motions, relaxed the quorum requirement for the Committee of the Whole so that it could transact more business, and streamlined the order of activity, such as the use of the "morning hour" to hear committee reports. Armed with rules that maximized the power of the House leadership and that linked it to the majority party through the Rules Committee, which the Speaker chaired and packed with his lieutenants, William McKinley and Joseph Cannon (chairs of Ways and Means and Appropriations, respectively), Reed positioned the Fifty-first Congress to give Americans "legislation such as they need" ("Obstructions in the House," p. 425). The resulting "Billion Dollar" Congress compiled an impressive record, which included higher duties in the McKinley Tariff, the Sherman Anti-Trust Act, liberalized pensions for military veterans and their dependents, authority for the president to protect national forests, creation of federal appeals courts, cash grants to the state agricultural colleges, and the prohibition of interstate lotteries. The Senate frustrated Reed's hope to protect the voting rights of southern blacks, and the Speaker was unable to prevent the enactment of a silver purchase act. Although its appropriations did not reach $1 billion, the Fifty-first Congress did outspend its predecessors.

Reed had less interest in the substance of these measures than in protecting the ability of the majority to enact them. He was determined that Democrats accept the logic of his position when they returned to power after the 1890 elections. When Democrats restored the old rules in the Fifty-second and Fifty-third Congresses, Reed led Republicans in filibusters until frustration drove the majority to adopt Reed's principles. This action coincided with a depression that threw the economy into a tailspin and contributed to massive Democratic losses in the congressional elections in 1894. The consensus choice of Republicans for the Speakership, Reed reinstituted his package of rules with little opposition from the Fifty-fourth Congress. Its primary preoccupations lay in the division among Democrats over President Cleveland's determination to keep the currency on the gold standard and political opportunism among Republicans, who sensed a new presidential victory ahead. Encouraged by Henry Cabot Lodge (1850–1924) and Theodore Roosevelt (1858–1919), Reed was among the aspirants for the nomination. Despite his prominence in Congress and in the nation, Reed lacked the attributes necessary to attract wide Republican support. Besides his acerbic tongue, a two-edged sword, Reed resisted political deals and refused to solicit large financial donations for his campaign. His candidacy was overwhelmed by the juggernaut that Mark Hanna assembled on behalf of McKinley.

Republicans scored a clean sweep of the national offices in 1896 and renewed Reed's reign in the House. The Speaker was at the peak of his power, manifested by his spiriting the Dingley Tariff through the House before committee assignments were announced and his muzzling of critics by denying them recognition. Yet the Speaker's influence could not overrule Congress's determination to free the Cubans from Spanish rule and to plant the American flag on new insular possessions. Although Reed had supported improvements in the navy, he opposed war with Spain and the acquisition of a colonial empire. Nonetheless, he deferred to McKinley's request for war rather than oppose the president. He absented himself when Congress annexed Hawaii but refrained from joining anti-imperialists, who sought his assistance. Instead of attacking Republican foreign policy, he resigned following his reelection in 1898, claiming the need to provide for his retirement. Reed remained with the New York law firm of Simpson, Thatcher, and Barnum until his death in Washington, D.C.

Reed was recognized in his time as one of the late nineteenth century's dominant political personalities. Admirers noted that, in an age reputed for corruption, no personal scandal tainted Reed's public career or personal life. He was an accomplished intellectual who learned French at middle age, read poetry and philosophy, wrote more than three dozen articles, and acquired a large personal library. Reed was instrumental in securing the congressional authorization for the construction of the modern Library of Congress. The barbed sarcasm that could humiliate an unlucky victim on the floor of the House became engaging conversation in private, a talent that made him a favorite at Washington dinner parties. His love of politics and his skill at it enabled him to make a career of lawmaking when short stays in Congress were the norm.

Reed also modernized the way the House of Representatives conducted its business. He broke through ancient bottlenecks caused by an increase in members, growth of the legislative work load, and intense partisan rivalry, and streamlined the order of business. By ensuring that a majority could enact legislation, his rules facilitated the expansion of national governmental power in the twentieth century. Reed was also an unembarrassed champion of the Republican party who fused the prerogatives of institutional position in the House with the power of party leadership to guarantee governance by the majority during his three terms as Speaker, when party voting conflict reached record levels. Yet his version of parliamentary democracy sanctioned the silencing of the minority, who labeled the Speaker a despot.

• A small collection of Reed papers is located at Bowdoin College, Maine. Reed's articles in the *North American Review* include "Obstructions in the National House, Oct. 1889, pp. 421–28, and "Spending Public Money," Mar. 1892, pp. 319–28. A listing of his writings and writings about him appears in Donald R. Kennon, ed., *The Speakers of the U.S. House of Representatives: A Bibliography, 1789–1984* (1986). Reed's principal biographers are William A. Robinson, *Thomas B.*

Reed: Parliamentarian (1930); Richard S. Offenberg, "The Political Career of Thomas Brackett Reed" (Ph.D. diss., New York Univ., 1963); and Samuel W. McCall, *The Life of Thomas Brackett Reed* (1914). Barbara W. Tuchman provides a delightful sketch in *The Proud Tower: A Portrait of the World before the War* (1966). Randall B. Ripley, *Party Leaders in the House of Representatives* (1967), and Ronald M. Peters, Jr., *American Speakership: The Office in Historical Perspective* (1990), place Reed in the historical development of Congress. David W. Brady analyzes Congress during the McKinley presidency in *Congressional Voting in a Partisan Era* (1973), and he compares legislative behavior in the 1890s to other periods in *Critical Elections and Congressional Policy Making* (1988). Homer E. Socolofsky and Allan B. Spetter, *The Presidency of Benjamin Harrison* (1987); Allan Nevins, *Grover Cleveland: A Study in Courage* (1932); and Lewis L. Gould, *The Presidency of William McKinley* (1980), review presidential politics when Reed was Speaker.

BALLARD C. CAMPBELL

REED, Walter (13 Sept. 1851–23 Nov. 1902), U.S. Army medical officer and bacteriologist, was born in Belroi, Virginia, the son of Lemuel Sutton Reed, a Methodist minister, and Pharaba White. After a year as an undergraduate, Reed entered medical school at the University of Virginia in 1868 at the age of seventeen; when he received an M.D. in July 1869, he was the youngest to receive this degree in the school's history. After a year of study at the Bellevue Hospital Medical College in New York City, he earned a second M.D., although this degree was not officially awarded until he turned twenty-one. In 1871, after a brief time on the staff of the Kings County Hospital at Brooklyn, he accepted a residency at Brooklyn City Hospital and then served as an assistant sanitary officer for the Brooklyn Board of Health.

In January 1875 Reed passed the entrance examinations for the U.S. Army Medical Department. After receiving his commission as first lieutenant, he was sent to Willet's Point in New York Harbor. In 1876 he married Emilie Lawrence, with whom he had two children. After service at several posts in the West, he was promoted to captain in 1880 and sent to Fort Ontario in Oswego, New York; in 1881 he was assigned to Fort McHenry in Baltimore, Maryland, before returning to the West in 1882. In July 1887 he was assigned to the Mount Vernon Barracks in Alabama, where he became responsible for the health of both the garrison and the disease-ridden Apache Indians held prisoner there. Reed attracted the attention of Surgeon General Jedediah H. Baxter, who, eager to improve the capabilities of promising members of his department, in 1890 reassigned Reed to Fort McHenry, with the understanding that his duties there would be light enough to permit him to devote most of his time to the study of pathology and bacteriology at Johns Hopkins Hospital under the famous William Henry Welch.

After completing seven months of study at Hopkins, Reed was again assigned to duty in the West, where he was called on to care for some of the casualties of the Battle of Wounded Knee, fought in December 1890. At this time he began working with the use of throat cultures in the diagnosis of diphtheria. In 1893 he was promoted to major and ordered back to Washington, D.C., to become curator of the Army Medical Museum, director of its pathology laboratory, and professor of bacteriology and clinical microscopy at the newly-opened Army Medical School. In 1895 he also joined the faculty of the Columbian University Medical School in Washington, D.C., to teach pathology and bacteriology. In 1896, while still at the museum, Reed succeeded in obtaining an X-ray machine for the laboratory only months after the first public demonstration of this device in Germany. He continued his research on diphtheria and was eventually able to prove the value of antitoxin in treating this disease as well as in preventing it.

In the summer of 1898 disease ravaged the camps where troops were being trained for possible participation in the Spanish-American War. Army Surgeon General George M. Sternberg created a Typhoid Board under Reed's direction to study the role played by typhoid fever in the camps and the ways in which it was spread. The surgeon general assigned two volunteer medical officers, Victor C. Vaughan and Edwin O. Shakespeare, to serve under Reed. After interviewing physicians who had served at the camps and conducting an exhaustive examination of sanitation, housing, and hospital conditions there, the board undertook to trace the movements of every soldier who might have had typhoid fever. During the height of the epidemic, physicians at the camps had not been supplied with the microscopes that could have made accurate identification of the prevalent diseases possible, but the Typhoid Board established laboratories at each camp and assigned experienced bacteriologists to them. As a result of these efforts, the board concluded that the major disease at these camps was not malaria, as many had believed, but typhoid fever, and that this disease had been spread principally by flies and the unsanitary habits of patients and their contacts, rather than by contaminated drinking water.

In 1900, before the typhoid board could issue its final report, Surgeon General Sternberg, a widely-respected authority on yellow fever, assigned Reed to head the tropical disease group that came to be known as the Yellow Fever Board or the Yellow Fever Commission. Reed directed the effort to identify the organism that caused yellow fever and the means by which it spread. This disease was a serious danger to occupying American forces in Cuba and periodically struck U.S. communities; from 1793 to 1901 it took more than 100,000 lives in the United States alone. Although many scientists had studied the disease in the decades before the Spanish-American War, few had suggested that mosquitoes might play a role in its transmission; most experts believed that it was spread by bedding and clothing contaminated by the bodily discharges of its victims.

Three contract surgeons, Aristides Agramonte, James Carroll, and Jesse W. Lazear, were assigned to work with Reed. Lazear's death as a result of the accidental bite of an infected mosquito was the only fatali-

ty to cast a pall over the work. Despite strenuous efforts, the board failed to identify the causative organism of yellow fever, a virus too small to be detected by the microscopes of the period; however, they soon discovered that the organism popularly blamed was actually the bacillus that caused hog cholera. The board's greatest accomplishment was proving by a series of carefully-controlled experiments conducted—using human subjects who were fully informed of the risk they were taking—not only that yellow fever was transmitted by the mosquito now known as *Aedes aegypti*, but also that it could not be spread by contact with body fluids. Board members also studied the life cycle of *Aedes aegypti*, gaining the precise information needed to make quarantine procedures more effective and to guide those seeking to develop practical means of eradicating the insect. As a result of the efforts of the Yellow Fever Board and of the medical officers who built on their work, the disease was eliminated as a serious threat to health and commerce both in the Caribbean and in the United States.

The discovery of the way in which yellow fever was transmitted was not completely accepted at first. Some denied the possibility that a mosquito could spread the disease, and others refused to believe that the mosquito's bite was the only way in which it could be spread. Furthermore, dissension arose concerning the extent to which Reed should be given credit for the work of the Yellow Fever Board. Surgeon General Sternberg managed to give the impression that he had known all along that a mosquito was the vector, even though this was far from the truth, and Carroll was embittered because he believed that Reed had received more credit than he deserved. Nevertheless, Leonard Wood, who was deeply involved in efforts to eradicate yellow fever from Cuba and was himself a physician, noted that Reed's was "the originating, directing, and controlling mind in this work" (*Yellow Fever*, 1911, 20).

Whether because of exhaustion from his work, discouragement spawned by the controversy, or the first symptoms of chronic appendicitis, Reed was in less than robust health when he returned to his position at the Army Medical School and the Columbian Medical School in February 1901. In June 1902, in spite of his personal magnetism and distinguished reputation as a scientist, an effort to have him named surgeon general after Sternberg's retirement failed. Reed's accomplishments were recognized, however, when in August he became chairman of the department of pathology at the Columbian University Medical School, and the following November was appointed librarian of the Surgeon General's Library. By this point his physical condition was very poor. When his illness was finally diagnosed as appendicitis, he was operated on at the hospital of the Washington Barracks, where he died of peritonitis a few days after surgery.

In the golden age of medicine that followed the acceptance of germs as a cause of disease, Reed was one of the brightest stars of the Army Medical Department and of his profession. By identifying the ways typhoid fever and yellow fever were spread, he laid the foundation for others to devise practical measures that led to a significant reduction in the toll taken by typhoid fever, and to the conquest of yellow fever. By making it possible to maintain a healthy work force to construct a canal through the once disease-ridden jungles of Panama, his identification of the yellow fever vector had profound economic consequences. Like most scientific breakthroughs, the discovery of the key to the spread of yellow fever depended on the accomplishments of many men, a fact that Reed never denied; but his was the driving force that brought the labors of his predecessors to fruition. Furthermore, his accomplishments encouraged young scientists, arousing the determination to attack the mysteries posed by a host of other deadly diseases.

• A large collection of Reed's papers is held by the University of Virginia, Charlottesville; the National Library of Medicine in Bethesda, Md., has a small collection. A valuable collection of articles by Reed and other members of the Yellow Fever Board is the U.S. Senate, *Yellow Fever, a Compilation of Various Publications: Results of the Work of Maj. Walter Reed, Medical Corps, United States Army, and the Yellow Fever Commission* 61st Cong., 3d sess. (1911), 20. Before being named to the Typhoid Board, Reed published "Typhoid Fever in the District of Columbia," Part III(A): "Diagnosis: the Value of Widal's Test, the Dried Blood Method," *National Medical Review* 7 (1897): 144–46; his most important work concerning typhoid is the two-volume *Reports on the Origin and Spread of Typhoid Fever in U.S. Military Camps During the Spanish War of 1898* (1904), written with Vaughan and Shakespeare.

Reed's life is the subject of several biographies, including Albert E. Truby, *Memoir of Walter Reed* (1943); Walter D. McCaw, *Walter Reed, a Memoir* (1904); and Aristides Agramonte, "The Inside Story of a Great Medical Discovery," *Scientific Monthly* 1 (1915): 209–39. William B. Bean, the author of *Walter Reed: A Biography* (1982), has also published a number of articles that flesh out his book's somewhat abbreviated narrative, including "Walter Reed and the Ordeal of Human Experiments," *Bulletin of the History of Medicine* 51 (1977): 75–92, and "A Note on the Association of Walter Reed and William Osler," *Johns Hopkins Medical Journal* 129 (1971): 346–50.

MARY C. GILLETT

REEDER, Andrew Horatio (12 July 1807–5 July 1864), lawyer and first governor of Kansas Territory, was born in Easton, Pennsylvania, the son of Absolom Reeder, a merchant, and Christiana Smith. Reeder received his education at an academy in Lawrenceville, New Jersey; later he read law and was admitted to the Pennsylvania bar in 1828. He married Amelia Hutter in 1831 and fathered eight children, five of whom lived to adulthood.

An ardent Democrat and advocate of Stephen A. Douglas's popular sovereignty doctrine, Reeder was appointed governor of Kansas Territory in June 1854. A successful lawyer, he had never held political office before, had only a local reputation, and was not suited to govern a brawling frontier community. Unaware of the tense political situation developing there, he delayed his arrival until October. Ignoring proslavery requests to hold an election for a territorial legislature,

Reeder instead decided on a tour in order to understand better Kansas's problems and economic potential; however, his enemies claimed his real purpose was to inspect land for speculative purposes. At the close of the tour the new governor drew up election districts and, contrary to proslavery hopes for a legislative election, authorized an election for delegate to Congress, which proslavery forces carried. He conducted a census of the territory that winter, and it was not until March 1855 that an election for a territorial legislature was held. Because evidence of fraud was too evident to be ignored, Reeder set aside election results in six districts, called for new elections in them, and summoned the legislature to meet at Pawnee. Meanwhile Reeder traveled to his home in Pennsylvania and to Washington, D.C., where friends of the proslavery faction were demanding his removal from office.

In June Reeder returned to Kansas, where he faced a hostile legislature angered by his call for new elections in the six districts and his selection of Pawnee, at the western edge of territorial settlement, as the capital. When it met in July, the legislature immediately unseated the more recently elected members and relocated the capital at Shawnee Mission, near the Missouri border. The governor irritated the group further by vetoing several bills on the grounds that the legislature's actions had negated its authority to act as a lawmaking body. Bolstered by the decision of Samuel D. LeCompte, chief justice for Kansas Territory, invalidating the governor's action, members of the legislature decided to secure his removal by petitioning President Franklin Pierce to discharge him. Influenced by southern politicians, notably Secretary of War Jefferson Davis and Senator David Atchison of Missouri, the president caved in and dismissed Reeder in August 1855.

Reeder now openly cooperated with the antislavery Free State movement, which wrote a state constitution at Topeka and applied to Congress for admission to the Union. At a separate election in October, held under the auspices of the Free State movement, he was elected congressional delegate, but the House eventually declared the seat vacant. Along with James H. Lane (1814–1866), a leader in the movement, in March 1856 Reeder was elected senator from Kansas by the "Free State" legislature but never took his seat because Congress denied the territory admission under the Topeka constitution. Angered by the activities of the antislavery forces, the proslavery legislature convened a grand jury, which brought charges of high treason against Reeder and other Free State leaders. Fearing assassination, Reeder fled Kansas Territory in disguise and resumed his law practice in Pennsylvania. He campaigned for John C. Frémont in 1856, won some support for the Republican vice presidential nomination at the national convention in 1860, and chaired the Pennsylvania Republican delegation to the presidential nominating convention in 1864. During the Civil War he rejected a commission as brigadier general, citing his lack of military experience as the reason, but indicated willingness to serve in a nonmilitary capacity.

Possibly because he was governor for so short a time, Reeder's impact on Kansas was minimal. The only legacy of his presence in the territory is Reeder Township in Anderson County. He died in Easton, Pennsylvania.

• There is no separate collection of Reeder papers, but letters written by Reeder in the 1850s can be found in the Thomas B. Cuming Papers, Nebraska State Historical Society; the David R. Atchison Papers, University of Missouri Library; and the John A. Halderman Papers, Kansas State Historical Society. Information on Reeder can be found in Homer E. Socolofsky, *Kansas Governors* (1990); William Connelley, *Kansas and Kansans*, vol. 1 (1918); *Transactions of Kansas State Historical Society* (1883–1885); William Phillips, *Conquest of Kansas* (1856); and Daniel W. Wilder, *Annals of Kansas* (1875).

EUGENE H. BERWANGER

REESE, Abram (21 Apr. 1829–25 Apr. 1908), inventor and manufacturer, was born Abram Rees in Llanelly, Wales, the son of William Rees, a skilled ironworker, and Elizabeth Joseph. After immigrating to the United States in 1832, the family relocated often as his father pursued his trade throughout Pennsylvania, including Phoenixville, at a forge he erected in Huntington County, and at Bellefonte. In 1837 the family finally settled in Pittsburgh, which was becoming a center for iron production, and his father soon changed the family name to Reese.

Reese went to school for a few years but soon followed his father into the city's iron mills. Two older brothers went on to highly successful careers in business. Jacob Reese helped build and manage ironworks in Sharon, Pittsburgh, and Johnstown, Pennsylvania, as well as a petroleum refinery in Pittsburgh. Also a prolific inventor and holder of 175 patents, he developed methods permitting Bessemer and open-hearth production of steel from basic iron ores. Isaac Reese pursued many ventures, but his most successful was production of refractory brick used to line industrial furnaces. He built several plants that eventually became the core of Harbison & Walker Refractories, the industry leader. In December 1854 Abram Reese married Mary Godwin; the couple had five children. Three of their sons followed Reese into the iron and steel industry.

From his start in Pittsburgh's iron works, Reese's career exhibited a restless streak. In 1854 he moved to Johnstown as the first labor boss at the Cambria Iron Works, joining brother Jacob, the plant's superintendent. Abram puddled—a refining process that converted brittle pig iron into more usable wrought iron—the first heat of iron there. Puddling was one of the more highly skilled jobs in the iron industry, requiring considerable strength and stamina. In 1857 Abram joined brother Isaac in an abortive coal-mining venture. By 1860, Reese was back in Pittsburgh; as the city developed into an early oil refining center, he became manager of Jacob's company, Petrolite Oil

Works. This position seems to have been an interim post, however, as Jacob was also one of the proprietors building Reese and Graff Iron Works (later the Fort Pitt Iron Works). When the ironworks plant opened in 1862, Abram worked for the firm helping to produce armor plates for the government's Civil War gunboat fleet. He soon moved on to become general manager of the Excelsior Iron Works, also in Pittsburgh, before serving as superintendent of the Vulcan Iron Works in St. Louis, Missouri, in 1870. Vulcan rolled the first railroad rails west of the Mississippi in June 1871. Some years later, Reese built and operated a rerolling mill for steel rails in Louisville, Kentucky. He managed that mill until his retirement and then moved back to Pittsburgh, where he died.

Although an effective manager, Reese was acclaimed mainly as an inventor. A number of his patents were connected to the iron and steel industry and drew on his knowledge of rolling, the last step in the puddling process. He received his first patent in 1859 for rolling street railroad rails. A year later he devised a rivet-and-bolt-making machine that, along with many improvements that followed, was widely adopted. During the years 1867–1870 Reese was one of many inventors who tackled machine production of horseshoes, and he took out eight patents on that process. The outcome of Reese's improvements was a remarkably ingenious machine that shaped horseshoes in a single pass through a set of rolls. As important was the flexibility of his process, which was eventually adopted in the manufacture of fifty other products, including ax heads, which could be rolled with the hole for the handle. Reese continued inventing into the 1890s, taking out more than twenty patents on such items as a railroad car stove, air brakes, a machine for making corrugated iron sheets, and another machine for making garden hoes. He also invented a gas conduit. In 1892 he patented perhaps his most important device—a universal rolling mill. The timing was perfect, for the mill could be used to produce structural beams, a product just coming to prominence with the development of the steel-framed skyscraper.

Reese is typical of the people whose efforts made possible the rapid advance of American industry and technology after 1850. His immigrant background was common, as were the links to a community of like-minded workers, including family members. Like other innovators of his time, he was involved in numerous enterprises in more than one industry. Reese and many early industrial developers like him left their marks as skilled workers, inventors, and managers. Such achievements were as important as the more widely acclaimed efforts of the captains of industry who employed them for their technical knowledge and skills.

• Information on Abram Reese is quite limited. A description of the achievements of the family, including Abram, can be found in John W. Jordan, *A Century and a Half of Pittsburgh and Her People*, vol. 3 (1908), pp. 128–37. Studies prepared during the nineteenth century, including local histories such as George H. Thurston, *Pittsburgh's Progress, Industries, and Resources* (1886), and the general overview by James M. Swank, *History of the Manufacture of Iron in All Ages* (1884), describe the development of the Pittsburgh iron industry of which Reese was a part. Also see John N. Ingham, *Making Iron and Steel: Independent Mills in Pittsburgh, 1820–1920* (1991). An obituary is in the *Pittsburgh Dispatch*, 26 Apr. 1908.

BRUCE E. SEELY

REESE, Charles Lee (4 Nov. 1862–12 Apr. 1940), research chemist, was born in Baltimore, Maryland, the son of John Smith Reese, a merchant, and Arnoldina Olivia Focke. Reese began his long career in chemistry at Johns Hopkins University in 1880. The following year he transferred to the University of Virginia, from which he graduated in 1884. To pursue a Ph.D. in chemistry, Reese went to Heidelberg, Germany, to study with Robert Wilhelm Bunsen, an inorganic analytical chemist and the inventor of the Bunsen burner. He also briefly studied with the organic chemist Victor Meyer at Göttingen. At this time, however, not even Bunsen's aegis could land Reese a good academic job in the United States. Upon returning to Baltimore in 1886 Reese became an assistant in chemistry at Johns Hopkins for two years. In the fall of 1888 he taught at Wake Forest before moving to the South Carolina Military Academy in Charlestown. Reese taught chemistry and physics there until he returned to Baltimore in 1896. While in South Carolina he published a pioneering paper in the *American Journal of Science* (1892), "Origin of Carolina Phosphates," which set forth the theory, later validated, of the formation of Carolina phosphates. In Baltimore, Reese was an instructor at Johns Hopkins while he sought other jobs in academia and industry. Finally, in 1900 he landed a job as chief chemist with the New Jersey Zinc Company. By this time many American companies had hired chemists to solve process and product problems. The New Jersey Zinc Company was having trouble with the new German contact sulfuric acid process. Using his skills in chemical analysis, Reese discovered that an impurity in the ore, arsenic oxide, was the culprit and developed a process to remove it. In 1901 he married Harriet Stedman Bent; they had five sons.

Reese's work for New Jersey Zinc brought him to the attention of one of their sulfuric acid customers, the Du Pont Company. In 1902 Du Pont executives hired Reese to be the director of a new experimental laboratory at Repauno, New Jersey. The new Eastern Laboratory was one of the first industrial research laboratories in the United States. General Electric had established its pioneering laboratory only a year earlier. Reese immediately set to work to build up a staff of competent chemists and to prove the value of chemical research for the explosives industry. Over the next few years Reese's small group made significant process and product improvements that impressed the Du Pont executives. Attempting to quantify the value of research, Reese reported in 1910 that four improve-

ments had saved the company $840,000 over the past three years. For example, the consumption of glycerin in the manufacture of dynamite had been decreased by 20 percent.

In 1911 Reese was named chemical director and put in charge of all Du Pont research activities, which included the company's other major laboratory, the Experimental Station near Wilmington, Delaware. In the following years Du Pont's research activities expanded as the company sought to diversify beyond explosives. Reese became one the first industrial research managers. He established procedures for organizing and reporting on research programs. Most important, he had to hire a large number of chemists. Reese excelled in this activity and brought many talented individuals into the company who would have long and productive careers as researchers and managers. Reese and his staff were pushed to the limit during World War I as the Du Pont Company simultaneously developed new explosives and related chemicals for the war, initiated a systematic plan to diversify into new lines of business, and attempted to develop the capability to manufacture synthetic dyestuffs. This last enterprise was the most difficult and costly research initiative Du Pont had undertaken to that date. Up until World War I Germany had dominated the U.S. market for dyestuffs. The war had interrupted international trade, even before the United States entered it in 1917, and supplies of dyestuffs soon ran critically short. The Du Pont Company took on the task of learning the secrets of dyestuff manufacture that the Germans had carefully accumulated over fifty years. By 1919 Du Pont had spent $11 million dollars on dyestuff research and had more than 500 chemists and technicians working on the problem. Overall, Du Pont research expenditures increased from $250,000 in 1914 to $3.5 million in 1919 and the staff increased to 1,200. Since 1902 Reese had presided over a dramatic expansion of Du Pont research that securely established its importance to the future of the firm. He was elected to the board of directors in 1917.

Exactly how research could best be managed and evaluated had become a troubling problem for the Du Pont executives. In 1921 Du Pont decentralized its organization by creating five product divisions—Explosives, Dyestuffs, Cellulose Products, Paint, and Pyralin (plastic)—to manage its now diverse businesses in a more effective manner. The company executives decided that in addition to production and sales, each division needed its own research capability. Over Reese's objections, Du Pont dismembered the Chemical Department, leaving it with few resources and no clear mission. It fell to Reese's protégé, Charles M. A. Stine, to rebuild the central Chemical Department in the 1920s. Reese served as titular head until his retirement in 1924.

After 1920 Reese used his organizational talents to serve the chemical community more broadly. He was president of the Manufacturing Chemists Association (1920–1923), the American Institute of Chemical Engineers (1923–1925), and the American Chemical Society (1934–1935). He was a founder in 1923 and chairman until 1931 of the Directors of Industrial Research, an informal association of research directors who met periodically to discuss issues of mutual interest. He also served in numerous other professional and technical associations. Until his death in Florida, Reese was one of the grand old men of the chemical industry who had participated in the early hectic and heady days of industrial research and chemical enterprise generally.

• There are Reese family papers in the Historical Society of Delaware. Documents on Reese's career at Du Pont are in the Du Pont Company accessions at the Hagley Museum and Library in Wilmington, Del., which also has imprints of many of his articles and copies of his talks. Two significant articles by Reese not mentioned in the text are "Developments in Industrial Research," *Proceedings of the American Society of Testing Materials* 18, pt. 2 (1918): 32–39, and "Scientific Ideals," *Science* 80 (1934): 299–303. He is the topic of a chapter in Maurice Holland, ed., *Industrial Explorers* (1928). Arthur M. Comey prepared an interesting biographical article in *Industrial and Engineering Chemistry* 20, no. 2 (1928): 224–26. An obituary by Robert E. Curtin, Jr. (with a bibliography) is in the *Journal of the American Chemical Society* 62 (1940): 1889–91.

JOHN KENLY SMITH

REESE, Curtis Williford (3 Sept. 1887–5 June 1961), Unitarian minister and religious Humanist, was born in Madison County, North Carolina, the son of Patterson Reese and Rachel Elizabeth Buckner. Reese was raised in a devoutly Southern Baptist family, and after graduating from Mars Hill College in North Carolina, he entered the Baptist ministry in Bellwood, Alabama, in 1908. After a brief stint of supply preaching there, he entered the Southern Baptist Theological Seminary at Louisville in 1908, meanwhile holding pastorates at Gratz and Pleasant Home, Kentucky.

Exposure during his seminary training to the higher criticism of the Bible began to undermine Reese's faith in biblical literalism and initiated a process of doubt and reformulation of his religious belief. He graduated from seminary in 1910 and worked first as state evangelist for the Illinois State Baptist Association and then as pastor of the First Baptist Church of Tiffin, Ohio, from 1911 to 1913. His doubts about conservative theology continued to grow, and feeling that he could no longer remain a Baptist, Reese entered the Unitarian denomination in 1913. Reese's conversion was a gradual one, and as Mason Olds has written, he "moved from a Southern Baptist fundamentalism to a vague type of liberal Protestantism and finally to a nontheistic humanism." He married Fay Rowlett Walker in 1913; they had three children.

After holding Unitarian pastorates at Alton, Illinois (1913–1915), and Des Moines, Iowa (1915–1919), Reese moved to Chicago to become secretary of the Western Unitarian Conference (1919–1930). He rose to prominence within the Unitarian denomination as one of the chief advocates of Humanism, a version of religious liberalism that attempted to turn religious be-

lief away from a focus on the traditional conception of a supernatural God and emphasize the grounding of all religion in human and social experience. In a 1920 article for the *Christian Register*, Reese described "the basic content of most religions" as a "monarchic view of religion" in which "the submission of persons to supernatural agencies" was a key element. He felt that liberal religion must revise that view by discovering the ways in which humanity is able to "cooperate" with cosmic processes "and in a measure control them." This empirically oriented, antidogmatic stance, which included a populist stress on the right of private judgment and the dignity of the individual, was the hallmark of his version of religious Humanism.

Reese was an important spokesman for the noncreedal and antisupernatural tradition in western Unitarianism, which was in frequent conflict with the longer established and more conservative Unitarianism of Boston and the East. Under the leadership of Jenkin Lloyd Jones, the Western Unitarian Conference had emphasized from its beginning in 1852 a stringently noncreedal and antisupernatural form of religious liberalism, and western Unitarianism had accordingly been hospitable to Humanism, with its deemphasis on, or in some cases denial of, the existence of God. Although his beliefs were similar to those of his fellow Humanist leader John H. Dietrich, Reese was less inclined than Dietrich to focus on the most contentious implication of Humanism, its denial of the centrality of a belief in God. In his preface to a 1927 collection of *Humanist Sermons*, Reese stressed that Humanism was not the equivalent of atheism and that the Humanist stance toward God was one of inquiry rather than denial. Yet he also affirmed the Humanist's fundamental faith in scientific method as a form of intellectual inquiry.

In an exposition of the "Program of Humanism" published in *The Meaning of Humanism* (1945), Reese outlined four basic goals: (1) a broadened "conception of the development of personality," which included the "revamping of our understanding of the educational process" to take account of the interaction between the individual and "his environing situation, including his physical and especially his cultural setting"; (2) a "frank abandonment of mystic practices" in deference to a pragmatic sense of means and ends in accomplishing goals—"the institutions designed to cultivate good wishes are reluctant to invent the means necessary to make the good wishes effective"; (3) an equal participation of people in "the goods of life"; and (4) a general "reorganization of social processes and redistribution of social forces" in the creation of a free and harmonious social order. Such a program elevated questions of social responsibility and political ethics to the forefront of religious concerns.

Reese served briefly as president of Lombard College (1928–1929) and was dean of the Abraham Lincoln Centre in Chicago from 1930 to 1957. He had a long association with the liberal religious periodical *Unity*, serving as associate editor from 1925 to 1933, managing editor from 1933 to 1944, and editor from

1945 to 1961. In recognition of his service to the denomination, the American Unitarian Association presented Reese with the Weatherly-Holmes Award in 1959. He died in Chicago.

• Reese's several expositions of humanism can be found in "Do You Believe What He Believes?" *Christian Register* 99 (9 Sept. 1920): 883–84; *Humanism* (1926); *Humanist Religion* (1931); and *The Meaning of Humanism* (1945). He edited a collection of *Humanist Sermons* in 1927, which is one of the most valuable introductions to religious humanist thinking at its high tide in the late 1920s. The best biographical sketch is Mason Olds, *Religious Humanism in America: Dietrich, Reese, and Potter* (1978), which is based in part on Reese's unpublished autobiographical manuscript, "My Life among the Unitarians" (1961). The Old book is also the most thorough assessment of his thought, detailing his involvement in the rise of humanism in Unitarian circles. His involvement with the Western Unitarian Conference is discussed in Charles H. Lyttle, *Freedom Moves West: A History of the Western Unitarian Conference* (1952); his place in twentieth-century Unitarianism is discussed in David Robinson, *The Unitarians and the Universalists* (1985).

DAVID M. ROBINSON

REESIDE, James (1789?–3 Sept. 1842), mail contractor and stagecoach proprietor, was born in Scotland, the son of Edward Reeside and Janet Alexander. His parents moved to Baltimore County, Maryland, shortly after his birth. Because the family had limited financial resources, Reeside received little formal schooling. In 1816 he married Mary Weis, and they had one son and two daughters.

Reeside began his career as a wagoner hauling merchandise between Baltimore, Philadelphia, and Pittsburgh. Later he also transported goods in Ohio from Zanesville to Columbus. Reeside eventually bought his own teams and, shortly thereafter, obtained a military contract for hauling artillery.

During the War of 1812 Reeside was commissioned as a forage master to coordinate the transportation of supplies under the command of General Winfield Scott. During the battle of Lundy's Lane, in which losses on both sides totaled the highest for the entire war, Reeside fought alongside the soldiers.

After the war, while managing a stage line from Hagerstown, Maryland, to McConnellstown, Pennsylvania, Reeside obtained his first government mail contract. In 1818 Reeside—in conjunction with Stockton & Stokes of Baltimore, Simms & Pemberton of Wheeling, Virginia, and several other partners—helped to establish the first regular stage line to carry mail along the Cumberland Road between Baltimore and Wheeling. Shortly thereafter he moved to Cumberland, Maryland, and, in addition to his stage line, managed a tavern. In 1820 Reeside quit the tavern-keeping business to concentrate his energy on expanding both his mail contracts and stage lines.

In 1827, at the request of Postmaster General John McLean, Reeside moved to Philadelphia to manage the mail service between Philadelphia and New York City. He quickly shortened the mail delivery time from twenty-three to twelve hours. Reeside soon purchased most of the stage lines running out of these two cities and became the largest mail contractor in the United States, with more than 400 employees and 1,000 horses. In recognition of his ability to manage such an extensive operation, the press nicknamed Reeside the "land admiral." Joseph Chandler, of the *United States Gazette*, quipped that "the Admiral would leave Philadelphia on a six-horse coach with a hot johnny-cake in pocket and reach Pittsburg before it could grow cold."

Reeside's coaches became famous for their luxury accommodations and, in particular, their bright red color. On warm summer afternoons people would often travel to southern Manhattan to watch the arrival of Reeside's spectacular coaches. "The driver [of the coach] would herald his approach by a melodious winding of his horn." Then, "he would harmlessly crack [his whip] over the heads of the spirited steeds with a noise that, on a clear day, could be 'heard a mile.'"

According to legend, vice president Richard Johnson encouraged Reeside to sport a red tie and vest to match his red coaches. Reeside agreed on the condition that Johnson would do the same. From then on, the two men were often seen strolling down streets together, showing off their red ties and vests. Johnson considered the "admiral" a powerful political ally on account of Reeside's influence over the electorate in the interior of Pennsylvania. Their matching red attire was an unmistakable declaration of a political connection.

Under McLean's successor, William Barry, Reeside became embroiled in a financial scandal. A combination of factors, including a congressional decision to expand mail service and lavish mail contracts awarded by Barry's subordinates, led to the insolvency of the general post office. In order to conceal his inability to cover expenses, Barry privately borrowed money from banks—a measure of dubious legality since the Constitution only granted Congress the authority to borrow money against the credit of the general treasury. Reeside, along with several other mail coach proprietors, also helped to raise large sums of money, as well as to lend personal funds to help Barry cover his costs. A legal battle resulted when Barry's successor, Amos Kendall, refused to repay the mail contractors. Reeside and several others brought suits against the U.S. government for the repayment of these debts. In 1841 a jury awarded Reeside nearly $190,000 in compensation for the personal outlays of money that he had made. A sixteen-year legal battle ensued, however, delaying repayment of the debt until 1857, long after his death.

Just before Reeside's mail contract expired under Kendall, Reeside placed the Philadelphia and New York mail on the Camden & Amboy railroad—one of the earliest instances of railroad mail delivery. Ironically, Reeside had ridiculed the locomotives when they had first come into use. He once offered $1,000 to any man who could build a machine that could drag a stagecoach from Washington to Baltimore faster than a team of his prized Virginia-bred horses. When his contract ended in 1836, he quit the mail service business.

That same year Reeside bought the stage line along the Cumberland Road from Cumberland, Maryland, to Wheeling, Virginia. Three years later he sold his entire interest in the Cumberland Road lines and focused his attention on his legal suit against the federal government. Shortly thereafter Reeside died in Philadelphia.

Quick-witted, friendly, and capable, Reeside was an esteemed friend of many prominent individuals in various political camps, including Andrew Jackson, Richard Johnson, and Henry Clay. His ability to straddle political fences enabled him to take advantage of patronage opportunities offered by the federal government. His influence over parts of the Pennsylvania electorate also made him an indispensable ally. Reeside's hard work and eagerness to maximize new opportunities ultimately made his success possible.

• No personal papers of Reeside are known to exist. The most extensive discussion of him can be found in Thomas B. Searight, *The Old Pike: A History of the National Road* (1894). On Reeside's involvement in the postal financial scandal, see Richard R. John, *Spreading the News: The American Postal System from Franklin to Morse* (1995). Other sources include Benjamin Perley Poore, *Perley's Reminiscences of Sixty Years in the National Metropolis* (1886); and the *Pennsylvania Census* (1840). For information on Reeside's legal suit against the government, see House Committee of Claims, *Report on the Petition of Mary Reeside*, 34th Cong., 1st sess., 1856; and Senate Committee of Claims, *Report on "An Act for the Relief of Mary Reeside,"* 34th Cong., 3d sess., 1857.

PAMELA BAKER

REEVE, Tapping (Oct. 1744–13 Dec. 1823), jurist, legal educator, and author, was born in Brookhaven, Long Island, New York, the son of Abner Reeve, a Presbyterian minister, and Deborah Tapping. In 1759, a year clouded by his mother's death and his father's bout with alcohol, Reeve entered the College of New Jersey (later Princeton University). There he distinguished himself academically, graduating first in his class in 1763. Reeve then entered teaching, serving at a Presbyterian grammar school and as a private tutor. In 1769 he secured a tutorship at his alma mater, where he served until 1771. In that year Reeve also moved to Hartford, Connecticut, to study law under Judge Jesse Root. He was admitted to practice in 1772.

The young lawyer quickly established himself at the bar and enjoyed the fruits of a burgeoning practice. In June 1773 he married Sally Burr, the granddaughter of Jonathan Edwards and the sister of Aaron Burr. They had one son. Stridently patriotic, Reeve accepted an officer's commission in December 1776 and took his place on a committee appointed by the Connecticut Assembly to generate public support for the American cause. In 1783 Reeve was appointed justice of the peace for Litchfield County, a position to which he was reappointed annually for the next four years.

As early as 1774 Reeve, who enjoyed a sterling reputation for his intellect and legal acumen, had also begun offering instruction in his home to students of law. In 1784 he erected a one-room building adjacent to his home designed to accommodate his library, law lectures, and moot court exercises. An extension of Reeve's law office, the Litchfield Law School offered eminently practical rather than theoretical instruction in the tradition of the legal apprenticeship, then the most popular means of preparing for practice. As such, the school cannot rightfully be considered the archetype of the modern legal academy; nevertheless, it has the honor of being America's first private law school. But more significant, from its inception Reeve's school was the most influential force in legal education until the publication of David Hoffman's *Course of Legal Study* and the opening of Harvard's law school, both of which occurred in 1817. An instant success, Reeve's institution attracted students from every state and territory in the country by offering the most thorough and systematic legal instruction of the day. After opening the Litchfield Law School, Reeve spent little time at the bar, devoting the next fourteen years primarily to teaching.

In 1788 Reeve was named state's attorney for Litchfield County. He served subsequently in the state legislature, and in 1792 he was appointed to the state council. The year 1798 marked a turning point in Reeve's life. In April 1798, one year after the death of his first wife, he married his devoted housekeeper, Elizabeth Thompson, a woman thirty years his junior. They had no children. That same year he accepted an appointment to the Connecticut Superior Court and turned over many of his teaching responsibilities to James Gould, a Yale graduate and recent Litchfield alumnus.

In political matters Reeve evinced decidedly Federalist sympathies. Frustrated by the policies of the Jefferson administration, Reeve, a man of ardent temperament, took up the pen. Writing under the names Phocion, Asdrubal, and Marcellus, he produced at least twenty-six articles for the Federalist newspaper *The Monitor* between 1801 and 1803. Reeve disdained Republican policies and perceived the party and its leader as blasphemous, immoral, and despotic, bent on undermining both the Constitution and the clergy. One of his earliest articles resulted in an indictment for seditious libel against President Thomas Jefferson. Grand jury proceedings, which did not commence until 1806, were, however, summarily dismissed by the defamed president himself.

Reeve enjoyed a successful tenure on the bench, and in May 1814, after sixteen years on the court, he was elevated to chief judge. One year after his promotion, however, Reeve reached the compulsory age of retirement, and in May 1815 he tendered his resignation. The former chief judge returned to the classroom, while his associate, James Gould, received an appointment to the superior court. Reeve took advantage of his retirement from the bench to publish his principal work, *The Law of Baron and Femme* (1816).

The jurist's health deteriorated steadily beginning in 1816, and by 1820 he was compelled to retire from teaching. Gould returned to the classroom full time and struck an agreement with his mentor whereby the latter continued to receive one-third of the school's proceeds. As attendance waned, however, the residuals proved too meager, and Reeve returned to publishing to supplement his income. Still, it was not until 1825, two years after Reeve's death, that his second work, *A Treatise on the Law of Descents in the Several United States of America*, was published.

This celebrated pedagogue and judge was also a deeply religious man, a devoted representative of the Connecticut Bible Society and stalwart layman who labored with Lyman Beecher to foster revival in Litchfield and to preserve morality and orthodoxy. He was a generous and devoted family man as well. Although he had no children by his second wife, his home was remembered as a bustling haven. Following the death of his son, Reeve moved his daughter-in-law and grandson into his home, accepting guardianship for the young boy. There they joined Amelia Ogden, an orphan whom the Reeves counted as a daughter, and Polly Barnes, the family's friend, nurse, and cook. Reeve died in Litchfield.

Reeve is best remembered as the new republic's most influential legal educator. By the time the Litchfield Law School closed its doors in 1833, the institution boasted more than 900 alumni, including two vice presidents, three U.S. Supreme Court justices, twenty-eight senators, 101 congressmen, fourteen governors, and at least sixteen state court chief justices. No contemporary academy could claim a more distinguished legacy, and "no educator," recalled one alumnus, "was ever more generally beloved by his pupils" (Lewis, p. 15). Reeve was also renowned as a jurist, and his retirement prompted "the regret of all admirers of legal learning and lovers of impartial justice" (Lewis, p. 16).

• Papers and correspondence relating to Tapping Reeve are gathered in several collections. The Reeve Family Papers, 1767–1866, are at the Fairfield Historical Society; the Reeve manuscripts are at Yale University and Princeton University; and the Gould Collection and numerous documents regarding Reeve and the Litchfield Law School are at the Litchfield Historical Society. The most recent account of Reeve and his contribution to legal education is Marian C. McKenna, *Tapping Reeve and the Litchfield Law School* (1986). For an earlier account see Samuel Fisher, *The Litchfield Law School, 1775–1833: Biographical Catalogue of Students* (1933). Other useful biographical sketches, along with many reminiscences, appear in Lyman Beecher, D.D., "Sermon Preached at the Funeral of Hon. Tapping Reeve," *Christian Spectator*, Feb. 1827, pp. 62–71; G. H. Hollister, *The History of Connecticut* (2 vols., 1857); J. W. Lewis, *History of Litchfield County, Connecticut with Illustrations and Biographical Sketches of Its Prominent Men and Pioneers* (1881); Dwight C. Kilbourn, *The Bench and Bar of Litchfield County, Connecticut, 1709–1909* (1909); and David Boardman, *Sketches of the Early Lights of the Litchfield Bar* (1860). Further discussion of Reeve and the Law School may be found in sundry sources, including Albert J. Harno, *Legal Education in the United States* (1953; repr. 1980), and Alfred Z. Reed, *Training for the Public Profession of the Law* (1921). Other useful sources include *Autobiography, Correspondence, Etc., of Lyman Beecher, D.D.*, ed. Charles Beecher (2 vols., 1864); Alain C. White, *The History of the Town of Litchfield Connecticut, 1720–1920* (1920); and Charles Moore, "The Litchfield Law School," *Law Notes* 4 (Feb. 1901): 208. Reeve's obituary is in the *Connecticut Courant*, 23 Dec. 1863.

KEVIN R. CHANEY

REEVES, David Wallis (14 Feb. 1838–8 Mar. 1900), bandmaster and composer, was born in Owego, New York, the youngest son of Lorenzo Reeves and Maria Clarke. His earliest musical training was on the alto horn, which he played in the Owego Municipal Band before switching to the cornet. He began studying with noted bandmaster and cornetist Thomas G. Canhan of Binghamton at about age fourteen. For the next several years Reeves played in traveling bands that were headquartered in Elmira, New York, and directed by his teacher. During the summers the bands played for the Don Rice Circus, and during the winters they played dances. He returned to direct the Owego Band in 1857.

In 1860 Reeves moved to New York City and became a member of the Dodworth orchestra. A European tour as cornet soloist with the Rumsey and Newcomb Minstrel Troupe followed. In England he met distinguished brasswind maker and cornetist Henry Distin, who gave him an engraved archetype piston-valve cornet. While in London, he acquired the technique of double and triple tonguing and was billed as the first American cornetist to triple-tongue in performance. Reeves returned to the United States in 1862, became a soloist in Dodworth's band in New York City, and played in the orchestra at the Lucy Rushton Theatre.

In 1866 Reeves was invited to succeed Joseph C. Greene as director of the American Band of Providence, Rhode Island, then primarily a marching band that traced its roots to the War of 1812 and the first completely civilian band in the United States. Reeves expanded the band's membership to include woodwinds, increasing its flexibility while standardizing the instrumentation of the parade and concert band. During Reeves's thirty-four years as its leader, the band consisted of a core of thirty full-time professional musicians, with almost no turnover. Throughout Reeves's tenure, the American Band remained financially independent and solvent. After achieving success in New England and Canada, Reeves took the band on tours to Baltimore, New Orleans, Chicago, Milwaukee, Minneapolis, and Portland, Oregon.

In addition to his conducting responsibilities, Reeves began composing, primarily marches; appearing as a guest soloist with other bands; and teaching the cornet. He married Sarah E. Blanding in 1871; they had one child, a son. In the summer of 1878, using a real ship as a set, Reeves staged an epic production of Gilbert and Sullivan's *HMS Pinafore*.

In the fall of 1892, following the death of Patrick Gilmore, Reeves was summoned, while on tour with the American Band in Tacoma, Washington, to become the director of Gilmore's celebrated Twenty-second Regiment Band. Reeves hurried to St. Louis, where he was welcomed at the train station by the Gilmore band, was escorted to his hotel by the Jefferson Barracks Army Band in a parade through streets lined with cheering admirers, and was presented with a lyre-shaped gold medal upon his public acceptance of his new role.

Reeves led the band for the rest of the season, performing at the World's Columbian Exposition in Chicago in 1893 and at the Western Pennsylvania Exposition in Pittsburgh. But the tour ended abruptly in Cincinnati. The financial hardship of touring with a 100-member band, coupled with the defection of several of Gilmore's key players to the newly formed John Philip Sousa band, hastened the band's demise. Reeves relinquished the conductorship but supported the continuation of the Gilmore band, now directed by Victor Herbert. He joined in an exchange of somewhat hostile words among former Gilmore bandsmen, chronicled in letters to the *Musical Courier*. He returned to Providence in October 1893 and resumed leadership of the American Band, a position he maintained for the remainder of his life.

As a composer, Reeves wrote 175 known works, including 136 marches, and was dubbed "the father of band music in America" by Sousa. As a forerunner to the "March King," Reeves combined extreme simplicity with utmost sophistication in creating the modern, contrapuntal military march. Reeves also crystallized the formal structure of the march, extended the range of its melodies to more than an octave and a half, and imbued the march with a rhythmic inventiveness extending beyond the percussion section.

Best known among his marches is the *Second Regiment Connecticut National Guard*, a favorite of Charles Ives, composed in 1876 for one of the several military units to which the American Band was attached. The playing of Reeves's 1895 "Marche Funebre," *Immortalis*, became a Memorial Day tradition at the Soldiers' and Sailors' Monument on Old Exchange Place in Providence. His *Brown University Commencement* march of 1869 was created to lead the school's annual academic procession. Reeves's marches were kept alive through regular performances by the American Band, including a memorial concert on the fiftieth anniversary of his death.

Reeves also wrote three operas, *The Ambassador's Daughter* (1880), *The Mandarin Zune* (1888), and *West Point* (1882), which includes additional marches; several programmatic pieces, such as *The Night Alarm* (1890), a chronicle of a fire company's call to arms; and *The Evening Call* (1894), a humorous depiction of an interrupted kiss; plus arrangements of other composers' works. Reeves's compositions were published by several eastern publishers, notably the W. H. Cundy Company in Boston.

Reeves's contributions as both a bandmaster and composer are significant. The American Band's musical growth and financial stability under his leadership provided a model for his successors, and his tripart, contrapuntal marches predate Sousa's by more than twenty years. David Stackhouse concludes that "Reeves' music is often deceptively simple; but like Mozart's, never naive. His soundness of musicianship is always in evidence; and his feeling for the movement of marching, his awareness of the musical complexities involved in writing for that movement, which some take for granted, amount to the most extreme sophistication" (Stackhouse, p. 23).

Reeves died in Providence. The David Wallis Reeves Amphitheatre, built in 1920, and a fountain dedicated to his memory are located in Providence's Roger Williams Park.

• Reeves's manuscripts, along with photographs, programs, correspondence, phonograph recordings, and other memorabilia, are in the Reeves American Band Collection at the Providence Public Library. A biography and catalog of his works was compiled by David L. Stackhouse in the *Journal of Band Research* 5, no. 2 (1969): 15–28, and 6, no. 1 (1969): 29–41. An updated list of his known works is included in *The Heritage Encyclopedia of Band Music*, vol. 2 (1991). Commentary from his contemporaries is found in F. O. Jones, *A Handbook of American Music and Musicians* (1886); "David Wallis Reeves," *Musical Courier* 26 (1893): 13; and Alfred M. Williams and William F. Blanding, eds., *Men of Progress: Biographical Sketches and Portraits of Leaders in Business and Professional Life in the State of Rhode Island and Providence Plantations* (1896). See also H. Barker, "The Father of American Band Music," *Providence Magazine* 28 (1916): 726; Arlan R. Coolidge, "How Rhode Island Nearly Lost Reeves and the American Band," *Rhode Island History* 22 (1963): 35; F. M. Marciniak and J. Stanley Lemons, *Strike Up the Band* (1979); H. W. Schwartz, *Bands of America* (1957); and Margaret Hindle Hazen and Robert M. Hazen, *The Music Men: An Illustrated History of Bands in America, 1800–1920* (1987). An obituary is in the *Providence Journal*, 9 Mar. 1900.

H. G. YOUNG III

REEVES, Jim (20 Aug. 1924–31 July 1964), country music singer, was born in Panola County, Texas, near the county seat of Carthage, the son of Thomas Middleton and Bulah Adams, cotton farmers. His father died when he was ten months old. He attended elementary school in the two-room schools located in Baptist churches, first in Deadwood and Galloway, and then in Deberry, where the family moved. "I learned early," he told an interviewer, "that farm life is hard, almost too hard unless you find diversions." His was the guitar, which he began playing at age six. However, he didn't see any future at first as a musician or singer and much preferred baseball.

Beginning in junior high at Carthage (Tex.) High School, he was a star athlete and graduated with a sports scholarship to the University of Texas. He was in college about six weeks when he was drafted into service for World War II. In his army physical, however, he was diagnosed with an athlete's heart (in which muscles surrounding the heart are too large) and rejected. He found work in the Galveston shipyards, then resumed his studies. In college, he was scouted by the St. Louis Cardinals. He was signed and shipped to their farm team, the Virginia Cardinals, in Lynchburg. He played from 1944 to 1947, first breaking a finger, then injuring his collarbone, and finally injuring a leg sliding into second base. He was farmed out to the Evangeline League in Alexandria, Louisiana, who sold his contract to a club in Marshall, Texas. There he met Mary Elizabeth White, a part-time waitress, drugstore clerk, and salesperson at Woolworth's. They married in 1947.

Singing became Reeves's "second choice, when I had to trade my glove in for a guitar." His widow said, "That might have been the case at first, but once he got a taste he wanted it so bad." She recalled they undertook a six-week tour of the Northwest in the winter of 1953, taking turns driving, sometimes through snowstorms, overnight to dates hundreds of miles apart.

Back home, when he wasn't singing in clubs on weekends, Reeves worked as an announcer and disk jockey for Henderson, Texas's KGRI Radio, which he later purchased. Famed honky-tonk pianist Moon Mullican hired him to play lead guitar in his Beaumont, Texas, band.

He was signed in 1954 by radio station KWKH as an announcer and artist on the Louisiana Hayride in Shreveport, where he got his first break filling in for former regular Hank Williams on the weekly Saturday night broadcast. Reeves was greatly influenced by Williams's style and attempted to follow in his footsteps. He recorded for a small label, Abbott Records. His first record, which he "threw off in an hour," was "Mexican Joe." "Nobody was as surprised as I was when it made the country hit parade and stayed there," Reeves told an interviewer.

Reeves made guest appearances on the Grand Ole Opry and Los Angeles's "Home Town Jamboree." He received acceptance from a wide spectrum of fans and soon learned his voice was much more in league with Bing Crosby's. An astute businessman, Reeves found country's hayseed and hillbilly image distasteful and was determined to see it progress and expand. Country music historian Bill Malone noted: "Of all the country-pop singers of the late fifties and early sixties, he had the greatest ability to appeal to popular (music) audiences without at the same time losing his sense of country identity. . . . He had a mellow, resonant quality [which many described as] a touch of velvet."

The singer was recognized in a poll of country disk jockeys in 1953. He was the only country performer selected to accompany a USO tour to U.S. bases in Europe. On his return, he appeared with several of the tour's artists on Ed Sullivan's television program "Toast of the Town." His popularity didn't escape RCA recording artist and producer Chet Atkins, who, with Decca Records producer Owen Bradley, was in the process of ushering in the country-pop era known as the Nashville Sound. When Reeves moved to Nashville in 1955 to join the Opry, Atkins was quick to sign him.

With "Four Walls" (1957), a plaintive ballad of longing and waiting and the first of several million-selling gold records, and his self-composed "Am I Losing You?" (1957), he became one of the earliest exponents of the new sound.

Reeves, who preferred tuxedos to rhinestone western wear, was termed a "smooth crooner" and nicknamed "Gentleman Jim." Music publishers frequently sought him out as their artist of first choice to record a song. He and his band the Blue Boys toured cross-country in a show bus. Other hits were: "Bimbo" (1954), "I Love You" (1954), "Yonder Comes a Sucker" (1955), "Billy Bayou" (1959), "He'll Have to Go" (1959), "Partners" (1959), "Guilty" (1963), "I Guess I'm Crazy" (1964), "Love Is No Excuse" (1964), and "Welcome to My World" (1964).

According to Melvin Shestack in *The Country Music Encyclopedia* (1974), from 1955 to 1968 (four years after his death) Reeves had one or more Top Ten chart records—and is still in the Top Ten list of artists with the most charted records.

Onstage and in the recording studio, Reeves was a perfectionist. "I'm most particular about what I record," he said, "I won't do a song unless I'm convinced it's very top quality and has commercial potential. I'm not attracted to frivolous songs or 'pot-boilers.' The songs I get sold on are those that have heart and emotional pull."

Reeves had his own radio show on the ABC network in 1957. Besides appearances on television with Steve Allen, Dick Clark, and Jimmy Dean, he hosted the popular (Ozark) "Jubilee, U.S.A." on ABC in the summer of 1958. With a Grand Ole Opry troupe, he played New York's Carnegie Hall in December 1961. He toured Europe extensively, where his popularity soared forth from American military bases. He starred in the movie *Kimberley Jim* (1965), shot in South Africa.

On the international appeal of country music, Reeves wrote in *Billboard's World of Country Music* (1964), "A country boy strumming a guitar and singing a story in which an American and a Russian share a common interest will do more to ease tension(s) than all the threats and counter threats of the past decade."

With his schedule expanding more and more, and tiring of long bus rides, Reeves learned to fly and bought a four-seater plane. On a real estate scouting trip, it crashed in Tennessee, killing Reeves and his manager/pianist Dean Manuel. Reeves was a prolific entertainer and at his death had a huge backlog of unreleased masters, which RCA continued to release on albums and compact disk. In 1967 Reeves was named to the Country Music Hall of Fame. His widow maintains the Jim Reeves Museum in Nashville.

• Jim Reeves is featured in Robert Shelton, *The Country Music Story* (1966), and the Country Music Foundation's *Country: The Music and the Musicians* (1988). An extensive description of his career appears in Irwin Stambler and Grelun Landon, *The Encyclopedia of Folk, Country & Western Music*, 2d ed. (1983). Bill Malone, *Country Music, USA* (1985), contains useful information as well as a bibliography. Obituaries are in the *Nashville Banner* and *Nashville Tennessean*, 1 Aug. 1964.

ELLIS NASSOUR

REEVES, Joseph Mason (20 Nov. 1872–25 Mar. 1948), U.S. Navy admiral, was born in Tampico, Illinois, the son of Joseph Cunningham Reeves and Frances Brewer, farmers. As a high school senior Reeves took an exam for admission to the U.S. Military Academy. Failing to receive an appointment, he accepted a position as a midshipman at the U.S. Naval Academy. After graduating in 1894, Reeves served two years as assistant engineer aboard the cruiser *San Francisco*. In 1896 he married Eleanor Merrken Watkins; they had three children. That same year he was assigned to the battleship *Oregon*, where he was responsible for operating and maintaining its main engines throughout the Spanish-American War. With the amalgamation of the Engineer Corps and the line, in 1899, Reeves received a line commission as lieutenant junior grade. From 1899 to 1906 he served as a gunnery officer aboard the battleships *Wisconsin* and *Kearsarge* and later returned to the cruiser *San Francisco*. While aboard these vessels, Reeves drilled the gun crews to fire rapidly and with accuracy. Reeves next taught at the Naval Academy from 1906 to 1908. He then became gunnery officer of the battleship *New Hampshire*. In 1913 Reeves received his first command, the collier *Jupiter*, and two years later he assumed command of the battleship *Oregon*. During World War I he commanded the battleship *Maine*, in the Atlantic, and later he served as naval attaché to Rome. From 1921 to 1923 Reeves commanded the battleship *North Dakota*, after which he attended the Naval War College and stayed on as a faculty member from 1924 to 1925.

Because of the navy's need for senior aviation officers, Reeves volunteered to attend a three-month naval aviation observer's course at Pensacola Naval Air Station in 1925. In October 1925 he became commander, Aircraft Squadrons, Battle Fleet, in the Pacific. This position enabled him to have tactical and operational command of the Battle Fleet's air squadrons, based in San Diego. Although not a pilot, Reeves had formed a keen insight into the capabilities and applications of the airplane and the aircraft carrier from his studies at the Naval War College and in Rome. Because of his ideas about and desires for experimentation with carrier aviation, Reeves, after arriving aboard the carrier *Langley*, gave his aviators more specifically military tasks, ordering them to increase flight deck operations, which resulted in a high number of takeoffs and landings in 1925 and the summer of 1926. In addition, he ordered more planes be carried on the *Langley* in order to enhance its operational effectiveness. The following year, additional pilots began training on board the *Langley* in order to fill the squadrons aboard the two new carriers *Saratoga* and *Lexington*. However, instead of overseeing this training, Reeves was, in 1927, ordered to temporary duty as aviation adviser for the United States at the Geneva Naval Con-

ference. After six weeks of unsuccessful disarmament negotiations among the world's leading naval powers, the conference concluded.

When Reeves returned from Switzerland, he was promoted to rear admiral on 16 August 1927. Resuming command of Aircraft Squadrons, Battle Fleet, he strove to prove the tactical applications of the carrier and its air squadrons to naval officers who maintained that battleships should be the backbone of the fleet. In simulated exercises for Fleet Problems VII and VIII (1927, 1928), Reeves established the tactical potential of his carriers and aircraft by deploying individual carriers to designated points and then launching the aircraft for dawn and daylight surprise attacks. In 1929, during Fleet Problem IX, he obtained permission to use the carrier *Saratoga* as an independent task force with only one additional ship acting as plane guard. When the carrier was in position, it launched its planes, which carried out a successful dawn attack on the preassigned target, the Panama Canal's Pacific locks. However, after recovery of the aircraft, enemy battleships located and, according to umpires, sank the *Saratoga*. Despite this unfortunate conclusion, the importance of naval aviation had been established.

After this exercise, Reeves served on the General Board, a body of senior naval officers who advised and recommended on matters such as intelligence, ship design, and war plans. While on the General Board, he played a role in decisions about the location of an airship base and, in the London Naval Conference, the last naval arms limitation treaty before World War II. Later in 1930 when his tour in Washington ended, Reeves returned to naval aviation's major post as commander carriers, Battle Fleet. In contrast to the success he experienced in the fleet problem in 1929, Reeves's participation in Fleet Problem XI proved less than successful. Because of excessive distances, pilots had difficulty locating their ships and his carriers burned exorbitant amounts of fuel. The closing of these maneuvers marked the end of Reeves's direct command association with naval aviation.

After briefly serving as commandant of the Navy Yard at Mare Island in 1931, Reeves became commander, Battleships Divisions, in 1932. Shortly thereafter, the navy assigned him to the second-highest sea command, commander, Battle Fleet. Because Japan increased its commercial maritime movement on the U.S. West Coast and terminated the Washington Naval Treaty of 1922, Reeves began placing an emphasis on fleet security and mentally prepared his men for war. Then in June 1934 he became commander in chief, U.S. Fleet. From 1934 to late 1936 Reeves conducted maneuvers to test fleet readiness for war, stressing operations in the Pacific. Foreshadowing future naval engagements, he ordered exercises around Pearl Harbor and Midway Island. Then on 1 December 1936, Reeves retired.

Within four years the navy recalled him to serve during the prewar national emergency and later for duty in World War II. Following duty in the office of the secretary of the navy, Reeves was assigned to the

Roberts Commission, which was established to examine the debacle at Pearl Harbor. From 1941 to 1945 he served as lend-lease liaison officer for the Navy Department and as a member of the Munitions Assignment Board. In 1946 Reeves retired once again and two years later died in Bethesda Naval Hospital. Admiral Reeves's involvement in and strong advocacy of naval aviation, along with other officers such as Admirals William F. Halsey and Ernest J. King, promoted the efficiency, experience, and growth of carrier-based operations, all of which were critical to carrier aviation's successes during World War II.

• Papers pertaining to Reeves are located in both Navy Department Records in the National Archives and in the Naval War College Archives. The best-detailed and most concise sources are John D. Hayes, "Admiral Joseph Mason Reeves, USN (1872–1948): Part One—To 1931, the Engineering, Gunnery, and Aviation Years," *Naval War College Review* 23 (Nov. 1970): 48–57, and Hayes's "Admiral Joseph Mason Reeves, USN (1872–1948): Part II—1931 to 1948, Commanding the U.S. Fleet and in World War II," *Naval War College Review* 24 (Jan. 1972): 50–64. Adolphus Andrews, Jr., "Admiral with Wings, the Career of Joseph Mason Reeves" (senior diss., Princeton Univ., 1943), also furnishes valuable information. An excellent article describing events in 1927 and 1928 is Eugene E. Wilson, "The Navy's First Carrier Task Force," U.S. Naval Institute *Proceedings* 76 (Feb. 1950): 158–69. See also Richard K. Smith, *The Airships Akron and Macon: Flying Aircraft Carriers of the United States Navy* (1965); Gerald F. Bogan, "The Navy Spreads Its Golden Wings," U.S. Naval Institute *Proceedings* 87 (May 1961): 96–119; Archibald D. Turnbull and Clifford L. Lord, *History of United States Naval Aviation* (1949); and Charles M. Melhorn, *Two-Block Fox: The Rise of the American Carrier, 1911–1929* (1974).

R. BLAKE DUNNAVENT

REGAN, John (1818–5 May 1893), newspaper editor and author, was apparently born in northern England, near the Lune River, of Irish parents. He attended school in Ayrshire, Scotland, and later taught there for a few years. Early in 1842 he married a woman named Elizabeth (last name unknown) and sailed for the United States. They eventually had four children.

In the summer of 1842 Regan established a homestead in Virgil—a rural hamlet that no longer exists—in Fulton County, Illinois, not far from the village of Ellisville. While there he raised crops, worked as a harvest hand, taught school during the winter months, and traveled throughout the western Illinois region. In late 1843 or 1844 Regan moved to the Mormon community of Nauvoo, fifty miles farther west, but he apparently had a bad experience there and did not stay long. (That theocratic city-state was in sometimes violent conflict with non-Mormon pioneers during 1844 and 1845.) Regan then moved to Knoxville, a village not far from Galesburg, where he lived for twenty months.

In 1847 Regan returned to Scotland, where he taught school at Whitletts, a village in Ayrshire, and wrote *The Emigrant's Guide to the Western States of America*, a record of his experience as a settler in Ful-

ton County and an account of conditions on the Illinois frontier. The work first appeared serially in the *Ayrshire Advertiser*, probably in 1850–1851, but no copy survives. Regan produced a second, expanded version in 1852, which was published in Edinburgh and called the "second edition."

The book is a lively compilation of scenic descriptions, character sketches, autobiographical episodes, and factual information. Despite its expansive title, *The Emigrant's Guide* focuses entirely on western Illinois, and although intended as a guide for emigrants, it includes much highly literary writing. Regan views the Illinois landscape in Edenic terms and vividly portrays several frontier communities. His character sketches frequently record the language spoken by his subjects, so the book is a remarkable record of the English dialects of early Illinois. Perhaps influenced by J. Hector St. John de Crèvecoeur's *Letters from an American Farmer* (1782), *The Emigrant's Guide* is as much a celebration of the American social experiment as it is a guide to the frontier. Moreover, by showing how he fit into western culture and by emphasizing the uniqueness of the United States, Regan creates a myth of the European who blends into New World society at its formative edge, the frontier. In other words, he presents himself as a representative emigrant who successfully undergoes the process of becoming that newest and most remarkable of humankind's manifestations, an American. The title of *The Emigrant's Guide* has, in fact, two meanings: it is a guide *for* emigrants, and it is an account produced *by* "the emigrant," Regan, whose experience is a model for others to follow, regardless of where they settle in "the Western States of America."

Regan and his family returned to Illinois in 1852 and settled at Knoxville, where he operated a book bindery. In 1855 he purchased the *Knoxville Journal*, which he edited for two years. After selling it, he founded the first newspaper at nearby Elmwood, the *Observer*, and soon supplied editions of it for the villages of Yates City and Maquon, under the titles *Western Watchman* and *Maquon Times*. Regan was in and out of the newspaper business for the rest of his life. In 1874 he launched his most successful newspaper, the *Elmwood Messenger*, which he edited, along with the revived *Maquon Times*, until 1890, when failing health forced his retirement.

In January 1893 Regan entered the Illinois Central Hospital for the Insane at Jacksonville, where he later died. He is buried at Elmwood.

• *The Emigrant's Guide* was reprinted in 1859 as *The Western Wilds of America*, but since then it has been out of print. Partly for that reason, Regan has remained a little-known figure. However, his book has received some attention in recent years. See John E. Hallwas, "John Regan's *Emigrant's Guide*: A Neglected Literary Achievement," *Illinois Historical Journal* 77 (1984): 269–94; Hallwas, *Illinois Literature: The Nineteenth Century* (1986), which reprints a section of Regan's book; and James Hurt, *Writing Illinois* (1992).

JOHN E. HALLWAS

REHAN, Ada (22 Apr. 1857–8 Jan. 1916), actress, was born Ada Delia Crehan in Limerick, Ireland, the daughter of Thomas Crehan and Harriett Ryan. Her family moved to Brooklyn, New York, when Ada was five years old and although she displayed no predisposition toward the theater as a young girl and received a somewhat scattered education, she followed her siblings to the stage. Her older sister Kate married actor-manager Oliver Doud Byron and joined his company, joined later by another sister Harriet; brother Arthur also became an actor. In 1873 Ada joined her sisters on tour helping out backstage. When the company was scheduled to perform in Newark, New Jersey, a young actress became ill so Ada appeared, for one night only, in the role of Clara in *Across the Continent*. A close family, the Crehans discussed Ada's talent and decided that she should pursue a theatrical career, so she embarked for New York City. She made her New York debut later that year in a small part in *Thoroughbred* at Wood's Museum. This brief exposure brought her to the attention of Louisa Lane Drew, an actress and the manager of the Arch Street Theatre in Philadelphia, and Ada Crehan became a member of the stock company there in late 1873. She remained in Philadelphia for the next two seasons gaining valuable experience and appearing most notably as Ophelia in *Hamlet* (with Edwin Booth, 1873) and Virginia in *Virginius* (with John McCullough, 1874). During her first season at the Arch Theatre, a typographical error in the program listed her as "Ada C. Rehan," and she kept the name for the rest of her career.

Like most actors of the time, Rehan moved from company to company in her early career, often playing with some of the most established stars of the day. In 1875 she joined the company at Macauley's Theatre in Louisville, Kentucky, for one season, then returned to the North to act for two seasons in Albany, New York, with John W. Albough's Company. In 1877, while appearing in Albany as Bianca in David Garrick's adaptation of Shakespeare's *Taming of the Shrew*, she came to the attention of manager and producer Augustin Daly. Two years later he saw her again appearing as Mary Standish in *Pique* at the Grand Opera House in New York City. Rehan signed with Daly and acted with his company for the next twenty years. She debuted with Daly in May 1879 at the Olympic Theatre in New York as Big Clemence in Daly's version of *L'Assomior*. The following September Daly opened his own theater at the corner of Broadway and Thirtieth Streets with Rehan making her first appearance there as Nelly Beers in *Love's Young Dream*; a few weeks later on 30 September Daly remounted his popular *Divorce* with Rehan as Miss Lu Ten Eyck. Rehan quickly became the leading comedienne and one of Daly's "Big Four" with John Drew, Anne Hartley Gilbert, and James Lewis. Recognizing and developing her ability as a comic actress, Daly gave Rehan contemporary roles such as Sylvia in Farquhar's *The Recruiting Officer* (1885) and Hippolyta in Colley Cibber's *She Would and She Would Not* (1882). As would be the case

for most of her career, her reviews at this time were mixed. Of her role as Hippolyta, critic John Ranken Towse said, "She frolicked through the part of the disguised Hippolyta with infinite vivacity and pretty audacity, making a fascinating cavalier. But as a bit of old comedy her performance was utterly insignificant" (p. 16). However, two years later Otis Skinner described her performance as "buoyant, scintillant, with a manner unlike other women, a voice that melted and caressed as it drawled, an awkward grace, an arch expression, a look of mischief in her gray Irish eyes, she was a young goddess of laughter—a modern Peg Woffington" (p. 138).

In 1884 Daly took his company to London for the first time where it performed at Toole's Theatre. Beginning in 1886 Daly, wishing to expand Rehan's repertoire, began producing revivals of Shakespeare's comedies beginning with *Merry Wives of Windsor* at Daly's Theatre in New York. She first played Katherine in *Taming of the Shrew* in 1887, often considered one of her greatest roles. Daly recalled that the "Katherine of Miss Rehan was one of the most individual and striking figures of the time" (p. 28), while Towse suggested that Rehan "started her performance at the highest pitch of quivering indignation at her command, and thereby secured a most picturesque and effective entrance. She maintained herself at this level, or near it, with amazing energy, but the effort left her without any reserve force for climaxes. Consequently her performance was lacking in light and shade, and grew weaker instead of stronger toward the end" (pp. 348–49). She perhaps rectified this as she played the role for the next decade, for the author of her obituary in the *New York Times* noted that "she raised the character of Shakespeare's Shrew from the level of turbulent farce, and made it a credible, consistent, continuously interesting and ultimately sympathetic image of human nature." During her tenure with Daly, Rehan played over 200 roles including the best of Shakespeare's comic heroines, including Helena in *A Midsummer Night's Dream*. Rosalind in *As You Like It*, Viola in *Twelfth Night*, Julia in *Two Gentlemen of Verona*, and Beatrice in *Much Ado about Nothing*. Other than Katherine, her most well-known portrayal was that of Rosalind. "She embodied it," noted critic William Winter, "charming every observer by the copious and prodigal exuberance of her sweetness and her brilliancy, and winning the honor that is due to royal achievement in dramatic arts. . . . When she spoke the epilogue, which she did with zest and finish that gave point and glitter to that inadequate tag, she had vindicated her rank among the great comedians of the century" (*Shadows*, pp. 161–64). Rehan also gained a European following with Daly's company making eight separate tours to Europe, acting in London, Paris, Dublin, Edinburgh, and Berlin, and in 1891 Daly opened his own theater in Leicester Square in London, at which Rehan regularly performed.

With Daly's death in 1899 Rehan retired from the stage, but returned a year later to play Nell Gwynn in *Sweet Nell of Old Drury* only to retire again after her mother's death in 1901. In 1903 she returned to the stage a final time touring with Otis Skinner in a repertoire of her most popular Shakespearean comedies and the following season began to tour on her own. But the tour was cut short in May 1905 because of illness and she never returned to the stage. She died in New York City having never married.

Rehan's portrayals of established roles, particularly Shakespearean, were fresh. Rather than relying on standard conventions she made each role wholly individual. She was known for her insight into characters and for her natural energy, which came through every part she played—Winter called it "buoyant glee." After seeing Rehan in various roles, the great English actress Ellen Terry said, "I can only exclaim, not explain! . . . She understood, like all great comediennes, that you must not pretend to be serious so sincerely that no one in the audience see through it!" (Ellen Terry, *The Story of My Life*, p. 293). Rehan's rise to stardom and recognition in the theater was a longer process than for many other stars of the time, and for most of her career she experienced qualified praise. Winter suggested that Rehan "was a prodigy of original force. Her influence, accordingly, was felt more than it was understood, and being elusive and strange, it prompted wide differences of opinion" (*Wallet of Time*, p. 135). At a time when a large portion of the theatrical community had come to the United States from England, Rehan followed Charlotte Cushman to become one of the first American actresses to gain a following outside of the United States and was known as one of the greatest actresses of her day. Along with other female stars such as Julia Marlowe and Viola Allen, Rehan is often credited with helping to instill a sense of middle-class morality to the American stage.

• Clippings and other memorabilia are in the Billy Rose Theatre Collection at the New York Public Library for the Performing Arts, Lincoln Center. William Winter's *Ada Rehan* (1891) was intended as a publicity tool for the actress and is highly complimentary. Information may be found in Winter, *Shadows of the Stage* (1892) and *Wallet of Time*, vol. 2 (1913). She is also included in Lewis C. Strang, *Famous Actresses of the Day in America* (1899), Otis Skinner, *Footlights and Spotlights* (1924), John Ranken Towse, *Sixty Years of the Theater: An Old Critic's Memories* (1916). She is discussed in Marvin Feldheim, *The Theatre of Augustin Daly* (1958), and Joseph Francis Daly, *The Life of Augustin Daly* (1917). An obituary is in the *New York Times*, 9 Jan. 1916.

MELISSA VICKERY-BAREFORD

REICH, Wilhelm (24 Mar. 1897–3 Nov. 1957), psychoanalyst and natural scientist, was born in Dobrzcynica, Galicia, Austro-Hungarian Empire, the son of Leon Reich, a cattle farmer, and Cecile Roniger. Reich, whose family was Jewish but nonobservant, always insisted that he did not adhere to any organized religion. He had a privileged if somewhat isolated childhood. Tutored at home until he was fourteen, he then entered a German Gymnasium. Shortly before this time, Reich suffered a tragedy that would profoundly influence his later views on sexuality. He told

his jealous and authoritarian father about an affair he had observed between his tutor and his mother. The father fiercely berated the mother, who committed suicide. Grief-stricken, the father died several years later.

After serving in the Austro-Hungarian army during World War I, Reich in 1918, at the age of twenty-one, attended medical school at the University of Vienna. Here he encountered psychiatrist Sigmund Freud and psychoanalysis. By 1920 he was a practicing analyst, an achievement due to both to his brilliance and to the loose analytic training system of that time. He earned an M.D. from the university in 1922. That same year he married Annie Pink, a psychoanalyst, with whom he had two children. Their marriage ended in 1933. In 1945 he married Ilse Ollendorff; they had one child before their divorce in 1951.

Within psychoanalysis, Reich's most recognized achievement was his development between 1920 and 1930 of "character analysis" described in his text of the same name (1933, English edition published in 1949). Here he focused on the way the "character armor," or defensive character traits such as evasiveness, overpoliteness, or coldness, developed in childhood to bind feelings of anger, anxiety, and sadness. Character analysis had a profound influence on the growth of psychoanalytic ego psychology, especially evident in Anna Freud's *The Ego and the Mechanisms of Defense* (1936).

During this same period Reich elaborated his most controversial psychiatric concept—that of "orgastic potency" as the basis of mental health. By orgastic potency he meant the full surrender of the organism to the emotions of love and the sensation of pleasure during the sexual embrace. Several prominent psychoanalysts have made use of this concept (Otto Fenichel in *The Psychoanalytic Theory of Neurosis* [1945] and Erik Erikson in *Childhood and Society* [1950]). However, it has received far more ridicule than appreciation.

Between 1927 and 1933 in Vienna and Berlin, Reich contributed to the integration of psychoanalysis and Marxism. His practical work, *The Mass Psychology of Fascism* (1933), in which he coined the term "sex-politics" and which was aimed at understanding and defeating Nazism, brought sex education and counseling to large numbers of people in a way that connected emotional issues with social concerns. Of this work social psychologist Paul Goodman has written: "The most trenchant political ideas of [Herbert] Marcuse and [Erich] Fromm . . . were stated first and more powerfully by Reich" (quoted in Ilse Ollendorff Reich, *Wilhelm Reich: A Personal Biography* [1969]). Reich's work in this area would later influence the way the women's movement "politicized the personal." It should be noted that whereas in his work Reich strongly emphasized the sexual rights of women, in his personal life he could be extremely jealous and authoritarian, like his father.

Following his expulsion from the German Communist party in 1933 because of his psychodynamic and sexual emphases and from the International Psychoanalytic Association in 1934 for his social stance Reich moved to Oslo, Norway. There he delineated "muscular armor," which represents the bodily aspect of rigid characterological attitudes. Thus, a stubborn, "stiff-necked" person might literally have a stiff neck. This work provided the originating impulse for such latter-day therapies as bioenergetics, Gestalt therapy, and primal therapy.

When Reich's work was attacked in Oslo by the press and organized medicine, he moved in 1939 to the United States, where he devoted the 1940s and 1950s mainly to natural science. He investigated an energy he termed "orgone," which, he asserted, functioned as the life energy (or what Freud had called "libido") inside the organism and in nature at large. In 1940 Reich invented and distributed a device, the "orgone energy accumulator," which he believed had therapeutic and preventative properties for a number of illnesses.

The Food and Drug Administration obtained an injunction against the accumulator in 1954, claiming it was worthless. Reich in turn argued that the FDA lacked jurisdiction over the accumulator and disobeyed the injunction. He was found in contempt and sentenced to jail on 12 March 1957 for two years. The FDA destroyed the accumulators and burnt many of his books, including ones that had nothing to do with the accumulator.

On 18 November 1957 *Time* published an obituary that reads in part: "Died, Wilhelm Reich, 60, once-famed psychoanalyst, associate and follower of Sigmund Freud . . . lately better known for unorthodox sex and energy theories; of a heart attack in Lewisburg Federal Penitentiary, Pa. . . . "

Among Reich's publications, *The Sexual Revolution* (1936) represents the sharpest critique of traditional sexual morality and the clearest affirmation of the healthy genital impulses of children, adolescents, and adults. His *The Function of the Orgasm* (1942) is a one-volume summary of his psychiatric work. *The Cancer Biopathy* (1948) is a concise and clear presentation of his laboratory and clinical-medical work. *The Murder of Christ* (1953) relates the attacks on Christ to those on other pioneers, including himself. His *Reich Speaks of Freud* (1967) is a vivid statement of the relationship between Reich and Freud. *Sex-Pol Essays* (ed. Lee Baxendall [1972]), a collection of Reich's sex-political papers written during his Marxist phase, remains relevant.

Reich's psychiatric contributions have influenced the practice of modern psychotherapy. On the other hand, his work on orgone energy has been dismissed by most scientists. Reich's audacious journey across scientific boundaries nevertheless merits serious evaluation of both its fruitfulness and its error.

• Reich's papers, including his manuscripts, are stored in Countway Library, Harvard Medical School. For a fine summary of his work, see David Boadella, *Wilhelm Reich: The Evolution of His Work* (1973). Orson Bean, *Me and the Orgone* (1971), is an amusing account by a patient of Reichian therapy. Colin Wilson, *The Quest for Wilhelm Reich* (1981), is an intriguing and well-written amalgam of insight and error. Myron Sharaf, *Fury on Earth* (1983), interweaves Reich's life and work in a comprehensive biography.

MYRON SHARAF

REICHARD, Gladys Amanda (17 July 1893–25 July 1955), anthropologist, was born in Bangor, Pennsylvania, the daughter of Noah W. Reichard, a doctor, and Minerva Ann Jordan. Reared in an intellectually oriented Quaker household, Reichard finished high school in 1911 and began teaching elementary school. In 1915 she entered Swarthmore College, where she majored in classics. During her senior year she discovered anthropology, and after graduating with Phi Beta Kappa distinction in 1919 she enrolled at Columbia University to study anthropology with Franz Boas. Gladys received an M.A. in 1920, then won a research fellowship from the University of California to conduct fieldwork among the Wiyot in northeastern California. This became the basis of her dissertation on Wiyot grammar, and Reichard earned her doctorate in 1925. When she returned from California in 1923, Boas arranged for her to take a full-time instructor's position in anthropology at Barnard College, where she had begun assisting him in 1921. Reichard taught at Barnard for the rest of her life.

While at Columbia, Reichard grew extremely close to Boas, whom she (like his other graduate students) called "Papa Franz." Like Boas and many of his students, Reichard engaged in "salvage ethnology": recording as much as possible of Native American culture before it was changed beyond recognition by life on reservations, missionization, and acculturation. Boas's interest in linguistics helped shape Reichard's research, and she remained loyal to his ideas throughout her career, perhaps to the detriment of her work. In the 1920s Reichard lived for many years with his family, almost as a daughter. And many of her closest friends—including Elsie Clews Parsons (who supported her field research), Alfred Kroeber, and Robert Lowie (both of whom she met in California)—were also Boas's students.

In 1923 Reichard began a close relationship with Pliny Goddard, a curator of ethnology at the American Museum of Natural History in New York and another of Boas's students. She accompanied Goddard on a field trip to the Navajo Reservation that year, and they returned the next two years. Reichard wrote a monograph, *Social Life among the Navajo Indians* (1928), as a result of her summers in the field with him. It is rumored that Reichard had an affair with Goddard, who was much older and was married (Reichard never married). He died quite suddenly in 1928, at Reichard's house in Newtown, Connecticut. While there is no clear evidence about the nature of their relationship, the two remained close throughout the 1920s, and Reichard continued Goddard's work after his death.

In 1926–1927 Reichard took her only professional break from the American Southwest, traveling to Hamburg, Germany, to study Melanesian art under a

Guggenheim fellowship. Her analysis of units of design and principles of composition became *Melanesian Design* (1932), for which she won the New York Academy of Sciences A. Cressy Morrison Prize in Natural Sciences.

Reichard spent her summers in the field and the remainder of each year at Barnard. From 1930 to 1934 she lived with a Navajo family, apprenticing herself to the women in order to learn weaving, an unusual arrangement for an anthropologist at the time. While she learned and practiced this craft, she also collected data on social organization and ritual life. The books that came out of this experience were unusual in their straightforward, novelistic style and in their inclusion of the anthropologist as a character in the proceedings. *Spider Woman* (1934) describes Reichard's experiences as a novice weaver, and *Dezba, Woman of the Desert* (1939) details the life of the family with whom she lived; both books were intended for, and found, a popular audience. As a woman participating in a matrilineal society, Reichard likely was able to get closer to certain aspects of Navajo society than could a male anthropologist. However, her work was generally overshadowed by that of Harvard University professor Clyde Kluckhohn, who also worked on the Navajo and with whom she had a series of disagreements over the classification of Navajo ceremonies.

In 1934, with funding from the Bureau of Indian Affairs, Reichard began to teach adult Navajos to write their language. Designed to provide an educational structure compatible with Navajo culture and to address some of the difficulties in adjusting to the dominant society, her Hogan School was an early example of the kind of bilingual, bicultural school that began to flourish on reservations in the 1970s.

Reichard's interest turned increasingly to Navajo religion, and by the end of the 1930s her work had shifted from the study of women in a family context to a broader analysis of Navajo language, belief, and religious practice. In 1944 she published *Prayer: The Compulsive Word*, a structural analysis of Navajo prayer. She collaborated with Franc Newcomb, the wife of a local trader, and Mary Wheelwright, a wealthy Bostonian, to collect records of Navajo sandpaintings, an essential element of Navajo rituals. Her magnum opus, *Navajo Religion: A Study of Symbolism* (1950), is an encyclopedic presentation of a people's symbol system seen in its own terms and in all its complexity. Reichard did not try to fit her research into a single pattern, making it rather hard to digest. The book also expressed her unwavering advocacy for the Navajo; in it, she contended that their religion was a "system which has for years enabled the Navajo to retain their identity in a rapidly changing world."

In her final work, *Navajo Grammar* (1951), Reichard created some controversy by rejecting the most recently developed method of transcription in favor of one she had designed earlier. This did nothing to strengthen Reichard's position among her colleagues, many of whom considered her "difficult." However, a number of women anthropologists received their initial training from her, and many held their first job as her assistant at Barnard. In this way, Reichard had a large impact on the subsequent development of the field.

In her personal writings, Reichard came across as an enthusiastic but unsophisticated woman, and she appears to have been more comfortable among the Navajo than at Barnard, where she became a full professor in 1951. The Navajo called her "Asdzaan naadlohii," which means "Laughing or Smiling Woman."

Reichard's work now appears have been a precursor of methodological and theoretical trends in anthropology of the 1960s and 1970s. Her holistic view of Navajo life was emulated in the work of more recent scholars. However, Reichard's intellectual commitment of Franz Boas's style of description steered her away from theory at a time when theory was becoming more important in the field of anthropology. Her eclectic empiricism allowed her to grasp Navajo categories on their own terms, but she never developed a theoretical framework in which to place her findings. Her work always remained personal on some level, bearing the stamp of her personality to an unusual degree for an academic.

Reichard died in Flagstaff, Arizona.

• Reichard's papers are at Barnard College. Among her works not already mentioned in the text are *Navajo Shepherd and Weaver* (1936), *Navajo Medicine Man, Sandpaintings and Legends of Miguelito* (1939), and "An Analysis of Coeur d'Alene Mythology," American Folk-Lore Society, *Memoirs*, no. 41 (1947). Louise Lamphere, "Gladys Reichard among the Navajo," in *Hidden Scholars*, ed. Nancy J. Parezo (1993), gives an excellent overview of her life and career. See also Eleanor Leacock, "Gladys Amanda Reichard," in *Women Anthropologists: Selected Biographies* (1989), which includes a bibliography; William H. Lyon, "Gladys Reichard at the Frontiers of Navajo Culture," in *American Indian Quarterly* (Spring 1989); and Lessie Jo Frazier, "Genre, Methodology, and Feminist Practice: Gladys Reichard's Ethnographic Voice," in *Critique of Anthropology* (1993). Obituaries are in the *New York Times*, 26 July 1955, and *American Anthropologist* 58 (1956).

BETHANY NEUBAUER

REICHEL, Charles Gotthold (14 July 1751–18 Apr. 1825), Moravian bishop and educator, was born in Hermsdorff, Silesia, the son of Carl Rudolph Reichel, a Lutheran minister, and Eleonore Sophie Müller. His parents, who were sympathetic to Nicholas Ludwig von Zinzendorf and the Moravians, entrusted him to the Moravian boys' school at Grosshennersdorf at the age of four. In 1764 he entered the Moravian *Paedagogium* at Niesky and became a member of the Moravian church, committing himself both to its introspective christocentric faith and a communal life ordered around worship and service.

Having received theological training at the Moravian seminary at Barby, Saxony, from 1771 to 1774, Reichel began his service in the Moravian church as a teacher at Niesky. In 1775 he was assigned the task of editing the *Periodical Accounts*, an internal Moravian chronicle, and returned to Niesky in 1777 as assistant superintendent of the Moravian educational institutions. In 1780 he was asked to serve the Unity Elders' Conference (the governing board of the Moravian church) as secretary. In the same year he married Anna Dorothea Maass; they had six children.

Having been ordained a deacon of the Moravian church in 1782, Reichel was called in 1783 to become the minister of the Moravian congregation at Nazareth, Pennsylvania, and to head the projected Moravian boys' school there. In the summer of 1784, shortly after his ordination as a presbyter, Reichel and his wife traveled to North America and assumed their new responsibilities. In October 3 1785 Nazareth Hall, a boys' school, was opened, and Reichel began instruction with eleven pupils. Although Nazareth Hall was primarily intended to serve Moravian families, Reichel also made an appeal to parents who, although not members of the Moravian church, desired their children to be brought up "in the nurture and admonition of the Lord, preserved from seduction and the prevailing vices of the age" ("Regulations of the Boarding School at Nazareth," 1785). Combining high scholarly standards with strict moral discipline and sympathetic spiritual guidance, Reichel soon secured the reputation and the growth of Nazareth Hall. Students came from as far as the southern states and the West Indies, and in 1797 the state government placed John Konkaput, a Housatonic Indian from Stockbridge, Massachusetts, at Nazareth Hall to be educated at the expense of the state. That year the school had a student body of sixty-two boys.

In addition to his responsibilities as principal, Reichel took part in the founding of the Moravian Society . . . for Propagating the Gospel among the Heathen in 1787, serving between 1788 and 1816 as vice president and then as president. Having written a geographical textbook while still in Germany, Reichel published in 1795 an American edition of C. G. Otterbein's *Lesebuch für Deutsche Schulkinder*. In the fall of 1801 Reichel received the call to become the pastor of the Moravian congregation at Salem, North Carolina. Having been ordained a bishop of the Moravian church by Johannes Ettwein on 6 December 1801 in Bethlehem, Pennsylvania, he left Nazareth in May 1802 and assumed his new duties in Salem.

Besides his pastoral responsibilities to the Salem congregation, Reichel in 1803 began serving as the president of the General Directing Board, which had oversight over all the Moravian congregations and missionary activities in North Carolina. In this capacity, Reichel officiated at the ceremony of the laying of the cornerstone for the Salem Female Academy and explicitly affirmed at that occasion his belief that the instruction of children of non-Moravian parents was an important ministry of the Moravian church. Reichel's wife died in 1806, and in 1809, during a visit to Pennsylvania, he married Catharina Fetter; they had three sons. In 1810 Joseph Caldwell, president of the University of North Carolina, was a guest at Salem and called on Reichel. In the following year Reichel received an honorary doctor of divinity degree from the University of North Carolina.

In 1811 Reichel was called from North Carolina to Pennsylvania to serve as the pastor of the Moravian congregation at Bethlehem and as the president of the northern Provincial Elders' Conference. His appointment came at a time when the relations between the Bethlehem congregation and the central governing board of the Moravian church in Herrnhut, Germany, became increasingly strained over the issue of provincial sovereignty. In preparation for the scheduled Unity Synod of 1818, a provincial synod chaired by Reichel convened in the summer of 1817 in Bethlehem. It proposed several measures toward more "home rule" and adaptation to the American environment, including the abrogation of the inhibition of military service, the abolition of the use of the lot for marriages, and the empowerment of the Provincial Elders' Conference to make ministerial appointments without consulting the central Moravian governing board in Germany.

Being a delegate to the Unity Synod, Reichel left Bethlehem in the fall of 1817 and traveled by way of New York and England to Herrnhut, where the Unity Synod took place from June to August 1818. In spite of Reichel's presence, the synod ruled against the proposed changes (which were not fully implemented until 1848). His poor health made it impossible for Reichel to return to the United States after the conclusion of the synod, and he retired to Niesky. After the death of his second wife in 1820, he began to compile a history of the Moravian church for the years 1801 to 1818; this work, however, remained unfinished. He died in Niesky.

In an autobiographical memoir written shortly before his death, Reichel expressed both thankfulness for countless blessings and humble contrition for numerous shortcomings and failures during his 33-year ministry in America. He was in many respects quite successful as an educator and administrator, yet in guiding the American Moravian church from the eighteenth into the nineteenth century he also faced problems and conflicts too momentous to be solved by him and his generation, chief among them the disruption of the Moravian community through a decline of religious zeal and through the impact of the American ideals of freedom and independence. Reichel's significance as a church leader is in the fact that he contributed to the compromises that preserved the transatlantic unity of the Moravian church and yet allowed for the transformation of its American branch.

• Reichel's correspondence and other manuscripts, as well as manuscript material relating to his ministry, can be found in the Moravian Archives in Bethlehem, Pa.; Salem, N.C.; and Herrnhut, Germany. His autobiographical memoir, which is also the best source about his life, was published as "Lebenslauf des am 18ten April 1825 in Niesky selig entschlafenen verwitweten Bruders Carl Gotthold Reichel, Bischofs der Brüderkirche," *Nachrichten aus der Brüdergemeine* 8 (1826): 756–79. Reichel's textbook is *Geographie zum Gebrauch der Schulen in den evangelischen Brüdergemeinen* (2 vols., 1785). He also is believed to be the author of an informative essay,

"Early History of the Moravians in North Carolina," in William L. Saunders, ed., *Colonial Records of North Carolina*, vol. 5 (1887). For further information on Reichel, see Adelaide L. Fries, ed., *Records of the Moravians in North Carolina* vols. 6 and 7 (1943, 1947); William C. Reichel, *Historical Sketch of Nazareth Hall* (1869); and Joseph M. Levering, *A History of Bethlehem, Pennsylvania* (1903).

PETER VOGT

REICHEL, William Cornelius (9 May 1824–25 Oct. 1876), Moravian educator and historian, was born in Salem, North Carolina, the son of Gotthold Benjamin Reichel, a principal of Salem Female Academy, and Henriette Friederike Vierling, a housemother. Belonging to a family of high standing in the Moravian church (Charles Gotthold Reichel was his grandfather), Reichel received the customary thorough education for ministry within the church. Orphaned by the age of nine, he entered Nazareth Hall, a Moravian boy's school in Nazareth, Pennsylvania, in 1834. In 1839 he progressed to the Moravian Theological Seminary in nearby Bethlehem, graduating with a bachelor of divinity in 1844.

Beginning his service in the Moravian church as an educator, Reichel taught Latin and drawing at Nazareth Hall from 1844 to 1848. He was then called to Bethlehem, where he first taught in the Moravian parochial school and in the theological seminary and college. In 1851 he married Mary Jane Gray and was appointed professor of natural sciences at the Moravian Seminary for Young Ladies in the following year. Apparently, Reichel first showed signs of his gift as a historical writer during his tenure at the female seminary, for in 1854 he was asked to write an account of the school's history, which appeared in 1858 under the title *A History of the Rise, Progress, and Present Condition of the Bethlehem Female Seminary* and went through five editions until 1901. Reichel also participated in the founding of the Moravian Historical Society in 1857 and in his second book, *A Memorial of the Dedication of Monuments . . .* (1860), recorded the society's discovery and marking of historical sites of the Moravian Indian Mission in New York and Connecticut.

In 1858 Reichel became a professor at Moravian Theological Seminary and College and taught natural sciences as well as Hebrew, Greek, and Old Testament exegetical theology. In 1862 he was called to be principal of Linden Hall Seminary, a Moravian school for girls in Lititz, Pennsylvania, and in the course of this appointment was ordained a deacon of the Moravian church on 29 June of the same year. Taking charge of Linden Hall Seminary under difficult circumstances, Reichel proved himself to be an able headmaster. Under his leadership, Linden Hall was incorporated by the legislature of Pennsylvania (1863), expanded considerably in size, and came to enjoy financial stability. In keeping with the Moravian tradition, Reichel declared it as his pedagogical aim "to *educate*, as well as to instruct," so that "the heart may be influenced by the precepts of morality and the lessons of Eternal Truth, while the mind is being stored with useful knowledge" (*Linden Hall* [1863], p. 4). His particular responsibilities included religious instruction, the leading of daily worship, and the spiritual care of the students.

In 1863 Reichel's wife died and left him with three children. He was ordained a presbyter of the Moravian church on 30 May 1867. In October of the same year he married Addie G. Harkins, but within a few weeks some estrangement occurred between him and his wife, causing him to resign his position at Linden Hall at the beginning of December. He returned to Bethlehem, where he taught temporarily at Moravian Theological Seminary for Young Ladies but continued to teach at Moravian Theological Seminary and College several hours a week.

The return to Bethlehem, where he was less occupied and had access to the extensive Moravian archival collections, enabled Reichel to resume his literary and historical pursuits. He renewed his involvement with the Moravian Historical Society and also participated in the Historical Society of Pennsylvania and the short-lived Moravian Book Association. On behalf of the Reunion Society of Nazareth Hall, he published *Historical Sketch of Nazareth Hall from 1755 to 1869* in 1869. His next and most scholarly book was a collection of annotated translations of important eighteenth-century Moravian documents, which appeared in 1870 under the title *Memorials of the Moravian Church*. In the following years Reichel published several historical studies of local landmarks and further editions of Moravian manuscript documents, some of which appeared as part of the *Transactions of the Moravian Historical Society*. For the Historical Society of Pennsylvania he prepared a new and annotated edition of John Heckewelder's *History, Manners, and Customs of the Indian Nations Who Once Inhabited Pennsylvania and Neighboring States* (1876; repr. 1990) and was, at the time of his death, working on a history of Bethlehem and Northampton County.

In the summer of 1876 Reichel was considered for the position of president of Salem Female Academy in Salem, North Carolina. However, before an official call was extended, he died of typhoid fever in Bethlehem, Pennsylvania.

Although not a historian by profession, Reichel distinguished himself as the leading nineteenth-century author on the history of the American Moravian church. His friend John W. Jordan correctly remarked that Reichel did "more to elucidate the early history of the Moravian Church . . . than has been attempted by any of his predecessors or contemporaries" ("Memorial Notice," p. 105). In contrast to earlier Moravian historiography by European authors, Reichel approached his subject matter with a novel sense of historical distance and from a distinctly American point of view. His works conformed substantially to the goal of the Moravian Historical Society "to cull many interesting memoirs from the manuscript archives of the Church, illustrating Moravianism in its most popular and engaging features, by unfolding to a new generation of men the beauty of that Christian life which adorned the age that has nearly passed away" ("The Moravian Historical Society: Its Organization and Aims," *Transactions of the Moravian Historical Society* 1 [1876]: 12). Reichel pioneered in the translation and editing of Moravian manuscript documents and, in his own writings, succeeded in combining accurate historical description with a literary elegance that secured his popularity beyond the Moravian church. While Reichel was the major interpreter of Moravian history to the nineteenth-century American audience, most of his writings are now only of local interest. His publications concerning Moravian education and Indian mission, however, remain significant historical sources.

• A number of Reichel's manuscripts are in the collection of the Historical Society of Pennsylvania. In addition to the works mentioned above, his publications include *The Crown Inn, near Bethlehem, Penna. 1745* (1872), *A Red Rose from the Olden Time; or, A Ramble through the Annals of the Rose Inn, on the Barony of Nazareth* (1872), and *The Old Sun Inn, at Bethlehem, Pa., 1758* (1873; six eds. until 1981). He edited John Heckewelder, "Names Which the Lenni Lennape or Delaware Indians Gave to Rivers, Streams and Localities within the States of Pennsylvania, New Jersey, Maryland and Virginia, with Their Significations," *Transactions of the Moravian Historical Society* 1 (1876): 227–82; and Abraham Reincke, "A Register of Members of the Moravian Church and of Persons Attached to Said Church in This Country and Abroad, between 1727 and 1754," *Transactions of the Moravian Historical Society* 1 (1876): 283–426. Reichel also contributed a historical account of Northampton County to *Illustrated History of the Commonwealth of Pennsylvania*, ed. William Egle (1876). Two unpublished essays were posthumously edited by John W. Jordan, "Friedensthal and Its Stockaded Mill," *Transactions of the Moravian Historical Society* 2 (1886): 1–36; and "The Old Inn at Nazareth," *Transactions of the Moravian Historical Society* 2 (1886): 301–10. Jordan also published several of Reichel's short historical sketches in *Something about Trombones, and the Old Mill at Bethlehem* (1884). Obituaries are in the *Moravian*, 2 Nov. 1876, and Jordan, "Memorial Notice of the Rev. William C. Reichel (with Portrait)," *Pennsylvania Magazine of History and Biography* 1 (1877): 104–7.

PETER VOGT

REICHELDERFER, Francis Wilton (6 Aug. 1895–25 Jan. 1983), meteorologist, was born in Harlan, Indiana, the son of Francis Allen Reichelderfer, a methodist minister, and Mae Olive Carrington. He received a B.S. from Northwestern University in 1917 and worked briefly as a chemist. In 1918 he enlisted in the U.S. Navy and was assigned to aviation ground school at the Massachusetts Institute of Technology. He also took an intensive course in meteorology at Harvard's Blue Hill Observatory. In 1919 he was certified as a naval aviator. His assignments included forecasting the weather for the transatlantic crossing of naval airships, balloon racing in Europe and the United States as a member of a navy team, and demonstrating the bombing and sinking of a captured German battleship with General Billy Mitchell (1879–1936). He was promoted to lieutenant in 1921. The previous year he married Beatrice Hoyle; they had one son.

In 1923 the navy sent him to study at the meteorological offices of Britain, France, and Germany. Upon his return, he was assigned to Washington, D.C., as chief of naval meteorology in the Bureau of Aeronautics. There he established standards for weather map analysis, investigated the use of static for detecting storms at sea, and helped develop a program of postgraduate meteorological training at MIT, which was aimed at meeting the needs of aeronautics. In the 1930s Reichelderfer served as executive officer at the naval air station in Lakehurst, New Jersey. He made four transatlantic crossings on the German dirigible *Hindenburg* as U.S. Navy observer and weather analyst. In 1931 he spent six months at the Geophysical Institute in Bergen, Norway, studying with the founders of "air mass analysis" and the "polar front theory." He returned to the Bureau of Aeronautics with the rank of lieutenant commander. In 1938 he was second in command on the battleship USS *Utah*.

Reichelderfer resigned his commission to become acting head of the U.S. Weather Bureau in the Department of Agriculture in 1938. His position was made permanent one year later. He brought the Norwegian methods of meteorological analysis to the bureau and standardized the acquisition of upper air data by the use of balloon-borne radiometeorographs. He also instituted a liberal training program that allowed employees to take college courses and participate in conferences and seminars. In 1940 the Weather Bureau was transferred to the Department of Commerce.

During World War II Reichelderfer helped establish a worldwide system of weather analysis in support of military operations. He also reduced the time it took to disseminate weather observations from four-and-a-half to one-and-a-half hours. For his war service he was awarded the U.S. Air Force International Service Award. In the 1950s he promoted the use of electronic computers for weather analysis and prediction and contributed to the design of the nation's first meteorological satellite, TIROS I, launched in 1960.

Reichelderfer was active in many scientific societies. He served as president of the American Meteorological Society in 1941 and 1942 and was elected first president of the World Meteorological Organization in 1951. He was a member of the National Advisory Committee for Aeronautics, National Academy of Sciences, and was a fellow of the Institute of Aeronautical Sciences. In 1964 he was awarded the International Meteorological Organization Prize. Though he retired in 1963, Reichelderfer maintained an office at the National Weather Service until 1978. President John F. Kennedy cited him for presiding over "the evolution of meteorology and weather forecasting from an art to a science." Reichelderfer died in Washington, D.C.

• Reichelderfer's personal papers are in the Library of Congress. His official correspondence as chief of the Weather Bureau is in the National Archives. Both series are described in James Rodger Fleming, *Guide to Historical Resources in the Atmospheric Sciences: Archives, Manuscripts, and Special Collections in the Washington, D.C. Area* (1989). Notable among his personal papers are manuscripts titled "Norwegian Methods of Weather Analysis" (1932) and "Historical Resume of Naval Aerology, 1917–1928" (n.d.). Reichelderfer wrote the article "Meteorology" for the *Encyclopedia Britannica* (1980).

A necrology, by George P. Cressman, is in *Bulletin of the American Meteorological Society* 64 (1983): 398–400. Biographical sketches include Patrick Hughes, "Francis W. Reichelderfer, Part 1: Aerologists and Air-devils" and "Part 2: Architect of Modern Meteorologic Services," *Weatherwise* 34 (1981): 52–59 and 148–57. Reichelderfer was interviewed in the *WMO Bulletin* 31 (1982): 171–84.

JAMES RODGER FLEMING

REICHENBACH, Hans (26 Sept. 1891–9 Apr. 1953), philosopher of science, was born in Hamburg, Germany, the son of Bruno Reichenbach, a prosperous wholesale merchant, and Selma Menzel, a teacher. His father was Jewish at birth but converted to the Reformed church in his early twenties. His mother's family belonged to the Reformed church. Reichenbach was an outstanding student and showed precocious independence of thought. He studied engineering for one year (1910–1911) at the Technische Hochschule in Stuttgart. He then studied mathematics, physics, and philosophy at the universities of Berlin, Munich, and Göttingen. His teachers included Max Planck, Arnold Sommerfeld, David Hilbert, and Max Born. He received his Ph.D. in 1915 from the University of Erlangen, with a dissertation on the problems of applying the concept of probability to the physical world. After serving in the German Army Signal Corps for two and a half years during World War I, he returned severely ill from the Russian Front. From 1917 to 1920 he worked as an engineer with a Berlin radio firm. During this period he attended Albert Einstein's seminars at the University of Berlin.

Reichenbach married his first wife, Elisabeth Lingener, in 1921. They had two children. He obtained a divorce shortly before his marriage in 1946 to his second wife, Maria Leroi (née Moll), who had a son by her previous marriage. She and Reichenbach had no children.

He taught both technical and philosophical courses at the Technische Hochschule in Stuttgart from 1920 to 1926, first as Privatdozent and then as associate professor. In 1926 he went to the University of Berlin as an associate professor for philosophy of physics. Opposition of some faculty because of his socialist views was overcome by supporters such as Planck, Einstein, and Richard von Mises. Reichenbach was a leader of the logical empiricist movement, which sought to show how scientific knowledge could be based on logical constructions built from particular experiences. This opposed the views of Immanuel Kant and Kant's Idealist followers. He was the leading force in organizing the Berliner Gesellschaft für Empirische Philosophie. The Berlin group worked with the Vienna Circle, a discussion group centered around Moritz Schlick, Rudolf Carnap, and Otto Neurath, which held similar views under the label "logical positivism."

While in Berlin, Reichenbach was noted for his clear presentation of modern theories of physics and their philosophical implications, both in periodicals and in frequent radio lectures. The latter served as the basis of his very popular book *Atom und Cosmos* (1930, Eng. trans. 1932). A more substantial treatment of his philosophy of physics is given in *Philosophie der Raum-Zeit-Lehre* (1928, Eng. trans. *The Philosophy of Space and Time*, 1958). Here he argued that our perception of space and time does not fit certain necessary forms, as Kant had believed. Reichenbach contended that there was an element of convention in our understanding of space and time structure.

In 1933 he was dismissed from the University of Berlin by the Nazi regime. Foreseeing the danger of Adolf Hitler, he had already accepted an invitation to be head of the philosophy department at the University of Istanbul. While in Istanbul he developed a comprehensive theory of probability based on the frequency interpretation in *Wahrscheinlichkeitslehre* (1935; 2nd ed. as *Theory of Probability*, 1949). This interpretation holds that statements about the probability of an outcome cannot be known a priori, independently of experience. Such statements serve only to summarize the observed frequency of that outcome in past events. In distinction from many other empiricists, he held that all empirical knowledge is only of probabilities. For Reichenbach the probable nature of knowledge was not a matter of human limitations, but reflected an indeterminacy in the facts of the world. He emphasized that many physical laws, such as those of statistical and quantum mechanics, are statements of probability. In 1938 he was appointed professor of philosophy in the University of California at Los Angeles. He was president of the Western Philosophical Association in 1946–1947.

Throughout his career Reichenbach was noted as a teacher. His writings corroborate that he was able to create striking examples and stories to illustrate often esoteric theories of physics, probability, and philosophy. A good example is his popular work *The Rise of Scientific Philosophy* (1951), which gives an overview of his philosophy.

Many of his treatments of specific issues are still referred to. Thus he distinguished the "context of justification" of scientific theories, which is the proper study of the philosophy of science, from the "context of discovery" of theories, which is a matter for historical investigation. In a noted criticism of David Hume (1711–1776), who had argued that there is no rational basis for the "principle of induction," that future events will follow past patterns, Reichenbach offered his "pragmatic" justification of the principle. If we guide our actions using the principle of induction and it is correct, then we are at an advantage. If the principle fails to give us correct beliefs about the future, then we are no worse off than we would have been anyway, since there is no alternative guide for forming beliefs about the future.

He died of a heart attack at his home in Pacific Palisades, a suburb of Los Angeles. At the time of his death he had been invited to present the William James lectures at Harvard in the fall of 1953. They were to be on the topic of his posthumously published book, *The Direction of Time* (1956). This addresses the question of why time seems to go in one direction, from past to future, even though the basic laws of physics don't treat time as directional.

Reichenbach's most enduring influence comes from the strength his work gave to the logical empiricist movement. This movement overthrew the domination of academic philosophy in the beginning of the twentieth century by Kantian Idealism. Reichenbach contributed significantly to the rejection by many philosophers of the Kantian claim that scientific knowledge of nature presupposes an a priori understanding of the basic structure of the world.

• Reichenbach's papers are kept at the University of Pittsburgh Library. More detailed biographical information, a complete bibliography, and a selection of both popular and technical articles by Reichenbach can be found in Maria Reichenbach and Robert S. Cohen, eds., *Selected Writings, 1909–1953* (2 vols., 1978). His *Gesammelte Werke* (collected works) is published in nine volumes, beginning in 1977. His most thorough development of empiricist epistemology is in *Experience and Prediction* (1938). Besides those works mentioned above, his other major books are *From Copernicus to Einstein* (1942), *Philosophical Foundations of Quantum Mechanics* (1944), *Elements of Symbolic Logic* (1947), *The Theory of Relativity and a Priori Knowledge* (1965), and *Laws, Modalities, and Counterfactuals* (1976). Assessments of his work by other philosophers can be found in Wesley C. Salmon, eds., *Hans Reichenbach: Logical Empiricist* (1979), and in *Erkenntnis* 35, nos. 1–3 (1991), which is a collection in honor of the centennials of Reichenbach and Rudolf Carnap.

MICHAEL SCANLAN

REID, Christian. *See* Tiernan, Frances Christine Fisher.

REID, David Settle (19 Apr. 1813–18 June 1891), governor and U.S. senator, was born in Rockingham County, North Carolina, the son of Reuben Reid, a yeoman farmer, and Elizabeth Settle. Through his mother, Reid was related to the distinguished Settle-Martin political dynasty, which included Stephen A. Douglas of Illinois and, with the exception of Reid himself, who was a Democrat, prominent Whig and Republican leader in North Carolina for three generations. Shortly after Reid's birth, his father moved to the nearby north-south stage road, opening a store and ordinary that soon attracted other settlers to the village that would become Reidsville. Although he was primarily self-educated, Reid did attend the plantation school of his wealthy uncle Thomas Settle, Sr., a noted superior court judge. As a youth of twelve Reid began clerking in another uncle's store in Wentworth, but in 1829 he returned home to assist his father in his expanding business and was appointed the first postmaster of Reidsville. Over the next decade he acquired a tobacco plantation of 600 acres and three slaves. Although his family was Baptist and Reid attended Baptist churches, he never formally joined the church.

Just over five feet in height, the slightly built Reid never outgrew the sobriquet "Little Davy." Yet with his shock of black hair and flashing blue eyes, he was a dynamic speaker, developing into an indefatigable campaigner. Possessing natural political talent and adhering throughout his life to strict Jeffersonian principles, Reid commenced his political career in 1835, winning election as colonel of the county militia and as a state senator. Always an advocate of public education, he devoted his most important service in his six-year tenure in the state senate to the Education Committee that drafted the act establishing the state's public school system. The first school opened in his home county.

Persuaded by the Democratic leaders of his district to run for Congress, Reid was defeated in his initial campaign in 1841 but succeeded two years later, serving two terms in the House of Representatives (1843–1847). The year prior to his successful race he spent in reading law, passing the bar in April 1843. In Washington Reid supported the James K. Polk administration's expansionist program regarding Texas, Mexico, and the Oregon boundary. In his first session he met Stephen A. Douglas, with whom he formed a lifelong friendship. Reid introduced Douglas to his cousin Martha Martin, who became Douglas's first wife.

As early as 1846 Reid was perceived by the state party leadership as an energetic and progressive candidate who might wrest control of the state house from the Whigs, who had never lost a gubernatorial election. Reid forged a partnership with the powerful William W. Holden, editor of the *North-Carolina Standard*, which was the most influential Democratic newspaper in the state. Nominated in 1848, Reid accepted on the condition that he be allowed to campaign on the issue of free suffrage for white males, the removal of the last property qualification on the electorate—a fifty-acre requirement for voting for the state senate. In what was then the closest election in the state's history, Reid narrowly lost to the Whig candidate Charles Manly, but the stage was set for a decisive victory in 1850. Also in 1850 Reid began an eighteen-year tenure on the board of trustees of the state university. That year he married Henrietta Williams Settle, the daughter of his uncle Thomas Settle, Sr. The Reids had four children.

Achievements of Reid's administrations included the chartering of railroads and plank roads, the appointment of a superintendent of public schools, and a geologic and agricultural survey. To his chagrin, conservatives of both parties delayed the free suffrage constitutional amendment until 1857. Nevertheless, Reid effected a permanent political revolution. Not only did the Whigs never win another state election, but the Democrats would dominate North Carolina politics until the late twentieth century.

In the last month of his second term Reid was elected by the legislature to the U.S. Senate. Serving on the Committees on Indian Affairs, Commerce, the District of Columbia, and Revolutionary Claims, he also chaired the committee that oversaw the patent office. Reid's most significant contribution to floor debate was his spirited defense of southern rights during the passage of the Kansas-Nebraska Act. His Senate service was shortened by incidents of serious illness, especially in 1858, when he survived a prolonged attack of pneumonia in Richmond, Virginia. Although highly regarded by the party rank and file, Reid lost touch with the Democratic leadership, which led to his defeat for renomination in 1858.

Reid willingly retired to his expanding family, his law practice, and the management of twenty-two slaves on his 700-acre Dan River tobacco plantation, which had been a wedding gift from his father-in-law. Not even the growing secession crisis could entice Reid to public office, but he continued to defend slavery and southern rights in his private correspondence. In January 1861 North Carolina initially rejected secession in a convention delegate election, and Reid was sent by the legislature as a delegate to the unsuccessful Washington Peace Conference. After the firing on Fort Sumter, secession delegates won a majority in a second state constitutional convention election. Reid was elected to the convention and voted with the majority for secession. He was also active in the convention that organized the state government under the Confederacy. He supported the defense of the state, yet he did not seek office in the Confederacy, consenting to serve only on a local soldiers' welfare committee.

In 1870, during the postwar Reconstruction era, Reid joined his cousin Thomas Settle, Jr., a state Republican leader, in denouncing, through letters to statewide newspapers, the violent political intimidation of the Ku Klux Klan. Shortly thereafter, the Klan disbanded in his home county. Reid came out of political retirement only one more time, when he was elected to the state constitutional convention of 1875, where he had a pivotal role in organizing and managing the convention. He maneuvered behind the scenes to break an initial convention deadlock that had blocked election of a chairman.

In 1871 Reid moved to Wentworth, the county seat, and established a law partnership with his son Thomas Reid, who lived in Reidsville. After a severe stroke left him partially paralyzed in 1881, Reid moved to Reidsville, where, after a decade of declining health, he died.

• The North Carolina State Archives has the official papers and most of the personal papers of Reid. Smaller personal collections are in the libraries of Rockingham Community College in Wentworth, N.C., and Duke University, Durham, N.C. For aspects of his public life see the state legislative papers and the papers of the state conventions of 1861 and 1875, which are in the state archives and the *Congressional Globe*. His official and personal correspondence has been published in *The Papers of David Settle Reid, 1829–1852*, ed. Lindley S. Butler (2 vols., 1993, 1997), which includes a detailed biographical sketch. A contemporary sketch is in John H. Wheeler, *Reminiscences and Memoirs of North Carolina and Eminent North Carolinians* (1884). A study of his years as governor is Paul A. Reid, *The Gubernatorial Campaigns and Administrations of David S. Reid, 1848–1854* (1953). For background see Clarence C. Norton, *The Democratic Party in Ante-Bellum North Carolina, 1835–1861* (1930); Marc W. Kruman, *Parties and Politics in North Carolina, 1836–1865* (1983); and Thomas E. Jeffrey, *State Parties and National Politics: North Carolina, 1815–1861* (1989). His obituary is in the *Reidsville Weekly Review*, 24 June 1891.

LINDLEY S. BUTLER

REID, Harry Fielding (18 May 1859–18 June 1944), geophysicist, was born in Baltimore, Maryland, the son of Andrew Reid, of unknown occupation, and Fanny Brooks Gwathmey. When Reid was nine years old, his family moved for some years to Lausanne, Switzerland, where he attended school and developed an interest in glaciers and in mountain climbing. On his return to the United States, he attended the Pennsylvania Military Academy, at which he studied civil engineering. He then entered Johns Hopkins University in 1877, the second year after its opening; he received an A.B. in 1880 and a Ph.D. in physics in 1885. He married Edith Gittings in 1883; they had two children. Reid studied in England and Germany from 1884 to 1886 when he became professor of mathematics at Case School of Applied Science in Cleveland, Ohio. In 1889 his position at Case changed to professor of physics. He taught courses and published a number of papers on glaciers.

Reid returned to Johns Hopkins in 1894 as a lecturer; in 1895 he became associate professor of geology at the University of Chicago but continued his appointment at Johns Hopkins. In 1896 he moved permanently to Johns Hopkins, as associate professor of geological physics, and in 1911 became professor of dynamic geology and geography. He became professor emeritus in 1930. The variety of titles held by Reid indicates the changing of status of the field of geophysics, which was not recognized by that name until later. Some scholars consider Reid, whose interest in and approach to geology was based on physics and mathematics, to have been the first American geophysicist (Lawson and Byerly, p. 4).

Reid began his scientific career by studying glaciers, both in Europe and, during the 1890s, in the western United States. In southeastern Alaska he mapped Muir Glacier and its tributaries, and he named many of the glaciers, fiords, and bays of Glacier Bay. Later the principal fiord at the head of that bay was named for him. From stakes set in Forno Glacier in the Alps he determined horizontal and vertical movements of the ice. This enabled him to define the internal structure of a glacier and its progressive deformation from differential movements. He advocated the systematic annual observation of glaciers. When the International Glacier Commission was established in 1894 by the International Geological Congress, Reid was named the U.S. representative. He was president of that commission from 1903 to 1906.

Reid published twenty-four papers on glaciers between 1892 and 1909, by which time his interests had shifted. After the 1906 earthquake in San Francisco, the governor of California appointed him one of eight scientists to investigate the disaster. He was a contributor to the first volume (1908) of the State Earthquake Investigation Commission's two-volume *The California Earthquake of April 18, 1906* and was author of its second volume (1910) on the mechanics of the earthquake. In it he proposed what he called the elastic rebound theory of earthquakes, which states that potential energy is stored in crustal rocks during a long period of increasing stress and strain. When the stress finally exceeds the shear strength of the rocks, the rocks move back toward equilibrium abruptly, releasing the stored energy as an earthquake, followed by aftershocks. Reid's analysis was based on triangulations repeated after the 1906 earthquake and compared with ones that had preceded it. Generally accepted by geologists after Reid's presentation, the concept of elastic rebound has been incorporated into the concept of plate tectonics, which may be assumed to create the strain.

Reid presented a definition of the manner in which a seismograph operates in "On the Choice of a Seismograph" (*Bulletin of the Seismological Society of America* 2, no. 1 [Mar. 1912]: 8–30), the first complete treatment of the subject in English. In it he analyzed all effects, displacements, tilts, and friction on the half a dozen kinds of instruments for recording earthquakes then available from various manufacturers throughout the world. He also maintained two seismographs at Johns Hopkins.

From 1909 Reid published more than forty papers on earthquakes, their mechanism, their waves and vibrations, the geometry of faulting, earth movements, and the constitution of the earth. He was a strong advocate of isostasy, first defined in 1889 by Clarence Edward Dutton as the balance between the elevated lighter rocks of the continents over the heavier rocks beneath them. Some geologists maintained that mountains were raised by compressional forces related to the cooling of the Earth and in response to weight from sediments. Reid believed that mountains had been raised primarily by unknown vertical forces from below, and that gravity measurements indicated isostatic equilibrium in areas as different as high mountains and low coastal valleys. Later knowledge of crustal movements and of the effects of pressure on deep crustal materials has clarified the nature of mountain building and has validated Reid's points.

In work for other agencies, from 1898 to 1905 Reid was adviser to the highway division of the Maryland Geological Survey, for which he published reports on the state's highways and methods of testing road materials. As expert in charge of earthquake records for the U.S. Geological Survey from 1902 to 1914 he compiled an extensive card catalog and set of newspaper clippings on earthquakes. These were used by researchers of the U.S. Coast and Geodetic Survey to publish successive historical lists, especially of West Coast earthquakes. The files were provided to that agency after Reid's death. Reid served as a member of a committee appointed by President Woodrow Wilson in 1915 to recommend ways of controlling landslides alongside the Panama Canal, which had just been completed.

Shortly after the 1906 San Francisco earthquake, Reid helped found the Seismological Society of America, of which he was president in 1912–1913. He was president of the American Geophysical Union from 1924 to 1926 and was active in several other scientific societies. He was elected to the National Academy of Sciences in 1912. Although somewhat remote with strangers, Reid was considered charming and an "exceptionally clear thinker" by colleagues. He died in Baltimore, Maryland.

• No repository is known for Reid's papers; some correspondence is at Johns Hopkins University in the files of Daniel Coit Gilman. A significant paper by Reid on isostasy was "Isostasy and Earth Movements," *Bulletin of Geological Society of America* 33 (1922): 317–26. Biographies of Reid are by George D. Louderback, in *Bulletin of the Seismological Society of America* 35 (1945): 95–97; by Edward W. Berry, in *Geological Society of America Annual Report for 1944* (May 1945), pp. 293–98); and by Andrew C. Lawson and Perry Byerly, in *National Academy of Sciences, Biographical Memoirs* 26 (1951): 1–12, which includes a bibliography.

ELIZABETH NOBLE SHOR

REID, Helen (23 Nov. 1882–27 July 1970), publisher, was born Helen Miles Rogers in Appleton, Wisconsin, the daughter of Benjamin Talbot Rogers, a hotel proprietor with additional business interests in the mining and lumber industries, and Sarah Louise Johnson. The eleventh and youngest child, Helen Rogers was three years old when her father's death created financial hardships for the family. Nevertheless, she was given a good education in public school and then at Grafton Hall, an Episcopal girls' boarding school in Fond du Lac, Wisconsin. Subsequently, she paid her own way through Barnard College in New York City, which she entered in 1899, working as a tutor, housekeeper, and office assistant. She received her A.B. in 1903 with a double concentration in Greek and zoology. In her senior year she was appointed business manager of the college yearbook. Under her management, the yearbook did not have a deficit for the first time in its history.

After graduation, Rogers was hired as social secretary to Elisabeth Mills Reid, whose husband, Whitelaw Reid, was the owner and publisher of the *New York Tribune*. In 1905 Whitelaw Reid was appointed ambassador to the court of St. James's, and his wife was accompanied by Helen Rogers on the couple's frequent trips between England and New York. In this period Rogers met Ogden Mills Reid, the Reids' only son, who had recently graduated from Yale University, and the couple was married in 1911. The following year Whitelaw Reid died, leaving his son the ownership of the *Tribune*.

Between 1912 and 1918, with the exception of her lifelong commitment to woman suffrage and economic equality, Helen Reid's interests were centered on her home. She had two children during this time, a son and a daughter. In 1917 she accepted the position of state treasurer for the suffrage campaign in New York, and she was instrumental in raising half a million dollars because, as she said, a "woman needs suffrage for her own spiritual and intellectual development." Reid also believed in the necessity of women's financial independence, both within and outside marriage, in the importance of men's increased involvement in the home and in child-rearing, and in the personal and national benefits of women's increased contribution to the war effort during World War I. The success of her work in the movement—and ultimately in women's campaign for the right to vote—motivated her to work outside the home. In 1918 she entered the family newspaper business, selling advertising for the *Tribune*, which was floundering. In the previous two decades, the Reid family had reportedly subsidized the publication with $15 million of their own funds, yet the newspaper was still struggling to show a profit. Ogden Reid was not proving to be a dynamic manager; his wife, on the other hand, had all the qualities necessary to turn the enterprise around.

After only two months in advertising sales, Helen Reid became advertising director, a position she was to occupy—even as her titles changed—until 1947. She supervised and encouraged her sales staff and courted prospective advertisers with such zeal and effectiveness that the advertising space in the *Tribune* doubled by 1924. That same year, her advice to purchase Frank A. Munsey's *New York Herald* was crucial to its merger with the *Tribune* into the *New York Herald Tribune*. With a larger staff and broader circulation, the new paper soon became one of the best-known and most influential dailies in the United States. Helen Reid's interest in the newspaper intensified despite her last pregnancy, which resulted, in 1925, in the birth of her second son. In 1930 Reid, working in conjunction with Marie Mattingly Meloney, organized the first annual Forum on Current Problems, a conference featuring lectures by prominent public figures on current issues in world affairs. The forum, described as an extension of Reid's vision for the *Herald Tribune*, was intended to be an "intelligent, dispassionate presentation of world news and events."

Though her nominal responsibility with the paper remained advertising, and her husband's position as publisher covered everything else, Helen Reid was soon leaving her imprint on every aspect of the publication, from the typeface to its social and political (independent Republican) agenda. She exercised her influence in the hiring of columnists, the purchase of rights from other sources, and the syndication of *Tribune* material. Faithful to her lifelong interest in women's causes, Reid encouraged a concentration on topics women would find valuable, including gardening and culinary articles, as well as features on suburban life. She hired a number of women for important staff positions, including Irita Van Doren as editor of the Sunday book review section, Clementine Paddleford as food writer, and Meloney as editor of the Sunday magazine supplement, *This Week*. By World War II,

the *Herald Tribune*'s staff contained a greater percentage of women than any other U.S. metropolitan daily.

In addition to her prominence in the world of journalism, Reid wielded considerable influence in New York State and national politics. While taking sides on some issues—the *Herald Tribune* endorsed the presidential bids of Wendell L. Willkie in 1940 and Dwight D. Eisenhower in 1952 and 1956—Reid's paper was generally known for its impartial reporting. Along with the *New York Times* and the *Christian Science Monitor*, the *Herald Tribune* was judged the fairest in a survey by the *Saturday Review of Literature* of the media coverage of the debate over President Truman's recall of General Douglas MacArthur in 1951. Reid was well known for her political soirées and dinners, which often featured debates on political topics.

In 1947 Ogden Reid died, and his widow became the president and publisher of the Herald Tribune Corporation. At that time, the paper's weekly circulation was more than 343,000, and the Sunday circulation approached 600,000. Reid became chair of the board of directors in 1953, at the age of seventy, and resigned two years later. Her older son, Whitelaw, who had succeeded her to the presidency, followed her to the chair upon her retirement. Her younger son, Ogden, became editor, publisher, and president in 1955.

Reid's activities outside the paper included wartime service on the Advisory Committee on Women in the Services during World War II, a membership on the U.S. Committee on Government Contracts from 1953 to 1961, the vice presidency of the New York Newspaper Women's Club, a trusteeship of the Metropolitan Museum of Art, and a trusteeship of Barnard College from 1914 to 1956. After her retirement, she lived quietly until her death in New York City. The newspaper to which she had devoted much of her life had not prospered without her and had predeceased her by three years, closing its doors in 1967.

Reid was one of the earliest women to become a major influential force in American journalism. She used her position to encourage many other female newswriters. She was also prominent in Republican political circles, both in New York City and, through her paper, nationally.

• The largest collections of Reid's papers are in the Reid Family Collection of the Library of Congress and in the archives of Barnard College. For other biographical sources see the *Saturday Evening Post*, 6 May and 13 May 1944, and *Today*, 11 July 1936. Reid's role in the management of the *Herald Tribune* is chronicled in Richard Kluger's *The Paper: The Life and Death of the New York Herald Tribune* (1986). An obituary is in the *New York Times*, 28 July 1970, and in the *Barnard Alumnae* 60, no. 1 (1970): 16–19.

ELIZABETH ZOE VICARY
BARBARA STRAUS REED

REID, Ira De Augustine (2 July 1901–15 Aug. 1968), African-American sociologist and educator, was born in Clifton Forge, Virginia, the son of Daniel Augustine Reid, a Baptist minister, and Willie Robertha

James. He was raised in comfortable surroundings and was educated in integrated public schools in Harrisburg, Pennsylvania, and Germantown, a Philadelphia suburb. Reid's academic promise was as apparent as his family connections were useful. Recruited by President John Hope of Morehouse College in Atlanta, Georgia, in 1918 Reid completed the college preparatory course at Morehouse Academy and in 1922 received his B.A. from Morehouse College.

Reid taught sociology and history and directed the high school at Texas College in Tyler from 1922 to 1923. He took graduate courses in sociology at the University of Chicago the next summer. From 1923 to 1924 he taught social science at Douglas High School, Huntington, West Virginia. Reid then embarked on a model apprenticeship that George Edmund Haynes, cofounder of the National Urban League, had established for social welfare workers and young social scientists as part of the Urban League program. Selected as a National Urban League fellow for the year 1924–1925, Reid earned an M.A. in social economics at the University of Pittsburgh in 1925, and that same year he married Gladys Russell Scott. They adopted one child.

Also in 1925 Reid was appointed industrial secretary of the New York Urban League, a position he held until 1928. In this role he worked with Charles S. Johnson, director of research and investigations of the National Urban League, helping the league position itself as a source of information about the economic conditions of African Americans as well as an agency for social reform. Reid surveyed the living conditions of low-income Harlem Negro families, conducted a study that was published as *The Negro Population of Albany, New York* (1928), and served as Johnson's research assistant in a National Urban League survey of blacks in the trade unions.

Reid also served as Johnson's assistant in collecting data for the National Interracial Conference of 1928 held in Washington, D.C. This conference represented a popular front of "new middle-class" social welfare activists and social scientists, white and black, who were professionally concerned with the race problem in the United States. The conference produced the landmark *Negro in American Civilization: A Study of Negro Life and Race Relations in the Light of Social Research* (1930). It was a volume that witnessed the emergence of a liberal consensus on race that would be reaffirmed by Gunnar Myrdal in 1944 in *An American Dilemma* and certified by the U.S. Supreme Court a decade later.

Reid's three-year tenure as industrial secretary completed another phase of his apprenticeship. In 1928 he succeeded Johnson as director of research for the national body, a position he held until 1934. As part of the league's procedure for establishing local branches, Reid's work included surveying seven black communities, which resulted in two important reports, *Social Conditions of the Negro in the Hill District of Pittsburgh* (1930) and *The Negro Community of Baltimore—Its Social and Economic Conditions* (1935). Drawing on earlier Urban League research, Reid also published one of the first reliable studies of blacks in the workforce, *Negro Membership in American Labor Unions* (1930).

Reid was enrolled as a graduate student in sociology at Columbia University throughout the period 1928–1934. While employed by the Urban League he began the research on West Indian immigration on which his Ph.D. dissertation would be based.

In 1934 Hope, then president of Atlanta University, encouraged W. E. B. Du Bois, chair of the Department of Sociology, to hire Reid. Du Bois complied happily. Reid, he remarked in 1937, "is the best trained young Negro in sociology today." Six feet four inches tall, confident, well dressed, and witty, Reid was an impressive figure. His biting intelligence was acknowledged—if not always appreciated—and his urbane manner made him an effective interracial diplomat in an era when black equality was an implausible hypothesis for most white Americans.

Reid worked closely with Du Bois at Atlanta University until the latter's forced retirement in June 1944, at which time he ascended to chair of the Department of Sociology, serving from 1944 to 1946. Having served under Du Bois as managing editor of *Phylon: The Atlanta University Review of Race and Culture* since 1940, the year of its founding, Reid also succeeded his senior colleague as editor in chief of the journal (1944–1948).

From 1934 until his departure from Atlanta University in 1946, Reid's work as a social scientist also had important policy implications. Under the auspices of the Office of the Adviser on Negro Affairs, Department of the Interior, Reid directed a 1936 survey of *The Urban Negro Worker in the United States, 1925–1936* (vol. 1, 1938), an undertaking financed by the Works Progress Administration. Three years later *The Negro Immigrant: His Background, Characteristics and Social Adjustment, 1899–1937* (1939) was published; it was based on the dissertation that had earned him a Ph.D. in sociology from Columbia University that same year. In 1940 Reid published *In a Minor Key: Negro Youth in Story and Fact*, the first volume of the American Youth Commission's study of black youths. This was a cooperative endeavor of anthropologists, psychiatrists, and sociologists to study the impact of economic crisis and minority-group status on the development of youngsters in black communities. From the standpoint of the history and politics of the social sciences, the project—funded by the Laura Spelman Rockefeller Memorial—reflected the Social Science Research Council's endorsement of a "culture and personality" paradigm that would support liberal policy initiatives.

While at Atlanta Reid also drafted "The Negro in the American Economic System" (1940), a research memorandum used by Myrdal in *An American Dilemma* four years later. In 1941, in collaboration with sociologist Arthur Raper of the Commission on Interracial Cooperation, Reid published *Sharecroppers All*, a pioneering study of the political economy of the South. The text reflects the emerging characterization of the depression South by social scientists and New Dealers as the country's number one economic problem; it signaled their growing impatience at the public costs of the region's class and race relations and dysfunctional labor market.

After Du Bois's retirement from Atlanta University, Reid grew restless there. As a result of his desire for more congenial academic surroundings, on the one hand, and the cracks emerging in the walls of segregation, on the other, Reid became one of the first black scholars to obtain a full-time position at a northern white university (New York University, 1945).

This was again an exemplary chapter in his life. Under the racial regime of "separate-but-equal," job opportunities for black scholars, however well trained and qualified, were restricted to historically black institutions in the South. However, in the early 1940s, as tactical Trojan horses in a foundation-sponsored campaign to desegregate the ranks of the professoriat, a handful of accomplished black academics—among them anthropologist Allison Davis and historian John Hope Franklin—were installed at northern institutions. Reid became visiting professor of sociology at the New York University School of Education (1945–1947) and, sponsored by the American Friends Service Committee, was visiting professor of sociology at Haverford College, Haverford, Pennsylvania (1946–1947). In 1948 Reid became professor of sociology and chair of the Haverford Department of Sociology and Anthropology, a position he held until his retirement in 1966.

Reid and his wife joined the Society of Friends in 1950, and over the next fifteen years he was involved increasingly in the educational activities of the American Friends Service Committee. Though Reid's scholarly output decreased during this period, his important earlier contributions were gradually acknowledged. He was named assistant editor of the *American Sociological Review* (1947–1950). Ironically, with the coming of the McCarthy era, Reid was honored for professional contributions that now earned him public suspicion. His passport was suspended from 1952 to 1953 by State Department functionaries for suspected communist sympathies. When he firmly challenged this action, the passport was soon returned. Reid served as vice president and president of the Eastern Sociological Society from 1953 to 1954 and from 1954 to 1955, respectively. He was elected second vice president of the American Sociological Association itself from 1954 to 1955.

After the milestone 1954 Supreme Court decision in *Brown v. Board of Education*, Reid was invited to edit "Racial Desegregation and Integration," a special issue of the *Annals of the American Academy of Political and Social Science* (304 [Mar. 1956]). This was another indication of his new visibility within the social science fraternity.

Reid's wife died in 1956. Two years later he married Anna "Anne" Margaret Cooke of Gary, Indiana.

Late in his career Reid enjoyed a wider public. Among other activities, he served on the Pennsylvania Governor's Commission on Higher Education and was a participant in the 1960 White House Conference on Children and Youth. In 1962 Reid was visiting director, Department of Extra-mural Studies, University College, Ibadan, Nigeria. From 1962 to 1963 he was Danforth Foundation Distinguished Visiting Professor, International Christian University, Tokyo, Japan. Reid retired as professor of sociology at Haverford College on 30 June 1966. He died in Bryn Mawr, Pennsylvania.

In addition to his personal achievements, Ira Reid is an important representative of the first numerically significant cohort of professional black social scientists in the United States.

• No comprehensive collection of Reid manuscript materials exists. However, information about Reid, the various projects and organizations with which he was associated, as well as relevant memoranda and correspondence may be found in *The Papers of W. E. B. Du Bois* (1877–1963), microfilm; in the John Hope Presidential Papers and the *Phylon* Records, Editorial Correspondence (1940–1948), Special Collections/ Archives, Robert W. Woodruff Library, Atlanta University; and in the Charles S. Johnson Papers and the Julius Rosenwald Fund Archives (1917–1948), Special Collections, Fisk University Library, Nashville, Tenn. See also the National Urban League Records (1910–1960), Library of Congress; Race Relations Department, United Church Board for Homeland Ministries Records (1943–1976), Amistad Research Center, Tulane University, New Orleans, La.; Ira De A. Reid File, Office of College Relations, Haverford College, and Ira De A. Reid File, Quaker Collection, Haverford College Library, Haverford, Penn.; Ira De Augustine Reid Papers, Schomburg Center for Research in Black Culture, Rare Books, Manuscripts, and Archives Section, New York City; and Urban League of Philadelphia Records (1935–1963), Urban Archives, Temple University, Philadelphia.

The biographical sketch on Reid in James E. Blackwell and Morris Janowitz, eds., *Black Sociologists: Historical and Contemporary Perspectives* (1974), pp. 154–55, is untrustworthy. A bibliography of his writings (1925–1959), prepared by Reid himself in 1960, is available in the Ira De A. Reid File, Office of College Relations at Haverford College. Obituaries are in the *New York Times*, 17 Aug. 1968, and the *Philadelphia Evening Bulletin*, 19 Sept. 1968.

PAUL JEFFERSON

REID, Mayne. *See* Reid, Thomas Mayne.

REID, Neel (23 Oct. 1885–14 Feb. 1926), architect, was born Joseph Neel Reid in Jacksonville, Alabama, the son of John Whitfield Reid, Sr., and Elizabeth Adams. At the age of eighteen Reid moved with his family to Macon, Georgia, where his father owned the John Reid Shoe Company. Neel Reid completed high school in Macon and then apprenticed with a local architect, Curran R. Ellis, who had been responsible for remodeling Reid's parents' home. Reid showed an early architectural talent, and in 1904, on the advice of Ellis, he moved to Atlanta, Georgia, where he worked in the office of Willis F. Denny. In Denny's office he met Hal F. Hentz, who became a lifelong friend and with whom he later entered into partnership.

During 1905 and 1906 Reid and Hentz lived in New York City and enrolled in architecture classes at Columbia University before their departure in 1906 for the École des Beaux-Arts in Paris. Reid studied in the atelier libre of Laloux but was unable to complete his Paris studies, having been summoned back to the United States by his father in 1907 because of family financial problems. Reid then worked as a draftsman at the New York firm of Murphy and Dana for a short while before setting up practice in Atlanta in 1908. He soon induced Hentz, who had continued his studies and travels in Europe, to join him, and the two entered into partnership with the well-established, older Atlanta architect Godfrey L. Norrman, who helped the new firm secure a number of early commissions. Norrman died soon after the formation of the firm, but in 1913 the partnership expanded to include Rudolph Adler, a German-born and Columbia University–educated architect Hentz and Reid had met in New York. The three worked well together, with Adler largely responsible for construction supervision, Hentz having responsibility for marketing and public relations, and Reid undertaking the bulk of the design, especially for the firm's many residential commissions.

Many of Reid's early commissions were located in the subdivision of Druid Hills in Atlanta (designed by Frederick Law Olmsted) and also in the slightly older subdivision of Ansley Park. Other early commissions were located in Macon, Georgia, and were often undertaken for family friends or for his father's business associates. During this period Reid designed houses in a variety of styles, including Tudor, neoclassical, and English and American Georgian. Reid became known for simple, clapboarded houses with obvious Georgian detailing, and his designs were noted for their mannered and educated use of traditional architectural elements. The house he designed for himself, on Fairview Road in Druid Hills (1914), provides a good example of his early work. Reid lived in the Fairview Road home until 1916, when he purchased the nineteenth-century Greek Revival "Mimosa Hall" in Roswell, Georgia. Other examples of his early work include the Joseph N. Neel House (1910) in Macon and the Frank Adair House (1911), the Will Campbell House (1914), and the Sigmund Montag House (1915) in Atlanta.

In 1916 the firm of Hentz & Reid received its largest residential commission, the Fuller Callaway House in LaGrange, Georgia. The Callaway house, known as "Hills & Dales," was built on the site of an earlier home that had been surrounded by gardens created by its former owner, Sarah Coleman Ferrell. The Italian character of the gardens was echoed in the Georgian-Italianate villa that Reid designed.

After 1915 many of the commissions of Hentz & Reid (later Hentz, Reid & Adler) were located in northwest Atlanta, where new enclaves of the city's elite were taking shape. Reid's work during this period was influenced by his contemporary Charles Platt, who promoted the integration of house and grounds to form Italian-style "villa" estates. Although Reid left no writings describing his more theoretical views on architecture and few complete site plans have survived, his completed works attest to the great importance he placed on this successful integration of houses and landscapes. The country house aesthetic promoted by Hentz, Reid & Adler, with its flowing expanses of lawn, uninterrupted by walls or fences, all of which serve to unify eclectic architectural styles, is still apparent in the neighborhoods he helped to define and has significantly influenced the look of suburban Atlanta. Examples of Reid's residential work in Atlanta during this period include the C. C. Case House (1918), the W. F. Manry House (1921), and the Philip McDuffie House (1922).

While specializing in residential design, the firm also designed commercial and public buildings, such as the Michael Brothers' Store (1922) in Athens, Georgia, a Palladian-inspired commercial block; the Massee Apartments in Macon, Georgia (1924); and the Atlanta Athletic Club (1926). Again, these were highly mannered buildings, employing richly defined classical details derived largely from the late Italian Renaissance.

During the early decades of the twentieth century, when Atlanta was experiencing rapid expansion due to its importance as a regional transportation hub, the work of Neel Reid was largely responsible for shaping the look of the city's high-style residential architecture. Greek Revival, the dominant historical style of the South, is conspicuous in its absence from Reid's architectural repertoire. Instead, he provided for his clients a connection with older architectural traditions of the United States and Europe, effectively sidestepping the often negative associations of the antebellum Greek Revival tradition.

Reid was an important figure in Atlanta society, readily accepted into the circles of his well-to-do clients. He belonged to the Piedmont Driving Club and the Nine O'Clocks (another social organization) and took an active interest in civic affairs.

Reid died of a brain tumor at Mimosa Hall in Roswell, Georgia. He was succeeded in the firm by Philip Trammell Shutze, who both continued and expanded upon Reid's design tradition. In its various forms, the firm begun by Neel Reid and Hal Hentz in 1909 survived until the death of Philip Shutze in 1982, making it the longest continuous architectural practice in Atlanta.

• Papers of the firms of Norrman, Hentz and Reid; Hentz & Reid; Hentz, Reid & Adler; and Hentz, Adler & Shutze are held by the Atlanta Historical Society and by the Architecture Library of the Georgia Institute of Technology. Reid's life and work is described in Stephanie A. Kapetanakos, "The Architecture of Neel Reid: A Study of the Residential Architecture of Neel Reid in Atlanta" (M.A. thesis, Univ. of Georgia); H. Stafford Bryant, Jr., "Two Twentieth Century Domestic Architects in the South: Neel Reid and William L. Bottomleg," *Classical America* 1, no. 2 (1972): 30–36; Lewis Paul, "Neel Reid, 1885–1926," *Atlanta Historical Bulletin* 16, no. 1 (1971): 9–30; James Grady, *Architecture of Neel Reid in Georgia* (1973); Catherine Howett, "A Georgian Renascence in Georgia: The Residential Architecture of Neel Reid," in *The Colonial Revival in America*, ed. Alan Axelrod (1985); and Catherine Howett, "The Residential Architecture of Neel Reid," *Georgia Journal* 2, no. 2 (1982): 15–25. Individual buildings are discussed in Annie Hornaby Howard, ed., *Georgia Homes and Landmarks* (1929); Franklin M. Garrett, *Atlanta and Environs* (1954); Herbert Wheaton Congdon, "A Shot at Two Targets," *American Architect*, 24 May 1916, pp. 329–34; Fiske Kimball, "The American Country House, Part II, Artistic Conditions: Traditions and Tendencies of Style; Part III, The Solutions: Disposition and Treatment of House and Surroundings," *Architectural Record* 46 (Oct. 1919): 299–329, 350–400; "The Scottish Rite Hospital for Crippled Children, Atlanta, Georgia," *American Architect*, 15 Sept. 1920, pp. 341–43; "House of C. C. Case, Esq.," *Southern Architect and Building News*, Aug. 1926, pp. 45–48; and Mrs. John W. Reid, Sr., "Mimosa Hall, Roswell, Georgia," *Southern Architect and Building News*, Nov. 1926, pp. 49–54. Obituaries are in the *Atlanta Constitution* and the *Macon Telegraph*, both 15 Feb. 1926, and the *A.I.A. Journal* (Apr. 1926).

WILLIAM R. CHAPMAN

REID, Ogden Mills (16 May 1882–3 Jan. 1947), newspaper editor and publisher, was born in New York City, the son of Whitelaw Reid, a journalist, politician, and diplomat, and Elisabeth Mills. The only son of a socially prominent New York family, he was raised in circumstances of wealth and privilege. His father, the editor and publisher of the *New York Tribune*, was the Republican vice presidential candidate in 1892 and later served as ambassador to England; his maternal grandfather, Darius Ogden Mills, was a financier and philanthropist. Reid graduated in 1899 from the Browning School, a private preparatory school in New York City, attended the University of Bonn in Germany for a year, and then returned to the United States to both complete his undergraduate studies (B.A., 1904) and earn a law degree (LL.B., 1907) at Yale University. A year after graduating from law school, he was admitted to the New York bar. In 1911 he married Helen Miles Rogers; raised in Racine, Wisconsin, and educated at Barnard College, Rogers had worked for his mother as a social secretary. They had three children.

Though trained as an attorney, Reid's chosen career as a journalist began in 1908 when he joined the reporting staff of his father's *New York Tribune*. After a succession of jobs, including copy editor, assistant night editor, and city editor, he was promoted to managing editor in 1912. With his father's death in England later that year, the ownership of the newspaper passed to his mother, and a few months later, Reid, at age thirty, became the editor, a position he would hold for the rest of his life. More interested in the journalistic than the commercial aspects of the newspaper profession, he welcomed the participation of his family in the paper's often precarious business affairs. His wife, Helen, a woman of exceptional enterprise and ability, was formally named advertising director in 1918 and within a few years was overseeing the paper's business management. His mother, whose family fortune had helped secure his father's original control of the *Tribune*, often played an active role in important financial decisions. She regarded the newspaper as a "family obligation" and, despite many years of losses, loaned it several million dollars shortly after her son was named editor.

The *Tribune* was moribund when Reid became editor in 1913. Staid in appearance, dull in tone, and predictable in outlook, the paper was known as "the little old lady of Park Row." It also faced stiff competition; Adolph Ochs's *New York Times*, with its greater readership and revenues, was an especially formidable rival. Lacking his competitors' resources, Reid's strategy for reviving the paper emphasized vivid reporting and stylish prose. "If it couldn't match its competitors in covering the news," recalled a former copy editor, "the *Tribune* would take the alternative course; it would write its way to success." World War I provided a unique opportunity, and Reid hired such established reporters as Richard Harding Davis, Will Irwin, and Heywood Broun, as well as columnist Frank H. Simmons, to cover the war. Davis and Irwin, both accomplished stylists, helped set the new tone Reid wanted. Davis's dispatch on the Germans' march into Brussels and the first reports by Irwin from the Ypres battlefield were widely noted and added to the paper's new reputation. Other important contributors of Reid's first decade included W. O. McGeehan, sportswriter Grantland Rice, political columnist Mark Sullivan, and cartoonists Clare Briggs and H. T. Webster. The light essays of Franklin Pierce Adams's regular feature, "The Conning Tower," also proved popular.

The scion of an august Old Guard Republican family, Reid nevertheless moved to moderate some of the archconservatism in the *Tribune*'s editorials. Despite this broadening of its political stance, the paper remained one of the nation's most influential conservative voices. Disapproving of many of the social changes of the 1920s, the *Tribune* was, for example, so outspoken in its opposition to Congressman (and later New York mayor) Fiorello La Guardia, a fellow Republican, that he sued the paper for libel.

By 1924 Reid's efforts had increased the *Tribune*'s circulation from 50,000 in 1912 to over 140,000. Success brought an offer to buy the paper from Frank Munsey, a publishing entrepreneur and owner of the *New York Herald*, another morning daily with a similar readership. When Reid declined, Munsey asked, "Do you buy us or do we buy you?" Reid's mother answered for the family: "We buy you." The agreed price, $5 million, also included the Paris edition of the *Herald*. "With Mr. Reid," Munsey wrote the next day, "the continuance of his ownership of the *Tribune* was a deep sentiment and a duty, as it was a family heritage. . . . I had no such obligation."

With a combined circulation of 275,000, the merger allowed the newly named *Herald Tribune* to become the *Times*'s chief competitor; it also gave Reid an energetic *Herald* reporter, Stanley Walker, whom he soon promoted to city editor. Excellent prose remained central to the paper's persona, and Reid and Walker assembled "a brilliant, gallant troop of journalistic cavalrymen," which included Joseph Alsop, Lincoln

Barnett, Lucius Beebe, James T. Flexner, Alva Johnston, George S. Kaufman, John Lardner, Joseph Mitchell, and Geoffrey Parsons. During World War II, Homer Bigart and Marguerite Higgins distinguished themselves as frontline correspondents. Most influential of all was Walter Lippmann; the success of his *Herald Tribune* "Today and Tomorrow" column, which first appeared in 1931 and was soon widely syndicated, signaled that the authority of the editorial page had been eclipsed by the op-ed essay. During the 1930s and 1940s, *Herald Tribune* writers won eight Pulitzer prizes, and the Paris edition, closed during the war but reopened by Reid in late 1944, soon became Europe's leading American newspaper.

As his health declined in the last years of his life, Reid turned over much of the responsibility for the paper to his wife. At the time of his death in New York City, the *Herald Tribune*'s daily circulation was 358,000, and 700,000 on Sunday. His family retained control of the paper until 1958, when it was sold to John Hay Whitney, who, faced in 1966 with mounting losses and a newspaper strike, chose to cease publication.

During his newspaper career of thirty-five years, Reid both reflected and in part shaped the changing attitudes of the eastern Republican establishment. Though socially and politically conservative, Reid and the *Herald Tribune* often represented the interests of the more centrist elements of the Republican party. A proponent of internationalism, his support of Franklin D. Roosevelt's foreign policies was an important counterforce to the isolationism of the prewar period. Under Reid's editorship, the *Herald Tribune* earned its reputation as "a newspaperman's newspaper," and his encouragement of gifted reporters and contributors produced stylishly written reportage and analysis that established a significant literary standard for twentieth-century journalism.

• The Reid family papers are at Manhattanville College in Purchase, N.Y. Microform copies of the *New York Herald Tribune* (1924–1966) are at the New York Public Library. Richard Kluger, *The Paper: The Life and Death of the New York Herald Tribune* (1986), contains a thorough assessment of Reid's editorship. See also Royal Cortissoz, *The New York Tribune: Incidents and Personalities in Its History* (1923), and Harry W. Baehr, Jr., *The New York Tribune since the Civil War* (1936), on the early history of his newspaper; Bingham Duncan, *Whitelaw Reid: Journalist, Politician, Diplomat* (1975), and Royal Cortissoz, *The Life of Whitelaw Reid* (1921), on his family background; Charles L. Robertson, *The International Herald Tribune: The First Hundred Years* (1987), on his paper's Paris edition; and Edwin Emery and Michael Emery, *The Press and America: An Interpretive History of the Mass Media*, 7th ed. (1992), Jean Folkerts and Dwight L. Teeter, Jr., *Voices of a Nation: A History of Media in the United States* (1989), Michael Schudson, *Discovering the News: A Social History of American Newspapers* (1978), Catherine Covert and John D. Stevens, eds., *Mass Media between the Wars: Perceptions of Cultural Tension, 1918–1941* (1984), Frank Luther Mott, *American Journalism*, 3d ed. (1962), and Kenneth Norman Stewart, *Makers of Modern Journalism* (1952), on the interwar in journalistic milieu. See also Fred C. Shapiro, "The Life and Death of a Great Newspaper," *American Heritage*, Oct. 1967, pp. 97–112, and Sean McCullough, "Trib after Greeley: Until Merger Do Us Part," *Media History Digest* 11, no. 2 (1991): 48–52, 57. Obituaries are in the *New York Herald Tribune*, 4–8 Jan. 1947; the *New York Times*, 4–5 Jan. 1947; and *Editor & Publisher*, 11 Jan. 1947.

DAVID ABRAHAMSON

REID, Robert Lewis (29 July 1862–2 Dec. 1929), impressionist and mural painter, was born in Stockbridge, Massachusetts, the son of Jared Reid, Jr., and Louisa Dwight. His father was the founder of the Edwards Place School for boys in Stockbridge and was headmaster until its failure in 1878, when he went to work as a salesman and dispersed his children among relatives. Reid spent his late adolescence partly with his parents in Andover, Massachusetts, and partly with his brother Charles in Hartford and Westfield, Connecticut. Limited financial resources were the backdrop against which Reid struggled until he was well established as an artist.

Reid was educated at his father's school and at Phillips Academy in Andover. He entered the School of Painting and Drawing at the Museum of Fine Arts, Boston, in the winter session of 1880–1881. He immediately became an assistant instructor and served as such for three of his four years at the museum school. Reid's education was conservative; his teachers included Otto Grundmann and Frederic Crowninshield, both of whom demanded anatomical accuracy in portrait and figure drawing. In fact, competence in drawing took precedence over painting. Crowninshield also introduced his students to stained glass design.

Reid's fellow students included Edmund C. Tarbell and Frank W. Benson, with whom Reid would later be professionally associated in the group known as Ten American Painters. While an art student, Reid was ambitious and noticed as something of a maverick. He founded and wrote for *Art Student*, a magazine for the students of the museum school.

Early in 1885 Reid moved to New York City to study at the Art Students League. By autumn he had decided to go to Paris, although his letters from Europe reveal that his going abroad entailed "substantial family sacrifice" (Weinberg, p. 4). He studied at the Académie Julian, where instruction continued in the conservative academic tradition to which he was accustomed. By 1887 he was working with Gustave-Rodolphe Boulanger and Jules-Joseph Lefebvre, the favorite teaching team of Americans at Julian's. In company with Tarbell and Willard Metcalf, another museum school alumnus, Reid also took classes taught by the American expatriate William Turner Dannat. For the three years he was in France Reid spent nine months of the year in Paris and summered at Etaples, a fishing village on the coast of Normandy. This pattern was broken only by a tour of Italy during the winter of 1886–1887.

The immediate goal to which Reid and all American students in Paris aspired was to have their paintings chosen for exhibition in the annual Paris Salon. In 1887 Reid submitted for the first time a painting to the

Salon jury. His letters home while he awaited the decision of the judges reveal his character to be ambitious and confident, yet in no way grandiose. Reid's submission, *The First Communion*, was accepted for the Salon of 1887. Painted at Etaples, it represented a local peasant girl about to take her first communion. *Flight into Egypt*, exhibited at the Salon of 1888, and *Blessing the Boats*, exhibited the following year, also used Etaplesian fisherfolk as their models.

Reid returned to New York in 1889, bringing with him some of his paintings executed abroad. *Flight into Egypt* was included that year in the autumn exhibition at the National Academy of Design. *Death of the First Born*, when exhibited at the Society of American Artists in 1889, won him election to that organization. He taught at Cooper Union and the Art Students League and shared a studio for a time with Metcalf in the Sherwood Studio Building.

Reid's conversion to impressionism occurred between his storytelling paintings executed in France and *Reverie*, painted in the United States in 1890. The subject of *Reverie*—a woman in a lush garden setting—exhibits an impressionist's choice of subject as well as an impressionist's technique in the rendering of light and color. From 1892 Reid was regularly referred to as an impressionist.

Reid's paintings were included in the annual exhibitions of the National Academy of Design, where he won the Thomas B. Clarke prize in 1897 and the first Hallgarten prize in 1898; the Pennsylvania Academy of the Fine Arts; and the Society of American Artists until his break with that organization in 1899. He was also a frequent contributor to the regular juried exhibitions sponsored by the Art Institute of Chicago; the Corcoran Gallery of Art in Washington, D.C., where he won the Clarke prize of $1,000 in 1908; and the Carnegie Institute in Pittsburgh.

Reid's first opportunity to paint a mural came in 1892, when he was commissioned to decorate one of eight domes in the entrance pavilion to the Manufactures and Liberal Arts Building at the World's Columbian Exposition in Chicago. Reid's painting of female allegorical figures representing the decorative arts earned him a Special Medal for Decoration.

For years Reid pursued the dual careers of easel painter and muralist. He painted murals for the Fifth Avenue Hotel (1892–1893), the Imperial Hotel, and the Apellate Division Court House of the New York State Supreme Court (1899), all in New York; the Massachusetts State House (1901); the Library of Congress in Washington, D.C.; the U.S. Pavilion at the Exposition Universelle in Paris (1900), for which he received a gold medal; the dome of the Fine Arts Palace at Panama-Pacific International Exposition in San Francisco (1914–1915); and an altarpiece for the Church of St. Paul the Apostle in New York. Reid's mural subjects were figural, and his style was to render them large, firmly drawn, and solidly colored. Around 1901, in order to accommodate the large canvases on which he had to work, he took a studio on East Thirty-third Street that was so large his friends nicknamed it the "Golf Links."

Reid's easel paintings most often featured young women singly or in groups of two or three amidst a flowering garden on a sunny spring or summer day. Nude or clothed in light-colored frocks, they blend into their lush surroundings rendered in the broken brushwork of impressionism. Reid minimized depth, combining figure with setting on the same plane to create a two-dimensional, decorative effect. Picture titles were more often inspired by the setting than the figure, such as *Gladiolas* (c. 1898), *Fleur-de-Lis* (c. 1899), and *Breezy Day* (c. 1898).

Between 1901 and 1905 Reid was occupied with the design and execution of some twenty stained glass windows for the H. H. Rogers Memorial Church in Fairhaven, Massachusetts. It was a time-consuming project, with much trial and error going into the artist's attempt to master the unfamiliar medium. By 1908 Reid began to paint women indoors, still in light-filled settings, their images often reflected in a mirror. *The Open Fire*, which won the Bronze Medal at the Corcoran Gallery in 1908, is one such indoor painting in which the glow from a fireplace plays off the figure's skin and dress. The model for this painting was Elizabeth Reeves, whom Reid had married in 1907. The marriage ended in divorce in 1916.

From 1898 until 1917 Reid exhibited nearly every year with the Ten American Painters, a group of artists who resigned in protest from the Society of American Artists and organized themselves for the mutual promotion of their work. Until about 1909 Reid spent summers painting at Medfield, Massachusetts, and Somers Center, New York. From 1920 to 1927 he taught at the Broadmoor Art Academy, Colorado Springs, Colorado. After suffering a stroke that paralyzed his right side in 1927, Reid lived in a sanatorium at Clifton Springs, New York, and taught himself to draw and paint with his left hand. He died at Clifton Springs.

In addition to the honors mentioned above, Reid became an associate of the National Academy of Design in 1902 and an academician four years later. He was given a one-man show at the academy the year before his death. There were also one-man shows at Grand Central Galleries and the Brooklyn Museum in 1929.

• The Robert L. Reid Papers are in the Archives of American Art, Smithsonian Institution, Washington, D.C. For appraisals of Reid's work by his contemporaries, see Henry W. Goodrich, "Robert Reid and His Work," *International Studio* 36 (Feb. 1909): cxiii–cxxii, and James W. Pattison, "Robert Reid, Painter," *House Beautiful* 20 (July 1906): 18–20. H. Barbara Weinberg discusses Reid's life and work in "Robert Reid: Academic 'Impressionist,'" *Archives of American Art Journal* 15 (1975): 2–11, and *The Lure of Paris: Nineteenth-Century American Painters and Their French Teachers* (1991). See also William H. Gerdts et al., *Ten American Painters* (1990), and Ulrich W. Hiesinger, *Impressionism in America: The Ten American Painters* (1991). An obituary is in the *New York Times*, 3 Dec. 1929.

CYNTHIA SEIBELS

REID, Samuel Chester (25 Aug. 1783–28 Jan. 1861), naval officer, was born at Norwich, Connecticut, the son of John Reid and Rebecca Chester. His father, a lieutenant in the British navy, was captured in the American Revolution, joined the rebels, and settled in America. Samuel Reid went to sea at the age of eleven, and his early experience was in the West Indies. After his ship was taken by a French privateer, he was imprisoned for a time at Guadalupe. He later served as acting midshipman on the sloop of war *Baltimore* and commanded his first merchant ship at the age of twenty. In 1813 Reid married Mary Jennings; they had eight children.

Reid achieved fame in the War of 1812 as commander of the privateer brig *General Armstrong*. On 26 September 1814 Reid's ship entered the neutral Portuguese harbor of Fayal in the Azores for water and provisions. On the same day the *General Armstrong* was discovered there by a British naval squadron consisting of the ship of the line *Plantagenet*, the frigate *Rota*, and the brig *Carnation*. Against this powerful squadron, the *General Armstrong* could muster less than 100 officers and men and carried only nine guns.

During the night of 26–27 September, the *General Armstrong* twice engaged in action with boats from the British ships. On the first occasion, Reid ordered his gunners to fire when he was convinced that the British boats were preparing to attack, and a brief engagement ensued. Later the British launched a full-scale attack with additional boats and made a determined attempt to board the American ship. They were beaten off and suffered heavy casualties. On the morning of the twenty-seventh, after renewed fighting with the *Carnation*, Reid ordered his ship to be scuttled and, with his men, abandoned it. The British lost more than 100 men killed and wounded, the Americans only nine. This fiercely fought engagement against overwhelming odds made Reid a national hero on his return to the United States. As the battle was in a neutral port, it led to an extended diplomatic correspondence between the United States, England, and Portugal over questions of responsibility and possible indemnities. In the 1850s the U.S. claim against Portugal was rejected, but ultimately one of Reid's sons received compensation from the U.S. government.

Apart from the battle at Fayal in the War of 1812, Reid's main claim to fame was his role in creating the modern design of the U.S. flag. The original U.S. flag of thirteen stripes and thirteen stars had been altered on the admission of new states by the addition of both stripes and stars, although after the official flag had been established in 1795 as fifteen stripes and fifteen stars, this was not done consistently because of the design problems it created. With more territories ready for admission to the Union after the War of 1812, it was proposed in Congress that there should be an inquiry into the possibility of altering the design of the flag. Consulted by the House Committee on Naval Affairs, Reid suggested that the design consist of thirteen stripes to represent the thirteen original states while the number of stars would increase as new states were added to the Union. He proposed two forms of this flag: one with the stars in one large star to be used on merchant vessels, the other with the stars in parallel lines to be used on warships and on land. The new design became law in April 1818, and a flag made to the new design by Reid's wife and others was raised over the Capitol in that month.

In the years after the War of 1812, Reid became harbor master of the Port of New York. This was a lucrative post, because its holder received fees from the vessels entering the port. He was active and creative in this position; he devised marine and land telegraph systems, reorganized the system of pilots for the port, published a code of signals for the telegraph on Staten Island, and took the lead in persuading the government to place a lightship off Sandy Hook. Reid's long service in peace and war was recognized by his appointment as sailing master in the navy.

Although best known for his bravery, Reid showed himself to be a man who combined imagination with considerable practicality. After a long and useful career, he died in New York City.

• Reid's son, Samuel Chester Reid, Jr., did much to make the public aware of his father's contributions in *The History of the Wonderful Battle of the Brig-of-War General Armstrong with a British Squadron, at Fayal, 1814* (1893). There is also information in Samuel C. Reid, Jr., ed., *The Case of the Private Armed Brig of War General Armstrong* (1857) and *A Collection of Sundry Publications and Other Documents in Relation to the Attack Made during the Late War upon the Private Armed Brig General Armstrong* (1833). See also Edgar S. Maclay, *A History of American Privateers* (1899), and Boleslaw and Marie-Louise D'Otrange Mastai, *The Stars and Stripes: The American Flag as Art and History from the Birth of the Republic to the Present* (1973).

REGINALD HORSMAN

REID, Thomas Mayne (4 Apr. 1818–22 Oct. 1883), author and soldier, was born in Ballyroney, County Down, Ireland, the son of Thomas Mayne Reid, a Presbyterian minister, and his wife, whose maiden name may have been Rutherford. Reid studied at the Royal Academical Institution in Belfast from 1834 to 1838 in preparation for the ministry. He quit, opened a day school in Ballyroney, and taught there in 1838 and 1839. From this point on, details concerning Reid's life are uncertain, because he boasted about himself, much of his fiction is wrongly regarded as autobiographical, and his widow's biography of him is sometimes vague and inaccurate.

Reid sailed in December 1839 for New Orleans, Louisiana, where he worked as a corn factor in 1840. He became the tutor for a family in Nashville, Tennessee, that same year and briefly taught in his own school there from December until June 1841. Later in 1841 he was a clerk for a provision dealer either in Natchitoches, Louisiana, or in Natchez, Mississippi, and then probably went on trading trips with Red River Indians and then with a group of trappers to the Pacific Coast. In 1843 he may have departed from St. Louis, Missouri, and traveled either to Fort Union, in

North Dakota, or to Wyoming. He published a poem, by "a Poor Scholar," in *Godey's Lady's Book* in August. After a stint as an actor in Cincinnati, he moved in the fall of 1843 to Philadelphia, where he met Edgar Allan Poe. Reid probably stayed in Philadelphia, perhaps doing newspaper work during the summer in Newport, Rhode Island, until 1846, during which time he published more poems and some tales in *Godey's* and also in *Graham's Magazine.*

When the Mexican War began, Reid obtained a commission in December 1846 as a second lieutenant with the First New York Volunteer Regiment, under the command of Colonel Ward B. Burnett and went to Veracruz, Mexico, in March 1847. During the attack on Chapultepec in September 1847, Reid sustained a serious thigh wound and was soon thereafter promoted to first lieutenant. He was also active as a war correspondent whose dispatches appeared, signed "Ecolier," in *Spirit of the Times* (1 May–18 Dec. 1847). After convalescing in Mexico, he resigned from the army in May 1848 with the rank of captain. Reid may have returned to Philadelphia and Newport or may have summered in Ohio. His five-act tragedy, *Love's Martyr,* perhaps written in 1846, was briefly staged in Philadelphia in October 1848. Evidently he was in New York City early in 1849 and while there may have established friendships with volunteers seeking to aid the revolutionary movement in Bavaria. He sailed to Liverpool, England, in June, visited family members and friends in Ireland in July and August, and settled in London.

While in London, Reid published *The Rifle Rangers; or, Adventures of an Officer in Southern Mexico* in 1850; a year later published *The Scalp Hunters; or, Romantic Adventures in Northern Mexico,* written in Ballyroney; became involved in liberal political issues; and did more rapid writing. The first of what he called his "boys' books" was *The Desert Home; or, The Adventures of a Lost Family in the Wilderness* (1852). In 1853 he married Elizabeth Hyde, age fifteen, in London; the couple may have had one child. They moved three years later to Gerrard's Cross, Buckinghamshire, where Reid designed and built "The Ranche," his own Mexican-style hacienda. He wrote nonfiction and produced plays based on his fiction. He was outraged when Dion Boucicault plagiarized *The Quadroon* (1856), his novel about miscegenation, for Boucicault's 1859 play *The Octoroon; or, Life in Louisiana.* In England during the years of the American Civil War, Reid denounced the slave states, espoused the Union cause, and rashly accused the English establishment of enslaving its own less fortunate. Reid's play *The Maroon* enjoyed a long run in London beginning in 1865. His extravagances sent him into bankruptcy in 1866. Recovering quickly, he returned to London, where in 1867 he established an evening daily newspaper, titled the *Little Times,* which failed in less than a month.

Reid and his wife, who disliked America, sailed for Newport in October 1867. The following year he published *The Child Wife,* a novel based on the wooing of his own teenage bride and on his relationship with Louis Kossuth, a Hungarian revolutionary he befriended in London. In advertising this novel, his New York publisher announced that Reid was now an American citizen and that his writings therefore would be protected for the first time by American copyrights. No proof of his citizenship, however, has been found. In 1868 Reid signed a contract with Beadle & Co. of New York City, publishers of sensational "dime novels." With incredible speed, he wrote and the firm published *The Helpless Hand* (14 Jan. 1868), *The Scalp Hunters* (19 May 1868), *The Planter Pirate* (6 Jun. 1868), and *The White Squaw* (24 July 1868). More followed. Among Reid's most popular fellow writers for Beadle were James Fenimore Cooper, William Frederick "Buffalo Bill" Cody, Prentiss Ingraham, Edward Zane Carroll "Ned Buntline" Judson, and Frederick Whittaker. In 1869 Reid and his wife moved to New York City, where he founded and edited the monthly *Onward: A Magazine for the Young Manhood of America,* which Charles Ollivant, a British admirer, coedited but which ceased publication in 1870.

In the summer of 1870 Reid was hospitalized with a leg infection, an aftermath of his war wound. That fall, after his release but chronically depressed, he and his wife returned to London. He purchased copyrights of his earlier publications, revised and reprinted them, and also wrote short pieces but at a slower pace and sometimes self-plagiarized. In October 1874 blood poisoning developed in his leg, after which he was able to walk only with a crutch. He and his wife moved to Ross, Herefordshire, where he raised sheep, grew potatoes, took in a boarder for needed income, coedited and published some fiction in the *Boys' Illustrated News* in 1881 and 1882, and wrote twenty-six articles on English rural life for the *New York Daily Tribune* (1882). In 1883 he returned to London shortly before his final illness and death there.

In addition to about sixty novels and collections of stories, Reid published more than thirty poems and nonfictional pieces in American and British periodicals. Widely translated, he was especially popular in France, Norway, and Poland. Although he was the most admired Englishman to write about the American West in the nineteenth century, and although he thrilled countless readers of all ages during that time, his fiction is now regarded as too unrealistic and melodramatic to be taken as more than symptomatic of the culture in which it flourished.

• Many of Reid's few and scattered papers are at the University of Illinois, Urbana; the Houghton Library, Harvard University; and the Library of Congress. Joan Steele, "Mayne Reid: A Revised Bibliography," *Bulletin of Bibliography* 29 (July–Sept. 1972): 95–100, is comprehensive; her *Captain Mayne Reid* (1978) is thorough and exact. Elizabeth Reid, *Mayne Reid: A Memoir of His Life* (1890), is tender but unreliable; Elizabeth Reid and Charles H. Coe, *Captain Mayne Reid: His Life and Adventures* (1900), is a revision of her earlier book. Both are partly plagiarized from a manuscript biography of Reid by Charles Ollivant. K. Jack Bauer, *The Mexican War 1846–1848* (1974), mentions the part Colonel W. A. Burnett's regiment played at Chapultepec. Martha A. Sand-weiss et al., eds., *Eyewitness to War: Prints and Daguerreotypes of the Mexican War, 1846–1848* (1989), quotes two of Reid's dispatches to the *Spirit of the Times* (24 Apr. and 11 Dec. 1847). Roy W. Meyer, "The Western Fiction of Mayne Reid," *Western American Literature* 3 (Summer 1968): 115–32, is excellent. Ray Allen Billington, *Land of Savagery Land of Promise: The European Image of the American Frontier in the Nineteenth Century* (1981), comments, often adversely, on Reid's impact. An account of Reid and the "dime novel" is in Albert Johannsen, *The House of Beadle and Adams and Its Dime and Nickel Novels: The Story of a Vanished Literature* (3 vols., 1950–1962). Edmund Pearson, *Dime Novels; or, Following an Old Trail in Popular Literature* (1929), and Daryl Jones, *The Dime Novel Western* (1978), place Reid in context. Frank Luther Mott, *A History of American Magazines, 1865–1885* (1967), names magazines in which Reid published. Obituaries are in the *New York Daily Tribune*, 23 Oct. 1883; *The Times* (London), 24 Oct. 1883; and the *Newport Mercury*, 27 Oct. 1883.

ROBERT L. GALE

REID, Whitelaw (27 Oct. 1837–15 Dec. 1912), journalist, politician, and diplomat, was born near Xenia, Ohio, the son of Robert Charlton Reid, a farmer and a devout Reformed Presbyterian, and Marion Whitelaw Ronalds. Whitelaw Reid attended Xenia Academy, which was presided over by his uncle, and at the age of fifteen he was enrolled as a second-year student at Miami University in Ohio. He especially enjoyed the study of Latin and modern foreign languages and while in college contributed articles to local newspapers. A superb student who was highly competitive and a perfectionist, Reid did well and graduated with scientific honors in 1856. Subsequently he headed a grade school in South Charleston, Ohio, for a year. After holding various other jobs, he turned to journalism and with his brother purchased in 1857 the *Xenia News*, which he edited for almost two years.

Reid was a committed adherent of the new Republican party, and in 1860 he supported Abraham Lincoln for the presidency. In 1861 Reid left for Columbus to cover the state legislature for the *Cincinnati Times*. He also wrote reports for the *Cleveland Herald* and the *Cincinnati Gazette*, using at the last paper the pseudonym "Agate." He first won acclaim, however, for his coverage of the Civil War, especially of the campaigns of Generals George McClellan and William S. Rosecrans in what is now West Virginia. He was granted the title aide-de-camp and the rank of captain. Reid's brilliant descriptions of the battles at Shiloh and Gettysburg were praised for their clarity, color, and accuracy. Edmund Clarence Stedman used Reid's dispatches as the basis for his commemorative poem on Gettysburg, completed in 1872. Already prominent at the young age of twenty-five, Reid was viewed by many of his contemporaries as driven by the need for fame, recognition, and wealth. While Reid was somewhat reserved, self-controlled, and detached, he could be assertive in his personal relationships, showing himself to be motivated by the work ethic and endowed with a powerful critical intelligence and a sense of public stewardship.

Because of his strong Republican ties, Reid was appointed librarian of the House of Representatives during 1863–1866. He was also named clerk of the House Committee on Military Affairs in the third session of the Thirty-seventh Congress. By 1863 Reid was one of the first eastern correspondents for the newly founded Western Associated Press. In 1864, disenchanted by what he viewed as Lincoln's weak leadership, he supported fellow Ohioan Salmon P. Chase for the Republican nomination for president. After the GOP convention he joined with Benjamin F. Wade, Henry W. Davis, and others in trying to get Lincoln to withdraw his candidacy at that late date.

After the war Reid remained an established figure in Republican circles. In May 1865 he traveled with Chief Justice Chase on an inspection tour of several southern states. His writings were collected in a volume titled *After the War* (1866), which discounted the notions that the Republicans could establish a viable party in that region and that sentiments of secession were really dissipating. The next year he tried his hand as a cotton planter in the Deep South but soon quit that venture after becoming disillusioned, in part, with free black laborers. During that period Reid was also involved in finishing a two-volume history, *Ohio and the War* (1868), which brought him further renown.

In 1868, at the age of thirty-one, Reid joined Horace Greeley's *New York Tribune*, serving under editor John Russell Young and later taking over Young's duties. Reid improved coverage of foreign affairs, brought John Hay to the editorial staff, and invited luminaries such as Mark Twain, Bret Harte, and William Dean Howells to be contributors. In 1872 Reid became Greeley's campaign manager when the latter accepted the splinter Liberal Republican nomination and then the Democratic nomination to run against President Ulysses S. Grant. Less than a month after the election Greeley died, and Reid borrowed money from the controversial financier Jay Gould to take control of the *Tribune*. The *Tribune*'s criticisms of Gould and his speculative activities soon became muted.

In the years that followed Reid invested his energies in increasing the newspaper's daily circulation to more than 60,000 in 1876. He added major reporters and commentators and acquired a building to accommodate the paper's expansion. Reid was also an innovator in the use of machines for printing and distributing. He was among the first to employ the Barr typesetting machine, was the first to adopt the Mergenthaler linotype machine, and initiated the use of Richard Hoe's new web presses in New York. His domineering management style led to a long and bitter struggle to curtail labor unions in his newspaper's operation.

During this period the *Tribune* became a major organ of opinion nationally as it devoted considerable coverage to the Whiskey Ring scandal, the Pacific Mail investigations, the overthrow of the Canal Ring, and the "cipher dispatches" that charged Samuel J. Tilden's nephew with election fraud in the disputed 1876 presidential election. Reid, however, portrayed the *Tribune* as a newspaper written by gentlemen for gentlemen, and he avoided much of the sensationalism that came to characterize the newspapers of William Randolph Hearst and Joseph Pulitzer. Reid concentrated on building a conservative and responsible Republican newspaper that would be respected locally and nationally. In the post-Reconstruction years, the *Tribune* loyally supported James G. Blaine for president and was highly critical of Democrat Grover Cleveland when he ran for president. Over the years Reid opposed New York Republican bosses Roscoe Conkling and Thomas C. Platt. In addition, he was at times rather unsympathetic toward American imperialism, especially outside of the Western hemisphere.

Reid was close to several Republican presidential candidates, especially President James A. Garfield, also from Ohio. Twice Reid was offered a diplomatic post in Germany by Garfield and then by Benjamin Harrison, but he refused those offers, seeking to stay home and further strengthen the financial position of the *Tribune* and increase his own economic security. In 1881 he married Elizabeth Mills; they had two children.

Finally, in 1889 Reid accepted without much enthusiasm the position of minister to France. While in office he opposed French protectionism, seeking to open up European oil markets and end a French prohibition on American pork imports (initially justified by the 1881 trichinosis scare). He was also generally noncommittal about U.S. involvement in conferences dealing with colonial problems in Africa. Reid did argue in favor of coaling stations in Africa to support the new, large navy that was being built. Secretary of State Blaine, however, vigorously opposed any such participation, and Harrison agreed. Reid also concluded a reciprocal trade agreement with France aimed at limiting the high duties under the McKinley Tariff and also concluded an extradition treaty. After having been rather successful in his diplomatic post, Reid returned to the United States to accept the vice presidential nomination on the Harrison ticket. While the president ran a lackluster campaign, Reid campaigned vigorously and was disappointed at the defeat of the GOP.

From 1892 to 1896 Reid retired from public life and left the newspaper's day-to-day operations to subordinates. During the William McKinley administration, he was seriously considered for both the secretary of state position and for the ambassadorship to Great Britain, but the strong opposition of Senator Platt of New York made McKinley hesitant, leaving Reid bitter and disillusioned. The president sent him to England in June 1897 as his special ambassador to the Queen's Jubilee. While there, Reid spoke informally with the Spanish representatives about the possible sale of Cuba, and he became committed to a modest sort of expansionism. In 1898 McKinley appointed him to the American commission to negotiate peace with Spain after the war, and Reid supported U.S. retention of the Philippines. He was also named a member of the board of trustees of Stanford University in

1902 and was a longtime member of the New York State Board of Regents.

Theodore Roosevelt's ascension to the presidency ended Platt's power, and in 1902 Reid was made special ambassador to the coronation of King Edward VII. In 1905 he became ambassador to Great Britain. Very little of substance happened during his term, but he and his wife enjoyed the stellar social life of London. He died in London. His wife continued a life of philanthropy and established an institute for working men in London named after her late husband.

During his life, Reid was criticized for being a determined self-promoter, an antiunion conservative, and a lackey for the Republican party. In fact he established a standard of quality in journalism in a time of sensationalism, was moderate and measured in his embrace of U.S. imperialism, and exhibited an ambition that was premised on the values of achievement and hard work. Henry Adams said that Reid was one of the best examples of success in his time and in his social circle. Reid stressed the importance of "the scholar in politics," and his newspaper was unrivaled during his stewardship for its intelligent treatment of foreign affairs. He practiced the virtues that he praised.

• Reid's papers are in the Manuscript Division of the Library of Congress. The best modern biography is Bingham Duncan, *Whitelaw Reid: Journalist, Politician, Diplomat* (1975). The most comprehensive and friendly account is Royal Cortissoz, *The Life of Whitelaw Reid* (2 vols., 1921). Also see William R. Thayer, *The Life and Letters of John Hay* (2 vols., 1915); and Elizabeth Reid's obituaries in the *New York Herald Tribune* and the *New York Times*, both 30 Apr. 1931. Of lesser interest are Lawrence Powell, *New Masters: Northern Planters during the Civil War and Reconstruction* (1980); Joseph B. Bishop, *Notes and Anecdotes of Many Years* (1925; repr. 1970); Earle Dudley Ross, *The Liberal Republican Movement* (1919; repr. 1971); and William Harlan Hale, *Horace Greeley, Voice of the People* (1950). An obituary is in the *New York Tribune*, 16 Dec. 1912.

MICHAEL P. RICCARDS

REIFF, Anthony, Jr. (11 May 1830?–6 Oct. 1916), conductor, musical director, and composer, was born in New York City, the son of Anthony Reiff, a bassoonist, and Ann Dobbs. Some sources list his birth year as 1836. His father immigrated to the United States from Mainz, Germany, in 1825 and settled in New York City, where he quickly became a pillar of the musical community as a member of the orchestra at the Park Theatre, a tenor singer at St. Patrick's Cathedral, and a music teacher at the Institution for the Blind. In 1842 Reiff, who also played the oboe, French horn, and piano, helped to organize the Philharmonic Society of New York. He was a charter member of the orchestra and served as its first vice president; in 1849 he also was named one of the vice presidents of the newly formed American Musical Fund Society in New York. Because of this vigorous and healthy musical environment, it is not surprising that Anthony Reiff, Jr., followed in his father's professional footsteps. As a young man Reiff studied violin with Ureli Corelli Hill and piano with the conductor and pianist Henry C. Timm; both of these men were associates of his father, and both were also connected with the early Philharmonic Society.

Anthony Reiff, Jr., seems to have launched his professional career in 1850 in the orchestra that accompanied Jenny Lind in her concerts at Castle Garden in New York. For the rest of the century Reiff was successful at securing musical employment in a steady succession of performing, conducting, or teaching jobs that continued until he retired in the early twentieth century. In February 1852 he commenced an engagement as leader of the orchestra at the National Theatre in New York; he subsequently moved to the Bowery Theatre, where he served in the same capacity from 1854 through September 1855. In autumn of 1855 Reiff was hired as musical director by the Pyne and Harrison English Opera Company, which immediately began a six-month tour to the American South and West; during this trip he kept a detailed journal that provides insight into the activities of an itinerant opera company of the antebellum period. Reiff describes performance venues, methods of transportation, illnesses, and tensions experienced by troupe members as a result of the stress of constant travel and performance. He also vividly recounts some of the perils experienced by the troupe, including the threat of a duel from an individual who was not a member of the company, a fire that broke out on a cotton-bale-loaded steam packet en route from Mobile to New Orleans, and traveling on a steamship that became trapped in ice on the Ohio River in January 1856.

From 1856 to 1858 Reiff taught piano, violin, and voice in New York City and led the orchestra at the New Olympic Theatre; in 1857 he became a violinist in the Philharmonic Society. In 1858 Reiff was hired as the musical director for the Lyster and Durand English Opera Company and accompanied that troupe on tours to the American South, Old West, and Far West; in California, the troupe was in residence at Maguire's Opera House in San Francisco and also performed in Stockton, Sacramento, and Marysville and in mining camps in the Sierras. From California the Lyster Company traveled to Australia, arriving in Melbourne in March 1861 and subsequently performing in various towns and cities, including Sydney. Reiff left Australia in 1863 for Europe and returned to New York in March 1864. In January 1865 he married Annie McBeth Nichols; the couple had two children. In subsequent decades Reiff was associated with various other opera troupes that toured the United States, including the New English Opera Company, Maguire's Italian Opera Company, and the opera troupes of Clara Kellogg and Teresa Parepa-Rosa. Reiff also served as associate conductor to Jacques Offenbach when he performed at the Centennial Exposition in Philadelphia in 1876. According to his obituary, Reiff was associated with the first American Gilbert and Sullivan company; at the time of his death he was the oldest living member of the American Institute.

Like most musical directors of nineteenth-century opera troupes, Reiff had myriad responsibilities, including the hiring of chorus and orchestra musicians, conducting rehearsals and performances, preparing operatic arrangements, and composing or arranging songs or instrumental compositions to be performed in benefit concerts or before, during, or after operas. Reiff apparently was an undemonstrative but quite accomplished conductor; he also played viola in string quartet performances with string section leaders and accompanied singers on the piano when required. He was sufficiently accomplished at the keyboard to perform in concert (in Australia) Louis Moreau Gottschalk's "The Banjo." Reiff also was a respectable composer. In his 1855–1856 journal he occasionally mentions the completion of vocal or piano works and his communications with publishers about them; he also wrote cantatas in Australia to celebrate the wedding of the Prince of Wales and the funeral of the Australian explorers Robert O'Hara Burke and William John Wills. When the Lyster and Durand Opera Company first arrived in San Francisco in 1859, the troupe discovered that its music trunk inadvertently had been left behind in New York, and on short notice Reiff successfully orchestrated (from piano-vocal score) several operas so that the season could start on time.

Reiff served as vice president of the New York Philharmonic Society and later acted as both chairman of the board of trustees and chairman of the orchestra's music committee. He also served at least two terms as president of the Musical Mutual Protective Union in New York City. In 1905 he began to write his memoirs, evidently based on journals he had kept as an itinerant musician; whether he finished this project is unknown, but several chapters are extant in manuscript. Reiff died in New York. As a conductor and a performer, Reiff has been almost completely forgotten by music historians. But his active and successful musical career belies the widespread stereotype that Americans of the nineteenth century could not support themselves as musicians; as such his career is worth further research.

• Reiff's two unpublished journals (1855–1856 and 1905), each of which contains a wealth of primary-source information about music making in the antebellum United States, are located, respectively, in the Department of Archives and Manuscripts, Louisiana State University Library, Baton Rouge, La., and in the Manuscripts and Rare Books Department, Swem Library, College of William and Mary, Williamsburg, Va. Isolated sheet-music copies of his compositions can be found in the Music Division of the Library of Congress, the New York Public Library, and other major sheet music collections. Genealogical information about the family is located in the Beatrice Reiff file in the Surrogates' Court records in New York City. Information about Reiff's life and career can be gleaned from a number of sources. Particularly useful are Katherine Preston, *Opera on the Road: Traveling Opera Troupes in the United States, 1825–1860* (1993), which includes a detailed examination of the 1856 American tour by the Pyne and Harrison Opera Company; and Harold Love, *The Golden Age of Australian Opera: W. S. Lyster and His Companies, 1861–1880* (1981). Howard Shanet's edition of the *Early Histories of the New York Philharmonic* (1979) also has some useful information, as does an article by Ludwig Weilich, "Philharmonic Society's Early Days," *Opera Magazine* 1, no. 2 (Feb. 1914): 26–28. An obituary is in the *New York Times*, 7 Oct. 1916.

KATHERINE K. PRESTON

REIGNOLDS, Catherine Mary (16 May 1836–11 July 1911), actress, was born near London, England, the daughter of Robert Gregory Taylor Reignolds, an officer in the British army, and Emma Absolon, a theatrical performer. Her father died when Catherine—better known as Kate—was a child. She and the rest of the family immigrated in 1850 to Chicago, Illinois, where her mother had been offered an acting job by John B. Rice. Her mother's American debut came in February 1851, in a production of *Cinderella* at Tremont Hall. The same performance also marked the first stage appearance for Kate, who received a minor role. Reignolds later wrote that her youthful debut was "an utter failure, most awkward, unpromising and uninspired." Nevertheless, she continued acting at the Tremont for four years.

Unable to improve her lot in Chicago, Reignolds moved to New York City in 1855. A personal appeal to Edwin Forrest, the preeminent actor of the day, won her the opportunity to play Virginia to his Virginius in Sheridan Knowles's *Virginius*. Her performance was so impressive that she subsequently cast at William E. Burton's Chambers Street Theatre. She soon acted with other notables, including Laura Keene and John Brougham. Reignolds moved to St. Louis, Missouri, in 1857 to join Ben De Bar's company at the Opera House. De Bar's company wintered in New Orleans's St. Charles Theatre, and there she met the great Charlotte Cushman, whom Reignolds credited for invaluable coaching and advice. She also met Henry Farren, a fellow company member, and married him in December 1857. Perhaps because of her marriage, she turned down an offer from Barry Sullivan to tour the English-speaking world as a leading lady.

Farren died in St. Louis in January 1860, and Reignolds joined E. F. Keach's stock company at the Boston Museum later the same year. She played there five years, gaining popularity quickly for her performances in *The Colleen Bawn* and other plays by Dion Boucicault, the celebrated melodrama writer. In Boston she also met her second husband, Alfred Erving Winslow, a businessman later known for his involvement in the anti-imperialist movement at the time of the Spanish-American War. They wed in 1861; they had one child.

Although Boston remained her permanent home, Reignolds began to tour as a star in 1865. The following year a critic in New York praised her performance as Donna Violante in *The Wonder*. "Grace, elegance, vivacity, the true spirit of laughing mischief, and withal a vein of earnest and tender sentiment, underlying archness and glitter, meet and blend in her temperament, and her manner," he wrote. In 1868 Reignolds traveled to England, where she had successful performances at London's Princess Theatre and at venues in Manchester, Liverpool, Glasgow, Weymouth, and Exeter. In the last place, however, she suffered a serious fall and injured her back during a performance of *Nobody's Daughter*. The remainder of the tour was canceled, but Reignolds later resumed touring in the United States with a company of her own.

After the birth of her son in 1877, Reignolds became less active on the stage. She gave dramatic readings from Shakespeare and from writers of the day considered controversial, including Henrik Ibsen, Hermann Sudermann, and Maurice Maeterlinck. The *New York Tribune* (11 Mar. 1890) noted her series of readings from Ibsen at the parlor of the Hotel Brunswick, where a "large and favorable audience listened to *The Pillars of Society* and frequently gave vent to their admiration in outbursts of applause." After 1890 she also began privately tutoring young women in acting and elocution. Her most recognized student was Josephine Hull.

In 1887 Winslow (who used her married name after retiring from the stage) published *Yesterdays with Actors*, a compilation of articles that originally appeared in the *Boston Herald*. The book gives personal accounts of some of the great actors of the day, including Cushman, Forrest, Brougham, and Keene. In 1895 she edited a two-volume work, *Readings from the Old English Dramatists*, that combined interpretive essays and plays from the Middle Ages through the eighteenth century.

Winslow died at her summer house in Concord, Massachusetts. She is noted as an accomplished actress who sustained a successful theatrical career for the majority of her life. She played a significant role in the cultural life of Boston and shared her skills and knowledge through teaching and publishing.

• No collection of personal papers is known to exist. *Yesterdays with Actors* includes an autobiographical sketch. John B. Clapp and Edwin F. Edgett, eds., *Players of the Present*, pt. 3 (1901), gives a view from her contemporaries. Other perspectives are offered by T. Allston Brown, *History of the American Stage* (1870), and George C. D. Odell, *Annals of the New York Stage*, vols. 6–8 (1931–1936). An obituary is in the *Boston Globe*, 12 July 1911.

KENT NEELY

REIK, Theodor (12 May 1888–31 Dec. 1969), psychoanalyst, was born in Vienna, Austria, the son of Max Reik, a civil servant, and Caroline Trebitsch. The family had limited means but valued education and the arts. After finishing secondary school, Reik worked his way through the University of Vienna, where he studied literature and psychology and planned to become a psychiatrist. He graduated in 1910.

In 1910 Reik met Sigmund Freud, and their ensuing friendship was probably the most important of Reik's life. As Reik's mentor, Freud helped him become a member of the Vienna Psychoanalytic Society and introduced him to his associate Karl Abraham, who analyzed him without charging a fee. Freud encouraged Reik to forgo his medical studies in favor of a career in research and writing and gave him financial support while he completed graduate studies in psychology.

Reik earned his doctorate in 1912 with the first psychoanalytic dissertation to be accepted by the university: a study of Flaubert's *The Temptation of St. Anthony*. He practiced and did research for several years, interrupting his career to serve in the German army during World War I. In 1914 he married his first wife, now known only as "Ellie O.," the name he gave to her in his writings; they had one son. After the war Reik lived and practiced in Vienna for a decade as part of Freud's inner circle.

In 1928 Reik moved to Berlin and taught at the Psychoanalytic Institute there for five years. In 1933, threatened by the rise of the Nazis, he fled to The Hague. About this time Reik's first wife died, and shortly afterward he married Marija Cubelik, with whom he had a daughter while living in the Netherlands. After intensive effort on Reik's part, he obtained U.S. entry visas for himself and his virtually penniless family—his son and daughter, and his wife, pregnant with another daughter—and came to New York City in 1938.

Reik had become a well-established psychoanalyst in Europe and had published fifteen books by the time he arrived in America, but he was not welcomed by the New York Psychoanalytic Institute because he had not earned an M.D. Reik therefore struggled during his first years in America to establish himself professionally and to support his family. Turning his back on the institute, he set up an independent practice and founded a clinic that offered analysis to people who could not afford high fees. In 1946 he organized the National Psychological Association for Psychoanalysis, which accepted analysts with and without M.D.'s.

Reik was a warm and kindly man, known for his gentleness and generosity. Throughout his career, he emphasized the importance of intuition on the part of the analyst in understanding the patient's problems and cautioned against strict reliance upon psychoanalytic theory. He differed with Freud in his belief that neuroses did not necessarily have a sexual basis; they were more often the result of a weak ego, he argued, and the inner conflict that resulted from that state.

Reik was naturalized as a U.S. citizen in 1941. During his years in America he continued to write books, which numbered more than fifty, and numerous articles on neurosis and its relationship to a variety of subjects, including sex, crime, myth and ritual, and religion. His best-known works were written for a general audience and include *Masochism in Modern Man* (1941), *Listening with the Third Ear* (1948), and *The Search Within* (1956). His anecdotal, nontechnical style in these works attracted many readers who had previously been unfamiliar with the general principles of psychoanalysis. Reik also wrote *From Thirty Years with Freud*, a collection of reminiscences published in 1949.

Reik continued to write and to see patients at his private clinic until he was in his mid-sixties, at which point he retired. After the death of his second wife in 1959, he became a virtual recluse, living alone in a modest apartment on the Upper West Side of Manhattan.

Reik's death in New York City brought him the public attention that he had not received for many years. In obituaries throughout the United States and Europe he was remembered as one of Freud's most important pupils and a major figure in the history of the psychoanalytic movement; in particular, he was cited for his nondoctrinaire approach to analysis and for his efforts to enhance public understanding of the psychoanalytic process.

• Information on Reik can be found in his autobiography, *Fragment of a Great Confession* (1949). Additional biographical information is in *Who Was Who in America*, vol. 5 (1973). For a largely appreciative assessment of Reik's contributions to the psychoanalytic movement, see Robert M. Lindner, ed., *Explorations in Psychoanalysis: Essays in Honor of Theodor Reik on the Occasion of His Sixty-fifth Birthday* (1953). See also Frederick Redlich and Daniel Freedman, *Theory and Practice of Psychiatry* (1966). An obituary is in the *New York Times*, 1 Jan. 1970.

ANN T. KEENE

REILLY, Marion (16 July 1879–27 Jan. 1928), leader in women's higher education, was born in Altoona, Pennsylvania, the daughter of John Reilly and Anna Lloyd. Her father was an entrepreneur in railroad development and an official of the Pennsylvania Railroad; he also served a term in the U.S. Congress from 1875 to 1877. The family moved to Philadelphia in 1881. Reilly was educated at the Agnes Irwin School, an academic preparatory school for girls in Philadelphia, and then at Bryn Mawr College. She was president of her class at Bryn Mawr, where she was awarded an A.B. degree in 1901. She remained at Bryn Mawr until 1907, pursuing a doctorate in mathematics and physics. She also did advanced study at Göttingen university in Germany, at Newnham College, Cambridge (1907–1908), and at the University of Rome (1910–1911). Her research was described by a colleague as "in the borderline between mathematics, physics and philosophy." The product of her research abroad was published in Germany by another scholar before Reilly was able to present the dissertation at Bryn Mawr. The theft of her work resulted in Reilly's not being awarded an advanced degree. Thus, to her bitter disappointment, her years of scholarly work and her contributions to theory in mathematics were never officially recognized.

Bryn Mawr appointed Reilly dean of the college in 1907, a position she held until 1916. These were years of expansion and innovation in both the college and women's higher education in general. As dean, Reilly assumed duties that had earlier been performed by Martha Carey Thomas, president of the college, who had for many years served as both president and dean. During her tenure as dean, Reilly assumed academic and administrative responsibilities within Bryn Mawr while Thomas, in a division of labor agreeable to both, took increasing leadership nationally as an advocate for the expansion of opportunity for women in higher education, particularly in graduate and professional study. In the early part of the century, many professions, including business, medicine, and law, were virtually closed to women. Along with others in higher education, Reilly and Thomas sought to further the advancement of women in new professions. For example, in 1910 Bryn Mawr opened graduate study for careers in the education of children and young adults. Influenced in part by the laboratory school work of John Dewey at the University of Chicago and the formative ideas that became progressive education, a "model school" was inaugurated on the campus at Bryn Mawr as a base for graduate study and research in education. Then, in 1915, a new professional program in social work was created as the Graduate Department of Social Economy and Social Research to open careers for women in yet another dimension. These innovative programs were widely imitated at other institutions, at women's colleges as well as coeducational ones, in following years. Though Reilly was always in the shadow of Thomas, a role Reilly apparently accepted as proper for herself, the close, effective work of Reilly and Thomas made possible these innovations at Bryn Mawr, which influenced the direction of women's higher education nationally.

Reilly's skills in leadership served to good effect on a number of boards and committees of varied academic, social, and civic organizations. Upon relinquishing the Bryn Mawr deanship in 1916, she was elected to the governing board of the college and continued to serve as an active member to the end of her life. Before 1920 she was also a major organizer and contributor to the National American Woman Suffrage Association. Following ratification of the Nineteenth Amendment, Reilly chaired the Philadelphia League of Women Voters during the 1920s. As a board member of the American Association of University Women (AAUW), Reilly chaired a committee to establish and promote interchange between American and European university women. Her work with AAUW contributed significantly to the opening of opportunity internationally for women in higher education. The general focus of Reilly's volunteer work during these years was on expanding opportunities for women in ever wider and more varied contexts. Reilly was consistently and ardently an internationalist.

As a woman of means, Reilly was able to travel abroad extensively and to acquire works of art in her diverse areas of interest. She developed two particularly distinguished collections, one of Japanese blockprints, the other of Napoleonic prints and cartoons. Reilly bequeathed both collections to the Brooklyn Museum of Fine Arts in New York. In her travels and her years of work abroad, Reilly learned to speak several languages comfortably, and she spoke Italian with native fluency. Italy, she said, was her spiritual home. She was remembered for her generous support to young scholars in need and, personally, for her considerable charm as well as her sharp wit—a combination of qualities that Reilly might have characterized as Italian.

Reilly remained unmarried and died in Philadelphia at the age of forty-eight. In a memorial following Reilly's death, M. Carey Thomas remarked, "She was magnificently independent. She had no 'entangling alliances'. She was a truly distinguished spirit, walking alone, and judging life after her own standards of excellence."

• Papers for the era of the M. Carey Thomas presidency are in the archives of the Bryn Mawr College Library, Bryn Mawr, Pa. No separate collection of Reilly's papers exists at Bryn Mawr or elsewhere. "Commemorative Service," *Bryn Mawr Alumnae Bulletin*, May 1928, includes remarks about Reilly made by M. Carey Thomas. For information about the college during the time Reilly was there, see Cornelia Meig, *What Makes a College? A History of Bryn Mawr* (1956). An obituary is in the Philadelphia *Inquirer*, 28 Jan. 1928.

JOHN HARDIN BEST

REINAGLE, Alexander (1756?–21 Sept. 1809), composer, theater manager, and pianist, was born in Portsmouth, England, the son of Joseph Reinagle, an Austrian trumpeter listed as a musician in the British royal house. His mother's name is unknown. Reinagle grew up in a musical environment; two of his brothers were professional cellists, and his sister married the cellist Johann Georg Schetky. It is believed that Alexander studied with organist and composer Raynor Taylor in Edinburgh, where the family lived from 1763 to 1774. By 1780 Reinagle was living in London, where he published "Twenty four short and easy pieces intended as the first lessons for the piano forte or harpsichord" (1780). In 1784 he visited Carl Philipp Emanuel Bach in Hamburg and accompanied his brother Hugh to Lisbon, primarily in the hopes of improving Hugh's health. Following Hugh's death there on 19 March 1785, Reinagle returned to England. He apparently wrote to C. P. E. Bach for permission to publish some of Bach's rondos in England; the Library of Congress retains Bach's two cordial but negative letters of response.

In early 1786 Reinagle left England for the United States. His years of performing, teaching, and publishing in London served him in good stead. In eighteenth-century London, music had grown as an industry, and both London and the new American nation were beginning to sell music as a leisure commodity. As soon as he arrived in New York, Reinagle advertised in a New York newspaper that he was offering pianoforte, harpsichord, and violin lessons, and was selling instruments and music. He first performed in New York on 20 July 1786. Recognizing that Philadelphia, the largest American city at the time, offered more musical opportunity than New York, he relocated to Philadelphia. On 21 September 1786 Reinagle played and sang in Henri Capron's cello concert in Philadelphia, and the next month he gave his own concert.

Reinagle became an important figure in the development of musical and theatrical taste in Philadelphia.

By October 1786 he had reinstituted the City Concerts, which had been established in 1783. The series continued through 1788, and records indicate that it was revived again in 1791 and 1792. Through these concerts Philadelphians became familiar with the music of Mozart, Abel, J. C. Bach, Haydn, Grétry, Reinagle, and many others. Reinagle also performed in benefit concerts during this period. He visited New York as director of and participant in some subscription concerts in 1788 and 1789.

Reinagle was active as a music teacher in Philadelphia. George Washington, who had attended Reinagle's concerts in 1787, hired him in 1789 to teach his granddaughter Nellie Custis. Reinagle wrote several compositions directly relating to the general, including "Federal March, as performed in the grand procession in Philadelphia, the 4th of July, 1788," and the "Chorus sung before Gen. Washington as he passed under the triumphal arch raised on the bridge at Trenton, April 21, 1789."

During the last two decades of the eighteenth century, Reinagle continued to compose and publish works for pianoforte or harpsichord. In addition to sonatas most likely written for his own performance, he published teaching pieces, arrangements of popular tunes, light compositions that appealed to amateurs, and piano arrangements of works performed in theater.

Reinagle made his most important contribution to the cultural life of the new country in the area of musical theater. As comanager with Thomas Wignell of a theatrical company, he brought the best of musical theater to Philadelphia, and the Wignell-Reinagle company was a major factor in Philadelphia's earning the designation "the western Athens." In 1793 Reinagle and Wignell founded the New Company, and for the next ten years they produced the most popular English operas, pantomimes, dramas, and plays with incidental music. Their company was a stellar collection of actors, actor-singers, dancers, and orchestral musicians. Many members were recruited directly from the Haymarket, Drury Lane, and Covent Garden theaters in London. In Wignell's first recruiting trip to London, he brought back a 56-member troupe for his company. The group comprised the best dramatic corps and group of singing actors yet seen in the United States. It included not only the obvious members (managers, actors, master painters, choreographer, orchestra) but also a treasurer, a propertyman, a housekeeper of the theater, a mistress of the ladies' wardrobe and assistant, a master tailor in the gentlemen's wardrobe, and a master carpenter. Wignell also brought back from London an extensive wardrobe and a library of plays and music.

Before establishing their company, both Wignell and Reinagle had admirable reputations in their fields—Wignell as an actor and Reinagle as a musician—so the Wignell-Reinagle company was able to attract financial backers. This enabled them to build the New Theatre in Chestnut Street, a magnificent 2,000-seat building designed by John Inigo Richards, who had furnished the designs for the remodeling of Covent Garden. The interior was modeled after the Theatre Royal in Bath. According to contemporary reports, the performances at the New Theatre attracted "most brilliant and numerous audiences." Vocal stars from London included Miss George of the Haymarket and Drury Lane theaters and Miss Broadhurst of Covent Garden. Among the more notable dancers and choreographers were William Francis, James Byrne, and John Durang. Reinagle directed the orchestra from the "grand square pianoforte" in the stage pit. He arranged most of the music for the performances, since full scores were not available.

From 1794 through 1800 the company produced almost 500 operas, pantomimes, and plays with music at the New Theatre. In addition, the group spent part of each year performing in Baltimore, and available newspaper accounts indicate it produced at least 156 events there from 1793 to 1795. In 1797, during a three-months stint in New York, the company performed twenty-five musical theater pieces. In 1800 the New Company performed in a new theater in Washington called the United States Theatre. Despite financial difficulties, the company continued performing for several more years.

Reinagle died in Baltimore. Although little information is available about his personal life, he had been married twice. He had two children by his first wife (name unknown) and one child by his second wife, Ann Duport.

Reinagle is believed to have written fifty complete works for the stage, but only thirty-one single numbers survive. The works include overtures to plays and pantomimes, arrangements of operas by other composers, incidental music to plays, and original compositions for light opera. He is credited with being the first to use piano in the American stage orchestra and the first to use organ in an American theater.

• Reinagle's *Memorandum Book* describing his trip with his brother to Lisbon (1784–1785), manuscripts of his two letters from C. P. E. Bach, and an autographed manuscript of his "Philadelphia Sonatas" are at the Library of Congress. The "Philadelphia Sonatas" are published with an extensive analysis and resume of Reinagle's life and work in Robert Hopkins, ed., *Recent Researches in American Music*, vol. 5 (1978). Personal anecdotes of Reinagle and Wignell are found in the published diaries of Reinagle's contemporaries: John Bernard, *Retrospection of America, 1797–1811* (repr. 1969), William Dunlap, *Diary of William Dunlap (1766–1839): The Memoirs of a Dramatist, Theatrical Manager, Painter, Critic, Novelist, and Historian* (1930), and John Durang, *Memoir of John Durang, American Actor (1785–1816)* (1966). For specific dates and programs arranged chronologically, see George Odell, *Annals of the New York Stage*, vol. 1 (1927), and Oscar Sonneck, *Early Concert-Life in America* (1907) and *Early Opera in America* (1915).

MARY JANE CORRY

REINER, Fritz (19 Dec. 1888–15 Nov. 1963), conductor, was born in Budapest, Hungary, the son of Ignatz Reiner, a textile merchant, and Vilma Pollak. Reiner was brought up in a cultivated, music-loving, middle-class household. His parents were Jewish, but he later renounced that faith and became a Roman Catholic. In deference to his father's wishes, Reiner studied law at the University of Budapest. But his real ambition was to become a conductor, and he abandoned his legal studies in 1905, the year that his father died. By then he was a music student at the Academy of Music in Budapest, where he studied composition, music history, and the piano with several illustrious teachers, including Hans Koessler, István Thoman, and Béla Bartók. (There were, at that time, no courses offered in conducting.) Reiner graduated from the academy in 1909. He then worked as a piano accompanist and teacher and as a rehearsal conductor at the short-lived Vígopera in his native city. Here he conducted in public for the first time when the regular conductor fell ill. The opera was *Carmen*. Between October 1910 and March 1911 he conducted at the Opera House in Laibach (now Ljubljana), the capital of Slovenia. This enabled him to conduct opera and operetta in repertory for the first time. In 1911 he married Angela (Elça) Jelačin; they had two children.

Reiner soon returned to Budapest, where he conducted many operas at the Népopera and where his abilities attracted wider attention. In 1914 he was engaged as a leading conductor by the Dresden Semper Opera House, one of the most prestigious operatic companies in Europe. Over the next seven years he conducted more than five hundred performances of opera there, as well as a number of symphonic concerts. He specialized in the works of Giuseppe Verdi, Richard Wagner, and Richard Strauss and conducted several contemporary German operas. But his years in the capital of Saxony were marred by a divorce in 1916, by intrusions into his autonomy as a conductor and limitations on his guest conducting, and by political turmoil in Germany after the First World War. Reiner married his second wife, Berta Gerster-Gardini, in 1921; they underwent a second marriage ceremony in 1922; they had no children. However, Reiner had one more child outside of his marriages; the child's mother's name is unknown.

From 1922 onward Reiner's career was mainly concentrated in the United States. He held a succession of important appointments as a conductor, both with orchestras and in the opera house, and undertook some significant teaching. Between 1922 and 1931 he was music director of the Cincinnati Symphony Orchestra, which he built up into a fine ensemble by hiring new musicians and concentrating on technical precision in rehearsals and performance. Always interested in contemporary music, he took great care with program building. He introduced Cincinnati audiences to new works by Paul Hindemith, Bartók, Igor Stravinsky, Ottorino Respighi, and George Gershwin, among others. During the 1920s he spread his reputation by appearing as a guest conductor with the Philadelphia Orchestra, with the New York Philharmonic Symphony Orchestra, and at La Scala, Milan, and the Teatro Colón, Buenos Aires. In 1928 he became an American citizen. Unfortunately, his later years in Cincinnati were marred by disagreements with the orchestra's

management and by a divorce from his second wife in 1930. In that same year he married Carlotta Irwin, an actress; they had no children.

Reiner resigned from his position in Cincinnati in 1931 and spent most of the 1930s working in Pennsylvania. He carried out a number of important guest engagements at this time, notably as an operatic conductor at the San Francisco Opera, at Covent Garden between 1936 and 1938, and as joint conductor, with Alexander Smallens, of an illustrious operatic season with the Philadelphia Orchestra in 1934–1935. For a decade after 1931 he was head of the opera and orchestral departments at the Curtis Institute of Music, Philadelphia. Here his teaching of conducting technique left an indelible mark on his pupils, who included Leonard Bernstein, Lukas Foss, Max Goberman, and Walter Hendl. He also trained the accomplished Curtis student orchestra to a very high standard. Probably no other conductor in the United States at that time devoted so much attention to music students as part of a curricular course.

In 1938 Reiner was appointed music director of the Pittsburgh Symphony Orchestra, a position he kept for a decade. He completely revitalized an ailing ensemble by hiring good players, offering interesting programs, and insisting on high musical standards. His programs mixed the mainstream classical and romantic repertoire with contemporary music. He performed works by a number of American composers, including William Schuman, Gershwin, and Aaron Copland, and championed music by Bartók, Stravinsky, and Hindemith. He recorded a wide repertoire with the Pittsburgh Symphony Orchestra for Columbia Records, including the premiere recording of Bartók's Concerto for Orchestra (which he had helped to commission). He appeared in a movie (*Carnegie Hall*) for the first and only time in 1947. Reiner resigned his position in 1948 after a falling out with the management over proposed cuts to the orchestra he had sedulously built up.

From 1949 to 1953 Reiner served as a leading conductor at the Metropolitan Opera, where he concentrated on the German repertoire. He made an illustrious debut in a famous performance of *Salome*, with Ljuba Welitsch as the heroine, and gave acclaimed performances of operas by Wolfgang Amadeus Mozart, Verdi, Wagner, Richard Strauss, and Georges Bizet, as well as the American premiere of Stravinsky's *The Rake's Progress*. He was not altogether happy, however, with the frequent changes of cast at the Met or with the policies of its chief impresario, Rudolf Bing, and so, when an opportunity arose to become music director of the Chicago Symphony Orchestra, Reiner seized his chance.

Reiner's decade in Chicago (1953–1963) was the peak of his career. For a third time he rebuilt a demoralized orchestra and restored its standards of playing. The perfection achieved was widely recognized by many musicians, including Stravinsky, who wrote that under Reiner the Chicago Symphony had become "the most precise and flexible orchestra in the world." In

1957 Reiner helped to found the Chicago Symphony chorus, the first permanent choral organization attached to an American orchestra. He also made many bestselling recordings with Chicago for RCA Victor. While in Chicago, Reiner undertook selective guest engagements, which included directing *Die Meistersinger* at the reopening of the Vienna State Opera House in 1955. In 1959 his position in Chicago was weakened by the fracas following the cancellation of a prestigious European tour scheduled for his orchestra. In the following year he suffered the first of a series of heart attacks that restricted his conducting. He died in New York City after extensive rehearsals of *Götterdämmerung* that were planned to mark his return to the Met after a decade's absence.

Reiner was a conductor's conductor, someone who was widely admired by fellow practitioners for the depth of his musical knowledge and for his high principles. Influenced in his conducting style by the spare movements of István Kerner, Artur Nikisch, and Strauss, he developed an economical but highly effective technique based on a "vest-pocket beat." His technical skills with the baton have probably never been rivaled by any other conductor. He had a vast repertoire, all of which was performed with an understanding of the need to differentiate varying musical styles. Equally at home in the concert hall and in the opera house, he made a great contribution to the building of orchestras and to the teaching of conducting in the United States. But his talents were never appreciated fully during his lifetime because he was an unshowy, introspective, private man who did not court publicity. In Virgil Thomson's words, he was "as calculable as the stars and about as distant." He argued with managers, did not tolerate poor musicianship, and was unwilling to please the social sets in the cities where he worked. From 1938 onward he and his third wife ensconced themselves as much as possible in their house, "Rambleside," near Westport, Connecticut, and cut down travel to a minimum. But if Reiner was hardly an endearing man in public, privately he was witty, courteous, and a genial host. Though the public conception of his character was, to his detriment, almost completely divorced from musicians' perceptions of his skills, he has now received his due with the reissue of recordings that testify to his stature as a conductor.

• Reiner's papers and memorabilia are in the Deering Music Library at Northwestern University. A smaller collection of his correspondence is in the Special Collections of the Butler Library at Columbia University. Reiner did not write his memoirs, but he discussed the conductor's art in several articles: "Reiner Discusses the Making of a Conductor," *Musical America*, 25 Oct. 1941, p. 29; "The Secrets of the Conductor," *Etude*, July 1936, pp. 417–18; and "The Technique of Conducting," *Etude*, Oct. 1951, pp. 16–17. For a full-length study of his career see Philip Hart, *Fritz Reiner: A Biography* (1994). Reiner's teaching at the Curtis Institute of Music is analyzed in Kenneth Morgan, "Fritz Reiner and the Technique of Conducting," *Journal of the Conductor's Guild* 14, no. 2 (1993): 91–100. Illuminating assessments of Reiner as a conductor can be found in Hope Stoddard, "Fritz Reiner:

'The Quality of Leadership'," *International Musician*, Nov. 1955, pp. 10–14; Boris Goldovsky, *My Road to Opera* (1979); Roger Dettmer, "Fritz Reiner," *Fanfare*, Nov.–Dec. 1981, pp. 60–69; Sebastian Caratelli, *A Musician's Odyssey* (1983); and Kenneth Morgan, "Fritz Reiner as Opera Conductor," *Opera Quarterly* 12, no. 3 (Spring 1996): 59–77. Much additional information can be gleaned from issues of the *Podium: Magazine of the Fritz Reiner Society* (1976–1988). For Reiner's recordings see John Holmes, *Conductors on Record* (1992), and Kenneth Morgan, "Reiner in Pittsburgh: A Survey of the Great Conductor's Earlier Commercial Recordings," *International Classical Record Collector* 2 (Autumn 1996): 24–30. An obituary of Reiner is in the *New York Times*, 16 Nov. 1963.

KENNETH MORGAN

REINHARDT, Ad (24 Dec. 1913–30 Aug. 1967), painter, was born Adolf D. Frederick Reinhardt in Buffalo, New York, the son of Frank Reinhardt, a garment worker who emigrated from Lithuania to the United States in 1907, and Olga Melitat. When he was a young child he and his family moved to New York City, where he attended public schools in Queens. He entered Columbia University in 1931 and was the editor of the humor magazine, *Jester*. One of his classmates at Columbia was Thomas Merton, who later became a Trappist monk and renowned spiritual writer; they remained life-long friends. After graduating from Columbia in 1935, Reinhardt, who had always wanted to be an artist but had never formally studied art, took courses at both the National Academy of Design and the American Artists' School and worked as a freelance illustrator.

Interested in abstract art, Reinhardt became a charter member of the American Abstract Artists organization in 1937. The following year, Burgoyne Diller, a proponent of abstract art and administrator for the Works Progress Administration's Federal Art Project, hired him as an easel artist; he worked for the project until 1941.

In the late 1930s Reinhardt painted in a cubist style influenced by Stuart Davis. He described his work from the 1940s on as "rococo-semi-surrealist fragmentation" and "all-over baroque-geometric-expressionist patterns." But Reinhardt was also a keen draughtsman. It was this skill, as well as his biting wit, that led to a position as a political cartoonist for the New York newspaper *PM* in 1943. He also ran an innovative series, "How to Look," which were cartoons that both critiqued the art world and stated his own aesthetic ideas. For example, "How to Look at Modern Art in America" (*PM*, 2 June 1946) shows American art as branches, twigs, and leaves of the "Tree of Art," growing out of a European trunk. Reinhardt remained with *PM* until 1947 when he left after an editorial dispute over the satirical content of his cartoons.

Soon after his first solo exhibition at Frederika Beers's Artists Gallery, Reinhardt was drafted into the U.S. Navy in early 1944 and was stationed in San Diego, California. Assigned duty as a photographer's mate aboard the USS *Salerno Bay* in January 1945, he was given an honorable discharge as an "anxiety case."

That year he married Elizabeth Armand Decker, they had no children and were divorced in 1949.

He and his wife moved back to New York in 1946. Reinhardt studied art history, concentrating in Eastern art, at New York University. He continued his studies until 1952 but never earned a degree. His interest in Buddhism was also sparked at this time, though he considered it "an aesthetic, not a religion."

Reinhardt became affiliated with the Betty Parsons Gallery, which in November 1946 held its first solo exhibition of his work. Reinhardt's presence at the Parsons Gallery and his participation in group exhibitions such as "The Intrasubjectives" at the Kootz Gallery in 1949, as well as his participation in a protest by artists of the acquisitions policy of the Metropolitan Museum of Art, placed him firmly in the circle of the abstract expressionist artists. *Life* magazine reported the protest in a photo essay (6 June 1951).

A teaching position at Brooklyn College (1947–1967) allowed Reinhardt the economic freedom to pursue his art. During these years he also taught at the California School of Fine Arts (1950), the University of Wyoming (1951), the School of Fine Arts, Yale University (1952–1953), and Syracuse University (1957).

By the late 1940s Reinhardt's work consisted of large canvases often covered in vibrant colors, highlighted by short, calligraphic strokes. Art historian Lucy Lippard has described such pieces as "light- and color-filled lyricism" (p. 58). Beginning in the early 1950s he worked in an expressionist style dominated by jagged, slashing strokes. The major works he had created to this point include *Abstract Painting* (1948, Allen Memorial Art Museum, Oberlin College), *Number 111* (1949, Museum of Modern Art, New York City), *Number 88* (1950, Hirshhorn Museum and Sculpture Garden, Smithsonian Institution), and *Number 5 (Red Wall, 1952)* (1952, Corcoran Art Gallery, Washington, D.C.).

Reinhardt made his first trip to Europe in 1952. The following year he married Rita Zyprokowski; they had one child. In 1958 he traveled around the world for about a year. The thousands of photographic slides he took during this trip served as the basis for both his classroom lectures and a talk at the Artists Club in New York City in 1959.

Reinhardt's works became more hard-edged, often simple monochromatic fields with similarly hued rectangles laid out in geometric patterns on the canvas. According to Lippard, he "established the five-foot square black canvas, systematically trisected by one vertical and one horizontal, as the single basis for his own, and, by inference, for all painting" (p. 11). Reinhardt completed numerous variations of the work *Abstract Painting, Black* between 1960 and 1966. Commenting on these works, Reinhardt described his concept of the black painting as "a free, unmanipulated and unmanipulatable, useless, unmarketable, irreducible, unphotographable, unreproducible, inexplicable icon. A non-entertainment, not for art commerce or mass-art publics, non-expressionist, not for one-

self" (Rose, p. 83). He died of a heart attack at his New York City studio.

Called the "black monk" of the art world for his impersonal, austere painting style, Reinhardt was a fierce critic of the corruption of the art world who considered himself its "conscience." A prolific writer on aesthetics, he was inclined toward aphoristic formulations on art, ethics, education, and politics. He discussed his aesthetics in a series of essays, "Art-on-Art," proclaiming, "Art is Art. Everything Else is Everything Else" and "The end of art is art-as-art. The end of art is not the end." Reinhardt contributed a sense of the purity of color and the idea that philosophy, particularly that of Asia, could play an important role in modern art. His paintings and writings were an important influence on the next generation of artists, particularly the minimalist artists of the 1960s.

• Reinhardt's works are in the Museum of Modern Art, the Hirshhorn Museum and Sculpture Garden, the Metropolitan Musem of Art, Yale University Art Gallery, and the Whitney Museum of American Art. His papers are at the Archives of American Art (Smithsonian Institution). The major biographical resource is Lucy Lippard, *Ad Reinhardt* (1981). See also Lippard's catalog, *Ad Reinhardt: Paintings* (1966), for the exhibition of the same title at the Jewish Museum in New York City and *Ad Reinhardt* (1991), the catalog for the exhibition at the Museum of Modern Art. Selections from Reinhardt's copious writings have been edited by Barbara Rose as *Art-as-Art: The Selected Writings of Ad Reinhardt* (1975). See also "Master of the Minimal," *Life*, 3 Feb. 1967, pp. 45–53. Obituaries are in the *New York Times*, 1 Sept. 1967, and the *Washington Post*, 2 Sept. 1967.

MARTIN R. KALFATOVIC

REINSCH, Paul Samuel (10 June 1869–24 Jan. 1923), educator and diplomat, was born in Milwaukee, Wisconsin, the son of George J. Reinsch, a clergyman, and Clara Witte. Reinsch was raised in a strict, Lutheran, German-speaking household and obtained a rigorous, gymnasium-style education at Concordia College. He received a B.A. in 1892 and an LL.B in 1894 from the University of Wisconsin, Madison. Disenchanted with the practice of law in Gilded Age Milwaukee and lured by the emergence of the University of Wisconsin at Madison as a major graduate institution in the social sciences and history, Reinsch decided on an academic career. Working under Frederick Jackson Turner, he received a Ph.D. in history in 1898. After a year of study and travel in Europe, Reinsch was appointed assistant professor of political science at Madison. The publication of his impressive and highly praised *World Politics at the End of the Nineteenth Century as Influenced by the Oriental Situation* (1900) established his reputation as a scholar and won him a promotion to full professor in 1902. Despite efforts to recruit him to other institutions, he remained in Madison until 1913. With his future secure, in August 1900 he married Alma Marie Moser; they had three children.

During the remainder of his academic career, Reinsch published seven additional books and dozens of scholarly and journalistic articles. Reinsch pioneered the systematic study and teaching of world politics, and he was probably the first scholar to examine colonialism from the standpoint of both the colonial powers and the subjected peoples. He was regarded as an authority on East Asia for his extensive reading on the subject and his inventive use of informants. Reinsch's interests were notably catholic, and his views were independent and eclectic. In domestic affairs, he was a Progressive who reflected the Wisconsin Idea's emphasis on efficiency and administration, and he had a New Nationalist bent. In foreign affairs, he was an ardent economic expansionist who believed in the China market, a severe critic of formal colonialism, and a nonpacifist, liberal internationalist. Outgrowing his narrow upbringing, Reinsch was a true humanitarian, a fighter for social justice, tolerance, and equality.

Like so many of his Progressive Era colleagues, Reinsch was not an isolated scholar. He led the movement to establish political science as a discipline that was distinct from history, organized the American Political Science Association, and eventually served as its president in 1920. He advised Wisconsin Progressive officials and consulted with businessmen and bankers. Reinsch participated actively in the international arbitration movement, the American Society of International Law, and, especially, the Carnegie Endowment for International Peace. He served as a delegate to three Pan-American conferences and actively sought a regular diplomatic appointment in Latin America or the Far East.

In 1913, thanks to the patronage of Charles R. Crane, a Chicago millionaire and Democratic party leader, and Reinsch's friend Joseph Davies, a Wisconsin attorney and chief of the Democratic party's western headquarters in the 1912 election, President Woodrow Wilson named Reinsch U.S. minister to China. For the next six years, he worked tirelessly and compulsively to achieve three interrelated goals: to establish and expand American markets, investment opportunities, and cultural influence in China; to protect China's integrity and independence from other nations, especially Japan; and to assist China in modernizing its political, economic, and social systems. In this, Reinsch sought to realize in fact rather than theory the American Open Door policy and the Wilson administration's declared support for independent economic action and the new Chinese republic.

In specific terms, Reinsch obtained many generous concessions for American firms for bank loans, petroleum development, naval facilities and training, railroad construction, and conservancy work. Chinese officials collaborated because they recognized Reinsch's genuine sympathy for China and saw these concessions as a means of using the United States to counter the more dangerous "barbarian" powers. Reinsch encouraged the Chinese to create a modern, efficient administrative state and move slowly toward political democracy. He exposed and helped to block the most dangerous features of Japan's infamous Twenty-One Demands, which was designed to make China a Japanese protectorate. In perhaps his most controversial and desperate initiative, he took advantage of a break in cable communications with Washington to make promises of American financial and moral support to get China to break relations with Germany in 1917 and enter World War I on the side of the Allies. Once the United States entered the war, he badgered the Wilson administration to provide China, as an ally, with funds to avoid total dependence on Tokyo. When that effort failed, he switched tactics and supported the establishment of the American-controlled Second Chinese Consortium. A private venture backed by the U.S. government, the consortium was meant to funnel money for China's development and neutralize Japan's attempt to control China's government and economy.

Reinsch's plans were thwarted by a number of factors: the inability, unwillingness, and fears of American businesses to fulfill the contracts he obtained; the breakdown of the balance of power in East Asia that resulted from the war in Europe, which gave Tokyo a free hand in China; the collapse of the central government in China, the emergence of civil war and the warlord system; and the failure of the Wilson administration to back his efforts. In fact, Washington occasionally undermined him, notably by the signing the Lansing-Ishii Agreement. But the cruelest blow was delivered by President Wilson himself, when he "sold out" China over the Shantung issue at the Paris Peace Conference. In 1919, angry and exhausted, Reinsch resigned in protest.

In Reinsch's last years his physical and mental health deteriorated, and he worried about money. He resumed his law practice but functioned primarily as a lobbyist and consultant for businessmen who were interested in China and the Pacific. His major client was the Peking government, which retained him as its counselor. In that capacity he advised the Chinese delegation to the Washington Conference in 1921–1922. Although it dovetailed with his ongoing crusade to drum up American political and economic support for China, his work essentially entailed public relations for the corrupt and bankrupt Peking regime, which generally ignored his reports and failed to pay his salary on time. Reinsch hastily wrote his oft-cited memoir, *An American Diplomat in China* (1922), to tell the story of his China experience and to collect royalties. In 1920 Reinsch suffered another embarrassment when he came in third as the Democratic candidate for the Senate race in Wisconsin. During a trip to China in late 1922, he had a complete physical and mental breakdown. He died of pneumonia in a Shanghai sanitarium.

Historians have been quite critical of Reinsch's diplomacy. Some have considered it inconsequential or irrelevant. His more severe detractors have labeled him naïve and idealistic; they have scolded him for antagonizing Japan, complicating matters for American foreign policy makers, and holding out false hopes to China and American businessmen. While these criticisms have some validity, they also distort the man and his record. Although he showed ignorance of China and had unrealistic expectations of American businessmen, he was also carrying out the guidelines of the Wilson administration and the principles of the U.S. Open Door policy. His program to establish American influence in China was actually logical and hard-headed; while he understood that the United States would not use force to uphold the Open Door, he also felt that it had leverage if Washington would only employ it effectively. He was willing to compromise, even with Japan, in return for a genuine quid pro quo. In spite of Reinsch's efforts, America was not ready for China; neither was China ready for America.

• Reinsch's papers, including the Horatio Bates Hawkins tape recordings, are at the State Historical Society of Wisconsin; Reinsch's voluminous dispatches are in the Department of State decimal file (RG 59) at the National Archives. Significant selections may be found in *Foreign Relations of the United States*. Reinsch also left considerable correspondence in the Peking Post records (RG 84). Reinsch's enormous literary output included, in addition to the publications mentioned above, *Colonial Government* (1902), *Colonial Administration* (1905), *Intellectual and Political Currents in the Far East* (1911), and *Secret Diplomacy: How Far Can It Be Eliminated?* (1922).

The only full-length biography of Reinsch is by Noel H. Pugach, *Paul S. Reinsch: Open Door Diplomat in Action* (1979). Pugach's "Progress, Prosperity and the Open Door: The Ideas and Career of Paul S. Reinsch" (Ph.D. diss., Univ. of Wisconsin, 1967) provides additional information and a complete bibliography of Reinsch's publications. See also Patrick J. Scanlon, "No Longer a Treaty Port: Paul S. Reinsch and China, 1913–1919" (Ph.D. diss., Univ. of Wisconsin, 1973). For important biographical sketches, consult John V. A. MacMurray, "Dr. Paul S. Reinsch," *American Consular Bulletin*, 15 May 1923, p. 138. Reinsch's diplomatic activities are covered in Nemai Sadhan Bose, *American Attitude and Policy to the Nationalist Movement in China* (1970); Roy W. Curry, *Woodrow Wilson and Far Eastern Policy 1913–1921* (1957); and Jerry Israel, *Progressivism and the Open Door: America and China, 1905–1921* (1971). Major obituaries are in the *New York Times* and the *Milwaukee Journal*, 26 Jan. 1923.

NOEL H. PUGACH

REIS, Irving (7 May 1906–3 July 1953), radio and film director, was born in New York City, the son of Austrian immigrants Philip Reis, a tinsmith and construction worker, and Rose Lipkowitz. Already a ham radio operator at the age of thirteen, Reis showed an early enthusiasm for sound technology and experimentation. Although he received a scholarship to study bacteriology at Cornell, Reis lacked credits for admission, so in order to acquire the necessary courses, he attended Columbia University extension classes. But his interest in broadcasting—and the financial demands of supporting the family—won out, and he quit college after two years to take a job with the radio division of the telephone company in 1928.

In 1929 Reis secured a position as a log engineer with CBS, but he soon rose to the position of studio engineer, which he held for the next six years. As he learned more about radio technology, he became interested in its narrative potential. In 1932 he wrote and broadcast his first radio drama, "Split Seconds," for *Columbia Dramatic Guild*, but it was not well received. He continued to submit scripts that featured sound effects, however; the radio dramas he encountered during a trip to Europe in 1934 only confirmed his belief that such experimentation could be narratively successful. This success came in 1934 and 1935, when three of the dramas that he wrote and produced for *Columbia Dramatic Guild*—"The Half-Pint Flask," "St. Louis Blues," and "Meridian 7-1212"—gained wide critical recognition. "Meridian 7-1212," in particular, won the National Radio Award, was translated into several languages, and became one of the most frequently repeated radio sketches on the air.

With these accomplishments, Reis approached CBS about creating a weekly series that would provide a forum for original dramatic material and experimental radio techniques. Eager to try new shows and capture new audiences, William B. Lewis, the vice president for programming, accepted Reis's suggestion and launched *Columbia Workshop*, which first broadcast in July 1936. The series was a huge success and became a training ground for some of the most prominent names in the business, including composer Bernard Herrmann and writer Norman Corwin. For two years Reis directed and produced the series, which often stressed the use of technical devices, such as sound filters and echo chambers. The *Workshop* rebroadcast "Meridian 7-1212," for example, which was penned as dramatic material for a new filter that could simulate the sound of a voice heard through the telephone. For an adaptation of Edgar Allan Poe's "The Tell-Tale Heart," Reis combined a microphone and a stethoscope to broadcast the sound of a human heartbeat.

Other plays experimented with writing style and subject matter. The *Workshop* adapted to radio for the first time such authors as William Shakespeare, William Saroyan, Ernest Hemingway, and T. S. Eliot. In 1936 Reis traveled to Dublin, Ireland, for a month to direct the first transatlantic dramatic broadcast, a production of John M. Synge's "Riders to the Sea" with the Abbey Theatre Players. In 1937 he produced and directed for the *Workshop* Pulitzer Prize–winning poet Archibald MacLeish's "The Fall of the City" to great success. This verse play for radio had a historic impact in two ways: it began a fruitful collaboration between radio and poetry that lasted for several years, and it brought the voice of Orson Welles to national prominence for the first time.

Reis's work in radio also attracted the attention of filmmakers interested in experimenting with sound recording. Dutch documentarist Joris Ivens, who was looking for a sound director for his classic documentary of the Spanish civil war, *The Spanish Earth* (1937), hired Reis at the suggestion of MacLeish, a writer for the film. Working closely with Ivens's editor, Helen van Dongen, Reis earned his first film credit by adding sound effects to the silent footage. The motion picture industry soon took notice of his writing skills. In

1937 Reis sold "Meridian 7-1212" to 20th Century–Fox, which produced it as *Time Out for Murder* (1938). On the basis of his successful radio plays, Paramount offered him a screenwriting position in 1937. Reis moved to Hollywood in 1938 and married Meta Arenson (they were divorced in 1942, and she later married Hollywood agent George Rosenberg). At Paramount, Reis worked on several "B" pictures, including *King of Alcatraz* (1938), a box office success that improved his position with the studio.

Yet Reis was eager to experiment with motion pictures in a way that was not possible as a screenwriter. The opportunity to direct films at Paramount eluded him, however, so he took a cut in pay to direct "B" films for the rival studio RKO. While he defended the low-budget film as the best forum in which to test new techniques, he was consistently frustrated in his own efforts. "The 'B' is the logical field for experiments to forward the motion picture entertainment art, and yet it is the most hidebound form of movie," he is quoted in one studio publicity release. He directed seven "B"s for RKO from 1940 through 1941, including the first three installments of the very successful "Falcon" series, starring George Sanders. He graduated to "A" features in 1942 with Damon Runyon's *The Big Street*, starring Henry Fonda and Lucille Ball.

After the United States entered World War II, Reis began producing documentaries for various branches of the federal government. He was vice president of Film Associates, which produced such films as *Hidden Hunger* (1942), a short documentary on the importance of good nutrition for the war effort. He also produced a series of institutional documentaries, titled "Brave New World," for the Department of Interior. He entered the U.S. Army Signal Corps at the end of 1942, rose to the rank of captain, and served with fellow Hollywood directors George Stevens and Anatole Litvak, filming the Normandy invasion and the first shuttle bombing mission to the Soviet Union.

Reis returned to RKO in 1946 to direct his two biggest hits, *Crack-Up*, with Pat O'Brien, and *The Bachelor and the Bobby-Soxer*, with Cary Grant, Myrna Loy, and Shirley Temple. The success of these features brought him a lucrative contract with Universal-International, which gave him a certain measure of independence and creative control. Only one film, *All My Sons* (1948), came out of this union, however, as Reis sought even more distance from the studios through collaborations with independent producers, such as Samuel Goldwyn and Stanley Kramer. From 1948 through 1951 he directed seven films—notably *Enchantment* (1948) and his last film, *The Four Poster* (released in 1953)—but he was unable to parlay this independence into his dream of a truly experimental Hollywood film. Cancer cut Reis's career short; he died in Woodland Hills, California, survived by his second wife, Vanessa Idu (whom he had married in 1948) and their three children.

• The Academy of Motion Picture Arts and Sciences Center for Motion Picture Study in Beverly Hills, Calif., holds the Irving Reis Collection. See also Douglas Coulter, Columbia Workshop Plays (1939), for a discussion of Reis's involvement with the *Columbia Workshop*. The entry in Ephraim Katz, *The Film Encyclopedia* (1979), provides an overview of his film work. An obituary is in the *Los Angeles Times*, 4 July 1953.

SCOTT CURTIS

REISCHAUER, Edwin Oldfather (15 Oct. 1910–1 Sept. 1990), educator and diplomat, was born in Tokyo, Japan, the son of August Karl Reischauer, a missionary of long residence in Japan, and Helen Sidwell. He lived in Japan until his graduation from the American School in Tokyo in 1927. That year, Reischauer entered Oberlin College, where he earned an A.B. degree, and from there went to Harvard University for graduate study. By the time he entered Harvard, in 1931, he knew that he wanted to become an expert in East Asian studies; in order to receive further specialized training, which was not then available in the United States, he went in 1933 to the University of Paris, where he continued his study of Japanese and Chinese. Two years later he returned to Japan to conduct research for his dissertation. The contrast between the more open, cosmopolitan Japan he remembered from the 1920s and the militaristic and chauvinistic Japan he experienced in the 1930s made a deep impression on Reischauer and provided the point of departure for his thinking about modern Japanese history. For the time being, however, he concentrated on his studies, working on a translation of the diary of Ennin, a ninth-century Buddhist monk who traveled and studied in China. While in Japan, Reischauer married Adrienne Danton, an alumna of Oberlin, in 1935. They were to have three children.

In 1938 he returned to Harvard, where he received a doctorate in Far Eastern languages a year later and was appointed an instructor of Chinese and Japanese. His academic career was interrupted, however, by the Japanese bombing of Pearl Harbor. Reischauer had expected a clash between the two countries; he had come to believe that Japanese militarism and aggression would ultimately have to be stopped by the United States, by force if necessary, if Japan were to return to its more open, cooperative days. He did his part in frustrating Japanese ambitions by spending the war years in Washington, D.C., where he trained the army's language officers and cryptanalysts to enable them to read decoded Japanese messages. Reischauer also sought to influence wartime policy toward Japan, stressing the desirability of aiming propaganda at less chauvinistic Japanese, of the kind he had known in the 1920s.

Released from the army in November 1945, he briefly worked for the U.S. State Department, writing policy memoranda concerning the treatment of Japan and Korea. In 1946 he returned to Harvard University, where he was given tenure. From then on until his departure for Japan in 1961 as American ambassador, Reischauer devoted his energies to developing an East Asian curriculum at Harvard and training graduate students who would emerge as future leaders in the field. He worked closely with John K. Fairbank, a historian of modern China, and together they succeeded in making the United States the world's center for research and training in modern East Asian history.

During this time he developed a perspective on Japanese history that came to be known as the "Reischauer thesis." It argued that there had been two Japans, the old, feudal, closed, chauvinistic, and militaristic Japan and the modern, developed, cosmopolitan Japan. The latter had been steadily gaining on the former when aggression and war started in the 1930s. But because the roots of liberalism and democracy already existed, postwar changes and the future direction of the country were simply building on those trends. He called these trends "modernization," which he took pains to explain as a value-free concept, basically quantifiable in terms of such indicators as productivity, literacy, and per capita income. Japan, he argued, was closer to Western countries in its modernizing efforts than to other Asian countries.

This interpretation found a niche in the then developing Cold War ideology; the Reischauer thesis seemed to rationalize Japan's postwar alliance with the advanced Western countries, in particular the United States, against the socialist nations. For this, he was criticized by those in Japan who opposed the American alliance and viewed Japan as still very feudalistic; the country, they asserted, could never be truly modern until it went through a socialist revolution. Reischauer viewed such views as doctrinaire, but he considered it imperative that American officials take them seriously so as to maintain a dialogue with Japanese of all opinions, for he firmly believed that no solid foundation could be built between nations unless it was grounded on intellectual communication and understanding.

The maintenance of a dialogue with Japanese of many classes and persuasions became the cornerstone of Reischauer's diplomatic career when he served as ambassador in Japan (1961–1966). By then he had been remarried to Haru Matsukata (his first wife had died in 1955), a granddaughter of a prominent Japanese statesman of the late nineteenth century. This marriage was childless. The Reischauer-Matsukata combination gave the ambassador and his wife an unusual degree of influence among Japanese, and he was immensely popular in Japan. Besides promoting dialogue with Japanese, he was instrumental in persuading Washington to begin the process of returning Okinawa (still under American occupation although the occupation of other parts of Japan had ended in 1952) to Japanese rule. The reversion did not come until 1972, but he is credited with having initiated the process. One unfortunate incident while he was ambassador occurred in 1964 when a mentally deranged Japanese youth stabbed him in the abdomen. Reischauer received many blood transfusions, some of which were contaminated and caused further complications. In his characteristic good nature, and deeply conscious of the

symbolism of such an event, Reischauer told the press that now he was truly a man of two bloods.

He resigned as ambassador in 1966 and returned to Harvard, where he taught courses in Japanese politics and American relations with East Asia. He continued to be a very effective public lecturer and writer, publishing an enormously popular introduction to Japan, *The Japanese*, in 1975. (A revised edition was published in 1980 under the title *The Japanese Today*.) In these and other publications, he continued to present a sympathetic portrait of Japan, always eager to enlighten his countrymen about the culture and history of the country of his birth. His fundamental optimism about U.S.-Japanese relations, that the two countries shared so many ideals and interests that temporary disagreement over security, trade, and other issues would never again separate them, remained with him to the very end. His autobiography, *My Life between Japan and America* (1986), eloquently reiterated this theme. He died in San Diego, California.

Reischauer was the single most influential individual in the history of U.S.-Japanese relations after the Second World War. Through his teaching, writing, and service as U.S. ambassador, he contributed to bridge building across the Pacific and left a lasting legacy of cross-national understanding.

• The best source on Reischauer's life is his autobiography. To understand his contributions to scholarship, see his *Ennin's Diary: The Record of a Pilgrimage to China in Search of the Law* (1955) and its companion volume, *Ennin's Travels in T'ang China* (1955). His more general views of Japanese society, including the "Reischauer thesis" on modernization, may be found also in his *Japan Past and Present* (1946 and subsequent editions). There exists no systematic study of Reischauer's life and thought, but a family portrait by his wife, Haru Reischauer's *Samurai and Silk* (1986), contains interesting glimpses into his personality and lifestyle. Revisionist critiques of his interpretations of Japanese history can be sampled in Edward Friedman and Mark Selden, eds., *America's Asia: Dissenting Essays on American-Asian Relations* (1969). A memorial article was published in the *Harvard University Gazette*, 22 Nov. 1991.

AKIRA IRIYE

REISNER, George Andrew (5 Nov. 1867–6 June 1942), Egyptologist, was born in Indianapolis, Indiana, the son of George Andrew Reisner and Mary Elizabeth Mason. He was a descendant of one of Napoleon's German soldiers who immigrated to America. Reisner took his undergraduate and graduate education at Harvard University, where he obtained a B.A. in 1889 and a Ph.D. in Semitic language and literature in 1893. He continued his studies in Germany, first at Göttingen and then at Berlin. At Berlin the great Egyptologist Adolph Erman turned him in the direction of Egyptology.

Reisner returned to the United States in 1896 to join the faculty at Harvard, where he was made a professor of Egyptology in 1914. Beginning in 1897, however, when he was invited to become a member of the International Cataloging Committee for the Cairo Museum,

Reisner spent most of his academic career as a field archaeologist in Egypt. His first excavation opportunity came in 1898. Reisner started his long archaeological career by directing the University of California excavations at the cemeteries of Deir el-Ballas (Dayr al-Ballas) and Naga ed-Deir. These projects were financed by Phoebe Hearst of the California newspaper family.

Reisner's excavation methodology was shaped by that of the best fieldworker of the era, the British archaeologist Flinders Petrie. Petrie stressed the need for trained workmen, careful recording of all finds, and rapid publication. Reisner was famous for the care and precision of both his excavation and recording. He was also a pioneer in the application of photography to the process of excavation recording.

In 1904 Hearst ended her support for the University of California excavations. Reisner rejoined the faculty of Harvard, but his teaching career there was again brief. He was by 1905 appointed director of the Harvard University–Boston Museum of Fine Arts excavations in the necropolis surrounding the Old Kingdom pyramids at Gizeh (Giza). This association with Harvard, the Museum of Fine Arts (where from 1910 Reisner was curator of the Egyptian department), and the Gizeh Pyramid complex continued for the rest of his life.

Reisner's fieldwork was not limited to Gizeh. From 1907 to 1909 he surveyed and recorded sites in Nubia that would be flooded by the first Aswan Dam in one of the first dam-related archaeological survey projects. It involved not just excavation but also locating, mapping, test excavating, and recording of a range of sites soon to be forever inaccessible to archaeologists. Reisner's comprehensive and careful recording of sites set standards that would influence field survey and excavation of this type not only in Nubia but also in other parts of the world.

During this period Reisner also excavated a series of sites in the Sudan, including major Egyptian forts at Kerma and Semna. This work provided important information on the interactions between the Egyptians and their neighbors to the south and on the cultural and political history of Egypt's southern neighbors. He also directed the Harvard excavations at Samaria in Palestine (Reisner, Clarence S. Fisher, and David G. Lyon, eds., *Harvard Excavations at Samaria* [1908–1910]).

During 1905–1942 most of Reisner's research focused on the systematic exploration of the Gizeh necropolis. The most important and dramatic discovery there was the 1926 unearthing of the tomb furnishings of Hetep-heres, mother of Cheops, builder of the Great Pyramid. Again Reisner's slow, careful excavations provided the information that allowed for the recovery and reconstruction of the tomb furniture.

Reisner followed Petrie in his field methodology, but not always in his policy of rapid publication. Reisner's German-inspired methodological perfectionism slowed his productivity. Many of his excavations remained unpublished at his death, and important volumes such as *The Tomb of Hetep-heres*, vol. 2 (1955) and *Semna Kumna* (1960) were posthumous. This slowness to publish in later years was due partly to declining eyesight. Still such studies as *Excavations at Kerma* (1923), *Mycerinus Temple of the Third Pyramid of Gizeh* (1931), and *The Development of the Egyptian Tomb down to the Accession of Kheops* (1936) became classics in the field.

Reisner became fluent in Arabic and identified early with the welfare and advancement of his Egyptian workers. Important excavation tasks such as photography were assigned to Egyptians. He also supported the political aspirations of the Egyptian people. The Egyptian government expressed its appreciation for his support by letting the Boston Museum of Fine Arts keep some of the finest pieces found during Reisner's excavations.

Reisner married Mary Putnam Bronson in 1892; they had one daughter. For much of his later life he lived in his field house by the pyramids of Gizeh, where he died. In his will, he bequeathed to Harvard among other things his collection of 13,000 detective stories.

Reisner, along with the University of Chicago Egyptologist James Breasted, was the scholar most responsible for development of Egyptology in the United States. While Breasted concentrated on the decipherment and interpretation of ancient Egyptian texts, Reisner made his mark as an archaeologist and art historian. His careful field methodology not only raised the general standard of Egyptian archaeology but also influenced archaeologists working in regions as distant and different as the southwestern United States.

• Reisner's papers are located at the Museum of Fine Arts, Boston. Among his other major publications are *The Hearst Medical Papyrus* (1905), *Amulets* (1907), *Models of Ships and Boats* (1913), and *History of the Giza Necropolis* (1942–1955). Biographical and obituary references are in Walter M. Whitehill, *Museum of Fine Arts, Boston: A Centennial History* (2 vols., 1970); W. Dawson and E. Uphill, *Who Was Who in Egyptology*, 2d ed. (1972); *Bulletin of the Museum of Fine Arts* (1942): 92–93; *Yearbook of the American Philosophical Society* (1942), pp. 369–74; and the *American Journal of Archaeology* 46 (1942): 410–12.

STEPHEN L. DYSON

REISS, Winold Fritz (16 Sept. 1886–29 Aug. 1953), portrait painter, illustrator, and interior designer, was born in Karlsrühe, Germany, the son of Fritz Mahler Reiss, a landscape painter and portraitist; his mother's name is not known. His early training with his father was followed by enrolling in the Academy of Fine Arts in Munich, where he was influenced by Franz von Stuck, who also taught Paul Klee and Wassily Kandinsky. Later Reiss enrolled in the School of Applied Arts, where he learned commercial design skills. While at the School of Applied Arts, he met and married fellow art student Henrietta Lüthy. From his classes and the exhibitions of Die Brücke and Der Bläue Reiter, Reiss synthesized elements of cubism, fauvism, and jungendstil into his own work.

As a child Reiss developed a romantic obsession with tales of Native Americans as popularized by James Fenimore Cooper and the German author Karl May. His desire to paint Native Americans and to avoid the escalating political tensions of prewar Germany led him to immigrate to New York City in 1913. He was followed a year later by his wife and only child. Because of his training, Reiss was recognized as an expert on German modernism and invited to lecture at the Art Students' League. By 1915 Reiss had established his own art school and cofounded *M.A.C.* (*Modern Art Collector*), a magazine geared toward advertisers and commercial art buyers. Published from 1915 to 1917, the magazine was short-lived due to the anti-German sentiment of World War I. Reiss supported his family by creating illustrations for other magazines and interior designs for restaurants and hotels. His well-received designs for the Crillon Restaurant in New York City combined a modernist aesthetic with the American taste for art nouveau. This success led to other commissions for commercial chains, including Longchamps and Lindy's Restaurants and the Roger Smith Hotels.

In 1919 Reiss visited Browning, Montana, to paint portraits of Native Americans. His depictions of members of the Blackfeet nation were not romanticized visions; he approached his subjects objectively, focusing on their individual characteristics. In 1920 his interest in Native American ethnography led him to travel to Mexico, where he hoped to document the descendants of the Aztec and Mayan civilizations. These portraits were incorporated into an article on the Mexican revolution published in *Century Magazine*. This trip was followed in 1922 by his only return to Germany. His exposure to social realism of the Neue Sachlichkeit (New Objectivity) strengthened his interest in truthfully recording individual character. The artist executed a series of portraits based on the folk types of Germany—particularly of note are the Oberammergau Passion Players.

Because of his sensitive handling of physiognomy, Reiss was asked to illustrate the Harlem issue of *Survey Graphic*, "Harlem: Mecca of the New Negro" (Mar. 1925). For the cover, he juxtaposed a portrait of the musician Roland Hayes with an abstract border based on African motifs. Alain Locke, a Howard University philosophy professor, used the series "Harlem Types" and several abstract designs to illustrate *The New Negro: An Interpretation* (1925), a collection of literary works by Harlem authors such as Langston Hughes. The portraits were immediately recognized as an accurate treatment of African-American physiognomy, replacing the racist stereotypes that proliferated popular culture. While working in Harlem, Reiss influenced several young artists, including Aaron Douglas, Richmond Barthé, and Lois Mailou Jones.

During the summer from 1927 to 1948 Reiss's trips to Glacier National Park in Montana to study and draw the Blackfeet were sponsored by the Great Northern Railway. The railway purchased the majority of Reiss's portraits to illustrate a calendar distribut-

ed to customers. In 1934, to help defray expenses, Reiss established an art school in the park. However, Great Northern stipulated that Reiss and his students accommodate tourists, and as a result Reiss disbanded the school in 1938. His connection with the railway led to the 1933 commission to create a series of mural mosaics for the rotunda of the Cincinnati Union Terminal Building. Reiss methodically researched Cincinnati industry, photographing the factory laborers on whom he based his designs. The mural mosaics were dismantled and moved when the building was cited to be razed in 1972, and they were subsequently reinstalled in sections throughout the Greater Cincinnati International Airport. Reiss was appointed assistant professor of mural painting and design at New York University in 1933. He continued to work in this medium, creating works for the Theater and Concert Building for the 1939 World's Fair in New York City and for the Woolarc Museum in Bartlesville, Oklahoma, completed in 1946. In 1939 he co-authored *You Can Design*, an influential summary of his aesthetic principles. His work was widely exhibited throughout his life and is included in the collections of the National Portrait Gallery, the Smithsonian Institution, and the Minneapolis Institute of Arts. Concerned for the continued study of America's diverse cultures, Reiss donated his portraits of African Americans to Fisk University in 1951. Reiss died in New York City, and his ashes were scattered in Montana by the Blackfeet Indians.

• Reiss's interior designs are thoroughly discussed in Fred Brauen, *Winold Reiss (1886–1953): Color and Design in the New American Art*, an unpublished manuscript (1980) held at the New York Public Library, Main Reading Room. For the most complete and critical discussion with an extensive bibliography, see the National Portrait Gallery retrospective exhibition catalog by Jeffrey C. Stewart, *To Color America, Portraits by Winold Reiss* (1990). Also from this exhibition, Stewart, *Winold Reiss: An illustrated Checklist of His Portraits* (1990), documents the breadth of the artist's subjects. John C. Ewers, *The Blackfeet: Raiders on the Northwestern Plains* (1958), provides an ethnographic study for Reiss's illustrations. Other significant exhibition catalogs include Elisabeth Kashy, *Winold Reiss, 1886–1953, Centennial Exhibition: Works on Paper: Architectural Designs, Fantasies and Portraits* (1987), Paul Raczka, "Art Has No Prejudice," *Winold Reiss: Portraits of the Races* (1986), and Kennedy Galleries, *Winold Reiss: Plains Portraits* (1972).

AMY M. MOONEY

REMEY, George Collier (10 Aug. 1841–10 Feb. 1928), naval officer, was born in Burlington, Iowa, the son of William Butler Remey, a merchant and county official, and Eliza Smith Howland. George entered the U.S. Naval Academy in 1855 and graduated fourth in a class of twenty in 1859. Among his classmates were Alfred T. Mahan and Samuel Dana Greene, who would win fame as the executive officer aboard the USS *Monitor*. After graduation from the Naval Academy, Remey served aboard the *Hartford*, which sailed to both China and Japan during 1860–1861.

Remey's first exposure to combat came aboard the gunboat *Marblehead* during Major General George B.

McClellan's ill-fated Peninsula campaign. The *Marblehead*'s primary tasks were shelling Confederate shore batteries and supporting Union land forces with gunfire. During the campaign, Remey participated in the siege of Yorktown from March until July 1862. Afterward, he and the *Marblehead* were dispatched to the protracted Union siege of Charleston, South Carolina.

The Union attempt to take the city of Charleston was more than an effort to gain an important harbor. The city was the birthplace of secession and the site of the humiliating Federal surrender of its guardian bastion, the island fortress Fort Sumter. Driven by Secretary of the Navy Gideon Welles, Rear Admiral John A. Dahlgren was determined to regain the fort, and Remey had the misfortune to become involved in a Dahlgren blunder. Initially, Remey's role was limited to executive officer duties aboard the *Canandaigua* and a ten-day stint as the skipper of the *Marblehead*, both ships engaged in shelling Confederate shore positions. On 23 August 1863 Remey went ashore to command a battery of landed naval guns as the Federal siege slowly advanced on the Confederate outer defensive works. In September he and about 450 other members of Dahlgren's command volunteered to take Fort Sumter by storm.

Since Sumter had been bombarded by nearly 5,000 shells per week for almost a month, Dahlgren believed the fort was ripe for the picking. He told his doubting subordinates that they had only to take possession of the fort since its garrison was "nothing but a corporal's guard." However, the northern admiral did not know that the rebel defenders had deciphered the Union flag code, had correctly perceived the reason for concentrating a number of boats around Union ships near the fort, and had made ready for an assault. After darkness fell on 7 September, Remey and his fellow volunteers entered their boats and, with oars muffled, made way for Fort Sumter. The assault was a disaster. The 300 Confederates at the fortress waited for the right moment and placed a withering fire on the attackers. Guns from surrounding Confederate positions joined in. More than 100 Federals, including Remey, were captured.

Remey was confined in the infamous Libby Prison and the Columbia, South Carolina, jail for thirteen months. He made a near-successful escape attempt by tunneling. He was eventually exchanged and served out the last few months of the war aboard the *De Soto* as its executive officer.

In comparison with his Civil War adventures, the remainder of Remey's long career was relatively unexciting, but it reflected the respect his superiors and contemporaries accorded him. He was one of the few chosen by the navy to draw White House duties immediately following Abraham Lincoln's assassination, and he was selected as an aide to Admiral David G. Farragut at the president's funeral. He saw tours of duty in Latin American and Mediterranean waters in the late 1860s and early 1870s. In 1873 he married Mary Josephine Mason, the daughter of Charles Mason, the chief justice of Iowa. The couple had two daughters and four sons. Remey was promoted to captain in 1885 and commanded the USS *Charleston* of the Pacific Squadron from 1889 until 1892.

When the United States went to war with Spain in 1898, Remey was commanding the navy yard in Portsmouth, New Hampshire, and was chosen to perform many of the navy's logistical tasks associated with operations in and around Cuba. Taking command of the Key West, Florida, naval facilities, he organized the troop convoy carrying the American invasion force and supervised naval logistical and repair support. Following the war, he resumed his duties at Portsmouth, and in November 1898 he was promoted to rear admiral.

In April 1900 Remey took command of the Asiatic Station, a scene of active American military operations. At the time, the U.S. Army was engaged in counterguerrilla operations in the Philippines. In 1901 the United States, in conjunction with contingents from other nations, suppressed the Boxer Rebellion in China. Remey, aboard his flagship the *Brooklyn*, provided essential support to these American actions.

Admiral Remey retired from the navy on 10 August 1903. His death in Washington, D.C., was marked by a tribute from Secretary of the Navy Curtis D. Wilbur, who stated that Remey's whole career was characterized by good judgment and close attention to duty.

• The Library of Congress holds sixteen volumes of Remey's papers, including a memoir written by the admiral and his wife. The latter is also available at the New York Public Library, the Naval Academy Library, and the library at the Department of the Navy. The Remey family history is summarized in B. F. Johnson, "A Brief Historical Sketch of the Remey Family," a typescript at the Library of Congress. Remey's career is traced in L. R. Hamersly, *The Records of Living Officers of the U.S. Navy and Marine Corps*, 5th ed. (1894). An account of the failed 1863 assault on Fort Sumter is in Thomas Stevens, "The Boat Attack on Sumter," *Battles and Leaders of the Civil War*, vol. 4 (1887). Obituaries are in the *Washington Post* and the *New York Times*, 12 Feb. 1928.

ROD PASCHALL

REMICK, Lee (14 Dec. 1935–2 July 1991), actress, was born Lee Ann Remick in Boston, Massachusetts, the daughter of Frank Remick, the owner of a department store in nearby Quincy, Massachusetts, and Margaret Patricia Waldo, an actress who used the stage name Patricia Remick. When Remick was seven years old her parents separated, and she moved with her mother to New York City, where she attended Miss Hewitt's School. She also studied ballet for ten years, hoping to become a professional dancer. Remick's first foray into show business came in 1952 as a chorus member in several summer stock musicals at the Music Circus Tent in Hyannis, Massachusetts. Later that same year Remick was introduced to playwrights Reginald Denham and Mary Orr while having lunch with her mother at Sardi's, a New York restaurant popular with theater people. Denham and Orr suggested that Remick, a striking honey blonde with pale blue eyes, audition for the "smart-aleck teenager" role in their new comedy *Be Your Age*. Remick was cast in the part, but the play, which opened on Broadway in January 1953, closed after five performances. Remick graduated from Miss Hewitt's School that spring and attended Barnard College for one semester before deciding to pursue an acting career full time. She found work in live television dramas. In 1956 the prominent director Elia Kazan noticed her on the "Robert Montgomery Presents" program and offered her a part in the film *A Face in the Crowd* (1957). A satirical look at the power of the media, *A Face in the Crowd* featured Andy Griffith as a southern backwoods drifter who is turned into a television idol and Remick as an admiring high school cheerleader. Remick, a Manhattanite, spent two weeks in Arkansas learning how to twirl a baton and speak with a southern accent. So convincing was her performance that she was repeatedly cast as a nubile southern girl in her early film career. Her somewhat patrician bearing gave these portrayals an interesting dimension and kept them from turning into caricature. Shortly after completing *A Face in the Crowd* in 1957, Remick married William Colleran, a television and film director. The couple had two children.

Remick signed a contract with 20th Century–Fox and appeared for that studio in *The Long Hot Summer* (1958), an adaptation of several William Faulkner stories costarring Paul Newman, Joanne Woodward, and Angela Lansbury. Her next film, *These Thousand Hills* (1959), was a western based on a novel by A. B. Guthrie, Jr., costarring Don Murray. *Wild River* (1960), a second collaboration with Kazan, cast Remick as a young Tennessee widow torn between loyalty to her family and love for the Washington bureaucrat (Montgomery Clift) assigned to confiscate her family's land in order to make way for a hydroelectric dam. (It was Remick's personal favorite of all her films.) *Sanctuary* (1961) was another adaptation of William Faulkner material, costarring Yves Montand. Remick's most highly regarded films of this period were made for other studios. These are the courtroom drama *Anatomy of a Murder* (1959), directed by Otto Preminger and starring James Stewart, with Remick as a young woman of dubious moral reputation who maintains that she has been raped; and *The Days of Wine and Roses* (1962), starring Remick and Jack Lemmon as a newlywed couple who descend into alcoholism. Remick received an Academy Award nomination for best actress for the latter film.

Remick's fast-rising star slowed down as the 1960s progressed, and substantial film roles for women were becoming scarce as the movie industry moved toward more violent and youth-oriented stories. The placid Remick was disinclined to fight for the few good roles available. "I don't quite know what stardom means," Remick told *Films in Review* (Nov. 1988, p. 515). "It was never something I went after, as such. I love to work, I always have; and I love trying to do the best. I suppose stardom means *power*, basically—and I'm not too good at that." In 1964 she returned to Broadway to costar with Angela Lansbury and Harry Guardino in Stephen Sondheim's musical *Anyone Can Whistle*. In this unconventional work Remick played an emotionally repressed nurse at a psychiatric hospital. *Anyone Can Whistle* survived for only nine performances but developed a cult following through its original cast recording, one of the highlights of which is Remick's plaintive rendition of the title song. Remick found greater commercial success on Broadway as a blind woman who unwittingly becomes involved in a drug-smuggling operation in Frederick Knott's *Wait Until Dark* in 1966. Remick stayed with the popular thriller for a year and received a Tony Award nomination for best actress.

Divorced from William Colleran in 1969, Remick married British director William "Kip" Gowans in 1970 and moved to England, where she lived until 1982. The couple had no children. Remick continued to appear in feature films, including screen versions of Joe Orton's play *Loot* (1972) and Edward Albee's play *A Delicate Balance* (1973), in which she played the daughter of Katharine Hepburn and Paul Scofield. She also appeared in film adaptations of well-known novels such as Iris Murdoch's *A Severed Head* (1971), Ken Kesey's *Sometimes a Great Notion* (1971), and Henry James's *The Europeans* (1979). During the latter part of her career, however, Remick worked mostly in television, where her greatest success was *Jennie: Lady Randolph Churchill* (1974), a British-produced seven-part series in which she starred as Jennie Jerome, the beautiful and flamboyant American mother of Winston Churchill. Remick won the best actress award from the British Society of Film and Television Arts for her work in this series, which was also shown to great acclaim on public television in the United States. Other notable television appearances include *Ike* (1979), featuring Robert Duvall as General Dwight Eisenhower and Remick as his wartime British driver and mistress Kay Summersby, and *Haywire* (1980), a biography of ill-fated actress Margaret Sullavan. In 1985 Remick participated in a well-received all-star concert version of Stephen Sondheim's musical *Follies* at New York's Lincoln Center.

Diagnosed with kidney cancer in 1989, a gravely ill but still cheerful Remick made a final public appearance in April 1991, when she was awarded a star on Hollywood's Walk of Fame. She died two months later at her home in Los Angeles.

Remick was a talented and versatile performer who never quite reached the top level of stardom. Although a great beauty, her earnest and guileless acting persona lacked passion and charisma.

• Michael Buckley's detailed article in *Films in Review*, Nov. 1988, pp. 514–33, is the most complete source of information on Remick's career and includes the actress's own comments on her films. Also of value are Lillian Ross and Helen Ross, *The Player: A Profile of an Art* (1962), and Michael J. Bander, "Lee Remick's Quiet Fight," *Ladies' Home Journal*, May 1990, pp. 62–65, which includes a late interview and photograph. An obituary is in the *New York Times*, 3 July 1991.

MARY C. KALFATOVIC

REMINGTON, Frederic (4 Oct. 1861–26 Dec. 1909), illustrator and artist, was born Frederic Sackrider Remington in Canton, New York, the son of Seth Pierre Remington, a newspaper editor, and Clara Sackrider. The details of his early years are poorly recorded. During the Civil War, his father served as a cavalry major and brevet colonel in the Union army; as a result, martial themes and scenes of conflict between men on horseback became an important component of Remington's art. In 1877 Remington attended Highland Military Academy at Worcester, Massachusetts, where he chafed under the military discipline of that institution but loved the thought of war and the soldier's life. He entered Yale University in 1878 to study art, but his passion for the details and techniques of this subject were second to his enthusiasm for football. In 1879 he was a starting forward on the Yale team captained by Walter Camp, the father of American football. While at Yale, Remington published his first illustration, an injured football player recovering in his dormitory room, in the *Yale Courant*. His father's death in February 1880 and the resulting financial pressure on his family brought to an end his formal education.

Remington became a clerk in the office of the governor of New York, Alonzo B. Cornell, in March 1880. Restless in spirit, he held several clerkships in state agencies but found no satisfaction in any of them. His personal life was equally unfulfilled; in 1881 his proposal of marriage to Eva Adele Caten was accepted by her but rejected by her father. To overcome this rejection Remington made his first trip to the West in August 1881. His experiences in Wyoming and Montana awakened in him an interest in the American frontier and an awareness of the rich potential the West possessed as a subject for artists and illustrators. On 25 February 1882 *Harper's Weekly* published Remington's sketch of a Wyoming cowboy, his first commercial publication and his first western illustration.

Remington sought his future in the West after he received his inheritance in October 1882. On the advice of a friend from Yale, he purchased in the spring of 1883 a quarter section of land in Kansas and embarked on a career raising sheep. Dissatisfied with the constant demands of ranching and missing the companionship of family and friends, he sold his ranch and returned to New York in early 1884. He married Caten in 1884, her father having consented to the marriage, and they returned to Kansas City, Missouri, where he had part interest in a saloon. They had no children. By the summer of 1885 Remington had lost his investment in the saloon and had squandered his father's bequest. His wife returned to her family in New York, and Remington traveled through the Southwest. In Mexico, New Mexico, Arizona, Texas, and Oklahoma, Remington had his first sustained opportunity to sketch and to observe Native Americans, including the Apache, Cheyenne, Kiowa, and Cherokee. He abandoned clerking, sheep raising, and saloon keeping, and art became his career.

In 1886 Remington moved to Brooklyn, New York, where he enjoyed almost immediate success selling his drawings of western subjects to many of the nation's leading magazines. Wishing to be more than just an illustrator for major periodicals, Remington enrolled in courses at the Art Students League and began to work for the first time with watercolors. To gain recognition as an artist, he exhibited in 1887 in the juried shows of the National Academy of Design and the American Water-Color Society. His growing prominence caught the attention of Theodore Roosevelt, who asked that Remington provide illustrations for an article he had prepared on western ranch life and hunting for *Century Magazine*. Thus began an enduring friendship between the two.

Publishers then began sending Remington forth each summer to collect sketches and materials for their magazines. He often augmented his field sketches with photographs of scenes and subjects he later planned to paint. In 1887 he spent part of the summer traveling through Canada, and in 1888 *Century Magazine* commissioned him to travel through Kansas, Colorado, New Mexico, Arizona, Texas, and the Indian Territory. Remington became an illustrator at a propitious time in the history of American journalism, for the number of magazines published in the United States had increased from approximately 700 in 1865 to more than 3,000 in 1885. The demand for illustrations was insatiable and almost impossible to meet. By the end of the 1880s Remington had published more than 400 illustrations in the nation's ten leading periodicals. He had also begun illustrating popular books, and his work appeared in Elizabeth B. Custer's *Tenting on the Plains* (1887), Theodore Roosevelt's *Ranch Life and the Hunting Trail* (1888), Thomas Janvier's *The Aztec Treasure-House* (1890), and in later editions of Henry Wadsworth Longfellow's *Song of Hiawatha* (1855).

Although he was a talented illustrator, Remington wished to be acknowledged as a painter who worked in oils and watercolors. In the late 1880s he devoted more energy to this dimension of his career. In 1889 Remington exhibited a major painting, *A Dash for Timber*, at the National Academy of Design's annual exhibition, and he also received a silver medal at the Paris Universal Exposition for his *Last Lull in the Fight*.

In 1890 Remington moved into a new home in New Rochelle, New York; it was quickly filled with saddles, guns, blankets, animal skulls, and other western accouterments that he collected on his annual western trips. In the summer of 1890 he sketched and photographed the sun dance of the Blackfeet in western Canada, and in October and December of that year he traveled to the Pine Ridge Agency to observe the ghost dance. In June 1891 he was elected an associate member of the National Academy of Design. By this time his larger paintings commanded prices of up to $5,000. In 1892 Remington began work on illustrations for Francis Parkman's *The Oregon Trail*. In 1898 Remington witnessed the charge of Theodore Roosevelt's Rough Riders up San Juan Hill.

Always willing to experiment in art, Remington began to work in clay, and by October 1895 he cast his first bronze, the famous *The Bronco Buster*. By 1898 he had cast three more bronzes, and in 1902 he cast his most famous and most popular multifigured bronze, *Coming through the Rye*. His skills in this medium were abundant, and he demonstrated as much talent as a sculptor as he had earlier demonstrated as an illustrator and painter. By his death, which occurred as a result of complications following an appendectomy performed at his home, he had created twenty-five bronze sculptures.

As the nineteenth century came to an end Remington sensed that the West had been changed by the advance of industrialized America. In his lament over the passing of the frontier West, his paintings of western themes were nostalgic and romantic. Remington's paintings of this era are intensely narrative and seek to capture the passing of the frontier for Native Americans and white frontier settlers. In these works, the horse and men on horseback often play a signal role; and he began to be recognized as the most adept painter of these subjects. He ultimately produced more than 700 paintings with such a specific focus. He was praised for his knowledge of western horses and his skill in capturing on canvas their speed, strength, and dexterity; he often used photographs to allow him to capture the details of horses in motion. The majestic topography of the West was not emphasized in his paintings as it was in the works of Albert Bierstadt and Thomas Moran, because in his work landscape was subordinate to the activities of men. Women were marginal figures in his art.

In the early years of the twentieth century, Remington's works had begun to be subtly influenced by impressionism in technique, mood, and color, and his work became more painterly. The obsession with detail that once characterized his paintings began to be replaced by an emphasis on the fundamental elements of the subject. His moonlight and nocturnal scenes of western subjects were particularly innovative.

Remington created an image of the frontier West in his illustrations, paintings, articles, stories, and bronzes that indelibly shaped the perception America had of the people and activities of that region. Remarkably prolific, he produced more than 2,700 paintings and provided illustrations for forty-one periodicals and 142 books. No nineteenth-century American artist surpassed his productivity.

• Collections of Remington's letters and papers are at the Owen D. Young Library, St. Lawrence University, Canton, N.Y.; Frederic Remington Art Museum, Ogdensburg, N.Y.; Missouri Historical Society, St. Louis, Mo.; and the Library of Congress, Washington, D.C. Paintings, drawings, and bronzes are found in the collections of many museums, including the Frederic Remington Art Museum; the Whitney Gallery of Western Art, Cody, Wyo.; the Amon Carter Museum of Western Art, Fort Worth, Tex.; National Cowboy Hall of Fame, Oklahoma City; and the Thomas Gilcrease Institute of American History and Art, Tulsa, Okla. Many of his letters have been published in *Frederic Remington—Select-ed Letters*, ed. Allen P. Splete and Marilyn D. Splete (1988). Articles and short stories that he wrote can be found in *The Collected Writings of Frederic Remington*, ed. Peggy Samuels and Harold Samuels (1979). He published one novel, *John Ermine of the Yellowstone* (1902), and compiled seven books that reprinted approximately half of his articles. His short stories may be read in his *Pony Tracks* (1895), *Crooked Trails* (1898), and *Sundown Leflare* (1899). A perceptive examination of his life and career is Ben Merchant Vorpahl, *Frederic Remington and the West* (1978). Alexander Nemerov, *Frederic Remington and Turn-of-the-Century America* (1995), provides a cultural context for his career, art, and accomplishments. Peter Hassrick, *Frederic Remington* (1973), offers a succinct appraisal of his life and career with examples of his paintings, drawings, and bronzes. A popular appraisal of Remington with examples of his art may be found in Harold McCracken, *Frederic Remington/Artist of the Old West* (1947).

PHILLIP DRENNON THOMAS

REMINGTON, Philo (31 Oct. 1816–4 Apr. 1889), manufacturer, was born in Litchfield, Herkimer County, New York, the son of Eliphalet Remington, a farmer and mechanic, and Abigail Paddock. His parents soon moved to his grandfather's farm, on Steele's Creek, near Ilion, New York, a farm that included shops and a foundry. Remington received his formal education locally in public schools and then at the Cazenovia Seminary, but his real education came at home, in the family shops and foundry. His father, supposedly refused a rifle by Remington's grandfather, gathered up scraps of iron, forged a barrel, and walked to Utica to have it rifled. The resulting quality was so high that his neighbors asked him to make more barrels, and later government contract permitted expansion into producing the entire gun. Thus, Remington grew up amidst an expanding, successful gunsmith business. By age twenty-four he was in charge of manufacturing, and when his father died in 1861, he took over as president, assisted by his two brothers. He married Caroline A. Lathrop in 1841; they had two daughters.

The Civil War brought Remington large orders for armaments and initial financial success. But the company was unprepared for the end of the war, when it was left holding large inventories and a factory too large for the civilian market to support. Remington responded by seeking international orders and expanding into other lines of manufacturing. To facilitate this process, he reorganized the company, creating E. Remington & Sons to handle the gun business and a separate entity, in partnership with his brother Eliphalet, for manufacturing other products. In 1866 his brother Samuel went to Europe to represent the gun company; he stayed until 1877, and from 1870 he served as France's procurement officer for American ordinance. In 1867 the Danish government placed an order for nearly $40,000 of armaments after sending inspectors to Ilion. The Swedish government soon followed. In the next few years Remington signed contracts with Spain, Egypt, Mexico, Japan, and other countries, and by 1875 he had delivered over 1,000,000 arms to foreign governments.

For the civilian market, Remington concentrated on pistols that offered the highest profits. By 1875 the company offered eighteen sizes and patterns, from a .50 caliber single shot to a "vest pocket companion" of 3.5 ounces. In rifles Remington was first to introduce steel barrels for sporting guns, and he pursued experimental work on a breech-loading design, one of which was eventually adopted by the United States and many European armies.

To utilize manufacturing capacity fully, Remington began producing farm implements, principally mowers and cultivators. But these had limited success, and the business was sold in 1887. With assistance from a former Singer executive, Remington developed the Remington Empire sewing machine in 1870. As with the farm machinery, it was never a true commercial success, and it was organized into the Remington Sewing Machine Company and sold in 1882.

In 1873 Remington began working on what was arguably his most influential business activity. Early that year he had received a letter from James Densmore, asking to exhibit his typewriter. On 1 March Remington signed a contract with Densmore and his partner G. W. N. Yost to manufacture the machine and handle distribution and sales. On 30 April 1874 the first Remington-made typewriter arrived. Although well made, it was a cumbersome affair, with all type in uppercase. Moreover, Densmore and Yost did a poor job distributing and selling the machine. But Remington saw the potential, and on 1 November 1875 he signed a new contract that gave his company exclusive rights to manufacture and sell typewriters under the patents held by Densmore and Yost. In 1876 Remington built a special display model for the Centennial Exposition in Philadelphia, which drew considerable notice but did little to strengthen sales.

Remington introduced the redesigned Remington No. 2, the first typewriter to offer upper and lowercase type, in 1878. He arranged an exclusive sales agency with Fairbanks & Company, famous scale manufacturers of St. Johnsbury, Vermont, believing that its well-developed distribution network would generate larger sales. But offices in which typewriters would find their primary market were not places where Fairbanks typically sold scales, and in 1881 Remington reestablished its own sales department, headed by Clarence W. Seamans, aged twenty-seven, who had handled typewriter sales for Fairbanks. Then, in 1882 Seamans, in partnership with Yost's former salesman William O. Wyckoff, and Henry H. Benedict, a Remington official critical to recognizing the potential of the typewriter in 1873, contracted to sell all Remington typewriters. In spite of numerous new competitors entering the market because of the typewriter's increasing acceptance, Wyckoff, Seamans, & Benedict did well, more than doubling sales in two years.

By the mid-1880s, due in part to a severe economic recession, Remington was in deep financial trouble. He had sold off the sewing machine business in 1882, and in March 1886, in a bid to stave off bankruptcy of the firearms company, Remington sold the typewriter business, including the Ilion plant, to Wyckoff, Seamans & Benedict, who reorganized as the Remington Standard Typewriter Company. This ended Remington's connection to the typewriter. In 1887 he also sold the agricultural implement business, but he was unable to avoid bankruptcy. Hartley & Graham of New York City bought the firearms company at auction in 1888, which they then operated under the name Remington Arms Company.

Although Remington's career ended in business failure, his companies played a central role in pushing development of the machine tool industry through his innovations in production techniques; the design of Remington firearms had an enduring influence on both civilian and military arms; and he played a central role in the development and adoption of the typewriter. But because he focused narrowly on production, failing to make critical investments in management and distribution, others captured leadership.

Remington served as mayor of Ilion for many years, and he was a generous supporter of the Methodist Episcopal church. Along with his brother, he gave Syracuse University $250,000. He died in Silver Springs, Florida, where he had gone to try to regain his health after bankruptcy.

• There are apparently no original manuscript sources about Philo Remington or his companies, although Richard N. Current had access to privately held correspondence dealing with some critical aspects of the typewriter industry's development. Even so, there is useful material available about Remington, his businesses, and his products. For the typewriter industry, see Wilfred A. Beeching, *Century of the Typewriter* (1974); Richard N. Current, *The Typewriter and the Men Who Made It* (1954); and Donald R. Hoke, *Ingenious Yankees* (1990). James M. Utterback's *Mastering the Dynamics of Innovation* (1994) discusses the emergence of dominant designs in a variety of industrial products, including typewriters. For information about firearms, see Louis A. Garavaglia and Charles G. Worman, *Firearms of the American West, 1866–1894* (1985); and Charles H. Fitch, *Report on the Manufacturers of Interchangeable Mechanism* (1883). For the importance of investments in management and distribution, see Alfred D. Chandler, *Scale and Scope* (1990).

FRED CARSTENSEN

REMOND, Charles Lenox (1 Feb. 1810–22 Dec. 1873), abolitionist and civil rights orator, was born in Salem, Massachusetts, the son of John Remond and Nancy Lenox, prominent members of the African-American community of that town. His father, a native of Curaçao, was a successful hairdresser, caterer, and merchant. Charles attended Salem's free African school for a time and was instructed by a private tutor in the Remond household. His parents exposed him to antislavery ideas, and abolitionists were frequent guests in their home. He crossed the paths of a number of fugitive slaves while growing up and by the age of seventeen considered himself an abolitionist. He had also developed considerable oratorical talent.

Remond was impressed by William Lloyd Garrison's antislavery views, particularly the notion of slaveholding as a sin. He heard Garrison speak in 1831 in Salem, and the two became longtime associates when in 1832 Remond became a subscription agent for Garrison's abolitionist newspaper, the *Liberator*. This move helped launch his career as a professional speaker and organizer at a time when the antislavery movement was gaining large numbers of new adherents. Remond traveled in Rhode Island, Massachusetts, and Maine in 1837, soliciting subscriptions and encouraging abolitionists to form local antislavery societies. The *Weekly Anglo-African* depicted Remond's early abolitionism: "He labored in its early movements most faithfully: he bore the brunt of the calumnies and oppression, the mobbings, the hootings, the assaults which were heaped upon that noble band in the times of 1834–7" (1 Feb. 1862).

The American Anti-Slavery Society hired Remond as its first black lecturing agent in 1838. He brought a new authenticity to the speakers' platform; his charm and eloquence aroused and impressed the predominantly white audiences. An associate of Garrison's wing of the antislavery movement, Remond recommended immediate emancipation through moral suasion rather than political action or colonization, positions that isolated him from a growing group of black abolitionists. He opposed Henry Highland Garnet's call for slave insurrection at the 1843 National Convention of Colored Citizens. Citing a flawed U.S. Constitution that sanctioned slavery, Remond advocated the dissolution of the Union, a view unpopular with former slaves. While Remond claimed that none of his ancestors had been slaves, he consistently declared southern slavery and northern discrimination dual violations of the Bill of Rights. He urged blacks to protest the discrimination they experienced daily. "We need more radicalism among us," he wrote to the *Liberator*. "We have been altogether too fearful of martyrdom—quite too indifferent in our views and sentiments—too slow in our movements" (21 May 1841).

The highlight of Remond's career came in 1840, when the American Anti-Slavery Society selected him as a delegate to the World's Anti-Slavery Convention in London. Financed by female antislavery groups, Remond welcomed women's involvement in the movement and refused to take his seat at the convention when it voted to bar women's participation. In the eighteen months following the convention, he lectured to great acclaim throughout the British Isles on such topics as slavery, racial prejudice, and temperance. The antislavery press commented widely on Remond's gracious reception in England, in contrast to the discriminatory treatment he endured on his passage abroad and upon his return to Boston. His comparison between travel in the United States and Britain formed the basis of his noted 1842 address to the Massachusetts legislature, "The Rights of Colored Persons in Travelling," with which he became the first African American to speak before that body. His address is an important document of the widespread campaign to end segregated seating in railway cars in the 1840s. Throughout his career he reminded whites of the pro-

scriptive laws and practices against blacks in northern states.

Remond was the most renowned African-American orator until 1842, when Frederick Douglass began speaking to American audiences. The two men often toured together in the 1840s, and in the fall of 1843 they sustained a heavy lecturing schedule in the Midwest, amid fears of antiabolitionist riots. On 28 October 1845 Douglass wrote Garrison of Remond's effective antislavery oratory: "His name is held in affectionate remembrance by many whose hearts were warmed into life on this question by his soul-stirring eloquence" (Carter G. Woodson, *The Mind of the Negro as Reflected in Letters Written during the Crisis 1800–1860* [1926]). Remond's and Douglass's friendship deteriorated when Douglass publicly broke with Garrison in 1852. Contemporaries remarked that Remond felt shunned when Douglass swiftly rose to eminence in antislavery circles. Remond's corresponding decline in stature may be due to the fact that he suffered from tuberculosis, which forced him to abandon the lecture field for long periods of time.

Remond became increasingly impatient with the progress of antislavery, prompting him to reevaluate the utility of moral suasion in the antislavery struggle. The Fugitive Slave Act of 1850, which strengthened slaveholders' ability to reclaim their human property, prompted Remond to defend forcible resistance, to relax his opposition to slave insurrection, and to endorse political action. He became increasingly critical of white abolitionists for not attacking racial prejudice as vehemently as they did slavery. Though he remained ambivalent about the Republican party, Remond welcomed the outbreak of the Civil War. When Massachusetts opened enlistment to African Americans in January 1863, Remond, Douglass, Garnet, William Wells Brown, and other black leaders traveled through the northern states and Canada to recruit African Americans to the ranks of the Fifty-fourth Massachusetts Infantry Regiment. With the war's end Remond supported the continuation of antislavery societies to secure civil and political rights for blacks, a position that divided him from Garrison. He rejected the inclusion of women's rights issues in the campaign for black suffrage, arguing that their inclusion would hinder the achievement of black male enfranchisement, on which the eventual success of woman suffrage depended. Remond made his final lecture tour for a New York State Negro suffrage campaign in 1867. His poor health permitted him to appear only sporadically at civil rights meetings thereafter.

Remond spent most of his time lecturing rather than writing on behalf of antislavery. As one of the earliest black orators, he served as a role model, yet his ideological proximity to the predominantly white Garrisonians isolated him from other black abolitionists. Contemporaries extolled his oratory and compared his style to that of Wendell Phillips. However, as a black man who had never been a slave, his appeal and value to the antislavery movement were limited. Fellow abolitionists remarked upon his increasingly querulous demeanor, bitterness, and irascibility.

Beginning in 1865 Remond worked as a streetlight inspector and was appointed as a stamp clerk in the Boston Custom House in 1871. He died of tuberculosis at his home in Wakefield, Massachusetts. He was married twice, first to Amy Matilda Williams, who died on 15 August 1856, and then to Elizabeth Thayer Magee, who died on 3 February 1872. He and his second wife had four children.

• No substantial collection of Remond's personal papers exists. Many speeches and letters can be found in the microfilm edition of C. Peter Ripley and George Carter, eds., *The Black Abolitionist Papers, 1830–1865* (1981). For information on Remond's life and career, see William E. Ward, "Charles Lenox Remond: Black Abolitionist, 1838–1873" (Ph.D. diss., Clark Univ., 1977), and Dorothy B. Porter, "The Remonds of Massachusetts: A Nineteenth Century Family Revisited," *Proceedings of the American Antiquarian Society* 95 (Oct. 1985): 259–95. On Remond's tour of the British Isles, see Miriam L. Usrey, "Charles Lenox Remond: Garrison's Ebony Echo," *Essex Institute Historical Collections* 56 (Apr. 1970): 112–25.

STACY KINLOCK SEWELL

REMOND, Sarah Parker (6 June 1826–13 Dec. 1894), abolitionist, physician, and feminist, was born in Salem, Massachusetts, the daughter of John Remond and Nancy Lenox. Her father, a native of Curaçao, immigrated to the United States at age ten and became a successful merchant. Her mother was the daughter of African-American revolutionary war veteran Cornelius Lenox. Sarah grew up in an antislavery household. Her father became a life member of the Massachusetts Anti-Slavery Society in 1835, and her mother was founding member of the Salem Female Anti-Slavery Society, which began as a black female organization in 1832. Sarah's brother, Charles Lenox Remond, was a well-known antislavery lecturer in the United States and Great Britain.

Sarah Parker Remond attended local public schools in Salem until black students were forced out by committee vote in 1835. Determined to educate their children in a less racist environment, the Remond family moved to Newport, Rhode Island, in 1835. After the family returned to Salem in 1841, Remond's education was further developed at home with English literature and antislavery writings. She was an active member of the Salem Female Anti-Slavery Society, the Essex County Anti-Slavery Society, and the Massachusetts Anti-Slavery Society. Her experience with the Salem school committee led to early activism against racial segregation. She was awarded $500 by the First District Court of Essex after being forcibly ejected from her seat at a public place of entertainment in 1853.

In 1842 Remond began touring on the antislavery circuit with her brother Charles who was the first black lecturing agent of the Massachusetts Anti-Slavery Society. Sarah and Charles toured New York State with Wendell Phillips, Abigail Kelley Foster, Stephen Foster, and Susan B. Anthony in 1856. Remond ac-

cepted an appointment as a lecturing agent of the American Anti-Slavery Society in 1858. On 28 December 1858 she sailed to Great Britain with three goals: to work for the antislavery cause, to pursue an education, and to live for a time away from American racism. She attended the Bedford College for Ladies in London while traveling as an antislavery lecturer to more than forty-five cities in England, Scotland, and Ireland between 1859 and 1861. Her approach on the antislavery circuit was different from black male American abolitionists. She won over the British public by drawing on her demeanor as a "lady," while recounting stories of sordid sexual exploitation forced on female slaves. She was popular in Great Britain, where lectures by women were rare. She was one of the first women to lecture in Great Britain to "mixed-sex" audiences. Because she was removed by both her race and nationality from British class politics and gender conventions, she was able to appeal to both the working class and the social elite.

Perhaps her popularity as an abolitionist in London caused the American legation in London to deny her request for a visa to travel to France in November 1859. The legation claimed that because of her race she was not a citizen of the United States. Support for her included editorials in most of the major London papers. The *Morning Star* compared the "visé affair" to the Dred Scott decision, which had been used by the United States as a basis for its actions. Benjamin Moran, the American assistant secretary of legation, wrote on 10 December 1859 that George Dallas, the American minister to Great Britain, threatened to go home should any more attacks of the kind appear, and if he went, he would be the last American minister in England for some time. Moran believed that public opinion on this matter reached Buckingham Palace. On 25 February 1860 he wrote, "on the subject of darkies, I am reminded that the queen looked at me very [oddly] on Thursday, & I now suspect the Remond affair was dancing about in her mind, and that she wished to know what kind of person (if she thought of the matter at all) the Secretary was that refused that lady of color a visé."

Remond's manner and standing in American antislavery circles made her a great many friends in the "upper circle" of British abolitionists. She lived for a time at the home of Peter Alfred Taylor, a member of Parliament and treasurer of the London Emancipation Committee. A center for London radicals, the Taylor home was also the meeting place for many of London's early female reformers because Taylor's wife Mentia was active in the woman suffrage movement. Remond worked with the Taylors in establishing the first two emancipation groups in London. In June 1859 concerned individuals, including famed runaway slaves William and Ellen Craft, formed the London Emancipation Committee. Remond was active in this group until 1 August 1859. After the committee failed to invite her to address a public meeting held in London to celebrate the twenty-fifth anniversary of the abolition of British colonial slavery, Remond stopped attending its meetings. The London Emancipation Committee concluded operations in February 1860 at a meeting attended by men only.

Four years later Remond and Mentia Taylor were founding members of the London Ladies Emancipation Society, which claimed that slavery was a question especially and deeply interesting to women. In 1864 the society put into circulation more than 12,000 pamphlets printed by the feminist publisher Emily Faithful. Remond's contribution was entitled *The Negroes and Anglo-Africans as Freed Men and Soldiers*. After the end of the Civil War, Remond was a member of the Freedman's Aid Association along with Ellen Craft. In 1865 she wrote a letter of protest to the *London Daily News* when the London press began attacking blacks after an insurrection in Jamaica.

Remond returned to the United States later in 1865 and worked for a short time with the American Equal Rights Association. She had served as a delegate to the National Woman's Rights Convention in 1858. In 1866 she moved to Florence, Italy, to attend a medical training program at Santa Maria Nuovo Hospital. After receiving a diploma for "professional medical practice" in 1871, she started a medical practice in Florence. On 25 April 1877 she married an Italian named Lazzaro Pintor. Sarah Parker Remond is buried in the Protestant Cemetery in Rome, Italy.

• Remond's autobiography, "Sarah Parker Remond," appears in *Our Exemplars, Poor and Rich; or, Biographical Sketches of Men and Women Who Have, by an Extraordinary Use of Their Opportunities, Benefited Their Fellow-Creatures*, ed. Matthew Davenport Hill (1861). The Remond family is described in Dorothy B. Porter, "The Remonds of Salem, Massachusetts: A Nineteenth-Century Family Revisited," *Proceedings of the American Antiquarian Society* 95 (1985): 259–95. Remond's letters and speeches appear in C. Peter Ripley, ed., *The Black Abolitionist Papers*, vol. 1, *The British Isles, 1830–1865* (1985). Remond's life and career are documented in Ruth Bogin, "Sarah Parker Remond: Black Abolitionist from Salem," *Essex Institute Historical Collections* 110 (Apr. 1974): 120–50, and Dorothy B. Porter, "Sarah Parker Remond," *Dictionary of American Negro Biography* (1982). An excellent overall discussion of Remond in London is in Clare Midgley, *Women Against Slavery: The British Campaigns, 1780–1870* (1992). Additional sources include Dorothy Sterling, *We Are Your Sisters* (1984); *The Second Annual Report of the London Ladies Emancipation Society* (1864); *The Journal of Benjamin Moran, 1857–1865*, vol. 1, ed. Sarah Agnes Wallace and Frances Elma Gillespie (1948); and the *Morning Star* (London), 10 Dec. 1859.

KAREN JEAN HUNT

REMSEN, Ira (10 Feb. 1846–4 Mar. 1927), chemist and educator, was born in New York City, the son of James Vanderbilt Remsen, a merchant, and Rosanna Secor. At age fourteen he entered the Free Academy (now the City University of New York), where he emphasized Latin and Greek. He left before graduating and, at the urging of his father, began an apprenticeship to a homeopathic physician and studies in a homeopathic medical school. He found this unsatisfactory and transferred to the College of Physicians and Surgeons in New York City, receiving an M.D. in 1867 and a prize for his thesis, "Fatty Degeneration of the Liver." He later commented critically on his medical education, "I had in fact never seen a liver that had undergone fatty degeneration nor a patient who . . . was supposed to possess one."

During his medical education Remsen became interested in chemistry, and the fame of Justus Liebig attracted him to Munich. This was a time of great excitement and advances in chemistry because confusion about atomic weights had been clarified by Stanislao Cannizzaro and because the mysteries of organic chemistry were being solved by application of the new structural theories. In his first laboratory research there with Jacob Volhard, Remsen was trained in methods of analysis, then an essential skill in research. When Friedrich Wöhler visited Munich, Remsen arranged to continue his studies in Göttingen. There he did research with Rudolph Fittig and received his doctorate in 1870. In that year Fittig became professor at Göttingen and asked Remsen to join him as his lecture and laboratory assistant. During his four years with Fittig Remsen published nine research articles, three authored jointly with Fittig and six alone. Remsen's research emphasized sulfobenzoic acids and included the observations that led to Remsen's Law: neighboring groups on a benzene ring inhibit oxidation by nitric and chromic acids.

In 1872 Remsen returned to the United States, translated Wöhler's *Outlines of Organic Chemistry*, and obtained a position as professor of chemistry and physics at Williams College in Williamstown, Massachusetts. When he arrived there he found no laboratories and a classical curriculum in which science played a peripheral role. Students were discouraged from participation in research. In addition to his teaching, Remsen continued his research, published a series of research articles, and wrote *Principles of Theoretical Chemistry* (1876), an important text that went through five editions and was translated into German and Italian; it gained wide recognition for Remsen because of the clarity of the writing and the chemical reasoning. His research at Williams included a study that concluded that $POCl_3$ was pentavalent and therefore that phosphorus had two valencies, a concept now recognized as correct but which violated the paradigm of that time. In 1875 Remsen married Elizabeth Hilliard Mallory; they had two sons.

Daniel Coit Gilman, president of the newly-established Johns Hopkins University, was recruiting an outstanding faculty that emphasized research and scholarship, a concept that would influence all American universities. His choice for professor of chemistry was Remsen. Remsen quickly established laboratories and a research program; he and his colleagues published thirteen articles between 1876 and 1878. The department blossomed, attracting students from many colleges—some from Germany. From its inception to 1913 Johns Hopkins awarded 202 Ph.D. degrees in chemistry, most of them to students of Remsen.

Constantine Fahlberg came from Leipzig to Johns Hopkins to do research with Remsen, who suggested that Fahlberg investigate permanganate as an oxidizing agent for a methyl group adjacent to a sulfonamide group. These experiments resulted in a cyclic derivative called benzoic sulfinide, now known as saccharin. Fahlberg patented this discovery without consulting Remsen, but Remsen never contested the matter. However, in a letter dated 12 March 1887 to William Ramsay, his friend from their days together in Tübingen, Remsen said, "I object most decidedly to the constant references to *Fahlberg's* Saccharin."

Remsen founded the *American Chemical Journal* in 1879. It quickly became the preferred medium for research publications by American chemists. All of Remsen's early publications appeared in German journals, but after 1879 most of his work appeared in his new journal. Beginning about 1890, a large number of publications from Remsen's research group started appearing with only the student's name on the title page. In 1913, when Remsen retired, the *American Chemical Journal* merged with the *Journal of the American Chemical Society*.

Remsen influenced graduate instruction in chemistry throughout the United States, mostly through his reputation and his emphasis on research. At Johns Hopkins he started weekly meetings for discussion of current literature, later a tradition in most American doctoral programs in chemistry. Remsen wrote several influential texts after his successful 1876 treatise on theoretical chemistry, including *An Introduction to the Study of Organic Chemistry* (1885), *An Introduction to the Study of Chemistry* (1886), *The Elements of Chemistry* (1888), *Inorganic Chemistry* (1889), *A Laboratory Manual* (1889), *Chemical Experiments Prepared to Accompany Remsen's "Introduction to the Study of Chemistry"* (1895), and *A College Text-book of Chemistry* (1901). The combined sales of the multiple editions and translations (even into Chinese and Japanese) were approximately 500,000, so Remsen may have taught more than a million students.

Remsen also contributed much public service. He helped to plan new chemistry laboratories for the University of Chicago. In 1881 he helped to solve a problem with Boston's water supply. After a disastrous 1904 fire in Baltimore, he was a key member of the commission that supervised construction of sewers. He served the government in investigations of the glucose industry, denatured alcohol, pollution of room air, and food contamination.

Remsen was acting president of Johns Hopkins in 1889–1890 and became president in 1901. Despite the university's financial problems, Remsen supervised planning for a new campus. He also supported the development of the College for Teachers and the School of Engineering. He felt that his most important duty was to foster the original objective of Johns Hopkins University: excellence in research and graduate instruction. As president, Remsen's motto was, "Every man does his best work when . . . allowed to do it in his own way." He continued to teach and lead the chemistry department during his tenure as president.

Remsen was president of the American Chemical Society (1902), the American Association for the Advancement of Science (1903), and the National Academy of Sciences (1907–1913). He received many honors, notably the Priestley Medal of American Chemical Society. The Maryland section of the American Chemical Society established the Remsen Lectures to celebrate the centennial of his birth and commemorate his contributions.

Remsen retired in 1913 and spent his time in consulting for industry and government, writing, and traveling. He died at Carmel, California. His ashes were placed in a crypt in Remsen Laboratory at the new campus of Johns Hopkins University. When the building was remodeled in the 1990s, care was taken to preserve this memorial to Remsen.

• Most of Remsen's manuscript materials are in the libraries of Johns Hopkins University. Correspondence between Remsen and Sir William Ramsay is in the manuscript collections of University College, London. Remsen's contributions to chemistry are summarized in National Academy of Sciences, *Biographical Memoirs* 14 (1932): 207–57, with a list of publications and major addresses. Two appendices describe Remsen's teaching and work on the commission for sewers. F. H. Getman, *The Life of Ira Remsen* (1940; repr. 1980), emphasizes nonchemical aspects of Remsen's life, including his time in Europe and his public service. Remsen's influence on the development of American chemistry is the subject of a chapter in D. S. Tarbell and A. T. Tarbell, *Essays on The History of Organic Chemistry in the United States, 1875–1955* (1987). An obituary is in the *New York Times*, 6 Mar. 1927.

PAUL HAAKE

RENFROE, Stephen S. (1843–13 July 1886), noted Alabama outlaw, was born in Georgia, the son of J. G. and M. A. P. Renfroe, farmers. The family moved to Butler County, Alabama, around 1853. Poorly educated but intelligent, Renfroe was quick-tempered, handsome, powerful, and athletic. An expert shot and accomplished horseman, he served as a private in the Civil War, was wounded, and then deserted in 1864.

In 1865 he married Mary E. Shepherd of Butler County. He and his wife lived in Lowndes County with Mary's sister and her husband, who was a physician. During a family argument in 1867, Renfroe shot and killed his brother-in-law. He fled to Livingston in Sumter County. A Black Belt county bordering Mississippi, Sumter County had become a Republican stronghold after the war. The county's native white Democrats fought bitterly with northern whites ("carpetbaggers") and their local white allies ("scalawags"), although former slaves provided the Republicans' real voting strength.

Renfroe's wife died, and in 1869 he married Mary M. Sledge. After his second wife's death (1871), he married Cherry V. Reynolds of nearby Meridian, Mississippi, in 1873. Their son was born the following year. Meanwhile, Renfroe became a respected farmer by day, but at night he rode with the Ku Klux Klan in opposition to Radical Reconstruction leaders. Renfroe was involved in Klan beatings, murders, and intimidation of Republican voters that made a tangible contribution to statewide Democratic victories in 1870. The Republicans won in 1872, however, and the Klan's excesses led to its demise. Nevertheless, Renfroe remained a hero to many white Democrats.

In 1874 Renfroe and two other men were arrested for murder in violation of the Enforcement Acts. Tried in Mobile, the men became martyrs. When all charges were dropped due to a lack of evidence, Renfroe returned home in triumph. In statewide elections the Democrats won political control of the state. Renfroe resumed farming, and in 1877 he was elected sheriff of Sumter County. Within a year the sheriff's courthouse office was robbed. Renfroe was suspected, but no charges were made. By 1880, Renfroe had burned the county clerk's office, embezzled money, misused trust funds, released prisoners, and committed an assault. On 19 April, he was indicted and imprisoned. Although friends posted bond, Renfroe's behavior resulted in his re-arrest.

On 19 June, he cut a hole through the outside wall of his cell and escaped. He hid out in the heavily timbered flatwoods bordering Mississippi. By letter he formally resigned as sheriff and awarded his property to his wife. In 1881 Renfroe allegedly joined the Harrison Gang, a band of robbers who operated in Louisiana and Mississippi. He secretly visited his family and, hoping to reform, returned to Livingston in 1884 and surrendered to authorities. Friends raised his bond, but again Renfroe began drinking and fighting and was locked up. His attempted escape caused authorities to transfer him to a more secure jail at Tuscaloosa. The resourceful ex-lawman burned his way out of this jail, making a brilliant escape on 7 July 1884.

Renfroe fled to New Orleans and from there to Texas and Mexico. He returned to Sumter County in 1885 but then decided to go to Central America. Before leaving Renfroe stole a horse and saddle. After he left Alabama, a detective tracked him through Mississippi and arrested him at Slidell, Louisiana. Renfroe was returned, physically debilitated, to Livingston's new jail (an unacknowledged tribute to him). An escape effort failed, and in August 1885 Renfroe pled guilty to two charges and received a five-year sentence. Under Alabama's notorious convict lease system he was consigned to the mines of a coal company near Birmingham. On 3 October, he broke out, eluded pursuers, and fled to the flatwoods. A massive manhunt failed to locate him, even as Renfroe gave out interviews to newspaper reporters.

Rewards for his capture were offered when he was accused of stealing horses and mules, and in July 1886 three farmers wounded and captured him near Meridian. Renfroe was returned to Livingston on 13 July and, when interviewed, asked that his wife change his son's last name. After dark, a small group of armed but undisguised men appeared before the jail and took charge of Renfroe. They marched with him down the main street, stopping south of town at the Sucarnat-

chie River. A noose was placed around the stoical Renfroe's neck, and he was hanged from the limb of a chinaberry tree. He was buried later in a pauper's grave in Livingston. The lynchers were well known, but no arrests were ever made. The incorrigible but able Renfroe has become an Alabama legend.

• The only biography of Renfroe is William Warren Rogers and Ruth Pruitt, *Stephen S. Renfroe, Alabama's Outlaw Sheriff* (1972). An inaccurate sketch of Renfroe, based on the Renfroe legend, is in Carl Carmer, *Stars Fell on Alabama* (1934), pp. 126–33. The book is worthwhile for evoking the mood and atmosphere of Alabama during Reconstruction. The most recent work is Ruth Rogers Pruitt, *Wind along the Waste* (1991), a work of fiction whose central character is based on Renfroe. See also Louis Roycraft Smith, Jr., "A History Of Sumter County, Alabama, through 1886" (Ph.D. diss., Univ. of Ala., 1988).

WILLIAM W. ROGERS

RENICK, Felix (5 Nov. 1770–27 Jan. 1848), cattleman, was born in Hardy County, Virginia, the son of William Renick (his mother's name is unknown). Renick's father worked for a time as a deputy surveyor for Lord Fairfax and taught Renick the skills of the trade. As a young man, Renick supported himself probably as a farmer. In or about 1795 he married Hannah See, with whom he had nine children.

Like many other young Virginians, the Renicks became enthusiastic about the idea of reestablishing themselves in the Ohio country. In late 1798 and early 1799 Renick and two friends explored the Ohio country to evaluate its agricultural potential. Not surprisingly, he was happiest with the Scioto Valley, which was becoming a magnet for Virginians trying to re-create a society of landed gentlemen without legal slavery. In 1801 Renick and his brother George returned to the area, accompanied by two servants, and Felix bought a sizable amount of land about four miles south of Chillicothe.

Combining a considerable amount of capital with sheer determination, the Renicks demonstrated the viability of cattle raising in the Ohio Valley. Initially, they purchased cattle locally; soon Renick was traveling as far away as Tennessee to increase his herd. According to George Renick's son, his father and uncle owned "much the largest stocks of thoroughblood . . . cattle" in Ohio (*Memoirs*, p. 19). In 1805 George supervised the first overland drive of cattle from Ohio to the East Coast, taking sixty-eight head to market in Baltimore. This was the beginning of a remarkably durable trade. In 1816 Renick purchased 100 steers in Kentucky for approximately $75 a head. The next year, after fattening them to an average weight of 1,300 pounds, he had them driven to Philadelphia. There he sold 100 head for an average price of $133, with about twenty of them fetching as much as $160.

In the 1830s the enterprising Renicks expanded their business to Great Britain. The brothers played major roles in the formation of the Ohio Company for Importing English Cattle in 1833. Forty-eight stockholders (of whom nine were named Renick) purchased ninety-two shares (of which Renicks held nineteen) at $100 each. Renick and two assistants left Chillicothe in January 1834, visited the cattle markets in Baltimore and Philadelphia, and arrived in Liverpool in March. They spent the next two months cultivating contacts in England and purchasing shorthorn cattle. In May 1834 nineteen shorthorns (seven bulls and twelve cows) departed Liverpool for Philadelphia and arrived in Chillicothe in October; their total cost was $2,404.26. Seven more were shipped in 1835 and thirty-five in 1836.

Renick prepared a catalog of fifty-four English cattle and hosted a successful auction at Indian Creek Farm on 29 October 1836. Buyers from throughout south-central Ohio paid $34,540 for forty-three of the imported cattle. The following October, another fifteen went for a total of $16,075; one cow and calf sold for $2,225. The panic of 1837 brought a halt to the imports, but not before the stockholders of the Ohio Company had netted a tidy profit. In 1837 the company paid a liquidating dividend of $280 per share. The profitability of the enterprise should not obscure the fact that the company's imports "exercised a strong beneficial influence on the character of the stock in the Scioto Valley" (Jones, p. 109). The Renicks may not have been as high-minded as their descendants would have us believe, but their efforts at improving the feeding, breeding, and marketing of cattle had an impact on the economy of the region as a whole.

Renick's success as a cattleman provided him with leisure time to explore other interests. He devoted a good deal of his time to learning about American Indians and the history of the Ohio Valley. He was the first president of the Logan Historical Society and contributed two articles to its publication, the *American Pioneer*, in 1842. He also served as an associate judge of Ross County. Renick's lifelong devotion to progress and profit led him to accept the presidencies of the Portsmouth and Columbus Turnpike Company and the Belpre and Cincinnati Railroad Company.

Renick was typical of the successful rural businessman in the early nineteenth century. He expended considerable money and effort on leading a refined life and ensuring that his children would be able to do the same. He invested in education, paying for the construction of what was known as the Felix Renick Schoolhouse for the use of his children and those of his neighbors. Meanwhile, the Renicks lived in an elegant style that transformed the aristocratic style and ethos of eighteenth-century Virginia gentry into the more private and slaveless world of nineteenth-century midwestern economic elites.

Renick died when a log securing the Paint Creek ferry came loose and crushed him while he was sitting in his carriage. Renick was perhaps the most prominent agricultural businessman in south-central Ohio in the early nineteenth century. The obituary in the Chillicothe *Scioto Gazette* called him "one of the most enterprising and public-spirited men of this section of the state," a "useful" citizen, and a staunch advocate of "progress" (quoted in Plumb, p. 57). Renick was the very model of a large-scale rural capitalist, blending the pursuit of private profit with a deep belief in the efficacy of scientific and economic progress.

• No collection of Renick papers exists, although the Western Reserve Historical Society has George Renick's account book from 1808 to 1829. Renick wrote articles for *American Pioneer*, including "A Trip to the West," Feb. 1842; "Anecdotes of Joe Logston," June 1842; "Second Trip to the West—Logan," Oct. 1842; and "Mr. Renick's Letter," Jan. and Aug. 1843. He also compiled *A Catalogue of the Improved Short-Horned Cattle, Imported from England in the Years 1834, 1835, and 1836 by the Ohio Importing Company* (1836). The main biography is Charles Sumner Plumb, "Felix Renick, Pioneer," *Ohio State Archaeological and Historical Society Publications* 33 (1924): 1–66. George Renick's son William Renick's *Memoirs* (1880) has some information about the cattle business but little about Felix. Robert L. Jones, *History of Agriculture in Ohio to 1880* (1983), is a helpful secondary source.

ANDREW CAYTON

RENO, Don (21 Feb. 1927–17 Oct. 1984), bluegrass banjo player, was born Donald Wesley Reno in Spartanburg, South Carolina, the son of subsistence farmers. Reno was raised on a farm in rural Haywood County, North Carolina. Like fellow Carolinian Earl Scruggs, Reno began experimenting with playing the banjo in a new style—using three fingers to pick the strings rather than the traditional two and picking melodic and chord runs in a rapid style. He was inspired by local banjo player Arthur "Snuffy" Jenkins, who also influenced Scruggs. Reno would later develop a unique style that combined chord rolls with picked single-note leads in the manner of tenor banjo playing. He worked as a sideman with the Morris Brothers and Fiddlin' Arthur Smith in the late 1930s, when he was still a teenager, before being drafted into World War II, where he served in Burma. When he returned from the war, he was employed from 1948 to 1949 by Bill Monroe as a replacement for Scruggs.

Reno met guitarist-vocalist Arthur Lee "Red" Smiley, who was originally from Asheville, North Carolina, when both were employed by fiddler Tommy Magness as members of his group the Tennessee Buddies in late 1949. The group was based out of Roanoke, Virginia. They recorded with Magness in 1951 for the Cincinnati-based King label and then moved on to work with another local band. The duo hit it off and formed their own band, the Tennessee Cut-Ups (or Cutups), by the end of 1951. They went into the studio to record in early 1952, again for King, but the band fell apart before the records were released. From this session came their first minor country hit, "I'm Using My Bible for a Roadmap," written by Reno. Reno's "I Know You're Married (But I Love You Still)," from the same session, was successfully covered by country duo Bill Anderson and Jan Howard, as well as by Red Sovine. Despite the band having ended, their records sold well, and King owner Syd Nathan urged them to continue to record, which they did, despite the fact that they had hung up their performing hats as a duo.

Between 1952 and 1955 Smiley was semiretired, although he returned to the studio to work with Reno as needed. Meanwhile, Reno formed a partnership with guitarist Arthur "Guitar Boogie" Smith (not the same person as Fiddlin' Arthur Smith). The duo cut one famous recording in 1955 called "Feuding Banjos," with Smith on tenor banjo and Reno on five-string. This was later revived as "Duelin' Banjos" in the 1970s and was used as the theme for the popular film *Deliverance* (1972). Reno's string wizardry was a featured element on all of the Reno and Smiley recordings of this period, and he created many breathtaking instrumentals, including "Banjo Signal" and "Choking the Strings." Also a talented guitarist, Reno later recorded many fine guitar leads at the urging of King's Nathan, including the popular "Freight Train Boogie."

Finally, in October 1955, the duo formally reunited with a new band. In the Reno-and-Smiley lineup, Smiley sang baritone lead and played rhythm guitar while Reno sang tenor harmony and primarily played banjo, although he was also an excellent lead guitarist. Besides performing on the Roanoke-based "Old Dominion Barn Dance" radio show, they also began appearing on TV station WDBJ, filling the early morning "farm-and-feed" slot. The duo continued to be popular on the King label, as well as working the local Virginia country music market and the burgeoning bluegrass and folk-revival circuit of colleges, small festivals, and concert halls. The group was as famous for their comedy routines as their music, with Reno proving a natural comedian. In the early 1960s he brought in his young son Ronnie Reno, a mandolinist and guitarist, to join the band. In 1961 the band enjoyed a top-twenty country hit with "Don't Let Your Sweet Love Die," which had been recorded by Roy Hall some twenty years earlier.

However, Smiley began to suffer from complications of diabetes and was unhappy with the expanding touring schedule of the group. The duo broke up in 1964, with Smiley continuing to head a local band under the name of the Bluegrass Cut-Ups. Reno was without a band for a while and worked sessions until he teamed with singer-guitarist Bill Harrell in December 1966, a partnership that lasted a decade. The group was most popular on the bluegrass circuit, although Reno on his own had a fluke, minor country hit in the late 1960s with the patriotic tearjerker "A Soldier's Prayer in Viet Nam."

After Harrell and Reno split in late 1976, Reno relocated to Lynchburg, Virginia, bringing together his sons mandolinist Dale Reno and banjo-bass player Don Wayne Reno, along with fiddler Bonny Beverley, to form a new band. Older half brother Ronnie had left his father's employment in 1968 and worked as a Nashville-based session picker, although he occasionally returned to work with the new family band. Reno continued to perform despite declining health and died in Lynchburg. By this time the three Reno sons were reunited and kept the family band going, achieving some success on the bluegrass circuit and keeping their father's unique style alive.

• For additional information on Reno's life and career, see Don Reno, *The Musical History of Don Reno: His Life, His Songs* (1975); P. Kuykendall, "Don Reno and Red Smiley and the Tennessee Cutups," *Disc Collector*, no. 1 (n.d.): 18; and Bob Artis, *Bluegrass* (1975). Reno's contribution to bluegrass music is described in Bill Malone, *Country Music, USA*, 2d ed. (1975). Reno and Smiley's 115-track output for King records has been reissued in a collector's box set (Starday 7001), incorporating most of their best material from the early 1950s through the early 1960s.

RICHARD CARLIN

RENO, Jesse Lee (20 June 1823–14 Sept. 1862), soldier, was born in Wheeling, Virginia (now West Virginia), the son of Louis Reno and Rebecca Quinby. About 1832 his family moved to Venango County, Pennsylvania. In 1842 Reno received an appointment to the U.S. Military Academy at West Point. He graduated in 1846, along with classmates Thomas J. Jackson and George B. McClellan, ranking eighth in a class of fifty-nine. Posted to the artillery as a second lieutenant, he participated in the Mexican War, distinguishing himself at the battles of Cerro Gordo and Chapultapec, where he was wounded while commanding a battery. For his conduct he received the brevet ranks of first lieutenant and captain.

Reno subsequently rose slowly in rank, performing routine duty in a variety of posts. He served as an assistant professor of mathematics at West Point (1849) and on various ordnance boards (1849–1853). After his marriage to Mary Blanes Cross in November 1853, Reno served successively on the coastal survey (1854); on topographical duty in Minnesota (1854), where he assisted with the construction of a military road from the Big Sioux River to St. Paul; and at Frankfort Arsenal (1854–1857). In 1857 as a first lieutenant (rank dating from 1853), Reno joined General Albert Sidney Johnston's Utah Expedition as chief ordnance officer. After his return East in 1859 and promotion to captain in 1860, he commanded the Mount Vernon Arsenal in Alabama until its seizure by Alabama state forces in January 1861. He then superintended the arsenal at Fort Leavenworth until his recall to Washington, where he was commissioned brigadier general of volunteers on 12 November 1861.

After his appointment to brigade command in Brigadier General Ambrose E. Burnside's expeditionary force in December 1861, Reno participated in Burnside's successful North Carolina campaign (Jan.–July 1862). In February he performed capably in the capture of Roanoake Island, and in March played a prominent role in the battle of New Berne. On 19 April Reno superintended the Union victory at the engagement of South Mills, North Carolina. In August Reno received promotion to major general of volunteers and commanded troops of the Union Ninth Corps participating in the second Manassas campaign. In the debacle of 29–30 August at the second battle of Manassas, Reno calmly and efficiently covered the retreat of the

Union Army as it streamed back to Washington. Reno also commanded the field in the latter stages of the battle of Chantilly on 1 September.

Assuming command of the full Ninth Corps in early September, Reno joined the Army of the Potomac in its campaign to repel the first Confederate raid into Maryland. On 14 September 1862 Reno led his troops into the battle of South Mountain. While attempting to force a passage through Fox's Gap, he was mortally wounded. As he was carried to the rear, he yelled to a friend, "Hallo, Sam, I'm Dead! . . . Yes, yes, I'm dead—good by!" (*Harper's New Monthly Magazine*, Feb. 1868, p. 278). His body was returned to his wife's home in Boston, and he was buried at Trinity Church. His remains were later moved to Oak Hill Cemetery in Washington, D.C. Described by a fellow officer as "a short, stout man with a soldierly look" (Cecil Eby, ed., *A Virginia Yankee in the Civil War* [1961], p. 82), Reno provided capable but unspectacular performance at every rank and in each of his battles. The city of Reno, Nevada, is named after him.

• Scattered Civil War–period letters from Reno are found in the George Hay Stuart Papers, Library of Congress. A brief biography of Reno appears in William J. Bolton's "War Journal," Civil War Library and Museum, Philadelphia. See also George W. Cullum, *Biographical Register of the Officers and Graduates of the United States Military Academy at West Point, New York* (3 vols., 1879), and Ezra Warner, *Generals in Blue* (1964). Obituaries are in *Harper's Weekly Magazine*, 4 Oct. 1862; the *Boston Daily Advertiser*, 16 Sept. 1862; the *New York Tribune*, 16 Sept. 1862; and the *Albany Evening Journal*, 16 Sept. 1862.

JOHN HENNESSY

RENO, Milo (5 Jan. 1866–5 May 1936), farm leader, was born near Agency, Iowa, the son of John Reno and Elizabeth Barrice, farmers. He attended a one-room country school and then completed high school in Batavia, Iowa. In 1883 he married Christine Good. The couple had three children, but only one daughter survived to maturity. After drifting through a series of jobs from South Dakota to California, Reno studied for the ministry one winter. Although never ordained, he often delivered fiery sermons on social justice in country churches.

Reno joined the Grange, campaigned for the Union Labor party in 1888, and was active in organizing the National Farmers' Alliance in Iowa. He championed the Populists and ran unsuccessfully for the Iowa legislature. After the farm revolt of the 1890s declined, he quietly engaged in farming for the next two decades near Agency.

In 1918 Reno found a new cause in the National Farmers' Union (NFU), which had been founded in Texas in 1902. The Iowa union was chartered in 1917, and Reno soon joined. He was elected state secretary-treasurer in September 1920, just as commodity prices began a rapid decline from wartime highs. Shortly thereafter, as a delegate to the national convention of the NFU, Reno called for farmers to withhold their crops from market until prices reached the cost of production plus a reasonable profit. This would remain a central principle for the rest of his life.

Reno was elected president of the Iowa Farmers' Union in 1921. He retained that position until 1930 when he hand picked a successor. During the twenties he established several successful farmers' mutual insurance companies and livestock commission houses. At the same time, Reno continued his battle to improve farm incomes. In 1925 he issued a call that resulted in the formation of the Corn Belt Committee, a coalition of most major midwestern farm groups. Two years later the committee adopted Reno's proposal that if justice for farmers could not be achieved through legislation, then organized refusal to deliver goods would be justified.

Reno's supporters had proposed him for president of the NFU several times during the 1920s, but conservative elements deemed him too radical. He endorsed Alfred E. Smith for president in 1928, and, as the worldwide depression set in after 1930, many of his allies solicited his support for Franklin Roosevelt. But he refused to disguise his belief that both parties were corrupt and that farmers could win necessary changes only through direct action. He had become, as his friend the writer Dale Kramer later said, "a man of the barricades."

By the late winter of 1932 conditions for farmers had become severe. In various localities ad hoc groups rose up to block tax sales, foreclosures, and evictions. Reno would wait no longer for political action, and on 3 May he presided over a mass meeting in Des Moines that organized the National Farmers' Holiday Association. Reno chose the word holiday in conscious mockery of those who were declaring "bank holidays" in order to prevent runs on banks. By the end of a summer of organizing, Reno claimed to have some 180,000 pledges from farmers to "buy nothing, sell nothing, stay at home" until cost-of-production prices had been achieved for farm commodities. He called for peaceful action to begin on 8 August, but within a couple of days farmers in northwest Iowa had established picket camps on highways leading into Sioux City, a major commodities market. Their purpose was to inform drivers carrying farm goods to turn back. Within days, however, as blockade runners became more obstinate, picketers began to throw logs and other obstacles in front of speeding trucks. What had been intended as a peaceful holiday became a forceful strike that spread elsewhere in Iowa and into other states. By the end of August the strike had become front-page news in major newspapers.

Reno emerged as a national leader who voiced the desperation of millions of farmers. He recognized that the strike in itself would not bring major price increases, and he called a truce while midwestern governors met in September 1932 to discuss the problem. The governors, distracted by the general election, failed to agree on a program. Most were defeated in November. Reno, for his part, already had a more important goal in mind. As winter set in, a large percentage of farmers stood in danger of dispossession. Reno ordered members and friends of the Farmers' Holiday Association to block evictions. When millions of acres of land were threatened with tax sales early in 1933, determined bands of farmers gathered at courthouses and prevented bidding. Throughout the winter Farmers' Holiday Association councils arbitrated disputes over rents and mortgages wherever possible. When peaceful methods failed they used intimidation and force to break up foreclosure sales. They also resorted to what became known as "penny sales" when livestock and implements were being sold to satisfy a debt. They bid a few cents for each item, prevented others from bidding, and then gave the items back to the original owner. Mass marches on state legislatures forced passage of mortgage moratorium legislation.

Reno had hoped that Roosevelt's emergency session of Congress would pass cost-of-production legislation, but after nearly two months it seemed stalled. Violence flared again in northwest Iowa, where hotheads threatened to lynch a judge. A Farmers' Holiday Association convention threatened a new strike on 13 May. On 12 May Congress passed the Agricultural Adjustment Act, and although it did not propose the cost-of-production plan, Reno grudgingly accepted it and called off the strike. During the summer Reno was subdued as enemies forced his insurance company into reorganization, but by fall he was denouncing New Deal legislation. He believed that the nation's problem was not one of overproduction, but one of underconsumption caused by poor distribution and a deflated monetary system manipulated by the Federal Reserve Banks. Much of his ire was focused on a fellow Iowan, Secretary of Agriculture Henry A. Wallace, who seemed to dislike Reno as much as Reno disliked him. Reno proclaimed a new strike in October 1933, but it rapidly failed. A majority of farmers were willing to give the New Deal a chance to prove its mettle, particularly after it made cash payments to those who signed contracts pledging to cut their planted acreage in 1934. It amused Reno to bring in as speakers to his annual convention such New Deal foes as Father Charles E. Coughlin and Senator Huey Long. He remained staunchly devoted to democracy, however, and he viewed the rise of fascism and the prospect of war with abhorrence. Although he had earlier traded bitter insults with Communists, Reno cautiously sought rapprochement with rural Communists during the last months of his life, after the party began to pursue cooperation with all antifascist elements in its "popular front" period.

Milo Reno was a man of great energy and a passion for causes such as that of the small farmer. His philosophy was a mishmash of the Gospels, the Declaration of Independence, the French Revolution, and Edward Bellamy, the utopian socialist author. A rural newspaper once headlined a story recounting a speech, "Milo Reno in General Denunciation of Everything!" He sympathized with the underdog and fought for years to remove the prohibition against blacks in the NFU. He insisted on integrated meetings when he spoke in Mississippi. His greatest achievement undoubtedly was to bring national attention to the desperate plight of American farmers. But his unwillingness to recognize the positive features of the New Deal undermined his influence and his place in history. Milo Reno died in Excelsior Springs, Missouri.

• A small collection of Reno papers are in the University of Iowa Library, including his correspondence files for 1933 and a couple of recorded radio addresses. There is no adequate biography, but Roland A. White's hurried job, *Milo Reno: Farmers Union Pioneer* (1941), contains material not available elsewhere. See also Lowell K. Dyson, "The Farm Holiday Movement" (Ph.D. diss., Columbia Univ., 1968); John L. Shover, *Cornbelt Rebellion* (1965); William C. Pratt, "Rethinking the Farm Revolt of the 1930s," *Great Plains Quarterly* 8, no. 3 (1988): 131–44; and Michael W. Schuyler, "The Hair-Splitters: Reno and Wallace, 1932–1933," *Annals of Iowa* 43, no. 6 (1976): 403–29.

LOWELL K. DYSON

RENOIR, Jean (15 Sept. 1894–12 Feb. 1979), film director, novelist, and playwright, was born in Paris, France, the son of Pierre Auguste Renoir, an impressionist painter, and Aline Charigot. Raised in Paris and Provence, Renoir graduated college in 1913 and became a cavalry officer. With the outbreak of World War I, he went to the front as a second lieutenant, was wounded, and later served as an aerial reconnaissance pilot. Shortly after his father's death, in 1920 he married Andrée Heuschling, one of Pierre Auguste's models who soon after, as Catherine Hessling, became the star of Jean's earliest films. Renoir and Hessling had one child before they separated in the early 1930s.

For a few years, Renoir worked as a ceramicist, but his interest in films and filmmaking had been growing for some time. It was first sparked, as he recounts in *My Life and My Films* (1974), when he was recovering from his war wounds, and it was revived when he showed his father Charlie Chaplin films during his last illnesses. After a frustrating experience as the scriptwriter for *Une Vie Sans Joie*, directed by Albert Dieudonné and starring Hessling, Renoir wrote and directed his first film, *La Fille de l'Eau* (1924), financing it with the sale of several of his father's paintings. Renoir's film career was fully launched with *Nana* (1926), a lavish, Franco-German coproduction in which Hessling also starred.

Throughout his career Renoir constantly experimented with genres and styles, often within the same film. Equally fascinated by stylized sets and location shooting, he freely mingled artifice and realism in both his plots and his images. Even his work during the silent period was enormously varied, including literary adaptation (*Nana*), costume drama (*Le Tournoi* [1929]), social comedy (*Tire-au-Flanc* [1928]), historical epic (*Le Bled* [1929]), contemporary drama (*Marquitta* [1927]), and visual experiment (*Charleston* [1927], *The Little Match Girl* [1928]). By the end of the silent period he was considered too expensive a director to hire, and new projects had dried up. To demonstrate both his virtuosity with sound and his economical methods, he made the short film *On Purge Bébé* (1931), which took only five weeks to go from script-writing to breaking even. His extravagant reputation was effectively disposed of, and Renoir became one of the few French silent directors to make the transition to sound successfully.

The 1930s inaugurated what many critics believe to be the greatest period of his work. One critical cliché about Renoir's films associates them with the effusive natural benevolence of the dappled, rosy nudes of his father's late paintings. But in the 1930s, in both subject matter and pictorial style, they more closely resemble the harsh urban interiors of Toulouse-Lautrec or the shimmering uncertainties of Monet's gardens, bound together by a deep affinity for the Parisian street scene. Once, when asked what his favorite scent was, Renoir replied, "the smell of tar in Paris streets."

Once again, the film styles and genres that attracted him were extraordinarily varied, but throughout the films, even at their most comic and surreal, runs a pervasive attention to the details of a social reality that Renoir perceived with both irony and sympathy. As he explained, "I try to work close to nature—but nature is millions of things, and there are millions of ways of understanding its propositions." Perhaps the two most prominent of Renoir's films of the 1930s are *La Grande Illusion* (1937), set in a World War I prisoner of war camp, and *The Rules of the Game* (1939), which deals with a weekend party at a French Château.

But beyond these two acknowledged masterpieces, Renoir's films of the 1930s show a creative prescience that made him a great influence on other filmmakers. *La Chienne* (1931), the story of a meek clerk who kills his mistress, is a forerunner of the tales of betrayal that would preoccupy film noir fifteen years later. *La Nuit du Carrefour* (1932) exploits even more the shadows, mists, and water-slick streets of a detective thriller. *Boudu Saved from Drowning* (1932) highlights the anarchic character of a Parisian clochard, played by Michel Simon, and demonstrates another important element of Renoir's aesthetic: his acute interest in the energy and movement of performers. *Toni* (1935), set among Italian laborers in the south of France, presaged Italian neorealism by its use of natural settings and nonprofessional actors. One of the most intriguing, *The Crime of M. Lange* (1936), bears Renoir's name not only as director but also as a member of a radical culture collective, the Groupe Octobre. *Lange*'s comic story of a publishing cooperative, whose center is a meek young Frenchman who writes stories about an American West he has never seen, is an early version of the sometimes sardonic, sometimes affectionate view of popular culture that would inspire the New Wave directors in the late 1950s.

In one of the ironies of history, *The Rules of the Game*, which was fiercely picketed by right-wing French groups who considered it to be an insult to their patriotism, became after World War II an inspiration for the revival of the French film industry, especially with a younger generation of filmmakers committed to the film artist who both writes and directs (the auteur). Meanwhile, Renoir had left France, first to work briefly in Italy, and then to live in the United States, where he settled in a Beverly Hills home that resembled in architecture and setting his family's in Provence. In 1944 he married Dido Freire, a Brazilian whom he had met in the late 1930s. They had no children. Despite his weak English, Renoir soon made close friends in both the native and émigré Hollywood communities. Rejecting studio efforts to typecast him as a director of "foreign" films, he sought American subjects instead, most strikingly in *Swamp Water* (1941) and *The Southerner* (1945).

With the war's end, and after five American films, Renoir went to India to make *The River* (1950) and then returned to Europe for the rest of his filmmaking career. Increasingly, he also branched out into theatrical directing as well as into the writing of plays and novels, in addition to making films such as *The Golden Coach* (1953), *French Cancan* (1955), and *Elena et les Hommes* (1956). In 1959, following his interest in new forms, he made two films for television, *Le Testament du Dr. Cordelier*, a modernized version of Jekyll and Hyde, and *Picnic on the Grass*, a tribute to the sunny world of Provence. *The Elusive Corporal* (1962), set in World War II, returned to some of the situations of *La Grande Illusion*, but with a decidedly modern sensibility. In 1962 Renoir also published a memoir of his father. He died in Beverly Hills and is buried in Essoyes, France.

Despite his commitment to the auteur director, Renoir himself acted as well, notably in *Rules of the Game*. Similarly, from his earliest films his camera plays the role of an observer within the scene rather than a Godlike eye above it. As he often remarked, "One discovers the contents of a film only in the process of making it." Appropriately enough, in the final film of his career of thirty-six films made in four countries over the span of nearly fifty years, Renoir in 1969 appeared as the narrator in *The Little Theatre of Jean Renoir*, an anthology of three stories and a song, demonstrating one final time his fascination with the infinite variety of film possibility.

• Renoir's *My Life and My Films* is the basic biographical text, as are the letters contained in *Lettres d'Amérique* (1984) and *Letters* (1994). *Ecrits, 1926–1971* (1974) and *Oeuvres de cinéma inedites* (1981) collect much unpublished writing, while *Jean Renoir: Entretiens et Propos* (1979) contains the texts of several print and television interviews. Two recent biographies are Ronald Bergan, *Jean Renoir: Projections of Paradise* (1992), and Célia Bertin, *Jean Renoir: A Life in Pictures* (1991). For further bibliographic and archival material see Christopher Faulkner, *Jean Renoir: A Guide to References and Resources* (1979). Among the many critical works on Renoir are Pierre Leprohon, *Jean Renoir* (1967); André Bazin, *Jean Renoir* (collected by François Truffaut, 1971); Leo Braudy, *Jean Renoir: The World of His Films* (1972); Raymond Durgnat, *Jean Renoir* (1974); Claude Beylie, *Jean Renoir: Le spectacle, la vie* (1975); Alexander Sesonske, *Jean Renoir: The French Films, 1924–1939* (1980); Claude Gauteur, *Jean Renoir: La Double Méprise, 1924–1939* (1980); Daniel Serceau, *Jean Renoir, l'Insurgé* (1981); and Christopher Faulkner, *The Social Cinema of Jean Renoir* (1986). An obituary is in the *New York Times*, 14 Feb. 1979.

LEO BRAUDY

RENSSELAER. *See* Van (*or* van) Rensselaer.

RENWICK, Edward Sabine (3 Jan. 1823–19 Mar. 1912), engineer, inventor, and patent expert, was born in New York City, the son of James Renwick and Margaret Anne Brevoort. James Renwick was an eminent teacher, engineer, and writer whose career was closely tied with the early history of Columbia University. Edward had two older brothers, Henry Brevoort Renwick, who also became an engineer and patent expert, and James Renwick, Jr., who became a world-famous architect. Edward Renwick attended school in New York and, at the age of thirteen, entered Columbia College, where he was the youngest in his class. He received an A.B. in 1839 and stayed on to receive an A.M. in 1842.

After graduation, Renwick became an assistant and bookkeeper to the superintendent of the New Jersey Iron Company at Boonton, New Jersey. In 1844 he was hired to examine and report on some mining properties in Maryland. In the process of preparing his report he traveled to England and Wales. While there he visited several of the better iron works. Upon his return to the United States, in the fall of 1845, Renwick became superintendent of the Wyoming Iron Works in Wilkes-Barre, Pennsylvania. The works were comprised of a merchant mill for rolling bars, a sheet mill for rods and hoops, and a nail factory. He later added a small blast furnace and began the production of pig-iron. All of these experiences helped him in his future career as an inventor and patent expert.

In 1849 Renwick went to Washington, D.C., as a solicitor of patents and an expert in patent cases in the U.S. courts. While he was in Washington he associated himself with Peter H. Watson, who later became assistant secretary of war under Edwin M. Stanton during the Abraham Lincoln administration. While establishing himself as a patent expert, Renwick worked on several inventions in conjunction with Watson. Most important was a design for the original self-binding reaper (U.S. Patent 8,083, 13 May 1851), which cut the grain, gathered it in gavels, compressed it, and bound it with wire or twine. Although he never executed the design, his ideas were widely used by manufacturers of harvesting machines after his patent expired. He subsequently secured, over the course of his life, around twenty-five patents, ranging from a wrought-iron railway chair for holding rails to the cross-ties to a steam valve (U.S. Patent 1576, 19 Aug. 1856), a tumbler lock, a domestic furnace grate, and a breech-loading firearm.

In 1855 Renwick moved back to New York, opened his own office as a patent expert, and served as consulting engineer to Harrison Gray Dyer, who was then acting as president of the New York & New Haven Railroad. After the resignation of Dyer, Renwick devoted himself full time to the practice of consulting engineer and patent expert. In 1862 he married Elizabeth Alice Brevoort, his second cousin; they had three children.

Also in 1862, in conjunction with his brother Henry Brevoort Renwick, he performed one of the more remarkable engineering feats of the period: the repair of the *Great Eastern* steamer while afloat. The *Great Eastern* was an enormous iron ship constructed in England by the great English engineer I. K. Brunel. Launched in England in 1858, it was 693 feet long, had a beam of 120 feet, and a draft of 26 feet. On 27 August 1862, off Montauk Point, New York, an 83-foot-long hole was ripped in her flat bottom, near the turning of the starboard bilge keel. With the help of his brother Henry, Renwick offered to repair the ship under water, on "salve and pay." This meant that if they did not succeed, there would be no charge. Their offer was accepted. They built a cofferdam of wood, 102 feet long and 16 feet wide, and fitted it over the hole. After the water was pumped from the vessel, they were able to repair the damage from inside the double hull. The repairs remained sound for the rest of the life of the ship.

From 1865 on, Renwick was almost in constant demand as an expert in patent cases. Many of the cases were long and tedious. In one case his cross-examination lasted twenty-one days, in another the cross-examination, by the complainant's counsel, was carried on in sessions of one to three days, separated by intervals, over six months, for a total of twenty-two days. The case was finally compromised for $15.00. Another, the Leffel waterwheel case, was the longest, with the cross-examination lasting thirty-five days.

Renwick's interest in his own inventions did not lag over the years. Many of his ideas were well in advance of the then current technology. For example, in 1868 he received a patent for a balanced-compound steam engine and a system of encasing that portion of the shaft of a twin propeller, which extends beyond the vessel, with a casing of sufficient size to permit this portion of the shaft to be inspected to the stern bearing. Such a system was not utilized by steamship builders until nearly the turn of the century.

Even more indicative of Renwick's broad interests and ability to patent needed inventions was his work between 1877 and 1886, when he was granted ten patents on incubators and chicken brooders. In 1883 he wrote *The Thermostatic Incubator: Its Construction and Management*, which became the foundation of today's poultry industry.

In 1893 Renwick published *Patentable Invention*, in which he endeavored to present an inventor's views of the rules of the courts regarding inventions. In its preface he listed as his qualifications as an expert witness his practice as a Solicitor of Patents, and as Expert in patent cases for forty-three years, and his engagement as Expert in probably a greater number of patent suits than it has fallen to the lot of any other expert to have been connected with, has brought him into intimate relations with inventors; and besides, he is an inventor himself, one of the inventions in which he was concerned, the original self binding harvester (patented to Watson, Renwick & Watson, May 13, 1851, and to Watson & Renwick, August 16, 1853) of which he was a joint and principal inventor, being of such importance that the present grain crops in the United States could not be harvested without its use.

Renwick was a member of the American Chemical Society, the Engineers Club, the Union Club, the New York Yacht Club, the St. Nicholas Society, the Metropolitan Museum of Art, and American Museum of Natural History, among other organizations. He died in Short Hills, New Jersey.

• Records of some of Renwick's patents and cases are in various Patent Office reports. A review of his illustrious family and its background is H. H. McIver, *Genealogy of the Renwick Family* (1924). The best contemporary review of Renwick's career is in the *National Cyclopaedia of American Biography* vol. 11 (1901), pp. 102–3. One of the best tributes after his death appeared in the *Transactions of the American Society of Mechanical Engineers* 34 (1912): 1438–39. An obituary is in the *New York Times*, 21 Mar. 1912.

ROBERT J. HAVLIK

RENWICK, James (30 May 1792–12 Jan. 1863), engineer and educator, was born in Liverpool, England, the son of William Renwick, a manufacturer, and Jean Jeffrey, who in her youth had inspired some poems of Robert Burns. In 1794 the family moved to New York City, where Renwick grew up in the highest social circles; Washington Irving and Henry Brevoort were his close friends. Renwick attended Columbia College and received a classical and scientific education. He graduated in 1807 at the top of his class and obtained his A.M. in 1810. Renwick's scientific talent was apparent by 1812, when he started teaching natural philosophy courses at Columbia. In 1814 he obtained a commission as a major in the U.S. Army and served as a topographical engineer. Following the War of 1812 he traveled with Washington Irving to Europe; Irving noted that Renwick's knowledge made travel books unnecessary. Renwick married Margaret Anne Brevoort, Henry's sister, in 1816; they had a daughter and three sons.

In 1817 Renwick was appointed colonel of engineers in the New York state militia and a trustee of Columbia College, but he supported his growing family by attempting to run his late father's business. Following the Panic of 1819 this enterprise failed, and Renwick had to move his family into his father-in-law's residence while searching for new employment. His misfortune was short-lived: in 1820 he received a faculty appointment at Columbia College in natural philosophy and experimental chemistry.

Renwick focused his subsequent career at Columbia on disseminating and applying scientific knowledge of direct economic relevance for the early American republic. In addition to educating students, he served as a scientific consultant on numerous engineering projects and brought in new scientific knowledge through editing and writing.

Renwick dominated Columbia College's science program. In addition to engineering mechanics courses, he taught up-to-date classes in chemistry, physics, mineralogy, and geology. He was the first to provide American university students with significant laboratory experience in electricity and magnetism as well as in chemistry. The success of this curriculum is evidenced by the careers of its students: Horatio Allen became a pioneering railroad engineer, Alfred Craven a hydraulic engineer, William Mitchell Gillespie the first professor of civil engineering at Union College, and Oliver Wolcott Gibbs emerged a leading chemist. Nonetheless Renwick failed to institutionalize science at Columbia. At the time of his retirement, he and a minor mathematician remained the only members of the science faculty. Only after the Civil War did Columbia College's trustees succeed in filling the gap by establishing the School of Mines.

Renwick contributed to critical engineering developments, including canal and railroad construction. In 1826 the Delaware and Hudson Canal Company hired him to verify John Jervis's plans for linking those rivers, and he caught Jervis's design errors in the inclined-plane system used for elevating canal boats. Renwick patented an improved version of this mechanism in 1813, for which he received the Franklin Institute's Silver Medal in 1826. As a consultant for New York State in 1827, he also worked on weights and measures issues. During the 1830s the U.S. government received Renwick's recommendations on a proposed site for the Bergen Naval Yard and on innovations for preventing boiler explosions. They also commissioned him to help survey the disputed boundary between New Brunswick and Maine. Following this topographical project, Renwick assisted with the Webster-Ashburton Treaty of 1842 through his correspondence with Sir Edward Sabine. Other projects included hydraulic investigations for an association of Rochester millers and evaluating Jervis's design proposals for the Mohawk and Hudson Railroad Company. The success of such work gave Renwick a reputation for resolving the most demanding engineering-science issues of his era. At the height of his career, few engineering projects of significance were executed without consulting him.

Although Renwick did not engage in significant basic research, his scientific publishing output was extensive. He translated H. Lallemand's *Treatise on Artillery* (1820) and edited Samuel Parke's *Rudiments of Chemistry* (1824), *Lardner's Popular Lectures on the Steam Engine* (1828), J. Frederick Daniell's *Chemical Philosophy* (1840), and Henry Moseley's *Illustrations of Practical Mechanics* (1844). Renwick's original work included the first full treatise on natural philosophy published in the United States, *Outlines of Natural Philosophy* (2 vols., 1822–1823), as well as the scientific and historical *Treatise on the Steam Engine* (1830), the calculus-based *Elements of Mechanics* (1832), and the popular *Applications of the Science of Mechanics to Practical Purposes* (1842). For his students, he privately published *First Principles in Chemistry* and *Outlines of Geology* (both 1838). Renwick disclosed his political interests in articles for the *New York Review*, the *American Whig Review*, and the *American Quarterly Review*, and wrote biographies of DeWitt Clinton, John Jay, and Alexander Hamilton. Renwick became Columbia's first emeritus professor following his retirement in 1853. He was also a member of the American Academy of Arts and Sciences. His death probably occurred in New York City.

• The Renwick Family Papers are in the Columbia University Library. For biographical references, see Stanley M. Guralnick, *Science and the Antebellum American College* (1975), pp. 205–6; J. K. Finch, *Early Columbia Engineers* (1929); Horace Coon, *Columbia: Colossus on the Hudson*; and Robert V. Bruce, *The Launching of American Science* (1987). F. Daniel Larkin, *John B. Jervis* (1990), and Daniel Hovey Calhoun, *The American Civil Engineer* (1960), shed light on Renwick's consulting career. Edwin Layton evaluated the historical relevance of Renwick's mechanics texts in "Mirror Image Twins: The Communities of Science and Technology in 19th-Century America," *Technology and Culture* 12, (1971): 565–67. Descriptions of Renwick's inclined plane invention are in the *Franklin Journal and American Mechanics Magazine*, Nov. and Dec. 1826. For insights into Renwick's dynamic character see George S. Hellman, ed., *Letters of Washington Irving to Henry Brevoort* (2 vols., 1915). An obituary is in the *New York Times*, 14 Jan. 1863.

BRETT D. STEELE

RENWICK, James, Jr. (1 Nov. 1818–23 June 1895), architect and engineer, was born in Bloomingdale, New York, the son of Margaret Brevoort, who came from a well-established New York family, and James Renwick, a distinguished engineer and professor of natural philosophy at Columbia College (now Columbia University). In this literate, socially prominent family, advanced education was assumed. James entered Columbia at the age of twelve and graduated in 1836; three years later he received an M.A. In 1851 he enhanced his enviable position by marrying Anna Lloyd Aspinwall, the daughter of one of the wealthiest men in the country. They never had any children.

Renwick had no professional training as an architect, nor did he serve an apprenticeship in an architect's office. His knowledge of architecture came to him through his father, who combined engineering with broad cultural interests that included architectural history; above all, he was an able water colorist with demonstrable skill in architectural design. Guided by his father and nurtured by his academic environment, Renwick acquired intellectual strengths and cultural and social advantages that were unmatched by any other American architect of his generation.

Renwick developed four special attributes as an architect. First, his knowledge of historical architecture was broad and detailed and, since he worked at a time when eclecticism was the dominant mode of design, that knowledge proved to be a rich functional resource. Second, he had the artistic talent to energize his extensive knowledge by coherent but expressive designing. Third, he was trained as an engineer and thus was alert to developments in building technology. Finally, his finely tuned social and cultural sensibilities made him responsive to the most sophisticated of his clients' needs. At the start of his career, American architecture was struggling to establish its identity as a mature profession with its own national character, and Renwick's pragmatic vision and highly trained intelligence put him in the mainstream of that effort.

For half a century Renwick produced religious, public, institutional, commercial, and domestic works of distinction, some so innovative as to be in the vanguard of the most important architectural developments of his time. His achievement can be characterized by a few of his most prominent works, beginning with his first commission. In 1843 he won the competition for Grace Church, the wealthiest and most fashionable Episcopal parish in New York City. Renwick's design was an inspired mix of English Gothic elements that was precisely what the church authorities then recognized as the only appropriate form for Episcopal church architecture. An informed essay in Gothic authenticity, it stands together with Richard Upjohn's Trinity Church (begun in 1841) at the beginning of a wholly new episode in the American Gothic revival.

Renwick's informed eclecticism made it natural for him to use historical style as a means of expression, as he did in his Congregational Church of the Puritans on Union Square in New York, commissioned in 1846. The Congregationalists, in order to be competitive in an expanding nation, deliberately abandoned their traditional classical meetinghouse in favor of a more dynamic architectural image, which they found in the Romanesque. The Church of the Puritans was among the first to be cast in this new mode, and thus Renwick again proved to be an innovator in a movement that would become national in scope.

Beyond this seminal building, Renwick turned to the Romanesque in a variety of churches and other building types, including the most demanding and influential commission of his career, the Smithsonian Institution in Washington, D.C. Devoted to the "increase and diffusion of knowledge among men," the Smithsonian was a new and challenging concept in the developing national culture. A competition for the design of its building was announced in September 1846, and through the help of his father the young architect was invited to compete. His design was chosen by the board of regents because his intellectual and cultural sophistication made it possible for him to understand better than any of the competing architects the complex nature of the regents' demands. The various components of his asymmetrical design, the first of its kind in the United States, were shaped and arranged according to function, and by subtle modulations of massing, proportion, and ornamental treatment, each part was made expressive of its function. To make the building "as nearly as possible fireproof," Renwick recommended for the most vulnerable areas a British technique of cast-iron beams with segmental brick vaults sprung between. A section of that structural method still remains in the lower part of the great west tower as the first application of the new technique to a major building in Washington. To meet the regents' final condition, Renwick's design was in "the Lombard (Romanesque) style, as it prevailed in Germany, Normandy, and in southern Europe in the twelfth century." Functionally conceived and richly orchestrated in the dark, vibrant tones of red sandstone, the expressive ensemble of the Smithsonian Institution was an aggressive challenge to Washington's entrenched classicism and opened the way for new directions in American architecture.

Of his many Gothic churches, the one that best reveals Renwick as an architect is St. Patrick's Cathedral in New York. Begun in 1853 and widely regarded as Renwick's finest achievement, the church was conceived of by the ambitious Archbishop John Hughes not only as the center of the "ancient and glorious Catholic" faith in New York but also as "worthy, as a public architectural monument, of the present and prospective crown" of the nation as a whole. Renwick gave the archbishop the largest, most sophisticated Gothic church that had yet been designed by an American-born architect. Based largely on the cathedral at Cologne but with sensitively interwoven French and English elements, the original design was a masterpiece of intelligent eclecticism; if it had been built as originally designed, it would have been one of the most advanced Gothic revival churches in the Western world. Unfortunately, for reasons beyond Renwick's control, radical changes had to be made, and the church that materialized was but a shadow of his brilliant conception. The superb vaults, however, though built in plaster rather than the specified stone, were completed as designed and still form, visually at least, one of the most moving Gothic spaces in America.

Renwick's command of historical styles also made him a leader in the introduction of the Second Empire style into the United States. Inspired by the additions to the Louvre in Paris by Visconti and Lefuel (1852–1857) and characterized by steeply pitched mansard roofs and a richly plastic treatment of classical details, it was an extravagant mode that would dominate American public and domestic architecture of the 1860s and 1870s. Renwick's Corcoran Gallery (1859–1871) in Washington was the first public building in the United States in which both the elements and the energy of this monumental style were persuasively displayed. Renwick's design was based directly on the new Louvre, but it was more prim than its grandiose Parisian model, it was built not of stone but of brick, a traditional American material that was then regaining popularity for institutional buildings.

Always alert to the changing directions of American architecture, Renwick also designed buildings in the high Victorian Gothic style, a mode popularized by the English critic John Ruskin. This style came to dominate American church architecture of the 1860s and 1870s and vied in popularity with the Second Empire in other forms of public building. Although Renwick cannot be said to have been a leader in this movement, he did design in the style with the same authority and imagination that he displayed in his handling of his earlier Gothic buildings. His most distinguished work in this mode was All Saints' Roman Catholic Church in Harlem (1882–1893), remarkable for the richness of its polychromy.

Renwick's intellectual approach to architecture placed him squarely in the line of descent between Thomas Jefferson and Richard Morris Hunt. All three were highly educated men whose works were born of a profound knowledge of historical architecture. It is poignantly appropriate, therefore, that Renwick's last project would link him directly with his luminous forebear. In 1890 he was commissioned to prepare the plans for the National Galleries of History and Art in Washington. Conceived by the visionary amateur architect Franklin Webster Smith, this monumental axial scheme was a grandiloquent mirror image of Jefferson's design for the University of Virginia. The project was never built, but by participating in its planning the aging Renwick had a final opportunity to address himself to the shaping of the nation's cultural identity. Inherited from Jefferson, this was the driving force that energized his entire creative life. Renwick died in New York City in his home at 28 University Place, a building he had designed and which had been his residence for many years.

• A considerable number of Renwick drawings are to be found in the archives of the Avery Architectural and Fine Arts Library at Columbia University; the Library of Congress; the New-York Historical Society; the Roman Catholic Diocese of New York; and the Smithsonian Institution. No definitive study of the life and work of James Renwick, Jr., has yet been published. The best account to date is that of Selma Rattner in the *Macmillan Encyclopedia of Architects* (1982). Five other published works are useful: Kenneth Hafertepe, *America's Castle: The Evolution of the Smithsonian Building and Its Institution, 1840–1878* (1984); Rosalie Thorne McKenna, "James Renwick, Jr., and the Second Empire Style in the United States," *Magazine of Art* 44 (1951): 97–101; William H. Pierson, Jr., "James Renwick, St. Patrick's Cathedral, and the Continental Gothic Revival," *American Buildings and their Architects: Technology and the Picturesque, the Corporate and Early Gothic Styles* (1978); and Bannon McHenry, "James Renwick, Jr.: Institutional Architect in New York," *Newsletter*, Preservation League of New York (Winter 1987). In addition, Rattner lists several unpublished theses on Renwick in her *Macmillan Encyclopedia* entry. An obituary is in the *New-York Daily Tribune*, 25 June 1895.

WILLIAM H. PIERSON, JR.

REPPLIER, Agnes (1 Apr. 1855–15 Dec. 1950), essayist, was born in Philadelphia, Pennsylvania, the daughter of John George Repplier, a coal retailer, and Agnes Mathias. Repplier cared about words. Although she reportedly could not read until almost ten years old and was expelled from two schools for refusing to conform to discipline (in one case refusing to read a book she considered stupid), her recalcitrance seemed to stem more from an innate sense of taste and a distinct taste for mischief than from any opposition to learning. In her essay "Woman Enthroned" (from *Points of Friction* [1920]), she wrote, "it is awkward to be relegated to the angelic class, and to feel that one does not fit." Repplier did not fit the good student image, yet she read voraciously, started writing early, and became one of the best-known essayists of her time. She lived her entire life in Philadelphia, leaving only to lecture, visit friends, or vacation in Europe, sometimes for extended periods. She never married and never held a salaried job, but when Repplier was sixteen years old, her formerly wealthy father suffered financial setbacks and, urged on by a rather demanding mother, Repplier helped to support herself and her family by writing literary, often humorous, essays about her responses to the world around her. She was to continue helping family members financially for the rest of her life and reportedly left an estate valued at $100,000 when she died. Her writing was encouraged by Agnes Irwin, director of the second school to expel Repplier and later a dean at Radcliffe, and by her girlhood companion, Elizabeth Robins, who later married artist Joseph Pennell and herself became a well-known writer.

Repplier's first markets were Philadelphia newspapers, particularly the *Sunday News*. From there, she moved to the *Catholic World* magazine, who paid her fifty dollars for her first article ("In Arcady") in January 1881. In August 1882, when Repplier's mother died of cancer, the author wrote, "My mother, who pushed me steadily on, died before anything was gained; and nothing has been the same to me since, because no one cared as she cared." In spite of this setback, Repplier continued to publish regularly in *Catholic World*, and in April 1886, at the age of thirty-one, she finally achieved her goal of publishing an article ("Children, Past and Present") in the *Atlantic Monthly*. This began a long relationship between the esteemed magazine and the talented essayist. It also opened up a new world of correspondence and meetings with other intellectuals, of travel and friendships. She met the famous poets John Greenleaf Whittier and James Russell Lowell as well as such other female writers as Sarah Orne Jewett and Mary Wilkins Freeman. She spent time with Walt Whitman, who, according to biographer George Stewart Stokes, "served Miss Repplier whiskey in a china toothbrush mug. She drank it heroically." A thin, chain-smoking woman without benefit of physical beauty, the essayist charmed with her quick mind and good humor. These helped her establish longtime friendships with Shakespearean scholar Horace Howard Furman and English essayist Andrew Lang, among others. Most of Repplier's relationships and interests centered on literature. This was enough for Repplier, who once said, "My niche may be very small, but I made it by myself."

Repplier's father died in 1888, and a need for money may have given her the impetus to offer her first essay collection for publication. *Books and Men* appeared in October of 1888 and eventually went into twenty editions. In 1890 Repplier gave the first in a long career of public lectures during the season of Lent, when she figured "people will have nothing better to do with their time than to come to hear me." In fact, she was a popular speaker because of her wideranging knowledge, brilliant language, and infectious sense of humor. Lecturing did not slow down her literary output. A remarkable series of published essay collections were praised by her contemporaries for their elegant phrasing. Her essays were meticulously writ-

ten, and her approach, although not scholarly, was well informed. These collections were interspersed with four biographies. The first of these, published in 1919, paid tribute to J. William White, M.D., the doctor who had operated on Repplier's cancer and whom she credited with saving her life. The other biographies focused on important figures in the history of the Catholic Church (*Père Marquette* [1929], *Mère Marie of the Ursulines* [1931], and *Junípero Serra* [1933]). Her only autobiographical writings were *Our Convent Days* (1905), a charmingly funny account of her first school experience that reads like humorous fiction and is rich in character development and twists of plot, and *Eight Decades* (1937).

Although her reputation has dimmed over time, Repplier was much admired during her lifetime for her gaiety and her polished prose. She was one of the first women offered membership in the National Institute of Arts and Letters. Mary Ellen Chase called her "the dean of American essayists." Repplier's subjects ranged widely, including everything from war policy to cats. She wrote an entire collection on the benefits of drinking tea (*To Think of Tea!* [1932]), which one reader called "a sheer delight. It is compact with learning and wisdom—which is not the same thing—and it is ironical and witty." Her essay "Woman Enthroned" argues that women can vote as sensibly as men. Repplier wrote, "No sane woman believes that women, as a body, will vote more honestly than men; but no sane man believes that they will vote less honestly. . . . They are neither the repositories of wisdom, nor the final word of folly." She opposed zealotry in all forms, including feminist activism, but through her words and her ability to earn a living by them, she proved that women can equal men.

Repplier continued writing for publication until 1940 when she was eighty-five years old. She died in Philadelphia. Although now virtually forgotten, Repplier was a well-known and highly esteemed writer in the late nineteenth and early twentieth centuries. Witty and prolific, she created work that invites review by modern critics.

• Repplier's manuscripts and correspondence are collected in the library of the University of Pennsylvania and at the American Institute of Arts and Letters. The University of Pennsylvania also holds two of her journals, a bibliography of her works for periodicals, and reviews. Besides the works discussed in the text, Repplier published *Points of View* (1889 or 1891), *Essays in Miniature* (1892), *Essays in Idleness* (1893), *In the Dozy Hours* (1894), *Varia* (1897), *The Fireside Sphinx* (1901), *Philadelphia: The Place and the People* (1901), *Compromises* (1904), *A Happy Half-Century* (1908), *Americans and Others* (1912), *The Cat* (1912), *Counter Currents* (1915), *Under Dispute* (1924), and, with J. W. White, *Germany and Democracy* (1914). Two biographies worth consulting are George Stewart Stokes, *Agnes Repplier: Lady of Letters* (1949), and Emma Repplier Witmer, *Agnes Repplier: A Memoir* (1957). Repplier receives significant attention in Nancy Walker and Zita Dresner, *Redressing the Imbalance: American Women's*

Literary Humor from Colonial Times to the 1980s (1988). Extensive obituaries are in the *New York Times* and the *Philadelphia Inquirer*, 16 Dec. 1950.

ELAINE FREDERICKSEN

REQUIER, Augustus Julian (27 May 1825–19 Mar. 1887), poet and lawyer, was born in Charleston, South Carolina. His parents (names unknown) were French; his maternal grandfather had been a planter in Haiti, and his father had emigrated from Marseilles. He received a classical education in Charleston; he then studied law and was admitted to the bar in Charleston in 1844. *The Spanish Exile* (1842), a blank-verse drama, was Requier's first published work and was performed on the stage. *The Old Sanctuary*, a romance set in South Carolina before the revolutionary war, was published in 1846. Around that time, Requier was living in Marion, South Carolina, where while trying to develop a law practice, he worked as editor of the *Marion Star*. During his years in Marion Requier married Mary Elizabeth Evans, who apparently predeceased him. He was married a second time, reportedly to a woman from Charleston. Both marriages were childless.

Although Requier wrote drama, essays, and fiction, his primary literary interest was poetry. In 1860 Requier published a collection entitled *Poems*; some of the more popular verses in this collection are "Marco Bozzaris," "The Dial Plate," "The Charm," and "The Image." In 1862, he published *Ode to Shakespeare*, a poem in which he praises the Elizabethan dramatist. It begins:

> He went forth into Nature and he sung,
> Her grandest terrors and her simplest themes,
> The torrent by the beetling crag o'erhung,
> And the wild-daisy on its brink that gleams
> Unharmed, and lifts a dew-drop to the sun!

It later continues:

> Bard, priest, evangelist! from rarest cells
> Of riches inexhaustible he took
> The potent ring of her profoundest spells,
> And wrote great Nature's Book!

The poem ends with the assurance that Shakespeare's name would remain immortal.

Requier's longest poem, *Crystalline*, reflects Swedenborgian philosophy. Developed by the Swedish scientist, philosopher, and theologian Emanuel Swedenborg, the theory distinguishes three spheres (divine mind, spiritual world, and natural world) that correspond to degrees of being in God and in humanity (love, wisdom, and use). Unification with each degree takes place through devotion to it, and a person is believed able to obtain union with creator and creation, a goal that is each person's destiny. In *Crystalline*, a young, atheistic artist is converted to Christianity. At the end of a discussion in the opening scene, the artist announces to an old hermit (the family's attaché who gave the artist religious instruction years before):

> There is no super-terrestrial sphere,
> Where the Dead shall arise, and reappear
> In the bosom of Him who placed them here.
> I hate the fanatic, and scorn the lie,
> That madly peoples a vacant sky;
> And brand the whole mysterious scheme
> A coward's hope and an idiot's dream!

However, by the end of the poem, the artist is converted to Christianity, and the hermit tells him:

> So, saved by His redeeming grace
> From that serpent's slimy trace,
> With His glory on thy face,
> Live, for thou art born to be
> Heir of His immortality.

In *The Legend of Tremaine* (1864), a sample of Requier's romanticism, the Lady Violet of Tremaine devotes herself to liberating from enchantment the Knight Ivor, her lover who is trapped in a cave guarded by a monster; Lady Violet succeeds at her task, and the two live happily ever after. Requier also wrote war poetry during and after the Civil War. His best-known war poem, "Ashes of Glory," represents a sorrowful South after suffering defeat.

As a lawyer, Requier won distinction while practicing law in Mobile, Alabama, where he had settled in 1850. He was appointed U.S. district attorney for Alabama by President Franklin Pierce in 1853. President James Buchanan renewed the appointment, and Requier held the position for a total of eight years. He was a superior court judge when Alabama seceded from the Union, and newly elected Confederate president Jefferson Davis appointed Requier to serve as district attorney for the Confederacy. In 1866 he moved to New York City, where he practiced law and, for a time, served as assistant district attorney. He died in New York City.

• Requier's other poems include "Clouds in the West," "Ode to Victory," and "Baby Zulma's Christmas Carol." James Wood Davidson, *Living Writers of the South* (1869), includes a discussion of some of Requier's poems. The *Library of Southern Literature*, vol. 10 (1909), also includes a discussion of Requier and his work.

SANDRA M. GRAYSON

RESE, Frederic (6 Feb. 1791–30 Dec. 1871), Roman Catholic missionary and bishop, was born in Vienenburg, Hanover, the son of John Gotfried Reese and Caroline Alrutz. In later life Rese altered the spelling of the family name, evidently so as to approximate its German pronunciation, which was *ray-zay*; Rese himself spelled the name with two grave accents, but contemporary documents nearly always omit them. Rese and his siblings were orphaned early, and Frederic was apprenticed to a tailor. He subsequently traveled as a journeyman. He joined a cavalry regiment in 1813 and fought during the War of Liberation under Gebhard Leberecht von Blücher at Waterloo.

Anxious to become a priest despite his scanty education, Rese presented himself to the College of the Propaganda at Rome as a candidate for the foreign missions and was accepted as a student in 1816. He was ordained a priest on 15 March 1823. After brief service in Africa, he returned to Rome for reasons of health and there met Cincinnati's Bishop Edward Fenwick. Fenwick needed a German-speaking priest for his diocese, and Rese accompanied him to the United States in the fall of 1824. He was a successful pastor to Cincinnati's German Catholics and an occasional itinerant missionary to German-speaking Catholics in the Cincinnati hinterland. He showed administrative aptitude, too, serving first as Fenwick's secretary and then as his vicar general. In this latter capacity he made two trips to Europe, in 1827 and again in 1829, recruiting clergy, raising funds, and tending to personal business for his bishop. In the course of his 1827 travels, he was instrumental in the formation of the Leopoldine Foundation in Vienna, a society dedicated to the support of Catholic missions in North America. He also traveled for Fenwick within the then-vast Diocese of Cincinnati, visiting missions as distant as Green Bay and Sault Ste. Marie in 1830.

Rese was named administrator of the Cincinnati diocese in December 1832, shortly after the death of Bishop Fenwick, and was named first bishop of Detroit on 8 March 1833. Bishop Fenwick had recommended him for this latter position, aware that a new diocese was about to be formed in the soon to be states of Michigan and Wisconsin. Rese was ordained a bishop on 6 October 1833 in the cathedral at Cincinnati and traveled to Detroit in January 1834. He thus became the first German-born bishop to serve in the United States.

Rese's new diocese was poor both in resources and in Catholic population. Though he had evidently hoped to be made bishop of the more prosperous and prestigious Diocese of Cincinnati, he nonetheless embarked on his Detroit career with energy and enthusiasm. He made a partial visitation of the diocese in 1834 and probably in each of the next four years, though almost no records of his Detroit years have survived. He brought the Poor Clares to Detroit to open what became a fashionable convent school, founded a classical academy for boys and St. Philip Neri's College, renovated the modest cathedral, and purchased a church for Detroit's growing number of Irish Catholics. He raised funds in Europe for his impoverished diocese and recruited additional priests, raising the number of his clergy to a record twenty-two. He even laid plans for a diocesan paper.

Despite its energetic beginnings, the Rese episcopate was soon in crisis. The reasons for this cannot be determined from the extant record, though it is likely that Rese's strong will and ambition played a part. In April 1837 he submitted an evidently forced resignation as bishop to his confreres at the Third Provincial Council in Baltimore; they in turn recommended its acceptance to the Holy See. Rese then went to Rome to argue in favor of his continued service in Detroit.

Pope Gregory XVI was unwilling to force Rese's resignation, apparently because the case against him was vague and circumstantial. Rese then traveled for a time in Europe, collecting funds for his diocese, prior to his return to Detroit in June 1838. His fundraising activities incurred the displeasure of the Lyons-based Society for the Propagation of the Faith and of certain members of the Propaganda. Summoned again to Rome, Rese was disabled in the exercise of his episcopal authority in August 1840, though he retained his title as bishop of Detroit until he died.

Rese's activities and whereabouts in the 1840s and 1850s are largely unknown. He was found ill and mentally impaired in Switzerland in 1859 and brought to his native Vienenberg. He was subsequently sent to the hospital kept by the Sisters of Mercy at Hildesheim, where he was cared for until his death there.

• Almost none of Rese's personal papers have survived. Several of his letters, written in the late 1820s and early 1830s, appear in various issues of *Annales de l'Association de la Propagation de la Foi* and *Berichte der Leopoldinen Stiftung im Kaiserthume Oesterreich*. Documents relating to his removal from Detroit are found in the archives of the Propaganda Fide at the Vatican; an excellent account, based on those records, is Robert F. Trisco, *The Holy See and the Nascent Church in the Middle Western United States, 1826–1850* (1962). George Paré, *The Catholic Church in Detroit, 1701–1888* (1951; repr. 1983), has the most accurate biographical information. See also Richard H. Clarke, *Lives of the Deceased Bishops of the Catholic Church in the United States* (3 vols., 1888), and Francis X. Reuss, *Biographical Cyclopedia of the Catholic Hierarchy* (1898). On Rese's career in Cincinnati, see John H. Lamott, *History of the Archdiocese of Cincinnati* (1921).

LESLIE TENTLER

RESHEVSKY, Samuel Herman (26 Nov. 1909–4 Apr. 1992), chess player, was born Samuel Herman Rzeszewski in Ozierkov, Poland, the son of Jacob Rzeszewski, a linen merchant, and Shaindel Eibeschitz. His year of birth is often incorrectly given as 1911, an inaccuracy brought about by Reshevsky's parents' desire to make their child seem even more extraordinary than he was. Often described as the most remarkable child prodigy in the history of chess, Reshevsky learned the game at age four and could play blindfolded by the age of eight. By age nine he was touring the capitals of Europe, giving simultaneous exhibitions in which he (as a master) took on many opponents. During one two-year period, he lost only eight of the 1,500 games he played.

Reshevsky continued his travels and simultaneous exhibitions in the United States until, following a late-night exhibition, his parents were charged with "improper guardianship." The charges against his parents were dismissed, but a guardian was appointed by the court to prevent "undue exploitation." At age twelve, Reshevsky settled with his family in Detroit, and in 1925 he was naturalized as an American citizen. The spelling of his last name was changed shortly after he settled in the United States. After passing an entrance examination, Reshevsky entered Northern High

School, graduating in 1929. He immediately entered the University of Detroit, where he majored in accounting. After returning to Chicago in 1931, Reshevsky finished his studies at the University of Chicago and graduated in 1934.

The former child prodigy was then faced with a difficult choice: to return to the exciting but uncertain world of competitive chess or to earn a stable and comfortable living as an accountant. In his May 1933 column in *Chess Review*, Isaac Kashdan set forth the dilemma: "Sammy is at a crossroads. If he continues in chess he has every prospect of repeating his triumphs as a child wonder. But as a young man looking for his place in the business world, he would have little time for serious chess playing. The time is at hand when he must choose. The chess world is keenly interested in his decision, as it must be in following the career of its most famous prodigy." Reshevsky never chose between his professional life and his chess career; instead he divided his energies between the two. Many believe that this is what ultimately prevented him from becoming the major contender for world champion that everyone expected him to be.

Despite his semiprofessional status, Reshevsky remained the strongest player outside the U.S.S.R. and Eastern European countries for over a decade. The first tournaments in which he played after resuming chess were the Western Open, which he won in 1931, and a tournament in Pasadena, where he tied for third in 1932. His first major success was in a 1934 tournament in New York City, which he won by placing ahead of Kashdan and Reuben Fine. He went on to win international tournaments in Margate and Great Yarmouth in England in 1935 and the U.S. championship tournament in 1936, again finishing ahead of Kashdan and Fine. Reshevsky finished only a half-point out of first place in the international tournament held in Nottingham, England, in 1936, a tournament described as the strongest ever held because of the presence of so many great players, including Machgiels Euwe, Fine, Mikhail Botvinnik, José Raul Capablanca, Alexander Alekhine, and Salomon Flohr.

First places at Hastings, England, in 1937–1938 and at the U.S. championship tournaments in 1938 and 1940, as well as a shared first at the U.S. championship in 1942, increased Reshevsky's reputation as a world-class player. His position at the top of U.S. chess was cemented by his defeat of Israel Horowitz (three to zero, with thirteen draws) in a 1941 U.S. championship match, and of Kashdan in a similar match the next year (scoring six wins, two losses, and three draws). In June 1941 Reshevsky married Norma Mindick; they had three children. He did not compete in the U.S. championship in 1944 because he was studying for his C.P.A. exam, but he did win the less prestigious U.S. Open that year. He regained the U.S. championship title in 1946. Reshevsky won the title of international grandmaster in 1949.

Although never qualifying for the world championship, Reshevsky had many impressive results in candidates' tournaments and international matches. In 1952

he won matches against Miguel Najdorf, finishing with eight wins, four losses, and six draws, and against Svetozar Gligoric with two wins, one loss, and seven draws. He tied for second at the candidates' tournament in Zurich in 1953. He defeated Pal Benko in a 1960 match with three wins, two losses, and five draws. Qualifying for an interzonal playoff in 1964, he was defeated by Lajos Portisch. Four years later he lost a quarterfinal match against Victor Korchnoi. In 1961 he was declared the winner by default of an aborted match with the young Bobby Fischer; Fischer had withdrawn, complaining of Reshevsky's bad manners while playing, when the score was tied at two wins each and four draws. His last impressive result was winning the Reykjavik Open in 1984 at age seventy-four. Reshevsky died in Suffern, New York.

After Fischer, Reshevsky ranks as the most important American chess player in the second half of the twentieth century. Although generally well liked, he was often accused of cheating and misconduct over the years. His style of playing was primarily strategic, favoring complicated, blocked positions that required subtle maneuvering. In a 1989 poll conducted by the *British Chess Magazine*, Reshevsky's playing style was rated by readers as the second most boring behind Russian player Anatoly Karpov. His theoretical knowledge was not outstanding, but he was praised for original opening ideas. He was also well known for his feats of memory, including record-setting simultaneous blindfolded games, which he continued well into his later years.

• Reshevsky's first book, a memoir titled *Reshevsky on Chess* (1948) that includes many of his games, was ghostwritten by Fred Reinfeld. He did author the second book that appeared under his name, *How Chess Games Are Won* (1962). The best source of information is Stephen W. Gordon, *Samuel Reshevsky: A Compendium of 1768 Games with Diagrams, Crosstables, Some Annotations, and Indexes* (1997). Articles on Reshevsky are in David Hooper and Kenneth Whyld, *The Oxford Companion to Chess* (1984), and Harry Golombek, *Golombek's Encyclopedia of Chess* (1977). An obituary is in the *New York Times*, 7 Apr. 1992.

ELIZABETH ZOE VICARY

RESNICK, Judith A. *See* Challenger Shuttle Crew.

RESOR, Stanley Burnet (30 Apr. 1879–29 Oct. 1962), advertising executive, was born in Cincinnati, Ohio, the son of Isaac Burnet Resor, a stove manufacturer, and Mary Wilson Brown. After receiving his early education in the Cincinnati public school system, Resor enrolled at Yale University, where he worked his way through school by tutoring and selling subscriptions to a history of the Bible door-to-door. He had hopes of teaching economics, but by the time he received his Bachelor of Arts degree in 1901, his father had lost control of the family's stove manufacturing firm. Thus, Resor could devote no more time to schooling and instead went to work in a Cincinnati bank for a $5-a-week wage.

After brief stints as a shipping clerk in a tool factory and as a worker in a print shop, Resor entered the field of advertising in 1904 at the Cincinnati firm of Proctor & Collier, the house agency for Proctor & Gamble. He wrote some advertisements for soap that captured the attention of Charles E. Raymond, the vice president in charge of the Chicago office of the J. Walter Thompson Company. In 1908 Raymond selected Resor (along with Resor's older brother, Walter) to head the newly opened Cincinnati office of the company. Resor was so successful in running the Cincinnati branch that he was transferred to the New York headquarters in 1912, where he was named to the positions of vice president and general manager in 1914.

In 1916 J. Walter Thompson, the founder and owner of the company, retired and sold the firm to Resor, Raymond, and Harry E. Ward, a banker who had been a friend of Resor's at Yale, for the sum of $500,000. Raymond provided the bulk of the purchase price, with Ward supplying most of the balance. Shortly thereafter, Raymond himself retired, leaving Resor in full control as president of the company.

While working as a copywriter in the Proctor & Collier office in Cincinnati, Resor had met Helen Lansdowne, who was also employed with the advertising firm. In March 1917, the two were married; the couple had three children. Helen Resor would eventually serve on the board of directors of the J. Walter Thompson Company.

Also in 1917 Resor, together with others in his business, established the American Association of Advertising Agencies, which had as one of its stated purposes the furtherance of high ethical standards in promotion. He was president of the association in 1923–1924, when membership included 135 firms creating eighty percent of all national advertising.

In addition to his duties at the J. Walter Thompson agency, Resor began writing articles dealing with the subject of advertising, including "Individual Effort Has Had Its Day" (*Fourth Estate*, Nov. 1921) and "What the American Association of Advertising Agencies Does to Make Advertising Scientifically More Effective" (*Annals of the American Academy of Political and Social Science* 1924). Additionally, he contributed an article to the book *An Outline of Careers* (1927), edited by Edward L. Bernays, which was entitled "Advertising as a Career." Although he usually shied away from public speaking, Resor also delivered the occasional lecture on his field before professional groups and on college campuses, including "The Press in Its Relation to Public Opinion" at Yale in 1930, and "A Plea for Education" at Harvard in 1938.

As president of J. Walter Thompson, Resor transformed the company into the largest advertising agency in the world. When he took over the firm, it was placing less than $3 million a year in advertising, had a mere five offices, and employed only 177 people. By 1927 the annual billing had increased to $23 million and the payroll included 432 employees. In 1947 the company became the first advertising agency with yearly billings of more than $100 million. In 1954, the

year before Resor resigned as the company's president to become chairman of the board, the volume of advertising placed reached $200 million; by 1961, the year Resor stepped down as chairman of the board, billings soared to greater than $370 million. At that time, the company had a staff of 6,225 people in fifty-five cities.

As an advertising executive, Resor believed strongly in applying ideas of scientific market research and promotion. He gave his clients more than the traditional copy and artwork usually supplied by ad agencies, and he provided them with services for analyzing business problems and studying prices and distribution. He also supplied services that tried to mesh advertising campaigns into the specific sales strategy of a particular client. Reflecting his dependence on statistical data in determining buying trends, he created in 1939 the J. Walter Thompson consumer panel, which was responsible for compiling such information on the company's behalf.

An editorial in the trade publication *Advertising and Selling*, commenting on Resor's introduction of market analysis to the field of advertising, stated, "Facts have been his constant weapon. . . . The research function has been paramount in his advertising planning" (repr. in *Current Biography*, July 1949, p. 48). This approach stemmed from Resor's days at Yale, when he became familiar with the works of British historian Henry Thomas Buckle. Convinced that all human behavior was scientifically predictable, as Buckle argued, Resor carried this concept with him into the advertising field. He described his philosophy succinctly in the article he wrote for *An Outline of Careers*: "Advertising is based on a study of habit."

Some of the other advertising innovations introduced by Resor were the testimonial and its well-known offspring, the celebrity endorsement. First used in a 1917 ad campaign for Pond's Skin Cream, the testimonial concept was expanded upon in 1926 when the queen of Spain lent her name to the selling of the product. In the 1940s the technique grew further in a series of ads featuring a young engaged woman recommending the skin cream. The advertisement contained what became a very popular slogan of that era: "She's engaged! She's lovely! She uses Pond's."

In addition to Pond's, at its height the J. Walter Thompson agency boasted such accounts as Eastman Kodak, Shell Oil, Cream of Wheat, Lux, Guinness, and Standard Brands. Despite all its success, the company continued to adhere to rigorous business standards. Resor refused to try to entice new clients by preparing potential ad campaigns for them, because he felt that doing so would take away from the needs of the company's already established clients. The company maintained firm ethical boundaries as well. For example, Resor did not allow the firm to market products with a high alcohol content. Furthermore, the agency once relinquished the account of a popular brand of cigarette—thereby freeing the cigarette company to sign with a competitor—simply because of a disagreement over the proper method of promotion. Resor's moral uprightness even transcended beyond his business: He once made the suggestion that every golf course in America should put up a certain poem on the bulletin board that reminded golfers not to utter any profanities after hitting a poor shot.

Resor attempted throughout his career to clean up the sullied image that the advertising business had acquired. He believed that "advertising must play a leading role not only in selling products but in selling elements in the social structure itself" (*Current Biography*, July 1949). Due in part to these efforts, in 1948 Resor received the Gold Medal Award bestowed annually by *Advertising and Selling* magazine to the Advertising Man of the Year. The award was given in recognition of Resor's "leadership in making advertising the essential and powerful force it is." After presenting the medal to Resor, Eugene Meyer, chairman of the *Washington Post*, said that no one had done more than Resor to remove the prejudice against advertising that had existed at the time. "In fact," Meyer continued, "he may be said to be a perfectionist because his standards are so high that he is never quite satisfied with the results as achieved. But let it be understood the one he is most critical of is Stanley Resor" (*New York Times*, 30 Oct. 1962).

Resor died in New York City, survived by his wife and three children.

• The archives of the J. Walter Thompson Company in New York City contains a significant amount of published information about Resor's life and career. For biographical profiles, see "This Man Resor," *Advertising and Selling*, 25 Nov. 1931; *New Outlook*, Jan. 1935, pp. 28–29; "J. Walter Thompson's Company," *Fortune*, Nov. 1947, pp. 94–101; "A Pioneer in Marketing: Stanley Resor," *Journal of Marketing*, Oct. 1961; and "Advertising Loses a Titan as Resor Dies," *Advertising Age*, 5 Nov. 1962. See also Martin Mayer, *Madison Avenue, USA* (1958). An obituary is in the *New York Times*, 30 Oct. 1962.

FRANCESCO L. NEPA

RESTELL, Madame. *See* Lohman, Ann Trow.

RETHBERG, Elisabeth (22 Sept. 1894–6 June 1976), soprano, was born Lisbeth Sättler in Schwarzenberg, Germany, a town near Dresden in the Erz Mountains of Saxony, the daughter of Charles Sättler, a schoolteacher, and Jenny Müller. The family was musical, and despite limited means all the children began piano lessons as soon as they could sit comfortably at the instrument.

By her early teens Lisbeth Sättler had decided to pursue a career in music, and around 1910 she enrolled at the Royal Conservatory in Dresden to study both voice and piano. Student life was a struggle: she had limited means, often went hungry, and supplemented the meager assistance she received from her family by accepting singing engagements at churches and social functions. Though her impoverishment grew even worse after the outbreak of World War I, she managed to continue her studies and graduated with honors from the conservatory in 1915. Shortly afterward, having decided to become a singer, she made her operatic debut as Arsena in *Der Zigeunerbaron* at the Dresden Opera.

Adopting Elisabeth Rethberg as her stage name, she remained with the company (renamed the Dresden State Opera after the war) for seven years. During this time she reportedly mastered more than one hundred roles in operas by Verdi, Mozart, Wagner, Puccini, and both Strausses. To augment her small salary she continued her engagements as a paid soloist and also formed a vocal quartet that performed in several German cities.

Rethberg's struggle to build a career in the upheaval of postwar Germany attracted the attention and encouragement of several prominent musical figures, including the conductor Fritz Reiner. Word of her beautiful *lirico spinto* voice spread, and in 1922 Giulio Gatti-Casazza, the general manager of the Metropolitan Opera in New York City, invited her to perform there. Rethberg, assuming that this would be a routine engagement, made her debut at the Met on 22 November of that year in the title role of *Aïda*. Her performance was a sensation and was widely acclaimed. Virtually overnight Rethberg went from poverty to international acclaim, and she remained a star of the Metropolitan Opera for the remainder of her singing career.

Equally at home in both German and Italian, Rethberg created more than thirty memorable heroines at the Met, among them Wagner's Sieglinde, Elsa, and Elisabeth; Strauss's Marschallin; Verdi's Desdemona and Amelia; and Mozart's Countess and Donna Anna. But she was most renowned as Aïda, and many critics consider her portrayal of that role the finest of her generation. She starred with many of the leading singers of the early twentieth century—Beniamino Gigli, Lauritz Melchior, Kirsten Flagstad, Lawrence Tibbett, and Ezio Pinza, among others—but in an era when operatic superstars attracted devoted public followings and lavish press attention, Rethberg was among the most celebrated.

Fame apparently never turned her head. Perhaps because she remembered all too keenly the deprivations of her youth, Rethberg gave generously to charitable causes, frequently performed at benefits for ailing children and mistreated animals, and provided scholarship assistance to needy students. A negative incident in her career occurred in 1935, when Ezio Pinza's wife sued Rethberg for alienation of affection. The widely publicized suit was subsequently dropped.

During her two-decade career at the Met, Rethberg sang with the company in other U.S. cities and also appeared often at the Dresden State Opera, where in 1928 she premiered Strauss's *Die aegyptische Helena*, singing the title role. Rethberg also appeared at Covent Garden, at the Salzburg Festival, and at major opera houses in Italy. She gave her farewell operatic performance at the Met on 6 March 1942 as Aïda, the same role she had debuted with there twenty years earlier. During the next two years she gave several lieder recitals before retiring in 1944. The opera-loving public did not forget her, however, and her many recordings were cherished. Twenty-two years later, at a farewell gala that closed the first Metropolitan Opera House, Rethberg made a rare public appearance with many other great singers of the past; she received the greatest ovation of the evening.

Rethberg became a U.S. citizen in 1939. She was married twice; she had no children. Her first husband was Ernst Albert Dormann, a businessman whom she married in 1923; the marriage ended in divorce after five years. In 1956 she married George Cehanovsky, a veteran baritone at the Metropolitan Opera. For many years Rethberg lived in Riverdale, New York; at the time of her second marriage she moved to nearby Yorktown Heights, and she died at her home there. Posthumous tributes to Rethberg appeared in newspapers throughout the world, nearly all of them echoing the assessment of *New York Times* music critic Harold Schonberg, who called Rethberg "one of the supreme sopranos of the century."

• For biographical information on Elisabeth Rethberg, see H. Henschel and E. Friedrich, *Elisabeth Rethberg: Ihr Leben und Künstlertum* (1928; rev. ed., 1977). For an analysis of her singing, see J. B. Steane, "Elisabeth Rethberg," in his *Voices: Singers and Critics* (1992). An obituary and an appreciative essay by Harold Schonberg are in the *New York Times*, 7 June 1976.

ANN T. KEENE

REU, Johann Michael (16 Nov. 1869–14 Oct. 1943), Lutheran church historian, author, and educational theorist, was born in Diebach, Bavaria, the son of Johann Friedrich Reu, a stone mason, and Margarete Henkelmann. As a child, his parish pastor tutored him in Latin, Greek, and Hebrew. He attended the Latin School in Oettingen and from 1887 to 1889 the Seminary for Mission Workers at Neuendettelsau, from which he graduated. He emigrated to America in 1889 and was ordained by the German Evangelical Lutheran Synod of Iowa and Other States on 1 September 1889 as assistant pastor of St. John Lutheran Church in Mendota, Illinois. In October 1890 he accepted a call to serve Immanuel Lutheran Church in Rock Falls, Illinois, and from 1891 on was also pastor at St. Paul Evangelical Lutheran Church in Yorktown, Illinois. He married Marie Wilhelmine Schmitthenner in 1892; they had four children.

In 1899 Reu was called to assume the chair of systematic theology at Wartburg Seminary in Dubuque, Iowa. He became an American citizen in 1902 and two years later was appointed editor of the *Kirchliche Zeitschrift*, the faculty journal of theology at Wartburg, serving as editor until his death. He received an honorary Th.D. in 1910 from the University of Erlangen, Germany, for his work on the origin and history of the use of Luther's Small Catechism in sixteenth-century German-speaking lands, which was published as *Quellen zur Geschichte des kirchlichen Unterrichts in der evangelischen Kirche Deutschlands zwischen 1530 und 1600* (9 vols., 1904–1935), and he also contributed portions to several volumes of the Weimar Edition of Luther's

works. He was awarded the doctor of literature degree from Capital University in Columbus, Ohio, in 1926.

Reu was prominent in church union negotiations following World War I that brought together various Lutheran denominations in the United States. He was the Iowa Synod's last official delegate of the Evangelical Lutheran Church in North America, serving until Iowa's fellowship ties to the General Council were severed in 1917. He also served as Iowa's representative to the National Lutheran Council from 1918 until 1920, when the synod withdrew. Reu was responsible for sending hundreds of thousands of dollars in relief funds and supplies to Europe and especially to Germany after World War I. He also represented his church as delegate to three Lutheran World Conventions— 1923 at Eisenach, 1929 at Copenhagen, and 1935 at Paris—giving major presentations at the 1929 and 1935 meetings. He took part in the drafting and adoption of the Toledo Theses (1907), a protocol that established church fellowship ties between the Iowa Synod and the Joint Synod of Ohio, and also participated as the voice of the Iowa Synod with representatives of Ohio, the Norwegian Lutheran church, and the Buffalo Synod in formulating the Minneapolis Theses (1925), a first step that led to the founding of the American Lutheran Conference (1930). Reu served for thirteen years on the executive board of the Iowa Synod; for twenty years he was a member of both the synod's board of education and its board of Sunday schools and young people's societies.

Reu had a pivotal role in union negotiations that led to the formation of the American Lutheran church in 1930, opposing the new church body's proposed constitution that mandated complete biblical inerrancy. Although Reu opposed a dictation theory of inspiration and believed that absolute inerrancy of Holy Scripture was not an article of faith taught in the Bible, he personally never questioned the divine authority or the inerrancy of the canonical Scriptures and by the end of his life asserted that affirmation of biblical inerrancy was a prerequisite to altar and pulpit fellowship among Lutheran church bodies.

Besides his expertise in the fields of Renaissance and Reformation studies, Reu was considered North America's foremost Luther expert. *Thirty-five Years of Luther Research* (1917) provides Reu's synopsis and notations from European scholarship on Luther studies; his *Luther's German Bible* (1934) offers important source materials on the use of the Bible in medieval times as well as on the problems of translation Luther confronted. His *Luther's Small Catechism: A History of Its Origin, Its Distribution, and Its Use* (1929) contains Reu's exhaustive researches into both pre-Reformation educational history and the historical development of the Small Catechism, while his *Luther and the Scriptures* (1944) is a scholarly compilation of Luther sources that demonstrates conclusively that Luther had a high view of the Bible's authority and reliability and that he rejected a historical-critical approach to biblical interpretation.

Reu was the second American to produce single-handedly an entire graded Sunday school curriculum for the Lutheran church, which appeared in two editions as the *Wartburg Lesson Helps* (8 vols., 1914, 1930–). His thetic *An Explanation of Luther's Small Catechism* (1904) became the standard catechism used for more than forty-five years, throughout the Iowa Synod and later the American Lutheran church. His *How I Tell the Story to My Sunday School* volumes (1918, 1926, 1935) pioneered the use of the children's sermon as part of Sunday worship in Lutheran churches in the United States.

In honor of the four-hundredth anniversary of the Augsburg Confession, Reu produced a volume of historical introduction as well as translations of source materials leading up to the Augustana as *The Augsburg Confession* (1930), with sources and historical research unrivaled in any English publication. His *Christian Ethics*, a work of systematic theology (with Paul H. Buehring, 1935), was a bestseller.

A talented preacher, Reu also won renown for his homiletic theory and style, which were widely studied in the American Lutheran church. His first books, *Die Alttestamentlichen Perikopen* (1901, 1903), were exegetical studies of the Thomasius Old Testament pericopes, adapted for homiletical use. His encyclopedic *Homiletics*, issued in five editions between 1922 and 1944, served as a standard text in Lutheran seminaries for four decades. Reu's complete English-language sermons have been published as *Anthology of the Sermons of J. Michael Reu* (ed. Paul I. Johnston, 1995).

Reu was an exponent and adapter of Heilsgeschichte theology as it was understood by the theologians of the Erlangen school, most notably J. C. K. von Hofmann and Theodor Zahn. Reu's elaboration of the concept of Heilsgeschichte emphasized the normative authority of Scripture and divine monergism more than the Erlangen exegetes did, but Reu followed historic Heilsgeschichte thinking in his emphasis on the gradual development of truth over time and in his conception of the organic wholeness of reality. His educational theories, especially his ontology and epistemology, were grounded in the work of Johann Friedrich Herbart, but Reu differed markedly from Herbart in his understanding of the nature of man and of the end of religious education, claiming faith in Jesus Christ, not external moral actions, to be the goal of education. Reu made biblical history the content of religious instruction. He elaborated his philosophy of education in his *Catechetics* (1918, 1927, 1931), the only scientific and comprehensive survey of the subject written by a Lutheran in America.

Reu died in Rochester, Minnesota, after undergoing surgery. His dream and lifework to accomplish a unified Lutheran church in the United States based on a mediating position that included both scientific progress in exegesis as well as biblical and confessional integrity were not to be realized. He was the last major exponent of the mediating position.

• Reu's papers are in the Johann Michael Reu Collection at the Wartburg Seminary Archives, Dubuque, Iowa. His scholarly contributions are profiled in Lowell C. Green, "J. M. Reu and Reformation Studies," *Concordia Historical Institute Quarterly* 42 (Nov. 1969): 147–56. Green gives a listing of the structure and contents of Reu's multivolume *Quellen* in his "Introduction and Index to the *Quellen* of J. M. Reu," *Bulletin of the Library, Foundation for Reformation Research* 6 (1971): 9–11, 17–24, 25–32; 7 (1972): 1–7. English translations of a number of Reu's more important theological treatises, book reviews, and exegetical studies are provided in *Anthology of the Theological Writings of J. Michael Reu*, ed. Paul I. Johnston (1997). Reu's importance in church union negotiations of the 1920s is discussed in Fred Meuser, *The Formation of the American Lutheran Church* (1958). Biographical information is provided in *Johann Michael Reu: A Book of Remembrance: Kirchliche Zeitschrift, 1876–1943* (1945). An obituary is in the *New York Times*, 16 Oct. 1943.

PAUL I. JOHNSTON

REULBACH, Edward Marvin (1 Dec. 1882–17 July 1961), baseball player, was born in Detroit, Michigan, the son of Edward J. Reulbach, a bookkeeper, and Catherine M. Paulus. Reulbach attended grammar school in Detroit, but the family moved to St. Louis, where he finished high school. In an unusual move for ball players of his era, Reulbach attended college; he matriculated first at Notre Dame, where he spent three years studying electrical engineering and pre-medicine. He then transferred to the University of Vermont, but he did not graduate from either school.

While at Notre Dame, Reulbach pitched for the Fighting Irish and played minor league baseball under a variety of names to preserve his college eligibility. He played three summers in the Missouri Valley League and, after he had enrolled at Vermont, one summer (1904) in the Green Mountain League. At the university he won four games without a loss, after which he received an offer from the Chicago Cubs.

In 1905, Reulbach's rookie year in the major leagues, he compiled an 18–14 record, completed 28 of 29 games he started, and pitched five shutouts. He struck out twice as many batters as he walked, and in 291 innings he stood out with an earned run average of only 1.42, the best he ever recorded as a major leaguer and second that year only to Christy Mathewson in either league. That season he held opposing hitters to a league-leading .201 batting average. In 1906 he reduced that figure to .175. His winning percentage for 1906 was .826; for 1907, .810; and for 1908, .774. In each year these percentages led the league. During those three seasons he won 60 games and lost 15, and the Cubs won the National League pennant all three of those years and the World Series twice. In several seasons he pitched more than 200 innings yet gave up only one or two home runs, astonishing even in the dead ball era in which he pitched.

The year 1908 was especially notable for Reulbach. The Cubs won the pennant by one game over the New York Giants, and Reulbach had his best season, winning 24 games. Late in the season, in order to help rest Mordecai "Three Finger" Brown, Reulbach pitched a doubleheader against the Brooklyn Dodgers; he won both games and held Brooklyn scoreless in each game, a feat achieved only once or twice in major league history. At one point during the season he also pitched 44 consecutive scoreless innings.

In four World Series Reulbach's record was less consistent. He won two games, including a one-hitter against the Chicago White Sox in 1906, and lost none. But in three other games, especially in 1910 against the Philadelphia Athletics, he was not impressive, although he did not receive a losing decision.

Reulbach pitched only eight full seasons for the Cubs, winning more games than he lost each year, but his steadily rising earned run average and declining strikeout record led to speculation that his famed curve ball was becoming less effective. Possibly he was worn out from the heavy burden he assumed with the Cubs in his young years. In 1913 he was traded to Brooklyn after winning only one game for the Cubs, and 1914 was also a bad year for him. In 1915 he joined a number of other dissident major leaguers in the Federal League. He performed credibly, but the league died that year, and Reulbach joined the Boston Braves the following season. In what was probably another reflection of his unhappiness with players' salaries during this time, he helped found and served as secretary of the Baseball Players Fraternity, which lasted only in 1914–1915. He retired from baseball following the 1917 season.

In his 13 years in the major leagues Reulbach won 182 games and lost 106, and he completed 201 games out of 300 that he started. He finished with a lifetime ERA of only 2.28. After retiring from baseball Reulbach worked in piano manufacturing and later ran his own tire business. He had married Nellie (maiden name unknown), and they had at least one child. As early as 1910 Reulbach had missed part of a season to care for his ailing son, who died in 1931. The prolonged expenses forced Reulbach into bankruptcy, and he lost his tire business. A Chicago newspaper described him as a sad, quiet man. For the last twenty years before his death he worked for a construction company in New York. He died in Glens Falls, New York.

Contemporaries described Reulbach as an intelligent, introspective man, much better educated than most of his teammates. Obviously dissatisfied with the management of baseball in his era, he also faced much personal affliction. During his most productive years Reulbach was considered only the third best pitcher in Chicago, for his superb record was generally surpassed by his teammate Mordecai "Three Finger" Brown and White Sox pitcher Ed Walsh. (Walsh and Reulbach were both called "Big Ed," yet most Chicagoans thought of Walsh when they heard that nickname.) Reulbach was even upstaged in death. He and Ty Cobb died on the same day, and while newspapers gave Reulbach a typical one-column obituary, Cobb's death made the front page.

• Material on Reulbach is scarce. An argument for the election of Reulbach into the National Baseball Hall of Fame is Cappy Gagnon, "Ed Reulbach Remembered," *Baseball Research Journal* (1982): 77–79. Gene Karst, *Who's Who in Professional Baseball* (1973), makes accurate, if very brief, mention of Reulbach. His pitching record is thoroughly explored in John Thorn and Pete Palmer, eds. *Total Baseball*, 3d ed. (1993). Reulbach's flirtation with the Federal League is described in Marc Okkonen, comp., *The Federal League of 1914–1915* (1989). An obituary is in the *New York Times*, 19 July 1961.

THOMAS L. KARNES

REUTHER, Walter Philip (1 Sept. 1907–9 May 1970), prominent labor leader, was born in Wheeling, West Virginia, the son of Valentine Reuther, a socialist and an iron and brewery worker, and Anna Stocker. Both German-born, Anna and Valentine met in a workingmen's saloon where Val delivered beer and Anna worked in the kitchen. The second of five children, Walter grew up in a strict but loving household, marked by a heavy emphasis on self-improvement, self-discipline, and duty. He received an early education in socialist politics and unionism from his father, who regularly moderated dinnertime debates between his sons on contemporary political issues. According to one of Reuther's biographers, by the time he was an adolescent, having accompanied his father to visit Eugene Debs in prison at age eleven, the young Reuther had become a Debsian socialist and was thus committed to a kind of socialism rooted in American political and cultural traditions such as republicanism, liberty, and self-government.

Reuther received his early education at the Ritchie grammar school and Wheeling High School, though he left before graduation at age sixteen to work. First taking a position as a handyman, Reuther eventually worked his way into an apprenticeship as a tool and die maker at Wheeling Corrugating. In 1927, beckoned by Ford Motor Company's high wages and five-day workweek, Reuther moved to Detroit. Within a short time, Reuther's skill and conscientiousness had earned him a position as one of the highest paid mechanics at Ford's huge River Rouge complex. At this point Reuther took night-shift work and went back to school at the relatively opulent Fordson High School in Detroit. A committed student, Reuther's school work revealed an unlimited, if unfocused, idealism and an enormous ambition for self-improvement. Earning his high school diploma at age twenty-two, Reuther then enrolled in the Detroit City College (now Wayne State University), where he was joined by his younger brothers, Victor and Roy Reuther.

In the early 1930s, as Reuther and his brothers were politicized by the Great Depression, Reuther's idealism and activism became more focused. Detroit was hit especially hard by the depression. Ford alone laid off nearly half of its workforce. Although Reuther did not lose his well-paying job, he and his brother Victor, like so many other aspiring labor leaders of their generation, were deeply affected by the social dislocations and suffering they witnessed. Reuther and Victor took photographs of "Hoovervilles" and interviewed hobos and unemployed workers. The brothers also became political and social activists. On campus, Reuther, Victor, and some friends founded a Social Problems Club (affiliated with the Socialist League for Industrial Democracy), and organized protests against the establishment of a campus Reserve Officers' Training Corps unit and the segregationist policies of a local swimming pool leased by the college. In 1932 Reuther traveled over 3,000 miles campaigning for Socialist party presidential candidate Norman Thomas. The following year, Reuther left Ford and, with his brother Victor, embarked on a nine-nation tour of Europe, which began with a visit to Germany and concluded with a lengthy stay in the Soviet Union. Deeply affected by events they witnessed in Germany, Reuther and his brother were radicalized by their encounter with Nazism. In the Soviet Union, Reuther spent two years working as a tool and die maker and training Russian peasants in his craft at the Soviet Union's massive automobile factory in Gorky. Although Reuther would later become an avowed anticommunist, he returned from the Soviet Union initially an enthusiastic defender of what he believed to be a genuine proletarian democracy.

When Reuther arrived home in 1935, the labor scene in Detroit and the rest of the nation had been transformed by the depression and the New Deal. The Wagner Act, passed in the spring of 1935, provided federal recognition of the right to organize and soon spurred the formation of the Committee for Industrial Organization (later the Congress of Industrial Organizations, CIO) within the American Federation of Labor (AFL). CIO leaders, who set up their own rival labor federation in 1936, were committed to organizing the unorganized, such as the thousands of auto workers in Detroit, without regard to skill or craft into industrial unions. Finding his prospects for reemployment at Ford negligible anyway, Reuther became active in labor education, labor organizing, and socialist politics. Within Detroit's progressive political circles, he met May Wolf, a physical education teacher and activist in the Detroit Socialist party. May and Walter were married in 1936. In 1941 they bought a home in Detroit where they raised two children.

In 1936 Reuther began organizing full-time for the CIO's United Auto Workers (UAW). Although Reuther was technically ineligible for UAW membership because he was unemployed, he attended the 1936 UAW convention in South Bend, Indiana, as a delegate from a General Motors local in Detroit. At this historic convention the UAW declared its independence from AFL leadership, and Reuther was elected to membership on the executive board. He returned to Detroit a paid official of the UAW. His first efforts focused on the Kelsey-Hayes Wheel Company, a manufacturer that held a key position in the industry as the supplier of parts used by Ford. In December 1936 Reuther and a handful of activists conducted a successful sit-down strike at Kelsey-Hayes and established the roots of UAW Local 174. Although this sit-down was less prominent than the massive General Motors strike in Flint, Michigan, that began just two weeks later, its success marked a turning point in the organization of Detroit's workers. Within eight months of the Kelsey-Hayes strike, Reuther's UAW Local 174, an "amalgamated local," represented 30,000 workers and seventy-six shops. Reuther assumed a prominent role in two of the UAW's major depression-era offensives—the planning of the 1937 Flint sit-down, and the organization of Ford's workers. In the words of biographer Nelson Lichtenstein, Reuther was transformed from 1936 to 1937 from a "radical organizer to [a] nationally recognized labor leader." In 1937, after a beating by Ford company goons, Reuther appeared in a photo spread in *Time* magazine. The UAW quickly became the nation's largest union, and Reuther became its most influential leader.

In 1940, as Americans debated the question of intervention in World War II, Reuther again seized national media attention with his "500 planes a day" proposal. That was but the first of many proposals that became so characteristic of Reuther and the corporatist vision he provided to modern labor liberalism. The plan entailed setting up an aircraft production board, administered by representatives of government, labor, and industry, and giving that board authority to reorganize production in existing factories for war production, without consideration for traditional corporate boundaries or prerogatives. Though Reuther attempted to sell the plan in the interest of efficiency and liberal support of the war effort, he was also indirectly proposing a radical restructuring of the political economy. If Reuther's plan had been carried out, it would have given the federal government and labor unprecedented control and authority over production, sustained the New Deal's activism in industry, and seriously undermined management's traditional authority. In spite of the federal government's New Deal industry codes, management decisions about production had traditionally been the exclusive and jealously guarded privilege of private capitalists. American businessmen and automobile executives, who understood precisely the radical implications of Reuther's proposal, bitterly opposed the plan. Such seemingly innocuous, but structurally radical, proposals led automobile executive George Romney in 1945 to identify Reuther as the "most dangerous man in Detroit" because no one, in his words, was "more skillful in bringing about the revolution without seeming to disturb the existing forms of society" (Lichtenstein, p. 230).

Ambition, as well as a keen ability to read and respond to the popular concerns of the rank and file, eventually placed Walter Reuther in the presidency of the UAW. Since the inception of the union, the UAW leadership had been deeply divided along political lines. A vocal anticommunist who had broken his ties with the Communists and Socialists in 1938, Reuther was supported by a spectrum of factions on both the political right and left. With his mastery of building organizational and political influence, and his authoritative post as the emergent leader of Detroit's Local 174, Reuther was well positioned to move into executive leadership. Reuther became the UAW's vice president in charge of the General Motors division during World War II, and in 1946 he won the presidency of the UAW.

The 1946 victory, by a narrow margin, stemmed from Reuther's skilled handling of a 1944–1945 UAW wildcat strike movement during World War II. Although the UAW officially agreed to the wartime no-strike pledge, rank-and-file resentments quickly emerged in reaction to government regulation and what many workers perceived to be management's wartime opportunism. Fearing that management was using the war emergency to roll back union gains, UAW members across the nation conducted a series of wildcat strikes, pulling half of the workers in the auto industry off the job. While Communist leaders in the UAW adhered to the Soviet party line and condemned the movement as breaking the no-strike pledge and damaging the war effort, Reuther championed the cause of the strikers. In 1945–1946, when militant voices among the rank and file demanded a strike to end wartime wage controls, Reuther backed the proposal. Reuther's subsequent leadership of the 113-day General Motors strike secured the loyalty of the rank and file and finally his ascension to the presidency.

The 1946 General Motors strike also provided an opportunity for Reuther to make his boldest proposal yet, securing his place in the annals of labor history. Combining contemporary liberal faith in Keynesian economics, an appreciation of the public's anxieties about postwar depression, a sensitivity to workers' demands, and his characteristic brand of corporatist liberalism, Reuther proposed that GM raise wages 30 percent without raising the price of its cars. Reuther argued that his proposal would raise consumption levels among the masses of UAW members, maintain consumption levels among the general public, and thus contribute to the purchasing power deemed necessary to avoid a second postwar Great Depression. Moreover, Reuther challenged GM to "open the books" to the UAW and the public to demonstrate that GM could afford to pay workers higher wages. Although Reuther never achieved his goal of making collective bargaining a tool to promote economic planning or to give the union more authority in production and pricing, he did win historic concessions from GM in 1948. The UAW's 1948 contract with GM included an automatic "cost of living adjustment" determined by the general price index, and a second wage increase, "the annual improvement factor," that theoretically tied raises to increases in productivity. The 1948 agreement, dubbed the "treaty of Detroit" by *Fortune* magazine, set a standard for postwar collective bargaining.

In 1947 Reuther won a solid victory for reelection, and in the following years he consolidated his control, bureaucratized the union structure, eliminated opposition, and channeled political activism into more mainstream electoral pursuits. Although Reuther himself was often critical of the federal government's rigid anticommunist policy, and his own circle of advisers continued to include a number of radicals and socialists, Reuther made anticommunism a central and popular issue of his presidency. Passage of the 1947 Taft-Hartley Amendment requiring noncommunist affidavits from all union officers vindicated Reuther's stance. His popularity mushroomed within the union, as many UAW members believed that Reuther's staunch anticommunism was necessary to insulate the union from conservative political attacks. An assassination attempt on Reuther in 1948 also dramatically increased his popularity.

Under Reuther's leadership and the union's postwar "treaty" with automakers, the UAW became a much more bureaucratized, business-minded union. In the 1950s UAW officials tried to channel shop-floor militancy into grievance procedures rather than strikes, and collective bargaining increasingly focused on money issues and fringe benefits. Emblematic of postwar prosperity, UAW members achieved all the hallmarks of working-class affluence, with pensions, health benefits, and supplemental unemployment benefits. In the same years, when other leaders of "big labor" were charged with corruption, Reuther's modest lifestyle and the integrity of his officers placed the UAW beyond reproach.

Over his lifetime, Reuther, the former Debsian socialist, became increasingly conservative in politics. Abandoning the radical politics of his youth, Reuther shifted his support to Democratic candidate Franklin Roosevelt in 1940 and 1944. As a founding member of the Americans for Democratic Action (ADA), Reuther, like many of his contemporaries, had once envisioned an American labor party, but this vision was abandoned after the failed campaign of Progressive party candidate Henry Wallace in 1948. After that year, Reuther's political energies were focused within the Democratic party on attempts to make it the party of liberal causes such as labor, the war on poverty, civil liberties, and civil rights.

In 1952, after the death of CIO president Philip Murray, Reuther became the president of the federation and served as an enthusiastic facilitator of the 1955 AFL-CIO merger. However, differences of politics and style soon divided Reuther and AFL-CIO president George Meany. Reuther, as a leader in the Industrial Union Department of the AFL-CIO, retained a broad activist vision that included plans for a large-scale organizing campaign that never materialized. He also became increasingly critical of what he believed to be Meany's complacency and the AFL-CIO's relatively uncritical stance toward U.S. foreign policy. Criticizing what he perceived to be the federation's apathy and its failure to organize, Reuther pulled the UAW out of the AFL-CIO in 1968. The UAW formed a short-lived alliance with the Teamsters, in the Alliance for Labor Action. But the UAW's unlikely association with the Teamsters, by then notorious for corruption, ended in 1971.

Finding himself for the first time on the margins of social movements for change, Reuther experienced the 1960s with frustration. By the late 1960s, the civil rights movement, black power, the antiwar movement, and women's liberation had well eclipsed the labor movement on the cutting edge of activism. Among younger activists, Reuther and other members of his generation of labor leaders were often viewed as marginal at best and enemies at worst, as the AFL-CIO under Meany was increasingly identified with conservatism. Within his own union, Reuther found it difficult to deal with increasingly strident demands of black UAW activists. Always a strong supporter of black civil rights, Reuther was an adamant enforcer of desegregation, but he was less responsive to the demands of the "revolutionary union movement," a militant group of black nationalists within the UAW in Detroit. By the 1960s Reuther had emerged as a centrist on several fronts, promoting compromise and reform within traditional electoral politics, and promoting order within his union. In 1967, when a wildcat strike by a GM local in Mansfield, Ohio, halted production in fifty-seven other plants, Reuther declared the strike illegal, ordered strikers to return to work, and finally obtained executive board permission to seize the local.

In 1970, as Walter Reuther contemplated retirement, his life ended abruptly in a tragic accident. On the way back to Detroit from the construction site of the UAW's Family Education Center on Michigan's Black Lake, Reuther's chartered plane crashed, instantly killing Reuther, his wife, and four passengers. Reuther's life coincided with a period of unprecedented labor activism and success, and his leadership of the UAW in many ways set the postwar standard for collective bargaining, labor politics, and personal integrity. At the height of his influence in the late 1940s, Reuther was ranked by his contemporaries with Stalin and Churchill as among the ten most influential men in the postwar world. Reuther's life, his idealism, and his creative vision of collective bargaining as a means of social change likewise ensured that, long after his death, his legacy has remained a powerful symbol for the American labor movement.

• Walter Reuther's papers and the records of the UAW are in the Archives of Labor History and Urban Affairs, Wayne State University, Detroit, Mich., in a library named in honor of Reuther. Reuther's career and his life are the subject of several biographies. Nelson Lichtenstein, *The Most Dangerous Man in Detroit: Walter Reuther and the Fate of American Labor* (1995), provides a thorough biography of Reuther, as well as a thoughtful assessment of Reuther's leadership role, his thought, and the significance of "Reutherism" within American labor history. Lichtenstein is also the author of a concise biographical sketch in *Labor Leaders in America* (1987). An earlier and standard biography is John Barnard, *Walter Reuther and the Rise of the Auto Workers* (1983). Walter's brother Victor G. Reuther provides an interesting account of Reuther's childhood in *Brothers Reuther and the Story of the UAW: A Memoir* (1976). Contemporary biographies by Reuther's peers such as Eldorous L. Dayton's conservative critique, *Walter Reuther: The Autocrat of the Bargaining Table* (1958), and Irving Howe and B. J. Widick's socialist critique, *The UAW and Walter Reuther* (1949), provide contemporary perspectives on Reuther from the right and the left. Other standard biographies published just after Reuther's death include Frank Cormier and William J. Eaton, *Reuther* (1970), and Jean Gould and Lorena Hickok, *Walter Reuther: Labor's Rugged Individualist* (1972).

MICHELLE BRATTAIN

REVEL, Bernard (17 Sept. 1885–2 Dec. 1940), educator and leader of modern Orthodox Judaism, was born in Pren, a suburb of Kovno, Lithuania, the son of Rabbi Nahum Shraga Revel and Leah Gittelevitch. Identified at age six as a budding talmudic prodigy, Revel's precociousness manifested itself at the yeshiva in Telshe, where Revel was ordained at the age of sixteen. While still in Lithuania, Revel became a devotee of the Jewish Enlightenment, which whet his interest in Jewish history, Hebrew literature, and Semitic Languages. In addition, he acquired a solid grounding in secular disciplines when he earned the equivalent of a Gymnasium education. He was also attuned to the sociopolitical currents that augured change in Russia. In fact, it was his arrest during the Russian Revolution of 1905 for supporting Jewish Socialist activities that hastened his departure for the United States the following year.

Between 1906 and 1915, Revel deepened his talmudic erudition while further broadening his general knowledge. He found the informal study environment of the Rabbi Isaac Elchanan Theological Seminary (RIETS) on New York City's Lower East Side reminiscent of the yeshiva in Telshe and conducive to his continued rabbinic studies. Revel would later publish learned treatises on questions of Jewish civil law, rules regarding ritual purity and impurity, laws affecting Jewish priestly behavior, and a host of other theoretical talmudic issues. Revel also studied comparative religion, philosophy, and Semitics at New York University, earning in 1909 an M.A. for a work on the medieval Spanish Jewish philosopher Bachya Ben Joseph ibn Pakudah. He then studied at Dropsie College in Philadelphia where, in 1911, he wrote his doctoral dissertation, "Karaite Halakah and Its Relation to Sadducean, Samaritan and Philonian Halakah." Concomitant with these Jewish studies, in 1907–1908, he studied American law at Temple University and ancient Hindu philosophy, oriental languages and economics at the University of Pennsylvania. In 1909 Revel married Sarah Travis, the daughter of Oklahoma oil magnates. Their union would produce two children.

In 1911 Revel entered his brother-in-law's petroleum business in Tulsa but reserved all of his spare time for continued personal scholarly quests. Revel's professional involvement in Jewish communal and educational life began in 1915, when he was approached by leaders of the RIETS to serve as first president of their reorganized school. Revel's appointment represented the end of a decade of internal strife at the seminary as the school was transformed from a transplanted East European yeshiva to an American Orthodox seminary, still rooted in the traditions of Torah learning but now also dedicated to training young men to serve the modern communal and intellectual needs of acculturating Jews. For the students and their supporters within the immigrant community who had pushed hard for modernization against resistant founders and faculty, Revel was the ideal man to institutionalize change.

Revel began by developing and implementing a diversified course of study. Beginning in 1915, RIETS students were required to study, in addition to Talmud and Codes, Jewish history, the Bible and its medieval and modern commentaries, Jewish history, philology, homiletics, and pedagogy. Revel himself taught Talmud and Codes. The following year, Revel founded the Talmudical Academy, a "High School Department of the Rabbinical College." This endeavor, the second phase of his modernization plan, transcended the goal of simply recruiting potential rabbinical students. With its integrated curriculum of yeshiva learning and New York State Regents–certified high school general studies, the Talmudical Academy ensured that both future rabbis and Jewishly educated laymen would possess the educational balance that modernity demanded and that Jewish teachings permitted.

Also in 1916, Revel attempted to form, under the auspices of RIETS, a society of Jewish academicians to further the ideals of traditional Judaism and to promote Jewish scholarship in the United States. But this endeavor, which would have linked professors at the Jewish Theological Seminary, Hebrew Union College, and Dropsie College, among other institutions, foundered due in part to intradenominational competition.

Revel's wide-ranging initiatives—facilitated in part by Travis family funding—were met with less than universal approbation. Old line rabbis from Eastern Europe, including some Talmud faculty members, wondered out loud about the necessity of disciplines like history and philology and philosophy, unheard of in old world yeshivas, within the curriculum, and they frequently questioned the religious reliability of some of the Jewish professors Revel had brought in to teach these subjects. Revel did not confront his critics head-on. His strategy was to bring in and appoint to his core Talmud faculty men like Rabbis Solomon Polachek of the Lida yeshiva and Moses Soloveitchik of Warsaw's Tachkemoni Rabbinical Seminary.

In 1919 Revel took temporary leave in order to return to Tulsa to help save the Travises' faltering oil business. In his absence, Rabbi Meyer Berlin, leader of the Mizrachi movement (Religious Zionists) in America, was appointed acting president of RIETS. Berlin quickly moved to append the Mizrachis' own fledgling Teachers Institute to Revel's school. Upon his return to the presidency in 1923, Revel did not undo what Berlin had initiated. He saw in the Teachers Institute the potential to produce well-trained Orthodox teachers, which was a necessary element of his plan to raise up many "Torah-informed" Jewish lay people as well as the "exceptional students" who would become the American Orthodox rabbis of the future.

This widening of the Orthodox seminary's purview was only a prelude to Revel's most dramatic undertaking: the establishment in 1928 of Yeshiva College, a liberal arts college under American Orthodox auspices. For Revel, Yeshiva College had a twofold mission, both practical and ideological. It had become clear to him that many of his Talmudical Academy graduates wanted to pursue a college education while also continuing to learn Torah at RIETS. With religious classes running from morning to midafternoon, night school sessions at schools like the City College of New York were the only options for these graduates. Students quickly realized, however, that part-time attendance delayed them greatly in earning their college degrees. Moreover, once on the college scene, they discovered that rarely, if ever, were their particular religious needs taken into account. Thus, many Talmudical Academy students were choosing not to pursue advanced Jewish education. Revel solved this practical problem by designing Yeshiva College to merge the logistical and socioreligious aspects of seminary and college life. But in addition, Revel believed in the intellectual and spiritual compatibility of religious and general education. For him, it was logical, if not imperative, that the college forcefully promote the synthesis of Torah study with study of the liberal arts. This philosophy, which later would be characterized as "Torah U'Mada" (literally, Torah and science), became the ideological bedrock of Yeshiva University, founded in 1946, six years after Revel's death.

Revel encountered opposition from many different directions. American Jewish Committee president and Reform Jewish lay leader Louis Marshall (1856–1929) was perturbed by Yeshiva College's self-segregation of Jewish students and feared that unsympathetic college admission officers would use Yeshiva's existence as an additional rationale for their discriminatory quota systems. From fundamentalist Orthodox quarters came a reinforced version of the complaint that was first articulated when Revel began to reorganize RIETS: the college was diminishing student commitment to traditional studies and was unconscionably equating the ways and teachings of the Gentile world with that of the traditional Jewish community. Revel persevered, and in 1929, a year after its founding, Yeshiva College and RIETS moved from the Lower East Side to the newly built Washington Heights section of Manhattan.

During the 1930s financial problems rather than ideological questions threatened to undo Revel's grand designs. Plans for Yeshiva College called for the construction of five buildings on campus, but only one was built (in 1929), as neither the Travises nor the larger Orthodox Jewish community had the financial wherewithal during the Great Depression to back continued growth. Meanwhile, Revel found it very difficult to pay faculty and support the many indigent students. Nevertheless, in 1937 he founded the Graduate School for Jewish Studies which, after his death, was renamed the Bernard Revel Graduate School. Revel died in New York City.

• The only full-length biography is Aaron Rothkoff, *Bernard Revel: Builder of American Jewish Orthodoxy* (1972), which contains a full bibliography. See also Jeffrey S. Gurock, *The Men and Women of Yeshiva: Higher Education, Orthodoxy and American Judaism* (1988), chapters 3–7.

JEFFREY S. GUROCK

REVEL, Harry (21 Dec. 1905–3 Nov. 1958), composer of popular music, was born in London, England. Nothing is known of his parents. He studied piano at the Guildhall School but left when his favorite teacher died. By the age of fifteen, Revel was an itinerant pianist and songwriter, roaming Europe as a performer in several eclectic bands. One Parisian group was "Hawaiian" and another, the "New York Jazz," included two Englishmen, two Italians, three Russians, two Frenchmen, and a Texan. At seventeen he published a song ("Oriental Eyes") in Italy; he wrote an operetta (*Was Frauen träumen*) that was staged in Berlin in 1922.

In England Revel collaborated in 1928–1929 with Rowland Leigh to create André Charlot's cabaret revues at the Grosvenor House and the Hotel Splendide. His interests turned toward American popular music. With Noble Sissle he wrote "Just Give the Southland to Me," "Guiding Me Back Home," "I'm Going Back to Old Nebraska" (which sold 500,000 copies), and a staccato novelty song, "The Little Dutch Doll."

In 1929 Revel came to the United States, where he collaborated with several lyricists. He formed a vaudeville act, accompanying a young Polish singer, comic, and lyricist named Mack Gordon, but they abandoned vaudeville to write songs. In 1930 Revel and Gordon interpolated a song in the show *Meet My Sister* and in 1931 were hired by the ailing Florenz Ziegfeld, whose fortunes were suffering the effects of the depression. It was his last *Follies*, however, and "Cigarettes, Cigars" for Ruth Etting and "Help Yourself to Happiness" for Harry Richman did not outlast it. Gordon and Revel's score *Fast and Furious* sank after six performances, and the demand for their black revues also collapsed. *Everybody's Welcome* included the Dorseys' orchestra, but the single Gordon-Revel song was upstaged by Herman Hupfeld's "As Time Goes By."

In 1932 Gordon and Revel placed one song in *Marching By*, which ran only thirty-one performances, and another in *The Little Racketeer*, which closed after forty-eight shows. Another score (including "Quick Henry, the Flit," which adapted an insecticide's current advertising slogan to the needs of a comic number, and a typical novelty number, "I Stumbled Over You and Fell in Love") accompanied *Smiling Faces*, a faded finale for its dancing comic star, Fred Stone. It managed thirty-three performances. Outside Broadway, their "On a Certain Sunday" was bright and slangy, "I Played the Fiddle for the Czar" was an upbeat specialty for Ben Bernie, the "yowsah" man, and

"Underneath the Harlem Moon" became a runaway hit that brought a Paramount Pictures contract.

By this time Revel's characteristic song style was set. Writing in a conventional 32-bar *a a b a* format, he employed repetitions of simple phrases or of single notes (which could be catchy or, at their worst, annoying) surging up the scale in the song's release and sometimes again in the climax. "Underneath the Harlem Moon" added razzmatazz tempo; Gordon's lyrics transplanted to Harlem with light satire the African-American stereotypes typical of the pseudo-southern popular songs of recent decades. Somehow it all worked together.

Perhaps the challenge of writing entire scores—on a virtual assembly-line basis but for guaranteed salary—without necessarily knowing the film's story line was exactly what Revel and Gordon needed. From 1933 to 1939 they were among the most successful songwriters in the second and most significant wave of Hollywood musical motion pictures, writing all or most of the music for thirty films. They worked for Paramount until 1936, providing Bing Crosby and Ethel Merman with their earliest screen material, as well as some of Al Jolson's last. They made the Hit Parade quickly with "Did You Ever See a Dream Walking?," written for Ginger Rogers in *Sitting Pretty* in 1933. Revel and Gordon so typified their craft that in this motion picture they were also cast as actors—a pianist and a song publisher, respectively. Later they played singing coaches in *Collegiate*. In 1935, when they won nine bonus awards from the American Society of Composers, Authors, and Publishers (often writing a half-dozen film songs without the benefit of a script), they maddened the nation with the jerkily repetitious "(Lookie Lookie Lookie) Here Comes Cookie." In 1936 they moved to Twentieth-Century Fox, where, in *Poor Little Rich Girl*, they had a number one Hit Parade song for Shirley Temple ("When I'm with You") and, in *Stowaway*, another for Alice Faye ("Goodnight, My Love"). Gordon and Revel were among the many American songwriters who wrote for Britain's mercurial Jessie Matthews. They composed the score for her 1936 film *Head Over Heels*, including a "looniest-Juniest" title song ("Head Over Heels in Love") and "May I Have the Next Romance with You?," which became a British hit. Among the Gordon-Revel standards are "Paris in the Spring," "Love Thy Neighbor," "Never in a Million Years," "Stay as Sweet as You Are," the musically inventive "There's a Lull in My Life" and "Without a Word of Warning," the set piece "My Grandfather's Clock in the Hallway," the rollicking "Take a Number from One to Ten," and a depression chaser, "You Can't Have Everything." After 1937 the hits slowed, and their partnership ended in 1939. Though Gordon's new teaming with Harry Warren was productive, Revel's efforts with a variety of lyricists were not.

Revel threw himself into home-front action during World War II. Antedating organizations such as the USO and the Stage Door Canteen, he created touring shows for military bases and hospitals; he also edited a magazine for hospitalized veterans. His reward was two Academy Award nominations for best song. Unfortunately, they were inferior songs with some stiff competition: "There's a Breeze on Lake Louise" (with Mort Greene) lost in 1942 to "White Christmas," and "Remember Me to Carolina" (with Paul Francis Webster) lost in 1944 to "Swinging on a Star."

Revel finally conquered Broadway in 1945. *Are You with It?*, written with Arnold Horwitt, ran 268 appearances and produced the hit "Here I Go Again." Revel, who shared the show's profits, returned to Hollywood and began to write a different sort of music. This was popular song's twilight; its metamorphosis into "background music" paved the way for rock and roll.

The darkly dramatic "Jet My Love" (1949) acquired words after an instrumental version proved popular. In 1949 Revel founded the Realm Music Publishing Company and moved to New York. In 1953 the Gordon-Revel song "With My Eyes Wide Open I'm Dreaming," composed twenty years earlier, became a hit thanks to modern recording techniques that allowed Patti Page to sing it as a duet. In 1954 Revel's commercially sponsored suite "Perfume Set to Music" was a Carnegie Hall Pops selection. It was billed as "probably the only successful attempt to capture and reproduce with musical instruments and the human voice the 'sounds' of fragrance and scent." He wrote further relaxation-enhancing mood music: "Music out of the Moon," "Music for Peace of Mind," "Music from out of Space," and "And So to Sleep."

A dapper, lifelong bachelor who remained close to his family, Revel died of a cerebral hemorrhage in his New York West Side apartment. Although throughout his career Harry Revel proved himself a highly adaptable composer, he achieved permanency through his motion picture songs which evoked the lighthearted side of the depression.

• No biography of Harry Revel exists. His life and works are covered to some extent in biographical dictionaries dealing with music and musicians. The sheet music of Revel's songs is collected in sources such as the University Library in Cambridge, England, the Americana Collection at the New York Public Library, and the Archive of Popular American Music at the University of California, Los Angeles, Library. Revel's work for André Charlot is documented in the private collection of Charlot's daughter, Mrs. Joan Midwinter, of Pacific Palisades, Calif. Revel's screen career can be partially adduced from Clive Hirschhorn, *The Hollywood Musical* (1981) and his stage career from various works by Stanley Green, including *Broadway Musicals of the 30s* (1971), originally published as *Ring Bells, Sing Songs!* Underpinning all such works is the Theatre Collection of the New York Public Library.

JAMES ROSS MOORE

REVELL, Fleming Hewitt, Jr. (11 Dec. 1849–11 Oct. 1931), publisher, was born in Chicago, Illinois, the son of Fleming Hewitt Revell, a shipbuilder, and Emma Manning. He left public school at an early age, perhaps as early as nine, to help support the family by selling dry goods and, later, pharmaceuticals.

Revell began his publishing career in Chicago in 1869, when his brother-in-law, well-known evangelist Dwight L. Moody, persuaded him to take over as editor of a weekly religious publication, *Everybody's Paper*, which Moody had begun. Revell traveled through the Midwest securing subscriptions. On the strength of Revell's hard work and Moody's growing fame, the paper's circulation grew to 145,000. In 1870 Revell founded the company that still bears his name, opening a retail bookstore and publishing books for other retailers.

Revell married Josephine Barbour in 1872; they had a son and a daughter. In the same year, his company published its first full-length book, a collection of sermons by Scottish preacher W. P. Mackay that stayed in print more than seventy years. After Moody authorized Revell to publish his sermons, the Fleming H. Revell Company continued to produce Moody's books even after his death in 1899, eventually releasing some thirty titles under his name. Revell's association with Moody undoubtedly contributed to the company's quick growth. By 1880 Revell's list contained more than a hundred titles from a broad range of genres, including religious fiction, missionary biography, tracts, booklets, hymnbooks, and Sunday school periodicals. By the 1890s Revell was publishing more than 300 titles in a year.

Revell expanded his firm to include a branch in New York City in 1887. Revell's early success won him the respect of others in the publishing industry; his company was one of only twenty-seven invited to join the American Publishers' Association when it was founded in 1900. Fleming moved to New York in 1906 and eventually transferred his company headquarters there from Chicago.

In the years before World War I, Revell began publishing titles aimed at broader audiences. One of his most popular authors was Presbyterian minister Newell Dwight Hillis, whose books *Studies of the Great War*, *The Blot on the Kaiser's 'Scutcheon*, and *German Atrocities* encouraged Americans to get involved in the war, a cause Revell himself supported. Nevertheless, the bulk of Revell's titles continued to be aimed at evangelical audiences. After the war the Revell Company became a major source of material supporting the fundamentalist cause during the modernist-fundamentalist controversy from 1918 to 1929, publishing works by William Jennings Bryan and others.

Revell was an active member of the religious and civic community. He served as director of the Presbyterian Church USA Board of Home Missions from 1908 to 1923 and as a board member of the Moody Bible Institute, Wheaton College, Northfield Seminary, the New York Young Men's Christian Association, and American Missions to Lepers.

Despite having lost a great deal of his personal fortune during the stock market crash of 1929, Revell retired the same year, leaving his son to take his place as president. He died at his home in Riverdale-on-Hudson, New York. His company went on to publish such major religious authors as Dale Evans Rogers, Corrie ten Boom, Charles Colson, Hal Lindsey, Elizabeth Elliot, and Catherine Marshall.

Fleming H. Revell Company faced increasing competition from other Christian publishers after Revell's death, losing ground to firms such as Zondervan, Word, and Baker. The company was still flourishing when it was purchased by Scott, Foresman and Company in 1978, a move that helped Revell expand into trade publishing. Scott, Foresman sold Revell in 1983 to one of its greatest rivals, Zondervan. Zondervan sold off Revell to Guideposts Associates, publisher of Guideposts Magazine. In 1992 the company was sold for the fourth time in twelve years to Baker Book House.

Revell is remembered as a friendly man who has not received recognition as a major force in publishing. Allan Fisher, historian and publisher, has written that "if Revell had begun a general [rather than a religious] publishing company and enjoyed comparable success, he would be accorded far greater honor today."

• Information on Revell's early family life can be found in Paul D. Moody, *My Father* (1938), and J. C. Pollock, *Moody: A Biographical Portrait of the Pacesetter in Modern Mass Evangelism* (1963). The best sources of information on Revell's life and publishing career are Allan Fisher, *Fleming H. Revell Company: The First 125 Years, 1870–1995* (1995) and "The Early Years of Fleming H. Revell: A Preliminary Report" (1996), both available on request through Fisher at Baker Book House in Grand Rapids, Mich. Several articles appear in *Publishers Weekly*, including "Revell: Seventy-Five Years of Religious Book Publishing," 9 Dec. 1944, pp. 2232–36, and "Fleming Revell: A New Thrust," 4 Mar. 1988, pp. 42–45. See also George Doran, *Chronicles of Barabbas* (1935). Obituaries are in the *New York Times*, 12 Oct. 1931, and in *Publishers Weekly*, 17 Oct. 1931, pp. 1807–8.

EDWIN J. MCALLISTER

REVELL, Nellie McAleney (13 Mar. 1873–12 Aug. 1958), journalist and publicist, was born in Riverton, Illinois, the daughter of Hamilton H. McAleney and Elizabeth Evans. While Revell in later life referred to her father as editor and publisher of the *Springfield (Ill.) Republican*, there is no firm evidence this was the case. At the time of his death in 1909 in Springfield, he was described as a former army captain and bookkeeper for the U.S. government. According to Revell, she began her reporting career at age sixteen, over her father's objections. She claimed that when he would not hire her, she scooped his newspaper on her first assignment for a rival editor, forcing her father to give her a job.

She was married at an early age, first to Charles Smith, an advance agent for P. T. Barnum's circus. The couple had twin daughters, one of whom died in early adulthood. After her divorce from Smith she married Joseph Revell. Her second marriage may have ended in divorce, although Revell referred to herself as a widow, and friends believed that her husband had been killed in the Spanish-American War. The Revells had no children together, and she continued to use the name Revell throughout her life. In 1913 she married Arthur J. Kellar, a theatrical press agent, who died in 1940; they had no children.

After leaving Springfield in the late 1880s for a job on the *Chicago Journal*, Revell moved across the country, establishing a reputation as a flamboyant general assignment reporter in an era of sensational coverage and emotional writing. She worked for the *Denver Post*, the *Seattle Post-Intelligencer*, the *San Francisco Chronicle*, and the *Chicago Times*, covering police and court trials and claiming to be the first woman to cover a prize fight. Revell insisted on attending the Jim Corbett–Bob Fitzsimmons fight even though Corbett initially objected to the presence of a woman. "If I don't come neither will Fitzsimmons," she reportedly said. "I don't think he has to anyway. He could lick you by mail." She covered other front-page events such as the coronation of Czar Nicholas II in 1895, Queen Victoria's funeral in 1901, and the Harry K. Thaw murder trial in 1906.

Weary of reporting, in 1906 Revell took a job as press agent for a vaudeville show in Chicago. She found the atmosphere congenial, and contemporaries said she seemed to have been "brought up on P. T. Barnum's lot." By 1911 she was living in New York and employed as a publicity director for Percy Williams, who owned a string of theaters. An offer from the *New York World*, which then represented the apex of journalism, brought her back to reporting. A determined individual, she demanded to be treated equally with male reporters in assignments and respect for herself as a journalist. Years later she told an interviewer how she had reacted when the *World* city editor, Charles Chapin, criticized her work. "I threw a bottle of ink at him once. In telling the story, he used to say, 'Nellie threw it at me? Hell, she hit me.'" Around 1910 she left the *World* to go to the *Evening Mail*.

Supposedly annoyed when her column was put on the women's page, which Revell considered beneath her talents, in 1915 she left journalism to launch a remarkably successful career as a theatrical publicist. Her first client was Al Jolson. Other Broadway stars followed, including Lily Langtry, Lillian Russell, and Will Rogers as well as six circuses. She was head of publicity for the Keith-Orpheum motion-picture circuit and business manager for the Winter Garden and leading producers. She referred to herself as the world's first woman press agent.

Tragedy struck in 1919 at the height of her career. First, she lost her life's savings in a bad investment. Second, a severe spinal illness kept her hospitalized for five years with doctors fearing that she would never walk again. Notable friends, including Russell, George M. Cohan, Arthur Brisbane, Heywood Broun, and Bernard Baruch visited her in the hospital. Her theatrical friends also held benefit performances for her on Broadway and in Chicago to help pay her medical expenses. When she finally left the hospital in a wheelchair in 1924, the Friars, an actors' club founded by Cohan, made her its first woman member. In addition, she was made the only honorary member of the

New York Newspaper Women's Club. Revell was referred to in obituaries as the nation's "most famous invalid" in the 1920s and was described by Ishbel Ross in the 1930s as "one of the town [New York] characters."

Displaying an indomitable will, Revell published three inspirational books dealing with her fight for recovery: *Right Off the Chest* (1923), written while she was flat on her back in her hospital bed; *Fightin' Through* (1925); and *Funny Side Out* (1925). She also wrote a column on theatrical news and gossip for *Variety* while in the hospital. The strength of her nonfiction lay in its color and personal testimony rather than in its style or insight. She also wrote a novel about the circus, *Spangles* (1926), which became a motion picture.

Radio broadcasting marked a third phase of her career. In 1930, after she was able to walk again, Revell joined the National Broadcasting Company. She conducted fifteen-minute weekly interviews with celebrities from stage, screen, sports, and politics. She was known for her sharp wit and cracker-barrel philosophy. In her book *Fightin' Through*, she wrote, "The best lessons are taught by misfortune, for there is no such thing as free tuition in the University of Life." At the time of her retirement in 1947, Revell was conducting a program called "Neighbor Nell." During her years as a radio personality, she continued to write freelance magazine articles. When she underwent cataract operations in 1950, newspapers wrote human interest stories about her life. She received 30,000 pieces of fan mail.

Revell died in a New York hospital after breaking her hip, having lived the last eighteen years of her life at a hotel in the Times Square area. She is buried in the McAleney family plot in Springfield.

Her significance lies in the example that she presented to others. She established herself in journalism at a time when relatively few women were accepted, and she went on to prove that a woman could succeed in the male field of press agentry. She displayed pluck and courage, both personally and professionally.

• Scrapbooks and newspaper articles are in the Billy Rose Theater Collection of the New York Public Library, Lincoln Center. Jane Barton of Esperance, N.Y., also provided material. A feature story on Revell appeared in the *New York World-Telegram and Sun*, 1 Feb. 1950. References can be found in Ishbel Ross, *Ladies of the Press: The Story of Women in Journalism by an Insider* (1936), and Stanley Walker, *The City Editor* (1934). Some information on the family was obtained from Nancy McAleney of St. Louis, Mo., the widow of Revell's nephew. Obituaries are in the *New York Times* and the *New York Herald-Tribune*, both 14 Aug. 1958.

MAURINE H. BEASLEY

REVELLE, Roger Randall Dougan (7 Mar. 1909–15 July 1991), oceanographer, was born in Seattle, Washington, the son of William Roger Revelle, a lawyer and schoolteacher, and Ella Robena Dougan. In 1917 the family moved to Pasadena, California, where Revelle attended public schools and became interested in journalism. In 1925 he entered Pomona College (Claremont, Calif.), where he was attracted to geology by Professor Alfred O. Woodford. He received an A.B. in geology in 1929, had a year of graduate study at Claremont College, and in 1930 entered the University of California (Berkeley). In 1931 he married Ellen Virginia Clark; they had four children.

Thomas Wayland Vaughan, director of Scripps Institution of Oceanography (SIO), a research station of the University of California in La Jolla, wanted a graduate student to examine sediment cores taken from the Pacific Ocean floor by scientists on the research ship *Carnegie* in 1928–1929. Revelle got permission from his adviser, George Davis Louderback, to do the task, and the family moved to La Jolla in 1931. He had his first taste of scientific work at sea as a graduate student and relished it. He received his Ph.D. from the University of California in 1936, with a dissertation on the marine bottom samples he had been studying. He then spent a year in Norway studying with oceanographer Bjørn Helland-Hansen and returned to Scripps Institution of Oceanography as an instructor. There he participated in two research expeditions to the Gulf of California and pursued researches in marine geology.

From 1941 to 1947 Revelle served in the U.S. Naval Reserve, rising from lieutenant (j.g.) to commander, in science-related assignments in Washington, D.C., with the Hydrographic Office and the Bureau of Ships. In 1946 he helped establish the Office of Naval Research and served as head of its geophysics branch. That same year he was in charge of the oceanographic program of the first postwar atomic test at Bikini Atoll, Operation Crossroads, which involved many of the nation's oceanographers. The scientists measured the waves produced by the explosions, the diffusion of radioactive waters, the unique base surge produced by the underwater explosion, and the effects on marine organisms. The following year Revelle organized another survey of Bikini Atoll, during which scientists drilled deep into the coral and, in Revelle's opinion, confirmed Charles Darwin's idea that atolls are sunken islands.

In 1948 Revelle returned to Scripps Institution of Oceanography as a professor of oceanography. He became director of the institution in 1951, after a year as acting director, and led it into a major expansion. Through Revelle's military connections, the institution had already acquired surplus military vessels for research. Revelle led two of the institution's major Pacific expeditions in 1950 and 1952, and he helped arrange many others. On the 1950 trip Revelle participated with Arthur Eugene Maxwell in taking and analyzing the first measurements of the flow of heat from the earth's interior through the floor of the ocean, with an instrument devised chiefly by British geophysicist Edward Crisp Bullard.

That program was an early example of Revelle's keen interest in all aspects of ocean-related geology and geophysics. He kept abreast of possibilities in this field, and, at an unusually productive time of ocean exploration because of federal support, he was able to arrange for scientists to participate in expeditions to gather new information. The geological/geophysical trips investigated deep-sea trenches, sea-floor sedimentation, heat flow, the nature of guyots (flat-topped, submerged volcanoes), and magnetism. These early researches formed a basis for later theories of sea-floor spreading and plate tectonics that became established during the 1960s. Revelle was aboard the drilling ship *CUSS I* in 1961 when it acquired the first sample of basalt rock from beneath 600 feet of sea-floor sediments off Mexico. Then in 1964 he and the directors of three other oceanographic institutions set up the Deep Sea Drilling Project, a program for extensive drilling throughout the world's oceans. Revelle and Hans Eduard Suess became much concerned with the possible increase in carbon dioxide in the atmosphere from the use of fossil fuels, so Revelle enticed Charles David Keeling to SIO in 1956 to pursue the problem; Keeling's research established a baseline of data for continuing studies.

Revelle was an international scientist. He helped plan the oceanographic program of the International Geophysical Year from 1957 to 1958, which involved many Scripps scientists on three expeditions and on island monitoring of sea levels. In 1957 he was the first chairman of the Special (later Scientific) Committee on Oceanic Research, which worked with other scientific agencies to conduct the first International Oceanographic Congress at the United Nations in New York in 1959, a congress for which he served as president. The congress proposed an International Indian Ocean Expedition that involved forty ships and scientists from many nations from 1959 to 1965 in a comprehensive oceanographic study of the Indian Ocean. Revelle organized a cooperative program with the Thai and South Vietnamese governments, for which the SIO vessel *Stranger* was in the South China Sea and the Gulf of Thailand from 1959 to 1961. There scientists from Southeast Asia worked with Scripps Institution oceanographers on fisheries and marine resources. Revelle served on various commissions of UNESCO (United Nations Educational, Scientific, and Cultural Organization), and he attended the Pugwash conferences on science and world affairs from 1958 to 1981. He was the first chairman of the National Academy of Sciences committee for the International Biological Program (1966), which organized studies of major ecosystems and the interactions between humans and the environment.

He also expanded Scripps Institution of Oceanography, first by increasing the graduate program and then by working with university officials and the city of San Diego to establish the University of California San Diego (UCSD) in the late 1950s. For that campus Revelle recruited leaders in their field to set up each department, and he established the concept of individual colleges within the campus. The first of these, with an emphasis on science, was named Revelle College in his honor.

From 1961 to 1963, on leave from Scripps Institution, Revelle was science adviser to Secretary of the Interior Stewart Udall. One of his significant contributions was advising the government of Pakistan on methods of improving agricultural yields.

In 1964 Revelle became the Richard Saltonstall Professor of Population Policy at Harvard and director of the new Harvard Center for Population Studies, where he organized research efforts on population and development. After retirement in 1975 he returned to UCSD as professor of science and public policy until his death. He advised university officials and inspired students.

Revelle received many scientific honors, including membership in the National Academy of Sciences (1957) and the National Medal of Science (1990).

Described as "imaginative, energetic, forthright," and "one of the two or three most articulate spokesmen for science in the western world," Revelle's primary ability was promoting scientific inquiry. He died in La Jolla, California.

• Revelle's extensive archival papers are in the archives of Scripps Institution of Oceanography, University of California San Diego, La Jolla (collections MC6 and MC6A), including a nearly complete bibliography. Oral histories by Revelle are at the University of California at Berkeley, Scripps Institution of Oceanography, and Texas A&M University. Revelle provided autobiographical material in "The Age of Innocence and War in Oceanography," *Oceans* 1, no. 3 (1968): 6–16, and in "How I Became an Oceanographer and Other Sea Stories," *Annual Review of Earth and Planetary Sciences* 15 (1987): 1–23. Biographies are Sanford Lakoff et al., University of California, *In Memoriam* (1991), pp. 159–69, especially on Revelle's role in founding UCSD; William A. Nierenberg, *Proceedings of the American Philosophical Society* 136, no. 4 (1992): 597–600; and Robert L. Fisher, Geological Society of America, *Memorials* (March 1993): 35–38. Additional material about Revelle as director of Scripps Institution of Oceanography is in Elizabeth Noble Shor, *Scripps Institution of Oceanography: Probing the Oceans* (1978).

ELIZABETH NOBLE SHOR

REVELS, Hiram Rhoades (27 Sept. 1827?–16 Jan. 1901), senator, clergyman, and educator, was born in Fayetteville, North Carolina, the son of free parents of mixed blood. Little is known of his family or early years. At eight or nine he enrolled in a private school for black children, where he was "fully and successfully instructed by our able teacher in all branches of learning" (Revels, p. 2). About 1842 his family moved to Lincolnton, North Carolina, where Revels became a barber. Two years later he entered Beech Grove Seminary, a Quaker institution two miles south of Liberty, Indiana. In 1845 he enrolled at another seminary in Darke County, Ohio, and during this period may also have studied theology at Miami University in Oxford, Ohio.

Revels's preaching career with the African Methodist Episcopal (AME) church began at this time. He was ordained as a minister in the Indiana Conference at some point between 1845 and 1847 and was confirmed as an elder by the same organization in 1849. His first pastorate may have been in Richmond, Indiana, and he is known to have served the Allen Chapel

Church in Terre Haute during the 1840s. In the early 1850s he married Phoeba A. Bass, with whom he had six children.

Revels traveled extensively, becoming a noted preacher in the Indiana-Ohio-Illinois area before the end of the 1840s. An urge to carry the gospel to slaves led him to expand his circles, and in the 1850s he journeyed to lecture and teach in Missouri, Kansas, Kentucky, and Tennessee. His freedom of movement suggests that Revels was not a known abolitionist, but he later recounted that he "always assisted the fugitive to make his escape" when in a free state (Thompson, p. 31).

In late 1853 Revels moved his ministry to an AME church in St. Louis, but because of a dispute with the bishop during the following year, he left both the congregation and the AME denomination, accepting the pastorate of Madison Street Presbyterian Church in Baltimore, Maryland. He stayed in that position for two years before entering Knox College in Galesburg, Illinois. In 1857 he returned to Baltimore and to his former denomination, becoming the pastor of an AME church in the city. He also was named principal of a high school for blacks, beginning his career as an educational administrator.

With the outbreak of the Civil War, Revels helped organize black work battalions for the Union army. In 1863 he moved back to St. Louis to teach at a high school for blacks and there continued his efforts to aid the North, participating in the organization of the first black regiment from Missouri. Again he did not stay long, moving to Mississippi in 1864 to work with the freedmen. Based primarily in Jackson, he was instrumental in the establishment of several schools and churches in the Jackson-Vicksburg area. Some sources claim that he was also a regimental chaplain and worked with the Vicksburg provost marshal's office.

In late 1865 Revels aligned himself with the AME Church North, the denomination with which he would be associated for the rest of his career. He held pastorates in Leavenworth, Kansas, Louisville, Kentucky, and New Orleans, Louisiana, before becoming the presiding elder at a church in Natchez, Mississippi, in June 1868. That summer Adelbert Ames, military governor of Mississippi, appointed Revels to the city board of aldermen. Although little is known about his term of service, his primary focus was apparently on improving the city educational system.

As his prominence in the community grew, Revels, who was one of the most highly educated African Americans in the state, was encouraged to seek higher office, and in late 1869 he agreed to run as a Republican for the Adams County seat in the state senate. With the military Reconstruction government assuring black voting privileges, Revels won easily, as three-fourths of the people in the county were African Americans. He was one of thirty-six blacks chosen for the legislature from across the state.

Revels was invited to offer the invocation at the opening of the legislative session. One participant later recalled that the prayer "made [him] a United States Senator, because he made a deep, profound and favorable impression upon everyone who was fortunate enough to be within the sound of his voice" (*Journal of Negro History* 16:107). Two unexpired Senate terms, dating from before the Civil War, did have to be filled, and the black legislators were insistent that at least one seat be given to an African American. Their preferred candidate, James Lynch, had been appointed secretary of state, so they turned to Revels. After three days and seven ballots, Revels was elected on 20 January to fill the seat vacated by Jefferson Davis in 1861.

The nation's first African-American senator arrived in Washington ten days after his election. He could not present his credentials until Mississippi was formally readmitted to the Union, which finally took place on 23 February. Three days of contentious debate over whether to seat Revels followed, with the Senate voting forty-eight to eight in favor of accepting his credentials on 25 February. Revels was then sworn in and seated.

Although his brief Senate term was relatively undistinguished, Revels's skill as an orator, honed through decades in the pulpit, earned favorable attention from the national press. He introduced three bills, but only one passed—a petition for the removal of civil and political disabilities from an ex-Confederate. He favored amnesty for white southerners "just as fast as they give evidence of having become loyal men and of being loyal," a stance that drew criticism from some in the black community. Revels served briefly on the District of Columbia Committee and nominated the first African American for enrollment at West Point (the candidate failed the entrance examination).

Revels returned to Mississippi upon the completion of his term in March 1871, and Governor James L. Alcorn asked him to oversee the establishment of a college for black males. The legislature suggested that the school be named Revels University, but the former senator declined the honor, recommending that the governor's name be used. In 1872 Alcorn University opened in Claiborne County, Mississippi, with Revels as the first president. His duties were interrupted briefly in 1873, when he was named secretary of state ad interim.

The new governor, Ames, who had given Revels his start in politics, pressured Revels into resigning the Alcorn presidency in July 1874, apparently because of Revels's political ties with ex-governor Alcorn. A third of the student body and a number of faculty members left in protest against the action. Revels was reappointed as president two years later, when John M. Stone became governor. In the interim he served churches in Holly Springs and New Orleans and briefly edited the *Southwestern Christian Advocate*.

Health problems and Alcorn's financial woes led Revels to resign again in 1882. He moved back to Holly Springs, where he taught theology at Rust College for a few years and assisted the pastor of the local AME North church. He died while attending a religious conference in Aberdeen, Mississippi.

• Collections of Revels's papers are at the Schomburg Center for Research in Black Culture, New York, N.Y., and at Alcorn State University. Revels's "Autobiography" is in the Carter G. Woodson Collection, Library of Congress. The most thorough examination of his life and career is Julius E. Thompson, "Hiram R. Revels, 1827–1901: A Biography" (Ph.D. diss., Princeton Univ., 1973), which includes an extensive bibliography. Other biographies include Elizabeth Lawson, *The Gentleman from Mississippi, Our First Negro Senator* (1960), and Gerald E. Wheeler, "Hiram R. Revels: Negro Educator and Statesman" (M.A. thesis, Univ. of California, Berkeley, 1949). William B. Gravely, "Hiram Revels Protests Racial Separation in the Methodist Episcopal Church (1876)," *Methodist History* 8 (1970): 13–20, mentions Revels's work in the Methodist Episcopal church. Obituaries are in the *Natchez (Miss.) Daily Democrat*, 18 Jan. 1901, and the *Southwestern Christian Advocate*, 31 Jan. 1901.

KENNETH H. WILLIAMS

REVERE, Paul (Dec. 1734–10 May 1818), craftsman, patriot, and businessman, was born in Boston, Massachusetts, the son of Paul Revere, a goldsmith, and Deborah Hichborn (or Hitchborn). Revere's father, born Apollos Rivoire, emigrated from France to Boston in 1715 at the age of thirteen and apprenticed with John Coney, a prominent local gold/silversmith. Shortly before his marriage he changed his name, first to Paul Rivoire and then to Paul Revere. The son's birth date has long been the source of confusion since only his baptismal date, 22 December 1734 OS and 1 January 1735 NS, is recorded. Revere's early life, fairly typical of boys of his day and economic status, included basic schooling at the North Writing School. During his teens he entered into a formal agreement with fellow North End youths to ring the bells at Christ Church for a fee. Revere's own words, "My Father was a Goldsmith. . . . I learned the trade of him," confirm that as the eldest surviving son, he apprenticed with his father, thus beginning his most enduring occupation. Though overshadowed by the fame of his son, the elder Revere's skill as a gold/silversmith may actually have equaled that of his son. The younger Revere noted that his father died "in the year 1754, he left no estate, but he left a good name." Just nineteen years old, Revere ran the shop with the help of his mother. In 1756 he received a commission as a second lieutenant of artillery and spent the better part of a year on an unsuccessful expedition to capture the French fort at Crown Point on Lake Champlain.

Once home from his military service, Revere took over the management of the silver shop, which his mother had operated with the help of a journeyman in his absence. In 1757 he married Sarah Orne. Luckily, Revere's father had left not only his "good name" but also a fully equipped silver shop and customer base. Surviving business ledgers for the silver shop, dated 1761–1797, reveal a great deal about his business operation. His patrons included middle-class artisans like himself as well as politically and socially prominent New Englanders. Ranging from simple spoons to elaborate tea services and from shoe buckles to commemorative tankards, silver bearing the mark "REVERE" or "*PR*" is prized.

In 1760, with his initiation into St. Andrew's Lodge, Revere began what would be a lifelong affiliation with Freemasonry. This association had an impact on his businesses, social life, philanthropic attitudes, and political ideals. It also provided early opportunities for him to develop his leadership potential. His skill as a craftsman and his standing as a Freemason made him the logical choice for the production of masonic silver—seals, ladles, and jewels (emblems of office)—and engravings for certificates and meeting notifications.

While the silver shop would be the cornerstone of Revere's professional life, he also expanded into other trades as circumstances and financial need demanded. By the early 1760s he had begun to turn to copperplate engraving as an important and profitable aspect of his business and a means of supporting his large family. He engraved trade cards, bookplates, certificates, political cartoons, and illustrations for the *Royal American Magazine*. Not an artist, he generally copied freely from available print sources, both English and American. In the years after the Stamp Act of 1765, he increasingly used this skill for political purposes. His shop accounts and newspaper advertisements indicate that he also practiced dentistry sporadically from 1768 to 1775. According to a 1770 newspaper advertisement, his abilities as a dentist included selling dentifrice, cleaning teeth, and wiring false teeth "as well as any Surgeon Dentist whoever came from London." Though surprising in the modern age, this was not such an unusual career option for someone skilled in the manipulation of silver and/or gold wire, which was used to hold replacement teeth (animal or ivory) in place. However, making a full set of false teeth, an accomplishment with which he is often credited, was beyond his abilities.

During the 1760s and 1770s, years of heightened political agitation, Revere's silver business suffered, and much of his time was given over to political groups, including the Sons of Liberty, the Long Room Club, and the North Caucus. Yet his skills as a craftsman were put to good use advancing the patriot cause with key propaganda pieces, such as the *Liberty Bowl*, which he made and published in 1768, and his response to the Boston Massacre, a 1770 engraving entitled *The Bloody Massacre Perpetrated in King Street Boston on March 5th 1770*. This work inaccurately depicts soldiers firing in unison at their commander's order on a group of helpless Bostonians, with shots from revenue officers issuing from the customhouse. The print made good propaganda, thanks to these misleading details. It remains the most reprinted image of the event. In that year he moved his family into an old but roomy home in North Square. His young wife died in 1773, shortly after the birth of their eighth child. Revere, left with several small children, his elderly mother, and businesses to run, married Rachel Carlisle Walker later that same year. They had eight children.

One of the defining events in prewar Boston was the 16 December 1773 Boston Tea Party. According to tradition, this action was planned during meetings of the North Caucus at the Green Dragon Tavern. Though Revere's participation in the actual destruction of tea cannot be documented, he certainly played a key role in planning and responding to it. Following this event, Parliament issued the Intolerable Acts, which revoked the Massachusetts Charter and closed the port of Boston. At this time Revere began his work as an express rider in the employ of the various committees of the Massachusetts government. In his role as trusted courier he brought news of Boston events, messages, and copies of legislation to other colonies. From late 1773 until 1775 he made more than a dozen rides to New York, Philadelphia, and Portsmouth, New Hampshire.

The best-known but least-understood event in Revere's life was his ride on 18–19 April 1775, which was made famous by Henry Wadsworth Longfellow's wonderful but largely inaccurate 1861 poem "Paul Revere's Ride." On the previous Sunday, the 16th, Revere made a ride to alert John Hancock and Samuel Adams in Lexington and passed the word to warn the locals to hide their stores of ammunition in Concord. For the next few days, Revere and a group of "upwards of thirty, cheifly [sic] mechanics, who formed our selves in to a Committee" continued to watch and wait, as they had done since the autumn of 1774, for evidence of British movements. On the evening of the 18th Dr. Joseph Warren, Revere's close friend, sent for him and instructed him to ride to Lexington to warn Hancock and Adams that the British troops were marching west from Boston. Warren also dispatched a second rider, William Dawes, by a different route. By his own account, Revere was rowed across the Charles River to Charlestown, where he borrowed a horse from Deacon John Larkin and verified that the local Sons of Liberty had seen the signals: two lanterns hung in the bell tower of Christ Church to indicate that the troops would row "by sea" across the river to Cambridge rather than march "by land" over Boston Neck. Revere had arranged for a friend, probably Robert Newman but possibly Captain John Pulling or both, to hang the lanterns so that other riders would be dispatched if he were prevented from leaving Boston. As Revere rode, he warned the countryside, stopping at several houses, and arrived at Lexington about midnight to alert Hancock and Adams that the troops were on the way. After a brief rest, Revere and Dawes decided to continue on to Concord. They were overtaken by Dr. Samuel Prescott, who agreed to join them. All three were stopped by a British patrol. Prescott and Dawes escaped; Revere was held for a time and released. His horse taken by the patrol, he returned to Lexington on foot in time to witness the skirmish on Lexington Green. Unable to return to Boston, Revere set up shop in Watertown, sending word to his wife to bring the children and join him. He once again put his considerable engraving skills to good use, printing currency for the Massachusetts Provincial Congress.

While remembered for his heroic work as a courier, Revere's regular military service was unspectacular at best. Though hoping for a commission in the Continental army, in November 1776 he settled for one as a lieutenant colonel in the Massachusetts State Train of Artillery and command of Castle William at the mouth of Boston Harbor. From there he was involved in three campaigns, one to return captured British troops from Worcester to Boston, a second to try to dislodge the British from Newport, Rhode Island, and a disastrous expedition to engage the British in Castine, Maine, the worst naval loss of the Revolution. In this last instance, Revere, in command of the artillery, was a part of an unwieldy American force sent in 1779 to lay siege to a smaller British force at a fort on the east side of Penobscot Bay. Confusion and lack of leadership allowed the British to organize a relief expedition, thus sealing the Americans' defeat. Revere was charged with cowardice and insubordination and forced to resign from the service. He demanded a court-martial, and in 1782, after almost three years and numerous petitions, delays, and hearings, he was acquitted of any wrongdoing, thus clearing his name. Controversy about this battle and Revere's actions continues, however.

After the war, Revere, ever the businessman, returned with fervor to his silver shop. The records for the shop indicate an active business that included the creation of fine silver, repairs, and engraving. Neither Boston's only nor its best silversmith, Revere was an exceptionally talented and innovative artisan. Some of his finest pieces, fluted teapots, were purchased by other smiths for resale. In the late eighteenth century, though still the master goldsmith, Revere increasingly left the shop to his eldest son, Paul Revere, as he explored other business ventures: "My dependence for a living will chiefly depend upon the Goldsmiths business, which will be carried out by my Son, under my inspection." Financed by his successful silver shop business, he in 1783 opened "a large Store of hard ware," which operated until around 1789. At times run from the same location as his silver shop, the store sold ready-made local and imported wares, such as looking glasses, cookware, tools, and copper kettles. Revere found that his first venture as a merchant was fraught with problems inherent in a business that relied on smooth seas and uninterrupted trade with England.

In 1788 Revere opened an iron foundry on the corner of Lynn and Foster streets in Boston's North End. This marked his expansion from the finer metals into baser ones, iron, brass, and eventually copper. Quickly the foundry moved into the casting of bells and cannon. Revere cast his first bell in 1792 for his own church, the Second Church of Boston. Over the years, Paul Revere & Son cast hundreds of bells, many of which survive both in use and in museum settings. By 1794 the foundry was producing ordnance for the new nation's defense, including howitzers, mortars, land artillery, and naval weaponry. In the late 1790s Congress commissioned six naval frigates, one of which,

USS *Constitution*, was to be made in Boston. Revere supplied large heavy fasteners (bolts or pins); barrels of smaller fittings, including spikes, staples, and nails; and other metal parts, such as rudder braces and pintles.

Revere, who now referred to himself as a gentleman, actively pursued "gentlemanly" pursuits and politics as well as his many business enterprises. He rallied the local mechanics in support of the ratification of the Constitution in 1788. In keeping with his business success and elevated economic position, he aspired to the recognition and prestige that accompanied civic activities. He was a member of the Massachusetts Charitable Fire Society and the Boston Library Society and served as the first president of the Massachusetts Charitable Mechanic Association. Though he never held a major elected office, Revere accepted an appointment from Governor Samuel Adams to serve as Suffolk County coroner from 1795 to 1801. He was also involved in the creation of Boston's first board of health, serving as its president (1799–1800).

Revere's affiliation with Freemasonry spanned nearly fifty years. He left his mark as an active member and frequent officeholder in St. Andrew's Lodge and Rising States Lodge, culminating with his election to the position of grand master of the Massachusetts Grand Lodge (1795–1797). In this role he chartered many lodges and presided over the laying of the cornerstone for the new Massachusetts State House in 1795. Revere wrote that serving as grand master was the "greatest happiness" of his life.

In 1800, though a man of sixty-five, Revere embarked on the most significant and ambitious business venture of his life, a copper-rolling mill in Canton, Massachusetts. Over the years the mill supplied the copper for the recoppering of the hull of USS *Constitution* in 1803, the dome of the new state house, boilers for several of Robert Fulton's early steamboats, and numerous more commonplace requests. As early as 1801 the firm had become Paul Revere and Son. In 1804 he formally made his son Joseph Warren Revere his business partner, and in 1811, though it seems Paul Revere never really retired, a new contract further divided the firm between son Joseph Warren Revere and grandsons Paul Revere and Thomas Stevens Eayres, Jr. Though he still owned a home on Charter Street in Boston, Revere and his wife spent a great deal of their time in Canton at their country home on the mill property.

In 1813 Revere endured the loss of both his beloved wife Rachel and his eldest son Paul. A man of strong will and constitution, Revere lived five more years and died in Boston. He was praised at his death as "a man of ingenuity and exertion." The son of an immigrant artisan, Revere died a moderately well-to-do businessman. At the time he was remembered more for his leadership ability, his business pursuits, and his service in the revolutionary era than for his midnight ride. He was once called an "ingenious mechanic," as his inventive spirit and financial ambitions combined to make him an innovative craftsman and manufacturer as well as successful businessman. History, too, would do well to remember his many contributions and achievements rather than focusing exclusively on Henry Wadsworth Longfellow's legendary rider crying an alarm in the night.

• The largest collection of Revere papers and business records, the Revere Family Papers, is held by the Massachusetts Historical Society. Many archives/libraries and museums own and display works by Revere, silver, engravings, and other metal items. Key collections are held by the Museum of Fine Arts in Boston and the American Antiquarian Society in Worcester, Mass. The Paul Revere Memorial Association, which owns and operates the Paul Revere House on Boston's Freedom Trail, has Revere-related artifacts and archival materials in its collection. The association publishes the *Revere House Gazette*, which often features articles on Revere, and its small in-house/staff library contains numerous unpublished manuscripts on important Revere themes. Works on the midnight ride include primary sources and secondary analyses. The best source is Revere's own description, with an introduction by Edmund S. Morgan, *Paul Revere's Three Accounts of His Famous Ride* (1961). Analyses of the ride include Jayne Triber et al., *History to Folklore* (1981), and David Hackett Fischer, *Paul Revere's Ride* (1994). Major biographical works on Revere, produced at somewhat regular intervals, each have a different emphasis, so they are all worth examining. Probably the earliest, Joseph Buckingham, "Paul Revere," *New England Magazine* 3 (1832): 304–14, appeared well before Longfellow's poem and is the best evidence of Revere's pre-poem stature. See also Elbridge Henry Goss, *The Life of Colonel Paul Revere* (2 vols., 1891); C. F. Gettemy, *The True Story of Paul Revere* (1905); and Esther Forbes, *Paul Revere and the World He Lived In* (1942). Nina Zannieri et al., *Paul Revere—Artisan, Businessman, and Patriot: The Man behind the Myth* (1988), is a series of essays on aspects of his life. Genealogical information is in Donald M. Nielsen, "The Revere Family," *New England Historical and Genealogical Register* 145 (1991): 291–316. Other sources examine his work, including Clarence S. Brigham, *Paul Revere's Engravings* (1954); Edward Stickney and Evelyn Stickney, *The Bells of Paul Revere and His Sons and Grandsons* (1976); Katheryn C. Buhler, *American Silver 1655–1825, in the Museums of Fine Arts* (2 vols., 1972) and *Paul Revere, Goldsmith 1735–1818* (n.d.); and *Paul Revere's Boston 1735–1818* (1975). The only complete work on Revere's active Masonic career is Edith Steblecki, *Paul Revere and Freemasonry* (1985). An obituary is in the Boston, Mass., *Columbian Centinel*, 13 May 1818.

NINA ZANNIERI

REVSON, Charles Haskell (11 Oct. 1906–24 Aug. 1975), founder, president, and chief executive officer of Revlon, Incorporated, was born in Somerville, Massachusetts, the son of Samuel Morris Revson, a Russian immigrant and cigar roller for the R. G. Sullivan Company, and Jeanette Weiss, a part-time saleswoman and store supervisor. Revson grew up in Manchester, New Hampshire, and after graduating from Manchester Central High School in 1923, he left for New York City, where he sold dresses for the Pickwick Dress Company. In 1930 he moved to Chicago, and after an unhappy stint there as a salesman he returned to New York and sold nail polish for Elka, a firm based in Newark, New Jersey.

Nail polish at this time was just a thin, translucent coating, available in different shades of just one color—red. Elka, although a small outfit, offered an opaque nail polish, and Revson was quick to see the revolutionary potential in this product. In 1932, when Elka refused Revson's request to make him a national distributor, he left the company. Revson then met Charles Lachman, who worked for Dresden, a chemical company in New Rochelle, New York. In 1932 Revson, his older brother Joseph, and Lachman formed the Revlon company—the "l" in Revlon stood for Lachman—to buy Dresden's nail polish, made to Revson's specifications. What Revlon offered was a creamy, opaque, nonstreak nail polish that came in a variety of colors. Revson became the president of Revlon, a title he was to keep until 1962, when he became chairman and chief executive officer, positions he held until his death. Three years after Revlon was founded, Revson's younger brother Martin joined the company as a sales manager.

Even though Revlon was born during the dark economic days of the Great Depression, it grew at a torrid pace because Revson sold his nail polish to beauty salons, which were enjoying a boom because of the permanent wave. In just four years sales multiplied forty-four times. By 1941 Revlon not only was selling to almost all of the nation's 100,000 beauty salons but also had a virtual monopoly over lipstick sales to them. The previous year saw the first of many additions to Revlon's product line with the introduction of Revlon lipstick, which was sold with the catchy advertising line "matching lips and fingertips." (Before then, women did not coordinate their lipstick and nail polish colors. Revlon offered different colors and shades for the season, the mood, or the occasion and encouraged color coordination.) During World War II Revson founded and served as president of the Vorset Corporation, which manufactured first-aid kits, pyrotechnics for the navy, and hand grenades for the army. Vorset was awarded an Army-Navy "E" award for its wartime production.

The 1950s saw Revson's masterful advertising strategies come of age and boost his company's earnings. Revson liked to advertise heavily relative to sales because that gave competitors the impression that Revlon was bigger than it really was. In 1935 Revlon first advertised outside trade journals, beginning in the *New Yorker* magazine. The 1940 "matching lips and fingertips" campaign was a smashing success, and Revlon ads appeared in magazines in full color and spread over two pages. In 1952 the brilliant "Fire and Ice" campaign began to promote a new line of cosmetics by that name. The campaign, considered a classic in the beauty business, saturated both general-circulation and fashion magazines with lush ads featuring model Dorian Leigh. Revlon also sponsored Fire and Ice beauty contests across the country. The campaign

generated a sensational response to the new Fire and Ice line.

What ultimately propelled Revlon above its competitors during the 1950s was its shrewd television advertising. In 1955 Revson agreed to become the sole sponsor of the game show "The $64,000 Question," which rose rapidly to the top of television ratings and became closely identified with its sponsor. Revson became a celebrity, and within just one year Revlon's sales increased by 54 percent and its earnings by 200 percent. Revlon stock, which in December 1955 was initially offered to the public at $12 per share, rose to $30 within weeks. The television advertising campaign created a momentum that kept Revlon ahead of its competitors for years to come.

As his company grew, Revson expanded and diversified his product line to include skin care products, shampoos and hair spray, perfumes, lotions, and men's products. He also branched out into unrelated business ventures by acquiring various companies. His first major acquisition came in 1957, when he bought the firm that made Esquire shoe polish, Knomark, Inc., which he sold a decade later. Revson's 1962 acquisition of sportsware manufacturer Evan-Picone for $12 million proved to be a major blunder when he had to sell it at a substantial loss four years later. Revson made other fruitless forays into plastic flowers, Schick shavers, and loungewear made in Hong Kong. But a major coup was his 1966 purchase of U.S. Vitamin and Pharmaceuticals Company for $67 million, a transaction he made against the advice of many associates. It was a risky venture because the drug company was a small-time operation with modest sales. But, as he did with Revlon, Revson advertised aggressively and diversified the company's products, and within ten years the company had grown enormously, accounting for 27 percent of Revlon's total earnings.

Revson transformed Revlon from a small company that netted $11,000 in profits during 1933, its first full year of operation, into a cosmetics empire that boasted profits of $606 million in 1974, his last full year as head of the company. Revson had notable gifts and qualities as an entrepreneur that enabled him to achieve such success. He was visually articulate and had a highly developed sense of color; his eye for subtleties in color was so sharp that he could spot one imperfect lipstick in a production line of hundreds. He possessed vision, a far-ranging imagination, and an instinct that enabled him to anticipate trends long before they became hot. This uncanny ability to read markets led him to develop separate cosmetic lines to satisfy individual markets. For example, his Revlon line was the popular-price line; his Natural Wonder line appealed to younger women; his Moon Drops line was directed at sufferers of dry skin. The exotic names Revson devised for his lines and color shades evinced his promotional flair—before Revlon, lipstick was simply called dark red, medium red, or some other staid variation. By creating new colors and market lines Revson also created demand, in much the same way as Detroit automakers created demand with annual model changes in their cars.

Revson was also fastidious about creating a theme to accompany every product and arranged a carefully orchestrated advertising and marketing blitz around the theme. "Theme is my religion," he once commented. One of the last perfume lines he introduced was "Charlie," an improbable theme that raised eyebrows among skeptical associates and competitors alike. But the perfume was a raging success, selling over $10 million in its first year and far outpacing any other fragrance. This kind of success was no accident: Revson took a high personal stake in all of his products, devoting considerable time to developing the perfect name or precise shade for a new lipstick or nail polish, personally choosing models and their clothing and letting few details escape him. In his early days as company president, he would often put nail polish on his own nails or apply lipstick to his hands to test them. Moreover, Revson made a fetish out of quality. His perfectionism as well as his onslaught of new products pushed Revlon continually ahead of competitors.

But there was a dubious side to Charles Revson. By some accounts he was abrasive, truculent, and profane, a man with a ravenous sexual appetite who had few inhibitions about satisfying it. Many of his business practices were eccentric as well as autocratic. Revson was known to tap employees' telephone lines to keep tabs on their performance. A Procrustean corporate ruler, he was intolerant of facial blemishes, beards, and brown shoes among male workers and frowned upon slacks among female employees. He was said to distrust women and employed few women in high posts, an irony since his empire's sales were directed at women. And while Revson demanded unrelenting standards from employees, he seldom expressed praise or appreciation for their work. He had no compunction about openly and severely rebuking executives, and the turnover rate in the upper echelons of his company was frightfully high. In 1958 there was a public falling-out when his brother Martin left the company and sued Revson on a number of charges emanating from a dispute over stock ownership; they eventually settled out of court, but their relationship remained frigid for years afterward. Revson harshly treated rivals in the cosmetics business as well, harboring a particularly intense dislike for Estee Lauder, his chief competitor. When cosmetics maker Elizabeth Arden referred to him icily as "that man," Revson retaliated by naming a line of men's fragrance "That Man."

Revson also lived a life of extreme opulence. A prized possession was his 257-foot yacht, the *Ultima II*, which he bought in 1967, refurbished, and used to host many soirees for the rich and famous. A large personal staff waited on him, and he was chauffeured about in a Rolls-Royce. His residences included a Park Avenue triplex and a Waldorf Towers suite in Manhattan, as well as a country estate at Premium Point, New York. A notable indulgence of his earlier years was cigarettes, as he consumed up to five packs per day, a habit he reliquished after a 1955 heart attack.

Revson married and divorced three times. His first marriage, to showgirl Ida Tompkins in 1930, was brief. In 1940 he married Johanna Catharina de Knecht, a model for Saks Fifth Avenue and the daughter of a Dutch publisher. They had two sons and adopted a daughter. The couple divorced in 1960. In 1964 Revson married Lyn Fisher Sherensky, whom he divorced in 1974.

Revson died in New York City.

• A brutally candid and unflattering portrayal of Revson is in Andrew Tobias, *Fire and Ice: The Story of Charles Revson—The Man Who Built the Revlon Empire* (1976). Profiles include D. Seligman, "Revlon's Jackpot; $64,000 Question," *Fortune*, Apr. 1956, pp. 136–38ff; "Unflabbergasted Genius," *Time*, 16 Nov. 1959, p. 106; "What I Don't Know about Women," *Cosmopolitan*, June 1960; and K. Lloyd, "Charles Revson: The Man from Beauty," *Vogue*, Apr. 1973, pp. 184–85ff. Obituaries are in *Time*, 8 Sept. 1975, and the *New York Times* and the *Washington Post*, both 25 Aug. 1975.

YANEK MIECZKOWSKI

REXROTH, Kenneth (22 Dec. 1905–6 June 1982), poet and translator, was born Kenneth Charles Marion Rexroth in South Bend, Indiana, the son of Charles Rexroth, a pharmaceuticals salesman, and Delia Reed. Owing to Charles's rocky career, the family moved frequently throughout the northern midwest until Delia died in 1916 and Charles in 1919. For the next three years, Rexroth lived with an aunt in Chicago. After his expulsion from high school, he educated himself in literary salons, nightclubs, lecture halls, and hobo camps while working as a wrestler, soda jerk, clerk, and reporter. In 1923–1924 he served a prison term for partial ownership of a brothel.

During the 1920s, Rexroth backpacked across the country several times, visited Paris and New York, taught in a religious school, and spent two months in a Hudson Valley monastery. Reflections on these experiences appear in his later poetry, but his early work was cubist and surrealist—often opaquely so. In 1927 he married Andrée Schafer, an epileptic painter, and they moved to San Francisco. In the late 1920s Rexroth's first poems appeared in *Pagany*, *Morada*, and Charles Henri Ford's *Blues*. He read much of Alfred North Whitehead's philosophy around this time.

During the 1930s, Rexroth studied mysticism and Communism. Readings of Jacob Boehme, St. Thomas Aquinas, and John Duns Scotus influenced revisions to his long poem, *Homestead Called Damascus*, published by New Directions in 1963. He also participated in the Communist party's John Reed Clubs, organizations supporting working-class writers and artists. Although skeptical about internal party politics, Rexroth helped organize clubs on the West Coast until 1938. He corresponded with other leftist poets, such as Louis Zukofsky and George Oppen, who wanted to save poetry from sentimentality and impressionism. In the mid-1930s, Rexroth participated in the Federal Arts Projects. In 1936 he spoke at the Western Writers

Conference and was published in *New Masses, Partisan Review, New Republic,* and *Art Front.* A long-standing association began in 1937 when Rexroth's poetry appeared in the second volume of James Laughlin's *New Directions in Poetry and Prose.* Rexroth would be a lifelong friend, guru, and skiing companion to this influential publisher.

In 1938 Rexroth shifted his political attention to an ecologically based pacifism. His first volume of poetry, *In What Hour* (1940), was tepidly received—a response he blamed on the literary establishment of the urban East Coast. After Andrée died in 1940, he married Marie Kass, a public health nurse who shared his passions for politics and camping. When the United States entered World War II, Rexroth registered as a conscientious objector and served as a psychiatric orderly. Objecting to war measures, he helped a number of Japanese Americans evade internment. During this period, he practiced Buddhism, Taoism, and yoga.

In 1944 his collection *The Phoenix and the Tortoise* appeared. The title poem is a long philosophical narrative interspersed with concrete sensual images. This kind of earthy Jeremiad was central to Rexroth's postwar aesthetic. He took the social role of the poet quite seriously, writing in a 1958 review of Kenneth Patchen's work, "If no one cried, 'Woe, woe to the bloody city of damnation!' and nobody listened to the few who cry out, we would know that the human race had finally gone hopelessly and forever mad" (*Kenneth Patchen: A Collection of Essays,* ed. Richard G. Morgan [1977], p. 23). In the late 1940s Rexroth established a Friday-evening salon and a Wednesday-night philosophy club to discuss his theories of politics and poetry; in attendance were friends such as Robert Duncan, William Everson, Richard Eberhart, Philip Lamantia and, later, Allen Ginsberg, Lawrence Ferlinghetti, Gary Snyder, and other Beats.

After receiving a Guggenheim fellowship in 1948, Rexroth traveled across Europe and the United States, making sociological observations that resurfaced in *The Dragon and the Unicorn* (1952). During the 1950s Rexroth continued to serve as father figure to the Beats, partly through a weekly radio show. He also became the biological father of two daughters; their mother was philosophy student Marthe Larsen. In 1953 he wrote what is probably his most well-known poem, "Thou Shalt Not Kill," in honor of Dylan Thomas. A passionate indictment of standardized culture, the poem asks who is responsible for Thomas's death; its answer implicates the cocktails and Brooks Brothers suits of this world. This piece became a standard in Rexroth's repertoire when, with the Beats, he began to read poetry with musical accompaniment. Actress Shirley MacLaine attended a poetry-and-jazz performance in the late 1950s and concluded that Rexroth resembled "John Donne in the fourth dimension."

After Kass divorced him in 1955 Rexroth legally married Larsen in 1958 (they had been illegally married in France in 1949); they divorced in 1961. His live-in secretary, Carol Tinker, became his fourth wife

in 1974. In the 1960s Rexroth supported civil rights struggles and the anti-war movement. His *Collected Shorter Poems* appeared in 1967 and *Complete Collected Longer Poems* in 1968. Increasingly recognized by mainstream critics, he wrote a series of essays for *Saturday Review* and received a National Institute of Arts and Letters award in 1964. This later work was dominated by Eastern philosophy—a theme that appealed to the students he taught at the University of California, Santa Barbara (1968–1974). Partly on the strength of his translations of Asian poets, Rexroth won a Fulbright to Japan (1974–1975) and a Copernicus Award for lifetime achievement. His last major project was a series of poems presented as translations of a fictional Japanese poet named Marichiko. In later years Rexroth maintained friendships with younger writers, such as his literary executor Bradford Morrow, and feminist poets such as Carolyn Forché and Denise Levertov. Rexroth died in Santa Barbara, and, characteristically, Catholic eulogies, Buddhist chants, and Beat poems were performed at his funeral.

Kenneth Rexroth's distinctive poetic voice emphasized sexuality, ecology, and mysticism and provided an aesthetic alternative to social realism and New Critical formalism. Although some feminists have objected to his philandering and dated representations of women, as a writer and editor, Rexroth generously promoted both male and female radical writers. His contributions energized postwar American poetry.

• Rexroth's papers are located at the University of California, Los Angeles and the University of Southern California. Rexroth's collections of poetry also include *The Signature of All Things* (1949), *In Defense of the Earth* (1956), *Natural Numbers* (1963), *Elastic Retort* (1973), *New Poems* (1974), and *Flower Wreath Hill* (1991). His translations include *100 Poems from the Chinese* (1956), *100 Poems from the Japanese* (1964), Pierre Reverdy, *Selected Poems* (1969), *Love and the Turning Year* (1970), *Orchid Boat* (1972), *100 Poems from the French* (1972), and *100 More Poems from the Japanese* (1976). His play *Beyond the Mountains* was published in 1951. His essays include *Bird in the Bush* (1959), *Assays* (1961), *Classics Revisited* (1968), *The Alternative Society* (1970), *With Eye and Ear* (1970), *American Poetry in the Twentieth Century* (1971), *Communalism* (1974), and *More Classics Revisited* (1984). *An Autobiographical Novel* was published in 1966. Lee Bartlett, ed., *Kenneth Rexroth and James Laughlin: Selected Letters,* appeared in 1991. See Bradford Morrow, "An Outline of Unpublished Rexroth Manuscripts, and an Introductory Note to Three Chapters from the Sequel to *An Autobiographical Novel,*" *Sagetrieb* 2, no. 3 (Winter 1983): 135–44. The major biography is Linda Hamalian's *A Life of Kenneth Rexroth* (1991). Critical studies include Morgan Gibson, *Kenneth Rexroth* (1972), Gibson, *Revolutionary Rexroth: Poet of East-West Wisdom* (1986), and Ken Knabb, *Relevance of Rexroth* (1990). James Laughlin and Denise Levertov wrote a moving tribute to Rexroth after his death; see "Remembering Kenneth Rexroth," *American Poetry Review* 12, no. 1 (1983): 18–19.

CAREN IRR

REY, H. A. (16 Sept. 1898–26 Aug. 1977), author and illustrator, was born Hans Augusto Reyersbach in Hamburg, Germany, the son of Alexander Reyersbach and Martha Windmuller. Rey's childhood revealed his early talent for drawing. Shortly after his second birthday he created his "first recognizable" picture of a man riding a horse. In his neighborhood was a zoo, which gave him a familiarity with nonfarm animals. He often drew in school instead of doing his schoolwork.

After being drafted into the army, Rey designed and lithographed posters for a circus. He attended the University of Munich and the University of Hamburg before moving to Brazil, where he worked for the family's import firm. There he met Margret Waldstein, also an artist, and in 1935 they married. The couple had no children. With her encouragement he decided to make a career in art.

In 1936 the Reys journeyed to Paris, where their honeymoon became an extended stay. *Raffy and the Nine Monkeys* (1939), the first picture book that he wrote and illustrated, was published in France and England. This book would later be published in the United States as *Cecily G. and the Nine Monkeys* (1942). Although this was one book of six published while the Reys lived in Paris, it is notable because one of the nine monkeys was named George; it was this little monkey who would make the Reys famous.

To escape the 1940 Nazi occupation of Paris, the Reys left on bicycles that Rey had pieced together. Tucked under their arms were their manuscripts. One of them, *Curious George*, so charmed the border guard that he let them pass out of France without difficulty.

They traveled to Lisbon, to Rio de Janeiro, and eventually to New York, where H. A. Rey's manuscripts were immediately accepted by publishers. *Curious George*, the manuscript that escaped France with them, appeared in 1941. Six more volumes of Curious George tales were written by Rey, four of them with his wife.

The working relationship of Hans and Margret Rey was collaborative. Generally, Margret wrote the text, and Hans did the illustrations, but the balance shifted from book to book and was reflected in how the work was attributed on the title page.

Rey also wrote and illustrated three books under the pseudonym "Uncle Gus" in 1942. Nonseries books constituted the bulk of his illustrative and writing career. He illustrated three books that Margret wrote: *Pretzel* (1944), *Spotty* (1945), and *Pretzel and the Puppies* (1946). He illustrated two books by Margaret Wise Brown, *The Polite Penguin* (1941) and *Don't Frighten the Lion!* (1942), and one by Charlotte Zolotow, *The Park Book* (1944). Emmy Payne's *Katy No-Pocket* (1944), the story of a kangaroo without a pouch, contained his drawings.

Rey's interest in astronomy led to two books about the stars—one for adults, *The Stars: A New Way to See Them* (1952), and one for children, *Find the Constellations* (1954). Both are considered standard informational books about astronomy. In total, Rey wrote and/or illustrated thirty-eight books. Additionally, in 1951 Rey and his wife produced a page for children in *Good Housekeeping* called "Zozo," the name by which Curi-

ous George was known in England. The Reys' publishing efforts also extended into short films about Curious George. These films, in turn, prompted more books that were made from the films.

Curious George appeals to children because of his impishness. He does not set out to be bad; rather, his youthful inquisitiveness propels him into predicaments that lead to trouble. All works out well in the end, often with George unintentionally solving a related problem, and he returns to the safety of his home with the Man in the Yellow Hat. His situations parallel those of young children who, like George, inadvertently get into trouble because of their native and very natural curiosity.

George's story follows the traditional structure of a cautionary tale in which a warning is issued and disregarded, and the circumstances that result from disobeying authority challenge the protagonist's survival abilities. Yet the tale ends with the traditional return to home that marked children's literature in the mid-twentieth century, as the wayward protagonist is welcomed back and forgiven.

Although the Curious George books are only a small part of Rey's lifetime achievement, they are the titles with which Rey is primarily identified. The balance maintained between George's tendency to mischief and the overwhelming good humor and capacity for forgiveness of the people in the stories imbues the series with a characteristic and identifiable warmth.

Rey died in Boston, Massachusetts.

• The bulk of H. A. Rey's papers are in the de Grummond Children's Literature Research Collection, University of Southern Mississippi (Hattiesburg). Lee Bennett Hopkins interviews Rey and his wife in his *Books Are by People* (1969), pp. 230–33. Julie Berg, *H. A. Rey* (1994), provides a short biography intended for young readers. Grace Hogarth offers her remembrances of her editor-writer relationship with Rey in "A Publisher's Perspective," *Horn Book* 65 (1989): 526–28. Margret Rey contributes to the fiftieth anniversary of the publication of the first Curious George title in Dennis Gaffney, "Curious George Hits 50," *Christian Science Monitor*, 31 May 1988, p. 23. Elizabeth Segel, "Beastly Boys: A Century of Mischief," *Children's Literature in Education* 18 (1987): 3–11, examines the theme of naughtiness in four characters from children's literature, including Curious George. In a similar theme, William Moebius examines the mischievous child in "*L'Enfant Terrible* Comes of Age," *Notebooks in Cultural Analysis* 2 (1985). An obituary is in the *New York Times*, 28 Aug. 1977.

JANET SPAETH

REYNOLDS, Bertha Capen (11 Dec. 1885–29 Oct. 1978), social worker and educator, was born in Stoughton, Massachusetts, the daughter of Franklin Stewart Reynolds, a manufacturer of organs, and Mary Capen, a teacher. She graduated Phi Beta Kappa from Smith College in 1908 and was one of the early recipients (1914) of a certificate in social work from the Boston School for Social Workers, later part of Simmons College. In 1919 she was in the first class to graduate from the Smith College School for Social Work's summer program.

Reynolds was an intellectually inclined young girl whose childhood had been marred by her father's early death (1887) and her mother's unpreparedness for widowhood. She took up teaching, but a period of ill health put an end to that. In 1912, after recovering, she decided on social work as a career and enrolled in Simmons College. Reynolds began her career as a social worker for the Children's Aid Society in Boston (1913–1918). She spent the following six years working at the Danvers State Hospital, with a special focus on preschool children, and in newly established clinics for preschool children in Boston.

In her memoirs she states that during these years she wished to marry but found it difficult to relate to men or even to cultivate a few friendships with male acquaintances. She was very successful in her career, if rather more reticent (even with women) than she wished to be.

Her most significant contributions to the field came when, in 1925, she was appointed associate director of the Smith College School for Social Work. For the next seven years she was pivotal in shaping and directing the curriculum of this increasingly prestigious program of graduate study. She was an outstanding educator who possessed extraordinary vision and foresight regarding the direction that social work should take. Her increasing commitment to radical politics, especially during the depression years, convinced her of the importance of enlarging social work aims to include social reform, union organizing, and political action. This would have involved organizing clients for political action, demonstrating with them for increased benefits, educating them to political action, and championing workers' goals.

All of these tactics and aims fit poorly with the narrower professional goals of the graduate program in social work, which emphasized a one-on-one psychotherapeutic approach to client problems as opposed to group political action. It also put her into direct conflict with the program director, Everett Kimball. His early enthusiasm and support for her work eroded under their continued disagreement about these professional differences. Her increasing political radicalism further alienated him, and the relationship continued to deteriorate, ultimately leading to her resignation in 1937.

Ostensibly, she was made to leave because of a curriculum dispute regarding her "Plan D." This was a proposal for broad advanced training for social workers with master's degrees. Her intention was to upgrade the status of the profession by making this a transition to a doctoral program. But her relationship with Kimball had by then been strained to breaking by her active and vocal adherence to radical politics. Ironically, it had been his advice to her, in an earlier and friendlier stage of their relationship, to enter psychoanalysis that set her life on a different course. Analysis (1927–1928) changed her sense of self as well as her view of her role in social work. Increasingly, she gained the self-confidence to move away from viewing individual counseling of clients and the case work method as sufficient in themselves. She believed that union organizing of social workers, community organizing for political action, and client self-help groups also were important in helping clients and improving the effectiveness of the profession.

All of this was quite radical for the time and led to a permanent breach with Kimball and the Smith School for Social Work. She subsequently worked as a self-employed consultant for staff development for various social work agencies (1939–1942). She was appointed by the United Seamen's Service of the National Maritime Union as a case supervisor (1943–1947), but she was effectively marginalized as a social work leader once her academic institutional base was gone. In 1948 she retired to her family home in Stoughton, where she studied Marxist works, maintained a small clinical practice, and was active in local volunteer work. She was the author of several textbooks published in the 1930s, 1940s, and 1950s, which continued to be used and reissued as late as the 1970s, but her influence on the profession was diminished.

Public recognition of her contributions came late in life and waited on the emergence of the women's liberation movement in the mid-1960s. In 1968 Reynolds received recognition from the Smith School for Social Work Alumni Association. She was honored with a degree of humane letters from Boston University School of Social Work (1969). Various social work schools in New York City and other organizations also honored her. On her ninetieth birthday the Hunter College School of Social Work held a colloquium in her honor. In her retirement years she continued to fight passionately for the poor and powerless, for workers' rights, and for social justice and world peace. She died at home in Stoughton, Massachusetts.

• Reynolds's papers are in the Sophia Smith Collection at Smith College and in the files of the Alumnae Association of the Smith College School for Social Work. Her unpublished autobiography and other memorabilia are also in the Sophia Smith Collection. Some materials are in the Schlesinger Library, Radcliffe College, Harvard University. In addition to many articles in the *Family* and *Social Work Today*, Reynolds published several books: *Between Client and Community: A Study in Responsibility in Social Case Work* (1934); *Learning and Teaching in the Practice of Social Work* (1942), her major work for social work educators; and *Social Work and Social Living* (1951). Her autobiography, *An Uncharted Journey*, was published in 1963. Sharon Freedberg, "Bertha Capen Reynolds: A Woman Struggling in Her Times" (Ph.D. diss., Univ. of Massachusetts, 1984), is a book-length biographical study of her life and work. A discussion of her Smith College years can be found in Penina M. Glazer and Miriam Slater, *Unequal Colleagues: The Entrance of Women into the Professions, 1890–1940* (1986).

MIRIAM SLATER

REYNOLDS, Charles Alexander (20 Mar. 1842–25 June 1876), soldier and scout, was born in Warren County, Illinois, the son of Joseph Boyer Reynolds, a physician, and Phebe Bush, both of pioneering Virginia families. Reynolds received schooling at the preparatory division of Abingdon College, Abingdon, Illinois. In 1859 the family moved to Kansas, where the boy worked on his father's farm, gaining a knowledge of animals and other frontier skills.

Reynolds left his family on his first western adventure in 1860, apparently working as a teamster on a wagon train headed for Denver. The following year he returned home, becoming a private in the Fourth Kansas Volunteer Infantry on 16 July. Reorganized in March 1863 as the Tenth Kansas Infantry, the unit saw hard service in the campaigns along the Kansas-Missouri border, the principal confrontation occurring on 7 December 1862 in the battle of Prairie Grove, Arkansas. He later served along the Santa Fe Trail and as a guard at the Alton, Illinois, prison for Confederates. Discharged on 19 August 1864, he went west and for several years made his living as a buffalo hunter on the plains of Kansas, Nebraska, and Colorado. In 1869 he traveled to the upper Missouri to pursue his trade and soon became known for his plainsman's skills.

Of stocky build with auburn hair and wide-set blue eyes, Reynolds stood five feet six inches tall. Unlike many of his contemporaries in the same occupation, he was neat in appearance, clean-shaven except for a trim mustache, and modest in demeanor, and he rarely smoked or drank. He enjoyed the company of scientists, who often rode with military expeditions that he guided, and shared with them his impressive knowledge of animals, geography, geology, and Indian ways. Called "Charley" by his friends, he received the nickname "Lonesome" because of his solitary habits and retiring disposition.

His career as an army scout began in July 1872 when he was employed as a guide for General David S. Stanley's initial Yellowstone Expedition. The troops had been detailed to escort surveyors for the North Pacific Railroad, then working west along the Yellowstone River. The following summer, while Reynolds served Stanley in the same capacity, he made the acquaintance and earned the respect of the general's subordinate, Lieutenant Colonel George Armstrong Custer of the Seventh Cavalry.

In the summer of 1874 Custer chose Reynolds to be the chief scout for his expedition into the Black Hills of South Dakota, where he was to find an appropriate site for a military post and investigate stories of the presence of gold. It was Reynolds who reached Fort Laramie on 8 August with dispatches confirming the rumors and precipitating a gold rush that eventually set in motion the circumstances that led to his death. In December he led troops to Standing Rocky Agency to arrest the Sioux Warrior Rain-in-the-Face, who had bragged of murdering two members of the 1873 Stanley expedition. Reynolds spent the following summer guiding Captain William Ludlow's engineering reconnaissance of Yellowstone National Park, where he became friends with the park's first superintendent, Philetus W. Norris.

On 3 March 1876 Reynolds was the first scout hired to guide General Alfred E. Terry's column in the campaign to bring in the Northern Sioux under Sitting Bull. After gathering Indian intelligence, he left Fort Abraham Lincoln on 17 May with Terry's troops, which included Lieutenant Colonel Custer and the Seventh Cavalry. On reaching the valley of the Little Bighorn almost five weeks later, Custer divided his command, sending Reynolds with Major Reno's battalion to attack the Indian village. After warriors circled Reno's flank, the troops headed for high ground across the river. In the retreat to the bluffs, Reynolds's horse fell, pinning him to the ground, where he was killed. Buried two days later on the site, his remains were exhumed in July 1877 by Philetus Norris, who, after not being able to find any of the scout's relatives, had his friend reburied in his home cemetery in a Detroit suburb. Remembered for his consummate competence and quiet courage, Reynolds remains best known for his association with Custer and his life as the premier scout in the Dakota Territory from 1872 to 1874.

• The only known writing of Reynolds is a terse diary, kept from 17 May to 22 June 1876, reproduced in Michael J. Koury, *Diaries of the Little Big Horn* (1968). Accounts by men who knew Reynolds include those by John Henry Taylor in *Sketches of Frontier and Indian Life* (1889) and George Bird Grinnell in two articles published in *Forest & Stream Magazine*: "Recollections of Charley Reynolds," 26 Dec. 1896, and "Reminiscence of Charley Reynolds," 30 Jan. 1897. Also important is John E. Remsburg and George J. Remsburg, *Charley Reynolds: Soldier, Hunter, Scout and Guide* (1931), which reproduces the biography of the frontiersman originally published as a series of twenty newspaper articles in the *Potter Kansan* in 1914–1915. This volume was reprinted in 1978 with a preface by John M. Carroll, which includes a Reynolds bibliography, and an excellent introductory sketch by John S. Gray. See also Gray, "On the Trail of 'Lonesome Charley Reynolds,'" *Chicago Westerners Brandbook*, Oct. 1957.

JOHN D. MCDERMOTT

REYNOLDS, Frank (29 Nov. 1923–20 July 1983), pioneer broadcast journalist and network television anchorman, was born in East Chicago, Indiana, the son of Frank James Reynolds, a manager at Inland Steel Company, and Helen Duffy. He attended Wabash College in Crawfordsville, Indiana, but left when he was drafted into the U.S. Army during World War II. He served as a staff sergeant from 1943 until 1945, receiving a purple heart for wounds sustained in Kassel, Germany, when shrapnel lodged in his left thigh. After a medical discharge, he attended Indiana University but never graduated. A practicing Roman Catholic, he married Henrietta Mary Harpster in 1947. They had five sons, two of whom also became broadcast journalists.

Reynolds began his career in 1947 as a sportscaster for radio station WJOB in Hammond, Indiana. In 1950 he became a news reporter for WBKB-TV (now WLS-TV) in Chicago, and from 1951 to 1963 he was a reporter at WBBM-TV, the CBS affiliate station in

Chicago. While at WBBM, he accompanied President Dwight D. Eisenhower on his 1960 trip through the Far East and the Philippines. In 1963 he returned to WLS-TV, the ABC Chicago affiliate, as a reporter and anchorman. In 1965 he filmed a special report in Vietnam, recording his vivid reflections of the war there. The program, well received in Chicago, was broadcast nationally on the ABC television network. Later in 1965 he took a 50 percent cut in salary to join the Washington Bureau of ABC's Network News Division. He was the network's White House correspondent from late 1965 to 1968, accompanying President Lyndon Johnson on major trips and to conferences throughout the world.

From May 1968 until December 1970 Reynolds (in New York) and Howard K. Smith (in Washington) were coanchors of the "ABC Evening News." In 1969 Reynolds received the George Foster Peabody Award for meritorious service to broadcast news.

In the late 1960s and early 1970s, before the development of cable news, the three network evening newscasts were the primary source for television news. The anchormen of these daily half-hour newscasts symbolized the credibility of the news department. Polls of viewers conducted at the time indicated the public perception of the anchorman to be the single most important element by far in gaining and retaining viewers.

ABC News was the youngest, smallest, and least-watched news division of the three networks. It operated with the fewest resources. Reynolds was not as popular as Walter Cronkite of CBS News or Chet Huntley and David Brinkley of NBC News, but the integrity of his reporting and his dedication to broadcast journalism earned him the respect of his colleagues. Occasionally that dedication resulted in strong on-air commentary. For example in 1969, Vice President Spiro Agnew attacked news commentators for registering their disapproval of a speech on the Vietnam War delivered by President Richard Nixon. Agnew, in a November 1969 address to the Midwest Regional Republican Committee in Des Moines, Iowa, complained that Nixon's words had been "subjected to instant analysis and querulous criticism . . . by a small band of network commentators." Reynolds reacted to Agnew's attack in a strongly worded commentary, saying, "There is something much worse than a public official attempting to frighten a broadcaster, and that is a broadcaster who allows himself to be frightened." In 1970, ABC News, still last in the ratings, had an opportunity to hire Harry Reasoner, a popular correspondent with CBS; ABC management replaced Reynolds with Reasoner.

After his removal as an anchor for the evening news, Reynolds returned to ABC News in Washington as a reporter and an anchorman for special reports. In 1972 he remained in Washington as coanchorman of ABC's coverage of President Nixon's visit to the People's Republic of China. In 1973 he anchored ABC News coverage of the Senate Watergate committee hearings, and in 1974 he traveled with the campaigns of congres-

sional and gubernatorial candidates. In 1976 he reported on the unsuccessful presidential campaign of Ronald Reagan—beginning a professional relationship and friendship with the future president that continued until Reynolds's death—covering the Republican and Democratic national conventions and reporting results on election night. During the administration of Jimmy Carter, he anchored coverage of the Camp David summit meeting between the president, Egyptian president Anwar Sadat, and Israeli prime minister Menachem Begin.

In 1978 the new president of ABC News, Roone Arledge, created the network's "World News Tonight," and Frank Reynolds returned as chief anchorman for the broadcast, based in Washington. In 1979 he also anchored ABC's series of late night specials, "The Iran Crisis: America Held Hostage," which developed into "Nightline," one of the most successful news programs, eventually broadcast five times a week. In 1980 Reynolds reported and anchored ABC's political coverage, receiving an Emmy for the network's "Post Election Special Edition." He anchored ABC's live coverage of Reagan's inauguration, the return of the American hostages from Iran, and the 1981 assassination attempt on the president. With new technology, ABC was able to report the assassination attempt moments after it occurred. During the live midday coverage, Reynolds became furious when it was incorrectly reported that Press Secretary James Brady, who also had been shot, was dead. Still on camera, Reynolds angrily demanded of the news staff, "Let's get it nailed down. Somebody! Let's find out." The new technology allowed quicker response to breaking stories but also meant less time to verify facts and avoid errors. Journalistically, Reynolds's anger was justified, but such reactions had rarely been seen on the air.

In March 1983 Reynolds received a blood transfusion at a Washington hospital during surgery on his left femur, which had been injured in a fall. He developed viral hepatitis from the transfusion and later died of liver failure. After his death, friends, colleagues, and the public learned that his condition had been complicated by multiple myeloma, a form of bone cancer from which he had suffered for several years. Reynolds is buried in Arlington National Cemetery.

• A transcript of a 24 July 1983 ABC News Special Tribute to Frank Reynolds, including recorded segments of his memorial service at St. Matthew's Cathedral in Washington, D.C., is available from ABC News. Transcripts of "ABC Evening News" from May 1968 until December 1970, containing the text of Reynolds's numerous commentaries, are available through ABC News, as is corporate biographical material. Barbara Matusow, *The Evening Stars: The Making of the Network News Anchors* (1983), and Edward Bliss, Jr., *Now the News: The Story of Broadcast Journalism* (1991), discuss the connection between Agnew's attack on television commentators and ABC News' decision to relieve Reynolds from his duties as anchorman. Obituaries can be found in the *New York Times*, *Washington Post*, *Los Angeles Times*, and *Chicago Tribune*, 21 July 1983, and a tribute from television columnist Tom Shales appears in the *Washington Post* on the same date.

JOAN BIEDER

REYNOLDS, Jeremiah N. (1799?–25 Aug. 1858), explorer and writer, was born in Cumberland County, Pennsylvania. His parents' names are unknown. He, his mother, and his stepfather, Job Jefferis, moved to Clinton County, Ohio, in 1808. Here Reynolds spent time in the forests, dressing as a woodsman and learning the value of self-reliance. Reynolds attended subscription schools and eventually became a teacher. In 1819 he enrolled at Ohio University, left to pursue a teaching position, returned, and left again. He then made arrangements to continue his uncompleted studies with his mentor, Francis Glass.

While serving as editor of the *Wilmington Spectator* in 1824, Reynolds became acquainted with the thinking of John Cleves Symmes. Reynolds followed Symmes from Ohio to cities in the East. Symmes's theory, bold for its time, held that the earth was hollow and at the poles beyond the ice barriers was a warmer climate and entrances to the earth's core. Armed with wooden globes as visual aids, Reynolds and Symmes were often laughed out of lecture halls: "Symmes' Hole" had become an object of jest for some. Discouraged, Symmes returned to Cincinnati, while Reynolds persisted, publishing *Remarks on a Review of Symmes' Theory* (1827). Here Reynolds admitted to weaknesses in Symmes's hypotheses, but he defended his own belief that icy circles surround both poles and that these circles diminish significantly approaching the poles.

Others expounded on Symmes's hypotheses, but Reynolds's defense had the greatest impact on the popular imagination. Especially notable was his influence on American romantics such as Edgar Allan Poe and to a lesser degree Herman Melville and James Fenimore Cooper. Whether Poe actually met Reynolds is uncertain, but there were opportunities for such a meeting. Reynolds knew Poe's editor at the *Southern Literary Messenger*, Thomas Willis White, who described Reynolds as "a most fascinating dog" and may have encouraged Poe's interest. While at the *Messenger*, Poe reviewed Reynolds's introduction to Glass's biography of George Washington (Dec. 1835) and Reynolds's "Address to Congress" (Jan. 1837) and cited an essay Reynolds had written on autography (Feb. 1836). Later, at *Graham's Magazine*, Poe wrote a review of Reynolds's account of the Wilkes expedition (Sept. 1843) in which Poe's admiration of Reynolds is evident: "With mental powers of the highest order, his indomitable energy is precisely of that character which *will not admit* of defeat" (p. 165).

The influence of Symmes's theory is evident in Poe's first success, "Ms. Found in a Bottle" (1833), and in the later works "The Unparalleled Adventure of One Hans Pfaall" (1835) and "The Descent into the Maelstrom" (1841). Poe borrowed directly in *The Narrative of Arthur Gordon Pym* (1838) from both Symmes's theory and Reynolds's "Address to Congress." Apparently Reynolds's influence on Poe extended beyond the literary. Biographers have long puzzled over why the delirious poet shouted "Reynolds" continuously the night before his death. Arthur Hobson Quinn speculates that Poe envisioned a voyage, a chasm similar to that in *Pym*, and thus called to "Jeremiah Reynolds, protector of the voyages of the South Seas, whose very language he used in that tale" (p. 640).

In 1828 Reynolds was asked by the secretary of the navy to conduct interviews with sea captains and to study logbooks, journals, and charts to generate information for a government-sponsored voyage to the South Seas. The voyage was canceled in 1829 because of costs. Refusing defeat, Reynolds organized a private expedition. Sailing under the command of Captain Nathaniel B. Palmer, the man credited with the discovery of Antarctica, expeditions were made in the South and Antarctic seas. The ill-fated voyage, struck by scurvy and desertion, was forced back to Chile.

Again Reynolds's accounts provided fodder for romantic writers. Records of one inland expedition on which the crew was stranded in bad weather may have provided source material for James Fenimore Cooper's novel, *The Sea Lions*. A sailor's yarn about a white whale off the coast of Chile led to an article by Reynolds in *The Knickerbocker Magazine* (May 1839), "Mocha Dick or the White Whale of the Pacific: A Leaf from a Manuscript Journal," that is a probable source for Herman Melville's *Moby Dick*.

In 1830 Palmer left Reynolds in Chile while returning cargo to the United States. Reynolds devoted himself to exploring Chile and southern South America. Reynolds boarded the *Potomac* at Valparaiso in 1832, becoming personal secretary to the ship's captain, Commodore John Downes. Upon his return to the United States, Reynolds published his accounts in 1835 as *The Voyage of the United States Frigate Potomac, 1831–34*. This volume established Reynolds's reputation as an explorer and a writer.

In 1836 Reynolds again sought public support for a government-sponsored expedition. On 3 April he addressed Congress in a three-hour oration and received a $300,000 appropriation. Americans responded enthusiastically to the opportunity for their country's growth as a global oceanic power, and Reynolds provided a catalyst for America's second age of discovery between 1830 and 1860.

Reynolds was appointed head of the scientific corps for the voyage and recruited many prestigious scientists, but his enthusiasm irritated the secretary of the navy, Mahlon Dickerson. The hostility between the two undermined the voyage's spirit and energy, and an exchange of angry letters ended in Reynolds's removal. The expedition sailed without Reynolds under the command of Lieutenant Charles Wilkes in August 1838. Reynolds's exclusion marked the end of both his advocacy and his explorations.

Reynolds devoted the remainder of this life to law and politics. Attracting large audiences in 1840, he toured Connecticut as a campaign speaker. In 1841 he joined a Wall Street law firm and practiced maritime law. Returning to Ohio in 1843, he lectured on the Indian problem, and in 1848 he organized a stock company for Mexican mining investments. Succumbing to failing health, he died in St. Catherine Springs, Ontario. He had remained a bachelor throughout his life.

• Three brief biographies of Reynolds's life are Mrs. R. B. Harlan, *The History of Clinton County* (1882); Robert Almy, "J. N. Reynolds: A Brief Biography with Particular Reference to Poe and Symmes," *Colophon* 2 (1937): 227–45; and Gerald McDonald's entry on Reynolds in *Ohio Authors and Their Books: Biographical Data and Selective Bibliographies for Ohio Authors, Native and Resident, 1796–1950,* ed. William Coyle (1962). Accounts of Reynolds's contribution as a scientist and explorer are in William H. Goetzmann, *New Lands, New Men* (1986), and in Edwin Swift Balch, *Antarctica* (1902). Reynolds's literary contributions are discussed in Aubrey Starke, "Poe's Friend Reynolds," *American Literature* 11 (1939): 152–66; Arthur Hobson Quinn, *Edgar Allan Poe: A Critical Biography* (1941); and Carl Van Doren, "Mr. Melville's *Moby Dick,*" *Bookman* 59 (1924): 154–57.

DEBRA WESTON

REYNOLDS, John (1713?–3 Feb. 1788), colonial governor, was born in England. His parents are unknown. He followed a naval career and served as first colonial governor of Georgia (1754–1758). Reynolds entered the Royal Navy in 1728 and was promoted to lieutenant in 1736. In 1745 he commanded the fireship *Scipio* in home waters. During the War of Austrian Succession (1744–1748) he convoyed vessels engaged in the North American trade. Lord Hardwicke, the lord chancellor, used his influence with the Board of Trade to secure Reynolds's appointment as royal governor of Georgia in 1754.

Reynolds's mission was to set up a model government in Georgia that would be an example for errant older colonies. He arrived in Savannah on 29 October 1754 to a general acclamation. Ominously, the end of the government house collapsed during his first meeting with his Council. Also inauspicious was Reynolds's decision to lavish seven political appointments on William Little, the naval surgeon who accompanied him to Georgia. Council members, who had hoped for offices for themselves, turned against the governor. During the ensuing feud between Little and the Council, Reynolds sided with Little and suspended three members of his Council.

Reynolds had trouble with the Commons House of Assembly, also. Edmund Gray, a delegate from Augusta, challenged the election returns when the first Assembly met in January 1755. Gray and three of his friends boycotted the sessions and were subsequently expelled. When Gray called for a meeting of friends of liberty, Reynolds issued a ban on unlawful assemblies and proscribed Gray as a rebel. Gray and his followers left the province and settled in the area below the Altamaha claimed by both Spain and Britain. The Grayites who remained in Georgia contended that their motives were misunderstood: they opposed the aristocratic Savannah-based Council, not the governor. In a political about-face, Little joined the Gray faction and was elected to the House and chosen Speaker of that body. Subsequently the House supported the governor in his ongoing dispute with the upper chamber. Little drew his support from the districts farthest removed from Savannah where the dangers of an Indian war were most felt.

The members of the Council carried their complaints against the governor to London. Councilor Jonathan Bryan, whose plantations were scattered across the low country, informed Lord Halifax, president of the Board of Trade, of Reynolds's many failings. Councilors Alexander Kellert and Patrick Graham presented a list of grievances to Lord Halifax. In August 1756 Reynolds was recalled and Henry Ellis was sent to Georgia as lieutenant governor.

On his arrival in Savannah on 16 February 1757, Ellis was accorded an enthusiastic reception. Little dared Ellis to interfere with the pro-Reynolds Commons House and prepared to deliver a fiery speech summoning Georgians to defend their liberty against an aristocratic cabal. He never had his chance. Ellis simply prorogued the assembly and waited until Reynolds and Little departed the province. Reynolds's bad luck continued. When his ship was captured by a French privateer, he lost the papers he and Little had prepared for his defense. After his release from a French prison, Reynolds made his way to London. Not until 8 March 1758 was he informed of the charges against him. He presented a plausible response on 7 April 1758, accusing the Council of fomenting trouble. However, his removal from the governorship was a foregone conclusion; Ellis was named governor on 21 April 1758.

Reynolds resumed his interrupted naval career and, thanks to seniority rather than talent, advanced in rank. He was made a rear admiral in 1775, a vice admiral in 1778, and in 1787, at the age of seventy-four and despite being incapacitated by a stroke, was promoted to the rank of admiral. He died in London a year later.

The historians who have characterized Reynolds as a failure are undoubtedly correct, though something positive could be made of his efforts to help the people in the backcountry. Reynolds had a plan of defense drawn up and authorized the raising of the troops of rangers, but he had no idea of how to pay the expenses. His assignment was to establish a constitutional government in Georgia, but Reynolds's concept of governing was that of a commander of a quarterdeck of a warship. The frontier province needed the alliance of the Indian tribes, but Reynolds was uncomfortable in dealing with Indians. The best that can be said is that he prepared the way for Ellis's successful tenure by providing a list of things not to do. Except that he was married, details of his personal life are not known.

• Reynolds's correspondence with the Board of Trade is in Kenneth Coleman and Milton Ready, eds., *The Colonial Records of the State of Georgia,* vol. 27 (1977). For narrative descriptions of his administration, see W. W. Abbot, *The Royal Governors of Georgia, 1754–1775* (1959), and Kenneth Coleman, *Colonial Georgia: A History* (1976).

EDWARD J. CASHIN

REYNOLDS, John (26 Feb. 1788–8 May 1865), fourth governor of the state of Illinois, was born in Montgomery County, Pennsylvania, the son of Protestant Irish parents, Robert Reynolds and Margaret Moore, farmers. The family soon moved to Tennessee and, in 1800, to Illinois, settling first in the Kaskaskia neighborhood and later southwest of Edwardsville near Cahokia. Growing up in this pioneer atmosphere, young Reynolds received the fragmentary education then available on the Illinois frontier.

After studying briefly at a school in Knoxville, Tennessee, he read law in both Tennessee and Illinois, and soon (probably in 1813), under the informal procedures of prestatehood days, he was admitted to the bar in Illinois. Although his law practice, which he opened in 1814 in Cahokia, appears to have been undistinguished and of little concern to him, it provided a vehicle for success in two major areas, land speculation—he bought and sold real estate, including the abundant government land for sale in Illinois after 1820—and politics.

Reynolds saw limited service in the War of 1812 on the territorial governor's staff and as a scout in Captain William B. Whiteside's company, which ranged the frontier to keep the Illinois tribes under surveillance. There he acquired the nickname of the "Old Ranger," which he used to political advantage for the remainder of his life. In 1817 he married Catherine Dubuque LaCroix Manegle, daughter of Julien Dubuque, the French Canadian trader who gave Dubuque, Iowa, its name. After Catherine's death in 1834, Reynolds married in 1836 Sarah Wilson, whom he had met during his congressional career. He had no children.

As the new state government took shape in 1818, Reynolds found himself elected an associate justice of the Illinois Supreme Court, a position he insisted he had not sought. He next won election to the general assembly in 1826 and reelection two years later, launching a long and wide-ranging political career.

A highly prejudiced man of many idiosyncrasies and opinions, Reynolds drove himself by what he called "a savage self-will to succeed" (*My Own Times*, p. 173). He was able to stretch his meager smattering of education to the appearance of erudition, but his political success depended primarily upon his ability to recognize and espouse those policies that were popular among the rough frontiersmen, upon whose votes he depended.

When Reynolds became a candidate for the governorship of Illinois in 1830, the popularity of President Andrew Jackson was at flood tide. Both Reynolds and his chief rival, Lieutenant Governor William Kinney (1781–1843), advertised themselves as "Jackson men," while the dispirited opposition failed to produce a candidate. Reynolds campaigned vigorously, covering much of the state on horseback, alternately charming and amusing the pioneer voters with repetitious speeches laced with Irish blarney and good common sense. By capturing the support of moderate Democrats and many of the Whig partisans, he won handily (60 percent of the vote) over Kinney.

In his inaugural address Governor Reynolds recommended legislation promoting public education, internal improvements, and the completion of the state penitentiary then under construction in Alton. He strongly urged the construction of the Illinois and Michigan Canal (for which a congressional grant of public land had been secured) and the building of roads leading to the Galena lead mines. However, a general assembly not in sympathy with the governor's views held achievements to a minimum.

Midway into his term (1832), difficulties with the Sauk and Fox tribes in the Rock River valley escalated into the Black Hawk War. Governor Reynolds acted as head of the Illinois militia volunteers, but federal troops from St. Louis and the East quickly drove the native warriors and their families across Wisconsin and back into Iowa, punishing them unmercifully along the way. Treaties that followed removed the last obstacle to white settlement in northern Illinois.

Ever the office seeker, Reynolds had sought and won election to Congress (1834) even before his gubernatorial term had ended. His congressional career was not particularly distinguished, and he failed to be reelected in 1836. He continued to be in and out of Congress and the Illinois General Assembly for the next twenty years. He was reelected to Congress in 1838 and 1840 and to the Illinois General Assembly in both the 1840s and the 1850s. In the history of Illinois to date, Reynolds alone has the distinction of having held the highest position in each of the three branches of state government: governor, chief justice of the Supreme Court of Illinois (1818–1824), and Speaker of the house of representatives (1852–1854).

As the Civil War approached, Reynolds's behavior became increasingly erratic and unpredictable. Although a lifelong Democrat, he became an implacable foe of Stephen A. Douglas, refusing to support him in his spirited contest with Abraham Lincoln for the U.S. Senate seat in 1858. Running for office for the last time, Reynolds appeared on the James Buchanan ticket that year as a candidate for superintendent of public instruction in Illinois. Among the three candidates, he finished last.

Chosen a delegate to the Democratic National Convention (1860) to oppose Douglas, he was denied a seat. Some of Reynolds's actions during the Civil War seem to border on the treasonable. Once the war came, he sympathized with Jefferson Davis and the southern Confederacy, opposed the Emancipation Proclamation, and continued to argue the merits of slavery. Though roundly criticized for giving aid and comfort to the enemy, he was neither charged nor prosecuted, thanks largely to his age and the general respect he commanded for his past services to the people of Illinois.

In his later years Reynolds became a prolific author, though the attractions of public life never left him. His writings, at times crude in style and not always reliable as to historical facts and events, are nevertheless priceless reservoirs of information, containing details about the settlement and early history of Illinois unavailable elsewhere. He had a remarkable, if disorganized, memory for names, faces, dates, and places, which adds to the charm of his best-known works: *The Pio-*

neer *History of Illinois* (1852) and its largely autobiographical sequel, *My Own Times, Embracing Also the History of My Life* (1855).

The ex-governor continued to live comfortably in his last home, in Belleville, Illinois, where he died. Following his death it was discovered that all of his private papers, correspondence, documents, and a will that he was supposed to have made had disappeared, never to be found.

• Executive documents for the Reynolds years may be found in Evarts Boutell Green and Clarence W. Alvord, eds., *The Governors' Letter-Books, 1818–1834,* vol. 4, Collections of the Illinois State Historical Library (1909). The only modern scholarly treatment of Reynolds is Josephine L. Harper, "John Reynolds: the Old Ranger of Illinois" (Ph.D. diss., Univ. of Illinois, Urbana-Champaign, 1949). As is true of all studies of Illinois governors, Robert Howard, *Mostly Good and Competent Men: Illinois Governors, 1818–1988* (1988), is indispensable. Several early state histories, all produced in the nineteenth century, are especially valuable for their attention to basic politics, candidates, campaigns, and elections: Alexander Davidson and Bernard Stuvé, *A Complete History of Illinois from 1673 to 1873* (1874); and Thomas Ford, *A History of Illinois from Its Commencement as a State in 1818 to 1847* (1854).

ROBERT M. SUTTON

REYNOLDS, John Fulton (20 Sept. 1820–1 July 1863), Union general, was born in Lancaster, Pennsylvania, the son of John Reynolds, a publisher and legislator, and Lydia Moore. He was educated at John Beck's school at Lititz, Pennsylvania, and Long Green Academy located near Baltimore, Maryland. He subsequently returned to Lancaster to enroll in the county academy. In 1837 he entered the U.S. Military Academy, graduating in 1841, twenty-sixth in a class of fifty-two. Breveted a second lieutenant and posted to the Third Artillery, from 1841 to 1846 Reynolds served with his regiment at a succession of posts in Baltimore, St. Augustine, Florida, and Fort Moultrie, South Carolina. By the outbreak of the war with Mexico, Reynolds was a first lieutenant in Captain Braxton Bragg's battery. He saw action at Monterrey, for which he was breveted captain, and bloody combat at Buena Vista, where he received the praise of his superiors and a major's brevet.

Following the Mexican War, Reynolds served garrison duty in Maine, New Orleans, and Fort Lafayette, New York. In 1854 he accompanied troop-transfer expedition overland to Salt Lake City. On 3 March 1855 he was promoted to captain. That spring he marched with his command from Salt Lake City to the Pacific and then was reassigned to Fort Orford, Oregon, where he participated in combat with the Rogue River Indians. In the fall of 1856 Reynolds was assigned to command Battery C, Third Artillery, Bragg's old battery. He joined his command at Fortress Monroe, Virginia, and remained there until 1858, when he and his command marched overland to Salt Lake City in the campaign against the Mormons. In June 1859 he marched 838 miles in 71 days with his command from near Salt Lake City to Fort Dalles, Washington. He subsequently shipped to Fort Vancouver, Washington, where he remained until August 1860. Reassigned to be commandant of cadets at West Point, he also taught artillery, cavalry, and infantry tactics and served as chief disciplinary officer.

At the outbreak of the Civil War, Reynolds was assigned to the Fourteenth Infantry with a promotion to lieutenant colonel and was sent to recruit a regiment in New London, Connecticut. Before he could settle into his new rank and position, he was promoted to brigadier general of volunteers and, at the request of General George McClellan, was assigned to the Army of the Potomac. He commanded a brigade in the Pennsylvania Reserve Division. In June 1862 his command joined the army in its campaign on the Virginia peninsula. He was lightly engaged at Mechanicsville and severely at Gaines' Mill, where on 28 June 1862 he was taken prisoner after attempting to post a battery and becoming separated from his command. He was taken to Libby Prison in Richmond. When the citizens of Fredericksburg, Virginia, where Reynolds had been military governor in May 1862, learned of his capture, a citizens' committee, including the mayor, petitioned the secretary of war that he be paroled. On 13 August 1862 he was released in a general exchange of prisoners. On 21 August he was placed in command of the Pennsylvania Reserve Division, joining it at Fredericksburg. During the disastrous Second Manassas campaign, Reynolds displayed aggressive and bold leadership. General John Pope, who was sparing of praise, wrote that Reynolds was "prompt, active, and energetic, he commanded his division with distinguished ability throughout all the operations." In the ensuing Maryland campaign, Governor Andrew Curtin of Pennsylvania requested that Reynolds be assigned to prepare the state militia to resist Robert E. Lee's anticipated invasion. Although he performed his duties with customary energy, Reynolds was disgusted with the poor discipline and disorganization of the militia and welcomed his return to his division in late September. On 29 September he was promoted to command the First Army Corps, and on 29 November 1862 he was promoted to major general of volunteers. At the battle of Fredericksburg in December, his corps was severely engaged and lost heavily. Although he was present at Chancellorsville the following May, his corps missed the principal part of the engagement.

Following Chancellorsville, Reynolds was considered as a replacement to Joseph Hooker in command of the Army of the Potomac. He was summoned to Washington, D.C., on 31 May and reputedly offered command of the army, which he was said to have declined because he was not promised a free hand in its maneuver. During the opening stages of the Gettysburg campaign, he commanded the right wing of the army, but on 30 June General George G. Meade assigned him to command the left wing of the army. It was Reynolds's wing and his own First Corps that led the advance of the army to Gettysburg on 1 July 1863. When Reynolds reached the field, John Buford's Union cavalry was already engaged with Lee's advance. In a bold decision, Reynolds determined to engage Lee with his advance troops in an attempt to purchase time to permit the rest of the army to move to his support and complete its concentration. Reynolds personally placed his leading infantry division and struck Lee's advance. He greatly exposed himself, and while leading the Second Wisconsin forward into McPherson's Woods, he was killed instantly by Confederate fire.

Reynolds never married, although there was a woman, Katherine Hewitt, with whom he was involved at the time of his death. As a commander, he may never have realized his full potential, although his aggressive leadership at Gettysburg helped lay the foundation of the Union victory there. He loved the outdoors, particularly hunting and fishing. He was six feet tall, erect in bearing, and of a somewhat retiring, reticent nature. Charles Veil, a member of Reynolds's staff, left a fitting description of the type of soldier and man his chief was: "Wherever the fight raged the fiercest, there the General was sure to be found, his undaunted courage always inspired the men with more energy & courage. He would never order a body of troops where he had not been himself, or where he did not dare to go."

• Reynolds's personal papers are located at Franklin and Marshall College in Lancaster, Pa. His official reports and correspondence are in *The War of the Rebellion: A Compilation of the Official Records of the Union and Confederate Armies* (128 vols., 1880–1901). An excellent biography is Edward J. Nichols, *Toward Gettysburg: A Biography of General John F. Reynolds* (1958). See also Henry S. Huidekoper, *Address at the Unveiling of the Statue of Major General John F. Reynolds at Gettysburg, July 1, 1899* (1899); Pennsylvania Historical Society, *Reynolds Memorial* (1880); and Joseph G. Rosengarten, *William Reynolds, Rear-Admiral U.S.N., John Fulton Reynolds, Major-General U.S.V.* (1880). For Reynolds's military service record, see G. W. Cullum, *Biographical Register of Officers and Graduates of the U.S. Military Academy* (1891). An observant and highly detailed account of service in the Union First Corps with Reynolds is Allan Nevins, ed., *A Diary of Battle: The Personal Journals of Col. Charles S. Wainwright 1861–1865* (1962). The best account of the Gettysburg campaign with ample information about Reynolds's role is Edwin Coddington, *The Gettysburg Campaign* (1979). Obituaries are in the *New York Times*, 3 July 1863, and the *Lancaster Weekly Examiner*, 8 July 1863.

D. SCOTT HARTWIG

REYNOLDS, Joseph Jones (4 Jan. 1822–25 Feb. 1899), Civil War general and Plains Indian fighter, was born in Flemingsburg, Kentucky, the son of Edward Reynolds, a hatter, and Sarah Longley. The family moved to Lafayette, Indiana, in 1837, and the next year young Reynolds attended Wabash College at Crawfordsville. In 1839 he received an appointment to the U.S. Military Academy, graduating in 1843, tenth in a class of thirty-nine. Classmate Ulysses S. Grant was his lifelong friend.

Commissioned as a brevet second lieutenant in the Fourth Artillery, Reynolds spent his first years at Fortress Monroe, Virginia. In 1845 he joined General Zachary Taylor's command, employed in the occupation of Texas. While on march from Corpus Christi to Fort Brown in 1846, Reynolds was ruptured in his right side. In later life he wore a powerful truss to prevent protrusion of the intestines. He married Mary Elizabeth Bainbridge at Fortress Monroe in 1846; they had five children. Promoted to second lieutenant on 11 May 1846, Reynolds became principal assistant professor of natural and experimental philosophy at West Point in August and remained there nine years. He became a first lieutenant on 3 March 1847. In 1855 Reynolds returned to the field, serving with his regiment at Fort Washita, Indian Territory. Two years later, apparently missing academic life, he left the service to become professor of mechanics and engineering at Washington University, St. Louis. In 1860 he went back to Lafayette to start a grocery business with his brother.

With the outbreak of the Civil War, Reynolds returned to military duty. Obtaining a commission as colonel of the Tenth Indiana Volunteers on 25 April 1861, he became a brigadier general a month later. In charge of the Cheat Mountain District in the Department of western Virginia, he successfully withstood an attack by a strong Confederate force under Robert E. Lee in mid-September, thereby securing that portion of the state to the Union. The death of his brother caused him to resign his commission on 23 January 1862 to take care of family business.

On 21 August 1862 Reynolds returned to the army as colonel of the Seventy-fifth Indiana Regiment. Recommissioned as a brigadier general of volunteers on 17 September, he became a major general on 29 November and was assigned to the Army of the Cumberland. In succession he commanded the Fifth Division, Center, Fourteenth Corps (11 Nov. 1862–9 Jan. 1863); the Fifth Division (9 Jan.–8 June 1863); and the Fourth Division (8 June–9 Oct. 1863) at Hoover's Gap and at Chickamauga, where he earned a brevet for gallant and meritorious conduct. Becoming chief of staff of the Army of the Cumberland in October 1863, Reynolds played a prominent part in the battles of Chattanooga, Lookout Mountain, and Missionary Ridge, for which he received a second brevet in 1867. From January to June 1864 he was in command of the defenses of New Orleans and afterward commanded the Nineteenth Army Corps (7 July–7 Nov. 1864). From 22 December 1864 to 1 August 1865 he commanded the Department of Arkansas and the Seventh Corps. Mustered out on 1 September 1866, he was one of eighteen major generals who lost their commissions.

In the meantime Reynolds had been appointed colonel of the Twenty-sixth Infantry, which he accepted on 21 September. From 1867 to 1872 he successively commanded the Subdistrict of the Rio Grande; the District of Texas; the Fifth Military District, comprising Louisiana and Texas; and the Department of Texas. He enforced Reconstruction policies in the region with skill and tact, prompting the Democratic Texas Legislature in 1871 to elect him U.S. senator. However, the U.S. Senate awarded the contested seat to his opponent, Republican Morgan C. Hamilton. During 1870 Reynolds changed regiments twice, transferring to the Twenty-fifth Infantry on 8 January and to the Third Cavalry on 15 December.

Reynolds lived in the West during 1872–1876, serving successively as the commander of Fort McPherson, Nebraska; Fort D. A. Russell, Wyoming; and the District of South Platte. From 23 February to 3 April 1876 he commanded troops in the Big Horn expedition, sent north from Fort Fetterman, Wyoming, to bring in the northern Sioux and their allies. On 17 March cavalry under Reynolds surprised a northern Cheyenne camp on the Powder River, succeeded in burning the village, and captured many horses. However, the Indians rallied, recaptured their stock, and drove the troops back. Failure to hold the field brought charges of incompetence and cowardice, resulting in a court-martial hearing for Reynolds and two subordinates early in 1877. The court found all of them guilty in varying degrees. Reynolds was sentenced to be suspended from the service for a year. Not unexpectedly, President Grant remitted the sentence in view of past service.

Suffering from a variety of ailments, Reynolds retired on 25 June 1877. He died in Washington, D.C., where he had lived for many years. Reynolds is remembered principally for his Civil War career, his devotion to duty in perilous times, and his administrative and organizational skills.

• For personal details of Reynolds's life and his military career see J. J. Reynolds, Military Service File, Records of the Office of the Adjutant General, Record Group 94, National Archives; and J. J. Reynolds, Pension File Number 495144, Record Group 15, National Archives. For Reynolds's testimony concerning his experience as an American Indian fighter, see Court-martial of Joseph J. Reynolds, 1877, Case QQ #26, Records of the Judge Advocate General, Record Group 153, National Archives, Washington, D.C. Covering this episode in detail is J. W. Vaughn, *Reynolds Campaign on Powder River* (1961). An obituary is in the *New York Times*, 27 Feb. 1899.

JOHN D. MCDERMOTT

REYNOLDS, Richard Joshua, Sr. (20 July 1850–29 July 1918), tobacco manufacturer and philanthropist, was born at "Rock Spring," the family estate near Critz, Patrick County, Virginia, the son of Hardin William Reynolds, a farmer and tobacco merchant, and Nancy Jane Cox. In addition to his other activities, his father engaged in both banking and chewing tobacco production; as one of the largest slaveholders in the state, his family was socially prominent and financially secure. As a boy Richard attended local country schools and worked on his father's farm. He also worked intermittently in his father's plug tobacco factory, gaining valuable practical experience that he would later put to good use.

Reynolds entered Emory and Henry College in Emory, Virginia, in 1868, only to drop out two years later in order to work full-time in his father's manufacturing operation. While he later attended Bryant and Stratton Business College in Baltimore, Maryland, early in 1873, he gained additional experience by soliciting orders for his father's factory in his spare time. After his return to Patrick County, he entered into a formal partnership with his father on 1 July 1873. Ever restless, Reynolds was soon dissatisfied in the position. His father's plant was located sixty miles from the nearest railroad, and he also chafed under his father's control of the operation. Consequently, he purchased a 100-foot lot on Depot Street (in what is today Winston-Salem, N.C.) in October 1874 and soon erected his first factory. His new location not only provided railroad connections but was also physically closer to the "Old Bright" tobacco belt of North Carolina. A new variety, the so-called flue-cured tobacco, was gaining in popularity among local farmers because of its adaptability to local soils; both the new tobacco and the rail connections played a vital role in Reynolds's later success.

Reynolds's factory began production in a modest fashion. During its first year it produced 150,000 pounds of Southern flat plug chewing tobacco. Prepared from flue-cured leaf, the end product provided a long-lasting chew, although it did not absorb sweetening agents (a common practice among manufacturers of the day) as readily as tobaccos prepared with the more traditional burley leaf. In one of the first of his many innovations, Reynolds pioneered the use of saccharin as a sweetener. Although the date of this innovation is unclear, the process resulted in a product far superior to its burley leaf–based competitors.

Buoyed by the increase in sales resulting from his innovation, Reynolds soon built a new manufacturing plant with the capacity to produce five times his current sales figures. Seeking improved transportation facilities, he helped to complete the Roanoke and Southern Railway in late 1891. The new line ran between Winston and Salem, North Carolina, and Roanoke, Virginia, providing the cities with ready access to both eastern and western markets. Although the line was almost immediately assumed by the Norfolk and Western Railway, it gave local manufacturers freedom from their former dependency on the Richmond and Danville system.

Shortly after the railroad line's completion, Reynolds initiated an advertising campaign. Seeking to utilize the most modern equipment in his facilities, Reynolds also installed new Adams Duplex automatic tobacco presses and Proctor Redrying systems. While the latest technology helped to make production more efficient, it was also costly. With production on the increase—it exceeded five million pounds of chewing tobacco by 1898—Reynolds needed still more capital for further expansion, but he was unable to generate the needed funds. Former sources of capital, including his family and associates in Baltimore, proved inadequate. Reynolds and his firm—formally incorporated in February 1890 as the R. J. Reynolds Tobacco Company, with his brother William Neal Reynolds as a partner (another brother, Walter R. Reynolds, joined them in 1893)—faced a difficult situation, complicated by an additional challenge in the form of James B. Duke's American Tobacco Company trust, which utilized cutthroat pricing to drive out the competition in the chewing tobacco market.

While fond of neither the Duke family nor the trust, Reynolds faced even less pleasant alternatives. Consequently, Reynolds Tobacco became a part of the American Tobacco trust in April 1899. Although nominally under the direction of the Continental Tobacco Company within the complex trust arrangement, Reynolds had no intention of relinquishing control of his firm, telling concerned friends, "You will never see the day when Dick Reynolds will eat out of Buck [James B.] Duke's hand" (Tilley, *Reynolds Homestead*, p. 155). True to his word, Reynolds Tobacco retained both its name and management team and actually prospered under the control of the trust. Access to the vast capital resources of the trust facilitated badly needed plant expansion, and Reynolds used the power of the trust (which had more or less allotted the chewing tobacco market to his firm) to establish a dominant position in that product line. He took time from his battles with the trust to marry Mary Katherine Smith of Mount Airy, North Carolina, in February 1905; they had four children.

Although prevented by the trust from entering the smoking tobacco market, Reynolds remained undeterred and developed several brands of smoking tobacco in hope of defying the trust. In 1907 he got his chance when the U.S. government launched an antitrust suit against American Tobacco, and Reynolds promptly launched the soon-to-be-famous Prince Albert brand. After a modest start, the brand—which featured a blend of both burley and flue-cured tobaccos—became enormously popular; by the end of 1917 more than 500,000 two-ounce "tidy red tins of P.A." were produced daily. Production soon required the use of a special train each night to transport the day's production; dubbed the "Prince Albert Special," it averaged thirty-five cars in length. Ironically, Reynolds was initially reluctant to use blended tobaccos; his brother Walter convinced the suddenly conservative entrepreneur to compromise his devotion to fluecured tobacco by incorporating burley leaf in the blend.

Having successfully overcome threats by the trust to sue his firm over its issuance of Prince Albert, Reynolds further expanded his product line into the newly emerging cigarette market upon the trust's final dissolution in November 1911. His most popular effort by far was the introduction in 1913 of the Camel brand of cigarettes. Featuring a blend of flue-cured, burley, and Turkish tobaccos, the Camel was the result of many years of experimentation with different tobacco blends. Its appeal was such that it eventually constituted one-third of all cigarettes sold in the United States.

Reynolds's hard work and vision made him an enormously wealthy man. Relatively progressive in his outlook toward labor for his time, Reynolds developed numerous employee benefits following the turn of the century that complemented his company's growth. He built lunchrooms for both sexes and races and initiated a popular profit-sharing plan in 1912 that allowed employees to purchase company stock. Known to his employees as "R. J." or "Dick Reynolds," he helped keep his firm remarkably free from labor strife. Also noted for his philanthropy, he contributed to the endowment of the first hospital in Winston-Salem as well as Slater Hospital (for African Americans) in that same community. Reynolds's efforts on behalf of African Americans included a critical donation that resulted in the founding of Slater Industrial and Normal School (now Winston-Salem State University).

Ill from pancreatic cancer, Reynolds gradually withdrew from active management of his firm until his death, which occurred at his massive estate, "Reynolda," on the outskirts of Winston-Salem. At the time of his death, his firm employed 15,000 workers in over forty-three buildings and enjoyed annual sales worldwide of $100 million. Reynolds's widow continued his philanthropic efforts following his death, while the family mansion later became a cultural center. Part of the Reynolds estate served as the site of the new campus of Wake Forest University, which relocated to Winston-Salem in 1956.

Although blessed with a wealthy background, Richard Reynolds created his own tobacco industry empire through hard work and sound management. His firm continues in operation today as part of RJR-Nabisco, and he deserves to be remembered as a leading figure in the industrial development of the postbellum South.

• The papers of Richard Joshua Reynolds are held at the Reynolda House archives in Winston-Salem, N.C. The best secondary source of information on Reynolds's life and career is Nannie M. Tilley, *The R. J. Reynolds Tobacco Company* (1985); Tilley's *Reynolds Homestead, 1814–1970* (1970) is also informative and contains a full genealogical sketch of the family. The best study of Reynolds's nemesis, James B. Duke, is Robert F. Durden, *The Dukes of Durham, 1865–1929* (1975). An obituary is in the *Winston-Salem Journal*, 30 July 1918.

EDWARD L. LACH, JR.

REYNOLDS, Richard Samuel, Sr. (15 Aug. 1881–29 July 1955), industrialist, was born in Bristol, Tennessee, the son of Abraham David Reynolds, the owner of a profitable tobacco business, and Senah Ann Hoge. After graduating in 1898 from King College in Bristol, Reynolds studied law at Columbia University and, subsequently, at the University of Virginia. However, his uncle Richard J. Reynolds convinced him to join his tobacco firm, the R. J. Reynolds Company in Winston-Salem, North Carolina. When Reynolds joined his uncle's firm in 1903, the company relied on a single product line, chewing tobacco, leaving the market for smoking tobacco to the Tobacco Trust, a powerful coalition of tobacco interests that then dominated the industry. Reynolds convinced his uncle to compete with the trust by putting out a smoking product made from mild leaf tobacco. The new Prince Albert brand was the first sold in tins, which helped preserve tobacco moisture. Despite determined efforts by the large firms to exclude the Reynolds Company from new markets and product lines, Prince Albert proved an immediate success for the firm, which Reynolds built on by initiating a national advertising campaign and introducing the Camel cigarette brand. Yet at the height of his success, Reynolds chose to leave his uncle's company, probably realizing that the company's future lay with his uncle's two sons. Reynolds married Julia Louise Parham in 1905, and they had four children. Concerned for his children's future, Reynolds decided to strike out on his own.

In 1912 Reynolds returned to Bristol and launched the Reynolds Corporation, which manufactured soap. The young entrepreneur again exhibited a talent for new product lines and merchandising as his company successfully produced a wide variety of household cleansers. But as his company expanded into the national market, Reynolds faced two serious challenges. First, his plant burned down, forcing him to relocate to Louisville; then, the outbreak of World War I created shortages in raw materials and transport bottlenecks that drove his business to the brink of bankruptcy. Once again, Reynolds's innovative talent salvaged his business career. He developed a new, waterproof gunpowder container that replaced existing steel vessels with drums made of steel and asphalt felt paper. The new containers won him a government contract and restored prosperity to his business. When the armistice eliminated the demand for wartime products, Reynolds once again shifted direction and entered the metal foil business.

Reynolds's past ties to the tobacco industry served as the basis for this venture. Foil was in increasingly heavy demand as packaging for cigarettes, and the Tennessee entrepreneur secured financing from the British-American and R. J. Reynolds tobacco companies, both of which were interested in expanding a tin foil market then dominated by a handful of firms and marked by serious shortages of the product. Once again, Reynolds successfully penetrated a tightly controlled market by relying on innovation and intense merchandising efforts. His U.S. Foil Company, incorporated in 1919, dramatically reduced production costs by introducing techniques for eliminating much of the labor-intensive handling of heavy lead ingots. Lower costs enabled the company to survive a price war launched by the established powers in the industry.

By the mid-1920s Reynolds became convinced that aluminum would replace heavier metals like tin and lead as the principal type of foil. Accordingly, he built a plant in Louisville devoted to the production of aluminum foil, although the company also produced other products such as pastes for paint. Through an aggressive merchandising campaign, the firm expanded the domestic market for foil packaging. As a part of that strategy, U.S. Foil moved directly into the consumer products industry with its acquisition of the Eskimo Pie Corporation. In 1928 Reynolds reorganized his business interests, creating the Reynolds Metals

Company, leaving U.S. Foil to function as a holding company. Reynolds Metals provided the platform from which the aluminum foil magnate launched his most ambitious undertaking.

While the aluminum foil business remained competitive, production of aluminum was monopolized by the Aluminum Company of America (Alcoa). By 1939 Alcoa could no longer supply Reynolds Metals with the ingots it required to produce an increasingly diverse range of products. Anticipating the problem, Reynolds had traveled to France in 1937 to secure aluminum pig for his foil business. While in Europe, Reynolds took note of Germany's emergence as the world's leading aluminum producer and the use of the metal in Hitler's rearmament program, particularly in the manufacture of aircraft. Sensing an opportunity to expand his own business and serve his country's interests, Reynolds urged Alcoa's chair of the board, Arthur Vining Davis, to triple the company's output. After Davis rejected the proposal, Reynolds attempted to enter the aluminum production industry directly with government backing. After his initial appeals to the federal government were rejected, Reynolds turned to his political connections as a southern Democrat to secure the backing of Senator Lister Hill of Alabama. At Hill's urging, the Reconstruction Finance Corporation agreed to loan Reynolds $15.8 million in return for a mortgage on the eighteen plants he owned. Reynolds employed that initial line of credit to build a smelter and mill in Sheffield, Alabama, and additional facilities in the state of Washington. Even with government-sponsored financing, the new venture represented considerable risk for Reynolds. The company had to integrate backward from consumer products into primary aluminum manufacturing and bauxite mining, areas where its employees had little experience. Furthermore, Alcoa responded to Reynolds's entrance into production with a price war. In turn, Reynolds continued to build additional capacity and survived the challenge. But he would be unable to compete seriously with Alcoa until the United States entered World War II. Both defense contracts and subsequent policies of the federal government created an exceptional opportunity for him.

While the entry of Reynolds Metals into aluminum production dramatically increased domestic output, plants controlled by the federal government accounted for half of U.S. aluminum production by the end of the war. The restoration of peace raised the question of what to do with the government-owned factories in light of the drastic reduction in demand. Most experts suggested closing or dismantling the federally owned facilities. Reynolds, however, argued in favor of selling the plants to private interests, asserting that the excess capacity would be absorbed in less than five years.

Reynolds's suggestion elicited a positive response within the government, where antitrust sentiment was running high. Specifically, in March 1945 a federal court decision declared Alcoa a monopoly—a finding that effectively prohibited it from acquiring any of the government plants. Alcoa strenuously resisted government plans to sell those factories that Alcoa itself had built and operated on behalf of the federal government, particularly the large refinery at Hurricane Creek, Arkansas, that used Alcoa's new "combination process," allowing the processing of low-grade bauxite ore. Under government pressure Alcoa relented, and Reynolds secured control of the refinery and use of the new process, which would allow him to compete effectively with Alcoa. Reynolds eventually acquired a total of six plants from the government for $57 million, about one-third of their original construction cost. In order to feed this vastly increased production capacity, Reynolds Metals acquired bauxite deposits in Jamaica and Haiti.

In the postwar boom economy, Reynolds's gamble that rising demand would soon absorb the production capacities created during the war paid off. But his success was not due solely to the general rebound of the national economy. His company had launched an intense consumer advertising campaign designed to convince the American public of the usefulness of aluminum in their daily lives. In the postwar years, Reynolds Metals generated a dizzying array of aluminum consumer products that ranged from sports equipment to home appliances. Its flagship product in this effort was aluminum foil, sold under the brand name Reynolds Wrap. Thanks in part to Reynolds's aggressive merchandising efforts, aluminum also gained wide acceptance for industrial uses ranging from building construction to automobile manufacture. That strategy helped establish Reynolds Metals as the second largest producer of aluminum in the United States. Once again, Richard Reynolds had successfully challenged a monopoly.

In 1948 Reynolds had stepped down as president of the Reynolds company to assume the post of chair of the board. He was replaced by his son Richard S. Reynolds, Jr., while his other three sons also held important management positions in the company. By the time of Reynolds's death in Richmond, Virginia, he was already recognized as a corporate pioneer who blended product innovation, astute consumer advertising, and risk taking to successfully challenge monopolistic enterprises.

• Reynolds's papers remain the property of the Reynolds family. Some correspondence regarding his entry into the aluminum production industry can be found in the Harry S. Truman Papers and the Truman Library. The best biographical essays are Richard Samuel Reynolds, Jr., *Opportunity in Crisis: The Reynolds Metals Story* (1956); Robert Sheehan, "Look at the Reynolds Boys Now," *Fortune*, Aug. 1953, pp. 106–13, 170, 172–78; and Peter Martin, *I Call on the Reynolds Brothers* (1961). George David Smith, *From Monopoly to Competition: The Transformation of Alcoa, 1888–1986* (1988), focuses on Reynolds's competitor but provides a balanced analysis of factors that enabled him to break the Alcoa monopoly. Other scholarly treatments of the industry include Merton J. Peck, *Competition in the Aluminum Industry, 1945–1958* (1961), and Charlotte F. Muller, *Light Metals Monopoly* (1946). For biographical information on the extended Reynolds family, see Nannie M. Tilley, *Reynolds Homestead, 1814–1970* (1970). An obituary is in the *New York Times*, 30 July 1955.

THOMAS F. O'BRIEN

REYNOLDS, Robert Rice (18 June 1884–13 Feb. 1963), lawyer and U.S. senator, known as "Our Bob," was born in Asheville, Buncombe County, North Carolina, the son of William Taswell Reynolds, a businessman and court clerk, and Mamie Spears. Reynolds's great-grandfather, James M. Smith, (1784–1853), was the first white child born west of the Blue Ridge Mountains and was a pioneer builder of Asheville.

Reared in a family of modest means, Reynolds early became obsessed with a desire to travel and ran away from home at age fourteen. He recounted his adventures in a book, *Wanderlust* (1913). He attended the University of North Carolina from 1902 to 1905 but did not obtain a degree. The friendly, gregarious Reynolds spent several summers in Europe, as described in his book *Gypsy Trails* (1925), and spent his academic career engaged in athletics and social events. After editing a magazine and coaching football, he read for the bar and was admitted to the practice of law in 1907.

In 1910 Reynolds married Fannie Menge Jackson, the first of his five wives. Fannie died in 1913, leaving Reynolds the responsibility for raising their two children. In 1914 he wed Mary Bland, with whom he had one child; he divorced her in 1917. He married Denise D'Arcy in 1920 and obtained a divorce from her in 1930. Reynolds's marriage to *Ziegfeld Follies* dancer Eva Grady in 1931 ended with her death in 1934.

In 1910 Reynolds entered politics, winning the post of district solicitor of Buncombe County. He then ran unsuccessfully in the Democratic primaries for Congress in 1914, for lieutenant governor of North Carolina in 1924, and for the U.S. Senate in 1926. In the U.S. Senate Democratic primary campaign of 1932, the perpetual candidate participated in a prolonged vaudeville in which he literally laughed his opponent out of the Senate. Reynolds portrayed his wealthy opponent, incumbent senator Cameron Morrison, as a man who ate "red Russian fish aigs" (caviar) at a posh Washington restaurant instead of "good ole' North Carolina hen eggs." Campaigning as a poor man of the people during the depth of the depression, the demagogic Reynolds played on people's fears by attacking entrenched wealth and big business. He also opposed prohibition and was the first statewide "wet" candidate since state prohibition was adopted in 1908. Although handicapped by a lack of funds and a weak organization, Reynolds's colorful and energetic campaign captured the attention of the voters, and he was victorious by a vote of 227,864 (65.4%) to 120,428 (34.6%) over the heavily favored Morrison. This was the largest majority ever obtained in a Democratic primary up to that time, and the state papers called his triumph a "miracle" and "without a parallel for sensation in North Carolina politics." In November he defeated his Republican opponent, Jake F. Newell.

In the Senate, Reynolds became chairman of the District of Columbia Committee and the Military Affairs Committee. Reynolds was an atypical southern senator as an isolationist and was also an ardent supporter of almost all of Franklin D. Roosevelt's New Deal legislation before 1938. His most important legislative goal during his two terms was the restriction of immigration into the United States. He sponsored bills to register and fingerprint all aliens and to deport habitual alien criminals. Convinced that foreigners were taking badly needed jobs from Americans and were responsible for a crime wave, Reynolds worked assiduously to control the alien menace at the gate. In 1939 he organized the Vindicators Association, Inc., an isolationist, nationalistic, antialien, anti-Semitic group, which was characterized by critics as pro-Nazi and racist. Reynolds then began a long and unwise association with such controversial individuals as George Deatherage, Gerald L. K. Smith, Father Charles Coughlin, and Nazi propagandist George Sylvester Viereck and isolationist groups like America First, contributing to the impression that he was pro-Nazi. Reynolds was a fervent noninterventionist who feared that defending Britain and France would destroy America. Though he consistently favored the neutrality legislation of the 1930s and voted against the World Court, Lend-Lease, and any other activity that might get the United States into a war, the pro-Nazi charges were unfair and unwarranted. His lack of discretion and his unyielding belief in nonintervention, however, led to a rapid decline in his popularity.

When the Japanese attacked Pearl Harbor, Reynolds abandoned his isolationism to work for victory. As chairman of the vital Military Affairs Committee, he cooperated fully with Roosevelt and worked hard to pass the necessary legislation. Roosevelt, however, did not trust Reynolds and generally found a way to bypass his committee. In 1942 Reynolds abolished the Vindicators Association and began publishing the *National Record,* which advocated a decisive victory over the Nazis and the outlawing of the Communist party. He reverted to his unilateralist concepts as the war drew to an end and was one of only five senators voting against the Connolly Resolution committing the United States to participation in a postwar organization, the United Nations, to maintain the peace.

As a senator, the colorful Reynolds engaged in a constant search for publicity. He kissed movie star Jean Harlow on the steps of the Capitol, endorsed Lucky Strike cigarettes, bagged a walrus in Alaska, and traveled around the United States in a trailer advertising North Carolina. In 1941, at age fifty-seven, the debonair Reynolds married his fifth wife, twenty-year-old Evalyn Washington McLean, whose wealthy parents owned the Hope diamond and the *Washington Post.* They had a daughter. Evalyn died of an overdose of barbiturates in 1946.

Due to his inflexible isolationist stance, which did not play well back home, the pro-Nazi charges, and his general dereliction of senatorial duties to travel the world on government junkets, Reynolds was now unpopular, and on 8 November 1943 he chose not to run for reelection. He practiced law briefly in Washington, D.C., but after his wife's death he retired to Asheville with his daughter and lived on Reynolds Mountain. In his last hurrah, he entered the 1950 Senate Democratic primary race in North Carolina. Although he campaigned infrequently, his 58,752 votes were enough to prevent incumbent senator Frank P. Graham from winning the first primary, and Graham subsequently lost in a runoff. Reynolds spent his final days traveling and raising his daughter. He died in Asheville.

• According to the Library of Congress and friends, Reynolds's papers were destroyed when he left the Senate. A few letters and clippings remain with family members. Letters from and about Reynolds are in the Josiah W. Bailey Papers at Duke University and in the Frank P. Graham, Jonathan Daniels, and O. Max Gardner papers at the University of North Carolina. Copies of the *American Vindicator* and the *National Record* are in the Library of Congress. See also Julian M. Pleasants and Augustus M. Burns, *Frank Porter Graham and the 1950 Senate Race in North Carolina* (1990); Pleasants, "The Last Hurrah: Bob Reynolds and the U.S. Senate Race in 1950," *North Carolina Historical Review* 65 (Jan. 1988): 52–75; Pleasants, "Carolina Casanova: The Five Marriages of Senator Bob Reynolds," *The State,* Aug. 1988, pp. 26–31; Pleasants, "The Beginnings of Buncombe Bob," *The State,* Aug. 1977; Pleasants, "Buncombe Bob and Red Russian Fish Eggs," *Appalachian Journal* 4 (Autumn 1976): 51–62; Pleasants, "The Senatorial Career of Robert Rice Reynolds" (Ph.D. diss., Univ. of North Carolina, 1971); Allan Michie and Frank Ryhlick, *Dixie Demagogues* (1939); and Elmer L. Puryear, *Democratic Party Dissension in North Carolina, 1928–1936* (1962). Obituaries are in the Raleigh *News and Observer,* the *Asheville Citizen,* and the *Washington Post,* 14 Feb. 1963.

JULIAN M. PLEASANTS

REYNOLDS, William Neal (22 Mar. 1863–10 Sept. 1951), tobacco manufacturer and philanthropist, was born at "Rock Creek," the family estate near Critz, in Patrick County, Virginia, the son of Hardin William Reynolds, a farmer and tobacco merchant, and Nancy Jane Cox. After receiving his early education in local schools, he entered King College in Bristol, Tennessee, in 1882. Reynolds attended King for only a few months before transferring to Trinity College in Durham, North Carolina, following the death of his father. The transfer placed Reynolds closer to Winston (later Winston-Salem), North Carolina, where older brother Richard Joshua Reynolds had established a tobacco manufacturing operation in 1875. Reynolds worked part-time at his brother's plant; beginning as a leaf-hanger in 1881, he quickly mastered all facets of the operation after leaving Trinity College in 1884. He took charge of tobacco purchasing in 1886, and two years later he formed a formal partnership with his brother and company bookkeeper Henry Roan. The elder Reynolds served as president with 75 percent ownership; his younger brother and Roan split the difference. In 1889 William Neal Reynolds married Kate Gertrude Bitting; they had no children.

Reynolds's responsibilities grew rapidly with the continued growth of his family's firm, which became the R. J. Reynolds Tobacco Company upon receiving a state charter on 11 February 1890. He served as a director and vice president of the new firm and retained both positions when the company became part of the American Tobacco Company trust on 4 April 1899. The Reynolds brothers entered the trust with mixed emotions and soon chafed under the control of the Duke family of Durham, North Carolina. The Reynoldses had entered the tobacco industry as producers of plug chewing tobacco, and although they desired to add smoking tobaccos to their product line, they were prevented from doing so by the trust.

Trust restrictions notwithstanding, the Reynolds firm developed three brands of smoking tobacco in anticipation that opportunities in the market would improve. With the instigation of federal antitrust legislation against American in 1907, the Reynolds brothers took advantage. At the insistence of Walter Robert Reynolds, the firm began production of the "Prince Albert" brand, which contained a blend of both flue-cured and burley tobacco. William Reynolds played a critical role in this new product line. As head of purchasing, he journeyed to Louisville, Kentucky, and purchased sixteen hogsheads of burley tobacco at a very favorable price. From these beginnings the "Prince Albert" brand became an immediate success; by 1911, the year in which the trust was finally dissolved, the brand was well established. Independent again by 1912, the firm entered the cigarette market in the following year with the introduction of the "Camel" brand, which soon became an industry leader.

William Neal Reynolds assumed the presidency of R. J. Reynolds upon his brother's death in 1918. He retained that position until April 1924, when he resigned because of poor health. He remained active in company affairs, however, serving as chairman of the board (1924–1931) and then as chairman of the executive committee (1931–1942). Although recognized as an expert in tobacco purchasing throughout his career, his methods occasionally came under scrutiny. After years of legal action, he was fined (along with executives of the American and Liggett and Myers firms) a total of $225,000 by the U.S. government for violating antitrust laws regarding price-fixing.

Reynolds did not allow his business activities to interfere with a major interest of his later years: the training and breeding of horses for harness racing. His first notable success in this area came during the 1909–1910 racing season, when one of his fillies, My Shady Bell, won fifteen of seventeen races. In 1922, following a doctor's advice that he receive a lot of fresh air while recuperating from an operation, he began training horses personally, often riding up to twenty-five miles a day at his estate, "Tanglewood," which was located on the Yadkin River near Clemmons, North Carolina. He also owned a breeding farm, "Arrowpoint," out-side of Lexington, Kentucky, and in 1927 he acquired part-ownership of Seminole Park. Located outside of Orlando, Florida, the latter property proved to be a popular location for winter horse training.

Reynolds's interest in the sport of harness racing extended beyond his own immediate success. His financial support of Grand Circuit racing was critical during the 1920s, and his efforts were recognized in 1926, when he became the first president of the Union Trotting Association. Perhaps his most memorable association in the sport revolved around the Hambletonian Stakes. He was active in the establishment of the race, which remains the sport's premier event, and gained an individual triumph when his filly Mary Reynolds won the event in 1933.

Philanthropy became increasingly important to Reynolds as the years went by. He made numerous financial contributions to his alma mater, by then known as Duke University and located in Durham, North Carolina, and he also served during the 1930s on its board of trustees. Reynolds formed the Z. Smith Reynolds Foundation in 1936 to honor the memory of his brother Richard's youngest son. The foundation immediately undertook two huge projects; it not only assisted the city of Winston-Salem in the construction of its airport, but it also provided the financial backing that enabled Wake Forest College (now University) to move in 1956 from Wake Forest, North Carolina, to its present location on the former estate of R. J. Reynolds. Reynolds also provided generous support to North Carolina State College (now University); donations of $100,000 toward construction of the D. H. Hill Library were accompanied by a grant of $340,000 to augment faculty salaries. A gift of $100,000 from his niece, Mary Reynolds, resulted in the naming of William Neal Reynolds Coliseum (State College's new basketball arena) in his honor; the state-of-the-art facility opened in 1946. In that same year Reynolds honored his late wife by financing the construction of the Kate Bitting Memorial Hospital for Negroes in Winston-Salem.

Reynolds became ill at Goshen, New York, the site of the Hambletonian, while attending to racing business; he died a month later in Winston-Salem. Possessing the traditional southern beliefs of his era, he bequeathed his estate to the "white race" as a park and playground; this stipulation was later removed. The remainder of his estate went to the Reynolds Foundation, which continues to support a wide range of charities. William Neal Reynolds is remembered for his role in building up the R. J. Reynolds Tobacco empire as well as for his philanthropy and for his assistance to the world of harness racing.

• Some of Reynolds's correspondence can be found among the William K. Boyd, William P. Few, and Robert L. Flowers Collections in the Duke University archives, Durham, N.C. An excellent study of the Reynolds family is Nannie M. Tilley, *Reynolds Homestead, 1814–1970* (1970), and the founding of the Z. Smith Reynolds Foundation is covered in Brian Haislip's *A History of the Z. Smith Reynolds Foundation*

(1967). Obituaries are in the *Winston-Salem Journal*, the *Winston-Salem Sentinel*, and the *New York Times*, all 11 Sept. 1951.

EDWARD L. LACH, JR.

REZANOV, Nikolai Petrovich (28 Mar. 1764–1 Mar. 1807), colonial administrator, was born in St. Petersburg, Russia, the son of Petr Gavrilovich Rezanov, a judge; his mother's name is unknown. He received his primary education at home. After short service in the army and civil duties of little significance, Rezanov became chief clerk in the office of Count Ivan G. Chernyshev, vice president of the Admiralty College. After his family friend Gavriil R. Derzhavin was appointed secretary for senate reports, Rezanov became chief clerk in Derzhavin's office. For some time Rezanov served also in the office of Empress Catherine's favorite prince, Platon A. Zubov, and carried out several special assignments for the empress.

The turning point in Rezanov's life occurred on 24 January 1795 while he was sent on a mission to Irkutsk. He married the fourteen-year-old Anna Grigoryevna Shelikhova.

After the death later that year of his father-in-law, Grigory I. Shelikhov, Rezanov had to defend not only his family interests but also had to carry forward extensive Shelikhov enterprises on the Northwest Coast of the American continent. In 1797 he was appointed chief secretary of the senate, and he played a leading role in the formation of the monopolistic Russian-American Company "under the Highest protection of His Imperial Majesty." This company monopolized hunting and fur trading over a wide area of North America south to 55° north latitude. The principal director of the company became Mikhail M. Buldakov, and Rezanov received the position of correspondent, performing the function of "protector" and "solicitor" on behalf of the Russian-American Company in St. Petersburg. He had close ties with the central government, and in order to limit the influence of native Irkutsk merchants, the headquarters of the company was moved in autumn 1800 to St. Petersburg.

Rezanov and his wife had two children, but in October 1802 their happy family life was interrupted by the death of young Anna Grigoryevna.

As a way out of this tragic situation, Rezanov accepted appointment in summer 1803 as the head of the first Russian round-the-world voyage aboard the ships *Nadezhda* and *Neva* and as the official envoy extraordinary and plenipotentiary to Japan. Arriving in Nagasaki in the autumn of 1804, Rezanov discovered that his office was not accepted by Japanese authorities and he was put under house arrest. The Russian diplomat was released only in the spring of 1805 and went to Petropavlovsk-on-Kamchatka. One result of his stay in Japan was that he compiled *A Dictionary of the Japanese Language* and *A Handbook of the Japanese Language*.

From Petropavlovsk Rezanov took the vessel *Sv. Mariia Magdalina* for an inspection visit of Russian colonies in America. Together with hieromonk Gede-on, the Orthodox Church envoy in the colonies, Rezanov reorganized the Kodiak school. The number of pupils soon rose to fifty and then to a hundred. They were taught reading and writing, arithmetic, geography, and sacred and secular history. Together with the chief manager of Russian possessions in North America Aleksandr Baranov, Rezanov enlarged trade connections with the Boston fur traders and bought the American vessel *Juno* from its captain, John D'Wolf. In spring 1806 he went aboard the ship *Juno* to California to obtain food supplies.

Rezanov's stay in San Francisco and his negotiations with Spanish authorities on the establishment of trade relations led to one of the most romantic episodes in early California history. Warmly welcomed into the house of the Spanish commandant José Darío Argüello, Rezanov became an admirer of his beautiful daughter María de la Concepción. His affections were reciprocated by the fifteen-year-old Concepción, and Rezanov asked for Concepción's hand in marriage. The final decision was postponed, however, until the pope granted permission.

Fate did not give Rezanov a chance to carry out his intention. On his way to St. Petersburg, he "contracted a cruel fever" and suddenly died in Krasnoyarsk. In his last letter to Buldakov written on 24–26 January 1807, Rezanov, who was already critically ill, reaffirmed his love for his prematurely deceased wife, and unbosoming himself before his death, he deemed it necessary to add "Concepción is sweet like an angel, beautiful, kind-hearted, she loves me, I love her and cry, because there is no place for her in my heart; here my friend, like a repentant sinner, I must confess it, but you, as my pastor, will keep my secret" (Bolkhovitinov, 153). The beautiful Concepción remained touchingly faithful to her sweetheart and, refusing to believe the tragic news, patiently awaited the return of her beloved. She spent her last years in a convent, where she died in 1857.

The romantic love story of "Concepción and Nikolai" has been retold in several literary forms, including a poem by Bret Harte, a novel by Gertrude Etherton (1906), the poem *Avos'* by Andrei Voznesenckii (1970), and at last the rock opera *Juno and Avos'* by Aleksei Rybnikov.

Having a premonition of his death, on the eve of his departure from Novo-Archangelsk Rezanov left "confidential instructions" for Aleksandr Baranov. First he drew attention to the importance of having a permanent population in the colonies and suggested the establishment of a sawmill, a hospital, and a church. He stressed the importance of trade connections with California, Japan, the Philippine Islands, and a number of other places. To encourage the settlers to build houses and start farms he suggested that land plots be assigned in their "hereditary possessions in perpetuality." The Russian colonies were to be "protected by a military garrison," for which Rezanov planned "for the first time" to send "57 cannons and 4 mortars with a decent number of military shells," and then annually "with every transport from Petersburg" to send 250 poods (9,000 pounds) of gunpowder and 600 poods (22,000 pounds) of lead.

In general, Rezanov belonged to that galaxy of Russian statesmen (Nikolai P. Rumiantsev and Nikolai S. Mordvinov, for example) who, following Peter the Great, saw vast prospects for Russia in the Far East, in North America, and the whole North Pacific. Like Grigory I. Shelikhov, Rezanov was a real builder of empire, one of the last who attempted to put his program in this region into practice.

• Rezanov's papers are in the Archive of the Foreign Policy of the Russian Empire in Moscow, the Russian State Archive of the Navy in St. Petersburg, and several other repositories. See also Hector Chevigny, *Lost Empire: The Life and Adventures of Nikolai Petrovich Rezanov* (1937); Victor P. Petrov *Kamerger dvora* (Chamberlain of the Court) (1973); Nikolai N. Bolkhovitinov, "The Will of the Russian Ambassador," *Lepta*, 1994, no. 2: 148–54.

NIKOLAI N. BOLKHOVITINOV

REZNIKOFF, Charles (31 Aug. 1894–22 Jan. 1976), poet, was born in a Jewish ghetto of Brooklyn, New York, the son of Russian immigrants Nathan Reznikoff, a businessman, and Sarah Yetta Wolvosky. A precocious student, he graduated from the Brooklyn Boys' High School when he was fifteen, spent one year studying journalism at the University of Missouri, and entered the law school of New York University in 1912. He graduated with an LL.B. in 1915 and was admitted to the bar of the state of New York in 1916, but Reznikoff practiced law only briefly. In 1918, the United States having entered the First World War, he joined the officers' training corps at Columbia University. Before he could begin training, however, the war ended, and he turned to work as a salesman in the family business of manufacturing hats. Following this he worked for a law publishing firm, helping to write an encyclopedia of law, and then went to Hollywood for three years as a writer for Paramount Pictures. For most of his life he chose to make his living by freelance writing, research, translating, and editing, in order to have time to write poetry.

Reznikoff never traveled outside the United States and, apart from his stint in Hollywood in the 1930s, never left New York. He was deeply attached to New York City and spent his early mornings walking, up to twenty miles a day, in the streets and parks. While singing the city's glories in many of his poems, Reznikoff also depicted its inhumanity. "Early History of a Writer," in *By the Well of Living and Seeing, and the Fifth Book of the Maccabees* (1969), for example, relates his encounters with anti-Semitism in the non-Jewish neighborhoods.

In 1930 Reznikoff married Marie Syrkin, a struggling writer and high school teacher who shared his passionate social concern and supported his commitment to poetry. The couple had no children.

Reznikoff wrote eighteen books of poetry (including the two volumes of his collected poems), numerous plays, memoirs, translations, and two novels, one of which, *The Lionhearted: A Story about Jews in Medie-*

val England (1944), was about medieval England's expulsion of the Jews. His poetry is characterized by an aesthetic of transparency. His model seems to be the photograph rather than the lyric, whether in the naive rhythms and rhymes of his first book, *Rhythms* (1918), or, more obviously, in the proselike, longer lines of the bulk of his work. Reznikoff tends not to foreground the linguistic as so many of his modernist contemporaries did; instead, he gives the effect of presenting objective reality, eschewing the artifices of style and refusing to sentimentalize. In the much later *Holocaust* (1975), for example, Reznikoff bases his poem entirely on the U.S. government's publication *Trials of the Criminals before the Nuremberg Military Tribunal* and the records of the trial of Karl Adolf Eichmann in Jerusalem. Other than line breaks, there is no suggestion of converting "reality" into "poetry."

Such a style, with its warring lyric and narrative impulses, raises problems. John R. Reed commented that "Reznikoff's poetry never fully succeeds," that it "lack[s] lyric intensity" ("Narrative as Poetic Structure: Richard Howard, John Hollander, James Merrill, and Others," *Ontario Review* [Fall–Winter 1976–1977]: 86). However, Reznikoff's work was admired by many American poets, including William Carlos Williams, Robert Creeley, Louis Zukofsky, and Allen Ginsberg. Sanford Pinsker wrote that Reznikoff's work "has provided a shaping force to the urban Jewish imagination, [bringing] Jewish concerns and Modernist technique into a juxtaposition" ("On Charles Reznikoff," *Jewish Spectator* 43 [Spring 1978]: 60).

Reznikoff was self-published for sixteen years, until the "Objectivist" Press brought out *Jerusalem the Golden* in 1934. The press was founded by Louis Zukofsky, George Oppen, and Reznikoff himself, following a special "Objectivist" issue of *Poetry* magazine in February 1931. "Objectivism" (always in quotation marks) was an offshoot of Ezra Pound's imagist directives. Reznikoff, in 1970, explained "Objectivist" verse as concerned with the projection of clear images, unstated meaning, and simple language; themes were to be principally Jewish, American, and urban. As with testimony in a trial, he explained, one must not state conclusions but facts. Later in his career, New Directions began to publish his work, beginning with *By the Waters of Manhattan: Selected Verse* (1962). Most of his last books were published in beautiful editions by Black Sparrow Press, beginning with *By the Well of Living and Seeing: New and Selected Poems, 1918–1973* (1974) and including *Holocaust* and the two volumes of his collected poems, *Poems, 1918–1936* (1976) and *Poems, 1937–1975* (1977).

Reznikoff's other books of poetry are *Rhythms II* (1919); *Poems* (1920); *Uriel Accosta: A Play, and a Fourth Group of Verse* (1921); *Five Groups of Verse* (1927); *In Memoriam: 1933* (1934); *Going to and fro and Walking up and Down* (1941), which contains the eleven poems of "Kaddish," dedicated to his mother, who died of cancer in 1937; *Inscriptions: 1944–1956* (1959); *Testimony: The United States, 1885–1890: Recitative* (1965); *Testimony: The United States, 1891–*

1900: Recitative (1968); and *Testimony: The United States, 1885–1915: Recitative* (2 vols., 1978–1979). The *Testimony* volumes, having some continuity with Reznikoff's 1934 prose account of the same title, now stand with *Holocaust* as the poet's major works. In writing them, he drew on legal records of various regions of the United States between 1815 and 1915 to recount, dispassionately and usually with names removed, a series of injustices and disasters. While some critics felt the writing was too simplistic and bare, the *Testimony* books combined Reznikoff's training as a lawyer and his sensitivity as a poet to produce results unlike anything else in American literature. The poems are painful records of arbitrary suffering at the same time that they are statements of irreducible human worth.

While Reznikoff has not been regarded, either in his own time or since his death, as a major American poet, his populism and social awareness as well as his open style and sense of history place him in a genealogy with Walt Whitman and Carl Sandburg. What sets him apart from most poets is the depth of his concern with Jewish culture and experience.

Following a heart attack at his apartment, Charles Reznikoff died at St. Vincent's hospital in New York City while the first volume of the *Complete Poems* was in press. On his tombstone is engraved a line from "Heart and Clock" (*Separate Way* [1936]): " . . . and the day's brightness dwindles into stars."

• Charles Reznikoff's papers are housed in the Archive for New Poetry at the University of California, San Diego. Milton Hindus, *Charles Reznikoff: A Critical Essay* (1977), is a book-length treatment of Reznikoff and his work. Hindus has also edited a collection of essays, *Charles Reznikoff: Man and Poet* (1984), which includes an interview with Reznikoff conducted by Reinhold Schiffer. At least two other interviews exist, one by L. S. Dembo, "The Objectivist Poet: Four Interviews, Charles Reznikoff," *Contemporary Literature*, Spring 1969, pp. 193–202, and one by Janet Sternburg and Alan Ziegler, "A Conversation with Charles Reznikoff," *Montemora*, Summer 1976, pp. 113–21. Mary Oppen's autobiography *Meaning: A Life* (1978) offers valuable information about Charles Reznikoff, George Oppen, and the "Objectivist" Press. Reznikoff may be said to have written his own autobiography in symbolic form in *The Manner "Music"* (1977), a novel about a composer to whose music no one has learned to listen. There are numerous essays and book reviews, among them Louis Zukofsky, "Sincerity and Objectification: With Special Reference to the Work of Charles Reznikoff," *Poetry*, Feb. 1931, pp. 272–84; Hayden Carruth, "A Failure of Contempt," a review of *Testimony: The United States, 1885–1890*, *Poetry*, Mar. 1966, pp. 396–97; and David Lehman, review of *Holocaust*, *Poetry*, Apr. 1976, pp. 37–45. An obituary is in the *New York Times*, 23 Jan. 1976.

JEFFREY GRAY

RHEA, John (1753–27 May 1832), congressman, was born in Langhorn, County Londonderry, Ireland, the son of Joseph Rhea, a Presbyterian minister, and Elizabeth McIlwaine. Rhea's family immigrated to the American colonies in 1769 and initially settled in Philadelphia, Pennsylvania, before moving to Piney Creek, Maryland, in 1771. Joseph Rhea later purchased land in Sullivan County, North Carolina, near the present location of Blountville, Tennessee, and despite the elder Rhea's death in 1777, the family relocated there in 1778. Little else is known about Rhea's earliest years. He is known to have fought in the revolutionary war at the battles of Brandywine and King's Mountain. Between these battles, he apparently attended the College of New Jersey, which later became Princeton University. Family tradition maintained that he attended the college, and Princeton's records indicate that a John Rhea graduated in 1780; he also displayed an interest in higher education throughout his life and served as a trustee for Washington, Greeneville, and Blount colleges. How Rhea managed to leave the military to complete his degree, however, is unclear. His last military service occurred in 1790, when he commanded a battalion of the territorial militia in General Arthur St. Clair's campaign against the Miami Indians in the Northwest Territory.

At the conclusion of the revolutionary war, Rhea returned to Sullivan County, where he served as county court clerk from 1785 until 1790. He was licensed to practice law in 1789, and the next year he became county attorney. In 1789 he also won election both to the North Carolina House of Commons and to the Fayetteville convention, where he voted with the majority in favor of ratifying the U.S. Constitution. Rhea opposed the move to establish the state of Franklin out of North Carolina's western counties, and he voted against the act ceding the state's western lands, including Sullivan County, to the federal government. Despite this opposition, he was elected in 1796 to the convention at Knoxville to write a constitution when those lands were organized as the new state of Tennessee. Although Rhea supported a plan for a government with a unicameral legislature, in which a two-thirds vote would be required for the passage of all bills and resolutions, he ultimately joined the unanimous vote in favor of a constitution with a bicameral assembly. He then served as one of Sullivan County's representatives in Tennessee's first two general assemblies before his election to Congress in 1803.

During his first six terms in Congress, Rhea loyally supported the administrations of Presidents Thomas Jefferson and James Madison. Along with a strict construction of the constitution, states' rights, and fiscal responsibility, he championed the promotion of agriculture and commerce as the sources of national prosperity. This view, joined with a vehement hostility toward Great Britain, made him one of the leading proponents of retaliation against British violations of American trade and neutrality; thus he strongly supported the Embargo of 1807–1809, continued nonimportation after the embargo's repeal, increased military preparations, and the American declaration of war in 1812. For unknown reasons, Rhea was defeated for reelection in 1815. Upon this loss, Rhea allowed his name to be presented to the Tennessee General Assembly as a candidate for the U.S. Senate. The assembly selected another candidate, however, and President Madison in 1816 appointed Rhea to commissions to superintend the sale of stock for the second Bank of the United States and to negotiate a treaty with the Choctaw Indians. In 1817 he was again elected to Congress. During his later years as a congressman, Rhea concentrated mostly on his duties as chair of the committee on pensions for revolutionary war veterans, though he did speak in favor of American neutrality in the Greek Revolution and against protective tariffs. A slaveholder himself—the 1830 census showed him possessing nineteen, the second largest number in Sullivan County—he adamantly opposed attempts to restrict slavery in territories west of the Mississippi River, and he voted against the division of the Louisiana Territory at 36°30′ into slave and non-slave regions as part of the Missouri Compromise of 1820.

Rhea is remembered mostly for his possible involvement with Andrew Jackson's 1818 invasion of Spain's Florida territory, in which Jackson sparked an international controversy by capturing Spanish fortresses and summarily executing two British subjects. Ordered by President Monroe to enter Florida only to prosecute a war against the Seminole Indians, Jackson wrote to Monroe asking for authorization to seize the territory and proposing, in order to limit the government's involvement, that permission "be signified to me through any channel, (say Mr. J. Rhea)." Monroe received this letter but until his death denied that he acted upon it. Jackson, however, later claimed that he had received a letter from Rhea indicating Monroe's approval but that he had destroyed the letter at Rhea's and Monroe's request. In Congress, Rhea defended Jackson's actions as "authorized by the supreme law of nature and nations, the law of self-defence" (*Annals of Congress*, 15th Cong., 27 Jan. 1819: 867), but he made no public or private reference to having written Jackson about the invasion; Monroe, in fact, stated that, when he asked Rhea directly, the congressman denied having written to Jackson about Florida. Several years later, with Jackson himself as president, Rhea claimed no recollection of having written such a letter, but at Jackson's urging he wrote to Monroe saying that he had done so. By this time Rhea was quite elderly, and his family was questioning his mental capacity. Scholarly interpretations of the "Rhea letter" incident have ranged from blaming Jackson for fabricating a "hoax" to suggesting that he misinterpreted Rhea's reference to some other subject as administrative authorization.

In 1822 Rhea was again nominated and defeated in the Tennessee legislature for the Senate, and in 1823 he chose not to seek reelection to Congress. Because he never married, he retired alone to his plantation near Blountville, though he remained close to his brothers and sisters and their descendants. He died in Blountville.

• Private papers are available in the Rhea Family Papers, the Overton-Murdock Collection, and the John Overton Papers, all in the Tennessee State Library and Archives, Nashville; and in James A. Padgett, ed., "Letters from John Rhea to Thomas Jefferson and James Madison," *East Tennessee His-*torical Society's Publications 10 (1938): 114–27. Circular letters written by Rhea to his constituents are printed in the *Knoxville Register*, 11 and 18 June 1822; and in *American Historical Magazine*, Apr. 1900, pp. 173–79. Several of Rhea's congressional speeches are recorded in the *Annals of Congress*. Biographical sketches of Rhea can be found in Oliver Taylor, *Historic Sullivan: A History of Sullivan County, Tennessee with Brief Biographies of the Makers of History* (1909); *Families and History of Sullivan County, Tennessee*, vol. 1: *1779–1992* (1992); and Marguerite B. Hamer, "John Rhea of Tennessee," *East Tennessee Historical Society's Publications* 4 (Jan. 1932): 35–44. On the "Rhea letter" controversy, see the *Correspondence of Andrew Jackson*, ed. John Spencer Bassett (7 vols., 1926–1935); Richard R. Stenberg, "Jackson's 'Rhea Letter' Hoax," *Journal of Southern History* 2 (Nov. 1936): 480–96; and *The Papers of Andrew Jackson*, ed. Harold D. Moser et al., vol. 4 (1994). An obituary is in the *Knoxville Register*, 6 June 1832.

JONATHAN M. ATKINS

RHEES, Rush (8 Feb. 1860–5 Jan. 1939), Baptist minister and university president, was born in Chicago, to John Evans Rhees, a merchant, and Annie Houghton McCutcheon. He was christened Benjamin Rush Rhees after the noted Dr. Benjamin Rush, whom his great grandfather had met in Philadelphia upon emigrating from Wales in 1794. Rhees dropped the "Benjamin" as a youth. His grandfather, Morgan John Rhees, Jr., was a Baptist minister and in 1852 received one of the first honorary degrees granted by the University of Rochester, where his grandson would later serve as president. His father died in 1862, and his mother eventually settled with the children in Plainfield, New Jersey. Upon graduating from Plainfield High School, Rhees studied for nearly two years to prepare for Amherst College, from which he received an A.B. in 1883. For the next two years he remained at Amherst teaching mathematics, though his focus of study had been Greek. He then enrolled in the Hartford Theological Seminary, where he made the New Testament his field of expertise and completed the ministerial course in 1888.

After a summer of study at the University of Berlin, in 1889 Rhees was ordained and called to the pastorate of Middle Street Baptist Church in Portsmouth, New Hampshire. He remained there until 1892 when the Newton Theological Institution in Massachusetts named him to the newly introduced position of associate professor, with particular responsibility for teaching New Testament interpretation. After another summer of study at Berlin, he became a full professor in 1894 and stayed at Newton until 1900, during which time he published a number of brief essays and his one book, *The Life of Jesus of Nazareth* (1900). Meanwhile, Rush met Harriet Chapin Seelye, the daughter of L. Clark Seelye, the president of Smith College. As their romance developed, Rhees came to the attention of the search committee for the presidency of the University of Rochester. With the support of President Seelye, Rhees was elected to the Rochester presidency on 6 July 1899. That same day he married Harriet; they had three children.

Assuming his new office in 1900, Rhees arrived at "a small college fifty years old, with two hundred students, seventeen teachers, four buildings, twenty-five acres, a tall iron fence, and a small endowment" (Slater, p. 54). Over the next thirty-five years, Rhees quietly and unobtrusively led a transformation of the institution. The curriculum was gradually modernized by the introduction of applied science and engineering, among other subjects. The College for Women was opened in 1914, the Eastman School of Music in 1919, the College of Arts and Sciences in 1921, and the School of Medicine and Dentistry in 1925, the same year that the university granted its first Ph.D.

In 1930 a new, $10 million campus was opened on the banks of the Genesee River. This last accomplishment, which occurred soon after the beginning of the Great Depression, demonstrates the support that the unassuming Rhees engendered in the Rochester business community, and particularly in George Eastman, the founder of Eastman Kodak Company. When he resigned in 1935, the University of Rochester had become a nationally recognized university, renowned for the study of medicine and music. Its $50 million endowment ranked fifth among universities in the United States. He retired to his summer home at Islesford, Maine, and died of a heart attack on a return trip to Rochester. Rhees's great success as president was widely attributed to his calm, deferential manner, which—combined with a commonsensical approach to problems—attracted the support of business and financial leaders.

• Arthur J. May, *A History of the University of Rochester 1850–1962* (1977), is an abridged and undocumented version of the original, annotated manuscript, which is held in the Rare Books Collection at the University of Rochester library, where Rhees's presidential papers are also reposited. The only book-length biography is John R. Slater, *Rhees of Rochester* (1946), to which is appended a bibliography of Rhees's published writings and addresses. An obituary is in the *New York Times*, 6 Jan. 1939.

BRUCE A. KIMBALL

RHEES, William Jones (13 Mar. 1830–18 Mar. 1907), government administrator and archivist, was born in Philadelphia, Pennsylvania, the son of Benjamin Rush Rhees, a physician, and Margaret Grace Evans. Rhees's grandfather, the Reverend Morgan J. Rhees, had come to America from Wales, and his father was a direct descendant also of Benjamin Rush, a signer of the Declaration of Independence. Rhees's mother's forebears included Evan Evans, a colonel of militia in the Revolution, and John Lukens, a member of the commission appointed in 1781 for the extension of the Mason-Dixon Line.

Rhees graduated in 1847 from Philadelphia's Central High School, of which he remained a loyal alumnus all his life. Beginning that year he worked for three years as a clerk for the Holland Land Company, Meadville, Pennsylvania, during which period he wrote to his family that he had become a member of the Baptist faith. In 1850 he moved to Washington, D.C., as clerk in the Census Office, where he was in charge of the Division of Social Services, which monitored schools, libraries, and religious institutions.

In 1852 Rhees was hired to be private secretary by Joseph Henry, secretary of the Smithsonian Institution, and by 1853 his title was chief clerk. For the next thirty-nine years he had charge of all routine areas of administration of the institution. There was a short interruption in Rhees's Smithsonian service in 1870, when he moved with his family to Springfield, Massachusetts, and established a business merchandising stationery, magazines, and other publications. He returned to the Smithsonian in 1871 and remained there until his death, probably in Washington, D.C.

After Secretary Henry's death in 1878, Rhees was second in command to Secretary Spencer F. Baird and by a special legislative act was named acting secretary in the event of Baird's absence. A prolific writer and keeper of files, Rhees was assigned by Baird in 1878 to prepare a history of the Smithsonian, and the resulting publication, *The Smithsonian Institution: Documents Relative to Its Origin and History* (still of inestimable value to researchers), was published in 1879. Samuel Pierpont Langley, who succeeded Baird as secretary in 1887, adopted a different system of administration, abolished the position of chief clerk, and appointed Rhees archivist, a position he held until his death. In 1900 Langley assigned Rhees the task of revising and updating his 1879 history, which he accomplished with his usual thoroughness; the revised edition was published in 1901 in two volumes totaling 1,856 pages.

During his entire professional career Rhees found time for philanthropic work. In 1852 he and two associates of kindred interests formed the District of Columbia YMCA. Rhees was elected recording secretary of the association in 1852 and its librarian in 1853. In 1854 he was a delegate to the first national convention of the YMCA in Buffalo, New York, and was elected secretary of the convention. A year later he was made president of the convention and in 1856 president of the D.C. association. During the Civil War he was a member of a committee that worked with other religious and civic organizations distributing religious material to the troops. Rhees's interest in young people resulted in his election as trustee of the D.C. public schools from 1862 to 1868, again from 1873 to 1874, and again in 1877, and he intervened frequently with police and correctional institutions on behalf of youthful offenders.

Rhees transferred his religious affiliation in 1866 to the Presbyterian Church of the Covenant in Washington, where he remained an active parishioner for the rest of his life. He was also a Freemason and a supporter of temperance movements. In 1891 he was one of the founders of the D.C. branch of the Sons of the American Revolution, in which he served as registrar from 1895 to 1899 and as vice president in 1900. In that year he was also an active member of the National Capital Centennial Commission.

Rhees's first wife, Laura O. Clarke, with whom he had one daughter, died in 1864. (The date of their marriage is unknown.) In 1866 he married Romenia Fontanette Ellis, with whom he had three sons (two of whom predeceased him) and two daughters. Rhees was devoted to the hobby of autograph collecting, and during his lifetime he built up a substantial collection of autographs from prominent individuals, many of whom had corresponded with Smithsonian officials. In 1922 Rhees's widow sold the collection to Henry E. Huntington for the Huntington Library in San Marino, California, where it is available to scholars as the Rhees Collection.

• Archival information is available at the Smithsonian Archives, Research Unit 7081. Also see Nathan Reingold, "The Anatomy of a Collection: The Rhees Papers," *American Archivist* 27, no. 2 (Apr. 1964): 252–59. In addition to the two Smithsonian histories, Rhees's published works include *A List of Public Libraries, Institutions and Societies in the United States and the British Provinces of North America* (1859), *The Smithsonian: Journals of the Board of Regents, Reports of Committees, Statistics, etc.* (1879), *James Smithson and His Bequest* (1880), *The Scientific Writings of James Smithson* (1879), *Visitor's Guide to the Smithsonian Institution and the National Museum, Washington, D.C.* (1880), and *A Catalog of the Publications of the Smithsonian Institution* (1882), and supplements through 1906. Additional information about Rhees is included in E. F. Rivinus and E. M. Youssef, *Spencer Baird of the Smithsonian* (1992).

EDWARD F. RIVINUS

RHETT, Robert Barnwell (21 Dec. 1800–14 Sept. 1876), secessionist politician, was born Robert Barnwell Smith in Beaufort, South Carolina, the son of James Smith and Marianna Gough, planters. In 1837 Robert and his brothers changed the family name to Rhett to honor an ancestor whose male line had died out. Although his father had studied law in England, economic reverses meant that Rhett could only attend the meager Beaufort College while living with his grandmother. He left school upon her death in 1818. In 1820 he began the study of law with Thomas Grimké in Charleston and was admitted to the bar in 1822. Establishing a successful practice with his cousin Robert Barnwell in Colleton in 1823, he married in 1827 Elizabeth Washington Burnet, with whom he had twelve children prior to her death in 1852. In 1854 he married Catharine Herbert Dent, and they also had children, although the exact number is unknown. Like many southern professionals, Rhett acquired a slave plantation as soon as he was able, even though its operation kept him perennially in debt.

In 1826 Rhett was elected to the state legislature, representing a low-country district, of whose population more than 80 percent were enslaved African Americans. Such districts were rare even in the South, and Rhett understood implicitly his white constituents' obsession with power and control. Self-confident, aggressive, and easily excited, Rhett quickly became a legislative extremist, refusing to budge on the grounds of principle.

Rhett's legislative career (1826–1833) coincided with South Carolina's dispute with the federal government over the tariffs of 1828 and 1832, which culminated in South Carolina's attempt to nullify both. Among the most radical "nullifiers," Rhett in 1828 called disunion a patriotic act reminiscent of the revolution. His outspokenness was popular locally and won him a place on the committee that issued John C. Calhoun's anonymously written *Exposition and Protest* (1828), urging the state to nullify the tariff, and on the committee that called the nullification convention in 1832, to which he was also elected. Disappointed when the convention, at the end of the dispute in 1833, refused to admit that South Carolina had not been vindicated by the compromise tariff, he resigned from the legislature.

Rhett, however, had already been selected state attorney general (1833–1835). The rapprochement between nullifiers and Unionists during his term gave him few opportunities to promote disunion.

In 1837 Rhett began the first of six consecutive terms in the U.S. House of Representatives as a States' Rights Democrat. In response to abolitionist petitioning of Congress, he demanded constitutional amendments prohibiting debates on slavery and denying Congress power over slavery in the territories and the District of Columbia. He urged South Carolina to withdraw its congressional representatives or secede if agitation on slavery continued. While wildly popular in parts of South Carolina, Rhett's actions seemed ill considered elsewhere. Calhoun, conscious of Rhett's connections with influential South Carolina newspapers, bankers, and politicians, guided him toward controlling the national Democratic party as an alternative means of protecting southern interests. For the next decade Rhett dedicated himself to advancing Calhoun's presidential ambitions. Acting as Calhoun's campaign manager, he sounded out northern support for him in 1843, edited Calhoun's campaign newspaper, the Washington *Spectator*, and pushed for popular election of convention delegates to compensate for Calhoun's lack of organizational support. Angered when the Democrats in 1844 instead nominated Tennessean James K. Polk, who, Rhett believed, would seek to broaden his northern support by compromising on the tariff, Rhett proclaimed at Bluffton that, if the Union ignored South Carolina's interests, the state should secede. The Bluffton speech popularized resistance to the national government among a new generation of South Carolinians but confirmed other southern leaders' beliefs that Rhett was too rash.

When Polk did keep the tariff down, Rhett supported his administration, although, like Calhoun, he considered the Mexican War likely to increase national power without materially benefiting the South. Faced with the Wilmot Proviso, which proposed to exclude slavery from lands acquired from Mexico, Rhett denied its constitutionality. Although pleased to see northern Free Soil Democrats leave the party on the issue in 1848, Rhett reluctantly supported the Democratic nominee, Lewis Cass of Michigan, again disappointed at Calhoun's failure to capture the nomination.

Remaining convinced that South Carolina's interests could best be met out of the Union and that other states would eventually follow its lead, Rhett chafed at his failure to convince others of what seemed so obvious to him. For the next decade he worked to find the right means to create a southern nation. Leaving Congress in 1849, he was elected a delegate to the 1850 Nashville Convention, intended to unite southern Whigs and Democrats in defense of southern rights. At the final session, he secured passage of a radical address rejecting the Compromise of 1850's concession of popular sovereignty in the territories and abolition of the slave trade in the District of Columbia. Few delegates remained, however, and even those claimed to disagree with Rhett's arguments. Refusing to admit defeat, Rhett insisted that great enthusiasm for radical action existed and urged South Carolina's governor to begin secession proceedings. Rhett's enthusiasm and his depiction of Calhoun, who had recently died, as an advocate of secession in whose footsteps he was treading, won him election that year to the U.S. Senate, a position he had long coveted. He worked to set up an organization of States' Rights Associations throughout South Carolina to work for secession and, seeking to provoke the North, recommended that the governor seize federal property in the state. Rhett's opponents stressed the dangers of seceding without the support of other states and accused Rhett of personal ambition. As support for the Compromise of 1850 increased throughout the country, the radical spirit could not be maintained. In Congress southern senators called Rhett a traitor. When even the States' Rights Associations could not agree to secede, Rhett resigned his Senate seat in 1852.

The revival of sectional anxieties over Kansas in mid-decade brought Rhett out of retirement. In 1857 he arranged for his son, Robert Rhett, Jr., to assume with a partner (whom the Rhetts bought out in 1858) the editorship of the *Charleston Mercury*. Now recognizing the importance of preparing public opinion for so drastic a solution as disunion, they used the paper to highlight alleged northern injustices and demonstrate the inability of the national Democratic party to protect southern interests. In this they acted in harmony with William Lowndes Yancey of Alabama and Edmund Ruffin of Virginia. They refused to be distracted by tangential (and divisive) issues, such as reopening the African slave trade, and chose to undermine the Democratic party, rather than attack it openly, by insisting on extreme proslavery policies and candidates. In July 1859 Rhett made his first public address since retirement, seeking to foster a sense of southern nationalism by describing the South as a unique civilization poorly protected by the U.S. Constitution. In the aftermath of John Brown's (1800–1859) raid on Harpers Ferry in 1859, Rhett directed anger toward planning for secession. Rhett participated in the split up of the Democratic party in Charleston in 1860, and after Abraham Lincoln's election, he

goaded the South Carolina legislature into acting quickly to call a secession convention before anger subsided. As a convention delegate, Rhett wrote the "Address to the Slaveholding States," which discouraged compromise by justifying secession as an assertion of nationalism rather than a response to specific grievances. Although aided by national events and a receptive audience, few had done more to exploit those events to accomplish secession.

When the first six states to secede met in Montgomery to form a Confederate government in 1861, Rhett attended as a delegate. Rhett wanted a constitution that would protect slavery and slaveholders and include a free trade policy, which he hoped would bring recognition from Great Britain. As chair of the committee preparing the constitution, however, Rhett was unable to ban free states, open the slave trade, or grant slaveholders representatives on the basis of slave population. Opposition from his own state cost him the desired posts of secretary of state and commissioner to England. Fearing that Confederate president Jefferson Davis might compromise with the North, Rhett, a member of the Provisional Congress, tried unsuccessfully to force overtures to Britain. Convinced of the necessity of a rapid and massive offensive before the North could organize, the Rhetts criticized southern inaction in the *Mercury*. When the Confederates failed to follow up their victory at Manassas, Rhett blamed Davis. Although he supported crucial financial and military measures, he became increasingly critical of the conduct of the war. Unable to win a Senate seat in 1861 and defeated for the House of Representatives in 1863, Rhett stayed on the sidelines, his final protest being over proposals to arm slaves for military service.

As southern resistance crumbled in 1865, Rhett fled to his wife's family in Eufala, Alabama. Suffering from skin cancer, he played little role in Reconstruction. In 1872 he went to New Orleans, where his son was editing a newspaper, and from there to St. James Parish, Louisiana, where he died. His history of the Confederacy, written in retirement, was never published. In it he argued that the South would have succeeded had it followed his advice. Defiant to the end, Rhett symbolized the extremes to which slaveholder politics could go.

• Rhett's papers are at the University of North Carolina, South Carolina Historical Society, University of South Carolina, and Duke University. Laura A. White, *Robert Barnwell Rhett: Father of Secession* (1931), is the only biography. See also Eric H. Walther, *The Fire-Eaters* (1992), John McCardell, *The Idea of a Southern Nation* (1979), George C. Rable, *The Confederate Republic* (1994), and John Barnwell, *Love of Order: South Carolina's First Secession Crisis* (1982).

PHYLLIS F. FIELD

RHINE, J. B. (29 Sept. 1895–20 Feb. 1980), parapsychologist, was born Joseph Banks Rhine in Waterloo, Pennsylvania, the son of Samuel Ellis Rhine, an itinerant shopkeeper, schoolteacher, and farmer, and Elizabeth Vaughan. Starting in 1915, Rhine attended Ohio Northern University for two years and then switched to the College of Wooster, where his childhood friend (and future wife) Louisa Ella Weckesser was a student. Rhine's intended vocation was the ministry, but he abandoned this after less than a semester at Wooster and dropped out of college. He served in the marines in World War I and then decided to pursue a science-related career. His initial choice was forestry, in preparation for which he followed Weckesser to the University of Chicago to study botany. Rhine completed his undergraduate degree there and continued on to do graduate work in plant physiology, as had his wife. They were married in 1920. They had three daughters and adopted a son. Louisa Rhine received her Ph.D. in 1923; Joseph Rhine received his M.S. in that year and his Ph.D. in 1925. Louisa Rhine was J. B.'s intellectual partner and a major researcher in parapsychology in her own right. After they briefly held research positions at the Bryce Thompson Institute in Yonkers, New York, Rhine accepted a post at West Virginia University in 1924. They remained there until 1926.

While they were still at Chicago, the Rhines had begun to explore psychical research, the original name for the study of paranormal phenomena. Rhine latterly recounted incidents of psychic happenings in his childhood, but what seems to have inspired the mature interest was his (their) continued concern with religious issues as they related to modern materialistic science. Psychical research seemed to offer a way of studying topics outside this latter domain through the method of experimental science.

In 1923 Rhine had explored possibilities for a part-time career in psychical research. The responses were not encouraging, but by the start of 1926 the Rhines had decided to abandon West Virginia University for retraining in psychical research at Harvard under psychologist William McDougall. Although McDougall was, in fact, setting out on a sabbatical leave when they arrived, the Rhines stayed in Cambridge for the academic year 1926–1927. Rhine attended classes of psychologist E. G. Boring, psychiatrist Morton Prince, and philosopher Alfred North Whitehead. Rhine also became close friends with psychical researcher Walter Franklin Prince.

Through some of these connections, Rhine was put in touch with a man who wanted scientific investigations carried out on the purported mediumistic utterances of his deceased wife. This undertaking took the Rhines to Duke University, for Rhine acceded to the suggestion that the study be done under the supervision of McDougall. During his sabbatical, McDougall had accepted the chairmanship of the psychology department of the recently founded Duke University, where he went in 1927. The Rhines followed him to Durham, North Carolina, where they remained for the rest of their lives.

By 1930, after a place had been made for him in the Department of Psychology at Duke, Rhine commenced the card-guessing tests for clairvoyance and telepathy through which he established his reputation. His subjects were primarily Duke students (in particular, eight good subjects), and the testing material was a 25-card deck composed of an equal number of five geometrical symbols. A variety of testing procedures was employed: for example, "D.T." ("down through"), whereby the subject guessed the order of a deck from top to bottom without anyone handling or disturbing the deck until after the guesses were recorded. This procedure tested for clairvoyance (the apprehension of external information without the use of the senses or the mediation of another mind); to test for telepathy (the apprehension of information from another mind without sensory intermediaries), a tester simply imagined a sequence of card symbols to be guessed by the subject.

Rhine tried not only to demonstrate his subjects' psychic abilities but to correlate variation in test scores with changes in test conditions and in the subjects' own psychophysiology—for example, through the administration of stimulants and depressants. The scores were evaluated statistically and yielded enormous odds against being due to chance.

The research was published in April 1934 by the Boston Society for Psychical Research in a monograph titled *Extra-Sensory Perception*. This experimental work was the most elaborate and purportedly successful research in what had been an important but hitherto not dominant tradition in psychical research. Among psychical researchers, *Extra-Sensory Perception* made the greatest impact in England, where, by the end of the decade, Rhine had found experimental support and his work had largely been accepted.

The experimental approach had always been recognized as the surest route to success with scientists; it was by American scientists, particularly psychologists, that his work was first judged. The initial reception was not very hospitable: many psychologists were hostile to the subject, Rhine himself was not a professional psychologist, and replication at the level of Rhine's claims was exceedingly hard to come by. Yet psychologist Gardner Murphy, himself a longtime student of physical research, reacted very favorably; there soon developed a close association between the two men.

By the late 1930s, parapsychology, the name by which Rhine had denominated his work in the 1934 monograph, appeared to be successfully developing as a nascent academic scientific field. Rhine had drawn to his research students from both within and without Duke; Murphy was working closely with some of Rhine's students; a specialized quarterly journal, the *Journal of Parapsychology*, was founded; and some psychologists were expressing interest in the research.

But the traditional hostility toward the field was still strongly in evidence among many psychologists, and this had been reinforced by the great amount of national publicity parapsychology received. Parapsychologists had the opportunity to make their case at a symposium on the subject at the September 1938 meeting of the American Psychological Association. They were able to show that their statistical methods were basically sound (and at this time received support from the president of the Institute of Mathematical

Statistics). Although the parapsychologists certainly did not persuade all their opponents on every issue, the APA was subsequently willing to appoint an advisory committee of APA members for the *Journal of Parapsychology*.

Buoyed by what appeared to be the dawning of scientific acceptance, the Duke parapsychology group published the most ambitious survey of the experimental tradition of the field in *Extra-Sensory Perception after Sixty Years* in 1940. However, in fact, parapsychology did not succeed academically much beyond the point reached in 1940; one can surmise that the endemic skepticism of the scientific community and methodological difficulties in parapsychology combined to keep parapsychology from participating in the tremendous growth of post–World War II academic science. Nevertheless, the parapsychology community itself continued to organize along lines similar to other scientific fields by founding the Parapsychological Association in 1957. Rhine himself continued to be recognized as the founder and spokesperson for the field. In October 1978, just months before his death in Hillsborough, North Carolina, Rhine was elected president of the Society for Psychical Research in London.

During the 1930s Rhine's group investigated two other purported psychical abilities: precognition (the apprehension of future information) and psychokinesis (to cause physical action without mechanical mediation), using the same experimental and statistical paradigm that was used for clairvoyance and telepathy.

In 1948 the Duke Parapsychology Laboratory was established for Rhine's research group; in 1962 this became independent of Duke (but adjacent to one of the campuses) as the Foundation for Research on the Nature of Man. Throughout Rhine's life, the foundation was the chief training center for parapsychologists.

Rhine's strong personality and commitment to his subject sustained him against the hostility and ridicule that continued, sporadically, until the end of his life.

• For biographical information on Rhine, see Denis Brian, *Enchanted Voyager: The Life of J. B. Rhine* (1982), and K. Ramakrishna Rao, *J. B. Rhine: On the Frontiers of Science* (1982). Sources for information on Rhine's area of research include John Beloff, *Parapsychology: A Concise History* (1993); Ivor Grattan-Guiness, ed., *Psychical Research: A Guide to Its History, Principles and Practice* (1982); James McClenon, *Deviant Science: The Case for Parapsychology* (1984); Seymour H. Mauskopf and Michael R. McVaugh, *The Elusive Science: Origins of Experimental Psychical Research* (1980); and Louisa E. Rhine, *Something Hidden* (1983). An obituary is in *American Psychologist* 36, no. 3 (Mar. 1981): 310–11.

SEYMOUR H. MAUSKOPF

RHODES, Eugene Manlove (19 Jan. 1869–27 June 1934), author, was born in Tecumseh, Nebraska, the son of Hinman Rhodes and Julia Mae Manlove. His father was a Mexican War veteran, a prospector during the early days of the California gold rush, a colonel of Illinois volunteers during the Civil War, and by 1869 an unsuccessful Nebraska farmer and merchant. In debt, the family moved to Beatrice, Nebraska (1871–1873), and Cherokee, Kansas (1873–1880), where his ailing father became a salesman and his mother a dressmaker. When Rhodes was four, he permanently damaged one eye trying to imitate a farmhand who showily removed and rinsed his glass eye. Rhodes left school and moved with his family to Columbus, Kansas (1880), and Engle, New Mexico (1881). His father, who tried homesteading (1886), became a Mescalero Apache Indian reservation agent near Engle (1890–1892).

Rhodes, who was an accomplished horseman from childhood, wrangled horses at age thirteen, worked at the Bar Cross Ranch near Engle, and was a civilian scout for the army at seventeen. He studied at the University of the Pacific, in San Jose, California (1888–1890); but lacking money, he returned to New Mexico and supported himself in various ways, including well digging. Mostly he was a cowboy for the Bar Cross Ranch (until 1898) and an independent rancher near Tularosa, New Mexico. Having a fierce temper, he also enjoyed boxing, wrestling, and brawling, despite being only 5′8″ and 150 pounds; but he "let whiskey alone," as he once put it, since drink led to most of the thirteen fatal gunfights he saw. He associated with lawmen and outlaws alike. He read voraciously, his favorite authors including Lewis Carroll, Omar Khayyam, Robert Louis Stevenson, and Rudyard Kipling.

In 1896 Rhodes published a poem, "Charlie Graham," in Charles Fletcher Lummis's *Land of Sunshine* (later called *Out West*). He combined sporadic writing and steady labor on his horse ranch outside Tularosa, in the San Andrés Mountains. Then fate stepped in. May Davison Purple, a young widow with two little boys in Apalachin, New York, on the Susquehanna River near Pennsylvania, read one of his poems in 1896, wrote him appreciatively, and thus generated a spirited correspondence and then a visit by him in 1899. Twenty-two days after they met, they were married. Their son, Rhodes's only surviving child, was born in Tularosa in 1901. (Their second child died in infancy.)

Rhodes sold his first short story to *Out West* in 1902. Later that year his wife, with all three boys, moved back to Apalachin to care for her parents. Rhodes followed four years later, farmed unhappily with his father-in-law in Apalachin and on his own, and continued to write in his limited spare time. He hit pay dirt when the *Saturday Evening Post* began accepting his writings in 1907. By 1926 he had written eight novels, several of which were serialized in the *Post*, thirty or so short stories, and many of his nearly fifty essays and nearly fifty poems. In 1919 Rhodes contracted influenza, which left him with asthma, damaged his heart, and caused him to move alone to Los Angeles (1919–1922) for its milder climate. While there, he sold three of his story plots to Hollywood for $2,500 each.

After May Rhodes's parents died in 1925, the Rhodeses moved West permanently—to Tusuque,

Tularosa, and Santa Fe (1926), Alamogordo (1927), and Pacific Beach, California (1931). Rhodes continued to write and to correspond and associate with many admiring friends, including Mary Austin, Harry Carey, Henry Herbert Knibbs, Alan LeMay, and Walter Prescott Webb. Rhodes's greatest financial success came when he serialized *The Trusty Knaves* in the *Post* for $7,500 in 1931. In leaner times, he and his wife sometimes had less than a dollar between them. Rhodes died in Pacific Beach and was buried two miles from his old ranch in what is now known as Rhodes Pass. Musing about his life in the Southwest, he once told a friend, "I have lived in exactly that place and time I would have chosen from all recorded history."

Through his fiction, not his essays or poems, Rhodes has earned a high place among writers of westerns. He reworked several of his short stories into parts of his novels. The artistry of his work lies in his uncanny, photographic rendering of scenes and his loving, phonographic capture of western lingo. His plotting is melodramatic, often rambling, and occasionally hurt by digressions. Many of his characters, sometimes with names unchanged, come from the author's horde of pals or from history. His twin themes are that the West is a finer place than the East, which has exploited the West commercially, politically, and financially and has snubbed it socially and culturally to boot; and that most lowly westerners are courageous, generous, reverent, and fun-loving. Accordingly, Rhodes's villains are bankers, grabbers, lawyers, manipulators, and speculators, while his heroes are ordinary, tough, fun-loving, tolerant, generous men who value loyalty to each other and chivalry toward women.

Three of Rhodes's best novels are *Bransford in Arcadia; or, The Little Eohippus* (1914), *Pasó por Aquí* (1926), and *The Proud Sheriff* (1932). In *Bransford*, Jeff Bransford, who is elevated to hero status after appearing in Rhodes's first novel, *Good Men and True* (1910), is falsely set up as a bank robber and flees the inept arm of the law into Mexico to avoid compromising the heroine, who could instantly prove his innocence—though at the expense of her reputation. His miniature turquoise eohippus, a tiny horse, brings Jeff good luck when he follows the heroine into New York State. *Bransford* is marred by too much witty, sarcastic dialogue and too little action. In *Pasó por Aquí*, usually acclaimed as Rhodes's masterpiece, a bank robber, based on an acquaintance of the author, could escape real-life sheriff Pat Garrett, another of Rhodes's friends, but he stops to nurse a Mexican family helpless with diphtheria. Garrett generously lets him go, and a Mexican is left to explain western mores to an incredulous nurse from the East. The hero of *The Proud Sheriff* is Spinal Maginnis, old and "sun-puckered about the eyes," but honest—thus unusual among Rhodes's lawmen. He is canny enough to solve a double murder in sleepy Sierra County, south of Albuquerque, circa 1905, once he rides his wonderful horse Sleepycat into bone-dry Apache Canyon. When

quizzed by cronies about concealing evidence, Maginnis replies: "Me, I sort of aim to deal out justice— which isn't exactly the same thing [as abiding by the law]." Rhodes will always remain timely.

• Most of Rhodes's personal papers are located in the Harold B. Lee Library, Brigham Young University, Provo, Utah; the Knox College Archives, Henry M. Seymour Library, Galesburg, Ill.; the New Mexico State University Archives, Las Cruces; and the Southwest Museum Library, Los Angeles, Calif. *The Hired Man on Horseback: My Story of Eugene Manlove Rhodes* (1938) is May Davison Rhodes's anecdotal, zestful biography of her husband. More thorough is W. H. Hutchinson's *A Bar Cross Man: The Life & Personal Writings of Eugene Manlove Rhodes* (1956), which has a detailed primary bibliography. The best monograph on Rhodes is Edwin W. Gaston, Jr.'s *Eugene Manlove Rhodes: Cowboy Chronicler* (1967); excellent also is Gaston's chapter on Rhodes in *Fifty Western Writers: A Bio-Bibliographical Sourcebook*, ed. Fred Erisman and Richard W. Etulain (1982). James K. Folsom's "A Dedication to the Memory of Eugene Manlove Rhodes 1869–1934," *Arizona and the West* 11 (Winter 1969): 310–14, is a glowing tribute. In "Two Views of the American West," *Western American Literature* 1 (Spring 1966): 34–43, James L. Fife finds differences in Rhodes and Sinclair Lewis, while in "Eugene Manlove Rhodes: Ken Kesey Passed by Here," *Western American Literature* 15 (Summer 1980): 83–92, Mark Busby finds similarities in *Pasó por Aquí* and Kesey's *One Flew over the Cuckoo's Nest*. Jon Tuska and Vicki Piekarski, eds., in *Encyclopedia of Frontier and Western Fiction* (1983), identify eight movies based on fiction by Rhodes. The University of Oklahoma Press has reissued the following novels by Rhodes, each with an introduction by Hutchinson: *The Proud Sheriff* (1968, with the original 1935 introduction by Knibbs), *Stepsons of Light* (1969), *Copper Streak Trail* (1970), *The Trusty Knaves* (1971), *Pasó por Aquí* (1973), and *Bransford in Arcadia; or, The Little Eohippus* (1975). A detailed obituary is in the *New York Times*, 28 June 1934.

ROBERT L. GALE

RHODES, James Ford (1 May 1848–22 Jan. 1927), historian, was born near Cleveland, Ohio, the son of Daniel Pomeroy Rhodes and Sophia Lord Russell. The senior Rhodes, a New Englander, was a prosperous iron and coal merchant and a capitalist with diversified investments in banking, railroads, and real estate; a lifelong Democrat, and a cousin of Senator Stephen A. Douglas of Illinois, he opposed the Republican administrations during the Civil War and Reconstruction. His son, reared among Cleveland's elite and surrounded by affluence and political conservatism, studied with private tutors, attended Cleveland public schools, and was enrolled briefly (1865–1866) at the University of New York (now New York University) and the following academic year at the University of Chicago that was established in 1857 (not the institution of the same name founded 1891 and now of great stature). From his earliest schooling James Ford Rhodes read voraciously and became infatuated with history. His father, however, had other plans for him, and James never earned a college degree, obliged instead to manage the substantial firm that he would inherit. The two men went abroad in the late 1860s to examine European iron and steel production. James studied metallurgy in Germany and, on his return to the United States in 1869, toured the South to determine the potential of its iron and coal deposits.

In 1872 Rhodes married Ann Card, whose father had been one of Daniel Rhodes's business associates. The couple had one son. Determined to conclude his career as an industrialist as quickly as possible in order to become a historian, Rhodes worked until 1884 to amass a fortune that was adequate enough to allow him to retire and write a history of the United States. Though without training in the field of history, Rhodes asserted that "a business life" provided "an excellent school for the study of human character," and he compensated for his lack of formal training by bringing tireless energy and ample time and finances to his research.

From 1885 to 1890 Rhodes, aided by Ph.D.-trained research assistants in Cleveland, researched extensively the last decade before the Civil War. He began writing in 1888 and, with the help of a professional editor, completed the first two volumes of his history in 1891, the same year that Rhodes moved to Cambridge, Massachusetts, ostensibly to take advantage of Boston's research facilities and intellectual life. There he quickly won acclaim as one of America's most respected historians and gained acceptance into Boston society, which better suited Rhodes's elite, epicurean life-style than had Cleveland's.

Published in 1892, volumes one and two of Rhodes's influential *History of the United States From the Compromise of 1850* concentrated on the sectional crises that led to the coming of the Civil War. Over the next dozen years Rhodes published three more volumes, which covered the Civil War era. In 1906 he added two volumes that treated the history of Reconstruction. In addition to three other books (a collection of essays, a set of lectures, and a general history of the Civil War), Rhodes published *History of the United States from Hayes to McKinley, 1877–1896* (1919) and *The McKinley and Roosevelt Administrations, 1897–1909* (1922). Though his early volumes received considerable praise (even from academic historians) for their use of sources, fairness in treatment, and literary style, Rhodes's last two volumes were criticized harshly for their shallowness, lack of interpretation, and intolerance of alternative social and economic views. Nevertheless, the sheer volume of Rhodes's writing was unsurpassed in his day. He was elected president of the American Historical Association in 1898 and received the Pulitzer Prize in history in 1918.

Rhodes's outpouring of scholarship and the arguments that he presented made him one of America's most popular historians during the Progressive Era. He espoused a "nationalist" interpretation that deemphasized blame for the sectional conflict, explaining it instead as a necessary stepping stone to national reconciliation, to a stronger, greater America. Unlike other northern writers, Rhodes referred to the armed conflict not as a "Rebellion" but rather as a "Civil War." Determined to be objective and fair to both North and

South, Rhodes nonetheless identified slavery as the cause of the war but reminded readers that Great Britain and its New England colonies held responsibility for slavery's establishment and expansion. He described the South's "peculiar institution" as a tragedy, not a crime. Like other neo-abolitionist historians, however, Rhodes denounced the horrors of slavery and was the first to identify slavery's institutional features and to examine the institution as a system of economic exploitation and social control.

For all his criticisms of slavery, Rhodes was remarkably balanced in his assessments of the South. He praised individual southerners, including Confederate generals, and wrote approvingly of the "Southern way of life." Ironically, Rhodes sympathized openly with the South in his treatment of Reconstruction. Though his own political allegiances shifted back and forth between the Democrats and the Republicans, Rhodes consistently opposed black suffrage and regretted that the Radical Republicans had not allowed white southerners to deal with the freedmen in their own way. Throughout his works Rhodes wrote condescendingly about blacks, Jews, immigrants, and other minorities. He endorsed the gold monetary standard, wrote approvingly of America's "captains of industry," and praised civil service reform. Somewhat of a mugwump, Rhodes also opposed tariff protection and American imperialism (especially annexation of the Philippines). Rhodes viewed organized labor and radicals and dissenters as dangerous obstructionists who stood in the way of American "progress." During his final years Rhodes revised earlier volumes of his *History* (a new edition appeared posthumously, in 1928), traveled to Europe, and cared for the family of his son Daniel. He died in Boston.

Rhodes was an important transitional figure between the "literary" historians of the early and mid-nineteenth century and the "scientific," academic historians who dominated American historical scholarship after World War I. He identified race as a major theme in American history both before and after the Civil War. Methodologically, he dug deeply in printed primary materials (newspapers, travel accounts, government records) and often allowed these sources to speak for themselves. Rhodes, however, never shunned interpretation. The advantage of writing about events that had occurred during his own life and about individuals whom he knew personally provided him with certain insights. But Rhodes failed to distance himself from the concerns of the men he admired, such as Grover Cleveland, Mark Hanna (his brother-in-law), William McKinley, and Theodore Roosevelt (his friend). Indeed, Rhodes was acquainted intimately with many of America's leading political and industrial figures. In the end he employed history to bolster moral judgments, whereas historians trained in the emerging graduate schools used history to analyze and to explain change. Nevertheless, until at least the 1920s, Rhodes's "nationalist" interpretation appealed to Americans who sought to put the bitter sectionalism of the Civil War behind them and to revel in the triumphs of American capitalism.

• Rhodes's papers are in the Massachusetts Historical Society, Boston, and at Duke University. His letters appear in manuscript collections at many institutions, including the Library of Congress and Harvard, Yale, Columbia, and Cornell Universities. Many letters appear in M. A. De Wolfe Howe, *James Ford Rhodes: American Historian* (1929). The standard biography is Robert Cruden, *James Ford Rhodes: The Man, the Historian, and His Work* (1961). For Rhodes and race relations, see Cruden, "James Ford Rhodes and the Negro: A Study in the Problem of Objectivity," *Ohio History* 71 (July 1962): 129–37, and the important collection of correspondence between Rhodes and his black Cleveland barber, *The Barber and the Historian: The Correspondence of George A. Myers and James Ford Rhodes, 1910–1923*, ed. John A. Garraty (1956). For analyses of Rhodes's contributions as a historian of slavery, see John David Smith, "James Ford Rhodes, Woodrow Wilson, and the Passing of the Amateur Historian of Slavery," *Mid-America* 64 (1982): 17–24, and *An Old Creed for the New South: Proslavery Ideology and Historiography, 1865–1918* (1985). Thomas J. Pressly provides an influential assessment of Rhodes's writings on the cause of the Civil War in *Americans Interpret Their Civil War* (1954).

JOHN DAVID SMITH

RIBAULT, Jean (c. 1520–12 Oct. 1565), French Huguenot sea captain and explorer, was born near Dieppe, France, the son of Jean Ribault Sieur du Mesnil and d'Ornanville, a local squire, and Isabeau du Bust. The family's proximity to the thriving Atlantic port of Dieppe influenced Ribault in choosing a maritime career. In all likelihood, Ribault married, but no records of whom and when remain. He had a son, Jacques, also a sea captain. Ribault's early birth date makes it impossible for him to have been born a Protestant. Although there is no record of Ribault's conversion, it is assumed that he converted to Calvinism in early adulthood. Ribault was alternately a mariner, holding captain's rank in the French royal navy, and a privateer, raiding Portuguese and Spanish galleons. He spent much of his early career, from 1546 to 1555, in England, acquiring there the reputation of being a skilled, experienced sea captain. In 1558, as a captain in charge of a supply convoy, Ribault took part in the successful seizure of Calais from the English. In 1559 he participated in a French naval operation in Scotland, where France attempted to protect Marie de Guise, wife of the late James V, from the English.

Given Ribault's experience, Gaspard de Coligny, admiral of France, chose him to lead an expedition to Terra Florida to explore the coast in the name of France. On 18 February 1562 Ribault left the port of Le Havre-de-Grâce with a fleet of three small ships carrying 150 men, half of whom were soldiers. René Goulaine de Laudonnière was appointed second in command. They reached the coast of Florida on 30 April at about the latitude of present-day St. Augustine. From that day until 11 June, Ribault explored the coast northward until he came to a large estuary, which he named Port Royal (in present-day South Carolina). There Ribault built a small wooden fortifi-

cation (believed to be located on Parris Island, South Carolina) that he called Charlesfort, in honor of Charles IX of France. Ribault left about thirty men there under the command of Albert de la Pierra and arrived back in France with the French fleet by 20 July.

At that time, the first of the eight French wars of religion, which began in March 1562, was still raging. Ribault took an active part in the defense of Dieppe, which was threatened by the Catholic royal troops. Despite English reinforcements, Dieppe surrendered, and Ribault returned to England in the winter of 1562–1563.

In Terra Florida, de la Pierra had begun to tyrannize the Native Americans and his own men; famine and mutiny racked the colony, and eventually de la Pierra was killed. Most of the colonists sailed back to Europe on a makeshift boat, and after months of starvation and the cannibalization of one of their own during the return voyage they reached the European coast and were rescued by Englishmen in the fall of 1562.

In May 1563 Ribault published his account of the Florida expedition, entitled *The Whole and True Discoverye of Terra Florida*. In the hopes of leading a new expedition to Florida, he then entered a three-way partnership with the English Crown and Thomas Stukeley, an English Roman Catholic and probably a double agent for Spain. The association collapsed, and Ribault, accused of planning to abscond to France on one of the jointly financed ships with survivors of the first expedition, was imprisoned in the Tower of London.

Meanwhile, the Spanish Crown, knowing of Ribault's first expedition to the southeast coast of North America, instructed the governor of Cuba to take action against the French intrusion. The governor sent Hernán Henrique de Rojas, who, aided by information from Guillaume Rouffi, a captured survivor of Ribault's first expedition who had remained with the Indians, found Charlesfort and destroyed it in June 1564.

With the return of peace in France and Ribault still in England, Coligny chose Laudonnière to lead a second expedition to Terra Florida. The fleet consisted of three ships carrying 300 people and left France on 22 April 1564. Laudonnière arrived in Terra Florida in June and decided to build a fort at the entrance of the Rivière de Mai (St. Johns River in present-day Florida), a location he favored over Port Royal. The fort was named La Caroline. Despite the fort's supposed better location, a more diversified group of settlers, and reinforcements brought by a certain Captain Bourdet in the fall of 1564, the second colony fared no better than the first.

Released in 1564, Ribault returned to France and prepared a third expedition, consisting of seven ships (one of which his son, Jacques, commanded) bearing 700 people; they sailed from Dieppe on 22 May 1565. He arrived at La Caroline on 28 August and at Coligny's behest replaced Laudonnière, who had apparently mismanaged the colony. Less than a week later arrived the fleet of Pedro Menéndez de Avilés, the Spanish captain sent by Madrid to dislodge the French from Florida. Leaving Laudonnière in command of the fort, Ribault decided to attack Menéndez's embryonic settlement of St. Augustine from the sea, but a violent storm dispersed and wrecked his four ships as they approached the Spanish post on 10 September. Knowing that Ribault had left La Caroline, and taking advantage of the stormy weather, Menéndez marched north and destroyed the French fort on 20 September. Laudonnière and a handful of settlers, including cartographer Jacques le Moyne de Morgues and Jacques Ribault, escaped to France. In the following weeks, Menéndez, with the help of local Indians, located the stranded Frenchmen. After hours of negotiations, he talked (or perhaps deceived) Ribault and most of his men into surrendering. Except for a few Catholics and individuals whose skills Menéndez needed, all the French were slain on the Matenzas Inlet.

Jean Ribault was a courageous, charismatic leader, a fervent Calvinist, and a devoted servant to his king. However, he could also be unyielding, such as when he left Fort Caroline unprotected and embarked on his last conflict with the Spanish, despite warnings by his subordinates.

• For primary sources relating to the early European settlement of Florida, see Jean Ribault, *The Whole and True Discoverye of Terra Florida*, ed. Jeanette T. Connor (1927; repr. 1964); René de Laudonnière, *Three Voyages*, ed. and trans. Charles Bennett (1964); Charles Bennett, ed., *Laudonnière and Fort Caroline: History and Documents* (1964); and Joseph Stevenson and Alan James Crosby, eds., *Calendar of State Papers: Foreign Series; The Reign of Elizabeth, 1558–1603* (11 vols., 1863–1880). Discussions of the sixteenth-century settlement of the southeastern coast of North America by Europeans include Paul E. Hoffman, *A New Andalucia and a New Way to the Orient: Sixteenth-Century Settlement in the Southeast* (1990); Eugene Lyon, *The Enterprise of Florida. Pedro Menéndez de Avilés and the Conquest of 1565–1568* (1976); Henry Folmer, *Franco-Spanish Rivalry in North America* (1953); and Lowery Woodbury, *The Spanish Settlements within the Present-Day Limits of the United States* (2 vols., 1901–1911).

BERTRAND VAN RUYMBEKE

RICE, Abraham Joseph (1802–29 Oct. 1862), rabbi and businessman, was born in Gochsheim, Bavaria, Germany, the son of Meir Rice. His mother's name is unknown. Abraham Rice received an intensive Jewish education, studying under the guidance of Rabbi Abraham Bing at the Würzburg yeshiva and with Rabbi Wolf Hamburger in Furth. After obtaining rabbinical ordination from Rabbi Bing, Rice served as a Talmud instructor in Zell, Germany.

Rice immigrated to the United States in 1840. With the hope of developing Orthodox Jewish life in America, Rice traveled to Rhode Island, where he tried unsuccessfully to rejuvenate the old Yeshuat Israel congregation (originally Nefutzoth Israel, now known as the Touro Synagogue) at Newport. Accepting the position of rabbi at Congregation Nidche Israel (also known as Baltimore Hebrew Congregation) in Balti-

more, Maryland, Rice served as spiritual leader of that congregation from 1840 until 1849, when he resigned from the rabbinate to pursue his livelihood as a merchant in dry goods. Forming a small synagogue, Shearith Israel, near his Baltimore home, Rice served as spiritual leader without compensation until 1862, when he assumed his former position as rabbi of the Baltimore Hebrew Congregation.

By virtue of his talmudic scholarship and personal piety, Rice emerged as one of the few noteworthy scholars of Jewish law in the United States during the mid-nineteenth century. Responding to religious queries from congregations throughout the United States regarding matters of family law, Sabbath observance, and dietary laws, Rice offered direction to the small community of American Jews who were eager to preserve Orthodox Jewish law and custom. Offering more than spiritual counsel and legal guidance to American Jews, Rice supported the efforts of various charitable organizations in Baltimore and abroad.

As one of the few Orthodox rabbis in the United States at that time, Rice also emerged as an important defender of the Orthodox tradition in the face of the growing religious Reform movement. He inveighed against what he considered to be Reform's religious deviations, and he excommunicated Isaac M. Wise, a leading Reform clergyman, for questioning aspects of the traditional Jewish belief of messiah and resurrection. Although his polemics failed to curtail the growth of Reform Judaism in the United States, his perspective reflected the concerns of Orthodox Jews regarding the preservation of Jewish tradition in America and regarding religious reform in particular.

At his death in Baltimore, Rice was mourned by many admirers throughout the United States. A former resident of Baltimore recalled with reverent affection that "Rabbi Rice was one of those pious and learned men whose influence, though silent, is nonetheless powerful, and that the city of Baltimore is even to this day favorably known for the true religious spirit of its Jewish inhabitants is perhaps in no small degree due to Rabbi Rice's early teachings and practice" (*The Occident*, p. 424).

• A collection of Abraham Rice's writings and correspondence is located in the Abraham Rice Collection, Jewish Theological Seminary Library, New York City. Additional communications of Rice can be found in the Minute Books of the Trustees, Congregation Shearith Israel, New York, bk. 5 (25 Aug. 1834–29 June 1849), p. 425. Some of Rice's sermons and polemics were published in *The Occident*. The only full-length study of Rice is I. Harold Scharfman, *The First Rabbi: Origins of the Conflict between Orthodox and Reform: Jewish Polemic Warfare in Pre–Civil War America* (1988). For information on certain aspects of Rice's life and career see Adolph Guttmacher, *History of the Baltimore Hebrew Congregation 1830–1905* (1905); Israel Tabak, "Rabbi Abraham Rice of Baltimore," *Tradition* 7 (Summer 1965): 100–120; Isaac Fein, *The Making of an American Jewish Community* (1971); Moshe Davis, "Igrot ha-Pekidim v'ha-Amrachlim me-Amsterdam," in *Salo W. Baron Jubilee Volume*

(1975); and Shmuel Singer, "From Germany to Baltimore," in *The Torah Personality*, ed. Nisson Wolpin (1980). An obituary is in *The Occident* 20 (Dec. 1862): 424–25.

MOSHE SHERMAN

RICE, Alice Caldwell Hegan (11 Jan. 1870–10 Feb. 1942), author, was born in Shelbyville, Kentucky, the daughter of Samuel Hegan, a businessman, and Sallie Caldwell. She was raised in Louisville, where poor health initially kept her from school. Home tutoring encouraged her interests in writing and sketching. At age ten, she began formal studies at Hampton College, a private academy in Louisville. There she continued to draw, but local publication of some of her short works convinced her to concentrate on writing. At sixteen, she volunteered as a teacher for boys at a local mission. The work stimulated her interest in the lives, language, and humor of Louisville's underprivileged white citizens. She continued charitable activity after graduation and also joined the Authors Club, a workshop of young women writers. Club members read their work aloud and offered each other friendly advice. With such support, Alice Hegan developed her observations of Louisville slum life into *Mrs. Wiggs of the Cabbage Patch* and submitted the manuscript to a New York publisher. The novel was published by Century Company in 1901.

Timing of the book's appearance was excellent, as President Theodore Roosevelt (1858–1919) (an eventual reader of *Mrs. Wiggs*) and reformers stirred interest in social problems. The novel sympathetically portrayed one family's struggle with urban poverty. Folksy dialogue conveyed the simple plot and reflected the author's fascination with people of "lower social scale" who "not only shared their emotions, but expressed themselves with spice and originality" (*Inky Way*, p. 39). Much of the book's appeal derived from its pairing of realistic descriptions of poverty ("Cabbage Patch" with a slum in Louisville's factory district) with advocacy of good cheer as the best way to cope with social ills. The title character, a widow, gamely fought to raise her children, avoiding self-pity and defeatism even as one died. The novel humanized poverty but did little to expose its causes or promote political agendas to address them. Although some critics (including Charlotte Perkins Gilman) dismissed *Mrs. Wiggs* as a romanticization of poverty, the book sold very well, remaining on the bestseller list for at least two years after its first appearance. Numerous editions, dramatizations, and film versions were produced.

On 18 December 1902, Alice Hegan married Cale Young Rice, a published poet and dramatist. The first years of their childless marriage set patterns that lasted four decades. Both formed friendships in the literary world and maintained them through correspondence and frequent travels. They toured Asia and visited Europe several times (inspiring *The Honorable Percival* [1914] and *The Lark Legacy* [1935]). Louisville remained their home, where Alice devoted mornings to writing and afternoons to community service (volunteer work at settlement houses).

Cale Rice never attained his wife's degree of fame or financial success, but this imbalance did not seem to damage their close partnership. In his autobiography, he occasionally took credit for "suggesting" ideas that resulted in his wife's bestsellers, and he called his own work more "aesthetic," but such notes of possible envy were fewer than proud references to her accomplishments.

Alice Rice never topped the success of *Mrs. Wiggs*, but her later works generally repeated much of its winning formula. Honesty, courage, and kindness were rewarded in her tales, though seldom with money. Poverty was a common theme, most sharply in *Calvary Alley* (1917). Such optimistic characters as *Sandy* (1905) and *Mr. Opp* (1909) used Wiggsian high spirits to conquer obstacles or survive heartache. Romance was often a theme, beginning with *Mrs. Wiggs*, but typically (*A Romance of Billy-Goat Hill* [1912] and *The Buffer* [1929]) the lovers developed mutual affection while working together to overcome social ills.

Rice produced almost a dozen novels by 1920, but her simplistic treatment of social ills began to lose favor with readers, who turned increasingly to grittier fiction that left conflicts unresolved. In the 1930s, the depression cut sharply into investments made by Cale Rice with his wife's earnings, and both Rices suffered ill health. Alice Rice wrote several books with Cale's editorial aid (they officially coauthored three over their lifetimes), but the books were uneven in quality, suggesting that they were written more from financial need than artistic inspiration. She died in Louisville; her husband's suicide the following year was cited as testimony to the intensity of their relationship.

Alice Rice published close to two dozen books, including several short-story collections and some nonfiction devotional works. Styles of adult fiction never returned to the rosy storytelling that she preferred, but her simple style and light humor remained attractive to younger readers. *Mrs. Wiggs* and *Lovey Mary* (1903), its sequel, emerged by the 1950s as children's favorites. Her most influential legacy was to juvenile fiction, a genre she deliberately attempted only with *Captain June* (1907), but into which changing tastes recategorized her work.

• Correspondence to Rice, business papers, notes and research materials, clippings, and several manuscripts are in the Alice Hegan Rice and Cale Young Rice Collection in the Kentucky Building at Western Kentucky University, Bowling Green. The most informative biographical data on Rice can be found in William Dix, "Alice Caldwell Hegan," *Outlook*, 6 Dec. 1902, pp. 802–04; Laban Lacy Rice, "Alice Hegan Rice—Homemaker," *Filson Club History Quarterly* 28 (July 1954): 233–38; Mary Boewes, "Back to the Cabbage Patch: The Character of Mrs. Wiggs," *Filson Club History Quarterly* 59 (April 1985): 179–204; and in Cale Rice's autobiography, *Bridging the Years* (1939). Her autobiography is *The Inky Way* (1940). An obituary is in the *New York Times*, 11 Feb. 1942.

BETH KRAIG

RICE, Charles (4 Oct. 1841–13 May 1901), pharmacist, journalist, and linguist, was born in Munich, Germany, the son of Austrian parents with the surname of Reis. He claimed to have changed his name to Rice when he came to the United States in 1862. Because Rice was intensely secretive about his personal life, especially his past, few details are known about his family or early education other than that he received intense instruction in classical and modern languages while in Germany and at the age of twelve began a lifelong study of Sanskrit. When family finances became tight, Rice followed the advice of an uncle who had emigrated to the United States and turned to more practical studies of science. On the death of his parents and in the face of continuing economic difficulties, Rice came to the United States, where he joined the U.S. Navy in 1862.

Rice's pharmacy career began in 1865, when he entered New York City's Bellevue Hospital as a patient. He had been a member of the crew of the U.S. sloop *Jamestown*, and he was sent to Bellevue with a malarial fever after discharge. On his recovery, he asked for a job and was assigned to bottle washing. Eventually his learning and expertise became obvious, and he was appointed assistant to the head of the hospital's drug department, John Frey, in 1867. Frey's health soon deteriorated, but Rice refused to take the title of director while his old mentor still lived, even though Rice had taken over the actual management of the department by the 1870s. In 1885 Rice was finally named chief pharmacist. Later that year he became head of the General Drug Department for all public charities in New York—more than twenty institutions—with responsibility for inspecting the city's milk supply. At the time this was the largest pharmacy operation in North America.

Rice was elected a member of the New York College of Pharmacy in 1867 and became a trustee just three years later. He quickly proposed the establishment of a pharmaceutical laboratory at the college and chaired the college's library committee for more than twenty years. He did not become a member of the faculty, however, choosing to devote himself primarily to the work of the General Drug Department.

In 1870 Rice joined the American Pharmaceutical Association (APhA) and soon became active in its scientific affairs but rarely left New York to attend conventions. In 1877 he was elected chairman of an APhA committee to consider reform of the *United States Pharmacopoeia*, the national compendium of drug standards (founded in 1820). From this committee, Rice sprang to national prominence in the area of drug standardization. His recommendations for reforms included the use of English without Latin (except for titles), the introduction of an alphabetical rather than drug-class ordering system, tests for drug identity and purity, and the addition of known chemical formulas for drugs.

In 1880 Rice was selected as chairman of the revision committee of the *United States Pharmacopoeia*, and he set out to organize a far-flung committee of twenty-five physicians and pharmacists. He did this through hectographed circulars sent out to the revision committee and its subcommittees. In 1882 the sixth revision of the *USP* was published, setting the model for the next sixty years for American drug standards. In 1885 Rice pushed hard and got the APhA to agree to publish a secondary compendium of medicine recipes, the *National Formulary*, which would supplement the *USP*. The first *NF* was published in 1888.

In 1876 Rice was asked by F. A. Castle to become associate editor of the journal *New Remedies*, for which Castle was editor and which became *American Druggist* in 1884. As he had with the Bellevue drug department, Rice soon took over managing the periodical, perhaps the most influential in the American drug trade because it covered all aspects of pharmacy and had the most eminent collection of pharmacy authors. Rice stepped down from his position in 1891, probably over a controversy with Castle about who would print the *USP*.

From the early 1880s until his death in New York City, Rice assisted physician editors John Shaw Billings and Robert Fletcher with the pharmacy sections of *Index Medicus* and the *Index Catalogue of the Library of the Surgeon-General's Office*. Rice also acted as a volunteer proofreader, reading all entries except those in the Slavic languages, Hungarian, or English. During his career, he was recognized through academic word of mouth as one of America's foremost Sanskrit scholars, attracting private students from across the country.

An exceedingly humble, proper, and private man, Rice never married and spent what little spare time he had reading Greek classics or doing Sanskrit studies. He spent all of his waking hours in work, never vacationing, and seldom leaving the grounds of Bellevue hospital. His crowning professional achievement was the reformation of the revision process of the *United States Pharmacopoeia*, accomplished in stages over the period from 1879 to 1900, for which he became recognized as the greatest pharmaceutical mind in the United States of his time. His innovations included the use of circulars to ensure national participation and the establishment of ongoing committees to provide continuous work on the revision process. Almost singlehandedly, he created the modern, scientific pharmacopoeia.

• Perhaps at Rice's request, the heir to his estate, Bellevue staff pharmacist Clarence Fountain, apparently destroyed all the personal papers that came into his hands. A nearly complete set of Rice's hand-written pharmacopoeial circulars are housed at the State Historical Society of Wisconsin and the University of Wisconsin's Rare Book Collection. The papers of the United States Pharmacopeial Convention, also housed at the State Historical Society of Wisconsin, contain a smattering of Rice correspondence. Some Rice letters are in the John Uri Lloyd Papers of the Lloyd Library in Cincinnati and in the John Shaw Billings Papers of the New York Public Library. Biographies include H. George Wolfe, "Charles Rice

(1841–1901), An Immigrant in Pharmacy," *American Journal of Pharmaceutical Education* 14 (1950): 285–305, which discusses the conflicting information available about Rice, and the hagiographical booklet, *Charles Rice*, printed for private circulation by J. B. Lippincott in 1904, and probably edited by Joseph Remington, which contains a bibliography of his publications. For details about Rice's work on the *United States Pharmacopeia*, see Lee Anderson and Gregory J. Higby, *The Spirit of Voluntarism: A Legacy of Commitment and Contribution, The United States Pharmacopeia 1820–1995* (1995). An obituary is "Death of Charles Rice," *American Druggist* 38 (1901): 283–85.

GREGORY J. HIGBY

RICE, Charles Allen Thorndike (18 June 1851–16 May 1889), editor, publisher, and journalist, was born in Boston, Massachusetts, the son of Henry Gardner Rice, a merchant, and Elizabeth Francis Thorndike. Although the marriage of Henry Rice and Elizabeth Thorndike merged two wealthy mercantile families of New York and Boston, it was not a happy one. They obtained a divorce in 1859, and Rice won custody of young Charles in an 1860 case heard before the Massachusetts Supreme Court. Elizabeth Thorndike responded by arranging for the kidnapping of her son. Charles's playmate Henry Cabot Lodge witnessed the crime and helped police apprehend the two men Thorndike had hired. In the meantime mother and son escaped to Canada, where Charles was disguised as a girl and hidden in a convent until transportation to Europe could be arranged. After five years in Germany and France, Thorndike died, and Charles returned to America for three years, only to witness his father's death. At age eighteen he moved to England, entered Oxford, and earned a B.A. in 1874 and an M.A. in 1878. Rice then returned to America with a considerable fortune and few definitive plans. After several desultory years of anonymous writing for journals and magazines, he purchased the *North American Review* in 1876 for $3,000.

First published in Boston in 1815, the *Review* was one of the longest-running American periodicals. Through the editorship of such notables as Edward Everett and James Russell Lowell, it had exerted considerable influence in antebellum literary culture. But by the 1870s, its provincial orientation and dry, pedantic tone seemed outdated, and the quarterly was losing both readers and profits to the more lively *Atlantic Monthly* and *Harper's*. Rice transformed the *Review* into a monthly and moved its offices from Boston to New York. He broadened the range of contributors and solicited articles on timely and controversial topics. Harriet Beecher Stowe wrote on Reconstruction. Julia Ward Howe and Wendell Phillips advocated woman suffrage, while Francis Parkman attacked it. William Gladstone wrote on Christianity, Cardinal Manning defended the Catholic church, and Robert G. Ingersoll denounced all creeds. Henry George floated his single tax plan, and General Ulysses S. Grant promoted a Nicaraguan Canal. Richard Wagner described his life and career; Walt Whitman speculat-

ed on the future of poetry; and Andrew Carnegie wrote his famed essay "Wealth," which appeared in an 1889 edition of the *Review* and which Rice declared to be the finest article he had ever published.

Rice's policy of publishing diverse and contrary viewpoints established the *Review*'s reputation as "the highest and most impartial platform upon which current public issues can be discussed" ("Prospectus," *North American Review* 125 [Nov. 1877]). His editorial practices were also good business. During his thirteen years as editor, circulation grew from 1,200 to over 17,000, and annual profits reached $50,000. Rice soon embarked upon other profitable ventures. In 1884 he purchased a controlling interest in *Le Matin*, a successful Parisian newspaper, and helped establish a foreign press syndicate. Two years later he edited and published *Reminiscences of Abraham Lincoln*, which went through eight editions in less than three years.

Rice also sought adventures beyond the world of publishing. In 1879 he helped organize and secure French and American patronage for the Charnay expedition to the Mayan ruins, a journey that earned Rice the French Legion of Honor. He later described the expedition in his 1880 *Ruined Cities of Central America*. Several years later he traveled the proposed route for the Panama Canal to describe its logistical impossibilities to *Review* readers.

Rice made a less successful foray into politics in 1886, when he lost a narrow race for Congress to General Francis B. Spinola, a New York City Democrat. Rice became convinced that ballot fraud within his own party had cost him victory, and he embarked on a campaign for election reform that advocated the printing and distribution of secret (or "Australian") ballots at public expense. Though he decried the practice of candidates "mortgaging their official acts in advance to the persons or organizations that defray their campaign disbursements" (Rice, "The Next National Reform," p. 84), Rice was a liberal contributor to the Republican national campaign fund. His largesse was rewarded in 1889 when President Benjamin Harrison appointed him as minister to Russia. While preparing to embark for his new post, he suddenly took ill and died several days later in his New York home.

Though associates frequently made note of Rice's charm, conviviality, and handsome appearance, he never married. He left a controlling interest in the *Review* to Lloyd Bryce, his close friend and Oxford University roommate. His large Maryland estate, his western ranch, and his prized art collection were auctioned off. The historical legacy of Rice was more enduring yet intangible. His wealth and enthusiasm for ideas provided an open forum for some of the most important social critics of his time. Indeed, the many seminal essays that appeared in his *North American Review* are critical to twentieth-century writing of the intellectual and cultural history of the Gilded Age.

• Rice's writings are scattered throughout issues of the *North American Review* between 1876 and 1889. See, for example,

"The Next National Reform" (148 [Jan. 1889]: 82–85), his article on ballot fraud. For information concerning his early life, see Henry Cabot Lodge, *Early Memories* (1913), and Joseph Foster, *Alumni Oxonienses, 1715–1886* (1888). John Tebbel and Mary Ann Zuckerman, *The Magazine in America* (1991), places Rice's work in the context of late nineteenth-century publishing. Detailed reminiscences of Rice written by William Astor, Edwards Pierrepont, General W. T. Sherman, and Lloyd Bryce are in the *North American Review* 149, no. 392 (July 1889): 110–17. An obituary is in the *New York Times*, 17 May 1889.

MARK G. SCHMELLER

RICE, Dan (23 Jan. 1823–22 Feb. 1900), clown and circus owner, was born in New York City, the son of Daniel McLaren, a grocer, and Elizabeth Crum, a Methodist minister's daughter. After Elizabeth's parents had the runaway marriage annulled, "Rice" (there are conflicting theories on the choice of name) remained in New York, attending school until his debut, at age nine, as a jockey. After 1837 Rice worked his way west to Pittsburgh and south to Kentucky as stable driver, jockey, hackney coachman, and riverboat gambler.

After a circus apprenticeship, Rice began his showman's life in 1840 as part owner of an "educated" pig named Sybil. In 1841, after a time in Nathan Howe's Philadelphia winter circus, Rice learned weightlifting and cannonball tossing, becoming a strongman ("The Yankee Samson") for P. T. Barnum's New York museum. He spent the 1842 season in Europe. Returning to the United States, Rice tried his hand at minstrelsy, popularizing "Root Hog and Die," which became a theme song. He married Margaret Ann Curran in 1842 in Pittsburgh. They had two daughters, one eventually an equestrian in Rice's circus. Rice made his debut as a clown ("Yankee Dan, the Jester") in either Davenport, Iowa, or Galena, Illinois, in 1844.

Rice was a dominating figure in the days of the one-ring circus. He wore chin whiskers, red, white, and blue striped tights, a top hat, and a star-spangled cloak. His contemporaries believed that cartoonist Thomas Nast had based his classic drawing of Uncle Sam on Rice. A cracker-barrel philosopher who often sat horseback, he wisecracked and chatted over the ringmaster's head. One contemporary wrote, "He takes you right by the hand with the heartiness of his humor, and at once hits you under the ribs with some rich quaintness, and moves around like an electric eel, tickling everything he touches."

In an era awash with Shakespeare, Rice was from 1846 a "Shakespearean" clown. He learned this specialty from the English clown William Wallett ("the Queen's jester"), who sometimes worked alongside him. While Wallett answered audience heckling with Shakespearean quotes, Rice burlesqued the Bard, peppering broad humor with critiques of contemporary actors. Late in his "Multifarious Account of Shakespeare's *Hamlet*," Rice says:

> He jumped into Ophelia's grave and said,
> "Just pile a million acres on my head."
> Of course they didn't do it, 'cause they couldn't;
> And if they could, rather guess they wouldn't;

> Because of time 'twould take a precious sight,
> And so they all agreed to go and fight.

For several springs and summers, the man who became known as "The King of American Clowns" worked for G. R. Spalding's midwestern circus; in the fall and winter Rice played such New York venues as John Tryon's Bowery Amphitheatre and Palmo's Opera House. In 1847 Spalding and Rice became partners. Under Rice's name, their circus (the partnership dissolved in 1849) toured along the Mississippi and Ohio rivers, from St. Paul to Pittsburgh to New Orleans. Rice introduced "The Battle of Buena Vista," based on the firsthand experience of his new friend, General Zachary Taylor. Following Taylor's election to the presidency, he made Rice an honorary colonel ("for great service rendered in entertaining mankind").

In 1851 the Dan Rice Circus, traveling by canalboat and steamers such as the *Allegheny Mail* but playing on the riverbanks, toured New York State and the Ohio and Mississippi rivers; it stayed on the southern Mississippi in 1852, and later that year Rice had to start over after losing a slander case. Having accused a rival manager of moving his buoy, Rice spent a week in jail. His circus was foreclosed. Rice wrote a song about the incident, borrowed money, and started his One Horse Circus.

In 1853 the Dan Rice Ampitheatre was established in New Orleans, where Rice claimed to have "discovered" the peanut, bringing it to national prominence soon afterward. By this time Rice's wife was an equestrian in the Rice circus, often appearing in a costume evoking the American flag. (They were divorced in 1861; she began her own circus, and in 1862 he married Charlotte Rebecca McConnell of Girard, Pennsylvania, where Rice had wintered his circus since 1852. Their only child died at six months. This marriage ended in divorce in 1881.)

Rice's 1858 engagement at New York's Niblo's Garden was called "sensational," featuring performing mules, a ropewalking elephant named Lala Rookh, and a dancing camel. Over the years there were other "educated" pigs, a trained black rhino, and horses named Aroostook, who "occupied the disputed boundary between man and horse," Excelsior, and Excelsior Junior, a blind animal that "understood English."

Though Rice had fraternized with Jefferson Davis and Robert E. Lee, associations that caused accusations of disloyalty, during the Civil War he became a great favorite of Abraham Lincoln's by speaking as a strong Unionist:

> I would like North and South to leave slavery alone
> And stand by the Union until the last stone.
> To settle the quarrel by war, blood and vice
> Is like burning your house to scare out a few mice.

During these years, when the diversions of the circus were much in demand, Rice made as much as $1,000 weekly. He published his songs and sketches, his parodying "stump speeches," political doggerel, and advertisements for himself ("Take your gal to a Dan Rice show, she'll marry you"). He "invented" pink lemonade. After the Civil War, he was first to restart showboat entertainment on the Mississippi. Showboat historian Philip Graham says Rice kept intact during the Reconstruction "the traditions—even the very possibility—of showboating" (p. 39).

By 1868 the owner of Dan Rice's Great Show, Circus and Menagerie was full enough of himself to advertise a "farewell tour" and seek a presidential nomination—either party would do. As early as 1859 Rice had been called—half-seriously—presidential material, and in 1866 he had lost a Pennsylvania campaign for Congress. Rice's "campaign" was eventually revealed as a (highly profitable) publicity hoax to rival P. T. Barnum. By 1869 he was back in the circus business, with "a bevy of belles" and "monarchs of muscle."

Rice began to miss performances. He gave money to friends and confidence men alike. At his own expense he erected in 1865 the Dan Rice Soldiers and Sailors Monument in Girard, and he built black churches there. It is generally agreed that alcohol proved his downfall, although even in middle age he could reputedly catch cannonballs on the back of his neck and wrestle three men at a time. But such former circus luminaries as Tony Pastor sensed the change in public taste and moved into variety.

In 1871 the huge Dan Rice Grand Paris Pavilion Circus opened in Baltimore, intending a tour to Europe. Two weeks later it closed, losing $60,000. A large frame building had been built, incorporating fountains, thousands of gas jets, heavy carpets, and handsome furniture. Most of the effects were stored—and later auctioned—and Rice took the show on the road, where it quickly collapsed. He was bankrupt by 1874. In 1878 Rice embarked on the temperance lecture tour, though it was widely suspected that his water pitcher held gin. He ran a small riverboat circus, but he could afford only "one half-starved lion"; the *Damsel* snagged and burned on the Missouri. There was a far western tour in 1882.

Constructing *The Floating Opera* at Cairo, Illinois, Rice made his final tour in 1885–1886. This return to the lower Mississippi also failed, and he moved to Long Branch, New Jersey. As late as 1890 he showed a one-ring circus in Brooklyn, where, billed as "The Clown of Our Daddies," he also lectured and organized benefit performances. His last ten years were quiet. Rice died in Long Branch, bypassed by time, finally smaller than life.

• Though much has been written about Dan Rice, he remains somewhat legendary. Rice's own works include *Dan Rice's Great American Humorist Song Book* (1863). Most recent among his biographies are John C. Kunzog, *The One Horse Show: The Life and Times of Dan Rice* (1962), which is particularly good on circus lore, and Don C. Gillette, *He Made Lincoln Laugh* (1967). Also see Eric Engdahl's (Ph.D. diss., Univ. of California, Los Angeles, 1979). George C. D. Odell, *Annals of the New York Stage* (1927–1949), is invalua-

ble for its nearly day-to-day coverage, particularly in vols. 5–8 and 14. George L. Chindahl, *A History of the Circus in America* (1959), details the successive forms of Rice's circuses. Beryl Hugill, *Bring on the Clowns* (1980), and Lawrence Senelick, *A Cavalcade of Clowns* (1977), describe the nature of Rice's performances. Philip Graham, *Showboats: The History of an American Institution* (1951), sets Rice in his riverboat context.

JAMES ROSS MOORE

RICE, David (29 Dec. 1733–18 June 1816), Presbyterian minister, was born in Hanover County, Virginia, the son of David Rice. (His mother's name is not cited in sources.) As a child Rice was devoted to the Church of England, but after the death of his father he became a Presbyterian and a protégé of the famed Presbyterian itinerant Samuel Davies. Rice studied with Davies at the College of New Jersey when Davies became president there and graduated in 1761. Licensed to preach by Hanover Presbytery in 1762, Rice served first as a missionary, helping pioneer families start congregations in small communities in Virginia and North Carolina. Married in 1763 and ordained later that year, Rice settled with his wife, the former Mary Blair, daughter of Presbyterian minister Samuel Blair, in Hanover County, Virginia, where he served a group of churches. The Rices eventually had eleven children.

In 1769 Rice became pastor of the Peaks of Otter Presbyterian Church in Bedford County, Virginia. Rice remembered these years most fondly, as the church grew and families attended to his instruction. He also was supportive in 1776 of the founding of Hampden-Sydney College in Prince Edward County, Virginia.

In 1783 Rice visited Kentucky at the urging of another Presbyterian, James Michel, who had been doing mission work in the Bluegrass area. Although at first he was repulsed by the greed of those he visited, Rice acceded later that year to their petition that he move his family to serve among them. In October 1783 the Rice household moved to what became Mercer County, Kentucky, and he became one of the first Presbyterian ministers in the region. He helped to organize a number of the nascent Presbyterian congregations—Concord at Danville, New Providence at McAfee Station, Cane Run at Trigg Station, and Fork of Dick's (Dix) River, among them. Rice was instrumental also in the forming of Transylvania Presbytery out of Hanover Presbytery in 1786 and in the founding of the Synod of Kentucky in 1802.

Rice was likewise a pioneer in the opening of schools in Kentucky. Transylvania Seminary, later Transylvania University, envisioned as a "public school" in the West and funded initially in 1783 with land donated by Virginia legislators, began in the home of Rice in 1785, with Michel, now Rice's son-in-law, as the first instructor in 1787. When Transylvania Presbytery lost control of this institution in 1794, Rice again helped to found the new Kentucky Academy at Pisgah Church in 1797.

Rice was among the candidates elected in 1792 to form a convention and frame a constitution for the new state of Kentucky. He attempted to persuade colleagues in the assembly to prohibit slavery as a part of that constitution. The pamphlet he wrote for the assembly, *Slavery Inconsistent with Justice and Good Policy* (1792), argued that no one should be forced into bondage or forfeit freedom without just cause. "A slave is a member of civil society, bound to obey the laws of the land; to which he has never consented . . . and to perform services to a society, to which he owes nothing, and in whose prosperity he has no interest." Even in their own interest, he argued, white Americans had no business holding slaves. Rice's arguments, among the first unequivocal antislavery statements by a Presbyterian leader, went unheeded by the constitutional convention. Rice retired from state politics after that convention.

He did not retire from church controversy, however. For example, in the early nineteenth century he opposed the relaxing of ordination requirements and other consequences of the Great Revival that began among Presbyterians in southern Kentucky in 1799 and moved throughout much of the United States. These ongoing revivals gave rise to calls for less doctrine and more preachers, calls that were heeded by Methodists and Baptists; by the "Christian" movement (1803–1823) among some Presbyterians, which eventuated in the Christian church (Disciples of Christ); by Finis Ewing and those who formed the Cumberland Presbyterian church (1810); and by the Shakers, who started a community in the area in 1805. Rice and some other Presbyterians, however, objected to the lack of decorum in revivals, to the doctrines of external signs of salvation and falling from grace that were taught, and to the general loss of discipline in church life. He was remembered for "shouting down" a revival at the Walnut Hill Presbyterian Church in 1801. "Holy, Holy, Holy! is the Lord God Almighty," he exclaimed. Rice and those opposing the excesses of revivals managed to keep those Presbyterians who remained in the Synod of Kentucky from depending strongly upon such meetings; but many, if not most, Presbyterians were drawn to the freer worship, and less Calvinistic denominations presented an alternative.

Personally disheartened by the unwillingness of Danville Presbyterians to pay his salary and to fulfill their promise to purchase property for him and his family, Rice moved in 1797 to Green County in western Kentucky. He preached occasionally at various churches during the early nineteenth century, but generally he remained depressed until his death there. One biographer speaks of his enduring "a disorder in his head," another of "an affection [affliction?] of the head." John Opie's study of Rice characterizes his later life in particular as one of "melancholy."

• A fascinating, self-disclosing autobiography is offered in Robert H. Bishop, *An Outline of the History of the Church in Kentucky . . . containing the Memoirs of the Rev. David Rice* (1824). The early, standard study, Robert Davidson, *History of the Presbyterian Church in the State of Kentucky* (1847), has been supplemented by John P. Opie, "The Melancholy Career of 'Father' David Rice," *Journal of Presbyterian History* 47 (1969): 295–319.

LOUIS WEEKS

RICE, Edgar Charles. *See* Rice, Sam.

RICE, Edwin Wilbur, Jr. (6 May 1862–25 Nov. 1935), electrical engineer and industrialist, was born in La Crosse, Wisconsin, the son of Edwin Wilbur Rice, a Congregational minister and an editor, and Margaret Eliza Williams. His family moved to Philadelphia, where he attended the Boys' Central High School. The school, which then gave its four-year graduates the bachelor's degree and the master's degree for a fifth year of study, conferred A.B. and M.A. degrees on him. This was the extent of his formal education. In school he came under the tutelage of Elihu Thomson, who taught physics and chemistry. When Thomson moved in 1880 to New Britain, Connecticut, to found the American Electric Company, which manufactured dynamos and electric arc lamps, Rice joined him. Taken over in 1883 by investors from Lynn, Massachusetts, the company, under the name of the Thomson-Houston Company, moved to that city. At the age of twenty-two, Rice became plant superintendent of the company. In 1892 a merger with Edison General Electric created the General Electric Company, with headquarters at Schenectady, New York.

Considered one of the three fathers of General Electric (along with Thomson and Charles A. Coffin), Rice was originally its technical director. He became, in 1896, vice president in charge of manufacturing and engineering, and eventually senior vice president. In 1913 he was chosen president of the company, and when he retired in 1922 was made honorary chairman of the board. His career has been described as one "devoted to making electricity understood and available" (Whitney, p. 3), a devotion that was already discernible in his high school graduation essay on the utilization of electricity.

Rice's managerial skill and vision contributed a great deal to the organizational methods, factory routine, technical development, and engineering and scientific inventions at General Electric. He consulted with the entire engineering staff and assisted in every form of engineering development. The over one hundred patents credited to him embrace practically the whole field of electrical operations and include systems of distribution, synchronous converters, arc lamps, incandescent lamps, oil switches of high capacity, both alternating- and direct-current generators, train control systems, and transformers. Some of these were fundamental; the oil switches, for example, "overcome a serious limiting factor in the development of electrical systems on an extensive and economical plan" (GE Source Book"). Recognizing within two months after Roentgen announced his discovery in December 1895 the commercial importance of the X-ray tube and apparatus, Rice provided the initiative and management that brought General Electric into the field.

During his vice presidency Rice advocated innovative forms of industrial organization and was largely responsible for his company's policy of employee representation, the recognition of the shop worker's part in the success of the company, and the importance of advancing the welfare of employees. Relations among employees and promotions "were governed more by what became known as the Rice sense of justice than by rules, rituals, or precedents" (Broderick, p. 62). A "manufacturing committee" composed of factory managers, of which Rice was chairman for twenty years, illustrated the principle of group action then characteristic of General Electric's industrial management. Nevertheless labor unrest coincided with Rice's becoming president of the company. In 1913 there was a strike in Schenectady, and in 1918 the Wobblies led "walk-outs" at five company sites. In 1916 Rice told the National Industrial Conference Board that the "day of extreme individualism is past . . . the time has come for co-operation in the broadest sense," and the postwar years saw the further development of the enlightened—and patronizing—company policy toward labor.

Rice added Charles P. Steinmetz, the mathematician and electrical "Wizard of Schenectady," to the engineering staff in 1893 and is credited with being a prime mover in the creation of the General Electric Research Laboratories in 1900. Rice's belief in the importance of science was further indicated when, on a trip to Germany in 1922–1923, he personally made up the year's deficit of the journal of the Mathematical Society and after his return spearheaded the financing of pure electrophysical research by General Electric and the large electrical manufacturing companies.

Rice was not a frequent contributor to the literature of his profession. Two articles worthy of note were his "Reminiscences of Early Arc Lighting Apparatus," in the *General Electric Review* (12 [Apr. 1909]: 158–62), and, with Samuel Crowther, "Pioneer Days of a Great American Industry," in the *Magazine of Business* (54 [1928]: 233–36, 298–99). Both are illustrated accounts describing firsthand, basic developments in electrical engineering. The most important of his addresses to appear in print, *The Field of Research in Industrial Institutions*, was given at the 1924 centenary celebration of the Franklin Institute.

The recipient of many honors, Rice was elected president in 1917 of the American Institute of Electrical Engineers, his tenure marked by his championing of the establishment of engineering standards. In 1931 the institute awarded him the Edison Medal "for his contributions to the development of electrical systems and his encouragement of scientific research in industry." He was the recipient of several honorary degrees; after the Paris Exposition of 1900, France made him a Chevalier de la Légion d'Honneur; and Japan bestowed The Third Order of the Rising Sun on him in 1917. He was elected to the Royal Society in 1934.

Among the professional organizations to which Rice belonged were the American Institute of Electrical Engineers, the Illuminating Engineering Society, and two British societies, the Institution of Civil Engineers and the Institution of Electrical Engineers. He held directorships in the General Electric Company, the International General Electric Company, the Electric Bond and Share Company, the British Thomson-Houston Company, Ltd., the Schenectady Trust Company, the Detroit Edison Company, and the Radio Corporation of America. His club memberships included the Engineers and University Clubs of New York, the University Club of Boston, and The Pilgrims.

Rice became a trustee of Union College in 1903 and chairman of the board in 1931. An ardent supporter and benefactor of the college, he was credited with invigorating its physics, chemistry and electrical engineering programs.

In 1884 Rice married Helen K. Doen, with whom he had three children. After her death Rice married her sister, Alice M. Doen, in 1897. He died in Schenectady, New York.

• The Edward W. Rice Papers are in the Special Collections of the Schaffer Library of Union College. They include correspondence, clippings, photographs, and lists of talks that mainly pertain to his activities at General Electric. Historical records of the General Electric Company are in that company's Hall of History Museum in Schenectady, N.Y. The best accounts of Rice's work at General Electric are (anonymous) "Career of the New President," *Electrical World* 61 (1913): 1345–46; J. T. Broderick, *Forty Years with General Electric* (1929); W. B. Carlson, *Innovation as a Social Process: Elihu Thomson and the Rise of General Electric, 1870–1900* (1991); R. R. Kline, *Steinmetz: Engineer and Socialist* (1992); and G. Wise, *Willis R. Whitney, General Electric, and the Origins of U.S. Industrial Research* (1985). A personal evaluation is W. R. Whitney, "A Tribute to Edwin W. Rice, Jr.," *General Electric Review* 39 (Jan. 1936): 3–6. A full obituary is in the *Schenectady Union-Star*, 26 Nov. 1935.

DAVID L. COWEN

RICE, Elmer (28 Sept. 1892–8 May 1967), playwright, was born Elmer Leopold Reizenstein in New York City, the son of Jacob Reizenstein and Fanny Lion, the children of German-Jewish immigrants who had come to the United States in the mid-nineteenth century. Jacob Reizenstein was a bookkeeper and traveling salesman, although epilepsy reduced him to reliance on relatives and friends for work. After leaving high school at fourteen without a diploma, Elmer Reizenstein had two jobs in quick succession in small business firms, a sampling of the world of commerce that left him unhappy. He next took a position as an office boy in a law firm headed by an older cousin. After one year on the job, with a promotion to clerk secured, he made the decision to study law—not out of a passionate interest in the legal profession, but for want of a suitable means of earning a living.

As a first step in obtaining his law degree, he was required to pass the New York State Board of Regents' examinations to make up for the two years of high school that he had missed. Since it was not then necessary for a would-be lawyer to equip himself first with an undergraduate degree, in 1910 he enrolled in New York Law School. He received an LL.B. with honors in 1912 and in the fall passed the New York State bar examinations, although he could not be admitted to the bar until he reached age twenty-one.

From an early age Reizenstein had taken pleasure in attending the theater, and during his law school years his love of playgoing intensified as he began to read and see the plays of modern British and continental playwrights. He admired above all others George Bernard Shaw, not only for his plays but also for his dramatic criticism and socialist political views. Literature, not law, was Reizenstein's true interest. Although he had done well in law school, he had never warmed to his legal studies, and the clerical work to which he was confined in his firm soon began to bore him. To offset the tedium of his job, he took evening courses in literature and sociology at Columbia University and began to write.

Reizenstein's apprentice works, composed before he reached the age of twenty-one, included poetry, short stories, one one-act play, and two full-length ones. Of this early writing, only one short story saw print. He wrote the longer plays, *A Defection from Grace* and *The Seventh Commandment*, in collaboration with Frank Harris, a friend and colleague. Neither was published or performed, but the first received honorable mention in a contest to which the young men submitted it. *The Passing of Chow-Chow*, a short play about a pet dog, later received some amateur productions.

In 1913, having had as much of the law profession as he could bear, Reizenstein resigned his position. Deciding on playwriting as a career, he composed *On Trial*, which was produced in 1914 by George M. Cohan and Sam H. Harris, shortly before Reizenstein's twenty-second birthday. A courtroom melodrama that gripped the audience, it was an immediate success, and its use of flashback brought something new to live theater.

On Trial altered its author's life. Not only were royalties plentiful, but any new play Reizenstein wrote was likely to find a willing producer. Over the years that followed, twenty-three more of his plays would be produced on Broadway. In addition, he would create one-act and full-length plays for production off Broadway along with still other plays completed but discarded before production. Success also enabled him to renew his earlier engagement to Hazel Levy, whom he married in 1915. They had two children.

In the years immediately following the closing of *On Trial*, Reizenstein audited courses at Columbia, taught at the University Settlement in (as he put it) "the heart of the ghetto" on the Lower East Side, directed the Morningside Players at Columbia, and, although not a member of the Socialist party, spoke on behalf of socialist causes. *The Iron Cross*, a play reflecting his anguish over the bloodshed of World War I,

was scheduled for Broadway, but casting difficulties held it up until the audience for war plays was sated. It received an off Broadway production, however, by the Morningside Players in 1917. He also wrote a short one-act satiric comedy, *A Diadem of Snow*, on the Russian revolution; it was produced by an amateur group and published in *The Liberator*, a leftist magazine.

In 1918, after prolonged deliberation, Reizenstein shortened his name to Rice. Accused in some quarters of attempting to disguise his Jewish roots by this move, he was quick to deny the charge. In addition to being difficult to spell, the original name, he believed, carried too heavy a reminder of the Old World.

Summoned to Hollywood by Samuel Goldwyn in 1918, Rice soon discovered that scenario writing and the daily routine of studio life held little pleasure for him, and he asked to be released from his contract after two years. Meanwhile, he continued to write plays. *Wake Up, Jonathan*, a comedy written in collaboration with Hatcher Hughes and starring Minnie Maddern Fiske, reached the stage in 1921. It was followed in 1922 by *It Is the Law*, a mystery melodrama. Neither play was a success.

Rice's fourth Broadway play, *The Adding Machine* (1923), ran a mere nine weeks but reestablished him as a leading dramatist. An expressionist work, its protagonist, Mr. Zero, is a bookkeeper hard pressed by the drudgery of his job and the nagging of his wife. In time, the play achieved the status of a classic. Before the decade reached its end, Rice offered five more plays: *Close Harmony* (1924), an unsuccessful collaboration with Dorothy Parker about another henpecked husband; *Cock Robin* (1928), a mystery play written with Philip Barry that enjoyed a respectable run; *See Naples and Die* (1929), an unsuccessful romantic comedy; *The Subway* (1929), a second, but unsuccessful, expressionist play about an office worker; and *Street Scene* (1929), a powerful naturalistic drama of life in a crowded New York tenement. *Street Scene* won the Pulitzer Prize for drama and proved to be Rice's one other contribution to the American classic repertory. Rice directed the play himself and thereafter directed all his own plays.

The severity of the Great Depression strengthened Rice's already acute awareness of social injustice in American life as had been demonstrated in both *The Adding Machine* and *Street Scene*. Not always, however, was he able to give effective dramatic form to his feelings; many of his plays of the 1930s create the impression that he struck while the iron was too hot. He began the new decade with two successes: *The Left Bank* (1931), on young American expatriates in Paris, and *Counsellor-at-Law* (1931), starring Paul Muni, on a severely troubled lawyer. But they were followed by five other plays that fell short: *Black Sheep* (1932), *We, the People* (1932), *Judgment Day* (1934), *Between Two Worlds* (1934), and *American Landscape* (1938). *Black Sheep*, a comedy written in the 1920s, was dismissed by critics as feeble and closed after a mere four performances; the others, all dealing at least in part with social issues, fared somewhat better in reviews but failed at the box office nevertheless.

The rejection of *Judgment Day* and *Between Two Worlds* so angered Rice that while lecturing at Columbia he savagely denounced the critics and declared that he would write no more plays for the commercial theater. The papers picked up and published his outburst, causing him great embarrassment, but he canceled plans to offer a comedy about the theater itself, *Not for Children*. The play was eventually produced for limited runs in London in 1935 and in Pasadena, California, in 1936. Rice's last play of the decade, *Two on an Island* (1940), a romantic comedy, enjoyed moderate success.

In 1935 Rice accepted the post of director of the New York region of the Federal Theatre Project, an arm of the Works Progress Administration. His tenure was brief, however. Although Harry Hopkins, national director of the WPA, had promised him that the Federal Theatre would not be subject to censorship, early in 1936 the performance of a documentary play on the Italian invasion of Ethiopia prepared for production by the New York unit was forbidden by the national office, on the demand of the State Department. Rice resigned immediately. A more satisfactory venture for him was the Playwrights' Company, which he helped to found in 1937, along with Maxwell Anderson, Sidney Howard, Robert E. Sherwood, and S. N. Behrman, for the production of their own plays. Rice remained a member of the company until its dissolution in 1960.

For many years Rice had been unhappy in his marriage. He and the rising young actress Betty Field fell in love when she was cast in *Two on an Island*, and they began an affair. Field also appeared in Rice's well-received *Flight to the West* (1940), a suspenseful play on refugees hastening by air to the New World from war-torn Europe. Rice obtained a divorce in 1942, and within days he and Field were married. Three children were born to the couple. During the course of their marriage, Field divided her time between Hollywood and Broadway. Rice wrote two plays specifically for her: *A New Life* (1943), an unsuccessful melodrama on whether the mother of a newborn child or the mother's wealthy parents-in-law should raise the child, and *Dream Girl* (1945), a romantic comedy on the fantasy life of a young woman that became one of Rice's major successes.

Rice had been frequently importuned by composers for the right to base an opera on *Street Scene* since its opening in 1929. He had always withheld permission, however, until approached by his friend Kurt Weill, whose music he had long admired. In 1948, with revisions of the text by Rice and lyrics by Langston Hughes, the work opened on Broadway, where it was billed as a musical. The reviews, although mixed, were essentially positive, but not so laudatory as to enable the production to regain its cost. Eventually, however, the Weill-Rice-Hughes *Street Scene* became a staple of the international operatic repertory.

In the years remaining to him, Rice was not destined to score another success. Each of his last five plays—*Not for Children* (1951), *The Grand Tour* (1951), *The Winner* (1954), *Cue for Passion* (1958), and *Love among the Ruins* (1963)—received only a brief run. The 1950s also brought a disappointment of another sort: the breakup of his marriage to Betty Field in 1956. In 1966 he married Barbara Ambrose Marshall, who survived him.

Although Rice is remembered chiefly as a playwright, he was also the author of many nondramatic works. They include the novels *A Voyage to Purilia* (1930), *Imperial City* (1937), and *The Show Must Go On* (1949), as well as a fictional adaptation of *On Trial* (1915); a nonfiction work, *The Living Theatre* (1959), on the forces that shape the writing and production of a play; his memoirs, *Minority Report* (1963); pamphlets on the arts and politics; and short stories and screenplays.

In addition to his writing Rice devoted much of his time and energy to professional and public service organizations. A lifelong advocate of civil rights and the advancement and protection of minorities, he was a member of the board of the American Civil Liberties Union and chairman of the National Council on Freedom from Censorship. He was active in the Dramatists Guild (president, 1939–1943), the Authors League of America (president, 1945–1946, and member of the board), the American National Theater and Academy (member of the executive committee), the International Association of Poets, Playwrights, Editors, Essayists and Novelists (PEN). He was also a member of the National Institute of Arts and Letters. Whenever an opportunity to teach came his way, he was quick to take advantage of it. In 1954 he lectured at the University of Michigan, and in the academic year 1957–1958 he taught at New York University. S. N. Behrman, his colleague in the Playwrights' Company, described him as "socially charming and humorous," but added that he was "apt to be strident when arguing for his plays at company meetings." Rice enjoyed frequent travels abroad, both for professional reasons and for recreation, and was an enthusiastic collector of modern art. He died in Southampton, England.

• Rice's manuscripts and papers, including correspondence, are in the collection of the Humanities Research Center, University of Texas, Austin. The Playwrights' Company papers, in the collection of the Wisconsin Center for Film and Theater Research, Madison, include letters from Rice. The New York Public Library for the Performing Arts has files on each of Rice's plays and a file of clippings on his career. His *Minority Report* (1963) provides a full and candid account of his public and private life. Robert Hogan offers well-written commentary on the plays and their reception in *The Independence of Elmer Rice* (1965). Rice's experience in the Federal Theatre is chronicled by Hallie Flanagan in *Arena* (1940). On the Playwrights' Company, see John F. Wharton, *Life among the Playwrights* (1974), and S. N. Behrman, *People in a Diary* (1972). An obituary is in the *New York Times*, 9 May 1967.

MALCOLM GOLDSTEIN

RICE, Grantland (1 Nov. 1880–13 July 1954), sports journalist, was born Henry Grantland Rice in Murfreesboro, Tennessee, the son of Bolling Hendon Rice and Beulah Grantland, farmers. He was named for his maternal grandfather, former Confederate major and cotton merchant Henry Grantland, who was an important influence in Rice's childhood. Rice and his parents resided in Henry Grantland's Nashville home for several years before they moved to their own home on Vaughan Pike in eastern Nashville in 1888. In the same year, according to Rice's autobiography, he acquired the instruments that directed his life—his first football, baseball, and glove. While completing his secondary education at the Nashville Military Academy and the Wallace University School, Rice was also an avid participant in baseball and football. In 1897 he began college at Vanderbilt University where he played both sports competitively. Even though his tall, slim frame made him an unlikely football player, and he sustained several serious injuries, the six-foot, 120-pound Rice lettered in varsity football his junior year. As a member and eventually the captain of the Vanderbilt baseball team, Rice was a power hitter and adept shortstop. His talents led to a short stint with a semiprofessional baseball team after graduating from college, but football-related shoulder injuries dashed his hopes for a professional career.

In 1901, at his father's urging, Rice turned to a career in journalism. Although Rice had never written for student publications in college, his interest in sports, his college major in Greek and Latin, and his academic proclivity for the arts rather than the sciences made sports journalism a natural choice. But when Rice went to the *Nashville Daily News* and requested a job as sports editor, he was informed that no such position existed. Although the *Daily News* hired him as a reporter at a salary of $5 per week, Rice's duties were those of a traditional newsman who also wrote about sports. A few months later Rice moved to Washington, D.C., to take a job with *Forester* magazine, but an attack of appendicitis forced him to return to Nashville.

After a brief stint back at the *Daily News*, the ambitious Rice moved through a series of increasingly prestigious and higher-paying positions as sports editor for the *Atlanta Journal*, from 1902 to 1905; the *Cleveland News*, from 1905 to 1906; and the *Nashville Tennessean*, from 1907 to 1910. By the time he moved to Cleveland, Rice's salary had increased tenfold, to $50 per week, which afforded him the financial security to start a family. In 1906 he married Katherine Hollis, whom he had been seeing in Atlanta. According to Rice's autobiography, the young couple spent their wedding night on a Pullman coach car en route to Louisville, where Rice was to begin coverage of the major league baseball season. The Rices had one daughter, Florence, who was born in Cleveland. In 1911 Rice moved to New York City, took a position as a sports writer with the *New York Evening Mail*, and began writing his column, "Sportlight." In 1914 he moved to the *New York Tribune*, where his column was syndicated nationwide. When the United States entered World War I, Rice put his career on hold and volunteered for service in the U.S. Army. In 1918 he was shipped overseas to France as a second lieutenant of artillery. Initially assigned to the army's paper *Stars and Stripes*, the superpatriotic Rice, at his own insistence, joined his unit at the front. Discharged in 1919, Rice returned to the *Tribune* and remained there until 1930, when he joined the National Newspaper Alliance.

In the 1920s, when Rice—or "Granny" as he was known to his contemporaries—returned to sportswriting, he was already well on his way toward becoming as famous as the athletes who inspired his prose. A part-time poet, an enthusiastic fan, and a writer with a penchant for florid, extravagant prose, Rice developed a distinctive style of writing on sports that built players into heroes and portrayed sports contests as great dramas. A central figure in what historians have labeled the "Gee whiz" school of sportswriting, Rice's columns frequently lapsed into poetry, alliteration, or grand literary metaphors that likened sportsmen to classic figures of military or mythical lore. Most famously, when writing on the 1924 Notre Dame–Army game, Rice compared the Notre Dame backfield to the four horsemen of the apocalypse. In the 1920s, a time when professional sports were reaching new heights of popularity, such names became commonplace, contributing to the fame of Rice as well as that of his subjects. Rice also specialized in inventing popular nicknames for famous players, such as the "Big Train" for Walter Johnson and the "Galloping Ghost" for Red Grange. In 1925 he took over the selection of the All-American football team for *Collier's* magazine, a position he would hold for the next twenty-seven years.

Rice's fame as a sports commentator extended to other media as well. He delivered the play-by-play broadcast of the World Series on nationwide radio in 1922 and 1923, and he hosted his own weekly radio show from the 1920s to the 1930s. Rice also helped form Sportlight films, a company that produced hundreds of short films on sports, many of them hosted by Rice himself. Sportlight films earned six Academy Award nominations and twice won in the category of best single reel. Given the great number of activities Rice pursued, he was an astonishingly prolific writer who authored, coauthored, or edited more than a dozen books of prose and poetry in addition to his weekly column. By his own estimate, Rice wrote about 67 million words, consisting of 22,000 columns, 7,000 verses, and 1,000 magazine articles over the course of his career. Rice's most famous, though often misquoted, verse was penned early in his career. Writing on a Vanderbilt alumnus football game in 1908, Rice observed, "When the Great Scorer comes / To mark against your name, / He'll write not 'won' or 'lost' / But how you played the game" (*Nashville Tennessean*, 16 June 1908).

Well liked by his journalistic colleagues and the athletes he covered, Rice's affable and self-effacing manner earned him a lasting reputation for courtesy and humility. Friendships with many of the famous sports figures of his generation permitted Rice an easy access to his subjects that was considered unusual at the end of the twentieth century. His columns and memoirs were spotted with references to golf games and casual conversations with stars such as New York Giants pitcher Christy Mathewson and heavyweight boxing champion Jack Dempsey. Although Rice's style of sportswriting had become somewhat old-fashioned by the end of his life, major newspapers continued to subscribe to his column in the 1950s, and frequent tributes, such as his 1948 appearance on the radio program "This Is Your Life," indicated the degree to which Rice himself had become a sports legend. Rice worked up until the day that he died in New York City.

• Rice's autobiography, *The Tumult and the Shouting: My Life in Sport* (1954), provides an inside look at Rice's career and his ideas about sports. Other essential sources include Charles Fountain, *Sportswriter: The Life and Times of Grantland Rice* (1993), and Mark Inabinett, *Grantland Rice and His Heroes: The Sportswriter as Mythmaker in the 1920s* (1994), both of which provide insight into Rice's popularity and place in the golden age of sports. For a more critical view of Rice's style, see Robert Lipsyte, *Sports World: American Dreamland* (1975). Other important sources on Rice include edited collections of his writings, such as *Sportlights of 1923* (1924) and *The Best of Grantland Rice*, ed. Dave Camerer (1963). Contemporary appraisals of Rice are Stanley Walker, *City Editor* (1934), and Stanley Woodward, *Sports Page* (1949). An obituary is in the *New York Times*, 14 July 1954.
MICHELLE BRATTAIN

RICE, Helen (16 Oct. 1901–22 Apr. 1980), violinist and advocate of chamber music, was born in New York City, the daughter of Edwin T. Rice, a lawyer, and Margaret Rood. From an early age, Helen's musicianship was encouraged by her artistic mother and by her father, an avid amateur cellist. When she was two years old, the family moved to a studio apartment near Central Park; there Helen Rice would spend the rest of her life, leaving it only for the family summer home in Stockbridge, Massachusetts, for occasional trips to Europe, and, during four years in the 1930s, to teach music and run a residence hall at Bryn Mawr College.

Though she began studying violin as a child, Helen's youthful accomplishments were not musical but athletic. Attending Bryn Mawr, she became a major player on nearly every college team. In 1918 and 1919, she won both single and doubles junior titles at the Forest Hills tennis tournament, achieving a national rating. After graduating from Bryn Mawr in 1923, she traveled for most of a year before confronting her father with her determination to find a salaried job. Although she could not shake his conviction that salaried work was unladylike—as well as unfair to the men who might be displaced by it—she became for a while a professional chamber music coach, spending a dozen years out of the next twenty teaching at Bryn Mawr, the Brearley School in New York, and Greenwood Music Camp in Cummington, Massachusetts. Her fa-

ther's disapproval did not prevent him from continuing to support her through his investments and, later, a modest legacy.

Rice's simple beauty and dignity, her friendliness, and her impeccable musicianship attracted hundreds of friends and admirers. At the same time, she frankly conveyed the highest expectations of each person who knew and played with her. As her musical friendships accumulated, Rice became renowned in both New York City and the Berkshire region as an organizer and hostess of chamber music gatherings both large and small. Her diary records the names of 1,150 different musicians, both amateur and professional, with whom she played; most of them returned again and again. Dozens of children and college students also joined her for the special Brandenburg and concerto grosso sessions she held at her New York apartment two or three times each year. Unfortunately, she kept no records of these events.

Rice materially encouraged numbers of professional musicians, seeing amateurs and professionals as "two sides of a single coin: one could not flourish without the other." The Juilliard quartet played an evening of Haydn quartets in her home during her last illness. Before her death, she gave its members first choice of her own and her father's chamber music collection of some 1,500 works.

Although Rice came to know the classical chamber music literature so well that she knew by heart all four parts of the standard string quartets, she was never complacent about her own playing and practiced continually to improve. She also loved gardening, woodworking, and walking in the Berkshire hills. Throughout World War II, she spent virtually every summer morning and afternoon helping a short-handed neighbor milk his cows. She found equal enjoyment in initiating children into chamber music and tennis.

The work of founding and sustaining the Amateur Chamber Music Players, Inc., became Rice's unpaid career after 1947. The ACMP was originally conceived in 1946 by Leonard A. Strauss of Indianapolis, an ardent amateur violinist who found himself too frequently traveling in the service of his family clothing business, away from the chamber music groups of his home city. Strauss wrote to several acquaintances, most of them professionals, asking if they would help to organize a directory of chamber musicians ready to welcome strangers who also played for pleasure. One was the writer Catherine Drinker Bowen, an amateur violinist and a close friend of Rice's. It was through Bowen that Strauss's plan reached Rice. She then did more than anyone to carry it out.

The ACMP was organized as an association in March 1947, with Strauss as chairman and Rice as secretary. Rice insisted from the beginning that there be no mandatory dues, saying that no one should be excluded because of inability to pay. Voluntary donations (with 70–80 percent of the members contributing yearly or biannually) kept the ACMP going. Members rated themselves as "pro," "A," "B," "C," or "D," so that those of like skill could find each other.

Seven years after Strauss's death in 1962, the ACMP was incorporated as a nonprofit charitable organization in New York State. Rice's home continued to serve as the ACMP office; she carried on a correspondence with members and potential members that eventually grew to about 1,000 letters a year. She arranged for the printing of each year's member directory and organized volunteers to address every one. She wrote the group's annual newsletter, collecting anecdotes from the hundreds of members who had enjoyed the hospitality of other musicians or had tendered it with happy result.

Continually signing up the friends she made on her travels abroad and inviting foreign players to stay with her when they visited the United States, Rice was the prime mover in expanding the ACMP's international membership. It grew remarkably fast in the 1950s and 1960s, as idealistic musicians from many nations sought ways to set war and Cold War aside and make new contacts through the language of music.

By 1970 ACMP membership had reached about 5,000, and the volume of routine work had grown proportionately. That year the organization's directors agreed to move the offices out of the Rice apartment and to secure paid parttime assistance in bookkeeping, printing, and mailing. This move gave Rice, the group's most important host and correspondent, more time to bind members together. ACMP membership continued to grow through the last decade of her life; it had doubled in size from about 2,500 in 1950 to about 5,000 verified members in 1980. Rice continued as an active violinist, host, newsletter editor, and letter writer until the last month of her life. Rice died in New York City. She had never married. She was posthumously given Chamber Music America's prestigious Naumburg Award.

In the decade following the death of their founding secretary, the Amateur Chamber Music Players' directors had to nearly double their number in order to continue Rice's essential work for the organization. The objectives of the organization were expanded as well to enlarge the lists of "rarely played but eminently playable" chamber music that she had initiated and to establish a large chamber music collection in her memory under the auspices of the Hartford (Connecticut) Public Library. In 1993 Clinton Ford, an amateur violinist who had played often at the Rice home, left the ACMP over $4 million in his will, allowing the organization to establish a foundation devoted to chamber music education and outreach programs.

• Rice's only formal writing can be found in the 1951–1979 editions of the annual newsletter published by the Amateur Chamber Music Players. Many samples of her enormous volume of correspondence survive in ACMP archives. Shortly after her death, her close friends Ruth Hill McGregor and Rustin McIntosh, M.D., compiled a memorial biography, *Helen Rice: The Great Lady of Chamber Music* (1981). McIntosh's narrative text is twenty-four pages; letters from Rice's friends, many of them unusually frank and detailed, make up the remainder of the book. An obituary is in the *New York Times*, 23 Apr. 1980.

SUSAN M. LLOYD

RICE, Henry Mower (29 Nov. 1816–15 Jan. 1894), Indian trader and commissioner, Minnesota territorial delegate, and U.S. senator, was born in Waitsfield, Vermont, the son of Edmund Rice and Ellen Durkee. After his father died in 1828, Rice lived with the family of Justus Burdick. He completed an academy education and studied law in Rutland, Vermont, before moving to Michigan with the Burdick family in 1835. He worked as a chainman in the surveying of the Sault Ste. Marie Canal and for Kalamazoo merchants until 1839. That year he traveled to St. Louis, Missouri, where he was hired by Kenneth MacKenzie, a prominent commission and forwarding merchant and fur trader, who sent him to Fort Snelling, in present-day Minnesota, to assist the post sutler. The next year he was appointed sutler at the newly created Fort Atkinson near the Winnebago reservation in northeastern Iowa. In 1842 he moved to Prairie du Chien, Wisconsin, to join Hercules L. Dousman, a longtime partner in the Western Outfit of the American Fur Company, in trade with the Winnebago and Ojibwa of the upper Mississippi region. Five years later he was sent to Mendota near Fort Snelling as an agent of Pierre Chouteau, Jr., and Company, the successor of the American Fur Company.

While engaging in the Winnebago and Ojibwa trade, Rice received federal government contracts to remove the Winnebago to their new agency at Long Prairie, Minnesota, and served as a commissioner in making two treaties with Ojibwa bands in 1847. (In 1853 his great influence among the indigenous peoples would be demonstrated again when he persuaded the reluctant Dakota to move to newly established reservations on the upper Minnesota River.) Rice's trading expeditions convinced him that St. Paul would emerge as the metropolis on the upper Mississippi. Consequently, in 1848 he bought eighty acres in the downtown area. The tract for which he paid about $400 was said to have been worth $3 million some forty years later. As one of the most important developers of St. Paul, which became the capital in 1849 when Minnesota Territory was created, he constructed many buildings and donated liberally to hospitals, churches, and the city. He would later, in 1856, found Bayfield, Wisconsin, on the shores of Lake Superior to try to cement St. Paul's trade links with the Great Lakes.

Rice ventured into politics in 1848 when residents of the St. Paul–Stillwater area claimed to be living in the residuum of Wisconsin Territory and were therefore entitled to representation in Congress; he challenged rival fur trader Henry Hastings Sibley for the supposed territorial delegacy. Although he was defeated, Rice enhanced his political stature by lobbying in Washington, D.C., for the creation of Minnesota Territory. On 29 March 1849, he married Matilda Whitall of Richmond, Virginia. The couple had nine children. After seizing the leadership in Minnesota's Democratic party, he succeeded Sibley as territorial delegate in 1853 and was reelected two years later. Rice performed distinguished service during his two terms in the House of Representatives. He acquired federal funds for territorial roads, post offices, and land offices and pleased his land-hungry frontier constituents by persuading Congress to authorize the preemption of unsurveyed lands in Minnesota Territory. Mainly because of his efforts, Congress in 1857 made a generous railroad land grant to Minnesota and approved the Minnesota enabling act. By introducing the enabling act, Rice played the key role in determining Minnesota's boundaries. As an advocate of a north-south state, which bordered Canada, he thwarted many Republicans, who favored an east-west state running from the Mississippi River to the Missouri River with a northern boundary lying a short distance north of St. Paul. Rice believed the north-south state would assure Minnesota's access to Lake Superior, help develop a diversified economy by opening the northern coniferous forest and presumed copper deposits, and preserve the capital for St. Paul. His opponents favored a state devoted to agriculture, which might attract a major east-west railroad and result in the transfer of the capital from the Democratic stronghold of St. Paul to a central location to its southwest.

As Minnesota's most prominent Democrat, Rice was selected by the first legislature to represent the state in the U.S. Senate. Early in his term (1858–1863) he became a business associate and friend of Senator John C. Breckinridge of Kentucky. He supported Breckenridge's presidential bid in 1860, but after the outbreak of the Civil War he was an ardent Unionist. He worked diligently on the Senate's military affairs committee to ensure sufficient recruitment and outfitting of Union forces. Recognizing the dominance of Republicans in Minnesota, he chose not to run for reelection in 1862. However, in 1865, after refusing an invitation to join the Republican party, which probably would have assured his continuance in major political positions, he was an unsuccessful Democratic gubernatorial candidate.

After leaving the Senate, Rice managed his considerable holdings, which included property in St. Paul and Bayfield and railroad investments. A director of four railroads, he was particularly interested in rail links between St. Paul and the Lake Superior ports of Duluth and Bayfield. Consistently active in civic affairs, he served on the University of Minnesota's Board of Regents, as president of the Minnesota Historical Society, as chairman of the St. Paul Chamber of Commerce, and as city treasurer of St. Paul. Because of his long-standing relations with the Minnesota Ojibwa, he was appointed by President Benjamin Harrison to head the U.S. Chippewa (i.e., Ojibwa) Commission. In 1889–1890 his group negotiated settlements with the Minnesota bands (which parceled out tribal lands to individuals) under the provisions of the Dawes Act and also procured additional cessions of Ojibwa land and consolidation of the various bands as authorized by other congressional legislation.

Rice's success in politics and business was generally attributed to his shrewdness and efficiency as well as his gracious manner. His personal charm was effectively complemented by that of his wife. Especially during his senatorial career, when the Rices were neighbors of Breckenridge and Stephen A. Douglas, they were reputed to be among Washington's most genial hosts. As one of Minnesota's most prominent pioneer leaders, Rice was recognized both during and after his life. In 1855 the territorial legislature named a county in his honor, and in 1916 the state legislature selected him as the first Minnesotan to represent the state in the Statuary Hall of the U.S. Capitol. Late in life, when his health was failing, Rice spent summers in Bayfield to enjoy the Lake Superior coolness and winters in San Antonio, Texas, where one of his daughters lived. Stricken with pneumonia, he died in San Antonio.

• The Rice papers are in the Minnesota Historical Society, St. Paul, which also has an unpublished typescript by John Alfton, "Henry Mower Rice" (1932). The most scholarly treatment of Rice is in William Watts Folwell, *A History of Minnesota* (4 vols., 1921–1930). For Rice's role in developing St. Paul, see T. M. Newsom, *Pen Pictures of St. Paul, Minnesota, and Biographical Sketches of Old Settlers* (1886), and J. Fletcher Williams, *A History of the City of Saint Paul and of the County of Ramsey, Minnesota*, vol. 3 of *Collections of the Minnesota Historical Society* (1876). A biographical sketch by Rice's friend and political rival William R. Marshall is in *Collections of the Minnesota Historical Society*, vol. 9 (1901). An obituary is in the *St. Paul Pioneer Press*, 16 Jan. 1894, and tributes including extensive biographical information were published in the newspaper on 28 Jan. 1894.

WILLIAM E. LASS

RICE, Isaac Leopold (22 Feb. 1850–2 Nov. 1915), attorney and entrepreneur, was born in Wachenheim, Bavaria, the son of Mayer Rice, a language tutor, and Fanny Sohn. The family emigrated to Philadelphia about 1855. A brilliant student, Rice at sixteen left Philadelphia's famed Central High School to study music and literature in Paris; at eighteen he became the Paris correspondent for the Philadelphia *Evening Bulletin*. Beginning in 1869 he taught piano, first in London, then in New York, where he also wrote for newspapers and played chess professionally. The publication of two books, *What Is Music?* (1875) and *How Geometrical Lines Have Their Counterparts in Music* (1880), the first an ontological study, the second a mathematical analysis of rhythmic and harmonic motifs, closed his active musical career. Intellectual restlessness led him to Columbia University Law School, where, after taking his law degree in 1880, he became a law instructor and the librarian of Columbia's School of Political Science. In 1886 he left the university to found *The Forum: A Magazine of Politics, Finance, Drama, and Literature*. Rice began *The Forum* as a wedding present to his bride, Julia Hyneman Barnett, whom he had married in 1885; together they edited the influential journal, soon known for a moderately liberal and activist approach to a wide range of cultural and business topics, until 1910.

The cost of raising six children led Rice to practice corporate law as an independent attorney, first in New York, then in other states. Victory in his first big case, an 1886 suit on behalf of the bondholders of a Brooklyn transit company, encouraged him to specialize in the restructuring of debt-ridden railroads such as the St. Louis and Southwestern and the Texas & Pacific. His reorganization of the Richmond and West Point Terminal Railway, of which he became counsel and director, and his consolidation of it with other lines into the Southern Railway earned him considerable wealth but also the enmity of powerful banking houses like J. P. Morgan's. Rice's European connections allowed him to draw on German-Jewish and British-Jewish sources of capital, and the rivalry between those interests and eastern American financial institutions was intense. In 1893, after the directors of the Philadelphia and Reading Railroad elected Rice chairman with a mandate to rescue the ailing corporation, Morgan took advantage of Rice's absence while he was in London seeking funds from Rothschild to adopt the lawyer's own scheme to reorganize the railroad into the Reading Company and to force him out.

Defeat simply pushed Rice into new enterprises. Noticing that most of the numerous electrical inventions he saw at the World's Columbian Exposition of 1893 ran on batteries, Rice bought controlling interest in the Electric Storage Battery Company of Philadelphia, a firm crippled by patent litigation. With capital from German financiers, Rice purchased virtually every battery patent in the United States and formed what he called "cognate companies," that is, those that could use batteries and hold additional electrical patents in the railroad, chemical, and refrigerating industries. The Electric Storage Battery Company was soon vertically integrated with the Quaker City Chemical Company, the Lindstrom Brake Company, the Consolidated Railway Electric Lighting and Equipment Company, the Car Lighting and Power Company, and the Railway and Stationary Refrigerating Company. By 1895 Rice held a monopoly on the chloride battery and annually sold a million dollars' worth of the "Exide," as the brand was named. In a series of chess matches held that same year the energetic entrepreneur also perfected the Rice Gambit, a risky strategy in which white sacrifices a knight; it has not proved popular. While not a grand master, Rice was highly regarded in chess circles for sponsoring tournaments around the world.

In 1897 Rice added to his empire the Electric Vehicle Company (EVC), manufacturer of the electric taxicabs pioneered by Henry G. Morris and Pedro G. Salom, two Philadelphia inventors. He also bought the Consolidated Rubber Tire Company, which furnished the EVC a cheap supply of automobile tires (marketed as the Kelly brand). Rice's electric cabs threatened the New York surface transit monopoly of Thomas F. Ryan and William C. Whitney, the latter a former secretary of the navy. The two had bought the Pope Automobile Company and then, finding that Rice controlled the price of batteries, mounted a proxy battle for the Electric Storage Battery Company. Having learned from his defeat by J. P. Morgan, Rice set in motion a corporate version of his chess gambit. He

"sacrificed" the Electric Storage Battery Company, selling his holdings in that firm for several millions. Only after the sale did Ryan and Whitney learn that Rice had amended the company's by-laws so that it was contractually obligated to sell batteries at cost to Rice's Electric Vehicle Company. That revelation forced Ryan and Whitney to buy the EVC as well, for an additional inflated cost of $2 million. Rice then checkmated Whitney, who had his eye on John P. Holland's submarine patents, by buying the rights himself and creating the Electric Boat Company. Between 1900 and 1906 Rice bought the Electro-Dynamic Company (manufacturer of electric motors), the Electric Launch Company (maker of luxury yachts), the Industrial Oxygen Company (supplier of compressed air), and the National Torpedo Company, and built three additional industrial research companies with more than 600 mechanical, marine, and armament patents, integrating all of these enterprises with Electric Boat to corner the market on submarines. As a sideline, he founded a second monopoly, the Casein Company of America, whose entire product was consumed by its paint, paper-sizing, and glue subsidiaries.

The U.S. Navy bought a dozen submarines between 1900 and 1905, and Japan purchased another four in 1904, but the contracts barely covered the cost of the complex vessels, and Rice began licensing construction to France, Russia, Portugal, the Netherlands, Austro-Hungary, Great Britain, and Germany. Although these agreements required the foreign licensing companies to put up all the capital and to pay most of the profits to Electric Boat, the banker's panic of 1907 compelled Rice to sell shares in Electric Boat to the Vickers Sons and Maxim Company of Britain. Rumors of excessive foreign investment in Electric Boat, of influence peddling and political corruption, and of Rice's increasing involvement in the international arms trade resulted in a congressional investigation in 1908. Rice spent all his political capital ensuring that the House report was equivocal. Tired of business, Rice returned to the arts; he launched the Poetry Society of America in 1910 and, ironically, considering his enterprises, the Peace Society in 1912. Patent litigation and weak demand for submarines eroded Electric Boat's finances. On 22 September 1914, however, the German U-9, modified from original Holland designs, torpedoed three British cruisers off the Dutch coast. American neutrality notwithstanding, Rice filled a British admiralty order for twenty submarines before illness forced him to step down as president of Electric Boat. He sold his stock just as the price began to soar and died in New York City before unrestricted submarine warfare brought the United States into the war. In 1952, thirty-seven years after Rice's death, the Electric Boat Company and its subsidiaries became the General Dynamics Corporation.

• Most of Rice's papers have disappeared, although some are in the archives of General Dynamics. Of the many articles Rice himself wrote, two are notable, "Suggestions for

Amendments to Our Patent Law," *The Forum*, Mar. 1909, pp. 193–98, and "A Remedy for Railway Abuses," *North American Review*, Feb. 1882, pp. 134–48. The most comprehensive study of Rice is Joseph W. Slade, "Bringing Invention to the Marketplace," *American Heritage of Invention and Technology* 2 (Spring 1987): 8–15. Rice receives only brief mention in the official history of General Dynamics, *Dynamic America* (1960), ed. J. Niven et al. Better accounts of his diverse enterprises are contained in Samuel Wyman Rolphe, *Exide, the Development of an Engineering Idea: A Brief History of the Electric Storage Battery Company* (1951); John B. Rae, "The Electric Vehicle Company: A Monopoly That Missed," *Business History Review*, Dec. 1955, pp. 298–311; Charles Edward Russell, *Lawless Wealth* (1908); Richard Knowles Morris, *John P. Holland, 1841–1914: Inventor of the Modern Submarine* (1966); Frank T. Cable, *The Birth and Development of the Modern Submarine* (1924); John Dick Scott, *Vickers: A History* (1962); and J. Herbert Duckworth, "A War-made Millionaire," *American Magazine*, Jan. 1916, pp. 48–49. The best account of Rice's editorship of *The Forum* is "Our Thirty-fifth Anniversary," *The Forum*, Jan. 1921, pp. 104–8. *The American Chess Bulletin* published a special supplement to vol. 12 (Dec. 1915) as a memorial to Rice; and two editions of *The Rice Gambit*, ed. S. Lipshutz (1898) and E. Lasker (1910), analyze Rice's chess strategies. Rice's testimony on railroad reorganization can be found in *Report of the Industrial Commission*, vol. 9 (1901), pp. 737–40, and on Electric Boat in *Report of the Select Committee Appointed Pursuant to House Resolution 288*, 60th Cong. (1908). An obituary is in the *New York Times*, 3 Nov. 1915.

JOSEPH W. SLADE

RICE, John Andrew (1 Feb. 1888–17 Nov. 1968), educator and author, was born in Lynchburg, South Carolina, the son of John Andrew Rice, a Methodist minister, and Anna Bell Smith. During his childhood, Rice moved with his family to various towns in South Carolina, where his father was assigned to Methodist churches. After his mother died when he was twelve, Rice was sent to Webb School, a coeducational preparatory academy in Bell Buckle, Tennessee, where his formal schooling and his ideas about education began. His relationship with masterful teacher John Webb led him to a lifelong commitment to Socratic questioning in the classroom and to a conviction that the teacher is the most important factor in the educational process.

Rice observed firsthand a range of early twentieth-century postsecondary educational philosophies. He received bachelor's degrees from Tulane University (1911) and from Oxford University as a Rhodes Scholar (1914), where he achieved first honors in law; he studied for, but never received, a Ph.D. in classics at the University of Chicago (1916–1918). He taught Latin and Greek at Webb School (1914–1916), at the University of Nebraska (1919–1927), and at the New Jersey College for Women (1927–1929). After a year in England on a Guggenheim fellowship, he joined the faculty at Rollins College in Winter Park, Florida. He married Nell Aydelotte, the sister of Frank Aydelotte, president of Swarthmore College, in 1914, and they had two children.

Rice's three years at Rollins were marked by frequent displays of brilliance, humor, and insensitive candor. Students applauded his Socratic approach when it led them to challenge assumptions and define values, but many also viewed his manner as arrogant and abrasive. Colleagues were polarized by his determination to voice his opinions honestly, no matter how stinging they might be. In 1933 Rollins president Hamilton Holt terminated Rice's appointment. A highly publicized investigation by the American Association of University Professors eventually exonerated Rice and censured the college. During the investigation several of Rice's supportive colleagues also were fired and several others resigned. Some of these joined with Rice to plan a new college.

In September 1933 the group opened Black Mountain College, near Asheville, North Carolina, an experimental and coeducational liberal arts school that became noted for its commitment to individualized programs of study, creative expression in the classroom, development of artistic abilities to support learning in any subject, and establishment of a living and learning community among faculty and students. It embodied an educational philosophy Rice described in an article for *Harper's* (May 1937): "Education, instead of being the acquisition of a common stock of fundamental ideas, may well be a learning of a common way of doing things, a way of approach, a method of dealing with ideas or anything else. What you do with what you know is the important thing. To know is not enough."

The college, with Rice as its "rector," was in the vanguard of progressive educational experiments that included no letter grades, no board of trustees, student representation in policymaking, outside examiners to administer comprehensive examinations for graduation, and four years divided into lower and upper divisions. Rice was the first to bring a German Bauhaus master to the United States when he hired Josef Albers to head the college art program in 1933. Albers agreed with Rice that the practice of art was essential not only for future artists but also for all students as experience in process, discipline, and observation. Rice insisted that "the job of a college is to bring young people to intellectual and emotional maturity; to intelligence, . . . not merely to an arbitrarily selected amount of cramming" (Adamic, p. 615).

Rice frequently spoke and wrote about education, including an angry debate in *Harper's* with Robert Maynard Hutchins during 1936 and 1937. At Black Mountain many of his colleagues and students viewed him as brilliant but insensitive. One student, Morton Steinau, later characterized him as "charismatic, direct, and often demeaning" (interview with author, 1993). In 1940 the faculty asked for his resignation. Rice left the college, began a new career as a writer, and was divorced from his first wife (date unknown). In 1942 he married Dikka Moen, with whom he had two children. Black Mountain closed in 1956 for a variety of reasons, including lack of funds and student recruitment, faculty departures, and mismanagement.

Rice's autobiography, *I Came Out of the Eighteenth Century*, was published in 1942 to critical acclaim and won him the Harper and Brothers 125th Anniversary Prize. He wrote short stories for the *New Yorker, Collier's, Harper's,* and other publications, many focusing on race relations in the South. He wrote for the Carnegie Corporation anthology, *American Panorama* (1957), and he served as a consultant to the Guggenheim Foundation. *Local Color,* a collection of his short stories, was published in 1955. Rice died in Silver Spring, Maryland.

John Andrew Rice provided, through Black Mountain College, a case study of the implementation of progressive ideals in higher education. His commitment to placing artistic practice in the general curriculum was particularly innovative, and his writing about the aims and means of education enriches ongoing debate and discussion.

• Papers concerning John Andrew Rice are in the North Carolina State Archives (Black Mountain College Papers), the Rollins College Archives, and the Swarthmore College Archives (Aydelotte papers). A revised edition of Rice's autobiography was published in 1957. Two books about Black Mountain College that include discussions of Rice's founding role and early influence are Martin Duberman, *Black Mountain: An Exploration in Community* (1972), and Mary Harris, *The Arts at Black Mountain College* (1987). For Rice's discussion of his educational philosophies, see Louis Adamic, *My America* (1938), and Rice himself in "Fundamentalism and the Higher Learning," *Harper's,* May 1937, pp. 572–82. Biographical detail about Rice is in Katherine C. Reynolds, "Visions and Vanities: The Educational Biography of John Andrew Rice" (Ph.D. diss., Univ. of Utah, 1994).

KATHERINE C. REYNOLDS

RICE, John Holt (28 Nov. 1777–3 Sept. 1831), Presbyterian pastor, educator, and ecumenist, was born near New London, Virginia, the son of Benjamin Rice, a lawyer, deputy clerk of court, and Presbyterian elder, and Catharine Holt, a distant relative of the Presbyterian revivalist Samuel Davies. Rice was also the nephew of the Anglican clergyman John Holt and the Presbyterian pastor David Rice. His mother died in 1789, when he was twelve, and his father soon married the widow of Patrick Henry's brother. For about eighteen months each, Rice studied under William Graham at Liberty Hall Academy (later Washington and Lee University) and at George Baxter's academy in New London.

Rice began his early career as a teacher. At age eighteen he conducted a family school at Malvern Hills, thirty miles downriver from Richmond. In 1796 Hampden-Sydney College hired nineteen-year-old Rice as a tutor, but he left in 1799 for successive positions in the family schools of Major James Morton of Willington and Josiah Smith of Montrose. He briefly studied medicine but returned to Hampden-Sydney in 1800.

In 1802 he married a former Willington student, Anne Smith Morton. She survived him, and they had no children. Shortly before his marriage, Rice began private theological studies under mentor and friend Archibald Alexander. On 8 September 1803 Hanover Presbytery licensed Rice to preach at the three-point parish of Cub Creek Presbyterian Church in Charlotte County, and they ordained him on 29 September 1804. Rice served there until 1812.

He undertook several other activities to supplement his salary as a part-time pastor. He farmed, opened a boy's school in his home, and frequently contributed to the *Virginia Religious Magazine.* In 1805 and 1810 Rice represented Hanover Presbytery at the General Assembly of the Presbyterian Church; the General Assembly repeatedly appointed him as a missionary to Charlotte County blacks for two or three months at a time. From 1806 to 1808 he solicited books and money for Hanover Presbytery's proposed seminary. As his sermons at Cub Creek became less "learned" and "argumentative" and more popular, the parish grew from barely 100 to nearly 500 members.

On 12 March 1812, the First Presbyterian Church in Richmond called Rice as its organizing pastor. He served there for twelve years, combining his influential position as pastor with a career as an editor and ecumenist. Within weeks of his arrival in Richmond in early May, colleagues urged him to begin a periodical. Rice acquiesced and edited the weekly (later biweekly) *Christian Monitor* from 8 July 1815 to 30 August 1817. He edited its successor, the monthly *Virginia Evangelical and Literary Magazine,* from its 1818 debut to its 1828 demise. In 1819 he established and operated a printing press for Christian literature.

Rice established and supported a variety of ecumenical protestant organizations for what he described in the first issue of the *Christian Monitor* as "the promotion of vital piety." He founded the Virginia Bible Society in 1813 and later urged its auxiliary societies to join him as founding delegates of the American Bible Society in 1816. His 1819 impromptu speech led to the establishment of the "Young Men's Missionary Society of Richmond," a voluntary society whose dues continued to support home missionaries throughout Virginia until 1864. He championed the founding of the University of Virginia, but he diverged from Thomas Jefferson's design by proposing that its faculty be endowed and nominated by their respective Jewish, Catholic, or Protestant organizations. Rice consistently supported the American Colonization Society but eventually despaired of a political solution to slavery; in a 24 February 1827 letter to William Maxwell he described slavery as "the greatest evil in our country, except whiskey," but concluded that "the only possible chance of deliverance is by *making the people willing to get rid of it.*"

Rice gained national prominence in the Presbyterian church. He represented Hanover Presbytery again at the 1816 General Assembly. In 1819 the General Assembly elected him moderator, asked him to preach a missionary sermon, named him to a committee to investigate the state of religion in Europe, and elected him as a director of the (Princeton) Theological School. He preached the opening sermon at the 1820 General Assembly, urging the delegates "to hold fast unto death the great and precious doctrines of the gospel; and at the same time to let little things pass for little things." After he attended the 1822 Assembly, he took a three-month tour of New England to represent the Presbyterian church at the Connecticut and Massachusetts Congregational Associations and visit the theological faculty at Yale, Andover, and Harvard.

Rice is credited with founding Union Theological Seminary in Virginia. His earlier fundraising efforts led to the engagement of Moses Hoge as theology professor at Hampden-Sydney, but Hoge's death in 1820 left the project defunct. On 26 September 1822 the College of New Jersey (later Princeton University) unanimously elected him president. Before he could respond, on 11 November 1822 he was unanimously named professor of theology at Hampden-Sydney. In a 5 March 1823 letter to Archibald Alexander he declined the Princeton position, explaining that "it would at once be said, 'Ah! this is what his love to Virginia has come to. Northern gold has bought him, and it can buy any of them.' And thus my influence at the South would be greatly lessened, if not destroyed." He resigned from First Presbyterian Church on 2 June 1823 and assumed his new duties at Hampden-Sydney on 1 January 1824. The theology department soon became a separate but affiliated school and was renamed Union Theological Seminary (relocated to Richmond in 1896).

During Rice's tenure, Union Seminary became firmly established. It acquired a healthy endowment and the support of the Synods of Virginia and North Carolina. It added three instructors and grew to nearly fifty students. Three new buildings included two new faculty residences, named North Carolina House and Boston House after their respective benefactors; and a new hall to house a library, a chapel, three lecture rooms, and rooms for fifty students.

In 1830 Rice wrote a series of anonymous open letters to James Madison in the *Southern Religious Telegraph*, arguing that the progress of the Christian religion was in the best interest of the country. That same year he delivered the "Murray Street Lectures" in New York; both were later published. The next year, during an extended illness, he drafted a proposal that became the basis for the 1837 creation of the Presbyterian Board of Foreign Missions. His illness persisted for several months, and he died at his Hampden-Sydney home, surrounded by his family and students.

His colleagues remembered Rice as an advocate for religious liberty and Christian unity. Rice once lamented, "When will the time come when the churches will have peace among themselves? I am sick to the heart of controversy" (Maxwell, p. 50). Archibald Alexander's son James lamented that "No man of the South was so well known in New England" as John Holt Rice (*Annals of the American Pulpit*, vol. 4, p. 335). The president of Andover Theological Seminary, Leonard Woods, described his respect for Rice in a 30 October 1832 letter to William Maxwell: "I never knew a man who had more zeal for the great truths of the gospel, or less zeal for unessential matters, or less bitterness against those who, in such matters differed from him. I never knew a man who showed less selfishness, or a more pure, disinterested attachment to the cause of the church."

• Rice's papers are located at Union Theological Seminary in Virginia, the Presbyterian Church (U.S.A.) Department of History (Montreat), the North Carolina State Archives, and the Historical Society of Pennsylvania. Rice preached from sketchy notes and left few sermon manuscripts, but he wrote extensively (and often anonymously) for the journals that he edited. Many of his letters are included in William Maxwell's *Memoir of the Rev. John H. Rice, D.D.* (1835) and in Julius W. Melton, "Pioneering Presbyter: A Collection and Analysis of the Letters of John Holt Rice" (master's thesis, Union Theological Seminary, 1959). His publications are inventoried in Morton H. Smith's *Studies in Southern Presbyterian Theology* (1962).

Biographies include Maxwell's *Memoir* and a series of 1886–1887 articles in the *Central Presbyterian* reprinted as P. B. Price, *The Life of the Reverend John Holt Rice, D.D.* (1963). W. H. Foote, *Sketches of Virginia: Historical and Biographical* (1850 and 1855) and E. T. Thompson, *Presbyterians in the South: Volume I, 1607–1861* (1963), place Rice in historical context. Significant explorations of Rice's life and thought include David E. Swift, "Thomas Jefferson, John Holt Rice, and Education in Virginia, 1815–25," *Journal of Presbyterian History* 49, no. 1 (Spring 1971): 32–58; and Louis B. Weeks III, "John Holt Rice and the American Colonization Society," *Journal of Presbyterian History* 46 (Mar. 1968): 26–41.

DAVID B. MCCARTHY

RICE, Joseph Mayer (20 May 1857–24 June 1934), physician, journal editor, and education critic, was born in Philadelphia, Pennsylvania, the son of Mayer Rice, a private tutor of languages, and Fanny Sohn. Rice's parents had emigrated from Bavaria in 1855 and had settled in the German community in Philadelphia. Rice attended public schools in Philadelphia until 1870, when the family moved to New York City. He finished his secondary education in the public school system there and then attended the City College of New York. In 1881 Rice received a degree in medicine from the College of Physicians and Surgeons of Columbia University. After practicing in local hospitals for a three-year period, in 1884 Rice established a successful private practice in pediatrics. During this period he became interested in the physical fitness programs offered by the New York City schools.

In 1888 Rice left his medical practice and traveled to Germany, where for the next two years he studied psychology and pedagogy at the universities in Jena and Leipzig. In addition, he traveled throughout Europe observing school systems and pedagogical practices. While the impetus for Rice's decision to leave his successful medical practice and travel to Germany to study education is a topic of speculation, his actions were in keeping with numerous American academics and educators who traveled to Germany to learn the rudiments of empirical research and the foundations for scientific pedagogy. Rice would observe the first laboratory of experimental psychology, directed by Wilhelm Wundt in Leipzig, and became fully introduced to Herbartism as it was taught at the University of Jena and its laboratory school. The theories of German philosopher Johann Friedrich Herbart, who viewed the purpose of education to develop character, greatly influenced American education during the late nineteenth and early twentieth centuries; based on them, the American movement formalized a very specific curricular and instructional method. Rice, who never matriculated in Germany, was viewed as a Herbartian by American educators, although his writings do not necessarily suggest this narrow a view.

Rice returned to the United States in 1890 with strong beliefs concerning the improvement of elementary education. In 1891 he first presented his views in an interview in *Epoch*, a New York City weekly, and in an article for the *Forum*, a New York monthly magazine owned by Rice's brother Isaac Leopold Rice. Rice's recommendations for American education involved better training of teachers, a curriculum based on sound psychological principles, and the scientific management of education, in which clearly defined goals and standards mandated the scientific measurement of outcomes.

Forum's editor became intrigued with Rice's German experiences and his critique of American schools and, seeing an opportunity to publicly expose a little-examined system, proposed that Rice conduct a school survey-study tour for the *Forum*. Rice began the project on 7 January 1892 and proceeded over the next six months to travel to thirty-six cities, visiting six to eight schools in each city. He observed classrooms, talked to approximately 1,200 teachers, met with school officials and school boards, interviewed parents, and visited twenty teacher-training institutions. A specific focus of Rice's was the comparison of traditional schools, with their narrow curricula and recitation, with that of the progressive "new pedagogy" of modern schools, characterized by an integrated approach to curriculum and instruction. Rice devoted the summer of 1892 to writing up his observations and data; from October 1892 to June 1893 the *Forum* published a series of nine articles by Rice.

As foreseen by Page, the exposé created an electrifying reaction among a public that had previously had much faith in the educational system. Rice's articles reported some of the most tedious, pedantic teaching imaginable in the traditional schools. He described unassisted superintendents responsible for the supervision of hundreds of teachers, and he quoted at length from board of education reports portraying the deplorable conditions of schools and the senselessness and ineffectiveness of educational practices. The general public became outraged at educators with each succeeding *Forum* essay. Noted twentieth-century historian Lawrence Cremin has described professional educators' reactions to Rice as ranging from "chilling disdain to near-hysteria." Rice's articles earned him a reputation for bringing the topic of schooling to the public's eye and, in so doing, introducing "muckraking" to the field of education.

Rice undertook a second survey tour in the spring of 1893 (while the first series of articles was still being published). This tour lasted only five weeks and, instead of exposing the deplorable conditions of education at the traditional schools as did the first survey, Rice investigated those schools deemed to represent New Education (progressive education). He visited schools in Indianapolis, Minneapolis, St. Paul, La Porte (Ind.), and Cook County (Ill.). This study was reported in *The Public-School System of the United States* (1893) along with the original *Forum* essays and continued Rice's critique of "unscientific or mechanical schools" and his faith in the boundless promise of scientific progress.

Rice traveled to Jena in the summer of 1893 and, upon returning to the United States, continued to visit schools. In February 1895 he embarked on another *Forum*-sponsored tour of classrooms. However, this time he conducted a school/student survey—often considered the first comparative test ever used in American education or psychology. This sixteen-month survey examined nearly 33,000 fourth- to eighth-grade children, tabulating age, nationality, environment, and type of school system. One aspect of the test results involved the pedagogy of spelling, deemed by Rice the "futility of the spelling grind"; he concluded that there was no correlation between the amount of spelling drill and the degree of success in the actual act of spelling. This comparative test was widely applauded and, while the results were not universally supported by educators, Rice received acknowledgment for helping to initiate the movement that advocated objective study of education. Stemming from this work are Rice's works *The Rational Spelling Book* (1898) and *Scientific Management in Education* (1913). *The Rational Spelling Book* was largely ignored, but Rice's methods portrayed a scientific and progressive methodology for the pedagogy of spelling and the "passing of the recitation"—a methodology that was well ahead of its time.

By early 1896 Rice had assumed many of the *Forum*'s editorial responsibilities, and in 1897 he became the editor, remaining in that capacity until 1907. Unfortunately, Rice was unable to maintain the *Forum*'s level of circulation, and in 1902 the journal changed from a monthly to a quarterly publication. Rice retired to Philadelphia in 1915, the same year that he published his last book, *The People's Government*. At this time Rice withdrew from public involvement in education. He devoted the last eighteen years of his life to writing, but no manuscripts were published. Rice had married Deborah Levinson in 1900; they had two children. He died in Philadelphia.

• Rice's unpublished manuscripts are housed in the special collections of the Milbank Memorial Library, Teachers College, Columbia University. His *Forum* articles are excerpted in sections of Lawrence Cremin, *The Transformation of the School* (1961), and in Herbert Kliebard, *The Struggle for the American Curriculum* (1986). One of the more provocative analyses of the significance of Rice's work is in Robert M. W. Travers, *How Research Has Changed American Schools*

(1983). See also C. M. E. Houston, "Joseph Mayer Rice: Pioneer in Educational Research" (M.A. thesis, Univ. of Wisconsin, Madison, 1965). An obituary is in the *New York Times*, 25 June 1935.

CRAIG KRIDEL

RICE, Luther (25 Mar. 1783–25 Sept. 1836), Baptist missionary and missionary agent, was born in Northborough, Massachusetts, the son of Amos Rice and Sarah Graves, farmers. He grew up on the family farm and in March 1802 joined the local Congregational church. Rice became an avid reader of classic and popular religious books. In 1805 he entered Leicester Academy and in 1807 matriculated at Williams College. While there, he helped to organize a prayer society called the Brethren, who were devoted to foreign missions. While still enrolled at Williams College, he jointly enrolled in Andover Theological Seminary. In the summer of 1810 Massachusetts ministers organized the American Board of Commissioners for Foreign Missions to support foreign missionaries. In August 1810 Rice graduated from Williams College and asked Rebecca Eaton to marry him. She initially accepted but later refused to become the wife of a foreign missionary. Both of them remained unmarried for the rest of their lives. In January 1812 the American Board of Commissioners appointed four men from among the Brethren to be their first missionaries. Rice wished to join the group, a request granted with the stipulation that he raise his own funds. Successful at procuring support, he was commissioned with the others in a service at Salem, Massachusetts, on 6 February 1812.

The missionaries left Philadelphia, Pennsylvania, aboard two ships in February and arrived in Calcutta, India, in August 1812. Aboard the ship, Rice spent much of his time discussing the issue of baptism with another passenger, British Baptist missionary William Johns. Soon after Rice arrived in Calcutta, he learned that one of his fellow Massachusetts missionaries, Adoniram Judson, had converted to the Baptist position. After struggling with the issue further, Rice was baptized by immersion on 1 November 1812 by British Baptist missionary William Ward. A few weeks later the British colonial governor informed the American missionaries that they could no longer remain in India. Rice and Judson decided that Rice should return to the United States to explain their change of beliefs and secure support from the Baptists for their missionary labors. Judson and his wife were to begin missionary work in Burma, where Rice would join them after his trip back to the United States.

Rice reached New York City in September 1813 and informed the Congregationalists of his and Judson's change of views. Instead of returning to the foreign mission field, however, Rice became a missionary agent. For the next two decades, he traveled throughout the country promoting missions and education among Baptists, while simultaneously laying the foundations for national Baptist unity. While traveling in Virginia, Rice determined that a national organization was necessary to sustain these efforts. In May 1814 Baptist delegates met in Philadelphia and organized the General Missionary Convention of the Baptist Denomination in the United States of America, for Foreign Missions, popularly known as the Triennial Convention. Rice became the official agent of the convention, the first national body of Baptists in America. While many Baptists applauded Rice's efforts on behalf of foreign missions, detractors questioned his failure to return to Asia as a missionary himself.

At its 1817 meeting, the Triennial Convention began to expand its function to include support for domestic missions to Indians, slaves, and settlers in frontier regions. The convention also started to promote religious publications and higher education. In 1818 Rice became the founding editor of the Triennial Convention's monthly periodical, *Latter Day Luminary*. Four years later he established the *Columbian Star*, a Baptist weekly newspaper published in Washington, D.C. Rice also served as treasurer of the Baptist General Tract Society, organized in 1824, a precursor of the American Baptist Publication Society. He was also instrumental in the founding of Columbian College (George Washington University after 1903), which opened in 1821 in Washington, D.C.

As the purposes of the Triennial Convention multiplied, support waned and opposition to Rice, one of the chief architects of this expansion, intensified. Baptists in the South generally favored the broader initiative and Rice's labors, but New England Baptists insisted that the convention should be devoted solely to the promotion of foreign missions. Poor planning and inadequate support quickly led Columbian College into deep debt. At the 1826 meeting of the Triennial Convention, the majority of delegates were from New England and New York. The convention, under their control, voted to return to exclusive concentration on foreign missions; domestic missions and education were left to other Baptist societies. The national organization investigated Rice's disorganized financial records and severed its relationship with Columbian College. Although it found Rice guilty of no immorality, the convention dismissed him as agent because of his financial "indiscretions."

For the last decade of his life, Rice traveled thousands of miles each year as an itinerant, raising money among Baptists for Columbian College. He spent most of this time in the South, the region where he was most popular. He died near Edgefield, South Carolina; long years of travel and old illnesses, aggravated by appendicitis, led to his death.

Rice was instrumental in the creation of the first national body of Baptists. His efforts in support of foreign missions, domestic missions, and publication efforts yielded institutions that bound American Baptists together for a generation. However, the controversies that arose over his ambitious plans for coordinated denominational effort helped to create sectional animosities that destroyed national Baptist unity in 1844–1845.

• Rice produced no published works, but portions of his manuscript journals as well as numerous letters have survived in two major collections at the American Baptist Historical Society in Rochester, N.Y., and at George Washington University in Washington, D.C. William H. Brackney edited many of these materials for his *Dispensations of Providence: The Journal and Selected Letters of Luther Rice, 1803–1830* (1984). James B. Taylor published the first biography of Rice, *Memoir of Rev. Luther Rice, One of the First American Missionaries to the East* (1840), which contains many letters to and from Rice. Edward B. Pollard and Daniel G. Stevens, *Luther Rice, Pioneer in Missions and Education* (1928), is a brief biography. Rice's role in the establishment of Columbian College is the subject of Elmer Louis Keyser, *Luther Rice: Founder of Columbian College* (1966). A complete biography is Evelyn W. Thompson, *Luther Rice: Believer in Tomorrow* (1967). Michael T. Justus, "Ties That Bind? Baptists and the First Church System in America, 1784–1830" (Ph.D. diss., Univ. of Florida, 1993), explores Rice's role in the creation and the demise of national Baptist unity.

DANIEL W. STOWELL

RICE, Oscar Knefler (12 Feb. 1903–7 May 1978), physical chemist, was born in Chicago, Illinois, the son of Oscar Guido Rice and Thekla Knefler. The elder Rice died before the birth of his son, who was raised by his mother and his aunt Amy Knefler. He received a B.S. and a Ph.D. in chemistry from the University of California at Berkeley in 1924 and 1926, respectively. Following several years of postdoctoral appointments at California Institute of Technology, the University of Leipzig, and the University of California, he joined the faculty of Harvard University as instructor of chemistry in 1930 and then moved to the University of North Carolina as associate professor of chemistry in 1936. In 1946–1947 he was principal chemist at the Oak Ridge Laboratory in Tennessee, where he met Hope Ernestyne Sherfy, whom he married in 1947. The Rices adopted two daughters, both born in Germany.

From 1959 until his retirement in 1975 Rice was Kenan Professor at UNC, after which he became Kenan Professor Emeritus. He also held the Stewart Lectureship at the University of Missouri in 1948, the Reilly Lectureship at the University of Notre Dame in 1957, the Barton Lectureship at the University of Oklahoma in 1967, the Robert A. Welch Foundation Lectureship in 1971, and the Distinguished Lectureship at Howard University that same year. He remained vigorously active in his scientific work until shortly before he died in Chapel Hill, North Carolina. An award conferred on him posthumously by UNC in 1978 described him as "very likely the most distinguished chemist ever to have lived in North Carolina."

To physical chemists of the last half-century, Rice is best known for his contributions to the theory of unimolecular reactions: the process by which a molecule acquires enough energy in a succession of collisions with other, dissimilar molecules or atoms to dissociate into smaller molecular fragments. He first addressed this problem in 1926–1927 while in Berkeley to explain measurements by Herman C. Ramsperger, also at the University of California, on the thermal decomposition of azomethane. Rice and Ramsperger first formulated a classical mechanical description of the process. After discussions with Louis S. Kassel at Caltech, Rice and Kassel reformulated the problem in quantum mechanical terminology, and for years the theory was known as the RRK (Rice-Ramsperger-Kassel) theory (later renamed the RRKM theory after refinements to the theory in 1951 with Rudolph A. Marcus). The theory has been one of the physical chemist's most useful tools in predicting the rates and products of reactions or extrapolating rates to temperatures and pressures beyond the range of experimental measurements.

During the late 1920s Rice also contributed pioneering work on the subject of predissociation—the process by which molecules can dissociate under conditions that would at first seem to provide insufficient energy to split them apart—and diffuse spectra—the impact such a process has on the spectrum of the molecule. In 1932 Russian physicist Lev Landau noted that Rice had been the only one until then who correctly recognized the role that the interaction of multiple potential energy surfaces played in the process, and later evaluations also praised his early insights. In the 1960s Rice made important contributions to what was then a lively topic among chemical kineticists, namely the validity of the commonly used simplification known as the "steady state assumption" in determining the relationship between the forward and reverse rate coefficients for a series of chemical reactions and the equilibrium constants for those processes. Prior to the ubiquity of high-speed computers and sophisticated numerical programs, this technique greatly facilitated the interpretation of the behavior of complex chemical systems that involve many reactions.

In 1934–1935, with Harold Gershinowitz at Harvard, Rice published several papers contributing to the early development of transition-state theory, thereafter the leading theoretical description of the mechanism that accounts for the rates of chemical reactions. Rice continued to address this topic well into the 1960s. From the 1950s, though, his major focus was on the problem of phase transitions and critical phenomena—the details accompanying the process whereby a liquid transforms into a gas, a solid into a liquid, or the reverse of these. In 1955 he was the first to demonstrate that compressibility, specific heat, and the shape of the coexistence curve (the set of pressures and temperatures for which the liquid and vapor phases of a pure component are in equilibrium) are thermodynamically related to one another.

In the early 1940s, in another area of physical chemistry, Rice was the first to treat seriously the fundamental problem of determining intermolecular forces from the properties of bulk materials. In 1942–1944 he was also among the earliest researchers to recognize the usefulness of a simple hard-sphere model in solving the problem of the structures of simple liquids.

Rice's career was long and productive. According to an oft-recounted anecdote from his days at Oak Ridge, "the Army officer in charge of the laboratory was much concerned about the productivity of this man who sat all day in an armchair thinking. When it was time to review what had been produced, the quality of the work that Dr. Rice had generated in the armchair was so impressive that the officer recommended stuffed armchairs for every scientist whom he supervised" (Bursey, p. 151). Rice's prolific publication record of more than 180 articles and essays also included two books, *Electronic Structure and Chemical Bonding: With Special Reference to Inorganic Chemistry* (1940; repr. 1969) and *Statistical Mechanics, Thermodynamics, and Kinetics* (1967).

Rice was highly regarded by colleagues and students as a generous and supportive mentor and accomplished scientist. He was outspoken in defending the civil rights of many unpopular individuals or groups: "He is remembered for his concern for the rights and freedoms of people everywhere, for his tolerance, for his patience with persons with whom he disagreed, for his unwillingness to be reconciled to injustice. . . . [He] championed scholars who were denied academic freedom, he worked for the elimination of racial segregation, he defended the rights of all citizens to freedom of expression and action in the redress of grievances" (UNC Faculty Council Memorial Statement, 15 Sept. 1978). For example, he vigorously worked to secure justice for convicted atom spies Julius and Ethel Rosenberg but also defended the right of the Ku Klux Klan to hold an outdoor meeting.

Rice accumulated numerous honors and awards during his distinguished career. In 1932 he became the second recipient of the American Chemical Society's Award in Pure Chemistry. He received the Southern Chemist Award in 1961; the North Carolina Award in Science in 1966; an award from the Florida section of the ACS in 1967; the ACS's Debye Award in 1970; and the ACS's Charles H. Stone Award (Carolina-Piedmont section) in 1973.

• The most useful sources on Rice are the biography by Benjamin Widom and Rudolph A. Marcus in National Academy of Sciences, *Biographical Memoirs* 58 (1989): 425–56; Widom, "*In Memorium*: Oscar Knefler Rice, 1903–1978," *Journal of Statistical Physics* 21 (1979): 341; a University of North Carolina Faculty Council Memorial Statement, prepared by Rice's colleagues W. F. Little, E. Merzbacher, J. C. Morrow, R. G. Parr, and J. W. Straley (15 Sept. 1978); and a biographical sketch by Maurice M. Bursey in his anecdotal departmental history, *Carolina Chemists: Sketches from Chapel Hill*, University of North Carolina Dept. of Chemistry (1982), pp. 150–53.

NORM COHEN

RICE, Sam (20 Feb. 1890–13 Oct. 1974), major league baseball player, was born Edgar Charles Rice in Morocco, Indiana, the son of Charles Rice and Louise Christine Newmyre, farmers. Rice attended only a few years of school in Iroquois County, Illinois, where the family moved soon after his birth. Classmates remembered him as a good athlete and fast runner who loved baseball, but one whose family experienced many tragedies, including deaths, fires, and crop failures.

Rice married Beulah Stam in 1908 and moved to Watseka, Illinois, where they had two children. He played baseball with several local teams, at the same time seeking unsuccessfully to become a pitcher in the Central Association. In April 1912 his life was forever changed by the greatest calamity in county history. While his wife and children went to stay with his parents, Rice was in Galesburg for another baseball tryout. A tornado struck, killing seventy-five people, including his wife, children, siblings, and mother. His father died shortly afterward, some said from the shock of losing his family. Rice never spoke of the tragedy, and it did not come to light until his election to the National Baseball Hall of Fame.

Despite his losses, Rice made one more attempt to become a pitcher for Galesburg. When this failed, he began wandering the United States working odd jobs. He joined the U.S. Navy in 1913 and was sent to Vera Cruz aboard the *New Hampshire* to quell an uprising following the overthrow of Mexican president Francisco Madero. Nineteen of Rice's shipmates died in the fighting, but he escaped harm.

At that time and during his career Rice stood 5′9″ and weighed 140 pounds. As well as playing on the ship's baseball team, he played winter ball in Cuba. In 1914 he left the navy to become a pitcher for Petersburg of the Virginia League. He compiled a 9–2 record, winning his first five games. He finished 11–12 with Petersburg in 1915, but the club was in financial trouble and unable to repay a debt of about $500 (sources disagree on the amount) to Clark Griffith, owner of the Washington Senators. The Petersburg owner offered Rice as payment; Griffith agreed and canceled the debt. Rice then acquired the name Sam. Announcing the acquisition to reporters, Griffith forgot Rice's first name and identified the new pitcher as Sam. Without such unusual circumstances, a 27-year-old pitcher who could not make the Galesburg team probably never would have gotten a chance at the major leagues.

Rice reported to the Senators in August 1915. During the next two seasons he pitched nine games, winning one. Since he experienced more success as a left-handed pinch hitter than as a pitcher, the Senators moved him to right field. In 58 games in 1916 he batted .299. He played his first full major league season in 1917. After missing part of the 1918 season while serving in the army, he returned to the Senators in 1919 and batted .321. He finished his twenty-year major league career with a .322 batting average.

Even though a contemporary of superstars Babe Ruth, Lou Gehrig, and Ty Cobb, Rice led the American League in hits in 1924 and 1926, and he twice led the league in putouts by an outfielder. He finished in the top four in base stealing eight of the ten seasons between 1919 and 1928, leading the league with a career high of 63 in 1920. He helped the Senators to the pennant in 1924, but he batted only .207 in the World Series, which the Senators won, defeating the New York Giants four games to three. His best year was 1925, batting .350 with a career high 227 hits, when the Senators again won the pennant. He batted .364 in the 1925 World Series, driving in three runs, although the Senators lost the seven-game series to Pittsburgh.

A controversial event during the 1925 Series made Rice more famous than any of his statistical achievements. In the third game he chased down a line drive and tumbled over a barrier into the bleachers, disappearing from view. Ultimately he emerged with the ball in his glove, and the runner was called out. Debate raged, but Rice made no further statements concerning the incident. In 1965 he presented an affidavit to baseball's Hall of Fame that was to be opened after his death. It stated that he had made the catch.

He made his last World Series appearance in 1933, getting a hit in his one time at bat. Rice played for the Senators through 1933 and in 1934 for the Cleveland Indians. Although age had slowed him, he hit a respectable .293. When he retired, he was thirteen hits short of 3,000, a fact of which he was unaware at the time. Griffith offered to let him return in 1935 to collect the hits, but Rice declined, saying he was too old and his career was behind him.

In 1929 he had married Mary Kendal, with whom he had one daughter. Although Rice never made more than $18,000 a year, he invested wisely. He purchased a farm in Maryland where he and his family enjoyed a comfortable retirement.

He was elected to the Hall of Fame in 1963. At his induction ceremonies he was nearly at a loss for words, and the *Newton County Enterprise* of Kentland, Indiana, carried a full-page spread about his honor. Rice's last public appearance was as a guest at the 1974 Cooperstown induction ceremonies three months before his death at Rossmor, Maryland.

• Rice's career statistics and official baseball records, as well as clippings and other data, are located at the National Baseball Hall of Fame and Museum, Cooperstown, N.Y. The best article about his life is John Yost, "Edgar Charles 'Sam' Rice, Enterprise Profile," *Newton County* (Indiana) *Enterprise*, 7 June 1964. Other sources include Martin Appel and Burt Goldblatt, *Baseball's Best: The Hall of Fame Gallery* (1977), and Rick Wolff, ed., *The Baseball Encyclopedia*, 8th ed. (1990). An obituary is in the *New York Times*, 15 Oct. 1974.

MARY LOU LECOMPTE

RICE, Stuart Arthur (21 Nov. 1889–4 June 1969), sociologist, statistician, and government administrator, was born in Wadena, Minnesota, the son of Edward Myron Rice and Ida Emelin Hicks. He graduated from high school in Puyallup, Washington, in 1907, enrolled at the University of Washington, and graduated in 1912. He was employed as a social worker in Washington state and New York City from 1913 through 1919 and received his masters degree in sociology in 1915 from the University of Washington. In 1914 Rice married Chimeta Williamson; the couple had one son. Rice received his doctorate from Columbia in 1924.

Stuart Rice was a leading member of the "objectivists" in interwar sociology, a group who stressed quantification and value neutrality in opposition to what they perceived as the reform orientation of previous sociologists. Rice's position was ironic since he claimed to have been a radical activist during his college and immediate postcollege years, working as a social settlement worker in New York City and an organizer for the Farmer-Labor party in Washington. After the collapse of the Farmer-Labor party in 1920, he came to Columbia to study sociology under Franklin Giddings and quickly adopted Giddings's scientist and quantitative perspective. Rice, who appeared even more enamored of "The Chief" than his peers, became one of the leaders in the development and utilization of what he called "political statistics." In his dissertation, "Farmers and Workers in American Politics" (1924), Rice asked whether an American farmer-labor party was possible or whether the two groups were irreconcilable opposites. Using extensive voting records from state legislatures, Rice noted that in many cases farmer and worker representatives had remarkably similar voting records on economic issues but differed considerably in cultural concerns, such as Prohibition. From such analysis, Rice concluded that a farmer-labor party could rationally work, but that a strong alliance was questionable.

After receiving his doctorate, Rice served as an instructor and assistant professor of sociology at Dartmouth from 1923 to 1926. He then moved to the University of Pennsylvania, where he was professor of sociology and statistics. During the next several years he wrote dozens of articles and reviews praising social statistics and elaborating upon their uses. Rice summarized his thinking on the matter in *Quantitative Methods in Politics* (1928), "a case book on quantitative methods," which had as its goal the elevation of statistics in political studies to their position in economics. In it he attempted to show how one could use electoral returns and political attitudes to predict future events. Harold Lasswell, one of his supporters at the time, later referred to Rice as someone who had won renown for "writing books in which they said social facts could be counted and then counting some."

Certainly, organized social science at the time was attracted to the apparent certainty of statistics. The Social Science Research Council commissioned Rice to edit a case book, *Methods in Social Science* (1931), commenting on the utility of different methods used by a number of scholars. Beginning from Karl Pearson's remark that the unity of all sciences lay in their method rather than their material, Rice argued that the three ascending goals of social science were definition, determination of sequence and change, and discovery of relations among the variables. Indeed, Rice declared that for some social scientists—and implicitly for himself—the last type of research was the only one that merited the name "science." This coincided with his mentor Giddings's insistence upon the discovery of the "how" of social change.

The infatuation with statistics among social scientists of the period was further demonstrated by the centrality of statistics in the government-sponsored *Recent Social Trends*. In 1929 President Herbert Hoover, long a champion of social scientists as technical experts, established the President's Research Committee on Social Trends, headed by prominent social scientists to report on developing social trends within the United States. Directors of research were Giddings's students, William Ogburn and Howard Odum, and they brought emphasis upon quantification, fear of connection with social reform, and their fellow Columbia graduates to the committee. Rice and his close friend Malcolm Willey composed both a chapter and an extended monograph on "communication agencies," which consisted primarily of statistical surveys and tables. More importantly, from 1931–1932 Rice held a position as special investigator of social statistics, heading a research group that composed a highly influential report. In it, Rice pointed out how the collection of social statistics was necessarily the province of national governments, and the United States was hindered by lack of a coordination agency and the absence of standardization of enumerated objects.

Rice's report coincided with the origins of the New Deal and its belief in a more activist and centralized federal government. Although nominally a Republican like most leading social scientists of the time, Rice was quickly recruited as an adviser on government statistics by the new administration and served in progressively more important positions. He served as an assistant director of the Bureau of the Census from 1933 to 1936. Following his divorce from Chimeta, Rice married Sarah Alice Mayfield in 1934. He then became chairman of the Central Statistical Board from 1936 to 1940. In 1940 he officially left the University of Pennsylvania to become assistant director of the Bureau of the Budget for Statistical Standards, a position he occupied until retirement in 1955. He simultaneously served as the government's official international expert on statistics, serving on numerous United Nations commissions, including the U.N. Statistical Commission from 1946 to 1955, and advising many Asian and African nations on the need to establish governmental statistical bureaus. After retirement he became president of the Washington firm, Surveys and Research Corporation. Among his many academic honors, Rice was chosen president of the American Statistical Association in 1933 and a fellow of the American Academy of Arts and Sciences. He died in Washington, D.C.

Throughout his long and distinguished career Rice focused on the importance and utility of quantitative information for the efficient operation of government and society and the absolute need for objectivity. In one of his last public appearances before his death, he noted his dissatisfaction with the direction of contemporary sociology and especially the decision of the American Sociology Association to condemn the Vietnam War. He feared that such actions would bring back the years of his youth when the public lumped sociology and socialism together. Rice's career reflected the growing recruitment of social scientists as technical experts into the national government and the growing reliance on statistics to qualify and validate social programs.

• Rice's fairly extensive papers are at the Harry S. Truman Library in Independence, Mo. See also Stuart Rice and Malcolm Macdonald Willey, *Communication Agencies and Social Life* (1933), and Rice, "Why I Wanted to Become a Sociologist," *American Sociologist* (Nov. 1968): 284–85. Robert Bannister, *Sociology and Scientism: The American Quest for Objectivity, 1880–1940* (1987), deals well with the Giddings school and includes some material on Rice's position within the debates on scientific method of the time. An excellent source on the significance of the Recent Social Science Trends is Barry Karl, "Presidential Planning and Social Science Research: Mr. Hoover's Experts," *Perspectives in American History*, ed. Donald Fleming and Bernard Bailyn, vol. 3 (1969). Useful for understanding the centrality of the debate over statistics and the possibility of an objective social science for the 1920s and 1930s is Mark C. Smith, *Social Science in the Crucible: The American Debate over Objectivity and Purpose, 1918–1941* (1994); while Ellen Herman, *The Romance of American Psychology: Political Culture in the Age of Experts* (1995), explores the mutual attraction between social scientists and the federal government in the postwar era. Rice is eulogized in Philip Houser, "In Memorium: Stuart A. Rice," *American Sociologist* (Feb. 1970): 48–49.

MARK C. SMITH

RICE, Thomas Dartmouth (20 May 1808–19 Sept. 1860), actor, was born in New York City. Few details of his early life, including his parentage, are known, except that he was born in abject poverty. Rice was apprenticed to a wood carver for a time in the 1820s but so disliked the work that he ran off to become an itinerant actor. He made his theatrical debut in 1828 in small roles with Ludlow and Smith's Southern Theater in Louisville, Kentucky. Between acts of the plays Rice appeared in blackface imitations. In his memoirs, Rice's manager Noah M. Ludlow provides an anecdote about the most significant breakthrough in Rice's career. While standing in the doorway of a Louisville theater during a rehearsal, Rice watched what Ludlow described as "a very black, clumsy Negro" singing. Rice paid the man to teach him the song, which he combined with an eccentric dance (some accounts suggest that the man was a crippled stableman and that Rice copied his movements as well as his song). When Rice appeared in New York at the Bowery Theater as "Jim Crow" in *The Kentucky Rifle* in 1832, his "Jump Jim Crow" comic song and dance done in blackface became phenomenally popular. His widely imitated style catapulted "Daddy" Rice, as he was often known, to stardom.

Rice, billed as an "Ethiopian delineator," was not the first white actor to appear in blackface, but he is usually credited with widely popularizing this performance tradition, which profoundly influenced generations of American entertainers. Minstrel shows

("Ethiopian operas") began featuring white actors in blackface; later, African-American actors in similarly exaggerated makeup appeared in comparable entertainments. Minstrel shows and blackface were enthusiastically received throughout the United States and predominated as a favored popular entertainment for one hundred years, firmly establishing racial stereotypes of African Americans that were not shattered until the middle of the twentieth century. Audiences unfamiliar with blacks or those threatened by racial difference found enjoyment, and perhaps security, in Rice's outrageous characterization.

Rice played variations of "Jim Crow" in numerous entertainments and derivative plays, including *Bone Squash Diablo*, *The Virginia Mummy*, *Oh! Hugh!*, *Long Island Juba*, *Jumbo Jim*, *Jim Crow in London*, and *Ginger Blue*. The nineteenth-century audience's taste for the "Jump Jim Crow" routine was so great that when Rice occasionally appeared in different roles they still demanded that he give them a turn as "Jim Crow." In the twentieth century the name "Jim Crow" (like "Uncle Tom") took on a significant sociopolitical meaning as it was applied to describe repressive laws in the South preventing African Americans from attaining equal rights and status with whites. In the nineteenth century, however, "Jim Crow" made Rice one of the most beloved and celebrated popular entertainers of his day.

Rice introduced actor Joseph Jefferson to the stage at the age of four when he made up the youngster in blackface makeup and costume identical to his own. When Jefferson imitated Rice, to the great amusement of the audience at the Washington Theater in Washington, D.C., this embellishment on the "Jim Crow" act caused a sensation. Rice toured theaters throughout the United States with his routine, and in 1836, 1838, and 1843 he also appeared in England, where he achieved a popular following equal to what he had attained in America. Between tours to England, Rice married Charlotte B. Gladstone in 1837, but their marriage ended abruptly with her death in 1847. All of their children died in infancy.

Sometime in the early 1850s, Rice was stricken with a form of paralysis (possibly the result of a stroke) that affected his speech and movement and that would end his life a few years later, but for a time he recovered sufficiently to return to the stage. Regarded as reclusive and eccentric by his contemporaries, Rice became increasingly isolated after his illness. As the best-known blackface actor of his day in the United States, it was inevitable that Rice would eventually play "Uncle Tom." He appeared in the role in a stage adaptation of *Uncle Tom's Cabin* at New York's Bowery Theater in 1858. Later Rice performed with Henry Wood's Minstrels, until his death in New York City, at a time when a significantly increased number of minstrel shows, which he had so influenced, were drawing his own audience away.

• For additional information on Rice see the memoirs of his manager, Noah M. Ludlow, *Dramatic Life As I Found It* (1880). See also William C. Young, ed., *Famous Actors and Actresses on the American Stage*, vol. 2 (1975); Dailey Paskman and Sigmund Spaeth, *Gentlemen, Be Seated* (1928); "Jump Jim Crow! The Opening of an Era," *New York Times Magazine*, 13 Nov. 1932, pp. 8, 15; Edward LeRoy Rice, *Monarchs of Minstrelsy* (1911); Carl Wittke, *Tambo and Bones: A History of the American Minstrel Stage* (1930); and Francis Courtney Wemyss, *Theatrical Biography of Eminent Actors and Authors* (n.d.). Obituaries are in *Frank Leslie's Illustrated Newspaper*, 6 Oct. 1860, and the *New York Times*, 20 and 21 Sept. 1860.

JAMES FISHER

RICE, William Marsh (14 Mar. 1816–23 Sept. 1900), merchant and founder of Rice University, was born in Springfield, Massachusetts, the son of David Rice, the inspector of the watershops at the Springfield Armory, and Patty Hall. Although he later financed several relatives' educations, Rice left school at fifteen to work as a clerk in a grocery store. By the time he was twenty-one he bought a store near the watershops and in less than two years cleared $2,000 in his first business venture. Despite two serious setbacks, his business success was to continue for more than sixty years.

In the aftermath of the financial panic of 1837, Rice left Massachusetts to seek his fortune trading in the young Republic of Texas. By October 1838 he appears in Texas records, having lost his first cargo at sea. Nevertheless, four months later he acquired 320 acres in the raw new town of Houston, which was to become a market center for all of Texas. Quick to see business opportunity, Rice became a liquor broker, although he was a teetotaler. He also began buying and selling real estate and lending against mortgages, and eventually he owned thousands of acres in Texas and Louisiana. Little is known of his military service, but he was a private in the militia in 1842, when Mexico invaded Texas.

Rice formed several profitable partnerships in the 1840s and 1850s, importing and trading whatever merchandise the booming state demanded. By 1848 the enterprising young man owned the brig *William M. Rice*, which made the run from Galveston to Boston to pick up New England ice during the fearsomely hot Texas summers. Rice's brother David Rice joined him in business for a time, but David was less successful than their younger brother Frederick Allyn Rice, who remained in Houston as an active partner in many ventures.

Seeing the importance of transportation for commerce, Rice helped to found the Houston and Texas Central Railroad and a stagecoach line connecting Houston to Austin. In 1851 he created the Houston and Galveston Navigation Company to bring goods up Buffalo Bayou from the port of Galveston for overland transport elsewhere in Texas.

In 1850 Rice married Margaret Bremond. Their reception at the Capitol Hotel was described by the newspaper as "the most splendid affair ever given in the city." Rice's fortune was reported as more than $25,000, an impressive sum for the time. By 1860 Rice was the second richest man in Texas; the census lists him with $750,000 in property and fifteen slaves. He was involved in nearly every major business enterprise in Houston.

In his forties Rice entered civic life as alderman and grand juror. He also became an incorporator of the Houston Academy, board member of the Houston Educational Society, and trustee of the Second Ward Free School and Texas Medical College.

The Civil War uprooted Rice for the second time. He opposed secession but remained in Houston and donated generously to war relief efforts organized by his wife. After her death in August 1863, he went to Mexico and made another fortune in cotton, trading through Monterrey and Matamoros. He later said, "The war broke up my business." He sold his Houston firm in 1864 at auction, his Confederate bonds were worthless, and his warehouses and storage depots were taken over by the U.S. government after Appomattox. After the war, Rice moved to New York but maintained business interests in Houston in insurance, real estate, and railroads.

In 1867 Rice married Julia Elizabeth "Libbie" Baldwin Brown, the widowed sister of Frederick Rice's wife, Charlotte Baldwin. Although the couple visited Houston for several months a year, they lived most of the time on their country estate in Dunellen, New Jersey.

As he reached seventy-five, the childless Rice said: "Texas received me when I was penniless, without friends or even acquaintances, and now in the evening of my life I recognize my obligation to her and to her children. I wish now to leave to the boys and girls, struggling for a place in the sun, the fortune that I have been able to accumulate." He first considered founding an orphanage or a high school, but by May 1891 he had determined to create the William M. Rice Institute for the Advancement of Literature, Science, and Art. Rice endowed the fledgling college with $200,000 and promised it the bulk of his estate (eventually nearly $5 million) after his death. Not surprisingly for the time, Rice intended his institute to serve whites only; he was progressive in creating it for both sexes, "free and open to all, . . . non-sectarian and non-partisan." In 1960 Rice Institute became Rice University, and in 1967 the first black students were admitted and tuition was charged after the trustees petitioned the court to amend the charter.

After Libbie Rice's death in 1896, Rice spent his last years in Manhattan, attended only by a young manservant, Charles F. Jones. The philanthropist's generosity was nearly derailed by a conspiracy between his valet and a crooked attorney, Albert T. Patrick. As the old man's health declined, Patrick decided that his vast fortune would be better entrusted to himself than to the students of Rice's institute. Enlisting the gullible valet to poison Rice with mercury tablets, Patrick forged a will in his own favor. When Rice persisted in living despite the mercury, Patrick insisted that Jones hurry him along, first with bitter oxalic acid, which Rice spat out, and then with chloroform.

Fortunately for justice, Rice's banker questioned a $25,000 check the greedy lawyer had forged, payable to himself, and telegraphed Rice's attorney in Houston, Captain James Baker. Baker raced to New York on the first train, prevented cremation of the body, and, after an autopsy showed that Rice had been murdered in his own apartment, began an investigation to fight the "Patrick will." Jones soon confessed to the murder and accused Patrick as the mastermind. Jones ultimately committed suicide. Although he was convicted of murder and forgery and sentenced to death, Patrick was pardoned in 1912, the year Rice Institute opened.

• Rice's papers are in the archives of Fondren Library, Rice University, Houston, Tex. The William Marsh Rice Papers and the Rice Litigation Papers contain most of the original source material available; the Andrew Forest Muir Papers contain the notes the late historian had taken in preparing to write a full-length biography. Sylvia Stallings Morris, ed., *William Marsh Rice and His Institute* (1972), is a biography created from the papers and research notes of Muir and was also published in *Rice University Studies* 58, no. 2 (Spring 1972). See also Edgar Odell Lovett, "The Foundation: Its History," in *The Meaning of the New Institution*, Rice Institute Pamphlet 1, no. 1 (Apr. 1915): 52–54; James A. Baker, *Reminiscences of the Founder*, Rice Institute Pamphlet 18, no. 3 (July 1931): 127–44; Fredericka Meiners, *A History of Rice University: The Institute Years 1907–1963* (1982); Jim Hutton and Jim Henderson, *Houston: A History of a Giant* (1976); and WPA, *Houston: A History and Guide* (1942). A play by J. D. Killgore, *The Rice Murder* (1987), produced as a videotape titled *The Trust* (1992), treats Rice's murder and Patrick's trial. An obituary is in the *Springfield* (Mass.) *Daily Republican*, 26 Sept. 1900.

KATHLEEN MUCH

RICH, Arnold Rice (28 Mar. 1893–17 Apr. 1968), pathologist, was born in Birmingham, Alabama, the son of Samuel Rich, a prosperous merchant, and Hattie Rich. After finishing elementary school in Birmingham, Rich entered the Bingham School, a military academy in North Carolina. Despite his very erect posture and trim physique, both apparently acquired while at the Bingham School, military training did not appeal to Rich. Neither did mathematics. His dislike of the latter caused him to reject a career as a mining engineer, and instead he chose to study biology while at the University of Virginia, earning an A.B. in 1914 after only two years and an M.A. one year later. Toward completion of his master's degree Rich undertook a project concerned with the reactions of the probiscus of the flatworm *Planaria albissima* Vejdovsky. In 1915 he entered the Johns Hopkins Medical School, where William H. Howell directed him toward studies on blood coagulation. A paper that Rich wrote on this subject was published while he was a medical student. Also published while he was in medical school was the research he had conducted for his master's degree. In 1918, during World War I, Rich served as a sergeant in the Johns Hopkins Unit of the Students Army Training Corps.

After graduating from medical school in 1919, Rich decided to follow the career of an experimental surgeon. He was advised by William Halstead, the professor of surgery, to prepare for a surgical residency by first studying pathology for a year. While working in the pathology laboratory, under William MacCallum, he decided instead to concentrate on pathology, and he remained a member of the pathology department at Hopkins for the remainder of his life. In 1944 he was appointed professor of pathology and three years later was made Baxley Professor of Pathology and chairman of the department as well as pathologist in chief to the Johns Hopkins Hospital. He became a professor emeritus in 1958 and served in that capacity until his death, ten years later.

Rich's first important contribution to the field was demonstrating the origin of bilirubin and bile pigment as summarized in "The Formation of Bile Pigment" (*Physiological Reviews* 5 [1925]: 182–224). Rich's novel discovery was that hemoglobin liberated by the digestion of erythrocytes by the Kupfer cells in the liver's reticuloendothelial system is the source of bile pigment and that epithelial cells of the liver help to excrete bile pigment but play no role in its formation. On the basis of this research Rich was able to divide jaundice into two types: retention jaundice, which is caused by overproduction of bile pigment resulting from conditions associated with decreased excretory processes, and regurgitation jaundice, which is caused by the reflux of bile from the liver canaliculi into the blood stream as the result of direct obstruction of bile ducts or liver necrosis.

Rich also devoted many years to the study of tuberculosis, specifically the hypersensitive inflammatory reactions associated with it, and determined that these reactions are independent of the host's immunity to the disease. Rich's work on this problem was summarized in another important article, "The Significance of Hypersensitivity in Infections" (*Physiological Reviews* 21 [1941]: 70–111), as well as in his book *The Pathogenesis of Tuberculosis* (1944; rev. ed., 1951). Expanding his work on hypersensitivity of tissues, Rich uncovered information concerning pneumococcal infections and syphilis. Of particular importance was his demonstration that the lesions of periarteritis nodosa, rheumatic carditis, pneumonitis, and some forms of glomerulonephritis were the result of anaphylactic sensitivity. In his studies of portal cirrhosis in the rabbit Rich found that the condition could be caused by diets deficient in B_1, B_2, B_6, and nicotinic acid, and through the use of time-lapse cinemicrography he was able to demonstrate how spleen tumor cells move. Rich's work also elucidated the pathogenesis of acute hemorrhagic pancreatitis by showing that trypsinogen activated by enterokinase is not always associated with the production of this lesion, rather, that it results from the liberation of inactivated pancreatic enzymes after rupture of the pancreatic ductules. Rich also demonstrated that tubular lesions can occur in the renal cortex as a result of acute infection, and he described a focal form of nephritis that occurs in acquired syphilis. In addition, Rich was the first to describe the obstructive pulmonary lesion of Tetralogy of Fallot. With Louis Hamman he described the idiopathic interstitial fibrosis of the lung that has since become known as Rich-Hamman disease. His numerous awards include the certificate of honor from the American Academy of Tuberculosis (1947), the Kober Medal of the Association of American Physicians (1958), membership in the National Academy of Sciences (1954), and recognition as an honorary fellow of the British Royal Society of Medicine (1956).

In addition to his scientific endeavors, Rich had a wide array of interests in the fields of history, politics, music, and literature. A composer of music as well as an accomplished musician, he was a regular member of the chamber music quartet that included Baltimore's ascerbic editor and critic, H. L. Mencken. Rich had been married to Helen Jones, a pianist and composer, since 1925. They had two daughters, one of them the poet Adrienne Rich. Rich died in Baltimore in the Johns Hopkins Hospital.

• Rich's papers are in the archives of the Johns Hopkins Medical School. A long, detailed memoir by Ella Oppenheimer is in the National Academy of Sciences, *Biographical Memoirs* 50 (1979): 330–50. A shorter one, also by Oppenheimer, is in the *Archives of Pathology* 66 (1968): 433–34. A short death notice is in the *Journal of the American Medical Association* 204 (1968): 32.

DAVID Y. COOPER

RICH, Buddy (30 Sept. 1917–2 Apr. 1987), musician, was born Bernard Rich in Albany, New York, the son of Robert Rich and Bess Skolnik, vaudeville entertainers. Endowed with an uncanny sense of rhythm, Rich was only eighteen months old when he made his debut in show business, playing drums in his parents' act. Soon afterward he began to be billed as "Traps, the Drum Wonder," quickly becoming one of the highest paid child performers of the day. At four he appeared in a pair of Broadway revues; at six he toured Australia. Rich never completed his elementary education. The demands of childhood stardom interfered with his spending significant time in public school, and such private tutoring as he received was haphazard at best. In 1929 he starred in his first film, *Sound Effects with Traps the Drum Wonder*, a Vitaphone short that exhibited his talents as a drummer, dancer, and singer. While still in his teens, Rich fronted a band of older musicians, enjoying some success on the vaudeville circuit.

The early 1930s, however, were difficult years for Rich. Child star no longer, he was compelled to perform on excursion boats and in cheap nightclubs. In the meantime, he had begun to develop a passion for jazz, haunting little clubs in Brooklyn and availing himself of every opportunity to sit in with the house band at the Crystal Café. In October 1937 Rich secured his first jazz job, playing with Joe Marsala's combo at the Hickory House on "Swing Street" (Fifty-second Street) in New York City. Very early the following year he initiated his recording career by sitting in on a session with Adrian Rollini, an esteemed jazz veteran. (It is possible that Rich is the drummer on the Andrews Sisters' bestselling recording of "Bei Mir Bist du Schön," cut in November 1937.)

Rich left Marsala in June 1938. After a short stint with conductor Leith Stevens on the CBS radio series "Saturday Night Swing Session," he led his own combo for a brief engagement at the Piccadilly Roof in New York. In the late summer of that year Rich joined the orchestra of Bunny Berigan, gaining his first experience in a big swing band. He spent most of 1939 with Artie Shaw, his dynamic drumming igniting the ensemble and securing the band's dominance in the music popularity polls that year. With Shaw, he appeared in a pair of movie shorts, *Class in Swing* (1939) and *Symphony in Swing* (1939), and in a full-length picture, *Dancing Co-ed* (1939), starring Lana Turner. In November 1939 Rich became a featured player in the outstanding Tommy Dorsey orchestra that showcased the trumpet solos of Ziggy Elman, the vocals of Frank Sinatra, and the arrangements of Sy Oliver. Rich's performances on Dorsey recordings such as "Quiet Please," "Not So Quiet, Please," "Swing High," "Deep River," and "Yes, Indeed!" proved that he deserved a place in the front rank of swing percussionists. With Dorsey, Rich also appeared in three motion pictures, *Las Vegas Nights* (1941), *Ship Ahoy* (1942), and *Du Barry Was a Lady* (1943), and, according to some sources, played on the soundtracks of *Presenting Lily Mars* (1943) and *Girl Crazy* (1943). In 1941 he easily won top place in the drums category of the *Down Beat* poll. He enjoyed an even greater margin of victory in the 1942 poll.

Rich parted ways with Dorsey late in 1942. After playing briefly with Benny Carter's band, he saw active duty stateside with the U.S. Marine Corps. Upon his discharge in June 1944, Rich rejoined Dorsey until October 1945. (In the fall of 1944, while the Dorsey band was in Hollywood for the filming of another motion picture, Rich found time to play for more than a week with Count Basie at the Plantation Club in Los Angeles.) Also in 1945 Rich married Jean Sutherland; they divorced after only a few months.

Rich's next undertaking was an orchestra of his own, made possible with financial backing from Frank Sinatra. The band, which premiered in December 1945, featured good sidemen and fine modern arrangements as well as the leader's own vocals and superb drumming. It was not a commercial success, however, and Rich was forced to disband a little more than a year later. After touring with Norman Granz's Jazz at the Philharmonic (JATP) in early 1947, Rich then organized a new orchestra, one he was able to hold together until the spring of 1949. That summer he played for several weeks with the band of Les Brown, closing out the year with more JATP engagements, recording sessions, and a brief return to the Dorsey fold.

The 1950s were particularly hectic for Rich. In addition to leading groups of all sizes, ranging from trios

to big bands, he was a mainstay with JATP, engaging in audience-pleasing "drum battles" with Gene Krupa. Rich was also a frequent participant in all-star recording sessions. Other ventures included a tour with famed entertainer Josephine Baker in 1951, a short-lived quartet called "The Big Four" with Charlie Ventura, Chubby Jackson, and Marty Napoleon that same year, and year-long stints with Harry James from 1953 to 1954 and Tommy Dorsey from 1954 to 1955. In 1953 Rich married Marie Allison, a dancer with stage and film experience. His only child, a daughter, was born a year later. Rich was back with James from 1956 to 1957 for a stay that included a tour of Europe. During this period Rich also worked briefly as a solo vocalist and occasionally acted on national television.

Despite significant signs of heart trouble by 1959, Rich maintained the demanding pace he had earlier set for himself. He organized various combos and in 1961 took a sextet to the Far East on a tour sponsored by the State Department. From late 1961 until 1966 Rich worked mainly with Harry James. During his occasional absences from the James orchestra, he led different small bands and participated in other musical activities. In 1965 he appeared with fellow drummer Louie Bellson in Tokyo and later gave what was described as a "phenomenal performance" at the Newport Jazz Festival. In April 1966 Rich left James in order to launch yet another big band of his own. This band featured what Rich called "the sound of today." It enjoyed huge success in the United States and won highest acclaim in its tours of both Europe and Japan. Rich suddenly found himself a "name" in the wider world of popular entertainment, sharing bills with Sammy Davis, Jr., Tony Bennett, and Sinatra. He was also in heavy demand for television appearances and became a regular on Johnny Carson's "The Tonight Show," pleasing audiences with his rapid-fire wit as well as with his drumming.

Rich dissolved the big band early in 1974 and put together a combo for the opening in Manhattan of "Buddy's Place," a club only nominally his own. A year later he was at the helm of another very successful big band. Rich underwent quadruple bypass surgery in 1983 but refused to curtail his activities. He died in Los Angeles. After his death, his daughter organized the Buddy Rich Memorial Brain Tumor Research Foundation at UCLA Medical Center and inaugurated a scholarship fund in his name for promising young drummers.

Rich is widely regarded as one of the all-time greats of jazz drumming. As the driving force behind an ensemble, he had few peers. As a soloist of sheer technical prowess, he was unsurpassed. In 1965, following his overwhelming performance at Newport, jazz critic Dan Morgenstern called him "without a doubt, the greatest drummer who has ever lived." Rich's accomplishments are all the more astonishing in that he never took a lesson, never practiced, and never learned to read music. Despite his lack of any real training as a drummer, Rich was not without early direct influences. The styles of Tony Briglia of the Casa Loma band,

Gene Krupa, and Chick Webb made a particularly strong impression on him, but he also admired the work of Dave Tough, Sid Catlett, O'Neil Spencer, and Jo Jones. Rich, in turn, influenced outstanding modern percussionists such as Alvin Stoller and Louie Bellson. The drums Rich used in his last years are now part of the collection of the Smithsonian Institution in Washington, D.C.

• There is considerable oral history material concerning Rich in the National Sound Archive of the British Library. The fundamental source on Rich's life and art is Mel Tormé, *Traps, the Drum Wonder* (1991). Tormé, a capable drummer himself, was Rich's friend for more than forty years, but he manages to provide an account that is well balanced and objective. Further biographical and musical details, especially on Rich's big bands of the post–1966 period, are in Doug Meriwether, Jr., *We Don't Play Requests* (1984), which also contains a career discography that is comprehensive (excluding the James and Dorsey stints) through mid-1983. Whitney Balliett's *Super Drummer: A Profile of Buddy Rich* (1968) is a candid description that makes extensive use of the drummer's own verbatim opinions, observations, and recollections. Burt Korall, *Drummin' Men* (1990), offers a colorful portrait of Rich based on anecdotal material from the subject himself and from a variety of music professionals who were associated with him over the decades. Also available is an excellent in-depth biographical documentary, *Buddy Rich: Jazz Legend*, pts. 1 and 2 (DCI Music Video, 1994). An obituary appears in the *New York Times*, 3 Apr. 1987.

STEVEN M. KANE

RICH, Charles Coulson (21 Aug. 1809–17 Nov. 1883), Mormon apostle and colonizer, was born in Campbell County, Kentucky, the son of Joseph Rich and Nancy O'Neal, pioneers and farmers. Shortly after his birth, Rich's parents purchased land across the Ohio River in Indiana. His early family life typified the hard existence of antebellum midwestern farmers: perpetual grinding labor punctuated by religious camp meetings, contending sects, Indian conflicts, modest education (Rich got more than some—three months each year until age seventeen), temperance crusades, and abolition and antiabolition strife. Following the family's move to Illinois in 1829, Rich became less typical when in 1832, along with his mother, father, and sister, he embraced the proclamations of Mormon missionaries then passing through Tazewell County. From that point on his existence was inexorably enmeshed with the emerging drama of the Latter-day Saints.

Ineloquent but tireless, astute, transparently sincere, and unhesitatingly obedient to his church's considerable demands, Rich was more responsible than any other individual for Mormonism's growth in central Illinois in the 1830s. One month after his baptism he embarked on the first of his proselytizing journeys, which included a stay in Kirtland, Ohio, where he deepened his religious allegiance by encountering Joseph Smith, Mormonism's founder. In 1834 Rich was elected a captain in Zion's Camp, an armed Mormon military expedition led by Smith and designed, in the wake of futile efforts at legal redress, to relieve fellow

Saints suffering pillage in Jackson County, Missouri. A costly, 300-mile march failed to restore the Saints to their lands but did launch Rich's career as a leader of Mormon military defenses and afforded him the opportunity to study the prophet whose cause he espoused for life. Returning home to Illinois, Rich organized and presided over branches of the flourishing church and spent fourteen of the next thirty-two months preaching the Mormon gospel during short missions.

Mormon revelations declared the crucial role of families in heaven and on earth. Apart from such prompting, Rich seemed uneager to seek a mate. As he later noted in a typically laconic sermon, "It was some years before I learned the fact that I could not do much good without a wife, and without posterity. I therefore concluded to marry," which he did (Sarah DeArmon Pea, 1838). When the revealed doctrine of "plural marriage" was subsequently introduced, Rich, with Sarah Rich's aid, married additional wives in 1845 (Eliza Graves, Mary Ann Phelps, Sarah Jane Peck), in 1846 (Emeline W. Grover), and in 1847 (Harriet Sargent); from these six unions fifty-one children eventually issued.

Even before and apart from polygyny, Mormon ways evoked ridicule, fear, and sometimes persecution from the wider culture. Tensions flared wherever the Saints concentrated their population (and their political power) by "gathering" to build a righteous society. In 1837 Rich gathered with the Saints in Missouri, whose legislature had organized Caldwell County especially for the Mormons. Hearing reports of persecution, Rich volunteered for Mormon defenses, becoming second in command when troubles crescendoed in 1838. Governor Lilburn Boggs ordered that the Mormons "be exterminated or driven from the state." Rich helped lead the resistance, personally killing one foe in battle. But Joseph Smith was soon captured, the Missouri military authorities sought to try Mormon resisters for murder, and—after the surrender of the Mormon headquarters at Far West—the Missouri militia-mob ransacked houses and raped women.

Fleeing "Missouri justice," Rich risked starvation while leading an escape to Illinois. The state at first welcomed the Mormon refugees, who purchased land at Nauvoo, which quickly became the state's largest settlement. Rich was appointed to the half-religious, half-civil high council (1839), served several church missions (1842, 1843, 1844), and from 1844 was prominent in the Council of Fifty, a semisecret shadow government regulating temporal affairs. In 1841 alone he was elevated to the "stake presidency" (thus becoming one of three presiding Nauvoo church authorities), elected to the city council and as school warden, named to the board of regents for the future University of Nauvoo, and appointed brigadier general in the Nauvoo Legion, which performed the functions of a regular state militia. In 1844 Rich assumed command of the entire legion, the prominence of which, along with rumors of polygamy and rivalries in state politics, also precipitated anti-Mormon sentiment, leading eventually to Joseph Smith's murder in 1844 and the exile of his followers from Illinois in 1846.

As the toil- and death-filled exodus developed, Rich took charge first of Mt. Pisgah, Iowa, a temporary settlement aiding the thousands trekking west, and then of the military organization of the emigration companies, defending primarily against Indian raids. General Rich continued as commander in chief while the Saints established themselves in the Salt Lake Valley (1847–1849), and a decade later he helped direct the Mormon response to the encroachments of one-third of the U.S. Army, dispatched by President James Buchanan to enforce federal will on Utah territory.

In the interim, Brigham Young integrated Rich fully into the central leadership of the church by ordaining him as one of the twelve ruling apostles in 1849, by which time the Salt Lake colony, with economic stimulus from the nation's rush to California gold, had proved its viability. Young then called Rich to lead in the great Mormon expansion that followed. From 1851 to 1857 he accepted the grueling task of establishing a colony in California at San Bernardino, the end link in the Mormon "highway to the sea." From 1860 to 1862 Rich was co-"President of the Church in Europe," orchestrating a vast missionary effort, aiding the emigration of converted thousands, and establishing Mormon organizations throughout Britain and Scandinavia. After 1863 he moved his families (thirty-six souls) north of Salt Lake City, to beautiful, harsh Bear Lake Valley, where he spent his last twenty years before dying in Paris, Idaho, as judge, counselor, temple builder, architect, territorial legislator, Indian agent, and religious authority—having ensured the survival of a ring of Mormon outposts, some of which still bear his name (St. Charles, Idaho; Rich County, Utah).

Rich was loyal, deferential, practical, terse, intelligent, and dogged. His career epitomizes not the Mormon life of the mind but the incessant spiritual, ecclesiastical, political, social, and martial rigors of those who cast their lots with the Latter-day Saints in the nineteenth century.

• The most extensive collection of Rich's correspondence and diaries is gathered at the Church Archives, Historical Department, Church of Jesus Christ of Latter-day Saints, Salt Lake City, Utah. His few published sermons are collected in *Journal of Discourses* (26 vols., 1855–1886). Leonard J. Arrington, *Charles C. Rich: Mormon General and Western Frontiersman* (1974), is the standard biography. Hagiographic but still useful is John Henry Evans, *Charles Coulson Rich: Pioneer Builder of the West* (1936).

PHILIP L. BARLOW

RICH, Daniel Catton (16 Apr. 1904–17 Oct. 1976), art museum director, was born in South Bend, Indiana, the son of Daniel Rich, a lawyer, and Martha (maiden name unknown). Rich attended the University of Chicago from 1922 to 1926, receiving a bachelor of arts degree in English. He received his graduate degree in English and art history from Harvard University in 1927. That same year he married Bertha Ten Eyck James, with whom he had four children.

After completing his education, Rich was hired in the fall of 1927 as editor of the *Bulletin of the Art Institute of Chicago*, a monthly membership newsletter. Rich's duties included writing articles about the museum's exhibitions and acquisitions, as well as editing the work of other contributors. The following year, 1928, Rich was promoted to the position of assistant curator of painting and sculpture by the museum's director, Robert B. Harshe. In 1930 his title was changed to associate curator, a reflection of his growing responsibilities. In these positions, Rich began to organize exhibitions and pursue research on the museum's permanent collection. His first exhibition was "Paintings, Pastels, and Drawings by Odilon Redon," held at the Art Institute from 27 December 1928 until 27 January 1929. Rich also wrote the catalog for this exhibition.

During the late 1920s and early 1930s, the Art Institute received several important art collections as gifts, and Rich was actively engaged in researching and cataloging these collections, including the Arthur Jerome Eddy Collection, the Mr. and Mrs. L. L. Coburn Collection, and the Mr. and Mrs. Martin A. Ryerson Collection.

In 1933, as part of the Century of Progress Exposition, the Art Institute of Chicago staged one of the largest loan exhibitions ever held. With over 1,000 objects, mostly loans from American museums, the Art Institute illustrated the history of Western art from the thirteenth century until the present. Rich played an important part in selecting and acquiring these loans and installing the exhibition. He also prepared the catalog, a monumental work of scholarship, which included detailed entries on each object in the exhibition. The following year, Rich published *Seurat and the Evolution of "La Grand Jatte"* (1935). This study of painter Georges Seurat's masterpiece, which belonged to the Art Institute's collection, was the first full-length study done on the painting.

In 1938, following the sudden death of Harshe, Rich was named director of fine arts for the Art Institute. He soon embarked on a program of improving the professional staff of the museum by hiring several additional curators, creating new departments, and reorganizing many of the existing departments. One of Rich's most ambitious projects involved completely overhauling the Department of Museum Education by integrating it more fully into the museum's curatorial decisions. In a 1955 lecture, Rich stated that museum education should be made the "core, rather than the fringe of a museum program." Under his guidance, the Gallery of Art Interpretation was created as the first permanent interpretative space for adults established by an American art museum.

Rich's greatest contributions to the museum came in the form of the many exhibitions he helped organize and the important works of art he acquired for the museum's permanent collection. Rich was an ardent modernist, and he was responsible for acquiring many important examples of twentieth-century art, including Pablo Picasso's portrait, *D. H. Kahnweiler* and Henri Matisse's *Bathers by a River*. He was also an admirer of Italian and Spanish baroque art, and he purchased fine examples in that style.

Although Rich was widely admired by his colleagues in the art world, he was also a target for criticism, both locally and nationally. Following a 1947 exhibition of abstract and surrealist American painting and sculpture held at the Art Institute, Rich was denounced as a Communist by Congressman George A. Dondero of Michigan, who stated that Rich was an encourager of "international art thugs" who were intent on destroying American art and culture. Again in 1958 Rich was criticized for refusing to exhibit the paintings of Sir Winston Churchill at the Art Institute. His stance that a museum should not show the work of amateur artists was derided in the press as elitist and disrespectful to Churchill. This controversy may well have been the one that convinced Rich to leave the Art Institute, for shortly after the Churchill episode, he announced that he had accepted a position as director of the Worcester Art Museum, in Worcester, Massachusetts. He served in this position until his retirement in 1970. His achievements in Worcester parallel those in Chicago: he doubled the size of the education department staff, extensively increased the holdings of twentieth-century art, developed a photography collection, and more than doubled the museum's membership. Following his retirement, Rich moved to New York City, where he later died.

Rich was one of the central figures in shaping the American art museum in the twentieth century. His achievements at the Art Institute of Chicago continue to inform the museum's agenda today. He created new departments, such as photography and primitive art, as a response to the twentieth-century's changing sense of what represented fine art. His dedication to the centrality of education to the fine arts redefined the museum's approach to acquisitions, exhibitions, and other programming. As a defender of modern art, Rich successfully engaged museum audiences in Chicago and later in Worcester with the latest currents in the visual arts.

• The Archives of the Art Institute of Chicago contain Rich's office files and correspondence from his time as director, including typescripts of most of his articles and lectures. The Worcester Art Museum has his records from his tenure there. His personal papers have been lost. The only published account of Rich's career focuses only on his Art Institute years. Titled "The Nervous Profession: Daniel Catton Rich and the Art Institute of Chicago, 1927–1958," it is in *The Art Institute of Chicago Museum Studies* 19, no. 1 (1993): 58–79. Rich was a frequent contributor to art periodicals and exhibition catalogs. Among his most notable works are *Seurat and Evolution of "La Grande Jatte"* (1934), *Henri Rousseau* (1942), *Georgia O'Keeffe* (1943), and *Degas* (1952). An obituary is in the *New York Times*, 18 Oct. 1976.

JOHN W. SMITH

RICH, Obadiah (1783–20 Jan. 1850), diplomat and book dealer, was born in Truro, Massachusetts, the son of Obadiah Rich, a ship captain, and Salome Lombard. About 1789 his family moved to the Boston area, where Rich resided until 1816. Although the details of Rich's schooling are not known, an acquaintance described him as "a gentleman by birth and education" and "really learned" (Henry Harrisse, *Bibliotheca Americana Vertustissima* [1880; repr. 1958], p. xxxi). This observation, along with his language and writing skills, suggest that Rich had at least a secondary education. He appears to have developed an interest in antiquarian materials early in life, having joined the Massachusetts Historical Society in 1805 and the Boston Athenaeum in 1807. He later became a member of the American Antiquarian Society.

Rich began his diplomatic career in 1816, when he accepted a position as U.S. consul in Valencia, Spain. Shortly after relocating to Spain he married Ann Montgomery, with whom he had six children. His brother, William, who was under his care after the death of their parents, also resided with him there. While in Valencia, Rich began collecting rare books and manuscripts. Although he remained the consul in Valencia until 1829, by 1823 he had moved to Madrid, where he took charge of the U.S. legation's archives during the second French invasion. During his stay in that city, books and manuscripts from a number of private and ecclesiastical libraries began to be offered for sale as a consequence of the social and economic disruption of the Peninsula Wars and Liberal Uprising of 1820. Rich began purchasing some of these materials, and he soon amassed an impressive collection of rare books and manuscripts, most of which related to Spain and Latin America.

Washington Irving, who resided in Rich's home in 1826, described his library as a "literary wilderness abounding with curious works and rare editions" (Justin Winsor, *Narrative and Critical History of America*, vol. 1 [1889], p. iii). Irving acknowledged the importance of Rich's library in conducting the research for his work *A History of the Life and Voyages of Christopher Columbus*. Other historians, including George Ticknor and William Prescott, also have acknowledged their debt to Obadiah Rich.

By 1819 Rich had begun reselling some of his manuscript and printed materials to American collectors. At this time the export of books from Spain was heavily regulated and closely monitored by government authorities; Rich's diplomatic position aided him in resolving difficulties that arose with customs.

In 1828 Rich moved to London, where he wrote and published *A General View of the United States* (1833), a gazetteer, and opened a shop to distribute American books and periodicals that were not then readily available in England. He continued to travel to Spain periodically and held the position of U.S. consul to Port Mahon, Spain, from 1834 to 1845. However, this does not appear to have been a full-time vocation. He continued to maintain a residence and storefront business in London, and much of his time in Spain was devoted to the acquisition of books and manuscripts.

Rich continued dealing in rare books and manuscripts, which he advertised through a series of descriptive catalogs published between 1827 and 1846, some of which were issued under the Spanish title *Bibliotheca Americana Nova*. Among the more significant materials he acquired and sold during this period was the library of Don Antonio de Uguina, which included the notes and transcripts of unpublished documents collected by the Spanish historian Juan Bautista Muñoz for his *Historia del nuevo mundo*. Rich acquired this collection from Henri Ternaux de Compans, a French book dealer, in 1844. These, along with other rare books and manuscripts, including a collection acquired from Lord Kingsborough, were sold to American book collectors and libraries through Henry Stevens, an American book dealer. The bulk of the manuscripts were purchased by James Lenox in 1848 and now constitute the Obadiah Rich Collection at the New York Public Library. Other materials collected by Rich were acquired by the John Carter Brown Library, the Library of Congress, the British Library, and the Boston Athenaeum Library.

By 1849 Obadiah Rich had fallen into ill health; he died in London. His book-dealing business was carried on initially by his sons and later by Edward G. Allen.

Today Obadiah Rich is primarily known as a bibliographer. His descriptive catalogs, one of which was reprinted as recently as 1967, continue to be used as primary sources in researching the provenance of rare books and manuscripts.

• Collections of correspondence and other materials relating to Obadiah Rich are at the Boston Public Library, the New York Public Library, the William L. Clements Library (Univ. of Mich.), the Workingmen's Institute (New Harmony, Ind.), and the Library of the Boston Athenaeum. The most comprehensive biographical account of Rich is Norman Tucker, "Obadiah Rich (1783–1850): Early American Hispanist" (Ph.D. diss., Harvard Univ., 1973). See also Tucker, "Obadiah Rich (1783–1850): American in Spain," in *Studies in Honor of Ruth Lee Kennedy* (1977); Edwin Blake Brownrigg, *Colonial Latin American Manuscripts and Transcripts in the Obadiah Rich Collection: An Inventory and Index* (1978); and Henry Stevens, *Recollections of James Lenox and the Formation of His Library* (1951).

RICHARD HOLLINGER

RICHARD, Gabriel (15 Oct. 1767–13 Sept. 1832), Catholic missionary and educator, was born in Saintes, France, the son of François Richard, a small landowner, and Marie Geneviéve Bossuet. Trained at Sulpician seminaries in Angers, he was admitted to the Society of St. Sulpice in 1789 and ordained a priest in October 1791. As a nonjuring member of the French clergy, he faced an uncertain future in his native country during the French Revolution and was soon sent with other Sulpicians to serve in the Diocese of Baltimore, which then encompassed the entire United States. Although trained for the classroom, Richard was assigned by Bishop John Carroll as a missionary priest to three French settlements in Illinois, where he remained from 1792 until 1798, when he was transferred to Detroit. He was stationed at St. Anne's in Detroit for the rest of his life, responsible also for missions elsewhere in Michigan and northeast Wisconsin. He was the only Catholic priest in the Michigan Territory from 1805 until 1819.

Richard was throughout his career primarily a pastor, serving not only the mostly French-speaking Catholic settlers in Michigan, but various Native-American groups and even many of Detroit's Protestants, to whom he often preached. He was not an ecumenist by present-day standards, but he shared Bishop Carroll's desire to cultivate good relations with Protestants and the Sulpician conviction that natural and revealed religion had important affinities. His work as an educator reflects this same orientation. He hoped throughout his time in Detroit to establish a Sulpician seminary, and establishing schools was for him invariably linked to evangelization and the recruitment of candidates to the priesthood. He was also a determined advocate for public education.

Richard is credited with the founding of a number of schools in Michigan, although due to the region's poverty most were short-lived. He is best known today for his contributions to the 1817 act of the territorial government that made legal and limited financial provision for a territorial university, dubbed a "Catholepistemiad." Recognized today as the ancestor of the University of Michigan, it was in its own time an important precedent for state sponsorship of education. Richard was also active in the cause of Native-American schooling, which he championed in an 1809 memorial to the Congress. Here he gave voice to a humane and optimistic pedagogy—he was an admirer of Swiss educator and reformer Johann Heinrich Pestalozzi—and to an acculturationist's perspective on Native-American issues. His short-lived school at Springwells, near Detroit, emphasized agricultural and vocational training for Native-American students but was open to all races—"one and the same people," in Richard's view, "and one family." In later years he promoted education for deaf-mutes.

Closely linked to Richard's role as school-founder was his role as frontier intellectual. He brought a printing press to Detroit in 1809, from which issued, until 1817, devotional and literary reprints in French and English as well as the territory's first newspaper, which probably did not survive its initial 1809 edition. He imported books for himself and others, tutored young men, pursued long-standing interests in mathematics and science, and was a founder of the Michigan Historical Society. His personal library, among the largest in the Old Northwest, bespeaks his broad intellectual interests and optimism about the human prospect. Strong not only in theology, but in literature, history, mathematics, science, and pedagogical theory, the library suggests a man who plausibly could be called a moderate proponent of the Enlightenment.

The gregarious Richard was an influential presence in Detroit even after the growth of Protestant in-migration. He was twice detained by the British during their occupation of Detroit (1812–1813) because of his republican sympathies. Asked to be a candidate for territorial delegate to the U.S. Congress in 1823, he prevailed in a four-man race and served a single term in Congress (1823–1825), where his principal achievement was to secure appropriations for a road from Detroit to Chicago. Although he had hoped by his election to influence federal Indian policy in directions favorable to Catholic missionary enterprises, he seems to have had little success. He narrowly missed reelection in 1825 and lost again in 1827 and 1829.

By the early 1820s the Vatican was debating the creation of a diocese coextensive with the Michigan Territory. Richard was recommended as bishop of this new see by influential American churchmen, and he was named to head the newly created Diocese of Detroit early in 1827. Decrees to this effect were subsequently suppressed, evidently due to debts incurred by Richard as the result of a lawsuit brought against him by a disgruntled parishioner. The Michigan Territory remained for all practical purposes part of the Diocese of Cincinnati until 1833, shortly after Richard's death in one of Detroit's worst cholera epidemics. A pastor to the end, he apparently contracted the disease in the course of his round-the-clock visits to the sick and dying.

• Transcripts of Richard's personal papers are held by the Michigan Historical Collections, Ann Arbor, with the originals variously located in the Catholic diocesan archives of Baltimore, Detroit, St. Louis, and Quebec; the Burton Historical Collections, Detroit Public Library; the Archives of the University of Notre Dame; and the Archives of the Society of St. Sulpice, Paris. The best biography is M. Dolorita Mast, *Always the Priest: The Life of Gabriel Richard, S.S.* (1965). See also Vladimir Honsa, "Gabriel Richard: A Bibliographical Essay," *Orbis: Bulletin International de Documentation Linguistique* 6, no. 1 (1957): 48–67, 327–41; Frank B. Woodford and Albert Hyma, *Gabriel Richard: Frontier Ambassador* (1958); Leonard Coombs and Francis X. Blouin, eds., *Intellectual Life on the Michigan Frontier: The Libraries of Gabriel Richard and John Monteith* (1985). Colorful but less reliable are Pierre Guerin, *Le Martyr de la Charité* (1850); N.-E. Dionne, *Gabriel Richard: Sulpicien, Curé et Second Fondateur de la Ville de Détroit* (1911).

LESLIE WOODCOCK TEUTLER

RICHARDS, Alfred Newton (22 Mar. 1876–24 Mar. 1966), pharmacologist, was born in Stamford, New York, the son of Reverend Leonard E. Richards, a Presbyterian minister, and Mary Elizabeth Burbank, a schoolteacher. From the beginning, religion played an important part in Richards's life: his mother named him for her best friend's father, Reverend Alfred Newton. Not only did his father have religious training, but his mother held a degree from Granville Female Seminary. Richards himself attended the Stamford Seminary and Union Free School, graduating as the valedictorian in 1892.

In the fall of 1893 Richards began his studies as an undergraduate at Yale University. He became interested in chemistry in his third year and graduated with honors in chemistry in 1897. During his senior year Richards took a course with Russell H. Chittenden in physiological chemistry that was designed for students planning to attend medical school after graduation. Richards had to abandon his plans for medical school because he did not have the money for tuition, but Chittenden, known as the leading American authority in the new field of physiological chemistry, offered him a scholarship to study the subject for one year at Yale's Sheffield Scientific School. Richards's work there led to a joint paper with Chittenden titled "Variations in the Amylolytic Power and Chemical Composition of Human Mixed Saliva," which was published in the first volume of the *American Journal of Physiology*.

When Chittenden left Yale in 1898 for the Department of Physiological Chemistry in the College of Physicians and Surgeons at Columbia University, Richards went with him as his assistant. While working in the laboratory there, Richards continued his graduate studies, and in 1901 he became the first person to receive a Ph.D. from the Department of Physiological Chemistry at Columbia.

Christian Herter, who was a Columbia faculty member and a trustee of the new Rockefeller Institute, became interested in Richards's laboratory work with inulin separated from dahlia bulbs. Partly through Herter's influence, Richards obtained one of the first scholarships given by the Rockefeller Institute, which from 1901 until 1904 enabled him to study epinephrine with Herter in the Laboratory of Physiological Chemistry at Columbia. When Herter and John Abel founded the *Journal of Biological Chemistry* in 1904, they invited Richards to become associate editor; after Herter's death in 1910, Richards became managing editor, a position that he held until 1914.

While at Columbia, Richards began teaching an elective course in pharmacology in 1904 for medical students; in 1907 the popularity of the course caused it be incorporated into Columbia's regular medical curriculum. Richards's success with the pharmacology course at Columbia led to a position in 1908 as professor of pharmacology at Northwestern University's medical school. The increased income allowed him to marry Lillian Woody in December 1908; they later had one son. After two years of work at Northwestern, Richards accepted a professorship in pharmacology at the University of Pennsylvania Medical School, where he immediately began reorganizing the pharmacology courses and also began laboratory studies of the perfusion of mammalian kidneys.

After the United States entered World War I, Richards went to Britain to study with Henry H. Dale and the staff of the British Medical Research Committee, with whom he did research on histamine and its role in wound shock. In 1918 he was appointed a major in the Sanitary Corps of the U.S. Army and was sent to France to set up a laboratory for the study of the effects of gas warfare. The war ended before equipment for the laboratory arrived, and Richards returned to Philadelphia, receiving an honorable discharge in December 1918. He resumed his laboratory investigations into kidney function, work that laid the foundation for kidney studies. Richards (with Joseph T. Wearn) used the technique of kidney micropuncture to attain results that supported the concept of filtration in the glomerulus and reabsorption in the nephron. Richards was elected a member of the National Academy of Sciences in 1927.

In 1939 Richards was named vice president in charge of medical affairs at the University of Pennsylvania. Two years later, he became chairman of the Committee on Medical Research (CMR) of the Office of Scientific Research and Development (OSRD), an office founded during World War II by President Franklin D. Roosevelt to encourage participation by America's scientists in the war effort. The OSRD decided which proposals for scientific research to fund and then entered into contracts with various institutions, including universities, hospitals, and private firms. One of Richards's main accomplishments during his tenure as chairman of the CMR was to help make penicillin widely available to troops (especially to the casualties at Normandy) and to the public. His decision to promote production of penicillin by natural fermentation with cultures of Alexander Fleming's original mold instead of through a synthetic process meant that penicillin was made available in greater amounts and at a lesser cost. From 1941 to 1946 Richards divided his time between his duties at the University of Pennsylvania and his duties at the CMR. A year after the OSRD was officially terminated in 1946, Richards was elected president of the National Academy of Sciences, a position that he held for three years.

In 1948 Richards was appointed to the Medical Affairs Task Force of the Commission on the Organization of the Executive Branch of the Government, a group that prepared the Report on Medical Services. That same year, Richards retired as vice president in charge of medical affairs at the University of Pennsylvania and became a member of the board of directors of Merck and Company. He had been a consultant to the company since 1931; later, between 1953 and 1955, he served as chairman of the scientific committee of the board of directors.

Throughout his life, Richards received numerous awards and honorary degrees and was a member of many professional and honorary organizations. In 1960 the University of Pennsylvania named after him the Alfred Newton Richards Medical Research Building, designed by the prominent architect Louis I. Kahn. Richards died in Bryn Mawr, Pennsylvania.

• Richards's papers are at the University of Pennsylvania Archives. "Alfred Newton Richards: Scientist and Man," an issue of *Annals of Internal Medicine* 71, suppl. 8 (1969), ed. Isaac Starr, includes a curriculum vitae, bibliography, excerpts from some of Richards's works, and biographical articles by students and colleagues. A chapter on Richards appears in Martin Meyerson and Dilys Pegler Winegrad, *Gladly Learn and Gladly Teach* (1978). Obituaries include Joseph T. Wearn, "Alfred Newton Richards," *Transactions of the Association of American Physicians* 79 (1966): 68–73; C. F. Schmidt, "Alfred Newton Richards," *Biographical Memoirs of the Royal Society* 13 (1967): 327–42; Detlev W. Bronk, "Alfred Newton Richards," American Philosophical Society, *Yearbook* (1971): 143–53; and Carl F. Schmidt, "Alfred Newton Richards," National Academy of Sciences, *Biographical Memoirs* 42 (1971): 271–318. The *New York Times* of 25 Mar. 1966 also has an obituary.

MIRIAM B. SPECTRE

RICHARDS, Dickinson Woodruff (30 Oct. 1895–23 Feb. 1973), physician and scientist, was born in Orange, New Jersey, the son of Dickinson Woodruff Richards, a lawyer, and Sally Lambert. He attended the Hotchkiss School, where he registered a remarkable scholarly performance, excelling in Greek. He received an A.B. in 1917 from Yale University, where again he chalked up an impressive record. Shortly after graduation, he enlisted in the U.S. Army and served with the American Expeditionary Force in France in 1918. After the war he received an M.A. in physiology from Columbia University in 1922 and an M.D. from Columbia University College of Physicians and Surgeons in 1923. His internship and residency in medicine at the Presbyterian Hospital in New York were followed by a one-year fellowship at the National Institute for Medical Research in London, where he worked with Sir Henry Dale, learning the basics of scientific medicine and clinical investigation. He returned in 1928 to the Columbia-Presbyterian Medical Center, where he served as an attending physician and teacher until 1945. In 1931 he married Constance Riley; the couple had four daughters.

Richards's colleague André Cournand, in paying tribute to his contributions to the study of the physiology and physiopathology of respiration and circulation in humans, identified several consecutive phases in Richards's scientific career. The first phase, from 1928 through 1932, was dominated by research that reflected the strong influence of Lawrence Joseph Henderson of Harvard University, who pictured the heart, lungs, and circulation as a unified system for the exchange of the respiratory gases between ambient air and the tissues of the body. During this period Richards published a classic study, "Oxyhemoglobin Dissociation Curves of Whole Blood in Anemia" (with M. Strauss, *Journal of Clinical Investigation* 4 [1927]: 105). He also undertook research with A. L. Barach into the effects of oxygen therapy in chronic cardiac and pulmonary disease. This collaborative effort helped lay the foundations for modern oxygen therapy.

The second phase of Richards's career, extending through 1940, centered on his collaboration with Cournand on studies of pulmonary function. It began with the introduction of Cournand, then chief resident of the Chest Service at Bellevue Hospital, to both the techniques and the disciplined scientific approach that Richards had mastered in the course of his training and research. The result of their subsequent collaboration was an outpouring of original papers dealing with innovative approaches to the study of pulmonary function in patients with different types of pulmonary diseases and the standardization of pulmonary function tests. These papers appeared in many journals, including *Medicine, Circulation,* and *Circulation Research.*

The next phase of Richards and Cournand's collaboration focused on the development of cardiac catheterization. The technique was introduced as a means of sampling mixed venous blood from the right side of the heart in order to apply the Fick principle, a mathematical formulation used to determine the cardiac output. After the technique had been improved and standardized, it was extended to a variety of hemodynamic studies. It turned out to be rewarding beyond all expectations. In rapid succession, Richards and Cournand applied the technique to shock, heart failure, assisted ventilation, acquired and congenital heart disease, and the effects of cardiac surgery. Later cardiothoracic surgery owed much of its progress to the application of this technique in various laboratories in this country and abroad.

Richards and Cournand's development of a research laboratory at Bellevue Hospital proved to be a landmark in the evolution of cardiology and chest medicine. It marked the transition from empiricism to scientifically grounded disciplines in diseases of the heart and lungs. The laboratory attracted national attention not only because of the scientific rigor with which it applied cardiac catheterization to the study of humans but also because it opened the way for modern medical and surgical interventions on the heart and lungs. Beginning in 1942, Richards organized at Bellevue a team of clinicians, physiologists, and surgeons from Columbia and New York Universities to study shock in humans. The pioneering results of these studies were summarized in his Harvey Lecture of 1944. These studies laid the physiological groundwork for the modern management of seriously ill patients in circulatory collapse. Pulmonary function tests were devised and standardized; the laboratory gained international acclaim for its original contributions to the understanding of the normal and abnormal pulmonary circulations, chronic pulmonary disease, and a wide variety of cardiac diseases. Trainees flocked to the Cardiopulmonary Laboratory from the United States and abroad. Many of these individuals subsequently became, in their own right, outstanding leaders in medicine, cardiology, and pulmonary disease.

In 1945 Richards moved his center of operations to Bellevue Hospital, becoming the director of the First Medical Division (Columbia). However, he continued to maintain close ties with the Presbyterian Hospital and in 1947 was designated Lambert Professor of Medicine at Columbia University. He promoted cardiopulmonary research not only at Bellevue but at Columbia-Presbyterian, where he encouraged the growth of a laboratory under the successive directorships of Drs. Eleanor Baldwin, John R. West, and Alfred P. Fishman. From the two laboratories Richards and collaborators issued papers addressing a wide variety of topics related to the physiology and physiopathology of circulation and respiration, including the oxygen-carrying pigment of the blood, the control of breathing and consequences of its derangement, and the oxygen consumption of the lung under normal conditions and in pulmonary disease.

In 1956 Richards and Cournand shared with Werner Forssman of Germany the Nobel Prize for medicine and physiology. The prize cited their "discoveries concerning heart catheterization and pathological changes in the circulatory systems." Richards received many other honors, including the John Phillips Memorial Award of the American College of Physicians in 1960, the Chevalier de la Legion d'Honneur in 1963, the Trudeau Medal in 1968, and the Kober Medal of the Association of American Physicians in 1970.

Richards retired from his positions at Bellevue and Columbia in 1961. For many years, he also served as a consultant to Merck, Sharp and Dohme Company, in which capacity he promoted fruitful research among scientists in government, industry, and the universities. He edited the *Merck Manual*, a synoptic textbook of medicine published by the Merck Company, as well.

In addition to being a pioneering physician, Richards was an analytical philosopher, classical scholar, distinguished lecturer, and social critic. He drew upon his experiences in the clinic, on the wards, and in the laboratory to develop a broad perspective on the workings of the body that extended far beyond the conventional integrative philosophy of his day. Based on his background, education, and delvings into medical history and philosophy, he also endeavored to trace the evolution of the modern physician from ancient Greek times to the present day. The development of his ideas along both lines can be seen in his small book *Medical Priesthoods* (1970), which consists of ten favorite lectures culled from the many he delivered over a stretch of forty-five years. He also coedited, with Alfred P. Fishman, *Circulation and Blood: Men and Ideas* (1964), in which prominent scientists each described the growth of understanding in a particular field of cardiovascular physiology.

A strong and vocal advocate of public health reform, Richards brought pressure to bear on New York City authorities to improve the care of the sick at Bellevue, thereby paving the way for the hospital's reconstruction. He also challenged the American Medical Association for its resistance to improving health care benefits for the elderly.

Richards died in Lakeville, Connecticut.

• For discussions of Richards's life and work, see André Cournand's autobiography, *From Roots to Late Budding* (1986), and Cournand's tribute in the *Transactions of the Association of American Physicians*, when Richards was awarded the Kober Medal in 1970. This tribute is also in the *American Journal of Medicine* 57 (1974): 312–30. A selected bibliography is included in National Academy of Sciences, *Biographical Memoirs* 58 (1989). An obituary is in the *New York Times*, 24 Feb. 1973.

ALFRED P. FISHMAN

RICHARDS, Ellen Henrietta Swallow (3 Dec. 1842–30 Mar. 1911), chemist and home economist, was born on a farm outside of Dunstable, Massachusetts, the only child of two schoolteachers, Peter Swallow and Fanny Gould Taylor. The family moved to nearby Westford so that Ellen could attend the coeducational Westford Academy. After graduation, she taught school briefly before returning home to nurse her ailing mother and work as a bookkeeper for her father, who had opened a general store. These years were marked by depression and despair. Richards was diagnosed as suffering from neurasthenia, which quickly subsided when her parents agreed to send her to the newly opened Vassar College for women.

In 1868 at the age of twenty-five Richards entered the junior class at Vassar, where she studied astronomy with Maria Mitchell and chemistry. Upon her graduation in 1870, she planned to go to the Argentine Republic as a teacher, but the plan was quashed by a political uprising. Instead she sought work, unsuccessfully, as a chemical analyst. One firm suggested she apply to the Massachusetts Institute of Technology. Founded in 1865, MIT was eager for qualified students and admitted her in December 1870, waiving her tuition because it did not wish to have a female student on the official rolls. Richards said later, "Had I realized on what basis I was taken, I would not have gone" (quoted in Hunt, p. 68).

Richards was the first woman to receive a degree from MIT, earning her B.S. in 1873. That same year she submitted a thesis on mineralogy to Vassar and received an M.A. Richards had planned to pursue a doctorate, but MIT did not wish to grant its first Ph.D. in chemistry to a woman and discouraged her studies. She stayed on as a laboratory assistant. In 1875 she married Robert Hallowell Richards, a professor of mining and metallurgy at MIT. The couple had no children. Richards continued her career in chemistry after her marriage. Working in the field of sanitary chemistry, she undertook the first scientific testing of America's water supply. Her survey of 40,000 samples of Massachusetts drinking water completed in 1887–1888 has stood as a benchmark for pollution studies.

Richards devoted her leisure to the promotion of higher education for women, founding in 1882 along with Marion Talbot the American Collegiate Association, precursor to the American Association of University Women. Intent on helping women achieve scientific education, she personally set up a woman's laboratory at MIT in 1876 and taught as a volunteer. In 1883, largely thanks to her efforts, women gained equal admission to the institute. The women's lab was torn down, and the following year Richards won an appointment as instructor of sanitary chemistry, the rank she held until her death. Informally she served as dean of women, setting up a woman's club and helping women students obtain financial aid.

In 1889 in an uncharacteristic moment of self-pity, she complained to a Vassar classmate, "I might have made a name and fame for myself. I have helped five men to positions they would not have held without me" (*Journal of Home Economics* 23 [Dec. 1931]: 1125). Frustrated and seeking an outlet for her prodigious energy, Richards put her talents to work in the service of domestic science, or home economics. While working in the women's lab she had begun to apply the principles of science to daily living, publishing *The Science of Cooking and Cleaning* (1880) and *Food Materials and Their Adulterations* (1885). She published seventeen books during her career, most of them related to domestic and sanitary science, where she spoke as an important pioneer in both fields. She also lectured extensively on topics ranging from "Chemistry in Relation to Household Economy" (1879) to "The Elevation of Applied Science to Equal Rank with the So-Called Learned Professions" (1911).

In 1890 Richards became involved in an experiment funded by Pauline Agassiz Shaw to provide nutritious food to Boston's poor. Working with Mary Hinman Abel she established the New England Kitchen, a food station where patrons could purchase meals to take home. Emphasis on bland New England cooking won few converts among Boston's Irish and Italian immigrants, but the experiment took her to the World's Columbian Exposition held in 1893 in Chicago, where she set up a model kitchen and developed a reputation as one of the early pioneers in nutrition.

More and more involved in domestic science, or home economics as it was coming to be called, Richards worked to professionalize the field by establishing the Lake Placid conferences (1899–1907), which met each summer to define and develop the field of home economics. Her work culminated in December 1908 with the founding of the American Home Economics Association, which elected her its first president. Richards herself favored the name "euthenics," which she defined as "the science of right living" and promoted in *Euthenics* (1910).

Under Richards's leadership home economics moved beyond emphasis on the household arts of cooking and sewing to train women in scientific principles and develop careers for college-educated women in university teaching and institutional management. Isabel Bevier, professor of household science at the University of Illinois, observed of Richards, "It is safe to say no university department has been organized, no important step taken, in which her ideas and her counsels have not had a part" (*Journal of Home Economics* 3 [June 1911]: 215). Richards had hoped to see home economics gain a place in the curriculum of the Seven Sisters colleges, but in 1890 and again in 1905 the American Collegiate Association, at the prompting of Bryn Mawr's M. Carey Thomas, ruled that home economics had no place in a college course for women. Richards did, however, receive an honorary doctor of science degree from Smith College in 1910.

Although she is considered the twentieth-century "mother of home economics," Richards never had the opportunity to teach a course in the subject. Instead, as instructor of sanitary chemistry at MIT, she trained hundreds of young men as sanitary engineers and chemists.

• Richards's papers are in the Edward Atkinson Papers, Massachusetts Historical Society, Boston; the MIT archives; the Vassar College archives; the Sophia Smith Collection, Smith College; the American Home Economics Association archives, Washington, D.C.; and the Schlesinger Library, Radcliffe College. Robert H. Richards, *His Mark* (1936), written by her husband, offers personal reflections on their life together. See also Robert Clarke, *Ellen Swallow: The Woman Who Founded Ecology* (1973); Caroline Hunt, *The Life of Ellen H. Richards* (1912); Sarah Stage, "From Domestic Science to Social Housekeeping: The Career of Ellen Richards," in *Power and Responsibility: Case Studies in American Leadership*, ed. David M. Kennedy and Michael E. Parrish (1986); and Margaret Rossiter, *Women Scientists in America: Struggles and Strategies to 1940* (1982).

SARAH STAGE

RICHARDS, I. A. (26 Feb. 1893–7 Sept. 1979), literary critic, poet, and educator, was born Ivor Armstrong Richards in Sandbach, Cheshire, England, the son of William Armstrong Richards, a chemical engineer, and Mary Ann Haigh. Richards studied moral sciences under J. M. E. McTaggart, W. E. Johnson, and G. E. Moore at Magdalene College, Cambridge, and received first-class honors in 1915. Shortly afterward, he suffered his third attack of tuberculosis, which kept him out of World War I. He recuperated in the mountains of North Wales where he met Dorothea Eleanor Pilley, a journalist and mountaineer, whom he married in 1926. They had no children. In 1919 he was invited to teach modern novels and literary theory in the recently founded English program at Cambridge.

About this time, together with C. K. Ogden, Richards began work on what has been called the best-known book ever written on semantics, *The Meaning of Meaning* (1923). Indebted to British philosophical psychology and pragmatism, but also incorporating new trends such as behaviorism, the authors advanced a theory of meaning based on the contextual situation, which they discussed in psychological and physical terms. Words "'mean' nothing by themselves"; it is only when someone "makes use of them that they stand for anything." Only context, that is, has meaning. Abstractions, universals, classes, all are so much "symbolic machinery," potentially useful for analysis, as long as one does not treat them as real; the rest are mere verbiage or "Word Magic." Two broad uses of language were outlined: emotive (expressing desires and feelings) and referential or symbolic (asserting or describing facts). In addition they distinguished five functions or jobs, each more or less present in a given utterance. In later works Richards would analyze as many as eight. One may choose "as many functions as one likes," Richards said, "provided each is given its specific work within the context."

Building on the semantics and psychology of *The Meaning of Meaning*, Richards turned to an examination of the nature and scope of literary language. *Principles of Literary Criticism* (1924) offers a theory of value and communication, and it champions a poetry that involves the widest interplay of ideas and emotions ("poetry of inclusion" with its "extraordinary hetero-

geneity"). Such a conflict of idea and emotion leads ideally to a synthetic resolution, an "equilibrium of opposed impulses," or "wholeness." Tragedy and literature with a high degree of irony were seen as bringing in the complementary or oppositional impulses or attitudes, Richards's favorite examples being literature in the "high modernist mode" such as Joyce's *Ulysses* and T. S. Eliot's *The Waste Land* or Dostoevsky.

Science and Poetry (1926) presented Richards's ideas in a popular form. He painted the postwar situation in the bleakest terms: the advancement of humanity has been blocked, while voices of propaganda, dogmatic philosophies, and wildly conflicting traditions assail us on all sides. History and science have stripped innumerable "beliefs" of their authority and created what appears to be an endless relativism. Language, meanwhile, has become debased and trivialized by the new media, and the age is awash with vulgarity and deceit. Yet the extreme suddenness, complexity, and danger of the situation can serve to increase awareness and shed light all around: "We shall be thrown back, as Matthew Arnold foresaw, upon poetry. It is capable of saving us." Richards meant that the immensely rich and varied body of world literature must be restudied and absorbed, not by the few, but by the many, and at a far deeper level of linguistic comprehension, for its emotional and intellectual insight and its internal debate over central human themes. Then individuals would be better prepared to assess the contemporary situation and legislate their future.

In 1929 Richards published what many consider to be his masterpiece, *Practical Criticism*. In one of the most famous experiments in the history of criticism, students at Cambridge were presented with poems varying greatly in their quality (the names of their authors being withheld) and asked to interpret them. Richards wanted to assess the problems that even honors students at a major university were encountering in their reading of not especially cryptic works of art. The book consists of Richards's analyses of their comments, grouped under type of error, his corrective method of "close reading," and a broad social and educational commentary. Some of the errors he identified are the interference of personal belief, stock responses, hobbyhorses, sentimentality, and irrelevant associations; the correctives include the analysis of tone (author as distinct from narrator), intention, feeling, and metaphor. The book also contained a penetrating critique of the media, as they then existed. Richards saw in the media's diffusion of ideas and information an inevitable leveling down, a reduction in the subtlety and refinement of ideas through the necessity of getting them across easily; he also saw the situation growing worse "as world communications, through the wireless and otherwise, improve."

Practical Criticism secured Richards's reputation, and together with his other books it exerted a potent influence on literary theory and practice—for example, of William Empson (one of Richards's students) and F. R. Leavis (who attended his lectures). Richards has been called the father of American New Criticism, the academic movement that dominated the teaching of literature in the universities from the 1940s to the 1960s and stressed the objective status and formal unity of the work of art. A typical New Critical analysis of a poem seeks to identify a poetic narrator; to locate tensions, ironies, and ambiguities among themes, images, and words; and to show thereby the structural integrity and internal equilibrium of the whole.

In the 1930s Richards's attention shifted from higher education to second-language training and beginning reading. He became increasingly involved with the movement surrounding Ogden's Basic English, a simplified version of English based on 850 key words and grammatical patterns, and he went to China for several years to attempt its implementation on a large scale. Among the results of these sojourns were *Mencius on the Mind* (1931), a study in the art of translation and the multiple definition of words, and *A First Book of English for Chinese Learners* (1938). After the Japanese invasion, which he witnessed in Beijing, cut short his larger plans, he accepted a position at the Harvard School of Education in 1939, eventually becoming university professor (1944–1963). There he pioneered the use of media in promoting literacy and in teaching reading and English as a second language with pictures, records, film, television, videotapes, and audiocassettes. His *English through Pictures* (1945), coauthored by Christine M. Gibson, was the pilot for the successful *Language through Pictures* series in seven languages. He translated Plato's *Republic* (1942), Homer's *Iliad* (*The Wrath of Achilles* [1950]), and other works into simplified English to provide beginning readers with major works of literature. He courted failure and misunderstanding through much of his second career because of what he considered the humanitarian goals at stake.

During this time Richards did not abandon his theoretical studies, and in 1936 he brought out his *Philosophy of Rhetoric* with his revolutionary theory of metaphor. Hitherto it was customary to define metaphor in terms of an idea and an image, the main value going to the idea. Richards named the two parts "tenor" and "vehicle," giving them equal weight in the making of the metaphor, seen now as a two-part unit. In the most successful metaphors, he showed, neither tenor nor vehicle go through the process unchanged: hence, his definition of metaphor as "a transaction between contexts." *Interpretation in Teaching* (1938) was intended to do for expository prose what *Practical Criticism* had done for the teaching of poetry, namely the close reading of prose. Although Richards preferred *Interpretation in Teaching* above all his books, it was not nearly as successful as his earlier works.

Nearing sixty, with two fruitful careers behind him, Richards began writing poetry. Showing the influence of Hardy and metaphysical wit, his poems display formal and linguistic variety and deal with philosophical issues, aspiration, old age, language, and high mountaineering, which was a lifelong passion. They were collected in *Internal Colloquies* (1971) and *New and Selected Poems* (1978); although they generally were given mixed reviews, Robert Lowell praised them warmly. In 1974 Richards published his humanistic testament, *Beyond*, a close reading of dialogues with deities from Homer, Plato, and the Book of Job, to Dante and Shelley. In the same year he returned to Cambridge, England. In 1979, in his eighty-seventh year, he accepted an invitation to tour China and lecture on the teaching of English. After several weeks on tour he fell seriously ill and was taken back to Cambridge, where he died.

In many ways Richards is the most representative critic of this century in the English-speaking world. One can point to his primary focus on language (so common today we almost forget the critical practice of 1914); his systematic spirit; his concern with science, psychology, and technology; his critical and experimental interest in modern media; his interdisciplinary approach; his perspectivism; his studies in translation and classical humanism; his internationalism. Similarly, his contributions to education extend from the most elementary to the most sophisticated levels. In one way, however, he can never be representative: his comprehensiveness. His criticism covers most phases of the communication process, from the artist, to the work, to the reader's response, and *Practical Criticism* ranks among the major texts in the history of twentieth-century criticism.

• Richards's letters and papers are housed in Magdalene College, Cambridge; letters and materials relating to his years in the United States are at the Widener and School of Education Libraries, Harvard University. For an annotated bibliography, see John Paul Russo, "A Bibliography . . . ," in *I. A. Richards: Essays in His Honor*, ed. Reuben Brower et al. (1973). For his biography, see John Paul Russo, *I. A. Richards: His Life and Work* (1989). Additional studies are W. H. N. Hotopf, *Language, Thought and Comprehension: A Case Study of the Writings of I. A. Richards* (1965); Jerome P. Schiller, *I. A. Richards's Theory of Literature* (1969); John Needham, *"The Completest Mode": I. A. Richards and the Continuity of English Criticism* (1982); and Ronald Shusterman, *Critique et poésie selon I. A. Richards: de la confiance au relativisme naissant* (1988). An obituary is in the *New York Times*, 8 Sept. 1979.

JOHN PAUL RUSSO

RICHARDS, Joseph William (28 July 1864–12 Oct. 1921), metallurgist and university professor, was born in Oldbury, Worcestershire, England, the son of Joseph Richards, a manufacturing metallurgical chemist, and Bridget Harvey. When he was approximately seven years old, Richards moved with his family to Philadelphia, where his father subsequently owned and operated a scrap metal recovery and evaluation facility. He was an excellent student and graduated from Lehigh University in 1886 with an analytical chemist degree. He then returned to his father's Delaware Metal Refinery in Philadelphia, where he served as superintendent for approximately a year. In 1877 Richards married his second cousin Arnamarie Gadd; they had three children.

Richards's senior thesis on the metallurgy of aluminum was published as *Aluminium* in 1887 and became recognized as the standard English-language treatise on the subject. It was revised and expanded in 1890 and 1896 and translated into a number of foreign languages. On the strength of this work Richards was invited to return to Lehigh to pursue graduate study and to serve as an assistant instructor in metallurgy and blowpiping in the mining and metallurgy curriculum. He received in 1891 the university's first M.S. and in 1893 its first Ph.D. (both in metallurgy), the latter with a thesis entitled "A Calorimetric Study of Copper." With the exception of a year's study in 1897–1898 in Heidelberg and Freiburg, Germany, Richards devoted his entire career after 1887 to metallurgical teaching and research at Lehigh, where he rose through the ranks to full professor of metallurgy.

As a teacher, Richards was able to inspire and stimulate the best from his own students, even when he dealt with the driest of technical subjects. His revision of a complex series of metallurgical course problems appeared as a series of articles in *Electrochemical Industry* and was later published as *Metallurgical Calculations* (1906–1908). Subsequently revised and widely translated, this three-volume work became a standard text on the subject and was perhaps his most important publication.

Richards frequently delivered lectures to professional scientific organizations and published extensively in their scholarly journals. He also translated into English from the original German and Italian five works on metallurgical and electrochemical subjects. Richards's own research and his frequent European trips, during which he acquired firsthand knowledge of industrial practices, made him one of the country's leading authorities on metallurgy, especially of aluminum and the electrochemical industry. He was a frequent consultant to industry and worked especially closely with Charles Martin Hall, the discoverer of the aluminum electrolytic reduction process, who worked for the Pittsburgh Reduction Co., which became Aluminum Company of America (Alcoa) in 1907. Richards both informally promoted the new industry by giving it visibility through his technical publications and provided a steady flow of students to Alcoa, especially after his creation in 1901 of a new electrometallurgy course at Lehigh, which led to the degree of El.Met. He also frequently served as an expert witness in patent litigations. Richards's proprietary knowledge of the industry was such that at one point he was receiving a princely annual retainer of $5,000 from Alcoa to keep his knowledge from competitors. In short, Richards served as one of the important scientific gatekeepers for the industry.

Richards's service to the professional technical community was equally important to his research publication and teaching of students. He was a founding member of the American Electrochemical Society, serving in 1902–1903 as its first president and from 1907 until his death as secretary and the editor of the society's *Transactions*. He also helped found in 1902

the allied industry-oriented journal *Electrochemical Industry*, which later became *Chemical Engineering*. In a 1902 inaugural address to the American Electrochemical Society and in a subsequent editorial in the first volume of *Transactions*, Richards noted that the changing face of scientific endeavor was creating the need for ever more specialized scientific societies.

Despite the increasing specialization of science and engineering, Richards retained an active interest in a wide range of fields and organizations. He was particularly active in the American Institute of Mining Engineers, serving it in a number of official capacities, including twice as its vice president (1910–1911 and 1916–1917). He also served as vice president of the American Chemical Society (1902) and as president of the Chemical Section of the Franklin Institute (1897 and 1899). He was a member of the Faraday Society, the Iron and Steel Institute of Great Britain, the American Iron and Steel Institute, the American Institute of Chemical Engineers, the Chemists' Club of New York, and the Engineers' Club of Philadelphia. He was also a member of the National Research Council and the Board of Engineering Foundation. In 1893 Richards received a medal at the Chicago World's Columbian Exposition for an exhibit that depicted the metallurgy of aluminum, and during World War I he served on the U.S. Navy Consulting Board as a dollar-a-year man (1915–1918).

An enthusiastic member of the National Geographic Society, Richards frequently gave slide-illustrated talks to a local geographic group that met monthly in his home. He was a member of the First Unitarian Church of Philadelphia, there being no formal church in Bethlehem, and his home was also the site for group meetings for religious discussion. He was a charter member of the renowned Bach Choir of Bethlehem, founded in 1898, for which he sang first bass at an annual May festival.

In an early 1895 essay entitled "Recent Advances in Electrochemistry," which was published in the Franklin Institute's *Journal* just as the field of electrochemistry was beginning to coalesce, Richards noted that in order "to be qualified as an electro-chemist," the scientist must be well versed both in chemistry and in theoretical electricity. He found "the scientist who is master in both sciences . . . a *rara avis*." By almost any measure, Richards was one of those rare birds. Well educated in several scientific fields, an eminent scholar, teacher, and author, he personified the turn-of-the-century era when scientific Ph.D.'s could still be less specialized yet make major contributions to the founding and development of whole new specialized fields of endeavor. In 1930, nine years after Richards's sudden death from heart failure at his home in Bethlehem, the American Electrochemical Society established an endowed lecture series in his name honoring his many contributions to the field of electrometallurgy.

• No central collection of Richards's personal papers is known to exist; however, a file entitled "Dr. Joseph W. Richards Correspondence, 1891–1901, AA, env. 119," pertaining to some of his Alcoa consulting work, is held at the corporate archives in Pittsburgh. In addition to Richards's books and translated works, an extensive set of his printed and published lectures and scientific papers can be found in the Special Collections Section of the Lehigh University Libraries. There is no full-scale biography of Richards, but helpful sources on his career include the third Richards lecture given in 1934 by his student Walter S. Landis, "Joseph W. Richards: The Teacher—The Industry," *Transactions of the American Electrochemical Society* 66 (1934): 6–14; and Robert D. Billinger's "America's Pioneer Press Agent for Aluminum—J. W. Richards," *Journal of Chemical Education* 14 (1937): 253–55. W. Ross Yates, *Lehigh University: A History of Education in Engineering, Business, and the Human Condition* (1992), provides both specific information on Richards as well as the overall setting in which he pursued his career, while George David Smith, *From Monopoly to Competition: The Transformation of Alcoa, 1888–1986* (1988); Margaret B. Graham and Bettye H. Pruitt, *R&D for Industry: A Century of Technical Innovation at Alcoa* (1990); and Martha Moore Trescott, *The Rise of the American Electrochemicals Industry, 1880–1910* (1981), provide useful overviews of the electrochemical and aluminum industries. Also useful is Robert M. Burns, *A History of the Electrochemical Society, 1902–1976* (1977). Obituaries are in *Mining and Metallurgy* 2 (Dec. 1921): 27–29 and *Transactions of the American Electrochemical Society* 40 (1921): 4–7.

STEPHEN H. CUTCLIFFE

RICHARDS, Laura Elizabeth Howe (27 Feb. 1850–14 Jan. 1943), author and biographer, was born in Boston, Massachusetts, the daughter of Samuel Gridley Howe, an educator, physician, and cofounder of the Perkins Institute for the Blind, and Julia Ward, a poet (the author of "The Battle Hymn of the Republic") and suffragist. Her namesake was Laura Bridgman, a student at the Perkins Institute and the first blind deaf-mute to learn to communicate. Educated first at home by her parents and tutors and then at private schools in Boston, Laura Howe and her five siblings were raised in relative wealth. When she was seventeen she traveled through Europe with her parents. In 1871, at the age of twenty-one, she married Henry Richards, a Boston architect and her brother Henry's classmate at Harvard. Laura and Henry Richards had seven children, one of whom died in infancy.

The couple lived in Boston until 1876, when, as a result of the panic of that year, Henry Richards had to close his architectural firm. They then moved to his childhood home in Gardiner, Maine, where he took over the management of the family paper mill. Although Richards had been writing all of her life, it was during this period, after the birth of their first child, that she began her professional writing career, presumably in part to assist the family financially.

A number of her nursery songs and nonsense rhymes had been published as early as 1873 in *St. Nicholas* magazine. Later they were compiled into a book, which Henry Richards illustrated, called *Sketches and Scraps*, published in 1881. The first book of nonsense rhymes to be written by an American and published in the United States, *Sketches and Scraps* marked the beginning of what was to be a prolific ca-

reer. Richards published more than ninety books, more than half of them for children, and during the course of her career she became known affectionately as the "Queen of Nonsense Verse."

Richards's writing, both in style and content, changed as her children grew and their interests changed; from the outset her stories were created to fit the particular developmental needs of her children. *Queen Hildegarde* (1889), for example, was the first in a series of books that Richards geared to young girls, the most popular of these being one of her more famous, *Captain January* (1890), about a lighthouse keeper who rescues a shipwrecked baby and raises her. Whether she wrote about pigs that swim or sharks that sing from the rooftops or feisty, outspoken little girls, all of her writing was marked by its strength, its simplicity, its fascination with sound, and its whimsy.

Interestingly, however, Richards is best known not for her children's nonsense verse but for the books she published about her own parents. She was responsible for editing her father's papers, which ultimately were published in two volumes as *The Letters and Journals of Samuel Gridley Howe* (1906–1909). She also wrote *Two Noble Lives* (1911), a book about her mother and father. Her most notable work, a collaboration with her sister Maud Howe Elliott, *Julia Ward Howe: 1819–1910* (1915), a biography of their mother, won them both the first Pulitzer Prize for biography, in 1917.

As if a writing career that spanned six decades did not demand enough of her time, Richards, and her husband, were active in local civic and philanthropic affairs. Richards was in part responsible for establishing the Gardiner library, through which she organized children's reading clubs, and from 1905 to 1911 she served as president of the Maine Consumers' League. She and her husband helped to establish the town high school, were successful in bringing public health nurses into the area, and worked to end abusive child labor practices. In 1893 the family paper mill burned and, though rebuilt, was closed permanently in 1900. The Richardses then opened a summer camp for boys on Lake Cobbosseecontee; Camp Merryweather, which operated for nearly thirty years, was one of the couple's most successful endeavors.

What is most curious, given Richards's ability as a writer, is that little of this information is included in her unrevealing autobiography, *Stepping Westward* (1931). It says nothing about the failures and financial hardships she experienced; neither does it focus on her greatest and most noble achievements. It is not even a book about herself or her feelings; rather, it chronicles what she and her husband did with their lives without offering more than a hint of how remarkable a woman she was. Richards died at her home in Gardiner, Maine.

• Richards's papers are at Colby College Library (Waterville, Maine) and at the Gardiner (Maine) Public Library. Her other books include *Five Mice in a Mouse Trap by the Man in the Moon, Done in Vernacular, from the Lunacular* (1880); *Little Tyrant* (1880); *Our Baby's Favorite* (1881); *The Joyous Story of*

Toto (1885); *Tell-Tale from Hill and Dale* (1886); *Kaspar Kroak's Kaleidoscope* (1886), written with Henry Baldwin; *Toto's Merry Winter* (1887); *In My Nursery* (1890); *Hildegarde's Holiday: A Sequel to Queen Hildegarde* (1891); *Hildegarde's Home* (1892); *Glimpses of the French Court: Sketches from French History* (1893); *Melody* (1893); *Marie* (1894); *When I Was Your Age* (1894); *Narcissa* (1894); *Five Minute Stories* (1895); *Hildegarde's Neighbors* (1895); *Jim of Hellas; or, In Durance Vile [and] Bethesda Pool* (1895); *Nautilus* (1895); *Isla Heron* (1896); *"Some Say" [and] Neighbors in Cyrus* (1896); *Hildegarde's Harvest* (1897); *Three Margarets* (1897); *Margaret Montfort* (1898); *Rosin the Beau* (1898); *Love and Rocks* (1898); *Sundown Songs* (1899); *Chop-Chin and the Golden Dragon* (1899); *The Golden-Breasted Kootoo* (1899); *Peggy* (1899); *Quicksilver Sue* (1899); *For Tommy, and Other Stories* (1900); *Rita* (1900); *Fernley House* (1901); *Geoffrey Strong* (1901); *The Hurdy-Gurdy* (1902); *Mrs. Tree* (1902); *The Green Satin Gown* (1903); *More Five Minute Stories* (1903); *The Golden Windows: A Book of Fables for Young and Old* (1903); *The Merryweathers* (1904); *The Armstrongs* (1905); *Mrs. Tree's Will* (1905); *The Piccolo* (1906); *The Silver Crown: Another Book of Fables* (1906); *Grandmother: The Story of a Life That Never Was Lived* (1907); *The Pig Brother and Other Fables and Stories* (1908); *The Wooing of Calvin Parks* (1908); *Florence Nightingale, the Angel of the Crimea* (1909); *A Happy Little Time* (1910); *The Naughty Comet and Other Fables and Stories* (1910); *On Board the Mary Sands* (1911); *Jolly Jingles* (1912); *Miss Jimmy* (1913); *The Little Master* (1913; republished in 1922 as *Our Little Feudal Cousin of Long Ago*); *Three Minute Stories* (1914); *The Pig Brother Play-Book* (1915); *Elizabeth Fry, the Angel of the Prisons* (1916); *Fairy Operettas* (1916); *Pippin, a Wandering Flame* (1917); *Abigail Adams and Her Times* (1917); *A Daughter of Jehu* (1918); *Joan of Arc* (1919); *Honor Bright* (1920); *In Blessed Cyrus* (1921); *The Squire* (1923); *Acting Charades* (1924); *Seven Oriental Operettas* (1924); *Honor Bright's New Adventure* (1925); *Star Bright, a Sequel to Captain January* (1927); *Laura Bridgman: The Story of an Opened Door* (1928); *Tirra Lirra: Rhymes Old and New* (1932), considered by some to be a collection of the best nonsense verse for children ever written by an American; *Merry-Go-Round: New Rhymes and Old* (1935); *E. A. R.* (1936), a book about poet Edwin Arlington Robinson, to whom Richards had become a close friend and adviser; *Harry in England* (1937); *I Have a Song to Sing to You* (1938); *The Hottentot, and Other Ditties* (1939), with words and melodies by Richards and piano notation by Twining Lynes; and *What Shall the Children Read?* (1939). For a fine critical analysis of Richards, see Anne T. Eaton's review in *Horn Book*, July-Aug. 1941, and Ruth Hill Viguers four-part article "Laura E. Richards: Joyous Companion," *Horn Book*, Apr., June, Oct., and Dec. 1956. Obituaries are in the *New York Times*, 15 Jan. 1943, and *Publisher's Weekly*, 23 Jan. 1943.

ALI LANG-SMITH

RICHARDS, Linda (27 July 1841–16 Apr. 1930), nursing leader and pioneer, was born Melinda Ann Judson Richards near Potsdam, New York, the daughter of Sanford Richards and Betsy Sinclair. No information on her early life and education is available. Evangelical religious roots and missionary habits, however, provided foundation, character, and purpose to Richards's nursing life. As she wrote in her autobiography of 1911, "Quite early in my teens I was called upon for such service . . . " In an era that preceded any sort of formal nurses' training, when minimal hospital sick-care was provided by charwomen, unemployed men,

or recovering patients, Richards worked at Boston City Hospital and "learned how little care was given to the sick, how little their groans and restlessness meant to most of the [untrained] nurses . . . the majority [of whom] were thoughtless, careless, and often heartless." Determined to reform sick-care, Richards embarked upon her nursing career, which lasted forty years and included superintendencies at myriad institutions: four major hospitals, four smaller ones, four mental institutions (one of which she returned to for a second time), one Visiting Nurse Service, and one foreign school. In addition, she visited three British hospitals and consulted on the founding of other schools, including the first hospital school for nursing the insane in America.

In 1873 Richards graduated from a nurses' training course, which was started by Dr. Susan Dimock, at the New England Hospital for Women and Children in Roxbury, near Boston. As the first applicant and graduate of this course, the first formal training course for nurses in America, Richards became known as America's first trained nurse. There were other significant "firsts" in Richards' career. In 1874 she wrote the first nurses' informational note in a patient record. From 1874 to 1877 Richards was the first superintendent of nurses at the Boston Training School, later the Massachusetts General Hospital Training School of Nursing. In 1878 she established the Boston City Hospital Training School for Nurses and placed it under medical authority rather than under a board of women, a decision that angered some of her nursing contemporaries because it violated Florence Nightingale's advice to keep nursing separate from the hospital. While at Boston City Hospital, Richards was among the first to inaugurate asepsis protocols. She also helped found the first Japanese nurses' training school at Doshisha Hospital in Kyoto while she served there with the Congregational Missions from 1885 to 1890. She became the first president of the American Society for the Superintendents of Training Schools (now the National League for Nursing), which formed in 1893. In 1900, when the nursing profession established its first journal, *The American Journal of Nursing*, association leaders urged members to purchase stock in the journal company to finance the venture, and Richards purchased the first share.

Richards's reforms of nursing care took place through schools of nursing because, prior to World War II, schools were the nursing service departments of hospitals, and pupils were the predominant providers of patient care. Drawing on Victorian and missionary ideals, and eager to raise the class and character of care providers, Richards's reforms included teaching nurses to be subservient and self-sacrificing as well as knowledgeable care providers. A rural person, unused to the patronage of sophisticated women who constituted the boards of women that founded and directed other early nurses' training schools, Richards developed schools that were separate from philanthropic sponsors. Instead she made nursing an integral department of the hospital, relying on physicians whom she trusted because of her early experiences with Dr. Dimock. Other nursing leaders, who found physicians hostile toward nurses, disagreed with Richards's approach. Consequently, although Richards greatly influenced the development of nursing as an art, she was seen as a marginal, or even negative, contributor to nursing's emergence as an autonomous profession.

In 1911, the year following the deaths of two other nursing legends, Florence Nightingale and Isabel Hampton Robb, Richards retired to Providence to live quietly with one of her sisters. In 1925 she suffered a cerebral hemorrhage and moved to the Frances Willard Home in Northboro, Massachusetts. Five years later she returned to the New England Hospital for Women and Children and died in the place where she had begun her nursing career. Perhaps a fitting epitaph is found in the words of Dr. Alfred Worcester, a physician prominent in promoting nursing education, at the time of her death: "In the advance of the science of nursing she had been left far behind; but in the art of nursing she never lost her pre-eminence."

• Richards's autobiography, *Reminiscences of Linda Richards, America's First Trained Nurse* (1911), as well as several letters, notes, and articles by or about her, are available in *The History of Nursing* Microfiche Collection in the Archives of the Department of Nursing Education at Teachers College, Columbia University. Several articles by or about Richards can be found in *The American Journal of Nursing* in 1900, 1901, 1903, 1915, 1920, and 1948. See also Meta R. Pennock, ed., *Makers of Nursing History* (1940). An obituary by Dr. Alfred Worcester appeared in the *New England Journal of Medicine* 202 (29 May 1930): 22. For a comparison of Richards to other early nursing leaders, see Ellen D. Baer, "Nursing's Divided House—An Historical View," *Nursing Research* 34, no. 1 (1985): 32–38.

ELLEN D. BAER

RICHARDS, Paul Snelgrove (25 Nov. 1892–20 Nov. 1958), physician, was born in Salt Lake City, Utah Territory, the son of Willard Brigham Richards and Louise Snelgrove, farmers. Overcoming serious childhood ailments, inflammatory rheumatism, and stammering, Richards served a proselytizing mission for the Church of Jesus Christ of Latter Day Saints in Scotland in 1911–1912. Although diphtheria cut his mission short, he had, through the experience, overcome his stammering and acquired an eagerness for education. He married Ethel Bennion in September 1916; they had three children. Richards graduated from Harvard University with an M.D. in 1920, interned at Cincinnati General Hospital in 1920–1921, and served residencies in obstetrics and gynecology at Boston Free Hospital for Women and Boston Lying-in Hospital in 1921–1922.

On 7 October 1922 Richards assumed control of the Bingham Canyon Hospital and Clinic in Bingham, Utah. His service to the hospital, which served three mines, including a large open-pit copper mine, was the advent of his career in industrial medicine. During the years 1922–1948 the clinic expanded from a dozen beds to a 35-bed hospital, with sixty-seven employees and five physicians.

Concern over lingering complications from silicosis tuberculosis, an industrial disease, caused Richards to encourage the local mines to introduce occupational safety measures, such as steps to improve mine ventilation and wetting down dust to prevent inhalation of the fine silica particles into the lungs. He also successfully lobbied the local mining companies to jointly hire an expert in industrial hygiene, Oscar A. Glaser. Their collaboration, which involved collecting X-rays and other clinical information, resulted in an industrial health research project under the auspices of the U.S. Public Health Service. In 1953 Richards earned a presidential citation for these activities.

Promoting a "Safety First" program, Richards's efforts led, on a national scale, to improved sanitation, lighting, ventilation, compulsory helmets, and safety goggles. In the 1930s Richards contributed to the design of the goggles by making plaster faces, exposing them to dynamite blasts, and analyzing the patterns formed by the embedded particles. A well-respected community leader, Richards was a major force in convincing mining officials of the advantages of safety programs. From 1938 to 1940 Richards served on the Utah Medical, Labor and Industrial Council and, in 1941, served on a committee that drafted the first occupational disease law for Utah. He was also the first clinical professor of industrial medicine at the College of Medicine, University of Utah, from 1944 to 1947.

Medical practice in a mining town included a great deal of surgery for traumatic injury resulting from falls, blasting, fires, floods, snowslides, and cave-ins. A snowslide in February 1926 killed thirty-nine town members and buried another 150. The victims, frozen into immobility, were removed hours later, with faintly beating hearts. Placing the victims in a cold room, Richards and his staff used towels to wipe away the snow. Richards then instructed volunteers to gently massage the entire body of each victim, using the warmth of their hands to gradually melt away the frost. At times, sixty to eighty people were working over the victims. Every victim who had a discernible heartbeat, even as slow as eight beats per minute, was revived and recovered. Later accounts of this experience at medical conferences were often disbelieved by other physicians.

Richards was also active in rehabilitative surgery. At the time, a fracture of the spine was thought to lead to permanent disability. Richards disproved this theory by demonstrating that injured workers could recover with the correct surgery and care. In conjunction with this theory, Richards was a pioneer in performing intervertebral disc operations. His skill became so renowned that, in the course of a year, he performed surgery on cases from twenty-two states. He was also sought out for his skill in repairing ruptured supraspinatus tendons in the shoulder, another common cause of disability. In 1953, along with Dr. Louis E. Viko, he received another presidential citation for outstanding service in rehabilitation.

As a member of the Jordan (Utah) School Board, which he served ten years as president, Richards expanded vocational education, introduced and taught sex education, and organized the first mass immunization campaign in a Utah school district.

In 1948 cancerous lesions on his hands from overexposure to radium and X-rays forced Richards to leave his Bingham practice. After operations and painful recuperation, he began to practice again in 1951 with the eldest of his three children, Dr. Lenore Richards. In 1953 they opened the Memorial Medical Center in Salt Lake City, naming it in honor of Richards's paternal grandfather, William Richards, and uncles, all three of whom were physicians. He founded the Richards Memorial Medical Foundation in 1958 to fund future medical research. Richards died in Salt Lake City of cancer.

While Richards did not make a major contribution to any one particular field, his interests and activities contributed to smaller advances in a number of fields, refining the work of others in industrial medicine and rehabilitative surgery. His concern for miners and their job-related health problems led to significant work in safety reform. A caring, compassionate man as well as a gifted surgeon, he spent his entire life striving for health reform in the mining industry.

• Scant information is available on the life of Richards. An invaluable source is "The Memoirs of Dr. Paul" (1963), left by Richards for his family. It is available at the University of Utah. A brief biography can be found in the *Dictionary of American Medical Biography*, ed. Martin Kaufman et al. (1984).

ERIC G. SWEDIN
MICHELLE E. OSBORN

RICHARDS, Theodore William (31 Jan. 1868–2 Apr. 1928), chemist, was born in Germantown, Pennsylvania, the son of William Trost Richards, a noted artist, and Anna Matlack, a Quaker author and poet. His father's predilection for seascapes took the family to Newport, Rhode Island, every summer. It was there, at the age of six, that Richards became inspired to the study of science through his acquaintance with Josiah Parsons Cooke, the founding father of academic chemistry at Harvard University. After graduating from Haverford College he joined the senior class at Harvard with the goal of earning a second bachelor's degree. He graduated in 1886 with highest honors in chemistry. Richards continued to study under Cooke's direction, earning the Ph.D. two years later at the early age of twenty. A one-year postdoctoral fellowship allowed him to study in Göttingen, under the tutelage of Victor Meyer and Paul Jannasch. Upon his return he joined the faculty at Harvard and began his rise through the academic ranks. His last promotion, to full professor in 1901, was occasioned by the unusual offer of a chair in physical chemistry at Göttingen. In 1896 Richards married Miriam Stuart Thayer, the daughter of a faculty colleague; they had three children.

Cooke had long been interested in increasing the precision of measurements of atomic weights, and Richards continued this work in his doctoral dissertation and thereafter. Accuracy was important not only for conventional and fiducial reasons, but it was also fundamental to the theory of matter. Since the origin of the chemical atomic theory nearly a hundred years earlier, the notion that all elemental atomic weights might be integral multiples of that of the lightest element, hydrogen, had been contested. If this thesis were true, it would be reasonable to suppose that all elements are composed of hydrogen more or less condensed to form atoms of the heavier elements. Earlier work, including that of Cooke, had suggested that most elements have atomic weights that are close to, but by no means precisely, integral values. Richards's first research, carried out under Cooke's direction, provided the most accurate determination to date of the single most critical measurement—the atomic-weight ratio of oxygen to hydrogen. His value, after subsequent correction of a subtle physical factor noted by Lord Rayleigh, the English mathematician and physicist, was accepted as definitive by the scientific world and in fact stands within 0.02 percent of the currently accepted figure.

It is important to note that this determination was carried out with means little different from those used by chemists dating back to the eighteenth century—namely, gravimetric "wet-chemical" methods. Such procedures are subject to many sources of error that are exceedingly difficult to eliminate. The accuracy achieved by Richards was attainable only by application of his many scientific skills and human virtues, chief among which were manipulative skill, wide understanding of physics and chemistry, methodological inventiveness, painstaking attention to detail, intellectual honesty, and extraordinary patience. Only a few years later, with the advent of mass spectrography, such measurements became, in principle, simpler and more precise.

Richards went on to determine the weights of twenty-five particularly important elements, once more achieving accuracies that far outdistanced earlier efforts and in several cases correcting values that were in significant error. Two of his students, Gregory P. Baxter and Otto Hönigschmidt, soon added thirty additional atomic weight determinations to the list. About half of Richards's 292 research papers concerned atomic weights. Perhaps his most dramatic finding was his verification that lead associated with uranium has a slightly different atomic weight from lead found in its usual geological deposits, thus helping to confirm the novel theory of radioactive decay.

By the turn of the century Richards's work with atomic weights had made him world famous. In 1903 he became chairman of the chemistry department at Harvard, and in 1912 a large new teaching and research laboratory was completed for his use; in the latter year he was also appointed to the Erving Professorship. Two years later he was awarded the Nobel Prize in Chemistry, becoming the first American to receive that honor (and the last until 1932).

When Cooke died in 1894, Harvard provided Richards with funds to support study at the laboratories of Wilhelm Ostwald in Leipzig and Walther Nernst at Göttingen (Germany then formed the focal point of the relatively young discipline of physical chemistry, and Ostwald and Nernst were the only two full professors in that field). Because of these sojourns in Germany—including a third visit in 1907, when he spent six months as exchange professor in Berlin—Richards is sometimes considered to have been essentially German-trained. In any case, his exposure to the breadth of interests of Ostwald and Nernst led to an expansion of his research agenda into thermochemical and electrochemical problems, research that was carried out concurrently with his continuing work on atomic weights. For instance, his development of a novel adiabatic calorimeter led to a fine series of investigations into specific heats and heats of solution, evaporation, combustion, and neutralization.

In 1902 Richards published an investigation into the free energies and enthalpies of electrochemical reactions at low temperatures. His extrapolations of these data to absolute zero stimulated several European chemists toward an idea first enunciated four years later by Nernst—what has come to be known as the third law of thermodynamics. Richards and a few latter-day defenders have argued that this law was first revealed in his 1902 paper. However, it is doubtful that Richards fully understood the thermodynamic implications of his data; his actual purpose for the research was to provide support for his own theory of the compressibility of atoms. The latter became an idée fixe for Richards; although he devoted much of the last ten years of his life to investigating the notion, he was never able to convince his colleagues in the field of its importance.

A key to the understanding of Richards's career and its significance is to note that although his research interests broadened considerably after 1894, his style never really changed from his first remarkable research performed as a student. No one in the world was superior to Richards in the art of measurement and the painstaking elimination of even the most subtle sources of error. On the other hand, he was uninterested in many theoretical issues that were engaging his colleagues, and his mathematical skills were quite modest. His approach was instinctively inductive, and he had a visceral suspicion of theoretical models, especially highly mathematized ones. When an undergraduate named J. Robert Oppenheimer took Richards's course in 1925, he regarded it as "a very meager hick course. . . . It was formal and tentative and timid; Richards was afraid of even rudimentary mathematics."

Despite this negative reaction of a brilliant and headstrong young man, Richards was in fact a dedicated and extraordinarily successful teacher. In addition to the students already named, Richards was doctoral advisor to Ebenezer Henry Archibald, James B. Co-

nant, Farrington Daniels, Norris Hall, Gilbert N. Lewis, Hobart Willard, and many other future leaders of American academic chemistry—more than sixty in all. In sum, he made Harvard into a mecca of physical and analytical chemical research. The research of his students, both while under his direction and subsequently, was of enormous quantity and the highest quality. Always working with a limited group of around a dozen students, Richards dedicated himself to their education in the fullest sense. He was a fine lecturer of imposing presence and appealing diction; his exposition was invariably marked by the highest standards of clarity, logic, and organization.

Richards's career was motivated, in his own words, by "an intense desire to know something more definite about the material and energetic structure of the universe." He had an engaging personality and cultivated wide interests in sports, music, literature, and art; he was as devoted to his family as he was to his profession. His guiding principles in life were kindliness and common sense, and he always maintained that the moral conditions for success in science were "perfect sincerity and truth." Those who knew him always averred that he approached closely the standards of his own ideal.

Richards died in Cambridge, Massachusetts.

• Richards's voluminous papers are held in the Harvard University Archives. A full historical study of his career is provided in Sheldon Kopperl, "The Scientific Work of Theodore William Richards" (Ph.D. diss., Univ. of Wisconsin, 1970). The best biographies are Harold Hartley, "T. W. Richards Memorial Lecture," *Journal of the Chemical Society* (1930) pp. 1937–68, and J. B. Conant, "T. W. Richards," *National Academy of Sciences, Biographical Memoirs* 44 (1974): 251–70 (followed by a bibliography of Richards's scientific papers, on pp. 271–86). The historical context for Richards's career is provided by John Servos, *Physical Chemistry from Ostwald to Pauling: The Making of a Science in America* (1990).

ALAN J. ROCKE

RICHARDS, Vincent (20 Mar. 1903–28 Sept. 1959), tennis player, was born in New York City, the son of Edward A. Richards, a building contractor, and Mary Frances McQuade. His family moved to South Yonkers, New York, while he was still small, and his father died when he was eight years old. Given a battered tennis racket, he hit a rubber ball against a brick wall interminably until he acquired pinpoint accuracy. By retrieving strayed tennis balls he gained entrance into nearby Lowerre Tennis Club and soon defeated the club champion. In 1915 Richards won the Yonkers junior championship, and one year later he became the runner-up in a boy's tourney at Sleepy Hollow (New York) Country Club after noted tennis player Fred B. Alexander sponsored his entry. Richards won numerous younger-age United States championships, including boys' singles in 1917 and 1918; junior singles in 1919, 1920, and 1921; and junior doubles with Harold Taylor in 1918. After graduating in 1919 from Fordham Preparatory School, Richards attended Fordham University two years, and, in 1922, studied a year at Columbia University School of Journalism. During this time Richards held various jobs: as a chalk boy on Wall Street; as a salesman and racket stringer at Alex Taylor's sporting goods store in New York City; as an assistant sports editor for the *Yonkers Statesman*; and as a copy boy and assistant rewrite man for the *Evening Mail* in New York City.

Bill Tilden and Richards became friends in 1916. Two years later Tilden asked the youngster to be his partner in the national championship. The pair captured U.S. doubles crowns in 1918, 1921, and 1922 and lost a 1922 Davis Cup challenge round match to Australasians Pat O'Hara Wood and Gerald Patterson. Richards, the small, 105-pound "Boy Wonder," became the youngest player to win a U.S. men's singles match by defeating Frank Anderson. Subsequently he earned five U.S. top-ten rankings: fourth in 1923; third in 1921, 1922, and 1925; and second in 1924. At the time, Richards was generally considered the world's best volleyer, but his chopped and sliced groundstrokes were average at best. Tilden advised him to strengthen his baseline game, but he reasoned that his strong serves, smashes, and magnificent net attack ultimately would prevail. In other Davis Cup challenge rounds, he vanquished O'Hara Wood and Patterson in singles in 1924 and, with Dick Williams, scored two brilliant doubles victories over the French "Four Musketeers": Rene Lacoste and Jean Borotra in 1925, and Henri Cochet and Jacques Brugnon in 1926. Richards and Williams also won the 1925 and 1926 U.S. doubles championships, never extending beyond four sets in any of their matches.

Richards made his first European trip in mid-1923, utilizing $400 raised by New York Tennis Club friends. His only victories during this time came in the London championship, a warm-up event before Wimbledon, in which he won the singles and the doubles with Frank Hunter, his closest friend among players. One opponent, Francis Marion Bates Fisher, who then headed the sports department at Dunlop Tire & Rubber Company of London, asked Richards to test Dunlop's new ball and racket. Richards tested them thoroughly and furnished a full written report.

In January 1924 Richards married Claremont Gushee, named for her father's fashionable Claremont Inn, in New York City. They had three children before her death in 1950. Also in 1924 Richards captured the doubles title with Hunter at Wimbledon and at the Olympic Games in Paris he won the gold medal in singles, besting Mohammed Sleem, Manuel Alonso, Umberto de Morpurgo, and Cochet; the gold medal in doubles, with Hunter; and the silver medal in mixed doubles, with Marion Zinderstein Jessup.

Richards supported his tennis career by writing magazine articles and reporting on tournaments he entered. He worked for King Features Syndicate from 1924 until 1927, when Arthur Brisbane fired him for refusing a non-tennis assignment. He reached the U.S. singles semifinals three times but lost to Tilden in 1924 and 1925 and to Borotra in 1926. Richards lost his $8,000 journalist's salary in early 1925 as the result

of a decision by the U.S. Lawn Tennis Association (USLTA) to prohibit players from being paid for writing about tournaments in which they were competing. He compensated partially by selling insurance for the Equitable Life Assurance Society.

During 1926 Richards's singles record clearly surpassed Tilden's. Richards defeated Tilden in three of four outdoor matches, lost to no other American, and won six tournaments. To support his family, Richards accepted, for a reputed $35,000, Charles C. Pyle's offer to play professionally on the "Suzanne Lenglen North-American Tour." Announcement of the plan was withheld until 30 September 1926 after Richards had completed his season's play, in order to protect his anticipated number one ranking as an amateur. However, while the USLTA Ranking Committee complied with this expectation, the Executive Committee ruled Richards ineligible for ranking because the 1926 schedule of all sanctioned tournaments extended beyond 30 September; hence, Richards had actually made his announcement before the end of the season.

The tour included Richards, Lenglen, Mary K. Browne, Paul Feret, Howard Kinsey, and Harvey Snodgrass. Beginning on 9 October 1926, the players performed in forty cities before the tour was terminated on 14 February 1927. That September, thirteen professionals, including Richards, founded the Professional Lawn Tennis Players Association of the United States. Richards won PLTA singles championships in 1927, 1928, 1930, and 1933, as well as six doubles titles with various partners.

In 1929 Fisher persuaded the president of Dunlop's U.S. operation to add sports equipment manufacturing to tire production, as the British parent company had done, and to install Richards to furnish his expertise. The enterprise flourished, and ultimately Richards became vice president of the sporting goods division, remaining in this position until his death. He retired from tennis competition in 1930 but returned intermittently. During World War II he played to benefit patriotic causes. He won one more title in 1945, the PLTA doubles championship; fittingly, his partner was Bill Tilden.

Richards died in New York City. In 1961 he was elected to the National Lawn (later International) Tennis Hall of Fame. He fulfilled his early potential in doubles but not in singles. According to an obituary in *Lawn Tennis and Badminton*, "He failed to stabilise a good baseline game." He never reached a singles final of a major annual world-class championship, yet he defeated Tilden eight times in amateur tournaments, more than anyone else (while losing to him fifteen times). A strong advocate for open tennis, he strove to establish season circuits of professional tournaments long before they actually materialized.

• Early parts of an autobiography, never completed, appear in *World Tennis*, July 1957, pp. 16–19; Aug. 1957, pp. 54–58; Nov. 1957, pp. 46–49; Dec. 1957, pp. 32–35; and Jan. 1958, pp. 35–37. A comprehensive biographical sketch is in Bud Collins and Zander Hollander, eds., *Bud Collins' Modern En-*

cyclopedia of Tennis, 2d ed. (1994), pp. 438–39. Richards provided personal background and commentary on the state of tennis in "Ex-Amateur," as told to John Tunis, *Liberty*, 8 July 1933, pp. 20–23, and 15 July 1933, pp. 28–31. Critical analyses of Richards's playing style are in Lawrence Rice, "Youth Will Be Served: Vincent Richards," and Wallis Merrihew, "Another Viewpoint of Richards," both in *American Lawn Tennis*, 15 July 1922. Obituaries are in the *New York Times*, 29 Sept. 1959, and *Lawn Tennis and Badminton*, 15 Nov. 1959, p. 488. Arthur Daley, "Sports of the Times: The First Wonder Boy," *New York Times*, 3 Nov. 1959, supplements the obituary by recalling memories of Richards.

FRANK V. PHELPS

RICHARDS, William Trost (14 Nov. 1833–8 Nov. 1905), landscape and marine painter, was born in Philadelphia, Pennsylvania, the son of Benjamin Moore Richards, a Welsh immigrant, and Anna Trost. Little is known about Richards's parents or his early childhood. His formal education was limited. In 1846 he entered Philadelphia's rigorous and innovative Central High School, where he may have received some formal art instruction, but his time there was brief. He withdrew from the school in October 1847, presumably because of the death of his father and the resulting pressure to contribute to the family income.

By 1850 Richards had found employment designing ornamental metalwork for a Philadelphia manufacturing firm. Yet he had already set his sights on a career as a landscape painter, devoting his evenings to drawing and his vacations to sketching the countryside around Philadelphia and further afield. He also sought instruction from the German-born landscape and portrait painter Paul Weber, with whom he studied from about 1850 to 1855. His work during this period was strongly influenced by the large-scale, realistic landscape paintings of artists of the Hudson River School such as Frederic Church and Jasper Cropsey. Through both their example and Weber's instruction, Richards absorbed a concern with the meticulous delineation of natural details and a belief in the morally and spiritually uplifting power of landscape art.

In 1852 the Pennsylvania Academy of the Fine Arts exhibited Richards's work for the first time. After exhibiting at the academy the next year, he was so encouraged by the critical response to his paintings that he gave up his full-time employment to concentrate on his art. In 1854 he described his artistic ambitions in a letter to his friend James Mitchell, writing of his "desire that will not rest satisfied till landscape can tell stories to the human heart and be a medium of noble and powerful expression even as the human countenance."

In the summer of 1855 he embarked on the first of many European sojourns, spending nine months in France, Switzerland, and Italy sketching scenery and looking at art. In 1856 he returned to Philadelphia to marry a young Quaker woman, Anna Matlack. Though her parents opposed the union, theirs was a long and affectionate marriage, resulting in the birth of eight children, five of whom lived to adulthood.

During the 1860s Richards committed his energies to the advancement of his career, exhibiting widely, taking on pupils, and seeking membership in various artistic organizations, all with considerable success. He established a solid reputation and won election to both the Pennsylvania Academy of the Fine Arts (1863) and the National Academy of Design (1871). In 1863 he joined the American Association for the Advancement of Truth in Art, a group of American Pre-Raphaelites. These young men and women were committed to reforming American art and architecture according to principles expounded by the British critic John Ruskin. For painting, Ruskin advocated an artistic "truth to nature," urging young artists to faithfully replicate the observed appearance of the natural world as an avenue to spiritual truth. Richards's paintings of these years epitomize the American Pre-Raphaelite style. They include *In the Woods* (1860, Bowdoin College Museum of Art), *Landscape* (1860, Yale University Art Gallery), *Red Clover, Butter-and-Eggs, and Ground Ivy* (1860, Walters Art Gallery, Baltimore, Md.), and *Forest Scene* (1866, Brooklyn Museum). Most represent forest interiors or close-up studies of plants and rocks executed in high-keyed colors with painstaking attention to detail.

In the late 1860s and 1870s Richards's life and art underwent a change. He announced his withdrawal from "art politics" and began spending increasing amounts of time at the seashore, purchasing a home in Newport, Rhode Island, in 1875. His subject matter gradually shifted from woodland scenery to coastal and marine themes, while watercolor, then enjoying a newfound prestige in American art circles, became for him an increasingly important medium. Although Newport provided many of his subjects during these years, he continually sought out new motifs, finding inspiration up and down the East Coast from Cape May, New Jersey, to Mount Desert, Maine, his interest in these sites corresponding to their growing popularity as vacation resorts. Richards's images of these years continued to be rooted in an intense study of his subject; one of his sons recalled that he would stand in the surf for long periods of time trying to catch the precise motion of the waves. Yet his concern was always as much with the mood and meaning of the scenery as it was with the facts. His paintings of this time period include *Seascape* (1870, Wellesley College), *East Hampton Beach* (1871–1874, High Museum of Art, Atlanta, Ga.), and *On the Coast of New Jersey* (1883, Corcoran Gallery of Art, Washington, D.C.). Through his consummate evocation of luminous light and varied atmospheric effects, he defined the poetic, spiritual, and symbolic content of his paintings.

The later 1870s marked the beginning of a more difficult period in Richards's career. At that time the American art scene was undergoing dramatic changes as patrons shifted their attention from native artists and native subjects to more cosmopolitan, European works. Many American landscape painters of this era fell under the influence of the French Barbizon and impressionist styles, but Richards deliberately clung to the style of meticulous realism he had mastered in his youth. Recognizing his apparent obsolescence, he wrote in 1879, "I feel that I am an old fogy." Perhaps under the influence of these new imported styles, his paint handling became a bit looser, but his only major concession to the new European orientation of the market was to turn abroad for some of his subjects and sales, spending long periods of time in England, with shorter trips to Scotland, Ireland, France, Italy, and Norway. These trips resulted in works such as *Mythical England: Stonehenge* (1882, Vassar College Art Gallery), *The Beach at Tenby, Wales* (c. 1885, Pennsylvania Academy of the Fine Arts, Philadelphia), and *League Long Breakers Thundering on the Reef* (1887, Brooklyn Museum), a view of the Cornwall coast.

His gambits seem to have been successful, for two decades later he was still painting for an appreciative, if conservative, audience. In 1898 he expressed himself "full of grateful astonishment at the unaccountable fact that there persists a vogue for the Richards pictures." When he died at Newport he was still painting, still solvent, with a reputation still intact, one of the few artists of his generation who could make such a claim.

• Richards's papers are available on microfilm through the Archives of American Art, Smithsonian Institution, Washington, D.C. The artist's works are scattered in public and private collections throughout the United States, with concentrations in the Vassar College Art Gallery; the Pennsylvania Academy of the Fine Arts, Philadelphia; the Brooklyn Museum; the Museum of Fine Arts, Boston; and the Metropolitan Museum of Art, New York City. Linda S. Ferber, *William Trost Richards (1833–1905): American Landscape and Marine Painter* (1980), offers the fullest treatment of Richards's life and art and contains an extensive bibliography. Also valuable is Ferber's earlier exhibition catalog, *William Trost Richards: American Landscape and Marine Painter* (1973), which contains a likeness of Richards. Ferber and William H. Gerdts, *The New Path: Ruskin and the American Pre-Raphaelites* (1985), discusses Richards's involvement in the American Pre-Raphaelite movement. On Richards's drawings, see Ferber, *"Never at Fault": The Drawings of William Trost Richards* (1986).

REBECCA BEDELL

RICHARDSON, Anna Euretta (5 Sept. 1883–3 Feb. 1931), home economist and educator, was born in Charleston, South Carolina, the daughter of William H. Richardson and Euretta Miller. In 1887 the family moved to Summerville, South Carolina, where her father served as mayor for many years. In 1900 she graduated from the Memminger High and Normal School in Charleston and three years later received a B.S. from Peabody College for Teachers in Nashville, Tennessee. During the next few years, Richardson took graduate courses at the University of Chicago and Columbia University while teaching at secondary schools in Summerville and in Ocala, Florida. She earned an M.A. in nutrition from Columbia University in 1911.

After obtaining her master's degree, Richardson began teaching at the Agnes Scott College for Women in Decatur, Georgia, where she held the rank of professor of home economics from 1911 to 1912. The next academic year Richardson was employed as an in-

structor of home economics at the University of Texas, and from 1913 to 1917 she served as adjunct professor, conducting research on the chemistry of foods. Home economics as an academic discipline had only developed as recently as the mid-nineteenth century. Influenced by Catharine Beecher and the Morrill Land-Grant Act (1862), as well as by advances in science, agriculture, and higher education for women, home economics quickly became a woman's field. Developed as the female component in agricultural schools, home economics brought the "application of science to the home environment for the purpose of bettering the living of all people" (Marie Negri Carver, *Home Economics as an Academic Discipline: A Short History* [1979], p. 3). During the era of progressivism, these studies were redefined and presented in a manner that made the care of the house more efficient, and by 1912 the term "home economics" had expanded to include "domestic sciences and arts, home sciences, and household arts and sciences" (Carver, p. 21). The "family" thus became the overwhelming theme to home economics education.

In 1917 Richardson declined a fellowship in nutrition at Yale University to accept a civil service position as a federal agent of home economics with the newly created Federal Board for Vocational Education in Washington, D.C. As a result of federal legislation in 1917, home economic and vocational education became a component of secondary school curriculum. As the federal board organized a national program of vocational education, Richardson utilized anything applicable to home economics from the studies of agricultural education, trade and industrial education, and commercial education. She saw home economics as an important part of a woman's life and advocated for "vocational home economics." Commenting on Richardson's thoughts concerning the education of women, Anna Lalor Burdick, a federal agent and contemporary of Richardson, wrote, "Miss Richardson was well aware that homemaking and wage-earning were not two mutually exclusive fields of work for a woman, but that increasingly, in every social level, her life cycle included both experiences." Richardson became assistant director of home economics education for the federal board in 1919; her position, however, changed in 1921, and she became the chief of the home economics education service.

In December 1922 Richardson left the federal board to become dean of home economics at Iowa State College in Ames. Over the next four years Richardson built the school's home economics department into one of the most prestigious in the United States. Her philosophy allowed for training in preliminary course work, followed by training in a specialty area. In this way the field of home economics was opened to more than just cooking and sewing. Under her influence the school's curriculum included courses that focused on childbearing and child rearing, as well as personal relationships within the home, thus providing education for home and family life. Her enthusiasm and devotion to the study of home economics did much to further the discipline at Iowa State College, as well as at other institutions. Under Richardson's leadership, Iowa State began a successful graduate program in home economics; additionally the establishment of a nursery school allowed graduate students to practice the skills they learned in the classroom.

In 1926 Richardson left academia and joined a private organization. In her efforts to develop home economics education at Iowa State College, she had discovered the connections between home economics and parental education. Richardson attracted the attention of the American Home Economics Association as it planned a program combining child development and parental education. Richardson joined the association as a fieldworker in child development and parental education. There she studied the home economics courses found in colleges and schools, held local and regional conferences with teachers and administrators, served on national boards and committees, and made the study of home economics easy to understand through her publications.

In an article in the *Journal of Home Economics* (1931), Richardson stated her own philosophy, which also embodied the aim of the movement that she championed much of her adult life. In the publication "Home Management in Relation to Child Development," Richardson discussed the manner by which a successful home should be run, while simultaneously outlining the objectives necessary in proper child development. Arguing that human satisfaction and development were the primary goals of home economics, Richardson believed that a "good home manager must, first, clearly see her objectives; second, she must organize the major responsibilities which must be carried out in achieving these objectives; and third, she must develop principles and methods for the use of the family's resources in the discharging of these responsibilities." These skills were to then be utilized in proper child development, which included the following concerns or objectives: physical and social behavior, character traits, intellect, and religious ideals. Above all, parents would be able to run a successful home by utilizing the resources of the family and community.

At the time of her death in Washington, D.C., Richardson, who never married, was working on the White House Conference report on education for home and family life. In a 1931 issue of the *Journal of Home Economics*, Richardson discussed her views of "Elementary and Secondary School Education for Home and Family Life," arguing that home economics "involves a recognition both of the place of home life and family responsibility in the education of youth and a program of education in the schools which aims at fitting youth for more effective home and family living at all stages of development." For Richardson, home economics was a cooperative effort—a responsibility of both the home and the school system. Thus, Richardson's views concerning education for home and family life sprung from Progressive ideals. Modern educational principles were in place to create "socially

adjustable individuals." Richardson assisted with bringing the study of home economics and the awareness of the nation to the topic through her work and teaching.

• A collection of Richardson's papers is housed in Special Collections, Parks Library, Iowa State University, Ames. The collection includes news clippings, press releases, and professional announcements of Richardson's work as dean at Iowa State College, as well as information concerning her subsequent employment and death. Many of Richardson's publications appear in the *Journal of Home Economics*, which defined the field of American home economics in the twentieth century. Her significant publications include "Future Administrative Problems in Vocational Education in Home Economics," *Journal of Home Economics* 12 (July 1920): 299–307; "Fundamental Problems of Home Making in the High School," National Education Association, *Addresses and Proceedings* 60 (1922): 1465–66; "Progress in Child Development and Parental Education," *Journal of Home Economics* 19 (Oct. 1927): 562–65, and 20 (Oct. 1928): 725–26; "Coordination of Educational Interests in Developing a Program for Child Development and Parent Education," National Education Association, *Addresses and Proceedings* 66 (1928): 223–26; "Progress in Child Training and Parent Education," National Education Association, *Addresses and Proceedings* 66 (1928): 988–92; "The School's Share in the Program of Child Development and Parent Education," *Hospital Social Service* 19 (Feb. 1929): 161–64; and "Suggestions for Courses in Family Relationships," *Journal of Home Economics* 23 (Jan. 1931): 39–41. For biographical information see Mary E. Sweeny et al., "Anna Richardson, the Woman," *Journal of Home Economics* 23 (June 1931): 517–31. Obituaries are in the *New York Times*, 5 Feb. 1931, and the *Washington Evening Star* 4 Feb. 1931.

STEPHANIE A. CARPENTER

RICHARDSON, Ebenezer (c. 1718–?), Loyalist, customs official, and informer, was born in Woburn, Massachusetts. Almost nothing is known of his parentage or early life, but he moved to Boston, Massachusetts, by the beginning of the 1750s. He earned the dubious distinction of breaking out of jail in both Boston (1751) and Cambridge, Massachusetts (1753), in the latter case his offense being the procurement of stolen tools for his brother. Around 1754 he also became involved in a scandal in which he accused the Reverend Edward Johnson of Woburn of fathering a bastard child by his wife's sister. It was later suggested that the child was Richardson's own.

Despite Richardson's background, local authorities did not scruple against making use of his services. In 1758 he received £25 from Massachusetts for detecting counterfeiters. Three years later Massachusetts attorney general Edmund Trowbridge, "perceiving he was well appraised of the manner in which goods and merchandizes were illegally imported into the province," recommended Richardson to the customs service. He was employed as a tidewaiter and soon came to be known as an informer. He sided with Charles Paxton in a dispute with fellow customs officer Benjamin Barrons, whom they thought negligent and overly friendly with local merchants, including those engaged in illegal trade. Richardson's loyalty to Paxton, who was committed to strict enforcement of customs duties, only added to the former's unpopularity. By mid-decade, Richardson enjoyed a distinctly sordid reputation. John Adams dubbed him "the most abandoned wretch in America" and included adultery, incest, and perjury among his offenses. Samuel Adams denounced him as "a detestable Person" and "an informer . . . as were never encouraged under any administration but such as those [of] Nero and Caligula." Yet leading royal officials, including Francis Bernard and Thomas Hutchinson, seem also to have disliked him.

Nevertheless, Richardson was a firm Loyalist, either through principle, interest, or both. As such, he was at the center of two important incidents of colonial protest in the decade preceding the American Revolution. On 24 September 1766 Customs Collector Benjamin Hallowell and Deputy Collector William Sheaffe appeared at the house of Colonel Daniel Malcom, a prominent patriot, to search for an illegally imported cargo of liquors. Malcom threatened to shoot them if they entered. Demonstrating that Bostonians would not allow the laws of trade to be enforced, the militia refused the governor's order to back up the customs officers, and a mob formed to support Malcom, who got off scot-free. The schoolboys in the crowd made it known that Richardson had informed on Malcom, whereupon a number of people set out after him. Richardson somehow escaped from the crowd of about 200.

Richardson was not so fortunate on 22 February 1770. A crowd formed at the shop of merchant Theophilus Lillie, a neighbor of Richardson, to erect a post informing the world that Lillie was importing goods from England in violation of colonial nonimportation agreements. In a rage, Richardson tried to persuade a farmer and a carter to use their horses to knock down the post. When they refused, he seized a third team and tried to level it himself. Richardson's effort caught the crowd's attention. Schoolboys began to pelt Richardson with rocks and wood and then besieged his home. Having earlier expressed the wish that British soldiers stationed in Boston would "cut up the damned Yankees," Richardson and George Wilmot, a British mariner trying to protect him, fired into the crowd, wounding one boy slightly and another, Christopher Seider or Snider, mortally. Seizing Richardson, the mob dragged him through the streets and may well have lynched him were it not for the intervention of Whig leader William Molineaux. Molineaux persuaded the outraged inhabitants to take Richardson to a justice of the peace, who imprisoned him pending trial for murder. The incident exacerbated an already volatile situation in Boston. Sam Adams choreographed an elaborate and very political public funeral for Richardson's victim. Whigs suggested darkly that Richardson had intervened on Lillie's behalf on orders of royal officials.

Richardson's fate became enmeshed with that of the British soldiers accused of firing on a crowd less than two weeks later in the famous Boston Massacre. Like the soldiers, Richardson claimed self-defense, but un-

like the soldiers, who at least generated some sympathy as unfortunate tools of corrupt politicians, he had few defenders. The superior court had to order patriots Josiah Quincy, Jr., and Sampson Salters Blowers to take Richardson's case when even Loyalist lawyers refused. Richardson came to trial on 20 April. Despite the judges' suggestions that manslaughter was the worst crime of which he could be convicted and Chief Justice Peter Oliver's blunt assertion that he ought to be acquitted and the fomenters of mobs indicted, jurors found Richardson guilty of murder after deliberating amid cries of "Hang that dog" from without the jury room.

Richardson endured equal opprobrium with the massacre soldiers. The "Monumental Inscription of the Fifth of March," which memorialized the massacre and featured Paul Revere's famous if inaccurate engraving of the soldiers firing into a helpless crowd of civilians at their officer's command, was accompanied by a poem condemning the "Murd'rer! Richardson! With their latest breath, Millions will curse you when you sleep in death!" In this atmosphere, the superior court, in consultation with Governor Hutchinson, postponed sentencing until September, when, instead of fighting the jury's verdict, they petitioned the king for a pardon. It was granted, and Richardson was finally released on 3 March 1772. He wasted no time in fleeing Boston. He was appointed to the customs service in Philadelphia, Pennsylvania, shortly before the Revolution broke out, after which no record of his life remains.

An especially obnoxious and belligerent Loyalist, Richardson was a sore trial to officials like Hutchinson, who were trying to cool tensions in troubled Boston. His spying, outspokenness, and propensity for violence could serve as prime exhibits for revolutionaries who wished to demonstrate the tyranny they anticipated the British would inflict if resistance were not stoutly maintained.

• A Richardson deposition dated 27 Feb. 1761 and a petition dated 14 Jan. 1775 in Treasury documents at the Public Record Office in London contain some personal information. Maurice H. Smith, *The Writs of Assistance Case* (1978), and Hiller Zobel, *The Boston Massacre* (1970), are good published sources. See also L. Kinvin Wroth and Zobel, eds., *The Legal Papers of John Adams*, vol. 2 (1965), pp. 396–430, for legal documents relating to *Rex v. Richardson*, Richardson's case.

WILLIAM PENCAK

RICHARDSON, H. H. (29 Sept. 1838–27 Apr. 1886), architect, was born Henry Hobson Richardson at Priestley Plantation in St. James Parish, Louisiana, the son of Henry Dickenson Richardson, a cotton merchant, and Catherine Caroline Priestley. He was raised on the Priestley Plantation and in New Orleans. Although he had hoped to attend West Point, he failed to qualify due to a speech impediment. After a year at the University of Louisiana, he entered Harvard College in February 1856, joining the class of 1859. As a student Richardson was unexceptional, but the friendships he made during his Harvard years endured throughout his life and proved critical to his professional success. After graduation he traveled to Europe and after several months of preparation was accepted as a student at the École des Beaux-Arts in Paris in November 1860. After his family's support was cut off by the outbreak of the American Civil War, he found employment as a draftsman in the offices of Theodore Labrouste and J. I. Hittorf and could pursue his studies only intermittently thereafter.

In October 1865, Richardson returned to the United States and settled in New York. Confident of his capabilities, he opened his own architectural office on 1 May 1866. In November he won the commission for Unity Church, Springfield, Massachusetts, and within a year he had three buildings under construction. In January 1867, Richardson married Julia Gorham Hayden to whom he had been engaged since his years at Harvard. They had six children. In October 1867, he formed the partnership Gambrill & Richardson with Charles Dexter Gambrill. In the new office, Gambrill was generally responsible for administrative and business concerns, an arrangement that allowed Richardson the freedom to develop his talent in design.

The first years of Richardson's career can best be described as a period of exploration. His early buildings are generally indistinguishable from those of his contemporaries. At this time the primary influences on American architecture came from England and France; both styles are evident in Richardson's designs. His early churches—Unity Church, Springfield (1866–1869; demolished 1961), and Grace Church, Medford, Massachusetts (1867–1869)—draw on English parish church conventions and Victorian Gothic precedent, while the Western Railroad Offices, Springfield (1867–1869; demolished 1926), and the William Dorsheimer house, Buffalo (1868–1871), show his knowledge of French prototypes and the Second Empire style.

By the early 1870s, however, Richardson's explorations began to move in an original direction. The relatively simple forms and application of round arches in the Brattle Square Church, Boston (1869–1873), indicate Richardson's initial consideration of Romanesque precedents as means of creating an architecture of coherence, gravity, and repose. Subsequent works, particularly the New York State Hospital (Asylum), Buffalo (1869–1880; 1895), and the Hampden County Courthouse, Springfield (1871–1874), show Richardson's continuing experimentation with forms and elements based on Romanesque precedent. The hospital commission was also the first collaboration between Richardson and landscape architect Frederick Law Olmsted. Richardson's relationship with Olmsted was among the most important of his career; they became close friends, neighbors (both on Staten Island and later in Brookline), and frequent collaborators.

Trinity Church, Boston (1872–1877) marked a critical turning point in Richardson's career. Richardson's design was chosen over five others on 1 June 1872, but almost two years of revisions and refinements followed before construction began. For the trapezoidal site facing Copley Square in Boston's Back Bay, Richardson designed a volumetrically additive but nonetheless unified composition, including a sanctuary and a parish house connected by an open cloister. The building can clearly be read as a series of attached, three-dimensional spaces that together create a total composition that is more than the sum of its parts. Built of granite with brownstone trim, Trinity applies motifs and details based on the Romanesque architecture of southern France. Although the nave, tower, and parish house can be read as independent elements, they are controlled within an implied overall pyramidal volume. In this design, Richardson achieved a synthesis of the hierarchical planning principles he had learned in Paris and the picturesque forms of contemporary English and American work. The attention given to this building following its dedication in February 1877 propelled Richardson to the front rank of American architects.

When the construction of Trinity Church began, Richardson moved to the Boston suburb of Brookline, but he continued his partnership with Gambrill, and the office remained in New York. Richardson maintained his design involvement in the firm's projects by creating initial schemes in preliminary sketch form in Brookline and sending these to New York, where they were developed into detailed drawings by his office staff. This method reflected his training at the École des Beaux-Arts, where he had learned to present a sketch showing a project's organization quickly (often in just a few hours) and then to develop his design based on this initial direction. Richardson adapted the École approach as a working method for his office by turning the development of each design after his initial sketch over to his staff; thereafter, his role was that of reviewer and critic. In the mid-1870s, when Richardson was separated from his office, this method allowed him to retain design control over the firm's projects. In the 1880s, as his practice grew, he was thus able to control a much larger office working on an expanding volume of work.

Richardson moved the office to Brookline in 1878, ending the partnership with Gambrill. He continued to live and work in the house he had rented in 1874, and between 1878 and 1885 he built a series of additions, nicknamed "the Coops," at the back of the house to serve as drafting rooms. This home studio was the setting in which he practiced for the rest of his career.

The synthesis of order and picturesqueness that Richardson realized in Trinity Church formed the basis for his further architectural development. His continuing simplification of form and elimination of extraneous ornament and historically derived detail is clearly reflected, for example, in his series of five library designs. His first library, the Winn Library, Woburn, Massachusetts (1876–1879), presents a clear articulation of program elements—stacks, reading room, picture gallery, and museum. The Ames Library, North Easton, Massachusetts (1877–1879), with a simpler program, is a much more tightly integrated design. The Crane Library, Quincy, Massachusetts (1880–1882), generally considered the best of Richardson's libraries, shows the full integration of stacks, reading room, and entry hall under a simple gable roof. The essential features are its simple, elemental forms, massive stone walls, and well-articulated window design. Historically derived detail is almost entirely absent.

The extent of Richardson's mastery by 1880 is demonstrated by the range of his designs at that time. Sever Hall, Harvard, Cambridge (1878–1880), is a simply detailed red brick classroom building set in Harvard Yard. Richardson's design of the facades, with their symmetrically placed half-round towers and horizontally grouped windows, and his use of an unbroken roofline fit the building into the context established by the existing Georgian buildings. The Ames Monument, Sherman (Buford), Wyoming (1879–1882), a simple two-step granite pyramid measuring sixty feet square and sixty feet high, lacks any historical detail and may be understood as an abstraction of nearby geological formations. Richardson's informally planned Ames Gate Lodge, North Easton, Massachusetts (1880–1881), is constructed of glacial boulders trimmed with brownstone and roofed with bright, red-orange tile, creating one of his most romantic designs. His Senate Chamber in the New York State Capitol, Albany, completed in 1881, a nearly cubic volume finished in a variety of rich materials including granite, onyx, marble, and oak, is considered one of the finest nineteenth-century architectural interiors in America.

Richardson's residential architecture similarly reflects his move toward simplicity and coherence and his elimination of extraneous detail. The F. W. Andrews house, Newport, Rhode Island (1872–1874; demolished 1920), was planned around a large central living hall and reintroduced shingles as an exterior sheathing material. The living hall reappears in Richardson's William Watts Sherman house, Newport (1874–1876), but its exterior, although detailed in American vernacular materials, reflects some influence from English architect Richard Norman Shaw. In his series of suburban and rural houses in the 1880s, such as the Dr. John Bryant house, Cohasset, Massachusetts (1880–1881), and the Mrs. M. F. Stoughton house, Cambridge, Massachusetts (1882–1883), Richardson's designs feature increased interior volumetric continuity and the use of plain shingles over virtually all exterior surfaces—innovations that contributed to the development of the shingle style. Richardson's urban houses show more difficulty in achieving a balance of domesticity and monumentality. The best of these, the J. J. Glessner house, Chicago (1885–1887), is located on a corner lot and features an unusual E-shaped plan enclosing a courtyard.

In the last six years of Richardson's life, his practice expanded both in geographic range and in the number of commissions. Richardson was responsible for houses in Washington, D.C., Buffalo, Chicago, and St. Louis, as well as other buildings in Cincinnati, Pittsburgh, and Detroit. He also took on new building types. For example, between 1881 and 1886, Richardson was responsible for the design of twelve railroad passenger stations, including nine for the Boston & Albany Railroad. Typically these were planned as simple rectangles or other basic geometric shapes, built of granite, trimmed in brownstone, and topped with slate roofs that sometimes extended to form a train shed or a porte-cochère. These stations functioned as shelters for waiting passengers and as gateways to the adjoining communities.

Richardson was besieged with commissions over the last years of his life, and two of his finest and most influential works were designed in this period. The Allegheny County Courthouse and Jail, Pittsburgh (1883–1888), fills two full blocks in downtown Pittsburgh. The courthouse is a four-story rectangular structure around an open courtyard, with a tower over the main entrance. The walled compound of the jail is connected to the courthouse by a "bridge of sighs." Both are executed in pinkish-gray granite with minimal ornamentation in order not to accumulate grime. Richardson foresaw that this would be among his most influential buildings; for almost a decade it served other architects as a model for public buildings of all types.

The Marshall Field Wholesale Store, Chicago (1885–1887; demolished 1930), is recognized as Richardson's finest design. This seven-story, U-shaped building, in granite and red sandstone, filled a full block in downtown Chicago. The power of Richardson's design resulted from its simplicity, unbroken mass, and controlled pattern of windows regularly grouped under arches, which doubled and quadrupled at the higher floors. This solution had been prefigured by Richardson's Cheney Building, Hartford (1875–1876), where he first designed a facade divided into zones with fenestration grouped under arches. The Field store had a direct impact on buildings subsequently designed by the leading commercial architects of the Chicago school, particularly Louis Sullivan.

Richardson's health deteriorated considerably over his last years under the constant demands of his practice. Part of the difficulty was Richardson's interest in every kind of design problem. He told J. J. Glessner, "I'll plan anything a man wants, from a cathedral to a chicken coop." Over the course of his career he took on all types of problems. He was responsible for the design for furniture in a number of his projects; he developed sketches for a lighthouse and design ideas for railroad passenger cars, and he expressed interest in the design of grain elevators and river boats.

Richardson was never completely healthy during any part of his career. Although he was warned about his health in 1882, he continued to work at a hectic pace until his death, probably from kidney failure, at his home in Brookline. Richardson's architectural practice was carried on by his three chief assistants, George Foster Shepley, Charles Hercules Rutan, and Charles Allerton Coolidge, under the name Shepley, Rutan & Coolidge. Nearly all of the projects under construction at the time of Richardson's death were completed under their supervision.

The architectural career of Henry Hobson Richardson spanned a period of only twenty years, from 1866 to 1886, but in that time he transformed American architecture. Even before his premature death Richardson was recognized as a leader in his profession. A fellow of the American Institute of Architects, he was nominated for the gold medal of the Royal Institute of British Architects. In 1885, a list of America's ten best buildings compiled in a survey by the *American Architect and Building News* included five of his designs. Few American architects in succeeding decades escaped his influence. After 1885, many architects copied the Romanesque elements of his buildings and created almost a decade of Romanesque revival architecture, sometimes called "Richardsonian Romanesque." Historians have argued that these architects too often copied the surface features of Richardson's designs and missed their real virtues. Richardson was also an inspiration to a generation of eclectic architects who usually did not copy Richardson's forms but learned from his use of historic precedent as a starting point for new design. Several of Richardson's assistants, such as Charles McKim, Stanford White, George Shepley, and John Galen Howard, went on to have significant careers as eclectic designers. Finally, Richardson's move toward simplified form and restrained detail, as exemplified in his best works, provided inspiration for the innovative architects of the Chicago school and through them for the development of a modern American architecture.

• The collection of drawings from Richardson's office is found at the Houghton Library, Harvard University. Other drawings relating to Richardson's projects are found at the F. L. Olmsted National Historic Site, Brookline, Massachusetts. Account books, ledgers, and similar materials are found in the archives of Shepley, Bulfinch, Richardson & Abbott, Inc., Boston. Some of Richardson's letters are held by the Massachusetts Historical Society, Boston. Collections of photographs of Richardson's buildings are found at the Houghton Library, the Boston Athenaeum, the Society for the Preservation of New England Antiquities, and the Library of Congress. Marianna Griswold Van Rensselaer, *Henry Hobson Richardson and His Works* (1888; repr. 1969), an early biography, has been the foundation for all subsequent research. A lengthy descriptive account from soon after Richardson's death is Henry Van Brunt, "Henry Hobson Richardson, Architect," *Atlantic Monthly* 58 (Nov. 1886): 685–93. Henry Russell Hitchcock, *The Architecture of H. H. Richardson and His Times* (1936; repr. 1966), is a full-length critical study that is supplemented by James F. O'Gorman, *H. H. Richardson: Architectural Forms for an American Society* (1987). Jeffrey Karl Ochsner, *H. H. Richardson: Complete Architectural Works* (1982) is a catalog raisonné of his architecture. See also O'Gorman, *H. H. Richardson and His Office, A Centennial of His Move to Boston: Selected Drawings* (1974), on his drawings and the workings of his office; Hitchcock, *Richardson as a Victorian Architect* (1966), for his early career; and Vincent J. Scully, Jr., *The Shingle Style and the Stick Style* (1971), for his shingled residential architecture. O'Gorman, *Three American Architects: Richardson, Sullivan and Wright, 1865–1915* (1991), traces Richardson's influence on Louis Sullivan and Frank Lloyd Wright, and Leonard K. Eaton, *American Archi-*

tecture Comes of Age: European Reaction to H. H. Richardson and Louis Sullivan (1972), traces his influence in Europe. An obituary is in *American Architect and Building News* 19 (1 May 1886): 205–6.

JEFFREY KARL OCHSNER

RICHARDSON, James Daniel (10 Mar. 1843–24 July 1914), congressman, was born in Rutherford County, Tennessee, the son of John Watkins Richardson, a physician and state legislator, and Augusta Mary Starnes. After attending local schools, he pursued studies at Franklin College near Nashville but withdrew before earning a degree to enlist in the Confederate army as a private. Richardson served throughout the duration of the Civil War, participating in the battles of Vicksburg, Baton Rouge, Murfreesboro (Stones River), Chickamauga, and Missionary Ridge. He left military service in 1865 as adjutant of the Forty-fifth Tennessee Volunteer Infantry. In 1865 he married Alabama Pippin; they raised five children.

At the close of the Civil War, Richardson read law to prepare for a legal career. Admitted to the bar in 1867, he practiced at Murfreesboro, Tennessee, with Joseph B. Palmer for twelve years and with a younger brother, John E. Richardson, for five years. While practicing law, he developed an interest in politics. In 1871 he was elected to the Tennessee state legislature, where he became Speaker of the house on the first day of the session. He then served in the state senate in 1873 and 1874. Two years later he was a delegate to the 1876 Democratic National Convention in St. Louis, Missouri, that nominated Samuel J. Tilden for president.

Richardson entered national politics in 1884 with his election to the U.S. House of Representatives, where he served until 1905, representing the Fifth District of Tennessee. Defeating Representatives William Sulzer of New York and John H. Bankhead of Alabama for the leadership of the Democrats in the House, Richardson was the Democratic caucus nominee for Speaker of the Fifty-sixth and Fifty-seventh Congresses. Because Republicans controlled the House of Representatives, he lost the contest for the Speakership to Representative David B. Henderson of Iowa. Richardson was chairman of the Democratic Congressional Committee in 1900 and minority leader of the House from 1901 to 1903. He also served on various committees, including the Committee on War Claims, the Printing Committee, and the Committee on the District of Columbia, in which he strove to beautify the nation's capital. As a legislator, Richardson methodically researched his topics and cogently presented his arguments in his addresses to the House. Notable were his speech on Hawaiian annexation and American foreign policy on 14 June 1898 and on trade with Puerto Rico on 19 February 1900. Active in national politics, he attended the Democratic National Convention in Chicago in 1896 and was permanent chairman of the party's 1900 national convention in Kansas City, which nominated William Jennings Bryan for president and Adlai E. Stevenson for vice president.

In addition to his congressional service, Richardson gained attention for researching and compiling multivolume primary source material on the presidency and the Confederacy. He collected and put together in ten volumes, including an index, *A Compilation of the Messages and Papers of the Presidents, 1789–1897* (1896–1899), a project authorized and published by Congress and later republished with additions. These masterful volumes immediately became standard reference sources and continue to be used widely by presidential scholars, guaranteeing Richardson a solid reputation in the historical profession. In addition, Richardson compiled and edited *A Compilation of the Messages and Papers of the Confederacy*, a two-volume work that was approved by Congress and published in 1905.

Richardson's career in politics and his publications were augmented by his Masonic duties. Attaining the thirty-third degree, he was grand master of the order in his state in 1873 and 1874. In 1883 he published *Tennessee Templars*, dealing with the Masonic organization in the Volunteer State. Upon the expiration of his tenth term in the House of Representatives in 1905, he voluntarily vacated his seat to accept the office of sovereign grand commander of the ancient and accepted Scottish rite of Masons for the southern jurisdiction. Holding this position for approximately thirteen years, he advocated internationalism, emphasized pacifism, and promoted the building of the Scottish Rite Temple in Washington, a structure recognized for its architectural design and beauty. In 1907 he was a delegate to the International Conference of Supreme Councils in Brussels, Belgium. Richardson died at his home in Murfreesboro, Tennessee.

Logical and earnest, Richardson attracted national attention during his two decades in Congress. He rose to leadership in his party during a contentious time of intraparty dissension over the currency issue and Bryan's controversial candidacy for the presidency. Richardson loyally endorsed Bryan and sought legislation, such as tariff reductions and a more flexible currency, to improve the lives of ordinary people. He was a southerner who gained northern respect. On more than one occasion, he was seriously considered by southern Democrats as a presidential possibility. Although he was not an outstanding orator, Richardson was a sharp and skillful debater, a politician of principle, and an unwavering advocate of what he deemed right whose firmness and intelligence enabled him to rise to the heights of political and editorial achievement.

• Richardson left no personal papers. His letters are scattered among the manuscript collections of various contemporaries, including the Grover Cleveland Papers in the Manuscripts Division of the Library of Congress. Two volumes (453 items) of letters Richardson received in 1898 from members of Congress, newspaper editors, and other prominent persons relating to *A Compilation of the Messages and Papers of the Presidents* are in the Southern Historical Collection, Wilson Library, University of North Carolina at Chapel Hill. Richardson's speeches are in the *Congressional Record* from 1885 to 1905. The best book on Gilded Age Tennessee is Roger L. Hart, *Redeemers, Bourbons and Populists: Tennessee, 1870–1896* (1975). Obituaries are in the *New York Times* and the *Washington Post*, 25 July 1914.

LEONARD SCHLUP

RICHARDSON, Joseph (17 Sept. 1711–Oct. 1784), silversmith, was born in Philadelphia, Pennsylvania, the son of Francis Richardson, a silversmith, and Elizabeth Growden. His grandfather was one of the original settlers of Pennsylvania in 1681. Joseph Richardson served his apprenticeship in his father's shop. When his father died in 1729, Joseph inherited the business. He married Hannah Worril in 1741; they had two children before her death in 1746. Two years later Richardson married Mary Allen, with whom he had three daughters and two sons, who were trained in his shop. After Richardson's retirement in 1777, his sons took over, continuing the family trade until Nathaniel Richardson became an ironmonger in 1790 and Joseph Richardson, Jr., was appointed assayer of the U.S. Mint in Philadelphia by George Washington in 1795.

A Quaker by birth and commitment, Richardson was active in the Society of Friends throughout his life, eventually becoming an overseer of the meeting. He was generous in supporting the needs of others. A champion of individual freedom, he was a signer of the nonimportation agreement in 1765. While holding pacifist views, he was still able to avoid alienating both patriots and Loyalists in the city. In 1779 he was active in the Friends effort to promote the manumission of slaves. He was remembered as a man of "marked excellence and uprightness" in *Family Sketches*, published by Julianna R. Wood in Philadelphia in 1870.

Over the years, Richardson had a number of apprentices and workers in his shop, including his sons and his older brother Frank, who subsequently became a merchant. John S. Hutton of New York was in his fifties when he became a day worker in Richardson's shop. Apprentices included Jeremiah Elfreth, Jr., and William Young.

Most of Richardson's customers were Friends in the Philadelphia area, although he made a pair of trays for the Devonshire parish in Bermuda in 1737. He produced hundreds of silver ornaments and struck medals for the Quaker organization to give to the Indians to promote peace. Domestic wares such as spoons, drinking vessels, porringers, salt dishes, sauce boats, and tea and coffee vessels constituted a large part of his production. Their designs followed the current fashions for late baroque and rococo shapes and motifs and were handsome in their simplicity. In the late 1750s and 1760s he made some of the finest examples of restrained yet exuberant rococo silver, his masterpiece being the elaborate teakettle-on-stand fashioned for the widow of Mayor Clement Plumsted, now in the Garvan Collection at Yale University Art Gallery. Few teakettles were made in colonial America, most being imported from England.

In addition to the silver made in his shop, Richardson imported silver and related goods from England for resale, often through Quakers such as clockmaker Thomas Wagstaffe and agents How & Masterman. These imports included silver tablewares and small items like buckles, thimbles, buttons, and chains, many of which were more economically made in the large specialized shops of London. Tools for his trade and small pocket sets of weights and scales were also ordered from England. Richardson died in Philadelphia and was buried on 4 October 1784; his exact date of death is unknown.

Richardson was not only one of the best silversmiths in the American colonies but is today one of the best documented members of his trade. He took pains to ensure that his silver was of proper alloy, even though an assay office was not allowed in Philadelphia, despite repeated petitions to Goldsmith's Hall in London by Richardson and other Philadelphia goldsmiths. He marked his silver with his initials *IR* in an oval or a rectangle (during this time, *I* was used instead of *J*). Several of his account books survive, enabling his silver to be authenticated and original owners to be identified. The letterbook containing his correspondence with his English suppliers survives as well. Similar materials relating to his father and two sons have also been preserved. Collectively they provide a unique record of three generations of one family of silversmiths in early America.

• Richardson's letterbook (1758–1774) and other family papers are in the library of the Henry Francis du Pont Winterthur Museum, Wilmington, Del. His account books for 1733–1740 and 1745–1748 are at the Historical Society of Pennsylvania. His biography, Martha Gandy Fales, *Joseph Richardson and Family, Philadelphia Silversmiths* (1974), includes 182 illustrations of silver made by the family and related materials, a complete transcription of the letterbook, and an extensive discussion of their lives and work.

MARTHA GANDY FALES

RICHARDSON, Sid Williams (25 Apr. 1891–30 Sept. 1959), oilman and entrepreneur, was born in Athens, Texas, the son of Nancy "Nannie" Bradley and John Isidore Richardson, a farmer and cattleman. He was named for an itinerant evangelist. Richardson's father reportedly got the better of him in Sid's first attempt at making a business deal, but the youth learned quickly. While still in high school he traveled to Louisiana and maneuvered local cattlemen into underbidding each other, resulting in cheap calves for Richardson and a $3,500 profit when he sold them in Texas.

After attending Baylor University and Simmons College (later Hardin-Simmons University) for about a year and half, Richardson left school in 1912 to work in the oil business. He started by selling supplies for well drilling and soon became an oil scout and lease purchaser and trader in the Wichita Falls area. A broken bone suffered when he was fifteen had left one leg shorter than the other and kept Richardson out of World War I. The small fortune he had accumulated disappeared during a 1921 bust, but he quickly started

to rebuild it, working with boyhood friend Clint Murchison as his partner. Oil speculation remained rampant, and in a legendary deal he and Murchison parlayed $50,000 into $200,000 in one day thanks to a tip that a wildcat well near the Oklahoma border was about to come in. A 1923 oil strike in West Texas's Permian Basin became the basis of Richardson's second fortune, but the wealth evaporated in 1930 when oil from East Texas flooded the market and dropped prices to ten cents a barrel.

Undaunted, Richardson turned to cattle, only to lose his herd to tick fever. So he started over once again, obtaining drilling equipment on credit to look for oil in West Texas while most wildcatters were concentrating on the eastern part of the state. He was able to pay his laborers only once a month, if at all, but he won their loyalty by working and playing right alongside them. Richardson was reportedly so broke during this period that he had to talk a railroad conductor into giving him free passage, but he remained convinced that luck would turn in his favor. "Luck has helped me every day of my life," he said. "I'd rather be lucky than smart, because a lot of smart people ain't eatin' regular. . . . Some people get luck and brains mixed up, and that's when they get in trouble" (Reston, p. 158).

With financial backing from Austin publisher Charles Marsh, Richardson drilled a successful test well in West Texas in 1935 on land leased from the Keystone Cattle Company. His luck was beginning to change, and with additional capital supplied by Fort Worth publisher Amon Carter he opened the Keystone field for regular production in 1937. More success followed, and by the end of 1940 he had 125 wells in three contiguous West Texas counties. When a messy divorce tied up Marsh's funds, Richardson took advantage of the situation and bought out his partner, greatly increasing his fortune.

As his holdings grew, Richardson in 1936 let Murchison talk him into buying his own private island, St. Joseph, just off Rockport, Texas. He raised Longhorn cattle on this 28-by-6-mile strip, and he also built a $250,000 retreat where he entertained many notables, including Franklin D. Roosevelt and Dwight D. Eisenhower. Richardson attended the 1940 Democratic convention as a personal guest of Roosevelt, and he became a financier for the investments of the president's son Elliott. He developed an even closer relationship with Eisenhower, beginning when a mutual friend introduced them on a Washington-bound train in December 1941. Richardson forgot the officer's name, but he and Eisenhower renewed acquaintances after the war, with the general investing in some of Richardson's oil properties.

By that point Richardson's holdings were considerable. In 1943 he had another major find in the Elllenberger lime field, with reserves estimated at 250 million barrels. After the war he discovered yet another substantial deposit, in Louisiana's Cox Bay. As he diversified into refining, carbon black production, cattle, radio, drugstores, and hotels, Richardson's fortune became perhaps the largest in the country, estimated at close to $1 billion. He acquired numerous powerful and famous friends, but chose to remain out of the limelight, simply stating "I do not like publicity." Interviews were rarely granted, as he informed one reporter that "you ain't learning nothing when you're talking" (*Houston Post*, 1 Oct. 1959).

Although he was at one time romantically linked with movie star Joan Crawford, Richardson remained "the billionaire bachelor," living modestly in two rooms at the Fort Worth Club from the 1930s on. In the 1940s his nephew Perry Bass became a partner in his businesses, and the following decade Richardson brought in future governor John Connally to supervise his affairs. Other than for high-stakes poker games, Richardson rarely entertained, and Connally remembered him as being "more at home with cowboys in a country cafe than . . . in a fine restaurant in New York" (Dippie, p. 2). Murchison, who settled in Dallas, remained a close friend, and the two called each other at 6:00 nearly every morning. One passion that Richardson did develop was an interest in western art, resulting in a sizable collection of the works of Frederic Remington and Charles M. Russell.

According to Connally, Richardson "could be coarse and stubborn in some of his dealings, but his political instincts were often subtle and shrewd" (Connally, p. 144). He had supported Sam Rayburn and Lyndon B. Johnson from early in their careers. In early 1952 he traveled to Paris in an attempt to convince Eisenhower to run for president. Although a Democrat, Richardson contributed roughly $1 million to Eisenhower's campaign as well as paying the general's living expenses in New York. Soon after his old friend was inaugurated, Richardson visited Eisenhower at Camp David, writing him the following week that "when I see you still have your sense of humor and your giggle it makes me have a lot of confidence in your being able to do the job ahead of you over the next four years" (*Eisenhower Papers*, vol. 14, p. 369). Richardson's investment paid dividends as Eisenhower signed legislation returning the oil-rich Tidelands to Texas and named Richardson's friend Robert B. Anderson as secretary of the navy.

In 1954 Richardson and Murchison purchased the Del Mar Turf Club in La Jolla, California, with the profits arranged to go to a charitable organization known as Boys, Inc. The two spent their summers at the racetrack in the company of J. Edgar Hoover and other notables. Three years after buying Del Mar, the pair joined fellow Texan Robert Young in the acquisition of the New York Central. "What was the name of that railroad again?" Richardson is supposed to have inquired after the deal was completed (Connally, p. 140).

When Richardson died while vacationing at his island, his will gave Perry Bass's four sons the nest eggs that they later turned into billions, but the majority of his estate went to the Sid W. Richardson Foundation, which he had established twelve years earlier. The foundation became his most lasting legacy, providing funds for not-for-profit organizations in Texas. Buildings at university campuses across the state bear his name, as do hospital additions, Boy Scout camps, and children's homes. Grants by the foundation through 1995 totaled nearly $200 million.

• A collection of Richardson's correspondence with Eisenhower is part of the Ann Whitman File, Names Series, at the Eisenhower Library in Abilene, Tex. Several of these documents are published in *The Papers of Dwight D. Eisenhower* (1970–). The Richardson Museum in downtown Fort Worth, Tex., houses the western art collection and the offices of the foundation. The collection is depicted in Brian W. Dippie, *Remington and Russell: The Sid Richardson Collection* (1982; rev. ed., 1994). Information on the foundation is available in the organization's annual reports. Books by and about John Connally contain useful background on Richardson. These include Connally, with Mickey Herskowitz, *In History's Shadow: An American Odyssey* (1993); James Reston, Jr., *The Lone Star: The Life of John Connally* (1989); and Ann Fears Crawford and Jack Keever, *John B. Connally: Portrait in Power* (1973). Roger M. Olien and Diana Davids Olien, *Wildcatters: Texas Independent Oilmen* (1984), has details on Richardson's early wells. Although he actively avoided publicity, there are photographs and several mentions of Richardson in an article about Murchison by Freeman Lincoln, "Big Wheeler-Dealer from Dallas," *Fortune* Jan. and Feb. 1953. Obituaries are in the *New York Times*, 1 Oct. 1959, as well as Texas newspapers on the same date.

KENNETH H. WILLIAMS

RICHARDSON, Thomas (10 Sept. 1680–28 Apr. 1761), merchant and Rhode Island treasurer, was born in New York. Richardson's early life and parentage are uncertain. By the early eighteenth century he had joined the mercantile community in Boston. A Quaker, and perhaps unhappy because of inhospitable conditions in Boston, Richardson moved to Newport, Rhode Island, in 1712. Newport, he thought, would present greater opportunities in the transatlantic, Long Island, and West Indies trades. No doubt the substantial Quaker presence in the vicinity of Newport also attracted him.

It was not long before Richardson was disabused of his notions of Newport's commercial advantages. He was unable to compete with Boston traders, who undercut his prices in Newport for British goods by temporarily absorbing the cost of transshipment. The hinterland near Newport also proved insufficient for his ambitions, especially when Boston merchants purchased local commodities through Newport intermediaries. Like other Newport merchants, Richardson turned to the West Indian trade, sending Rhode Island products like barrel staves south and receiving sugar products in return. He purchased British products through Boston and turned to fellow Quakers on Nantucket for whale oil and other products of the expanding whale fishery there. For the balance of his life Richardson carried on an active business focusing on Newport. There is evidence that he did break into the transatlantic trade, dealing directly with such merchants as London Quaker Richard Partridge, who doubled as agent for Rhode Island with Crown officials. In that as in other cases, Richardson's fellow

Quakers provided a measure of security in a world without banks and with limited international oversight on trade.

Richardson's Quaker connections abroad reflected his importance in the New England Quaker community. At first active in Boston Quaker affairs, when he moved to Newport, the center of New England Quakerism, he was able to use his considerable political talents on behalf of Friends. From 1713 he was named by local Quaker meetings as a representative to superior meetings. By 1719 he had joined with fellow Newport Quaker merchant John Wanton to help with the appeals of southeastern Massachusetts Quakers who had resisted taxes levied to support Congregational churches. He was eventually successful in that effort. In 1727 the New England Yearly Meeting named him clerk, a position he retained until 1760. The clerk was essentially the presiding officer and had great influence in the yearly meeting for he named committee members, recognized participants in discussions, and drew up minutes in a meeting that came to its decisions by consensus, not majority vote. Richardson presided over considerable numerical growth among New England Friends from the 1720s to the 1760s. Toward the end of his clerkship, reform of Quakerism in New England effectively reversed the relatively tolerant policies of Richardson and other leaders of his generation. Within a decade after his death new behavioral standards for members led to a decline in membership, especially because of the expulsions of younger members. The decline continued well into the nineteenth century.

Paralleling his significant role in Quaker affairs was the political leadership that Richardson brought to Rhode Island politics. In 1748, soon after fellow Quaker Gideon Wanton left the office of colony treasurer, Richardson was elected treasurer, a reflection of the respect fellow colonists had for both his financial ability and his integrity. Like Gideon Wanton before him, however, he compromised his pacifism by paying out and collecting funds for military purposes, although he suffered no censure from his fellow Quakers. While other Quakers may not have openly acted against him for these activities, the office occasionally carried great risk. In 1757, after he had received specie from the Crown to reimburse Rhode Islanders for war-related expenses, his home was broken into, presumably because of the cash he had there, and personal items were taken. Happily, the colony reimbursed him. He seems to have avoided the political strife between the Wantons and the Wards and perhaps because of that neutrality remained treasurer when that office changed hands from one faction to another.

Richardson was the last of the Rhode Island Friends able to combine a prominent mercantile position, religious leadership, and political acumen to sustain a leading position in the colony at large. After Richardson's death many Friends began to withdraw from political activity and looked critically on those who did not. In the same period, the crisis between the colonies and Britain moved steadily toward independence.

Thereafter leading Rhode Island Quaker politicians like Stephen Hopkins found themselves at odds with their faith as they attempted to deal with a growing imperial crisis. Richardson married twice, to Anne Newbury in 1704 and to Mary Wanton in 1729. He had six children in his second marriage. He died in Rhode Island, presumably in Newport.

• Richardson's extensive business correspondence is in the Newport Historical Society. Secondary sources are limited, although Sydney V. James, *Colonial Rhode Island: A History* (1975), provides a useful discussion of Richardson's early mercantile activities in Newport, and Arthur J. Worrall, *Quakers in the Colonial Northeast* (1980), supplies Quaker background. Information on Richardson's activities as treasurer are in John Russell Bartlett, ed., *Records of the Colony of Rhode Island and Providence Plantations in New England*, vol. 5 (1860), and vol. 6 (1861).

ARTHUR J. WORRALL

RICHARDVILLE, Jean Baptiste (c. 1760–13 Aug. 1841), American Indian leader also known as Peshewa or Wildcat, was born at Kekionga (now Fort Wayne, Ind.), the son of Antoine Joseph Drouet de Richardville, a French trader, and Tacumwah (The Other Side), a Miami Indian woman. Jean Baptiste Richardville's father was a trader at Kekionga, the major portage between the Wabash and the St. Marys rivers and the site of two large Miami villages, from about 1750 to 1770. His mother was the sister of Pacanne, the civil chief of the villages. Jean Baptiste Richardville served as chief of the Miami at Kekionga during the long absences of Pacanne in Spanish Louisiana beginning in the 1780s.

During Richardville's early manhood, skirmishes between American settlers in eastern Ohio and Kentucky caused rising tensions, as did poorly negotiated treaties that assumed the defeat of various Indian tribes along with the British during the American Revolution. Warfare broke out from 1790 to 1794. The Miami under Little Turtle helped repulse American armies twice, but in 1794 General Anthony Wayne defeated the American-Indian forces of the Old Northwest at Fallen Timbers. In 1795 Richardville came to prominence as one of the Miami signers of the Treaty of Greenville, by which various tribes ceded about half of Ohio to the United States. At that time he and his mother lost control of the lucrative portage business at Fort Wayne, the American name for Kekionga. Within a few years, he became allied to Little Turtle in negotiating treaties with William Henry Harrison, the governor of Indiana. Between 1803 and 1809 Harrison pushed through a series of Indian treaties by which the Miami and other tribes relinquished the southern third of what became the state of Indiana by bribing favored "American chiefs" and including tribes with no claims to the land in the negotiations.

Bribed by Harrison, Little Turtle became too closely identified with American demands for land. By 1805 Richardville was withdrawing from Little Turtle's pro-American stance and moving toward the position of his uncle Pacanne, who resisted American pressures. In the fall of 1809 Pacanne, Richardville, and other chiefs strongly resisted Harrison's demand for more land in southern Indiana. Little Turtle, who had invited Potawatomi warriors to the negotiations to pressure the Miami chiefs to sign yet another treaty, was instead driven from authority. Richardville and the other Miami chiefs agreed to the 1809 Fort Wayne treaty ceding land in southern Indiana only after Harrison acknowledged the Mississinewa council as the seat of authority for the Miami tribe.

After the outbreak of the War of 1812, Richardville moved to Canada and did not return until the conclusion of hostilities. He then settled at the Forks of the Wabash, near present-day Huntington, Indiana, where he entered trade with the Miami and Potawatomi Indians. As a *metis*, or mixed-blood, he acted as an intermediary between the Miami tribe and American officials. In 1824 Governor Lewis Cass of Michigan sent his private secretary Charles Christopher Trowbridge to interview Richardville and another Miami chief, Le Gros, concerning the history and traditions of the Miami tribe. The interviews, later published as *Meearmeear Traditions*, are the most complete ethnography of the Miami existing.

During the 1830s Richardville's influence was at its height when he led Miami treaty negotiations as American officials sought to extinguish Indian title to the northern third of Indiana, then facing rapid settlement. As a trader, Richardville was well aware of the high value of Miami lands and achieved large cash settlements for the tribe as well as a delay in removal of the Miami to Kansas Territory. He was himself granted 28,320 acres but maintained the loyalty of the Miami village chiefs by taking a firm position on tribal sovereignty and proper payment for land with Indiana and federal officials. Indian agent John Tipton characterized Richardville as "one of the most shrewd men in North America" (*Tipton Papers*, vol. 2, p. 400).

The Miami finally accepted removal of the tribe to Kansas Territory in 1840 when certain chiefs and their families were exempted and a five-year delay was allowed for settlement of tribal debts to powerful trading firms. Richardville and his family were allowed to stay in Indiana, as were two other chiefs and the family of a white captive. These groups became the nucleus of the modern Indiana Miami tribe.

Richardville died at his home on the banks of the St. Marys River southeast of Fort Wayne. He was said at the time of his death to be the richest Indian in America. Most of his land had already been sold to white advisers such as Indian agent Allen Hamilton and the influential traders and land speculators George W. and William G. Ewing, however, and much of his wealth was used to assist needy tribespeople. As a metis intermediary during a harsh transition period for the Miami, his actions were at times controversial, but his success in delaying and frustrating federal removal policy enabled many of the Miami to return to Indiana from west of the Mississippi to take refuge with the Indiana chiefs who were exempted from removal. Most of the Miami remain in their homeland to this day.

• A number of letters, reports, and other documents concerning Richardville are in the W. G. and G. W. Ewing Papers and the Allen Hamilton Papers at the Indiana State Library, Indianapolis. The National Archives, Record Group 75, Records of the Bureau of Indian Affairs, holds many items pertaining to Richardville in the papers of the Fort Wayne Agency, Indiana Agency, Indiana Agency Emigration, Miami Agency, Miami Agency Emigration, and Special Files of the Office of Indian Affairs, 1807–1904. Richardville's life is discussed in Bert Anson, *The Miami Indians* (1970), and in Harvey Lewis Carter, *The Life and Times of Little Turtle* (1987). Nellie Armstrong Robertson and Dorothy Riker, *The John Tipton Papers* (1942), contains many documents concerning Richardville's activities.

STEWART RAFERT

RICHBERG, Donald Randall (10 July 1881–27 Nov. 1960), lawyer and government official, was born in Knoxville, Tennessee, the son of John Carl Richberg, an attorney, and Eloise Olivia Randall, a physician. Richberg graduated from the University of Chicago (B.A., 1901) and Harvard Law School (LL.B., 1904). His first two marriages, to Elizabeth Herrick in 1903 and Lynette Mulvey Hamlin in 1918, ended in divorce (in 1917 and 1924), but his third, to Florence Weed in 1924, endured, and they had one child (he had no children with his first two wives).

Richberg launched his political career in Chicago reform circles in the early 1900s and supported Theodore Roosevelt's (1858–1919) Progressive party in 1912. He subsequently entered the field of labor law, representing the railway unions and fighting Attorney General Harry Daugherty's injunction in the 1922 shopmen's strike. In due course he became general counsel for the Railway Labor Executives Association (1926–1933). He was the principal draftsman of the Railway Labor Act of 1926 and assisted in writing the Norris–La Guardia Anti-Injunction Act of 1932.

Though regarded by many in the corporate world as radical, Richberg's strategy on behalf of labor was to gauge the realities of the Harding-Coolidge-Hoover era and to proceed accordingly. He believed that protection for labor was to be found in the courts and in legislation defining the right to organize, to bargain collectively, and to strike—that is, in safeguards enabling labor to act for itself. Richberg wanted labor and management to settle their differences without the direct intervention of the state, because in the 1920s the latter was too often predisposed to favor business. After the New Deal, however, Richberg believed that the balance had been reversed—and unfairly so.

It was Richberg's role in the administration of Franklin Roosevelt, rather than his association with railway labor, that most advanced his fortunes as a national figure. Anxious to play a part in the New Deal, he worked for Roosevelt in the 1932 campaign. Hugh Johnson recruited Richberg to help draft the National Industrial Recovery Act of 1933, particularly the labor clauses (Section 7a). When Johnson became National

Recovery Administration (NRA) head the same year, he made Richberg general counsel.

Once inside the administration, Richberg identified with colleagues from the business world and adopted their perspective on Section 7a of the law, guaranteeing labor's right to bargain collectively. For example, in August 1933 he and Johnson ruled that individual persons as well as any type of labor organization (so long as it was freely chosen by employees) might bargain with employers, thereby permitting open shops and even company unions under the NRA.

The NRA proved to be short-lived. By 1934 Johnson's disruptive administrative style led to his retirement. Richberg succeeded him in an acting capacity and also assumed a number of other offices, albeit in the face of rising opposition to the NRA from both business and labor. Though dubbed "Assistant President" by the press, Richberg was only a caretaker until the Supreme Court declared the NRA unconstitutional on 27 May 1935. He then returned to the practice of law, joining one of Washington's leading firms and acquiring a number of major corporate clients. He published three novels, two autobiographies, and numerous articles. He also wrote book-length polemics against "labor union monopoly" and lobbied for fundamental revisions in American labor law. By the time of his death in Charlottesville, Virginia, Richberg's identification with right-wing politics was complete and unambiguous.

• The principal collection of Richberg papers is at the Library of Congress and covers Richberg's entire life; it is supplemented by a substantial body of material at the Chicago Historical Society on his work as a labor lawyer. Numerous references to Richberg are in the presidential papers at the Franklin D. Roosevelt Library and in the National Recovery Administration Papers at the National Archives. Richberg's autobiographies are *Tents of the Mighty* (1930) and *My Hero: The Indiscreet Memoirs of an Eventful but Unheroic Life* (1954); his novels are *The Shadow Men* (1911), *In the Dark* (1912), and the semiautobiographical *A Man of Purpose* (1922); and his polemics include *Labor Union Monopoly: A Clear and Present Danger* (1957) and, with Albert Britt, *Only the Brave Are Free: A Condensed Review of the Growth of Self-Government in America* (1958). The basic biography is T. E. Vadney, *The Wayward Liberal: A Political Biography of Donald Richberg* (1970). Also see Peter Irons, *The New Deal Lawyers* (1982), and the references in John Kennedy Ohl, *Hugh S. Johnson and the New Deal* (1985), and T. H. Watkins, *Righteous Pilgrim: The Life and Times of Harold Ickes, 1874–1952* (1989). An obituary is in the *New York Times*, 28 Nov. 1960.

T. E. VADNEY

RICHMAN, Julia B. (12 Oct. 1855–24 June 1912), educational reformer, was born in New York City, the daughter of Moses Richman, a painter and glazier, and Theresa Melis. She attended school in Huntington, Long Island, and then went to New York City public schools. After graduating from P.S. 50, she attended the two-year teacher-training program at the Normal College of the City of New York (later Hunter College). She often clashed with her father, who ruled the family with an iron hand, but she prevailed against his objections to her becoming a teacher.

Richman started her career as a teacher in New York City, at P.S. 50, where she remained until 1881. Viewed as an excellent teacher, she advanced rapidly, moving on to P.S. 73 and then P.S. 78, at which she taught until 1884. When she was promoted to the position of principal at P.S. 77, she became the first Jewish principal in the city's school system as well as the first woman to hold such a position; she was also one of the youngest principals. She served in her post at P.S. 77 for almost nineteen years, from 1884 to 1903, and was regarded as a "benefactor of pupils."

In September 1903 Richman was assigned to the district level of the school system as a superintendent, the first woman in the borough of Manhattan to rise that far (Brooklyn had previously had a woman superintendent). Given supervision of the Second and Third School Districts on the Lower East Side, she quickly attracted attention from the press; the *New York Times* cited Julia Richman as a "doer of things." Despite the role that she played in school affairs, she did not like to be called a "reformer," saying, "I am not a builder of air castles." Until her retirement in 1912 she had the reputation as an "enlightened educator." Her genius was for ferreting out the basic needs of a growing school system, and the New York City system was growing fast. Not everyone in Richman's districts was keen about her social programs and efforts, however. Some in the Seward Park neighborhood, for example, interpreted her enthusiasm and resourceful energy for children's welfare as a "degrading influence." The complaints seem to have lacked substance, and the school trustees, after a long review of the neighborhood complaints, dismissed all the charges against her and gave her their commendation.

None of the criticisms dampened Richman's spirit for reform in educational matters. She was instrumental in establishing a probationary day school for delinquents and school truants. She worked hard to provide special classes for intellectually backward and mentally handicapped children. And she was interested in and developed new curricula for physical and vocational education. One of her favorite projects was the Teacher's House, where, from 1899 onward, she organized social gatherings for teachers, which often included the parents of pupils. A champion of exercise and sport for young women, she established a female athletic league that in later years was named in her honor. She made an overt effort to encourage athletics for young girls in all the schools in her jurisdiction. One of Richman's biggest projects was the Consumptive Outdoor Home, a place for children with weak lungs headquartered on a boat in New York harbor. She established an employment bureau or agency for school dropouts to help those young people who were forced by their circumstances to leave school as soon as the law allowed. She was able to convince the school trustees to provide free eye examinations for all students. She established the Bureau of Child Guidance, which became a permanent fixture of the New York City school system, as did the school lunch program that she had put into most of the daily elementary school programs.

The unvarying focus of Richman's efforts was the moral welfare of young boys and girls, and she always emphasized ethical conduct and civil behavior. This concern for the well-being of children motivated her active role in the establishment of the Educational Alliance, one of her most important activities. Formed in 1880 to aid in the Americanization of Jewish immigrants, the organization conducted special classes for immigrant children to teach them English and prepare them to attend public school. From 1893 on, Richman served as the link between the school system and the Educational Alliance. Some Jewish immigrants resented her efforts, as is explained in Moses Rischin's *The Promised City* (1977): many of the nearby residents (mostly Eastern European Jewish immigrants) on the Lower East Side claimed that she had a "paternalistic attitude toward them and their culture" (p. 239), and it was even bruited about that she was behind the move to abolish pushcarts on city streets. Rischin contends that the resentment toward Richman stemmed from a perception of her as a "self-constituted censor of our morality" (p. 239). Nevertheless, she retained her public reputation as "defender of the welfare of the immigrant children."

Richman's numerous other causes and involvements included the Young Ladies Charitable Union (1876–1881); the Young Women's Hebrew Association (starting in 1886), of which she was the first president; the Hebrew Free School Association (1886–1900), for which she served as director; and the Educational Council of the Jewish Chatauqua Society (1897–1898). She also found time to write, with Eugene H. Lehman, a book titled *Methods of Teaching Jewish Ethics*, which was published posthumously in 1914. In addition, she coauthored *Pupil's Arithmetic*, a six-volume textbook series put into use in the New York City school system in 1911, and, with Isabel Richman Wallach, a textbook called *Good Citizenship* (1908).

In 1912 the load of activities that Richman had taken upon herself came to seem too much. After nearly suffering a nervous breakdown, she took a leave of absence. Her plan was to go abroad and visit Paris, where—while on vacation—she would improve her French. She was in fair health but needed a rest. Her intention on returning to the United States was to work on improving conditions for the immigrants in the Jewish-Russian neighborhoods of New York City. Richman crossed the Atlantic Ocean on the SS *Victoria Louise* with Richard Gotthell, who handled her affairs. She became ill in mid-June, however, and was taken to the American Hospital at Neuilly, where she died. According to the attending doctor she evidently had contracted appendicitis, which brought on the peritonitis that caused her death. A funeral was held in the synagogue on the rue Copernia in Paris. The day after her death the city superintendent of the New York schools ordered all school flags to be put at half-mast, and the *New York Times* ran six memorials praising Julia B. Richman as a "true educator."

• Some of Richman's papers are in the New York City School District Headquarters Archives, which also hold an informative pamphlet by her sister Bertha R. Proskauer et al., *Julia Richman* (1916). See Richman's article "Social Needs of the Public School," *Forum* 48 (Feb. 1910): 161–67. Other useful sources are J. M. Cattrell et al., eds., *Leaders in Education* (1974); Robert A. Woods et al., *Handbook of Settlements* (1916); Moses Rischin, *The Promised City: New York's Jews, 1870–1914* (1972); Selma Cantor Berroll, "Immigrants at School, New York City, 1898–1914" (Ph.D. diss., College of the City of New York, 1967); and the entry on Richman in the *Jewish Encyclopedia*, vol. 10 (1925). See also Selma C. Berroll, "Superintendent Julia Richman: A Social Progressive in the Public Schools," *Elementary School Journal* 71 (May 1972): 402–11; "Julia Richman, Friend of the East Side Schools," *Literary Digest* 45 (18 July 1912): 65ff.; and the entry by Kathryn D. Lizzard on Richman in *Biographical Dictionary of American Education*, ed. John F. Ohles (1978), vol. 3. Concerning her illness, death, and legacy, see the *New York Times*, 20, 24, 25, and 26 June, 12 Oct., and 10 Nov. 1912.

NICHOLAS C. POLOS

RICHMOND, Charles Wallace (31 Dec. 1868–19 May 1932), ornithologist and museum curator, was born in Kenosha, Wisconsin, the son of Edward Leslie Richmond, a railway mail clerk and federal government employee, and Josephine Ellen Henry. He developed an interest in birds as a young child and began collecting bird eggs around his Kenosha home. His mother died in 1880, and shortly thereafter the family moved to Washington, D.C., where his father took a position with the U.S. Government Printing Office and remarried. Once in Washington Richmond began visiting the Smithsonian Institution and became acquainted with Robert Ridgway, the curator of birds, who helped him identify birds and eggs in his collection. Ridgway became a mentor to Richmond and reinforced his interest in ornithology.

Richmond attended the public schools of Washington, but his education was sporadic, as he was often required to leave school and find employment to supplement the family income. During 1881–1882 Richmond was a page in the House of Representatives in the forty-seventh congress, and at age fifteen he left school for good to accept a position as a messenger with the U.S. Geological Survey. In 1888 Richmond was chosen to accompany a Geological Survey expedition to Montana on which he made a collection of birds. After a short tenure with the U.S. Census Office collecting statistics on mineral waters, Richmond was appointed ornithological clerk in the Division of Economic Ornithology and mammalogy (later to become the Bureau of Biological Survey) in the U.S. Department of Agriculture in 1889.

Richmond left government service in 1892 to accompany his brother and several friends on an expedition to Central America with the idea of pursuing horticultural work. Although the trip was plagued by various problems, and he was continually battling malaria, Richmond remained in the tropics for a year and made extensive bird collections in Jamaica and Nicaragua. After returning to Washington in 1893 Richmond sold his collection to the U.S. National Museum and used the proceeds to enter the medical school of Georgetown University. He graduated with the degree of M.D. in 1897, but he never practiced medicine.

On 1 July 1893 Richmond was appointed night watchman in the telephone room of the U.S. National Museum (USNM), and the following year he joined the department of birds as scientific assistant to Robert Ridgway. He remained at the USNM the rest of his life as assistant curator of birds (1894–1918) and associate curator of birds (1918–1932). In 1929 Richmond was appointed curator, but after two months he was reappointed associate curator at his own suggestion to allow for the appointment of a new curator.

Richmond's scientific work mostly concerned issues in ornithological nomenclature and bibliography, fields in which he was considered an international authority. Around 1889 he began compiling a card catalog of all described species and genera of birds, with names as originally spelled, complete references and dates of publication, type locality, name of collector, present location of type, and other pertinent data. He continued work on the catalog until his death, and it became an invaluable reference tool for ornithologists around the world. Richmond's knowledge of ornithological literature was vast, and he was constantly consulted by ornithologists embarking on field expeditions and writers of scientific papers. Richmond published around 150 papers, mostly short taxonomic descriptions of new birds. He was not fond of field work, participating on his final trip in 1900, when he accompanied Leonhard Stejneger to Puerto Rico to collect specimens for the USNM. Elected an associate member of the American Ornithologists' Union (AOU) in 1888, Richmond served on the AOU Committee on Classification and Nomenclature of Birds from 1901 to 1922. He was also a member of numerous other scientific groups including the British Ornithologists' Union, the Cooper Ornithological Club, and the Washington Academy of Sciences.

Richmond's greatest contribution to ornithology was his card catalog of generic and specific names, which is still maintained in the division of birds at the National Museum of Natural History. Using his superb bibliographic skills, Richmond produced the definitive catalog of ornithological literature—a service to his science that is still in use today. According to Witmer Stone, Richmond's catalog and bibliographic work "did more to stabilize nomenclature than perhaps any other single effort."

Richmond was married in 1898 to Louise H. Seville; they had no children. He died in Washington, D.C., after several years of failing health.

• Correspondence documenting Charles Wallace Richmond's curatorial career at the U.S. National Museum, as well as his work on ornithological nomenclature and bibliography, is maintained in the Smithsonian Institution Archives. Field notes, catalogs, notes, lists, and his card catalog of generic and specific names, are housed in the Division of Birds, National Museum of Natural History. Despite his expertise on nomenclatural issues and ornithological bibliography, Richmond published little on the subjects. His primary contribution was a four-volume list of generic terms proposed for birds from the years 1890 to 1922, published between 1902 and 1927 in the *Proceedings of the United States National Museum*. The best biographical article is Witmer Stone, "In Memoriam: Charles Wallace Richmond, 1868–1932," *The Auk* 50 (Jan. 1933): 1–22, which gives a complete assessment of his professional career, as well as information on his childhood, family life, personality, and private life. Another biographical sketch of Richmond can be found in G. M. Mathews, *The Birds of Australia*, supp. no. 4 (1925): iv–viii. An obituary is in the *Washington Evening Star*, 19 May 1932.

WILLIAM E. COX

RICHMOND, Cora L. V. Scott Hatch Daniels Tappan (21 Apr. 1840–2 Jan. 1923), spirit medium and trance lecturer, was born near Cuba, in Allegheny County, New York, the daughter of David W. Scott, Jr., a miller and free thinker, and Lodencia Veronica Butterfield, who followed her daughter into mediumship and whose name provided her daughter's middle initials. The Scotts were reform-minded religious nonconformists. When Cora was ten they moved to the Christian socialist community of Hopedale, Massachusetts, where abolition and women's rights mixed easily with water cure and spirit-rappings. The following year they moved to Wisconsin to start a new community modeled on Hopedale. When Cora was eleven she began showing the unusual abilities that were interpreted as spirit communication. She would "write in her sleep" on her school slate—her family and neighbors believed her hand was controlled by spirits of dead friends who wished to send them messages. Soon both Cora's hand and voice were controlled by the spirit of Adin Augustus Ballou, the recently deceased son of Hopedale's founder, Adin Ballou. At this point her father abandoned his dream of a western Hopedale to promote her mediumship. When he died two years later, Cora returned to western New York and became the regular speaker at a Spiritualist society in Buffalo.

At age sixteen Cora L. V. Scott married Benjamin Hatch, a man nearly three times her age, who became her manager. They moved to New York City, where her trance lectures attracted increasing attention. She would enter the lecture hall already in trance, then deliver a spontaneous lecture on a subject selected by a committee from the audience. Believers attributed these lectures not to the medium but to external intelligences who spoke through her. In addition to Adin Augustus Ballou, her controls included Andrew Jackson, Benjamin Rush, and Theodore Parker, who addressed a variety of political, scientific, and religious topics. For the most part, however, her trance lectures concerned metaphysical and poetic subjects. The extraordinary fluency of speech emanating from the unconscious teenage girl, along with her golden curls, enchanted believers and skeptics alike. Thus began a seventy-year career as a beloved trance medium.

In 1858 Cora Hatch was awarded a divorce from Benjamin Hatch, whom she accused of frequenting prostitutes, of sexual misconduct, and of exploiting her financially. The divorce became a cause célèbre among Spiritualists and feminists who viewed her refusal to remain with an abusive husband as proof of the purity of their favorite medium. Henry James heard her speak in 1863 and used her as a model for the character of Verena Tarrant in *The Bostonians* (1886). She continued to attract adoring audiences in the hundreds and thousands throughout the cities of the North. In 1865 she married Colonel N. W. Daniels, who had recently distinguished himself in the cause of the Union. She continued to lecture until within three months of the birth of a daughter in 1866. The family moved to New Orleans to participate in the reconstruction of that city. While Colonel Daniels fulfilled his commission, Cora wrote to the antislavery press about political and economic conditions in Louisiana. Within months yellow fever took the lives of both her husband and their baby.

Cora recovered from the fever, and by January 1868 she was back on the lecture circuit. In addition to speaking in trance for Spiritualist societies, she lectured on what she had seen in Louisiana and solicited funds as an agent of the Louisiana Homestead Association "to secure homes for the poor of Louisiana, white and black." Later that year her lectures began to focus on the plight of the Indian. For the next two years she served as a vice president of the American Anti-Slavery Society, which, following emancipation of the slaves, had turned its attention to Indian rights. She became a passionate critic of government policy toward Native Americans and a vocal advocate for the position espoused by Indian rights advocate Colonel Samuel F. Tappan. Claiming to have been aided by spirit guides, she turned his accounts of army misconduct into poetic narratives of martyred chiefs and murdered innocents. In 1869 she and Tappan were married.

In 1872 Cora L. V. Tappan left for the first of several extended tours of England, where her trance lectures gained her the same popularity she enjoyed in the United States. In 1876 she became minister of the First Society of Spiritualists in Chicago, from which she received an "all-life call" in 1878. After twenty years of itinerant lecturing, she now turned her attention to pastoral concerns. She divorced Tappan and married a member of her Chicago congregation, William Richmond, in 1877. After their marriage, he learned stenography and devoted himself to recording her trance lectures, which he did every week from 1886 to 1890 for publication in the *Weekly Discourse* as well as in a number of collections. True to her radical roots, Cora L. V. Richmond met with the governor of Illinois to plead for the lives of the Haymarket anarchists in 1887. In 1893 she gave a paper representing spiritualism at the World Parliament of Religions held in conjunction with the World's Columbian Exposi-

tion. That same year she reversed her earlier opposition to organizing Spiritualism as a denomination and helped to found the National Spiritualists Association, of which she became vice president. She died at her home in Chicago.

• Major collections of Richmond's trance lectures and writings appear under all of her married names except Daniels and include *Discourses on Religion, Morals, Philosophy and Metaphysics* (1858), *Hesperia* (1871), *Discourses through the Mediumship of Mrs. Cora L. V. Tappan* (1875), *The Nature of Spiritual Experience* (1884), *The Soul* (1887), *Psychopathy; or, Spirit Healing* (1890), and *My Experiences While Out of My Body and My Return after Many Days* (1915). Harrison D. Barrett's biography, *Life Work of Mrs. Cora L. V. Richmond* (1895), provides useful accounts of her childhood and early mediumship and of her later career in England and Chicago, but it ignores her first three marriages and many other particulars. Her life and work can be followed through the periodical press, especially the *Banner of Light* (Boston), the *National Anti-Slavery Standard* (New York), and the *Practical Christian* published at Hopedale (Millford, Mass.). For modern interpretations of her life see Ann Braude, *Radical Spirits: Spiritualism and Women's Rights in Nineteenth-Century America* (1989), and Howard Kerr, *Mediums, and Spirit-Rappers, and Roaring Radicals: Spiritualism in American Literature, 1850–1900* (1972).

ANN D. BRAUDE

RICHMOND, Dannie (15 Dec. 1931?–16 Mar. 1988), jazz drummer, was born Charles Daniel Richmond in New York City. Details of his parents are unknown. Richmond gave his birth year as 1935, a date reproduced in nearly all sources, but the *New York Times* obituary gives 1931, which fits better with his activities before joining bassist Charles Mingus in 1956. Richmond was raised alternately in New York City and Greensboro, North Carolina. Although his memory of his upbringing was contradictory in locating important events—for example, where he took up the tenor saxophone and where he switched to drums—the essential story is clear.

It was probably while Richmond was in Greensboro that he first played saxophone; the instrument had been given to his older brother, who had chosen football over music and consequently left it unused. He studied mainly tenor saxophone in high school, but for student ensembles he also was asked to play xylophone and timpani, and he began to acquire a command of percussion technique. As a teenager he worked professionally in rhythm-and-blues groups, and at one point he dropped out of high school to play with saxophonist Paul Williams. His mother made him finish school. His graduation, which was somewhat delayed, was presumably around 1949 or 1950, if he was born in 1931.

After graduating Richmond returned to New York. At the Music Center Conservatory in the Bronx, he studied saxophone, clarinet, flute, piano, vibraphone, and timpani with the conservatory's distinguished faculty of jazz musicians, which included drummers Max Roach and Kenny Clarke and pianist John Lewis. He also learned to maintain a simple beat on the drum set.

After at least two years Richmond moved back in with his mother and continued his musical studies at the Agricultural and Technical College of North Carolina in Greensboro. In the course of jam sessions with fellow students, including alto saxophonist Jackie McLean, Richmond took over the drum chair on a day when the regular drummer failed to appear. He played so well that his friends encouraged him to switch instruments. Richmond immediately bought a drum set and practiced incessantly at home.

About six months later, in October 1956, Richmond was back in New York. That month he sat in with Mingus's Jazz Workshop band in place of drummer Willie Jones, who was failing to keep up a furiously fast version of "Cherokee." Mingus hired Richmond immediately, and over the next decade he held a reasonably stable position in the otherwise ever-changing Jazz Workshop. Mingus said, "Dannie . . . gave me his complete open mind to work with as clay. . . . I didn't play drums so I taught Dannie bass. Dannie is me with his own sense of will" (quoted in Case, p. 27). Thus his career during this period closely paralleled Mingus's own, with club work mainly in New York, occasional concerts and festivals, a European tour in 1965, and a series of monumental recordings, including *Blues and Roots and Mingus Ah Um* (both 1959), *Charles Mingus Presents Charles Mingus* (1960), *The Black Saint and the Sinner Lady* (1962), *Mingus, Mingus, Mingus, Mingus, Mingus* (1963), *Town Hall Concert* (1964), and *Mingus at Monterey* (1965).

Apart from Mingus, Richmond recorded on pianist Herbie Nichols's trio album *Love, Gloom, Cash, Love* (1957), and he performed with tenor saxophonist Zoot Sims, trumpeter Chet Baker (on and off for about a year from 1958 to 1959), and pianist Freddie Redd. Richmond was also away from Mingus briefly because of his arrest in Philadelphia for possession of drugs in 1962.

By 1966 Mingus was in semiretirement, owing to severe personal problems, and Richmond moved back and forth between work in the Greensboro area and jobs with Mingus in New York. Around this time he married Juniata (maiden name unknown), a high school principal in Greensboro; they had a daughter. As Mingus stopped working altogether, Richmond formed a cooperative band, LTD, which toured with rhythm-and-blues singer Johnny Taylor. Then in 1970 Mingus reformed his band, with Richmond rejoining briefly for performances at Ronnie Scott's nightclub in London.

While at Scott's, Richmond sat in with the then-drummerless folk- and jazz-rock group of singer and guitarist Jon Mark and multi-instrumentalist Johnny Almond. As with Mingus years before, his contribution was so useful that he was immediately asked to join the band. He toured Canada and the United States with the Mark-Almond band, made recordings, including *Mark-Almond 2* (1972), and performed in England. He also accompanied rock singer Joe Cocker and toured with pianist and rock singer Elton John.

Richmond rejoined Mingus in 1974. He remained with the band until Mingus's death in 1979, often taking over its direction as the leader's health deteriorated. His British experience made him well suited to Mingus's turn toward jazz-rock during this period, but the recorded results are consistently unsatisfying. Turning back toward the hard bop, soul jazz, and semifree jazz styles in which Mingus's music flourished, Richmond attempted to carry on in the posthumous Mingus Dynasty, but he found it frustrating to deal with frequent changes in group size and instrumentation that undermined his efforts to adhere to Mingus's conception. He left to focus on his own quintet, which he had first led in 1978 with Mingus's sidemen Jack Walrath (trumpet), Ricky Ford (tenor saxophone), and Bob Neloms (piano), and with bassist Eddie Gomez replacing Mingus. Cameron Brown had replaced Gomez by 1980, when they made their finest album, *Dannie Richmond Plays Charles Mingus*. The group remained intact, touring Europe and the United States until 1983, when Richmond began leading a quartet.

Still more successful was Richmond's membership from 1979 onward in the quartet of tenor saxophonist George Adams and pianist Don Pullen, again with Cameron Brown. Their recordings, including *Don't Lose Control* (1979) and *Earth Beams* (1980), convincingly present the stylistic amalgam that the Mingus Dynasty had attempted to capture. Richmond also recorded several albums with tenor saxophonist Bennie Wallace, including *Bennie Wallace Plays Monk* (1981), and appeared on tenor saxophonist Lew Tabackin's album *Angelica* (1984). Richmond died of a heart attack in New York City shortly after returning from a West Coast tour with the Adams-Pullen quartet.

After his experiences with rock music, Richmond played a number of ostentatious drum solos, but he may be heard in tasteful and lyrical settings on a variety of solos recorded earlier with Mingus, including "Better Git It in Your Soul" on *Mingus Ah Um* and "Folk Forms, No. 1" on *Charles Mingus Presents Charles Mingus*. It was, however, as an accompanist that he was most distinguished, both for his explicit and detailed manner of supporting Mingus's compositions by accenting melodies and counter-melodies and for his almost telepathic reactions to Mingus's bass playing. This involved for example, abrupt changes in volume and tempo on pieces such as "Fables of Faubus" on *Mingus Ah Um* and the album-length suite *The Black Saint and the Sinner Lady*.

• Interviews and surveys are by Dan Morgenstern, "Mingus' Man Dannie Richmond," *Down Beat* 33 (24 Mar. 1966): 18, 49; Mark Plummer, "Danny: From Mingus to Mark-Almond," *Melody Maker*, 13 Nov. 1971, pp. 30–31; Pete Senoff, "New Bands: Mark-Almond," *Jazz and Pop* 10 (June 1971): 18–20; Bret Primack, "The Gospel According to Mingus: Disciples Carry the Tune," *Down Beat* 45 (7 Dec. 1978): 12–13, 39–42; and Brian Case, "Minus Mingus," *Melody Maker*, 22 Mar. 1980, p. 27. See also Bill Shoemaker, "Danny [sic] Richmond," *Coda* 179 (June 1981): 4–7; Brian Priestley, *Mingus: A Critical Biography* (1982); Howard Mandel,

"Dr. Dannie Richmond: Rx for Swing," *Down Beat* 52 (Nov. 1985): 27–29, 59, which includes a detailed list of selected recordings; and Mathieu Mowlett and Dominique Roustain, "Les riches mondes de Dannie," *Jazz Magazine* 371 (May 1988): 24. For musical analysis, see Priestley; Don Locke, "Jazz Paradox," *Jazz Monthly* 11 (Nov. 1965): 23–25; and Barry Kernfeld, *What to Listen for in Jazz* (1995). Obituaries are in the *New York Times*, 18 Mar. 1988, and the *Independent*, 30 Mar. 1988.

BARRY KERNFELD

RICHMOND, Dean (31 Mar. 1804–27 Aug. 1866), businessman and politician, was born Elkanah Dean Richmond in Barnard, Vermont, the son of Hathaway Richmond, a manufacturer, and Rachel Dean. He never used his first name. He received only a few years of formal education during childhood, and after 1816, when the family moved to Salina (now Syracuse), New York, he learned the skills of salt production from his father and three uncles, who together operated a salt manufacturing concern. In 1821 Richmond's father died, and Richmond took his father's place in the salt business. Richmond married Mary Elizabeth Mead in 1833, and the couple had eight children. In 1842, after twenty-two years as a moderately successful businessman in Syracuse, Richmond moved to Buffalo, New York, and opened a new concern as a grain transporter. He also cofounded and directed the Buffalo & Rochester Railroad.

As one of the leading businessmen of western New York, Richmond was often called upon to run for political office or to take part in party organization. In the 1840s he was a member of the New York Democratic faction known as the "Barnburners," a group that favored an end to the expansion of slavery but also hoped for compromise with proslavery politicians in the South. Like other New York railroad owners, Richmond probably believed that the Democrats more than the Whigs would protect railroad interests in the state. After the Barnburner delegation bolted the national convention in Baltimore in May 1848, Richmond acted as a delegate to the independent Barnburner convention in Utica, New York, the next month. In August of that year Richmond was also a delegate to the Free Soil National Convention in Buffalo. Both of these conventions nominated for president Martin Van Buren, who ultimately lost to the Whig candidate, Zachary Taylor. Although Richmond attended the Free Soil convention, he never left the Democratic party. His sympathy for the Free Soilers naturally led to his affiliation in the early 1850s with the "Soft Shells," the Democratic faction in New York that, in opposition to the "Hard Shells," advocated conciliation with those Barnburners who had bolted the party. In addition to becoming a leader of the Softs, Richmond became, along with Peter Cagger, a leader of the Albany Regency, one of the most powerful factions in the New York Democratic party.

Beginning in 1850, Richmond was the chairman of the state Democratic committee. After helping to block the nomination of Fernando Wood for governor in 1856, he and Wood frequently feuded, but generally during the 1850s he avoided confrontation with most of the major Democratic factions. As a leader of the Albany Regency, Richmond was in the eye of the storm that struck the Democratic party in 1860. The party threatened to break along sectional lines that year, and at the Charleston convention in April, delegations from eight southern states bolted. Richmond tried to appease the extreme proslavery faction by casting his vote for the rule dictating that a presidential candidate had to be nominated by two-thirds of the original delegations. In the wake of the withdrawal of the southern delegates, this rule, which passed, ensured that no candidate would be nominated. As a result, the party reassembled in Baltimore in June. This time Richmond did not act as compromiser; rather, he swayed the New York delegation to support the motion excluding the delegates who had bolted at Charleston. Moreover, he insisted upon the nomination of Stephen A. Douglas as the presidential candidate despite the demands of southern delegates for a candidate more firmly committed to positive protection of slavery. Even when Douglas privately offered to withdraw his name from consideration, Richmond concealed the offer and demanded Douglas's nomination. Ultimately, Richmond's hard line at Baltimore helped lead to a separate southern convention of Democrats that nominated John C. Breckinridge for president.

During the Civil War, Richmond supported the Union, but his main efforts were directed toward restoring the strength of the New York Democracy. Through editorials in the *Albany Argus*, the leading newspaper of the Regency, he tried to unite the separate factions of the Democracy by generating opposition to two Republican policies: emancipation and suppression of civil liberties. These issues were central to the successful campaign of Horatio Seymour for governor in 1862, a campaign that Richmond helped to manage. Richmond did not support Seymour's campaign for the presidency, however, because he felt Seymour would be more likely to settle for immediate peace than would George B. McClellan, Richmond's favorite and the eventual Democratic nominee. Richmond continued to try, unsuccessfully, to heal relations between the prowar and propeace factions.

During the last months of the war and the immediate postwar period, Richmond used innovation and chicanery to try to rejuvenate the Democratic party. During the final voting by the House of Representatives on the Thirteenth Amendment abolishing slavery, Richmond advised that the Democratic leadership allow Democratic representatives to vote as they wished. By not making a vote against constitutional abolition a test of party discipline, Richmond hoped he might sway ex-Democrats who had left the party because of the slavery issue to resume their old affiliations. During late 1865 and 1866, Richmond joined with the Republican Thurlow Weed in planning a coalition National Union party that would join Democrats and conservative Republicans in support of President

Andrew Johnson and in opposition to the Radical Republicans. Richmond was in fact not interested in a genuine coalition party. His real motives in this effort were twofold: to obtain a monopoly of New York State patronage for affiliates of the Albany Regency instead of Tammany Hall and to split the Republican party permanently so that ex-Democrats would rejoin their old organization.

During his tenure as chairman of the state Democratic party, Richmond continued to expand his business interests. In 1853 his Buffalo & Rochester Railroad incorporated with six other lines in the state to form the New York Central Railroad. Richmond used his political influence to secure this incorporation in the face of massive opposition. He became a vice president of the New York Central, and in 1864 he succeeded Erastus Corning as president of the line. Although his professional life reveals a great success story, his political endeavors were not as fruitful. Richmond and Weed planned for a National Union Convention in Philadelphia in 1866, but just days before the convention Richmond died suddenly in the home of Samuel J. Tilden in New York City. As a result, Tammany Hall dominated the National Union Convention, and when the Tammany delegates nominated as governor John T. Hoffman, a candidate unacceptable to conservative Republicans, the National Union movement collapsed.

• No single collection of Richmond's papers exists, but letters written by him are found in the Samuel L. M. Barlow Papers in the Henry E. Huntington Library, San Marino, Calif.; in the Manton M. Marble Papers in the Library of Congress; and in the Samuel J. Tilden Papers in the New York Public Library. Some of Richmond's business endeavors are traced in Josephus Nelson Larned, *A History of Buffalo* (1911), and Frank Walker Stevens, *The Beginnings of the New York Central Railroad* (2 vols., 1926). Two of the most valuable books that discuss Richmond's political activities were written by Jerome Mushkat, *The Reconstruction of the New York Democracy, 1861–1874* (1981) and *Fernando Wood: A Political Biography* (1990). Especially helpful on Richmond's pre–Civil War political career is Roy Franklin Nichols, *The Disruption of the American Democracy* (1948). For Richmond's activities during the Civil War and Reconstruction, LaWanda Cox and John H. Cox, *Politics, Principle, and Prejudice, 1865–1866: Dilemma of Reconstruction America* (1963) is thorough. Also helpful is DeAlva Stanwood Alexander, *A Political History of the State of New York* (3 vols., 1909). Obituaries are in the *Albany Evening Journal*, 27 Aug. 1866, and the *New York Times* and *New York Herald*, both 28 Aug. 1866.

MICHAEL VORENBERG

RICHMOND, John Lambert (5 Apr. 1785–10 Oct. 1855), physician, was born on a farm in Chesterfield, Massachusetts, the son of Nathaniel Richmond and Susannah Lambert, farmers. The family moved to western New York State when John was three years of age. Except for two weeks' attendance in a country school, his early education was all self-acquired and self-taught. In 1806 he married Lorana Sprague Patchin, who encouraged and guided him in his educa-

tion; they had ten children. In 1816 he was ordained as a Baptist minister. Believing, like many other Americans, that his future was in the West, he traveled to Pittsburgh, Pennsylvania, then down the Ohio River by flatboat to Cincinnati, Ohio.

In 1818 Daniel Drake organized in Cincinnati the Medical College of Ohio, with state approval. After finding space for the college and organizing a faculty, the first class was held in the fall of 1820. After working for a time as a janitor at the school, Richmond convinced Drake to allow him to enroll in the medical college, offering half of his salary for tuition. Richmond graduated on 4 April 1822, having written his thesis on the medicinal plant Indian arrow-wood. He then established a practice in Newtown, Ohio. In addition to his general practice and his obligations as a preacher, he was appointed surgeon of the Second Regiment of the Ohio State Militia in 1825.

On Sunday evening, 22 April 1827, he was summoned by two midwives to see a pregnant woman who was in labor. It was a dark and rainy night, the Miami River was flooding, and he was able to get to the patient's log cabin only by rowboat. When he arrived, he saw that the woman was convulsing. He used every medicinal agent available to him to control the convulsions and was totally unsuccessful. He thoroughly examined the woman and found that she had a vaginal abnormality with no cervical dilatation. Richmond was convinced that he could not safely deliver the infant vaginally. At 1:00 A.M., on Monday, 23 April, with the help of the two midwives, he performed a cesarean section. This was before the advent of any anesthesia. When he opened the uterus, he found that the infant's back was to the incision, a transverse lie, and it was impossible for him to deliver the baby through the incision, where the back was the only presenting part. He then decided to do a transverse incision across the back of the stillborn baby. Once the baby was cut in half, it was possible to deliver the infant safely without damage to the mother.

Richmond's description of the surgery in the *Western Journal of Medical and Physical Sciences* (3 [1830]: 485) was excellent. The surgical repair was also well described. The wound was sutured, leaving a small opening for drainage, a very important procedure to prevent infection and fluid collections. No mention was made of what was used for suture material, but in that era linen thread was the most commonly used material.

This patient made a complete recovery and was back to work in twenty-four days. This was the first successful cesarean section in the United States that resulted in a live patient. However, because of the complications of the surgery and the anatomical anomaly, the woman never was able to become pregnant again.

Richmond continued his general medical practice in Newtown, Ohio. True to his dedication to medicine, Richmond was among the first physicians to volunteer to take care of the victims of the cholera epidemic that occurred in Cincinnati in 1831. Richmond contracted cholera himself, and though he recovered, he was left in very poor health. This made it very difficult for him to continue his robust and active practice. In 1834, because of his reduced physical status, he moved to Pendleton, Indiana, and settled there for one year to convalesce from his illness. In 1835 he moved again, this time to the city of Indianapolis, Indiana, where he continued to practice medicine and preached as a minister at the First Baptist Church. In 1842, however, he suffered from a stroke that left his left leg totally paralyzed. Because of this physical disability, he gave up both his medical practice and the ministry and moved to Covington, Indiana, to live with some of his surviving children. His wife died in 1854, and Richmond followed her one year later in Covington. On 22 April 1912 a monument in his memory was erected in Newtown.

• For additional information on Richmond, see Fielding H. Garrison, *An Introduction to the History of Medicine* (1924), p. 544, and Howard A. Kelly and Walter L. Burrage, eds., *American Medical Biographies* (1920), pp. 978–80. For details of the first successful cesarean, see G. W. H. Kempner, "The Celebrated Richmond Cesarean Case," *Indianapolis Medical Journal* 11 (Sept. 1909). One of Richmond's speeches has been transcribed by Otto Juettner as "John L. Richmond—Western Pioneer Surgery Address before McDowell Medical Society" (1912) and can be found at the University of Cincinnati Medical School library. Entries on Daniel Drake provide helpful information about Richmond's career; see, for instance, the section on Drake in James G. Wilson and John Fiske, eds., *Appletons' Cyclopedia of American Biography*, vol. 2 (1887), p. 223. Providing additional biographical information is Juettner, *Daniel Drake and His Followers: Historical and Biographical Sketches, 1785–1909* (1909), pp. 121, 174, and 460.

W. ROBERT PENMAN

RICHTER, Charles Francis (26 Apr. 1900–30 Sept. 1985), seismologist and inventor of the magnitude scale for measuring earthquakes, was born Charles Francis Kinsinger on a farm near Hamilton, Ohio, the son of Frederick W. Kinsinger, and Lillian Richter. Richter's parents separated while he was still an infant, and his mother resumed her maiden name after their divorce. Richter had little contact with his father and only remembered meeting him once. Because his mother went through periods of mental instability, he was raised by his maternal grandfather, Charles Otto Richter, a farmer who also worked at a firm that manufactured stationary engines. Richter later claimed that he owed everything to his grandfather. In 1926 Richter legally adopted his mother and grandfather's surname.

Richter moved with his family to Los Angeles in 1909. His mother educated him at home for a time, but at age twelve he entered the Southern California Academy and later University High School, a preparatory school for the University of Southern California. Richter entered USC at the age of sixteen and spent one year there before moving to Stanford University, where he completed a degree in physics. He wanted to pursue a career in astronomy, but soon after graduating Richter suffered what he termed a nervous break-

down and was limited for several years to pursuing odd jobs in Los Angeles. Upon hearing of Nobel laureate Robert Millikan's arrival at the California Institute of Technology, however, Richter decided to resume his studies. He entered the graduate program at Caltech in 1923 and studied for a Ph.D. in physics under Paul Epstein. He graduated with a dissertation on atomic theory in 1928, the same year that he married Lillian Brand; the couple had no children.

Even before his graduation from Caltech, Richter had accepted a position as a research assistant in seismology at the Carnegie Institution's newly established Geophysical Laboratory in Pasadena. Richter remained for a time quite ambivalent about this migration from physics to seismology and some years later claimed that he had still not accepted his new field "wholeheartedly." At the geophysical lab, Richter assisted Harry Oscar Wood, who had recently developed (with John Anderson) the torsion seismometer, an instrument that reliably recorded the short period vibrations of small, local earth tremors. With this device, Richter spent the next several years recording and measuring California's numerous minor earthquakes. In 1930 Caltech hired Beno Gutenberg, one of the leading seismologists in Europe and author of a well-respected *Handbook of Geophysics*, to join the Pasadena Seismological Laboratory. Together with Gutenberg, Richter began work on a scale that could measure the relative magnitude of earthquake tremors.

At the time, earthquakes were generally measured in subjective terms, by recording the damage sustained by structures of different types. The only existing scale, the Mercalli scale, judged a tremor according to how its effects were felt by people in various places. Such effects generally decreased as a function of the distance from the earthquake's source. Richter had the idea of creating a quantitative scale for seismic events, one that would enable scientists to make comparisons between shocks regardless of the location of their epicenter. On a suggestion from Gutenberg, Richter plotted the data he had recorded over the past several years on a logarithmic scale and found that the data points of different quakes lined up in roughly parallel sets of curves. Each event could then be assigned a numerical value based on its overall size, rather than on the intensity of the quake at a given point. Richter called his invention "the magnitude scale." Although Richter had developed the scale in collaboration with Gutenberg, seismologists took to referring to it as "the Richter scale." This name persisted, although later in his life Richter began to emphasize the role that Gutenberg had played in aiding in the scale's development. In a speech in 1977 he suggested that the name "Richter scale" did "less than justice" to Gutenberg's role in the creation of this widely used seismological measure.

In 1937 the Pasadena Seismological Laboratory was officially transferred to Caltech, and Richter was appointed assistant professor in the Department of Geology. In 1947 he was promoted to associate professor and in 1952 attained a full professorship. During his career, Richter produced two important works in seismology. The first, *The Seismicity of the Earth*, a comprehensive survey of geophysical research on earthquake activity around the globe, was published in 1941 in collaboration with Gutenberg. In 1958 Richter completed an introductory textbook for what he called his "young science," *Elementary Seismology*, which was used to introduce an entire generation of students to the latest findings in his rapidly growing field of research.

Richter spent his entire career at Caltech, with the exception of one year he spent as a Fulbright Research Scholar at Tokyo University in 1959–1960. He accumulated numerous honors for his work in earthquake research, including the medal of the Seismological Society of America; he also served as president of that organization. Richter was elected a fellow of the American Academy of Arts and Sciences and was a member of Sigma Xi. In 1971 he also founded a consulting firm, Lindvall, Richter and Associates, which offered seismic evaluations of buildings.

A very private individual, Richter was often somewhat awkward in social situations. He grew to love his work, however, and was most at ease pouring over seismic data and talking about the nature and effects of earthquakes. He spent most of his time engaged in research and produced many professional papers. In addition to creating the scale that bears his name, Richter helped to transform seismology from a qualitative survey of earthquake damage into a study focused on the forces that cause seismic events and the devastating energies that result from them. He was particularly instrumental in shaping the understanding of the seismology of southern California, where he spent his entire adult life. He retired in 1970 and died in Altadena, only a few miles from his institutional home of Caltech.

• Richter's papers, including his extensive collection of science fiction magazines and an oral history interview with him are in the Institute Archives at the California Institute of Technology. Of his more than one hundred journal articles (many in collaboration with Beno Gutenberg), the most significant relate to the magnitude scale of earthquakes: "An Instrumental Earthquake Magnitude Scale," *Bulletin of the Seismological Society of America* 25 (1935): 1–32; and, with Gutenberg, "Magnitude and Energy of Earthquakes," *Science* 83 (1936): 183–85. Historical assessments of Richter's work have just begun to appear. The best source is the chapter on "Earthquakes" in Judith Goodstein, *Millikan's School: A History of the California Institute of Technology* (1991). For a view of Richter from a Caltech colleague see Clarence R. Allen, "Charles F. Richter: A Personal Tribute," *Bulletin of the Seismological Society of America* 77, no. 6 (Dec. 1987): 2234–37. Obituaries are in the *Los Angeles Times* and the *New York Times*, both 1 Oct. 1985.

DAVID A. VALONE

RICHTER, Conrad Michael (13 Oct. 1890–30 Oct. 1968), novelist and essayist, was born in Pine Grove, Pennsylvania, the son of John Absalom Richter, a general merchant and later a Lutheran minister, and Charlotte Esther Henry, daughter, niece, and sister of Lutheran ministers. Both religion and family strongly influenced Richter's writing by providing him with subjects, character models, and idealistic themes.

In 1906 Richter graduated from high school in Tremont, Pennsylvania, where his father served his first Lutheran parish, and worked at several different jobs, including teamster, farm laborer, bank clerk, timberman, and subscription salesman, occupations that figure in his first works of short fiction. Richter's writing career did not begin, however, until 1910, after the twenty-year-old youth had chanced upon a series of articles about the American newspaper. The discovery quickened a latent writing interest to the point that Richter applied for and received a reporter's job on the Johnstown, Pennsylvania, *Journal*. Later he worked for newspapers in Patton and Pittsburgh, Pennsylvania. As it did for Ernest Hemingway, journalism taught Richter concise and concrete expression that manifested itself, among other ways, in the compressed length of his novels, most of which are fewer than 200 pages in length.

From newspaper work, Richter moved to a job as private secretary in Cleveland, Ohio, where, in his spare time, he began writing short works of fiction. His first published story, "How Tuck Went Home," appeared in *Cavalier* (6 Sept. 1913). About six months later, his "Brothers of No Kin" was published in *Forum* (Apr. 1914); very well received, it was later reprinted in *Reedy's Mirror, Illustrated Sunday Magazine*, and, finally, in *The Best Short Stories of 1915*. Also in 1915, Richter married Harvena Achenbach, daughter of a Pine Grove, Pennsylvania, squire; they had one child, a daughter named Harvena, who became a story writer and poet.

From 1915 to 1928 Richter engaged in magazine editing and publishing as well as in continued creative writing. Under his own name and pseudonyms, he wrote stories for *John Martin's Book*, a children's publication, and for his own juvenile publication, *Junior Magazine*, for which he also served as editor, publisher, copywriter, and advertising salesman. In his limited spare time he wrote adult short stories for *Outlook, Ladies' Home Journal, Saturday Evening Post, American*, and *Every Week*. Simultaneously Richter engaged in a process of reading and reflection about the meaning of life, an investigation that resulted in two book-length essays, *Human Vibration* (1925) and *Principles in Bio-Physics* (1927); both advance recondite ideas about physical and psychological energy and seek to reconcile the seeming contradictions of mind and matter, science (physics) and spirit (metaphysics). Despite their philosophical weaknesses, the theories developed in these essays became what Richter called "the overtones" of his fiction, and indeed they undergird both the action and themes of his later stories and novels.

In 1928, because of his wife's poor health, the Richters moved from Pennsylvania to the warmer, dryer climate of Albuquerque, New Mexico. The move forced Richter to adjust his writings to a new cultural orientation. It was difficult: the American Southwest, he later said, was a "hard place to love" and "so loved the more." Nevertheless, the region provided Richter with the material, most of it gleaned from tedious library research and from interviews with pioneers (New Mexico had been a state only since 1912), for his first novel, *The Sea of Grass* (1937), as well as three other novels and numerous works of short fiction.

A graphic fictional account of the actual conflict between ranchers who had tamed the area and lately arrived farmers—"nesters" to the ranchers—over the best use of the land, *The Sea of Grass* depicts the demise of prairie grasses caused by improvident farming. Published by Alfred A. Knopf, who would publish all subsequent book-length works by Richter, *The Sea of Grass* was one of six Richter novels that would be adapted for motion picture and television.

Like *The Sea of Grass*, the remainder of Richter's novels set in the West concern the conflicts and other hardships of pioneering. They include the collected stories *Early Americana* (1936) and *The Rawhide Knot and Other Stories* (collected posthumously 1978); and the novels *Tacey Cromwell* (1942), the story of the struggle of a mining town prostitute to achieve respectability and to be a worthy foster mother, and *The Lady* (1957), an account of an aristocratic woman's resistance to the violence perpetrated against her sheep-ranching family and property by neighboring cattle ranchers. Richter's only other book-length work set in the Southwest is the novel *The Mountain on the Desert* (1955), a philosophical treatise (affiliated with the two earlier book-length essays) that centers around a mystic named Michael.

During his southwestern residence, Richter continued to write about subjects concerning his native eastern America. *The Trees* (1940) became the first volume of a trilogy including *The Fields* (1946) and the Pulitzer Prize–winning *The Town* (1950). These three novels later were collected in one volume as *The Awakening Land* (1966). Graphically describing the arduous and heartbreaking process of bringing European customs to the eighteenth- and nineteenth-century wilderness in western Pennsylvania and eastern Ohio, the trilogy revolves around an archetypical frontier heroine named Sayward Luckett, who rescues the erudite but wayward Portius Wheeler from a wasted life prompted by a failed romance in his native Boston. The trilogy was televised in 1979 by the National Broadcasting Company and again in 1993. While working on the trilogy, Richter sandwiched two minor novels between the major ones: *The Free Man* (1943), an American revolutionary war story actually inspired by Richter's desire to join other American writers in supporting his nation's World War II effort, and *Always Young and Fair* (1947), the story of a young American soldier who died in the Philippines during the Spanish-American war.

For *The Sea of Grass* and *The Trees*, Richter in 1942 received the gold medal for literature from the Society of Libraries of New York University. In 1946 the Pennsylvania German Society awarded him a certificate of merit for *The Fields*, and in 1947 the Ohiana Library awarded Richter a medal for *Always Young and Fair* (1947). He was also the recipient of four honorary doctorates.

In 1950 the Richters returned from Albuquerque to Pine Grove, where they took up permanent residence. Working steadily, Richter produced eight novels, a novelette, several short stories, and some magazine articles in the final eighteen years of his life. His *The Light in the Forest* (1953), a tale of the Indian captivity of an American colonial white boy, was filmed by Walt Disney Studios. Its sequel, *A Country of Strangers*, was published in 1966.

The major achievement of Richter's later years was the first two volumes of an unfinished trilogy of novels. Winner of the 1960 National Book Award for fiction, Richter's *The Waters of Kronos* recalls Thornton Wilder's *Our Town* in the way it hauntingly cuts across space and time. Its central character, an author, grown old and ill, miraculously returns to his childhood home in a quest to understand his ministerial father and his father's religion. The events and people closely resemble those of Richter's own family. Likewise resembling familial events and people, *A Simple Honorable Man* (1962), a fictional account of the life of a Lutheran minister, is the second volume of the unfinished trilogy. Lesser works written by Richter in his final years are *The Grandfathers* (1964), a folkloric novel; *Over the Blue Mountain* (1967), a folkloric novelette appealing mainly to children; and *The Aristocrat* (1968), an awkwardly constructed novel about a spinster who refuses to tolerate mediocrity.

Richter died in Pottsville, Pennsylvania, and was buried in Pine Grove. A private person, he had carefully avoided the self-indulgent lifestyles generally associated with authors of his day. He did so in fidelity to the ideals he espoused and in the interest of his personal and familial privacy and of the integrity of his art.

Into the nearly six decades of his writing career, Richter had packed an impressive amount of writing—including fifteen novels and three collections and numerous uncollected works of short fiction. His works reflect the remarkable scientific and technological changes that occurred in the United States during his lifetime and especially his continuing concern with those changes he found at variance with the values of earlier generations. Richter's reputation rests mainly on the historical masterpieces, *The Sea of Grass*, *The Trees*, *The Fields*, and *The Town*, and on his autobiographical *The Waters of Kronos* and *A Simple Honorable Man*. Those six novels establish him clearly in the front ranks of American historical novelists, and they leave as a legacy a paean to simple goodness.

• Six book-length studies and numerous articles have been devoted to Conrad Richter's life and works. The primary analytical-biographical investigation has been Edwin W. Gaston, Jr., *Conrad Richter* (1965; rev. ed., 1989). Harvena Richter provides an illuminating analysis of her father's personality, motivation, and work habits in *Writing to Survive: The Private Notebooks of Conrad Richter* (1988). Focusing only on Richter's southwestern American works, Robert J.

Barnes, *Conrad Richter* (1968), demonstrates the author's careful attention to event, place, and people. Clifford Edwards, *Conrad Richter's Ohio Trilogy* (1970), examines the author's only triptych *The Trees, The Fields,* and *The Town.* Finally, Marvin J. LaHood, *Conrad Richter's America* (1975), examines some major themes in Richter's fiction and the literary affiliation of Richter with Willa Cather, Elizabeth Madox Roberts, and Caroline Miller.

EDWIN W. GASTON, JR.

RICHTER, Curt Paul (20 Feb. 1894–21 Dec. 1988), psychobiologist and educator, was born in Denver, Colorado, the son of Paul Ernst Richter, an engineer and iron and steel firm owner, and Martha Dressler. After completing his high school education in Denver, Richter studied engineering at the Technische Hochschule in Dresden, Germany, from 1912 to 1915. When his stay in Germany was interrupted by World War I, he attended Harvard University and graduated with a B.S. in 1917. There, he was introduced to behavioral psychology by Robert M. Yerkes. After two years of military service, Richter went to graduate school at the Johns Hopkins University, where he worked especially with John B. Watson and Adolf Meyer and completed his Ph.D. in psychology in 1921. His doctoral dissertation and first publication dealt with the "Behavioristic Study of the Spontaneous Activity of the Rat" and presaged a career of research on the behavior of that species.

Richter's life is a study in long-term dedication to research in psychobiology. In 1919 he began research in Watson's laboratory at the Phipps Psychiatric Clinic of the Johns Hopkins Hospital, where Richter continued to conduct research for over sixty-five years. He became the director of the psychobiology laboratory in 1922, associate professor in 1923, professor of psychobiology in 1957, and professor emeritus in 1960. Richter married Phyllis Greenacre, and they had two children; little mention of her is made in his papers, and the date of the marriage and how it ended are unknown. He married Leslie Prince Bidwell in 1937; they had one child.

A master experimenter, Richter made major contributions to a diverse array of areas within behavioral psychology. He studied behavioral patterns in a variety of species that included bullfrogs, alligators, chickens, ground squirrels, beavers, porcupines, sloths, and primates as well as rats. He had a genius for designing apparatus, such as the first running wheel to record spontaneous activity that would enable the recording and quantification of significant behavioral patterns in the life of the animal.

Richter's skills and lifelong dedication yielded nearly 300 publications. His earliest work was in the study of spontaneous activity in rats and how it was affected by such factors as age, illumination, and temperature. He became well known for his career-long research on biological clocks, the internal timing mechanisms that affect mood, sleep patterns, and physiological activity, begun in the 1920s. Richter had strong interests in how the central nervous system is organized to produce movement and in the functions of the sympathetic nervous system, in both normal and pathological states.

Richter's name is firmly associated with the role of behavior in maintaining the relatively steady conditions within the body—behavioral homeostasis. He was especially interested in the self-selection of diets, whereby, for example, a rat that lacks adrenal glands and needs to ingest sodium in order to live displays taste preferences for sodium. He also found that rats that lack parathyroid glands ingest much-needed calcium.

Interested in wild as well as domesticated rats, Richter studied their reactions to stress and the phenomenon of sudden death in the laboratory. He helped in the development of poisons for rats but also studied the phenomenon of poison avoidance that they display. Through all of these diverse fields of interest, Richter investigated the environmental, hormonal, and neural regulation of behavior, but emphasized the individual organism and its regulatory abilities. His clinical research dealt with such subjects as peripheral nerve damage in soldiers, "voodoo" death, and abnormal biological rhythms in psychiatric patients.

Richter remained an active researcher until shortly before his death in Baltimore. Along the way he received many recognitions. He was a member of the National Academy of Sciences, the American Philosophical Society, and the American Academy of Arts and Sciences. He received the Warren Medal of the Society of Experimental Psychologists in 1950, the Lashley Award in Neurobiology from the American Philosophical Society in 1980, and the Passano Award in Medicine and Biology in 1977.

Called the "compleat psychobiologist" by Paul Rozin because of the range and richness of his studies, Richter was interested in both the physiological mechanisms controlling behavior and the significance of behavior for the adaptation of the organism to its environment as an individual and in an evolutionary context. At the same time, he was interested in pathology and the clinical relevance of biological and behavioral phenomena. His work was strongly empirical and programmatic, reflecting the skills of a dedicated and skilled laboratory scientist.

• Richter's papers are in the Alan Mason Chesney Medical Archives of the Johns Hopkins University, although they were not yet available for use as of 1994. An excellent source that includes many of Richter's key papers is E. M. Blass, ed., *The Psychobiology of Curt Richter* (1976). Richter's autobiography is in *Leaders in the Study of Animal Behavior* (1985) and *Studying Animal Behavior* (1989), ed. D. A. Dewsbury. Biographical sketches include those by E. M. Blass in *American Journal of Psychology* 104 (1991): 143–46; and A. McGehee Harvey, *Adventures in Medical Research: A Century of Discovery at Johns Hopkins* (1976), pp. 340–47. Obituaries and tributes are in the *New York Times,* 22 Dec. 1988; *Time,* 2 Jan. 1989; *Journal of the American Medical Association* 261 (1989): 3174; and *Psychobiology* 17 (1989): 113–14.

DONALD A. DEWSBURY

RICHTER, Gisela Marie Augusta (14 Aug. 1882–24 Dec. 1972), classical archaeologist and art historian, was born in London, England, the daughter of Jean Paul Richter, a historian of Italian Renaissance art, and Louise Schwab, a novelist, translator, and historian of Italian Renaissance art. Gisela Richter's sister, Irma, an artist and also a historian of Italian Renaissance art, worked closely with her sister, teaching her to see like an artist and about the value of the "practical side" of art, as Richter called it. Gisela Richter later studied pottery with Maude Robinson and learned the techniques of marble carving and bronze casting. This knowledge was invaluable to her in purchasing antiquities and writing her published works. The family's background was German, but it was cosmopolitan and multilingual. They traveled frequently in continental Europe, with lengthy stays in Italy.

Richter's father was associated with the Italian art historian Giovanni Morelli from 1876 and introduced the young American art historian Bernard Berenson to him in 1890. Morelli's approach to connoisseurship, especially his concentration on artists' depiction of anatomical details, had a profound impact on Jean Paul Richter and through him on Gisela Richter's approach to Greek and Roman art history. Examination of the object was primary to Richter. She grouped objects stylistically and then dated the groups chronologically, using both external and internal criteria, including comparisons of sculpture to vase painting and anatomical accuracy.

The Richter family lived in both Rome and Florence, although they traveled a great deal, before they moved back to London in 1892. Richter's education was at Maida Vale School, one of the finest for women at the time, but she later recalled that it was her attendance at Emmanuel Loewy's lectures at the University of Rome around 1896 that convinced her to become a classical archaeologist. In 1901 Richter entered Girton College, Cambridge University. Her don there was Katherine Jex-Blake, a prominent classicist and a co-translator of Pliny the Elder's chapters on the history of art. In 1904 Richter left Cambridge, where as a woman she was ineligible for a degree, to study at the British School in Athens. Although Richter was not allowed to live at the school, she was befriended by its director, Charles Bosanquet, who encouraged her to publish her first article, in the *Annual of the British School at Athens* (1904–1905). During 1905 Richter traveled in the Peloponnese, Attica, Euboea, and the Greek islands, as well as to Constantinople, Pergamon, Priene, and Mytilene in the Ottoman Empire. However, Richter's most important visit was to the island of Crete. There she met Harriet Boyd, the first woman to direct an archaeological excavation, Gournia. Illness prevented Richter from seeing much of Crete, but she saw much of Boyd, and the two became lifelong friends. After a vacation with the Richter family, Boyd persuaded Richter to come to the United States, and the two women landed in Boston in 1905. Richter's first attempts to find employment were unsuccessful, but she did meet Edward Robinson, director of the Museum of Fine Arts, Boston. When he moved to become vice director of the Metropolitan Museum of Art in New York, Robinson invited Richter to catalog a newly purchased collection of Greek vases. In 1906 Richter agreed to become a permanent member of the Metropolitan's staff, negotiating three months off each summer to travel to Europe, not only to see family but also to immerse herself in the great collections and make valuable contacts with colleagues.

The years 1906–1928 were heady ones for the Metropolitan, as Robinson and his agent, John Marshall, vastly increased the museum's holdings in Greek and Roman art. Richter was promoted to assistant curator in 1910, and in 1911 her rich flood of publications, inspired by the Metropolitan's classical collection, began. In 1917 Richter became an American citizen, and in 1921 she founded the American Archaeological Club with several friends. Richter's willingness to share her knowledge with others throughout her career was an important reason for her success in keeping abreast of the latest developments in scholarship. Although Richter held only one teaching position, the Annual Professorship at the American School of Classical Studies in Athens (1961), her help to student colleagues was invaluable. She also contributed generously to the financial support of archaeological expeditions.

Richter's rise at the Metropolitan was steady. In 1922 she was promoted to associate curator then in 1925 to curator, the first woman to hold that high a rank. She arranged for the acquisitions of many masterpieces, among which the Kleitias stand and Lydos krater (1931), the Metropolitan kouros and the Landsdowne Amazon (1932), a Roman portrait of Caracalla (1941), and a Hellenistic Sleeping Eros (1943) particularly stand out. Richter's range of publications expanded as well. In addition to Greek ceramics, she wrote on Roman glass and portraits; Greek, Roman, and Etruscan engraved gems; furniture; bronzes; and above all, Greek sculpture. She dominated the field of Greek sculpture from 1929, when the first edition of *Sculpture and Sculptors of the Greeks* appeared, until her death.

Richter retired from the Metropolitan in 1948 but remained as honorary curator until 1952, when she fully retired and became curator emerita. In 1952 Richter moved to Rome with her sister Irma. Richter's retirement was remarkably fruitful, allowing her to update existing books and write new ones. Her greatest works come from this period: *Attic Red-Figured Vases: A Survey*, 2d ed. (1958); *Portraits of the Greeks* (3 vols., 1965–1972); *Furniture of the Greeks, Etruscans and Romans*, 2d ed. (1966); *Korai* (1968); *The Engraved Gems of the Greeks, Etruscans and Romans* (2 vols. 1968, 1971); *Kouroi*, 3d ed. (1970); *Perspective in Greek and Roman Art* (1970); *Sculpture and Sculptors of the Greeks*, 4th ed. (1970); and posthumously, *Handbook of Greek Art*, 7th ed. (1974). Richter received numerous honors over the course of her career, including the AAUW Achievement Award (1944), the American

Academy Medal (1955), the Isabella d'Este Award (1965), and the gold medal for distinguished archaeological achievement of the Archaeological Institute of America (1968). She died in Rome, never having married.

Richter's descriptions of works are detailed yet concise. She seldom hypothesized. Her categories are so convincing that readers forget that some subsequently discovered works may not fit into her groupings. Her works of synthesis, such as *Sculpture and Sculptors of the Greeks*, depend on the compilation of references from classical texts and reject unprovable attributions based on Roman copies. Richter did not try to relate Greek art to external factors such as history, literature, or philosophy. She saw Roman art through Greek eyes. However, Richter's contributions to the study of Greek art, especially sculpture, are basic for all subsequent scholarship in that field. Her writings and their collections of photographs are fundamental tools in art history.

• Richter's personal papers are on deposit in the library of the American Academy in Rome. Documents on her work at the Metropolitan Museum are in the files of the Department of Greek and Roman Art. The most complete primary sources are those written by Richter herself: *My Memoirs: Recollections of an Archaeologist's Life* (1972) and "The Department of Greek and Roman Art: Triumphs and Tribulations," *Metropolitan Museum Journal* 3 (1970): 73–95. Short biographies have appeared: Ingrid E. M. Edlund et al., "Gisela Marie Augusta Richter (1882–1972): Scholar of Classical Art and Museum Archaeologist," in *Women as Interpreters of the Visual Arts, 1820–1979*, ed. Claire R. Sherman (1981; with selected bibliography); and Evelyn Harrison, "Gisela Richter," in *Notable American Women*, ed. Barbara Sicherman and Carol H. Green (1980). Mary Allsebrook, *Born to Rebel: The Life of Harriet Boyd Hawes* (1992), written by Harriet Boyd Hawes's daughter, has information on Richter not found elsewhere. Perceptive obituaries are in Frank E. Brown, *Studi Etruschi* 41 (1973): 597–600; Homer Thompson, *American Philosophical Society Yearbook* (1973): 144–50; and Cornelius C. Vermeule III, *The Burlington Magazine* 115 (1973): 329.

JOHN STEPHENS CRAWFORD

RICHTMYER, Floyd Karker (12 Oct. 1881–7 Nov. 1939), physicist, was born of German and Dutch ancestry on a farm near the town of Cobleskill, New York. His only sibling, an older half brother, Edgar Richtmyer, and Edgar's wife Louise served as Floyd's foster parents after the early death of young Richtmyer's own parents. Upon graduating from high school in Cobleskill in 1900, he put himself through college at Cornell University by waiting tables and other menial employment. He received an A.B. in 1904 and that same year married Bernice Davis, with whom he would have four children, one of whom died in infancy. After teaching for two years at Drexel University in Pennsylvania, he returned to Cornell in 1906 for graduate study and received a Ph.D. in physics in 1910. In 1911 he joined the faculty at Cornell, where he spent the rest of his life, except for two sabbaticals and occasional summers spent at other universities.

During the First World War, Richtmyer worked for the Signal Corps of the U.S. Army (with the reserve officer rank of major) on the development of radio for communication between aircraft and ground stations. He spent his first sabbatical, during the academic year 1919–1920, in Schenectady, New York, where he worked at the General Electric Research Laboratory and taught at Union College. During his second sabbatical, 1927–1928, he spent the first semester at the University of Göttingen in Germany and the second at Uppsala University in Sweden, where he conducted research in X-rays at the laboratory of physicist Manne Siegbahn.

One of Richtmyer's early experimental results, published in 1909 in the *Physical Review*, established a strict proportionality between a photoelectric current and the intensity of the light falling on the photoelectric surface, for given wavelength of the light and given atomic number of the material of the surface. This finding had not been expected. According to classical (nonquantum) theory, the electric field strength (also the magnetic field strength) of the light wave varied as the square root of the intensity of the light. It was supposed that the electric field had to be of at least a certain limiting strength in order to eject electrons from the atoms, so that the light would have to be of at least a certain limiting intensity to produce any photoelectric current at all. According to quantum theory, however, a light beam is a stream of photons. For a given wavelength of the light, all photons are identical with respect to electric field strength; it is only the *number* of photons that varies with the light intensity. Hence the proportionality of light intensity and photoelectric current. Richtmyer's result thus provided a confirmation of the quantum theory.

The 1909 result also illustrated Richtmyer's strong belief that precise determination (by measurement) of functional relations among physical quantities was fundamental to any theory, either as leading to the theory or as confirming an existing theory. Though this belief may seem a truism, he felt that it needed emphasizing, to other scientists, to the public, and to government supporters of scientific research.

Many of Richtmyer's researches and publications dealt with X-rays. One result of this work was a precise formula for the absorption coefficient in its dependence on the atomic number Z and wavelength λ for wavelengths between two absorption discontinuities, namely $KZ^4 \lambda^3$.

Richtmyer also participated in several solar eclipse expeditions led by astronomer S. A. Mitchel, including one in New England and one on Canton Island in the Pacific, in which he made studies of the solar corona.

An advocate of nationwide organizations for scientists, he served for several years as editor of the *Journal of the Optical Society of America* and of the *Review of Scientific Instruments*. At times he held administrative positions in the National Research Council, the American Institute of Physics, the American Association of Physics Teachers, the National Academy of Sciences,

Sigma Xi (honor society for excellence in scientific work), and the Association of American Universities.

Richtmyer was a man of great drive and energy who had no use for frivolities. He tended an extensive garden on a lot adjacent to the lot containing his family home, where he raised enough fruit and vegetables to supply the family all year. The only sport he indulged in was a little fishing, now and then, and that only to the extent that the fish were used to feed the family. He liked camping, which he regarded as healthful, especially for the children. The Richtmyers were members of the Unitarian Church; home life was not religious, but rather strict. He died of heart failure at home in Ithaca, New York.

Richtmyer was best known as author of the text *Introduction to Modern Physics* (1928) for physics majors at the first-year graduate level, which emphasized the relation between theory and experiment in physics, from early times to the present. It went eventually through six editions, the last four of which were published after Richtmyer's death, with a succession of coauthors. It was still in use nearly fifty years after the publication of the first edition.

• In addition to Richtmyer's principal publication, *Introduction to Modern Physics*, he published many research articles, too numerous to cite individually, in various scientific journals, primarily the *Physical Review*. For a description of his work with X-rays, see Arthur H. Compton and Samuel K. Allison, *X-rays in Theory and Experiment* (1934). An obituary is in the *New York Times*, 8 Nov. 1939.

ROBERT D. RICHTMYER

RICKARD, Clinton (19 May 1882–14 June 1971), Indian rights advocate, was born on the Tuscarora Reservation, near Lewiston, New York, the son of George Rickard and Lucy Garlow, farmers. Rickard's family frequently suffered hardship, and food was often scarce as he was growing up. His mother supplemented a meager family income by taking in washing. Rickard went to reservation schools until age sixteen, completing the Third Reader.

In 1901 Rickard enlisted at Fort Niagara in the Eleventh Cavalry of the U.S. Army. In December his squadron departed for the Philippines, arriving two months later. There he fought on the island of Luzon against Filipino insurgents and contracted malaria. Rickard reenlisted upon his return to the United States in 1904, but while on leave on the Tuscarora Reservation he met a white woman, Ivy Onstott, purchased his discharge, and married her in December of that year.

Rickard did some farming on the Tuscarora Reservation but also took employment off the reservation. His wife died of tuberculosis in early 1913; the younger of their two children died a month later. In 1916 the parents of Elizabeth Patterson approached Rickard's parents to arrange a marriage, arranged marriages then still customary on the Tuscarora Reservation. Rickard and Patterson agreed; they had three children before she died in 1929. In 1931 Rickard married Beu-

lah Mt. Pleasant, also a Tuscarora and the daughter of one of Rickard's classmates. They had seven children. The eldest was killed in a hunting accident at the age of thirteen in 1945.

In the early 1920s Rickard became acquainted with Levi General (Deskaheh), a nationalist chief from the Six Nations Reserve in Canada who had argued the sovereignty of the Six Nations before both the British government in London and the League of Nations in Geneva. General became ill in Rochester, New York, and took residence in Rickard's home on the Tuscarora Reservation, hopeful of regaining his health. Traditional healers from the Six Nations Reserve helped restore General's health, but he is said to have suffered a relapse and died on 27 June 1925 after learning that, under terms of the U.S. Immigration Act of 1924, Indians from Canada would no longer be allowed into the United States, including those from the Six Nations Reserve who had been treating his illness.

To combat such restrictions at the border, Rickard formed the Indian Defense League of America in 1926. It argued that the right of Indians to freely cross the international border was recognized in the Jay Treaty of 1794. The Indian Defense League supported congressional legislation to recognize this right. Rickard claimed to have written 500 letters in five months to congressmen and other influential individuals. This campaign helped pass the bill affirming the right of Indians born in Canada to enter the United States, which was signed by President Calvin Coolidge in 1928.

Despite this victory, Rickard was accused by individuals from his own community and from other Iroquois reservations in the United States of working for Canadian Indians. Conservative chiefs from other reservations objected that he was a Christian and a Mason. Rickard also continued to encounter government hostility on both sides of the border; he was jailed briefly in Canada in 1931, charged with soliciting funds for the pursuit of an Indian claim, such activity still being illegal in Canada at the time. Charges were later withdrawn. Rickard never accepted the Indian Citizenship Act of 1924 that gave U.S. citizenship to Indians. Hence he opposed conscription of his people during World War II, arguing that they were not citizens of the United States. He also opposed the attempts of the Bureau of Indian Affairs to sever connections with New York Indians after World War II, leaving the state of New York with jurisdiction over the reservations in the state. As sovereign nations, he believed, Indians in New York should deal with the government in Washington, D.C., not with state officials. Despite Indian protests, the federal Bureau of Indian Affairs withdrew from New York in 1948.

Rickard experienced defeat in another major battle with government. The New York State Power Authority decided in 1956 to take a portion of the Tuscarora Reservation to use for a reservoir in a power project. Rickard was indeed vocal in opposition, but a far more prominent role was taken by his son William Rickard. The Tuscarora argued that confiscation of lands violated treaties. They lost their case before the U.S. Supreme Court in a decision rendered 7 March 1960. In his dissenting opinion, Justice Hugo Black concluded, "Great nations, like great men, should keep their word."

Throughout his life, Clinton Rickard expressed consistent and strong views on Indian sovereignty, Indian rights, and the injustice of any actions that might compromise these. On the other hand, he viewed his service in the U.S. Cavalry as a rewarding and pleasurable period in his life. He continued to be active in veterans' organizations. In addition he was a steadfast Christian and found in the Masonic Lodge considerable fellowship. Possibly his ease in acting in the white world helped him to pursue so vigorously his convictions on Indian rights.

It was in the Veterans Administration Hospital in Buffalo, New York, that Rickard died. He was buried with a military funeral at the Mount Hope Cemetery on the Tuscarora Reservation. At their annual Border Crossing Celebration held each July at Niagara Falls to demonstrate the right of Indians to freely enter the United States, the Indian Defense League on 17 July 1971 included a riderless horse to represent the departure of its founder.

• Clinton Rickard dictated his autobiography, *Fighting Tuscarora: The Autobiography of Clinton Rickard*, ed. Barbara Graymont (1973), which he saw in typescript before his death. Actions of Rickard and other leaders are discussed in Laurence M. Hauptman, *The Iroquois and the New Deal* (1981) and *The Iroquois Struggle for Survival: World War II to Red Power* (1986). An obituary is in the *New York Times*, 17 June 1971.

THOMAS S. ABLER

RICKARD, Tex (2 Jan. 1871–6 Jan. 1929), sports promoter, was born George Lewis Rickard in Clay County, Missouri, the son of Robert Woods Rickard, a struggling millwright, and Lucretia (maiden name unknown). His family moved to Texas when he was four years old, and he grew up in the small town of Cambridge. After his father died in 1882, Rickard left school and worked as a cowboy and trail driver. By the time he reached adulthood he was a good horseman, shooter, and gambler. In 1894 he was elected city marshal of Henrietta, Texas, and soon afterward he married Leona Bittick, the daughter of the local physician; she died in childbirth in 1895.

Shortly thereafter Rickard resigned his job as marshal and went to the Alaska goldfields. He dragged a sled over Chilkoot Pass to the Yukon River and briefly owned a saloon in Circle City, Alaska. In 1897, when the Klondike gold rush began in the Yukon Territory of Canada, he went there to mine gold but found it hard, unrewarding work. In Dawson City, Yukon, he worked for fifteen months in saloons, then briefly operated one himself in Rampart, Alaska. He then went to Nome, setting up a gambling tent near the beach where gold was discovered soon after. His business thrived in the gold rush that followed and he eventually opened the biggest gambling house in Nome, "The Northern." Later, he estimated that he had cleared a

half million dollars in the four years he spent in Nome, but he lost most of it through gambling. Finally, in 1902, he sold The Northern and left for the states with $65,000 in his pocket.

Rickard's character was formed during his Alaska years. In the vernacular of the time, he was a "sporting man," making his living by gambling, and he was not averse to taking advantage of "suckers" who did not know how to hold on to their money. Yet, he was scrupulously honest and was never accused of cheating; in fact, the miners actually used his saloon in Nome as a bank. Generous to others, he was a good listener who was always interested in what others had to say, although he said little himself. Tall and calm in demeanor, he was generally trusted and liked wherever he went.

Rickard went to South Africa in 1902 to mine diamonds, but without success. Returning to the United States, he married Edith Mae Myers in Sacramento, California. The couple went to Nome, and Rickard bought back an interest in his old saloon, but his wife disliked the Alaskan cold and they left there for good in 1904.

In 1905 Rickard opened a saloon in remote Goldfield, Nevada, and soon became a leading citizen and booster of the town. Some local men conceived the idea of publicizing the town, the leading industry of which was the sale of worthless gold mining claims, by staging a world title fight. Rickard was selected to promote it even though the only fights he had ever seen were crude slugging matches held in his Alaska saloons to attract gambling patrons. Rickard arranged a world lightweight title fight between Joe Gans and Battling Nelson. In so doing he proved to be a publicity genius, offering a record purse of $33,500 in gold coins to the fighters. The stacks of coins were displayed at a local bank and drew much attention. On 3 September 1906 Gans won the fight on a foul in 42 rounds. Almost 8,000 persons made their way to Goldfield to view the fight, producing a gate of nearly $70,000. Rickard and his backers made a handsome profit.

The Goldfield boom soon became exhausted, and Rickard sold his saloon there and moved to Rawhide, Nevada. There, as previously in Goldfield, he was closely associated with George Graham Rice, who sold worthless gold stock and later became infamous as the "Jackal of Wall Street" for his gigantic frauds during the 1920s. Rickard's ballyhoo would attract the "suckers" to Nevada, and Rice among others would then swindle them. Rickard moved on to Ely, Nevada, and entered the bidding to hold the fight between the much-hated black heavyweight champion Jack Johnson and the "White Hope" and former champion James J. Jeffries. Rickard inveigled Johnson into signing a contract with him for the fight, which was to be held in San Francisco. However, Governor J. N. Gillett of California prevented the fight from being held there, and it took place instead at Reno, Nevada, on 4 July 1910. With Johnson winning by knockout in the

15th round, the fight drew a record gate, and Rickard and his co-promoter split a profit of $120,000.

At the end of 1910 Rickard went to South America with his wife, leased a large area of land in the Grand Chaco of Paraguay, and became a rancher. He lived there until April 1915, the owner of 35,000 cattle and, as a sideline, a traveling circus. However, when he tried to sell his cattle to the British government, he was blocked by the strong German influence in Paraguay. Impulsively selling out, he returned to the United States and promoted a no-decision fight between heavyweight champion Jess Willard and Frank Moran in New York City on 25 March 1916. From this venture he made a $42,000 profit. Rickard's next major project was to promote a world heavyweight title fight between Willard and Jack Dempsey. This fight occurred in Toledo, Ohio, on 4 July 1919, with Dempsey stopping Willard after three rounds. A terrible heat wave caused attendance to fall far below expectations, and Rickard and his backer had a small loss, the only one of his major boxing promotions that failed to make money.

In 1920 Rickard secured backing from circus owner John Ringling to operate Madison Square Garden in Manhattan. The Garden had a history of losing money, but Rickard soon turned it into a moneymaker by promoting boxing programs, circus performances, rodeos, and numerous other popular events. In 1921 he promoted the world heavyweight title fight between Dempsey and Georges Carpentier of France in Jersey City. A huge wooden stadium was constructed especially for the fight at a site called Boyle's Thirty Acres. The presence of Carpentier, a war hero who was charming and graceful but fragile-looking, along with a steady stream of clever publicity, attracted a crowd of 80,000. The stadium swayed alarmingly during the fight, whenever the crowd became excited. Dempsey knocked out Carpentier in four rounds and the fight drew the first $1 million boxing gate, resulting in a profit of $400,000 for Rickard.

On 21 January 1922 Rickard was arrested in New York City for "immoral relations" with seven underage girls, all juvenile delinquents from poor families who had been allowed to swim at the Garden pool. He was later tried for having had sex with one of them. Many details of the girl's allegations were shown to be false, and Rickard was acquitted by the jury after only ten minutes of deliberation. This controversy may have been developed in order to discredit Rickard and thus force him out of his position at Madison Square Garden, but if so the perpetrators were never discovered.

In 1923 Rickard promoted Dempsey's title defense against Luis Angel Firpo of Argentina at the Polo Grounds in New York City. The fight was a sensational one, with Dempsey winning by a knockout in the second round after being knocked out of the ring in the first round. It was Rickard's second million-dollar gate and was followed in 1925 by his third, the heavyweight championship fight in Philadelphia between Dempsey and Gene Tunney, in which Tunney won the title before a record crowd of 120,000. In 1927 Rickard promoted the second Tunney-Dempsey fight at Chicago. This was the famous battle of the "long count," held before a crowd of 105,000. The gate receipts exceeded $2.5 million, which set a longstanding record for any fight ever held.

Rickard continued to oversee Madison Square Garden promotions after a new and larger structure, often called "The House That Tex Built," was opened in 1925. Following the death of his wife in October 1925, he married Maxine Hodges, a 24-year-old actress, in 1926, and they had one daughter. He died of acute appendicitis in Miami, Florida, and his body was returned to New York City to be viewed by 15,000 persons at Madison Square Garden. Although Rickard was considered America's greatest promoter, with his name being synonymous with everything big, he was always careless of his own finances; when probated, his net estate was found to be only $166,662.

Rickard played an important role in making professional sports in the United States into big business. His use of publicity and showmanship revolutionized the promotion of all large entertainment events, and he brought boxing to its highest level of popularity. He was an inaugural inductee into the International Boxing Hall of Fame in 1990.

• The principal source of information on Rickard is Charles Samuels, *The Magnificent Rube: The Life and Gaudy Times of Tex Rickard* (1957). Maxine Elliott Rickard with Arch Oboler, *Everything Happened to Him: The Story of Tex Rickard* (1936), is a somewhat fictionalized biography. Nat Fleischer wrote two articles on Rickard: "Six Years Ago," *The Ring*, Feb. 1935, and "Rickard, the Man with the Golden Touch," *The Ring*, Jan. 1948. Details of some of Rickard's most important promotions are given in two books by Randy Roberts: *Papa Jack: Jack Johnson and the Era of White Hopes* (1983), and *Jack Dempsey, the Manassa Mauler* (1979). Obituaries are in the *New York Times* and the *New York Sun*, both 7 Jan. 1929.

LUCKETT V. DAVIS

RICKENBACKER, Edward Vernon (8 Oct. 1890–23 July 1973), aviator and airline executive, was born in Columbus, Ohio, the son of William Rickenbacher, a construction worker and bridge builder, and Elizabeth Baseler. The son of Swiss immigrants, "Eddie" Rickenbacker's formal education ended when he was thirteen and in seventh grade, after his father was fatally injured in a construction accident. He dropped out of school and began working twelve-hour night shifts in a factory to help support his family. His only academic preparations after that came from correspondence courses in mechanical and automotive engineering. He worked in a machine shop, an automobile garage, and for the Frayer-Miller Company, which manufactured automobiles.

A quick learner, a hard worker, and mechanically talented, Rickenbacker in 1908 moved on to the Firestone-Columbus automobile manufacturing company. That led to maintenance and sales accomplishments in Texas, Arizona, Nebraska, and Iowa. As an extension of his sales activities, Rickenbacker (by then nineteen years old and 6′2″ tall) began entering local car races—and winning. The racing cars he drove had their share of mechanical breakdowns and accidents, but Rickenbacker won victories. He drove in his first Indianapolis Speedway races in 1911 and 1912 and turned to racing full time. Victories in major races brought him prize money, fame, and contacts with influential people. He never stopped learning from his experiences.

A chance meeting with aviation pioneer Glenn Martin in 1916 provided Rickenbacker with his first airplane ride—and pointed him in the direction his career was to take later. Driving a Duesenberg, Rickenbacker won his final racing victory on Thanksgiving Day 1916 at Ascot Park in Los Angeles.

A short visit to England at the end of 1916 gave Rickenbacker a look at that country in wartime and at Royal Flying Corps planes in flight. That confirmed his growing aviation interest. After returning to the United States early in 1917, he urged American entry into the war against Germany. In May 1917, after the United States had declared war, Rickenbacker joined the army as a sergeant and sailed to England and on to France as a staff driver with General John J. Pershing's American Expeditionary Force. He drove for Colonel William "Billy" Mitchell, who became America's most famous air-power advocate.

Mitchell helped Rickenbacker get orders to flight training in France. After a couple of dual flights, he soloed; after twenty-five hours in the air he was commissioned a lieutenant in the Army Air Service. Assigned as engineering officer at the Issoudun flying school, where he did his advanced flight training, he completed gunnery training at Cazeau. In March 1918 he was ordered to the newly formed Ninety-fourth Aero Pursuit Squadron, the first American squadron in combat on the western front. It adopted the "hat-in-the-ring" insignia that grew famous along with Rickenbacker.

Rickenbacker scored his first victory in the skies on 29 April 1918. Before the end of May he had shot down his fifth German plane, becoming an ace. He changed the spelling of his name to make it appear less German. On 24 September Rickenbacker became commanding officer of the Ninety-fourth Squadron.

By the time the fighting ended on Armistice Day, 11 November 1918, Captain Eddie Rickenbacker had fought 134 air battles and had shot down a total of twenty-six German airplanes and balloons, making him America's top ace (Ace of Aces) in World War I. Rickenbacker's Ninety-fourth had more victories than any other American squadron. His numerous medals included the French Croix de Guerre with four palms, the American Distinguished Service Cross with nine oak leaf clusters, and the Congressional Medal of Honor. He was a charter member of the American Legion.

Back in the United States for a Liberty Bond drive in 1919, Rickenbacker was received with wild enthusiasm across the country. Both his earlier racing successes and his heroic accomplishments in the air during the war enabled him to meet prominent and

powerful people in government and business; he never lacked contacts in business and finance to support his later ventures. In 1922 he married Adelaide Frost Durant, whom he had met in California before the war. The couple had two children.

After the war he organized the Rickenbacker Motor Company, which manufactured automobiles. Though the vehicles were innovative and of good quality, the venture failed in the mid-1920s and left Rickenbacker $250,000 in debt.

In 1927 he took over and revitalized the Indianapolis Speedway. He closed it during World War II and sold it after that war for the same amount he had paid for it originally.

Rickenbacker never lost his interest in aviation. Like Mitchell, he was frustrated by the failure of the government and military to develop American air power. In 1934 he took over management of Eastern Airlines. In 1938 he became president and general manager of Eastern, and in 1953 he became chairman of the board and continued as chief executive officer. He retained roles in Eastern's operation until he retired in 1963.

As a devotee of free enterprise, Rickenbacker insisted that Eastern accept no government subsidies. His was a "hands on" management that extended down to the smallest detail and lowliest employee. He revitalized and expanded the airline, built worker morale, assured that the company kept up with developing aviation technology, accomplished an impressive safety record, and put Eastern in the black financially.

A conservative on domestic issues and an air-power and preparedness advocate, Rickenbacker had no use for President Franklin D. Roosevelt and his New Deal "socialism." Visits to Europe in 1935 and 1939 alerted him to the alarming dangers posed by Adolf Hitler's Nazi Germany. Originally Rickenbacker was a member of the national committee of the noninterventionist America First Committee, but he resigned early in 1941. With American involvement in World War II, Eastern Airlines made facilities and personnel available for the war effort.

Early in 1942 General Henry H. Arnold and Secretary of War Henry L. Stimson asked Rickenbacker to tour Army Air Corps bases in the United States to bolster morale and advise on improvements. He spoke to thousands of airmen and their leaders and provided helpful suggestions for improvements. That tour was so successful that Stimson asked him to go on a similar mission to England and then on one to the Pacific.

In 1942, on a flight from Hawaii en route to New Guinea, the plane on which Rickenbacker was a passenger missed the tiny Pacific island where it was to refuel and went down at sea. Though all eight people on board survived the ditching in the ocean, they floated in life rafts for twenty-four days before they were spotted from the air and rescued. One of them died, but Rickenbacker (the oldest) survived the terrible ordeal.

He had scarcely recovered from that adventure when Stimson asked Rickenbacker to go on another mission across the South Atlantic to North Africa, the Middle East, India, China, and the Soviet Union. Again he met with thousands of airmen as well as top military and political leaders. In the Soviet Union he conferred with Molotov, Litvinov, Marshal Zhukov, and other top military and aviation leaders. He flew over front lines and inspected Soviet aircraft. He provided Stimson, Arnold, and other American officials with a unique portrait of the Soviet war effort in 1943. After the war he resumed his peacetime responsibilities, as well as various philanthropic efforts on behalf of boys' clubs and the Boy Scouts of America.

Eddie Rickenbacker was a daring racing driver and combat pilot. But he was much more. He became a highly skilled corporation executive and manager who contributed constructively to the economic life and strength of the United States and to the development of modern aviation transportation. He died in a Zurich hospital on a trip to Switzerland.

• The best place to start in studying Rickenbacker's life may be with his own book, *Fighting the Flying Circus* (1919), *Seven Came Through* (1943), and *Rickenbacker* (1967). For a scholarly volume on the American air war in World War I, see James J. Hudson, *Hostile Skies: A Combat History of the American Air Service in World War I* (1968). For a history of Eastern Airlines see Robert J. Sterling, *From the Captain to the Colonel: An Informal History of Eastern Airlines* (1980).

WAYNE S. COLE

RICKER, Marilla Marks Young (18 Mar. 1840–12 Nov. 1920), lawyer and suffragist, was born in New Durham, New Hampshire, the daughter of Hannah Stevens and Jonathan B. Young. Her freethinking father introduced her to women's rights doctrines, and, as a central part of her education, she accompanied him to town meetings and court proceedings. Beginning at age sixteen she taught school. In 1863 she married John Ricker, an elderly farmer who also believed in gender equality. His death five years later left her with no children and with an inheritance that rendered her financially independent. For four years in the 1870s she lived in Europe, where she learned foreign cultures and languages and absorbed progressive beliefs about birth control and political equality.

In the late 1870s Ricker moved to Washington, D.C., where she studied law with Arthur B. Williams and Albert G. Riddle. In 1882 she was admitted to the District of Columbia bar; in the same year President Chester A. Arthur appointed her as a notary public in the district. Through the 1890s she continued to live most of each year in the nation's capital, although she typically spent summers in New Hampshire.

Her District of Columbia law practice reflected her commitment to prisoners' rights. For example, she won a test case designed to secure a ruling that ended a law in the district requiring that pauper convicts who could not pay their fines remain indefinitely in jail.

Ricker teamed with women's rights activist Belva Lockwood in various activities in the 1880s and 1890s. Lockwood, when the Supreme Court refused to admit her to its bar, secured a federal law in 1879 that per-

mitted her to become the first woman to practice before the federal courts, and Ricker herself was admitted to the Supreme Court bar in 1891. When Lockwood ran for the U.S. presidency on the Equal Rights ticket in 1884, Ricker was an elector for that party on the New Hampshire ballot.

Just as Lockwood took action to break down the male monopoly of the legal profession in some states, among them Virginia in 1894–1895, Ricker petitioned the New Hampshire Supreme Court for the right to practice law in that state. Lelia J. Robinson, the first woman admitted to the Massachusetts bar, represented Ricker. Their petition relied on the language of the New Hampshire statute, which spoke of how "any citizen . . . shall be admitted to practice as an attorney."

The chief justice, speaking for a unanimous court (*Ricker's Petition*, 1890), broke new ground when he determined that, in the absence of a statute expressly prohibiting the admission of a woman, the decision on the question Ricker raised fell to the judiciary's discretion. He then drew a distinction between official employment as an officer of the state government, a role that a woman could not play in New Hampshire, and the position of an attorney as an officer of the court, a role that a woman might play. Women's "exclusion from the exercise of legislative, executive, and judicial authority," he concluded, did not "prevent their being licensed to practise as physicians or attorneys." He suggested that perhaps the question had become "not whether women could lawfully be admitted, but whether they could lawfully be kept out." Thus the court granted her petition in 1890, subject only to her supplying the kind of evidence ordinarily offered by men. In view of her previous admission to practice elsewhere, she did not even have to take an examination. Ricker was thus the first woman admitted to the practice of law in New Hampshire.

The distinction that the court had drawn, although it served Ricker's immediate purpose in expanding women's professional opportunities in New Hampshire, failed to satisfy her. It left women with no political rights in New Hampshire, and she argued that women should be able to vote in elections and hold elective and appointive office. For the final half century of her long life, Ricker campaigned for equal political rights for women. From 1870 through 1919 she contested her exclusion from voting rights on the grounds that she paid taxes and therefore was being taxed without representation. Only in her final year did the law change to grant her the right to vote. She was a member of the National Woman Suffrage Association, for many years the New Hampshire delegate to its national conventions, and a life member of the National American Woman Suffrage Association from its establishment in 1890.

Ricker sometimes failed in her efforts to blaze new paths for women. In a bid to open diplomatic posts to women, for instance, she unsuccessfully sought an appointment as a minister to a South American nation during the presidency of William B. McKinley. In 1910 she announced her candidacy for the governorship of New Hampshire, but the state attorney general ruled that she could not run for an office for which she could not vote.

After concentrating for nearly her entire adult life on expanding the professional and political opportunities of women in the United States, Ricker devoted her eighth decade to her freethinking beliefs. She published *Four Gospels* (1911), in which her heroes, Tom Paine and Robert Ingersoll, bested John Calvin and Jonathan Edwards. She also published two other critiques of conventional religion, *I Don't Know, Do You?* (1916) and *I Am Not Afraid, Are You?* (1917). She died in Dover, New Hampshire.

• Obituaries of Ricker are in the *New York Times*, 13 Nov. 1920, and in two Dover newspapers, *Foster's Daily Democrat*, 12 Nov. 1920, and the *Dover Tribune*, 18 Nov. 1920.

PETER WALLENSTEIN

RICKETTS, Howard Taylor (9 Feb. 1871–3 May 1910), pathologist, was born on a farm near Findlay, Ohio, the son of Andrew Duncan Ricketts, a grain merchant, and Nancy Jane Taylor. In 1873 the family moved to Illinois and settled near Fisher, where Ricketts spent his childhood. He entered Chicago's Northwestern University in 1890, but when his parents moved in 1892 to Lincoln, Nebraska, he transferred to the University of Nebraska, where he graduated in 1894 with a degree in zoology.

Although his family had been hard hit by the panic of 1893, Ricketts, determined to work his way through, entered Northwestern University Medical School. Because he possessed an undergraduate degree, he was placed in the second-year class. Constant overwork and worry about financial problems led to a nervous breakdown during his senior year, but he recovered, graduated in 1897, and won an internship at Cook County Hospital in Chicago. In 1900 he was appointed a fellow in pathology and cutaneous diseases at Rush Medical College in Chicago. In 1900 the financial stability provided by this position enabled Ricketts to marry Myra Tubbs, the daughter of a physician; they had two children.

At Rush, Ricketts accomplished his first important research, a study of blastomycosis, the first disease known to be produced by a yeast. This work brought him to the attention of Ludvig Hektoen, chairman of the department of pathology and bacteriology at the University of Chicago. At Hektoen's suggestion, Ricketts spent a year visiting major research institutes in Berlin, Vienna, and Paris, where he perfected his laboratory technique and broadened his understanding of theoretical microbiology. After his return to the United States in 1902, he was appointed instructor in Hektoen's department and launched studies in the new field of immunology. A series of his papers in the *Journal of the American Medical Association* were collected and published in 1906 as *Infection, Immunity, and Serum Therapy*, a textbook that went through three editions.

That same year Ricketts initiated his most important research, an investigation of Rocky Mountain spotted fever, a mysterious malady that had exacted an especially high mortality among residents of the Bitterroot Valley in western Montana. Scientific understanding of spotted fever was muddled when Ricketts entered the field. One earlier investigation had indicated that it was caused by a protozoan and transmitted by the bite of a tick, but other experts had discounted both the causative organism and its putative vector. Ricketts chose to test the tick transmission theory independently. Having developed a method to maintain spotted fever in guinea pigs, he permitted a tick to feed on a sick guinea pig and then attached it to a healthy pig, which developed typical spotted fever signs. He thus demonstrated that the disease was indeed transmissible through the bite of a tick, and in so doing, he identified the first human tick-borne disease known in the United States.

During the next two years, Ricketts conducted an imaginative multipronged research program on Rocky Mountain spotted fever. Through painstaking and tedious experiments that required raising ticks from eggs, he demonstrated that the organism was transmitted to new generations of ticks in the eggs of the female and that infected ticks existed in nature. To diminish incidence of the disease, he outlined a plan for controlling ticks on their mammalian hosts. He suggested that ranchers dip cattle and horses, on which the mature stages of the tick fed and mated, in an arsenical solution that would kill the ticks. In addition, he called for destruction of ground squirrels and other small rodents that served as hosts during immature stages of the tick. This two-pronged strategy, aimed at decreasing the tick population in inhabited areas, was implemented in part by later investigators. Unfortunately, the harsh Montana climate, biological considerations of which Ricketts was unaware, and political interference in the program militated against its success. Ricketts also identified hitherto unknown microorganisms as the potential cause of the disease, although he was unable to prove causation conclusively. He also pursued, unsuccessfully, techniques for producing a vaccine and antiserum against the disease.

In 1909 funding for these investigations by the state of Montana was suspended because of budget problems; hence Ricketts accepted an offer from the Mexican government to investigate typhus, whose etiology was unknown but whose victims exhibited symptoms similar to those of Rocky Mountain spotted fever. Only after arriving in Mexico did Ricketts learn that other investigators had recently demonstrated that the body louse was the vector of typhus and had transmitted it to an experimental animal. Gamely proceeding with his work even though he had lost the chance to claim priority, Ricketts confirmed their findings and also described an organism similar to the spotted fever organism that was consistently found in the blood of patients, in the lice that fed on these patients, and in the feces of the infected lice. As Ricketts prepared to conclude this work and return to the United States to accept the chair in pathology at the University of Pennsylvania, he became infected with typhus and died in Mexico City.

Ricketts's contributions to the understanding of Rocky Mountain spotted fever and of typhus were recognized by his scientific peers when the taxonomic genus to which these diseases belong was named *Rickettsia* in his honor. The organism that causes spotted fever also carries his name in its species designation, *Rickettsia rickettsii*.

• The Howard Taylor Ricketts Papers are in the Department of Special Collections, Joseph Regenstein Library, University of Chicago. Letters from Ricketts can also be found in the Montana State Board of Health Records, 1908–1977, Record Group 28, Montana State Archives, Helena. A *Scrapbook* prepared by Ricketts's family was deposited in selected libraries, including the National Library of Medicine, the Library of Congress, and the Regenstein Library. An account of his life and most of his published papers were collected in a memorial volume, *Contributions to Medical Science by Howard Taylor Ricketts, 1870–1910* (1911). See also William K. Beatty and Virginia L. Beatty, "Howard Taylor Ricketts—Imaginative Investigator," *Proceedings of the Institute of Medicine of Chicago* 34 (1981): 46–48; Paul F. Clark, *Pioneer Microbiologists of America* (1961), pp. 285–91; and Victoria A. Harden, *Rocky Mountain Spotted Fever: History of a Twentieth-Century Disease* (1990), pp. 47–71. An obituary is in the *Journal of the American Medical Association* 54 (1910): 1640.

VICTORIA A. HARDEN

RICKETTS, James Brewerton (21 June 1817–22 Sept. 1887), soldier, was born in New York City, the son of George R. A. Ricketts and Mary Brewerton. He received an appointment to West Point in 1835 and graduated sixteenth in his class in 1839. He was commissioned a second lieutenant and assigned to the First U.S. Artillery. Soon after his graduation, in 1840, he married Harriet Josephine Pierce; they had one child. Ricketts's first six years in the service were spent in northern New York and northern Maine, where his regiment provided military muscle to a border disturbance with Canada. He was transferred to Fort Pike, Louisiana, from which point his regiment joined General Zachary Taylor's army in its invasion of Mexico. Ricketts saw action at Monterrey (21–23 Sept. 1846), and Buena Vista (22–23 Feb. 1847). Following the war he served garrison duty at Fort Columbus, New York, and then served as the regimental quartermaster until 1852. During the later part of his tenure as quartermaster, he accompanied elements of his regiment to New Orleans and took part in operations against the Seminoles in Florida in 1852. He spent the next eight years in Louisiana or Texas on garrison, recruiting, or frontier duty. His first wife died in the 1850s, and in 1856 Ricketts married Frances Lawerence, an uncommonly strong-willed woman. They had five children, of whom two survived childhood.

At the outbreak of the Civil War Ricketts returned east, serving in the garrison at Fort Monroe, Virginia. Called to Washington, he served in the defenses of that city from April through July 1861 and commanded a battery in the capture of Alexandria, Virginia, on 24 May 1861. At the first battle of Bull Run (Manassas) on 21 July 1861, he commanded Battery I, First U.S. Artillery. In fierce fighting on Henry House Hill, his battery was effectively destroyed, and Ricketts was badly wounded in the knee and captured. Ricketts's wife was in Washington the day of First Bull Run. When she learned of her husband's wounding, she immediately set out to join him, passing through Confederate lines to the hospital where he was being treated. She accompanied him to Libby Prison in Richmond and remained with him for six months, helping to nurse him until he was exchanged. Besides being blessed with a most remarkable wife, Ricketts possessed an iron constitution and strong recuperative powers. During his imprisonment he was promoted to brigadier general of volunteers, to date from 21 July 1861.

By 8 May 1862 Ricketts had returned to the army in command of a division in the First Army Corps. His division took part in active campaigning in northern Virginia during the Second Manassas campaign and was active in the fighting at Thoroughfare Gap on 28 August 1862 and Second Bull Run (Second Manassas) on 29–30 August 1862. Following the defeat at Bull Run, Ricketts's division moved into Maryland, seeing some action at South Mountain (14 Sept. 1862) and bloody fighting at Antietam (17 Sept. 1862), where his division lost 1,051 men. Ricketts was wounded again, although he remained in the field with his division until October, when he was quietly relieved in order to recover. For the next sixteen months he served on courts-martial, including the celebrated case of Fitz-John Porter, and on commissions.

On 18 March 1864 Ricketts assumed command of a somewhat demoralized division in the Sixth Army Corps. His command took part in fierce fighting at the Wilderness (5–6 May 1864), where elements of the division were roughly handled. They also participated in nearly constant fighting from Spotsylvania Court House, through North Anna, to Cold Harbor. In the fighting at Cold Harbor on 1 June 1864 Ricketts's command "broke and ran as usual," wrote General George G. Meade's aide, Colonel Theodore Lyman; "but Ricketts, their new commander, a man of great personal courage, pitched into them and kept at them, till finally, on the 1st of June, he got them to storm breastworks. . . . Such are the effects of good pluck in generals" (Agassiz, p. 139). Ricketts did such a fine job with his division that when Jubal Early invaded Maryland and threatened Washington, D.C., in July, Ricketts's was the first unit of the Army of the Potomac sent north to counter Early's threat. The battle of Monocacy, 9 July 1864, was a Confederate victory, but Ricketts's division significantly delayed Early's advance on the capital. When Early withdrew to the Shenandoah Valley, Ricketts accompanied the Sixth Corps and General Philip Sheridan in pursuit. His division took part in heavy fighting at Winchester (19 Sept. 1864), Fisher's Hill (22 Sept. 1864), and Cedar Creek (19 Oct. 1864). At Cedar Creek Ricketts received a severe wound in the lung, his sixth in the war.

He spent nearly seven months recuperating but returned to duty and command of his division on 7 April 1865. Through the course of the war, Ricketts received five brevets for gallant and meritorious service.

Following the war Ricketts reverted to the rank of major in the First Artillery. Although he commanded a district in the Department of Virginia from July 1865 to April 1866, his wounds rendered him unfit for active field service, and on 3 January 1867 he retired. He made his home in Washington, D.C. Throughout the rest of his life Ricketts suffered greatly from his wounds, particularly the one received at Cedar Creek. Time and again, however, he astounded physicians by rallying from illnesses that would have killed a man of weaker constitution. He died in Washington and was buried in Arlington National Cemetery. Not a brilliant or flashy soldier, Ricketts was always reliable, possessed unquestionable courage, and set an example of devotion to duty for others to live up to.

• Some of Ricketts's papers are at Manassas National Battlefield Park Library. His official reports and some correspondence are in U.S. War Department, *The War of the Rebellion: A Compilation of the Official Records of the Union and Confederate Armies* (128 vols., 1880–1901). His military record is in George W. Cullum, *Biographical Register of the Officers and Graduates of the U.S. Military Academy* (1879). The character of his wife is revealed in an excerpt from a wartime diary edited by Marshall Bond, "The Indomitable Mrs. Ricketts," *Civil War Times Illustrated*, Nov. 1982. See also George R. Agassiz, *Meade's Headquarters, 1863–1865: Letters of Colonel Theodore Lyman from the Wilderness to Appomattox* (1922). An obituary is in the *National Tribune*, 29 Sept. 1887.

D. SCOTT HARTWIG

RICKETTS, Palmer Chamberlaine (17 Jan. 1856–10 Dec. 1934), university administrator, was born in Elkton, Maryland, the son of Thomas C. Ricketts, an editor, and Elizabeth Getty. He was educated in a private school and tutored in Princeton, New Jersey, after his family moved there during his early youth. He arrived at Rensselaer Polytechnic Institute (where he was to spend the rest of his life) in 1871 when he was fifteen years old. He was awarded the degree of C.E. (civil engineer) in 1875 after a successful and nearly uneventful career as a student. His record was impeccable except for an event during his junior year while on the editorial board of the school yearbook. He helped to produce an unusually irreverent volume that treated faculty, staff, and fellow students satirically and caused the faculty to consider expulsion for the entire editorial board.

Upon graduating, Ricketts was appointed instructor of mathematics and astronomy at Rensselaer. In 1882 he was promoted to the rank of assistant professor, and two years later he became the William Howard Hart Professor of Rational and Technical Mechanics. In 1892, when a vacancy occurred in the directorship of the institute, he was selected from among four finalists for that position. The directorship effectively made him head of the faculty. In 1901 he became the first member of the Rensselaer faculty to be chosen president. Up to that time outstanding members of the local community were appointed president. In 1902 he married Vjera Conine Renshaw.

Rensselaer is, by Ricketts's reckoning, "the first school, having a continuous existence, to be established in any English speaking country primarily for the teaching of science and engineering." Its founding in 1824 by the Patroon Stephen Van Rensselaer and by Amos Eaton, first senior professor, represented a departure from traditional higher education in featuring the practical and the applied.

During his presidency Ricketts built the modern Rensselaer and was a force in engineering education nationally for nearly a half century. He was not an inspired revolutionary but a methodical builder. In May and June 1904 Rensselaer suffered two fires; the one in its main building caused major destruction. Ricketts saw this as an opportunity and acquired an adjacent estate uphill from the soon-to-be former campus. Earlier he had begun to do what he called advertising and what we would call development, particularly with the alumni. The combination of the fires and his development efforts resulted in the construction of two new buildings almost immediately: one funded by Andrew Carnegie and the other by the mother of a deceased young graduate. Russell Sage's widow, Margaret Olivia Slocum Sage, contributed $1 million to endow departments of electrical and mechanical engineering and to construct a building to house them. Under Ricketts ten buildings or complexes were erected, and at the moment of his death a building, later named for him, was being constructed to house new departments of metallurgical, aeronautical, and industrial engineering.

Ricketts was a charter member of the Society for Promoting Engineering Education and unsuccessfully espoused the idea that engineering should be a postgraduate pursuit. Recognizing the limits placed on preprofessional education, he also advocated a broad education for engineering students. Concerning engineering course work itself, he favored a grounding in theory, leaving application to engineering practice. He saw mathematics as the key discipline in engineering education. He expanded engineering education at Rensselaer from civil engineering alone to most of the modern fields of engineering study. In 1933 he introduced the programs in metallurgical, aeronautical, and industrial engineering. Although he introduced graduate programs, he insisted that all faculty teach undergraduate courses as well.

As an engineer, Ricketts was bridge consultant for both the Troy and Boston Railroad and the Rome, Watertown and Ogdensburg Railroad. He was chief engineer of the Troy Public Improvement Commission and designed the sewer system of Troy. He held two patents and produced three editions of his history of Rensselaer. In the Troy community he served as a director of the National City Bank, vice president of the Troy Public Library, and trustee of the Dudley Observatory, the Albany Academy, Albany Medical College, and the New York State College for Teachers.

He was also a director of Samaritan Hospital and vice president of the Rensselaer County Tuberculosis and Public Health Association.

In 1933 Temple Beth El named Ricketts Troy's outstanding citizen. In 1924, during the celebration of Rensselaer's centennial year, he was made a commander of the Crown of Italy and of the Legion of Honor of France. He was also made an honorary member of the Association of Mechanical Engineers. Ricketts died in Baltimore, Maryland.

E. W. Siple, Ricketts's private secretary and director of admissions and publicity, said of him that he had a "surprising ability to judge people." He was "firm," but he had a "warm and generous heart." He had a "retentive memory" but always gave a little more credit than was really due. To the faculty he was an autocrat. To students he was both a firm taskmaster and a caring friend who knew each one of them and their needs. He often called needy students into his office and gave them money to help them through the depression years. He was the builder on whose shoulders the modern Rensselaer, a technological university, was built.

• Ricketts's papers are to be found in Archives and Special Collections, Richard G. Folsom Library, Rensselaer Polytechnic Institute, Troy, N.Y. He wrote a textbook, *Notes on Mechanics, Machines and Structures* (1906). "The Engineer and the Intellectual Life," his basic note on the limits of engineering education, is published in the Rensselaer Engineering and Science Series, no. 25; it is reprinted from the magazine section of the *New York Herald-Tribune* of 8 Sept. 1929. The Rensselaer Engineering and Science Series, no. 45 (1933), carries an article by Ricketts on the history of Rensselaer: "Rensselaer Polytechnic Institute: Amos Eaton, Author, Teacher, Investigator: The First Laboratories for the Systematic Individual Work of Students in Chemistry, Physics and Botany, to Be Created in Any Country: B. Franklin Greene and the Reorganization in 1849–50." The first edition of Ricketts's *Rensselaer Polytechnic Institute: A Short History* was published in 1895. The second edition appeared in 1914 and carried the history through that year, and the third, *History of Rensselaer Polytechnic Institute, 1824–1934*, carried it through to the year of Ricketts's death.

THOMAS PHELAN

RICKEY, Branch (20 Dec. 1881–9 Dec. 1965), baseball executive, was born Wesley Branch Rickey near Lucasville, Ohio, the son of Jacob Franklin Rickey and Emily Brown, farmers. His parents named him after John Wesley, the founder of Methodism, and instilled in him a staunch respect for religious devotion, education, and diligent work.

After teaching for two years in a one-room schoolhouse, Rickey won a partial scholarship to Ohio Wesleyan University. There he played and coached baseball and football and completed a five-year course in just over three years, graduating with a B.Litt. in 1904. Two years later he earned a bachelor of arts degree from Ohio Wesleyan.

In 1903 Rickey played minor league baseball and semiprofessional football. In 1904 he was a catcher for Dallas in the Texas League when the Cincinnati Reds bought his contract. Because Rickey refused to play on Sunday, the Reds released him. He played for the St. Louis Browns in 1905 and 1906. During the off-seasons, he taught and coached at Allegheny College (Pa.), Delaware College (Ohio), and Ohio Wesleyan. In June 1906 he married Jane Moulton. They had six children, including Branch Rickey, Jr., who also became a baseball executive.

The Browns traded Rickey to the New York Highlanders (later the Yankees), but he retired after batting only .182 in 1907 and contracting tuberculosis. After his recovery in a sanatorium, he enrolled at the University of Michigan Law School. He coached baseball again and squeezed three years of study into two, graduating in 1911.

Rickey moved to Boise, Idaho, for his health and to help establish a new law firm, but in 1913 Browns owner Robert Hedges hired him to be second in command of the ball club, creating a position later known as general manager. Rickey moved to St. Louis in June, and in September he was named field manager as well. Rickey tried to approach his work as a teacher, but he found it difficult to develop an easy rapport with his players, many of whom did not appreciate his lectures on baseball and temperance. After the 1915 season, he stopped managing the Browns, who did not improve, and new owner Philip Ball let Rickey move to the St. Louis Cardinals in 1917 as manager and president.

Rickey entered the Chemical Warfare Service in 1918, during World War I. Upon leaving the service, he served as the Cardinals' field manager from 1919 through 1925 without much success. Thereafter, as vice president and business manager, he introduced a number of significant innovations that have marked him as one of baseball's original thinkers.

Rickey popularized Ladies' Days and started the "Knot Hole Gang," letting youngsters into games for free with the hope that they would grow into paying fans. He lectured his players in great detail on baseball fundamentals during spring training and introduced the batting cage and the sliding pit as instructional aids. In 1927 he authorized the first regular radio broadcasts of major league games.

Even before leaving the financially strapped Browns, Rickey had signed a working agreement with a minor league team that would guarantee a cheap supply of young players for the Browns. With the Cardinals also short of investment capital, he constructed a network of minor league clubs that became known as a farm system. Other teams copied Rickey, but none matched the extent or productivity of the Cardinals. By 1940 St. Louis either owned or had working agreements with more than thirty teams, a network that led to six pennants and four World Series championships while Rickey was at the helm.

Rickey's fine eye for evaluating talent created a surplus of players whom he could trade and sell to other teams. The Cardinals made money on these transactions, as did Rickey, since his contract paid him a percentage of player sales. His prosperity, though, rankled St. Louis owner Sam Breadon, who dismissed him in 1942.

Rickey then became president, general manager, and later co-owner of the Brooklyn Dodgers. While the Cardinals team he had built continued to win pennants in 1943, 1944, and 1946, he expanded the Brooklyn farm system in order to challenge St. Louis for National League supremacy.

In October 1945, Rickey shocked the baseball world by breaking the sport's unwritten but firm color line. He signed Jackie Robinson to a minor league contract with the Montreal Royals, Brooklyn's top farm team, and prepared him to play in the major leagues. Rickey's motives were complex, but they included his recollection of Charles Thomas, an African American who played for Rickey at Ohio Wesleyan and had repeatedly been refused hotel accommodations with the rest of the team. In addition, Rickey believed that black ballplayers were good enough to play major league baseball and to attract new fans to major league ballparks.

Rickey advanced Robinson to the Dodgers in 1947. Brooklyn won the pennant that year and again in 1949, but a year later Rickey was forced to sell his share of the club by co-owner Walter O'Malley, who resented Rickey's leadership style. In so doing Rickey engineered a clever deal that resulted in an estimated $850,000 profit for himself.

In 1951 Rickey signed a five-year contract as general manager of the Pittsburgh Pirates. He applied his proven methods to this woeful team, but improvement in the Pirates' performance occurred more slowly than in St. Louis and Brooklyn. Pittsburgh did not win a pennant until 1960, five years after Rickey had been named chairman of the board, a position with little authority.

Rickey could have retired and rested on his considerable laurels, but in 1959 he accepted the presidency of the Continental League, a proposed third major league that threatened to challenge baseball's existing structure by placing teams in cities that had never seen major league baseball. The Continental League never played a game, but it forced the National League and the American League to undertake expansion in short order.

In 1963 Rickey returned to the Cardinals as adviser to the club president, a nebulous position from which he resigned in 1964. He suffered a heart attack on 13 November 1965 while delivering a speech accepting his induction into the Missouri Sports Hall of Fame. He died in Columbia, Missouri, never having regained consciousness. Celebrated as the "Mahatma" for his ability to talk articulately and at length on baseball and many other subjects, Rickey was elected to the Baseball Hall of Fame in 1967.

• The Branch Rickey Papers are in the Manuscript Division of the Library of Congress. There are extensive clipping files in the archives of the *Sporting News*, St. Louis, Mo., and at the National Baseball Library and Archive, Cooperstown, N.Y. Some of Rickey's thoughts on baseball are in his *Ameri-* *can Diamond* (1965), written with Robert Riger. For biographical details, see Arthur Mann, *Branch Rickey: American in Action* (1957), and David Lipman, *Mr. Baseball: The Story of Branch Rickey* (1966), both of which are useful, as are many of the books about Jackie Robinson. Obituaries are in the *New York Times*, 10 Dec. 1965, and the *Sporting News*, 25 Dec. 1965.

STEVEN P. GIETSCHIER

RICKOVER, Hyman George (27 Jan. 1900–8 July 1986), nuclear engineer and naval officer, was born in Makow, Russian Poland, the son of Abraham Rickover, a tailor, and Rachel Unger. Because of poverty and the persecution of Jews, Abraham Rickover fled to the United States. His wife, son, and daughter followed in 1906. They lived in Brooklyn, New York, in straitened circumstances. The family moved to Chicago in 1909 or 1910.

Hyman entered the Chicago public school system and worked at various part-time jobs, among them that of a Western Union messenger. After graduating from high school in February 1918, he determined to continue his education, but he needed money. Entry of the United States into World War I gave him a chance. The navy had increased the number of midshipmen at the Naval Academy at Annapolis, Maryland. Through the political influence of a relative, Rickover received a nomination on 6 February 1918. Never having thought of a naval career, he was poorly prepared academically, and his cultural and social background were against him. But after barely passing the entry examination, he was admitted on 29 June 1918. He graduated on 2 June 1922, standing 107th in a class of 540. Rickover's later clashes with the navy have often been traced to anti-Semitism he suffered while at the academy. Although subjected to prejudice, he was not as badly treated as some Jewish midshipmen.

During his first years at sea, Rickover established a reputation for working hard and disregarding procedures and protocol. From 5 September 1922 until 3 December 1924 he served as an engineer in the destroyer *La Vallette*. From 21 January 1925 until 28 April 1927 he was in the battleship *Nevada*, winning praise for his initiative in rewiring the system controlling the fire of the guns. Professionally ambitious, he took brief courses on range finders and torpedoes and a correspondence course on strategy and tactics from the Naval War College.

For his first shore duty Rickover studied electrical engineering in the navy's postgraduate program from 1 July 1927 to 30 September 1929, first at Annapolis and then at Columbia University, New York. Graduating with distinction and awarded a master of science degree, he was always to credit Columbia with teaching him the principles of engineering, a great change from the practical training gained at sea.

Rickover had applied for submarine duty on 3 April 1929. Although warned he was older and more senior than most officers beginning their service in submarines, he saw this as the quickest way to gain command. From 10 October 1929 to 2 January 1930 he served in the *S-9*, operating out of New London, Connecticut. Beginning 5 January 1930 he attended the submarine school at New London, graduating 6 June 1930 and standing fourth in a class of thirty-seven. On 21 June 1930 he reported to *S-48*, usually operating off the Panama Canal, first as engineer, then as executive officer. He qualified for submarine command on 4 August 1931 but left the ship on 5 June 1933 without having received a command.

On 5 July 1933 Rickover reported to the inspector of naval material at Philadelphia, Pennsylvania. He oversaw the navy's interest in components manufactured for submarines and played a part in improving batteries and diesel engines used in American submarines during World War II. Off duty, he completed a translation, begun on the *S-48*, of *The Submarine: Its Importance as Part of a Fleet; Its Position in International Law; Its Employment in War; Its Future*, a work by Admiral Hermann Bauer of the German navy. He also completed "International Law and the Submarine," which appeared in the U.S. Naval Institute *Proceedings* (61 [Sept. 1935]).

Rickover joined the battleship *New Mexico* of the Pacific fleet in April 1935 as assistant engineer officer. For two consecutive years he raised the ship to first place in the intense competition for engineering efficiency by stringent economy in operating the propulsion plant, by cutting back on the use of electricity and heating, and by carrying these measures to extremes that became legendary. Throughout his career he argued that wasting energy was squandering irreplaceable natural resources. Detached on 2 June 1937, he was sent to the Asiatic fleet, where on 17 July 1937 he received what was to be his only command, the minesweeper *Finch*.

Because of Rickover's reputation in engineering, his love of the discipline, and the urging of other engineers, he became an engineering duty only officer on 5 October 1937. It was a major change in his career. An elite, such officers specialized in engineering but could not command at sea.

Rickover served in the Cavite navy yard in the Philippines from 30 October 1937 to 26 May 1939 while waiting duty in the Bureau of Ships in Washington, D.C. Reporting to the bureau on 15 August 1939, he was assigned to the electrical section, responsible for providing electrical equipment to a rapidly expanding navy. In December 1940 he became chief of the section. For the first time he had an opportunity to work with industry, learning lessons that were to prove invaluable. The urgency of World War II let him take quick actions; under his leadership the section grew quickly in size and responsibilities. An aggressive if unorthodox administrator, he achieved outstanding results.

On 24 March 1945 Rickover left the electrical section to command the planned naval repair base at Okinawa, which was to repair ships damaged in the impending invasion of Japan. First visiting other Pacific repair installations, he arrived on Okinawa on 20 July 1945. After the Japanese capitulated on 14 August 1945, Rickover closed up the uncompleted base.

On his return to the United States, Rickover was assigned temporary duty on the West Coast from 18 December 1945 to 8 May 1946, laying up ships no longer needed. He was uncertain of his future in a much smaller postwar navy.

When atomic fission was discovered in late 1938, navy scientists quickly realized its energy might be used for ship propulsion, particularly for submarines. These were propelled by diesel engines on the surface and by battery-powered electric motors when submerged. Running at high speed beneath the surface quickly exhausted the batteries. Atomic energy, not requiring oxygen, offered the possibility of far longer undersea voyages at sustained high speed. However, all atomic research and development during World War II was assigned to the army's Manhattan Project to produce atomic bombs. With the return of peace, the navy resumed its efforts to explore the technology and sent Rickover, along with four other officers, to Oak Ridge, Tennessee, one of the Manhattan Project installations. Arriving on 4 June 1946, he was soon convinced nuclear propulsion was feasible.

The technical problems were immense. Atomic energy had not yet provided power in the quantity and with the reliability needed to drive machinery. Research and development was necessary to produce materials and components that would maintain their integrity and function for long periods of time in an environment of intense radiation, devise shielding to safeguard personnel, and design a propulsion plant that would fit in a ship's hull and operate as the ship pitched and rolled at sea.

By law, only the Atomic Energy Commission, which came into existence on 1 January 1947, could develop atomic energy. By great skill in assessing the policies and goals of the navy and by mastering the technology, Rickover outmaneuvered other officers to become head of the joint navy-commission nuclear propulsion program on 15 February 1949. His dual position often made it possible for him to take swift administrative actions.

Usually the navy set specifications, and contractors made technical decisions. Rickover reversed this procedure. He made the technical decisions with the help of engineers he had selected and trained; the laboratories and contractors provided technical data, made recommendations, and carried out the work. He decided the propulsion plant for the first nuclear ship, the submarine *Nautilus*, would be fabricated in two steps: a land prototype and the shipboard plant, and he determined that both should be developed almost concurrently. Because the land prototype had the same layout and dimensions of the shipboard plant, he was able to save time and to force technical decisions early in the development. Lessons learned in the prototype were promptly applied to the submarine as it was being built. Consequently there was little margin for error, and the pressure to solve technical problems quickly was immense.

Progress was amazingly swift. Construction of the prototype plant began in August 1950, the keel of the *Nautilus* was laid 14 June 1952, and the prototype generated the world's first useful atomic power on 25 June 1953. The *Nautilus* was launched on 21 January 1954 and went to sea on 17 January 1955, beginning a profound revolution in naval operations. When Rickover left the program on 31 January 1982, the navy had in operation thirty-three ballistic missile submarines, eighty-eight attack submarines, one deep submergence research vehicle, four aircraft carriers, and nine cruisers—all powered by nuclear propulsion plants he and his organization had designed and developed. These ships had to be refueled only every ten to fifteen years. In addition, he designed and developed at Shippingport, near Pittsburgh, Pennsylvania, the world's first full-scale civilian atomic power station. He received the assignment in 1953 as part of the effort of the United States to show its leadership in developing the peaceful uses of atomic energy. The plant began generating electric power for commercial use on 18 December 1957 and was shut down on 1 October 1981.

Rickover aroused intense antagonism during his career. As a commission official he was responsible for safe operation of the navy's nuclear propulsion plants. He used this authority to impose strict technical and high personnel standards and to interview and select officers for nuclear training. Although nuclear-powered ships had significant military advantages over conventionally powered ships, their initial construction costs were much higher. At a time of tight budgets, many navy officers and civilian officials opposed building them, particularly for the surface fleet. Nonetheless, Rickover fought hard for nuclear ships in the annual shipbuilding programs. By demanding high standards of work at low cost, Rickover also made enemies in private industry, especially among shipbuilders.

Because Rickover's program was vital to national defense; because the propulsion plants worked superbly, making possible achievements such as passing beneath the North Pole and even a submerged voyage around the world; and because Shippingport contributed to civilian nuclear power, Congress supported him. Members of Congress intervened to assure his promotion over navy protests and enabled him to lead the program long after he would ordinarily have been retired.

When Rickover left the program at eighty-two, his short term memory was failing, and death or retirement had removed most of the congressional figures who had supported him. A few years later he admitted having accepted gratuities from contractors; some were personal but most were for travel associated with business. Critics and admirers alike agreed the gratuities did not lessen his demand for technical excellence. The navy changed after his death, particularly with the collapse of the Soviet Union. Many nuclear ships were being laid up, and the future of nuclear propulsion was under debate. Some officers and civilians familiar with Rickover's leadership assert his greatest legacy was training people how to achieve technical excellence, not only in the navy but in industry and other walks of life. President Jimmy Carter was one of many who credited Rickover with having a great influence on their lives.

Rickover often spoke on education and wrote three books: *Education and Freedom* (1959), *Swiss Schools and Ours: Why Theirs Are Better* (1962), and *American Education: A National Failure* (1963). His writing stressed the need for setting national standards for American high school children by arguing that other countries were giving their children a better education. He also wrote a series of biographical essays, *Eminent Americans: Namesakes of the Polaris Submarine Fleet* (1972), and *How the Battleship Maine Was Destroyed* (1976), a technical investigation of the event leading to the Spanish-American War. In his retirement he established the Rickover Foundation, which raised funds for the Rickover Science Institute. The institute gave intensive instruction for six weeks in summers to a limited number of outstanding high school students. On 5 February 1986, in ill health, he resigned from the foundation and no longer allowed his name to be associated with it. It has continued under the name of the Center for Excellence in Education.

In 1931 Rickover had married Ruth Masters, a student of international law whom he had met at Columbia. They had one child. His wife died in 1972. In 1974 Rickover married Eleonore Ann Bednowicz, a commander in the navy nurse corps.

Because of Rickover, the United States had the first nuclear-powered ship in operation in 1955. Other nations followed: the Soviet Union in 1958, Great Britain (with American help) in 1963, and France in 1971. Most of his technical decisions have stood the test of time, both in naval propulsion and civilian power. Demanding and often abrasive on technical issues, he usually saw nontechnical matters with sympathy and wry humor. In speeches on social and industrial issues, he strongly asserted that ethical solutions lay in personal responsibility, not in organizations. Rickover died in Arlington, Virginia; his ashes are interred in the Arlington National Cemetery.

• Rickover's widow has possession of his papers. Norman Polmar and Thomas B. Allen, *Rickover* (1982), is a biography that must be used with care. Richard G. Hewlett and Francis Duncan, *Nuclear Navy 1946–1962* (1974), and Duncan, *Rickover and the Nuclear Navy: The Discipline of Technology* (1990), historians in the Atomic Energy Commission, describe Rickover's achievements, organization, and philosophy. Theodore Rockwell, *The Rickover Effect: How One Man Made a Difference* (1992), is a portrait by an engineer who worked for him for many years. Patrick Tyler, *Running Critical: The Silent War, Rickover, and General Dynamics* (1986), is a dramatic account of the last years of Rickover's professional career. An obituary is in the *New York Times*, 9 July 1986.

FRANCIS DUNCAN

RICORD, Frederick William (7 Oct. 1819–12 Aug. 1897), public official and educator, was born on the island of Guadaloupe, the son of Jean Baptiste Ricord, a physician, and Elizabeth Stryker, an educator and writer, and the brother of Philippe Ricord, the famous specialist on venereal diseases. Ricord's grandfather, a Girondist, left France in 1794, migrated to Italy and Guadaloupe, and arrived in Baltimore in 1798. When Ricord's father, who was educated in the United States and naturalized in 1810, died in 1827, the family moved to Woodbridge, New Jersey, a farming community near the small ports of Elizabeth and Perth Amboy. A year or two later, the Ricords moved to Geneva, New York, where Ricord's mother operated a school for girls. At fourteen Ricord entered the school that became Hobart College and later transferred to Rutgers College. For unknown reasons, he did not finish his course and returned to Geneva, where he read law. He then settled in Newark, New Jersey, the home of his maternal grandparents. In 1843 he married Sophia Bradley, with whom he had four children.

Ricord's early professional career, as a teacher and scholar who read fourteen languages and enjoyed translating, coincided with the emergence and growth of the publicly supported common school system in Newark. In 1836 the city charter was amended to furnish $3,000 a year for public education. A board of education administered the system, which funded pauper children in both private and public schools. The educational system of Newark grew with the city's population, expanding into four sectors: elementary, secondary, adult education, and a teacher training school. In 1853 Ricord was asked to administer the new system, a job for which both policymaking and institutional management skills were needed in dealing with elected officials who funded the schools. He had exhibited these skills as the librarian of the Newark Library Association, a position he assumed after beginning work in 1849 as an assistant. Ricord kept both his library and board of education positions until 1869. While engaged in these management positions, he also wrote three Roman history books and *The Youth's Grammar* (1853), all widely used as textbooks.

On 15 January 1861 Ricord was appointed by the New Jersey State Board of Education as state superintendent for public instruction. Created in 1846, this was the sole position for the enforcement of the state education law. Although his annual reports to the state board often called for greater state legislative initiative and funding for common schools, his major emphases were on improvement of teaching staffs and instructional methods. Ricord served the state board until 1865, when he returned to Newark and successfully ran for the sheriff's office in Essex County. In Newark Ricord resumed his career as educational manager. He was appointed secretary to the board of education in 1867 and became its president in 1868 and 1869. He was also elected mayor of Newark, serving two terms from 1870 to 1873. As mayor Ricord gained both fame and enemies when he resisted members of his own political party and influential contractors who wanted to use wood as a street pavement material in Newark. Paving streets with wood was a craze in numerous American cities and had caused a city bankruptcy in neighboring Elizabeth. Ricord refused to sign a city council bill, which was later passed over his veto. He then refused to sign the contracts obligating the city for the paving. The city council passed an ordinance empowering the city treasurer to pay, and Ricord took the case to court, which supported his executive position.

In 1875 he was appointed a judge in the Essex County Court of Pleas, where he served for five years, followed by another five-year term as a judge of the city court. Ricord returned to institutional management from 1881 until his death in Newark. He was the treasurer/librarian of the New Jersey Historical Society, whose collection he cataloged and increased while editing publications. He also continued his own writing with *English Songs from Foreign Tongues* (1879) and *The Self-Tormentor from the Latin of Publius Terentius Afer, with More English Songs from Foreign Tongues* (1885).

Ricord was a popular, professional civic worker whose career spanned both elective and appointive politics and the institutional management of new civic enterprises in public education, public libraries, state education, and the state historical society. In an era of "improvement" when the population of Newark grew from nearly 39,000 in 1850 to 105,000 in 1870, Ricord's managerial career evolved as new institutions were created to extend and expand a new educational and intellectual culture. By airing his ideas of increased public education and improved teacher training, Ricord influenced education in his state and elsewhere, linking popular beliefs in common schools with an elite intellectual tradition fostered through public institutions and private societies.

• Ricord's annual reports are in *Reports of State Superintendent of Public Instruction to State Board of Education* (1861–1864). For information on Ricord and his career, see his *Biography and General History of the City of Newark* (1898); *Proceedings of the New Jersey Historical Society* 2 (Jan. 1902): 194–95; and J. T. Cunningham, *Newark* (1988). An obituary appears in the *Newark Daily Advertiser*, 12 Aug. 1897.

HARRY STEIN

RIDDELL, John Leonard (20 Feb. 1807–7 Oct. 1865), botanist, microscopist, and geologist, was born in Leyden, Massachusetts, the son of John Riddell and Lephe Gates. Riddell's father, successively a schoolteacher, constable, and justice of the peace, subsequently moved his family to New York State near the town of Preston. Here Riddell received his early education at a school kept by one of his uncles. He then attended Oxford Academy for four months, served briefly as a schoolmaster, and later enrolled in Rensselaer School in Troy, New York, receiving a B.A. degree in 1829 and an M.A. in 1832. While acquiring his degrees, he supported himself by giving lectures on geology, botany, and chemistry in New York State and Ontario, Canada. His growing reputation as a lecturer led in 1832 to his appointment as professor of chemistry and botany at Ohio Reformed Medical College. Two years later he began lecturing on botany at the Cincinnati Medical College, where in 1836 he was awarded a medical degree. While in Ohio he published a series of papers on botany and geology and wrote *A Synopsis of the Flora of the Western States* (1835). As the first study devoted to western flora, this work is of major importance to botanists.

In 1836 Riddell married a young woman who was an orphan and who at various times called herself Mary Elizabeth Knocke (her father's name), Mary Bone, and Mary Schrager (her uncle's name). She bore two children, one of whom died shortly after birth, before her death from tuberculosis in 1840. Also in 1836 Riddell accepted the professorship of chemistry in the newly organized Medical College of Louisiana in New Orleans, where he would remain for the rest of his life. Shortly after moving to New Orleans he began a relationship with Ann Hennefin, who gave birth to one child in 1841 and another in December 1844. Apparently Ann Hennefin was Riddell's mistress; he never mentioned her in his diary, and the New Orleans archives have no record of a marriage. When the relationship ended is not known, but in 1846 he married Angelica Eugenia Brown by whom he had five children.

In New Orleans, Riddell continued his research in geology, botany, and chemistry and, in addition, experimented in physiology and microscopy. He chaired the Geological Committee of the state of Louisiana, published a study on the geology of Trinity County, Texas, and compiled a catalog of Louisiana plants. Regrettably, most of this catalog was lost in the state printing office, but a part of it was published in the *New Orleans Medical and Surgical Journal*. Riddell is regarded as the outstanding Louisiana botanist of the nineteenth century. He identified a number of new plants and mosses, and collections of his botanical specimens are located in museums in Paris, Oxford, and Tulane University in New Orleans. The largest collection can be found in the Natural History Museum in London.

In the late 1840s he became interested in microscopy and secured the best microscopes available. He was soon publishing accounts of his studies of infusoriae, blood corpuscles, sputum, and feces from Asiatic cholera, tuberculosis, and yellow fever patients. Although unable to demonstrate that specific minute organisms, or "morbific agents," were responsible for cholera or yellow fever, Riddell was convinced that the explanation for contagious diseases lay in the "animalculae [or germ] theory." His work in microscopy led to his appointment to a commission to investigate the origin, causes, and nature of the 1853 New Orleans yellow fever epidemic, the most devastating of all epidemics to strike the city.

He was active in professional and scientific associations and was a charter member of the American Association for the Advancement of Science, the original Louisiana State Medical Association, and the New Orleans Academy of Science. Riddell supplied much of the leadership for the latter organization during its early years and served as vice president in 1854 and president in 1855.

Not content with his scientific research, he dabbled in many areas, ranging from making cement to constructing musical instruments. As early as 1830–1831 he drew plans for a typewriter. While in New Orleans he analyzed the well water, theorized about atoms and matter, and became interested in the mechanics of microscopes. In 1851 he devised a binocular microscope, using four glass prisms to divide the light from a single object. He ground and polished the lens himself and demonstrated the principle before the New Orleans Physico-Medical Society in 1852 and the American Association for the Advancement of Science in 1853. Subsequently he commissioned Grunow Brothers of New Haven, Connecticut, to construct a binocular microscope based on his plan. This microscope was presented by his widow in 1879 to the U.S. Army Medical Museum in Washington, D.C. Riddell's microscope, although of limited value, brought him a measure of international recognition.

On a personal level he was described as eccentric, outspoken, pompous, and cynical, but despite these qualities he was quite active in public and political life. He helped persuade the Louisiana state legislature to undertake a geological survey of the state, and in 1844 he was appointed to a state commission to study methods for preventing the perennial flooding of the Mississippi River. From 1839 to 1848 he held a presidential appointment as melter and refiner for the U.S. Mint in New Orleans. He was active in politics and opposed secession, a stand that probably accounts for his appointment as postmaster for New Orleans in 1860. A few days before his death in New Orleans, probably from a vascular problem, he served as presiding officer of the Louisiana State Democratic Convention in New Orleans. Although Riddell wrote many articles and was knowledgeable in a wide range of subjects, his chief contribution was to promote an interest in science at a time when few Americans were concerned with what they considered abstruse knowledge. His most original work lay in the fields of botany, microscopy, and geology.

• The John Leonard Riddell Papers in the Special Collections division of the Howard-Tilton Memorial Library of Tulane University contain his 28-volume diary. Among Riddell's many articles are the first reports of his binocular microscope published in the *New Orleans Monthly Medical Register* 1 (Oct. 1852): 4, and 2 (Apr. 1853): 78. He postulated the animalculae (germ) theory in the *New Orleans Medical and Surgical Journal* 7 (July 1850–1851): 127–29 and expanded on it in a "Memoir on the Nature of Miasm and Contagion," *New Orleans Medical and Surgical Journal* 16 (May 1859): 348–69. For an excellent account of Riddell's microscopic studies, see James H. Cassedy, "John Riddell's Vibrio Biceps: Two Documents on American Microscopy and Cholera Etiology 1849–59," *Journal of the History of Medicine and Allied Sci-*

ences 28 (Apr. 1973): 101–8. The best biography is a monograph by Karlem Riess, *John Leonard Riddell*, Tulane Studies in Geology and Paleontology, no. 13 (1977). Additional material on his medical career can be found in John Duffy, ed., *The Rudolph Matas History of Medicine in Louisiana*, Vol. 2 (1962). Short biographies can be found in L. H. Bailey, Jr., "Some North American Botanists," *Botanical Gazette* 8 (Aug. 1883): 269–71, and H. A. Kelly and W. L. Burrage, *American Medical Biographies* (1920). For further information see Leslie D. Stephens, "Scientific Societies in the Old South," and James H. Cassedy, "Medical Men and the Ecology of the Old South," in *Science and Medicine in the Old South*, ed. Ronald L. Numbers and Todd L. Savitt (1989). A good obituary was written by John T. Scott, "Necrological Essay," *New Orleans Medical and Surgical Journal* 19 (Sept. 1866–1867): 284–87.

JOHN DUFFY

RIDDLE, Almeda (21 Nov. 1898–1986), singer, was born in lower Cherburne County, Arkansas, the daughter of J. L. James, a timber merchant, singing-school instructor, and fiddler, and Martha "Mattie" Francis Wilkerson. Almeda was exposed to singing from an early age by her father, who would sing each morning from his "ballad book," a collection of songs—many of them older American or British ballads. One of the first songs she remembers him singing is the British ballad "The House Carpenter," which she herself continued to perform throughout her life. A distant relation of the outlaw brothers Frank and Jesse James, her father traveled locally both as a purveyor of railroad ties and as a singing teacher, teaching classes at local schools or churches in the evenings. Her father's repertoire included ballads, hymns, folksongs, and popular songs of the day. Another influence on the young singer was her mother's brother John Wilkerson, who wrote out the lyrics to a number of songs for her to learn, including "Black Jack Davey," a British folksong about a wayward wife and her gypsy lover, which Riddle continued to sing throughout her performing years. Her mother and uncle also taught her many charming children's songs, including the classic "Go Tell Aunt Nancy" and "Froggie Went a-Courtin'." She later performed unique versions of both songs.

Almeda married a local boy, H. P. Riddle, in 1917, and they settled on a farm near Heber Springs, Arkansas. Tragically, in November 1926 a cyclone hit the area, killing her husband and baby and seriously injuring her three other children. Almeda Riddle moved back to her family's farm, where she raised her children. She worked professionally as a nurse and a companion for the elderly and invalids through the late 1950s. Although continuing to sing, she never performed professionally until the early 1960s.

In 1952 Riddle was discovered by folklorist John Q. Wolf of Memphis, who eventually introduced her to Alan Lomax. In 1959 Lomax recorded her, and several of these recordings were issued as part of two series of record albums of traditional southern music that he oversaw for Atlantic and Prestige Records in the early 1960s.

At this time, thanks to a revival of interest in folk music, many traditional singers were invited to perform on the folk circuit, Riddle among them. In 1965 Riddle made an album for Vanguard, which further cemented her popularity. Roger Abrahams, a prominent academic folklorist, befriended the singer and helped her compile a combination autobiography and songbook, published in 1970. Riddle preferred to go by the name "Granny" and was often referred to this way on record and in print.

In the 1970s Riddle continued to perform and record. She made two albums for Rounder Records and another for a smaller local label, recording most of her repertory. She performed at a number of festivals, including the Newport Folk Festival in the 1960s and the Bicentennial Smithsonian/American Folklife Festival in 1976, and also at smaller clubs and colleges. Her unusual interest in collecting songs led her to purchase a small tape recorder so that she could accurately learn new songs as she heard them. In 1983 she was honored with a National Endowment for the Arts Heritage award. She died in Arkansas.

• Riddle's autobiography/songbook was compiled by Roger D. Abrahams and published as *A Singer and Her Songs: Almeda Riddle's Book of Ballads* (1970). Her recordings for folklorist Alan Lomax were reissued on Sounds of the South (Atlantic 82496), a four-CD set; sadly, her Vanguard and Rounder albums are out of print.

RICHARD CARLIN

RIDDLE, Matthew Brown (17 Oct. 1836–30 Aug. 1916), New Testament scholar, was born in Pittsburgh, Pennsylvania, the son of David H. Riddle, a Presbyterian clergyman, and Elizabeth Blaine Brown. Riddle received biblical instruction from his mother and was tutored in other subjects outside the home. He entered Jefferson College's sophomore class at thirteen, graduated three years later, and then attended Western Theological Seminary in Allegheny, Pennsylvania (now Pittsburgh) intermittently (1853–1854 and 1855–1857). In 1855 Jefferson awarded him an M.A. He left Western Seminary because of Presbyterian Old School–New School controversies and taught as adjunct professor of Greek at Jefferson in 1857–1858. Riddle completed his seminary education at New Brunswick Theological Seminary in 1859. In 1860 he studied in Germany, primarily at Heidelberg. He returned to the United States in 1861.

During the Civil War, Riddle served briefly as chaplain to the Second New Jersey Volunteers, but malarial fever forced his resignation. In 1862 he was ordained by the Dutch Reformed Bergen Classis and married Anna M. Walther, whom he had met at Heidelberg. They had three children.

Riddle was pastor of the First Reformed Church of Hoboken, New Jersey, from 1862 to 1865 and the Second Reformed Church in Newark, New Jersey, from 1865 to 1869. He resigned to return to Germany for a year, and there he formed a lifelong friendship and collaboration with the church historian Philip Schaff.

In 1871 Riddle returned to Hartford, Connecticut, to become professor of New Testament exegesis at the then small, and relatively unknown, seminary. Riddle's New Testament acumen, deep piety, and frenetic style of pacing during lectures captured the respect of Hartford students and resulted in an invitation from Schaff to serve on a New Testament committee commissioned to revise the English Bible in an American standard edition. In 1908 he wrote *The Story of the Revised New Testament, American Standard Edition,* an account of the committee's work.

Riddle moved to Western Theological Seminary in 1887 as professor of New Testament literature and exegesis. He refused numerous speaking engagements that would have required his absence from classes and only accepted church assignments that he deemed essential. He served on committees for revising the doctrinal standards of the Presbyterian Church in the United States; in 1889 he assisted in emending the prooftexts of the Westminster Confession and Larger and Shorter Catechisms and 1890 in the revision of the Confession itself. His health began to fail in 1911, but he continued to teach and conduct chapel services until 1913. He died in Edgeworth, Pennsylvania.

Although Riddle possessed a keen sense of humor, his blunt and outspoken style often offended strangers. His teaching regimen reflected his father's close discipline. Riddle insisted that scholarship must be done for Christ's, not scholarship's, sake, and he encouraged students to "get the facts first, and then formulate your theory." He resisted modernist theology because he considered it too loosely tied to scripture, but he was equally disdainful of biblical literalism or interpretations reputedly arising from direct spiritual inspiration. He characterized these interpretive modes as "Brother Boanerges Blatherskite," "Dr. Hardheaded Theology," and "Mr. Mystical Effervescence." Such colorful imagery enlivened his central message that gospel revelation does not lie on the text's surface to be skimmed off by the casual reader. Rather the Bible was in his view a deep mine whose every detail must be examined and charted before its treasures could be fully extracted.

• Riddle wrote, edited or co-edited volumes in Johann Peter Lange's *Commentary* (1869, 1870), the *International Popular Commentary* (1879), the *International Revision Commentary* (1881, 1882, 1884), the *Illustrated Commentary* (1882), and the American edition of Heinrich A. W. Meyer's *Commentary* (1884). He contributed to Bishop A. Cleveland Coxe's *Ante-Nicene Fathers* 1885–1896, Schaff's *Nicene and Post-Nicene Fathers* (1886), and the *Schaff-Herzog Encyclopedia of Religious Knowledge* (1882–1884). He wrote regularly for the *Sunday School Times* (1875–1916) and *Notes on International Sunday School Lessons* (1877–1881).

For a bibliography of Riddle's work, see *List of Publications, Edited, Translated, or Written. Printed privately for the information of students of Western Theological Seminary* (1900). Extensive biographical material is in the *Bulletin of the Western Theological Seminary* 9 (Jan. 1917): 73–120. For biographical sketches, see Western Theological Seminary, *General Biographical Catalogue* (1927), E. T. Corwin, *A Manual of the*

Reformed Church in America (1902), and Peter N. Vandenberge, *Historical Directory of the Reformed Church in America* (1978).

MILTON J COALTER, JR.

RIDDLE, Nelson (1 June 1921–6 Oct. 1985), composer and arranger, was born Nelson Smock Riddle, Jr., in Oradell, New Jersey, the son of Nelson S. Riddle, a commercial artist, and Marie Albertin. He inherited a love of popular music from his father, who played trombone and piano, and an appreciation of classical works from his mother, a Frenchwoman who had been raised in Alsace-Lorraine. He attended public schools in Ridgewood, New Jersey, where he studied piano from the age of eight; he turned his attention to the trombone at fourteen.

In 1938–1939, Riddle began studying with Bill Finnegan, who later became famous as an arranger for the Glenn Miller and Tommy Dorsey big bands. "He showed me how to go about writing some simple things for dance orchestra," Riddle later recalled. On weekends, he would often listen to broadcasts of the Philadelphia Orchestra on his father's car radio.

Riddle's studies took a practical turn when, at the age of nineteen, he went to work briefly for Jerry Wald's band as a trombone player and arranger, then for Charlie Spivak's band in the same capacities. He credited his two-year stint with the Spivak group with giving his arranging technique a "degree of polish [and] distinctiveness." He then spent eighteen months in the merchant marine, where he was assigned to the orchestra and learned how to write for strings—a talent he further honed after joining the Tommy Dorsey Orchestra in May 1944 as an arranger and trombone player.

Riddle spent fifteen months in the army, from April 1945 to June 1946. In 1945 he married Doreen Moran; they had seven children. At the end of 1946 he moved to Los Angeles to be an arranger for the Bob Crosby Orchestra; he then became a staff arranger for NBC Radio in Hollywood, where he stayed until 1950. During this period he also studied symphonic orchestration and composition with the renowned Italian expatriate composer Mario Castelnuovo-Tedesco, and with former Glazunov pupil Victor Bay he studied conducting and music history.

The year 1950 marked a turning point for Riddle. After he created a memorable arrangement of the song "Mona Lisa" for Nat "King" Cole, "the pace of my commercial assignments suddenly and dramatically quickened," Riddle later said. (Riddle's 1951 arrangement of Cole's "Unforgettable" was resurrected when daughter Natalie Cole sang a "duet" with her late father on a 1991 hit record.) Nat "King" Cole was a Capitol Records artist, so Riddle became the "virtual music director" at the label from 1951 to 1962. He arranged and conducted for many other Capitol performers, notably crooner Frank Sinatra starting in 1953.

Riddle's facility with the orchestra and his creative, sometimes unconventional arrangements made him

Hollywood's most sought-after arranger. He wrote for Sinatra off and on up until the early 1980s; among their celebrated album collaborations were *Songs for Swingin' Lovers* (1956), *Only the Lonely* (1958), and *Strangers in the Night* (1965). He also provided orchestral backgrounds for Peggy Lee.

His other well-remembered classics of arranging included the albums *Judy* for Judy Garland (1956), Ella Fitzgerald's *George and Ira Gershwin Song Books* (1959), and *Oscar Peterson–Nelson Riddle* (1965) for the great jazz pianist. In the liner notes for *'Round Midnight* jazz expert Jonathan Schwartz wrote:

In those days, the '50s and '60s, everyone wanted Riddle. He worked himself to exhaustion, hammering out, frequently in the middle of the night, masterpieces of invention and wit . . . Nelson worked at the piano, and most always under pressure. It is astonishing to find no lapses of taste, no distortion of judgment, no cheap tricks posing as nuance. His immense body of work stands as one of the great achievements in American arts.

Riddle also brought a fresh sound to musical variety shows on television, receiving seven Emmy nominations between 1954 and 1967 for arranging, conducting, and adapting music for that medium. (Five of the nominations were for Sinatra programs.) He served as musical director for weekly variety series headlined by Cole (1956–1957), Rosemary Clooney (1956–1957), Sinatra (1957–1958), the Smothers Brothers (1967–1969), Julie Andrews (1972–1973), and several other singers and comedians.

Riddle began scoring movies in the mid-1950s, both writing original music and adapting the music of songwriters for movie musicals. He received five Oscar nominations, four of them for scoring musicals (*Li'l Abner* in 1959, *Can-Can* in 1960, *Robin and the Seven Hoods* in 1964, and *Paint Your Wagon* in 1969). He won an Academy Award in 1974 for his adaptation of period tunes for *The Great Gatsby*.

He worked on other film musicals such as *Guys and Dolls* (1955), *Carousel* and *High Society* (both 1956), *Pal Joey* and *The Pajama Game* (both 1957), *How to Succeed in Business Without Really Trying* (1967), and *On a Clear Day You Can See Forever* (1970). His original dramatic film scores included *Lolita* (1961), *What a Way to Go* (1964), and *El Dorado* (1967).

Riddle composed the scores for some of the most popular television shows of the 1960s. He composed the themes and weekly underscores for "The Untouchables" (1959), "Route 66" (1960), "Sam Benedict" (1962), "The Rogues" (1964), and "Profiles in Courage" (1964). Later, he scored "Emergency" (1972), "City of Angels" (1976), and the three miniseries "The Blue Knight" (1973), "Seventh Avenue" and "79 Park Avenue" (both 1977). He also composed considerable music for "Naked City" (1962), "Batman" (1966), "Newhart" (1982), and "Cagney & Lacey" (1984).

Riddle's "Route 66" theme became a top-40 hit record in 1962 and brought him two of his eleven Grammy nominations. He won three: for composing

Cross-Country Suite in 1958; and for arrangements on two of his three albums with Linda Ronstadt, *What's New?* (1983) and *Lush Life* (1985). Pop singer Ronstadt turned to Riddle for rich orchestral treatments of many old standards for her trilogy of LPs (the last was the 1986 *For Sentimental Reasons*), all of which were critically praised and brought him extensive and surprising media coverage after toiling for years in the relative obscurity of television background music. *What's New?* went double platinum, selling an estimated 3.5 million copies; *Lush Life* sold more than 1.5 million.

In addition to his "Route 66" hit, Riddle's arrangement of the song "Lisbon Antigua" became a gold record in 1956. His concert works included *Three-Quarter Suite* (1962), *British Columbia Suite* (1968), and *Santa Monica Suite* (1975). His first marriage ended in divorce in 1970. That same year he married his second wife, Naomi Tennenholtz.

Riddle was music director for the inaugural ceremonies of President John F. Kennedy in 1961 and of President Ronald Reagan in 1985. From 1973 to 1982 he also served as musical director for the American Film Institute's annual Life Achievement Award ceremonies and was a frequent guest conductor at the Hollywood Bowl. He died in Los Angeles.

Nelson Riddle's sophisticated arrangements made great singers—Sinatra, Fitzgerald, Ronstadt—sound even better. Astute observers of the recording scene recognize Riddle as one of the finest arrangers of popular music ever. Riddle's music for television (notably his jazz-oriented scores for "Route 66") was underrated in an era when many fine composers were active in Hollywood. His study of the classics and his big-band background made both his original music and his creative orchestrations of popular standards truly timeless.

• Riddle's own anecdote-filled account of his early life and major accomplishments is in *Arranged by Nelson Riddle* (1985), his definitive study of arranging. Jonathan Schwartz's liner notes for *'Round Midnight* (1986), the collection of Riddle's complete album trilogy with Linda Ronstadt, provide an assessment of his life and career. A concise overview of Riddle's work is available in *The New Grove Dictionary of American Music* (1986). Bruce Rhodewalt's interview with Riddle for the *Los Angeles Herald-Examiner*, 30 Sept. 1983, conducted at the height of the resurgence of interest in Riddle (due to the Ronstadt collaboration), is insightful. The most accurate of the many published Riddle obituaries is Todd McCarthy's, in the *Daily Variety*, 8 Oct. 1985.

JON BURLINGAME

RIDDLE, Oscar (27 Sept. 1877–29 Nov. 1968), zoologist, was born in Cincinnati, Indiana, near Bloomington, the son of Jonathan Riddle and Amanda Emeline Carmichael, farmers. His father died in 1882, and from the age of nine Oscar helped to support his family by trapping and working on neighboring farms. He matriculated at nearby Indiana University in 1896 to study biology but left in 1899 to collect specimens for the U.S. Commission of Fisheries in Puerto Rico. After his arrival he was recruited to teach biology at the Model and Training School in San Juan, and chemistry, zoology, and physiology at several teachers' institutes. In 1901 he traveled to Trinidad and the Orinoco River delta to collect fish specimens for his own use. He returned to Indiana University later that year and received his A.B. degree in 1902. He then joined the University of Chicago's graduate zoology program as a student and teaching assistant. Under the tutelage of Charles O. Whitman, the department chairman, Riddle began experimenting with the evolution of color patterns in domestic fowl; however, economic considerations forced him to leave the program in 1903 to teach physiology at Central High School in St. Louis, Missouri. He resumed his studies three years later and in 1907 received his Ph.D. in zoology.

Riddle remained at the University of Chicago as an associate in zoology and embryology and a research assistant in experimental therapeutics; he was promoted to instructor the next year. However, in 1911 he was forced to leave because of a reorganization in the zoology department. Out of a job, he assumed responsibility for maintaining Whitman's pigeon colony and preparing his voluminous papers for publication. In 1912 he became a research associate at the Carnegie Institution of Washington, and the next year he moved to the Institution's Station for Experimental Evolution at Cold Spring Harbor on Long Island. Except for serving as a captain in the U.S. Army Sanitary Corps during World War I, Riddle remained at the station for the rest of his career.

In 1914 the Institution published Riddle's three-volume compilation of Whitman's papers, essentially an anti-Mendelian approach to such problems as inheritance of feather patterns, sexual behavior, and reproductive activities. Riddle devoted his own scientific career to explaining organic development and heredity, particularly such phenomena as pigment distribution and sexual determination and reversal, in terms of biochemistry and physiology rather than Mendelian genetics. This decision can be attributed to the filial devotion he felt for Whitman as well as to his self-confessed traits of scientific dogmatism and overconfidence. Consequently, most of the findings in his more than 200 research articles were superseded by the findings of geneticists. He made one important contribution, however—the discovery of a hormone produced by the anterior pituitary gland, which stimulates mammaries to produce milk. Scientists had believed that lactation was triggered by either the placenta, the corpus luteum, or the ovaries. In 1930 George W. Corner discovered that an aqueous extract of the pituitary gland induced lactation in spayed rabbits that had never ovulated; however, he failed in his attempts to isolate a lactogenic hormone. Two years later Riddle and his associates succeeded in discovering and purifying this substance, which they identified as a protein and named prolactin. By 1937 Riddle had demonstrated that prolactin also induced production of milk in rats and crop milk in pigeons.

Having taught high-school biology during his early career, Riddle retained a lifelong interest in how this subject was taught in U.S. public schools. In 1936 he contended that major advances in the life sciences were not being properly conveyed to high-school students because of the anti-evolutionary stance of dogmatic clergymen and their uninformed congregations. While making an address in St. Louis as vice president of the American Association for the Advancement of Science and chairman of its zoology section, Riddle attacked this attitude as well as the supernaturalism that spawned it. This address, "The Confusion of Tongues," created a great deal of controversy, especially after it was discussed at length in the *New York Times* the next day and published shortly thereafter in its entirety in *Science*. It quickly led to the establishment by the Union of American Biological Societies of a committee, chaired by Riddle, that in 1942 substantiated his accusations that religious strictures were responsible for preventing the presentation of the theory of evolution to many publicly-educated students. Over the next twenty-three years Riddle wrote a dozen articles for publications such as *Science Education* and *American Biology Teacher*, urging the faculty in secondary schools to stand up to religious dogmatism and make their students biologically literate.

Riddle served as president of the Association for the Study of Internal Secretions (1928–1929), vice president of the American Academy of Arts and Sciences (1935–1936), and president of the American Rationalist Federation (1959–1960). He chaired the American delegation to the Second International Congress for Sex Research in London, England (1930), and represented the Carnegie Institution at the Second Pan-American Congress of Endocrinology in Montevideo, Uruguay (1941). He was section editor of *Biological Abstracts* (1926–1946) and on the publication board of *Endocrinology* (1931–1934, 1939–1942). He received the American Institute of the City of New York's Gold Medal (1934), the American Humanist Association's Humanist of the Year Award (1958), and the National Association of Biology Teachers' Distinguished Service Award (1958). He was elected to the American Academy of Arts and Sciences in 1934 and the National Academy of Sciences in 1939.

Riddle married Leona Lewis in 1937; they had no children. In 1945 he retired to Plant City, Florida, where he continued to study and write about biology until his death.

With the exception of prolactin, Riddle's work did not result in any significant revelations because he insisted on explaining genetic phenomena in other terms. Ironically, his only other important contribution consisted of educating the public to accept the correctness of new scientific discoveries, something he himself failed to do.

• Riddle's papers are in the American Philosophical Society Library in Philadelphia, Pa. A biography, including a bibliography, is George W. Corner, "Oscar Riddle," National Academy of Sciences, *Biographical Memoirs* 45 (1974): 427–65. Obituaries are in the *New York Times*, 1 Dec. 1968, and *American Biology Teacher*, Feb. 1969).

CHARLES W. CAREY, JR.

RIDENOUR, Louis Nicot, Jr. (1 Nov. 1911–21 May 1959), research physicist and science administrator, was born in Montclair, New Jersey, the son of Louis N. Ridenour and Clare Wintersteen. He graduated from the University of Chicago in 1932 with a B.S. in physics. While at Chicago, Ridenour was editor of the student newspaper, which aided in his facility as a writer. In 1934 he married Gretchen Hinkley Kraemer; they had two daughters.

Ridenour received his Ph.D. from the California Institute of Technology in 1936. Meanwhile in 1935 he had begun a year of work in Princeton, New Jersey, at the Institute for Advanced Study, where he had been hired to be an assistant to future physics Nobel laureate Enrico Fermi. However, Fermi did not show up for his appointment, and Ridenour became an instructor of physics at Princeton University. While at Princeton, he helped build their early cyclotron.

In 1938 Ridenour joined the faculty of the University of Pennsylvania to develop their electrostatic accelerator. He remained there until 1947, except for several leaves granted during World War II. In 1941 he was called to work as assistant director of the Massachusetts Institute of Technology (MIT) Radiation Laboratory, which had just been established by the National Defense Research Committee. There he lead an enthusiastic team of young men who called themselves "Ridenour's Rangers"; the group worked on the use of airborne microwave radar and directed the development of the first experimental unit of the target-following radar later known as SCR 584. In 1943 he became a special consultant to the staff of General Carl Spaatz, U.S. air commander in Europe. He spent most of 1944 integrating radar into air force operations in England and on the Continent. During this period he also visited the Pacific theater of war. For his war work he was awarded the Bronze Star and later, in June 1949, received the Presidential Medal of Merit for his contribution to the development of radar.

As an expression of his varied talents and concern for the future uses of science, Ridenour coauthored a grim, prophetic, one-act play, *Open Secret* (1947, with Robert Adler and George Bellak), about flocks of satellite atomic bombs orbiting above a doomed earth. Later, as a result of his work on radar, he served as editor in chief of the *Radiation Laboratory Series* (28 vols., 1947–1953), which detailed wartime advances in radar and associated fields. These books remained in use at the end of the twentieth century in many engineering schools. During this same period he encouraged the American Institute of Physics to establish a "house organ" for members of the institute. This eventually evolved into the journal *Physics Today*.

In 1947 Ridenour became professor of physics and dean of the Graduate College at the University of Illinois, where he was instrumental in the development of the Illinois Digital Computer (ILLIAC), one of the first reliable university computers. His work with computers also led him to early proposals into the possibility of using computers to solve library growth problems. Other projects he was involved in at Illinois included founding of a solid-state group, a microbiology group, the Control Systems Laboratory, and the Radio Carbon Laboratory.

Military research, however, was never far from Ridenour's interests. In 1949, under the direction of General Hoyt Vandenberg, air force chief of staff, and with the assistance of physicist Theodore Von Karman, Ridenour was appointed to chair a special committee to study the air force research and development efforts and recommend improvements to the air force research and development organization. The resulting "Ridenour Report" recommended the establishment of a separate research and development command and a new air staff deputy chief of staff for research and development. The report was approved, and Ridenour was appointed the first chief scientist of the air force to help implement the recommendations of the report. One of his achievements in this position was his sponsorship of the establishment of the MIT Lincoln Laboratory along the lines of the MIT Radiation Laboratory. This laboratory, in conjunction with the Air Research and Development Command (ARDC), developed WHIRLWIND, the largest digital computer of the early 1950s.

In 1950, instead of returning to the University of Illinois, Ridenour became vice president of the International Telemeter Corporation in Los Angeles, where he worked on early stages of magnetic core memory for the IBM 704 computer, as well as on pay-as-you-go television devices. In 1955 Ridenour joined the Lockheed Aircraft Company, where he rose in rank and responsibility to become vice president of the company and general manager of the Electronics and Avionics Division shortly before his death. During this time he worked on the development of the Polaris and the X-17 missiles. While on a trip to Washington, D.C., to address the National Missile Industry Conference, Ridenour died of a cerebral hemorrhage.

Ridenour was posthumously awarded the Exceptional Civilian Service Medal by the U.S. Air Force. It has been reported that the medal was accompanied by, "perhaps the longest and most highly classified document of justification ever written." Because of his brilliant and complex career and personality, Ridenour acquired many enemies as well as devoted friends during his life. He was best described by a colleague, Francis Wheeler Loomis, who said, "His influence was felt in all phases of the war because of his ability to analyze complex tactical situations, see which possible devices might help, persuade the powers that be by the logic of his presentations, and follow through in the laboratory and in the field to see that the necessary steps were accomplished. This ability, in a variety of endeavors, characterized his life."

• Ridenour published many papers and reports, most of which have remained classified. Memorials published by colleagues after his death include F. W. Loomis, "Louis Nicot Ridenour, Jr., 1911–1959," *Physics Today* 12 (Sept. 1959): 19–21, and Frederick Seitz and A. H. Taub, "Louis N. Ridenour, Physicist and Administrator," *Science* 131 (1 Jan.

1960): 20–21. A summary of Ridenour's contributions to the development of computers is James W. Cortada, *Historical Dictionary of Data Processing: Biographies* (1987). His work at the University of Illinois is summarized in Alan Kingery, *Men and Ideas in Engineering: Twelve Histories from Illinois* (1967). His role in the foundation of the Air Research and Development Command is discussed in Arthur D. Tubbs, "Establishing Air Research and Development Command: Two Civilian Scientists Played Key Roles," *Student Report*, Air Command and Staff College, Maxwell Air Force Base, Ala., Apr. 1986 (AD-A166-671-8-XAB-8608). The most complete obituary may be found in the *New York Times*, 22 May 1959.

ROBERT J. HAVLIK

RIDEOUT, Alice Louise (? Oct. 1871–18 Apr. 1953), painter and sculptor, was born in Marysville, California. Rideout's exact birth date is still unknown, but, according to the *San Francisco Chronicle*, Rideout was born "two months more than twenty years ago" from its publication date of 6 December 1891. She was the daughter of Captain James Ransom Rideout. No information regarding her mother's name and background has been found. From 1868 to 1870 her father was county treasurer, and he and one of her brothers, Ernest V. Rideout, ran a fleet of freight and passenger steamers that traveled the San Francisco Bay and up the Sacramento and Feather rivers to Sacramento.

Beginning at age four, Alice Rideout lived in San Francisco. In 1889, following high school, Rideout began studying with the German sculptor Rupert Schmid, who was active in San Francisco. A story recounted in the *San Francisco Chronicle* in 1891 stated that Rideout was passing the open door of Schmid's studio when her dog bounded in, damaging a clay sculpture. She remodeled the broken section and, when Schmid returned to see her at work, took her as his student. Rideout also attended the San Francisco School of Design (later Art Institute) and, according to the *Chicago Inter-Ocean*, she may also have studied in Boston. She modeled a bust of President Benjamin Harrison (location unknown) "with which the subject," according to the *Chicago Inter-Ocean*, "is said to be much pleased." She also modeled a bust of Sitting Bull (location unknown) before entering the sculpture competition to decorate the exterior of the Woman's Building at the World's Columbian Exposition to be held in Chicago in 1893.

Rideout was announced the winner of this competition in November 1891, but she did not travel to Chicago to commence work until April 1892. At that time she executed the large-scale sculptures, based on her winning models, for the pediment and cornice groups (all destroyed) of the Woman's Building. For this work she was awarded a contract of $8,200 for her original models, plus $2,205.04 for their enlargement.

The pediment (forty-five by seven feet), called *Woman's Place in History*, is also referred to as *Woman's Work* (i.e., in the various walks of life). The figures, modeled in high relief, depict a central allegorical figure flanked by representations of the relatively new professions for women in the public sphere (teacher, nurse, student, and professional artist) while also retaining the more traditional aspects of women's role in society in the domestic sphere (motherhood and home life).

The two attic cornice groups are known as *Woman's Virtues* and *Woman as the Spirit of Civilization*. These groups, modeled in the round, both depict a central winged figure ten feet high supported by smaller seated figures, one to either side. All are allegories. *Woman's Virtues* presents a central figure of Virtue flanked by Charity to her left and Sacrifice to her right. *Woman as the Spirit of Civilization* presents the central figure of Civilization or Wisdom flanked by Dark Age to her left and Enlightenment to her right. A detailed description of these works in Rideout's own words appeared in the *San Francisco Chronicle* (18 Nov. 1891).

Once her work in Chicago was completed, Rideout returned home to San Francisco and, shortly after, married John Frederick Canady, a locomotive and combustion engineer; they had no children. They moved to Manhattan in 1905 and in 1918 permanently settled in Staten Island. There they were charter members of the Oakwood Heights Community Church (incorporated 1925); Alice Rideout was its first Sunday school superintendent and its first choir director. She also directed several theatricals for the church. She continued her art interests by giving painting lessons in her home. She is not known to have created any sculptural works following those of the Woman's Building, but a portrait painted by her of Reverend Pearse Pinch (c. 1927), first pastor of the Oakwood Heights Community Church, is still owned by the church.

Rideout died in Staten Island. Her obituary makes no reference to her early work as a sculptor. Rideout's grandniece, Sybil Willis Keating, described her in a newspaper interview with the *San Francisco Examiner and Chronicle* as a "slight, beautiful woman, more a loving aunt than a famous sculptor."

• Primary sources on Rideout are the World's Columbian Exposition, Board of Lady Managers Collection, and the Palmer Collection, Manuscripts Division, Chicago Historical Society. Works on her life and sculpture include "California Models: Miss Rideout's Sculpture," *San Francisco Chronicle*, 18 Nov. 1891; "She Gains the Prize: Miss Rideout's Triumph," *San Francisco Chronicle*, 5 Dec. 1891; "A Fair Sculptress: Pen Sketch of Miss Alice Rideout," *San Francisco Chronicle*, 6 Dec. 1891; "The Prize Statuary," *Chicago Inter-Ocean*, 5 Dec. 1891; [anon.], "General Backus at Mechanics Fair," *Wave*, 12 Dec. 1891, p. 6; Daniel Burnham, *Final Official Report of the Director of Works of the World's Columbian Exposition, 1894*, vol. 4 (repr. 1989), p. 2; Penny Dunford, *A Biographical Dictionary of Women Artists in Europe and America since 1850* (1990), p. 251; Mildred Hamilton, "A Place That Women Could Call Their Own," *San Francisco Examiner & Chronicle*, 5 July 1981; and James Todhunter, *Jubilee: An Oral History of the Oakwood Heights Community Church, Staten Island, New York, 1925–1975* (n.d.). An obituary is in the *Staten Island Advance*, 20 Apr. 1953.

CHARLENE G. GARFINKLE

RIDGE, John (1803–22 June 1839), Cherokee leader, was born in Oothcaloga, Georgia, the son of Major Ridge, a Cherokee leader, and Susanna Wickett. As a young man Ridge was slight, delicate, and walked with a limp because of a hip problem, but he appeared to be a bright and eager student. His parents stressed education early in the boy's life, and he attended a mission school at age seven. Ridge was a quick learner and felt that the school system, which called for advanced students to tutor younger, slower students, was retarding his education. Therefore, he, with several other Cherokee students, attended a school in Cornwall, Connecticut, in 1818. There they received religious and agricultural training and studied geography, history, rhetoric, surveying, Latin, and natural science.

After three years Ridge's hip problems increased, and he was removed from the dorm and sent to be lodged under the care of a nurse, Mrs. John Northrup. He met and fell in love with the nurse's daughter Sarah Bird Northrup, and with her help his condition improved rapidly. Sarah's family discouraged the relationship until Ridge had recovered his strength. By late 1823 he was able to walk without crutches, and in January 1824 he and Sarah were married with the support of Sarah's parents but against the protest of the Connecticut town. The newlyweds fled immediately after the wedding to avoid being mobbed. They would have seven children.

Back in Georgia, Ridge gained much influence by working to abrogate a treaty that had ceded Creek lands. He also supported missionaries and educational efforts among the Cherokee tribe. His successes made him many enemies, including Creeks who disagreed with him, Cherokees who were jealous of his ability and influence, and government officials whom he had defeated. During this period Ridge was an adamant supporter of Indian land ownership and supported a Cherokee law calling for the death penalty for any Cherokee giving up Cherokee land without the consent of the tribe.

As Georgians increased pressure on the Cherokee to remove to lands west of the Mississippi, Ridge made several trips to Washington, D.C., to argue the tribe's case. In 1831–1832 he made a speaking tour in Philadelphia, New York, New Haven, and Boston, hoping to excite public support against President Andrew Jackson's removal policy. When Ridge visited Jackson and was informed by the president that the federal government would not act against Georgia to prevent removal, Ridge began to waver in his stance. Realizing that the Cherokee could not possibly hope to succeed against Georgia without government support, John Ridge; his father, Major Ridge; his cousin Elias Boudinot; and several others held a council at "Running Waters," Ridge's plantation, in November 1834 to draft a memorial to Congress announcing their decision to remove to the West.

In December 1835 the Ridge party signed the Treaty of New Echota, exchanging Cherokee land in the East for 13.8 million acres in the West, plus a payment of $4.5 million and an annual annuity to support a school fund within the nation. After the ratification of the treaty, Ridge and his supporters moved to the new lands, in present-day Oklahoma, where they quickly carved out a prosperous new plantation and opened a school and a store to assist new arrivals. A significant portion of the Cherokee tribe, however, refused to acknowledge the legality of the Ridge party's treaty, remained in Georgia, and blamed Ridge and his followers for all of their problems. This began a propaganda war between the two factions. Ridge defended his position as the only realistic choice for the Cherokee to survive as a nation.

By 1838 the government had forced the remaining Cherokee to move west along the infamous Trail of Tears. The new arrivals, having suffered privation and death along the trail, resented the prosperity of Ridge and his followers. In addition, the new arrivals, led by John Ross, wanted to put their own government in charge rather than accept the government already in place. Ross suggested holding a council to solve the problem, but the two groups failed to reach an agreement. Several of Ross's followers blamed Ridge and Boudinot for the failure to reach a satisfactory conclusion and held their own meeting, concluding that the men should be assassinated.

On 22 June 1839 three squads of executioners set out to carry out their missions. Twenty-five men approached Ridge's house at dawn and surrounded it. Three men broke in and tried to shoot Ridge in his bed, but their gun misfired. They then dragged him from his house, stabbed and beat him, and left him dying in his yard. He died shortly thereafter. Major Ridge and Elias Boudinot were assassinated the same night.

John Ridge was an important American Indian leader. He fought for the rights of his people until he felt that to continue to resist white encroachment would lead to their destruction. At that point he determined to make the best deal possible, from a position of strength, rather than wait and have the federal government dictate the terms once the Cherokee had lost their bargaining power. He also realized the importance of education for his people's survival. Perhaps his greatest failing was in not convincing the entire Cherokee nation that his path was the best under the circumstances. This failure eventually cost him his life.

• John Ridge's personal papers are scattered in several locations. The best collections are in the Western Historical Collections at the University of Oklahoma, the Manuscripts Division of the University of Texas, and the Georgia Department of Archives and History, which has a John Ridge folder. Thurman Wilkins, *Cherokee Tragedy: The Story of the Ridge Family and the Decimation of a People* (1970), has substantial information and puts Ridge's life in the context of Cherokee removal. James W. Parins, *John Rollin Ridge: His Life and Works* (1991), a biography of Ridge's son, gives a good summary of Ridge's life.

JEFFREY D. CARLISLE

RIDGE, John Rollin (1827–1867), poet, novelist, and journalist, was born in the Cherokee Nation (present-day Georgia) to John Ridge, a leader of the Cherokees, and Sarah Bird Northrup. At the time, the Cherokee Nation was being pressed by the U.S. government and Georgia settlers to leave their lands and move to territories in the West not yet reached by the advancing frontier. Ridge's family played an important role in Cherokee affairs; both his father and grandfather, Major Ridge, were leaders in the tribe, and they at first opposed leaving their well-tended farms and plantations in Georgia for the uncertainties of Indian Territory. After a time, however, they came to see that resistance to the growing pressure was futile, since President Andrew Jackson's policy was clearly to remove, peacefully or otherwise, all of the southeastern tribes to west of the Mississippi. Accordingly, the Ridges and other Cherokees entered into negotiations with the federal government, made the best bargain they thought they could, and in 1835 signed a treaty that ceded their lands in the East for land in what is now Oklahoma. This began the time in Cherokee history known as the Trail of Tears (1838–1839), during which U.S. troops forcibly removed the majority of the tribe, most of whom did not agree with the treaty the Ridges had signed. In 1839 Ridge's father was dragged from his bed and brutally assassinated in front of his son and the rest of the family. As part of the same revenge conspiracy, Ridge's uncle Elias Boudinot and his grandfather were killed on the same day. These events were to influence Ridge for the rest of his life.

John Rollin Ridge was educated in Arkansas, where the family fled after the assassinations, and later in Massachusetts. On his return to Arkansas, he studied law for a time. His education was rich in literature and history, and he began writing poetry and political essays as a young man. He continued his literary ambitions after his marriage to Elizabeth Wilson in 1847 and even after he settled down to a life as a farmer and rancher. He, his wife, and daughter settled down at Honey Creek, Cherokee Nation, just across the line from Southwest City, Missouri. At this time Ridge's intention was to rebuild the social and economic prominence his family had lost since his father's death. But Cherokee affairs were still unsettled; in 1849 Ridge was involved in a fight with a man from the faction of the tribe still hostile to his family. The altercation ended when Ridge shot and killed his adversary. Forced to flee as a fugitive, he first went to Missouri; then, in early 1850, Ridge joined a wagon train for California, never to return to the Cherokee Nation.

Once in the gold fields, Ridge tried mining. Finding this hard and largely unprofitable employment, he soon found work as a writer. He reported from the gold rush towns for newspapers in San Francisco and New Orleans and later edited several of the newspapers springing up in northern California. As an editor, he became involved with politics and allied himself with the Democratic party. Before and during the Civil War, he was a bitter opponent of Abraham Lincoln and the abolitionist cause in general. Ridge was a supporter of the states' rights policies of Stephen Douglas. After the war, Ridge traveled to Washington, D.C., to participate in the peace negotiations between the Cherokee Nation and the United States. He was one of five delegates from the Cherokee faction that supported the South during the war.

While Ridge pursued his career in journalism, he was writing poetry and publishing it in newspapers and in San Francisco literary journals. Many of these works were signed "Yellow Bird," a translation of his Cherokee name Chees-quat-a-law-ny. His reputation as a writer grew and was greatly enhanced when in 1854 he published *The Life and Adventures of Joaquín Murieta, the Celebrated California Bandit*. Ridge's novel is considered to be the first written in California and the first written by an American Indian anywhere. This romance was read widely, as were subsequent pirated editions. Ridge died in Grass Valley, California.

John Rollin Ridge achieved some regional fame during his lifetime as a writer and political figure. He was well known throughout northern California as an organizer and fundraiser for the Democratic party, especially during the Civil War. His poetry and essays were widely published, and his *Joaquín Murieta* was extremely popular. Ridge's literary work is a prime example of early Native American writing in English. Ridge's work was largely in the romantic vein and resembled that of mainstream writers during the period.

• Ridge's *Poems* (1868) were collected by his wife and published posthumously in San Francisco. The volume includes a biographical note written by the poet. *The Life and Adventures of Joaquín Murieta, the Celebrated California Bandit*, first published in 1854, has been reprinted with an introduction by Joseph Henry Jackson (1955). The only full-length biography is James W. Parins, *John Rollin Ridge: His Life and Works* (1991), which contains discussions of his literary and political writing.

JAMES W. PARINS

RIDGE, Lola (12 Dec. 1873–19 May 1941), poet and social activist, was born Rose Emily Ridge, in Dublin, Ireland, the daughter of Joseph Henry Ridge and Emma Reilly. Taking Rose Emily with her, Emma Reilly immigrated to New Zealand in 1887. Mother and daughter lived in New Zealand and Australia for the next twenty years. At age twenty-one, Rose Emily married Peter Webster, manager of a gold mine, but the relationship was short-lasting. She subsequently moved to Sydney and attended Trinity College and the Académie Julienne, where she studied painting under Julian Ashton and wrote poetry.

Upon immigrating to the United States in 1907, Rose Emily Ridge changed her name to Lola Ridge. She also revised her date of birth to 1883. This pretense of being younger than her years would later increase the perception of sickliness and fragility that she inspired by making her worn appearance seem due to illness rather than age. Lola Ridge published her first poems in North America in the *Overland Monthly* (Mar. 1908) and later in the radical journal *Mother*

Earth (Apr. 1909). She lived in self-chosen poverty in a bare and cold apartment in Greenwich Village, New York, supporting herself by writing advertising copy and popular magazine fiction. After three years of this work, she decided it was detrimental to her life as an artist and chose to earn her living as a factory worker, an artist's model, and an illustrator. In October 1919 she married David Lawson, whom she met at a gathering of the Ferrer Association, a radical political organization.

Ridge's first major poem, "The Ghetto," was published in the *New Republic* on 13 April 1918. Reviewing her work in the same magazine (16 Nov. 1918), Francis Hackett called this poem "the most vivid and sensitive and lovely embodiment that exists in American literature of that many-sided transplantation of Jewish city-dwellers which vulgarity dismisses with a laugh and a jeer." With the success of her collection *The Ghetto and Other Poems* (1918), Ridge began to publish more frequently, not only in the *New Republic* but also in major literary magazines, including *The Dial*, the *Literary Digest*, and *Poetry*.

In the role of associate editor and guiding spirit, Ridge was heavily involved with the socially conscious magazine *Others*, published by the poet Alfred Kreymborg. Meetings of the social circle that surrounded the magazine frequently convened at her New York apartment. Among the participants were writers who would become prominent literary figures, such as Conrad Aiken, William Carlos Williams, Marianne Moore, and Waldo Frank.

After the dissolution of *Others* in 1919, Ridge became the American editor of *Broom*, an avant-garde literary magazine, which she coedited with Harold Loeb, the European editor based in Rome. The magazine's associated salon, hosted by Ridge, drew such regular participants as John Dos Passos, Elinor Wylie, Jean Toomer, Edwin Arlington Robinson, Monroe Wheeler, Marianne Moore, and Louis Ginsberg. But Ridge left the magazine in late 1922 because of growing ideological differences with Loeb and frustration over the increasingly modernist, surrealist content of the magazine. Her interests leaned more toward social reform and Marxist political revolution. An editorial battle over the inclusion of a short piece by Gertrude Stein in the January 1923 issue was the final impetus for Ridge's resignation. Ridge described the notorious American expatriate and experimentalist Stein as "mostly blah! blah! . . . In a few years her work will be on the rubbish heap with the rest of the literary tinsel that has fluttered its little day and grown too shabby even for the columns of the daily."

In the meantime, Ridge's standing as a poet had risen with the publication of *Sun-Up and Other Poems* (1920); according to the *New York Times Book Review* (9 Jan. 1921) Ridge was now in the "foremost place among American women writing poetry." Although she had continued to write political poems akin to her earlier work, she had also adopted a highly personal lyricism. *Sun-Up* contains memories of Ridge's childhood in Australia. A similar dichotomy marks her next collection, the sonnet sequence *Red Flag* (1927), which is composed of political poems celebrating heroes of the Russian Revolution and other political martyrs and, in sharp contrast, of personal poems often focused on her own illness and fragility.

In 1927 Ridge was arrested while protesting the controversial execution of Nicola Sacco and Bartolomeo Vanzetti, two anarchists on death row whose guilt on a charge of murder was much in question. The 200-page epic poem *Firehead* (1929), written while Ridge stayed at the artist's colony Yaddo near Saratoga Springs, New York, and acclaimed as her masterpiece, was written in reaction to the Sacco and Vanzetti executions. It retells the story of the Christ's crucifixion from the perspectives of the Virgin Mary, Mary Magdalene, Judas, Peter, and others. An ambitious work, which at its best impresses the reader with its vividness of detail and its attempted scope, nonetheless suffers from a lack of focus and clarity. Her poem "Three Men Die," published in the magazine *Left* (Spring 1931) and included in her final book, *Dance of Fire* (1935), is a more direct response to Sacco and Vanzetti's fate. Ridge won *Poetry*'s Guarantor Prize in 1923 and the Shelley Memorial Award in 1935 and 1936; she also received a Guggenheim fellowship in 1935. She died at her home in Brooklyn.

Ridge's poetry tends to be either vehement political polemic or personal poetry filled with abstract, ethereal language and images. Both the political and the personal are emotionally charged and heartfelt; passion, rather than an interest in language itself, inspired her work. Unlike many writers who profess an interest in working-class life, she chose to live in the milieu and nearly in poverty.

• Ridge's papers are in the Sophia Smith Collection at Smith College. Obituaries are in the *New York Times*, 21 May 1941, and the *Saturday Review of Literature*, 31 May 1941.

ELIZABETH ZOE VICARY

RIDGE, Major (c. 1771–22 June 1839), Cherokee leader, was born in Hiwassee, Cherokee Nation, on the Hiwassee River in present-day Polk County, Tennessee. His parentage is unknown. His Cherokee name was Kah-nung-da-cla-geh (variously spelled), which loosely translates as "the man who walks on the mountaintop"; thus he became, in English, "the Ridge." In the 1790s Ridge earned his livelihood through farming operations that were worked by black slaves. He also maintained a profitable ferry near his home at Oothcaloga (near present-day Calhoun, Gordon County, Georgia) and carried on a thriving trading business with his partner, George M. Lavender. He became one of the wealthier men in the Cherokee Nation. Around 1792 Ridge married Susanna Wickett; they raised four children to adulthood.

As a young man he was a noted warrior, and during the Creek War of 1814 he served as a major of Cherokee forces. From then on he took the name Major Ridge. In time, Ridge dedicated himself to white cultural influences. He sent his children to mission schools in the Cherokee Nation and in the East, but he apparently never converted to Christianity. It appears that he could neither read nor write English and that he spoke it only haltingly.

As he assumed an increasing role in Cherokee affairs in the 1810s, Ridge joined others who wanted the tribe to modernize and acculturate. These reformers pushed for missionaries, schools, technological improvements, and a newspaper in the Cherokee written language. They also desired a modern government with a constitution, a judicial system, and elected officials. Finally, they took a firm stand against removal of the tribe to the West and opposed further land cessions to the United States. When constitutional government was established in the 1820s, Ridge served as speaker of the Cherokee legislature. He also became a member of the executive council and signed documents as a recognized Cherokee authority. He and his family were clearly a part of the modernizing element of the tribe, but Ridge stoutly resisted further encroachments by surrounding states and the federal government.

Sometime in the early 1830s the Ridge family, including the major, his son John Ridge, and his nephew Elias Boudinot, began to doubt the wisdom of resisting federal demands for the tribe's removal. The Ridge faction, as they came to be called, sincerely believed that salvation for the Cherokees lay in moving beyond the sphere of white influence. They hoped to convince their people of the logic of this decision and then negotiate the best treaty possible with the federal government for the tribe's removal. While John Ross and other leaders of the majority faction, the Ross party, were in Washington, D.C., in 1835 condemning the forceful tactics of federal negotiators, the Ridges acted on their convictions. On 29 December 1835, with 300 to 400 supporters present, from a nation of perhaps 20,000 individuals, the Ridge faction signed the Treaty of New Echota relinquishing the native lands for a new home in the West. The Cherokee majority called the compact a fraud, and Congress debated it intensely. It passed despite its questionable legality, however, and President Andrew Jackson enthusiastically signed it.

Soon after the treaty was concluded, the Ridge family and their followers, often called the Treaty party, left the eastern Cherokee Nation for the West. There in Indian Territory (now Oklahoma) they joined previous Cherokee settlers to form a new nation. Later, their eastern kinsmen who had resisted removal were forced to leave under the 1835 treaty provisions and followed what has aptly been called the Cherokee "Trail of Tears." Blaming the Ridges for their great losses in life, property, and self-esteem, and accusing them of disrupting attempts to establish unity in the West, the Ross supporters determined to extract revenge. On 22 June 1839 they retaliated in coordinated attacks against the Ridges, killing the principal signers of the New Echota agreement, among them Major Ridge. The assassins caught him alone, just across the state line near present-day Cincinnati, Arkansas. Others marked for execution escaped. A period of civil war ensued until peace returned in the 1850s, but it was not until the 1860s after the American Civil War that the Cherokees regained the unity they had lost over the removal issue.

Major Ridge was a traditional Cherokee leader who became a prominent figure during one of the most crucial eras of Cherokee history. He was a guiding personality as the Cherokees tried to accommodate themselves to the American republic and as they moved from a tribal pattern of behavior to a future of quickening modernization. Ridge was also a controversial figure. His Cherokee enemies saw him as a traitor to his people, a man who sold the tribal homeland for personal gain. Indian and white friends viewed him as a hero who was willing to take an unpopular and perilous position. When he signed a treaty with the United States in 1835 that caused the removal of the Cherokees, he symbolically signed his death warrant and paid the price with his life.

• The majority of Ridge's papers are at Western History Collections, University of Oklahoma, Norman; Oklahoma Historical Society, Oklahoma City; and the Thomas Gilcrease Museum, Tulsa, Okla. Biographical studies and sketches of Ridge are found in Edward Everett Dale and Gaston Litton, eds., *Cherokee Cavaliers* (1939); William G. McLoughlin, *Cherokee Renascence in the New Republic* (1986); Henry Thompson Malone, *Cherokees of the Old South: A People in Transition* (1956); James Mooney, *Historical Sketch of the Cherokee* (1900; repr. 1975); and Thurman Wilkins, *Cherokee Tragedy: The Ridge Family and the Decimation of a People* (1970, rev. 1986).

GARY E. MOULTON

RIDGELY, Charles Goodwin (2 July 1784–4 Feb. 1848), naval officer, was born in Baltimore, Maryland, the son of Lyde Goodwin, a physician, and Abigail Levy. He took the surname Ridgely in order to qualify for an inheritance from his uncle Charles Ridgely. Ridgely entered the U.S. Navy during the Quasi-War with France. He was appointed a midshipman on 17 October 1799. His first assignment was to the newly launched sloop of war *Patapsco*. He remained on board this sloop while it was in the West Indies with Commodore Silas Talbot's squadron. *Patapsco* returned to Philadelphia in the spring of 1801 and was sold.

On 1 April 1801 Ridgely was ordered to the frigate *President*, which was preparing for a cruise in the Mediterranean to protect American trade against attacks from the Barbary corsairs. Ridgely remained with the *President* until it returned to Hampton Roads the following April.

After returning from the Mediterranean, Ridgely took a two-month furlough. For the next year (July 1802–July 1803) he served aboard the frigates *General Greene* and *New York*, both inactive at Washington, D.C. On 6 July 1803 he was ordered to the frigate *Constitution*, which was then preparing for a cruise to the Mediterranean under the command of Captain Edward Preble. Ridgely was aboard as a midshipman when the *Constitution* sailed from Boston on 14 August.

Preble thought very highly of Ridgely, referring to him as one "of the smartest Officers" serving under his command. As soon as it was possible (19 Aug. 1804) Preble promoted Ridgely to acting lieutenant on the schooner *Nautilus*. While Ridgely was aboard, *Nautilus* participated in Preble's bombardments of Tripoli. It was the *Nautilus* that stood offshore when Lieutenant Richard Somers took the ketch *Intrepid* into Tripoli harbor in an attempt to blow up the frigate *Philadelphia*, which had earlier been captured by the Tripolitans. A premature explosion destroyed the *Intrepid* and killed all the crew. Ridgely viewed the disaster through his spyglass and in 1836 published an account of the scene in the *Naval Magazine* (vol. 1, pp. 172–75).

On 23 January 1805, while ashore in Messina, Ridgely killed George Hutchinson, the mate of an English transport, in a fight. Apparently Ridgely and Hutchinson had been drinking. Ridgely was tried and acquitted. Ridgely remained in the Mediterranean until May 1806 when at his own request he returned home.

Shortly after returning home Ridgely was furloughed from the navy. Early in 1807 he sailed to the East Indies aboard a merchantman. While he was away Congress confirmed his appointment as lieutenant. On 16 August 1807 Ridgely was given command of *Gunboat 58* stationed at Baltimore.

Between 1807 and the opening days of the War of 1812 Ridgely served brief stints aboard the frigates *Constellation* and *Constitution* as well as several weeks on furlough. Ridgely was serving aboard the *Constellation* when war broke out. Ordered to Hampton Roads, the frigate was soon blockaded by a superior British force and remained at anchor for the entire war.

On 7 August 1813 Ridgely was ordered to Baltimore to take command of the sloop of war *Erie* being built in that port. The *Erie* got to sea on 20 March 1814 but was unable to get past the British blockaders and returned to Baltimore. The following month Ridgely was ordered to Sackets Harbor on Lake Ontario to serve with Commodore Isaac Chauncey's squadron. Little of importance happened on that station, and Ridgely returned to Baltimore shortly after the end of the war.

After returning to Baltimore, Ridgely was promoted to the rank of captain (28 Feb. 1815) and was once again given command of the *Erie*. He sailed with the *Erie* in Commodore William Bainbridge's squadron for the Mediterranean. Ridgely was back home early in 1816, but in September of that year he was posted back to the Mediterranean, serving under Commodore Chauncey. Ridgely remained in the Mediterranean for nearly three years. After returning to the states in 1819 he was given command of the Baltimore station. In 1822 Ridgely married Cornelia L. Livingston; they had three children.

Ridgely remained ashore until 27 October 1826, when he was given command of the West Indies Squadron with the sloop of war *Natchez* as his flagship. Ridgely remained at this post for about two years, after which he took an extended four-year furlough. He returned to active duty on 10 June 1833 as commandant of the New York Navy Yard.

Ridgely undertook his last sea duty on 28 October 1839, when he received orders to command the Brazil Squadron from the flagship *Potomac*. He was relieved on 30 April 1841 and ordered home to again command the naval station at Baltimore. He remained there until 11 November 1843 when he was detached, temporarily returning to the same post on 2 May 1844. This was his last assignment. He was detached on 20 September 1845. Ridgely remained inactive for the next three years and died in Baltimore.

• Ridgely's career may be followed in *Naval Documents Related to the Quasi War between the United States and France* (7 vols., 1935–1938); and *Naval Documents Related to the United States Wars with the Barbary Powers* (6 vols., 1939–1944). For specific service information see the "Z File," Naval Historical Center. Among the general naval histories of this period see William M. Fowler, Jr., *Jack Tars and Commodores: The American Navy 1783–1815* (1984), and Gardner W. Allen, *Our Navy and the Barbary Corsairs* (1905).

WILLIAM M. FOWLER, JR.

RIDGELY, Frederick (25 May 1757–21 Nov. 1824), physician and surgeon, was born in Anne Arundel County, Maryland, the son of Greenberry Ridgely and Lucy Stringer, substantial landholders. After studying at the Newark Academy in Delaware, he served an apprenticeship with Dr. Philip Thomas in Fredricktown, Maryland (1774–1775). In the revolutionary war he was a surgeon's mate in Continental army hospitals during the siege of Boston (1775–1776) and a regimental and hospital surgeon at Brandywine, Germantown, and Philadelphia (1777–1778). Late in 1778 he left the army and attended lectures at the medical department of the College of Philadelphia. For a few months in 1779 he was a surgeon on a privateer. Back in Philadelphia he rejoined the army as surgeon and served in that capacity until the end of hostilities. He then returned to Maryland and practiced general medicine.

In 1790 he moved to Lexington, Kentucky, where he developed a large practice and became co-owner of a drugstore in 1792. During 1793–1795 he once again served as army surgeon with Major General Anthony Wayne. Leaving the army for the last time, he reentered private practice in Lexington with Dr. James Watkins. The partnership ended in 1797 when Ridgely married Eliza Short, to whom were born eight children. With the creation of the Medical Department of Transylvania University in 1799, he became professor of materia medica, midwifery, and the practice of physic, and during 1801–1804 he served only as professor of medicine. He and his colleagues offered the first medical lectures in the western states. In 1801–1802 he and the Transylvania colleague who had introduced the technique to Kentucky, Dr. Samuel Brown, performed small pox vaccinations on 500

Lexington residents. In the two years before he resigned from the university (1804), he practiced with Dr. James Fishback, who would later replace him at Transylvania. He served on the university's board of trustees in 1798 and for some years after his resignation to enter private practice.

Among Ridgely's many apprentices were two future professors at Transylvania, the renowned surgeon Benjamin Winslow Dudley and Ridgely's nephew, Charles Wilkins Short, the well-known botanist. His son William Ridgely (M.D., 1825) also pursued a medical career.

With extensive property holdings, including twenty-seven slaves in 1810, he was an organizer of the Lexington Library in 1795 and was benefactor of the Fayette Hospital (later the Eastern State Lunatic Asylum) in 1816. By 1820 he was practicing in Montgomery County, Ohio. After his wife's death in 1822, his health deteriorated, and he died in Dayton two years later.

• Some Ridgely manuscripts are available on microfilm in the University of Louisville, *Kentucky Medical History, 1801–1940: Microfilm Edition. A Guide to the WPA Research Project Records* (1985). Details of Ridgely's life and medical practice are revealed in Charles Wilkins Short, "Obituary of Frederick Ridgely," *Transylvania Journal of Medicine and Associate Sciences* 1 (1828): 442–48; Robert Peter and Johanna Peter, *The History of the Medical Department of Transylvania University* (1905); and Philip Cash, *Medical Men at the Siege of Boston April, 1775–April, 1776* (1973), pp. 158–59, 162.

ERIC HOWARD CHRISTIANSON

RIDGWAY, Matthew Bunker (3 Mar. 1895–26 July 1993), army officer, was born at Fort Monroe, Virginia, the son of Thomas Ridgway, an army officer, and Ruth Starbuck Bunker. Raised at several army posts, Ridgway graduated from the U.S. Military Academy at West Point, New York, in 1917 and was commissioned a second lieutenant in the infantry. That year he married Julia Caroline Blount. They had two children before they divorced in 1930. Promoted to first lieutenant in May 1917, Ridgway spent World War I in the United States, serving as a company commander and adjutant with the Third Infantry Regiment at Eagle Pass, Texas, and then, beginning in September 1918, as a romance language instructor at West Point. Promoted to captain in July 1919, he remained at West Point until 1924, becoming executive for athletics in 1921 and graduate manager of athletics in 1922.

During the remainder of the interwar period Ridgway rotated through a variety of peacetime assignments, earning a reputation as a bright and zealous officer. He attended the Infantry School at Fort Benning, Georgia, from 1924 to 1925. He then commanded a company in the Fifteenth Infantry Regiment at Tientsin, China, for a year and served as a company commander and adjutant with the Ninth Infantry Regiment at Fort Sam Houston, Texas, from 1926 to 1927. Over the next two years Ridgway worked with Major General Frank McCoy on the American Electoral Commission in Nicaragua and the Commission

of Inquiry and Conciliation, which was charged with resolving a boundary dispute between Bolivia and Paraguay. From 1929 to 1930 he again was a student at the Infantry School. In 1930 he married Margaret Howard Wilson; they had no children and divorced in 1947.

After serving with the Thirty-third Infantry Regiment in the Panama Canal Zone from 1930 to 1932, Ridgway, who was promoted to the rank of major in October 1932, was a technical adviser to the Philippine insular government from the spring of 1932 to the spring of 1933. A student at the Command and General Staff School at Fort Leavenworth, Kansas, from 1933 to 1935, he was appointed assistant chief of staff, G-3 (operations officer), with the VI Corps in Chicago, Illinois, and briefly served as operations officer with the Second Army. From 1936 to 1937 Ridgway studied at the Army War College in Washington, D.C., and from 1937 to 1939 he was operations officer with the Fourth Army in San Francisco, California. In May 1939 Ridgway was assigned to a special mission to Brazil with army deputy chief of staff and chief of staff designate Brigadier General George C. Marshall, who had served with Ridgway in China and was impressed with his abilities and knowledge of Latin American affairs. Later that year Marshall, now chief of staff, appointed Ridgway to the War Plans Division of the War Department General Staff, where he remained until the United States entered World War II. During that time he was promoted to colonel.

In January 1942 Ridgway became assistant commander of the newly activated Eighty-second Division with the rank of brigadier general, and later that year, in August, he became division commander with promotion to major general. When the division was redesignated the first American airborne division in August 1942, Ridgway remained in command and eventually won his paratrooper wings. During the next months he put his troops through a vigorous training program, and in April 1943 he and his division went to North Africa. On 10 July 1943 he led the introduction of American airborne troops into combat in Operation Husky, the invasion of Sicily, where they performed well and demonstrated that parachute forces were a valuable tactical asset.

After the Sicily operation, Ridgway's division participated in the Allied landing at Salerno, Italy, in September 1943, then they were deployed to England. On 6 June 1944 Ridgway and his division parachuted onto the Cotentin Peninsula as a leading element of the Allied invasion of Normandy. Following the invasion, he was appointed commander of the XVIII Corps, which consisted primarily of three American airborne divisions. During the remaining months of World War II, his corps saw heavy fighting in Holland, the Battle of the Bulge, the crossing of the Rhine River, and the battle of the Ruhr pocket before linking with the Russians in May 1945. Promoted to lieutenant general in June 1945, Ridgway emerged from the war as one of the army's most highly regarded combat commanders. He had led his men from the front lines, often exposing himself to enemy fire, he showed a tremendous concern for the ordeals and dangers of the common soldier, and he inspired his men to perform gallantly and successfully.

Following the war, Ridgway was named commander of the Mediterranean theater of operations, and in January 1946 he became a member of the Military Staff Committee of the United Nations, an advisory body to the Security Council. From 1946 to 1948 he was chairman of the Inter-American Defense Board, a multinational board that worked on plans for the defense of the Western Hemisphere and the standardization of military organization, training procedures, and equipment. In 1947 he married Mary Princess Anthony Long; they had one child. In 1948 Ridgway was appointed head of the Caribbean Command, and in October 1949 he became deputy chief of staff for administration and training, the assignment he held when the Korean War broke out in June 1950.

In December 1950 Ridgway was named commander of the Eighth Army in Korea. At the time it was a defeated and demoralized force. The Eighth had been severely bloodied by the Chinese Communist onslaught in November 1950 that forced it to retreat from the Yalu River, the boundary between North Korea and China, and threatened to push United Nations (UN) forces completely from Korea. Until this time General Douglas MacArthur, commander of the UN troops, had been directing the war effort from his headquarters in Tokyo, Japan. But shaken by the defeat in North Korea, he gave Ridgway complete control of the ground war in Korea.

Ridgway soon stabilized the situation by retreating to prepared defense positions south of Seoul, South Korea, where he brought the Chinese onslaught to a halt. Equally important, he restored the morale of the Eighth Army. Spending much of his time at the front with his trademark grenade and first-aid kit worn on paratrooper shoulder straps, he visited as many units as possible to encourage the troops with his presence and to demonstrate his concern for their welfare. He replaced officers who failed to measure up to his standards of competence with men eager to take the fight to the enemy. Under Ridgway's firm leadership, the Eighth Army exhibited a new fighting spirit, and by the end of March 1951 it recovered Seoul and pushed beyond the thirty-eighth parallel, the line dividing North and South Korea, effectively redeeming the UN position in Korea.

When President Harry S. Truman relieved MacArthur in April 1951, Ridgway, with the rank of general, became the UN commander. During the next thirteen months Ridgway, in effect, presided over a stalemate. Negotiations to end the fighting began in July 1951 while UN and Communist forces engaged in attacks against each other with little to show for their efforts except heavy casualties. Unlike MacArthur, Ridgway closely adhered to Truman's policy of limiting the war to Korea and used firepower to destroy enemy forces rather than to capture territory. He emphasized continued pressure on the Communists, hoping to force them to make concessions at the negotiating table.

In May 1952 Truman appointed Ridgway to replace General Dwight D. Eisenhower as supreme commander of the North Atlantic Treaty Organization (NATO) military forces, headquartered in Belgium, and in October 1953 Ridgway returned to the United States to become army chief of staff. As head of the army, Ridgway participated in the formulation of President Eisenhower's "New Look" defense policy. Based on the assumption that a strong national economy was the best defense against the Soviet threat and that overspending on defense actually weakened the nation, it called for significant reductions in spending for conventional forces and primary reliance on the threat of massive retaliation with nuclear weapons as a deterrent to aggression. From the outset, however, Ridgway expressed strong reservations about the New Look to Eisenhower and its most forceful military advocates, Admiral Arthur W. Radford, chairman of the Joint Chiefs of Staff, and General Nathan F. Twining, Air Force chief of staff, both of whom, contrary to Ridgway, contended that air power and nuclear weapons could substitute for large armies. To Ridgway a strategy based on massive retaliation was morally indefensible and would leave the United States incapable of dealing with threats that did not warrant the use of either strategic or tactical nuclear weapons. Instead, he advocated developing a flexible strategy centered on carefully measured responses to aggression with conventional forces to minimize the possibility of nuclear war. Ridgway also strongly objected to the proposed limited American military intervention in the Indochina war at the time of the Dien Bien Phu crisis in 1954. Convinced from the experience of Korea that the United States should not again commit itself to a limited war in Asia and that the proposed use of air and naval action alone could not turn the tide in favor of the French against the Communists, he said that a successful intervention would require a large American ground force and the possible extension of the war to Communist China. Given the global overextension of American forces and the likely high cost in money and lives, Ridgway's objections helped persuade Eisenhower to reject intervention.

In June 1955, frustrated by the battles over the New Look and close to the end of his two-year term as chief of staff, Ridgway retired from the army and became an executive with the Mellon Foundation, an industrial research organization in Pittsburgh, Pennsylvania. When the United States began to escalate its involvement in the Vietnam War in the 1960s, Ridgway was an early critic. Repeatedly expressing concern about the cost in American lives and the failure of the American government to define a viable political goal, he called for negotiations to end the war and was one of the "wise men" who influenced President Lyndon B. Johnson in March 1968 to reject the military's proposed escalation of the war and to order a partial bombing halt over North Vietnam as a means to initiate negotiations.

Courageous, a brilliant leader, and principled, Ridgway stands out as a pioneer in airborne warfare, for his success in reversing the tide of the Korean War, and as a prominent critic of American military involvement in Vietnam. He died in Fox Chapel, Pennsylvania.

• Ridgway's papers and an oral history are in the U.S. Army Military History Institute, Carlisle Barracks, Pa. His most important writings are *Soldier: The Memoirs of Matthew B. Ridgway as Told to Harold H. Martin* (1956), *The Korean War* (1967), and "Indochina: Disengaging," *Foreign Affairs* 49 (1971): 583–92. For a bibliography of writings by and about Ridgway see Paul M. Edwards, comp., *General Matthew B. Ridgway: An Annotated Bibliography* (1993). For Ridgway's service during World War II see Clay Blair, *Ridgway's Paratroopers: The American Airborne in World War II* (1985). His service during the Korean War is examined in Roy E. Appleman, *Ridgway Duels for Korea* (1990); Blair, *The Forgotten War: America in Korea, 1950–1953* (1987); and D. Clayton James with Anne Sharp Wells, *Refighting the Last War: Command and Crisis in Korea, 1950–1953* (1993). Ridgway's opposition to the New Look is described in Mark Perry, *Four Stars* (1989), and his opposition to American involvement in Vietnam is discussed in Robert Buzzanco, "The American Military's Rationale against the Vietnam War," *Political Science Quarterly* 101 (1986): 559–76. See also Buzzanco, *Masters of War: Military Dissent and Politics in the Vietnam War* (1996). An obituary is in the *New York Times*, 27 July 1993.

JOHN KENNEDY OHL

RIDGWAY, Robert (2 July 1850–25 Mar. 1929), ornithologist and museum curator, was born in Mount Carmel, Illinois, the son of David Ridgway, a pharmacist, and Henrietta Janes Reed. The eldest of ten children, he was educated in the local school and by his parents, who encouraged his interests in natural history. At the early age of ten Ridgway demonstrated considerable ability in collecting birds and other animals near his home and in painting them with watercolors he mixed himself at his father's pharmacy.

Lacking many books about birds, Ridgway got in touch in 1864 with Spencer F. Baird, the assistant secretary of the Smithsonian, for aid in their identification. Baird encouraged the young man, who soon joined the informal network of individuals around the nation who collected specimens for the United States National Museum. In 1867 Baird placed young Ridgway with Clarence King's Geological Survey of the Fortieth Parallel in the western territories as a zoologist. Ridgway came to Washington, D.C., for a brief training session, then spent much of the next two years with Sereno Watson, the survey's botanist, and photographer Timothy O'Sullivan in parts of California, Nevada, Idaho, Utah, and Wyoming. Ridgway's affiliation with the King Survey continued until 1876; his "Ornithology," *Report of the United States Geological Exploration of the Fortieth Parallel*, volume 4, part 3 (Professional Paper no. 18 of the Engineer Department, U.S. Army [1877]), was consulted for some years thereafter as a useful source of data on western birds.

In 1869 Ridgway returned to Washington with his many specimens; there he was trained by Baird in taxidermy, curatorial procedures, and scientific techniques. He was placed on the Smithsonian staff as assistant in charge of bird collections from 1869 until 1874. Ridgway wrote a number of descriptions with Thomas M. Brewer and, in conjunction with Henry Wood Elliott, another Smithsonian artist-naturalist, prepared illustrations for Baird's *A History of North American Birds: Land Birds* (3 vols., 1874) and *The Water Birds of North America* (2 vols., 1884). These two works were considered standards for a number of years. Ridgway was appointed ornithologist at the United States National Museum in 1874, and he spent the next five years classifying falcons. In 1880 he was named curator in the Department of Ornithology and, in 1881, curator of the Division of Birds, a post he held for forty-eight years until his retirement in 1929. Only his distaste for administration prevented further promotion for Ridgway within the Smithsonian hierarchy. Ridgway married Julia Evelyn Perkins in 1875. They had one son, himself a promising young ornithologist, who died at the age of twenty-four.

Ridgway's great abilities as an ornithologist did not go unrecognized elsewhere. In 1874, not long after he joined the Smithsonian Institution staff, Ridgway was offered a position on the staff of the American Museum of Natural History in New York City, at what would have been a substantial increase in salary, with assurances of periodic increments. He declined out of loyalty to his mentor Baird. "Brookland," for many years Ridgway's home in Washington, D.C., was a haven for birds, and he spent considerable time maintaining the shrubs, trees, and other plantings about the property. In 1915, while continuing his association with the Smithsonian in a nonresident capacity, Ridgway moved permanently to Olney, Illinois, where he established a home and an eighteen-acre bird and plant sanctuary that he called "Bird Haven." Here again Ridgway demonstrated his considerable botanical skills, and this property became a sanctuary and memorial to Ridgway following his death.

At the request of the Smithsonian, Ridgway began an extensive system of cataloging North American birds in the collections of the National Museum in 1884. To facilitate this project, he carried on field work in various parts of the United States between 1895 and 1897, in Alaska with Louis Agassiz Fuertes as part of the Harriman Alaska Expedition in 1899, and in Costa Rica with José Zeledon in 1904–1905 and 1908. In the 1890s he also assisted Smithsonian secretary Samuel Langley's experiments on powered flight by providing information on the wing characteristics of soaring birds. Ridgway published more than 500 books, articles, catalogs, checklists, and other works over a period of sixty years (1869–1929). These included "A New Classification of the North American Falconidae, with Descriptions of Three New Species" (*Proceedings of the Academy of Natural Sciences of Philadelphia* [1870]); "The Birds of Colorado" (*Bulletin of the Essex Institute* 5 [1873]); "Song Birds of the West" (*Harper's New Monthly Magazine* [1878]), one of many popular articles he wrote; "Nomenclature of North American Birds Chiefly Contained in the United

States National Museum" (*Bulletin, United States National Museum* 21 [1881]), then a major work of revision; *Nomenclature of Colors for Naturalists and Compendium of Useful Knowledge for Ornithologists* (1886), in which he described sone 200 different colors; *A Manual of North American Birds* (1887; 2d ed., 1896; repr. 1900), long a standard work in its field; *The Ornithology of Illinois, Part I: Descriptive Catalog* (1889); "The Humming Birds" (*Report of the United States National Museum for 1890* [1892]); "Birds of the Galapagos Archipelago" (*Proceedings of the United States National Museum* 19 [1897]); and *Color Standards and Color Nomenclature* (1912), long the standard work in its field. In *Color Standards* Ridgway included descriptions of approximately 1,100 colors, though he indicated that it was possible to designate six times that number. He also suggested a means of scientifically classifying colors, which proved to be a substantial aid to naturalists in various fields in addition to ornithology. Ridgway's magnum opus was "The Birds of North and Middle America" (*Bulletin, United States National Museum* 50, parts 1–8), published between 1901 and 1919. This work won him the coveted William Brewster Award of the American Ornithologists' Union (AOU) in 1921. Manuscripts and notes left by Ridgway were used by Herbert Friedmann, Ridgway's successor as Curator of Birds at the National Museum (1929–1957) in publishing parts 9 to 11 between 1941 and 1950; parts 12 and 13 were never finished. In addition, Ridgway published a large number of descriptions of birds collected by other ornithologists. He also edited Frank H. Knowlton's *Birds of the World: A Popular Account* (1909) and several papers concerning the trees of the Lower Wabash River Valley of southwestern Indiana. Ridgway was noted not only for the amount of work he turned out, but also for its accuracy, which was achieved despite working under conditions that were sometimes less than ideal.

Ridgway played an important role during the formative years of the AOU. He was a longtime member of its Checklist Committee, assisting with the first three editions of the AOU *Checklist of North American Birds* (1886, 1895, and 1910). He served the AOU as vice president (1883–1891) and president (1898–1900). From the beginning of the twentieth century until his death, he was regarded as the nation's preeminent ornithologist. He won a number of awards, including the Walker Grand Prize from the Boston Society of Natural History (1913), the Daniel Giraud Elliott Medal of the National Academy of Sciences (1920), and membership in the National Academy of Sciences (1926).

A generous and supportive person, Ridgway was noted for his kindness to colleagues. He was, however, not interested in social activity for its own sake, and was loathe to make public appearances or presentations at scientific meetings. He accepted the presidency of the AOU only after having been assured that he would not be obliged to preside at its annual meetings. Ridgway died in Olney.

• Ridgway's papers are held in the Records of the Division of Birds, United States National Museum, Smithsonian Institution Archives. There are also some Ridgway letters in the Academy of Natural Sciences of Philadelphia, and the George N. Lawrence Collection, American Museum of Natural History, N.Y., and some Ridgway papers in the Blacker-Wood Library, McGill University, Montreal, Quebec, Canada. Other pertinent records include the Spencer F. Baird Papers and the United States National Museum Bulletin 50 Collection, Smithsonian Institution Archives, and the Clarence King Survey Papers, National Archives and Records Service, Washington, D.C. The best biographical sources include "Robert Ridgway," a detailed biographical account by Harry Harris in *Condor* 30 (1928) and Alexander Wetmore, "Biographical Memoir of Robert Ridgway," in National Academy of Sciences, *Biographical Memoirs* 15 (1932). The bibliography of Ridgway's publications in Harris was updated and corrected by Wetmore. See also Harry C. Oberholser, "Robert Ridgway: A Memorial Appreciation," *Auk* 50 (1933); "Robert Ridgway," an anonymous account in Charles G. Abbot, "Report of the Secretary," *Annual Report of the Board of Regents of the Smithsonian Institution . . . for the Year Ending June 30, 1929* (1930); and William A. Deiss, "Spencer F. Baird and His Collectors," *Journal of the Society for the Bibliography of Natural History* 9 (1980). An obituary is in the *New York Times*, 26 Mar. 1929.

KEIR B. STERLING

RIEGEL, Byron (17 June 1906–20 May 1975), organic chemist, was born in Palmyra, Missouri, the son of William Henry Riegel and Mary Beagle, farmers. Riegel attended Central Methodist College in Fayette, Missouri, and received a bachelor's degree in chemistry and physics in 1928. After serving as instructor of chemistry there for one year, he began graduate study at Princeton University. In 1930 he transferred to the University of Illinois to work with Roger Adams, under whom he earned a master's degree in 1931 and a doctorate in 1934. He married Belle Mae Huot in 1934; they had one child. He served as a research assistant at George Washington University for one year before becoming a National Research Council fellow, first at the Danzig Technical Institute in 1935 and then at Harvard University in 1936. The Danzig year introduced him to steroid research and the Harvard year to the study of carcinogens with Louis Fieser. In 1937 he joined the Northwestern University faculty, rising through the ranks to become a professor of chemistry in 1948. From 1951 to 1971 he was director of chemical research for the Chicago pharmaceutical company G. D. Searle.

Riegel's researches display a consistency of purpose over a three-decade period. His studies on carcinogens, cancer chemotherapy, vitamin K, saxitoxins (paralytic shellfish poisons), and steroid hormones are all concerned with the relationship between chemical structure and biological activity. Fieser influenced his earliest researches. Riegel broadened Fieser's study of carcinogens to include the synthesis of what he termed their antagonists. This was a joint effort with the Department of Pathology of the Northwestern Medical School in which he prepared the chemicals and the pathologists tested them on mice to see if they could counter the effects of carcinogens. Fieser synthesized vitamin K in 1939, and Riegel developed a process for the separation of the vitamin from other plant substances to obtain enriched vitamin concentrates. In 1943 he received a patent for the process and licensed it to Abbott Laboratories. During World War II, at the request of the Navy Department, he investigated the saxitoxins, isolating them from clams and mussels and establishing their chemical structure. This was part of a biological warfare project that he continued after the war under Department of Defense contracts. Another wartime and postwar investigation involved steroid hormones. As part of a large wartime cooperative program, he studied the adrenocortical hormones, contributing to their purification and isolation. Among his last researches at Northwestern was the preparation of the sex hormone progesterone labeled with a radioactive tracer in order to study the intermediate metabolism involving this steroid.

Riegel was not the only chemist intrigued by steroids. By the end of the 1930s organic chemists had isolated the female sex hormones, estrogen and progesterone, demonstrated that they were steroids, and begun to explore methods to synthesize them for clinical use. Interest quickened in the 1940s when Russell Marker, a Pennsylvania State University chemist, developed a method to prepare steroids from substances occurring naturally in Mexican yams. In 1944 Marker moved to Mexico and founded the Syntex Company to exploit this discovery. Marker converted a yam substance into progesterone, making it the most widely available steroid hormone. Although he left Syntex in 1945, the company prospered. Another American chemist, Carl Djerassi, joined Syntex in 1949. Progesterone both inhibited ovulation during pregnancy and regulated menstrual disorders. Since it was orally inactive, Djerassi searched for a related substance by means of organic synthesis and in 1951 prepared norethindrone, an orally active progestational agent. By then Syntex was a commercial success making a variety of hormones for clinical use.

The work underway in Mexico City and elsewhere stimulated interest in steroids among established makers of pharmaceuticals, most especially the Searle Company. In 1951 Searle's president decided to expand a modest research program on steroids, especially on corticoid steroids, which had recently been shown to have anti-inflammatory properties, and on the sex hormones. Riegel was a natural choice to lead this effort because his work at Northwestern had focused on both cortisone and progesterone. Arriving at Searle in 1951, Riegel hired a number of talented chemists, including Frank B. Colton, a former student, and directed his team toward finding methods to modify steroid molecules so as to produce useful and unique drugs. Riegel and Colton first focused on corticoid research, but in 1952 Searle's medical research director, Irwin Winter, returned from a physicians' conference where he was told of the need for an orally effective progestin for treatment of problems such as menstrual disorders and habitual abortion. Riegel and

Colton now focused on the synthesis of such an agent. In 1952 Colton prepared norethynodrel, another orally active progestin.

Riegel and Colton turned to outside consultants to evaluate the biological properties of their promising new molecule after Searle's endocrinologists demonstrated its progestational activity. Gregory Pincus became consultant to Searle. Pincus had founded a research center in Massachusetts to engage in fertility research. He hoped to develop a mass consumption pill to control fertility. Riegel and Colton supplied Pincus with their new subtance as did Djerassi at Syntex with his norethindrone. Pincus evaluated both progestins on rabbits, finding that both agents were effective. Riegel and Colton then supplied the Harvard gynecologist, John Rock, with norethynodrel, and Rock demonstrated in 1954 that women did not ovulate while on the progestins. In 1957 both Searle and Syntex received Food and Drug Administration (FDA) approval to market their oral agents under the trade names of Enovid and Norlutin for the control of menstrual disorders.

Pincus and Rock also recognized the potential of progestins as oral contraceptives and with the approval of Searle devised large field tests of Enovid with volunteer women in Puerto Rico and Haiti. In the course of their studies, Pincus and Rock found that the side effects associated with the progestin could be reduced by the addition of small amounts of an estrogen. The formulation of the contraceptive decided on by Riegel, Colton, and Winter consisted of 98.5 percent progestin and 1.5 percent estrogen.

Having established Enovid's efficacy, Searle obtained FDA approval in 1960 for marketing Enovid as the first commercial oral contraceptive. Searle had a two-year monopoly on what came to be known as "the Pill" because Syntex did not obtain a licensing partner in the United States before 1962 due to several pharmaceutical companies' fear of a religious reaction to it. Riegel and Colton created a new progestin in the 1960s. Enovid proved inferior to newer drugs and disappeared from use. Riegel and Colton, using the experience and insight gained in their 1950s studies, developed a new compound, Ovulen, which became available to women in the mid-1960s as a contraceptive at much lower dosage and with fewer side effects.

In 1971 Riegel retired. The following year he suffered a stroke and was an invalid until his death in Evanston, Illinois. He was highly active in scientific organizations, holding more than fifty elective offices. In 1970 he was president of the American Chemical Society. His contributions to chemistry were relatively modest until he joined Searle at age forty-five. By leading the research group that produced the first commercial oral contraceptive, he became associated with one of the most important events of the postwar decades. The Pill revolutionized the control of fertility and had a major impact on society by facilitating the women's movement of the 1970s.

• The archives of Northwestern University, Evanston, Ill., and the G. D. Searle Company in Chicago have only a small amount of material on Riegel. There is very little published information on his life. A brief essay is in *Chemical and Engineering News*, 18 Nov. 1968, p. 71. Riegel and Victor Drill summarized the work of the Searle research group in "Structural and Hormonal Activity of Some New Steroids," *Recent Progress in Hormone Research* 14 (1958): 29–76. See Louis Fieser and Mary Fieser, *Steroids* (1959) and *Topics in Organic Chemistry* (1963), for a discussion of Riegel's steroid researches. For the chemistry behind the Pill, see Carl Djerassi, "The Making of the Pill," *Science 84*, Nov. 1984, pp. 127–29. Djerassi considers the rivalry between Syntex and Searle in *The Politics of Contraception* (1979) and devotes two chapters of his autobiography, *The Pill, Pygmy Chimps, and Degas' Horse* (1992), to the birth, development, and reaction to the Pill. Richard A. Edgren recalls in "Memoir—The Beginning of Oral Contraceptives," *Endocrinology* 129 (1991): 1144–45, how Searle initiated the research leading to Enovid. See Alfred Burger, "Biomedical Science: The Past 100 Years," *Chemical and Engineering News*, 6 Apr. 1976, pp. 160–62, for the broad biomedical context of progesterone research. For information on the Pill's side effects and risks, see Bernard Asbell, *The Pill: A Biography of the Drug that Changed the World* (1995). Loretta McLaughlin in *The Pill, John Rock, and the Church* (1982) provides information on the relation between the Searle scientists and Pincus and Rock. Obituaries are in the *New York Times*, 22 May 1975, and *Chemical and Engineering News*, 26 May 1975, p. 5.

ALBERT B. COSTA

RIEGGER, Wallingford (29 Apr. 1885–2 Apr. 1961), composer, was born in Albany, Georgia, the son of Constantin Riegger, the owner of a lumber mill, and Ida Wallingford. The family moved to Indianapolis when he was three, and several years later, encouraged by his parents, themselves accomplished amateur musicians, he began taking violin lessons. At the age of fifteen Riegger moved with his family to New York City and began playing the cello. In 1905, after attending Cornell University for one year as a scholarship student, he withdrew and returned to New York City to continue his music studies. He enrolled at the forerunner of the Juilliard School, the Institute of Musical Art, where he studied cello and composition. Following graduation in 1907, Riegger went to Berlin, where he studied at the Hochschule für Musik, again concentrating on cello and composition. He made his conducting debut with the Blüthner Orchestra in Berlin in the spring of 1910 and returned to the United States shortly thereafter.

In June 1910 Riegger was married to Rose Schramm; the couple would have three daughters. To support his family, Riegger joined the cello section of Minnesota's St. Paul Symphony, where he played until 1913. That same year he returned to Germany for further study and in 1914 was appointed assistant conductor of the state theater orchestra in Würzburg. Riegger remained in that post for three years, during which time he also conducted the opera house orchestra in Königsberg and the Blüthner Orchestra in Berlin.

Riegger and his family returned to New York in April 1917—three days before the United States entered World War I. A year later he joined the music department at Drake University (Des Moines, Iowa) as a teacher of cello and music theory. After three years he returned to New York and in 1924–1925 was a faculty member at his alma mater, the Institute of Musical Art. After teaching for two years at the Ithaca (N.Y.) Conservatory (1926–1928), Riegger again returned to New York and made the city his permanent home. He taught at several local schools before joining the Metropolitan Music School faculty in 1936; he later became president of the school.

Riegger had begun composing in his youth, and he continued to write music in between and during his periods of conducting and teaching. His earliest work to achieve recognition was the Trio in B Minor, for violin, piano, and cello, written in 1920, which won both the Paderewski Prize and the Society for Publication of American Music Award; it received its premier performance in New York ten years later. His 1923 setting of Keats's poem "La Belle Dame sans Merci," for four solo voices and chamber orchestra, received the Elizabeth Sprague Coolidge Award, and was the first work by an American-born composer to be so honored; it was premiered at the Coolidge Festival in Pittsfield, Massachusetts, in September 1924. These and other early Riegger works were written in a formal idiom that made use of traditional, melodic harmonies, and they were generally well received by audiences.

Riegger's first composition to include atonality was his *Rhapsody for Orchestra*, written in 1925 and played publicly for the first time in October 1931 by the New York Philharmonic under the direction of Erich Kleiber. Audiences were less enthusiastic about this and later Riegger works, but critics for the most part applauded his break with tradition. There were similar responses to his 1927 *Study in Sonority*, a totally atonal piece written for ten violins or multiples thereof; it was introduced by the Philadelphia Orchestra under Leopold Stokowski in March 1929. Riegger was one of the first American composers to adopt Arnold Schoenberg's twelve-tone system; he used it initially for part of *Dichotomy*, a work for chamber orchestra written in 1932 and performed that same year in Berlin; two later works, the String Quartet no. 1 (1938–1939) and *Duos for Three Woodwinds* (1943), are entirely twelve-tonal. Thereafter Riegger wrote mostly atonal or twelve-tone compositions. His concert works generally found favor with both critics and fellow composers—his Symphony no. 3, which premiered in 1946, won the New York Music Critics Circle Award that year—but did not please audiences.

Riegger found greater public acceptance for a series of scores he wrote in the 1930s and 1940s for dances by leading American choreographers, including Martha Graham and Doris Humphrey. Riegger also created popular concert versions of some of his dance music, including *New Dance*, written for Humphrey. To supplement his income from teaching, Riegger moonlighted as an arranger of choral and vocal music for the commercial market. Under various pseudonyms he turned out dozens of arrangements for such popular standards as "Short'nin' Bread."

Riegger's seventy-fifth birthday in 1960 was the occasion for performances of his major works in cities throughout the United States. Following his death, which occurred in a New York City hospital after he underwent emergency surgery for a brain injury suffered in a street accident, Riegger was cited in numerous obituaries as a major influence on American composers in the mid-twentieth century.

• For additional biographical information see Stephen Spackman, *Wallingford Riegger: Two Essays in Musical Biography* (1982). See also Virgil Thomson, *American Music Since 1910* (1971); Elie Siegmeister, ed., *The Music Lover's Handbook* (1943), pp. 775–76; R. F. Goldman, "The Music of Wallingford Rieger," *Musical Quarterly*, Jan. 1950, and "Wallingford Riegger," *Hi-Fi/Stereo Review*, Apr. 1968; and Henry Cowell, "Wallingford Riegger," *Musical America*, 1 Dec. 1948. An obituary is in the *New York Times*, 2 Apr. 1961.

ANN T. KEENE

RIGDON, Sidney (19 Feb. 1793–14 July 1876), restoration preacher and early Mormon leader, was born in St. Clair Township, Allegheny County, Pennsylvania, the son of William Rigdon and Nancy Briant, farmers. Rigdon learned to read in a rural schoolhouse but taught himself grammar and constantly borrowed books from neighbors, in particular books on history; these, along with the Bible, he liked best. In 1817, after a conversion experience that a local congregation found convincing, Rigdon joined the United Baptists and began to preach as a skillful orator. In 1919, his widowed mother having sold the farm and gone to live with her daughter, Rigdon set out on his own. From 1919 until 1921 he lived in the home of Adamson Bentley, a Baptist minister in Warren, Ohio, and during this period became an ordained minister. Also while living with Bentley, Rigdon met and in 1820 married Bentley's sister-in-law, Phebe Brooks; the couple had at least ten children.

Soon after Rigdon was named minister of the First Baptist Church in Pittsburgh in 1821, he brought growth and stability to the congregation. Stability would never characterize his own ministerial life, however. In the summer of 1821 he met Alexander Campbell, the religious reformer whose movement to restore the first-century church would lead, in 1830, to the formation of the Disciples of Christ. Scriptural discussions with Campbell led Rigdon to question the tenets of every denomination with which he was familiar, and to the dismay of his more orthodox parishioners, he began to preach his newly formed ideas on what the primitive church of Christ had been like.

Rigdon's determination to preach the "ancient order of things" offended many in the congregation, yet in a pattern he repeated many times over the course of his life, he was not hindered by the potential consequences. In 1824, as a result of doctrinal differences between him and the congregation, Rigdon resigned his pastorate, and over the next two years, while working as a tanner, he continued to develop his spiritual beliefs and his association with Campbell. After moving to Bainbridge, Ohio, in 1826, Rigdon founded churches in Mantua and then at Mentor. Over the next few years, largely as a result of Rigdon's increasing fame as an orator and as a "reasoner of the Scriptures," the Mentor church grew and became prosperous. But once again stability was short-lived. Rigdon began to develop his own theology, which, though similar to Campbell's, differed in several respects, in particular over the issues of a communal society and the doctrine of the millennium. Convinced he would be unable to establish "the true church of Christ" through Campbell's movement, in 1830 Rigdon withdrew from the Mentor church.

That fall, former members from Mentor asked Rigdon to pastor their independent congregation in Kirtland, Ohio. Once again he found himself part of a congregation that was able to provide for his material as well as spiritual needs, and once again the situation did not last. It was about this time that Rigdon received four visitors, among them Parley Parker Pratt, a former disciple of Rigdon's who had gone to New York; there he had encountered and joined the group that later came to be known as the Church of Jesus Christ of Latter Day Saints, led by the self-proclaimed latter-day prophet Joseph Smith. Initially Rigdon was skeptical of the Book of Mormon that Pratt handed to him, but soon he embraced the story of its discovery and translation and once again set out to explore the unknown.

Rigdon met Smith in New York early in 1831 and persuaded him to move the church headquarters to Kirtland. There, as a member of the church's three-man presidency, Rigdon was extremely influential in developing the ecclesiastical structure and theological positions of the church. He also edited two Mormon papers, the *Elders Journal of the Church of Latter Day Saints* and the *Latter Day Saint's Messenger and Advocate*. Largely as a result of Rigdon's abilities and influential position in the area, the Latter Day Saints came to be seen as a major threat to mainstream Protestantism in the northeastern section of Ohio known as the Western Reserve. The price of success was high. In addition to the physical violence that was directed against them, the communitarian group had to struggle to survive, a situation that was exacerbated by the group's determination to build a temple, which finally was dedicated in March 1836. Less than two years later, however, the community was torn apart, partially as a result of a financial scandal involving church leaders. To escape legal action as well as mob violence, Smith and Rigdon fled to Missouri.

When Smith and Rigdon arrived in Missouri in January 1838, they joined other Mormons—as the Latter Day Saints had come to be called—in Far West, a village in Caldwell County. The earlier Mormon settlement that Pratt and others established in Independence had collapsed in 1833 when the group was run out of Jackson County. Persecution soon followed them to Far West, where the group was plagued by internal problems as well. In June Rigdon delivered what was called the "salt sermon." Taking as his text Matthew 5:13, he compared disloyal members to salt that has lost its taste and is no longer good for anything except to be thrown out or trampled under foot, thus initiating a purge of the ranks. In a companion sermon, delivered on the Fourth of July, Rigdon took the "Gentiles" to task. Indicating that it was "better . . . to sleep with the dead than to be oppressed by the living," he outlined the Mormon Declaration of Rights and stirred his normally pacifistic listeners to resistance.

Word of these sermons spread throughout the area, and a virtual war ensued. Far West was occupied by a militia group—actually a mob that burned, looted, raped, and destroyed the village—and on 30 October 1838 Missouri governor Lilburn Boggs issued an order calling the Mormons enemies of peace who must be "driven from the state or exterminated." Rigdon and other church leaders would have been executed on the spot had Brigadier General Alexander Doniphan not refused to carry out the order. In November, at his trial on charges of treason, murder, arson, and robbery, Rigdon took the stand in his own defense. Initially he was jeered, but soon the crowd began to listen as he spoke of the numerous injustices to which he had been subjected. When he was finished, the judge dismissed the case and the crowd took up a collection of about $100, which he used to flee the state.

Rigdon and other Mormons arrived in Quincy, Illinois, in February 1839. That spring they were joined by Smith and others who had escaped from Missouri, and the community set about implementing Smith's plan to build a city where the Latter Day Saints could live in peace. The site, situated along the Mississippi River about sixty miles north of Quincy, was called Nauvoo, a Hebrew word meaning, "the beautiful place."

Although he retained his position in the church presidency and served as postmaster, Rigdon was not as active or as influential in church affairs in Nauvoo as he had been before, due mainly to ill health and personal conflicts with Smith. In 1844, however, despite his growing distrust for Rigdon, Smith selected him as his vice presidential running mate for the U.S. presidency. Their brief campaign ended in June 1844, when Smith and his brother Hyrum were murdered by a mob in Carthage, Illinois. Rigdon sought to lead the church after Smith's death, but Brigham Young won the bitter battle for control and Rigdon was squeezed out.

In October Rigdon returned with a few followers to Pittsburgh, where he cofounded and edited the *Latter Day Saint's Messenger and Advocate*. Through it he castigated Smith as a "fallen prophet" who in his later years had led his followers astray. Rigdon, however, retained his belief in the divinity of the Book of Mormon, and in 1845, in Franklin County, Pennsylvania, he and about 150 followers established "a gathering" based on the tenets that had been practiced in Kirtland. Called the Church of Christ, it broke up after two years. Rigdon's last years were spent in Friendship, New York. He always denied claims that he had fabricated the Book of Mormon by rewriting a novel by Solomon Spaulding.

• A collection of Rigdon papers does not exist, but a few dozen of his letters are at the Church of Jesus Christ of Latter-Day Saints historian's office in Salt Lake City, Utah. John W. Rigdon, Sidney Rigdon's son, wrote a useful though inaccurate biography of Rigdon titled "Lecture on Early Mormon Church," which was delivered to the Washington State Historical Society in 1906. Daryl Chase, "Sidney Rigdon—Early Mormon" (master's thesis, Univ. of Chicago, 1931), is a historically accurate account dealing exclusively with Rigdon. A more recent study is F. Mark McKiernan, *The Voice of One Crying in the Wilderness: Sidney Rigdon, Religious Reformer, 1793–1876* (1971); it includes a comprehensive biographical essay and reprints Rigdon's 1 January 1844 petition of grievances to the Pennsylvania legislature, which is essentially a handwritten autobiography. The best official Mormon account of Rigdon's participation in the early church is the "Journal History of the Church of Jesus Christ of Latter-Day Saints," a day-by-day account of the church since its founding that ran in the Nauvoo *Times and Seasons*. After Rigdon adopted the Mormon faith, he was attacked repeatedly by his former mentor, Alexander Campbell, in the *Millennial Harbinger*, a paper Campbell edited in Bethany, Va. Campbell attacked the Mormon faith in *Delusions: An Analysis of the Book of Mormon; With an Examination of Its Internal and External Evidences, and a Refutation of Its Pretences to Divine Authority* (1832). The claim that Rigdon invented the Book of Mormon by rewriting a manuscript by Solomon Spaulding originated in E. D. Howe, *Mormonism Unveiled . . .* (1834). Spaulding's manuscript, however, which was discovered in 1886 and given to Oberlin College, bears no relationship to the Book of Mormon.

F. Mark McKiernan

RIGGS, George Washington (4 July 1813–24 Aug. 1881), banker, was born in Georgetown, District of Columbia, the son of Elisha Riggs, a wealthy merchant and banker, and Alice Lawrason. In 1815 Riggs moved with his family to Baltimore, Maryland. Before entering Yale in 1829, he attended the famous Round Hill School in Northampton, Massachusetts, run by George Bancroft and Joseph G. Cogswell. Leaving Yale in his junior year, Riggs went abroad and upon his return worked in his father's New York City firm, Riggs, Taylor & Company. In 1840 he married Janet Madeleine Cecilia Shedden of Glasgow, Scotland. They had nine children.

Also in 1840 Riggs became a banking partner of William Wilson Corcoran, who in 1837 had started a brokerage firm in Washington, D.C. Through his family, which owned banks in Baltimore, Philadelphia, St. Louis, and New York, Riggs brought financial connections to the new bank, which was called Corcoran & Riggs. His father was said to be a silent partner in the bank and received half of the profits when his money was involved in transactions.

Corcoran and Riggs were "men with dominant personalities . . . who moved in the proper circles, were acquainted with influential people, and had the vision necessary to be more than routine bankers" (Cole, p. 526). Their bank grew rapidly. In 1844 it became a depository for federal government funds and in 1845 purchased the Washington branch of the defunct Second Bank of the United States (BUS), including its building on the corner of Fifteenth Street and New York Avenue. Federal officials turned to Corcoran & Riggs for many of the services the BUS had performed. "Corcoran & Riggs are bankers of large capital," Secretary of the Treasury George M. Bibb declared, "doing business from Boston to Mobile and New Orleans, from Washington to St. Louis, having the confidence of mercantile men" (Cole, p. 265).

Basking in their government's approval and with foreign legations generally using their banking facilities, Corcoran & Riggs "captured the imagination of the public and the business of the right people" (Cole, p. 277). The leading financier of the Mexican War, Corcoran & Riggs took on a loan of $5 million in 1846 and one of more than $14 million in 1847. The next year the bank, on behalf of itself, Baring Brothers & Co. of London, and others, again took on a loan for more than $14 million.

Riggs withdrew from his partnership in July 1848. He differed with Corcoran over the wisdom of their last loan; he disapproved of his country's participation in the Mexican War; and he was uncomfortable with the reputation their bank had earned among bankers throughout the United States and abroad for making large profits from financing that war. The bank's name, however, remained the same, for Riggs's 22-year-old half brother, Elisha Riggs, Jr., who had started working in the bank six months earlier, became Corcoran's junior partner.

When Corcoran retired from the bank in April 1854, Riggs reentered the firm. He bought Corcoran's share with an inheritance from his father the year before, renamed his bank Riggs & Co., and to accommodate his late father's customers opened a branch in New York that lasted until 1889. Riggs & Co. soon became "familiar all over the globe"; in 1896 it became Riggs National Bank. Riggs & Co. advanced a half million dollars to army contractors in the first year of the Civil War and continued to help finance the northern cause. It operated on such a large scale that in 1868, when the United States purchased Alaska from Russia, that government upon presenting Riggs & Co. with a U.S. government draft received $7.2 million in gold.

Riggs was deeply involved in the affairs of the District of Columbia. He helped finance the construction of early telegraph lines emanating from the capital and was among those organizing the Washington & Georgetown Street Railroad Company, which soon after its 1862 charter began running horsecars from the Navy Yard to a point beyond Rock Creek. In 1865 Riggs headed a local board of trade, formed that year to stem the area's loss of jobs and businesses following the Civil War. Deciding that Washington's greatest need was better railroad connections, the board

worked to obtain them. In 1868 Riggs was on a committee that prepared a new plan for the district, making some of its officials elective, but Congress was too absorbed with the impeachment of President Andrew Johnson to take notice of the plan.

As a member of the board of aldermen of the district, Riggs chaired the 1873 committee that early the next year petitioned Congress to investigate again the Board of Public Works. Congress had investigated and exonerated that board in 1872, despite cost overruns and "miles of incomplete sewers, half-graded streets and half-paved sidewalks" (Bryan, vol. 2, p. 607). Having purchased from the federal government much of its vacant Washington real estate, Riggs, like other big property owners, felt that tax assessments made by the district government were excessive and suffered from the unfinished state of streets and sidewalks fronting his property. The congressional investigation spurred by Riggs's committee ran from February to June 1874 and made the capital's management an issue of national significance. As a result of the investigation, Congress ended the district's territorial status and arranged for a temporary government, administered by a three-member commission appointed by the president and confirmed by the Senate, and for four members of Congress to draft a bill providing for a permanent government for the district. Riggs was chair of the Committee of One Hundred, which bolstered the district's credit by securing from Congress a 50 percent contribution to the expenses of the district and a promise to assume responsibility for district bonds.

Riggs and his close associates were cited as examples "of what men of business should be, showing that the pursuit of wealth need not . . . make men hard and narrow" (Cole, p. 279). Riggs generously supported orphan asylums in the Washington area and was a trustee of the Peabody Educational Fund, which was used to combat illiteracy among southern blacks and whites. Known for his hospitality and artistic taste, he had numerous interests outside of banking. He was the second vice president of the Washington Horticultural Society, which was organized, founded, and gave its first exhibition in 1857. That same year, after it had arranged to purchase the home of George Washington, the Mount Vernon Ladies' Association asked Riggs to be its treasurer and a member of its executive board. For the remainder of his life, except for a brief period in the 1870s, he held these positions (and his son E. Francis Riggs, who took over his banking house, also succeeded him as treasurer of the association). The association later recalled its "rare good fortune" in having its finances "in his experienced hands" and remembered gratefully how during the Civil War he "came nobly to the relief of Mount Vernon . . . by advancing the funds" needed to maintain it (King, pp. 81, 174). Riggs had a handsome home and a splendid collection of paintings, which he shared in 1865 at the "1st Art Soiree" of the Metropolitan Club. He became a trustee of the Corcoran Gallery of Art, which his former partner opened in 1872 (it had been incorporated by an act of Congress in 1870).

Appearing in good health until his last three months, Riggs died at "Green Hill," his country home in Montgomery County, Maryland. Although he was raised an Episcopalian, his immediate family was Roman Catholic, and he died a communicant of that faith.

• Riggs's papers form a significant part of the Riggs Family Papers, Manuscript Division, Library of Congress. For the importance of Riggs in banking, see David M. Cole, *The Development of Banking in the District of Columbia* (1959). Personal and professional information on him can be found in *Third Record of the Class of 1833 in Yale College* (1870); Wilhelmus Bogart Bryan, *A History of the National Capital: From Its Foundation through the Period of the Adoption of the Organic Act*, vol. 2 (1916); Constance McLaughlin Green, *Washington Village and Capital, 1800–1878* (1962); William Benning Webb and John Wooldridge, *Centennial History of the City of Washington* (1892); Allan Nevins, *Ordeal of the Union*, vol. 1 (1947); Donald B. Cole and John J. McDonough, eds., *Benjamin Brown French: Witness to the Young Republic, a Yankee's Journal, 1828–1870* (1989); and Grace King, *Mount Vernon on the Potomac: History of the Mount Vernon Ladies' Association of the Union* (1929). Obituaries are in the *Washington, D.C., Evening Star*, 24 Aug. 1881, and the *New York Times*, 25 Aug. 1881.

OLIVE HOOGENBOOM

RIGGS, Lutah Maria (31 Oct. 1896–8 Mar. 1984), architect, was born in Toledo, Ohio, the daughter of Charles B. Riggs, a physician, and Lucinda C. Barrett. She attended public school and the Manual Training High School in Indianapolis. In 1914 she moved to Santa Barbara, California, with her mother and stepfather, Theodore Dickscheidt. There she attended the local teachers' college. After receiving her teaching certificate, she obtained a scholarship that enabled her to enter the architectural program at the University of California at Berkeley. She studied at Berkeley in a Beaux Arts program developed by John Galen Howard. She received her architectural degree in 1919 but continued on with her studies through 1921. After working as a draftsperson in several San Francisco and northern California architects' and engineers' offices, she returned to Santa Barbara in late 1921.

While working in northern California, Riggs came across the October 1920 issue of *Architectural Record*, which contained an illustration of a house designed by the Santa Barbara architect George Washington Smith. She was deeply impressed with the abstract qualities of this design, and soon after returning to Santa Barbara she applied for work in his office. At first she was refused, but she finally obtained a position with Smith in 1921. Within a short time she emerged as Smith's chief designer. By 1924 she was a partner in the firm, and in 1928 she received her architectural license.

With her remarkable talent for rendering, Riggs was responsible for the steady stream of sketches and presentation drawings that substantially contributed to Smith's national reputation. The Smith office not only produced a wide array of country houses in California, Arizona, Texas, and even as far away as New York, but it also was intensely involved in the replanning of Santa Barbara, which by 1930 had turned the community into an idealized seaside city, designed in a Spanish colonial style.

During the 1920s she traveled and made sketches in Mexico, Spain, Italy, and France, both alone and with Smith. From these sketches Riggs produced a number of drawings for a book on traditional Mexican architecture that she and Smith planned to publish, but they never completed it due to the pressure of their practice.

When Smith died in 1930, Riggs, in partnership with Harold Edmondson, completed his remaining projects and started her own practice. As became characteristic of her independent work, she divided her time between designs for architecture and for landscape. In landscape design, among other projects, she worked with landscape architect A. E. Hanson to redesign the extensive formal Italian garden of Mrs. Daniel Murphy in Los Angeles (1932–1933). In architecture, her domestic and commercial designs during the 1930s ranged in style from the Spanish colonial revival to the Monterey (a blend of early nineteenth-century Spanish and Anglo architecture), including eighteenth-century French, Anglo-colonial revival, and even Art Deco and Streamline Moderne.

Riggs's practice during the depression years of the 1930s was divided between Los Angeles and Santa Barbara. Along with African-American architect Paul R. Williams, she designed a number of Anglo-colonial and California ranch houses for Rolling Hills (1939–1941), a suburban development designed by Hanson. Her largest and most important commission of the 1930s was the country villa for Baron Maximilian von Romberg in Montecito (1937–1938). As with Smith's designs of the 1920s, the house played off the traditional Spanish against the Moderne.

Because of America's entry into the Second World War at the end of 1941 and the subsequent dearth of architectural commissions, Riggs turned her attention to the designing of Hollywood film sets. Her most famous sets were the Regency-style sets for the MGM film *The Picture of Dorian Gray* (1943) and the English medieval set for the MGM film *The White Cliffs of Dover* (1943).

After the war in 1945, she formed a partnership with Arvin Shaw that lasted until 1950. Much of their work of these years reflects a warm, woodsy modernism, as exemplified in the often-published Alice Irving house (1949–1951; garden by Thomas Church) and the Doyle C. Cotton house (1947–1948), both in Montecito. In 1947 Riggs and Shaw worked with Brazilian architect Oscar Neimeyer and landscape architect Roberto Burle Marx on a beach house for Burton G. Tremaine, Jr., at Serena Beach, California, but unfortunately this was never built. After Shaw's departure Riggs continued to produce modernist designs such as the post-and-beam Pardee Erdman house in Montecito (1957–1959; garden by Church).

After 1951 Riggs slowly returned to the use of traditional images. The Vedanta Temple in Montecito (1954–1956) reflects Japanese influences, while her two country houses for Wright Ludington (1957–1959; 1973) combine the Spanish and English Regency. Her elaborate garden for Daniel J. Donohue in Los Angeles was the largest of California's formal Italian designs of the 1950s and early 1960s.

Remaining unmarried, architecture became her life, and in addition to her practice Riggs was active in the American Institute of Architects, being one of the first women chapter presidents (1941, 1953) and one of the first women to be made a fellow of the AIA (1960). She was a member of the State Board of Architectural Examiners (1961–1964) and was active on a local and national level in historic preservation. She died in Santa Barbara.

• The papers and drawings of Lutah Maria Riggs are on permanent loan to the Architectural Drawing Collection, University Art Museum, University of California, Santa Barbara. A biography, accompanied by a complete bibliography, is David Gebhard, *Lutah Maria Riggs: A Woman in Architecture, 1921–1980* (1992). Other writings about her are Art Seidenbaum, "Lutah Maria Riggs Lines Up the Future," *Los Angeles Times*, 4 Jan. 1967; Harriet Rochlin, "A Distinguished Generation of Women Architects in California," *Journal of the American Institute of Architects* 66 (Aug. 1977): 38–42; Esther McCoy, "A Walk with Lutah Maria Riggs," *L.A. Architect* 5 (July 1979): 3; Stella Haverland Rouse, "Lutah Maria Riggs," *Noticias* 30 (Summer 1984): 36–39; and Terre Ouwehand, "Lutah Maria Riggs," *Santa Barbara Magazine*, Jan.–Feb. 1990, pp. 36–41, 53, and 62. Obituaries are in the *Santa Barbara News-Press*, 18 Mar. 1984, the *Los Angeles Times*, 21 Mar. 1984, *Progressive Architecture* 65 (May 1984): 29, and *Architecture* 73 (May 1984): 378.

DAVID GEBHARD

RIGGS, Stephen Return (23 Mar. 1812–24 Aug. 1883), missionary and linguist, was born in Steubenville, Ohio, the son of Stephen Riggs, a blacksmith, and Anna Baird. He was educated at the Latin school in Ripley, Ohio, at Jefferson College, and for one year at Western Theological Seminary. On 6 April 1836 he was ordained by the Chillicothe Presbytery at West Union, Ohio. He preached for a year in Hawley, Massachusetts, where in February 1837, he married Mary A. C. Longley, to whom he had become engaged while she was teaching school in southern Indiana. The couple had eight children. Her father, General Thomas Longley, was for many years in the General Court of Massachusetts, and her grandfather, Colonel Edmund Longley, had served under Washington.

Under appointment by the American Board of Commissioners for Foreign Missions, the newlyweds set out in early March 1837 for their lifelong work in the American Board mission to the Dakota (Sioux) Indians, which had begun in 1835. Journeying by stage to Pittsburgh, then by boat down the Ohio and up the Mississippi, they arrived at Fort Snelling on 1 June 1837. Stationed at Lac qui Parle, 150 miles to the west

among the Isanti Sioux, Riggs made the acquisition of the local language his first priority. He and his wife taught in small mission schools for boys and girls and held regular Sunday services with hymn singing, which the Indians loved. By 1841 a few women were baptized, as was the first Dakota man, who afterward put on white man's clothes and began to farm. In the following year the Riggses visited the East and had Dakota literature printed in Boston and Cincinnati. Upon returning in 1843 they opened a new station at Traverse des Sioux. In 1846 they moved back to Lac qui Parle. They began to develop a better understanding with the Indians, and Riggs found his preaching far more effective as Dakota became a "heart language" for him. In 1851 Riggs saw his Dakota grammar and dictionary through the press in Boston; it was then published by the Smithsonian Institution (1852). He had previously published in the Dakota language, either alone or in cooperation with others, *The Dakota First Reading Book* (1839), *Wowapi Mitawa: Tamakoce Kaga*, a primer, and *Dakota Tawoonspe*, two books of Dakota lessons (1850). A trader with Indian blood gave him crucial help in translating the books of Genesis and part of the Psalms (1842), the Acts of the Apostles, the epistles of Paul, and Revelation (1843) from the French Bible into Dakota. In 1853 Riggs published *Dakota Odowan*, a hymn book that played a central part in worship; it went through four editions in thirteen years. He also published translations of *Pilgrim's Progress* (1857) and the Constitution of Minnesota (1858).

After the accidental burning of the Lac qui Parle buildings in 1854, the Riggses and their colleagues the Williamsons established a settlement of Christianized Indians organized as a separate band with elected officers; the enterprise took the name Hazelwood Republic. A boarding school was established and the churches grew, but in August 1862 Indian anger at government policy and white encroachments led to massacres at several white border settlements. Riggs and his wife and other missionaries escaped, saved by the help of Indian friends.

Riggs was then appointed chaplain of a military force sent to pacify the territory. The Dakotas were subdued, many fleeing west, with hundreds of others imprisoned and summarily sentenced to be hanged. For three years Riggs sojourned at St. Anthony, Minnesota, making frequent visits to Indian prisoners at Mankato, Fort Snelling, and Davenport, Iowa, and lobbying for them in Washington. During their years in prison many of the Dakota became responsive to missionary ministrations, feeling that their old gods and ways of life had proven a failure and that they must come to terms with the white man's culture and religion. President Abraham Lincoln ultimately commuted most of the prisoners' sentences. When the prisoners and their families were relocated to northeast Nebraska in 1866, Riggs was active in reestablishing churches among them.

In 1865 Riggs had settled his family in Beloit, Wisconsin, where he spent winters translating amd publishing, and summers visiting the Indian churches in Minnesota and Nebraska, preaching and arranging for Indian pastors and elders to assume leadership. His account of missionary success among the prisoners was published in 1869 as *Tahkoo Wakan: The Gospel among the Dakotas*.

In 1864 Riggs had published a catechism *Dakota Wiwicawangapi Kin*, and in the Beloit years most of the New Testament, translated into Dakota directly from Greek, the Psalms translated from Hebrew, and several primers. When Mary Riggs died in 1869 their Beloit home broke up, and Riggs launched a new station named Good Will on the Sisseton reservation in South Dakota. For several summers his camp meetings led to many accessions to the church. Riggs's oldest son Alfred joined the mission in 1870 and became its leading educator. When a Presbyterian mission board was formed in 1871, the Riggs and his son remained with the American Board while others transferred to the Presbyterians; the Dakota churches, however, retained their unity.

In 1872 Riggs married Annie B. Ackley, who had served in the Hazelwood Republic, and reopened his Beloit home. Riggs and Ackley had one child. Again devoting winters to literary work, Riggs produced a Dakota first reader (1875) and a translation of Guyot's *Elementary Geography*. In 1880 his *Dakota Wowapi Wakan, The Holy Bible in the Language of the Dakotas* appeared, as well as his memoir, *Mary and I: Forty Years with the Sioux*.

When Riggs died in Beloit, five of his nine children were serving in mission fields, four among the Dakotas and one in North China.

• Riggs's papers are at the Minnesota Historical Society; his correspondence with the mission agency in the American Board of Commissioners for Foreign Missions Papers at Houghton Library, Harvard University. The annual reports of the American Board for the years 1837–1883 have numerous reports of Riggs and his work, as does the *Missionary Herald*. His other publications include "The Dakota Mission," *Collections of the Minnesota Historical Society*, vol. 3 (1880) and "Protestant Missions of the Northwest," *Collections*, vol. 6 (1894), as well as many articles in religious periodicals and newspapers. His "Dakota-English Dictionary" was printed in *Contributions to North American Ethnography* vol. 7 (1890) as was "Dakota Grammar Texts and Ethnography" (Ibid., vol. 9, 1893). An obituary is in the *Missionary Herald*, Oct. 1883, pp. 378–79.

DAVID M. STOWE

RIGGS, William Henry (22 Mar. 1837–31 Aug. 1924), collector of European arms and armor, was born in New York City, the son of Elisha Riggs, a merchant and banker, and his second wife, Mary Ann Karrick. Educated in private schools in New York and Hartford, Riggs displayed an early interest in collecting Native American artifacts. After his father's death in 1853, he moved to Europe to study engineering, a career intended to prepare him to take over the family's mining interests. He attended the Institut Sillig in Vevey, Switzerland, the University of Heidelberg, and

the Technische Hochschule in Dresden. At Vevey he was the classmate of J. Pierpont Morgan, the two youths sharing a mutual interest in collecting objects d'art. In Dresden Riggs was deeply impressed by the display in the Saxon Royal Armory, and he was encouraged in the study of ancient weapons by curators and collectors in the field. Arms and armor rapidly supplanted his other interests and became his life's vocation.

Riggs settled in Paris about 1857 and that city was to remain his home for the rest of his life, with only infrequent visits to the United States in 1858, 1863–1864, 1870, and 1913. As a beneficiary of his father's estate, he had sufficient income to devote his energies exclusively to collecting. He never married. The decade of the 1860s witnessed a rapid growth of his collection, as he made repeated visits to Spain, France, Germany, and Italy in search of medieval and Renaissance arms. He bought entire private collections as well as individual items sold at public auction and is said to have acquired during his lifetime as many as eight thousand items. The era of the Second Empire (1852–1870) was a golden age for arms and armor collecting, with Emperor Napoleon III and his superintendent of fine arts, the Count de Nieuwerkerke, setting the standards at the pinnacle of French society. Riggs played an active role in this milieu and himself entertained the leading collectors, artists, and musicians in his home.

In 1871, following the collapse of the empire, Riggs bought the luxurious house on rue Murillo, near the Parc Monceau, that had formerly belonged to Nieuwerkerke. There he continued to collect until the end of his life. With age Riggs became increasingly reclusive, and his armor was seen by few visitors. The collection nonetheless enjoyed a considerable international reputation, as numerous pieces served as models for illustrations in such notable antiquarian publications as Viollet-Le-Duc's *Dictionnaire Raisonné du Mobilier Français de l'époque carlovingienne à la Renaissance* (1858–1875) and the first volume of Victor Gay's *Glossaire Archéologique du Moyen Âge et de la Renaissance* (1887), and many of his finest arms were lent for display in Paris at the international exhibitions of 1878, 1889, and 1900.

As early as 1870 Riggs made known his intention to donate his collection "to instruct and please the art-loving people of his country." After initially considering the Smithsonian Institution, he decided on the Metropolitan Museum as its ultimate home. Riggs was a vice president of the museum during its first years (1870–1874), and his decision was influenced by his lifelong friendship with Morgan, the museum's president from 1904 to 1913, and by the guidance and friendship of the museum's curator of arms and armor, Bashford Dean. Riggs visited his native land for the last time in 1913, when he deeded his entire collection to the museum and undertook to supervise personally all aspects of the galleries designed to receive it. The collection was opened to the public in January of 1915.

Riggs was the most distinguished American collector of arms and armor of his generation. Comprising about 2,000 arms intended for use in battle or the tournament, for the hunt, or for parade, most dating between 1400 and 1700, the Riggs collection is the only one of its time to remain essentially intact and on display in an American institution. Riggs's donation to the Metropolitan Museum is especially noteworthy in that it was made during the collector's lifetime and was given without conditions; this allowed his pieces to be combined with others already in the museum, thereby ensuring a coherent and complete arrangement. Following his death at his country house at Bagnères-de-Luchon in the Pyrénées, the Riggs collection was supplemented with objects he had acquired since 1913, together with a comprehensive library on the subject.

• Riggs's papers concerning his collection, including receipts, correspondence, and manuscript catalogs, are in the Department of Arms and Armor in the Metropolitan Museum of Art; papers relating to the gift of his collection to the Metropolitan Museum are in that museum's archives. Extensive business and personal papers relating to the Riggs family, including William Henry Riggs, are in the Library of Congress. The most important biographies of Riggs, drawn largely from his own recollections, are those by Bashford Dean, "Mr. Riggs as a Collector of Armor," *Bulletin of the Metropolitan Museum of Art* 9 (Mar. 1914): 66–74, and the obituary in the *Bulletin* 19 (Dec. 1924): 300–307. The most comprehensive genealogical reference to the family is John Beverley Riggs, *The Riggs Family of Maryland* (1939). Further notices of Riggs's collection are also found in the *Bulletin* 10 (Jan. 1915): 2 and 32, and 20 (Sept. 1925): 213–15 and 288–89. Illustrations of many Riggs pieces are included in Dean's *Handbook of Arms and Armor, European and Oriental, including the William H. Riggs Collection* (1915) and subsequent Metropolitan Museum publications.

STUART W. PYHRR

RIIS, Jacob August (3 May 1849–26 May 1914), journalist and social reformer, was born in Ribe, Denmark, the son of Niels Edward Riis, a Latin teacher, and Carolina Lundholm. After studying in his father's school, Riis was apprenticed for four years to a carpenter in Copenhagen. Unable to find steady employment and spurned by Elisabeth Gortz, the young woman who in 1876 would marry him, Riis emigrated in 1870 to the United States. For the rest of his life he regularly compared the sociability and the close relationships of life in Ribe with the impersonality and harsh precariousness of American urban life.

For several years Riis found and lost a series of jobs in the Northeast—carpenter, miner, farm laborer, peddler, salesman. He was often hungry and sometimes reduced to sleeping in a field or in a police station house. By his own account, however, he was never completely demoralized. His artisanal skills; his rapid acquisition of literacy in English; his sense that a Danish American was a breed superior to the blacks, Orientals, and southern and eastern European immigrants; and his inbred self-confidence all allowed him to continue to scorn "pauperism." But he would be preoccupied throughout his life with the plight of the urban poor.

Riis had written for a newspaper in Ribe; after several abortive stints with New York newspapers, he was hired in 1877 as a police reporter by the *Tribune* (he subsequently worked for the *Sun*). He quickly demonstrated the ability to "cover," with pathos, a stream of human disasters. He was also impressed by the detailed indictment of New York slum conditions developed by Felix Adler for the Tenement House Commission.

Riis complemented his newspaper reports with lectures—often to church groups—asking Christians how they could remain indifferent to the soul-destroying character of slum life. In 1890 Riis expanded on a magazine article he had written the year before. The result was his most influential book, *How the Other Half Lives*.

For over a generation, critics like Charles Loring Brace had warned about the threat posed by the "dangerous classes" trapped in the slums of the new metropolis. Riis, too, was alarmed. But his own experiences as a casual laborer and as a police reporter evoked in him less concern about a class than sympathy for the individual, less fear of social revolution than outrage at the consequences of having to live in a tenement. The strength of *How the Other Half Lives*, and of most of Riis's books, derived from his deeply felt—always picturesque, sometimes sentimental—vignettes of the lives of slum-dwellers. (Landlords, police, government officials, if they appear at all, were usually not named.)

Riis, proud to be a reporter, felt no need to support his implied generalizations about tenement life with "statistics," or "theory," or "sociology." But he found, and relied on, a new kind of authority. A number of technical innovations in photography in the 1880s enabled Riis to take pictures in dark interiors and alleyways at night as well as in daylight. He did not claim to be an artist. His pictures were effective just because they were spontaneous and unsophisticated. Riis himself contentedly observed that his *words*, spoken or written, had made little impression until his "negatives" came "dripping from the dark-room. . . . From them, there was no appeal" (*Making of an American*, p. 176). Riis was thus a pioneer in the development of the documentary.

The popularity of *How the Other Half Lives* made it possible for Riis to give up his job as a police reporter and to devote himself to writing and to lecturing. In 1892 he published *The Children of the Poor*, which protested that the tenements jeopardized family life, cut children off from life in Nature, and robbed them of their natural innocence. For the rest of his life Riis supported "fresh-air" funds to carry children into the country. He advocated more city parks and worked to keep school playgrounds and assembly halls open for long hours daily and on weekends. A member of the Public Education Society, he campaigned both for "industrial schools" and for enriched public schools. He helped found a settlement house. At his death, Theodore Roosevelt called Riis "the staunchest, most efficient, friend the children of New York City have ever had" (*Outlook*, 6 June 1914).

For a dozen years after *How the Other Half Lives*, Riis was engrossed in the battle for "Good Government" in New York City. Riis had no difficulty identifying Tammany Hall as the enemy of every worthy reform, but he always disclaimed "political partisanship" just as strenuously as he disavowed commitment to a reformist ideology. His *A Ten Years' War* (1900) provided additional vignettes of the devastating effect of life in the tenements rather than a systematic interpretation "of the battle with the slum in New York."

Shortly after *How the Other Half Lives* was published, Theodore Roosevelt had volunteered to help Riis, and the two men collaborated for the next twenty years. In 1902 Riis dedicated to Roosevelt *The Battle with the Slum*, an account of "some battles in which we fought back to back, and counted it the finest fun in the world." Riis's biography, *Theodore Roosevelt, the Citizen* (1903), verged on idolatry. Both men, though celebrated for their criticisms of malefactors, remained optimistic about the promise of American life. Riis certainly shared Roosevelt's impatience with what seemed to them to be the indiscriminate negativism of the "muck-rakers." In his writing, Riis went out of his way to acknowledge the good deeds of at least one Tammany boss and the compassion of some tenement landlords. Neither Roosevelt nor Riis had any sympathy with socialism, and both men were fiercely patriotic. Riis's autobiography was proudly titled *The Making of an American* (1901). Roosevelt called him "the ideal American citizen."

Despite failing health, Riis continued through the last decade of his life to write and to lecture. His first wife died in 1905; five of their six children survived her. He married Mary Phillips in 1907. In 1913 he moved to a farmstead he had bought in Barre, Massachusetts, where he died.

Riis's reportage of the miseries of life in the tenements moved large numbers of Americans who shared his progressive hope for a bridge between the classes, a bridge that was built "of human hearts" and "founded upon justice."

• Major collections of Riis's papers are in the New York Public Library and the Library of Congress. The Museum of the City of New York holds a large collection of Riis's negatives, prints, and slides. Robert J. Doherty, ed., *The Complete Photographic Work of Jacob A. Riis*, was published in microfiche in 1981. For a collection of Riis's fictional stories taken "fresh from the life of the people," see *Children of the Tenements* (1903). A new and useful edition of *How the Other Half Lives*, ed. David Leviatin, was published in 1996. Louise Ware drew on the memories of Riis's children and friends in *Jacob A. Riis: Police Reporter, Reformer, Useful Citizen* (1938; repr. 1975). A more scholarly biography is James B. Lane, *Jacob A. Riis and the American City* (1974). Among the more judicious interpretations of Riis's work are Roy Lubove, *The Progressives and the Slums* (1962); Sol Cohen, *Progressives and Urban School Reform* (1964); the introduction by Sam Bass Warner to his edition of *How the Other Half Lives* (1970); and Alexander Alland, *Jacob A. Riis, Photographer and Citizen*

(1974; repr. 1993). An annotated bibliography of writings about Riis from 1889 to 1975 is in Lewis Fried and John Fierst, *Jacob A. Riis: A Reference Guide* (1977). An obituary is in the *New York Times*, 27 May 1914.

ROBERT D. CROSS

RIIS, Mary Phillips (29 Apr. 1877–4 Aug. 1967), financier and social welfare reformer, was born in Memphis, Tennessee, the daughter of Richard F. Phillips, a cotton broker and later president of the Cotton Exchange in St. Louis, and Lina Rensch. She was educated in England and France but held no college degree. She moved to New York and was acting in small parts on Broadway when, at the age of twenty-six, she met the social reformer Jacob Riis. In 1905, though she was preparing to return home to her family in St. Louis, she was persuaded by Riis to remain in New York to act as his secretary. Mary Phillips shared his interest in social services, particularly for children, and accepted his offer. She worked as his secretary until they married in July 1907 in Ipswich, Massachusetts. She was his second wife. They had one child who died in infancy, but Mary became a second mother to Jacob Riis's youngest child from his first marriage, Roger William Riis.

Before and during her marriage, Riis helped her husband with both his writing and his work at the Jacob A. Riis Neighborhood Settlement in New York. In the fall of 1911, they bought a run-down farm near Barre, Massachusetts. Mary Riis wished to turn the farm into an example of progressive modern farming. She proved to be an able farmer, planting potatoes and apple trees, reconditioning the soil, and eventually acquiring horses, cows, and pigs. Even then, she exhibited a wise investment sense, and under her guidance the farm became self-supporting. In 1913 Jacob Riis entered a sanitorium, and in 1914 he died.

At the time of her marriage Mary Phillips was twenty-eight years younger than her husband. She insisted that her husband leave most of his assets in trust to his children. Therefore, three years after her husband's death, Mary Riis realized that she needed a job to support herself. She was turned down by employment agencies but was hired by Bonbright and Company, a firm willing to employ a woman in business. She sold bonds for $75 a month. In 1919 she was asked to head the uptown branch of the company. She organized the firm's first women's department and in time had ten other women working for her selling bonds.

Though she did not have a college degree, Riis attended evening courses at New York University and was an avid reader in economics. In October 1922 she began teaching a principles of investments class at Columbia University. It was aimed at inexperienced investors, particularly women, to enable them to handle their money wisely. In the 1920s Riis also wrote several articles on investing that were published in women's magazines.

Her successful career in finance enabled Riis to live in a 22-room mansion called "Whitefields" near Bedford Village, New York. She attributed her success as a financial adviser to her ability to evaluate facts unemotionally. In response to questions about the fitness of women to compete in business, she replied, "The brain has no sex." However, she felt that a woman was required to be "at least 10 percent better than a man to achieve the same results. She will need that margin to overcome prejudice." She was one of the few brokers who, early in 1929, advised her customers to get out of the stock market or to at least use caution. She herself suffered financially during the Great Depression because of a bad loan decision.

Riis continued her support for and work among the poor. For many years after the death of her husband she served as president of the Jacob A. Riis Neighborhood Settlement. The settlement house was established for relief work and provided a play space for children. It included game and reading rooms, classes in cooking, sewing, and music, and socials, lectures, and entertainment. Over the years, newspapers published a number of letters of appeal written by her, asking for needed equipment, supplies, or money for the house. Riis believed that the true meaning of democracy and the American spirit was embodied in working for others. Her view of the role of settlement work was that it should teach people their duty, not just to themselves, but to family, neighborhood, city, and country.

Riis's continued interest in social welfare was a reason that she supported Franklin D. Roosevelt in 1936 after years of supporting the Republicans. She argued that Roosevelt, under the New Deal, was successfully relieving much of the economic hardship caused by the Great Depression. "The money spent is not going into destruction of wealth but is staying safely in this country, saving lives and courage," she said. Her concern for people extended beyond the United States. In 1938 she wrote in an open letter to President Roosevelt, "It is as an American woman who for twenty years has given her time to the study of our financial and economic problems that I venture to suggest to you that it would be to our economic as well as moral advantage to open our gates to the 600,000 harassed Jews in Germany" (quoted in the *New York Times*, 17 Nov. 1938).

Riis continued selling stocks into her eighties, working at the firm of MacQuoid & Coady and, later, at Shearson, Hammill & Company. She was honorary chair of the Jacob A. Riis Settlement at the time of her death at the Dresden Madison Nursing Home in New York City.

• Articles by Mary Riis include "How to Watch Your Investments," *Woman's Journal*, Apr. 1929, and "Is It Safe to Buy on Margin?" *Woman's Journal*, Feb. 1929. Information on her and her marriage to Jacob A. Riis and some insight into her personality can be found in the epilogue to Jacob A. Riis, *The Making of an American* (1901; new ed. 1970, with an epilogue by his grandson J. Riis Owre), and Edith Patterson Meyer, *"Not Charity, But Justice": The Story of Jacob A. Riis* (1974). See also Elizabeth M. Fowler, "Social Reformer Also Sells Stock," *New York Times*, 29 Sept. 1957. An obituary is in the *New York Times*, 5 Aug. 1967.

MARY FRANCES GROSCH

RILEY, Alice Cushing Donaldson (18 Mar. 1867–10 Aug. 1955), playwright and theater association founder, was born near Morrison, in Whiteside County, Illinois, the daughter of Sereno Edward Donaldson, a farmer and railroad worker, and (Frances) Ellen Cushing. She attended public school in Chariton, Iowa, and studied French and music at the Park Institute in Chicago. In 1889, at the age of twenty-two, she married Harrison Barnett Riley of Chicago, an attorney and the founder and president of the Chicago Title and Trust Company. They were married for fifty-five years, until his death in 1944, and had two children.

Riley developed a strong interest in the theater, even though raising a family limited her ability to attend plays. As a result, in 1901 she began inviting a few woman friends to read plays at her Evanston, Illinois, home every Thursday. The Riley Circle met regularly for play reading for almost twenty years, permitting the women to familiarize themselves with a great number and wide range of plays while in the company of friends. In 1906 the group sponsored a drama lecture course. Their profit of $154 encouraged them to incorporate into a new association, taking the name Drama Club of Evanston and embracing additional dramatic challenges. Club members not only read and discussed plays but performed occasionally for each other and even for small audiences, such as Young Women's Christian Association members. In addition, they alerted each other to top-notch professional touring productions in nearby Chicago so they could be sure to enjoy the best theatrical fare available.

The Evanston Drama Club's enthusiasm for the theater led it to criticize the sometimes mediocre quality of commercial productions traveling throughout America under the auspices of the consolidating drama syndicates. The low standards of popular burlesque and vaudeville shows also troubled the club's members. They sought a higher level of drama for themselves and the rest of the population and began to organize to improve drama standards by building a market for more intellectually challenging and morally uplifting entertainment. At the Pasadena Playhouse in California, for example, the largest audiences came for plays written by William Shakespeare, Henrik Ibsen, and George Bernard Shaw. First, the members visited other women's clubs throughout the region, persuading them to study drama, both classics and contemporary works, as their group did. Next, in a move that was to have important repercussions for American theater history, they called together sixty representatives, from clubs totaling a membership of 10,000, to an April 1910 conference in Chicago. Assembled there were delegates from a range of women's clubs who came to support the work of the budding theater organization, including the Evanston Woman's Club, the Catholic Women's League, and college clubs and civic societies from Louisville, Kentucky, and Milwaukee, Wisconsin. At this initial meeting, under the leadership of the theater lover and volunteer administrator Marjorie Ayres Best, Riley's circle launched the Drama League of America. The main focus of the new league was to unite like-minded theater enthusiasts in small women's clubs into a national pressure group for better theater fare for all American audiences. Before the Drama League of America folded in 1931, it also served to inspire and inform countless new "little theater" groups, or amateur community drama associations. The organization achieved enormous success in persuading a broad audience of the value of viewing plays that were more challenging than those afforded by popular culture and in nurturing extraordinary numbers of amateur thespians to form local drama clubs to perform plays for their own and their neighborhood audiences' enjoyment.

Riley's attraction to organized cultural activity spilled into many other areas. Broad-minded, with varied interests, high energy, and rapport with other volunteers, she became involved in the Garden Club, the MacDowell Club, the Northwestern University Guild (for writers), the Chicago Art Institute, the Midland Authors, and Omega Epsilon, the last a physical-education sorority at the Comstock School of Oratory in Evanston.

She also made time to author a variety of works. She wrote lyrics to *Songs of the Child World* (1897) for Froebel Kindergartens, setting them to music by Jessie L. Gaynor. The following year, she wrote lyrics to several *Playtime Songs* with Gaynor, including "A Tiny Fish I'd Like to Be," "Gingerbread Man," "Japanese Doll," and their most successful hit, "Slumber Boat." In addition, she published *Lilts and Lyrics for the School Room* (1907); *Welcome Spring! A Spring or Easter Program for Sunday or Day Schools, for Primary and Intermediate Grades* (1909); and, with her daughter Dorothy, *Tunes and Runes* (1925). Riley also found time to assemble numerous bibliographies on the drama for other theater lovers and run Chicago's Municipal Pier Children's Theater. She collaborated with Gaynor on an operetta, *The House That Jack Built* (1902); with William Otto Miessner on *Dryad's Kisses*; and with Frederick Fleming Beale on *Fatima*. She wrote pageants as well, including *The Lover's Garden: A Flower Masque Arranged from Shakespeare for the Tercentenary* of 1916 and *The Brotherhood of Man: A Pageant for International Peace* (1924). Some of her numerous nonmusical plays for children were included in *Ten Minutes by the Clock* (1928), in which were collected *Poet's Well*, *Tom Piper and the Pig*, *Blue Prince*, and the title play. Such works provided roles for great numbers of amateur actors and enabled them to entertain their communities.

When Riley's husband retired in 1927, the couple moved the next year to Pasadena, California, where they had formerly spent winter vacations. There she again involved herself in many clubs, to which she carried her enthusiasm for theater and in which she linked members of the Pasadena Art Institute, the Society of Artists, the Women's City Club, the Garden Club, the Town Club, the California Writers Guild, the Dramatists' Guild, and the Authors League to theater activities in southern California. It is of no small importance that Riley's retirement community was home to the renowned Pasadena Community Playhouse, the site of an ambitious amateur theater. Her involvement in the theater continued, and she began to write plays to serve the many amateur thespians she met. Some of her plays, performed regularly on the amateur theater circuit, were published in *Mandarin Coat* (1925), a collection including *Sponge* and *Their Anniversary*. *Radio* (1925), a one-act play, was broadcast on NBC. After a European vacation, she wrote *Skimming Spain, in Five Weeks, by Motor* (1931). She died in Pasadena.

Alice C. D. Riley's immense creative output fueled her era's passion for amateur dramatics, providing the vehicle for theatrical expression for multitudes of adult and children's little theater groups. A notable exponent of community cooperation, Riley ingeniously tapped the energy, creativity, and goodwill in groups and associations of her day to forge social alliances of great significance to participants.

• The Riley story must be assembled from the Riley scrapbooks in the Evanston Historical Society, Evanston, Ill.; the Riley file, Newberry Library, Chicago; and Riley's "The Incredible Years," an unpublished autobiography in the possession of her great-granddaughter Alison Blake Ramsey of Portland, Oreg. See also the unpublished manuscript at the Evanston Historical Society: Isabelle J. Meaker, "Thirtieth Anniversary of the Drama Club: October 13, 1937." In addition to the plays and children's works already mentioned, see Riley's study guide for clubwomen, *The Drama League of America: The Evolution of Social Ideals, a Modern Drama Course* (1917); "French Drama Chronologically Studied," *Drama Monthly* 1, no. 4 (1916): 198–205; "Study Course Outline on One-Act Plays," *Drama Monthly* 2 (Feb. 1918): 617–29, 2 (Mar. 1918): 639–46, and 3 (Apr. 1918): 8–13; *The Elements of English Verse* (1905); and *Rival Peachtrees*, in *Seven to Seventeen*, ed. Alexander Dean (1931). Several of her plays are collected in *The Book of Plays for Young People* (1923), *Let's Pretend* (1934), and *The Mandarin Coat and Five Other Plays for Little Theaters* (1925). See also William Blair, *Pasadena Community Book* (1947), pp. 504–5; Lillian Brand, "Songs for Children Grow out of Mother's Own Life," *Pasadena Star-News*, Dec. 1938; and Karen J. Blair, *The Torchbearers: Women and Their Amateur Arts Organizations, 1890–1930* (1994), chap. 6. Obituaries are in the *Evanston Review* and the *Pasadena Star-News*, both 11 Aug. 1955.

KAREN J. BLAIR

RILEY, Bennet (27 Nov. 1787–9 June 1853), army officer and military governor of California, was born probably in St. Marys County, Maryland. Although little is known of his parentage, his birthplace is also ascribed to Alexandria, Virginia. Riley was commissioned ensign in the elite Regiment of Riflemen on 19 January 1813 and assigned to the company of Captain Benjamin Forsyth. Forsyth was the most notorious partisan officer of the War of 1812, and Riley distinguished himself in several engagements. He rose to third lieutenant on 12 March 1813, became a second lieutenant on 15 April 1814, and was present at the 28 June skirmish at Odelltown, Lower Canada, in which Forsyth was killed. Riley subsequently commanded a detachment of riflemen who, on August 10, avenged their fallen commander by ambushing and fatally wounding Captain Joseph St. Valier Mallioux, a noted Canadian officer. One month later he fought in the 11 September 1814 defense of Plattsburgh, New York, and won commendation from General Alexander Macomb.

In 1815 Riley was retained in the peacetime establishment and advanced to first lieutenant on 31 March 1817. Between 1816 and 1817 he functioned as adjutant of the Regiment of Riflemen and was promoted captain on 6 August 1818. When the riflemen were disbanded in 1821, Riley transferred to the Fifth Infantry and commenced a far-ranging western career. In 1823 he commanded the left wing of Colonel Henry Leavenworth's Arikara expedition, and in 1825 he accompanied Colonel Henry Atkinson's (1782–1842) Yellowstone expedition. Riley received brevet promotion to major on 6 August 1828 and the following year commanded the first armed escort on the Santa Fe Trail. For defeating the Indians in two pitched battles he was voted a ceremonial sword by the Missouri state legislature. Riley was present throughout the Black Hawk War, 1831–1832; acquired his majority on 26 September 1839; and rose to lieutenant colonel, Second Infantry, on 1 December 1839. Shortly afterward he was ordered to fight in Florida's Second Seminole War and, for gallant conduct in the 2 June 1840 battle of Chakotta, received brevet promotion to colonel.

The onset of war with Mexico in 1846 afforded Riley additional opportunities for advancement. He commanded the Second Infantry during the capture of Veracruz in March 1847 and, for distinguishing himself at the 18 April 1847 battle of Cerro Gordo, obtained brevet promotion to brigadier general. As the army of General Winfield Scott approached Mexico City, Riley assumed command of the Second Brigade of General Persifor Frazer Smith's Second Division. On 19 August Riley's brigade reached Contreras, where it repulsed several determined attacks by Mexican cavalry. The following day he personally led a spectacular charge down a slope in the rear of the enemy's position, routing them. Riley was commended by Scott in the general's official report and received his fourth and final brevet promotion, to major general. At the war's end Riley led the Second Infantry back to Louisiana and Missouri, where they remained until the fall of 1848.

One consequence of the Mexican War was acquisition of large tracts of western territory. Vast, hostile, and thinly populated, it represented major administrative problems for any military force occupying it. On 12 April 1848 Riley arrived at Monterey, California, to assume responsibility for the Tenth Military District. Until the territory's formal admission into the Union, he also functioned as its ex officio civil governor. When the national Congress adjourned without authorizing formation of a territorial government, Riley authorized a state convention to draw up a constitution. He also took direct steps to maintain order by deploying troops to protect Indian tribes against rapacious settlers and miners. On 1 October 1849 Riley

turned over civil power to Peter Hardeman Burnett, the first governor of California, and confined himself to duties of the Tenth Military District. On 31 July 1850 he became colonel of the First Infantry, but soon resigned because of cancer. Riley settled in Buffalo, New York, where he died. He was survived by his wife Arbella (marriage date and maiden name unknown); they had five children.

Riley was part of an important military cadre that distinguished itself in the War of 1812 and facilitated the growth of professionalism in the years that followed. He compiled an exemplary 37-year career, of which 25 years were spent on the frontier. As the battles of Contreras and Cerro Gordo demonstrate, Riley was a combat officer of great tactical adeptness. His tenure in California, though beset by logistical and communication difficulties, was marked by administrative flair and respect for civilian authority. These qualities, coupled with his natural honesty and directness, made him an ideal candidate to lead California out of chaos and into statehood. This archtypical frontier officer was commemorated in the naming of present-day Fort Riley, Kansas.

• Riley's official correspondence is in RG 98, Records of the Tenth Military District, and RG 107, Records of the Secretary of War, National Archives. Caches of personal letters are at the Bancroft Library, University of California, Berkeley, and the Beinecke Library, Yale University. Scattered material is located at the U.S. Military Academy Library, West Point. For published material consult Otis E. Young, *The First Military Escort on the Santa Fe Trail* (1952); James S. Hutchins, ed., "'Dear Hook': Letters From Bennet Riley, Alphonzo Wetmore and Reuben Holmes, 1822–1823," *Missouri Historical Society Bulletin* 36 (1980): 203–20. The only biographical sketch remains Carolyn T. Foreman, "General Bennet Riley," *Chronicles of Oklahoma* 19 (1941): 225–44. Details on his career are in Fred S. Perrine, "Military Escorts on the Santa Fe Trail," *New Mexico Historical Review* 2 (1927): 175–93, and Dale L. Morgan, *Jedediah Smith and the Opening of the West* (1971). For discussion of Riley's brush with civilian office, consult Rockwell D. Hunt, "Legal Status of California, 1846–1849," *Annals of the American Academy of Political and Social Science* 12 (1898): 63–84, 387–408; Joseph Ellison, "The Struggle for Civil Government in California, 1846–1850," *California Historical Society Quarterly* 10 (1931): 129–64; and Theodore Grivas, *Military Governments in California* (1963). Obituaries are in the *Buffalo Commercial Advertiser*, 10 June 1853, and the *New York Times*, 11 June 1853.

JOHN C. FREDRIKSEN

RILEY, Charles Valentine (18 Sept. 1843–14 Sept. 1895), entomologist, was born in London, England, the son of Charles Edmund Fewtrell Wylde, an Anglican clergyman, and Mary Louisa Cannon. An illegitimate child, Riley was reared by his mother and her family, who were middle-class people with strong family ties and an appreciation of education. His mother selected his surname. Riley attended school at Walton-on-Thames, then boarding school in London. At thirteen years of age he was enrolled in private schools at Dieppe, France, and then in Bonn, Germany. His formal education ended in his seventeenth year, when he emigrated to the United States to join family friends in livestock farming on the prairie frontier at Kankakee, Illinois.

Riley's career in the United States had seven chapters: farm laborer, reporter with the *Prairie Farmer*, soldier, Missouri state entomologist, chief of the U.S. Entomological Commission, entomologist with the U.S. Department of Agriculture, and honorary curator of the Smithsonian Institution. His farm experience taught him about community life in rural America and the vicissitudes of farming, including losses caused by insects. In 1863 in Chicago, with the *Prairie Farmer*, he understudied its progressive editorial leaders and honed his talents as writer and illustrator. His work for the *Prairie Farmer* revealed his literary style, philosophy of insect control, and control recommendations and earned him membership in the scientific community of Chicago. His job as journalist was interrupted in 1864 by a six-month stint of military duty with the 134th Illinois Volunteer Regiment, which he spent in routine guard duty, venturing as far as Columbus, Kentucky.

In 1868 Riley moved to St. Louis to become Missouri's state entomologist. In this position he coursed the state via rail, studying the insect fauna and its injury to agriculture. Between 1868 and 1876 he published nine annual reports and promoted them through the international network of entomologists. Often cited as the foundations of applied entomology, these volumes became classics because of their appealing style, completeness, quality of illustrations, practical philosophy, and recommendations for insect control. In 1869 he became a U.S. citizen.

Based on this success, in 1877 Riley was named chief of the Department of Interior's U.S. Entomological Commission, which was formed to cope with devastating outbreaks of the Rocky Mountain locust. He and two able colleagues organized an extensive program that combined the spirit of the western explorations and the Missouri investigations. The vast geographical scope of the locust work and the skillful enlisting of cooperators from many sources established a new style of government work in insect control. In 1878 Riley was named entomologist with the Division of Entomology of the Department of Agriculture, while still heading the USEC. His free-wheeling operational style offended Commissioner of Agriculture William G. LeDuc, and Riley resigned after less than a year. Change of government in 1881 brought a new commissioner, George B. Loring, who restored Riley to office. The USEC was phased out in 1882 and its duties assumed by the Division of Entomology under Riley. He served in this role until his resignation in 1894. In 1881 Riley was invited to become honorary curator of the Department of Insects of the Smithsonian Institution. He skillfully melded holdings of the two agencies into a national insect collection, which became an invaluable resource for American entomologists.

The hallmarks of Riley's leadership of the Division of Entomology were superb organization, strong advocacy, able personnel, field agents at key agricultural locations, and comprehensive publications of new findings. Among these publications was *Insect Life* (7 vols., 1888–1895), which provided a medium for contributions from the applied entomological community and profoundly influenced the organization of professional entomologists.

Plagued by ill health from 1880, Riley was forced to delegate work to his able assistant, L. O. Howard, during his extensive absences. Despite these distractions, he retained control of even routine details. A hard taskmaster, Riley was intense, competitive, and often embroiled in controversy.

Riley, who had an international view of entomology, dispatched agents to foreign countries in search of beneficial parasites and predators and was honored for his novel assistance to the French government in control of the grape phylloxera.

Riley almost single-handedly organized in 1889 the American Association of Economic Entomologists, wrote its mandate, and through his office as Department of Agriculture entomologist published its transactions in *Insect Life*. He perceived this organization as a semiofficial lobbying group for entomology in the framework of the Hatch Act, which provided federal funds for research at the State Agricultural Experiment Stations. AAEE members continued to dominate economic entomology long after Riley's death. In 1878 Riley had married Emily Conzelman, daughter of a prosperous merchant and businessman of St. Louis; they had seven children, one of whom died in infancy. Riley was a devoted family man with strong ties to his immediate family and relatives in England. He died in Washington following a bicycle accident a few blocks from his home.

Riley's reputation as a contentious colleague and oppressive supervisor, while perhaps deserved, has overshadowed his contributions to the discipline of entomology. In this formative period of the American scientific community, he was an articulate advocate for science in support of agriculture and high professional standards. He recognized the role of publications such as *Insect Life* as the glue that held professional groups together and kept them focused on worthy goals. A skilled writer, illustrator, investigator, and advocate, Riley was without peer in overall influence on the emerging field of applied entomology and held the highest positions in this field of his day.

• A useful inventory of Riley archives is National Agricultural Library, *The Papers of Charles Valentine Riley* (1990). Clippings of entomological events of his day as reported in the popular press comprise eighty-eight scrapbooks at the Smithsonian Institution (Record Unit No. 7076). His work as the first Missouri state entomologist is well documented in his nine Missouri reports, *Report on Noxious, Beneficial and Other Insects of the State of Missouri* (1868–1876). The work of the U.S. Entomological Commission is fully reported in the five volumes, circulars, and bulletins issued by the commission between 1878 and 1890. Riley's work for the Department of Agriculture is covered by its annual reports of 1878, and 1881–1893. His work as honorary curator is in the annual reports of the Smithsonian Institution (1881–1895). The dominance of Riley's publications in the field of economic entomology in his time is revealed in Samuel Henshaw, *Bibliography of the More Important Contributions to American Economic Entomology*, pts. 2 and 3 (1889), which was published by the Division of Entomology at Riley's instigation. Assessments of Riley's life and work include L. O. Howard, *A History of Applied Entomology* (1930); James Fletcher, "Charles Valentine Riley," *Canadian Entomologist* 27 (1895): 274; and W. C. Sorensen, *Brethren of the New American Entomology, 1840–1880* (1995).

EDWARD H. SMITH

RILEY, Isaac Woodbridge (20 May 1869–2 Sept. 1933), philosopher and educator, was born in New York City, the son of Isaac Riley, a Presbyterian minister, and Katherine Southmayd Parker. Riley's father was pastor of the Thirty-fourth Street Reformed Church in New York City, and then of the Westminster Presbyterian Church, in Buffalo, New York, where the family moved in 1875. After studying at the English School in Florence, Italy, Riley returned and attended Yale University, graduating in 1892 with a bachelor's degree. He taught English at New York University from 1897 to 1898. In 1898 he presented a thesis, "The Metaphysics of Mormonism," for his M.A. in philosophy at Yale and expanded this work to earn his Ph.D. in philosophy in 1902. That same year he was appointed professor of philosophy at the University of New Brunswick.

His doctoral dissertation was published as *The Founder of Mormonism: A Psychological Study of Joseph Smith* (1902) and contained a preface by well-known philosopher and head of the Yale philosophy department, George T. Ladd. Riley's study is an exposition and critique of certain religions, most notably Mormonism and Christian Science. The book drew immediate fire; Riley presented a quite unfavorable portrait of Joseph Smith, and his work was publicly denounced by the president of the Mormon church in Salt Lake City.

In 1904 Riley accepted an appointment at Johns Hopkins University as Johnston Research Scholar under the direction of James Mark Baldwin, the well-known psychologist. Three years later he published the work for which he was best known in his own lifetime, *American Philosophy: The Early Schools* (1907), which covered the period between 1680 and 1820.

In this work Riley identifies five major schools of thought in American philosophy: puritanism, idealism, deism, materialism, and realism. The book is an expository work, that provides, in Riley's words, a portrait of "the psychological characteristics and intellectual development of each of the more important thinkers . . . a summary of his doctrines, and the transitional relations to predecessors and successors, both at home and abroad" (p. vii). Riley's study was a very important contribution to the philosophical literature because it presented for the first time material that previously had been scattered, inaccessible, or almost unknown. Among the figures discussed are Jonathan Edwards, Joseph Buchanan, Joseph Priestley, Thomas

Cooper, and Samuel Miller. The chapter on deism is unusual in that it is arranged by college rather than by philosopher, with Yale, Harvard, and Princeton all represented.

In 1908 Riley accepted the position of professor of philosophy at Vassar College, a position he held for the rest of his career. The following year he married Laura Brooks Troth; they had five children.

Riley followed up his pathbreaking work with another major study of the history of American philosophy, *American Thought from Puritanism to Pragmatism* (1915; rev. ed., 1923). In it he summarizes his earlier study, adding chapters on transcendentalism, evolutionism, modern idealism, modern realism, and pragmatism and discusses Ralph Waldo Emerson, Josiah Royce, Charles Sanders Peirce, John Dewey, and William James.

During the next few years, Riley continued to lecture and publish on topics in his discipline as well as on the subject of normal and abnormal speculative movements. One article, in particular, brought him a brief period of notoriety. In 1917 his essay "The Faith of Christian Science" appeared in the *Cambridge History of American Literature*, a work that was considered the most significant publication on American literature to date. Riley's analysis was very critical of Christian Science, particularly of the character of Mary Baker Eddy, its founder, and the light and flippant tone of the article angered many. The controversy surrounding the article reached the front page of the *New York Times* and caused the volume to be withdrawn by the publisher, G. E. Putnam's Sons, until Riley's article could be replaced with a more sympathetic study. He later published the original article in *The Faith, the Falsity, and the Failure of Christian Science* (1925), which he wrote with Frederick W. Peabody and Charles E. Humiston.

In 1920 Riley was a visiting lecturer at the Sorbonne in Paris, France, and his lectures there on representative American philosophers were published as *Le Génie américain* (1921). This book included an introduction by French philosopher, Henri Bergson, who at this time was one of the most influential and best-known philosophers in the world, an indication of the high regard in which Riley's philosophical work was held. In 1929 Riley published *Men and Morals*, a more general study, tracing the history of ethics all the way from Greek myth and philosophy up to William James. The book ends with a favorable essay on James, a philosopher who had a significant influence on Riley's thinking. Riley published his last work, *The Meaning of Mysticism*, in 1930. He died at Cape May, New Jersey.

Riley was primarily a responsible and careful historian of philosophy and an insightful critic rather than an original thinker. It is, however, beyond doubt that his major historical works represent a valuable and indispensable contribution to the study of the history and development of American thought.

• Riley's major work, *American Philosophy: The Early Schools*, was republished in 1958. His *American Thought from Puritanism to Pragmatism* was republished in 1959 and again in 1969. A limited edition of *The Meaning of Mysticism* appeared in 1975. *The Faith, the Falsity, and the Failure of Christian Science* contains an essay by Frederick Peabody describing the events leading up to the suppression of Riley's article on Christian Science. The *New York Times* article on this subject appeared on 19 Apr. 1921. An obituary is in the *New York Times*, 4 Sept. 1933.

BRENDAN SWEETMAN

RILEY, James (27 Oct. 1777–18 Mar. 1840), mariner, slave, and author, was born in Middletown, Connecticut, the son of Asher Riley, a farmer of reduced means, and Rebecca Sage, the daughter of an old Wethersfield family. Riley received a limited education, and from the age of eight he had to earn his keep helping local farmers. When he was fifteen, "tall and stout for my age," Riley went to sea, working his way up until he gained command of his own ship at the age of twenty and subsequently acquired responsibility for trading the cargoes. Sailing mainly from New York, he made "voyages in all climates usually visited by American ships" and gained "a fair share of prosperity" (*Narrative*, pp. 16–17). In January 1802 he married Phebe Miller, daughter of Hosea Miller and Mary Stow, with whom he had five children.

Like most American merchants, Riley fell victim to the Napoleonic wars. In January 1808 the French authorities seized his ship and its cargo as it took shelter from British naval vessels. Stranded in France, Riley traveled widely, learning French and Spanish. Returning home late in 1809, he tried unsuccessfully to retrieve his fortunes by trading mainly throughout the Americas. During the War of 1812 he remained at home, unable to secure command of a naval ship or privateer and unwilling to break the wartime embargo. When peace came, he secured appointment as master and supercargo of the brig *Commerce*, out of Hartford, Connecticut, and set off in May 1815 on his notoriously ill-fated voyage.

In August, as the ship sailed from Gibraltar to the Cape Verde Islands, unfavorable winds and currents swept it past the Canary Islands in foggy weather and wrecked it on the barren coast of Cape Bajador, in what later became Spanish Sahara. A band of nomadic Arabs captured the eleven survivors, stripped them naked, and marched them off into the Sahara as slaves. With skins roasted off and feet cut raw, they survived on a meager daily allowance of camels' milk, supplemented by camel urine. In this desperate situation, despised and unvalued, Riley managed to communicate with their captors and even picked up some Arabic. When the nomads chanced upon a caravan of traders returning from Timbuktu, Riley persuaded one of them, Sidi Hamet, to buy him and four of his men, and take them to Mogadore (now Essaouira) in Morocco, where he mendaciously claimed he had a wealthy friend who would ransom them. After a journey of nearly a thousand miles over difficult and treacherous terrain, the British consul in Mogadore, William Willshire, saved Riley's throat by ransoming the five exhausted, diseased, ravaged, and emaciated "skeletons of men" for $920 and two double-barrelled shotguns. Riley's weight had dropped from 240 to 90 pounds, and his bones "appeared white and transparent through their thin and grisly covering" (*Narrative*, pp. 154–55).

Returning to the United States in March 1816, Riley persuaded Secretary of State James Monroe to reimburse Willshire for redeeming both his party and two other shipmates who turned up the following year. Riley became a celebrity in Washington, where prominent public figures urged him to publish the account he had written while recuperating in Mogadore. After Anthony Bleeker had polished and simplified Riley's somewhat careless prose, the book—*An Authentic Narrative of the Loss of the American Brig Commerce*—appeared in New York in 1817, with its accuracy endorsed by other participants. Combining harrowing adventure with acute observation of an alien world, and challenging white attitudes by inverting racial relationships, the *Narrative* became an immediate bestseller on both sides of the Atlantic. At least seven editions came out within two years, some with extra corroborating material, and at least sixteen more American editions appeared between 1820 and 1859. In 1851 a million Americans then alive were said to have read the book, including Abraham Lincoln, who listed it as one of his favorite works.

Immediately following his return, Riley spent the best part of three congressional sessions in Washington as agent for James Simpson, the U.S. consul at Tangier, who had longstanding financial claims against the U.S. government. In 1818 Riley toured the West on horseback, and in 1819 he secured temporary appointment as deputy surveyor responsible for surveying lands in northwestern Ohio and northeastern Indiana. In September 1820 he bought land on Ohio's western border, moved his family in January 1821 to this "wilderness, environed by wolves and other beasts of prey," and in 1822 laid out the town of Willshire (*Sequel*, p. 21). Despite sickness and hardship, Riley and his sons raised a two-story cabin, carved out a farm, and built both a gristmill and a sawmill. Becoming well-acquainted with local Indians, he tried in 1822–1823 to secure the Indian agency at Fort Wayne but failed because his residence, only thirty miles away, did not lie in Indiana. Riley's ambitious projects soon exhausted his funds, floods destroyed his mills in 1823, and finally a severe and prolonged bout of "ague" and "phrenitis" brought him to death's door and forced his family to move him by boat to New York in July 1826 (*Sequel*, pp. 25–27).

While recovering, Riley revised and reissued the *Narrative*, rekindling interest in his tale. He took to the seas again in November 1828, trading at first with southern ports and the West Indies and then with the western Mediterranean. In 1832 he and Willshire entered a partnership to develop trade between the United States and Morocco, and on several occasions Riley acted as a go-between for the respective governments. Working strenuously at his business with little rest, he died at sea after years of failing health.

Following his great adventure, Riley believed he had been saved for some great purpose. Picking up on the antislavery message of his book, he campaigned in 1819–1820 against the admission of Missouri to the Union as a slave state. In 1823–1824 he advocated the election of John Quincy Adams specifically as a non-slaveholding president, in preference to his friend Henry Clay, and he spoke out for the cause of national independence in Greece and Latin America. But despite his powerful denunciations of slavery, Riley always insisted on the need to win the cooperation of the slaveholders and warned of the danger of releasing "a race of men incapable of exercising the necessary occupations of civilized life" (*Narrative*, p. 261). Thus he never supported abolitionism, and actively worked for the American Colonization Society and its Liberian experiment.

Although he was a large and impressive figure with a natural air of command, Riley never developed the political career his fame indicated. Serving in the Ohio Assembly in 1823–1824, he alienated some colleagues by overly hasty and ill-considered interventions, and on occasion he clumsily embarrassed causes he supported, notably internal improvements. Lacking the literary and verbal skills considered necessary at the time, he was reportedly "laughed at" when he ran for Congress in western Ohio in 1824 (Charles Hammond to J. C. Wright, 1 Oct. 1824, Hammond papers, Ohio Historical Society). Yet in his day no private citizen who had never held national public office was "so extensively or so favorably known" in the United States. In Washington drawing rooms, even in the 1830s, he appeared "an exciting object," although he had "no talents for conversation." A "kind, warm-hearted man" who had "mingled in every grade of human society," he made many strong friendships, business and personal (*Sequel*, pp. 326–27; Hunt, pp. 367–68, 372). Above all, he possessed unusual courage and initiative, a gift for understanding alien languages and cultures, and a power of close observation and precise recall. These considerable qualities made possible his great achievement: to extricate part of his crew from their sufferings in Africa, and then to produce a book that captured the imagination of his contemporaries and taught them to ponder the moral implications of his extraordinary tale.

• Riley's correspondence is scattered, but for a revealing letter of July 1824, see *Northwest Ohio Quarterly* 16 (1944): 41–44; his business papers are at the Mercer County Historical Museum, Celina, Ohio. The key document is Riley's *An Authentic Narrative of the Loss of the American Brig* Commerce (1817), later editions of which vary in small ways. References here are to the 1859 New York edition. The 1965 abridged edition, entitled *Sufferings in Africa*, contains an introduction by Gordon H. Evans that, like most brief treatments of Riley, is inaccurate. His subsequent career was described in W. Willshire Riley, *Sequel to Riley's Narrative* (1851); and in "Reminiscences by W. Willshire Riley," *History of Van Wert and Mercer Counties, Ohio* (1882), pp. 244–53. Margaret Bayard Smith's personal glimpses of Riley are in Gaillard Hunt, ed., *The First Forty Years of Washington Society, 1800–1840* (1906). For a comparison of his experiences as slave and western pioneer, see Donald J. Ratcliffe, "The Strange Career of Captain Riley," *Timeline* 3, no. 4 (1986): 36–49. The significance of Riley's tale for contemporaries is discussed in R. Gerald McMurtrie, "The Influence of Riley's Narrative upon Abraham Lincoln," *Indiana Magazine of History* 30 (1934): 133–38; and Ratcliffe, "Captain James Riley and Antislavery Sentiment in Ohio, 1819–1824," *Ohio History* 81 (1972): 76–94. For Riley as an example of the white slave experience, see John W. Blassingame, *The Slave Community*, rev. ed. (1979). For an invaluable collection of biographical materials, see Joyce L. Alig, *Ohio's Last Frontiersman: Connecticut Mariner Captain James Riley* (1997).

DONALD J. RATCLIFFE

RILEY, James Whitcomb (7 Oct. 1849–22 July 1916), poet, was born in Greenfield, Indiana, the son of Reuben Alexander Riley, an attorney, and Elizabeth Marine. The Riley home, built by Reuben Riley, was a log house on the Old National Road. Riley's mother had a poet's spirit and encouraged young Bud, as he was known, in writing, music and art. Riley's father was a lawyer and an orator of note and perhaps passed some of his platform skills to his son. Both mother and father were talented writers of verse.

Few boys have had a happier childhood than young Bud. There was excitement on all sides for this lively, bright, impressionable young lad. Boredom was never a problem. At hand was a primitive forest with all its mysteries, as well as creek bottoms, country roads, and farm lands. He was surrounded by chums who knew where the best swimming and fishing holes were and who shared in the treasured joys of childhood. The community was busy and growing, and thousands streamed westward in front of the Riley home seeking gold and new land. Young Riley was quick to note the odd and unusual. His keen mind retained in detail all aspects of his childhood.

Riley cared little for school until his teenage years, when Captain Lee Harris became his schoolmaster and directed his education, particularly his reading. Riley plunged eagerly into the works of Charles Dickens, Sir Walter Scott, Washington Irving, Nathaniel Hawthorne, and others. In addition, Harris encouraged young Riley in his poetry writing and declamation. Riley also enjoyed acting, drawing, painting, and music. His acting ability was honed first in shows in the barnloft and later with the "Adelphian Society," a dramatic club that Riley helped promote. Plays, including Shakespeare's and Goldsmith's, were performed in the Masonic Hall. Riley traveled with several medicine shows, painting ads, reciting his poetry and stories, and playing the violin, guitar, and banjo.

As a young man, Riley wanted desperately to be a poet, but poems he submitted to magazines and papers usually were returned or ignored. He sought advice from the poet he liked best, Henry W. Longfellow, and from Captain Harris. They both counseled him to write about the things around him and what was closest to his heart. He did just that. His poems celebrate everyday life and everyday people and the everyday glories of a beautiful place. Riley said, "I will sing of black haws, mayapples, and pennyroyal; of hazel thickets, sycamores, and shellbark hickories in the pathless woods."

In 1875 Riley received his first check for a published poem, and he became the unpaid editor of the local paper, the *Greenfield News*. Newspapers began to publish his poems, and in 1877 he was hired to edit the *Anderson Democrat*. Two years later he joined the staff of the *Indianapolis Journal*, and in 1883 his first volume of poetry, *"The Old Swimmin'-hole," and 'Leven More Poems*, was published.

This was the time of the Chautauqua and lecture platform. Riley became a solo performer on the Redpath Lyceum Bureau circuit, reading his poetry. Audiences loved him. In the 1880s he was hailed as one of its brightest stars. Sir Henry Irving, the famous English actor, heard Riley perform and said, "The American stage lost a great actor when Riley refused to take the profession seriously as a life work."

Riley's poems began to burst forth in large numbers, sometimes 100 per year; they were in great demand. In all, some 1,011 of Riley's poems were published; the majority (roughly 55 percent) were in dialect. Riley was often compared to Robert Burns because he frequently wrote in dialect and sang of ordinary folks in simple words. He was not only the Hoosier poet, but a true poet of the people.

Between 1890 and 1902 eleven more volumes of Riley's previously unpublished work appeared. His poems were enormously popular, and he became rich and famous, one of the first American poets to become wealthy from his writing. Although Riley never attended college, Yale University presented him with a master of arts degree, the University of Pennsylvania and Wabash College presented him with doctor of letters degrees, and Indiana University presented him with a doctor of laws degree. He was elected into the American Academy of Arts and Letters, and in 1911 the National Institute of Arts and Letters made him a member. The following year the National Institute of Arts and Letters conferred upon him the medal for poetry, a prestigious award.

At the turn of the century Riley was probably the most popular poet in the United States. James Russell Lowell called him "a true poet"; Mark Twain said of Riley's work, "This is art—and fine and beautiful, and only a master can compass it"; William Lyon Phelps said, "Riley's contributions to American folklore are imperishable, . . . he was a lyrical poet of high quality"; and William Dean Howells called Riley "one of our greatest poets." Riley particularly enjoyed the acclaims tendered him by Twain and Rudyard Kipling.

Riley never married. While he had a few serious romances, he was later to say that when he had the right girl, he didn't have the money, and when he later had the money, he couldn't find the right girl. For awhile he lived with his sister, and he also tried living in hotels and boardinghouses. In 1893 he was invited to join the household of his good friend Major Charles Holstein, on Lockerbie Street in Indianapolis. Riley agreed to do so only as a paying member of the household. The beautiful Victorian home, which he loved, was to be his home the last twenty-three years of his life. Literary greats and other distinguished visitors made up a steady stream of callers. He died in his sleep there.

After his death, Riley's fame as a national poet waned, and today he is considered a regional poet at best. Characterized by some critics as a local color versifier or as an oversentimental rhymester, he nevertheless left a lasting and memorable account of the life and times in the Midwest in the nineteenth century. His poetry is still treasured in his beloved state of Indiana.

• The largest collection of Riley papers and memorabilia is in the Lily Library, Indiana University, Bloomington. Other materials may be found in the Indiana State Library, the Indianapolis City Library, the Riley Memorial Association in Indianapolis, the Riley Home on Lockerbie Street in Indianapolis, and the Riley Birthplace Home in Greenfield. For his writings, see Edmund Henry Eitel, ed., *The Complete Works of James Whitcomb Riley* (6 vols., 1913); Donald C. Manlove, ed., *The Best of James Whitcomb Riley* (1982); and *The Complete Poetical Works of James Whitcomb Riley* (1993). The most complete biography is Marcus Dickey's two-volume biography, *The Youth of James Whitcomb Riley* (1919) and *The Maturity of James Whitcomb Riley* (1922). See also Jeannette Covert Nolan, *James Whitcomb Riley: Hoosier Poet* (1941) and Minnie Bell Mitchell, *James Whitcomb Riley as I Knew Him* (1949).

DONALD C. MANLOVE

RILEY, William Bell (22 Mar. 1861–5 Dec. 1947), Baptist preacher and fundamentalist leader, was born in Greene County, Indiana, the son of Branson Radish Riley, a farmer, and Ruth Anna Jackson. Riley's father was a proslavery Democrat, and he took his family to Kentucky soon after the start of the Civil War. Riley grew up in Boone and Owen Counties.

Riley's parents were devout Baptists, and in 1878 he underwent conversion and baptism. Riley performed a variety of farm chores from an early age, but he decided to get an education rather than remain a farmer. He received a teaching certificate from Valparaiso (Indiana) Normal School in 1879 and a B.A. from Hanover (Indiana) College in 1885. While at Hanover, Riley decided to pursue a career in law, but during the summer after graduation he felt a call to the ministry. Riley graduated from Southern Baptist Theological Seminary in Louisville, Kentucky, in 1888. That same year, he received an M.A. from Hanover College.

From 1888 to 1892 Riley served rural pastorates in Kentucky, Indiana, and Illinois. In 1890 he married Lillian Howard; they had six children. After her death, Riley in 1933 married Marie R. Acomb; they had no children. In January 1893 Riley became the pastor of Calvary Baptist Church in Chicago. There he learned of the growing theological divisions between liberals and conservatives in the Northern Baptist Convention (NBC) through contacts with modernist faculty members from the University of Chicago Divinity School. In 1897 Riley moved to Minneapolis, Minnesota, to become the pastor of the First Baptist Church, where he remained until his retirement in 1942.

Riley was a commanding figure in the pulpit, possessing considerable rhetorical skill. Early in his ministry he angered some of the wealthier parishioners by attracting members of humbler backgrounds, ending pew rentals and consolidating administrative control in his hands. Riley made himself known in Minneapolis by opposing the Spanish-American War and by supporting prohibition and the enforcement of anti-vice laws.

Riley traveled a few months each year across Minnesota as an evangelist. His travels introduced him to the many struggling congregations in the countryside and small towns. In 1902 he founded the Northwestern Bible and Missionary Training School to train men (and some women) to serve these churches. The school taught dispensational premillennial theology, emphasizing biblical inerrancy, prophecy, and the imminent return of Jesus. Dispensational premillennialism was a philosophy of history that presented a Christian counterpart to Marxism and Darwinism. The dispensations referred to various periods in history commentators saw described or predicted in the Bible. History would end, commentators said, when Jesus returned to defeat his enemies and establish a thousand-year reign on earth, the millennium. Riley taught himself the system after graduating from seminary, probably through books and tracts, and perhaps through attendance at one of the numerous prophecy conferences held in the late nineteenth century.

Throughout the early 1900s, tensions between conservatives and advocates of liberal theology and the Social Gospel divided the Northern Baptist Convention. In 1919 Riley helped launch the Modernist-Fundamentalist controversy as a founder of the World's Christian Fundamentals Association (WCFA), serving as its president until 1929. Membership in the WCFA was open to individuals, congregations, and Bible schools in the United States and Canada. Most members were from the United States and were Baptists and premillennialists. The organization's goal was to rout liberals from control of the NBC and other denominations, but by the mid-1920s this program had failed. The WCFA turned its attention to evolution, and in 1925 Riley persuaded William Jennings Bryan to help prosecute John Scopes in the Tennessee antievolution trial. The evolution crusade also stalled; the WCFA, twice defeated, was moribund by the end of the decade when Riley resigned from its presidency.

After 1929 Riley turned to the organizing and empire building that defined his real accomplishment. Devoted to training warriors against modernism, the Riley empire could be viewed as a series of concentric circles. At the center were the schools: the Northwestern Bible and Missionary Training School, the Evangelical Theological Seminary (1935), and the Northwestern College of Liberal Arts (1944). These schools trained pastors and teachers to serve within the next circle: fundamentalist churches. While the schools were interdenominational, the students and churches tended to be Baptist, mostly Northern Baptist. One result of Riley's work was that numerous NBC churches in Minnesota that had been moderate or liberal became fundamentalist. The outer circle consisted of Vacation Bible Schools, Bible conferences, and publications. Through these activities Riley established a surrogate denomination for fundamentalist Baptists in the Upper Midwest who were nominally members of the NBC. Riley's was typical of other regional empires that kept grassroots fundamentalism going after it disappeared from the national scene.

Throughout the 1930s Riley presented an anti-Semitic message. Linking Jews to theological modernism and to international communism, he even expressed support for Adolf Hitler. The idea of a Jewish conspiracy provided Riley with an explanation for fundamentalist failures in the 1920s. It also reflected the undercurrent of anti-Semitism in the Twin Cities at this time. Anti-Semitic messages largely disappeared from Riley's writings after about 1940, partly as a result of pressure from other fundamentalist leaders disturbed by his pronouncements. But even when he criticized Hitler in the 1940s, he did not denounce the Nazi leader's Jewish policies, and he never repudiated his anti-Semitic statements. Riley also shifted his political allegiance from the Democratic to the Republican party, opposing Al Smith for president in 1928 because Smith was a Roman Catholic and rejecting Franklin Roosevelt's New Deal as communist.

Fundamentalist success came in 1936 when the Riley forces gained control of the Minnesota Baptist Convention. Riley himself became its president in 1944. The fundamentalists removed liberals from state boards and worked against policies of the national convention. In 1947 Riley left the NBC, and the next year, after Riley's death, the state convention also separated from the national body.

In 1947, ill and knowing he was near death, Riley appointed as his successor at the Northwestern Schools the young evangelist Billy Graham. Graham reluctantly accepted and served for almost four years before leaving to pursue his own evangelistic career. Riley died at his home in Golden Valley, Minnesota, and within a few years his empire broke apart; but his institution building helped set the stage for the late twentieth-century revival of Protestant conservatism.

• Riley's papers are in the Northwestern College Library in Roseville, Minn. Representative works by Riley are *The Finality of the Higher Criticism* (1909), *The Menace of Modernism* (1917), *The Only Hope of Church or World* (1936), and *Wanted: A World Leader* (1939). Marie Acomb Riley, *The Dynamic of a Dream* (1938), is as much Riley's autobiography as his wife's memoir of her husband. William Vance Trollinger, *God's Empire: William Bell Riley and Midwestern Fundamentalism* (1990), is a fine biography with a bibliography of Riley's works. C. Allyn Russell, *Voices of American Fundamen-*

talism (1976), has a good chapter on Riley. George Marsden, *Fundamentalism and American Culture* (1980), is a thoughtful interpretation of the movement.

STUART D. HOBBS

RIMMER, Harry (9 Sept. 1890–19 Mar. 1952), itinerant evangelist and sometime pastor, was born in San Francisco, California, the son of English immigrants William Henry Rimmer and Katherine Duncan. Rimmer's father died shortly afterward, and his mother married a widower named Stubbs, who turned out to be a lazy, unfaithful husband who often beat Rimmer and his mother. When Stubbs abandoned his wife a few years later, Rimmer, who had been expelled from school in third grade for poor behavior, hunted game for cash and worked as a laborer. An engineer whom he met while working in a mining camp saw potential in the young Rimmer, who was always reading books despite his lack of formal education. He encouraged Rimmer to study science, helped him form a reading list, and suggested that entering the military would be a good avenue to obtain an education. Thus, in 1908 Rimmer enlisted in the army, serving in the Coast Artillery until 1911 or 1912 and learning to box well enough to win several intraservice matches and to fight for purses on the side.

Shortly after his discharge, Rimmer earned a nearly perfect score on an entrance examination at the Hahnemann Medical College in San Francisco, a homeopathic school where he completed one or two semesters before dropping out for financial reasons. While returning from a prize fight one night, probably on New Year's Day, 1913, Rimmer was converted to Christianity at a street meeting in San Francisco. He gave up boxing, decided to become a missionary, enrolled for a semester at San Francisco Bible College, and began preaching on the waterfront. There he met Mignon Brandon of Oakland, California, a fellow student who accompanied him to evangelistic meetings. They were married in 1915 and had three children.

Late in 1915, Rimmer moved to southern California in order to become pastor of the Friends Church in Lindsay. The next year he accepted a similar post at the First Friends Church of Los Angeles, a job he combined with evangelistic work for the Young Men's Christian Association (YMCA). Meanwhile, he ended his formal education with single semesters at Whittier College and the Bible Institute of Los Angeles, never earning enough credits to obtain a degree.

In 1919 Rimmer gave up his pulpit to focus entirely on his work for the YMCA. Young men, especially students and servicemen, would be the focus of his ministry for the next fifteen years. But he had not forgotten his interest in science: indeed, his conviction that science supported the literal truth of the Bible at several points was the distinguishing characteristic of his career as an evangelist. Although other fundamentalist leaders of his generation also spoke against the theory of evolution and used what they took for genuine science in support of the Bible, only Rimmer sought to establish himself as a "scientist" with "cre-dentials" appropriate to the role. In March 1921, with financial backing from a few friends, he made himself president of the Research Science Bureau, an august façade for a one-man team working out of a backyard shed that was little more than a darkroom.

Under the auspices of the bureau, Rimmer published more than two dozen pamphlets and thirty books, while giving thousands of lectures, sermons, and debates at schools, colleges, churches, public auditoriums, and other locations. Although he also spoke and wrote on traditional biblical topics, such as salvation and prophecy, he gained his national reputation from his sermons (later published as books) on science and the Bible, often delivered in a series over several days at large urban churches (including Calvary Baptist Church in New York City, Church of the Open Door in Los Angeles, and Arch Street Methodist Church in Philadelphia) or, during the summer, at various fundamentalist Bible conferences throughout the nation. His extensive travels continued even after he was installed in 1934 as pastor of the First Presbyterian Church of Duluth, Minnesota, an important conservative pulpit with heavy responsibilities that only increased two years later when he became moderator of the Duluth Presbytery. Eventually his absences undermined his effectiveness, and he resigned in 1939, moving to New York City and resuming his itinerant ministry full time.

During World War II, Rimmer worked at a Christian recreation center for soldiers near Fort Dix, New Jersey, headed by an evangelist from Philadelphia, Pennsylvania, George A. Palmer. He continued to work closely with Palmer after the war on various aspects of Palmer's Morning Cheer ministry, until shortly before he died, at home, in Pacific Palisades, California, where he had moved in the late 1940s.

Rimmer was the most visible antievolutionist in America after the death of William Jennings Bryan in 1925. He viewed himself as a champion for the Bible, someone willing and able to defend fundamentalist Christian beliefs against the assaults of biblical critics, scientists, and other academics, whom he loved to ridicule, bait, and debate. His sarcasm, simplicity, and pugilistic manner endeared him to many who were put off by the smug sophistication and secular ways of thinking of many academic professionals. Through his many books (the most famous being *The Theory of Evolution and the Facts of Science* [1935], *The Harmony of Science and Scripture* [1936], and *Modern Science and the Genesis Record* [1937]), pamphlets, and personal appearances, Rimmer reached millions of Americans and ultimately inspired the antievolutionism of the self-styled scientific creationists of the postwar generation, led by Henry Morris.

• No archive of Rimmer's papers exists. The many letters he wrote to his wife were destroyed after she wrote *Fire Inside: The Harry Rimmer Story* (1968), which quotes extensively from them and is therefore a crucial source. Rimmer's biographical novel of his father, *In the Fullness of Time* (1948), reprinted as *Harry* (1973), is useful for background information. For details of his life and a list of his publications, see Roger Daniel Schultz, "All Things Made New: The Evolving Fundamentalism of Harry Rimmer, 1890–1952," (Ph.D. diss., Univ. of Arkansas, 1989). For short biographies that emphasize Rimmer's career as an antievolutionist, see the introduction to *The Antievolution Pamphlets of Harry Rimmer*, ed. Edward B. Davis (1995), and Ronald L. Numbers, *The Creationists* (1992), pp. 60–71. Rimmer's activity as a folk scientist and his tactics as a debater are examined in two articles by Edward B. Davis, "A Whale of a Tale: Fundamentalist Fish Stories," *Perspectives on Science and Christian Faith* 43 (Dec. 1991): 224–37, and "Fundamentalism and Folk Science between the Wars," *Religion and American Culture* 5 (Summer 1995): 217–48.

EDWARD B. DAVIS

RIMMER, William (20 Feb. 1816–20 Aug. 1879), artist and teacher, was born in Liverpool, England, the son of Thomas Simon Rimmer, a shoemaker and laborer, and Mary Elizabeth Borroughs. His father believed himself to be the younger son of Louis XVI and rightful heir to the throne of France after the death of his older brother in 1789. This supposed royal heritage, which is historically unverifiable, provided the source for recurring themes and motifs in Rimmer's later work. Rimmer was brought to the United States in 1818 and never returned to Europe. Raised in poverty, he spent most of his life eking out a living to support himself and his large family. In 1840 he married Mary Hazard Corey Peabody, with whom he had eight children. Rimmer was virtually unknown as an artist until he was forty-five. Partially educated by his father and partially self-taught, his diverse activities and talents extended beyond those of sculptor, painter, draftsman, printmaker, and teacher to include writer and physician. A learned anatomist, Rimmer practiced medicine in the Boston area from the late 1840s to the early 1860s, and through his study of art anatomy, he fashioned a personal grammar of form in which the male nude became a metaphor for themes of heroic struggle.

In addition to lecturing on art anatomy in Boston, New York, Providence, and other East Coast cities during the 1860s and 1870s, Rimmer served as director of the School of Design for Women at Cooper Union in New York from 1866 to 1870. He published two highly illustrated and important books—*Elements of Design* (1864) and *Art Anatomy* (1877)—and taught several of the next generation's major artists, notably John La Farge and Daniel Chester French.

Rimmer was familiar with European artistic traditions, and his work reveals the influence of Michelangelo, William Blake, Antonio Canova, Antoine Barye, Gustave Doré, and Jean Léon Gérôme. Rimmer's art and writings—particularly the *Art Anatomy* drawings—evince his awareness of contemporary scientific and pseudoscientific areas of investigation, including physiognomy, phrenology, typology, comparative anatomy, and Darwinian thought. Far from being derivative, most of Rimmer's sculptures, paintings, drawings, and prints exhibit creative assimilation of their divergent thematic and formal sources. His

books and teaching earned him many admirers: the sculptors Gutzon Borglum and Leonard Baskin rank among Rimmer's most enthusiastic exponents during the twentieth century.

Only about two-thirds of Rimmer's approximately 600 known works have been traced, and the quality of most of those that survive is high; several of these works are located at the Boston Museum of Fine Arts. Although Rimmer was especially well known in the Boston area after 1860, fewer than a quarter of his works were commissions. He was not well paid even for such works as his only surviving public monument, the granite statue of Alexander Hamilton on Commonwealth Avenue in Boston (1865), and his drawings for the eighty-one plates in *Art Anatomy*. His gypsum statuette *Seated Man* (1831) was the first nude sculpture in the United States. With his *Head of a Woman* (c. 1859) and bust of St. Stephen (1860), Rimmer became probably the first American sculptor to create granite carvings for other than utilitarian purposes.

Rimmer's emphasis on and exploration of powerfully expressive anatomy, dynamic composition, and animated surfaces are evidenced in his finest sculptures—*Seated Man, St. Stephen, Falling Gladiator* (1861), *Dying Centaur* (1869), *Fighting Lions* (c. 1871), and the plaster *Torso* (1877). His sculptures foreshadow the work of the great French Romantic sculptor Auguste Rodin and are a fitting embodiment of Rimmer's repeated statement that "anatomy is the only subject."

In both subject and style, Rimmer's paintings reflect the influence of such English artists as Charles Robert Leslie and such American artists as William Morris Hunt. Similarly, his well-known *Flight and Pursuit* (1872) and *Sunset/Contemplation* (1876) are comparable to the works of Washington Allston and Albert Pinkham Ryder.

Rimmer was once seen as a predominantly enigmatic and isolated artist, but scholars are increasingly recognizing his special achievements in the context of his own time. Although an amateur in many respects, he is recognized today as one of the most gifted sculptors of his generation in the United States, a painter of compelling and evocative images, a powerful and imaginative draftsman, and an inspiring teacher. Rimmer died in South Milford, Massachusetts.

• Letters to Rimmer from his patron, Stephen Higginson Perkins, as well as Rimmer's manuscripts of his philosophical narrative "Stephen and Phillip" and of his poetry, are at the Boston Medical Library in the Francis A. Countway Library of Medicine. Rimmer's musical manuscripts are housed in Special Collections at the Oberlin College Library. Because of its publication during the artist's proximate lifetime, Truman H. Bartlett, *The Art Life of William Rimmer: Sculptor, Painter and Physician* (1882; repr. 1970), is a useful study. Lincoln Kirstein, "Who Was Dr. Rimmer?" *Town & Country*, July 1946, pp. 72–73, 118, 132–33, and an exhibition catalog from the Whitney Museum of American Art entitled *William Rimmer, 1816–1879* (1945) further amplify knowledge of Rimmer's art and life. The most detailed and comprehensive study of Rimmer's life and work is Jeffrey

Weidman, "William Rimmer: Critical Catalogue Raisonné" (Ph.D. diss., Indiana Univ., 1982). Also informative are Weidman, "William Rimmer: Creative Imagination and Daemonic Power," in *The Art Institute of Chicago Centennial Lectures: Museum Studies 10* (1983), pp. 146–63; and the exhibition catalog for the Brockton Art Museum/Fuller Memorial entitled *William Rimmer: A Yankee Michelangelo* (1985).

JEFFREY WEIDMAN

RIND, Clementina (1740?–25 Sept. 1774), colonial printer and editor of the *Virginia Gazette*. Little is known of her childhood and early adult years. She is thought to have been a native of Maryland, although no record of her birth or marriage is extant. Her husband, William, was apprenticed as a young boy to the owner and publisher of the *Maryland Gazette*; he became a partner in the firm in 1758. After her marriage, Rind would have had easy access to her husband's circulating library; through it she would have been exposed to his political views as well as those of the most popular writers and thinkers of her time.

In 1765 the Rinds moved to Williamsburg, Virginia, at the urging of Thomas Jefferson. In the aftermath of the Stamp Act crisis, the editor of the first *Virginia Gazette* had been under the control of the royal governor and would not print attacks on the Stamp Act in the newspaper. Jefferson offered financial backing for a printer who would publish a "nonpartisan" newspaper or at least a paper that would publish the patriot viewpoint. William Rind accepted the offer and established his new printing office in Williamsburg on 9 May 1766. A week later he published the first edition of a rival *Virginia Gazette* under the motto Open To All Parties, But Influenced By None.

The young family lived in a brick building that served as both house and print shop, giving Rind a chance to learn the technical aspects of printing in addition to providing maternal comfort to their five children. The household also included a relative, John Pinkney.

On 19 August 1773 William Rind died and was buried with full Masonic honors in Bruton Parish Church graveyard. Rind immediately assumed full responsibility for her husband's public business. Within one week of becoming a widow, she announced plans to resume publication of the *Virginia Gazette*.

As the new editor, Rind had the opportunity to expand the paper's contents beyond the usual news accounts from foreign and domestic sources. The extant issues of the gazette that she edited include essays and poems, as well as articles with a special interest in science, philanthropy, and educational improvements. She also seems to have made a deliberate attempt to educate and entertain her female readers by publishing letters of advice to them and poetic tributes in acrostic form to individual ladies. The gazette continued to carry articles on the major political and constitutional issues of the day. As tension between the colonies and Great Britain mounted, it reported on nonimportation resolutions, resolves against taxation

by Parliament, and warnings of Parliament's encroachments upon colonial liberties.

In December 1773 Alexander Purdie, a rival printer, accused Rind of violating the paper's principles of free expression by refusing to publish a libelous piece submitted by an anonymous author. In her reply published on 30 December 1773, Rind explained that the article dealt with an incident that should be aired in a court of law rather than in her paper. She did agree, however, to print the author's writing if he would be willing to disclose his name.

Rind's management of the print shop associated with the *Virginia Gazette* proved so successful that in April 1774, she announced the purchase of "an elegant set of types from London." The next month, when she petitioned the House of Burgesses to be appointed to her husband's former position as printer of the colony, she was selected by sixty votes out of eighty-seven and was granted a salary of £450 per year.

In addition to publishing the *Virginia Gazette*, Rind sold books, almanacs, religious pamphlets, and operated a commercial printing business. Although only five publications have been attributed to her press, one was a work of major importance: Thomas Jefferson's *A Summary View of the Rights of British America* (1774).

Rind died in Williamsburg "after a tedious and painful illness." Her brief obituary paid tribute to her as "a Lady of singular Merit, and universally esteemed." Pinkney continued the printing business and used the revenues toward the care of her orphaned children. After his departure from Williamsburg, the local Masons assumed financial responsibility for the clothing and schooling of the Rind boys.

Although she lived roughly only thirty-four years and assumed sole responsibility for her print shop for only thirteen months, Rind made a significant contribution to her community during that time. Her legacy lies in the extant works she published that reveal a glimmer of her character—the deference she practiced in her role as public printer to the colony, her constant concern for the security and care not only of herself but of other widows and orphans as well, and her growing consciousness of the political nature of events influencing the Williamsburg community in the years preceding the Revolution.

• The available primary sources relating to Rind's life include Purdie & Dixon's *Virginia Gazette*, 25 Sept. 1774; "Inventory of the Estate of William Rind," *William and Mary Quarterly* 17 (Jan. 1937): 53–55; John Pendleton Kennedy, ed., *Journals of the House of Burgesses of Virginia 1773–1776, Including the Records of the Committee of Correspondence* (1905); Lyon G. Tyler, "Williamsburg Lodge of Masons," *William and Mary Quarterly*, 1st ser., 1 (1892): 1–33. The available secondary published and unpublished sources are Richard L. Demeter, *Primer, Presses, and Composing Sticks: Women Printers of the Colonial Period* (1979); Leona M. Hudak, *Early American Women Printers 1639–1820* (1978); Martha J. King, "Making an Impression: Women Printers of the Southern Colonies, 1767–1797" (Ph.D. diss., College of

William and Mary, 1992); Norma Schneider, "Clementina Rind: 'Editor, Daughter, Mother, Wife'," *Journalism History* 1 (1974–1975): 137–40.

MARTHA J. KING

RINDGE, Frederick Hastings (21 Dec. 1857–29 Aug. 1905), philanthropist and collector, was born in Cambridge, Massachusetts, the son of Samuel Baker Rindge, a woolen importer and manufacturer, and Clarissa Harrington. He attended public schools in Cambridge and developed an interest in travel and foreign cultures at an early age. In 1870 he traveled to California, and between 1871 and 1872 he made his way through Europe. He entered Harvard College in 1875; there his interest in North American native peoples was stimulated through contact with Frederic Ward Putnam, who was then curator of American Archaeology and Ethnology at the Peabody Museum. Because Rindge became ill during his senior year and had to take a leave of absence to Florida, he did not receive his degree until 1890. After his return from Florida, he spent eighteen months in Colorado, New Mexico, and California.

In 1881 Rindge entered the Boston commission house of Parker, Wilder and Company but quit in a few months because of poor health. During the next few years he traveled extensively in the United States, primarily in California, and spent the winter of 1883 and 1884 in the Hawaiian Islands, where his appreciation of the Pacific area and its native cultures grew. In 1887 Rindge inherited $3 million from his father and determined to aid institutions in the Cambridge area. He gave money to build a manual training school, a public library, a city hall, and land for a new high school. These donations demonstrate his generous commitment to public education. The next year he purchased fifteen acres for the Children's Island Sanitarium at Salem, Massachusetts.

Rindge moved to southern California in 1887, and on 27 May that same year he married Rhoda May Knight of Trenton, Michigan; they had three children. Three years later he purchased a 13,000-acre ranch near Santa Monica on which he built "Laudamus Farm" (destroyed by fire two years before his death), raised fruit, cattle, and angora goats, and became greatly interested in collecting tools and implements used by native peoples of the area. Rindge also invested in a variety of companies in southern and central California, all of which improved the quality of life for local residents and made money for his philanthropic interests. Among his companies were the Middle River Navigation & Canal Company, which reclaimed for farming 25,000 acres of bottomland near Stockton, and the Artesian Water Company, which was involved in real-estate and colonization efforts in the state of Sinaloa, Mexico.

Some of the religious and educational institutions that benefited from these ventures were American University in Washington, D.C., the University of Southern California, Los Angeles, Sunday schools of the South, and the Young Men's Christian Association

(of whose the Los Angeles branch he was the president). Renowned as a benevolent and honest businessman, he was a deeply religious, lifelong member of the Methodist church. Rindge built Methodist churches in both Cambridge and Santa Monica and was the author of numerous privately printed books expressing his religious convictions. One of these, published in 1889, was *Can You Read Your Title Clear to a Mansion in the Sky?*

Rindge's extensive business and religious activities did not prevent him from pursuing his other interests. Chief among these was collecting ethnographic and archaeological objects from Mesoamerica, North America, and Europe. Proud of his New England heritage, Rindge housed most of these objects in the Peabody Museum at Harvard University and gave his collection of more than 5,800 coins to the Museum of Fine Arts in Boston. To display his Pacific coast archaeological collections and the materials he had gathered on the early history of California, Rindge—who was vice president of the Southwestern Branch of the Archaeological Institute of America—built an annex to his Los Angeles home in 1905. Despite his illnesses, Rindge remained a person with a youthful spirit and vitality, a person determined to preserve objects from the past for the benefit of future public interest. He died at Yreka, California, while on a business trip.

• Several letters of correspondence in 1884 and 1903 between Rindge and Frederic Ward Putnam, curator of the Peabody Museum of Archaeology and Ethnology, are housed in the Peabody Museum, Cambridge, Mass. Information can also be found in *Class Notes*, Harvard College, Secretary's Report (1890); *Class Notes*, Harvard College, Fiftieth Anniversary (1929); and A. R. Willard, "The Rindge Gifts to Cambridge," *New England Magazine*, Feb. 1891. Obituaries are in the *California Independent*, 7 Sept. 1905; the *Los Angeles Times*, 2 Sept. 1905; *Conservative News*, Sept. 1905; *Boston Transcript*, 30 Aug. 1905; and *New England Historical and Genealogical Register*, Apr. 1906, supp.

ANNE S. HENSHAW

RINEHART, Mary Roberts (12 Aug. 1876–22 Sept. 1958), novelist, playwright, and journalist, was born in Allegheny, Pennsylvania, the daughter of Thomas Beveridge Roberts, a sewing machine salesman, and Cornelia Gilleland. After high school, disappointed in her desire to study medicine, she entered the Pittsburgh Training School for Nurses. At this time, her father's business career, already marginal, slipped further until, in 1895, he committed suicide. The next year, she married Dr. Stanley Rinehart, a surgeon, and between 1897 and 1902 gave birth to three sons.

Although Rinehart was occupied with housekeeping, child rearing, and assisting in her husband's medical practice, she found time at night to write, sending first poems and then stories to newspapers and magazines. In 1904 she published about a dozen minor pieces. Only two years later she was writing full-length mystery novels; *All-Story* serialized *The Man in Lower 10* in 1906 and *The Circular Staircase* in 1907–1908.

She began to publish in book form when Bobbs-Merrill issued *The Circular Staircase* in 1908.

America's major mass-market magazines published Rinehart's short and long fiction, as well as her articles on the American West, a favored vacation spot after her first trip in the summer of 1916. Rinehart's longest and most satisfactory publishing relationship began in 1909, when the *Saturday Evening Post* published "The Borrowed House," the first of her famous "Tish" stories.

It was through the *Post* that Rinehart found her opportunity to work as a war correspondent. Early in 1915 she sailed for England; at a time when all reporters were barred from Allied lines, Rinehart crossed the Channel and spent several weeks with the English and French armies. To cap her triumph, she interviewed the king and queen of Belgium and, unprecedentedly, the queen of England. The *Post*'s circulation soared by 100,000 as her articles, later collected as *Kings, Queens and Pawns* (1915), appeared.

By the 1920s Rinehart was already established as one of America's most successful and popular writers of fiction and nonfiction. In addition, she scored a considerable success in the theater. With Avery Hopwood she collaborated on *Spanish Love* and *The Bat* (a dramatization and modification of *The Circular Staircase*); both plays opened in 1920 and ran, respectively, for 307 and 878 performances.

In 1922 Rinehart moved the family to Washington, D.C., where her husband had taken a job with the Veteran's Bureau. Dr. Rinehart, however, was to give up the job to become his wife's business manager. Three years after her husband died in 1932, Rinehart took up residence on Park Avenue in New York City.

Rinehart's popularity continued through the 1930s and 1940s. Collections of her stories now appeared under the imprint of the new firm of Farrar and Rinehart; the company was at least partially subsidized by Rinehart as a business for her sons. Her autobiography, *My Story*, was published in 1931 as a book after it had been serialized in *Good Housekeeping* (1930–1931); it was updated and reissued in 1948. Among her most successful works in this period were such mystery novels as *The Door* (1930), *The Album* (1933), and *The Wall* (1938).

Although after World War II Rinehart's energy diminished somewhat, as did her audience appeal, she produced *The Swimming Pool* in 1952, and as late as 1953 published stories in the *Post* and *Collier's*. She died in New York City.

• Rinehart's papers are housed in Special Collections, Hillman Library, University of Pittsburgh. She published more than sixty books, primarily fiction. For a full biography, see Jan Cohn, *Improbable Fiction: The Life of Mary Roberts Rinehart* (1980), which provides details about Rinehart's writings besides those mentioned in the text. Other biographical sources include D. C. Disney and M. Mackaye, *Mary Roberts Rinehart* (1948); G. H. Doran, *Chronicles of Barabbas* (1935); G. Overton, *When Winter Comes to Main Street* (1922); and G. Overton et al., *Mary Roberts Rinehart: A Sketch of the Woman and Her Work* (1921?). There are useful references in

American Magazine, Oct. 1917; *Boston Evening Transcript*, 12 June 1926; *Good Housekeeping*, Apr. 1917; *Life*, 25 Feb. 1946; and *Writer*, Nov. 1933. An obituary appears in the *New York Times*, 23 Sept. 1958.

JAN COHN

RINEHART, Stanley Marshall, Jr. (18 Aug. 1897–26 Apr. 1969), publisher, was born in Pittsburgh, Pennsylvania, the son of Stanley Marshall Rinehart, Sr., a physician, and Mary Roberts, a former nurse who became a bestselling novelist under the name Mary Roberts Rinehart. Her royalties enabled the family to live in Vienna in 1910–1911, so that Dr. Rinehart could pursue studies leading to a specialty. Rinehart attended the Morristown School, a private New Jersey institution, and then Harvard, beginning in 1915. In 1917, when the United States entered World War I, he quit school, enlisted in the U.S. Army as a private, and went to France with an infantry division. He was commissioned second lieutenant and trained troops in trench warfare.

In 1918 Rinehart returned home, and in early 1919 he joined George H. Doran's publishing house in New York. He married Doran's daughter Mary Noble Doran later the same year; the couple had two children. Rinehart, whose father-in-law greatly admired his commercial acumen, joked that marriage to the boss's daughter enabled him to work his way down in the firm. In truth, his wealthy mother helped his position by buying him a share in the company. On his own, however, Rinehart proved himself as advertising manager, secretary, and director. From the start, he worked closely with John Farrar, who became editor in chief in 1925. In 1927, when the company merged with Doubleday, Page, & Company to form Doubleday, Doran & Company, Rinehart was one of the managers of the new organization. In June 1929 Rinehart, his brother Frederick Rinehart, and Farrar established their own publishing house—Farrar & Rinehart—with Stanley Rinehart as president and his brother as treasurer. The company issued its first four books in September, one being *The Romantics*, by the Rinehart brothers' bestselling mother. They also published *Speculation: The Wall Street Gamebook*, which challenged readers to guess how certain stocks would move on a given day. The book was a disaster since it appeared on Black Tuesday, the day of the crash of 1929. According to an office legend, 5,000 copies were printed but 5,500 were returned.

Rinehart and his partners at first sold their books by personally placing them in bookstores. By the fall of 1930 their sales totaled $46,000. They developed price-cutting strategies by selling reprinted novels for a dollar each. In 1931 they bought the Cosmopolitan Book Company, one of William Randolph Hearst's many ventures, and thus acquired profitable authors such as Faith Baldwin, Rex Beach, Louis Bromfield, James Oliver Curwood, DuBose Heyward, Fannie Hurst, Anita Loos, and Ruth Suckow. Other Farrar & Rinehart writers included Stephen Vincent Benét, Floyd Dell, Upton Sinclair, and Philip Wylie.

In 1930 Rinehart and Mary Noble Doran were divorced. In 1933 he married Frances Alice Yeatman. The couple had one child.

When the Rinehart brothers and Farrar left Doubleday, Page, they purchased not only the Doubleday, Page stock of Hervey Allen's biography of Edgar Allan Poe, which the firm had published in 1926, but also the right of first refusal of Allen's next work. This was a great stroke of fortune, because Allen had just finished writing *Anthony Adverse*, a romantic, picaresque novel that Farrar & Rinehart published in 1933 and that immediately became a bestseller. Other successes ranged from Rex Stout's Nero Wolfe detective fiction beginning in the mid-1930s to Henry Pringle's *The Life and Times of William Howard Taft* (1939). In 1934 Farrar & Rinehart also began to publish textbooks. In 1936 they tried, without success, to organize a distribution system to handle books published by university presses. In 1937 they began their Rivers of America Series, the first title being *The Kennebec* by Robert P. Tristram Coffin. In 1943 the firm received the first Carey-Thomas Award, from *Publishers' Weekly*, for developing its Rivers series, which ultimately included more than fifty titles. The editors recruited many notable authors. Struthers Burt wrote on the Powder River; Henry Seidel Canby on the Brandywine; Hodding Carter, the lower Mississippi; Donald Davidson, the Tennessee; Harry Hansen, the Chicago; Edgar Lee Masters, the Sangamon; and Stanley Vestal, the Missouri. The books, illustrated by attractive drawings and well documented, combined scientific and pictorial descriptions with relevant social history.

During World War II the publishing partners began to part ways. Farrar took a leave of absence to join the Office of War Information. Rinehart in 1942 headed the New York State "Draft [Wendell] Willkie" Committee. After the war, Rinehart bought Farrar out, dissolved the firm, and with his brother Frederick formed Rinehart & Company in 1946. Notable publications immediately followed, with Frederick Wakeman's *The Hucksters* (1946) and Norman Mailer's *The Naked and the Dead* (1948) being the most popular. In 1948 the firm broke into the college and university market with its inexpensive paperback Rinehart Editions. In 1952 it printed the first book by "photon," the innovative Higonnet-Moyroud photographic type-composing process. Throughout the 1950s its list grew less impressive. So in 1960 Rinehart & Company merged with Henry Holt & Company and the John C. Winston Company, the result being Holt, Rinehart, and Winston. Three years later, having served as senior vice president and director, Rinehart retired. Also in 1963, in an instance of an early merger by a book publisher and a communications giant, Holt, Rinehart, and Winston became a subsidiary of the Columbia Broadcasting System. Rinehart died in South Miami, Florida.

• Some of Rinehart's relatively few papers are mingled with those of his mother, Mary Roberts Rinehart, in the Hillman Library, University of Pittsburgh. Reminiscences concerning Rinehart are in Mary Roberts Rinehart, *My Story* (1931), and in George H. Doran, *Chronicles of Barabbas, 1884–1934* (1935). Rinehart's professional career is summarized in John Tebbel, *Between Covers: The Rise and Transformation of Book Publishing in America* (1987). An obituary is in the *New York Times*, 27 Apr. 1969.

ROBERT L. GALE

RINGGOLD, Cadwalader (20 Aug. 1802–29 Apr. 1867), naval officer, was born at "Fountain Rock," his family's estate near Hagerstown, Maryland, the son of Samuel Ringgold, a prominent Democrat and congressman, and Maria Cadwalader. Ringgold entered the navy as a midshipman in 1819. His most interesting early experience, probably from 1823 to 1825, was aboard the shallow-draft schooner *Weasel*, in the so-called Mosquito Fleet that effectively controlled piracy in the West Indies. In 1828 Ringgold became a lieutenant and served until 1831 in the sloop of war *Vandalia* in the Brazil Squadron. He next served from 1834 to 1835 on the frigate *John Adams* as part of the Mediterranean Squadron.

When Ringgold was asked by Charles Wilkes to be part of the great U.S. exploring expedition (1838–1842), he readily agreed. The nation's first marine exploring venture, it surveyed Pacific Ocean routes and South Sea whaling grounds and charted part of Antarctica. Ringgold commanded the 224-ton, two-year-old hermaphrodite brig *Porpoise*. The ship sailed well. With a crew of sixty-five it was the fastest in the six-vessel squadron. During the long voyage, Ringgold heeded the instructions of Wilkes, a difficult commander, even though at times this complicated the work of the scientists aboard his brig; on at least one occasion, adhering to Wilkes's instructions subjected Ringgold to ridicule by some of his officers.

But maintaining good relations with Wilkes (who, at the expedition's end, pronounced Ringgold "always the officer and Gentleman in his intercourse with others") had its rewards. Ringgold was entrusted with independent cruises and projects, and his judgment was not questioned when bad weather made it necessary for him to postpone or eliminate surveys. When Wilkes on 18 August 1840 ordered reprisals against Fijians who had killed two of his officers, he took command of one of the landing parties himself and entrusted the other to Ringgold. Ringgold restrained his impulsive men and kept at least one from being killed by shouting that they were there "to punish the natives and not ourselves."

Near the close of the expedition Ringgold helped survey the West Coast of North America, and during 1849 and 1850 he conducted additional coastal surveys in California. In 1851 he published *A Series of Charts, with Sailing Directions . . . to the Bay of San Francisco*, which sold out five printings the following year, and *Correspondence to Accompany Maps and Charts of California*.

When American merchants and their sea captains agitated for a survey of the passage from California to the Far East, Ringgold was asked to head the North

Pacific exploring expedition (1853–1856). Planned in conjunction with the expedition of Captain Matthew C. Perry, it was to explore waters north of China and Japan and to gather pertinent scientific material. Two of Ringgold's five ships and at least two of his officers were veterans of the Wilkes expedition.

Leaving Norfolk on 11 June 1853 the expedition rounded the Cape of Good Hope and sailed across the Indian Ocean on its way to "the Coral Archipelago and its approaches." From the day of its departure the expedition observed winds and currents, and while in the Indian Ocean, and especially Melanesia in the South Pacific, it charted numerous islands and shoals. When the squadron arrived at Hong Kong in March 1854, Ringgold and some of his officers were suffering from malaria. Perry, on his return to China after making his treaty with Japan, found Ringgold's fleet in disarray. Feeling duty bound to interfere, Perry ordered Ringgold home, after appointing a board of surgeons, which in August 1854 reported that he needed rest and quiet. Ringgold, who to some observers had appeared insane, grew angrier and angrier at Perry, as his own health rapidly improved en route back to the United States, where a medical board declared him completely recovered. In September 1855 a naval board that included Perry and Samuel Francis Du Pont put Ringgold on the reserve list. Infuriated, he insisted on a review of his case, which in 1857 won him a place on the active list and a retroactive promotion to captain (2 Apr. 1856).

Working under his successor John Rodgers, Ringgold's expedition continued the important work he had begun. Its plant specimens were so extensive that when joined with those from the Wilkes expedition they enabled Asa Gray, America's leading botanist at the time, to become the first botanist in the world to have a comprehensive knowledge of Northern Hemisphere plants. Certain that Ringgold bore him "ill will" and admiring neither "his morals" nor "his intellect," Rodgers, after sending charts and records to Washington, pleaded with the navy secretary to keep them out of Ringgold's hands.

Commanding the frigate *Sabine* during the Civil War, Ringgold was part of Du Pont's expedition to capture Port Royal, South Carolina, for the Union. When in early November 1861 a furious gale lashed the fleet en route, Ringgold rescued 400 marines in the steam transport *Governor*. As the steamer buried "her sharp bow deep into the trough of the sea, each plunge seemed to be her last." Displaying daring and innovative seamanship, Ringgold secured his sailing vessel to the sinking steamship with a heavy chain, and, before it parted, 30 of the marines reached the *Sabine*. One hawser fortuitously held and 30 more marines leaped to safety after "the wreck [was] hauled up on the starboard quarter" (*Official Records*, vol. 12, p. 241). Rescue efforts were suspended when the thumping of the plunging vessels threatened to sink the steamer. Early the next morning, as the storm abated, a line was passed from a boat of the *Sabine* to the steamer, enabling the remainder of the marines in groups of 15 to

jump overboard one by one and swim and pull themselves to the boat and then be rowed to the *Sabine*. All were saved except seven.

In March 1862 Ringgold in the *Sabine* searched for and found the store-and-receiving ship *Vermont*, which was drifting after suffering severe damage from a violent northwest gale. Ringgold supplied it with a main-topsail, jib, and other lost articles and worked with its crew for five days, making it sufficiently fit to sail on its own to Port Royal.

In 1862 the Life-Saving Benevolent Association of New York presented Ringgold a gold medal, and the Common Council of New York City and the legislature of Maryland commended him for "saving the lives of so many human beings." Already smarting over the attention paid Ringgold and getting wind of a proposed congressional resolution of thanks to him, Du Pont complained, "Ringgold has made more capital out of an ordinary act of humanity than has yet been accorded to any human being in this war for military services" (Hayes, vol. 1, p. 331). Despite Du Pont's fulmination, on 7 March 1864 the U.S. Congress approved a resolution thanking Ringgold "for the daring and skill displayed in rescuing . . . a battalion of United States marines" and in finding and rescuing the disabled *Vermont*.

In July 1862 Ringgold was made a commodore, and from October of that year until June 1863, still commanding the *Sabine*, he cruised the Azores and Cape Verde Islands, then to Brazil, and back to New York in search of Confederate commerce destroyers.

Remaining unmarried, Ringgold retired from the navy as a rear admiral two years before he died suddenly in New York City, after suffering a stroke at his club.

• For Ringgold's part in the Wilkes Expedition, 1838–1842, see William Stanton, *The Great United States Exploring Expedition of 1838–1842* (1975), and *Autobiography of Rear Admiral Charles Wilkes, U.S. Navy, 1798–1877*, ed. William James Morgan et al. (1978). Information about Ringgold's North Pacific exploring expedition, 1853–1856, is in *Report of the Secretary of the Navy* (1860), pp. 18, 44–48. For more on this expedition, see Allan B. Cole, ed., *Yankee Surveyors in the Shogun's Seas: Records of the United States Surveying Expedition to the North Pacific Ocean, 1853–1856* (1947), and A. W. Habersham, *My Last Cruise; or, Where We Went and What We Saw: Being an Account of Visits to the Malay and Loo-Choo Islands, the Coasts of China, Formosa, Japan, Kamtschatka, Siberia, and the Mouth of the Amoor River* (1857). Information on Ringgold's Civil War service is in *Official Records of the Union and Confederate Navies in the War of the Rebellion* (30 vols., 1894–1922) and *Samuel Francis Du Pont: A Selection from his Civil War Letters*, ed. John D. Hayes (3 vols., 1969). For information on the vessels Ringgold served on, see *Dictionary of American Naval Fighting Ships* (8 vols., 1959–76) and Henry P. Bakewell, Jr., "U.S.S. *Sabine*," *American Neptune*, 23 (1963): 261–63. A death notice is in the *New York Times*, 30 Apr. 1867, and an obituary is in the *Army and Navy Journal*, 4 May 1867.

OLIVE HOOGENBOOM

RINGLING, Charles (2 Dec. 1864–3 Dec. 1926), circus founder and manager, was born Karl Edward Ringling in McGregor, Iowa, the son of August Ringling (formerly Rüngeling), a harness maker, and Marie Salome Juliar. Charles Ringling and four of his brothers were inspired to enter show business after seeing a performance of Dan Rice's riverboat circus in 1870. Their first public performance, that same year in Iowa, was a makeshift, homespun, backyard affair that ran for just a single performance, but it was the date from which the Ringlings calculated their anniversaries in show business.

In 1882 the five brothers began their show business careers in earnest. They combined their various talents for song, dance, and comedy to produce an entire evening of entertainment that toured the nearby states as the Ringling Brothers Classic and Comic Concert Company, playing indoor engagements. Charles, something of a child prodigy on the fiddle, eventually added other stringed instruments and the trombone to his repertoire. Eventually he also learned to walk the tightrope and tumble.

The brothers' first tented tour took place in 1884. Their partner in that venture was the popular circus impresario Yankee Robinson. The show boasted three wagons, two horses, and a tent seating 600. Robinson died before the end of the tour, but the Ringlings persevered without their mentor, putting whatever profits they earned from the summer tour of the circus and the winter tour of their concert company into buying more equipment and exotic animals, the first of which was a hyena. Their first two elephants were added in 1888. Two years later the show had grown to such an extent it began traveling on its own eighteen-car train. Within three years their circus, then known simply as Ringling Brothers' World's Greatest Shows, was a serious competitor of their largest rival, Barnum & Bailey, which had been touring Europe between 1897 and 1901 while the Ringlings grew more powerful.

In 1904 James A. Bailey, P. T. Barnum's surviving partner, agreed to divide the territory between the Barnum & Bailey and Ringling shows (neither show would tour in the area designated for the other), and he sold the brothers half interest in the Forepaugh and Sells Bros. Circus. A year later the Ringlings owned that show outright and after Bailey's death in 1906 became a major stockholder in Barnum & Bailey's Greatest Show on Earth. They bought it in 1907 for $410,000 and toured the two circuses separately for a dozen years.

The Ringlings' success is credited to their ability to appear in all places at all times—which, given the fact that there were five of them, was not entirely illusionary. They had direct control over every aspect of the business and were thus able to keep track of every penny spent and earned.

In the division of labor among the brothers, Charles was first put in charge of the advertising. Although, like his brothers, his formal schooling concluded with grammar school, Charles was fascinated with words, and he used his verbal talent to create the circus's extravagant verbal style that made a virtue of grandiose exaggeration. Thus, until the size of the circus could speak for itself, the show was billed as nothing less than the United Monster Circus, Museum, Menagerie, Universal World Exposition and Roman Hippodrome. Although this approach to advertising might be construed as basically dishonest, the circus-going public not only understood it for what it was but also expected and enjoyed such excesses. The public may have been inclined to indulge such practices because in every other respect the Ringling brothers, unlike their predecessors in the business, operated a clean show, so honest in fact that it was known as a "Sunday school" show. Grafters, gamblers, pickpockets, and bunco artists, so plentiful around other circuses, were not permitted to ply their trade around the Ringling show.

In the early twentieth century Charles functioned as the circus's general manager, although he never carried that title. During the touring season he made copious notes on details that would need attention during the winter. These were recorded in what came to be called the "Book of Wonders." In later years, when success had crowned the brothers' efforts, Charles remained adamant about running a clean show and would dismiss even the most popular act if the individuals in it did not live up to high standards of sobriety and morality.

Throughout his life Charles maintained an avid interest in music, and it is through his efforts that the musical accompaniment for a Ringling performance always met the highest standard. For many years, until just before his death, he made it an annual custom to appear with the circus band in a preshow concert, playing "The Lost Chord" on his gold-plated baritone saxophone. He collected old violins, many of which he carried on the circus train. His private railroad car featured a reed organ. He and his brother Alfred T. Ringling were responsible for having created the famous Ringling bell wagon.

By the time the Ringlings decided to combine their two giant circuses in 1919, which became known as Ringling Bros. and Barnum & Bailey Combined Shows, Inc., only Charles and brother John Ringling were left to run the show, the other brothers having died. John frequently traveled the world, leaving Charles with the circus to oversee its operation. On the circus lot and in the "backyard," where the performers lived, he saw and made note of everything that was going on. He was, nevertheless, a popular and trusted figure, thanks to the concern he evidenced for his performers and laborers.

By 1876 the Ringling family had taken up residence in Baraboo, Wisconsin. Charles Ringling married Edith Conway, the daughter of a minister there, in 1889. They had two children, one of whom, Robert Ringling, ran the circus between 1943 and 1946. Charles moved his family to Sarasota, Florida, in 1911 at the urging of his brother John. Together the two men did much to bring their adopted state to national prominence, including moving their circus's winter quarters there in 1926.

In Sarasota Charles was the founder and president of the Ringling Trust and Savings Bank, the Chamber of Commerce, and the Charles Ringling Co., which specialized in real estate development. He died in Sarasota.

After 1916 Charles's fame outside the circus was easily overshadowed by the media attention paid to his younger brother John, but his contributions toward the creation of an honest, spectacular American-styled circus that was always bigger and better are unsurpassed.

• The Baraboo Public Library in Baraboo, Wis., maintains an extensive clipping file from the *Baraboo News* and *News Republic* on all the Ringlings from their beginnings in show business, while the Circus World Museum, also located in Baraboo, maintains a far-ranging collection of artifacts relative to the career of the Ringling brothers and their circus. There are several accounts of the Ringling brothers' rise to fame and fortune written by those who were either members of the family or prominent members of the circus troupe. Chief among them are Henry Ringling North, *Circus Kings* (1960) and Fred Bradna, *The Big Top* (1952). Charles Philip Fox, *A Ticket to the Circus* (1959), contains a personal history written by John Ringling and a reminiscence by Alice Ringling Coerper, a niece. Gene Plowden, *Those Amazing Ringlings and Their Circus* (1967), dedicates itself entirely to the earliest segments of the Ringling story, and Ernest Albrecht, *A Ringling by Any Other Name* (1989), takes up the story and brings it into the next generation. Earl Chapin May, *The Circus from Rome to Ringling* (1932, repr. 1963), provides many insights into the lives of the various Ringlings. An obituary is in the *New York Times*, 4 Dec. 1926.

ERNEST ALBRECHT

RIORDAN, Patrick William (27 Aug. 1841–27 Dec. 1914), second archbishop of the Archdiocese of San Francisco, was born in Chatham, New Brunswick, Canada, the son of Matthew Riordan, a ship carpenter, and Mary Dunne, both Irish immigrants. In 1848 the family moved to Chicago, where Riordan studied at the Academy of St. Mary's of the Lake, followed by two years at the University of Notre Dame in South Bend, Indiana. In 1858 he began his studies for the priesthood for the Archdiocese of Chicago. That year he was sent to Rome as one of the first twelve students at the newly established North American College, but poor health forced him to withdraw. After studying for a brief time in Paris in 1860, Riordan enrolled in 1861 at the American College at Louvain, Belgium, where he received his licentiate in sacred theology in 1866. He was ordained to the priesthood in Mechlin, Belgium, on 10 June 1865 by Cardinal Englebert Sterckx.

Riordan returned to Chicago, where he was assigned to teach canon law and ecclesiastical history at St. Mary's of the Lake Seminary. In 1868 he was appointed pastor of Woodstock, Illinois, and later that same year was transferred to Joliet, Illinois. In 1871 he was appointed pastor of St. James Parish in Chicago, where he distinguished himself as an administrator, builder, and fundraiser, qualities that led to his appointment in 1883 as coadjutor archbishop for the Archdiocese of San Francisco, with the right of succession, and titular archbishop of Cabesa in Egypt. He was consecrated bishop by Archbishop Patrick Feehan on 16 September 1883 in Chicago. He succeeded Joseph Alemany as archbishop of San Francisco on 28 December 1884.

Riordan's reputation as a builder and fundraiser was tested early, as he inherited a $600,000 archdiocesan debt, which he succeeded in retiring before 1906. In addition, he built and funded a new cathedral, St. Mary's of the Assumption, replacing Old St. Mary's Cathedral, which was located in an increasingly unseemly part of town, replete with opium dens and houses of prostitution. The new cathedral was built in a better part of town and dedicated on 11 January 1891. Riordan also provided for the creation of a local clergy by establishing an archdiocesan seminary; St. Patrick's Seminary in Menlo Park opened in September 1898 under the direction of the Sulpician Fathers.

The beginning of the twentieth century brought Riordan two legal victories. On 6 November 1900 Riordan's campaign to amend the California state constitution to eliminate taxes on church buildings was endorsed by the California voters. Two years later, the archdiocese was victorious in its prolonged dispute with the government of Mexico over the Pious Fund, a trust that had been established in the seventeenth century to fund missionary work in Alta and Baja California. When California was ceded to the United States in 1848, the fund, which had been absorbed by the Mexican government in 1842, became a source of conflict between the Catholic church in California and Mexico. After a partial settlement was reached in 1869, the case floundered until 1902, when Riordan brought it before the Permanent Court of Arbitration at the recently established Hague Tribunal. It was the first case argued before this body, and the court decided in favor of Riordan. After 1910, however, the Mexican Revolution once again disrupted the payment schedule.

For the last fifteen years of his episcopate, Riordan, burdened by the heavy demands of his missionary archdiocese, sought to obtain a coadjutor bishop to assist him in his work. On 8 February 1903 George Montgomery was appointed, but after serving impressively for only four years, he unexpectedly died, forcing Riordan to resume his search for an assistant. His subsequent nomination of Edward Hanna of Rochester resulted in a long and bitter dispute with the Vatican, which denied Hanna's appointment on the grounds that he was a "modernist." Ironically, Hanna was reconsidered and appointed auxiliary bishop in 1912 and ultimately succeeded Riordan as archbishop of San Francisco in 1915.

The main work of the last decade of Riordan's life was dictated by the great fire and earthquake that leveled San Francisco in 1906. Twelve parishes suffered severe damage, as did scores of other institutions, including St. Patrick's Seminary. Estimates of damages ranged from $2 to $6 million. Riordan was not in San

Francisco at the time of the earthquake; he was notified of the disaster while in Omaha, Nebraska. Upon his return, Riordan rallied the residents in an emotional speech to the Citizens' Committee of San Francisco in which he asserted, in the words of St. Paul, "I am a citizen of no mean city, although it is in ashes," and he vowed, "We shall rebuild." Although personally devastated by the tragedy, Riordan rallied his people, and within two years all of the earthquake-damaged parishes, save one, were reopened.

Riordan's thirty-year episcopate was one of enormous growth for the archdiocese, even with the earthquake. Seventy new parishes were established, bringing the total to 200, the number of clergy rose from 100 to 350, and numerous charitable and educational institutions were established. When Riordan died, in San Francisco, the church was firmly established there.

• Riordan's papers are housed in the Archives of the Archdiocese of San Francisco in Menlo Park, Calif. Equally important are the collections in the Archives of the Sacred Congregation de Propaganda Fide in Rome. An impressive biography of Riordan has been written by James Gaffey, *Citizen of No Mean City: Archbishop Patrick Riordan of San Francisco* (1976). Obituaries are in the *San Francisco Chronicle*, 28–31 Dec. 1914, and in a Catholic newspaper in San Francisco, the *Leader*, Jan. 1915.

JEFFREY M. BURNS

RIPLEY, Edward Payson (30 Oct. 1845–4 Feb. 1920), railroad executive, was born in Dorchester, Massachusetts, the son of Charles Pinckney Ripley, a merchant, and Anne Robinson Payson. After graduating from Dorchester High School, Ripley clerked in a dry-goods store in Boston for four years before joining the Star Union Line, a freight-forwarding firm. Quickly mastering the details of freight rates and dispatching, he accepted a higher paying position with the Chicago, Burlington and Quincy Railroad (CB&Q) in 1870. In 1871 Ripley married Francis E. Harding, with whom he had four children.

Ripley devoted himself to the CB&Q and was subsequently promoted to various positions in the Boston office. Recognizing Ripley's talents and work ethic, the management of the CB&Q named him general manager in 1888. Ripley moved to Chicago, the railroad's headquarters, and promptly found himself embroiled in a major labor dispute. He acted quickly to mitigate the carrier's reputation as militantly antilabor by trying to resolve the issues raised by the workers through negotiation rather than confrontation. When the CB&Q was restructured in 1890, company president Charles Elliott Perkins offered Ripley the position of vice president for traffic. But disapproving of the new organizational scheme, Ripley left to join the rival Chicago, Milwaukee & St. Paul as third vice president.

The St. Paul, or Milwaukee Road as it was known later, fought for business in the highly competitive Chicago-Omaha and Chicago–Twin Cities corridors. Ripley's knowledge of traffic and rate making provided the carrier with an able and experienced executive. Even as the dynamic and vigorous Ripley sought to generate revenues for the railroad, he accepted numerous civic responsibilities, helping to organize the World's Columbian Exposition in 1893 and serving as a trustee and later president of the Chicago suburb of Riverside, where he lived.

Ripley's reputation brought him to the attention of the bankers attempting to reorganize the Atchison Topeka and Santa Fe Railroad, which had fallen into bankruptcy in 1893 after more than a decade of overexpansion. English and Dutch investors, J. P. Morgan, and Boston security holders agreed that Ripley possessed the experience, personality, and leadership qualities necessary to lead this fallen giant. When the reorganized "Railroad" became the "Railway" in 1895, Ripley became its first president on 1 January 1896.

Stretching from Chicago to Kansas City, Galveston, Denver, San Diego, and Los Angeles before its reorganization, the Santa Fe had also acquired the Colorado Midland and St. Louis–San Francisco railroads prior to the stock market collapse in 1893. The lengthy and tumultuous reorganization led to it shedding the Midland and the Frisco, reducing fixed charges, and eliminating some security issues. Ripley inherited a leaner railroad but one desperately in need of modernization and vibrant leadership.

From 1896 until 1920 Ripley led the Santa Fe Railway, determined to make it the premier carrier in the Southwest. He assembled a talented team of junior executives, rebuilt hundreds of miles of mainline, cautiously expanded into new territories, built major cutoffs in Texas and New Mexico to reduce costs, and he traveled constantly over the carrier's territory soliciting traffic. His able lieutenants spent nearly $300 million on improvements, and the operating ratio (the cost of doing business) fell dramatically.

New locomotives, freight and passenger cars, yards, and shops helped produce greater revenues. Modern signaling systems, safety couplers, and air brakes on all equipment reduced accidents and raised employee morale. By 1915 the Santa Fe had become a highly profitable giant, some 11,000 miles long. Security analysts referred to the Atchison, Topeka and Santa Fe Railway as the "Pennsylvania of the West," a high accolade. Ripley was viewed as a decisive executive, but much of his success came as a result of his ability to select a highly skilled management team and then delegate considerable responsibility to it.

During the Progressive Era, Ripley responded to criticism of the railroad's rate structure by dispatching "Harmony Specials" over the line. Company executives, engineers, and agricultural specialists rode these trains and met with community leaders, farmers, and government officials to offer advice on engineering projects, farm problems, and traffic-generating ideas. He gave speeches and published articles describing efforts to lower rates and improve service. Likewise, he tried to promote good relations with employees by expanding company hospitals, building reading rooms, swimming pools, and new Young Men's Christian Associations, and providing death and disability insurance. Although Ripley sought to create a "spirit of teamwork," his institution of the "Brown System" (a disciplinary concept supposed to create greater efficiency and to provide workers with a sense of security by awarding merits and demerits based on job performance), his use of East Asian strikebreakers, and the introduction of merit pay led to labor disputes and strikes. Employees, nevertheless, referred to him as "the old man" with respect, if not affection.

Ripley created one of the nation's premier carriers, but in 1917, when the nation's railways were federalized, "the stern old lion" lost control of the Santa Fe, resigning as president in January 1920. The Ripleys wintered each year in Santa Barbara, California, so that he could play golf, a passion that paralleled his love for the Santa Fe. While Ripley often said, "I just happened into the railway business," only two years before his death in Santa Barbara, a major trade journal proclaimed him "the greatest living railroad man."

• The major collection of Ripley manuscripts and correspondence is in the Atchison, Topeka and Santa Fe Railway Collection at the Kansas State Historical Society in Topeka. Among Ripley's published writings are "The Railroads and the People," *Atlantic Monthly*, Jan. 1911, pp. 12–23, and "How I Got Customers to See My Side," *System* 29 (Apr. 1916): 339–45. Analysis of his presidency can be found in Edward Hungerford, "Edward Payson Ripley," *System* 27 (Feb. 1915): 155–59, and "Nineteen Years' Development Work on the Santa Fe," *Railway Age Gazette* 58 (25 June 1915): 1403–6 and 1465–68. Other sources for Ripley's career are Keith L. Bryant, Jr., *History of the Atchison, Topeka and Santa Fe Railway* (1974), and James H. Ducker, *Men of the Steel Rails: Workers on the Atchison, Topeka and Santa Fe Railroad, 1869–1900* (1983). An obituary is in the *New York Times*, 5 Feb. 1920.

KEITH L. BRYANT, JR.

RIPLEY, Eleazar Wheelock (15 Apr. 1782–2 Mar. 1839), army officer and politician, was born in Hanover, New Hampshire, the son of the Reverend Sylvanus Ripley, a professor of theology at Dartmouth College, and Abigail Wheelock, daughter of the founder of that school. Ripley attended Dartmouth and graduated in 1800. He studied law and subsequently established a practice in Waterville, Maine, then administered by Massachusetts. In 1807 Ripley was elected to the state house of representatives and by 1811 had succeeded future Supreme Court justice Joseph Story to the Speakership. That year he also married Love Allen of Pittsfield, Massachusetts; they had two children. Early in 1812 Ripley relocated to Portland, Maine, and was elected state senator. However, in anticipation of renewed conflict with Great Britain, he resigned from public office to be commissioned lieutenant colonel of the Twenty-first Infantry on 12 March 1812.

Once the War of 1812 commenced, Ripley was commanded by Major General Henry Dearborn to assume command of coastal fortifications in the Saco district of Maine. In September 1812 he marched his regiment from Portland to Plattsburg, New York, as part of Brigadier General Joseph Bloomfield's brigade. In this capacity Ripley accompanied Dearborn's aborted invasion of Lower Canada and wintered in Burlington, Vermont, to train his troops. He was one of the first regimental officers to recognize the need for systematic discipline and, by drilling the men along British lines, transformed the Twenty-first Infantry into a model unit. On 12 March 1813 Ripley was promoted to colonel and marched to Sackets Harbor, New York, to join Brigadier General Zebulon Pike's brigade. He was slightly wounded during the 27 April capture of York (now Toronto), Upper Canada, and restored order following the death of Pike. Ripley was present during the 27 May capture of Fort George, Niagara, and later accompanied the ill-fated Montreal expedition of Major General James Wilkinson. He fought with distinction at the 11 November defeat of Crysler's Farm and was praised in Wilkinson's official report. Consequently, on 14 April 1814 Ripley became brigadier general assigned to the Left Division of Major General Jacob Jennings Brown at Buffalo, New York. This promotion rendered him, after Winfield Scott, the second youngest commanding general in the army.

Ripley's military career had thus far proved exemplary, but his performance throughout the ensuing 1814 Niagara campaign was fraught with controversy. He openly doubted its chances for success, owing to a lack of manpower, and incurred Brown's enmity. Ripley's Second Brigade was marginally involved in the 5 July victory at Chippewa, when Brown ordered him forward too late to fall upon the British right flank. However, three weeks later, at the desperate 25 July battle of Lundy's Lane, Ripley scored a resounding tactical success by orchestrating the capture of the British battery at night. He had skillfully repulsed three determined efforts to recapture them when a severely wounded Brown ordered him to fall back to camp. The Americans, fatigued and lacking horses, could not bring off the British cannon, which were recaptured. The next morning, Ripley refused to renew the conflict with his battered and weary survivors. The Americans then fell back to Fort Erie and entrenched, but Brown angrily summoned Brigadier General Edmund Pendleton Gaines to assume command of the Left Division.

Ripley, meanwhile, was actively employed in the defense of Fort Erie. He had supervised the construction of fortifications and on 15 August bloodily repulsed a desperate British night attack. On 17 September he commanded the reserves during Brown's successful sortie and sustained a musket ball in the neck. For his Niagara services, Ripley received brevet promotion to major general, the Thanks of Congress, a gold medal struck in his likeness, and swords from New York and Georgia.

In 1815 a furor developed over the laurels accorded Ripley when Brown, who regarded him as insubordinate, publicly questioned his moral courage. A spate of affidavits and anonymous publications ensued from both sides. The contretemps escalated until Ripley demanded and received an official court of inquiry. This convened briefly in Albany when it was suddenly dissolved by President James Madison; Ripley was the highest-ranking New England war hero, and the Republicans, facing an election in 1816, did not want to further alienate that important region. Ripley emerged exonerated in most circles, although political enemies delayed presentation of his gold medal until 1834, two decades after it had been struck.

Ripley was retained in the peacetime establishment but transferred to Major General Andrew Jackson's Southern Division to distance himself from Brown. He erected coastal fortifications throughout the South but resigned his commission on 1 February 1820. Ripley thereupon took up residence in New Orleans, resumed his legal activities, and served several terms in the Louisiana State Senate. In 1834 and 1836 he was elected to the U.S. House of Representatives from Louisiana's Second District. Ripley was a strong supporter of his former commander, Jackson. As such, he favored the annexation of Texas and opposed nullification and the national bank. Declining health precluded completion of his second term, and he died in West Feliciana Parish, Louisiana.

Ripley was the most controversial military figure of the War of 1812. A fine regimental officer, his performance at Lundy's Lane and Fort Erie also suggests he was a talented defensive general. However, he was also a stubborn, opinionated individual whose recalcitrance bordered on insubordination. Throughout the 1814 Niagara campaign, Ripley's main shortcoming proved his style of command: cool and self-possessed under fire, he nonetheless leaned toward caution, which placed him at odds with aggressive contemporaries like Brown and Scott.

• Ripley's official correspondence is in the National Archives, Records of the Adjutant General, RG 94. Scattered Ripley correspondence is at the Lilly Library, Indiana University; the Clements Library, University of Michigan; the Historical Society of Pennsylvania; and the Forbes Library, Northampton, Mass. Opinions respecting his Niagara performance are in the Jacob Brown Papers, Massachusetts Historical Society. The best source of published materials concerning his activities is Eleazar W. Ripley, *Facts Relative to the Campaign on the Niagara* (1815). An anonymous article also appeared, "Biographical Memoirs of Major General Ripley," *Port Folio* 14 (Aug. 1815): 108–36, that was much criticized. Two favorable accounts are Nicholas Baylies, *Eleazar Wheelock Ripley and the War of 1812* (1890), and C. R. Corning, "General Eleazar Wheelock Ripley," *Granite Monthly* 17 (July 1894): 1–23. Modern evaluations of his career are in John C. Fredriksen, "Niagara, 1814: The United States Army Quest for Tactical Parity in the War of 1812 and Its Legacy" (Ph.D. diss., Providence College, 1993); Richard V. Barbuto, "A Fair Experiment: The Niagara Campaign of 1814" (Ph.D. diss., Univ. of Kansas, 1996); Donald E. Graves, *The Battle of Lundy's Lane* (1993); and Joseph A. Whitehorne, *While Washington Burned: The Battle of Fort Erie* (1992). Information on his postwar activities are recorded in various volumes of *The Papers of John C. Calhoun*, ed.

Edwin W. Hemphill (13 vols., 1959–1980). Finally, an excellent overview of the officer corps in which he served is William B. Skelton, *An American Profession of Arms* (1992).

JOHN C. FREDRIKSEN

RIPLEY, Ezra (1 May 1751–21 Sept. 1841), minister, was born in Woodstock, Connecticut, the son of Noah Ripley and Lydia Kent, farmers. In 1762 the Ripley family moved to Barre, Massachusetts, where Ripley engaged mainly in farm labor until he was sixteen years of age. His father, probably concerned about his inability to pass on substantial landholdings to his nineteen offspring, determined that young Ezra needed an education that would enable him to teach grammar school. Ripley studied under the tutelage of the Reverend [Eli?] Forbes of Gloucester, providing labor in return for instruction, clothing, and books. In 1772, determined on schooling that would enable him to take up a more prominent public role, he entered Harvard College. At the age of twenty-one, he was considerably older than most students. He took his degree in 1776 and went on to teach and to study for the ministry, to which he was ordained as pastor in the First Church of Concord, Massachusetts, on 7 November 1778. He served the church as its pastor for almost sixty-three years.

Ripley married the widow of his predecessor in the Concord pulpit, Phebe Bliss Emerson, in 1780. Together they had three children; in addition, Ripley at various times provided support and assistance to Phebe's five children by her first marriage and to their offspring. To judge from the accounts of contemporaries, Ripley's tenure in the Concord pulpit was in many ways unremarkable. Installed at a time when revolutionary inflation had devalued his salary, he supported himself throughout his life in part by farming several acres of valuable land that came to him through his marriage. He was the consummate pastor, knowing his flock of almost 2,000 by name and ancestry and taking great pleasure in visiting with them and instructing them in their moral duties. Such was the trust and respect that he engendered in his congregation that he is credited with healing a bitter split in the Concord church early in his pastorate and with warding off until a relatively late date (1826) the kind of split between liberal and conservative religionists rampant in New England communities of the era. He himself had been ordained a Calvinist and a Trinitarian but moderated his views over time, ending his life a Unitarian. Never, however, were the fine points of theology particularly an issue for him: not much of a scholar or a theologian, Ripley's forte was his understanding of the practical necessities of day-to-day life in a country town. When he prayed for rain, it seemed to come. When birth or death touched Concord's families, he was there with the appropriate words. In 1816 he was awarded an honorary doctor of divinity degree from Harvard College.

Ripley's memory for particulars and his interest in the history of his region led to his writing and publishing a *History of the Fight at Concord* (1827), an attempt to demonstrate that the first significant forcible resistance to the British in the revolutionary war had taken place in Concord, not Lexington, as some had claimed. During the course of his ministry, Ripley wrote about 3,000 sermons, some 16 of which were published. He was also instrumental in setting up the Concord Lyceum (1829), the first and most successful institution of its kind; in generating support for the cause of temperance, especially through his membership in the Massachusetts Society for the Suppression of Intemperance; and in assuring the success of Concord's common schools.

Assessing Ripley's place in history presents us with a curious problem: although he was the exemplar of a type of old-fashioned, patriarchal country ministry that even by his own time had begun to die out, he does not stand out as an extraordinary example of that breed. His claim to fame probably lies in the longevity of his tenure in Concord as well as in his relationship to the Emerson family, particularly to his famous stepgrandson, the philosopher and essayist Ralph Waldo Emerson. His remembrances depict him from one of these two points of view.

Those who knew him as a pastor of long standing recalled him as did Concordian G. W. Hosmer: "arbitrary and imperious but . . . a MAN, fearless in his duty and determined to walk in the ordinances of his God and Saviour, blameless" (Sprague, vol. 8, p. 120). Many of his memorialists remarked on his appearance: he wore small clothes, neckcloths, and knee buckles far into an era when they had come to seem outmoded and was both physically and temperamentally the survivor of a time long gone. Because he died in his ninety-first year, however, his eulogies were written by individuals several generations younger than himself, and few clues exist as to what his contemporaries may have thought of him. Tellingly, however, at Harvard his classmates had dubbed him "Holy Ripley."

The Emersons, particularly Ralph Waldo Emerson, provide us with a decidedly ambivalent image of the patriarch. He seems to have been generous to a fault, always contributing liberally to charitable endeavors and taking in Ruth Emerson (his stepson's widow) and her four young sons in 1814 in a period of famine and misfortune for them. "No waste, & no stint," Emerson wrote of Ripley in his journal just before Ripley's death. "My little boy, a week ago, carried him a peach in a calabash, but the calabash brought home two pears." On the other hand, the cultured and erudite Emersons seemed to think of Ripley as a bit below their station, both intellectually and socially. "I am sure all who remember . . . will associate his form with whatever was grave and droll in the old, cold, unpainted, uncarpeted, square-pewed meetinghouse," his stepgrandson remarked of him in a memoir written for the Social Circle in Concord after Ripley's death. He had "a very limited acquaintance with books," and although Emerson saw him as "manly and public-spirited" with "his house open to all men," the compliment was surely a backhanded one. For Emerson went on to

say that "he had no studies, no occupations, which company could interrupt." Ripley died in Concord.

• Letters to and from Ripley are included in various of the Emerson family papers in the Houghton Library, Harvard University, and some of Ripley's manuscript sermons are available at the Library Company in Concord. Of the several contemporary assessments, the best include Ralph Waldo Emerson, "Ezra Ripley, D.D.," in *The Complete Works of Ralph Waldo Emerson*, vol. 10 (1911); William B. Sprague, *Annals of the American Pulpit*, vol. 8 (1865); *Christian Register*, "Reverend Dr. Ripley," 9 Oct. 1841, p. 163, and "Dr. Ripley," 16 Oct. 1841, p. 167; and "Critical Notices," *Christian Examiner*, Jan. 1842, pp. 403–4. Biographies of Emerson often deal with Ripley at various points in the narrative. See especially John McAleer, "Ezra Ripley: An Old Semi-Savage," chapter 13 in *Ralph Waldo Emerson: Days of Encounter* (1984).

MARY KUPIEC CAYTON

RIPLEY, George (3 Oct. 1802–4 July 1880), reform writer, literary reviewer, and communalist, was born in Greenfield, Massachusetts, the son of Jerome Ripley, a businessman, and Sarah Franklin. After attending private academies in the area, in 1819 Ripley went on to Harvard, where his personal and philosophical education was tumultuous. He tried desperately to hold onto the conservatism his parents had encouraged, but he was also attracted to liberal ideas in social reform and theology. When his transformation did not happen quickly enough to suit his classmates, he was ridiculed in one of Harvard's student riots as "Ripley the pious, fickle as the wind, / For nine times an hour he changes his mind." When he entered Harvard's divinity school in 1823, Ripley was still trying to reconcile his inherited Calvinist beliefs with the new views that saw humanity's inward nature as the source of all beauty and truth.

Ordained in 1826, he became minister of Boston's (Unitarian) Purchase Street Church and married Sophia Willard Dana the next year; the couple did not have children. In 1830 Ripley began to publish controversial essays that represented very radical Unitarian views in the *Christian Examiner*. He quickly became a writer known not so much for his insight or genius as for ably expressing new ideas being developed in America and giving them a solid scholarly footing in British, French, and German thought. In the 1830s he published a collection of European writings as *Specimens of Foreign Standard Literature* as well as his own theological opinions in *Discourses on the Philosophy of Religion*. He also joined the Transcendental Club in 1836 with his cousin Ralph Waldo Emerson and became one of *The Dial*'s editors and contributors. However, the economic hardship caused by the panic of 1837 prevented Ripley from being as idealistically oriented as Emerson; his Transcendentalism became a philosophy engaged in social activism more like that of his friends Margaret Fuller and Theodore Parker. As he witnessed the suffering around his parish, he chastised his congregation for not responding more actively and compassionately, and he visited several contemporary experiments in communal life to study alternative modes of social organization. When Andrews Norton, a powerful Unitarian so conservative that some of his enemies called him "Pope Norton," accused Transcendentalism of being "the latest form of infidelity" in 1839, Ripley represented radical Unitarians in an exchange of controversial essays that became known as the Norton-Ripley Debate. In 1840 he resigned as minister, thus ending the formative stage of his career, and set forth to start his most famous project.

In 1841 Ripley founded Brook Farm, a six-year experiment in Transcendentalism and communal socialism that was probably more responsible for his continued fame than anything he did before or after. In one of his *Dial* articles, he wrote that "what the age requires is not books but experience, high, heroic example; not words but deeds," and Brook Farm was meant to be precisely one such example. Rather than discuss spirituality at a club, people would live it; rather than just writing about political reform, communards would practice it. Margaret Fuller in 1840 had warned that the experiment would fail because Ripley was only "a captain, not a conqueror," but captaincy was precisely what Ripley intended. Other than some general notions that Brook Farm would "combine the thinker and the worker as far as possible" and would "permit a more simple and wholesome life than can be led amidst the pressure of our competitive institutions," Ripley mostly tended Brook Farm as a garden to see what crop it could best support. Its members were expected to share in the necessary labors as they not only farmed but produced oil lamps, teapots, shoes, boots, window sashes and blinds, doors, and nature books. A school under the supervision of Ripley's sister Marianne became an important source of income, and its graduates included a prominent lawyer (Arthur Sumner), Civil War general (Francis Barlow), and publishing house founder (George Curtis).

By January 1844, however, Brook Farm had changed despite the objections of Sophia Ripley and Orestes Brownson from a Transcendentalist idyll to a socialist commune based on the ideas of Charles Fourier as interpreted by Arthur Brisbane's recent book, *The Social Destiny of Man* (1840). Ripley accepted the change advocated by about half the commune's one hundred members because it would defuse accusations of "schoolboy dilettantism" and because it would receive financial support from New York backers such as Marcus Spring, Horace Tweedy, and Ellis Gray Loring as well as favorable and extensive publicity from Horace Greeley's *New York Tribune*.

Brook Farm life became more disciplined (requiring sixty hours of labor per communard per week, which was carefully tabulated), and members were expected to promote Fourierist socialism more aggressively by lecturing and writing for journals and newspapers. In 1845 *The Harbinger* was published at Brook Farm as a reform periodical and lasted until 1849. It supported labor unions, woman suffrage, civil rights, abolition, popular education, and other specific liberal

movements, but its main ambition was to rewrite the American economic-political system and make it more socialistic. The commune attracted hundreds of visitors and much public attention. Its account books showed a respectable profit for 1844, and in March 1845 Ripley arranged for Brook Farm to be incorporated into the state of Massachusetts, but the next year it could not survive a smallpox scare and a disastrous fire that destroyed a large communal structure into which they had invested most of their capital. Ironically, Ripley had established Brook Farm as an example of cooperative living because what America needed most "was not words but deeds," yet what best survived the blaze—other than a few flower books and dilapidated buildings—was words. *The Harbinger* outlasted the commune by two years, but eventually it too succumbed, forcing Ripley to begin another phase of his career.

In the last thirty years of Ripley's life his interests were so scattered that no one event stands out as particularly noteworthy. After Brook Farm's demise, he spent some time as a journeyman writer earning only a penny a line, but soon he established himself as a man of letters. Although not as eminent in that position as Oliver Wendell Holmes or James Russell Lowell or Margaret Fuller (his predecessor on Greeley's *New York Tribune*), Ripley published thousands of essays and reviews on every conceivable topic in magazines and newspapers from Boston to San Francisco but primarily for the *New York Tribune*. As a popularizer of ideas and arbiter of public opinion, Ripley made interesting comments in passing but produced no sustained commentary. He wrote opinions on literature, reform, psychology, history, science, economics, and philosophy, he observed sweeping changes in American life from 1850 to 1880, and he regularly offered many interesting insights, but his thoughts had no cohesive development or central thesis.

Ripley appeared to welcome this more casual life after the intensity of his earlier philosophical deliberations and reform efforts. With Bayard Taylor he published *A Handbook on Literature and the Fine Arts* in 1852 and with Charles Dana a *New American Cyclopaedia* (1858–1863; reissued in 1873), and he helped found *Harper's New Monthly Magazine* in 1850. All projects proved to be as popular as they were dilettantish compared to his previous work. In 1861 Sophia died after seeming to have survived surgery. She was buried at Ripley's old Purchase Street Church, which had become a Roman Catholic parish. Four years later Ripley married Louisa Schlossberger, a woman much his junior with whom he twice toured Europe and enjoyed a bubbly social life. This former heretic and social reformer died peacefully in New York City.

Emerson had claimed that Ripley's life is a "fine historiette of the age." His life represents a "historiette" not of transcendent genius but of America's changes from 1820 to 1880 as embodied in a well-educated, intelligent, middle-class man responding sensitively to the forces that defined his times.

• Ripley's letters and manuscripts remain uncataloged and are housed in many places, including the Boston Public Library, the Fruitlands Museum, the Houghton Library at Harvard, the Massachusetts Historical Society, and the New York *Herald Tribune* files. Samples of his published articles appear in anthologies such as *The Transcendentalists*, ed. Perry Miller (1950), *Autobiography of Brook Farm*, ed. Henry W. Sams (1958), and *Selected Writings of the American Transcendentalists*, ed. George Hochfield (1966) as well as in his first biography, Octavius Brooks Frothingham's *George Ripley* (1882), half of which consists of Ripley's writings. More recent biographies are Charles Crowe, *George Ripley: Transcendentalist and Utopian Socialist* (1967), and Henry Golemba, *George Ripley* (1977).

HENRY GOLEMBA

RIPLEY, James Wolfe (10 Dec. 1794–15 Mar. 1870), soldier, was born in Windham County, Connecticut, the son of Ralph Ripley and Eunice Huntington. He was an uncle of future Confederate general Roswell S. Ripley. After getting his early education in the public schools of his county, Ripley received an appointment in May 1813 to the U.S. Military Academy. The army's need for officers because of the War of 1812 resulted in Ripley's graduation from West Point on 1 June 1814; he stood twelfth in his class of thirty and was commissioned as a second lieutenant in the corps of artillery.

From his graduation until the end of the war, Ripley served on garrison duty at Sackets Harbor, New York. He continued on duty at various garrisons until ordered in 1817 to report to General Andrew Jackson in Florida. Ripley participated in Jackson's war with the Seminoles and his invasion of Spanish East Florida the following spring. His service from December 1816 to June 1821 was as a battalion quartermaster. Promoted to first lieutenant on 20 April 1818, he transferred to the Fourth U.S. Artillery on 1 June 1821. After additional garrison duty, Ripley joined James Gadsden in 1823 as an assistant commissioner to draw boundaries for the American Indian reservations in Florida. Both Gadsden and territorial governor William P. Duval spoke highly of Ripley's performance in this task.

In 1824 Ripley married Sarah Denny; they had nine children. Ripley received promotion to captain on 1 August 1825 and spent another eight years on recruiting and garrison duty. On 30 May 1832 he transferred to the Ordnance Department, which had just been formed. Later that year, he joined the staff of General Winfield Scott, who was ordered to Charleston, South Carolina, when that state's government threatened to nullify the federal tariff act. Scott commended Ripley's service in a letter to the secretary of war, saying he had "no superior in the middle ranks of the Army . . . in general intelligence, zeal, or good conduct" (Cullum, p. 120).

After the Nullification Crisis, Ripley was assigned to command the arsenal at Kennebec, Maine. He held that post for eight years and was promoted to major on 7 July 1838. In 1841 Ripley transferred to the Springfield Armory, which he supervised until 1854. He succeeded in rebuilding the armory and making it a model facility for producing modern small arms. His efforts there during the Mexican War earned him a brevet as lieutenant colonel to date from 30 May 1848. Ripley took over the Watertown, Massachusetts, arsenal in 1854, and his promotion to the full rank of lieutenant colonel occurred on 31 December of that year. In 1855 he assumed the position of chief of ordnance of the Pacific Department in California. Two years later Ripley became inspector of arsenals.

When the Civil War began, Ripley was on an inspection tour in the Far East, but he returned to the United States as quickly as possible. On 23 April 1861 he received an appointment as head of the Ordnance Department and was commissioned as a brigadier general on 3 August. Ripley's main task was the testing and procurement of weapons for the Union armies. Although he worked energetically and honestly, he opposed many innovations in small arms and artillery, particularly breechloaders. He did have several accomplishments as chief of ordnance. His department had become disorganized and bogged down in red tape, and he brought some order to its administration. Ripley strove to standardize both the small arms and ammunition used by the army, and he was able to get the government armories to increase their production. Whenever people brought unworkable inventions before the War Department, Ripley fended them off, and he opposed political influence and favoritism.

Some of Ripley's opposition to improvements in weaponry stemmed from his desire to avoid having to supply ammunition for a wide variety of arms, but most of it can be attributed to his lack of imagination and stubbornness. He is said to have been short-tempered, arrogant, and rude to both businessmen and subordinates. At times Ripley approved wasteful contracts without going through the standard process of accepting written proposals and taking bids. His continuing failure to approve contracts for breechloading rifles for the infantry and repeating carbines for the cavalry brought him into conflict with Secretary of War Edwin M. Stanton and eventually with President Abraham Lincoln. Using a law passed in 1842, they forced Ripley to retire on 15 September 1863, since he had been in the army for more than forty-five years.

Ripley continued to act as an armaments inspector for forts on the coast of New England until 1869. On 13 March 1865 he was breveted a major general for his long, faithful service to the army. He died at his home in Hartford, Connecticut.

• No collection of Ripley's personal papers exists, and a biography of him has yet to be published. The outlines of his career can be pieced together from the standard reference works, particularly George W. Cullum, *Biographical Register of the Officers and Graduates of the United States Military Academy at West Point, New York, from Its Establishment, March 16, 1802, to the Reorganization of 1866–67* (1868), and *The War of the Rebellion: A Compilation of the Official Records of the Union and Confederate Armies* (128 vols., 1880–1901). An obituary is in the *Hartford* (Conn.) *Daily Courant*, 17 Mar. 1870.

ARTHUR W. BERGERON, JR.

RIPLEY, Martha George (30 Nov. 1843–18 Apr. 1912), physician and feminist, was born Martha George Rogers in Lowell, Vermont, the daughter of Francis Rogers, a local politician, and Esther Ann George, an ardent abolitionist. Of Irish stock, Francis traced his roots to the *Mayflower*, while Esther's father, a Scotsman, had served in the revolutionary war. Although her father had two daughters from a previous marriage, Martha was the oldest of Esther's five children. Soon after her birth, the family moved to Iowa, where her father eventually became a county supervisor, and both parents continued their abolition work. Schooled at home in her early years, she helped out with the effort by carrying food to escaping slaves. Although she eventually entered the local high school, she never graduated.

At the age of seventeen, Martha Rogers secured a job as a rural teacher. In addition to her teaching duties, she acted as a nurse for many of her students and their families who contracted diphtheria. When the Civil War started, she volunteered to work with the U.S. Sanitary Commission. In 1867 she married William Warren Ripley, a well-off easterner. The couple soon moved east to Lawrence, Massachusetts, where her husband secured a managerial job at his uncle's mill. Later, he bought a paper mill of his own in Middleton while Ripley started raising their family of three girls. In addition, she volunteered as a nurse to the mill workers and became an active member of the New England Woman Suffrage Association.

Inspired by fellow suffragists who were women physicians, such as Marie Zakrzewska and Mercy Jackson, Ripley began considering a medical career. When a young child in her care choked to death from membranous croup, she resolved to either acquire additional training or leave nursing altogether. At the age of thirty-seven Ripley entered the Boston University School of Medicine in October 1880, joining a class that was one-third female. During her second year of medical school, she led a protest against the school's policy that prevented women from watching operations. Although the board of trustees did not officially change the policy, from that point on they did allow women into the operating rooms. This rabble-rousing behavior notwithstanding, when Ripley graduated with honors in 1883, a faculty member announced that she was one of the most thorough physicians the school had produced.

Tragedy struck her family in Ripley's final year of medical school when her husband was injured in a mill accident. Left with the onus of supporting the family, Ripley decided to open a medical practice in Minneapolis, where her husband had relatives. Within six months of her move to Minneapolis, she had not only opened a thriving medical practice, specializing in obstetrics and pediatrics, but she had also been elected president of the Minnesota Woman Suffrage Association. She was instantly recognized because of the strong recommendations from Boston suffragists with whom she had arrived. Within a few years, Ripley had forged an alliance with the temperance movement and brought the seventeenth annual convention of the American Woman Suffrage Association to Minneapolis through her ties with the Boston members.

Ripley argued stridently for women's rights. She started a public information campaign against male infidelity, arguing against the conventional Victorian wisdom that men needed regular sex to stay healthy. What both men and women needed to stay healthy, she countered, was for husbands not to bring sexual diseases into the home. Among other feminist causes she championed was an increase in the age of sexual consent for young girls, the need for women on the police force, the right of maids to unionize, and the right of women to serve on boards of education. She also belonged to the Women's Rescue League and the Minneapolis Improvement League through which she led a movement against dirt and contaminated water.

Ripley carried her reformist tendencies into her medical practice. One of eight female doctors in the city and twenty in the state, she cut a familiar figure as she made her house calls, her husband often by her side in their buggy. She saw a diverse group of patients. Before her arrival in Minneapolis, the city had had only one maternity hospital and a home for women pregnant out of wedlock. Inspired by the diversity of her first three patients—a teacher, a clergyman's daughter, and a girl on her own—Ripley in 1886 started another hospital for mothers-to-be from all walks of life. The hospital opened in a small house and within months had moved to an eighteen-room house. Within its first decade, the hospital moved twice more, each time to larger quarters.

The Maternity Hospital tended patients' needs, both physical and emotional. Ripley insisted on aseptic practices in her hospital and refused to admit patients with contagious diseases. She encouraged patients to attend Sunday services—she herself belonged to the Plymouth Congregational Church—and offered instruction in infant care. Eleven years after the first hospital opened, Ripley could boast that no child under her care had been lost in childbirth and that the hospital's death rate was quite low compared with similar institutions in the state. Her hospital was also first to establish a social service department to help patients with nonmedical problems.

Never one to shy away from the moribund, Ripley had lobbied for a city crematory to ease the unsanitary crowding found in municipal cemeteries. She requested that her body be shipped back to Boston if she died before the city had made cremation an option. Such precautions turned out to be unnecessary. The crematory opened three years before Ripley died of a respiratory infection. Ever concerned about her patients, her last words were, "Is everything all right at the hospital?" Three years after she passed away, the board of the hospital built a new maternity facility, which they named in her memory.

• For a thorough biography of Ripley, see Winton U. Solberg, "Martha G. Ripley: Pioneer Doctor and Social Reformer," *Minnesota History* 39 (1964): 1–17, for which the author interviewed family members and pored over documents in their possession. More circumspect accounts of her life are in Robert Rosenthal's entry in *The Dictionary of American Medical Biography*, ed. Martin Kaufman et al. (1984), and in Frances E. Willard and Mary A. Livermore, eds., *American Women: Fifteen Hundred Biographies* (1973). See also Mary Roth Walsh, *Doctors Wanted: No Women Need Apply, Sexual Barriers in the Medical Profession, 1835–1975* (1977).

SHARI RUDAVSKY

RIPLEY, Robert LeRoy (26 Dec. 1893–27 May 1949), cartoonist and creator of the newspaper feature "Believe-It-or-Not," was born LeRoy Ripley in Santa Rosa, California, the son of Isaac Davis Ripley, a carpenter, and Lily Belle Yucca (or Yocka). Throughout his life he claimed 25 December as his birthday because, he said, he preferred it that way.

From an early age LeRoy (he was in his teens before he added Robert to his name) claimed there was travel and adventure in his blood. His father at age fourteen had left his West Virginia home and roughed it to California; his mother, who was part Portuguese, had been born in a covered wagon on the Santa Fe Trail. Ripley was only twelve when his father died, leaving the family in poor financial circumstances. He worked at odd jobs, including polishing tombstones, and never finished high school.

Young Ripley had two great ambitions: to be a professional baseball pitcher and to be a successful cartoonist. An arm injury wiped out the first, and he concentrated on drawing, at which he had earlier shown talent. In 1907 *Life* magazine paid him $8 for one of his humorous drawings, and he knew then what he could and would do as his life's work. Two years later, before he was sixteen, with the help of a San Francisco newspaperwoman, Carol Ennis, he got a job as a sports cartoonist for the San Francisco *Bulletin*. Two years after that he moved to the San Francisco *Chronicle*, which already had several noted sports cartoonists. In 1913, when Ripley asked for a raise, he was fired.

Ripley had just received $100 for book illustrations; with that money he moved to New York City and landed a job at the *Globe*. His sports illustrations were very popular there, but it was largely by chance that he began drawing and writing about oddities. Finding himself without an idea for one of his December 1918 drawings, Ripley grouped together nine small drawings of sports oddities—including a Canadian who ran backward 100 yards in 14 seconds, a Frenchman who remained under water for 6 minutes and 29.8 seconds, and an Australian who jumped rope 11,810 times in four hours—and published them under the heading "Believe It or Not!" With that Ripley launched his extremely successful series of the same name, which soon went from a weekly to a daily feature.

After the *Globe* ceased publication in 1923, Ripley started drawing the feature for the *Evening Post*. In 1929 a book-length selection of his drawings and sketches published by Simon and Schuster was so quickly and widely a bestseller that William Randolph Hearst directed his King Features Syndicate to imme-

diately sign up Ripley for national distribution. Ripley began, as he said, "drawing real oddities from the whole world." Some of his surprising claims—"George Washington was not the first president of the United States"; "The Battle of Waterloo was not fought at Waterloo"—outraged a few educators, but Ripley's feature was nationally popular, and he was satisfied that he had plausible explanations for his assertions. A deluge of protests poured in to newspapers after Ripley published a cartoon stating that Charles Lindbergh was the sixty-seventh, not the first, man to make a nonstop flight over the Atlantic. Ripley then pointed out that Lindbergh's trip was the first *solo* flight; two men in one airplane and sixty-four men in two dirigibles had crossed the Atlantic before him.

According to his biographer, Ripley's personal favorites included a drawing of the Panama Canal with a caption reading, "A postage stamp built the Panama Canal." Ripley's involved account of how he came to that conclusion had to do with the 1902 procedure by which a young French engineer stopped passage of a bill being seriously considered by Congress to build a canal through Nicaragua, not Panama. The engineer distributed to congressmen hundreds of Nicaraguan postage stamps showing the country's coastline and, not far back from it, one of the area's many volcanoes in full eruption. With each stamp was a brief letter asking if it was wise to build, at great cost to the American taxpaper, a canal through a country filled with active volcanoes. Congress refused to vote funds for a canal through Nicaragua; in 1904 it approved the canal project through Panama. Another Ripley favorite was "Neils Paulsen of Uppsala, Sweden, died at the age of 160 and left two sons—one nine years old and the other 103 years of age." Many of Ripley's readers were most delighted with his discovery and drawing of "a one-armed paperhanger," Albert J. Smith of Dedham, Massachusetts.

During the depression of the 1930s, Ripley's operation remained prosperous. He had built up a large staff of researchers, artists, translators, and secretaries to process letters from around the world, most with suggestions for Believe-It-or-Not subjects. Ripley himself spent a large part of each year traveling the globe, seeking curiosities wherever they might be, and enjoying every minute of it. In addition to his syndicated feature he made twenty-six movie shorts for Warner Brothers. In 1933 he began a "Believe It or Not" radio program, had new book collections of his features published, and sponsored "odditoriums" of his curiosities, which were displayed in a circus atmosphere at several world's fairs. Ripley's syndicated cartoon feature was published in 326 papers, in thirty-eight countries, and in seventeen languages. By the late 1930s he had a net annual income of $500,000.

In 1919 Ripley had married Beatrice Roberts, a *Follies* showgirl and New York model. They separated a few months later but were not divorced until 1925. A large, energetic man, he never lacked female companionship but "never came close," a friend said, to marrying again. Ripley had two fine homes, one named

"Bion" (acronym for "Believe It or Not") on his large estate on New York Sound, the other a winter home in Palm Beach, Florida. He enjoyed entertaining lavishly in them and showing off his $2-million collection of curios, which included a Chinese junk.

Ripley died of a heart attack in New York City and was buried in Santa Rosa, his hometown. Three decades after his death, museum-type displays of his collected curiosities were still operating in the United States, Canada, and England.

Once when Ripley was traveling in England, the duke of Windsor referred to him as "the modern Marco Polo." Shortly before his death Ripley said that of all the great sights he had seen in his world travels, the Grand Canyon of the American West was the greatest.

• Ripley's papers are at King Features Syndicate in New York City. For additional information see Bob Considine, *Ripley: The Modern Marco Polo* (1961).

PEGGY ROBBINS

RIPLEY, Sarah Alden Bradford (31 July 1793–26 July 1867), scholar, Transcendentalist, and teacher of Ralph Waldo Emerson, was born in Boston, Massachusetts, the daughter of Gamaliel Bradford III, a sea captain and penal reformer, and Elizabeth Hickling. Her father traced his ancestry to William Bradford, the first governor of Plymouth, and to Priscilla Alden, a lineage that gave Sarah considerable status in nineteenth-century New England. After her father's death when she was nine, Sarah, because of her mother's unspecified illness, had primary care of her eight younger siblings. Nevertheless, at her grandfather's home in Duxbury during the summers and in school in Boston the rest of the year, she was able to get a good education, learning French and Italian as well as Greek and Latin.

When Sarah Bradford was sixteen, Mary Moody Emerson, although twenty years older, heard of the remarkable young scholar, sought her out, and, according to Sarah, "did not give up till she had enchained me entirely in her magic circle" (Hoar, p. 176). Thus began one of the most intense intellectual relationships between two educated women of the era. In 1814 Mary Emerson introduced twenty-year-old Sarah to her precocious nephew, Ralph Waldo Emerson, who was then only eleven. Sarah also recognized Waldo's potential, and she did what she could to encourage his intellectual and physical growth. She took him horseback riding and urged him to send her his own poetic translations of Greek and Latin classics.

In 1818 Waldo was delighted when his friend and "wisest, soberest tutor" became his aunt after marrying the Reverend Samuel Ripley, Mary Emerson's half brother. Thus Sarah joined the extended Emerson family. Between helping with her husband's Waltham congregation, teaching in his small boarding school, and raising seven children, she gained a reputation for being the most learned member of that notable family. An enthusiastic collector and identifier of wild plants, particularly lichens and mosses, she shared with Hen-ry David Thoreau what she called "a kind of botanic mania." But her duties as minister's wife, schoolteacher, and mother constantly interrupted her studies and kept her busy. "I would there were any hole to creep out of this most servile of all situations, a country clergyman's wife," she wrote once to her brother (Eisler, p. 104). In another letter, she looked forward to the sabbath as a day of "comparative" leisure—"if it can be called leisure to rise at half-past six, wash three babies before breakfast, look after the tidiness of fifteen boys, and walk half a mile to meeting under a burning sun" (Hoar, p. 149).

Although she never published, Ripley engaged in extended correspondence, most notably with Mary Moody Emerson, whom the family called "Aunt Mary." These two women "engaged each other in genuine dialogue," challenging each other in an attempt to get the most out of their different readings and religions. Emerson was a passionate Calvinist iconoclast who did not hide her disdain for her nephew's Transcendentalism. On the other hand, Ripley was well read in the new German idealism, and she helped to shape young Emerson's Transcendentalism by encouraging him from a young age to have faith in his "intuitions and capabilities." For this, Mary Emerson accused her of helping to destroy her nephew's faith and called her "a radical—fixed in unbelief." But like most of the family, Emerson valued her correspondence with Ripley too much to break from the one other woman whose independence and intellect she respected. At the time of Ripley's wedding, Mary Emerson wrote beseeching her to "be yourself and play no part." Though no feminist, Emerson realized the tragedy of this superior woman's having to play a secondary part in a man's world. You "who have known the wonders of language," she once praised her, "you who have been unfortunate in your connections with men who seek to please you and gather strenght [*sic*] for their speculations & non inspiration." Ralph Waldo Emerson himself remembered her as "one of the best Greek scholars in the country," and another admirer called her "a Greek goddess in a Yankee wrapper." President Edward Everett of Harvard insisted that she could have filled any professor's chair.

After their oldest child left home, the Ripleys in 1846 moved from Waltham to Concord to live in the "Old Manse," the Emerson family home that Nathaniel Hawthorne was then renting. After Samuel Ripley's death in 1847, Sarah Ripley remained at the Old Manse, reading, writing, teaching, caring for children, and even tutoring Harvard boys who had been suspended. The Harvard botanist Asa Gray, visiting once, "found her instructing a student in differential calculus, correcting the Greek translation of another, and at the same time shelling peas and rocking her grandchild's cradle with her foot" (Allen, p. 26). She read and approved of Darwin's speculations, finding in them nothing to jar her theology. At the age of seventy, she learned Spanish in order to be able to read *Don Quixote*. She died in Concord and is buried in the Sleepy Hollow Cemetery.

Sarah Ripley's primary contributions were secondary. Her enthusiasm for botany, classical literature, and the new romantic philosophy inspired those with whom she came in contact: Harvard undergraduates, her own family, and her Concord neighbors, including eminent men such as Waldo Emerson and Thoreau. She was one of those remarkable nineteenth-century women who struggled within the limits of the domestic roles assigned to her gender to create and sustain an intellectual life for herself around the edges of long days of domestic duty.

• More than two hundred letters by Ripley are in the Schlesinger Library, Radcliffe College. The most extensive publication of these letters is Elizabeth Hoar, "Mrs. Samuel Ripley," in *Worthy Women of Our First Century*, ed. Sarah Wister and Agnes Irwin (1877; repr. 1975). See also Joan Goodwin, "Sarah Alden Ripley, Another Concord Botanist," *Concord Saunterer*, n.s., 1 (Fall 1993): 77–86; Benita Eisler, "'Up to the Mind's Elbows': The Instructive Friendship of Emerson's Aunts," *American Voice* 3 (Summer 1986): 96–107; Frances Knickerbocker, "New England Seeker: Sarah Bradford Ripley," *New England Quarterly* 30 (Mar. 1957): 3–22; *Selected Letters of Mary Moody Emerson*, ed. Nancy Craig Simmons (1993); and Gay Wilson Allen, *Waldo Emerson* (1981).

DAVID R. WILLIAMS

RIPLEY, Sophia Willard Dana (6 July 1803–4 Feb. 1861), Transcendentalist and early feminist, was born in Cambridge, Massachusetts, the daughter of Francis Dana, Jr., and Sophia Willard Dana. The eldest of four children, Sophia Dana grew up in an atmosphere of alternating uncertainty and stability. Her straying father, a black sheep son of the illustrious and prosperous Dana flock, which included a chief justice, lawyers, professors, seafarers, and merchants, was frequently "out west or away somewhere." Her mother was from the academic Willard family, which included a Harvard College president and any number of influential liberal-thinking ministers. From early in her youth, Sophia was probably aware of her immediate family's precarious financial arrangements. Because of her father's irresponsible spending habits, her mother pragmatically opened a school in her Willard family home, "Fay House" (which stood on the edge of the grounds of Harvard College), where Sophia and her only sister, Mary Elizabeth Dana, later taught. In time, her grandfather largely disowned his namesake son for creating so many debts, noting in his will that while he was leaving him "one hundred dollars and no more" as his share of the family estate, he was bequeathing one sixth of his fortune to his grandchildren, with the provision that his son have no stake in the money. Sophia Dana's share of that inheritance seems not to have substantially eased her later straitened circumstances, but her growing years in Fay House were comfortable and promising.

After completing her formal training at the famous Dr. Parks School in Boston, where she excelled in Latin and Greek, at twenty Sophia Dana opened her own elementary school with her sister, first on Mason Street and then in Fay House in Cambridge with their mother. Among her early pupils were Mary Lowell (sister of editor and poet James Russell Lowell), Mary Channing (the only child and daughter of the great Unitarian minister William Ellery Channing), the daughters of the Parkman and Tuckerman families who were eminent Unitarians and scholars in town, and "all the best girls in Cambridge." Mary Elizabeth reportedly took charge of conduct and manners while Sophia did the teaching. Through social gatherings of the parishioners at the Unitarian church and the proximity of close-knit Cambridge friends and neighbors, Sophia met George Ripley in 1825 when she was in her early twenties. He too came from stock that included American statesmen, scholars, and reforming Calvinist and Unitarian ministers tending to abandon Trinitarian tenets. On his mother's side he was related to Benjamin Franklin; on his father's was the minister Ezra Ripley, Ralph Waldo Emerson's stepgrandfather.

Swayed by the introspective and intellectual iconoclasm and the religious unorthodoxy of her husband's family, Sophia was drawn to one who seemed to share her ideals, a man with an average intelligence and a passion for intellectual thoughts, one who in his youth had been an "earnest, introspective, sickly, and pious boy preoccupied with religion, books, and personal relationships" (Crowe, p. 7). Later becoming one of the Harvard Divinity School classmates who dared to change the tenets of Unitarian thought, George Ripley immersed himself in the challenging company of his distant cousin Emerson, and of Frederic Henry Hedge, Augustus Brownson, James Freeman Clarke, and especially Theodore Parker, a core group of thinkers who led the Unitarian movement into Transcendental and ultimately utopian thought. His marriage to the "tall and rather prim" Sophia, whom peers described as possessing "an angular grace and compelling vivacity" in her youth (Crowe, p. 40), took place in Fay House on 22 August 1827; they were married by Oliver Wendell Holmes.

It appeared to be a solid marriage as far as lineage and mutual interests were concerned. The Ripleys' Cambridge home became a center of heated discussions on Transcendentalism and utopianism, a domestic refuge where new and radical thoughts could be safely examined and where notions of a changing church and utopian visions were raised. Dissatisfied with filling the pulpit at the Purchase Street Church, a Unitarian congregation in Boston, George Ripley decided to apply his emerging spiritual and social beliefs to everyday life. In 1841 the Ripleys and fifteen others established an experimental community in West Roxbury called Brook Farm, which began as a Christian agricultural association but over the course of its six-year history devolved into a communitarian outpost testing the utopian theories of French economist and reformer Charles Fourier. Between 1841 and 1847, the years of Brook Farm's existence, Sophia Ripley experienced perhaps her own best years as well as the zenith of the short-lived Transcendental movement in

New England. Transcendentalism had in good part been inspired by members of her family on both her parents' and her husband's sides, and during these years—her late thirties through mid-forties—Sophia was an intellectual guide in expressing the highest claims of Unitarianism, a tireless worker at Brook Farm, a contributor to the Transcendental journal *The Dial* (published between 1840 and 1844), and an early advocate of feminist claims to woman's independence and autonomy, stating controversially that "not until a woman moulded herself to her own ideals" would she be truly liberated.

Sophia Ripley may have initially been "attracted by her husband's displaying both the genial nature of her father and the responsibility which he lacked" (Crowe, p. 40), but in coming years, when Brook Farm was sapping her energy and drying up the funds to maintain the bold venture, she may also have fully realized that her husband's temperament was dogged in his determination to prove utopian theories at the expense of common sense. Indeed, she may already have been aware of a slowly growing sense of marital stress as she and her husband prepared to move to the farm in West Roxbury. An outspoken member of Margaret Fuller's Boston Conversations circle (1839–1844) and exhilarated by Fuller's powerful call for woman's autonomy, during the first year of Brook Farm's existence Sophia wrote an original, powerful single essay entitled "Woman," published in 1841 in *The Dial*, a first assessment of woman's secondary place. The essay also said a great deal about her own circumstances. Thirty-seven years old and childless, she observed critically what very few women of her era and station dared express openly: "Woman is educated with the tacit understanding that she is only half a being, an appendage. Her life is usually bustle and hurry, or barren order, dreary decorum and method, without vitality . . . His wish is law, hers only the unavailing sigh uttered in secret" (p. 364).

Brook Farm served as a surrogate family for both George and Sophia Ripley. The union appears to have been heavily dependent on group activity, a substitute for their deepest emotions about each another—and a common situation in that straitlaced era when marriages of convenience rather than passion were perhaps the unacknowledged norm. As she became enmeshed in causes and spiritual concerns that began in Transcendental ideals and moved to the communal tenets of Fourierism, Sophia Ripley found that despite high-minded philosophical claims to the contrary, wives were peripheral to decision-making even though they were essential to Brook Farm's practical daily operations. Handling endless chores and attending to a myriad of kitchen duties, nursing sick Brook Farmers and teaching their children, Sophia was totally caught up in maintaining the well-being of a community where she had envisioned woman's sphere being expanded and transformed. She "worked until exhausted," caring for an ersatz family that included "ministers who rejected the pulpit, bankrupt businessmen, religious cranks, occasional bluestockings, several tal-

ented writers, artists, farmers, reform leaders, mechanics, laborers, and young men and women out for a lark" (Crowe, p. 147), while her husband cleared brush, cleaned and repaired buildings, fed farm animals, planted and reaped crops, took the produce to sell at the village market, planned farm operations, kept accounts, and taught at his wife's Brook Farm School. In his leisure he "conducted conversations, organized pageants and proposed summer outings" (Crowe, p. 147). As cofounders of Brook Farm, the Ripleys did a disproportionate amount of manual labor to make a go of George Ripley's dream.

For Sophia, Brook Farm proved to be a profound source of disappointment, from her cumulative fatigue from hours of overwork to a moral letdown in her zeal to belong unquestioningly to the Fourierist phalanx. Having hoped to achieve "self-communion" in a locale she had initially described in a letter to another would-be Brook Farmer, John Sullivan Dwight, as an oasis with "birds & trees, sloping green hills & hayfields as far as the eye can reach—and a brook clear running, at the foot of a green bank," she experienced none of the "separation from worldly care and rest to the spirit" that she prayed "was in waiting for me somewhere" (letter to John Sullivan Dwight, 18 May 1841, Boston Public Library). On the contrary, her fear that the place contributed to a "desolate feeling" she had told Margaret Fuller about the day she arrived at Brook Farm, a melancholy sense that she "belonged to nobody, [and had] a right to nobody" (quoted in Rose, p. 190), had grown alarmingly over the days and months. The venture did not end well. With the change from being an association to a socialist phalanx in 1844 came another new building, which exemplified the highest of Fourier's ideals: the Phalanstery contained parlors, reception rooms, a dining hall, an assembly hall seating three hundred (there were never more than around one hundred Brook Farmers), a printing plant for *The Harbinger*, the official publication of the Fourierist movement, a kitchen, and a bakery. Failing to attract wedded couples and families, perhaps an outcome of its increasing overemphasis on an artificially extended family and a denigration of monogamy, an increasingly antimarriage message dominated the venture. The Phalanstery burned to the ground in 1846, and the reality of Brook Farm went up in flames. The following year the experiment ended.

Discovering that "all through my life my ties with others were those of the intellect & imagination, & not warm heart ties," Sophia confessed "that I do not love anyone and never did, with the heart, & of course could never have been worthy in any relation" (quoted in Rose, p. 196). Deciding that her existence at Brook Farm had been "childish, empty, and sad," before 1847 Sophia decisively converted to the Roman Catholic church, a religious antithesis to the uncluttered and etherial tenets of Unitarian and Transcendental thought. Her sense of need was perhaps partly the outcome of Brook Farm's spiritual, intellectual, and moral letdowns, but it seems also to have been linked to her uneven girlhood and a binding but lackluster marriage. Having been, in essence, abandoned by her father and suffering a subtle but persistent estrangement from her husband, Sophia Ripley may have been unable to find completion in a social or psychological climate that did not provide for woman's missing sense of self-worth. She was surrounded outside and consumed inside by circumstances that weighed her down and deprived her of self-satisfaction. Disillusioned and resigned, she moved to New York City with her husband, who unsuccessfully tried one career after another, and retired within herself. Her life thereafter was one "in which virtually all waking hours were spent in prayer, contemplation, and charitable work, the translation of religious tracts, and visits to hospitals, prisons, and insane asylums" (Crowe, p. 225). She would continue to be dominated by religious motives and the need to do good works, but never with the same creative zeal and healthy energy as during the earlier freethinking period.

Sophia Ripley died of breast cancer in New York City, with her insolvent and struggling husband at her side. Though emotionally separated, the two of them had lived together for thirty-four years. George Ripley went on to lead a totally different life after his wife's death. He married again, this time a woman thirty years his junior, and scratched his way out of insolvency by serving as literary critic for the *New York Herald Tribune*, ultimately making a small fortune by editing popular books until his death.

Although Sophia Dana Ripley's understanding of an expanded woman's sphere, gained in her youth and tested at Brook Farm, did not become manifest in her own life, it helped to ignite the coals of a social and spiritual revolution containing greater personal promise for women. Editorials in *The Harbinger* in 1846–1847 vowed that the phalanx would not countenance "women's holding rank in creation several degrees below the autocrats of the Universe" and encouraged woman to "shake off the paralysis with which long ages of subjection have benumbed her" (quoted in Delano, p. 47). This language was indebted to Sophia, who many years earlier had noted in "Woman" that:

There have been no topics for the last two years, more generally talked of than Woman, and the "sphere of Woman." Even the clergy have frequently flattered "the feebler sex" by proclaiming to them from the pulpit what lovely things they may become if they will only be good, quiet, and gentle, attend exclusively to their domestic duties and the cultivation of religious feeling, which the other sex very kindly relinquish to them as their inheritance. Such preaching is very popular! . . . Woman may be soothed by [man's] sweet numbers, but she cannot be helped by his counsels, for he knows her not as she is and must be. . . . When most needed, he is most impotent. (Pp. 362 and 364)

The story of the struggles at Brook Farm cannot be told without a study of the Ripley marriage. The sense that women in the last years of the twentieth century have of themselves in history is strengthened by Sophia Ripley's early and potent pleas for her own and all women's self-reliance against great personal and social odds.

• The Dana papers in the Schlesinger Library at Radcliffe College include the manuscript of the *History of Fay House* by Christina Hopkinson Baker (1929) and letters and papers from members of the Dana family. The collection also includes letters and manuscript excerpts of works pertaining to the family written by Octavius Brooks Frothingham, Elizabeth Dana, Isabella Dana, and Mary Caroline Crawford, some of which have been published. Another collection of Dana family papers is at the Massachusetts Historical Society in Boston. Ripley's essay, "Woman," appeared in *The Dial* 1, no. 4 (1841): 362–66. For more on the Ripleys and Brook Farm see Matthew David Fisher, "A Selected, Annotated Edition of the Letters of George Ripley, 1828–1841" (Ph.D. diss., Ball State Univ., 1992); Charles Crowe, *George Ripley: Transcendentalist and Utopian Socialist* (1967); Sterling F. Delano, *The Harbinger and New England Transcendentalism* (1983); Henry L. Golemba, *George Ripley* (1977); Georgiana Bruce Kirby, *Years of Experience, an Autobiographical Narrative* (1887; repr. 1971); Joel Myerson, ed., *The Brook Farm Book: A Collection of Firsthand Accounts of the Community* (1984); Elizabeth Palmer Peabody, "Christ's Idea of Society," *The Dial* 2, no. 2 (Oct. 1841): 214–28; Anne C. Rose, *Transcendentalism as a Social Movement, 1830–1850* (1981); Henry Sams, *The Autobiography of Brook Farm* (1974); Lindsay Swift, *Brook Farm: Its Members, Scholars and Visitors* (1900); Perry Miller, ed., *The Transcendentalists: An Anthology* (1950); and "Digging Brook Farm," *Harvard Magazine*, Jan.–Feb. 1992, p. 8.

JUDITH STRONG ALBERT

RIPLEY, William Zebina (13 Oct. 1867–16 Aug. 1941), economist and authority on railroads, was born in Medford, Massachusetts, the son of Nathaniel L. Ripley, a manufacturer of jewelry in Boston, and Estimate R. E. Baldwin. After attending the public schools in the nearby town of Newton, Ripley became a student at the Massachusetts Institute of Technology in Cambridge. He graduated from the institute in 1890 with an A.B. in civil engineering and then remained for a year of graduate work in economics. He then attended Columbia University, where he received an A.M. in 1892 and a Ph.D. in political economy in 1893. His doctoral dissertation was published as *The Financial History of Virginia, 1609–1776* in 1893. That same year Ripley married Ida Sabine Davis of Boston. They had four children.

Ripley's early academic appointments ranged over a variety of disciplines. His first position was in 1893 as an instructor in political science at MIT. In 1895 he shifted to sociology and economics at the same school, where he was promoted to professor in 1901. In the same years he held part-time positions at Columbia University; from 1893 until 1899 he was a "prize lecturer" in physical geography and anthropology there. From 1899 until 1901 he taught sociology at Columbia. During 1901–1902 he was a lecturer in economics at Harvard, where in 1902 Ripley was appointed a professor of political economy. Within a few years he was named the Nathaniel Ropes Professor of Economics, a position he held until his retirement in 1933.

Much of Ripley's first research and publishing was in anthropology rather than economics. While at Columbia he had offered a unique course reviewing the role of geography in human development. He was convinced that environmental conditions were important in the development of the human race. In his studies he carefully reviewed the work of many European anthropologists in the decades after 1860. Ripley summarized his own views in a series of lectures delivered both at Columbia and at the Lowell Institute in Boston. Later he wrote *The Races of Europe: A Sociological Study*, a large scholarly volume published in 1899. It was accompanied by a smaller work, *A Selected Bibliography of the Anthropology and Ethnology of Europe*. In this study Ripley divided the people of Europe into three white racial groups: a northern group of tall, blond longheads called Teutonic; a central group of stocky roundheads called Alpine; and a southern group of slender, dark longheads called Mediterranean.

Like many Americans at the turn of the century, Ripley had a certain preference for the Teutonic (or Nordic) races of northern Europe. His writings on European anthropology may have had some influence on his contemporary, Madison Grant, an active advocate of immigration restriction. Ripley was a member of the anthropological societies of Paris and Rome. He received the Huxley Memorial Medal of the Royal Anthropological Institute of Great Britain and Ireland for a series of lectures given in London in 1908.

In 1900 President William McKinley appointed Ripley to the U.S. Industrial Commission, a group of five U.S. senators, five representatives, and nine laymen, who were directed to study the effectiveness and value of the Anti-trust Act of 1890. Ripley in 1900–1901 investigated the relations of the nation's railroads with the anthracite coal industry. After his appointment at Harvard in 1902, Ripley gave his major attention to economics, especially in the field of railway transportation. During his early years at Harvard he published in the *Railroad Gazette* and the *Railway Age Gazette* several lengthy serialized articles on railway freight rates and railroad securities. During the same years Ripley served as the general editor of *Selections and Documents in Economics*, a ten-volume series that made technical economic material more available for the general public. He edited two of the ten volumes; the first was *Trusts, Pools, and Corporations* (1905) and the fifth was *Railway Problems* (1907). A few years later Ripley was the author of two volumes about American railroads, *Railroads: Rates and Regulation* (1912) and *Railroads: Finance & Organization* (1915). These two books plus the earlier *Railway Problems* were among the most significant works on American railroads written in the generation before World War I. As of 1915 Ripley believed the struggle to bring the nation's rail system under public and governmental control had been clearly achieved. He was not convinced that the newer regulations adequately protected the railway system from the new competing modes of transportation that had appeared in the early twentieth

century. He felt that an adequate rail service with reasonable rates could be maintained if the public was informed, rail management enlightened, and regulation restrained. Ripley was firmly opposed to any government ownership of the nation's railroads.

In 1916 the rapidly increased cost of living that accompanied World War I caused the four operating railroad brotherhoods (engineers, firemen, conductors, and trainmen) to demand an eight-hour day instead of the ten-hour workday then in effect. Later that year Congress passed the Adamson Act, which gave the railroad operating unions the eight-hour day. In 1917 President Woodrow Wilson appointed Ripley to make a report to the U.S. Eight-Hour Commission, which was to implement the Adamson Act. For many weeks he visited railroad yards, cabooses, engine cabs, and roundhouses to learn all he could concerning the wages and hours of various railroad workers. Later, in 1918, he worked for the War Department on labor standards in the procurement of army uniforms and equipment. In 1919–1920 he was chairman of the National Adjustment Commission formed to settle labor disputes for the U.S. Shipping Board.

On 1 March 1920, after more than two years of federal governmental management, American railroads were turned back to private control, under the terms of the Transportation Act of 1920. An enlarged Interstate Commerce Commission was directed by the 1920 act to prepare a master plan of railroad mergers, creating several giant railroad systems. In 1920 the ICC selected Ripley to prepare a tentative consolidation plan as a basis for public hearings from which a definitive group of mergers could be established. Ripley conferred with the presidents of major railroads and corresponded with hundreds of people with an interest in the project. He concentrated first on the New England lines, then the Trunk Line region, and finally on the roads in the South and the West. In the summer of 1921 he submitted a proposal consisting of twenty-one major systems. The plan contained more than 200 lines, including nearly all the Class I roads, but very few of the smaller Class II and Class III lines.

By September 1921 the commission had reduced the proposal to nineteen giant systems, with the belief that each newly created system would benefit from profitable long-haul traffic. Lines such as the New York Central, the Pennsylvania, the Baltimore & Ohio, the Norfolk & Western, the Atlantic Coast, the Santa Fe, and the Union Pacific headed up several of the nineteen newly formed groups. Ripley continued to assist the commission until 1923. To his disappointment legislative approval for the consolidation plan was delayed until 1932. By this time the numerous railway receiverships resulting from the depression of the 1930s prevented the implementation of the proposal. In the early 1930s Ripley had urged the necessity of railroad mergers as a defense against the growing competition from buses, truck lines, waterways, airways, and pipelines.

In the mid-1920s Ripley returned to an earlier concern with American corporate finance. He saw a growing danger in the popular corporate practice of issuing nonvoting common stock and the increasing establishment of holding companies. Ripley believed that such practices increased the gap between company stockholders and corporate control and management. In a series of articles with titles such as "Stop, Look, Listen" and "From Main Street to Wall Street" Ripley expressed his views on American business in the *Atlantic Monthly* in 1925 and 1926. The public reaction was strong. The magazine received hundreds of letters from readers of the articles.

The protest reached Wall Street, and soon members of the board of governors of the New York Stock Exchange were debating whether they should permit future issues of nonvoting common stock to be listed in their trading lists. Ripley published a collection of his essays on company finance in a book, *Main Street and Wall Street* (1927). In June 1927 Ripley received $500 and a gold medal from the Harmon Foundation for his views on American business. In 1931 and 1932 he testified before U.S. Senate banking committees on the subject. Many of his recommendations were included in the 1934 act that created the Securities and Exchange Commission.

Ripley was long active in the American Economic Association, of which he became the thirty-fifth president in 1933. For years it had been his custom at annual meetings to introduce new younger members to his older associates. Because of failing health Ripley retired from Harvard on 1 March 1933. In the same year he gave up his seat on the Board of Directors of the Chicago, Rock Island & Pacific Railway Company, a position he had held since 1917.

Even in retirement Ripley remained a forceful writer and diligent student, both versatile and thorough. He had gained his broad knowledge of American railroads not only from company reports and accounts, but also from covering thousands of miles on dozens of American lines, often traveling incognito in day coaches, engine cabs, and cabooses, as well as in official business cars. With iron-gray hair, imperial beard, and rugged outdoor complexion he had a bearing not often associated with the classroom or research library. Ripley was at ease with his scholarly associates and also with railroad workers and mill hands. He drowned near his summer home at East Edgecomb, Maine.

• A collection of Ripley's papers are at Harvard. Much material on Ripley's interest in anthropology is in Carleton S. Coon, *The Races of Europe* (1954), and John Higham, *Strangers in the Land* (1955). For a review of Ripley's railroad activities see Albro Martin, *Enterprise Denied: Origins of the Decline of American Railroads, 1897–1917* (1971); Sidney L. Miller, *Inland Transportation* (1933); *Railway Age Gazette*, 23 Mar. 1917; and *Railway Age*, 15 Oct. 1921. For a summary of Ripley's views on corporate finance see the *New York Times*, 26 Sept. 1926. Obituaries are in the *New York Times*, 17 Aug. 1941, and *Railway Age*, 23 Aug. 1941.

JOHN F. STOVER

RISING, Johan Classon (1617–Apr. 1672), last governor of Sweden's colony in America and the first Swede to publish important treatises on national commerce, was born in Risinge Parish in Östergötlandslän, Sweden, the son of the Reverend Clas Botvidi, the local pastor (mother's name unknown). Johan and his two brothers took as their last name the name of the district where he was born. Johan's middle name was sometimes latinized as Claudius. Rising studied history and the law and received his doctorate from the University of Uppsala in 1640. He spent the next eleven years traveling and studying the economic policies of other countries. He particularly admired the Dutch system and considered it a commercial model for Sweden.

In 1651 he was appointed secretary of Sweden's new trade organization, the Commercial College, which governed Sweden's colonies. He was soon appointed head of Sweden's ninth expedition, to send two ships to New Sweden on the Delaware River. Rising was to have served as Governor Johan Printz's commissary, but news of Printz's departure from America reached Sweden just as the *Eagle* (*Örn* in Swedish) sailed. Whether the colony had been captured was not known. Just before Rising's departure, Queen Christina knighted him and gave him a long and detailed list of instructions for managing the colony. A young engineer, Peter Lindstrom, was ordered to accompany Johan and to keep a journal of all that transpired.

In February 1654 the *Eagle* left Sweden with many more people—350—and much less food and water than planned. The *Golden Shark* (*Gyllene Haj* in Swedish), which was also to have sailed then, was pronounced unseaworthy. More than 100 families who had sold their property had to be left behind. After a terrible three-and-a-half month voyage, during which more than 100 people died, the *Eagle* reached the Dutch Fort Casimir (present-day New Castle, Del.) on 21 May 1654.

This fort had been built in 1651 by Peter Stuyvesant, governor of the Dutch colony at New Amsterdam. Sweden considered the fort an invasion of its territory and planned to claim it. By the time Rising arrived the fort was in a state of disrepair; fewer than a dozen men occupied it.

The proper steps were taken to arrange the surrender, but on the next day, Trinity Sunday, Rising forced the Dutch out at sword's point before terms had been signed. He had had no military training and evidently did not realize the significance of his hasty actions; a few hours' wait might well have postponed Sweden's subsequent loss of the colony. Rising, who was fluent in Dutch, immediately wrote Governor Stuyvesant of his arrival and of his friendly intentions. Stuyvesant did not reply but wrote to his superiors in Holland for instructions.

Rising assumed the governorship, renamed the fort Fort Trinity, and reversed two of his predecessors' extremely unpopular policies, allowing private colonists to trade with Europeans and Native Americans and to buy land directly from the Native Americans or from the company.

On 17 June Rising met with ten Lenape chiefs at Tinicum, about twenty miles north of the main settlement at Fort Christina (now Wilmington, Del.), and gave them cloth, kettles, hoes, knives, powder, and lead. They agreed to warn each other of danger and to help protect each other. He also rebutted rival territorial claims from English Maryland and Connecticut with tactful diplomacy and with Sweden's deeds from the Native Americans.

His first report, sent back to the Commercial College on the *Eagle* in July 1654, requested skilled people and supplies needed by the colony, especially cannons, powder, bullets, and lead, as well as priestly vestments, an altar painting, and two or three bells. Rising also asked the head of the Commercial College to send him a suitable wife who could look after the garden and cattle, spin and weave, keep nets and seines in order, make malt, brew ale, cook food, milk cows, and make cheese and butter. No wife and very few workers or goods ever arrived. Rising never married.

Help would have arrived on the *Golden Shark* that September, but because of the Dutch navigator's mistake, or collusion, the ship sailed into Raritan Bay (near modern Staten Island, N.Y.) rather than Delaware Bay and was seized by Stuyvesant in retaliation for the taking of Fort Casimir. The Netherlands's peace treaty with England in July 1654 meant that Stuyvesant could afford to commence hostilities against the Swedes in order to disrupt their trade and give Dutch shipping the upper hand. Before the treaty, England had not allowed Dutch ships to trade with the English colonies but had allowed Swedish ships to buy goods in Holland and sell to any of the colonies.

Governor Stuyvesant received orders the following summer to retake his fort from the Swedes. Rising decided to concentrate his strength downriver at Fort Trinity, leaving his headquarters at Fort Christina with few men and no ammunition. On 31 August 1655 seven Dutch ships with hundreds of soldiers commanded by Governor Stuyvesant captured Fort Trinity when its commander inexplicably surrendered without firing a shot. Rising, also inexplicably, had remained at Fort Christina and thus had no say in the terms of surrender. Four days later, the Dutch surrounded the severely weakened Fort Christina and demanded its surrender. While Rising stalled, some of the Dutch raided nearby farms, killing cattle and poultry, taking everything of value, and burning houses. He surrendered on 15 September in return for liberal terms.

Having learned that Native Americans had raided Dutch settlements at New Amsterdam and Staten Island, possibly to avenge the expedition against New Sweden, Stuyvesant was eager to return to New Amsterdam. To expedite matters, he offered to turn the fort back over to Rising in return for an alliance. Rising rejected the offer in the hope of filing claims against the Dutch for material losses during the raids. If the Swedes had held out a few days longer at either fort, Governor Stuyvesant would probably have had to drop the siege and take his soldiers back to defend his settlements. Rising did not know that a Swedish ship with supplies and more settlers would soon be on its way.

In fear of his disgrace in Sweden, Rising went to London and then to Holland, where, as an enemy of the state, his books, manuscripts, and clothes were confiscated. He was eventually given a job in Sweden as a toll collector, a job he hated and eventually quit. He finished a book on agriculture and several shorter economic treatises but did not finish his life's work, the "Treatise on Commerce." Much of his time and strength was spent trying unsuccessfully to exonerate himself for losing the colony and suing to collect salary he thought he was owed. He died in Stockholm, alone and penniless.

Rising's failures cannot be ignored, but his accomplishments, in the colony and in Sweden, should be acknowledged. He doubled the amount of cleared land, procured food from other colonies, and held courts. He greatly improved the lives and well-being of his colonists through his careful economic direction, through the trust he earned from the Native Americans, and through his strong diplomatic stands against English claims. He occupies a conspicuous place in Swedish literature of that period. His theories on trade were far ahead of their time and became the foundation of Swedish free trade.

• Johan Rising's 1654 treaty with the Native Americans, his journals, reports, and letters are kept in the Royal Archives in Stockholm, Sweden. The reports were translated into English by Amandus Johnson and are printed in Albert Cook Myers, *Narratives of Early Pennsylvania, West New Jersey, and Delaware, 1630–1707* (1912). A typed translation of Rising's journal is among the Amandus Johnson Papers at the Balch Institute in Philadelphia, Pa. Johan Rising's "Relation of Surrender" was translated into English by George P. Marsh and published in *Collections of the New-York Historical Society*, 2d ser., vol. 1 (1841), pp. 443–48. Translations of the instructions to Johan Rising, his deeds with Native Americans, and various other official documents are in Amandus Johnson, *The Swedish Settlements on the Delaware, 1638–1664* (1911). Peter Lindstrom's journal, *Geographica Americae*, was translated by Amandus Johnson in 1925. Information on Rising also appears in Israel Acrelius, *A History of New Sweden* (1874); Christopher Ward, *New Sweden on the Delaware* (1938); and two books by C. A. Weslager, *New Sweden on the Delaware, 1638–1655* (1988), and *The Swedes and the Dutch at New Castle* (1987).

DOROTHY ROWLETT COLBURN

RISKIN, Robert (30 Mar. 1897–20 Sept. 1955), screenwriter, was born in New York City, the son of Jakob Riskin, a tailor, and Bessie (maiden name unknown). Riskin dropped out of school after the eighth grade to go to work. While he was still in his teens and working for a shirtmaking firm, his early attempts at writing came to the attention of his bosses, who were investing in short comedy films. They asked his opinion of the films they backed, and he told them how bad they were. Instead of being fired for his candor, he was sent to Florida to supervise the production of the films, which meant that he wrote, produced, and directed them.

After serving in the navy during World War I, Riskin and his older brother, Everett, tried to produce films on their own, but they met with no success. They then turned their attention to writing for the New York stage and had several indifferently successful plays produced in the twenties. Riskin went broke in the 1929 stock market crash and came to Hollywood to work in films. His play *Bless You, Sister* (1927) had been sold to Columbia Pictures, then a small studio. The play was made into *The Miracle Woman* (1931). Riskin had nothing to do with the making of the movie, but he did meet its director, Frank Capra, who would become his most important collaborator.

Capra put Riskin to work writing dialogue for the 1931 film *Platinum Blonde*. From the beginning, Riskin's dialogue had bite and energy, although the picture suffers from the miscasting of Jean Harlow as a society girl. The following year, Riskin wrote the first distinctly Capra-Riskin collaboration, *American Madness*. In the heart of the depression, Riskin had the wit and daring to write a populist script in which the head of a bank is the hero. Riskin made the banker, played by Walter Huston, sympathetic to audiences by showing his sincere concern for his customers. Huston's banker is clearly a forerunner of the George Bailey character in Capra's post-Riskin *It's a Wonderful Life* (1946).

In 1934 Riskin adapted Samuel Hopkins Adams's short story "Night Bus" into the Capra-directed *It Happened One Night*. Studio executives at Columbia recommended against a comedy about a runaway heiress who falls in love with a man on a bus, since there had been recent, unsuccessful bus comedies. Riskin and Capra, whose working pattern was to discuss the story structure in depth before Riskin wrote the first-draft screenplay on his own, changed Adams's plot and characters. In the story the heiress is running away because she is not being allowed to marry the man of her choice, but in the film she hopes to avoid a marriage forced on her. In the story the man on the bus has no occupation, but in the film he is a reporter who may or may not be writing a story about her. Riskin also elaborated on scenes, such as the "Walls of Jericho" episode in which the couple have to share a motel room. The "Walls" refer to the blanket they hang between them, but Riskin added a funny monologue/demonstration for Clark Gable in which he explains how to undress. The montage in which Gable demonstrates different hitchhiking methods, none of which work, is not in the story at all.

Riskin's scenes gave Capra the opportunity to get the most out of the actors, and Capra, experienced in directing comedy performances since silent film days, rose to the challenge, obtaining uniformly excellent performances. Riskin won an Academy Award, as did Capra and the two stars, Gable and Claudette Colbert; the film also won an Oscar for best picture, thus helping to turn Columbia into a major studio.

Capra decided he wanted to go beyond the escapist comedy of *It Happened One Night*, and in their next two films he and Riskin moved to social satire. *Broadway Bill* (1934) is the weaker of the two, but *Mr. Deeds Goes to Town* (1936) is probably their best collaboration and the most perfectly balanced of their films. Longfellow Deeds (played by Gary Cooper), who writes poems for greeting cards, suddenly inherits a fortune from a long-lost uncle, and city slickers in New York try to get the money from him. When Deeds proposes to give his money to the poor, lawyers try to have him declared insane. Riskin again provides playable moments, such as Deeds's lack of reaction when he is told about the inheritance, and Capra directs those scenes skillfully. Riskin and Capra find the balance between the comedy (Deeds playing the tuba at odd times) and the social comment (the insanity hearing, where Riskin inventively keeps Deeds silent until the end, letting the others reveal themselves through their dialogue and behavior). Screenwriter Philip Dunne said of the Capra-Riskin collaboration: "Frank provided the schmaltz and Bob provided the acid. It was an unbeatable combination. What they had together was better than *either* of them had separately."

Their next collaboration, a change from their previous work, was an adaptation of James Hilton's best-selling novel *Lost Horizon* (1937). Film historian Sam Frank writes that the film "is certainly the supreme example of Riskin's talent for shaping basically uncinematic material into an escapist epic with popular appeal, improving on the original in the process." Riskin's script has more humor and warmth than Hilton's novel, elements that Capra's direction captured.

In 1938 Capra and Riskin collaborated on an adaptation of the George S. Kaufman and Moss Hart Broadway hit *You Can't Take It with You*. The script places more emphasis on the two young lovers than the play did, and the film won an Academy Award for best picture. Riskin had begun to chafe a bit in their creative relationship, at least partly because Capra was getting nearly all the credit for their films. Riskin wrote scripts for other directors, such as *The Whole Town's Talking* (1935), a gangster comedy directed by John Ford. In 1937 he wrote and directed *When You're in Love*, but he decided he was not happy directing. He left Columbia in the late thirties and worked as a writer-producer for Samuel Goldwyn, a job and relationship he did not enjoy.

In 1940 Capra and Riskin formed an independent production company, and the following year they made *Meet John Doe*, a populist comedy with a darker edge than their previous work. A woman newspaper columnist creates a fictional common man and then hires a hobo to pretend to be that man. A cynical business mogul manipulates John Doe for his own political ends, then exposes Doe as a fraud. The film suggests that common people can be easily manipulated by the powerful, although in Capra and Riskin's fifth and final ending, the common people come to Doe's rescue.

In 1942 Riskin became chief of the Overseas Motion Picture Bureau of the Office of War Information, supervising production of documentary films for use abroad, as well as distributing foreign newsreels in the United States. That same year he married actress Fay Wray; they had three children. Riskin stayed at OWI until the end of the war, then joined RKO as a writer-producer. His first film was *Magic Town* (1947), the story of a pollster who discovers the perfect American town so he can do all his national opinion sampling in one place. Although he does not let the townspeople know what he is doing, it eventually is revealed. Riskin's lively script has much of his 1930s populist feel, but, like *Meet John Doe*, its impact is darker. *Magic Town* is marred by two personnel decisions: the miscasting of the usually genial and unsophisticated James Stewart as the "city slicker" pollster, a role in which Stewart is not believable, and the choice of director, William Wellman, who, although good at other things, lacked Capra's warmth and comic skill. Wellman realized early that he was wrong for the film, saying, "this is the kind of picture only Capra can do. It's not my kind of film." Nevertheless, the film has charming moments, and one can see what it might have been under different circumstances.

Riskin's last two films, *Mister 880* (1950) and *Half Angel* (1951), were rather bland. Riskin also received a story credit on Capra's 1951 film *Here Comes the Groom*, but it was adapted from a story he had developed years earlier and shows only a few flashes of his skill. In 1950 Riskin suffered a stroke that left him paralyzed on his left side until his death in Woodland Hills, California.

In the thirties the general critical assumption was that Riskin's contributions to the Capra films was reasonably substantial, and other screenwriters in Hollywood gave him even greater credit. However, his reputation waned as critics and historians increasingly paid attention to directors rather than writers. Riskin's devaluation was fueled by Capra's autobiography, *The Name above the Title* (1971), in which the director downplayed *all* other contributors to his films. Joseph McBride's monumental biography, *Frank Capra: The Catastrophe of Success* (1992), attempts to reestablish Riskin's contributions, going so far as to claim that "Robert Riskin became the social conscience of Frank Capra's films in the 1930s."

• The majority of Riskin's papers are in the Fay Wray Collection at the University of Southern California, Los Angeles. Some Riskin materials are at the Margaret Herrick Library of the Academy of Motion Picture Arts and Sciences, Beverly Hills, California. As yet there is no full-scale biography, although Joseph McBride's *Frank Capra* covers Riskin's collaboration with Capra in great and sympathetic detail. Additional material on Riskin is in Bob Thomas, *King Cohn* (1967).

TOM STEMPEL

RITCHARD, Cyril (1 Dec. 1898–18 Dec. 1977), theatrical comedian, dancer, and director, was born Cyril Trimnell-Ritchard in Sydney, New South Wales,

Australia, the son of Herbert Trimnell-Ritchard, a hotel owner, and Margaret Collins. After Jesuit schooling, in 1916 Ritchard entered Sydney University, where for one year he pursued a medical career. At nineteen he was a chorus boy in Oscar Straus's *A Waltz Dream* (1917); between 1917 and 1924 he continued as a dancer-comedian in contemporary American and British musical comedies such as *Oh, Lady Lady!*, *Going Up*, *The Cabaret Girl*, and *So Long, Letty*. He was briefly in New York for *Puzzles of 1925* before making his London debut for producer André Charlot in *Bubbly* and later editions of *Charlot's Revue*. A toppered dandy, he also performed cabaret at the Hotel Metropole.

In 1927 Ritchard and Madge Elliott, a graceful and athletic team, began a series of yearly "dancing comedies" in London. These lightly plotted, highly topical shows costarred Leslie Henson. They were *Lady Luck* (1927), *So This Is Love* (1928), *Love Lies* (1929), *The Love Race* (1930), and *The Millionaire Kid* (1931). Ritchard appeared in two films and a revival of the revue *The Co-Optimists* before returning to Australia for musical comedy in 1932. Ritchard and Elliott married in 1935. They had no children. They returned to London and appeared in several Herbert Farjeon revues. In 1936's *Spread It Abroad*, once more lauded as "wizard dancers," they earned from Noël Coward the title of "the musical Lunts." *Nine Sharp*, which ran throughout 1938, provided Ritchard a swooping comedy pastiche, "When Bolonsky Danced Belushka Antigua."

Ritchard's range expanded rapidly during World War II. In revues, he costarred with Beatrice Lillie and assumed roles as a fan dancer and a fusty armchair soldier. In 1942 he directed his first revue and made his first appearance with John Gielgud, as the inventive Algernon Moncrieff in Oscar Wilde's *The Importance of Being Earnest*. In 1943 he was Prince Danilo in a long-running revival of *The Merry Widow*; a version of it produced by Ritchard, Elliott, and Jack Hylton for the British armed forces toured Egypt and the Mediterranean. Ritchard's *Gay Rosalinda (Die Fledermaus)* ran for more than 400 performances in 1945. After a season of Noël Coward plays in Australia, he returned in 1947 with Gielgud to New York and began an unforeseeable and remarkable new career in Restoration comedy.

Ritchard played the vain, dim-witted Tattle, marrying the wrong woman in Congreve's *Love for Love*. After a London appearance as the wily beau Sir Novelty Fashion in Vanbrugh's *The Relapse*, he appeared in New York as the effeminate Georgie Pilson in John Van Druten's *Make Way for Lucia* (1948). His American reputation growing, in 1950 he was the too-credulous Sparkish in Wycherly's *The Country Wife* in Massachusetts, and he repeated *The Relapse* in New York. In 1952, as Adrian Blenderbland, he costarred with Katharine Hepburn in George Bernard Shaw's *The Millionairess* in both New York and London. The critic Brooks Atkinson praised his "airs and graces, stylized condescension and fripperies." The theatrical historian Gerald Bordman wrote that he had become his era's consummate portrayer of fops. Ritchard and Elliott settled in New York and Connecticut.

Ritchard's abstracted Mr. Darling and the preposterously dandified Captain Hook were born on the road in Los Angeles and San Francisco; by the time *Peter Pan*, costarring Mary Martin, opened in New York, they were classic. Ritchard won a 1954 Antoinette Perry (Tony) award. Plotting Peter's demise, Hook dances a mincing tango and a sweeping tarantella. Celebrating his own "swinishness," he waltzes extravagantly. With his large face, upturned nose, and exaggerated expressions, he seemed a fine period cartoon come to life. Ritchard's nasal, bleating voice helped create in Hook a gurgling, pompous, and insecure villain. British audiences would have recognized its source in pantomime.

In 1954 he also directed sketches for a John Murray Anderson revue and staged *The Barber of Seville* at the Metropolitan Opera. Olin Downes wrote that his version was "swift, light and comedic, hand in hand with the tempo of the score." At the American Theatre Wing, Ritchard taught Restoration manners. In 1955 his wife died. He recorded an album, *Odd Songs and a Poem*, and became much in demand on American television, reprising *Peter Pan* and *Gay Rosalinda* and starring in children's programs.

For the rest of his life, Ritchard was rarely away from the United States and rarely at liberty. He directed the operas *The Gypsy Baron* (1959) and *The Marriage of Figaro* (1959), the plays *The Reluctant Debutante* (1956) and *The Happiest Girl in the World* (1961, playing six parts as well). He was Krton from outer space in Gore Vidal's *Visit to a Small Planet* (1957) on Broadway. His longest-running role was in the contemporary light comedy *The Pleasure of His Company* (1958). He created Sir, the ruling-class authority figure, in the musical by Anthony Newley and Leslie Bricusse, *The Roar of the Greasepaint, the Smell of the Crowd*, which opened in the English provinces but bypassed London for New York success in 1965. He was in the film version of the David Heneker musical *Half a Sixpence*, and he narrated Prokofiev's *Peter and the Wolf* at the Met.

In his seventies, Ritchard continued in Broadway musicals: *Lock Up Your Daughters* (1968), *Sugar* (1972), and *The Jockey Club Stakes* (1973). As *Sugar*'s lecherous Osgood Fielding, Jr., he was lauded by Clive Barnes for his "geriatric jauntiness and style." In 1975 Ritchard donned a medieval doublet for another revue, *A Musical Jubilee*. There was more television. He said, "I live far beyond my means, which is about the only way to live."

In November 1977 Ritchard was hosting the musical anthology *Side by Side by Sondheim* in Chicago when he suffered a heart attack onstage. He remained in a coma until his death in Evanston, Illinois.

• Reviews of Ritchard's theatrical performances can be found in the New York Public Library for the Performing Arts, the British Library, and the archives of the Victoria and Albert Theatre Museum in London. Discussions of individual British musical comedies appear in Kurt Ganzl, *The British Musical* (1987). An excellent pictorial study of the British revue is Raymond Mander and Joe Mitchenson, *Revue: A Story in Pictures* (1971).

JAMES ROSS MOORE

RITCHEY, George Willis (31 Dec. 1864–4 Nov. 1945), maker, designer, and prophet of large reflecting telescopes, was born in Tuppers Plains, Ohio, the son of James Ritchey, a cabinetmaker, and his wife, Eliza Gould. Ritchey made his first small telescope as a young boy. He wanted to be an astronomer but had to work to earn a living, particularly after he married Lillie Gray in 1885. Ritchey studied at the University of Cincinnati for only two years, one of them in the course in drawing and the other in the course in science. During that second year he worked as a student assistant at the Cincinnati Observatory. There he read the publications of the pioneer makers of reflecting telescopes, Henry Draper and Andrew A. Common. In 1886 Ritchey left Cincinnati for a job as a teacher of shop at the Chicago Manual Training High School. There the Ritcheys' two children were born.

In Chicago in 1890, Ritchey met George Ellery Hale, the scion of a very wealthy family and an astronomer. Their careers were to be closely intertwined for the rest of their lives. Hale owned his own private Kenwood Observatory, provided by his father and located in the rear of their family mansion. Its telescope and auxiliary instruments were superior to those of most university observatories of the time. Ritchey began working for Hale, first as a part-time volunteer doing instrumental repair and photographic jobs, then as a full-time instrumental assistant, his salary paid by Hale's father. Although in 1891 Hale had helped persuade tycoon Charles T. Yerkes to provide the money to build the world's largest refractor for the University of Chicago, Ritchey and Hale were both convinced that large reflecting telescopes were the real future of astronomy. Ritchey had already made the mirrors for several small reflectors in his own home laboratory, and he now began making larger ones, including two 24-inch parabolic mirrors, for the University of Chicago. In 1895 Hale's father bought a 60-inch glass disk, the specifications provided by Ritchey, for a future very large reflecting telescope.

In 1896 or 1897, as Yerkes Observatory approached completion, Ritchey moved to its site in Williams Bay, Wisconsin. He soon was transferred from Hale's father's payroll to the University of Chicago as head of the Yerkes optical shop, later superintendent of instrument construction, and still later instructor, then assistant professor, in practical astronomy. At the dedication of Yerkes Observatory in 1897, the visiting astronomers saw Ritchey rough grinding the 60-inch disk, the first step in turning it into a parabolic mirror. He was an expert photographer, who had begun taking direct photographs of the moon with Hale's 12-inch refractor at Kenwood. As soon as the 40-inch went into operation at Yerkes, Ritchey began using this very long focal length instrument to obtain superb images of features on the moon and of star clusters.

Ritchey's outstanding achievement at Yerkes was building the 24-inch reflector, the first modern American reflecting telescope. He had made the parabolic mirror for it in Chicago, and when he took over the project he was saddled with parts from an existing design, which he could therefore modify only slightly, but he did get some of his own ideas into it. With this optically fast telescope, he obtained spectacular photographs of many nebulae, including the rapidly expanding shell around Nova Persei in 1901. Ritchey also made several long-focus mirrors for fixed, horizontal solar telescopes, fed by heliostats or coelostats, including one that E. E. Barnard and he used to obtain superb images of the chromosphere and corona at the solar eclipse of 1900.

In 1903 Hale moved to Pasadena, soon bringing his "first team" of Ritchey, Ferdinand Ellerman, and Walter S. Adams to found with him on Mount Wilson a remote observing station of Yerkes Observatory. By 1905 he had obtained a grant from the Carnegie Foundation that enabled him to break away from the University of Chicago and establish the Mount Wilson Solar Observatory. Ritchey became the superintendent of construction, superintendent of instruments, and head of the optical shop. He designed and built the 60-inch telescope and with his assistants ground, figured, tested, and polished its mirrors. It was a great success, the first large American reflector. Ritchey himself used it to take excellent direct photographs of the moon, globular clusters, and nebulae, including many that now are known to be galaxies. In the hands of Adams and others the 60-inch produced a stream of important spectroscopic results.

In 1910 Ritchey and his volunteer assistant from France, Henri Chrétien, invented the coma-free reflecting mirror system that they called their "new curves" system, later known as the Ritchey-Chrétien design. Ritchey wanted to make a 100-inch reflector as the world's first Ritchey-Chrétien, but Hale vetoed the idea. Ritchey then appealed to John D. Hooker, who had given the money for a 100-inch mirror, to change this decision. Furious, Hale took the design of the 100-inch telescope out of Ritchey's hands but had him make the mirrors for it. The 100-inch disk was badly flawed, but in the end Ritchey produced a superb parabolic mirror from it. The telescope was essentially completed in 1917 but was held up by World War I and only went into operation in 1919. Hale then fired Ritchey for disloyalty; he received no separation benefits or pension. No other American observatory would hire the optician whom the powerful director of Mount Wilson Observatory had discharged, and no American journal would consider publishing his papers. Ritchey could only eke out a living on his orange and lemon ranch in Azusa and dream of great reflecting telescopes of the future.

Hoping to build a large reflecting telescope, the French in 1924 brought Ritchey to Paris to do so. Their idea was to build a 102-inch reflector (which

would be the largest telescope in the world), but Ritchey had much more grandiose ideas. His first plans were to build a 4-meter (160-inch) or 6-meter (240-inch) Ritchey-Chrétien on an equatorial (conventional) mounting or, preferably, as a fixed vertical telescope, fed by a coelostat. Later he projected a similar 8-meter design. These systems were designed to allow rapid changes in the focal length and in the auxiliary instruments to make best use of the available seeing. The proposed observatories, telescopes, and mirrors were designed to minimize temperature changes and to get the telescopes as much as possible into the open air, to minimize what is now called "dome seeing." Ritchey proposed, and tried to make, lightweight built-up mirrors instead of solid glass disks. He experimented with systems to interrupt the exposure during moments of poor seeing.

His ideas were very advanced; most were far ahead of the technology of his time. He did not succeed in bringing them into practice, and he was ridiculed as a dreamer or even as insane, but most of his ideas have become accepted practices in the large telescopes of the post-Palomar era. The prospective donor of the French telescope turned out not to be the "Macaenas" the organizers had thought he would be, and the whole project collapsed in recriminations and lawsuits, terminated by his death under mysterious circumstances. The large telescope was never built, but Ritchey did have a laboratory and in 1927 built the world's first Ritchey-Chrétien reflector, a little 0.5-meter (20-inch), which he and Chrétien exhibited at the French Academy of Sciences. Ritchey realized that he would have to take spectacular photographs with it to validate it (as he had with the earlier Yerkes 24-inch and Mount Wilson 60-inch reflectors). However, with little money, a borrowed, poorly made mounting, the cloudy French skies, and his own disabilities (he was by then blind in one eye and too old and infirm to work effectively at the demanding task of operating a telescope all night long), Ritchey failed completely. He produced no spectacular photographs, and most American astronomers simply ignored the Ritchey-Chrétien system.

At the end of 1930, with the French telescope project completely out of money, Ritchey returned, nearly destitute, to the United States, where, through a complicated series of events, he did get his chance to build the world's first operating research Ritchey-Chrétien reflector, for the U.S. Naval Observatory. It was a 1-meter (40-inch) telescope, originally designed for the latitude of Paris but modified for erection in Washington, D.C. Ritchey completed it in 1934, but again in the poor climate and light-polluted skies of the nation's capital, operated by Naval Observatory astronomers who had no previous experience in photography or reflecting telescopes, it was an apparent failure. Ritchey returned to Azusa in 1937 or 1938, spending his last years writing manuscripts for popular books on astronomy, which he hoped would bring him the fame and fortune that had always eluded him. They were never published. Ritchey died in Azusa, California.

Only after World War II, when John S. Hall, an experienced research astronomer, took over the 40-inch Ritchey-Chrétien and succeeded in having it moved to a clear, dark-sky site near Flagstaff, Arizona, were its true potentialities realized. With it Arthur A. Hoag, another skilled astronomical researcher, produced spectacular direct photographs of nebulae and galaxies. Astronomers could see for themselves that the large coma-free field of view of the Ritchey-Chrétien was a great improvement over a conventional prime-focus, Newtonian or Cassegrain reflector. Aden Meinel, himself an expert in optics and observational astronomy, adopted the Ritchey-Chrétien design for the 84-inch Kitt Peak reflector, completed in 1963. Nearly all large research telescopes have since been built to this design.

• There is no single collection of Ritchey's scientific correspondence, but many letters to and from him can be found in the Yerkes Observatory Archives, Williams Bay, Wis.; the Mount Wilson Observatory Collection in the Henry Huntington Library, San Marino, Calif.; the George Ellery Hale Papers in the California Institute of Technology Archives, Pasadena; the Henri Chrétien Papers in the Cercle Henri Chrétien, Nice, France; the Records of the Naval Observatory in the National Archives, Washington, D.C.; and the Elihu Thomson Papers in the American Philosophical Society Library, Philadelphia. His own best published summary of his ideas is *L'Evolution de l'Astrophotographie et les Grands Téléscopes de l'Avenir* (1929), with the text in French and English in parallel columns. Ritchey was almost completely forgotten at the time of his death, and no adequate biographical articles were written until years later. Two excellent ones are Deborah J. Mills, "George Willis Ritchey and the Development of Celestial Photography," *American Scientist* 54 (1966): 64–93, and John S. Hall, "The Ritchey-Chrétien Reflecting Telescope: Half a Century from Conception to Acceptance," *Astronomy Quarterly* 5 (1987): 227–51. The only book-length biography is Donald E. Osterbrock, *Pauper and Prince: Ritchey, Hale and Big American Telescopes* (1993), which contains a complete bibliography of Ritchey's published scientific papers.

DONALD E. OSTERBROCK

RITCHIE, Albert Cabell (29 Aug. 1876–24 Feb. 1936), politician and governor of Maryland, was born in Richmond, Virginia, the son of Albert Ritchie, a judge, and Elizabeth Caskie Cabell. After graduation from Johns Hopkins University in 1896, Ritchie attended the law school of the University of Maryland, where he received his law degree in 1898. He was a noted early legal activist for consumer rights against utility companies.

Following admission to the Maryland bar in 1899, Ritchie practiced law in Baltimore, first with the prestigious firm of Steele, Semmes, Carey & Bond (1898–1903) and later as senior partner of Ritchie & Janney (1903–1920). As a respected legal theoretician and practitioner, he held an appointment as professor of law at his alma mater, the University of Maryland Law School, from 1907 to 1920. Ritchie married Elizabeth Catherine Baker in 1907. They had no children and divorced in 1916.

Ritchie entered public service in 1903 as assistant city solicitor for Baltimore, Maryland. In 1910 he was appointed assistant general counsel of the Maryland Public Service Commission, where he won wide public notice as an adversary of utility companies and an advocate of lower utility rates for consumers. Largely on the basis of the reputation he earned in the utility rate fights, he was elected attorney general of Maryland as a Democrat in 1915.

During World War I, in 1917, Ritchie served as general counsel for the War Industries Board under board chairman Bernard M. Baruch. Elected governor of Maryland in 1919, in 1921 he broke a longstanding Maryland tradition of single-term governorships and ran successfully for reelection. He eventually served four consecutive terms.

Ritchie regarded himself as a Jeffersonian Democrat, strongly supportive of decentralized decision making and states' rights. From that philosophical position he opposed the Volstead Act, the basis for the Eighteenth Amendment to the U.S. Constitution that mandated Prohibition. He believed Prohibition was a drastic federal infringement on the rights of state and local governments to regulate the production and sale of alcoholic beverages as they saw fit. At a conference of the nation's governors, convened by President Warren G. Harding in 1922 to rally public support for Prohibition, Ritchie stood virtually alone in opposition. His articulate defense of his position brought him to national prominence.

In 1924, 1928, and 1932 Ritchie unsuccessfully sought the Democratic party's presidential nomination. In 1932 he emerged as a major contender for the nomination before losing to Governor Franklin D. Roosevelt of New York. At the 1932 convention Ritchie played an influential role in the drafting of the party platform, which included two of his most ardently held positions: the repeal of Prohibition and a balanced federal budget.

Although Ritchie loyally supported the Roosevelt-Garner ticket in 1932, his philosophical differences with Roosevelt were wide and deep. In 1934 he suffered a humiliating defeat for reelection as governor of Maryland, losing to Republican Harry Whinna Nice, the man whom he had defeated in 1919 to launch his long tenure as governor. Ritchie suspected that the popular president had a hand in his downfall and grew increasingly bitter toward his party's leader.

In a series of speeches delivered in 1935, Ritchie attacked the New Deal as a "failed experiment" that threatened the ability of states to govern and the freedom of the people to direct that governance. In increasingly strident terms, he attacked the Roosevelt administration for eroding the self-governing function of the states, reckless deficit spending, and failure to implement the 1932 Democratic party platform, which, not incidentally, Ritchie largely wrote. He expected to take a leading role, perhaps as a candidate himself, against the renomination of President Roosevelt at the 1936 Democratic National Convention in Philadelphia. However, Ritchie died unexpectedly of a stroke in Baltimore, Maryland, before the convention.

• Ritchie's papers are at the Maryland Historical Society in Baltimore. Ritchie's anti–New Deal views are best expressed in his public speeches during 1935, especially "The Threatening Destruction of Self-Government among the American States," *Vital Speeches of the Day* 1 (22 Apr. 1935): 456–59, and "Which Way, America?" *Vital Speeches of the Day* 1 (12 Aug. 1935): 723–25. During the year before his death Ritchie wrote two articles that summarized his accomplishments as governor of Md. and expanded upon his political philosophy, "Fifteen Years a Governor," *American Magazine*, Aug. 1935, pp. 56–57; and "Balance of Powers," *Survey Graphic*, Apr. 1936, pp. 228–29. Notable articles detailing his life and career are "Albert C. Ritchie Dies Suddenly in Baltimore Home," *Washington Evening Star*, 24 Feb. 1936, and "Ex-Gov. Ritchie Is Dead; Stricken in Night in Home," *New York Times*, 24 Feb. 1936. Obituaries, including assessments of his career, are in *Time*, 2 Mar. 1936, p. 34; *Scholastic*, 14 Mar. 1936, p. 24; and *Christian Century*, 18 Mar. 1936, pp. 56–57.

FREDERICK J. SIMONELLI

RITCHIE, Thomas (5 Nov. 1778–3 July 1854), newspaper editor and Democratic party activist, was born in Tappahannock, Virginia, the son of Archibald Ritchie, a prominent immigrant Scots merchant, and Mary Roane, a member of one of Virginia's leading legal and political dynasties. After a number of false starts in law and medicine, Ritchie became a schoolteacher and then a bookseller in Richmond. In 1807 he married the daughter of a doctor, Isabella Foushee, with whom he had seven daughters and five sons. Encouraged and supported by his Roane relations he agreed, as an avowed promoter of the Jeffersonian administration, to buy and edit a Richmond newspaper, the *Enquirer*. It first appeared in 1804, and Ritchie ran it for the next forty-one years, usually supported by public patronage, such as state printing contracts.

From the first, Ritchie spoke in strong partisan terms while, at the same time, being himself heavily involved in running Virginia's Republican party. He ultimately became secretary of the party's state central committee and a member of the Republican leadership cadre, the Richmond Junto. Ritchie's early views were reformist in state politics: he advocated extending educational opportunities and expanding voting rights (to most white males). But he was ambivalent, sometimes negative, about slavery, hoping that it would gradually disappear yet never supporting any attempt to upset the racial status quo in Virginia. In national politics he served as spokesman for the Virginia dynasty and its states' rights tradition, supporting William Harris Crawford in the presidential election of 1824. With Crawford's passing, Ritchie joined with Martin Van Buren behind Andrew Jackson and against the centralizing ideas of John Quincy Adams (1767–1848) and Henry Clay. The long alliance between Ritchie and Van Buren represented, in the latter's words, the coming together of "Southern planters and plain republicans of the North" dedicated to preserving the Jeffersonian ideological tradition.

In the new democratic politics, involving a mass electorate and sustained party battles over policies, partisan newspaper editors became the prime channels of policy articulation and electoral mobilization. Ritchie was recognized as one of the leaders, along with Francis Preston Blair (1791–1876), Thurlow Weed and Horace Greeley, in the arts of editorial politics in this era. The *Richmond Enquirer* published Ritchie's views on policies, reprinted material from Democratic newspapers elsewhere, and denounced the National Republicans and their Whig successors. By arguing for a politics that subordinated immediate personal, local, and regional interests to national ones, the newspaper helped to define the party and promoted cooperation and unity against a common enemy. As a result, the *Enquirer*'s influence reached well beyond Virginia. "Father" Ritchie, as he was called, was universally considered the most powerful advocate of Jacksonian–Van Buren Democracy, and his editorials were reprinted by other Democratic newspapers throughout the Union.

Ritchie's expressed views represented the mainstream Democracy and unionism of his day. Loyal to the national party and committed to its advocacy of limited government intervention and free trade, as well as its opposition to a national bank, Ritchie was a moderate on the slavery issue whenever it appeared on the national scene. He advised caution and always sought compromise, as in the nullification and gag rule controversies. Along with Van Buren he was quick to denounce sectional extremists who challenged the national party's views and who demanded more attention to the slavery question. In 1836, even in the face of some southern resistance to Van Buren as Jackson's successor, Ritchie remained loyal to the New Yorker and to the national Democracy both of them represented.

During Van Buren's presidency after 1837, Ritchie's role as a national spokesman for the Democratic party expanded. But in the 1840s, with great reluctance, Ritchie and Van Buren split apart. Committed to the annexation of Texas and fearful that Van Buren's resistance to it was encouraging southern extremism, Ritchie broke with him to support James K. Polk as Democratic presidential nominee in 1844. After his victory, Polk invited Ritchie to Washington to become the editor of the new Democratic administration organ, the *Union*, in succession to the long established *Globe* of Van Buren's close friend Blair. Ritchie reluctantly agreed, turned the *Enquirer* over to two of his sons, and for the next six years powerfully defended the traditional Democracy in an increasingly troubled political climate, as he and others were drawn into debates over the extension of slavery. As always, Ritchie sought middle ground, looked for a national unionist position, and was quick to condemn those who spoke in sectionalist terms, even when such positions seemed increasingly out of step with the new directions of national political controversy. Ritchie supported the Compromise of 1850, his swan song on the national stage. He retired from the *Union* the next year and died, probably in Washington, D.C., three years later.

• Small amounts of Ritchie's correspondence are in the Library of Congress and in the library of the College of William and Mary. There are also many letters from Ritchie in the Martin Van Buren papers in the Library of Congress. The only full-scale biography is outdated: Charles H. Ambler, *Thomas Ritchie: A Study of Virginia Politics* (1913). There is a great deal of information about him in Karen Cook Janes, "From Ally to Enemy: Thomas Ritchie and Martin Van Buren, 1835–1848" (M.A. thesis, Cornell Univ., 1973). Two recent biographies of Martin Van Buren have much on Ritchie: Donald B. Cole, *Martin Van Buren and the American Political System* (1984), and John Niven, *Martin Van Buren: The Romantic Age of American Politics* (1983). On Virginia politics in Ritchie's day, there are useful insights in two articles by Harry Ammon: "The Jeffersonian Republicans: An Interpretation," *Virginia Magazine of History and Biography* 61 (Oct. 1953): 395–418, and "The Richmond Junto, 1800–1824," *Virginia Magazine of History and Biography* 71 (April 1963): 153–67.

JOEL H. SILBEY

RITT, Joseph Fels (23 Aug. 1893–5 Jan. 1951), mathematician, was born in New York City, the son of Morris Ritt and Eva Steinberg. He studied at the College of the City of New York (now City College of the City University of New York) from 1908 until 1910. He then accepted a position at the Naval Observatory in Washington, D.C., in part to help support his parents. While at City College he received the Belden Mathematical Prize for two consecutive years. He managed to continue his studies at George Washington University, where he received his Bachelor of Arts degree in 1913. In a summer graduate course in mathematics Ritt took at Columbia University, his talents were immediately recognized by Edward Kasner. Offered a place at Columbia as a University Fellow, Ritt resigned his position in Washington. In 1917 he received his Ph.D. from Columbia University, having completed his dissertation on differential equations of infinite order.

Following a brief stint as a master computer for the Ordnance Department around the end of World War I, Ritt returned to Columbia as an assistant professor in 1921 and was promoted to associate professor in 1927. In 1928 Ritt married Estelle Fine, and for most of his career she worked closely with him, preparing his mathematical publications for press. Both were avid travelers, and Ritt, who visited Asia and Europe frequently, was fluent in a number of languages. Several of his early papers were published in French. He reached the rank of professor in 1931 and served as head of the department of mathematics from 1942 to 1945; after that tenure he was named Davies Professor of Mathematics.

Reflecting the early and high regard his colleagues had for his work, Ritt was invited to be a colloquium lecturer for the American Mathematical Society in 1932 and later was a member of the AMS Colloquium Editorial Committee (1943–1948). He was elected vice president of the society in 1938 for a two-year term, having already been a trustee (1923–1924) and a member of the council (1926–1928). He was also on the editorial board of the *American Journal of Mathematics* (1936–1940). In addition to being a member of the National Academy of Sciences, he served on the National Research Council (1938–1941).

As a teacher, Ritt's talents were impressive: "His lectures were etched on the minds of his hearers who carried away a feeling of masterfulness" (Lorch, p. 308). Just as remarkable was his wit. Despite the fact that he was meticulous in the preparation of his lectures, Ritt managed to give the impression of spontaneity, and according to Paul Smith, "He believed that every teacher should be something of an actor" (p. 255).

Despite his energy in the classroom, Ritt was apparently a mathematician who preferred to work alone, although on rare occasions he collaborated on papers with students or colleagues, including Eli Gourin, J. L. Doob, H. W. Raudenbush and E. R. Kolchin. For the most part he worked by himself; perhaps his innate shyness made it difficult for him to work comfortably with others, as Lorch suggested. It is clear that Ritt took an unusual interest in reading the great mathematical works of his predecessors. He drew substantial inspiration from his careful study of classic texts, especially those by the great figures of the eighteenth and nineteenth centuries. Among his heroes were Niels Henrik Abel, Augustin-Louis Cauchy, David Hilbert, Carl G. J. Jacobi, Joseph-Louis Lagrange, the marquis Pierre-Simon de Laplace, Joseph Liouville, and Jules-Henri Poincaré. Their works set the standards Ritt tried to reach in his own mathematics, and were they to judge his work, he hoped it would be found worthy (Lorch, p. 309).

Consequently, Ritt preferred to work on classical subjects—areas already well-established in the nineteenth century, complex function theory and differential equations. Nevertheless, he appreciated the great power of abstract algebra, especially the value of structures, which he exploited with great finesse in much of his seemingly more conventional mathematical research. Much of his work, in fact, depended on decompositions and unique factorization theorems.

Ritt's dissertation, "On a General Class of Linear Homogeneous Differential Equations of Infinite Order with Constant Coefficients" (1916), was published the following year in the *Transactions of the American Mathematical Society* (18 [1917]: 21–49). In this early work Ritt was interested in properties of linear homogeneous differential operators of infinite order with constant coefficients. This was followed by two important studies, both published in the same journal in 1922: "Prime and Composite Polynomials" (23: 51–56) concerned the problem of factoring polynomials into primes, along with a thorough analysis of all possible decompositions; the other was "On Algebraic Functions Which Can Be Expressed in Terms of Radicals" (24: 21–30). Both exhibit his mastery of monodromy groups of Riemann surfaces, especially those associated with trigonometric polynomials and elliptic functions. Another important early paper, "Permutable Rational Functions" (*Transactions of the American Mathematical Society* 25 [1923]: 399–448), was devoted to the problem of determining when, given two rational functions ϕ (z) and Ψ(z), $\phi(\Psi(z)) = \Psi(\phi(z))$. Although Europeans like Gaston Julia and Pierre Fatou had been working on this subject with limited success, Ritt's approach was far more conclusive and marked a high point of his early career. Equally impressive were results Ritt in 1925 began to obtain in the theory of elementary functions, beginning with "Elementary Functions and Their Inverses" (*Transactions of the American Mathematical Society* 27 [1925]: 68–69). Following more or less directly in the steps of Liouville, whom he read with great care, Ritt developed Liouville's idea of factorization. In determining the structure of the elementary functions y=f(x) whose inverses x=g(y) are also elementary, he found that these were functions that could be factored in terms of $e(x)$, log x, or some algebraic function of x.

Over the years Ritt regularly offered courses on elementary functions, about which he wrote a short monograph, *Integration in Finite Terms* (1947). He was especially interested in studying exponential polynomials and problems of factorization, which led him to a definitive solution in the case of irreducible exponential polynomials in "A Factorization Theory for Functions $\sum_{i=1}^{n} a_i e(\alpha_i x)$" (*Transactions of the American Mathematical Society* 29 [1927]: 584–96). Over the next few years Ritt published several more papers devoted to exponential polynomials, notably results related to algebraic combinations of exponentials and on the zeros of exponential polynomials, which were published in 1929.

Ritt's best-known and most outstanding work is undoubtedly a long series of studies he began in the 1930s. These were devoted to creating a theory of ordinary and partial algebraic differential equations, first advanced in "Manifolds of Functions Defined by Systems of Algebraic Differential Equations" (*Transactions of the American Mathematical Society* 32 [1930]: 569–98). Over the next two decades, along with his students, he explored nearly every aspect of this subject. What he accomplished is summarized in two books spanning the entire history of Ritt's work on this subject: *Differential Equations from the Algebraic Standpoint* (1932) and his last major publication, *Differential Algebra* (1950).

A major discovery related to Ritt's algebraic approach to the theory of differential equations was made by one of his students, H. W. Raudenbush, who found a "definitive" formulation known as the "intersection theory," which was based on ideals. Ritt later acknowledged his earlier failure to appreciate sufficiently the role ideal theory might play in studying differential equations.

Ritt devoted much of the last three years of his life to applying Lie theory to the study of homogeneous differential polynomials. In a remarkable series of papers he achieved a bold generalization of the classic concept of continuous group. When asked to deliver an invited address at the first International Congress of Mathematicians after World War II, held in Cambridge, Massachusetts, in 1950, Ritt discussed his most recent research devoted to developing a Lie theory of differential groups. He died suddenly in New York City.

• In addition to works discussed in the text, Ritt published "Algebraic Aspects of the Theory of Differential Equations," *American Mathematical Society Semi-Centennial Publications* 2 (1938): 35–55, and two books, *Theory of Functions* (1947) and *Integration in Finite Terms* (1948). Ritt's last publications were devoted to generalizing Lie theory applied to homogeneous differential polynomials: "Associative Differential Operations," *Annals of Mathematics* 51 (1950): 756–65; "Differential Groups and Formal Lie Theory for an Infinite Number of Parameters," *Annals of Mathematics* 52 (1950): 708–26; and "Differential Groups," *Proceedings of the International Congress of Mathematicians*, vol. 1 (1950), pp. 207–8. For an assessment of Ritt's last papers see W. Nichols and B. Weisfeiler, "Differential Normal Groups of J. F. Ritt," *American Journal of Mathematics* 104 (1982): 943–1003. On Ritt's life and works see E. R. Lorch, "Joseph Fels Ritt," *Bulletin of the American Mathematical Society* 57 (1951): 307–18; and Paul A. Smith in National Academy of Sciences, *Biographical Memoirs* 29 (1956): 253–64.

JOSEPH W. DAUBEN

RITT, Martin (2 Mar. 1914–8 Dec. 1990), film director, was born in New York City, the son of Jewish immigrants from Eastern Europe, Morris Ritt, an emigration consultant, and Rose Lass, a theatrical agent. Ritt was raised in the Lower East Side milieu of "Europe in the home and America in the streets." After cheder each day, he and his classmates were usually assaulted by gangs of young anti-Semites. In later years he said such experiences toughened him and made him sympathetic to victims of prejudice. A good athlete, he went to Elon College in North Carolina in 1932 to play football for the "Fighting Christians," a comic and ironic experience for a first-generation American Jew.

During the depression Ritt witnessed the long bread lines in New York, and in North Carolina he saw the injustices perpetrated on blacks. Both experiences helped to develop in him strong feelings of social consciousness. He believed the federal government, both under Herbert Hoover and under Franklin Roosevelt, was not doing enough to help the "down-and-outers" and concluded that a socialist solution to America's problems was called for. He left Elon without graduating, and after a short stint at St. John's University in Brooklyn, he went on the "Borscht Circuit" in the Catskills, playing a nonsinging role in *Porgy and Bess*. Afterward he participated in the Theater of Action and then became affiliated with Harold Clurman's Group Theatre (1937–1942), where he was befriended by both Lee Strasberg and Elia Kazan. He married Adele Cutler Wolfe (also known as Adele Jerome, a dancer of some note) in 1940. They had two children.

After a stint (13 Apr. 1943–3 Jan. 1946) in the Army Air Corps (where in 1943 he produced a Sidney Howard play, *Yellow Jack*), Ritt began to direct plays on and off Broadway, two of which were Dorothy Heywood's *Set My People Free* (1948) and Mel Dinelli's

The Man (1950). He also acted in more than 150 tele-plays and directed about 100. For some time he direct-ed and acted in CBS's "Danger" series. Then in 1951 he went to work and found that he had been fired, hav-ing become a victim of the infamous television black-list of the early 1950s, when the House Un-American Activities Committee and Senator Joseph McCarthy were running roughshod over much of America's ar-tistic and creative community. Whether Ritt was ever a "card-carrying" member of the Communist party in the 1930s is problematic, because he gave different an-swers to this question in later years. His wife said that while he was quite sympathetic with socialist goals in the 1930s, he never became an official member of the Communist party. From 1951 to 1956 Ritt and his wife survived by selling ads for telephone directories and by winning at the racetrack. He was also on the staff of Actor's Studio and occasionally directed plays—Arthur Miller's *A Memory of Two Mondays* (1955), for example.

In 1956, though shunned by television producers, Ritt was offered a job by producer David Susskind to direct a movie about black-white relations and the con-ditions of labor unions in the United States. Starring John Cassavetes and Sidney Poitier, it was titled *Edge of the City*. This movie could not be shown in certain parts of the country, because it avoided racial stereo-types and depicted a close friendship between a black man and a white man. The success of *Edge of the City* prompted Abe Skouras of Twentieth Century Fox to invite Ritt to direct *No Down Payment* (1957), a scath-ing portrait of America's middle class in the immediate post–World War II era, when easy credit and social climbing were important characteristics. In this movie Ritt made it clear that the American dream came at a price, which included high divorce rates, neighbor-hood trysts and quarrels, and alcohol and gambling addictions. Ritt's movie career was all but assured af-ter *No Down Payment*.

Ritt was an inveterate reader of everything from comic books to philosophy. He loved the American South, though he abhorred its racism. He said that fer-ment and drama characterized the South more than any other part of the country. Thus he welcomed the chance to film William Faulkner's *The Long Hot Sum-mer* (1958) and *The Sound and the Fury* (1959), two films that identified him not just with black-white rela-tionships in the South but with all-white class struc-tures and struggles as well. Both of these films had mixed receptions from moviegoers and critics.

Ritt's most significant film in the early 1960s—and some admirers say of his entire career—was *Hud* (1963), starring Paul Newman and Patricia Neal. Ritt and his writers, Irving Ravetch and Harriet Frank, Jr., wanted to portray Hud as a person without any moral compulsions, someone who would be abhorred by "decent" people. To some extent, exactly the oppo-site happened: Hud's rebellious nature fit well into the growing "anti-establishment" mood of the early 1960s. Thus, with many moviegoers, Hud was a hero, not a villain.

Another milestone for Ritt was *The Spy Who Came in from the Cold* (1965), starring Richard Burton. In this film, Ritt demonstrated that the Western democ-racies were just as capable as the Soviets of using wick-ed ploys to have their way in the Cold War. In this respect, the British MI-5, the American CIA, and the Soviet KGB were more alike than different.

In 1979 Ritt released what many critics believed to be his signature film, *Norma Rae*, starring Sally Field (for which she won a Best Actress Oscar), about efforts to unionize a textile mill in North Carolina. Critics claimed that *Norma Rae* exemplified Ritt's themes of the loner, the outsider, individualism, the underdog, and social justice better than any of his other efforts.

In the 1980s Ritt continued his socially conscious themes, not permitting car chases or rampantly violent scenes to intrude on his creativity. Movie audiences, he believed, were sophisticated enough to understand and appreciate pictures that would make them think and reflect on their world. The "pensive necessity" of Ritt's films, however, probably accounted in large part for his never winning an Oscar as best director. His 1983 movie *Cross Creek* was a treatment of the famed novelist Marjorie Kinnan Rawlings's autobio-graphical account of rural Floridians in the 1920s. *Murphy's Romance* (1986) showed a sixty-year-old man (James Garner) winning the heart of a woman in her thirties (Sally Field), a development that won praise for Ritt from groups like the American Association of Retired People. In 1987 he joined with Barbra Strei-sand in making *Nuts*, a psychological treatment of child abuse in the United States. Continuing with themes of the day, in 1990 Ritt directed *Stanley and Iris*, a movie about widespread illiteracy in the United States.

In addition to directing, Ritt also acted in a number of films. *The End of the Game* (1976) was a psychologi-cal thriller in which Ritt played Inspector Hans Bar-lach. In *The Slugger's Wife* (1985), Ritt played Burley Devito, loosely based, some critics believed, on the life and career of the Los Angeles Dodger skipper Tommy Lasorda. Ritt also appeared in a documentary movie, *Hollywood on Trial* (1977), dealing with the blacklist, and a documentary for PBS titled *The Group Theatre* (1985).

After *Stanley and Iris*, Ritt retired to his home in Pa-cific Palisades, California, ill with diabetes and heart trouble and suffering from exhaustion. He died in a Santa Monica hospital. Some critics called him "the last" of the socially conscious directors; others disa-greed with this thought, saying that, in time, such movies will make a comeback.

• Letters, interviews, press clippings, memoranda, memora-bilia, and production notes on Ritt may be found in the col-lections at the Margaret Herrick Library of the Academy of Motion Picture Arts and Sciences in Beverly Hills, Calif. There is a small collection on Ritt at Boston College. Adele Ritt has a sizable collection of his materials at her home in Montecito, Calif. A full-length biography of Martin Ritt is Carlton Jackson, *Picking Up the Tab: The Life and Movies of*

Martin Ritt (1995). Another useful work is Sheila Whitaker, *The Films of Martin Ritt* (1972). Obituaries are in the *New York Times*, 11 Dec. 1990, and *Time*, 24 Dec. 1990.

CARLTON JACKSON

RITTENHOUSE, David (8 Apr. 1732–26 June 1796), astronomer, mathematician, and maker of mathematical instruments, was born at Paper Mill Run near Germantown, Pennsylvania, the son of Matthias Rittenhouse, a farmer, and Elizabeth Williams. Naturally talented in mathematics and mechanics, Rittenhouse constructed a model of a water mill at the age of eight, a wooden clock at about the age of seventeen, and a brass clock a short time later. He was fascinated with mathematics from his early years but, with little opportunity for schooling, was largely self-taught from books on elementary arithmetic and geometry and a box of tools inherited from an uncle, David Williams, a skilled furniture maker. From a translation of Isaac Newton's *Principia* (1687) and other scientific works procured for him by a brother-in-law, he managed to obtain a sound knowledge of the physical sciences. Despite the limitations of his environment, Rittenhouse eventually developed a remarkable capability for theoretical and observational astronomy.

At the age of nineteen Rittenhouse constructed a shop on his father's farm along the road to Norriton. There he made additional tools required for his adopted trade of clockmaker and produced and sold a number of tall case clocks, three of which incorporated small orreries, as well as mathematical instruments. He successfully experimented with the expansion of steel and wood for the development of a compensated pendulum of his own design for regulating his clocks with greater accuracy.

Between 1756 and 1785 Rittenhouse made a variety of astronomical instruments, which were highly prized, including transit and equal altitude instruments, zenith sectors, and telescopes. Particularly interesting was a collimating telescope he invented for the purpose of adjusting instruments in the meridian when intervening structures prevented visibility of a distant mark. He was also the first in the United States to utilize spider web as the filament for cross hairs in the telescope's eyepiece. His other instruments included barometers, a pocket metallic thermometer, and at least one hygrometer. In 1786 he experimented with diffraction, which had been described in Newton's *Opticks* (1704) as "the inflection of light in passing near the surfaces of bodies," and designed a plane transmission grating, made of fine wire fitted into a frame, that resolved a problem in the inflexion of light. With one of these he was able to observe six orders of spectra and to formulate the law that governed their displacement.

By 1770 there was a constant market for surveying instruments, and Rittenhouse's instruments were eagerly sought by surveyors and men of science as the finest available in America. The volume of his work required that at various times he employ shop assistants, including his brother Benjamin. Rittenhouse also made at least one variation compass and numerous plain surveying compasses and levels. Often cited as the inventor of the vernier surveying compass, he was among the very first to make them from about 1770. Featuring a nonius or vernier scale that enabled the surveyor to compensate for the angular difference between true north and magnetic north, "Rittenhouse's improved compasses," as they were known, became the basic instrument specified by the government for surveys of national public lands and remained in official use until the mid-nineteenth century. In 1766 Rittenhouse married Eleanor Coulston; they had two children. Two years after her death during childbirth in 1770, he married Hannah Jacobs; they had one child, who died in infancy.

For part of the year 1774, Rittenhouse held the post of city surveyor of Philadelphia, and throughout his career he served on commissions engaged in boundary surveys. These included surveys of portions of the boundaries of Pennsylvania with Maryland, New York, and what became the Northwest Territory as well as portions of New York's boundaries with New Jersey and Massachusetts. In 1784 he assisted in surveying a ninety-mile westward extension of the Mason-Dixon line, and in late 1772 or early 1773 he set the southwest corner of Pennsylvania, a point from which a line was run north in 1785 to establish the Pennsylvania-Virginia boundary. Experienced in common or terrestrial surveying, he also undertook topographical surveys of canals and rivers and was skilled in the use of astronomical observations for surveying.

Although Rittenhouse worked primarily as a maker of clocks and mathematical instruments, his major contributions to the sciences were in astronomy, for which his early studies of mathematics and the physical sciences served him well. He became closely involved with the transit of Venus in 1769, a scientific event of worldwide importance. Based on the preliminary calculations Rittenhouse had provided in 1768, the American Philosophical Society made elaborate plans to observe the event from three sites. For the occasion Rittenhouse constructed an observatory at his home in Norriton to serve as one of the sites, and he made most of the instruments used by himself and other observers at the Norriton observatory. These included a transit and equal altitude instrument, a regulator clock, and a transit instrument, which may have been the first telescope made in America. He also assisted in assembling the instruments for the other sites. Both Nevil Maskelyne, the British Astronomer Royal, and later Simon Newcomb, superintendent of the *American Ephemeris and Nautical Almanac* (authorized by Congress in 1849), attested to the accuracy of the observations of the transit made by Rittenhouse and his associates.

In 1770 Rittenhouse moved permanently to Philadelphia, where he constructed another observatory from which he regularly conducted observations. He maintained detailed records and published data on transits of Mercury and the satellites of Jupiter. He made observations of Uranus following its discovery, and of various solar and lunar eclipses, and calculations on meteors, comets, and other celestial phenomena. By this time his work as an astronomer had become recognized overseas, and in his *Traité d'astronomie* (1764) Jérome Le Français de Lalande noted that Rittenhouse's was the only American observatory of which he had knowledge. In 1770 Rittenhouse published "An Easy Method for Deducing the True Time of the Sun's Passing the Meridian" (*Transactions of the American Philosophical Association* 1 [1771]: 47–49), which the German astronomer Baron Franz Xaver von Zach included as part of his *Tabulae Motuum Solis* in 1792. Among Rittenhouse's important published works was a paper that provided his original solution for locating the place of a planet in its orbit, and he also published on the subjects of meteorology and geology and on the concept of magnetic dipoles.

Rittenhouse solved various problems in mathematics, producing the first of his mathematical papers in 1792, in which he sought to determine the period of a pendulum. He experimented with magnetism and electricity and in about 1784 produced the Rittenhouse Stove, an improvement on Benjamin Franklin's Pennsylvania fireplace.

Among Rittenhouse's best-known achievements was the construction of two orreries of his own design. Familiar with published descriptions and illustrations of orreries produced by several English makers, he based his design on John Rowning's *Compendious System of Natural Philosophy* (1758) and completed the instrument in early 1771. Although originally intended for the College of Philadelphia (now the University of Pennsylvania), it was purchased by the College of New Jersey (now Princeton University). In the summer of 1771 Rittenhouse built a second orrery on the same principle; it was purchased by the Pennsylvania General Assembly for the College of Philadelphia.

Thomas Jefferson, who saw the latter instrument during his sojourns in Philadelphia in 1775 and 1776 as a delegate from Virginia to the Continental Congress, was so intrigued with it that in 1783 he initiated a proposal to have it renamed "Rittenhouse" and to commission a similar instrument to be made for King Louis XVI of France, partly as an expression of gratitude for France's support during the American Revolution but primarily as evidence of American ingenuity. Rittenhouse agreed to make a third instrument, but poor health and other priorities interfered, and the project was abandoned.

Between 1773 and 1780 Rittenhouse calculated ephemerides for a number of almanacs published in Virginia, Pennsylvania, and Maryland. During this period he was in charge of the State House clock and of the scientific instruments and apparatus of the College of Philadelphia, and he served as librarian of the American Philosophical Society. In 1775 he delivered the society's annual address. The society's plans to erect a public astronomical observatory with Rittenhouse as its director had been submitted to the state legislature just as the American Revolution erupted, which caused its postponement and eventually its cancellation.

As one of the most prominent mechanicians of his time, Rittenhouse became involved at the outset of the Revolution with a variety of military responsibilities. He served as an engineer with the Committee of Safety in 1775, as its vice president in 1776, and as its president in 1777. He supervised the local casting of cannon and the manufacture of saltpeter, and he arranged for the substitution of iron for lead weights in clocks throughout the city to provide lead for making ammunition. He selected sites for a gunpowder mill and a magazine for military stores, supervised production of chains for protecting the Philadelphia harbor, and experimented with rifling of cannon and musket balls. During this period he was also a member of the Pennsylvania General Assembly and of the state constitutional convention of 1776. He served as a member of the Board of War, a trustee of the Loan Fund, and from 1779 to 1787 was the state treasurer.

From 1779 to 1796 Rittenhouse served as a member of the Board of Trustees of the University of Pennsylvania, where he held the position of professor of astronomy in 1780–1781. He was a member of the committee to organize the United States Bank, and in 1792 President George Washington appointed him the first director of the newly established U.S. Mint, a position he held until 1795.

Among the first elected to membership in the American Philosophical Society in 1768, Rittenhouse was active from the time of its founding, having served as curator, librarian, secretary, vice president, and as a member of many of its committees, and he contributed numerous articles to its publications. In 1791 he was elected the second president of the society, succeeding Benjamin Franklin on the latter's death. He received many honors, including three master of arts degrees; a privately owned ship was named for him; and in 1795 he was appointed a foreign member of the Royal Society of London.

Rittenhouse, who suffered poor health constantly throughout his lifetime, died at his home in Philadelphia. His body was laid beneath the floor of his observatory, the place later marked with a marble slab inscribed only with his name, age, and date of death. (His remains were later moved to a local cemetery.) Next to Franklin, Rittenhouse was the leading figure in eighteenth-century American science. His achievements reflect an unusual combination of theory and practice: while his major contributions were primarily observational and experimental, his name has become synonymous with precision instrumentation.

• The collections of the American Philosophical Society contain three of Rittenhouse's manuscript notebooks, and other Rittenhouse papers are in the society's minutes, archives, and miscellaneous manuscripts. Letters, receipts, and orders are scattered in the collections of the Historical Society of Pennsylvania, primarily among the Benjamin Smith Barton Papers. The University of Pennsylvania Archives contain minutes of its board of trustees for the period during which Rittenhouse served and other related materials. Papers relating to the various Pennsylvania state committees and the Treasury on which Rittenhouse served are part of the state archives of the Pennsylvania Historical and Museum Commission in Harrisburg. Other Rittenhouse items are among the papers of Thomas Jefferson in the Manuscripts Division of The Library of Congress. All of Rittenhouse's papers on astronomy, the physical sciences, and mathematics were published in the first four volumes of the *Transactions of the American Philosophical Society*. The most important of these are "Projection of the Ensuing Transit of Venus," 1 (1771): 4; "Calculation of the Transit of Venus Over the Sun as It Happened June 3rd, 1769 in Lat. 40 N. Long 5h. West from Greenwich," "Apparent Time of the Contacts of the Limbs of the Sun and Venus; with other Circumstances of Most Note, in the Different European Observations of the Transit, June 3rd, 1769," "Delineation of the Transit of Venus," 1 (1771): 4–38; "New Method of Placing a Meridian Mark," 1 (1771): 181–83; "A Description of a New Orrery," 1 (1771): 1–3; "An Account of Some Experiments in Magnetism," 2 (1786): 178–81; "A Method of Finding the Sum of the Several Powers of the Sines," 3 (1793): 155–56; and "To Determine the True Place of a Planet," 4 (1799): 21–26. His writings on natural history appeared in the *Columbian Magazine* 1 (1786–1787), and an article coauthored with Francis Hopkinson on electricity was published in the *Philadelphia Medical and Physical Journal* 1, pt. 2 (1805): 96–160.

Rittenhouse's *Memoirs of the Life of David Rittenhouse, LL.D., F.R.S., Late President of the American Philosophical Society, &c., Interspersed with Various Notices of Many Distinguished Men: With an Appendix Containing Sundry Philosophical and Other Papers, Most of Which Have Not Hitherto Been Published* (1813), remains one of the most useful sources about his life and work. Also useful is Benjamin Rush, *An Eulogium Intended to Perpetuate Rittenhouse Delivered . . . on the 17th Dec. 1796* (1797). The most recent biography, Brooke Hindle, *David Rittenhouse* (1964), emphasizes Rittenhouse's scientific activities and achievements. See also Hindle, *The Pursuit of Science in Revolutionary America 1735–1785* (1956). A comprehensive family history, although containing errors, is provided by Daniel K. Cassel, *A Genea-Biographical History of the Rittenhouse Family and All Its Branches in America. With Sketches of Their Descendants . . .* (2 vols., 1893). Articles that relate to specific scientific achievements include Thomas D. Cope, "The Rittenhouse Diffraction Grating," *Journal of the Franklin Institute* 214 (July 1932): 99–104; Simon Newcomb, "Discussion of Observations of the Transits of Venus in 1761 and 1769," *Astronomical Papers Prepared for the Use of the American Ephemeris and Nautical Almanac*, vol. 2 (1891), pp. 259–405; and W. Carl Rufus, "David Rittenhouse as a Mathematical Disciple of Newton," *Scripta Mathematica* 8 (Dec. 1941): 228–31.

SILVIO A. BEDINI

RITTENHOUSE, Jessie Belle (8 Dec. 1869–28 Sept. 1948), critic and poet, was born in Mount Morris, New York, the daughter of John E. Rittenhouse and Mary J. MacArthur, farmers. Her childhood was spent on a farm in the Genesee Valley, where she was an avid reader. The generosity of Rittenhouse's aunt enabled her to attend Genesee Wesleyan Seminary in Lima, New York, which she entered as a sophomore after attending the Nunda Academy for two years. Rittenhouse excelled in languages, thrived in the literary society, and graduated in 1890. She then returned to her family in Cheboygan, Michigan, where they had re-

cently moved so that Mary Rittenhouse, who was chronically ill, could be closer to her mother. Family finances precluded any further formal education.

Rittenhouse described her own interests in her autobiography, *My House of Life* (1934), as including "from the outset two passions—reform and poetry" (Rittenhouse, p. 116). After a winter with an aunt in St. Augustine, Florida, Rittenhouse somewhat reluctantly took a job teaching Latin and English at a private school in Cairo, Illinois; likewise, the next year she taught at Akeley Institute for Girls in Grand Haven, Michigan. Subsequently she began writing feature stories for newspapers, but her career really took off when she reviewed Clinton Scollard's *The Hills of Song* for the *Buffalo Express*. Scollard was then a young poet and a professor of English at Hamilton College. Rittenhouse's review caught the attention of Copeland and Day, a poetry publishing firm in Boston, which began sending her collections of verse by other young poets for reviews. After other publishers began to send her their books, Rittenhouse started to establish herself as a writer, going to work as a reporter for the *Rochester Democrat and Chronicle*. Although she was successful as a reporter, Rittenhouse still wanted to spend more time writing literary criticism; consequently, in 1895 she moved to Chicago and resumed freelance writing.

Four years later Rittenhouse moved to Boston, the literary mecca of the day, where a "new spirit of poetry was stirring" (Rittenhouse, p. 139). While in Boston, Rittenhouse developed her literary reputation by editing two volumes of translations of the Rubáiyát of Omar Khayyám for Little, Brown and Company. In order to remedy the common perception that American poetry was dead, she published *The Younger American Poets* (1904), a volume of critical essays on contemporary poets. In essence creating a new field, the novelty of her approach generated much discussion and garnered praise from many newspapers, including the *New York Times Book Review*. Her criticism focused on analyzing the verse and the feelings that it evoked rather than on biographical details of the author's life.

Rittenhouse decided to try her luck in New York in 1905. After moving there she began to review poetry regularly for the *New York Times Review of Books*, a position she retained for the next ten years. In 1910 she played a pivotal role in founding the Poetry Society of America, a combination society and salon for leading contemporary poets and their ideas. As the first secretary, Rittenhouse spent the next ten years developing it into a forum for intellectual exchange, friendship, and support of emerging poets and their work. After supporting Amy Lowell in the advancement of the imagist movement in poetry, in 1913 Rittenhouse published the first of her anthologies, *The Little Book of Modern Verse*. The only anthology at the time that featured living poets, Rittenhouse included writers of the 1890s and the first decade of the twentieth century. She organized the anthology by theme, the first volume with poetry arranged according to content rather than chronology or author. It was quite successful, and Rittenhouse followed with *The Little Book of American Poets* in 1915, volumes two and three of *Modern Verse* in 1919 and 1925, and *The Little Book of Modern British Verse* in 1924. In 1914 she also began to give popular lectures on poetry, which continued for the next ten years.

Rittenhouse's activities as a critic and anthologist kept her from her own creative work until 1917, at which time she began writing her own lyric verse. *The Door of Dreams* appeared in 1918, followed by *The Lifted Cup* (1921) and *The Secret Bird* (1930). Her verse, written in conventional rhyme and meter, has been largely overlooked on account of modernists' critical emphasis on poetic complexity, free verse, and irony. Ironically, while Rittenhouse embraced the energy and spirit of poetic modernism in her own criticism and teaching, her own work never followed its precepts.

In 1924 Rittenhouse married Clinton Scollard in Carmel, California; they had no children. The couple spent part of each year in Kent, Connecticut, and part in Winter Park, Florida, where Rittenhouse gave an annual lecture course at Rollins College. She also organized the Poetry Society of Florida and with Scollard edited *Patrician Rhymes: A Resume of American Society Verse* (1932) and *The Bird-Lovers Anthology* (1930). After Scollard's death in 1932, she moved to Grosse Point Park, Michigan. She was also awarded a bronze medal by the Poetry Society of America in 1930 for her service to poetry, and in 1940 the National Poetry Center gave her a gold medal for *The Moving Tide: New and Selected Lyrics* (1939). Rittenhouse died in Detroit.

Rittenhouse was recognized among her peers as a strong force behind the development of poetry; Edwin Markham, in *The Book of American Poetry* (1934), declared her an "immense force in the onward march of poetry" (Markham, p. 530). Although many of her contributions to poetry have been overlooked and largely forgotten, there is no doubt that her intellectual, creative, and organizational energies were significantly influential in the establishment of public interest in contemporary poetry and criticism at the beginning of the twentieth century.

• Jessie Belle Rittenhouse left her library and correspondence to Rollins College. For the letters of Sara Teasdale and Rittenhouse, see Edward H. Cohen, *Resources for American Literary Study* 4 (1978): 224–27. Rittenhouse's own autobiography is still the most informative source concerning the details of her growth and career. Rittenhouse also edited numerous collections in addition to the ones mentioned above, including *The Poetry of Clinton Scollard* (1911), *Selected Poems of Edith M. Thomas* (1926), *Rollins Book of Verse* (1929), and *The Singing Heart: Selected Lyrics and Other Poems by Clinton Scollard* (1934). A book-length consideration of Rittenhouse and her circle is Margaret Widdemer, *Jessie Rittenhouse: A Centenary Memoir-Anthology* (1969). For earlier mention of Rittenhouse, see also Howard Willard Cook, *Our Poets of Today* (1918); Gustav Davidson, *In Fealty to Apollo* (1950); and Louis Untermeyer, *The New Era in American Po-*

etry (1919). Obituaries appear in the *New York Times*, 30 Sept. 1948; *Detroit News*, 29 Sept. 1948; and the *Saturday Review of Literature*, 30 Oct. 1948.

HEATHER HEWETT

RITTENHOUSE, William (1644–17 Feb. 1708), paper manufacturer and Mennonite bishop, was born in Mülheim on the Ruhr River near Essen, in the lordship of Broich and the duchy of Berg, the son of Maria Hagerhoffs and George Rittenhausen (also spelled Rüddinghuysen and Rittinghausen). Almost nothing is known about his early life. His father may have been involved in papermaking, an important industry in Mülheim since at least the early sixteenth century. William married a local woman (name unknown), with whom he had three children, all of whom were born between 1666 and 1674, presumably in Mülheim.

About 1678 Rittenhouse moved his family to the Netherlands, where he engaged in papermaking. They lived for a while in Arnhem, then in Amsterdam, where in June 1678 Rittenhouse became a Dutch citizen. Ambitious to improve his fortune, and perhaps influenced by William Penn's broadsides publicizing his new colony of Pennsylvania, Rittenhouse immigrated with his wife and three children to Pennsylvania about 1688. He had come under the influence of the pietistic Anabaptists while living in Mülheim or in Holland (the details are not known); by the time he immigrated to Pennsylvania he had become a devout follower of Menno Simons. There was no paper mill at the time in any of the British American colonies, and he found the possibility of gaining a monopoly of paper production in such a potentially large market quite appealing.

Rittenhouse settled in Germantown, a hamlet situated on high, hilly ground a few miles north of the rapidly growing town of Philadelphia. Germantown was already a thriving community of German immigrants when the Rittenhouses arrived. Although Pennsylvania was a Quaker colony, Germantown was the cradle of American Mennonitism. In April 1689 Rittenhouse was awarded a town lot. His oldest son Claus, who married a Dutch woman from New York the following month and joined his father in the paper manufacturing business, was granted two half-lots in Germantown.

Lacking the capital to construct the paper mill alone, Rittenhouse formed a company to underwrite the venture. Three Philadelphia residents joined Rittenhouse, including William Bradford, the colony's only printer. The company acquired a twenty-acre parcel of land on a branch of Wissahickon Creek, later known as Paper Mill Run, in what is now Roxborough Township and built the mill in 1690. What difficulties Rittenhouse encountered in getting the operation underway are unknown, but the business was successful. Within two years tracts publicizing Pennsylvania spoke glowingly of the mill at Germantown that made fine white paper from castoff rags. One of the conditions of the partnership was that Rittenhouse would give Bradford first claim on the purchase of the paper he produced, an arrangement that ensured access to a ready market for his product. In 1691 William and Claus Rittenhouse became naturalized citizens by swearing fealty to the English sovereigns William and Mary. Two years later Bradford departed for New York. Thereafter he leased his quarter share in the mill to the Rittenhouses, father and son. They continued to honor their contractual arrangement to give Bradford first claim to the paper they produced. That monopoly ended about 1700 when a spring freshet swept the wooden mill completely away. Along with the structure they lost a considerable quantity of paper, materials, and tools, reducing them to great distress. They rebuilt. But Bradford declined to give his aid, with the result that Rittenhouse terminated the monopoly Bradford had enjoyed and began selling the mill's paper goods to others.

About this time Claus, who was gradually taking over the mill's operation, began to buy out the other partners. In 1704 the last holdout, Bradford, sold his share, so that fourteen years after it was established the Rittenhouses became sole proprietors of the only paper-making factory in America. The mill, built on or directly over Paper Mill Run in order to provide water to keep the mass of decomposing rags wet and to operate the triphammer that pounded the pulp, was a small operation. Its annual output probably did not exceed fifteen hundred reams of paper of all kinds, but that was all-important in supplying much of the local need for high-quality paper.

In addition to pioneering the manufacture of paper in America, Rittenhouse served as minister and the first bishop of the Mennonite faith in America. Mennonite records are sparse, but it appears from one surviving document that Rittenhouse was chosen minister of the Germantown Mennonites in 1690 and commenced ministerial duties at the same time he began building his paper mill. Rittenhouse planned to print an English translation of the eighteen-article Mennonite Confession of Faith, which was available only in the German and Dutch languages. But the cost was greater than the Germantown Mennonite community, which grew only slowly, could afford, and Rittenhouse abandoned the project.

Mennonite practice stipulated that only a bishop could administer holy communion and baptism; thus the Germantown Mennonites were without those Christian sacraments for more than a decade. The Germantown brethren in 1701 appealed to church fathers in Hamburg to send them a bishop. The fathers responded by authorizing the Germantown communicants to elect their own. Rittenhouse was chosen but declined to serve, believing himself to be unworthy of the office. In 1706 the desperate congregation again appealed to church fathers abroad to send relief and in 1707 were again told to elect their own bishop. Rittenhouse was promptly chosen. This time the reluctant minister accepted the important position, but he died at his Germantown home before he could assume the office. Rittenhouse's wife survived him only a short

time. His son Claus carried on the paper-making business and in time became a Mennonite minister himself.

• No Rittenhouse papers are known to exist. The fullest account of his life and career is Milton Rubincam, *William Rittenhouse and Moses Dissinger, Two Eminent Pennsylvania Germans* (1959), vol. 58 of the Publications of the Pennsylvania-German Society series, but it is limited by the dearth of documentary sources. The *Mennonite Quarterly Review*, especially for the years 1933 and 1934, has scattered information about the Germantown Mennonites. The history of the paper mill is covered in a rather dated article by H. G. Jones, "Historical Sketch of the Rittenhouse Paper Mill," *Pennsylvania Magazine of History and Biography*, 20 (1899), and in James N. Green's brief monograph, *The Rittenhouse Mill and the Beginnings of Papermaking in America* (1990). D. K. Cassel, *A Genealogical-Biographical History of the Rittenhouse Family and All Its Branches in America* (1893), discusses the family's German roots.

CHARLES LOWERY

RITTER, Frédéric Louis (22 June 1834–6 July 1891), composer, conductor, and author, was born in Strasbourg, France. His father (full name unknown) was of Spanish extraction, the family name having originally been Caballero. (His mother's identity also is unknown.) Ritter studied music as a youth with Hans Schletterer and Franz Hauser and then went to Paris to study with J. Georges Kastner, his cousin. In 1852 Ritter was appointed professor of music at the Protestant seminary of Fénéstrange in Lorraine.

Ritter emigrated to the United States in 1856 with his parents and settled in Cincinnati. There he founded the Cecilia Society chorus and the Philharmonic Orchestra and successfully worked to promote classical music performance. In 1861 he left Ohio for New York, where he accepted directorship of the Sacred Harmonic Society and the Arion male choir. With the latter group he conducted a series of seven annual concerts, and in 1867 he organized and conducted, in Steinway Hall, the first musical festival held in New York.

Also in 1867, Ritter became professor of music at Vassar College in Poughkeepsie, New York, serving as administrator of the music program, offering historical lectures, and conducting choral ensembles. He continued to conduct in New York and devoted time to writing. He was married to Francis "Fanny" Raymond (1840–1890), who was also a musician (mezzo-soprano) and author. She wrote *Woman as a Musician* (1877), translated Schumann's *Gesammelte Schriften* and Ehlert's *Briefe über Music*, and gave lecture recitals in New York and at Vassar. After 1874 he resided in Poughkeepsie, holding his professorship at Vassar until his death. He was awarded a Mus. D. from New York University in 1878. Ritter died while on a trip to Antwerp.

Ritter is remembered for his choral conducting in Cincinnati and New York and for his service as a guest conductor and adjudicator at other venues. He is credited with introducing a number of choral works to

American audiences and with providing leadership at a time when many felt it important to raise the standard of musical taste in the United States. Of equal interest are his numerous writings and articles; the latter appeared in American, French, and German periodicals and were apparently well known on both sides of the Atlantic. Ritter's books include *History of Music* (2 vols., 1870 and 1874), *Music in England* (1883), *Music in America* (1883), and *Music in Its Relation to Intellectual Life* (1891). The text on American music is one of the first to deal with that subject, though its scope is limited: part one covers seventeenth- and eighteenth-century Anglo-Saxon music in New England; part two focuses on social and musical life in New York and Boston in the nineteenth century. Ritter's belief in European musical and aesthetic superiority is evident in his writings. In his concluding survey of American musical activity to that time, he claims that "There is, at present, only one city in the United States in which all these features of modern musical culture are to be found—New York" (*Music in America*, p. 475). Regarding American composers, he states, "The history of music in America is apparently now entering on a new epoch, and, it is to be hoped, a most important one. So far the divers labors in the music field have been, more or less, preparatory ones" (*Music in America*, p. 503).

Ritter's pedagogical works include *Musical Dictation, a Practical Method for Instruction of Choral Classes* (2 vols., 1887–1889) and *Manual of Musical History* (1886). He edited an English edition of *The Realm of Tones* (1883), a collection of more than 300 brief biographies and portraits of celebrated European musicians. To this edition he added an appendix of biographical sketches of American musicians "who have done most to cultivate in America a taste for the best class of music" (*The Realm of Tones*, preface). Discussed among the nearly fifty entries are John S. Dwight, Theodore Thomas, George Bristow, Louis M. Gottschalk, Dudley Buck, Clara Kellogg, and himself. Ritter collaborated with Rev. J. Ryland Kendrick on *Laudamus: A Hymnal* (1877).

Ritter's compositions, which are European in style, include three symphonies; an overture entitled *Othello*; a symphonic poem, *Stella*; concertos for piano and cello; a fantasia for bass clarinet and orchestra; and several chamber, keyboard, and choral works. He also composed a number of German art songs and songs for children. His cello concerto was performed by the New York Philharmonic Society during the 1864–1865 season; the same group presented his Symphony no. 2 in 1871.

Ritter's contribution to American music is threefold. He provided leadership in organizing choral ensembles with high performance standards, was instrumental in introducing American audiences to classical choral repertoire, and initiated the study of music in the United States. His shortcoming was his belief that American music should imitate its European heritage; he saw little value in the cultivation of indigenous styles.

• A Complete listing of Ritter's compositions is found in F. O. Jones, ed. *A Handbook of American Music and Musicians* (1971), an unabridged republication of the first edition published in 1886. Information about Ritter is contained in Johannes Riedel's introduction to the 1970 reprint of Ritter, *Music in America* (1883), and in Louis C. Elson, *The History of American Music* (1925). A lengthy obituary is in the *New York Tribune*, 7 July 1891.

LINDA L. POHLY

RITTER, Joseph Elmer (20 July 1892–10 June 1967), Roman Catholic cardinal, was born in New Albany, Indiana, the son of Nicholas A. Ritter, a baker, and Bertha Luette. While a seventh grader in parochial school, he decided to become a priest. Two years later he enrolled in St. Meinrad's Abbey, a Benedictine seminary near Evansville, Indiana, where he completed his high school and college education while studying for the priesthood. In 1917 he was ordained and appointed assistant pastor of St. Patrick's Parish in Indianapolis, and six months later he was made assistant pastor of the diocesan cathedral in Indianapolis. He became rector of the cathedral in 1920 and pastor of the cathedral parish in 1925.

In 1930 Ritter was made a consultor to Joseph Chartrand, the bishop of Indianapolis. In this position he advised Chartrand concerning the management of diocesan affairs and spoke out forcefully against the activities of the Ku Klux Klan, which at the time was particularly strong in Indiana. Ritter also served briefly as vice president of the *Indiana Catholic and Record*, the diocesan newspaper. In 1933 he was named Chartrand's auxiliary bishop, and in 1934, following Chartrand's death, he was consecrated bishop of Indianapolis. Despite the ill effects of the Great Depression, the diocese under Ritter's direction reduced its debt by considerably more than $3 million while expanding significantly its charitable activities and completing construction of its cathedral. He also established a home missions board that redistributed contributions from the wealthier parishes to the poorer ones and implemented a special ministry for evangelizing rural areas. His most noteworthy achievement came in the area of race relations. In addition to establishing the De Paul Center in downtown Indianapolis to provide cultural and recreational opportunities for blacks, he effected the integration of the diocese's parochial schools, a task that was completed with little fanfare in 1941. When Indianapolis was designated an archdiocese three years later, he was made its archbishop and given jurisdiction over the new dioceses of Evansville and Lafayette, Indiana.

In 1946 Ritter was appointed archbishop of St. Louis, Missouri. At the time only one St. Louis parochial school was completely integrated, so the next year he ordered the desegregation of all Catholic schools in the archdiocese. The order inspired vehement protests by many parents of white students who appealed to the Vatican's apostolic delegate in Washington, D.C., to rescind the order. When this appeal failed, those parents threatened to seek a federal court injunction barring desegregation. Ritter responded by formally notifying every Catholic in the archdiocese that anyone who opposed the order in any way would be excommunicated, which brought the protests to a complete halt. Once the schools were integrated Ritter implemented the desegregation of hospitals and other archdiocesan facilities. Throughout his tenure in St. Louis he urged white Catholics to reach out to blacks by inviting them to move into their communities and to join their organizations.

In 1949, Ritter implemented a major building program that resulted in the construction of forty-one churches, sixteen high schools, and two hospitals. In 1955 he dispatched three archdiocesan priests to La Paz, Bolivia, where they established the first foreign mission sponsored by a U.S. diocese, inspiring other U.S. prelates to follow suit. Three years later, following a papal decision to encourage greater lay participation during religious services, he became head of the Bishops' Commission on the Liturgical Apostolate that permitted laymen to serve as lectors and ministers of the eucharist during the celebration of the mass.

Proclaimed a cardinal in 1961, Ritter attended every session of the Second Vatican Council, a series of meetings of the Roman Catholic hierarchy held in Rome, Italy, from 1962 to 1965 to renew and reform the church. He joined with the more liberal cardinals to pass resolutions recognizing the rights of individual conscience in religious liberty, absolving the Jews of blame for the death of Jesus Christ, and reaffirming the right of the bishops to participate actively in the decision-making process concerning every aspect of the church's affairs. He also opposed the conservative faction's efforts to bring the council to a close without discussing nuclear warfare, birth control, and other contemporary topics. He played a major role in gaining approval for a resolution to permit saying mass in the vernacular instead of Latin and saw to it that the first mass said in English in the United States took place in 1965 in St. Louis. Despite his liberal leanings, he declared in 1962 that Catholics in his archdiocese should attend secular colleges only to study curricula not available in Catholic schools, and then they must enroll in their college's Newman Club, a Catholic campus organization.

Ritter served as president of the National Catholic Educational Association in 1952. He was a member of the governing board of the National Catholic Welfare Conference from 1953 to 1967 and became the head of its legal department in 1959. He died in St. Louis. As a leader of the more liberal element of the U.S. hierarchy, Ritter pioneered the participation of the Roman Catholic church in the civic and social welfare of the community and in the struggle to eradicate racial intolerance in the United States.

• Ritter's papers are in the archives of the archdiocese of St. Louis. A biography is in Francis Beauchesne Thornton, *Our American Princes: The Story of the Seventeen American Cardinals* (1963). An obituary is in the *New York Times*, 11 June 1967.

CHARLES W. CAREY, JR.

RITTER, Tex (12 Jan. 1905–2 Jan. 1974), singer and actor, was born Woodward Maurice Ritter in Murvaul, Texas, the son of James Everett Ritter, a farmer and cowboy, and Elizabeth Matthews. Ritter attended school in his church, "which was partitioned into two rooms." When he was fifteen, the family of eight resettled in Nederland, southwest of Beaumont and Port Arthur. After the harvest, he attended "singing schools" conducted by itinerant teachers, one of whom was P. O. Stamps, who formed the Stamps Quartet. Ritter sang bass in the Methodist choir and performed at "play parties" in churches. "However," he told an interviewer, "singing was a hobby. I never thought about getting paid. My two brothers were the singers. When I'd sing with them, they'd ask Mother to make me stop!"

His parents often left Ritter with his grandfather, an attorney and county clerk in Carthage. He was fascinated by law and sat in on trials. By the time he was graduated from Beaumont's South Park High School, he was a strong debater, inspired by hours of watching summations. He enrolled at the University of Texas at Austin. Intent on a law degree, he majored in political science and economics. Ritter joined the glee club and led a campus quartet, eventually singing the cowboy songs he had grown to love. He entered law school in 1928, dropping out after a year to sell insurance and sing.

Ritter worked in Houston radio, becoming the first major western singer on a weekly program. Growing restless, his brother-in-law suggested going east. He joined a choral group "which took me to New York at the height of the Depression. People were jumping out windows and selling apples. I had no money and tried to find work. An oil company wanted to send me to Venezuela, but I stayed and studied voice." He shared an apartment and bought food by selling his books. He enrolled in Columbia School of Law and sang nights, an activity "frowned upon by the faculty." He withdrew, joining a Chicago company of his choral group. He studied law at Northwestern University, but less than a year later left on a road tour.

Ritter returned to New York in 1930 and landed a part singing four traditional cowboy songs in *Green Grow the Lilacs* (on which Richard Rodgers and Oscar Hammerstein based *Oklahoma!*). He understudied the lead played by Franchot Tone. After the run, he took his act to Ivy League colleges. Soon he was much in demand on the lecture/recital circuit. He appeared in several short-lived Broadway shows, then in *Mother Lode*, a play about the discovery of San Francisco. Ritter became a popular cowboy singer in clubs and on radio programs.

When Gene Autry and Roy Rogers ushered in musical westerns in Hollywood, Ritter moved west and starred as a singing cowboy. Ritter married Dorothy Fay Southworth, his leading lady in three westerns, in 1941 in Prescott, Arizona, her hometown. They had two sons: Tom, afflicted with cerebral palsy, became an attorney, and John became a popular television star. The Ritters became active spokespersons for United Cerebral Palsy.

In two decades Ritter starred in eighty-five second features, including *Song of the Gringo* (1936); *Trouble in Texas* (1937), which featured Rita Cansino, later Rita Hayworth; *Sing, Cowboy, Sing* (1938); *Where the Buffalo Roam* (1938); *Ridin' the Cherokee Trail* (1941); *The Old Chisholm Trail* (1943); and *Marshal of Gunsmoke* (1946).

In the 1940s, billed as "America's most beloved cowboy," he formed Tex Ritter's Hollywood Western Revue. As the popularity of musical westerns faded with the advent of television, Ritter became a regular performer on "Town Hall Party," broadcast from Compton, California, a Los Angeles suburb, as NBC's answer to ABC's (Ozark) "Jubilee, U.S.A."

A larger-than-life character with a gruff bass voice, Ritter did not provide any major firsts as a recording artist. He made his first recordings for Columbia in Chicago in 1932. "They gave me one hundred dollars for four sides," he told an interviewer in 1973. His first recording was "Goodbye Ole Paint." "There were no royalties. It was just me and my guitar. One of the songs, 'Rye Whiskey,' became a hit." He was signed by Decca Records and recorded for their Vocalion label. In 1942 Ritter joined Capitol Records, where he recorded for thirty-three years.

Ritter's hits (many of which he wrote) are a list of country western classics: "Jingle Jangle Jingle," "Have I Told You Lately That I Love You?," "When You Leave, Don't Slam the Door," "We Live in Two Different Worlds," "Bad Brahma Bull," "I Dreamed of a Hillbilly Heaven," "Boll Weevil," and "Blood on the Saddle" (his recording, sung by an animated grizzly bear, is featured in Disney World's All American Jamboree). His million-selling "High Noon (Do Not Forsake Me, Oh, My Darling)," written by Dimitri Tiomkin and Johnny Mercer, which Ritter sings on the soundtrack of the 1952 film *High Noon*, won the Academy Award for best song.

In October 1964 Ritter became the first living inductee into the Country Music Hall of Fame. His plaque reads, "One of America's most illustrious and versatile stars of radio, television, records, motion pictures and Broadway stage. Untiring pioneer and champion of the Country and Western music industry. His devotion to his God, his family and his country is a continuing inspiration."

In 1965 the Ritters settled in Nashville, the center of country music, and Tex joined the Grand Ole Opry. A staunch Republican, Ritter ran against Tennessee's Al Gore, Sr., for the Senate in 1970, but he was defeated. On his death in Nashville, there were tributes from President Richard Nixon, senators, representatives, governors, and industry peers. In April 1980 he was inducted into the National Cowboy Hall of Fame in Oklahoma City. In his hometown of Carthage the Tex Ritter Museum was established. Ritter, an American treasure in the mold of Will Rogers, was dubbed "country music's roving ambassador of good will."

• Johnny Bond wrote *The Tex Ritter Story* (1976), and there is extensive research material on file at the Country Music Foundation Library and Media Center at Nashville's Country Music Hall of Fame. An obituary is in the *New York Times*, 3 Jan. 1974.

ELLIS NASSOUR

RITTER, William Emerson (19 Nov. 1856–10 Jan. 1944), naturalist, philosopher, and administrator, was born in Hampden, Wisconsin, the son of Horatio Emerson and Leonora Eason, farmers. He spent most of his boyhood on the farm, where he gained an early love of nature. Ritter attended local public schools and began teaching in Wisconsin public schools in 1877. He graduated from the State Normal School in Oshkosh, Wisconsin (1884), then served as principal of the Oconto, Wisconsin, high school (1884–1885), before continuing his education at the University of California, Berkeley, where he earned a B.S. (1888). At Berkeley, Ritter studied under the geologist Joseph LeConte and the philosopher George H. Howison, whose influence did much to mold his later writings. Following brief postgraduate studies with LeConte and at the Cooper Medical College, San Francisco, Ritter continued academic training at Harvard, earning an A.M. (1891) and a Ph.D. (1893), both in zoology. He returned to Berkeley to become an instructor of biology (1891–1893), assistant professor of biology (1893–1898), associate professor of zoology (1898–1902), and professor of zoology (1902–1923). As head of the zoology department, one of his major accomplishments was the establishment of postgraduate studies in biology at the University of California. In 1891 he married Mary E. Bennett, a physician; they had no children.

In 1894 and 1895 Ritter studied at the Stazione Zoologica at Naples and at the University of Berlin. He returned with the desire to establish a field research station on the California coast. Later he traveled to England, Japan, and various Pacific islands. Ritter was among the naturalists who participated in the Harriman Alaska Expedition of 1899. He was president of the California Academy of Sciences (1898–1900), a fellow of the American Association for the Advancement of Science, an elective associate of the American Ornithologists' Union, president of the Biological Society of the Pacific (1912–1913), a member of the American Academy of Arts and Sciences, American Society of Naturalists, American Society of Zoologists, and National Institute of Social Science, and an honorary member of the Berkeley chapter of Phi Beta Kappa.

Ritter's scientific research and writings ranged from anatomical to physiological and ecological work. At first he studied the sensory systems and ecology of a diversity of vertebrates. His first scientific paper was "The Parietal Eye in Some Lizards from the Western United States" (*Bulletin of the Museum of Comparative Zoology* 20 [1891]: 209–28); his doctoral dissertation was "On the Eyes, the Integumentary Sense Papillae, and the Integument of the San Diego Blind Fish

(*Typhlogobius californiensis* Steindauchner)" (1893). On returning to California, Ritter studied the life history and habits of the Pacific coast newt. Once on the faculty at Berkeley, however, he quickly shifted his focus to the marine environment and published extensively on marine invertebrates, especially sea squirts (ascidians) and acorn worms (enteropneusta).

Ritter set himself the goal of surveying the fauna of the Pacific waters adjacent to southern California. Along with several colleagues in the Department of Zoology, he made attempts at different sites to set up a marine biological station. At each site, faculty and students conducted summer investigations. In 1903 the site was at La Jolla, near San Diego, where the newspaper magnate E. W. Scripps helped to found the San Diego Marine Biological Association and provided some financial support for the summer research. Scripps and Ritter quickly became good friends and partners in a number of ventures. Ritter took up permanent residence at La Jolla in 1906 and became the station's first director (1909–1923). Scripps provided the funding, and Ritter the scientific leadership. The initial focus of the biological station shifted: the word "marine" was dropped from its name, allowing for inclusion of other studies at the station. In 1912 the station was officially transferred to the University of California as the Scripps Institution for Biological Research. In 1925 the name was changed to the Scripps Institution of Oceanography, returning the focus to the marine environment. While at Scripps, Ritter retained his position at Berkeley as professor of zoology, retiring to become professor emeritus in 1923. In 1927, a year after Scripps died, Ritter retired from Scripps Institution and returned to Berkeley, where he remained until his death there.

Scripps's interests were in "human problems" and in science as it related to humans, and under his influence Ritter's writings took on a more philosophical nature, looking at science as it related to human society. Among his more prominent works are the primarily philosophical books *War, Science and Civilization* (1915), *The Probable Infinity of Nature and Life* (1918), *The Unity of the Organism, or the Organismal Conception of Life* (2 vols., 1919), *The Natural History of Our Conduct* (with Edna W. Bailey, 1927), and *Natural vs. Supernatural, or a Man as a Unified Whole and as Part of Nature as a Unified Whole* (1933) and the articles "The Organismal Conception: Its Place in Science and Its Bearing on Philosophy" (with Edna W. Bailey, *University of California Publications in Zoology* 31 [1928]: 307–58) and "Why Aristotle Invented the Word *Entelecheia*" (*Quarterly Review of Biology* 7, no. 4 [1932]: 377–404). His last book, *The California Woodpecker and I* (1938), combined his basic observations on the behavioral ecology of the woodpecker with broad anatomical comparisons and philosophical consideration of human behavioral ecology.

In collaboration with Scripps, Ritter was also a founder of the Foundation for Population Research at Miami University (1921) and a founder and first president (1921) of Science Service (initially called Science News Service) in Washington, D.C. Science Service was begun as a science news agency to provide interpretations of science to the public. It initiated the weekly *Science News Letter* (now *Science News*) and weekly radio broadcasts and provided science news articles for the popular media and editorial assistance for science-related books. Science Service also sponsored searches for American youth with aptitudes in science, continued as the Westinghouse Science Talent Search. Ritter was honorary president of Science Service until his death. In May 1944 the U.S. Maritime Commission launched a Liberty Ship christened the SS *William E. Ritter* in his honor.

• Collections of Ritter's papers are archived at the University of California libraries in San Diego and Berkeley; photographs and Mary Ritter's diaries are archived at the University of California, San Diego. Some biographical material is included in Mary Bennett Ritter, *More Than Gold in California, 1849–1933* (1933), and Oliver Knight, ed., *I Protest: Selected Disquisitions of E. W. Scripps* (1966). Among numerous obituaries are Francis B. Sumner, *Science* 99 (1944): 335–38; W.D., *Science News Letter* 45, no. 4 (1944): 60–61; T. S. Palmer, *Auk* 64 (1947): 665–66; and the *New York Times*, 11 Jan. 1944.

JEROME A. JACKSON

RITZ BROTHERS, comedy team, known individually as Harry Ritz (28 May 1907–29 Mar. 1986), Jimmy Ritz (22 Oct. 1904–17 Nov. 1985), and Al Ritz (27 Aug. 1901–22 Dec. 1965), were born with the surname Joachim in Newark, New Jersey, the sons of Max J. Joachim, a haberdasher who had emigrated from Austria. Their mother's name is unknown. The brothers grew up in Brooklyn, New York, where during their high school years they became increasingly interested in finding their way into some facet of show business. Al, the eldest, led the way after winning an amateur talent contest and entering vaudeville as a dancer. Following their graduation from high school, Harry and Jimmy joined Al on the theatrical circuit but as separate acts. In the mid-1920s the brothers became a team, billed themselves as the Collegians, and made their debut appearance at the College Inn nightclub on Coney Island. Costumed in exaggerated collegiate dress, they performed the sort of comic mayhem that was to become their trademark. For their first genuine vaudeville appearance, in September 1925 at the Albee Theater in Brooklyn, they were billed as the Ritz Brothers; the new name was appropriated from the side of a passing truck after their agent suggested that Joachim would be too hard for audiences to remember.

Having gained a foothold in vaudeville, the Ritz Brothers appeared in the 1926 edition of George White's *Scandals*, in which they continued their comic assault on college men and introduced the song "Collegiate." In March 1929, and again in March 1932, they headlined at New York's Palace Theater and also toured in *The Florida Girl*, a musical comedy that featured them as Harry Aristotle, Al Socrates, and Jimmy Plato. They also appeared in several editions of Earl Carroll's *Vanities*. Their act changed very little over the course of their careers. Led by Harry, they sang and danced in manic fashion, performed zany clowning that bordered on theatrical anarchy, and developed broad physical comedy that made them the equal of similar acts such as the Runaway Four and the Slate Brothers. They dressed in outrageous drag (with their trousers rolled up under their skirts), made grotesque facial contortions, and accelerated the speed and volume of everything they did. Some critics found their performances vulgar, but it was the lack of subtlety that made the act popular in vaudeville and especially in burlesque.

The 1934 Al Christy short *Hotel Anchovy* marked the beginning of the Ritz Brothers' sixteen-feature screen career (excluding an appearance that Al had made alone in the 1918 feature *The Avenging Trail*). The brothers were first contracted to 20th Century–Fox, for which they appeared in the musical comedy *On the Avenue* (1937), with a score by Irving Berlin and a cast featuring Dick Powell, Madeleine Carroll, and Alice Faye; *One in a Million* (1937), costarring skating star Sonja Henie; *The Goldwyn Follies* (1938), an all-star musical revue; and a broadly comic version of *The Three Musketeers* (1939), with the brothers in the title roles. After their contract with Fox ended in 1939, the brothers signed on for four low-budget features at Universal; the oddest of these pictures was a curiosity called *The Gorilla* (1940), in which the brothers played detectives tracking a murderer played by screen horror legend Bela Lugosi. After the early 1940s most of their movie roles were comic cameo appearances.

In the late 1940s, as their movie career began to wind down, the brothers went back on the vaudeville and nightclub circuit with an act that featured a parody of Walt Disney's popular animated feature *Snow White and the Seven Dwarfs* (with Harry as the wicked witch and Al and Jimmy as two of the dwarfs), a lampoon of Latin music, considerable interplay with the audience and the orchestra, and the sort of general onstage chaos that audiences—if not all critics—enjoyed. In 1939 *Billboard*'s critic had described their act as "zany heckling that defied classification." Harry, often referred to as "the one in the middle," was the most admired of the three for the sheer lunacy of his style. Many later comedians, including Mel Brooks, Jerry Lewis, and Albert Brooks, acknowledged Harry's influence.

In the mid-1960s the brothers made a highly successful comeback as a nightclub act, but their triumph ended abruptly with Al's death from a heart attack in New Orleans, Louisiana. Harry and Jimmy continued to make occasional nightclub and television appearances. They also made brief appearances in *Blazing Stewardesses* (1975) and *Won Ton Ton, the Dog Who Saved Hollywood* (1976), both of which featured cameos by many screen stars from the 1930s and 1940s. Harry appeared alone in Mel Brooks's 1976 feature, *Silent Movie*, to which he contributed his famous "crazy walk." Jimmy died in Los Angeles, followed by Harry, who died less than six months later in San Die-

go. Although their comedy lacked the timeless artistry of the Marx Brothers, their absurd antics ensured the Ritz Brothers a prominent place in the history of screen comedy teams.

• For more information on the Ritz Brothers, see *Billboard*, 3 June 1939; Frank Condon, "Triple Hysterics," *Collier's*, 27 Feb. 1937; Leonard Maltin, "The Ritz Brothers," in his *Movie Comedy Teams* (1970); Jeffrey Robinson, "Ritz Brothers," in his *Teamwork* (1982); Anthony Slide, *The Encyclopedia of Vaudeville* (1994); and Bill Smith, "Harry Ritz," in his *The Vaudevillians* (1976). An obituary for Harry Ritz is in the *New York Times*, 1 Apr. 1986.

JAMES FISHER

RIVÉ-KING, Julie (31 Oct. 1854–24 July 1937), concert pianist, was born Julie Bell Rivé in Cincinnati, Ohio, the daughter of Leon Rivé, a portrait painter, and Caroline Staub, a professional musician. Evidence regarding her general education is sketchy. She began musical studies with her mother at the age of five or six. Because both parents taught at private women's schools in Hamilton, Ohio, she may have enrolled at the Glendale Female College, the Ohio Female College, or the Cincinnati Conservatory. She may also have attended Woodward High School, a public school in Cincinnati. Later she worked with Henry George Andres, who was one of the original faculty members at the Cincinnati Conservatory and who also served as musical director of that institution. From fall 1870 to spring 1873 she studied in New York, primarily with Sebastian Bach Mills and briefly with William Mason (1829–1908). In May 1873 she went to Europe to work with Carl Reinecke in Leipzig and Franz Liszt in Weimar.

After her return to the United States in 1874, she began a performance career managed by Frank H. King, who became her husband in 1877. (They did not have children.) Despite the fact that European and American women were encouraged to study and perform music only as amateurs, Rivé-King pursued a professional career that proved to be more successful than those of most American male pianists of her era. Between 1874 and 1900 Rivé-King performed with prominent conductors and orchestras throughout the United States. Devoted to educating the musical public, she played in large and small cities throughout the United States and Canada. Her major tours included a seven-month tour featuring 136 concerts with the Rivé-King Concert Company in 1881–1882; a solo transcontinental tour in 1882; and a transcontinental tour including seventy-three concerts in thirty cities in 1883 as the featured soloist with Theodore Thomas and his orchestra. The *New York Daily Tribune* (Apr. 1883) declared this last tour to be "the most remarkable concert tour ever made in this country." In 1886 Rivé-King undertook what the *American Art Journal* (Oct. 1886) called "one of the most successful tours of any pianist for years," which included at least 126 concerts in fourteen states and two Canadian provinces. Rivé-King was the featured soloist on tours with conductor Anton Seidl in 1896 and 1897. Piano manufacturing companies including Steinway, Chickering, Decker Brothers, and Weber sponsored many of her concerts and tours.

In a feature article in *Music* (Dec. 1897), W. S. B. Mathews wrote: "To Madame Julia Rivé-King belongs the honor of having contributed to a greater extent than almost any other artist to the elevation of the standard of piano playing in this country." Reflecting back over Rivé-King's career, T. P. Currier (*Musician* [Dec. 1912]) remarked: "No American pianist, except [William H.] Sherwood, did more to establish the new standard of piano playing in the United States than this highly talented woman."

Many concert pianists during the late nineteenth century also composed. Recognizing this tradition, Frank King persuaded Rivé-King to publish his works under her name in order to enhance her reputation. During her lifetime six different publishing companies released compositions written by Frank King but bearing Rivé-King's name. In addition, the couple allowed its major publisher, Charles Kunkel of St. Louis, Missouri, to publish Kunkel's transcriptions under Rivé-King's name.

Rivé-King performed many of the aforementioned compositions on her recitals, and in 1887 James Huneker, in *Etude* (July 1887), declared Rivé-King to be "the best composer among the fair sex" in America. Rivé-King helped her husband in composing the passagework in his most popular piece, "Bubbling Spring," which continued to be published in original and simplified editions through 1950. Piano roll companies also recorded at least fourteen of the works attributed to Rivé-King on both hand-cut and machine-cut rolls during the early twentieth century.

After Frank King's death in February 1900, Rivé-King found that she was not able to manage her own concert career. She instead turned to teaching privately in New York, performing on a much more limited basis and in smaller, less prestigious halls. In 1908 she accepted a contract to teach full time at the Bush Conservatory in Chicago, where she worked until 1937. She died in Indianapolis.

• The Helen King Boyer Collection, Georgetown University, has letters, photographs, programs, and a scrapbook documenting Rivé-King's career. Additional clippings and programs can be found in the Frederick Grant Gleason and W. S. B. Mathews collections at the Newberry Library, Chicago. For articles that discuss Rivé-King's teaching ideals see Julie Rivé-King, "Thoughts on Music Teaching, Music Study and the Preparation for a Musical Career," *Musician* 18 (Dec. 1913): 805, as well as Grace Dickinson Patterson's interviews with her in *Musician* 19 (July 1914): 446, 494–95; and *Musician* 23 (July 1918): 460. The most complete modern assessment of Rivé-King is M. Leslie Petteys, "Julie Rivé-King, American Pianist" (Ph.D. diss., Univ. of Missouri–Kansas City, 1987). See also Karin Pendle, "Cincinnati's Musical Heritage: Three Women Who Succeeded," *Queen City Heritage* 41 (Winter 1983): 41–55, and the Arlan Coolidge article in *Notable American Women* for a more detailed discussion of Rivé-King's family and personality.

LESLIE PETTEYS

RIVERA, Tomás (22 Dec. 1935–16 May 1984), novelist, poet, and university administrator, was born in Crystal City, Texas, the son of Florencio Rivera Martínez and Josefa Hernández Gutiérrez, migrant farmworkers. From his early years until 1954, Rivera traveled with his family, joining the migrant stream that left Crystal City around mid-April, searching for farm work as far north as Michigan and Minnesota and returning around the beginning of November. Years later, in much of his writings, and especially in his novel *. . . y no se lo tragó la tierra* (1970), he would document the experiences that he underwent and witnessed as a migrant worker.

The irregularity of Rivera's schoolwork caused by his nomadic life motivated his concern for his people and their education, and he sought a career as a teacher. After receiving his B.S. in English education in 1958 from Southwest Texas State University, he taught high school Spanish and English in San Antonio, Crystal City, and League City. He returned to Southwest Texas State, where he received an M.Ed. in 1964, and continued his graduate studies at the University of Oklahoma, receiving his Ph.D. in Spanish literature in 1969, completing a dissertation on the modern Spanish poet León Felipe. In the early 1960s he married Concepción "Concha" Garza, with whom he had three children.

Rivera's ascent through the professorial ranks and into university administration was rapid. Beginning as an associate professor of Spanish at Sam Houston State University in 1969, he became professor of Spanish and director of foreign languages at the University of Texas-San Antonio in 1971. By 1976 Rivera had become vice president for administration, leaving this post in 1978 for the University of Texas-El Paso, where he assumed the position of executive vice president of academic affairs. One year later Rivera became chancellor of the University of California, Riverside, a position he held for five years, until his sudden death in Fontana, California, of a heart attack.

Rivera was active in minority organizations and educational associations and was a founder of several important programs in the education of minorities: a founding contributing editor in 1973 of *Revista Chicano-Riqueña* (now *The Americas Review*); president of the Chicano Council on Higher Education, which distributed significant grants to Mexican-American scholars in the 1970s; and board member of the American Association of Higher Education (AAHE). The keynote address to the annual AAHE convention is now known as the Tomás Rivera Lecture. Shortly after Rivera's death, the Clarement Colleges established the Tomás Rivera Center, a national policy center and think tank on issues facing Latinos in the United States.

Rivera's *. . . y no se lo tragó la tierra*, winner of the Quinto Sol Literary Prize in 1970, is a product of the Chicano social movement of the 1960s and a landmark in Chicano literary history. This novel gave considerable impetus to Chicano writers and brought wide recognition to the Hispanic creative process in the United

States. Taking place within the context of the experiences of the Chicano migrant farmworker between 1945 and 1955, the theme of this episodic *bildungsroman* deals with a young boy's quest for his identity. Functioning as the novel's central consciousness—either as protagonist, narrator-protagonist, narrator-witness or as a character who overhears but does not narrate—the boy recoups his past, discovers his history, and affirms his own singular being and his identity as a collective person. By discovering who he is, this adolescent becomes one with his people. Through his quest, he embodies and expresses the collective consciousness and experiences of his society. As Ramón Saldívar has written, . . . *y no se lo tragó la tierra* "represents the first milestone in Mexican American literary history after the turbulent events of the 1960s and sets itself explicitly within the political and social contexts of the post–World War II agricultural worker's life. . . . Rivera's novel immediately established itself as a major document of Chicano social and literary history" (p. 74).

The adolescent protagonist, in the solitary darkness beneath his house (as the final episode reveals), struggles to recall and to make sense of the events of the previous year ("El año perdido" / "The Lost Year"). On the narrative level, he strings together the histories that make up that year but that, essentially, are *all* his life and *all* the life of his people. Inspired by his people's oral tradition and influenced by the laconic prose of the Mexican writer Juan Rulfo, whose subject is the Mexican peasant, Rivera achieves in his novel an overwhelming sense of a communal oral history. Rivera not only artistically captures the speech of his people, he employs it structurally in the form of anonymous dialogues that function as a chorus commenting—often ironically—on the actions and outcomes of various episodes. As Nicolás Kanellos has noted, the novel's Chicano language, "considered by some as a regional dialect of Spanish, is represented here in its most universal and artistic form, while exhibiting the flexibility and expressiveness to reproduce the argot called for in each social situation" (in Olivares [1986], p. 53).

Rivera's concern for education, especially that of minorities, and his extensive administrative duties curtailed his creative efforts. After the publication of *Tierra*, he published but five short stories in journals and anthologies, two of which were episodes omitted from the novel; a chapbook of poetry, *Always and Other Poems*; and a handful of poetry, including his epic poem *The Searchers*. It is believed that Rivera was working on a second novel, "La casa grande del pueblo" (The People's Mansion), when he died, but various archival searches have not uncovered it. One such search, by Julián Olivares, uncovered two unpublished short stories, "La cosecha" (The Harvest) and "Zoo Island," and thirty unpublished poems. These stories, along with the five others that Rivera did publish, have appeared in a bilingual edition titled *The Harvest: Short Stories by Tomás Rivera / La Cosecha: Cuentos de Tomás Rivera* (1989). Rivera's poetry, written in English and Spanish, was collected and published as *The Searchers: Collected Poetry* (1990). Rivera's entire literary production, including his essays on Chicano literature (three of which have been instrumental in the ethical and aesthetic appreciation of much of Chicano literature of the 1970s: "Into the Labrynth: The Chicano in Literature," "Chicano Literature: Fiesta of the Living," and "Remembering, Discovery and Volition in the Literary Imaginative Process") and his essay "Richard Rodriguez' *Hunger of Memory* as Humanistic Antithesis," have been collected in *Tomás Rivera: The Complete Works* (1992).

Rivera's literary production, while slim, will continue to be one of the landmarks of modern U.S. Hispanic literature. . . . *y no se lo tragó la tierra*, critically acclaimed for its originality because its episodes can be read individually as short stories and collectively as a novel, documents a people and a parcel of American experience that would have passed into oblivion had it not been for the determination of its author to preserve it in literature. Speaking of the novel's intent and his own role as a writer, Rivera told an interviewer, "In . . . *Tierra* . . . I wrote about the migrant worker in [the] ten-year period [1945–1955]. . . . I began to see that my role . . . would be to document that period of time, but giving it some kind of spiritual strength or spiritual history. . . . I felt that I had to document the migrant worker *para siempre* [forever], *para que no se olvidara ese espíritu tan fuerte de resistir y continuar under the worst of conditions* [so that their spirit of resistance and willingness to endure should not be forgotten]" (Bruce-Novoa, pp. 148, 150–51).

• The Tomás Rivera Archives is housed at the University of California, Riverside. Two bilingual editions of Rivera's major novel have appeared: . . . *y no se lo tragó la tierra / . . . and the earth did not part*, trans. Herminio Ríos and Octavio I. Romano-V (1971), and . . . *y no se lo tragó la tierra / And the Earth Did Not Devour Him*, trans. Evangelina Vigil-Piñón, 3d ed. (1992). Vernon Lattin et al., eds., *Tomás Rivera, 1935–84: The Man and His Work* (1988), contains articles on Rivera's life and work and a complete bibliography. Juan Bruce-Novoa published an interview with Rivera in *Chicano Authors: Inquiry by Interview* (1980). Rafael Grajeda, "Tomás Rivera's . . . *y no se lo tragó la tierra*: Discovery and Appropriation of the Chicano Past," *Hispania* 62, no. 1 (1979): 71–81, places Rivera's novel in its social and historical context; the article was reprinted in *Contemporary Chicano Fiction*, ed. Lattin (1986). Literary analyses of Rivera's novel include Lattin, "Novelistic Structure and Myth in . . . *y no se lo tragó la tierra*," *Bilingual Review/Revista Bilingüe* 9, no. 3 (1982): 220–26; Julián Olivares, "Los índices primitivos de . . . *y no se lo tragó la tierra* de Tomás Rivera y cuatro estampas inéditas," *Crítica* 2, no. 2 (1990): 208–22; and Olivares, "'La cosecha' y 'Zoo Island' de Tomás Rivera: Apuntes hacia la formación de . . . *y no se lo tragó la tierra*," *Hispania* 74, no. 1 (1991): 57–65. Important sociocritical studies of his novel include José D. Saldívar, "The Ideological and Utopian in Tomás Rivera's . . . *y no se lo tragó la tierra* and Ron Arias' *The Road to Tamazunchale*," *Crítica* 1, no. 2 (1985): 100–114, and Ramón Saldívar, "Beyond Good and Evil: Utopian Dialectics in Tomás Rivera and Oscar Zeta Acosta," in *Chicano Narrative: The Dialectics of Difference* (1990). Joseph Sommers, "From the Critical Premise to the Product: Critical Modes and Their Applications to a Chicano Literary Text," *New*

Scholar 6 (1977): 67–75 (repr. as "Interpreting Tomás Rivera," in *Modern Chicano Writers*, ed. Joseph Sommers and Tomás Ybarra-Frausto [1979]), discusses problems of interpreting Chicano literature with particular application to Rivera's work. Thomas Vallejos, "The Beetfield as Battlefield: Ritual Process and Ritualization in Tomás Rivera's 'Las salamandras,'" *Americas Review* 17, no. 2 (1989): 100–109, investigates one of Rivera's short stories. Olivares, ed., *International Studies in Honor of Tomás Rivera* (1986), considers Rivera and his place in modern Chicano literature.

JULIÁN OLIVARES

RIVERS, Mendel (28 Sept. 1905–28 Dec. 1970), U.S. congressman, was born Lucius Mendel Rivers in Gumville, Berkeley County, South Carolina, the son of Lucius Hampton Rivers, a farmer and turpentiner, and Henrietta Marion McCay. Following his father's death in 1914, young Rivers worked at a series of odd jobs to help support his family. He was educated in the public schools of Charleston County, where he was a star athlete. He played semiprofessional baseball before attending the College of Charleston from 1926 to 1929 and the University of South Carolina School of Law from 1929 to 1931. Although he did not receive a degree from either institution, he gained admission to the South Carolina bar in 1932. After a brief stint as a private attorney in Charleston, he was elected to the state legislature in November 1933. A lifelong Democrat, he served three years in the legislature before taking a position as a special attorney with the U.S. Department of Justice in 1936. In 1938 he married Margaret Simons Middleton; they had two daughters and one son.

In 1940 Rivers left the Justice Department to run for Congress. Buoyed by the support of Senator James F. Byrnes and Governor Burnet Rhett Maybank, the former mayor and political boss of Charleston, he won handily in both the Democratic primary and the general election. During the following three decades, he won reelection fifteen times, rarely facing serious opposition. On several occasions he ran unopposed.

During his early years in Washington, Rivers maintained close ties with Byrnes and other New Deal leaders and generally supported the Franklin D. Roosevelt administration. However, as his career progressed he grew increasingly conservative and independent. In 1948 he gained national attention by challenging the dairy lobby with a bill that repealed federal taxes on oleomargarine, and in later decades he surprised his colleagues by voting for public housing, food stamps, and antipoverty legislation. In general, however, he practiced a neo-Bourbon style of politics that allowed little room for social reform or populistic activism. A paternalist by nature, he supported the Taft-Hartley Act and other measures that restricted the power of organized labor. On the race issue, he was a staunch segregationist and white supremacist who vehemently opposed antilynching and other civil rights legislation. In 1948 he openly sympathized with the Dixiecrat revolt led by fellow South Carolinian Strom Thurmond, and in 1952 and 1956 he defied Democratic leaders by supporting the Republican presidential candidate Dwight Eisenhower. An inveterate Cold Warrior, Rivers strongly endorsed the national security and antisubversive acts of the Harry S. Truman and Eisenhower years. Though generally an internationalist in foreign affairs, from the late 1950s onward he was a sharp critic of foreign aid and United Nations–style multilateralism.

Rivers's greatest passion, for which he became justly famous, was the oversight of the American military. From the outset of his congressional career, he was a tireless advocate of military preparedness and expansion. During World War II, he held a seat on the powerful House Committee on Naval Affairs, and with the aid of Byrnes, who was appointed director of war mobilization in 1943, he was remarkably successful in his efforts to expand the military presence in and around Charleston. By 1945 several major military facilities punctuated the South Carolina low country, including the Charleston Naval Shipyard and the Parris Island Marine Corps training center.

After the war Rivers's reputation as a military powerbroker continued to grow. While many of his congressional colleagues turned away from a single-minded preoccupation with military matters, he became even more absorbed with the technology and politics of the defense establishment. As a vocal member of the powerful House Committee on Armed Services, he played an increasingly important role in the formulation of weapons policy, the determination of military appropriations, and the selection of military sites and defense contractors. During the late 1950s and early 1960s, he worked closely with the committee's chairman, Carl Vinson of Georgia, expanding the committee's authority and touting a strong and vigilant military as the only realistic deterrent to Communist aggression. He also made sure that South Carolina received more than its share of military largesse. At one point even Vinson quipped, "You put anything else down there in your district, Mendel, it's gonna sink" (*New York Times*, 29 Dec. 1970).

By the beginning of the John F. Kennedy administration, Rivers was the third-ranking Democrat on the committee and the chair of two important subcommittees. However, he did not achieve national attention until January 1965, when he replaced Vinson as chairman of the committee. For the remainder of the decade, the tall, silver-haired congressman from Charleston was one of the most powerful and controversial figures in American politics, a symbol of hawkish militarism and pork-barrel politics. Shuttling between Capitol Hill, the Pentagon, and countless military installations, he unhesitatingly embraced his new role as a visible architect of the American war effort in Southeast Asia. Seemingly impervious to the widening criticism of American involvement in Vietnam, he became an increasingly strident proponent of domestic repression and military escalation. Indeed, his militant rhetoric and enthusiasm for expensive military hardware often outstripped that of even the most bellicose Pentagon officials. Not only did he call for the use of nuclear weapons in Vietnam, as he had during the Korean War, but when the intelligence vessel *Pueblo* was captured by North Korea in 1968, he was ready to launch an invasion north of the thirty-eighth parallel.

By almost any standard, Rivers was a devout militarist, and whenever American interests were challenged abroad—as in Cuba in 1961–1962—he invariably advocated massive armed retaliation. As one Republican congressman wryly remarked, "If Mendel was running things, we'd be in World War V" (*New York Times*, 29 Dec. 1970). Although it sometimes appeared that Rivers was indeed running things, his power was often circumscribed by Defense Department officials, who resented his uncompromising advocacy of congressional power and prerogatives where military policy was concerned. As the self-appointed champion of the common soldier, he also frequently clashed with military leaders over their treatment of enlisted personnel and other subordinates. In two celebrated cases, Rivers, who had never served in the military himself, persuaded administration officials to suspend prosecution of soldiers who had allegedly committed atrocities in Vietnam. Such interference drew praise from archconservatives but did not always endear him to other members of the defense establishment. He was also roundly criticized for representing the interests of his district at the expense of the general national welfare. By the late 1960s the numerous military facilities and defense contractors located in Rivers's district reportedly accounted for more than half of the area's total payroll. As the new decade began, some observers complained that Rivers's appetite for local military expansion seemed to have no limit, but in the fall of 1970 his ambitious plans were cut short by a serious heart condition. On 11 December he had open-heart surgery at a Birmingham, Alabama, hospital, where he died of heart failure.

Far more than most politicians, Rivers left a considerable material legacy, especially in the military enclaves of South Carolina. But he is best remembered for his spirited, unrelenting style of military advocacy. As F. Edward Hebert, the Louisiana Democrat who replaced his longtime friend as chairman of the House Committee on Armed Services, declared in 1970: "Mendel was a very fierce advocate. What he believed in, he believed in—he never backed off. He was outspoken, rambunctious, flamboyant. . . . His objective was defense—whatever it took, he was for it. Mendel'll leave his stamp, all right" (*New York Times*, 29 Dec. 1970).

• Rivers's papers are in the Library of Congress. The most comprehensive source is Will F. Huntley, "Mighty Rivers of Charleston" (Ph.D. diss., Univ. of South Carolina, 1993). Marion Rivers Ravenel, *Rivers Delivers* (1994), is a biography written by his daughter. A useful biographical sketch is in *Current Biography Yearbook 1960* (1961). Charley B. Brassell, "The Rhetorical Strategy of L. Mendel Rivers" (Ph.D. diss., Univ. of Utah, 1973), is an important specialized study. See also Robert G. Sherrill, "L. Mendel Rivers," *Nation* 19 Jan. 1970, pp. 40–47; Don Oberdorfer, "Rivers Delivers," *New York Times Magazine*, 29 Aug. 1965, pp. 30–31, 86, 88–91;

Charles McCarry, "Ol' Man Rivers," *Esquire*, Oct. 1970, pp. 168–71, 211–12; Robert Yoakum, "The Power People—Rep. L. Mendel Rivers," *Look*, 26 Aug. 1969, pp. 22–23; Marshall Frady, "The Sweetest Finger This Side of Midas," *Life*, 27 Feb. 1970, pp. 52–60; "New House Foe Fires on McNamara," *Business Week*, 3 July 1965, pp. 24–25; "Congressman Rivers on the Rampage," *Christian Century*, 18 Jan. 1967, p. 70; "Now It's Rivers vs. McNamara," *U.S. News and World Report*, 27 June 1966, p. 15; "Mendelian Domain," *Time*, 21 June 1968, pp. 21–22; Luther J. Carter, "Representative Rivers: Military Spokesman Hopes to See McNamara Revolution Upset," *Science*, 15 Mar. 1968, pp. 1217–19; "Southern Gothic," *Nation*, 29 Dec. 1969, pp. 715–16; "Mendel Rivers," *Newsweek*, 11 Jan. 1971, p. 18; and "Tribune for the Military," *Time*, 11 Jan. 1971, pp. 10–11. A lengthy obituary is in the *New York Times*, 29 Dec. 1970.

RAYMOND O. ARSENAULT

RIVERS, Pearl. *See* Nicholson, Eliza Jane Poitevent Holbrook.

RIVERS, Richard Henderson (11 Sept. 1814–21 June 1894), Methodist clergyman, was born in Montgomery County, Tennessee, the son of Edmund Rivers and Sarah "Sallie" Henderson, affluent farmers who also raised and raced horses. He grew up on the family farm, but after his religious conversion at a revival in Hardeman County, Tennessee, in 1830, he sought ordination as a minister in the Tennessee Conference of the Methodist Episcopal church, which admitted him on trial in 1831 and ordained him as a deacon in 1833. After serving a large Methodist circuit in Alabama, he entered LaGrange College in LaGrange, Alabama, from which he graduated with honors in 1835. He immediately returned to the school as an assistant professor and the following year became the professor of ancient languages. Also in 1836 he married Martha Bolling Cox Jones; they had nine children, only three of whom survived him.

In 1843 he became president of the Tennessee Conference Female Institute (later renamed Athens College) in Athens, Alabama. After five years there he moved to Centenary College in Jackson, Louisiana, as professor of moral science and then as president from 1849 to 1854, but the poor health of his wife convinced him to leave Louisiana. In 1854 he accepted the presidency of LaGrange College, which moved the next year to Florence, Alabama, where its trustees renamed it Wesleyan University. A carriage accident there in 1856 left him crippled and in pain for the rest of his life. His friend J. H. Young wrote that his sufferings were "terrible to witness."

At the outset of the Civil War most of the students and faculty at Wesleyan enlisted in the Confederate army, and the school closed its doors. Rivers moved to Summerfield, Alabama, where he served as president of Centenary College for Girls. After the war he moved to Somerville, Tennessee, to care for his widowed mother and directed a small school for women from 1865 to 1868. He presided for a year over the Logan Female College in Russellville, Kentucky, before accepting an appointment in 1869 as pastor of the Broadway Church in Louisville, Kentucky.

In 1872 Rivers moved to the Chestnut Street Methodist Church in Louisville. The Methodists normally transferred ministers to new positions every two years, so in 1874 he moved back to the Tennessee Conference, where he again became president of a school for women, the Martin Female College in Pulaski, Tennessee. When the local parish beckoned again, he moved to the Alabama Conference, which appointed him to pastorates in Auburn, Eufaula, and Greenville. Another transfer to the Louisville Conference brought him back to the Broadway Church, where he remained four years before moving in 1888 to the Shelby Street Church in Louisville, from which he retired from the ministry later in the same year.

Rivers made his mark among Southern Methodists as a talented preacher, a biographer, a correspondent for church periodicals, and a popularizer of philosophy who wrote two textbooks for students and teachers in the denomination's colleges. The first, *Elements of Moral Philosophy* (1859), used the methods of the Scottish philosophers Thomas Reid and Dugald Stewart to describe such modes of consciousness as remorse and obligation and thus to exhibit the reality of conscience as an original moral power that could sustain right intentions and obedience to a divine moral law. He argued that actions were virtuous insofar as they were performed out of an intention to obey the divine law revealed in Scripture, the natural law revealed in creation, a just civil law, or even the laws of human health and hygiene. The argument enabled him to find both biblical and civil warrants for southern slavery.

Rivers's moral thought reflected the widespread reaction among the teachers of moral science in antebellum American colleges against utilitarian ethical theory. He believed that utilitarian theorists, who judged actions as morally sound when they produced the greatest possible good for the largest possible number of persons, promoted ethical relativism and ignored the moral quality of motives and intentions.

In the second textbook, *Elements of Mental Philosophy* (1861), Rivers presented conventional descriptions of the faculties and acts of intellect, sensibility, and will. His adherence to Methodist theology prompted him to emphasize such topics as moral duty and the freedom of the will and to criticize Jonathan Edwards's (1703–1758) deterministic theory of volition. This book also drew heavily on the Scottish philosophers, particularly on their theories of epistemology, which were designed to show that the mind had a direct and immediate knowledge of the world. American theologians often admired Scottish Common Sense philosophy because it echoed their distaste for epistemological skepticism and supported their confidence that reason could confirm religious truth.

A student of the Methodist bishop Robert Paine (1799–1882), who had introduced him to the works of the Scottish realists, Rivers expressed his debt to his mentor in his *Life of Bishop Robert Paine* (1884).

Rivers embodied the growing desire for respectability and education within a religious denomination that had originally flourished by identifying itself with the common people and with rural culture. His career illustrated the burgeoning enthusiasm of religious denominations for education, especially their emergence as sponsors of education for women. He took no public stand on the debate in the *Quarterly Review of the Methodist Episcopal Church, South* between 1853 and 1857 over the proper rationale for women's education, but his support for women's colleges allied him with the Methodists who argued that women deserved the same education as men, including the study of mathematics and metaphysics, so that they might cultivate "the highest powers of mind" for their "station" as wives and mothers. Methodist conservatives argued against calling the women's schools "colleges" because they thought it wrong to copy them after the schools for men or to allow men and women the same course of study.

Rivers died in Louisville, where Methodists honored his memory by designating one of their churches as the Rivers Memorial Church.

• Biographical information is available in the *Minutes of the Annual Conferences of the Methodist Episcopal Church, South* (1894); J. H. Young, "Memoir of Richard Henderson Rivers," *Nashville Christian Advocate*, 26 July 1894; and *Appleton's Cyclopaedia of American Biography* vol. 55 (1888). Nell Peerson, "The Life of Richard Henderson Rivers" (1933), available from the Collier Library of the University of North Alabama, Florence, drew on correspondence with Rivers's relatives and acquaintances. An obituary is in the Louisville *Courier-Journal*, 22 June 1894.

E. BROOKS HOLIFIELD

RIVERS, Thomas Milton (3 Sept. 1888–12 May 1962), medical scientist and research administrator, was born in Jonesboro, Georgia, the son of Alonzo Burrill Rivers, a farmer, cotton buyer, and warehouse owner, and Mary Martha Coleman. Rivers spent his childhood on the family farm and received only the barest education at the Middle Georgia Military Academy in Jonesboro. He enrolled at Emory College in Oxford, Georgia, in the fall of 1904, beginning as a "subfreshman" because of the limitations of his previous education. After five years, he graduated first in his class, with a higher average than any previous Emory student.

As an undergraduate, Rivers came under the influence of a biology professor, Frederick N. Duncan, who convinced him to pursue a career in medicine and to apply for admission to Johns Hopkins Medical School in Baltimore. Rivers won acceptance at Johns Hopkins and began his medical education in the fall of 1909. In the middle of his second year, Rivers began to notice some muscle degeneration in his left hand. A Johns Hopkins faculty member diagnosed him as suffering from progressive muscular atrophy of the Aran-Duchenne type and told the 22-year-old that he could expect a rapid and probably fatal decline. On the advice of his professors, Rivers withdrew from medical school and returned to Jonesboro. Shortly thereafter, however, he grew restless and, through a friend, secured a job as a laboratory assistant at San Tomas Hospital in Panama. Rivers spent eighteen months working in Panama, where he gained extensive clinical experience (the hospital superintendent quickly pushed him to assume responsibilities well beyond those of a laboratory assistant). In addition, Rivers's muscular affliction mysteriously disappeared, and in the fall of 1913 he resumed his medical studies at Johns Hopkins. In 1915 he received his M.D., again finishing first in his class.

Despite Johns Hopkins's strong research tradition, Rivers originally had little interest in medical investigation either as a student or during his subsequent internship at the Johns Hopkins Hospital; he was firmly committed to a career as a practicing pediatrician. World War I, however, brought a dramatic change to Rivers's career path. Commissioned an army medical officer in January 1918, with the cooperation of a friend on the Baltimore medical examining board who was willing to overlook Rivers's recent brush with muscular disease and his missing right eardrum (which had been removed during a childhood operation), he was assigned to serve with commission organized to investigate a dangerous outbreak of both measles and pneumonia at Fort Sam Houston in San Antonio, Texas. This commission included several senior members of the American medical research community, but Rivers was particularly influenced by the head of the commission, Rufus Cole, who was also director of the hospital at the Rockefeller Institute for Medical Research in New York City.

When Rivers returned to Johns Hopkins after the war, he obtained a transfer from the pediatrics ward to the bacteriology department. In the spring of 1922 Rufus Cole, now back in New York, invited Rivers to establish a laboratory for the investigation of viral diseases at the Rockefeller Institute. Rivers quickly accepted and, over a 33-year career at the institute, established an extraordinary scientific reputation. In 1922, just before going to New York, he had married Theresa Jacobina Riefele; they had no children.

When Rivers went to the Rockefeller Institute, viruses were not well understood and virology was not well established as a discipline. Over the next few decades, Rivers would play a pivotal role in the effort to increase medicine's understanding of viruses and to solidify the standing of virology as a field of scientific inquiry. Rivers's own research at the Rockefeller Institute brought improved fundamental understanding on a number of fronts within virology. A partial list of the diseases affected by his research gives some sense of the wide range of subjects on which he published in more than 100 scientific papers: chickenpox, smallpox, herpes, psittacosis (parrot fever), louping-ill (which affects sheep), Rift Valley fever, lymphocytic choriomeningitis, and epidemic encephalitis (sleeping sickness). But Rivers's greater—and more exceptional—talent was his ability to offer broad answers to basic questions within the discipline of virology. At a

symposium on virology that Rivers organized as part of the 1926 meeting of the Society of American Bacteriologists, he included the following insight in a general overview of virology: "Viruses appear to be obligate parasites in the sense that their reproduction is dependent on living cells," which colleague Frank L. Horsfall, Jr., would label as "one of the most important single statements ever made in the history of virology." According to Horsfall, "Rivers's stubborn insistence on this fundamental point of difference between viruses and bacteria did much to establish virology as a separate discipline and to foster the development of knowledge about the nature of viruses and viral infections" (Horsfall, pp. 270–71). Continuing to employ his powers of insightful generalization throughout his career, Rivers would publish sixty-eight review articles and edit two classic textbooks, *Filterable Viruses* (1928) and *Viral and Rickettsial Diseases of Man* (1948; rev. eds., 1952, 1959).

In arguing for his own positions, Rivers did not shrink from controversy or pointed scientific discourse. Colleague Richard Shope observed that "many of those of us who have known Dr. Rivers best have felt the sting that he could so picturesquely deliver in an argument. . . . It is my feeling that Dr. Rivers believed that verbal chastisement of the sort that he occasionally delivered was good for the younger virologists among us" (Shope, p. 387).

Under the leadership of Rivers, the virology laboratory at the Rockefeller Institute became by the early 1940s the world's leading center for virus research and an important training locus for many virologists who went on to work elsewhere around the globe. The recipient of many honors, Rivers was elected a member of the National Academy of Sciences in 1934 and during the 1930s served year-long terms as the president of the American Society for Clinical Investigation (1932), the Society of American Immunologists (1934), and the Society of American Bacteriologists (1936).

During the Second World War, Rivers served in the navy as commander of the Naval Medical Research Unit Two in the South Pacific, leading a talented team of scientists in attacking a number of infectious diseases of military significance, including malaria and scrub typhus. For this service, Rivers was eventually promoted to the rank of commodore and was awarded the Legion of Merit. After the war, Rivers returned to the Rockefeller Institute, where he continued for ten years as an active and effective research administrator, eventually becoming director of the institute in 1953.

In 1955 Rivers left the Rockefeller Institute to become medical director for the National Foundation for Infantile Paralysis, which he had served since 1938 in a voluntary capacity as chairman of its Committee on Research. As both volunteer and employee, Rivers applied his vast knowledge of virology, his powers of critical thinking, and his administrative skill to play a leadership role in the massive, high-profile effort that eventually resulted in the development of an effective polio vaccine in the 1950s. In 1958 Rivers became the foundation's vice president for Medical Affairs, and he remained in this position until his death in New York City. Shortly after Rivers's death, fellow virologist Shope remarked that "it was he who most of us looked upon as the natural leader of our science" (Shope, p. 385).

• Rivers's papers are at the American Philosophical Society in Philadelphia, Pa. In the last several months of his life, he recorded his own professional legacy in an oral history skillfully conducted, edited, and annotated by Saul Benison. The book that resulted from the joint efforts of Benison and Rivers, *Tom Rivers: Reflections on a Life in Medicine and Science* (1967), contains a wealth of information on Rivers's professional activities and relationships. Another major source of biographical information is a tribute by Frank L. Horsfall, Jr., in the National Academy of Sciences, *Biographical Memoirs* 38 (1965): 262–94, which includes a lengthy bibliography. Richard E. Shope's unusually frank biographical account is in the *Journal of Bacteriology* 84 (Sept. 1962): 385–88. See also James Bordley and A. McGehee Harvey, *Two Centuries of American Medicine, 1776–1976* (1976), pp. 639–44. Obituaries are in the *Baltimore Sun* and the *New York Times*, 13 May 1962.

JON M. HARKNESS

RIVES, Amélie (23 Aug. 1863–16 June 1945), novelist and playwright, was born in Richmond, Virginia, the daughter of Colonel Alfred Landon Rives (CSA), a civil engineer, and Sarah Catherine Macmurdo. Amélie Rives spent much of her youth near Charlottesville, Virginia, at "Castle Hill," the estate of her paternal grandparents, William Cabell Rives and Judith Page Walker. Because Civil War hostilities bypassed Castle Hill, after the war it functioned largely as it had before, thus affording her a leisured, aristocratic, and cultured environment that few southerners were privileged to know after 1865. William Cabell Rives had been a friend of Thomas Jefferson, a U.S. senator, and twice minister to France, and he played a significant role in his granddaughter's education. Governesses and tutors were provided, and Rives was given free access to the several thousand volumes in her grandfather's library.

Rives's reading was broad and eclectic. A precocious child, she was reading by the age of four and produced much juvenilia, none of it intended for publication. However, in 1885, when Rives was twenty-three, a visitor from Boston discovered one of her manuscripts and recommended it to Thomas Bailey Aldrich, editor of the *Atlantic Monthly*. "A Brother to Dragons" was published in the March 1886 issue of the *Atlantic*. Although it exhibited a youthful naivete, as well as numerous flaws in language and structure, this first publication was well received; it appealed to the popular taste for romantic fiction that was still thriving in Gilded Age America. Set in Shakespearean England, this was one of several Rives plots to deal with faraway times and places.

However, the story gave only a limited indication of what was to come in her later work. In 1888 Rives published a novel that, like most of her subsequent work, was given a contemporary setting, obviously modeled upon Castle Hill. This novel, *The Quick or the Dead?*, also features the first in a long line of heroines whose background, physique, and temperament resemble those of their author. (The first edition of the novel, published in *Lippincott's Monthly Magazine* in April 1888, contained a steel engraving of Amélie Rives, as if to suggest this connection.) This character is beautiful yet self-effacing, vivacious yet sensitive, passionate yet somewhat tempered by social mores. In subsequent novels the heroine gradually matures and, after enduring trying vicissitudes, becomes wiser and more capable in matters of the heart.

However, in *The Quick or the Dead?* the protagonist, Barbara Pomfret, is a young widow faced with the dilemma of whether to remarry or remain loyal to the memory of her husband. This vexing question illustrates the changing tide of American literary tastes of the time: whether to adhere to sentimental custom or to follow a more independent course, one informed by reason. Probably unaware of the censurings leveled upon such realists as William Dean Howells and Mark Twain whose protagonists often veer from accepted norms of behavior, Rives allowed Barbara to come dangerously close to following the dictates of her heart rather than society's conventions of widowhood. She also had Barbara express sensual urgings by entreating her suitor, "Kiss me! Kiss me!" As a result, *The Quick or the Dead?* became a *succès de scandale*, calling forth a pious barrage from moralistic critics and ministers and eventually resulting in sales of over 300,000 copies in America and 100,000 in England.

While *The Quick or the Dead?* was in production, Amelie Rives had made her debut in Newport, where she met John Armstrong Chanler, a New York attorney and an Astor descendant, whom she married in June 1888. Balancing the furor generated by the novel with marriage to the eccentric Chanler proved something of an ordeal. However, she was warmly received on her belated wedding trip to Europe the following year. She was introduced to many of the British literati, such as George Meredith and Thomas Hardy, and became friends with George Curzon and "the Souls," a fashionable intellectual coterie that also included Arthur Balfour. She also began to study painting in Paris. In 1894 her marriage all but over as a result of Chanler's erratic behavior, Oscar Wilde introduced her to Prince Pierre Troubetzkoy, a young portrait painter recently arrived in London. In 1895 Rive returned to America and received an amicable divorce from Chanler; she married Prince Troubetzkoy in February 1896. The success of this marriage is reflected in an interview in the *New York Times* of 19 April 1914 concerning her views on feminism. The ideal for a woman, Rives asserted, was to realize in marriage equality with her husband; there should be "complete comraderie," with husband and wife friends as well as marriage partners.

Marriage to Prince Troubetzkoy marked the beginning of the happiest segment of Rives's life, but during this period her writing diminished in volume and quality. The uncertain, maudlin plot of *A Damsel Errant* (1898) was her weakest, and the narrative poem *Selene* (1905) was derivative of Greek myth and aesthetic poetic tradition. However, a decade after her marriage she began to publish more accomplished works: *Augustine the Man* (1906), a closet drama, and *World's End* (1914), her most mature—and realistic—novel. *World's End*, *Shadows of Flames* (1914), and *Firedamp* (1930) embody a variant of the "international theme" associated with such contemporary American authors as Henry James (1843–1916) and Edith Wharton. Rives's typical heroine in such novels is depicted in a European setting, as much at home in London, say, as in her native Virginia, and still as striking and vital as in her earlier manifestations.

For almost two decades following their marriage the Troubetzkoys divided their time between Castle Hill and Europe. They enjoyed celebrity on both sides of the Atlantic: he through prestigious portrait commissions and she through literary reputation and physical beauty (she was one of the most frequently photographed women of her era). Always interested in spiritualism, and claiming to be psychic, Rives later avowed that in the spring of 1914 she had a premonition of an imminent cataclysm in England. Though not intending to travel abroad that summer, she and the Prince hastily changed their plans. During their stay at Lord Curzon's estate, Archduke Francis Ferdinand was assassinated in Sarajevo. They never returned to Europe.

After 1914 the Troubetzkoys' lives underwent major changes. Throughout the 1920s and into the depression years finances were often strained, though Rives enjoyed a certain success as a dramatist in New York in the late 1910s and early 1920s, and the prince obtained what painting commissions he could. By 1930, fifteen years before her death, Rives's creative years were nearly over. Although she completed *The Young Elizabeth*, perhaps her finest work, in 1938, this drama was neither published nor professionally produced. The sudden death of Prince Troubetzkoy in 1936 was catastrophic for Rives. Being childless, she all but lost the will to live. Though her health and spirits improved temporarily during the late 1930s, they declined steadily during World War II. She died in a Charlottesville nursing home. Obituaries and later commentators noted her striking beauty, her provocative body of fiction, and her courage in asserting an independence of mind while embodying the style of the international *haut monde*.

• There is no single, all-inclusive collection of Amélie Rives's extant papers (most were burned at her request), but limited holdings are in the archives of the University of Virginia, the Virginia Historical Society, the Valentine Museum (Richmond), Harvard University, and Duke University (in the John Armstrong Chanler Papers). In addition to the works discussed above, other important titles are the novels *Barbara Dering* (1893, a sequel to *The Quick or the Dead?*), *The Golden Rose* (1908), *The Queerness of Celia* (1926), and *Trix and Over-the-Moon* (1909); the plays *The Sea-Woman's Cloak and November Eve* (1923); and the poetry collection *As the Wind Blew* (1920). The only published biography is Welford Dunaway Taylor, *Amélie Rives (Princess Troubetzkoy)* (1973); however, George C. Longest's unpublished dissertation, "Amélie Rives Troubetzkoy: A Biography" (Univ. of Ga., 1969), also is a full-length study. The most comprehensive source for bibliographical information is George C. Longest, *Three Virginia Writers; Mary Johnston, Thomas Nelson Page and Amélie Rives Troubetzkoy: A Reference Guide* (1978).

WELFORD DUNAWAY TAYLOR

RIVES, Hallie Erminie (2 May 1876–16 Aug. 1956), novelist, was born at "Post Oak Plantation," Christian County, Kentucky, the daughter of Colonel Stephen T. Rives, a prosperous tobacco farmer, and Mary Ragsdale. Rives's family was steeped in the affluent plantation South that she would romanticize in many of her novels; she took pride in a Cavalier ancestor's escape to Virginia after the downfall of Charles I and in her father's service with General Robert E. Lee. Educated at home by tutors, Rives averred that her secret reading of her kinswoman Amélie Rives's then-shocking novel *The Quick or the Dead?* (1888) inspired her at age fifteen to become a writer. At sixteen she won a prize for her short story "The Treasure of a Feud," based on her father's recollection of a Civil War incident.

During Rives's childhood, Post Oak Plantation still had its "quarters," occupied by former slaves working as servants on the property, and Rives turned to the question of race for her first novel, *Smoking Flax* (1897). Dedicated to Rives's "mother and the South" and espousing white supremacist sentiments like those of Thomas Dixon's 1905 romance of the Ku Klux Klan, *The Clansman*, Rives's novel details the conversion of Elliot Harding, a northerner who resettles in his family's Kentucky home, from ardent antilynching sentiments to a prolynching stance after the rape and murder of his fiancée by Ephriam Cooley, an African-American schoolteacher. Rives's mother, impressed by the manuscript, persuaded Colonel Rives to allow Hallie to travel unaccompanied to New York to find a publisher for the novel. After unsuccessfully visiting a string of publishers, Rives placed the book with F. Tennyson Neely.

Although the controversy over Rives's polemical defense of lynching proved profitable for Neely, Rives found notoriety troubling. Nonetheless, in her next novel, *A Furnace of Earth* (1900), she turned to an equally controversial subject, a woman's sexual awakening and the resultant guilt that she feels. Citing English psychologist Havelock Ellis, Rives avowed that "your good woman disrespects her body"; the heroine comes to terms with her passionate nature by the novel's end. Convinced of the story's commercial appeal, Post Wheeler, whom Rives had met in 1898 and would marry in 1906, agreed to place the manuscript with a publisher for her. After a series of rejections, Wheeler formed the Camelot Company for the sole purpose of publishing the novel. Although Rives's depiction of women's sexual needs seems tame by later standards, and despite her insistence that she had written an essentially moral story, contemporary audiences found the book, in the words of the *Detroit Free Press*, "heated red-hot with the lurid flame of love." It was removed from library shelves and placed on the Catholic church's list of banned books. Thanks to this infamy and an aggressive advertising campaign, the first edition sold out after four days, and five weeks later the novel was selling 3,000 copies per week.

For the publication of her third novel, *Hearts Courageous* (1902), Wheeler advised Rives to turn to Bowen-Merrill (later Bobbs-Merrill). Rives had finally hit upon an inoffensive subject: a historical romance set in Virginia during the American Revolution, with the erotic elements sugared and sanitized. Nonetheless, Wheeler—on behalf of Bowen-Merrill—directed a series of publicity stunts so audacious that Rives again achieved bestseller status. *Hearts Courageous* was adapted into a play and a silent film, with William S. Hart, later a cowboy hero of the silent screen, playing the part of Patrick Henry in both versions. In her next two novels, *The Castaway* (1904; a fictionalized biography of Lord Byron) and *Satan Sanderson* (1907; a tale of a reformed-rake minister)—as in all her fiction—Rives continued to blend genteel eroticism with fast-moving, sensational plots.

Rives's 1910 novel *The Kingdom of Slender Swords* is set in Japan, where she and Wheeler lived while he held the first of many diplomatic posts. Although not devoid of racialism, the novel demonstrates a respect for Japanese customs and religions uncharacteristic of its time; the Japanese minister of education, N. Makino, was so impressed with Rives and the novel that he wrote a laudatory preface. With *The Valiants of Virginia* (1912), Rives returned to upper-class white plantation society in the turn-of-the-century South. While the overtly white supremacist theme of *Smoking Flax* is absent, Rives's demeaning depiction of African Americans as "good-natured friendly savages" is still in the vein of her earlier work.

Rives's subsequent books took a variety of forms. *The Long Lane's Turning* (1917; serialized in *Redbook* as "The Heart of Man") is a temperance tale; *The Magic Man* (1927) is science fiction; and *The Golden Barrier* (1934) is a story of class conflict in a depression-era marriage. The two former novels were filmed, the latter dramatized for the stage. Rives also produced *The Complete Book of Etiquette* (1926; all editions after 1939 appear under the title *The Modern and Complete Book of Etiquette*) as well as several volumes of tales and short stories.

In 1955 Rives and Wheeler published their joint autobiography, *Dome of Many-Coloured Glass*, which remains the most complete source of biographical information about Rives. In prose more energetic and less turgid than that of her novels, Rives recounts her life as a writer, world traveler (she lived abroad much of her adult life), and diplomat's wife who met many of the political luminaries and crowned heads of Europe and the Americas in the early twentieth century. Rives died in New York City.

Rives was a well-known writer during her own time. Her sales were consistently high, and her books, even if failing to garner literary acclaim, were reviewed in prestigious publications like the *New York Times* and the *New Yorker*. As with most twentieth-century romance novelists, however, her reputation has proved ephemeral. Beyond the critics' refusal to take seriously the romance genre, two factors have worked against Rives's critical acceptance: her ornate prose style seems overwrought, and her preference for fast-moving plots over psychologically complex characterization seems shallow. Viewed historically, however, Rives's texts demonstrate cultural anxieties and fantasies about race, class, and sexuality in early twentieth-century America.

• Rives's papers remain uncollected. For biographical information, see (in addition to *Dome of Many-Coloured Glass*) "Hallie Erminie Rives," *Wilson Library Bulletin*, Mar. 1956, p. 496, and Rives's obituary in the *New York Times*, 18 Aug. 1956.

TESS LLOYD

RIVES, John Cook (24 May 1795–10 Apr. 1864), journalist and printer, was born in Franklin County, Virginia, the son of George Rives. His mother's name is not known. His father had died by 1806, when Rives moved to Kentucky to live with his uncle Samuel Casey. Rives later moved to Illinois, where he worked in the Edwardsville branch of the Bank of the United States and was admitted to the bar in Shawneetown, after studying law there.

Rives went to Washington in 1824 to testify before a congressional committee concerning the Bank of the United States. He first worked as a clerk in the office of the *United States Telegraph*, whose editor, Duff Green, recommended him to other influential Democrats. Without making an application, Rives was made a clerk in the Treasury Department, under its fourth auditor, Amos Kendall, who was a close adviser to President Andrew Jackson. After holding that job for about three years, Rives resigned in April 1832 to work as a clerk and office manager for Francis Preston Blair, whom Kendall had brought to the capital to establish and edit the *Washington Globe* as an administration newspaper. Rives and Blair became full partners in the paper in 1834. Neither man was handsome, and they were soon calling themselves "the ugliest looking pair in the country" (Hudson, p. 239).

A master of sarcasm, Rives used his pen to wound political enemies. His favorite topic was the tariff, and his "notions" on collecting it were unlike "those of any person that ever wrote on that subject" (Hudson, p. 247). "Take, *in kind*, one sixth—sixteen and two thirds per cent—of all the goods imported," was his formula, "and sell them on the wharf at auction, for cash" (Hudson, p. 247). This simple method, he claimed, would dispense with "the services of nineteen-twentieths of custom-house officers in the large cities" (Hudson, p. 248).

As his columns on the tariff indicate, Rives's prime interests were finance and organization, and he used his genius to lift the *Globe* out of its early financial troubles and to build a printing empire. In the summer of 1833 Rives (who at first had used "his own strong arm" to turn the wheel that moved the *Washington Globe* presses) purchased a modern Napier press for his and Blair's establishment. In December of that year they started a second publication, the *Congressional Globe*. At first summarizing congressional debates, Rives and Blair soon found that condensations were unsatisfactory and gradually moved to printing them in full. Earlier publications had offered detailed summaries of debates, but the *Congressional Globe* was the first to print a complete record and to be bound in book form. A quasi-official, nonpartisan, inexpensive journal (subsidized by Congress, it required no postage and in 1852 cost only $3 a year), it became a vital force in the political education of the nation. In it could be found the proceedings of Congress, the president's messages, the reports of department heads, and the laws of the session. Congress continued to subsidize the *Congressional Globe* until 1873 (after Rives's death it was published by his son Franklin) when Congress replaced it with the *Congressional Record*. In 1835 Rives married Mary (maiden name unknown), a "bindery girl" in his printing establishment; they had seven children.

In 1842 Rives began a third undertaking. "Buoyed up with the hope that" his children might "reap some profit," he became a partner of Peter Force in the reprinting of historical documents. Aided by a contract with the State Department and authorized by an act of Congress, the *American Archives* prospered until 1853.

On 30 April 1845 the last issue of the *Washington Globe* appeared. For fifteen years the *Globe* had flourished on conflict, but over the past four years during the John Tyler administration it had lacked political patronage. After consulting with former presidents Andrew Jackson and Martin Van Buren and with Governor Silas Wright of New York, Rives and Blair bowed to the inevitable. They sold the *Globe* to the journalists Thomas Ritchie and John P. Heiss, who had come to Washington to establish and edit the *Washington Union* as the organ of the new Polk administration. After a three-year hiatus, Rives began publishing, in conjunction with the *Congressional Globe*, a *Daily Globe*, which also appeared when Congress was in session and lasted until 1873.

Rives and Blair both esteemed Andrew Jackson. To keep their old hero and early benefactor from suffering embarrassment from the extravagances of his adopted son, they lent Jackson $18,000 in two lump sums, beginning in 1841. Through the Democratic Association, which Rives headed in 1845 and 1846, they helped erect a statue of Jackson (made from a cannon he had captured at Pensacola) and placed it in Lafayette Square. And when in 1845 they used their $20,000 election winnings (earned from betting that Henry Clay would not carry certain states) to erect

buildings, they named the one fronting their new three-story printing plant Jackson Hall.

Less a "vehement party man" than Blair, Rives usually agreed with Jackson's policies and gave large sums to the Democratic party, but he sometimes sided with Henry Clay on internal improvements and foreign affairs. Although a Union man, Rives did not want the federal government "to meddle with slavery in the States." Having purchased his own ten slaves "at their own request," he insisted he would not part with them "upon compulsion" (Hudson, p. 251). In 1844 Blair's activities to gain Van Buren the Democratic nomination embarrassed Rives, who was working hard to secure it for Lewis Cass. When Blair followed what Rives called Van Buren's political "*misfortunes*" into the Free Soil party in 1848, the partners' split the next year became inevitable. They both knew that Blair's antislavery stand would make it impossible for them to secure the bipartisan backing necessary for publication of the *Congressional Globe*. For Blair (who continued to leave his personal finances in the hands of Rives) the partnership ended "most satisfactorily," with Rives wanting "to do more" for him than he "would allow" (W. E. Smith, vol. 1, p. 246).

Rives was devastated in 1853 when his wife died suddenly after giving birth to a dead premature baby. When the Civil War came, Rives, who was anxious to preserve the Union, gave more than $30,000 to the wives of men who enlisted in the Union army from the District of Columbia. He died on his Bladensburg, Maryland, farm.

• Rives's autobiography is reprinted in Frederic Hudson, *Journalism in the United States, from 1690–1872* (1873; repr. 1968). Much material on Rives is also in the biographies of his partner: William Ernest Smith, *The Francis Preston Blair Family in Politics* (2 vols., 1933) and Elbert B. Smith, *Francis Preston Blair* (1980). Information on Rives can also be found in the following: Donald B. Cole and John J. McDonough, eds., *Benjamin Brown French: Witness to the Young Republic, A Yankee's Journal, 1828–1870* (1989); Allan Nevins, *Ordeal of the Union*, vol. 1 (1947); Arthur M. Schlesinger, Jr., *The Age of Jackson* (1946); Rufus Rockwell Wilson, *Washington: The Capital City and Its Part in the History of the Nation* (2 vols., 1902); Constance Mc Laughlin Green, *Washington Village and Capital, 1800–1878* (1962); Wilhelmus Bogart Bryan, *A History of the National Capital: From Its Foundation through the Period of the Adoption of the Organic Act*, vol. 2 (1914–1916); William Benning Webb and John Wooldridge, *Centennial History of the City of Washington* (1892); James Rives Childs, *Reliques of the Rives (Ryves) . . .* (1929), which reprints a detailed obituary written by Francis Preston Blair. A short obituary is in the *New York Times*, 13 Apr. 1864.

OLIVE HOOGENBOOM

RIVES, Richard Taylor (15 Jan. 1895–27 Oct. 1982), judge of the U.S. Court of Appeals for the Fifth Circuit, was born in Montgomery, Alabama, the son of William Henry Rives, a law enforcement officer and county road construction supervisor, and Alice Bloodworth Taylor. Rives, whose ancestors had lost their considerable land holdings as a result of the Civil War, was born into a family of modest means. He earned a scholarship at Tulane University but, because of financial constraints, attended for only one year (1911–1912). He then studied law with Montgomery attorney Wiley Hill, a friend of his father, and in 1914 was admitted to the bar at the age of nineteen. Rives began work for Hill's law firm (Hill, Hill, Whiting, & Stern), with which he remained affiliated for the next thirty-three years. He served on the Mexican border as a member of the national guard in 1916–1917 and then as a first lieutenant in the U.S. Army during World War I. In 1918 Rives married Jessie Hall Dougherty, with whom he had two children.

Rives became quite active in state Democratic party politics, preferring to organize support for candidates rather than to run for office himself. He successfully directed several statewide campaigns, including Hugo Black's run for the U.S. Senate. Rives was closely associated with Alabama's long-time senators, Lister Hill and John Sparkman. Although many urged him to run for office, Rives believed that his progressive racial attitudes imposed a significant barrier to a successful candidacy. His commitment to fundamental human fairness kept him from advocating segregationist policies. In 1946 he opposed the Boswell amendment, a proposal to allow local voting registrars the ability to deny the franchise to those without "sufficient understanding" to vote intelligently. The clear purpose of the amendment was to deny voting rights to blacks. The amendment was approved by the state's voters but later overturned in the courts. Rives's public opposition to the proposal permanently branded him a liberal on the race issue.

Rives left the Hill law firm in 1947, anticipating a legal partnership with his son, then a law student at the University of Michigan. The partnership plans were dashed, however, when Richard, Jr., was killed in an automobile accident in 1949. Rives was devastated by his son's death. The two had been exceptionally close. Before law school the younger Rives had attended Harvard University and served in the navy during World War II. His experiences outside the South had led him to adopt very progressive racial views, and to impress these attitudes on his father. After his son's death, Rives invited a young attorney, John Cooper Godbold, to join his new firm.

In 1951 long-time friend Leon McCord announced his retirement as judge from the Fifth Circuit Court of Appeals. McCord wanted Rives to fill his vacancy, and Rives was agreeable. Rives and McCord enlisted the help of Senators Hill and Sparkman to persuade President Harry S. Truman to appoint Rives to the bench. The effort was successful, and Rives took his seat in May 1951.

When the Supreme Court handed down its decision in *Brown v. Board of Education* (1954), the significance of the Fifth Circuit became apparent. With jurisdiction over the six states of the Deep South, the court was crucial to the implementation of the *Brown* mandate. Rives joined judges Elbert Tuttle of Georgia, John Brown of Texas, and John Minor Wisdom of Louisiana to form a liberal core that vigorously enforced desegregation principles. The decisions of these four judges became legendary in civil rights history.

Rives is probably best known for his majority opinion in *Browder v. Gayle* (1956). This case arose from the Montgomery bus boycott, a civil rights protest against laws that required racial segregation in public transportation. The boycott is often cited as the beginning of the modern civil rights movement and the incident that established Martin Luther King, Jr., as a civil rights leader. At issue in *Browder* was whether the *Brown* precedent applied only to public education or controlled other areas as well. Rives's opinion gave *Brown* a broad construction. The Supreme Court affirmed, holding that state-sponsored racial segregation was unconstitutional wherever it occurred. Decisions such as this earned Rives considerable criticism. Old friends shunned him. Members of his Presbyterian church made him feel unwelcome. Vandals desecrated his son's grave.

In 1959 Rives became chief judge of the Fifth Circuit. He served only until 1960, however, preferring to turn the position over to Elbert Tuttle, a man Rives considered to be much better suited for administrative tasks. From 1963 to 1966 Rives joined forces with Judge Wisdom to fight a proposal to divide the Fifth Circuit into two separate courts. Proponents believed that the circuit had become unmanageable because of the growth in caseloads and judgeships. Rives and Wisdom, however, feared that division would result in two excessively small and parochial circuits and would have a detrimental effect on civil rights cases by gerrymandering the liberal judges into separate circuits. They were able to delay the restructuring until 1980, when Congress created a new Fifth Circuit consisting of Texas, Louisiana, and Mississippi, and a new Eleventh of Alabama, Georgia, and Florida.

Rives took senior status in February 1966 after reaching the age of seventy. He was replaced by John Godbold, his friend and former law partner. Rives continued to hear cases while in retirement until his health failed some years later. After the death of his wife in 1973, Rives married Martha Blake Frazer in 1976; they had no children. He died at his Montgomery home.

Rives's career on the federal bench was a distinguished one. His sense of fairness and human dignity led him to champion the cause of racial change in the South. Although a quiet man, Rives was widely regarded, even by his enemies, as a person of strength, courtesy, and integrity.

• Rives's life and judicial career are included in a number of works on southern federal courts. The historical development of the U.S. Court of Appeals for the Fifth Circuit can be found in Harvey C. Couch, *A History of the Fifth Circuit, 1891–1981* (1984). Jack Bass, *Unlikely Heroes* (1981), and Frank T. Read and Lucy S. McGough, *Let Them Be Judged: The Judicial Integration of the Deep South* (1978), chronicle Rives's role in the southern desegregation cases. Rives's opposition to the division of the Fifth Circuit is examined in Deborah J. Barrow and Thomas G. Walker, *A Court Divided* (1988). An obituary is in the *New York Times*, 30 Oct. 1982.

THOMAS G. WALKER

RIVES, William Cabell (4 May 1793–25 Apr. 1868), politician, diplomat, and author, was born in Amherst County, Virginia, the son of Robert Rives, a revolutionary war veteran and merchant, and Margaret Jordan Cabell. Rives was educated at Hampden-Sydney College and graduated from William and Mary in 1809. He studied law with Thomas Jefferson and was subsequently admitted to the Charlottesville bar in 1814. In 1819 Rives married Judith Page Walker, with whom he had five children. His marriage brought him into possession of the "Castle Hill" plantation, located about twenty miles north of Charlottesville. From this inheritance, Rives became a planter and slaveholder. By the outbreak of the Civil War in 1861, Rives owned 104 slaves.

Rives's political career began in 1816, when he represented Nelson County, which was formed from Amherst County, in the Virginia constitutional convention in Staunton. From 1817 to 1821 he represented Nelson County in the Virginia House of Delegates and in 1821–1822 served as delegate from Albemarle County. In 1823 Rives was elected to the U.S. House of Representatives, where he served until 1829. Throughout the 1820s Rives displayed a firm loyalty to the principles of Jefferson. He adhered strongly to a states' rights interpretation of the Constitution, advocated a limited role for the federal government, and envisioned an agrarian society of yeoman farmers. As a true Jeffersonian, Rives opposed the nationalizing tendencies of both Henry Clay's "American System" and the administration of John Quincy Adams. Rives's rather strict republicanism was somewhat moderated in the late 1820s under the influence of James Madison. Led by this Founding Father of Virginia, Rives came to cherish the value of the Union and accept nationalistic measures such as a protective tariff.

Rives became an influential national political figure during the age of Andrew Jackson. In the 1820s he worked with Thomas Ritchie, editor of the Richmond *Enquirer*, to build the foundations of the Democratic party in Virginia that helped elect Jackson to the presidency in 1828. Rives was a loyal Jackson supporter and consequently was named minister to France. During his first tour, from 1829 through 1832, he helped negotiate those American claims that had been raised against Napoleonic France.

Rives was elected to the U.S. Senate as a Democrat in 1832, but he resigned his seat in 1834 rather than obey the instructions of the Virginia legislature to vote against Jackson's removal of federal deposits from the Second Bank of the United States. On the controversial issue of nullification, however, Rives sometimes broke with the president and many of his Democratic followers. Rives also opposed the subtreasury system of Jackson's successor, Martin Van Buren. As part of the revolt of the "Conservative" Democrats in the late 1830s, Rives favored paper money and insisted that federal monies should be deposited in state banks instead of independent federal treasuries. In January 1841 Rives was reelected to the Senate, where he became chair of the Committee on Foreign Relations. By 1844 he switched his political allegiance to the rival Whig party, whose support of economic modernization fit well with his hopes for economic diversification and manufacturing in Virginia. In 1845 his term in the Senate ended.

Rives served a second stint as minister to France from 1849 to 1853. During the rise to power of Louis-Napoléon, he witnessed the civil turmoil that led him toward Unionism in 1861. He became a prominent spokesman in the upper South for the preservation of the Union, opposing those radical secessionists who argued that slavery was safe only in a separate confederacy of southern states. Rives suggested the name for the Constitutional Union party, which ran John Bell during the presidential election of 1860. Rives remained a strong Unionist after the election of Abraham Lincoln and the secession of the seven slave states of the lower South. Throughout the secession winter of 1860–1861 Rives sought to protect the slaveholding rights of the South within the Union. He participated in the Peace Convention of 1861 that sought congressional compromises between the North and South. After the bombardment of Fort Sumter in April 1861 and Lincoln's call for troops, Rives accepted the secession of Virginia and became one of the first five delegates from the state to the provisional Confederate Congress. In 1864 he served in the Confederate House as a member of the Foreign Affairs Committee.

In addition to being a politician and diplomat, Rives was also the biographer of his former mentor Madison. His *History of the Life and Times of James Madison* (3 vols., 1859–1868) combined careful scholarship and documentary editing with a veneration of the ideals of the Founding Fathers. It remained the standard biography of Madison for years.

The importance of Rives lies primarily in his long participation in American politics from the Jeffersonian Era through the Civil War. Educated by Jefferson and Madison, Rives carried on the spirit of eighteenth-century republicanism within a changing political culture. Underlying his later moderation in politics was an overriding belief in reason and restraint, an inheritance of the Enlightenment. His suspicion of parties and vision of an idealized and harmonious society, characteristic of republicanism, ran against the main currents of nineteenth-century political development. By the end of his career, Rives was considered part of a passing generation that revealed its ultimate inability to reconcile slavery with the ideals of the American Revolution and the demands of a modern party system. He died in his plantation home in Albemarle County, Virginia.

• The voluminous William Cabell Rives Papers are in the Manuscript Division of the Library of Congress. Other Rives letters are in the Hugh Blair Grigsby Papers, the William Cabell Rives Papers, and the Rives Family Papers at the Virginia Historical Society. Drew McCoy, *The Last of the Fathers: James Madison and the Republican Legacy* (1989), offers the fullest and most perceptive account of Rives's public life. On Rives as biographer of Madison, see Ralph L. Ketcham, "William Cabell Rives: Editor of the *Letters and Other Writ-*

ings of James Madison," *Virginia Magazine of History and Biography* 68 (Apr. 1960): 131–36. His participation in the high politics of the Jacksonian Era can be traced most fully in John Niven, *Martin Van Buren: The Romantic Age of American Politics* (1983). For Rives's role during the secession crisis, see Robert G. Gunderson, "William C. Rives and the 'Old Gentlemen's Convention,'" *Journal of Southern History* 22 (Nov. 1956): 459–70; and Patrick Sowle, "The Trials of a Virginia Unionist: William Cabell Rives and the Secession Crisis, 1860–1861," *Virginia Magazine of History and Biography* 80 (Jan. 1972): 3–20. Some background on the personal life of Rives is in Raymond C. Dingledine, "The Education of a Virginia Planter's Son," in *America: The Middle Period; Essays in Honor of Bernard Mayo*, ed. John B. Boles (1973).

MITCHELL SNAY

RIVINGTON, James (17 Aug. 1724–4 July 1802), journalist and newspaper publisher, was born in London, England, the son of Charles Rivington, a publisher, and Eleanor Pease. Following his father's death in 1742, James joined his brother John in continuing the family printing business. In 1752 Rivington married Elizabeth Minshull. They had only one child, who died as an infant. In 1756 he entered a successful partnership with James Fletcher. However, Rivington enjoyed an expensive lifestyle that included gambling at the horse races. Gambling losses, combined with a number of lawsuits for illegally printing books, forced him to file for bankruptcy in 1760. Shortly thereafter, Rivington left for New York, hoping to retrieve his fortunes in the colonies.

After his arrival, Rivington opened bookstores in Philadelphia and New York and advertised himself as the only London bookseller in the colonies. In 1762 he opened a third bookstore in Boston. However, by 1765 he had confined his activities to New York alone. In 1766 he moved to Annapolis briefly, where he engaged in a land scheme, the "Maryland lottery." This plan failed, and Rivington returned to New York, bankrupt for a second time. His finances once more improved, partially because of his marriage, after the death of his first wife, to a wealthy New York widow, Elizabeth Van Horne, in 1769. They had three children.

In 1773 Rivington established his newspaper, *Rivington's New-York Gazeteer or the Connecticut, Hudson's River, New-Jersey, and Quebec Weekly Advertiser*. At first, Rivington's gazette was successful, primarily because it was well written and well edited. It contained the best coverage of foreign news in any colonial paper and carried transcripts of Parliament's debates as well as continental European news. By 1775 Rivington claimed 3,600 subscribers. His contemporaries praised his efforts. Isaiah Thomas, in the *Massachusetts Spy*, stated that "few men, perhaps, were better qualified . . . to publish a newspaper" and concluded that "no newspaper in the colonies was better printed, or more copiously furnished with foreign intelligence."

Rivington promised that his newspaper would present all sides of issues being debated by the public, and originally he attempted to honor that promise. He emphasized the importance of a free press in political discussions, but many colonials, increasingly distrustful of the British, did not agree. Increasingly, Rivington's attempts to print multiple viewpoints received criticism. As a result, his own Tory convictions became clearer in his paper. Thomas, who had earlier praised Rivington for his abilities as a journalist, called him "that Judas." In May 1775 Rivington narrowly survived an attack on his press by the Sons of Liberty. By November 1775 his luck had run out for on the 20th a mob led by Isaac Sears wrecked his presses and carried off his types, which were supposedly later melted down and made into bullets. Shortly after, Rivington and his family sailed for London.

Rivington returned to New York in September 1777 after the British army occupied the city. Having received an appointment as the king's printer, Rivington resumed his newspaper in October under the title *Rivington's New York Loyal Gazette*. Changing the name to *Royal Gazette* in December 1777, Rivington strongly advocated the British cause and attacked the patriots at every opportunity. Rivington's previous desire to present all sides of controversies had disappeared, and he used whatever means available to advance the Royal cause. The patriots quickly labeled his paper "The Lying Gazette," and even many Loyalists questioned his journalistic veracity at times. The paper continued until war's end, but Rivington's attacks on the Americans became fewer and weaker as the fighting slowed and it became clear that the patriots would win. Following the withdrawal of the British from New York in 1783, Rivington remained, to the surprise of many. The fact that Rivington escaped major retribution from the patriots for his support of the Tory cause has been the subject of much debate over the years. Some evidence indicates that he may have been spared punishment because he spied for George Washington in the latter years of the war. The factual support for this story is slim, but not totally without merit. Whatever the reason, Rivington did not leave with the British Army. He changed the name of his paper to *Rivington's New-York Gazette and Universal Advertiser*. He clearly desired to continue publishing his gazette, but he no longer had the support needed to maintain the paper. The last issue appeared on 31 December 1783. Rivington returned to bookselling as his primary source of income, but success eluded him. He spent 1797 to 1801 in debtor's prison. Rivington died in poverty in New York.

Rivington's legacy is somewhat difficult to adequately evaluate because of the strong hatred that he generated among many of his contemporaries. For example, Philip Freneau, a fellow printer during the 1780s, described Rivington as "the Inventor, as well as the Printer of Lies!" As a consequence of the invectives hurled at him in his own time, Rivington's successes are often overlooked. From May 1778 to July 1783, while publishing the *Royal Gazette*, Rivington established a publishing schedule with other New York newspaper printers that, in effect, produced the first daily newspaper in America. He also led the way in urging freedom of the press during the early years of the Revolution. His failure to adhere to this ideal throughout the conflict does not erase his faithfulness to it during the early 1770s. Rivington's career reflects many contradictions. He is remembered primarily as the most famous, most successful, and most hated Tory printer during the Revolution, but he was also one of the earliest colonial advocates of freedom of the press, a legacy that finally reached fruition many years later.

• The New-York Historical Society has a complete run of Rivington's newspaper. Good overall discussions of Rivington's life and career include Robert M. Ours, "James Rivington: Another Viewpoint" in *Newsletters to Newspapers*, ed. Donovan H. Bond and W. Reynolds McLeod (1977), and Michael Sewell, "James Rivington," *Dictionary of Literary Biography: American Newspaper Journalists, 1690–1872* (1985). A lengthy consideration can be found in Leroy Hewlett, "James Rivington, Loyalist Printer, Publisher, and Bookseller of the American Revolution" (Ph.D. diss., Univ. of Michigan, 1958). Discussion of Rivington's spying activities can be found in John L. Lawson, "The 'Remarkable Mystery' of James Rivington, 'Spy,'" *Journalism Quarterly* 35 (1958): 317–23, 394; and Catherine Snell Crary, "The Tory and the Spy: The Double Life of James Rivington," *William and Mary Quarterly* 16 (1959): 61–72.

CAROL SUE HUMPHREY

RIZZO, Frank Lazzaro (23 Oct. 1920–16 July 1991), police officer and politician, was born in Philadelphia, Pennsylvania, the son of Raffaele "Ralph" Rizzo, a police officer and tailor, and Theresa Erminio. Both of his parents were Italian immigrants. Rizzo was raised in predominately Italian South Philadelphia, where he attended local schools but failed to graduate from high school. He joined the navy in 1938 and received a medical discharge just one year later. Returning to Philadelphia, he worked in the steel and construction industries. In 1942 he married Carmella Silvestri; they had two children.

Rizzo joined the Philadelphia Police Department on 6 October 1943. An aggressive officer, he caught the eye of his superiors and was promoted to acting sergeant. Assigned to a center city district, Rizzo eventually became his own father's supervisor. In 1952 the Democratic party took control of city hall after decades of Republican rule. A new home rule charter was adopted, giving city employees civil service protection. Rizzo was officially promoted to sergeant and assigned to the highway patrol. Continuing to ascend the promotional ladder, he became an inspector in 1959. He entered the 1960s with a strong law and order reputation, but he was also known for his quick use of force and poor record in dealing with African Americans. The Democrats stayed in power, but the city was now under the control of the Irish Catholics and James H. J. Tate. Rizzo and Tate used each other to advance their careers. Rizzo made quite an impression during his testimony before Senator John McClellan's Senate Subcommittee on Crime in Washington, D.C., in June 1962, when he made his first public comments attacking the courts and the American Civil Liberties Union (ACLU) for being "soft" on crime.

In 1963 Rizzo became a deputy commissioner and Tate was reelected mayor. In August of that year Philadelphia experienced urban riots, but unlike in other major metropolitan areas, the police handled the situation with only one death and few injuries. Deputy Rizzo and Commissioner Howard Leary, a low-key liberal, did not see eye-to-eye on keeping the peace and constantly clashed. In February 1966 Leary left to become police commissioner of New York City. Later that year Arlen Spector was elected district attorney, the first Republican victory in the city in fifteen years, and he was a threat to unseat Tate as mayor. Rizzo, ever present on the streets of Philadelphia, led his police force in confrontations with civil rights and anti–Vietnam War protestors.

In May 1967, a year of more urban unrest throughout the country, Rizzo was named commissioner of police, and the city council granted Mayor Tate emergency powers. Philadelphia remained quiet through the summer, and with Rizzo's help, Tate defeated Spector for mayor by a small margin. On 4 April 1968 Martin Luther King was assassinated, but again Philadelphia remained calm. Rizzo's reputation for law and order caught the eye of Republican presidential candidate Richard Nixon, who was running in part on law and order himself. Rizzo made plans to run for mayor in 1971, and the two major parties vied for the honor.

Rizzo preferred to run for mayor as a Republican but chose the Democratic party as his best chance to win. Law and order was becoming an issue in urban and national politics beyond Philadelphia. While Rizzo was a unique politician, he also represented that national trend. The Democrats needed Rizzo to hold onto the white blue-collar voters, who were defecting to the law and order Republicans. Rizzo won the Democratic primary, then defeated his Republican opponent with 71 percent of the vote. Just two weeks later Rizzo visited President Nixon and J. Edgar Hoover in Washington, becoming one of the best-known mayors in the United States.

In 1975 Rizzo ran for reelection and defeated a prominent black independent candidate, who finished second, and the Republican candidate, who was a distant third. Mayor Rizzo's major campaign issue was his fulfilled promise not to raise taxes during his first term. However, keeping this pledge forced him during his second term to enact the largest tax increase in Philadelphia history to that date. This tax increase was the catalyst for a recall movement begun in 1976 by a coalition of labor unions, black leaders, and liberal groups such as the Americans for Democratic Action, the ACLU, and the newly created Philadelphia party. Rizzo was a symbol of blue-collar, white ethnic pride to his supporters and a brutal, racist police force to his detractors. The recall effort needed more than 145,000 signatures and collected at least 211,000, but Rizzo's supporters challenged the validity of the signatures. The Pennsylvania Supreme Court settled the issue in a

September 1976 decision that struck down the entire Philadelphia recall process.

Rizzo wanted to run again, but the Philadelphia city charter limited the mayor to only two consecutive terms. Rizzo began an unsuccessful campaign to change the charter. On 11 September 1980 a committee was formed to revise the Philadelphia Home Rule Charter to allow the mayor to serve for more than two consecutive terms, and the question was placed on the November ballot. The vote was 85 percent against the measure. The 1980s began with a new mayor in city hall. The incumbent decided not to run again in 1983, and Rizzo, courted by the Republicans, ran as a Democrat. He lost the primary to the former city managing director, W. Wilson Goode, who defeated the Republican in the general election to become the city's first elected black mayor. In 1987 Rizzo ran again, this time as a Republican, but he lost the election to Goode by less than 3 percentage points.

Rizzo, sixty-seven years of age, went into semiretirement. At the end of 1988 he accepted a spot as a radio talk show host on one of the local stations, and with this exposure a movement urging his candidacy for mayor began to build. With the support in the black community, which was plagued by the crack cocaine epidemic, he decided to run in the Republican primary against a popular Republican district attorney and Vietnam War hero, Ron Castille. A third candidate split the vote, but Rizzo ran a brutal campaign against Castille and won the primary. With his momentum building, Rizzo died in Philadelphia just three months before the general election. His funeral was one of the largest in Philadelphia history. Thousands waited in the July heat for hours to view for the last time one of Philadelphia's most famous citizens.

Rizzo was one of the last of the powerful big city mayors. From his first days on the police force to his last days running for office, he was a major presence in the everyday lives of the citizens of Philadelphia. A biographer concluded that few men in history have been their own political party. Rizzo's admirers followed him not because he was a Democrat or a Republican but because he was Rizzo.

• S. A. Paolantonio, *Frank Rizzo: The Last Big Man in Big City America* (1993), a complete biography of Rizzo written by a Philadelphia newspaper reporter, is objective and well written. Theodore H. White, *The Making of the President, 1972* (1973), discusses the relationship between Richard Nixon and Rizzo. Jonathan Rubinstein, *City Police* (1973), is a detailed study of the Philadelphia police and Rizzo written by an author who worked the streets with Rizzo's beat cops. Fred Hamilton, *Rizzo* (1973), and Joseph R. Daughen and Peter Binzen, *The Cop Who Would Be King* (1977), are mostly negative and concentrate on his political career. Extensive obituaries are in the *Philadelphia Inquirer* and the *Philadelphia Daily News*.

MICHAEL A. CAVANAUGH

ROACH, Hal (14 Jan. 1892–2 Nov. 1992), movie producer and director, was born Harold Eugene Roach in Elmira, New York, the son of Charles Roach, a jeweler-ry salesman, and Mabel Bally, who ran a boardinghouse. Roach attended public and Catholic schools until the age of sixteen, when his father advised him to leave home and educate himself by traveling.

Roach headed west and worked a series of temporary jobs: ice cream vendor in Seattle, postman and gold prospector in Alaska, and mule skinner in California's Mojave Desert. In 1912 he became an extra in westerns produced at Universal Studios in Hollywood and rapidly progressed through the roles of stuntman, minor actor, cameraman, writer, director, and, finally, producer.

While at Universal Roach became friends with Harold Lloyd, another minor actor at that studio. Roach's receipt of a $3,000 inheritance in 1915 provided the financing for them to leave Universal and start making one-reel comedy "shorts" on their own. Their first featured Lloyd as "Willie Work" in *Just Nuts* (1915). The pair had problems finding a film distributor, so Lloyd went to work for Mack Sennett's Keystone Studios, and Roach began directing films for Essanay. Roach eventually secured a distribution and financing deal with the Pathé Exchange—one of the largest film distributors, Pathé Exchange also helped finance other companies' productions—so he organized the Rolin Film Company and began working again with Lloyd on *Lonesome Luke* (1915) and *Lonesome Luke's Movie Muddle* (1916). Roach also produced, and frequently coscripted, other comedies in which Lloyd developed his best-known characterization, a befuddled fellow with prominent eyeglasses who was subjected to continuous and highly dangerous mishaps. *Safety Last* (1923) was one of their most popular collaborations. The film's image of Lloyd hanging on to the hands of a giant clock high above the streets of Los Angeles has become one of the best-known icons of American silent comedy.

During this period Roach married the movie actress Marguerite Nichols. The couple had two children; Hal, Jr., became a movie director, and Margaret became a movie actress. The couple separated in 1940. Roach then married Lucille Prin, a secretary for the American Society of Composers and Publishers, in September 1942. They had three children.

During the early 1920s Roach's studio employed numerous other comedians. Roach teamed up Stanley Laurel, an English music-hall veteran who was writing and directing some of Roach's films, with Oliver "Babe" Hardy and created one of the nation's most popular comedy teams. Their first film was *45 Minutes from Hollywood* (1925), and it led to a long series of hits, including the Oscar-winning *The Music Box* (1932), *Pardon Us* (1931), in which Roach appeared as a prisoner on a chain gang, *Way Out West* (1937), *A Chump at Oxford* (1940), and *Saps at Sea* (1940). Roach also developed the "Our Gang" comedy series, which served as a training ground for numerous young actors and actresses who later became comedy stars in their own right, including Jackie Cooper and Nanette Fabray.

During most of the 1920s Roach and Sennett were Hollywood's two leading producers of comedy shorts and represented different styles of humor. Sennett's productions featured comedy stereotypes and relied heavily on slapstick, sight gags, and frantic car chases (e.g., the Keystone Kops). Roach's comedians, on the other hand, were developed as individuals with their own unique personalities, and while their films contained slapstick and sight gags they relied more on story structure and character development. Sennett's heavy-handed style of comedy eventually fell out of favor with movie audiences, who were demanding more sophisticated comedies by the end of the 1920s. Roach also expanded production into drama, westerns, and adventure stories.

The expenses incurred with the transition to talking movies and the subsequent onset of the Great Depression bankrupted many Hollywood studios, including Sennett's, but Roach survived and continued to prosper. He reviewed his studio's output and eliminated the less popular series. He focused on such proven audience-winners as Laurel and Hardy and "Our Gang," whose *Bored of Education* (1936) won an Oscar.

During the late 1930s Roach noted that movie theaters were dropping traditional comedy shorts in favor of cartoons, which had been raised to new levels of sophistication by Walt Disney and the animation departments of the major studios. He shifted to the production of longer, second feature "B" films. He sold the rights to "Our Gang" to Metro-Goldwyn-Mayer (MGM) Studios in 1938, and expanded the Laurel and Hardy films into feature-length productions. *Topper* (1937) initiated a series of sophisticated, full-length comedies featuring Roland Young as a stuffy banker pestered by the ghosts of a debonair, and frequently inebriated, society couple modeled on Nick and Nora Charles from MGM's "The Thin Man" films. Roach also produced films featuring a female comedy team starring Thelma Todd, initially teamed with Zasu Pitts and later with Patsy Kelly. Roach also produced serious films, including *One Million B.C.* (1940), directed by his son, and *Of Mice and Men* (1939), a film version of John Steinbeck's novel.

After America's entry into World War II, Roach enlisted in the U.S. Army, where he produced training and propaganda films for the army and army air corps. The Roach Studios were taken over by the army air corps, which constructed an enormous relief map of Japan on the sound stages. This was filmed from overhead by camera crews mounted on cranes to produce simulations of the views pilots and navigators would see on their bombing runs. Roach was discharged in 1945 with the rank of colonel.

Problems in obtaining financing for films caused Roach to shift into television production in the late 1940s. He and his son organized the Hal Roach Television Corporation and used the movie studio facilities to produce a number of successful television series during the 1950s, including "The Life of Riley," "My Little Margie," "Public Defender," "Racket Squad," and "The Amos and Andy Show."

Roach sold his studio to his son in 1955 and went into semiretirement. But his son lost financial control of the company in 1958, and the firm later entered bankruptcy proceedings. The Hal Roach studios were sold and demolished in 1963 to make way for an automobile dealership. Soon afterward Roach attempted to reenter the movie business. He obtained financing from English investors to coproduce a remake of *One Million Years B.C.* in 1966 and compiled a sequence of shots from his comedies for *The Crazy World of Laurel and Hardy* (1967).

In 1984 the American Academy of Motion Picture Arts and Sciences awarded Roach an honorary Oscar for lifetime achievement. He died in Los Angeles.

• Roach's business papers are at the Cinema-Television Library, University of Southern California, Los Angeles, Calif. The Library of Congress has a collection containing many of his silent films. He wrote "Living with Laughter," *Films and Filming*, Oct. 1964. An informative interview is in Mike Steen, *Hollywood Speaks! An Oral History* (1974). Roach was profiled in the *Washington Post*, 24 Jan. 1992. See also William K. Everson, *The Films of Hal Roach* (1971); Tom Dardis, *Harold Lloyd: The Man on the Clock* (1983); Adam Reilly, *Harold Lloyd* (1977); Leonard Maltin, *Our Gang: The Life and Times of the Little Rascals* (1977); and Randy Skretvedt, *Laurel and Hardy: The Magic Behind the Movies* (1987), which is based on extensive interviews. See also Walter Kerr, "The Roach Lot: A Bit More Method in the Madness," in his *The Silent Clowns* (1975), pp. 108–16; "The Men Who Make and Sell TV Film," *Television*, July 1953; Anthony Slide, "Hal Roach on Film Comedy: An Interview," *Silent Picture* (Spring 1970): 3–7; and "Hal Roach" in Gerald Mast, *The Comic Mind: Comedy and the Movies* (1973), pp. 183–93. Obituaries are in the *New York Times*, 3 Nov. 1992, and the *Washington Post*, 8 Nov. 1992.

STEPHEN G. MARSHALL

ROANE, Archibald (7 July 1759?–4 Jan. 1819), lawyer and governor of Tennessee, was born in Lancaster (now Dauphin) County, Pennsylvania, the son of Andrew Roane, a weaver who emigrated from Ireland in 1739, and Margaret Walker. Roane's parents died in about 1767, and his paternal uncle John, a Presbyterian minister, assumed supervision of Roane's upbringing and education. He attended for a time Dickinson College near Carlisle, and later he was admitted to the Pennsylvania bar. In 1780 he enlisted as a private in the Lancaster County militia and witnessed Lord Cornwallis's surrender at Yorktown in 1781. (An unverified family tradition also places Roane with George Washington during the crossing of the Delaware River on Christmas Day 1776.)

Following the war Roane moved to Rockbridge County, Virginia, where he first studied and then taught languages and mathematics at the Presbyterian-sponsored Liberty Hall Academy. Undoubtedly Roane's reputation for scholarship dates to this period. During this sojourn in Virginia, Roane probably met his future wife, Anne Campbell. They married in 1788 and settled in Washington County, North Carolina (after 1790, the Southwest Territory), where Roane had previously relocated. They had no children.

Roane was admitted to the county bar; from 1790 to 1794 he was county attorney, and from 1794 until Tennessee's statehood in 1796 Roane was territorial attorney general for the Hamilton District. Roane represented Jefferson County at the Tennessee state constitutional convention in 1796. The new state's legislature elected Roane as one of three judges for the Superior Court of Law and Equity, a post he held until his inauguration as governor on 23 September 1801.

Tennessee politics during the territorial and early statehood years revolved around personalities, and two factions dominated the scene. One faction, led by territorial governor (later U.S. senator) William Blount, included, among others, Roane and Andrew Jackson. The other group was led by revolutionary war hero John Sevier, who became the state's first governor. When Sevier completed three consecutive two-year terms (the constitutional maximum), Roane was elected to the governorship over nominal opposition. Few substantive issues divided the two factions, and Roane's legislative program was remarkably similar to his predecessor's. Roane supported road construction, increased compensation for judges, and settlement of the state's borders with Virginia, Kentucky, and North Carolina, although only the Virginia dispute was resolved during his administration.

Despite similar legislative aims, the personal quality of Tennessee politics brought the Roane and Sevier factions into conflict, and the flash point involved one of the new state's most flamboyant and enduring political figures, Jackson. Tennessee militia major general George Conway's death in late 1801 opened the door for Sevier's return to the militia, where he had served as brigadier general during the territorial period. Yet when the state militia officers voted on 5 February 1802 for a new commander, Sevier and Jackson tied, though Jackson had little military experience. By law the governor would cast the deciding vote. Previously Jackson, a former colleague of Roane on the Superior Court of Law and Equity, had discovered evidence that implicated Sevier in extensive land fraud and bribery. Some time during the day set for Roane to cast the deciding ballot (it is not certain whether before or after), Jackson showed this evidence to the governor. Roane voted for Jackson, marking a fateful turn in both their lives. Jackson began a long and important military career. Sevier, however, was outraged at his defeat and shortly thereafter determined to retake the gubernatorial chair. During the contest in 1803, Jackson campaigned vigorously for Roane, making public his charges against Sevier. Nevertheless, Sevier handily defeated Roane, 6,780 to 4,923. On 23 September 1803, shortly before leaving office, Roane transmitted copies of Jackson's evidence to the state legislature. Prolonged investigation, while tending to confirm Sevier's guilt, resulted in no action against the governor, and modern historians have differed on the truth of the charges. It apparently mattered little to most Tennessee voters, for in 1805 Sevier again defeated Roane (10,733 to 5,909), and he was reelected to a third term

in 1807. In the meantime, Roane returned to private life for eight years.

Always interested in education, Roane had been appointed in 1794 a trustee of Greeneville College and Blount College (now the University of Tennessee) and, a year later, of Washington College, the state's first three incorporated institutions of higher learning. Among those who read law with Roane was Hugh Lawson White, subsequently U.S. senator from Tennessee and presidential candidate in 1836.

Roane returned to public life in 1811 as a state senator representing Knox County but resigned that post after only two months to accept appointment as judge of the Second Circuit Court of Law and Equity. He remained there until 1815, when he was appointed to the state Supreme Court of Errors and Appeals, a post he held until his death at his home near Knoxville. His grave in the Pleasant Forest Cemetery near Knoxville was unmarked until 1918, when the state erected a monument to his memory.

Roane's chief contribution to Tennessee history was his vote securing Jackson's command of the state's militia, yet it was also his own personal, political undoing. Most observers agree that, had Sevier returned to the militia in 1802, he probably would not have challenged Roane in 1803. More important, Jackson's military career might never have begun.

• Roane's papers are housed at the Tennessee State Library and Archives; a number of his letters are also found in the David Campbell Papers, Duke University. A few letters are printed in two selected editions of Jackson's papers, *Correspondence of Andrew Jackson*, ed. John S. Bassett (7 vols., 1926–1935); and *The Papers of Andrew Jackson*, ed. Sam B. Smith et al. (4 vols., 1980–). Roane's official messages with a commentary and overview of his administration are found in Robert H. White, ed., *Messages of the Governors of Tennessee*, vol. 1 (1952). Charles W. Crawford, ed., *Governors of Tennessee, 1790–1835* (1979), is the most complete treatment of Roane's life. For other biographical information and for Roane's gubernatorial years, see especially *Roster of the Texas Daughters Revolutionary Ancestors*, vol. 4 (1976); *Historical Sketches of the Campbell, Pilcher and Kindred Families* (1911); Robert M. McBride and Dan M. Robison, eds., *Biographical Directory of the Tennessee General Assembly*, vol. 1 (1975); John Trotwood Moore, *Tennessee: The Volunteer State, 1769–1923* (1923); Philip M. Hamer, *Tennessee: A History, 1673–1933* (1933); Carl S. Driver, *John Sevier, Pioneer of the Old Southwest* (1932); and Joshua W. Caldwell, *Sketches of the Bench and Bar of Tennessee* (1898).

GEORGE H. HOEMANN

ROANE, Spencer (4 Apr. 1762–4 Sept. 1822), member of the Virginia Court of Appeals, was born in Essex County, Virginia, the son of William Roane and Elizabeth Ball. Affluent and influential, William Roane owned plantations in both Essex and King and Queen counties and a sawmill in Tappahannock, and he served as a member of the House of Burgesses and as a colonel in the militia during the Revolution. Trained at home under a Scottish tutor named Bradfute, Spencer Roane developed a taste for classical literature and music. In 1776, at the age of fourteen, he entered William and Mary College, where he became a member of the original Phi Beta Kappa Society. After graduation from college in 1780, he attended the lectures of Chancellor George Wythe, one of the most distinguished jurists of the period. In 1782 Roane was admitted to the bar.

Roane grew up during the constitutional debate over the nature of the British empire when the meaning of liberty was incessantly discussed. George Mason's Declaration of Rights and Thomas Jefferson's bill for the establishment of religious freedom, which Roane called "sublime," particularly touched him. Elected to the House of Delegates in 1783, Roane arrived just in time to take part in the great debates over religious freedom. Although Essex County was an Episcopalian stronghold and although he usually was a follower of Patrick Henry, Roane voted against both the incorporation act, which settled the legal status of the Episcopal church created by the separation from the Anglican church after the Revolution, and the assessment act, which required that the people of the Commonwealth of Virginia pay a tax to support the Christian church of their choice and made the Christian faith the official religion of the Commonwealth, proposed by Henry and joined the opposition in its fight for a more complete separation of church and state. Roane served on the Council of State as an adviser to Governor Henry for a little over two years. With the enthusiastic approval of Henry, he in 1786 married Henry's eldest daughter Anne Henry. They had nine children.

The new Constitution generated a heated debate in the summer of 1787. Governor Edmund Randolph's shift from the Antifederalist to the Federalist side provoked an attack by Antifederalists in the form of a public letter written by Roane to Randolph. Under the pseudonym of "Plain Dealer," Roane attacked Randolph's inconsistent position with cutting sarcasm. He explained that he opposed the Constitution because powers reserved to the states and to the people were not reserved with sufficient explicitness, and, therefore, he advocated the addition of a Bill of Rights as a condition for ratification.

After two sessions in the state senate in 1788 and 1789, Roane was notified of his appointment by the legislature as a judge in the general court in 1789. In 1794 the Court of Appeals had a vacancy, and despite the fact that all the judges of the general court were nominated for the post, the legislature elected Roane on the first ballot.

Brilliant, contentious, and controversial, Roane took the oath of office on the Virginia Court of Appeals on 13 April 1795 and held that post for the rest of his life. In *Kamper v. Hawkins* he helped lay the foundation for the Court of Appeals to declare unconstitutional legislative acts that interfered with the independence of the judiciary. Roane argued that the state constitution "fixed" the fundamental laws of Virginia and that the legislature could not tamper with those laws. The Court of Appeals agreed with Roane's views and by so doing took the first step in asserting the concept of judicial review. No doubt John Marshall, who appeared frequently before the Court of Appeals in this period, learned much from its judges. Years later, in *Marbury v. Madison* (1803), Marshall did for the Supreme Court what Roane and his colleagues had done for the Virginia court.

Roane supported the Kentucky and Virginia resolutions (1798–1799) written by Jefferson and James Madison in opposition to the Federalist-sponsored Alien and Sedition acts. He agreed that the Union created by the Constitution was a Union of the people of the states and the federal government; therefore, a state government could nullify an act of Congress that was contrary to the Constitution. His first wife died in 1799, and that year he married Elizabeth Hoskins.

According to some authorities, if Oliver Ellsworth, the chief justice of the Supreme Court, had not resigned during the administration of outgoing president John Adams, who appointed Marshall, President Jefferson would have appointed Roane as chief justice. Question of this appointment remains a matter of speculation. However, by 1800 Roane was active as a judge on the Court of Appeals, and he was also deeply involved in local and national politics.

Roane, his cousins Thomas Ritchie and John Brockenbrough, and others formed a secret Republican clique, the "Essex Junto," designed to combat the "Old Party," a secret Federalist group led by Randolph and the Nicholas family. During the War of 1812, the "Old Party" and the "Richmond Junto" merged into the "Richmond Party" to combat antiwar sentiment. By 1822 the "Richmond Party" controlled state government and the state's financial system, and Roane controlled the "party."

The great political questions of the day produced Roane's most outstanding decisions, many of which were in direct conflict with the decisions of the U.S. Supreme Court. In *Turpin v. Locket* (1804) Roane upheld the constitutionality of a statute that deprived the Episcopal church of its glebes. He understood the political value of religion, but he believed that the Revolution had changed the character of religious freedom in the United States by establishing the principle of separation of church and state.

Although Roane owned plantations in Essex, Hanover, and Goochland counties and more than thirty slaves, he, like many other southerners, favored emancipation. In *Pleasants v. Pleasants* (1800) he freed the slaves involved in the dispute because he was able to do so under the rules of common law. However, in other decisions, he made it clear that he believed emancipation was contingent upon whether the slaves could be freed within the rules of private property and without expense to the public.

Roane sensed that the explosive issue in Virginia society was slavery, not religion. He reacted to the Missouri Compromise of 1820 with a combination of fear, anxiety, and distrust. In a letter to President James Monroe on this subject, Roane cautioned him to "resist the menaced restriction." Except for this letter, Roane took no part in the controversy. He explained that the Missouri dispute was a "practical" question that, unlike the decisions of the Supreme Court, did not involve "basic principles."

From *Martin v. Hunter's Lessee* (1815) to *McCulloch v. Maryland* (1819) to *Cohens v. Virginia* (1821), Roane and Marshall engaged in a running battle in the pages of the court reports and newspapers. Clearly both men were using the press as a means of educating the public on the legitimacy of their constitutional views of the power of the judiciary in a republican society. The debate between Roane and Marshall was rooted in the compromise character of the Constitution. The framers of the Constitution maintained that sovereignty resided in both the state and federal governments without explaining where the ultimate sovereignty resided if a conflict developed between these governments. Marshall attempted to solve the difficulty by giving a broad interpretation of powers granted the federal government. The chief justice believed in a national Union, while Roane believed in a federal Union. Marshall's view of the Union rested on a Hamiltonian construction of the Constitution; Roane's rested on a Jeffersonian interpretation of that document.

In a case involving the Fairfax lands, *Mumford* (1815), the Virginia Court of Appeals had the rare opportunity to review a decision of the Supreme Court and in the process to discuss the constitutionality of the Supreme Court's practice of reviewing state court decisions. After the Virginia court refused to execute the federal Court's order, the case returned to the Supreme Court as *Martin v. Hunter's Lessee.* Marshall recused himself because he had a financial interest in the outcome, but he played an active role behind the scenes, consulting extensively with Justice Joseph Story, who wrote the opinion. In this decision the Supreme Court reasserted its authority over the Virginia court on both theoretical and practical grounds.

In *McCulloch v. Maryland* and *Cohens v. Virginia*, Roane and Marshall continued their battle over the nature of the Union and the Supreme Court's authority to review state court decisions, and Roane took to the columns of the Richmond *Enquirer.* In *McCulloch v. Maryland* Marshall was interested in establishing the constitutionality of the Bank of the United States and in asserting the supremacy of the federal Court over the state courts. He discussed at length the origins of the federal compact and the meaning of the Necessary and Proper Clause. Especially determined to quell state court opposition to his decisions, which was becoming nationwide, in *Cohens v. Virginia* Marshall forcefully reasserted the authority of the Supreme Court over state judiciaries.

Marshall's *McCulloch* and *Cohens* decisions were attacked in a series of letters written to the Richmond *Enquirer* under the pseudonyms of "Amphictyon," "Hampden," and "Algernon Sidney." Scholars believe that the "Amphictyon" letters were probably written by Judge William Brockenbrough and the "Hampden" and "Sidney" letters by Roane. In these letters Roane contended that it was not necessary to determine whether the people or the states were the source of federal power. Such an inquiry, although pertinent to a consideration of judicial review of state court judgments, was not relevant in these cases. He declared that the people themselves were the only common arbitrator set up by the Constitution and concluded that the Supreme Court had done everything but "claim power by divine right."

To check Marshall's nationalistic decisions, Roane proposed an amendment to the Constitution allowing the Senate to have appellate jurisdiction in cases involving a conflict between a state law and the Constitution. His proposal failed, and the "Sidney" essays were Roane's last important work. He died in Warm Springs in Bath County, Virginia.

An implacable enemy of Marshall and a political leader of Virginia, Roane aroused the admiration of his friends and the animosity of his enemies. His writings on judicial review and his political activities make it clear that his goal was to save the Union by applying Jeffersonian principles to the state and federal courts. Tragically, the Civil War and not the courts determined the nature of the Union.

• Roane's personal papers have not been preserved. The best primary source on Roane is the *John Branch Historical Papers of Randolph-Macon College*, ed. William E. Dodd, vol. 2 (1905, 1906). Reprinted in this collection are the "Amphictyon," "Hampden," and "Sidney" letters and part of Roane's correspondence. Additional correspondence is in "Letters of Spencer Roane, 1788–1822," *Bulletin of the New York Public Library* 10 (1906); *Virginia Colonial Abstracts*, ed. Beverley Fleet, vol. 6 (1939); and "Letters to James Barbour, Senator of Virginia in the Congress of the United States," *William and Mary College Quarterly*, 1st ser., 10 (1901–1902). Letters to Roane from Thomas Jefferson are scattered throughout *The Writings of Thomas Jefferson*, ed. Paul Leicester Ford, vol. 10 (1892–1899). His Virginia Court of Appeals decisions are in *Reports of Cases Argued and Adjudged in the Court of Appeals of Virginia*. A biography is Margaret Horsnell, *Spencer Roane: Judicial Advocate of Jeffersonian Principles* (1986). Comments on Roane's career by his contemporaries are in *The Writings of James Madison*, ed. Gaillard Hunt, vols. 8 and 9 (1900–1910); *The Memoir of John Quincy Adams*, ed. Charles Francis Adams, vol. 5 (1874–1877); and "The Correspondence of John Marshall," ed. Charles C. Smith, *Massachusetts Historical Society Proceedings*, 2d ser., 14 (1900). Frank Gildart Ruffin, "The Roane Family," *William and Mary College Quarterly*, 1st ser., 18 (1910), has information about his private life.

MARGARET HORSNELL

ROBACK, A. A. (19 June 1890–5 June 1965), psychologist, educator, and linguist, was born Abraham Aaron Roback in Goniondz, in what is now Poland, the son of Isaac Roback, a tailor, and Leba (maiden name unknown). He was raised in Montreal, Canada, from the age of two. Roback developed an early interest in comparative linguistics, mastering French, Greek, and Latin by the time he was thirteen years old and soon adding German, Hebrew, Yiddish, and Arabic. He attended McGill University, where he earned an A.B. with honors in 1912, winning the Prince of Wales Medal for exceptional scholarship. He received an M.A. from Harvard University in 1913 for a thesis specializing in psychology, having been denied the opportunity to do interdisciplinary work by his professors. Roback spent a year at Princeton as a Traveling Fellow in 1916–1917. He received a Ph.D. from Harvard in 1917; he wrote his dissertation, *The Interference of Will-Impulses*, under Hugo Münsterberg, but it was signed by Herbert S. Langfeld because of Münsterberg's untimely death. The work was published in 1918 as a monograph by the Psychological Review Company.

Roback was married briefly and had one daughter, but no information is available on his wife. He was described at his memorial as a hermit-scholar who occasionally published under a pseudonym, Anton de Borca, and who lived most of his life in Cambridge, Massachusetts, in a succession of attic apartments stacked from floor to ceiling with books, letters, and manuscripts. Roback began his teaching career at the University of Pittsburgh in 1917. He was professor of psychology at Northeastern University in Boston from 1918 to 1921, and he taught as an instructor at Harvard and Radcliffe from 1920 to 1923. He was a National Research Council Fellow in the biological sciences from 1923 to 1925 and taught at the Massachusetts Institute of Technology in 1926. Thereafter, he was a lecturer in the Extension Division of the Commonwealth of Massachusetts from 1926 to 1948. From 1959 to 1965 and from 1949 to 1959 he was professor and chairman of the psychology department at Emerson College in Boston.

Although Roback appears to have had a checkered career as a teacher, editor, and writer, his acquaintances were wide ranging and included many well-known figures. Sigmund Freud, Carl Jung, George Bernard Shaw, Havelock Ellis, Albert Einstein, and Albert Schweitzer were among his correspondents, and he counted among his friends Gordon Willard Allport, the pioneer psychologist in personality and social theory; Morton Prince, the psychopathologist; and Henry James, Jr., the lawyer, Harvard overseer, and son of the famous Harvard philosopher-psychologist William James.

Roback's two principal fields were psychology and Yiddish culture, subjects on which he wrote prolifically. The connecting thread was psycholinguistics, which remained his lifelong passion. According to the assessment by Allport, Roback produced several important works in psychology. One was *The Psychology of Character* (1927), which went into three editions. Roback's most enduring idea in it was that character was produced by the unique ways in which the individual restrained the instinctual drives in a consistent direction. Another of his important works was *The History of American Psychology* (1952), which was printed in a new and expanded edition the year before Roback died. In a lucid, if idiosyncratic, style, Roback packed extensive new information into this volume, which proved to be the first such text devoted exclusively to psychology as it had developed on the American scene.

Roback wrote extensively on Freud, believing that there were important parallels between psychoanalysis and the mystical teachings of the Jewish Kabbalah. He also wrote *Behaviorism and Psychology* (1923), taking issue with the "rat psychology" of J. B. Watson that was just being developed as well as works such as *Business Psychology* (1928), *Self-Consciousness and Its Treatment* (1933), *Personality in Theory and Practice* (1950), *Destiny and Motivation in Language* (1954), and *Aspects of Applied Psychology* (1964). He was the author of numerous paper-and-pencil tests, among them the "Roback Superior Adult Tests," which went through eight editions between 1919 and 1948, and the "Sense of Humor Test," which went through two editions between 1946 and 1948.

It was in the field of Yiddish studies, however, that Roback was best known: the greater portion of his professional achievements was recognized exclusively in learned Jewish circles. His father and mother had instilled in him at an early age a love of Jewish colloquialisms and folktales that led him to master Yiddish at a time when it was fashionable among assimilated Jews in late nineteenth-century Montreal to let all remnants of Old World culture disappear. He was heavily influenced by his maternal grandmother, who taught him the older linguistic patterns of the Lithuanian and Polish Jews, which later allowed him to make expert comparisons in both the evolution and corruption of the Yiddish language. As a teenager, he was an ardent Zionist, reader of the Torah, and student of the Kabbalah. More important, having determined that Yiddish, in language, folklore, and customs, was the binding agent that preserved all popular Jewish culture throughout the diaspora, Roback, by the time he had left Montreal for Harvard in his early twenties, was already a recognized scholar and pioneer in the introduction and preservation of Yiddish in the New World. With this background to prepare him, for the next half century he would be a fiery exponent, linguistic watchdog, interpreter, and defender of Yiddishism and world Jewry.

Among Roback's more important accomplishments in this area are "Characteristics of Yiddish Proverbs," *Canadian Jewish Chronicle* (1914); *Bastait-Schultz von Delitzsch* (1916); "The Euphemism in Yiddish: A Study in Folk Psychology," *Jewish Forum* (1921); *Jewish Influence in Modern Thought* (1929); *I. L. Peretz: Psychologist of Literature* (1935), an in-depth study of the Polish poet and playwright and the model for Roback's theory of personality; *The Story of Yiddish Literature* (1939); *Contemporary Yiddish Literature* (1957); *Die Imperye Yiddish* (1958); and *Der Folks Geist in der Yiddish Sprach* (1964).

Roback edited numerous Jewish periodicals, contributed to Jewish encyclopedias, was the editor in chief of *Who's Who in American Jewry* beginning in 1925, and even launched his own publishing company, which he called Sci-Art. Following in the footsteps of Leo Weiner, the true pioneer in Yiddish studies, Roback also developed the Yiddish collection at Harvard from 400 to 10,000 pieces. In 1929 he instituted the first course on Yiddish in an American university. The wealth and diversity of his vocabulary was remembered as astounding, while his style, imagery, and idiom were considered the richest among Yiddish prose writers. Ever a rationalist and "possessed of a Jew's sense of burning justice," Roback was remembered by Yiddishists as "Streitbar," disputatious. He was also called an unyielding polemicist, the "Romantic Knight of Mamme Loshen," "Guardian of the Walls," and the "High Priest of Yiddish." Once asked why he had taken this life path, he replied that there were several reasons, all inherited: impracticality, individualism, sympathy for the humiliated, a consistent logic, and an interest in language. By the time he died, he had authored more than thirty books and 2,000 articles, the majority of them either on or in Yiddish.

A polymath and master of several fields, Roback was even compared to Chaucer. He died in Cambridge, Massachusetts.

• Roback's collected papers are at the Harvard College Archives (restricted by the Judaica Department). Biographical sources on Roback include Joseph Berger, *The Destiny and Motivation of Dr. A. A. Roback* (1957); F. DeHovre, *Paedagogische Denkers van onzen Tijd* (1936); and *Canadian Jewish Archives*, n.s., 41 (1988): 60–132.

EUGENE TAYLOR

ROBB, Isabel Hampton (26 Aug. 1860–15 Apr. 1910), nursing educator and leader, was born Isabel Adams Hampton in Welland Ontario, Canada, the daughter of Samuel Hampton, the owner of a tailoring business, and Sarah Mary Lay. Young Isabel (nicknamed "Addie") preferred reading to almost anything and was a good student in the local public school. After graduation she taught in a rural public school, where she was very successful at controlling unruly students and getting them to work together. While teaching, she also studied with a Mr. Henderson, the headmaster of the Collegiate Institute at St. Catherines, Ontario. He tutored her in the liberal arts or perhaps mathematics. Isabel was ambitious; she felt "wound up" much of the time and confided to a sister, "If I were a man I would stop at nothing; I would be prime minister of Canada."

In 1881 Hampton went to New York City to attend the new Bellevue Hospital Training School for Nurses. In the first months after her graduation from Bellevue in 1883 she served as a supervising nurse in New York's Women's Hospital. She then went to St. Paul's House in Rome, Italy, where for eighteen months she served as one of two American nurses in this small Episcopal hospital that provided nursing care for English-speaking travelers. Hampton worked in the operating room and in various other capacities as a hospital nurse (sister) at St. Paul's. In addition to her hospital work, she also cared for several private patients with whom she traveled extensively. Through these wealthy, well-educated patients she was exposed to music and to great literature and thus developed her interests in art, music, and history. After returning to the United States, Hampton stayed with the Astor

family at Newport, Rhode Island. In 1887 Hampton left the Astors to become superintendent of nurses at the Illinois Training School for Nurses at Cook County Hospital in Chicago.

This was Hampton's first major administrative and teaching position, and it was difficult, primarily because the physicians were accustomed to having a say in how the nursing component of hospital work was to be managed and thus were resistant to Hampton's authority. For example, after she expelled a student for a legitimate reason, the physicians took up the student's cause. Hampton persevered, however, and with the support of her board of lady managers the student was forced to leave. As superintendent Hampton developed political skills and learned the importance of building a strong base of support. Her awareness of the issues in nursing and American health care sharpened as well.

Historically nursing had been unpaid work performed by women who became known in their communities as healers and health care providers. Hampton and others, as part of the great social reform movement at the turn of the century, were attempting to create an educated discipline and to professionalize nursing. There were major hurdles to overcome in upgrading nursing to a profession. For one thing, there were no standards for nursing education and no mechanism to determine which nurses were educationally prepared to do the work or licensure laws to protect the public from unqualified impostors. Another problem was the exploitation of nursing students in the hospital training programs where their dual position as student and worker was ambiguous at best. (Graduate nurses were not employed by hospitals but were expected to work as private duty nurses in people's homes, referrals coming from physicians, alumni registries, or by word of mouth.) In addition to the social status of the nurse and nursing as a profession, Hampton also continuously concerned herself with the future direction of nursing as a women's profession.

Having been successful at the Illinois Training School, and characteristically restless for a new challenge, Hampton was chosen from among nearly 100 candidates to become the founding principal and superintendent of the Johns Hopkins Training School for Nurses when it opened in 1889. Hopkins, America's first university medical school founded in the European tradition, represented state of the art in health care and education. Hampton administered both nursing service and the School of Nursing as well as taught the "pupil nurses." Believing that women should have the same educational opportunities as men to qualify for and to work in any field they chose, she was also influential in facilitating the admission of women to the Johns Hopkins Medical School. As her assistant she hired the keen-minded social activist Lavinia Lloyd Dock, a Bellevue graduate who wrote the first nursing textbook on pharmacology and wrote or co-wrote several nursing history textbooks. Although Hampton and Dock were very different, they worked well together.

Hampton and several others at Hopkins were involved in planning the World Congress of Charities, Correction, and Philanthropy, which met during the World's Columbian Exposition held in Chicago in 1893. Hampton chaired the subsection on nursing that led to the founding of the American Society of Superintendents of Training Schools for Nurses of the U.S. and Canada, the first national nursing organization in the United States. It was renamed the National League for Nursing Education in 1912. The superintendents society sponsored the founding of another organization for nurses, the Nurses Associated Alumni of the United States and Canada, which also was renamed in 1912, as the American Nurses Association. Hampton served two consecutive terms as the first president of the Nurses Associated Alumni.

Hampton's first book, *Nursing: Its Principles and Practice*, was published in 1893. The next year she left Hopkins to marry Hunter Robb, a physician. The couple were married in London. After a wedding trip that included visits to many European hospitals, they settled in Cleveland, Ohio, where they had three sons, one of whom died in infancy. In Cleveland Robb taught as a volunteer in the local Lakeside Hospital Training School and served on the board of directors of the Cleveland Visiting Nurse Association. She also was a member of the Board of Lady Managers for the Lakeside Hospital Training School and became one of the first women to serve as a hospital trustee.

In 1899 Isabel Hampton Robb organized a graduate program for nurses at Teachers College, Columbia University. She also taught, whenever possible, the nursing administration course, offered each spring as part of the two-year hospital economics program at Teachers College. Robb was also very involved in founding the American Journal of Nursing Company, which published its first issue of the *American Journal of Nursing* in October 1900. In addition to these projects, she continued to write and to deliver papers in the United States and abroad. These papers were later collected and published as *Educational Standards for Nurses* (1907). Her second book, *Nursing Ethics for Hospital and Private Use*, was published in 1900.

Isabel Hampton Robb, Ethel Benford Fenwick, Lavinia Dock, and other nurses from around the world met during the Pan-American Exposition held in Buffalo, New York, in 1901 and founded the International Congress for Nurses (ICN). As Robb discovered, the issues in American nursing were not unique. Nursing leaders from several countries had been meeting for several years to try to develop solutions to the problems of standardizing nursing education, protecting patients from unqualified nurses, and improving working conditions and the status of nurses around the world. The papers presented at the first ICN meeting, which Robb and Dock coedited, give an interesting view of how the nursing discipline was evolving around the world.

Robb believed that the education of nurses belonged in the educational mainstream of higher education, not in hospitals. For graduate nurses to try to learn more sophisticated skills and to learn to be leaders as teachers and superintendents while practicing was a disservice to them as well as to their patients. Around 1906 Robb, along with public health nurse Lillian D. Wald, convinced reform-minded philanthropist Helen Hartley Jenkins to finance the Department of Nursing Education at Teachers College, Columbia University. Richard Olding Beard of the University of Minnesota later credited Robb with persuading him that nurses should be taught as undergraduates within the university. Such a program was implemented at the University of Minnesota in 1909, and degrees were granted by 1919.

Philosophically Robb believed that a good education coupled with a disciplined life were the keys to reforming society. She believed that nurses had the opportunity to profoundly shape the health of families and communities by educating people to live healthy, disciplined lives, and she charged nurses of her era to look beyond their work in hospitals. At her death in a street car accident in Cleveland in 1910, Robb was still at the center of the movement to professionalize nursing, having been elected president of the superintendents society the previous year. Although she helped to develop many opportunities for women, particularly nurses, to work together to transform health care, her legacy has yet to be fully realized.

• Isabel Hampton Robb's papers are primarily in the archives of the Department of Nursing Education, Special Collections, Teachers College, Columbia University, and in the archives of the Johns Hopkins School of Nursing, Welch Medical Library, Baltimore, Md. She coedited, with L. L. Dock and Maud Banfield, *Third International Congress of Nurses* (1901). The most complete contemporary assessment is Nancy L. Noel, "Isabel Hampton Robb: Architect of American Nursing" (Ph.D. diss., Teachers College, Columbia Univ., 1979). Robb's contributions to nursing are documented by nurse historians in virtually every history of nursing textbook. See in particular, Ethel Johns and Blanche Pfefferkorn, *The Johns Hopkins Hospital School of Nursing, 1889–1949* (1954). Susan M. Reverby, *Ordered to Care: The Dilemma of American Nursing, 1850–1945* (1987), and Barbara Melosch, *"The Physician's Hand": Work Culture and Conflict in American Nursing* (1982), include Robb in their explorations of how nursing evolved as women's work over the course of the twentieth century. Obituaries are in the *Cleveland Plain Dealer* and the *Cleveland News*, both 16 Apr. 1910, and the *New York Herald Tribune*, 17 Apr. 1910.

NANCY L. NOEL

ROBBINS, Jane Elizabeth (28 Dec. 1860–16 Aug. 1946), settlement house worker and physician, was born in Wethersfield, Connecticut, the daughter of Richard Austin Robbins, a prosperous seed merchant who was active in the Congregational church and also a member of the Connecticut legislature, and Harriet Welles. Jane Robbins belonged to the first generation of women to graduate from college in significant numbers. After attending Smith College for the 1879–1880 academic year, she worked for five years as a teacher in Kentucky and New Jersey. Partly out of a desire to help the poor, she then decided to become a physician.

Even though she had a lifelong loyalty to Smith, she chose to enter the New York Infirmary's Women's Medical College in 1887, graduating in 1890. She then interned for a year at the New York Infirmary before setting up a medical practice in the Italian ghetto around New York's Mulberry Street.

While a medical student, Robbins became one of the pioneers of the social settlement house movement in the United States. She began by teaching Sunday school at Five Points Methodist Mission, named after the notoriously poor New York neighborhood in which it was located. She then joined a friend from Smith, Jean Fine, in establishing a sewing club for children at Neighborhood Guild, which had been established in 1886 as the first social settlement in the United States. Founder Stanton Coit soon left to devote the rest of his career to the Ethical Culture movement in England, and Neighborhood Guild changed its name to University Settlement. Its largely male staff, residents, and volunteers focused primarily on serving the men and boys of the surrounding Lower East Side. The sewing club was an anomaly. In order to maintain the settlement practice of actually living in the neighborhood served (in most cases in the settlement house itself), Robbins moved to a nearby tenement in 1888. Thus, she may be regarded as the first woman settlement resident in the United States. In 1889 she assisted Fine in organizing the second American settlement house, College Settlement. Located near University Settlement and in some ways its "sister," College Settlement attracted women as settlement workers and focused on serving the female population of the neighborhood. Robbins served as headworker from 1893 through 1897.

The years of Robbins's leadership coincided with one of the worst depressions in American history. During these difficult years, Robbins made College Settlement into a center for relief work. Her house also worked with University Settlement on an experimental cooperative in 1893. In addition, College Settlement did an 1894 study of unemployment, provided data for New York's Tenement House Committee, and furnished testimony before housing commissions about poor housing conditions. At the same time, the settlement took part in a neighborhood publicity plan of the commissioner of streets while also protesting the unfair way pushcart peddlers were being treated. Both issues involved streets and refuse. In 1894 the settlement provided support to garment makers who were seeking a minimum wage and a ten-hour work day; it tried to foster other union efforts as well. As the economy improved, Robbins channeled her efforts toward campaigning for more playgrounds, parks, and the expanded use of schools as neighborhood centers. In 1897 she visited Cleveland to help launch the second settlement house there, Goodrich House.

The early settlement house leaders saw themselves as reformers as well as providers of a daily program of clubs and classes for their neighborhoods. Robbins was an energetic practitioner of the reform side of the settlement's mission. While Robbins shared a wealthy, old New England family background with a number of other settlement workers, she was unusual in learning to speak Italian, the language of many of her settlement neighbors. Her contemporaries commented on her cheerfulness, common sense, and quiet dignity.

In 1898 Robbins resumed the practice of medicine, and for the next several decades her interests vacillated among medicine, education, and settlement house work. During the Spanish-American War, she helped meet the shortage of nurses for typhoid patients. She headed Normal College Alumnae House in New York in 1901, then moved to Cleveland in 1902 to direct Alta House (a settlement in Cleveland's Little Italy). From 1905 to 1911 she was executive secretary of New York's Public Education Association, and she headed Little Italy Settlement in New York in 1911 and Jacob A. Riis's Neighborhood Settlement in 1914. During World War I, her knowledge of Italian was a motivation for her joining the Red Cross in Italy. Following the war, she became the substitute superintendent of a temporary hospital in Macedonia, one of a number that women doctors organized throughout Greece. She also periodically attended meetings of the Medical Women's International Association, which was founded in 1919.

By 1920 Robbins was an acknowledged leader of the American settlement house movement, and a series of settlements hired her to advise them on reorganization. They included Alta House (1920) and East End Neighborhood House (1921) in Cleveland; Minneapolis's Margaret Barry House (1923); and Neighborhood House in Denver (1924). She also served on the executive committee of the National Federation of Settlements from 1917 to 1922. In 1927 she returned to Greece for two years to work in the American Women's Hospital in Athens helping refugees from Turkey. The National Federation of Settlements made her an honorary president in 1934, a post she held until her death in Hartford, Connecticut. As one of the pioneers of the early settlement house movement, Robbins was unique in the way she moved from one settlement house to another while maintaining her professional involvement in education and medicine.

• The National Federation of Settlements Records at the Social Welfare History Archives Center, University of Minnesota, contain some material on Robbins. See also the reports of the College Settlements Association for 1893–1897 and Robert A. Woods and Albert J. Kennedy, eds., *Handbook of Settlements* (1911) for information on College Settlement under Robbins's leadership. Robbins published at least ten articles; the most important are: "The First Year at College Settlement," *Survey*, 24 Feb. 1912, pp. 1800–1802; "A Maker of Americans," *Survey*, 6 June 1914, pp. 285–86; and "Bureaucratic and Political Influences in Neighborhood Civic Problems," *Proceedings of the National Conference of Social Work* (1925), pp. 391–95. Notable obituaries are in the *New York Times* and *Hartford Times* 17 Aug. 1948, and the *Smith Alumnae Quarterly*, Nov. 1946.

JUDITH ANN TROLANDER

ROBBINS, Marty (26 Sept. 1925–8 Dec. 1982), country and pop musician, was born Martin David Robinson in Glendale, Arizona, the son of Jack Joe Robinson, a Polish immigrant who worked at a number of jobs and deserted his family when Robbins was young, and Emma Heckle. Robbins identified most closely later in life with his grandfather "Texas Bob" Heckle, who died in 1931. Texas Bob had carried dispatches for General Nathan Bedford Forrest and General Jo Shelby in the Civil War and then joined the Texas Rangers. He became a philosopher, poet, and storyteller and had published two books, *Rhymes of the Frontier*, volumes 1 and 2, that he hawked at medicine shows. His gift for storytelling and love of western lore had a profound influence on his young grandson.

Robbins never graduated from school, and by the early 1940s he was getting into trouble for petty crime. He later addressed the struggles of his early life in a song called "You Gave Me a Mountain," an epic of trial and redemption, which pop stars Frankie Laine and Elvis Presley later recorded. Robbins joined the navy in May 1943 and saw active service in the Pacific, participating in the landings on Bougainville in the Solomon islands. He was discharged in February 1946 and worked at various jobs around Phoenix, never staying long at any one job. He finally gravitated toward a career in music and in 1948 landed a spot singing with his guitar on radio station KOY, Phoenix. The fact that he made his start in country music, rather than in his true love, pop music, was largely a reflection of the fact that it was easier to play solo or cheaply organize a small group in country music.

After starting on KOY, Robbins began playing with western swing bandleader Frankie Starr. The chronology of Robbins's early career in and around Phoenix while he played with Starr and immediately after he quit is a little blurred. He married Marizona Baldwin in 1948, and their son, Ronnie (who later recorded as Marty Robbins, Jr.), was born in 1949; their daughter was born in 1959.

By 1950 Robbins's band was one of the hottest draws in and around Phoenix. He secured a radio show on KTYL, Mesa, three afternoons a week, then returned for his regular showdate at Fred Kare's club. The show on KTYL was parlayed into a spot on KPHO, Phoenix, where Robbins hosted a morning show five days a week called "Chuck Wagon Time." Shortly afterward he started working at KPHO-TV, where he guested on a show called "Western Caravan." His success on "Western Caravan" led to Robbins being offered his own television show, "The Marty Robbins Show."

In July 1950 Robbins copyrighted his first songs, "H-e-a-r-t-s-i-c-k" and "I Wish Somebody Loved Me," the first of which was recorded by country rocker Ricky Riddle for Tennessee Records in 1950. Robbins's first commercial recording session was held for Columbia Records in November 1951. He was signed by Art Satherley in a deal that probably was initiated by Harry Stone, who had moved to KPHO from radio station WSM.

After Robbins's first single was released, he quit Kare's club in Phoenix and worked a round of club dates throughout the West as a solo act. His third single, "I'll Go on Alone," was released on 10 October 1952 and became a number one country hit. On 19 January 1953 Robbins was granted full membership at the Grand Ole Opry and moved to Nashville.

Without a trace of regionality in his accent, Robbins sounded more like a West Coast country singer, but he obviously saw his long-term future in Nashville, although he never really grew to love the city or its climate. "I like to drive where you can just see for miles and miles," he told interviewer Bob Allen. "I don't care anything for hills. . . . They're beautiful, but they're blockin' my view! . . . I felt trapped down here. I almost went back to Arizona. . . . I couldn't handle the cold weather [and] couldn't take the humidity." Later, Robbins used his distance from the West to build a series of albums that reinterpreted traditional western themes and drew heavily on the stories and myths that his grandfather had told him.

In 1954 Robbins's career seemed to stall. His records failed to chart until, in December 1954, he recorded a cover version of Elvis Presley's first record, "That's All Right Mama." The song brought Robbins back into the charts for eleven weeks, peaking at number seven. During the following two years, Robbins flirted with rock 'n' roll music, especially after working a tour with Presley in Florida during July 1955. He covered Chuck Berry's "Maybellene" for the country market and later recorded a complete ten-inch LP of rock 'n' roll songs, *Rock 'n' Rollin' Robbins*.

Robbins's career was entering another trough when he recorded "Singing the Blues," a song that had been pitched to him backstage at the Grand Ole Opry by its composer, Melvin Endsley, a songwriter from Drasco, Arkansas. By November 1956 Robbins's version of "Singing the Blues" had reached the number one position on the country charts, where it remained until February 1957. Unfortunately for Robbins, the song was rerecorded by Guy Mitchell, who recorded it for the pop division of Robbins's label, Columbia. Robbins's version sold more than a half-million copies, but Mitchell's cover version sold between two and three million.

From Robbins's viewpoint, Mitchell's success could have been his. Robbins's voice was not identifiably country; only his backup musicians identified him as a country artist. He confronted Columbia Records and was allowed to record pop music in New York starting in January 1957. His first New York pop session included "A White Sport Coat and a Pink Carnation," a song he had written himself. It bore out Robbins's assertion that he could record pop as well as country music, and for two years he went to New York to record what was essentially pop music (as opposed to rock 'n' roll music) with Mitch Miller and Ray Conniff as his producer and arranger. Robbins's accomplishment was comparable to that of country crooner Eddy Arnold in the mid-1950s; his music was rooted in country forms, but with his smooth, easygoing delivery and lack of regionality he was able to find a broader market.

The pop recordings were part of a broad range of experimental career moves that Robbins undertook between 1956 and 1958. He sensed correctly that the market was opening up, and in addition to the New York pop recordings, Robbins recorded vocal-guitar folk sessions in Nashville as well as regular country LPs and a Hawaiian LP.

Robbins's ambitions ran beyond performing. He wanted greater autonomy over every aspect of his career. He realized that if he had owned a publishing company when Melvin Endsley had come backstage with "Singing the Blues," and if he had signed Endsley to *his* publishing company rather than to Acuff-Rose, his earnings from "Singing the Blues" would have been in the hundreds of thousands of dollars instead of barely twenty thousand. So in late 1956 Robbins and his rhythm guitar player Hillous Butrum (who earlier had played with Hank Williams) formed a music publishing company, Be-Are Music ("Be" was Butrum; "Are" was Robbins). Robbins himself was still under contract to Acuff-Rose, but it was clearly his intention to search for new material that he could publish and record. One of the first of his own copyrights that Robbins was able to assign to his companies after his Acuff-Rose contract ended was "Cigarettes and Coffee Blues," a composition that he placed with Lefty Frizzell, who had a fair-sized hit with it in late 1958. Robbins cut the song later.

Robbins also branched into talent management and booking. In August 1957 he started the Lee-Mart Agency in conjunction with Lee Emerson. It booked Robbins and other leading country stars George Jones, Johnny Horton, Bobby Helms, and Jimmy Newman, but the venture did not outlast the year. Robbins also saw that the restructuring of the music business in the mid- to late 1950s had opened the doors to independent labels, and he thought that this too was an opportunity for him. In 1957 he launched Robbins Records. The releases continued for a year, but the only artists that showed any promise were the Glaser Brothers, who later were major country stars. In 1958 he sold the Glasers' contract to Decca and folded the label.

Robbins Records was not a strictly country label, and although Robbins continued to base his career out of Nashville and clearly cherished the security that the country market afforded, he was determined to challenge the established patterns of a "country" artist. This inevitably brought him into conflict with the Grand Ole Opry, and in March 1958 Robbins had a well-publicized dispute with the Opry management over television sponsorship. He was dismissed on 1 March, but both parties reconciled a few days later. He would never happily subjugate himself to the strictures that the Opry imposed (for instance, that he be present almost every Saturday night), although he never broke away from the show again. In 1968 he began closing the Opry, a tradition that would continue until his death. Often he continued performing for the

audience long after the show went off the air at midnight.

The arrangement that had brought Robbins to New York for some recording sessions started to fall apart in 1958. The New York recordings were still successful, but both Mitch Miller and Ray Conniff were becoming absorbed in their own projects, and Robbins returned to Nashville to record.

After the success of "White Sport Coat and a Pink Carnation," Robbins had worked with background vocalists. In September 1958 he hired Bobby Sykes, who stayed with him as a harmony vocalist and rhythm guitarist until Robbins's death. He also used the Glasers as part of his show (Robbins had discovered Chuck, Jim, and Tompall Glaser on local television in Spalding, Nebr.). Jim Glaser and Bobby Sykes accompanied Robbins into the studio on the afternoon of 7 April 1959 with the idea of recording a complete album of cowboy songs. Glaser and Sykes were to provide Sons of the Pioneers–style vocal harmony. Robbins had no real faith in the sales potential of the album; he simply wanted to do it and told producer Don Law that Columbia Records owed him a favor. The instrumental group was led by Grady Martin playing acoustic guitar. Robbins, Glaser, Sykes, and Martin combined on a five-minute epic called "El Paso" that, against all the odds, went on to become the bestselling record of Robbins's career.

During the early 1960s the pop-country fusion that Robbins had pioneered became codified into what was known as the "Nashville Sound." Robbins was one of the most successful Nashville Sound artists, and his records continued to cross between the pop and country markets throughout the early 1960s. Among those hits were "Devil Woman," "Ruby Ann," "Begging to You," and "Ribbon of Darkness." He was arguably the most consistently successful country artist of the early to mid-1960s.

After the success of "El Paso," Robbins inevitably recorded more albums of western music and found great success with them. He also returned to Hawaiian music and recorded several albums of pop standards as well as hymns. He tried writing a western novel, a self-published book, *The Small Man* (1966), as well as producing his own television series, "The Drifter" (1965; thirteen episodes), "The Marty Robbins Show" (1969; thirty-nine episodes), and "Marty Robbins Spotlight" (1978–1979; forty-eight shows). After confessing to a profound unease appearing on television in Phoenix in the early 1950s, Robbins became a gregarious and engaging television performer, and he found that it was a medium well adapted to his talents.

Robbins also appeared in a number of motion pictures. These included *The Badge of Marshall Brennan* (1957), *Raiders of Old California* (1957), *Buffalo Gun* (1958), *Ballad of a Gunfighter* (1963), *Country Music Caravan*, also known as *Country Music Carnival* (1964), *Tennessee Jamboree* (1964), *The Road to Nashville* (1966), *Hell on Wheels* (1967), *From Nashville with Music* (1969), *Country Music* (1972), *Guns of a Stranger* (1973), and *Honky Tonk Man* (1982). In addition,

Robbins composed or sang songs for *The Hanging Tree* (1959), *The Young Rounders* (1960s), *Moonfire* (1970), and *Emperor of the North Pole* (1973).

Robbins also had a deep involvement in stock car (NASCAR) racing. Beginning in 1966, he competed regularly. His first event was the NASCAR Grand National Championship Circuit Race No. 36, held at the fairgrounds in Nashville. He appeared in thirty-four other competitions, the last at the Winston Cup Grand National Race No. 29 at the Atlanta Raceway in Atlanta, Georgia, just a month before his death.

Robbins's musical career tailed off somewhat in the early 1970s, leading him to leave Columbia Records in 1972 and switch to Decca Records (which later became MCA Records). He later admitted that this had been a mistake and returned to Columbia Records when his MCA contract expired in 1975. His first Columbia single after he returned to the label was "El Paso City," a song that developed the mystical element inherent in "El Paso" and touched on themes of reincarnation that intrigued Robbins. It became a number-one hit for him in the country market, and he was still scoring country hits when he died.

Robbins's first sign of heart disease came on 1 August 1969 when he complained of chest pains traveling to a show in Cleveland, Ohio. When he stopped at a hospital after the show, it was revealed that he had suffered a heart attack. He underwent what was then experimental bypass surgery for three blocked arteries but ignored doctors' instructions that he not overexert himself. He returned to the stage (starting at the Grand Ole Opry on 28 Mar. 1970) and to the NASCAR circuit. In 1981 he suffered a second heart attack. On 11 October 1982 Robbins was inducted into the Country Music Hall of Fame (the only living inductee that year), and although he stated that there were perhaps others more worthy of induction, he recognized that heart disease could claim him at any point and said, "It might not happen again, so I'm gonna take it tonight." Robbins arrived back in Nashville on 2 December 1982 with the intention of attending a screening of *Honky Tonk Man*, in which he sang and made a cameo appearance. He suffered another heart attack the morning before the screening and underwent another heart bypass operation, but his lungs and kidneys failed.

Robbins was a true musical eclectic, perhaps more of an eclectic than any other performer in country music. "I was never ashamed of singing country music," he told interviewer Alanna Nash, "and I was never ashamed of buying it. The same as I was never ashamed of saying I liked Perry Como . . . or Eddy Arnold, or Hank Williams, or Fats Domino or anybody else." Robbins had an intuitive musicality that gave him what appeared to be an innate understanding of his strengths as a performer, which in turn imparted a consistency to his work that was all the more surprising because of its variety. The manner in which he was able to regenerate his career and renew his audience base was reflected in the fact that he scored hits in the 1950s, 1960s, 1970s, and 1980s.

• An invaluable source is Barbara J. Pruett, *Marty Robbins: Fast Cars and Country Music* (1990), which painstakingly lists every reference to Robbins in the music trade and consumer press from 1948 until 1988. It also details his movies, television series, NASCAR starts, record releases, and Library of Congress copyrights. Also noteworthy is Alanna Nash's interview in *Behind Closed Doors* (1988). By far the best interview with Robbins was conducted by Bob Allen in 1981. It was published in part in "Marty Robbins Doesn't Sweat the Small Stuff," *Country Music*, Sept. 1981, and in *Hustler*, Jan. 1982. The complete transcription is on file at the Country Music Foundation in Nashville.

COLIN ESCOTT

ROBBINS, William Jacob (22 Feb. 1890–5 Oct. 1978), botanist, physiologist, and institution director, was born in North Platte, Nebraska, the son of Frederick Woods Robbins, a schoolteacher and administrator, and Clara Jeanette Federhof, a journalist. When he was two, his family moved to Muncy, Pennsylvania. Robbins graduated from high school in 1906 and then attended Lehigh University in Bethlehem, Pennsylvania, graduating in 1910 with Phi Beta Kappa honors. After teaching at Lehigh and at the Mining and Mechanical Institute at Freeland, Pennsylvania, for one year, he entered graduate school at Cornell University in Ithaca, New York. Originally Robbins planned to train as a plant pathologist and a scientific farmer, but he changed the focus of his studies to plant physiology. He worked as an instructor at Cornell from 1912 to 1916; he earned his doctorate there in 1915. On 15 July 1915, Robbins married Christine Faye Chapman, a botanist who later became a scientific biographer. They had three sons, one of whom, Frederick Robbins, won the Nobel Prize in medicine in 1954.

In 1916 Robbins accepted the positions of professor and chairman of the Department of Botany and plant physiologist in the Agricultural Experiment Station, both at the Alabama Polytechnic Institute, Auburn. He initiated research on the effect of growth factors on cultivation of excised plant roots. His research abruptly ended, however, when he moved to Springfield, Massachusetts, in 1917, to manage his ill father-in-law's hardware store. In 1918 Robbins enlisted in the U.S. Army; after completing training in bacteriology at Yale's Army Laboratory School, he served as a second lieutenant in the U.S. Sanitary Corps. World War I ended before Robbins was deployed abroad.

After his military service, Robbins worked briefly as a soil biochemist at the U.S. Department of Agriculture in Washington, D.C., before accepting in 1919 the positions of professor and chairman in the Department of Botany at the University of Missouri. He resumed research on the cultivation of excised roots, research critical for the developing field of tissue culture, a method of propagating virus-free plants in large quantities. He demonstrated that vitamins, especially B1 (thiamine), are essential for the growth of fungi and agricultural crops such as peas, corn, and cotton. Robbins also examined the effects of pH on the toxicity of some dye substances. During this period he coauthored with H. W. Rickett three editions of a widely used botany textbook. From 1928 to 1930 he traveled throughout Europe, accepting applications and interviewing candidates for Rockefeller Foundation–sponsored research grants and postdoctoral fellowships. Between 1931 and 1937, he served as chairman of the Fellowship Board of the National Research Council, which administered these postdoctoral awards. Robbins, who had gained worldwide recognition as both a scientist and an administrator, in 1930 became the dean of the graduate school at the University of Missouri; from 1933 to 1934 he also served as the acting university president. In the latter capacity he secured Works Progress Administration (WPA) support for the construction of a new library, classroom buildings, and a research facility.

In 1938 Robbins became director of the New York Botanical Garden and professor of botany at Columbia University. As a plant and fungal physiologist, he was the botanical garden's first director from outside the field of systematic botany. Early in his tenure, he revitalized the garden's staff by encouraging retirements and hiring new botanists, using scientific productivity as the main criterion. Robbins developed training courses for professional gardeners, encouraged the investigation of South American flora, and promoted horticulture through flower shows and displays. He also trained WPA workers to assist in the preparation of herbarium specimens. WPA workers also assisted in the six laboratories he developed for studies of plant physiology, mycology, virology, and plant biochemistry.

Despite his busy administrative schedule, Robbins spent at least one hour a day in his laboratory. During World War II, his research group screened antibiotics produced by more than 3,000 cultures of basidiomycetous fungi (mushrooms). Their efforts isolated a dozen new antibiotic substances, as well as metabolites with antibacterial, antifungal, antitumor, antileukemic, and cardiotonic properties. After World War II, his research continued under a grant from the National Foundation for Infantile Paralysis. Robbins and his coworkers also identified natural sources of the vitamin B12 in soil bacteria and fungi such as the actinomycetes. In addition, the garden staff under his direction worked for various government agencies on the production of quinine, rubber, and insecticides, and identified tropical plants that could be used as food sources. In 1956 the laboratories moved into a new research facility, the Charles B. Harding Research Laboratory, funded by private donations. During this period Robbins also taught botany classes at Columbia University and developed degree programs with both Columbia and Fordham Universities.

In addition to his work at the garden, Robbins served on the advisory council of the National Arboretum in Washington, D.C. He was active in developing the Fairchild Tropical Garden in Montgomery, Florida, serving on its board of trustees (1948–1962) and as its president (1962–1969). He hosted a National Academy of Sciences Conference on Tropical Botany there in May 1960. On 8 March 1967, Fairchild Tropical Garden honored his long association by dedicating the William J. Robbins Plant Science Building, with a herbarium, reference library, and laboratories.

In 1940 Robbins was elected to membership in the National Academy of Sciences (NAS), where he was chairman of the botany section (1944–1947) and treasurer (1948–1960). He served as a member of the executive board of the National Research Council between 1941 and 1960. Perhaps as a result of his own academic experiences, he opposed the NAS's recommendation for concentrating federal educational funds in the elite research institutions; he strongly recommended that at least 25 percent of funds be retained to support education at less well-known schools.

In 1958 Robbins retired as director of the New York Botanical Garden after a diagnosis of severe heart disease. In 1962 he moved briefly to Washington, D.C., to serve as assistant director of international science activities at the National Science Foundation. After returning to New York in 1964, he remained active in retirement, conducting research at the New York Botanical Garden and in a laboratory he developed at Rockefeller University. He isolated fungi that leaf-cutting ants cultivated as food in their underground gardens, and in collaborative research he first showed that some of these fungi were species of the mushroom *Lepiota*. At Rockefeller University he turned his research to tissue culture and topophysis, propagational differences in juvenile and adult stages of plants. Robbins continued his research until his death in New York City.

Robbins served on a scientific advisory commission to Japan in 1947, to evaluate and give advice on development of scientific research and to reestablish contact with Japanese scientists after the war. He was elected to membership in the American Philosophical Society and served as its president (1956–1959) and executive officer (1960). He was a fellow of the American Association for the Advancement of Science and the New York Academy of Sciences, as well as a member of many other scholarly and professional societies. He was active in the Torrey Botanical Club and served as its president (1943). He was a member and director of the Boyce Thompson Institute for Plant Research and served on its executive committee. He was a trustee of Rockefeller University (1956–1965) and until his death a trustee emeritus.

Robbins guided the New York Botanical Garden during a critical period. The garden, founded in 1891, had long been under the nominal direction of its founder Nathaniel Lord Britton and, after 1930, a series of acting directors. In the years immediately preceding Robbins's appointment, the institution had experienced extreme administrative neglect and as a result had both a depleted scientific staff and a large backlog of unprepared plant collections that threatened its scientific productivity. Robbins rejuvenated the garden by increasing both the quantity and the quality of its scientific staff. He used WPA workers to reduce the backlog of plant collections and to repair the museum building, display houses, and gardens.

Robbins was a man of high standards in both his personal and his administrative actions. He valued scientific research, believing that the results from even one-tenth of one percent of the research conducted could have critical importance for the development of society. Although his demanding administrative schedule left little time for scientific pursuits, he published more than 200 influential scientific publications with diverse coauthors and at least forty popular articles.

• The New York Botanical Garden's archives contain documents concerning Robbins's years at the garden and at Rockefeller University and a transcript of his 20 July 1973 interview in the New York Botanical Garden Oral History Program of Columbia University. The American Philosophical Society in Philadelphia holds biographical materials and documents concerning his years at the University of Missouri, and the National Academy of Sciences archives contain documents concerning his work with that organization. A biographical sketch is Frederick Kavanagh and Annette Hervey, National Academy of Sciences, *Biographical Memoirs* 60 (1991): 292–328. See also Kavanagh and Hervey, "William Jacob Robbins, February 22, 1890–October 5, 1978," *Bulletin of the Torrey Botanical Club* 108 (1981): 95–121; and S. Nixon, "William J. Robbins: Indomitable Scientist," *Fairchild Tropical Garden Bulletin*, Oct. 1978, pp. 29–31.

PAULA DePRIEST

ROBERDEAU, Daniel (1727–5 Jan. 1795), merchant and revolutionary war general, was born on St. Kitts (St. Christopher), West Indies, the son of Isaac Roberdeau and Mary Cunyngham. Nothing is known about his parents' occupations. His father was a Huguenot from La Rochelle, France; his mother was of Scottish ancestry. Roberdeau was sent to England for his education but on his father's death moved to Philadelphia with his mother and completed his studies there. He soon began a successful career in the West Indian trade. He entered politics as a warden of the city and in 1756 was elected to his first of five annual terms in the state assembly. He married Mary Bostwick of Philadelphia in 1761 and, adopting her devout Presbyterianism, became an elder of the Second Presbyterian Church. The couple had nine children.

As the Revolution approached Roberdeau advocated nonimportation. In 1775 the Pennsylvania Assembly appointed him to the committee of safety, and in that capacity Roberdeau conducted a mass outdoor meeting in Philadelphia in May 1776. John Adams (1735–1826) described his performance as done "with great order, decency and propriety." Roberdeau joined the Pennsylvania Associators, a voluntary militia, at first serving as a colonel of the Philadelphia City Second Battalion. In 1776 he was elected brigadier general and led the Associators in the New Jersey campaign. He helped prepare the defenses of New Jersey in the summer of 1776 but fell ill in the fall and was taken to Lancaster, Pennsylvania, to recuperate. He did not participate in George Washington's retreat across New Jersey in November-December 1776 or in the counterattacks at Trenton and Princeton. Rober-

deau also helped outfit two privateers that preyed on British shipping.

Roberdeau was appointed to the Continental Congress by the assembly in 1777 and served for two years. He was identified with the radical wing of Pennsylvania patriots: Thomas Paine served as his secretary for a time, and in 1779 Roberdeau chaired a Philadelphia assembly of soldiers demanding price controls in order to counteract wartime inflation. While the congress was at York, Pennsylvania, he rented one of the town's largest houses and entertained many guests.

During the war Roberdeau's personal fortunes suffered. His wife died early in 1777, and in the following year he led an expedition of fifty soldiers into central Pennsylvania to open a lead mine and build a smelter to supply the Continental forces with munitions. Although he erected a stockade, named Fort Roberdeau, in Sinking Spring Valley in modern Blair County, his heavy investment in the operation was a total loss when his workers abandoned the site because of Indian attacks in the vicinity.

Roberdeau married Jane Milligan of Philadelphia in 1778 and was in that city for the remainder of the war. In 1783–1784 he traveled to Great Britain and the West Indies to reestablish business associations. In 1785 he moved to Alexandria, Virginia. In 1794 he purchased a home in Winchester, Virginia, where he died.

• A letterbook, 1764–1771, and a receipt book, 1761–1767, recording Roberdeau's business activities are at the Historical Society of Pennsylvania. The most complete sketch of Roberdeau's life is in Roberdeau Buchanan, *Genealogy of the Roberdeau Family* (1876). Roberdeau's revolutionary war activities may be traced in the *Pennsylvania Archives*, vols. 5–12 (1852–1856); Worthington C. Ford et al., eds., *Journals of the Continental Congress*, vols. 8–11 (1908–1909); *Papers of the Continental Congress*, National Archives, Washington, D.C.; and *Letters of Delegates to Congress, 1774–1789* (1976).

DARWIN H. STAPLETON

ROBERDEAU, Isaac (11 Sept. 1763–15 Jan. 1829), civil and military engineer, was born in Philadelphia, Pennsylvania, the son of Daniel Roberdeau, a revolutionary war general, and Mary Bostwick. He was educated in Philadelphia and by 1783 was one of four clerks under Joseph Nourse, registrar of the Treasury Department. The same year Roberdeau visited the West Indies with his father before embarking for London, where he studied engineering until 1787. In 1792 Roberdeau married Susan Shippen Blair; they had three daughters.

Roberdeau is most often remembered as Pierre Charles L'Enfant's assistant in laying out the city of Washington. He was originally hired by Andrew Ellicott on 4 February 1791 to supervise the field team that surveyed the ten-mile-square federal district carved out of Maryland and Virginia in which the federal city was located. In November 1791 the federal city's commissioners ordered Roberdeau to stop tearing down Daniel Carroll of Duddington's house, the first indication that Roberdeau was then working directly with L'Enfant. (L'Enfant had ordered the demolition on the grounds that the house's erection had contravened the agreement made between the government and the original proprietors of land.)

While L'Enfant was in Philadelphia during the winter of 1791–1792, Roberdeau wrote him frequently to inform him of both the physical and the political progress of the city's affairs. In January 1792 Roberdeau was arrested by the commissioners for refusing to stop digging the foundations for the Capitol after they had formally dismissed him. Roberdeau claimed he took his orders directly from L'Enfant; neither accepted the authority of the commissioners. After L'Enfant was dismissed in March 1792, Alexander Hamilton hired him as the engineer for a new manufacturing town at Paterson, New Jersey. However, no position was found for Roberdeau, who wished to continue working for L'Enfant. In 1793 Roberdeau may have done additional surveying work in the District of Columbia, for he was paid eight and a half pounds that year, but his insubordination blocked many of his later attempts to secure a government position.

Beginning in 1792, Roberdeau was involved for several years in surveying canals in Pennsylvania, Delaware, and New Jersey, principally the one connecting the Schuylkill and Susquehanna Rivers under the direction of the English engineer William Weston. In 1798 he applied for the position of superintendent of a proposed national cannon foundry, citing not his direct experience, but rather his wide knowledge of people in the field. Two years later he applied to the War Department for the job of purveyor of public supplies. On 22 February 1800, while directing a brigade building a canal near Trenton, New Jersey, Roberdeau (who had dined at Mount Vernon in 1785) delivered an oration on Washington's death. In 1808 he sought a presidential appointment in the U.S. Army and was disturbed to learn that Thomas Jefferson did not consider him politically sound.

The War of 1812 offered Roberdeau the opportunity he had been seeking. In 1813 he was appointed a major in the topographical engineers and assigned to fortification work, principally at Fort Mifflin near Philadelphia. When the corps was abolished on 15 June 1815, Roberdeau was retained as a civilian employee. From June until December 1815, he and John Anderson led the team that surveyed that part of the boundary between the United States and Canada lying between Whitehall, New York (the headwaters of Lake Champlain), and Niagara Falls. The Treaty of Ghent set the boundary in the middle of the waterways; Roberdeau and Anderson may have carried their survey through part of Lake Ontario. They also examined the fort at Crown Point, New York, reported on its condition, recounted its history, and made recommendations for its repair.

On 2 May 1816 Roberdeau was commissioned a major in the army's revived Topographical Corps of Engineers. His time was divided between West Point, New York, and Washington as a surveyor and administrator. In May 1818 he met with the commissioners appointed to examine Hampton Roads, near Old Fort Comfort, Virginia, and in July he was ordered to undertake a survey of Annapolis, Maryland. On 1 August 1818 the headquarters of the Topographical Corps were moved permanently to Washington, and Roberdeau was named its chief. He was breveted a lieutenant colonel in 1823.

Roberdeau prospered after John C. Calhoun was appointed secretary of war in 1820. Roberdeau accompanied Calhoun on many of his official inspection tours; Peter Hagner kept a diary of their visit to military installations in New York, New England, and Montreal in 1820. Roberdeau's own account book records the expenses incurred in this and other trips, including one in August 1822 through the Shenandoah Valley with Calhoun. In May 1820 Calhoun ordered that Roberdeau receive five months of extra pay retroactively for preserving the department's maps, plans, and mathematical instruments. Thereafter he was in charge of caring for the government's surveying and weighing instruments. In 1820 the costly instruments ordered from Europe by Ferdinand R. Hassler, the first superintendent of the U.S. Coast and Geodetic Survey, were placed under Roberdeau's care. In 1821 he aided the astronomer William Lambert, who borrowed Hassler's instruments, to calculate the longitude and latitude of the Capitol. Under Roberdeau the Topographical Corps of Engineers became a clearinghouse for accurate geographical information about the entire country. Private individuals and government agents used the office's resources when planning expeditions or seeking cartographic information for the publication of atlases and maps. Roberdeau apparently redrew or made composite maps from charts and maps deposited with him by both military and civilian personnel. His office was working toward a definitive map of the American frontier.

As early as 1819 Roberdeau became involved with the seacoast survey originally proposed by Thomas Jefferson in 1807 and officially launched in 1816. On 9 December 1826 Roberdeau read a paper, "Observations on the Survey of the Sea Coast of the United States," before the Columbian Institute, Washington's only learned society, of which he was a member. The full text appeared in the newspaper the *National Journal*; he argued that the coast survey should be carried out by the Topographical Corps of Engineers and that a national observatory in Washington was necessary to ensure its accuracy. In 1825 he had discussed the importance of a national observatory with John Quincy Adams. Roberdeau's account of the history of the coast survey was challenged by Hassler. Both their texts were subsequently published together in pamphlet form.

Roberdeau's scholarly interest in the history of his profession led him to order for the department in 1823 several French books on the military sciences, particularly surveying. In 1828 he unsuccessfully sought support to publish his substantial illustrated essay on canal design and construction, "Mathematics and

Treatise on Canals," the manuscript of which is in the Library of Congress. He died in Georgetown, D.C.

• Most of the documents recording Roberdeau's career are in the National Archives, RG 77, with a few others scattered among record groups, including RG 42, RG 46, and RG 59. His personal and professional correspondence is among the W. Robert Leckie Papers at Duke University, the Timothy Pickering Papers at the Massachusetts Historical Collections, University of North Carolina at Chapel Hill. Roberdeau's grandson deposited his account book and other minor journals and memorabilia at the Historical Society of Pennsylvania, and his treatise on canals at the Library of Congress. Supplementary information is in Roberdeau Buchanan, *Genealogy of the Roberdeau Family* (1876), and Todd Shallat, *Structures in the Stream: Water, Science, and the Rise of the U.S. Army Corps of Engineers* (1994). An obituary is in the *Washington Daily National Intelligencer*, 16 Jan. 1829.

PAMELA SCOTT

ROBERT, Henry Martyn (2 May 1837–11 May 1923), army engineer and parliamentarian, was born on his grandfather's plantation near Robertville, South Carolina, the son of Reverend Joseph Thomas Robert, a Baptist minister and teacher, and Adeline Elizabeth Lawton. Before the Civil War his family moved to Ohio, from which state Robert received an appointment to the U.S. Military Academy at West Point. He graduated in 1857, briefly taught at the academy, and in 1858 traveled to the Washington Territory as a second lieutenant in the Corps of Engineers. He was in charge of the engineering defense of San Juan Island during a border dispute with Great Britain in 1859.

Robert returned to the East and on 24 December 1860 married Helen M. Thresher; they had five children. With the outbreak of the Civil War, Robert chose to remain with the North in spite of his southern background and briefly worked on the defense of Washington, D.C. He was promoted to first lieutenant, but the debilitating effects of the "Panama fever" he had caught while traveling to the West Coast forced his removal to Philadelphia and in 1862 to New Bedford, Massachusetts. At New Bedford, presumably because of his education and position, Robert was elected to chair a public meeting. He was embarrassed because he did not know what to do and thus began his lifelong interest in parliamentary procedure.

Promoted to captain in 1863, he returned to West Point two years later, where he taught military engineering and served as treasurer for the academy. With a promotion to major in 1867 he traveled to San Francisco to serve as chief engineer in the Military Division of the Pacific. There he worked on harbors and lighthouse construction.

San Francisco was a chaotic boom town of about 150,000 people wherein Robert became involved in the administration of the First Baptist Church and the YMCA. Good intentions, he realized, could be thwarted by disagreements over rules of order, and the mixed population had differing thoughts about how to proceed in meetings. Robert investigated the available manuals, found them inadequate, and tried without success to write his own. He was transferred to Portland in 1871, again for work on harbors and lighthouses, and then to Milwaukee in 1873. The long winters of inactivity in the Great Lakes region gave him an opportunity to try once more to construct some universal rules of procedure.

Drawing from his experience and study, Robert put together a 176-page manual of rules whereby the majority would prevail, the minority would be heard, and courtesy would control emotions. Rejected by publishers, Robert paid for the first 4,000-copy printing and arranged for distribution in 1876 by S. C. Griggs and Company of Chicago. Demonstrating a flair for promotion, Robert sent out 1,000 free copies of *Robert's Rules of Order* to legislators and civic leaders across the country. The book was practical, handy, widely approved, and it sold out in four months. Robert invited questions and commentary, added new sections and examples, and provided new editions. He published a major revision in 1915, *Robert's Rules of Order Revised*, and later additional commentary with *Parliamentary Practice* in 1921 and *Parliamentary Law* in 1923.

In his professional field Robert directed the writing of *The Water-Jet as an Aid to Engineering Construction* in 1881 and assembled *Analytical and Topical Index to the Reports of the Chief of Engineers and the Officers of the Corps of Engineers, United States Army, upon Works and Surveys for River and Harbor Improvement, from 1866–1892* from 1881 to 1895. Robert became a lieutenant colonel in 1883 and for the remainder of the century worked on projects related to the Great Lakes, St. Lawrence, Lake Champlain, Cumberland River, Tennessee River, New York Harbor, Long Island Sound, Gulf of Mexico, Philadelphia, and Washington, D.C. In 1889 he led a board to select a suitable harbor on the western Gulf of Mexico for development. He chose Galveston, Texas, which started a long-term relationship with that island city. He was also involved in the engineering improvements that led to harbor development at Texas City, Aransas Pass, Sabine Pass, and Houston. He gained promotion to full colonel in 1895, the same year his wife died. Three days before Robert's retirement on 2 May 1901, President William McKinley promoted him to brigadier general and chief of the Corps of Engineers, a reward for long and loyal service. Within a week of retirement Robert married Isabel Livingston Hoagland at their hometown of Owego, New York, and settled into a life of consulting and revising the *Rules of Order*.

In 1900 Galveston, Texas, suffered the worst hurricane disaster in the history of the United States in terms of loss of life, and civic leaders turned to Robert as an engineering consultant to devise a plan for revival and protection. With two other civil engineers, Alfred Noble and H. C. Ripley, Robert drew up a successful design for a concrete seawall and provided advice about grade raising and a causeway to the mainland. In 1911 he planned the harbor improvements at Frontera, Mexico. Robert died in Hornell, New York.

The work at Galveston stands as Robert's greatest engineering achievement. It saved the city from future hurricane destruction, and his seawall became one of the finest marine boulevards in the nation. More widely known is *Robert's Rules of Order*, which has become so thoroughly accepted among democratic organizations that hardly anyone challenges the reasoning or process. Trained in logical building methods, Robert was able to construct a procedure whereby the will of an assembly could be determined in an orderly manner.

• Robert's personal papers are in the Library of Congress, and his military papers are in the National Archives. The best recent assessment of the *Rules of Order* was written by Don H. Doyle, "Rules of Order: Henry Martyn Robert and the Popularization of American Parliamentary Law," *American Quarterly* 32 (Spring 1980): 3–18. Other accounts of Robert's work include Ralph C. Smedley, *The Great Peacemaker* (1955), and the introductory portions of Henry M. Robert, *Robert's Rules of Order Newly Revised* (1970; repr. 1981), which contain commentary about parliamentary law and Robert's role in its development. Also see the extensive interview with E. J. Mehren, "Henry Martyn Robert," *Engineering News-Record*, 22 Apr. 1920, pp. 798–802. An obituary is in the *Oswego Gazette*, 17 May 1923.

DAVID G. MCCOMB

ROBERTS, Benjamin Stone (18 Nov. 1810–29 Jan. 1875), soldier, was born in Manchester, Vermont, the son of Martin Roberts and Betsey Stone. He graduated in the West Point class of 1835, ranking fifty-third in a class of fifty-five cadets. Despite his standing, he managed to avoid a posting to the lowly infantry, gaining a commission in the First U.S. Dragoons. Also in 1835 he married Elizabeth Sperry; they had three children. After four years of desultory service on the frontier, he resigned his commission, moved to upper New York State, and entered the fledgling railroad industry. Following a stint as chief engineer of the Champlain & Ogdensburg, he was appointed in 1841 geologist of New York. In 1842 he relinquished this post to accompany the railroad pioneer G. W. Whistler to Russia, where he helped build a rail line from St. Petersburg to Moscow.

Roberts's multidirectional career took another turn when he returned to the United States in 1843, relocated to Des Moines, Iowa, studied law, and became active in the state militia. Upon the outbreak of war with Mexico in May 1846, he reentered the army; by the following February he was captain of Company C, Regiment of Mounted Rifles. In Mexico, under Winfield Scott, Roberts distinguished himself in several battles, including Veracruz and Molino del Rey. His most conspicuous service occurred during the attack on Chapultepec on 13 September, when he was second in command of a storming party that captured a pair of artillery positions guarding the approach to the fortified castle. The success of this operation—celebrated in Scott's report of the campaign—made the position's capture inevitable. Roberts's heroics at Chapultepec

and later at Matamoros and Pass Gualaxara won him the brevets of major and lieutenant colonel.

Following the war, Roberts remained with the Mounted Rifles, serving in garrison at Washington, D.C., and in the field against Native Americans in the Southwest. Promoted to major of his regiment (redesignated the Third U.S. Cavalry in Aug. 1861), he joined Colonel E. R. S. Canby in opposing the Confederate invasion of the New Mexico Territory. Roberts's experience in the region made him one of Canby's most trusted subordinates, and Canby recommended him for command of a force of regular and volunteer cavalry and light artillery. After helping defend Fort Craig, the key stronghold along the Rio Grande road, Roberts accompanied Canby to the Val Verde ford, where Brigadier General Henry Hopkins Sibley's army attacked on 21 February 1862. Although the battle ended in a Union retreat, Roberts won favorable notice and the brevet of colonel for leading his command over the river at a point considered unfordable, then striking the enemy's right flank in a spirited counterattack. Sibley's setback at Roberts's hands foreshadowed the ultimate failure of his invasion.

Eager to serve in a more active theater, Roberts seized the opportunity to go east in the spring of 1862. In July he became chief of cavalry, with the rank of brigadier general of volunteers, in John Pope's newly formed Army of Virginia. Roberts's service in the disastrous campaign of Second Bull Run (Second Manassas) was of a minor nature; he gained greater notice in the aftermath of the debacle, when Pope accused one of his subordinates, Major General Fitz John Porter, of disobedience and misconduct during the recent fighting. At Porter's highly publicized court-martial, Roberts's legal training and his prominent position on Pope's staff gained him the dubious honor of preferring charges against the accused.

Pope's failure at Second Bull Run resulted in his being transferred to the Department of the Northwest, where he waged war against the Sioux and other American Indian nations. Accompanying his commander to Minnesota, Roberts served as his inspector general, then led an expedition against the Chippewas in the northern part of the state.

Recalled to Washington in February 1863, Roberts briefly commanded the defenses on the upper Potomac. Subsequently he served in West Virginia, where he failed to defend portions of the Baltimore & Ohio Railroad against Confederate raiders under Brigadier Generals John D. Imboden and William E. Jones. After being outfought and forced to retreat from the railroad, Roberts lost his field command and was exiled to a desk job in the Milwaukee, Wisconsin, headquarters of the Department of the Northwest. In the summer of 1864 he was rescued from this assignment and sent to Louisiana to command a division in the XIX Corps, then to serve as chief of cavalry in the Department of the Gulf. He closed his multifaceted wartime career in Memphis, where he commanded the District of West Tennessee. By the conflict's end, despite the small extent of his military contributions from mid-1862 onward, Roberts was a brevet brigadier general in the regular army and a brevet major general of volunteers.

In 1865 Roberts returned to the Third U.S. Cavalry, and from 1867 to 1868 he served in the New Mexico Territory as lieutenant colonel. From 1868 until his retirement from the army in December 1870, Roberts taught military science at Yale College. In civilian life he moved to Washington, D.C., and returned to his legal practice, specializing in prosecuting claims against the government and in his spare time designing firearms. He died in Washington.

Roberts was one of a multitude of Civil War commanders who forged generally undistinguished careers—albeit in his case a peripatetic and colorful one. Already in his fifties when the shooting started, he appears to have lacked the energy and initiative that had won him honors in the prewar army. His limited success at Val Verde marked the zenith of his service against the Confederacy. Largely ineffective as an administrator and field leader of cavalry—an arm monopolized by younger, more enterprising officers—his career after mid-1862 suffered from his close association with Pope, whose humiliating defeat at Bull Run soiled not only his own reputation but those of many of his subordinates.

• The only body of Roberts's papers known to exist is a small collection in the Iowa State Department of History and Archives in Des Moines. The salient facts of his military career can be gleaned from Francis B. Heitman, comp., *Historical Register and Dictionary of the United States Army* (1903), and Ezra J. Warner, *Generals in Blue* (1964). His Civil War correspondence and reports are sprinkled throughout *The War of the Rebellion: A Compilation of the Official Records of the Union and Confederate Armies* (128 vols., 1880–1901). Roberts's service in Mexico receives brief mention in K. Jack Bauer, *The Mexican War, 1846–1848* (1974), and George Winston Smith and Charles Judah, *Chronicles of the Gringos* (1968); while his service under Canby merits detailed attention in Robert Lee Kerby, *The Confederate Invasion of New Mexico and Arizona, 1861–1862* (1958), and Martin H. Hall, *Sibley's New Mexico Campaign* (1960). Roberts's association with Pope and his role in the Porter court-martial are chronicled in Wallace J. Schutz and Walter N. Trenerry, *Abandoned by Lincoln* (1990), as well as in Otto Eisenschiml, *The Celebrated Case of Fitz John Porter* (1950).

EDWARD G. LONGACRE

ROBERTS, Benjamin Titus (25 July 1823–27 Feb. 1893), founder and first general superintendent of the Free Methodist church, was born in Cattaraugus County, New York, the son of Titus Roberts, a general merchant, and Sally Ellis. Roberts taught school by age sixteen and worked in a law office by eighteen. While studying law, he delivered an antislavery speech and remained a lifelong abolitionist. After a religious conversion in July 1844, he decided on a career in ministry. In April 1845 he enrolled at Genesee Wesleyan Seminary in Lima, New York, and by autumn was attending Wesleyan University in Middletown, Connecticut. He was licensed to preach on 19 April 1847, graduated Phi Beta Kappa in August 1848 with

B.A. and M.A. degrees, and in September was admitted on trial to the Genesee Conference of the Methodist Episcopal church. Before leaving college, he had met Ellen Lois Stowe, whom he married in 1849; they had seven children.

Upon affiliation with Genesee, Roberts served seven appointments in upstate New York from 1848 to 1858, a period in which the Methodists were mired in conflict. Slaveholding, membership in secret societies, pew rent, the Holiness Revival, and the role of the laity had become key issues in a church that Roberts felt had grown formal, backslidden, cold, and worldly. By 1852, Roberts was advocating free churches versus pew rent. In 1857 he published "New School Methodism" in the *Northern Independent*, charging that the denomination, intoxicated by its high status in society, had departed from the "old path" and become infested with "noxious weeds." He also complained that oyster suppers, festivals, and stock churches had become more important than a spiritual life cultivated by deep and thorough revivals. "Benevolence," a popular concept, was not the "root," but the "fruit" of Christian faith, he insisted; repentance, bolstered by faith in Christ and the loving God, was decisive for true spirituality.

Church leaders satirized Roberts and his associates—called Nazarites—as "beardless and brainless boys." It did not matter that some of Genesee's most respected and time-honored clergy supported him. These Nazarites, the critics charged, met in "secret conclave" and valued "a long face," "sanctimonious airs," and "plainness in dress" more than the Golden Rule. Consequently, the conference gave Roberts a strong reprimand in 1857 and expelled him for "unchristian and immoral conduct" in 1858. Many Genesee Conference laity were appalled by the happenings. The Pekin (N.Y.) congregation reaffirmed its faith in Roberts by granting him an exhorter's license. One hundred and ninety-five laymen from forty-seven circuits then gathered in Laymen's Convention at Albion, New York, in December 1858 and denounced the expulsion of Roberts as "one of the most oppressive and tyrannical abuses of power" ever. Additional expulsions followed in 1859 for "contumacy."

In 1860 elected representatives of the Methodist Episcopal church gathered in Buffalo, New York, for General Conference, the primary policy-making and ruling body of the Methodist connectional system, which convened once every four years. On 15 May the general body referred Roberts's case to its Committee on Appeals for trial. After closely divided actions, the committee decided to let stand the Genesee Conference action as "the final adjudication of the case." Roberts had presented his appeal, but to no avail; traditionalists and antiabolitionists controlled the conference.

In August, about eighty laymen and fifteen preachers gathered in Pekin and organized the Free Methodist church. Stressing John Wesley's doctrine of entire sanctification as an instantaneous work of God's grace rather than a gradual process of growth, they deemed that the church's primary task would be the salvation of souls. Roberts was elected general superintendent, but the church held that power should be shared by clergy and laity.

As superintendent, Roberts traveled extensively, preached once or twice daily, and prepared material for publication. He advocated camp meetings and grove meetings in summer and protracted meetings in winter as vital methods of Christian nurture. He edited the *Earnest Christian*, a monthly magazine of "devotional thought, holy aspiration, and fearless advocacy of the right." For a time, he also edited the *Free Methodist*.

The new church soon experienced troubling disruptions, however, including a dispute over Roberts having organized the Susquehanna Conference in Central New York and Pennsylvania. His opponents believed that the conference had been irregularly and illegally organized, and they reacted to what they called Roberts's "one man power." Accepted discipline gave the superintendent authority to travel at large but did not clarify whether he had the means to organize conferences. Roberts insisted that he had done nothing inconsistent with previous practices. Events culminated in October 1862, when Genesee delegates refused to recognize Susquehanna delegates at a church conference in St. Charles, Illinois.

Free Methodist leader Benjamin Hackney, a former U.S. congressman, helped in the resolution of the conflict.

As superintendent, Roberts worked to make Christian education a strong element in Free Methodism. In 1866 in North Chili, New York, he opened Chili Seminary as an alternative to modernization in what he called "fashionable schools." At Chili, students could take preparatory or graduating courses, study in an environment that retained basic scriptural values, and benefit from "influences that would tend to foster, and not discourage, a life of devotion to God." Renamed A. M. Chesbrough Seminary, it became Roberts Wesleyan College in 1949.

A reformer at heart, Roberts was deeply engaged in his times. Before the Emancipation Proclamation, when the primary issue between North and South was separation rather than the liberation of human beings, Roberts condemned the War between the States, and he then hailed President Abraham Lincoln for freeing the slaves. Roberts also stood for equality between the sexes and affirmed women in ministry. Toward the end of his life, he called attention to the economic plight of farmers and warned against unequal distribution of wealth, business combinations that promoted monopolies, and inconsistent railroad freight fares. In short, Roberts sought to remind the church of its responsibility to promote social justice and the redemption of society.

Roberts died in Cattaraugus, New York, while en route to a quarterly conference. According to statistics culled from reports a year after his death, Free Methodism had grown to twenty-nine conferences in North America with 22,112 members, 4,030 probationers, and roughly 1,000 preachers.

Within twenty years, Methodist Episcopal church perspective had shifted regarding Roberts. In 1910, Ray Allen, representing Genesee Conference as its official conference secretary, raised the motion that "ordered" Roberts's credentials be posthumously restored, saying it had acted against one of its "best" and thus had been "unjust and exceedingly unwise" (Genesee Minutes, pp. 42, 177).

• Microfilms of Roberts's family papers, copies of the *Earnest Christian*, journals of the Free Methodist church, and other resources are in Roberts Room Rare Books, Kenneth B. Keating Library, Roberts Wesleyan College, Rochester, N.Y. General records of the Methodist Episcopal church are kept under the auspices of the General Commission on Archives and History of the United Methodist Church, Madison, N.J. The archival and historical documents of the Genesee and the East Genesee conferences of the Methodist Episcopal church are kept under the auspices of the Committee on Archives and History of the Western New York Conference of the United Methodist church in Buffalo, N.Y. E. S. Smail, "Forbears of Some Roberts Cousins" (1959), located in the archival collections of Roberts Wesleyan College, has genealogical information.

Benjamin Titus Roberts's published books include *Fishers of Men* (1878); *Why Another Sect* (1879); *Spiritual Songs and Hymns for Pilgrims*, a compilation (1879); *Hymn Book of the Free Methodist Church*, prepared by William Gould (1883); *First Lessons on Money* (1886); *Ordaining Women* (1891); a collection of articles and editorials, *Holiness Teachings* (1893); and a collection of editorials, and *Pungent Truths* (1912).

Benson Howard Roberts, *Benjamin Titus Roberts, Late General Superintendent of the Free Methodist Church: A Biography* (1900), is a standard resource. Francis W. Conable, *History of the Genesee Annual Conference of the Methodist Episcopal Church* (1876); Matthew Simpson, *Cyclopaedia of Methodism* (1876); and Ray Allen, "Historical Sketch of Genesee Conference," in *Official Minutes [of] Genesee Annual Conference of the Methodist Episcopal Church* (1910), pp. 174–78, provide materials from the Methodist Episcopal church's perspective of Roberts's legacy.

See also Clarence Howard Zahniser, "Earnest Christian: Life and Works of Benjamin Titus Roberts" (Ph.D. diss., Univ. of Pittsburgh, 1951); James Arnold Reinhard, "Personal and Sociological Factors in the Formation of the Free Methodist Church 1852–1860" (Ph.D. diss., Univ. of Iowa, 1971); Leslie R. Marston, *From Age to Age a Living Witness: A Historical Interpretation of Free Methodism's First Century* (1960); and Walter W. Benjamin, "The Free Methodists," in *The History of American Methodism*, ed. Emory Stevens Bucke, vol. 2 (1964), pp. 339–60. H. A. Snyder, "An End to Tyranny: B. T. Roberts on Woman's Rights," *Light and Life* 114, no. 2 (1981): 12–13, discusses his views on women.

DUANE W. PRISET

ROBERTS, Brigham Henry (13 Mar. 1857–27 Sept. 1933), Mormon leader, writer, and politician, was born in Warrington, Lancashire, England, the son of Benjamin Roberts, a blacksmith and ship plater, and Ann Everington, a seamstress. The year of his birth, Roberts's parents converted to the Church of Jesus Christ of Latter-day Saints (commonly known as the Mormon or LDS church). An alcoholic, Benjamin Roberts later abandoned the family, but when Roberts was five his father sent his mother money that she used to take two of their children to Utah. Roberts and a sister remained in England under cruel conditions until April 1866 when, assisted by the LDS Perpetual Emigrating Fund, they left Liverpool for Utah. In July they joined a wagon team in Nebraska and proceeded to walk, for much of the way barefoot, to Salt Lake City, where they were met by their mother.

Roberts's youth in the mining district west of Salt Lake Valley was characterized by rough company, gambling, and drinking—he once was disciplined by a Salt Lake bishop. From a local tutor, Roberts finally learned how to read and write, and he worked as a farmhand, a brick maker, an ox-team grader, and, with his new stepfather, as a silver miner. To rescue her son from his self-destructive habits his mother apprenticed Roberts to James Baird, a blacksmith in Centerville, Utah. During this time Roberts began to develop intellectually. He attended school three months each year, reading literature as well as Bible commentaries; he also began to record short "Truth Gems" and studied extensively the Book of Mormon and Parley P. Pratt's *Key to the Science of Theology*. In 1878 Roberts married Sarah Louisa Smith, with whom he would have seven children. The couple lived with her parents in Centerville until Roberts graduated, that same year, from the University of Deseret, finishing first in his class and delivering the valedictory speech before church and territorial dignitaries.

In 1879, after the birth of the couple's first child, Roberts was called to the Northwestern States Mission for the LDS church; he returned in 1882 only to be called as president of the Southern States Mission in 1883. Public lectures, missionary training, traveling, and writing filled the next three years. Opposition to his work, which included harassment and the burning of a school, climaxed with the murder of four Mormons. Disguised as a tramp, Roberts retrieved the bodies and returned them to Utah for burial. In the meantime, encouraged both by LDS president John Taylor and by his own wife, Roberts entered into plural marriage by marrying Celia Dibble during a short visit home in October 1884; his second marriage would produce eight children.

Returning to Utah in 1886, Roberts assumed an editorial position with the *Salt Lake Herald*. While at work on 5 December 1886, Roberts was arrested on bigamy charges. His lawyer and bondsmen agreed to sacrifice the bond, and that same night, after a brief goodbye to his family, he left for England to become editor of the *Millennial Star*, an important LDS publication. In England Roberts traveled and wrote widely, producing weekly editorials and publishing *The Gospel* (1888), a popular book on faith, repentance, and baptism that went through many printings. Roberts returned to Salt Lake City as full-time editor of the *Contributor* in 1888, and that October, at the LDS General Conference, he became one of the seven presidents of the First Council of the Seventy, the third highest governing body in the LDS church.

Early in 1889 Roberts pled guilty to the charge of unlawful cohabitation and was imprisoned for four months. The following year he showed his support for Mormon principles by marrying Margaret Shipp, his third wife, thus making himself responsible for the maintenance of three households. (His third marriage was childless.) He worked as an editor of the *Salt Lake Herald* and wrote books, including a detailed biography of former LDS church president Taylor. The LDS First Presidency, comprising the president of the church and two counselors, asked him to make a presentation before the World Parliament of Religions to be held in conjunction with the World's Columbian Exposition in Chicago in 1893. Although the leaders of the parliament rejected his proposal, this experience, as well as campaigning successfully for John T. Caine of the People's party in 1889, prepared Roberts for a brief career in politics. In 1895 he was elected as a delegate from Davis County to the Utah constitutional convention. While there Roberts spoke in opposition to woman suffrage, probably because he was concerned that such a provision would jeopardize Utah's admission into the Union—Utah women were granted the franchise in 1870, but that right had been revoked by Congress in 1887. Although his speeches were recognized for their logic and eloquence, the woman suffrage provision was passed, and despite his concerns, Utah became a state in 1896. Two years later, running as a Democrat, Roberts was elected to the U.S. House of Representatives, but because he had three wives, House members debated whether or not he should be seated. At a hearing in Washington, D.C., Roberts cited cases in which the House had not expelled members for offenses that had been committed before a particular member's election, but in January 1900, after a month of debating the issue, a closed committee voted to exclude him.

Roberts returned to Salt Lake City and devoted his time to writing—often argumentatively. His exchanges with two local Protestant ministers and a Jesuit priest were later published as *The Mormon Doctrine of Deity* (1903). He also published a rejection of biblical higher criticism (1912) and a series of articles responding to Theodore Schroeder on LDS history; this series, which appeared in the *New York Historical Magazine* (1911), paved the way for his monumental *Comprehensive History of the Church* (1930). In addition Roberts served as editor of another church magazine, the *Improvement Era*, and wrote manuals for youth programs, his *Seventy's Course in Theology* (1907–1912), and *New Witnesses for God* (1909–1911), a case for the logical, spiritual, and historical plausibility of the Book of Mormon.

After U.S. entry into World War I, Utah governor Simon Bamberger appointed Roberts chaplain of the First Utah Light Field Artillery unit, activated in September 1917. Because he was sixty, Roberts was discouraged from serving, but he insisted and qualified as an officer. At Camp Kearney, in California, Roberts conducted LDS and nondenominational services, and in France he gave open-air sermons and ministered to sick soldiers. His unit had orders to report to Verdun days before the armistice. They were released from their duties in 1919, and Roberts kept contact with the men in his unit for the rest of his life.

Early in 1922 Roberts was asked by President Heber J. Grant and Elder James E. Talmage to serve on a committee to respond to questions about the Book of Mormon. He drafted a lengthy answer and went on to pose further questions (reprinted in Brigham D. Madsen, ed., *Studies of the Book of Mormon* [1985]) that he believed future defenders of the faith should seek to answer. Some have interpreted the magnitude of his questions as a sign of doubt, but others view it as a testimony to the resoluteness of his faith. Also in 1922, at his request, Roberts became a mission president over the area that included western New York, where in 1830 in Fayette the LDS church had been organized and where that same year, in Palmyra, the Book of Mormon was published. In 1923 he was diagnosed with diabetes and returned to Salt Lake City for rest; a few months later, with renewed determination, he returned to New York and served there until May 1927, innovatively basing much of his teaching on the Book of Mormon.

In 1924 Roberts became senior president of the First Council of the Seventy. A powerful orator, he typically spoke without notes on subjects ranging from religion and philosophy to politics. His favorite topics were Joseph Smith, the Book of Mormon, and a return to basic principles, prayer, and study. Roberts considered the manuscript of *The Truth, the Way, the Life*, written in 1927–1928 but not published until 1994, to be his crowning theological achievement. A synthesis of the gospel of Jesus Christ and natural theology, the work assumes a continuity between human and divine experience, draws heavily on the Bible and all LDS scripture, and subscribes to an optimistic view of human purpose and progress. Because the LDS church would not give the work its official endorsement (one member of a committee objected to some of Roberts's positions), Roberts preferred that his opinions not be published if he had to make certain changes in his statements about pre-Adamic death on earth.

In April 1931 part of Roberts's right foot was amputated due to complications related to diabetes. Though ill, he continued to serve and write until his death two years later in Salt Lake City.

• A collection of Roberts's papers and letters, as well as his library, is at the LDS Church Archives in Salt Lake City, Utah. For additional information see Truman G. Madsen, *B. H. Roberts: Defender of the Faith* (1980), and John W. Welch, ed., *B. H. Roberts: The Truth, the Way, the Life*, 2d ed. (1996). An obituary and related stories are in the *Deseret News*, 28 Sept. 1933, and the *Salt Lake Tribune*, 28 and 29 Sept. 1933.

JOHN W. WELCH

ROBERTS, Elizabeth Madox (30 Oct. 1881–13 Mar. 1941), poet, short story writer, and novelist, was born in Perryville, Kentucky, the daughter of Simpson Roberts, a teacher, shopkeeper, surveyor, and engineer, and Mary Elizabeth Brent, also a teacher. Both parents were descendants of the early settlers of Kentucky. Roberts spent her early life first in Perryville, then in Willisburg, and finally, by 1884, in Springfield, seat of Washington County, where she would finally make her permanent home. Since Springfield did not have public schools at the time, her early education was in private schools, including "Professor" Grant's Academy and the Covington Institute. She also learned, informally, from her father, who told stories of her pioneer ancestors and recited passages from his "phantom library" (his books had been destroyed in a fire) of Greek and Roman mythology and history. In 1896 Roberts went to Covington, Kentucky, to live with relatives, so she could attend high school. There, her maternal grandmother told the family tales and folk legends about Kentucky, which would later become a part of Roberts's writing. Following graduation in 1900, she briefly attended the State College of Kentucky (now the University of Kentucky) but was forced to withdraw because of financial problems and illness. Throughout her life Roberts would be plagued with health problems.

From 1901 to 1914 Roberts taught school, first with her mother in a private school for young children, which they set up in their own home in Springfield, and later, in 1904, in the newly established Springfield public school. Roberts would later teach in Pleasant Grove and in Maude, both located far into the country. During her teaching years, Roberts met many of the people of the farming communities who would later be fictionalized in her books.

By 1914 Roberts had incipient tuberculosis and as a result relocated to Colorado to stay with relatives, hoping the mountain air would cure her respiratory problems. Her health did improve, and she contributed seven poems to a book of photographs of mountain flowers by Kenneth Hartley entitled *In the Great Steep's Garden* (1915), her first published work.

Returning to Kentucky in 1916, Roberts took classes at the University of Kentucky, where her poetry was highly praised by Professor James Noe who wrote about her work to Robert Morss Lovett of the University of Chicago. Lovett invited Roberts to come to Chicago, and, at the age of thirty-six, she registered in January 1917 as a freshman. Roberts's years at the University of Chicago were crucial to her development as a writer, not only because of her course work but also because of the friends she made. The Chicago years also gave her the perspective to see Washington County, Kentucky, as her "Little Country," a phrase derived from Willa Cather. Kentucky and its people became the focus of Roberts's work.

At Chicago, Roberts became part of a group of talented writers, the University Poetry Club, which included Glenway Wescott and Ivor Winters, and by her senior year, Roberts was president of the club. While a student she also met Harriet Monroe, editor of *Poetry* magazine, who encouraged her and accepted some of her poems for publication. Other poems were published in the *Atlantic Monthly*. Roberts graduated Phi

Beta Kappa in 1921. She was also awarded the Fiske prize for her poetry, and the following year her poems were published in *Under the Tree* (1922). Roberts wrote, "The book is autobiographical, probably the only autobiography I shall ever write" (Slavick, p. 756). This collection of poems, told from the perspective of a child, was, indeed, her only "autobiography."

After graduation Roberts returned to Springfield to devote herself to writing. She had experienced some success with her poetry and felt, originally, that it answered her needs for a creative outlet. As she observed in a letter to Harriet Monroe, "Until I fell upon 'Poetry' I had grasped about rather blindly, unhappily" (Slavick, p. 754). However, Roberts soon realized that she would best be able to recreate the world of her "Little Country" through the novel.

At Chicago she had started writing out memories for class assignments; these would become the nucleus of her novels. During the summer of 1920 Roberts had tried her hand at writing her first novel. "Sallie May" was never completed, yet Roberts described the characters as "less than an essence out of the soil. They are a word out of the clods" (Campbell and Foster, p. 35). This concept of characters and their relationship with the soil became the tenant farmers of her first and highly successful novel *The Time of Man* (1926), which took her three years to write. The novel was initially stalled when Roberts became ill, but her Chicago friends came to her aid by sending her to the Riggs Foundation for holistic medicine in Stockbridge, Massachusetts, in 1923. During her stay at Riggs, Roberts learned the craft of hand weaving, which was not only a recreation but a symbol for her of the intricacies of the creative process. To Roberts, "weaving is handwork." As in a story, "you have certain things you want to say. You may say them with words, or notes, or colors, or lines . . . or colored yarn" (McDowell, p. 26).

At Stockbridge, Roberts regained her health and was then able to finish *The Time of Man*, which was a Book-of-the-Month Club selection and both a popular and critical success. The book had been in her mind since 1919. Roberts wrote, "I began to think of the wandering tenant farmer of our region as offering a symbol for an Odyssey of man as wanderer buffeted about by the fates and the weathers" (Campbell and Foster, p. 129). Stylistically, the novel is, as Roberts wrote to Harriet Monroe, "as much within the province of poetry as it is within that of the novel." Her heroine, Ellen Chesser, is a woman wedded to the soil but not bound by it, who, despite poverty and disappointments, continually moves forward with her life. As Luke Wimble remarks in the novel when discussing Ellen Chesser, "She's got the honey of life in her heart."

Critics were enthusiastic about *The Time of Man*. Ford Madox Ford said it was "the most beautiful individual piece of writing that has yet come out of America" (Tate, p. 25). Success and relatively good health encouraged her, and Roberts rapidly completed three more novels: *My Heart and My Flesh* (1927), *Jiggling in the Wind* (1928), and *The Great Meadow* (1930). In *My Heart and My Flesh* another strong heroine, Theodosia Bell, travels from a world of aristocratic, privileged innocence through a series of deprivations and a near-death experience to a final rebirth. According to Roberts, "It is a story of a woman who went to hell and returned to walk among you."

As in *The Time of Man*, Roberts explores, much like Henry James and Herman Melville, the consciousness of her heroines. *My Heart and My Flesh* with its representation of sexuality also shows Roberts's familiarity with Freud. In the prologue to this novel, Roberts introduces an archetypal city and the character Luce. Both were to be the basis for a series of future novels spanning Kentucky's history; this plan never came to fruition.

Roberts saw *Jiggling in the Wind* as her *Midsummer-Night's Dream* between the *Hamlet* of *The Time of Man* and the *Romeo and Juliet* of *The Great Meadow*. But the critics did not like it. Louis Auchincloss described it as "one of the dullest novels ever written by a first-rank American novelist" (p. 130). *The Great Meadow*, however, was well received by critics and public alike and was a March 1930 Literary Guild selection.

In terms of conception, *The Great Meadow* was Roberts's earliest novel. As early as 1913 the idea of this novel had come to her, based on recollections of her Grandmother Brent describing how her Virginia ancestors came over the Wilderness Road, past Indians, through forests to "the great meadow" of Kentucky, where they founded forts at Boonesborough and Harrodsburg. Roberts also did a lot of research for this novel and crafted the story of yet another strong heroine, Diony Jarvis, who had to leave her home and travel into the unknown. As noted by J. Donald Adams in the introduction to Harry M. Campbell and Ruel E. Foster's study of Roberts, "Outwardly, its theme is the settlement of Kentucky by the pioneers who followed in the path of Daniel Boone; inwardly, it is the power of mind and will over the material world." In 1931 Metro-Goldwyn-Mayer produced a film version of the novel, starring John Mack Brown, which was described as "dim."

As a change of pace, Roberts turned to a lighthearted tale about a farm couple who discover a kettle filled with old coins. The inspiration for *A Buried Treasure* (1931) came from a brief news item, and the novel first appeared as a long short story in *Harper's*. Critics saw the novel as "dreary" and felt it signaled a downward turn in her writing.

While working on the novels, Roberts continued to write poetry and short stories. The stories were published in the *American Caravan*, *Harper's*, and *American Mercury*. In 1930 her short story "The Sacrifice of the Maidens" won second prize in the O. Henry Memorial Award contest for that year. This story, which was first published in *Letters*, the literary magazine of the University of Kentucky, was included in her first book of collected short stories, *The Haunted Mirror* (1932).

Roberts published two more novels: *He Sent Forth a Raven* (1935) and *Black Is My Truelove's Hair* (1938). Unfortunately, her health was rapidly deteriorating. In 1936 Roberts had been diagnosed with Hodgkin's disease. She published a second book of poems, *Song in the Meadow* (1940), and was working on an epic for stage or radio on Daniel Boone as well as a novel about the Great Louisville Flood of 1937, which she had actually experienced. As Frederick McDowell notes, "she was physically exhausted before she had exhausted her creative resources" (p. 28). Because of her health problems, Roberts, who never married, had begun wintering in Orlando, Florida. She died there of anemia, and her second book of collected short stories, *Not by Strange Gods* (1941), was published posthumously.

Despite a lifetime of illness, Roberts created a significant body of work. Unfortunately, Roberts is read little today. Only one novel, *The Great Meadow*, and both collections of short stories are in print. Initially a poet, Roberts is best known for her novels and short stories. In her fiction it is her poetic use of language, her strong female characters, and her Kentucky settings that make her writing unique. Yet her novels are not just about Kentucky and its people. They are timeless and universal in their treatment of the human condition and man's struggle with his world. Her work should be rediscovered not only because of her innovative style but also for her depiction of social history. Her knowledge of psychology contributed to the creation of strong female characters. Like the pioneer women of this country, Roberts's heroines suffer relocation, defeat, and despair, yet they also develop the inner strength to rebuild a life for themselves and their families on the land.

• The papers of Elizabeth Madox Roberts are at the Library of Congress. Three book-length studies that include biographical material and criticism are Harry M. Campbell and Ruel E. Foster, *Elizabeth Madox Roberts: American Novelist* (1956); Earl H. Rovit, *Herald to Chaos: The Novels of Elizabeth Madox Roberts* (1960); and Frederick P. W. McDowell, *Elizabeth Madox Roberts* (1963). For more information see the *Southern Review* 20 (Fall 1984), which includes ten essays devoted to her. Of particular interest are William H. Slavick, "Taken with a Long-Handled Spoon: The Roberts Papers and Letters," pp. 752–73, Lewis P. Simpson, "The Sexuality of History," pp. 785–802. Also in the same issue are personal remembrances, including Janet Lewis, "Elizabeth Madox Roberts: A Memoir," pp. 803–16, and Gladys Campbell, "Remembering Elizabeth," pp. 821–23. More recent critical articles are Linda Tate, "Against the Chaos of the World: Language and Consciousness in Elizabeth Madox Roberts' *The Time of Man*," *Mississippi Quarterly* 40 (Spring 1987): 95–111, and John J. Murphy, "Coming of Age and Domesticating Space in the Wilderness: Roberts' *The Great Meadow* and Cather's *Shadows on the Rock*," *Willa Cather Pioneer Memorial Newsletter* 33 (Fall 1989): 26–31. Chapters on Roberts are included in Louis Auchincloss, *Pioneers and Caretakers: A Study of 9 American Women Novelists* (1965), and Lewis P. Simpson, *The Fable of the Southern Writer* (1994). For a bibliographic essay see Linda Tate, "Elizabeth Madox Roberts," *Resources for American Literary Study* 18 (1992): 22–43. An obituary is in the *New York Times*, 14 Mar. 1941.

MARCIA B. DINNEEN

ROBERTS, Ellis Henry (30 Sept. 1827–8 Jan. 1918), editor, congressman, and financier, was born in Utica, New York, the son of Watkin Roberts, a factory worker, and Gwen Williams, immigrants from Wales. His father died in 1831, and consequently Roberts experienced a difficult childhood. He attended local schools. To support himself and earn money for more education, he learned the printer's trade in the office of William Williams in Utica. Roberts did the usual work assigned to beginners and had mastered the trade and saved money by the time his brother Robert W. Roberts, under whom he continued to work, purchased the office. Roberts attended Whitestown Seminary for two terms in 1845 before enrolling in 1846 at Yale College, where he won a scholarship, took prizes for English composition, and edited the *Yale Literary Magazine*. He graduated with honors from Yale in 1850 and returned to Utica, where he was principal of the Utica Free Academy and also taught Latin at the Utica Female Seminary in 1850 and 1851. He received a master's degree from Yale in 1853.

In 1851 two important events impacted Roberts's life. That year he married Elizabeth Morris; they had no children. He also became editor and part proprietor with his brother of the *Oneida Morning Herald*, a daily newspaper later known as the *Utica Morning Herald*. Because of political differences with his brother and dissension among stockholders, Roberts briefly left his position in 1854. Upon the urging of certain stockholders four months later, however, he returned as the sole editor, in which capacity he remained until 1889. His well-written editorials conveyed a sense of hopefulness and encouragement during the Civil War. Under his leadership, the strongly Republican newspaper became one of the most influential and widely circulated dailies in New York State.

In addition to his career in journalism, Roberts gained recognition for his political activities. In 1852 he gave his first political campaign speech in support of General Winfield Scott, the Whig candidate for president. In 1856 Roberts delivered several speeches in Oneida County for John C. Frémont of California, the Republican presidential standard-bearer. Four years later he campaigned for Abraham Lincoln for president. Devoted to Republicanism, he was a delegate to the 1864 and 1868 national conventions.

Roberts had a varied political career. In 1866 he was elected to the New York General Assembly from the Second Oneida District, garnering 3,193 votes to 2,643 for his Democratic opponent, James G. Preston. As a state legislator, Roberts played an active role as a member of the Committees on Ways and Means, Education, and Printing, and he went on record in favor of African-American suffrage. He also assisted in the successful candidacy of New York congressman Roscoe Conkling, his political ally, for the U.S. Senate. In

1870, after two earlier failed attempts to obtain the Republican nomination, Roberts won election to the U.S. House of Representatives from the Oneida district, receiving a plurality of 1,716 votes over Abraham B. Weaver, a Democrat. Two years later he was returned to the House, defeating Richard U. Sherman, the Liberal Republican and Democratic challenger.

Serving in Congress from 1871 to 1875, Roberts, a member of the important Ways and Means Committee, championed the refunding of the national debt, the redemption of bonds, the reduction of war taxes, and protective tariffs to shield American industries from foreign competitors. His speeches were especially noteworthy for their concise descriptions and analyses of national finance. On more than one occasion, he advised President Ulysses S. Grant on financial matters.

In 1874 the Democratic resurgence and Roberts's feud with Conkling cost Roberts his House seat. He lost the election to Democrat Scott Lord, a Utica lawyer, former Livingston County judge, and law partner of Conkling. The intraparty factional feud between the "Stalwarts," who befriended Senator Conkling, and the "Half Breeds," reformers who supported Roberts—a feud that concerned primarily the spoils of office and civil service reform, as well as Ulysses S. Grant's possible candidacy for a third presidential term—mirrored on the state level the fight that eventually disorganized the Republican party across the country. The breach between Roberts and Conkling never healed.

Roberts traveled widely throughtout his life and wrote books partly influenced by his travels. During his sojourns abroad in 1868 and 1873, he observed other governments, and he recorded his experiences in published essays and letters. After delivering a series of lectures at Cornell University in Ithaca in 1884, he put together a book, *Government Revenue: Especially the American System; An Argument against the Fallacies of Free Trade* (1884), which four years later was in its fourth edition. Roberts also compiled a two-volume study entitled *New York: The Planting and the Growth of the Empire State*, which was published in 1887 in the American Commonwealth series.

On 1 April 1889 President Benjamin Harrison appointed Roberts assistant U.S. treasurer, and during the subsequent four years, Roberts directed the subtreasury at New York City. In 1892 the presidential victory of Democrat Grover Cleveland ended any hopes Roberts harbored for continuing his work in New York City. He left his position in 1893, receiving praise from Secretary of the Treasury John G. Carlisle, a Kentucky Democrat, for the efficiency and admirable manner in which he had conducted the affairs of his office. That summer, at the beginning of a national economic depression, Roberts accepted the presidency of the Franklin National Bank of New York, where he remained until 1897. When Republicans regained the White House that year, President William McKinley chose Roberts to be treasurer of the United States. He continued in that office until 1905,

serving under Presidents McKinley and Theodore Roosevelt.

Upon his retirement in 1905, Roberts returned to Utica. For several years he contributed a weekly letter to the *Utica Daily Press*, in which he expressed his views on questions of the day. He closely followed the course of world and national events and addressed various groups, carefully memorizing most of his speeches. He remained active in several organizations, such as the Fort Schuyler Club, Oneida Historical Society, National Geographic Society, Cymreigyddion Society, Men's Society of the Church of the Covenant, and Washington Economic Society. Roberts died at his niece's home in Utica. His was a career of notable and distinguished achievement as an editor, writer, educator, politician, and statesman. He was a forceful factor in the affairs of his times and one of the most prominent citizens of Utica and New York.

• Roberts left no papers. Two of his letters are in the Boston Public Library. Others are in the manuscript collections of his contemporaries, including the papers of Benjamin Harrison, William McKinley, and Theodore Roosevelt in the Manuscripts Division of the Library of Congress. His speeches are in the *Congressional Record* from 1871 to 1875. For primary sources relating to Roberts, see James G. Blaine, *Twenty Years of Congress: From Lincoln to Garfield* (1884). For relevant secondary sources, see H. J. Cookinham, *History of Oneida County, New York* (1912), and David M. Jordan, *Roscoe Conkling of New York: Voice in the Senate* (1971). Obituaries are in the *New York Times* and the *Utica Daily Press*, 9 Jan. 1918.

LEONARD SCHLUP

ROBERTS, Frank H. H., Jr. (11 Aug. 1897–23 Feb. 1966), archeologist and government administrator, was born Frank Harold Hanna Roberts, Jr., in Centerburg, Ohio, the son of Frank Harold Hurd Roberts, a university professor and administrator, and Lou Ella Hanna.

Roberts received undergraduate training at Las Vegas (N.M.) Normal College and the University of Denver, where he received his B.A. in 1919. He majored in English and history. After a brief career as a Las Vegas journalist, he studied political science at the University of Denver, earning his M.A. in 1921, and at the same time studying anthropology under Etienne B. Renaud. He spent the next three years serving as an instructor of archeology at the University of Denver, performing archeological field work under Etienne B. Renaud and Jean Allard Jeançon, and working with the State Historical and Natural History Society of Colorado (whose collections would later form part of the Colorado State Museum holdings). Roberts then undertook graduate work in anthropology at Harvard University, where he received his M.A. in 1926 and his Ph.D. in 1927. He joined the staff of the Smithsonian Institution Bureau of American Ethnology (BAE) in 1926, and soon after he received his doctorate he married Linda Buchardt. The couple had no children.

Roberts's archeological career was divided into three phases. Between 1921 and 1933 his primary focus was the Southwest, especially the early development of Pueblo cultures. For this study he explored the Piedra-Pagosa region of southwestern Colorado. In 1926 he joined Neil Merton Judd's work at Pueblo Bonito and was assigned to work out the sequence of pottery. In 1927, as a newly appointed archeologist with the Bureau of American Ethnology, he excavated Shabik'eshchee Village in Chaco Canyon; in 1929 he was at Kiathuthlunna in Arizona; and in 1930 he was at the Village of the Great Kivas in Arizona. Roberts participated in the first Pecos Conference that worked out the time frame of Basketmaker-Pueblo cultures, and his explorations that followed demonstrated the validity of that sequence. For a brief time at the end of this period, Roberts was diverted from his main concerns to excavate mounds at Shiloh National Military Park in Tennessee.

In the second phase of his career, Roberts concentrated on the problem of early man in America. As early as 1927, he had become involved in this study when he was asked to examine the site of the original Folsom find. His examination convinced Roberts of the error of the widely held view—in the past stoutly defended at the Smithsonian—that man was a relatively recent arrival to the Americas. He began to collect all the supporting evidence he could find, corresponding widely with professional and amateur archeologists and following up promising reports by visiting sites. Thus he became an outstanding authority on the matter.

In 1934 Roberts began work at the Lindenmeier site in northern Colorado, a site with a particularly long period of occupation back to Folsom man. Lindenmeier occupied Roberts off and on until 1941. He also worked at an early site at San Jon in New Mexico in 1941, in the Agate Basin in Wyoming in 1942 and 1961, and at the Clear Fork site in Texas in 1943.

The third phase of Roberts's career began in 1944 when he and several other prominent archeologists became concerned with U.S. government plans to carry out a large-scale program of dam construction after World War II. Such a program troubled archeologists because many early settlements lay near streams and rivers, and these sites would disappear under the waters of newly created reservoirs. Concerned archeologists formed the Committee for the Recovery of Archaeological Remains. Roberts became their liaison with the Smithsonian as the committee began to urge action by government officials. The result was the Interagency Salvage Archeological and Paleontological Program (1946), involving the Smithsonian, the National Park Service, the Bureau of Reclamation, and the U.S. Army Corps of Engineers.

Roberts had become assistant chief of the BAE in 1944, and in 1947 he also became the director of the River Basin Surveys (RBS), the Smithsonian's part of the salvage program. Eventually the RBS became involved directly or indirectly in several thousand sites in twenty-five states. Not only did the RBS collect specimens and data and issue many publications, it also provided on-the-job training for a new generation of American archeologists. The RBS also became involved in the development of new methods, most notably C14 tests to aid in archeological dating.

Roberts was an associate editor of the *American Anthropologist* from 1932 to 1944 and an assistant editor of *American Antiquity* from 1935 to 1950. For much of the period between 1935 and 1949 he was the representative of the American Anthropological Association to the National Research Council (NRC) and served as an NRC vice president and chairman of the section for anthropology and psychology in 1952. In 1939 he became the U.S. representative on the League of Nations International Commission on Historic Sites and Monuments. In 1947–1948 he was on the visiting committee of Harvard College. In 1949 he was elected president of the Washington Academy of Sciences, and the following year he became president of the Society for American Archaeology (SAA). In 1951 he was selected by the SAA to receive its highest tribute, the Viking Fund Medal and Award. In 1952 he became a vice president of the American Association for the Advancement of Science. He became associate director of the BAE in 1957 and director in 1958. In the latter years he was also named a member of the advisory board for the National Park Service Weatherill Mesa project. He received LL.D. degrees from the University of New Mexico in 1957, the University of Colorado in 1959, and the University of Denver in 1962. He died in Washington, D.C.

Roberts was a man with a combination of admirable traits. His contemporary admirers attest to his great energy and considerable intelligence, both set to advantage by his scientific connections and social skills. His contributions to Southwestern archeology have been lasting. His studies of early man not only helped give legitimacy to an area of archeological concern but were also brave, considering that the center of opposition to the idea of early man in America was among senior colleagues at the Smithsonian. In addition, Roberts was a personification of the idea of the scholar-administrator. For many years he ran the central office of the RBS with minimal help, effectively taking care of broad planning, oversight of scientific work, and many detailed administrative arrangements. Robert L. Stephenson, a close professional associate, wrote that Roberts was an aristocrat in his own field, a man "universally respected and admired by all who knew him, . . . one of the most influential and most honored of American archaeologists."

• Most of Roberts's professional papers are in the National Anthropological Archives. These include Lindenmeier materials that reflect his own work and that of Edwin Wilmsen, who had been engaged to prepare a publication on the site; a fairly large set of his other archeological papers; documents in the records of both the Bureau of American Ethnology and the River Basin Surveys. The last named include a series that started as Roberts's file long before the RBS came into being. There is little about his personal life included in these sources.

The best single source concerning Roberts's life is Edwin Wilmsen's introduction to *Lindenmeier, 1934–1974: Concluding Report on Investigations* (1978). Obituaries include those by Neil M. Judd in the *American Anthropologist* 68 (1966): 1226–32; Robert L. Stephenson, in *American Antiquity* 32 (1967): 84–94; and Omer Stewart and John Greenway in *Southwestern Lore* 25 (1959): 1–6.

JAMES R. GLENN

ROBERTS, George Brooke (15 Jan. 1833–30 Jan. 1897), civil engineer and fifth president of the Pennsylvania Railroad, was born at the family estate, "Pencoyd Farm," near Bala, Montgomery County, Pennsylvania, the son of Isaac Warner Roberts and Rosalinda Evans Brooke. Roberts was born into an old and distinguished Philadelphia family of Welsh ancestry whose interests included coal, railroads, ironmaking, and farming. His early education was completed at the Lower Merion Academy, and at age fifteen he enrolled in the technical course at Rensselaer Polytechnic Institute in Troy, New York, where he completed the three-year course in just two years. This was followed by a year's postgraduate studies there, which he completed in 1851 at age eighteen.

Roberts accepted his first railroad job in March 1851 as a rodman in the Pennsylvania Railroad's engineering corps, then engaged in surveying and locating the railroad's mountain division through the Alleghenies. In 1852 Roberts became assistant engineer in charge of locating the route of the Sunbury and Erie Railroad, an independent line chartered in 1837. Roberts left the Sunbury and Erie in the spring of 1853 to spend a year and a half as principal assistant engineer of construction on the North Pennsylvania Railroad, laying out a line from Philadelphia to Bethlehem, Pennsylvania. In 1854 he moved to the Northwestern Railroad of Pennsylvania, where he spent three years as principal assistant engineer of construction. This line had been chartered in 1853 to connect Johnstown, Pennsylvania, with the Ohio state line.

Roberts moved to eastern Pennsylvania in 1857 to become chief engineer of the stillborn Allentown Railroad, and then from 1857 to 1862 he served as chief engineer for several small lines, including the Mahanoy and Broad Mountain, the Lorberry Creek Railroad (both anthracite coal hauling railroads in eastern Pennsylvania), and the Cape May Railroad in New Jersey. Through changing employment frequently, Roberts gained valuable professional experience and advanced his reputation as a talented and hard-working civil engineer.

In 1862 Roberts returned to the Pennsylvania as assistant to its president, J. Edgar Thomson. His duties included special assignments in engineering and construction and the acquisition of feeder lines. His work earned him the post of fourth vice president in 1869. In 1873 Roberts was advanced to second vice president and in 1874 was appointed first vice president under Pennsylvania Railroad president Thomas Scott. In this post Roberts had broad and varied responsibilities, including oversight of the company's many leased and subsidiary railroads. He also was in charge of construction, extension, and improvement of PRR lines and general supervision of the comptroller's department.

With Scott's resignation in 1880, Roberts was elected to fill the post. His extensive engineering experience and his work in managing finances, plus extensive tutelage under both Thomson and Scott, well qualified Roberts for the position of president, a post he held until his death.

As president, Roberts oversaw the workings of the United States' largest and busiest railroad, a system that reached from New York to Chicago and St. Louis, boasting more than 6,100 miles of main line track and serving the country's densest centers of population and industry. His term was marked by periods of tremendous traffic growth (freight volume tripled, passenger volume doubled) brought on by headlong industrialization. He also endured a terrible flood that wiped out the city of Johnstown, Pennsylvania, in addition to miles of railroad main line and branches, a severe economic recession in the early 1890s, and continuous national labor unrest.

During Roberts's term the Pennsylvania was relatively unscathed by strikes, a fact partially attributable to the company's relatively high wages, improving safety record, and paternalistic practices. Although he was accused of being tight-lipped, hard-headed, and aloof, Roberts took more than usual interest in the welfare of his employees. He was an active promoter of the railroad department of the Young Men's Christian Association, hoping to improve "the moral and intellectual condition of such of our employees as are brought under their influence." Roberts also founded the Employees Voluntary Relief Department to help support workers disabled by sickness or accident and to provide death benefits to families of deceased employees. (Employees made monthly contributions based on their wages.)

Perhaps Roberts's most serious challenge was maintaining the PRR's status as the nation's leading railroad in a period of unbridled, cutthroat competition among railroad corporations. This destructive competition took the form of rate wars (which drove revenues down) and rampant overbuilding, spawned by a desire to take over others' territory. In spite of these obstacles Roberts slowly and methodically developed the Pennsylvania system to handle expanding traffic. This included adding tracks to the railroad's main line, in many places four tracks wide; eliminating dangerous grade crossings; building new rail yards to expedite the handling of freight; constructing "cut off" tracks to bypass congested yard tracks and industrial zones in Philadelphia; and adding connecting tracks and freight lines around Pittsburgh.

Roberts also pushed the extension of feeder lines to serve coal mines, coke ovens, steel mills, and factories. He added 230 miles of new track in western Pennsylvania's bituminous coal fields, acquired a line to Wilkes Barre, Pennsylvania, the anthracite fields of northeast Pennsylvania, and coal fields and coke ovens in southwestern Pennsylvania. He constructed new harbor facilities on the New Jersey coast to handle increased exports of coal, grain, and manufactured products.

The PRR also acquired railroads linking Camden, New Jersey, with Atlantic City, providing Philadelphia and points west with access to the country's most popular seaside resort. In all, Roberts added about 3,000 miles of main line track to the railroad's system. The greatest triumph of his term, however, was the acquisition of the Philadelphia, Wilmington and Baltimore Railroad, which gave the PRR direct access to Washington and the South from Philadelphia and New York.

Roberts also engaged in some competitive building of his own. As part of an ongoing bitter feud with the Reading Railroad, he directed the construction of a branch line up the Schuylkill Valley to tap coal mines and other local traffic generated in the lower anthracite coal fields north of Reading. The Schuylkill Valley line was within sight of the Reading tracks for almost all of its 101-mile length.

Roberts oversaw construction and later expansion of Philadelphia's Broad Street Station, a massive monument to the power of the Pennsylvania Railroad, situated directly across from City Hall. The station was called the "Grandest Railway Terminal in America" by the railroad's publicity department.

During the 1880s Roberts faced the most serious threat to the stability of the PRR since the railroad's charter in 1846. Pittsburgh industrialists, finding that the PRR's virtual monopoly on transportation meant high-handed dealings, shortages of cars, and high shipping rates, joined with New York Central and Reading Railroad interests to finance, survey, and partially grade a new railroad line, the South Pennsylvania Railroad, across southern Pennsylvania. Completion of the line would have dealt a severe blow to PRR hegemony in its industrial heartland. Roberts vowed publicly to "smash the South Penn like a bubble." The Pennsylvania began acquiring an interest in the West Shore Railroad, a line in direct competition with the New York Central in the Hudson Valley.

This corporate warfare was disrupting the railroad securities market. In 1885 financier J. P. Morgan stepped in and arranged a conference between Roberts and New York Central president Chauncey Depew aboard Morgan's yacht, the *Corsair*. While sailing down the Hudson and off Sandy Hook the men reached an agreement, and the South Penn project was dropped.

In 1883 the New York Central did succeed in extending its lines into another Pennsylvania-dominated region, the Clearfield coal district of north-central Pennsylvania. To the south the Reading completed connections with the Western Maryland Railway, the West Virginia coalfields, and, ultimately, Pittsburgh and the Midwest. While these lines provided competition to the PRR, they did not challenge the railroad's dominance in the region.

In his personal life Roberts was involved in Philadelphia-area civic and church affairs. A devout Episcopalian, he was a member of the vestry of Saint Stephens in Philadelphia and was rector's church warden of Saint Asaph's in Bala, a church he supported generously. He was a director of the Free Library of Philadelphia and vice president of the Fairmount Park Art Association, and he held membership in the Pennsylvania Historical Society, the Sons of the American Revolution, and several social clubs. He was twice married, first in 1868 to Sarah Lapsley Brinton, who died in 1869 giving birth to their only child, and in 1874 to Miriam Pyle Williams, with whom he had five children. Held in high esteem by officials of other railroads, he served several terms as chairman of the Board of Presidents of the Trunk Line Association.

In politics Roberts shied away from public appearances but actively supported hard-money policies (the dollar backed by the gold standard) and opposed government control of railroads. On the former he remarked in 1895, "I tell you fellow laborers, that when you find that the dollar or dollar and a half which you receive for your day's labor . . . will buy you but one half the amount of flour . . . wheat . . . or beef that you can buy at present, then you will begin . . . to realize that while money is plenty, its value, is gone." On government control of railroads, he commented, "the history of such undertakings might be summed up in two words; partisanship and peculation."

In August 1896, while on a vacation trip, Roberts had a heart attack. He had a history of heart trouble resulting from his contraction of typhoid fever while working on the PRR's mountain division in 1851. After a long illness, he died at Pencoyd Farm. After his death, his archrival, Chauncey Depew of the New York Central, remarked, "a great railwayman, a conscientious and chivalrous gentleman and a patriotic citizen has been lost to the country."

Described by his contemporaries as modest and gentle "with a willingness to hear all sides of a question," Roberts slowly and unpretentiously kept pace with the nation's growing transportation demands. He was characterized as "quiet but effective" with "a sense of justice so keen that no one ever feared to leave to his decision the determination of what was right." Although called weak and cautious by his detractors, Roberts was committed to steady growth. He maintained the financial stability and preeminence of the Pennsylvania Railroad in an era of railroad failures, bankruptcies, and receiverships, a record many of his more flamboyant competitors could not equal.

• A summary of Roberts's life and career is in the official Pennsylvania Railroad histories, George Burgess and Miles Kennedy, *Centennial History of the Pennsylvania Railroad Company 1846–1946* (1949); William Bender Wilson, *History of the Pennsylvania Railroad Company* (2 vols., 1899); and briefly in H. W. Schotter, *The Growth and Development of the Pennsylvania Railroad Company* (1927). For a less complimentary view of Roberts, see Patricia Davis, *End of the Line: Alexander Cassatt and the Pennsylvania Railroad* (1978). A brief account of Roberts's involvement in the South Penn project is in William H. Shank, *Vanderbilt's Folly* (1964). An obituary is in the *American Engineer*, Mar. 1897.

ROBERT L. EMERSON

ROBERTS, Howard (9 Apr. 1843–18 Apr. 1900), sculptor, was born in Philadelphia, Pennsylvania, the son of Edward Roberts, a successful merchant, and Mary Elizabeth Reford. He was educated at the Classical Institute of the Reverend John W. Faires in Philadelphia. He probably began to study sculpture with Joseph Alexis Bailly at the Pennsylvania Academy of the Fine Arts in the same city in 1860 or 1861. Roberts exhibited a bas-relief titled *Cordelia* in the academy's 1863 annual exhibition and a piece titled *Cupid* in the 1864 exhibition. In 1864 he was elected an associate of the Pennsylvania Academy, a designation that allowed him free entry to the academy's school. He was active in the Philadelphia Sketch Club, which was formed in 1860 by students and alumni of the Pennsylvania Academy to promote comraderie among Philadelphia's artists and to hire live models once a week. Roberts served as the club's treasurer in 1865, as its vice president in 1871–1872, and as its president from 1873 to 1877.

Following the Civil War, in April 1866, Roberts and his friend, the painter and art critic Earl Shinn, departed Philadelphia for Paris. At the time, Paris was replacing Florence and Rome as the mecca for young sculptors. The Parisian or École des Beaux-Arts style, with its new naturalism and vigorous surface modeling, was quite different from the restrained, smooth surfaces associated with the neoclassical schools of Italy. In choosing to study in Paris rather than in Italy, Roberts allied himself with the vanguard American sculptors of his day. While awaiting entry to the École des Beaux-Arts in Paris, Roberts and Shinn spent the summer at the American art colony at Pont-Aven in Brittany. Prior to his admittance to the École that fall, Roberts studied for a short time in the private atelier of Charles Alphonse Achille Gumery. At the École des Beaux-Arts, under the tutelage of Augustin Alexandre Dumont, Roberts gained a sound understanding of the human figure and adopted the traditional academic interest in rendering the body with lifelike accuracy. Before returning home in 1869 he and Shinn toured Italy.

Back home, Roberts took a studio at 1731 Chestnut Street and was quickly favored with commissions from Philadelphia's high society. Although his works are primarily in marble, not bronze, they do display the active surfaces associated with the École des Beaux-Arts style. According to the custom of the time, Roberts usually employed skilled marble carvers to assist him in his work. However, he was an adept carver and often carried out some of the final carving and polishing himself. He was fond of calling his original clay model "the life," the subsequent plaster cast "the death," and the final marble piece "the resurrection."

In the early 1870s Roberts produced several ideal pieces drawn from literature. *Eleanore* (1870), an ideal

bust named after an Alfred, Lord Tennyson poem, was purchased by the Philadelphia art collector Henry C. Gibson and later bequeathed to the Pennsylvania Academy of the Fine Arts. Another early ideal bust, *Lucille*, was inspired by the work of author Owen Meredith, and a statuette of Hester Prynne and baby Pearl at the pillory (1872, location unknown) was drawn from Nathaniel Hawthorne's *The Scarlet Letter*. Although it wasn't carved in marble until 1877, Roberts modeled his lifesize *Hypathia* (Pennsylvania Academy of the Fine Arts) in 1873. Inspired by Charles Kingsley's 1853 novel, it is a stunning work that depicts the beautiful pagan philosopher turning to face the murderous band that has driven her into a church to slay her.

In 1873 Roberts returned to Paris for an eighteen-month-long sojourn to create *La Premiere Pose* (Philadelphia Museum of Art), his virtuoso depiction of a female nude supposedly captured at her very first sitting. When it was exhibited at the Centennial Exhibition in Philadelphia in 1876 it won Roberts one of three medals awarded to American sculptors. Despite its many admirers, it was criticized for its lack of a narrative content and for the immodesty of the figure's pose, which was thought to conflict with its title.

Roberts married Helen Pauline Lewis in 1876. They had one son, who was the model for *Napoleon's First Battle* (1876, location unknown). The sculpture depicted the young conqueror with his head propped on a pillow surveying the wreckage of wooden sodiers around him. In 1878 Roberts completed another major full-length figure, *Lot's Wife* (private collection), which captures the character being turned into a pillar of salt. Stylistically it is his most forward-looking work and exhibits a greater emphasis on geometry. The critic William J. Clark wrote of the piece, "It cannot be called beautiful, but it is most original in conception and execution, and, in spite of its grotesqueness, it is full of power and impressiveness" (Clark, p. 103). In 1878 Roberts also won a competition held among Pennsylvania's sculptors for a statue destined for Statuary Hall in the U.S. Capitol. Roberts's finished marble, which depicts the Pennsylvania inventor Robert Fulton, was installed in 1883. He returned to Paris often throughout his career and was on an extended stay there with his family when he died.

Roberts bridged the neoclassical and Beaux-Arts eras. He remained enamored of the polished white marble of the neoclassicists and shared with them a delight in the small details and accessories that provide narrative context. However, in his major works the paramount emphasis in not on sentiment or storytelling but simply on his technical mastery of the human figure. His tour-de-force representations of nudes in twisted and contorted poses is thoroughly Beaux-Arts modern.

• Howard Roberts's scrapbook (c. 1867–1894) filled with numerous newspaper clippings is preserved on microfilm at the Archives of American Art, Smithsonian Institution. David Sellin, *The First Pose: 1876, Turning Point in American Art;*

Howard Roberts, Thomas Eakins and a Century of Philadelphia Nudes (1976), is an important source. Biographical accounts appear in Lorado Taft, *The History of American Sculpture* (1903); Abigail Schade, "Howard Roberts," *Philadelphia: Three Centuries of American Art* (1976); and William J. Clark, Jr., *Great American Sculptures* (1878). An obituary is in the *Philadelphia Public Ledger*, 19 Apr. 1900.

MARY MULLEN CUNNINGHAM

ROBERTS, Jack (8 Dec. 1916–2 Apr. 1990), anthropologist and ethnologist, was born John Milton Roberts in Omaha, Nebraska, the son of John Milton Roberts, Sr., a roads engineer and contractor, and Ruth Kohler. The young Roberts attended public schools in Lincoln, Nebraska. He graduated from the University of Nebraska in 1937 and entered the University of Chicago Law School. After a disenchanting term, he took anthropology courses. He left in 1939 for Yale University, where he studied principally under Clellan Ford, Cornelius Osgood, and George Peter Murdock while working on the Cross-Cultural Survey, which evolved into the Human Relations Area Files. In 1941 Roberts married Marie Kotouc of Nebraska; they had two children.

An ROTC reservist, Roberts was mobilized in 1942 for World War II, receiving the Silver Star for gallantry in action and the Bronze Star for meritorious service and achieving the rank of captain on Europe's battlefield. Returning to Yale in late 1945, he conducted research for his dissertation among the Navajo of New Mexico in 1946, receiving a Ph.D. in 1947. That fall he joined the University of Minnesota's faculty. A year later he moved to Harvard University, but he did not receive tenure, and in 1953 he accepted a faculty position at the University of Nebraska. In 1958 Cornell University recruited him. That year his wife died suddenly; in 1961 he married Marilyn Skutt, with whom he had two more children.

Meanwhile, Roberts's Yale mentor had moved to the University of Pittsburgh, where an exceptional anthropology program was being built. After Murdock's retirement in 1971, Roberts accepted the distinguished Andrew W. Mellon Chair with a joint appointment in sociology; sixteen years later he was awarded emeritus status. In addition, he was a visiting scholar at the Center for Advanced Study in the Behavioral Sciences, Palo Alto, California; at the Naval War College, Newport, Rhode Island; and at the University of California's San Diego and Irvine campuses. Roberts served as president of the American Ethnological Society (1960), the Northeastern Anthropological Association (1965), the Society for Cross-Cultural Research (1974), and the Association for the Anthropological Study of Play (1979), and he ran twice for the presidency of the American Anthropological Association.

Roberts conducted relatively little field investigation after his early participant-observation among the Navajo and Zuñi, but throughout the 1980s he took research trips to Mexico with his Pittsburgh colleague Hugo Nutini, coauthoring several books. Roberts was a notable collaborator, drawing on extensive ethnographic data about numerous societies and subcultures—from East Asia and Latin America, to trapshooting women, African Americans, and other American ethnic groups—through joint efforts with more than sixty researchers of diverse disciplines and national origins over more than forty years.

Roberts's methodology was an eclectic one, transcending the observational frontiers of traditional anthropology. For example, introducing imaginative statistical correlations arrived at with the aid of then-incipient computer programs, Roberts rehearsed even experimental techniques—particularly in his studies of games in culture—which are normally more typical of psychology and other more experimentally prone disciplines. He was equally versatile in the topics he covered, from classical kinship, rituals, and child training, to values and questions of political and legal anthropology. Some of his intriguing findings had unsuspected practical applications, including the rehabilitation of gambling addicts, management, marketing, pilot training, and traffic safety.

In the perennial debate over whether anthropology belonged in the sciences or the humanities, Roberts decisively sided with the position that anthropology ought to be an objective behavioral science aiming at uncovering cross-culturally valid sociocultural (nomothetic) generalizations as universally valid as possible. This preoccupation drove him to develop the theory that he considered the epitome of what was then called "Newer Anthropology," a concept he identified as expressive culture and that he, more than anyone else, popularized in the sociobehavioral sciences. He proposed that all social institutions and cultural complexes—including material culture—have an emotional (not necessarily utilitarian) significance to the individual. His analyses engendered the Conflict-Enculturation Theory of Model Involvement, according to which affective (or expressive) activities such as ritual, performance, and games project subconscious archetypes of real-life situations. With other researchers, Roberts legitimized the anthropological study of play; a poker strategist himself, he generated the standard classification system of games into those of physical skill, strategy, and chance. He also brought into the academic mainstream the study of the culture of small, even temporary, groups, such as tourists and drivers.

Additionally, Roberts advanced the recognition of the complexity or diversity of cultural forms within every society. Culture theory now has to account for the mechanisms that keep such internal variation within limits, despite its dynamism. Roberts proposed, further, the seminal notion of culture as an information management system and thus redefined anthropology as "the science of cultural management." Moreover, he broke ground in documenting how individuals differ in processing their sets of accumulated cultural knowledge of their larger plural societies and their various subgroups.

Roberts's innovative approach made it difficult for him to publish in conventional anthropology journals;

he was better received among related disciplines—notably social psychology—and in interdisciplinary journals. He also faced obstacles in securing research funding, although shortly before his death, the National Science Foundation awarded him and an associate a grant to study the impact of technological change among Pennsylvania machine-shop workers.

In 1981 a group of colleagues and former students gave Roberts a surprise gathering. The resulting Festschrift contained twenty-eight papers by thirty-eight contributors and highlighted Roberts's pioneering contributions to anthropology as well as to other fields. In 1982 he saw his creativity acknowledged when he was inducted into the National Academy of Sciences. He served as its anthropology section chair until he became ill with cancer in late 1989; he died the following spring in Pittsburgh.

Paradoxically, while a methodological rebel, Roberts was rather conformist privately. Professionally, he lamented that his holistic vision for anthropology was challenged by fragmentation and politicization after the 1960s. In spite of personal reverses, he considered himself lucky; and despite his unusual accomplishments, there was a boyish shyness and humility to him, combined with self-deprecating humor and extraordinary gentlemanliness.

• Some of Roberts's most significant writings are "Three Navaho Households: A Comparative Study in Small Group Culture," *Papers of the Peabody Museum of American Archaeology and Ethnology* 40, no. 3 (1951): 1–88; with Watson Smith, "Zuñi Law: a Field of Values," *Papers of the Peabody Museum of American Archaeology and Ethnology* 43, no. 1 (1954): 1–175; with Eric Lennenberg, "The Language of Experience: A Study in Methodology," supp. to the *Journal of Anthropological Linguistics* 22, no. 2 (1956); with Malcolm Arth and Robert Bush, "Games in Culture," *American Anthropologist* 61, no. 4 (1959): 597–605; "The Self-Management of Cultures," in *Explorations in Cultural Anthropology: Essays in Honor of George Peter Murdock,* ed. Ward H. Goodenough (1964); "Belief in the Evil Eye in World Perspective," in *The Evil Eye,* ed. Clarence Maloney (1976); with Susan Natrass, "Women and Trapshooting: Competence and Expression in a Game of Physical Skill with Chance," in *Play and Culture,* ed. Helen B. Schwarzman (1980); and the posthumously published, with Hugo G. Nutini, *Bloodsucking Witchcraft: An Epistemological Study of Anthropomorphic Supernaturalism in Rural Tlaxcala* (1993). Biographical material on Roberts and overviews of his expressive culture approach, as well as a bibliography of his works, are in Ralph Bolton, ed., *The Content of Culture* (1989), a Festschrift for Roberts by a number of his colleagues and students. An informative obituary by G. Chick and H. Nutini appears in the *Anthropology Newsletter,* Sept. 1990, and a sketch by W. Goodenough in National Academy of Sciences, *Biographical Memoirs* 67 (1995): 1–15.

ROLAND ARMANDO ALUM
RALPH BOLTON

ROBERTS, Kenneth (8 Dec. 1885–21 July 1957), author, was born Kenneth Lewis Roberts in Kennebunk, Maine, the son of Frank Lewis Roberts, an unsuccessful businessman, and Grace Tibbets. Most of his boyhood was spent in suburban Boston, with different relatives of his mother. An aunt paid his way through a local private school and then Cornell University, where he managed to graduate in 1908 in spite of multiple extracurricular activities capped by editing the *Cornell Widow,* an agreeable chore that netted him $5,000. Within a year he joined the *Boston Post,* writing occasional news stories but specializing in humor, and by 1915 felt secure enough to marry Anna Mosser. They had no children. His income and literary output increased when the three famous humor magazines, *Puck, Life,* and *Judge,* began competing for his work, notable for its flip character and momentary pertinence. He soon found it wise to slacken his pace, moving to Kennebunk Beach and producing longer pieces for *Collier's* and the *Saturday Evening Post.*

When the United States entered the war in Europe in April 1917, Roberts joined the army as a captain in military intelligence, but was soon so bored by assigned duties in Washington that he volunteered for the American Expeditionary Force in Siberia, where he found copious material for articles. At war's end, the editor of the *Saturday Evening Post,* George Horace Lorimer, gave him a roving assignment to report postwar conditions in Europe. His first contacts, in Great Britain, were congenial, but when he moved on to Central and Southern Europe he was increasingly ill at ease, revealing in the reports he sent to Lorimer a strong conservative if not reactionary bias. (Later, he was in the front ranks of people who hated Franklin Delano Roosevelt.) The people in countries such as Hungary and Italy struck Roberts as being not only unable to govern themselves but far below Americans genetically and unqualified for American citizenship. Lorimer, an ardent opponent of unrestricted immigration, was delighted and encouraged Roberts, who was never one to mince words, to express his views at congressional hearings. He has been credited, in some quarters, with passage of the McCarren–Walter Act of 1924 that imposed severe limits on immigration from the countries he deprecated.

A quite different result of that same roving assignment, prompted by his discovery of how much he and his contacts in Great Britain had in common, was an impulse to learn all he could about his English forebears in Maine and immortalize them in fiction firmly grounded in history. Theodore Roosevelt, learning of that interest, issued a virtual order: "You write those books! I want to see those books written!" Of more practical significance was the readiness of Booth Tarkington, a summer resident of Kennebunkport and at the time the nation's highest paid author, to tutor him in the art of fiction. As Roberts insisted in one essay, "The Truth about a Novel," he wrote not a single word of *Arundel* (1930) until both he and Tarkington agreed that every narrative element—plot, setting, and character—was firmly and clearly established. The actual writing, of that and its sequels—*The Lively Lady* (1931), *Rabble in Arms* (1933), and *Captain Caution* (1934)—were then managed alone in a house on the west coast of Italy he virtually rebuilt by hand to serve as a winter retreat.

Superpatriots were indignant that he made Benedict Arnold the hero of *Arundel* and that later, in *Oliver Wiswell* (1940), he reported the Revolution as Tories must have viewed it. Such carping meant nothing to Roberts and little to serious reviewers and most readers. What did matter was that he maintained reader interest by his plot development; it was so rapid that only slow readers were likely to notice that his fictional narrators were usually types, his historical figures were one-dimensional, and his female characters were commonly insipid.

In 1935 Roberts turned from fiction to air his opinions on authorship in *For Authors Only, and Other Gloomy Essays*, which he followed in 1938 with his caustic *Trending into Maine*, excoriating the billboards lining its major highways. By then he could bask in the popularity of his finest novel, *Northwest Passage* (1937), which recorded the exploits of Robert Rogers and his Rangers, first in fighting the Indians and then in their search for the Northwest Passage. The book's longer first part was made into a successful motion picture, enabling Roberts to have a fine stone house built at "Rocky Acres," his Kennebunkport farm of more than a hundred acres bordering Tarkington's estate.

It was there that his final major interest, dowsing, developed after he needed reliable groundwater and found it with the help of a local dowser, Henry Gross. He promptly created a company, Water Unlimited, that successfully found groundwater not only in Maine but in distant places, for a fee. Gross even located veins of potable water in Bermuda by holding his forked stick over a map of that island. Skeptics were numerous, but Roberts responded to their derisive comments in letters to editors, extended articles, and even in three final books. "I can do more for my country by writing about my dowsing experiences," he once wrote, "than I can by writing fiction." It was a fitting conclusion to the career of this Kennebunk native renowned for his stubbornness, hot temper, profanity, virtually unlimited capacity for making enemies of friends and neighbors, and mastery of different kinds of writing. If there was one trace of sentimentality in his makeup it may have been his decision, in spite of the duties he had hated as an army officer, to be buried with fellow veterans in Arlington National Cemetery. He died at Rocky Acres in Kennebunkport.

In the year of his death, 1957, Roberts received a special Pulitzer Prize citation from Columbia University for excellence in historical writing. But he was deeply offended that neither *Northwest Passage* nor *Oliver Wiswell* was considered an important enough novel to be awarded the Pulitzer Prize for fiction.

• The Dartmouth College library contains the largest collection of Roberts material and includes typescripts, galley proofs, and/or page proofs of fifteen of his twenty-five published books. The library also has a special collection devoted chiefly to correspondence and other private papers, but it is sealed until the year 2006 because the documents contain material potentially slanderous. Yale has a respectable collection in the Beinecke Rare Book and Manuscript Library, and the Library of Congress also has an extensive holding.

The most detailed and comprehensive source of information about Kenneth Roberts is Jack Bales, *Kenneth Roberts: The Man and His Works* (1989), which includes a copiously annotated biographical essay. Roberts wrote what he called "Autobiography" in 1919; it was intended for the *Saturday Evening Post* but was never printed. "The Truth about a Novel" was published first in his *For Authors Only, and Other Gloomy Essays* and then again in his autobiographical *I Wanted to Write* (1949). It may be noted that Arundel was no toponymic invention by Roberts but the actual name of Kennebunkport prior to 1821. His three late books on dowsing, *Henry Gross and His Dowsing Rod, The Seventh Sense*, and *Water Unlimited* are all partly autobiographical. See also John Ira Fitch, Jr., "From History to Fiction: Kenneth Roberts as an Historical Novelist" (Ph.D. diss., Univ. of Illinois, 1965).

Roberts could hardly have complained about his work receiving inadequate attention from literary critics. He was reviewed by important critics such as Carl Van Doren, Frank Luther Mott, Ernest Leisy, and Howard Mumford Jones.

WILLIAM PEIRCE RANDEL

ROBERTS, Luckey (7 Aug. 1887?–5 Feb. 1968), ragtime, theatrical, and jazz pianist and composer, was born Charles Luckeyeth Roberts in Philadelphia, Pennsylvania, the son of William Roberts, an unaccredited veterinarian, and Elizabeth (maiden name unknown). His birth year is widely given as 1887, but writer Henry T. Sampson gives 1893. Roberts's mother died three weeks after he was born, and he was raised with the Ringolds, a family active in African-American show business. They brought him up as a Quaker, and accordingly he abstained from tobacco and alcohol throughout his subsequent career, even when running his own saloon.

In the 1890s Roberts toured in the role of a sleeping toddler with a troupe performing *Uncle Tom's Cabin*. He next appeared as a singer and dancer with Gus Selke (or Sulky) and His Pickaninnies, and the following year he joined Mayne (or Mamye, according to Sampson) Remington's Black Buster Brownies Ethiopian Prodigies, with which he remained for almost ten years, touring the United States and three times visiting Europe. In the course of his affiliation with Remington, Roberts added tumbling and juggling to his singing and dancing, and, far more significantly, at around age seven he began to teach himself to play piano. For some time he could only play in one key, F-sharp (that is, on the black keys), which served well enough to accompany the drum corps at Philadelphia's First Regiment Armoury one summer but caused some complaints from girl singers he accompanied in a carnival the following summer.

Around 1905 Roberts spent the summer in Baltimore, Maryland, where he exchanged ideas with pianist Eubie Blake at Joe Gans's saloon; took fighting lessons from Gans, a former lightweight champion boxer; and performed at Billy Williams's restaurant. During another vacation from annual vaudeville touring, he performed at the Green Dragon saloon in Philadelphia.

Roberts continued to tour in vaudeville, sometimes leading Luckey and His Brown and Blues and also serving as musical director and pianist in the Southern Smart Set Company of Salem Tutt Whitney and J. Homer Tutt. While touring with J. Leubrie Hill's My Friend for Dixie Company, he met singer Lena Stanford. They married late in 1911. Writer Terkild Vinding reports that Roberts raised ten children, but as the *New York Times* obituary mentions only one, it might be that Vinding conflated the daughter and the Robertses' several grandchildren and great-grandchildren.

Roberts composed "Junk Man Rag" in 1911. He could not yet notate music, but with ragtime pianist Artie Matthews's help he published the piece in 1913. Writers Rudi Blesh and Harriet Janis speculate that Matthews's involvement accounts for this composition's Joplinesque sound, uncharacteristic of Roberts. He also wrote "Pork and Beans" (also published in 1913), "Shy and Sly" (1915), and "Music Box Rag" (1914). William J. Schafer writes,

The three early Roberts rags share a paradoxical combination of Mozartian delicacy and driving rhythm. There are foreshadowings of the familiar "stride" bass in them, balanced against filigreed treble melodies of considerable intricacy. The printed scores do not convey the degree to which Roberts and the Harlem pianists would decorate the rags in performance [the sheet music to "Junk Man Rag" bears the label "simplified"], but the basic contrast of light and harsh sounds creates a brilliant pattern.

As a soloist in New York City, Roberts worked informally with Willie "the Lion" Smith, James P. Johnson, and others at the Jungles Casino in midtown, and he held a job at Baron Wilkins's nightclub in Harlem. Johnson recalled,

Luckey Roberts was the outstanding pianist in New York in 1913—and for years before and after. . . . Luckey had massive hands that could stretch a fourteenth on the keyboard, and he played tenths as easy as others played octaves. His tremolo was terrific, and he could drum on one note with two or three fingers in either hand. His style in making breaks was like a drummer's: he'd flail his hands in and out, lifting them high. A very spectacular pianist. [Davin, p. 12]

Throughout these years Roberts doubled as a pool hustler whose skills in this endeavor were as formidable as his playing.

While at Wilkins's, Roberts studied technical aspects of music with Melville Charlton, a pianist, organist, and choir director. He became involved in musical theater, writing individual songs and full comedies in partnership with lyricist Alex Rogers. Their work, extending into the late 1920s, was not especially lucrative or notable, apart from *My People*, for the fact of its being among the first African-American revues (1917). Around 1927 Rogers and Roberts also wrote for and acted in a popular weekly radio comedy, "The Two Black Crows," on WABC.

Even more obscure are Roberts's piano rolls. He punched three titles, including "Railroad Blues" for the Vocalstyle company in 1919 and two further titles

for QRS in 1923. Although he could reputedly outplay Johnson, Smith, and other jazz greats, Roberts did not participate in the first decade of jazz recordings, by one account because he did not need the money. Having earlier performed as an accompanist for the famous dance team of Irene and Vernon Castle, he gained entrance into American high society, and through the 1920s and 1930s he made huge fees leading dance orchestras in New York, Newport, Nantucket, Palm Beach, and other resort areas for America's wealthiest families and their visitors, including the Vanderbilts, the Carnegies, the Roosevelts, the Hearsts, the du Ponts, and the prince of Wales. Banjoist Elmer Snowden recalled playing for millionaires as a member of Roberts's group as late as 1935 to 1939.

Roberts took a stab at a blend of African-American and European orchestral music in compositions performed in concerts in New York at Carnegie Hall on 30 August 1939 and Town Hall on 28 May 1941. In the interim he suffered a serious automobile accident. Pianist Claude Hopkins recalled, "Both his hands were crushed. . . . He was wired up so each hand looked like a banjo for months, but afterwards he could play again" (Dance, p. 32).

For some time Roberts had been performing his "Ripples of the Nile," a composition so complicated that no other pianist attempted it. Around 1940 he slowed it down drastically to teach it to a student, and he realized that it sounded good as a ballad. With lyrics added by Kim Gannon and a new title, "Moonlight Cocktail," the piece was popularized by Glenn Miller's big band, which recorded it in 1941, and by Bing Crosby, who also recorded a version; members of the armed forces voted "Moonlight Cocktail" the number one hit in America in April 1942.

Roberts owned, operated, and often performed at Luckey's Rendezvous, a Harlem saloon, from 1940 to 1954. Known for his generosity, he had given out Christmas baskets anonymously during the Great Depression, and now he paid for a medical library at Harlem Hospital. He encouraged hopeful young musicians to perform at his saloon, and according to his piano-playing friend Smith, Roberts gave away so many free drinks that the business eventually failed.

On 18 January and 8 February 1946 Roberts was the pianist in an all-star traditional jazz group for the first two shows in the radio series "This Is Jazz," hosted by Blesh. That May, for Blesh's Circle label, he recorded "Railroad Blues" and his five durable compositions: "Ripples of the Nile," "Pork and Beans," "Shy and Sly," "Music Box Rag," and "Junk Man Rag."

Roberts's wife died in 1958, and that same year he suffered a stroke shortly before recording an album, *Harlem Piano Solos*. Later, a second stroke impaired his control of his left hand. In his final years he was writing a show, *Old Golden Brown*, to be presented concurrently with and without music. He did not realize this venture before his death in New York City.

Hopkins recalled that Roberts "was small, but he was a powerful man. He very seldom got angry, but when he did he was dangerous. . . . He was a swimming and boxing instructor at the Y.M.C.A., and I couldn't understand it when he took sick and died. He didn't look any eighty-one."

Roberts is a legendary figure in the transition from ragtime to jazz. By reputation he was potentially one of the giants of twentieth-century American music, but unfortunately he left little documentation in support of this position, owing to the absence of early recordings and the obscurity of his compositions and piano rolls.

• Henry T. Sampson, *Blacks in Blackface: A Source Book on Early Black Musical Shows* (1980), gives many unique details of Roberts's life. Surveys and interviews are Rudi Blesh and Harriet Janis, *They All Played Ragtime* (1950; rev. 4th ed., 1971), pp. 200–202; George Hoefer, "Luckey Roberts," *Jazz Journal*, Mar. 1963, pp. 7–9, 40; Dill Jones, "August in New York: Birdland, Charles Luckeyeth 'Lucky' Roberts," *Jazz Beat*, Sept. 1965, pp. 14–15; Bob Kumm, "Charles Luckeyeth Roberts: Discovery of a Disc," *Storyville*, Dec. 1967–Jan. 1968, pp. 30–31, 39; Terkild Vinding, "Forgotten People," *Second Line*, May–June 1970, pp. 329–31, 340; and William J. Schafer, "'Fizz Water': Ragtime by Eubie Blake, Luckey Roberts and James P. Johnson," *Mississippi Rag*, Dec. 1975, pp. 1–2. See also Tom Davin, "Conversations with James P. Johnson: 1912–1914," *Jazz Review*, July 1959, p. 12; Willie "the Lion" Smith, with George Hoefer, *Music on My Mind* (1964; repr. 1975), pp. 33–34; Claude Hopkins and Elmer Snowden in *The World of Swing*, by Stanley Dance (1974; repr. 1979), pp. 32, 61; and Al Rose, *Eubie Blake* (1979). A list of piano rolls is Mike Montgomery, "Luckey Roberts Rollography," *Record Research*, no. 30 (Oct. 1960): 2. Edward A. Berlin, *Ragtime: A Musical and Cultural History* (1980), gives a music example. Obituaries are in the *New York Times*, 7 Feb. 1968, and *Down Beat*, 21 Mar. 1968, p. 13.

BARRY KERNFELD

ROBERTS, Lydia Jane (30 June 1879–28 May 1965), home economics educator and nutritionist, was born in Hope Township, Barry County, Michigan, the daughter of Warren Roberts, a carpenter, and Mary McKibbin. She attended grade school and high school in Martin, Michigan. After graduating from high school (1898), Roberts obtained a Limited Teaching Certificate (qualification for teaching in only certain elementary schools) from Mt. Pleasant Normal School in 1899 and began teaching in rural Michigan. Her adventuresome nature led her to teaching positions in Miles City and Great Falls, Montana, before she returned to obtain her Life Certificate (qualification for teaching in all rural and urban schools) from Mt. Pleasant in 1909. She then taught third grade and served as a critic teacher, or supervisor of student teachers, in the local normal school in Dillon, Montana. Having observed a relationship between the health of her students and the quality of their diets, Roberts wanted to know more about the nutritional needs of children. To pursue this knowledge she entered the University of Chicago in 1915 at the age of thirty-six, ending her seventeen-year career as an elementary school teacher.

Roberts completed her baccalaureate degree in home economics in 1917 and remained at the universi-

ty as an instructor to contribute to a child nutrition education project. The project results enabled her in 1918 both to obtain a master's degree for work in applied nutrition and to be promoted to assistant professor.

As a member of the home economics faculty, Roberts collaborated with the university nursery and local clinics to provide the opportunity for her many students to do research and develop new education programs in child nutrition. After pursuing her own research on child nutrition for ten years, Roberts wrote her best-known work, *Nutrition Work with Children* (1927; rev. ed., 1935). On the basis of this book, which became a nutrition classic, the university awarded her a Ph.D. in 1928 and promoted her to associate professor.

In 1929 Roberts became head of a three-person committee to administer the department after the previous chair, Katharine Blunt, accepted the presidency of the Connecticut College for Women. After a national search, Roberts was promoted to professor and made departmental chair, a position she held until her retirement. During her years at the University of Chicago, Roberts, who never married, was supported in her work by her sister Lillian, with whom she lived.

Starting while at the University of Chicago, Roberts served on several important national committees, the most influential of which was the committee that established the first Recommended Dietary Allowances (RDAs) for the Food and Nutrition Board of the National Research Council, National Academy of Sciences. Roberts chaired the group that proposed the first recommendations in 1941 and continued to serve as chair of the RDA committee and as a member of the Food and Nutrition Board for several years. Roberts later wrote in the *Journal of the American Dietetic Association* (Sept. 1958) that the difficult task of consensus on the RDAs was accomplished because "the first allowances were developed democratically . . . all persons who had a basis for judgment concerning them had an opportunity to express it" (p. 904). Roberts also made important contributions as a member of the American Medical Association's Council on Food and Nutrition from 1934 to 1948. On both committees she was active in encouraging the nutritional enrichment of foods such as flour and bread.

With her many students, Roberts undertook both laboratory and community-based human nutrition studies, often conducted in normal living situations. In her 1937–1938 study of the value of increasing the daily milk consumption of children in a boarding school, she demonstrated that the growth, bones, and teeth of children drinking additional milk were improved over those who were not. For this work she received the Borden Award of the American Home Economics Association in 1938.

Roberts retired from the University of Chicago in 1944 and became the head of the University of Puerto Rico's home economics program. Building on her earlier survey of nutritional problems in Puerto Rico sponsored by the U.S. Department of Agriculture,

Roberts, with Rosa Luisa Stefani, associate head of the Department of Home Economics at the University of Puerto Rico, undertook a major survey of living conditions and food habits on the island. Their results served as the basis for subsequent teaching and research at the university and for nutrition education workshops. In 1952 Roberts received the Marjorie Hulsizer Copher Award from the American Dietetic Association, which honored her as an outstanding leader and teacher of human nutrition.

After retiring from the University of Puerto Rico in 1952, thereby ending her 35-year career as a university professor, Roberts continued public health work in Puerto Rico. She conceived and administered the widely emulated Doña Elena Project, named for an isolated village of about 100 families. Although it was a broad community development project, including work on roads, schools, homes, and electrification, the project was centered around nutrition education. A brother and a sister, he an agronomist and she a nutritionist and both graduates of the university, lived in the community for five years to supervise day-to-day work on the project. Impressive results led the Puerto Rican government to provide funds for similar projects in many other communities. Officials in international development agencies, including the Organization of American States and the Food and Agricultural Agency of the United Nations, learned of Roberts's work in Puerto Rico and sought her counsel. Stricken at her desk while working on a nutrition textbook in Spanish, she died in Rio Piedras, Puerto Rico. Roberts, who dedicated her life to the well-being of children, first as a teacher, then as a scholar, and finally as a public health worker, is recognized as an outstanding pioneer in the study of the nutrition of children.

• Roberts's papers are in the Sala Roberts, School of Home Economics, University of Puerto Rico. Bibliographies of her publications are in Margaret D. Doyle and Eva D. Wilson, *Lydia Jane Roberts: Nutrition Scientist, Educator, and Humanitarian* (1989), and Ethel Austin Martin, "The Life Works of Lydia J. Roberts," *Journal of the American Dietetic Association* 49 (1966): 199–302. Biographical accounts are by Doyle and Wilson (above) and Franklin Bing, "Lydia Jane Roberts—A Biographical Sketch," *Journal of Nutrition* 93 (1967): 3–13. Two later editions of *Nutrition Work with Children*, updated by Ethel Austin Martin, are *Roberts' Nutrition Work with Children* (1954; 1978). Among Roberts's other works are *The Child Health School* (1923), *What Is Malnutrition?* (1927), and, with the staff of the U.S. Children's Bureau, *The Road to Good Nutrition* (1942, 1944, 1947), all bulletins for the U.S. Children's Bureau, and, with Rosa L. Stefani, *Patterns of Living in Puerto Rican Families* (1949). The results of Roberts's work in the Puerto Rican village are given in her *The Doña Elena Project—A Better Living Program in an Isolated Rural Community* (1963).

PATRICIA B. SWAN

ROBERTS, Oran Milo (9 July 1815–19 May 1898), secessionist, governor of Texas, and jurist, was born in Laurens District, South Carolina, the son of Oba Roberts and Margaret Ewing, slaveowning farmers. At the age of three, Roberts moved with his family to St.

Clair County, Alabama. He graduated from the University of Alabama in 1836 and was admitted to the bar in 1837. The same year he married Frances Edwards; six of their seven children survived infancy. The young lawyer initially practiced in Talledega, then in Ashville, Alabama. Partial to the doctrines of John C. Calhoun, he was elected to the Alabama legislature in 1840. Seeking further professional and political opportunity, however, Roberts departed for the Republic of Texas the next year, settling in San Augustine. His practice thrived, and in 1844 Texas president Sam Houston appointed him district attorney. Roberts enthusiastically supported the annexation of Texas by the United States, and in 1846 the state's first governor, J. Pinckney Henderson, named him district judge. Roberts returned to private practice in 1851 and subsequently lived on a Shelby County farm. In 1857 voters elected him to the Texas Supreme Court.

Supporting southern unity against "freesoil aggression" (Bailey, p. 70), Roberts aligned himself in the 1850s with states' rights Democrats against more nationally minded Texans who identified with Sam Houston. Though not counted among Texas's fire-eaters, he apparently became convinced by 1860 that the election of a Republican president would warrant southern independence. Accordingly, as Abraham Lincoln's victory became apparent, Associate Justice Roberts began to plot strategy with similarly inclined politicians and made a much-publicized speech in Austin supporting secession. Now governor, Houston opposed precipitate action, so Roberts and his allies issued their own unsanctioned call for a secession convention. Gathering in late January 1861, the delegates chose Roberts convention president by acclamation. Roberts appointed a committee on public safety, which arranged for volunteer forces to seize federal property, evict U.S. soldiers from the state, and raise troops. After the electorate endorsed the convention's secession ordinance, the body deposed Houston because the venerable governor refused to swear allegiance to the Confederacy. Roberts had wished secession to be an orderly process and afterward made much of its constitutional justifications, but he never shrank from declaring that its essential object was to perpetuate the enslavement of an "inferior" race. Not a planter himself, neither was Roberts disinterested. He owned eight slaves in 1860.

Having done much to lay the groundwork for Texas's secession, Roberts left the court and in 1862 raised the Eleventh Texas Infantry. Colonel Roberts's regiment served in the trans-Mississippi and, in November 1863, saw action at Bayou Bourbeau. In 1864 Texans remanded Roberts to civilian life, electing him chief justice. The Texas Supreme Court dissolved with the Confederacy the following year, but Roberts remained politically active during "presidential" Reconstruction, his prominence suggesting Texas secessionists' unwillingness to step aside despite military defeat. Chairing the judiciary committee at the 1866 constitutional convention, Roberts introduced a measure allowing freedpeople limited legal rights, while also proposing that black southerners be resettled outside the region. During the subsequent legislative session, other erstwhile secessionists, less disposed to be conciliatory than Roberts himself, made the provocative choice of electing him to the U.S. Senate instead of a conservative who had opposed disunion in 1861. Roberts journeyed to Washington, D.C., in late 1866 but, like other southern senators and representatives–elect, was not seated by Congress. He spent the remaining years of Reconstruction practicing and teaching law in East Texas.

In January 1874 Richard Coke, the newly installed Democratic governor, returned Roberts to the helm of Texas's high court, and voters affirmed the choice in 1876. One of Roberts's distinguishing features on the bench was, a friend recalled, "his implacable hostility . . . to judge-made law" (Wooten, "Life and Services," p. 8). Roberts's predilection for judicial restraint prevailed most prominently in *Bledsoe v. The International Railroad Co.* (1874). By denying judges the right to compel the state comptroller to sign railroad bonds against his better judgment, the court refused to resolve a subsidy controversy that had badly divided Texas Democrats.

Four years later, a deadlocked Democratic convention turned to the respected but rather pedantic chief justice—a man, one party member declared, "that everybody laughed at and everybody loved" (Barr, p. 42)—as a compromise candidate for governor. Facing Greenback and "straight-out" Republican opponents, Roberts won 67 percent of the vote.

As governor, Roberts pushed "Redeemer" Democrats toward sterner choices than they had been accustomed to making. Having attacked both high taxes and the ballooning state debt during Reconstruction, Democrats had thereafter proved loathe to increase one in order to lower the other. Insisting on a "pay as you go" policy, Roberts set out to eliminate deficit spending and reduce the existing debt while holding the line on state property taxes. He sought to scale back spending on what he regarded as secondary tasks of government, most notably by vetoing the biennial public school appropriation. This dismayed many "progressive" or "young" Democrats and not simply Republicans and Greenbackers. The post-Reconstruction school system, already languishing in many areas, could ill afford cutbacks as Texas's population boomed.

Roberts's second "pay as you go" strategy proved equally controversial. Under the terms of annexation, Texas's vast public domain had remained under state control. Many Democrats hoped that by selling land to fund schools and by granting it to railroads and settlers, the state could promote a variety of worthy interests without making politically unpopular demands on taxpayers. But Roberts chose to emphasize sales over railroad and homestead grants, wishing that more land be disposed of quickly and the proceeds applied to the debt and schools in lieu of tax revenue. Laws were passed to allow sale of larger tracts at low prices with fewer requirements that purchasers settle what they

bought. Many condemned this policy, believing it favored speculators over actual settlers and squandered Texas's birthright for short-term gain.

Despite the uproar, many Texans endorsed Roberts's unflinching ordering of the state's priorities, and he easily won renomination and reelection in 1880. By the end of his second term, Texas had indeed reduced property taxes, cut its bonded debt, and eliminated the floating debt, but the state seemed unwilling to continue taking Roberts's medicine in its original dosage. The governor himself allowed educational appropriations to rise after 1880. Shortly after he left office, the legislature provided for a state tax for schools and for the more deliberate disposition of public land through price increases and further limits on the amounts that nonsettlers could acquire.

His grudging attitude toward common schools stood in distinct contrast to his enthusiasm for higher education, one of the signal accomplishments of his second term being the establishment of the University of Texas. After retiring in 1883, Roberts joined the university's faculty as professor of law. Ten years later he retired to Marble Falls, Texas, having married Catherine Border in 1887, after the death of his first wife in 1883. The "Old Alcalde" died in Austin.

If Roberts might be regarded as a statesman in insisting Texans choose slavery *or* the Union, retrenchment *or* a generous cultivation of education and economic development, he might also be seen as embodying tendencies that continued to hobble Texas long after his death: profound racial prejudice, the treatment of the state's rich human resources as secondary objects of public concern, and an excessive dependence on natural wealth—rather than any politically unpalatable marshaling of the power to tax—to underwrite government.

• The Center for American History at the University of Texas at Austin has a large collection of Roberts's personal papers. Official correspondence is in the Governors' Records (RG 301) at the Texas State Library (Archives Division) in Austin. For his supreme court opinions, see *Texas Reports*, vols. 19–27, 40–49. On secession, see Ernest Winkler, ed., *Journal of the Secession Convention of Texas 1861* (1912). Roberts's "The Political, Legislative, and Judicial History of Texas for Its Fifty Years of Statehood, 1845–1895," in *A Comprehensive History of Texas 1685 to 1897*, ed., Dudley Wooten, vol. 2 (1898), covers many developments in which Roberts himself played an important role. Other of his published writings include *A Description of Texas, Its Advantages and Resources, with Some Account of Their Development, Past, Present, and Future* (1881); *Our Federal Relations, from a Southern View of Them* (1892); the section on Texas in vol. 11 of Clement Evans's *Confederate Military History* (1899); and "The Experiences of an Unrecognized Senator," *Quarterly of the Texas State Historical Association* 12 (1908–1909): 87–147. Wooten, "The Life and Services of Oran Milo Roberts," *Quarterly of the Texas State Historical Association* 2 (1898–1899): 1–20, offers a contemporary assessment. The most extended biographical account is Lelia Bailey, "The Life and Public Career of O. M. Roberts, 1815 to 1883" (Ph.D. diss., Univ. of Texas, 1932). For more judicious discussions of his role in Texas political history, see Walter Buenger, *Secession and the*

Union in Texas (1984), and Alwyn Barr, *Reconstruction to Reform: Texas Politics, 1876–1906* (1971). Hans W. Baade, "Law at Texas: The Roberts-Gould Era (1883–1893)," *Southwestern Historical Quarterly* 86 (1982–1983): 161–96, treats Roberts's later years.

PATRICK G. WILLIAMS

ROBERTS, Owen Josephus (2 May 1875–17 May 1955), U.S. Supreme Court justice, was born in Germantown, Pennsylvania, the son of Josephus R. Roberts, a hardware merchant, and Emma E. Lafferty. Roberts was educated at the Germantown Academy and the University of Pennsylvania, where he was a Phi Beta Kappa graduate in 1895 at the age of twenty. He entered the University of Pennsylvania Law School, becoming an associate editor of the *American Law Register* in 1897–1898 and graduating with the highest honors in 1898. On his admission to the bar he joined a law firm in Philadelphia while also teaching at the University of Pennsylvania Law School. During his twenty-two years at the law school, Roberts taught the basic courses in contracts and real property, among others, and attained the rank of full professor in 1907. In 1903 he was appointed first assistant district attorney for Philadelphia County, a position he held for three years before resigning to continue his private law practice. Roberts married Elizabeth Rogers in 1904, a union that produced one daughter. In 1918 Roberts accepted appointment as special deputy U.S. attorney and prosecuted violations of the Espionage Act of 1917.

Roberts first came to national attention in 1924, when President Calvin Coolidge appointed him a special U.S. attorney with the responsibility, in association with fellow special U.S. Attorney Atlee Pomerene, of prosecuting those involved in the Teapot Dome oil reserve scandals that had occurred during the administration of President Warren Harding. Roberts mustered the evidence that led to the successful prosecution and conviction for bribe-taking of Albert B. Fall, the former secretary of the interior in the Harding administration.

In 1930 the sudden deaths of Chief Justice William Howard Taft and Justice Edward T. Sanford created two vacancies on the U.S. Supreme Court. President Herbert Hoover nominated Charles Evans Hughes to become the new chief justice and Judge John J. Parker of the U.S. Court of Appeals for the Fourth Circuit to replace Sanford. The U.S. Senate confirmed the nomination of Hughes, but after a rancorous battle rejected Parker, 41 to 39.

Two days later the president nominated Roberts for the Sanford vacancy. The Senate Judiciary Committee unanimously endorsed the nomination, and on 20 May the Senate confirmed in less than a minute and without a roll-call vote. Roberts took the oath of office and assumed his seat on the Supreme Court on 2 June 1930. Within a few years he became a central figure in the constitutional crisis of the New Deal era.

The Supreme Court had been dominated during the 1920s by a solid, six-member conservative bloc, but the deaths of Taft and Sanford reduced the conservative bloc to four justices—George Sutherland, Pierce Butler, James McReynolds, and Willis Van Devanter. Considered more liberal on constitutional issues were Justices Louis Brandeis, Oliver Wendell Holmes, Jr., and Harlan F. Stone. The retirement of Holmes in 1932, and his replacement by Benjamin N. Cardozo, did not change the ideological makeup of the Court. With the Court divided four to three along ideological lines, Chief Justice Hughes and Justice Roberts were the Court's "swing votes," because their votes when added to either the conservative or liberal bloc would determine the outcome of the Court's decisions in closely divided cases.

With Roberts on the Court, the trend of decisions indicated that the Court was quite different from the conservative Court of the 1920s. In 1931, for example, it explicitly held in *Stromberg v. California* and *Near v. Minnesota*, with Hughes and Roberts in the majority, that freedom of speech and freedom of the press were rights guaranteed from impairment by the states by the Fourteenth Amendment of the Constitution. The rights in the Bill of Rights had hitherto been held to apply as restrictions on the federal government alone, but after the *Stromberg* and *Near* decisions the trend was to make most of the rights in the Bill of Rights applicable to the states via the Fourteenth Amendment.

Decisions by the Hughes Court in the area of criminal procedure were also marked by a liberal departure from prior decisions. In *Powell v. Alabama* (1932), the Court for the first time ruled that the Fourteenth Amendment guaranteed to indigent defendants the right to have counsel appointed for their defense in state criminal trials for capital offenses, and in noncapital cases as well if the lack of counsel for the defendant would lead to an unfair trial. In *Brown v. Mississippi* (1936), the Court held for the first time that the use of coerced confessions against criminal defendants in state trials denied due process of law and required the reversal of convictions obtained by such methods.

On questions of the constitutional validity of governmental regulation of economic affairs, which would constitute the central constitutional question during the 1930s, the Hughes Court also deviated, at least for a time, from the trend of decisions in the 1920s. In 1934, with Justice Roberts writing for a narrow majority of five, the Court upheld a New York law fixing the minimum price of milk, which was intended to rescue the state's depression-plagued dairy farmers. That same year, with Roberts again in a narrow majority of five, the Court upheld a Minnesota law allowing extensions of time during which real estate owners could pay off their mortgages.

With the election of Franklin D. Roosevelt as president in 1932 and the initiation of his New Deal programs to combat the depression, however, the Court was confronted with the problems of determining the scope of the federal government's power to control the economy and whether to construe the congressional power to regulate commerce and to tax and spend broadly or narrowly. As challenges to New Deal legislation came before the Court in 1935 and 1936, Hughes or Roberts or both joined the four conservatives to invalidate key parts of Roosevelt's program.

With Roberts writing for the majority, the Court invalidated the Railroad Retirement Act of 1933, which provided pensions to railroad employees. The act was based on the commerce power, but the majority followed precedent that narrowly construed congressional power over commerce and held that the act was not a valid regulation of interstate commerce. A unanimous Court in *Schechter Poultry Corp. v. United States* (1935) again adopted a narrow interpretation of the commerce power and invalidated the centerpiece of the New Deal, the National Industrial Recovery Act of 1933. The Court held that Congress had not only overreached its power to regulate commerce but had also unconstitutionally delegated power to the executive branch.

The Agricultural Adjustment Act of 1933, designed to alleviate the depression in agriculture by payments to farmers to reduce the acreage producing major agricultural commodities, was based on the congressional power to tax and spend rather than the commerce power. Writing for a majority of six in *United States v. Butler* (1936), Roberts held that the power to tax and spend was an independent grant of power to Congress to promote the general welfare, thus adopting a broad view of that congressional power. However, Roberts held that agricultural production was a local activity beyond the legitimate reach of congressional power and the Agricultural Adjustment Act was therefore unconstitutional. Defending the Court's power of judicial review, Roberts asserted that in exercising that power the Court's only duty was to lay "the article of the Constitution which is invoked beside the statute which is challenged and to decide whether the latter squares with the former." This characterization of judicial power was attacked as an example of "mechanical jurisprudence" that denied or concealed the policy-making power the Court in fact exercised through judicial review.

In 1936 the Court also invalidated the Bituminous Coal Conservation Act, which regulated coal production and labor relations in the coal fields. With Roberts once again in the majority, the Court held that coal production and labor relations associated with it were local activities beyond the legitimate scope of congressional power to regulate interstate commerce. In *Morehead v. New York* (1936), with Roberts joining a narrow majority of five, the Court invalidated New York's minimum wage law for women as violating the due process right to liberty of contract. The *Morehead* decision was based on the Court's earlier decision in *Adkins v. Children's Hospital* (1923) that had invalidated a similar minimum wage law for women in the District of Columbia.

Although the Court appeared to be an insuperable barrier to the implementation of many of his New Deal programs, President Roosevelt nevertheless overwhelmingly won reelection in 1936. In February 1937 Roosevelt proposed legislation that would authorize him to appoint six additional justices to the Court. During the spring and summer of 1937 this "court-packing" plan became the central issue in an increasingly contentious national debate while additional New Deal programs were challenged before the Court.

Although Roberts had joined the majority to invalidate New York's minimum wage law in 1936, on 29 March 1937, in *West Coast Hotel v. Parrish*, he joined the dissenters in *Morehead* to uphold a Washington State minimum wage law for women. Roberts's change of position on the validity of minimum wages was soon heralded as the "switch in time that saved nine" from Roosevelt's court-packing scheme. In a memorandum published after his death, Roberts maintained that counsel for New York in the 1936 *Morehead* case had not asked the Court to reverse its decision in the 1923 *Adkins* case, but rather had sought to distinguish it. When the reversal of *Adkins* was squarely presented in the *Parrish* case, he voted to reverse *Adkins* and uphold minimum wages, an action he contended he was prepared to take all along.

If that were indeed his position, Roberts need only have concurred in the *Morehead* case on the narrow basis on which he joined the majority, but he failed to do so. It was nevertheless inaccurate to attribute his apparent about-face on minimum wages to the court-packing plan. The vote in the *Parrish* case with Roberts joining the majority had in fact occurred well before Roosevelt's introduction of the court-packing measure. The decision in the *Parrish* case was delayed until March 1937 because of the illness of Justice Stone, who joined the majority in upholding minimum wages.

The Court continued to dismantle the barriers it had erected against the New Deal programs when Hughes and Roberts aligned themselves with the liberal bloc. In April the Court upheld the validity of the National Labor Relations Act of 1935, now adopting a broad interpretation of the commerce power that it had previously rejected. Subsequently, the Court upheld the Social Security Act of 1935 as a valid exercise of the power of Congress to tax and spend to promote the general welfare. In 1941 the Court additionally sustained the validity of the Fair Labor Standards Act of 1938 and a reenacted Agricultural Adjustment Act in 1942, relying on a broad view of the congressional commerce power.

After the "constitutional revolution" of 1937, Justice Willis Van Devanter, one of the staunch conservatives on the Court, announced his retirement. President Roosevelt was thus assured of his first appointment to the Court, and indeed by the early 1940s he had appointed a majority of the justices and had guaranteed the permanence of the Court's 1937 shift in constitutional doctrine. Van Devanter's retirement also diminished support for the court-packing plan, which was defeated in the Senate during the summer of 1937.

As a member of the reconstituted Court during the 1940s, Roberts was confronted with issues of civil rights and civil liberties that increasingly became the focus of the Court's agenda. Writing for a unanimous Court in 1940, Roberts held that religious freedom was protected from deprivation by the states, thus continuing the trend of applying the Bill of Rights to the states. In 1935 Roberts had written the opinion upholding the validity of white primaries in the South, despite their obvious use as a method of excluding blacks from the electoral process, and he strongly protested when the Court repudiated that ruling in 1944 and held the white primary unconstitutional. Roberts joined the majority in upholding compulsory flag salutes and pledges of allegiance in the public schools in 1940, over objections that the practice violated religious liberty, and he dissented when the Court reversed its position on that issue in 1943.

In 1942 Roberts wrote the majority opinion in *Betts v. Brady*, limiting the right to counsel recognized by the Court in *Powell*. The right to counsel in state criminal cases, he held, applied only in those cases in which the lack of counsel for an indigent defendant would result in an unfair trial, a rule that prevailed until reversed in *Gideon v. Wainwright* (1963). Also in 1942, however, he again supported civil liberties, vehemently dissenting from the Court's decision upholding the forced evacuation of Japanese Americans from the West Coast during World War II. Roberts was also chosen by President Roosevelt to chair the commission that investigated the American disaster at Pearl Harbor.

In June 1945 Roberts announced his resignation from the Court, and Chief Justice Stone drafted a customary letter of farewell. Apparently because of Roberts's controversial role in the constitutional crisis of 1937, Justice Black objected to Stone's expression of regret at Roberts's resignation and to a phrase that Roberts had "made fidelity to principle your guide to decision." Other justices, particularly Felix Frankfurter, refused to sign a letter that deleted the language Black objected to; in the end the customary letter of farewell to Roberts was not sent.

In retirement, Roberts served as dean of the University of Pennsylvania Law School from 1948 to 1951 and as the chair of the security board of the Atomic Energy Commission. He also served as the president of the Pennsylvania Bar Association, president of the 1946 general convention of the Episcopal house of deputies, and president of the American Philosophical Society. In 1951 Roberts delivered the Holmes lectures at Harvard University, which were subsequently published that same year as *The Court and the Constitution*, and in 1953 he served as chair of the Fund for the Advancement of Education. Most of his energy in his later years was devoted to the cause of world federalism as a means of ensuring world peace. Roberts died in West Vincent Township, Chester, Pennsylvania.

The service of Owen J. Roberts as a member of the Supreme Court would always be remembered for his famous "switch in time that saved nine" during the constitutional crisis of 1937, an event that affected his treatment by the Court at his resignation in 1945. Roberts was a solid lawyer with relatively moderate positions on major constitutional issues, but it was his fate to serve on the Court when the constitutional doctrines of an earlier era proved inadequate to the needs of a national economy in crisis. While he contributed to the constitutional crisis in 1937, it is to his credit that he recognized that a modification of constitutional law was required to meet the exigencies of the time, and albeit belatedly he came to support that necessary modification. Himself a modest individual, Roberts perhaps best summed up his career on the Court when on the occasion of his retirement, he remarked that he had "no illusion about my judicial career." Said Roberts, "Who am I to revile the good God that did not make me a Marshall, a Taney, a Bradley, a Holmes, a Brandeis, or a Cardozo?"

• There appear not to be any Roberts papers; nor is there a full-length biography of Owen J. Roberts. An overall assessment of his judicial career may be found in Charles A. Leonard, *A Search for a Judicial Philosophy: Mr. Justice Roberts and the Constitutional Revolution of 1937* (1971). An explanation of his behavior during the constitutional crisis of 1937 and his votes in the 1936 and 1937 minimum wage cases was offered by Roberts in a memorandum he left in the keeping of Justice Felix Frankfurter. This memorandum was published after Roberts's death in Frankfurter, "Mr. Justice Roberts," *University of Pennsylvania Law Review* 104 (1955–1956): 311–17. Further assessments of various facets of Roberts's life may be found in Erwin N. Griswold, "Owen J. Roberts as a Judge," and Robert T. McCracken, "Owen J. Roberts—Master Advocate," both in *University of Pennsylvania Law Review* 104 (1955–1956): 322–31; 332–49. Other assessments of Roberts are Jay S. Bybee, "Owen J. Roberts," in *The Supreme Court Justices*, ed. Clare Cushman (1993), and David Burner, "Owen J. Roberts," in *The Justices of the United States Supreme Court: Their Lives and Major Opinions*, ed. Leon Friedman and Fred L. Israel, vol. 3 (1969), pp. 2253–63. An extensive, substantive obituary is in the *New York Times*, 18 May 1955.

RICHARD C. CORTNER

ROBERTS, Richard Brooke (7 Dec. 1910–4 Apr. 1980), physicist and biochemist, was born in Titusville, Pennsylvania, the son of Erastus Titus Roberts, a banker, and Helen Troth Chambers. The family moved to Princeton, New Jersey, in 1916 and to New York City in 1921. Roberts attended private schools in both locations and developed an interest in science and mathematics.

Roberts received his A.B. in 1932 and his Ph.D. in 1937 from Princeton. In 1935 he married Adeline Furness; they had two children. After their divorce in 1946, he married Irena Zuzanna Eiger in 1948; they had a son. After Irena's death in 1966, he married Josephine Taggart Rice in 1967; they had no children. He joined the Department of Terrestrial Magnetism at the Carnegie Institution of Washington, D.C., in 1936, where he entered research in nuclear physics in a small group led by Merle Tuve. Roberts and Norman Heydenburg discovered the radioisotope beryllium-7 (^7Be), concerning which there had been substantial conjecture because of its theoretical importance in one of the proposed methods for stellar energy generation. This isotope decays by capturing one of its orbital atomic electrons, a process that directly emits only a neutrino and an X-ray for detection—both of which were impossible to observe with the apparatus available at the time. Ten percent of the decays of ^{7}Be leave the residual lithium-7 (^{7}Li) in an excited nuclear state, which decays with an easily observed gamma ray.

Two days after Niels Bohr reported at a Washington conference the radio-chemical evidence of Otto Hahn and Fritz Strassmann for uranium fission, Roberts demonstrated the phenomenon to Bohr and Enrico Fermi, among others. Two weeks later he discovered delayed neutrons. Generally the uranium nuclei emit neutrons the instant they undergo fission, but a few of the beta fission fragments decay to an isotope that emits a neutron. As a result, a few fission neutrons are delayed. Without delayed neutrons it is possible to make nuclear explosives but not nuclear reactors.

Because of his fission work, Roberts took part in the first meetings of President Franklin D. Roosevelt's Advisory Committee on Uranium, which initiated the atomic bomb program. He and Tuve were greatly affected by the Battle of Britain during the summer of 1940 and saw a greater need for improving antiaircraft defense than for making a weapon that even if feasible would not in their opinions alter the outcome of the war. When Roberts demonstrated that an electron tube could withstand the accelerations experienced by projectiles of modern artillery, he and Tuve sketched the design of their "proximity fuze" and immediately initiated its development at their Carnegie department.

The research was continued later at the Johns Hopkins University Applied Physics Laboratory, which Tuve organized. The fuze had a small radio transmitter and utilized the reflections of its waves from an aircraft target to detonate an artillery shell when near enough to cause damage. This fuze, along with gun-laying radars and electronic directors, made antiaircraft artillery deadly accurate—an enormous change from 1939, when it was generally disregarded as an effective mode of defense. Introduced into combat only twenty-eight months after the first preliminary experiments, the fuze reduced greatly the danger to the fleet from air attack. It altered the course of the war in the Pacific and helped put an end to the flying bomb attacks on London and Antwerp in 1944.

By September 1946 Roberts was in charge of a military research group numbering 1,000, but along with Tuve he chose to return to the Carnegie Institution, where he remained for the rest of his life. Before the war Roberts had developed an interest in applying isotopes to research in biology, having made an experiment with L. B. Flexner on the rates of placental transfer of sodium-24 (^{24}Na) from the maternal to the fetal circulation. His interest in biology increased after he participated in a bacteriophage course given at Cold Spring Harbor, New York, in 1947; in 1946 he had joined P. H. Abelson and D. B. Cowie in the Department of Terrestrial Magnetism's new biophysics sec-

tion. Before leaving nuclear physics, however, he and Abelson reported the first unequivocal experimental evidence that some deuteron-induced reactions do not pass through a compound nucleus. This model for nuclear reactions had been proposed by Niels Bohr and asserts that a bombarding particle such as a proton, neutron, or deuteron first forms a compound nucleus that exists so long that all memory of the manner of its formation is lost. Later explanations of their data resulted in a completely new theory of nuclear reactions.

Roberts was attracted to the simple system of the bacterium *Escherichia coli* and used it with carbon-14 (^{14}C) to deduce the pathways of synthesis in cells and calculate the carbon flow along each pathway. Two processes of synthesis were recognized: feedback inhibition and enzyme repression. In 1955 he and his colleagues published the monograph *Studies of Biosynthesis in Escherichia coli*, which remains a handbook of the many researchers using this bacterium. While following closely the work of his associates in the study of macromolecules, nucleic acid interactions, and repeated DNA sequences, Roberts's personal investigations shifted to the biochemical basis of long-term memory in the brain, once again in collaboration with L. B. Flexner and J. B. Flexner. They observed that protein synthesis proceeded at a sufficiently rapid pace in the brain to account for the connections among neurons. This led to the discovery of memory inhibition and restoration techniques through the use of catecholamines and peptides.

Roberts devoted a great deal of time to the problems of disarmament. He became an organizing member of the Science and Technology Committee of the Democratic Advisory Council in 1957, which in turn initiated the organization of the Arms Control and Disarmament Agency, on which he served as a consultant. He was a member of the National Academy of Sciences, received the Presidential Medal of Merit in 1947, and was president of the Biochemical Society in 1964–1965.

Roberts distinguished himself in three greatly different fields of endeavor: experimental nuclear physics, weapons technology, and biophysics. He enthusiastically attempted research in other subjects and was not troubled when they failed to yield a new insight. His approach to science was always that of a happy amateur. Roberts died in Washington, D.C.

• Roberts's life is portrayed with a list of his scientific publications in Roy J. Britten, "Richard Brooke Roberts," in National Academy of Sciences, *Biographical Memoirs* 62 (1993): 327–48. His important papers on nuclear physics are Roberts and N. P. Heydenburg, "Formation of ^{7}Be," *Physical Review* 53 (1938): 929; Roberts et al., "The delayed neutron emission which accompanies fission of uranium and thorium," *Physical Review* 55 (1939): 664; and Roberts and P. H. Abelson, "(d,n) reactions at 15 MeV," *Physical Review* 72 (1947): 76. The invention of the proximity fuze is described in Ralph B. Baldwin, *The Deadly Fuze: Secret Weapon of World War II* (1980). Other important biochemical papers are L. B. Flexner and Roberts, "The measurement of placental permeability with radioactive sodium," *American Journal of Physiology*

128 (1939): 154–59; L. B. Flexner et al., "Loss of recent memory in mice as related to regional inhibition of cerebral protein synthesis," National Academy of Sciences, *Proceedings* 52 (1964): 1165–69.

LOUIS BROWN

ROBERTS, Robert Richford (2 Aug. 1778–26 Mar. 1843), bishop in the Methodist Episcopal church, was born in Frederick County, Maryland, the son of Robert Morgan Roberts and Mary Richford, farmers. In 1785 the large family moved to the Ligonier Valley of western Pennsylvania, settling in Westmoreland County. Roberts attended school in Maryland from age four to seven, and with the exception of one winter in his late teens, he received no other formal instruction. Before they left Maryland, their Anglican priest had warned them against Methodists; he could not have imagined that their seven-year-old boy would later shepherd the church the priest found "peculiarly dangerous." Roberts's mother, however, took him to a Methodist service in 1778, and she converted; despite their father's objections, several of the children began to frequent Methodist worship. Within two or three years their home was hosting a constant traffic of itinerant preachers, who began to cultivate young Roberts as a prospective minister. At age fourteen he listened to one of his sisters praying for her salvation in the woods and believed his heart, too, must be changed, and earnestly prayed to that end. He described his May 1792 conversion as a singular sensation: as he rose from prayer, nature itself "wore a new aspect," and he enjoyed a cheerfulness and calm previously unknown to him.

Roberts's restful feeling was soon replaced with a persistent urge to preach. He lacked certainty, but, as became typical of his career, others settled the matter for him. Fellow believers in Roberts's home church designated this spiritually serious young man a preacher. Roberts evaded this call by leaving for Shenango, a hundred miles north in Mercer County, Pennsylvania, in the spring of 1796. He spent the next two and a half years converting his 400-acre claim into a farm. His family soon joined him, organized the first Methodist society in the region, and appointed him class leader. He returned to Ligonier in January 1799 to market his stock of furs and to marry Elizabeth Oldham; they had no children. Roberts's anxiety about preaching began to manifest itself in bouts of depression, and at his wife's urging, he pursued a license to exhort in the summer of 1800. Having assuaged his conscience by securing the license, however, he proceeded to avoid preaching.

In 1802 Roberts finally surrendered to the call to full-time ministry. Although married itinerants were uncommon at that time, he was immediately licensed to preach and assigned a circuit. He easily negotiated the mandatory four-year probation period and was ordained an elder in 1806. Roberts eventually traveled circuits encompassing portions of Ohio, Pennsylvania, New York, Maryland, and Virginia. In the process he became acquainted with the leading figures of the denomination, especially Francis Asbury (who affectionately called him "mountain-headed Roberts"). Asbury advanced Roberts's promotion by altering the rules of appointment in his favor on at least one occasion. Roberts was present at the pivotal General Conference of 1808 that established delegated representation and locked into perpetuity its "restrictive rules." For Roberts, however, it proved significant by introducing him to Baltimore's elite Methodists. Roberts, dressed in the "coarse garb of a backwoodsman" (Simpson, p. 176), preached against pride and ostentation to the people of the Light Street Church. The congregation was pleased by the searching sermon and entreated Asbury to station Roberts there; two months into a western assignment, Roberts was transferred to Baltimore. An anonymous donor outfitted him with new clothes. He spent much of the next eight years serving urban congregations throughout the East. Roberts occasionally shared pulpits with clergy of different denominations (especially Episcopalians), and while stationed in Georgetown he attracted the attention of President James Madison.

Election to the office of bishop in 1816 began the final phase of Roberts's life. Though the youngest presiding elder present, he had been elected to chair the Philadelphia Conference when no bishop arrived. Several delegates to the General Conference (which convened less than four weeks later) attended and observed Roberts's skill as a parliamentarian. With the recent death of Bishop Asbury and his only associate, Bishop McKendree, in ill health, it was common knowledge that at least one bishop would be selected at the impending General Conference. The delegates elected Roberts (along with Enoch George, a North Carolinian and presiding elder in Virginia), but characteristically, he hesitated to accept the office. Many, like James Quinn, marveled at Roberts's meteoric rise: "Thus fifteen years after I heard him deliver his first exhortation, I saw him placed in the episcopacy by the election of the General of conference, and the ordination of Bishop McKendree" (Elliot, p. 167).

Despite his rapid rise to the pinnacle of church leadership, little is known about the balance of Roberts's career. He certainly exhausted himself over the next twenty-seven years, crisscrossing the nation from one conference assembly to another. In 1819 he relocated to the White River area of Lawrence County, Indiana. Moving in part for financial and family reasons, Roberts also wanted to call attention to the untapped potential for the church in the West. When he died on his Indiana farm, three conferences sought possession of his remains, a measure of his eminence within the church. Originally buried on his farm, Roberts was reinterred at Indiana Asbury (now DePauw) University in January 1844. A marble monument was erected in 1858.

• Biographies of Roberts include Charles Elliot, *The Life of the Rev. Robert R. Roberts* (1844); Benjamin St. James Fry, *The Life of Robert R. Roberts* (1856); and Worth Marion Tippy, *Frontier Bishop: The Life and Times of Robert Richford*

Roberts (1958). Valuable sketches by contemporaries include William C. Larrabee, ed., *Asbury and His Colaborers*, vol. 2 (1854); Douglas P. Gorrie, *The Lives of Eminent Methodist Ministers* (1852); Thomas A. Morris's entry in *Annals of the American Pulpit*, ed. William B. Sprague, vol. 7 (1857); and Matthew Simpson's entry in *Lives of Methodist Bishops*, ed. Theodore L. Flood and John W. Hamilton (1882).

FRANK E. JOHNSON

ROBERTS, William Henry (31 Jan. 1844–26 June 1920), Presbyterian minister and church administrator, was born in Holyhead, Wales, the son of William Roberts, a minister, and Catherine Parry. His family immigrated to the United States in 1855. Roberts graduated from New York Free Academy, later called the College of the City of New York, in 1863. From 1863 to 1867 he worked as a statistician for the U.S. Treasury Department in the nation's capital. He married Sarah Esther McLean in June 1867; the couple had four children. In the same year he became an assistant librarian for the Library of Congress, until 1872. While working as a librarian he decided to enter the ministry and began studying at Princeton Theological Seminary. He graduated in 1873 and on 5 December was ordained by the presbytery of Elizabeth, New Jersey. After a four-year pastorate at the Presbyterian Church of Cranbury, New Jersey, he served nine years as librarian at Princeton Theological Seminary. In 1880, while still serving as Princeton's librarian, he was elected permanent clerk of the General Assembly, the national governing body of the Presbyterian church, and in 1884 he was elected its stated clerk, a principal administrative position he held for thirty-six years.

In a period of strong theological disagreement within the Presbyterian church about biblical interpretation, Roberts assumed the chair of practical theology at Lane Theological Seminary in Cincinnati, Ohio, in 1886 as a mediator with conservative sentiments. When heresy cases arose, first with Charles Augustus Briggs at Union Seminary in New York City and then with Henry Preserved Smith at Lane, Roberts sided with those supporting biblical inerrancy. What some scholars called "higher criticism" of the Bible he termed "negative criticism." "Their actual purpose, whether intentional or unintentional," he wrote, "is to discredit the Bible" ("Notes on the Negative Criticism," *Timely Topics* [1892]). His position found favor with many in the larger church, but Lane's trustees resisted, and Roberts's position was eliminated in 1893. He moved to Philadelphia, Pennsylvania, preaching nearby at the Second Presbyterian Church in Trenton, New Jersey, from 1894 to 1899. However, when permanent offices for the stated clerk were established in Philadelphia, Roberts assumed the position full time.

As the Presbyterian church's chief administrator Roberts gained a reputation for organizational ability and parliamentary skill and was viewed as an authority on Presbyterian law, history, and doctrine. He helped regularize procedures, for instance in his production of a *Manual for Ruling Elders*, which was requested by the General Assembly of 1894 and was published under his name in 1897 and in several revised editions thereafter. A committee headed by him compiled *Laws Relating to Religious Corporations* (1896), a nearly 600-page listing of state laws about the incorporation and management of churches and other religious institutions. During his tenure church membership grew from 600,000 to 1,310,000 communicants, with contributions rising from $10 to $22 million annually. In 1907 he was elected moderator of the General Assembly, the highest honor Presbyterians can bestow.

Roberts also was deeply involved in ecumenical activity. He viewed himself as a conservative, loyal Calvinist and was not interested in theological dilution, but he supported ecumenical cooperation for the sake of more efficient, effective Christian witness. Although he was interested in organic union among Calvinist bodies, he advocated only federation with other denominations. He was a delegate to the Alliance of the Reformed Churches Throughout the World, Holding the Presbyterian System and served as its American secretary for over thirty years and as its president in 1896. A Committee on Church Cooperation and Union, formed by the Presbyterian General Asembly in 1903, named Roberts as chairman. The committee negotiated the church's reunion with the Cumberland Presbyterian church in 1906, with Roberts playing a central role. He presided over negotiations that led to the establishment of the Federal Council of Churches in 1908, served as its acting president in the council's first year, as chair of its executive committee from 1908 to 1912, and as a member of its administrative committee until his death, in Philadelphia.

• The Presbyterian Historical Society in Philadelphia, Pa., holds manuscript materials pertaining to Roberts and his work. In addition to the books mentioned above, Roberts published *A History of the Presbyterian Church* (1888), *The Ecclesiastical Status of the Theological Seminaries* (1891), *The Presbyterian System: Its Characteristics, Authority, and Obligation* (1895), *Manual of the Alliance of the Reformed Churches . . . with a Brief History of the Alliance* (1898), and *A Concise History of the Presbyterian Church in the United States of America* (1917), plus articles, addresses, and sermons. A significant article is "The Reunion of the Cumberland Presbyterian Church with the Presbyterian Church in the U.S.A.," *Journal of the Presbyterian Historical Society* 54 (Sept. 1906). Discussions of Roberts's life are in Bruce David Forbes, "William Henry Roberts: Resistance to Change and Bureaucratic Adaptation," *Journal of Presbyterian History* (Winter 1976), and J. Ross Stevenson, "The Churchmanship of William Henry Roberts," *Princeton Theological Review* 18 (Oct. 1820). An obituary is in the *Philadelphia Public Ledger*, 27 June 1920.

BRUCE DAVID FORBES

ROBERTS, William Randall (6 Feb. 1830–9 Aug. 1897), merchant, politician, and Fenian, was born in Mitchelstown, county Cork, Ireland, the son of Randall Roberts and Mary Bishop. Nothing is known about his parents' occupations. William received only a little education, and at the age of nineteen he immigrated to the United States. He went to work in New York City as a dry goods clerk. In 1857 Roberts went into business for himself but was financially ruined in the panic of that same year. He began again, however, and ran his own store in the Bowery so successfully that by 1869 he was able to retire from business as a wealthy man.

During the 1860s Roberts participated in New York's Irish societies and was a generous benefactor of charitable and patriotic causes. In 1865 he was elected president of the Knights of St. Patrick. Roberts was particularly active in the Fenian Brotherhood, which he joined in 1863, and became a leader in the movement against its president, John O'Mahony. When the brotherhood's senate deposed O'Mahony in 1865, Roberts became president.

The Fenians, organized in 1858, descended from earlier Irish-American societies. Their goal was to win Ireland's independence from Great Britain, but the movement gained momentum only as the American Civil War drew to its conclusion. Playing on Canadians' uneasiness over the large Union armies to their immediate south, the restlessness of American veterans, and England's sympathy toward the Confederacy, the Roberts wing of the Fenians undertook to win Ireland's freedom by invading Canada from the United States, while the O'Mahony wing sought revolution in Ireland itself.

Roberts, along with General Thomas William Sweeny, led this wing of the brotherhood in drumming up public support for invasions and in organizing concentrations of men at several points along the United States–Canadian border. Roberts's plan was to have these men invade Canada and hold it as a base for operations against England. From 1866 to 1871 several border incursions did incite fear and tension, but the net result was a fiasco for the cause and for its leaders.

Roberts was among the leaders arrested in 1866 for a foray into Canada in the Niagara area. The charge was breaching neutrality laws, and Roberts "lodged for some time in Ludlow Street Jail" (*New York Times*, 13 Aug. 1897). Prosecution did not follow arrest, however, as congressional elections were at hand in the United States, and anti-English sentiment ran high among Americans.

In 1867 Roberts was in Paris discussing cooperation with representatives from the Fenian Brotherhood in the British Isles and hoping that they would combine efforts with his own organization. Although they entered into an agreement with the impressive title of the Treaty of Paris, no action resulted. Roberts resigned his presidency and became less active in the Fenian Brotherhood. While the Fenian conspiracy kept Canadians in a state of "nerves" for four or five years and kindled a feeling of nationalism among them, Roberts's plan failed (Stacey, p. 254).

Turning his energies toward national politics, in 1870 Roberts was elected to the Forty-second Congress as a Democrat from New York City. He was reelected to the Forty-third Congress in 1872, but he declined renomination in 1874. In Congress, Roberts opposed the Radical Republicans' oppressive policies toward the former Confederate states and any proposals that would deplete the federal treasury. As a matter of principle, he voted against a "back pay" bill in Congress. When the bill passed, he returned his $5,000 to the federal Treasury, and several other members followed his example. He also opposed the increasing power of corporations and railroads. He promoted protection for Americans in foreign countries, especially Fenians imprisoned in Canada, and civil rights for black people, being one of only two Democrats who voted for an 1873 supplemental bill guaranteeing those rights.

Congressman Roberts vehemently attacked British foreign policy. In a speech to the House of Representatives on the *Alabama* claims, 20 May 1872, he eloquently described the injuries inflicted by a supposedly neutral Great Britain on Union shipping during the Civil War, for which the United States was then claiming indemnity. Contemporaries called Roberts's speech "one of the ablest presentments of the attitude of Great Britain" on this subject.

On leaving Congress, Roberts turned from national to city politics, becoming a member of the Tammany Society. More popularly known as Tammany Hall, this New York Democratic party organization controlled city and state politics from the early 1800s to the mid-1900s. Roberts was elected to the New York Board of Aldermen in 1878 and 1879, serving as president during his first year. He then ran for sheriff but was defeated. In 1881 Roberts and others seceded from Tammany to form a rival organization, the New York County Democracy.

When Grover Cleveland campaigned for the governorship of New York in 1882, Roberts was his faithful supporter. In 1884, when Cleveland won the presidential nomination over Tammany Hall opposition, Roberts again backed him. For his support, Roberts was rewarded in 1885 with an appointment as envoy extraordinary and minister plenipotentiary to Chile. While serving in Chile, he suffered a paralytic stroke in May 1888. The secretary of the legation, C. M. Siebert, brought him back to New York City. Although he lived eight more years, Roberts never regained either his mental or physical health. He died in New York after losing his considerable financial wealth in the panic of 1873. He was married and had at least one son, but nothing more is known of his family life.

• Roberts's congressional remarks are in the *Congressional Globe*, 42d and 43d Congs., 1871–1873. For his diplomatic correspondence from Chile see *Papers Relating to the Foreign Relations of the United States, 1888* (1889). Biographical information on Roberts is scarce. Details on his role in the Fenian Brotherhood are in John Rutherford, *The Secret History of the Fenian Conspiracy: Its Origins, Objects, and Ramifications* (2 vols., 1877). C. P. Stacey, "Fenianism and the Rise of National Feeling in Canada at the Time of Confederation," *Canadian Historical Review* 12 (1931): 238–61, is essential for understanding Roberts's focus and for appreciating the unintended results of the Fenian raids. Stacey is also valuable for the bibliography provided by the extensive footnotes, which cite newspapers, government documents, and reports and correspondence of the Fenians. New York City politics during Roberts's years is detailed in Matthew P. Breen, *Thirty Years of New York Politics* (1899). An obituary is in the *New York Times*, 13 Aug. 1897.

SYLVIA B. LARSON

ROBERTSON, Alice Mary (2 Jan. 1854–1 July 1931), U.S. congresswoman, was born at the Tullahassee Mission in the Creek Nation, Indian Territory, the daughter of William Schenck Robertson and Ann Eliza Worcester, missionary schoolteachers. Robertson was proud of her missionary heritage, especially of her grandfather Samuel A. Worcester, who championed the political autonomy of the Cherokee Nation in the landmark Supreme Court case *Worcester v. Georgia* (1832).

Robertson's early activities were in keeping with her family's interests in American-Indian welfare. In 1873, after two years at Elmira College in New York, she left for financial reasons to become a clerk in the Office of Indian Affairs in Washington, D.C. Bored with the work, she resigned in 1879 and returned to Tullahassee Mission. A year later, she went east again to take a position as secretary to Henry Pratt at Carlisle Indian School. Shortly after her father's death in 1881, Robertson returned to Indian Territory, where she worked to raise funds for a new school for the Creeks, established in 1885 and named Nuyaka. Also in 1885 Robertson became head of the Minerva Home, a boarding school for American-Indian girls. The Minerva school evolved into the University of Tulsa but under Robertson's supervision specialized in the "domestic arts." She taught there until 1899.

Robertson's work in American-Indian education linked her to a national network of reformers and brought her other opportunities. In 1889 the federal government hired her to be part of the commission to negotiate the sale of the Cherokee Outlet, and in 1900 she was appointed Federal Supervisor of Creek Schools, despite many objections as to whether a woman could handle such a position. When speaking at the 1891 Lake Mohonk Conference, a national gathering of American-Indian reformers, Robertson had the good fortune to meet and impress Theodore Roosevelt (1858–1919). Robertson's enthusiastic support for the Spanish-American War and her motherly attention to two Creek students who joined the Rough Riders cemented their friendship. In 1905 Roosevelt appointed Robertson U.S. postmaster at Muskogee, Oklahoma, a position she held until President Woodrow Wilson took office in 1913. Robertson first entered politics as a candidate in 1916, when the local Republican party asked her to run for the office of county superintendent of public instruction. She lost the election but seemed not to mind, for other activities kept her occupied. She operated a farm and a successful cafeteria in Muskogee, and during World War

I she was busy at the train station, where on her own initiative she distributed food to soldiers.

In 1920 Robertson became a candidate for office again, this time challenging the Democratic incumbent W. W. Hastings, a Cherokee lawyer, to his seat in the U.S. House of Representatives. Robertson won by a slim margin in what was a good year for Republicans in general. Robertson's promises to help women, children, soldiers, and American Indians may also have earned her the necessary votes. However, two years later, when Hastings regained his seat, he did so with a substantial majority. "Miss Alice," as she was called by her constituents, was overwhelmingly voted out of office, probably by many of the same people who had voted her into office.

Robertson's record in Congress was true to her campaign slogans: "Christianity, Americanism and Standpattism," "I cannot be bought; I cannot be sold; I cannot be intimidated," and "I am a Christian; I am an American; I am a Republican" (Spaulding, p. 91). Since Jeanette Rankin had left the House in 1919, Robertson was the only woman in Congress for the 1921–1923 term and the second woman ever to serve in the U.S. Congress. As such, she became a minor celebrity in Washington, D.C., but her conservatism, especially during House debates on the Bonus Bill and the Sheppard-Towner Bill, angered many of her constituents. The Bonus Bill would have allowed World War I veterans to receive earlier payments on their pensions. Despite Robertson's long history of supporting soldiers and war veterans, she voted against the Bonus Bill because it meant big government and would encourage dependency. The Sheppard-Towner Bill, passed in 1921, was to set up child hygiene and prenatal centers to be administered by the Federal Children's Bureau. Robertson opposed it because it would infringe on states' rights, encourage dependency, and spread information about birth control.

Soldiers were surprised and outraged at Robertson's opposition; supporters of the Sheppard-Towner Bill were merely outraged. As one woman in the Oklahoma League of Women Voters said, "Herself a political accident, in her contempt of women and their ability, her total ignorance of women and women's affairs, she fortunately in no way represents women, though she sits as the only woman in Congress" (Spaulding, p. 153). Before entering Congress, Robertson had alienated many women's organizations by her vehement antisuffrage stance. While serving in Congress, she continued to condemn woman suffrage and "deplore woman's tendency to drift away from the home" (Spaulding, p. 152). Although attacked by the majority of women's organizations, she had two wealthy, conservative patrons, Mary C. Thaw and Elizabeth Lowell Putnam, who gave her important emotional and financial assistance throughout her life.

After losing her 1922 reelection campaign, Robertson returned permanently to Muskogee. Her financial fortunes declined, and favors from friends sustained her until she died in the Muskogee Veterans' Hospital. Robertson, who often referred to herself as an "old maid," never married; however, she informally adopted or fostered several American-Indian girls.

• Robertson's papers are at the University of Tulsa Library. The most thorough biographical and bibliographical resource is Joe Powell Spaulding, "The Life of Alice Mary Robertson" (Ph.D. diss., Univ. of Okla., 1959). Also see Ruth Moore Stanley, "Alice M. Robertson, Oklahoma's First Congresswoman," *Chronicles of Oklahoma* 45 (1967): 259–89. An obituary is in the *Chronicles of Oklahoma* 10 (1932): 12–17.

NANCY SHOEMAKER

ROBERTSON, Eck (20 Nov. 1887–17 Feb. 1975), fiddler, born Alexander Campbell Robertson in Delaney, Madison County, Arkansas, the son of Joseph Robertson, a farmer and Campbellite preacher. His mother's name is unknown. His father was one of the more respected old-time fiddlers in the area but gave up the instrument when he became a preacher; young Eck learned much of his early fiddling from an uncle and an older brother named Quince. He also learned many tunes and techniques from Civil War veterans, such as Polk Harris. Though his first instrument, used at age five, was a long-necked gourd with tanned cat hide, he was soon playing on real instruments and perfecting tunes like "Ragtime Annie" and "Done Gone," both of which he would later record and popularize.

Though his uncle, brother, and friends often plied their trade at country dances and at marathon Texas fiddling contests, Robertson as a teenager determined to try to make better money with his fiddle. He joined a traveling medicine show when he was sixteen years old and for the next several years traveled the "kerosene circuit," gaining entertaining experience and learning new tunes. In 1906 he married his childhood sweetheart, Jeanetta "Nettie" Belle Levy, who was herself a skilled musician; for the next several years the two traveled around eastern and central Texas putting on musical shows and slide shows with musical accompaniment. Robertson also worked as a piano tuner in towns like Clarendon and Big Spring, Texas. The pair started a family that would eventually include two sons and eight daughters; later, certain members, including Daphne, Dueron ("Eck, Jr."), and Marguerite, would go on stage with Robertson and his wife, and they would perform as a family band.

By the end of World War I the family was living in Vernon, Texas, where Robertson had established a reputation as a serious contest fiddler and where he often performed with two neighbors, fiddlers Lewis Franklin and A. P. Howard. He might have remained a respected but unrecorded regional performer save for a chance encounter in early 1922 with a newsreel crew from Fox Movietone films. The film crew made motion pictures of the three fiddlers and impressed Robertson by saying they would be shown around the country. He liked this idea but was upset that the movie fans would not hear his fiddling. A remedy presented itself in June 1922, when he and a friend, fiddler and Civil War veteran Henry Gilliland, attended an Old Confederate Soldiers Reunion in Richmond, Virginia. Gilliland had a friend in New York City who worked for the Victor Talking Machine Company, and he and Robertson took the train and decided to see if they could make some records.

Wearing cowboy garb, Robertson, accompanied by Gilliland, appeared at the Victor offices and auditioned for the recording executives; they were dutifully impressed by the two fiddlers and promptly set up the studio and recorded some twelve sides by them on 30 June and 1 July. Four unaccompanied fiddle duets by Robertson and Gilliland thus became the first southern fiddle tunes put on record: "Arkansas Traveller," "Apple Blossom" (never released), "Forked Deer" (never released), and "Turkey in the Straw." One of Robertson's solos, "Sallie Gooden," proved to be the most popular of all these early records.

Though the Robertson-Gilliland 1922 records sold quite well and initiated the company's first old-time music catalog in 1924, Robertson seemed either unwilling or unable to capitalize on the situation. Following his lead, other fiddlers from around the South began to record during the period from 1923 to 1929, with many of them winning fame and riches. Robertson seemed content with doing his regional schoolhouse and auditorium shows in Texas. Finally, in 1929, he and his family string band entered the portable Victor studios in Dallas to record a total of eight string band sides. These were far less successful than his earlier efforts, and while he tried to get the company to record him yet again in the 1930s, the new western swing craze had hit, and Victor felt his old-time fiddle tunes were behind the times. Robertson was frustrated, but he did appear often on radio, and in the late 1930s he recorded a series of more than 100 transcriptions for radio use for the Sellers company, but these have not been traced.

In later years Robertson returned to the fiddle contest circuit and in 1963 was rediscovered by some members of the New Lost City Ramblers, a young folk music string band then popular on college campuses. They recorded long interviews with him and some of his fiddle tunes (later issued on an LP as *Eck Robertson: Famous Cowboy Fiddler*). He also traveled to several folk festivals, including ones at the University of California at Los Angeles and in Newport, Rhode Island. After his house and fiddle shop burned in Amarillo, Texas, he moved to a nursing home, where he died. He was interred in Fritch, Texas, with a tombstone that appropriately reads "World's Champion Fiddler."

• Some of Robertson's interviews are in the archives of the Southern Folklife Collection at the University of North Carolina, Chapel Hill. The brochure accompanying the County 201 LP *Eck Robertson: Famous Cowboy Fiddler* contains a good account of Robertson's life, as well as a bibliography of other writings about him. An article derived from the Robertson family papers and scrapbooks is Charles Wolfe, "Eck Robertson," in his *The Devil's Box* (1996). An important early source is John Cohen, "Fiddlin' Eck Robertson," *Sing Out!* 14, no. 2 (Apr.–May 1964): 55–59.

CHARLES K. WOLFE

ROBERTSON, Howard Percy (27 Jan. 1903–26 Aug. 1961), mathematical physicist, was born in Hoquiam, Washington, the son of George Duncan Robertson, a county engineer, and Anna McLeod. His father died when he was fifteen, and despite the ensuing financial difficulties he entered the University of Washington in 1918 with the intention of becoming an engineer. There his unusual mathematical abilities attracted the attention of his professors, notably Eric T. Bell, who persuaded him to change his course of studies to mathematics and physics. He received his B.S. in 1922 and M.S. in 1923 in mathematics from Washington. Also in 1923 he married Angela Turinsky; they had two children. Again with Bell's encouragement, he transferred to the California Institute of Technology for graduate work. He attended Caltech from 1923 to 1925, and there he received his Ph.D. in 1925 with a dissertation on general relativity, "On Dynamical Space-Times Which Contain a Conformal Euclidean 3-Space," directed by Harry Bateman. He then was awarded a National Research Council Fellowship for the years 1925–1928, which he spent at the Universities of Göttingen and Munich and Princeton, where he met a number of outstanding mathematicians, such as John von Neumann, Hermann Weyl, Luther P. Eisenhart, and Oswald Veblen, who were to influence his career and research interests. He then served Princeton as an assistant professor, 1929–1931; associate professor, 1931–1938; and professor of mathematical physics, 1938–1947. While there he mastered the differential-geometric theories of Eisenhart and Veblen and was closely involved in some of the work of Albert Einstein and his collaborators, Banesh Hoffmann and Leopold Infeld, at the Institute for Advanced Study.

In late 1939 Robertson's Caltech colleague, Richard Tolman, persuaded him to get involved in national defense work, and Robertson was subsequently involved in such activities for the rest of his life. From 1940 to 1943 he served on the National Defense Research Council and the Office of Scientific Research and Development; and during 1943–1945 he was liaison officer at the London Mission of the latter organization and technical consultant for the Department of War. During 1944 he was active in the Allied efforts to assess and combat the German secret weapons program, such as the V-1 and V-2 attacks on England. The war's end found him the chief of the Scientific Intelligence Advisory Section of the Supreme Headquarters of Allied Expeditionary Forces in Europe. In recognition of his services he was awarded the Medal of Merit in 1946. In 1947 he returned to Caltech as professor of mathematical physics and held that position until his death. Concurrently he served as a member of the Air Force Scientific Advisory Board (1949–1950); director of Weapons System Evaluation Group for the secretary of defense (1950–1952); chairman of the "Robertson Panel" that investigated UFO activity for the Office of Scientific Intelligence (the Central Intelligence Agency) in 1953; scientific adviser to the North Atlantic Treaty Organization commander, General Alfred

M. Gruenther (1954–1956); and chairman and member at large of the Defense Science Board (1956–1961). During his final years he was a member of the Presidential Scientific Advisory Committee (1957–1961). Little is publicly known about the specific details of Robertson's postwar governmental service, except that after his death it was widely hailed as being exemplary. However, it did affect his purely academic scientific productivity, and there is a conspicuous gap in his list of publications from 1940 to 1949. He was elected a member of the National Academy of Sciences in 1951 and served as its foreign secretary from 1958 until his untimely death.

Robertson's research encompasses some of the most mathematically demanding areas of theoretical physics: quantum theory, cosmology, and general relativity. His quantum work included a study of coordinate systems in which the Schrödinger equation was separable (1928); one of the first rigorous mathematical discussions of the Heisenberg uncertainty principle (1929); and an expert translation from the German of Weyl's *Theory of Groups and Quantum Mechanics* (1931). Next his attention was turned to cosmology (1928–1933), and in 1928 he was one of the earliest to propose a linear cosmological redshift. In 1929 he gave a careful examination of the assumption of physical uniformity in the universe and deduced possible cosmological models that included the famous Robertson-Walker line element. In 1936 Arthur G. Walker independently derived this result by other means. Robertson's work was lucidly summarized in his 1933 paper "Relativistic Cosmology" in *Reviews of Modern Physics*, which had broken new ground by the use of group-theoretic methods. This paper was long regarded by many as one of the best expositions of the application of general relativity to cosmology. Then followed a lively series of dialogues (1933–1936) with Edward A. Milne on Milne's theory of kinematic relativity and world structure. This greatly helped to clarify the distinction between Milne's theory and general relativity. In 1937 Robertson deduced the relativistic version of the Poynting effect dealing with moving bodies that both absorb and reemit solar radiation. This is now commonly known as the Poynting-Robertson effect. He also became deeply involved in the study of the equations of motion in general relativity and played a significant role in the development of the Einstein-Infeld-Hoffmann approximation. One of his most important results was his detailed analysis of the geometric properties of the Schwarzschild radius in general relativity. This was subsequently shown to play an essential role in the theory of black holes. Curiously, this work was done and announced in 1939 but only formally published in the posthumous book, *Relativity and Cosmology* (1968), which was prepared by his former student, Thomas W. Noonan, and based on Robertson's Caltech lectures. While the Robertson-Noonan book is not what Robertson would himself have written, it nevertheless succeeded in bringing the spirit of his work to a later generation of students. Most of Robertson's postwar publications were of lesser importance but still provided valuable insight into the observational aspects of relativity and cosmology. His final paper, "Relativity and Cosmology," which appeared in *Space Age Astronomy* (1962), is now regarded as one of the seminal papers on the use of the now-popular post-parametrized Newtonian approximation in general relativity.

During his time, although his list of publications is remarkably short (fewer than forty research papers), Robertson was one of the leading world authorities on relativity and cosmology. His writings were elegant and insightful, and among American relativists he probably had the deepest understanding of not only the mathematics, but also the cosmological and observational aspects of Einstein's theory. In person, "Bob," as he was commonly known, was a big, jovial man with an outgoing personality and witty sense of humor. He was especially known for his fondness for limericks and his collection of stories. Scientifically, he had a remarkable ability to get to the heart of a problem and present his conclusions in a lucid manner that all could understand. He had a wide circle of friends and was always ready to lend assistance to them in their problems, although such activities were often inconvenient and detrimental to his own research.

Robertson died unexpectedly in Pasadena of a pulmonary embolism brought on by injuries sustained in an automobile accident.

• Robertson's scientific papers are held by the Institute Archives at the California Institute of Technology. Robertson wrote little that is accessible to the general reader, but two expository articles are noteworthy: "Geometry as a Branch of Physics," in *Albert Einstein: Philosopher-Scientist*, ed. Paul A. Schilpp (1949), pp. 313–32, and "The Geometries of the Thermal and Gravitational Fields," *American Mathematical Monthly* 57 (Apr. 1950): 232–45. Appendix B of the posthumous Robertson-Noonan text has a valuable guide to Robertson's relativity papers. The Society of Industrial and Applied Mathematics published a memorial volume to Robertson in 1963, which includes a short biography. Obituaries are in National Academy of Sciences, *Biographical Memoirs* 51 (1980): 343–63, the *New York Times*, 28 Aug. 1961, and the *Quarterly Journal of the Royal Astronomical Society* 3 (June 1962).

JOSEPH D. ZUND

ROBERTSON, James (29 June 1717–4 Mar. 1788), British general and royal governor of New York, was born at "Newbigging," the family estate near Burntisland, Scotland, the son of George Robertson, a laird, and Christian Dundas. Little is known of his childhood. Robertson enlisted in the British army as a common soldier, very unusual for a future general. In 1739 he became an officer. During 1747 he married Ann White; they had one child. Slowly rising in rank, he gained the earl of Loudoun, John Campbell (1705–1782), as his patron. When Lord Loudoun became the commander in America, Robertson moved there during 1756, serving in various posts in the army bureauc-

racy. Each succeeding commander valued his work. He became a lieutenant colonel in 1760, thanks to the influence of General Jeffrey Amherst.

After General Thomas Gage (1721–1787) took charge, Robertson warned him about possible future problems in obtaining quarters for the army. Some lawyers, Robertson cautioned, doubted whether there existed sufficient legal grounds to force the colonies to provide barracks. Robertson feared that troublemakers would take advantage of the issue and urged that Parliament forestall such difficulties by passing legislation before a crisis developed. Gage agreed with Robertson, and the Quartering Act (1765) ensued. Robertson became barrackmaster general, allegedly enriching himself in the office. During the 1770s he rose rapidly in rank to colonel, then brigadier, and, in 1776, to major general.

In the campaign to seize southern New York (July–Sept. 1776), Robertson's advice was important because he had been based there for much of his American career. His suggestion of Staten Island as the initial landing site was a wise one, since its Loyalist population and geographic position made it a useful British base.

Robertson had become a confidant of British minister Lord George Germain, and in June 1779 Germain invited the general to appear before Parliament to support the government. Robertson backed the ministry and insisted that most Americans were Loyalists. But during questioning by the opposition, his assertions were torn to shreds. At least one observer concluded that Robertson was becoming senile, an assertion that, while untrue, would hound him during the rest of the Revolution. Nevertheless, his health was declining, and he may have suffered a stroke.

Robertson was named the governor of occupied New York and began his duties there in March 1780, knowing that New Yorkers had been disturbed by the harshness of military law. He hoped to restore the colonial government, thus placating the New Yorkers and possibly convincing other rebellious Americans to abandon the revolt. Although Sir Henry Clinton, the commander, promoted Robertson to lieutenant general in 1780, he refused to end martial law. Robertson's failure to end military rule brought him much hostility from bitter Loyalists. Tory historian Thomas Jones would lambaste Robertson over many things, including his sexual affairs. The general's fondness for young women had long been widely known.

After Yorktown, Robertson dreamed of becoming commander in chief, and in 1782 Germain authorized him to succeed Clinton temporarily. But Clinton, who believed Robertson had schemed against him, refused to surrender his authority. The new ministry, frightened by Robertson's failing health, ordered Sir Guy Carleton to rush to America. He arrived before Clinton's departure, frustrating Robertson. In April 1783 Robertson turned over his government to Lieutenant Governor Andrew Elliot and left America. He died in London.

James Robertson was not a great soldier, and his administrative experience did not enable him to defeat or conciliate the American rebels. But the martial skills of his more robust colleagues failed just as badly.

• Robertson's letters are found among manuscripts of his correspondents. The William L. Clements Library, University of Michigan, Ann Arbor, has Robertson letters in several collections. The Library of Congress has copies of the Frederick Haldimand Papers. More items are possessed by the Henry E. Huntington Library, San Marino, Calif. The British Public Record Office has substantial holdings. Robertson's Colonial Office letters are calendared in K. G. Davies, ed., *Documents of the American Revolution*, vols. 10, 13, 16, 19 (1972–1981). Milton M. Klein and Ronald W. Howard, eds., *The Twilight of British Rule in Revolutionary America: The New York Letter Book of General James Robertson, 1780–1783* (1983), is valuable and includes an extensive biography in the introduction. See also Sir Henry Clinton, *The American Rebellion* (1954); William H. W. Sabine, ed., *The Historical Memoirs . . . of William Smith* (3 vols., 1956–1971); Thomas Jones, *History of New York During the Revolutionary War* (1879). Books covering his career include John Shy, *Toward Lexington: The Role of the British Army in the Coming of the American Revolution* (1965); Ira D. Gruber, *The Howe Brothers and the American Revolution* (1972); Philip Ranlet, *The New York Loyalists* (1986); and William B. Willcox, *Portrait of a General: Sir Henry Clinton in the War of Independence* (1964). A death notice is in *Gentleman's Magazine* 58 (Mar. 1788): 275.

PHILIP RANLET

ROBERTSON, James (28 June 1742–1 Sept. 1814), soldier and pioneer, was born in Brunswick County, Virginia, the son of John Robertson, a planter and merchant, and Mary Gower. He has been variously described as the "Father of Tennessee," the "Father of Middle Tennessee," and the "Founder of Nashville." He was among a group of Scotch-Irish descendants who played a prominent role in the settlement of the American frontier.

Robertson was married in 1768 to seventeen-year-old Charlotte Reeves, in Wake County, North Carolina, where he and his parents probably were living. A little more than a year later the first of their thirteen children was born. Robertson may have farmed briefly in nearby Orange County, but by 1771 the family had crossed the Blue Ridge mountains. They settled in the vicinity of Sycamore Shoals on the Watauga River, not far from present-day Johnson City, and Robertson immediately became active in the development of the first major settlement in what later became the state of Tennessee.

Transient hunters and traders preceded Robertson by several decades, but those who came when Robertson did planned to stay permanently. Numbers increased dramatically after the battle of Alamance Courthouse (1771) in North Carolina, in which a motley army of more than 1,000 North Carolina "Regulators" was defeated by supporters of Sir William Tryon. Robertson may have been a Regulator; if not, he certainly had "regulating principles" and was willing to fight against eastern domination of the government.

Far removed from the centers of government in both Virginia and North Carolina, the "Wataugans" developed a frontier government known as the "Watauga Association." Robertson became one of five who, as a council, had executive, legislative, and judicial powers over the small but rapidly growing settlement. He also fought and negotiated with nearby tribes and served as North Carolina's and Virginia's agent to the Cherokee Nation.

After nearly a decade on the Watauga, Robertson migrated 200 miles westward to establish a settlement on the Cumberland River. He had explored the area as early as 1778, and in the spring of 1779 he returned to plant a crop of corn and establish the nucleus of "Fort Nashborough." When he returned for his family in the summer of 1779, he recruited scores of others to join him in the venture. That fall, Robertson and a party of more than 100 drove cattle, sheep, and hogs overland to Fort Nashborough; John Donelson departed at the same time by flatboat, bringing women and children. In May 1780 the settlers developed the "Cumberland Compact," a crude constitution to which 256 men attached their signatures. It established a frontier government similar to the one developed earlier at Watauga. In 1783 North Carolina recognized the settlement as "Davidson County," and the House of Commons received Robertson as the county's representative.

Until his death Robertson was active in the development of the Tennessee frontier. Although he attained the rank of brigadier general during Tennessee's territorial period, his place in history was earned because of his leadership as a civilian, not as a soldier. Indeed, writers have questioned why he moved westward to found a new settlement soon after the Revolution began instead of remaining to fight the Tories and the British, as did John Sevier and others among his associates. He resigned his general's commission in 1795 and devoted the final years of his life to government service and personal affairs. Throughout the territorial period he was active in the movement for statehood and was chosen as a delegate to the Constitutional Convention of January 1796, which prepared fundamental law for the new state. He served briefly in the state senate from 1798 to 1799.

When not at war, Robertson viewed Indians kindly and was frequently called upon to represent Tennessee and the United States in conferences to settle boundary and other disputes requiring his skill as a mediator. In 1811 he was appointed agent to the Chickasaws on behalf of the federal government; he had taken up temporary residence at the Chickasaw Bluffs when he died. His remains were removed to the Old City Cemetery of Nashville in 1825.

Although limited in formal education and writing skills, as his correspondence indicates, Robertson was a firm believer in the importance of education. He became a trustee of Davidson Academy of Nashville in 1785. Until his death he annually cleared acreage for cultivation and engaged in such kindred enterprises as saw- and gristmilling and whiskey manufacture. A contemporary, Judge John Haywood, described him as a person of "sound mind, healthy constitution, a robust frame, a love of virtue, an intrepid soul, and an emulous desire for fame."

• Accounts of Robertson's pioneer activities are included in all of the standard works concerned with Tennessee state history. Two book-length accounts are Thomas E. Matthews, *General James Robertson, Father of Tennessee* (1934), and Albigence W. Putnam, *History of Middle Tennessee; or, Life and Times of General James Robertson* (1859; repr. 1971). Much of his limited correspondence is included in William R. Garret, ed., "The Correspondence of General James Robertson," *American Historical Magazine* 1–5 (1896–1900). Articles include Eugene C. Lewis, "James Robertson, Nashville's Founder," *American Historical Magazine* 8 (July 1903): 285–94, and Margaret Burr Des Champs, "Early Days in the Cumberland Country," *Tennessee Historical Quarterly* 6 (Sept. 1947): 195–229.

ROBERT E. CORLEW

ROBERTSON, James (1747–24 Apr. 1816), Loyalist printer and journalist, was born in Stonehaven, Scotland, the son of Alexander Robertson, a printer, and possibly Elizabeth Anderson. (Records show that she was at some point married to his father but not whether she was the mother of his children.) James learned the trade of printing in his father's shop in Edinburgh, but he did not remain in Scotland. In 1766 he sailed for America, seeking better opportunities for economic success. Robertson became a journeyman printer in the shop of John Mein and John Fleming, printers and booksellers in Boston.

Having become a competent printer through his years as an apprentice in Edinburgh and a journeyman in Boston, Robertson joined with his brother Alexander in 1768 to establish a printing business in New York. While in New York, the brothers did job printing (contracted small productions such as special forms or institutional records), published pamphlets, and printed the third American edition of William Livingston's *Review of the Military Operations in America from 1753–1756*. They began publication of a newspaper, the *New-York Chronicle*, on 8 May 1769 and continued it until 1770. Although the paper did not last long, it published several important articles by the King's College faculty, discussing the theory of comets and the transit of Venus.

In 1771 Robertson and his brother moved to Albany to establish a new printing office, the first in the colony of New York outside New York City. Sir William Johnson, superintendent of Indian Affairs in America, encouraged the Robertsons in this effort and provided money to purchase a press and type for the new venture. Besides the usual job printing done by almost all eighteenth-century printers, the Robertsons once more established a weekly newspaper, the *Albany Gazette*, which continued publication until 1775.

In 1773 Robertson and his brother established a second printing office in Norwich, Connecticut, in partnership with John Trumbull. In October 1773 they published that town's first newspaper, the *Norwich Packet*. Trumbull handled the business of the Norwich office, while the Robertsons remained in Albany to run the business there. With two printing offices well established, the Robertson brothers seemed destined for financial success.

Permanent success in America was not to be, however, because of the growing conflict between Great Britain and the colonies. The Robertsons remained loyal to the British Crown and sought to use their printing establishment to further that cause. In 1776 rebels in Albany attacked the two brothers for their support of the British. To escape permanent injury, the Robertsons fled to Norwich, leaving their printing equipment with a friend who buried it for safekeeping. In Norwich, they discovered that their partner, Trumbull, supported the rebel cause. Selling their interest in the partnership to Trumbull, the brothers returned to Albany, "where they imagined they could be of more immediate service to Government." Continuing to publish in support of Great Britain, the brothers were once more attacked by rebels. James Robertson fled his house to hide in the woods and then, fearing discovery, went to New York City. Alexander Robertson was arrested and spent the next year in prison.

After safely reaching New York, Robertson once more established himself as a printer, but he was to be continually disappointed. He rented a printing press and began publishing a weekly newspaper, the *Royal American Gazette*. His patrons included General William Howe and Governor William Tryon, and success and prosperity seemed assured. However, in 1777, James Rivington arrived in New York as His Majesty's Printer and Robertson lost all the government printing. With his brother's safe arrival in New York in December 1777, Robertson decided to leave the New York office in his hands and sailed with the British army to Philadelphia in February 1778. James Robertson established a printing shop and published the semiweekly newspaper, the *Royal Pennsylvania Gazette*, from March to May 1778. When the British army evacuated Philadelphia, he returned to New York and continued to work with his brother in their New York office.

In 1780 Robertson once more followed the British army, this time to Charleston. He established a printing office in April 1780, but he was frustrated in his desire to acquire the government printing when Robert Wells was appointed the King's Printer for South Carolina. Robertson again turned to a newspaper for financial support, establishing the *Royal South Carolina Gazette* in June 1780. The paper ceased publication in September 1782, just before the British departure from Charleston.

Robertson returned to New York to rejoin his brother in the publication of the *Royal American Gazette*, in partnership with Nathaniel Mills and John Hicks. The New York newspaper finally ceased publication on 31 July 1783, following the departure of the Robertsons from New York in April 1783.

After deciding to leave New York, the Robertson brothers joined the company of Captain Andrew Barclay, a fellow Scot and one of sixteen captains chosen to lead the Port Roseway Associates, a group of American Loyalists who chose to move to Nova Scotia rather than remain in the United States. James Robertson quickly built a printing office and store to ply his trade. In July 1783 he was appointed one of five justices of the peace for the new community of Shelburne. By September, he and his brother were partners in the publication of a weekly news sheet, the *Royal American Gazette*, the first newspaper in Shelburne. Alexander Robertson died in November 1784. James Robertson continued to publish the newspaper and operate the printing office until 1786, when he made plans to move his printing operation to Prince Edward Island. Before his brother's death, Robertson had gone to England to present the claim of the Robertson brothers to the royal commission investigating the losses of American Loyalists. The brothers claimed losses of £650, but they were awarded only £200 in August 1784. As late as December 1788, Robertson had still not received any compensation for his wartime losses.

Moving to Charlottetown on Prince Edward Island Robertson again sought the position of King's Printer. He opened a print shop and began publishing the *Royal American Gazette* in September 1787. Robertson received the recommendation of the colonial governor, but he was once more disappointed. The Crown responded that Robertson could be named the official printer, but there would be no salary to accompany the title.

In 1789 Robertson closed his business in Charlottetown and returned to his native Scotland. He and his brother-in-law, Walter Berry, established a printing and bookselling business in Edinburgh. Robertson ran the printing establishment, while Berry managed the bookshop. In 1793 Robertson printed and sold a pamphlet (apparently written by someone else) entitled *The Political Progress of Great Britain*. As a result of this publication, which decried political developments in Britain that sought to stifle the free expression of personal opinions about the government, Robertson was tried before the High Court of Scotland and thrown in jail. While in prison, he continued to challenge the government by writing and publishing an account of three men who had been sent to Australia for their radical political views. Following his release from jail, Robertson remained in the printing business until 1805, when his estate was sequestrated for debt. He died bankrupt in Edinburgh.

Robertson married twice. His first wife, Amy (maiden name unknown), died while in Norwich in 1776, while Robertson and his brother were in exile from Albany. Nothing is known of Robertson's second wife except her first name, Mary, which appears in documents related to his bankruptcy.

Robertson was a capable printer who happened to side with the losers in the American Revolution and then failed to gain recognition from the British through receipt of an official printing position. Time and time again Robertson proved his loyalty by following the British army throughout the colonies, establishing a printing office, and publishing a newspaper supporting the Royal cause. Isaiah Thomas described him as "a worthy man and a very good printer." Unfortunately, Robertson has seldom received recognition for his abilities as a printer because his professional accomplishments have been overshadowed by the brand of loyalism.

• The primary sources are the newspapers published by James Robertson and his various partners. Another important primary source is the Memorial of Alexander and James Robertson, presented to the Loyalist claims commission, series A6, Prince Edward Island, M. 404-E, p. 183, Public Archives of Canada. The primary secondary source is a journal article by Marion Robertson, "The Loyalist Printers: James and Alexander Robertson," *Nova Scotia Historical Review* 3, no. 1 (1983): 83–93.

CAROL SUE HUMPHREY

ROBERTSON, Oswald Hope (2 June 1886–23 Mar. 1966), physician and biologist, was born in Woolwich, England, the son of Theodore Robertson, a former artillery officer, and Kathleen Conlan. In early 1888 the family moved to the San Joaquin Valley in California, but Robertson would not become a naturalized U.S. citizen until 1920. He completed high school in San Francisco and had planned to study biology, but a visit with an American medical student studying in Germany caused him to change his mind. He enrolled in premedical studies at the University of California, where he completed both a B.S. and an M.S. before transferring into the penultimate year of the medical program at Harvard University. He graduated with an M.D. in 1913, winning a Dalton scholarship for postgraduate study of pernicious anemia as part of his internship at Massachusetts General Hospital. There he was influenced by hematologist Roger I. Lee, who had studied transfusion and blood-clotting. He stayed a second year as a trainee in pathology, before accepting a position in 1915 as assistant bacteriologist and pathologist at the Rockefeller Institute in New York City. With the future Nobel laureate Francis Peyton Rous, he conducted experiments on red blood cell survival. In 1916 Robertson married Ruth Allen, a nurse, with whom he would have three children.

In 1917 Robertson joined the medical team from Massachusetts General Hospital led by Harvey Cushing to serve the American and British forces in France. During this World War I experience, he made the contribution for which he is remembered by hematologists: a method for safely collecting and storing donor blood to treat hemorrhagic shock in the battlefield. When a need was projected, he began collecting half-liter donations from healthy soldiers with group O^+ blood (the universal donor) into vessels containing an equal amount of the sodium citrate (to prevent clotting) and dextrose (to nourish the red blood cells). The mixture was stored in an icebox, ready for quick administration, without crossmatching, to wounded soldiers. His technique, frequently cited as "the first blood bank," was published in the *British Medical Journal* in 1918, but Robertson recognized his debt to earlier researchers, including those at the Rockefeller Institute. For this achievement, he was decorated by the British government (Distinguished Service Order of Great Britain, 1919).

Following the war, Robertson returned briefly to the Rockefeller Institute but soon moved to Peking (Beijing), China, first as associate professor (1919–1923) and later as professor and head (1923–1927) of the Department of Medicine in the newly established Peking Union Medical College. Initially, he had planned to study pernicious anemia, but his research interests were diverted to pneumonia because of the prevalence of that disease.

After a bout of typhus fever, Robertson decided to return to the United States to become professor and head of the Department of Medicine at the University of Chicago, a position he held from 1927 to 1951. At the time, the department was conducting one of the earliest experiments with "full-time" medicine, a project that met with some resistance. He continued to study lung infections and participated in the development of a heart-lung machine that could induce artificial pneumonia. Using a dog model, Robertson proved that the bacterial cause of pneumonia, the pneumococcus, was carried throughout the lung by infected fluids. He also explored the use of aerosols in controlling the spread of disease among hospitalized patients. These interests brought him back into service for the U.S. Army, as civilian director of the Commission on Air-borne Infections, from 1941 to 1950. With his former associate Rous, he also acted as a consultant to the formation of the Cook County Hospital blood bank, generally thought to have been the first of its kind in the United States.

Robertson became professor emeritus in 1951, but the year before he had already moved back to California to embark on a new stage in his career: fish physiology. Former associates traced this interest to a set of observations about fish populations that he had made while on vacation in the Wyoming lakes in the 1930s. After 1950 he lectured in biology at Stanford University and built a research laboratory for surgical experimentation on salmon and trout near Santa Cruz. This work resulted in the description of an endocrine syndrome produced by the pituitary gland of salmon, analogous to Cushing's syndrome in humans. He died in Santa Cruz.

Robertson was recognized for having made important contributions to both medicine and biology. A member of the U.S. National Research Council (from 1937 to 1940), the Association of Clinical Investigation, and the National Academy of Sciences (from 1943), he also belonged to the Association of American Physicians, over which he presided in 1951. With Rous, he shared the 1958 Landsteiner Award of the American Association of Blood Bankers, and in 1961 he received the Kober Medal, the highest honor of the American Association of Physicians. His friends described him as a humble aristocrat, a rigorous, creative scientist, and a solitary yet warm personality. Thirty years after his death, his work in blood banking stands

as his best-known medical achievement, but his articles on fish endocrinology constitute the most frequently cited of his 127 publications.

• Robertson's papers were donated to the American Philosophical Society in Philadelphia. Other papers are in the Rockefeller Archive Center, North Tarrytown, N.Y. For an account of his early blood-banking experience, see his "A Method of Citrated Blood Transfusion" and "Transfusion with Preserved Red Cells," *British Medical Journal* 1 (Apr. and June 1918): 477–79 and 691–95. A three-part article on lung infection, coauthored with L. T. Coggeshall and E. E. Terrell, is "Experimental Pneumococcus Lobar Pneumonia in the Dog," *Journal of Clinical Investigation* 12 (1933): 393–493. For his early work on fish migration, see "An Ecological Study of Two High Mountain Lakes in the Wind River Range, Wyoming," *Ecology* 28 (1947): 87. See also, with B. C. Wexler, "Histological Changes in the Organs and Tissues of Migrating and Spawning Pacific Salmon (genus *Oncorhynchus*)," *Endocrinology* 66 (1960): 222–39, and with M. A. Krupp et al., "Physiological Changes Occurring in the Blood of the Pacific Salmon (*Oncorhynchus tshawytscha*) Accompanying Sexual Maturation and Spawning," *Endocrinology* 68 (1961): 733–46. L. T. Coggeshall, "Oswald Hope Robertson," National Academy of Sciences, *Biological Memoirs* 42 (1971): 319–38, includes a bibliography and a portrait. See also the tributes by former associates, F. Peyton Rous, "Presentation of the Kober Medal," *Transactions of the Association of American Physicians* 74 (1961): 49–56; and J. Garrott Allen, "O. H. Robertson—An Inquiring Mind: From Blood Bank to Cutthroat Trout," *Pharos* 48 (1985): 25–27. An obituary is in the *New York Times*, 25 Mar. 1966.

JACALYN DUFFIN

ROBERTSON, Sterling Clack (2 Oct. 1785–4 Mar. 1842), founder of Robertson's Colony in Texas, was born in Nashville, Tennessee, the son of Elijah Robertson, a planter, and Sarah Maclin. He received a liberal education under the direction of Judge John McNairy.

From 13 November 1814 to 13 May 1815 Robertson served as deputy quartermaster general, with the rank of major, under Major General William Carroll, who had fought the British at the battle of New Orleans. Robertson, whose name was missing from the muster rolls at the time of the battle, took care of the wounded and bought supplies and medicines for them on the return march to Nashville. He became a planter in Giles County, Tennessee. He had two children, one with Rachael Smith and one with Frances King. There are no records of any marriage.

On 2 March 1822 Robertson was one of seventy citizens of Tennessee and Kentucky who signed a memorial addressed to the Independent Government of Mexico, asking for permission to settle in Texas. In November 1825 he set out for Texas as a member of a party to explore and survey Leftwich's Grant, which initially consisted of all or part of nineteen present-day counties in central Texas. He remained in Texas until August 1826. In the spring of 1830 he signed a subcontract with the Texas Association to bring 200 families to Texas, but the association lost interest in the project so he obtained a colonization contract in his own name in 1834 and served as *empresario* (contractor) of Robertson's Colony in 1834 and 1835. As *empresario* Robertson was granted permission by the state government of Coahuila and Texas to bring in up to 800 families, and, for each 100 families thus introduced, he was to be granted five leagues and five labors of premium lands, or nearly 200,000 acres for all 800 families. He helped pay moving expenses to Texas, and he furnished guns, gunpowder, lead, and food to keep his settlers going during the early years of the colony.

Robertson became the captain of a Texas Ranger company on 17 January 1836, served as a delegate from the municipality of Milam to the convention at Washington-on-the-Brazos (1–17 Mar. 1836), signed the Texas Declaration of Independence and the Constitution of the Republic of Texas, took part in the battle of San Jacinto, then served as a senator in the first and second congresses of the Republic of Texas (3 Oct. 1836–24 May 1838), after which he retired to his home in Robertson County, Texas, where he became the earliest known breeder of Arabian horses in Texas. He died there, but in 1935 his remains were reinterred at the Texas State Cemetery in Austin. The area of Robertson's Colony covered all or part of thirty present-day Texas counties. In all, Robertson was responsible for settling 600 families in Texas.

• Everything that is known about Sterling Clack Robertson, the Texas *empresario*, is contained in the nineteen-volume series compiled and edited by Malcolm D. McLean and published under the title *Papers Concerning Robertson's Colony in Texas* (1974–1993).

MALCOLM D. MCLEAN

ROBERTSON, Thomas Bolling (27 Feb. 1779–5 Oct. 1828), third governor of the state of Louisiana, was born in Prince George's County, Virginia, the son of William Robertson, a Petersburg merchant, and Elizabeth Bolling. There is confusion regarding the year of his birth. Family tradition places it as 1773, but some scholarly sources list it as six years later. Robertson's family played a major part in Virginia affairs, his father serving as member and secretary of the council for many years, his brother John Robertson as attorney general, chancellor, and congressman, and another brother, Wyndham Robertson, as governor in 1836. A 1797 graduate of the College of William and Mary, Robertson practiced law in Virginia until Thomas Jefferson on 12 August 1807 appointed him secretary of the Territory of Orleans. In that office he also acted as one of three federal land commissioners and as attorney general of the territory from March to September 1808.

Opinionated and contentious, Robertson quarreled continuously with territorial governor William C. C. Claiborne and sent regular reports to his Washington superiors criticizing what he deemed the ignorance and backwardness of the Latin creole population among whom he served. But when the territory became the state of Louisiana in 1812 he readily accepted election as its first and for a time its only member of the national House of Representatives, where he worked primarily to defend the tariff protecting the state's young sugar industry.

Resigning from Congress in April 1818, Robertson returned to Louisiana and successfully campaigned to succeed the native Jacques Villeré as governor in 1820, profiting from a community consensus to alternate the position between contending creole and Anglo-American factions. Instead of promoting ethnic harmony, Robertson's election introduced a "time of troubles" in Louisiana politics, for he steadfastly committed his administration to advancement of the American community at the expense of the native French, especially promoting favoritism toward Americans in patronage and encouraging the pervasive cultural antagonisms, and he did so in such arrogant and insensitive fashion that even some within his own ethnic group christened him "King Thomas," a play on his oft-boasted supposed descent from Powhatan.

The conflict deepened in January 1823 when Robertson supported an effort to move the state capital from New Orleans to Baton Rouge, in the American-dominated Florida parishes (so called because they had once been part of the British colony of West Florida), upriver from the metropolis. Creoles and their French immigrant allies responded with attempts in the legislature to expel Florida members from the senate, and the state moved close to civil war, averted only when both sides recoiled from the extreme positions that threatened to plunge them into violence.

The return to an uneasy peace did little to improve the atmosphere of Robertson's governorship. His veto of a usury bill in 1823 opened him to charges that he favored "shavers" and usurers, the preponderance of whom, the Gallic press claimed, figured among Robertson's American favorites. A renewed quarrel in militia companies, triggered by conflict between American and unnaturalized foreign officers and sustained in large part by Robertson's refusal to address the problem, kept the community in turmoil during the last months of his term.

Despite these obvious failures, Robertson's administration was not without its accomplishments, including internal improvements such as the opening of the Red and Pearl rivers to navigation, the building of Louisiana's segment of the national road from Madisonville to Nashville, creation of the Bank of Louisiana in 1824, initiation of planning for a new state penitentiary, and increased funding for the College of Orleans and the state's Charity Hospital. His gubernatorial messages, as well, spelled out a broad program of liberal reforms, calling for abolition of imprisonment for debt, expansion of eleemosynary services, and speedier transfer of national lands to state and private ownership. But these laudable expressions did little to improve his popularity, eroded more and more by his increasingly violent temper joined to intemperate denunciation of those who opposed him, with explications of his actions that bordered on paranoia and mental derangement. Bedeviled by financial problems as well, Robertson resigned the governorship in November 1824 to become judge of the federal eastern district of Louisiana. His judicial career proved decidedly lackluster, and a final collapse in his reputation came in 1826 when he reported to the Louisiana legislature that election returns, which he had previously denied ever having received, had accidentally been found in the bed of his greyhound bitch.

A champion of Henry Clay and John Quincy Adams in national politics, Robertson vigorously supported Latin American independence but opposed the Adams-Oñis treaty, which he thought surrendered legitimate U.S. claims to Texas. He resigned his federal judgeship in 1828, dying shortly thereafter at White Sulphur Springs, Virginia. The cause of his death is unknown. In the mid-1820s he had married Lelia Skipwith, daughter of Fulwar Skipwith, governor of the short-lived Republic of West Florida. They had no children.

• There is no collection of Robertson papers, but a fragmentary diary covering the few months just prior to his governorship is held by the Virginia Historical Society. He is mentioned, as well, in many of the letters in the Josiah Stoddard Johnston Collection at the Historical Society of Pennsylvania. His report of experiences in France while a congressman appears in the Richmond *Enquirer*, 30 Sept.–23 Dec. 1815, and in book form as *Events in Paris* (1816). There is no Robertson biography, but he figures in James S. Patton, *The Family of William and Elizabeth Bolling Robertson* (1975), and Wyndham Robertson, *Pocahontas and Her Descendants* (1887). His portrait and an account of his career may be found in Joseph G. Tregle, Jr., "Thomas Bolling Robertson," in *The Louisiana Governors*, ed. Joseph G. Dawson III (1990), pp. 91–96.

JOSEPH G. TREGLE, JR.

ROBERTSON, William (19 Sept. 1721–11 June 1793), minister and historian, was born in the parish of Borthwick near Edinburgh, Scotland, the son of William Robertson, a minister, and Eleanor Pitcairne. Apart from several visits to London and an abortive attempt to join the Jacobite Pretender's army in 1745, Robertson spent his entire life in or around Edinburgh. From 1735 to 1741 he attended the University of Edinburgh. After the completion of his studies, he was granted a license to preach and spent the next decades in various parishes. In 1751 he married his cousin Mary Nisbet; they had three sons and two daughters.

Parallel to his career as a minister, Robertson became an increasingly important public figure in the Scottish Enlightenment. He first gained prominence in the 1751–1652 debate over whether ministers should be appointed by their parishioners or by patrons. Robertson advocated the latter because he believed that the alternative would subvert the authority of the church and therefore undermine society. This debate resulted in the formation of what came to be called the Moderate party, a group that also wrote for the new *Edinburgh Review* and in which Robertson played a leading role. In another debate in 1757, he defended the theater against charges that it was morally dangerous—a progressive position for his time. In general, Robertson's political views can be described

as guardedly liberal with a strong emphasis on the maintenance of public order and stability.

These Enlightenment views, especially concerning progress and tolerance, were also worked out and presented by Robertson in his historical writings. In 1759 he published his first large historical work, *The History of Scotland during the Reigns of Queen Mary and of King James VI till his Accession to the Crown of England*. This work was an immediate success and brought Robertson much political and social prestige. *Scotland* traced the country's development from feudalism to an emergent capitalist society and the rule of law. Robertson's Enlightenment view of history included what he described in 1755 as the "plan of God's providence, . . . a skilful [sic] hand, directing the revolutions of human affairs" (*Situation of the World*, p. 4).

In the early 1760s, Robertson became more active as a public figure. He was appointed as the principal of Edinburgh University in 1762 (a position he held until 1792) and one year later was elected as the moderator of the General Assembly of the Church of Scotland. In 1763 he was also named the "historiographer to his Majesty for Scotland." In these positions, Robertson wielded great influence over academic, ecclesiastical, and public discourse in Edinburgh, which he tried to use with statesmanlike impartiality.

Robertson's next major historical work was *The History of the Reign of Emperor Charles V*, which was published in 1769. It was followed by the first part of *The History of America* in 1777, which was immediately translated into French and German. This work, divided into eight books, presented "an account of the discovery of the New World, and of the progress of the Spanish arms and colonies there" (vol. 1, p. vi). It gives extensive descriptions of Native-American cultures and moves on to narrate the Spanish colonization of America, which Robertson interpreted as a means of bringing progress to the peoples of the New World. *America* was part of a larger project that was to cover the Spanish, British, and Portuguese colonizations of the New World. This project was interrupted by the American Revolution, which forced Robertson to "wait for times of greater tranquillity, when I can write and the public read with more impartiality and better information than at present" (letter to Robert Waddilove, July 1778). In 1796 Robertson's son posthumously published two fragments of Robertson's history of the British colonization of America, which treated Virginia until 1688 and New England until 1652. This was the first section of *America* to actually appear in the United States, where *Charles V* had been published in 1770.

After 1780, Robertson did not do much original historical work and retired from politics. His international reputation continued to grow, and he became a member of the Academy of Sciences at Padua and of the Russian Academy. In Edinburgh he worked to improve the university and was one of the founders of the Royal Society in 1782. However, Robertson lost much of his prestige in the city because of the changing political climate. He spent the years after 1785 continually revising his earlier historical works. Robertson's last work that was published before his death was *An Historical Disquisition concerning the Knowledge Which the Ancients Had of India* (1791), which oscillates between a tolerance of Indian culture and support of the British Empire.

Although his importance has waned since the nineteenth century, Robertson is still considered one of the founders of modern historiography. With David Hume and Edward Gibbon, he formed the Edinburgh "triumvirate" of historians. Of these three writers, Robertson covered the greatest variety of subjects. In *America*, he described some of the qualities he desired in a historian: "patient industry," an "impartiality which weighs evidence with cool attention," and the ability to participate in a "critical discussion" (vol. 2, p. 440). Robertson insisted on the use of historical sources and documents to an extent that was unknown at the time. He declared that it was not "by theory or conjecture that history decides, with regard to the state of character of nations. It produces facts as the foundation of every judgment which it ventures to pronounce" (*America*, vol. 2, p. 273), and that these facts should be learned from original documents. In *Scotland*, he wrote that history should "relate real occurrences, and . . . explain their real causes and effects" (vol. 1, p. 165). Although Robertson's individual histories have been superseded by later works, his theoretical contributions to historiography, influenced by Enlightenment thinking, still endure.

• Most of Robertson's papers and manuscripts are held in the Robertson-McDonald Collection at the National Library of Scotland, in the Edinburgh University Library, and in the British Library. Several of his sermons were published during his lifetime, including *The Situation of the World at the Time of Christ's Appearance* (1755). Others appeared posthumously, such as the *Sermon on the Centenary of the Glorious Revolution* (1788). Robertson also wrote a number of occasional pieces, including contributions to *The Principal Acts of the General Assembly of the Church of Scotland, Convened at Edinburgh the 26th Day of May, 1763*, the "Dedication to the King" in the first volume of the *Transactions of the Royal Society of Edinburgh* (1788), and a number of reviews in the *Edinburgh Review*. Two contemporary biographies are Dugald Stewart, *Account of the Life and Writings of William Robertson* (1801), and George Gleig, *Some Account of the Life and Writings of Robertson* (1812). Important recent material on Robertson includes David Spadafora, *The Idea of Progress in Eighteenth-Century Britain* (1990), which provides excellent background to his life and thought; Mark Duckworth, "An Eighteenth-Century Questionnaire: William Robertson on the Indians," *Studies in the Eighteenth Century* 11, no. 1 (Feb. 1987): 36–49; and Mark Kingwell, "Politics and the Polite Society in the Scottish Enlightenment," *Historical Reflections* 19, no. 3 (Fall 1993): 363–87, which tries to reclaim Robertson as a "practical genius." Stewart J. Brown, ed., *William Robertson and the Expansion of Empire* (1997), includes ten essays on a wide range of topics as well as an extensive bibliography of secondary literature by Jeffrey Smitten.

NORBERT SCHÜRER

ROBESON, Paul (9 Apr. 1898–23 Jan. 1976), actor, singer, and civil rights activist, was born Paul Leroy Robeson in Princeton, New Jersey, the son of William Drew Robeson, a Protestant minister, and Maria Louisa Bustill, a schoolteacher. Robeson's mother died when he was six years old, and he grew up under the influence of a perfectionist father, a former runaway slave who fought in the Union army. During his senior year at the Somerville, New Jersey, high school, he achieved the highest score in a statewide scholarship examination to attend Rutgers College (later Rutgers University). The lone black at Rutgers as a freshman in 1915 and only the third African American to attend the institution, Robeson was an outstanding student and athlete. A varsity debater, he won class prizes for oratory all four years, was elected to Phi Beta Kappa as a junior, was one of four seniors chosen for membership in the Cap and Skull honorary society, and was named class valedictorian. The 6'3", 215-pound Robeson earned twelve varsity letters in four sports (baseball, basketball, football, and track) and was twice named football All-America (1917 and 1918). According to former Yale coach Walter Camp, "There never has been a more serviceable end, both in attack and defense, than Robeson." Despite his popularity with fellow students, a series of social slights and racial incidents in football brought to the fore longstanding concerns about race. Robeson's senior thesis predicted the eventual use of the Fourteenth Amendment to advance civil rights, and his commencement address boldly combined the accommodationist philosophy of Booker T. Washington with the more militant views of W. E. B. Du Bois.

Robeson received the B.A. degree in 1919 and moved to Harlem preparatory to entering the Columbia University Law School in 1920. He helped finance his legal education by playing professional football for three seasons (1920–1922) with the Akron Pros and the Milwaukee Badgers. In 1921 he married Eslanda "Essie" Cardozo Goode, a member of a prominent Washington, D.C., black family, who worked as a laboratory pathologist at Columbia's medical school; they had one child. Recognizing Robeson's lack of enthusiasm for the law and football, his wife urged him to take up acting. After playing the lead in a Harlem YMCA production of *Simon the Cyrenian* in 1920, he appeared in several other local productions and became acquainted with the Provincetown Players, a Greenwich Village theatrical group that included Eugene O'Neill. He debuted professionally in a short-run Broadway play, *Taboo*, in 1922. Robeson, meanwhile, finished his legal studies, received the LL.B. degree in February 1923, and joined a New York City law firm headed by a Rutgers alumnus. But discouraged by discrimination within the firm and the legal profession generally, he quit a few months later, before taking the bar exam, to pursue an acting career.

Robeson launched his stage career in 1924 in the lead roles in two O'Neill plays, *The Emperor Jones* and *All God's Chillun Got Wings*, the latter a daring drama about interracial marriage. He achieved a spectacular triumph in London in 1930 when he not only became one of the first black actors to play Othello but also rendered the finest portrayal of the character yet seen.

Robeson was also an accomplished singer, and at Essie's urging he performed at Carnegie Hall in 1925. The first soloist to devote an entire concert to Negro spirituals, Robeson both enthralled the sell-out audience and boosted the popularity of the musical genre. Robeson steadfastly refused to sing operatic and classical music, preferring to emphasize Negro spirituals and international folk songs. In time his rich basso-baritone voice was familiar to millions through national and international concert tours, radio performances, and more than 300 recordings. He combined singing and acting in several musicals and was best known for his rendition of "Ol' Man River" in *Show Boat* (London, 1928; New York, 1932; Los Angeles, 1940). Robeson also appeared in eleven motion pictures, including film versions of *The Emperor Jones* (1933) and *Show Boat* (1936) and Hollywood extravaganzas such as *King Solomon's Mines* (1937). Robeson chafed at the stereotyping and racial slights suffered by blacks in the movie industry and demanded positive leading roles; he was most proud of his work in *Song of Freedom* (1936) and *The Proud Valley* (1940). Robeson's legacy, as actor/director Sidney Poitier noted, was profound: "Before him, no black man or woman had been portrayed in American movies as anything but a racist stereotype" (quoted in *Current Biography* [1976], pp. 345–46).

Robeson's political ideas took shape after George Bernard Shaw introduced him to socialism in 1928. To escape American racism, he lived during most of the 1930s in Europe, returning to the United States only for movie and concert appearances. Impressed by the absence of racial and class discrimination in the Soviet Union during a concert tour in 1934, Robeson subsequently spent extended periods in Moscow, learned Russian, and enrolled his son in Soviet schools. He became politically active in opposing fascism, imperialism, and racism. He gave benefit performances in England for refugees from fascist countries, associated with British left-wing political groups, became acquainted with key figures in the West African Political Union, including Jomo Kenyatta and Kwame Nkrumah, and in 1938 traveled to Spain to support the republican troops engaged in the civil war against Francisco Franco's fascists.

When forced by the outbreak of World War II to return to the United States in 1939, Robeson was as well known as a critic of American racism and champion of the Soviet Union as an entertainer. He protested the segregation of organized baseball, appeared frequently at union and labor meetings, delivered antiracist lectures during concerts, joined the pan-Africanist Council on African Affairs, and quit Hollywood because "the industry is not prepared to permit me to portray the life or express the living interests, hopes, and aspirations of the struggling people from whom I come." Robeson's political activism drew criticism but did not hurt his career, primarily because of the U.S.–Soviet military alliance. Indeed, he enjoyed his greatest hour as a performer in October 1943 when he became the first black actor to play Othello in the United States. Following a then record-setting 296 performances for a Shakespearean drama on Broadway, the company undertook a nationwide tour and Robeson received the Donaldson Award as the best actor of the year. In 1945 the National Association for the Advancement of Colored People (NAACP) awarded him the prestigious Spingarn Medal.

However, when Robeson continued to use the Soviet Union as a hammer to pound against racism in the United States, he suffered the fate of other political leftists during the anti-Communist hysteria of the Cold War. In 1946 he denied under oath to a California State Legislature committee that he was a member of the Communist party but thereafter refused as a matter of conscience and constitutional right to comment on his political beliefs or affiliation. Instead, he continued to speak out against American racism and to praise the Soviet "experiment in socialism," associated openly with Marxist organizations, and, as a founder and chairman of the Progressive party, campaigned for Henry Wallace in the 1948 presidential election. While addressing the World Peace Congress in Paris in 1949, he said: "It is unthinkable that American Negroes could go to war on behalf of those who have oppressed us for generations against a country [the Soviet Union] which in one generation has raised our people to the full dignity of mankind." He was immediately denounced by the black and white press, repudiated by most black civil rights organizations, and attacked by government agencies and congressional committees. The U.S. House of Representatives Committee on Un-American Activities labeled him a "Communist" and a "Communist sympathizer" and enlisted Jackie Robinson, who in 1947 had integrated organized baseball, to "give the lie" to Robeson's statement. He was hounded by the Federal Bureau of Investigation, and in 1950 the State Department took away his passport, refusing to issue a new one until he signed a non-Communist oath and pledged not to give political speeches abroad. He refused, and his persistent use of the Fifth Amendment during House and Senate hearings and the Soviet Union awarding him the International Stalin Peace Prize in 1952 only exacerbated the public's perception of him as a subversive. Outraged Rutgers alumni demanded that his name be excised from the school's athletic records and that the honorary master of arts degree awarded to him in 1930 be rescinded. He was blacklisted as an entertainer, and his recordings were removed from stores. His income fell from over $100,000 in 1947 to $6,000 in 1952. Unable to travel abroad to earn money, Robeson was forced to sell his estate, "The Beeches," in Enfield, Connecticut.

By the late 1950s the burgeoning civil rights movement along with the lessening of Cold War paranoia and the demise of McCarthyism led to a rehabilitation of Robeson's reputation, particularly among African Americans. Critical was *Here I Stand* (1958), a brief autobiography as manifesto in which Robeson reaffirmed his admiration for the Soviet Union and in which he stated, "I am not and never have been involved in any international conspiracy." He also declared his "belief in the principles of scientific Socialism" as the basis for a society "economically, socially, culturally, and ethically superior to a system based upon production for private profit." Although essentially a recitation of the stands he had taken all along, as the first sentence of the foreword—"I am a Negro"—made clear, the book was primarily a declaration of allegiance to the black community. Here Robeson presaged the Black Power politics of the 1960s by rejecting gradualism in civil rights, insisting that "the Negro people's movement must be led by Negroes," and advocating change through the "mass action" of "aroused and militant" black masses. He performed several concerts, recorded an album, and after being reissued a passport in 1958 (following a Supreme Court decision in a related case that confirmed his contention that the right to travel was independent of political views), left for Europe to revitalize his career.

But fifteen years of persistent harassment and political attacks had taken its toll, destroying not only his career but also his health and, ultimately, his sanity. Despite a tumultuous welcome, his sojourn in the Soviet Union was bleak. He was frequently hospitalized for exhaustion and a circulatory ailment as well as emotional instability. He attempted suicide; excessive drug and electric shock therapy likely caused permanent brain damage. He returned to the United States in 1963 and went into seclusion. His wife's death in 1965 ended their long marriage of convenience. Robeson's numerous infidelities had led to several separations, but Essie, who obtained a Ph.D. in anthropology and wrote *African Journey* (1945), resignedly managed his career in exchange for economic and social status. Robeson then moved to Philadelphia, where he lived with a sister. Virtually an invalid and suffering from acute depression, he refused interviews and was seen only by family and close friends. Too ill to attend the "75th Birthday Salute to Paul Robeson" staged at Carnegie Hall in April 1973 by leaders in the entertainment and civil rights fields, he sent a recorded message: "I want you to know that I am still the same Paul, dedicated as ever to the worldwide cause of humanity for freedom, peace and brotherhood." Three years later he died in Philadelphia.

Paul Robeson is an American tragedy. He was an enormously talented black man whose imposing personality and uncompromising political ideals were more than a racist and anti-Communist United States could appreciate or tolerate. One of the major performing artists of the twentieth century, his achievements as a stage actor, movie star, and singer are individually outstanding but collectively astounding. He was easily the most influential black entertainer of his day. Because he spent so much time abroad, Robeson never established close political associations in black America and thus served the African-American community more as a symbol of black consciousness and pride than as a spokesperson. A victim of character assassination during the Cold War, Robeson—unlike many black (and white) entertainers who maintained silence to protect or advance their careers—courageously combined art and politics. If he was politically naive and oblivious to the realities of Stalinist Russia, he astutely connected American racism and the international oppression of colored peoples. And Robeson proved to be ahead of his time in rejecting both the black nationalism of separation and repatriation as well as the assimilationism of the NAACP in favor of a cultural pluralism in which ethnic integrity was maintained amid international solidarity. For all his achievements, Robeson's pro-Soviet stance continues to preclude just recognition. He remains the only two-time All-America not in the College Football Hall of Fame.

• By far the largest and most important collection of manuscript materials pertaining to Paul Robeson's life and career is the Robeson Family Archives, featuring the writings of his wife, in the Moorland-Spingarn Research Center, Howard University, Washington, D.C. An excellent guide to published material by and about Robeson is Lenwood G. Davis, comp., *A Paul Robeson Research Guide: A Selected Annotated Bibliography* (1982). Indispensable is Robeson's autobiography, *Here I Stand* (1958), and a compendium of his views, Philip S. Foner, ed., *Paul Robeson Speaks: Writings, Speeches, Interviews, 1918–1974* (1978). There is no wholly satisfying biography of Robeson. Eslanda Cardozo Robeson, *Paul Robeson, Negro* (1930), is hagiographic but provides intimate information about Robeson's ancestry, personality, and personal life not available elsewhere. Marie Seton, *Paul Robeson* (1958), an "authorized" biography by a London journalist who was close to the Robeson family, is valuable for firsthand information and for Robeson's "corrections" to the original manuscript. Dorothy Butler Gilliam, *Paul Robeson: All-American* (1976), is a sprightly written and perceptive survey of his life. Martin Bauml Duberman, *Paul Robeson* (1988), is an exhaustively researched and richly detailed encyclopedic work that more effectively recounts than analyzes Robeson's life. Also important is an anthology of topical essays and tributes that initially appeared in *Freedomways* magazine, *Paul Robeson: The Great Forerunner* (1975; rev. ed., 1978). Important obituaries are in the *New York Times*, 24 Jan. 1976, and the *Amsterdam News* (New York City), 31 Jan. 1976.

LARRY R. GERLACH

ROBEY, Don D. (1 Nov. 1903–16 June 1975), entertainment entrepreneur and rhythm-and-blues record label owner, was born Don Deadric Robey in Houston, Texas, the son of Zeb Robey and Gertrude (maiden name unknown). Little is known of his childhood. Robey dropped out of high school in the eleventh grade, reportedly to become a professional gambler in Houston nightspots frequented by African Americans; later he was suspected of being involved in the city's numbers operation. He also entered the taxi business prior to World War II and established a business in entertainment promotion, bringing name bands and celebrity attractions into segregated sections of the Houston area.

Though Robey opened his first nightclub in 1937, it was the postwar Bronze Peacock Dinner Club (1946) that he parlayed into a connecting set of entertainment and music businesses that made him, according to the

Houston Informer, one of the city's "foremost black business wizards." Robey's skill as a promoter in booking talent for the Bronze Peacock led to his activity first in the talent management business and eventually into records and music publishing. He established Peacock Records in 1949 to launch the blues career of Clarence "Gatemouth" Brown, a relatively unknown guitarist from San Antonio, and soon signed other secular and gospel acts.

Robey's first big record was released in 1950, when the religious song "Our Father" by the Original Five Blind Boys (Peacock 1550) became a national jukebox hit. Robey once claimed that it was he who "put the beat" in gospel music. Eventually he had so many religious groups under contract that he established an additional gospel label, Song Bird.

In 1952 Robey became a partner, then owner, of Duke Records of Memphis, Tennessee, moving its operation to Houston and establishing ballad singer Johnny Ace as a black crooner and a nationally known rhythm-and-blues performer. Robey carefully cultivated the polished, uptown image that Berry Gordy would later emulate at Motown. The next year Willie Mae "Big Mama" Thornton's "Hound Dog" (Peacock 1612) made her famous in the national blues community and established Peacock Records as a major independent label in black secular music. Robey is also credited with discovering Bobby "Blue" Bland, Little Junior Parker, and the Dixie Hummingbirds.

With Evelyn Johnson, his business partner and common-law wife from 1953 to 1960, Robey helped establish the Buffalo Booking Agency in Houston to arrange personal appearances for his recording artists. Eventually, Buffalo Booking was able to send Duke and Peacock acts to California and large cities in the East and Midwest.

After Johnny Ace shot himself playing Russian roulette on Christmas night 1954, his new record, "Pledging My Love," became the most played R & B record of 1955. It was a crossover hit on the popular music charts as well, the first ballad by a black male performer signed to an independent label to attract a white audience in the postwar era. "Pledging My Love" established Duke Records as an important cultural force in the transition between rhythm-and-blues and rock-and-roll.

In 1957 Robey developed a new label, Back Beat, and signed young white performers in an attempt to court the white teenage market. In 1963 he added the Sure-Shot label to his operation, but in the mid-1960s, as R & B became more popular, Robey's importance as an independent entrepreneur in the field of black secular music began to diminish. In addition, his hold on black gospel was threatened by an eleven-year lawsuit with Chess Records of Chicago.

When the courts ruled against him, Robey sold all his music business interests to ABC/Dunhill in 1973 for a reported $1 million. By this time Robey's Lion and Don publishing companies controlled 2,700 copyrights, and his various record labels had 100 contracted artists ($250,000 of unrecouped advanced royalties on active contracts), with approximately 2,000 unreleased masters. Robey, who had been able to acquire writer credit on many of the songs he recorded, ended up as the author of 1,200 published songs.

It is alleged that Robey was a "black godfather," "a czar of the Negro underworld," and "a character out of *Guys and Dolls*." Evelyn Johnson admitted that while he did everything his way, "he did far more good than he did bad." Robey was a pioneer in the history of black music in the United States. Galen Gart calls him "the first successful black entrepreneur to emerge in the music business after World War II."

Robey married for the first time in 1921 or 1922 (Beatrice Sherman, one child) and for the last time in 1960 (Murphy Louise Moore, three children). In between, he married, divorced, and remarried Sadie Malone (no children) and entered into common-law marriages with Naomi Parks (two children) and Evelyn Johnson (no children). He was an avid sportsman and hunter who raised thoroughbred horses and promoted, and sometimes participated in, rodeos. He helped establish the first golf course for blacks in Houston, and in his later years he became a community leader in the United Negro Fund Drive. Robey continued to work as a consultant to ABC/Dunhill (now MCA) until his death in Houston.

• For the most complete account of Robey's career, see Galen Gart and Roy C. Ames, *Duke/Peacock Records: An Illustrated History with Discography* (1990). Alan Govenar's *Meeting the Blues* (1988) and *The Early Years of Rhythm & Blues: Focus on Houston* (1990), provide valuable information about Robey and excellent photographs of him and the performers signed to his record companies. See the chapter titled "The Black-Owned Texas Company" in Arnold Shaw's *Honkers and Shouters: The Golden Years of Rhythm & Blues* (1978) and "The Success Story of Duke & Peacock Records" in *Nothing But the Blues*, ed. Mike Leadbitter (1971), for overviews of the complete Robey operation. The only known published interview with Robey is Craig Fisher's "Don Robey—A Lifetime of Music," *Record World*, 24 Mar. 1973, pp. 3, 24, 49, which is reprinted in Mike Sigman, ed., *Record World Dialogues* (1974). For a negative account of Robey from the point of view of the founder of Duke Records see George A. Moonoogian and Roger Meeden, "Duke Records—The Early Years: An Interview with David J. Mattis," *Whiskey, Women, and . . .* , June 1984, pp. 20–21. James M. Salem, "Death and the Rhythm-and-Bluesman: The Life and Recordings of Johnny Ace," *American Music* (Fall 1993): 316–67, provides a full account of Robey as music producer and marketer. In addition, Nelson George, "Why I Promote the Blues: Dave Clark Was a Promotion Man before the Term's Creation. To Him, James Brown Is a Kid," *Village Voice*, 26 Aug. 1986, pp. 74–77, treats Robey as an R & B hero. Obituaries are in *Rolling Stone*, 31 July 1975; *Variety*, 9 July 1975; *Living Blues*, Sept.–Oct. 1975; and the *Houston Forward Times* and the *Houston Informer*, both 21 June 1975.

JAMES M. SALEM

ROBIE, Thomas (20 Mar. 1689–28 Aug. 1729), tutor, mathematician, and physician, was born in Boston, Massachusetts, the son of William Robie and Elizabeth Greenough, laborers. Baptized in Increase Mather and Cotton Mather's North Church where his father was a full member, Robie was influenced by the Mathers during a period when they were increasingly interested in scientific pursuits, especially astronomy. Robie was early inclined toward science, but coming from an impecunious family, he could not satisfy his inclination without patronage from the Mathers, Thomas Brattle, and others in the scientific community who had influence at Harvard College.

Robie was able to graduate from Harvard College with the class of 1708 through the help of scholarships and teaching a half year in Watertown during his senior year. Returning to Boston, he joined the Mathers' church and began writing a series of almanacs. Eleven were published before 1720, supporting him financially and nourishing his inclination toward mathematics and astronomy. Robie also joined with the library keeper and future president of Harvard, Edward Holyoke, in calculating the course of solar eclipses through to 1845. Robie's studies and scientific calculations after 1708 qualified him for an A.M. degree in 1711.

One of Robie's principal patrons during his undergraduate and graduate years was Thomas Brattle, the treasurer of the college and New England's most talented mathematician and astronomer. In 1711 Robie assisted Brattle in studying the recurrence of smallpox epidemics, attempting to find a mathematical pattern that would allow them to predict future epidemics. The recurrance of epidemics, however, does not have patterns like comets and eclipses. The attempt failed but is important for showing that Robie learned—probably from Brattle—the crucial scientific importance of discovering mathematical relationships in nature. Later as a tutor at Harvard, Robie asserted that knowledge of mathematics was "useful for Solving all questions in any Science Phylosophy Medicine etc. to help men to think true and know when they doe so."

Careers in science were not available in New England, and Robie reluctantly cast about for a job as minister while also accepting an appointment in 1712 to the college sinecures of Librarian and Scholar of the House. In 1713 he was appointed a tutor, a job that paid little and required that he remain unmarried; however, it was the closest thing to a scientific career available. Although tutors were required to be eclectic, they were encouraged to pursue special areas of knowledge. Robie specialized in astronomy and created an observatory on the top floor of Massachusetts Hall where people in the community were invited to learn and assist in observations. One recorded public exhibition was the observation of a solar eclipse from Massachusetts Hall on 27 November 1722, which he preceded with an essay in the two local newspapers "For the Entertainment of the Country and the Promoting of Knowledge."

During his years as tutor, Robie joined with Cotton Mather, Thomas Prince, and others in educating the community through almanacs and essays on earthquakes, lightning, and other matters of popular scientific interest. He also became one of the Royal Society's correspondents. Scientifically minded men in

New England were cultivated by William Derham, a fellow of the society and influential proponent of buttressing religion with science. Derham often presented information from New Englanders to the Royal Society, and Robie's communications include careful descriptions of astronomical and meteorological phenomena. Robie, however, was more dedicated to science than were his fellow New Englanders, and he did more than serve Derham. One of his publications, "An Account of a large Quantity of Alcalious Salt Produced by Burning Rotten Wood" (*Philosophical Transactions of the Royal Society* 31 [1720–1721]: 121–124), was the first chemical analysis published by a British American.

Because of his inclinations and his position at Harvard, Robie pursued mathematics and science more single-mindedly and productively than had any previous New Englander. Increasing cosmopolitanism allowed Robie to have better access to newer books and periodicals, and his writings show consistent reliance on the best English scientists and mathematicians he could find. Boston, however, was still a provincial society. Robie had to rely on popularizations of Newtonianism and other scientific works of varying quality. Understanding the provincialism of New England, Robie filled an important role as New England's most serious scientist. In the context of that role, Robie, in 1720, laid claim to and was awarded an income from Thomas Brattle's endowment at Harvard, which supported a mathematician who carried on scientific correspondence with overseas scholars.

Robie's influence on the formal Harvard curriculum is difficult to trace. Thomas Brattle, who never showed any knowledge of calculus, had informally taught algebra and higher levels of geometry to interested students although the formal curriculum required only arithmetic and a low level of geometry. Commencement theses during Robie's tenure as tutor indicate that algebra was being taught; the first indication of the teaching of Newton's Method of Fluxions (calculus) appears in 1719. Commencement theses do not necessarily reflect what was required of every student in the formal curriculum, but given the obscurity of the sources, Robie may be credited with introducing calculus into the provincial college.

While a tutor, Robie was sometimes a controversial figure. Beginning in 1720 he joined with fellow tutors Henry Flynt and Nicholas Sever in an attempt to preserve the power and status of tutors on the Harvard Corporation at a time when these were threatened. The essential question was whether tutors would continue to help govern the college as colleagues of the president or become mere employees. When by 1723 this controversy refused to end and became entwined with religious factions allied for and against the autocratic president, John Leverett (1662–1724), Robie resigned from the college. That year he also married Mehitable Sewall, with whom he had four children.

Robie could not always avoid religious controversy. His college sermons seemed to some "only Heathenish Discourses, no better Christianity than was in Tully."

Also, his inclination to separate science from religion seemed a dangerous strategy. Robie was forthright about the separation. In 1719 he had published *A Letter to a Gentleman*, which gave an account of a "wonderful meteor" that was really an aurora borealis and which included a caveat that he wished only to explain "natural" causes and leave divinity and philosophy to others. This separation encouraged fears that the Harvard tutor was neglecting the important religious aspects of science. Knowing of these criticisms, President Leverett arranged for Robie to preach and publish a conspicuously orthodox sermon: *A Sermon Preached in the College at Cambridge . . . to a Society of Young Students* (1721).

Like Thomas Brattle, Cotton Mather, Thomas Prince, and other men caught up in science in early eighteenth-century New England, Robie embraced Christianity. But unlike them he symbolized to many Puritans the advance of science separated from religion in higher education. For this reason, he seems more modern than some of his contemporaries, and historians have viewed him as an important step in the progress of science at Harvard and in New England.

Certainly Robie was an important link in the development of mathematics education. As an heir to Thomas Brattle, who informally taught higher mathematics to Harvard students, Robie passed on Brattle's idealism concerning the use of mathematics in solving all types of questions and giving certainty to logic. To what he learned from Brattle, he added an understanding of Newtonian fluxions. One of Robie's students, Isaac Greenwood, would become the first Hollis Professor of Mathematics and Natural Philosophy at Harvard. Greenwood's obituary in 1745 reports that "Mr. Roby" was "famous for his skill in Mathematicks" and that Greenwood often reflected on his former tutor's directions and encouragements. Overall, Robie was most important as a mathematics teacher. As a science teacher to the community and a source of pride because of his correspondence with the Royal Society, he also helped increase interest in science. President Leverett wrote that Robie "was no small honour to Harvard College, by his Mathematical Performances and by his Correspondence thereupon with Mr. Derham & other Learned persons in those Studys abroad."

Although Robie was one of Harvard's most important tutors, he was never satisfied with the constrained and ill-paying job that was also being demoted from its former prestige in the early 1720s. He lasted longer at the job than most because it offered the chance to indulge his science and mathematics.

Robie had long been interested in medicine and practiced it conspicuously during the smallpox outbreak of 1721–1722. Called "Dr. Roby" of Cambridge, he joined with two other doctors willing to experiment with the innoculations that most doctors and many of the leaders of New England condemned.

In Salem, Robie observed the transit of Mercury on 29 October 1723. He wrote that he was eager to determine the presence of an atmosphere around Mercury and continue his astronomy. Having left his teaching post, however, Robie apparently no longer had as much time for science. On 15 April 1725 Robie was elected to the Royal Society of London. He died four years later in Salem.

• Robie's scientific papers, letters, and publications are scattered among the Royal Society of London, the New York Historical Society in New York, the Massachusetts Historical Society in Boston, and the Harvard University Archives in Cambridge, Mass. Two important communications not cited in previous bibliographies are his study of smallpox in the *Journal Book of the Royal Society*, vol. 11, p. 275 (housed at the Royal Society in London), and his calculations of eclipses (MS 49) in the Holyoke Family Papers at the Essex Institute, Salem, Mass. Robie also appears often and is quoted in the 1713–1724 diary of fellow tutor Henry Flynt housed at the Massachusetts Historical Society. For sketch biographies of Robie with bibliographical references see Raymond Phineas Stearns, *Science in the British Colonies of America* (1970), pp. 426–35; Frederick G. Kilgour, "Thomas Robie (1689–1729), Colonial Scientist and Physician," *Isis* 30 (1939): 473–90, which includes a transcription of Robie's "Journal of the Inoculation at the Hospital on Spectacle Island," and Clifford K. Shipton, *Sibley's Harvard Graduates*, vol. 5 (1937), pp. 450–55.

RICK KENNEDY

ROBINS, Elizabeth (6 Aug. 1862–8 May 1952), actress, author, and suffragist, was born in Louisville, Kentucky, the daughter of Charles Ephraim Robins, a financier who later became a metallurgist, and Hannah Mariah Crow. After a move to Staten Island, New York, in an unsuccessful attempt to regain his failing business interests, Robins's father was forced by severe financial difficulties to make a desperate move to Colorado to mine for metals, leaving his family in the care of his wife. In 1872, after the deterioration of her mother's mental faculties and subsequent removal to an asylum, Elizabeth Robins and her five younger siblings were sent to live with their paternal grandmother, Jane Hussey Robins, in Zanesville, Ohio. This distinguished albeit impoverished side of the family provided Robins with a stable and refined atmosphere, enabling her to receive a superior education at the Putnam Seminary for Young Ladies in Zanesville, from which she graduated in 1880. As she developed strong interests in acting and writing, her performances and essays won praise from fellow students and teachers.

Although her family strongly disapproved of her choice of a career, Robins was determined to realize her dream of becoming an actress. On 24 August 1881 she boldly set out alone for New York City. Immediate success eluded her, but her acting in America provided the dramaturgical training she would need for her later career in London. She toured with several companies, including those of Lawrence Barrett, James O'Neill (playwright Eugene O'Neill's father), and the Boston Museum. While she was with the Boston Museum Company, she met George Richmond Parks, whom she married in a private ceremony in January 1885. Their union proved brief and childless. Parks, suffering from a severe mental depression brought on by financial insecurity and the anxieties of an acting career, committed suicide in 1887. Shocked and devastated, Robins found solace in a trip to Norway, where she became fascinated with the culture and made an effort to learn the language.

On her return voyage to the United States in 1889, Robins made a detour in London. This "detour" lasted sixty years, although she never officially became a British citizen. Tempted by the chance to act on the English stage, she canceled the remainder of her trip back to America and made appearances in several minor London productions over the next two years. Dismayed by the scarcity of intelligent, substantial roles for actresses, Robins and her American friend Marion Lea formed the Robins-Lea Company. Their production of Henrik Ibsen's *Hedda Gabler* debuted on 20 April 1891. Though attracted to the dramatic potential of Ibsen's modern heroines, Robins and Lea were aware that the production ran a considerable risk of ending in failure because Ibsen's themes were not thought fit by Victorian audiences for public discussion. However, the risky venture paid off handsomely. Despite her two years of experience on the English stage, Robins was relatively unknown to London theatergoers before the premiere of *Hedda Gabler*. Her production and portrayal of Ibsen's play (aided by her ability to translate and thus interpret Ibsen's native Norwegian) firmly established her dramatic reputation. Hailed as the first actress of intellectual standing, acute enough to stimulate a new generation for Ibsen, she received much critical acclaim in London. When *Hedda Gabler* closed after a successful run, she continued to perform other "risky, non-traditional" roles, such as that of Mme Cintré in the stage adaptation of Henry James's novel *The American* (1891), which James and Robins had collaborated on. Her primary fame as an actress, however, was reserved for her interpretation of Ibsen heroines. After her production of *Hedda Gabler*, she also acted in Ibsen's *A Doll's House* (1892), *The Master Builder* (1892, 1893, 1894), *Rosmersholm* (1893), *Little Eyolf* (1894, 1896), *John Gabriel Borkman* (1896, 1897), and *When We Dead Awaken* (1899). In a brief but triumphant return to the American stage, she introduced New York City to her production of *Hedda Gabler* (1893). By the beginning of the twentieth century, Ibsen had written his last play. Robins, having discovered a talent for writing when she sold short stories to supplement her meager income in the early years before she became famous, decided to retire from the stage to pursue a full-time writing career.

Initially fearful that her fame on the stage would overshadow her efforts as an author, she wrote under the pseudonym C. E. Raimond. Veiled by this pen name, she published numerous short stories in both American and English magazines as well as the widely acclaimed novel *The Open Question* (1898), following the appearance of which her identity as the author was discovered. Her three-week journey in 1900 to Alaska to visit her youngest brother, Raymond Robins (famous in his own right as a political activist), provided material for her novel *The Magnetic North*, which was published in 1904 under her own name. This second novel, an adventure story, achieved widespread popularity on both sides of the Atlantic and elicited praise from Mark Twain. She produced an equally popular sequel, *Come and Find Me* (1908).

With her literary reputation established, Robins began to explore the social and feminist concerns that she had become aware of during her acting career. Her earlier literary work had tentatively demonstrated a growing interest in women's equality, but now she began to make woman suffrage her central theme. Although she permanently lived in England, her ties to the United States assured that her ideas would circulate among and influence American as well as English readers. In 1907 she became a member of the Women's Social and Political Union (WSPU), which encouraged her to write *Votes for Women!* This controversial play debuted on 9 April 1907, virtually creating suffrage theater. The novel adapted from the play, titled *The Convert*, was published in October 1907, and like the play, it presents compelling and intelligent arguments in favor of women's right to vote. Although Robins feared that the propagandist material would damage her literary reputation, both *Votes for Women!* and *The Convert* were lauded. She also wrote political pamphlets for the WSPU, including *Woman's Secret* (1907), *Why* (1910), and *A Defense of Militant Suffrage* (1913). Her theatrical abilities made her an invaluable speaker, and she lectured at events where record amounts of money were collected for the cause.

Although she resigned from the WSPU in 1912 because of political infighting among factions, Robins continued to involve herself deeply in the concerns and welfare of women. Prefiguring feminists of the latter part of the century, she probed the motivating factors and consequences of a male-dominated world. In 1913 she published *Where Are You Going To . . . ?*, a sensational novel about prostitution and white slavery that examines the role of men in the continuation of both trades. In *Ancilla's Share: An Indictment of Sex Antagonism* (1924), which was not well received, Robins anticipated future arguments on sexist language and the silencing of women throughout history. In 1927 Robins converted her house in Sussex (Robins herself moved to London) into a convalescent home where women who were exhausted from professional and domestic duties could regain their strength. The home remained in operation until 1989.

In her later years Robins did not cease her prolific writing and activity. She produced several books about her theater years, including *Ibsen and the Actress* (1928), which was published by her friends Leonard Woolf and Virginia Woolf. Her *Theatre and Friendship* (1932) served as a means of reminiscing about her friendships with Henry James, Florence Bell, and others who had been important in her stage career. She spent the duration of World War II in the United States, where she completed her memoirs, *Both Sides of the Curtain* (1940), and was invited to lecture on Ibsen at Princeton University and Vassar College. At the end of the war Robins returned to England. She died at her home in Brighton, England, leaving behind eight unpublished stories.

Elizabeth Robins was a pioneer on the stage and a powerful advocate of woman suffrage. The feminist ideas in her literary work, while unpopular in her own day, have become central, if not commonplace, in modern debate. Yet her work has largely been ignored. In the 1990s scholars became increasingly aware of Robins's intuition and foresight in her writings as well as of her ground-breaking contributions to the stage. Although recognition of her work has come slowly, feminist scholarship has raised her from historical obscurity.

• Robins's personal papers are housed in the Fales Library, New York University. The most complete modern assessment is Angela V. John, *Elizabeth Robins: Staging a Life, 1862–1952* (1995). Another important text is Joanne E. Gates, *Elizabeth Robins, 1862–1952: Actress, Novelist, Feminist* (1994). Robins's feminist scholarship is discussed in Jane Marcus, "Art and Anger," *Feminist Studies* 4 (Feb. 1978): 69–97. For a detailed treatment of Robins's production of *Hedda Gabler*, see Gay Gibson Cima, "Elizabeth Robins: The Genesis of an Independent Manageress," *Theatre Survey* 21 (Nov. 1980): 145–63, and Joanne E. Gates, "Elizabeth Robins and the 1891 Production of *Hedda Gabler*," *Modern Drama* 28 (Dec. 1985): 611–19. Obituaries appear in the *New York Times* and *The Times* (London) 9 May 1952.

LAURA C. RUDOLPH

ROBINS, Margaret Dreier (6 Sept. 1868–21 Feb. 1945), social reformer and labor leader, was born in Brooklyn, New York, the daughter of Theodor Dreier, a prosperous businessman, and Dorothea Adelheid. As a teenager Margaret suffered from various physical ailments that left her weak and depressed. Rather than retire to a life of semi-invalidism, however, she threw herself into volunteer work, starting at the age of nineteen when she became treasurer of the women's auxiliary at Brooklyn Hospital, where her father was a trustee. She did not attend college but sought out private tutoring in philosophy, history, and public speaking. In 1902 Margaret Dreier joined the State Charities Aid Association and the recently established Women's Municipal League (WML). Soon afterward she and social worker Frances Kellor spearheaded a successful drive by the WML to expose and regulate employment agencies that had been recruiting girls for prostitution. Dreier and Kellor also founded the New York Association for Household Research (entirely financed by Dreier), which helped provide women seeking domestic work with safe lodgings and reliable placement services.

In 1904 Dreier joined the organization to which she would devote most of her career and much of her wealth: the Women's Trade Union League (WTUL). This group had been founded only a few months earlier by a coalition of labor leaders and upper middle-class female reformers who hoped to improve the conditions of female workers by encouraging them to join unions. The organization was designed as a cross-class

alliance, with the upper-class members (called "allies") providing financial and organizational support to their trade-unionist sisters. Within a few months she had become both president of the New York League and treasurer of the national WTUL; by the end of 1905 her infusion of energy, talent, and money had given new life to the New York branch.

The year 1905 brought an equally important change in her personal life: within just three months she met, became engaged to, and married Raymond Robins, a handsome and wealthy young minister who was then serving as head resident at the Northwestern University Social Settlement in Chicago. Revivified by her marriage and her role in the WTUL, Robins suffered no more from the physical problems that had plagued her. The couple had no children; instead they devoted their lives to social reform. Robins's husband wrote her in later years that the WTUL was like "one of your children that you raised from feeble infancy to maturity and power."

Moving to Chicago, the Robinses set up housekeeping in a tenement not far from America's most famous settlement—Hull-House, founded by the revered Jane Addams. The Hull-House circle dominated the local WTUL, but Robins soon established her own ascendancy. In 1907 she was elected president of both the national organization (based in Chicago) and the Chicago branch; the following year she persuaded the members to move their meetings from Hull-House to the Chicago Federation of Labor (CFL) building. The new location made many union members feel more at home; it also served Robins's purpose by giving the League greater independence from the formidable Addams. When, soon after, Robins became the only middle-class female member of the CFL executive board (she served until 1917), the election affirmed her position as the central mediating figure between the WTUL's upper- and working-class members, and also between the WTUL and the broader labor movement. She edited the organization's journal, *Life and Labor*, for several years, but her greatest contribution was to sustain an effective coalition between her fellow allies and the WTUL's wage-earning members. Robins also worked heroically to keep alive the often problematic connection between the WTUL and the male-dominated American Federation of Labor (AFL).

Guided by Robins, the WTUL played a major role in the historic garment strikes of 1909–1911. In New York, Philadelphia, Chicago, and Cleveland, WTUL allies raised funds, marched on picket lines, and galvanized public attention by the very fact of their participation. Robins herself took a central part, donating large sums of money, serving on the Chicago strike committee, and providing powerful leadership to the whole WTUL effort. In 1914 she spearheaded the establishment of a pioneering program that during the next twelve years trained forty working women as union leaders. Robins also worked actively for woman suffrage and municipal reform, served on the state executive committee of the Progressive party in 1912, and campaigned for Republican Charles Evans

Hughes in 1916. By this time the AFL had discontinued its stipend to the League, but with a combination of tireless fundraising and her own inheritance, Robins kept the organization going.

During World War I, Robins served on the Illinois Committee of Women and Children in Industry, part of the Women's Council of National Defense. After the peace she served for two years on the Republican National Committee's women's division. She convened the first International Congress of Working Women in Washington in 1919 and in 1922 organized the International Federation of Working Women (IFWW). She retired as WTUL president that year, hoping to dedicate herself to this new project, but she resigned from the IFWW the following year when the group voted to become part of another international organization that had few contacts with the American labor movement.

When Robins retired from the WTUL, she insisted that it appoint its first trade-unionist president as her successor. A few years later she and her husband moved to an estate in Hernando County, Florida, where they had vacationed for many years. Besides working for such causes as the Red Cross and the League of Women Voters, Robins served on the Republican National Committee in 1928, and during the 1930s she became a strong supporter of the New Deal. By this time the WTUL had grown much smaller and weaker, but Robins rejoined the executive board in 1934 and in 1937 chaired its committee to investigate labor conditions in the south. She died on her Florida estate, which she and her husband donated to the state of Florida as a retreat for intellectuals and activists.

Because the WTUL was always in shaky financial state, Robins's continual donations were central to its survival; she once said she felt as if she were "nothing but a money machine." But she was far more. She was the driving force behind a remarkable organization with a remarkable agenda: to empower working women to improve the conditions of their lives through their own collective efforts, and to harness the wealth and influence of some of the country's most privileged women to support them in that effort. If the WTUL did not achieve all it hoped, it nevertheless represents a vital chapter in the history of American women and American labor.

• Robins's papers are at the University of Florida, Gainesville. See also her husband's papers and those of Alexander Gumberg at the State Historical Society of Wisconsin in Madison; the WTUL papers in the Library of Congress and at Radcliffe College; the papers of Leonora O'Reilly, Mary Anderson, Ethel Dummer, and Mary E. Dreier at Radcliffe; and the papers of Rose Schneiderman at Tamiment Library, New York University. The fullest—though wholly uncritical—account of her life is written by her sister, Mary E. Dreier, *Margaret Dreier Robins: Her Life, Letters and Work* (1950). See also the memoirs of colleagues like Agnes Nestor, *Woman's Labor Leader* (1954); Mary Anderson, *Woman at Work* (1951); and Samuel Gompers, *Seventy Years of Life and Labor* (1925). Other useful material appears in Philip S. Foner, *Women and the American Labor Movement* (1979); William L.

O'Neill, *Everyone Was Brave* (1969); Gladys Boone, *The Women's Trade Union Leagues in Great Britain and the United States of America* (1942); Clarke A. Chambers, *Seedtime of Reform* (1963); Allen F. Davis, *Spearheads for Reform* (1957) and *American Heroine: The Life and Legend of Jane Addams* (1973); Nancy Schrom Dye, *As Equals and as Sisters: Feminism, the Labor Movement, and the Women's Trade Union League of New York* (1980); Ellen Condiffe Lagemann, *A Generation of Women: Education in the Lives of Progressive Reformers* (1979); and Eleanor Flexner, *Century of Struggle* (1959). An obituary is in the *New York Times*, 22 Feb. 1945.

SANDRA OPDYCKE

ROBINS, Raymond (17 Sept. 1873–26 Sept. 1954), social reformer, politician, and diplomat, was born on Staten Island, New York, the son of Charles Ephraim Robins, a businessman, and his second wife, Hannah Mariah Crow. After his father went bankrupt and moved to Colorado to mine for metals and his mother went into a mental asylum, Raymond grew up with relatives in Zanesville, Ohio; Louisville, Kentucky; and Brooksville, Florida. In the early 1890s Robins took coal mining jobs in Coal Creek, Tennessee, and in Leadville, Colorado. In 1893 he took a position as manager of a Florida phosphate company, where he became interested in phosphate mining and discovered a rich deposit of kaolin clay, used for porcelain production. He purchased land options worth $10,000 at once, but he sold the property to a New York company for $3,000 in 1893. The company's lawyer, by using his knowledge and legal skills, outmaneuvered Robins, who, as a result, had to absorb a severe financial loss on what had looked like a sound investment. This experience convinced him to study law. Working as a lawyer, Robins felt, suited both his personal temperament and his social and political inclinations. In 1896 he graduated with a law degree from Columbian University (now George Washington University). He moved to San Francisco, where he was admitted to the bar in 1896.

In San Francisco he entered the realm of politics and soon received the opportunity to make a mark for himself. He became actively involved in Democratic politics, and when the city and county organization chairman defected to the Republican party Robins assumed the leadership of both and campaigned on behalf of William Jennings Bryan in 1896. Robins successfully used his legal talents to help a bipartisan effort to halt municipal corruption.

In July 1897 Robins joined the gold rush to the Klondike in Alaska, where he not only made a little fortune but also embraced Christianity. He became pastor of a Congregational church in Nome but could not let go of his social and political commitments and became active in Alaskan politics. In 1900 his sister Elizabeth came to Nome and convinced him to return to Chicago.

During the years in Chicago, Robins became involved in a variety of reform causes that gave him the opportunity to merge his social and political commitments with his religious convictions. Chicago was one of the centers of the settlement house movement in the

United States at that time and was especially suited to provide Robins with an outlet for his social, religious, and political ideals. Unlike other reformers, who often blamed the poor and destitute for their own misfortune, participants in the settlement house movement emphasized environmental causes of poverty, placing effective remedies of their plight beyond the control of the affected. Settlement house workers, such as Jane Addams and Graham Taylor, offered a mix of practical help and political advocacy to immigrants and working-class Americans in whose neighborhoods settlement houses were founded. Robins joined the Commons Social Settlement House founded by Taylor, became head worker of the Northwestern University settlement house, and eventually served as superintendent of the Municipal Lodging House from 1902 to 1905.

His active role in reform causes soon drew him again into municipal politics. In 1906 mayor Edward Dunne appointed Robins to the city's board of education, but his thorough work and success in exposing wrongdoings in the city's public school system led to his removal by Dunne's successor, Fred Busse. In 1907 Robins and the other committee members ousted with him carried their case to the Illinois Supreme Court, which ordered them to be reinstated.

After an unsuccessful attempt to gain the interest of the recently widowed Anita McCormick Blaine, Robins found a soulmate in Margaret Dreier, whom he married on 21 June 1905. Margaret came from a wealthy background, and her political and reform interests matched Robins's quite well. Their relationship, which remained childless, was founded on deep mutual affection, respect, and commitment to the same political and reform causes. Despite their secure financial standing, they moved into a tenement flat in the Seventeenth Ward, known for its rampant political corruption.

The years in Chicago were a both politically rewarding and personally trying time for Robins. In 1907 he was severely beaten up and left for dead in the gutter as a retaliation for his attacks on Martin B. "Skinny" Madden, who played a key role in the Building Trades Council, the Chicago Federation of Labor, and the Democratic party machine.

In subsequent years Robins became more involved in religious work and took on a more prominent role in political life. In 1911 and 1912 he became a leader in the YMCA-organized Men and Religion Forward Movement. In 1915 and 1916 he spoke at the National Christian Evangelical Camp. In 1912 he took part in Theodore Roosevelt's presidential campaign as candidate of the newly founded Progressive party. Two years later, he became chairman of the Illinois State Committee of the Progressive party and ran for the Senate. Robins became chairman of the Progressive party's Bull Moose Convention in 1916.

During World War I, Robins went with the army to Russia, where he attempted to foster diplomatic relations between the United States and the Russian government. Robins served as a major in the U.S. Army and was also placed second in command of President Woodrow Wilson's Red Cross mission to Russia. The intention behind this mission was to keep the Kerensky government in power and in the war. Once the Bolshevik Revolution had succeeded, however, Robins opposed the counterrevolutionary intentions of the United States' intervention. Robins himself was opposed to socialism and communism, but he saw that a large part of the Russian population supported the Revolution and that, therefore, the U.S. government should recognize the Bolshevik government.

His unsuccessful attempt to foster cooperative relations between his own country and the Soviet government made him many enemies at home, resulting in charges of disloyalty. A government-ordered silence about his mission kept him from helping to defend several radicals indicted for treason, such as the radical journalist John Reed and the New York anarchists around Jacob Abrams. In 1919 the restraining order was eventually lifted when the government wanted him to testify before the Overman Committee on Bolshevik propaganda, which had been formed to gather evidence about the radical attempts to overthrow the U.S. government. Robins, however, used the opportunity to advocate cooperation between the two governments despite public vilification by his enemies.

During the 1920s Robins's political allegiance began to undergo a radical transformation, which ultimately led him back to the Democratic party. During the Great Depression, Robins and his wife, together with other former progressives, moved more closely into the orbit of the New Deal Democrats. In 1933 he received the opportunity to pursue old diplomatic interests. From April to June 1933 Robins made a visit to the Soviet Union, studying mass production methods in industry and agriculture and Soviet education. Although he did not serve as an official emissary of the U.S. government, Robins's visit is credited with convincing the Roosevelt administration to exchange ambassadors with the Soviet Union. Robins's hopes to be named the first ambassador himself went unfulfilled, but he thought that William C. Bullitt was "a good selection . . . I am glad Roosevelt sent him" (Salzman, p. 361). Robins himself withdrew from national politics.

On 21 September 1935 Robins fell from a ladder, breaking three vertebrae in his back. The accident left him paralyzed from the waist down. However, Robins remained connected to political events. He received many visitors seeking his advice, and he kept up an extensive correspondence about domestic and world events. He died on his estate, "Chinsegut Hill," which he had bought with money he had made in the Klondike gold rush, near Brooksville, Florida.

Robins's significance is twofold: as a former progressive who came to support the New Deal, he, with many others, symbolizes the continuity between the two reform eras. And although he did not immediately succeed in convincing the Wilson administration to recognize the Soviet Union, the personal relationship he forged with Lenin and Trotsky laid the foundation for diplomatic recognition more than a decade later.

• Essential sources on Robins's life are the Margaret Dreier Robins Papers, University of Florida Library, Gainesville; the Raymond Robins Papers and the Alexander Gumberg Papers, both at the Wisconsin State Historical Society, University of Wisconsin, Madison; and the Elizabeth Robins Papers at Fales Library, New York University, N.Y. In addition, material pertaining to Robins can be found in the collections of several Progressive leaders, such as Theodore Roosevelt. For a biography, see Neil V. Salzman, *Reform and Revolution: The Life and Times of Raymond Robins* (1991). Other published sources on Robins's life include Elizabeth Robins, *Raymond and I* (1956); Mary Dreier, *Margaret Dreier Robins* (1950); and William Hard, *Raymond Robins' Own Story* (1920), an account of Robins's activities in the Soviet Union during World War I. Other works containing information on Robins are Allen F. Davis, *Spearheads for Reform* (1967); William Appleman Williams, *American Russian Relations, 1781–1947* (1952); and Richard Polenberg, *Fighting Faiths: The Abrams Case, the Supreme Court, and Free Speech* (1987). An obituary is in the *New York Times*, 27 Sept. 1954.

THOMAS WINTER

ROBINSON, Beverly (11 Jan. 1723–9 Apr. 1792), land proprietor and Loyalist officer, was born in Middlesex County, Virginia, probably at his family's Hewick plantation, near Urbanna. He was the son of John Robinson, president of the Virginia council and acting governor (1749), and Catherine Beverley. The Robinsons had strong alliances and kinship ties with Virginia's gentry. Little is known of Beverly (also spelled Beverley) Robinson's early life, but he was probably educated by tutors. In June 1746 he raised a company of 130 men, which he took to join British troops at Albany, where they remained without seeing battle action during King George's War. Robinson stayed in New York City after the war and became a mercantile partner of Oliver De Lancey. On 7 July 1748 he married Susanna Philipse, daughter and an heiress of Frederick Philipse II, one of New York's wealthiest landlords. Around 1750 Robinson built as his family residence a large wooden house, which he called "Beverly" (a change he preferred in his own name once he took up residence in New York), on the east bank of the Hudson River two miles south of West Point. The home, which was destroyed by fire in 1892, was noted for its beautiful grounds and orchards; during the revolutionary war it served as both an American army headquarters and as a hospital. George Washington visited "Beverly" on a return trip from Boston in 1756, borrowing £91 from Robinson to help him return to Mount Vernon.

With the death of his father-in-law in 1751, Robinson acquired a large estate. Along with Roger Morris and Philip Philipse, he purchased the 205,000-acre Highland Patent in Dutchess County, New York. In 1757 the three partitioned their holdings, with Robinson's share being 60,000 acres of the Highland Patent. In his role as a landlord, Robinson held nearly every local office, including colonel of the Dutchess County militia and judge of the court of common pleas. He also served as a commissary and paymaster for New York troops during the French and Indian War.

The Highland Patent was a source of much litigation for Robinson. It was first deeded by the crown on 17 June 1697 to Adolph Philipse, who did not clear the Indian rights to the land. The Wappinger Indians claimed much of the territory covered by the patent, and they sold or leased land to settlers, mostly from Massachusetts, to help support this claim. Alarmed, the three proprietors—Philipse, Morris, and Robinson—seized lands occupied by the Indians while the Wappinger men were serving in the British armed forces in 1756. By 1761 the proprietors had begun ejectment suits against those who held Indian land titles. Many tenants had renounced their leases with the proprietors and took lands from the Wappingers. The Wappinger chief, Daniel Nimham, twice appealed in vain to the governor and council of New York (the crown refusing to hear the case), and no lawyer in New York would take the Wappinger case. Late in 1765 the displaced tenants, who were considered as squatters and wanted long-term leases and reasonable rent, rioted in the proprietaries from Westchester County to Albany. Mobs forced Highland Patent tenants off their lands and burned their barns. Robinson, for his own protection, fled to New York City on 21 November 1765. In 1766 the rebellion was put down by the New York government.

Robinson kept close watch over his 146 tenancies, which increasingly became more productive, and thereby raised his rental income. Annual rents expected by 1777 amounted to over £1,250. Robinson also profited from fees when tenants sold their rights.

At the beginning of the revolutionary war Robinson was not hostile to the Whig cause, having earlier cooperated with the economic boycott against Great Britain. Given more time to make up his mind he might have supported the Revolution, but probably expected to remain neutral. Refusing to take the patriot oath of allegiance, he was told by John Jay of the New York Commission for Detecting and Defeating All Conspiracies on 22 February 1777 that he had to declare loyalty to one side or the other. Thus he sought refuge with the British in New York City.

Robinson recruited about 400 men, chiefly from among his tenants and neighbors, to form the Loyal American Regiment; he served as colonel and commander of this unit. He was also put in charge of a corps of guides and pioneers for the British army. Of the officers in the Loyal American Regiment, 72.7 percent were American born. With this unit Robinson served in General Henry Clinton's expedition to the Highlands along the Hudson River, 3–22 October 1777, and took part in the storming of Fort Montgomery just above Peekskill on the west bank of the Hudson, on 6 October 1777.

During the war Robinson played an important role in Clinton's espionage network. His operative plied information from his tenants, friends, and acquaintances in the lower Hudson River region. Clinton used Robinson in an attempt to lure Ethan Allen to bring Vermont into the British fold. In June 1780 Robinson wrote Allen that "you may obtain a separate government under the king and constitution of England," an offer that the British ministry had authorized. Allen did not respond, hoping to sustain pressure on the Confederation Congress to recognize Vermont as a state. Robinson also made a faint effort to bring General Israel Putnam, whose Highlands command headquarters were in the Robinson house, over to the British side.

Robinson also volunteered to be a liaison between Clinton and General Benedict Arnold in the West Point treason plot, a mission that was ultimately assigned to John André. To this end Robinson arranged the meeting between André and Arnold. After the plot unraveled, Robinson wrote to George Washington entreating him to spare André's life, and he accompanied Clinton's commissioners for that purpose to Washington's headquarters in order to attest to André's innocence.

In August 1782 Robinson left New York City for England. Although he was appointed in 1784 to the council of New Brunswick, he did not serve. For the rest of his life Robinson resided quietly at Thornbury, near Bath, England. After his lands were confiscated by acts of the New York legislature during February and March 1780, Robinson sought £79,980 compensation from the royal claims commission for the loss of his estate; he was awarded £17,000.

Robinson died at his home at Thornbury, survived by his wife and their seven children. Four of his five sons served in the British army during the Revolution, and two of them were knighted. Robinson admitted to no regrets in becoming a Loyalist military officer. "I acted from upright and conscientious principles, in doing my duty to my king and Country," he wrote Clinton on 8 August 1782. That decision made Robinson an exile from his native country and cost him his considerable American estate.

• Robinson's letters are in the Sir Henry Clinton Papers, William L. Clements Library, University of Michigan. For Robinson as a Loyalist claimant and witness, see the Library of Congress's microfilm edition of the American Loyalist Papers, 1783–1790, the originals of which are in the Public Record Office, and the American Loyalist Transcripts, New York Public Library. The Philipse proprietary case against the Wappinger Indians, presented from the Indian point of view by a contemporary, is in Oscar Handlin and Irving Mark, eds., "Chief Daniel Nimham v. Roger Morris, Beverly Robinson, and Philip Philipse—an Indian Land Case in Colonial New York, 1765–1767," *Ethnohistory* 11 (Summer 1964): 193–246. Sung Bok Kim, *Landlord and Tenant in Colonial New York: Manorial Society, 1664–1775* (1978); Irving Mark, *Agrarian Conflicts in Colonial New York* (1940; 2d ed., 1965); and Edward Countryman, *A People in Revolution: The American Revolution and Political Society in New York, 1760–1790* (1981), relate Robinson to the landlord-tenant problems. Carl Van Doren, *Secret History of the American Revolution* (1941; repr. 1968); Willard S. Randall, *Benedict Arnold: Patriot and Traitor* (1990); and Robert M. Hatch, *Major John André: A Gallant in Spy's Clothing* (1986), treat the Robinson-Arnold-André connection. Robinson's letter to Ethan Allen of June 1780 is in Charles A. Jellison, *Ethan Allen: Frontier Rebel* (1969), pp. 245–46. Brief biographies of Robinson and

his five sons are in Lorenzo Sabine, *Biographical Sketches of Loyalists of the American Revolution*, vol. 2 (1869), pp. 221–28. The Robinson-Washington relationship is mentioned in Douglas S. Freeman, *George Washington*, vols. 1 and 5 (1949, 1952). A death notice is in *The Gentleman's Magazine*, May 1792, p. 479.

HARRY M. WARD

ROBINSON, Bill (25 May 1878–25 Nov. 1949), African-American tap dancer, known as "Bojangles," was born Luther Robinson in Richmond, Virginia, the son of Maxwell Robinson, a machinist, and Maria (maiden name unknown), a choir director. After both parents died in an accident around 1885, Luther and his brother William lived with their grandmother, Bedilia Robinson, a former slave who sought salvation through faith and disavowed dancing of any kind in her house. Too old and infirm to care for the boys, she entrusted them to a local judge, John Crutchfield.

Robinson appropriated his brother's name, calling himself Bill, and took to the streets to earn nickels and dimes by dancing and scat-singing. In Richmond, he got the nickname "Bojangles," from "jangler," meaning contentious, and he invented the famous phrase "everything's copasetic," meaning everything's tip-top or first-rate. Robinson ran away to Washington, D.C., picking up odd jobs dancing in beer gardens around town. He got his first professional break in 1892 as a pickaninny in the chorus line of Whallen and Martel's *South Before the War*, a touring show that featured Mayme Remington, a former French burlesque dancer who became a top headliner in the 1890s. Shortly after arriving in New York in 1900, Robinson challenged "In Old Kentucky" star dancer Harry Swinton to a Friday night buck-and-wing dance contest and won. With a gold medal and the valuable publicity attendant to winning, he was quickly targeted as the man to challenge.

Robinson worked wherever and whenever he could, and with a variety of partners, including Theodore Miller, Lula Brown, and Johnny Juniper. Bound by the "two-colored" rule in vaudeville, which restricted blacks to performing in pairs, he teamed with George W. Cooper from 1902 to 1914. They played the classiest tours in white vaudeville, the Keith and Orpheum circuits, without the blackface makeup expected of African-American performers at the time. They also toured London with great success. Robinson married Lena Chase in 1907, although touring and professional activities kept them apart and forced them to separate around 1915 and divorce in 1922.

Robinson was a staunch professional, adamant about punctuality and a perfectionist with his routines. He was also known to anger quickly, gamble, and carry a gold-plated revolver. After an assault charge in 1908 that split up his act with Cooper, Robinson decided to launch his solo career and became one of the few blacks to perform as a soloist on the Keith circuit. He was a headliner at New York's Palace Theatre, the undisputed crown jewel of vaudeville theaters. At one point in his career, he made $6,500 a week in vaudeville and was billed as the "World's Greatest Tap Dancer." Being billed as a champion dancer meant winning dance competitions of the toughest kind to stay on top. Contests were audited by a panel of judges who sat under the stage, in the wings, and in the house, judging the dancer on the tempo and execution of steps. Robinson was challenged to dozens of contests and won, and according to tap dance lore competed against dancers such as James Barton, Will Mahoney, Jack Donahue, Fred Astaire, and Ray Bolger. Robinson's stair dance, first performed in 1918, was distinguished by its showmanship and sound, each step emitting a different pitch and rhythm. Onstage his open face, twinkling eyes, and infectious smile were irresistible, as was his tapping, which was delicate and clear. Buck or time steps were inserted with skating steps or crossover steps on the balls of the feet that looked like a jig, all while he chatted and joked with the audience. Robinson danced in split clog shoes, ordinary shoes with a wooden half-sole and raised wooden heel. The wooden sole was attached from the toe to the ball of the foot and left loose, which allowed for greater flexibility and tonality.

In 1922, Robinson married Fannie Clay, who became his business manager, secretary, and partner in efforts to fight the barriers of racial prejudice. He was a founding member of the Negro Actors Guild of America. Hailed as the "Dark Cloud of Joy" on the Orpheum circuit, Robinson performed in vaudeville from 1914 to 1927 without a single season's layoff. Yet Broadway fame did not come until he was fifty years old, with the all-black revue *Blackbirds of 1928*, in which he sang and danced "Doin' the New Low Down." Success was instantaneous and he was saluted as the greatest of all dancers by at least seven New York newspapers. Broadway shows that followed included *Brown Buddies* (1930), *Blackbirds of 1933, All in Fun* (1940), and *Memphis Bound* (1945). The opening of *The Hot Mikado* (1939) marked Robinson's sixty-first birthday and he celebrated by dancing down Broadway, from 61st Street to the Broadhurst Theatre at 44th Street.

In the 1930s Robinson also performed in Hollywood films, a venue hitherto restricted to African-American performers. His first film, *Dixiana* (1930), had a predominantly white cast, but *Harlem Is Heaven* (1933) was one of the first all-black films ever made. Other films include *Hooray for Love* (1935), *In Old Kentucky* (1935), *The Big Broadcast of 1937* (1935), *One Mile from Heaven* (1937), *By an Old Southern River* (1941), and *Let's Shuffle* (1941). The well-known all-black film *Stormy Weather* (1943) featured Robinson, Lena Horne, Cab Calloway, and Katherine Dunham and her dance troupe. Robinson and Shirley Temple teamed up in *The Little Colonel* (1935), *The Littlest Rebel* (1935), *Just Around the Corner* (1938), and *Rebecca of Sunnybrook Farm* (1938), in which he taught the child superstar to tap dance.

In 1936, Robinson opened the downtown Cotton Club in New York (south of the more famous uptown Harlem Cotton Club) and introduced a new dance, the "Suzi-Q"; he was later featured in several Cotton Club shows. Claiming to have taught tap dancing to Eleanor Powell, Florence Mills, Fayard and Harold Nicholas, and Astaire, Robinson profoundly influenced the next generation of dancers at the Hoofers Club in Harlem, where he also gambled and shot pool. Throughout his lifetime, he was a member of many clubs and civic organizations and an honorary member of police departments in cities across the United States. Robinson was named "Mayor of Harlem" in 1933. His participation in benefits is legendary and it is estimated that he gave away well over $1 million in loans and charities. During his long career, he never refused to play a benefit, regardless of race, creed, or color of those who were to profit by his performance. In 1943 he divorced Fannie Clay and married the young dancer Elaine Plaines.

"To his own people," Marshall Stearns wrote in *Jazz Dance*, "Robinson became a modern John Henry, who instead of driving steel, laid down iron taps." Although he was uneducated, Robinson was accepted in high places that were previously beyond the reach of most African Americans. He commanded the respect due to a gifted artist and became the most famous tap dancer of the twentieth century. Robinson's exacting yet light footwork was said to have brought tap "up on its toes" from an earlier flat-footed shuffling style. Although he invented few new steps, he presented those he used with technical ease and a sparkling personality, turning relatively simple tap dancing into an exciting art.

When Robinson died in New York City, newspapers claimed that almost 100,000 people witnessed the passing of the funeral procession, a testament to the esteem in which he was held by members of his community. The founding of the Copasetics, a fraternity of male tap dancers formed the year Robinson died, ensured that his excellence would not be forgotten.

• For short biographies of Robinson see Tom Fletcher, *100 Years of the Negro in Show Business* (1954), and Jim Haskins and N. R. Mitgang, *Mr. Bojangles* (1988). Marshall and Jean Stearns, *Jazz Dance: The Story of American Vernacular Dance* (1968), offers a critical biography. A list of recordings of Robinson's singing and dancing can be found in Rusty Frank, *Tap! The Greatest Tap Dance Stars and their Stories, 1900–1955* (1990).

CONSTANCE VALIS HILL

ROBINSON, Charles (21 July 1818–17 Aug. 1894), first governor of Kansas and reformer, was born in Hardwick, Massachusetts, the son of Jonathan Robinson and Huldah Woodward, farmers. For two years he attended Amherst Academy, dropping out at age twenty because of an eye inflammation. In 1843 he received a degree in medicine from Berkshire (Mass.) Medical School and set up practice in Belchertown, Massachusetts. His marriage that year to Sarah Adams was followed by the death of two children in infancy and of Sarah in 1846. He moved to Springfield, Massachusetts, where with Dr. J. G. Holland he opened a private hospital. A physical breakdown caused Robinson to abandon his practice. Seeking a change and travel, he became physician for a group of fifty-one Massachusetts men who were traveling to California in quest of gold. On the overland journey the rolling prairie and the rich and fertile soil of eastern Kansas deeply impressed him. In California he took up the stormy cause of squatters' rights and was elected president of a squatters' association. When violence flared, he was wounded and briefly imprisoned. His constituents sent him to the state legislature in 1850, where he strongly supported John C. Frémont for U.S. senator and Frémont's stand against the extension of slavery. The California years gave early evidence of a lifelong commitment to reform causes, including those of blacks.

In 1851 Robinson returned to Massachusetts and married Sara Tappan Doolittle Lawrence; they had no children. Well educated and related to Amos A. Lawrence, the Boston industrialist and philanthropist, Sara became a lifelong helpmeet, writing an antislavery account of the Kansas controversy and defending her husband's reputation after his death. For more than two years the couple lived in Fitchburg, Massachusetts, where Charles practiced medicine part-time and edited the Fitchburg *News*.

Inspired by Eli Thayer, organizer of the New England Emigrant Aid Company, Robinson in 1854 journeyed to Kansas Territory, opened to settlement by the disastrous Kansas-Nebraska Act of that year, to gather information helpful to settlers. He wrote a pamphlet for prospective settlers and in August accepted appointment as a general agent for the company in Kansas. In September he led a party of emigrants, all hopeful to improve their economic lot and at the same time make Kansas a free state. He established headquarters at a site he named Lawrence.

Robinson became a key figure during the violence known as "Bleeding Kansas." Leader of a free-soil faction that considered blacks as potential equals, he opposed accepting the results of the fraudulent election of a proslavery legislature. During the statehood controversy and thereafter he faced a rival in James H. Lane (1814–1866), a political opportunist who favored excluding blacks from the territory. Concerned about the emigrant aid company's investment as well as his own land speculation and the free-state cause, Robinson in 1855 urged Thayer to send Sharps rifles to Kansas. He took part in the faction-torn conventions at Big Springs, which formed a Free State party favored by Lane, and at Topeka, which drafted a free-state constitution, favored by Robinson, that proposed a referendum on excluding blacks, favored by Lane and opposed by Robinson.

When violence flared in the so-called Wakarusa War between proslavery and free-state elements, Robinson took a hand in avoiding bloodshed that enhanced his reputation among moderate free-state groups. Early in 1856, in a contest against Lane, he was elected governor under the Topeka constitution adopted by free-state voters. He now headed a rump government that became the storm center of presidential politics in 1856.

During the crucial years 1856–1857, Robinson played the roles of both sacrificial lamb and moderate. Early in 1856 President Franklin Pierce denounced the Topeka government and offered federal troops to maintain public order. To this Robinson, in his inaugural address, responded with a defense of republican principles and squatter sovereignty. A grand jury, instructed by an anti-free-state federal judge, indicted Robinson and others for treason. Robinson was arrested and detained for four months. During this period Kansas was the scene of the notorious events that helped shape the newly formed national Republican party: the "sack of Lawrence" and John Brown's (1800–1859) "Pottawatomie massacre." The Republican party platform, denouncing violence and fraudulent voting in Kansas, demanded immediate admission as a state under the Topeka constitution.

In 1857, when an election for territorial legislature impended, Robinson abjured force and nonparticipation and in October took satisfaction in a free-state victory. His leadership—entailing courage and peaceful participation in politics—had done much to dampen the prospect of Kansas becoming a slave state.

The Free State party in Kansas yielded to the Republican party and the Topeka constitution to the freshly drafted Wyandotte constitution. In 1861, with the admission of Kansas, Robinson became the state's first governor. He faced the demands not only of organizing a new state but also of meeting Washington's war needs. His administration suffered a heavy blow when his rival, Lane, became U.S. senator. Lane successfully claimed both the state's political patronage and authority to recruit in Kansas. Dissatisfaction with the governor, fomented by Lane, found expression in attempts to unseat him by a new election and to evict him by impeachment for mishandling state bond issues. He survived both attempts but left office in 1863 under a cloud that shadowed his future in politics.

The succeeding three decades saw Robinson engaged in virtually every Kansas reform movement. He held a strong belief in what he called "universal freedom," derived from "the immutable laws of God" and the Declaration of Independence. He took up the causes of suffrage for women and blacks, political reform, currency reform, and opposition to prohibition and business monopoly. A supporter of the Liberal Republican movement, he was elected to the Kansas House in 1872 as an Independent candidate; elected in 1874 to the state senate as an Independent Reform party candidate; and reelected in 1876 and 1878 as an Independent Greenbacker. His strong stand against prohibition, which he believed unworkable, contributed in 1882 to his failed gubernatorial candidacy on the National Labor Greenback ticket.

Sympathetic to the Democratic party's stand on liquor, labor, and money, Robinson in 1884 ran as a Democrat for the state senate, losing by a narrow margin. Two years later he became the party's nominee for

Congress in his district but lost in a Republican landslide. In 1890 he accepted the nomination for governor on a ticket fusing Democrats and persons favoring resubmission of the prohibition question and ran third against the victorious Republican incumbent and the Populist candidate.

During these post–Civil War years, Robinson played an active part in other aspects of Kansas life. He served as regent of the University of Kansas, which as governor he helped establish in Lawrence; sponsored reform of the public school system; served as president of the state historical society, which he had helped organize; and from 1887 to 1889 was president of Haskell Institute. In retirement he wrote *The Kansas Conflict*, published in 1892. He died in Lawrence. Throughout his long life, while eschewing organized religion, he pursued liberal measures and often was ahead of his time on such matters as suffrage, prohibition, and currency reform. His greatest achievement lay in his moderate and persevering work toward quelling violence in Kansas and making it a free state.

• Robinson's papers, with those of his wife Sara, are in the Kansas City, Kansas, Public Library; Kansas State Historical Society, Topeka; and the University of Kansas, Lawrence, Spencer Library. The Kansas State Historical Society has miscellaneous materials. Don W. Wilson, *Governor Charles Robinson of Kansas* (1975), is a full, scholarly life with a good bibliography. Sara Robinson, *Kansas* (1856), is helpful, though not impartial. G. Raymond Gaeddert, *The Birth of Kansas* (1940), treats Robinson as the state's first governor. Paul W. Gates, *Fifty Million Acres* (1954), has some material on Robinson's land speculations.

JAMES A. RAWLEY

ROBINSON, Christopher (15 May 1806–3 Oct. 1889), lawyer and diplomat, was born in Providence, Rhode Island, the son of Benjamin Robinson and Ann Pitts (occupations unknown). Educated initially in Oliver Angell's private academy, he graduated from Brown University in 1825, after which he taught for several years at Kent Academy in East Greenwich and preached in local Universalist societies.

While still teaching, Robinson studied law in the office of U.S. senator Albert C. Greene. Admitted to the bar in 1833, he settled in Woonsocket, where he was active in establishing a public school system and, as a respected civic leader, worked unsuccessfully to promote the construction of a railroad to Boston. He was married three times: first to Mary A. Tillinghast, whose one child died; second to Mary A. Jencks, who had no children; and finally to Louisa Aldrich, with whom Robinson had four children.

Following the death of his third wife in 1853, Robinson entered politics. His first public office was that of attorney general of Rhode Island (1854–1855). As a member of the American (Know Nothing) party, he was elected in 1858 to the Thirty-sixth Congress. During a single unobtrusive term in the House of Representatives (1859–1861), he was a member of the Judiciary Committee and a staunch antislavery man. Serving on the Select Committees of Thirty-three dur-

ing the secession winter of 1860–1861, he deprecated disunion but voted with the "irreconcilables" on the committee against Charles F. Adams's compromise resolution proposing statehood with slavery for New Mexico.

Defeated for reelection in 1860, Robinson was able, through the personal intervention of Senator James F. Simmons with President Abraham Lincoln, to obtain an appointment as the U.S. minister to Peru. Assuming this position in January 1862 and holding it until December 1865, he was able successfully to settle a large backlog of claims of American citizens against Peru that had led the administration of James Buchanan in 1860 to break off diplomatic relations with that country. So ably did he combat Confederate influence in Peru that its leaders never yielded to the pleas of the large number of southern sympathizers in that country to grant official recognition to the slaveholders' rebellion. Vociferously expressing the opposition of his government to Spain's seizure in 1864 of the guano-rich Chincha Islands, Robinson shared the gratitude of the Peruvian government for the vigorous representations of the United States, resulting in Spain's evacuation of the islands early in 1865. Upon his resignation from his ministerial position, Robinson was asked to become Peru's diplomatic agent in Europe.

Robinson chose instead to return to private life in Rhode Island. Although he went to Philadelphia in August 1866 as a delegate to the Union party loyalist convention supporting President Andrew Johnson, he otherwise lived quietly and comfortably in Woonsocket until his death there.

Robinson's public career was unexceptional. Neither in the writings of his congressional and diplomatic colleagues nor in contemporary newspapers is one provided more than a fleeting glimpse of this Rhode Islander. Yet he performed his duties competently, if not with distinction, in difficult circumstances.

• Robinson has yet to attract a scholarly biographer. Information about him may be obtained from Rhode Island newspapers, from legal records regarding his law practice as well as from wills and tax records pertaining to his family and himself, from the *Congressional Globe* for 1859–1861, from the archives of the U.S. Department of State for 1861–1865, and from occasional references to him in the journals, letters, and memoirs of contemporaries. L. C. Nolan, "The Diplomatic and Commercial Relations of the United States and Peru, 1826–1875" (Ph.D. diss., Duke Univ., 1935), treats his tenure at Lima. An obituary is in the *Providence Daily Journal*, 5 Oct. 1889.

NORMAN B. FERRIS

ROBINSON, Conway (15 Sept. 1805–30 Jan. 1884), lawyer, historian, and author, was born in Richmond, Virginia, the son of John Robinson, a respected local superior court clerk, and Agnes Conway Moncure. Educated in local schools, Conway was the only one of his father's six sons not to attend college. Instead, he followed in John Robinson's footsteps and was apprenticed at age fourteen to Thomas C. Howard, clerk of the Richmond City Hustings Court. In 1826 Conway Robinson himself became deputy clerk of the Virginia general court and in the same year published an updated edition of *A Collection of Forms Used by the Clerks of the Courts of Law and Equity in Virginia*, previously issued by his father in 1809.

Robinson read law while clerking and qualified for the bar in 1827. The following year he made his first appearance before the Virginia Supreme Court, where he later dominated the state's antebellum appellate practice. He joined the bar of the U.S. Supreme Court in 1839 and practiced there for most of the rest of his life. His contemporaries celebrated Robinson's clarity of thought and expression as an attorney, his skills as a meticulous and indefatigable researcher, and his unswerving personal and professional integrity.

In 1829 Robinson ventured into historical writing, submitting an edited document he discovered in the archives of the General Court concerning New Netherland's governor Peter Stuyvesant to the *Virginia Literary Museum and Journal of Belles Lettres*. Two years later he joined a cadre of influential educators and legislators in forming the Virginia Historical and Philosophical Society. He served as the first treasurer of this organization and was later named to head its executive committee, which he did until 1870. In 1848 he launched the institution's *Annals of Virginia* series with the publication of his own work, *An Account of Discoveries in the West until 1519, and of Voyages to and Along the Atlantic Coast of North America, from 1520 to 1573*.

Robinson published an article in 1831 on "The Right of an Accused to Argument by Counsel before the Jury Both on the Law and Fact" in the *American Jurist and Law Magazine*. This piece gave the legal community a hint of important things to come, for in the following year appeared the first book of his three-volume series, *Practice in the Courts of Law and Equity of Virginia* (1832–1839). Hailed for its precise and encyclopedic coverage of Virginia law, the *Practice* became one of the primary legal treatises consulted and cited by practicing attorneys in the commonwealth until after the Civil War.

During this same period Robinson took a brief hiatus from his law practice. In 1834 he had been elected to the board of directors of the Richmond, Fredericksburg and Potomac Railroad (RF&P), to which his older brother Moncure had been named chief engineer. Faced with crucial financial problems, his fellow directors turned to Robinson in 1836 to lead the company out of potential ruin. This he did, resigning within two years upon the announcement of a 3½ percent dividend by the railroad. Thereafter he often represented the RF&P, as well as other internal improvement companies, in various courts. His successful leadership as president of the RF&P resulted from a variety of factors, including his full-time commitment to the position (which the previous president had not done and which allowed him to monitor the road's employees and business affairs closely), the expansion of the road under his direction, and the successful securing of a U.S. mail contract from the federal government.

In 1836 Robinson married Mary Susan Selden Leigh, the daughter of Benjamin Watkins Leigh, one of Virginia's most successful attorneys and later a U.S. senator. The couple had eight children, six of whom survived infancy. Robinson assisted his father-in-law in compiling several volumes of Virginia superior court case reports in the 1830s, and when the older man resigned the post of court reporter, Robinson took over, issuing two volumes in his own name (1842–1844). Several years later the Virginia legislature selected Robinson and his colleague, John Mercer Patton, to revise the state's civil and criminal codes. The final draft of the new Virginia code, completed in 1849, represented a greatly modified and streamlined system of judicial procedure, along with a significantly consolidated body of statute law. Shortly, however, the new code itself needed modification to bring it into conformity with the state constitution adopted in 1851. A large group of Richmonders supported Robinson for a seat in the legislature, which would enable him to take charge of that procedure, and he was elected to serve one term in the House of Delegates (1852).

This was not Robinson's first venture into politics, although he always intensely disliked election campaigns and political infighting. A supporter of the Whig party, he had been elected to the Richmond City Council in 1849. Chairing the council's committees of finance and police, he was instrumental in developing the city's water and natural gas system, creating city parks, and establishing a municipal library and lecture hall.

Robinson at this time also launched a new book series, the seven-volume *Practice of Courts of Justice in England and the United States* (1854–1874). Based in style on his earlier *Virginia Practice* series, this study reflected Robinson's broadened interest in Anglo-American jurisprudence. Similarly lauded for its breadth and accuracy, the series garnered praise from both sides of the Atlantic as well as from both sides of the Mason-Dixon line. Its scope, however, forced Robinson to leave his native city in 1858 to resettle with his family in the District of Columbia. There he continued his practice in the U.S. Supreme Court while being close to the law libraries of the national capital that were essential to his research.

This personal move came at a crucial time in the nation's history. Slavery had always posed ethical and intellectual problems for Robinson, but he had defended the institution, and the South, on legal and constitutional grounds. In 1835 he contributed a chapter on the slave laws of Virginia to James K. Paulding's *View of Slavery in the United States*. In response to agitation about the fugitive slave law, he published an article, "Slavery and the Constitution," in Richmond's *Southern Literary Messenger* in 1841, in which he avoided any question of the right or wrong of bondage and instead focused on the legal rights of slaveholders. Although opposed to secession on principle, he could not renounce his native state. He refused to take the so-called "test oath" and thus could not practice in the Supreme Court during the Civil War. Instead he initially wrote articles for newspapers and journals offering constitutional and legal defenses for Southern secession. While he did not practice in the federal courts of Washington, he did continue his research for the *Practice* series. While he remained in the District of Columbia, three of his four sons went south to join the Confederate army, and two of them died in the conflict. He and his wife and daughters were briefly detained by federal authorities following the assassination of Abraham Lincoln.

After the war Robinson returned to his appellate practice in the Virginia Supreme Court and the U.S. Supreme Court. As counsel in some forty-two postwar cases before the Court, Robinson specialized in railroad and transportation law, along with banking and insurance issues. He appeared for the Commonwealth in *Paul v. Virginia* (1869), in which the Court ruled in favor of state regulation by declaring that the insurance business was not "commerce" in the context of the Constitution, while he argued unsuccessfully for the RF&P in *Railroad Co. v. Richmond* (1878) against regulation as a deprivation of property by imposing excessive expenses on the roads.

Robinson completed his "new" *Practice* series in 1874. Still greatly interested in Anglo-American legal history, he subsequently researched and published his first (and ultimately only) volume in a projected multivolume series, *History of the High Court of Chancery and Other Institutions of England*, in 1882. He died on a visit to the home of his brother Moncure in Philadelphia and was buried in Richmond's historic Hollywood Cemetery.

• Major collections of Robinson's papers may be found in the Special Collections Division of the College of William and Mary and at the Virginia Historical Society, Richmond. Some additional materials of note are in the Brock collection at the Huntington Library, San Marine, Calif. Contemporary assessments of Robinson's life and career abound, including John Selden, "Conway Robinson," *Virginia Law Register* 1 (Jan. 1896): 631–46; Alexander H. Sands, "Conway Robinson," *Virginia Law Journal* 8 (1884): 257–66; Edward B. Merrill, "Conway Robinson," *Albany Law Journal* 29 (1884): 165–66 (reprinted in *Washington Law Reporter* 12 [1884]: 145–47); and perhaps most importantly, Thomas Harding Ellis, "In Memory of Conway Robinson, Esquire" (unpublished mss., Virginia Historical Society). See also Richard A. Claybrook, "Conway Robinson," in *The Virginia Law Reporters Before 1880*, ed. W. H. Bryson (1977). Obituaries are in the *Richmond Dispatch* and *Richmond State*, both 1 Feb. 1884.

E. LEE SHEPARD

ROBINSON, Earl Hawley (2 July 1910–21 July 1991), composer, was born in Seattle, Washington, the son of Morris Robinson, a department store executive, and Hazel Beth Hawley. Robinson received his B.A. in music at the University of Washington in 1933, there composing *Rhapsody in Brass* (1932) and *Symphonic Fragment* (1933).

Influenced by poet Carl Sandburg's folk-song anthology *American Song Bag* (1927), Robinson sang his way across the country in 1934, meeting socially active folksingers such as Woody Guthrie and Pete Seeger. Settling in New York City, Robinson became the musical director for a workers' theater, joining the Cultural Section of the Communist Party of the U.S.A. and the Composers Collective of the Pierre Degeyter Club (named for the composer of "The Internationale"), whose members included Aaron Copland and Marc Blitzstein. Early songs appeared in the *First Workers Songbook* (1934). His classical studies continued under Copland, Hanns Eisler, and George Antheil.

At a Communist party summer camp in 1936, Robinson, a slender, sandy-haired man who believed, in musicologist David Ewen's words, that "a socially conscious musician had to ally his art to the labor movement and the class struggle," set to music Alfred Hayes's poem "Joe Hill." The poem asserts that Joe Hill, the Industrial Workers of the World labor leader who was executed by a Utah firing squad in 1915, lives on in all workers who fight for their rights.

In 1937 Robinson married Helen Wortis; they had two children. That year he wrote songs for the satirical revue *Pink Slips on Parade* (1937). He also created the score for a 1937 Federal Theatre version of John Howard Lawson's 1925 play about industrial unionism, *Processional*; the score was praised by Brooks Atkinson in the *New York Times* (14 Oct. 1937) for its authentic "hard, shrill, 'corny' jazz." Robinson also formed the American People's Chorus in 1937.

In 1938 Robinson, who had claimed in an article in *New Masses* that African Americans "were the most important sources of folk music," set to music "Abe Lincoln," Hayes's strongly pro-Negro poem based on Abraham Lincoln's words. The next year he and Alex North scored *The Life and Death of an American*, an expressionistic history. The Federal Theatre's *Sing for Your Supper* (1939) provided the springboard for Robinson's 1938 setting of John Latouche's 1935 poem "The Ballad of Uncle Sam." Robinson's composition was heard by radio writer Norman Corwin, who induced Robinson and Latouche to retitle it as *Ballad for Americans*. In 1939 Corwin included it in his CBS radio series "The Pursuit of Happiness."

Ballad for Americans, a cantata Robinson called a progressive version of American history, features antiphonal passages between a soloist and chorus, dialogue and recitative, all in narrative form. Corwin persuaded African-American actor and singer Paul Robeson to be its soloist and narrator. By the middle of 1940, *Ballad for Americans* was performed thrice daily at the New York World's Fair. That year the cantata also opened the conventions of both the Communist and Republican parties—a seeming paradox that delighted Robinson. Ewen wrote that Robinson had "emerged as the song laureate of the radical left." Of his uncomplicated music Corwin wrote: "I always felt Earl was a kind of latter-day Stephen Foster, in that his idiom was folksy, easily assimilable, and singable . . . simple, instinctive and direct."

For the rest of his career, Robinson regularly returned to the cantata form, creating *In the Folded and*

Quiet Yesterdays (1940); *Tower of Babel* (1941); *The People, Yes* (1941), a setting of Sandburg's poetry for Corwin's radio program, written when Robinson held a Guggenheim Fellowship; *Battle Hymn* (1942); *The Town Crier* (1947); *When We Grow Up* (1954); *Preamble to Peace* (1960); *Illinois People* (1968); *Strange Unusual Evening: The Santa Barbara Story* (1970); and *Ride the Wind* (1974), based on the environmental writings of Supreme Court Justice William O. Douglas.

The Lonesome Train (1942), a Robinson cantata with Millard Lampell's words partly based on Sandburg's biography of Lincoln, was played at the death of President Franklin Roosevelt (1945) and regularly revived. As Corwin said, "Earl . . . twice accomplished something few American composers of any category have succeeded in doing even once—he aroused in millions of people a rare kind of patriotic emotion."

While directing the Almanac Singers, a folk-protest group, Robinson contributed "The House I Live In" (lyrics by Lewis Allan) to the revue *Let Freedom Sing* (1942). Called by the *New York Times* "a quiet and homely invocation to America," the song appeared in many venues before becoming a short film, *The House I Live In* (1945), starring Frank Sinatra. The film won a special Academy Award for its contributions to racial tolerance.

Robinson composed *It's Up to You* (1943), a U.S. Department of Agriculture revue that urged a patriotic approach to wartime food consumption. In 1945 Robinson's and E. Y. Harburg's "Free and Equal Blues" appeared in *Blue Holiday*, an African-American revue. In Hollywood they collaborated on the score for the film *California* (1946). In 1946 Robinson also became a director of People's Songs, Inc., a music publishing company formed to promote a progressive social agenda in post–New Deal circumstances.

Between 1945 and 1948, Robinson often accompanied Robeson, whose left-wing political views were increasingly at odds with the national temper. Robinson wrote incidental music for the anti-witch-hunt play *Dark of the Moon* (1947), ballet music for *Bouquet for Molly* (1949), and the song "Good Morning" (1949).

In 1949 People's Songs was labeled a Communist front. By the early 1950s Robinson stopped receiving film commissions, although he was not named as suspicious by the House Un-American Activities Committee until 1957. He continued to write, returning to New York, where he gave guitar lessons.

Robinson collaborated with Waldo Salt on the short-lived off-Broadway musical *Sandhog* (1954), the tale of an Irish immigrant tunnel laborer blown to the surface of the North River (New York) in the 1880s. In 1954 his song written with Dave Arkin, "Black and White," was occasioned by the Supreme Court ruling against school segregation; it later became a children's book with illustrations by Arkin. A participant in the folk-song revival of the later 1950s, Robinson helped found the Woody Guthrie Children's Fund Trust in 1956. Between 1958 and 1965 he taught at Elisabeth Irwin High School in New York. After the death of his

first wife in 1963, Robinson married Ruth Martin in 1965; they had no children and were divorced c. 1973.

Robinson edited five books: *Young Folk Song Book* (1963), *Folk Guitar in Ten Sessions* (1966), *Songs of the Great American West* (1967), *The Brecht-Eisler Song Book* (1967), and *German Folk Songs* (1968). During the years of national disquiet over the war in Vietnam, Robinson, who had left the Communist party, again became popular. In 1969 "Joe Hill," sung by Joan Baez at the Woodstock Festival in New York, became an anthem for that era's counterculture.

Between 1967 and 1981 Robinson taught at branches of the University of California. His music, such as the abstract *Banjo Concerto* (1967), gradually became less overtly programmatic. Among other compositions were the symphonic *Soul Rhythms* (1972); a piano concerto titled *The New Human* (1973); and *To the Northwest Indians* (1974), written for singing narrator, folk instruments, and orchestra. Robinson and Harburg's theme song written for but not used in the race-relations film *Hurry Sundown* (1967) became popular. Robinson regularly composed for television drama. In 1972 came a bestselling rock recording of "Black and White." There followed *Earl Robinson's America* (1976), an anthology drama; *David of Sassoon* (1978), a folk opera; *Listen for the Dolphin* (1981), an environmental musical; and *Song of Atlantis* (1983), a musical drama. In 1986 "The House I Live In," uncredited, was the theme of the national rededication of the Statue of Liberty.

In 1989 Robinson returned to his native Seattle. That year Governor Booth Gardener of Washington made a proclamation noting his contributions to "our musical heritage." Robinson involved himself in environmental causes and was writing his autobiography when he was killed in an automobile accident in Seattle.

• Robinson's papers are at the University of Washington in Seattle. Corwin's comments are contained in a letter to the author, 29 Mar. 1996; other information was obtained from letters to the author from Pat Arkin and Sandy Arkin, Apr. and May 1996. Robinson's autobiography is *Ballad of an American* (1998), cowritten with Eric A. Gordon. Other sources setting Robinson in his social and historical context are Timothy E. Scheurer, *Born in the USA: The Myth of America in Popular Song from Colonial Times to the Present* (1991); Robbie Lieberman, *My Song Is My Weapon: People's Songs, American Communism and the Politics of Culture* (1989); David Ewen, *All the Years of American Popular Music* (1977); Bruce Jackson, ed., *Folklore and Society* (1966); and Eric Winship Trumbull, "Musicals of the American Workers' Theatre Movement, 1928–1941: Propaganda and Ritual in Documents of a Social Movement" (Ph.D. diss., Univ. of Maryland, 1991). Also useful are Pete Seeger, *The Incompleat Folksinger* (1972); Joe Klein, *Woody Guthrie: A Life* (1981); and Martin Duberman, *Paul Robeson* (1989). Obituaries are in the *New York Times* and the *Los Angeles Times*, 23 July 1991.

JAMES ROSS MOORE

ROBINSON, Edgar Munson (15 May 1867–9 Apr. 1951), educator and youth group leader, was born in St. Stephen, New Brunswick, Canada, the son of an area merchant (his parents' names are unknown). Educated in local schools, he grew up working in the family store, which he eventually took over. At the same time, however, he developed an early interest in volunteer youth work. Over the next few years he achieved some renown for his work at camp meetings and evangelical conferences. He married Serena Truman (marriage date unknown), with whom he had four children, and in 1893 formed a boys' camp, which he successfully operated.

About 1894, after much indecision, Robinson gave up his interest in the store and migrated with his family to Springfield, Massachusetts. There he met with Dr. Frank N. Seerley at the International Conference of the YMCA, thus beginning a lifelong association with that organization. In 1898 he accepted the half-time position of boys' work secretary for Massachusetts and Rhode Island. At the same time he enrolled as a student at Springfield College, where he came under the influence of the more liberal, progressive educational philosophies promoted by faculty members William G. Ballantine and college president Laurence L. Doggett. By the time he graduated in 1901, Robinson had largely been transformed from an "intolerant," dogmatic evangelical to an open-minded believer in the Social Gospel. Luther H. Gulick and other YMCA workers encouraged him to apply a liberal, more flexible approach to his work with boys.

In September 1900 Robinson became the first boys' work secretary for the International Committee of the YMCA, which encompassed the youth of both the United States and Canada. In that position he toured the continent, encouraging the growth and development of YMCA boys' work, with particular emphasis on character building. Along with Gulick and others, Robinson came to embrace G. Stanley Hall's "recapitulation" theory, that basically a child's life stages parallel the history of the human race, culminating in civilized adulthood, and he sought to apply this theory to their regimented programs. As a pioneer camp director, he believed that summer outdoor camping experiences would help lead adolescent boys "out into a noble Christian life." In February 1902 he started *Association Boys*, a magazine that became an effective organ of information for the progressive ideas of youth leaders. By 1913 Robinson had five associates and nearly 400 boys' workers under his supervision. One colleague described him as "a stimulant to all searchers of truth. To the contented and complacent he was a constant irritant and a troublesome person to have around."

Along with his YMCA work, Robinson was sympathetic to other new youth movements, notably Ernest Thompson Seton's Woodcraft Indians and Dan Beard's Boy Pioneers. As early as 1909 he supported initial efforts of YMCA units to organize Boy Scout troops based on Lord Baden-Powell's approach in England. But after he, Seton, William D. Boyce, and others formed the first National Boy Scout Committee at New York City in 1910, he soon came to the conclusion that the Boy Scouts of America (BSA) should be self-supporting and independent of the YMCA. Nevertheless, Robinson agreed to serve for a year as the organization's first chief executive secretary, and even after resuming his YMCA work in 1911, he remained a staunch BSA backer. Unlike most BSA executives, including his conservative successor, James E. West, Robinson favored Seton's less-centralized woodcraft mode of scouting, allowing more democratic control by local leaders and members; when William D. Murray published his *History of the Boy Scouts of America* in 1937, Robinson argued that Seton and Beard had not received the full credit they deserved for their roles in starting the Boy Scout program. Indeed, later historians consider Robinson one of the foremost instigators of that movement in America.

In 1920, at the second assembly of boys' work secretaries, Robinson and Charles R. Scott were chosen to make a world tour on behalf of the YMCA. In 1922 Robinson was made boys' work secretary of the YMCA World Alliance. In that position he was instrumental in the planning of the 1923 Pörtschach conference, which enhanced the World Alliance considerably.

Robinson was a member of the board of the Home for Elderly People at his hometown of St. Stephen; on the board of directors of Goodwill Homes in Hinchley, Maine; an honorary life member of the Canadian YMCA and the Canadian Maritime Commission; and an honorary member of the YMCA World's Committee. In addition, Robinson held many honorary titles and received the Tarbell Medallion for citizenship, named after journalist Ida Tarbell and given by New York businessmen, in honor of his outstanding humanitarian achievements.

After retiring in 1927, Robinson became honorary head of the Springfield College faculty and head of its boys' work division. He maintained the college as his principal interest through the years and was instrumental in obtaining a pueblo, which was named in his honor, for the college campus. He published a historical account of his YMCA youth work, *The Early Years*, in 1950. Robinson died at his home in Springfield.

• Papers and correspondence of Edgar M. Robinson can be found in the YMCA Historical Library in New York City, the Springfield College Library and Connecticut Valley Historical Museum in Springfield, Mass., and the Ernest Thompson Seton Memorial Library at Philmont Scout Ranch near Cimarron, N.M. See also A. G. Kniebel, *Four Decades with Men and Boys* (1936); C. Howard Hopkins, *A History of the YMCA in North America* (1951); and David I. Macleod, *Building Character in the American Boy* (1983). An obituary is in the Springfield (Mass.) *Union*, 10 Apr. 1951.

H. ALLEN ANDERSON

ROBINSON, Edward (10 Apr. 1794–27 Jan. 1863), biblical scholar, was born in Southington, Connecticut, the son of William Robinson, a clergyman, and Elisabeth Norton. He graduated from Hamilton College in 1816. After a year reading law at Hudson, New York, at the office of James Strong, he returned to Hamilton in 1818 as a tutor in Greek and mathematics. There he married Eliza Kirkland; they had no children. After her death in 1819, Robinson spent three years farming and in private study, preparing an edition of parts of the Iliad (*Iliadis Libri Novem Priores Librique XVIII et XXII* [1822]).

On a visit to Andover Seminary in 1821 to see his book through the press, Robinson was encouraged by Moses Stuart, a professor of Hebrew, to devote his energies to biblical Hebrew. Consequently, Robinson remained at Andover from 1823 to 1826 as instructor in Hebrew. As Stuart's assistant, Robinson helped to prepare a second edition of Stuart's *Hebrew Grammar* (1823) and to translate and revise G. Winer's *A Greek Grammar of the New Testament* (1825). In 1825 Robinson published a *New Testament Lexicon*, translated and revised from C. A. Wahl's *Clavis Philologica Novi Testamenti* (2d ed., 1855).

Stuart was one of the first American biblical scholars to become familiar with German biblical philology and criticism. Through his inspiration Robinson not only read extensively in German scholarship but resolved to continue his studies in Germany. Robinson spent 1826 to 1830 studying Hebrew and theology at Göttingen, Halle, and Berlin with F. Gesenius, E. Roediger, A. Tholuck, and A. Neander. In 1828, while in Germany, he married Therese Albertina Louise von Jakob, a distinguished scholar of German and Slavic languages and a well-known writer. They had four children.

Returning to the United States in 1830, Robinson became professor extraordinary of biblical literature and librarian at Andover. In 1831 he founded the *Biblical Repository*, which became an important medium for translation and dissemination of German biblical scholarship in America. Robinson wrote and translated a substantial number of the contributions himself. In 1832 he published a revised version of A. Calmet's *Dictionary of the Bible* and a translation of P. Buttmann's *Larger Greek Grammar* (2d ed. 1839, rev. ed. 1850). He also founded a second journal, *Bibliotheca Sacra*, which appeared as a collection of essays by that title in 1843 and began as a periodical with the same name in 1844. For reasons of ill health, he resigned his professorship at Andover in 1833 and moved to Boston, where he served as first vice president of the newly formed American Oriental Society. (Robinson would later serve as president from 1849 to 1863.) In 1836 Robinson completed a translation of Gesenius's *Hebrew Lexicon*, with extensive revisions and additions. He later made further revisions and updatings in 1849, 1850, and 1854. This was the standard dictionary of biblical Hebrew in English for the last half of the nineteenth century, the 1854 version being reprinted twenty-nine times. In 1845 he also published *Harmony of the Four Gospels*, based on the Greek text, and in 1848 a *Harmony of the Four Gospels in the Authorized Version*, a work intended for students and ministers not conversant with Greek. Through this monumental publication program, Robinson put American biblical

philology, grammar, and lexicography on a sound scholarly footing.

Robinson's most original contributions to biblical studies, however, were his researches on the geography of Palestine and Syria. Having thoroughly mastered biblical and classical Greek and Latin sources for Near Eastern geography, Robinson journeyed to Palestine, Syria, and the Sinai in 1837, having accepted in the same year a professorship in biblical literature at the Union Theological Seminary, New York, with an agreement to delay his appointment until his explorations were completed and written up (1840). With the collaboration of an Arabic-speaking American missionary, Eli Smith, Robinson made a detailed survey of the region, recording the Arabic toponyms and proposing and discussing numerous identifications with localities known from the Bible and other ancient sources. He also carefully evaluated the evidence for the reliability of traditional locations of the birthplace, trial, crucifixion, and burial of Jesus, as well as other celebrated pilgrimage sites. His work was characterized by scrupulous personal observation of the terrain and profound knowledge of the written evidence.

In 1841 Robinson published *Biblical Researches in Palestine, Mount Sinai and Arabia Petraea* in three volumes, which established a scholarly foundation for historical geography of the region. Returning to Palestine in 1852, he produced in 1856 a revised edition of his *Researches*, together with a supplementary volume, *Later Biblical Researches in Palestine and the Adjacent Regions* (rev. ed. of both works combined in 1867). This was the most important American scholarly contribution to biblical studies prior to the Civil War. He planned a much larger geographical work but was hindered by failing eyesight and poor health, so that only his *Physical Geography of the Holy Land* appeared posthumously in 1865. Robinson died in New York City.

Robinson's extraordinary linguistic and scholarly attainments were pervaded by his personal religious outlook, which accepted the divine inspiration of the Hebrew and Greek scriptures, but which also permitted the use of critical techniques regarded as heretical by many clergy and students of the Bible of the period. He saw the need to provide dictionaries, grammars, reliable texts, and handbooks for serious students of the Bible, thus opening to Americans the extensive resources and developments of nineteenth-century German biblical scholarship. He was methodical, exact, and cautious, manifesting a certain inflexibility and intolerance of dissenting viewpoints or what he considered inferior work. He was the most distinguished and influential American biblical scholar of his time.

• Robinson's scholarly papers, including his travel diaries, are in the library of the Union Theological Seminary. About four hundred letters to his family describing his studies in Germany are in the possession of Jay G. Williams of Hamilton College. Robinson's biography of his father, *Memoir of the Rev. William Robinson . . .* (1859), contains autobiographical information, with particulars on his immediate family. The fullest account of his life is Henry B. Smith and Roswell D. Hitchcock, *The Life, Writings and Character of Rev. Ed-*

ward Robinson, D.D., LL.D. (1863). Individual aspects of his work are considered by Julius Bewer, F. M. Abel, Albrecht Alt, and William Stinespring in a group of essays published in the *Journal of Biblical Literature* 58 (1939): 355–87. Information on his career at Andover is in Leonard Woods, *History of the Andover Theological Seminary* (1885), and Henry K. Rowe, *History of Andover Theological Seminary* (1933). His career at the Union Theological Seminary is discussed by G. L. Prentiss, *Fifty Years of the Union Theological Seminary in the City of New York* (1889), and in Prentiss, *Another Decade in the History of the Union Theological Seminary in the City of New York* (1899). Robinson's place in American biblical criticism and theology is discussed by Jerry Wayne Brown, *The Rise of Biblical Criticism in America, 1800–1870* (1969). Personal recollections of Robinson can be found in Edward E. Salisbury and Elijah Barrows, "Proceedings at Boston and Cambridge, May, 1863," *Journal of the American Oriental Society* 8 (1863), iii–vii. An obituary is in the *New York Tribune*, 29 Jan. 1863.

BENJAMIN R. FOSTER

ROBINSON, Edward G. (12 Dec. 1893–26 Jan. 1973), actor, was born Emanuel Goldenberg in Bucharest, Romania, the son of Morris Goldenberg, a builder, and Sarah Guttman. He immigrated to the United States in 1902. The family settled in Manhattan's Lower East Side, where his father ran a candy store and Emanuel attended P.S. 137, graduating in 1906. That year the family moved to the Bronx, where his father opened an antique shop and Emanuel attended P.S. 20 before being accepted at Townsend Harris High School. In 1910 Emanuel enrolled at the New York City College. He joined the campus drama club, the Elizabethan Society, and worked part time at an etching and lithograph printing shop, where he acquired the foundation for his extensive knowledge of the art world. In 1911 he was awarded a scholarship to the American Academy of Dramatic Arts. His closest friend at the academy was Joseph Schildkraut, son of Rudolf Schildkraut, famous as a leading actor of the Yiddish Theater and a future successful actor in his own right. At the academy Emanuel changed his name to Edward G. Robinson, the *G* standing for his original surname.

When the United States entered the First World War in 1917, Robinson enlisted in the U.S. Navy, where he served briefly but was never shipped overseas.

Robinson spent the first sixteen years of his acting career (1913–1929) on the New York stage, during which time he appeared in thirty plays. Some of the more important were Booth Tarkington's *Poldekin* in 1920, with George Arliss; Henrik Ibsen's *Peer Gynt* in 1923, with Joseph Schildkraut; and Elmer Rice's *The Adding Machine* in 1923. In the same year he made his first film, *The Bright Shawl*, starring Richard Barthelmess, Mary Astor, and William Powell. It was a silent film, and it left Robinson very disappointed with the medium. He returned to New York, where in 1925 he appeared in George Bernard Shaw's *Androcles and the Lion* and *Man of Destiny*.

In 1927 Robinson married Gladys Cassell (stage name Gladys Lloyd), who had a daughter from a previous marriage. They had one son, Edward Robinson, Jr.

Robinson returned to the movies in *Hole in the Wall*, with Claudette Colbert, and *Night Ride*, with Joseph Schildkraut, both made in 1929. In 1930 he brought the play *The Kibitzer* to New York. He starred and shared the authorship credits with Jo Swerling. Its success introduced the verb "to kibitz" into the English language. He appeared in New York in one more play, *Mr. Samuel*, in 1930, then moved to California. He did not return to the New York stage until 1951.

Irving Thalberg hired Robinson to star with Vilma Banky in *A Lady to Love* (1930), but First National gave him a jump into stardom when they cast him in *Little Caesar* (1931). The film, based on a novel by William Burnett, was directed by Mervyn Le Roy. Robinson's part was created around the character of Al Capone. Although the film was mediocre, Robinson provided such a convincing performance of a criminal type that the role defined him as an actor for many years.

Following this success, Robinson was cast in a string of "B" movies in which he played Italian gangsters, Chinese hatchet men, and gamblers. Occasionally he was on the right side of the law as a newspaper reporter, an editor, or a district attorney. The stories, however, revolved around crime. These parts were interspersed with roles as a farmer, a tuna fisherman, an art student, and a stage director. Nevertheless his screen image remained well entrenched.

Robinson struggled to be cast in a variety of other roles than the assorted criminals he was given. Although he was often compared in this category to James Cagney and Paul Muni, Robinson's hope was to transcend to other roles similar to those that had helped him make his reputation on the New York stage. He starred with Kay Francis in *I Loved a Woman* (1933), with Jean Arthur in *The Whole Town's Talking* (1935), with Miriam Hopkins in *Barbary Coast* (1935), and with Joan Blondell in *Bullets or Ballots* (1936), none of which were crime movies. But these roles did not erase the screen image that had stuck to him since *Little Caesar*.

Robinson reached another peak in his career when he starred in *Kid Galahad* (1937) with Bette Davis and Humphrey Bogart. Robinson played the part of Nick Donati, a prizefighter manager. Called by the critics his "best part since *Little Caesar*," it pulled Robinson out of the "B" movies. He now commanded a higher salary, and many offers were coming his way. He appeared in *The Amazing Dr. Clitterhouse* (1938), based on a play by Barre Lyndon. It was followed by *Blackmail* (1939), in which Robinson's performance led the *New York Times* to describe his character as "one of the screen's greatest criminals."

Robinson was given the opportunity to expand his horizons as a serious actor in the title role of *Dr. Ehrlich's Magic Bullet* (1940), the biography of Paul Ehrlich, discoverer of the cure for syphilis. The critics called Robinson's performance "a round gem of a portraiture," "most dramatic and moving," and "one of the most distinguished performances" on the screen. Robinson also rendered a notable performance in *The Sea Wolf* (1941), based on the Jack London novel. Robinson's films became more expensive, the casts larger, the directors more prominent; nevertheless, in essence, Robinson was still associated primarily with crime movies.

As news began arriving from occupied Europe regarding the fate of the Jews there, the entrepreneur Billy Rose organized a mass memorial for them at the Madison Square Garden. Participating in the ceremony were, besides Robinson, Paul Muni, Frank Sinatra, John Garfield, Luther and Stella Adler, Jacob Ben-Ami, and fifty Orthodox rabbis. Music was provided by Kurt Weill, and words were written by Ben Hecht.

During the 1940s Robinson made several "war movies," none of which received enthusiastic critical acclaim. They included *Destroyer* (1943) and *Mr. Winkle Goes to War* (1944). In 1946 he appeared in *Journey Together*, which was produced by the Royal Air Force Film Unit. Also in 1946 he starred in *The Stranger*, a Nazi-chasing espionage movie directed by Orson Welles. Of the other films that he made during that decade, several stand out in particular. *Double Indemnity* (1944), directed by Billy Wilder, was based on a novel by James M. Cain that was adapted to the screen by Wilder and Raymond Chandler; it costarred Fred MacMurray and Barbara Stanwyck. In 1948 Robinson transferred to the screen one of the most moving stage roles of that decade. As Joe Keller, the factory owner who sells defective airplane parts to the government in Arthur Miller's play *All My Sons*, Robinson once again received rave reviews. He followed it with another fine performance as the gangster in the screen adaptation of Maxwell Anderson's play *Key Largo* (1948). Critics again compared his performance to his achievement in *Little Caesar*, finding his work "expertly timed" in a "top-notch style." As a result of this success, for the next two years crime and mystery scripts came to him from the studios, the most worthwhile of which was *House of Strangers* (1949), an intense drama of family rivalries. His friend Ben Hecht, who produced, directed, and wrote the screenplay for the film *Actors and Sin* (1952), cast Robinson in the leading role; Marsha Hunt costarred.

Robinson's next noncrime role was that of an aging baseball player in *Big Leaguer* (1953). It was followed by more crime, mystery, and sleuthing films in which Robinson repeated the same role in many different guises. In view of his typecast character over the years, it seemed somewhat surprising that Cecil B. De Mille chose him to appear in his biblical epic *The Ten Commandments* (1956) in the part of Dathan. In 1956 Robinson made his last New York stage appearance in *Middle of the Night*. After the play closed in New York he took it on a tour (1957) that ended in San Francisco (1958). He lost the film role to Frederic March when the play was adapted to the screen in 1959.

In *A Hole in the Head* (1959) Robinson starred with Frank Sinatra. The film was directed by Frank Capra. The *New York Times* found Robinson's performance "superb" and called him an actor "whose sense of timing in dialogue is fascinating to watch."

Quite noteworthy among the films that he made during the 1960s are a Kirk Douglas vehicle, *Two Weeks in Another Town* (1962), and *The Prize* (1964). In 1965 he enacted a memorable characterization in *A Boy Ten Feet Tall*; then he starred with Steve McQueen in *The Cincinnati Kid* (1965). Approaching the end of his career, Robinson appeared in just two more films before his death, *MacKenna's Gold* (1969), with Gregory Peck and Omar Sharif, and *Song of Norway* (1970), the life story of composer Edvard Grieg.

In Robinson's personal life a major change occurred when his wife sued him for divorce in 1956. She insisted on sharing Robinson's extensive art collection. Rather than split the collection, Robinson sold the major part of it to Greek shipping tycoon Stavros Niarchos and split the proceeds with his wife. The sale made headlines in much of the press and created a sensation in the art world, with art collectors and museums clamoring to bid on the items that were put on the auction block. The collection specialized in French artists of the impressionist era and of the twentieth century. A few years later, when Robinson offered to buy back his collection, Niarchos refused to sell. But in due course Robinson managed to assemble another fine collection of paintings. In 1958, after his divorce from Gladys Lloyd became final, he married Jane Adler (maiden name Bodenheimer), a divorcée who worked as a director for the Nettie Rosenstein Group; she was twenty-six years his junior.

Robinson had strongly held opinions and was often intolerant of opposing views. As a lifelong Democrat he actively distanced himself from Republicans. Hecht's support of the Irgun in Palestine was sufficient cause for Robinson to stop seeing Hecht for several years. In the 1950s Robinson was accused of being connected with a variety of procommunist causes. The allegation was based on contributions that he had made to communist fronts and on his financial support of Dalton Trumbo's family while the latter was in prison for "un-American activities." In 1950, to counter the risk that he might be blacklisted in Hollywood, Robinson insisted on appearing before the House Un-American Activities Committee (HUAC) to clear his name. He submitted to the committee a twelve-page list of all the contributions that he had made over the previous ten years, indicating a wide variety of purposes, and a detailed description of his war record in both world wars, but during the sixteen months of the congressional investigation Robinson could not get employment in Hollywood. He accepted an offer to go on a tour with the successful Broadway hit *Darkness at Noon* (1951–1952), a fiercely anticommunist play by Sidney Kingsley and Arthur Koestler based on a novel by Koestler. Finally, on 30 April 1952, HUAC pronounced him "a good, loyal and intently patriotic American citizen."

Robinson was an active supporter of the state of Israel, especially as concerned the Israel bond drive. In recognition of his efforts, on his fifty-seventh birthday, at a special ceremony at Madison Square Garden during the annual Chanukah Festival, the Israel Bond Agency presented him with the Tree of Life Award. Eighteen years later Israel honored him with a Distinguished Artist Award. Robinson's only professional award was given him at the 1949 Cannes Film Festival for his portrayal of Gino Monetti in *House of Strangers*. On 19 May 1952 he was presented with the French Legion d'Honneur, making him the first American film actor to receive this award. When in late 1972 it became known that Robinson was dying of cancer, the Academy of Motion Picture Arts and Sciences announced that it planned to bestow on him the award for lifetime achievement at its March 1973 ceremonies. But by then Robinson had already died at his Beverly Hills home. The Oscar was awarded him posthumously.

• The serious researcher may profit by reference to the collection of Robinson's papers at the University of Southern California Department of Motion Pictures Special Collections. Robinson wrote his memoirs twice, first in *My Father, My Son* (1958), when he was not even halfway through his career, and then again in Edward Robinson, *All My Yesterdays* (1973), which was published posthumously. In addition, one may want to consult Alan Gansberg, *Little Caesar: A Biography of Edward G. Robinson* (1983), which boasts voluminous research. It also contains a fairly comprehensive listing of all of Robinson's appearances on stage, motion pictures, radio, and television. Another biography was published soon after his death by Foster Hirsch, *Edward Robinson* (1975). Comprehensive listings of Robinson's stage appearances, filmography, short films, radio work, and dramatic television roles, with excellent film synopses, can be found in James Robert Parish and Alvin H. Marill, *The Cinema of Edward G. Robinson* (1975). Mervyn Le Roy, who had directed Robinson in four films, including the milestone *Little Caesar*, wrote the biographical introduction to the book. Obituaries are in the *Los Angeles Times* and the *New York Times*, both 27 Jan. 1973, and in all the trade papers of the motion picture industry.

SHOSHANA KLEBANOFF

ROBINSON, Edward Stevens (18 Apr. 1893–27 Feb. 1937), psychologist and educator, was born in Lebanon, Ohio, the son of Clinton Cooke Robinson and Carrie Isabella Stevens. He attended the University of Cincinnati, where he majored in psychology, earning his A.B. in 1916. He earned his A.M. in psychology one year later at the Carnegie Institute of Technology, Pittsburgh, Pennsylvania. In 1917 Robinson was accepted for doctoral work in psychology at the University of Chicago, where he worked with James Angell and Harvey Carr. His graduate studies were briefly interrupted by service in the Trade Test Division of the War Department during the First World War. His services in the military were directed toward personnel classification and in the development of intelligence and trade tests. After the war Robinson returned to his graduate studies at Chicago. Prior to the receipt of his

doctoral degree in 1920, he spent the academic year of 1919–1920 as an instructor in psychology at Yale University. Robinson married Florence Richardson, a psychologist, in 1921; the couple had no children.

Robinson was appointed to an assistant professorship at the University of Chicago after completion of his doctoral work. He was promoted to assistant professor in 1923 and remained at Chicago until 1927. Robinson was named a visiting associate professor at Yale University in 1926 and a visiting lecturer at Harvard University in 1927. He returned to Yale in 1927 as a full professor in the Department of Psychology. He remained there until his death.

Robinson was a steady contributor of scholarly research and writing, publishing frequently in psychology journals and the professional literature of law, education, and the museum. His published writings included six books and fifty-seven papers. While at the University of Chicago, Robinson's research interests were in experimental psychology—primarily in learning and memory, mental fatigue, and mental efficiency. He produced a number of research reports based on his experimental work, several of which were under joint authorship with his wife. Most notable of his early work was a book of readings in psychology, coauthored with his wife, *Readings in General Psychology* (1923; rev. ed., 1929), which was widely adopted as a textbook for college undergraduates.

After Robinson moved to Yale University in 1927, his academic interests shifted away from experimental research and toward psychology in the social sphere. His psychological writing in this last period of his life ranged over a variety of topics: from play to Gestalt psychology to psychological jurisprudence to the psychology of the museum. His *Association Theory Today* (1932) traces the continuing influences of associationist models of learning through the work of Janet, Freud, Jung, and Pavlov and into the then mainstream behaviorist psychology of American academic psychology.

During his career at Yale, Robinson was involved in the development of the Institute of Human Relations, a multidisciplinary approach to graduate education and scientific investigation initially funded by the Rockefeller Foundation. Robinson served at the Institute as a professor of psychology with close ties to the Law School, where he offered seminars in ethics and the psychology of jurisprudence. In his *Law and the Lawyers* (1935), Robinson calls for an empiricizing of jurisprudence based upon the contributions of psychological science. It was considered at the time to be a seminal contribution on the psychological aspects of legal practice. At the Institute Robinson also pioneered a new approach to adult education under the Division of General Graduate Studies. This approach, designed to facilitate breadth of preparation among those already at work in some professional field, was a marked success under his chairmanship (1935–1937).

From the late 1920s until his death, Robinson was involved in extending the range of social psychology. Two examples may serve to illustrate his efforts. His work on the place and function of public museums in American social life was a pioneering effort to apply social psychology principles to everyday life: Do museums reach their educative goals through their displays? Robinson's investigation of political judgment by voters during the presidential election of 1932 was a landmark of careful social psychological research and presaged later attempts to understand voter preferences on political issues. His interests in this area also included studies of radio, social work, and the effects of propaganda.

Beyond his research and scholarly writings, Robinson was active as an editor of psychological journals. He was editor of the *Psychological Bulletin*, 1930–1934, and an editor of the *Journal of Social Psychology* from 1935 until his death. He served as a cooperating editor of the *American Journal of Psychology* (1925–1935).

Robinson was involved in a variety of social, educational, and scientific organizations. These included the vice presidency of the American Association for the Advancement of Science and chairman of its section on psychology. He was the treasurer of the American Psychological Association (1925–1930) and a member of its governing council (1934–1937); a member of the National Research Council's (NRC) Division of Anthropology and Psychology (1930–1933); and chairman of the NRC Committee on Personality in Relation to Culture (1936–1937). His honors included membership in the Society of Experimental Psychologists, Sigma Xi, Beta Theta Pi, and fellow of the American Association for the Advancement of Science.

Robinson died in New Haven, Connecticut, of cerebral injuries received in a freak accident. He apparently stepped into the path of a bicyclist while carrying a large package and was thrown to the pavement, striking his head. His place in psychology is that of one of the members of the broad middle of the discipline in a time of its expansion. He made no great discovery, nor was he an especially adept leader. Rather, he utilized his keen insight and gracious wit as a corrective to the perceived excesses of those psychologists too eager to promise the arrival of a new psychological millennium. His attitude of encouragement to students and younger members of the discipline endeared him to many who later made more salient contributions to psychology and society.

• A small amount of archival material on Robinson may be found at the Sterling Library, Yale University. His published works include "Some Factors Determining the Degree of Retroactive Inhibition," *Psychological Monographs* vol. 28, no. 128 (1920); "A Concept of Compensation and Its Psychological Setting," *Journal of Abnormal and Social Psychology* 17 (1923): 383–94; "Two Factors in the Work Decrement," *Journal of Experimental Psychology* 9 (1926): 415–43; "The Contributions of Psychology to Social Work," *Proceedings of the National Conference on Social Work* 57 (1930): 536–43; "Psychological Studies of the Public Museum," *School and Society* 33 (1931): 121–25; "Trends of the Voter's Mind," *Journal of Social Psychology* 4 (1933): 265–84; and, with L. W. Doob, "Psychology and Propaganda," *Annals of the*

American Academy of Political and Social Science (1935). Biographical sketches were prepared after his death by Harvey Carr (*American Journal of Psychology* 49 (1937): 488–89); James Angell (*Psychological Bulletin* vol. 34, no. 10 (Dec. 1937): 801–05; and Roswell Angier (*Psychological Review* vol. 44 (July 1937): 267–73.

WADE E. PICKREN

ROBINSON, Edwin Arlington (22 Dec. 1869–6 Apr. 1935), poet, was born in Head Tide, Maine, the son of Edward Robinson, a timber merchant and civic leader, and Mary Elizabeth Palmer. Shortly after his birth the family moved to nearby Gardiner, where he grew up; the town later provided the model for a series of poems that he wrote throughout his career. The third of three sons, Robinson had been considered a disappointment by his mother, who had wanted a daughter. While his oldest brother, Herman, was destined to manage the family fortune and his middle brother (Dean) to become a doctor, Robinson was free to turn to poetry. He began writing regularly at the age of eleven and in high school attended meetings of the town's poetry society as its youngest member. But while Robinson was willing to be taught the rudiments of the various poetry forms, one of his contemporaries recalled that "he was one of those persons whom you cannot influence *ever*, he went his own way" (quoted in Smith, p. 85). This strength of purpose would mark his character throughout his life.

Robinson attended Harvard from 1891 to 1893 despite his father's doubts about the value of a higher education. During the early 1890s the family's fortunes began to decline, triggering a series of tragedies that influenced Robinson's life and poetry. In 1892 his father died, and the panic of 1893 and the lingering aftermath slowly bankrupted the family over the next seven years. Robinson's brother Dean became addicted to morphine and returned home in failing health. Robinson was forced to leave Harvard because of the family's financial difficulties and his mother's failing health. She died in 1896 of "black diphtheria," and because no mortician would handle the body, the brothers had to lay out their mother, dig the grave, and bury her. During this time Robinson wrote the poems that were later published in 1896 as *The Torrent and the Night Before* and in 1897 as *The Children of the Night*. (The publishing costs of both were borne by friends.)

From the first, Robinson's poetry was noted for mastery of conventional forms, be it the sonnet, the quatrain, or the eight-line stanza. The characters of works like "Richard Cory," "Luke Havergal," "Aaron Stark," and "John Evereldown" are faced with failure and tragedy, but Robinson, as Louise Bogan noted, "with the sympathy of a brother in misfortune, notes their failures and degradations without losing sight of their peculiar courage" ("The Line of Truth and the Line of Feeling," *Achievement in American Poetry: 1900–1950* [1951], pp. 19–27). His hometown of Gardiner, renamed Tilbury Town, also appears for the first time in these poems. As Robinson saw it, the town's Puritan ethic, portrayed as repressive and critical, combined with the materialistic aspects of society, conspires to beat down its citizens. He would return to this theme of public failure, counterbalanced by the subject's life-affirming belief in a higher power, throughout his career.

In Gardiner, Robinson's relations with his brother Herman became strained. Robinson had first met Emma Shepherd, the great love of his life, while taking dancing lessons in 1887, and in her he found a companion he could talk to and who encouraged his poetry. Although he loved her, he believed he could either write poetry or raise a family but not do both. He introduced Emma to Herman, who married her in 1890. It was not a happy marriage, strained by financial difficulties and Herman's drinking. Robinson's love for Emma during this difficult time resulted in his leaving Gardiner for New York City in 1897. In 1899 his brother Dean died, possibly of an intentional drug overdose. As executor of their mother's estate, Herman had agreed to support Robinson with a monthly stipend that allowed him to barely get by, but he was left penniless when the family fortune finally vanished in 1901.

For the next quarter-century Robinson chose to live in poverty and write his poetry, relying on scraps of temporary work and charity from friends. In 1902 he published *Captain Craig*, again with friends paying the bill. Despite some earlier warm reviews for *The Torrent*, critics had either ignored or disliked *The Children of the Night* and *Captain Craig*. As a result, Robinson fell into a depression, neglecting his poetry, drifting from job to job and drinking heavily.

In 1905 he received help from an unexpected source. President Theodore Roosevelt's son Kermit had read *The Children of the Night* in school and encouraged his father to read it as well. Roosevelt liked the book and arranged a job for Robinson at the New York Customs House. The president bullied Scribner's into republishing *The Children of the Night* and co-wrote with Kermit an article for *Outlook* magazine, explaining, "It is not always necessary in order to enjoy a poem that one should be able to translate it into terms of mathematical accuracy . . . and to a man with the poetic temperament it is inevitable that life should often appear clothed with a certain sad mysticism. . . . I am not sure I understand 'Luke Havergal,' but I am entirely sure that I like it" (quoted in Hagedorn, p. 218). Literary critics did not appreciate the president's judgment of Robinson's poetry, for the most part they reviewed the new edition of *The Children of the Night* with phrases like "a very pleasant little book" (*Nation*) and "the product of a wholesome faith" (*New York Times*).

Robinson's job at the customs house was deliberately structured to enable him to do as little work as possible and to devote his time to poetry. "The strenuous man," Robinson wrote, referring to Roosevelt, "has given me some of the most powerful loafing that has ever come my way" (quoted in Hagedorn, p. 221). His duties, in biographer Chard Smith's words, "consisted of opening his roll-top desk, reading the paper, closing the desk, leaving the paper in his chair to show he had been there, and going home" (p. 220). The job left him ample time to write poetry, and his salary of $2,000 a year made it possible to support himself and Herman until the latter's death in 1909. But, ironically, Robinson found the poetry he created during this time to be second-rate. "The stuff that I have been writing of late," he wrote to a friend, "has been so bad that I have been ashamed of it and of myself. I shall do better pretty soon. At any rate I am not likely to do any worse" (quoted in Hagedorn, p. 222). The major magazines remained closed to him despite Roosevelt's patronage, and when the president left the White House in 1909, Robinson quit the customs house after being ordered to do his job, keep regular hours, and wear a uniform.

Back in Gardiner living with a friend, Robinson set to work full time, revising old poems and writing new ones. In 1909 he also published *The Town down the River*, which he dedicated to Roosevelt. The review in the *New York Times* was generally favorable, its critic describing the title poem as "an elusive imagination . . . an apparent simplicity, veiling a subtle and curious wisdom, a wisdom content to question, ponder, doubt, yet conscious of a sublime answer somewhere." In the *Boston Transcript*, writer and editor William Stanley Braithwaite went further, hailing Robinson in a large headline as "America's Foremost Poet."

In 1911 Robinson began spending his winters at the homes of New York friends and his summers at the MacDowell Colony in Peterborough, New Hampshire. The colony, originally a 200-acre farm owned by composer Edward MacDowell, was founded by MacDowell's widow to provide a refuge where composers, artists, and writers could create. Despite an initial prejudice against a gathering of artists, Robinson discovered he could devote his full energies to writing and revising his poetry. He also gave up alcohol. During this time, he tried playwriting; but his play *Van Zorn* (1914) was unsuccessfully produced, and *The Porcupine* (1915) never made it to the stage.

In late 1916 Robinson received a measure of financial security through a monthly stipend from an anonymous source. This, he wrote to the bank handling the gift, would let him "go on with a rather exacting piece of literary work without worry or interruption" (Hagedorn, p. 316). A book of poetry, *The Man against the Sky* (1916), broadened his reputation. While most of the critics at the major magazines were not wholeheartedly behind him, some were, and that he was being noticed at all was better than being ignored. The most glowing review came from Amy Lowell of the *New Republic*, who wrote that *The Man against the Sky* was a book of "great power . . . dynamic with experience and knowledge of life." Her lengthy essay about Robinson in her book *Tendencies in Modern American Poetry* (1917) established him as a poet worth reading.

In 1917 *Merlin* appeared, the first of three long Arthurian-related poems, followed by *Lancelot* in 1920 and *Tristram* in 1927. In 1919, on his fiftieth birthday, Robinson was the cover subject of the *New York Times*

Review of Books, and he was praised by Lowell, Vachel Lindsay, and Edgar Lee Masters, among others. Through Braithwaite, Robinson was convinced the time was right to publish a collection edition of his poems. In 1921 his *Collected Poems* was awarded the first Pulitzer Prize for poetry. He was awarded a second Pulitzer Prize in 1924 for *The Man Who Died Twice*.

Aided by a push from the Literary Guild and critical notices by Mark Van Doren, *Tristram* (1927) became a bestseller, earning Robinson his third Pulitzer. Critical reception to it was equally favorable. In the *Nation*, Lloyd Morris called *Tristram* "the finest of Mr. Robinson's narrative poems" and "among the very few fine modern narrative poems in English." For the first time in his life, Robinson was financially independent, and the success exhilarated him. After years of self-denial, he surprised friends by the attention he paid to his clothes and the generosity he paid to others in need. In what he called a protest against Prohibition, he began drinking again. Otherwise, his habits remained unchanged: summers at the MacDowell Colony and winters in New York City, with his full attention paid to his poetry.

Robinson published regularly for the rest of his life, mostly long verse narratives, including *Avon's Harvest* (1921); *Roman Bartholow* (1925); *Dionysus in Doubt* (1925); *Cavender's House* (1929); *Matthias at the Door* (1931); a collection of shorter poems, *Nicodemus* (1932); *Talifer* (1933); and *Amaranth* (1934). These psychological studies did not attempt to capitalize on the popularity of his Arthurian cycle, and sales were a tenth of that of *Tristram*. Robinson also worked himself to exhaustion on these poems, and according to later critics the deliberation shows. "He lost the power of compression and precision; he lost much of the control of structure," wrote Hoyt C. Franchere, "That he produced anything at all after 1930 testifies to the strength of the man's spirit, when his body had failed him" (*Edwin Arlington Robinson* [1968], p. 146). Robinson died in a New York City hospital while revising the galleys of his last work, *King Jasper* (1935).

Robinson was the first major American poet of the twentieth century, unique in that he devoted his life to poetry and willingly paid the price in poverty and obscurity. As for his works, his once-popular Arthurian trilogy has fallen in favor, criticized by William H. Pritchard as having "occasional purple patches, fine lines here and there, but on the whole prolix, fussy, and somehow terribly misguided—the long poems are stone-dead" (*Twentieth-Century Literary Criticism*, vol. 5 [1981], p. 418). The poems from his earlier period, especially the Tilbury Town cycle, have held critical esteem. In his shorter works, Robinson excelled in limning characters who failed on a materialistic level but somehow succeeded, though at great cost on a moral or spiritual level. In an age of free verse and experimentation, his technical expertise is considered intolerably old-fashioned, but there is no doubt he was a master of many forms.

"Robinson's poems, the best of them and those that will last," Radcliffe Squires wrote, "emerge from an awareness that life is continuously menaced: that innocence and experience alike are threatened by the bland modular construction of society and the soulless press of industrialism" (*Poetry Criticism* 1 [1991]: 496).

• Robinson's papers are in collections at Colby College Library in Waterville, Maine, the Houghton Library at Harvard University, the New York Public Library, and the Library of Congress. Robinson's *Collected Poems*, rev. ed. 1937), remains the standard edition of his work. His *Selected Letters* was published in 1940. Emery Neff, *Edwin Arlington Robinson* (1948), is the standard biography, while Chard Powers Smith, *Where the Light Falls: A Portrait of Edwin Arlington Robinson* (1965), and Hermann Hagedorn, *Edwin Arlington Robinson: A Biography* (1938), are a combination of memoir and biography. Ellsworth Barnard, *Edwin Arlington Robinson: A Critical Study* (1969), is the best critical introduction.

BILL PESCHEL

ROBINSON, George Dexter (20 Jan. 1834–22 Feb. 1896), governor of Massachusetts, congressman, and attorney, was born in Lexington, Massachusetts, the son of Charles Robinson and Mary Davis, farmers. His original name was George Washington Robinson, but he changed it in 1855 because it was too similar to someone else's in Lexington. After graduating from Harvard in 1856, he studied at his brother's law practice, moved to Chicopee, Massachusetts, taught and served as principal at the local high school, and was admitted to the bar in 1866. In 1859 he married Hannah E. Stevens; they had one child before Hannah died in 1864. In 1867 he married Susan E. Simonds; they had one child. Throughout his life, Robinson was actively involved in the Unitarian church in Chicopee and in the American Unitarian Association.

Robinson's political career began in 1873, when he was elected as a Republican to the General Court of Massachusetts, where he was appointed to the Judiciary Committee. In 1875 voters elevated him to the state senate, where he chaired both the Judiciary Committee and the Committee on Constitutional Amendments. The following year he was elected to the Forty-fifth Congress, and he held his seat during the next three elections. During his congressional career, Robinson served on several committees, including the Committee on Mississippi Levees, the Committee on Expenditures in the Justice Department, the Judiciary Committee, and the Committee on Revision of the Laws. He was well regarded for his regular attendance and his command of parliamentary procedure. While he actively participated in many debates, his speeches regarding a bill for the improvement of the Mississippi River and the Culbertson Court Bill, which limited the jurisdiction of the federal courts, are considered the most noteworthy.

In 1883 the Republican State Convention nominated Robinson for governor to run against incumbent Benjamin F. Butler. Following a campaign in which he advocated reform of the spoils system, the hiring of government employees based on political affiliation rather than merit, Robinson defeated Butler 160,092 to 150,228. Robinson defeated opponents William C. Endicott in 1884 (159,345 to 111,829) and Frederick O. Prince in 1885 (112,243 to 90,346). Several reform laws were enacted during Robinson's administrations. In his inaugural address in 1884, he called for an end to the patronage system, and the General Court obliged. The law created a bipartisan Civil Service Commission to establish rules for the selection of state and city government employees. In 1884 Robinson also signed acts requiring that school committees provide textbooks to students free of charge and preventing insurance companies from discriminating on the basis of race.

In 1885 a Gas Commission was created to investigate complaints regarding the rate and quality of service. Robinson also approved an act that prohibited discrimination on the basis of race in public places; violations were punishable by a $100 fine. During his last year as governor he signed an act that required the weekly payment of wages by corporations. That year he cooperated with the legislature to create a state board of arbitration that would seek negotiated resolutions to disputes between employees and employers.

Not all measures Robinson actively supported were enacted during his administration. He had repeatedly called for a constitutional amendment to provide for the biennial election of the governor and other state officers and stressed the importance of putting the issue directly to the voters in a referendum. Robinson also made repeated calls for greater equity in state funding for public schools and for a higher level of assistance for smaller schools, though no legislation was passed during his administration.

Declining to run for reelection in 1886, Robinson retired from the office of governor in 1887 to return to his private law practice in Chicopee. President Grover Cleveland offered him an appointment to the Interstate Commerce Committee in 1887, and in 1889 President Benjamin Harrison offered him an appointment on the Cherokee Commission. Robinson turned down both of these positions. In 1889 he presided at the Republican State Convention.

The most notorious case of his legal career involved his role in the defense of Lizzie Borden, who was accused of brutally killing her father and stepmother with an ax in Fall River, Massachusetts, on 4 August 1892. Because of the violent and gruesome nature of the murders, the case was closely followed statewide and nationally. Borden's family attorney was Andrew Jennings, but Robinson was asked to join the defense team. The trial became a media circus, and Robinson was often in the limelight. Among the factors making Robinson so valuable was that, as governor, he had appointed Justice Justin Dewey, one of the judges who presided at the trial.

Robinson shared the trial work with Jennings and achieved some important victories for the defense. For example, Robinson successfully argued for the exclusion of Borden's testimony at the inquest. The prosecution was anxious that this testimony be included, because she made many contradictory statements regarding her whereabouts on the day of the murder. Robinson's argument for the exclusion centered on the fact that Borden was not represented by an attorney during the inquest. The judges in the case held that, though she was not formally charged with a crime during the inquest, she did stand accused, and her testimony was not voluntary. The exclusion of this evidence was seen as a great blow to the prosecution.

Robinson also played a key role in the cross-examinations of Bridget Sullivan, the Borden family maid, and Assistant Marshal John Fleet of the Fall River police. During these interrogations, Robinson confused the witnesses and raised doubts about the accuracy of their testimony. Borden was acquitted of the murder charges on 20 June 1893. After the trial, Robinson continued his legal career, and in April 1895 he was appointed solicitor for the city of Springfield.

Robinson died in Chicopee. While he did not live to see Massachusetts adopt a biennial election system, his career was distinguished by both his record of public service and his work as a private attorney. His administration was in keeping with the movement toward political reform.

• No major collection of Robinson's papers exists. For Robinson's views on the issue of biennial elections and woman suffrage, see his *Biennial Elections Opinions and Arguments* (1886) and *Is It Expedient That Municipal Suffrage Be Granted to Women?* (1895). *The Layman's Responsibility for the Church* (1885) is a published copy of Robinson's address at the Annual Missionary Meeting of the American Unitarian Association. *The Memorial of the Harvard College Class of 1856* (1906) contains information about Robinson's life, as does Henry Cabot Lodge's tribute in *The Fighting Frigate* (1902). Sources for Robinson's role in the Lizzie Borden trial are David Kent, comp., *The Lizzie Borden Sourcebook* (1992), and Michael Martin and Dennis Binette, *The Commonwealth of Massachusetts vs. Lizzie Borden* (1994). Albert Bushnell Hart, *Commonwealth History of Massachusetts* (1930), provides some background on the gubernatorial elections and on civil service reform. An obituary is in the *Boston Herald*, 23 Feb. 1896.

LAURA RUNDELL

ROBINSON, Harriet Jane Hanson (8 Feb. 1825–22 Dec. 1911), textile mill worker, suffragist, and author, was born in Boston, Massachusetts, the daughter of William Hanson, a carpenter, and Harriet Browne. When Harriet was six, her father died. Her mother then ran a boarding house in Industrial Lowell, Massachusetts, with the help of her children.

Harriet attended school until she was ten; she then entered the mills at her own wish, working as a doffer, a child who replaced the full bobbins on the spinning frames with empty ones. She worked fifteen minutes an hour for fourteen hours a day. Later she worked briefly at a spinning frame and then for about ten years as a drawing-in girl, preparing the beams for the weavers' looms by hooking the individual threads of the warp through the harness and the reed.

In her memoir of this period, *Loom and Spindle* (1898), Robinson identified the mill girls as the first female workers whose labor had monetary value. According to her, the women were healthy, well paid, and thrifty, with access to the cultural benefits of evening schools and lending libraries; they reflected spirit and independence rather than oppression and went on to productive later lives. Her account stressed the literary creativity of the women involved in publishing *The Lowell Offering*, but it ignored the unionizing effort of the Female Reform League in 1845 and 1846. Robinson led the workers from a room during a strike to maintain benefits, but in general she identified with the positive aspects of mill life, refusing to see herself as a wage slave.

For Robinson, the path to improvement was education. She attended school, as state law required, three months a year after entering the mills, and she also passed a competitive examination to spend two years in high school. After she went back to the mills, she took private lessons in German, drawing, and dancing, a remarkably aristocratic education for a mill worker.

In 1848 she married William Stevens Robinson, a newspaperman from Concord, Massachusetts. He was a founder of the Free Soil party and set up his own newspaper, the *Lowell American*. He served two terms (1852–1853) in the Massachusetts House of Representatives. Never profitable, the paper failed after five years. Both Robinsons were firm abolitionists, and Harriet Robinson belonged to the Concord Anti-Slavery Society. However, she and other suffragists opposed giving the vote to black citizens before it was given to women. After the beginning of the Civil War, when her husband's views became popular, he was given a party sinecure as clerk of the Massachusetts House of Representations; he also wrote a regular column for the influential *Springfield Republican*.

The Robinsons had four children, one of whom died young when the homeopathy his mother espoused failed to save him. The household moved to Concord to care for William Robinson's mother, and after her death the family moved to Malden, Massachusetts.

While Harriet Robinson blossomed as a creative mother and housekeeper, she also read widely and studied literature, taking the train into Boston almost daily to shop and to attend cultural events. With her daughters she founded the Old and New Club in Malden. The members studied literature and wrote papers that were read and criticized. She was also a member of the New England Women's Club and a founder and officer of the General Federation of Women's Clubs.

Robinson's husband lost his clerkship for political reasons in 1873. His friends sent the couple to Europe as a reward for his service. Harriet Robinson reveled in this journey, but after their return her husband fell ill and died in 1876.

Robinson's literary work was all accomplished in her thirty-five years of widowhood. She collected her husband's works as *"Warrington" Pen Portraits* (1877), with a long biographical introduction. She published the book at her own expense and set off on the road to sell it.

Massachusetts in the Woman Suffrage Movement (1881), a highly readable and partisan account, resulted from Robinson's conversion to woman suffrage in 1868. Originally attracted by the eloquence of Lucy Stone and her husband H. B. Blackwell, she held office in their Middlesex County Woman Suffrage Association in 1875. She broke with them over a lack of recognition and allied herself with Elizabeth Cady Stanton and Susan B. Anthony of the National Woman Suffrage Association, in which she also held office in 1878. In 1882 she was recording secretary of a state group, the National Woman Suffrage Association of Massachusetts, under her daughter Hattie's presidency. Thus, she held office at three levels.

Robinson's essay *Early Factory Labor in New England* (1883) was expanded to become *Loom and Spindle* (1898), her best book. She also wrote two plays, *Captain Mary Miller* (1887), a charming suffrage melodrama, and *The New Pandora* (1889), a serious feminist play. Her writing was fresh and lively, but none of her six books sold well. She died in Malden. While real fame eluded her during her lifetime, she received considerable appreciation and notice. She has since come to be seen as an articulate and clear-eyed, if self-centered, chronicler of her age.

• Besides the books cited in the text, all of which are largely autobiographical, Robinson kept regular and extensive diaries and scrapbooks and saved her correspondence. These papers, and those of her daughter Harriet Lucy Robinson Shattuck, are housed in the Arthur and Elizabeth Schlesinger Library on the History of Women in America, at Radcliffe College, Cambridge, Mass.
An extended biographical account is Claudia L. Bushman, *"A Good Poor Man's Wife": Being a Chronicle of Harriet Hanson Robinson and Her Family in Nineteenth Century New England* (1981).

CLAUDIA L. BUSHMAN

ROBINSON, Jackie (31 Jan. 1919–24 Oct. 1972), baseball player, was born Jack Roosevelt Robinson in Cairo, Georgia, the son of Jerry Robinson, a farmworker and sharecropper, and Mallie McGriff, a domestic worker. Six months after Robinson's birth, his father deserted the family. Faced with severe financial difficulties, Robinson's mother moved her family to Pasadena, California, in pursuit of a better life. The Robinsons settled in a white Pasadena neighborhood—where they received a chilly reception—and Robinson's mother supported her family in modest fashion as a domestic worker.

Robinson demonstrated his athletic prowess from an early age. After graduating from high school in Pasadena in 1937 as one of the city's most celebrated athletes, he entered Pasadena Junior College. He established himself as an exceptional multi-sport athlete at Pasadena and won junior college All-American honors in football. By the time of his graduation from Pasadena in 1939, he was one of the most widely recruited athletes on the West Coast. Robinson eventually decided to enter the University of California at Los Angeles (UCLA) which he attended from 1939 to 1941.

Playing four sports at UCLA, Robinson continued to display extraordinary athletic ability, causing one sportswriter to label him "the Jim Thorpe of his race" (Tygiel, p. 60). He twice led the Southern Division of the Pacific Coast Conference in basketball scoring, averaged 11 yards per carry as an All-American running back during his junior year on the football team, and won the National Collegiate Athletic Association (NCAA) broad jump championship in track and field. Ironically, Robinson's weakest performance came in baseball; he played only one season at UCLA and had minimal success, batting only .097. Robinson was not the only athlete in his family; his older brother Mack finished second to Jesse Owens in the 200-meter sprint at the 1936 Berlin Olympics.

Robinson dropped out of college during his senior year at UCLA to help support his family. After brief stints as an assistant athletic director at a National Youth Administration camp in California and as a player with two semiprofessional football teams—the Los Angeles Bulldogs and the Honolulu Bears—Robinson was drafted into the U.S. Army in the spring of 1942.

The U.S. Army of the 1940s was a thoroughly segregated institution. Although initially denied entry into the army's Officers Candidate School because of his race, Robinson, with the assistance of boxer Joe Louis, successfully challenged his exclusion and was eventually commissioned a second lieutenant. Robinson spent two years in the service at army bases in Kansas, Texas, and Kentucky. During this time Robinson confronted the army's discriminatory racial practices; on one occasion he faced court-martial charges for insubordination arising from an incident in which he refused to move to the back of a segregated military bus in Texas. A military jury acquitted Robinson, and shortly thereafter, in November 1944, he received his honorable discharge from the army.

Following his discharge, Robinson—who continued to enjoy a reputation as an extraordinarily gifted athlete—spent the spring and summer of 1945 playing shortstop with the Kansas City Monarchs in the Negro Leagues. Robinson proved to be a highly effective player, batting about .345 for the year. At this time major league baseball did not permit black players to play on either minor league or major league teams, pursuant to an unwritten agreement among the owners that dated back to the nineteenth century. Pressure to integrate baseball, however, had steadily increased. Many critics complained of the hypocrisy of requiring black men to fight and die in a war against European racism but denying them the opportunity to play "the national pastime." During the early 1940s a few major league teams offered tryouts to black players—Robinson had received a tryout with the Boston Red Sox in 1945—but no team actually signed a black player.

In the meantime, however, Branch Rickey, president of the Brooklyn Dodgers baseball team, had secretly decided to use African Americans on his team. Rickey was convinced of the ability of black ballplayers, their potential gate attraction, and the injustice of their exclusion from major league baseball. Using the ruse that he wanted to develop a new league for black players, Rickey deployed his scouts to scour the Negro Leagues and the Caribbean for the most talented black ballplayers during the spring and summer of 1945. In particular Rickey sought one player who would break the color line and establish a path for several others to follow; he eventually settled on Robinson. Although Robinson was not the best black baseball player, his college education, experience competing in interracial settings at UCLA, and competitive fire attracted Rickey. In August 1945 Rickey offered Robinson a chance to play in the Dodgers organization but cautioned him that he would experience tremendous pressure and abuse. Hence Rickey extracted from Robinson a promise not to respond to the abuse for his first three years.

Robinson spent the 1946 baseball season with the top Dodgers minor league club located in Montreal. After leading the Montreal Royals to the International League championship and winning the league batting championship with a .349 average, he joined the Dodgers the following spring. Several of the Dodgers players objected to Robinson's presence and circulated a petition in which they threatened not to play with him. Rickey thwarted the boycott efforts by making clear that such players would be traded or released if they refused to play.

Robinson opened the 1947 season as the Dodgers' starting first baseman, thereby breaking the long-standing ban on black players in the major leagues. During his first year he was subjected to extraordinary verbal and physical abuse from opposing teams and spectators. Pitchers threw the ball at his head, opposing baserunners cut him with their spikes, and disgruntled fans sent death threats that triggered an FBI investigation on at least one occasion. Although Robinson possessed a fiery temper and enormous pride, he honored his agreement with Rickey not to retaliate to the constant stream of abuse. At the same time he suffered the indignities of substandard segregated accommodations while traveling with the Dodgers.

Robinson's aggressive style of play won games for the Dodgers, earning him the loyalty of his teammates and the Brooklyn fans. Despite the enormous pressure that year, he led the Dodgers to their first National League championship in six years and a berth in the World Series. Robinson, who led the league in stolen bases and batted .297, was named rookie of the year. Overnight, he captured the hearts of black America. In time he became one of the biggest gate attractions in baseball since Babe Ruth, bringing thousands of African-American spectators to major league games. Five major league teams set new attendance records in 1947. By the end of the season, two other major league teams—the Cleveland Indians and the St. Louis Browns—had added black players to their rosters for brief appearances. By the early 1950s most other major league teams had hired black ballplayers.

In the spring of 1949, having fulfilled his three-year pledge of silence, Robinson began to speak his mind and angrily confronted opposing players who taunted him. He also enjoyed his finest year, leading the Dodgers to another National League pennant and capturing the league batting championship, with a .342 mark, and the most valuable player award. Off the field, Robinson received considerable attention for his testimony in July 1949 before the House Committee on Un-American Activities in opposition to Paul Robeson's statement that African Americans would not fight in a war against the Soviet Union. During the next few years Robinson, unlike many other black ballplayers, became outspoken in his criticism of segregation both inside and outside of baseball.

Robinson ultimately played ten years for the Dodgers, primarily as a second baseman. During this time his team won six National League pennants and the 1955 World Series. Robinson possessed an array of skills, but he was known particularly as an aggressive and daring baserunner, stealing home nineteen times in his career and five times in one season. In one of the more memorable moments in World Series history, Robinson stole home against the New York Yankees in the first game of the 1955 series. Robinson's baserunning exploits helped to revolutionize the game and to pave the way for a new generation of successful basestealers, particularly Maury Wills and Lou Brock. Robinson batted .311 for his career and in 1962 became the first black player to win election to the National Baseball Hall of Fame. On 15 April 1997, the fiftieth anniversary of Robinson's first major league game, Major League Baseball, in an unprecedented action, retired Robinson's number 42 in perpetuity.

After the 1956 season, the Dodgers traded Robinson to the New York Giants, their crosstown rivals. Robinson declined to accept the trade and instead announced his retirement from baseball. Thereafter, Robinson worked for seven years as a vice president of the Chock Full O'Nuts food company handling personnel matters. An important advocate of black-owned businesses in America, Robinson helped establish several of them, including the Freedom National Bank in Harlem. He also used his celebrity status as a spokesman for civil rights issues for the remainder of his life. Robinson served as an active and highly successful fundraiser for the National Association for the Advancement of Colored People and conducted frequent fundraising events of his own to support civil rights causes and organizations. He wrote a regular newspaper column throughout the 1960s in which he criticized the persistence of racial injustice in American society, including the refusal of baseball owners to employ blacks in management. Shortly before his death, Robinson wrote in his autobiography *I Never Had It Made* that he remained "a black man in a white world." Although a supporter of Richard Nixon in the 1960 presidential campaign, Robinson eventually became involved with the liberal wing of the Republican party, primarily as a close adviser of New York governor Nelson Rockefeller.

Robinson had married Rachel Isum in 1946, and the couple had three children. Robinson suffered from diabetes and heart disease in his later years and died of a heart attack in Stamford, Connecticut.

Probably no other athlete has had a greater sociological impact on American sport than did Robinson. His success on the baseball field opened the door to black baseball players and thereby transformed the game. He also helped to facilitate the acceptance of black athletes in other professional sports, particularly basketball and football. His influence spread beyond the realm of sport, as he emerged in the late 1940s and 1950s as an important national symbol of the virtue of racial integration in all aspects of American life.

• The National Baseball Library and Archive in Cooperstown, N.Y., contains extensive material on Robinson. The Arthur Mann and Branch Rickey papers, both located in the Library of Congress, also contain documentary material on Robinson. Robinson published three autobiographies: *I Never Had It Made*, with Alfred Duckett (1972); *Wait Till Next Year*, with Carl Rowan (1960); and *Jackie Robinson: My Own Story*, with Wendell Smith (1948). Robinson also published a fourth book, *Baseball Has Done It* (1964), that contains the reaction of various players to the integration of baseball. Robinson's newspaper columns, written with Duckett, were published in both the *New York Post* and the *Amsterdam News*. The most complete assessments of his life are David Falkner, *Great Time Coming: The Life of Jackie Robinson, from Baseball to Birmingham* (1995); and Jules Tygiel, *Baseball's Great Experiment: Jackie Robinson and His Legacy* (1983). Other Robinson books include Maury Allen, *Jackie Robinson: A Life Remembered* (1987); Harvey Frommer, *Rickey and Robinson: The Men Who Broke Baseball's Color Barrier* (1982); and Arthur Mann, *The Jackie Robinson Story* (1950). See also Rachel Robinson, *Jackie Robinson: An Intimate Portrait* (1996), by Robinson's wife. An obituary is in the *New York Times*, 25 Oct. 1972.

DAVISON M. DOUGLAS

ROBINSON, James Harvey (29 June 1863–16 Feb. 1936), historian and educator, was born in Bloomington, Illinois, the son of James Harvey Robinson, a banker, and Latricia Maria Drake. Enjoying a comfortable youth, he was educated in the public schools of Bloomington and the Illinois State Normal School. Robinson early displayed a strong fascination with natural science, especially biology and astronomy. He interrupted his studies in 1882 to spend a year traveling through Europe. Upon his return home, Robinson worked in the family bank, but in 1884 he determined to follow his younger brother Benjamin to Harvard University. There he received his A.B. in 1887 after only three years of study and then earned his A.M. in 1888. While at Harvard, he came under the influence of William James, who developed his interest in pragmatic philosophy and psychology. In 1887 he married Grace Woodville Read, the daughter of a merchant from his hometown. They had no children.

Accompanied by his wife, Robinson in 1888 returned to Europe to be with his brother Benjamin, who was studying botany at the University of Strasbourg. He spent a semester perfecting his German and then transferred to the University of Freiburg, where he prepared his doctorate. While at Freiburg, Robinson took courses from the eminent scholar Hermann von Holst, himself a specialist in American political history. Robinson wrote a dissertation, "The Original and Derived Features of the Constitution of the United States of America" and received his doctor of philosophy degree in 1890. He spent the following year touring Germany. At Halle Robinson met Simon N. Patten, a professor of political economy at the University of Pennsylvania, who, impressed by his intellect, invited him to teach there.

Robinson began his academic career in 1891, giving courses in European history and rising from lecturer to associate professor within a year. The school published his study, *The German Bundesrath: A Study in Comparative Constitutional Law*, soon after he arrived. His undergraduate courses covered the Middle Ages, Renaissance, Reformation, French Revolutionary and Napoleonic Era, and Europe since 1815. As a teacher, Robinson held his students' interest through his lively lecture style.

Strongly influenced by his studies in Germany and convinced that direct consultation of primary documents was essential, Robinson, along with his colleagues Dana C. Munro and Edward P. Cheney, initiated the series Translations and Reprints from the Original Sources of European History in 1894. The five volumes that Robinson edited demonstrated the high standards of scholarship that he had developed. Robinson also sought to promote improved teaching of history by accepting membership in 1892 on the subcommittee on history, civil government, and political economy of the Committee on Secondary School Studies of the National Education Association.

Robinson's reputation as a scholar persuaded Columbia University to hire him as a professor of European history in 1895. He remained there until 1919, establishing himself as one of America's most eminent historians. His fame rested on his classroom teaching, voluminous writings, and a theory of a "New History."

In both his undergraduate lectures and graduate seminars, Robinson proved an original, stimulating instructor. He regarded the course of European history as an evolutionary process without sudden breaks between ancient, medieval, and modern periods, emphasizing general causes rather than eminent individuals. He constantly challenged received ideas and established truths. With humor and insight, he sought to awaken his students' interest in the subject, encourage them to examine the original sources, and then let them form their own conclusions. His approach owed much to the eighteenth-century *philosophe* Voltaire, whose wit and skepticism Robinson deeply admired. He never wrote out his lectures but spoke freely in somewhat drawling tones, usually standing, arms folded, rarely looking directly at his class, but interspersing his delivery with flashes of humor that stirred general laughter.

Robinson developed an innovative course on the history of the intellectual class in Europe. It evolved from simply linking the thought characteristic of the Middle Ages, Renaissance, Reformation ("Protestant Revolt"), and Enlightenment into a far-reaching examination of ideas, beginning with the ancient world, and ultimately into a study of comparative psychology and animal behavior. He stressed the growth of science and its impact on material culture and thought patterns.

During the near quarter century that he remained at Columbia, Robinson inspired numerous students who would later become celebrated in their own right, among them Harry Elmer Barnes, Charles A. Beard, Carl Becker, Carlton J. Hayes, Lynn Thorndike, John H. Randall, Jr., Arthur M. Schlesinger, Sr., and J. Salwyn Schapiro. The influence he exerted proved one of his lasting legacies.

Robinson gained wider fame through his efforts to improve the quality of history teaching, particularly by producing better textbooks. In 1900 he published "Popular Histories, Their Defects and Possibilities," an article that called for greater emphasis on historical method as well as more attention to the accurate, objective, and comprehensive explanation of human accomplishments in economic, social, cultural, and intellectual fields and not simply the political and military. In 1904, at a meeting of the Association of History Teachers of the Middle States and Maryland, Robinson suggested that history might prove valuable in explaining contemporary problems. He urged that high school teaching place stronger emphasis on recent historical events so as to help explain the pressing questions of the day. Six years later, addressing a meeting of the American National Education Association, Robinson declared that "history in one sense is not fixed or immutable but ever changing. Each age has a perfect right to select from the annals of mankind those facts that seem to have a particular bearing on the matters it has at heart." Robinson went even further, contending that historical study could contribute to needed social reform and provide information about how technology might transform daily lives.

Reacting against traditional college textbooks that emphasized political, dynastic, and military matters almost exclusively, Robinson produced a series of volumes that widened students' views of the past. In 1902–1903 he published *An Introduction to the History of Western Europe* and then in 1904–1906 followed this successful venture with the two-volume *Readings in European History*. The latter presented original documents so arranged as to accompany chapters in the textbook. He collaborated with Charles A. Beard on *The Development of Modern Europe: An Introduction to the Study of Current History*, which appeared in 1907–1908. With Beard he also produced a high school text, *Outlines of European History: From the Opening of the Eighteenth Century* (1912). Robinson eliminated unimportant facts, as well as extraneous names and dates, while expanding upon cultural and intellectual developments. In addition, he stressed science, medicine, industry, and social questions that had hitherto been slighted. Widely hailed by critics, these volumes won Robinson both recognition within the academic community and financial success. (The *History of Western Europe* alone sold a remarkable 250,000 copies.)

Robinson's most important work appeared in 1912. Called *The New History*, it was, in fact, not especially "new." The term "new history" itself had been employed in 1900 by Edward Eggleston, president of the American Historical Association, in his address to the organization. Eggleston had called upon his colleagues to place less emphasis on military and political matters in their work. Nor was the content of Robinson's volume original. A collection of eight separate essays, only one had not been previously published as an address or journal article. The volume took its title from the first chapter, based on his essay of 1900, "Popular Histories: Their Defects and Possibilities." In it Robinson attacked traditional forms of historical writing and called for a discipline grounded in the social sciences, the "discoveries that are being made about mankind by anthropologists, economists, psychologists—discoveries which have . . . served to revolutionize our ideas of the origin, progress, and prospects of our race." These "new allies" of historians would enable them to reinterpret the past in dramatically fresh ways. Robinson particularly emphasized the importance of intellectual history. If properly understood, he explained, it "enables us to reach a clear perception of our duties and responsibilities by explaining the manner in which existing problems have arisen [and] promotes that intellectual liberty upon which progress fundamentally depends." The ultimate purpose of historical writing, therefore, was to "promote the social betterment of humanity." Warmly received by reviewers, the volume enjoyed healthy sales and exerted a strong influence on younger scholars.

Ironically, vocal as Robinson became in advocating his "new history," he produced no original scholarly works, only textbooks such as his *Medieval and Modern Times: An Introduction to the History of Western Europe from the Dissolution of the Roman Empire to the Opening of the Great War of 1914* (1916).

The outbreak of World War I did not immediately dash Robinson's hopes for human progress. At first he sympathized with the Allied cause. In his article "War and Thinking" (Dec. 1914) he blamed German scholars for supporting militarism and conquest. But as the conflict widened, he became no less unhappy with the "absurd lust of the allies and the wild and unreasoning patriotism of many of our leaders." By December 1917, he could warn in "The Threatened Eclipse of Free Speech" of the dangers of repressing free inquiry and discussion, which retarded progress. Indeed, Robinson's *Medieval and Modern Times* became the target of superpatriots who considered its treatment of the origins of the war too pro-German. He had already grown disillusioned when, in October 1917, Columbia dismissed two colleagues for having opposed American entry into the war.

Resenting this assault on academic and personal freedom, Robinson, in 1918, began to develop plans for a new institution of higher learning where such constraints did not exist. It would be, in his words, "a free and independent school of social science, designed to bridge the gap between the intellectual and capitalistic classes and the so-called working classes." With the cooperation of Beard and such prominent intellectuals as John Dewey, Alvin Johnson, and Thorstein Veblen, he created a college without admissions requirements or academic degrees. Nor would there be any professional administrators, since the school was to be run democratically by the faculty members themselves. When, in early 1919, the New School for Social Research was launched and Robinson named chairman of its board of directors, he resigned his professorship at Columbia.

For two years Robinson taught classes in intellectual history and worked strenuously to make the new venture succeed. Despite his sincere efforts, however, the lack of degree programs, disagreements among the board of directors over curriculum, and lack of finances, as well as outside criticism of its innovative programs, led Robinson to withdraw from the New School in 1921. Thereafter, he devoted himself entirely to his own writing.

That same year Robinson published *The Mind in the Making*, a book synthesizing his views on the development of western thought. Its subtitle, *The Relation of Intelligence to Social Reform*, reflected his desire to link intellectual development to the progress of society. Robinson impressed upon his readers the absolute need for clear thinking that would eliminate what he styled the "gross stupidity and blindness which characterize our present thought and conduct in public affairs."

Robinson followed this volume with *The Humanizing of Knowledge* (1922), which argued that the rapid rise of science had not yet been understood by even the best educated, and *The Ordeal of Civilization: A Sketch of the Development and World-wide Diffusion of Our Present-Day Institutions and Ideas* (1926), which reprinted large sections of his textbook *Medieval and Modern Times*.

By 1929 Robinson had gained such renown that he was elected president of the American Historical Association. The presidential address he delivered, "The Newer Ways of Historians," revealed how much his thinking had changed from his *New History* of seventeen years earlier. Robinson's former liberalism and confidence in human progress had been shaken by World War I. No longer did he worship the original document as the key to historical understanding. His old assumptions about the past had been swept away, while he placed increasing emphasis on "up-to-date" history. Yet Robinson concluded optimistically that "Never before has the historical writer been in a position so favorable as now for bringing the past into such intimate relations with the present."

At his sudden death from a heart attack in New York City, Robinson left an incomplete manuscript that his friend Harry Elmer Barnes published in 1937. Titled *The Human Comedy as Devised and Directed by Mankind Itself*, the book represented a compilation of published articles and selections drawn from earlier works, arranged from prehistory to his own day. It reaffirmed his old belief that someday history "may well become the most potent instrument for human regeneration."

Apart from the *New History*, all of Robinson's writings have sunk into respectable obscurity. Only the term itself and his suggestion that historical methodology should incorporate the various social sciences have retained their interest.

• A small collection of Robinson's papers is in the Columbia University library. The intellectual biography by Luther V. Hendricks, *James Harvey Robinson: Teacher of History* (1946), contains a substantial bibliography. See also Hendricks's article "James Harvey Robinson and the New School for Social Research," *Journal of Higher Education*, Jan. 1949. Appreciations are Harry Elmer Barnes, "James Harvey Robinson," in Howard W. Odum, ed., *American Masters of Social Science* (1927); Crane Brinton's review of *The Human Comedy* in the *Nation*, 9 Jan. 1937, pp. 48–50. "The New History: Twenty-Five Years After," *Journal of Social Philosophy*, Jan. 1936; See also Rae Wahl Rohfeld, "James Harvey Robinson and the New History" (Ph.D. diss., Western Reserve Univ., 1965). Obituaries are in the *New York Times*, 17 Feb. 1936, and *American Historical Review*, Apr. 1936.

JAMES FRIGUGLIETTI

ROBINSON, Jane Marie Bancroft (24 Dec. 1847–29 May 1932), church leader, was born in West Stockbridge, Massachusetts, the daughter of George C. Bancroft, a Methodist clergyman, and his second wife, Caroline M. Orton. The early years of her life were spent in the towns of New England where her father served. She graduated from the Emma Willard School, Troy, New York, in 1871 and the New York State Normal School (now the State University of New York at Albany) in 1872. Following her graduation she worked as a preceptress at Fort Edward (New York) Collegiate Institute until 1876, when she entered Syracuse University. She earned a bachelor's degree in 1877, a master's degree in 1880, and in 1884 a Ph.D. degree. Her dissertation was published under the title *A Study of the Parliament of Paris and Other Parliaments of France* (1884). These degrees were earned while she was dean of women and professor of French language and literature at the Woman's College of Northwestern University. During her tenure there (1877–1885) she also founded the Western Association of Collegiate Alumnae, a forerunner of the American Association of University Women.

In the fall of 1885 she resigned to become the first fellow in history at Bryn Mawr College. Her work was directed by the head of its history department, Woodrow Wilson. A year later, accompanied by her parents, she traveled to Europe for two years of study. The first was spent at the University of Zurich and the second at the University of Paris at the Sorbonne and L'École Practique des Hautes Études, to which she was one of the first women to be admitted. Her special interest in deaconess work began during the year in Zurich when she became friends with Sister Myria of the Deaconess House of that city. Having for years

been active in the work of the Woman's Home Missionary Society (WHMS) of the Methodist Episcopal church, she was greatly impressed with Sister Myria's work and wrote of it to the corresponding secretary of the WHMS, Elizabeth Lownes Rust. Rust encouraged her to study the work and organization of deaconesses in Europe in order to be prepared to offer assistance upon her return. Bancroft's study was published by the Methodist Episcopal church in 1889 as *Deaconesses in Europe and Their Lessons for America*.

The WHMS quickly formed a Deaconess Bureau, and Bancroft was named to lead it in October 1888. In the meantime she had been appointed to the faculty of Ohio Wesleyan University but given leave to promote the deaconess movement. She never actually served on the faculty.

Under the leadership of Lucy Rider Meyer, the Methodist Episcopal church was developing a second deaconess organization. Meyer, however, was committed to a scheme in which independent deaconess homes reported broadly to the annual conferences in which they were located. Robinson and the WHMS sought to maintain centralized control over the work of all deaconesses, and a conflict ensued. The final resolution was not obtained until the creation of the Methodist church in 1939, when responsibility for all deaconess work was placed under a single board.

In 1891 she married George Orville Robinson of Detroit, a wealthy lawyer and loyal Methodist, who had founded the *Michigan Christian Advocate*. The couple did not have children. After her marriage Robinson continued her leadership in the WHMS, serving as its vice president from 1893 to 1908 and president from 1908 to 1913. She was instrumental in the establishment of Lucy Webb Hayes National Training School, Sibley Hospital, and the National Training Schools in Kansas City, Washington, D.C., and San Francisco.

In 1918 Robinson moved to Pasadena, California, and in 1923 she helped found the Robincroft Rest Home for Deaconesses and Women Missionaries and Robinson Park for retired ministers. A member of Phi Beta Kappa, Robinson was the first woman to receive the honorary LL.D. from Syracuse University, and she was honored with a second by the University of Southern California in 1929. She was also an associate of the California Institute of Technology and a delegate to the General Conference of the Methodist Episcopal church in 1908 and 1920. She died in Pasadena.

The formation of the deaconess movement enabled Methodist women to find official status and recognition for their work. It was, in many ways, a prelude to the larger movements of the early twentieth century that broadened the rights and presence of women in the society and workplace.

• Carolyn De Swarte Gifford, ed., *The American Deaconess Movement in the Early Twentieth Century* (1987), outlines the history of the work in the Methodist Episcopal church and contains sections on the work done by Robinson. Her obituary is in the *New York Christian Advocate*, 9 June 1932, and the Pasadena *Post*, 30 May 1932.

JAMES E. KIRBY

ROBINSON, Jim (25 Dec. 1892–4 May 1976), jazz trombonist, was born Nathan Robinson in Deer Range, Louisiana, the son of a church deacon. Robinson gave one biographer his year of birth as 1890, but often in interviews he moved events forward a few years. His parents' names are unknown. In Deer Range he played blues guitar, and three brothers were musicians. He moved to New Orleans in 1914 to work as a longshoreman for the Southern Pacific Steamship Company. There he acquired the nickname "Jim Crow," referring to his Native American features, not to southern racism. Drafted into the U.S. Army in 1917, he served in France, where a brother of bassist Pops Foster quickly taught him to play trombone, to avoid his having to dig ditches.

On returning to New Orleans in 1919, Robinson worked for many years as a longshoreman for the Southern Pacific Railroad. At first he performed music only occasionally, but, after filling in for Kid Rena's trombonist, he began performing regularly at night and on weekends. After playing with banjoist Jesse Jackson's Golden Leaf Orchestra and Papa Celestin's Tuxedo Band, he joined Isiah Morgan's band in 1923. Three years later, Sam Morgan took over the band's leadership. The group made celebrated recordings in 1927, including "Boogalusa Strut." Sam Morgan was unable to march, and on Sundays Robinson played in brass bands under other leaders. Morgan's group toured mostly in the vicinity of New Orleans, but it held an engagement in Chicago for one week in 1929.

Robinson played for seven years at the La Vida dance hall in New Orleans with different bands, including those of Captain John Handy and Kid Howard, and one under his own leadership. Eventually, the effects of the depression and the popularity of the swing style forced him to return to work as a longshoreman, but in 1940 he played trombone at Kid Rena's recording session, a landmark in the revival of New Orleans jazz. As a consequence of this session, Robinson began playing regularly with Bunk Johnson and Johnson's clarinetist George Lewis. By this time his nickname had become "Big Jim," to distinguish him from "Little Jim," his nephew Sidney Brown, a bassist; together in Lewis's band they recorded "Two Jim Blues" in 1943. Other recordings from this period include "Panama" and "Weary Blues," under Johnson's leadership in 1942; "Climax Rag" and "Just a Closer Walk with Thee," under Lewis in 1943; a jazzed-up and joyous version of "Ice Cream" ("I scream, you scream, we all scream for ice cream"), when Robinson nominally led trumpeter "Kid Shots" Madison's band (including Lewis as a fellow sideman) for a few titles in 1944; and "Far Away Blues" with the Eclipse Alley Five, again including Lewis, in 1946. Robinson was with Johnson at the Stuyvesant Casino in New York in 1945 and 1946, although Johnson would have preferred a swing-style orientation and tried, unsuccessfully, to replace Robinson with Sandy Williams. After Johnson's death, Robinson remained with Lewis, touring the United States and Europe into the 1960s and making recordings, including the album *George Lewis at San Jacinto Hall* (1964). He also recorded the album *Blues and Spirituals* as a leader in 1961, and perhaps he married around this time. Although the date of the marriage is unknown, his wife's name was Pearl, and a child was born when Robinson was about seventy-one years old.

From 1961 into the 1970s Robinson played at Preservation Hall in New Orleans with De De and Billie Pierce, Percy Humphrey, his own bands, and with others. He remained active until the age of eighty-three, having played concerts at Lincoln Center and in Boston at Symphony Hall with the Preservation Hall Jazz Band only a few weeks before his death in New Orleans. Throughout his life he took great pleasure in his music and was known to burst out laughing on finishing a passage that he felt had pleased the audience.

Robinson was, after Kid Ory, one of the best of the jazz trombonists in the New Orleans "tailgate" style. He played with a powerful, rough sound, a hefty dose of sliding pitches, and an unselfish approach that complemented the trumpet and clarinet while driving the rhythm forward. He rarely played solos, but when he did he was likely to use the same stuttering, punching, spurting style that made his work in collective improvisations so effective.

• A brief autobiography appeared as Jim Robinson, "New Orleans Trombone," in *Selections from the Gutter: Jazz Portraits from "The Jazz Record,"* ed. Art Hodes and Chadwick Hansen (1977), pp. 124–26. He was interviewed by Max Jones for *Melody Maker*, Jan. 1959 (repr. in Jones, *Talking Jazz* [1987], pp. 175–77); Valerie Wilmer, "Robinson: Eighty Years On," *Melody Maker*, 19 June 1971, p. 16; and Frederick Turner, *Remembering Song: Encounters with the New Orleans Tradition* (1982), pp. 90–108. Karl Koenig, "Nathan 'Big Jim' Robinson: Jazz Trombonist," *Second Line* 35 (Winter 1983): 24–35, includes excerpts from interviews held in the archives of Tulane University; further excerpts appear on microform as *New York Times Oral History Program: New Orleans Jazz Oral History Collection*, no. 40 (1978), and no. 46 (1979), chap. 146. See also William Carter, *Preservation Hall: Music from the Heart* (1991); Tom Stagg and Charlie Crump, *New Orleans: The Revival* (1973); Alan Barrell, "Jim Robinson: A Biographical Sketch," *Footnote* 7, no. 2 (1975–1976): 4–10; Eberhard Kraut, "Jim Robinson," *Jazz Podium*, Feb. 1982, pp. 12–13; and Austin M. Sonnier, Jr., *William Geary "Bunk" Johnson: The New Iberia Years* (1977), pp. 12–13. Obituaries are in *Down Beat*, 15 July 1976, p. 11; by Dave Donohoe, "Jim Robinson: A Tribute," *Footnote* 7, no. 5 (1976): 29–31; and by Chris Hillman, "Big Jim: 1892–1976," *Jazz Journal* 29 (Aug. 1976): 16, 41.

BARRY KERNFELD

ROBINSON, John (3 Feb. 1704–11 May 1766), planter, Speaker of the House of Burgesses, and treasurer of Virginia, was born at "Hewick" plantation, Middlesex County, Virginia, the son of John Robinson, a planter and a member of the Virginia Council, and Catherine Beverley. Young Robinson studied at the College of William and Mary. In 1723 he married Mary Storey, who apparently died within a few years, probably in childbirth. They had no surviving children. By 1727 Robinson had moved to King and Queen County, possibly at the time of his marriage to Lucy Moore. Although the dates of both the wedding and the construction of the house are unknown, the Robinsons subsequently resided at "Pleasant Hill" across the Mattaponi River from "Chelsea," the home of Lucy's father, Augustine Moore. The new couple had at least two children. The date of Lucy Robinson's death is uncertain, possibly 1755. Robinson married Susanna Chiswell in 1759. They also had at least two children.

Robinson was well placed politically. His great uncle was bishop of London, and his father represented Middlesex as a burgess from 1711 to 1720, when he was appointed to the council, where he served until his death in 1749, at the end as president and acting governor. The younger Robinson became a burgess from King and Queen County in 1727 and quickly rose in favor with Speaker John Holloway and his successor, Sir John Randolph. Robinson succeeded to the office at Randolph's death in 1738 and concurrently became treasurer, holding both posts for twenty-eight years, the longest tenure in the colony's history. Elected Speaker seven times, he had no opposition on the last four ballots. He continued the policy of his two immediate predecessors, who had been educated in England, of modeling the burgesses' procedures on those of the House of Commons. Some compared Robinson to a renowned contemporary, Arthur Onslow, who served a similarly lengthy term as Speaker of the British house. But whereas Onslow set the British model of the impartial, nonpartisan moderator of a legislative assembly, Robinson presaged the American pattern of the all-powerful chair acting in the dual role of majority leader.

Robinson became a major player in the contest for lands beyond the Blue Ridge Mountains. As early as 1736 he and Speaker Randolph joined William Beverley in obtaining the 118,491 acres that eventually formed Beverley Manor. In 1745 Robinson secured 100,000 acres on the Greenbrier River and with Thomas Nelson founded the Greenbrier Company six years later. In 1749 Robinson helped engineer an 800,000-acre grant for the Loyal Land Company, whose members largely resided south of the Rappahannock River, to offset an award of up to 500,000 acres for the Ohio Company, entirely based in the Northern Neck between the Rappahannock and Potomac rivers. On good terms with Governor William Gooch, Robinson fell out with Gooch's successor, Robert Dinwiddie, over imposition of a fee of one pistole (a Spanish coin used in Virginia) for processing land patents. Although Dinwiddie had authority for his action, his predecessors had not exercised the right, and in Virginia's eyes the imposition constituted levying a new tax without the legislature's consent. On appeal, the Privy Council affirmed Dinwiddie's right

but advised him to accommodate the issue. The quarrel continued over Robinson's efforts to pay the attorney general, Peyton Randolph, for journeying to London to defend the burgesses in defiance of the governor. The outbreak of hostilities with France over the Ohio Valley in 1754 finally forced Dinwiddie to accede. During the war Robinson supported George Washington and the western campaigns against the French but often with less alacrity and smaller appropriations than Dinwiddie wanted. The Speaker said the reason was a slim treasury, but Northern Neck speculators suspected he did not want to advantage the Ohio Company, to which Dinwiddie belonged.

Northern Neck resentment against Robinson climaxed in May 1765 when Richard Henry Lee moved for an audit of the treasury because of rumors that Robinson had not retired wartime currency as the law required but had reissued it as loans to his friends. Although the auditors, mostly Robinson supporters, found no malfeasance, the council vetoed the Speaker's proposal for a government loan office to mitigate retirement of the currency. The proposal, which also required imperial sanction, may have influenced Robinson on another issue that session. At the news that Parliament had imposed a stamp tax on the colonies, Patrick Henry delivered a fiery speech introducing resolutions that bordered on threatening armed resistance. Although the previous December the burgesses under Robinson had adopted firm resolutions against the tax, their language had been circumspect, and in May the Speaker moved to suppress the most extreme of Henry's resolves. Newspapers, however, reported them all and propelled Virginia to the forefront of opposition to the tax.

Robinson's death the next year uncovered a political scandal that cast doubt on the integrity of the planter class and its worthiness to govern. Investigation of the treasury's records proved Richard Henry Lee's intimations correct: Robinson had reissued more than £100,000 of the wartime currency in personal loans to hard-pressed associates. Another effort to establish a remedial loan office failed in 1767. Robinson's defenders blamed his compassion. Most debtors, in fact, did live in his home county, King and Queen, or its neighbor, King William; at least half the shortage originated during the economic downturn of 1763–1766; and nearly half the cases involved less than £100. But to critics, the revelations seriously undermined the claim of the elite to disinterestedness. A tenth of the loans exceeded £1,000, many to Robinson's allies. His brothers-in-law, Bernard and Thomas Moore, owed £8,500 and £3,442 respectively, his protégé Edmund Pendleton, £1,020. Debtors included more than twenty burgesses and four council members, led by William Byrd III, whose loan topped the list at £14,921. By 1781 Pendleton, Robinson's executor, had satisfied the estate's liability to the treasury, but ten years later he had yet to recoup from two out of five of the borrowers. The political reverberations affected the Revolution. Robinson supporters never forgave Lee, and Robert Carter Nicholas's moralistic campaign to separate Robinson's two posts—a move that British administrators had planned to curb the power of the Speakership but dared not attempt while Robinson's image remained unsullied—fostered enmity between the new Speaker, Peyton Randolph, who had expected the treasurership, and Nicholas, who obtained it. Robinson died probably at Pleasant Hill and was buried at Stratton Major Parish Church, King and Queen County.

• A convenient source for details of the Robinson family is William Minor Dabney, "John Robinson: Speaker of the House of Burgesses and Treasurer of Virginia" (M.A. thesis, Univ. of Virginia, 1941). *The Diary of Colonel Landon Carter of Sabine Hall, 1752–1778*, ed. Jack P. Greene, vol. 1 (1965), pp. 65–124, which covers the years 1752–1755 when Carter was a burgess, affords insight into Robinson's style as Speaker, and Edmund Randolph, *History of Virginia*, ed. Arthur H. Shaffer (1970), pp. 173–74, affords insight into the esteem in which many contemporaries held the Speaker. Richard L. Morton, *Colonial Virginia*, vol. 2, *Westward Expansion and Prelude to Revolution, 1710–1763* (1960), recounts the contest for western lands. Joseph Albert Ernst, *Money and Politics in America, 1755–1775: A Study in the Currency Act of 1764 and the Political Economy of Revolution* (1973), and Marc Egnal, *A Mighty Empire: The Origins of the American Revolution* (1988), describe the tension between Robinson and the Northern Neck. David John Mays exhaustively analyzes the defalcation of treasury funds in *Edmund Pendleton, 1721–1803* (1984). Rhys Isaac, *The Transformation of Virginia, 1740–1790* (1982), discusses the political and ideological division between the Randolphs and Robert Carter Nicholas.

JOHN E. SELBY

ROBINSON, John C. (1906–27 Mar. 1954), aviator who promoted flight training for African Americans but gained his greatest fame as a pilot for Ethiopian emperor Haile Selassie, was born in Gulfport, Mississippi. All that is known of his parents is that his mother was born in Ethiopia. Robinson graduated from Tuskegee Institute in Alabama in 1924. For the following six years, he was a truck driver in Gulfport. Then he moved to Chicago, where he and his wife, Earnize Robinson, operated a garage. In 1931 he graduated from the Curtiss-Wright Aeronautical Institute in Chicago. He taught at Curtiss-Wright Institute and organized African-American men and women pilots in the Chicago area into the Challenger Air Pilots Association.

Early in 1935 the Tuskegee Institute invited Robinson to organize the first course in aviation entirely for African Americans. By that time, he held a transport flying license and had piled up 1,200 hours of flight time, much of it as an instructor at South Side Chicago airports. At about the same time as the Tuskegee offer, a nephew of Emperor Haile Selassie invited Robinson to come to Ethiopia. Benito Mussolini's Italian legions were threatening, and Ethiopia needed experienced aviators, even though some press reports at the time said that none of the emperor's twenty-five airplanes was flyable. Robinson appeared to have selfless motives, in contrast with the many intriguers and opportunists who flocked into Addis Ababa during Ethiopia's futile attempts to repel the Italians. He "had come to Ethiopia to testify to the solidarity of the colored peoples" (Del Boca, p. 86).

Soon after arriving, Robinson displayed what would become a familiar penchant for prickly behavior toward others. He clashed with the only other African-American pilot on the scene, Col. Hubert Julian, a Harlem native who had renounced his U.S. citizenship to serve in the Ethiopian air force. Julian, known as the "Black Eagle," apparently lost the contest, because he was banished to a far-off province to drill infantry recruits. That left Robinson, the "Brown Condor," in charge of the ragtag air force. Now a colonel, he had to deal with an Italian air force that controlled the skies over Ethiopia during the invasion in 1935 and 1936. In an unarmed monoplane, he repeatedly flew courier missions between the front lines and Addis Ababa. Robinson escaped from Ethiopia on 4 May 1936, the day before the country capitulated. Returning to the United States, he toured the country on behalf of United Aid for Ethiopia. That fall, he returned to Tuskegee Institute to teach the aviation course he had given up before he left for Ethiopia.

When World War II ended, Robinson returned to Ethiopia, where Selassie granted him his old rank of colonel. Within a year, however, he was at odds with a group of Swedish technicians who were in Ethiopia to work with equipment sent by Swedish munitions makers. In August 1947 the conflict exploded into violence. Robinson was arrested and jailed for an assault on Swedish Count Carl Gustav von Rosen, who was then commander in chief of the Ethiopian air force. Robinson was found guilty by a jury, lost his appeal, and spent an undetermined amount of time in prison.

In 1951 *Ebony* magazine reported that Robinson—still the best-known African American in Ethiopia—had become disillusioned by his conviction and was thinking of returning to the United States. "But," said *Ebony*'s reporter, "despite Selassie's apparent indifference to him, he remains something of a national hero to the Ethiopian people."

Robinson died as a result of severe burns sustained on 13 March 1954, when the training plane he was flying crashed and burned at the Addis Ababa airport, after narrowly missing a nurses' home. The apparent cause of the accident was engine failure. Also killed in the accident was Bruno Bianci, an Italian engineer.

Although Robinson was a glamorous figure in Ethiopia's highly publicized resistance to Mussolini, his greatest legacy may have been his attempt to increase African-American interest in aviation in the United States. Had he remained in his native country after World War II, he would have witnessed the integration of the armed forces—perhaps by some of the pilots he helped train.

• The Robinson bibliographical record is meager, thanks almost certainly to his race and the fact that he spent a good part of his adulthood in another country. He is barely mentioned in accounts of the Italian-Ethiopian War, the only exception being Angelo Del Boca, *The Ethiopian War, 1935–*

1941 (1965; Eng. trans., 1969). Robinson is mentioned briefly in Dwight L. Smith, ed., *Afro-American History, a Bibliography*, vol. 2 (1981). "Americans in Ethiopia," *Ebony*, May 1951, pp. 79–81, includes a discussion of Robinson and a photograph of him with an Ethiopian eunuch. The obituaries in the *Chicago Tribune* and the *New York Times*, both 28 Mar. 1954, differ to some extent, particularly with respect to key dates. The *Times*'s obituary is more detailed and is likely more reliable, but the *Tribune*'s obituary has the advantage of being accompanied by the colonel's picture.

DAVID R. GRIFFITHS

ROBINSON, John Cleveland (10 Apr. 1817–18 Feb. 1897), soldier, was born in Binghamton, New York, the son of Tracy Robinson, a physician and druggist, and Sarah Cleveland. In 1835 he entered the U.S. Military Academy, but an infraction of the rules led to his expulsion in 1838. After a year of studying law he succeeded in getting a commission as second lieutenant in the Fifth Infantry. In 1842 Robinson married Sarah Maria Pease, with whom he had seven children.

Robinson's service in the Mexican War involved fighting in the battles of Palo Alto, Resaca de la Palma, and Monterrey and the capture of Mexico City. He served also as both brigade and regimental quartermaster. Robinson was promoted to first lieutenant in 1846 and to captain in 1850. He was the Fifth's quartermaster in 1847 and 1849–1850 and was stationed for most of this period in Indian Territory. Service in the 1850s included Indian campaigns in Texas and Florida and participation in the Utah Expedition (1857–1858). He later wrote that the expedition was part of a scheme devised by southerners to pave the way for secession by weakening the eastern United States militarily.

At the outbreak of the Civil War Robinson was in command of a small body of troops at Fort McHenry, Maryland. Pro-Confederate rioting in Baltimore threatened the post, and city officials tried to pressure Robinson into surrendering it. He saved the fort for the Union by training its guns on the city and by giving the impression that he had more soldiers than were actually there.

While on recruiting duty, in September 1861, Robinson was elected colonel of the First Michigan Volunteers. He was promoted to major in the Second Infantry of the regular army in February 1862 and to brigadier general of volunteers in April. After service at Newport News, Virginia, Robinson was given command of a brigade in the Army of the Potomac. He fought with distinction in George B. McClellan's Peninsular campaign and the battles of Seven Days and Second Bull Run. He missed the battle of Antietam, the corps to which his division was attached having been sent toward Washington.

As a division commander, Robinson engaged in the battles of Fredericksburg and Chancellorsville. On the first day at Gettysburg his division held at Oak Ridge, earning him a brevet to lieutenant colonel in the regular army. For his actions at the Wilderness he was brevetted to colonel.

Robinson received a brevet to brigadier general for personally leading the charge on Laurel Hill at the battle of Spotsylvania. Believing the opposing forces to be too strong and his own troops too exhausted and spread out to justify the charge, he had argued against it. However, his corps commander, Gouverneur K. Warren, assumed that the hill was lightly defended and insisted that he go forward. Events proved that Robinson's assessment of the situation had been sound. He was driven back, and a bullet to the knee cost him his leg, taking him out of combat for the remainder of the war. He had been, at age forty-seven, the oldest division commander in the Army of the Potomac.

For the remainder of the conflict Robinson commanded military districts in New York. In 1865 he became military commander of North Carolina, where he was also commissioner of the Freedmen's Bureau. He was awarded brevets to major general and major genral of volunteers. Promoted to colonel, Robinson commanded the Forty-third Infantry of the regular army, 1866–1869. Other postwar duties included command of the Department of the South in 1867 and of the Department of the Lakes, 1868–1869. At his own request he was retired in 1869 with the regular army rank of major general.

Robinson, a Republican, was lieutenant governor of New York (1873–1874). Active in veterans' affairs, he served as commander in chief of the Grand Army of the Republic (1877–1878), and as president of the Society of the Army of the Potomac (1887–1888). In his later years he also wrote articles about his experiences in Utah and at Fort McHenry, in which he insisted that the United States be always prepared militarily. In 1894 Robinson received the Medal of Honor for his gallantry at Laurel Hill. A posthumous honor was the erection of a statue at Gettysburg. He died in Binghamton, where he had been pursuing various business ventures. A few years before his death he became totally blind.

Shelby Foote has characterized Robinson as "a large hairy New Yorker with an outsized beard and shaggy brows, a crusty manner, and a solid reputation earned in practically all of the major eastern battles" (Foote, vol. 3, p. 200). Had his wound not removed him from the battlefield, Robinson might have been given a higher command. Nevertheless, he was among the most dependable and courageous brigade and division leaders in the Union army.

• Robinson gave accounts of two major events of his life in "The Utah Expedition," *Magazine of American History* 11 (1884): 335–41, and "Baltimore in 1861," *Magazine of American History* 14 (1885): 257–68. A helpful biographical sketch is in *Broome County Biographical Review* (1894). Information on promotions and honors is in Francis B. Heitman, *Historical Register and Dictionary of the United States Army, from Its Organization, September 29, 1789, to March 2, 1903*, vol. 1 (1903). Details of some of his Civil War engagements are in Shelby Foote, *The Civil War: A Narrative* (1958–1974).

MICHAEL J. BRODHEAD

ROBINSON, Joseph Taylor (26 Aug. 1872–14 July 1937), general assemblyman, congressman, governor of Arkansas, and senator, was born on a farm near Lonoke, Arkansas, the son of James Madison Robinson, a physician and Baptist minister, and Matilda Jane Swaim. With almost no formal schooling, Robinson passed the Arkansas teacher's examination in 1889 and began teaching in rural schools near Lonoke. He later attended the Industrial University of Arkansas (now the University of Arkansas) at Fayetteville for two years, returned to Lonoke, and studied law with Judge Thomas C. Trimble. He attended the University of Virginia School of Law and received his law degree in 1895. By 1897 he had formed a law practice with Judge Trimble. In 1896 he married Ewilda Gertrude Miller; they had no children.

Even before receiving his law degree, Robinson was elected to the state legislature. In 1894 he successfully ran for the office on the Democratic ticket, and during his one term in the Thirtieth Arkansas General Assembly (1894–1896), before returning to Lonoke and opening a private law practice, he allied himself with those in favor of railroad regulation, an issue of considerable controversy in the late nineteenth century. In 1902 he returned to the political arena, again on the Democratic ticket, and was elected to Congress from the Sixth Congressional District of Arkansas. He remained in that office for five terms (1903–1913), and although he was a Democrat, he often aligned himself with progressive Republicans. He favored the regulation of railroads and child labor, and he supported the imposition of the income tax and suffrage for women.

While still a congressman, Robinson announced his candidacy for governor of Arkansas in 1912, and in the Democratic primary he defeated the incumbent governor, George W. Donaghey. He then won the office in the general election. After resigning his congressional seat on 14 January 1913, he was inaugurated the twenty-third governor of the state of Arkansas on 16 January 1913. He was not destined to serve as governor for very long. When Senator Jeff Davis of Arkansas died suddenly on 3 January 1913, Robinson began to pursue the vacated Senate seat. The legislature elected him to that office on 28 January 1913. Despite his election to the Senate, Robinson remained in the governor's office until his resignation on 10 March 1913. For a fourteen-day period, therefore, Robinson enjoyed the unique position of being congressman, governor, and senator. Although his governorship was short-lived, he actively pursued legislation in connection with some of his campaign issues, especially economic and financial reform; he was largely responsible for the creation of a state banking department.

On 10 March 1913 Robinson began a distinguished career in the U.S. Senate. He was reelected four times to that office, serving until his death. He supported the major initiatives of his party, including the New Freedom legislation. He supported President Woodrow Wilson's declaration of war against Germany in 1917 and Wilson's effort to secure ratification of the League of Nations. He became the Democratic minority leader in the 1920s and led the opposition against Republican economic policies. An internationalist, he supported the expansion of the navy and advocated increased benefits for veterans. He came close to being the Democratic presidential candidate in 1924, and in 1928 he was Alfred E. Smith's running mate on the Democratic ticket. It was hoped that his presence on the ticket would attract southerners uncomfortable with Smith, who was Catholic, antiprohibitionist, and a New Yorker.

When the Democrats came into control of the Senate in the 1932 election, Robinson became Senate majority leader and was key to Franklin D. Roosevelt's relationship with southern Democrats. Robinson helped secure passage of certain key features of Roosevelt's New Deal, providing enthusiastic support for agricultural policies and defusing opposition to works programs. Robinson remained loyal to Roosevelt when the president attempted to "pack the court" with his Judiciary Reorganization Bill, which was designed to dilute the influence of justices who were ruling against certain features of the president's New Deal. It was during the intense struggle over this bill that Robinson died in Washington, D.C.

Although only one major piece of legislation actually carries his name—the Robinson-Patman Act of 1936, an antimonopoly bill designed to eliminate price discrimination—Robinson was a major force in the Senate and was crucial to Roosevelt's success in securing passage of his New Deal programs. Robinson owed much of his success to his oratorical skills, and perhaps therein lies his most well-known legacy. A raconteur in the southern tradition, he regularly peppered his speeches and lobbying efforts with colorful stories. In one story-telling contest during a trip down the White River with a couple of boatmen, Robinson told a particular tale that has endured in the folk history of his state. He bested the boatmen with a story concerning the fish in his Prairie County home area:

Up there the streams back up when it floods and when the water goes down again there'll be a pond out in cotton fields as big as a lake. And in these ponds there'll be fish. In one of these ponds last year there was something so big nobody could catch it. Broke their tackle and went away with their rods. So one day we took an anchor and baited it with a dead calf and tossed it in on the end of a two-inch rope tied to a grandpappy of all cottonwood trees in Prairie County. Pretty soon the cottonwood begins to buckle and we knew we had him. We hitched on six pair of oxen and we pulled him out. He was a catfish. And when we cut him open, what do you think we found? We found a pair of harnessed mules and a wagon and seven acres of burnt ground.

One of the two boatmen conceded the contest by remarking, "Hell, I ought to have known a Senator would tell the biggest lie."

• Robinson's papers are housed at the University of Arkansas Special Collections Division in Fayetteville. Despite his long tenure in the Senate and his popularity within his home state, no full-length biography of Robinson currently exists. Details of his route from congressman to governor to senator are in Stuart Towns, "Joseph T. Robinson and Arkansas Politics: 1912–1913," *Arkansas Historical Quarterly* 24 (Winter 1965): 291–307. The fate of his vice presidential race with Smith in Arkansas in 1928 is the focus of Nevin E. Neal, "The Smith-Robinson Arkansas Campaign of 1928," *Arkansas Historical Quarterly* 19 (Spring 1960): 3–11. Despite his short tenure in the governor's office, an excellent biographical sketch on Robinson by Jerry Vervak was included in *The Governors of Arkansas*, ed. Timothy P. Donovan and Willard B. Gatewood, Jr. (1981). Also helpful is Vervak, "The Making of a Politician, Joe T. Robinson, 1872–1921" (Ph.D. diss., Univ. of Arkansas, 1990). The Robinson "fish" story is quoted in Kenneth R. Hubbell, "Always a Simple Feast: Social Life in the Delta," in *Arkansas Delta: Land of Paradox*, ed. Jeannie Whayne and Willard B. Gatewood (1993). Hubbell found the quote in Archibald MacLeish, "Robinson," Joe T. Robinson Papers, vol. 1, ser. 1, subser. 9. Obituaries are in the *Arkansas Gazette* and the *Arkansas Democrat*, both 15 July 1937.

JEANNIE M. WHAYNE

ROBINSON, J. Russel (8 July 1892–30 Sept. 1963), ragtime, jazz, and popular pianist and composer, was born Joseph Russel Robinson in Indianapolis, Indiana, the son of Mark L. Robinson, a factory worker and later a hotel engineer, and Elizabeth Eleanor Hoover. His father played jew's harp and harmonica, and his mother, piano. In infancy Robinson contracted polio, which permanently crippled his right arm. As a consequence of this disability he later developed an acrobatic left-hand technique on piano, but like hunchback drummer Chick Webb, Robinson clearly had a special musical talent that would have made him distinctive irrespective of this physical anomaly.

Robinson took piano lessons briefly, but he chiefly learned his craft by playing in a duo with his brother, drummer John C. Robinson. He dropped out of Shortbridge High School to play music. The duo started entertaining in theaters in 1906, and from 1908 the family toured, as the brothers performed for six months each in Macon, New Orleans, and Memphis (the six-month period, writer John Hasse explains, was the upper limit that each local union allowed to outsiders). As talented as Robinson was, his self-esteem was even greater. Of the period in New Orleans, he told writer Ralph auf der Heide, "Most of the playing was crude, and had little musical content or inventiveness. My brother and I were the hottest musicians around . . . white or black." Although no ragtime or early jazz recordings from this era exist to provide hard evidence one way or the other, most historians of music are disinclined to accept this view, when considered against the testimony of Robinson's contemporaries and the subsequent profound achievements of African-American New Orleans players.

Robinson's success as a composer began with "Sapho Rag," published in 1909 by Scott Joplin's publisher, John Stark. Robinson married Marguerite Kendall in the fall of 1909 in Macon, and together they wrote "I Feel Religion Coming On" (1910), a racist take-off, typical of its day, on a black Baptist church meeting in Georgia. This "coon" song and Robinson's "Dynamite Rag" were published by the Southern California Music Company in 1910. Further publications with Stark included "The Minstrel Man" (1911) and the waltz ballad "Shadows of Flame." In 1912 he wrote "Eccentric" (originally "That Eccentric Rag"), which in the following decade would become a Dixieland jazz standard. Early in 1913 he began working in motion picture theaters and with his wife in vaudeville as "The Two Robinsons: The Piano Wizard and the Beautiful Doll." They coauthored ragtime songs, including "Te Na Na," which reportedly sold 200,000 copies, and "On the Eight O'Clock Train," sung by Sophie Tucker. Robinson's tour of the South ended in 1914.

Robinson's formidable skills made him a favorite of piano roll makers. After an association with the Imperial Piano Roll Company in Indiana, he performed by day for the U.S. Piano Roll Company in 1917 while working at night with brass player Merritt Brunies's Original New Orleans Jazz Band at Casino Gardens in Chicago. From 1918 to 1926 he had an exclusive contract with the QRS company of Chicago but worked at their piano roll plant in New York City, his base during most of this period.

The pianist Henry Ragas of the Original Dixieland Jazz Band had been sick since the fall of 1918, and he would die in February 1919. Upon arriving in New York in January 1919, Robinson sat in with the band and was immediately hired for their ongoing engagement at Reisenweber's Restaurant. After a vaudeville tour on the Keith Circuit, the band embarked for London for an engagement beginning early in April. Robinson left the group on 11 October 1919 and returned to New York, where he played in society dance orchestras.

Robinson's composing continued. From 1917 to 1918 he wrote the songs "Jazzola" and "Lullaby Blues." After his arrival in New York, Robinson and African-American songwriter Spencer Williams coauthored "Ringtail Blues," in which Robinson claimed to have been the first to use the boogie-woogie pattern; the song was recorded by a Dixieland jazz band, the Louisiana Five, around September 1919. On 25 September 1920 he rejoined the Original Dixieland Jazz Band for a long engagement at the Folies Bergère above New York's Winter Garden Theater. Around this time, in association with Con Conrad, Robinson wrote "Margie," based on the harmonic structures of "Lullaby Blues," and "Singin' the Blues." Early in December 1920, with an alto saxophonist brought into the studio, the six-piece Original Dixieland Jazz Band recorded a medley, "Margie (Introducing Singin' the Blues)." This became a hit record, and alongside the contemporary work of Paul Whiteman, it marked the beginning of the integration of hot Dixieland jazz and sweet pop songs. "Singin' the Blues" would have a life of its own after the definitive recording by alto saxophonist Frankie Trumbauer's group with cornetist Bix Beiderbecke. The reverse side of "Margie (Introducing Singin' the Blues)," without alto saxophone, presented Robinson and Conrad's "Lena from Palesteena," which also entered the Dixieland repertory. Additionally credited as composers are, for "Margie," Benny Davis, and for "Singin' the Blues," Sam M. Lewis and Joe Young.

While spending nights with the Original Dixieland Jazz Band, Robinson managed the career of blues songwriter W. C. Handy by day, and at some point later in his career, he wrote lyrics for Handy's "Memphis Blues." In a financial dispute evidently prompted by the success of "Margie," pianist Frank Signorelli replaced Robinson in the Original Dixieland Jazz Band at the Folies Bergère on 11 April 1921. Robinson's wife died that year.

Chasing after the theatrical success of African-Americans Flournoy E. Miller, Aubrey Lyles, Noble Sissle, and Eubie Blake in *Shuffle Along*, which had its debut on Broadway in 1921, Lew Leslie, the so-called black Ziegfeld, staged the *Plantation Revue*, the first "all-colored" production to be scored by white men: Robinson and lyricist Roy Turk. Their song "Sweet Man o'Mine" was a modest success, but the show was remembered for the sensational performances of singer and comedienne Florence Mills rather than for its musical content.

Robinson accompanied cabaret singer Marion Harris and blues singer Lucille Hegamin, the latter on a few recordings in June and November 1923. He said that he also used Spencer Williams's name when accompanying blues singers, including Lizzie Miles, and claimed that Williams could not play well enough to do it himself. Indeed, Williams called Robinson "the white man with colored fingers" (Hasse, p. 166). Miles was one of many artists to record Robinson's hit song "Aggravatin' Papa (Don't You Try to Two-Time Me)"; her version dates from the beginning of 1923. In April 1923 Bessie Smith recorded another of Robinson's hits, "Beale Street Mama."

Robinson contributed nothing of great significance after the mid-1920s, with musical fashion moving toward the swing era as he remained based in older styles. He remarried and divorced, but details are unknown. While working for NBC radio, Robinson helped reorganize the Original Dixieland Jazz Band, beginning with a successful performance on Ed Wynn's network show on 28 July 1936. There followed a brief attempt to remake the group into a big band to accord with current styles, a series of nostalgic five-piece rerecordings of their pioneering titles, some further appearances on radio shows, and touring through 1937, with diminishing success. Robinson left the group in February 1938. In the late 1940s he settled in the Los Angeles area and married Gertrude (maiden name unknown). He died at home in Palmdale, California.

Robinson held an ambivalent attitude toward African-American musical creations. His deep and genuine understanding seemed to be inseparable from a desire to appropriate them and to claim priority. The unpleasant side of this complex relationship—evident in his description of New Orleans musicians, his faux-Baptist coon song, his assertion about boogie-woogie piano, and his involvement in controversies over the place of the Original Dixieland Jazz Band in the creation of jazz—is counterbalanced by his collaborative work with African-American songwriters and singers and outweighed by his significant contributions as a composer of ragtime music, Dixieland jazz themes, blues, and pop songs.

• Important sources include J. Russel Robinson, as told to Ralph auf der Heide, "Dixieland Piano," *Record Changer*, Aug. 1947, pp. 7–8, 15; and H. O. Brunn, *The Story of the Original Dixieland Jazz Band* (1960). John Edward Hasse, "The Creation and Dissemination of Indianapolis Ragtime, 1897–1930" (Ph.D. diss., Indiana Univ., 1981), places Robinson within the context of the ragtime era and includes information from Robinson's unfinished autobiography and from an interview with his widow. See also Barry Singer, *Black and Blues: The Life and Lyrics of Andy Razaf* (1992). An obituary is in the *New York Times*, 2 Oct. 1963.

BARRY KERNFELD

ROBINSON, Julia (8 Dec. 1919–30 July 1985), mathematician, was born Julia Bowman in St. Louis, Missouri, the daughter of Ralph Bowers Bowman, a machine tool and equipment businessman, and Helen Hall. She grew up in Arizona and California and graduated from San Diego High School in 1936. She then entered San Diego State College (later San Diego State University), where she studied for three years with the intention of receiving a teaching certificate in mathematics. During this time she developed a greater interest in mathematics, and she transferred to the University of California at Berkeley for her senior year. She received an A.B. in 1940 and an M.A. in 1941 from Berkeley. On 22 December 1941 she married Raphael Mitchel Robinson, then an assistant professor at Berkeley. Possessing similar mathematical interests, they had a very happy marriage; however, nepotism rules in effect for most of her working lifetime made it impossible for her to obtain a regular position at Berkeley for many years.

During World War II Robinson worked at the Berkeley Statistical Laboratory for Jerzy Neyman. Following the war she became the first Berkeley doctorate of Alfred Tàrski, obtaining her Ph.D. in 1948 for the dissertation, "Definability and Decision Problems in Arithmetic." In her doctoral thesis she proved that the notion of an integer can be defined arithmetically in terms of the notion of a rational number and the operations of addition and multiplication on the rationals. This appeared in 1949 and, apart from a statistical paper (based on her war work), was her first publication.

During 1949–1950 Robinson was a junior mathematician at the RAND Corporation; as a consequence of her work there, she solved a basic question in game theory by the so-called iterative method (1951).

Robinson devoted the remainder of her work to a subtle application of the methods of number theory to the solution of problems in mathematical logic. Her most famous result was her contribution to the resolution of Hilbert's tenth problem, namely to find an effective method (an algorithm) for determining whether a given Diophantine equation is solvable in integers. Her first step in this direction occurred in her work on the existential definability in arithmetic (1952), and she reported the result in a joint paper written with Martin Davis and Hilary Putnam (1961). This showed that every recursively enumerable set is existentially definable in terms of exponentiation. The paper also contained the Julia Robinson Hypothesis, to which, it was immediately recognized, the solvability of the Hilbert problem was inextricably linked. This hypothesis remained unproven until Yuri Matijasevich, a 22-year-old Russian mathematician, provided a proof in 1970 showing that Hilbert's tenth problem was unsolvable. Delighted by Matijasevich's feat, Robinson subsequently collaborated with him on two papers (1974, 1975). One of her final projects was a joint paper with Davis and Matijasevich (1976), in which they discussed the positive aspects of the negative solution of the Hilbert problem. In the academic years 1963–1964 and 1969–1970, as well as in 1966 and 1975, she was a lecturer in mathematics at Berkeley. In 1975 she was elected a member of the National Academy of Sciences (the first woman to be a member of the Mathematics Section), and in 1976 she was appointed a professor of mathematics at the University of California at Berkeley. She was the colloquium lecturer of the American Mathematical Society in 1980 (the second woman to be so honored), and president of that organization for 1983–1984 (the first woman to hold that office). In 1983 she received a five-year MacArthur Fellowship to pursue her research interests. Robinson retired from her Berkeley professorship less than a month before her death.

During her life Robinson repeatedly suffered from ill health. She had scarlet fever at the age of nine, and this was followed by rheumatic fever. These caused a scar tissue buildup which would impair her heart function and lead ultimately to open heart surgery in 1961. She then had about a decade of reasonable health, but this required a restricted schedule and effort on her part. In 1984, at the height of her fame, she was diagnosed with leukemia. After a temporary remission, she died in Oakland, California.

Robinson survived all the difficulties that confronted her and her career with grace and style. Her compassion and dedication were exemplified by her courage and unfailing optimism. At the time of her death she was the most visible and highest honored woman mathematician in America, and has been cited often as a role model for women in mathematics. A very modest person, however, she preferred to be remembered for her mathematical achievements, namely the theorems she proved and the problems she solved. On such a level her reputation and fame was secured.

• Robinson's papers are published in *The Collected Works of Julia Robinson*, ed. Solomon Feferman (1996). A full-length biography is Constance Reid, *Julia: A Life in Mathematics* (1996). The most detailed biographical sketch, including a list of her publications, is in Louise S. Grinstein and Paul J. Campbell, eds., *Women of Mathematics: A Biographical Sourcebook* (1987). A unique item is Constance Reid (Robinson's sister), "The Autobiography of Julia Robinson," in *More Mathematical People* (1987), and in *The College Mathematics Journal* 17 (Jan. 1986): 3–21, which contains numerous family photographs. Two expository articles give a very lucid presentation of the Hilbert problem and Robinson's efforts to resolve it: Martin Davis and Ruben Hersh, "Hilbert's 10th Problem," *Scientific American* 229 (Nov. 1973): 84–91, and Martin Davis, "Hilbert's Tenth Problem Is Unsolvable," *American Mathematical Monthly* 80 (Mar. 1973): 233–69. Obituaries are in National Academy of Sciences, *Biographical Memoirs* 63 (1994): 452–75, and the *New York Times*, 2 Aug. 1985, with errata 14 August 1985. The *Notices of the American Mathematical Society* 32 (Oct.–Nov. 1985) also contain an obituary and personal recollections of her colleagues.

JOSEPH D. ZUND

ROBINSON, Lelia Josephine (23 July 1850–10 Aug. 1891), lawyer and author, was born in Boston, the daughter of Daniel Robinson, a trader, and Mary (maiden name unknown). She was educated in the Boston public schools, where she became primarily interested in journalistic writing. At the age of seventeen, she married a tinsmith, Rupert J. Chute, and began a journalistic career, working for several of Boston's newspapers. Her marriage, however, ended when she charged her husband with adultery and was granted a divorce and the right to resume her maiden name by the Supreme Judicial Court of Massachusetts in 1877. The stigma endured by divorced women in Robinson's day was so great that Robinson tried to erase this marriage from her life completely. She never mentioned it in her autobiographical writings, and only one of the many eulogies and obituaries after her death mentioned it.

Robinson's divorce was a turning point in her life. This personal experience with the court opened her eyes to the legal system, and she enrolled at the Boston University School of Law in 1878. The only woman in a school of 150 students, she related well with her male classmates. In 1881 she became the first woman to graduate from the law school, receiving the LL.B. cum laude and placing fourth in a class of thirty-two students.

Upon graduation, Robinson became the first woman to apply for admission to the Massachusetts bar. While awaiting the court's decision, she opened a law office in Pemberton Square in Boston. After the Supreme Judicial Court rejected her equal rights argument for admission to the bar in 1881, the Massachusetts legislature passed a bill enabling women to practice law on the same terms as men. It was signed by the reform-minded Republican Governor John D. Long in 1882. Robinson passed the bar in 1882, becoming the first woman to practice law in Massachusetts.

Though a pioneer in breaking the barriers to women in the legal profession, Robinson preferred to keep a low profile in her legal practice. Avoiding the public scrutiny of the courtroom, she maintained a discreet office practice, focusing primarily on claims work. In her first three and a half years of law practice, she appeared in court only once, to argue a claim for separate maintenance and custody for a deserted wife.

Unhappy with customs and restrictions that impeded her career in Boston, Robinson moved to Seattle in the Washington Territory in 1884, hoping to find a more hospitable atmosphere for women lawyers. The openness toward women's rights there buoyed Robinson's spirits, and her law practice thrived. She began to do court work, including arguing cases before mixed juries of men and women. Despite the growing success of her career, however, she missed her family and in 1885, when it became clear that they could not join her in the West, she returned to Boston.

In Boston, Robinson drew on her journalistic skills to write a book making the law accessible to the general public. In 1886, she published *Law Made Easy: A Book for the People*, which summarized the law of contracts, real property, wills, marriage, divorce, criminal law, and tort for a popular audience. The following year, she worked as a legal stenographer for an established lawyer in order to refamiliarize herself with Massachusetts law. Her legal skills did not go unnoticed, and before the year was out, her employer encouraged her to open her own office.

This time, six years after her initial lonely foray into the Boston legal establishment, Robinson had the company of a handful of women also interested in the law. Two women were enrolled at Boston University Law School at the time, and Robinson assisted two other women in studying law in her office. Robinson appreciated the importance of professional women's associations in furthering her legal career. In 1887 she joined the Equity Club, a national correspondence club of women lawyers, and in 1888, she helped found the Portia Club, a local dinner and discussion club of women lawyers and law students. She was also a founder of the Pentagon Club, an association of professional women in theology, medicine, teaching, law, and journalism.

Nurtured by this thriving community of professional women, Robinson began to focus her writing and legal work more specifically on the needs of women. With an eye to making family law accessible to women, she published *The Law of Husband and Wife* in 1889. In order to meet the legal needs of women who could not afford her services, she opened her office on Saturday afternoons to women only, offering them free legal consultations. By 1890, nearly a decade after graduating from Boston University, Robinson had come to believe that women's place in the legal profession was secure. Her article "Women Lawyers in the United States," published that year in *The Green Bag*, proudly surveyed the achievements of women lawyers across the nation.

Even as Robinson's professional life thrived, she was well aware of the dilemmas of women lawyers of her day and raised them for discussion among the members of the Equity Club. In 1888 she addressed the delicate question, "Shall the woman attorney wear her hat when arguing a case or making a motion in court, or shall she remove it?" The question was a difficult one because it was customary for women to always appear in public with their heads covered, whereas lawyers always removed their hats when addressing judges. The following year, as Robinson privately pondered marriage, she confronted the Equity Club with a more enduring dilemma: "Is it practicable for a woman to successfully fulfill the duties of wife, mother and lawyer at one and the same time? Especially a young married woman?"

Robinson answered this question for herself when she married Eli Sawtelle, a piano dealer, in 1890. Sawtelle fully supported Robinson's professional career and aspirations. His wedding gift to her was a rolltop desk for her office. On their wedding trip to Washington, D.C., the couple took time out while Robinson was admitted to the bar of the U.S. Supreme Court. Their marriage, however, was brief. Only a year after their wedding, Robinson died from an overdose of sleeping medication while vacationing at her husband's family homestead in Amherst, New Hampshire.

• No collection of Robinson's papers exists. Original briefs containing legal arguments Robinson used are "The Petitioner's Brief in Support and Petitioner's Supplemental Brief in Support," *Lelia J. Robinson's Case*, 131 Mass. 376 (1881), located in the Supreme Judicial Court, Boston. The fullest discussion of Robinson is Douglas Lamar Jones, "Lelia J. Robinson's Case and the Entry of Women into the Legal Profession in Massachusetts, in *The History of the Law in Massachusetts: The Supreme Judicial Court, 1692–1992*, ed. Russell K. Osgood (1992). A biographical sketch of Robinson is in Virginia G. Drachman, ed., *Women Lawyers and the Origins of Professional Identity* (1993), which also reprints her Equity Club letters. Additional sources include Mary A. Greene, "Lelia Robinson Sawtelle: First Woman Lawyer of Massachusetts," *Women Lawyers' Journal* 7 (Apr. 1918): 51; and "Women Lawyers: Judge Gray's Decision," *Woman's Journal* 12 (Nov. 1881): 373. An obituary is in the *Chicago Legal News*, 22 Aug. 1891.

VIRGINIA G. DRACHMAN

ROBINSON, Max Cleveland (1 May 1939–20 Dec. 1988), television newscaster, was born in Richmond, Virginia, the son of Maxie Cleveland Robinson and Doris Griffin, schoolteachers. Robinson attended Oberlin College in 1957–1958 and Virginia Union University, his father's alma mater, briefly in 1959.

That year Robinson made his first venture into broadcast journalism when he answered a newspaper advertisement for a newsreading job in Portsmouth, Virginia. The ad was for whites only, but Robinson, an African American, answered it anyway. He was allowed to audition with four white candidates. Surprisingly he was hired, but when he read the news his face was not shown, and instead a slide with the station's logo appeared. One day, wanting his family and friends to see him read the news, Robinson told the crew to remove the slide, which they did. The next day Robinson was fired after the station received a myriad of negative telephone calls.

Robinson joined the U.S. Air Force in 1959, hoping to become a pilot. Poor vision ended that dream, and the air force sent him to Indiana University to learn Russian in 1959–1960. In 1965 Robinson resumed his journalism career as a cameraman and correspondent for WTOP-TV in Washington, D.C. He learned early that the life of a black news journalist would not be an easy one: at WTOP he earned $50 per week, $25 less than his white counterparts.

Seeking advancement, Robinson left WTOP and became a news correspondent for rival station WRC-TV from 1965 to 1969. While at WRC he won six journalism awards, including two regional Emmys for a documentary on black life in Anacostia titled *The Other Washington*, and an award for his coverage of the 1968 riots after civil rights leader Martin Luther King, Jr., was assassinated. Despite the many accolades bestowed upon Robinson while at WRC, the news director told him that he didn't think Washington was ready for a black news anchor.

Robinson returned to WTOP in 1969 in search of an anchor position. He became the first black anchor in Washington, D.C., coanchoring the midday newscast. In 1971 he was promoted to coanchor of the prestigious 6:00 P.M. and 11:00 P.M. news. He helped make WTOP's the top-rated newscast in Washington.

In 1977 Robinson received international attention when Hanafi Muslims seized three federal buildings and the B'nai B'rith headquarters in Washington. One of the sect leaders' first telephone calls was to Robinson, who helped negotiate the release of the hostages. Impressed with seeing Robinson so calm under fire, ABC-TV approached him about a network anchor position.

In 1978 Robinson moved to Chicago to become a prime-time coanchor at ABC. This broke the color barrier for the most prestigious job at the major networks. He served as a national desk anchor of ABC's *World News Tonight*. While at ABC he reported on major events such as the American space laboratory, Skylab, falling to earth and the accident at the Three Mile Island nuclear plant, both in 1979. In 1981 he won an Emmy award for his coverage of the 1980 national election.

Robinson's career at ABC was mired by controversy. In a 1981 speech at Smith College in Massachusetts, he verbally attacked the networks (ABC in particular). He was upset at the networks for not including black journalists in the coverage of Ronald Reagan's inauguration and the simultaneous release of U.S. hostages in Iran. Robinson claimed that the network officials were racist and said they promoted racially biased news coverage. He went on to say that the news media was a "crooked mirror" through which "white America views itself."

Robinson further embarrassed ABC by failing to appear at the 1983 funeral of colleague Frank Reynolds (one of the anchors of *World News Tonight*). He was supposed to have sat with First Lady Nancy Reagan. After he missed the funeral, Robinson was demoted, and Peter Jennings was made the sole anchor of *World News Tonight*. Frustrated about his demotion, Robinson became deeply depressed, grew bitter, and drank heavily. He left ABC in 1983.

In 1984 Robinson joined WMAQ-TV in Chicago as an anchor. While at WMAQ he voluntarily hospitalized himself for depression and alcoholism; after his frequent absences from the air, the station bought out his contract in 1987. This marked the end of Robinson's career as a television news anchor, even though he did some freelance journalism from 1985 to 1988.

Robinson was married three times. His first wife was Eleanor Booker; they had three children. His second wife was Beverly Hamilton; they had one child. This 1973 marriage was annulled after two months. His last marriage was to Hazel O'Leary, later an energy secretary in the Clinton administration; they had no children.

Robinson died of AIDS at Howard University Hospital in Washington, D.C. The Reverend Jesse Jackson eulogized him, telling the audience of Robinson's dying request: that everyone know he contracted AIDS through sexual promiscuity. Robinson had hoped that his death would energize the efforts to educate minorities about the disease.

• Biographical information on Robinson can be found in Dhyana Zeigler, "Max Robinson, Jr.: Turbulent Life of a Media Prophet," *Journal of Black Studies* (Sept. 1989): 97–112, and Peter J. Boyer, "The Light Goes Out," *Vanity Fair*, June 1989, pp. 68–84. Obituaries are in *Broadcasting*, 26 Dec. 1988, p. 86; *Jet*, 9 Jan. 1989, p. 17; and the *Chicago Tribune* and the *Los Angeles Times*, both 21 Dec. 1988.

DARREN RHYM

ROBINSON, Moses (26 Mar. 1742–26 May 1813), politician and jurist, was born in Hardwick, Massachusetts, the son of Samuel Robinson and Mercy Leonard, farmers. Little is known of his youth or education, but in 1761 he followed his father to the northern New England frontier when the elder Robinson led the members of Hardwick's Separatist Congregational church to the newly founded town of Bennington in the area then known as the New Hampshire Grants. In 1762 he married Mary Fay, with whom he had seven children.

Moses Robinson served as Bennington's first town clerk, holding office from 1762 to 1781, while his father became the town's leading citizen and played a prominent role in the opposition of New England settlers on the Grants to New York's attempt to establish control over the territory between the Hudson and Connecticut rivers. Following Samuel Robinson's death in England in 1767 while acting as the Yankee settlers' agent to the Crown, Moses and his brothers continued the family's support of Ethan Allen, the Green Mountain Boys, and the rest of the westside faction that New York characterized as "the Bennington mob" in the Grants jurisdictional dispute. When the onset of the American Revolution and the example of the colonies' break with England set the stage for Yankee autonomy east of the Hudson, Moses was especially active in the 1776–1777 series of local conventions that culminated in the January 1777 creation of the state that became Vermont.

As the head of the most powerful family in independent Vermont's principal town, Robinson became a key figure in the Green Mountain republic's government. He saw action against John Burgoyne's invading army in the summer of 1777 as a colonel in the Vermont militia, but his chief contributions to the new state's survival were political rather than military. He was a member of Vermont's first Council of Safety, which governed the state from July 1777 to March 1778, a judge on the revolutionary courts of sequestration and confiscation, chief justice of the state supreme court from 1778 to 1784, and a member of the powerful governor's council from 1778 to 1784. He also served Vermont as occasional agent to Congress, where he worked effectively to counter New York's insistence on jurisdiction to the Connecticut River but failed to gain sufficient support for Vermont's admission to the Union. Near the end of the Revolution, Robinson was part of the small group of Green Mountain leaders who entered into secret negotiations with Frederick Haldimand, governor general of the British forces in Canada, to discuss Vermont's rejoining the Empire as a semiautonomous province. A political rather than personal ally of the state's three most influential leaders, brothers Ethan and Ira Allen and longtime governor Thomas Chittenden, and never part of the large-scale speculation in Champlain Valley lands that drove their vision of Vermont's future, Robinson was nonetheless a significant force in revolutionary Vermont's successful defiance of its internal and external enemies.

After the war, when some of Vermont's pioneer leaders gave way to younger, more sophisticated newcomers, Robinson maintained his position near the top of the state's political pyramid. He accepted annual, albeit largely symbolic, reappointment as the state's agent to a still-hostile Congress and retained his seat on the supreme court until 1789. That year Yale granted him an honorary M.A. degree, an example that Dartmouth College followed in 1790. More consequential recognition also came in 1789, when the public furor over a land speculation deal involving Ira Allen kept Chittenden from achieving a majority in Vermont's gubernatorial election and the legislature chose Robinson, who had received less than 30 percent of the popular vote, to fill the vacancy. The change was significant for Vermont's future: Chittenden had been unenthusiastic about joining the Union, but Robinson used his year in office to push for a settlement with New York that would clear the way for national recognition of Vermont. By the time Chittenden regained the governorship in October 1790, the momentum toward statehood was unstoppable. In January 1791 Robinson served as vice president of the Bennington convention that ratified the Constitution, and when Vermont became the fourteenth state later that year the legislature named him as one of Vermont's two U.S. senators.

As a senator, Robinson quickly distinguished himself as a Francophile and as a staunch ally of Thomas Jefferson and James Madison on national issues. Opposed to Alexander Hamilton's plan for closer American ties to England, he voted against the Jay Treaty in the summer of 1795 and encouraged local meetings in Vermont to petition the Senate to withhold the appropriation necessary for the treaty's implementation. Vermont, however, had a Federalist majority, and in October 1796 Robinson resigned from the Senate and returned to Bennington. He held public office only twice thereafter, serving as a member of the state council of censors in 1799 and as Bennington's representative in the legislature in 1802, but he remained a vocal Jeffersonian through the embargo years and the War of 1812. The administration should continue the embargo and enforce it vigorously, he wrote in February 1809, rather than submit to Federalist opposition and risk losing "that Just and Righteous Energy which at all times ought to Characterise a Government of a nation."

His wife died in 1801. Two years later he married Susannah Warner Howe. In his last years Robinson maintained his family's tradition of local leadership, gaining a lasting reputation as the wealthiest man in Bennington and a pillar of the Congregational church. He died there, reportedly with remarkable composure after a painful illness of six days, of the spotted fever epidemic that swept Vermont in 1812–1813.

• There is no substantial body of Moses Robinson manuscripts; a few letters and documents at the Vermont Historical Society, the Vermont State Archives, the Bennington Museum, and the Special Collections department of the University of Vermont Library are all that have survived. Published biographical sketches and family genealogical sources include Abby M. Hemenway, ed., *The Vermont Historical Gazetteer* (5 vols., 1867–1891), vol 1, pp. 170–71; Jacob G. Ullery, comp., *Men of Vermont* (1894), pp. 54–57; Harry Parker Ward, *The Follett-Dewey-Fassett-Safford Ancestry* (1896), pp. 179–83; Jane Bancroft Robinson, *A Historical Sketch of the Robinson Family of the Line of Ebenezer Robinson* (1903); Prentiss C. Dodge, ed., *Encyclopedia Vermont Biography* (1912), pp. 28–29; and Walter H. Crockett, *Vermont: The Green Mountain State* (5 vols., 1921–1923), vol. 5, pp. 47–48. For background on early Bennington and Robinson's local leadership, see Isaac Jennings, *Memorials of a Century* (1869); Richard G. Wood, "Moses Robinson—Town Clerk," *American Archivist* 25 (1962): 189–91; and John Page, "The Economic Structure of Society in Revolutionary Bennington," *Vermont History* 49 (1981): 69–84. Among the more useful secondary sources on eighteenth-century Vermont are Hiland Hall, *The History of Vermont* (1869); Matt B. Jones, *Vermont in the Making* (1939); Chilton Williamson, *Vermont in Quandary: 1763–1825* (1949); Michael Sherman, ed., *A More Perfect Union: Vermont Becomes a State, 1777–1816* (1991); and Michael Bellesiles, *Revolutionary Outlaws: Ethan Allen and the Struggle for Independence on the Early American Frontier* (1993).

J. KEVIN GRAFFAGNINO

ROBINSON, Prince (7 June 1902–23 July 1960), jazz clarinetist and tenor saxophonist, was born in Portsmouth, Virginia. Nothing is known of his parents. Largely self-taught, Robinson began playing clarinet at age fourteen and, while in high school in Norfolk, worked with the Ben Jones band. Between 1919 and 1921 he played with Lillian Jones's Jazz Hounds in Norfolk and in 1922 went to Atlantic City, New Jersey, as a member of pianist Quentin Redd's band.

In 1923 he moved to New York City, where he worked with Lionel Howard's Musical Aces and then with banjoist Elmer Snowden's highly regarded Nest Club band, which included cornetist Rex Stewart, trombonist Te Roy Williams, alto and baritone saxophonist Joe Garland, pianist Freddy Johnson, bassist Bob Ysaguirre, and drummer Walter Johnson. In 1924 he also worked with cornetist June Clark and along with Garland and trumpeter Harry Cooper, made his first records with a small group called the Seminole Syncopators. In the spring of 1925 Robinson joined Duke Ellington's Washingtonians at the Kentucky Club, and in September, on "I'm Gonna Hang around My Sugar" and "Trombone Blues" from this fledgling band's second recording session, Robinson displayed equal ability on both clarinet and tenor sax. In November on a freelance date with a group called the Gulf Coast Seven, led by Willie "the Lion" Smith, he shared reed responsibilities with the formidable Buster Bailey on "Santa Claus Blues" and "Keep Your Temper." In March and June 1926 Robinson appeared on four more titles with Ellington and may also be present on the eight successive sessions recorded through April 1927. During the summer of 1926 Robinson worked in saxophonist Billy Fowler's band, and in May 1927, after a recording date with Te Roy Williams, he joined Leon Abbey's orchestra for a South American tour.

In late 1927, possibly at the urging of his childhood friend and trumpeter-arranger John Nesbitt, Robinson joined the Detroit-based McKinney's Cotton Pickers, then a major attraction at Jean Goldkette's Graystone Ballroom in Detroit. With two bandstands and a capacity of 2,000, the Graystone was also home to Goldkette's other orchestras, including the "Number One" band that featured Bix Beiderbecke, Frank Trumbauer, Don Murray, and other highly rated white jazzmen. Although Goldkette forbade drinking on the job and discouraged fraternization between the members of his racially segregated orchestras, the musicians themselves enjoyed each others' styles and often found opportunities for informal camaraderie after work.

As he did with the other bands his agency handled, Goldkette also booked the Cotton Pickers on far-ranging tours. In the fall of 1927 they substituted for the Fletcher Henderson orchestra at New York City's Roseland Ballroom, playing opposite the popular white dance band of Sam Lanin. The Cotton Pickers also did battle with the redoubtable Henderson crew at the Graystone, as well as performing at private campus clubs for Princeton's house-party weekend in May 1929, where, with jazzmen from many other bands also in evidence, Robinson must certainly have had ample occasion for spirited after-hours jamming. With the harmonically advanced, challenging arrangements of Don Redman and Nesbitt, coupled with the group's excellent ensemble skills and a nucleus of inventive soloists, the Cotton Pickers invariably made a good impression wherever they appeared. However, despite their musical successes, both on record and off, dissension grew within the ranks over their treatment by the Goldkette office. Following a May to July 1931 booking at Frank Sebastian's Cotton Club in Culver City, California, the band broke up in late 1931, with Robinson returning in 1932 to a McKinney contingent led by drummer Cuba Austin.

It was on the many bright-tempo, richly intoned records that the Cotton Pickers made between July 1928 and September 1931 that Robinson earned a reputation as a jazz tenorman second only to his idol Coleman Hawkins, at the time Fletcher Henderson's star soloist and the universally acclaimed master of his instrument. Sharing improvised jazz solos equally with trumpeters Nesbitt and Joe Smith, trombonists Claude Jones and Ed Cuffee, and pianist Todd Rhodes, Robinson was a competent clarinetist, but because of his powerful attack, heated timbre, urgent rhythmic sense, and fluent technical command on tenor sax he enjoyed the respect and admiration of virtually all who heard him. His artistry is especially apparent on "Crying and Sighing," "Cherry," "Some Sweet Day," "Shim-Me-Sha-Wabble," "Birmingham Breakdown," "It's a Precious Little Thing Called Love," "I've Found a New Baby," "Okay Baby," "I Want a Little Girl," "Hello," and "Do You Believe in Love at First Sight?" In 1929 and 1930, and once again in 1937, Robinson participated as a freelance sideman on several recording sessions organized by pianist Clarence Williams, but it was his work on the Cotton Pickers records that marked his greatest achievement.

After leaving the Cotton Pickers in Boston in early 1935, Robinson joined singer Blanche Calloway's orchestra in the summer and remained with her through early 1937. Along with trumpeter Shirley Clay and clarinetist Buster Bailey, in July 1937 Robinson recorded a freelance session with vocalist Lil Armstrong during which he played tenor in a style somewhat influenced by Chu Berry, Hawkins's then most advanced disciple. Reverting to clarinet for another freelance session in November with Teddy Wilson and Billie Holiday, Robinson appeared in a rather subdued role, but he acquitted himself well despite his limited opportunities for expression. Between April 1937 and November 1938, Robinson worked with entertainer Willie Bryant, recording one session with his band in April 1938. In November 1938 Robinson began an extended engagement with Roy Eldridge's orchestra at New York City's Arcadia Ballroom, and while there recorded two studio sessions with the band in October and December 1939. Broadcast performances from the preceding August and September have also been issued on record. In 1940 Robinson replaced Bingie Madison in Louis Armstrong's orchestra and was present at the three sessions recorded between

March 1941 and April 1942. He was the sole reedman on the first date by the septet and can be heard in solo on clarinet on "Leap Frog" from November 1941. In this band the tenor sax solos were the domain of Joe Garland, Armstrong's musical director and chief arranger.

After a brief turn with Lucky Millinder's orchestra in 1942–1943, Robinson spent the remainder of his career as a freelancer in and around New York City. In the fall of 1944 he played in trombonist Benny Morton's sextet at Café Society Downtown and recorded a session with the group in 1945. Between 1945 and 1953 Robinson worked both casual jobs and residencies in New York City with such swing band veterans as pianist Claude Hopkins and tenor saxophonist Sam "the Man" Taylor, and in 1954 he went on tour with trumpeter Henry "Red" Allen. Between 1955 and 1959 Robinson worked in Queens with Freddie Washington's Dixiecrats, taking time out in July 1958 for an appearance with the Fletcher Henderson Reunion Band. Robinson's last recorded performance was as a clarinet soloist on arranger Andy Gibson's 1959 LP-length "Blue Print." He died of cancer in New York City.

Despite Robinson's early promise and the high plateau he reached as a soloist in the late 1920s and early 1930s, he does not seem to have been able to keep up with the competition offered by younger jazz saxophonists during the swing era. By the mid- and late 1930s, with the advent of such distinctive stylists as Chu Berry, Herschel Evans, Dick Gibson, Ben Webster, and Lester Young, it was clear that Robinson had fallen behind. Two years older than Hawkins, at his peak he had been a brilliant improvisor in the "stomp" style, but as with some others of his generation, he found it difficult to make the transition to modern swing. As an alternative, he could have concentrated on clarinet, particularly after the mid-1940s revival of interest in earlier jazz styles. But then he would have had to compete with such specialists as Omer Simeon, Barney Bigard, Albert Nicholas, Edmond Hall, and Buster Bailey. Although highly regarded by his contemporaries for his early jazz work and his continuing ability as a big-band section man, Robinson spent the last two decades of his life in obscurity.

• The best comprehensive source of information about Robinson's most productive period is John Chilton, *McKinney's Music: A Bio-Discography of McKinney's Cotton Pickers* (1978), while supplemental data can be found in Walter C. Allen, *Hendersonia: The Music of Fletcher Henderson and His Musicians* (1973). Gunther Schuller, *The Swing Era: The Development of Jazz, 1930–1945* (1989), includes an insightful analysis of the McKinney recordings and discusses Robinson's role as an improvising jazzman. Stanley Dance, *The World of Swing* (1974), provides commentary on Robinson by a number of his colleagues. See also Albert McCarthy, *Big Band Jazz* (1974), and Rex Stewart, *Boy Meets Horn* (1991). Complete discographical information is in Brian Rust, *Jazz Records, 1897–1942* (1982), and Walter Bruyninckx, *Swing Discography, 1920–1988* (12 vols., 1989).

JACK SOHMER

ROBINSON, Rowland Evans (14 May 1833–15 Oct. 1900), author and farmer, was born in Ferrisburg, Vermont, the son of Rowland Thomas Robinson and Rachael Gilpin, farmers. Both parents were Quakers. The prominent abolitionist William Lloyd Garrison was a friend of the family. During young Rowland's childhood the Robinsons' farmhouse provided accommodations for slaves fleeing to Canada via the Underground Railroad. Memories of his parents' abolitionist activities later served Robinson in his writing.

Robinson was educated in a rural one-room school and at Ferrisburg Academy. His home was well stocked with books, which he read eagerly, especially the novels of Sir Walter Scott and histories by Francis Parkman. At an early age he became interested in the history of Vermont, particularly that of the Lake Champlain valley in which he lived. Events from the French and Indian Wars, the American Revolution, the War of 1812, and Vermont's struggle to win independence from New York found a place both in his historical fiction and in his *Vermont: A Study of Independence* (1892), which was included in Houghton Mifflin's American Commonwealth series.

Robinson possessed an untrained talent for drawing. In an effort to improve his natural talent, he spent several years in New York City as a draftsman, doing commercial work, and also managing to place several drawings in magazines. In 1870 he married Anna Stevens of East Montpelier, Vermont, with whom he had two daughters and a son. For a time he continued his drawing with some success, but he was mainly occupied in farming. Following a suggestion by his wife, he wrote an essay, "Fox-Hunting in New England," which appeared in *Scribner's Monthly* (Jan. 1878). From then on his numerous essays, sketches, and stories found ready publication in various magazines, among them the *Atlantic Monthly*, *Lippincott's Magazine*, and *Century*, and soon collections of his work were published as books—for example, *Danvis Folks* (1894), in which all but one of the twenty-six pieces had previously been printed in the magazine *Forest and Stream*. Altogether fourteen such collections were printed.

In his mid-fifties Robinson's eyesight began to fail, and soon he was totally blind, but with the aid of a grooved writing board he continued his prolific writing with no diminution of his knack for vivid description of people and natural scenes. For the subjects and settings of his writing, Robinson drew almost exclusively from the area in which he had lived all his life. Thus he belonged to the group of regionalists and local-color writers who flourished in the decades after the Civil War, among them Sarah Orne Jewett, Mary E. Wilkins Freeman, and Hamlin Garland. Writing in this genre, Robinson focused on three aspects of his region aside from its history: its physical and natural features, the way of life of its people, and the patterns and phonetics of local speech. As Van Wyck Brooks wrote, "His sensitiveness to sounds . . . caused him to observe the varieties of speech he recorded all too faithfully" (*New England: Indian Summer* [1940]:

458); at times, as Brooks suggests, readers may have difficulty understanding what is being said.

In Robinson's work there is a strong strain of the nostalgia frequently found in local colorists. He wrote in *Danvis Folks* that in Vermont "manners have changed, many customs have become obsolete, and though the dialect is yet spoken by some in almost its original quaintness, abounding in odd similes and figures of speech, it is passing away." Though he finds much that is admirable in both past and present Vermont, he avoids the sentimentality that often informs local-color writing. His sense of humor goes far in accomplishing this. Also, much that is far from admirable receives his attention—for example, the plight of paupers in a New England poorhouse and the bigotry, greed, and meanness that characterize many of his country folk.

Much of Robinson's writing is set in the fictional town of Danvis, which is closely modeled on towns near Ferrisburg in the foothills of the Green Mountains. Robinson knew this area well and thought the old ways had lingered there longest. Danvis is home to a group of characters typical of the area, who meet at the shop of the cobbler Uncle Lisha to exchange news, gossip, and yarns. Accounts of these gatherings are scattered throughout Robinson's writing; they occur most notably in *Uncle Lisha's Shop: Life in a Corner of Yankee-Land* (1887) and in *Danvis Folks*. Though Robinson's characters represent village types, he is careful to individualize them. Among them are Uncle Lisha, who had moved to Wisconsin but soon returned homesick; Gran'ther Hill, a veteran who claimed to be a major participant in the Battle of Bennington and the campaign against Fort Ticonderoga; Solon Briggs, the malaprop of the group, "a man of big if not weighty words"; the Quaker Joel Bartlett, the "clark of the deestrick" and a worker on the Underground Railroad; and the French-Canadian Antoine (pronounced Ann Twine) Bissette, a bigger liar than Gran'ther Hill.

As a local colorist Robinson was highly esteemed during his lifetime. His gentle realism, humor, and evocation of a passing way of life pleased readers and reviewers alike. After his death in Ferrisburg, Vermont, his reputation declined, and his books gradually went out of print. Then, during the four years following the hundredth anniversary of his birth, the Charles Tuttle Company of Rutland, Vermont, published a Centennial edition of Robinson's works, including in seven volumes twelve of his fourteen books. Each of the Centennial volumes contains prefaces and forewords by various authors and critics, among them Dorothy Canfield Fisher, Sinclair Lewis, Arthur Wallace Peach, and Fred Lewis Pattee. The critical assessments of these commentators are generally favorable. More recently Robinson has received attention from literary historians and folklorists, the latter finding his writings to be a rich source of material.

• Robinson's letters are in the Sheldon Museum in Middlebury, Vermont; other papers, including manuscripts, notebooks, and sketchbooks are in the Rokeby Museum in Ferrisburg, Vermont. A concise biographical essay by Mary Robinson Perkins, "Rowland Evans Robinson," is in *Out of Bondage and Other Stories*, ed. Rowland E. Robinson (1936). Further biographical material and discussions of Robinson's writing may be found in Ronald L. Baker, *Folklore in the Writings of Rowland E. Robinson* (1973), and in Perry D. Westbrook, *Acres of Flint: Sarah Orne Jewett and Her Contemporaries*, rev. ed. (1981). Terence Martin, "Rowland Evans Robinson, Realist of the Outdoors," *Vermont History* 23 (1955): 3–15, discusses Robinson as a nature writer. Hayden Carruth, "Rowland E. Robinson: Vermont's Neglected Genius," *Vermont History* 41 (1973): 181–97, is mainly concerned with Robinson's rendition of Vermont dialects.

PERRY D. WESTBROOK

ROBINSON, Ruby Doris Smith (25 Apr. 1942–7 Oct. 1967), civil rights leader, was born in Atlanta, Georgia, the daughter of John Thomas Smith, a furniture mover and Baptist minister, and Alice Banks, a beautician. She did well in high school and in 1959 entered Spelman College. Halfway through her freshman year, Smith was deeply stirred by news of the restaurant sit-in organized by black college students in Greensboro, North Carolina. When Atlanta's college students formed a civil rights organization, Smith joined. She experienced her first arrest soon after, while trying to desegregate the state capitol building's cafeteria. A few months later she went to Shaw University in Raleigh to attend the conference at which the Student Non-Violent Coordinating Committee (SNCC) was founded. In February 1961 she and three others from SNCC joined a sit-in in Rock Hill, South Carolina, using a new tactic: "jail, no bail," which made them the first civil rights protesters to serve their full sentences. She spent thirty days in jail, acquiring a stomach ailment that remained with her the rest of her life.

In May 1961 the Congress on Racial Equality (CORE) began its Freedom Rides, testing the recent court decision outlawing segregation in interstate bus terminals. When violence in Alabama forced CORE to end the ride in Birmingham, SNCC members determined to carry it on, and Smith flew to Birmingham to join them. After several days of intimidation and violence, the riders were arrested in Jackson, Mississippi. Refusing bail, they served forty-five days in Parchman State Prison. Smith remained in Mississippi after her release, working on SNCC's voter registration project. At a seminar for student activists that summer, she argued in defense of several blacks who had thrown rocks at their assailants during a demonstration.

Throughout the spring of her freshman year and all of her sophomore year, Smith spent more time on SNCC than her school work. She was arrested a dozen times and spent many weeks in various jails. Spelman College authorities were sympathetic, but in fall 1961 they asked her to reapply for admission. Smith acknowledged the disruptive effects of her past activities but affirmed her intention to concentrate on college in the future. Granted readmission, she remained in school for two more years. She was still active in SNCC, however, serving on its executive committee;

working in Cairo, Illinois, during summer 1962; and helping to organize demonstrations in Albany, Georgia, that December. In 1963 she withdrew from Spelman to work for SNCC full time.

Serving primarily in SNCC's Atlanta office, Smith spent most of her early years as administrative assistant to the executive secretary, James Forman, though she also managed personnel, kept the accounts, and maintained SNCC's fleet of 100 cars in eight states. Developing into what one observer called "the administrative and logistical center of SNCC," Smith experienced continual stress in seeking to impose discipline and structure on a loosely organized, independent-minded staff. Both her dedication and her rages over unsatisfactory staff work were legendary. "You could feel her power on a daily basis," recalled one colleague. Said another, "Ruby just stood up to *anybody*." White volunteers were terrified of her, yet as one of them said, "Ruby was a woman I had the greatest respect for, and in a way, loved."

By 1964 Smith had begun to feel that SNCC was ignoring the fundamental economic questions that concerned most black Americans. In addition, the organization was becoming increasingly dependent on financial and political support from whites, and it was recruiting hundreds of white volunteers. This troubled Smith, who argued that blacks must continue to dominate SNCC. According to one colleague, she "had been anti-white for years." She also spoke out on the subordination of women within SNCC, though her willingness to protest this issue diminished as the organization became more polarized racially. In fall 1964 her commitment to black nationalism was intensified when she joined an SNCC delegation to Guinea's independence celebrations. Meanwhile, her personal life was placing new demands on her. She reentered Spelman in 1964 and graduated with a bachelor of science degree in physical education in 1965. She had married Clifford Robinson, an SNCC employee, in November 1964 and gave birth to a son, Kenneth Touré (named for the president of Guinea), two months after graduation.

During this period the South's continuing intransigence and the bitter disappointments of Freedom Summer led many SNCC members, like Ruby Robinson, to question the value of white liberal allies, nonviolence, and integration itself; by spring 1965 few whites still felt welcome in the organization. In spring 1966 Robinson was chosen to succeed Forman, becoming SNCC's first female executive secretary. Her election was perceived as an affirmation of separatism, particularly because black nationalist Stokely Carmichael was elected chair at the same time. Robinson's election was also seen as a victory for tighter administration because she and Forman had fought to hold staff more accountable. Nevertheless, her administrative efforts drew what Forman called "vicious attacks from the SNCC leadership." Some of her opponents had long fought any centralization of authority, while others explicitly objected to having a woman assert such power. Robinson's racial views also caused dissension; just as many of her colleagues were hardening their views on race, she was easing hers. Though she supported the goals enunciated by Black Power spokesmen, she told her staff that she had gone through a period of hating whites and "there's nothing to it." She insisted that they all had more important things to do than, she said, "sit around talking about white people."

By the time she was elected executive secretary, Robinson had little more than a year to live. Hospitalized in January 1967, she was diagnosed with cancer in April and died in Atlanta that fall. So contested had her administration been that some SNCC members believed she was murdered. Her friend Kathleen Cleaver, who disagreed, said, "It wasn't necessary to assassinate her. What killed Ruby was work, work, work, with being married, having a child, the constant conflicts, the constant struggles that she was subjected to because she was a woman. . . . She was destroyed by the movement." Yet if Cleaver was right, Robinson made her sacrifice with passion and conviction, and her dedication inspired hundreds of people who worked with her. Alice Walker based her novel *Meridian* in part on Robinson's life. Forman described her as "one of the few genuine revolutionaries in the Black liberation movement." Stanley Wise, her successor at SNCC, called her "the nearest thing I ever met to a free person."

• Although Ruby Smith Robinson's personal papers remain with her family, the archives of both Spelman College and SNCC (Martin Luther King Center for Nonviolent Social Change, Atlanta) shed light on her career. Discussions about her by colleagues and acquaintances include James Forman, *The Making of Black Revolutionaries* (1972); Cleveland Sellers, *The River of No Return* (1973), with Robert Terrell; Jessica Harris, "An Interview with Alice Walker," *Essence*, July 1976, p. 33; and Howard Zinn, *SNCC: The New Abolitionists* (1964). See also "Builders of a New South: Negro Heroines of Dixie," *Ebony*, Aug. 1966, pp. 27–37; Paula Giddings, *When and Where I Enter: The Impact of Black Women on Race and Sex in America* (1984); Emily Stoper, *The Student Non-Violent Coordinating Committee: The Growth of Radicalism in a Civil Rights Organization* (1989); Jacqueline Jones Royster, "A 'Heartbeat for Liberation': The Reclamation of Ruby Doris Smith," *Sage* Student Supplement 1988, pp. 64–66; Clayborne Carson, *In Struggle: SNCC and the Black Awakening of the 1960s* (1981); and Sara Evans, *Personal Politics* (1979). An obituary is in the *New York Times*, 10 Oct. 1967.

SANDRA OPDYCKE

ROBINSON, Solon (21 Oct. 1803–3 Nov. 1880), author, agricultural journalist, and Indiana pioneer, was born in Tolland, Connecticut, the son of Jacob Robinson, a farmer and cooper, and Salinda Ladd. His father died when Solon Robinson was about six, and then his mother married James Robinson, one of her deceased husband's cousins. After his mother died and her second husband refused further responsibility for his stepchildren, Solon Robinson was in the care of William Bottom. He worked on his guardian's farm, got a little education in a country school near Lisbon, Connecticut, and briefly worked as a carpenter's apprentice, which was harder labor than his health could stand. In 1818, for unknown reasons, Solon successfully petitioned that Vine Robinson, an uncle in Brooklyn, Connecticut, be his guardian. Solon's later devotion to temperance may have been learned from his uncle, but little more is known about the next few years of his life.

Family tradition holds that young Solon Robinson became a traveling peddler and then sold tickets in a Cincinnati theater; he is listed as a clerk in Cincinnati's 1829 city directory. In 1828 he married Mariah Evans, from Germantown, Pennsylvania. Two years later Robinson moved to Madison, Indiana, and then bought eighty acres in Jennings County, between Madison and Indianapolis, where he planned the town of Solon and tried to sell lots to settlers. In 1834 he abandoned the enterprise and became one of the first settlers of Lake County, in Indiana's northwest corner.

The Robinsons lived in a cabin, and Solon started, in partnership with his brother Milo, a store that traded with Potawatomi Indians and settlers. Because no sale of land had yet been conducted, the settlers, including Robinson, were squatters who feared that they might lose their new homes when the land was formally sold. That fear inspired Robinson to call a meeting on 4 July 1836 that began a squatters' union. He also helped to write the union's constitution, described the squatters' land claims, and attended the official land auction in 1839. The armed squatters bought their land for $1.25 an acre without having to exceed competing bids. In honor of his leadership Robinson became known as the "Squatter King." Crown Point, which soon became Lake County's seat, may have gotten its name because the "king" lived there.

In 1837, when Lake County was organized, Robinson became its first county clerk and for several years thereafter served as a justice of the peace, postmaster of the county seat, a devoted Whig partisan, and an organizer of the Lake County Temperance Society. He also owned the county's first printing press, published a newspaper, and in 1837 began to contribute essays, including vivid descriptions of the northwest Indiana frontier, to the widely read *Cultivator* of Albany, New York, and other agricultural magazines. Increasingly devoted to journalism and to organizations that promoted agricultural improvement, Robinson presided over an 1840 meeting in Washington, D.C., that called for a national agricultural society. In 1841 the organization began its brief life and its unsuccessful campaign to get a share of the Smithson bequest from Congress. Robinson also helped to organize other agricultural societies, spoke at fairs, and became an assistant editor of the *American Agriculturist*, a New York magazine, in 1851, just before its publication was suspended.

In 1852 the *American Agriculturist*'s publisher began a new monthly, *The Plow*, which Robinson edited with assistance from Anthony Benezet Allen and Richard Lamb Allen, who had edited the suspended journal. An ambitious project that lasted only one year before the *American Agriculturist* returned to successful life, *The Plow* required Robinson to leave Indiana, where he had spent little time since becoming an agricultural journalist, and his wife and five children, who remained in Crown Point. Robinson stayed in New York after *The Plow*'s year of publication ended. First he edited a weekly newspaper, the *New-York Agricultor*, which his colleagues at *The Plow* briefly published, and then the agricultural department that Horace Greeley added to the *New York Tribune*'s weekly edition in 1853. Robinson provided the *Tribune* with articles based on experiments that he conducted just north of the city, on the eight Westchester County acres to which he moved in 1859, and his poignant observations of the city's suffering poor. Some of his New York essays, republished in 1854 as *Hot Corn: Life Scenes in New York Illustrated*, had a popular success. The little book sold about 50,000 copies in half a year. Dedicated to Greeley and Robinson's other colleagues at the *Tribune*, the "Friends of the Working Man," it described street vendors of roasted corn, including "Little Katy," a twelve-year-old girl who had to peddle and beg until midnight so that her mother would have money to buy rum. The publisher's preface claimed that the book was an unequaled "temperance tale." Two years later, in 1856, Robinson recycled some of his *Tribune* essays in a pamphlet, sold for a dime, called *The Economy of Food; or, What Shall We Eat*. Its preface mentioned that Robinson was secretary of the American Widows' Relief Association and then described the achievement of a widow who fed herself and her four children on a dime a day. Dimes could go a long way, but too many of them were wasted, Robinson observed, on liquor and cigars. Moreover, Americans separated consumers from farmers; they needed more opportunities for farmers to market their products in cities and more use of cheap, nutritious foods such as hominy and oatmeal.

Robinson's other literary efforts included *Me-Won-I-Toc*, an 1867 recollection of frontier Indiana and, especially, of the Potawatomi who mostly left the state soon after Robinson arrived, and some practical agricultural books, including *Facts for Farmers*, a thousand-page volume published in 1864. He also wrote, under the pseudonym Blythe White, Jr., a novel, *The Green Mountain Girls: A Story of Vermont* (1856), about pioneer life and troubles, notably including alcohol abuse.

Robinson's travels as an agricultural journalist took him to the South. Enjoying Florida's hot climate, he resigned from the *Tribune* and moved to Jacksonville in 1868. Continuing to send essays to the *Tribune*, he also wrote for Jacksonville papers, particularly the *Florida Republican*, which may have published his lost novel, *Osceola; or, The Last of the Seminoles*. In 1872, after the death of his first wife, who had filed a request for divorce in 1871, he married Mary Johnson, who had been his secretary in New York. They had no children. Robinson died in Jacksonville. Mary Robinson inherited his Florida home, but fire destroyed the house and Solon Robinson's papers and library in

1901. His career as a pioneer, author, agricultural journalist, and reformer is recorded, almost exclusively, in his published works.

• Herbert A. Kellar, who wrote about Robinson for the *Dictionary of American Biography*, also wrote "Solon Robinson," *Indiana History Bulletin* 7 (Apr. 1930): 223–28, and a substantial introduction to his *Solon Robinson, Pioneer and Agriculturist* (1936), a two-volume collection of Robinson's published writings and surviving manuscripts. Other helpful sources are Timothy Horton Ball, *Lake County, Indiana, from 1834 to 1872* (1873); "Solon Robinson, an Address Delivered by A. F. Knotts at Crown Point, August 27, 1921" (typescript, Indiana State Library); and Robinson's own books, especially *Hot Corn* and *Facts for Farmers*.

DONALD B. MARTI

ROBINSON, Stuart (14 Nov. 1814–5 Oct. 1881), Presbyterian minister, was born in Strabane, Ireland, the son of James Robinson, a linen merchant, and Martha Porter. When his father went bankrupt in 1816, the family immigrated to the United States from Northern Ireland, settling finally outside Martinsburg, in what became West Virginia. When his mother died, Robinson was informally adopted by the Troutman family, German Presbyterians, and educated by their pastor, Reverend James M. Brown. After completing Brown's preparatory school and another in Romney, Robinson entered Amherst College, where he graduated in 1836. He studied at both Union Theological Seminary in Virginia and Princeton Seminary in New Jersey, was licensed by Greenbrier Presbytery in Virginia in 1841, and ordained on 8 October 1842 to be the pastor of the Presbyterian congregation in what is now Malden, West Virginia. In 1841 he married Mary Elizabeth Brigham of Massachusetts; of their eight children, five died in infancy or early childhood.

Robinson, having earned a reputation as a literate and attractive preacher, was called to the Presbyterian church in Frankfort, Kentucky, in 1847. Called to the Fayette Street Church in Baltimore, Maryland, in 1852, he started a year later in Baltimore the Central Presbyterian Church and served it until asked in 1856 to become professor of pastoral theology and church government at the recently begun Danville Theological Seminary in Kentucky. During his tenure there, he quarreled frequently with another member of the faculty, Robert J. Breckenridge, about the nature of the church; signs of the debate continued in Robinson's two major books, *The Church of God, an Essential Element of the Gospel* (1858) and *Discourses of Redemption* (1868). Breckenridge argued that the church should be involved in all of life, whereas Robinson increasingly held that individual Christians should be involved in worldly affairs but that churches should not. From 1858 until only months before his death, Robinson served as pastor of Second Presbyterian Church in Louisville, Kentucky, though he served from exile in Canada during a portion of the Civil War.

From the time of his service in Frankfort onward, Robinson gained fame also as a sagacious businessman. He served on the city council in Frankfort as well as on the boards of banks in the cities where he ministered, and his advice was generally sought in matters of commerce and industry. He gained a modest fortune in land speculation, and he counseled city leaders, especially in Louisville, where he came to be known as "pastor to the city" throughout the 1870s.

Through most of his ministry Robinson also edited and sometimes published religious journals, the *Presbyterial Critic and Monthly Review* in Baltimore in the mid-1840s and the *Presbyterian Herald*, the *True Presbyterian*, and the *Free Christian Commonwealth* successively from Louisville in the 1860s. When several of his articles and sermons were deemed to be pro-Confederate, Robinson went into exile in Toronto, Canada, from 1862 to 1866. Nonetheless his articles helped convince most Presbyterians in Kentucky and Missouri to side with southern Presbyterians after the war had ended. In 1865 and 1866 he collaborated with Louisville ministerial colleague Samuel R. Wilson to offer the "Declaration and Testimony" for signing among Presbyterians in the Old School Assembly; the complaint asserted that, in demanding that ex-Confederates repent of their stance, the church had engaged in presumption and idolatry. The thousands of new members of the (southern) Presbyterian Church in the United States (PCUS) from border states helped enormously in reconstruction efforts in the deep South. In part for this leadership, he was elected moderator of the PCUS in 1869.

Robinson helped form the southern Presbyterian doctrine of "the spirituality of the church," an interpretation of the Bible which held that denominations and congregations ought to distance themselves from political involvement. Before the Civil War, he had eschewed antislavery actions of Presbyterian governing bodies in the North, but he came to fight any church action involving social issues. He considered his own ministry to include political involvement, however, and he led at least two attempts to elect members of reform slates to public office in Louisville. The reform slates he supported sought tighter Sabbath laws and an end to political corruption in the city.

Robinson also engaged in mission efforts wherever he went. During his tenure in Louisville especially, he helped Second Presbyterian Church begin at least three other Presbyterian congregations. He also encouraged his son-in-law, Bennett Young, to challenge Kentucky Presbyterians to undertake mission projects in Appalachia, and Confederate veteran E. O. Guerrant was called to lead them. Although much of the mountain ministry of Presbyterians took place after his death, Robinson's imprint remained firmly on the enterprise. Robinson died in Louisville.

• The Stuart Robinson Collection in the Presbyterian Historical Foundation, Montreat, N.C., contains scrapbooks and other documents. Also see Thomas E. Peck, *A Memorial of the Life and Labors of the Rev. Stuart Robinson* (1882); Alfred Nevin, *Encyclopaedia of the Presbyterian Church in the United States of America* (1884); and Louis Weeks, *Kentucky Presbyterians* (1983).

LOUIS WEEKS

ROBINSON, Sugar Ray (10 July 1922–12 Apr. 1989), professional boxer, was born Walker Smith, Jr., in Detroit, Michigan, the son of Walker Smith, a laborer, and Leila Hurst, a seamstress. In 1927 his mother left his father and later, in 1932, moved with her children to New York City. There, the boy helped support the family by collecting and selling driftwood, delivering groceries, and dancing in the streets for coins; he received little formal schooling. At the age of fifteen he began boxing for George Gainford at the Salem Crescent Club and soon was competing in amateur programs. When he made his debut, he had no American Athletic Union card, and Gainford gave him the card of another boy, Ray Robinson, whose name he kept throughout his career. He acquired the nickname "Sugar Ray" after unexpectedly scoring his first knockout over a Canadian opponent at Watertown, New York, when a local sportswriter used it in his report of the fight.

After a very successful amateur career, during which he won Golden Glove championships in 1939 and 1940, Robinson turned professional on 4 October 1940, boxing in the lightweight division. Tall, at five feet eleven inches, graceful, and with great hand speed and elusiveness, he was immediately successful and rose to main event status in only a few months. Within a year and a half he had defeated a former world champion, Fritzie Zivic, and two future champions, Sammy Angott and Marty Servo, and grown into a welterweight.

Because of his unusual height, reach, and ability, Robinson sometimes fought middleweights, defeating the young Jake LaMotta in 1942. In a return fight, LaMotta gave him his first defeat on 5 February 1943 in Detroit. In three more meetings in 1943 and 1945, Robinson won each time, although two of the decisions were disputed. Another middleweight, José Basora, held Robinson to a draw in 1945, but Robinson won all of his other fights in this period and came to be called "the uncrowned welterweight champion."

In July 1943 Robinson (who had been married briefly while a teenager and fathered a son by his first wife) married Edna Mae Holly, a former dancer; they would have one child. That year he entered the U.S. Army and was assigned mainly to a boxing exhibition touring troop with Joe Louis. On one occasion in Alabama, when Louis was assailed by a military policeman for using a telephone reserved for white persons, Robinson came to his defense in a tense situation. Robinson refused to appear before service audiences from which black troops were excluded. In March 1944 he was assigned to go abroad but failed to appear for departure. In his autobiography, he states that he had fallen, received a head blow that resulted in temporary amnesia, and regained his memory three days later in a hospital. He was given an honorable discharge in June 1944.

Robinson returned to the ring in peak form, winning twenty-three of his next twenty-four fights, including a thrilling tenth-round knockout of middleweight Artie Levine at Cleveland after twice being almost knocked out himself. On 20 December 1946 Robinson survived a knockdown and defeated Tommy Bell for the welterweight title that had been vacated by Servo. He then successfully defended the title five times, against Jimmy Doyle, Chuck Taylor, Bernard Docusen, Kid Gavilan, and Charley Fusari, before finally vacating it in 1950. The defense against Doyle, at Cleveland on 24 June 1947, ended in tragedy, when Doyle died of brain injuries. At the inquest, when asked, "Did you intend to get Doyle in trouble?" his memorable response was "Mister, it's my business to get him in trouble."

In 1950, having had difficulty in reducing to the welterweight limit, Robinson moved into the middleweight division. He gained limited recognition as champion by defeating Robert Villemain in Philadelphia and defended his claim successfully against Basora and Carl "Bobo" Olson. On 14 February 1951 in Chicago he became undisputed middleweight champion by stopping LaMotta in the thirteenth round after a tremendous battle. Soon afterward he departed for a boxing tour of Europe with an entourage of ten, including his wife, Gainford, and his flamingo-colored Cadillac. Always inclined to live luxuriously, he headquartered himself in Paris and defeated several minor opponents. Wherever he went he was received as a major celebrity and showered with attention. Having signed to defend his title against Randolph Turpin in London, he moved his headquarters there but was unable to train properly; on 10 July Turpin trounced him decisively.

Robinson was quickly rematched with Turpin in New York and on 12 September regained the middleweight title by rallying from the verge of defeat to win by a knockout in the tenth round. He followed with successful title defenses against Olson and Rocky Graziano. On 25 June 1952 Robinson challenged champion Joey Maxim for the world light-heavyweight title in New York. Under the ring lights in Yankee Stadium the temperature was 104 degrees Fahrenheit, and both men suffered heavily from the excess heat. Maxim conserved his energy at the expense of falling badly behind on points. In the thirteenth round Robinson lost his coordination and collapsed at the end of the round, unable to continue. Suffering from heat exhaustion, he did not recover until many hours later. He then decided to retire from boxing and relinquished the middleweight title.

Known as a master of footwork in the ring and having been a street dancer as a boy, Robinson became a professional dancer. However, he soon found that he could not support his usual lifestyle by this means and decided to return to boxing in 1955. After winning his first comeback fight he suffered a bad defeat from Ralph "Tiger" Jones, but he persevered and was given a title fight with Olson, the reigning middleweight champion. On 9 December 1955 Robinson scored a sensational two-round knockout to regain the title. He then defended it successfully against Olson, again winning by a one-punch knockout at Los Angeles on 18 May 1956.

After his return to the ring, Robinson was inconsistent, achieving several remarkable victories interspersed with defeats. He lost the middleweight title to Gene Fullmer at New York on 2 January 1957 but regained it with a one-punch five-round knockout in Chicago the following May. Before the year was over, he had lost the title again on points to Carmen Basilio, but he regained it from Basilio in Chicago on 25 March 1958. After a long period of inactivity, he lost the title again to Paul Pender in Boston on 22 January 1960, and four months later he failed to regain it from Pender. The title having fallen into dispute, Robinson then twice fought Gene Fullmer for championship recognition, the first result being a draw and the second a victory for Fullmer on 4 March 1961 in Las Vegas, Nevada.

Throughout his long career, Robinson was usually his own manager and was noted for driving hard bargains. Often he would refuse to fight if his physical condition was less than perfect. He represented himself in contract disputes and often displayed a better grasp of rules and laws than boxing officials and lawyers representing his opponents. He invested his money in Harlem businesses and, at one time, owned nearly an entire city block. A regular churchgoer, he often gave substantial amounts of money to charities. Twice he showed conspicuous mercy to opponents, once in 1943, when he refused to knock out former triple champion Henry Armstrong, and again in 1950, when he permitted challenger Fusari to last fifteen rounds in a title fight, while donating his entire purse to charity.

Despite his generosity, Robinson was one of the mostly widely disliked figures in boxing history. His self-serving behavior offended his neighbors in Harlem, who longed for his defeat. Reporters found him to be evasive and overbearing and were among his most severe critics. Although his fights were almost always exciting, boxing audiences usually rooted against him. Robinson continued to box until 1965, evidently sustained by his immense ego and convinced that he might yet regain a world title. Despite winning most of his fights, he suffered ten defeats and descended into mediocrity. In his final fight, a loss to Joey Archer in Pittsburgh on 10 November 1965, Robinson was knocked down and nearly out by an opponent who was a notoriously light hitter. His professional career spanned twenty-five years and 202 fights, of which he won 170, 110 by knockout. At his peak, he was unbeaten in ninety-one consecutive fights.

Having divorced his wife in 1960, Robinson married Millie Wiggins Bruce in May 1965; they had no children. He had squandered most of his $11 million in ring earnings through extravagant living and eventually had to sell his Harlem property, which was rapidly losing value. He moved with his wife to Los Angeles, where he worked as an actor in television and movies. In 1969 he founded the Sugar Ray Robinson Youth Foundation for inner city children. In his remaining years he lived comfortably but modestly. Suffering from diabetes and Alzheimer's disease, he died in Culver City, California.

Robinson is regarded by some authorities as the greatest fighter of all time, pound for pound. He has often been rated at or near the top of all middleweights, but better-informed ring historians place him instead at the top of the welterweight division, in which he fought during his best years. His style was the perfect combination of boxer and puncher. He hit cleanly and effectively with either fist. His speed afoot, quickness of hand, and defensive skills were second to none. However, the qualities that made him so good were less obvious: supreme self-confidence, the ability to quickly analyze an opponent's style and adjust his own tactics accordingly, and the ability to launch a sudden, devastating attack. In more recent years imitators have borrowed the cognomen of "Sugar Ray," but none has matched the original. Robinson was elected to the International Boxing Hall of Fame in 1990.

• Robinson wrote an autobiography, *Sugar Ray* (1970), with Dave Anderson. He was the subject of many articles in *The Ring* magazine, the best of which is W. C. Heinz, "Sugar Ray Robinson: Boxing's Greatest Pound-for-Pound," Feb. 1980, pp. 22–33, which also appears in Heinz, *Once They Heard the Cheers* (1979). Other useful articles in *The Ring* are Nat Fleischer, "Worshipped but Not Loved," Apr. 1959, pp. 8–9, 36, 56–57; "Why Does Robinson, at 44, Go On Fighting?" Dec. 1964, pp. 24–26, 47; Hardy Westerveld, "Sugar Ray Very Big in Acting Nowadays," Nov. 1968, pp. 12–13; Michael Silver, "Who Hit Robinson the Hardest? 'Artie Levine,' says Sugar Ray," Dec. 1975, pp. 28–31; and Fleischer, "Meet Mrs. Robinson," Sept. 1951, pp. 28, 30. A good article on Robinson is in Peter Heller, *In This Corner! The Candid View of the Champion's Corner* (1973), pp. 272–79. Robinson's complete record is in Herbert G. Goldman, ed., *The Ring Record Book and Boxing Encyclopedia* (1986–1987). An obituary is in the *New York Times*, 13 Apr. 1989.

LUCKETT V. DAVIS

ROBINSON, Theodore (3 June 1852–2 Apr. 1896), painter, was born in Irasburg, Vermont, the son of Elijah Robinson, a Methodist minister, and Ellen Brown. In 1855 the family moved west, settling eventually in Evansville, Wisconsin, where Robinson received most of his schooling. Beginning in childhood he showed a marked aptitude for drawing and painting, and his mother encouraged his talent. At the age of eighteen he studied art briefly in Chicago, but poor health—asthma and other respiratory ailments—forced his return to Evansville. As a competent organist, Robinson was able to earn a living at his father's former church while doing crayon portraits on the side. When Robinson's health did not improve, he was urged by his doctor to go to Denver, Colorado, then a refuge for those suffering from lung ailments, and he spent some months there in the early 1870s.

Robinson's western stay improved both his health and his spirits and revived his interest in pursuing a career as a painter. In 1874 he moved to New York City and enrolled at the National Academy of Design. During the next few years he studied at the academy, became friendly with other aspiring painters, and helped found the Art Students League of New York; he is credited with naming the organization.

Realizing that study abroad was a necessity for all aspiring American artists, Robinson went to Paris in 1876. There he became a pupil of the academic painters C. E. A. Carolus-Doran and Jean-Léon Gérôme while forming friendships with Scottish writer Robert Louis Stevenson and the American artists John Singer Sargent and J. Alden Weir. In the summer of 1879 Robinson traveled to Venice, where he spent some weeks in the company of James McNeill Whistler. Late that year Robinson returned to New York, confident of his abilities and intending to return someday to France.

In New York Robinson began to exhibit both figure paintings and landscapes, and in 1881 he was invited to join the newly formed Society of American Artists. To support himself, he taught art for a while at a private school. He disliked teaching, however, and left that job to accept assignments for interior decoration from wealthy clients like the Vanderbilts, for whom he painted murals at their New York mansion as an assistant to fellow artist John La Farge. He also freelanced as an art critic, contributing articles to various local publications. Finally in 1884 he was financially able to return abroad.

For the next eight years Robinson spent much of his time in France, alternating residence in Europe with brief periods in New York and visits to his Wisconsin home. From 1884 to 1886 he painted mostly in Barbizon, where his style grew broader as he moved beyond academic realism and drew closer to the new school of impressionism. In 1887 he moved to Giverny, in Normandy, Claude Monet's place of residence and the center of the impressionist movement. There, painting alongside Monet and his followers, Robinson developed his own impressionist style in both watercolors and oils. His debt to Monet is nevertheless apparent in many of his landscapes, including *The Valley of Arconville* (1887–1889) and *On the Tow Path* (1893–1894).

Robinson painted the countryside around him, but he not only depicted the landscape. A recurring theme in his work beginning around 1880 was the figure of a young woman in a natural setting, an idea he may have borrowed from his contemporaries Winslow Homer and Eastman Johnson, and from the idealized female figures then prevailing in popular American art. Critics later noted that Robinson's women, particularly in such paintings as *The Girl with the Dog* (1880) and *Girl Lying in Grass* (1886), were shown as though posed for a photograph, and the belief that he probably painted from photos was supported by his known interest in the camera and his frequent picture taking. These suspicions were confirmed in the early 1940s, when a cache of Robinson's photographs—many of them obvious antecedents of his artworks—was discovered in an old hotel in Giverny where he had once lived.

In late 1892 Robinson returned permanently to the United States, settling at a studio on East Fourteenth Street in Manhattan that had formerly belonged to Weir. That same year Robinson published an article on Monet in *Century* magazine. Living frugally and in declining health, he struggled in the last four years of his life to paint American landscapes in an impressionist style. He made several trips in 1893, visiting fellow artist John Twachtman in Connecticut and attending the Columbian Exposition in Chicago, where several of his paintings were exhibited. That summer he stayed in Napanoch, New York, where he painted one of his better-known landscapes, *Port Ben, Delaware and Hudson Canal*.

In 1895 Robinson had his first one-man show, at the Macbeth Gallery in New York City. The show later traveled around the country, and it continued to do so after his death. Robinson spent the summer of 1895 in Vermont, painting happily in the belief that he had at last discovered an American equivalent of Giverny. He planned to return, but he died the following spring at his studio in New York, two months before his forty-fourth birthday. He had never married. His death was officially attributed to asthma as well as poverty. In 1897 a poem he had written called "A Normandy Pastoral" was published posthumously in *Scribner's Magazine*.

In his lifetime Robinson had little success selling his work, although he won two major awards: the Webb Prize in 1890 for the best landscape painting shown by a young American artist at the Society of American Artists' annual exhibition in New York; and the 1892 Shaw Prize for figure painting. Robinson is credited with introducing and adapting the techniques of Monet and his followers to American art, but he did not live to see the flowering of American impressionism in the works of Weir, Twachtman, Childe Hassam, and their contemporaries.

A revival of interest in Robinson occurred in the 1940s following the discovery of his photographs, and a major show of his work was given at the Brooklyn Museum in 1946. In the early 1970s a retrospective organized by the Baltimore Museum of Art traveled to several U.S. galleries.

Today critics vary in their assessment of Robinson: Most of them, while valuing his work at Giverny over his American canvases, contend that all his paintings have a certain static quality; they lament his inability to capture the energy and liveliness of Monet's impressionistic style and criticize him for never quite eliminating a sentimental strain from his work. Despite these reservations, Robinson's place in art history as a pioneering American impressionist is assured, and today his works hang in the permanent collections of major U.S. museums.

• Biographical information on Theodore Robinson can be found in John I. H. Baur, *Theodore Robinson* (1946); Eliot Clark, *Theodore Robinson: His Life and Art* (1979); Sona Johnston, *Theodore Robinson* (1973); and Will H. Low, *A Chronicle of Friendships* (1908). See also "Theodore Robinson, Pioneer Impressionist," *Scribner's Magazine*, Dec. 1921, pp. 763–68; Florence Lewison, "Theodore Robinson: America's First Impressionist," *American Artist*, Feb. 1963, pp. 40–45, 72–73; and Lewison, "Theodore Robinson and

Claude Monet," *Apollo*, Sept. 1963, pp. 208–11. For an assessment of Robinson's place in American art, see William H. Gerdts, *American Impressionism* (1984).

ANN T. KEENE

ROBISON, Carson Jay (4 Aug. 1890–24 Mar. 1957), singer, musician, and songwriter, was born in Oswego, Kansas, the son of Albert Robison, a fiddler and dance caller, and Maggie Andrews, a singing pianist. The family moved to Chetopa, Kansas, during his early childhood. He may have had only a grade school education. Surrounded by the music of his parents, Robison got his first guitar at age twelve. His first composition is said to have been an Easter hymn written for his church choir. By age fifteen, he was singing and performing on the guitar professionally in the Midwest despite never having had a formal lesson. He worked in the Texas and Oklahoma oil fields and served in the army during World War I. Robison married Bernice Rucker in 1907, and they had one son. His wife died of tuberculosis when their son was five years old.

At age thirty Robison decided to pursue a career in music. In 1920 he began playing guitar for dance bands in Kansas City, including the Kansas City Nighthawks and the Coon-Sanders Band. Two years later he was performing on the pioneering radio station KDAF in Kansas City. It was at KDAF that he met Wendell Hall, "the Red-Headed Music Maker." Hall encouraged Robison to accompany him to Chicago and New York City, where they both found work in the recording industry. Later, in reflecting on his career, Robison attributed his success to Hall, whose biggest achievement as an entertainer was his 1923 hit, "It Ain't Gonna Rain No Mo."

In New York City Robison quickly found work as a studio guitarist and whistler for Victor Records. Robison had the amazing ability of whistling two tones in harmony, which can be heard on Hall's recordings of "Songbirds in Georgia" (1924) and "Whistling the Blues Away" (1924). Robison had a hit as a whistler with pianist Felix Arnoltin's novelty song, "Nola" (1926). On 13 August 1924 Robison played guitar on Vernon Dalhart's historic recording of "Wreck of the Old '97/The Prisoner's Song," which became country music's first million-selling recording. Robison accompanied other country artists besides Dalhart, but by 1926 he had emerged as Dalhart's regular duet partner, singing tenor harmony and, for the first time, receiving joint credit with Dalhart on the label. Dalhart, whose real name was Marion Try Slaughter, had a musical background in opera but recorded in many different styles. It was his hillbilly recordings that made him an internationally known singer and eventually landed him in the Country Music Hall of Fame.

Robison not only performed with Dalhart but also wrote many of his hits in the 1920s, including "The John T. Scopes Trial (The Old Religion's Better After All)" (1925), written under the pseudonym Carlos B. McAfee; "The Miami Storm" (1926); and "My Blue Ridge Mountain Home" (1927). He was a master at writing topical songs about natural disasters and news events. In the beginning of country recordings, performers were responsible for finding their own material, and many relied upon banjo and fiddle tunes, traditional folk ballads, and songs from Tin Pan Alley. Robison was one of a handful of songwriters who supplied country music with new songs to record, sometimes writing under pseudonyms such as Maggie Andrews and Carlos B. McAfee. He has been called the most versatile country songwriter of the 1920s and 1930s. In his essay on Robison, Robert Coltman wrote of him, "As an artist Robison stands curiously alone, a member of no easy category. He fathered an approach, a musical point of view, but never a style." Robison met his second wife, Catherine Barrett, at RCA Victor, where she worked as a secretary. The couple married in 1927 and had four children.

In 1928 Robison broke bitterly with Dalhart. He later explained that he was upset that violinist Murray Kellner had been replaced by Adelyne Hood while Robison was on vacation, but he objected even more to Dalhart's insistence on receiving half, rather than a third, of the royalties from the sheet music and recordings of Robison's songs.

The following year Robison teamed up with fellow Kansan Frank Luther, sometimes recording under the name "Bud and Joe Billings." Robison wrote one of their well-known songs, "Barnacle Bill the Sailor" (1929), in which Luther played the Fair Young Maiden and Robison played the lustful sailor. "Left My Gal in the Mountains" (1929) was another popular song from the duo. During this time, the duo, joined by Luther's wife Zora Layman, sometimes recorded as the Carson Robison Trio. Robison worked with Luther until 1932, and his musical style became more varied as he continued to experiment. Under the name "Carson Robison's Kansas City Jack-Rabbits," he recorded some jazz that was released on Victor's "race" series in 1929. "Race" is the name that the recording industry at that time gave music with black influences. Robison continued to stretch his musical style. Even a country song like "Going to the Barn Dance Tonight" (1932), which Robison recorded but did not write, stands out against other contemporary recordings with its introduction of crowd noise and the shout, "Partners for a quadrille!" Musically, Robison was far different from the rural music of the time, but the settings and themes of his songs were ones to which country folk could relate and which rural and urban buyers alike enjoyed. He issued his first songbook folio, *Carson J. Robison's Folio of Hill Country Songs and Ballads* (1929), which was sold through Sears.

Robison was one of the first country performers to turn to western imagery. The Carson Robison Trio experimented with the sound but without much success, and other bands would surpass them in popularizing the western element. In 1932, fully committed to the western image, he formed Carson Robison's Buckaroos, also performing under the name Pioneers. The group undertook a national tour, including a performance at the White House. They were the first country band to tour Britain and also toured Australia. The tour of Britain was extensive, and the band was very popular, playing London's Berkeley Hotel for thirteen weeks. Robison recorded for some British labels and, with the possible exception of Jimmie Rodgers, was the most popular country recording artist in Britain. Robison toured Britain again in 1936 and 1939 and hosted programs on Radio Luxembourg during this time period.

By the 1940s, Robison's performing career had crested, but he continued to record with a group named after his 140-acre farm in Pleasant Valley, New York, the Pleasant Valley Boys. During World War II, Robison, always the enterprising entertainer, recorded songs with titles like the self-penned "Hirohito's Letter to Hitler and Hitler's Last Reply to Hirohito" (1945) and "We're Gonna Have to Slap That Dirty Little Jap (And Uncle Sam's the Man That Can Do It)" (1941), which was written by Bob Miller. One of Robison's biggest hits was "1942 Turkey in the Straw" (1942). At the height of the McCarthy hearings Robison recorded "I'm No Communist" (1952), composed by Scott Wiseman. In 1948 Robison recorded his personal favorite and his highest charting song, the recitative "Life Gets Tee-jus, Don't It," which reached number three on the country charts and was even a number fourteen pop hit. Robison, the consummate professional songwriter adapting to the times, wrote "Rockin' and Rollin' with Granmaw " in 1956.

An all-around talent—singer, songwriter, guitarist, and arranger—and businessman, Robison was involved in the music business at a time when country music was steadily becoming more professional. He could not read music but was a masterful songwriter nonetheless. Not confined by genre or style, Robison's catalog numbers over 300 songs, including the western standard "Carry Me Back to the Lone Prairie" (1934). He was nominated for the Country Music Hall of Fame in 1970 and was inducted into the Nashville Songwriter's Hall of Fame in 1971. Robison's place in country music was unofficially recognized by his mention in the hit song, "Hillbilly Heaven" (1961).

The son from Robison's second marriage, Robert Robison, especially remembers his father's tremendous sense of humor, which included practical jokes, and his abilities as a storyteller. He also remembers the excitement of Friday night rehearsals in his family's New York City apartment and begging to be allowed to stay up and observe the musicians in action. Robison remained active up until his death in Poughkeepsie, New York.

• The Carson J. Robison Collection at the Leonard Axe Library, Pittsburg State University, consists of manuscripts, sheet music, recordings, business correspondence, and copyright records. For biographical information on Robison, see Robert Coltman, "Carson Robison: First of the Rural Professionals," *Old Time Music*, no. 29 (1978), a substantial source on Robison. Hugh Leamy, "Now Come All You Good People," *Collier's*, 2 Nov. 1929, discusses Robison's approach to writing topical songs. His songwriting is also discussed in Bob Dumm, "Two Men Who Sell New Songs for Old," *Farm and Fireside*, May 1927, and Elmore Peltonen, "Covered Wagon Songs," *Rural Radio*, Dec. 1938. Jim Walsh, "Favorite Pioneer Recording Artists: Vernon Dalhart," *JEMFQ* (Fall/Winter 1982), includes detailed information on Robison and Dalhart's collaboration and breakup, including excerpts of letters from Robison to the author.

An exhaustive discography of Robison's work would be a huge undertaking, but R. D. Morritt has published a partial discography in *New Amberola Graphic*, no. 29 (1979), no. 30 (1980), no. 32 (1980), no. 33 (1980), no. 38 (1981), no. 40 (1982), no. 42 (1982), no. 44 (1983), no. 45 (1983), and no. 49 (1984). *The Complete Encyclopedia of Popular Music and Jazz, 1900–1950* (1974) lists Robison's albums.

MARILEE BIRCHFIELD

ROBSON, Mark (4 Dec. 1913–20 June 1978), film director, was born in Montreal, Quebec, Canada, the son of George Robson, a real estate agent. His mother's name is not known. He attended Montreal public schools and secondary school at the Army and Navy Academy in San Diego, California. While a student at the University of California at Los Angeles, Robson got a part-time job in the Fox Pictures property department, an experience that turned him toward a career in the motion picture industry. Graduating from the University of California at Los Angeles in 1935 with a degree in political science, Robson briefly studied law at Pacific Coast University. He immediately returned to the movie industry with a full-time job carrying film cans at RKO Pictures and soon became apprenticed as a film editor at RKO. In 1936 he married Sara Riskind, with whom he had three daughters.

As an assistant to RKO film editor Robert Wise, Robson helped with the editing of *Citizen Kane* (1941) and *The Magnificent Ambersons* (1942), both directed by Orson Welles. Wise and Robson's work on *The Magnificent Ambersons* was especially extensive since Welles had moved on to another project and was not involved with the film during its post-production stages. Using the reactions of preview audiences as a guide, Wise and Robson reduced the playing time of Welles's version of the film by forty-five minutes. "I must say that the original version was simply marvelous: it was truly *The 'Magnificent' Ambersons* . . . but it was so advanced, so ahead of its time, that people just didn't understand it," Robson later explained in *The Celluloid Muse* (Higham and Greenberg, p. 206). Robson was also the editor of another Welles project, *Journey into Fear* (1943), directed by Norman Foster.

In 1942 RKO reassigned Robson to a low budget horror film unit, where he worked with Val Lewton and Jacques Tourner, masters of the genre. His first directorial assignment was *The Seventh Victim* (1943), a tale of devil worship in Greenwich Village. Robson's other films for the Lewton unit include *The Ghost Ship* (1943), *Youth Runs Wild* (1943), and two films starring Boris Karloff—*Isle of the Dead* (1945) and *Bedlam* (1946), which Robson co-wrote as well as directed. After Robson completed the last film, his contract with RKO was not renewed. He later said that his years with the poorly financed but critically admired Lewton unit taught him that a quality film could be made on a shoestring budget through the use of inventive direction, editing, and sound effects.

Robson worked for a time as an acting coach and story editor, returning to his career as a film director with *Champion* (1949), a moral tale about a disillusioned young veteran who becomes a sadistic prize fighter. The cheaply made film was popular with critics and audiences, giving Robson his first major success. It also made a star out of Kirk Douglas, who played the film's "anti-hero" leading man. Robson followed up with the equally well-received *Home of the Brave* (1949). Based on a play by Arthur Laurents, the drama examines racism in the U.S. military. Robson then directed three lackluster dramas for producer Samuel Goldwyn: *My Foolish Heart* (1949), with Susan Hayward; *Edge of Doom* (1950), with Dana Andrews; and *I Want You* (1951), with Dorothy McGuire. Robson returned to "message pictures" with *Bright Victory* (1951), starring Arthur Kennedy as a blinded soldier whose affliction helps him overcome his racial bigotry.

Robson's first big budget film was the unsuccessful *Return to Paradise* (1953), starring Gary Cooper as an American in the South Seas. After two more poorly received efforts—*Hell Below Zero* (1954), an adventure yarn with Alan Ladd, and *Phffft!* (1954), a comedy about a divorcing couple with Judy Holliday and Jack Lemmon—Robson had a major success with *The Bridges at Toko-Ri* (1955), starring William Holden as a World War II fighter pilot called up from the reserves during the Korean War. The film offered Oscar-winning flying sequences and a plot suggesting that American involvement in Korea was a futile endeavor. Even more successful was Robson's screen version of Grace Metalious's lascivious bestseller, *Peyton Place* (1957), with Lana Turner, Hope Lange, and Lloyd Nolan. Robson, producer Jerry Wald, and screenwriter John Michael Hayes earned high praise for crafting a fine film out of a trashy book. One of the biggest box office draws of the year, *Peyton Place* received nine Academy Award nominations, with Robson nominated for best director. His tastefully effective reworking of *Peyton Place* exemplified his positive attitude toward the production code. Robson believed that imaginative and conscientious filmmakers were not hindered by the code's restrictions.

The bespectacled and soft-spoken Robson earned a second Academy Award nomination for best director with *The Inn of the Sixth Happiness* (1958), a prestigious and moderately successful production starring Ingrid Bergman as a middle-aged English housemaid who becomes a missionary in China in the 1930s. A series of poorly received efforts, including *From the Terrace* (1960), with Paul Newman and Joanne Woodward; *The Prize* (1963), with Newman and Edward G. Robinson; *Von Ryan's Express* (1965), with Frank Sinatra; and *Valley of the Dolls* (1967), with Patty Duke and Susan Hayward, caused Robson's career to decline. In 1971 he formed a producing corporation, the Filmmakers Group, with Wise, who was now a prominent director, and Bernard Donnenfeld. For this company Robson made *Happy Birthday, Wanda June* (1971), a black comedy based on *Limbo* (1972), a drama about three women whose husbands are missing-in-action in Vietnam. Robson also directed *Earthquake* (1974), a "disaster" movie with an all-star cast including Charlton Heston and Ava Gardner. Dismissed by critics, *Earthquake* was a hit at the box office and won a special achievement Academy Award for visual effects. The film used "sensurround," a low frequency sound process that made theater seats seem to rumble during quake sequences. Although Robson took advantage of special effects when appropriate, he thought that first-rate directors should not emphasize technical wizardry but should focus their attention on working effectively with actors.

Other notable Robson films include *Roughshod* (1949), a western; *The Harder They Fall* (1956), a stark look at corruption in professional boxing; *The Little Hut* (1957), a comedy about a married couple and their best friend marooned on a tropical island; *Nine Hours to Rama* (1963), a story of events leading up to the assassination of Mahatma Gandhi; and *Daddy's Gone A-Hunting* (1969), a suspense thriller about a happily married woman being terrorized by a former boyfriend.

Robson died in London while making *Avalanche Express* (1979), a negligible spy picture with Robert Shaw and Lee Marvin. He was a skilled and versatile director, like many in Hollywood, but his distinctive work on *Champion, Home of the Brave, Bright Victory, Trial,* and *The Harder They Fall* sets him apart from countless other directors. These hard-hitting dramas brought a liberal, moralistic perspective to divisive social, economic, and racial issues that Hollywood studios typically avoided.

• The Mark Robson Papers, including scripts, production information, and correspondence, are in the Arts Library-Special Collections at the University of California at Los Angeles. See also Jerry Wald and Mark Robson, "The Code Doesn't Stultify," *Films in Review,* Dec. 1957, pp. 503–6, and Mark Robson, "Why You Hear What You Hear at the Movies," *Good Housekeeping,* July 1955, pp. 99–102. Charles Higham and Joel Greenberg, *The Celluloid Muse: Hollywood Directors Speak* (1969), offers an interview with Robson. Herbert G. Luft, "Mark Robson: Did Not Dally Overlong with Message Films," *Films in Review,* May 1968, pp. 288–97, is an overview of Robson's career. An obituary is in the *New York Times,* 22 June 1978.

MARY C. KALFATOVIC

ROBSON, Stuart (4 Mar. 1836–29 Apr. 1903), actor, was born Henry Robson Stuart in Annapolis, Maryland, the son of Charles Stuart, a lawyer, and a former Miss Johnson, whose given name is not known. The family moved to Baltimore soon after he was born. The young Robson became stage-struck when he saw John Owens perform, and his first attempt at drama was staging enthusiastic theatricals in a stable loft with his young friends, charging the neighborhood boys several pennies for admission. Robson claimed the Wilkes brothers and John Sleeper Clarke, popular performers, as his dramatic "chums" in Baltimore.

Robson's first employment was as a Congressional page, but he was not suited for the world of politics and returned to Baltimore for his acting debut with the Baltimore Museum. On 5 January 1852 he appeared in *Uncle Tom's Cabin As It Is*, written, according to Lewis C. Strang (1900), "to counteract the effect of Mrs. Stowe's work." He earnestly rehearsed his sole line, "Farewell, my mother—farewell, perhaps for ever!" but he suffered a violent attack of stage fright and moved the audience to roars of laughter. The debacle made him abandon his tragedian ambition and opt for comedy.

Robson turned his squeaky voice and other physical eccentricities into comic assets. He apprenticed in small and utility roles in the East and earned leading comic parts in a western tour in 1856, successfully returning to Baltimore the following year. During the early years of the Civil War he played in Cincinnati, St. Louis, Washington, and Richmond, then made his New York debut as Bob in *Old Heads and Young Hearts* in September 1862.

The following season Robson's career was boosted by his engagement with Mrs. John Drew, lessee of the prestigious Arch Street Theatre in Philadelphia. He was hired to replace Mrs. Drew's recently deceased husband, a popular Irish comedian, in the leading low comic roles. Of particular note was Robson's work with John's brother Frank Drew in *The Comedy of Errors*. Robson proved up to the job and remained in Philadelphia for three seasons, although he defied Mrs. Drew's house rules by smuggling both beer and friends into his dressing room. After an appearance in New Orleans, Robson acted for three seasons at the end of the 1860s at Selwyn's North Globe Theatre, Boston.

It was the comic policeman—usually Irish—at which Robson excelled, first in Philadelphia as the lead in *John Wopps, Policeman*, then as John Beat in the farce *Law in New York*, which ran at Boston's Howard Athenaeum. In the early 1870s he worked for three seasons at New York's Union Square Theatre; he then undertook an engagement at London's Gaiety Theatre, appearing with Charles R. Thorne, Jr., in *Led Astray*, among other pieces.

Robson suffered financially with a failed tour in 1876 of *Two Men of Sandy Bar*, by Bret Harte, but in 1877 he regained much of his $6,000 loss with a new collaboration with William Crane in a production of *Our Boarding House* at New York's Park Theatre. Robson and Crane continued to work together for a dozen more years, excelling in their version of *The Comedy of Errors* and in Bronson Howard's *The Henrietta* (1887). Eventually Robson bought out Crane's share of the partnership, and they parted on good terms, to pursue more lucrative solo careers. Robson built a repertory that included *Is Marriage a Failure?* and *She Stoops to Conquer*. One of the best-loved and most respected actors of the late nineteenth century,

Robson was also distinguished for the roles of Picard in *The Two Orphans*, Gaston in *Camille*, and Bob Acres in *The Rivals*.

Robson married twice. His first wife, whose maiden name was Johnson and with whom he had one daughter, died in 1890. The following year he married the Australian actress May Waldron, who had been a member of Daly's company and with whom he continued to perform. They had one son. Robson died in New York City.

Robson's appearance on stage was described by a contemporary, Charles M. Skinner, as having a sleek and youthful contour and countenance; his eyes are large and innocent; he is in a state of constant astonishment at the world he so recently came into; he has the solemnity of an infant; he walks with a deliberate teeter; and on facing his audience absently sways from side to side, sometimes with hands depending loosely from the wrists; his mouth is mobile and good-natured, and has a way of dropping slightly open whenever he intensifies surprise; all his movements, though quick, have an ease and softness. (McKay and Wingate, p. 356)

A fellow actor, Nat C. Goodwin, asserted that "analytically he was master of more of the fundamental rules of acting than even Lawrence Barrett who was an authority" (Goodwin, p. 30).

• Contemporary accounts of Robson include Lewis C. Strang, *Famous Actors of the Day in America* (1900); Frederick Edward McKay and Charles E. L. Wingate, *Famous American Actors of Today* (1896); Amy Leslie, *Some Players* (1899); and other actors' autobiographies, such as Nat C. Goodwin, *Nat Goodwin's Book* (1914). A particularly notable interview with him is in the *New York Dramatic Mirror*, 1 Feb. 1896; a good summary of his career and descriptions of performances were compiled in William Young, *Famous Actors and Actresses on the American Stage: Documents of American Theatre History*, vol. 2 (1975). Obituaries are in the *New York Times*, 30 Apr. 1903, and the *New York Dramatic Mirror*, 9 May 1903.

NOREEN BARNES-McLAIN

ROBUS, Hugo (10 May 1885–14 Jan. 1964), sculptor, was born in Cleveland, Ohio, the son of Edward Robus, an iron worker, and Anne Daniels. His family opposed his early desire to be an artist. Nonetheless, Robus graduated from Cleveland's Central High School in 1903 and from the Cleveland School of Art (now the Cleveland Institute of Art) in 1907, completing the "Regular Pictorial Art Course," which focused on easel painting. He studied design with Horace E. Potter, life drawing with Carl F. Gottwald, and impressionist techniques in oil painting with Henry G. Keller, who also taught Marsden Hartley, Charles Burchfield, and William Zorach. From 1905 to 1911 Robus handcrafted jewelry, carving tiny figures in ivory and setting them into articulated metal work, at Potter's arts and crafts design workshop, where he also lived. Potter, an influential mentor, provided financial support, a home, a profession, and lessons in design and art history.

From 1907 to 1909 Robus studied at New York's National Academy of Design with Emil Carlsen, who focused on painterly texture and color, and with Edgar Melville Ward (brother of sculptor John Quincy Adams Ward), who emphasized academic techniques of anatomical and life drawing. Robus appreciated the simplicity and sun-drenched colors of modern paintings he found in the galleries and museums, and he admired the swiftly executed figure drawings by the French sculptor Auguste Rodin on view at Alfred Stieglitz's the Little Galleries of the Photo-Secession (aka "291"). Equally prepared for careers in commercial design and painting, Robus decided on painting for his life's work.

In Europe from 1912 to 1914 Robus aligned himself with modern artists in Paris. He knew well the pioneering painters of color abstraction who emphasized musical analogies to color—the American synchromists Stanton Macdonald-Wright and Morgan Russell and the Czechoslovakian artist František Kupka. Robus evolved from using chiaroscuro and descriptive hues to a fauve palette of pure warm and cool colors juxtaposed for maximum intensity. He modeled clay figures at the École de la Grande Chaumière under the direction of Emile-Antoine Bourdelle, then the greatest modern teacher of sculpture in Paris. In France Robus lived and painted out-of-doors for five months in Brittany and Cassis and for two months in Vernon. He made trips to see art and architecture in Bremen, Düsseldorf, and Cologne, Germany; Pisa, Rome, Naples, Pompeii, Florence, and Venice, Italy; Tunis, Tunisia; and Algiers, Algeria. His later plans to return to Europe were thwarted by World War I, and he rarely traveled again.

In 1915 Robus married Irene Bogart Chubb, whom he had known at the Cleveland School of Art; they had one son. The paintings Robus created from 1915 to 1920 are avant-garde and the most experimental works of his career. He was part of three New York groups of vanguard artists and writers: the Modern Art School on Washington Square South (where he taught design and painting), the Sunwise Turn Book Shop on East Thirty-first Street (a center for contemporary and Asian art and literature that exhibited and sold the batik designs of Hugo and Irene Robus and Marguerite and William Zorach) and Fourteenth Street (where he lived). After 1918 the Robuses also lived in the artists' colony in New City, New York.

Modeling figurative sculptures in clay and casting and refining them in plaster preoccupied Robus after 1920. *Modelling Hands* (1920–1922, Forum Gallery) and *The General* (1922, Hirshhorn Museum and Sculpture Garden, Smithsonian Institution), show his knowledge of the work of the Italian futurist Umberto Boccioni. Also evident are the hallmarks of Robus's mature sculptures—human themes, abstract forms, smoothly curved planes, and serpentine contours.

Robus's eight full-length, life-size figures created in the 1920s are original in concept and form. *Blackbottom* (1925, Forum Gallery) concretizes the swift, whirling motion of an animated dancer, probably Josephine Baker. In *Vase*, Robus planted the female figure up to her ankles at the base and provided her with a detachable head that can be supported properly on her neck or hung nonchalantly on the headless woman's right index finger. She is sculpturally whole, even when figuratively she has lost her head. Robus's partial figures, *Despair* (1927, Whitney Museum), *Supplication* (1925), *Invocation* (1928–1929, Israel Museum), *North Wind* (1930), and *Dawn* (1931), are both individuals and personifications, expressing the duality of physical and spiritual being. Robus sold his first sculpture, *Summer Afternoon*, in 1925. It was commissioned in silver by Marjorie Content, then the wife of Harold Loeb, editor of the avant-garde magazine *Broom*. Its Art Deco characteristics include long, finely incised parallel lines describing strands of hair, decorative elongation of the arms, serpentine composition, brilliant reflective surfaces, elegance, and stylish languor. *Girl Washing Her Hair* (1933), Robus's white marble signature sculpture, was installed during the 1940s and 1950s near the entrance of the Museum of Modern Art. The continuous, curving contour of the sleek, streamlined head and torso, doubled in the mirrored surface of the polished stainless steel sheet on which it rests, completes a visual circle and embodies Robus's philosophy of the synthesis of motion with abstract human form. Robus resisted the appeal of the tribal sculptures and direct carving techniques that engaged contemporary American modern sculptors William Zorach, Robert Laurent, and John B. Flannagan. His article in *Critique* articulates his strong preference for modeling sculpture.

Robus did not exhibit his sculpture until 1933, but he was then included in every Whitney Museum sculpture annual or biennial from 1933 to 1964. He showed regularly in group shows in New York City at the Museum of Modern Art, the Sculptors Guild (he was a founding member in 1938), and the Brooklyn Museum, and in Philadelphia at the annual juried exhibitions of the Pennsylvania Academy of the Fine Arts and at the Philadelphia Museum of Art. His most important solo exhibitions were organized by the American Federation of Arts (sixteen venues, 1960–1962); the National Collection of Fine Arts, Smithsonian Institution (three venues, 1979–1980); and the Forum Gallery (1963, 1966, 1974, and 1980).

• Archival resources include the Hugo Robus Papers, diaries, letters, foundry records, and published documents at the Archives of American Art, Smithsonian Institution (partially recorded on microfilm N705–06); the Hugo Robus Scrapbook, compiled by Irene Robus and owned by the family; the negatives of photographs of Robus's sculpture by Consuela Kanaga (1930s), by Carroll Siskind (1940s and 1950s), and by eeva-inkeri (1970s); and the artist's records at the Forum Gallery, New York City, which has represented his work since 1961 and his estate since 1964. Two essays written by Robus were published as "The Sculptor as Self Critic," *Magazine of Art* 36 (Mar. 1943): 94–98, and "Artists and Sculptors," *Critique* 1 (Nov. 1946): 12–15. The key published resource for Robus is Roberta K. Tarbell, *Hugo Robus (1885–1964)* (1980), which includes a biographical essay, critical analyses of his works, his one-man and group exhibitions listed chronologically with citations for pertinent published critical reviews, and a catalogue raisonné of his sculpture and studies. See also Tarbell, "Hugo Robus Pictorial Works, 1912–20," *Arts Magazine* 54 (Mar. 1980): 136–40, and Wallace Putnam, *Manhattan Manners* (1935), the story of an unnamed sculptor who is Hugo Robus. An obituary is in the *New York Times*, 15 Jan. 1964.

ROBERTA TARBELL

ROCHAMBEAU, Comte de (1 July 1725–12 May 1807), French general, was born Jean-Baptiste-Donatien de Vimeur in Vendôme (now in the department of the Loir-et-Cher), France, the son of Joseph-Charles de Vimeur, the marquis de Rochambeau, governor of the Château of Vendôme, and grand bailiff of the region, and Marie-Claire-Thérèse Begon, the governess of the duc d'Orléans's children. As a younger son, he was first destined for the clergy and educated by Oratorian and Jesuit priests, until the death of his older brother opened the way for him to pursue a military career. Rochambeau's first military service came in the War of Austrian Succession. Commissioned on 24 May 1742, he saw considerable action, was wounded, and emerged at the end of the war a colonel of infantry. On 29 December 1749 he married Jeanne Thérèse da Costa, the daughter of a wealthy bourgeois family of Portuguese origins; they had two children. With the outbreak of the Seven Years' War, he returned to action in central Europe and reached the grade of major general in 1761, two years before the war's end. After 1763 Rochambeau devoted his energies to improving military training in the French army. He was appointed governor of Villefranche in 1776, and in 1779 he was named commander of the advance guard of a French army assembled for an aborted invasion of England.

The rebellion of England's American colonists provided French leaders with an opportunity to avenge the humiliating defeat of 1763. After providing limited, unofficial, surreptitious aid, France signed a treaty of alliance with the new republic in February 1778. The first French military operations, attacks on the British garrisons at Newport in the summer of 1778 and Savannah in the autumn of 1779, were disillusioning failures. In early 1780 King Louis XVI decided to send an expeditionary corps to serve in the United States under the orders of General George Washington. To command this force he selected the experienced Rochambeau whom he simultaneously promoted to lieutenant general.

Rochambeau had the daunting task of preparing this transatlantic operation. On 2 May 1780 his army of some 5,500 officers and men sailed from Brest for Newport, Rhode Island, where it arrived on 11 July. Their safe arrival by no means ended the problems of the French. When they reached America more than 700 men were ill, and scores died in the following weeks. By 21 July a British fleet blockaded Newport. Within a few days of their landing, the marquis de Lafayette came to Newport as Washington's personal envoy to urge an immediate attack on New York. Rochambeau, who was promoted to brigadier the year before Lafayette was born, patiently explained his problems and the dire consequences that precipitous action might have. Meanwhile, he had to contend with American prejudices and suspicions about the French, the consequence of generations of hostility and conflict.

Typically, Rochambeau was calm and methodical in dealing with these difficulties. He first saw to the health of his men and the establishment of defenses. He imposed exemplary discipline on his command and paid for his purchases in hard cash, thereby conciliating all but the most hostile Yankees. Still tensions continued, due to differences in language, customs, religion, even food. Also, some French officers felt that they were being charged excessively for goods of inferior quality. Occasionally during their stay in Newport conflicts arose, for example, the murder of an American by a French corporal in August 1780 (for which the corporal was executed) and the shooting of a French sentinel by an American a few months later. Rochambeau and American authorities were quick to hush up such incidents.

Meanwhile American military and political fortunes reached their nadir. Benedict Arnold's treason in September 1780, the mutinies of line units from New Jersey and Pennsylvania the following January, and growing British success in the South reflected and intensified disillusionment among both Americans and French with the American cause by 1781. Limited expeditions sent by Rochambeau to the Chesapeake in February and March provided no real relief. Even Washington was reaching the limit of his patience when he met with Rochambeau in Wethersfield, Connecticut, on 22 May 1781. The French commander agreed to join Washington in a combined attack on New York, the most important British position in North America.

The French forces began leaving Newport on 9 June and joined the American army outside New York four weeks later. On 14 August, as siege preparations were proceeding, Rochambeau received a dispatch from Admiral de Grasse, who wrote that he was leaving the Caribbean with a fleet of nearly thirty ships of the line and an army of more than 3,000 men for Chesapeake Bay, where he planned to remain until mid-October. Washington then made the most critical decision of the war: within four days the allied armies were on the march south to Virginia, an objective that Rochambeau clearly preferred to the English stronghold of New York.

Since early summer Lafayette's American corps had been harassing the British under Lord Cornwallis in Virginia. By August the English had taken up positions on the York River that would, they expected, allow them ready access to supplies, reinforcements, or, if necessary, evacuation by sea. De Grasse arrived in Chesapeake Bay at the end of August, and the troops aboard his fleet joined forces with the Americans under Lafayette in establishing positions around the British in Yorktown. On 5 September the French ships encountered the English fleet under Admiral Thomas Graves, fought them to a draw, and managed to retain control of Chesapeake Bay.

By the end of September Washington's and Rochambeau's armies had arrived from the north, and the siege commenced. The battle was a classical eighteenth-century operation, and no one was better fit to conduct it than Rochambeau, the veteran of more than a dozen European campaigns. His skills in handling people also contributed to military success by inducing the impulsive and independent de Grasse to cooperate fully, by minimizing Franco-American friction, and by ensuring a continuous flow of essential supplies. The inexorable advance of the allied lines reflected Rochambeau's expertise and personality. When the inevitable capitulation occurred, Cornwallis's representative, General Charles O'Hara, tried to surrender the British commander's sword to Rochambeau who, characteristically, referred him to Washington.

After victory celebrations the French settled into winter quarters in Virginia, where Rochambeau won the good will of the inhabitants by the same policies that had succeeded in Rhode Island. In July 1782 the French marched northward, again encamped with Washington's army near New York, and proceeded to Boston, whence they departed in December. Meanwhile Rochambeau had given up his command, and he sailed for France, arriving on 20 February 1783.

The disorder and violence unleashed by revolution in his own country in 1789 disturbed Rochambeau, but he remained at his duties and was promoted to the rank of marshal in 1791. In May of the following year, however, he resigned. Like many other nobles, Rochambeau was arrested during the Terror and was imprisoned from April to October 1794. He then resumed his retirement on the family estates near Vendôme and rarely visited Paris. A notable exception came in 1801 when Napoleon Bonaparte introduced some generals to the old marshal as his "pupils." With typical graciousness Rochambeau replied, "The pupils have far surpassed their master." A half-dozen years later he died quietly at his country home.

• Rochambeau's papers as well as other materials on France's role in the American Revolution are in the Manuscript Division of the Library of Congress, *The Papers of Jean Baptiste Donatien de Vimeur, Comte de Rochambeau, 1777–94*, in 15 volumes and containing about 1,800 items. Although an additional volume contains a handwritten inventory, the collection is poorly organized and contains much duplication; it is, nevertheless, an indispensable source. Less useful but more accessible is M. W. E. Wright, ed., *Memoirs of the Marshal Count de Rochambeau, Relative to the War of Independence of the United States* (1838; repr. 1971). A well-written, reliable biography is Arnold Whitridge, *Rochambeau* (1965). Howard C. Rice, Jr., and Anne S. K. Brown, eds., *The American Campaigns of Rochambeau's Army, 1780, 1781, 1782, 1783* (2 vols., 1972), is rare among such lavish productions in that its utility equals its beauty. The best account of Rochambeau's expedition is Lee Kennett, *The French Forces in America, 1780–1783* (1977).

SAMUEL F. SCOTT

ROCHE, Josephine Aspinwall (2 Dec. 1886–29 July 1976), social worker and New Deal administrator, was born in Neligh, Nebraska, the daughter of John J. Roche, a lawyer, banker, and mining executive, and Ella Aspinwall, a former teacher. Roche spent her childhood in Nebraska, where her father was a member of the state legislature. While Roche was at Vassar College, where she earned a B.A. in 1908, her parents moved to Denver, Colorado, which remained her hometown for much of the rest of her life. After working for a short while as a probation officer there, she returned east.

Roche did settlement work for the New York Probation Society, and in 1910 she earned a master's degree in sociology from Columbia University, where she became friends with Frances Perkins. Displaying her approach to the social problems of the time, she wrote her thesis on "Economic Conditions in Relation to the Delinquency of Girls." She returned to Denver, where, under police commissioner George Creel, she became the city's first policewoman. Events like the Triangle Shirtwaist fire in New York City in 1911 and the Ludlow massacre in Colorado in 1914 epitomized for her the social and industrial conditions that cried out for change. She campaigned for Bull Moose presidential candidate Theodore Roosevelt in 1912 but supported Democratic candidate Woodrow Wilson in 1916. Roche served as executive secretary of the Colorado Progressive Service (1913–1915), giving talks, for example, on why "all social workers should go into politics." She directed the Girls Department in the Denver Juvenile Court under Judge Ben Lindsey from 1915 to 1918.

Between 1915 and 1925 Roche's Progressive agenda on social policy took her to New York City and Washington, D.C. Her service began during World War I when she served in 1915 as a special agent for the Belgian Relief Commission. In 1917, after the United States entered the war, President Wilson appointed George Creel to head a Committee on Public Information with the task of mobilizing public opinion in support of U.S. participation in the war. Creel recruited Roche, "a strong right arm in my Colorado days," as a member of the committee and director of the Foreign Language Education Service, where, as one writer put it, she interpreted immigrants to America and America to immigrants. She continued to direct the Foreign Language Information Service as a private agency after the war. In 1923 she undertook the directorship of the editorial division of the U.S. Children's Bureau in the Labor Department. In 1920 she married Edward Hale Bierstadt, an advertising writer. They had no children and divorced in 1922.

In 1925, with her parents in failing health, Roche returned to Denver and served as a referee of the Denver Juvenile Court. Her father, president and general manager of the Rocky Mountain Fuel Company, a large coal mining concern in Colorado, died in January 1927, and she inherited his interest in the company. Not long afterward she hired Edward P. Costigan, former United Mine Workers (UMW) attorney and later U.S. senator from Colorado, as company counsel and John R. Lawson, a former president of the Colorado State Federation of Labor, as vice president. Next she proposed that the United Mine Workers be invited to unionize her company's employees, which was accomplished by September 1928. This development constituted a breakthrough in labor relations in the West. After the Ludlow massacre of 1914, the UMW had played no role in Colorado until Roche took control of Rocky Mountain. She served as company president from 1929 to 1934 and again from 1937 to 1950.

After Congress enacted the National Industrial Recovery Act in 1933, Roche participated in meetings in Washington, D.C., that established a national code for the bituminous coal industry. In 1934 she acceded to popular demand that she run in the Democratic primary for the Colorado governorship. Running on a campaign of "Roosevelt, Roche, and Recovery," she took Denver and won the labor vote but lost with 45 percent of the statewide vote to incumbent Edwin C. Johnson, who opposed the New Deal.

Roche then became a New Deal administrator. Treasury Secretary Henry Morgenthau recruited her for a position as assistant secretary in the Treasury Department, where she took charge of the Public Health Service from late 1934 through late 1937. That position led to other roles in shaping New Deal social policy. Roche served as the Treasury Department's representative on the President's Committee on Economic Security, which drafted the recommendations that emerged as the Social Security Act, and as a member of the Social Security Advisory Committee (1937–1939), on which she replaced Lucy Randolph Mason. From their establishment in 1935 she served as chair of the executive committee of the National Youth Administration and as a member and then the chair of the Interdepartmental Committee to Coordinate Health and Welfare Activities. While on the Interdepartmental Committee she continued the work she had begun in planning the Social Security Act, helped coordinate the federal government's public health programs, and turned her attention to developing a national health program. She convened a National Health Conference in July 1938, but her committee and the American Medical Association were unable to agree on a common proposal, and Senator Robert F. Wagner's national health bill died in committee in 1939.

Roche's New Deal service waned in the late 1930s, but her commitments continued. From 1939 to 1944 she served as president of the National Consumers' League, and she lectured widely on such topics as "Our Stake in Industrial Democracy," "Women and Industry," and "Health Security—For Some or All?" In 1948 she accepted John L. Lewis's invitation to become director of the UMW's new Welfare and Retirement Fund, which provided millions of dollars in pensions, hospitalization, and medical care for miners and their families. She held that position until her retirement in 1971.

Roche's career in social services and her commitment to a Progressive agenda ranged from before World War I through the New Deal to long after World War II. She labored to change prevailing attitudes and conditions regarding juvenile delinquency, child labor, adult wages and working conditions, old-age insurance, and medical well-being. In 1936 the magazine *American Women* selected her as one of the ten outstanding women in the nation. She was termed "Denver's Joan of Arc" in the 1910s and was mentioned as a credible candidate for the presidency in the 1930s. After her many years as a social worker, mining executive, and government administrator, she died in a nursing home in Bethesda, Maryland.

• The Josephine Roche Papers are in the Western Historical Collection at the University of Colorado in Boulder. The fullest rendition of her life is Marjorie Hornbein, "Josephine Roche: Social Worker and Coal Operator," *Colorado Magazine* 53 (1976): 243–60. Other good sketches are John H. Monnett and Michael McCarthy, "Josephine Roche," in *Colorado Profiles: Men and Women Who Shaped the Centennial State* (1987); Elinor M. McGinn, "She Made a Difference: The Work of Josephine Roche," a paper presented at the annual meeting of the American Historical Association's Pacific Coast Branch, Corvallis, Oreg., Aug. 1992; and Mabel Cory Costigan, "A Woman's Way with Coal Mines," *Woman's Journal* (Mar. 1929): 20–21, 37. Books touching on Roche's public life are George Creel, *Rebel at Large: Recollections of Fifty Crowded Years* (1947); Mary Van Kleek, *Miners and Management: A Study of the Collective Agreement between the United Mine Workers of America and the Rocky Mountain Fuel Company* (1934); and Susan Ware, *Beyond Suffrage: Women in the New Deal* (1981). An obituary is in the *New York Times*, 31 July 1976.

PETER WALLENSTEIN

ROCHE, Martin (15 Aug. 1855–4 Jun. 1927), architect, was born in Cleveland, Ohio. Nothing is known about his family beyond the fact that he moved with them to Chicago in 1857. It appears that the bulk of Roche's formal education took place in the Chicago public schools, although obituary writers mention private tutors and classes at the Art Institute of Chicago.

Roche was apprenticed to a cabinetmaker at age fourteen, but in 1871 he entered the office of architect William LeBaron Jenney as a draftsman. Jenney was the best-trained Chicago architect of the period immediately after the great fire of 1871, and in Jenney's office Roche met his future partners, Ossian Simonds and William Holabird. The latter two men left Jenney's employ in 1880 to found the firm of Holabird & Simonds. They were joined by Roche in 1881, and the firm was renamed Holabird, Simonds & Roche. As Simonds became more involved with his practice of landscape design, he spent less time at the firm, withdrawing altogether in 1883 at which date the firm became Holabird & Roche, the name it would retain until the time of Roche's death.

In the firm Roche was considered to be the designer, the man responsible for the artistic side of the practice, while Holabird devoted himself more to securing commissions, running the office, and working with the client on the practical aspects of the work. The exact assignment of responsibilities varied considerably over the years, however, and both men clearly had major roles in the appearance of almost all of the firm's most important buildings.

During the earliest years, which were slow ones for the firm, Roche designed furniture in addition to working on small architectural commissions. The first major commission, received in 1884, was for the planning of Fort Sheridan, an army base in Chicago's north suburbs. The initial phase of construction, completed about 1895, included dozens of buildings by the firm. It was soon followed by several large commercial buildings in the Chicago Loop, notably the Tacoma (1886–1889), Marquette (1891–1895), and Old Colony (1893–1894) buildings. In these buildings the firm successfully managed to design for its clients speculative office buildings that were inexpensive to build but boasted a rich and satisfying decorative treatment. By the early 1890s Holabird & Roche had emerged, along with Burnham and Root, as one of the largest firms in Chicago and in the United States.

The firm expanded its practice in the last years of the nineteenth century and early years of the twentieth century, producing works like the massive Cook County Courthouse/Chicago City Hall, the elegantly decorated LaSalle (1907–1909) and Sherman House (1906–1911) hotels and the University Club (1904–1908), all in Chicago. The latter, an essay in adapting the Gothic style to a highrise steel frame building, has usually been considered Roche's masterpiece. After the death of Holabird in 1923 Roche continued to guide the firm, joined now by Holabird's son, John Holabird, and John Wellborn Root, Jr., son of the partner of Daniel Burnham, until Roche's death in 1927, when the firm was reorganized as Holabird & Root. Although Roche continued to be active in the practice, the younger men increasingly took over day-to-day responsibilities in the mid-1920s. Major buildings in the 1920s included the Grant Park Stadium (Soldier Field, 1919–1926), the Palmer House (1919–1927), and the Stevens (later Conrad Hilton) Hotel (1922–1927), all in Chicago, the Nicollet Hotel in Minneapolis (1923–1924), and the Schroeder Hotel in Milwaukee (1925–1928).

Roche was a lifelong bachelor, living for many years with his sister and brother-in-law. At the time of his death in Chicago, most writers emphasized his enormous and eclectic output, ranging from simple loft buildings like the McCormick Buildings (later called the Gage Group, 1898–1900) to immense classical buildings like the Cook County Courthouse and Chicago City Hall to the convincingly solid Gothic of the University Club. Writers in sympathy with European avant-garde modernist ideas of the 1920s, notably Sigfried Giedion and Carl Condit, tended to focus on the more utilitarian works, claiming Holabird & Roche as precursors of the later European International Style. More recent scholarship has returned to a more inclusive view.

• A laconic diary Roche kept from 1888 to 1917 is at the Chicago Historical Society. Studies of his work from a modernist perspective include Sigfried Giedion, *Space, Time and Architecture* (1941), and Carl Condit, *Chicago School of Architecture* (1964). Further information about Roche and his firm is in Robert Bruegmann, *Holabird & Roche and Holabird & Root: An Illustrated Catalog of Works* (1991) and *The Architects and the City: Holabird & Roche of Chicago, 1880–1918* (1996). The major sources for his life are the obituaries in Chicago newspapers and the architectural press, notably an appreciation by his former employee and colleague Lucian Smith, *Architecture* (Aug. 1927), and one by Robert Craik McLean, the *Western Architect* (July 1927).

ROBERT BRUEGMANN

ROCK, John Charles (24 Mar. 1890–4 Dec. 1984), physician and advocate of planned parenthood, was born in Marlborough, Massachusetts, the son of Frank Sylvester Rock, a businessman, and Ann Jane Murphy. He and his twin sister benefited from the amenities of an upwardly mobile Irish Catholic household, where rugged older brothers were taught to respect John's interests in sewing, music, and theater, as well as his piety as a daily communicant at the Immaculate Conception Church. In 1906 he left home to attend the High School of Commerce in Boston. After graduation in 1909, he worked for the United Fruit Company on a banana plantation in Guatemala, where he was moved by the plight of the poor and was dismissed after nine months for his lack of enthusiasm. Another job as a cashier for an engineering firm in Rhode Island confirmed that he lacked an aptitude for business. In search of a vocation, he entered Harvard College; lettered in track; performed in Hasty Pudding, the theatrical society; and tried to revive Newman Club, the Catholic students' organization. He graduated in three years with the class of 1915, received his M.D. from Harvard Medical School in 1918, and spent World War I as a resident in surgery at Massachusetts General Hospital. He concluded his medical education with residencies in obstetrics at Boston Lying-In Hospital and in gynecology at the Free Hospital for Women. After he began private practice in 1921, Rock quickly became prominent in one of the world's most distinguished medical communities. In 1925 he married Anna Thorndike of Boston, a mathematics major from Bryn Mawr; they had five children.

In 1922 Rock was appointed assistant clinical professor in the Harvard Medical School. In 1924 he began an infertility clinic at the Free Hospital for Women, which served as a focus for his research until his retirement from Harvard in 1956. Rock became one of the leaders in the translation of advances in reproductive physiology into clinical medicine, with publications on the nature of the menstrual flow, the behavior and physiology of the human ovum, the role of hormones in the female reproductive cycle, and the mechanisms of conception. In collaboration with such colleagues as George Smith and Arthur Hertig, he developed the technique for dating samples of the endometrium, surgical maneuvers to open and reconstruct damaged oviducts, and techniques for artificial insemination. He collected a famous series of human embryos, extending until the seventeenth day, that became stock material in medical texts. In 1948 Rock, in collaboration with Miriam Menkin, claimed to have achieved the first in vitro fertilization of a human ovum. Although he probably mistook clumping of ova for cell division, his research got much publicity and helped win his promotion to the rank of clinical professor of gynecology in 1947.

From his early days as a resident delivering babies in Boston tenements, Rock expressed concern over the suffering associated with frequent, unwanted pregnancies. In 1931 he was the only Roman Catholic among fifteen leading Boston physicians who signed a petition to repeal the Massachusetts statute that prohibited giving contraceptive information. In 1936 he opened the first clinic in the United States devoted to the rhythm method of contraception, and in 1937 he was a member of an American Medical Association committee that recommended that contraceptive techniques be included in the medical curriculum. Experience had taught Rock that the female reproductive cycle varied enough to make the rhythm method unreliable, yet he believed that erotic fulfillment was essential to marital happiness. As one of Boston's most successful doctors and a leader in biomedical sex research, he became convinced that Catholic teaching on sexuality made unrealistic demands on married couples and had destructive effects on the quality of family life. Although Rock enjoyed his high status in cosmopolitan Boston society and defied the sexual teachings of clerics whom he regarded as out of touch with normal human beings, he maintained a strong emotional attachment to the church and was a daily communicant.

Rock's anomalous position as a Catholic sex researcher contributed to his intense interest in discovering means to predict and control ovulation. He used female sex hormones extensively in the treatment of infertility and discovered that when ovulation was suppressed in barren women, an encouraging percentage of them conceived when the hormone therapy ended. When orally active synthetic analogues of progesterone and estrogen became available in the early 1950s, Rock was one of the first to employ them in his medical practice.

In 1953 Rock accepted an invitation from Gregory Pincus of the Worcester Foundation for Experimental Biology to participate in an intensive effort to develop an oral contraceptive. Pincus and Rock had worked together since the 1930s because much of Pincus's research on ovulation and fertilization in rabbits paralleled Rock's work with humans. At the behest of the feminist birth-control advocate Margaret Sanger, and with generous funding from her ally Katharine Dexter McCormick, Pincus had begun systematic screening of ovulation-suppressing drugs in 1951, and he had reached the point in his research where clinical work with humans was necessary. Rock's reputation as a distinguished and conscientious physician proved essential to the effort to develop, test, and win approval for the first oral contraceptive, Enovid, which was approved by the U.S. Food and Drug Administration for use as a contraceptive in 1960. Rock played a crucial role in convincing chemists at G. D. Searle and Company, the manufacturers of Enovid, that large doses of synthetic hormones could be ingested by healthy women without prohibitive health risks, and his clinical data and immense prestige were essential to government approval of "the pill."

In 1960 Rock announced to a national meeting of fertility specialists that the pill had to be acceptable to the Catholic church as a morally permissible alternative to the rhythm method. In 1961 he published articles in *Good Housekeeping* and *Reader's Digest* repeating this claim. He fully developed his argument in *The Time Has Come: A Catholic Doctor's Proposals to End the Battle over Birth Control* (1963). A tall and elegant exemplar of Irish fey, Rock became the leader of an international effort among the laity to reshape the church's positions on marital sexuality. He received intense media attention during the period from June 1964, when Pope Paul VI disclosed the creation of a special commission on population, the family, and natality, until the optimism among liberal Catholics was dampened by the papal encyclical *Humanae Vitae* in July 1968. During this period of ferment, Rock was awarded an honorary doctor of laws degree by Harvard (1966), and a majority of U.S. Catholics concluded that the church's position on contraception was wrong.

In 1969 Rock sold his practice and moved to a farmhouse in Temple, New Hampshire, where he continued to receive academic friends and journalists and to defend oral contraceptives and his belief that the celibate hierarchy of his church failed to comprehend the profound role of human sexuality in spiritual bonding within the family. He died in Peterborough, New Hampshire.

• Rock's papers are in the Countway Library of Medicine, Boston. In 1949 he published, with David Loth, *Voluntary Parenthood*. Loretta McLaughlin's biography, *The Pill, John Rock, and the Church: The Biography of a Revolution* (1982), should be compared with John D. Biggers, "In Vitro Fertilization and Embryo Transfer in Historical Perspective," in *In Vitro Fertilization and Embryo Transfer*, ed. Alan Trounson and Carl Wood (1984), and with James Reed, *From Private Vice to Public Virtue: The Birth Control Movement and American Society since 1830* (1978). An obituary is in the *Boston Globe*, 5 Dec. 1984.

JAMES W. REED

ROCKEFELLER, Abby Aldrich (26 Oct. 1874–4 Apr. 1948), philanthropist, was born Abby Greene Aldrich in Providence, Rhode Island, the daughter of Nelson Wilmarth Aldrich and Abby Pearce Chapman. After establishing himself in business in Rhode Island, her father was elected to the U.S. House of Representatives. In 1881 he won a seat in the U.S. Senate, where he became a powerful chair of the Finance Committee. His political skills and passion for art were his legacy to Abby.

Until she was seventeen Abby Aldrich was tutored in the family schoolroom by a Quaker governess. From 1891 to 1893 she attended Miss Abbott's School for Young Ladies to pursue a rigorous academic curriculum. Following her debut in 1893 she took courses at the local lyceum, read widely in her father's library, and accompanied him to the museums and historic buildings of Europe. She worked in behalf of the Providence Day Nursery, the Rhode Island Exchange for Women's Work, the Dorrance Home for Aged Colored Women, and the Providence Young Women's Christian Association (YWCA). As her mother retreated from official life, Abby became her father's hostess in Washington.

In October 1894 Abby met John D. Rockefeller, Jr., a student at Brown University and the only son of the founder of the Standard Oil Trust. John was the triumphant product of his mother's Christian fervor, "home-made and hand-trained," in the words of a family adviser. He was stiff and inhibited and had no small talk and few social skills—a striking contrast to the impulsive, self-assured, adventurous daughter of an extroverted political clan. But they fell in love and as John would recall to his biographer sixty years later, "She treated me as if I had all the *savoir-faire* in the world and her confidence did me a lot of good" (Fosdick, p. 60). Indeed it did. They were married seven years later in 1901, and the marriage perpetuated a business dynasty and founded a political one.

For fifteen years Abby's life was shaped by John's reclusive personality and the bitter public hostility toward the Standard Oil monopoly, epitomized by the figure of John D. Rockefeller, Sr. Abby and John studiously avoided gratuitous displays of great wealth, the one exception being their mansion on West Fifty-fourth Street, the largest private residence in Manhattan in 1913. Publicity was anathema, especially as regards the six Rockefeller children. Abby, with her gregarious, affectionate ways, was able in some measure to soften the impact on the children of her husband's unbending expectations and stern discipline. Unlike women of other wealthy families she was intimately involved in all corners of their daily lives. In a fundamental sense she humanized both the fortune and the Baptist rectitude. As one Aldrich cousin phrased it, "She was the yeast in the bread."

In every aspect of his public and private life, John D. Rockefeller, Jr., esteemed his wife for her sharp, intuitive judgment and her original insights and depended on her for emotional comfort and validation. He quite literally wanted her nearby whenever possible and was relaxed only in her presence. Abby met such needs unreservedly, whatever the price, and it can safely be stated that such a relationship brought her passion, satisfaction, and stress in equal measure.

When John decided in 1904 that he should build for his father a great country house overlooking the Hudson River at Pocantico, Abby brought her aesthetic skills, already honed, to the project. (In 1994 "Kykuit," under the aegis of the National Trust, was opened to the public.) Deftly and subtly she educated John in the world of art, closed to him during his barren childhood. She became his intimate, if unofficial, consultant when he restored Colonial Williamsburg and built Rockefeller Center. In 1914 a bitter strike of miners against the managers of the Colorado Fuel and Iron Company erupted in tragedy in a tent colony at Ludlow, Colorado. Thirteen members of miners' families were killed by the machine gun fire of hired militia. Both John and his father, major absentee stockholders in the company, became the targets of national outrage. In the aftermath of the crisis Abby worked closely with William Lyon MacKenzie King, a Canadian labor expert, to enlarge and solidify John's commitment to progressive industrial relations.

By the time the United States declared war on Germany in 1917, the Standard Trust had been formally broken up, and John D. Rockefeller, Sr.'s ruthless organization of the oil industry was acknowledged as a crucial factor in an Allied victory. The great fortune was largely disbursed—$500 million to philanthropy and $500 million to John. With the public perception of Rockefeller power softening, Abby was free to enter a decade of public service. She applied her personal vision and her respect for the new and the untried to social needs that might not be on a typical foundation agenda.

The dreary mining camps of Ludlow and the flimsy, overcrowded women's dormitories around the munitions factories convinced her of the dire need for cheerful, affordable housing. In 1919, with $4,000 of her own money and $7,000 from John, she built, furnished, and landscaped a model house for a working family near the Standard Oil refinery in Elizabeth, New Jersey. Discarding the idea of serving one family, she converted the Bayway cottage into a community center with rotating activities—a baby clinic, language and craft instruction, current events, and recreation. For twenty years she bore the general overhead costs, hired the staff, and shared intimate experiences with the immigrant mothers.

As chair of the National Housing Committee of the YWCA, Abby realized her dream of building a hotel in 1921–1922 for professional and business women in Washington, D.C. No commercial developer lavished more attention on a project than she did on the Grace Dodge Hotel. She worked closely on the design, both exterior and interior, with Duncan Candler, her favorite architect. She introduced many innovative conveniences and in perhaps another reflection of the Ludlow experience, insisted on special consideration for the health and welfare of the employees.

In 1924 Abby bought her first piece of modern art, a watercolor by German expressionist Erich Heckel. The contemporary works that she viewed in Germany under the guidance of William Valentiner, the director of the Detroit Museum of Art, were so different from the porcelains and medieval tapestries favored by John as to be from a different universe. John's Puritan upbringing was a formidable barrier between him and modern art. Throughout their marriage he had tried to follow her artistic enthusiasms for Italian primitives, Japanese prints, and Persian miniatures. But when her zest for discovery led her into the bewildering arena of twentieth-century art, he refused to follow. The artists' desire for self-expression seemed to him without humility or discipline.

Sensitive to his discomfort, Abby commissioned Donald Deskey to create a private gallery for her on the seventh floor of the Fifty-fourth Street mansion. There she arranged continually changing exhibitions of works in her collection so that she might study them. There, many of her friends and family saw modern American art for the first time. But John did not venture up there. The gallery was Abby's world, insulated from John's distaste for it.

The most compelling and demanding project in Abby's public life during the decade of the 1930s was the Museum of Modern Art. Lillie Bliss and Mary Sullivan joined her in founding it in 1929. A. Conger Goodyear was the first president, Alfred Barr the first director. But everyone who observed the institution in its formative years agreed that Abby was the moving spirit. Without her it would not have come into existence. Deprived of her persistence it would not have survived. It was her creation as much as Barr's, and her intelligent, albeit quiet, management carried it through to success.

Abby as treasurer raised the necessary capital, although she did not as yet have access to the vast Rockefeller fortune. Philip Johnson contended that it must have been painful to her to be Mrs. John D. Rockefeller, Jr., and not be able to make major contributions to her beloved museum. Instead she used her Aldrich "pin money" to build her private collection with the museum in mind. She bought the work of both American and European artists, employing her great eye and skill and foresight, concentrating on drawings, watercolors, and prints. Important oils were often too expensive. By 1940 she had transferred most of her holdings to the Museum of Modern Art, including works by Peter Blume, Walt Kuhn, Charles Sheeler, and Preston Dickinson. The Europeans were represented, among others, by Pablo Picasso, Amedeo Modigliani, and Henri Matisse. Her print collection made the Museum of Modern Art the greatest repository of twentieth-century prints in the world. In 1939 she gave her folk art collection—the most comprehensive in the United States—to Colonial Williamsburg, where it is housed in the Abby Aldrich Rockefeller Folk Art Center.

"Remember me most cordially to Mr. Rockefeller (who I find hard to forgive his granite indifference to what interests you so much)," Alfred Barr wrote after visiting Abby in Maine. Such granite indifference was troubling, but Abby understood the depth of John's needs and his disinclination to share her even with his own children, much less with an institution dedicated to art that alienated him.

But Abby plowed ahead, compromising here, staking out her position there. Her concept of the Museum of Modern Art went far beyond her personal aesthetic preferences. It was her deep conviction that art deserved to be brought into the lives of ordinary people and that even the most extreme and unpopular art has a right to be seen. "To me art is one of the great resources of my life," she wrote her son Nelson. "I feel that it enriches the spiritual life and makes one more sane and sympathetic, more observant and understanding."

John could not hold out against her forever. In 1933, when the museum was in danger of losing the Bliss collection, he stepped in with $200,000 to assure that it went to the museum. When the museum expanded in 1937–1939, John gave the property at 10 West Fifty-fourth Street for the Abby Aldrich Rockefeller Sculpture Garden. His implacable hostility toward modern art never softened, but his strong sense of fairness and his unequivocal love for Abby made it inevitable that he capitulate.

Following Abby Aldrich Rockefeller's death in Manhattan, the *New York Times* (7 Apr. 1948) editorialized, "Hers was the spirit that held [the family] together." An ailing Matisse designed the stained glass window for the Union Church of Pocantico as a memorial to her. Alfred Barr wrote Abby's son Nelson that although the outside world assumed she could do almost anything with her wealth and power, "few realize what positive acts of courage her interest in modern art required. Not only is modern art artistically radical but it is often assumed to be radical morally and politically and sometimes indeed it is. But these factors which might have given pause to a more circumspect or conventional spirit did not deter your mother."

• Abby Rockefeller's correspondence, diaries, and other significant papers are at the Rockefeller Archive Center, Pocantico Hills, North Tarrytown, N.Y. Additional manuscript sources are in the Museum of Modern Art Archives; the Colonial Williamsburg Foundation Archives, Williamsburg, Va.; the Nelson Aldrich Papers, Manuscript Division, Library of Congress; and the Winthrop Rockefeller Collection, University of Arkansas. Correspondence, as it pertains to the Museum of Modern Art, is available on microfilm through the Archives of American Art, Washington, D.C. Published works include *Abby Aldrich Rockefeller's Letters to Her Sister Lucy* (1957); Bernice Kert, *Abby Aldrich Rockefeller* (1993); Mary Ellen Chase, *Abby Aldrich Rockefeller* (1950); Raymond B. Fosdick, *John D. Rockefeller, Jr.: A Portrait* (1956); Russell Lynes, *Good Old Modern* (1973); and Aline Saarinen, *The Proud Possessors* (1958). An obituary is in the *New York Herald Tribune*, 6 Apr. 1948.

BERNICE KERT

ROCKEFELLER, John D. (8 July 1839–23 May 1937), industrialist and philanthropist, was born John Davison Rockefeller in Richford, New York, the son of William Avery Rockefeller and Eliza Davison. The family moved several times during his youth: to Moravia in 1843, to Owego in 1850, and to Ohio in 1853, settling in Strongsville, then in Parma in 1855, and finally in Cleveland. His father, an itinerant business-man, dealt in horses, lumber, salt, patent medicines, and herbal remedies and often lent money at profitable rates of interest. He gave his son practical training in business, but the father's frequent, long absences burdened young Rockefeller with larger responsibilities within the family and helped foster a close relationship with his mother, a devout Baptist whose emphasis on proper moral conduct, discipline, thrift, and hard work would remain with her son.

Rockefeller's formal education began at what he later called a "good country school" in Owego, followed by the Owego Academy in 1852. During 1853–1855 he boarded in Cleveland and attended Central High School. After taking a series of business courses at Folsom's Commercial College in Cleveland, followed by a six-week job search, Rockefeller began his business career on 26 September 1855 as a clerk and bookkeeper in the wholesale produce commission house of Isaac L. Hewitt and Henry B. Tuttle. In the spring of 1859, unhappy with his salary, Rockefeller resigned and, with a $1,000 loan from his father at 10 percent interest, formed a partnership with Maurice B. Clark to establish their own commission house. Clark & Rockefeller was profitable from the beginning and flourished during the Civil War.

Rockefeller was an earnest, disciplined, and ambitious young businessman in a growing city, and his pious upbringing provided a source of both strength and self-doubt. He used aphorisms to remind himself to follow the road of proper conduct. "Keep your own accounts. Speak evil of no man," he wrote on the front of an account book in January 1857. He later recalled holding nightly "intimate conversations" with himself, cautioning against the sins of greed, pride, and over-ambition. "I was afraid I could not stand my prosperity," he wrote later in *Random Reminiscences*, "and tried to teach myself not to get puffed up with any foolish notions." The Baptist church also helped fortify his faith and moral discipline. Baptized at the Erie Street Baptist Church in Cleveland in 1854, he took an active role in the leadership of the church.

Rockefeller's partner in church affairs was Laura Celestia Spelman, a former teacher in the Cleveland schools whom he married in 1864. The couple had three daughters and a son. Although he struck many of his business acquaintances as quiet, cold, and reserved, Rockefeller exhibited a patient, warm, and sociable personality at home and among friends. His recreations included driving and racing his horses, winter sleighing, ice skating, and later, bicycling.

In 1863 Rockefeller and Clark entered the oil-refining business in partnership with Samuel Andrews, an acquaintance of Clark's who was an expert in refining crude oil into illuminating oil. Andrews managed the technical operations while Rockefeller and Clark handled the firm's business affairs. By 1865 Andrews, Clark & Company had the largest refinery in Cleveland, but tensions had arisen over Rockefeller's plans to expand the business. This would not be the only time in his career that his expansive plans for the busi-

ness—and the borrowing and risk they entailed—put him at odds with more cautious colleagues. In February 1865 Rockefeller bought out Clark's interest for $72,500, and he and Andrews continued the business as Rockefeller & Andrews. He and Clark soon dissolved their commission merchant partnership as well, and Rockefeller entered the oil industry full time. Rockefeller's buyout of Clark represented "the beginning of the modern oil industry," according to industry historian Daniel Yergin (p. 35), for it began a process that ultimately brought order to the chaotic industry in the form of the Standard Oil Company.

Rockefeller proceeded with his plans for expanding the business, building a second refinery and in 1866 organizing a company in New York, managed by his brother William, to handle both the eastern trade and the export of kerosene. The company was reorganized in 1867 as Rockefeller, Andrews & Flagler after Henry M. Flagler and Stephen V. Harkness invested in it. Harkness remained a silent partner, but Flagler and Rockefeller developed a close personal friendship and a strong working relationship. Between 1867 and 1870, as increasing crude production drove down oil prices and as the railroads engaged in periodic rate wars, Flagler negotiated with the competing railroads to secure lower freight rates for his firm. He used the greater efficiency and capacity of his firm's refineries to guarantee a volume of freight that other refiners could not match. These lower rates helped mitigate against the advantages enjoyed by refiners in other areas who were closer to either the sources of crude oil or the markets for refined oil. Although such discounts and rebates were common in the railroad industry, many of Rockefeller and Flagler's competitors viewed the preferential rates as an unfair advantage.

To attract new capital for further expansion, the partnership was reorganized in January 1870 as the Standard Oil Company, a joint stock corporation with Rockefeller, the largest stockholder, as president. Worried about the overproduction of crude oil, excess refining capacity, and falling prices, Rockefeller began to develop a plan to bring order to the volatile industry. He envisioned a cooperative alliance of refiners, with a strong Standard Oil at the nucleus of the organization; such a combination of refiners, he believed, could effectively coordinate the industry to the mutual benefit of refiners, producers, and railroads. In January 1872 the capitalization of the Standard was increased from $1 million to $2.5 million as Rockefeller and Flagler began to acquire other Cleveland companies and implement their plan.

At the same time Rockefeller lent his support to the South Improvement Company, a plan launched by the railroads that aimed to end price wars, restore transportation rates to a profitable level, and guarantee each oil-carrying line an equitable share of the traffic while offering preferential rates to member refiners. Oil producers rebelled against the plan when it became public in February 1872. Especially troublesome was the provision for drawbacks, by which the participating railroads would pay to member shippers a portion of the higher rates charged to nonmember shippers. The producers vowed to boycott anyone associated with the scheme, and Standard's supplies of crude oil quickly dried up. In April the South Improvement Company was dissolved, and the boycott ended.

Rockefeller's reputation among the oil producers was severely damaged by his association with the South Improvement scheme, but he continued to implement his own plan for organizing the industry. By the end of 1872 he had acquired thirty-four former rivals, consolidated Standard's control of refining in Cleveland, and made inroads among New York's refiners. At the same time Flagler secured even lower shipping rates, and the Standard began to increase the products it manufactured beyond kerosene to include lubricants, candles, paints, and dyes.

Attempts by both refiners and producers to bring order to the industry continued without success in 1872–1873. In August 1872 Rockefeller became president of the National Refiners Association, an effort to allocate crude oil among member refiners and thus control production and prices, but the refiners' association lasted less than a year. In the meantime Rockefeller continued to expand the Standard. Acquisitions in 1873 increased its role in the retail trade, and it entered the pipeline business in 1874–1876, consolidating its holdings into the United Pipe Lines in 1877, one of the three major systems in the industry. Between 1874 and 1876 the Standard acquired major refiners in Philadelphia, Pittsburgh, New York, the oil regions of Pennsylvania, and Parkersburg, West Virginia. These new Standard firms were acquired secretly, no announcement was made, and they continued to be operated under their previous names by the old owners, now Standard stockholders, who were in a strategic position to learn about the plans of Standard's competitors and report them to Rockefeller and Flagler.

In 1877 Rockefeller and the Standard defeated a major challenge to its growing power. The Empire Transportation Company, a subsidiary of the Pennsylvania Railroad, entered the oil-refining business and sought to put together a network of independent refiners and producers. Rockefeller and his colleagues canceled the Standard's contract with the Pennsylvania, lowered the price of kerosene in markets served by the Empire and its allies, and persuaded Standard's allied railroads, the Erie and the New York Central, to reduce shipping rates to cut into their rival's business and profits. The rate war and the railroad strike of 1877 led to serious financial problems for the Pennsylvania, and in October 1877 the Standard bought the refining assets of the Empire, which went out of business. That same month the Standard acquired a major pipeline system and, in a new agreement with the railroads, became the refiner responsible for allocating oil shipments among the roads according to an agreed-upon formula in exchange for reduced rates. Over the next two years the Standard pushed its advantage and made other acquisitions. By 1879 Standard Oil controlled 90 percent of the nation's oil-refining capacity and domi-nated both the transportation of refined oil and the piping and storage of crude oil in Pennsylvania's oil regions. Rockefeller's plan for bringing discipline and order to the chaotic industry had been successfully, and profitably, implemented.

During the 1880s the Standard fended off challenges to its domination of the industry, continued to expand its domestic and export sales, and, at Rockefeller's insistence, aggressively acquired crude supplies in the Lima oil fields in Ohio and Indiana. His plan was vindicated in 1888 when Standard chemist Herman Frasch developed a method for adequately refining the sulfur-based oil from these fields, making the acquisitions highly profitable.

Rockefeller and his colleagues struggled to devise both an efficient management system and a satisfactory legal organization for their growing business. An innovative system of committees evolved during the 1870s to oversee specific aspects of the daily operations, with an executive committee directing the entire operation. This system permitted greater efficiency through the detailed analysis of operations and the coordination of the work among geographically dispersed plants. As an Ohio corporation, however, Standard Oil could not legally own property in other states or hold stocks in other companies. During the 1870s various Standard officials were designated as trustees and given responsibility for particular stocks in Standard subsidiaries, but this system grew unwieldy, and in 1879 Standard officials named three trustees to hold the stock of the various companies allied with the Standard of Ohio.

Problems with the trustee device led to a new innovation in 1882, the Standard Oil Trust agreement, which created the first modern trust in American business history. It established a nine-member board of trustees that held the stock of the Ohio company as well as that of its subsidiaries, and the trustees issued to the former stockholders certificates that entitled them to a proportionate share of the stock dividends. In 1890 the Ohio attorney general challenged this arrangement in court, and after the Ohio Supreme Court annulled the charter of the Ohio corporation in 1892, Standard officials moved control of the trust to the Standard Oil (New Jersey) and several other units coordinated by interlocking directorates. By 1899, however, officials realized that this arrangement also was unstable legally, and they reorganized the Standard Oil (New Jersey) as a holding company for all Standard Oil stock.

The methods by which Rockefeller and his associates gained control of the industry made them many enemies, who believed that Standard Oil's collusion with the railroads on freight rates, its secret acquisitions of other companies, and its use of threats and cutthroat price cutting to induce competing refiners to sell or join its combination were unfair and unethical manipulations of the marketplace. Beginning in the late 1870s Rockefeller and his colleagues faced a series of court challenges and legislative inquiries into the Standard's policies and practices. The first public revelations about Standard's business practices came in 1879 as a result of the New York legislature's investigation of railroad practices, led by Alonzo B. Hepburn. The findings of such investigations aroused public sentiment for both the Interstate Commerce Act of 1887, which prohibited discriminatory rates and practices in interstate shipping, and the Sherman Antitrust Act of 1890, which prohibited the restraint of free trade. The press also turned its attention to the Standard Oil, beginning with Henry Demarest Lloyd's "The Story of a Great Monopoly" in the March 1881 *Atlantic Monthly*. Although he testified at various hearings and in court, Rockefeller refused to respond in the press to public attacks on his business and his character, and many people believed his silence confirmed the accuracy of the charges.

In the 1890s the stress and strain of business, the growing demands on his philanthropy, and the public attacks began to affect Rockefeller's health, and in 1901 he lost all of his hair. In 1897 Rockefeller retired from the daily management of Standard Oil, relinquishing his duties to John D. Archbold. But his retirement was not announced publicly, and Rockefeller continued to personify the Standard Oil Company for its many critics and the general public during a period of intense investigation and publicity. He retained the title of company president until the end of 1911, when the Standard Oil trust was dissolved and reorganized into thirty-eight companies in compliance with the U.S. Supreme Court's antitrust decision of 15 May 1911.

As the Standard's largest stockholder, Rockefeller amassed a fortune that is estimated to have peaked at $900 million in 1913, making him one of the wealthiest men of the industrial era. He donated much of his wealth to charity and the philanthropic foundations he created. During his lifetime his philanthropic gifts totaled $540 million, 82 percent of which went to the endowment of the Rockefeller Institute for Medical Research (1901; renamed Rockefeller University in 1965) and three grant-making philanthropies: the General Education Board (1903), the Rockefeller Foundation (1913), and, in memory of his wife, who had died in 1915, the Laura Spelman Rockefeller Memorial (1918). Rockefeller thus became a pioneer in the development of a new entity in American society, the privately endowed general-purpose foundation.

The fact that Rockefeller's most notable philanthropic gifts occurred after 1900 has overshadowed his long and conscientious tradition of charitable giving. His correspondence and account books, beginning with Ledger A in 1855, reveal the extent of his giving to churches, missions, temperance work, old age homes, hospitals, schools and colleges, Young Men's Christian Associations, and other charitable societies. The Baptist church was at the heart of Rockefeller's philanthropic network, although he often gave to churches of other denominations. Between 1864 and 1903 in the Cleveland area alone he made charitable gifts totaling more than $1.6 million to 136 organizations and eighteen individuals. During the 1880s and

1890s, as his national reputation grew, requests for aid came in from farther away, and he became desperate in his attempt to keep up with the flood of appeals. In the early 1880s he turned to the American Baptist Home Mission Society (ABHMS) for help in evaluating appeals and in dispensing his charity. The head of the ABHMS, the Reverend Henry L. Morehouse, was especially concerned with the development of Baptist higher education, particularly for African Americans, and channeled more of Rockefeller's support toward these purposes. In early 1884, for example, Morehouse was influential in securing support from Rockefeller that allowed an Atlanta school for African-American women to preserve its single-sex status, and the founders renamed the school Spelman Seminary (Spelman College in 1924) in honor of Rockefeller's abolitionist in-laws.

In the late 1880s the wealthiest Baptist was caught up in the debate about where to locate the great Baptist university that denominational leaders advocated. In May 1889 the head of the new American Baptist Education Society (ABES), the Reverend Frederick T. Gates, persuaded Rockefeller to pledge $600,000 toward a $1 million endowment to establish the university in Chicago; by 1910 Rockefeller's contributions to the University of Chicago totaled $35 million. Between 1890 and 1914 Rockefeller also supported Baptist education more broadly, using the ABES to channel more than $800,000 to thirty-four different schools.

In 1891 Rockefeller hired Gates away from the ABES and brought him to New York to organize and oversee his philanthropic work. He soon entrusted Gates with the resolution of a number of problematic investments, including his holdings in the Mesabi iron range in Minnesota. Gates's astute management of the iron-ore interests enabled Rockefeller to sell his holdings to J. P. Morgan's U.S. Steel Corporation in 1901 for $88.5 million, with an estimated profit of $50 million.

Both Gates and John D. Rockefeller, Jr., who joined his father's office in 1897, played significant roles in shaping Rockefeller's twentieth-century philanthropy. The Rockefeller Institute for Medical Research, led by Simon Flexner, was the first institution in the United States devoted solely to biomedical research. Its earliest work was conducted through grants-in-aid to researchers in various laboratories, but by 1906 it had constructed its own laboratory in New York City and assembled a distinguished staff of investigators. The General Education Board worked for "the promotion of education within the United States, without distinction of race, sex, or creed," and it spent $324 million before ceasing operations in 1964. Rockefeller also established the Rockefeller Sanitary Commission for the Eradication of Hookworm Disease (1909), giving it $1 million for an aggressive five-year public health campaign in the South, led by Wickliffe Rose. In 1913 the commission's work was expanded to combat additional diseases worldwide with the creation of the International Health Board of the Rockefeller Foundation. The purpose of the foundation, incorporated in New York after public criticism thwarted attempts to obtain a congressional charter, was "to promote the well-being of mankind throughout the world." It focused on medicine and public health in its early years and in 1914 established the China Medical Board, which built the Peking Union Medical College to develop modern western medicine in China.

For all of the criticism Rockefeller received for unethical business practices, it was the controversy aroused by one of his philanthropic gifts that prompted him to abandon his policy of silence in the face of public criticism. In 1905 Washington Gladden denounced as "tainted money" Rockefeller's gift of $100,000 to the Congregational Board of Foreign Missions. The controversy abated following the revelation that the board had solicited the donation. At the urging of Gates and his son, Rockefeller began to increase his public presence, granting more interviews, appearing more frequently in public, and dispensing dimes to people he met. Between 1917 and 1920 he gave a series of interviews to journalist William O. Inglis that was to form the basis of a friendly biography, but the book was never published.

In retirement Rockefeller traveled between his estates in Cleveland (until the house, "Forest Hill," burned in 1917) and Pocantico Hills, New York, and homes in Lakewood, New Jersey, and Ormond Beach, Florida. His estates allowed him to indulge his interest in landscape architecture. After he took up golf in 1899, it became his favorite pastime. He died at his home in Ormond Beach and was buried in Lakeview Cemetery in Cleveland.

Although Standard Oil's domination of the oil industry and Rockefeller's enormous fortune made him one of the most controversial and hated men of the industrial age, Rockefeller's legacy includes one of the first fully integrated modern business corporations, an influential biomedical research institute, one of the largest private foundations in the United States, and a tradition of family philanthropy that has extended over four generations.

• Rockefeller's papers, including correspondence, letterbooks, account books, ledgers, and scrapbooks, form part of the Rockefeller Family Archives at the Rockefeller Archive Center in Sleepy Hollow, N.Y. The Archive Center also holds the records of the philanthropies Rockefeller established: Rockefeller University, the General Education Board, the Rockefeller Sanitary Commission for the Eradication of Hookworm Disease, the Rockefeller Foundation, and the Laura Spelman Rockefeller Memorial. Significant portions of Rockefeller's papers have been published in microform: *The William O. Inglis Interview with John D. Rockefeller, 1917–1920*, ed. David Freeman Hawke (microfiche, 1984; 2-vol. book, 1989); and *Papers of John D. Rockefeller, Sr.* (1991), a microfilm collection that includes incoming business correspondence, business investment correspondence, and office correspondence. Additional manuscript material has been published in *"Dear Father"/"Dear Son": Correspondence of John D. Rockefeller and John D. Rockefeller, Jr.* (1994), ed. Joseph W. Ernst, former archivist for the Rockefeller family.

Rockefeller's autobiography was serialized in the *World's Work* beginning in Oct. 1908 and was subsequently issued as *Random Reminiscences of Men and Events* (1909).

The standard biographies of Rockefeller remain the two works by Allan Nevins, *John D. Rockefeller: The Heroic Age of American Enterprise* (2 vols., 1940) and *Study in Power: John D. Rockefeller, Industrialist and Philanthropist* (2 vols., 1953). More recent appraisals of Rockefeller include Ron Chernow, *Titan: The Life of John D. Rockefeller, Sr.* (1988), John Ensor Harr and Peter J. Johnson, *The Rockefeller Century* (1988), and Hawke, *John D.: The Founding Father of the Rockefellers* (1980), a lively introduction for general readers.

The literature on Rockefeller and the Standard Oil Company is voluminous. For general readers, Daniel Yergin, *The Prize: The Epic Quest for Oil, Money and Power* (1991), offers a useful and readable introduction to Rockefeller's leadership of the Standard; scholars seeking a thorough analysis of Rockefeller's and Standard Oil's role in the development of the oil industry should consult Harold F. Williamson and Arnold R. Daum's two-volume history, *The American Petroleum Industry*, especially the first volume, *The Age of Illumination, 1859–1899* (1959). The most detailed study of this period is Ralph W. Hidy and Muriel E. Hidy, *Pioneering in Big Business: History of Standard Oil Company (New Jersey), 1882–1911* (1955). Edward N. Akin, *Flagler, Rockefeller Partner and Florida Baron* (1988), provides a detailed study of the Rockefeller-Flagler partnership and the early years of the Standard. Early critical works include Henry Demarest Lloyd, *Wealth against Commonwealth* (1894), and Ida M. Tarbell, *The History of the Standard Oil Company* (1904).

On specific aspects of Rockefeller's philanthropy, see Florence Matilda Read, *The Story of Spelman College* (1961), Thomas W. Goodspeed, *The Story of the University of Chicago, 1890–1925* (1925), and Richard J. Storr, *Harper's University: The Beginnings* (1966). See also George W. Corner, *A History of the Rockefeller Institute, 1901–1953: Origins and Growth* (1964), Raymond B. Fosdick, *Adventure in Giving: The Story of the General Education Board* (1962) and *The Story of the Rockefeller Foundation* (1952), and John Ettling, *The Germ of Laziness: Rockefeller Philanthropy and Public Health in the New South* (1981).

KENNETH W. ROSE

ROCKEFELLER, John D., Jr. (29 Jan. 1874–11 May 1960), philanthropist, was born John Davison Rockefeller, Jr., in Cleveland, Ohio, the son of John Davison Rockefeller, Sr., an industrialist, and Laura Celestia Spelman. Rockefeller was the third child born to his parents but the only son, the circumstance that defined his life and career. When Rockefeller was born, his father was already wealthy from the success of the Standard Oil Trust, and the boy was raised with the expectation that he would be his father's successor in business and philanthropy. Rockefeller, Jr., spent most of his childhood in Cleveland until his family moved to New York in 1884. With Rockefeller, Sr., frequently absent, the dominant influence in the home was Laura Spelman Rockefeller, a pious woman who gave her youngest child tender attention and a strict sense of moral obligation.

Rockefeller was first educated by private tutors and then at the Browning School in New York. He left home for Brown University in 1893 a painfully shy, deeply religious, and resolutely earnest young man. Family advisers had recommended Brown for Rockefeller on the assurance that its president, E. Benjamin Andrews, would oversee the young man's educational, social, and spiritual development. President Andrews impressed upon young Rockefeller the obligation of the Christian to engage the issues of day. Being part of a large community of equals was a challenge that Rockefeller would never face again, but he struggled to overcome his passion for unobtrusiveness. A member of the glee club and manager of the football team, he was elected to Phi Beta Kappa and graduated with a B.A. in 1897.

While attending college in Providence, Rockefeller met his future wife, Abigail Aldrich, the daughter of Winthrop Aldrich, the U.S. senator from Rhode Island. The young couple had an extended courtship that continued after Rockefeller's graduation. They were married in October 1901, and following a European honeymoon they moved into a brownstone next door to the senior Rockefellers. They had six children, all of whom became prominent as adults.

Upon graduation, Rockefeller joined his father's office as a junior associate with a modest salary. He was ill prepared for his responsibilities of participating in the management of Standard Oil and of superintending his father's many other investments and philanthropies. "Never in my business life," Rockefeller later wrote, "did my father give me directions." Rockefeller, Sr.'s principal adviser, Frederick T. Gates, filled that gap by instructing the son in the complexities of his father's overlapping affairs, and Rockefeller applied himself sedulously to all the tasks presented to him. Rockefeller's dedication, lack of self-confidence, and overwhelming desire to please his father, whose accomplishments he felt he could never equal, combined to bring on an emotional breakdown in 1904. Rockefeller took leave from the office for six months, languidly traveled through southern France with his wife, and concluded that his deepest interests lay in the philanthropic, not the business side, of the family fortune. Nevertheless, he held directorships in many corporations wholly or partly owned by his father and was from 1908 to 1910 a vice president of Standard Oil of New Jersey.

Rockefeller gradually withdrew from business and by 1910 was devoted almost completely to the management of philanthropies that his father, often with his advice, had established: the Rockefeller Institute for Medical Research (1901), the General Education Board (1902), and several Baptist benefactions. Still, the growth of Rockefeller, Sr.'s wealth continued faster than the increase in his giving, especially after the breakup of the Standard Oil Trust ordered by the Supreme Court in 1911 dramatically increased his net worth, thanks to the rapid rise in the value of the stock in the newly spun-off companies. Rockefeller and Gates convinced the elder Rockefeller to endow a major foundation that would continue support for established interests while exploring new philanthropic opportunities. Over two years, the Rockefellers and their associates sought to obtain a congressional charter for the Rockefeller Foundation, but increasing public dis-

trust of great wealth in general and of Rockefeller, Sr., in particular made that impossible. In 1913 the New York State legislature quickly chartered the foundation, with John D. Rockefeller, Jr., as president and member of the board.

After Rockefeller's recovery from his breakdown, his father had accelerated the transfer of wealth to his son; one-sentence notes signed "Affectionately, Father" would accompany the allocation of sums on the order of $65 million to the younger man. Now in control of vast wealth, Rockefeller began his own philanthropic ventures. One of the first grew out of his service in 1910 as chairman of a New York grand jury convened to investigate prostitution. Protesting his lack of "personal experience" with the issue, Rockefeller first sought to decline the service, but he went on to direct a searching examination of how police corruption and municipal connivance were involved in the "white slave trade." After the grand jury was dismissed, Rockefeller established and founded the Bureau of Social Hygiene in 1911 to conduct research and develop programs focused on the suppression of the sex trade and on the rehabilitation of prostitutes.

A violent strike in the Colorado coalfields interrupted Rockefeller's progress as a public philanthropist. As a major stockholder and director of the Colorado Fuel and Iron Company (one of the few corporate boards from which he had not resigned), he was called to testify before Congress in 1913 on the company's unwillingness to recognize the miner's union or to modify the conditions in the mining "camps." His artless and formulaic responses to congressional questions came back to haunt him when on 20 April a clash between miners and the state militia, called to keep order in the fields, resulted in the so-called Ludlow Massacre, in which thirteen women and children died. Facing public outrage, picketing, and death threats, the younger Rockefeller began to realize that unquestioning reliance on the company's management, made up of long-time business associates of his family, had not served him well. Hoping that the new Rockefeller Foundation could be useful in this connection, Rockefeller engaged the former Canadian minister of labor, William Lyon Mackenzie King, as a foundation officer to investigate the dispute and recommend a new means of addressing worker grievances.

King developed a plan for worker representation and participation in management that avoided union recognition, and he convinced Rockefeller to travel to Colorado in 1915 to meet the workers and to present the plan. Rockefeller did so, despite great misgivings on the part of his father and colleagues, and for the first time met the industrial workers whom he employed. The miners voted to adopt the proposed plan, but political consequences of the episode reverberated. A subpoena came from the Commission on Industrial Relations, appointed by President Wilson after the Ludlow violence, which was investigating both industrial conditions and the role of the newly invented endowed foundations in public affairs. Coached by both King and publicist Ivy Lee, Rockefeller gave creditable testimony, but public skepticism about the role of foundations was apparent. The Rockefeller Foundation suspended its program in industrial relations and economics. In 1917 Rockefeller resigned as its president to be chairman of the board, and a full-time president was appointed to oversee a less controversial program. Industrial relations remained a personal interest of Rockefeller's, and he founded a consulting firm to promote King's scheme.

Rockefeller continued to develop his sizable personal philanthropic giving, which for many years equaled the sum total of Rockefeller Foundation grants. A devout Christian, he disliked denominational sectarianism and was quite liberal theologically. He assiduously courted Harry Emerson Fosdick, one of the most vocal opponents of fundamentalism, for the pulpit of his home church, the Park Avenue Baptist Church, even though Fosdick was a Presbyterian. Fosdick agreed, with the understanding that Rockefeller would support a new nondenominational church open to an economically diverse congregation, which resulted in Riverside Church on the Upper West Side of Manhattan. In the 1920s Rockefeller actively supported the Interchurch World Movement, which attempted to raise funds through various denominations for ecumenical activity. When this movement failed, he backed the Federal Council of Churches, which brought mainline Protestant denominations together on social issues. In the 1940s and 1950s Rockefeller turned his attention to the successor National Council of Churches and made possible the construction of the Interchurch Center, headquarters building for the National Council and for individual Protestant denominations and organizations, located one block from Riverside Church. He also provided for the establishment of the Bossey Ecumenical Institute in Switzerland.

Conservation of scenic areas and restoration of monuments became prominent concerns of Rockefeller's philanthropy as well. In 1917 he purchased a large tract on the northern tip of Manhattan so that the city of New York could create Fort Tryon Park. Land that he acquired in Jackson Hole, Wyoming, eventually was turned into Grand Teton National Park. Another gift of land in Maine became the basis for Arcadia National Park. Rockefeller provided for the excavation of the Agora in Athens, the restoration of Rheims Cathedral and the palace at Versailles, and the endowment of the Oriental Institute at the University of Chicago for excavations in Egypt and the Near East. During the 1920s Rockefeller also became interested in international philanthropy. In 1923 he underwrote the International Education Board, which supported academic research institutions overseas. And some $15 million of Rockefeller money were used to construct and equip "International Houses," residences for foreign students near the campuses of Columbia University, the University of Chicago, the University of California at Berkeley, and the University of Paris. Various operating agencies of the League of Nations were beneficiaries of Rockefeller largesse, which also provided for building and equipping the league's library and the acquisition of the grounds surrounding its Geneva headquarters to prevent their commercial development.

Besides being engaged in the affairs of the Rockefeller Foundation and several of the foundations endowed by it, Rockefeller served from 1918 to 1929 as president of the Laura Spelman Rockefeller Memorial, a philanthropy devoted to women and children and to the encouragement of academic social science. He always tried to achieve consensus among board members, but he remained at the center of decisions regarding the overall direction of Rockefeller funds. He chaired a Monday lunch group of the heads of all the Rockefeller philanthropies that in 1928 started planning for a major reorganization and rationalization of their overlapping activities. In 1934 his close adviser Raymond Fosdick became president of the chief foundation, while Rockefeller continued as chair of the foundation board until 1939.

Family unity and identity were always of major concern to Rockefeller. By 1929 John D. Rockefeller, Sr., had allocated much of his wealth to his son and to his philanthropies, having given each roughly a half billion dollars. (Rockefeller's two sisters received small sums by comparison.) Rockefeller was an exacting parent to his own children—he insisted on weekly audits of the account books his children were required to keep—even as he remained the dutiful son to his much more relaxed and humorous father. When the chairman of Standard Oil of Indiana, Robert W. Stewart, was charged with perjury in 1928, Rockefeller concluded that the continued identification of the family name with the company obliged him to lead a proxy fight the next year to install new leadership, which proved successful even though he and his sisters controlled only 10 percent of the company's stock. In 1934 he established a series of seven trusts for his wife and each of his children. These trusts, with a single set of trustees, would provide the beneficiaries with financial independence while preserving the family fortune as a financial unit. When his father died in 1939, the younger Rockefeller publicly announced that he would continue to be styled "John D. Rockefeller, Jr.," because there could only be one "John D. Rockefeller."

The development and construction of Rockefeller Center (as it was later named) in midtown Manhattan began in 1928 when Rockefeller agreed to help support a new home for the Metropolitan Opera. Land was leased from Columbia University in 1928 on his personal liability just as the Great Depression was about to halt almost all real estate development. The Metropolitan Opera withdrew from the plan, but Rockefeller pressed ahead, recruiting RCA as prospective tenant for the new "Radio City." His philanthropy provided other New York landmarks. In the early 1930s he paid for and supervised the reconstruction of pieces of several French monasteries as the Cloisters Museum of medieval art in Fort Tryon Park. To preserve the westward view from northern Manhattan, he purchased much of the Hudson River shoreline north of the George Washington Bridge to begin the Palisades Interstate Park. When in 1946 the nascent United Nations was undecided about a permanent site, he bought $8.5 million worth of land on the East River and donated it as the grounds of the international organization's headquarters.

Rockefeller's other great construction project involved Colonial Williamsburg. In 1926, when he first visited the run-down village that had been the colonial capital of Virginia, he became excited about the idea of its restoration. He saw the possibility of applying to an American town the archaeological techniques that he had supported for the Agora and in Egypt, and his gifts (ultimately more than $50 million) and grants from the Rockefeller Foundation allowed for the creation of Colonial Williamsburg, Inc. The Williamsburg restoration, lasting into the 1950s, was probably the most emotionally consuming of all of Rockefeller's philanthropic ventures. He eventually turned over the chairmanship of the Colonial Williamsburg corporation to his namesake, John D. Rockefeller III, but they clashed over the younger man's desire to desegregate Williamsburg's tourist facilities and other matters.

Abby Aldrich Rockefeller died in 1948, and in August 1951 Rockefeller married Martha Baird Allen, a performing pianist whom he had known as the wife of one of his late college classmates. He died in Tucson, Arizona.

The most direct measure of Rockefeller's accomplishments is the sum of his philanthropic donations: $537 million, almost equal to his father's total of $540 million. Short, pale, and prim, he never became a vivid public figure of the sort his father was and his sons would be. He did, however, transform the Rockefeller fortune into a structured entity, linking the family to an intricate constellation of philanthropic agencies, which in turn linked the Rockefellers to an extraordinary number of beneficiaries.

• John Ensor Harr and Peter J. Johnson, *The Rockefeller Century: Three Generations of America's Greatest Family* (1988), is an admiring work by long-time associates of the Rockefeller family that takes into account scholarship on the family and draws on a wealth of archival sources. Raymond Blaine Fosdick, *John D. Rockefeller, Jr.: A Portrait* (1956), is a guarded but informative biography written before Rockefeller's death by the former president of the Rockefeller Foundation, who had worked with Rockefeller, his philanthropies, and the family for more than thirty years. Peter Collier and David Horowitz, *The Rockefellers: An American Dynasty* (1976), covers several generations. For different chapters of Rockefeller's career, see Howard M. Gittelman, *Legacy of the Ludlow Massacre: A Chapter in American Industrial Relations* (1991); Nancy Newhall, *A Contribution to the Heritage of Every American: The Conservation Activities of John D. Rockefeller, Jr.* (1957); and Albert F. Schenkel, *The Rich Man and the Kingdom: John D. Rockefeller, Jr., and the Protestant Establishment* (1995). Useful articles include John M. Jordan, "'To Educate Public Opinion': John D. Rockefeller, Jr., and the Origins of Social Scientific Fact-Finding," *New England Quarterly* 64, 2 (1991): 292–97, and Milton Goldin, "Why the Square?": John D. Rockefeller 3rd and the Creation of Lincoln Center for the Performing Arts," *Journal of Popular Culture* 21, 3 (1987): 17–30. The *New York Times* of 12 May 1960 has an extensive obituary.

STEVEN C. WHEATLEY

ROCKEFELLER, John D., III (21 Mar. 1906–10 July 1978), philanthropist, was born John Davison Rockefeller III in New York City, the son of John Davison Rockefeller, Jr., heir to the Standard Oil fortune and philanthropist, and Abby Greene Aldrich. Rockefeller attended the Browning School in New York City, the Harvey School in Hawthorne, New York, and the Loomis School in Windsor, Connecticut. He received his B.S. at Princeton University in 1929 and married Blanchette Ferry Hooker on 11 November 1932. They had four children.

Rockefeller—known as "JDR"—was shy and frail as a boy and so self-conscious of his unusual jaw line that he had it examined many times for correction. He majored in economics at Princeton with the approval of his father, "Junior," and completed the equivalent of an art minor. After his graduation, JDR became a trustee to several of his father's projects, including, in 1931, the Rockefeller Foundation, which was governed independent of the family. JDR wished to shift the foundation's contributions from European institutions toward the development of the world's poor countries. However, the old guard within the foundation rejected his new ideas. He remained in his father's shadow until war work from 1942 to 1945 gave him an opportunity to be recognized on his own merit. As a member of the Combined Civil Affairs Committee and the State-War-Navy Coordinating Committee, he gained policymaking experience and insight into the bureaucratic struggles that occur within and between large organizations. He helped develop plans for postwar Japan that included guidelines for military occupation, relief, and rehabilitation. In 1951 he was invited to join the Dulles Mission to Japan to negotiate a peace treaty between Japan and the United States that would end U.S. occupation of the island nation.

JDR had the means to become a philanthropist in his own right as a result of the 1934 trusts that Junior established for his seven children. In 1940 JDR and his brothers created the Rockefeller Brothers Fund as a means of organizing their philanthropy. But it was not until a disagreement over the direction of his father's pet project, the restoration of Colonial Williamsburgh, that JDR finally pursued his independence. In 1952 he became chairman of the Rockefeller Foundation and finally received the foundation's support of his projects.

Population control was an interest JDR developed while serving on his father's organization, the Bureau of Social Hygiene, and visiting China in 1929. He funded investigations that resulted in foundation grants for birth control education in foreign countries. To keep controversy surrounding research into human fertility and contraceptives away from the Rockefeller Foundation, JDR created the Population Council in 1952. He served as a trustee from 1953 to 1967 and as chairman from 1957 to 1978. His early investigation of overpopulation and his appointment of experts made the council the top private organization in the 1960s and JDR the most highly publicized philanthropist. In 1970 Nixon invited him to chair the United States Commission on Population Growth and the American Future.

JDR's fascination with Japanese culture led him in 1952 to revive the Japan Society, a bilateral cultural organization founded in New York City in 1907. To aid the Japanese economy, JDR established the Council on Economic and Cultural Affairs. Though originally planned to fund a variety of programs, the council ultimately focused on helping other Southeast Asian countries develop their agricultural base so that Japan could import agricultural goods and concentrate on building its industry. In 1963 JDR renamed the organization the Agricultural Development Council and founded the JDR 3rd Fund to sponsor projects that promoted other aspects of Asian culture, such as art. He then created the Asian Society as companion to the Japan Society. As a cultural rather than a political organization, the Asian Society served to strengthen U.S. cultural relations with all of the Far East and Southeast Asia. JDR was keenly aware of the international threat of communism and characteristically he focused on the positive: promoting democracy through the Asian Society rather than denigrating communism.

JDR showed his commitment to his native New York when, in 1955, he joined a committee to explore the possibilities of erecting a musical arts center alongside the new buildings for the Metropolitan Opera and the Philharmonic Orchestra, at Lincoln Square. Consistent with his democratic spirit, JDR wanted the public to have access to culture. He single-handedly raised from the private sector more than one half of the $184.5 million necessary to build the Lincoln Center for the Performing Arts. He contributed $1 million himself in 1957. Maintaining a Rockefeller tradition, JDR offered his leadership until 1969, when he felt the center was operating smoothly.

JDR was an effective public speaker who believed there was no substitute for personal contact. When traveling to foreign countries, he preferred spending time with civilians more than being chaperoned by members of government agencies. He turned down ambassadorships because his private citizenship enabled him to avoid the tension that arose from government conflicts with Asian countries. He often preferred to go by car to New York City from his New York estate rather than in the Rockefeller private jets used by his brothers. He was known for investing in private citizens who initiated projects that foreshadowed endeavors the government would later want to establish nationally. The Rockefeller Public Service Awards (1951) were his organized way of encouraging cooperation between the government and the private sector and nurturing the reform of public administration. The government, impressed by the success of the awards, established the Government Training Act to

aid in this reform. In 1971 JDR began coalescing his thoughts on philanthropy and current civil strife for his book *The Second Revolution: Some Personal Observations* (1973). He encouraged the nation to view the youth rebellion of the 1960s as positive. His focus was not on curtailing youthful enthusiasms but rather on answering the national cry to address problems of poverty, racism, and overpopulation. JDR, the senior member of one of the country's wealthiest families, died in a car accident near his Pocantico Hills estate north of New York City.

• The Papers of the Rockefeller Family and its affiliated organizations are held in the Rockefeller Archive Center in Pocantico Hills, N.Y. See John Ensor Harr and Peter. J. Johnson, *The Rockefeller Century* (1988), for an account of the Rockefellers' use of their wealth from 1889 to the early 1950s. The book contains a section on JDR's life from 1912 to 1929. *The Rockefeller Conscience: An American Family in Public and in Private* (1991), by the same authors, focuses on JDR, since as the oldest son he carried on the Rockefeller tradition in philanthropy. An obituary is in the *New York Times*, 11 July 1978.

BARBARA L. CICCARELLI

ROCKEFELLER, Nelson Aldrich (8 July 1908–26 Jan. 1979), forty-first vice president of the United States, was born in Bar Harbor, Maine, the son of John Davison Rockefeller, Jr., a businessman and philanthropist, and Abby Greene Aldrich, an art patron and philanthropist. He was the grandson of America's wealthiest individual, John D. Rockefeller, and a leading U.S. senator, Nelson Aldrich. Rockefeller was brought up on the Rockefeller family estates in Maine and Tarrytown, New York, and in New York City. He attended Dartmouth College from 1926 to 1930, graduating with a B.A. cum laude in 1930. That same year he married Mary Todhunter Clark; they had five children.

After graduation, Rockefeller took his expected place in the family's business office. He became president of Rockefeller Center in 1938. Having developed a passion for modern art because of his mother, Rockefeller became heavily involved in the Museum of Modern Art, of which he became president in 1939.

Another lifelong interest, the economic development of Latin America, drew Rockefeller into politics and public service. After a trip to check on his investments in a Venezuelan subsidiary of Standard Oil, Rockefeller became concerned about social and economic conditions in Venezuela. With some expert assistance, he produced a position paper arguing for greater U.S. economic involvement in Latin America. This came to the attention of President Franklin Roosevelt, who appointed Rockefeller coordinator of the Office of Inter-American Affairs (OIAA), directly responsible to the president, in 1940.

OIAA's primary responsibilities were to promote U.S. cooperation with Latin America and to counter Nazi influence there. The energetic Rockefeller succeeded in greatly expanding the scope and personnel of the agency and was rewarded by a promotion to assistant secretary of state for Latin American affairs in 1944. His most significant achievement was persuading the Latin American nations to sign the March 1945 Act of Chapultepec, providing for a regional mutual security pact that became the future Organization of American States. At the San Francisco conference to draft the United Nations (UN) charter, Rockefeller secured support from the U.S. delegation for Article 51, permitting regional security agreements such as Chapultepec, in defiance of the official State Department position.

Harry Truman, who had succeeded Roosevelt as president in April 1945, was not as receptive to Rockefeller's aggressive approach to diplomacy, leading to Rockefeller's resignation later in 1945. Guided, however, by a strong conviction that neglect of Latin America would encourage communism, Rockefeller as a private citizen founded the nonprofit American International Association for Economic and Social Development (AIA) in 1946 to channel private U.S. capital to improve social conditions, food production, and public health in underdeveloped nations—primarily Brazil and Venezuela. His International Basic Economy Corporation (IBEC), founded the following year, was a for-profit operation through which American corporations could promote Latin American economic development. Rockefeller was also instrumental in securing the permanent location of the newly established UN in New York City, persuading his father to purchase the East River site later donated to the world organization.

Following the election of President Dwight Eisenhower in 1953, Rockefeller was appointed chair of the President's Advisory Committee on Government Organization. Acting on one of the committee's recommendations, President Eisenhower sought legislation to create the Department of Health, Education, and Welfare (HEW) and appointed Rockefeller deputy secretary. The following year Rockefeller left this post to accept a White House appointment as special assistant to the president for Cold War strategy. Rockefeller's most important initiative in this position was the so-called "Open Skies" proposal presented by Eisenhower at the 1955 Geneva summit, by which the United States and the Soviet Union would allow each other to conduct aerial inspections of their nuclear installations, thereby precluding a surprise attack. After his promotion to secretary of defense was blocked by Treasury Secretary George Humphrey because of his reputation as a heavy spender, Rockefeller resigned his White House post at the end of 1955.

This hiatus from public life proved to be short-lived. In 1958 Rockefeller ran for governor of New York State as the Republican candidate against Democratic incumbent Averell Harriman and, in a generally disastrous election year for the Republicans, won an upset victory. Reelected three times, Rockefeller occupied the governorship for fifteen years.

Despite being a Republican, Rockefeller was a product of the New Deal era of strong governmental activism in domestic policy. As governor he presided over an unprecedented expansion in New York State government, increasing the state budget by more than 300 percent. His greatest legacy to the state was the expansion of the state university system, which increased from 38,000 students on 28 campuses to 246,000 students attending 71 campuses by the time Rockefeller left office in 1973. The Rockefeller administration also initiated a very large number of new programs and construction projects in other areas of state activity, particularly roads, parks, hospitals, and housing. The most visible of the governor's construction projects was the "Albany Mall," a vast state government complex that cost more than $1 billion to construct.

When the political imperative of a balanced state budget and the state constitutional requirement that all state bond issues be approved by the voters threatened to restrict his ambitious schemes, Rockefeller created an elaborate system of more than forty quasi-autonomous "state authorities" that were empowered to raise funds via bond sales and to pay their operating expenses out of charges imposed on the users of their facilities. In fact, this system was sustained only by Rockefeller's ties to the Wall Street financial community, and after he left office it collapsed, dragging New York into virtual bankruptcy. Most New Yorkers benefited greatly from Rockefeller's programs and projects, however, and this, combined with his energetic campaigning, engaging personality, and limitless financial resources, ensured his reelection in 1962, 1966, and 1970.

On the national scene, Rockefeller became a major figure from the moment of his first election to governor of New York. He never made any secret of his presidential ambitions, but in a party that had always celebrated the self-made man rather than inherited wealth, Rockefeller and his millions aroused great suspicion among "Main Street" as opposed to "Wall Street" Republicans. During the 1960s this suspicion was compounded by Rockefeller's fiscal profligacy and government expansionism in New York and his strong liberal positions on civil rights. Rockefeller remained a quintessential big government, "me-too," eastern establishment Republican of the New Deal era, while the Republican party was becoming increasingly fiscally and socially conservative at the grass roots as well as more western and southern in its geographical orientation.

Rockefeller considered challenging Vice President Richard M. Nixon for the Republican nomination in 1960 and conducted a nationwide tour in the fall of 1959 to assess his chances. While he received an encouraging response from the press and public, it soon became apparent that the key state and local Republican leaders around the nation were strongly committed to Nixon, and Rockefeller renounced his presidential aspirations at the end of the year. After the U-2 incident (the downing of a U.S. spy plane overflying Soviet territory) in May 1960, however, Rockefeller hinted at his availability for a draft at the convention unless his views on the necessity for increased defense spending and strong GOP support for black civil rights were reflected in the party platform. Anxious to avoid a damaging party split, Nixon acceded to Rockefeller's demands in the so-called "Treaty of Fifth Avenue," concluded after a meeting between the two at the governor's New York apartment.

Despite outrage from the growing ranks of Republican conservatives at the Treaty of Fifth Avenue following Nixon's defeat in the 1960 election, Rockefeller immediately became the front-runner for his party's nomination in 1964. At this point, however, Rockefeller's personal life intruded upon his presidential ambitions. Following a divorce from Mary Clark Rockefeller in 1962, Rockefeller married Margaretta Fitler "Happy" Murphy, a divorced mother of four children, in May 1963. Rank-and-file Republicans were outraged, and Rockefeller's huge lead over the other Republican contenders in the opinion polls disappeared overnight, never to return.

Nevertheless, Rockefeller soldiered on, attacking his main rival for the nomination, Arizona senator Barry Goldwater, as an "extremist." These tactics only alienated the New York governor even further from conservative Republican activists. After his victory in the Oregon presidential primary in May 1964, Rockefeller had one last chance to derail the Goldwater bandwagon in the California primary the following month. The birth of the first of Rockefeller's two sons from his second marriage just three days prior to the primary revived the divorce issue and was instrumental in Goldwater's narrow triumph.

Although powerless to prevent Goldwater's nomination, Rockefeller fought determinedly but unsuccessfully at the GOP convention in San Francisco to preserve the Republican platform commitment on civil rights. His refusal to be intimidated by prolonged booing from Goldwater supporters in the galleries when he addressed the convention won Rockefeller plaudits from the news media but did nothing to dispel his image as a "party wrecker," an image confirmed by his refusal to endorse Goldwater during the fall campaign.

After 1964 Rockefeller's presidential hopes seemed finished, and he had to spend almost ten times as much as his Democratic opponent to eke out a narrow victory in his 1966 reelection campaign for governor. He was also on poor terms with his fellow liberal Republican, New York City mayor John V. Lindsay, particularly after the governor personally settled a 1968 New York City garbage strike by overruling the mayor and capitulating to labor leaders.

Nevertheless, the failure of Lindsay or any other serious contender to emerge on the moderate-to-liberal wing of the party and the crisis atmosphere in the nation created by the Vietnam War and urban racial violence led Rockefeller to consider another presidential candidacy. After first declaring in March 1968 that he would not run, Rockefeller formally announced his candidacy at the end of April, claiming he had been influenced by the nationwide rioting that followed the assassination of Dr. Martin Luther King, Jr. Having

entered too late to challenge frontrunner Nixon in the primaries, Rockefeller's only hope was to persuade uncommitted GOP convention delegates that he would be a stronger candidate in November. To this end, Rockefeller spent lavishly on national television advertising to raise his opinion poll ratings. When the polls showed him doing no better than Nixon, Rockefeller's hopes were dashed once again at the convention.

Despite their longstanding rivalry, Rockefeller became a loyal and determined supporter of the Nixon administration at home and abroad. In 1969 he acted as the president's emissary to Latin America, but instead of a rapturous reception in a region to which he had devoted so much of his time, energy, and financial resources, Rockefeller was greeted by rioting students and widespread anti-American sentiment. Perhaps these events and the knowledge that only by changing his political profile among Republicans as a raging liberal and party wrecker would he have any chance of succeeding Nixon in the White House explain Rockefeller's more conservative tilt in his final years as governor. Always a staunch anti-Communist "Cold Warrior," Rockefeller strongly supported Nixon's Vietnam War policy. In 1971 he pointedly refused to meet with rioting prisoners who had taken forty guards as hostages at the state prison in Attica, New York, and subsequently ordered an assault on the prison that resulted in thirty-nine deaths and eighty wounded. Despite heavy criticism of his actions by liberal commentators and the news media, Rockefeller was unrepentant. In his final year in office, he confirmed his newfound social conservatism by proposing a Draconian antidrug law that included mandatory life sentences for drug possession.

After he resigned the governorship at the end of 1973 to concentrate on one final attempt at the White House in 1976, Rockefeller's career took an unexpected turn. Nixon's resignation in August 1974 elevated Vice President Gerald R. Ford to the White House, and Ford nominated Rockefeller to succeed to the vice presidency. After weeks of grueling confirmation hearings, during which the Rockefeller family finances were publicly investigated in detail by congressional Democrats, Rockefeller was finally confirmed by both houses of Congress in mid-December 1974. Despite the controversy surrounding Rockefeller's selection, his conception of his role as vice president was unprecedented in scope. Named head of the president's Domestic Council, Vice President Rockefeller expected to play a role in domestic policy similar to the dominance of his former protégé, Secretary of State Henry Kissinger, over foreign and defense policy. His ambitions were consistently thwarted by Ford's White House chiefs of staff, Donald Rumsfeld and Richard Cheney. Then when Ford was challenged in his quest for the Republican presidential nomination in 1976 from the right of the party by Ronald Reagan, it became apparent that Rockefeller, the longtime bogeyman of the Republican right, was a major political liability. In November 1975 Rockefeller announced that he did not wish to be considered for renomination in 1976. It was clear, however, that his departure from the ticket had not been voluntary.

After leaving the vice presidency in January 1977, Rockefeller retired completely from politics and attended to his young second family, his business affairs, and the marketing of his considerable art collection. Rockefeller died at his New York townhouse.

Despite his failure to attain the presidency, Rockefeller was a highly influential figure in post–World War II American politics. His activities in Latin America as U.S. diplomat and private citizen had a profound impact on that region and on U.S. hemispheric policy from 1940 onward. As governor of New York, Rockefeller expanded the scope of state government to an unprecedented degree, bringing tangible benefits to millions, although his fiscal irresponsibility had deleterious long-term effects. In the art world, Rockefeller was instrumental in creating the Museum of Modern Art and the Museum of Primitive Art, and as the de facto leader of his generation of the Rockefeller dynasty, he continued the family's extensive philanthropic and public service activities.

Yet in terms of the goal that Rockefeller had set for himself, the presidency, he failed spectacularly. While tactical errors and poor luck attended each of his failed attempts at the Republican presidential nomination, the explanations of his failure were more fundamental. In a party that was becoming ever more southern and western in its electoral support and that had never shed its deep-rooted aversion to a large, interventionist federal government, Rockefeller epitomized the big government policies of the New Deal/Cold War era. Despite his inveterate anticommunism and Baptist heritage, he also represented East Coast "high society" and wealth in a Republican party that was becoming increasingly averse to both. Had he rejected family tradition and become a Democrat, he might have had more success in the presidential stakes. Unfortunately for Rockefeller, by the time he made a serious attempt at the Republican presidential nomination, it was too late for a candidate with his progressive and expansionist views of government to prevail.

• Rockefeller's private and governmental papers are in the Rockefeller family's archive center at "Pocantico Hills," the Rockefeller estate near Tarrytown, N.Y. Many of these documents remain closed to the public, however. The most comprehensive work available on Rockefeller's life is Peter Collier and David Horowitz, *The Rockefellers: An American Dynasty* (1976), which devotes considerable attention to Rockefeller's political career and also places him in the context of the Rockefeller family history. Joseph E. Persico, *The Imperial Rockefeller* (1982), is an interesting personal portrait by a former Rockefeller speech writer. Of the various journalistic accounts, Michael Kramer and Sam Roberts, *"I Never Wanted to Be Vice-President of Anything!": An Investigative Biography of Nelson Rockefeller* (1976), and James Desmond, *Nelson Rockefeller: A Political Biography* (1964), are probably the most useful. Aspects of Rockefeller's long political career are well documented in several other works. Robert H. Connery and Gerald Benjamin, *Rockefeller of New York: Executive Power in the Statehouse* (1979), and James F. Underwood and William J. Daniels, *Governor Rockefeller in New York: The Apex of Pragmatic Liberalism in the United States* (1982), are studies of Rockefeller's administration in N.Y. from a political science perspective. His innovative vice presidency is examined in Michael Turner, *The Vice-President as Policy-Maker: Rockefeller in the Ford White House* (1982). His activities in Latin America are discussed in Elizabeth Anne Cobbs, *The Rich Neighbor Policy: Rockefeller and Kaiser in Brazil* (1992), and more critically in Gerard Colby with Charlotte Dennett, *Thy Will Be Done: The Conquest of the Amazon: Nelson Rockefeller and Evangelism in the Age of Oil* (1995). For an analysis of Rockefeller's failed campaigns for the presidency see Nicol C. Rae, *The Decline and Fall of the Liberal Republicans: From 1952 to the Present* (1989). An obituary is in the *New York Times*, 27 Jan. 1979.

NICOL C. RAE

ROCKEFELLER, William (31 May 1841–24 June 1922), industrialist and financier, was born in Richford, New York, the son of William Avery Rockefeller, an itinerant dispenser of cure-alls and self-proclaimed "botanic physician," and Eliza Davison. He grew up in rural New York State until the family moved in 1853 to Cleveland, Ohio, where he and his older brother John Davison Rockefeller attended Cleveland Central High School and became regular worshipers at the Erie Street Baptist Church. When not absent on his travels, their father introduced the boys to the ways of business, boasting that "I cheat my boys every time I get a chance. . . . I want 'em to be sharp" (Nevins, vol. 1, p. 93).

William and John were close friends, and William's career paralleled that of his older brother. After graduation he found work as a bookkeeper, then entered the produce business, and at the age of twenty-one became a partner in the commission house where he worked. In 1864 he married Almira Geraldine Goodsell, with whom he had six children. When in 1865 John wanted to open a second oil refinery, he convinced William to invest his savings and become a partner in the firm of Rockefeller and Andrews.

In 1866 William went to New York City to open the firm of Rockefeller and Company to handle eastern and export sales for the Cleveland partnership. William proved to be one of the ablest export managers in the business, establishing cordial contacts with merchants and dock workers, arranging shipments, and closely watching prices of kerosene and other petroleum products, which he telegraphed back to Cleveland so they could adjust production to the most profitable lines. Since money could be borrowed more cheaply in New York than in Cleveland, he cultivated bankers and became the financial expert for the organization.

In order to make mergers and acquisitions of competitors easier, the partnership in 1870 converted to a corporation, becoming the Standard Oil Company of Ohio. John became president and William vice president. William played a major role in support of John in the savage battles to unify the petroleum refining industry, which ended with Standard Oil in control of 90 to 95 percent of the refining capacity of the United

States. He persuaded the major refiners of the Eastern Seaboard to join the combination. When Standard organized as a trust in 1882, William Rockefeller was one of the original trustees, serving until the trust was ruled illegal by the Ohio courts. He became a director and major stockholder in Standard Oil of New Jersey, the holding company set up to replace the trust, and president of Standard Oil of New York, positions he held until the Supreme Court dissolved the holding company, as a violator of the Sherman Antitrust Act, in 1911, when he formally retired from management.

One of Rockefeller's closest friends was James Stillman, president of the National City Bank (two of Rockefeller's sons married daughters of Stillman). Rockefeller made National City the major depository for the corporation, so that most people thought of it as the Standard Oil Bank. By the late 1890s, as the monopoly began to pay enormous dividends, Rockefeller's interests began to shift from the oil business to the stock market, where he joined with Henry Huddleston Rogers, another leader of Standard Oil, and Stillman in a series of spectacular stock-market manipulations of mining and utility companies that earned the trio the envy of Wall Street and the name the "Standard Oil Gang." Most notorious was the flotation of the Amalgamated Copper Company for $75 million in 1899. The sponsors purchased the mining properties that would form the new concern for $39 million, with the understanding that the purchase money was to be left on deposit in the National City Bank until the stock was successfully floated, earning the promoters a profit of $36 million without investing any money. Violent swings in the price of Amalgamated stock, as well as in the stock of gas and electric companies and railroads controlled by the trio, marked their manipulations.

Rockefeller played a major role in the growth of Standard Oil into one of the most efficient industrial enterprises in the history of American business, yet he escaped the opprobrium aroused by the ruthless and unscrupulous methods of the trust. Stillman warned his successor that Rockefeller's "velvety politeness . . . masked a character accustomed to work in darkness" (Frank A. Vanderlip, *From Farm Boy to Financier* [1935], p. 272), but most saw only the genial face he turned to the world. His brother became "the most hated man in America," but even in Ida Tarbell's exposé of Standard Oil, William Rockefeller is described as "open-hearted, . . . not a man to suspect or fear" (*History*, p. 50). Thomas W. Lawson excoriates Rogers and Stillman for their role in mining and gas speculations, but terms Rockefeller "a good, wholesome man made in the image of his God" (*Frenzied Finance*, p. 22).

Unlike his somewhat puritanical brother, William Rockefeller enjoyed a lavish lifestyle. He built himself a mansion on Fifth Avenue and a great estate overlooking the Hudson in Tarrytown, New York, where he spent some $3 million erecting a baronial country house, lavishly furnished and set in elaborately landscaped grounds. He remained affiliated with the Baptist church but contributed little to it. When he died in Tarrytown, he left entirely to his children and grandchildren an estate estimated at between $150 million and $200 million. There were no bequests to charity.

• The William Rockefeller Papers and other manuscript material relevant to his life and career are held in the Rockefeller Archive Center, Pocantico Hills, North Tarrytown, N.Y. William is widely featured in biographies of his brother, including John T. Flynn, *God's Gold: The Story of Rockefeller and His Times* (1932); Allan Nevins, *John D. Rockefeller: The Heroic Age of American Enterprise* (2 vols., 1940); Grace Goulder, *John D. Rockefeller: The Cleveland Years* (1972); and David Freeman Hawke, *John D.: The Founding Father of the Rockefellers* (1980). For William's major role in Standard Oil, see Ralph W. Hidy and Muriel E. Hidy, *Pioneering in Big Business, 1882–1911* (1955). Contemporary opinion can be sampled in Henry Demarest Lloyd, *Wealth against Commonwealth* (1894); Ida M. Tarbell, *History of the Standard Oil Company* (2 vols., 1904); John Moody, *The Truth about Trusts* (1904); and Thomas W. Lawson, *Frenzied Finance* (1905). An obituary is in the *New York Times*, 25 June 1922, with a follow-up story on his will on 30 June 1922.

MILTON BERMAN

ROCKHILL, William Woodville (1 Apr. 1854–8 Dec. 1914), Orientalist and diplomat, was born in Philadelphia, Pennsylvania, the son of Thomas Cadwallader Rockhill, a lawyer, and Dorothy Anna Woodville. The death of his father when William was ten months old, the consequent decision of his energetic mother to move to France, and the near poverty in which he and his brother were raised shaped Rockhill's childhood, remarkable education, cosmopolitan outlook, and personality. While a cadet at the rigorous École Spéciale Militaire de St. Cyr, Rockhill began his lifetime fascination with the Orient and his serious study of its civilizations and languages, especially Chinese, Sanskrit, and Tibetan. After Rockhill graduated with honors from St. Cyr in 1873, this self-driven, stoical perfectionist served three years as sublieutenant in the French Foreign Legion in Algeria. In 1876 he resigned his commission, returned as a virtual stranger to the United States, and married Caroline Adams Tyson, with whom he had two children.

Rockhill has been described as an austere, solitary, and antisocial figure who preferred the company of his books and manuscripts to diplomatic protocol and mixing with what he believed were ignorant and narrow-minded superiors and colleagues. This image may be exaggerated. Both of his marriages were happy and agreeable: the first to Caroline, who died in Greece in 1898, and the second (childless) to Edith Perkins, whom he married in 1900. Rockhill also counted many colleagues as friends and moved easily within the fraternity of cosmopolites (including Theodore Roosevelt (1858–1919), Henry Cabot Lodge, Henry Adams (1838–1918), and John Hay) who sought a larger role for the United States in world affairs.

Rockhill's fame rests on his diplomatic career, but he was first and always a dedicated, pioneering, and prolific Orientalist. Whether he was uncovering and translating ancient Chinese and Tibetan classics or exploring remote parts of China and Tibet between 1888 and 1892, with amazing indifference to his personal safety, Rockhill was driven by the late nineteenth-century search for "objective," scientific truth and the love of knowledge for its own sake. Rockhill was one of a handful of Westerners to penetrate Tibet and Mongolia, and in 1908 he was honored by having several long conversations with the Dalai Lama, who sought the American's advice on his delicate relationship with the Manchu Court and Tibet's future. Over a period of thirty years Rockhill produced dozens of significant books, articles, and papers that vividly depicted the physical landscape and sought to understand Asian societies. Meanwhile, he deliberately cultivated his image as an authority on the Far East in an era that was beginning to recognize the need for professional expertise.

Penury, partially relieved by Caroline's subsequent inheritance, as well as his scholarly agenda, led to Rockhill's diplomatic career after a failed attempt at ranching in New Mexico from 1878 to 1881. With interruptions for expeditions to Tibet and writing projects, Rockhill served in a succession of posts: second secretary and secretary of the American legation in Peking (1884–1888); chargé d'affaires *ad interim*, Seoul, Korea (Dec. 1886–Apr. 1887); chief clerk in the State Department (1893–1894); third assistant secretary of state (1894–1895); assistant secretary of state (1896–1897); and minister to Greece, Romania, and Serbia (1897–1899). Rockhill's two years in Athens were perhaps the most miserable of his life: he found Greece absolutely boring, he suffered from poor health and Athens's oppressive heat, and he was shattered by Caroline's untimely death from typhoid. Fortunately, Secretary of State John Hay rescued Rockhill by securing his appointment in Washington as director of the International Bureau of American Republics, the U.S.-controlled commercial arm of the Pan American Union. Hay also made him a paid consultant to the State Department and his principal adviser on Far Eastern affairs.

It was an auspicious and critical moment, as the imperialist powers were scrambling for spheres of influence and concessions in the crumbling Manchu empire, while northern China was being swept by the violent Boxer Rebellion. Rockhill played a central role in formulating the U.S. response, which included the Open Door Notes of 1899 and 1900, the dispatch of a large military contingent to relieve the siege of the foreign legations in Peking, and active involvement in the Boxer peace negotiations. At Hay's request, and in collaboration with Alfred Hippisley, Rockhill composed the notes of 1899, which asserted the principle of equal commercial opportunity, and he drafted much of the diplomatic correspondence that followed. Rockhill's ideas informed the notes of 1900, which declared the commitment on the part of the United States to preserving the integrity of China. He was then sent to China as a commissioner to assist Minister Edwin Conger in the Boxer diplomatic settlement. He quickly supplanted Conger as the leading American

negotiator and was partially successful in mitigating the harsh terms of the Boxer Protocol and preserving at least the appearance of an independent China.

Afterward Rockhill returned to the Bureau of American Republics until 1905, when he was appointed minister to China. His tenure in Peking was marked by repeated crises in Sino-American relations over Chinese immigration to the United States, the boycott of American goods by resentful Chinese, and the embarrassing cancellation of the major railway concession to the American China Development Company. In 1909 Rockhill was transferred to St. Petersburg, where he became embroiled in the rivalry for concessions in Manchuria, partly provoked by the William Howard Taft administration's emphasis on Dollar Diplomacy. He ended his diplomatic career as ambassador to Turkey (1911–1913). Financial pressures, as well as his old attachment to Yuan Shih-k'ai as China's possible savior, induced Rockhill to accept an appointment as foreign adviser to the new Chinese president, even though he realized that his position was largely window dressing for the infant republic, in which he had little faith. Rockhill died suddenly in Honolulu on his way back to China.

Historians continue to argue over the assignment of credit for the Open Door notes among Rockhill, Hippisley, the viceroys of central China, and other individuals and governments. They also debate Rockhill's motives as well as the respective importance of commercial equality and Chinese integrity for the United States. There is little question, however, that Rockhill helped to shape American Far Eastern policy for several generations. He was instrumental in reframing the traditional and interrelated American principles of equal commercial opportunity and support for China's independence so as to meet the perceived threat to national interests from the crisis in China. He did this at a time when American leaders were seeking a domestically acceptable way to assert a larger U.S. role in world affairs. Rockhill understood that the political, economic, and financial dimensions could not be isolated, even as he insisted that the solution to the "Oriental question" rested on the preservation of a stable, independent China willing and able to carry out its obligations. While often frustrated by the ineptitude and duplicity of his diplomatic colleagues, Rockhill proved to be a "supreme realist," a tough bargainer, and a skilled diplomat in the service of his country. Finally, as a scholar, he represented the prototype of the foreign expert and the model for advocates of the professionalization of America's foreign policy apparatus.

• The William W. Rockhill Papers are at the Houghton Library, Harvard University, and provide the basic source of information on his life and career. Other important manuscript collections are those of John Hay, Philander C. Knox, Theodore Roosevelt, and Elihu Root at the Library of Congress. Students of Rockhill's diplomatic career should also consult the relevant files of the Department of State at the National Archives; some of Rockhill's diplomatic correspondence may be found in the appropriate volumes of *Foreign*

Relations of the United States. Among Rockhill's significant writings are the following: *Udânavarga, the Northern Buddhist Version of Dhammapada* (1883); *The Life of the Buddha* (1884); *The Land of the Lamas: Notes of a Journey through China, Mongolia, and Tibet* (1891); *Diary of a Journey in Mongolia and Thibet in 1891 and 1892* (1894); and *Treaties and Conventions with or concerning China and Korea, 1894–1904,* and a supplement covering the years 1904 to 1908 (1908).

The only full-length biography of Rockhill is the useful but dated work by Paul A. Varg, *Open Door Diplomat: The Life of W. W. Rockhill* (1952). See also A. E. Hippisley's memoir in the *Journal of the Royal Asiatic Society* 47 (May 1915): 367–74.

Rockhill's career and contributions are discussed and evaluated in a large number of secondary works, including Tyler Dennett, *Americans in Eastern Asia: A Critical Study of the Policy of the United States with Reference to China, Japan, and Korea in the Nineteenth Century* (1922); Michael H. Hunt, *Frontier Defense and the Open Door: Manchuria in Chinese American Relations, 1895–1911* (1973); A. Whitney Griswold, *The Far Eastern Policy of the United States* (1938); Harvey Pressman, "Hay, Rockhill, and China's Integrity: A Reappraisal," *Papers on China* 13 (1959): 61–79; and Peter W. Stanley, "The Making of an American Sinologist: William W. Rockhill and the Open Door," *Perspectives in American History* 2 (1978): 419–60.

An obituary is in the *New York Times,* 9 Dec. 1914.

NOEL H. PUGACH

ROCKINGHAM, Lord (13 May 1730–1 July 1782), twice prime minister of Great Britain during the era of the American Revolution, was born Charles Watson-Wentworth in England, probably at the family home in Yorkshire, the son of Thomas Watson-Wentworth, a member of the Whig aristocracy, and Mary Finch, the daughter of the seventh earl of Winchilsea. His father was the first baron Wentworth, was created the first marquess of Rockingham in 1746, had his family seat at Wentworth-Woodhouse in Yorkshire, and possessed estates in Britain and Ireland with a rent-roll of £20,000 a year. Charles later succeeded his father as second marquess of Rockingham. By 1739 Charles was the only survivor of five sons and styled viscount Higham as his father's heir (a courtesy title). Educated at Westminster School, he came to public notice when at the age of fifteen he enlisted in a volunteer force raised by his father to oppose the 1745 Stuart rebellion. He made a solitary and foolhardy journey to offer his services to the duke of Cumberland, younger son of George II and commander of the king's army. This naive enthusiasm reaped a rich reward in subsequent ministerial and royal favors. After school he went on a grand tour but not to Cambridge University as is sometimes stated. Styled earl of Malton from 1746, he succeeded his father in titles and estates on 14 December 1750. The entry of the young marquess into the ruling oligarchy was signified by a succession of honors. His appointment in 1751 as a lord of the bedchamber at the royal court was matched by the post of lord-lieutenant of the West Riding of Yorkshire, together with sundry lesser posts. Marriage followed in 1752 to Mary Bright, daughter of the late Thomas Bright and Lady Ramsden, wife of Sir John Ramsden. His intelli-

gent and cultivated wife was to be a great support to him, often acting as his political secretary. During this same period Rockingham joined the exclusive White's Club, was elected a fellow of the Royal Society (1751) and a fellow of the Society of Antiquaries (1752), and became a member of the Jockey Club; throughout his life many thought him more interested in horse racing than politics.

Rockingham took his seat in the House of Lords in 1751 but seldom spoke after a poor maiden speech on 17 March 1752. During the next few years he became the leading political figure in Yorkshire, England's largest county. He had inherited control of three House of Commons seats, two for Malton and one for Higham Ferrers (in Northamptonshire). He now built up a major "interest" in the county and several boroughs, notably York, where the local Whigs formed a Rockingham Club. In national politics he ignored all opposition enticements and attached himself to the head of the main Whig Party, the duke of Newcastle, who was prime minister 1754–1756 and 1757–1762. The seal of ministerial and royal approval came on 6 May 1760, with his nomination as a knight of the prestigious Order of the Garter.

The British political world changed with the accession of George III a few months later. The young king's disapproval of the Whig oligarchy and his desire to appoint his favorite, Lord Bute, as prime minister led to the enforced resignation of Newcastle in May 1762. Rockingham signified his adherence to the duke by resigning his court office on 3 November, a gesture followed by dismissal from his lord-lieutenancy and minor offices. Thereafter Rockingham spent three years in unaccustomed opposition, to the ministries of Bute and George Grenville. In 1765 a reluctant Newcastle was persuaded to step down as party leader in favor of Rockingham, who in July became prime minister without ever having held executive political office, for George III recalled to office "the old Whig Party" to rescue him from the by now obnoxious Grenville.

Rockingham's appointment therefore owed nothing to ability and achievements, and his supposedly inept performance as premier for long incurred the censure of historians. In debate he was inarticulate and timid, the despair of his friends, mocked by his opponents in the House of Lords. "How could you worry the poor dumb creature so," said one to another with great relish. But he possessed the requisite qualities for a prime minister of charm and tact and displayed practical sense when confronted with the first American crisis over the Stamp Act. Determined to be his own man, he excluded Newcastle, twice his age, from any effective say in policy making. Rockingham soon perceived that conciliation of the American colonies by repeal of Grenville's taxation was the only practical policy, since he knew that enforcement of the Stamp Act would be impossible. His problem was that British public opinion would not accept a simple surrender to mob violence. Rockingham devised an ingenious solution. His ministry accompanied repeal of the Stamp

Act with the Declaratory Act of 1766, asserting the right of Parliament to legislate for the colonies "in all cases whatsoever," including taxation. Having established that principle, Rockingham would abandon the practice. He displayed great political skill in persuading king, Lords, and Commons to accept this face-saving compromise that quieted America. George III was grateful but not sufficiently so to retain him in office when the monarch's preferred choice of William Pitt made himself available. Rockingham was unceremoniously dismissed in July 1766 and spent the next sixteen years as leader of the main opposition party. By 1770 he had become by conscientious effort a frequent speaker in Parliament: his papers contain many drafts of what he intended to say. He had the assistance of Edmund Burke, whom he had made in 1765 his private secretary and brought into the House of Commons, where he was the famous Rockinghamite spokesman.

The American question henceforth dominated Rockingham's career. The Declaratory Act was an expression of political faith as well as a tactical expedient. During the next decade his criticism of ministerial policies therefore centered on the folly of taxing and legislating for the colonies, while conceding Parliament's right to do so. In 1770 the Rockinghamite line was to favor repeal of the tea tax being retained by Frederick, Lord North. After that led to the Boston Tea Party in 1773 Rockingham, during debates on the consequent Intolerable Acts of 1774, urged the need of "temper" to reconcile Britain with America and argued that the economic benefits of colonial trade were more important than constitutional formalities. His dilemma, once the War of Independence began, was that he wished success to neither side; but after news of Saratoga (Oct. 1777), Rockingham was one of the first politicians to accept the fact of American independence. "I conceive that America will never again assent to this country's having actual power within that continent," he wrote to William Pitt, first earl of Chatham. "I cannot, therefore, so betray my trust to the public, as to act as if that was practicable, which I thought otherwise." Not until 1782, after Yorktown had brought majority British opinion round to this view, did the resignation of Lord North in March compel George III to summon Rockingham to form his second ministry. The marquess would not agree to do so until the king accepted a program that included the offer of independence to America. He did not live to implement it. Always plagued by ill health, including gallstones and a urinary tract infection, he died in London from influenza after barely three months in office.

Rockingham, an underrated prime minister, had a more realistic attitude toward the American Revolution than most British politicians. While his conciliatory attitude concealed a determination to retain the colonies under British rule if possible, he was unwilling to fight a war to do so.

• Lord Rockingham's papers, the Wentworth-Woodhouse Muniments, are in Sheffield City Archives, England. Numerous extracts were included in George Thomas, earl of Albemarle, ed., *Memoirs of the Marquis of Rockingham and His Contemporaries* (2 vols., 1852). The only full biography is R. J. S. Hoffman, *The Marquis: A Study of Lord Rockingham 1730–1782* (1973). The period until his first premiership is also covered by G. H. Guttridge, *The Early Career of Lord Rockingham 1730–1765* (1952). For that ministry see P. Langford, *The First Rockingham Administration 1765–1766* (1973); and, for his party, F. O'Gorman, *The Rise of Party in England: The Rockingham Whigs 1760–82* (1975). Rockingham's attitude toward the American Revolution may be studied in three books by P. D. G. Thomas: *British Politics and the Stamp Act Crisis 1763–1767* (1975), *The Townshend Duties Crisis: 1767–1773* (1987), and *Tea Party to Independence 1773–1776* (1991). Much important work is unpublished, notably three doctoral dissertations: W. M. Elofson, "The Rockingham Whigs in Opposition 1768–1773" (Oxford Univ., 1977); M. Bloy, "Rockingham and Yorkshire: The Political, Economic and Social Role of Charles Watson-Wentworth, Second Marquess of Rockingham" (Sheffield Univ., 1987); and S. M. Farrell, "Divisions, Debates and Dis-Ease: The Rockingham Whig Party and the House of Lords 1760–1785" (Cambridge Univ., 1993).

PETER D. G. THOMAS

ROCKNE, Knute (4 Mar. 1888–31 Mar. 1931), college football player and coach, was born Knute Kenneth Rokne in Voss, Norway, the son of Lars Knutson Rokne, a blacksmith and carriage maker, and Martha Gjermo. His father came to the United States in 1893 to exhibit his carriage designs at the World's Columbian Exposition in Chicago. Soon thereafter he was joined by his wife and five children, and the family took up residence in the United States. Rockne (the "c" was added to the surname in America) grew up in the Logan Square neighborhood of Chicago, where he attended Brentano Grammar School. He later was a student at North West Division High School, where he participated on the track team in the half-mile and pole vault events. Rockne played some football as a freshman, but he did not excel at the sport. As a senior, Rockne skipped classes to practice for an upcoming track meet. Consequently, school authorities expelled him in 1905.

Rockne nonetheless still dreamed of attending college, preferably the University of Illinois. He thus diligently took a series of miscellaneous jobs, saving as much money as he could, before working for three years in the Chicago Post Office as a postal clerk. With money in relatively short supply, Rockne decided to attend the University of Notre Dame, a small Catholic school in South Bend, Indiana. "What swung me to Notre Dame," he said, "was that my thousand dollars would go a longer way than at Illinois and that I could get a job very easily at South Bend." Because Rockne lacked a high school diploma, university authorities required him to take an entrance examination before admittance. He successfully completed the exam in 1910 and began working as a janitor in the chemistry lab to help pay for his expenses.

Quite active as a college student, Rockne contributed to various student publications, played the flute with the campus orchestra, and participated on the track team. Competing in the half-mile, long jump, shot put, and pole vault, he won a varsity letter as a freshman and recorded a pole vault of 12′4″, establishing a school record. Rockne also supplemented his income by boxing and playing with a semiprofessional football team in South Bend. Despite his relatively small stature (5′8″, 165 pounds), Rockne decided to try out for the football team. He played little as a freshman fullback under coach Frank "Shorty" Longman. In 1911, his sophomore year, Rockne became new coach John Marks's starting end.

In 1913 Rockne was elected captain of one of the Fighting Irish's most notable squads. The team went undefeated for the third consecutive season but became better known for the revolutionary impact Rockne and quarterback Charles "Gus" Dorais had on the game. Although the passing attack in football was rarely used at this time, new coach Jesse Harper allowed the two roommates to practice pass patterns on their own. Dorais had an exceptionally strong arm and was able to toss the large, oval-shaped ball with a good amount of accuracy. The pair planned to take advantage of the new and less restrictive rules on passing; no longer were incomplete passes regarded as fumbles. The Fighting Irish unleashed their new air game against a top-rated Army team. Catching the Cadets by surprise, Notre Dame scored a stunning upset, 35–13, as Dorais completed 14 of 17 passes, including 10 to Rockne. The victory put tiny Notre Dame on the football map and showed the potential of the "open" game. For his season's efforts, Rockne won third-team All-American honors from Walter Camp.

In 1914 Rockne graduated magna cum laude with a bachelor of science degree in chemistry and pharmacology. He soon landed a high school coaching job in St. Louis and entertained thoughts of becoming a doctor. St. Louis University administrators advised him, however, that he would be unable to pursue medical school while coaching. Discouraged, Rockne returned to Chicago. Notre Dame officials then contacted Rockne and offered him a position as chemistry instructor, head track coach, and assistant football coach to Jesse Harper. Rockne leapt at the offer of $2,500 per year. Later in 1914 he married Bonnie Gwendoline Skiles, with whom he would have four children.

Rockne spent four years as Harper's assistant, coaching a poorly funded team outfitted in ragged, hand-me-down uniforms. Rockne quickly established himself as a master motivator by giving inspirational pregame and halftime speeches to his team. The Fighting Irish lost only five of 33 games during that span (1914–1917). In early 1918 Harper unexpectedly resigned as head coach to run his family's cattle ranch. At Harper's insistence, the university named Rockne as his successor.

World War I shortened Notre Dame's schedule in Rockne's first year as head coach. His team, featuring the gifted halfback George Gipp, lost only one game of six. The following season Rockne hired former teammate Gus Dorais as an assistant, and the pair directed Notre Dame to an undefeated season and unofficial

recognition as national champions. Another perfect season followed in 1920, but the tragic death of Gipp at the end of the year dampened that achievement.

Rockne's squads from 1921 to 1924 lost only three games in 40 contests. Those teams featured the fabled "Four Horsemen" backfield—so dubbed in 1924 by sportswriter Grantland Rice—of Harry Stuhldreher, Jim Crowley, Don Miller, and Elmer Layden. Rockne maintained that the 1924 club "would always be my favorite team. I think I sensed that that backfield was to be a great one. They were a product of destiny." The Irish closed out the season with a New Year's Day victory over Pop Warner's Stanford team in the Rose Bowl and claimed another national championship.

With Notre Dame's success, Rockne had become a national celebrity whose public appearances became valuable to many groups throughout the country. He held coaching clinics, wrote magazine articles, and became a popular speaker for various business and athletic organizations. Later he became a sales promoter for the Studebaker Corporation of South Bend. With so many demands put upon his time, Rockne seriously considered leaving Notre Dame for Columbia University following the 1925 season. Although he signed an agreement with Columbia, he had second thoughts and returned to South Bend.

Thereafter Rockne kept Notre Dame at the top of the college football world, defeating major opponents regularly and losing a total of only two games in 1926 and 1927. The 1928 squad was Rockne's poorest at 5–4–0, but it achieved mythical status in a dramatic game against Army. After a scoreless first half against the potential national champions, Rockne gave a stirring halftime speech. He claimed that the late George Gipp wanted Rockne to win a big game for him. "Boys," Rockne said, "I'm convinced that this is the game George Gipp would want us to win." While most historians believe that Rockne fabricated Gipp's deathbed plea to motivate his team, the Fighting Irish would win an emotional 12–6 upset victory.

The 1929 season was a remarkable one for Rockne and the Notre Dame eleven. Rockne had finally convinced the university to build a new football stadium to replace Cartier Field, and the Irish played every game on the road while the new stadium was under construction. Early in the season a life-threatening case of phlebitis incapacitated Rockne. Although doctors warned him of the possibility of a heart attack or stroke, Rockne still insisted on guiding his squad through practices with the use of a microphone, loud speakers, and an observation tower. He even made appearances at a few games, coaching from the sidelines in a wheelchair. Despite Rockne's absence from most contests, Notre Dame won all its games and claimed another national championship. Rockne's health improved enough in 1930 to steer the Irish through another undefeated, national championship season.

Although Rockne did not have a reputation as a great football innovator, he developed the use of "shock troops" (substitutes who played early in games to wear down the opposition before the regulars played), and brush blocks that took advantage of a lineman's leverage to throw his opponent off balance. He also instituted the famed "Notre Dame Shift," whereby the backfield moved before the snap of the ball to confuse the defense. Rockne's brand of football consisted of speed and deception rather than size and brute strength. He was responsible for developing a demanding schedule that pitted Notre Dame against strong college teams from all regions of the country. Notre Dame's success against such formidable opposition as Army, Nebraska, and Southern California made the small Catholic college and Rockne himself household names. Notre Dame football had become an extremely popular and lucrative enterprise, with the team attracting huge crowds wherever it played. By the end of the 1920s, Catholics throughout America had established a strong identification with Notre Dame's football teams.

In 1931 Rockne agreed to accept $75,000 to help in the production of a Hollywood motion picture, *The Spirit of Notre Dame*. Before he ever made it to California, however, Rockne tragically died in an airplane crash near the small Kansas town of Bazaar. Rockne's death shocked a nation that had come to identify him as a national treasure, symbolic of big-time college athletics and success in American sport's "golden age." Rockne was lionized as a hero after his death, and his legend was reaffirmed in 1940 by the Warner Brothers' film, *Knute Rockne, All-American*, starring Pat O'Brien.

In his abbreviated career Rockne coached his teams to 105 wins, only 12 losses, and five ties, for a record-setting .881 winning percentage. He coached 20 All-American players for teams that claimed four national championships. In 1951 he became a charter member of the National Football Foundation Hall of Fame. That same year the Associated Press named him the top college football coach of all time.

• Rockne's papers are at the University of Notre Dame. Much inaccurate information has been published about Rockne, some of it by Rockne, an inveterate self-promoter, himself. Rockne wrote four books: *The Autobiography of Knute Rockne* (1931), which helped to establish a growing mythology; *Coaching: The Way of the Winner* (1925), explaining his philosophy of coaching; *The Four Winners—the Head, the Hands, the Foot, the Ball* (1925), a novel loosely based on the exploits of the "Four Horsemen"; and *Knute Rockne on Football*, ed. Christy Walsh (1931). Rockne also wrote numerous articles in *Collier's*, including "Coaching Men," 15 Nov. 1930, pp. 22–23 ff.; "From Norway to Notre Dame," 18 Oct. 1930, pp. 7–9 ff.; and "What Thrills a Coach," 6 Dec. 1930, pp. 20–21 ff. Many early biographies of Rockne, such as Harry Stuhldreher's *Knute Rockne, Man-Builder* (1931) and Robert Harron's *Rockne, Idol of American Football* (1931), perpetuate and add to some of the myths that Rockne had created about his life. Later biographies have worked to correct previous misconceptions. See, for example, Michael R. Steele, *Knute Rockne, a Bio-Bibliography* (1983); and Jerry Brondfield, *Rockne: The Coach, the Man, the Legend* (1976). Similarly, Coles Phinizy, in "We Know of Knute, Yet Know Him Not," *Sports Illustrated*, 10 Sept. 1979, pp. 98–112, and "Win One for the Gipper," *Sports Illustrated*, 17 Sept. 1979, pp. 40–48, demythologizes Rockne's career. Rockne is featured in many books and articles concerning Notre Dame football, including Ken Chowder, "When Notre Dame Needed Inspiration, Rockne Provided It," *Smithsonian*, Nov. 1993, pp. 164–77; Gene Schoor, *100 Years of Notre Dame Football* (1987); Murray Sperber, *Shake Down the Thunder: The Creation of Notre Dame Football* (1994); and Ken Rappaport, *Wake Up the Echoes: Notre Dame Football* (1975).

MARC S. MALTBY

ROCKWELL, Alphonso David (18 May 1840–12 Apr. 1933), physician and exponent of the use of electricity in medicine, was born Alphonso Elias Rockwell in New Canaan, Connecticut, the son of David Rockwell, a teacher who turned to farming later in life, and Betty Comstock. Alphonso Rockwell, one of nine children, left Kenyon College, Ohio, after two years because of family financial difficulties. He returned to Milan, Ohio, where his family owned a farm, and in 1861 began to study medicine under a Dr. Dean, the father of a former college roommate.

The following year, with the Civil War under way, Rockwell joined Company B of the Eighty-fifth Ohio Volunteer Infantry, a company otherwise made up entirely of students and professors from Hudson, Ohio, and was charged with guarding prisoners at Camp Chase, near Columbus, Ohio. After a four-month tour of duty, Rockwell began studies in the Medical Department at the University of Michigan from 1862 to 1863. Following another brief preceptorship under Dean, Rockwell enrolled at Bellevue Hospital Medical College in New York City in 1863 and graduated in March 1864. He returned to Ohio and was commissioned as assistant surgeon in the Sixth Ohio Volunteer Cavalry, assigned to the Army of the Potomac. Following discharge from the army after the war, he began a private medical practice in New York in 1866; two years later he married Sussanah Landon, with whom he had four children.

An acquaintance Rockwell made early in his medical practice, William Miller, introduced Rockwell to the possibilities of applying measured amounts of faradic, or alternating, current to medicine. Physicians had employed electricity empirically since the eighteenth century, primarily for cases of paralyzed limbs or digits. Electricity had entered the realm of medical quackery as well. (The first patent for a medical device in the United States was granted to Elisha Perkins in 1796 for his metallic tractors, which he said utilized a "pathological electroid fluid" that allegedly cured a variety of illnesses as the tractors were drawn over the skin.) The understanding of the physiological action of electricity had grown substantially by the mid-nineteenth century, due in large part to the work of Guillaume Benjamin Amand Duchenne and Robert Remak, who championed the use of faradic and galvanic (direct) currents, respectively.

Despite Miller's lack of formal instruction in the scientific principles underlying the application of electricity to medicine, Rockwell was so impressed by his results that he joined Miller's medical practice in 1867. George Beard, whom Rockwell had met while he was at Bellevue and Beard was a student at the College of Physicians and Surgeons in New York, sent charity patients from his practice at the Demilt Dispensary to the Miller-Rockwell practice. Beard himself already had some familiarity with the medical application of electricity, originating with his exposure to the subject when he was a student at Yale.

Miller soon retired, and by 1867 Rockwell and Beard began publishing the results of their electrotherapeutic procedures, initially in a series entitled "The Medical Use of Electricity," in the *Medical Record* of New York. Their results with more than 10,000 cases, and the experiences of others, were collected into *A Practical Treatise on the Medical and Surgical Uses of Electricity Including Localized and General Electrization* (1871), which became the most popular text on the subject in the United States, reaching four editions by 1884 and ten in all. Aware of the reputation of irregular practitioners in the field, the authors stated that "The somewhat deserved reproach against electrotherapeutists, that they publish only their most fortunate results, we have endeavored to avert by giving prominence to failures as well as to successes; by noting relapses as well as permanent recoveries."

Beard and Rockwell concluded their joint practice in 1876 by mutual consent, but disputes over specific credit for work cited in their text drove the two apart; they apparently reconciled before Beard's death in 1883. Rockwell continued to publish the results of his clinical experiences with electrotherapeutics in a wide variety of professional journals. Moreover, he was affiliated, as an electrotherapeutic specialist, with a number of academic institutions and hospitals, including Women's Hospital in New York in the 1870s, the New York Post–Graduate School of Medicine, from the late 1880s to the early 1890s, and the Flushing Hospital, from 1904 to 1912. Rockwell also served as president of the American Electro-Therapeutic Association. He applied his understanding of electricity in a radically different venue at the request of the state of New York, for which he developed a method of electrocution to carry out capital punishment.

Rockwell's work, including his collaborations with Beard, was respected by his peers for its honesty and attention to detail; he also helped establish the use of electrocautery in surgery. While at least some of his reported successes probably were more the result of the nature of self-limited illnesses, Rockwell nevertheless played a major role in the introduction of electrotherapeutics into legitimate medical practice in the United States. He died in Flushing, New York.

• The principal source for biographical information on Rockwell is his autobiography, *Rambling Recollections* (1920). For a comprehensive list of his monographs and journal publications, see the sections on or related to electricity in medicine in the various series of United States, War Department, Surgeon General's Office, *Index-Catalogue of the Library of the Surgeon General's Office* (1880–1961). Beard and Rockwell's overall results with electricity were originally published in

G. M. Beard and A. D. Rockwell, "The Medical Use of Electricity," *Medical Record* of New York (1866–1867), p. 514, and (1867–1868), pp. 1, 98, 148, 169. A brief assessment of Rockwell's work can be found in Margaret Rowbottom and Charles Susskind, *Electricity and Medicine: History of Their Interaction* (1984).

JOHN P. SWANN

ROCKWELL, George Lincoln (9 Mar. 1918–25 Aug. 1967), leader of the American Nazi Party, was born in Bloomington, Illinois, the son of George "Doc" Rockwell, a vaudeville comedian, and Claire Schade, a dancer. Rockwell was six when his parents divorced; from then on he lived with one or the other of his parents in Maine, Rhode Island, and New Jersey.

Rockwell graduated from Central High School in Providence, Rhode Island, then from Hebron Academy in Maine, and in 1938 enrolled at Brown University, but he never graduated from college. Enlisting in March 1941, he served as a U.S. Navy aviator throughout World War II, receiving several decorations and a promotion to lieutenant commander in 1945. In 1943 he had married Judith Aultman, with whom he had three children. They divorced in 1953.

On his return to civilian life, Rockwell studied commercial art at the Pratt Institute in Brooklyn. Between 1945 and 1950 he earned his living as a commercial photographer, painter, advertising executive, and publisher. In 1951, recalled to active duty, he trained naval fighter pilots throughout the Korean War. Horrified by the purported revelations of Senator Joseph R. McCarthy's investigations into subversive political activities during the early 1950s, but more puzzled by efforts to silence the senator, Rockwell became convinced that Adolf Hitler's National Socialism was the "doctrine of scientific racial idealism" and the "new religion." Influenced by Hitler and McCarthy as well as by Huey Long and the Reverend Gerald L. K. Smith (the self-proclaimed "rabble-rouser for the right"), Rockwell fervently believed that a Jewish-Communist conspiracy was attempting to subvert American society through racial integration and miscegenation. Assigned to one year of duty in Iceland in 1952, he consolidated his political beliefs and planned a campaign of political action based on his National Socialist philosophy.

In 1953 Rockwell remarried. He and his second wife (whose name is not given in published records) had four children and were divorced in 1959.

As a civilian again in 1954, Rockwell began to publish the periodical *U.S. Lady*, directed to the wives of American servicemen. Through this publication he hoped to subtly spread his views to what he believed was a receptive audience. He established personal contacts in right-wing circles, bought radio advertising, organized meetings and lectures, wrote letters, and created a paper organization, the American Federation of Conservative Organizations. Despite these efforts, however, the federation disbanded in 1956.

During 1957 and 1958 Rockwell worked for a management consulting firm, sold advertising, and produced political cartoons in collaboration with the publisher of a small racist magazine, *Newport News*. In 1958 the financial support of wealthy conservative Harold N. Arrowsmith, Jr., enabled him to establish the National Committee to Free America from Jewish Domination. The purpose of the committee was to print, publish, and distribute material that documented evidence of a widespread Jewish-Communist conspiracy in the United States. Rockwell set out to exert "agitation of such a blatant and revolutionary sort that the mass media could not ignore it." On 29 July 1958 he organized the first public protest since 1941 against alleged Jewish control of the U.S. government. His picketing of the White House in response to President Dwight Eisenhower's decision to send U.S. Marines to Lebanon was the first of several demonstrations and violent incidents. Although attracting media attention, Rockwell's radical tactics lost him Arrowsmith's financial and personal support. Meanwhile, constant harassment by the public, he claimed, forced him to send his wife and their children to Iceland to ensure their safety.

In 1959, alone and disillusioned by his failures, Rockwell claimed to have undergone a religious experience during which Adolf Hitler showed him "the way to survival." Rockwell became convinced that his life's task was to carry the Führer's ideas "to total, world wide victory." In March 1959 he founded the Union of Free Enterprise National Socialists (he later changed the name to the American Nazi Party), referred to himself as the "American Fuehrer," and proclaimed his renewed dedication to the establishment of an Aryan world order.

The American Nazi Party remained small throughout the 1960s—unable to raise more than a few dozen people for rallies—lacked sufficient funding, and had but negligible influence. Nonetheless, Rockwell's flamboyant personality and his outrageous methods (including driving a "hate bus" through the South to counter the influence of the integrationist Freedom Riders) often attracted media headlines. Summing up his methods during a lecture to a thousand students at Hofstra College in Hempstead, New York, he claimed to have attempted to build an image through his unit of uniformed "storm troopers" and the use of the swastika. "You never convert masses of people with reason and logic." According to the American Nazi Party, the "Jewish Bolsheviks" were aiding "the niggers rampaging in the streets" (who were led by "Martin Luther Coon"), the "queers," the anarchist students, and other enemies of "Decent White Christian America."

Rockwell attempted through various magazines (including the *National Socialist Bulletin* and *Rockwell Reports*) to promote the National Socialist movement. In 1962 he established the World Union of National Socialists to bring together similar movements in Great Britain, France, Germany, and Belgium in a common effort. Then, in 1966, he reorganized party activity; the following year he officially renamed the party as the National Socialist White People's Party,

and he shifted the focus of propaganda from anti-Semitism to harangues against blacks.

Rejected and discredited by the majority of mainstream conservatives, Rockwell nonetheless claimed the conservative right wing to be his ideological companions. By the late 1960s, however, the American Nazis no longer attracted media attention. At the time of Rockwell's death, the party numbered only a small group of adherents. Indeed, government officials were reported to have estimated that Rockwell's organization comprised fewer than a hundred members.

Rockwell was assassinated in Arlington, Virginia, near American Nazi headquarters by a man he had expelled from the party a few months earlier.

• In addition to the numerous magazines and newspapers that Rockwell contributed to throughout his career (including "From Ivory Tower to Privy Wall: On the Art of Propaganda," *National Socialist World*, Spring 1966), he wrote an autobiography, *This Time the World* (1961); also see his *White Power* (1967), which describes America's racial and national decay and Rockwell's plans to bring about an Aryan victory. *Lincoln Rockwell: A National Socialist Life* (n.d.), a tribute by a Nazi party member, William Pierce, reveals the admiration that the party leader won from his followers. Rockwell's American Nazi Party is examined in Charles U. Daly, "The Man Who Would Bring Back Hitler," *Cavalier*, June 1961; Charles Crause, "George Rockwell: A Myth or Real Threat to America's Peace," *Private Affairs*, June 1962; and Jack Anderson, "Why I Quit the American Nazi Party," *Parade*, 6 Dec. 1964. David H. Bennett, *The Party of Fear: From Nativist Movements to the New Right in American History* (1988), contains the section "Neo-Nazis and Other Extremists," which includes a discussion of Rockwell's affiliation with other right-wing groups, such as the John Birch Society. See also John Carpenter, *Extremism U.S.A.* (1964), for a discussion of Rockwell's views and methods as well as a brief outline of proposed social and political programs under an American Nazi Party administration. An obituary is in the *New York Times*, 26 Aug. 1967.

SHARON D. RUDY

ROCKWELL, Norman (3 Feb. 1894–8 Nov. 1978), illustrator, was born Norman Percevel Rockwell in New York City, the son of Jarvis Waring Rockwell, the manager of the New York City office of a textile firm, and Nancy Hill. According to Rockwell, his father was aloof and his mother was self-indulgent, and neither he nor his older brother enjoyed a warm relationship with either parent. His maternal grandfather, Howard Hill, was a sporadically successful artist, active from 1860 to 1870, who painted detailed scenes of woodland flora and fauna, especially bird subjects, and later in life Rockwell kept an example of his grandfather's work, a small painting of a quail, in his studio. The family moved frequently around Manhattan neighborhoods, but Rockwell thrived on summer holidays in the upstate New York countryside and formed a lifelong attachment to rural life. He described his youthful self as nonathletic, clumsy, skinny, and pigeon-toed, but his talent for drawing afforded him stature among his classmates. In his autobiography, he also recalled listening to his father read the works of Charles Dickens aloud in the evenings and sketching the characters from his imagination. He credited Dickens with influencing his own view of looking at the world. He loved novels rich in characterization and detail, and his painting style would reflect this penchant for detail.

Rockwell knew at a young age that he wanted to be an illustrator and sought the best training for his chosen career. He left Mamaroneck High School when he was fourteen and began a course of study at the Chase School; at sixteen he enrolled at the National Academy of Design, both in New York City. Seeking more progressive instruction he later enrolled at the Art Students League in New York City. Founded in 1875, the Art Students League was considered the most-progressive and exciting art school of its day. Rockwell was classically trained by George Bridgman and Thomas Fogarty, disciples of Howard Pyle, Rockwell's most-revered illustrator. While Bridgman taught him anatomy, perspective, and structure, skills that Rockwell would rely on throughout his long career, Fogarty insisted that his students learn how to "live" in a painting, to know and understand the figures and scenes they were illustrating. Rockwell, a disciplined and conscientious student, began to develop his distinctive style, an exacting technique rich with details and usually executed with gentle humor.

Rockwell worked in the tradition of the fine arts and admired many artists, from Old Masters to his own contemporaries. In his autobiography, he described his respect for artists such as Rembrandt, Jan Vermeer, Albrecht Dürer, Henri Matisse, Paul Klee, and Picasso but also humbly noted that they had no discernible effect on his work. However, throughout his career Rockwell referenced and included representations of well-known works by Vermeer, Michelangelo, Rembrandt, Dürer, Picasso, and even Jackson Pollock in his own pictures. On more than one occasion he "borrowed" directly from a great master. The woman factory worker in his 1943 piece *Rosie the Riveter*, for example, was patterned directly from Michelangelo's *Prophet Isaiah* in the Sistine Chapel. In his 1960 *Triple Self-Portrait*, Rockwell pinned portraits by Dürer, Picasso, Rembrandt, and van Gogh to his own canvas. Hundreds of study prints from museums around the world and an extensive art library served as his reference tools, and he kept abreast of the contemporary art world through journals such as *American Artist* and Museum of Modern Art bulletins. Lifelong professional art club memberships included the Art Director's Club, the Salamagundi Club, and the Society of Illustrators.

Workers of the artists in the golden age of illustration (1880s–1920s) had a significant impact on the development of Rockwell's style, approach, and subject matter, and he was proud to be an illustrator in the great tradition of the golden age masters. He admired the work of his mentors and colleagues and surrounded himself with reminders of the tradition he loved. He had a small collection of works by illustrators Maxfield Parrish, Arthur Rackham, Thomas Fogarty, and Edward Penfield, among others. His favorite illustrator was Howard Pyle, whom he described as "an historian with a brush" and whose "pictures always seemed to tell a story. When I looked at one of Pyle's pictures, it was always crammed with detail, each one important to the whole picture and the tale it illustrated."

Compulsive about his craft, Rockwell worked seven days a week, from dawn to dusk, and produced a prodigious number of drawings, sketches, and paintings. He typically went through at least five (and sometimes as many as fourteen) preliminary steps from idea to illustration, starting with thumbnail sketches, and moving to large detailed charcoal drawings, a color study, and then to the final oil painting. In the 1930s he succumbed to the lure of the camera and began using photography in the development of an idea, although he felt he was betraying artistic principles. "At first I used photographs only occasionally, trying to hang on to at least the shreds of my self-respect," he wrote. "But it was like a touch of morphine now and then. Pretty soon, before I knew it, I was an addict. A guilty, shamefaced addict, but an addict nonetheless" (*My Adventures as an Illustrator*, p. 289). Rockwell worked like a stage director when posing his models in a photography session. He acted out the poses and used only authentic locations, costumes, and props.

Success came early. Before his sixteenth birthday Rockwell had received commissions to do four Christmas cards. The earliest published Rockwell covers appeared in September and October 1913 on the Scout magazine *Boys' Life*. Thus began Rockwell's first important professional position, as illustrator and art director of *Boys' Life*, for which he produced more than 250 illustrations. This position began a lifetime association with Scouting; for a half century he painted the annual calendar scenes for the Boy Scouts of America. In his early years he also painted hundreds of illustrations for publications such as *American Magazine, Collier's, St. Nicholas*, and *Youth's Companion*.

At the age of twenty-one Rockwell moved from New York City to suburban New Rochelle, an active illustrators' colony, where he engaged in a busy social life and enjoyed the companionship of other successful illustrators, including Howard Chandler Christy, the brothers J. C. and Frank Leyendecker, and Coles Phillips. Before his marriage to Irene O'Connor in 1916 he shared a studio with artist and cartoonist Clyde Forsythe, whom he later credited with encouraging him to develop the style and subject matter for which he was to become best known, humorous pictures of children and families, and warning him to avoid the more popular style and subjects of the day, slick representations of sophisticated society types as painted by Christy and the Leyendeckers. With his architect friend Dean Parmelee, Rockwell designed his first studio, located on Lord Kitchener Road in New Rochelle, where he lived with his wife, her mother, and several of her siblings. During this period Rockwell also produced work for magazines such as *Life, Literary Digest*, and the *Country Gentleman*.

Rockwell's first *Saturday Evening Post* cover—a depiction of a disconsolate boy shoving a baby carriage past jeering friends who were suited up for baseball—was published on 20 May 1916, a date that signaled his arrival among the greats in American illustration. Rockwell went on to illustrate 321 *Post* covers over a 47-year period. Ken Stuart, a former *Post* art editor, observed that during the 1950s and early 1960s a Rockwell cover ensured an additional 50,000 to 75,000 copies in newsstand sales. At that time illustrations were still being reproduced primarily in black and white, with red occasionally added. Rockwell, who kept abreast of changes in reproduction processes over the course of his career, sometimes painted an illustration in full color in his early years with the *Post*, but most were executed *en grisaille*, using only gray or sepia and white for illustrations that would be printed in black and white. By 1926 magazines were publishing in full color, and Rockwell was painting rich, full-color canvases. From his early experience with black and white Rockwell had come to see the merit of using contrasting color tones and relative values of light and dark to tell his stories. An important step in the development of his illustrations was a meticulous black-and-white charcoal drawing in which he worked out the final composition, contrasts, and detail. In later years Rockwell prepared a color study, usually on a photograph of the detailed drawing, scaled to the size of the magazine, so that he could see how the illustration would appear in print.

During World War I Rockwell served in the navy. Stationed in Charleston, South Carolina, he worked as art editor of the base publication, *Afloat and Ashore*, and was sought after to paint officer portraits. He also continued his successful civilian career, painting several covers for the *Post*. After his one-year enlistment ended in 1918, he made several trips to Europe during the 1920s with friends. His childless marriage ended in divorce in 1930. That same year, while painting on location for a *Post* cover in Hollywood, he met and married Mary Barstow, with whom he had three sons. Despite the Great Depression, Rockwell made several trips to Europe in the early 1930s with his new family as he sought inspiration during an ebb in his career.

The 1930s and 1940s were the most productive decades of Rockwell's career. He was illustrating *Post* covers and story illustrations for other publications. Also, during his lifetime he produced advertisements, calendars, and other commercial art for more than 150 different companies, including Edison Mazda, Hallmark, and Ford Motor Company. In 1935 he received a commission from Heritage Press to illustrate the Mark Twain classics *The Adventures of Tom Sawyer* and *The Adventures of Huckleberry Finn*. His illustrations are among the best known depictions of these two famous literary characters.

Rockwell's work reflected small town America. In 1939 the family moved to Arlington, Vermont, where he used his neighbors and friends as models. Like New Rochelle, Arlington was home to numerous noted illustrators, such as Mead Schaeffer, John Ather-

ton, and George Hughes, with whom he developed close friendships. He once remarked, "I guess I have a bad case of the American nostalgia for the clean, simple country life as opposed to the complicated world of the city." A series based on scenes of rural Vermont life titled "Norman Rockwell Visits" became a regular feature in the *Saturday Evening Post* in the 1940s. The original paintings for this series, exemplified by *Family Doctor*, are some of Rockwell's finest works of this period. Despite his love for small town living, he maintained close professional ties to major urban centers, delivering his fresh canvases by train to Curtis Publishing Company in Philadelphia, working with Manhattan art editors, or continuing his travels to California to paint covers and movie posters.

Vignettes of small town life, barefoot country boys, and family moments constitute but one aspect of Rockwell's work, however. In 1943, as a contribution to the war effort, he created a series of four paintings based on President Franklin Roosevelt's "Four Freedoms" speech. Featured in the *Post* along with essays by respected thinkers of the day, Rockwell's *Four Freedoms* became symbolic of democracy and human compassion; the series also was used as the centerpiece of traveling World War II war bond shows, which raised more than $132 million. Rockwell's wartime paintings for the *Post* depicted scenes from the homefront, and his series on imaginary private Willie Gillis was enormously popular.

A fire in Rockwell's studio shortly after delivery of *Four Freedoms* to the *Post* razed the building and consumed his collection of period costumes, his working props and supplies, and an unknown number of paintings and sketches. The family moved shortly thereafter to a home in West Arlington, where he built a new studio. In 1953 the family moved again to Stockbridge, Massachusetts, so that Mary Rockwell could receive medical treatment for depression. In the 1950s Rockwell became best known for his paintings of warm and humorous scenes of American family life. His portrayals of familial relationships and situations are timeless and universal and transcend a given period of history or culture. Rockwell once wrote, "Without thinking too much about it in specific terms, I was showing the America I knew and observed to others who might not have noticed." Some of his most famous *Post* covers of this period include *The Marriage License*, *Girl at Mirror*, and *The Runaway*. Also in the 1950s and early 1960s the Massachusetts Mutual Life Insurance Company commissioned eighty-one advertisements for their American Family series campaign.

The death of his wife in 1959 deeply distressed Rockwell, and he sought relief from his grief by taking poetry and sketch classes, participating in men's social groups, and undergoing psychiatric therapy. It was in a poetry class that he met Mary "Molly" Punderson, a retired schoolteacher from Milton Academy (Milton, Mass.). They were married in 1961. Rockwell's relationship with the *Saturday Evening Post* ended in 1963, after a 47-year association that had catapulted him to fame and delivered his work into the homes of one out of four American families during the *Post*'s heyday. He and his third wife began to travel extensively in Europe, the Soviet Union, and throughout the United States, both for pleasure and on assignment for *Look* magazine. They also collaborated on a children's book, *Willie Was Different* (1967). The book, which features fourteen color oils and numerous black-and-white sketches, combined his best skills as an illustrator and storyteller with his fondness for children.

In the 1960s and 1970s Rockwell returned to his journalistic style of illustration with a series of topical illustrations for *Look* that depicted a changing America. Painted to accompany news stories, the *Look* group differs significantly from his more familiar subject matter. International politics involving the Middle East and the Soviet Union, the Peace Corps, the civil rights movement and racial integration, the NASA space program, and social issues, such as poverty, were his new subjects, and his work reflected the seriousness of these themes. Rockwell captured the civil rights movement in moving and often graphic paintings published in *Look*. His 1964 portrait of a young black girl being escorted to school by U.S. marshals is one his most powerful. *Southern Justice* presents in stark relief the murder of Freedom Riders in a small Mississippi town. He left future generations a clear and compelling picture of America in the midst of great social change.

Rockwell was also adept at portraiture. He painted a number of portraits of world leaders for the *Saturday Evening Post* during the late 1950s and early 1960s. In 1968 he completed portraits of all six major presidential candidates for *Look*, frequently traveling on location to sketch and photograph his famous subjects. Five U.S. presidents had their likenesses recorded by Rockwell: Dwight D. Eisenhower, John F. Kennedy, Lyndon B. Johnson, Richard M. Nixon, and Ronald Reagan. President Kennedy's profile appears alongside young volunteers in *The Peace Corps*, executed by Rockwell for *Look* in 1966. Celebrities including John Wayne, Frank Sinatra, and Arnold Palmer also sought out Rockwell, who selectively accepted occasional private commissions.

Having been largely ignored by the art world and disdained by the critics, Rockwell's work was finally accorded some professional appreciation in the 1970s. The Bernard Danenberg Galleries of New York City hosted, in 1972, a major sixty-year retrospective exhibition of works by the artist who as a boy in 1899 had observed Admiral George Dewey's flagship steaming victoriously into New York harbor at the end of the Spanish-American War and who as a septuagenarian in 1969 painted man's first step on the moon. The first major critical treatment of his work was written by Thomas Buechner, then director of the Brooklyn Museum, to accompany a national exhibition tour. Subsequently, Rockwell's work began to be featured in Madison Avenue galleries and New York auction houses, and private collectors started to acquire his paintings. Rockwell was not, however, deprived of

public recognition during his lifetime. The town of Stockbridge honored him with a parade in 1976. The following year President Gerald Ford presented him with the Presidential Medal of Freedom for his "vivid and affectionate portraits of our country." Rockwell was eighty-two when he painted his last and fiftieth Boy Scouts of America calendar and his final magazine cover, for *American Artist* in celebration of the nation's bicentennial in 1976. He died two years later at his home in Stockbridge.

The Norman Rockwell Museum in Stockbridge, one of only a few museums in the United States devoted to a single artist, houses the largest significant public collection of his original artwork and his last studio. His original paintings are widely collected, especially by private collectors. Museums and institutions with Rockwell originals in their collections include the Berkshire Museum, the Brandywine River Museum, the Brooklyn Museum, the Columbus Museum of Art, the Corcoran Gallery of Art, the Los Angeles County Museum of Art, the Metropolitan Museum of Art, the National Air and Space Museum, the National Baseball Hall of Fame and Museum Inc., the National Portrait Gallery, the National Scouting Museum, the New Britain Museum of American Art, the Virginia Military Institute, and the Wadsworth Athenaeum.

The name "Norman Rockwell" continues to be invoked by writers and politicians, sometimes reverently at other times sardonically. References to "Rockwell values" and to "Rockwellian small town images" are phrases in an American mythic shorthand that conjures up memories of a time when life was simpler. It is not uncommon for political cartoonists to lampoon current events by caricaturing Rockwell's iconic images, such as *Freedom from Want* or *Triple Self-Portrait*. A lifelong chronicler of personalities and events, Rockwell painted a model in honor of aviator Charles Lindbergh and also painted astronaut Neil Armstrong, a Negro porter from the 1940s and black civil rights activists from the 1960s, as well as international figures such as India's Jawaharlal Nehru, and Egypt's Gamal Abdel Nasser. He was an artist of remarkable accomplishments who possessed an extraordinary eye for detail and was beloved by the American people.

• The archive and papers of Rockwell are at the Norman Rockwell Museum Reference Center in the Norman Rockwell Museum at Stockbridge, Mass. The collection comprises more than 100,000 items, including photographs, letters, personal calendars, fan mail, and business documents. The center also houses film and tape footage about the artist, including an interview by Edward R. Murrow. Several bronze busts by Rockwell's son Peter are owned by the National Gallery in Washington, D.C., and by the Norman Rockwell Museum. Laurie Norton Moffatt, *Norman Rockwell: A Definitive Catalogue* (1986), is a complete and detailed record of individual Rockwell artworks and the source for identification and verification of Rockwell artwork. *Norman Rockwell, My Adventures as an Illustrator*, by Norman Rockwell as told to Thomas Rockwell, 2d ed. (1988), is filled with anecdotes and humorous reminiscences. Thomas S. Buechner, *Norman*

Rockwell, Artist and Illustrator (1970), contains fine reproductions and assesses Rockwell's work and contribution. Arthur L. Guptill, *Norman Rockwell, Illustrator* (1946), presents a richly detailed and personal look at Rockwell's career at its pinnacle. Susan E. Meyers, *Norman Rockwell's World War II: Impressions from the Homefront* (1991), combines Rockwell's storytelling ability with a visual record of the war's impact on civilian life. Stuart Murray and James McCabe, *Norman Rockwell's Four Freedoms: Images that Inspire a Nation* (1993), is primarily a reference work on the *Four Freedoms* paintings. *Norman Rockwell: A Centennial Celebration* (exhibition catalog, the Norman Rockwell Museum, 1993), with preface by Maureen Hart Hennessey, was published in connection with the 100th anniversary of Rockwell's birth and includes a representative sampling from almost every year of his career (1912–1976).

LAURIE NORTON MOFFATT

RODALE, J. I. (16 Aug. 1898–7 June 1971), health food publisher, was born Jerome Irving Cohen in New York City, the son of Michael Cohen, a capmaker and grocer, and Bertha Rouda. Both parents were Polish immigrants. Rodale studied at New York and Columbia Universities but did not earn any degrees. At age twenty he became an auditor for the Internal Revenue Service, and at twenty-one he moved to Pittsburgh, where he worked in a private accounting firm for three years. He wanted, however, for some vague reason that he never explained, to be a farmer and publisher. In 1920 he traveled to Kentucky on business and became enchanted with the Bluegrass State. "Being among farmers and in farm country I was more and more imbued with the ambition of some day having my own farm and riding to town with my children on a buck-board drawn by two trusty horses."

Because the New York publishing world at that time excluded Jews, he changed his name. He took a combination of old family names and came up with Rodale. Henceforth, he was known as J. I. or "Jerry" Rodale.

He married Anna Andrews in 1927, in both religious and civil ceremonies because Anna was not Jewish. They had three children, including one son, Robert, who took over the Rodale Enterprises at the time of his father's death.

Shortly after their marriage, the Rodales moved to Emmaus, Pennsylvania, where J. I. started his first magazine, the *Humorous Scrapbook*. It quickly folded, in part because not very many people in the Allentown, Pennsylvania, area understood all of the "inside" Jewish jokes. His second magazine, the *Clown* (later retitled the *American Humorist*), also failed.

Rodale bought a farm in Emmaus in 1940 and began experiments with organic methods. He started the magazine that was to make him wealthy, well known, and controversial: *Organic Gardening and Farming* (1942). Strongly influenced by Albert Howard's *An Agricultural Testament* (1943), which contained long descriptions about organic gardening, in time Rodale started other periodicals, including the most widely distributed health magazine in the United States, *Prevention* (1950).

In addition to magazine publishing at Rodale Press and experimenting on the Emmaus farm, Rodale wrote books relating to gardening, farming, and good nutrition. These included *Happy People Rarely Get Cancer* (1970), *The Hawthorne Berry for the Heart* (1955), *Lower Your Pulse Rate and Live Longer* (1971), and *Are We Really Living Longer?* (1955).

Rodale also wrote plays, some of which were performed in small theaters in New York City and in upstate New York. Most of his plays were health and nutrition oriented and were generally panned by the critics because he frequently turned plays and short stories of famous authors (Molière and Somerset Maugham, for instance) into his own one-act productions. Rodale retitled Molière's *Le Malade imaginaire* as *Toinette*, and the following lines encouraged critics in their disparagement of his playwriting abilities: "Our neglect may help kill 'em; But we won't neglect to bill 'em; That is one mistake we doctors never make."

Rodale was also scorned by the scientific community. For one thing, he had no credentials; for another, scientific farming had increased crop yield by using chemical fertilizers, pesticides, and insecticides. Even writers who might have been expected to support Rodale shied away from him. *Silent Spring* author Rachel Carson refused to appear on health and farming programs with him because, for reasons known only to her, she objected to the word *organic*. The Lehigh Valley (Pa.) Committee against Health Fraud constantly investigated Rodale, calling him a charlatan who only wanted to make money. The Federal Trade Commission (FTC) tried unsuccessfully to put him out of business, particularly because of one of his books, *The Health Finder*. The FTC accused Rodale of trying to practice medicine without a license.

Rodale wanted people to quit smoking; to stop drinking milk, coffee, and alcohol; to take large doses of natural food supplements; and to create a diet that eliminated most red meats. He wanted farms—even large ones—to be operated on an organic system. This meant the use of compost heaps composed of everything from animal manure to hair clippings.

Rodale was persistent, however, shrugging off criticisms. During the 1950s, actress Gloria Swanson visited his farm at Emmaus as did busloads of curiosity seekers and even politicians, such as former vice president Henry A. Wallace. In the mid-1960s and into the 1970s a large number of communal farms developed in the United States. At many of these places, Rodale was the "high guru."

Throughout his life and career, Rodale followed a dictum set by John Stuart Mill, that new ideas and methods are first met by ridicule and anger, then discussion, and finally approval. He believed in 1971 that he was entering the third phase of Mill's sequence. He was happy, therefore, to be a guest on the Dick Cavett Show in New York City on 7 June 1971. He and Cavett bantered back and forth for a time, and Rodale said he expected to live to the year 2000, when he would be 102 years old. Since he had been born in

1898, that would mean, he said, that he would live in three different centuries. About twenty minutes into the show, Cavett turned his attention to another guest and then noticed that Rodale's head had begun to droop. Everyone in the audience, including Cavett, thought Rodale was feigning sleep out of boredom and laughed. It did not take long to discover that Rodale was suffering a heart attack. He was rushed to a nearby hospital, where he died.

Many of the farming and health methods Rodale championed a quarter of a century ago had come into vogue by the 1990s. Medical studies regularly inveigh against alcohol, coffee, milk, tobacco, and other products that Rodale thought harmful to the human body. Even the U.S. Department of Agriculture, which disdained Rodale during his lifetime, today supports an "alternate" farming section in which organic farming is widely studied and applied in dozens of instances to big farms rather than just family units. Through his arguments against chemical fertilizers, insecticides, and pesticides and his other suggestions for improving nutrition and health, Rodale heralded new approaches to environment and lifestyles.

• Rodale wrote his *Autobiography* (1965). Some of his other books that provide an insight into the "Father of Organic Farming" in America are *Organic Front* (1948), *An Organic Trip to England* (1954), and *The Stones of Jehosaphat* (1954). Also consult *Organic Merry-Go-Around, Our Poisoned Earth and Sky*, and *My Own Technique for Health*, all published by Rodale Press. Some other Rodale books—all published by Rodale Press between 1955 and 1971—are *Smoke and Die: Quit and Live, Twenty Ways to Stop Smoking, How to Eat for a Healthy Heart, Natural Health, Sugar, and the Criminal Mind, Poison in your Pots and Pans, The Prostate, This Pace Is Not Killing Us, Walk, Do Not Run to the Doctor*, and *Conversations toward Better Health*. The only full-scale biography is Carlton Jackson, *J. I. Rodale: Apostle of Nonconformity* (1974). The most substantive obituary is in *The New York Times*, 8 June 1971.

CARLTON JACKSON

RODEHEAVER, Homer Alvin (4 Oct. 1880–18 Dec. 1955), evangelist, musician, and music publisher, was born in Cinco Hollow, Ohio, the son of Thurman Hall Rodeheaver, who was in the lumber mill business, and Francis "Fannie" Armstrong. As a young man growing up in the mountain logging village of Jellico, in East Tennessee, he was exposed to rural singing school music and fiddle dance music from the Scots-Irish settlers in the area. As a boy he also learned to play the cornet. He attended Ohio Wesleyan College in 1896; there he switched to trombone, played in the college band, took music courses, and served as a cheerleader. He interrupted college to serve in the Fourth Tennessee Band in the Spanish-American War, and after the war, though initially drawn to the law, in about 1904 he joined evangelist William E. Biederwolf as a music director.

Rodeheaver's buoyant, outgoing personality and rugged good looks made him popular as a song leader, and by 1910 he had been hired to work with Billy Sun-

day, at that time one of the most flamboyant and successful evangelists in the country. Rodeheaver was willing to try the newer, lively gospel songs that were being written, and he brought a sense of showmanship to the large crowds Sunday attracted. Often leading the singers with his trombone and pulling practical jokes onstage, he advised his choirs to "go at it like selling goods." His own "big-voiced baritone" (as his record company described it) popularized a number of songs during this time, including Ira David Sankey's "The Ninety and Nine," "Brighten the Corner," and "Bringing in the Sheaves."

Beginning in September 1913 Rodeheaver took his popular style into the Victor Talking Machine Company's studios and recorded the sentimental favorite "Mother's Prayers Have Followed Me." This initiated a long recording career that lasted, on Victor, until 1932. He also recorded for Columbia and for his own Rainbow label. Some of his records, such as "The Unclouded Day" and "The Great Judgement Morning," sold so well that they had to be rerecorded to keep up with demand. Other records featured Rodeheaver's recitations of works such as Paul Lawrence Dunbar's poem "When Malindy Sings" (1916).

Following the example of Sankey, Rodeheaver went into the publishing business in 1910, compiling songs both old and new to sell at revivals. From 1921 to 1941 he hired his older brother Joseph Newton Rodeheaver to work as his business and literary adviser and named his company the Rodeheaver Company. Though Rodeheaver employed veteran songwriters such as B. D. Ackley and Charles Gabriel, he also wrote a number of songs on his own, such as "Lonesome" and "Christmas in Your Heart." Several gospel songbooks also came from the Rodeheaver and the later Rodeheaver-Hall-Mack Company. Starting in about 1922, the company began issuing 78-rpm records on its own label, Rainbow, creating the nation's first record company devoted solely to gospel music. "Radiant Reflections of Religion," as their advertisements proclaimed, the records often featured Rodeheaver himself. The first issue on the label was apparently Rodeheaver's solo "Safe in the Arms of Jesus," released on Rainbow 1001. The company for a time had its own pressing plant, with headquarters on Wabash Avenue in Chicago. It was later moved to Winona Lake, Indiana, and although the Rainbow label was discontinued in the 1930s, it was revived in the late 1940s and continued to release gospel records.

The company remained active through the 1980s, publishing songbooks, sheet music, and inspirational books about the Winona Lake enterprise and the songwriters who worked there. Rodeheaver's venture was one of the first and most successful attempts to apply modern advertising and marketing techniques to gospel music and had a major impact on the landscape of American music.

Rodeheaver, who never married, died in Winona Lake.

• Much of the information on the Rainbow-Rodeheaver company comes from the files of Charles K. Wolfe and interviews with Bruce Howe, manager of the company. A collection of papers and songbooks belonging to Ruthella Feaster Rodeheaver, the sister-in-law of Homer, is at the Center for Popular Music at Middle Tennessee State University in Murfreesboro. Rodeheaver authored or compiled more than 120 books; representative titles include *Great Revival Hymns* (1911), *Songs for Service* (1915), *Victorious Service Songs* (1925), *Christian Service Songs* (1939), and *Glad Tidings in Song* (1945). Biographical data on Homer Rodeheaver is in Thomas Henry Porter, "Homer Alvin Rodeheaver, Evangelist, Musician and Publisher" (Ph.D. diss., New Orleans Baptist Seminary, 1981). An obituary is in the *New York Times*, 19 Dec. 1955.

CHARLES K. WOLFE

RODELL, Fred (1 Mar. 1907–4 June 1980), legal educator and journalist, was born Alfred M. Rodelheim, Jr., in Philadelphia, Pennsylvania, the son of Alfred M. Rodelheim, an engineer, and Florence Wolf Fleisher. Rodell's parents, members of prominent assimilated Jewish families, divorced when he was four, and he and his younger brother John went with his mother to live on the estate of his uncle, Howard Loeb, president of Tradesmen's National Bank. Rodell avoided contact with his father after he turned sixteen and changed his name to Fred Rodell in 1928. Attracted to journalism at an early age, Rodell edited his high school student newspaper and college yearbook. He entered Haverford College at the age of fifteen, received his B.A. in 1926 with high honors, and was elected a member of Phi Beta Kappa. During the winter of 1926–1927 he studied with Harold Laski at the University of London. He edited for the Century Publishing Company and wrote for *Time* magazine afterward.

In 1928 Rodell entered Yale Law School, where he served as student case and comments editor of the *Yale Law Journal*. He graduated in 1931 magna cum laude and was elected a member of the Order of the Coif. For two years he worked as legal adviser to Pennsylvania governor Gifford Pinchot. He married Geraldine Watt, a receptionist in the office, and was divorced from her five years later; they had no children. In 1933 he returned to Yale Law School to teach. He left teaching in 1937 to work as editor and writer at *Fortune* magazine, but he returned to Yale in 1939 after a feud with the publisher.

From the start of his career at Yale, Rodell was identified with legal realism, a movement that flourished at Yale Law School in the 1920s and 1930s. Legal realists combined a commitment to liberal politics with criticism of traditional legal scholarship and skepticism about the autonomy of legal rules. At Yale he taught constitutional law, taxation, labor law, and administrative law. Professor Charles Alan Wright recalled him as "the best teacher I ever had." His course on law and public opinion focused on legal writing and included many students who went on to distinguish themselves as journalists.

In 1936 Rodell published *Fifty-Five Men*, a history of the drafting and ratification of the Constitution, dedicated "to the school children and the politicians—for the same reason." In the same year he published "Goodbye to Law Reviews," a footnoteless article denouncing legal academic prose: "There are two things wrong with almost all legal writing. One is its style. The other is its content." Journalist David Margolick has written that it is "perhaps the most widely read—and most controversial—article in all of legal literature."

Rodell delighted in polemics. His most celebrated book, *Woe unto You, Lawyers!* (1939), opened "In tribal times, there were the medicine men. In the Middle Ages, there were the priests. Today there are the lawyers." More than a generation before it became commonplace, Rodell linked legal institutions and practices to the language of law. He argued that arcane and confusing language resulted from law's role in perpetuating irrational or undemocratic traditions. He objected that "most legal principles, too, are couched in such vague, general language that they cannot possibly be guides to a specific decision on a specific matter." He showed how such vagueness left judges to resort to their personal prejudices in resolving disputes.

Rodell promoted the use of plain language in both legal drafting and in writing about the law. He wrote his books in a popular style and contributed many articles on legal and other topics to popular magazines and periodicals.

In 1939 Rodell married Katherine Cowin Carr, a writer. They were divorced in 1953, and Rodell was awarded custody of their only child, Michael. The next year he married child psychologist Janet Learned, and they remained married till his death.

In *Democracy and the Third Term* (1940), Rodell discussed arguments for and against the reelection of President Franklin D. Roosevelt. He publicly championed the politics of the New Deal. In 1949, realizing an era was come to an end, he dubbed the preceding decade the "Supreme Court's Golden Age."

In *Nine Men: A Political History of the Supreme Court from 1790 to 1955* (1955), he recounted the history of the Supreme Court through a series of biographies of influential justices, noting especially how politics influenced judicial opinions. He insisted that "Laws are words, nothing more. Laws do not write or enforce or interpret themselves." He was one of the first to emphasize the legal importance of the Supreme Court's refusal to hear cases and exposed the political motivations behind judicial inactivity. He bluntly assailed the court's failure throughout its history to defend civil liberties.

Rodell admired his friends, liberal justices Hugo Black and William O. Douglas, but he preferred a plainspoken and courageous conservative over a "weak and weaseling liberal." In later years he denounced Justice Felix Frankfurter with special venom, for Frankfurter abandoned the liberal cause and came to represent the cautious academic reliance on technical rules that Rodell most despised.

With the changing political mood in the 1950s and declining prestige of legal realism, Rodell was increasingly viewed as an anachronism. Students fondly called him "Fred the Red" behind his back, and the administration repeatedly denied him salary increases and appointments to endowed chairs. He believed he was snubbed because of his outspoken politics and his criticism of sacred cows. But according to Dean Eugene V. Rostow, Rodell's popular writings were not the sort of scholarly achievements to justify academic recognition.

Critics detested Rodell's liberal politics and viewed him as something of a wasted intellect. But Justice William O. Douglas said, "His influence upon students was profound and his contributions to legal analysis and legal thought will, I think, be enduring."

Rodell suffered a series of illnesses in the late 1960s that eventually disabled him. He retired in 1973 and was housebound during his last years. His hobbies included fly fishing, photography, and dog breeding. He published some of his amateur photographs of female subjects as *Her Infinite Variety* (1966).

Rodell died at Yale New Haven Hospital. At his request, there was no funeral or memorial service. His widow scattered his ashes over the Seine in Paris together with the ashes of his favorite poodle.

• Rodell's papers are at the Haverford College Library, Haverford, Pa. A selection of his articles, reviews, and humorous poems is *Rodell Revisited: Selected Writings*, edited by Loren Ghiglione, Janet Rodell, and Mike Rodell (1994). The introduction has a biography and discussion. His obituary in the *New York Times*, 6 June 1980, claims he wrote more than 200 articles; the bibliography appended to Charles Alan Wright, "Goodbye to Fred Rodell," *Yale Law Journal* (1980), lists ninety-five popular and academic articles and forty-four book reviews. For biographical information and discussions of his works, see David M. Margolick, "Always the Rebel," *National Law Journal*, 5 May 1980; G. Beth Packert, "The Relentless Realist: Fred Rodell's Life and Writings," *University of Illinois Law Review* (1984); Neil Duxbury, "In the Twilight of Legal Realism: Fred Rodell and the Limits of Legal Critique," *Oxford Journal of Legal Studies* (1991); and Ken Vinson, "Fred Rodell's Case Against the Law," *Florida State University Law Review* (1996).

MICHAEL H. HOFFHEIMER

RODES, Robert Emmett (29 Mar. 1829–19 Sept. 1864), Confederate general, was born in Lynchburg, Virginia, the son of David Rodes, a general of Virginia state militia, and Martha Yancey. Rodes graduated from Virginia Military Institute in 1848 and spent the next two years on the institute's teaching staff. After some experience in Virginia as a civil engineer, he went to work for the Texas Pacific Railroad and then in 1855 moved to Alabama and worked as an engineer there. He married Virginia H. Woodruff of Alabama; they had two children.

In January 1861 Rodes entered Confederate service as captain of a company of Alabama volunteers, which he led to Fort Morgan. He won election to colonel of the Fifth Alabama Infantry on 11 May 1861 and in June took the regiment to Virginia. Although he had

no chance for distinction at the first battle of Manassas, Rodes received a commission as brigadier general to rank from 21 October 1861. His brigade, which eventually included five Alabama regiments, became a seasoned and reliable unit under Rodes's direction.

Rodes and his brigade earned high praise by their desperate and successful attack at Seven Pines (31 May–June 1862); the *Richmond Whig* soon thereafter published a lavish poetic tribute to the general and his men for their efforts in defense of the city. A severe wound at Seven Pines put Rodes out of action for almost three months. He returned to duty in time to win further plaudits for a tenacious stand on the north flank of Turner's Gap at South Mountain on 14 September. Three days later Rodes and his brigade stood bravely in a sunken road near Sharpsburg and christened it with their blood as the famous Bloody Lane. In a day-long succession of close calls for the Army of Northern Virginia, Rodes and his men played the key role in holding Robert E. Lee's center against heavy odds, buying time for A. P. Hill to arrive from Harpers Ferry and hold the Confederate right.

At the battle of Chancellorsville (29 Apr.–5 May 1863), Rodes commanded a large division, as the senior brigade commander present, in Stonewall Jackson's flank attack. His well-earned promotion to major general was fittingly dated from 2 May 1863. In his first battle at the new rank, Rodes organized an attack that did much to make 1 July at Gettysburg a spectacular victory. Two of his brigades were all but destroyed, however, and for the rest of the battle Rodes accomplished little.

During the operations of Lee's army in late 1863 and early 1864, Rodes and his division served competently, sometimes brilliantly. In May they opened the battle of the Wilderness and saved the army at Spotsylvania Court House. Rodes took his division to the Shenandoah Valley under Jubal A. Early in the summer of 1864, making the march to the outskirts of Washington and fighting in the lower valley in July and August. At the third battle of Winchester on 19 September, Rodes fell victim to an enemy bullet. His death had a major negative impact on Confederate fortunes that day and during the rest of the campaign.

Jedediah Hotchkiss, a veteran of staff duty under Stonewall Jackson and Early, called Rodes "the best Division commander" in the army and insisted that the general would have been capable of commanding the entire army. Most of his colleagues and subordinates loved and respected Rodes. A private in the Fourth Georgia called him "our beloved Maj. Genl." in a letter to his wife. General Bryan Grimes labeled Rodes "one of the bravest and best," and a member of another general's staff called him "intrepid & accomplished . . . a gentleman of many noble qualities, & of unaffected & attractive manner." Robert Rodes certainly was among the best division commanders in Lee's army—and may have been the very finest.

• Unfortunately no notable body of Rodes manuscripts survives. For that reason neither a full biography nor even a sizable biographical sketch has ever been written, and none seems possible. The best sketch of the general is Peyton Green, "Robert E. Rodes," in *Memorial, V.M.I.* (1875). See also Bryan Grimes, *Extracts of Letters of Major-General Grimes to His Wife* (1883); Rodes's Compiled Service Record in National Archives Microcopy M331, Roll 215; and the Jedediah Hotchkiss Papers, Library of Congress.

ROBERT K. KRICK

RODGERS, Elizabeth Flynn (25 Aug. 1847–27 Aug. 1939), labor leader and social reformer, was born in Woodford, County Galway, Ireland, the daughter of Robert Flynn and Bridget Campbell. When Elizabeth was seven, her family emigrated, first to New York City and then to London, Ontario, Canada. She attended Catholic schools until she was fourteen, at which time she became a tailoress. In 1864 she married George Rodgers, a Welsh-born iron molder whom she had known since childhood; they had twelve children. The couple moved to Toronto, then to Detroit. In 1876 they moved to the west side of Chicago.

Elizabeth's public career began with her marriage to Rodgers, who was a labor and women's rights activist. In her words, "My husband always believed that women should do anything they liked that was good and which they could do well." While in Detroit, she had operated a boardinghouse that was the family's primary income for six years since her husband was blacklisted for his union activities. She sold the family's furniture on three separate occasions to make ends meet. She also took an active part in her husband's union affairs.

When the Rodgers family moved to Chicago, Elizabeth organized a citywide union of working women (no official name cited in sources) and served as its president in 1876 and 1877. From 1879 through 1886 she organized female workers and agitated for improved working conditions. In each of those years she also served as a delegate to the Illinois State Trades Assembly. She supported the cause of Irish nationalism and served as president of the Eighth Ward Land League, a chapter of an Ireland-based organization that combined land reform with the cause of Irish nationalism.

By 1881 she was active in the Knights of Labor (KOL) and was reputed to have been the first Chicago woman to join the organization. She served as Master Workman of the all-female local assembly 1789, through which she reportedly organized housewives for the KOL. She was local 1789's delegate to KOL District Assembly 24 from 1882 to 1886, at which time she assumed the post as District Master Workman when J. P. Murphy died. She was the first woman to hold such a position in the KOL. Even though she had just given birth two weeks earlier, she served as a delegate to the KOL's 1886 convention. (Delegates jocularly initiated her new son as the youngest Knight.) At the convention she was nominated for the post of General Secretary Treasurer for the entire Order but declined the honor because of family commitments and pressing needs inside District Assembly 24.

Although the KOL upheld women's equality in its constitution, in its official journals, and in the utterances of its leaders, Elizabeth Rodgers tested the limits of the Order's rhetoric. Her methods and tactics often put her at odds with more cautious leaders. She was an ardent supporter of the 1 May 1886 nationwide eight-hour demonstrations sponsored by trade unions and anarchist organizations, even though KOL leader Terence Powderly ordered the Knights to take no part in them. When events in Chicago culminated in a bomb explosion in Haymarket Square on 4 May, she became a staunch defender of the eight men eventually arrested, convicted, and condemned for the crime. Because two of those men—Albert Richards Parsons and August Spies—were members of KOL District Assembly 24, Rodgers diverted monies from district funds for their defense and for clemency appeals. When ordered by Powderly to cease such activity, Rodgers ignored his directives.

In 1887 Rodgers joined with several other Chicago women to form an informal political club to agitate for the United Labor party and to promote woman suffrage. She also joined several socialist groups in Chicago. As District Master Workman of District Assembly 24, she was in charge of all the city's Knights except the stockyards workers, some 50,000 in all, and every two weeks she presided over a meeting of about 300 district delegates. When criticized for assuming such power and for her political work, Rodgers replied, "Knowing my duty to my sex, I thought it necessary to show our brothers how false the theory is that women are not good for anything. I will leave it to the delegates to say whether I performed my duty or not. I have always believed that women should be able to perform any duty that may devolve upon them."

Her high-principled statements and behavior led Powderly to attempt to undercut her power through his Chicago ally Richard Griffiths, but he proved no match for Rodgers. Ironically, the only Chicago Knights she did not control were the ones who eroded her power base. In late 1886 the KOL lost a disastrous strike in the city's stockyards when central leaders repudiated a settlement negotiated by one of its own board members. Thousands of local Knights felt betrayed and left the Order, a pattern common elsewhere. By 1889 KOL membership was a mere third of its 1886 level. The Order was very weak in Chicago, and Rodgers left the KOL shortly thereafter.

From 1889 through 1892 Rodgers worked in various jobs and was a partner in the printing firm of Leavell and Rodgers. She also immersed herself in the Catholic Order of Foresters, a fraternal organization and insurance society that followed a ritual based loosely on the Robin Hood legend. She joined the Foresters shortly after Pope Leo XIII relaxed the church's condemnation of secret societies. Her role with that organization was in keeping with her lifelong pattern of breaking out of women's traditional spheres. She and twelve others founded the Women's Catholic Order of Foresters, and she served as High Chief Ranger, the order's highest office. In most voluntary organizations of the time, women's sororities were little more than auxiliaries that planned social events for male fraternities. Under Rodgers's guidance, however, the WCOF paid death benefits and insurance premiums to female members. This was quite unusual considering that the Foresters did not officially recognize its female members until 1952.

Rodgers retired from public life in 1908. Her husband died in 1920, and she continued to live in Chicago until 1933, when she moved to Milwaukee to live with a daughter. She died in Milwaukee. Her obituaries note her work with the Foresters but give little hint of a life lived in defiance of prescribed roles. In an age in which women's rights and the position of women in organized labor were hotly contested, Rodgers's deeds surpassed rhetoric.

• Biographical sketches of Elizabeth Rodgers appear in several labor periodicals, including the *Labor Leaf*, 29 Dec. 1886; the *Knights of Labor*, 12 Feb. and 5 Mar. 1887; and the *National Labor Tribune*, 2 Apr. 1887. Her activities are discussed in John Andrews and W. D. P. Bliss, *History of Women in Trade Unions* (1974); Eleanor Flexner, *A Century of Struggle* (1972); Susan Levine, *Labor's True Woman* (1984); Philip S. Foner, *Women and the American Labor Movement* (1979); Barbara Mayer Wertheimer, *We Were There* (1977); and Frances Willard, *Glimpses of Fifty Years* (1889). Obituaries are in the *Chicago Daily News*, the *Chicago Tribune*, and the *New York Times*, 28 Aug. 1939.

ROBERT E. WEIR

RODGERS, George Washington (22 Feb. 1787–21 May 1832), naval officer, was born in Cecil County, Maryland, the son of John Rodgers and Elizabeth Reynolds. He was a younger brother of the noted commodore John Rodgers, Jr. On 2 April 1804 Rodgers entered the navy as a midshipman and cruised the Mediterranean aboard the frigate *President*. He witnessed the closing phases of the Tripolitan War and subsequently served on the frigates *Essex* and *United States* and the sloop *Vixen*. Rodgers was promoted to lieutenant on 24 April 1810; the following year he took post with Commander Jacob Jones of the sloop *Wasp*.

Rodgers was still serving with the *Wasp* when the War of 1812 commenced and distinguished himself during the 18 October 1812 victory over the British brig *Frolic*. Once the enemy had been riddled by cannon fire, Rodgers commanded one of the boarding parties that subdued them. Both vessels were recaptured soon after by superior forces, and he endured a brief captivity at Bermuda. Rodgers was exchanged, and following his return to America he received a congressional silver medal and a sword from his native state. In December 1812 he accompanied Jones to New London, Connecticut, to serve aboard the frigate *Macedonian*. British blockades confined them to port for nearly a year and a half before a transfer to Sackets Harbor, New York, was arranged. Rodgers spent the final months of the war onboard the frigate *Mohawk*,

then part of Commodore Isaac Chauncey's Lake Ontario Squadron.

In March 1815 Rodgers assumed command of the brig *Firefly* as part of Commodore Stephen Decatur's squadron. He was intending to sail against Algiers, but en route *Firefly* encountered heavy winds that sprung its mast, and the vessel took no part in the conflict. Rodgers returned home and in July 1815 married Ann Maria Perry, the sister of Commodore Oliver Hazard Perry; the couple had several children. On 27 April 1816 Rodgers became a master commandant and took charge of the sloop *Peacock* in the Mediterranean Squadron from 1816 to 1819. He then spent six years at the New York Navy Yard, until 3 March 1825 when the rank of captain was conferred. Between 1826 and 1830 Rodgers functioned on the Board of Examiners. In November 1831 he received appointment as commodore of the Brazilian Squadron aboard the flagship *Warren* and sailed to Argentina on a diplomatic mission. He died of illness at Buenos Aires and was buried there. In 1850 his remains were returned to the United States and reinterred on his property in Connecticut.

Rodgers was an active and enterprising sailor sired from one of the foremost naval families in U.S. history. His untimely death cut short a promising career but not before he contributed to the professionalism and traditions of the U.S. Navy.

• Rodgers's official correspondence is in RG 45, Captains' Letters, National Archives. Scattered materials also exist in the Isaac Chauncey letterbooks, New-York Historical Society, and the Oliver Hazard Perry Papers, Clements Library, University of Michigan. Family information can be gleaned from Charles O. Paullin, *Commodore John Rodgers* (1910), and C. B. Perry, *The Perrys of Rhode Island* (1913). Rodgers's War of 1812 activities are amply covered in George Gibbs, *Pike and Cutlass* (1900), pp. 106–17; Frederick S. Hill, *Twenty-six Historic Ships* (1902), pp. 80–98; and Joseph Leeming, *The Book of American Fighting Ships* (1939), pp. 115–21. Perspective into his diplomatic missions can be found in David F. Long, *Gold Braid and Foreign Relations* (1988).

JOHN C. FREDRIKSEN

RODGERS, George Washington (30 Oct. 1822–17 Aug. 1863), naval officer, was born in Brooklyn, New York, the son of George Washington Rodgers, a naval officer, and Ann Maria Perry. Rodgers joined the navy at age thirteen, when he was commissioned a midshipman on 30 April 1836. He first went to sea aboard the *Boston* and the *Constellation* in the West Indies and subsequently served in the Mediterranean on board the *Brandywine*. Upon his return to the United States in 1841, Rodgers entered the Philadelphia naval school, achieving promotion to passed midshipman on 1 July 1842. On 21 August 1842 he married Kate Margaret Lane. The marriage produced no children.

Rodgers spent the next three years serving with the African Squadron on board the *Saratoga*. During the Mexican War, he served in the Gulf of Mexico on the *Colonel Harney* and the *John Adams*. After the war he spent two years with the Coast Survey, finally achieving promotion to lieutenant on 4 June 1850. Thereafter he served on the *Germantown* with the Home and African squadrons from 1850 to 1853, saw shore duty at the New York Navy Yard from 1853 to 1856, and served with the Brazil Squadron on the *Falmouth* from 1856 to 1859. After another stint at the New York Navy Yard, Rodgers in September 1860 was ordered to the U.S. Naval Academy at Annapolis, where his brother Christopher Rodgers was serving as commandant of midshipmen, and was placed in command of the academy's training ship, the *Constitution*.

Although Maryland never joined the Confederacy, the strength of southern sentiment in that state greatly alarmed Federal authorities. In April 1861 rumors of a secessionist plot to seize the *Constitution* for the Confederacy led Superintendent G. S. Blake to order Rodgers to evacuate the ship, the midshipmen, and much of the school's memorabilia to New York on 21 April. After a week at the New York Navy Yard, the *Constitution* on 9 May 1861 reached its final destination, Fort Adams at Newport, Rhode Island, where it was joined by the rest of the school's faculty.

On 22 September 1861 Rodgers succeeded his brother as commandant of midshipmen. As Union war preparations intensified, however, he decided to seek more active duty. In May 1862 he was given command of the *Tioga*, then under construction at the Boston Navy Yard. On 30 June 1862 the *Tioga* was commissioned and assigned to duty with the North Atlantic Blockading Squadron, headquartered at Hampton Roads, Virginia. On 10 July the ship was transferred to the James River Flotilla, where it patrolled the river and occasionally shelled rebel positions along its banks. On 16 July 1862 Rodgers was promoted to commander. With the end of active Union operations along the James, the *Tioga* was ordered to duty with the West Indian Squadron, where Rodgers spent the fall of 1862 pursuing blockade runners and commerce raiders.

In February 1863 Rodgers was back at the New York Navy Yard overseeing construction of a new ironclad ship, the *Catskill*. On 5 March Rodgers and the *Catskill* reported to Admiral Samuel du Pont for duty with the South Atlantic Blockading Squadron. On 7 April 1863 the *Catskill* participated in an attack on Charleston Harbor. Despite taking some twenty hits, the *Catskill* came within 600 yards of Fort Sumter but was forced to withdraw with the rest of the fleet, with Charleston still defiant. It was yet another demonstration of the futility of relying solely on ships—even ironclads—to take shore fortifications. After a brief stint as senior officer at the Union naval post at North Edisto, South Carolina, Rodgers and the *Catskill* once again tested the guns of Charleston on 10–11 July 1863, this time in support of army operations against Fort Wagner on Morris Island. On the tenth the ship took sixty hits, its attractiveness to Confederate gunners no doubt heightened by Admiral John Dahlgren's decision to make it his flagship for the operation.

On 19 July 1863 Dahlgren, who had replaced du Pont in command, chose Rodgers as his chief of staff. Rodgers's performance as fleet captain greatly impressed Dahlgren, yet when given the choice between remaining with Dahlgren or resuming command of the *Catskill* for another operation against Fort Wagner in late August, Rodgers chose the latter. At 7:30 A.M. on 17 August 1863 the *Catskill*, along with the rest of Dahlgren's ironclads, was exchanging fire with the fort 1,000 yards away. Dahlgren then decided to bring his ships closer to the rebel stronghold and ordered his lead ship, the *Weehawken*, to weigh anchor. To his surprise, Rodgers had already decided on such a move and had the *Catskill* underway. Then tragedy struck. At approximately 8:30 A.M. a shot from the fort slammed into the pilothouse of the *Catskill*, shattering the interior lining. Rodgers was killed instantly.

The U.S. Navy's contribution to the northern victory in the Civil War was the product of the cumulative efforts of the officers and men who manned the ships that commanded the rivers and coastlines of the South. Rodgers was a prime example of the professional naval officer whose bravery, ability, and dedication to duty helped preserve the Union. If his exploits did not have a major impact on the course of the Civil War, he nonetheless lived up to the high expectations that came with being a member of one of the nation's most celebrated naval families.

• A collection of correspondence from Rodgers's Civil War service is in the Naval Records Collection of the Office of Naval Records and Library, entry 395, Letter Books of Officers of the United States Navy at Sea, item 64, RG 45, National Archives. See also George Washington Rodgers, Jr., File, ZB Series, Early Records Collection, Operational Archives, Naval Historical Center, Washington, D.C., and the Rodgers Family Papers, Naval Historical Foundation Collection, Manuscripts Division, Library of Congress. Rodgers's antebellum service can be traced through U.S. Navy Department, *Register of the Commissioned, Warrant, and Volunteer Officers of the United States, Including Officers of the Marine Corps and Others* (1837–1864). His Civil War operations are in *The Official Records of the Union and Confederate Navies in the War of the Rebellion*, ser. 1, vols. 1, 4, 7, 13, 14 (30 vols., 1894–1922). Additional information is contained in obituaries in the *Army and Navy Journal*, 29 Aug. 1863, and the *National Intelligencer*, 25 Aug. 1863.

ETHAN S. RAFUSE

RODGERS, Jimmie (8 Sept. 1897–26 May 1933), singer and musician, was born James Charles Rodgers in Meridian, Mississippi, the son of Aaron Rodgers, a foreman on the Gulf, Mobile & Ohio Railroad, and Eliza Bozeman. His father raised him alone after his mother died in 1901. Rodgers spent his youth in boardinghouses, switch shanties, and freight yards. These circumstances, according to biographer Nolan Porterfield, taught him the essentials that were to mark his life: "The human condition is a tough proposition and music helps lighten the load."

At age twelve Rodgers won a Meridian talent competition. He quit school at fourteen and worked in the rail yards as a water boy. Rodgers tried to follow in the footsteps of his father by working as his assistant foreman, but he was restless and drifted from one railroad job to another until, thanks to his older brother Walter, he became a regular on the New Orleans & Northeastern line. Rodgers learned how to play the guitar and banjo and developed his singing style from listening to black railroad workers. Rodgers often sang songs about the myth and adventure of the railroads, without accompaniment, to the tempo that kept the workmen laboring in unison.

In May 1917 the nineteen-year-old Rodgers married Stella Kelly, with whom he had one child, born in 1918. Marriage did not dampen his wandering spirit, however, and the following year the couple divorced. In April 1920, after a whirlwind courtship, Rodgers married Carrie Williamson. They had two children, the second of whom died in December 1923, less than six months following birth. At the time of his baby daughter's death, Rodgers was trying to find work in New Orleans. To get home for the funeral, he had to pawn his banjo.

Rodgers found railroad jobs in Utah and Colorado, which required long separations from his family. Traveling the rails in winter took a toll on his health, and by 1924 he had developed a persistent, hacking cough. After he began to spit up blood, he was diagnosed with tuberculosis. In 1925 a nearly fatal pulmonary hemorrhage required treatment, but he was so broke only a charity hospital would take him in.

Six months later, Rodgers was performing in blackface with a medicine show throughout Tennessee and Kentucky. He developed a flair for yodeling, derived, one researcher assumed, from touring Swiss musicians. Rodgers, however, restructured the yodel into a means of expression for rural white Americans and to reflect the wail of blues singers. He came to be called "America's blue yodeler," according to Ronnie Pugh of Nashville's Country Music Foundation, "because of his ability to fit his yodeling to the black blues." Rarely did he make enough money to send any home. In spite of his circumstances, he invested in 1926 in a tent carnival, where he played any kind of music requested, from dance tunes to waltzes, and even a Hawaiian revue. But, when he started to make money, a storm destroyed the tent.

Rodgers returned to railroading in Florida, where the damp climate brought back his bouts with tuberculosis. In 1927 he and Carrie decided to move to Arizona, and against doctors' advice he found work on the Southern Pacific line. Rodgers then moved to Asheville, North Carolina, to seek yet again a better climate and obtain work as a musician. He became a city detective, which enabled him to relocate his wife and one surviving daughter, but quit the job to work as an apartment house custodian.

In 1927 Rodgers formed a string quartet, the Jimmie Rodgers Entertainers, in which he played tenor banjo. The group got a job on radio but later lost its sponsor. Rodgers auditioned in Atlanta for Columbia Records and was turned down. Despite these setbacks, the group continued to barnstorm. Although

Rodgers's style and flair for yodeling helped develop a sizable following, times were hard and soon he was broke again. When Carrie saw an ad in the *Bristol News Bulletin* that read "Mountain Songs Recorded Here by Victor Company," the group began "playing" its way to Bristol.

Intrigue surrounded the audition. With four songs written in haste by his sister-in-law Elsie McWilliams, Rodgers along with Carrie met Ralph Peer, a Missouri sewing machine and record salesman and recording pioneer, who was looking for "local rustic types" for the Victor Talking Machine Company (later RCA Victor). When they arrived, Peer told Rodgers he was too late, but Rodgers talked Peer into letting him audition. Despite being physically weak, Rodgers sang with a confident voice. Members of his band, meanwhile, thinking that Rodgers had planned to audition without them, tried in vain to arrange their own audition. Shaken by what he saw as a potential double cross, Rodgers recorded two songs without the band. Wanting a fuller sound, Peer asked a waiting group, the A. P. Carter Family, to accompany Rodgers. Rodgers selected "Sleep, Baby, Sleep," one of his daughter's favorite lullabies, and "Soldier's Sweetheart," a simple ballad he had written about a friend who had died in World War I. Peer was impressed. However, when Rodgers pitched a novelty song, "T for Texas," with a twelve-bar blues patter and a trembling yodel, Peer refused to record it. Nonetheless, before Rodgers left, Peer paid him $20 and handed him a recording contract. Thus began a career that would forever change American music.

Rodgers relocated to Washington, D.C., where he and Carrie lived with his brother. He sang in theaters, and his wife worked as a waitress. That November, when he had yet to hear from Peer, Rodgers decided to seek him out in New York. Elsie McWilliams recalled in a 1970 interview: "On the trip, Jimmie talked about his daddy and home, that's what gave me the idea for 'Daddy and Home.' He told me about his home in New Orleans and I wrote that one ['Little Old Home in New Orleans']. By the time we arrived, I had them ready to put on paper."

In November 1927, having made contact with Peer, Rodgers recorded at RCA Victor's new Camden, New Jersey, recording studio (a converted Baptist church). The session—which included the songs "T for Texas," "Away Out on the Mountain," and "Rock All Our Babies to Sleep"—went off without a hitch, so well that Peer offered Rodgers a management deal. Afterward, at their hotel, Carrie cooked a turkey dinner to celebrate. According to Elsie McWilliams, "When Jimmie came in, he had his guitar in one hand and Carrie in the other. He said, 'Darling, with you and my old guitar, I've got the stars in my hand!' Well, I didn't even stop to eat. I went straight to the piano and wrote 'You and My Old Guitar.'" Elsie McWilliams did not like the way Rodgers slurred the words, but the trait endeared him to his public. Rodgers's 78 rpm acetates, even at seventy-five cents each (when steak cost forty cents a pound), quickly found an audience. By summer he was on radio and headlining with popular crooner Gene Austin at Washington's Earle Theater.

In November 1929, while recording at RCA, Rodgers made his only movie, a short titled *The Singing Brakeman* for Columbia-Victor. In it, a waitress flirts with Rodgers, dressed in a train engineer's outfit, strumming his guitar and singing three songs. Soon earning $2,000 a month, Rodgers was able to afford a new Cadillac and tailor-made suits. He also built a $50,000 home near Kerrville, Texas, and a tuberculosis sanatorium. Eventually his recordings about cowboys, the prairie, trains, hoboes, and love gone bad—111 in all—sold six million copies. For his recording of "Blue Yodel No. 9," RCA coupled him with jazz pianist Earl "Fatha" Hines and trumpeter Louis Armstrong. In 1933, when record sales were diminishing because of the depression, Rodgers outsold Enrico Caruso. Elsie McWilliams wrote many of Rodgers's hits, including "Hobo Bill's Last Ride," "Waitin' for the Train," "Home Call," "Mississippi River Blues," "My Little Lady," "Lullaby Yodel," and "A Sailor's Plea."

Rodgers was influential in affecting trends. As a musician he gave form, shape, and content to hillbilly music; as a balladeer, he laid the foundation for commercial country music. According to Carrie Rodgers, her husband touched many segments of society: families, grim-faced he-men, the poverty-stricken, the sick, the troubled, railroad men, even poolhall rowdies. In her biography of Rodgers, she wrote, "They knew he was a fellow who understood . . . Jimmie reached them, every one, with his sobbing, lonesome yodels; held them with his whimsy, with his deliberate audacity."

His recordings and America's fascination with the railroads gave Rodgers the opportunity to travel extensively. Rather than wear western outfits, he donned natty suits with polka dot bow ties and a straw hat. He became a regular in tent shows. On the vaudeville circuit, he toured with Will Rogers ("We were always having to tell people, 'No, we ain't brothers. There's a D separating us.'") and silent screen stars Clara Bow and Ben Turpin. While in Hollywood to record, he was received by the comedy duo of Stan Laurel and Oliver Hardy.

At the end of 1932, Rodgers moved to San Antonio, where he appeared twice weekly on radio programs from the Bonnet Hotel. But tuberculosis struck him again in February 1933, and because of medical bills he had to sell his mansion. He was far from defeated, even writing songs about his ailment, "The TB Blues" and "Whippin' That Old TB." With his recording contract up for renewal, he traveled to New York in May 1933 to record. Rodgers became so weak that his musicians had to carry him from the hotel to the sessions. He rested between songs and received morphine. During a song with the Carters, now his chief competition, Rodgers was so sick that Maybelle Carter had to imitate his guitar style. Yet his voice on his last two recordings, "I'm Free from the Chain Gang Now" and "Yodeling My Way Back Home," remained strong. On the night of 25 May, Rodgers began to

hemorrhage. He lapsed into a coma and died the next morning. His body was brought back to Meridian by train, where weeping fans met it.

Rodgers, now known as the "Father of Country Music," was the first inductee into the Country Music Hall of Fame in 1961. His plaque reads, "Jimmie Rodgers's name stands foremost in the country music field as the 'man who started it all.' His songs told the great stories of the singing rails, the powerful steam locomotives and the wonderful railroad people that he loved so well. Although small in stature, he was a giant among men, starting a trend in the musical taste of millions." In the late 1950s and early 1960s Rodgers's fame reached as far away as Japan. RCA reissues of his remastered originals sold 30,000 to 50,000 copies each. Meridian, which holds an annual Jimmie Rodgers festival, established the Jimmie Rodgers Memorial Park and Museum. The legend beneath his monument states: "His is the music of America. He sang the songs of the people he loved."

• Correspondence, music, and personal papers of Jimmie Rodgers are housed in the Country Music Foundation in Nashville and in the Mitchell Library at Mississippi State University. Nolan Porterfield, *Jimmie Rodgers: The Life and Times of America's Blue Yodeler* (1979), is a comprehensive biography. Carrie Rodgers wrote *Jimmie Rodgers' Life Story* (1935), which was reprinted, with a new introduction and a chronology, as *My Husband, Jimmy Rodgers* (1975). Johnny Bond, *The Recordings of Jimmie Rodgers: An Annotated Discography*, issued by the John Edwards Memorial Foundation (1978), offers a complete listing of the original Rodgers recordings, whereas Norm Cohen's article, "Jimmie Rodgers on Record: America's Blue Yodeler," *Journal of American Folklore* 102 (1989): 463–76, reviews reissues of these recordings and describes his career.

ELLIS NASSOUR

RODGERS, John (1773–1 Aug. 1838), naval officer, was born near Havre de Grace, Maryland, the son of John Rodgers and Elizabeth Reynolds, farmers who also kept a tavern and owned mills. Rodgers, after attending the village school, was apprenticed to a Baltimore shipowner. Like many of his contemporaries, he rose to command a merchant ship while still in his teens, trading to Western Europe. Rodgers spent eleven years in the merchant service before being commissioned a lieutenant in the new U.S. Navy in 1798. He was appointed second lieutenant of the frigate *Constellation* under Captain Thomas Truxtun, and when the first lieutenant resigned soon afterward, Rodgers became Truxtun's executive. From this most influential of the navy's first generation of captains Rodgers learned not only naval tactics but the art of managing the complex organization of a naval ship.

As *Constellation*'s first lieutenant, Rodgers took a prominent part in the capture of the frigate *Insurgente* in 1799, the most dramatic action of the Quasi War with France. He was promoted to captain in March 1799 and commanded the ship *Maryland* through the remainder of the war. As a very junior captain, he was nearly eliminated from the navy list in the Peace Establishment of 1801, but his early association with the Smith family of Baltimore stood him in good stead when Robert Smith became secretary of the navy in the Jefferson administration. Rodgers survived as the eighth of twelve captains on the list and was given command of the frigate *John Adams* in the squadron sent to the Mediterranean under Richard V. Morris in 1802. He headed the blockading ships on the coast of Tripoli and engaged in some skirmishes with the Tripolitan forces before succeeding Morris in command of the squadron; however, he was almost immediately superseded by the commander of the replacement squadron, Edward Preble. Rodgers swallowed his disgust and dismay long enough to support Preble with his ships in a successful negotiation at Tangier and then returned to the United States. He reached the Mediterranean again in the Samuel Barron squadron, sent in relief of Preble, and remained to command the squadron after Barron had concluded peace with Tripoli and returned home. Rodgers's squadron was withdrawn in 1806.

Rodgers was never involved in a duel, but he flirted with the prospect more than once. His closest call was in the fall of 1806 when, almost immediately after reaching the United States, he demanded satisfaction from Captain James Barron for alleged insults said to have been spread by the latter in Rodgers's absence. The real cause for the bad feeling between the two was Rodgers's suspicion that Barron had worked to dissuade his elder brother Samuel from turning his squadron over to Rodgers, even when Samuel Barron was seriously ill and unable to function. Before the duel could take place, Rodgers professed himself satisfied. His reluctance to duel may have been related to the fact that, on 21 October 1806, he married Minerva Denison of Havre de Grace; the couple eventually had eleven children, ten of whom survived infancy.

In spite of the bad feeling between the two captains, the small number of officers of that rank in the navy necessitated the selection of Rodgers to preside over James Barron's court-martial after the *Chesapeake-Leopard* incident in 1807. Barron was convicted on one charge and given a five-year suspension. When the navy's large vessels were ordered out again to enforce the Embargo and Non-Intercourse acts, Rodgers, now the navy's senior captain, took command of the northern cruising squadron in the *Constitution*. Dissatisfied with the frigate's performance, he exchanged with Isaac Hull in 1810, taking the frigate *President*, which remained his command until 1814.

Although Rodgers was greatly respected for his administrative abilities, heroism at sea evaded him throughout his career. Before and during the War of 1812 he displayed a curious inability to make an accurate estimate of the size of a potential opponent. In May 1811, while cruising off the Atlantic coast to protect American commerce, he engaged the much smaller British sloop of war *Little Belt* in a night action. In his first wartime cruise, his squadron pursued the frigate *Belvidera*, but the quarry escaped by superior management. Rodgers was wounded in the action, suffer-

ing a broken leg from the explosion of a cannon. In three subsequent cruises, Rodgers captured a significant number of merchant vessels but failed to encounter a naval ship. In the North Sea in 1813 he retreated from a British frigate that he mistook for a ship of the line, and off New York in 1814 he made a similar error. He then left the *President* to take command of the new frigate *Guerriere* under construction at Philadelphia, and while waiting for that ship to be finished he joined the land forces in the defense of Chesapeake Bay in the fall of 1814.

Both his skills and seniority made Rodgers the logical choice to head the new Board of Navy Commissioners constituted in 1815. The remainder of his naval service consisted of two terms as president of that board, from 1815 to 1824 and from 1827 to 1837, interrupted only by a two-year cruise in command of the Mediterranean squadron. The commissioners succeeded in giving the first systematic organization to naval administration, especially with regard to matters such as construction and supply. Rodgers's conservative temperament may have retarded some innovations, but the probity of his administration could never be faulted. He set the tone that prevailed throughout the history of the Board of Navy Commissioners, until it was replaced in 1842 by the system of bureaus.

Rodgers's health declined noticeably after he survived an attack of cholera in 1832. He progressively lost his memory and mental agility, until in 1837 he resigned from the Board of Navy Commissioners to travel to Europe for his health. He returned a year later and went to the Naval Asylum in Philadelphia, where he died.

• Important collections of Rodgers's papers can be found at the Historical Society of Pennsylvania and the New-York Historical Society. The only biography is C. O. Paullin, *Commodore John Rodgers* (1910). For additional information on Rodgers's last cruise, see James M. Merrill, "Midshipman Dupont and the Cruise of *North Carolina*, 1825–1827," *American Neptune* 40, no. 3 (1980): 211–25, based on S. F. du Pont's letters.

LINDA M. MALONEY

RODGERS, John (12 Aug. 1812–5 May 1882), American naval officer, was born at Sion Hill near Havre de Grace, Maryland, the son of Commodore John Rodgers (1773–1838), an American naval officer, and Minerva Denison. Rodgers entered the U.S. Navy as a midshipman on 13 February 1829 at age sixteen. His early service was in the Mediterranean on the frigate *Constellation* and the sloop *Concord*. He passed his exams for promotion in the spring of 1834, and while awaiting a vacancy for a lieutenant's billet, he enrolled at the University of Virginia, though he did not complete the academic year. He served for three years (1836–1839) in the Brazil Squadron on board the *Dolphin*, where he was acting master (or navigator), then aboard the razee *Independence*.

In November 1839 Rodgers was assigned to command the centerboard schooner *Wave* for service along the Florida coast during the Second Seminole War, and he participated in several army-navy expeditions into the Everglades during 1840–1841. After the Seminole War, Rodgers became first lieutenant on the brig *Boxer* (1842–1844) then spent two years in Pittsburgh, Pennsylvania, assisting Lieutenant William Hunter (1805–1863) in his unsuccessful effort to perfect a new propulsion device, called a Hunter's Wheel, for steam vessels.

Rodgers served for most of three years (1846–1849) in the Africa Squadron on board the frigate *United States* and the sloop *Marion* and in 1849 was posted to the Coast Survey, first in command of the *Petrel* and then the *Hetzel*. In command, Rodgers was a strict disciplinarian, often assessing more than the dozen lashes that were ostensibly the maximum punishment a captain could mete out to transgressors. He was disappointed in 1850 when the navy abolished the lash as a punishment for sailors.

From 1852 to 1856, Rodgers served with the North Pacific Surveying Expedition, first as its second in command (as captain of the steamer *John Hancock*) then as its commander. In that capacity, he led a squadron of U.S. vessels around the world, surveying Batavia, the Formosa Strait, the Bonins, the Kurils, and venturing into the Bering Sea. He was promoted to commander while on this expedition, his date of rank being 14 September 1855. He spent two more years compiling the results of the expedition, though they were never published. In 1857 he married Ann Elizabeth Hodge, with whom he had three children, including the future Vice Admiral William L. Rodgers.

After a brief tour in command of the *Water Witch* (1858–1859), Rodgers was assigned to the Japan Expedition Office in Washington, D.C., where he was serving when the secession of Virginia on 17 April 1861 led navy authorities to dispatch him to Norfolk the next day to help ensure that the navy facilities there did not fall into rebel hands. Rodgers was in the last boat to depart the Norfolk Navy Yard after it was set afire, and as a result, he was captured by Virginia forces. Since Virginia had not yet joined the Confederacy, however, he was released and allowed to return to Washington by train.

In May the Navy Department sent Rodgers to Cincinnati to aid Major General George B. McClellan (1826–1885) in preparing a squadron of gunboats for the Ohio and Mississippi rivers. Working with naval contractor Samuel Pook, Rodgers supervised the conversion of three wooden gunboats and the construction of seven ironclads that came to be known as "Pook's Turtles." He never commanded this riverine armada, however, being relieved by Captain Andrew Foote in October.

Rodgers returned to Washington and requested sea service. As an unofficial member of Flag Officer Samuel F. Du Pont's staff, he participated in the Union seizure of Port Royal (7 Nov. 1861), during which he personally raised the U.S. flag on South Carolina soil, and afterward took command of the converted merchant steamer *Flag* on the South Atlantic Blockade off Savannah. In command of the *Flag*, Rodgers led the expedition that captured Tybee Island off the Savannah River in November 1861 and participated in the expedition that seized Fernandina, Florida, in March 1862.

In April Rodgers returned to Washington and was assigned to command the ironclad *Galena*, an experimental vessel that was well armed but poorly armored—Rodgers called it "a most miserable contrivance." In the *Galena*, Rodgers led a naval squadron in ascending the James River but was repelled at Drewry's Bluff on 15 May 1862, his vessel sustaining forty hits and thirty-three casualties. With some understatement, Rodgers reported, "We have demonstrated that she [the *Galena*] is not Shotproof." In June Rodgers's *Galena* helped cover McClellan's withdrawal to Harrison's Landing and later his evacuation of the peninsula. Rodgers was promoted to captain dating from 16 July 1862.

Appointed to the command of the new ironclad monitor *Weehawken* on 14 November 1862, Rodgers participated in the unsuccessful naval attack on Charleston Harbor on 7 April 1863. Soon afterward, on 17 June, his vessel defeated the Confederate ironclad ram *Atlanta* in Wassaw Sound, for which Secretary of the Navy Gideon Welles recommended him for promotion to commodore, though the promotion was not forthcoming until 2 March 1864. After a short illness, Rodgers secured command of the newest monitor, the *Dictator*, but that vessel had so many design flaws that Rodgers never got back into the war.

After the war, Rodgers served as commandant of the Boston Navy Yard (1866–1869). Promoted to rear admiral, he commanded the Asiatic Fleet (1870–1872). In that capacity, Rodgers escorted U.S. Ambassador Frederick Low to Korea with a five-ship squadron in the spring of 1871. When one of the forts guarding Inchon Harbor fired on the *Palos*, Rodgers responded by shelling all the harbor forts. Failing to get the apology he demanded, Rodgers landed a party of 700 sailors and marines and captured three of the forts, killing 243 Korean soldiers in the process. His last command was as superintendent of the Naval Observatory in Washington, D.C., and he was serving in that capacity, still on active duty, when he died there.

• Rodgers's papers are in the Library of Congress; see the Naval Historical Collection and the Rodgers Family Papers. Rodgers's wartime service is chronicled in the relevant volumes of *The Official Records of the Union and Confederate Navies in the War of the Rebellion* (30 vols., 1894–1922). An excellent biography is Robert E. Johnson, *Rear Admiral John Rodgers, 1812–1882* (1967). Rodgers is prominently mentioned in John D. Hayes, ed., *Samuel Francis Du Pont: A Selection from his Civil War Letters* (3 vols., 1969).

CRAIG L. SYMONDS

RODGERS, John (15 Jan. 1881–27 Aug. 1926), naval officer and aviator, was born in Washington, D.C., the son of Rear Admiral John Augustus Rodgers and Elizabeth Chambers. The son and grandson of distinguished naval officers, Rodgers attended the U.S. Naval Academy from 1899 to 1903 and reached the rank of commander on 4 November 1920. At the time of his death, he was listed for promotion to captain.

Rodgers's interest in aviation can be dated to January 1911, when he participated in experiments with observation kites aboard the USS *Pennsylvania*. The kites, which were used throughout the First World War, carried men aloft to act as gunfire sighters, lookouts, or observers. A few weeks later he witnessed Eugene Ely's historic first airplane landing aboard the *Pennsylvania*. The success of Ely's flight led the navy to begin aviation operations. Lieutenant Rodgers was selected to train with Orville Wright in Dayton, Ohio, and in April 1911 became the second man in the U.S. Navy to qualify as a naval aviator. His skills as a pilot seem to have been marginal, prompting one officer to later recall that he "never showed good flying sense" (van Deurs, p. 48). He talked his cousin, Calbraith "Cal" Perry Rodgers—later known as the pilot of the famous *Vin Fizz*—into joining him at Dayton to learn to fly. After qualifying to fly, and while awaiting the delivery of the Wright factory's first airplane to the navy, Rodgers spent a few months barnstorming with his cousin Cal to make some extra money. He acted as Cal's mechanic, believing that the Navy Department would not approve of his flying at air meets. He also helped set up and plan Cal's attempt to win the Hearst prize for the first transcontinental flight. During the fall of 1911 Rodgers traveled in a special train, following Cal's route and helping to rebuild his airplane, the *Vin Fizz*—named for a popular soft drink—after its five major crashes, numerous hard landings, and mechanical failures.

In 1912 Rodgers returned East to begin naval experiments with the new Wright and Curtiss airplanes. During the summer of that year he took the first aerial photograph for the U.S. Navy. In the fall of 1912 he was ordered back to sea duty aboard the USS *Nebraska*, possibly as a result of several accidents with the Wright machine. His marital status—he had married Ethel Greiner in 1911—may also have played a role in the navy's decision to transfer him out of what was then hazardous duty. He did not return to aviation until 1922. The marriage ended in divorce in 1924; there were no children.

During World War I Rodgers served in submarines and on North Sea mine duty. Eventually he became executive officer aboard the USS *Nevada*. In 1922 he was put in command of the Naval Air Station at Pearl Harbor, Hawaii, a position that required little or no solo flying. Later he also commanded the USS *Wright*, flagship of the Aircraft Squadron, Scouting Fleet. He held this position when, in 1925, he was tapped to lead the navy's first San Francisco to Hawaii transpacific flight. On 31 August 1925 he left San Francisco in flying boat PN9-1, with a crew of four, and a second, similar aircraft. The second airplane went down about 300 miles into the flight. After twenty-five hours in the air, Rodgers's flying boat ran out of fuel and was forced down at sea. With no power for the radio and little food and water, Rodgers and his crew ripped fabric from the wings to make sails and set a course for Hawaii. On 10 September they were picked up by submarine R-4, fifteen miles from the island of Kauai. In nine days they had covered 400 miles. The incident brought Rodgers national acclaim.

In the summer of 1926 Rodgers was appointed assistant chief of the Bureau of Aeronautics in Washington, D.C. For unknown reasons, however, the position did not suit him. In the middle of August, after only a few weeks at the job, he requested a transfer and was given command of a new experimental seaplane squadron in San Diego. On 27 August while preparing for his new assignment, Rodgers flew to Philadelphia's Mustin Field to inspect some new aircraft. His aircraft stalled on his approach over the Delaware River and crashed into four feet of water, some hundred yards offshore. Rodgers died later that day of his injuries.

John Rodgers entered naval aviation at its inception and played a prominent role in its first year. His return to sea duty in 1912 occurred at a time when the navy was still testing the merits and applications of airpower to naval operations. By the time he returned to naval aviation in 1922, the navy had accepted the airplane as an observation tool for the fleet, and his subsequent flying career emphasized that aspect. But the navy was also to accept the results of General Billy Mitchell's 1921 bombing tests on captured German warships, and Rodgers was killed before the navy began to see the airplane as an offensive weapon. His preferred duty, however, like that of his illustrious forefathers, seems to have been at sea. Of his twenty-three years with the navy, Rodgers spent fifteen on sea duty.

• Rodgers's papers have not been located. The best published sources of his life and activities in naval aviation may be found in Rear Admiral George van Deurs (USN ret.), *Wings for the Fleet: A Narrative of Naval Aviation's Early Development, 1910–1916* (1966), and Theodore Roscoe, *On the Seas and in the Skies: A History of the U.S. Navy's Air Power* (1970). Biographies of each of the navy's early aviators are held by the Biographies Branch, Office of Information, Navy Department, Washington, D.C. The unpublished *Investigation into the Death of Commander John Rodgers at Philadelphia, 8/27/26* can be found in the National Archives, Navy Section, Washington, D.C. The San Francisco to Hawaii flight is recounted in the *New Times*, 11 and 12 Sept. 1925. An obituary is in the *New York Times*, 28 Aug. 1926.

JOSEPH E. LIBBY

RODGERS, Richard (28 June 1902–30 Dec. 1979), composer of the American musical theater, was born in Arverne, New York, the son of William Abraham Rodgers, a physician, and Mamie Levy. Rodgers showed an unusual ability to remember, pick out, and even harmonize melodies on his mother's piano from early on. He resisted formal training in piano, but throughout his career he used this instrument as his primary means of working out a song. His parents loved the musical theater and brought him to see Victor Herbert's *Little Nemo* at age six, an experience that affected him deeply. He began composing original tunes at age nine. He entered Columbia College in 1919 because of its amateur musical theater. His "varsity show" *Fly with Me* (1920), written with Lorenz Hart, a Columbia graduate, was the first effort of their long and productive collaboration. It was noticed by Broadway producer Lew Fields, who immediately engaged the two to write a new show for professional production, *A Little Ritz Girl* (1920).

Rodgers left Columbia in 1921 and entered the Institute of Musical Art in New York City, where he studied basic harmony, ear training, and music history until 1923. Two lean years followed during which entree into the professional musical theater seemed out of reach. At the point of taking a sales job, Rodgers was invited to contribute the score for *The Garrick Gaieties* (1925), a semi-amateur benefit show sponsored by the New York Theatre Guild. It was a hit, and Rodgers and Hart's already completed *Dearest Enemy* (1925) soon followed.

Rodgers wrote almost all his songs in collaboration with a lyricist, and his career can be conveniently divided into a Hart period (1919–1942), an Oscar Hammerstein II period (1942–1959), and a post-Hammerstein period (1960–1979).

Rodgers and Hart quickly established themselves as one of America's premier songwriting teams for theater and film. In the late 1920s they produced *The Girl Friend* (1926), *A Connecticut Yankee* (1927), and *Evergreen* (London, 1930), all with significant runs, as well as eleven other less successful shows. The best-known songs of these shows include "Manhattan," "The Blue Room," "Mountain Greenery," "My Heart Stood Still," and "Thou Swell."

In 1930 Rodgers married Dorothy Feiner; they eventually had two daughters. In that same year Rodgers, Hart, and Herbert Fields accepted a contract to write for First National Pictures. In 1932 Rodgers and Hart returned to Hollywood from New York City to write for Paramount and stayed two and one-half years, working for various film studios. These contracts, which retained the songwriting team for a set period, provided a secure income during four of the worst years of the Great Depression, when comparatively few shows were opening on Broadway. Nevertheless, Rodgers disliked the working environment and considered these years his most unproductive. The team had little control over the final product, and too often the work was summarily discarded. Of eight films from this period, only one was successful—*Love Me Tonight* (1932), for which they wrote "Mimi," "Lover," and "Isn't It Romantic."

A casual remark in the *Los Angeles Examiner*—"Whatever became of Rodgers and Hart?"—frightened them enough to send them back to New York as soon as their last contract expired in 1934. Thereafter Rodgers worked intermittently in the film industry, writing with both Hart and Oscar Hammerstein II. But he never returned to Hollywood full time.

In New York, however, Rodgers and Hart found it difficult to resume their career. They wrote an outline and several songs for a show about a vaudeville dancer working in ballet, called *On Your Toes*, but could find no producer. Finally, Billy Rose offered them the chance to write the score for his theatrical extravaganza about rival circus companies, to be produced in the renovated Hippodrome. *Jumbo* (1935) was not the kind of show that particularly interested Rodgers and Hart, but circumstances forced them to accept. Their songs, particularly "The Most Beautiful Girl in the World," "Little Girl Blue," and "My Romance," received good notices, and the team found itself reestablished on Broadway.

Jumbo inaugurated an unbroken string of Rodgers and Hart successes that spanned the rest of the decade: *On Your Toes* (1936), *Babes in Arms* and *I'd Rather Be Right* (1937), *I Married an Angel* and *The Boys from Syracuse* (1938), *Too Many Girls* (1939), and *Higher and Higher* and *Pal Joey* (1940). The productions involved a number of theater luminaries, including George Abbott, who wrote the books and undertook the direction for several of them, choreographer George Balanchine, and playwrights George S. Kaufman and Moss Hart. Rodgers's music during this half-decade was the best of the Hart period; the most famous titles include "There's a Small Hotel," "Where or When," "My Funny Valentine," "The Lady Is a Tramp," "Spring Is Here," "Falling in Love with Love," and "Bewitched, Bothered and Bewildered."

Although these songs and many others have survived as standards, the shows that first presented them have fallen out of the theater repertory and, with the possible exception of *Pal Joey*, do not seem capable of any revival beyond historical interest. Despite Rodgers's interest in the dramatic integrity of the musical theater, the integration of music and plot necessary for a truly dramatic music eluded the Rodgers and Hart musicals. Too many decisions about the book of the show were made by producers, stars, or the original writers. Only for *Babes in Arms* and *I Married an Angel* did Rodgers and Hart write the complete book themselves, and even those stories depend on formulaic twists of plot that are unacceptable today. The other limiting factor was the working habits of Lorenz Hart. Hart's lyrics—brilliant, clever, full of technical virtuosity—seemed to come to him without effort, once he was stimulated by a melody from Rodgers. However, his astonishing facility and speed may have been a dramatic hindrance. He would not rework a completed lyric, and since Rodgers usually had to corner him in a room with a completed melody just to finish a single song, extensive discussion of dramatic actions in the play was out of the question. Hart would suddenly disappear from these frantic work sessions, sometimes for many hours, even days, in his last years when his alcoholism became severe.

Rodgers began to consider his future career without the lyrics of Lorenz Hart. In September 1941 he proposed a collaboration to Oscar Hammerstein II. Hammerstein was unwilling to break up such a famous partnership, but told Rodgers that, should Hart become incapacitated, he would accept.

In 1942 Rodgers and Hart completed their last show, *By Jupiter*. To do it, Rodgers had to have Hart, himself, and a grand piano lodged at Doctors Hospital in New York in order to control Hart's alcoholism. The musical was written there. After its successful opening, Rodgers was approached by the Theatre Guild to make a musical of a play by Lynn Riggs, *Green Grow the Lilacs*; but Hart, showing no interest, was determined to go on "vacation." Rodgers, with great reluctance, dissolved the partnership and turned to Hammerstein. Lorenz Hart died in November 1943, eight months after the musical version of the Riggs play, now called *Oklahoma!*, opened.

Oscar Hammerstein II differed from Hart in almost every respect. He was a painstaking and methodical worker, sometimes taking weeks to compose a lyric. He was never at home with the light virtuoso comedy lyric, preferring direct and simple expressions of feeling. On the page his lyrics seem plain, hiding rather than flaunting his expert craft, and seem to beg for a musical setting.

Such characteristics suited Rodgers's melodic gifts perfectly. Rodgers composed in a simplified version of nineteenth-century Romantic style, in which chromatic delays of cadences build to melodic climaxes, usually toward the end of the song. He almost always employed the introductory verse-refrain pattern common in American popular music since the turn of the century, whose refrain consists of an *aaba* phrase pattern. The main compositional problem with this form is how to make the ending convincing, composed as it is of the same music as the beginning. Perhaps Rodgers's greatest melodic gift was for ending a melody, which he usually accomplished by an extension of the last phrase. This extension, while seemingly a fresh and unexpected departure, always has significant relationships with the original melodic material of the song. In this way, his melodic gifts coincided precisely with the natural proclivities of the Romantic style—the climactic close—which also fit the strong sentiments expressed so very well by Hammerstein.

Rodgers and Hammerstein composed their musical plays in three stages. First they would have extensive conversations about the dramatic nature and qualities of the material to be set, carefully placing the songs in the plot scheme. Second, Hammerstein would write the book and the lyrics to the songs. Finally, Rodgers would set the lyrics to music. This procedure gave them the control and the time for reflection and revision that were missing from the Rodgers and Hart collaboration.

More important, it produced a half-dozen musicals that form the core of the Broadway repertory. *Oklahoma!* (1943) has long been hailed as a milestone in American theater history, not only for its record-breaking run of 2,248 performances, but for setting new standards of drama for a musical play. Certain supposed innovations, such as Agnes de Mille's dream ballet and the killing scene, had already appeared in musicals of the 1930s. The true innovations were a means of integrating song and dialogue with frequent reprises, so as to make one a part of the other, and a faithfulness to dramatic logic that allowed convention and invention to work together credibly.

Their second effort, an adaptation of Ferenc Molnar's *Liliom*, became a serious musical and Rodgers's personal favorite, *Carousel* (1945). Although less popular, *Carousel* surpasses *Oklahoma!* with its treatment of Molnar's more substantial drama and its more tightly integrated and extended musical scenes. Serious dramatic issues became the hallmark of Rodgers and Hammerstein's most notable achievements thereafter: the problems of prejudice and race relations in *South Pacific* (1949), political power and morality in *The King and I* (1951), cultural adaptation in *The Flower Drum Song* (1958), personal integrity in the face of fascism in *The Sound of Music* (1959). Other plays, less successful, include *Allegro* (1947), *Me and Juliet* (1953), and *Pipe Dream* (1955). Rodgers and Hammerstein also collaborated on two films, *State Fair* (1945) and *Main Street to Broadway* (1953), and the excellent adaptation of *Cinderella* (1957) for television. This brilliant partnership ended when Hammerstein died of cancer in 1960.

Rodgers's post-Hammerstein period was characterized by an unsuccessful search for a new collaborator. In *No Strings* (1962), he wrote his own lyrics. There followed an abortive effort to work with Alan Jay Lerner and then an unpleasant experience writing *Do I Hear a Waltz?* (1965) with Stephen Sondheim and Arthur Laurents. In 1967 Rodgers contributed the score for an adaptation of George Bernard Shaw's *Androcles and the Lion* for television, once again writing his own lyrics. His last three musicals were *Two by Two* (1969), with lyrics by Martin Charnin; *Rex* (1974), with lyrics by Sheldon Harnick; and *I Remember Mama* (1979), with lyrics by Charnin and Raymond Jessel. None of these plays has achieved the critical stature of his earlier works with Hammerstein.

Rodgers also composed a "symphonic narrative" called *All Points West* (1936); two ballets, *Nursery Ballet* (1938) and *Ghost Town* (1939); and the score for the documentary *Victory at Sea* (1952).

Rodgers received two Pulitzer Prizes, seven Antoinette Perry ("Tony") Awards, the Donaldson Award, an Oscar, and the Kennedy Center and Lawrence Langner Awards for lifetime achievements. He established scholarships at the Juilliard School, the American Academy of Dramatic Art, and the American Theater Wing. He died in Manhattan.

• Principal papers and manuscripts of Rodgers may be found in the Performing Arts Research Center of the New York Public Library at Lincoln Center and the Library of Congress. There is an oral history at Columbia University. Other information may be sought at the Rodgers & Hammerstein Organization in New York City. His autobiography is *Musical Stages* (1975); there is no critical biography. Others, all rather anecdotal, include David Ewen, *Richard Rodgers* (1957), Samuel Marx and Jan Clayton, *Rodgers and Hart* (1976), and Deems Taylor, *Some Enchanted Evenings* (1953). For critical analysis of his work see Lehman Engel, *The American Musical Theatre: A Consideration* (1967), and Joseph P. Swain, *The Broadway Musical: A Critical and Musical Survey* (1990). An obituary is in the *New York Times*, 31 Dec. 1979.

JOSEPH P. SWAIN

RODIA, Simon (c. 1879–16 July 1965), artist, was born Sabato Rodia, in Rivatoli, Italy, a peasant community near Nola, twenty miles east of Naples, to Frank Rodia and Angelina (maiden name unknown). During much of his life in the United States, Rodia went by the nickname of Sam. He himself *never* used the name Simon, which was the result of a largely inaccurate *Los Angeles Times* newspaper article in 1937 in which the reporter among many other errors called Rodia "Simon Rodilla." While the last name was given correctly in later articles, the incorrect first name Simon stuck. Scholars who have worked on Rodia and the Watts Towers have consistently tried to reintroduce the name Sabato.

Rodia's family immigrated to the United States in the early 1890s and settled in central Pennsylvania. Little is known about Rodia's early life, except that he moved to the West Coast in his late teens and worked as an itinerant laborer in rock quarries, logging and railroad camps, and as a construction worker and a tiler. He married Lucy Ucci in 1902 in Seattle. They had three children, one of whom died in infancy. They divorced in 1912. In 1918 Rodia lived with a woman who used the name Benita Rodia, but it is not known if they were married.

In 1921 Rodia purchased an unusual triangular-shaped lot (151-by-69-by-137 feet) at 1765 East 107th Street in the Watts District of Los Angeles. He immediately set to work to construct a large assemblage structure that he called "Nuestro Pueblo," Spanish for "Our Town." He first built scalloped masonry walls around the lot. He then constructed seven towers and other arbor-like enclosures out of steel rods and reinforced cement. He decorated the walls of his structure with mosaics made from thousands of tile shards, broken dishes, seashells, and pieces of bottles. He covered the walls with impressions of handprints, work tools, automobile parts, corncobs, wheat stalks, and various types of fruit. He incised his initials into the wet cement as well as recurrent heart and rosette shapes. Humorous touches include teapot spouts sticking out of the walls and a cement foot with a cowboy boot. Using only a tiler's tools, Rodia designed and built the structure entirely by himself, working evenings and weekends. During the day he worked as a telephone-line repairman, tiler, or security guard. Over a quarter century he continued adding to and refining his piece until 1948.

Six years later, he suddenly gave his property to a neighbor, Luis Sauceda, who one year later sold the towers to Joseph Montoya, who planned to use the towers as a backdrop for a taco stand but was unable to get his business started. In 1959, after the towers were condemned as a public hazard, two young filmmakers, Nicholas King and William Cartwright, bought the property from Montoya for $3,000 and transferred the title to the towers to the Committee for Simon Rodia's Towers in Watts, a nonprofit coalition of citizens interested in preserving the towers for posterity. An engineer proved the towers safe, and in 1975 the state of California and the city of Los Angeles assumed responsibility for conservation and maintenance of the towers as a public heritage site.

After giving the towers to Sauceda, Rodia retired to Martinez, California, where his sister lived, and where he spent most of his time visiting friends and family. He did not continue any artistic work. After 1959, as greater international attention focused on the towers, he welcomed the visits of scholars and admirers. In 1961 he attended a conference on the towers at the University of California, Berkeley. He expressed satisfaction that his work had found recognition, but he never saw the towers again after he left in 1954. He died in Martinez.

In the 1920s Rodia had lived with a woman known to surviving neighbors only as Carmen; there is no evidence that they were married, and she left him in 1927. For the rest of his life Rodia lived alone, and the first news reporters to write about the towers assumed their creator was a reclusive eccentric. However, his neighbors later explained that Rodia participated in social clubs in the Watts area, and it is now known that he traveled to downtown Los Angeles to attend meetings of the Italo-American society. (He spoke Spanish fluently, and his Mexican neighbors thought he was Hispanic.) For most of the thirty-three years he lived in Watts, Rodia encouraged his neighbors to visit and use his project. Weddings and baptisms were celebrated under the towers.

Rodia told William Hale, who made a documentary film on the towers in 1952 as a student project, "I was going to do something big, and I did." He said he wanted Nuestro Pueblo to be a monument to himself: "You have to be good good or bad bad to be remembered." His heroes were Copernicus, Galileo, and Columbus, and he spoke of his work as celebrating their spirit of exploration. He also told interviewers that he started working on his project to keep himself busy after he quit drinking.

The triangular shape of the lot, created by the diagonal slash of railroad tracks running alongside his property, was ideal for the display he created. At the narrowest point, Rodia built "Marco Polo's Ship," a bench that resembles a four-tiered galley with seashell-encrusted masts. Then come three lofty towers, the highest 99½ feet tall, with four smaller companions, 10- to 15-feet high each. The towers create the outline of the composition and ensure that Nuestro Pueblo is visible for several blocks. The base of the triangle, the area closest to Rodia's house (which burnt down in the mid-1950s) contains the most park-like elements in the project: a gazebo-arbor, stalagmite groupings, fountains, birdbaths, and benches. The basic materials of the towers are steel beams surrounded by concrete over chicken wire. The towers' lacy use of space comes from the interlocking circular tiers of vertical columns, reinforced with woven spiral and elliptical horizontal rings and spokes connecting the individual towers to create delicate, lace-like shapes soaring into the sky. The mosaics, a veritable museum of valuable Batchelder and Malibu tiles, form a protective shell over the reinforced cement. The basic materials in Rodia's composition remain visible for what they are and the forms, while suggestive of imagery, have no specific program. The towers suggest both church spires and the modern skyscraper; the stalagmites, both the natural forms of a cactus garden and miniature apartment buildings; the arbor and incised designs speak interchangeably of parks, the industrial work of automobile parts and construction tools, agriculture, and pure purposeless beauty. Possible folk roots of the towers and ship may be ceremonial towers of wood and ribbon used for the Festa de Gigli, celebrating San Gennaro, the patron saint of Nola. Yet Rodia's forms, colors, and techniques are unique. Rather than nostalgically recreating memories from his early childhood, he reflected upon the rapidly changing world of the laboring immigrant.

Other works attributed to Rodia include a fireplace in a house in the Los Feliz District of Los Angeles, a tower covered with seashells in the yard of a house in Malibu, California, garden ornaments at the home of his sister in Martinez, California, and, most importantly, concrete and mosaic carousels constructed in the backyard of Rodia's home in Long Beach, California, in 1915. His Long Beach creations, which appear to be rehearsals for the Watts project, were demolished in 1961.

Though the Watts Towers of Simon Rodia barely escaped demolition, they are now recognized as one of the finest examples of American environmental art. Rodia's work inspired a generation of assemblage artists, and the towers were featured in the 1961 Museum of Modern Art exhibition, "The Art of Assemblage." Through the sheer force of the creative intelligence they manifest, the towers uplift the Watts community. They serve as an urban oasis, providing a dignified public space for ceremonies. The towers have become the site of the Watts Towers Arts Center, which offers classes in the arts to the community and sponsors several annual music festivals.

• Documentation of the Watts Towers of Simon Rodia, including correspondence and interviews, is located at the conservation office attached to the site. Published accounts of Rodia and efforts to preserve the Watts Towers can be found in Selden Rodman, "The Artist Nobody Knows," *New World Writing No. 2* (1952); "The Watts Towers," pamphlet published by the Committee for Simon Rodia's Towers in Watts (c. 1960); Kate Steinitz, "A Visit with Sam Rodia," *Artforum* 1 (May 1963), 32–33; Calvin Trilling, "'I Know I Want to Do Something,'" *New Yorker*, 29 May 1965, 72ff. A chronology of Rodia's life, an illustrated description of the towers, a review of conservation efforts, and a bibliography can be found in Leon Whiteson, *The Watts Towers of Los Angeles* (1989). Jon Madian's *Beautiful Junk: A Story of the Watts Towers* (1968) is a fictionalized account written for children of Rodia's life and his relationship with the Watts community. The relation of Rodia's work to modernist art in California is discussed in Richard Cándida Smith, "The Elusive Quest of the Moderns," in *On the Edge of America: Modernist Art in California*, ed. Paul J. Karlstrom (1995). Two obituary notices that consider the social and aesthetic relevance of the Watts Towers are "In Memoriam Simon Rodia," *Los Angeles Free Press*, 23 July 1965, p. 5, and "Death of an Enigma," *Architectural Forum*, Sept. 1965, p. 19.

RICHARD CÁNDIDA SMITH

RODMAN, Hugh (6 Jan. 1859–7 June 1940), naval officer, was born in Frankfort, Kentucky, the son of Hugh Rodman, a physician, and Susan Ann Barbour. The Rodmans were of the local slaveowning elite. Nothing is known of his early education. Probably more interested in fun than in matters intellectual, Rodman finished second from the bottom of sixty-one graduates in the class of 1880 at the naval academy at Annapolis. Like his contemporaries, Rodman moved up slowly, from midshipman in 1882 to lieutenant in 1897. His early sea duty included cruising on the gunboat *Yantic* to Nova Scotia and in the Caribbean (1880–1882), on the sloop *Wachusett* over wide areas of the Pacific (1882–1883), and on the sloop *Hartford* (famous as Admiral David Farragut's flagship during the Civil War) along the west coast of the Americas and westward to Hawaii (1883–1884). After a year at the Hydrographic Office (1885–1886), he cruised to the Far East on the wooden steamer *Essex* and served on the gunboats *Monocacy* and *Palos* in the Far East. In 1889 Rodman married Elizabeth Ruffin Sayre, also of Frankfort. They had no children.

After brief stints at the Hydrographic Office and at the Naval Observatory, Rodman spent five years with the U.S. Coast and Geodetic Survey (1891–1896). While with USCGS, he sailed on the Coast Survey steamers *Endeavor*, *Patterson*, *Batche*, and *Matchless* along the Atlantic and Gulf coasts as well as in the north Pacific. All of these assignments suggest Rodman's love of the sea and interest in marine life to a degree unusual even among naval officers.

During the Spanish-American War, Rodman was attached to the new steam and steel cruiser *Raleigh* in Commodore George Dewey's Asiatic Squadron. At the battle of Manila Bay on 1 May 1898, the *Raleigh*, with Rodman directing the forward guns, sank the old Spanish cruiser *Castilla*. Later the *Raleigh* forced the surrender of the Spanish fort at the entrance to Subic Bay.

From 1899 to 1901 Rodman served as executive officer and navigator on the U.S. Fish Commission steamer *Albatross*, which carried out exploration of the Pacific Ocean bottom under Professor Alexander Agassiz. Rodman's first command was of the naval tug *Iroquois* (1901–1904), during which he cruised through the Hawaiian Islands and westward to Midway. Advanced to the rank of lieutenant commander in 1903, Rodman from 1904 to 1907 was again on the Asiatic Station attached to the cruisers *New Orleans* and *Cincinnati* and to the battleship *Wisconsin*. His second command was of the former Spanish gunboat *Elcano* (1905–1907), on which he first cruised in southern Philippine waters and then patrolled the

Yangtze River as far inland as Hankow. He also served briefly as aide to Admiral Willard H. Brownson, the commander in chief of the Asiatic Fleet, on the armored cruiser *West Virginia*.

Rodman reported to the Naval War College at Newport in June 1907, but he was almost immediately given the additional duty of inspector in charge, Sixth Lighthouse District, with headquarters at Charleston, South Carolina. Six months as captain of the yard at Cavite in the Philippines (1909) were followed by a brief command of the protected cruiser *Cleveland* and by about two years (1910–1912) as captain of the yard at Mare Island in California.

Rodman's years in the rank of captain began auspiciously in 1911 with successive commands of the battleships *Connecticut* and *Delaware*. The *Delaware* under Rodman escorted President William Howard Taft to Panama and paid a courtesy visit to France. From January 1914 until October 1915 Rodman was in the Panama Canal advising General George Goethals, the army engineer-builder, and as marine superintendent drawing up regulations for the control of shipping through the canal. After a year in command of the battleship *New York*, Rodman moved to the general board in Washington, with additional duty on the board of directors of the Panama Railroad.

With the entry of the United States into World War I in April 1917, Rodman was moved into a succession of battleship division commands and advanced to the rank of rear admiral. In November 1917 he was placed in command of Battleship Division Nine, which consisted of the flagship *New York*, the *Texas*, the *Wyoming*, and the *Arkansas*, subsequently joined by the *Florida* and the *Delaware*. The division was ordered to join the British Grand Fleet, then based on Scapa Flow, Scotland, under Admiral Sir David Beatty. Without instructions to do so from the Navy Department, Rodman placed himself under Admiral Beatty's command. As the Sixth Battle Squadron of the Grand Fleet, the American battleships adopted British codes and signals and battle instructions on the common successful mission to keep the German High Seas Fleet confined to its home ports and thus to assure Allied control of the surface of the seas. After the war, Rodman vigorously denied before a Senate naval investigation the charges by Admiral William S. Sims, late commander of U.S. naval forces in Europe, that the navy was unprepared when the United States entered the war in 1917.

After Germany's surrender, Rodman in 1919 was named commander in chief of the new Pacific Fleet with the temporary four-star rank of full admiral. He led the major units of this new fleet from the Atlantic through the Panama Canal into the Pacific, the first passage by a fleet through the recently opened waterway. On completion of his tour with the Pacific Fleet in 1921, Rodman reverted to the rank of rear admiral and was named commandant of the Fifth Naval District, Naval Operating Base, Hampton Roads, Virginia. While in this command, he was sent on a special mission with rank of minister plenipotentiary to Peru.

In 1922 Rodman also chaired the Special Board on Shore Establishments, whose report in September 1922 stressed the importance of developing Pacific bases on San Francisco Bay, in Puget Sound, and at Hawaii comparable to those in the Atlantic at New York and Hampton Roads.

Rodman was retired from the navy in January 1923 after reaching the statutory age of sixty-four. He was recalled for temporary active service in 1923 to accompany President Warren G. Harding on an inspection of Alaska. By special act of Congress in 1930, Rodman was accorded the rank of full admiral (four stars) on the retired list. In 1937 he was ordered to Britain for the coronation of King George VI, at which he attended the naval review on his wartime flagship, the *New York*. Rodman died in Washington, D.C., where he had lived during his retirement. Among Rodman's numerous decorations from the American and foreign governments were the Spanish Campaign Medal, the Distinguished Service Medal for meritorious service during World War I, Knight Commander of the Order of the Bath from Britain, and the Legion of Honor from France.

Rodman was from the generation of naval officers who served during the navy's transition from ships of wood and sail to those of steel and steam. He identified with the seagoing officers of the navy, as distinguished from those who sat at desks pushing papers. Rodman was also one of the very few high-ranking U.S. naval officers who actually served afloat in the war zone during World War I. He successfully integrated U.S. battleships into the Grand Fleet so that the Americans and the British fought practically as brothers of the same service. Rodman was an outgoing, bluff sea dog, well known for his sense of humor. Once asked what he had done with a critical message from a superior, he responded that he had consigned it to the Rodman file—into the wastebasket.

• Apparently Rodman did not leave any significant private papers. There is a folder of materials at the Naval Historical Center, chiefly biographical sketches issued to the press. His memoirs, *Yarns of a Kentucky Admiral* (1928), are principally tales of human interest that Rodman picked up during many years of cruising in various parts of the world.

WILLIAM R. BRAISTED

RODMAN, Samuel (11 Nov. 1753–24 Dec. 1835), whaling merchant and Quaker leader, was born in Newport, Rhode Island, the son of Thomas Rodman, a ship captain, and Mary Borden. Samuel was apprenticed at the age of thirteen after the death of his father at sea. Remarkably for a young Quaker, whose denomination was attempting at this time to remain apart from other groups, he served his apprenticeship with Abraham Riveira, one of a number of successful Jewish merchants in Newport before independence. There Rodman learned the shipping trade and came into contact with Nantucket whaling merchants Joseph Rotch and William Rotch. This connection served Rodman well when external trade came to a virtual halt in Newport during the War for Independence. Like many other Newport residents, Rodman left Newport during the war and joined the Rotches' interests on Nantucket by 1780.

As Quakers dominated Nantucket socially and economically, the island was a congenial place for Rodman to settle. But there was more to his move than mere religious affinity, as his marriage to William Rotch's daughter, Elizabeth Rotch, in 1780 demonstrated. (They had nine children.) Ordinary Nantucket residents were moving to the Hudson River valley in New York and to Nova Scotia; Rodman must have seemed remarkably able for the Rotches to recruit him, although romance may have led to his move initially. The family alliance developed further when William Rotch, Jr., married Rodman's sister Elizabeth in 1782.

After peace with Britain in 1783, like other international businesses, the Rotch interests had to face substantially changed trading patterns. No longer would the British protect the American whaling trade. To survive in changed economic conditions, American merchants had to penetrate the protected markets of other nations. To develop this geographical diversification, William Rotch, Sr., left Nantucket in 1785, moving first to Britain and then to France, where he settled until 1793. He left William Rotch, Jr., and Rodman in charge of the family's Nantucket operations. Their shared control was short, for in 1787 William Rotch, Jr., took his part of the firm to Dartmouth, Massachusetts (renamed New Bedford in 1793). Rodman continued to manage the firm's affairs on Nantucket until 1798, when he too moved to New Bedford. Longstanding hostility to Rotch interests had grown among other Nantucket residents during the war and worsened with attempted geographical diversification after 1785. In this hostile climate, Rodman probably had no choice but to join the family firms in New Bedford.

While continuing active in the whaling business, Rodman, like his brother-in-law and many other contemporary New England businessmen, broadened his business efforts. He was among the early investors in the cotton mills of Fall River, Massachusetts, a center of the developing New England textile industry. He was also active in banking and served on the board of directors of the Bedford Commercial Bank. With William Rotch, Jr., he helped finance the reconstruction of the New Bedford–Fairhaven bridge. Not surprisingly, considering his and his family's involvement in international trade, Rodman was a staunch Federalist, strongly opposed to the policies of Thomas Jefferson's administration.

Like other members of his family, Rodman was active in New England Quaker affairs and served on many local and New England committees. In 1808–1810 and 1814, he served as clerk (essentially chair) of the New England Yearly Meeting, the chief decision-making body for New England Friends. He also served as clerk of the yearly meeting's executive committee, the Meeting for Sufferings, from 1802 to 1822.

He, William Rotch, Jr., and their wives (Quaker women ran their own meetings) exercised substantial influence on New England Quaker affairs from the late eighteenth century through the early 1820s. They were active in promoting Quaker causes: lobbying for peace, against slavery, for Quaker education, and, daringly, for general education in schools that mixed Quaker youths with others.

In economically developing New England, Rodman, like others of the Rotch clan, had frequent contacts outside the closed Quaker world, which many other Quakers resented. The family also held to views that harked back to early Quakerism and derived from the speeches and writings of Job Scott, an eighteenth-century Providence, Rhode Island, Quaker. Seventeenth-century Quakers challenged the doctrine of the Trinity. Scott continued the challenge, but by the late eighteenth century most Friends concerned about that position were trinitarians. To many early nineteenth-century Friends, Scott's positions and those of the Rotch-Rodmans were entirely too close to unitarian developments among Congregational neighbors. By 1823 the doctrinal split among Friends had festered so long that it could not be contained. The New Lights, as the Rotch-Rodman group and their allies were called, lost a power struggle to control the New Bedford Monthly Meeting. With the exception of William Rotch, Sr., they resigned their memberships, mostly joining the newly formed Unitarian church, thereby confirming the suspicions of the remaining Friends, who had attacked the New Lights as unitarian. While the family remained among New Bedford and southeast Massachusetts leadership for the balance of the period before the Civil War, Friends soon forgot their dominant role among the Quakers. Rodman died in New Bedford.

• Manuscript collections on Rodman are in the Old Dartmouth Historical Society, New Bedford, Mass. James Lawrence McDevitt, Jr., "The House of Rotch: Whaling Merchants of Massachusetts, 1734–1828" (Ph.D. diss., American Univ., 1978), and John M. Bullard, *The Rotches* (1947), provide material on Rodman's economic activities. Arthur J. Worrall, "New England Quakerism 1656–1830" (Ph.D. diss., Indiana Univ., 1969), provides material on Rodman's religious activities.

ARTHUR J. WORRALL

RODNEY, Caesar (7 Oct. 1728–26 June 1784), Speaker of the colonial assembly and president of the state of Delaware, was born on a farm near Dover in Kent County, Delaware, the son of Caesar Rodeney, a planter, and Elizabeth Crawford. (His father and grandfather both spelled their name Rodeney.) Little is known of Rodney's education except that in 1743 he attended the Latin school in Philadelphia.

Rodney's inheritance at his father's death in 1745 freed him to devote his life to public service. His early service was in Kent, where he was chosen sheriff in 1755 and returned to the office in 1756 and 1757. Over the following years he held a number of appointed clerkships, such as register of wills, recorder of deeds, clerk of the orphans' court, and trustee of the county loan office. He also served as a justice of the peace and, though not a lawyer, as a judge on the supreme court from 1769 to the end of the colonial government.

Rodney's long legislative service began in 1758 with his election to the unicameral assembly. Chosen again in 1761, he won reelection annually, except in 1771, to the conclusion of that assembly's existence. He became Speaker in 1769 and again in March 1773, retaining the office until 1776. In 1762 the assembly asked Rodney and Thomas McKean to revise and print the laws then in force, a task they completed in 1763.

Rodney's initial participation in intercolonial politics came in 1765, when he and McKean represented Delaware in the Stamp Act Congress, where they enthusiastically supported a petition (which some members would not sign) insisting on the right to trial by jury and taxation only with the agreement of their own assemblies, as well as threatening an embargo on all but the most necessary British goods until the Stamp Act was repealed. The Delaware assemblymen unanimously approved the work of Rodney and McKean and in 1766, when the Stamp Act was repealed, asked them, together with George Read, to prepare an address of thanks to the king. Pleased by this address, the assembly extended the commission of these three men, who, by a succession of resolutions, became a committee of correspondence that was active into the early years of the Revolution.

Rodney had entered Delaware politics as a member of the dominant court party, but gradually his ties to this group loosened and he became a leader of those opposing British policies. In 1774 after Parliament passed the Boston Port Bill, Rodney, as Speaker, took a leading role in summoning the assemblymen to a special meeting to choose delegates to attend a Continental Congress. Since only the governor could legally call the assembly into special session, participants termed this meeting a convention, and Rodney, presiding as usual, signed the resolutions as chairman, not as Speaker. The delegates sent to congress were the usual trio entrusted with intercolonial business: Rodney, McKean, and Read.

Meeting Rodney in Philadelphia, John Adams described him as "the oddest looking Man in the World; he is tall, thin and slender as a Reed, pale; his Face is not bigger than a large Apple, Yet there is Sense and Fire, Spirit, Wit, and Humour in his Countenance" (Smith, vol. 1, pp. 8–9). In March 1775 the assembly approved the actions of the irregular 1774 convention, accepted a report from the three congressmen, and reelected them to a second Continental Congress that was to meet in May 1775.

At home in Kent, Rodney took an active part in supporting the actions of Congress; he served on a committee of observation and inspection to enforce a boycott of British goods and on a council of safety that organized men and supplies for the army. Years earlier, during the French and Indian War, Rodney had been commissioned a captain in the militia, but his company was not called to active service. In the spring of 1775 the militia officers elected him colonel of a Kent County regiment, and in September the council of safety made him brigadier general.

In June 1776 the assembly, with Rodney presiding, responded to a recommendation from Congress by suspending all authority under the Crown and eliminating from the instructions of its congressmen previous references to a hope for reconciliation and peace. Though ordered to join in compacts, treaties, and other measures, the delegates were not specifically instructed to vote for independence.

When Congress took up the subject on 1 July, Rodney was absent and the Delaware vote was divided. Read did not wish to move so far so fast; consequently McKean, knowing Rodney to be more intrepid, sent for him to hurry to Philadelphia. Rodney, as Speaker, the ranking official in Delaware, had gone from the assembly meeting to Lewes to inquire into a threatened Tory uprising. He had returned to Kent when he received McKean's message, and he set off at once for Philadelphia. He rode eighty miles through the night of 1–2 July and arrived at the Pennsylvania state house, "tho detained by Thunder and Rain" (Ryden, p. 94), in time to join McKean in casting Delaware's vote for independence. The crucial voting occurred on July 2. A justification of this action, in the form of the famous Declaration of Independence, was adopted without any recorded vote on July 4. All three Delaware delegates signed the Declaration, but the signing did not take place until a fine copy was available in August.

A special session of the assembly that Rodney called ordered an election of delegates to a constitutional convention in August, the first in America with the specific function of writing a state constitution. In this election a conservative backlash against Rodney was apparent, for he was not included in the Kent delegation. Nor was he chosen in the fall to the first assembly under the new constitution. A crowning blow occurred in November 1776 when he and McKean were dropped from the congressional delegation in favor of delegates thought to be more conservative.

Rodney remained active in the council of safety and the militia. In January 1777 he joined the army in New Jersey and briefly commanded a post at Trenton. In the late summer he was again in the field, leading Kent militia removing supplies from the path of the British army as it advanced from the Chesapeake to Philadelphia. Promoted to major general in command of all the Delaware militia, Rodney shortly assumed even higher rank, as the legislature elected him president, or chief executive, in March 1778 by twenty of twenty-four votes. With a British army in Philadelphia and a British fleet on the Delaware River, the state's situation was perilous. In a term lasting three years and a few months, 1778–1781, Rodney did all in his power to rally the resources of his state to the weakened cause he fervently embraced. At the close of his term he was twice elected to Congress, but increasing fears for his health precluded his attendance.

Since the 1760s Rodney had suffered from skin cancer and asthma. After an operation in Philadelphia in 1768 a scar extended from the corner of his eye halfway down his nose. Though advised to travel to England for a cure, his public responsibilities kept him in America. As he grew older, the cancer became more worrisome, and in early 1782 he spent several months in Philadelphia under treatment. "The Doctor must conquer the Cancer, or the Cancer will conquer me," he wrote (Ryden, p. 431). In the spring of 1784 the upper house of the legislature, of which he had become Speaker the year before, met at his home to save him a journey. He died at "Poplar Grove," a farm near Dover. A memorial monument is in the yard of Christ Episcopal Church in Dover, of which he was a member. His will provided for the gradual emancipation of all his slaves.

Rodney never married. No likeness of him is known, probably because of his disfigurement from cancer; it is said that he wore a cloth over his face in his later years. An equestrian statue in the central square of Wilmington commemorates his famous ride of 1–2 July 1776, but it is likely that at least part of the ride was made in a carriage. For his ardent spirit and his leadership Rodney is the preeminent figure of the Revolution in Delaware. His zeal, and his restraint, made possible an unusually smooth transition for a small colony to statehood.

• Papers of Caesar Rodney are in the Historical Society of Delaware; the Historical Society of Pennsylvania; the Delaware State Archives, Dover; the Library of Congress; the New York Public Library; the New-York Historical Society; Rowan College of New Jersey, Glassboro; and elsewhere in collections of papers of signers of the Declaration of Independence. The major printed collection of Rodney's correspondence is George H. Ryden, ed., *Letters to and from Caesar Rodney, 1756–1784* (1933), which includes a sketch that is still the best biography of Rodney. Supplementary collections of Rodney papers, edited by Leon de Valinger, Jr., have been published in *Delaware History* 1 (1946): 99–110, and 3 (1948): 105–15, and by Harold B. Hancock in 12 (1966): 54–76 and 147–68, and 20 (1983): 185–221. William P. Frank, *Caesar Rodney, Patriot* (1975), is episodic but includes new material. Hancock, ed., "'Fare Weather and Good Health': The Journal of Caesar Rodney, 1727–1729," *Delaware History* 10 (1962): 33–70, provides details of Rodney's birth and, in the introduction, of his schooling. William P. Frank and Harold B. Hancock, "Caesar Rodney's Two Hundred and Fiftieth Anniversary: An Evaluation," *Delaware History* 18 (1978): 63–74, is very helpful. See also John M. Coleman, *Thomas McKean, Forgotten Leader of the Revolution* (1975), and John A. Munroe, *Colonial Delaware, A History* (1978). Claudia L. Bushman et al., eds., *Proceedings of the Assembly of the Lower Counties on Delaware, 1770–1776* (1986), provides a legislative record of the smooth transition from colonial to state government. Many Rodney letters appear in Paul H. Smith et al., eds., *Letters of Delegates to Congress, 1774–1789*, vols. 1–5 (1977–1979), but most have been published previously.

JOHN A. MUNROE

RODNEY, Caesar Augustus (4 Jan. 1772–10 June 1824), attorney general and diplomat, was born in Dover, Delaware, the son of Thomas Rodney, a scholarly merchant and politician, and Elizabeth Maud Fisher. In his youth the family moved between Dover, Philadelphia, and Wilmington. After his mother's death in 1783, he lived with relatives or friends when not away at school. He was the principal legatee of his uncle Caesar Rodney (1728–1784), for whom he was named, but the estate was encumbered by debt, and Thomas Rodney, its executor, spent fourteen months in debtors' prison in 1791–1792.

Caesar Augustus received an A.B. from the University of Pennsylvania in 1789 and from 1790 to 1793 read law in the Philadelphia office of Joseph B. McKean. Admitted to the bar in Philadelphia and in Delaware in 1793, the year of his marriage to Susan Hunn, he soon began to combine political activities with the practice of law, becoming a member of both the Democratic Society of Philadelphia and its sister society, the Patriotic Society of New Castle County, in 1794.

An active civic leader in Wilmington, where after 1802 he resided in a stone mansion called "Cool Spring," west of the town, he was a member of a fire company, a water company, the abolition society, and a Masonic lodge. He and John Dickinson (1732–1808) were the principal speakers in 1795 at a town meeting protesting the Jay Treaty. In 1796 Rodney was elected to the first of six successive one-year terms in the state legislature. Through these years he worked closely with Dickinson, Dr. James Tilton, Robert Coram, and young Hezekiah Niles in organizing the Democratic-Republican party, of which he soon became the acknowledged leader in Delaware. Through this role he also came to be in close contact with the national leadership of his party.

In 1802 President Thomas Jefferson persuaded him to oppose the Federalist champion, James A. Bayard (1767–1815), for a seat in the U.S. House of Representatives. Victorious by a narrow margin, he entered Congress with an éclat that brought him immediate prominence. He was appointed to the Ways and Means Committee and became one of the managers of both the John Pickering (c.1738–1805) and the Samuel Chase impeachments. With Speaker Nathaniel Macon, John Randolph (1773–1833), and Joseph Nicholson he was a leading spokesman for administration policy, urging acceptance of the Twelfth Amendment and of Jefferson's policy for Louisiana—while declaring his hostility to slavery.

In January 1805 he left Congress temporarily to prosecute a Pennsylvania impeachment case against three state supreme court judges, no Pennsylvania lawyer of equal reputation being available and willing to take the case. His argument was supported by a majority of the state senate but with too few votes for conviction. By this time he had lost his seat in Congress in another contest with Bayard. The two men, who were very close friends, sought election only to satisfy their parties, each preferring to concentrate on a more lucrative legal practice.

In his private practice Rodney was retained by such entrepreneurs as Stephen Girard and E. I. du Pont de Nemours, but he also defended the right of the cordwainers to organize. In January 1807 he again accepted public office when Jefferson appointed him attorney general. This was then a part-time post, with no department to supervise; indeed Rodney said he had neither an assistant nor a desk in Washington. He intended to move his family to the capital for part of the year, but a vessel carrying his library and some household goods was wrecked near Chincoteague and the move was given up.

In March 1807 Rodney attended the circuit court in Richmond at the beginning of the Aaron Burr (1756–1836) indictment trial. He directed the summoning of witnesses and gathering of depositions but left the prosecution to George Hay, the district attorney, and two assistants.

Reappointed by James Madison (1751–1836), Rodney continued commuting between Washington and his office in Wilmington until December 1811, when he resigned in a huff at being passed over for appointment to a vacant Supreme Court judgeship with responsibility for a circuit that included Delaware.

After outbreak of the War of 1812 Rodney joined a volunteer military company that elected him captain. Later he was commissioned major but saw no action. During the war, in 1814, he won election to a three-year term in the state senate. In 1816 he ran again for Congress but lost by one vote.

After James Monroe became president Rodney began to play a role in foreign affairs, as the negotiator, for instance, with the delegate from Brazilian revolutionaries. In 1817–1818 he went to South America as one of three commissioners to examine the state of the new governments there. Rodney's report on conditions in the Argentine provinces was the most favorable of the three reports submitted. His opinion that the new government had made as much progress as could reasonably be expected encouraged the administration to recognize its independence.

In 1820 Rodney was again elected to the House of Representatives, and as before he won immediate attention, receiving seventy-two votes, nine less than necessary, in the election of a Speaker. His outspoken opposition to the Missouri Compromise and to any extension of slavery may have cost him needed southern votes. In January 1822 he left the House for the Senate when the Delaware legislature chose him to fill a vacancy. He was the first Democratic-Republican elected to the Senate from Delaware.

Rodney's Senate service was brief. He resigned in 1823 to accept appointment as the first American minister to Buenos Aires. Taken seriously ill soon after arrival at his post in November 1823, Rodney seemed to recover, only to die suddenly after less than eight months' residence. The Buenos Aires government honored Rodney, their first minister from abroad, with a grand funeral and ordered a marble sepulchral monument, which stands on the porch of the Anglican church in the heart of the financial district.

Caesar A. Rodney was a cultivated gentleman, the possessor, it was said, of the largest library in Delaware, and one that was well used. Genial, good hearted, unaffected in dress or address, Rodney had a talent for friendships that transcended politics. A political liberal in the terms of his day, he supported republicanism here and abroad. Esteemed as a trial lawyer, Rodney enjoyed the luxuries of life but was careless of money, to the detriment of his wife and their large family. Thirteen children survived him; two other children had died in their youth. Rodney was the acknowledged leader of the Delaware Democratic-Republicans, who relapsed, after his death, into the minority position from which he had helped rescue them.

• Caesar A. Rodney's papers are numerous and are to be found at the Historical Society of Delaware and the Hagley Library, Wilmington; the American Antiquarian Society, Worcester, MA; Brown University; the New York Public Library; and the Library of Congress. See also C. A. Rodney and John Graham, *Reports on the Present State of the United Provinces of South America* (1819; repr. 1969). For biographical sketches, see William Plumer, "Caesar A. Rodney," *Delaware History* 4 (1951): 369–73, and William T. Read, *Life and Correspondence of George Read* (1870), pp. 230–43. Articles by men acquainted with Rodney are in *Niles' Weekly Register* 25 (1823–1824): 321–23, and 27 (1824–1825): 6–7 and 74–77. Further information on Rodney can be found in William B. Hamilton, *Thomas Rodney* (1953); George H. Ryden, ed., *Letters to and from Caesar Rodney* (1933), pp. 18–20; and John A. Munroe, "Party Battles, 1789–1850," in *Delaware, a History of the First State*, ed. H. Clay Reed, vol. 1 (1947), pp. 125–62.

JOHN A. MUNROE

RODNEY, Red (27 Sept. 1927–27 May 1994), jazz trumpeter, was born Robert Chudnick in Philadelphia, Pennsylvania. Details of his parents are unknown. After playing the bugle in a drum and bugle corps sponsored by the Jewish War Veterans, Rodney received a trumpet for a bar mitzvah present. At age fourteen he played in a band with Elliot Lawrence. At age sixteen, as older men were being drafted, Rodney dropped out of high school to spend one month with clarinetist Benny Goodman's big band before touring with Jerry Wald's dance band. He then played briefly in the bands of Tony Pastor, Jimmy Dorsey, and Les Brown.

Throughout 1945 Rodney and saxophonist Gerry Mulligan played with Lawrence's orchestra six nights a week on WCAU, a CBS radio affiliate in Philadelphia. Meanwhile, Rodney took a music course at Mastbaum Trade School and performed at Philadelphia's Down Beat club. Upon hearing trumpeter Dizzy Gillespie there, he became infatuated with bebop, and his feeling only intensified when Gillespie introduced him to the playing of alto saxophonist Charlie Parker.

Rodney joined drummer Gene Krupa's band at the Palladium in Hollywood, California, in January 1946. That year he recorded with Krupa, tenor saxophonist Charlie Ventura, and drummer Buddy Rich, as well as with his own Beboppers, producing a version of "Perdido" for which he supplied a now standard countermelody to the main theme. Around this time he married. His wife's name is unknown; they had a son.

Rodney remained with Krupa until early 1947. He then joined tenor saxophonist Georgie Auld's small group and recorded with Auld's sideman, baritone saxophonist Serge Chaloff. Rodney joined pianist Claude Thornhill's band in the fall of 1947. During 1948 he freelanced and played for a time in a cooperative sextet with Mulligan before joining Woody Herman's band, the Second Herd, in November 1948. He recorded another small group bebop session with Chaloff, then also with Herman, in 1949. Around this time Rodney's marriage fell apart.

Late in 1949 Rodney took Miles Davis's place in Parker's quintet. Somehow he had avoided joining the many heroin addicts who had been sidemen in the Second Herd, but while with Parker, he became addicted. Rodney performed at Carnegie Hall with Parker in December 1949 and toured the South, masquerading as an African American, "Albino Red," an experience later portrayed in Clint Eastwood's movie *Bird* (1988). When Rodney's appendix ruptured, he was obliged to leave Parker. In the mid-1950s, upon recovering, he joined tenor saxophonist Charlie Ventura, with whom he had recorded the previous year; he also served briefly as a substitute for Shorty Rogers in Stan Kenton's band in December 1950. In August 1951 Rodney rejoined Parker for a recording session that included "Blues for Alice," "Swedish Schnapps," and "Back Home Blues." He remained with Parker for a year.

Many of the details of Rodney's life are somewhat unbelievable, although the overall outline of events is reasonably consistent. Arrested and rearrested for narcotics violations, he spent periods in federal prisons and hospitals. At some point, perhaps in 1953, he lost two teeth in a fight. During a stay at a federal hospital in Lexington, Kentucky, he met his second wife. They married shortly after their discharge (probably spring 1953), and both resumed their heroin use; they had a child. Rodney last played with Parker in July 1953.

When not incarcerated, Rodney led society bands for weddings and bar mitzvahs in Philadelphia. Around 1957 he recorded his finest album in collaboration with multi-instrumentalist Ira Sullivan, *Red Rodney: 1957* (later reissued as *The Red Arrow*). He also supported himself through theft and various exploits as a con artist. But while in prisons and hospitals, he continued his education, finishing high school, taking courses from the University of Kansas and the Berklee School of Music in Boston, Massachusetts, and becoming proficient in the law, which he studied after becoming a friend of Melvin Belli and his partners.

Rodney spent a number of years during the 1960s and early 1970s performing in pit orchestras in Las Vegas, Nevada, and in television studio orchestras in Los Angeles, California. He won $12,500 playing keno in a casino and bought a house. He claimed to have made nearly $50,000 from a piece of real estate he had bought in 1954, but he lost it all in hospital bills after he suffered a paralytic stroke in 1972. Unable to talk or walk for a year, he finally returned to performing in 1973, expressing no regret for his adventures

but a deep regret for having abandoned modern jazz for the security of uninspiring musical jobs. He spent the remainder of his life leading a bebop group.

Rodney performed at the Newport Jazz Festival in New York in 1973 and began recording for the Muse label. He toured Europe with a memorial show, the Musical World of Charlie Parker (c. 1974) and also worked in Europe with Dexter Gordon. Over the course of about a decade he underwent a few unsuccessful surgeries for problems stemming from his broken teeth. His playing continued to suffer until 1978, when dental reconstruction finally worked.

The ending to Rodney's second marriage is unknown. Around 1978 he married Helene, her maiden name unknown. From 1980 to 1985 he co-led a quintet with Sullivan. They recorded the album *Live at the Village Vanguard* in 1980. During this period Rodney increasingly used the mellow, lower-voiced flugelhorn rather than trumpet.

Thereafter, Rodney continued leading bop groups, most notably with tenor saxophonist Chris Potter among his sidemen from around 1989. He served as an an adviser to Eastwood in the making of *Bird*. A regular performer at the JVC (formerly Newport) Jazz Festival in New York, he also recorded the album *Then and Now* (1992). He performed at a Jazz at Lincoln Center concert in August 1993 and that same summer played the White House lawn party in Bill Clinton's Presidential All Stars. He died in Boynton Beach, Florida.

Rodney led an eccentric and fascinating life. The extent to which he may have confused or embellished his account awaits laborious research into police, FBI, and military files, but no one questions the essence of his narrative or his skills as an engaging storyteller. Early on, Rodney the trumpet player was far less engaging, an aspiring bebop improviser whose solos sounded mechanical and cliché ridden, even into his years with Parker. Although he never became one of the exceptionally creative bop trumpeters, his 1957 album with Sullivan testified to an improved command of the idiom, and later in life he showed skill as a sensitive soloist on ballad melodies.

• Surveys and interviews of Rodney include Jack Tracy, "Make Jazz Respectable, Asks Rodney," *Down Beat*, 2 June 1950, p. 3; Dom Cerulli, "Narcotics 'Nearly Killed Me,'" *Down Beat*, 20 Feb. 1958, pp. 13–14, 18; Jimmy Burns, "Red Rodney: An Introduction," *Jazz Journal* 16 (Oct. 1963): 9–10; Mark Gardner, "Red Rodney Talks," *Jazz Monthly*, Apr. 1970, pp. 2–9; Michael James, "Red Rodney on Record," *Jazz Monthly*, Sept. 1970, pp. 4–7; Roland Baggenaes, "Red Rodney," *Coda*, Feb. 1976, pp. 13–16; Michael Smith, "Red Rodney," *Cadence*, July 1980, pp. 5–8, 24, and Sept. 1980, pp. 5–8; Larry Birnbaum, "Red Rodney: His Bite Is Back," *Down Beat*, Feb. 1981, pp. 20–24; Doug Long, "Red Rodney," *Cadence*, Dec. 1986, pp. 5–16; Martin Isherwood, "Red Rodney," *Jazz Journal International* 41 (June 1988): 19; Fred Bouchard, "Red Sails in the Limelight," *Jazz Times*, Dec. 1993, pp. 36–37; and Frank Gibson; "Red Rodney: A Discography," *Jazz Journal* 16 (Oct. 1963): 10–12, with additions and corrections in *Jazz Journal* 17 (Jan. 1964): 39–40. See also Ross Russell, *Bird Lives!: The*

High Life and Hard Times of Charlie (Yardbird) Parker (1973); Gary Giddins, *Riding on a Blue Note: Jazz and American Pop* (1981), pp. 228–44; Ira Gitler, *Swing to Bop: An Oral History of the Transition in Jazz in the 1940s* (1985); and Woody Herman and Stuart Troup, *The Woodchopper's Ball: The Autobiography of Woody Herman* (1990), pp. 76–78. An obituary is in the *New York Times*, 28 May 1994.

BARRY KERNFELD

RODZINSKI, Artur (1 Jan. 1892–27 Nov. 1958), conductor, was born in Spalato (now Split) on the Dalmatian coast of the Adriatic, the son of Josef Rodzinski, an army surgeon, and Jadwiga Wiszmiewska. In 1897 he moved to his father's home town, Lvov, Poland (then known as Lemberg), where he was raised. He began to study the piano at secondary school but then, in deference to his parents' wishes, studied law at the University of Lvov. Ill health prevented him from being called up for service in World War I. He therefore continued his education at the University of Vienna, earning a doctorate in law in 1916 but never practicing in that profession. Rodzinski's real love was music, and he enrolled at the Vienna Academy of Music, where he studied piano, composition, and music theory, and where he was taught conducting by Franz Schalk. Rodzinski earned a D.Mus. from the academy. In 1917 he married Ilsa Reimesch, a fellow pianist; they had one child before they divorced.

Rodzinski's career as a professional musician began in Poland between 1918 and 1925. He first worked as a pianist and coach with the Lvov Opera Company. In 1919 he conducted his first opera, Verdi's *Ernani*. After leaving Lvov in 1920 he spent five seasons as the principal conductor of the Teatr Wielki in Warsaw, at which he conducted many productions in German, Italian, French, Russian, and Polish. He also conducted the Warsaw Philharmonic Orchestra and gave concerts in Germany and Russia as well as in Poland. In 1925 conductor Leopold Stokowski heard Rodzinski conduct a performance of Wagner's *Die Meistersinger* in Warsaw and was sufficiently impressed to engage him as his assistant conductor with the Philadelphia Orchestra.

From 1926 until 1929, while serving as Stokowski's assistant, Rodzinski was responsible for preparing new scores for performance by the Philadelphia Orchestra. He conducted the orchestra and some Philadelphia Grand Opera concerts, and he spent two years (1927–1929) as director of the orchestral department of the Curtis Institute of Music. In 1929 Rodzinski was appointed conductor of the Los Angeles Philharmonic Orchestra, a post he held for four seasons. In Los Angeles he first demonstrated his skills as an orchestral trainer, raising the quality of playing to an admirable standard. He conducted seventy-eight performances of works, including five world premieres, new to Los Angeles audiences.

Rodzinski attained national prominence in his next position as music director of the Cleveland Orchestra. He accepted the post in 1933, the year he became a U.S. citizen, and he remained with the orchestra for a decade. Rodzinski built up the Cleveland Orchestra from a provincial ensemble to one of the half-dozen best symphony orchestras in the United States. He achieved this by hiring players of high quality, by rehearsing intensively, and by devoting close attention to the quality of music making. Rodzinski championed operas as part of the regular orchestral season. In the 1934–1935 season he presented six full operas. But by 1936 financial restrictions forced him to cut back the offerings to two per season. He also conducted many performances of new scores, including the premieres of Hindemith's Violin Concerto, Walton's Violin Concerto, Roy Harris's Third Symphony, and Walter Piston's *The Incredible Flutist*. In 1934 he married Halina Lilpop, a grandniece of the Polish violinist Henri Wieniawski; they had one child.

Rodzinski extended his own reputation and that of his orchestra by appearing on a series of coast-to-coast Saturday afternoon CBS radio broadcasts and by making several guest appearances in New York, notably at a gala performance of Shostakovich's opera *Lady Macbeth of Mtsensk* in 1935. Rodzinski made his debut at the Salzburg Festival in 1936, at which he impressed conductor Arturo Toscanini. In 1937 Toscanini selected Rodzinski to engage and train the players for the newly created NBC Symphony Orchestra. Rodzinski's final years in Cleveland were marked by quarrels with the manager and the orchestra's board of directors over budget restrictions, and he left his post in 1943 to begin a four-year association with the Philharmonic-Symphony Orchestra of New York.

Rodzinski's tenure in New York began controversially. As soon as he was appointed he fired fourteen players, including the concertmaster (five were later reinstated). His years in Manhattan continued in a stormy way, and he eventually quit at the end of the 1946–1947 season, accusing the manager, Arthur Judson, of interfering with his artistic privileges and responsibilities. Rodzinski established good discipline within the orchestra and conducted a wide repertory. Composer Virgil Thomson wrote that Rodzinski had done more to train the orchestra than any other conductor during the century (Rodzinski, *Our Two Lives*, p. 292). The repertoire presented by Rodzinski included contemporary music by Bartók, Hindemith, Martinu, Prokofiev, Shostakovich, Samuel Barber, Copland, and William Schuman. Rodzinski also provided a significant opportunity to the young Leonard Bernstein, whom he appointed assistant conductor of the orchestra in 1943.

Rodzinski's final permanent appointment lasted for a single season, 1947–1948, as music director of the Chicago Symphony Orchestra. He elicited precise and alert playing from the orchestra, which had suffered neglect for several years, and he was popular with Chicago audiences. But once again Rodzinski clashed with the orchestral board, which announced that he would not be reengaged for the next season because he had failed to conduct a subscription concert in January 1948 (he missed this owing to a mild heart attack, which he kept secret).

After leaving Chicago, Rodzinski performed as a guest conductor in Europe, the United States, South America, and Cuba. He led the Philharmonic season in Havana in 1949–1950 and settled in Italy in 1952. In 1953, at the Florence May Festival, Rodzinski conducted Prokofiev's opera *War and Peace*, the first performance of the work outside Russia. The final years of his career were interrupted by health problems. He had a severe heart attack in London in 1948, and by the mid-1950s he found the physical strain of conducting enormous. In 1958 he returned to Chicago to direct two memorable performances of Wagner's *Tristan und Isolde* at the Lyric Opera. Soon afterward, however, he died in Boston.

Rodzinski's career was troubled by his impulsive, contradictory, and eccentric behavior. He argued with orchestral managers over budgets and artistic policy and sometimes expressed his philosophical thoughts to musicians during rehearsal. He conducted with a loaded revolver in his pocket, for superstitious reasons, and he demanded to be pinched hard on the left arm before performances to boost his adrenalin. He was interested in oriental arts and customs and was a devout Roman Catholic. Rodzinski often read the Bible and for a time was involved in the Buchman Moral Rearmament movement. He was a conductor of considerable ability whose main achievements lay in training American orchestras to a high technical standard. He rehearsed until he achieved the desired perfection in execution, and he was most comfortable with directing music that required orchestral brilliance, color, and emotional intensity. Among his most effective performances were those of pieces by Wagner, Tchaikovsky, Richard Strauss, Prokofiev, and Shostakovich. He also excelled in presenting large-scale projects, notably opera; he was less attuned to the orchestral repertoire of the classical period.

Rodzinski recorded extensively. In the 1940s he made many records for Columbia with the Cleveland Orchestra and the New York Philharmonic. In the 1950s he recorded for EMI/HMV and Westminster Records, chiefly with the Royal Philharmonic Orchestra. He also delivered many live radio broadcasts. Rodzinski's earlier recordings tend to be literal and straightforward; his later recordings are more representative of his fresh and imaginative response to the romantic and twentieth-century repertoire.

• Photocopies of Rodzinski's personal papers are at the New York Public Library for the Performing Arts at Lincoln Center. The archives of the Cleveland Orchestra and the New York Philharmonic Orchestra contain scrapbooks that cover Rodzinski's years with those ensembles. His late widow recalls his personality and career in Halina Rodzinski, *Our Two Lives* (1976). Rodzinski's views on conducting and rehearsing orchestras are in Robert C. Marsh, "Artur Rodzinski and the Education of a Conductor," *Saturday Review*, 26 Jan. 1957, pp. 41, 43, and 62–63; and Rose Heylbut, "Developing the Orchestra," *Etude* (Apr. 1945): 185–86. His career is also covered in David Ewen, *Dictators of the Baton* (1943); Moses Smith, "Rodzinski Comes to New York," *Harper's Magazine*, Nov. 1943, pp. 509–16; Donald Brook, *International Gallery of Conductors* (1951); Marsh, *The Cleveland Orchestra* (1967); Howard Shanet, *Philharmonic: A History of New York's Orchestra* (1975); and Boris Goldovsky, *My Road to Opera* (1979). Rodzinski's recordings are discussed in John L. Holmes, *Conductors on Record* (1982), and are listed in Michael Gray, "Artur Rodzinski: A Discography," *Recorded Sound*, no. 73 (Jan. 1979): 10–19. An obituary is in the *New York Times*, 28 Nov. 1958.

KENNETH MORGAN

ROE, Edward Payson (7 Mar. 1837–19 July 1888), author and minister, was born in Moodna (now New Windsor), Orange County, New York, the seventh child of Peter Roe and Susan Williams. Peter Roe had moved to Moodna from New York City, where he had been a successful wholesale grocer and importer. In Moodna he became president of the Newburgh Whaling Company and a leading abolitionist. Young Edward learned lifelong standards of honor and moral integrity from his father. Susan Roe, an invalid, had an inquisitive mind and a strong reading interest in the Bible and the classics; from her, young Edward received his interest in religion and literature. He was educated at home and at private and boarding schools before President Mark Hopkins of Williams College advised him to enter the senior class in the fall of 1859. Because of troubling eyestrain, he temporarily withdrew from college, but he reentered and was graduated in 1861. He enrolled at Auburn Theological Seminary and was ordained in 1862.

In 1862 Roe became chaplain of the Harris Light Cavalry of New York. He then began his successful writing career as a battlefield correspondent for the New York *Evangelist*. He also married Anna Sands, with whom he had five children. In March 1864 Roe reported for his new duties as chaplain at Hampton Hospital in Virginia, immediately establishing a library and a productive garden tended by ambulatory patients.

In October 1865 Roe returned to civilian life and a small Presbyterian parish at Highland Falls, New York. To raise funds for a new church, he presented at least fifty lectures a year on his Civil War experiences. In October 1871 he read about the Chicago fire and immediately left for Chicago, hoping he could write about the fire's devastation. In Chicago, as Roe remembered, "the vague outline of my first story, *Barriers Burned Away*, began to take form in my mind."

When Roe's impulsive journey ended, his creative journey began. After writing eight chapters of *Barriers*, he took his incomplete manuscript to the *Evangelist* editors, who agreed to publish the novel as a serial. To the amazement of Roe and the editors, the series received much popular attention. When Dodd & Mead published *Barriers Burned Away* (1872), it was by popular demand. Within four months 13,000 copies were sold, and by 1888 over 130,000. Eventually Roe's first novel sold over one million copies; later, other Roe books were bought by millions of readers in the United States, Canada, and England. By combining a man-made or natural disaster, a bittersweet love affair, and an ecumenical religious theme, Roe had discovered a successful formula for his first novel and for almost all his later fiction. Roe's ecumenical religious themes, combined with his stimulating plots and action, substantially helped the American novel to become acceptable *and* respectable reading for millions of Americans, particularly women. Before Roe's novels were published, fiction (except for religious novels) was morally suspect—the same kind of prejudiced belief that was held about women acting on the stage.

The public's acceptance of *Barriers* and its commercial success were extraordinary, making Roe into what Fred Lewis Pattee called "the novelist of the great middle class." (After a trip to the United States, elitist English critic Matthew Arnold, lamenting the fact that Roe was more popular than Charles Dickens or Sir Walter Scott, in contemptuous rebuttal labeled Roe "America's Native Author.") *What Can She Do?* (1873), Roe's second novel, expressed his concern for a much-needed equal role for women in America's increasingly industrialized society. Roe condemned contemporaneous restrictions on adequate education and acceptable working conditions for women, stressing the need for equality of opportunity in all areas of life for both sexes. In his fiction, many of his heroines not only challenge men on their own terms, they frequently surpass their male counterparts. As he had done earlier, Roe interlaced this story with nondenominational religious concepts. Sales of *What Can She Do?* were phenomenal. Roe's next novel, *Opening a Chestnut Burr* (1874), incorporates a shipwreck with a religious theme. It, too, was a commercial success.

When Roe became ill from overwork, he gave up his pastorate and moved to Cornwall-on-the-Hudson, where he continued his highly profitable writing as well as his gardening. Each year, when his unusually large strawberries were at their peak, he invited the members of the New York Authors' Club to Cornwall.

At Cornwall, Roe wrote almost a book a year, some of them first published as periodical serials, generally to the praise of reviewers. *Without A Home* (1881) is noteworthy for Roe's pioneering efforts as a social critic. He condemned the deplorable working conditions for women and the undesirable living conditions in city tenements. And he was remarkably prescient in forewarning the American people of the almost uncontrollable personal and public problems to be brought about by drug addiction: "I am sure I am right in fearing that in the morphia hunger and consumption one of the greatest evils of the future is looming darkly above the horizon of society. Warnings against this poison of body and soul cannot be too solemn or too strong."

Roe's last novel, *"Miss Lou"* (1888), remained unfinished, for an unexpected heart attack suddenly took his life at Cornwall-on-the-Hudson. Dodd & Mead published it with a postscript. Besides his nineteen novels, Roe wrote novellas, short stories, and books and pamphlets on horticulture. When Roe died, his novels were still selling by the thousands. His publishers estimated that by 1888 over 1.4 million copies of his books had been sold, not counting the hundreds of thousands issued in pirated editions in foreign countries. (Roe had long advocated an international copyright law.)

The novels of Edward Payson Roe represent a much overlooked and important development in American literature, for his fiction, which highlighted a practical, everyday, and nondenominational religion, brought the American religious novel to its peak. Roe's ecumenical religious themes, combined with his stimulating plots and steadfast characters, even more significantly helped make the American novel acceptable and respectable reading for millions of Americans, especially women.

During the twentieth century, scholars failed to acknowledge that Roe was a well-informed and far-seeing critic of American life as illustrated by his novel *Without a Home* and other writings. But in his belief that a religious novel could also be enjoyable and appealing to its readers, he showed himself to be modern in his thinking. Not only was he a bestselling novelist; he convincingly confuted Matthew Arnold's sarcastic judgment of him by becoming indeed "America's Native Author."

• Roe published an autobiographical essay, "A Native Author Called Roe," *Lippincott's Monthly Magazine* 42 (Oct. 1888): 479–97. Essays by Roe on writing include "The Element of Life in Fiction," *Forum* 5 (Apr. 1888): 226–36; "How to Succeed in Literature," *Home and School Supplement: An Illustrated Educational Monthly*, Dec. 1886, pp. 165–69; and "My First Novel: *Barriers Burned Away*," *Cosmopolitan* 3 (July 1887): 327–29. "International Petty Larceny," *Publisher's Weekly* 15 (9 Jan. 1886): 47–48, presents Roe's views on the lack of international copyright laws. Biographical sources include Mary A. Roe, *E. P. Roe: Reminiscences of His Life* (1902), and Susan Roe, *Diary* (n.d., holograph manuscript). Katherine M. Babbitt, "E. P. Roe: A Preliminary Checklist" (M.A. thesis, SUNY, Albany, 1971), is the leading bibliographic source. Glenn O. Carey, *Edward Payson Roe* (1985), provides full coverage of Roe's life and writings. Other critical essays on Roe include Dennis E. Minor, "The New and Regenerated Adams of E. P. Roe," *Markham Review* 6 (Winter 1977): 21–26; Paul R. Cleveland, "Is Literature Bread-Winning?" *Cosmopolitan* 5 (June 1888): 312–20; Julian Hawthorne, "Edward Payson Roe," *Critic* 10 (28 July 1888): 43–44; and William S. Walsh, "Some Words about E. P. Roe," *Lippincott's Monthly Magazine* 42 (October 1888): 497–500.

GLENN O. CAREY

ROE, Gilbert Ernstein (7 Feb. 1865–22 Dec. 1929), lawyer and author, was born in Oregon, Wisconsin, the son of John Roe and Jane McKeeby, farmers. Educated at the University of Wisconsin, Roe graduated from its law school in 1890 and joined the law firm of Robert M. La Follette. Throughout La Follette's long political career, first as governor of Wisconsin and later as its U.S. senator, Roe frequently put aside his own legal practice to assist La Follette in his election campaigns, to serve as his personal lawyer, and to draft legislation and speeches. In 1899 Roe married Gwyneth King and moved to New York City. They had three children, and as a family they frequently socialized and took vacations with the La Follettes.

Commercial and personal injury cases dominated Roe's busy legal practice in New York, but he also devoted substantial time to civic affairs and to the defense of free speech. He tried in New York to duplicate the progressive legislative agenda he had helped La Follette enact in Wisconsin. In 1905 the governor of New York appointed him to a commission that wrote a direct primary law, and for many years Roe was active in efforts to pass workmen's compensation legislation. In his free-speech work, Roe represented many defendants at reduced or no pay, lectured and testified frequently about free-speech issues, and became a key member of the Free Speech League, the only organization in the country before World War I that defended free speech whatever the speaker's ideology.

Roe's free-speech clients in the prewar years included Max Eastman, who had been indicted for criminal libel after publishing an article in *The Masses* alleging that the Associated Press had misrepresented the facts of labor strikes; Upton Sinclair, who had been arrested for leading a demonstration in front of the offices of John D. Rockefeller; and an IWW activist who had been prosecuted for illegal advocacy during a strike in Paterson, New Jersey. In a 1915 Supreme Court case, Roe represented an anarchist editor convicted for advocating nude bathing. Justice Oliver Wendell Holmes, Jr., writing for a unanimous court in *Fox v. Washington*, rejected Roe's arguments and upheld the conviction. Roe was a good friend to Emma Goldman, who reported in her autobiography that he had provided her the refuge of his home, financial assistance, and free legal advice while most people shunned her as a dangerous radical. Roe lectured on the law of free speech at the 1914 annual meeting of the American Sociological Society, and, at the nationally publicized hearings of the Commission on Industrial Relations in 1915 he testified about the repression of free speech during labor unrest.

After the United States entered World War I in 1917, Roe was at the center of efforts to protect antiwar speech. He wrote Senator La Follette repeatedly and at length about the dangers to free speech in the bill that became the Espionage Act of 1917 and testified against the bill in Congress. Roe soon became the lawyer for many defendants prosecuted under the Espionage Act for antiwar speech. Most notably, he again represented Max Eastman when the New York postmaster claimed that antiwar articles and cartoons rendered *The Masses* "nonmailable" under the Espionage Act. Roe also submitted a lengthy friend of the court brief to the Supreme Court on behalf of Eugene Debs, who had been convicted of violating the Espionage Act following a speech expressing Socialist opposition to the war. During this period Roe represented La Follette while the Senate was considering a motion to expel him for an address to the Nonpartisan League urging high taxes on potential war profiteers.

Roe worked closely with Roger Baldwin throughout the war and remained one of a small group of key advisers to the American Civil Liberties Union (ACLU) after its founding in 1920. Continuing his civil liberties activities after the war, Roe collaborated with Charles Evans Hughes and Morris Hillquit as counsel for five Socialist assemblymen expelled from the New York legislature in 1920. As counsel to the Teachers Union in New York, he challenged the Lusk laws, which until their repeal in 1923 provided for inquiries into the "loyalty and morality" of teachers. Appointed as counsel to a Senate committee chaired by La Follette, Roe conducted an investigation of the oil industry in 1922 and 1923 that led to the Teapot Dome Scandal and other revelations of official misconduct within the Harding administration.

Roe never achieved his goal of a full-time position in public service. Louis Brandeis, who had met Roe when they both were key advisers to La Follette, made several attempts in 1913 to help Roe secure a judicial post in New York that ultimately went to Benjamin Cardozo. Roe suffered another disappointment in 1915 when La Follette almost convinced President Wilson to appoint Roe to the Federal Trade Commission. Despite regrets that he could not find more time for writing, Roe did publish one book, *Our Judicial Oligarchy* (1912), which contained an introduction by La Follette. Roe made the standard progressive argument that courts had exceeded their proper role in a democracy by invoking the property rights of the wealthy to invalidate reform legislation passed in the public interest. This book, however, was less important than Roe's work as a progressive reformer and a free-speech activist who provided an important link between the Free Speech League and the ACLU. Roe died in New York City.

• Roe's papers are part of the La Follette Family Collections in the Library of Congress and in the Wisconsin State Historical Society. Roe's close personal and professional relationship with La Follette is detailed in Belle Case La Follette and Fola La Follette, *Robert M. La Follette* (2 vols., 1953), and in Robert M. La Follette, *La Follette's Autobiography* (rev. ed., 1960). David M. Rabban, *Free Speech in Its Forgotten Years* (1997), describes Roe's work as a free-speech activist. Roe's friend of the court brief in *Debs v. United States* (1919), provides an excellent example of his legal arguments on behalf of free speech. An obituary is in the *New York Times*, 23 Dec. 1929.

DAVID M. RABBAN

ROEBLING, John Augustus (12 June 1806–22 July 1869), engineer and bridge-builder, was born in Mühlhausen, Prussia, the son of Christoph Polycarpus Roebling, a prosperous merchant, and Friederike Dorothea Mueller. He acquired an engineering education at the Royal Polytechnic Institute in Berlin (where he also studied under Hegel, whose favorite student he is reputed to have been). After working three years for the Prussian government, Roebling migrated to the United States with a group from Mühlhausen, who set up a farming community, Saxonburg, near Pittsburgh. There in 1836 he married Johanna Herting, daughter of another emigrant from Mühlhausen; they had nine children. After his wife's death in 1864, Roebling in 1867 married Lucia W. Cooper. They had no children.

Although he did some farming in Saxonburg, Roebling felt that the community should also engage in industrial enterprise. He designed a steam plow, which never got manufactured, and in 1837 he went to work for a canal company in western Pennsylvania, which used winch-driven hemp ropes to haul canal boats over hills from one canal to another. But the ropes sometimes broke under such heavy loads, and in 1841 he witnessed two men killed when a rope broke.

In 1841–1842, having read in a German technical journal about the possibility of producing wire rope, Roebling devised—and patented—a machine to make twisted-wire cables strong enough to pull canal boats up a ramp without breaking. His wire ropes were so strong that Roebling used them to construct between 1845 and 1950 a number of suspension aqueducts for the Delaware and Hudson Canal, eliminating the need to pull canal barges over hills. These wire-suspended aqueducts established Roebling's reputation as a builder.

Roebling's wire ropes could serve many purposes, and the demand for them became so large that in 1848 he moved to Trenton, New Jersey, where his company (formed in 1842) became extremely prosperous, producing everything from chicken wire to massive cables capable of sustaining great weights.

Roebling's successful use of wire ropes for suspending canal aqueducts had taught him a great deal about the characteristics of suspension bridges, and his mechanical ingenuity, structural imagination, and entrepreneurial ability eventually made him the leading builder of suspension bridges in the United States. His first major success was his design for a double-deck bridge over the Niagara River, with an upper deck for a railway and a lower deck for carriages.

In 1851 Roebling commenced construction of the Niagara bridge, but he changed his design when, in 1854, Charles Ellet's suspension bridge over the Ohio River at Wheeling, West Virginia—with the largest span length in the world (1,010 feet)—collapsed. To avoid such a catastrophe befalling his Niagara bridge, Roebling added trusses to stiffen and reinforce the heavy weight of the bridge spans. This significant contribution to bridgebuilding made suspension-bridge roadways rigid and impervious to varying loads as well as to destructive oscillations from changing wind pressures. Completed in 1855, Roebling's Niagara Falls Bridge was the first successful railroad suspension bridge. It brought Roebling other contracts and encouraged him to make further innovations in construction.

In constructing a bridge over the Allegheny River at Pittsburgh (1857–1860), Roebling employed a new method of spinning the cable on the site, using traveling sheaves that moved on temporary cables over the support towers from one anchor to the other. He then used this device on a bridge over the Ohio River at Cincinnati, with a 1,057-foot span, a record for that time. In addition to stiffening trusses, this bridge had bound cables of parallel wires, wire rope suspenders, and auxiliary stays radiating downward and outward from the tops of the tower to the deck, thereby providing additional aerodynamic stability. Those features, which became characteristic of Roebling's bridges, also possessed the unique ability to stir the aesthetic feelings of those viewing the bridges, making the bridges artistic creations as well as landmarks in civil engineering.

Although begun in 1856, Roebling's Cincinnati bridge was not opened until 1867, as a result of delays caused by financial difficulties, the Civil War, and natural disasters (ice, floods, and storms). A testimony to the bridge's strength was its use throughout the whole of the twentieth century.

The same holds true for the Brooklyn Bridge (originally referred to as the East River Bridge), which represents the acme of Roebling's combination of engineering and artistic skills. The idea for such a bridge had been around for some time, and in 1867 the New York state legislature chartered a private company, the New York Bridge Co., to raise money to build the bridge. Roebling's successful record of building major bridges made him the logical choice to design and build it.

The main span of the Brooklyn Bridge extends 1,595.5 feet between its two towers, and the two anchor spans each add another 930 feet. The four cables sustaining the bridge's roadway contain 5,434 galvanized steel wires, marking the first use of steel for that particular purpose; indeed, Roebling used steel for all parts of the bridge for which iron had been used in previous bridges, making it much stronger. Since the towers had to stand on bedrock, far below the alluvial sediments of the East River, they were built on top of caissons made of concrete and granite blocks weighing up to six tons each. When completed the towers stood 273 feet above water, the tallest structures in the country at that time.

But Roebling did not live to see his design achieve fulfillment. On 28 June 1869, while he was inspecting a site for locating one of the towers, a ferry hit the dock where he was standing, smashing the toes of his right foot between two timbers. Although doctors amputated his crushed toes, some three weeks later he died in Brooklyn of tetanus. Roebling's son, Washington Augustus Roebling, then thirty-two years old, took over as chief engineer and completed the project.

At the time of its opening, the Brooklyn Bridge was the largest in the world. Not only did it possess strength to carry much more traffic—and weight—than had originally been anticipated, but it had great economic, political, technological, and aesthetic implications. By connecting Brooklyn with lower Manhattan, for example, it created an economic surge in both communities, which helped bring about the consolidation of five boroughs to create the metropolis of New York City (1898). In addition to its socio-economic impact, the Brooklyn Bridge attracted attention as both a great technical artifact and aesthetic delight, utilizing new materials and techniques to create a beautiful and expressive artistic design and combining form and function, which it did with efficiency and economy. It also became a cultural symbol, attracting the attention of artists (from realists to abstractionists) and serving as a source of inspiration to poets and writers for over a century.

Although the bridge underwent some structural alterations in the 1940s, directed by David Steinman, it retained its basic technical and artistic elements, as created and constructed by John and Washington Roebling. The bridge's great impacts on American technology and culture were demonstrated anew when its 1983 centennial celebration again attracted the attention of the entire nation. In his final creation—the Brooklyn Bridge—John A. Roebling's splendid contributions to bridge-building, technical devices and materials, and engineering are epitomized.

• David McCullough, *The Great Bridge* (1972), provides the most complete account of Roebling's life and works. Utilizing primary source material from Roebling collections at Rutgers University and Rensselaer Polytechnic Institute McCullough gives a vivid account of the background and building of the Brooklyn Bridge. Margaret Latimer et al., eds., *Bridge to the Future: A Centennial Celebration of the Brooklyn Bridge* (1984), contains scholarly papers dealing with a wide range of topics, including the Roebling family, bridge-building technology, and the sociocultural context and implications of Roebling's work. Roebling's technical contributions are treated in some detail in Joseph Gies and Frances Gies, *The Ingenious Yankees* (1976), which devotes an entire chapter to Roebling's construction of the bridge over the Niagara gorge, and also in Carl W. Condit, *American Building: Materials and Techniques from the First Colonial Settlements to the Present* (1968). David Billington provides an insightful view of the aesthetic elements in Roebling's work in *The Tower and the Bridge: The New Art of Structural Engineering* (1983). See also Hamilton Schuyler, *The Roeblings: A Century of Engineers, Bridge-Builders and Industrialists* (1931), and David B. Steinman, *The Builders of the Bridge: The Story of John Roebling and His Son* (1945). Carroll W. Pursell, Jr., "A Trade Catalog on the Transmission of Power by Wire Rope," *Technology and Culture* 16 (1975): 70–73, describes a trade pamphlet, written in 1869 by Washington A. Roebling, for the firm of John A. Roebling's Sons, titled *Description of a New Means of Transmitting Power by Means of Wire Ropes*.

MELVIN KRANZBERG

ROEBLING, Washington Augustus (26 May 1837–21 July 1926), civil engineer, was born in Saxonburg, Pennsylvania, the son of John Augustus Roebling, a civil engineer, and Johanna Herting. After graduating in 1857 from Rensselaer Polytechnic Institute in Troy, New York, he returned to the family home in Trenton, New Jersey, to work in his father's wire-manufacturing mill. In 1858 he joined his father in Pittsburgh where the elder Roebling, who specialized in suspension bridge design and construction, was engaged in spanning the Allegheny River. When the work was completed in 1860, Washington Roebling returned to Trenton and the mill.

With the outbreak of the Civil War in April 1861, Roebling enlisted as a private in the New Jersey National Guard. Owing to his dislike of the routine dullness of garrison duty, he sought and obtained an early discharge. Hoping for a more active role in the war, he joined the Sixth New York Independent Battery in June as a private. He rose to the rank of second lieutenant before being discharged in 1864 to accept a commission as a major in the U.S. Volunteers. Serving until 1865, Roebling was breveted lieutenant colonel in 1864 and in the following year colonel for gallant and meritorious service. In addition to utilizing his skills as a civil engineer, his later military assignments offered excitement he had not found early on.

While on the staff of General Irvin McDowell, Roebling was responsible for the construction of a temporary suspension bridge across Virginia's Rappahannock River. Among the campaigns in which he participated were the Second Battle of Bull Run (29–30 Aug. 1862), Antietam (17 Sept. 1862), and South Mountain (14 Sept. 1862), during which he built a temporary suspension bridge across the Shenandoah River at Harpers Ferry. While serving at Chancellorsville, Virginia, during the battle of 1–4 May 1863, it was his duty to ascend each morning to view enemy troop movements from one of the Union army's tethered observation balloons. From this vantage point Roebling may have been one of the first to discover the start of Robert E. Lee's march to Gettysburg. During the action at Gettysburg he was on the staff of General G. K. Warren. It was while serving in that capacity that he met Warren's sister Emily, whom he married in 1865. The couple had one child.

Following his resignation from the army in 1865, he assisted his father in the construction of a suspension bridge across the Ohio River between Cincinnati, Ohio, and Covington, Kentucky. The bridge was completed in 1867, and in that same year Roebling's father was appointed chief engineer of the proposed East River Suspension Bridge (Brooklyn Bridge) in New York City.

The project to build a bridge between Manhattan and Brooklyn would yield the longest suspension bridge in the world at the time. One of the most challenging aspects of the Brooklyn Bridge was the proper founding of the massive granite towers that would support the cables. Because of variations in the characteristics and depth of the bedrock underlying the river, John Roebling determined that the towers would be best built on wooden caissons. The caissons would be sunk to bedrock or as close as possible to it. As the science of pneumatic caisson foundation work had only recently been developed in Europe, Washington Roebling left almost immediately to study it. He spent the next year visiting important bridge sites, especially those under construction, in England, France, and Germany to learn the principles and practice of using compressed air in subaqueous excavation work.

Returning to the United States in 1868, Roebling settled in Brooklyn to be near the project, and he assisted his father in preparing preliminary plans and specifications for the bridge. Final plans were approved and work was moving forward, when in June 1869 Roebling's father was fatally injured as he surveyed the location of the bridge's Brooklyn tower. Within a month, Roebling was named chief engineer. Having been involved in every aspect of the work up to that point, he was eminently qualified to take charge of the entire project, although he was only thirty-two years old.

The huge box-like caissons on which the towers would be built were floated into place in 1870. They slowly sank from the weight of the added courses of granite laid in place on their tops. Once the caissons reached bottom, workers excavated the river bed from their hollow undersides, and, as the weight above increased, the caissons sank deeper into the river bed. Compressed air was used to counterbalance the force exerted by the river as it tried to push the fluid mass of its bed into the work space.

Roebling spent long hours in the pressurized atmosphere of the caissons, guiding the effort so critical to the overall construction. Exposure to compressed air and its long-term effects were not fully understood, however, and the physically exhausted Roebling collapsed on several occasions, only to recover and return to the excavation. He continued to drive himself, until finally, in the spring of 1872, he collapsed unconscious and had to be carried from the caisson, a victim of the bends (nitrogen narcosis). The use of a recompression chamber to alleviate the condition and remove its symptoms was unknown; his situation was critical. Nonetheless, in time he appeared to recover and returned to work. But his health had been seriously and permanently damaged. By December he had become a physical invalid and could no longer go to the worksite. For the remainder of his life he suffered from debilitating ailments caused by the damage brought on by the compressed air.

Roebling was, however, still chief engineer and had the responsibility to see that work went forward. Intellectually unimpaired, he was able to direct activities from a room in his home in Brooklyn Heights. A telescope permitted him, at least, to observe the bridge as work progressed. As a result of his disablement, his wife Emily became actively involved in the effort. Serving as his secretary and courier, she carried instructions and relayed messages between him and his staff. At the same time, under his tutelage, she acquired an understanding of technical matters and a working knowledge of engineering principles. Roebling never again visited the site during the construction. He was too infirm to participate in the opening ceremonies in May 1883. With the bridge's completion, he retired from an active role in the civil engineering profession.

In 1884 Roebling temporarily moved his family to Troy, New York, while his son was a student at Rensselaer Polytechnic Institute. He permanently returned to Trenton in 1888. His wife died in 1903, and in 1908 he married Cornelia Witsell Farrow, a widow.

Roebling's writing was primarily in the form of reports and articles. One of the first items he authored came as a result of his military duties. It was a manual titled *Instructions for Transport and Erection of Military Wire Suspension-Bridge Equipage* (1862). He wrote several articles that appeared in *Scientific American* magazine during the 1860s. No doubt the influence of the family business played no small part in his writing a booklet (often reprinted) describing a new method of transmitting power by means of wire ropes. His study of foundation work resulted in the pamphlet *Pneumatic Tower Foundations of the East River Suspension Bridge* (1872). By far the greatest number of items generated by him were reports written while he was chief engineer of the East River bridge project. One of his last papers was a 1924 history of Saxonburg.

Roebling spent more than forty years in retirement, and his time was taken up in a variety of nonphysical activities. A voracious reader, there were few subjects not of interest to him, and as a result he developed a sizable library. Although not schooled in mineralogy, he became a well-respected authority on the subject. His lifelong interest in minerals led him to amass a study collection consisting of an estimated 16,000 specimens; only the rarest were lacking. As a benefactor of the Mineralogical Society of America, he endowed a fund for the society's journal. Roebling was honored when a mineral found only at Franklin Furnace, New Jersey, was named after him. Roeblingite is the only mineral known to contain sulphite. (Following his death, his son donated the collection to the Smithsonian Institution.)

Despite his physical condition, Roebling was able to render a degree of public service, acting as a presidential elector for the state of New Jersey on several occasions and as a director on the boards of several local corporations. Because it required little physical effort, he found assembling jigsaw puzzles to his liking, and this became one of his favorite activities. His specially made puzzles were cut from large photographs or copies of paintings.

At the time of their father's death, Roebling and his brothers had inherited the Roebling wire-manufacturing business. It was on his insistence that a branch store selling a complete line of the company's wire goods was opened in New York City in the late 1860s. He served briefly as president of the wire business when it was incorporated in 1876 as John A. Roebling's Sons Company. Thereafter operation of the company was for the most part in the hands of his brothers. After their passing he again felt obliged to take an active role in the management of the business, and in 1921 he once more became president despite his advanced age and infirmities. He plunged into the work with the fervor of his earlier activities, making a number of improvements to the physical plant and adding facilities for new processes. Roebling died in Trenton, New Jersey.

• There is a voluminous and detailed record of the bridge work, wire business, and private lives of the Roeblings. The major holdings pertaining to bridge work are in the Institute Archives and Department of Special Collections, Rensselaer Polytechnic Institute, while records of business and family matters are in the Department of Special Collections and Archives, Rutgers University. Hamilton Schuyler, *The Roeblings: A Century of Engineers, Bridge-builders and Industrialists* (1931), presents the most thorough discussion of Roebling's life and a good overview of the entire family. Information on building the Brooklyn Bridge can be found in the numerous reports written while he was chief engineer. But the essence of the process and his role has been concisely distilled in Robert M. Vogel, *Building Brooklyn Bridge: The Design and Construction 1867–1883* (1983). Elizabeth C. Stewart, ed., *Guide to the Roebling Collections at Rensselaer Polytechnic Institute and Rutgers University* (1983), provides a detailed listing of material generated by Washington Roebling. His interests are further revealed in the guide's accounting of the Roebling library. An obituary is in the *New York Times*, 22 July 1926.

WILLIAM E. WORTHINGTON, JR.

ROETHKE, Theodore (25 May 1908–1 Aug. 1963), poet, was born Theodore Huebner Roethke in Saginaw, Michigan, the son of Otto Roethke and Helen Huebner, owners of a local greenhouse. As a student at Saginaw's Arthur Hill High School, Roethke demonstrated early promise in a speech on the Junior Red Cross that was subsequently published in twenty-six languages. The poet's adolescent years were jarred, however, by the death of his father from cancer in 1923, a loss that would powerfully shape Roethke's psychic and creative lives. From 1925 to 1929 Roethke distinguished himself at the University of Michigan at Ann Arbor, graduating magna cum laude. Resisting family pressure to pursue a legal career, he quit law school after one semester and, from 1929 to 1931, took graduate courses at the University of Michigan and later the Harvard Graduate School, where he worked closely with the poet Robert Hillyer.

The hard economic times of the Great Depression forced Roethke to leave Harvard and to take up a teaching career at Lafayette College from 1931 to 1935. Here he met Rolfe Humphries, who introduced him to Louise Bogan; during these years Roethke also found a powerful supporter, colleague, and friend in the poet Stanley Kunitz. In the fall of 1935 Roethke assumed his second teaching post at Michigan State College at Lansing but was soon hospitalized for what would prove to be recurring bouts of mental illness. Throughout his subsequent career Roethke used these periodic incidents of depression for creative self-exploration. They allowed him, as he said, to "reach a new level of reality."

During the remainder of the decade Roethke enjoyed a growing reputation as a poet. He taught at Pennsylvania State University from 1936 to 1943, publishing in such prestigious journals as *Poetry*, the *New Republic*, the *Saturday Review*, and *Sewanee Review*. He brought out his first volume of verse, *Open House*, in 1941. Not insignificantly, the title piece of this first book stands as an early figure for the confessional aesthetic of Roethke's later poetry. "My secrets cry aloud," he writes, describing his psyche, or "heart," as an "open house" with "widely swung" doors.

Open House was an important beginning for Roethke as it was favorably reviewed in the *New Yorker*, the *Saturday Review*, the *Kenyon Review*, and the *Atlantic*; W. H. Auden called it "completely successful." Not surprisingly, this first work shows the influence of poetic models such as John Donne, William Blake, Léonie Adams, Louise Bogan, Emily Dickinson, Rolfe Humphries, Stanley Kunitz, and Elinor Wylie, writers whose verse had shaped the poet's early imagination and style. Yet the book's subjective focus on personal experience marked an important departure both from T. S. Eliot's doctrine of poetic impersonality, articulated in "Tradition and the Individual Talent" (1917), and from what the New Critics W. K. Wimsatt and Monroe Beardsley later deplored as the intentional fallacy.

The year after *Open House* was published Roethke was invited to deliver one of the prestigious Morris Gray lectures at Harvard University, and in 1943 he left Penn State to teach at Bennington College, where he joined such luminaries as Léonie Adams and Kenneth Burke. Bennington challenged Roethke to develop as a teaching poet. HIs collaboration with Burke, in particular, was crucial to the development of the second, and pivotal, volume of Roethke's career, *The Lost Son and Other Poems* (1948). In the book's opening fourteen lyrics, the so-called "greenhouse poems," the metaphor of the open house passes into the figure of the glasshouse as the dominant symbol of the self's interior, existential world. Roethke described the glasshouse, in "An American Poet Introduces Himself and His Poems" (BBC broadcast, 30 July 1953), as "both heaven and hell. . . . It was a universe, several worlds, which, even as a child, one worried about, and struggled to keep alive." The poet's close attention to the subhuman world of organic growth served as a scenic counterpart to Roethke's own imaginative development, and it staged Roethke's need as the "lost son" to work through his psychic ambivalence toward the absent patriarch Otto Roethke as well as the fathering "great dead" of the literary tradition.

The descent into the organic life of things themselves dramatized the theme of regression that is explored in psychoanalytic terms in the book's title piece. "Sometimes, of course, there is regression," Roethke said in "An American Poet Introduces Himself and His Poems." "I believe that the spiritual man must go back in order to go forward." "The Lost Son" presented this regressive aesthetic in terms of both a descent into the subhuman life of nature and a return to repressed, childhood scenes. Karl Malkoff was one of the first critics to interpret these so-called "developmental poems" in terms of Roethke's divided attitude toward his father Otto, depicted, for example, in his widely anthologized work "My Papa's Waltz." Apparently, Roethke's filial anxieties stemmed from the trauma of Otto's death, which interrupted the adolescent's successful passage through oedipal rivalry. The five sections of "The Lost Son" work through the poet's conflicted attitude toward the dead patriarch and, by extension, what Roethke described as his "spiritual ancestors" of the literary tradition. Indeed, in a telling *Yale Review* essay, "How to Write Like Somebody Else" (1959), Roethke described his relation to W. B. Yeats in terms of "daring to compete with papa." Roethke's drive to master his precursors, however, led him to forge significant literary innovations.

Building on modernist stream-of-consciousness narrative techniques, Roethke achieved an arresting poetic performance in an associative, and often surreal, verbal style, one that depicted primal and psychic states of mind. In his next volume, *Praise to the End!* (1951), Roethke's regressive aesthetic continued to explore further the prerational experience of early childhood and sexual discoveries of adolescence. The volume's title, as an allusion to Wordsworth's *The Prelude*, signaled the work's romantic celebration of the child's unity of being in the natural world. Employing nonsense lyrics, nursery rhymes, synaesthesia, and natural personifications, works such as "Where Knock Is Open Wide" were written "entirely from the viewpoint of a very small child"—as Roethke observed in "Open Letter" (1950). Such unmediated encounters with nature and the unconscious in, for example, "I Need, I Need" also characterize the poet's initiation into erotic sexuality in "Give Way, Ye Gates," "Sensibility! O La!," and "O Lull Me, Lull Me."

Praise to the End! was composed after the poet's move to the University of Washington, where he not only found talented protégés in Carolyn Kizer, David Wagoner, and James Wright (1927–1980) but loyal colleagues such as Robert Heilman who, as department head, helped Roethke manage his recurring bouts of depression. The early 1950s augured Roethke's growing stature with the award of a Guggenheim Fellowship (1950), *Poetry* magazine's Levinson Prize (1951), and major grants from the Ford Foundation and the National Institute of Arts and Letters in 1952. The following year Roethke married Beatrice O'Connell, whom he had met during his earlier stint at Bennington. The two spent the following spring at W. H. Auden's villa at Ischia, off the coast of Italy, where Roethke edited the galley proofs for *The Waking: Poems 1933–1953* (1953), a seminal volume that won the Pulitzer Prize the next year. Although thematically akin to Roethke's work of the late 1940s, this volume's title piece marked the poet's return to formalist verse, composed as it is in the complex villanelle pattern. *The Waking* also included such major works in the Roethke canon as "Elegy for Jane" and "Four for Sir John Davies," which was modeled on Davies's metaphysical poem "Orchestra."

Throughout 1955 and 1956 the Roethkes traveled in Italy, Europe, and England on a Fulbright grant. The following year he published a collection of works that included forty-three new poems entitled *Words for the Wind* (1957), which won the Bollingen Prize, the National Book Award, the Edna St. Vincent Millay Prize, the Longview Foundation Award, and the Pacific Northwest Writer's Award. Divided into five sections, the new poems included children's verse, love poetry (including his famous "I Knew a Woman"), poems on natural themes, and two long works entitled "Dying Man," an elegiac work in the Yeatsian mood, and "Meditations of an Old Woman," a verse commemoration of the poet's mother. Now at the height of his popularity and fame, Roethke balanced his teaching career with reading tours in New York and Europe, underwritten by another Ford Foundation grant. While visiting with friends at Bainbridge Island, Washington, Roethke suffered a fatal heart attack. During the last years of his life he had composed the sixty-one new poems that were published posthumously in *The Far Field* (1964)—which received the National Book Award—and in *The Collected Poems* (1966).

Roethke's historical significance rests both on his established place in the American canon and on his influence over a subsequent generation of award-winning poets that includes Robert Bly, James Dickey, Carolyn Kizer, Sylvia Plath, Anne Sexton, William Stafford, David Wagoner, and James Wright. Although Roethke's last works have been criticized for their indebtedness to such high modernists as T. S. Eliot, Wallace Stevens, and W. B. Yeats, contemporary poets and critics have also emphasized the expansive vision of self, at one with American place, that Roethke masterfully presented in the Whitmanesque catalogs of "North American Sequence." "There is no poetry anywhere," James Dickey wrote in the *Atlantic* (Nov. 1968), "that is so valuably conscious of the human body as Roethke's; no poetry that can place the body in an environment." Roethke's pioneering explorations of nature, regional settings, depth psychology, and personal confessionalism—coupled with his stylistic innovations in open form poetics and his mastery of traditional, fixed forms—have secured his reputation as one of the most distinguished and widely read American poets of the twentieth century.

• In addition to the volumes mentioned above, Roethke published *The Exorcism: A Portfolio of Poems* (1957), *I AM! Says the Lamb* (1961), *Party at the Zoo* (1963), *Sequence, Sometimes Metaphysical* (1963), and *Dirty Dinky and Other Creatures: Poems for Children* (1973). The standard edition of Roethke's verse remains *The Collected Poems of Theodore Roethke*, ed. Beatrice Roethke in collaboration with Stanley Kunitz (1975; repr. 1982). The standard biography is Allan Seager, *The Glass House: The Life of Theodore Roethke* (1968). Ralph J. Mills, Jr., ed., *On the Poet and His Craft: Selected Prose of Theodore Roethke* (1965), provides a comprehensive selection of Roethke's statements on poetics, pedagogy, and literary tradition. Other primary writings are collected in the *Selected Letters of Theodore Roethke*, ed. Ralph J. Mills, Jr. (1968), and *Straw for the Fire: From the Notebooks of Theodore Roethke, 1943–63*, ed. David Wagoner (1972). Students of Roethke's career will also find helpful *A Concordance to the Poems of Theodore Roethke*, ed. Gary Lane (1972); James McLeod, *Theodore Roethke: A Manuscript Checklist* (1971); and Keith R. Moul, *Theodore Roethke's Career: An Annotated Bibliography* (1977).

Ralph J. Mills, Jr., *Theodore Roethke* (1963), offers the earliest overview of the poet's career. Of the over twenty book-length studies of Roethke, see also Peter Balakian, *Theodore Roethke's Far Fields: The Evolution of His Poetry* (1989); Don Bogen, *Theodore Roethke and the Writing Process* (1991); Neal Bowers, *Theodore Roethke: The Journey from I to Otherwise* (1982); Jenijoy La Belle, *The Echoing Wood of Theodore Roethke* (1976); William Martz, *The Achievement of Theodore Roethke* (1966); Jay Parini, *Theodore Roethke: An American Romantic* (1979); Randall Stiffler, *Theodore Roethke: The Poet and His Critics* (1986); and Harry Williams, *"The Edge Is What I Have": Theodore Roethke and After* (1977). Seminal essays on the poet are anthologized in two major collections: William Heyen, ed., *Profile of Theodore Roethke* (1971), and Arnold Stein, ed., *Theodore Roethke: Essays on the Poetry* (1965). An obituary is in the *New York Times*, 2 Aug. 1963.

WALTER KALAIDJIAN

ROGAN, Bullet (28 July 1889–4 Mar. 1967), African-American baseball player and manager, known also as "Bullet Joe," was born Wilber Rogan in Oklahoma City, Oklahoma, the son of Richard Rogan and Mary (maiden name unknown). Rogan, whose first name is often misspelled as "Wilbur," was the heart and soul of the Kansas City Monarchs, perennial powerhouse of the Negro leagues in the 1920s and 1930s, their predominant pitcher, most powerful hitter, and (for seven years) manager. His imposing career is even more remarkable considering that when he joined the Monarchs in 1920 he was already 31 years old, having spent 10 prime years playing in the obscurity of military outposts in the Philippines, Hawaii, and Arizona.

While he was in his teens, Rogan's family moved to Kansas City, Kansas, where he dropped out of high school to play for the semipro Kansas City Giants, which won 54 consecutive games against local and semipro competition in 1909. Two years later, Rogan enlisted in the U.S. Army.

At a time when African Americans faced severe hardships in the United States, military life presented a relatively attractive alternative. The army encouraged its four segregated black regiments (the 9th and 10th Cavalry and the 24th and 25th Infantry) to field successful athletic teams to bolster morale. Superior black athletes were diligently recruited to form some of the strongest baseball teams in the service, winning many tournaments that included white regimental teams. Rogan played three years for the 24th Infantry Regiment in the Philippines, then reenlisted in the 25th Infantry Regiment, where he played at Honolulu's Schofield Barracks. In 1918 the 25th was transferred to Camp Stephen D. Little in Nogales, Arizona, on the Mexican border, where Rogan completed his military career.

Rogan, who was called "Cap" in the army, was the most storied player on the great 25th Infantry team known as the "Wreckers." Occasionally they played white civilian teams, even major leaguers. When John J. McGraw's New York Giants played the 25th in Hawaii during a world tour, he praised Rogan as a pitcher with major league ability. Casey Stengel was so impressed after facing Rogan in Arizona during a barnstorming tour that when he returned to Kansas City he notified J. L. Wilkinson, who was then forming the Monarchs. In July 1920 Rogan and five teammates left the army and joined the nascent Negro National League. With so many veterans of the 25th Infantry, the Monarchs were often called "the army team" in the early years.

The Monarchs won NNL championships in 1923, 1924, 1925, and 1929 and lost a playoff to the Chicago American Giants in 1926 (Rogan's first year as manager). Rogan's brilliance as a pitcher obscures his talent as an all-around player. He was the finest fielding pitcher in the Negro leagues, and, when not pitching, he skillfully played center field. His offensive accomplishments alone were remarkable during the Monarchs' glory years. At 5' 9" and 175 pounds, Rogan (who hit and threw right-handed) batted fourth. Standing deep in the batter's box and wielding an uncommonly heavy bat, he was productive in key situations. His regular season batting average through the 1920s was .340, while in championship play he hit a remarkable .410. In 25 recorded exhibition games against major league pitching he hit .329.

But it was on the mound that Rogan attained legendary status. He was called "Bullet" (later "Bullet Joe") because of a blazing fastball, which he threw from a sidewinding, short-arm delivery. Teammate Chet Brewer recalled that Rogan's curveball was faster than most pitchers' fastballs. And he was   ovator. His off-speed pitch was a palm ball, which Brewer credited him with inventing. And he threw without a wind-up, a then-unusual technique that Stengel later taught pitchers when he managed the New York Yankees. From 1920 to 1930 Rogan won 106 and lost 44 regular season games against Negro League competition, and he had an 8–3 record in championship play. Many contemporaries regarded him as the greatest pitcher they ever saw, and in overall versatility Martin Dihigo was his only equal in Negro League ball.

Rogan's military bearing as manager probably caused him to be disliked by some of his players. Yet others regarded him as easygoing and an effective instructor. He retired from baseball in 1938 and worked for the U.S. Post Office for 20 years, occasionally umpiring Monarchs' games until 1946. He spent his last years on a farm near a lake with his wife, Kathryn, whom he married in 1922. He died in Kansas City, Missouri, survived by a son, Wilbur, and daughter, Jean.

• Janet Bruce, *The Kansas City Monarchs: Champions of Black Baseball* (1985); John Holway, *Blackball Stars: Negro League Pioneers* (1988) and *Bullet Joe and the Monarchs* (1984); Robert Peterson, *Only the Ball Was White* (1970); James A. Riley, *The All-Time All-Stars of Black Baseball* (1983).

JERRY MALLOY

ROGAN, Wilber. *See* Rogan, Bullet.

ROGERS, Bruce (14 May 1870–18 May 1957), book designer, was born Albert Bruce Rogers in Linwood, Indiana, the son of George Rogers, a baker and confectioner, and Ann E. Gish. As a teenager, "Bert" (short for Albert) displayed an aptitude for book designing when he created a hand-lettered edition of William Cullen Bryant's "Forest Hymn," complete with imitation etchings bearing plate marks made by a kitchen iron. At the age of sixteen, Rogers entered Purdue University, where he pursued art as an academic interest and contributed artwork and lettering designs to university publications. Rogers graduated from Purdue with a B.S. degree in 1890.

Bruce Rogers (no longer "Bert") began to focus his talents on professional book design in 1893. In Indianapolis, Indiana, he worked with Joseph M. Bowles, the creator of the quarterly *Modern Art*, contributing decoration and design to almost every issue of the magazine until it ceased publication in 1897. While still working with Bowles, Rogers made his first contribution to book design when he created decorations for *Homeward Songs by the Way* by A.E. (George William Russell), published in 1895 by Thomas B. Mosher of Maine.

Rogers moved to Boston in 1895 to work for L. Prang and Company, to which the publication of *Modern Art* had been moved. At this time he also did freelance book designing. While Rogers was in Boston, his work was noticed by George H. Mifflin of Houghton, Mifflin & Company, who hired Rogers in 1896 to work at the Riverside Press. During Rogers's first few years at Riverside, he designed advertising and some trade books. He also learned about the mechanics of printing. In 1900 Mifflin created the Department of Special Editions and placed Rogers in charge, leaving him free to experiment with typography, paper, and binding. During the next twelve years, Rogers produced about sixty Riverside Press Editions, as the books issued by the special department were called, the first being the *Sonnets and Madrigals of Michaelangelo Buonarroti* (1900).

Rogers stopped working for Riverside Press in 1911 and decided to become a freelance designer of books. From 1912 to 1915 he worked mainly in New York. It was during this period that he designed his lauded typeface Centaur, which took its name from *The Centaur* (1915) by Maurice de Guérin, the book in which it first appeared.

From 1917 to 1919 commissions and an appointment to Cambridge University Press made it possible for Rogers to live and work in England, a situation he enjoyed immensely. At the Mall Press in Hammersmith, London, under difficult wartime conditions, Rogers designed and printed a translation of Albrecht Dürer's *Of the Just Shaping of Letters* (1917). Working at Cambridge he wrote a "Report on the Typography at the Cambridge University Press" (1917), in which he evaluated the type, equipment, paper, and presswork at Cambridge and proposed improvements. Rogers practiced his suggestions while working on twenty-four books and brochures for the press.

Rogers returned to the United States in 1919. He was then invited by William Edwin Rudge to pursue his commissions at Rudge's printing house in Mount Vernon, New York. He was also asked by Harvard University Press to become its printing adviser. It was at this time, too, that Rogers became known to his friends and associates, with respectful affection, as "B.R." He was admired for his artful combining of type and type ornaments, and he expressed this skill in a book he designed at the Rudge plant called *The Pierrot of the Minute* (1923) by Ernest Dowson. Rogers's greatest achievement at Mount Vernon, however, was his meticulously prepared reprint of Geofroy Tory's sixteenth-century, illustrated treatise on letter forms, *Champ Fleury* (1927). Like the translation of Dürer that he had printed in London on the same subject, *Champ Fleury* was made for the Grolier Club in New York and featured Rogers's Centaur type. Among the thirty or so books Rogers designed at the Harvard University Press during this period was *The Passports Printed by Benjamin Franklin at His Passy Press* (1925), an example of "allusive typography," in which Rogers employed Baskerville type to evoke the look of an eighteenth-century book for an eighteenth-century subject.

Rogers led a transatlantic life from 1928 to 1936, traveling between the United States and England. In England in 1928, he supervised the Monotype Corporation's cutting of his Centaur type for machine composition. In 1931 he restored an old house he had bought in New Fairfield, Connecticut, which he called "October House." Back in London he designed, illustrated, and saw through the press T. E. Lawrence's translation of the *Odyssey of Homer* (1932). In 1935 Rogers completed work on his highly regarded *Oxford Lectern Bible*, which had been commissioned six years earlier by the Oxford University Press.

Rogers spent the remaining two decades of his life working at his October House. He designed a dozen titles for George Macy's Limited Editions Club of New York, among which was a thirty-seven volume set of *The Comedies, Histories & Tragedies of William Shakespeare*, completed in 1940. One of the last books Rogers designed was *The Divine Comedy of Dante Alighieri*, a project he had always wanted to print. Rogers's opportunity came in 1955 when the printer A. Colish financed his edition.

Rogers married Anne Embree Baker in 1900. They had one daughter, who died in 1924 at the age of only twenty-three; he became a widower when Anne died in 1931.

Rogers was appreciated in his lifetime. In addition to several honorary degrees, in 1948 he was awarded a gold medal from the American Academy of Arts and Letters for distinction in the graphic arts. Over decades of accomplishment in which he designed approximately 500 books, many of which bore his famous printer's mark of the thistle, Rogers literally defined the profession of book designing in the United States. He died at his October House in New Fairfield.

• Letters of Bruce Rogers can be found at a number of institutions, among which are the Grolier Club, New York, and the Arts of the Book Room, Yale University Library. Rogers related some thoughts on typographical problems and the functions of the book designer in *Paragraphs on Printing* (1943). A miscellaneous collection of pieces written by Rogers was published as *PI: A Hodge-Podge of Letters, Papers, Addresses Written during a Period of 60 Years* (1953). Frederic Warde wrote about the early career of Rogers in *Bruce Rogers: Designer of Books* (1925). The comprehensive critical biography of Rogers is Joseph Blumenthal, *Bruce Rogers: A Life in Letters, 1870–1957* (1989). For a collection of essays by Rogers's friends about his work, see Paul A. Bennett, ed., *B.R. Marks & Remarks* (1946). A bibliographical listing of many books designed by Rogers can be found in *The Work of Bruce Rogers*, published in 1939 on the occasion of an important exhibition of his work in New York that was organized by the American Institute of Graphic Arts and the Grolier Club. An obituary is in the *New York Times*, 19 May 1957.

CHARLES ZAROBILA

ROGERS, Carl Ransom (8 Jan. 1902–4 Feb. 1987), psychologist, was born in Chicago, the son of Walter Rogers, a civil engineer, and Julia Cushing. Rogers characterized his parents as people with strong puritan convictions and his upbringing as austere puritanism. As an adolescent he was withdrawn, dreamy, and absent-minded, with no social life outside the family circle. His interest in farming brought him in 1919 to the agriculture program at the University of Wisconsin-Madison where, however, he graduated with a major in history (1924). He enrolled in the Union Theological Seminary in New York City, but because he enjoyed counseling more than religious work he transferred to Teachers College at Columbia University. Specializing in clinical and educational psychology, he developed as a doctoral dissertation a test for measuring personality adjustment in children (1931).

He married Helen Elliott in 1924; they had two children. In 1928 he became a child psychologist and then the director of the Rochester Society for the Prevention of Cruelty to Children (1930–1939). In Rochester he wrote *The Clinical Treatment of the Problem Child* (1939), in which he discussed the theory and practice of child guidance. This manuscript was the primary reason Ohio State University at Columbus offered him a full professorship in 1940. During his Ohio years Rogers wrote *Counseling and Psychotherapy* (1942) and established the first academic program of supervised psychotherapy or "practicum" in North America.

Many of Rogers's colleagues in Rochester had taken courses at the Pennsylvania School of Social Work that followed the orientation of the Austrian neo-psychoanalyst Otto Rank, who had been a student of Freud. In response to their enthusiasm for Rank's work, Rogers invited Rank to Rochester for a weekend. Rogers was impressed with Rank's description of therapy, particularly his emphasis on the importance of listening to the feelings behind the client's words and of "reflecting" them back to the client. Rank's claim that the person has potential for growth and that therapy should rely on human qualities rather than on intellectual skills became in Rogers's practice of psychotherapy an effective way of working with people in distress.

In *Counseling and Psychotherapy* Rogers integrated his own experience in counseling and the "relationship" or "passive" therapy of Otto Rank. Rogers argued that a therapist's nondirective, nonjudgmental attitude creates a permissive climate that enables the patient to freely express his or her own feelings, which leads to self-understanding and self-acceptance; these are, in their turn, the first steps toward personality reorientation and psychological growth.

In 1945 Rogers accepted the invitation of the University of Chicago to develop a counseling center there. In so doing Rogers digressed into the philosophical implications of his psychotherapy. In *Client-Centered Therapy* (1951) he argued that the primary goal of psychotherapy is to stimulate the organism's drive toward growth, health, and adjustment. He concluded that a constructive change in personality and behavior is possible if the client experiences in the counseling relationship "certain necessary and sufficient conditions": the realness and congruence of the therapist in the counseling relationship, and the therapist's unconditional positive acceptance and empathic understanding of the client's feelings and way of being in the world. Rogerian psychotherapy deliberately focused on the emotional aspects of the immediate existential condition of the client, rather than upon his or her intellectual or rational deliberations.

While in Chicago Rogers came under the influence of European existentialism. Reading the basic writings of Martin Buber and Søren Kierkegaard, he wrote many years later, had a "loosening up" effect that helped him discern the existential context of his views on psychotherapy.

Rogers was particularly impressed with Kierkegaard's assertion that the aim of life was "to be that self which one truly is." Rogers found a parallel experience in his practice of psychotherapy in the fact that when clients become their own self they not only hear inner messages and meanings but also deeply desire to be fully themselves (e.g., to become authentic) in all their complexity and richness. They also no longer withhold and fear anything that is part of the inner self.

Rogers had argued that in addition to unconditional positive regard and the immediacy and realness of the therapist, a deep sense of communication and unity between therapist and client was crucial. In this sense psychotherapy was a genuine person-to-person experience. This, Rogers argued, was exactly what Buber described in the "I-thou relationship." Buber thought that the mutual experience of meeting between two people and of speaking truly to each other without playing a role had a healing effect. Buber named this process "healing through meeting." It was a process Rogers experienced in the most effective moments of psychotherapy.

Building on these ideas, Rogers explained in *On Becoming a Person* (1961) that the human organism has an "actualizing tendency" to develop all its capacities in order to enhance its existence. The task of the psycho-therapist is to create conditions for the release of this capacity for self-reorganization, thus inducing psychological health and growth. People, he argued, have the capacity to understand their psychological complexities. They need only a climate that facilitates the unfolding of "organismic wisdom."

When in 1957 Rogers joined the departments of psychology and of psychiatry at the University of Wisconsin-Madison, he sought to expand his nondirective techniques to the treatment of psychotic individuals and to influence the training of psychiatrists with his theoretical perspective.

In Madison, however, disappointed with the skepticism of his colleagues, their behavioristic orientation, and the rigid structure of graduate education in psychology, he resigned from the department of psychology, retaining only his position in psychiatry. There he continued to study the impact of the client-centered therapeutic relationship upon schizophrenic patients. His and his associates' research was presented in *The Therapeutic Relationship and Its Impact* (1967).

Disappointed with the intellectual climate at Madison, Rogers joined the Western Behavioral Sciences Institute in California, where he applied his views to the practice of group psychotherapy in *Carl Rogers on Encounter Groups* (1970), to education in *Freedom to Learn* (1969), to marriage and intimate relationships in *Becoming Partners* (1972), and to politics in *Carl Rogers on Personal Power* (1977).

Despite his advancing years, Rogers remained active until his death, primarily exploring the theoretical and practical applications of client-centered techniques to group psychotherapy (e.g., the so-called encounter groups) to the solution of international conflicts in Central America, South Africa, Northern Ireland, and the Soviet Union.

Along with Abraham Maslow, Gordon Allport, and Rollo May, Rogers was a founder of humanistic psychology. He was instrumental in the theoretical formulation of humanistic psychology, and his life and work, along with Maslow's, was a cataclysm for the establishment of this American school of psychology. He was active in the Association for Humanistic Psychology until his last days. In spite of having been honored on many occasions by colleagues for having laid the foundations of the fields of counseling and psychotherapy, his lifework aroused much antagonism from mechanistic-atomistic quarters (e.g., behavioristic psychology) and from psychoanalysts. He was a president of the American Association for Applied Psychology and of the American Psychological Association (APA) and the recipient of the APA's Distinguished Professional Contribution Award and Distinguished Scientific Contribution Award. He died in La Jolla, California.

• Rogers's papers are at the Archives for the History of American Psychology at the University of Akron. Useful material may also be found at the Humanistic Psychology Archives at the University of California, Santa Barbara, and in the Manuscript Division of the Library of Congress. References to Rogers's publications can be found in his *A Way of Being* (1980) and in Roy J. deCarvalho, *The Founders of Humanistic Psychology* (1991). *Carl Rogers Reader*, ed. Howard Kirschenbaum and Valerie L. Henderson (1989), presents a useful selection of readings, and *Carl Rogers: Dialogues*, ed. Kirschenbaum and Henderson (1989), transcribes the philosophical encounters with Paul Tillich, B. F. Skinner, Gregory Bateson, Michael Polanyi, Rollo May, and others. Rogers's autobiography is in *A History of Psychology in Autobiography*, ed. Edwin G. Boring and Gardner Lindzey, vol. 5 (1967). Significant biographical information is in Howard Kirschenbaum, *On Becoming Carl Rogers* (1979), and Richard I. Evans, *Carl Rogers: The Man and His Ideas* (1975). Roy J. deCarvalho's *The Growth Hypothesis in Psychology: The Humanistic Psychology of Abraham Maslow and Carl Rogers* (1991) and *The Founders of Humanistic Psychology* (1991) place Rogers's life and work in the context of the history of humanistic psychology and the history and systems of psychology.

ROY J. deCARVALHO

ROGERS, Clara Kathleen (14 Jan. 1844–8 Mar. 1931), composer and singer, was born Clara Kathleen Barnett in Cheltenham, Gloucestershire, England, the daughter of John Barnett, a composer, and Eliza Lindley, the daughter of the eminent cellist Robert Lindley. Clara was to acquire the name Rogers when she married Henry Munroe Rogers, a prominent Boston attorney, in 1878; they had no children. John Barnett was, in Clara's proud words, the "Father of English opera," because his *The Mountain Sylph* (1834) was the "first English opera in complete form ever attempted up to that time" (*Memories*, p. 5). Rogers studied with her parents until she was twelve, at which time the family sought her admission to the Leipzig Conservatory. After being initially rejected because of her age, Rogers subsequently passed all the admissions tests and, elated with her achievement, pictured herself "already a great artist with the world at my feet!" (*Memories*, p. 102). Enrolled in piano, music theory, and voice classes at a musically conservative institution where Chopin and Schumann were "admitted only on sufferance," Rogers lamented that "there was no composition class for my sex, no woman composer having yet appeared on the musical horizon" (*Memories*, p. 108). Rogers's talent and industry led to a policy change in 1860, adding composition classes for girl students, when the faculty recognized the quality of her String Quartet, composed when she was only fourteen or fifteen. She graduated with honors in 1860 and continued her voice and piano studies in Berlin with the eminent pianist and conductor Hans von Bülow, who praised her "innate musical feeling and strong individuality" (*Memories*, p. 195).

Rogers pursued additional musical training in Milan with Antonio Sangiovanni and, after many disappointments because of difficulties with vocal tone, register, and fatigue, debuted in Turin as Princess Isabella in Meyerbeer's *Robert le diable* in 1863. She toured Italy for the next three years under her stage name, Clara Doria, and sang in several notable performances, including Donizetti's *Lucia di Lammermoor*, Bellini's *La Sonnambula*, Spontini's *La Vestale*, and Verdi's *Rigoletto*. Rogers returned to London in 1866 and performed regularly at concerts but seldom in opera. In 1871 her parents reluctantly allowed her to emigrate to the United States to perform with the Parepa-Rosa Opera Company.

She made her New York debut on 4 October 1871 as Princess Arline, the female lead in Balfe's *The Bohemian Girl*, and she appeared in various soprano roles (Donna Elvira in *Don Giovanni* and the Countess in *The Marriage of Figaro*) with Euphrosyne Parepa-Rosa during the 1871–1872 season. Her "habit of mental study through visualization" (*Memories*, p. 394) allowed her to learn the principal role in Boieldieu's *La Dame Blanche* overnight and perform it without rehearsal the next afternoon to a Washington audience. Rogers recalled that Rosa told her, "if you only had two more notes in your voice you would be one of the great artists of the world" (*Memories*, p. 395). She also performed with Max Maretzek's Italian Opera Company in New York in 1872–1873, but mostly as a last-minute substitute for regular performers. Favorable reviews of the private performances she gave in Boston in 1873 appeared in *Dwight's Journal of Music* and helped to establish her as a worthy member of Boston's social and cultural elite at a time when the city "was still the hotbed of literature, art, and science in America" (*Memories*, p. 417). Her Boston public debut occurred in 1873 at a Harvard Symphony concert, in which she sang "Selva Opaca" from Rossini's *William Tell* and a group of lieder. Intrigued by the prospect of new experiences, Rogers joined Camilla Urso's touring company for the 1875 season. During this season the company traveled to many states in the Northeast and Midwest and to Canada, and she observed that American audiences outside Eastern cities "could be appealed to by nothing but the most elemental stuff!" or by "an abnormally long, soft, high note . . . because it would seem impossible for any one to hold their breath so long!" (*Memories*, p. 439).

Having rejected an offer by Eben Tourjee, director of the New England Conservatory, to teach German lieder there in 1873, she finally accepted a faculty appointment there as a professor of voice in 1902. A proficient pianist, Rogers accompanied violinist Charles Martin Loeffler at the Boston premiere of her Sonata for Violin and Piano (1888). Her Sonata for Violoncello and Piano was performed publicly on 18 December 1895 in New York. She composed numerous songs, two song cycles on poems by Robert Browning (1893 and 1900), a string quartet (1866), and various other works. Inspired partly by her own history of vocal problems, she wrote several volumes on singing, including *The Philosophy of Singing* (1893) and a two-volume text entitled *English Diction in Song and Speech* (1912 and 1915). Her three-volume autobiography *Memories of a Musical Career* (1919) provides interesting reflections on American music taste and the life of a touring artist. Rogers's later years are recorded in her *Story of Two Lives: Home, Friends, and Travels*

(1932). Her Scherzo for piano op. 15 (1893) is reprinted in *American Women Composers, Piano Music from 1865–1915* (1990). She died in Boston.

Rogers's vocal and chamber compositions show a great gift for melody, a fine sensitivity to the texts she chose to set, and a good understanding of instrumental sonorities in the Violin Sonata. Her disappointment over her lack of training in orchestration limited her output, and her reputation rests largely on her songs and song cycles.

• Rogers's personal papers, manuscripts, and documents are in the Department of Rare Books and Manuscripts at Boston Public Library and in the Library of Congress. Bibliographical, biographical, and publication history of Rogers's works are in Adrienne Fried Block and Carol Neuls Bates, eds., *Women in American Music: A Bibliography of Music and Literature* (1979). Biographical information and brief discussions are in Christine Ammer, *Unsung: A History of Women in American Music* (1980), and Jane Bowers and Judith Tick, eds., *Women Making Music: The Western Art Tradition, 1150–1950* (1986). Performances of Violin Sonata and two songs are on *Women at an Exposition*, Koch International CD (3-7240-2H1). See also Arthur Elson, *Woman's Work in Music; Being an Account of Her Influence on the Art* (1904), and Louis C. Elson, *The History of American Music* (1925; rev. ed., 1935) and "Review of New Music: Six Songs for Soprano and Tenor," *Musical Herald* 4 (1883): 24. Obituaries are in the *New York Times* and the *Boston Herald*, both 9 Mar. 1931.

WILLIAM J. MAHAR

ROGERS, Daniel (28 July 1707–9 Dec. 1785), Congregational clergyman, was born in Ipswich, Massachusetts, the son of Reverend John Rogers and Martha Whittington. The grandson of Harvard's President Rogers, Daniel was something of a religious seeker during college. After graduating from Harvard in 1725 he served as a tutor and later unsuccessfully candidated for Cotton Mather's vacant pulpit at Second Church, Boston. In 1740 Rogers left his tutoring duties and put off an affirmative call from Boston's New North Church to travel with British evangelist George Whitefield, who refers positively to him in his journals. The call was eventually withdrawn, probably the result of Rogers's own dallying. The lure of itinerant preaching was stronger than that of settlement, however, and Rogers, marveling at the "very remarkable outpouring of the Holy Spirit," continued to itinerate across New England. In this endeavor he met with some success, especially in the more receptive North, where standards of proper Congregational behavior were less firmly entrenched. In late 1741 Rogers and his brother Nathaniel began a revival near their hometown of Ipswich, generating a controversy with the settled pastor, Theophilus Pickering, who considered them both interlopers. The ensuing epistolary exchange signaled the deterioration of Rogers's relationship with the settled clergy.

An invitation from supporters of the Great Awakening, or "New Lights," in Exeter, New Hampshire, moved Rogers to embark on a second successful northern tour, and their affirmation of his ministry turned his mind toward the possibility of ordination. This solemn ceremony took place in a York, Maine, field on 13 July 1742, with supporters of the revival assisting. It was a revolutionary event. New Englanders had long insisted that a minister without a settled church was a contradiction in terms; itinerancy, which typically meant preaching without invitation from local settled clergy, was a significant breach of ministerial propriety. Now "Old Light" opponents of the Awakening denounced Rogers's ordination as invalid and contrary to the churches' good order.

As the Great Awakening progressed, Rogers traveled on preaching tours between Exeter, Ipswich, and Kittery, Maine. More conservative than many of his New Light colleagues, he was reluctant to preach without explicit invitation; that he occasionally did so is a yardstick of his conviction that he was about God's work. In 1747 he received a call from a group of Exeter New Lights who had earlier seceded from the Old Light church in that town. The following year he accepted and was installed in August 1748. Like his ordination, this event was controversial, generating anger both at the new church's "illegal" separation and at its use of the term "installation," which gave the seal to the irregular status of Rogers's earlier ordination. Formal condemnation from an ecclesiastical council, however, changed neither Rogers's mind nor that of his new congregation.

Not a great deal is known of Daniel Rogers's later life and ministry. He married Anna Foxcroft of Boston soon after settling in Exeter. The incorporation of Exeter Second Parish in 1755 gave his church legal standing; and although he was boycotted by some neighboring clergy, he seems to have taken an active role in ministerial affairs thereafter. Reconciliation in some measure must have taken place, because Rogers joined the influential New Hampshire Convocation of Ministers after 1760 and eventually served as its speaker and moderator. He remained a New Light—George Whitefield preached his last sermon in Rogers's parish and Rogers prayed at his funeral service in 1770—but whatever "enthusiasm" remained to him was played out finally in the formal context of a regularly gathered church.

• Rogers's written material remains relatively obscure. There are manuscript sermons in the Congregational Library in Boston, the New Hampshire Historical Society, and the New York Public Library. An extensive and valuable diary (1740–1753), which provides a remarkable account of both Rogers's own pilgrimage and more generally the Great Awakening, is in the New-York Historical Society. A briefer account (1730–1785) is in the New England Historic Genealogical Society.

ELIZABETH NORDBECK

ROGERS, Edith Nourse (19 Mar. 1881–10 Sept. 1960), congresswoman, was born in Saco, Maine, the daughter of Franklin T. Nourse, the manager of a textile mill, and Edith Frances Riversmith. With both parents from old New England families and her father a leader in business and politics, Edith and her younger brother had comfortable childhoods in Saco. Educated

by a tutor until she was fourteen, Edith then attended Rogers Hall boarding school, a private girls' academy in Lowell, Massachusetts, and Madame Julien's finishing school in Neuilly, France. Returning to Lowell after her European schooling and travel, she became active, as was her mother, in social welfare and church work. In 1907 she married her neighbor and childhood sweetheart, Harvard law graduate John Jacob Rogers. With a thriving law practice in Lowell, her husband entered politics as a regular Republican in 1911. He won election to Congress in the Fifth Congressional District in 1912 and was reelected until his death.

Living in Washington, Edith's interests turned toward public affairs. In 1917, when her husband and other members of the House Foreign Affairs Committee journeyed to France and Britain, she accompanied them, volunteering briefly with the YMCA in London and then touring the battlefields. John Jacob Rogers, retaining his congressional seat, enlisted in the artillery, while Edith joined the Red Cross as a Grey Lady and worked at Walter Reed Army Medical Center in Washington, beginning her lifelong commitment to the welfare of veterans.

At the end of the war, Congressman Rogers joined the newly formed American Legion; Edith joined the auxiliary. In 1922 President Warren G. Harding appointed her as a dollar-a-year inspector of the new veterans' hospitals. She toured the country visiting hospitals and communicating their needs directly to the Harding, Coolidge, and Hoover administrations. She entered politics as a presidential elector for Calvin Coolidge in 1924.

When her husband died in March 1925, Edith yielded to pressure from Republicans and the American Legion to run for his seat and to continue their support of veterans. Commenting that "the office seeks the woman," 44-year-old Edith Nourse Rogers won the special election in June 1925, defeating a former governor with 72 percent of the vote, the first of eighteen lopsided electoral triumphs. Averaging 60 percent of the vote in elections throughout the New Deal years, she increasingly faced no Republican opposition and in three campaigns had no Democratic opponent. In several campaigns her only expenditure was the filing fee.

Although she served on the Committee on Foreign Affairs and the Civil Service Committee, her major energies were devoted to veterans' affairs. In 1947, when forced to choose service on one major committee, Rogers selected the Committee on Veterans' Affairs, becoming the ranking Republican member and serving as its chair in the Eightieth and Eighty-third Congresses. Of the more than 1,200 bills Rogers introduced in her long congressional career, more than half concerned veterans' and military affairs. She secured pensions for army nurses in 1926, a permanent Nurse Corps in the Veterans Administration (VA), and major appropriations to build VA hospitals. During World War II she successfully sponsored the legislation creating the Women's Auxiliary Army Corps (WAC) and the Navy Waves. One of the landmark measures she sponsored and helped to draft was the 1944 GI Bill of Rights, which established veterans' financial and educational benefits.

In the area of foreign affairs, Rogers was one of the first in Congress to speak against Hitler's treatment of the Jews, and she voted for preparedness measures in the Pacific. During the Cold War she supported appropriations for the House Committee on Un-American Activities and was a backer of Senator Joseph McCarthy, but she balked in 1954 at sending U.S. troops to Vietnam. She supported the United Nations but in 1953 urged American withdrawal of support and removal of UN headquarters from the United States if Communist China were admitted.

Rogers worked tirelessly for her constituents, explaining she could not "refuse to spend mere money when I know that people need it." She fought relentlessly to protect the textile and leather industries of Massachusetts, won flood control appropriations for the Merrimack River basin, and was successful in securing jobs through the billions of dollars in federal contracts garnered for her state.

When elected in 1925, Rogers had hoped that "everybody would forget that I am a woman as soon as possible." Yet her longevity and her legislative effectiveness made her the "dean" of congresswomen; her trademark was an orchid or gardenia on her shoulder. Colleagues described her as capable and aggressive. While insisting that, for a woman, home and children came first, she also worked for equal pay for equal work. Her motto was "fight hard, fight fair and persevere," adding, "when women fight to protect their rights, though, they hang on longer than the men" (*Boston Globe*, 11 Sept. 1960).

Rogers was childless and never remarried. In 1949 she was threatened with scandal when named in a divorce case brought by the wife of one of her aides, but the district court judge dismissed the allegations and ordered all references to Rogers stricken from the record. Throughout her long career she was recognized by honorary degrees, by the Distinguished Service Medal of the American Legion in 1950, and by the naming for her of the WAC museum in Alabama and the veterans hospital in Bedford, Massachusetts. In an interview near the end of her career she asserted, "The first 30 years are the hardest" (*Boston Globe*, 11 Sept. 1960). She died in Boston in the midst of her nineteenth congressional campaign, three days before the primary, ending thirty-five years in Congress.

• A massive collection of Rogers papers is in the Schlesinger Library, Radcliffe College; other papers are in the Harold A. Latta Lawrence Papers, Saco, Maine. Rogers's articles on preparedness and peace include: "A Women's Army?" *Independent Woman*, Feb. 1942, p. 38; "The Time Is Now," *Woman's Home Companion*, Aug. 1943, p. 25; "Does Naval Preparedness Prevent War?" *Congressional Digest* 8 (Jan. 1929): 18–19; and "How the Kellogg Peace Pact Can Be Made Effective," *Annals of the American Academy of Political and Social Science* 144 (July 1929): 51–54. A brief biography is in Hope Chamberlin, *A Minority of Members: Women in the U.S. Congress* (1973). Congressional colleagues memorialized Rogers in the *Congressional Record*, 16 Jan. 1961, pp. 784–94. Brief coverage of her personality and career is in Peter Gilfond, "Gentlewomen of the House," *American Mercury*, Oct. 1929, pp. 151–58; Frances Parkinson Keyes, "Seven Successful Women," *Delineator*, July 1928, pp. 16, 82–83; and "New Note in Scandals," *Newsweek*, 4 Apr. 1949, p. 24. Susan M. Hartmann, *The Home Front and Beyond: American Women in the 1940s* (1982), and Davis R. B. Ross, *Preparing for Ulysses: Politics and Veterans during World War II* (1969), cite her work for the WAC and veterans. Obituaries are in the *Boston Globe* and *New York Times*, 11 Sept. 1960, and the *Christian Science Monitor*, 12 Sept. 1960.

DOROTHY M. BROWN

ROGERS, Elizabeth Ann (2 Nov. 1829–20 Feb. 1921), Anglican sister and educator at St. Andrew's Priory in Honolulu, Hawaii, was born in Cornwall, England, the daughter of James Rogers, a carpenter, and Ann Ellis. Elizabeth Ann's early display of Catholic piety was encouraged by her family's friendship with the vicar of Porthleven, Reverend Thomas L. Williams, and as a grown woman she became interested in devoting herself to the church. Reverend Williams introduced her to an Anglican sisterhood known as the Congregation of Religious of the Society of the Most Holy Trinity, which was a recent outgrowth of an earlier organization that had been devoted to raising the orphaned daughters of British soldiers and sailors.

The Society of the Most Holy Trinity was the first Anglican sisterhood to establish foreign missions, and Hawaii was its first mission field. Responding to a request from King Kamehameha IV (Alexander Liholiho) and his consort Queen Emma, Mother Lydia Sellon, the society's founder, sent two sisters to Lahaina, Maui, where they established St. Cross School and administered to the sick, including lepers. In 1865 Queen Emma came to England seeking support for an Anglican cathedral in Honolulu and an associated preparatory school for Hawaiian girls. She visited the society's Ascot priory to consult with Mother Lydia as to curriculum and educators. The reverend mother promised to send three sisters to Honolulu to establish the priory school. Rogers met Queen Emma during her trip and grew interested in the Hawaiian mission.

In 1866 London was swept by cholera, and Rogers worked as a nurse in a temporary hospital established by the society in Spitalfields. The next year, taking the religious name of Sister Beatrice, she was received into the first order of the society as a Sister of Mercy dedicated to helping the poor and the sick by feeding, clothing, and educating destitute children; offering charity to those in hospitals, workhouses, and prisons; and helping those who needed to bury their dead. About the time she was received into the order, Sister Beatrice wrote her father that she would soon embark for the Sandwich Islands (Hawaii). By then, with the cholera epidemic over, Mother Lydia was ready to fulfill her promise to Queen Emma, and she began to plan the mission to Hawaii. The party, which was composed of Mother Lydia, three sisters who would remain in Hawaii, and three others who planned to return to England with Mother Lydia, set sail on 15 January 1867. After Sister Beatrice's father received her letter, he went to London to prevent her from going, but she had left already.

The sisters crossed the Isthmus of Panama, visited San Francisco, and arrived in Honolulu on 30 March 1867. Their arrival was greeted enthusiastically by Royalist and pro-British elements who sought to counter the growing American influence on the islands, hoping thereby to keep Hawaii independent. They were welcomed by Honolulu Anglican bishop Thomas Nettleship Staley and stayed in his home briefly. They were then offered residence in "Rooke House," Queen Emma's private home, pending completion of the priory school that was being built on the grounds of St. Andrew's, the Anglican cathedral, on land that had been donated by Kamehameha IV. Mother Lydia expended $7,000 of society funds to erect St. Andrew's Priory and the school opened on 30 May 1867 with forty students from the islands' chiefly (alii) class. The mother foundress then returned to England, leaving the sisters, including Sister Beatrice, to conduct the school. Under their direction the school became a distinguished preparatory academy and enrolled more than 600 young Hawaiian women. Queen Emma continued her patronage of St. Andrew's Priory, and she developed a close relationship with the sisters, taking tea with them on Sunday afternoons. After her husband's death, when Queen Emma sought the throne through the 1874 legislative election, she was given sanctuary in the parlor of the priory after threats had been made against her life by the political faction supporting her rival, David Kalakaua. The sisters also cared for the queen during her last illness in 1885.

In 1877 Sister Beatrice was professed, ending her novitiate. In addition to her teaching and guardianship duties at St. Andrew's Priory, she also supervised the youngest children's dormitory and ran a free school in Honolulu for poor Hawaiian children. By 1871 Bishop Wilberforce wrote that "schools conducted in the Hawaiian Mission were appreciated more than all the rest of the work done by the Anglicans throughout the islands." The life of the sisters "served to exalt and sustain the school teaching," he wrote; "their services, their separation to God told directly upon their work: they were felt to be not merely eminently successful schoolteachers, but women engaged in mission work for Christ and using their teaching powers to carry on their mission" (Williams, p. 241). But after 1890, because of lack of funds, the society withdrew its support from the Hawaiian mission and recalled sisters Beatrice and Albertina, but they refused to return out of devotion to their charges. They asked to be allowed to stay in Hawaii and continue to administer the priory as a boarding school. Permission was granted, and they continued to supervise the school until the American Anglican church in Honolulu took it over in 1902. The sisters remained close friends of the Hawaiian monarchy, and when Queen Liliuokalani was dethroned, and her enemies tried to kill her in 1893, she also sought the protection of the priory. In 1919 three generations of Hawaiian women who had been educated at the priory feted Sister Beatrice on her ninetieth birthday. She died in Honolulu at the priory.

• Information about Elizabeth Ann Rogers's life at St. Andrew's Priory can be found in letters written by the Hawaiian missionaries to the Ascot priory, which are housed in the archives of the Ascot priory in England. Other primary sources include "Sister Albertina's Story," *Hawaiian Church Chronicle*, June 1934, p. 5, Apr. 1935, p. 101, and Sept. 1936, p. 6; Reverend H. C. Potter, *Sisterhoods and Deaconesses at Home and Abroad* (1873); and Isabella Bird, *Six Months among the Palm Groves, Coral Reefs, and Volcanoes*, 5th ed. (1882). Useful secondary sources include Thomas Jay Williams, *Priscilla Lydia Sellon* (1950), and Henry Bond Restarick, *Hawaii 1778–1920 from the Viewpoint of a Bishop* (1924). See also, "Priscilla Lydia Sellon," in *Notable Women of Hawaii*, ed. Barbara Bennett Peterson (1984). Obituaries are in the *Honolulu Star-Bulletin* and the *Honolulu Advertiser*, 21 Feb. 1921, and in the *Hawaiian Monthly Chronicle*, Mar.-Apr. 1921.

BARBARA BENNETT PETERSON

ROGERS, Elymas Payson (10 Feb. 1815–20 Jan. 1861), clergyman, poet, and missionary, was born in Madison, Connecticut, the son of Abel Rogers and Chloe Ladue, farmers. His father, the son of an African slave who had survived a shipwreck off the coast of Connecticut, was raised as family by the Reverend Jonathan Todd, from whom he eventually inherited the farmland on which he made his living. In the early 1830s, Rogers left for Hartford, Connecticut, where he attended school and worked for his board in the home of a Major Caldwell. His first formal church affiliation was established in 1833 as a communicant of the Hartford Talcott Street congregation.

In 1835 Rogers went to Peterboro, New York, to study for the ministry at a school established by the philanthropist-reformer Gerrit Smith. The following year, to pay for his studies, he began teaching at the recommendation of Smith in a public school for black children in Rochester, New York, where he continued for five years. In the spring of 1837 he enrolled at Oneida Institute in Whitesboro, New York, while continuing to teach. Jermain Wesley Loguen, one of Rogers's students, who also went on to study at Oneida, became a prominent abolitionist and African Methodist Episcopal bishop. Rogers later wrote a poem, "Loguen's Position," which denounces the evils of slavery and affirms the legitimacy of Loguen's angry abolitionist stance.

Immediately after his graduation from Oneida in 1841, Rogers became principal of the Trenton, New Jersey, public school for black children. That year he married Harriet E. Sherman, and they settled in Trenton where Rogers pursued his career by teaching and studying theology. On 7 February 1844, he was licensed by the New Brunswick Presbytery and received full ordination to the ministry one year later. His first ministerial position was as pastor of the Witherspoon Street Church in Princeton, New Jersey, where he served for two years.

Rogers sought and obtained membership in the Newark Presbytery on 20 October 1846, when he accepted the pastorate at the Plane Street Church in Newark, New Jersey. The next fourteen years were among the most fruitful of his career. By 1857, the church had grown from 23 to 140 communicants and 130 Sabbath scholars. It was one of only two churches described as "prosperous" in the *Minutes* of the 1957 denominational meeting. Rogers served as moderator of the 1856 Presbyterian and Congregational Convention; the following year in Philadelphia, he delivered the opening sermon of the denominational meeting in Philadelphia, which passed a resolution denouncing the Dred Scott Decision and praising the two dissenting Supreme Court justices.

Rogers's abolitionist fervor is reflected in two published satires: "A Poem On the Fugitive Slave Law" (1855) and "The Repeal of the Missouri Compromise Considered" (1856). The former is an erudite exposition on law written in octosyllabic couplets. It argues that a higher law should take precedence over manmade rules advocated by such men as Blackstone, Witherspoon, and Cicero, when such rules violate human rights. The latter, a longer 925-line poem, also in octosyllabic couplets, is a dialogue between "Freedom" and "Slavery." In it he argues that national greed and expedience had motivated both legislation and popular opinion regarding slavery. Rogers's satires are unusual in antebellum black poetry for their erudition, wit, and courageous expression of moral indignation.

Rogers's active membership in the African Civilization Society led eventually to the fulfillment, albeit brief, of his dream to be a missionary in Africa. On 5 November 1860, he sailed from New York to Freetown, Sierra Leone. He visited Monrovia, Bassa, Sinoe, and Cape Palmas, where he died of fever and heart disease. His early death cut short a career that he had hoped would extend both the gospel of Christ and civilized life to much of Africa.

• Rogers's letters are held in the American Missionary Association Archives at the Amistad Research Center, New Orleans, La. Critical discussion of Rogers's life and work can be found in Joan R. Sherman, *Afro-Americans of the Nineteenth Century* (1974), and William Wells Brown, *The Black Man, His Antecedents, His Genius, and His Achievements* (1863). A testimonial and biographical sketch is found in Joseph M. Wilson, *The Presbyterian Historical Almanac . . . for 1862*, vol. 4 (1862), pp. 191–95.

MARILYN DEMAREST BUTTON

ROGERS, Fairman (15 Nov. 1833–23 Aug. 1900), civil engineer, was born in Philadelphia, Pennsylvania, the son of Evans Rogers, an iron merchant, and Caroline Augusta Fairman. In 1849 he graduated from preparatory school and matriculated at the University of Pennsylvania, where he studied mathematics and the physical sciences. After receiving his A.B. in 1853, he became a lecturer in mechanics at Philadelphia's Franklin Institute, a position he held for the next twelve years. In 1855 he received his A.M. from the university, joined its faculty as a professor of civil engineering, and became affiliated with the U.S. Coast Survey (USCS) as a volunteer engineer. In 1856 Rogers married Rebecca H. Gilpin, with whom he had no children. In 1857 he contributed to the work of the USCS by helping to establish the base line for the survey of the coast of Maine. Under the auspices of the Smithsonian Institution of Washington, D.C., in 1861 he delivered a series of lectures on the construction of highways and bridges, addressing the sorry state of roads in the United States and emphasizing the importance of such design features as proper width, roadbed, and drainage.

Shortly after the outbreak of the Civil War, Rogers, an accomplished horseman, joined the Philadelphia city cavalry for a ninety-day tour of duty, serving as the First Troop's first sergeant. Upon returning to civilian life, he completed a survey of the northern reaches of the Potomac River for the USCS, and in the fall of 1861 he joined the Pennsylvania militia as a volunteer engineer. He served on the staff of General William F. "Baldy" Smith, the Army of the Potomac's chief engineer, and saw action at the battles of Antietam and Gettysburg. While in the army he wrote "Horsemanship," *U.S. Service Magazine* (1864), in which he presented a scientific program for training both rider and horse to perform satisfactorily in either military or civilian pursuits. In 1865 he rejoined the Philadelphia city cavalry as captain of his old troop and finished the war in this capacity.

When the U.S. Congress established the National Academy of Sciences in 1863 to advise the government on matters related to science and technology, Rogers was selected to become one of its original fifty members. He served as the academy's treasurer for a number of years and was actively involved in the affairs of its governing council and various committees. As a member of the academy, he was invited to undertake a study of the compasses being used aboard the government's iron-hulled ships in order to determine the effect of the hulls on the accuracy of the compasses. The results of his study, published as *Terrestrial Magnetism and the Magnetism of Iron Ships* (1877; 2d ed., 1883), outlined the procedures by which a ship's officer might recognize and avoid relying on erroneous readings caused by an uncorrected compass or by unexpected shifts in the magnetic North Pole.

In 1871 Rogers resigned from the University of Pennsylvania as a teacher. He was immediately elected to its board of trustees and served on that body from 1871 to 1888. He developed a great interest in mechanical computing devices, particularly the Difference Engine, a calculating machine developed in 1871 by George Barnard Grant, which could perform a number of arithmetical computations. In 1875 Rogers, who had apparently inherited a substantial sum of money, agreed to underwrite the construction of a large Difference Engine, with the proviso that Grant would eventually donate it to the University of Pennsylvania. This calculator, which consisted of almost 15,000 parts and weighed one ton, was exhibited at the Philadelphia Centennial in 1876.

In addition to his scientific pursuits, Rogers devoted much time and attention to the civic improvement of Philadelphia. He oversaw the construction of the Centennial's main exhibition hall; in 1880 he presented the University of Pennsylvania with his valuable collection of books on civil engineering. In 1880 he turned down an offer to become the university's provost, choosing instead to accept a position as chairman of the Committee of Instruction of Philadelphia's Pennsylvania Academy of Fine Arts, the oldest school of its kind in the United States. Under his direction the academy continued to offer instruction in painting and sculpture to aspiring professional artists while implementing programs to improve the artistic ability of amateurs.

Rogers was a founding member of both the Union League, a Philadelphia social club, and the Philadelphia Coaching Club; he was reputed to have been the first person in Philadelphia to drive a four-in-hand, a coach pulled by a team of four horses. He also had an important part in popularizing polo, which was first played in the United States in 1876, in Philadelphia. In 1893 he resigned from the Pennsylvania Academy and spent the remaining years of his life touring Europe and writing *Manual of Coaching* (1900), an exhaustive treatise on horse-drawn coaches that combined his expertise as a civil engineer, his understanding of the principles of statics and dynamics, and his knowledge of horses and carriages. He died in Vienna, Austria.

Rogers was a member of the American Society of Civil Engineers and the American Philosophical Society. He contributed to American society by bringing scientific principles to bear on a variety of subjects without losing sight of those subjects' grace and beauty. As a charter member of the National Academy of Sciences, he played an important role in establishing that organization as a useful vehicle for the promotion of scientific research in the United States.

• Rogers's papers are in the archives of the University of Pennsylvania. A good biography, including a bibliography of his works, is Edgar F. Smith, "Fairman Rogers," National Academy of Sciences, *Biographical Memoirs* 6 (1904): 93–107.

CHARLES W. CAREY, JR.

ROGERS, Ginger (16 July 1911–25 Apr. 1995), actress, dancer, and musical comedy performer, was born Virginia Katherine McMath in Independence, Missouri, the daughter of William Eddins McMath and Lela Emogen Owens, a writer. Her parents soon divorced, and her mother (who died in 1977) became the most important person in Rogers's life, managing her career with force and confidence and often delivering pointed advice that Rogers says she countered only rarely, and then usually to her later regret. Her mother, she recalls in her autobiography, was variously "my writer, designer, seamstress, business manager, confidante, and chaperone" (Rogers, p. 50).

Stage-struck at an early age, Rogers's first break came in 1925 when she won a Charleston dancing contest in Texas that led to three years of touring in vaudeville in a song-and-dance act. By 1930 she had performed in several shorts and features filmed in New York. In the first of these, *Young Man of Manhattan* (1930), she delivered a sassy line, "Cigarette me, big boy," that quickly became a catch phrase. She also appeared successfully on Broadway. In *Top Speed* (1929–1930) she stole the show, and in George and Ira Gershwin's *Girl Crazy* (1930–1931) she introduced the memorable songs "Embraceable You" and "But Not for Me."

Rogers soon had a contract to go to Hollywood, where she appeared in eight feature films in 1931 and 1932. In 1933 she made nine more, scoring particularly as a wise-cracking chorus dancer in *42nd Street* and *Gold Diggers of 1933* at Warner Bros. and as pal, comedy foil, and dancing partner (in "The Carioca") to Fred Astaire in *Flying Down to Rio* at RKO.

The Astaire-Rogers combination showed excellent box-office promise, and RKO was quick to capitalize on it. *The Gay Divorcee* (1934) featured the pair as romantic leads and became a huge hit, leading to seven more pairings in the following years: *Roberta* and *Top Hat* in 1935, *Follow the Fleet* and *Swing Time* (probably Rogers's best in the series and her personal favorite) in 1936, *Shall We Dance?* in 1937, *Carefree* in 1938, and *The Story of Vernon and Irene Castle* in 1939. One of the legendary partnerships in screen history, it offered Astaire's casual, likable elegance pitched engagingly against Rogers's sometimes caustic, but arrestingly vulnerable, liveliness. Most important, these films preserve a series of dance duets choreographed by Astaire that stand out as a major highlight in the history of dance.

More than any of Astaire's other partners, some of whom were far better trained dancers than she, Rogers seemed instinctively to have grasped the dramatic point of each dance—whether joyous or doom-laden, celebratory or seductive, flirtatious or pensive. And as a skilled actress she found a way, without shattering Astaire's understated, intricate style, to contribute importantly to the dance's effect, not so much in the way of steps as in matter and point. Conventional gossip to the contrary, Rogers and Astaire appear to have gotten along quite well off screen. Although different personalities—Astaire tended to be a quiet homebody, Rogers a vivacious, outgoing admiration-seeker—both were dedicated, hardworking professionals whose relations remained businesslike, affectionate, and cordial.

During the years of her partnership with Astaire, Rogers also made twelve feature films without him, almost all at RKO. These were mostly lively comedies, and several were substantial successes, most memorably the witty *Stage Door* (1937), in which Rogers traded scene-stealing with Katharine Hepburn, and *Vivacious Lady* (1938), in which she appeared opposite James Stewart.

By 1939 the Astaire-Rogers pairing was losing some of its box-office appeal, and the films were beginning to lose money in major part because of the two stars' escalating salaries. In a disagreement over fees, Astaire left the studio while Rogers stayed on in vehicles that exploited her acting and comedy talents more than her musical abilities. In these she was paired with such leading men as Joel McCrea in *Primrose Path* (1940), David Niven in *Bachelor Mother* (1941), Burgess Meredith in *Tom, Dick and Harry* (1942), Ray Milland in *The Major and the Minor* (1942), Cary Grant in *Once Upon a Honeymoon* (1942), and Robert Ryan in *Tender Comrade* (1943). For the melodramatic and sentimental *Kitty Foyle* of 1940 she received the Academy Award for best actress. She became one of the highest-paid stars in Hollywood.

Rogers's film career began to go in something of a decline with *Lady in the Dark* (1944), an overcalculated and overelaborate film musical at Paramount Pictures. However, she made twenty-one more motion pictures in the next twenty years, including *The Barkleys of Broadway* (1949), in which she replaced the ailing Judy Garland and in which she was reunited with Astaire, as well as *Weekend at the Waldorf* (1945), *Storm Warning* (1950) opposite Ronald Reagan, *Monkey Business* (1952) opposite Cary Grant, and *The First Traveling Saleslady* (1956).

At the same time, Rogers returned to the stage. Between 1951 and 1984 she was featured in revivals and tours both of nonmusical plays and of such musicals as *Annie Get Your Gun*, *The Unsinkable Molly Brown*, *Mame*, and *Anything Goes*. In 1965 she successfully replaced Carol Channing in *Hello, Dolly!* on Broadway. Between 1975 and 1979 she was featured in *The Ginger Rogers Show*, which toured the United States and abroad. She also did a great deal of work on television, making her debut in 1954 in a ninety-minute version of Noël Coward's *Tonight at 8:30*.

Like her mother, Rogers was a devout Christian Scientist and a staunch Republican. She was married five times—to Edward Culpepper (1929–1931); to Lew Ayres, the actor (1934–1936); to Jack Briggs (1943–1949); to Jacques Bergerac, a law student (1953–1957); and to William Marshall (1961–1972). All her marriages ended in divorce, and she had no children. Among the men in her life whom she did not marry were Rudy Vallee, Harold Ross, Mervyn LeRoy, Fred Astaire (one date in New York in the 1920s, she says, ending with a long and passionate kiss), Howard Hughes, Alfred Vanderbilt, Cary Grant, George Gershwin, and James Stewart. Her greatest love may have been George Stevens, who directed her in *Swing Time* and *Vivacious Lady*. But he was married, she notes wistfully in her autobiography, and "it was not to be." In her later years she lived mostly on her ranch in Oregon. Rogers died at her home in Rancho Mirage, California.

• Rogers's autobiography, rather reticent but informative, is *Ginger: My Story* (1991). Her films and dances with Astaire are discussed in Arlene Croce, *The Fred Astaire and Ginger Rogers Book* (1972), and John Mueller, *Astaire Dancing: The Musical Films* (1985). See also Richard B. Jewell and Vernon Harbin, *The RKO Story* (1982). An obituary is in the *New York Times*, 26 Apr. 1995.

JOHN MUELLER

ROGERS, Harriet Burbank (12 Apr. 1834–12 Dec. 1919), educator of the deaf, was born in North Billerica, Massachusetts, the daughter of Calvin Rogers and Ann Faulkner, farmers. After receiving her early education in local public schools, she attended the Massachusetts State Normal School (later Framingham State College) in West Newton. Following her graduation in 1851, she taught at several country schools as well as at the Westford (Mass.) Academy.

Under the influence of her older sister Elisa Ann, a teacher at the Perkins Institution for the Blind, Rogers undertook a task that determined the course of her career. Elisa Ann, who had numbered Laura Bridgman (the first successfully educated deaf-blind child in the United States) among her pupils, convinced Harriet to take the position of private tutor to a deaf girl, Fanny Cushing. Initially hesitant to take the job because of her lack of training in the field, Rogers agreed to attempt to teach the child to speak and immediately set out to learn all she could about the subject. At the time almost all instruction of deaf students was conducted using the manual alphabet, or sign language, method.

Through a friend Rogers heard of a school in Germany where deaf students learned to reproduce vocal sounds by feeling the instructor's breath patterns as well as throat and chest vibrations and then attempting to duplicate the effect. Using the new method, Rogers achieved notable success in her initial efforts with her student.

Rogers's efforts soon gained the attention of Gardiner Greene Hubbard, a lawyer and businessman who also served as a member of the Massachusetts Board of Education. Hubbard's involvement in the area of hearing-impaired education became personal when, in 1863, he was unable to find anyone with the training or desire to instruct his own daughter, who had recently suffered the loss of her hearing. Unsuccessful in his efforts to obtain a charter for a school for the deaf (1864), Hubbard and his wife had instructed their daughter at home using the same methods employed by Rogers. Hubbard finally met Rogers in 1865 and encouraged her to open a school for deaf students.

The school, which opened in June 1866 with five students at Chelmsford, Massachusetts, was a success. By the end of the first year enrollment had increased to eight students, and the movement for education of the deaf had gained another ally in the person of John Clarke, who offered to endow a school offering such instruction in his home town of Northampton, Massachusetts. On the basis of this support, the state legislature granted a charter to the Clarke Institution for Deaf Mutes (later the Clarke School for the Deaf) on 1 June 1867. On 1 October of the same year Rogers was named as the school's first director, and she moved her students from Chelmsford to the new location.

The first school in the United States to offer instruction to the deaf using lipreading, the experimental program was not without its critics. Many traditional educators in the field, most of them male, believed that only the manual method of instruction was effective. Rogers gained many followers—mostly female—for her method, but the controversy simmered for years. Oralists tended to view deafness as an unfortunate social handicap to be overcome, while manualists tended to believe that the deaf merely needed to adapt to their deafness. Neither side gave the other much credence, however. Manualists thought oralists frauds, and oralists believed that manualists were condemning the deaf to a "deaf ghetto" of being able to communicate only with other deaf individuals. One man who supported Rogers in her efforts was Alexander Graham Bell, who not only lent his knowledge of phonetics to the school as an instructor for a short time but also married Hubbard's daughter.

Eager to expand her knowledge of teaching methods, Rogers journeyed to Europe, where she studied methods then in use in German schools in 1871–1872. Upon her return, she continued to run Clarke, assisted in this task after 1873 by Caroline A. Yale, who served as associate principal. With the passing of time, schools using the "oral" method multiplied, and many older institutions adopted the "combined system," which utilized vocal communication in the classroom but reverted to sign language in other situations.

Although poor health forced Rogers to relinquish her position in 1884, her methods were vindicated when the 1886 convention of the American Instructors of the Deaf issued a statement urging every school for the deaf to include her methods in the instruction of every student. In that same year Rogers formally resigned her post, having in the meantime relocated to Colorado for relief from chronic bronchial problems. She then returned to North Billerica and assumed the management of the local kindergarten. Never married, she died there following a long illness.

Rogers was important for starting the first oralist school in the United States, and her success undoubtedly led to the increasing popularity of oralism during her time. In many ways she typified the experience of many nineteenth-century educational reformers. Lacking extensive formal training in their fields, these pioneers nevertheless made substantial contributions to the development of modern educational theory and practice.

• The papers of Rogers are at the Clarke School for the Deaf, Northampton, Mass. Sources of information on her life and career include an autobiographical article, "Reminiscences of Early Days of Speech Training," in *Clarke School and Its Graduates* (1918), and Caroline A. Yale, *Years of Building* (1931). An obituary written by Yale appears in *Volta Review* (July 1920).

EDWARD L. LACH, JR.

ROGERS, Henry Darwin (1 Aug. 1808–29 May 1866), geologist, was born in Philadelphia, Pennsylvania, the son of Patrick Kerr Rogers and Hannah Blythe, Irish immigrants. His father had earned an M.D. after coming to Philadelphia but was unable to establish a practice that would support his family. In 1813 he moved his family to Baltimore, and then in 1819 they moved to Williamsburg, Virginia, when he accepted a teaching position in mathematics, natural philosophy, and chemistry at the College of William and Mary. Henry Rogers's education was provided primarily by his father, and he was well schooled in the sciences, especially chemistry and mathematics; he attended William and Mary briefly around 1825.

In 1825 Henry and his brother William Barton Rogers, who later founded the Massachusetts Institute of Technology, opened a high school in Windsor, Maryland, and in 1928 William opened a high school at the Maryland Institute in Baltimore. After the Windsor school closed in 1928, Henry taught at the Baltimore school. The school closed in the spring of 1829, and that winter Henry Rogers joined the faculty of Dickinson College in Carlisle, Pennsylvania, where he taught chemistry, mathematics, natural philosophy (physics), and some natural history. However, a deep interest in educational reform, particularly the ideas of Johann Heinrich Pestalozzi, led to his dismissal in 1831.

Rogers wanted education to be experiential and directed toward some practical end with less emphasis placed on teaching classical languages and ancient history. His interest in educational reform and a belief that knowledge of the practical importance of science could better the lot of humankind led him to join the followers of the Scottish social reformer Robert Owen in New York. He began lecturing and writing for the Owenites, and in 1832 he went to England, at the urging of the Owenites, to broaden his knowledge of the sciences. He studied geology while there, and by the time he returned to the United States in 1833 he had decided on a career in geology.

After returning he began to explore the geology of the eastern United States and arranged to teach a course on geology at the University of Pennsylvania in 1834. In 1835 he was appointed professor of geology and mineralogy. He was attracted to geological surveys and in 1835 was appointed director of the first state geological survey of New Jersey. The following year he also became the director of the first Pennsylvania state survey. The New Jersey survey was completed in 1836 and 1837, although the final report was not published until 1840. The Pennsylvania survey was expected to be completed by 1843; however, difficulties in assembling the materials and in securing funding postponed its publication. The survey was reopened in 1851, and the final report was published in 1858. The report was issued in Great Britain and in the United States.

Rogers's observations on the geology of Pennsylvania and New Jersey had no parallels at the time. He described the geological features and structure of the states in detail, and he unscrambled the Paleozoic sequence of rocks in the Appalachian Mountains. He recognized that layers of rock can be inverted in their order because of the severity of the folding found in mountainous areas and that even though formations like coal appear in isolated centers, they once were part of continuous deposits covering the area.

Rogers developed a theory of mountain elevation in 1837. It was first presented publicly with his brother William, who was the director of the Virginia Geological Survey, in 1842. The catastrophic theory argued that rocks were folded when molten material below the earth's crust was set in a wavelike motion by a sudden release of pressure. Although the brothers believed their observations of the geology of the Appalachians supported the theory, it was not successful. Rogers and his brother also worked out an elaborate nomenclature for Paleozoic rocks based on words signifying the passing stages of a day to indicate the passing of geologic time. Thus his nomenclature included *primal* (meaning early day or early history of the earth), *levant* (rising day), *meridian* (noon), and *cadent* (waning day), but it too was unsuccessful.

Between 1843 and 1851 Rogers received no salary from the state of Pennsylvania, although he continued to work on the preparation of the final report. Hailed as a brilliant lecturer, he supported himself, in part, by giving lectures. In 1845 he started to work as a consultant in geology, often doing surveys for mining companies. This developed into a regular source of income, and he was well known for his work as a consultant for developers in Pennsylvania's coal regions.

In 1845 Rogers had moved to Boston, but while in Scotland attending to the publication of his final report on the geology of Pennsylvania, he decided that he wanted to remain there. He sought a teaching position and in 1857 was appointed Regius Professor of Natural History at the University of Glasgow. He remained in Glasgow until his death. Rogers had married Elizabeth Stillman Lincoln in 1854. They had two children. Although Rogers considered his theory of elevation and his nomenclature to be his most significant achievements, his observations on geologic structure, particularly on the inverted order of rocks, represent his most lasting contribution.

• The principal sources of letters are the Rogers family papers at the Massachusetts Institute of Technology and Emma Rogers, ed., *Life and Letters of William Barton Rogers* (2 vols., 1896). Rogers's final reports of the New Jersey and Pennsylvania surveys are *The Geology of Pennsylvania. A Government Survey* (1858) and *Description of the Geology of the State of New Jersey. Being a Final Report* (1840). The theory of elevation was first published as "On the Physical Structure of the Appalachian Chain, as Exemplifying the Laws Which Have Regulated the Elevation of Great Mountain Chains, Generally," in *Reports of the First, Second, and Third Meetings of the Association of American Geologists and Naturalists at Philadelphia in 1840 and 1841, and at Boston in 1842* (1843). There are two published biographical studies: J. W. Gregory, *Henry Darwin Rogers, an Address to the Glasgow University Geological Society, 20th January, 1916* (1916), and Patsy Gerstner, *Henry Darwin Rogers, 1808–1866: American Geologist* (1994).

PATSY GERSTNER

ROGERS, Henry Huttleston (29 Jan. 1840–19 May 1909), oil tycoon, railroad builder, and capitalist, was born at Fairhaven, Massachusetts, the son of Rowland Rogers, a bookkeeper, and Mary Eldredge Huttleston. A high school graduate, Rogers worked in his hometown five years before leaving in 1861 for Pennsylvania, where oil had been discovered in 1859. Beginning with a $1,200 investment in a small refinery erected at McClintockville, Pennsylvania, Rogers and a partner, Charles Ellis, made $30,000 their first year. In 1866 Rogers met Charles M. Pratt, famous for his "Astral" high-quality illuminating oil. Because of a drop in the price of crude, however, the partners went into debt to Pratt, who had been buying the entire output of their refinery. In taking responsibility for the debt, Rogers so impressed Pratt that he became, in the words of Elbert Hubbard, Pratt's "hands and feet and eyes and ears" (*Little Journeys to the Homes*, 1909).

Now in partnership with Pratt, after selling out to Standard Oil in 1874, Rogers's astute next move was to get for himself and Pratt high positions within Standard, which by 1878 controlled 95 percent of oil production and distribution in the United States. Paradoxically, two years before the sellout, representing New York refiners, Rogers had been among the most vocal objectors to Standard Oil's conspiracy to drive independent oil producers out of business through secret railroad rate rebates to the rigged South Improvement Company. Negotiations preceding Rogers's and Pratt's merger gained Rogers a substantial block of Standard Oil stock and a directorship. Subsequently, Rogers served as chairman of the company's manufacturing committee and was a vice president by 1890.

Because of Rogers's reputation for aggressiveness, his critics would easily believe a charge that he was guilty of sabotage on behalf of Standard Oil in a case involving Vacuum Oil of Rochester, New York. In 1880, after Standard Oil gained control of Vacuum, two men left the company to pursue a refining process that Rogers believed belonged to Vacuum. Rogers's anger over the alleged patent infringement and consequent personal threats led to his later implication in a fire and explosion at the independent's refinery. In a subsequent controversial lawsuit—*Buffalo Oil Company v. Vacuum Oil Company*—Rogers and John Archbold were acquitted of conspiracy charges despite the direct involvement of a former employee of Vacuum's in conditions that led to the explosion. Rogers's business style, which earned him the sobriquet "hell hound," extended to his testimony under oath. Before the Hepburn Commission of 1878, investigating railroads of New York, he fine-tuned his circumlocutory, ambiguous, and haughty responses. His most intractable performance was later in a 1906 lawsuit by the state of Missouri, which claimed that two companies in that state registered as independents were actually subsidiaries of Standard Oil, a secret ownership Rogers finally acknowledged.

When it became clear that John D. Rockefeller favored Archbold as his successor, Rogers went his own way and headed a group within Standard Oil's top management that engaged in takeovers, speculations, and deals far beyond the company's interests. In the Marquis *Who's Who* for 1908, Rogers listed more than twenty corporations of which he was either president and director or vice president and director, and he secretly managed other enterprises, principally in mining and transportation. Although Rogers achieved no particular distinction in management or production, he did militantly push the expansion of his enterprises—Standard Oil included—to gain a personal fortune of more than $100 million.

Rogers knew the value of favorable public relations, and at the same time he was quite adept at working secretly to effect his ends. Muckrakers therefore could find little in Rogers to excoriate. But in *Frenzied Finance* (1905), first serialized in *Everybody's*, Thomas W. Lawson, one of Rogers's peers in finance, attempted to expose him. Lawson's subjectivity—especially his rambling style and self-aggrandizing persona—makes him an unreliable reporter of all that was amiss in Rogers's organizing of Amalgamated Copper (1889) and Consolidated Gas (1884), holding companies aimed at controlling copper and gas production and distribution. Nevertheless, Lawson's negotiations with Rogers, as Lawson records them, were unethical enough to have gotten them both indicted for insider trading and stock watering had there been, at the turn of the century, a Securities and Exchange Commission to expose fraudulent and unfair practices in the sale of stocks and bonds. Ida M. Tarbell, a respected *McClure's* staffer, let Rogers off rather easily in her *History of the Standard Oil Company* (1904), probably because Rogers had opened the corporation's files to her.

Rogers died in New York shortly after completing the Virginian Railway, a project in which his flair for gambling backfired. Rogers thought he could sell off the Deepwater Railway, a coal- and timber-hauling short line, by the same tactic he had employed successfully while president of the Ohio River Railroad. His strategy was to threaten to expand his road into coal fields considered future reserves by a competing railroad to force the larger road to buy him out. After the announced expansion of the Deepwater, neither threatened road would purchase it because, unknown to Rogers, both roads had signed a secret "community of interest" pact that prevented him from playing one against the other. Rogers, angered by their refusals, expanded the newly named Virginian to Tidewater to flaunt them both. In the panic of 1907, unable to obtain adequate financing, Rogers spent $40 million of his own funds to complete the road, which, although profitable until its merger with Norfolk and Western in 1959, was nevertheless an "investment disproportionate to the needs" (William Z. Ripley, *Railroads: Finance and Organization* [1915]).

A strange dualism characterized Rogers. Pitiless in business deals, in his personal affairs he was warm and generous, and at sixty, according to Tarbell, "by all odds, the handsomest and most distinguished figure in Wall Street" (Dias, *Henry Huttleston Rogers*). In 1862 he had married his hometown sweetheart Abbie Pal-

mer Gifford, with whom he had four children. Two years after her death in 1894, he had married Emelie Augusta Randel Hart, a New York socialite; they had no children together. Rogers aided financially both Booker T. Washington and Helen Keller and from 1893 to his death was a close friend of Mark Twain. Besides exchanging extensive correspondence, he and Twain were seen together on the streets of New York, at its theaters, and on trips aboard Rogers's yacht, the *Kanawha*. And as Twain's trusted business adviser, Rogers rescued the writer from near financial disaster in 1894.

Rogers delighted in outwitting his contemporaries and in exercising power that comes from great wealth. However, he flourished just as the Gilded Age was giving way to the Progressive Era, and therefore his drive to power was frustrated by reforms and changes to more acceptable management styles that the twentieth century was ushering in.

• Although his family reportedly has either destroyed or has not released Rogers's business papers, his personal papers—including family correspondence, diaries, journals, and memorabilia—are in the Millicent Library, Fairhaven, Mass. Illuminating a friendship that warmed Twain's later years are the 464 letters in *Mark Twain's Correspondence with Henry Huttleston Rogers, 1893–1909*, ed. Lewis Leary (1969). The only biography is Earl J. Dias, *Henry Huttleston Rogers: Portrait of a "Capitalist"* (1974). Rogers's relationships with John D. Rockefeller are briefly covered in Allan Nevins, *Study in Power: John D. Rockefeller, Industrialist and Philanthropist* (2 vols., 1953). A quaintly genteel account is Elbert Hubbard, *Little Journeys to the Homes of Great Businessmen*, vol. 25 (1909). Thomas W. Lawson, Wall Street broker and investor, "exposes" Rogers in *Frenzied Finance*, vol. 1, *The Crime of Amalgamated* (1906); there was no second volume. Stewart H. Holbrook, *Age of the Moguls* (1953), untangles Lawson's dealings with Rogers. And Ida Minerva Tarbell lightly touches on Rogers in *The History of the Standard Oil Company* (2 vols., 1904). Essential for Rogers's motives in completing the Virginian Railway are Joseph T. Lambie, *From Mine to Market: The History of Coal Transportation on the Norfolk and Western Railway* (1954), and the memoirs of a West Virginia governor and attorney, William A. McCorkle, *Recollections of Fifty Years of West Virginia* (1928). A moralistic obituary is in the *Nation*, 27 May 1909.

EUGENE L. HUDDLESTON

ROGERS, Isaiah (17 Aug. 1800–13 Apr. 1869), architect, was born in Marshfield, Massachusetts, the son of Isaac Rogers, a farmer and shipwright, and Hannah Ford. In 1817, encouraged by Edward Preble Little, a locally prominent kinsman by marriage, Rogers left the family farm and apprenticed himself to Boston housewright Jesse Shaw. From 1822 until 1825 Rogers assisted his second mentor, Solomon Willard, as he learned the art of architecture. Later, during the 1830s and 1840s, Rogers was involved with Willard in the granite business in Quincy. In 1822 Rogers successfully competed for the Mobile (Ala.) Theatre (erected 1824; burned 1829). The following year he married Emily Wesley Tobey of Portland, Maine. The couple had eight children, only four of whom survived infancy. In establishing himself independently in 1825, Rogers listed himself as "Architect," not as "Builder." Initially his Boston practice was devoted primarily to standard rowhouse design and commercial buildings, including those along the city's merchants' row.

In 1826, the year Rogers became a Mason, he won the competition to design the Augusta, Georgia, Masonic Hall (demolished 1888), locally misattributed to the builders John Crane and William Thompson. The front, minus the first story of shops, resembled Rogers's Tremont Theatre in Boston (1827; burned 1852), a design that critic H. R. Cleveland, Jr., writing in the *North American Review*, later described as "the most perfect piece of architecture in Boston . . . uncommonly chaste and dignified." The success of the beautiful Tremont Theatre brought Rogers the patronage of leading Bostonians, including the William Havard Eliot and Robert Bennet Forbes families and the Merchant Prince Thomas Handasyd Perkins, promoters of a hotel to replace architect Asher Benjamin's Exchange Coffee House, which had burned in 1818. Rogers's Tremont House (1828–1829; demolished 1895) has long been regarded as the pioneer among first-class luxury hotels. Behind its dignified granite front lay amenities that until then had not been available to most travelers. The ingenious plan masked an irregular site and provided elegant public spaces as well as ample bathing facilities. The lavishly illustrated *A Description of Tremont House* (1830), published anonymously by Rogers's friend and patron Eliot, established Rogers as a nationally noted architect.

Rogers practiced in Boston until 1834 and took Richard Bond as his partner in 1833–1834. During that first Boston period Rogers designed two Greek Revival churches, Pine Street (1827) and the First Methodist Church (1828), followed by the Lowell Town Hall (1829–1830). In 1830 Rogers revised the Old State House in Boston for use as city hall and added two fireproof rooms to the Bulfinch State House. All of Rogers's work had been in the Greek Revival manner until his Boston Masonic Temple (1830–1832), which demonstrated his naive unfamiliarity with the Gothic style. His "Carpenter Gothic" First Parish Church in Cambridge (1833) and his granite St. Peter's Church in Salem (1833–1834) were more successful; both still stand but in altered states. His Nahant Church (1832) marked a return to Greek Revival. His handsome Greek Revival granite Suffolk Bank (1833–1836) graced State Street in Boston until its demolition in 1900, and his still-extant but much-altered Bangor House (1833–1834), built in Bangor, Maine, was a smaller, brick version of the Tremont House; its plan, a mirror image of the Boston hostelry. Both the Joseph Andrews house in Lancaster, Massachusetts (1831), and the home he designed for Forbes in Milton, Massachusetts (1833–1834; altered by Peabody and Stearns in 1872–1873), are rare, extant examples of Rogers's Greek Revival residential work.

In 1834 Rogers went to New York City to design the Astor House, a majestic Greek Revival granite block situated on lower Broadway. Completed in 1836 and

demolished in 1913, for a generation it was the city's leading hotel, containing such novel amenities as central heating and running water on all five floors. On 6 December 1836 Rogers became a founding member of the short-lived American Institution of Architects, the first organized group that sought to attain recognition of architecture as a profession. His Bank of America, a granite *distyle in antis* composition, was built on Wall Street in 1835 and demolished in 1889; its two colossal monolithic columns still exist but have since been transported to a park in Methuen, Massachusetts. The Merchants' Bank on Wall Street, similar to the Bank of America, was completed in 1840 and survived until 1887. Two other long-vanished Wall Street banks that Rogers designed, the United States Bank (1838–1839) and the City Bank (1839), had less-impressive, three-story fronts.

The New York Merchants' Exchange, built at Wall and William streets between 1836 and 1842, was Rogers's structural masterpiece. Fronted by a colonnade of twelve immense Ionic granite monoliths plus six more within the entrance bays, the magnificent edifice contained a marble rotunda eighty feet in diameter vaulted by a brick dome larger than any other then in America. The splendid exterior still exists, but the interior was gutted in 1907 by the partnership of McKim, Mead and White, whose National City Bank added four stories atop Rogers's colonnade. The colonnade and rotunda combination may have been inspired by German architect Karl Friedrich Schinkel's Altes Museum in Berlin. Rogers contributed one other notable building to New York City over the six years he was based there, the Middle Collegiate Dutch Reformed Church (1837–1839; razed in 1887). A granite building with a monolithic Ionic portico, the church had a spire that resembled the one on British architect John Nash's All Souls, Langham Place, in London. Rogers's Exchange Hotel in Richmond, Virginia (1840–1841; razed 1900) had a tetrastyle engaged Ionic center flanked by curved bays (an elegant facade).

By 1840 Rogers had returned to Boston, where he essayed the ancient Egyptian style for his Old Granary Burying Ground Gate and Fence. The following year he used an almost identical design for his Jew's Cemetery Gate in Newport, Rhode Island. Rogers's Boston Merchants' Exchange (1841–1842; razed 1889) contained even more massive Quincy granite monoliths than did the New York Merchants' Exchange. The 45-feet-high pilasters and antae of the pedimented front weighed up to sixty tons apiece, and the central domed reading room (80 feet long) had Corinthian columns that stood twenty feet tall. All construction was fireproof, including the iron roof. Rogers's Brazer's Building (1842; razed c. 1890) was outstanding for its unornamented bowed front of trabeated granite. "Elmwood," Rogers's Enoch Reddington Mudge House (1843–1844; razed 1954) in Swampscott, Massachusetts, was a Gothic mansion that was one of the most impressive New England estates of its day, its granite walls laid in a unique pattern of upended lozenges. Willard paid Rogers for his plans but took charge of construction of the granite, Greek Revival Quincy Town Hall (1844–1845; extant). The plain brick Boston Female Orphan Asylum (1844–1845; demolished), a project dear to Rogers because of his four deceased children, was noteworthy for its fireproof construction. The Harvard Astronomical Observatory (partially extant) followed in 1844–1845.

By the mid-1840s his diary entries show that Rogers was suffering some hearing loss, which resulted in frequent confusion over proper names and in misunderstandings that affected his practice until his son clarified matters for him. His Howard Athenaeum in Boston (1846; razed 1962) had an unusual Gothic granite front. The theater also introduced a sloping parquet instead of a flat pit. After competing for the Smithsonian Institution project awarded to James Renwick in 1846, Rogers was awarded $250 for his design, which combined Romanesque and Gothic elements. He then returned to New York to supervise his Astor Place Opera House (1847; razed c. 1890).

In 1848 Rogers went to Cincinnati to design and supervise construction of the Burnet House, a major hotel. Completed in 1850, the building, which had a five-part Italianate front crowned with a dome, was razed in 1927. Rogers's house for George Hatch on Dayton Street in Cincinnati (1850–1851; extant) was only moderately altered throughout the twentieth century. St. John's Church (1849–1852), notable for its concentric-arched entrance bay and towers placed at 45-degree angles to the front plane, and the Tyler Davidson Store (1849–1850, both demolished) were early Rogers additions to Cincinnati. The Phillips House (1850–1852; razed 1926) in Dayton, Ohio, was another of his Italianate hotels. It was followed by the Battle House (1851–1852; burned 1905) in Mobile, Alabama, and the Capital Hotel (1852–1853; burned 1917) in Frankfort, Kentucky. In 1851 James Gallier's St. Charles Hotel in New Orleans, Louisiana, burned, and Rogers provided plans for which he was paid after an on-site consultation, although George Purvis carried out the rebuilding. In 1853–1854 Rogers designed "Hillforest," the home of Thomas Gaff at Aurora, Indiana. The Italianate estate, now a museum, is the only perfectly preserved and virtually unaltered example of Rogers's still-extant domestic work.

In 1853 Rogers took Henry Whitestone into a partnership that ended in 1857. Rogers's firstborn son, Solomon Willard Rogers—his name attesting to the bond between Rogers and Willard—became his partner on 14 February 1855, having assisted him since 1848. The firm maintained offices both in Cincinnati and in Louisville, Kentucky. The second Galt House (1853; burned and replaced c. 1870), the Newcomb Building (1854), the Fifth Ward School (1855; extant), the W. B. Reynolds Store (1855–1856), and the Louisville Hotel (1855–1856) were among the firm's Louisville works. During this same period, Rogers was the designing partner for the Robert B. Bowler house and the Gothic Reuben Resor house (extant), both in Cincinnati. The Metropolitan Hall in Chicago (1854; burned 1871) also appears to have been entirely by

Rogers, as was the Commercial Bank of Kentucky in Paducah (1855–1856; burned 1863), notable for its Corinthian front of terracotta, a remarkably early extensive use of that material. Longview State Hospital (1856–1860), a vast insane asylum near Cincinnati, was designed by both father and son. Its domed entrance rotunda was a particularly handsome feature. The Rogers firm also designed the Oliver House hotel in Toledo, Ohio (1859). The Italianate exterior remains, but the interior was gutted in 1920 to make room for a warehouse. Rogers also produced plans for the Maxwell House in Nashville, Tennessee; construction began in 1859 but the Civil War intervened. The hotel was finished in 1869 without Rogers's supervision, although his plans were followed. Rogers and son took Alfred Bult Mullett as a junior partner during 1859–1860. Until the outbreak of war in 1861, the firm was occupied with the Hamilton County Jail (1860–1861; razed 1884) in Cincinnati and the completion of the state capitol in Columbus (1858–1860).

On 23 July 1862 President Abraham Lincoln appointed Rogers to head the U.S. Treasury Department's Bureau of Construction. He moved to Washington, D.C., where he built the department's west wing (1862–1865). At least one example of his patented "burglar-proof" safe was manufactured and now remains in the U.S. Treasury building. On 30 June 1863 Rogers was made supervising architect of the Treasury Department, a post he resigned on 30 September 1865. Mullett, who had written letters to the secretary of the treasury against Rogers's work, succeeded to his post in 1866. Mullett's official reports positively seethe with sarcasm when discussing Rogers's work.

By 1865 Rogers's health had declined. Pike's Opera House in Cincinnati (1866; burned 1903) and the Lagonda House hotel in Springfield, Ohio (1869; burned 1895) were among the ailing architect's last works. Rogers had patented a metal spiral "cylinder" bridge in 1841 and other bridges in 1856 and 1862, but none was built. By the summer of 1867 Rogers was happily estivating at Marshfield in the old family homestead built in 1720 (which he had modernized in 1842). He died two summers later at his home in Cincinnati.

Although he was a farm lad with little formal schooling, Rogers had an innate, extraordinary talent that enabled him to become one of the few leading and prolific American architects of his generation. His diaries reveal him to have been a creative, industrious, honorable, kindly, and engaging man. Although he is remembered primarily as the architect of famous hotels, his banks too, as well as his exchanges and certain of his churches and residences, rank among the best of their time.

• Rogers's manuscript diaries (1838–1856, 1861, and 1867) are in the Avery Architectural Library, Columbia University, New York. Also see Denys Peter Myers, "The Recently Discovered Diaries of Isaiah Rogers," *Columbia Library Columns* 16 (1966): 25–31, and William W. Wheildon, *Memoir of Solomon Willard* (1865). For additional biographical information see *Biographical Encyclopaedia of Ohio of the Nineteenth Century* (1876), and Josiah H. Drummond, *John Rogers of Marshfield and Some of His Descendants* (1898). For his professional impact see Talbot Hamlin, *Greek Revival Architecture in America* (1944; repr. 1964); H. -R. Hitchcock, *Architecture: Nineteenth and Twentieth Centuries* (1963; repr. 1977); and Walter H. Kilham, Jr., *Boston after Bulfinch: An Account of Its Architecture, 1800–1900* (1946). Also see Cynthia Hagar Krussell and Betty Magoun Bates, *Marshfield: A Town of Villages 1640–1990* (1990).

DENYS PETER MYERS

ROGERS, James Gamble (3 Mar. 1867–1 Oct. 1947), architect, was born in Bryant's Station, Kentucky, the son of Joseph Martin Rogers, a lawyer and insurance broker, and Katherine Gamble. The Rogers family moved to Chicago some time during James's infancy. There, he grew up in the Buena Park subdivision on the North Side of Chicago. While his father sold insurance, Rogers made many contacts with the families of fellow Kentucky émigrés and local architects. One of the latter, William Bryce Mundie, gave him his first job in architecture, and other neighbors, the Wallers, gave him several important early commissions. Rogers attended the local high school and entered Yale College on a scholarship in the class of 1889. Though he did not excel academically, he became noted for his wit and sociability. Upon receiving his bachelor's degree, he returned home to Chicago and worked as a draftsman in the firm of William LeBaron Jenney (later Jenney & Mundie) until 1891, when he joined the firm of Burnham & Root. The following year he opened his own practice, probably after obtaining the commission to design the twelve-story Lees Building in Chicago's Downtown Loop district. Despite such rapid success, Rogers left Chicago in 1892 to study architecture at the École des Beaux-Arts in Paris. There, like numerous other American students at the École, he worked in the studio of Scelliers de Gisors until he received his diploma, along with awards in both design and construction, in 1898.

Again returning to Chicago, Rogers quickly established himself as a society architect, designing a house for the prominent doctor George Isham (1900). This commission was followed by houses for local businessmen H. S. Robbins (1902), Arthur Farwell (1902), Albert M. Day (1902), and A. B. Dick (1903) in Lake Forest as well as several other residential commissions in town. In 1901 Rogers married Anne Tift Day, daughter of Albert Morgan Day, the second president of the Chicago stock exchange. Rogers and Day had four children. Through his marriage, Rogers became related to the powerful Farwell and McCormick families, for whom he designed several houses on adjacent lots between 1902 and 1907. Rogers's brother-in-law, John V. Farwell III, later became chairman of the building committee of the Yale Corporation, in which position he was instrumental in obtaining commissions for Rogers. Rogers also continued to benefit from connections he had made in the neighborhood in which he grew up, designing an apartment building for James B. Waller and several small subdivisions near his former home.

In 1899 he received his first institutional commission, a school founded by Anita McCormick Blaine and headed by educational reformer Colonel Francis Wayland Parker. When the project was split into two, a school of education at the University of Chicago and the Francis W. Parker School on Chicago's North Side, Rogers designed both projects. The former was his first essay in the neo-Gothic, a style for which he was to become famous. It also brought him into contact with the philosopher and education specialist John Dewey and the pragmatist movement. Founded by William James, this school rejected then-prevalent German idealism as well as epistemology, preferring to focus on knowledge gained from direct experience. Dewey and his followers had a profound impact on the development of both liberal politics and institutions of higher learning in the United States. They created an ideology for the new wealth gained in the Midwest and for the American experience in general. Rogers was later to work for several of Dewey's pupils, including the presidents of Yale and Northwestern Universities, and his architecture represented their philosophy at the same time it housed their institutions.

Throughout the early years of the twentieth century, Rogers sought to expand his practice, entering competitions for large civic projects and associating himself in 1905 with New York architect Herbert D. Hale. In 1904 he was given the commission to design the Shelby County Courthouse in Memphis, Tennessee. In response, he designed a neoclassical envelope housing a southern veranda and a brick-lined court. This project was soon followed by the New Orleans Courthouse and Post Office (1909–1911) and the New Haven Courthouse and Post Office (1913–1917). Both projects sheltered their split programs behind neoclassical fronts but lacked the grand central spaces and formal axes usually associated with such a style of building. Rogers spent more and more time working out of New York and moved there in 1905. The partnership of Hale & Rogers, which handled most of this large institutional work, dissolved at the death of Hale in 1908. Rogers continued to seek institutional and commercial work, but during the 1910s he remained confined to residential commissions for wealthy clients.

In 1917 Rogers received his largest commission, the design of the Harkness Memorial Quadrangle at Yale University. Rogers had designed the New York home for the donor of this project, Edward S. Harkness, in 1908. He had also designed a Yale-affiliated hospital paid for by Harkness in China in 1915 and the Yale Club in 1915, as well as a small Yale boathouse in 1914, but the Quadrangle was by far his largest and most expensive design. Rogers assembled a team of seasoned neo-Gothicists to create a lavish world of courtyards, turrets, and a central clock tower, all built out of carefully chosen stone and covered with an elaborate iconography of carved figures and inscriptions. The sensuality of the material, the sophistication of the composition, and the efficiency of the design established Rogers's reputation.

Shortly after the completion of the Quadrangle in 1921, Rogers became the consulting architect to Yale University, the first of a series of positions from which he guided the phenomenal growth of that school's campus during the 1920s. Fueled both by a large bequest from lawyer John William Sterling and by continuous donations from Edward S. Harkness, Yale transformed itself into one of the most coherent neo-Gothic campuses in America. Rogers himself designed the academic core of Yale, consisting of the Sterling Memorial Library (1930), the Law School (1931), and the Hall of Graduate Studies (1932). He also devised, with the help of Harkness and several old friends, a scheme adopted in 1929 to split Yale College into a series of residential colleges; he then designed eight of these structures between 1932 and 1934. The buildings were almost all designed using the same stone and brick, and they exhibit a refinement of the combination of the episodic application of medieval detailing, picturesque building masses, and efficient functional arrangements that Rogers had developed for the Harkness Memorial Quadrangle. Eschewing monumental progressions, Rogers built up a rambling Oxford- or Cambridge-like village whose diverse purposes were united by an architecture meant to express the sophistication, historical awareness, and sense of community on which Yale prided itself. Working in both the neo-Gothic and a neo-Georgian variant that used much of the same massing, but with different details, Rogers created a nearly seamless image of collegiate fortresses of learning surrounding courtyards of cultural self-affirmation.

Rogers's work for Yale led to more commissions, making him one of the most visible designers of educational institutions in this country. In addition to his early designs for Sophie Newcomb College in New Orleans (1911–1919) and his neo-Georgian Southern Baptist Seminary in Louisville (1925–1928), Rogers also designed buildings for New York University (School of Education, 1930), Columbia University (Butler Library, 1934), Colgate-Rochester Divinity School (1932), Atlanta College (1933), the Taft School (1929), and St. Paul's School (New Schoolhouse, 1937). His largest educational commission outside of New Haven came in the form of the design of the downtown Chicago campus of Northwestern University (1923–1927). In addition, he designed a stadium (1927), a library (1931), a music school (1940), a social center (1939), and a series of women's dormitories (1923–1938) for the Evanston campus of Northwestern University. In many of these institutions he worked with educators who espoused pragmatist principles. Many of these buildings were also at least partially funded by Edward Harkness. One might say that Rogers's buildings represent the integration of midwestern wealth as an ideology into elite East Coast institutions. Rogers designed only a few residential commissions during this period, while the only major commercial structures he created were the Connecti-

cut General Life Insurance (1926) and Aetna Life Insurance Company (1931) buildings, both in Hartford.

In 1921, Edward Harkness asked Rogers to design the new Columbia-Presbyterian Medical Center in New York City. Rogers produced a series of soaring towers housing the various teaching, research, and hospital functions of the complex. This commission began a new line of work for Rogers. In addition to the Montgomery Ward Building at Northwestern's Chicago campus, Rogers also designed the New York Memorial Hospital for the Treatment of Cancer and Allied Diseases (now the Sloane-Kettering Cancer Clinic, 1937) and, starting in 1926, a series of rural medical centers for the Commonwealth Fund, the charitable organization set up by Edward Harkness to distribute his wealth. By the time Frank Rogers took over his father's firm after the Second World War, it had come to specialize in the design of medical buildings, a focus that remains the mainstay of a firm that is now known as Burgun, Shahide & Deschler. Rogers died in New York City.

James Gamble Rogers is not remembered as either a startling innovator or an idiosyncratic designer. He obtained most of his commissions through his friendships with a small group of wealthy individuals; gave the impression of wit, charm, and business acumen rather than of artistic brilliance; and ran an office capable of producing many complicated projects simultaneously. He created designs that combine a sensuous manipulation of material with an efficiency of form to create complex three-dimensional compositions that remain convincing to this date.

• The Manuscripts and Archives Collections of Sterling Memorial Library at Yale University contains the James Gamble Rogers Papers. In addition, the Architectural Collection at the same location is the repository of many of the drawings Rogers produced for Yale, and the papers of the Office of the Secretary contain correspondence that traces the design process in some detail. The University Archives at Northwestern University contain documentation on Rogers's work at that institution. The Chicago Historical Society is the source of most information on Rogers's early work and family life. Other material is dispersed among the various institutions for which Rogers worked. The only substantial published works on Rogers are Patricia D. Pierce, *Sparing No Detail: The Drawings of James Gamble Rogers for Yale University, 1913–1935* (1982), and Susan Ryan, "The Architecture of James Gamble Rogers at Yale University," *Perspecta* 18 (1982): 24–41.

AARON BETSKY

ROGERS, James Harvey (25 Sept. 1886–13 Aug. 1939), economist, was born in Society Hill, South Carolina, the son of John Terrel Rogers and Florence Coker, farmers. The family had banking connections and operated several hundred acres of farmland, and in later years the son referred to himself as a cotton farmer. After receiving a B.S. and an M.A. from the University of South Carolina in 1906 and 1907, Rogers matriculated as an undergraduate once again at Yale and obtained his bachelor's degree in 1909. At both institutions he specialized in mathematics. Additional graduate studies under Alvin Johnson at the University of Chicago resulted in Rogers's decision to combine his interest in math with economics. He returned to Yale, where he received an M.A. in math and economics jointly in 1913. He then went on to write a doctoral thesis on "Some Theories on the Incidence of Taxation" (1916).

While working on his doctorate, Rogers became deeply interested in sociology. Having been awarded Yale's traveling Cyler Fellowship in economics in 1914, he went to the University of Geneva to study with Vilfredo Pareto. Although Pareto was the leading mathematical economist of his day, he had retired from formal teaching and, like Rogers, had developed an interest in sociology. He welcomed the young American to his home, and during a ten-month period the two discussed Pareto's manuscript on general sociology. Rogers later arranged for and supervised its translation, which appeared in 1935 as *The Mind and Society*.

Rogers accepted his first position as an instructor in economics at the University of Missouri in 1916. He was promoted to associate professor in 1919. The following year he moved on to Cornell University, and after three years there as an assistant professor (1920–1923), he returned to Missouri as professor of economics (1923–1930). In 1930 he became professor of political economy at Yale and in 1931 was promoted to a Sterling professorship and made a fellow in Pierson College. Rogers also served five times (1926–1935) as lecturer at the Geneva School of International Studies.

While Rogers enjoyed a long and distinguished academic career, he also had a keen interest in government service. In 1917–1918 he had served as a statistician on the Council of National Defense and in 1918–1919 as a first lieutenant in the U.S. Army. From 1933 to 1937 he was a member of the League of Nations' Economic Committee. In addition, in 1934 he was a special representative of the U.S. Treasury in China, Japan, and India.

Service as one of President Franklin Roosevelt's monetary advisers during the first administration gave Rogers an opportunity to exert a direct influence on public policy during the early years of the Great Depression. A supporter, although not an uncritical one, of Irving Fisher's views on the close linkage between the quantity of money and prices, Rogers recommended a moderate policy of "controlled inflation" to encourage investment. Businesses would presumably have an incentive to invest at a relatively low price level so that they might profit from sales at the inflated level. In 1931 Rogers produced a bestseller, *America Weighs Her Gold*. Attacking a rigid adherence to the gold standard, the book treated the depression in terms of international economic relations. Excessive tariff barriers and intergovernmental debts had led to a concentration of gold in the United States and in France. Fearing inflation, however, the Federal Reserve Board had not permitted the inflowing gold to serve as the basis for an enlargement of credit by the nation's banks—an enlargement that would naturally be followed by price and currency expansion. Rogers urged the Federal Reserve to use its great open market powers, for example, the power to purchase government bonds. This would have the automatic effect of increasing the reserves of the member banks of the system, enabling them, in turn, to increase their loans to the business community. The resulting price and currency expansion would arrest the damaging price declines and the fall in spending and employment that followed. Unfortunately, the Federal Reserve did not respond adequately, and scholarly opinion holds that its failure to do so had much to do with the depth of the depressed economy of the 1930s. It should also be noted that Rogers suggested a huge public works program to put money in circulation.

Rogers never married. He died in a plane crash while engaged in private financial activity in Rio de Janeiro.

• Rogers's papers are at the Yale University Library. His other principal publications are *Stock Speculation and the Money Market* (1927), *The Process of Inflation in France* (1929), and *Capitalism in Crisis* (1938). For a sketch of Rogers's career, an evaluation of his economic ideas, and a list of his publications, see Joseph Dorfman, *The Economic Mind in American Civilization*, vol. 4 (1946). The standard critique of Federal Reserve policy at the onset of the Great Depression is in Milton Friedman and Anna J. Schwartz, *A Monetary History of the United States, 1867–1960* (1963). Rogers's experience as a statistician for the Council of National Defense is reflected in a monograph on the history of wartime prices that he prepared with the assistance of Grace M. Fairchild and Florence A. Dickinson, *Prices of Cotton and Cotton Products* (1919). He also wrote the section on foreign markets and foreign credits of the *Report on Recent Economic Changes* of the President's Conference on Unemployment (1929).

STUART BRUCHEY

ROGERS, John (1 Dec. 1648–17 Oct. 1721), founder of the Rogerenes, was born in Milford, Connecticut, the son of James Rogers, a miller and landowner, and Elizabeth Rowland. By the mid-1650s, the Rogers family had relocated to New London, where Rogers's father became one of the wealthiest men in the colony as well as a magistrate and town deputy to the Connecticut General Court. In 1670 Rogers married Elizabeth Griswold, the daughter of Matthew Griswold of Lyme and granddaughter of Henry Wolcott of Windsor, both prominent figures in Connecticut.

By 1674 Rogers and his wife had withdrawn from the New London Congregational church and had become members of a Baptist church in Newport, Rhode Island, after their study of scripture had convinced them that a number of Congregational beliefs and practices were nonbiblical. Within a short time, Rogers had converted his parents and several other members of his family and was presiding as pastor over his own New London Baptist church. His forceful and public propounding of his new views in favor of a seventh-day sabbath and against infant baptism and the authority and special regalia of Connecticut's ministers caused much upset in New London. One immediate result was the breakup of his own family as his wife, pressured by her family, left him, with their two children, and was granted a divorce on 12 October 1676. Subsequently, both children would return to their father and become Rogerenes.

Meanwhile, contact in 1675 with William Edmundson, an English Quaker, as well as his own study of the Bible, was leading Rogers and his small group of adherents to advance views with a decided Quaker flavor, such as pacifism, plain dress, a refusal to take oaths, and a discomfort with the pagan names for months and the days of the week. A sturdily independent-minded fellow, however, Rogers published thirteen pamphlets and books, in Boston and New York, including *An Epistle to the Church Called Quakers* (1705), which took issue with the Quakers for their stands against baptism by water and the Lord's Supper, even as he now embraced their designation of the first day of the week as the Lord's day instead of the seventh day, his earlier position. While the Rogerenes were sometimes referred to as Rogerene Quakers then, their theology was an admixture of traditional Christian, Baptist, and Quaker beliefs, all with a Rogers gloss. Never a very large group, some Rogerenes did establish communities in New Jersey in the mid-eighteenth century. In the following century, several Rogerene families moved west of the Mississippi River.

Rogers spent approximately one-third of his final forty-five years in prison in Connecticut and was fined often, usually because of his refusal to attend regular Sunday services and his insistence on plying his trades of shoemaker and shipbuilder on that day. Under Connecticut law, both of these actions were crimes. In one instance, he spent almost four years (1694–1698) in a Hartford jail and was whipped for reproaching Connecticut's ministers and then refusing to pay a fine or post a required bond not to disturb the colony's religious establishment. His particular nemesis was Gurdon Saltonstall, New London's Congregational minister (1687–1707) and later Connecticut's governor (1707–1724).

Years after his divorce, which he refused to recognize, contending it to be an illegitimate civil interference and groundless, in 1699 Rogers and Mary Ransford were married without any civil ceremony. The brief marriage was ended in 1703 when Mary Rogers gave in to pressure and the threat of a whipping to swear that Rogers was the father of their second child, an admission of their fornication in the eyes of the authorities. Fleeing to Block Island, Mary Rogers later married Robert Jones with Rogers's blessing, while Rogers married a Long Island Quaker, Sarah Coles, in 1714. Rogers died in New London from smallpox he had contracted in Boston. John Rogers, Jr., the son of John and Elizabeth Griswold Rogers, continued in his father's stead as leader of the Rogerenes until his own death in 1753. Small remnants of the group, principally in Connecticut, continued in existence into the early twentieth century.

While Rogers is not usually numbered in the company of such as Roger Williams, William Penn, and Lord Baltimore, he did play a lesser, but viable, role in the development of religious liberty and separation of church and state in the early American experience.

• Rogers's legal difficulties may be traced in the New London County Court records at the State Library, Hartford. A list of his writings and excerpts from several documents are included in the appendix of John R. Bolles and Anna B. Williams, *The Rogerenes: Some Hitherto Unpublished Annals Belonging to the Colonial History of Connecticut* (1904). A chapter of Frances M. Caulkins, *History of New London, Connecticut* (1852), deals with Rogers. See also John Rogers, 3d., *A Looking Glass for the Presbyterians of New London* (1767); James S. Rogers, *James Rogers of New London, Connecticut, and His Descendants* (1902); and two articles by Ellen Starr Brinton, "The Rogerene-Quakers," *The Friend* 113 (1939): 5–9, and "The Rogerenes," *New England Quarterly* 16 (1943): 3–19.

THOMAS W. JODZIEWICZ

ROGERS, John (30 Oct. 1829–26 July 1904), sculptor, was born in Salem, Massachusetts, the son of John Rogers, a graduate of Harvard College and a Boston merchant, and Sarah Ellen Derby. After attending high school in Boston, he worked briefly as a dry-goods clerk, studied engineering, and then served as surveyor for the Boston Water Works. Around 1849 he first took up modeling as a hobby. He learned the machinist's trade in a cotton mill in Manchester, New Hampshire, but then traveled to the Midwest to seek his fortune, working as superintendent of a railroad repair shop in Hannibal, Missouri, until the financial panic of 1857 left him without a job. Now with leisure time, he turned to modeling small, homey clay figures, which he exhibited at county fairs. From the beginning he preferred subjects taken from the everyday life he observed around him or scenes from the popular literature of the day, such as Charles Dickens's "Little Nell in the Curiosity Shop."

It is difficult to say precisely when Rogers began to think of turning to sculpture professionally, but in 1858 he left for Europe to study art. In Paris he was shown around by fellow New Englander Richard Greenough, who had already become a sculptor. Rogers studied for two months in the studio of the celebrated sculptor Jean Pierre Dantan, but he disapproved of both the French style of sculpture and of the practice of drawing endlessly from plaster casts of ancient statues. In December of that year he left for Rome, where he arranged to work in the studio of the English sculptor Benjamin Edward Spence. But Rogers rejected the rigid neoclassicism that prevailed there, preferring instead a simple, naturalistic style. In the spring of 1859 he returned to America.

Although Rogers took a job in Chicago in the city surveyor's office, the success of a small sculptured group at a charity bazaar led him to move to New York to become a sculptor. He took with him another piece, *The Slave Auction*, modeled in 1859, which reflected his own ardent abolitionist sympathies and which had broad appeal in the days preceding the outbreak of the

Civil War. From an Italian craftsman he learned how to make flexible molds that allowed him to reproduce his sculptures in plaster in considerable number, and he began selling them, first door-to-door, then through a shop he opened for the purpose. Three of his pieces were displayed at the National Academy of Design annual exhibition of 1860, and the acclaim he received established his reputation. Demand rose amid the upper middle-class for his plaster groups, painted gray in imitation of stone, to decorate its parlors. Here was an art for a democratic society that paralleled the popularity of Currier and Ives's lithographic prints. In 1865 Rogers married Harriet Moore Francis, daughter of Charles Stephen Francis of New York City. The couple had seven children. Their home was in New Canaan, Connecticut.

During the Civil War, Rogers produced several groups that glorified the Union cause, among them *The Picket Guard*, which he patented, mass-produced in his growing "factory," and sold for six dollars each. Even well after the war he continued to draw on its themes for some of his finest pieces, as in *The Council of War* (1868), with its excellent portraits of General Ulysses S. Grant, Secretary of War Edwin Stanton, and President Abraham Lincoln, or *The Fugitive's Story* (1869), depicting a young African-American mother telling her woeful tale of slavery to John Greenleaf Whittier, Henry Ward Beecher, and William Lloyd Garrison. Such groups averaged about twenty-four inches in height and could be purchased in general stores from New York to St. Louis or from an illustrated catalog that Rogers published. In 1863 Rogers was elected to the National Academy of Design, and at the great Centennial Exhibition at Philadelphia in 1876 he exhibited twenty-nine of his plaster groups.

Rogers's art reached the zenith of its popularity in the 1870s as he turned increasingly to ordinary scenes—that is, scenes of unremarkable people doing everyday things—often with a touch of good humor and wit but always with an underlying sentiment of the wholesomeness of American middle-class life. Among the most popular of these was *Coming to the Parson* (1870), which sold more than 8,000 copies at fifteen dollars each, and *Checkers Up at the Farm* (1877), the demand for which ran to over 5,000 replicas. Much of the appeal of these groups lay in the richness of homey anecdotal detail, which Rogers modeled with masterful exactitude. Late in the decade he began producing scenes from Shakespearean plays, while one of his last groups, *The Watch on the Santa Maria* (1892), was of the historical type, depicting a dramatic moment from Columbus's first voyage to the Americas.

In all, Rogers modeled and mass-produced more than seventy groups. An estimated 80,000 to 100,000 replicas were produced in his New York factory, where as many as sixty workers were employed. In addition, he modeled two life-size statues, which were cast in bronze—*General John Reynolds* (1884, Philadelphia) and *Abraham Lincoln* (1892, Manchester, N.H.). In 1893 a nervous affliction made it impossible for Rogers to continue sculpting, and he sold his business to his foreman. That same year, however, his work received a gold medal at the World's Columbian Exposition in Chicago. Rogers died in New Canaan.

Some contemporary sculptors and critics refused to admit that Rogers's groups were art at all, declaring that they were created for a mass audience that had no taste for high art. But "to the army of simple-minded admirers of 'Weighing the Baby' and 'Checkers on the Farm,'" wrote the sculptor Lorado Taft, "must be joined a smaller group of thoughtful men and women who see in Mr. Rogers's work something deeper than its indiscriminate realism and its misplaced attempts at humor. They find within its homely oddities a hint at an indigenous art, an art inspired by the life of our own time" (*The History of American Sculpture* [1903], p. 180). The most complete collections of his small plaster groups are found at the New-York Historical Society and the Essex Institute in Salem, Massachusetts. The appeal of Rogers's art was in its narrative reflection of a prospering, wholesome, good-natured America on the one hand, and in its strong appeal for social justice, from the abolitionist point of view, on the other.

• The largest collection of Rogers papers is at the New-York Historical Society. The most complete study of his life and work is David Wallace, *John Rogers, the People's Sculptor* (1967). A condensed assessment is available in Wayne Craven, *Sculpture in America* (1984), pp. 357–66. See also Wallace, "The Art of John Rogers: 'So Real and So True,'" *American Art Journal* 4 (1972): 59–70; D. C. Barck, "Rogers Groups in the New-York Historical Society," *New-York Historical Society Quarterly* 16 (1932): 67–87; and William Ordway Partridge, "John Rogers, the People's Sculptor," *New England Magazine*, n.s., 13 (1896): 705–21. Collectors should consult Paul Bleier, *John Rogers' Groups of Statuary: A Pictorial & Annotated Guide for the Collector* (1971); Vrest Orton, *The Famous Rogers Groups: A Complete Check-List and Collector's Manual* (1960); and Mr. and Mrs. Chetwood Smith, *Rogers Groups, Thought and Wrought by John Rogers* (1934). An obituary is in the *New York Times*, 27 July 1904.

WAYNE CRAVEN

ROGERS, John Almanza Rowley (12 Nov. 1828–22 July 1906), clergyman, missionary, and a cofounder of Berea College, was born of Puritan ancestry in Cornwall, Connecticut, the son of John Cornwall Rogers, a prominent farmer and landowner, and Elizabeth Hamlin. He attended Williams Academy in Stockbridge, Massachusetts, with the intention of attending Yale University. This hope was dashed when at age fifteen, a family move to Pittsfield, Ohio, placed Rogers close to Oberlin College. At Oberlin Rogers studied theology, Latin, and Greek, receiving his B.A. in theology in 1851 and his master's degree from Oberlin Seminary in 1855. In 1856 he married Elizabeth Lewis Embree, an Oberlin student; they had six children. She became his teaching partner in the one-room schoolhouse, "poorly fitted even for a stable," that was Berea College's earliest beginnings.

Having been exposed to traditional New England abolitionist sentiment early in his life, always seeking the "higher Christian ground," Rogers was greatly challenged by the antislavery movements of the antebellum United States. The Kentucky movement, of which Berea was born, was fired by the writings and speeches of Cassius Marcellus Clay, an antislavery candidate for Kentucky governor, and the speeches of the Reverend John Gregg Fee, an evangelical abolitionist and the disinherited son of a Kentucky slaveholder. These southern abolitionists had drawn interest from northern abolitionists and the Oberlin intellectual community long before Rogers's "calling" to Berea. Both Clay and Fee had prominent roles in the founding of Berea.

During Oberlin vacations Rogers worked summers in New York for the "Female Guardian Society," one of the earliest organizations of its kind devoted to the amelioration of the conditions of poor children in the slums of New York. During these summers in New York Rogers developed a deep respect for the work of the American Missionary Association through its secretary George Whipple.

"While yet a student at Oberlin, I had felt a great interest in the missionary work in Kentucky . . . I felt a longing to go to Kentucky . . . and start a school something like Oberlin," Rogers wrote to Berea College president William Goodell Frost on 17 February 1893. Repeatedly, Rogers heard of the heroic struggles of the missionaries in Kentucky from his brother-in-law, the Reverend James Scott Davis (also an Oberlin seminarian), while pastor of the Congregational church in Roseville, Illinois, in 1855. "Without saying anything to my church, I found a very desirable minister who was willing to take my place, and then told my congregation what was in my heart, and asked them to release me for the work to which my spirit was leading me" (Rogers to Frost, 17 Feb. 1893).

"Berea and Berea College are distinct things though closely united," Rogers wrote as he attempted to delineate the early evolution of church and school (Rogers to Frost, 17 Feb. 1896). Clay provided financial support and a large gift of land for Fee to establish a community in which "free speech could be maintained" after Clay was attracted to Fee's widespread preaching against slavery and his staunch beliefs in the freedom of speech. The Old Glade Church House, an antislavery church, was built, and John Fee named the colony Berea in 1855. Two years after the Berea colony was established, Rogers and his family settled in Berea to begin the permanent work of establishing a school that was to grow into a college of national and international renown for its "distinctive and unorthodox" approaches to education.

Rogers and his wife opened the school with just fifteen pupils—children of wealthy slaveholders and children of the "abject impoverished living in rude cabins." By the end of that first year Rogers was appointed to oversee the writing of a school charter. Guided by prayer, by his mentor professor at Oberlin, Edward Henry Fairchild, and by Oberlin's constitution, he established the founding by-laws of Berea College in 1858, and they have remained throughout its history. The school was founded especially to meet the needs of the poor, and no one was refused on account of the color of his skin if he was desirable otherwise. It was further agreed that the school would be nonsectarian and would provide "all the inducements and facilities for manual labor."

Widespread fear and suspicion of the school's teaching of liberty was exacerbated by the John Brown raid at Harpers Ferry, and in 1859, under threats of violence from a mob of some sixty of the local townsmen, Rogers was ordered to shut down the school. The "Berea Exodus" across the Ohio River was immediate and brought national attention. For the period Rogers was in exile, he continued his missionary outreach, lecturing for the American Missionary Society in the New York and New England area. He finally accepted a call to the Presbyterian church in Decatur, Ohio (two of his five sons were born there), all the while alerting his congregation that he would return to Berea at a moment's notice. Rogers continued his education work establishing the Ohio Valley Academy and serving as examiner to Marietta College and Lane Seminary.

After the Civil War Berea was reopened to an "epoch-making" event in 1866. Three African-American children applied for admission and were accepted. The school had come to be known as the place where freedmen were treated with kindness and where their children could obtain knowledge. In the earlier years after the war the influx of these "colored scholars" was such that for a time they slightly exceeded the number of whites.

Before Berea the schools and colleges of the rest of Kentucky were practically closed to the mountain people. To reach this "belated civilization," extension and settlement work became an integral part of the Berea curriculum as Rogers and some of the leading Bereans traveled on horseback into the mountains. From these forays Rogers wrote about the mountain people, their culture, and their needs. He published a series of letters in the *New York Independent* (c. 1858), the *New York Evangelist* (c. 1868), and the *American Missionary Magazine*. His ethnographic-like descriptions are believed to be the first to give cultural dignity and intellectual validity to the study of the people of this region, confirming that Berea College was the discoverer of the "noble mountain people" and of an area later to become known as Appalachian America.

Twelve years after his arrival at Berea Rogers relinquished leadership of the school to Fairchild. For the next decade (1869–1879) Rogers, a noted Greek scholar, gave untiringly of his energies to Berea as trustee, professor, and fundraiser, always keeping in the forefront its providential beginnings and its Christian mission. Berea gained national prominence and importance, and through its reputation it sparked major philanthropic interest from private northern donors and considerable support from the Freedman's Bureau. The "great meeting at Cooper Institute," a fundraiser at the Cooper Institute in New York that included addresses by such prominent men as Henry Ward Beecher and Horace Greeley, was a turning point in the marked growth in the Berea endowment and in the support of its principles. These speeches were revered by Rogers and accompany his earliest writings of the history of the college.

Increasingly fragile health forced Rogers to leave Berea in 1879. He settled with his family, including six children, in Shawano, Wisconsin, as pastor of the Presbyterian church. For the next twenty-five years Rogers devoted his full-time energies to his preaching, while maintaining an attachment to Berea as trustee, college historian, and confidante of Frost, Berea's second president. He continued his ministry in Hartford, Connecticut, and Wisconsin, and he became a preacher for the Apostolic church in the last years of his life. In 1884 Rogers's ministry took a more evangelical turn when he became preacher of the Catholic Apostolic church in Philadelphia and Hartford, an English church of which there were only three in the United States. Rogers returned to Berea in 1903 to deliver the semi-centennial address, and that same year he published what continues to be the most definitive history of the college for that time, *Birth of Berea College: A Story of Providence.*

In 1904 Rogers witnessed another turning point, another assault on the principles upon which the college was founded. The Kentucky legislature passed the Day Law, which forbade black and white students to attend the same schools, and consequently Berea faced the explusion of all of its African-American teachers and students. Berea lost its appeal in a United States Supreme Court decision upholding the Day Law in 1908.

Rogers and his wife moved to Woodstock, Illinois, in 1903 to live the final years of their lives near their only daughter. Rogers died in Woodstock. To John Rogers, Berea College was the creation of God's providence, "the same hand which gave it its origins has upheld it in all its history."

• Primary sources on Rogers are in the Berea College Archives. The Founders and Founding Collection of the Archives and Special Collections Department of the Hutchins Library holds major sources that focus on the early life and work of Rogers: unpublished manuscripts, letters, diaries, and newspaper clippings that include "Family Tree of J. A. R. Rogers"; "Diaries of J. A. R. Rogers" (2 vols., 1850–1867); unpublished manuscripts of Mrs. Elisabeth Embree Rogers, "Full Forty Years of Shadow and Sunshine: A Sketch of the Family Life of the J. A. R. Rogers Family" (1896) and "Personal History of Berea College" (1910?); "Fifty Years of Wedded Happiness," *Woodstock Sentinel,* 25 Jan. 1906; and "Founded Berea College . . . ," *Hartford Times,* 5 Feb. 1895. A better insight into Rogers's years after Berea and the process of his writing of the history of the college can be found in the J. A. R. Rogers correspondence to President Frost 1893–1904. Published works include the definitive early history of Berea College by Rogers, *Birth of Berea College: A Story of Providence* (1904); John Gregg Fee, *Autobiography of John G. Fee* (1891); and Cassius Marcellus Clay, *Letters of Cassius M. Clay: Slavery: The Evil—The Remedy* (1846?). Rogers, "Crossing the Lines of War," *Berea Quarterly* (Feb. 1896), tells the story of Rogers's return to Berea in 1862 after being exiled in Ohio. Secondary sources on the unusual history of slavery in antebellum Kentucky are W. J. Landrum, "Anti-Slavery in Kentucky," *Berea Quarterly* (Feb. 1896); Ivan E. McDougle, *Slavery in Kentucky, 1792–1865* (1918); and J. Winston Coleman, *Slavery Times in Kentucky* (1940). On the early history of Berea College and Rogers's role in it, see Richard Sears, "Rogers—A Modern Knight Errant" and "Administration of Principal Rogers," *Berea Quarterly* (Aug. 1904). The most extensive works recently published on Berea College include Sears, *"The Day of Small Things": Abolitionism in the Midst of Slavery, Berea, Kentucky* (1986) and *The Kentucky Abolitionists in the Midst of Slavery, 1854–1864: Exiles for Freedom* (1993); Elisabeth S. Peck, *Berea's First Century, 1855–1955* (1955); and Francis S. Hutchins, "Berea College: The Telescope and the Spade," a speech delivered on 17 May 1963 in Louisville, Kentucky. Obituaries are in the *Hartford Courant,* 25 July 1906, and the *Berea Citizen,* 26 July 1906.

JOYCE BICKERSTAFF

ROGERS, John Raphael (11 Dec. 1856–18 Feb. 1934), inventor, was born in Roseville, Illinois, the son of John Almanza Rowley Rogers, a clergyman, and Elizabeth Lewis Embree. His father was also a professor of Latin and Greek at Berea College, Kentucky, where Rogers studied for several years before he transferred to Oberlin College. He earned his A.B. from Oberlin in 1875. His first job was as a schoolteacher in Hancock, Michigan. After a year there he returned to Berea and served there for one year as acting professor of Greek. In 1877 he became superintendent of public schools in Lorain, Ohio. In 1878 he married Clara Ardelia Saxton; they probably had no children. In 1881 ill health caused him to take a civil engineering job on railroads in Iowa and Michigan. After two years he returned to his former position and remained superintendent at Lorain until 1888.

Rogers's interests and talents included mechanical experimentation as well as book learning. He built an operable bicycle at the age of eleven. During an 1881 visit to his brother Joseph, who worked on the editorial staff of a Philadelphia newspaper, he became acquainted with efforts to mechanize the typesetting process. Typesetting machines before the 1880s required workers to space, or "justify," words manually across a line of type for readability, an operation demanding a high degree of skill. Rogers developed an idea for a new kind of typesetting machine, one that could justify lines of type mechanically so that the type extended evenly across the line. His machine replaced hand spacing with a wedge-shaped character that permitted automatic variable spacing. On 4 September 1888 Rogers was awarded a patent for a machine that made stereotype matrices, that is, one that used negative molds instead of positive characters to cast a line of type in metal. After this award, he gave up teaching and moved to Cleveland, Ohio, to develop his invention. He founded the Rogers Typograph Company to manufacture his machine, which was capable, first, of setting a line of matrices, or engraved dies, and then of casting a line of type from molten metal.

At about the same time that Rogers filed for his first patent, two other inventors were working on similar machines. Ottmar Mergenthaler perfected his first Linotype machine in 1886 and earned a patent for the part of the machine that casts the slugs for each line. Jacob W. Schuckers experimented with mechanical typesetting, although he did not actually construct a machine. In 1885 Schuckers patented a double-wedge spaceband that could automatically justify a line of matrices. Rogers devised a similar spaceband, for which he also applied for a patent. The spaceband allowed operators to set type without stopping to insert extra blank characters between words by hand. Instead, the wedge-shaped spaceband lodged between words until the operator signaled the end of a line, at which time the wedges pushed text characters to each side, justifying the text. Recognizing that the spacing mechanism was essential for any mechanical typesetting machine, Rogers purchased Schuckers's patent. When litigation over this patent finally ended after several years, Schuckers was acknowledged as inventor, which gave Rogers the right to utilize the device. Meanwhile in 1891 the Mergenthaler Linotype Company of Brooklyn, New York, sued Rogers for infringement on the casting device used in his typograph. Mergenthaler's Linotype machine required the double-wedge spaceband, while Rogers's typograph required the casting device. The suit threatened both companies and lasted for several years. Finally, the Mergenthaler Linotype Company bought the Rogers Typograph Company and consolidated the two companies in July 1895. Rogers accepted the position of consulting engineer and chief of the experimental department.

Rogers continued to develop the Linotype machine, improving and broadening the scope of Mergenthaler's original one-letter Linotype machine. The Linotype machine continued as the industry standard until 1950. Rogers sought technical ideas from machinists and operators, many of which he developed and incorporated into commercially produced machines. In 1925 he published a book explaining the mechanism and operation of the Linotype machine, *Linotype Instruction Book*. He also lectured throughout the country on subjects related to printing. During his career he earned more than 400 patents in the United States and foreign countries for his inventions and improvements in the area of composing machines. Although the purchase of his company by Mergenthaler Linotype precluded the production of Rogers Typograph machines in the United States, they continued to be manufactured and used in Canada and Europe.

Rogers reaped significant financial reward from his inventions, much of which he donated to educational institutions. For many years he served on the board of directors of the American Missionary College. He was also trustee of both Oberlin College and Berea College. His wife died in 1932, after which he married Marion Rood Pratt, of Cleveland, Ohio. They had no children together. She and her two daughters from a previous marriage survived him. Rogers retained his position as chief of the experimental department at Mergenthaler

Linotype until he died in Brooklyn, New York. He was buried in Berea, Kentucky.

• For a technical history of composing machines including Rogers's, see John S. Thompson, *History of Composing Machines* (1904). See also *Oberlin Alumni Magazine*, Dec. 1924. Obituaries are in *Printing Equipment Engineer*, Mar. 1934; the *New York Times*, 19 Feb. 1934; and *Necrological Record of Oberlin Alumni* (1934).

HELEN M. ROZWADOWSKI

ROGERS, Moses (c. 1779–15 Nov. 1821), shipmaster and steamboat promoter, was born in or near New London, Connecticut, the son of Amos Rogers, a Groton, Connecticut, lumber- and brickyard owner, and Sarah Phillips. Born into a seafaring family claiming some forty sea-captain ancestors, Moses Rogers as early as 1800 commanded a vessel sailing on Long Island Sound. He already was a prosperous and well-regarded shipping operator by the time of his 1804 marriage to Adelia Smith; they had five children over the next ten years.

That Rogers, as commonly believed, was directly involved with or even briefly commanded Robert Fulton's *North River Steam Boat* (better known as *Clermont*) is doubtful and still a matter of dispute; however, Rogers's early interest in steamboats is well documented and significant. Following a brief period when he commanded two merchant sloops, Rogers in the spring of 1809 signed on as master of the steamboat *Phoenix*, owned by Fulton's rival, Colonel John Stevens (1749–1838), who previously had supported the steamboat project of John Fitch. With Rogers on board the small river steamer *Phoenix*, prohibited by Fulton's monopoly from competing on the Hudson River, departed Hoboken, New Jersey, on 10 June 1809 for a cautious thirteen-day coastwise run to Philadelphia for intended service on the Delaware River. The ship's arrival marked the first successful ocean voyage under steam power and officially launched Rogers's career as steamboat captain, first with the *Phoenix* and then, starting in 1813, with the *Eagle*, which ran between Philadelphia and Baltimore (not New York, as previously believed) and then between Baltimore and Norfolk. During this period Rogers developed a horse-powered ferry, or "teamboat," which he patented in 1814 and operated successfully across the East River between Manhattan and Brooklyn. Having earlier severed his ties with Stevens, Rogers increased his own financial investments in maritime steam enterprise and in 1814 took command of the steamboat *New Jersey*. Signaling Rogers's successive career shifts southward along the Atlantic Coast, his next steamboat, *Charleston*, made its maiden voyage from that principal South Carolina port to Savannah, Georgia, on 10 December 1817 to begin a weekly South Atlantic coastal service. During this period Rogers's family accompanied him, finally settling in Savannah.

In 1818 residents of the busy port of Savannah, with their leading citizen William Scarborough as primary promoter, organized a transatlantic steamship company (reputedly the world's first) and sent Rogers north to acquire a suitable vessel for their ambitious purpose. Traveling to New York, Rogers purchased from the Crockett and Fickett shipyards an oceangoing sailing packet then under construction. The ship would be suitably altered, by the combined efforts of several local machinery firms, for oceangoing steam propulsion. The result was a well-equipped but essentially hybrid vessel, effective under sail but small and underpowered for transoceanic steam travel and with an ingenious but troublesome propulsion system. The 320-ton, ship-rigged auxiliary steamship *Savannah* was launched 22 August 1818 and departed on its maiden voyage to its namesake port (with Rogers serving as both captain and chief engineer) on 28 March 1819.

With Rogers in command and also supervising the machinery, the SS *Savannah*'s famous, if endlessly controversial, transatlantic voyage from Savannah to Liverpool, England, lasted from 22 May to 20 June 1819, primarily under sail. *Savannah* then went on to Stockholm and St. Petersburg before departing for home by way of Copenhagen and Arendal, Norway. Again employing little steam power on the voyage, until arriving at home port on 30 November, Rogers's steamship had completed a six-month transoceanic voyage, although with virtually no passengers or cargo it was not a commercial success. How much of this sea voyage took place under steam power is still a matter of debate, which involves deciding whether or not the *Savannah* was an authentic transoceanic steamship—and whether or not Rogers, accordingly, should be given credit for an important achievement. The most detailed study, by Frank Braynard, decides emphatically in favor of Rogers's *Savannah* as eligible for recognition as the first successful transatlantic steamship; as engineer as well as vessel commander, Rogers thus would merit more recognition than he customarily receives. Opposing this view is Cedric Ridgely-Nevitt, whose briefer but more technical and equally authoritative examination of the *Savannah*'s history diminishes the historical significance of the steamship and its leading promoter. The *Savannah*, Ridgely-Nevitt argues, "was the wrong type of ship at the wrong place at the wrong time" (p. 67).

Governmental interest in the steamship and its voyage failed to offset serious financial difficulties of the *Savannah* Steam Ship Company. The company failed; the vessel was laid up; its machinery was removed; and it was converted into a sailing vessel. Rogers left Georgia, moving as far north as Philadelphia before once again venturing into steamboat service in South Carolina, where he became part owner and operator of a vessel named after the Pee Dee River. The *Savannah*, commercially successful as a sailing packet, was lost when it went aground on Fire Island, New York, on 5 November 1821. Unaware of his old vessel's fate, Moses Rogers on the next day began his last voyage on the highly profitable steamer *Pee Dee*; scarcely a week later he suddenly fell ill of a virulent fever that was complicated by a typhus infection. Despite close medical supervision, Rogers died at Georgetown, South Carolina. Rogers's historical reputation is so inextricably linked to that of the *Savannah* that since his death he has been, and undoubtedly will continue to be, celebrated or ignored in relation to the ongoing estimation of his steamship.

• Source material on Rogers is slight and incomplete, and most of it is in relation to his best-known steamship. See J. E. Watkins, "The Log of the *Savannah*," in the Smithsonian Institution, *Report of the National Museum for 1890* (1891); J. S. Rogers, *James Rogers of New London and His Descendants* (1902); and J. B. Marestier, *Memoir on Steamboats of the United States of America*, trans. S. Withington (1957; orig. pub. 1824). The most thorough discussion of Rogers's career and his historical reputation remains Frank O. Braynard's meticulously researched and well-annotated *S.S. Savannah: The Elegant Steam Ship* (1963), which argues for considerably greater importance of both man and vessel than most historians acknowledge. Braynard does correct a number of frequently repeated errors about Rogers's early life, such as those contained in H. C. Bolton, "The Log-Book of the 'Savannah'," *Harper's New Monthly Magazine*, Feb. 1877, and perpetuated in David B. Tyler, *Steam Conquers the Atlantic* (1939). In his authoritative and well-researched *American Steamships on the Atlantic* (1981), naval architect and historian Cedric Ridgely-Nevitt is critical of both Rogers and the *Savannah* and, accordingly, sees less of historical significance in them.

EDWARD W. SLOAN

ROGERS, Randolph (6 July 1825–15 Jan. 1892), sculptor, was born in Waterloo, New York, the son of John Rogers, a carpenter, and Sarah McCarthy. After spending his youth in Ann Arbor, Michigan, Rogers moved to New York City in 1847 in the hope of becoming a wood engraver. There he found employment in a dry goods store and began modeling and carving in plaster in his spare time. Rogers's portrait busts so impressed his employers that they financed his trip to Italy in 1848.

Once in Florence, Rogers sought instruction from the famed sculptor Lorenzo Bartolini at the Academy of St. Mark. In 1851 Rogers left for Rome and established a studio on the Piazza Barberini. Among his early works was an ideal bust of Night, which he sent to New York to be exhibited at the National Academy of Design in 1852. His first successful sculpture was *Ruth Gleaning* (1853), after which many replicas were made; twelve are in American museums, including the Detroit Institute and the Toledo Museum of Art. Although Rogers based the pose of the statue on a classical prototype, he created a female figure more real than ideal and carefully rendered each naturalistic detail. Such easily perceived narrative content is also found in his subsequent works *The Truant* (1854) and *Atala and Chactas* (1854).

Rogers's first public commission was a portrait statue of John Adams (1854–1859) for a Gothic chapel in Mount Auburn Cemetery in Cambridge, Massachusetts, now in Memorial Hall at Harvard University. In preparation for the project Rogers made one of many trips to the United States in 1855. After returning to Italy in August 1855 he created his famous sculpture *Nydia, the Blind Flower Girl of Pompeii* (1856). Basing his narrative on a popular novel by Edward Bulwer-Lytton, Rogers portrayed Nydia seeking her lost lover during the chaos that followed the volcanic eruption. The groping movement of the young woman listening intently for a guiding sound appealed to the Victorian taste for sentimental narrative. More than one hundred replicas were made, and the sculpture's popularity lasted long after the end of the Civil War. Copies are housed in several museums in the United States, including the Metropolitan Museum of Art and the Newark Museum.

Also in 1855 Rogers received a commission from Captain Montgomery C. Meigs to create a set of bronze doors for the rotunda of the newly erected Capitol in Washington, D.C. (1855–1859). Using the design of Ghiberti's *Gates of Paradise* on the Baptistery of Florence as his model, Rogers related the story of Christopher Columbus in eight panel reliefs united by a lunette depicting the discovery of America.

In 1857 sculptor Thomas Crawford died, leaving unfinished his monumental tribute to George Washington in Richmond, Virginia. That year Rogers returned to the United States to marry Rosa Ignatia Gibson of Richmond; they had eleven children, two of whom died in infancy. Rogers was chosen to complete Crawford's project. He added the heroic figures of Andrew Lewis and Thomas Nelson and attended to the casting of Crawford's models of John Marshall and James Mason in Munich, Germany. Rogers's figure of Lewis, Nelson, and the six female allegories created for the base are judged to be his finest works. The project was completed in 1869.

During this period Rogers's work became more idealized and less narrative, as exemplified in his standing *Isaac* (1858, New-York Historical Society), *Somnambula* (1861), a later, smaller version of which is in the National Museum of American Art, and the *Angel of Resurrection* (1863–1864, Samuel Colt Monument, Hartford, Conn.). Rogers's ability to heroize the military figure while attending to every detail of its uniform brought him several commissions for Civil War monuments, for which he commanded high prices: *Soldier of the Line* (1863–1865, Cincinnati), *Soldiers' National Monument* (1865–1869, Gettysburg); *Rhode Island Soldiers' and Sailors' Monument* (1866–1871, Providence); *Michigan Soldiers' and Sailors' Monument* (1867–1881, Detroit); *Abraham Lincoln Monument* (1868–1870, Philadelphia); and *Soldiers' Monument* (1871–1874, Worcester, Mass.). Rogers had one of the most active studios in Rome where he produced, among other works, a bronze seated figure of William Seward (1873–1875) for Madison Square in New York.

In *The Lost Pleiad* (1874–1875, Philadelphia Museum of Art), Rogers returned to mythology to create one of his most dramatic works, one that rivaled *Nydia* in popularity. As Merope drifts through the firmament looking for her lost sisters, drapery skims her almost nude body and trails off in a swirling mass into the space behind her. This flair for the dynamic is again displayed in *Genius of Connecticut* (1877–1878), commissioned for the state capitol in Hartford, and in Rogers's final work, *The Last Arrow* (1879–1880, Metropolitan Museum), a work depicting an equestrian group of Native Americans caught in violent action.

Illness cut short Rogers's activity during the last ten years of his life in Rome, where he died. He was the recipient of several awards. In 1873 he was given honorary membership in Rome's prestigious Academy of Saint Luke, the first such award given to an American, and he also received honorary memberships to the academies in Perugia and Urbino. In 1884 he was knighted by King Umberto I and was dubbed a knight of the Kingdom of Italy.

• Most of the primary documentation on Rogers is in the Michigan Historical Collections in Ann Arbor, including the Randolph Rogers Journal (1867–1891); an unpublished biography by Rosa G. Rogers; and a diary by Henry S. Frieze (1856). The collection also contains a catalog of the ninety-four plaster casts (only three of which survive) given to the University of Michigan. See Martin D'Ooge, *Catalogue of the Gallery of Art and Archaeology of the University of Michigan* (1892). A checklist by Rosa G. Rogers of her husband's work is in the New York Public Library, and material on the Lincoln memorial is in the Stille papers at the Historical Society of Pennsylvania. A comprehensive biography, extensive bibliography, and checklist of works are in Millard F. Rogers, Jr., *Randolph Rogers, American Sculptor in Rome* (1971). This book was reviewed by Wayne Craven in *Art Bulletin* 55 (Spring 1973): 158–59, and by William H. Gerdts in *Art Journal* 33 (Fall 1973): 75–76. For a concise biography see Craven, *Sculpture in America* (1968; rev. ed., 1984). For a discussion of *The Lost Pleiad* see Marina Elena Pacini, "The Lost Pleiad" (M.A. thesis, Univ. of Delaware, 1988). See also Millard F. Rogers, Jr., "Nydia, Popular Victorian Image," *Antiques* 97 (Mar. 1970): 374–77. An obituary is in the *New York Times*, 16 Jan. 1892.

SYLVIA L. LAHVIS

ROGERS, Robert (7 Nov. 1731–18 May 1795), soldier, was born in Methuen, Massachusetts, the son of James Rogers and Mary (maiden name unknown), farmers. Soon after his birth, his father, an Irish settler, moved the family to Dunbarton, New Hampshire, then the frontier, where he was raised. Rogers grew to be a skilled trader and frontiersman and became a colonial scout in the third French and Indian War, "King George's War." In 1755 he worked as a recruiter for Massachusetts colonial governor William Shirley until he enlisted in the New Hampshire regiment to free himself from prosecution on a charge of counterfeiting, one of many financial misdealings in his career. By the time of Sir William Johnson's Crown Point Expedition, an operation in 1755 to seize control of the Great Lakes, he was a captain. In March 1756 Johnson made him the leader of a group of irregular soldiers called rangers; these mobile units were composed of fighters who could work as individuals or in small groups in a way comparable to modern guerrilla warriors. Appointed major in 1758 by James Abercromby, the commander in chief of the British military forces, Rogers came to command nine companies comprising a total of 600 men known as "Rogers' Rangers," fighting in places such as Halifax (1757) and Ticonderoga (1758). In 1759 an expedition under his command destroyed the Saint Francis Indians at Crown Point. He participated in the attack on Quebec under General James Wolfe as well as in the defeat of Montreal in 1760. General Jeffrey Amherst sent him as far west as Detroit to take possession of the northwestern forts and posts from the French.

Rogers married Elizabeth Browne (daughter of the Reverend Arthur Browne) in 1761 and in the same year was promoted to captain and commanded a company fighting against the Cherokees of South Carolina. The year 1763 found him fighting with James Dalyell (formerly a subordinate in his Rangers) in Pontiac's War (1763–1764), including the Battle of Bloody Bridge. He dramatized these experiences in *Ponteach; or, The Savages of America* (1766). This play seemed crude to critics even at the time of its first presentation, but it was well received in London as an account of colonial exotica. It is regarded as an important part of the history of American drama and considered useful for its depiction of the Indian. Rogers also wrote about his campaigns in *Journals: Containing an Account of the Several Excursions He Made under the Generals Who Commanded upon the Continent of North America* (1765), and *A Concise Account of North America: Containing a Description of the Several British Colonies and an Account of the Several Nations and Tribes of Indians* (1765). These works were published in London after he fled America because of illegal trading with the Indians and a debt of some £13,000. Highly effective as a fighter and leader of men, he seems not to have been able to control his drinking or his own avarice, and his social position was not sufficiently high to protect him from the effects of the latter vice.

Tremendously popular as a highly successful colonial warrior, Rogers proposed an exploratory expedition from the Mississippi to the Pacific Ocean to find the much-sought Northwest Passage, but King George III refused to sponsor him. He was instead made commander of Fort Michilimackinac (1765–1768) at what is now Mackinac, Michigan. There he overstepped his authority and sent Jonathan Carver in 1766 to seek the fabled passage by way of the Upper Mississippi and Great Lakes region. Although many of the facts are uncertain, Rogers clearly quarreled with his fellow officials and was accused both of trying to sell out to the French and of trying to set up an independent administration. Arrested and conveyed to Montreal for court-martial, he was cleared of all charges but found himself unemployable in America.

Returning to England he was thrown into debtor's prison until bonded out by his brother James. He returned to America in 1775, apparently as a loyalist spy; at least he was so regarded by George Washington, who ordered his imprisoned in 1776. Rogers escaped, however, and then organized and led a Tory regiment called the Queen's American Rangers to fight in the environs of New York City, but his defeat at White Plains lost him the command, and his brother James took over.

In 1778 his wife divorced him and was awarded custody of their only child. He returned to England for the last time in 1780 and lived on half-pay from his former services to the Crown until he died in obscurity in London. His story is most popularly known from Kenneth Clark's novelistic portrait *Northwest Passage*.

• For additional information see John Cuneo, *Robert Rogers of the Rangers* (1988), and H. M. Jackson, *Rogers' Rangers: A History* (1953).

HENRY RUSSELL

ROGERS, Robert Empie (29 Mar. 1813–6 Sept. 1884), chemist and teacher, was born in Baltimore, Maryland, the son of Patrick Kerr Rogers, a teacher of science, and Hannah Blythe. Rogers was the youngest of four brothers, and soon after his birth the family moved to Williamsburg, Virginia, where Patrick Rogers took up the post of professor of natural philosophy and mathematics at the College of William and Mary. All four boys helped their father to make equipment for his lecture demonstrations, learning to work in metal and wood, but this close-knit family was soon struck by tragedy. When Rogers was seven, his mother died of malarial fever, and his father's colleagues, in particular the Reverend Adam Empie and his wife, acted almost as foster parents to young Robert, who adopted Empie as his middle name in gratitude for their care. In the summer of 1828 his father also died of malarial fever, and Robert's two oldest brothers, James Blythe Rogers and William Barton Rogers, became his guardians and guided his education.

In an initial and unsatisfying stint as a civil engineer in training, Rogers worked as an assistant surveyor for the Boston and Providence Railroad. In 1833 he began the study of medicine at the University of Pennsylvania as a student of Robert Hare, professor of chemistry. Rogers presented his thesis, *Experiments upon the Blood, Together with Some New Facts in Regard to Animal and Vegetable Structure, Illustrative of Many of the Most Important Phenomena of Organic Life*, which was published in 1836, and graduated with an M.D. in March 1836, but he had found that he preferred chemistry to medicine. For the next six years he was chemist to the first Geological Survey of Pennsylvania, of which his brother Henry Darwin Rogers was the head. In that capacity he carried out analyses of minerals and published his first article, coauthored with Martin Boyé, in the *Journal of the Franklin Institute* in 1840, on the determination of calcium in limestone. Robert Rogers had become a member of the Philadelphia Academy of Natural Sciences in 1837 and of the Franklin Institute in 1838, and he remained actively involved with both organizations throughout his career.

During the 1841–1842 academic year Rogers was invited to teach the chemistry course at the University of Virginia, replacing the ailing professor John P. Emmet; Rogers was elected to succeed Emmet as professor of general and applied chemistry and materia medica in March 1842. He taught successfully at Virginia for ten years, his clear lectures being illustrated with informative demonstrations. Rogers's brother William was professor of natural philosophy and geology at the University of Virginia from 1835 to 1853, and the two brothers collaborated in a range of chemical researches. Together they published several articles on potassium dichromate as an oxidant in the preparation of chlorine, of formic acid from sugar, and of acetaldehyde from ethanol and in the determination of carbon in graphite and in diamond. Other joint researches were on the volatility of alkali metal hydroxides and carbonates, on the decomposition of rocks by water, and on the solubility of carbon dioxide in a variety of liquids. With his brother James (then professor of chemistry at the University of Pennsylvania), Rogers conducted research into analysis of metal ores and compiled a textbook of inorganic and organic chemistry, based on works by William Gregory and Edward Turner, that was published in 1846. He married Fanny Montgomery in 1843; they had no children.

When James Rogers died in 1852, Robert Rogers was chosen to succeed him at the University of Pennsylvania, where the latter served as professor of chemistry until he was chosen dean of the medical faculty in 1856. He published his American edition of Karl Gotthelf Lehmann's *Physiological Chemistry* in 1855. During the Civil War Rogers served as an acting assistant surgeon at the West Philadelphia Military Hospital in 1862–1863. There he oversaw the installation of a steam mangle to speed up laundry work, but while he was demonstrating its use in January 1863 his right hand was crushed in the machine and had to be amputated above the wrist. He recovered rapidly and taught himself to write and do chemical manipulations with his left hand. That same year, his wife died, and in 1866 he married Delia Saunders; they had no children.

After the war Rogers, with H. R. Linderman, another chemist, was asked by the secretary of the U.S. Treasury to review the operations of the Melter and Refiner's Department of the Philadelphia Mint. Their careful and detailed report initiated a more scientific approach to the operations of the mint, and Rogers followed up with visits to the San Francisco Mint in 1873 and 1875 and to the New York Assay Office in 1874. He was also employed as a consultant for the Virginia and California Mine in Nevada and for the Gas Trust of Philadelphia.

In 1877, during a period of reform of medical education initiated by the board of trustees at the University of Pennsylvania that gave rise to uncertainty about his own position there, Rogers was asked to take the chair of medical chemistry and toxicology at the Jefferson Medical College in Philadelphia. He accepted and remained there, teaching courses on chemistry and materia medica, until his retirement in 1884. He died in Philadelphia. One of a quartet of remarkable brothers, each of whom made important contributions to American science and science education in the nineteenth century, Robert Rogers was the most considerable chemist of the group, making significant contributions to both pure and applied chemistry.

• A biography by W. S. W. Ruschenberger of Rogers and his father and brothers in *Proceedings of the American Philosophical Society* 23 (1886): 104–47, includes a bibliography of the writings of the Rogers brothers. Biographies by Edgar Fahs Smith are in the National Academy of Sciences, *Biographical Memoirs* 5 (1905): 291–309, and in his *Chemistry in America* (1914), pp. 235–41, which includes a bibliography.

HAROLD GOLDWHITE

ROGERS, Shorty (14 Apr. 1924–7 Nov. 1994), jazz trumpet and flugelhorn player, arranger, and bandleader, was born Milton Michael Rajonsky in Great Barrington, Massachusetts, the son of Abraham Rajonsky, an immigrant tailor from Romania, and Anna Sevitsky, from Russia. Rogers was raised in Lee, Massachusetts, where his father owned a tailor shop. He played bugle from age five. Four years later the family moved to the Bronx, New York. He took up trumpet at age twelve and on the strength of his playing he subsequently enrolled at the High School of Music and Art in New York City.

Rogers acquired his nickname, Shorty, while in high school. Upon graduating in 1942, he was hired into the big band of trombonist Will Bradley, with whom he toured. Late in 1942 Bradley disbanded, and Rogers joined xylophonist Red Norvo's small group. Drafted in May 1943, he served in the 379th Armed Service Forces Band, stationed at Newport News, Virginia.

In September 1945 trumpeter Conte Condoli was drafted, and Rogers, discharged, took Condoli's place in clarinetist Woody Herman's big band, the First Herd. That same year Rogers married Michele (maiden name unknown); they had three children. He remained with Herman until the First Herd disbanded in December 1946, at which point the couple moved to Burbank, California, and changed their surname to Rogers.

Rogers found sporadic work with lesser-known bands in the Los Angeles area until Herman organized his Second Herd in November 1947. Rejoining, Rogers played trumpet, composed and arranged "Keeper of the Flame" (recorded in 1948), and also supplied arrangements of "That's Right," "Lemon Drop" (also 1948), "More Moon" (1949; a version of "How High the Moon," featuring tenor saxophonist Gene Ammons), and "Lollypop" (1949).

When Herman broke up the Second Herd in December 1949, Rogers joined Stan Kenton's big band, for which he arranged "Jolly Rogers," "Viva Prado," and "Round Robin" (all recorded in 1950). In June 1951 he left Kenton and big band touring behind and thereafter worked almost exclusively in the Los Angeles area. He studied classical composition with Wesley La Violette, and he became involved in local bands that practiced a substyle of cool jazz that came to be known as West Coast jazz. In this setting Rogers worked mainly with former sidemen from Kenton's ensemble, including reed player Jimmy Giuffre, saxophonists Art Pepper and Bud Shank, and drummer Shelly Manne, although he also played with a few of the outstanding African-American jazz musicians in the area: pianist Hampton Hawes participated in Rogers's first recordings as a leader, in an octet modeled after the sound of trumpeter Miles Davis's "Birth of the Cool" nonet (October 1951); later, string bassist Curtis Counce was a member of Rogers's Giants.

In December 1951 Rogers began a long engagement in bassist Howard Rumsey's Lighthouse All Stars band at the Lighthouse Club in Hermosa Beach, California. In January 1953 he brought Shorty Rogers and his Giants, a nine-piece group including Pepper, Giuffre, Hawes, and Manne, into the studio to record two further sessions along the lines of Davis's nonet. He recorded as a soloist on the quintet album of vibraphonist and pianist Teddy Charles, *New Directions*, with Giuffre, Counce, and Manne, in August 1953. Late that same year, with pianist Russ Freeman taking Charles's place, the quintet Shorty Rogers and his Giants held an engagement at the Haig club on Wilshire Boulevard in Los Angeles.

By March 1954, when he recorded as co-leader of a quintet with Shank, Rogers had taken up flugelhorn in addition to trumpet. Around this time the Giants transferred from the Haig to Zardi's on Hollywood Boulevard. During this year the piano chair was shared by Freeman, Marty Paich, André Previn, and Pete Jolly. Under Manne's leadership, Rogers and Giuffre recorded the beautifully played trio album, *The Three* (Sept. 1954), made without chordal and bass instruments; thus the "pianoless" West Coast jazz of the Gerry Mulligan and Chet Baker quartet moved one step closer to a pristine and ascetic musical transparency. In 1955 the Giants quintet made Rogers's aptly named and best-known album, *The Swinging Mr. Rogers*, presenting "Martians Go Home," a sprightly blues theme that became a modest jazz hit. Concurrently Rogers helped to produce record sessions for the Atlantic and RCA Victor labels, and he became involved in writing for films. Most notable were his arrangements of Leith Stevens's compositions for portions of the soundtrack for the movie *The Wild One*, starring Marlon Brando (1953), and his arrangements of Elmer Bernstein's compositions for *The Man with the Golden Arm*, starring Frank Sinatra (1955).

While continuing to lead the Giants, whose new members included pianist Lou Levy, bassist Ralph Peña, and drummer Stan Levey, Rogers became increasingly involved in Hollywood studio work. By the 1960s he was focusing on writing for film soundtracks, and he gradually abandoned playing. During the 1970s he was mainly involved with television, writing scores for such series as "Felony Squad," "The Partridge Family," "Vegas," and "Starsky and Hutch."

Born Jewish, Rogers converted to Christianity in 1977. He began to suffer health problems as a consequence of the hectic life of writing for new television

shows week after week, and ultimately he decided to reduce his workload in the studio. In 1982 he started playing again, strictly on flugelhorn. Over the next decade Rogers organized performances around reunions with colleagues from the Lighthouse All Stars engagement of the early 1950s. Hospitalized with a blood clot in 1986, he had a recurring problem with internal bleeding for the remainder of his life but nonetheless continued touring internationally through the early 1990s. He died in Van Nuys, California.

Rogers was a leading figure in West Coast jazz, a contributor to the intelligent use of jazz as film music, and the first musician to make the flugelhorn—a mellower cousin of the trumpet—into a significant jazz brass instrument. Writer Ted Gioia characterized him as "a spiritual man, a gentle man, soft-spoken and quietly dedicated to his music" (p. 246), and Gioia argues that these characteristics were reflected in the emphasis on moderation and craftsmanship predominant in Rogers's version of the West Coast jazz style. Unfortunately this style was marketed in a contentious manner, with excessive claims for his significance and a consequent reaction by many critics who thought that he was overrated. The battle having subsided, it is possible to appreciate in a level-headed way Rogers's recorded legacy, which is consistently pleasant, polished, and well-played.

• The finest survey of Rogers's jazz career is by Ted Gioia, *West Coast Jazz: Modern Jazz in California, 1945–1960* (1992). See also interviews and surveys by Loward Lucraft, "The Gentle Giant," *Jazz Journal International* 32 (Feb. 1979): 4–6; Steve Voce, "Cool & Crazy," *Jazz Journal International* 35 (Oct. 1982): 14–15; and Les Tomkins, "The Shorty Rogers Story," *Crescendo International* 21 (Jan. 1983): 20–22, an article continued as "West Coast Jazz Was the Time of Our Lives," *Crescendo International* 21 (Mar. 1983): 12–13. Other sources include Robert Gordon, *Jazz West Coast: The Los Angeles Jazz Scene of the 1950s* (1986); Hal Hill, "Portrait of Shorty," *Coda*, no. 235 (Dec. 1990–Jan. 1991): 20–22; Doug Ramsey, "Shorty Rogers: Advancing the Freedom (and Fun) Principle," *Jazz Times* 21 (Dec. 1991): 23–24, 81; Jean Maggs, "Shorty Rogers: An Appreciation," *Crescendo & Jazz Music* 30 (May–June 1993): 12–14; and William D. Clancy with Audree Coke Kenton, *Woody Herman: Chronicles of the Herd* (1995). Gioia's dating of Rogers's association with Kenton is confirmed in William F. Lee, *Stan Kenton: Artistry in Rhythm*, ed. Audree Coke (1980). A two-volume catalog of recordings is by Coen Hofmann and Erik M. Bakker, *Shorty Rogers: A Discography* (1983). An obituary is in the *New York Times* 9 Nov. 1994.

BARRY KERNFELD

ROGERS, Will (4 Nov. 1879–15 Aug. 1935), entertainer and social commentator, was born William Penn Adair Rogers near Oologah, Oklahoma, in what was then the Cooweescoowee District of Indian Territory, the son of Clement Vann Rogers and Mary America Schrimsher, Cherokee ranchers. Rogers County, which contains both Oologah, site of the historic Rogers home, and Claremore, site of the Will Rogers Memorial and Museum, is named after the prominent father, not the prominent son. "Uncle Clem" was a major player in Oklahoma politics before and after statehood (1907), serving as a judge, as a member of the Dawes Commission (to distribute Indian lands prior to statehood), and as the first local banker. Will's loving wife, the former Betty Blake, whom he married in 1908, later remembered that "Will had everything he wanted. He had spending money and the best string of cow ponies in the country. No boy in Indian Territory had more than Uncle Clem's boy." (Yet being "Uncle Clem's boy" could have its downside, too.)

Myths surround every aspect of Will Rogers's life, but none conflicts with reality more than the myth of his ignorance. Because Rogers so often spoke about his lack of education and because his daily column began with the expression "All I know is what I read in the papers," many people, including biographers, have mistaken the *persona* for the *person*. Although he was certainly a frisky youth who left high school without completing the curriculum, he was a better-than-average student with special interests in social studies and history. Furthermore, he had grown up reading the *New York Times*, which was delivered by train to Oologah; at the dinner table, the family frequently discussed national and international issues. Clearly, Rogers knew much more than he read in the daily press, but he was successful at hiding his political awareness until he stumbled upon its expressive and commercial potential.

The four-year cowboy phase of Rogers's career began in 1898, immediately after he ran away from Kemper Military School in Missouri. Wishing to remain at a safe distance from Uncle Clem, he cowboyed on the Ewing Ranch near Higgins, Texas. He later returned home to manage cattle (loaned to him by his father) on a ranch near Oologah. All through this ranching phase Rogers was fascinated with roping but felt suffocated by the rustic life style; he was very much a young man in search of himself. In 1902 he sold his share in the ranch and left for South America to ride with the gauchos in Argentina. Once reality set in, he drifted to South Africa where his life as an entertainer began.

Billed as the "Cherokee Kid" in Texas Jack's Wild West Show, Rogers toured South Africa; soon thereafter, with the Wirth Brothers Circus, he performed in Australia and New Zealand. His act was strictly physical, a display of the riding and roping he had perfected during his lonely days on the Oologah ranch. For many outside the United States, the cowboy symbolized something particularly American, an unfettered man free of institutional restraints. With the world becoming more bureaucratized each day, the cowboy pose was fascinating, and Rogers's skill with a lariat evoked the dexterity and freedom of the disappearing frontier life. Once back in the United States, Rogers continued his trick-roping act in a variety of Wild West shows until he discovered that audiences were just as fascinated by his frontier, Oklahoma twang. He took the leap from "Ropin' Fool" to "Talkin' Fool" sometime around 1916.

The turning point for Rogers occurred in Baltimore in 1916 during a touring performance of the *Ziegfeld*

Follies. President Woodrow Wilson was in the audience, and Rogers decided to experiment with a ribbing technique, what later generations would call "roasting." General John Joseph Pershing had just conducted an unsuccessful punitive raid into Mexico, about which Rogers quipped: "I see where they have captured [Pancho] Villa. Yes, they got him in the morning editions, but the afternoon ones let him get away . . . We chased him over the line five miles, but run into a lot of government red tape and had to come back." When Wilson joined in the laughter, Rogers had arrived as a public commentator. For the remainder of his career he would exploit the premise implicit in his topical humor, which even a "roasted" official could appreciate. Whether on stage or in print he carefully cultivated the persona of a cowboy who, due to his innocent isolation from urban values, was constantly bemused by twentieth-century American mores and morals. His topical observations caught on with readers: in 1919 he collected his comments on the Versailles Treaty and on Prohibition into two slim books for Harper Brothers. In the meantime, he continued as a *Follies* performer, a frontier naïf among urbane sophisticates.

In 1920, while his show business career continued, Rogers ventured into the field of journalism by covering the presidential nominating conventions for the McNaught Syndicate—a practice he would continue until 1932. The next year he began to write a longer column. In 1926 he kicked off a daily item entitled "Will Rogers Says." His favorite journalistic exercise, it reached forty million readers each day.

Always one of editor George Horace Lorimer's favorite contributors to the *Saturday Evening Post*, Rogers was sent on special assignments to survey developments in Europe and Russia (1927) and the Far East (1934). Articles for the *Post* followed, garnished, as always, with fanciful illustrations by Herbert Johnson. Rogers advised Americans to embrace the frontier values of neighborliness and democracy on the domestic front while remaining clear of foreign entanglements. Nonetheless, he also advocated a strong military establishment, especially a strong air corps. Like his flying buddy General William "Billy" Mitchell, Rogers looked ahead apprehensively to aerial wars of the future.

Rogers was successful as well in the medium of motion pictures. In 1918, at the suggestion of Mrs. Rex Beach, who thought the Oklahoman would be perfect for the lead role in an adaptation of one of her husband's *Laughing Bill Hyde* stories, Rogers starred in the five-reel, fifty-minute film produced at Samuel Goldwyn's studio at Fort Lee, New Jersey. Although the film earned little money, it launched Rogers's motion picture career. From 1918 to 1929 he made forty-eight silent comedies and travel films, exploiting his persona as a wise innocent who can see through the malice and pretensions of self-styled sophisticates. His first sound film, *They Had to See Paris* (1929), finally gave him the chance to exercise his verbal magic, and after that film, his movie career really took off. Not surprisingly, his best sound-era movies feature Rogers as a down-to-earth farmer (*State Fair* [1933]), an old-fashioned physician (*Dr. Bull* [1933]), a small town banker (*David Harum* [1934]), and a rural politician (*Judge Priest* [1934], *County Chairman* [1935], *Steamboat 'Round the Bend* [1935], and *In Old Kentucky* [1935]). Many of these last great films benefited from the artistry of the black actor "Stepin' Fetchit" (Lincoln Perry) and director John Ford.

Also during the early 1930s, Rogers became a prominent radio personality. Using material from his articles, and combining it with extemporaneous horseplay, Rogers beguiled radio listeners on his "Good Gulf Show" from April 1933 until June 1935. (Transcripts exist for all fifty-three programs, and tapes are available for thirteen.) An additional series of twelve radio programs for the E. R. Squibb drug company focused on such major personalities as Charles Lindbergh, Herbert Hoover, Charles Curtis, Al Smith, and—never to be forgotten by Rogers—Henry Ford. (Ford symbolized for Rogers many of the paradoxes of industrialism; while a nineteenth-century man in many ways, Ford's inventions destroyed a prized way of life.)

Rogers often asserted that he was not a member of any organized political party, adding, for humorous effect: "I'm a democrat." In other words, as a public figure, he tried to avoid political squabbles in order to allow himself critical distance from both political parties. At the beginning of the depression, he went on the air for President Hoover; after Franklin D. Roosevelt was elected, Rogers did his best to promote the new president's progressive—some would say radical—domestic programs. Yet both in his columns and on the radio, Rogers found flaws in the New Deal—indeed, he often debunked the dogmatism of FDR's "brain trust." On the other hand, on his Sunday night show for 20 January 1935 he raked the "nine old men" of the U.S. Supreme Court over the coals for thwarting FDR's efforts to control the economy. On 7 April 1935 Rogers defended new taxes, observing that the Soviet experiment had little to offer Americans as a model: "There's no income tax in Russia, but there's no income." Rogers hoped that the New Deal would work; unlike his Republican friends, the Oklahoman endorsed deficit spending as a legitimate experiment to get America moving again. At such moments, Rogers crossed the line to become a partisan spokesman.

Will Rogers died in a plane crash in Alaska while en route to the Far East. An astute film reviewer, trying to account for the popularity of the Oklahoman, had come to the conclusion that Rogers has a "curious national quality. He gives the impression somehow that this country is filled with such sages, wise with years, young in humor and life, shrewd, yet gentle . . . He is what Americans think other Americans are like." After the erosion of traditional values in the 1920s, and after the economic disaster of the 1930s many Americans were indeed grateful to Rogers for his public faith in old-fashioned American common sense.

After the Will Rogers Memorial opened in 1938, his two surviving sons, Will Rogers, Jr., and James Rogers—their brother Fred had died in childhood—became directly involved in preserving the memory of their beloved father. Will Rogers, Jr., spent much of his early life trying to carve out a niche in show business and politics, yet he is probably best known for portraying his father in the 1952 film *The Story of Will Rogers*. His younger sister Mary, after a brief career in the movies, maintained a low profile until her death in 1989. The family donated its Santa Monica ranch, which served as the family home until Betty Rogers's death in 1944, to the state of California, which preserved it as a state park.

Americans old enough to recall 15 August 1935 remember what they were doing when they heard about the plane crash that killed the Oklahoma humorist and his fellow Oklahoman and pilot, Wiley Post. These aging Americans are the same people who revere Rogers today. For them, it is entirely appropriate that the award-winning Broadway musical *The Will Rogers Follies: A Life in Re-vue*, which debuted in 1992, opens with a tune entitled "Willamania," a musical tribute to his daily and weekly columns. In this opening number, Ziegfeld's "favorite girl" tells of being unable to drink her morning coffee without an accompanying serving of Will's "wit and wisdom." Millions of Americans shared her addiction. And yet an invisible glass wall seems to have separated his brand of humor from the cultural tastes of succeeding generations. Perhaps his appeal perished with him. Or perhaps it simply lies fallow, until such time as Americans once again find themselves in need of a wise—as well as wise-cracking—cultural counselor.

• Not only the papers of Will Rogers but thousands of photographs, hundreds of scrapbooks, films, videos—even some of his clothes—are preserved at the state-supported Will Rogers Memorial in Claremore, Okla. Many university libraries own *The Writings of Will Rogers* (1973–1984), a 22-volume series of authenticated versions of Rogers's books, articles, radio broadcasts, and essays backed by a cumulative index. The most scholarly work is Peter C. Rollins, *Will Rogers: A Bio-Bibliography* (1984), which contains a detailed overview of his life and career as well as a fifty-page bibliographical essay and such helpful items as credits for his films, plot summaries of his films and radio broadcasts, and an inventory of his papers held at the memorial in Claremore (as of 1984). The best biography is by Betty Rogers, *Will Rogers: His Wife's Story* (1941; repr. 1979). Lavishly illustrated, but without new insights, is Richard M. Ketchum, *Will Rogers: His Life and Times* (1973). The only work to probe the psyche of Will Rogers is an unpublished dissertation: Samuel F. Roach, "Lariat in the Sun: The Story of Will Rogers" (Oklahoma State Univ., 1972), a study that extends from cradle to grave. Roach was the first biographer to discuss openly some of the negative aspects of Rogers's upbringing, especially his ambivalent feelings toward his father. An article by Roach limns the outlines of his argument: "Will Rogers' Youthful Relationship with His Father, Clem Rogers: A Story of Love and Tension," *Chronicles of Oklahoma* 58 (1980): 325–42. Family footage and contemporary scenes from the Santa Monica ranch appear in the Peter C. Rollins documentary *Will Rog-*

ers' 1920s: A Cowboy's Guide to the Times (1976). An HBO special entitled Will Rogers: Look Back in Laughter (1987) also devoted considerable screen time to images from the ranch.

PETER C. ROLLINS

ROGERS, William Augustus (13 Nov. 1832–1 Mar. 1898), astronomer and physicist, was born in Waterford, Connecticut, the son of David Potter Rogers, a fisherman and farmer, and Mary Anna (her maiden name was also Rogers). Rogers entered Brown University in 1854. Upon his graduation in 1857, he was hired by the Alfred Academy in Alfred, New York, where he had prepared for college, to teach mathematics. In that same year, he married Rebecca Jane Titsworth, with whom he had three children. His wife also served as his research assistant, especially in correcting astronomical observations for known errors. In 1859 he became professor of mathematics at Alfred University, where he was also appointed to the chair in industrial mechanics in 1860.

Faced with the prospect in 1860 of becoming director of the planned astronomical observatory at Alfred University and without any formal training or experience in astronomy, Rogers applied to Harvard College Observatory, which offered a program in practical astronomy. He spent parts of 1860 and 1861 at Harvard, learning how to use astronomical instruments. In 1864 he returned to Harvard College Observatory, where as a student assistant he observed and reduced transit observations of stars and asteroids. After serving a one-year enlistment in the U.S. Navy at the close of the Civil War, Rogers returned to Alfred in 1865 and oversaw construction of its observatory. At Alfred, Rogers observed and computed orbits for a number of asteroids, a continuation of the research program he had begun at Harvard.

Rogers returned to Harvard College Observatory in 1870, this time as a member of the staff. He was soon put in charge of the new eight-inch meridian circle and of a research program to determine the positions of stars between fifty and fifty-five degrees north declination for the international survey organized by the Astronomische Gesellschaft. He completed the observations in 1879. The published observations filled six volumes of the Annals of Harvard College Observatory (vols. 10, 15 [pts. 1 and 2], 16, 25, 35, and 36) and appeared between 1877 and 1896. Rogers oversaw the completion of the publication of the star catalog both at Harvard College Observatory and at Colby College, where in 1886 he had become professor of physics and astronomy.

In the 1880s Rogers began receiving peer recognition. He was elected vice president of the American Microscopical Society in 1884 and president in 1887. In 1882–1883 he was vice president of the Mathematics and Astronomy Section of the American Association for the Advancement of Science. He became a member of the National Academy of Sciences in 1885.

While at Harvard, Rogers had become increasingly interested in questions of precision, physical constants, and accuracy in measurement. He published in a variety of journals over two decades, including the Proceedings of the American Academy of Arts and Sciences, the American Journal of Science, and the Proceedings of the American Association for the Advancement of Science, writing on the limits of accuracy in measurements with telescopes or microscopes and on the construction and comparison of standards of length. He became concerned with precision instruments, such as diffraction gratings. In 1879 he was selected by the American Academy of Arts and Sciences, of which he was a member, to travel to Europe to obtain copies of the imperial yard and the French meter.

These interests dominated his research program at Colby, where he established a model laboratory for research on physical constants and accurate measurement. The most important result to come out of that laboratory was the paper he coauthored with Edward W. Morley, published in the 1896 Physics Review, which described the application of optical methods for the detection of minuscule changes in the length of metals; the technique was quickly and widely adopted. He died in Waterville, Maine, only a month before he was to retire from teaching to become director of a new physics laboratory at Alfred University.

Contemporaries saw Rogers as a man of detail, precision, and dedication. In 1864 the director of Harvard College Observatory, George P. Bond, described Rogers as having "true zeal and entire honesty of character." Though not a scientist who strove for spectacular accomplishments, Rogers nevertheless advanced the frontier of knowledge slowly and systematically.

• For insight into Rogers's training in the pre-Ph.D. era of American science, the material in the Harvard University Archives is very useful. The only modern assessment of Rogers is in Bessie Zaban Jones and Lyle Gifford Boyd, The Harvard College Observatory: The First Four Directorships, 1839–1919 (1971). The standard biographical sources are the memoirs written by Edward W. Morley and Arthur Searle in National Academy of Sciences, Biographical Memoirs 4 (1902), pp. 185–99, and 6 (1909), pp. 109–17. Morley provides a bibliography of Rogers's publications in Biographical Memoirs 6, pp. 113–17.

MARC ROTHENBERG

ROGERS, William Barton (7 Dec. 1804–30 May 1882), geologist and educator, was born in Philadelphia, Pennsylvania, the son of Patrick Kerr Rogers, a Physician, and Hannah Blythe. William and his brothers, James Blythe, Henry Darwin and Robert Empie (all of whom became successful scientists), were educated in the public schools of Baltimore. When Patrick Rogers was elected professor of natural philosophy and chemistry at the College of William and Mary in 1819, the fifteen-year-old William immediately enrolled there, studying science until 1821. Thereafter he operated a school at Windsor, Maryland, with his younger brother Henry.

William Rogers began to lecture at Baltimore's Maryland Institute in 1827. Here he began to establish his reputation as an educator. His lectures on such diverse subjects as astronomy and railroads were so successful, and his ideas on education so persuasive, that the Institute's board of governors invited him to organize and manage a high school to be opened in 1828. When his father died of malaria in August 1828, however, Rogers was invited to succeed him at William and Mary, where he remained until 1835. His lectures on astronomy, chemistry, mathematics, and physics became famous for their clarity, elegance, organization, and animated delivery. They were illustrated by experiments, reportedly carried out with such a dramatic flair that they evoked spontaneous applause from his audiences. After his brother Henry returned from England with a great enthusiasm for geology in 1833, Rogers turned his attention to the study of minerals, rocks, and fossils. These early efforts culminated in the publication of several papers on artesian wells, the chemical analyses of carbonates, and the glauconitic greensands and calcareous marls of Virginia with a view to their use as fertilizers.

This practical application of Rogers's research findings to farming attracted the interests of the Virginia legislature, prompting Rogers to lobby for the establishment in 1835 of a Virginian Geological Survey. For this he secured resources and funding by promising economic returns from properly mapping the terrain for future railroad construction, locating more fertilizer sources, and revealing the existence of valuable mineral deposits. The same year he left Baltimore to become the state geologist and director of the Virginian Geological Survey; he was also appointed professor of natural philosophy and geology at the University of Virginia. His efforts with the Geological Survey from 1835 until 1842 provided the data for his most important geological publications.

The survey began its detailed study of the scientific and practical geology of Virginia with four specific goals: to produce an accurate geological map with topographic sections; to create a stratigraphic map without vertical exaggeration; to conduct chemical analyses of material found; and to assemble a collection of minerals. Although his workload was lightened by the aid of his brothers, Robert and James, and a group of assistants, Rogers found it necessary to oversee personally all aspects of the survey. He was a perfectionist, and there were not enough sufficiently-trained field geologists under his direction. Despite his exhaustive efforts, after 1837 the Virginia legislature responded to a drop in public revenues by cutting funding and more closely scrutinizing the survey, finally terminating support for the project altogether in 1841. Rogers was unable to persuade them to continue funding beyond 1842. As a result, few copies of Rogers's six annual reports were printed, and a final report was never published. The reports were not even combined into a single publication until Jed Hotchkiss compiled and published them with a map in 1884. Nevertheless, the short-lived survey had pioneered work in the study of Virginian deposits of infusorial earth, in chemical geology, in demonstrating the relation of coal beds to the amount of disturbance in surrounding strata, and in the geological mapping of Virginia.

During the same period William's brother Henry, then state geologist for Pennsylvania, directed geological surveys of Pennsylvania and New Jersey. The brothers collaborated to produce their most important geological works, on the Appalachian Mountain chain. The Rogers brothers were the first to map authoritatively this region's stratigraphy and structural geology. Their fieldwork, laboratory analyses, and careful recordings of observations were much admired. They effectively studied the solvent action of water on rocks and minerals, and their stratigraphic observations were extremely precise. In 1842 they jointly presented a paper on their findings at the third annual meeting of the Association of American Geologists and Naturalists; on the invitation of Charles Lyell, the paper was later presented before the British Association and published in both countries.

In the paper William and Henry Rogers proposed a new and controversial theory on mountain formation and the distribution and processes of faulting and folding. They demonstrated that any explanatory framework for the formation of mountain chains must incorporate elements that provide for the uniformity of forces over a vast area of land. As a result, they rejected prevailing theories of vertical uplift in favor of an explanation relying on the effects of tangential forces acting perpendicularly to the orientation of the mountain chain. Their resulting theory ultimately attempted to link orogenesis (mountain-building) to folding, wavelike motions in the crust that mirrored similar motions in the molten layer below. In Britain the structural and stratigraphic work was praised and many considered it the most important American contribution to geological theory of the day; others, however, vehemently opposed the brothers' views. Nevertheless, their theory paved the way for the more uniform tangential contraction theory of mountain formation developed by geologist James Dwight Dana, which dominated geological thought well into the twentieth century.

While Rogers conducted his pioneering efforts in geology and established his reputation as a scientist, he continued to teach at the University of Virginia, rising to the position of chairman of the faculty in 1844. His courses were popular, but the university experienced a decade of turbulence punctuated by student riots, during which Rogers was required regretfully to call the civil authorities to restore order on campus. At the same time, he frequently had to defend the university before the legislature. Suffering from exhaustion, intermittent severe illness, and disillusionment with the attitude toward education and research in Virginia, Rogers attempted to resign in 1848. Convinced by his colleagues to stay, however, he remained until 1853. He married Emma Savage of Boston in 1849; they had no children.

In 1853 Rogers moved to Boston, which he found more receptive to his views on the value of scientific research and its technical applications. While continuing to publish on a variety of scientific subjects, he became involved with scientific movements in Massachusetts and began to focus his efforts on popularizing useful scientific knowledge and on establishing a technical institute where students would learn by doing. During his work with the Virginia Geological Survey he had frequently lamented the lack of well-trained field geologists and had become convinced of the need to establish an institution to provide practical scientific training. He and his brother Henry had discussed how such a school should be formed and managed. After Henry moved to Scotland in 1857, Rogers was left alone to lobby for a technical college in Boston; in 1861, the same year he was appointed state inspector of gas meters, the legislature passed an act incorporating the Massachusetts Institute of Technology (MIT). The outbreak of the Civil War prevented it from opening until 1865. With the establishment of MIT, which initially offered degrees in mechanical engineering, civil and topographical engineering, practical chemistry, geology and mining, building and architecture, and general science and literature, Rogers provided the prototype of the modern engineering technical institute. With a slant toward applied science, it offered a curriculum that heavily emphasized laboratory work. During their first years students were to receive a thorough grounding in mathematics, physics, and chemistry, coupled with a broad exposure to the humanities.

At the opening of the new school Rogers was professor of physics and geology. He was also responsible for its early administration as its first president until he was forced to step down in 1870 owing to ill health. In 1878 he resumed the position until his retirement in 1881. During his presidency he did much to secure the future for and to give integrity to the college; meanwhile, he focused his own research on the study of such physical problems as variations of ozone in the atmosphere and binocular vision.

Rogers's influence was not restricted to the universities and institutions that employed him. He was able to reach a larger audience through his publications and activities with various scientific organizations. He published ninety-three papers and two textbooks on geological subjects, twenty-eight papers on physical subjects, and twenty-one on chemistry. He presented papers at numerous conferences and meetings and gave popular lectures, including a series delivered before the Lowell Institute in Boston in 1862.

Rogers played a significant role in the organization in 1840 of the Association of American Geologists and Naturalists, over which he presided as chairman in 1845 and as president in 1847. He was also a founding member of the Association of the Advancement of Science (1848), becoming its president in 1876. He also was a founding member and eventually president (1879–1882) of the National Academy of Sciences, and a prominent member in numerous other societies, including the American Academy of Arts and Sciences, for which he was corresponding secretary from 1863 to 1869. After an illustrious career during which he received many honors and awards, Rogers died of heart failure while addressing the graduates of the class of 1882 in Huntington Hall at MIT.

• A collection of Rogers's papers is in the archives of the Massachusetts Institute of Technology, Cambridge. The most comprehensive biographical works are Emma Rogers, ed., *Life and Letters of William Barton Rogers* (2 vols., 1896); and R. R. Shrock, *Geology at M.I.T. 1865–1965*, vol. 1, *The Faculty and Supporting Staff* (1977), pp. 1–19, 99–214. For his years in Virginia see M. L. Aldrich and A. E. Leviton, "William Barton Rogers and the Virginia Geological Survey," in *The Geological Sciences in the Ante Bellum South*, ed. J. X. Corgan (1982), pp. 83–104; W. Ernst, "William Barton Rogers, Ante Bellum Virginia Geologist," *Virginia Cavalcade* 24 (1974): 13–21; R. C. Milici and C. B. Hobbs, Jr., "William Barton Rogers and the First Geological Survey of Virginia, 1835–1841," *Earth Science History* 6 (1987): 3–13; and P. W. Roper, "Jed Hotchkiss and the Geological Map of Virginia," *Earth Science History* 10 (1991): 38–43. Also of interest are S. C. Bevan, "William Barton Rogers, a Pioneer American Scientist," *Scientific Monthly* 50, no. 2 (1940): 110–24; Patsy A. Gerstner, *Henry Darwin Rogers, 1808–1866: American Geologist* (1994); J. R. Killian, Jr., "William Barton Rogers," *Technology Review* 60 (1958): 105–8, 124–30; and N. A. Pierce, "The Rogers Brothers and Lyell," *Pennsylvania Geology* 9, no. 5 (1978): 7–14. For Rogers's role in the AAAS see Sally Gregory Kohlstedt, *The Formation of the American Scientific Community: The AAAS, 1848–1860* (1976), and Robert V. Bruce, *The Launching of American Science, 1846–1876* (1987).

TRENT A. MITCHELL

ROGGE, O. John (12 Oct. 1903–22 Mar. 1981), attorney, government prosecutor, and civil liberties activist, was born Oetje John Rogge in Cass County, Illinois, the son of Hermann Rogge and Lydia Ann Satorius, farmers. Schooled partly on threshing crews until his late teens, Rogge became the youngest person to earn a bachelor's degree from the University of Illinois in 1922 at the age of nineteen. Rogge's impressive academic achievements at Illinois were followed by a brilliant career at Harvard Law School, where he became an editor of the law review and in 1925 the youngest person to earn an LL.B. in the school's modern era. Returning to Harvard in the early years of the Great Depression, he took a doctor of laws degree in 1932 and soon followed other recent graduates to Washington, D.C., where, inspired by professors such as Felix Frankfurter, they practiced law for Franklin Roosevelt's New Deal.

Rogge first drew attention to himself as a first-class investigator and litigator in 1934 by representing the Reconstruction Finance Corporation in a successful five-year suit to recover millions of dollars in loans made to the Central Republic Trust Company of Chicago during the Herbert Hoover years. Other officials of the New Deal in the Securities and Exchange Commission, the Treasury Department, and the Justice Department soon also called on Rogge to handle their complex cases. With a shifting portfolio of titles, ranging from special counsel to assistant general counsel in charge of litigation, Rogge successfully prosecuted Moe Annenberg, the publishing tycoon, for income tax evasion and launched the inquiry that uncovered misconduct by A. P. Gianini's huge western banking empire. Promoted to assistant attorney general in charge of the Justice Department's Criminal Division, in 1939 he opened a wide-ranging probe into political corruption directed at the remnants of Huey Long's Louisiana machine.

Faced with the fact that members of the Long organization, then headed by Huey's brother Earl, had reported all income from graft and extortion on their tax returns, Rogge and his aides secured their conviction on charges of mail fraud by arguing that they had received payoffs through the U.S. Post Office, a theory ultimately endorsed by the federal courts that heard the cases. According to one historian of Louisiana politics, Rogge "ruined more reputations and more businesses, cracked apart more fortunes than the genius Huey [Long] himself."

After a brief respite from government service, during which time he represented the giant Associated Gas and Electric Company, Rogge returned to the Justice Department in 1943 as special assistant to Attorney General Francis Biddle. He assumed direction of the government's disastrous wartime prosecution of more than two dozen American fascists, including theoretician Lawrence Dennis and anti-Semitic leader Gerald L. K. Smith.

The trial, which lasted eight months, alternated between a riot and a circus. Five defense lawyers were cited for contempt. Death, illness, and various disruptions reduced the number of defendants. The judge's own death produced a mistrial. Sensing only further embarrassment for the government once the Supreme Court reversed a similar conviction for sedition, Rogge urged his superiors to drop the case. Attorney General Tom Clark pushed ahead, however, until the chief justice of the U.S. District Court finally quashed the effort in 1946.

Rogge again ran afoul of Attorney General Clark when in a speech at Swarthmore College in 1946 he alleged that his investigations had produced evidence of links between the defeated German Nazi regime and American fascists, including members of Congress. The proof, he said, was in a lengthy report he had prepared for the attorney general. Clark, apparently on orders from President Harry S. Truman, fired Rogge for divulging the contents of a confidential government document. "I am more afraid of fascism than communism in America," Rogge said at the time. He also noted that Federal Bureau of Investigation director J. Edgar Hoover regularly leaked the contents of official government documents when attacking American communists.

Returning to private practice in New York, disillusioned with Truman's liberalism, Rogge plunged further into left-wing politics and legal-defense efforts. He dropped his Democratic party affiliation and took out membership in the communist-dominated American Labor party (ALP) led by the charismatic New York congressman Vito Marcantonio. Rogge ran on the ALP's judicial slate in 1948, while also chairing the

New York campaign of Henry Wallace, whose 1948 Progressive party drew substantial support from domestic communists because of Wallace's call for rapprochement with the Soviet Union.

With the Cold War now in full swing, Rogge went as an American delegate in 1948 to the World Peace Congress in Poland, which denounced atomic bombs and, by implication, America's atomic monopoly. In Poland, however, he also made a rousing speech in defense of American institutions that had come under attack by Soviet delegates. Back in the United States he became vice president of the National Lawyers Guild and a major supporter of the Civil Rights Congress, two legal organizations with important ties to the Communist party.

Along with Emanuel Bloch, later the attorney for accused atomic spies Julius and Ethel Rosenberg, Rogge represented the Trenton Six, a group of black youths under death sentence in New Jersey who became a cause célèbre for the American left. He also argued on behalf of the Joint Anti-Fascist Refugee Committee in its successful legal actions against the attorney general of the United States, who had placed the group on his list of subversive and communist-dominated organizations. Rogge seldom missed an opportunity to attack the Truman administration's Loyalty and Security Program, the House Un-American Activities Committee, or FBI director Hoover.

Although a frequent critic of U.S. foreign policy in the Cold War, Rogge had not closed his eyes entirely to Soviet misconduct. Joseph Stalin's condemnation of the Tito regime in Yugoslavia in 1950 and the outbreak of the Korean War that same year confirmed Rogge's doubts about the Soviet ruler and led him back into the traditional liberal fold. He broke with the ALP when it failed to condemn North Korean aggression, and he rejoined the Democratic party.

Most significantly, O. John Rogge represented David Greenglass, Ethel Rosenberg's brother, who testified against his brother-in-law and sister at their trial for espionage in 1951. Greenglass's cooperation, encouraged by Rogge, secured the couple's conviction and spared his client, who also had been charged with espionage, from a death sentence. Rogge's former allies in the Communist party bitterly denounced his part in the Rosenberg case and even accused him of conspiring with government prosecutors. The FBI, however, continued to regard him as a dangerous radical throughout the trial, and Rogge was stunned by the severity of the sentences handed down by Judge Irving Kaufman—death for the Rosenbergs and fifteen years in prison for Greenglass.

Rogge came in for further abuse from his old left-wing associates in 1951 when he testified for the government in its unsuccessful attempt to prosecute W. E. B. Du Bois and his associates in the Peace Information Center for failing to register as agents of a foreign power.

For the remainder of his life Rogge continued his legal representation of minority groups and the poor and to write often of the threat posed to civil liberties by both the extreme right and left. He died in New York City. He had been twice married and had two children.

• Rogge's legal papers remain with his New York law firm, Rogge, Wright, Rogge and Weiner, which has made them available to scholars, especially his files on the Rosenberg case. Rogge wrote numerous law review articles and four books, *Our Vanishing Civil Liberties* (1949), *Why Men Confess* (1959), *The First and the Fifth: With Some Excursions into Others* (1960), and *The Official German Report: Nazi Penetration, 1924–1942* (1961). Rogge's relationship to the American communist movement is discussed in David A. Shannon, *The Decline of American Communism* (1959), pp. 204–5. Alva Johnson chronicled Rogge's legal battle with the Long machine in three *Saturday Evening Post* articles in two editions, May and June 1940. An obituary is in the *New York Times*, 23 Mar. 1981.

MICHAEL E. PARRISH

ROHDE, Ruth Bryan Owen (2 Oct. 1885–26 July 1954), congresswoman, diplomat, lecturer, and author, was born in Jacksonville, Illinois, the daughter of William Jennings Bryan, a lawyer, and Mary Elizabeth Baird. When Ruth was two, the family moved to Lincoln, Nebraska, and then to Washington, D.C., three years later, when her father was elected to Congress. Young Ruth became "the sweetheart of the House" as she sat with her father during fierce tariff debates (Ramsey, *Delineator*, p. 11). The family traveled with Bryan during his tumultuous campaign as the Democratic party's nominee for president in 1896. In 1901 Ruth entered the University of Nebraska, remained two years, and at eighteen married artist William Homer Leavitt. They had two children. Ruth Bryan Leavitt served as her father's secretary during his third and final presidential campaign in 1908. In May 1909 she divorced Leavitt and seven months later traveled to Germany to study voice. In 1910 she married Reginald A. Owen, an officer of the British Royal Engineers. They had two children. Posted to Jamaica until European tensions led to her husband's recall to England in 1913, Ruth Owen settled in London, where she worked with Lou Hoover, wife of Herbert Hoover for the American Woman's War Relief Fund. In 1915, while her husband fought in the Dardanelles campaign, she served as a volunteer operating room nurse for the British army in the Egypt and Palestine campaigns. At the end of the war, the Owens relocated in Florida with the Bryans.

With her husband left a permanent invalid from the war, Ruth Owen became the major breadwinner. Initially using her father's contacts to join the Chautauqua and lyceum circuits to lecture on her Middle East experiences, she was quickly acclaimed for her "magnetic and charming personality" and her "power as a speaker" (*Miami Herald*, 12 Nov. 1919). She joined organizations ranging from the National Consumers' League to the Daughters of the American Revolution (DAR) and served as Florida's member of the National Council on Child Welfare and as president of the Community Council of Civic Clubs. Named vice

chairwoman of the board of regents of the fledgling University of Miami in 1925, she also taught in the Public Speaking Department and wrote a well-regarded text, *Elements of Public Speaking* (1931).

In 1926 Owen failed in her campaign to win the Democratic nomination for Congress representing a district stretching from Jacksonville to Key West. She determined to try again in 1928. Widowed in 1927, but with a record strengthened by her relief work after the devastating hurricane of 1926, she campaigned with the energetic tactics of her father. A striking image in her green Model A Ford, she gave 500 speeches while touring the district. Winning the primary by a wide margin, Owen was the first woman elected to the House of Representatives from a southern state.

House colleagues were impressed by her talent and charm. One journalist asserted: "male colleagues are daft about her, and she has been rushed like the most popular co-ed on a campus" (Gilfond, p. 152). Her election was challenged because under a 1907 law, she had forfeited her U.S. citizenship when she married a British citizen. In 1922 women lobbyists had won passage of the Cable Act, which changed the status of an American woman who married a foreigner to that of a naturalized citizen. However, if she lived abroad for more than two years as had Owen, she "renounced" her citizenship and could apply for naturalization on her return to the United States after one year's residency. Owen had not petitioned for naturalization until January 1925 and technically did not meet the constitutional requirement of U.S. citizenship for seven years prior to her election to Congress. She persuasively argued her case, pointing out that the demands of her lecture schedule, which enabled her to support her husband and children, had precluded her appearance at the federal courthouse to file for citizenship at an earlier date. She insisted that the Cable Act had restored her status as a citizen and noted that American men marrying foreign women faced no loss of citizenship. She won overwhelming vindication from the House and eventual amendment of the Cable Act so that a woman who married a foreigner was "no longer subject to presumptive loss of her citizenship" (Lemons, pp. 235–36).

The House leadership, in recognition of her father and her own experience abroad, named Owen as the first woman member of the prestigious Foreign Affairs Committee. In the gathering economic crisis, she voted for the protectionist Hawley-Smoot Tariff of 1930, causing some wags to insist they heard Bryan rolling in his grave. In the area of social policy, she argued for a federal home and child department, explaining she had "to play a game of hide-and-seek with these government agencies, . . . whenever I seek answers to questions asked by the wives and mothers of my district" (Chamberlin, p. 77). She also won appropriations to send delegates to international conferences on health and child welfare and received private support from the DAR for a citizenship program to bring young leaders from each state to Washington. For her constituents she fought to make the Everglades a national park and won appropriations to battle the Mediterranean fruit fly. Reelected in 1930, her dry position on Prohibition caused her defeat in 1932. As a lame duck, she yielded to her constituents and voted for repeal of the Eighteenth Amendment.

When Franklin Delano Roosevelt named Owen minister to Denmark and Iceland in 1933, she became the first woman to hold such a post in the American foreign service. Ironically, one of her first duties was to allay the Danes' concerns over the Hawley-Smoot Tariff. She married Captain Börge Rohde of the Danish Royal Guards in 1936, embroiling herself again in a citizenship controversy. She became, through her marriage, a Danish citizen. Unable with dual citizenship to continue her diplomatic assignment, she resigned and returned to the United States to campaign for Roosevelt's reelection.

Residing in West Virginia, Ruth Rohde was appointed to the board of directors of nearby Alderson federal prison for women. She became one of the highest-paid lecturers in the country and served as a director of the American Platform Guild. She published four books on Scandinavia, *Leaves from a Greenland Diary* (1935), *Denmark Caravan* (1936), *The Castle in the Silver Wood and Other Danish Fairy Tales Retold* (1939), and *Picture Tales from Scandinavia* (1939), followed by *Caribbean Caravel* (1949). During World War II, she lectured on postwar peace and published her plan for a United States of the world in *Look Forward Warrior* (1943). In 1949 President Harry Truman appointed her an alternate delegate to the General Assembly of the United Nations. She died in Copenhagen, where she was to accept the Danish Order of Merit for her contribution to Danish-American friendship.

In many ways, Ruth Bryan Owen Rohde followed her distinguished father: as a popular lecturer, as a member of Congress, and, finally, in foreign affairs. However, as a woman she faced her own challenges in the legislature and foreign service and found her own issues for women, children, and world peace.

• There are a few letters from Rohde in the William Jennings Bryan Papers, and correspondence on her lecture tours and her third marriage is in the Bess Furman Papers at the Library of Congress. A short biography of Rohde is in Hope Chamberlin, *A Minority of Members: Women in the U.S. Congress* (1973). William Jennings Bryan and Mary Baird Bryan, *The Memoirs of William Jennings Bryan* (1925), treat her early years and marriage, as does Paolo Coletta, *William Jennings Bryan*, vol. 1: *Political Evangelist, 1860–1908* (1964). Duff Gilfond, "Gentlewomen of the House," *American Mercury*, Oct. 1929, pp. 151–59, J. Elliot Ramsey, "Double Helpings of Fame," *Delineator*, Jan. 1937, p. 11; "Mr. Hoover's Congress," *Literary Digest*, 28 Nov. 1928, pp. 10–11; "Mr. Roosevelt's New Deal for Women," *Literary Digest*, 15 Apr. 1933, pp. 22–24; "Lady Lame Duck's Farewell," *Literary Digest*, 25 Feb. 1933, p. 32; and "Ruth Bryan Owen: First Woman Diplomat," *Christian Century*, 26 Apr. 1933, pp. 549–50, cover her personality and career. J. Stanley Lemons, *The Woman Citizen: Social Feminism in the 1920s* (1973), discusses the Cable Act; for Rohde's argument see U.S. House of Representatives, Committee on Elections, *Arguments and Hearings in the Contested Election Case of William C. Lawson v. Ruth Bryan Owen*, 17 Jan. 1930, Committee Print 1. Obituaries are in the *New York Times*, 27 July 1954, and *Newsweek*, 9 Aug. 1954, p. 65.

DOROTHY M. BROWN

ROHÉ, George Henry (26 Jan. 1851–6 Feb. 1899), physician, was born in Baltimore, Maryland, the son of John Rohé and Mary Fuchs. He attended public schools in Baltimore and began his medical education with Augustus F. Erich, professor of gynecology at the College of Physicians and Surgeons in the same city. He continued his studies at the University of Maryland, earning a medical degree in 1873. Soon after graduation Rohé entered the U.S. Signal Service and was stationed in Atlanta, New Orleans, and Boston. In Boston he became interested in dermatology and worked as the assistant physician of the Boston Dispensary for Skin Diseases.

In 1877 Rohé returned to Baltimore and established a private practice. He also joined the faculty of the College of Physicians and Surgeons, renewing his affiliation with the institution that he would serve in various capacities until 1890. Starting out as a lecturer on skin diseases, he was soon asked to chair the department of hygiene; he subsequently headed the department of obstetrics. Displaying a wide range of medical expertise, he also worked as professor of therapeutics and mental disease. In 1890 he married Mary Laudermann Coffin; they had one child.

Rohé is perhaps best known, however, for his contributions to psychiatry. While serving as Baltimore's commissioner of health in 1891, he was asked to become superintendent of the Maryland State Hospital for the Insane in Catonsville. According to the *American Journal of Insanity*, he "entered with characteristic vigor upon this new field of work" (Apr. 1899). Eager to implement the latest techniques in sanitation and hygiene, he supervised the successful installation of a newly designed system of sewage disposal. He was praised by his contemporaries for his organizational skills and painstaking attention to details, and he devoted his first few years at the hospital to improving its management and efficiency. While he directed much of his time to administrative responsibilities, Rohé remained an active member of the medical staff as well. Through his regular interactions with female patients, he began to explore the widely believed allegation that diseased pelvic organs could contribute to insanity. Rohe followed the lead of many gynecologists who advocated surgical removal of reproductive organs, although most psychiatrists, who were less convinced of this association, rejected this treatment. His research in this area prompted many to question the relationship between physical and psychological well-being.

After four years at the Maryland asylum Rohé was chosen to establish a second state hospital, and he once again set eagerly to work. He labored in the planning and development of the new facility, and in 1898 the Springfield State Hospital at Sykesville received its first patients. Innovative in his treatment methods,

Rohé was a vocal advocate of the "open door" system and wanted no locks on any of the windows or doors. Reporting to the *American Journal of Insanity* in July 1898, he proudly claimed, "This institution is believed to be the most consistent example of the 'open-door' system in existence." He considered the lack of restraints to have a positive effect on patient morale, while possibly decreasing their desire to escape. He acknowledged that greater demands were placed on the attendants, but Rohé boasted of the diligence of his staff, and of the superior environment surrounding both patients and employees at the Springfield institution.

Rohé's achievements extended beyond his managerial and medical accomplishments. He was well known for his contributions to the medical literature, and he authored and edited numerous publications. His works, praised for their style, were widely distributed. In addition to many journal articles, he wrote several texts, including *Textbook of Hygiene* (1885), which was reprinted several times. He also wrote *Practical Notes on the Treatment of Skin Diseases* (1885) and coauthored, with G. A. Liebig, *Practical Electricity in Medicine and Surgery* (1890). He served as associate editor for the *Independent Practitioner* and the *Annual for Universal Medical Science*; he also edited the *Medical Chronicle* from 1882 to 1885.

Among the many organizations Rohé was active in were the Baltimore Medical and Surgical Society, the Southern Gynecological and Surgical Society, the American Academy of Medicine, and the American Medico-Psychological Association (later the American Psychiatric Association). He was president of the American Association of Obstetricians and Gynecologists (1893–1894), the Medical and Chirurgical Faculty of Maryland (1893–1894), and the American Public Health Association (1898–1899). A member of the first Pan-American Medical Congress, he was also a corresponding member of several foreign medical societies.

After experiencing symptoms of cardiac illness for a year, Rohé died while attending the National Prison Congress at New Orleans, Louisiana. He was remembered by many as an avid reader and his ability to speak several languages. He was particularly renowned for his extraordinary memory. Rohé was said to be "eminently successful" as a teacher of medicine; his unbounded energy and devotion, particularly toward the treatment of the mentally ill, earned him much recognition and respect.

• Brief biographical accounts of Rohé appear in Henry M. Hurd, ed., *The Institutional Care of the Insane in the United States and Canada*, vol. 4 (1917); and William B. Atkinson, ed., *The Physicians and Surgeons of the United States* (1878). Obituaries are in the *American Journal of Insanity*, Apr. 1899; the *Journal of the American Medical Association*, 18 Feb. 1899; and the *Baltimore Sun*, 7 Feb. 1899.

CHRISTINE CLARK ZEMLA

ROKEACH, Milton (27 Dec. 1918–25 Oct. 1988), social psychologist, was born in Hrubishow, Poland, the son of Lejb Rokeach, an Orthodox Jewish rabbi, and Han-

na Miriam Mischne. When he was seven years old, his family moved to Brooklyn, New York, where he grew up. In 1941 he graduated from Brooklyn College, where his influential teachers included Abraham Maslow, a leader in the humanistic psychology movement, and Solomon Asch, who promoted the perspective of Gestalt theory in social psychology. Entering graduate study at the University of California at Berkeley, he earned a master's degree in 1942 before serving four years as an enlisted man in the army in the Aviation Psychology Program. He married Muriel Weiner in 1942; they had three children and were divorced in 1968. Returning to Berkeley in 1946, he worked primarily with Else Frenkel-Brunswik and Nevitt Sanford, leaders in the research later reported in the classic *The Authoritarian Personality* (1950).

The Berkeley group had found anti-Semitic prejudice to be an aspect of a generalized readiness to reject minorities and out-groups. This brand of ethnocentrism, they claimed, was a reflection of a pattern of proto-Fascist dispositions of personality, or authoritarianism. The approach was inspired by psychoanalytic theorizing about the roots of Nazism in the authoritarian German family. Frenkel-Brunswik had particularly stressed the role of black-and-white thinking, or "intolerance of ambiguity," in authoritarianism. Rokeach saw the possible psychological equivalence of intolerance of ambiguity to Abraham Luchins's concept of mental rigidity in problem solving, to which Asch had introduced him. In his doctoral research with Sanford and Frenkel-Brunswik, he adapted Luchins's experimental procedure and related mental rigidity to prejudice. The ensuing article, "Generalized Mental Rigidity as a factor in Ethnocentrism," became an immediate center of psychological attention.

During the 1950s *The Authoritarian Personality* attracted much substantive and methodological criticism. When Rokeach joined the psychology faculty at Michigan State University in 1947, his initial research addressed two of the lines along which the book had been criticized: that the work focused on right-wing authoritarianism but ignored authoritarianism of the left, and that its psychoanalytic framework implied a characterological basis of prejudice inaccessible to educational impact. An important monograph, "Political and Religious Dogmatism," introduced the ideologically neutral concept of dogmatism, or closed-mindedness, as an alternative to the authoritarian personality. Its measurement also makes no assumptions about psychodynamics. *The Open and Closed Mind: Investigations into the Nature of Belief Systems and Personality Systems* (1960), which further developed his theory of belief systems, received wide attention.

Concurrent with this research on normal beliefs and attitudes, Rokeach carried out a unique study of paranoid psychotics. He managed to bring three patients, each of whom claimed to be Jesus Christ, to adjacent beds in the same mental hospital to challenge their central identity beliefs. *The Three Christs of Ypsilanti: A Psychological Study* (1964) was reissued in 1981; in an afterword to the new edition, Rokeach noted wryly that there was a "fourth Christ" at Ypsilanti—the investigator. From the perspective of his later work with self-confrontation, he renounced the manipulative approach on which this and some of his earlier work had been based.

In 1970, after his marriage to sociologist Sandra Ball, Rokeach left Michigan State and moved to Washington State University, where he remained until 1986. During his tenure at Washington State he did his classic survey and experimental research on values, much of it in collaboration with his wife, an independent scholar and researcher into the dynamics of media effects, violence, and values. This research, stemming naturally from his concern with people's belief systems of which values are hierarchically central components, was based on a simple but effective instrument according to which people ranked their "instrumental values"—desirable modes of conduct—and "terminal values"—desirable end-states of existence (*The Nature of Human Values*, 1973). In the experimental treatment, some of the Michigan State students were informed that students who rate "equality" above "freedom" were less likely to involve themselves with civil rights—with the stated implication that they were more concerned with their own freedom than with the freedom of others. Not only did this brief treatment raise their ranking of "equality," but it produced a greater-than-chance effect on behavioral measures, including response to recruitment appeals from a local civil rights organization (the National Association for the Advancement of Colored People) even one year later. Shalom Schwartz (1994) based his extensive research on values in world perspective on an adaptation of Rokeach's instrument.

Rokeach's most unusual research using the self-confrontational method showed methodological brilliance and audacity like that of the *Ypsilanti* study: *The Great American Values Test: Influencing Behavior and Belief Through Television* (1984), written with his wife and Joel W. Grube. This was a carefully controlled study of the effects on a normal home audience of a professionally produced program that induced self-confrontation of terminal value rankings—again freedom and equality, and also "a world of beauty." The results of the study, which was conducted among communities in eastern Washington, were essentially the same as had been obtained with the Michigan State students. The study has no equal in modern communications research.

In 1986 the Rokeaches moved to the University of Southern California with primary appointments as professors of communications in the Annenberg School. Rokeach and his wife continued to be active in their related research programs until his death in Los Angeles from a painful cancer of the spine, which he had endured for thirteen years without allowing it to disrupt his work.

Rokeach was honored internationally by visiting appointments at the Polish Academy of Science and Heidelberg University. He was the president of the Society for the Psychological Study of Social Issues (1966–1967) and received its coveted Kurt Lewin Memorial Award (1984). His most telling comment on the sources that inspired his contribution came in his remarks made while accepting the Harold Lasswell Award of the International Society of Political Psychology. He attributed his inspiration to "my adolescent and even pre-adolescent years growing up in Brooklyn when I was continually torn by demands, on the one side, to continue in the footsteps and traditions of my Orthodox Jewish forefathers and, on the other side, to embrace the humanistic values and anti-humanistic discipline of my orthodox Marxist friends. My work . . . can thus be said to represent both a personal and scientific statement designed not only to increase our theoretical understanding of ideological dogmatism but also to maintain my personal independence from the two kinds of ideological dogmatisms vying for my allegiance, one religious, the other political" (Campbell, p. 261).

Aspects of Rokeach's formulations concerning dogmatism and left-wing authoritarianism have remained contested, but the research career initiated by these personal concerns contributed largely to a social science focused on central human values and human problems. He was a creative innovator whose contribution hinged on his remaining apart from the mainstream. That won him great respect, even from the mainstream.

• Other significant works by Rokeach include "Generalized Mental Rigidity as a Factor in Ethnocentrism," *Journal of Abnormal and Social Psychology* 43 (1948): 259–78; *Political and Religious Dogmatism: An Alternative to the Authoritarian Personality*, Psychological Monographs, vol. 70 (1956); *Beliefs, Attitudes, and Values: A Theory of Organization and Change* (1968); and *Understanding Human Values: Individual and Societal* (1979). *The Authoritarian Personality* (1950) was criticized for ideological bias in Edward A. Shils, "Authoritarianism: 'Right' and 'Left'," in *Studies in the Scope and Method of 'The Authoritarian Personality,'* ed. Richard Christie and Marie Jahoda (1954). This book contains a variety of other contemporary criticism. For Schwartz's cross-cultural research on values see Shalom H. Schwartz, "Studying Human Values," in *Journeys into Cross-Cultural Psychology*, ed. Anne-Marie Bouvy et al. (1994). Challenges to Rokeach's conclusions about dogmatism and left-wing authoritarianism appear in Bob Altemeyer, *The Authoritarian Spectre* (1996.) An appreciative obituary is Donald T. Campbell, "In Memoriam, Milton Rokeach, 1918–1988," *Public Opinion Quarterly* 53 (1989): 258–61.

M. BREWSTER SMITH

ROLFE, John (1585?–1622), planter, was probably born in Heacham, Norfolk, England, the son of John Rolfe and Dorothea Mason. Rolfe and his first wife (name unknown) sailed for America with the great 1609 Virginia fleet. The *Sea Venture* was wrecked on Bermuda, where his daughter Bermuda was born and apparently died; he arrived in Jamestown on 23 June 1610. By 1612 Rolfe had begun experimentation with West Indian tobacco, *Nicotiana tabacum*, which became Virginia's cash crop and the colony's economic salvation. In 1614 Rolfe was made the plantation's secretary and recorder general.

In 1614 Rolfe, whose first wife died shortly after their arrival in Virginia, married Pocahontas (Mataoka), then a captive in Jamestown. Rolfe, disturbed by God's wrath against the sons of Levi and Israel "for marrying strange wives" and by accusations of lustfulness by the "vulgar sort," protested in a letter to Deputy Governor Sir Thomas Dale that in marrying Pocahontas he sought the plantation's good, God's glory, and salvation for his new wife and himself.

In 1616 the Rolfes, with their infant son Thomas, sailed for England where they created a sensation and were received at court. While there Rolfe wrote a "True Relation of the State of Virginia" (1617) attempting to counter the colony's negative image among discouraged investors and prospective emigrants. The "True Relation" added weight to calls by Sir Edwin Sandys's party for change in the Virginia Company.

Pocahontas died in March 1617 at Gravesend as the Rolfes were preparing to return to Virginia. Back in Virginia John Rolfe immediately wrote Sandys justifying his decision to leave Thomas in England and asked for continued payment of the company stipend granted his wife. He also hoped Sandys would "remember me for some place of commaund and some estate of land to be confirmed to me and my childe." This letter reiterated his estimate of the colony's economic well-being and promised that the Indians would consent to having their children raised as Christians.

In 1619 Rolfe moved from the secretaryship to the governor's council. Captain John Smith (1580–1631) printed "A relation from Master John Rolfe," dated June 1618 but covering events to 1620, in his *Generall Historie of Virginia, New-England, and the Summer Isles* (1624). Rolfe reported the death of Powhatan and various other events in the colony. He vigorously defended both Virginia's economic promise and its government, accusing English brokers of dishonestly denigrating Virginia tobacco. His account also reported the first general assembly and the purchase of "twenty Negars" from a Dutch vessel. Rolfe wrote Sandys in January 1620 covering many of these topics and describing his own role as emissary to the Indians. He depicted critics of the colony's government as "falseharted, envious and malicious people (yea amongst some who march in the better ranck)" and reported general satisfaction as lands were divided and granted to the "ancient planters." Rolfe himself received 400 acres in the "Territory of Tappahanna over against James Cittie" and, with unnamed others, 1,700 acres near Mulberry Island. In 1621 he was named to the Council of State.

Rolfe married his third wife, Jane Pierce, in 1619 or 1620; their child Elizabeth was born in 1621. He made his will in March 1622 and died of natural causes that same year in Virginia. Allegations that he died in the great Indian attack of 22 March 1622 are mistaken.

Through his marriage to Pocahontas and his successful experimentation with tobacco, Rolfe contributed to the establishment of Virginia. His writings provide an interpretation of struggles within the colony from the perspective of a Virginia Company loyalist who supported the experiment with martial law.

• John Rolfe's letter to Sir Thomas Dale was printed by Ralph Hamor as an appendix to *A True Discourse of the Present State of Virginia* (1615), pp. 61–68. A manuscript copy of this letter is transcribed in Philip L. Barbour, *Pocahontas and Her World* (1969). A paraphrase of Rolfe's "A True Relation of the State of Virginia" was printed by Samuel Purchas in *Purchas His Pilgrimage*, 3d ed. (1617). The "True Relation" was published in its entirety in *The Virginia Historical Register and Literary Companion* (1848) and in a modern edition (1971). Rolfe's letters of 1617 and 1620 to Sir Edwin Sandys are printed in Susan Myra Kingsbury, ed., *The Records of the Virginia Company of London* (1906–1935), vol. 3, pp. 70–73, 241–48. "A Relation from Master John Rolfe" is in Philip L. Barbour, ed., *The Complete Works of Captain John Smith*, vol. 2 (1986), pp. 265–69. A newly discovered Virginia Company grant issued to the departing Rolfes in 1617 is printed and analyzed in David R. Ransome, "Pocahontas and the Mission to the Indians," *Virginia Magazine of History and Biography* 99 (1991): 81–94.

The best modern treatment of Rolfe is in Barbour, *Pocahontas and Her World*. The significance of his marriage to Pocahontas is analyzed in J. Frederick Fausz, "An 'Abundance of Blood Shed on Both Sides': England's First Indian War, 1609–1614," *Virginia Magazine of History and Biography* 98 (1990): 3–56.

KAREN ORDAHL KUPPERMAN

ROLLINI, Adrian (28 June 1904–15 May 1956), bass saxophonist, was born in New York City; the names of his parents are unknown. A child prodigy on piano and xylophone, Rollini gave a Chopin recital at age four at the Waldorf Astoria Hotel and by age fourteen he was leading his own band. He joined the California Ramblers in 1922 at age eighteen, and it was only then that he took up the bass saxophone, becoming proficient in one week.

The Ramblers, a white dance band that could also swing, arrived in New York City from Ohio in 1921. Some scholars claim that their version of "Copenhagen" is as good as that of the Fletcher Henderson band. Rollini made a number of recordings with them from August 1923 through July 1927, playing with impressive clarity on his cumbersome instrument, and he won the admiration of other musicians for his facility on this most difficult of instruments. Coleman Hawkins expressed his respect, Budd Johnson actually bought a bass sax and mimicked Rollini's style before switching to tenor, and even Harry Carney, the great baritone player in the Ellington band, said that he tried to achieve a sound similar to Rollini's.

Even more important and widely influential were the recordings Rollini made with a variety of groups during a prolific eight-year span beginning in 1927. From August through October 1927 he recorded ten sides with Frankie Trumbauer and His Orchestra. In June and September of the same year, he excelled on sessions with Joe Venuti's Blue Four. In October he made six cuts with Bix Beiderbecke and His Gang, highlighted by his solo on "Jazz Me Blues." Throughout these sessions, his playing reflected a harmonic sophistication that was far advanced for the time, as well as the ability to perform with extraordinary facility on an instrument that frightened away most who even considered adopting it.

Rollini played in London with Fred Elizalde from 1927 to 1929. From 1927 through 1930 he also recorded with Red Nichols and His Five Pennies, and two of these sides included a young Benny Goodman on clarinet. Rollini played the "goofus" on one of these tunes, one of several novelty instruments he introduced (another, the "hot fountain pen," was a tiny, one-octave clarinet). He also led a marvelous saxophone ensemble passage on "Ida, Sweet as Apple Cider." In 1933 he made several sessions with different groups led by Venuti, and on 12 June he cut four sides under his own leadership as Adrian Rollini and His Orchestra, on which he also played vibraharp. The same group recorded four sides in October 1934 with Goodman. Rollini also founded his own club in 1934, Adrian's Tap Room, at the President Hotel in New York City. In March 1935 he cut six sides with another Venuti group, playing both vibraharp and baritone. On the impressive "Vibraphonia," Rollini showed off his four-mallet technique, an approach later championed by Gary Burton. In addition to these sessions, Rollini played with many other groups during the decade, including those led by Hawkins, Bunny Berrigan, and Bobby Hackett.

Rollini made his final jazz recordings of any significance on 14 June 1935, with a group called Adrian and His Tap Room Gang, cutting two sides on which he played both bass saxophone and vibes. He has a strong solo on "Bouncing in Rhythm," and he leads an excellent ensemble passage on "Honeysuckle Rose," shining on the vibraharp. During the 1940s he led a variety of small groups for long engagements at various New York hotels, and in the early 1950s he moved to Florida, where he played mostly commercial gigs for the remainder of his life and operated the Driftwood Lounge. He died from complications after a fall in Homestead, Florida.

Rollini was a harmonically advanced, melodically inventive, virtuosic musician with a strong rhythmic sense. He was an early swing musician, an amazing accomplishment considering the difficulties presented by the unwieldy bass saxophone. He could readily make the instrument sound like the tuba it often replaced, but he also soloed with a flexibility and grace that belied the limitations of an instrument whose range was a full octave below that of the tenor saxophone. And he made it all sound and look easy.

• Very little information is available on Rollini. The interested listener can best profit from T. Shoppee, "Adrian Rollini," *Jazz Journal* 23, no. 8 (1970): 20, and no. 100 (1970): 7; and S.-A. Worsfold, "The Forgotten Ones: Adrian Rollini," *Jazz Journal International* 24, no. 6 (1981): 21. See also Ar-

thur Rollini, *Thirty Years with the Big Bands* (1987). There is scattered but useful information in Max Harrison et al., *The Essential Jazz Records*, vol. 1: *Ragtime to Swing* (1984). Obituaries are in *Downbeat* 23, no. 13 (1956): 9, and the *New York Times*, 16 May 1956.

RONALD P. DUFOUR

ROLLINS, Edward Henry (3 Oct. 1824–31 July 1889), U.S. senator and congressman, and railroad executive, was born in Rollinsford, New Hampshire, the son of Daniel Rollins and Mary Plumer, farmers. Rollins attended the Franklin Academy in Dover, and the Berwick Academy in Maine, but lack of funds prevented him from enrolling at Dartmouth College. Aside from a brief tenure as a Rollinsford common schoolteacher, he worked as a drugstore clerk in Concord, New Hampshire, and Boston until 1847, when he bought his own establishment opposite the statehouse in Concord. Two years later he married Ellen Elizabeth West; they had five children.

Rollins ran the apothecary throughout the 1850s, during which time he also became an important figure in state politics. His drugstore became a well-known meeting place, and Rollins's political ascendancy was rapid. In 1850 he became a member of the Whig party's state committee, but he resigned in 1852, apparently disappointed by the party's failure to nominate Daniel Webster for president. By 1854, however, he was playing a vital role in building a new anti-Democratic coalition. Elected as a Know-Nothing to the state house of representatives in 1855, he was elected speaker of the house the following year, allegedly because he threatened to lead a party bolt if he was not.

As chairman of the American-Republican state committee in 1856, Rollins orchestrated a smooth organizational transition between Know-Nothingism and Republicanism through a fair distribution of patronage and a careful avoidance of the Republican party label until after the 1857 state elections. He was reelected to the chair annually until his election to Congress in 1861, only to serve in that capacity again between 1868 and 1872. Although New Hampshirites consistently chose Republican candidates in statewide elections, contests were nearly always close, making Rollins's role as party chairman of vital importance. He and his close associate, William E. Chandler, proved to be master strategists and party builders. Because New Hampshire's annual March gubernatorial elections were the first contests held in the nation each year, they acquired national attention as predictors of party fortunes elsewhere. Outside money and speakers poured into the state—especially during presidential election years—thus magnifying Rollins's fame and influence. National party figures credited his fundraising techniques, even-handed distribution of patronage, and tireless work—especially in 1868, when his efforts saved the state for the Republicans, foreshadowing Ulysses S. Grant's presidential election victory.

As a congressman between 1861 and 1867, Rollins was identified with the more radical wing of the Republican party. Early in the Civil War he authored an antidiscrimination statute for the District of Columbia. He supported the principal antislavery enactments of Congress during the war, including the Thirteenth Amendment, and he supported the congressional reconstruction program after the war.

To be sure, Rollins had his share of enemies, even within the Republican party. His seemingly dictatorial rule earned him and his Concord associates the derisive title of "the Drugstore Clique," while the Whiggish, probusiness wing of the party from which he hailed often put him at odds with Republicans of Free Soil Democratic antecedents such as George G. Fogg, John P. Hale, Amos Tuck, and Mason W. Tappan, who wished to distance the party more from the corporate interests. The executive positions Rollins held between 1869 and 1876 in the Union Pacific Railroad Company also furnished ammunition to his enemies, especially when the Crédit Mobilier scandal (with which he was not involved, apparently) came to light.

Rollins twice lost senatorial bids: in 1866, when Daniel Clark of Manchester was reelected—partly to fulfill an agreement in which Concord was permitted, two years earlier, to remain the state capital—and again in 1872, mainly because of his involvement with the Union Pacific. He won election to the Senate in 1876. Rollins opposed President Rutherford Hayes's abandonment of southern blacks and favored strict enforcement of the Fifteenth Amendment. On economic issues he favored hard money, high tariffs, and tax exemptions for savings banks. Although renominated in 1883, Rollins withdrew from the race when it became apparent that he could not win reelection. His role in politics diminished after that point.

In his retirement from politics Rollins became an executive of two banks, and from 1886 to 1889 he was a director and president of the Boston, Concord, and Montreal Railroad. He died at Isle of Shoals, off the New Hampshire coast.

• A small collection of the Edward H. Rollins papers is in the New Hampshire Historical Society, but letters from Rollins are better found in the William E. Chandler Papers and to a lesser extent in the Mason W. Tappan and James Lovering papers—all three of which are also at the society. James O. Lyford, *Life of Edward H. Rollins: A Political Biography* (1906), is detailed but also eulogistic. See also "Edward H. Rollins," *Granite Monthly*, Sept. 1877. Much about Rollins's role in state politics can be found in Lex Renda, "The Polity and the Party System: Connecticut and New Hampshire, 1840–1876" (Ph.D. diss., Univ. of Virginia, 1991). For obituaries, see the *Independent Statesman* (Concord, N.H.), 1 and 8 Aug. 1889.

LEX RENDA

ROLLINS, James Sidney (19 Apr. 1812–9 Jan. 1888), congressman, was born in Richmond, Kentucky, the son of Anthony Wayne Rollins, a physician, and Sallie Rodes. He was educated at Richmond Academy, matriculating at Washington College at the age of fifteen. Two years later he transferred to Indiana College (now

University), where he graduated summa cum laude in 1830. He then moved to Columbia, Missouri, where his parents now lived and which would remain his home for the rest of his life. He volunteered for service in the Black Hawk War in 1832, serving as aide-decamp to Colonel Richard Gentry, a Columbia lawyer. He studied law with Abiel Leonard and later returned to Kentucky to complete the law course at Transylvania University in 1834. Returning to Columbia, he established his law practice with Thomas Miller, with whom in 1836 he also established a Whig journal, the *Columbia Patriot*, which he continued to edit for several years. That same spring Rollins attended the first railway convention ever held west of the Mississippi River at St. Louis and was appointed chair of the Committee to Memorialize Congress for Land Grants for Internal Improvements. The promotion of railroad development with federal and state assistance would continue to be one of his major concerns throughout his political career. He married Mary E. Hickman in 1837; they had eleven children.

Rollins was elected to the lower house of the state legislature in 1838 as a Whig, serving until 1844. He was a delegate to the Whig National Convention in 1844. From 1846 to 1850 he was a member of the state senate. While in the lower house, he supported the passage of a bill in 1839 to establish a state university and then worked successfully to secure its location in Columbia. While in the state senate, he was successful in securing state aid for the university. He continued as its champion for the rest of his life, earning the sobriquet "Father of the University of Missouri."

Rollins was the Whig candidate for governor in 1848, losing to Democrat Austin A. King while securing the largest vote total for any Whig to that date. He was appointed to the board of examiners for the U.S. Military Academy in 1850. He returned to the legislature in 1854 at a time when Missouri was heavily involved in the controversy over the entry of slavery into Kansas Territory and when both of the state's political parties found themselves in disarray as a result. An advocate of Free Soil doctrines in the special gubernatorial election of 1857, Rollins was the candidate of a group known as "the Opposition," made up of a coalition of former Whigs, Know Nothings, and Benton Democrats, which evolved into the Missouri Republican party. He lost to Democrat Robert M. Stewart by only 334 votes.

In the election of 1860 Rollins supported the John Bell–Edward Everett ticket while gaining election to Congress as a constitutional Unionist. A slaveowner himself, Rollins, nevertheless, opposed secession and during his two terms in Congress gave President Abraham Lincoln strong support for his military policies. Although initially opposed to the various proposals for emancipation during the war, by 1865 he realized that slavery was doomed and voted for the Thirteenth Amendment. His major contribution while in Congress was his introduction of the Pacific Railroad Bill of 1862, which provided the impetus for the construction of the transcontinental railroad.

When the Radical Republicans gained control of the Missouri state government in 1864 and rewrote the constitution to their liking the following year, Rollins strongly opposed its extreme proscriptive measures against former Confederates and Confederate sympathizers. He joined with Frank Blair, James O. Broadhead, and others in organizing the Conservative party, which evolved into the postwar Democratic party in Missouri, although Rollins was never totally comfortable within the ranks of the Democrats. He returned to the state legislature in 1866 to champion the cause of the state university, which the Radicals were threatening to move. Not only was he successful in keeping that institution in Columbia, he also managed to incorporate the land grant function (a mechanical and agricultural college), established by the Morrill Act of 1862, within it, as opposed to creating a new college for that purpose.

A close friend of Blair throughout their respective careers, Rollins worked hard to secure for Blair the Democratic presidential nomination in 1868 and strongly supported the party's ticket that year with Blair in the second spot. He encouraged the active cooperation between the Democrats and the Liberal Republicans after the latter group broke from the Radicals in the election of 1870. In the aftermath of that coalition's triumph that year, he secured the election of Blair to the U.S. Senate. Two years later Rollins had his final political frustration when he lost the Democratic nomination for governor as the former Confederate element assumed control of the party in Missouri.

Early in 1874 Rollins was seriously injured in a train wreck and never regained full health. He spent his declining years in retirement from both the law and politics and died in Columbia.

• The James S. Rollins Papers are in the State Historical Society of Missouri, Columbia. A laudatory biography, William B. Smith, *James S. Rollins: A Memoir* (1891), contains some letters. A better source for his career is James Madison Wood, Jr., "James Sidney Rollins of Missouri: A Political Biography" (Ph.D. diss., Stanford Univ., 1952). Rollins's friendship with Blair is detailed in William E. Smith, *The Francis Preston Blair Family in Politics* (1933). His leadership of the prewar Missouri Whig party is discussed in John V. Mering, *The Whig Party in Missouri* (1967).

WILLIAM E. PARRISH

ROLLINS, Philip Ashton (20 Jan. 1869–11 Sept. 1950), author, bibliophile, and philanthropist, was born in Somersworth, New Hampshire, the son of Edward Ashton Rollins, a financier, and Ellen Chapman Hobbs, an author. His father, a Harvard-trained lawyer, was active in Republican politics and served as a high-level Treasury Department official in the Abraham Lincoln and Andrew Johnson administrations. In the 1870s, while president of an insurance company and later of a bank, both in Philadelphia, Edward Rollins acquired three vast western ranches. From 1874 on he regularly either took or sent his son out West during school vacations, where Philip had experi-

ences, especially among cowboys on the family ranches, that influenced much of his later life. After his mother died in 1881, followed by his father in 1885, Philip Rollins inherited an estate worth more than $1 million.

Matriculation in 1885 at the College of New Jersey (now Princeton University) ended his series of boyhood western adventures, which had included two cattle drives from Texas to Montana. (A photograph of him as a lanky, awkward-looking teenager, decked out in cowboy garb, suggests why Rollins as an adult said he lacked the physical attributes to become a real cowboy.) In 1889, with a B.A. in American history, Rollins left Princeton for Oregon on a paleontological expedition led by Professor William Berryman Scott, followed by hunting trips to Siberia and Alaska plus one more stay out West of more than a year. By 1892 he had earned an M.A. at Princeton in history and was in New York City, working in an uncle's law firm and studying law. In 1894 Rollins sold his last ranch, severing direct ties to the West.

In 1895 Rollins married Beulah Brewster Pack, a North Carolina woman of his social and economic class, with whom he had one child, and for over twenty years he practiced law in Manhattan. Near the end of World War I, Rollins became an aggressive collector of western American books, manuscripts, and maps, eventually accumulating not only "the finest collection of range literature in the world" (Dobie and Dykes, p. 8) but also an array of scarce and unique "narratives associated with overland journeys to the Pacific" (Streeter, p. 193), part of his efforts to recover and preserve two key periods of the nineteenth-century American West. Scott, his Princeton mentor, then challenged Rollins with advice that became his creed: "Don't be just a dilettante collector—make a study of your material and write a really accurate scientific study of that world" (Bentley, p. 184).

By the time that Rollins embarked on his avid accumulation of western memorabilia, the cowboy had become the dominant American folk hero, transformed from a "hired man on horseback" into a western version of the knight errant, a romanticized symbol of a bygone era. Reacting to false portrayals of cowboys and range life in various popular forms of entertainment, such as silent films and pulp fiction, Rollins set out to redress what he considered to be libel.

The result was Rollins's first book, *The Cowboy: His Characteristics, His Equipment, and His Part in the Development of the West* (1922). Peppered with illustrative anecdotes and packed with detailed descriptions, it was immediately and widely acknowledged to be an authoritative study of life on the range, receiving numerous favorable reviews in the United States and abroad. Soon published in an illustrated second edition, *The Cowboy* was reprinted seven times by the decade's end. The third edition, expanded and corrected, appeared in 1936 under the title *The Cowboy: An Unconventional History of Civilization on the Old-Time Cattle Range*. This version has been periodically reissued since then.

More than twenty-five years after the initial appearance of *The Cowboy*, Robert Glass Cleland, a distinguished historian of the American West, judged it this way: "The book's value lies in its great accuracy, its vivid and detailed descriptions, its correct historical appraisals, and the preservation of scores of humorous, colorful, and dramatic episodes. It is an indispensable source book on the cowboy and the cattle range and will survive as long as Americans have an interest in the history and tradition of the West" (pp. 206–7). Interest in the days of the open range has indeed continued, and no other study has superseded. Rollins's book, with its descriptions of cowboys and how they made their livelihood, remains an important source of evidence in serious discussions of the American range cattle industry. A notable endorsement appears in the book that accompanied the exhibition The American Cowboy, held in 1983 at the American Folklife Center of the Library of Congress: "Rollins's *The Cowboy* may still be the best single book written on cowboy work and life" (Taylor and Maar, p. 222).

Throughout the 1920s and 1930s Rollins continued to accumulate western Americana, competing with other avid, wealthy collectors. Unlike them, though, Rollins drew on his collection to reconstruct in writing different eras of the nineteenth-century West. Besides over a half-dozen periodical articles, he also wrote two juvenile novels, each popular enough to justify additional printings: *Jinglebob: A True Story of a Real Cowboy* (1927) and *Gone Haywire: Two Tenderfoots on the Montana Cattle Range in 1886* (1939). Clearly autobiographical, their plots feature wealthy eastern youths visiting the West in its open range heyday, as Rollins had, to experience ranch life firsthand and to share adventures with cowboys.

In the 1930s Rollins and his wife moved from New York to Princeton, where he completed his second significant book, an annotated edition of the journals of a Pacific Northwest fur trader, *The Discovery of the Oregon Trail: Robert Stuart's Narratives of His Overland Trip Eastward from Astoria in 1812–13* (1935). Meticulously researched, the book was still in print more than sixty years later. Based on his own retracing of the Oregon Trail as well as on careful study of period documents, Rollins's extensive notes provide revealing comments on everything that Stuart encountered along his route, including the landscape, the flora and fauna, and the Indian tribes. Like *The Cowboy*, Rollins's edition of Stuart's narratives is both encyclopedic and authoritative.

Although he had other writing and editing projects either in mind or under way, Rollins never finished them. With his wife's assistance he devoted himself, instead, to benefiting his alma mater. A founding member of the Friends of the Princeton University Library, he had long taken an active hand in enhancing the university's collections. In 1945 he and his wife donated to the university the Rollins Collection of Western Americana, along with endowments for maintaining and adding to it. They later endowed the Philip and Beulah Rollins Professorship of History. Rollins died in Princeton.

Philip Ashton Rollins is a striking example of an independently wealthy American who pursued a passion for scholarship related to his sense of the past. Although he was not a scholar per se, he emulated the best attributes of one. Blessed with the means to gather and preserve a mother lode of western Americana, he made himself an expert on parts of the country's history that had been to a considerable extent either ignored or grossly romanticized. Alive to the bygone worlds of the overland pioneers and of the open range, Rollins succeeded in vivifying those worlds for later generations. Through *The Cowboy* and *The Discovery of the Oregon Trail*, he will continue to be an important guide to the making of the American West.

• Rollins's papers are in the Princeton University Library. Donald Drew Egbert, *Princeton Portraits* (1947), provides a biographical profile and reproduces two likenesses of Rollins. The June 1948 *Princeton University Library Chronicle* (*PULC*), dedicated to Rollins, has three useful articles: Esther Felt Bentley, "A Conversation with Mr. Rollins," pp. 178–90; Thomas W. Streeter, "The Rollins Collection of Western Americana," pp. 191–204; and Robert Glass Cleland, "The Writings of Philip Ashton Rollins," pp. 205–10. Other views of the Rollins collection include Alfred L. Bush, "The Princeton Collections of Western Americana," *PULC* 33 (Autumn 1971): 6–12, and J. Frank Dobie and Jeff Dykes, *44 Range Country Books . . .* (1972). Appreciations of *The Cowboy* appear in J. Frank Dobie, *Life and Literature of the Southwest* (1952), pp. 107, 116; Lonn Taylor and Ingrid Maar, *The American Cowboy* (1983); and William S. Reese, *Six Score: The 120 Best Books on the Range Cattle Industry*, rev. ed. (1988), entry 92. For Rollins's seminal role as a benefactor of the Princeton library, see Stephen Ferguson, "Friends of the Princeton University Library, 1930–1980: A Photographic Essay," *PULC* 41 (Winter 1980): 121, and Mark R. Farrell, "Library Notes: A Chronicle of Gifts," *PULC* 51 (Spring 1990): 295–97; the primary source for the Friends' beginning is the first issue (June 1930) of *Biblia* (the predecessor of *PULC*). James R. Nicholl, "A Dedication to the Memory of Philip Ashton Rollins, 1869–1950," *Arizona and the West* 26 (1984): 301–6, includes a list of short works by Rollins. An obituary is in the *New York Times*, 12 Sept. 1950.

JAMES R. NICHOLL

ROLPH, James, Jr. (23 Aug. 1869–2 June 1934), mayor of San Francisco and governor of California, was born in San Francisco, California, the son of James Rolph, an English-born bank clerk, and Margaret Nicol, an immigrant from Scotland. After graduating from Trinity School, a private secondary school headed by an Episcopal priest, Rolph worked in a commission house then formed his own shipping and commission company in 1898. After 1900 he engaged in several additional business activities, including banking, shipbuilding, importing, and insurance. In his shipping and shipbuilding enterprises, he dealt only with union labor, a fairly common practice in San Francisco at the time. During the early twentieth century, Rolph became prominent in civic affairs, serving as chairman of the Mission Relief Committee after the earthquake of 1906, president of the Merchant's Exchange, trustee of the Chamber of Commerce, and vice president of the association sponsoring the Panama Pacific International Exposition.

Rolph married Annie Marshall Reid in 1900, and they had three children. Throughout his life, he was proud that they lived in the city's Mission District, the area that was home to many working-class and lower-middle-class San Franciscans and to many first- and second-generation immigrants.

In 1911 Rolph ran for mayor in San Francisco's first nonpartisan election. A Republican, Rolph received endorsements from both the Republican and Democratic parties and had support from much of the city's business leadership. Patrick H. McCarthy, the incumbent mayor, was head of the city's Building Trades Council and had been elected in 1909 as the candidate of the Union Labor party, the political arm of the city's labor movement. Rolph, however, secured support from several key union leaders, based in part on his deserved reputation as a "friend of labor" and in part because of divisions within organized labor. Promising to be mayor of "all the people" and to unify the city, Rolph received 60 percent of the vote, initiating an unrivaled tenure of nineteen years.

In his first four years as mayor, Rolph established a strong record of activism on behalf of urban growth and development: he tirelessly promoted the Panama Pacific International Exposition (1915), completed the first Municipal Railway (city-owned) streetcar line, finished several other Municipal Railway lines, secured approval of a bond issue for a new city hall and pushed it through to completion, and initiated construction of a new city reservoir in the Hetch Hetchy valley in the Sierra Nevada. At the same time, he exemplified the Progressive Era's emphasis on expertise and efficiency in city administration.

Rolph routinely won reelection at four-year intervals, usually taking 55 percent or more of the vote. His major opponent always drew most strongly from working-class and foreign-stock voters—Rolph's neighbors in the Mission District. Rolph, however, consistently tried to smother class and ethnic antagonisms with his gregariousness, the genial smile that earned him the nickname "Sunny Jim," and his repeated commitment to be "mayor of all the people." Always a showman, he loved to don his western hat and boots, mount a horse, and lead a parade. He experienced an undefined breakdown early in 1916, however, and his shipbuilding and shipping enterprises suffered serious losses after World War I.

Rolph never again matched the accomplishments of his first administration. In 1916, as the city became increasingly polarized between labor and business, he continued his support for unions. During a longshore strike that year, he refused a request from the city's business leadership that he hire 500 special police to protect strikebreakers; the same year, he cancelled city contracts with firms that insisted on the open shop. He did little to enforce Prohibition in San Francisco.

Throughout the 1920s Rolph continued to advocate municipal ownership of streetcars, water, and electricity but did not exercise the dynamic leadership of his early years in office. The city constructed an extensive Municipal Railway system but failed to buy out the privately owned lines until long after Rolph left city hall. After several failed attempts to secure public ownership of the electrical power system, Rolph accepted an arrangement that left sale of electricity within the city to private enterprise. In 1928 voters finally approved funds for public ownership of water distribution.

Rolph sought the governorship in 1918 and, under California's peculiar cross-filing system then in operation, won the Democratic nomination. He was ruled ineligible to run, however, because he lost the nomination of his own party, the Republicans. In 1930, as the economic depression deepened, he narrowly won the Republican nomination for governor, defeating the incumbent governor, and went on to a landslide victory in the general election. As governor he promoted a public works program to relieve unemployment and approved a state sales tax and a major water project for the Central Valley. For the most part, however, he made little effort to influence the legislature and often found himself in conflict with it. After condoning the lynching of two kidnappers by a mob in San Jose in November 1933, Rolph received nationwide criticism and was labeled "Governor Lynch." He died at "Riverside Farm" in Santa Clara County.

• The most important collection of Rolph papers is at the California Historical Society, San Francisco; smaller collections are in the San Francisco Public Library and the State Archives in Sacramento. The only published biography is highly laudatory: David Wooster Taylor, *The Life of James Rolph, Jr.* (1934). See also Herman G. Goldbeck, "The Political Career of James Rolph, Jr.: A Preliminary Study" (M.A. thesis, Univ. of California, Berkeley, 1936); Carole Hicke, "The 1911 Campaign of James Rolph, Jr., Mayor of All the People" (M.A. thesis, San Francisco State Univ., 1978); Moses Rischin, "Sunny Jim Rolph: The First 'Mayor of All the People'," *California Historical Quarterly* 53 (1974): 165–72; Morley Segal, "James Rolph, Jr., and the Municipal Railway: A Study in Political Leadership" (M.A. thesis, San Francisco State College, 1959); and the treatment of Rolph's mayoral administration in William Issel and Robert W. Cherny, *San Francisco, 1865–1932: Politics, Power, and Urban Development* (1986). The best obituary is the series by Tom Bellew, "The Life of James Rolph, Jr.," *San Francisco Chronicle*, 4–30 June 1934.

ROBERT W. CHERNY

RÖLVAAG, Ole Edvart (22 Apr. 1876–5 Nov. 1931), author and educator, was born on Dönna Island, near the coast of northern Norway, the son of Peder Benjamin Jakobsen, a fisherman, and Ellerine Petersdatter Vaag. From his early childhood Rölvaag was an excellent fisherman and spent many hours on the sea with the mountains towering above him. In his unfinished autobiography, "The Romance of a Life" (the only book he composed in English), his descriptions of the mountains and sea foreshadow his later ambivalent attitude toward the North American prairie. He describes the mountains as "so terrible that they made me shiver in my own insignificance. Even so they fascinated me." He attributes a dual nature to the sea: "On the sea we depended for sustenance as the farmer on his crops. The sea was kind and beneficent, treacherous and terrible, all depending on his mood." His family, although poor, was religious and literate. He attended school until age fourteen and afterward continued to read voraciously. Finally deciding that he did not wish to spend his life as a fisherman, Rölvaag emigrated to the United States.

Rölvaag landed in New York City on 20 August 1896 and went immediately to the farm where his uncle worked in Elk Point, South Dakota. After working as a farmhand for two years, he entered Augustana Academy in Canton, South Dakota, a Lutheran preparatory school, graduating in 1901. The following fall Rölvaag matriculated at St. Olaf College in Northfield, Minnesota, a school operated by Norwegian Lutherans. He considered the ministry but instead studied Norwegian literature. In 1905 he graduated with honors.

Rölvaag then returned to Norway for a year of graduate study at the University of Christiana (now the University of Oslo) after St. Olaf lent him $500 and offered him a job when a vacancy occurred. He made the highest grade possible on the final examination and was awarded a candidate of philosophy (the equivalent of an M.A.) in 1906. Returning to Northfield in September 1906, he began teaching in the Department of Norwegian at St. Olaf (both the academy and the college).

On 17 May 1907, Norwegian Independence Day, Rölvaag explained his ideas about the role of immigrants in their new land to a Norwegian-American audience. He believed that their Norwegian background enriched their lives and inspired contributions to the United States and that they should adopt the best of America's values.

In 1908, the year he was naturalized as a U.S. citizen, Rölvaag married Jennie Marie Berdahl; they had four children. Rölvaag dedicated himself during 1910 to the establishment of the Society for Norwegian Language and Culture, the goal of which was to safeguard Norwegian culture in the United States. This association, which was composed predominantly of educators, promoted improvements in Norwegian language instruction in American schools. As a result of Rölvaag's zeal, other Norwegian organizations were born and flourished; the Norwegian-American Historical Association, for example, was created in 1925.

During the next few years Rölvaag focused primarily on writing and teaching. He suffered chronic ill health and money problems, which were compounded by his concern about his family in Norway; nevertheless, he crusaded in a letter-writing campaign for the prosperity of Norwegians in America. In 1909 Rölvaag had produced *Ordforklaring*, a Norwegian-English dictionary, and he later published three Norwegian readers: *Deklamationsboken* (1918), *Norsk*

Læsebok I (1919), and *Norsk Læsebok II* (1920). Augsburg Publishing House published his first novel, *Amerika-Breve* (Letters from America) in 1912 under the pseudonym Paal Mörck. The book did not sell widely, but Rölvaag was acclaimed in the Midwest for representing the Norwegian people in the world of literature.

Rölvaag is most famous for his depiction of the midwestern prairie. He saw the prairie as a powerful presence, a mixture of good and evil, capable of destroying men or of making heroes of them. His next book, *Paa Glemte Veie* (On forgotten paths), was published in 1914 under his pseudonym. Here the prairie is not always malevolent and calamitous, but it is a force of nature superior to any person.

In 1916 Rölvaag left the United States for a short trip back to Norway, but he returned to St. Olaf, where he served as head of the Department of Norwegian. He saw St. Olaf as an ideal base of operations from which he could continue his campaign to bring Norwegian culture into the mainstream of American culture.

Although Rölvaag was busy with his teaching, he continued to write. *To Tullinger: Et Billede fra Idag* (Two fools: A scene from today) was published in 1920; a revision titled *Pure Gold* was published in 1930. *Længselens Baat* (The boat of longing) appeared in 1921 and *Omkring Fædrearven*, a book of essays, in 1922. Rölvaag, however, wanted to concentrate on his prairie saga, and so he took a sabbatical from St. Olaf from 1923 through 1924. In recalling the experiences gleaned from his two years on the farm in Elk Point, Rölvaag perceived that the struggle for the Norwegian settlers was not merely physical but also intellectual and emotional. To draw closer to their struggles, he spent part of his sabbatical in a cabin he had built in 1922 on the coast of Big Island Lake, Itasca County, Minnesota. There he imaginatively re-created the Norwegian settlers' lives, recalling stories that he had heard while in Elk Point. He later claimed that he could not have finished the novel without the tranquility and isolation of that interval in the woods. Rölvaag's novel was published in two parts, the first appearing in the fall of 1924 as *I De Dage—Fortælling om Norske Nykommere i Amerika* and the second in 1925 as *I De Dage—: Riket Grundlægges*. Lincoln Colcord, a journalist and short story writer, translated and combined the two parts into one volume as *Giants in the Earth: A Saga of the Prairie*, which appeared in 1927 as a Book-of-the-Month-Club selection. Before the end of the year it sold almost 80,000 copies and won critical praise for its recognition of the complexities of the frontier. This first book of Rölvaag's trilogy was translated into several other languages soon after its appearance in English. In 1926 the king of Norway honored Rölvaag by making him a knight of the Order of St. Olaf.

In 1928 Rölvaag's *Peder Seier* was published, and in 1929 this book appeared in translation as *Peder Victorious*, the second of the trilogy. The last of the trilogy, *Their Fathers' God* (in Norway it had the title *Den Sig-*

nede Dag [The blessed day]), was published in 1931. The respect that *Giants in the Earth* received upon its publication has endured, and Rölvaag has earned a place in American literature as one of the best portrayers of pioneer life. He died in Northfield, Minnesota, of heart disease.

• Rölvaag's papers are in the Rölvaag Memorial Library at St. Olaf College in the archives of the Norwegian-American Historical Association. A biography of Rölvaag was written by two of his St. Olaf colleagues, Theodore Jorgenson and Nora O. Solum, *Ole Edvart Rölvaag* (1939). It contains the only available translation of some of his writings, such as his letters. Paul Reigstad, *Rölvaag: His Life and Art* (1972), and Einar Haugen, *Ole Edvart Rölvaag* (1983), are excellent books on Rölvaag. Of the many articles, chapters, and dissertations on him, see Carol Spiller, "O. E. Rölvaag's Norwegian Immigrants: Rural Perspectives," *Ethnic Groups* 4 (1982): 1–2, 9–32; Einar Haugen, "Rölvaag and the Norwegian Heritage," in *The Prairie Frontier*, ed. Geoffrey Hunt (1984); Paul Reigstad, "Mythic Aspects of *Giants in the Earth*," in *Vision and Refuge: Essays on the Literature of the Great Plains*, ed. Virginia Faulkner (1982); and Michael Douglas Basinski, "Ethnicity and the Prairie Fiction of Hamlin Garland, Willa Cather and O. E. Rölvaag" (Ph.D. diss., Univ. of Michigan, 1996). Obituaries are in the *Northfield News*, 13 Nov. 1931; *Publishers Weekly*, 14 Nov. 1931; and the *New York Times*, 6 Nov. 1931.

SHIRLEY LAIRD

ROMAN, Charles Victor (4 July 1864–25 Aug. 1934), physician and medical educator, was born in Williamsport, Pennsylvania, the son of James William Roman, a former slave, and Anna Walker McGuinn, the child of a former slave. Roman's parents met in Canada, where his father had fled about twenty years before the Civil War. After the Emancipation Proclamation, a year and a half before Charles's birth, they had moved back to the United States, but making a living there was difficult, and by the time Charles was six, the family returned to Ontario where his father worked as a broom maker. From an early age Charles knew he wanted to be a physician. Soon after the move to Canada, he apprenticed himself to a local herbalist, possibly his grandmother. His practice ended when one of his patients' parents became nervous about the treatment Roman had administered and called in the local doctor, who pronounced the child cured and predicted that one day the young herbalist would become a physician himself.

At the age of twelve Roman moved with his family to Dundas, Ontario, and started working in a cotton mill to supplement the family's meager income. He continued this grueling work until an accident left him lame for life. He entered the Hamilton Collegiate Institute as its first black student and supported himself by selling small items. Despite these obstacles, he took only two years to finish a course of studies that usually took four. Later in life he would describe himself as "a factory boy—the product of the night school and public library, a triumph of democracy and a justification of its creed" (quoted in Cobb, p. 301). After graduating from the Canadian school, he wanted to attend McGill University's School of Medicine, but he did not have the money to pay tuition. At the advice of one of his teachers, he headed south and started teaching school.

After five months teaching first grade in Trigg County, Kentucky, Roman decided to spend another year teaching in the South. He still planned to return to Canada one day for medical school, but he happened to board with a physician who was an alumnus of Meharry Medical College. This doctor persuaded Roman to apply to his alma mater in Nashville, Tennessee, and in 1887 Roman entered Meharry. An able and popular teacher, he continued teaching during the day to fund his night medical classes. The Nashville Board of Education required its applicants for teaching jobs to take a competitive examination, and Roman finished first among one hundred white and seventy black teachers who took the test. After apprenticing with a local physician in his third year of medical school, he decided to give up teaching and pursue a career in medicine. He set to work completing a required graduate thesis on prophylaxis, or preventive medicine.

In 1890 Roman received his medical degree from Meharry and moved to Clarksville, Tennessee, where he opened a medical practice. In 1891 he married Margaret Voorhees, a Tennessee native, with whom he later had one child. The young couple moved to Dallas in 1893, and Roman practiced there. Like many physicians of that time, after a few years in practice, Roman decided he needed additional training. In 1899 he went to Chicago for a year of postgraduate study, and in 1904 he traveled to England's Royal Ophthalmic Hospital and the Central London Ear, Nose, and Throat Hospital for specialty training in ophthalmology and otolaryngology.

When Roman returned from abroad he contemplated opening a private practice specializing in diseases of the eye, ear, nose, and throat, but George Hubbard, dean of Meharry Medical College, made him a more attractive offer. While in Chicago, Roman had encountered the noted African-American physician Daniel Hale Williams, who had written to his good friend Hubbard of the younger physician's great promise. When the National Medical Association, the professional society for black physicians, gathered in Nashville in 1903, Hubbard met with Roman and tried to woo him back to Meharry. The following year Roman accepted Hubbard's offer and came to Meharry as the first chair of the ophthalmology and otolaryngology department, a post he retained until 1931.

At Meharry Roman lobbied for the construction of a teaching hospital attached to the university. Meharry used Mercy Hospital as a teaching hospital, but it was becoming increasingly crowded, and the school had no control over its operation. The faculty had long planned to build a hospital to honor Hubbard while he was still alive but had been uncertain where to start construction and how to fund the project. Roman presented a definitive schedule for construction. When the doors of Hubbard Hospital opened in 1912, he was considered one of the key forces behind its rapid completion. His influence in medical circles in Nashville extended beyond Meharry. From 1904 to 1933 he served as director of health at Fisk University, and he started and for a while conducted medical inspections in the city's black public schools.

Throughout his career Roman played an active role in the National Medical Association, founded in 1895. He served a year as its president, but perhaps his greatest contribution was founding and for ten years editing its journal, the *Journal of the National Medical Association*. His leadership role in the national organization of black medical professionals attests directly to the respect he was accorded within this community—respect that was well earned. In 1904, the year of his presidency, the association had only 250 members; four years later Roman proposed that the group start the journal to help raise professional standards and attract more members, and by 1912 membership exceeded 500. Roman described the group in a 1908 speech: "Conceived in no spirit of racial exclusiveness, fostering no ethnic antagonisms, but born of the exigencies of the American environment, the National Medical Association has for its object binding together for mutual cooperation and helpfulness the men and women of African descent who are legally and honorably engaged in the cognate professions of medicine, surgery, pharmacy, and dentistry."

Roman did not restrict his activities to medicine; in the later years of his life he became increasingly involved with the humanities and the state of blacks in America. During World War I, for instance, he lectured to black troops about social hygiene. Over the course of his life he wrote more than forty journal articles and two books, which cemented his intellectual reputation among both blacks and whites. After he stepped down as chair of the medical department in 1934, he became professor of medical history and ethics at Meharry.

Roman wrote a number of pamphlets and papers on health, race, and Christian ethics. In 1921 he published a book, *American Civilization and the Negro: The Afro-American in Relation to National Progress*. In this well-received work he discussed the nature of race relations in the United States and the place of blacks in American society. In the introduction he summarized his point of view, saying, "The writer of this volume believes that the differences in mankind are the differences between charcoal and diamonds—differences of *condition* and not of *composition*."

Roman, a resonant orator, did not confine his opinions to the printed page. His 1913 speech before the Southern Sociological Congress was described in one local newspaper as the "most significant utterance on the race question" of that year. A devout member of the African Methodist Episcopal church for his entire life, he was one of the pillars of Nashville's St. Paul A. M. E. Church community. He taught an adult Sunday school class that was so popular that the pastor invited him to address the entire congregation. Roman's lay sermons, as they came to be called, were imitated in other congregations throughout the country.

Throughout his life Roman enjoyed the respect of his peers, black and white, physicians and humanists. In a world rarely sympathetic to black men, he managed without compromising his ideals to pursue the work that interested him and to help others. He was aware, however, that few black men shared his experiences. In *A History of Meharry Medical College*, published in the year of his death, he wrote, "The young professional man of my race needs to be learned in the lore of the past and wholeheartedly committed to the principles of noblesse oblige. Without these virtues, scientific knowledge will become an individual delusion and a group danger—apples of Sodom that will turn to ashes in the hour of need." Roman continued writing and speaking until his death in Nashville.

• In *A History of Meharry Medical College* (1934), Roman traced his own career along with the development of the school. William Montague Cobb has a brief biography of Roman in the "Medical History" section of the *Journal of the National Medical Association* 45 (1953): 301–4. There are brief paragraphs on Roman's life in Frank Lincoln Mather, ed., *Who's Who of the Colored Race* (1915; repr. 1976); *Who's Who in Colored America* (1927–); and Clement Richardson, ed., *National Cyclopedia of the Colored Race* (1919–). Lily Hardy Hammond, *In the Vanguard of Race*, contains some stories about his early years. Herbert M. Morais, *The History of the Negro in Medicine* (1967), has a brief entry on him. James Summerville, *Educating Black Doctors: A History of Meharry Medical College* (1983), follows Roman's relationship with Meharry. An obituary is in the *Journal of the National Medical Association* 26 (1934): 174–75.

SHARI RUDAVSKY

ROMAN NOSE (1830?–18 Sept. 1868), Northern Cheyenne warrior, was called Sautie or the Bat as a boy; he later took the name Woquni or Hook Nose, which was translated by whites as Roman Nose. Little is known of his early life; the names of his parents have not been determined. His contemporaries described him as being well over six feet in height and possessing great physical powers. A man of fine character, quiet and self-contained, he was held in high esteem by all the Cheyennes, both men and women, and was so renowned among whites that they credited him with being a leader in a number of engagements in which he did not participate. Throughout his life he remained a fighter, refusing opportunities to become a chief or headman.

In his youth Roman Nose became a member of the Elk Soldiers or Elk-Horn Scrapers, a military society whose duty it was to police the Indian camp and participate in war activities. During much of the last part of his life, he lived with the Dog Soldiers, another military society to which he did not belong but whose aggressiveness he admired.

In battle Roman Nose wore a distinctive headdress made for him in 1860 by the medicine man White Bull, who had envisioned it many years earlier. Being careful to use only natural materials, White Bull fashioned a war bonnet that had a single buffalo horn in the center, with a kingfisher's skin above and behind it. Two long trains of eagle feathers, one red and one white, nearly reached the ground when the wearer rode on horseback. Attached to the crown were the skins of a barn swallow, a bat, and a hawk, each symbolizing a desirable power in battle. The invulnerability insured by the war bonnet depended on the warrior's adherence to two taboos: Roman Nose could not shake hands with anyone or eat food that had been taken from a dish with a metal utensil. Violation of either stricture meant certain death in battle.

Roman Nose apparently remained at peace with whites until after Colonel John Chivington's attack on Black Kettle's village at Sand Creek, Colorado, when he became a leader of native resistance. On 26 July 1865 he gained prominence in the battles at Platte River Bridge and Red Buttes, in present-day central Wyoming, which resulted in the death of Lieutenant Caspar Collins and the destruction of Sergeant Amos Custard's wagon train. On 5 September 1865 he was with the large party of Indians that attacked Colonel Nelson Cole's and Lieutenant Colonel Samuel Walker's segments of the Powder River Expedition, sent into central Montana to punish Plains Indian raiders. Mounted on a white war horse, Roman Nose rode three or four times across the soldier line within easy carbine shot but escaped unharmed, causing the battle to be known in Cheyenne history as Roman Nose's Fight.

In 1866 Roman Nose left for the plains south of the Platte River, where he remained until his death. In August he attended a council at Fort Harker, Kansas, denouncing the building of the Union Pacific through buffalo country, then attacked railroad facilities and workers. On 14 April 1867, when General Winfield S. Hancock approached the Cheyenne village near Fort Larned for a council, Roman Nose rode out to meet him. Although determined to kill Hancock, he was deterred by other Cheyennes. Following the conclusion of discussions, Roman Nose led Cheyenne and Kiowa warriors in a battle with U.S. troops near Prairie Dog Creek, Kansas. Two months later he participated in preliminary discussions with the Peace Commission of 1867 at Medicine Lodge Creek. However, he refused to take part in council deliberations and did not sign the resulting treaty, the purpose of which was to confine Indians of the southern plains to reservations in present-day Oklahoma.

In 1868 Cheyenne raids along the Saline and Solomon rivers brought soldiers into the field, resulting in the famous Battle of Beecher Island in northeast Colorado on 17 September. Several days before, Roman Nose had participated in a Sioux feast during which he ate a piece of fry bread that had been removed from the fire with a metal fork. Learning of this, he knew that he would die in his next encounter. When the Cheyennes surrounded Major George Forsyth and fifty-three scouts on a small sandbar in the Arickaree River, Roman Nose did not participate in the early fighting. Late in the afternoon, however, after repeat-

ed urging by other warriors, he mounted his war horse and led a charge in which he was mortally wounded, dying the next day. Today he remains a symbol of the proud spirit of the Fighting Cheyennes.

• Early works recounting the most important events in the life of Roman Nose are two by George Bird Grinnell based on interviews with Cheyennes who knew him: *The Fighting Cheyennes* (1915) and *The Cheyenne Indians: Their History and Ways of Life* (1923). For a good recent summary, see Stan Hoig, *The Peace Chiefs of the Cheyennes* (1980). The standard work on the classic battle in which Roman Nose died is John Monnett, *The Battle of Beecher Island, and the Indian War of 1867–1869* (1992).

JOHN D. McDERMOTT

ROMANS, Bernard (c. 1720–c. 1784), cartographer and naturalist, was born in Holland. Nothing is known about his parents or early childhood. He traveled to England in his youth and studied botany, mathematics, and engineering. Romans came to the United States around 1757, serving as a junior surveyor for the British government.

Arriving in St. Augustine, Florida, Romans was probably the first surveyor to settle in the region. His position involved extensive travel throughout the southern colonies. In 1766 he was appointed one of several deputy surveyors of Georgia, and in 1768 he was promoted to principal deputy surveyor for the Southern District of British North America. During this period he conducted numerous surveys throughout eastern and western Florida, producing navigational charts of many previously unrecorded inland waterways. He compiled the earliest known detailed maps of Pensacola Harbor, Mobile Bay, and Tampa Bay. Romans is credited with being the first cartographer to compile a chart of the entire Florida coastline based on personal observation.

Romans went north to New York in 1773, initially to obtain subscribers for a book he hoped to publish, *A Concise Natural History of East and West Florida*. He was elected a member of the Marine Society, a New York organization composed largely of sea captains. In 1774 he was made a member of the American Philosophical Society after he presented a paper to that body in Philadelphia, describing previously unknown Florida plants. He also contributed articles to Isaiah Thomas's *Royal American Magazine*.

In 1775 a first volume of Romans's *Concise Natural History* was published. It would be his most significant work. John Hancock was one of the subscribers, purchasing a copy for the Harvard Library. Volume two was never produced, perhaps in part because of the outbreak of the revolutionary war and Romans's active participation in the patriot cause. Disputes with the British government over his crown pension may have contributed to his revolutionary zeal.

Romans had settled in Hartford, Connecticut, in 1775, and shortly thereafter became involved in the effort to capture Fort Ticonderoga. He was employed by the New York committee of safety to construct fortifications on the Hudson River near West Point. It has been suggested, though not confirmed, that on the recommendation of General George Washington he was assigned to build fortifications at Fort Constitution. He resigned after a bitter dispute with the committee about the fortifications.

In 1776 Romans returned to Philadelphia to accept a commission as captain in the Pennsylvania Artillery. He served under General Horatio Gates in the northern campaign in Canada and resigned from the army in 1778 to retire to Wethersfield, Connecticut, near Hartford. During this time he earned a substantial income from publishing maps of various battle sites of the war, for which there was popular demand. In 1778 he also published *Annals of the Troubles in the Netherlands*, a historical compilation. In January 1779 Romans married Elizabeth Whiting; they had one son.

Despite his advanced age—Romans must have been nearly sixty at this time—two years of inactivity away from the war were more than he could tolerate, and he rejoined the military in 1780. He was ordered to South Carolina to join the southern army. What happened next is unclear. It is known that Romans set sail from Hartford for Charleston and was captured at sea by the British. His widow claimed that his ship was taken to Jamaica, where he was imprisoned for the duration of the war. His exchange was refused by the British, presumably because his specialized knowledge would be too valuable to the colonists. The British later claimed that he was imprisoned in England and lived for a time there after the war ended.

In 1784 Romans boarded a ship for the return trip to the United States, but he was never seen or heard from again. It was believed that he carried a large sum of money with him and was murdered for it, his body thrown into the ocean.

• Large collections of Romans's cartography are in the Library of Congress and the New York Public Library. His correspondence with the New York Committee of Safety, the New York Provincial Congress and Convention, and the Continental Congress is in the Peter Force Collection at the Library of Congress. Other Romans correspondence is at the American Philosophical Society Library in Philadelphia and at the New York Public Library. Lincoln Diamont, *Bernard Romans: Forgotten Patriot of the American Revolution* (1985), the best single source on Romans, contains an excellent bibliographical essay. See also Philip Lee Phillips, *Notes on the Life and Works of Bernard Romans* (1924). In 1789 an appendix to the *Concise Natural History* was published by others under the title *The Complete Pilot for the Gulf Passage*. It was reprinted several times with slight title changes, and a facsimile edition was published in 1961.

STEVE FISHER

ROMAYNE, Nicholas (?Sept. 1756–21 July 1817), physician and teacher, was born in New York City, the son of John Romeyn, a silversmith, and Juliana McCarty. Nicholas changed his name from Romeyn to Romayne when he was a young man to facilitate pronunciation. Romayne received an elementary education at Hackensack Academy in New Jersey and commenced his medical education in the medical school of

King's College in 1774. When the revolutionary war broke out a year later, Romayne traveled to Edinburgh to continue his medical studies. He received his medical degree from Edinburgh in 1780, with a dissertation on the formation of pus.

Romayne returned to America in 1782 after spending two years in London, Paris, and Leyden. Because British troops still occupied New York City, Romayne settled in Philadelphia, where he practiced medicine. Returning to New York City in 1783 after the British evacuation, Romayne embarked on a tempestuous career. He also married Susan Van Dam, who was the daughter of a prominent New York City merchant. Their marriage produced several children, all of whom died at an early age.

In 1784 Columbia College (formerly King's College) came under the control of the Board of Regents of the University of the State of New York, of which Romayne was a member. During the same year, Columbia's medical faculty was reorganized, and Romayne was appointed professor of the practice of physic. He was then appointed to Columbia's own Board of Trustees when it was restored in 1787, which made him ineligible to teach medicine at that institution. Precluded from teaching at Columbia, Romayne began to offer private courses at the New York Almshouse and at other locations within the city on anatomy, the principles and practice of medicine, chemistry, and botany. His private school was very successful, drawing students from as far away as Canada.

In 1791 Romayne, in view of the fact that his private school had many students and offered courses in all of the major branches of medicine, asked his colleagues on the Board of Regents to grant his private medical school a charter. Accordingly, the board granted a charter to the College of Physicians and Surgeons but then postponed action to open it when Columbia's trustees promised the board that they would offer the same courses. Angered by Columbia's opposition to the College of Physicians and Surgeons, Romayne resigned from the former's Board of Trustees and took many of his students with him. He worked out an arrangement with Queen's College (later Rutgers) to grant medical degrees to his students. Romayne was on the medical faculty of Queen's from the autumn of 1792 to late 1793, when the school closed owing to financial difficulties.

Deprived of a faculty appointment, Romayne in 1795 sailed to England, presumably for further study and to investigate the possibility of practicing there. Later that year Romayne became a licentiate of the Royal College of Physicians, which would have enabled him to practice medicine in England. It has been suggested by Byron Stookey, one of Romayne's biographers, however, that he may have traveled to England as an agent of William Blount (1749–1798), a signer of the Constitution from North Carolina, a U.S. senator from Tennessee, and a notorious land speculator, who was then deeply involved in a scheme to help Great Britain take over Spanish-controlled Florida and

Louisiana in order to protect his land investments in the Ohio River valley. Romayne, who had met Blount in Philadelphia in 1782, returned to the United States in 1797. Once he was back in New York City, Romayne, who was an investor in Blount's speculations, was asked by the senator to persuade his friends to purchase some of the latter's lands. Although Romayne refused, he was implicated in the Blount fiasco when it was discovered by the U.S. government. In July 1797 Blount was expelled from the Senate, and Romayne, on orders from President John Adams, was arrested and taken to Philadelphia to testify before a House of Representatives' committee investigating the conspiracy. Romayne spent a short time in prison for his activities in this affair.

In 1800 Romayne again traveled abroad. He was admitted that year as a licentiate of the Royal College of Physicians of Edinburgh. It is not known how long Romayne was out of the country, but he was again active in New York City's medical affairs in 1806 when he was elected president of the New York County Medical Society. Four years later, he was elected president of the New York State Medical Society.

The College of Physicians and Surgeons, which had been dormant since 1791, was revived in 1807, with Romayne as its first president. Romayne was not only a member of the faculty, teaching anatomy and the institutes and practice of medicine, but he also financed the medical school's operating expenses by writing personal notes worth $5,700 as well as largely financing the building of its new quarters. Yet Romayne could not escape controversy. In 1811, as the result of a bitter dispute with the faculty, which was controlled by his enemies, Romayne and those friendly to him resigned and went back to Queen's College. A year later Queen's College established a medical faculty, with Romayne holding the chairs of the institutes of medicine and forensic medicine. Queen's College was forced to close again in 1816 due to financial troubles. The closing of Queen's College brought Romayne's stormy teaching career to an abrupt end. He died in New York.

Romayne's career began with promise but ended in controversy and turmoil. Romayne possessed a brilliant mind and was an excellent teacher, yet he also had a difficult time getting along with people. An aggressive and combative personality made Romayne many enemies within New York City's medical profession. Despite his many contributions to the advancement of medical education in New York, especially his roles in the founding and the later revival of the College of Physicians and Surgeons, Romayne was shunned by many of his professional colleagues. His death was ignored by the faculty of the College of Physicians and Surgeons, which at the time was still controlled by his enemies.

• It does not appear that Romayne's personal papers have survived. The archives of Columbia University's Medical School contain information relating to Romayne's association with that institution. Useful biographical accounts include James Thacher, *American Medical Biography*, vol. 2 (1828), pp. 25–29; Fred B. Rogers, "Nicholas Romayne, 1756–1817: Stormy Petrel of American Medical Education," *Journal of Medical Education* 35 (1960): 258–63; and Byron Stookey, "Nicholas Romayne: First President of the College of Physicians and Surgeons, New York City," *Bulletin of the New York Academy of Medicine* 43 (1967): 576–97.

THOMAS A. HORROCKS

ROMBAUER, Irma (30 Oct. 1877–14 Oct. 1962), cookbook author, was born Irma Louise von Starkloff in St. Louis, Missouri, the daughter of Dr. H. Max von Starkloff, a physician, and Emma Kuhlmann. Her mother, who emigrated from Germany around 1873, had worked in one of the first St. Louis kindergartens, in addition to being a governess for a prominent family. In 1889, when Dr. Starkloff was appointed American consul in Bremen, Germany, the family moved to Europe. Irma studied in "finishing" schools in Lausanne and Geneva and spoke both French and German fluently. She recalled in her later years, "I was brought up to be a 'young lady'"—the thought of which made her smile and laugh. "I played the piano poorly, embroidered and sewed, painted on china and entertained 'gentlemen callers.'" After the family returned to St. Louis in 1894, she took art classes at Washington University.

In October 1899 Irma Starkloff married a young lawyer, Edgar Roderick Rombauer, with whom she was to have three children. As sepia-toned photographs of the time show, she had an elegant, refined face with a warmth and richness to her features, which she was to retain throughout her life. But she found herself ill prepared for household duties. She was later to tell a journalist that early in her marriage she did not even have an oven thermometer, and there were "stains on the kitchen sink which defied all treatment." One of Rombauer's most quoted lines is that as a bride-cook she placed "many a burnt offering on the altar of matrimony." In those first years her husband was a sportsman who enjoyed camping out, and she was to credit him with teaching her the ins-and-outs of cooking. An admirer of Rombauer's famous cookbook has said that her early mistakes with a skillet enabled her to save many a newlywed and amateur cook from similar disasters.

Rombauer did not give serious thought to publishing a cookbook until 1930, when her husband died. She was fifty-three years old at the time, and shortly afterward her son and daughter married and set up their own households. As a distraction from her recent loss, she began to write down favorite family recipes. She completed the selection in 1931, titled it *Joy of Cooking*, and paid for the publication herself. On a visit to Indianapolis shortly thereafter, she was playing bridge at the home of a cousin. One of the players was Laurance Chambers, president of Bobbs-Merrill publishing house, who leafed through a copy of Rombauer's book and politely admired it. In 1936 Bobbs-Merrill agreed to publish it.

Rombauer's *Joy of Cooking* was not, as many categorized it, an exclusively "American cookbook." Although it included hundreds of American recipes, it was in fact international in scope. Through a succession of revised editions, more and more foreign dishes were added, such as bagna cauda, cardoons, the codfish mousse called brandade de morue, Chinese firepot cooking, veal Orloff, hummus (chickpea) dip, fettucine, and huevos rancheros, the great Mexican breakfast dish. Among the numerous classic French recipes was one for puff pastry, conceivably the most complicated of all dishes to describe without hands-on preparation. Given her Germanic roots, the *Joy of Cooking* had curiously few recipes of German origin, among them Königsberger Klops (meatballs), Gefüllte Krautkopf (stuffed cabbage), Spaetzle (dumplings), Sachertorte, and Lebkuchen. When Rombauer was once asked to name her favorite dish for year-end entertaining, she said without hesitation that it was herring salad, a dish her German mother had always made on New Year's Eve. Rombauer's recipe called for milter herring (or sperm herring, which are the male of the species at breeding time) to be soaked overnight, skinned, with the "milt" and bones removed, and then blended with vinegar, cubed cooked veal, hard-cooked eggs, pickled beets, onions, boiled potatoes, diced apples, sugar, horseradish, and chopped parsley.

A highly adventurous traveler, Rombauer tasted the food of many countries. In an interview with the *New York Times* in December 1953, she described her diet during a brief visit to Mexico, a country for which she developed a passion. She spoke at length of tortilla-making and the dishes for which tortillas are the base, including enchiladas, tostadas, and chalupas; each such dish is called an antojito, a word meaning, she said, "a little, sudden, capricious and overwhelming desire." She was also fascinated by the widespread use of fried grasshoppers in Mexican cuisine. A year later, Rombauer noted to a newspaper columnist that in her opinion, "No dish is pedestrian if it is faultlessly prepared." To illustrate her point, she recommended as a first course the uncomplicated cheese fondue of Swiss cuisine (made with Swiss cheese, white wine, and kirsch), one of the first times the soon-to-be-popular dish was suggested to American cooks.

Rombauer frequently interlaced the recipes in her book with humorous remarks and anecdotes. "Is there anything better than a good coffee cake?" she asked her readers. "I am told that the deposed King of Spain 'dunked.' Perhaps that afforded him comfort." One of Rombauer's most widely quoted stories concerned the celebrated opera contralto Ernestine Schumann-Heink and the tenor Enrico Caruso. At a restaurant, Caruso passed by Mme Schumann-Heink's table when a huge steak was placed before her. "Stina," he exclaimed, "surely you are not going to eat that alone." "No," she replied, "no, not alone. With potatoes."

In 1943 Bobbs-Merrill published a revised and considerably enlarged *Joy of Cooking*, which Rombauer had prepared with the aid of her daughter, Marion Rombauer Becker. On its way to becoming a perennial bestseller, it surpassed in number of copies sold the previous standard American guide to the kitchen, Fanny Farmer's *Boston Cooking School Cookbook*. The third edition appeared in 1946; the fourth, published in 1951, was the first to credit Rombauer's daughter as coauthor.

Rombauer enjoyed a comfortable income but always claimed that she preferred to live modestly. She maintained her third-floor apartment in St. Louis until 1955. She also had a small cottage in the Ozarks near Antonia, Missouri, where she spent many weekends and much of her free time. Active in civic interests of various kinds—the St. Louis Symphony, the St. Louis Opera Guild, a lunch program for children, and the local Audubon Society, among them—she also collected antiques and enjoyed watching all sports, with the exception of wrestling. In her last years, she was bedridden. She died in St. Louis.

During Rombauer's lifetime and for several decades thereafter, as her daughter continued to make revisions and additions, *Joy of Cooking* came to be widely considered the finest cookbook published in the United States. The book succeeded on several counts. It was fascinating to browse through and read even by those who shun the kitchen; it was thoroughly reliable in the fine points of measurement, both of weight and volume; the recipes were varied and appealing; and *Joy of Cooking* became a model for cookbook authors who were born after the book's first publication. Although other cookbooks began to be favored, *Joy of Cooking* continued to be a standard at the end of the twentieth century, when Irma Rombauer's grandson, Ethan Becker, brought out yet another new edition in 1997.

• Besides the various editions of the *Joy of Cooking*, Rombauer published *Streamlined Cooking* (1939) and *Cookbook for Boys and Girls* (1946). The most useful published sources on Rombauer are Marion Rombauer Becker, *Little Acorn: The Story behind the "Joy of Cooking," 1931–1966* (1966), and Anne Mendelson, *Stand Facing the Stove: The Story of the Women Who Gave America the "Joy of Cooking"* (1996). See also the *New York Times*, 24 Dec. 1952, 31 Dec. 1953, 7 Nov. 1954, and 7, 26 Feb. 1956. Obituaries are in *New York Times*, 17 Oct. 1962, and *Time*, 26 Oct. 1962.

CRAIG CLAIBORNE

ROMBERG, Sigmund (29 July 1887–9 Nov. 1951), composer, was born in Nagykanizsa, on the Hungarian-Yugoslavian border, the son of Adam Romberg, an affluent sawmill manager and amateur musician, and Clara Fells, a poet and short story writer who used the pen name Clara Berg. In 1888 the family moved to the small village of Belisce on the Drava River. Romberg grew up in a musical household, and as a child he was captivated by Johann Strauss's waltzes. At age six he began violin lessons and two years later started studying the piano as well. He was educated at home by private tutors until 1897, when Romberg's parents enrolled him at the Realschule in the nearby city of

Osijek. Romberg joined the school's sixty-member band directed by Luigi Boggio, who assigned Romberg the C trumpet.

After graduating from the Realschule in 1905, Romberg attended a preparatory school in Pécs (1905–1906) and then the Realschule in Szeged (1906–1907). He then entered the Vienna Politechnische Hochschule. In Vienna he obtained a low-paying job as a stagehand at a musical theater, where he watched musicals and befriended Franz Lehar, the composer of the opera *The Merry Widow.* Romberg also took music lessons from Richard Heuberger, a leading music teacher and musician. Disregarding his parents' insistence that he concentrate on his engineering studies, in 1908 Romberg joined the Imperial First Hussar cavalry regiment, which guarded the Royal Palace in Vienna, and he continued to take music lessons. After being discharged from the army in 1909, he took another year off for travel to England and the United States. Once in New York, with its many theaters and large German-speaking population, Romberg never returned to live in Europe again.

In New York Romberg worked as a pianist, first at the Cafe Continental (1909) and then at the Pabst-Harlem restaurant, a popular nightspot (1910–1913). In 1913 Romberg obtained U.S. citizenship, joined the musicians' union, and brought his brother Hugo to the United States. The year 1913 proved to be a watershed year for Romberg in other ways. He was hired by the exclusive Bustanoby's restaurant to lead his own dance band. Renowned Broadway impresarios J. J. and Lee Shubert hired Romberg to write songs for them. His first operetta, *The Whirl of the Wind,* opened at the Shuberts' Winter Garden Theatre on 10 January 1914. Lyrics were written by Harold Atteridge, who became Romberg's most frequent lyricist.

When the United States entered World War I Romberg registered for the draft, and in February 1918 he was inducted into the army in Yaphank, Long Island. Composer Irving Berlin was inducted at the same time. Because of his knowledge of German, Romberg was assigned to military intelligence.

By 1919 Romberg had composed twenty-four operettas, including *Dancing Around* (1914), which starred Al Jolson in his first Broadway role at the Winter Garden; *Maytime* (1917), which later was made into a film starring Jeanette MacDonald and Nelson Eddy (MGM, 1937); and Jolson's third Winter Garden show, *Sinbad* (1918). Among Romberg's well-known songs from that period were "Auf Wiedersehn" from *The Blue Paradise* (1915), "Wedding Bells" from *The Show of Wonders* (1916), and "Wine, Women and Song" from *The Passing Show* (1916). His last two shows under his initial contract with the Shuberts, who paid him only a small flat fee for each operetta, were *Monte Cristo Jr.,* which opened on 12 February 1919, and *The Passing Show of 1919,* which opened on 23 October 1919. Although Romberg was under an exploitative contract with the Shuberts, other producers of his hits paid him considerable royalties. The Shuberts did not allow Romberg to produce his own complete operettas or to keep his copyrights and royalties for Broadway productions. As a result, in 1919 he terminated his contract but continued to receive assignments from them for new musical shows under improved conditions. Shortly thereafter Romberg formed the Wilner-Romberg firm with Max Wilner. Their first operetta was *The Magic Melody,* which opened at the Shubert Theater on 11 November 1919 and included such songs as "Love Makes the World Go Round," "Two's Company, Three's a Crowd," "I Am the Pasha," and "The Little Church around the Corner." In 1921 the Wilner-Romberg firm failed financially, and Romberg continued to freelance as an independent producer-composer, accepting commissions from Florenz Ziegfeld, George White, and Lawrence Schwab, in addition to the Shuberts.

New Romberg shows emerged steadily through the 1920s. In 1920 he composed the music for *Poor Little Ritz Girl,* for which Richard Rodgers wrote the lyrics. In 1921 Dorothy Donnelly adapted the Austrian hit *Das Drei Maedelhaus,* with music by Franz Schubert, for the American stage; Romberg adapted the music for the show, which was renamed *Blossom Time.* He boldly dispensed with the chorus; the show, therefore, was played *and* sung by twenty-eight characters. Also in 1921 Romberg wrote the music for the hit *Bombo,* starring Jolson. In 1923 he was hired by Universal International to write the background music for the silent movie *Foolish Wives.* The next year he composed *The Student Prince,* an operetta frequently produced by repertory theaters. The show, with lyrics by Donnelly, was presented by the Shubert brothers on 2 December 1924 at the Al Jolson Theater. Much of Romberg's childhood memories are depicted in this operetta, characterized by the bright colors and military pomp of Osijek and the gaiety and rhythm of the Viennese waltzes. Hit songs from this show include the "Drinking Song," "To the Inn We Are Marching," "You're in Heidelberg," "Deep in My Heart," "Serenade," and "Gavotte." Nine road companies traversed the country with *The Student Prince,* often playing across the street from two other Romberg hits that were touring at the same time, *Blossom Time* and *Louis the 14th.* In 1925 Romberg married Lillian Harris of Washington, D.C. They had no children.

As an independent freelance composer, Romberg created some of Broadway's greatest musicals of the era. He followed *The Student Prince* with *Princess Flavia* (1925), the musical version of *The Prisoner of Zenda.* Over time he collaborated with lyricist Oscar Hammerstein II in five stage shows and three films. The stage shows include *The Desert Song* (1926), for which Otto Harbach cowrote the lyrics with Hammerstein, *The New Moon* (1928), *East Wind* (1931), *May Wine* (1935), and *Sunny River* (1941). The films were *Viennese Nights* (Warner Bros., 1930), *Children of Dreams* (Warner Bros., 1931), and *The Night Is Young* (MGM, 1935), all box office hits.

Although both songwriters and music publishers belonged to the American Society of Composers, Authors, and Publishers (ASCAP), the organization did not often protect songwriters from exploitation by the publishers. On 28 August 1931 Billy Rose created the Songwriters Protective Association (SPA) to secure better negotiating conditions for songwriters. Romberg devoted much time to the new organization. In 1936 he became its president, remaining in this position for fifteen years.

In the 1930s sophisticated Broadway audiences were tiring of "schmaltzy" operettas and demanding shows that reflected life in the United States. But as the demand for old-fashioned operettas was declining in New York, it reemerged with renewed force among moviegoers. A good number of Romberg's operettas were adapted to the screen. In 1930 he moved to California to create film musicals, including *The Girl of the Golden West* (MGM, 1938), *They Gave Him a Gun* (MGM, 1937), and *Up in Central Park* (Universal International, 1948).

Rodgers and Hammerstein's musical *Oklahoma!* heralded a new era on Broadway, and the popularity of the operetta further waned. Romberg turned to conducting, touring with orchestras throughout the country. From time to time he was invited by the CBS radio network to conduct complete concerts of his own music. Although his recordings, most of them produced by RCA-Victor, continued to sell well, Romberg felt as if he had musically outlived his time.

Along with Victor Herbert and Jerome Kern, Romberg is considered one of the giants of American musical theater. During his lifetime he produced seventy-eight operettas, eight original films, and about two thousand songs. On 9 November 1951 the CBS network aired a television salute to Romberg. He died in New York City just minutes after the end of the program, only fifteen days before a gala tribute that the SPA was preparing in honor of his fifteen years as president of the organization.

• Romberg's papers are at the University of California at Berkeley, the Music Division and the Motion Picture, Broadcasting, and Recorded Sound Division of the Library of Congress, and the New York Public Library. Elliott Arnold, *Deep in My Heart* (1949), is a fictionalized account based on real incidents in Romberg's life. Romberg is discussed in Gerald Bordman, *American Musical Comedy* (1982); David Ewen, *New Complete Book of the American Musical Theater* (1970); and John Koedel, "The Film Operettas of Sigmund Romberg" (M.A. thesis, California State Univ., Northridge, 1984). Articles that provide additional information on Romberg include "Middle-Brow Music Master," *Look*, 8 July 1947; Ruth Harvey, "Sigmund Romberg Felicitated on Sixty-third Birthday," *Daily News*, 29 July 1950; John Keating, "Romberg Goes Zing-Zing, Zoom-Zoom," *Cue*, 17 Feb. 1951; and the *New York Times*, 16 Sept. 1973. Obituaries are in the *Los Angeles Times* and the *New York Times*, both 10 Nov. 1951.

SHOSHANA KLEBANOFF

ROME, Harold (27 May 1908–26 Oct. 1993), Broadway composer, was born in Hartford, Connecticut, the son of Louis Rome, the owner of the Connecticut Coal Company; his mother's name is unknown. As a child, Rome studied piano at home from local teachers. He attended Yale, where he studied architecture and law while playing in amateur dance bands on the side to raise extra money. He also mounted musical revues as a summer-camp counselor.

After graduation from the Yale School of Architecture in 1934, he took an unpaid job in an architect's office in New York City, while continuing to study piano and write songs for amusement. Most of his songs had topical content, commenting on the plight of the worker during the depression years, an unusual topic for popular songs of the day, so he met with little success in selling his music to the standard popular publishers. However, when the International Ladies Garment Workers decided to mount a show to tell the story of the poor working conditions of the sweatshops, Rome's socially conscious music seemed perfect to them. The show, *Pins and Needles* (1937), was an enormous success, running for four years; Rome's songs, including "Sunday in the Park" and "Sing Me a Song of Social Significance," became hits. While written in a typical pop style of the day, the topical content of his lyrics was daring, mirroring the work of left-leaning folk song writers like Woody Guthrie.

Rome followed this success with another political review, *Sing Out the News* (1939), which featured another hit song for him, "F. D. R. Jones," and won that year's American Society of Composers, Authors, and Publishers (ASCAP) award. He was then drafted into the army, where he served in the entertainment unit, writing songs for revues to entertain the troops, under the name *Stars and Gripes* (1943). His military experience inspired his first civilian revue after the war, *Call Me Mister* (1946), which featured the hit "South America, Take It Away." However, his next show, again in the social commentary mode, *That's the Ticket* (1948), closed out of town.

His greatest success in the commercial theater came in the 1950s with a string of hit shows that were in a more conventional Broadway style. This began with *Wish You Were Here* (1952), which was based on his experiences mounting shows at summer camps and which featured the novelty of a swimming pool on stage. It was followed by adaptations of a French novel, *Fanny* (1954), and the famous American western film, *Destry Rides Again* (1959), which featured a young Andy Griffith in the lead. Finally, *I Can Get It for You Wholesale* (1962) returned him to the garment worker's world and introduced Barbra Streisand to the Broadway stage.

In the 1960s Rome's output slowed, and his success rate dipped precipitously. His last Broadway show for which he provided the book, *The Zulu and the Zayda* (1965), suffered from an unfortunate marriage of the stereotyped Jewish role put into a South African setting and had a short run. He continued to compose, most notably his 1970s adaptation of *Gone with the Wind* called *Scarlett*, which was produced successfully in Tokyo and then, two years later, in London but never made it to the Broadway stage.

Rome spent the following decades in retirement from the music business. During this period, he garnered many awards, including election into the Songwriters' Hall of Fame (1981) and the Theater Hall of Fame (1991), ASCAP's Richard Rodgers Award (1985), and a Drama Desk Award (1990). He died in New York City in 1993. Rome was survived by his wife, Florence, and a son (Joshua) and daughter (Rachel).

• Adrienne Scholtz compiled a catalog of Rome's papers housed at the Yale University Music Library that was published by the library in 1990. Rome's contributions to the American musical stage are discussed in Gerald Boardman's *The American Musical, 1900–1950* (1972). Obituaries are in the *New York Times*, 27 Oct. 1993, and the *Los Angeles Times*, 28 Oct. 1993.

RICHARD CARLIN

ROMEIKE, Henry (19 Nov. 1855–3 June 1903), originator of a press-clipping service, was born in Riga, Latvia, the son of a German father, Albert Romeike, a merchant, and his Latvian wife, Henriette Szabries. Henry completed primary schooling in Memel, East Prussia, and at the age of thirteen was apprenticed to a draper (dry goods merchant). In 1870, at the age of fifteen, he absconded from Memel to Berlin, where he worked for almost a decade in various draper concerns. Seeking more remunerative employment, Romeike abandoned Berlin in 1880 to seek his fortune in other German and European cities and finally moved to Paris in 1881 or early 1882. According to his friend William Durrant, Romeike found employment in Paris with M. Gallois, who supplied artists and actors with press comments on their work. Gallois was apparently emulating M. Blum, who as early as 1875 provided celebrities with written copies, rather than the cuttings, of notices in foreign papers. However, according to Paul J. Morgan, former chairman of the Romeike and Curtice Press Clipping Service, the Argus de la Presse organization was the first to attempt a world press-clipping service.

On the basis of what he had apparently learned from Gallois and the examples of Blum and the Argus de la Presse, Romeike attempted to establish a press-clipping service in France. Lacking funds to make his venture a success and, as he later asserted, deciding that the English were more avid readers of newspapers than the French, Romeike left Paris for London in 1884. He opened a newspaper shop at 66 Ludgate Hill that sold Continental newspapers and periodicals, and he continued to serve some of his French clients with press clippings. The shop—with newspapers hanging on the walls—attracted actors, writers, musicians, and painters who came to read items about themselves. This affirmed Romeike's belief that he could turn the vanity of his customers to profit by supplying subscribers with press clippings about themselves.

To implement his scheme, Romeike formed a partnership with Edward Curtice, Sr., the proprietor of Curtice and Company. The Curtice firm was established in 1852 as a wholesale bookseller and news agent, printer, and engraver; by the 1880s it also included a bookshop and bookbinding facilities. Romeike brought the press-clipping service to the enterprise. The firm became Romeike and Curtice (later Romeike and Curtice, the Press Clipping Bureau) and took over two publications Romeike had begun in his shop: *The Wife-Beaters' Manual. A Guide to Husbands' Connubial Correctness. With a List of Prices Attached.* (which the British Library catalog lists as "compiled from statistics by H. Romeike") and *Romeike's Register*, which listed living accommodations available in London. The Romeike and Curtice partnership was quite successful and endured amicably until Romeike left London to establish a press-clipping service in New York. Indeed, Edward Curtice was proud at having been "the first to recognise the enterprise of Romeike" and at having "associated himself with him in a business which . . . [became] . . . worldwide" (*Times*, 1 Sept. 1898).

Increasingly, the ambitious Romeike was attracted to the possibilities offered by the vast expansion of the daily press and its varied uses in the United States. During 1885 he dispatched a business associate, Samuel Leavitt, to the United States to study the media and prospects for a press-clipping service in New York. Following Leavitt's report that American newspapers were read more widely and conveyed greater information than papers in Britain, Romeike financed Leavitt's establishment of a press-clipping service in New York and prepared to emigrate to the United States. In 1887 he sold most of his interest in Romeike and Curtice to Edward Curtice and left London for New York with his young wife, Jane Sarah Mary Ganther, whom he had married in 1884. They had no children.

Romeike's press-clipping service fulfilled a real need in the United States and, following a slow but steady growth, became a great financial success during the 1890s. The company and Romeike personally achieved considerable prominence as the press-clipping service proved useful to socialites, politicians, businessmen, theater personalities, literary figures, artists, musicians, corporations, and banks who desired information not only on how they were reported to the public but on the public image of their competitors and adversaries. In fact, Romeike's enterprise helped make prominent Americans more conscious of their image. His press-clipping service was also used by nonfiction and fiction writers and newspaper reporters and editors for their productions, thus giving rise to the verb *romeiked* in press and literary circles to describe publications based on press clippings.

By 1900 the Romeike press-clipping enterprise had established branches in Paris, Berlin, and Rome and was, of course, supplied with material by Romeike and Curtice in London. The company catered not only to American personages and institutions but to foreign governments, monarchs, princes, and presidents. Romeike became a prominent member of the New York Press Club and the International Press Club. While attending a press club convention in Berne during 1892 he was severely injured in a fall while mountain climbing.

His first wife having died, he had married Suzanne Dayes in 1892; the marriage, which produced two children, was dissolved a year before Romeike's death of apoplexy in New York City. One of Romeike's obituarists noted that "through the wide advertisements given his odd calling, he became a public character in America" (*Collier's Weekly*, 20 June 1903).

• The location of Romeike's papers and scrapbook of letters and press clippings, previously reported in the possession of his brother, Arthur, is unknown. Unfortunately the extensive archives and press-clipping library of Romeike and Curtice were destroyed in the bombing of London in 1941. Hence the major sources on his life are still the obituaries in the *New York Times*, 4 June 1903; *Collier's Weekly*, 20 June 1903; the *Baltimore Herald*, 6 June 1903; and the *Utica (N.Y.) Observer*, 8 June 1903; Gordon Beckles's flawed article, "Not for Nonentities: How Much Are You Worth to the Press-Cutting Agencies?" *Strand Magazine* 110 (1946): 33–35; the Edward Curtice, Sr., obituary in the *Times*, 1 Sept. 1898; and the correspondence of William Durrant and others in *World's Press News*, 7 Apr. and 5 May 1932. These were supplemented by information provided by Paul J. Morgan, Simon Lanyon (managing director, Romeike and Curtice, Ltd.), and David Linton, a newspaper historian.

J. O. BAYLEN

ROMER, Alfred Sherwood (28 Dec. 1894–5 Nov. 1973), paleontologist, was born in White Plains, New York, the son of Henry Houston Romer, a journalist, and Evelyn Sherwood. He lived with his family in New York City until his parents' divorce in 1904, after which he moved with his father to Torrington, Connecticut, and later to Waterbury, Connecticut. In 1909 he returned to White Plains to live with his father's mother while completing his secondary education. He worked for a year as a railroad clerk before matriculating at Amherst (Mass.) College, where he decided to pursue a career studying fossils after taking a course on evolution that was taught by a vertebrate paleontologist. In 1917 he received his A.B., joined the American Field Service, and drove an ammunition truck in France during World War I. When the United States entered the war later that year, he enlisted in the U.S. Air Service as a private. Discharged in 1919 as a second lieutenant, he entered Columbia University and received his Ph.D. in zoology in 1921. He then became an instructor in anatomy at the city's Bellevue Hospital Medical College while also serving as a research associate in the American Museum of Natural History's Department of Comparative Anatomy.

In 1923 Romer was appointed associate professor of vertebrate paleontology at the University of Chicago. In 1924 he married Ruth Hibbard, with whom he had three children. The University of Chicago possessed an excellent collection of fossils, and Romer developed a particular interest in its Permian tetrapods, four-legged creatures who lived approximately 250 million years ago. He spent much of his time searching for additional specimens in the fossil-rich sediment beds of

Texas and New Mexico in an effort to trace the evolution of vertebrates from their incarnation as fishes approximately 500 million years ago into amphibians and, during the Permian period, into reptiles. Because he regarded extinct vertebrates as once-living creatures, he also attempted to understand the evolution of their musculature and nervous systems as well as their skeletons. He made his findings accessible to people with a variety of scientific backgrounds. He wrote *Vertebrate Paleontology* (1933), one of the first textbooks for training would-be paleontologists, and *Man and the Vertebrates* (1933), aimed at the general educated public.

In 1931 Romer was promoted to full professor. His colleagues at Chicago viewed paleontology as a branch of geology and not a branch of zoology as he did. Therefore, three years later he accepted an appointment as professor of zoology at Harvard University and curator of vertebrate paleontology for its Museum of Comparative Zoology, also known as the Agassiz Museum. At the time of his appointment Harvard's fossil collection attracted little attention, largely because the museum's primary emphasis was directed toward modern reptiles and amphibians. As curator he implemented an aggressive acquisition campaign and eventually added a number of fossilized Permian tetrapods to the museum's collection, thus transforming it into a world center for paleontological research. In 1945 he became director of the university's biological laboratories but stepped down the next year to become the museum's director, a position he held for fifteen years. As director he increased the museum's endowment almost tenfold, which enabled him to improve significantly the scope of the museum's activities by employing a staff that was larger, better paid, and better trained. Meanwhile Romer produced several groundbreaking studies of extinct amphibians, particularly labyrinthodonts, lizard-like creatures resembling alligators and salamanders from whom all land vertebrates most likely evolved, and pelycosaurs, sail-backed reptiles that evolved into the therapsids, mammal-like reptiles from whom all mammals are thought to have evolved.

In 1947 Romer was appointed Harvard's Alexander Agassiz Professor of Zoology, a chair he occupied for the next eighteen years. Because of his background in anatomy he became one of the world's leading authorities on the skeletal structures of prehistoric reptiles, and his books shared this expertise with a number of audiences. *The Vertebrate Body* (1949), which was reprinted through a fourth edition in 1970, was used extensively as a college-level textbook on comparative anatomy. *The Vertebrate Story* (1959) and *The Procession of Life* (1968) again addressed the general educated reader, and *Osteology of the Reptiles* (1956) informed the thinking of the most knowledgeable paleontologists. He retired from Harvard in 1965 to participate in a decade-long dig in the Chañares region of Argentina. This area yielded a number of reptilian fossils dating to the Triassic period, the period immediately following the Permian and the one during which dinosaurs first appeared. Although many of these fossils closely resembled other forms Romer had uncovered in Africa in 1929, he knew from examining their skeletal structures that these creatures could not possibly have swum across the South Atlantic Ocean. He also had known since the mid-1940s of remarkable similarities between fossilized Permian tetrapods found in Texas and Czechoslovakia. His conclusion that approximately 200 million years ago Africa and South America must have been part of one large landmass contributed strong paleontological evidence for the geological theory of continental drift.

Romer served as a founder and first president of the Society of Vertebrate Paleontology in 1940. He was elected to membership in the National Academy of Sciences in 1944. He presided over the American Society of Zoologists in 1951, the Society of Systematic Zoology in 1952, the Society for the Study of Evolution in 1953, the Sixteenth International Zoological Congress in Washington, D.C., in 1963, and the American Association for the Advancement of Science in 1966. He was awarded the National Academy of Sciences' Thompson Medal in 1956 and its Daniel Giraud Elliot Medal in 1960, the Academy of Natural Sciences of Philadelphia's Hayden Geological Award in 1962, the Geological Society of America's Penrose Medal in 1962, the Paleontological Society Medal in 1967, the Linnaean Society of London Medal in 1972, and the Geological Society of London's Wollaston Medal in 1973. He died in Cambridge, Massachusetts.

Romer contributed to the advance of paleontology by applying the techniques of comparative anatomy to the study of fossils. His work shed much light on the evolution of vertebrates from sea- to land-dwelling creatures and contributed to a better understanding of the origin of the continents.

• Romer's papers are in the Harvard University Archives. A biography, which includes a bibliography, is Edwin H. Colbert, "Alfred Sherwood Romer," National Academy of Sciences, *Biographical Memoirs* 53 (1982): 265–94. An obituary is in the *New York Times*, 7 Nov. 1973.

CHARLES W. CAREY, JR.

ROMNEY, George Wilcken (8 July 1907–26 July 1995), industrialist and politician, was born in Chihuahua, Mexico, the son of Gaskell Romney, a construction contractor, and Anna Pratt. From the beginning, Romney's Mormon faith strongly influenced his life. His parents had moved to Mexico to escape American laws discriminating against Latter-day Saints. After Mexican revolutionary leader Pancho Villa expelled American nationals, Romney's family returned to the United States and eventually settled in Utah. Romney strictly adhered to church practices; he neither smoked nor drank, and he tithed freely. Although he attended Latter-day Saints University in Salt Lake City, the University of Utah, and George Washington University, he never earned a college degree. In the 1920s he served as a Mormon missionary in Great Britain. Friends detected a moralistic, evangelical zeal in his later undertakings. "Living the gospel of Jesus Christ," Romney intoned, "has as its prime purpose the perfection of all mankind through individual effort and divine aspiration. . . . Our responsibility for brotherhood is world-wide and our moral concern universal." In 1931 he married Lenore LaFount; they had four children.

Ambitious, Romney pursued political and business interests with predictable intensity. While a student at George Washington University, he joined the staff of Senator David I. Walsh (D.-Mass.). During 1930–1931 he worked for the Aluminum Corporation of America and from 1932 to 1938 served as Washington lobbyist for the Aluminum Wares Association. In 1939 Romney moved to Detroit to manage the local branch of the Automobile Manufacturers Association. The association's national board named him general manager three years later. In 1948 he joined Nash-Kelvinator Corporation. Six years later, when Nash-Kelvinator merged with Hudson Motor Car Company to form American Motors, Romney became the new corporation's first president.

Aggressive, innovative, and possessing a flair for salesmanship, Romney proved a successful corporate executive. He rescued AMC from near bankruptcy by promoting the company's compact, fuel-efficient Nash Rambler, introduced in 1950 to compete with the luxurious cars put out by General Motors, Ford, and Chrysler. "Who wants a gas guzzling dinosaur in his garage?" Romney asked. "Think of the gas bills!" The Rambler changed the automobile industry by forcing the "Big Three" into small-car production. In the process, the American Motors president became an industrial folk hero. "Romney," recalled one journalist, "was David taking on three Goliaths—and the public loved it."

Romney's service in the private sector combined with his religious fervor to spark a lifelong devotion to voluntarism. He concurred with President Woodrow Wilson's observation that "the most powerful force on earth is the spontaneous cooperation of a free people." In the 1950s Romney headed a citizens' committee to improve Detroit's schools. "I don't know of any substitute for what the volunteer can do," he later remarked.

Propelled by civic responsibility, Romney leaped into politics in the late 1950s. Concerned over the deadlock between Michigan's conservative Republicans and the union-controlled Democratic party, he helped to launch Citizens for Michigan, a campaign to convene delegates to rewrite the state's constitution. After selling the revised constitution to voters and stepping down as president of AMC in 1962, that same year Romney ran for the Michigan governorship as a Republican and won by a narrow margin. Voters reelected him in 1964 and 1966 by ever-widening margins. Columnist David S. Broder credited him with engineering "a revolution in Michigan politics that has no parallel, to my knowledge, in any major state." Before Romney assumed the governorship, Democrats had ruled the Wolverine State for fourteen years. Over the succeeding two decades, Romney and his Republican successor, William Milliken, set Michigan's agenda.

Romney's successes thrust him into the national limelight. During the 1960s he emerged as a leader of the moderate wing of the Republican party. Balancing market principles with concern for social problems, he secured tax reform and civil rights measures from the state legislature. To the dismay of conservative Republicans, Romney refused to support the presidential campaign of Senator Barry M. Goldwater of Arizona in 1964, when he denounced the Grand Old Party's platform as "extremist." Romney came to oppose U.S. intervention in Vietnam, later calling that war "the most tragic foreign policy mistake in the nation's history." In 1967 he announced his candidacy for the Republican presidential nomination.

Romney's campaign quickly fizzled. Having visited Vietnam in 1965, the Michigan governor remarked in 1967, during the campaign, that military officials had given him a "brainwashing" about the war's progress. Critics seized upon this comment, which made Romney appear witless and gullible. (Americans later learned that military brass had indeed attempted to mislead government officials as well as the public.) Faced with declining support, Romney withdrew from the presidential race in March 1968. Later that year President-elect Richard M. Nixon named him secretary of housing and urban development.

Independence characterized Romney's tenure as housing secretary. He continued to support voluntary action and sought new ways to produce low- and medium-income housing. Against the wishes of Nixon and the president's more conservative advisers, Romney defended federal programs to aid cities, pressed for racial integration of suburbs, and favored wage and price controls to arrest inflation. Not surprisingly, he never penetrated Nixon's inner circle, and his achievements proved limited. After campaigning for the president's reelection in 1972, Romney resigned as housing secretary.

Out of office, Romney remained active. He had founded the National Volunteer Center in 1970. In 1992 he formed Americans for America, a movement that urged voters to cast ballots on the "basis of citizenship" instead of partisanship or economic interest. Two years later he advised his son W. Mitt Romney during the latter's unsuccessful bid to unseat Senator Edward M. Kennedy (D.-Mass.). Romney loved to exercise, play golf, and participate in church activities. He died in Bloomfield Hills, Michigan.

Along with Wendell L. Willkie and H. Ross Perot, George Romney exemplified the civic-minded businessman turned politician. Commentators marked his passing by lauding his accomplishments, decency, honesty, and prescience, especially regarding the Vietnam War. Like others who entered politics from business, however, Romney was outspoken and often unwilling to compromise, qualities that limited his political success.

• Romney's papers are housed at the Bentley Historical Library, University of Michigan, Ann Arbor. The Bentley Library also possesses the papers of two Romney aides, Richard C. Van Dusen and Albert Applegate. Manuscript material on Romney's tenure as housing secretary is in the Van Dusen and Applegate files in RG 207 at the National Archives, Washington, D.C. Studies of Romney's career include Thomas Mahoney, *The Story of George Romney: Builder, Salesman, Crusader* (1960); T. George Harris, *Romney's Way: A Man and an Idea* (1967); and D. Duane Angel, *Romney: A Political Biography* (1967). Joseph Jeppson covers Romney's religious beliefs in "A Man's Religion and American Politics," *Dialogue: A Journal of Mormon Thought* 2, no. 3 (1967): 23–38. Andrew F. Wilson discusses Citizens for Michigan in "Citizenship vs. the Power Groups," *Chronicle: The Quarterly Magazine of the Historical Society of Michigan* 21, no. 3 (1985): 21–29. For Romney's governorship, consult "A Gathering of Governors," *Michigan History* 66, nos. 3–4 (1982): 16–23, 26–31. Romney's service in the Nixon administration is mentioned in John Ehrlichman, *Witness to Power: The Nixon Years* (1982), and H. R. Haldeman, *The Haldeman Diaries: Inside the Nixon White House* (1994). For assessments of Romney's place in history, see David S. Broder, "George Romney's Republican Party," *Washington Post*, 30 July 1995; and Godfrey Sperling, "The George Romney We Missed Out On," *Christian Science Monitor*, 22 Aug. 1995, p. 19. Obituaries are in the *New York Times*, the *Los Angeles Times*, and the *Washington Post*, all 27 July 1995.

DEAN J. KOTLOWSKI

RONNE, Finn (20 Dec. 1899–2 Jan. 1980), naval officer and Antarctic explorer, was born in Horten, Norway, the son of Martin Richard Ronne, an explorer, and Maren Gurine. Ronne studied mechanical and marine engineering at Horton Technical College and was active in several sports, including alpine and cross-country skiing.

In 1923 Ronne immigrated to the United States and applied for citizenship. He worked for Bethlehem Steel Company in New Jersey for one year and then moved to Pittsburgh, Pennsylvania, where he worked for the Westinghouse Corporation for fifteen years. His father had joined Richard E. Byrd's Antarctic Expedition (1928–1930). From Little America, Antarctica, Byrd sent a radio message inviting Ronne to join Byrd's next expedition.

The world depression delayed Byrd's return to Antarctica until 1933. Ronne's father had died in 1932, but Ronne himself joined the expedition as a ski expert and dog driver. Ronne helped to unload the supply ship and then took dog teams south on the Ross Ice Shelf to establish Advance Base, where Byrd would spend the winter alone. The following year he made sledging trips further south and east to the Rockefeller Mountains.

After his return from Antarctica, Ronne developed plans for his own expedition to the Antarctic (Palmer) Peninsula. Admiral Byrd also planned for another expedition to Little America, and other nations organized expeditions to establish territorial claims. In 1939 President Franklin D. Roosevelt created the United States Antarctic Service (USAS) to protect American claims in Antarctica. The proposed Byrd and Ronne expeditions were merged into one USAS expedition under the overall command of Byrd. Ronne became the second in command for the proposed base on the Antarctic Peninsula. He helped select the site and build East Base at Marguerite Bay on Stonington Island.

In November 1940 Ronne and his companion, Carl Eklund, began an epic 1,264-mile sledge journey south along the Antarctic Peninsula. Frequent fog and bad weather had prevented previous explorers from accurately mapping this area. During their journey the two men discovered that Alexander I Land actually was an island, and not mainland Antarctica. This meant that the 1819–1821 Russian expedition did not discover the antarctic mainland. On their return, the difficult ice surface caused the loss of most of their dogs, and bad weather prevented airplanes from reaching them. They returned to East Base on 28 January 1941, after exploring and surveying 500 miles of new coastline during their 84-day trip. The threat of war in early 1941 forced the hasty evacuation of East Base and return to the United States.

During World War II, Ronne served on active duty from May 1941 to February 1947 as an officer in the Bureau of Ships for the U.S. Navy. He also served on several military committees relating to polar affairs. In 1942 he met and married Edith "Jackie" Maslin; they had one child. As the war ended, Ronne formulated plans to continue his antarctic explorations from Stonington Island. From this base, he expected to map the largest remaining strip of unexplored coastline and conduct a variety of scientific studies. His naval experience enabled him to locate and obtain a ship and many other items from the mountains of surplus military equipment. Unlike most expeditions after the 1920s, Ronne put his expedition into the field without raising huge amounts of money or depending upon large cash subsidies from the government.

Ronne's expedition sailed from Beaumont, Texas, in February 1947, for his old base in Antarctica. His wife, Jackie, and Jennie Darlington, the recent bride of one of the pilots, accompanied the ship to South America. Jackie, who wrote the expedition's press dispatches, proved to be so valuable to the expedition that her husband decided to take the two women to Antarctica. One Norwegian woman had landed briefly on the frozen continent, but the two American women became the first to spend a winter there on an expedition.

When they reached Stonington Island, Ronne established a close working relationship with nearby British explorers. His expedition conducted the aerial mapping, while the British explorers established ground control survey points. As a result, they accurately mapped the southern half of the Antarctic Peninsula for the first time. Two major flights of 21 November and 12 December 1947 explored the large gap in the unknown coastline and identified a huge ice shelf, now known as the Ronne Ice Shelf, at the head of the Weddell Sea. The expedition explored about 250,000 square miles of new territory and accurately mapped for the first time another 450,000 square miles

of previously known areas. They took 14,000 aerial photographs over an area nearly the size of Mexico and conducted studies in geology, oceanography, meteorology, and other sciences. The expedition returned to the United States in 1948.

The Korean War and rivalry with Admiral Byrd for government support interrupted Ronne's plans for further exploration in the Weddell Sea during the following eight years. In 1957 he became the leader for the proposed Ellsworth Station in the Weddell Sea as part of the International Geophysical Year. His old friend, Eklund, was the scientific leader at the Wilkes Station on the opposite side of Antarctica.

The ice-clogged Weddell Sea nearly prevented the ship from reaching the Ronne Ice Shelf. After establishing the base, Ronne and his staff made several exploratory flights that discovered new mountains and land. After analyzing their flight data, Ronne realized that they had discovered a huge ice-covered island in the middle of the floating Ronne Ice Shelf. The staff scientists conducted detailed studies of glaciology, meteorology, and other fields during their year's stay. Ronne, who was both scientific and military leader of the base, experienced a number of personality clashes with staff members while they wintered at their isolated post.

After returning from Ellsworth Station in 1958, Ronne served again in the U.S. Navy until his retirement in 1962. Rather than stay home, he made trips to both the Arctic and Antarctic, and he helped to initiate the commercial Lindblad Cruises to the Antarctic. In 1971 he and his wife again visited Antarctica and the South Pole to celebrate the sixtieth anniversary of Roald Amundsen's great discovery. He died in Bethesda, Maryland.

Finn Ronne continued his family's exploring heritage. Between the day he saw his father sail with Amundsen to discover the South Pole and the day he retired from the navy, Antarctica had been completely explored. Ronne played a major role in this exploration, especially the mapping of the Antarctic Peninsula and the exploration of the great ice shelf that bears his name. During his nine trips to Antarctica, he personally experienced the transition from dogsled to the great snow vehicles and airplanes. Even after his death his family's connection with the frozen continent continued. In 1995 his widow, Jackie, and their daughter made a nostalgic visit to the old Ronne base on Stonington Island.

• Edith Ronne of Bethesda, Md., has his personal papers and provided oral information about his expeditions. Ronne's autobiography, *Antarctica, My Destiny* (1979), covers his early life and all his expeditions. Ronne wrote *Antarctic Conquest* (1949) about his 1947–1948 expedition and related articles in the *Geographical Review* 38, no. 3 (July 1948): 355–91; *Explorers Journal* 26, nos. 3 and 4 (Summer–Autumn 1948): 1–16, 45; *Scientific Monthly* 71, no. 5 (Nov. 1950): 287–93; and the *Annual Report of the Smithsonian Institution, 1949* (1950). He and Edith Ronne also wrote numerous articles for the North American Newspaper Alliance from 1946 to 1948. His experiences at Ellsworth Station during the IGY are related in *Antarctic Command* (1961). Admiral Richard E. Byrd described Ronne's 1933–1935 work in *Discovery* (1935). Ronne's 1940–1941 explorations are in his "Main Sledge Journey from East Base, Palmer Land, Antarctica," *Reports on Scientific Results of the USAS Expedition 1939–1941* (1945), and Richard B. Black's "Geographical Operations from East Base . . ." in the same publication. Kenneth J. Bertrand wrote an excellent appraisal of Ronne's 1947–1948 expedition in *Americans in Antarctica, 1775–1948* (1971).

TED HECKATHORN

ROOD, Ogden Nicholas (3 Feb. 1831–12 Nov. 1902), physicist, was born in Danbury, Connecticut, the son of Anson Rood, a minister, and Alida Gouverneur Ogden. Sometime during his childhood his family moved to Philadelphia, Pennsylvania, where he received his early formal education. In 1848 he matriculated at Yale College and studied there for two years before transferring to the College of New Jersey, known today as Princeton University, where he received his A.B. in 1852. With the exception of a brief teaching stint at the University of Virginia, he spent the next two years as a graduate student at Yale's Sheffield Scientific School, where he developed an interest in optics in general and light and color in particular that would be the object of much of his research throughout his academic career. From 1854 to 1858 he studied physics and chemistry in Germany at the Universities of Berlin and Munich and learned to paint with oils. In 1858 he married Mathilde Prunner, with whom he had five children, and returned to the United States to accept a professorship in chemistry at the fledgling University of Troy in New York State.

For the next five years Rood investigated subjects in optics such as spectrum analysis, light vibration in crystals, the relation between perception and color and between light and luster, and the visual effects produced by revolving disks. In the most important of these experiments he mounted a camera to a microscope in order to take photographs of *Pleurosigma angulatum*, boat-shaped diatoms whose sculpted silica-coated cell walls make them particularly attractive to microscopists. His work settled a dispute on the markings of these tiny creatures and made him a pioneer in the infant field of microscopic photography. He managed to photograph an electric spark by letting it pass through photographic film, which he then developed and enlarged. He also conducted experiments on the behavior of bullets fired from a rifle and investigated the circulation of the eye.

In 1863 Rood joined the faculty at Columbia College (now Columbia University) as a professor of physics, a position he held until his death. While at Columbia he dabbled in virtually every branch of physics and earned a reputation as an exceedingly able experimentalist. In 1867 he connected an induction coil, a device for producing high-voltage alternating current from low-voltage direct current, to a Leyden jar, a glass vessel lined inside and out with tin foil, and demonstrated that the duration of a spark, previously thought to be about one millionth of a second, was actually about

four ten-millionths of a second. Four years later, by refining the equipment and developing a ruled, lamp-black-coated plate of glass upon which to observe the spark, he determined its duration to be approximately forty-eight hundred-millionths of a second. Moreover, he showed that such an infinitesimal moment of light is sufficient not only to illuminate an object but also to detail its distinguishing features. Toward the end of his career he made improvements to the air pump to achieve higher vacuums than had been possible before, investigated the properties of X-rays, and developed a method for measuring high electrical resistance. However, he devoted most of his research to the physical laws governing light and optics, especially color.

Rood continued to paint after leaving Germany, and in 1866 he cofounded the American Water Color Society. In 1879 he published *Modern Chromatics, a Text-Book of Color*, a work that drew upon the results of many of his experiments with color as well as his experience as an oil painter. The book was intended to explain in the language of the layman how the physical laws that govern color might be put to artistic purposes and offers the insights of both a painter and a physicist into such important matters as the constants of color, complementary colors, color-mixing, and the duration of the impression of color on the retina of the eye. Perhaps its most startling revelation is Rood's declaration that, by changing ever so slightly the purity of all possible combinations of the colors of the spectrum, one may obtain 400 million visibly distinct variations. The book was seized upon by the artists of the day and eventually became the bible of the Impressionists, painters who emphasized color, tone, and texture over form by employing short brush strokes of bright and vivid colors. Ironically, Rood hated Impressionist art and was appalled by the suggestions that his book either endorsed it or contributed to its development in any way.

Rood's most significant contribution to science involved the photometric comparison of light of different colors. Before he investigated the subject, the brightnesses of two colors could not be compared because the wavelengths of the light reflected by surfaces of different color are unequal. In 1893, fifteen years after he first began considering the problem, he devised a simple method of solving it by using the flicker phenomenon, a property of the retina unknown to physicists at the time but of which he had apparently learned while investigating the circulation of the eye. When one's gaze shifts back and forth between two colors of different brightness the eye sees a flickering that disappears if the light illuminating the less bright color is intensified. He reasoned that the difference in intensity required to eliminate flicker should be equal to the difference in brightness between the two colors. This deduction, which was rigorously tested and proven in 1896 by F. P. Whitman, led to the development of flicker photometry, a principle used with great effectiveness by experimental psychologists and photometricians ever since.

Rood was elected to membership in the National Academy of Sciences in 1865. He was elected vice president of the American Association for the Advancement of Science in 1869 and received an honorary doctorate from Yale in 1901. He died in New York City.

Rood's work with color, the highlight of which was the publication of *Modern Chromatics*, inspired many of his artistic contemporaries to hail him as "one of the guiding lights of Impressionism." The ingenious experiments he conducted in other areas of physics induced many of his scientific contemporaries to hail him as the "father of American experimental physics."

• Rood's papers are in the Archives of the Columbia University Library. A good biography and a bibliography of his published work appear in Edward L. Nichols, "Ogden Nicholas Rood," National Academy of Sciences, *Biographical Memoirs* 6 (1909): 447–72. His obituary is in the *New York Times*, 13 Nov. 1902.

CHARLES W. CAREY, JR.

ROONEY, Arthur Joseph, Sr. (27 Jan. 1901–25 Aug. 1988), founder and owner of the Pittsburgh Steelers professional football team, called Art, was born in Coultersville, Pennsylvania, the son of Daniel and Kathleen Rooney. His father, who was of Welsh descent, operated a hotel-saloon on Pittsburgh's tough north side. Between 1917 and 1927 Rooney attended Duquesne Preparatory School, Duquesne University, Georgetown University, and Indiana (Pennsylvania) State Normal School, but he did not receive a college degree. A versatile and talented athlete, during the 1920s Rooney played amateur semiprofessional and professional sports in western Pennsylvania. In an era of lax enforcement of eligibility rules it was not uncommon for athletes such as Rooney to play for college teams and professional teams simultaneously. Rooney played football and baseball for Duquesne University in the early 1920s and football for Indiana of Pennsylvania in 1927, but the informality of college football and the large number of Rooneys (including Art's five brothers) who played in the area make it impossible to trace the details of his college career. He also played semiprofessional football for numerous Pittsburgh teams, including the James P. Rooney's, a team used to publicize his brother's political career.

While Rooney was an amateur boxer of note, his best sport was baseball. He played minor league baseball in 1921 for Flint in the Michigan-Ontario League and in 1925 for Wheeling, West Virginia, in the Mid-Atlantic League, where he was second in the league in hitting, with a .369 average. Rather than continue his career in the minor leagues, however, he offered his services to the highest bidder from among the better-paying small-town and coal league teams of Pennsylvania.

Rooney was also interested in horse racing. "For a period of years after 1927 I was one of the country's biggest and most successful horse players," he said in a 1985 interview. Later his interest in racing led Rooney to purchase racehorses, establish a farm, and by the 1950s become a racetrack owner. In 1931 Rooney married Kathleen McNulty. They had five children.

Rooney is best known as the founder and longtime owner of the Pittsburgh Steelers, which he began in 1933 when he purchased a franchise in the National Football League. He chose the 1933 season, at the height of the Great Depression, because in that year the Pennsylvania legislature repealed the state's blue laws prohibiting the playing of professional sports on Sunday. The new team, initially called the Pirates after the city's baseball team (they became the Steelers in 1941), struggled financially, along with the rest of the league, as a result of the depression and a general lack of fan interest. According to folklore, some of the team's financial problems were alleviated in 1936 when Rooney won the staggering sum of $300,000 during two days of betting on horses. The team's struggles on the field lasted longer, however; the Steelers did not win a division championship until 1972.

Rooney was involved in two of the more bizarre incidents in professional football history. He sold the Pittsburgh franchise to Alexis Thompson in 1940, but he missed the team so much that the following season he bought part ownership in the Philadelphia Eagles and then traded the Eagles to Thompson to get the Steelers back. Later, owing to a lack of available players during World War II, the Steelers and Eagles merged for the 1943 season, and similarly the Steelers and the Chicago Cardinals merged in 1944. The 1943 "Steagles" won five of ten games, but the 1944 "Carpits" were the joke of the league losing each of the season's ten games.

In the 1950s and 1960s, Rooney, who was fiercely loyal to his coaches and players, built a team that reflected many of the values of the strongly ethnic, heavily industrialized city of Pittsburgh. The Steelers worked hard, hit hard, and often drank too hard. Mediocrity and losing seasons were the rule. Fans admired Rooney's tenacity and loyalty but grew critical of the team's lack of success.

In 1969 Rooney turned over the day-to-day management of the team to his sons Daniel and Art, Jr., who promptly hired Chuck Noll as head coach. Noll led the team to its first division championship in 1972 and later to Super Bowl victories in 1974, 1975, 1978, and 1979.

Rooney was inducted into the Professional Football Hall of Fame in 1964 because he was a pioneer in the game and a supporter of many of the ideas that placed the good of the National Football League ahead of the wishes of key teams. Rooney never provided innovative ideas but was known in league circles as a soothing voice and a person who was willing to compromise. He supported ideas such as the college draft in 1936 and the share-the-wealth television package of the 1950s, and he allowed the Steelers, along with the Cleveland Browns and the Baltimore Colts, to be placed in the American Football Conference when the NFL and the American Football League merged in 1970.

Rooney was beloved in Pittsburgh because he had a politician's smile and handshake for everyone, he could tell a story, and he was genuinely kind and sincere. He was one of the last of the "sportsman" owners, who had the perseverance and love to stick, through good times and bad, with his team and the city where he spent his life.

• There is no biography of Rooney. His papers have not been collected, but the Professional Football Hall of Fame in Canton, Ohio, has an extensive clipping file and both audio tapes and film interviews with Rooney. Roy Blount, Jr., *About Three Bricks Shy of a Load* (1974), provides an interesting character sketch. Joe Tucker, *Steelers Victory After Forty* (1973), and Beau Riffenbargh, *The Official NFL Encyclopedia* (1986), place Rooney in the context of the Pittsburgh Steelers and the development of professional football. An obituary is in the *New York Times*, 26 Aug. 1988.

C. ROBERT BARNETT

ROONEY, Pat (4 July 1880–9 Sept. 1962), vaudeville, musical theater, and nightclub performer, was born Patrick James Rooney, Jr., in New York City, the son of Patrick James Rooney, Sr., and Josie Granger, entertainers. His mother had danced in the chorus of *The Black Crook*, a precursor of the American musical. His father performed as an "Irish single" in the era of variety entertainment (featuring, in Douglas Gilbert's words, "early Irish kick-in-the-bowels comedy" [Gilbert, p. 70]), and he helped make the slow transition to more respectable vaudeville entertainment. Although he appeared in the stereotypical Irish outfit of plug hat, cutaway coat, plaid checkered pants, and long side whiskers called "Galway sluggers," his humor and characterizations of the Irish were humane and genial. He died in 1892, around the same time that his son Pat and a daughter, Mattie, were appearing at Tony Pastor's Theatre in New York City in an act called "Two Chips off the Old Block."

Rooney had already danced professionally by the age of ten. Taking after his father, his specialty was dancing the waltz clog, a forerunner of tap dancing. Little is known of this early stage of his career, but he seems to have defined a stage personality early on. Most often described as "diminutive" (at five feet, three inches tall and approximately 125 pounds), the agile and light-footed Rooney played street-smart and likable urban types. These types were less pungent versions of the Irish characters his father's generation had played, thus appealing to audiences in areas where the Irish or their stereotypes were unknown. By the age of twenty he had appeared with success in a series of male-female duos, but it was not until 1904 that he met his performing and life's partner, Marion Bent, in a production of *Mother Goose*. They were married later the same year.

Vaudeville by 1905 had become America's greatest form of mass entertainment. Millions of people in hundreds of theaters each week attended shows divided into a series of unrelated acts. The acts varied greatly in quality, tone, and content, but vaudeville's main drawing cards were the variety of acts and the shows'

reputation as "respectable, family entertainment." In this context the act of "Rooney and Bent" became enormously successful. They appeared during the years in a series of comic song and dance sketches such as "Half and Half" (a winsome, fast-talking jockey meets a young woman at the race track) and "At the Newsstand" (a winsome, fast-talking newsstand clerk meets a young woman from out of town). In the sketches, Rooney played the comic and Bent played the straight. The sketches involved wordplay gags and comically contrived excuses to allow both performers to sing and dance, although Rooney was clearly the star in these departments. It was his dancing that truly stood out: W. C. Fields declared, "If you didn't hear the taps you would think he was floating over the stage."

The couple's career rose and peaked along with vaudeville's popularity. Rooney and Bent embodied the happily married performing couple, which fit perfectly with vaudeville's family appeal. This impression was only strengthened with the birth in 1909 of a son, Pat Rooney III (sometimes referred to erroneously as "Pat Rooney, Jr."), who was frequently carried onstage at the end of the act. By 1910 Rooney and Bent were headliners, the stars of the bills on which they appeared, a status they held for more than twenty years until vaudeville died.

Rooney was a pioneer in the late teens in creating "unit shows" with titles such as *Rings of Smoke* and *Shamrock*. Unit shows were minirevues of an hour or more that included large casts and elaborate scenery and costumes and filled fully half of a vaudeville bill. Rooney also explored other forms of entertainment. He signed short-term movie contracts with Lubin in 1915 and with Universal in 1916, but little of note came of these. In the 1920s he had successes both on Broadway and on the road in such musical comedies as *Love Birds* and *The Daughter of Rosie O'Grady*. He also had a sideline as a songwriter, composing such numbers as "I Got a Gal for Every Day in the Week" and "You Be My Ootsie, I'll Be Your Tootsie." In the 1930s, with the death of vaudeville and Bent's retirement due to arthritis, Rooney appeared steadily in nightclubs and on radio. He also coproduced and costarred in a revue with Herman Timberg.

Rooney's personal life took some sad and strange turns during this period. His marriage, troubled for some years, ended in separation in 1939, and on 28 July 1940 Bent died. In 1942 Pat Rooney III's marriage of seven years to Helen Rulon (stage name Janet Reed) ended in divorce, and on 21 July of that year the elder Rooney married her. She died seven months later, on 6 February 1943. Rooney married for a third time in 1943 to Carmen Schaffer who, like Bent and Rulon, had been a stage performer.

Rooney's last great moment in American stage history came in 1950. At the age of seventy he originated the role of Arvide Abernathy (appropriately, an Irish father figure) in the musical *Guys and Dolls*, singing the lilting ballad "More I Cannot Wish You." Rooney never truly retired, commenting once that "As long as

I can move my feet, I'm gonna keep working. It keeps you alive." Through the 1950s he appeared occasionally on television's "Ed Sullivan Show" and "Name That Tune," at benefits, and with his son in New York's Palace Theatre in 1956. He died in New York City.

Rooney's career parallels the rise and fall of vaudeville, the importance in vaudeville of individual stage personality, the shifting emphases of ethnicity on the American stage, and the durability of performers who came up through vaudeville's ranks.

• There is a slightly longer biography of Rooney and his family in Anthony Slide, *The Encyclopedia of Vaudeville* (1994). Much of the information on the careers of Rooney and his father is contained in contemporary periodicals (especially the *New York Dramatic Mirror* and *Variety*) and in collections in the New York Public Library for the Performing Arts at Lincoln Center, the Theatre Collection of the Ransom Humanities Research Center at the University of Texas at Austin, and the Theatre Collection of the Free Library in Philadelphia. Shirley Staples, *Male-Female Comedy Teams in American Vaudeville, 1865–1932* (1984), gives a number of helpful references in the notes. Douglas Gilbert, *American Vaudeville: Its Life and Times* (1940), although unfootnoted, contains useful information on Pat Rooney, Sr. For information about the Rooney-Bent marriage, see John B. Kennedy, "We've Forgotten How to Fight," *Colliers*, 11 May 1929, pp. 39–40, 42. Useful obituaries are in the *New York Times*, 11 Sept. 1962, and *Variety*, 12 Sept. 1962.

RICHARD CANEDO

ROOSEVELT, Alice Hathaway Lee (29 July 1861–14 Feb. 1884), first wife of Theodore Roosevelt, was born in Boston, Massachusetts, the daughter of George Cabot Lee, a banker, and Caroline Haskel. One of Boston's first families, the Lees had fled the encroachment of immigrants to the inner city for the fashionable suburb of Chestnut Hill while keeping their Beacon Street home for winter use. At seventeen, when she met her future husband, Alice was described as tall, athletic, a champion tennis player, graceful, with "golden curls," "dove-gray eyes," a piquant, slightly turned-up nose, and such a cheerful disposition that she was nicknamed "Sunshine."

Although Theodore Roosevelt wrote in his diary after he first met Alice Lee that he had found her a "very sweet, pretty girl," later he was to confess that, on first encountering her in October 1878, he "loved her as soon as I saw her sweet fair young face." She was not easily won, refusing his first proposal in June 1879. But he was undeterred, courted her confidently, relentlessly, saying once to a mutual friend, "You see that girl there?" pointing to Alice. "I am going to marry her. She won't have me, but I am going to have her." And in January 1880 he was able to record, "At last everything is settled. . . . I am so happy that I dare not trust my own happiness."

In February 1880 their engagement was announced, celebrated by a party at the Hasty Pudding Club, where Theodore was a member. They were married on his twenty-second birthday, 27 October, in the Unitarian Church, Brookline. The honeymoon was spent at "Tranquility," the Roosevelt summer home on Long Island. That winter they occupied an apartment on West Fifty-seventh Street in New York. Alice fit easily into the life of her new family and was much beloved and indulged, joining their Presbyterian church and attending parties in her honor, dinners, receptions, operas, and balls. Meanwhile, Theodore studied law at Columbia University and wrote his *Naval History of the War of 1812*. In his diary, he fervently said of his wife, "She behaved like a queen on every occasion." On 12 May 1882 they sailed for Europe, explored London and Paris, then spent five days in a Venetian palace and four on Lake Como. During their tour of the Alps, Theodore insisted on climbing the Matterhorn, while in their hotel in Zermatt Alice anticipated widowhood.

After returning to the United States fired with reforming zeal, Theodore caused Alice great dismay by becoming involved in what her Puritan relatives dubbed "dirty politics" and winning a seat in the New York assembly. Reluctantly she moved with him to Albany, missing the excitement of the social season in New York. Though she tried hard to understand his concerns, even sitting in the gallery at legislative sessions, she hated the noise and confusion.

Alice was secretly averse to Theodore's buying a large tract of land on Long Island and building a big house there modeled exactly on her home in Chestnut Hill, with all its gables and turrets, insisting that it be named "Leeholm" (a name later changed to "Sagamore Hill"). To Alice the house seemed lonely and far from city life. After she became pregnant in May 1883, she moved into his family's home on West Fifty-seventh Street, spending only weekends in the new brownstone Theodore had bought on West Forty-fifth Street. Theodore's assurances of devotion and adoring relatives did not allay her loneliness and feelings of neglect.

On 12 February 1884 Theodore went to Albany, leaving Alice in a stable condition. His sister Bamie seemed equal to any emergency, and the baby was not due until 14 February. It was a fateful day. Theodore's mother fell sick with typhoid, and Alice's labor pains started. Alice refused to have her husband wired because he had an important bill coming up on 13 February. That day he received a telegram. He had a daughter. Alice was doing well. Soon he received another message, indicating that Alice was in danger. He rushed to New York, groped his way through the densest fog the city had seen in years, and was met at the door by his brother Elliott. "There is a curse on this house. Alice is dying, and Mother is dying, too."

Both women died on the same day, 14 February. Theodore scarcely looked at his daughter, another Alice, who was to have her mother's gaiety and charm, but not her inhibitions, and would achieve fame as the unpredictable, redoubtable Alice Roosevelt Longworth. Theodore's diary that day was marked by a black cross and the words, "The light has gone out of my life."

• See Theodore Roosevelt's *Autobiography*, vol. 20 of *The Works of Theodore Roosevelt* (1926). See also Bradley Gilman, *Roosevelt: The Happy Warrior* (1921); *The Letters of Theodore Roosevelt*, ed. Elton E. Morison (1951); Edmund Morris, *The Rise of Theodore Roosevelt* (1979); Henry F. Pringle, *Theodore Roosevelt* (1936; repr. 1956, 1984); Carleton Putnam, *Theodore Roosevelt*, vol. 1 (1958); Michael Teague, *Mrs. L: Conversations with Alice Roosevelt Longworth* (1979); and Dorothy Clarke Wilson, *Alice and Edith: The Two Wives of Teddy Roosevelt* (1989).

DOROTHY CLARKE WILSON

ROOSEVELT, Archibald Bulloch (9 Apr. 1894–13 Oct. 1979), businessman and military officer, was born in Washington, D.C., the son of Theodore Roosevelt, then a U.S. civil service commissioner, and Edith Kermit Carow. In 1901 Roosevelt's father succeeded the assassinated William McKinley as U.S. president. A rambunctious youth, Archie made headlines by sliding down a White House banister into one diplomatic reception and by arriving at another on stilts.

In 1913 Roosevelt graduated from Andover Academy and entered Harvard University. He attended summer military training camp for civilians at Plattsburg, New York, in 1915 and 1916, and offended Harvard's pacifist president A. Lawrence Lowell by trying to form a preparedness drill team on campus. He received his B.A. from Harvard in 1917, shortly after the United States entered World War One. With help from his father, Roosevelt became one of the first American officers to be commissioned to France in 1917. Between graduation and shipping out, he married socialite Grace Lockwood in Boston; they had four children. Serving with the First Division, he rose to the rank of captain, becoming reportedly the youngest U.S. company commander in the war. Shortly after his brother Quentin was killed in aerial combat in July 1918, Roosevelt was badly wounded, almost losing his leg. He received the Croix de Guerre from Marshal Foch while still on the operating table and a bronze star somewhat later. Invalided home, he was with his father when the former president died in 1919. Archie cabled his two surviving brothers, Theodore, Jr., and Kermit, who were both still abroad, "The Old Lion is dead." His son Archibald, Jr., used to say that his father's "intellectual clock stopped" when Theodore, Sr., died.

After the war, Roosevelt took a job as vice president of the Sinclair Oil Company. Without Roosevelt's knowledge, Harry Sinclair and others had intrigued with Secretary of the Interior Albert Fall to drill for oil at the Elk Hills and Teapot Dome Naval Oil Reserves. Roosevelt's brother Theodore had been assistant secretary of the navy at the time; when the scandal broke, people suspected that there was some collusion between the brothers in the project. Archibald did his best to clear the family name by testifying before Congress in 1924, but to little avail. His revelations forced the resignation of Fall and the secretary of the navy, but helped lose Ted's race for governor of New York. After a brief spell of unemployment, Archie became a municipal bond salesman in a firm managed by his cousin W. Emlin Roosevelt.

Roosevelt and his wife became active social critics. Grace was a prominent opponent of Prohibition. Shortly after the Stock Market Crash in 1929, Archibald helped found the National Economy League, which called on President Herbert Hoover to cut spending in the crisis. In 1932 he denounced the proposal to pay his fellow World War I veterans their bonuses early. Roosevelt was an especially conspicuous critic of his cousin President Franklin Delano Roosevelt and the New Deal. The animosity between the "in-season" (Hyde Park) Democratic Roosevelts and the "out-of-season" (Oyster Bay) Republican wing was both personal and political. The rift was not healed for decades. He vocally opposed American entry into World War II before Pearl Harbor. After Japan attacked the United States, Roosevelt volunteered for service and, with the intervention of the president and Army Chief of Staff General George C. Marshall, was commissioned a lieutenant colonel—reportedly the oldest U.S. battalion commander in the war. He saw action in the South Pacific with the Forty-first Division, caught pneumonia and malaria, and was wounded grievously again—in the same leg. He was awarded a silver star for heroism. In 1945 the army forcibly retired him, the only U.S. soldier released on 100 percent disability in both world wars. He even met with President Roosevelt to appeal his case. FDR turned the matter over to General Marshall, who upheld the doctors. Both Theodore, Jr., and Kermit died in World War II, and Archie had apparently wished to join them. The meeting between cousins, however, did begin the process of rapprochement among the Roosevelt clan.

After the war, Roosevelt returned to New York to establish his own municipal bond firm, Roosevelt and Cross. He also became more outspokenly reactionary. In 1948 he claimed that President Harry Truman "encourages and protects the Communists and fellow travelers high in our government." He formed the Alliance Inc., to supply information on communist subversion to congressional committees investigating internal security and testified repeatedly before the House Committee on Un-American Activities. He accused State Department official Owen Lattimore of being "the number one Soviet agent in the U.S." He opposed, unsuccessfully, liberalization of the McCarran-Walter Immigration Act, which prevented alleged communists and assorted radicals from entering the country. He also tried, unsuccessfully, to keep nuclear physicist Robert J. Oppenheimer, whose patriotism he challenged, from teaching at his alma mater, Harvard. He was a leader of the National Committee to Preserve the Connally Resolution, which opposed making the United States subject to World Court decisions. In 1968 he edited a volume of his father's works, *Theodore Roosevelt on Race, Riots, Reds, Crime*, in order to prove that his father was far more reactionary than contemporary scholars suggested. Although some quotations were taken out of context (e.g., the "criminals" denounced in one passage were plutocrats, not footpads), others clearly were not, such as the elder Roosevelt's giddy demand that rioters be shot on sight.

Publicly acknowledging his family's problem with alcohol while denying his own, Roosevelt joined Alcoholics Anonymous and served as a treasurer of the organization from 1953 to 1966. He was also an active sportsman and conservationist. In 1957 he sued the state of New York unsuccessfully to stop it from spraying the pesticide DDT. In 1963 he was elected honorary president for life of the Boone and Crocket Club, which his father had founded. He retired from business in 1969 and moved to Hobe Sound, Florida, where he went into seclusion in 1971 after his wife died in an automobile accident in which he was driving. He died in Stuart, Florida.

• Roosevelt's papers are in the Houghton Library at Harvard University. Sources on his life and career include Peter Collier, with David Horowitz, *The Roosevelts: An American Saga* (1994); David M. Esposito, "Refulgent Thunderer: Archibald Bulloch Roosevelt, 1894–1979," in *Theodore Roosevelt: Many Sided American*, ed. Douglas Brinkley (1992); Archie Roosevelt, Jr., *For Lust of Knowing* (1988); and Grace Roosevelt, *We Owed It to the Children* (1935). An obituary is in the *New York Times*, 15 Oct. 1979.

DAVID M. ESPOSITO

ROOSEVELT, Edith Kermit Carow (6 Aug. 1861–10 Sept. 1948), second wife of Theodore Roosevelt, was born in Norwich, Connecticut, the daughter of Charles Carow, a wealthy shipping magnate, and Gertrude Elizabeth Tyler. The Carow (originally Quereau) family were French Huguenots who had come to America to escape persecution after the revocation of the Edict of Nantes in 1685. In Edith's childhood the Carow home was on Livingston Place in New York City, close to the Union Square mansion of Theodore Roosevelt's grandfather.

Theodore's sister Corrine was Edith's age and her best friend. Edith also had much in common with Theodore, who was two years older. They both had inquiring minds, a love of books, and a thirst for adventure. An old picture shows "Edie" reading to "Teedie" on the steps of the Roosevelt brownstone. Edith was reportedly somewhat shy and remote. She attended kindergarten with the Roosevelt children and received her formal education at Miss Comstock's private school.

Friends tacitly assumed that Edith and Theodore would marry, though there is no record of a proposal. Then during his junior year at Harvard Theodore met Alice Hathaway Lee and fell in love with her. Undoubtedly shocked and hurt, Edith nevertheless gave no sign of emotion. She attended the wedding and, a little more than three years later, the double funeral of Alice and Theodore Roosevelt's mother.

Still grieving for his wife, Theodore purposely avoided Edith, but one day they accidentally met, and the bonds of intellectual rapport were renewed. Love developed. After she moved with her family to London, he proposed, and they were married by the canon of York in December 1886. They honeymooned in France and Italy. "The most absolutely ideal time imaginable," Theodore wrote his sister Anna.

Back in the United States, they settled into Theodore's new house at Oyster Bay, New York, renamed "Sagamore Hill," since the original "Leeholm" had been in honor of Alice. At Edith's insistence Alice and Theodore's daughter, also called Alice, joined their family. Edith gave birth to two children, one in 1887 and one in 1889. In spite of her yearning for privacy, Edith became a proficient hostess. Though she would have preferred to remain at Sagamore Hill immersing herself in books, when Theodore became civil service commissioner she went with him willingly to Washington, D.C., where she developed greater social skills and won admiration from such scholars as Henry Adams.

By 1895, when Theodore became police commissioner for New York, there were two more children. Edith understood children, indulged their mischief, and imbued them with her love of nature and knowledge of poetry. One son declared, "When Mother was a little girl, she must have been a boy!" One last child was born to the couple. In 1897 they were again in Washington, where Theodore served as secretary of the navy. Then, though the four months of his Cuban adventure were a nightmare of fear and loneliness for Edith, she coped with domestic problems at Sagamore Hill and wrote him cheerful letters about the children and their antics.

As wife of the governor of New York, Edith emerged increasingly out of her shell of shyness and reserve to become both Theodore's social and political helpmate. She was with him at the Republican convention in 1900 when a roaring crowd insisted on nominating him for vice president. On 7 September 1901 news came of William McKinley's assassination, and Theodore Roosevelt became president of the United States.

The White House was now invaded by a family unlike any that that august residence had known: water-pistol fights in the East Room, spitballs affixed to the portrait of Andrew Jackson, an alligator in the bathtub. Yet never had a family in the mansion been so much beloved by officials and staff. Edith Roosevelt was the steady and gentle but subtly controlling manager of the brood, including Theodore, whom she sometimes called her sixth child. She was a self-effacing but competent first lady, guiding renovations, restoring the mansion to its early colonial style, entertaining often but not lavishly, hiring the first social secretary to serve a first lady. One of Roosevelt's aides once said of her, "She never made a mistake."

After his tenure as president, Theodore Roosevelt hunted lions in Africa and explored the jungles of South America. Edith adjusted quietly at Sagamore Hill to desperate loneliness, living for his letters and the visits of her children, seeing three of her sons give their lives in service to their country. But after her husband's death in 1919 she traveled extensively, wrote books, joined the first women voters at the polls, and became active in politics, even campaigning for Herbert Hoover. She died at Sagamore Hill.

Edith Roosevelt believed in order, duty, and discipline. She practiced them all, even planning the simple details of her last journey as carefully as those for previous destinations: "Simplest coffin possible . . . no flowers but a bunch of pink and blue blossoms from my children . . . processional hymn, 'The Son of God,' not slow tempo."

• The papers of Theodore Roosevelt, Kermit Roosevelt, and Theodore Roosevelt, Jr., are in the Library of Congress. See also the Theodore Roosevelt Collection, Widener and Houghton Libraries, Harvard University; the Cecil Spring-Rice Papers, Churchill College, Cambridge, England; the archives at the Sagamore Hill National Historic Site, Oyster Bay, N.Y., and the Theodore Roosevelt Birthplace National Historic Site, New York City; the National Archives, Washington, D.C., which include Edith Roosevelt's "White House Record of Social Functions," 1901–1909; and the archives at the White House Curator's Office, Washington, D.C. Edith Roosevelt's books include *Cleared for Strange Ports* (1927) and *American Backlogs* (1928). For personal details of Edith Roosevelt's life see Hermann Hagedorn, *The Roosevelt Family of Sagamore Hill* (1918); Earle Looker, *The White House Gang* (1929); Sylvia Jukes Morris, *Edith Kermit Roosevelt: Portrait of a First Lady* (1980); Lu Ann Paletta, *First Ladies* (1990); Mary Randolph, *Presidents and First Ladies* (1936); Theodore Roosevelt, Jr., *All in the Family*; and Dorothy Clarke Wilson, *Alice and Edith: The Two Wives of Teddy Roosevelt* (1989). Periodical sources include Mabel Potter Daggett, "Mrs. Roosevelt, the Woman in the Background," *Delineator*, Mar. 1909; A. Maurice Low, "A Day at the White House," *Harper's Weekly*, 2 Jan. 1904; Helena McCarthy, "Why Mrs. Roosevelt Has Not Broken Down," *Ladies' Home Journal*, Oct. 1908; Jacob A. Riis, "Mrs. Roosevelt and Her Children," *Ladies' Home Journal*, Aug. 1902; and Charles A. Selden, "Six White House Wives and Widows," *Ladies' Home Journal*, June 1927.

DOROTHY CLARKE WILSON

ROOSEVELT, Eleanor (11 Oct. 1884–7 Nov. 1962), first lady of the United States, social reformer, politician, diplomat, was born Anna Eleanor Roosevelt in New York City, the daughter of Elliott Roosevelt and Anna Hall. Her childhood was materially comfortable—both sides of her family were wealthy and prominent in New York society—but it was also emotionally arid. Her mother, beautiful but distant and so disappointed in the looks of her daughter that she called her "granny," died when Eleanor was eight. Her youngest brother died the following year. She clung to her father, the younger brother of Theodore Roosevelt, but he was an alcoholic so erratic that he was often forbidden to see her. He died when she was ten, leaving her and her surviving brother, Hall, in the care of maternal relatives whose interest in them was more dutiful than affectionate. From these misfortunes Eleanor Roosevelt drew three grim lessons: she was unattractive; no one's love for her was likely to last; and those whom she counted most could be counted on to let her down. From her earliest years she found solace in helping others. "As with all children," she wrote in

This Is My Story, "the feeling that I was useful was perhaps the greatest joy I experienced." It would remain her greatest source of joy all her life.

At age fifteen, she was sent away to the Allenswood School outside London. Its founder, Marie Souvestre, the daughter of the French radical philosopher Emil Souvestre, who saw in the tall, slender, diffident young American "the most amiable girl I have ever met" (Cook, p. 110), opened up to her the worlds of art and ideas and service to the less fortunate and encouraged her to think for herself. "Whatever I have become," Eleanor Roosevelt wrote in the first volume of her autobiography, "had its seeds in those three years of contact with a liberal mind and strong personality."

Eleanor returned to America at age eighteen because her relatives insisted she make her formal debut in New York society, but Souvestre's lessons were not forgotten. Eleanor joined the National Consumer's League, which championed health and safety standards for workers, and she began teaching calisthenics and "fancy dancing" to the children of immigrants at the Rivington Street Settlement House on Manhattan's Lower East Side.

In November 1902 her cousin Franklin Delano Roosevelt, whom she had known since childhood, began to court her. He was attracted to her intelligence and sympathy—and perhaps by her closeness to the man he admired most, Theodore Roosevelt. She in turn was drawn to his cheerful buoyancy. He was "perfectly secure . . . while I was perfectly insecure," she remembered. But she also confessed to a cousin her worry that Franklin was too "attractive" to remain in love with her for long.

They were married in 1905 and would have a daughter and four sons. Franklin's formidable widowed mother, Sara Delano Roosevelt, who controlled the family purse strings and often sought to control her son as well, dominated the early years of their marriage. She forbade her daughter-in-law to do settlement work for fear of bringing illnesses home, built and furnished the Roosevelt's New York home, and supervised the servants and the raising of her grandchildren. Eleanor, starved for maternal affection and unsure of her own skills as wife and mother, was grateful to her mother-in-law at first, but as the years went by grew increasingly resentful.

Then in 1911 Franklin won a seat in the New York State Senate as a Democrat and the Roosevelts moved to Albany, where Eleanor reveled in getting out from under her mother-in-law's rule and got her first taste of political combat as her home became headquarters for the doomed insurgency her husband helped lead against Tammany Hall. Two years later she accompanied Franklin to Washington where he joined the Woodrow Wilson administration as assistant secretary of the navy. She disliked Washington life at first and found especially wearying the formal Washington dinners that delighted her gregarious husband. When the United States entered into the First World War in 1917 she was grateful to be given a socially acceptable rationale for resuming volunteer work outside her home for the first time in twelve years. She threw herself into Navy Relief, regularly visited the wounded, and helped operate a Red Cross canteen. "I became . . . more determined to try for certain ultimate objectives," she recalled in *This Is My Story*. "I had gained a certain assurance as to my ability to run things, and the knowledge that there is joy in accomplishing good."

Then, she confided to a friend many years later, "the bottom dropped out of my particular world, and I faced myself, my surroundings, my world, honestly for the first time" (Lash, *Love Eleanor*, p. 66). In September 1918 she discovered that her husband was in love with a younger woman, her own social secretary, Lucy Mercer. According to family tradition, she offered FDR a divorce. He rejected it, fearing both that his political career would be ruined by a public scandal and that his mother would cut him off without a penny if he left his wife and children. He pledged never to see Lucy Mercer again. Her husband's betrayal was deeply wounding to Eleanor; it seemed to confirm all her girlhood fears about her own attractiveness. Marital intimacy ended: thereafter there was "no fundamental love to draw on" between her and her husband, she confided to a friend, "just respect & affection" (Scharf, p. 139).

But this personal crisis also liberated her. From 1918 onward, she and FDR would lead increasingly separate lives and she was free to pursue the host of social and political causes that soon consumed her. Her husband's paralysis, from polio, in the summer of 1921 and his subsequent seven-year withdrawal from active politics was the public explanation for her activism. She was acting as her invalid husband's "legs and eyes," she liked to say, just keeping his name before the public until he could return to public life. But in fact she was already active in her own right before he fell ill.

She had been unsure about woman suffrage before 1920, but now that women were armed with the vote she believed that "women must learn to play the game as men do" (Cook, p. 366). Soon her gift for organizing and her astonishing energy and determination to do good, combined with her famous name, had made her an influential figure in both social reform and partisan politics. She helped lead four important organizations—the League of Women Voters, the Women's Trade Union League, the Women's City Club, and the Women's Division of the New York State Democratic Committee. "Against the men bosses," she wrote, "there must be women bosses who can talk as equals, with the backing of a coherent organization of women voters behind them" (Cook, p. 368). Eleanor Roosevelt became such a boss and used her influence on behalf of causes on which many of her male counterparts preferred to waffle—the five-day week, an end to child labor, the League of Nations—but not the Equal Rights Amendment, which she saw as undercutting the hard-won rights of women workers to special protection.

She also wove around her a network of woman activists, among them Esther Lape, Elizabeth Reade, Mary Dewson, Mary Dreir, Maud Swartz, and Rose Scheiderman. With former suffragists Nancy Cook and Marion Dickerman, she bought the Todhunter School for Girls in New York City, at which she taught government and literature. She also shared with them "Val-Kill," the retreat FDR built for her near the Roosevelt estate at Hyde Park, New York, in 1926. It was the first home she had ever had and would remain her real home for the rest of her life. Cook and Dickerman were the first in a series of women and men with whom she would forge intense friendships and from whom she drew emotional sustenance when melancholy threatened to overwhelm her. They would eventually include Earl Miller, a New York State trooper; the journalist Lorena Hickock; her future biographer Joseph P. Lash; and, during her last years, a New York physician, David Gurewitsch.

By the time Al Smith ran for the presidency in 1928, she was the head of the Women's Division of the Democratic National Committee and not enthusiastic about her husband's bid for the New York governorship: she feared her role as governor's wife would curtail her hard-won independence. The prospect of becoming first lady in 1933 filled her with such dread that she spoke privately of divorcing FDR rather than accept its burdens and limitations, and she was bitterly disappointed when he rebuffed her offer to help handle his White House mail.

"I shall have to work out my own salvation" (Lash, *Eleanor and Franklin*, p. 355), she told a friend. In doing so, she set the standard against which president's wives have been measured ever since. Believing that "government has a responsibility to defend the weak" (Scharf, p. 93), she worked tirelessly to ensure that no group of Americans in need failed to benefit from New Deal programs. She saw to it that women joined the government in unprecedented numbers and that they were included in the programs of the Works Progress Administration (WPA). She was also instrumental in creating the National Youth Administration (NYA) to aid young people and personally helped organize a planned community for jobless West Virginia miners called Arthurdale. She was also the New Deal's most consistent champion of civil rights for blacks, working closely with Walter White of the National Association for the Advancement of Colored People to enact antilynching legislation that her husband hesitated to back, and lobbying for integration within the armed forces and defense industries. In 1939 she resigned her membership in the Daughters of the American Revolution when that body refused to allow the African-American soprano Marian Anderson to sing in Constitution Hall in Washington.

She acted as FDR's ally but also as his conscience and sometimes as his goad, making sure that he heard the views of people otherwise without access to him. "No one," wrote presidential advisor Rexford Tugwell, "who ever saw Eleanor Roosevelt sit down facing her husband, and, holding his eye firmly, say to him,

'Franklin, I think you should . . . ' or, 'Franklin, surely you will not . . . ' will ever forget the experience."

Between 1933 and 1945 she would dictate 2,500 newspaper columns, write 299 magazine articles, publish six books, make more than seventy speeches a year, and travel so many miles that no one ever tried to count them. Her activities won warm support—polls showed that she was often more popular than her husband—but they also inspired fierce opposition. She was denounced as naive, undignified, neglectful of her family, even subversive. When her husband ran for an unprecedented third term in 1940, his opponents wore buttons reading "We Don't Want Eleanor Either."

Her dramatic appearance at the turbulent Democratic National Convention that year won her friend Henry A. Wallace renomination as vice president. But after the United States entered World War II and her husband's attention turned from economic reform to military victory, her influence began to wane. Her brief tenure as assistant director of the Office of Civil Defense ended in embarrassed failure; her efforts to keep alive such New Deal programs as the NYA and WPA were thwarted. But her energies never flagged: she undertook grueling wartime visits to Britain, the Southwest Pacific, and the Caribbean, and even after FDR's health began to decline continued doggedly to exhort him to do more for the disadvantaged.

The shock of FDR's death in April 1945 was intensified for her when she discovered that his old friend Lucy Mercer (now a widow, Lucy Mercer Rutherfurd) had been with him when he died. "He might have been happier with a wife who had been completely uncritical," she would write in *This I Remember*. "That I was never able to be and he had to find it in other people. Nonetheless, I think that I sometimes acted as a spur, even though the spurring was not always wanted . . . I was one of those who served his purposes."

Convinced that "when you cease to make a contribution, you die" (Lash, *Eleanor Roosevelt: The Years Alone*, p. 102), she remained at the center of American and global politics for nearly two more decades. In 1946 President Harry S. Truman appointed her as a delegate to the United Nations, the institution that she believed to be her late husband's most significant legacy to the world. She served as chair of the United Nations Human Rights Commission and with her unique blend of grandmotherly tact and political realism helped hammer out the United Nations Declaration of Human Rights enacted by the General Assembly in 1948. She was now routinely hailed as "the First Lady of the World."

Although she was disappointed by what she saw as Truman's unwillingness to push for the liberal policies of her late husband and initially chagrined by the rapid collapse of the wartime alliance with the Soviet Union, she refused to join her old friend Henry A. Wallace's Progressive party in 1948: Wallace was "too idealistic" to be president, she wrote, and she helped found Americans for Democratic Action as a home for those Democrats like herself who favored liberal social and economic domestic programs but distrusted the Soviet Union.

She was an enthusiastic supporter of Democratic presidential candidate Adlai E. Stevenson, for whom she campaigned in 1952 and 1956, and an outspoken foe of the reckless anti-Communism of Senator Joseph McCarthy, whom she denounced as "the greatest menace to freedom we have in this country" (Black, p. 168). She resigned from the United Nations after President Dwight Eisenhower took office in 1953, although she maintained close ties to the American Association for the United Nations for the rest of her life. She divided the year between Val-Kill and New York City but traveled constantly at home and abroad, delivering more than 100 speeches a year urging greater opportunities for women, civil rights for blacks, civil liberties for all Americans, and a foreign policy built on economic rather than military aid to the Third World.

Although she had initially opposed the presidential candidacy of John F. Kennedy in 1960, she agreed to chair his Commission on the Status of Women. Now seventy-three years old and ill with what was later diagnosed as a rare form of bone-marrow tuberculosis, she also presided over Washington hearings by a citizen's Commission of Inquiry into the Freedom Struggle in the South. She sharply criticized the administration for being slow to desegregate federal housing and for failing to insure the safety of black and white Freedom Riders who had been attacked by white mobs while protesting segregation in interstate travel. She died in New York City.

Eleanor Roosevelt never conquered the self-doubt that gripped her during childhood. Her headlong pace and determination to do good were in part efforts to outpace the fear and anxiety she once called "the great crippler" (Roosevelt, *You Learn By Living*, p. 25). Slower than many of her contemporaries to see the value of votes for women, she nonetheless transformed herself into a tough and wily politician; famously timid and reticent as a girl, she became a fearless international champion of progressive causes and perhaps the most influential American woman of the twentieth century.

• Eleanor Roosevelt's papers are in the Franklin D. Roosevelt Library at Hyde Park, N.Y. Other collections at Hyde Park that cast important additional light on her life and career include those of Mary Dewson, Hilda Worthington Smith, Lorena Hickock, Anna Roosevelt Halsted, and the Women's Division of the Democratic National Committee. Her own autobiographical writings include *This Is My Story* (1937), *This I Remember* (1949), and *On My Own* (1958). A selection of her newspaper columns has been published in three volumes: *Eleanor Roosevelt's My Day: Her Acclaimed Columns, 1936–1945*, ed. Rochelle Chadakoff (1989); *Eleanor Roosevelt's My Day: Her Acclaimed Columns, 1945–1952*, ed. David Emblidge (1990); and *Eleanor Roosevelt's My Day: Her Acclaimed Columns, 1953–1962*, ed. Emblidge (1991). Her monthly question-and-answer column, "If You Ask Me," ran in the *Ladies' Home Journal* from June 1941 to spring 1949 and in *McCall's* from 1949 until her death. She is the subject of a number of biographies, including Allida M. Black, *Cast-*

ing Her Own Shadow: Eleanor Roosevelt and the Shaping of Postwar Liberalism (1996); Blanche Wiesen Cook, *Eleanor Roosevelt*, vol. 1: *1884–1933* (1992); Tamara Hareven, *Eleanor Roosevelt: An American Conscience* (1968); Joseph P. Lash, *Eleanor and Franklin* (1971) and *Eleanor: The Years Alone* (1972); and Lois Scharf, *Eleanor Roosevelt: First Lady of American Liberalism* (1987). Three volumes of her letters have been published: *Love, Eleanor* (1982) and *A World of Love* (1984)—both edited by Lash—and *Mother and Daughter: The Letters of Eleanor and Anna Roosevelt*, ed. Bernard Asbell (1982). She is also given major biographical treatment in biographies of her husband, especially Kenneth S. Davis, *FDR: The Beckoning of Destiny, 1882–1928* (1972), *FDR: The New York Years, 1928–1933* (1985), *FDR: The New Deal Years, 1933–1937* (1986), and *FDR: Into the Storm, 1937–1940* (1993); and Geoffrey C. Ward, *Before the Trumpet: The Young Franklin Roosevelt* (1985) and *A First-Class Temperament: The Emergence of Franklin Roosevelt* (1989). She and her husband are jointly the subject of Doris Kearns Goodwin, *No Ordinary Time: Franklin and Eleanor Roosevelt: The Home Front in World War II* (1994).

GEOFFREY C. WARD

ROOSEVELT, Elliott (23 Sept. 1910–27 Oct. 1990), advertising executive, public figure, and author, was born in New York City, the son of Franklin Delano Roosevelt, the thirty-second president of the United States, and Eleanor Roosevelt. He attended Groton Academy in Massachusetts (1923–1929) and Hun School in New Jersey (1929–1930). He declined to follow the family tradition and did not go to Harvard but entered the business world instead. He was an advertising account executive in one firm (1930), vice president of another (1931), and then an account executive in yet another (1932). He became aviation editor for the *Los Angeles Examiner* (1933–1935) and vice president of the Aeronautical Chamber of Commerce of America (1934). He was vice president and then president and general manager of Hearst Radio (1936, 1937–1939), owner of the Frontier Broadcasting System (beginning 1937), and radio commentator on and adviser for three radio networks (1938–1940). Critics felt that his rapid rise owed something to his father's friendship with the publisher-politician William Randolph Hearst.

In 1940 Roosevelt violated family tradition in another manner. Instead of joining the navy, he obtained a commission as a captain in the Army Air Corps. At 6'3" and 225 pounds, he was welcome. Those who thought that he would capitalize on his family name were soon proved wrong. He flew as a reconnaissance pilot over the North Atlantic. He and his younger brother Franklin Roosevelt, Jr., were aides to the president at the August 1941 Atlantic Charter conference with Prime Minister Winston Churchill; during the war, both brothers were aides to the president at the Casablanca conference in January 1943 and at the Cairo-Tehran conference in November 1944. In between, Roosevelt flew 300 combat missions; commanded a multinational photographic reconnaissance wing (1942–1944); participated in the invasions of North Africa (Nov. 1942), Sicily (July 1943), and Normandy (June 1944); was wounded twice; and rose to

the rank of brigadier general in late 1944. In 1945 he received several decorations—the U.S. Air Medal, the Legion of Merit, the Distinguished Flying Cross (with oakleaf cluster), and the French Croix de Guerre (with palm)—and was also made officier de la Légion d'Honneur and commander of the Order of the British Empire. In 1945 he was also, briefly, president of Empire Airlines.

Roosevelt displayed a restlessness and instability in his personal life that only intensified after the war. He had married Elizabeth Donner in 1932; living in Texas, the couple had one child and were divorced in 1933. He married Ruth Googins that same year; they had three children before divorcing in 1944. That same year—on the rim of the Grand Canyon—he married Faye Emerson, the recently divorced star of movies (1942–1945), then television (1948–1958), and Broadway (1950–1958). They were the first accredited correspondents to enter the Soviet Union after World War II ended and interviewed Joseph Stalin. Faye obtained a Mexican divorce from Roosevelt in 1950. Roosevelt married Minnewa Bell days after Bell's divorce in 1951. Four months after their divorce in late 1960, he married Patricia Peabody Whitehead and adopted her five children.

Roosevelt's first book was *As He Saw It* (1946), which describes eyewitness details of President Roosevelt at several international conferences. Reviewers criticized the author's careless handling of sources and quotations. Three years after Elliott and Patricia Roosevelt moved from Minneapolis to Miami, he was elected mayor of that city and served from 1965 to 1969. He was also on the Democratic National Committee. He and his wife moved to Portugal, where they bred Arabian horses during the early 1970s. Then they lived in England; Seattle, Washington; Palm Springs, California; and finally Scottsdale, Arizona. During these years he was writing again. With James Brough as coauthor, he prepared *An Untold Story: The Roosevelts of Hyde Park* (1973), which reveals the president's relationship with his secretary Marguerite A. "Missy" LeHand and asserts that after the birth in 1916 of their youngest child his parents "never again lived as husband and wife." Elliott Roosevelt's sister and three brothers publicly dissociated themselves from *An Untold Story*. Undaunted, Roosevelt wrote *A Rendezvous with Destiny: The Roosevelts of the White House* (1975), again with Brough; and *Mother R: Eleanor Roosevelt's Untold Story* (1978). Turning to a different topic, he wrote *The Conservators* (1984), in which he condemns military spending, the wasting of human and natural resources, the nuclear industry, the public education system, and much else; in the book, he favors a flat tax, "workfare" not welfare, and a United Nations–sponsored global government. His *Eleanor Roosevelt, with Love: A Centenary Remembrance* (1985) is aimed at a juvenile readership.

Roosevelt also wrote a series of popular mystery novels, for which he may ultimately be remembered with the greatest affection. The series startlingly features Eleanor Roosevelt as an astute detective in Hyde

Park, Washington, D.C., the Bahamas, Buckingham Palace, and elsewhere. It begins with *Murder and the First Lady* (1984). Later titles are *Murder in Hyde Park* (1985), *Murder at Hobcaw Barony* (1986), *Murder at the Palace* and *The White House Pantry Murder* (both 1987), *Murder in the Oval Office* and *Murder in the Rose Garden* (both 1989), and *Murder in the Blue Room* (1990). Continuations published after Roosevelt's death include *A First Class Murder* (1991), *Murder in the Red Room* and *Murder in the West Wing* (both 1992), *Murder in the East Room* and *New Deal for Death* (both 1993), and *A Royal Murder* (1994). The easy dialogue, fast-paced action, and Hollywood-style murder-scene evidence in these breezy novels reveal their author's intimate knowledge of his parents' behavior, White House protocol, and international politics. They mix invented characters with real ones so numerous that a tiny sampling must suffice: royalty (King George and Queen Elizabeth), statesmen (Winston Churchill), politicians (Harold Ickes), federal officials (J. Edgar Hoover), soldiers (Dwight D. Eisenhower), diplomats (Vyacheslav Molotov), financiers (Bernard Baruch), celebrities (Charles Lindbergh), entertainers (Josephine Baker), and White House habitués (Missy LeHand). Roosevelt also edited *Perfect Crimes: My Favorite Mystery Stories* (1989) and started a new series of mystery novels, to feature "Blackjack" Endicott, of which only *The President's Man* (1991) appeared. Roosevelt died at his home in Scottsdale, Arizona.

Inevitably, Elliott Roosevelt tried to be active outside the shadow of his father's towering figure. He succeeded best in the military, in creating a sequence of clever mystery novels, and in breeding magnificent horses. Less admirable are the writings on his controversial family in which he indulged himself.

• Correspondence from and to Roosevelt, interviews by and concerning him, and other items are in the Minnewa Bell Papers, the Eleanor Roosevelt Oral History Transcripts, the Eleanor Roosevelt Papers, and the Franklin D. Roosevelt Papers in the Franklin D. Roosevelt Library, Hyde Park, N.Y.; the George W. Goddard Papers in the Manuscript Division, Library of Congress; the Margaret Bayne Price Papers in the Bentley Historical Library, Michigan Historical Collections, University of Michigan; and the Albert F. Simpson Historical Research Center at the Air University, Maxwell Air Force Base, Ala. Otis L. Graham, Jr., and Meghan Robinson Wander, eds., *Franklin D. Roosevelt: His Life and Times, an Encyclopedic View* (1985), is informative in general and has many bibliographical leads. Eric Larrabee, *Commander in Chief: Franklin Delano Roosevelt, His Lieutenants, and Their War* (1987), makes use of Elliott Roosevelt's *As He Saw It*; Geoffrey C. Ward, however, in *A First-class Temperament: The Emergence of Franklin Roosevelt* (1989), which includes discussions of Roosevelt's relationship with his parents, concludes that his books on the Roosevelt family are of limited usefulness. Jesse H. Jones, head of the Reconstruction Finance Corporation, in his *Fifty Billion Dollars: My Thirteen Years with the RFC (1932–1945)* (1951), explains how he bailed Roosevelt out in 1942 after a bad investment in Texas. Thomas M. Coffey, *Hap: The Story of the U.S. Air Force and the Man Who Built It* (1982), discusses Roosevelt's friendship with General Henry H. "Hap" Arnold. Patricia Peabody Roosevelt, *I Love a Roosevelt* (1967), is helpful but not sufficiently objective. An obituary is in the *New York Times*, 28 Oct. 1990.

ROBERT L. GALE

ROOSEVELT, Franklin Delano (30 Jan. 1882–12 Apr. 1945), thirty-second president of the United States, was born on his family's estate in Dutchess County, New York, the son of James Roosevelt, a wealthy, landed gentleman who dabbled in but usually devoted no great effort to business, and Sara Delano. The couple lived their lives and raised their child in a manner reminiscent of the English aristocracy, and Franklin grew up, therefore, in a remarkably cosseted environment, insulated from the normal experiences of most American boys both by his family's wealth and by their all-encompassing love. Until he was fourteen years old, he lived in a world almost entirely dominated by adults: his Swiss tutors, who supervised his lessons at home or during the family's annual travels through Europe; his father, who sought to train his son in the life of a landowner and gentleman; and above all his mother, who devoted virtually all her energies to raising her only child.

It was a world of extraordinary comfort, security, and serenity but also one of reticence and reserve, particularly after 1891, when James Roosevelt suffered the first of a series of heart attacks that left him a semi-invalid. Franklin responded to his father's condition protectively. He tried to spare his father any anxiety by masking his own emotions and projecting a calm, cheerful demeanor. He would continue hiding his feelings behind a bright, charming surface for the rest of his life.

In the fall of 1896 Franklin left his parents to attend Groton, a rigorous boarding school in Massachusetts that was something of a shock to a boy who had never before attended school with other children. He had never had any close friends of his own age and had difficulty making them now. Physically slight, he attained little distinction in athletics, which dominated the life of the school, and went through his four years at Groton a lonely outsider.

Upon entering Harvard College in 1900, Roosevelt set out to make up for what he considered his social failures at Groton. He worked hard at making friends, ran for class office, and became president of the student newspaper, the *Crimson*. He also became conspicuous in his enthusiasm for his distant cousin Theodore Roosevelt, even affecting some of the president's famous mannerisms, such as wearing a pince-nez and frequent, hearty use of the well-known Roosevelt exclamations "Delighted" and "Bully." But he failed to achieve what he craved above all: election to the most exclusive of the Harvard "final clubs," the Porcellian. It was, he later said, "the greatest disappointment of my life."

During Roosevelt's first year at Harvard, his ailing father died, and Sara Roosevelt took a house in Boston to be near her son. Devoted to his mother, Franklin

Roosevelt was always attentive and loving toward her. Yet he was determined by now to create a life of his own, and Sara's intrusive presence made him intensely secretive. Indeed, he obscured from her the most important experience of his Harvard years, his courtship of his distant cousin, Eleanor Roosevelt, Theodore Roosevelt's niece, whom he had known slightly as a child. The couple began to spend time together during the 1902 social season, when Eleanor made her debut. Even though the handsome, charming, and somewhat glib Franklin seemed to have little in common with the quiet, reserved, and intensely serious Eleanor, the mutual attraction grew. By the time Franklin graduated from Harvard in 1904, they were secretly engaged. Despite the initial resistance of Franklin's mother, they married in March 1905. They had a daughter and four sons.

By the time of his marriage, Roosevelt was a student at Columbia Law School. He never completed the requirements for his degree, but he passed his bar exams and spent several years desultorily practicing law in New York City. Already he was principally interested in politics, and in 1910 he accepted the invitation from Democratic party leaders in Dutchess County to run for the state senate. The race seemed hopeless, but profiting from a split in the Republican party and from his own energetic denunciation of party bosses, Roosevelt won. He made few friends at first among his fellow legislators, most of whom considered him naive and arrogant. But he compiled a creditable if modest record protecting the interests of Upstate farmers, his own constituents among them, and opposing the New York City Democratic machine, Tammany Hall.

In 1912 Roosevelt won reelection easily, in part because he had by then enlisted the aid of a politically knowledgeable journalist, Louis M. Howe, who managed his campaign, taught him to drop many of his aristocratic mannerisms, and helped him make alliances with politicians of backgrounds very different from his own. Howe would be indispensable to Roosevelt's career for the next twenty years.

Roosevelt did not serve out his second term in the legislature. Early in 1913 Woodrow Wilson, the new Democratic president whom Roosevelt had energetically supported, offered him an appointment as assistant secretary of the navy. Roosevelt eagerly accepted, not least because it was from that same position that Theodore Roosevelt had launched his national political career fifteen years earlier. Franklin enjoyed the new job and the Washington social life that came with it, and he plunged into both with a sometimes reckless enthusiasm. In the Navy Department, he was brashly assertive and often almost openly insubordinate to his remarkably tolerant superior, Secretary of the Navy Josephus Daniels; but with the help of Howe, Roosevelt ran the day-to-day affairs of the fast-growing department with reasonable efficiency. He also kept his hand in New York politics and tried unsuccessfully in 1914 to seize the Democratic nomination for the U.S. Senate away from the Tammany candidate. From that experience he concluded that, while hostility to Tam-

many was good politics in Dutchess County, it was a serious, perhaps insurmountable, obstacle to statewide and national success. From 1914 on he worked to develop cordial relations with Tammany leaders.

Roosevelt lobbied strenuously for preparedness during the years preceding World War I and for American entry into the war in 1917. Later he successfully promoted the laying of a large barrage of antisubmarine mines in the North Sea, supervised the production of small vessels to defend the American coasts, and intruded himself into deliberations of naval strategy and tactics that were not normally the province of the assistant secretary. He also became involved, perhaps inadvertently, in a controversy that would haunt him for years. In 1918 the navy began an attempt to "clean up" the area around the large naval base at Newport, Rhode Island, after receiving complaints about prostitution and homosexuality. Enlisted men were dispatched to entrap sailors and others, including a prominent Protestant clergyman, in homosexual acts. The scandal that resulted when the operation became public simmered for years, and in 1921 a Senate investigation, dominated by Republicans, openly chastised Roosevelt for his part in the operation.

In the meantime, Roosevelt was experiencing a personal crisis that was even more threatening to his future. As a fixture in Washington's active social life, he often found himself at odds with his wife, to whom social events were seldom less than an ordeal. Perhaps as a result, he found himself drawn to the poised, attractive, gregarious young woman whom Eleanor hired as her social secretary, Lucy Mercer. Franklin and Lucy formed a romantic relationship, which continued until Eleanor discovered it late in 1918. Franklin refused Eleanor's offer of a divorce and promised to end all relations with Lucy Mercer, a promise he broke many years later when, during World War II, he began to see her occasionally again. Eleanor was deeply wounded and withdrew from any real intimacy with her husband. Their marriage survived on the basis of shared public commitments and residual respect and affection, but from 1918 on they lived increasingly separate lives.

Despite the occasional travails of his Washington experience, Roosevelt emerged from his eight years in the Navy Department with a significantly enhanced reputation, which, combined with his famous name, made him immediately attractive to national Democratic leaders. In 1920 he secured the party's nomination for vice president on the ill-fated ticket headed by Ohio governor James M. Cox. Roosevelt campaigned energetically and at times rashly, such as when, in defending the League of Nations, he falsely claimed that he had written the constitution of Haiti and thus had that nation's vote "in his pocket." Despite the Democrats' crushing defeat, he emerged with little of the blame for it and with many new friends among party leaders.

In 1921 Roosevelt returned to private life. He became a vice president of a bonding company and formed a legal partnership in New York, intending all the while to focus primarily on politics. In August 1921, however, a personal disaster seemed to shatter all his hopes. He developed polio while at Campobello Island, his family's summer home, and within days he had lost the use of both of his legs and was in excruciating pain. Months later his doctors told him that he would never walk again. But Roosevelt refused to believe them, and he spent most of the next seven years in a futile search for a cure, trying innumerable forms of therapy and becoming particularly attached to the spa-like baths he discovered in Warm Springs, Georgia. There he spent much of his personal fortune buying an old resort hotel and converting it into a center for polio patients. Eventually he became at least partially reconciled to his continuing paralysis and learned to disguise it for public purposes by wearing heavy leg braces, supporting himself with a cane and the arm of a companion, and using his hips to swing his inert legs forward. So effective was this deception (and so cooperative was the press in preserving it) that few Americans knew during his lifetime that he was largely confined to a wheelchair.

Roosevelt almost never talked about his own feelings, least of all about the impact of paralysis on him; but contracting polio was clearly one of the most important events of his life. His determination to hide his condition from those around him probably strengthened what was already his natural inclination to dissemble, to hide behind an aggressive public geniality, and to reveal as little about himself as possible. Eleanor Roosevelt later claimed that polio also gave him patience and increased his understanding of "what suffering meant." The ordeal certainly made him more serious and determined, and gradually he transferred his steely new resolve away from his efforts to walk and toward an attempt to resume a public career.

After the polio attack, Sara Roosevelt believed that her son should retire from politics and return to the family estate at Hyde Park to live as a gentleman invalid. Both Eleanor and Howe supported Franklin's own desire to resume a public life, and together they worked to keep his name alive in New York politics. During much of the 1920s Roosevelt maintained his ties to politics largely through correspondence, much of it orchestrated by Howe, and through the increasing public activities of his wife. He developed a close political although never personal relationship with Al Smith, the Tammany-supported governor of New York. He also forged ties to other groups in the Democratic party and presented himself as a bridge between its two bitterly divided wings: one, represented by Smith, largely eastern, urban, Catholic, and ethnic; the other, represented by William Jennings Bryan and William McAdoo, largely southern, western, rural, and Protestant.

At the 1924 Democratic National Convention, a grim-faced Roosevelt dragged himself laboriously to the podium on crutches and placed Smith's name in nomination. In 1928, when he again nominated Smith for president, he "walked" to the podium without crutches, one hand holding a cane and the other

clutching his son's arm. It was an important personal triumph, signaling his readiness to resume an active political career, which he did more quickly than even he had expected. After months of resisting pressure from Smith and other party leaders to run for governor of New York, he finally agreed in 1928. He campaigned energetically and buoyantly, partly to dispel the persistent rumors of weakness and poor health. Although Smith lost his home state to Herbert Hoover in the presidential contest by 100,000 votes, Roosevelt won his own race by a narrow margin.

Roosevelt's four years as governor coincided with the first three and a half years of the Great Depression. More quickly than most other political leaders, he concluded that the economy would not recover on its own and "that there is a duty on the part of government to do something about this." Roosevelt pushed for a series of modest reforms that included measures to develop public electric power, lower utilities rates, and reduce the tax burden on New York farmers. Later he also created a state agency to provide relief to the unemployed and began calling for national unemployment insurance and other government programs to assist the jobless. He was careful not to seem reckless or radical. He criticized President Hoover for failing to balance the budget and denounced excessive government intervention in the economy.

From the moment of his landslide reelection as governor of New York in 1930, Roosevelt was the obvious front-runner for the 1932 Democratic presidential nomination. With the help of Howe and James A. Farley, a talented New York political organizer who had helped orchestrate Roosevelt's two gubernatorial campaigns, he accumulated pledges from delegates throughout the country, particularly in the South and the West, where antipathy to Smith, Roosevelt's chief rival for the nomination, was strong. Even so, he approached the Democratic National Convention far from certain of nomination. Smith had defeated him in the Massachusetts primary, and House Speaker John Nance Garner of Texas had won the California primary. Their delegate strength, when combined with that of other candidates and favorite sons, denied Roosevelt through three ballots the two-thirds vote the Democratic party then required for nomination. On the fourth ballot Garner, after being promised the vice presidential nomination, released his delegates, and those additional votes gave Roosevelt the margin he needed. The following day he broke with tradition and flew to Chicago to become the first Democratic candidate ever to appear personally before a convention to accept its nomination. In his speech to the delegates, he pledged "a new deal for the American people," and within weeks the phrase became a widely accepted label for his program.

Roosevelt's task in the fall campaign was a relatively simple one: avoid doing anything to alarm the electorate while allowing Hoover's enormous unpopularity to drive voters to the Democrats. He traveled extensively giving speeches filled with sunny generalities; he was perpetually genial; and he continued to criticize Hoover for failing to balance the budget and for expanding the bureaucracy. But he only occasionally gave indications of his own increasingly progressive agenda. On one such occasion, at the Commonwealth Club in San Francisco, he outlined in general terms a new set of government responsibilities: for an "enlightened administration" to help the economy revive, to distribute "wealth and products more equitably," and to provide "everyone an avenue to possess himself of a portion of that plenty sufficient for his needs, through his own work."

The presidential campaign brought together people who had guided Roosevelt's career in the past and people who would shape his presidency thereafter. Howe and Farley remained his principal political strategists, Eleanor Roosevelt continued to serve as a surrogate for her husband, and Marguerite "Missy" LeHand, Roosevelt's personal secretary since 1920, remained the one constant, daily presence in his life. The 1932 campaign also brought him into contact with new aides and advisers, perhaps most notably a group of academic advisers dubbed the "brain trust" by reporters. Chief among them were three Columbia University professors, Raymond Moley, Adolf A. Berle, Jr., and Rexford G. Tugwell, who helped write his campaign speeches, including the Commonwealth Club address, and, more important, began developing ideas for his presidency.

Roosevelt won handily with 57 percent of the popular vote to Hoover's 40 and with 472 electoral votes to Hoover's 59. Democrats also won solid control of both houses of Congress. Most observers interpreted the results less as a mandate for Roosevelt, whose plans remained largely unknown to the public, than as a repudiation of Hoover. Many skeptics still shared Walter Lippmann's famously dismissive view of Roosevelt as "a pleasant man who, without any important qualifications for the office, would very much like to be president."

In the four months between his victory and his inauguration, Roosevelt did little to dispel those doubts. The depression worsened considerably, with more than 25 percent of the workforce unemployed, and early in 1933 a series of bank failures deepened the crisis. President Hoover, conservative Democrats, and leading business figures all urged the president-elect to restore confidence by pledging himself to fiscal and monetary conservatism. Roosevelt refused while offering few clues to his own plans. The most dramatic event of his "interregnum" was an attempted assassination in Miami in February, in which Roosevelt was not injured but the mayor of Chicago was killed. The president-elect responded to the incident with the same unruffled, genial calm he had displayed since the election.

Roosevelt assumed the presidency at a moment of great crisis for the nation. Millions were unemployed or underemployed, the agricultural economy was nearly in chaos, industrial production had fallen dramatically, new capital investment had almost ceased, and the banking system had become paralyzed as a widening panic drained banks of their deposits. The governor of Michigan had ordered all the banks in his state closed in mid-February, and by the beginning of March almost every state in the nation had placed some restrictions on banking activity.

The banking crisis provided the ominous backdrop both for Roosevelt's inauguration and for his first days in office. His inaugural address offered words of assurance, "The only thing we have to fear is fear itself," and stern warnings: "Rulers of the exchange of mankind's goods have failed through their own stubbornness and their own incompetence. . . . The money changers have fled from their high seats in the temple of our civilization." It was less a diagnosis of the national condition than a direct response to the banking crisis itself, and his first days in office were devoted largely to solving that crisis. On 6 March 1933 he ordered every bank in the nation closed—a "bank holiday," as he euphemistically described it. Three days later Congress met in special session to consider an emergency banking bill, drafted so hastily by holdovers from the Hoover administration that members did not even receive printed copies of it. Both Houses passed it, and the president signed it the same day. Stronger banks could now reopen with promises of government assistance; weaker ones remained closed until Treasury Department examiners could assure their viability. This was a modest and essentially conservative action, but it was enough to stop the panic. Nearly three-quarters of the nation's banks reopened within three days of the measure's passage.

Roosevelt also contributed to the restoration of calm on 12 March with the first of his avuncular "fireside chats" over national radio, during which he explained the provisions of the banking bill in simple terms and offered comforting assurances that it was "safer to keep your money in a reopened bank than under your mattress." The president continued to use radio throughout his administration and thus became the first national leader whose voice was a part of the country's everyday life.

Roosevelt promised in his 1932 campaign that he would end the deficits that had plagued the Hoover administration and restore a balanced budget. This he never did, and eventually he would come to consider deficit spending a useful and necessary response to recession. In 1933, however, he remained committed to fiscal orthodoxy, and on 10 March he asked Congress to pass legislation cutting government salaries and veterans' benefits. Both Houses passed the Economy Act within days, despite protests from some progressives who argued correctly that the measure would add to the deflationary pressures on the economy.

The New Deal soon departed from these conservative beginnings. Over the next three months, known then and later as the "Hundred Days," Roosevelt won passage of a series of bills that began to transform the role of the federal government in the workings of the nation's economy. The result was not a "revolution" as some liked to claim, but it was a significant turning point in the evolution of the American state. Roosevelt drew heavily from the progressive traditions with which he had grown up and in which his principal advisers had been schooled, and he also responded to genuinely new ideas born of the unprecedented problems of the Great Depression. In the end, the New Deal was an amalgam of many different ideologies with no single, consistent rationale. Roosevelt's only solid commitments were to what he called "bold, practical experimentation" and, of course, to his own political survival.

The crisis of the farm economy spurred the first of the innovative New Deal reforms, a comprehensive farm bill, the Agricultural Adjustment Act. Signed in May 1933, the new law reflected the longstanding demands of many of the leading farm organizations for government support for farm prices. The Agricultural Adjustment Administration (AAA), which the legislation created, helped farmers limit production of basic commodities; over production, farm experts agreed, was one of the principal reasons for tumbling agricultural prices. The AAA also created subsidies for farmers who left land idle. Much of the administration of the program fell into the hands of the American Farm Bureau Federation, which represented mostly commercial farmers. Unsurprisingly, therefore, the AAA tended to favor larger producers and weaken smaller ones. While farm income rose by almost 50 percent in the next three years, the dispossession of small farmers, tenants, and sharecroppers continued and even accelerated. Subsequently the New Deal experimented with a series of programs designed to help these marginal farmers, including the Resettlement Administration, established in 1935, and the Farm Security Administration, created in 1937, but the movement of the agricultural economy toward large-scale commercial farming continued inexorably. In 1936 the Supreme Court invalidated the original Agricultural Adjustment Act, declaring that Congress had no authority to compel individual farmers to reduce their acreage. The administration preserved the bill's major provisions in slightly altered form through the Soil Conservation and Domestic Allotment Act of 1936 and the Agricultural Adjustment Act of 1938, and federal support for farmers continued, in much the same form the New Deal created, through the rest of the century.

Another major concern during the Hundred Days was the health of the industrial economy. The U.S. Chamber of Commerce, Gerard Swope of General Electric, and other leading businessmen and industrialists urged the government to suspend the antitrust laws and allow corporations to work together to stabilize prices and production, forming a cooperative "associationalism" policed in some modest way by the government. In June 1933 the New Deal responded to these appeals and the demands of other constituencies with the National Industrial Recovery Act (NIRA), one of the largest and most complicated pieces of legislation in American history to that point. Roosevelt called it "the most important and far-reaching legislation ever enacted by the American Congress."

The NIRA established a National Recovery Administration (NRA), headed by the flamboyant Hugh Johnson, a retired general who had directed the selective service system during World War I. Its most important task was persuading the industrialists in major industries to join together under "code authorities" roughly analogous to the trade associations many of them had created in the 1920s and earlier. Through the code authorities, industries established price floors, production restrictions, and employment standards to check deflation and restore prosperity. The codes thus produced, when approved by the NRA, were to have the force of law and were to be enforced through governmental sanctions. In addition, Johnson created a public relations campaign behind a set of largely voluntary "blanket codes" for all the employers not covered by specific code authorities. The blanket code established a minimum wage of 30 to 40 cents an hour and a maximum work week of 35 to 40 hours.

Initially the NRA was successful in creating public enthusiasm for the new program. The agency's symbol, the Blue Eagle, soon appeared in shop windows, on banners, and in public parades and demonstrations around the country. But the NRA was less successful in solving the problems of industrial production. Administratively unprepared for the enormity of its task, the agency floundered as it tried to enforce the codes. Once it became clear that large producers would dominate the code-making process, smaller businesses—many of which relied on lower prices to be able to compete with larger firms—complained loudly about their deteriorating positions. Critics also objected to artificially raised prices, which in a depressed economy tended to dampen demand and reduce production. Organized labor protested the limited implementation of NIRA's Section 7a, which guaranteed workers the right to organize and bargain collectively. This stimulated an upsurge in trade union membership, but the lack of enforcement provisions and the administrators' disagreements about the section's requirements ensured that few employers were willing to recognize and bargain with the unions.

By the end of 1933 the failure of the NRA was already becoming clear. In 1934, after an external review board chaired by Clarence Darrow charged that the agency was dominated by big business and was encouraging monopoly, Roosevelt pressured Johnson to resign. Johnson's successors, however, made little progress in solving the NRA's problems, and in May 1935 the Supreme Court declared the NIRA unconstitutional. The president charged that in doing so the Court had adopted a "horse-and-buggy" interpretation of the Constitution. He was rightly concerned, for the Court's narrow construction of the Interstate Commerce Clause and its strict view of the limits on executive power called many other New Deal measures into question. Even so, the nullification of the NRA itself rescued the president from a failed experiment.

Roosevelt's first year in office produced other significant initiatives. The Tennessee Valley Authority, the culmination of years of progressive efforts to promote the development of public power, combined an ambitious program of flood control and regional development with the creation of large, government-owned hydroelectric power plants. The Civilian Conservation Corps created camps in national parks and forests and other nonurban settings where young, unemployed men from the cities found employment and training. The Federal Emergency Relief Administration and the Civil Works Administration provided funds to relief agencies and jobs for the unemployed. The Securities and Exchange Commission began regulating the stock market. A second banking reform bill established federal insurance of bank deposits.

By the end of 1933 economic conditions were showing signs of modest improvement, but Roosevelt was reaping political rewards far out of proportion to the actual results of his programs. His carefully cultivated relations with the Washington press corps, including weekly informal news conferences in the Oval Office, ensured that he received largely favorable news coverage despite the animus he attracted from most newspaper publishers. Above all, he conveyed an image of energy and compassion—a sharp contrast to the cautious, dour image Hoover had conveyed in his last years in office.

Within the White House itself, Roosevelt created an atmosphere of jovial camaraderie among the small circle of aides and advisers on whom he relied, while his relationship with his wife remained distant. Even when they were together in the White House, they lived largely separate lives, and the first lady communicated with her husband on public issues largely through memos. The president's most intimate companion was LeHand, who served as his secretary and as a surrogate wife and household manager when Eleanor Roosevelt was away. Roosevelt relied heavily on LeHand for companionship and support but probably not for romance. Several of the president's children came to live at the White House at various times, and some of them worked for him while they were there. Yet he remained, in the end, the same reserved, self-contained, and somewhat mysterious figure he had always been—to no one more than to those who knew him best.

The president's disability meant that he left the White House relatively seldom and traveled less than other presidents normally did. He continued to vacation occasionally in Warm Springs, to take cruises on the Potomac and the Chesapeake, and to make regular visits to his home in Hyde Park, where his mother still lived. Periodically he embarked on elaborately orchestrated "fact-finding" missions around the country, traveling on specially fitted trains and in specially designed automobiles with aides, who created elaborate subterfuges to hide his disability. The press was willingly complicit. Never during Roosevelt's public life did any newspaper or magazine publish a photograph of him in a wheelchair or being lifted in or out of a car.

By the middle of 1934 the New Deal, for which many had had great hopes in 1933, was experiencing serious difficulties. The economy was not improving fast enough to meet public expectations, resulting in the growth of popular and radical protest movements accompanied by one of the largest waves of strikes in the nation's history. These developments were jeopardizing the president's political future, and beginning in the spring of 1935 Roosevelt responded with a series of new proposals that historians have sometimes called the "Second New Deal." Dominating it were two landmark pieces of legislation that remain among the New Deal's principal legacies.

The Social Security Act of 1935 created the framework for the nation's first national system of social insurance and public assistance. More specifically, it created an old-age pension system funded by contributions from workers and employers, a system of unemployment insurance funded by employers alone, and several programs of social welfare supported by ordinary public funds for such particularly needy groups as single mothers with children in the home, the elderly poor, and the disabled. In operation it provided the framework for America's version of the modern welfare state.

The National Labor Relations Act of 1935, better known as the Wagner Act because Senator Robert Wagner of New York was the bill's principal sponsor, reaffirmed the guarantee of workers' right to bargain collectively as first stated in the now defunct NIRA. It also provided for enforcement of that right by creating the National Labor Relations Board, empowered to compel employers to recognize and bargain with unions that had won legitimate elections among a firm's workers.

Also in 1935 the New Deal launched the most extensive and innovative program of work relief in American history to that date, the Works Progress Administration. Directed by Harry Hopkins, this agency kept an average of 2.1 million workers employed between 1935 and 1941 and was responsible for constructing a remarkable number of public buildings and facilities. Tax reform, utilities regulation, and other measures, some of them largely symbolic, were also part of this new wave of legislative action.

The Second New Deal did not end the depression, but it did provide crucial short-term and long-term protections to large groups of Americans. In addition, it revived Roosevelt's political fortunes. In the 1936 presidential election, he faced the Republican governor of Kansas, Alf Landon, a moderate conservative with a dull public presence, and a third-party challenge from Congressman William Lemke of North Dakota, the hapless candidate of the short-lived Union party. Roosevelt campaigned energetically and effectively, and he won by an unprecedented landslide: 61 percent of the popular vote, the electoral votes of every state except Maine and Vermont, and increased Democratic majorities in both Houses of Congress. The election displayed clearly the fundamental political realignment the New Deal had created. The Democratic party now had the support of a broad coalition of southern and western farmers, the urban working class, the poor and unemployed, the black communities of northern cities, traditional progressives, and committed new liberals. This "New Deal coalition" would dominate American politics for a generation.

Few could have imagined in the glow of the November election how quickly the Roosevelt administration would move from its triumph into a quagmire of frustration and defeat. In February 1937, emboldened by his apparent mandate, Roosevelt introduced a Court "reform" plan designed to give him the authority to appoint additional, sympathetic justices to the Supreme Court, which he feared would otherwise invalidate virtually all of the legislative achievements of his first term. The "Court-packing" bill, as it quickly became known, was intensely controversial and energized the president's conservative opposition. Congress defeated it, humiliating the president in the process. But the Court itself, in the face of this assault, prudently moved toward the center and became more amenable to New Deal programs. At about the same time, Roosevelt also supported an ambitious proposal to reorganize the executive branch of the federal government, which his opponents charged was an attempt to consolidate still more power in the hands of the president. They defeated the original proposal in Congress and forced him to settle for a much more modest bill in 1939.

Most damaging of all to the administration was a serious recession that began suddenly in August 1937 and quickly wiped out most of the painfully won economic gains of the previous four years. The collapse was especially traumatic to New Dealers because it came at a point when they had begun to believe that the depression was over. Now, confronted with the hollowness of those claims, the president joined in an agonizing reappraisal of his policies and eventually launched two important new initiatives.

One was a newly energetic effort to combat "monopoly power." Opposition to monopoly had been a staple of New Deal rhetoric, although seldom of action, in 1935 and 1936, and now some of the most committed New Dealers convinced the president that the recession was a result of a deliberate effort by "economic royalists" to sabotage the economy—a "capital strike," as some called it. Roosevelt responded by calling for the creation of a new commission to investigate economic conditions. The Temporary National Economic Committee spent over three years studying the effects of monopoly power, but its final report, released after World War II had begun, had no effect on public policy. In addition, Roosevelt's new director of the antitrust division of the Justice Department, Thurman Arnold, began making more energetic use of the antitrust laws than had any of his predecessors. But Arnold's experiment, too, came to an end during the war.

At the same time, Roosevelt responded to pleas from liberal economists and others who argued that the recession was a result of the significant reductions in government spending he had approved early in 1937. In the spring of 1938, to the chagrin of Secretary of the Treasury Henry Morgenthau, Roosevelt abandoned further efforts to balance the budget and se-

cured emergency appropriations of $5 billion in spending and loans for relief and public works. It was the first time a president had explicitly endorsed the idea that stimulating mass consumption through deficit spending could promote economic growth. Ultimately the idea that federal fiscal policy was an effective tool by which government could regulate the economy, an idea associated with the British economist John Maynard Keynes, became one of the New Deal's most important policy innovations and one of its most significant legacies. Also in 1938 Roosevelt won passage of the Fair Labor Standards Act, which established a minimum wage, created a maximum forty-hour work week, and abolished child labor. It, too, was in part an effort to stimulate economic growth by increasing mass purchasing power.

By the end of 1938 Roosevelt was only about halfway through his presidency, but the New Deal he had created was close to completion. In retrospect, it has often seemed as significant for the things it did not do as for the things it achieved. It did not end the Great Depression and the massive unemployment that accompanied it; only the enormous public and private spending for World War II finally did that. The complaints of conservative critics notwithstanding, it did not transform American capitalism in any fundamental way. Except in the fields of labor relations and banking and finance, corporate power remained nearly as free from government regulation or control in 1945 as it had been in 1933. The New Deal did not end poverty or significantly redistribute wealth, nor did it do very much, except symbolically, to address the principal domestic challenges of the postwar era, among them the problems of racial and gender inequality. Despite the commitment to civil rights of Eleanor Roosevelt and other New Deal officials such as Secretary of the Interior Harold Ickes, the president shied away from issues that he feared would divide his party and damage his ability to work with Congress.

Even so, the achievements of the Roosevelt administration rank among the most important of any presidency in American history. First, the New Deal created new state institutions that significantly and permanently expanded the role of the federal government in American life. The government was committed to providing at least minimal assistance to the elderly, the poor, and the unemployed; to protecting the rights of labor unions; to stabilizing the banking system; to building low-income housing; to regulating financial markets; to subsidizing agricultural production; and to doing many other things that had not previously been federal responsibilities. As a result, American political and economic life became much more competitive, with workers, farmers, consumers, and others now able to press their demands upon the government in ways that in the past had usually been available only to the corporate world. Hence the frequent description of the government the New Deal created as a "broker state," a state brokering the competing claims of numerous groups. Second, the New Deal produced a political coalition that sustained the

Democrats as the majority party in national politics for more than a generation after its own end. Finally, the Roosevelt administration generated a set of political ideas, known to later generations as New Deal liberalism, that remained a source of inspiration and controversy for decades and that helped shape the next major experiment in liberal reform, the Great Society of the 1960s.

That the New Deal sputtered to something like a close in Roosevelt's second term was in part because the political tides were turning against him. In 1938 and again in 1942 the Democrats suffered considerable losses in congressional elections, and the emerging conservative coalition of Republicans and southern Democrats was capable of blocking almost anything liberals proposed. The New Deal faded as well, however, because of the president's growing preoccupation with the worst catastrophe of the twentieth century, the spiraling global crisis that led Europe, Asia, and ultimately the United States into World War II.

For the first five years of his presidency, foreign policy had been a distinctly secondary concern to Roosevelt. Shortly after taking office, he withdrew his support from the London Economic Conference, which was seeking a global solution to depression-induced problems of currency and trade. He was implicitly saying that the United States would go it alone, and he then devalued American currency by weakening its link to the gold standard. Subsequently he promoted American foreign trade and, not unrelated, improved U.S. relations with Latin America through a wide-ranging cluster of initiatives known together as the "Good Neighbor Policy."

Still, as a Wilsonian, Roosevelt was an internationalist at heart, as was his secretary of state, Cordell Hull, and from time to time they tried to nudge the United States into a more active global role. In 1935 Roosevelt asked the Senate to approve a treaty that would allow the United States to join the World Court. Spirited opposition from isolationists both in and out of Congress prevented ratification. In 1937, in response to Japanese attacks on China, he made a vague proposal to "quarantine the aggressors," only to be greeted with such savage denunciations from much of the press and the public that he drew back again. Although disturbed by the growing militarism in Europe and Asia, he was as yet uncertain about what role the United States could play in stopping it. In 1938, when British prime minister Neville Chamberlain met with Adolf Hitler at Munich and ceded Czechoslovakia to the Nazis in exchange for what turned out to be a hollow promise of peace, Roosevelt cabled Chamberlain congratulations.

When war finally broke out in Europe in September 1939, Roosevelt insisted that the conflict would not involve the United States, but he took pains to differentiate his policies from those of Wilson in 1914. Whereas Wilson had insisted that the United States would be neutral in "word and deed," Roosevelt declared, "This nation will remain a neutral nation, but I cannot ask that every American remain neutral in thought as

well." His support for Britain and its allies was clear and unequivocal from the start.

In the spring of 1940, as the war spread throughout western Europe, driving the British and French armies from the Continent, public opinion began to move slowly toward support for a more active American role in the conflict. Roosevelt moved with it and at times somewhat ahead of it. Despite organized opposition from powerful isolationist groups, he managed to persuade Congress to repeal the Neutrality Acts it had passed in the 1930s, thus making it possible for the United States to begin selling weapons and other supplies to Britain. He formed an extraordinarily intimate relationship with Britain's prime minister Winston Churchill that facilitated increasing aid to Britain. In September 1940 Roosevelt traded fifty American destroyers to the British in exchange for several British bases in the Caribbean. In December, shortly after winning an unprecedented third term in the White House by handily defeating Wendell Willkie, a prominent industrialist who had secured the Republican nomination, Roosevelt proposed what he called "lend-lease," a system designed to permit the nearly bankrupt British to continue receiving armaments from the United States without paying cash for them. Congress obliged him by passing the Lend-Lease Act of March 1941.

Gradually American assistance to the Allies grew even more overt. As German submarines made shipping material across the Atlantic increasingly difficult, American naval vessels began patrolling the ocean and escorting convoys of merchant ships. In August 1941 Roosevelt and Churchill met aboard an American cruiser off Newfoundland and signed the Atlantic Charter, a statement of war aims that called for an end to fascism and a guarantee of national self-determination throughout the world. In November 1941, shortly after Hitler invaded Russia, Roosevelt extended lend-lease assistance to the Soviet Union, the first step toward forging what would soon be an important wartime alliance.

In the meantime, the United States responded to continuing Japanese aggression in China by imposing a trade embargo on Japan and freezing Japanese assets in the United States. To meet this threat to their oil supplies, the Japanese laid plans to seize the oil-producing British and Dutch possessions in the Pacific. It was there, Roosevelt and most other American officials assumed, that Japan's next aggressive moves would be. The Americans had cracked the Japanese codes and knew an attack on the territory of one of the Western powers was coming. The intelligence information Washington received could have, if properly interpreted, alerted the United States to Tokyo's plans, but because no one anticipated that the Japanese would launch so bold an effort, no one predicted what they actually did. On 7 December 1941, without warning, a wave of Japanese bombers struck the American naval base in Pearl Harbor, Hawaii, killing more than 2,000 American servicemen and damaging or destroying dozens of ships and airplanes. The next day Roosevelt traveled to Capitol Hill to ask Congress for a declaration of war, which it passed within hours. Three days later Germany and Italy, Japan's European allies, declared war on the United States, and the American Congress quickly reciprocated. The United States was now fully engaged in the largest war in history.

Roosevelt was somewhat more detached from day-to-day decision making as a war leader than he had been as a domestic one. More than a year before Pearl Harbor, he had appointed men of great stature to supervise the military. Former secretary of state Henry Stimson was secretary of war, and Frank Knox, a distinguished Chicago publisher of strong internationalist credentials, was secretary of the navy. Both men were Republicans, and indeed Roosevelt made strenuous efforts throughout the war to attract bipartisan support for his policies, even to the point of permitting and at times encouraging the departure from government of New Deal liberals. During the war Roosevelt tended to defer to the judgment of his military leaders, but he participated actively and often decisively in major strategic decisions.

Almost immediately after Pearl Harbor Roosevelt made what was perhaps the most important of those decisions: although the United States would wage a two-front war, it would concentrate first on the conflict in Europe. Disagreement quickly emerged, however, over the best strategy for defeating Germany and Italy. The American leaders wanted to devote virtually all of their resources to preparing an invasion across the English Channel into France, the most direct route to Germany. Churchill and other British leaders, remembering the terrible carnage in France during World War I, preferred to delay the major invasion and begin with smaller incursions along the periphery of the Nazi empire. Roosevelt finally sided with Churchill and supported the British proposal to engage the Germans first in the territories they had seized in North Africa. An Allied invasion of North Africa began in November 1942. After Anglo-American forces drove the Germans from Africa, they continued across the Mediterranean, invading Sicily and Italy in the summer of 1943.

Although American forces in the Pacific received less than a fifth of the resources the nation devoted to the war in these early years, they pursued an active strategy against the Japanese. Having been driven from virtually the entire Pacific west of Hawaii (including the Philippines) within a few months of Pearl Harbor, American forces began striking back and soon won two critical victories—first in the battle of the Coral Sea in May 1942 and then in the battle of Midway a month later. From there the United States launched a series of offensives against Japanese outposts in the Solomon Islands just north of Australia, the first in several prolonged and savage island campaigns that continued for the rest of the war.

Throughout 1942 and 1943 Roosevelt was preoccupied with the ongoing debate over how and when to launch an Allied invasion of France. The Soviet Union was now bearing the brunt of the German war effort. Soviet leader Joseph Stalin argued that Anglo-American forces must move quickly to open another front in Europe. At a meeting with Churchill in Casablanca, Morocco, in January 1943, Roosevelt tried to mollify Stalin by declaring his support for nothing less than "unconditional surrender" by the Axis. In other words, the United States and Britain would not agree to a separate peace and leave the Soviet Union to fight alone.

In November 1943 Roosevelt and Churchill traveled to Teheran for their first meeting with Stalin. By then the war in eastern Europe had turned decisively in favor of the Soviet Union, which meant that Roosevelt now had only limited leverage over Stalin. Even so, Stalin agreed to enter the Pacific war after the fighting in Europe came to an end, and Roosevelt and Churchill promised to launch the long-delayed invasion of France in the spring of 1944. The meeting produced less agreement on other matters, but the Western leaders seemed inclined toward arrangements that would allow the Soviet Union to keep the areas of Poland it had seized in 1939.

Roosevelt turned his attention increasingly to the shape of the postwar world. He persuaded twenty-six nations to sign the United Nations Declaration, a statement of principles based on the Atlantic Charter. In July 1944 he convened an international monetary conference at Bretton Woods, New Hampshire, that created the International Monetary Fund, charged with stabilizing global currencies, and the International Bank for Reconstruction and Development, to assist the shattered nations of Europe and Asia in rebuilding after the war.

At home, massive wartime spending had ended the depression and launched a period of vigorous economic growth, while a new set of war mobilization agencies—staffed, like the comparable agencies in World War I, largely by corporate executives and attorneys borrowed from their firms—channeled manpower, materials, and capital into the production necessary for the war. Roosevelt's liberal allies complained constantly, but ineffectually, about the domination of the war effort by capitalists. Roosevelt promoted no significant domestic reform legislation during the war, and in 1943 he was unable to prevent an increasingly conservative Congress from dismantling many New Deal agencies. He did, however, support an ambitious vision of a peacetime society in which the government would ensure a minimal level of comfort and security for all Americans, and he helped craft the Servicemen's Readjustment Act of 1944, or the "G.I. Bill of Rights," which provided generous housing, educational, and other benefits to veterans when the war ended.

Roosevelt was less receptive to the demands of the many Americans who sought to harness the war effort to great moral causes. In 1940, largely because of heavy pressure by African-American leaders, he created the Fair Employment Practices Commission, the first federal agency since Reconstruction that was actively engaged in the effort to promote racial equality. He did not, however, respond to other black demands, and the armed forces remained segregated throughout the war. The president approved a proposal from military officials on the West Coast to "intern" the thousands of resident Japanese Americans, many of them native-born citizens, despite the absence of any evidence that they were disloyal. Most of them were not released until 1944. Even more troubling to many Americans, both at the time and since, was the administration's apparent unwillingness to take effective action to save the Jews of Europe, who were being systematically exterminated by Nazi Germany. In fairness, the United States could have done little other than win the war to save most of the Jews imperiled by the Holocaust, but the government gave minimal help even to those cases in which it might have made a difference at the margins.

Roosevelt agreed without any apparent resistance to be the Democratic party's candidate for president for the fourth time in 1944. Preoccupied with the war and in increasingly frail health, he took only slight interest in the campaign. At the convention, he acquiesced, almost passively, to the demand of party leaders that he abandon his controversial vice president, Henry Wallace, and run instead with the more moderate senator Harry S. Truman of Missouri. After the convention, he did virtually no campaigning until rumors of his declining health became a factor in the election. At that point he rallied for several vigorous and effective appearances. He defeated Governor Thomas E. Dewey of New York, a man he had come to despise, with 53 percent of the vote.

One of the many reasons for Roosevelt's political resilience was that the Allied war effort was by then clearly on the road to victory. On 6 June 1944 Allied forces landed on the Normandy coast and began a successful invasion of France. By August they had liberated Paris, and by mid-September they had driven the Germans almost entirely out of France. The invasion bogged down for a time later that fall, and not until early spring 1945 did the Anglo-American advance on Germany resume. Soviet forces also swept westward into central Europe and the Balkans. In the Pacific, American forces captured almost all the strategic islands east of Japan, retook the Philippines, and were closing in on Japan itself. Unknown to all but a few, the United States was by then far along in an effort Roosevelt had authorized early in the war, the Manhattan Project, which detonated the first atomic bomb two months after Roosevelt's death. There is little evidence to suggest how he would have used the new weapon had he lived.

In January 1945, with victory in Europe apparently imminent, Roosevelt traveled to Yalta for another meeting with Churchill and Stalin. Both men were shocked at the president's wasted physical appearance, a result of advanced arteriosclerosis that had been weakening him for over a year, forcing him to live much of the time as a virtual invalid. At Yalta, however, Roosevelt participated actively and capably in the negotiations. The three leaders agreed on the postwar occupation of Germany, the Soviet Union's participation in the Pacific war, and the creation of what became the United Nations. But they could reach no accord on other issues, most notably the future of Poland. Instead, they papered over their differences with a series of weak and unenforceable compromises. Roosevelt returned home still believing that he could eventually reach some accommodation with Stalin. Even though he did not realize it then, however, the outlines of the coming Cold War were already visible at Yalta.

Both because of his failing health and because of the distortions the war had caused in his family life, Roosevelt became even more isolated during the war years than he had been before. His mother died in 1941, his sons were serving overseas, and his wife traveled almost constantly. LeHand suffered a debilitating stroke in 1941 and died in 1944. The president turned for companionship to his daughter Anna, to two adoring and unmarried cousins who came to live at the White House, and to a rotating series of charming, attractive women who deferred to him in a way Eleanor had never been willing to do. He also began seeing Mercer (now Lucy Mercer Rutherford and a widow) again, nearly thirty years after the unhappy end of their World War I romance.

Early in April Roosevelt left Washington for a vacation at his retreat in Warm Springs, Georgia, accompanied by his cousins and several aides. On 12 April he received a visit from Rutherford, who brought with her an artist who wished to paint a portrait of the president. As he posed for the portrait while working on papers at a small table in his cabin, he suddenly looked up and complained of a "terrific headache." Moments later he collapsed. He had suffered a massive stroke, and he died several hours later.

In the half century after his death, Roosevelt's stature as one of the major figures of the twentieth century did not diminish. Even those critical of his achievements recognize their magnitude: the reshaping of American government, the transformation of the Democratic party, the redefinition of American liberalism, the leadership of the United States through the largest war in world history, and the reconstruction of America's relationship to the international order. Such achievements were not his alone, of course. But it is only necessary to look at some of those who contended with him for leadership of the United States in the 1930s, and some of those who actually assumed leadership of other major nations, to understand Roosevelt's critical importance to the great changes that America experienced during his unprecedented—and never to be repeated—twelve years as its leader.

• The Franklin D. Roosevelt Papers are housed in the Roosevelt Presidential Library in Hyde Park, N.Y., along with the papers of many other New Dealers. *The Public Papers and Addresses of Franklin D. Roosevelt*, ed. Samuel Rosenman, published in two multivolumed series (1938, 1941), contains speeches and other official documents through 1940. Biographies of Roosevelt are numerous. Among the most important are Frank Freidel, *Franklin D. Roosevelt* (4 vols., 1952–1973) and *Franklin D. Roosevelt: A Rendezvous with Destiny* (1990); James MacGregor Burns, *Roosevelt: The Lion and the Fox* (1956) and *Roosevelt: The Soldier of Freedom* (1970); Geoffrey Ward, *Before the Trumpet* (1985) and *A First-Class Temperament* (1989); and Kenneth S. Davis, *FDR* (4 vols., 1972–1993). Among the many informative studies of the New Deal are Arthur M. Schlesinger, Jr., *The Age of Roosevelt* (3 vols., 1957–1960); William E. Leuchtenburg, *Franklin D. Roosevelt and the New Deal* (1963); Ellis Hawley, *The New Deal and the Problem of Monopoly* (1966); and Alan Brinkley, *The End of Reform* (1995). "Revisionist" studies of the New Deal are relatively few, but among the more important are Barton Bernstein, "The New Deal: The Conservative Achievements of Liberal Reform," *Towards a New Past*, ed. Bernstein (1968); Thomas Ferguson, "Industrial Conflict and the Coming of the New Deal: The Triumph of Multinational Liberalism in America," *The Rise and Fall of the New Deal Order*, ed. Steve Fraser and Gary Gerstle (1989); and Colin Gordon, *New Deals* (1994). Major studies of Roosevelt's diplomacy include Robert Dallek, *Franklin D. Roosevelt and American Foreign Policy, 1932–1945* (1979), and Warren Kimball, *The Juggler* (1991). Doris Kearns Goodwin, *No Ordinary Time* (1994), provides an intimate portrait of the Roosevelts during World War II. For assessments of Roosevelt's posthumous legacy, see Robert Eden, ed., *The New Deal and Its Legacy* (1985), and William E. Leuchtenburg, *In the Shadow of FDR* (1983). Otis Graham and Meghan Robinson Wander, *Franklin D. Roosevelt: His Life and Times. An Encyclopedic View* (1985), is a valuable reference work.

ALAN BRINKLEY

ROOSEVELT, Franklin Delano, Jr. (17 Aug. 1914–17 Aug. 1988), politician and businessman, was born at the family's summer estate on Campobello Island, New Brunswick, Canada, the son of President Franklin Delano Roosevelt, then assistant secretary of the navy, and Anna Eleanor Roosevelt. Continuing the family's educational tradition, "Frank" Roosevelt, as his friends called him, graduated from the Groton School in Massachusetts in 1933. He completed his formal education at Harvard University in 1937. In 1940 he earned a law degree from the University of Virginia.

The so-called glamour boy of the family, Roosevelt bore a strong resemblance to his father in face and in voice. Perhaps in part because of such similarities, he was considered to be the most likely to follow in his father's footsteps. However, he never realized these expectations, in part because, as he said in a 1949 *New York Times* interview, "We are a very close but also a very independent family." Each child developed his or her own views through discussion and debate, at times differing with the opinions expressed by the father. Roosevelt's marriage to Ethel du Pont in 1937 was considered by many the social event of the season. They had two children before divorcing in 1949. That year Roosevelt married Suzanne Perrin; they had two children.

Roosevelt practiced law only briefly in 1940 before being called to military service in March 1941 as a member of the Navy Reserves. By the time of his discharge in October 1945, he had risen from ensign to lieutenant commander and had received the Purple Heart, the Silver Star, the Navy Cross, and the Legion of Merit along with numerous awards for meritorious service. Following his military service, he returned to the practice of law, joining the New York firm of Poletti, Diamond, Rabin, Freiden, and MacKay.

Roosevelt's wartime experiences in the navy led to his involvement with the American Veterans' Committee (AVC), a liberal organization of World War II veterans. Through his leadership role within the AVC, Roosevelt launched his career as a public figure. In 1947 he served as vice chairman of President Harry Truman's Committee on Civil Rights and was appointed to various committees by the mayor of New York City. After the death of Democratic representative Sol Bloom in 1949, Roosevelt was selected by the Liberal party to fill the vacant congressional seat for the Twentieth District of New York. He was reelected as the Democratic candidate and served in the House from 17 May 1949 until 3 January 1955. In addition, he was a delegate to the Democratic National Convention in 1952 and again in 1956.

In 1954 Roosevelt made an unsuccessful bid for the Democratic nomination for governor and was instead nominated for New York State attorney general. He lost the race and returned to his law practice. Despite the firm's original reluctance to hire the flashy young Roosevelt, the partners of Poletti, Diamond, Rabin, Freiden, and MacKay soon came to appreciate his legal mind and distinctive style for dealing with his clients. By 1958 Roosevelt had traded his legal practice for the automobile business. His distributorship, the Roosevelt Automobile Company, was considered the principal importer of Fiat and Jaguar automobiles for the United States.

Despite his failure to move from Congress to a governorship then on to the White House as his father had done, Roosevelt remained active in politics. In 1960 he assisted in the presidential campaign of Senator John F. Kennedy, using his name and likeness to his father to help Kennedy win key states, including West Virginia, in the Democratic primaries.

In return for Roosevelt's service during the campaign, President Kennedy appointed him under secretary of commerce in 1963. The appointment proved controversial because many questioned Roosevelt's ability to fulfill the responsibilities of the position. Nevertheless, Roosevelt's appointment was confirmed. In 1965 President Lyndon B. Johnson appointed him the first chairman of the Equal Opportunity Commission. He left that position in 1966 for a second attempt at the governorship of New York as a Liberal party candidate, but again he was defeated.

The unsuccessful race for governor in 1966 ended Roosevelt's political career. He left Washington for Millbrook, New York, where he was involved in farming and various business endeavors. In 1970 he and his second wife divorced. That year he married Felicia Schiff Warburg Sarnoff. They had no children and divorced in 1976. In 1977 he married Patricia Oakes, with whom he had one son. After their marriage ended, Roosevelt wed Linda Stevenson Weicker in 1984. Their childless marriage ended with Roosevelt's death, in Poughkeepsie, New York.

• Roosevelt is featured in numerous articles in the *New York Times*, 1937–1988, including 24 Apr. 1949, 21 Feb. 1963, and 11 Apr. 1965. Information regarding his aid to President Kennedy's campaign as well as his personal relationship with the president is in James N. Giglio, *The Presidency of John F. Kennedy* (1991). Obituaries for Roosevelt are in the *New York Times*, *Chicago Tribune*, and *Los Angeles Times*, all 18 Aug. 1988.

SHELLY L. LEMONS

ROOSEVELT, Kermit (10 Oct. 1889–4 June 1943), businessman and explorer, was born in Oyster Bay, Long Island, New York, the son of Theodore Roosevelt, twenty-sixth president of the United States, and Edith Kermit Carow. He spent his early years at family residences in New York State and Washington, D.C., as his father pursued a political career. He was nearly twelve years old when his father became president in September 1901.

A year later Kermit Roosevelt enrolled at the Groton School in Massachusetts. He graduated in 1908 and entered Harvard that fall. In contrast to his five siblings, Kermit was introspective and timid as a child, but he developed a great love of adventure through his close relationship with his father. Kermit accompanied the senior Roosevelt on western hunting and camping trips throughout his youth, and while at Harvard he served as the photographer on a lengthy expedition to East Africa led by his father.

Following graduation from Harvard in 1912, Roosevelt became an executive of the Brazil Railroad Company. A year later he accompanied his father, again serving as a photographer, on a dangerous expedition into the Brazilian wilderness to chart the River of Doubt. In 1914 Roosevelt traveled to Madrid to marry Belle Wyatt Willard, the daughter of the U.S. ambassador to Spain. The couple had four children. Roosevelt and his wife settled in Buenos Aires, Argentina, where he became the assistant manager of an American bank.

As the son of the hero of the battle of San Juan Hill, Roosevelt doubtless felt that military service was a family duty. Along with his three brothers, he eagerly joined Allied forces shortly after the United States entered World War I in 1917. He served first with the British in their campaign against the Turks, and for his gallantry he received the British Military Cross. In 1918 he transferred to the U.S. Army's First Division and served as a field artillery captain on the western front.

Upon returning to the United States in 1919, Roosevelt began his long career in the shipping industry, joining the Kerr Line as an executive. In 1920 he established the Roosevelt Steamship Co., which operated a shipping service between North America and India. In addition to his business activities, Roosevelt pursued his love of adventure. During the 1920s he hunted in Korea and India and led several collecting expeditions on behalf of the Field Museum of Natural History in Chicago with his brother Theodore Roosevelt. In the first, in 1925, he collected rare animals and birds in East Turkestan; in the second expedition, in 1928–1929, he traveled in China and brought back the first snub-nosed monkey and giant panda seen in the United States.

In 1931 the International Mercantile Marine Co. bought the Roosevelt Steamship Co., and Roosevelt became vice president of the firm. He continued in that post until 1938, when he resigned in response to the renewed German threat to peace. Roosevelt moved to England in September 1939, not long after war was declared in Europe, and he subsequently became a British citizen. He was commissioned a major in the British army that fall.

In early 1940 Roosevelt accepted a temporary commission as a colonel in the Finnish army and recruited volunteers in England to fight against the Nazis in Finland. That spring he served with the British in Norway and saw further service in Egypt during the summer. He became ill with dysentery in Africa, and its recurrence forced him to be invalided out in December and returned to England. He was evacuated to the United States for further treatment in June 1941 and subsequently rejoined his family at their home in Oyster Bay.

In April 1942, his health somewhat improved, Roosevelt enlisted in the U.S. Army as a major. He was sent with an intelligence unit to Alaska and served at Fort Richardson in Anchorage until his death there from complications of dysentery.

Roosevelt was the author of several books about his experiences as a soldier and an explorer, including *War in the Garden of Eden* (1919), an account of his service during World War I; *The Happy Hunting Grounds* (1920), a collection of his articles on hunting; *Cleared for Strange Ports* (1927); and *American Backlogs* (1928). He also wrote *Quentin Roosevelt: A Sketch with Letters* (1920), a tribute to a brother who was killed in World War I. With his brother Theodore he coauthored *East of the Sun and West of the Moon* (1926), an account of their collecting expedition in East Turkestan, and *Trailing the Giant Panda* (1929), which relates their adventures in China. Photographs by Kermit Roosevelt are included in his father's books *African Game Trails* (1910) and *Through the Brazilian Wilderness* (1914).

Like his father, Roosevelt was an avid conservationist, a member of the Dutch Reformed church, and a Republican, though he was not active politically. He served for a time as president of the Boone and Crockett Club, an organization of conservation-minded sportsmen that his father had cofounded in 1887.

• Roosevelt's papers are in the Harvard College Library and the Library of Congress. For biographical information about Roosevelt, see Hermann Hagedorn, *The Roosevelt Family of Sagamore Hill* (1954), and Theodore Roosevelt, Jr., *All in the Family* (1929). See also *The Letters of Theodore Roosevelt*, ed. Elting E. Morison and John M. Blum (8 vols., 1951–1954), selections of which are in *Letters to Kermit from Theodore Roosevelt, 1902–1908*, ed. Will Irwin (1946), and *Theodore Roosevelt's Letters to His Children*, ed. Joseph B. Bishop (1919). An obituary is in the *New York Times*, 6 June 1943.

ANN T. KEENE

ROOSEVELT, Nicholas J. (27 Dec. 1767–30 July 1854), engineer and inventor, was born in New York City, the son of Jacobus Roosevelt, a shopkeeper, and Annetje Bogard. Nicholas's brother Jacobus was the great-grandfather of Theodore Roosevelt. As a boy Roosevelt developed a great love for mechanics and built a model boat propelled by paddle wheels turned by springs and a cord. This experiment proved to be the start of his career in manufacturing steam engines and building some of the earliest steamboats. He persuaded friends to purchase land in what is now Belleville, New Jersey, and erect a metal foundry and shop. It was called Soho after the famous works of Boulton and Watt in Birmingham, England. Managing the enterprise alone, with several skilled mechanics imported from England, at first he had some success, building an engine for the Philadelphia waterworks and winning a federal contract to establish a rolling mill for copper to be used in the construction of warships. Unfortunately, the ships were never built, causing him a great financial loss.

Around 1797 he entered into an agreement with Robert R. Livingston, a wealthy New York lawyer and later minister to France, and Livingston's brother-in-law, John Stevens of Hoboken, New Jersey, another pioneer in steam propulsion for vessels, to build a steamboat. Roosevelt undertook to supply the engine, while Livingston contributed the financing and the design of the propelling apparatus, which consisted of wheels on a vertical axis submerged at the stern. Not until the middle of 1798 was the boat ready for a trial and then the *Polacca*, as it was called, could attain a disappointing speed of only three miles an hour on the Passaic River. Roosevelt tried to induce his patron to use paddle wheels on the sides, but Livingston would not change his design. Stevens and Roosevelt continued their experiments without finding a practical solution to propulsion. Despite the drawing up of a twenty-year partnership agreement, these efforts ceased when President Jefferson, in 1801, appointed Livingston minister to France.

Roosevelt's affairs were now in a precarious state and he had to close his foundry. Eight years passed before he again became engaged in the development of steamboats, this time in association with Livingston and Robert Fulton. The Louisiana Purchase in 1803, which Livingston had negotiated while serving in France, had opened up a vast new territory for settlement and commerce. No sooner had Fulton's *Clermont* made a successful trip up the Hudson in 1807 than he and Livingston acquired a monopoly on steamboat operation on the Mississippi, just as they had done in New York. They sent Roosevelt to Pittsburgh to undertake a survey. In the summer of 1809, accompanied by his wife, Lydia Latrobe—whom he had married the year before and with whom he eventually had nine children—he left Pittsburgh in a flatboat and continued to Cincinnati, Louisville, and Natchez. Most of his contacts scoffed at the idea of a little steamboat being able to overcome the strong, whirling currents. But Roosevelt gathered enough data on current velocity to conclude otherwise. So confident was he that he bought coal mines along the Ohio River and arranged to have supplies heaped upon the shore. His report encouraged his backers to go ahead, and in the spring of 1811 construction began on the banks of the Monongahela River on Fulton's plans for a side-wheeler 148 feet long with a 20-foot beam and a 7-foot draft. It was powered by a 34-inch-cylinder low-pressure engine that developed less than 100 horsepower. It was also fitted with two masts and sails.

After a short trial run up the Monongahela, the *New Orleans* commenced her maiden and historic voyage with Roosevelt and his pregnant wife as the only passengers. The crew consisted of a captain, an engineer, a pilot named Andrew Jack, six hands, two female servants, a steward, a cook, and a large Newfoundland dog named Tiger. They ran downstream between the heavily forested riverbanks for two days at a speed of eight to ten miles an hour, "as jolly a set as ever floated on the Ohio," according to the account written much later by J. H. B. Latrobe, Mrs. Roosevelt's brother. After stopping at Cincinnati and reaching Louisville on 1 October, they had to wait for nearly two months before the water was deep enough to navigate the Falls of the Ohio. Just as the water began to rise, Mrs. Roosevelt gave birth.

Finally, in the last week in November, the time had come to proceed. It was a tense moment as they put on maximum steam, and with safety valve shrieking the *New Orleans* headed into white water, flashing past black rocks and pitching forward. "Not a word was spoken; the two pilots directed the men at the helm by motions of their hands. Even the great Newfoundland dog" sensed the danger and crouched at Mrs. Roosevelt's feet. Fortunately, the passage was soon over and the boat rounded to safety below the falls.

That danger surmounted, Roosevelt and his party soon encountered others that threatened disaster. In the fall of 1811 violent earthquakes shook the Mississippi Valley. Mrs. Roosevelt recorded that she "lived in constant fright, unable to sleep or sew or read." Hostile Chickasaw Indians, who called the steamboat "fire canoe," pursued in their canoes but could not catch it. To them the vessel presaged evil, the sparks from the chimney like the comet preceding the earthquake and the revolving paddles like the rumbling of the earth. One night Roosevelt awoke to discover the *New Orleans* on fire, and part of the forward cabin was destroyed before the blaze could be extinguished.

From Louisville on no more coal was available, so every afternoon the steamer tied up to a bank and the crew went ashore to cut wood. At New Madrid terrified refugees, their homes swallowed up by the earthquake, begged to come aboard, a plea that had to be denied because of lack of room and food. The earthquake also caused many changes in the river's course that confused the pilot. Despite these incidents, the first steamboat on the Ohio and Mississippi rivers was able to reach New Orleans on 12 January 1812. A week later it started regular runs between New Orleans and Natchez with passengers and freight. In July 1814 it sank near Baton Rouge.

In the belief that he was entitled to a patent for use of vertical paddle wheels, Roosevelt applied for one, which was granted on 1 December 1814. He also applied to the New Jersey legislature for similar protection, but it was rejected because of the objections of Fulton and Livingston. Roosevelt withdrew from active work and spent the remainder of his life with his family in Skaneateles, Onondaga County, New York, where he died.

• There is no known collection of Roosevelt's papers. Some details of his life can be found in Charles Barney Whittelsey, *The Roosevelt Genealogy, 1649–1902* (1902). His work with the steamboat is covered by J. H. B. Latrobe, *A Lost Chapter in the History of the Steamboat* (1871). Roosevelt receives extensive coverage in G. H. Preble, *A Chronological History of the Origin and Development of Steam Navigation* (1883), and John H. Morrison, *History of American Steam Navigation* (1958). Some detail is filled in by Leonard V. Huber, "Heyday of the Floating Palace," *American Heritage* 8, no. 6 (Oct. 1957), pp. 15–25, 96–98.

ELLSWORTH S. GRANT

ROOSEVELT, Theodore (27 Oct. 1858–6 Jan. 1919), twenty-sixth president of the United States, was born in New York City. His father, Theodore Roosevelt, Sr., a partner in a prosperous family glass-importing firm, was a buoyant, dominant man with a self-described "troublesome conscience." He imbued his son with an acute sense of civic and moral responsibility. He also pressed him excessively. Father, wrote Theodore, "was the best man I ever knew" and "the only man of whom I was really afraid." To his son's enduring regret, he bought his way out of military service in the Civil War in deference to the sensibilities of his Georgian wife, whose brothers were active Confederates. His mother, companionable, intelligent, and pleasure-loving Martha Bullock, was neurasthenic and tended to avoid many responsibilities. From her came Theodore's humorous strain and delight in storytelling.

As a youth Theodore Roosevelt was frail, asthmatic, and nearsighted. He was educated by private tutors until he entered Harvard College in 1876, and he read voraciously even before glasses gave him almost normal vision. By his fourteenth year he had mastered Darwin. He also had begun to acquire the practical knowledge that enabled him to become an accomplished field naturalist. At Harvard, where he ranked twenty-first in a class of 171 and "second among the gentlemen," in his own phrase, he won election to Phi Beta Kappa, while gradually shifting his academic emphasis from natural history to political economy. He became a competent horseman, boxer, and marksman. He published (with a friend) a paper of professional quality on birds of the Adirondacks and wrote a senior thesis that called for limited voting rights for women and their "most absolute equality" in marriage. He also wrote the first two chapters of *The Naval War of 1812* (1882), a work of meticulous scholarship acclaimed in British and American naval circles alike.

By Roosevelt's graduation the qualities that were to attract, repel, or bemuse his countrymen for four decades became pronounced. He abounded in physical and mental energy, acted often on impulse and at times on shrewd calculation, and generally exuded warmth, affection, and charm. Yet he was rarely overly familiar; neither in college nor in the West, where cowboys addressed him as "Mister," did he lose his sense of station. He possessed the gift of words, though he limited their flow with difficulty; and even when he was moralizing, his force and imagery made him unfailingly interesting. A compulsive competitor, he could be, and sometimes was, ruthless. He was also resolute.

"See that girl," Roosevelt remarked at Harvard of Alice Hathaway Lee, a tall, graceful, and somewhat coquettish seventeen-year-old Brahmin from Chestnut Hill. "I am going to marry her. She won't have me, but I am going to have her." Four months after his graduation in June 1880 they were married. A few weeks earlier Roosevelt had enrolled in Columbia Law School. He was elected to the New York State Assembly the following autumn but continued to study law conscientiously. Only after Columbia raised its requirement to three years and the state changed its licensing procedure did he give up the formal study of law.

Politics at once gratified Roosevelt's craving for raw power and his urge to promote the common good. Nominally a Republican, he soon affronted party leaders by forcing an investigation of reports that a Republican-appointed justice of the state supreme court had colluded with Jay Gould and others in a "stock-jobbing" deal. He also pressed a bundle of "good government" measures on the GOP majority. Roosevelt, declared the mugwump *New York Evening Post*, had "accomplished more good than any man of his age and experience . . . in years." By the end of his third and last term his reputation for independence within a party framework was statewide. Furthermore, he had made a first break with laissez-faire. The extremes of poverty and wealth, he said of a union-sponsored measure to regulate working conditions, demand that we "modify the principles or doctrines on which we manage our system of government."

Midway through Roosevelt's third term in 1884, his wife died after giving birth to a daughter. He immersed himself in legislative matters to the end of the session, then sought solace on his ranch in western Dakota—"a land of vast silent spaces, a place of grim beauty." He wrote a deeply felt private memorial to his wife and never mentioned her again, not even to their daughter, Alice. For a while the 25-year-old widower considered a life of ranching, hunting, and writing.

He expanded his cattle operation, published *Hunting Trips of a Ranchman* (1885), and wrote *Thomas Hart Benton* (1887). He also began to prepare to write his magnum opus, the four-volume *Winning of the West* (1889–1896), a flawed and unevenly researched work with touches of brilliance.

Meanwhile politics and romance had drawn Roosevelt away from Dakota. In New York City in the fall of 1886 he ran as the Republican candidate for mayor, finishing a poor third to Democrat Abram S. Hewitt, the winner, and to Henry George, the author of *Progress and Poverty* and candidate of the United Labor party. Roosevelt then went to London, where on 2 December he married his childhood friend, Edith Kermit Carow. A handsome, strong-willed woman four years his junior, Edith, he noted, "was not only cultured, but scholarly." Quietly, with a rapier-like thrust at times, she both moderated and helped sustain him. She also accepted many of his more disruptive actions in the realization that they "were best for him." She raised Alice Lee and, between 1887 and 1897, had four sons and a daughter of her own: Theodore, Jr., Kermit, Ethel, Archibald, and Quentin.

Three months after his remarriage, Roosevelt joined the ineffectual U.S. Civil Service Commission in Washington, D.C. He soon became chairman. Not only did he regard appointment and advancement on merit as a tangible measure of an open society, he viewed it as a linchpin of scientific administration. His imaginative and energetic enforcement of the law did much to make merit an integral, if hardly inclusive, component of federal governance. Concurrently, Roosevelt's political philosophy continued to mature. Too astute a student of nature to believe that Darwin's theory of natural selection applied unqualifiedly to human social evolution, he concluded that we should "modify the principles or doctrines" of government to create a more just social environment.

Roosevelt returned to New York in 1895 to serve two turbulently constructive years as president of the New York City Police Board. He regularized discipline, upgraded the selection of officers, and increased dismissals almost ten-fold. He also instituted a formal training program and partially modernized the force and its equipment. As a patrolman remarked when Roosevelt left to become assistant secretary of the navy in 1897, "It's tough on the force, for he was dead square, was Roosevelt, and we needed him in the business."

Roosevelt's year in the navy department was in the same mode. He improved morale, administration, and tactical efficiency, and he publicized the case for increased naval power and technological improvement. He also argued behind the scenes for war against Spain. Acting on his own while Secretary John D. Long was away from his office one afternoon ten days after the battleship *Maine* sank off Havana, Roosevelt enjoined Commodore George Dewey in Hong Kong to prepare to engage the Spanish fleet in the Philippines in the event of war. The order accorded with standing policy and was not reversed.

Hardly had war come in April than Roosevelt resigned to organize the First U.S. Volunteer Cavalry Regiment under the command of Colonel Leonard Wood. It was soon dubbed the "Rough Riders." Roosevelt's "heart is right, and he means well," Secretary Long wrote, "but it is one of those cases of aberration-desertion-vain-glory." Actually, Roosevelt had been champing for war for years. As he later said, military combat afforded him the "chance to cut my little notch on the stick that stands as a measuring rod in every family." It was, furthermore, the ultimate test of national character. "No triumph of peace," he declared at the Naval War College in 1897, "is quite so great as the supreme triumph of war." The United States had to expand its influence or lose place, power, and prestige. "If . . . we lose the virile, manly qualities, and sink into a nation of mere hucksters . . . subordinating everything to mere ease of life, then we shall indeed reach a condition worse than that of the ancient civilizations in the years of their decay."

Promoted to commander of the regiment after the first skirmish in Cuba, Colonel Roosevelt led his unmounted cowboy and Ivy League volunteers to victory in a fierce battle for Kettle Hill, in the San Juan ridges outside Santiago. Alone on horseback, he was nicked on the elbow by a bullet as troopers fell on each side. Afterward he gloated that he had "doubled-up" a Spaniard and invited postbattle visitors to "look at these damned Spanish dead." In the field hospitals afterward, he acted with great sensitivity.

Less than two weeks after the Rough Riders were mustered out in September 1898, Colonel Roosevelt became the Republican gubernatorial candidate. Although New York State GOP leaders feared his independent strain, they deemed him the only Republican who could divert attention from charges of corruption in the administration of the Erie Canal. Predictably, his charisma and loudly trumpeted war record pushed him far enough ahead of the ticket to eke out a 17,794-vote victory.

The governorship foreshadowed Roosevelt's presidency. He deferred to the Republican leadership on small matters, fought it on large ones, and imbued officials with a heightened sense of the public trust. Convinced that many social and economic problems were beyond the capacity of cities and towns to solve, he inclined more and more toward centralized, interventionist government. He supported regulation of factories and limitations on the working hours of women and children. He approved an eight-hour day for state employees on the premise that the state should "set a good example as an employer." He spurred the legislature to repeal a law authorizing separate schools for blacks and whites on a local option basis. Terming light taxation of public utilities "an evident injustice," he also supported a franchise tax. Finally, he took important steps to conserve the state's forests, wildlife, and natural beauty. As the Democratic *New York World* conceded, "the controlling purpose and general course of his administration have been high and good."

Meanwhile the governor's alienation of utility and insurance interests prompted Republican leaders to ease him out of the state by supporting him for vice president in 1900. Roosevelt won election in the Republican landslide and became president on 14 September 1901, the day after William McKinley died of an assassin's bullet. Just a month shy of his forty-third birthday he was the youngest chief executive in the nation's history.

Although Roosevelt promised to continue McKinley's policies "absolutely unbroken," he soon chartered his own course. He believed that the nation needed to match its administrative capacity to its economic and political capacity, and he aspired to create an administrative state staffed by experts and committed to regulation of *all* corporations in interstate commerce. His first annual message tried to deflect the states' rights argument against such a program:

When the Constitution was adopted . . . no human wisdom could foretell the sweeping changes . . . which were to take place at the beginning of the twentieth century. At that time it was accepted as a matter of course that the several states were the proper authorities to regulate . . . the comparatively insignificant and strictly localized corporate bodies of the day. The conditions are now wholly different and wholly different action is called for.

Within months Roosevelt instituted antitrust proceedings against the Northern Securities Company, a western railroad combine organized by the J. P. Morgan and other interests. His motives were complicated. He sought to test the virtually defunct Sherman Antitrust Law, signal his independence from business and congressional leaders, and affirm his executive power. He hoped, furthermore, that the threat of dissolution would prompt sophisticated businessmen to support his regulatory program. Two years later the Supreme Court upheld the government, and some forty-three antitrust suits followed.

Despite Roosevelt's resultant image as "the great trustbuster," dissolution of trusts remained secondary to his larger object: continuous regulation. In 1903, while the Northern Securities Case was still in the courts, he prevailed on Congress to create a Bureau of Corporations empowered to inspect and publicize corporate earnings. Concurrently, he encouraged passage of the Elkins bill to prohibit railroad discrimination against small shippers.

Earlier Roosevelt had come perilously close to exposing his expansive conception of his office to a Supreme Court test. In October 1902 negotiations to end a bitter, five-month-long anthracite coal strike broke down. The president feared that a shortage of fuel that winter would provoke an urban crisis "only less serious than the civil war" and that failure to act might induce an "overturn" in the fall elections. He further persuaded himself that "the supreme law of duty to the republic" required him to act. Secretly he arranged for the army to take over the mines on signal. He then disclosed his intent to the mine operators, who agreed to appointment of an independent arbitration committee that he tipped in the miners' favor. This amounted to de facto recognition of the union and established a new precedent: federal intervention to foster negotiation of a labor dispute.

Roosevelt's election to a term "in his own right" in 1904 was a foregone conclusion. He overwhelmed his colorless, conservative Democratic opponent, Judge Alton B. Parker of New York, and swept dozens of GOP congressional candidates into office with him. Even Wall Street supported the president. As the *New York Sun* explained, businessmen preferred "the impulsive candidate of the party of conservatism to the conservative candidate of the party which business regards as permanently and dangerously impulsive." With characteristic moral earnestness, Roosevelt sapped much of his potential influence over Congress his last two years in office by announcing the night of his election that he would not run for reelection in 1908.

Concurrently, the president worked relentlessly to create a more just society based on "as well planned, economical, and efficient" a centralized administration as that of the great corporations. With consummate political skill, he persuaded Congress in 1906 to support the Hepburn railroad rate bill, the Pure Food and Drug bill, federal inspection of stockyards and packing houses, and limited employer's liability. He further oversaw expansion of the civil service and encouraged appointment of many men of quality to second-tier positions. On the other hand, his cabinet appointees were undistinguished except for Elihu Root as secretary of state and, in some respects, William Howard Taft, the secretary of war.

More crucially, Roosevelt failed to transform his party into a dynamic agency of change. Republican leaders recoiled from his imperious use of power. They resented his stridency, his shrewd manipulation of the press, his use of his office as a "bully pulpit." They shared only marginally his progressive views on labor and consumer issues. And they had limited sympathy, if that, for his effort to create a new administrative state. From 1907 to the end of his administration they stood in open rebellion against him. They sided with the corporate opponents of his regulatory program, ignored six separate messages on abuse of the labor injunction, and rejected calls for tariff reduction for the Philippines. They refused to enact a model child labor law for the District of Columbia or to nationalize marriage and divorce laws. They further disregarded key recommendations of the Keep Commission on Department Methods.

Virtually giving up hope of constructive compromise, the president concentrated much of his energy on educating the public. In words that resonated with the allegations of journalists he had earlier branded "muckrakers," Roosevelt charged that representatives of "predatory wealth" were foiling his program, that corporations were purchasing politicians, and that the courts were depriving labor of the right to organize "under the guise of protecting property rights." In the older tradition of noblesse oblige and the newer mode of reform Darwinism, he insisted that it was "hypocritical baseness to speak of a girl who works in a factory where the dangerous machinery is unprotected as having the 'right' freely to contract to expose herself to dangers to life and limb." He called for guarantees of "a larger share of the wealth" to labor, and he proposed income, and especially inheritance, taxes on the very rich. He also challenged the sincerity of the opponents of federal regulation: "There has been a curious revival of the doctrine of State rights . . . by the people who know that the States cannot . . . control the corporations."

On race, political and temperamental considerations compromised Roosevelt's marginally advanced views. Thus, in a notorious incident in 1906, he summarily discharged "without honor" three companies of black soldiers for engaging in a "conspiracy of silence" over the fatal shooting of a white bartender in Brownsville, Texas. None of the discharged soldiers was ever tried in a court of law, military or civil; sixty years later close historical investigation pointed to white civilians as the probable culprits.

Roosevelt continued, meanwhile, to push for rational use of the nation's natural resources. Driven by a holistic view of society and informed by his knowledge of nature as enriched by his experience in the West, his policies rested on a blend of applied science, administrative efficiency, and democratic ideals unexampled to that time. Central were the concepts, as propounded by Gifford Pinchot, chief forester of the United States, and others, that "every stream was a unit from its source to its mouth" and that natural resources had multiple uses: The forest should act as a reservoir, inhibit erosion of crop and grazing lands, and afford habitat to wildlife. It also should supply lumber for housing and other human purposes. Against the opposition of powerful members of his own party, and at times of both parties, Roosevelt pressed Congress and the states to place the future public interest above the current private interest. The reserves, he insisted, should be "set apart forever" for the benefit of all the people, not "sacrificed to the short-sighted greed of a few"; they should even provide "free camping grounds."

The first fruits of the multiple-use policy came with the Democratic-sponsored Newlands Reclamation Act of 1902. It encouraged federal construction of vast storage dams, ostensibly to irrigate small farms at low cost. Three years later Roosevelt induced Congress to transfer the forest reserves from the Department of Interior to the rehabilitated Forest Service under Pinchot in Agriculture. A small revolution followed. Selective cutting was mandated, fees imposed for grazing on the public lands, overgrazing was reduced far below the level on private lands, and development of waterpower sites by private utilities was subjected to enlightened controls. An act of 1906 established the principle of fees for grazing on public lands, and a second law enabled Roosevelt to proclaim a notable series of national monuments from Mount Olympus to the Grand Canyon.

By 1907 Congress was even more hostile to Roosevelt's conservation program than to his proposals for incremental social and economic reforms. It prohibited the president from creating new national forests in six western states. (Roosevelt capitalized on the ten days he had to sign the measure by proclaiming twenty-one new forests embracing sixteen million acres.) It disregarded the multipurpose river valley recommendations of the Inland Waterways Commission and refused to continue the commission itself. It even declined, on a loosely related matter, to publish the seminal report of the Country Life Commission.

All this struck a heavy blow at the president's grand design for a new administrative state. Nonetheless, the sum of his achievements was impressive. Besides eighteen national monuments, he created 150 national forests, fifty-one bird reservations, and four national game preserves. Altogether 230 million acres were placed under federal protection. By calling the first national conference of governors in history in 1908, he also stimulated the formation of forty-one state conservation commissions. As his bitter enemy Senator Robert M. La Follette of Wisconsin wrote, Roosevelt had inspired "a world movement for . . . saving for the human race the things on which alone a peaceful, progressive, and happy life can be founded."

Roosevelt also stamped his imprint on foreign policy with unusual force. He gloried in the opportunities for national expression afforded by world power, and he willingly shouldered the responsibilities thrust upon him. Occasionally he returned to the view that a far-flung empire was the hallmark of greatness. "Rome expanded and passed away," he wrote, "but all western Europe, both Americas, Australia and large parts of Asia and Africa to this day continue the history of Rome. . . . Spain expanded and fell, but a whole continent to this day . . . is covered with commonwealths of the Spanish tongue and culture. . . . England expanded and England will fall. But think of what she will leave behind her."

In practice, Roosevelt reacted far more to changes in the balance of power than to his own rolling periods. Assuredly, he maintained a hegemonic posture toward Latin America to the end of his presidency. But in the Pacific and elsewhere he sharply refined his conception of the national interest. He admitted an Asian country—Japan—into the group of "superior" nations sanctioned to dominate the world. He encouraged preparation of the Philippines for eventual independence. And he worked conscientiously to foster peace in both Europe and Asia. Even his vaunted buildup of the American navy was comparatively modest.

Roosevelt agreed with A. T. Mahan (*The Influence of Sea Power upon History*) and others that the United States needed a first-class navy to foster and protect its commercial and political interests. He also subscribed uncritically at first to Secretary of State Hay's Open Door policy. But neither his commitment to Mahanism nor his support of the Open Door proved wholly consistent. His own supervision of the navy department was erratic, though constructive on balance, and that of the department's several secretaries was lackluster. Roosevelt reinvigorated McKinley's program of two new battleships a year and maintained it to 1905. Satisfied that the buildup made the United States "a good second to France" and put it about on a par with Germany, he announced that a replacement policy would suffice. (Congress authorized two ships anyway.) Prompted by new international tensions in 1906, especially with Japan, Roosevelt returned to expansionism, including dreadnoughts. Significantly, he made no effort to increase the regular army's authorized strength of 85,555; his concern was tactical efficiency grounded on technological and administrative improvement, as exemplified by his earlier support of Secretary of War Root's modernization program.

From the beginning, Roosevelt's conviction that the Atlantic and Pacific oceans should be linked by a United States–controlled canal propelled him deep into Latin American affairs. In 1902 he apparently induced Kaiser Wilhelm II to resort to international arbitration of a dispute over payment of debts to German citizens. A year later he took the most controversial action of his presidency. Convinced that Colombia had played fast and loose in negotiations over United States construction of a canal through the Colombian state of Panama, he abetted a revolution by the Panamanians. One result was a legacy of ill will that Roosevelt himself augmented. "I took the canal zone," he declared in his autobiography, "and let Congress debate."

Thereafter, Roosevelt's resolve to restrict European influence in the Caribbean directly reflected his interest in the Panama Canal and its protection. In 1904, to preclude a debt-collection mission in Santa Domingo by Germany, Italy, and Spain, the president took over that revolution-wracked country's customs temporarily. He had, he explained, "about the same desire to annex it as a gorged boa constrictor might have to swallow a porcupine wrong-end-to." But he believed nonetheless that the United States had both the right and the duty to serve as a Western Hemisphere police force in the event of "chronic wrongdoing, or an impotence which results in a general loosening of the ties of civilized society." Under this formulation, which became known as the Roosevelt Corollary to the Monroe Doctrine, he sent troops into Cuba to avert revolution in 1907.

In the Pacific, where Roosevelt came to perceive the Philippines as "our heel of Achilles," he grew increasingly sensitive to the limits of American power as he maneuvered to create a balance of power. He viewed Japan as a counterpoise to Russia, and in 1902 he pledged the United States to silent partnership in the Japanese-British naval alliance. Three years later he fostered mediation of the Russo–Japanese War, partly to keep Japan from weighting the balance too heavily. The action earned Roosevelt the Nobel Peace Prize. Concurrently, he secretly acquiesced to Japanese suzerainty in Korea in return for a disclaimer of "any aggressive designs whatever" in the Philippines. In 1906 he denounced a decision by the San Francisco School Board to segregate Japanese schoolchildren as "a crime against a friendly nation" and then prevailed on the board and the Japanese government to accept a so-called "Gentlemen's Agreement" that provided for the board to rescind the segregation order and for Japan to curb the emigration of peasants and laborers.

The president made a final concession to Japan in 1908 while the American fleet was still on its world cruise. The nonbinding Root–Takahira Agreement implicitly recognized Japanese economic ascendancy in Manchuria in return for a reaffirmation of the status quo in the Pacific and the Open Door in China. Two years after he left office, Roosevelt tried to impress the limits of American power on his chosen successor, Taft, to accept the limits of American power. A successful war over the Open Door in Manchuria, he warned, "would require a fleet as good as that of England, plus an army as good as that of Germany."

On several other fronts, Roosevelt gave moderate support to international mechanisms. He did so without illusion; always his commitment to large American interests transcended his internationalist impulses. In 1903, for example, he virtually forced the British to support the American position in the Alaskan boundary controversy with Canada. Yet he also believed that power carried the responsibility to promote peace even when the national interest was not directly involved, and in 1906 he fostered the Algeciras Conference to resolve a dispute between France and Germany. By the end of his administration Roosevelt had sponsored twenty-four binding arbitration treaties, cosponsored the Central American Peace Conference of 1907, and endorsed Root's plan for the Hague Conference to create a permanent Court of Arbitral Justice.

Less than a month after Roosevelt left the White House in March 1909, he went to Africa to hunt and incidentally collect fauna for the Smithsonian Institution. The Colonel, as he then preferred to be called, returned in 1910 to a Republican party beginning to split openly into conservative and progressive factions. Taft, who had long disapproved of Roosevelt's broad construction of presidential power, was aligned with the conservatives, Pinchot with the progressives. Roosevelt soon drove the wedge deeper. "This New Nationalism," he declared in a militant statement of his still-evolving views, "regards the executive power as the steward of the public welfare"; it further holds that the judiciary should protect "human welfare rather than . . . property."

On 21 February 1912 the Colonel announced that his hat "is in the ring." He then embittered conservatives irreparably by endorsing the recall of state judicial decisions involving constitutional interpretation. Although he outpolled Taft by 2 to 1 in the Republican presidential primaries, he failed to win the GOP nomination because conservatives controlled the party machinery in nonprimary states. Reluctantly, for he knew that he could not win, he became the candidate of his fervent supporters, the newly formed Progressive ("Bull Moose") party.

The Progressive platform embodied much of the program Roosevelt had advocated in the last years of his presidency and amplified from 1910 to 1912. It called for "permanent active supervision" of corporations in interstate commerce, for income and inheritance taxes, and for medical, unemployment, and old age insurance. It also endorsed woman suffrage. Only on civil rights for blacks was it silent. Roosevelt won 27 percent of the popular vote in the general election—the highest ever recorded by a third-party candidate. But Woodrow Wilson, the moderately progressive Democratic governor of New Jersey, captured the presidency with 42 percent of the popular vote and forty states in the electoral college. Taft ran a weak third.

In the next two years, Roosevelt wrote his autobiography, made a memorable sally into art criticism (the necessary penalty of creativity, he wrote of the historic Armory Show of 1913, "is a liability to extravagance"), and explored the unmapped River of Doubt in Brazil, renamed the "Rio Roosevelt." He also campaigned for Bull Moose congressional candidates, though with scant enthusiasm; the outbreak of war in Europe in August 1914 had radically altered his priorities.

The former president first viewed the war as a strategic realist: He perceived that a decisive Allied victory would disrupt the balance of power in Europe, and he feared that German domination of the Continent would challenge American hegemony in the Caribbean. He soon concluded, however, that Germany was the greater threat and that President Wilson should have protested the invasion of Belgium at the outset. Muting his views in deference to antiwar Progressive congressional candidates in the Midwest, Roosevelt waited until after the elections to arraign Wilson. Meanwhile he embarked on a lonely and politically courageous crusade for military preparedness.

For Roosevelt, Germany's warning in February 1915 that neutral ships risked destruction in the war zone around the British Isles completed the metamorphosis of the war from a strategic to a moral struggle. National character and American rights now became the transcendent issue. "We owe it not only to humanity but to our national self respect" to act, the Colonel declared when the British liner *Lusitania* was torpedoed in the war zone with the loss of 124 Americans. Hence his searing indictments of peace-at-any-price pacifists, his insistent demands for universal military service, his poignant statement when his youngest son was shot down over German-occupied France in 1918: "It is very dreadful that he should have been killed, it would have been worse if he had not gone."

Without quite calling for war, the Colonel worked resolutely to move the nation to war. Privately asserting that Republican presidential candidate Charles Evans Hughes was somewhat more likely than Wilson to "rise to a very big height" in a crisis, he jettisoned the Progressive party in 1916 to support Hughes and the Republicans. With good cause, he blasted the Wilson administration for its demoralizing delays in industrial mobilization after the United States entered the war. He stiffened his demands "for one hundred percent, undivided loyalty," and he loosely read "Bolshevist" into labor strife. He even urged the public schools to stop teaching German. Yet he remained the progressive moralist on some issues. He scorned draft deferments for the privileged, fulminated against the making of "unearned and improper fortunes out of the war," and backed an effort by La Follette and others to increase an administration bill for a 60 percent excess profits tax. He further urged party and nation to pursue a moderately progressive course after the war.

Roosevelt's attitude toward a league of nations varied with his changing emphases on realism, nationalism, and internationalism. He had called for a world league to enforce peace in his Nobel Peace Prize address of 1910, and he had affirmed the concept in 1914, two years before President Wilson espoused it. In 1915 he said further discussion was "inopportune." Subsequently, he demanded unconditional surrender of Germany and dismissed Wilson's Fourteen Points as "Fourteen Scraps of Paper." He also deplored Wilson's failure to share his view of American dependence on British naval power. The Royal Navy, he insisted, "should be the most powerful in the world." Only after he decided to bring the GOP's nationalist and internationalist factions together in 1918 did he half-heartedly agree to support the idea of a league, and then only "as an *addition to*, . . . not as a *substitute for*," American military power. Had he lived, he probably would have been the Republican nominee for president in 1920. He died in his home, "Sagamore Hill," at Oyster Bay, Long Island.

In foreign affairs, Theodore Roosevelt's legacy is judicious support of the national interest and promotion of world stability through the maintenance of a balance of power; creation or strengthening of international agencies, and resort to their use when practicable; and implicit resolve to use military force, if feasible, to foster legitimate American interests. In domestic affairs, it is the use of government to advance the public interest. "If on this new continent," he said, "we merely build another country of great but unjustly divided material prosperity, we shall have done nothing."

• Roosevelt's letters and papers are at the Library of Congress, as is the Theodore Roosevelt Association Film Collection. The most complete collection of printed materials, photographs, and family papers is in the Harvard College Library. The collection also includes scrapbooks of newspaper clippings. *The Letters of Theodore Roosevelt*, ed. Elting Morison et al. (8 vols., 1951–1954), contains some 6,500 letters. Roosevelt's books, including his autobiography, voluminous nature writings, collected essays, and many speeches and messages are reprinted in *Memorial Edition: Works of Theodore Roosevelt*, ed. Hermann Hadedorn (24 vols., 1923–1926). *Theodore Roosevelt Cyclopedia*, ed. Albert Bushnell Hart and Herbert Ronald Ferleger (1941), as revised in 1989 by John A. Gable, is especially useful for students. The same holds for Gable, "The Historiography of Theodore Roosevelt," in *Theodore Roosevelt: Many-Sided American*, ed. Natalie A. Naylor et al. (1992), a compilation of recent essays on many of the more controversial aspects of Roosevelt's life, ranging from his study of law to his values as a hunter. Of importance also is the *Theodore Roosevelt Association Journal*, 1975–.

David G. McCullough, *Mornings on Horseback* (1981), offers psychological and social insights into young Roosevelt and his circle. Edmund Morris, *The Rise of Theodore Roosevelt* (1979), is a penetrating and superbly written account of Roosevelt's life to the eve of his presidency. The tone of William Henry Harbaugh, *Power and Responsibility: The Life and Times of Theodore Roosevelt* (1961), is described by its title. Nathan Miller, *Theodore Roosevelt: A Life* (1992), is a popular and reliable synthesis. Also see Edward Wagenknecht's richly diverse treatment, *The Seven Worlds of Theodore Roosevelt* (1958).

Of the short studies, John Morton Blum, *The Republican Roosevelt* (1954), is notably insightful. Lewis L. Gould's authoritative *The Presidency of Theodore Roosevelt* (1991) is the best book on the subject. George E. Mowry's seminal *Theodore Roosevelt and the Progressive Movement* (1946) is well complemented by Gable's analysis of the party on both state and national levels in *The Bull Moose Years* (1978). Paul Russell Cutright, *Theodore Roosevelt: The Making of a Conservationist* (1985), happily incorporates much of his earlier study of Roosevelt as a naturalist. Stephen Skowronek, *Building a New American State: The Expansion of National Administrative Capacities, 1877–1920* (1982), is a comparative analysis of the failure of Roosevelt, Taft, and Wilson to create a new administrative state.

Howard K. Beale, *Theodore Roosevelt and the Rise of America to World Power* (1956), is still worth reading. For a full bibliography see Gould's *The Presidency*. John Milton Cooper, Jr., offers a fascinating analysis of Roosevelt foreign policy views in *The Warrior and the Priest: Woodrow Wilson and Theodore Roosevelt* (1983). Two other challenging interpretive works, both favorable to Roosevelt, are Richard H. Collin, *Theodore Roosevelt, Culture, Diplomacy, and Expansion* (1985) and *Theodore Roosevelt's Caribbean: The Panama Canal, the Monroe Doctrine, and the Latin American Context* (1990). See also McCullough, *The Path between the Seas: The Creation of the Panama Canal, 1870–1914* (1977). A substantive obituary is in the *New York Times*, 7 Jan. 1919.

WILLIAM H. HARBAUGH

ROOSEVELT, Theodore, Jr. (13 Sept. 1887–12 July 1944), public official and military officer, was born in Oyster Bay, New York, the son of Theodore Roosevelt, twenty-sixth president of the United States, and Edith Kermit Carow. He grew up in the shadow of his presidential father, who pushed his son toward ever greater accomplishments. He entered Harvard University in 1905 and graduated in 1908. Two years later he married Eleanor Alexander; they had three sons and a daughter.

"Ted" Roosevelt worked in the carpet trade on the West Coast until 1912, when he switched to investment banking. He was one of the organizers of the Plattsburgh preparedness movement before U.S. entry into World War I. After the United States declared war on Germany in April 1917, thanks to the influence of his father, Captain Roosevelt went to France under General John J. Pershing and achieved a distinguished combat record. For gallantry he received the Croix de Guerre, the Distinguished Service Cross, and the Distinguished Service Medal.

Roosevelt was one of the founders of the American Legion. He saw the veterans' organization as a way to overcome the class, sectional, and racial divisions within American society. In 1919 he was elected to the New York Assembly and served two one-year terms. Politically conservative, he nonetheless argued against the expulsion of Socialist members from the legislature. He campaigned for Warren G. Harding and the Republican ticket in 1920. His distant relation, Franklin D. Roosevelt, was the Democratic vice presidential candidate, and Theodore Roosevelt called him "a maverick" who did not have "the brand of our family" (Snyder, p. 97).

In 1921 Harding appointed Roosevelt the assistant secretary of the navy, a post Roosevelt's father had held twenty years earlier. He worked closely with Secretary of State Charles Evans Hughes during the Washington Conference of 1922 that sought to limit naval construction. His emerging political career hit a snag, however, when he became entangled in the scandal involving the Teapot Dome oil deposits in Wyoming.

Roosevelt ran for governor of New York in 1924 against Alfred E. Smith and made an energetic campaign. The Democrats, in turn, had his cousin Eleanor Roosevelt, Franklin D. Roosevelt's wife, tour the state with a tea kettle to suggest that the Republican Roosevelt had been implicated in scandal. The episode further enhanced the bitterness between the two branches of the Roosevelt family. Ted Roosevelt lost his race to Smith by more than 100,000 votes.

Out of politics, Roosevelt traveled and hunted in Asia for the next several years. In 1929 President Herbert Hoover named him governor of Puerto Rico, where Roosevelt worked to improve education, sought to attract industry, and made gains in land distribution. Hoover selected him to be governor general of the Philippines in January 1932. Again, Roosevelt proved to be a capable administrator who stressed education and land reform. The election of Franklin D. Roosevelt to the presidency in 1932 meant that Ted Roosevelt's political career had once again ended. He told reporters, who asked about his family connection to the incoming president, that he was "fifth cousin, *about to be* removed" (Snyder, p. 99).

During the 1930s Roosevelt worked for the publishing house Doubleday, Doran and was active in a number of charitable causes, including the Boy Scouts and the National Association for the Advancement of Colored People. He became a strong critic of the New Deal. After the Second World War began, however, he came out for the Destroyer for Bases deal in 1940 and the introduction of the military draft. He returned to active duty in 1941 as a brigadier general with the U.S. Army.

Roosevelt fought in North Africa, Italy, and France. He won the affection of the troops for his bravery under fire and his evident concern for their survival and welfare. His superiors deemed Roosevelt a lax disciplinarian and relieved him of his command in Sicily. However, Roosevelt pressed to be included in the D-Day landings. His superiors knew of his fighting spirit, and when the Normandy invasion occurred on 6 June 1944, Roosevelt, as deputy commander of the Fourth Division, was in the first wave to hit Utah Beach. Landed at the wrong place, he nonetheless led the troops ashore. He told his men, "We're going to start the war from right here" (Nalty, p. 85). Throughout the day, he directed his men to move inland despite German fire aimed at his position. For this action, which General Omar Bradley called the bravest he had ever seen in combat, Roosevelt received the Congressional Medal of Honor posthumously. He died of a heart attack in his camp in Normandy.

Theodore Roosevelt, Jr.'s political accomplishments did not equal those of his father. He lacked the elder Roosevelt's sense of timing and ability to discern the popular mood. On the battlefield, however, the eldest son served with bravery and distinction in two major wars and won decorations that his presidential father never received. Friends recalled his bravery in combat and his infectious personality that inspired his troops. A secondary figure in politics and business, Roosevelt's record as a soldier was outstanding.

• The Theodore Roosevelt, Jr., Papers are at the Manuscript Division, Library of Congress; the Theodore Roosevelt, Sr., Papers, the Kermit Roosevelt Papers, and the Alice Roosevelt Longworth Papers, also at the Library of Congress, have important materials. Roosevelt wrote several books, including, with Kermit Roosevelt, *East of the Sun and West of the Moon* (1926) and *Trailing the Giant Panda* (1929), and, with Harold Coolidge, *The Three Kingdoms of Indo-China* (1933). See also his article "A Boy's Book Rambles," *Bookman* 60 (1925): 689–91. A memoir by his wife is Eleanor Roosevelt, *Day before Yesterday: The Reminiscences of Mrs. Theodore Roosevelt, Jr.* (1959). For further biographical information, see Lawrence H. Madaras, "The Public Career of Theodore Roosevelt, Jr." (Ph.D. diss., New York Univ., 1964); and Richard Loosbrock, "Worthy Son of a Worthy Sire—The Early Years of Theodore Roosevelt, Jr.," and Charles W. Snyder, "An American Original: Theodore Roosevelt, Jr.," both in *Theodore Roosevelt: Many-Sided American*, ed. Natalie A. Naylor et al. (1992). A more critical appraisal of Roosevelt is Michael Pearlman, *To Make Democracy Safe for America: Patricians and Preparedness in the Progressive Era* (1984). Roosevelt's place in his family is assessed in Peter Collier, *The Roosevelts: An American Saga* (1994). Bernard C. Nalty, ed., *D-Day: Operation Overlord from the Landing at Normandy to the Liberation of Paris* (1993), touches on Roosevelt's combat performance. The *New York Times*, 14 July 1944, has an extended obituary.

LEWIS L. GOULD

ROOSMA, John Seiba (3 Sept. 1900–13 Nov. 1983), athlete and army officer, was born in Passaic, New Jersey, the son of Simon Roosma, a building contractor, and Mamie Casteline. In his youth, Roosma was a standout basketball player on the Passaic High School "Wonder Teams" that won 159 straight games from 1919 to 1925. Roosma's teams initiated the streak, and

his ability to score was largely responsible for their success. Roosma played from 1919 to 1921, when his teams compiled the first fifty-seven victories of the streak. Roosma's 1918–1919 squad had won twenty games in a row before bowing to Union Hill High School in the state championship game. But then his teams rebounded to win New Jersey state high school basketball championships in 1920 and 1921. He averaged twenty-eight points per game during his senior season and was named to the all-state team for three years in a row. Ernest "Prof " Blood, coach of the Wonder Teams, considered Roosma his greatest player. Roosma, he said, was "smart, had basketball sense, could dribble, jump, guard and shoot with remarkable accuracy." Of equal importance for the team's success was his role as a leader who, according to Blood, "knew just how to adapt the team to certain conditions."

Roosma, who was 6'1½" tall and weighed 188 pounds, continued his athletic career at the U.S. Military Academy at the urging of General Douglas MacArthur, superintendent of the academy. A player and team captain during his senior year, Roosma led army basketball teams to a 70–3 record and one undefeated season, 1922–1923. During one stretch, his teams won thirty-three consecutive games. Reportedly the first collegian to score 1,000 points during his career, Roosma was named to several all-American teams. For his achievements, he was awarded the Army Athletic Sabre Award, which signifies all-around athletic excellence. As in high school, Roosma also played baseball at the academy and soccer and football as well.

Upon graduating from West Point in 1926, Roosma served as an army officer for thirty years. Following domestic tours of duty at Fort Benning, Georgia, he served in the Philippines and in China from 1931 to 1934. He returned to West Point in 1935 and served as provost marshal (chief of police) before being sent to Hawaii in 1940. Stationed at the Schofield Barracks near Pearl Harbor, Roosma and his family (in 1926 he had married Marjorie Henion, with whom he had three children) endured the Japanese bombardment before he was reassigned to Fort Benning to command the student training regiment in 1942. The following year in the European theater, he commanded the 334th Infantry Regiment, which attacked the Siegfried Line, German installations along the French border. He was then named provost marshal of the Delta Base at Marseilles, France. Following the war, he came home to serve as provost marshal of New York City and northern New Jersey. In 1950 he returned to Europe to serve the Seventh U.S. Army at Stuttgart, Germany, in the same capacity. Three years later he became chief of the First Army information office at Fort Jay on Governor's Island, New York. He retired from active duty in 1956 at the rank of colonel.

Following his retirement, from 1957 to 1958 Roosma was executive director of the local chapter of the United Fund in Passaic and the surrounding region and from 1959 to 1962 was commandant at the Bordentown, New Jersey, military institute. He died in

Verona, New Jersey, and was buried at West Point with full military honors.

Roosma was inducted into the Basketball Hall of Fame in 1961 for his outstanding career as a college player. Although the Hall of Fame generally honors individuals, Roosma believed that the six Passaic High School Wonder Teams deserved a spot there, too. He mounted a virtually single-handed crusade to get the Wonder Teams inducted. Working relentlessly, he provided Hall of Fame trustees and selection committee members with reams of evidence to support the nomination. His persistent efforts over a seven-year period led the Hall of Fame in 1974 to recognize the Wonder Teams' 159-game winning streak with a display in the shrine's high school room. Although this brought Roosma great satisfaction, he continued to call for the full induction of all the Wonder Teams.

• The best description of Roosma's life and career appears in Mike Moretti, "Basketball Was Young and He Was the Best," *Herald-News* (Passaic-Clifton), 15 Nov. 1983. The October 1969 issues of the *Herald-News*, the *Newark News*, and other northern New Jersey newspapers that covered the fiftieth anniversary of the Wonder Teams' streak have accounts of Roosma's playing career, as do the 1961 issues that covered his induction into the Basketball Hall of Fame. Additional information on his career appears in the April 1974 issues, which reported the Hall of Fame's recognition of the Wonder Teams' streak. Obituaries are in the *Herald-News* and the *New York Times*, both 14 November 1983.

J. THOMAS JABLE

ROOT, Azariah Smith (3 Feb. 1862–2 Oct. 1927), librarian and professor of bibliography, was born in Middlefield, Massachusetts, the son of Solomon Francis Root, the proprietor of a general store, and Anna Smith. Root's family traditions emphasized civic responsibility, Baptist and Congregational convictions, antislavery, higher education, and equal rights for men and women. These ideals influenced Root's choice of Oberlin College, which had admitted African Americans as early as 1835 and had achieved a national reputation as the nation's first coeducational college and a hotbed of abolitionist sentiment. Root earned an A.B. and an A.M. at Oberlin (1884, 1887), studied law at Boston University (1884–1885) and Harvard University (1886–1887), and studied analytical bibliography and the history of printing at the University of Göttingen (1898–1899). In 1887 he married a college classmate, Anna Mayo Metcalf; they had two children.

That same year Root was appointed Oberlin College library director and, in 1890, professor of bibliography, positions he held until his death. He pioneered in teaching the use of libraries as a natural extension of the liberal arts philosophy. His approach to librarianship, most apparent in his instructional program, attempted to give undergraduate colleges a unique place in higher education. In a profession that was then dominated by the rapid reconceptualization and unprecedented growth of university research libraries, Root sought to define the special role of the library in a liberal arts environment. Thus, he became the premier spokesperson for college librarianship during his era. He determined that Oberlin, though a small liberal arts college, should have the rich retrospective research collections needed to attract faculty in the social sciences and humanities. Given Oberlin's inadequate library budget, Root soon concluded that collection growth depended, in part, on gifts from exchange programs and from private collectors, many of them Oberlin alumni. By 1924 the Oberlin library had become the largest college (as distinguished from a university) library in the nation. A decade after Root's death, Oberlin still ranked among the ten fastest-growing research libraries in the United States (Rider, p. 6).

Root expanded his influence throughout the college and the local community. In 1893 he was appointed to a committee that handled the daily affairs of the college, which he chaired for many years; he also assisted the trustees with college investments. In 1908 he established a rare unified college-public library when a new Carnegie building was constructed. He spoke annually in Oberlin's black churches, facilitated the merger of two congregations, wrote a brief history of Congregationalism in Ohio, and served on the local board of commerce, the board of education, the Oberlin Mutual Benefit Association, and the Village Improvement Society.

Root was attracted to the social experiments and reform proposals that were constantly under discussion at Oberlin in the late nineteenth and early twentieth centuries. He raised funds for woman's rights advocate Lucy Stone and supplied the pulpit for Howard H. Russell, which enabled the latter to increase his prohibition activities. Root and his Oberlin colleagues founded the Anti-Saloon League of America at a meeting in his library office on 24 May 1893. He served prohibitionist causes in the movement's early years, when it was characterized by broad reforms, rather than later, when it concentrated on the liquor question alone and stressed law enforcement. He affirmed as college policy Oberlin's commitment to the "brotherhood of man of all classes and color" based on the "fundamental principles of righteousness and justice" (*Oberlin Alumni Magazine*, July 1910).

Root became a leader in his profession. In 1889 he was a founding member of the American Library Association's College Library Section (precursor of the Association of College and Research Libraries), which he also chaired in 1901–1902 and 1910–1911. He was a founding member of the Bibliographical Society of America, over which he presided (1909–1910, 1923–1926), and for which he helped obtain support to complete Joseph Sabin's *Bibliotheca Americana*, one of the nation's major retrospective bibliographies. He presided over the Ohio Library Association (1900–1901, 1914–1915) and the American Library Association (1921–1922) and served as librarian at Camp Sherman near Chillecothe, Ohio in 1918. He was the first secretary and a charter trustee of the Hayes Historical Society from 1925 to 1927, and he collaborated with Webb C. Hayes in establishing the Rutherford B. Hayes Memorial Library.

A skilled rhetorician, Root was much in demand as a library educator. He taught the history of books and printing at Western Reserve University from 1904 to 1927, served as acting principal of the New York Public Library School in 1916–1917, and presided over the American Correspondence School of Librarianship from 1923 to 1927. He lectured at the Carnegie Library School of Atlanta, Columbia University, Drexel Institute, Pratt Institute, and the University of Michigan, and he influenced a number of individuals to pursue library careers, including his brother-in-law, Keyes D. Metcalf, Harvard University librarian (1937–1955).

Root's home was a "rallying place" for his wife's large family and numerous other Oberlinians. He died in Oberlin. Known among townspeople as a promoter of good will and among the Oberlin College community as a symbol of its traditions, Root is also remembered by professional colleagues as a gifted speaker, scholar, and "Dean of American College Librarians."

• The Azariah Smith Root Papers, including speech texts and lecture notes, are in the Oberlin College Archives. Root's more important articles include "The Scope of an American Bibliographical Society," *Yearbook of the Bibliographical Society of Chicago* 3 (1902): 41–52; "Local Historical Societies: Their Uses and Beliefs," *Firelands Pioneer* n.s. 17 (1909): 1546–53; "The Present Situation as to the Origin of Printing," *Bibliographical Society of America Papers* 5 (1910): 9–21; and "The Library School of the Future," *Bulletin of the American Library Association* 11 (1917): 157–60. The principal interpretive study is John Mark Tucker, "Librarianship as a Community Service: Azariah Smith Root at Oberlin College" (Ph.D. diss., Univ. of Illinois, 1983). See also Tucker, "Azariah Smith Root and Social Reform at Oberlin College," *Journal of Library History* 16 (1981): 280–92, and Richard Rubin, "Azariah Smith Root and Library Instruction at Oberlin College," *Journal of Library History* 12 (1977): 250–61. Fremont Rider included Oberlin in his discussion of the growth patterns of American research libraries in *The Scholar and the Future of the Research Library* (1944). Obituaries are in the *Cleveland Plain Dealer* and the *New York Times*, 3 Oct. 1927.

JOHN MARK TUCKER

ROOT, Elihu (15 Feb. 1845–7 Feb. 1937), cabinet officer and U.S. senator, was born in Clinton, New York, the son of Oren Root, a professor of mathematics at Hamilton College, and Nancy Whitney Buttrick. He attended Hamilton College, finishing as class of 1864 valedictorian. After teaching for a year at the nearby Rome Academy, he enrolled in New York University Law School. He graduated in 1867 and was admitted to the bar. After a year's clerkship with the firm of Mann and Parsons, he started his own firm with John H. Strahan. In 1878 he married Clara Frances Wales; they had three children.

Root rapidly became one of the leaders of the New York bar. Although he played a minor role in 1871–1873 on the defense side in the criminal trial of New York City political boss William M. Tweed for corruption, the bulk of his practice involved civil matters.

The keys to his success were his painstaking preparation, absorptive memory, and mastery of detail. His forte was trial work, thanks to the lucidity and clarity of his arguments, which were often enlivened by his keen wit. His clients came to include many of the industrial and financial leaders of the time, including Henry O. Havemeyer and William F. Havemeyer of the so-called sugar trust and traction magnates William C. Whitney and Thomas Fortune Ryan.

Root served as U.S. attorney for the Southern District of New York from 1883 to 1885. He began his association with Theodore Roosevelt in 1886 when he was chairman of the Republican County Committee during Roosevelt's unsuccessful race for New York City mayor. Their ties were strengthened when Root successfully explained away the questions about Roosevelt's meeting the residency requirements when Roosevelt ran for governor of New York State in 1898.

In 1899 President William McKinley, in a surprise move, appointed Root secretary of war. The major reason for the appointment was McKinley's wish to have a top lawyer in the post to deal with the new overseas possessions acquired in the Spanish-American War. Root took a paternalistic approach to the colonies that emphasized economic development and material improvements for the inhabitants of those possessions. He was dubious about the capacity of the native peoples for self-government and thus wished to keep political control firmly in American hands.

The Foraker Act of 1900 allowed Puerto Rico more representation than Root had favored but gave island exports free access (after 1902) to the U.S. market. Root picked General Leonard Wood to head the American military government in Cuba and backed Wood's ambitious program of sanitary, road, and school improvements. He felt that the United States was bound by the no-annexation pledge of the Teller Amendment of 1898, but he insisted that the Cubans write into their new constitution safeguards to protect American interests—including recognition of the right of the United States to intervene in the event of the breakdown of law and order. He was largely responsible for the Platt Amendment to the Army Appropriation Act of 2 March 1901, which made Cuban acceptance of those conditions the prerequisite for the end of military occupation.

The Philippines presented a more difficult problem. The first priority was the suppression of the insurrection of Filipino nationalists. Root succeeded in overcoming the impediments presented by the army's cumbersome and inefficient machinery to build up American forces in the archipelago and put down resistance by 1902. Anti-imperialists in the United States seized upon and exploited reports of atrocities by American troops to embarrass the McKinley administration. Although he took disciplinary action against individual wrongdoers, Root defended the behavior of the American forces under the adverse conditions of a guerrilla-type jungle war. He drafted the instructions for the commission, headed by William Howard Taft, that was sent in 1900 to the Philippines to replace military rule. Those instructions became the basis for the Philippine Organic Act of 1902, which laid down the framework for U.S. rule in the Philippines.

The difficulties Root had faced in putting down the Filipino revolt led him to undertake a major overhaul of the War Department's administrative structure. His skill in dealing with Congress enabled him to carry through his program over the opposition of the commanding general of the army, Nelson A. Miles. His reforms included an increase in the authorized size of the army from its pre-Spanish-American War level of about 28,000 officers and men to a minimum of 60,000 enlisted men and a maximum of 100,000; extension of a larger degree of War Department control over the National Guards of the individual states; abolition of permanent staff jobs in Washington by instituting the principle of rotation from staff to line; and establishment of an Army War College to provide instruction in planning and strategy. His most significant innovation was his introduction of the nucleus of a general staff system to centralize responsibility for the planning and execution of military policy.

Root had the confidence and strong backing of President McKinley and, after McKinley's assassination, Theodore Roosevelt. He resigned as secretary of war in early 1904, partly because of his wife's dislike of Washington, partly because of health problems resulting from overwork. After the death of Secretary of State John Hay in 1905, however, Root yielded to Roosevelt's plea to accept that post.

As secretary of state, Root made a beginning toward taking consular appointments out of politics and establishing a professional career service. He promoted friendlier relations between the United States and the countries of Latin America. The high points of that effort were his 1906 goodwill tour of South America and his cosponsorship of the Central American Peace Conference in 1907, which established the Central American Court of Justice. He successfully negotiated twenty-two bilateral arbitration treaties providing for submission to the Permanent Court of International Arbitration at The Hague differences of a legal nature or relating to the interpretation of treaties that could not be resolved by diplomacy. He also resolved the long controversy with Canada over the North Atlantic coastal fisheries by an agreement in January 1909 to submit the dispute to The Hague court. Perhaps Root's major asset was his talent for getting along with the Senate; he lost no important treaty in the Senate during his term.

The most troublesome problems during Root's secretaryship of state were rivalries with Japan in the Far East, which were aggravated by the hostility toward Japanese immigrants in the Pacific Coast states. Root worked in tandem with Roosevelt to develop the "Gentlemen's Agreement" halting Japanese immigration to the continental United States and the political modus vivendi formalized in the Root-Takahira Agreement of 1908. The two powers agreed to maintain "the existing status quo" in the Pacific and support the Open Door policy in China and China's independence and integrity. Roosevelt was the major architect of the settlement with Japan; Root's role in this area was more to implement than to formulate policy. In 1912, Root was awarded the Nobel Peace Prize for his role in shaping the administration of the new colonies and his contributions to peace.

Root resigned as secretary of state in 1909 after his election to the Senate. As the breach between the progressive and standpat wings of the Republican party widened, he became identified, at least in the public mind, with the Old Guard. Much to his personal discomfort, he found himself caught in the middle of the conflict between President Taft and Theodore Roosevelt. He was repelled by Roosevelt's support for popular recall of judicial decisions as undermining the basis of American constitutional government. When his efforts to reconcile the two leaders failed, he lined up with the Taft forces and was their pick for temporary and permanent chairman of the 1912 Republican National Convention. Roosevelt never forgave Root for what he thought was Root's role in robbing him of the nomination.

Root opposed all the important domestic measures of President Woodrow Wilson. Although he supported the chief executive in the fight to repeal the exemption of American coastal shipping from Panama Canal tolls as a violation of the Hay-Pauncefote Treaty of 1901, he was contemptuous of what he thought was Wilson's blundering in Mexico. He had long been suspicious of German expansionist ambitions, but he tried to maintain an appearance of neutrality after the outbreak of war in Europe because of his position on the Senate Foreign Relations Committee. The Seventeeth Amendment for the popular election of U.S. senators—which he had opposed—had been ratified in 1913, and rather than undergo the physical strain of an election campaign, Root decided to retire from the Senate at the end of his term in 1915.

After leaving the Senate, Root became more and more openly pro-Allied and hostile to Wilson's neutrality policy. He did not advocate intervention in the war until after the severance of diplomatic relations with Germany in early February 1917. He reluctantly allowed supporters to put forward his name for the Republican presidential nomination in 1916, but a Root boom failed to materialize.

In April 1917, Wilson named Root to head a mission to Russia to investigate and report upon the situation there in the wake of the overthrow of the tsarist regime. The mission was a fiasco. Root lacked empathy and rapport with the leaders of the revolutionary forces gaining ascendancy in Russia, and Wilson, who had picked Root for reasons of political expediency, ignored his recommendation for funding a pro-Allied propaganda campaign in Russia and came to blame Root for failing to foresee the Bolshevik triumph. The resulting antipathy led Wilson to rebuff suggestions that he include Root on the American delegation to the Paris Peace Conference.

Root's attitude toward U.S. membership in the League of Nations was mixed. He acknowledged that the United States must cooperate with other nations to prevent future wars. The stumbling block was Article X, pledging the signatories to respect and preserve against external aggression the territorial integrity and political independence of all members. Root doubted the wisdom of such a commitment; he was even more dubious about the willingness of the American people to live up to such a blank check. He thus favored ratification with reservations to protect American independence of action. He cooperated with Massachusetts senator Henry Cabot Lodge (1850–1924), the chairman of the Senate Foreign Relations Committee, in lining up Senate Republicans behind this approach. However, ratification with reservations failed, partly because of the die-hard opposition of the irreconcilables to U.S. membership in the league under any conditions, and even more because of Wilson's stubbornness.

In the years that followed, Root became a widely respected elder statesman, but his influence was limited. Although named a member of the U.S. delegation to the Washington Conference of 1921–1922, he played only a minor role in the resulting naval limitation and four-power nonaggression agreements. His longtime favored solution to the problem of maintaining peace was through the codification of international law and the strengthening of the international judicial machinery for its enforcement. He was president of the American Society of International Law from its founding in 1907 until 1924. He was a member of the commission of international law experts appointed by the League of Nations in 1920 that drafted the governing statute for the new Permanent Court of International Justice (or World Court), but he turned down the invitation to serve as one of the court's judges. Despite his continuing advocacy of American membership in the World Court, opposition by Senate isolationists blocked approval. Root served as president or chairman of the board of the Carnegie Endowment for International Peace, the Carnegie Institution of Washington, and the Carnegie Corporation of New York. He died in New York City.

Root's long-term significance is difficult to assess. Although no die-hard reactionary, he made the maintenance of order and stability his top priority. In foreign affairs, he stood for an internationalism that coupled recognition of U.S. responsibility to play a larger role in world affairs with a realistic understanding of the limits of the commitments that the United States could and should undertake. As such, he became the patron saint of the foreign policy elite that largely shaped the role of the United States in the world from the late 1930s through the Vietnam War.

• The Root papers in the Library of Congress are fullest for the years 1899 to 1915. Supplementary materials are in his scrapbooks in the New York Public Library. Robert Bacon and James B. Scott edited eight volumes of Root's writings and addresses, including extracts from War Department reports and State Department instructions along with his 1907 Dodge Lectures at Yale University, "The Citizen's Part in Government," and his 1913 Stafford Little Lectures at Princeton University, "Experiments in Government and the Essentials of the Constitution." The titles are *Addresses on Government and Citizenship* (1916), *The Military and Colonial Policy of the United States* (1916), *Addresses on International Subjects* (1916), *Latin America and the United States* (1917), *Miscellaneous Addresses* (1917), *North Atlantic Coast Fisheries Arbitration at The Hague* (1917), *The United States and the War: The Mission to Russia, Political Addresses* (1918); and *Men and Policies* (1925). The standard biography remains the magisterial two-volume authorized biography by a younger associate and admirer, Philip C. Jessup, *Elihu Root* (1938). Richard W. Leopold, *Elihu Root and the Conservative Tradition* (1954), is a brief reappraisal that is more critical but still sympathetic. Julius W. Pratt, *America's Colonial Experiment: How the United States Gained, Governed, and in Part Gave Away a Colonial Empire* (1950), gives a handy summary of Root's role in formulating the policies for governance of the new colonial possessions; William R. Roberts, "Reform and Revitalization, 1890–1903," in *Against All Enemies: Interpretations of American Military History from Colonial Times to the Present* (1986), by Kenneth J. Hagan and Roberts, does the same for Root's army reforms. Biographical essays by James B. Scott in *American Secretaries of State and Their Diplomacy*, vol. 9, ed. Samuel F. Bemis (1927–1929), and Charles W. Toth in *An Uncertain Tradition: American Secretaries of State in the Twentieth Century*, ed. Norman A. Graebner (1961), are brief surveys of Root's term as secretary of state. Root's role in the resolution of the difficulties with Japan is more fully treated in Charles E. Neu, *An Uncertain Friendship: Theodore Roosevelt and Japan, 1906–1909* (1967). Root's presidency of the 1915 New York State Constitutional Convention is detailed in Thomas Schick, *The New York State Constitutional Convention of 1915 and the Modern State Governor* (1978). An obituary is in the *New York Times*, 7 Feb. 1937.

JOHN BRAEMAN

ROOT, Erastus (16 Mar. 1773–24 Dec. 1846), politician and lawyer, was born in Hebron, Connecticut, the son of William Root and Zeruiah Baldwin. After graduating from Dartmouth in 1793, he took a job as a school teacher; during his brief teaching career he published *An Introduction to Arithmetic for the Use of Common Schools* (1796). He also began reading law with Sylvester Gilbert of Hebron, was admitted to the bar in 1796, and opened a practice in the Catskill Mountain town of Delhi, New York. Root became extremely popular, with Martin Van Buren noting a few years later that Root "exercised undisputed and indisputable political sway" in the Delaware County area ("Autobiography of Martin Van Buren," p. 95).

In 1798 Root won election to the state assembly as a Democrat-Republican (Jeffersonian), serving two terms. He fought the legislature's rejection of the Kentucky and Virginia resolutions in 1798 and supported successful abolition legislation, despite opponents who, according to Root, "raved and swore by *dunder* and *blitzen* that we were robbing them of their property" (White, p. 20). By 1801 Root had emerged as a leading voice in the assembly. Early that year when senate Republicans, led by De Witt Clinton, attempted to block the patronage power of outgoing Federalist governor John Jay, Root insisted that the assembly maintain a stance of noninterference in the fight. In 1802 he won the first of four nonconsecutive terms in the House of Representatives. Root held a seat in Congress from 1803 to 1805 and from 1809 to 1811. During the interim, he got married in 1806, to Elizabeth Stockton, with whom he would have five children.

Root was a member of the state senate from 1812 to 1815, a period of upheaval for both New York and the country. He arrived in Albany in time to join Van Buren as an outspoken critic of the chartering of the Bank of America in New York City, a measure that the Federalists passed with "the most daring and unscrupulous bribery," according to Van Buren ("Autobiography of Martin Van Buren," p. 110). Root called for a committee to investigate the bank. When the Federalists in 1812 convinced Republican Clinton to become their peace candidate against incumbent president James Madison, Root spoke out against the nomination, believing that what he saw as a doomed effort would cost his party and his state the influence of one of its leaders. "Spare, oh, spare that great man!" Root opined (Bobbé, p. 186), an ironic remark since Clinton would soon be one of his most bitter political enemies.

A strong proponent of the War of 1812, Root was given high rank in the militia and was subsequently known as "General" for the rest of his career. During the conflict he was generally allied with Governor Daniel D. Tompkins and Van Buren in support of war legislation, fighting stiff state-level opposition from the Federalists. In 1814, however, he and Van Buren proposed competing senate bills to raise troops from the state. Root favored a volunteer system, while Van Buren wanted a draft, and remembered that Root "denounced [the draft bill] with great bitterness" ("Autobiography of Martin Van Buren," p. 56). Several Federalists backed Root, but Van Buren used the influence of war hero Winfield Scott to secure passage of what was known as the "classification bill." During the war Root also supported the idea of using African-American troops.

In late 1814 Root lost a controversial U.S. congressional race to John Adams, a state assemblyman from Durham, New York. Adams took his seat in Washington the following March, but Root successfully contested the election, and on 26 December he replaced Adams, serving until 1817. During the same period Root backed Van Buren's bid to unseat Ambrose Spencer as the leader of the New York Republicans. When Spencer allied with his brother-in-law Clinton to thwart the power play, it split the party. As Root returned to the state assembly (1818–1822), he joined Van Buren and Tompkins as members of what became known as the Bucktails, who took their name from the symbol for Tammany Hall. The elite of this group, the "Albany Regency," became the political machine that vaulted Van Buren to national prominence.

Root's influence reached its peak in 1821 during the state constitutional convention, which Root opened as temporary chairman. "We have no different estates having different interests, necessary to be guarded from encroachments by the watchful eye of jealousy," he eloquently proclaimed in defense of universal white manhood suffrage. "We are all of the same estate—all commoners" (Miller, p. 13). He did, however, oppose giving blacks the right to vote. Both positions were approved by the convention, but Root's suggestions of a one-year term for governors and veto override by simple majorities in both houses were not. His proposals for judicial reform were opposed by Van Buren, but the convention ultimately passed changes in the system that met the approval of both men. "Madcap democrats" was what Van Buren called Root and his liberal supporters (Mushkat and Rayback, p. 152).

In 1822 the Bucktails considered running Root for governor, but chose Joseph C. Yates instead, with Root winning election as lieutenant governor. He served in 1823–1824 but was unsuccessful in a reelection bid, losing by 32,409 votes. His cause had been irreparably damaged by a report in the *New York American* (25 Aug. 1824) that he had presided over the senate while drunk. Root sued editors Charles King and Johnston Verplanck for libel, winning in both the circuit court and the court of errors. Alcoholism had begun to affect Root, however, and was the primary reason that he did not reach the political heights of contemporaries Clinton, Van Buren, and Tompkins. The opposition characterized him during the 1824 campaign as an anti-Christian drunkard, "deplorably successful in contaminating public morals" (Hanyan and Hanyan, p. 238). His career was far from over, but he was no longer ascending.

He still had the support of Delaware County, however, and its voters returned Root to the general assembly in 1826. He served as Speaker in 1827, 1828, and 1830, noting when he first took the position that "if by impartiality [it] is meant to throw aside the principles which distinguish the party to which I belong, it must not be expected that I will be impartial" (Bobbé, p. 285). The Clinton camp referred to him as "the Root of all evil" (Bobbé, p. 271) as he continually opposed the governor's measures.

Root failed to gain party support for a gubernatorial bids in 1826 and 1828 or appointment to the Senate in 1829, and by the end of the decade he had begun to break with the Albany Regency. In the summer of 1830 he was chosen as a commissioner to negotiate with the Green Bay Indians, and that fall he won election to the House as a Jacksonian Democrat. His severing of ties with the New York machine was completed in 1832 when he spoke out in favor of rechartering the Bank of the United States, a measure that received stiff opposition from the Regency. Root became a Whig, opposed Andrew Jackson's reelection in 1832, and by 1834 feared that Jackson was turning into "an American Caesar." He wondered in a letter to Henry Clay if "the mad career" of the "military Chieftain" would ever be checked (*Papers of Henry Clay*, vol. 8, p. 688). His later-life conversion to the more conservative

Whig party was nearly as great a surprise to his friends as his decisions to give up drinking and swearing.

Although defeated in the 1838 U.S. congressional race, Root remained active in the Whig Party and from 1840 to 1844 he was back in the state senate. This proved to be his last political service, as he died in New York City while en route to Washington. Although he never attained high office, Root was a strong political voice and an influential figure in the nation's most populous state for nearly half a century of public life.

• There is no substantial collection of Root's papers. Some Root documents can be found in the manuscripts of others, including the Martin Van Buren Papers in the Library of Congress. A published speech is *Address of Erastus Root to the People of the State of New York* (1824). Root's involvement in the constitutional convention can be traced in Nathaniel H. Carter and William L. Stone, reporters, *Reports of the Proceedings and Debates of the Convention of 1821* (1821). Contemporary accounts of his political activities are Jabez D. Hammond, *The History of Political Parties in the State of New-York From the Ratification of the Federal Constitution to December, 1840* (2 vols., 1842), for which Root provided some of his notes; John C. Fitzpatrick, ed., "The Autobiography of Martin Van Buren," in *Annual Report of the American Historical Association for the Year 1918*, vol. 2; Charles Francis Adams, ed., *Memoirs of John Quincy Adams* (12 vols., 1877); and James F. Hopkins et al., eds., *The Papers of Henry Clay* (10 vols. and supplement, 1959–1992). Biographies of contemporaries that contain extensive mention of Root include John Niven, *Martin Van Buren: The Romantic Age of American Politics* (1983); Donald B. Cole, *Martin Van Buren and the American Political System* (1984); Jerome Mushkat and Joseph G. Rayback, *Martin Van Buren: Law, Politics, and the Shaping of Republican Ideology* (1997); Robert V. Remini, *Martin Van Buren and the Making of the Democratic Party* (1951); Craig Hanyan and Mary L. Hanyan, *De Witt Clinton and the Rise of the People's Men* (1996); and Dorthie Bobbé, *De Witt Clinton* (1933). Among the general state political histories are Alvin Kass, *Politics in New York State 1800–1830* (1965); Douglas T. Miller, *Jacksonian Aristocracy: Class and Democracy in New York 1830–1860* (1967); and Shane White, *Somewhat More Independent: The End of Slavery in New York City, 1770–1810* (1991). An obituary is in the *New York Herald*, 25 Dec. 1846.

DONALD M. ROPER
KENNETH H. WILLIAMS

ROOT, Frederick Woodman (13 June 1846–8 Nov. 1916), music teacher, author, and editor, was born in Boston, Massachusetts, the son of George Frederick Root, a Civil War songwriter and teacher, and Mary Olive Woodman, a gifted singer. Frederick grew up in musical surroundings and became absorbed in his father's educational and business pursuits. He studied piano with William Mason, voice with Carlo Bassini, and organ with James Flint in New York City.

In 1863 his father moved the family to Chicago, Illinois, where the music company Root & Cady had been in business since 1858. Root continued to study music and became an editor and arranger for Root & Cady. In 1863 he became a church organist, a role he was to play throughout most of his career, principally

at the Swedenborgian church and later at the First Church of Christ, Scientist. After the Civil War Root assisted his father in musical institutes for teachers held in a different place each summer. During 1869 and 1870 he traveled in Europe and studied voice with Vannuccini in Florence, Italy. In Rome he visited Franz Liszt and watched him work with a young composer.

From 1871 to 1875 he was editor of the *Song Messenger of the Northwest*, Root & Cady's music periodical. He edited or coedited collections of music for adults as well as *Our Song Birds* (1866–1867), a quarterly music periodical for children. After the Chicago fire of 1871 Root & Cady went through several reorganizations but never regained its former prominence. In 1874 he married Fanny Smith; they had one daughter and two sons.

Root became conductor of the Mendelssohn Club and for the 1877–1878 season planned an ambitious schedule of five concerts and "soirees." An amateur organization, the club included a large chorus, "its actual working strength being 100, and there were in the orchestra 30 instruments," according to Root. The club performed works of George Frederick Handel, Franz Joseph Haydn, Ludwig van Beethoven, Wolfgang Amadeus Mozart, and Felix Mendelssohn. He also conducted a festival chorus of 400 in a series of concerts given by Patrick Gilmore's band in 1889. In 1893 he conducted a chorus at the World's Columbian Exposition in Chicago.

In vocal music he was considered "one of Chicago's best teachers," according to the *Sunday Herald* (6 June 1885). Several of his students had successful singing careers. In addition to his private teaching, Root taught singing to large classes of adults. For some years he presented his classes in public concerts. A typical program, described in the Chicago *Sunday Herald* of 7 June 1885, began with Root's lecture-demonstration on vocal technique, featured a performance by the class of almost 200 women, and ended with solos by some of his private students. He also wrote books, articles, and pamphlets on voice training. The most comprehensive was his *Technic and Art of Singing* (1903–1906), a multivolume work including sight-singing, exercises and scales, voice culture, songs, and "analytical studies." He wrote that good singing is "a harmony of physical action, poise, grace, vigor, control" (Hubbard, vol. 11, p. 225).

As music critic for the *Chicago Herald* in 1885, Root wrote principally about opera performances. Reviewing a festival performance of the opera *Faust*, he praised the soprano's "grace, her quality of tone, which is rich and sensuous; her execution, which is so finished; the pose of her head—all is charming." Then he scolded, "But for the most part she is engaged less in delineation of character than in exerting her charms." He reasoned that "a great artist has special responsibilities in her influence upon the performance of students and the taste of the public" (18 Apr. 1885). In 1889 Root was named an examiner in voice for the American College of Musicians, an early attempt by the Music Teachers' National Association to set high standards through accreditation for music teachers.

Among his compositions were several in a series called "Piano Pictures" (1871–1872) and many songs, of which "Beyond" (1870), a serious dramatic solo, was evidently the best known. His arrangements of the works of other composers, including Stephen Foster, were well received. His cantata *The Landing of the Pilgrims* was performed in 1875 by the Beethoven Society of Chicago.

Preparations for the World's Columbian Exposition drew attention to America's ranking among the nations in science and industry and strengthened the desire for distinctively American music that would rank with European works. Root offered his advice in an article for *Music* magazine:

As soon as our composers conclude to learn all they can from European art without slavishly imitating its forms of thought and subjects of musical portrayal, they will, perhaps, come to realize that in our national history are some grand inspirations for the native artist; and that in our folk music there are melodies which, however unworthy they may seem from certain affected standpoints, are yet dear to the hearts of our people. . . . Moreover they may realize that in this direction lies something distinctively characteristic. We shall yet see him—the American composer who has acquired all the necessary musical erudition, but who has also the heart, brains and spirit to give musical expression to that which excites generous and loyal emotion on this side [of] the Atlantic. (May 1892, pp. 3–4)

In 1893 Root traveled to Europe again, studying the vocal methods used in several countries. In 1900 he joined the Church of Christ, Scientist, and for the 1910 edition of the Christian Science hymnal he wrote paraphrases of several hymns and new words for others. In this denomination, soloists have traditionally taken the place of choirs, and Root composed solos for the church, several of them settings of the poems of Mary Baker Eddy, founder of Christian Science. Root died in Chicago.

• A large collection of Root's music is housed in the Special Collections Division of the Chicago Public Library. Root and James R. Murray coedited *The Pacific Glee Book: A Collection of Secular Music* (1869), which included operatic arrangements. Root also edited *The Song Era: A Book of Instruction and Music, for Elementary and Advanced Singing Classes, Choirs, Institutes and Conventions* (1874). His works on voice training include *F. W. Root's School of Singing* (1873), *Studies from the Opera* (1896), and *Analytical Studies in Voice Culture* (1899). He was a contributor to Florence Ffrench, ed., *Music and Musicians in Chicago* (1899; repr. 1979), which contains a biographical sketch and photo of him, and W. L. Hubbard, ed., *The American History and Encyclopedia of Music* (1910). Among his piano pieces were "The Home Run Galop!" (1867), dedicated to a Chicago baseball organization, and "Crosby's Opera House Waltz" (1865), the cover of which pictured the exterior of the Root & Cady music company. Also see informative biographical information in W. S. B. Mathews, ed., *A Hundred Years of Music in America* (1889). A death notice is in the *Chicago Tribune*, 9 Nov. 1916.

POLLY CARDER

ROOT, George Frederick (30 Aug. 1820–6 Aug. 1895), composer and music educator, was born in Sheffield, Massachusetts, the son of Frederick Ferdinand Root and Sarah Flint, farmers. At age eighteen George decided to become a professional musician, although he apparently had no formal training. He moved to Boston, where he studied music with A. N. Johnson and George Webb, joined the Handel and Haydn Society, and assisted Lowell Mason in his public school music classes.

Root's gifts as a music teacher had already become evident when he departed for New York City in 1844. There he taught at various institutions, including Abbott's School for Young Ladies, Rutgers Female Institute, Union Theological Seminary, and the State Institution for the Blind. After a year in New York City, Root married Mary Olive Woodman, who became the star soprano of the Mercer Street Church Choir for which Root was the music director; they had two sons and four daughters. (Their son Frederick Woodman became a prominent musician and their daughter Clara Louisa was a well-known author.)

In 1850 Root traveled to Paris, where he studied voice and piano with Giulio Alary and Jacques Potharst. Upon his return the following year, Root began composing music in the parlor song tradition of Stephen Foster. His most successful songs were "Hazel Dell" and "Rosalie, the Prairie Flower," with the latter reportedly earning him over $3,000. Root also composed music for several cantatas, including *The Flower Queen; or, The Coronation of the Rose* (1852) and his most successful, *The Haymakers* (1857). The author of many of these early works was Fanny Crosby, one of Root's students at the State Institution for the Blind who later became an important author of Sunday school songs. For many of his early songs—some of which were written for Edwin Pearce Christy, founder of the blackface minstrel troupe Christy's Minstrels—Root employed the pseudonym G. Friedrich Wurzel (the last name of which is German for "root").

The highly energetic Root continued his interests in music education and, with Mason, Webb, and William Bradbury, established the New York Normal Institute in New York City (1853), the first systematic training facility for music teachers in the United States. By 1859, however, Root had moved to Chicago, where he soon became a partner with his brother Ebeneezer Towner Root and Chauncey Cady in the music firm of Root and Cady. The ensuing Civil War years proved to be highly successful for both the company and for Root, as the northern war effort elicited Root's best-known songs. These included "The Battle Cry of Freedom" (1862), "Just before the Battle, Mother" (1862), and "Tramp, Tramp, Tramp" (1864). Root usually wrote both the words and music for these songs; President Abraham Lincoln is reported to have said that through his work Root had "done more than a hundred generals and a thousand orators."

Closely related to Root's contributions to music education were his contributions to church music. In an age when educational material was often religious in nature, many of Root's over 200 songs and three dozen cantatas contained religious subjects. In addition, he composed several collections for the popular Sunday school song market. His best known religious songs include the tunes "Children" ("Jesus Loves the Little Children"), "Quam Dilecta" ("The Lord Is in His Holy Temple"), and "Ring the Bells" (of Heaven). Unlike most of his musical associates, whose religious affiliations were mainstream Protestant, Root was denominationally affiliated with the Swedenborgian church beginning in 1864.

In 1871 the Chicago fire devastated the firm of Root and Cady, and its assets were sold off. The John Church Company of Cincinnati purchased the book catalog, and Root established an association with that firm. Root traveled to England in 1886 at the invitation of his British publishers, making contacts that led to several commissions abroad. Throughout the remainder of his life he continued to compose music, produce pedagogical materials, and hold musical training institutes. He died in Bailey Island, Maine.

Root occupied an influential position during a critical period for American music during the nineteenth century. It was a time of transition from the colonial singing-school tradition of William Billings to a more European-based approach strongly espoused by Mason and his associates. Although sympathetic to Mason's ideas, which were based on the art music traditions of Handel, Mozart, and Beethoven, Root strongly favored the use of simple music that he felt was appropriate for the vast, unsophisticated American public. As a teacher and an editor-publisher he influenced a generation of sacred and secular songwriters—such as Philip P. Bliss and Henry Clay Work—to write music that would reach the widest possible audience.

• The two best examples of Root's own writing are his fascinating autobiography, *The Story of a Musical Life* (1891), and various articles he penned for Root and Cady's periodical, the *Song Messenger of the Northwest*, during the period between 1863 and 1872. A recording of Root's *The Haymakers: An Operatic Cantata* (New World Records, no. 234) provides valuable information on the composer and his work. The most complete scholarly biography is Polly H. Carder, "George Frederick Root, Pioneer Music Educator" (Ph.D. diss., Univ. of Maryland, 1971). Another important source is Dena Epstein, *Music Publishing in Chicago before 1871: The Firm of Root and Cady, 1858–1871* (1969). See also the biographical entries in *The New Grove Dictionary of Music and Musicians* (1980) and *The New Grove Dictionary of American Music* (1986), both of which contain a good list of Root's publications. For an excellent treatment of Root in the musical context of his times, see William Austin, *"Susanna," "Jeanie," and "The Old Folks at Home": The Songs of Stephen C. Foster from His Time to Ours* (1975). Also see Gilbert Chase, *America's Music from the Pilgrims to the Present* (1987), and J. H. Hall, *Biography of Gospel Song and Hymn Writers* (1914). An obituary is in the *Chicago Daily Tribune*, 8 Aug. 1895.

MEL R. WILHOIT

ROOT, Jesse (28 Dec. 1736–29 Mar. 1822), politician and jurist, was born in Coventry, Connecticut, the son of Ebenezer Root and Sarah Strong. As the youngest of eight children, Root was directed by circumstances to pursue his worldly fortune within the ranks of the growing professional classes rather than as a farmer amidst the mounting land shortage in mid-eighteenth-century Connecticut. In 1756 Root graduated from the College of New Jersey (later Princeton University) in preparation for the ministry. He continued his theological studies under the tutelage of the Reverend Samuel Lockwood, the Congregational minister for Andover, Connecticut, and was formally licensed as a Congregational preacher by the Hartford South Association on 29 March 1757. In May 1758 Root married Mary Banks of Newark, New Jersey; they would have nine children.

The sudden deaths of his brother in 1758 and his father in 1760 placed the Root family in unfavorable economic circumstances. As a result Root abandoned the ministry and, under the guidance of Connecticut lawyer-politicians such as future governor Jonathan Trumbull and revolutionary statesman Eliphalet Dyer, began to prepare for the law. Admitted to the bar in Windham County in 1763, he joined the swelling ranks of young, ambitious lawyers who flocked to Hartford, which along with New Haven was a co-capital of the colony and one of the two seats of Connecticut government and the court system. As a lawyer Root became noted for his specialization in tax matters and served as the colony's lawyer in several tax cases in 1771. He also supplemented his modest income during the late 1760s and early 1770s by tutoring aspiring young law students, including future U.S. chief justice Oliver Ellsworth. In 1775 and 1776 Root served as justice of the peace for Hartford County.

Early in the revolutionary war, Root was directed by Connecticut's Council of Safety to raise troops in the western counties of the state for the Continental army. In December 1776 he was appointed lieutenant colonel of this Connecticut regiment and later rose to the rank of adjutant general while serving as the aide-de-camp to General Israel Putnam during the latter's abortive New York campaign. By 1778 Root was serving the revolutionary cause more as a political figure than a military leader. From 1778 to 1780 he was a member of Connecticut's Council of Safety, which conducted the war during frequent legislative recesses, and the town of Coventry's representative to the lower house of the state legislature. During this time Root rose further within the ranks of Connecticut's political elite by serving as one of the state's delegates to the Continental Congress. At the congress, Root ardently supported a strong national government with the power to tax its citizens directly. He also presented the opening arguments for Connecticut before a special confederation commission in 1782 in the notable case involving the dispute between that state and Pennsylvania over territory in the Wyoming area of Pennsylvania.

Root continued his political ascendancy in 1780 with his election to the Governor's Council, the upper house of the state legislature, where he served until 1789. From 1785 to 1789 Root also was appointed as state's attorney for Hartford County. In 1788 Coventry elected Root as its delegate to the Connecticut ratifying convention on the U.S. Constitution. During the convention he vociferously supported the new plan of national government.

In 1789 Root abandoned his legislative career for the bench because of the rise of an agrarian faction bent on removing pro-mercantile lawyers from office. He served as an assistant justice of the Connecticut Superior Court from 1789 to 1796 and as the court's chief justice from 1797 to 1807. A 1784 Connecticut statute had forbidden any of the superior court's justices from serving in the legislature, thus forcing Root's resignation from the council. While serving on the superior court, Root made an important contribution to the development of the American legal system by compiling and publishing the official *Reports of Cases Adjudged in the Courts of Errors of Connecticut* (reprinted in 1952 as *Reports of Cases of the Connecticut Supreme Court*). Root's *Reports, 1789 to 1793* (1798) and *Reports, 1794 to 1798* (1802) continued the pioneering work of Ephraim Kirby for the court by providing an official compendium of the court's decisions to serve as case-generated legal precedents upon which the foundations of a distinct American system of common law would be based. As a result Root is considered one of the early fathers of American common law. In 1807 Root retired from the bench and resumed his legislative career when he was again elected as Coventry's delegate to the Connecticut legislature. In 1808 he cast his ballot as a presidential elector for the Federalist candidate Charles Pinckney, and in 1818 he called the Connecticut State Constitutional Convention to order. Root served in the town government of Coventry until his death there.

• Papers relating to Root's public career during the revolutionary and early republic periods are in the Connecticut State Library and the Connecticut Historical Society. In addition to the published papers found in Connecticut's *Public Records*, materials on Root are in Julian Boyd and Robert Taylor, eds., *The Susquehannah Company Papers* (1936–1971), and Edmund Burnett, ed., *Letters of Members of the Continental Congress* (1921–1938). Modern appraisals of Root's life are offered in James McLachlan, *Princetonians, 1748–1768* (1976), pp. 163–66, and U.S. Government Printing Office, *Biographical Directory of the American Congress 1774–1971* (1971), pp. 1632–33. For Root's military and political career in revolutionary Connecticut, see Richard Buel, Jr., *Dear Liberty* (1980); Christopher Collier, *Roger Sherman's Connecticut* (1971); and Collier, *Connecticut in the Continental Congress* (1973). For an assessment of Root's station in American legal history, see Morton Horwitz, *The Transformation Of American Law* (1977). Root's later political career in state politics is traced in Richard Purcell, *Connecticut in Transition, 1775–1818* (1918).

RONALD LETTIERI

ROOT, John Wellborn (10 Jan. 1850–15 Jan. 1891), architect, was born in Lumpkin, Georgia, the son of Sidney Root and Mary Clark. He was educated at home. When the family moved to Atlanta, they provided their son with a piano and a drawing studio, and his early proficiency in music and the visual arts later inspired his thinking about color in architecture. Following Atlanta's capture in 1864 by Union soldiers, fourteen-year-old Root was sent to Liverpool, England, where he was surrounded by the monumental stone, brick, and cast iron commercial architecture of a seaport. Studying at Clare Mount School, he matriculated at Oxford in June 1866, but his studies were interrupted when he was called back to New York, his family's home after the war. In September 1866 Root enrolled as a sophomore at New York University, graduating fifth in his class in 1869 with a B.S. in civil engineering.

Unable to afford architectural studies in Europe, Root apprenticed for a year with a successful New York office, Renwick & Sands, under the guidance of James Renwick, Jr., the designer of St. Patrick's Cathedral. In 1870 Root joined the office of John B. Snook, a London-born architect of New York residences and commercial buildings. While the Snook office was completing New York's first Grand Central Station (1869–1871), Root was made superintendent of construction for this structure, notable for its enormous, vaulted glass and iron train shed. To meet Chicago's urgent need for new buildings after the 1871 fire, Peter Wight invited Root to join Carter, Drake & Wight as chief draftsman early in 1872, the same year that Daniel H. Burnham joined the firm as a draftsman. Root and Burnham became friends quickly, and in July 1873 they left Wight's office to establish their architectural partnership, an influential collaboration lasting eighteen years.

The firm of Burnham and Root was involved at first with residential work, but the economic depression of 1873 curtailed their practice. Late in 1874 the wealthy Union Stockyards businessman John B. Sherman commissioned Burnham and Root to design a stylish and colorful Queen Anne style house and stable on the city's prestigious Prairie Avenue. This successful commission helped establish Burnham and Root's reputation. Throughout the 1870s and 1880s the firm was commissioned to design many Queen Anne style residences in the manner of British architect Richard Norman Shaw, as well as Romanesque revival style public and commercial buildings in the manner of architect Henry Hobson Richardson. Burnham and Root designed more than 270 projects across the country between 1873 and 1891, including as many as 216 private residences, 39 office buildings, and numerous apartments, hotels, railroad stations, stores, warehouses, schools, and other buildings. In 1880 Root married Mary Louise Walker, who died six weeks later of tuberculosis. In 1882 he married Dora Louise Monroe; they had two daughters and a son, John Wellborn, Jr., who became a prominent architect in the 1920s. Burnham and Root's partnership emerged during the 1880s to play a central role in conceiving the ten- to twenty-story-tall commercial building, then an astonishing height. Burnham's business sense and planning abilities were matched by Root's design abilities as an engineer and architect. Root advanced the stylistic and structural development of the early skyscraper by improving building technologies, fireproof construction materials, and secure foundations to carry heavy load-bearing and metal frame buildings. Architectural critic Henry Van Brunt believed that the work of Burnham and Root rivaled the work of Adler and Sullivan.

One of the earliest iron-frame structures to include fireproof terra cotta sheathing in Chicago, the ten-story Montauk building (1881–1882) owes much of its form and planning to the profit-driven limits imposed by the building's owners, Boston business brothers Peter and Shepherd Brooks and their Chicago real estate agent Owen F. Aldis. Peter Brooks insisted in an 1881 letter that "the building throughout is to be for use and not for ornament. Its beauty will be in its all-adaptation to its use" (quoted in Condit, p. 52, and in Hoffman, *Architecture*, p. 26, n. 10). Another Brooks and Aldis commission, the corner-sited Rookery building (1885–1888), illustrates Burnham's logical planning with its street-level shops and quadrangular office space arranged around a spectacular iron and glass central light court that provided natural light to the interior office façades. Richly ornamented inside and outside, the Romanesque-inspired red brick and granite building combines load-bearing masonry walls with iron skeleton construction, all resting on a reinforced concrete slab foundation. Describing this landmark in the January 1891 *Inland Architect*, Henry Van Brunt wrote, "The Rookery is not only a noted example of great fertility of design, but there is nothing bolder, more original or more inspiring in modern civic architecture either here or elsewhere than its glass-covered court."

The world's tallest and largest office building when completed, the sixteen-story Monadnock building (1889–1892) incorporated early wind-bracing technology into its massive brick walls. With battered six-foot-thick walls, the building was erected on a spread foundation of steel and concrete, a space-saving system that distributed enormous building loads horizontally and somewhat evenly across a concrete slab reinforced with criss-crossing steel beams. Root looked to ancient Egyptian sources for this tall office building's silhouette and unornamented form. Although Root had conceived of polychromatic walls of gradated bricks, client Peter Brooks chose a uniform dark color to express stability and verticality. Root's 22-story Masonic Temple (1890–1892) then became the world's tallest building until 1898. The building was demolished in 1939.

An influential neo-Gothic colorist familiar with John Ruskin's writings, Root was an innovative theorist interested in using color and ornament to create a reformed and indigenous American architecture. Root and other theorists believed that color and ornament applied to urban architectural form served to evoke

nature and its philosophical and emotional associations within the streets of the modern city. His ideas about color and light contributed to a theoretical basis for the organic architecture of his contemporary Louis Sullivan and, later, Frank Lloyd Wright. In his 1883 series of essays for *Inland Architect*, "Art of Pure Color," Root examined the psychological and emotional content of color in architecture as suggested by scientific color theory, French impressionist landscapes, and infamous colorist paintings by Turner and Whistler. Referring to Wagner's synaesthetic music theory and popular ideas about the *Gesamtkunstwerk* ("total work of art"), Root advocated a "symphony of colors" in urban architecture, sensitive to scale, local climate, and purpose. In an essay titled "Architectural Ornamentation" for the April 1885 *Inland Architect*, Root stated: "Unity of design we must have. But the unity must spring from within the structure, not without it. The great styles of architecture are of infinite value but they are to be vitally imitated, not servilely copied. Continually return to nature and nature's methods."

Although Root has been remembered most for his tall buildings, he was an influential contributor to urban residential architecture. In the October 1890 *Scribner's Magazine*, he published an essay titled "The City House in the West," which was included posthumously in the book *Homes in City and Country* (1893), coauthored with Russell Sturgis, Bruce Price, and others. Root commented that western city houses were noteworthy for their "openness," providing interior spaces well lit by large and numerous windows. Active in the service of the architectural profession, Root was elected secretary (1885) and then president (1886) of the Western Association of Architects, established in Chicago in 1884 to counter the dominating presence of the East Coast architects and the American Institute of Architects (AIA). In 1885 the Chicago Architectural Sketch Club was established to serve young draftsmen, and Root frequently supported the club's educational purposes as a competition juror and lecturer. In 1887 he was elected a director of the AIA. To settle professional conflicts between the two competitive organizations, Root helped consolidate the AIA and Western Association of Architects in 1889, when he was elected secretary to the reinvigorated AIA. In 1889 Root was also a lecturer for the architecture classes at the Art Institute of Chicago.

In 1890 Root was appointed consulting architect, Burnham the chief of construction, and Frederick Law Olmsted the consulting landscape architect for the 1893 World's Columbian Exposition in Chicago. Root developed the fair's site plan but did not live to implement it. Less than a year later, he died in Chicago of pneumonia, the result of a cold he caught after a dinner for the fair's architects. At the time of his death, Root had been reelected as secretary of the AIA.

• Archival materials for Root are not plentiful. An 1885 fire destroyed the firm's office and its contents; however, some of his plans, sketches, and drawings belong to the Department of Architecture at the Art Institute of Chicago. Meaningful (but inaccurate) for its proximity to Root's career, Harriet Monroe's 1896 memoir, *John Wellborn Root* (facsimile edition 1966), narrates her brother-in-law's life. The most thorough scholarship and bibliographic summary regarding Root's career is Donald Hoffman, *The Architecture of John Wellborn Root* (1973). For a study of the famous Monadnock building, see Hoffman's earlier article, "John Root's Monadnock Building," *Journal of the Society of Architectural Historians* 26 (Dec. 1967): 269–77. Some of Root's writings are collected in Donald Hoffman, ed., *The Meanings of Architecture: Buildings and Writings by John Wellborn Root* (1967). Important critical biographical pieces on Root include Henry Van Brunt's essay "John Wellborn Root," *Inland Architect* (Jan. 1891), and Theodore Starrett, "John Wellborn Root," *Architects' and Builders' Magazine* 13 (1912): 429–31.

For more about Burnham and his partnership with Root, see the two-volume biography by Charles Moore, *Daniel H. Burnham: Architect and Planner of Cities* (1921). Thomas S. Hines, *Burnham of Chicago: Architect and Planner* (1974), examines the partnership and Root's work through the world's fair, and he includes an appendix of Burnham buildings. For the Rookery, see Meredith Clausen's essay, "Paris of the 1880s and the Rookery," in *Chicago Architecture, 1872–1922: Birth of a Metropolis*, ed. John Zukowsky (1987). For a detailed examination of how Root's ideas about color and architecture developed from nineteenth-century color theory, see Lauren S. Weingarden, "The Colors of Nature: Louis Sullivan's Architectural Polychromy and Nineteenth-Century Color Theory," *Winterthur Portfolio* 20 (Winter 1985): 243–60. The broader development of tall office buildings in Chicago has been evaluated by Carl Condit, *The Chicago School of Architecture: A History of Commercial and Public Building in the Chicago Area, 1875–1925* (1964). For a revised and critical study of Chicago's urban landscape and architecture, see Daniel Bluestone, *Constructing Chicago* (1991).

R. STEPHEN SENNOTT

ROOT, Joseph Pomeroy (23 Apr. 1826–20 July 1885), physician and diplomat, was born in Greenwich, Massachusetts, the son of John Root and Lucy Reynolds. He graduated from Berkshire Medical College (Mass.) in 1850. The following year he established a medical practice in Hartford, Connecticut, and married Frances Evaline Alden, with whom he had five children.

In 1855 Root began his political life when he was elected to the Connecticut legislature as a Whig. Soon after, however, motivated by his antislavery views, Root joined the Connecticut-Kansas colony, a party of forty-nine emigrants who left for Kansas in March 1856. This group became better known as the "Beecher's Bible Rifle" colony after Henry Ward Beecher's congregation raised sufficient money to give each member of the colony a Bible and a Sharps rifle.

As a Free Soiler, Root was an active participant in Kansas's struggle for statehood. He was concerned with the ease of immigration and helped establish a road from Topeka to Nebraska City. In 1860 he also advocated a territorial convention to devise a system of railroad land grants to further develop Kansas's infrastructure. Root also actively worked to arm Free Soil settlers, helping transport two hundred Sharps rifles to the region under the escort of John Brown. Root contributed to free state propaganda as well, writing editorials for the Wyandotte *Register* (1857) and the Wyandotte *Gazette* (1858). Indeed, Root remained interested in Kansas and its history throughout his life and eventually wrote a memoir of his 1856 experiences.

But Root's greatest contribution to Kansas history was through his political service, especially during Kansas's troubled transition from territory to state. Root was most active at a time when Kansas had two rival governments. One government, organized under the territorial act and based in Lecompton, was proslavery and, despite concerns over electoral fraud, enjoyed the support of Presidents Franklin Pierce and James Buchanan. The other government, organized under a free state constitution and headquartered in Topeka, was backed by the Republican-controlled U.S. House of Representatives. Adamantly antislavery, Root was several times a member of the territorial council, a delegate to the Topeka constitutional convention, and served as the chair of the Free State Executive Committee. In 1857 he was elected to the territorial senate and served as a member of the Kansas Volunteers (called by "Governor" James Lane to protect the ballot boxes during the elections), serving as the superintendent of enrollment for the Fourth Division. In 1859 Root attended the first Republican party convention held in Kansas. He was elected the first lieutenant governor under the Wyandotte Constitution as a Republican and served the new state from February 1861 to January 1863. During the Civil War Root entered the army as a surgeon for the Second Kansas Cavalry and served as the medical director of the Army of the Frontier. After the war he settled in Wyandotte to practice medicine and served as surgeon general from 1878 to 1882. With the exception of two years spent in New York as chief surgeon of the Clifton Springs Sanitarium, from 1877 to 1879, he remained in Wyandotte for the rest of his life.

President Ulysses Grant appointed Root U.S. minister to Chile, where he served from 15 September 1870 to 14 March 1873. Taking an interest in Chilean culture, Root described the conditions he found in many missives to Secretary of State Hamilton Fish, devoting particular attention to Latin American Indians and the transportation conditions in the Straits of Magellan. Root's ministry was distinguished mainly by his actions during the smallpox epidemic that struck Santiago in the summer of 1872. At first unwilling to act publicly due to his political position, Root published newspaper articles under an assumed name urging changes in sanitary conditions, but, as the mortality rates rose, he attended the people of Santiago personally in his capacity as a doctor. He was especially solicitous to those of the poorer classes who disliked the smallpox institutions, and he treated without charge those unable to afford a physician. He diligently toured hospitals and made recommendations for improving sanitary conditions, eventually succumbing to smallpox himself. Root recovered, and in appreciation for his humanitarian services, which were widely praised as beyond the normal diplomatic purview, a street in Santiago, Calle de Root, was named in his honor in 1872. His interest in Chile continued after he was recalled from Santiago; he was named to the Chilean Centennial Commission in 1876.

Root remained interested in politics and reform after his diplomatic service. In 1867 he was named one of the vice presidents of the Kansas Impartial Suffrage Association. He was also involved in the temperance movement, serving as an officer of the Kansas State Temperance Society in 1861 and in 1874 as vice president of the Temperance Convention, which worked to include a prohibition plank in the 1874 Republican platform. Root was an active member of the Republican party and attended the 1884 convention as a delegate. In 1876 he published *Catechism of Money*, which urged the continued use of "greenbacks" to increase the supply of paper money. Root died in Wyandotte, Kansas, after three decades actively serving Kansas.

• Root's memoir can be found in the archives of the Kansas Historical Society. while U.S. minister to Chile are in U.S. Government Printing Office, *Papers Relating to the Foreign Relations of the United States, 1871–1873*. For bibliographic information, the most useful sources for Root's career are published in the *Kansas Historical Collections* (17 vols., 1881–1928) and in Perl Morgan, *History of Wyandotte County, Kansas, and Its People* (1911). Also see D. W. Wilder, *The Annals of Kansas* (1886). Obituaries are in the *Topeka Capital*, 22 July 1885, and the *Topeka Weekly Commonwealth*, 23 July 1885.

PEARL T. PONCE

ROOT, Waverley (15 Apr. 1903–31 Oct. 1982), writer and journalist, was born Waverley Lewis Root in Providence, Rhode Island, the son of Francis Solomon Root and Florence Mae Lewis. When Root was seven years old, his family moved to Fall River, Massachusetts, where he attended the public schools. In 1920 he enrolled in Tufts University, where he worked as a campus reporter for Boston newspapers and the Associated Press, wrote for the student paper, and began a major in English. Dissatisfied with the English department, Root changed his major to psychology and talked the college administration into allowing him to teach his own course in American literature. In 1923 he left Tufts without a degree and moved to New York City. For the next few years he wrote theater and music criticism and fiction for a number of publications and a few book reviews for the *New York World*. Describing his writing many years later, Root said that he wrote "*New Yorker* short stories before the *New Yorker* was there to publish them" (*Paris Edition*, p. viii). In 1927, on a whim, Root packed a tin suitcase and his typewriter and took ship to France. He planned to stay only a few weeks but remained in France for the next thirteen years. Although details on Root's personal life—most notably his four marriages—are lacking, his subsequent career as Paris correspondent, literary critic, and author is well documented.

After arriving in Paris, Root used his connections with the *New York World* to talk his way into a position with the Paris edition of the *Chicago Tribune*. From 1927 to 1930 he wrote news stories and features as well as literary and art criticism. Except for a brief stint in London, where he moved with the first of four French wives in 1928, Root spent most of his time in Paris. From 1930 to 1934 Root was editor of the Paris edition. When the *Tribune* merged with the European edition of the *New York Herald Tribune* and ceased publication, Root joined the Paris bureau of the United Press, and for a few months he edited his own weekly, *Paris Tribune*. From 1932 to 1940 he also worked as the Paris correspondent for the Danish newspaper *Politiken*. In 1937 he married Jeanne Rose Albinelli, with whom he would have one daughter.

While employed by the United Press, Root wrote a 1938 story on the Nazis that eventually cost him his job. Root's story predicted that Germany would invade Austria on 15 May, missing the actual date of the invasion by only two days. But United Press managers, under pressure from the Nazi Propaganda Ministry and German subscribers to their service, fired Root. From there he moved to the Paris bureau of *Time* magazine and then became a radio broadcaster with the Mutual Broadcasting System. He remained in Paris until June 1940, when the French surrender forced him to return to the United States. There Root worked as a news commentator at WINS radio from 1940 to 1945, as a world news editor at the *New York Daily Mirror* from 1941 to 1942, and as a syndicated columnist for the New York City Press Alliance from 1941 to 1953. In 1950 Root returned to Europe where he held a variety of writing jobs, including positions as a ghost writer while he lived at Villefranche-sur-Mer in France from 1950 to 1952 and as an editor of Fodor's Travel Guides while he lived in The Hague. In 1955 he returned to France and became the Paris correspondent for the *Washington Post*, a position he held until 1967. In 1959 he married his last wife, Colette Debenais.

Although Root often joked that he would title his autobiography "I Never Knew Hemingway," in reference to all the literary memoirs of Paris in the 1920s, he held strong opinions on literature and became involved, if only indirectly through his criticism, with many of the best-known Paris artists and writers of his day. His letters and reviews revealed an early irritation with self-conscious expatriatism, and he issued scathing criticism of writers who put style and indulgent literary experimentation above content. A 1931 review of Gertrude Stein's *Lucy Church Amiably* criticized Stein's spare, repetitive, and self-conscious style by parodying it in the structure of the review: "You can read sometimes *Three Lives*. Sometimes you can you can read sometimes *Conversation as Explanation*. You can read even you can read sometimes you can read if you have time sometimes you can read the *Making of Americans*. You cannot read *Lucy Church Amiably*. Not even sometimes" (*Paris Edition*, p. 40). In 1932 he disparaged the literary magazine *New Review* as one that harbored "an undue proportion of the dry-as-dust theorists, talking a language of their own and, as a rule, laboring points that everyone else perceives intuitively, if indeed they have succeeded in getting hold of any points at all."

In 1930 Root collaborated with Philip D. Hurn on his first and highly controversial book, *The Truth about Wagner*, which purported to expose the composer Richard Wagner's private life. In the mid-1940s he published a three-volume work, *The Secret History of the War*.

Root was best known, however, for his writing on food. Never an author of recipes or even one who enjoyed cooking, Root in his writing focused on the techniques, history, and peculiarities of regional cuisines. His first such book, *The Food of France* (1958), made him into a world-renowned authority and did much to popularize French cuisine in the United States. Once established as a food writer, Root produced similar books on Italian and American cuisine, but *The Food of France*, which remained in print for more than twenty years, was by far his most popular work. In the late 1960s and early 1970s, as Root worked as the Paris correspondent for *Holiday* magazine, he wrote and collaborated on several books and began work on his massive gastronomical dictionary, *Food: An Authoritative Visual History and Dictionary of the Foods of the World*, a work that took him nearly a decade to finish. As a writer Root was generally known for his energetic, prolific, and quickly produced prose, but he frequently clashed with editors and publishers. His later correspondence reveals a frustration with editors who tried to cut his prose and a suspicion of publishers who cut authors' profits. Root's writing tended toward complex sentences laden with subordinate, interrupting clauses and witty but lengthy asides. As he explained to one editor, "One of my difficulties . . . is that my style, for better or for worse, is somewhat leisurely. I need space in which to turn around" (*Paris Edition*, p. xi). Though Root completed his memoirs of life in Paris between 1927 and 1934 in the 1970s, disagreements with publishers about how to edit them delayed publication of the book until after his death. In the early 1980s he wrote several short pieces based on his memoirs for the *International Herald Tribune*. An epicure until his final days, Waverley Root described in some of his last letters a lunch of oysters cooked in a rich cream sauce and the luscious breakfast croissants that he had enjoyed at the Île de Ré, where he died in his sleep.

• The essential source on Root is his autobiography, *The Paris Edition: The Autobiography of Waverley Root, 1927–1934*, ed. Samuel Abt (1987). The introduction by Abt also provides a useful biography. See also Root's many books on food, including *The Cooking of Italy* (1968); *Paris Dining Guide* (1969); *The Food of Italy*, with Richard de Rochement (1971); *Eating in America: A History* (1976); *Herbs and Spices: The Pursuit of Flavor*, a collaboration with other authors (1980); and, with de Rochement, *Contemporary French Cooking* (1962). A biographical sketch in the *Dictionary of Literary Biography*, vol. 4: *American Writers in Paris, 1920–1939*, assesses Root as a literary critic and describes his connections to the literary world in the 1920s. Obituaries are in the *Chicago Tribune* and the *New York Times*, both 2 Nov. 1982.

MICHELLE BRATTAIN

ROPER, Daniel Calhoun (1 Apr. 1867–11 Apr. 1943), cabinet member, was born in Marlboro County, South Carolina, the son of John Wesley Roper, a plantation owner, and Henrietta McLaurin. Roper was only two and a half years old when his mother died. He was raised in his mother's ancestral home by his father and stepmother, Lucy McColl, during Reconstruction. His father, a slave owner and Confederate army veteran, was bitter toward Reconstruction. While the elder Roper was not an educated man, he was a voracious reader who firmly believed in education for his son. Roper attended high school in Laurinburg, North Carolina, where he boarded with his uncle. He attended Wofford College in Spartanburg, South Carolina, for two years before transferring to Trinity College (now Duke University) in North Carolina, from which he received a bachelor of arts degree in 1888.

Although educated, Roper remained untrained in any specific profession. With a vague idea of pursuing a legal career, he decided to earn money for law school by teaching and accepted a position as an instructor at a consolidated school near his home. It was during this time that he met his future wife, Lou McKenzie, at the wedding of a friend. The couple married in December 1889, and the union produced seven children.

Sensing greater opportunities, Roper left teaching to become a life insurance agent. Having become well known locally as a result of his insurance solicitations, he was soon urged by friends to run for the state legislature. Although Roper had joined the Farmers' Alliance in 1890, he remained a Democrat when the Populist party formed. He was elected to the South Carolina House of Representatives in 1892. That year a state referendum on Prohibition had passed, and upon taking his seat in the legislature Roper was invited to introduce a bill that instituted a statewide ban on alcohol. Although the measure passed the lower house, it succumbed in the senate, and a compromise measure was enacted that set up the state-controlled dispensary system; it was the first such system in the country.

Although Roper left the legislature at the end of his term, his only experience with elected office represented merely the beginning of his career in government. The Prohibition bill brought him to the attention of U.S. senator Matthew C. Butler of South Carolina and led directly to his first appointed position when Senator Butler asked Roper to act as clerk for the Senate Interstate Commerce Committee. During his tenure with this committee, Roper attended hearings during which issues such as shipping rates were discussed (he also managed, as a visitor, to attend the first public legislative hearing on woman suffrage). Following the defeat of Butler in 1896, Roper left the committee to manage the office of financier Charles E. W. Smith in New York. He followed this position with another stint in the insurance industry but in 1900 returned to public service as a cotton specialist for the U.S. Census Bureau. Roper used his childhood knowledge of cotton production in preparing an accurate survey of the number of cotton gins in operation and the amount of cotton being produced from the gins. At first confined to survey work by mail, he later oversaw a field force of 626 agents that traveled throughout the South collecting information. His carefully planned and executed study led to further opportunity in 1911, when Congressman Albert S. Burleson of Texas recommended him as clerk of the House Ways and Means Committee.

Burleson's support of Woodrow Wilson for the Democratic presidential nomination in 1912 was rewarded with his appointment as postmaster general. Eager to surround himself with competent assistance, Burleson soon offered Roper the post of first assistant postmaster general. His duties included appointing 58,020 new postmasters. Since the Democrats had been out of power for sixteen years, there was a clamor for positions. Roper's first contact with Franklin D. Roosevelt came during this appointment process. Roosevelt was assistant secretary of the navy at the time and had sent his assistant, Louis McHenry Howe, to help with arbitration for the appointments. During his tenure with the post office, Roper worked to implement the newly created Parcel Post and to create public education programs that would teach the general population how to more effectively use the Post Office. Roper left the Post Office to assist Wilson in his successful reelection bid. In 1917 the president appointed Roper commissioner of internal revenue, a post in which Roper worked closely with Secretary of the Treasury William Gibbs McAdoo, Wilson's son-in-law. As commissioner of internal revenue Roper was also responsible for the enforcement of Prohibition, which he called "Uncle Sam's incorrigible child." He attempted, to no avail, to remove enforcement from the Bureau of Internal Revenue. He resigned his position on 31 March 1920.

Roper spent the next thirteen years in private life as president of the Marlin Rockwell Corporation. As a reward for swinging the support of McAdoo and other former Wilson Democrats to his camp, Franklin D. Roosevelt invited Roper to be his secretary of commerce in 1933. Roper not only oversaw the numerous tasks of his department, which included the gathering and compiling of business statistics, but also instituted a Business Advisory Council to make recommendations to the president and to Congress. In addition to his duties at the Commerce Department, he also served on the Council for National Defense, the Federal Board of Vocational Education, and the National Emergency Council.

When Roper resigned as secretary of commerce in December 1938, he thought his career as a public servant was over, but he was called into service one more time when President Roosevelt asked him to temporarily serve as minister to Canada for the period coinciding with the visit of King George VI and Queen Elizabeth of England. Roosevelt was eager to make a good impression during the first-ever visit of an English ruling monarch to the New World. Roper was sworn in on 9 May 1939, which was forty-six years to the date of his first induction into federal service. After remaining in the position until September, Roper finally retired for good. He died in Washington, D.C.

Daniel Roper's career spanned fifty years and six different presidents. His integrity and administrative abilities were widely respected, despite being overshadowed by some of the more dynamic men of the Roosevelt administration.

• Roper wrote *The U.S. Post Office* (1917) following his appointment in that department. The main source of information on his life and career is his autobiography, *Fifty Years of Public Life* (1941), written with Frank H. Lovette. Arthur M. Schlesinger, Jr.'s series on Franklin D. Roosevelt, *The Crisis of the Old Order* (1957) and *The Politics of Upheaval* (1960), plus Arthur S. Link's *Wilson: The New Freedom* (1956) also provide valuable information. The *New York Times* is a good source of information on his career during the years 1933–1939, and his obituary appears in that paper on 12 April 1943.

MARTI SPECKMAN
EDWARD L. LACH, JR.

ROPER, Elmo (31 July 1900–30 Apr. 1971), market researcher and public opinion analyst, was born Elmo Burns Roper, Jr., in Hebron, Nebraska, the son of Elmo Burns Roper, a banker, and Coco Malowney. He attended the University of Minnesota (1919–1920) and the University of Edinburgh (1920–1921), but he did not receive a degree. In 1922 he married Dorothy Shaw; they had two children.

In 1921 Roper opened a jewelry store in Creston, Iowa, but was unsuccessful and closed it in 1928. For the next four years he worked as a traveling salesman, first for Seth Thomas Clock Co. and then for the New Haven Clock Co. He was a good salesman, later crediting his success to a willingness to ask customers about their likes and dislikes.

In 1933, in the midst of the Great Depression, Roper became a sales analyst for Traub Manufacturing Co., a jewelry company. His first task was to discover why sales of the firm's engagement rings fell. Interviewing jewelers across the country, he discovered that Traub's rings fell between two markets, being too old-fashioned for upscale jewelers but too expensive for smaller stores. This exercise fascinated Roper. In 1934 his friend Richardson Wood, who had been a researcher at the J. Walter Thompson advertising agency, introduced Roper to Paul T. Cherington, a former Harvard Business School professor and research director at Thompson. Later that year they founded the market research firm of Cherington, Roper, and Wood.

The firm did its first surveys for Engineers' Public Service, a utility holding company that hoped consumer surveys would help it improve service and therefore avoid government regulation. In 1935 Wood proposed to *Fortune* magazine that the publication commission a regular survey of economic, social, and political trends. The magazine's founder, Henry Luce, liked the idea, and in 1935 the first "*Fortune* Survey" appeared, the first national public opinion poll.

Unlike earlier straw polls, which chose respondents indiscriminately, the *Fortune* Survey relied on responses from a small sample, in some cases only a few hundred people, carefully selected to represent the entire population. Cherington, Roper, and Wood was not the only firm to develop this approach, however. The market researchers Archibald Crossley and George Gallup had been planning similar surveys, and by the end of 1935 they began syndicating their own public opinion polls to newspapers. Over the next few years Roper, Gallup, and Crossley proselytized for the new polls and soon became known as the "big three" of polling.

At first many questioned the new polls' accuracy, doubting that such small samples could adequately measure the nation's opinion. The most famous poll in the United States, the *Literary Digest*'s quadrennial presidential poll, relied on millions of mail-in ballots to predict the upcoming election. In 1936, however, the *Digest* predicted the Republican Alf Landon would win the presidential election, while the *Fortune* Survey and the Gallup and Crossley polls picked the Democrat Franklin D. Roosevelt. The *Digest* had been misled by its unscientific sample, skewed as it was toward middle and upper-class voters. This triumph legitimated the scientifically sampled poll as a measure of public opinion.

In 1936 Wood left the firm, and in 1937 Cherington and Roper split. Roper worked on his own first as Elmo Roper and after 1955 as Elmo Roper & Associates. The bulk of his business was always market research, and he once estimated that opinion polling was only 5 percent of his work. He developed a loyal client base that included RCA, Standard Oil of New Jersey, Spiegel & Co., and the American Meat Institute. Roper managed to keep in the public eye as director of the *Fortune* Survey (1935–1950), a regular commentator on CBS, columnist for the *New York Herald Tribune* (1944–1948), and editor at large of the *Saturday Review*.

During World War II Roper worked for General William "Wild Bill" Donovan, first as deputy coordinator of information for the Office of Facts and Figures in 1941–1942, then as deputy director of the Office of Strategic Services (OSS) in 1942–1945. His main task at the OSS was staffing the new agency, but along the way he convinced several military leaders of the value of survey research. He helped George Marshall assemble the team that produced the pioneering social science study *The American Soldier* (1949) and led Dwight D. Eisenhower to support pioneering surveys of American soldiers and English civilians in wartime Britain.

Roper resumed full-time market research in 1945. In 1948 he and other pollsters suffered a setback after predicting Thomas Dewey would win the presidency. That September Roper announced that Dewey was "so clearly ahead" that Americans should "get ready to listen to his Inaugural." In the wake of Harry S. Truman's victory, several firms dropped Roper's service, and opinion polls in general did not regain their credibility until after 1960. He suffered another blow in 1956, when his associate Louis Harris quit Roper and Associates to form his own polling firm, taking several clients with him and leaving a permanent enmity between the two men.

Except for voting for Socialist Norman Thomas in 1932, Roper was a loyal Democrat. He supported many liberal causes, serving as fundraising chair of the National Urban League in the 1940s; as president of the Atlantic Union and of the Fund for the Republic in the 1950s; and as Chester Bowles, another chair of the commission described him, a "tough-minded" chair of the Connecticut State Civil Rights Commission from 1957 to 1962. He retired in 1966, when his son Burns Roper took over his firm. Elmo Roper died in Norwalk Hospital near his home in West Redding, Connecticut.

Observers spoke of Roper's frank manner and subtle wit. He was firmly convinced that the opinion poll could be a "great tool for democracy" if used to discover areas where the electorate was misinformed. He helped shape modern America by carrying the tools of market research into politics and government, but Roper had his greatest influence and is best remembered as one of the inventors of the public opinion poll.

• A selection of Roper's papers and letters are in the Roper Center for Public Opinion Research at the University of Connecticut. An August 1968 oral history is in the American Association for Public Opinion Research (AAPOR) Collection, Regenstein Library, University of Chicago. For overviews on the development of opinion polling, see Jean Converse, *Survey Research in the United States: Roots and Emergence, 1890–1960* (1987); Susan Herbst, *Numbered Voices: How Opinion Polling Has Shaped American Politics* (1993); and David W. Moore, *The Superpollsters: How They Measure and Manipulate Public Opinion in America* (1992). For two contemporary views, see Lindsay Rogers, *The Pollsters: Public Opinion, Politics and Democratic Leadership* (1949), and Beverly Smith, "Who's behind That poll," *American Magazine* 130 (Nov. 1940): 31, 153–56. An obituary is in the *New York Times*, 1 May 1971.

HARWELL WELLS

ROPES, Joseph (15 Dec. 1770–29 Sept. 1850), shipmaster and privateersman, was born in Salem, Massachusetts, the son of David Ropes and Ruth Hawthorne. His father, a naval captain in the American Revolution, died of his wounds at Halifax, Massachusetts, in 1781. Joseph was raised by his mother, reputedly the only person he ever feared. As a youth Ropes made several voyages to the West Indies and in 1794 took command of his own ship, *Recovery*. In 1801 he married Sarah Burchmore, with whom he had two children. Ropes subsequently pursued far-ranging maritime activities and was among the first Americans to visit the distant ports of Mocha (Yemen), Arabia, and Sumatra.

In 1809 the Crowninshield family appointed Ropes master of their newest vessel, *America*, acknowledged as one of the fastest afloat. Sailing from Malta that year, he forsook the usual coffee trade and proceeded up the Dardanelles to Constantinople, where he remained ten months. This was the first American vessel to call upon the Ottoman Empire. Ropes favorably impressed the Turkish officials, who arranged an audience with the sultan. He declined an opportunity to initiate a commercial treaty between the respective countries but was later permitted to trade on the Black Sea.

After returning home, Ropes developed a taste for politics, and in 1811 he represented Salem in the state assembly. During the War of 1812 Salem became renowned for the prowess of its privateering community. Ropes had *America* lightened, cut down, and modified to carry twenty nine-pounder cannons. He departed Salem on 7 September 1812, cruised the English Channel, and in rapid succession took the brigs *James and Charlotte*, *Benjamin*, and *Ralph Nickerson* and the armed ships *Hope* and *Dart*. Running low on water and prize crews, Ropes made for home and captured an additional vessel, *Euphemia*, off the New England coast. *America* returned to Salem amid great fanfare on 7 January 1813, after cruising 122 days. The ship's six prizes were valued at $158,000; according to one observer, "The superior reputation of Capt. Joseph Ropes of the *America* & the better condition of his ship have taken from our other navigators that praise which in any other comparison they might have shared" (Bentley, vol. 4, p. 146). Ropes spent the rest of the war in Salem commanding a company of naval artillery, or "Sea Fencibles," in defense of the coast. His only active service was on 3 April 1814, when he led the march to Marblehead to protect the frigate *Constitution* from a British squadron.

After the war Ropes retired from active seafaring and pursued careers in business and politics. Staunchly Republican, he was active in his party's politics and served several terms as town selectman. Ropes was also elected to the state assembly from Salem four times between 1823 and 1826. As an indication of public trust, he was made president of a bank, an insurance company, and the East India Marine Society. He died in Salem.

Ropes was an accomplished maritime figure, even in a town famous for its sailing heritage. He plied uncharted waters fearlessly and conducted business affairs so honestly that employers granted him wide latitude in their foreign dealings. Ropes's War of 1812 career, though brief, was highly successful and compares favorably with other privateersmen. He was also unique among contemporaries by being a strict disciplinarian, drilling his gun crews vigorously between chases. Ropes was typical of the old-style Yankee sea captains who carried the flag to all corners of the globe and made it respected wherever they went. He was, in Rev. William Bentley's estimation, "a firm & good seaman" (Bentley, vol. 4, p. 111).

• Clippings about Ropes exist at the Essex Historical Institute, Salem, and the Massachusetts State Library, Boston. Facets of his civilian career are discussed in William A. Fairburn, *Merchant Sail*, vol. 1 (1945) and vol. 2 (1947). For information on Ropes's War of 1812 activities, consult Bowdoin B. Crowninshield, "An Account of the Private Armed Ship *America* of Salem," *Essex Institute Historical Collections* 37 (1911): 1–76; and George Coggeshall, *History of American Privateers* (1861). For greater historical context see William Bentley, *The Diary of William Bentley* (4 vols., 1905–1914); James D. Phillips, *Salem and the Indies* (1947); Walter M. Whitehill, *The East India Marine Society* (1949); and Reuben E. Stivers, *Privateers and Volunteers* (1975).

JOHN C. FREDRIKSEN

RORER, David (12 May 1806–7 July 1884), attorney, was born in Pittsylvania County, Virginia, the son of Abraham Rorer and Nancy Cook, farmers. After his early education Rorer moved to Franklin County, Virginia, to study law with Nathaniel Claiborne and Henry Calaway. During his two-year course of study, Rorer lived with the Claiborne family and taught school to support himself. He was admitted to the bar in Pittsylvania County in April 1826.

In the fall of 1826, Rorer, accompanied by a slave, traveled by horseback to Little Rock, Arkansas. His early career there included farming, law practice, and holding governmental offices. Rorer was appointed by the governor as a county judge and later became a prosecuting attorney. For a short time, he also worked in American Indian removal and supervised construction of a portion of the Memphis and Little Rock Military Road. Although born in a slave state and having owned slaves, Rorer became disgusted with the injustice of slavery. Consequently, in 1835 Rorer sold his farm, freed his slaves, and moved north to Burlington, Michigan Territory (now Burlington, Iowa). Shortly after his arrival in late March 1836, Rorer was admitted to the practice of law.

In 1827 Rorer married Martha Daniel Martin, who died in 1838. The couple had four children. In March 1839 Rorer married Delia Maria Viele; they had three children.

Rorer's legal career grew with the town of Burlington. The meeting called to incorporate Burlington was held in 1836 in his office. He drafted the town's articles of incorporation, wrote some of its first ordinances, and named many of its first streets. Rorer is credited with first giving to the citizens of Iowa the name "Hawkeye" in 1838, which he did to prevent citizens of other states from giving Iowans "a more opprobrious title." Profits from his practice enabled him to build the first brick house in Iowa in 1836.

During the course of his career in Burlington, Rorer became one of the area's most prominent attorneys. From 1839 to 1884, Rorer argued before the Iowa's high court more often than any other attorney. In May 1853 he became counsel for the Burlington & Missouri River Road Company and continued as counsel after its consolidation as the Chicago, Burlington & Quincy Railway Company. During the last twenty-five years of his life, Rorer specialized in railroad litigation, becoming an expert in railroad law. Rorer wrote three highly valued treatises known commonly as *Rorer on Judicial Sales*, *Rorer on Inter-State Law*, and *Rorer on*

Railroads. The last of those was a two-volume work that Rorer completed when he was in his late seventies; it was used as a text at the Columbia College Law School and the University of Wisconsin.

Rorer is remembered primarily for his appearances in fugitive slave cases. In 1839 he argued for the slave Ralph in the first case heard before Iowa Territory's Supreme Court, *In re Ralph.* Ralph contracted for the purchase of his freedom from his owner for $550 and was allowed to travel to the Dubuque lead mines to earn the money for his freedom. When Ralph failed to pay the debt, the owner sent slavecatchers to return him to Missouri. The slavecatchers were stopped before reaching Missouri, and a writ of habeas corpus was issued on Ralph's behalf. On facts similar to those cited in *Dred Scott v. Sandford* (1857), Rorer argued that Ralph, as a resident of Iowa Territory, was free because Congress prohibited slavery within Iowa's borders. The Missouri Compromise, which outlawed slavery north of the 36° 30′ parallel, further supported Ralph's argument for freedom. Ralph was not subject to the fugitive slave laws but instead was in Iowa indefinitely by the voluntary consent of his owner, "virtually manumitted." Rorer argued that the act of contracting with Ralph indicated his free status, concluding that any relief that was due to the owner would have to be granted under the contract. The court accepted Rorer's arguments unanimously, and Ralph obtained his freedom.

In another fugitive slave case, Rorer represented a slaveowner. In June 1848 nine slaves escaped from Ruel Daggs's Missouri farm. The slavecatchers found nine alleged slaves near Salem, Iowa, shortly thereafter. Through sheer numbers and legal maneuvering, the citizens of the Quaker community prevented the slavecatchers from taking their captives to Missouri. The alleged slaves escaped, and Daggs filed suit in the federal district court in Burlington against the persons in Salem who had helped them.

Rorer's closing argument in *Daggs v. Frazier* (1850) centered on Iowa's recent statehood and the duty of its citizens to uphold the Constitution and laws of the United States. Referring to the impending crisis of disunion that arose from the slavery question, he urged the jury to honor the contract that Iowa had made with all states, slave and free, when it entered the Union. He stated that "above all, the law should be vindicated—its supremacy confirmed.—The idea that any man or society of men, may be permitted to trample upon the plain letter of the law and Constitution, should be severely rebuked, and the offenders convinced that the impunity they have enjoyed in other places, will never be found in Iowa." The jury accepted Rorer's arguments and found for Daggs, whom they awarded $2,900 in damages.

Although early in the Civil War Rorer advocated emancipation of the slaves, as a lawyer he represented both sides of the issue. Chief Justice Charles Mason of the Iowa Supreme Court recalled that "Mr. Rorer [was] always . . . a devoted legal student. . . . I [do not] know of any who devoted himself more unreserv-

edly to the interests of his clients." Rorer died in Burlington, Iowa.

Rorer exemplified what it was to be a lawyer in Iowa during its early years of white settlement. His career followed the territory and the state's growth through its developing towns and expanding rail transportation. In the fugitive slave cases, Rorer was at the center of defining Iowa's role in the constitutional compact and reflected in his arguments a common northern attitude of avoiding disunion by placating the South. By representing both slave and slavemaster, Rorer played the role of a vigorous advocate within the law's bounds. Through his litigation and three treatises, Rorer left a legacy of experience for the generation of attorneys who followed him.

• The actual titles of Rorer's three treatises are *A Treatise on the Law of Judicial and Execution Sales* (1873), *American Inter-State Law* (1879), and *A Treatise on the Law of Railways* (1884). His closing arguments in *Daggs v. Frazier* are found in Paul Finkelman, ed., *Fugitive Slaves and American Courts*, vol. 1 (1988), pp. 495, 516–27 (reprinting George Frazee's report of the case). Rorer's legal career is described by J. A. Swisher, "Eminence at the Bar," *The Palimpsest* 26 (1945): 275–88. Personal recollections of Rorer and a letter from him to the author are found in Edward Holcomb Stiles, *Recollections and Sketches of Notable Lawyers and Public Men of Early Iowa* (1916), pp. 240–49. For a description of Rorer's work in the fugitive slave cases, see James Connor, "The Antislavery Movement in Iowa," 343 *Annals of Iowa* 40 (1970): 352, 354–56.

JILL M. GOSSIN

RORER, Sarah Tyson (18 Oct. 1849–27 Dec. 1937), cooking teacher and diet reformer, was born Sarah Tyson Heston in Richboro, Bucks County, Pennsylvania, the daughter of Charles Tyson Heston, a pharmacist, and Elizabeth Sagers. The family resided in Buffalo, New York, but Elizabeth Heston returned to her mother's home for the delivery of her firstborn. "Sallie," as she was called, grew up in the Buffalo area and attended East Aurora Academy, a female seminary. She later attributed the beginnings of her interest in cooking reform to her father's poor health and delicate digestion resulting from service in the Civil War. Around 1869 the family returned to eastern Pennsylvania, and in 1871 Sallie Heston married William Albert Rorer, a clerk/bookkeeper, in Philadelphia's Second Reformed Church. The couple had three children, one of whom died in early childhood.

To relieve household tedium, Sallie Rorer attended some lectures at the Woman's Medical College and in 1879 enrolled in a cooking course at Philadelphia's New Century Club. She proved such an apt pupil that when the instructor left, Sallie was asked to teach the cooking classes. Mrs. Rorer, as she was thereafter called, taught there for several years and then set out on her own, founding the Philadelphia Cooking School in 1882. Here people from all strata of society studied improved diet and cooking methods. Later a normal course to train teachers was added, and some of the first dietitians and home economists in the country received their education. At the urging of several well-known local doctors, Rorer added a "diet kitchen" in which special menu items were prepared for patients who came to Philadelphia for treatment but who stayed at local hotels where special foods were unavailable. She also carried her message of improved diet in outreach programs to institutions as diverse as finishing schools and refuges for "fallen women." Classes about diet therapy were also provided for doctors and nurses.

Rorer expanded her teachings into all the communications media of her time. *Mrs. Rorer's Philadelphia Cook Book* appeared in 1886. She wrote at least fifty-four cookbooks or booklets. Among her other major publications were *Mrs. Rorer's New Cook Book* (1902) and *Mrs. Rorer's Diet for the Sick* (1914). A perennial favorite that went through at least twenty printings was *How to Cook Vegetables* (1891), distributed as a premium by the W. Atlee Burpee Seed Company.

In 1886 Rorer began writing "Housekeeper's Inquiries" for *Table Talk*, a Philadelphia-based monthly. This feature attracted a large following, and the size of and subscriptions to the magazine increased rapidly. During her eight-year affiliation with the periodical she wrote more than 240 articles and answered more than 2,000 inquiries. After editing the magazine *Household News* from 1893 to 1896, she was asked by Edward Bok to write for the *Ladies' Home Journal*, in which she was introduced in 1897 as the "Most Famous Cook in America." By the time she left in 1911, the magazine was said to be read by 13 million women.

Beginning in 1889 Rorer's cooking demonstrations became a fixture at food expositions held annually in Philadelphia. With a carefully cultivated stage presence, she proved to be a consummate showwoman. To illustrate how neat and clean cooking could be, she always appeared in a silk gown. (Some commentators did point out that much of the "dirty work" was done by her assistant, who wore calico.) Reports tell of seats filled by two o'clock even though her lecture began at four, repeats of sessions by popular demand, and other evidence of her public success. Enthusiastic press coverage of these performances revealed Rorer's epigrammatic wit and superb audience rapport.

Rorer was an advocate of light, healthful cookery and of reducing kitchen drudgery. She gave advice and made pronouncements on a variety of topics: "Preserves are things people put up in the summer to make them sick in the winter." "If you can digest those things [fried potato cakes], you deserve to have a monument erected to your digestion at your death." "Fish is not brain food, because no fishermen of my acquaintance are overly brilliant." "Banish the frying pan and there will not be much sickness either in city or country." "Bad cooking is largely responsible for the crowded conditions of our insane asylums, almshouses, prisons and hospitals." "It is the hankering of the ill-fed stomach that induces men to drink." "It is deadly to follow a hearty meal with mental or physical exercise; many a man has died making his after-dinner speech." "There is nothing in a cake to give you brain

and muscle unless you get the latter from beating the cake." "I would feel my life work finished if I could emancipate women from coal cookery." "Exercise is wholesome, but a promenade in the open air is more beneficial than running all over the kitchen until you drop from exhaustion." "If your kitchen is the size of a barn, divide it into four imaginary rooms . . . use one for the kitchen."

Rorer was soon called on to take her cooking show to cities across the country, where she was equally well received. At the Woman's Building of the World's Columbian Exposition in Chicago in 1893, she presided over a "corn kitchen" that was visited by a quarter of a million people who watched her prepare dishes, all of which featured a form of corn as an ingredient. In 1904 at the Louisiana Purchase Exposition in St. Louis she drew large audiences to her model kitchen. She spent many summers at the Pennsylvania Chautauqua at Mount Gretna where a large building, Rorer Hall, was constructed for her demonstrations.

Rorer closed her cooking school in 1903; her last cookbook was published in 1917. Over the years her marriage had deteriorated, and she and her husband separated around 1896. She later moved to Colebrook near the Pennsylvania Chautauqua grounds. In retirement she became interested in politics and served several terms as president of the Lebanon County League of Democratic Women. At age seventy-nine she toured Pennsylvania making speeches supporting Al Smith. During the depression her investments failed, her book royalties dwindled, and she was left destitute. Former students organized a pension fund to assist her. Some professional organizations, realizing her importance as a pioneer cooking teacher and reformer, also contributed to the fund. She died in her Colebrook home.

Sarah Tyson Rorer has been widely acclaimed as an important figure in the home economics movement that culminated in the founding of the American Home Economics Association in 1908 (although she was not directly involved with the organization). She spread the word about improved cooking and diet to an audience that ranged from slum residents to society figures and worked passionately to reduce kitchen drudgery both for women who did their own cooking and for hired help. Many early home economists and dietitians were educated in her Philadelphia Cooking School. Because of the school and the diet kitchen attached to it, Rorer is widely acknowledged as the first American dietitian.

• A small collection of Roreriana is housed in the Schlesinger Library, Radcliffe College. Five letters by former students with recollections about Rorer are in the files of the American Dietetic Association in Chicago. During Rorer's active career several biographical sketches were published, including Mrs. Talcott Williams, "The Most Famous Cook in America," *Ladies' Home Journal*, Feb. 1897, p. 7, and Elise Biesel, "The First Cook in the Land," *Good Housekeeping*, Mar. 1914, pp. 420–22. A song, "Mr. and Mrs. Rorer," with lyrics by P. G. Wodehouse and music by Jerome Kern was featured in the 1924 Broadway musical *Sitting Pretty*. For discussion of Rorer's role as the first American dietitian, see Mary Pascoe Huddleson, "A New Profession Is Born," *Journal of the American Dietetic Association* 23 (1947): 573–78, and Huddleson, "Sarah Tyson Rorer—Pioneer in Applied Nutrition," *Journal of the American Dietetic Association* 26 (1950): 321–24. Rorer herself reminisced in "Early Dietetics," *Journal of the American Dietetic Association* 10 (1934): 289–95. The most complete assessment is Emma Seifrit Weigley, *Sarah Tyson Rorer: The Nation's Instructress in Dietetics and Cookery* (1977). See also Weigley's "The Philadelphia Chef: Mastering the Art of Philadelphia Cookery," *Pennsylvania Magazine of History and Biography* 96 (1972): 229–40. Obituaries are in the *Lebanon* (Pa.) *Daily News*, 29 and 31 Dec. 1937.

EMMA S. WEIGLEY

ROSA, Edward Bennett (4 Oct. 1861–17 May 1921), physicist, was born in Rogersville, New York, the son of the Reverend Edward David Rosa, a Methodist minister, and Sarah Gilmore Roland. He received a B.S. in physics from Wesleyan University in Middletown, Connecticut, in 1886, graduating first in his class. He then taught physics and chemistry at the English and Classical School, Providence, Rhode Island, for two years before entering the Johns Hopkins University in Baltimore, Maryland, for graduate study under the renowned experimentalist Henry A. Rowland. In 1891 Rosa received his Ph.D. from Johns Hopkins, where his research investigated the measurement of fundamental electrical constants. He was appointed assistant professor of physics at the University of Wisconsin in 1890 and accepted an associate professorship at Wesleyan in 1891, advancing to full professor of physics there the following year. Rosa taught at Wesleyan until recruited by Samuel Wesley Stratton in 1901 to become a physicist at the recently organized National Bureau of Standards (NBS) in Washington, D.C., where Stratton was director. Rosa became chief physicist there in 1910 and remained in that position until his death. He married Mary Evans of Harrisburg, Pennsylvania, in 1894. They had no children.

Edward Rosa contributed significantly to American science both as an imaginative experimentalist and as a research administrator at NBS, which had become, soon after its inception, the world's largest comprehensive laboratory for the physical and engineering sciences. His personal scientific research focused mostly on metrological problems in pure physics, including the electrical properties of inductance, capacitance, current, power, and resistance. Rosa was especially effective in helping develop international consensus on electrical measurements in his position as secretary of the International Technical Committee on Electrical Units and Standards. He also studied technical solutions to problems that bore specifically on large-scale public industries. These included the determination of flame standards for heating and illuminating gas and the difficult problem of electrolysis, which was the bane of early electric power industries and electric rail systems.

His career as an administrator both paralleled and helped to determine the agenda of NBS during its first two decades. The NBS came into existence at the same time that science-based industries began to rise to prominence in leading industrial economies. This was also when the industrial might of the United States began outpacing its nearest rivals of the Industrial Revolution, namely Great Britain and Germany. The electrical industries, including power generation and equipment manufacturing, and the large chemical industries of the day relied increasingly on research laboratories to produce innovations and to drive commercial expansion and competitiveness. Metrology was key to all research, and this was the specific charter responsibility of the NBS.

As broad and significant as metrology was for American science-based industries, several other factors moved NBS beyond this program, and Rosa was central to this expanded agenda as the highest-ranking administrator below the NBS director. First, it was Rosa who immediately oversaw the comprehensive NBS investigations of the major utilities industries of the day, which included electrical power, telephony, and natural gas. The results of these multiyear research projects produced major analyses of technical service standards, safety requirements, and cost-pricing guidelines that allowed local utilities commissions around the country to regulate these public services in their districts.

In addition, the First World War brought emergency powers for research and development of critical technologies to NBS in very short order. For the bureau as a whole, this new scientific territory included hundreds of investigations in virtually every emerging technology of the day, from novel synthetic chemicals to advanced optical systems to aeronautical engineering. Into Rosa's own division (electricity) the war brought forth one of the world's most advanced radio laboratories, whose pioneering work produced radio direction finders and advances in aviation and naval communications and navigations systems. Additionally, the new disciplines of X-ray and radioactivity measurements were organized under Rosa's direction.

As a result of the two themes at NBS of the scientific advising of regulatory commissions for the nation's utilities on the one hand, and the involvement of government science in producing innovations in high technology for the public good on the other hand, Rosa developed a strongly progressive philosophy of government-public interaction. In essence Rosa argued that scientific research, pure and applied, is a proper and publicly beneficial activity for the federal government to pursue. Rosa's efforts to move both public and legislative opinion in this direction were not mere polemical exercises. Instead, he applied the same rigor of research and execution toward this end as he had toward any of his laboratory investigations. His reconnaissance of the civil service, of the categorized expenditures and returns for government programs in general and for scientific research in particular, comprised the most comprehensive studies of their kind when they were published.

In 1900 Rosa received the Eliott Cresson Medal (for "service to humanity") of the Franklin Institute for his work at Wesleyan University with Wilbur O. Atwater in developing the "respiration calorimeter," a device useful in determining the available energy content of various foods. He was a member of many honorary organizations, including the American Philosophical Society, American Physical Society, American Association for the Advancement of Science (vice president in 1910), and the National Academy of Sciences (elected in 1913), among others. He died at work in his office of a heart attack.

• Miscellaneous papers and memoranda relative to Rosa's administrative career are located at the National Archives, Washington, D.C., RG 167. Rosa authored or coauthored ninety articles and published lectures. The majority of these are technical/scientific expositions in fundamental physics and metrology, published in leading scientific journals such as the *Physical Review*, the *Proceedings of the National Academy of Sciences*, the *Bureau of Standards Bulletin*, and the journals of many of the principal engineering societies. More than twenty articles were either popular articles or policy studies, and among the policy studies are his two most exhaustive analyses on government programs and government science. The first of these two essays, "The Economic Importance of the Scientific Work of the Government," ran in three installments of *Scientific Monthly* (July, Aug., and Sept. 1920). The companion piece, "Expenditures and Revenues of the Federal Government," was a book-length manuscript that was published in the *Annals of the American Academy of Political and Social Science* (May 1921). His career is discussed in several sections in Nelson R. Kellogg, "Gauging the Nation: Samuel Wesley Stratton and the Invention of the National Bureau of Standards" (Ph.D. diss., Johns Hopkins Univ., 1991), as well as Rexmond C. Cochrane, *Measures for Progress: A History of the National Bureau of Standards* (1966). His NBS colleague William Weber penned a biographical essay that includes Rosa's bibliography in National Academy of Sciences, *Biographical Memoirs* 16 (1936). Obituaries are in the *New York Times*, 18 May 1921, and *Science*, 24 June 1921.

NELSON R. KELLOGG

ROSATI, Joseph (12 Jan. 1789–25 Sept. 1843), Catholic bishop, was born Peter Louis Joseph Raphael Rosati in Sora, then in the kingdom of Naples, Italy, the son of Giovanni Rosati and Vienna Senese, aristocrats. He attended the local diocesan seminary but felt called to join the Congregation of the Mission, the religious community founded by St. Vincent de Paul and commonly called Vincentians. After completing his novitiate in Rome, he professed vows in 1808. He then pursued theological studies at the Vincentian seminaries in Naples and Rome and was ordained a priest in February 1811. He next engaged in the typical Vincentian work of preaching in parishes around Rome and Naples and giving retreats to seminarians preparing for ordination.

In 1816 Rosati joined the Roman Vincentians under the leadership of Felix DeAndreis, who accepted the invitation of Bishop Louis DuBourg of Louisiana to do missionary work in Missouri, then a part of the latter's diocese. After long stays in Baltimore, Maryland, and Bardstown, Kentucky, where he taught at the diocesan seminary, Rosati joined DeAndreis in Missouri in 1818. Rosati served as rector of the Vincentians' St.

Mary's Seminary at Perryville, Missouri's first chartered college, which opened in 1818. He also served as pastor of the local church. Following DeAndreis's death in 1820, Rosati became superior of the American Vincentians, a position of importance as the order's work began to expand.

As Vincentian superior, Rosati was a logical candidate for the episcopate. In 1824 he was appointed coadjutor bishop of Louisiana and continued to head the school at Perryville while exercising episcopal functions in the northern part of this vast diocese. After DuBourg resigned as bishop of Louisiana in 1825, the Holy See created the separate dioceses of New Orleans and St. Louis and appointed Rosati first bishop of St. Louis in March 1827 and administrator of the New Orleans diocese until 1829.

Taking up residence at St. Louis in 1830, Rosati began the institutional development characteristic of a diocese. He welcomed religious orders such as the Sisters of St. Joseph from France to staff schools, the Sisters of Charity from Maryland to conduct a hospital, and the Visitation Sisters to begin their educational work, first in nearby Illinois before moving to St. Louis. The Jesuits came to staff a college that became St. Louis University. Rosati also built the first St. Louis Cathedral and made plans for a diocesan seminary. Although he was a leader of an important religious order, he exercised a quiet, unobtrusive competence in laying the institutional foundations for an important American diocese.

In church affairs outside his diocese, Rosati participated in the American bishops' provincial councils in Baltimore in 1829, 1833, 1837, and 1840. When visiting Rome in 1840, Rosati received appointment from Pope Gregory XVI as apostolic delegate to Haiti to resolve church-state differences there. After his diplomatic mission to Haiti, Rosati returned to Rome with a draft treaty between the Holy See and the Haitian government. Having consulted with Roman officials, he began the return trip to Haiti to arrange for the agreement's completion. He was taken ill in Paris and returned to Rome, where he died.

• Rosati's extensive personal papers are in the Archives of the Archdiocese of St. Louis. Other papers are deposited in the DeAndreis-Rosati Memorial Archives, St. Mary's Seminary, Perryville, Mo. Rosati letters are held in the *Curia Generalizia della Missione* in Rome with a microfilm edition at the DeAndreis-Rosati Memorial Archives. Frederick John Easterly, C. M., *The Life of Rt. Rev. Joseph Rosati, C. M., First Bishop of St. Louis, 1789–1843* (1942), is a fine scholarly biography. For an account of the establishment of the Vincentians in the United States, see Joseph Rosati, "Recollection of the Establishment of the Congregation of the Mission in the United States," trans. R. Stafford Poole, C. M., serialized in *Vincentian Heritage*, vols. 1–4 (1980–1984), and John E. Rybolt, C. M., *The American Vincentians: A Popular History of the Congregation of the Mission in the United States, 1815–1987* (1988). William Barnaby Faherty, *Dream by the River: A History of the Archdiocese of St. Louis*, rev. ed. (1981), and John Rothensteiner, *History of the Archdiocese of St. Louis* (1928), treat Rosati's role as bishop.

JOSEPH M. WHITE

ROSE, Aquila (c. 1695–1723), poet, was born in England. Nothing is known of his life except the sketchy details supplied by friends and acquaintances in elegies and other brief references published after his death. We know from the most informative of those contemporary pieces, "To the Memory of Aquila Rose, Deceas'd," which has been attributed to fellow poet Joseph Breintnall, that Rose was educated in England. Breintnall's long poem notes that a "dissast'rous" love affair with "Silvia" and "cross affairs," the result of "some strange power, who envied his repose," drove Rose from England. He became a common seaman, traveling to Iberia, "Etruscan Ports," and Sardinia before making his way to North America. Rose probably arrived in Philadelphia sometime before 1717. When an illness forced him to remain for a few weeks, he acquired a local reputation for "his pleasing Conversation" and formed a friendship with James Logan, who was among the most influential of Pennsylvania's citizens in the first half of the eighteenth century. After Rose's health returned, he became a compositor in Andrew Bradford's printing office. He married "Maria," served for a time as clerk to the provincial assembly, and eventually became master of the ferry he established on the Schuylkill River. Both the clerkship and the right to develop the ferry were apparently rewards from Lieutenant Governor William Keith, who occasionally had the benefit of Rose's writing skills in support of his campaign to remove control of Pennsylvania from the Penn Proprietary. That Rose kept a degree of autonomy in the arrangement is suggested by the fact that one of his few extant poems is an ode to Richard Hill, a strong supporter of the proprietary interest.

Breintnall remarks repeatedly on Rose's comfort with doing common labor to earn his living, despite an education that would seem to fit him for other kinds of work:

Now he, disguis'd, assumes the lab'ring Swain,
And looks as when he lately plough'd the Main.
Great Spirits thus can brook an humble Shew,
And unobserv'd beneath their Burthens grow.

Rose did not have long to pursue his new trade. In 1723 a storm broke his boat loose from its moorings. While retrieving it, Rose was severely chilled. He became ill, apparently as a result, and died in Philadelphia soon after, at the age of twenty-eight, leaving a widow and a child. (One anonymous elegy printed in the *American Weekly Mercury* [4 Mar. 1725] alludes to two children—"two lovely pledges"—but Breintnall and Samuel Keimer mention only one.) Elegist Elias Bockett gives 22 August 1723 as the exact date of Rose's death, but Keimer has it as 24 June 1723.

This sketch of Rose's life, from humble and troubled beginnings to at least local fame, provides a story often preserved in American biography. Benjamin Franklin, whose life and autobiography followed the same trajectory, memorializes Rose as "a pretty Poet." Though he lived in Philadelphia for little more than six years, Rose had a significant impact on the development of literary culture there. His charismatic personality and educated tastes attracted others with interest in belles-lettres into an informal company gathering for the exchange of ideas and poetry. This group, the first circle of belletrists in Philadelphia, included such notables as William Allen, David French, Jacob Taylor, Breintnall, and Keith.

In 1740 Franklin printed a posthumous collection of Rose's verse gathered together by Rose's son Joseph: *Poems on several Occasions, by Aquila Rose: To which are prefixed, some other Pieces writ to him, and to his Memory after his Decease.* Joseph Rose prefaces the volume by remarking that his motivation for publishing his father's work derived from "the good Reception the poetical manuscript Writings . . . have met with." He goes on to explain that he has collected all the verses he could find, but "many of [Rose's] best Pieces were lent out, after his Decease, by my Mother, to Persons who have forgot to return them." What remains is twenty-six pages of poetry: two translations of selections from Ovid's *De Tristibus*, a drinking song "To His Companions at Sea," odes "To Richard Hill, Esq." and "To his Excellency Sir William Keith, Bart. on his Journey to Connestogoe, and Treaty with the Indians there," a poem of gratitude "To J———n C———dge, Esq." for his hospitality, a lament "To Mr. W———m C———r, on the Death of his Wife" and another "On the Death of his Friend's much-lov'd Child," a reminiscence "To the Memory of his Sister, who died on his Birth-Day," three occasional poems as New Year's gifts to local newspaper carriers, a humorous song "On the Gift of a Boat," and a brief piece "Written Extempore."

This slight body of work is apparently all that remains. The translations from Ovid include passages that may have reminded Rose of his own "exile" from England and trials at sea. They speak movingly of the dangers of ocean storm and of the pain of leaving loved ones and comfort behind. These translations, the best of Rose's extant work, document his strong sense of narrative and considerable skill with heroic couplet. Other poems are more conventional in both form and content, though that very conventionality suggests the depth of Rose's education in neoclassical texts and aesthetics. The lament "On the Death of his Friend's much-lov'd Child," for example, uses heroic couplet to bring the grieving process to its predictable end:

But Mourning's vain: No Tears will Death controul,
Or stop one Moment the departing Soul:
What Mortal dares with Providence contend;
He rul'd the Birth, and will command the End?

Rose frequently adopts the self-deprecatory descriptors common to eighteenth-century poets. He sends "these worthless Lines" as "a slender Tribute" "To the Memory of his Sister," apologizing for his "weak Verse" because it is no match for her "Due in Praise." Whatever Rose thought—and we think—of the value of these few poems, they form the first collection of poetry written and published in Pennsylvania.

• All extant work by Rose and much of what remains about him is gathered in *Poems on several Occasions . . .* (1740). At least six copies remain in special collections, but most readers will find access to the *Poems* in the microformed Early American Imprint Series. This volume prints Breintnall's elegy, mentioned above, and six other poems to Rose, mostly elegies, including Elias Bockett, "A Poem to the Memory of Aquila Rose," which had also been printed separately in London and included in the *American Weekly Mercury*, 2 July 1724, pp. 2–3. The text of Samuel Keimer's *Elegy to Aquila Rose* (1723), which Franklin's *Autobiography* describes as being composed and set in type simultaneously, is available in Samuel Hazard, *Register of Pennsylvania* (Nov. 1828), and Evert A. Duyckinck and George L. Duyckinck, eds., *Cyclopaedia of American Literature*, vol. 1 (1855; repr. 1875, 1965), pp. 110–11. *The Cambridge History of American Literature* (1917) gives it the distinction of being "perhaps the worst elegy ever written."

Modern readers will find easier access to a few of Rose's poems in reprinted or recent editions. The Duyckincks reprint two poems in their entry on Rose (vol. 1, pp. 107–09) and Kenneth Silverman includes two others in *Colonial American Poetry* (1968). Brief discussions of Rose's life and influence are available in Joshua Francis Fisher, "Some Account of the Early Poets and Poetry of Pennsylvania," *Memoirs of the Historical Society of Pennsylvania*, vol. 2, pt. 2 (1830); Francis Howard Williams, "Pennsylvania Poets of the Provincial Period," *Pennsylvania Magazine of History and Biography* 17 (1893): 5–10; M. Katherine Jackson, *Outlines of the Literary History of Colonial Pennsylvania* (1906); David S. Shields, "Wits and Poets of Pennsylvania: New Light on the Rise of Belles Lettres in Provincial Pennsylvania, 1720–1740," *Pennsylvania Magazine of History and Biography* 109 (April 1985): 122–33; and Shields, *Oracles of Empire: Poetry, Politics, and Commerce in British America, 1690–1750* (1990).

PATTIE COWELL

ROSE, Billy (6 Sept. 1899–10 Feb. 1966), songwriter, show business impresario, and philanthropist, was born on the Lower East Side of New York City, the son of David Rosenberg, a button salesman, and Fannie Wernick. He was born William Samuel Rosenberg, according to most biographical sources, though one source states he adopted that name in school after being born Samuel Wolf Rosenberg. He grew up in the Bronx and attended public schools there, winning junior high school medals for sprinting and English. Medals and honors were important as proofs of stature and worth to Rose, who never grew taller than five feet three inches. In the High School of Commerce, he became an outstanding student of the Gregg system of shorthand, winning first a citywide competition (1917) and then a national competition (1918). In 1918 he left high school shortly before graduation to become head of the stenographic department of the War Industries Board, headed by Bernard Baruch, in Washington. Baruch's money and influence and circle of similarly rich, powerful friends made a lifelong impression on Rose.

Though Rose was making $300 a week as a top stenographer by 1920, he wanted to gain real wealth. Through a girlfriend, he began to meet songwriters of Broadway's "Tin Pan Alley." They were not impressive, he recalled: "I saw they were unimportant, shod-

dy, second-rate compared to the men I had worked for during the war. Then I learned some of these song writers were making as much as $75,000 a year. And these boys weren't Kerns or Berlins." No musician, he decided to become a lyric writer. "I had no particular desire to write for music, but I saw no reason why I, with a little preparation and work, could not join the gold rush" (*New York Herald Tribune*, 11 Feb. 1966). He prepared by studying popular song lyrics at the New York Public Library for several months to see what the public most often responded to. Then he began turning out lyrics under the name of Billy Rose, a name he later adopted legally. His first real successes came in 1923, with "Ain't Nature Grand" and "Barney Google (with the Goo, Goo, Googly Eyes)."

Once established, Rose invariably collaborated with other songwriters, and his actual writing abilities have been questioned by many. His main gift seemed to be to galvanize his collaborators into giving their best efforts. In the view of songwriter Harry Warren, Rose "was a great feeder. He'd sit with the boys and say, 'Now come on, you can do better than that.' . . . He stimulated the real lyricists to produce" (Conrad, pp. 47–48). Rose worked with a number of teams concurrently and was accomplished at getting music publishers to accept the songs of the various teams. Many of the standard popular songs of the 1920s and 1930s bear Rose's name as a collaborator: "Me and My Shadow," "It Happened in Monterey," "Without a Song," "It's Only a Paper Moon," and "I Found a Million Dollar Baby (at the Five and Ten Cent Store)" are among a number of others. He earned the top AA rating of the American Society of Composers, Authors, and Publishers and a large annual income from royalties.

Using some of his earnings from songs, Rose opened the Back Stage Club—essentially a speakeasy—late in 1924. The small, crowded club was immediately profitable, though underworld figures cut themselves in on the takings. It also gave Rose a status on Broadway beyond that of Tin Pan Alley's denizens. He got to know the top celebrities, show business royalty, who came to the club. In particular, he met in 1926 Ziegfeld star, comedienne Fanny Brice. Though she was inches taller and several years older than he, and on the rebound from a previous marriage, he courted her with determination. The two wed in 1929.

Rose was determined to become a successful theatrical producer and equal his wife in professional status. Using Brice as his star, Rose in 1930 brought to Broadway a revue first called *Corned Beef and Roses*, then retitled *Sweet and Low*. Not really a success, the show hung on for several months. After revamping the revue and renaming it *Crazy Quilt*, he sent it on tour in 1931, despite conventional wisdom that in depression times the "road" was extinct. Using saturation publicity, with circus-like ads in flamboyant colors and unrestrained language, playing towns where no legitimate stage attraction had appeared in years, Rose turned his near-flop into a resounding financial success. In so doing he won the grudging respect of Broadway professionals who had previously dismissed him as "Mr. Fanny Brice."

Throughout the 1930s, Rose went from success to success, becoming a legend of hustle and audacity and innovation in the entertainment field—the veritable "Bantam Barnum" that his personal publicist dubbed him. He turned two empty New York theaters into nightclubs: the Casino de Paree (1930) and Billy Rose's Music Hall (1934). Both were highly successful until underworld figures who were his backers shut him out. He staged a giant musical comedy, *Jumbo* (1935), starring Jimmy Durante, which with its elephants and acrobats and aerialists was as much a circus as a stage show.

Rose's efforts next expanded from New York to the entire nation. In three months of 1936, he turned a sun-baked Texas plain into the Fort Worth Exposition, an attraction that rivaled the Dallas Texas Centennial a few miles away. The production team he had assembled for *Jumbo* created not only "The Last Frontier," a glittering combination of spectacle and rodeo, but also the Casa Mañana, a theater-restaurant seating four thousand. In 1937 he and his team created the first Aquacade, a combination of musical spectacle and synchronized swimmers, for the Great Lakes Exposition in Cleveland. In 1938, back in New York, he opened two new nightclubs, one called Billy Rose's Diamond Horseshoe, the other a transplanted Casa Mañana. The climax of his efforts with the production team was a much enlarged Aquacade at the 1939 New York World's Fair. Like all his other shows, it was fast-paced, eye-filling, and offered to the public at irresistibly low ticket prices.

That year the *New York Times* reported that Rose "has 1,400 people in his employ—more than any other producer in America. They range from singers to swimmers, from actors to athletes, from dancers to directors. Girls, seals, elephants, horses, cooks, waiters, busboys and orchestras are all performing under the wand of his showmanship." Rose commented regarding his success, "People everywhere want to be amused, and I try to give them what amuses them— girls, glamour, sentiment, gayety. . . . You must have something the people want, you must present it in a new way and you must not hesitate to tell the people you have the goods. [Ballyhoo is a must] for without shouting the best of shows may flop" (23 Apr. 1939). The Aquacade was a feature of the World's Fair again in 1940.

A further part of Rose's success and the fortune he was amassing was a careful eye on expenses. He was known to spend freely on big, important items but would bargain to the death to get small items for the lowest possible price, and he hired accountants to serve as watchdogs on all his enterprises. One big, important item he bought himself was a palatial 45-room townhouse in Manhattan's Beekman Place. He filled it with antiques and art works, all bought after careful bargaining for prices, and he did the same for a country house in Mount Kisco, New York. He developed the habit of spending most of his waking hours in his townhouse, in his pajamas, and directing his enterprises by telephone. His marriage to Brice had failed, as their careers pulled them in opposite directions, and in 1939 they divorced. Soon after, in 1939, he married the swimming star of his Aquacade, Eleanor Holm.

Through the remaining years of his life, Rose continued to pursue wealth and public respect. Success on Broadway had so far eluded him, since even the costly *Jumbo* had failed to make money. Straight drama was never congenial territory for him, and his productions of *Clash by Night* (1941), *The Immoralist* (1954), and *The Wall* (1961) were at best successes of esteem. His two hits were *Carmen Jones* (1943), Oscar Hammerstein II's modernized version of *Carmen* using a black cast, and *The Seven Lively Arts* (1944), a lavish revue. The latter was staged at the Ziegfeld Theatre, which Rose bought in 1944. He also bought the National Theatre in 1958 and renamed it the Billy Rose Theatre. In another endeavor, he publicized himself as a lovable Broadway character in his triweekly syndicated newspaper column, "Pitching Horseshoes." The column of rambling reminiscences and opinions ran in several hundred newspapers from 1946 to 1950. A collection of the columns appeared in book form as *Wine, Women and Words* (1949).

As times and public tastes changed—and even the long-profitable Diamond Horseshoe closed in 1951— Rose withdrew more and more into his luxurious homes and into increasing his fortune by shrewd investments. He set up a special "ticker room" in the Beekman Place townhouse for watching his portfolio. He became the largest single stockholder in American Telephone and Telegraph, acquired large holdings of International Business Machines, and was a director of the New York Central Railroad. He also continued the art collecting he loved: "Outside the fact that you can't cuddle up to art," he said, "I get very much the same sort of joy [from it] I get out of friendship with a beautiful girl" (*New York Times*, 11 Feb. 1966).

Large-scale philanthropic endeavors were also a feature of Rose's later years. In 1958 he set up the Billy Rose Foundation to further education and research in medicine and the arts; the Billy Rose Theatre Collection at the New York Public Library for the Performing Arts, Lincoln Center, is one result. Another philanthropy in 1960 was the Billy Rose Art Garden at the National Museum of Jerusalem, where his sculpture collection—valued then at $1 million—is displayed. The rest of his art collection, along with the bulk of a fortune estimated at up to $54 million, was bequeathed to the Billy Rose Foundation.

Rose's personal life never achieved tranquility. He and Holm divorced in 1954, and in 1956 he married showgirl Joyce Matthews, with whom he had been involved since at least 1951, when she tried to commit suicide at his home. They divorced in 1959, remarried in 1961, and divorced again in 1963. In 1964 Rose married Doris Warner Vidor, and they were divorced the same year. There were no children by any of his marriages.

Rose won his lifetime struggle for material success, wealth, and status. His life has been called by show business historian Anthony Slide "the ultimate American success story." He created a distinct new style of theater. "His ability to mix elements from such disparate sources as circuses, nightclubs, vaudeville, musical comedy, aquatics, and burlesque resulted in productions of a scale and sumptuousness seldom equaled in the commercial theatre" (Nelson, p. xiii), merging theatrical spectacle with an outdoor amusement tradition. Rose's own self-assessment was more quizzical. He seemed to see himself made up of as many disparate parts as his shows. When asked to describe himself on a 1965 radio program, he replied: "I don't quite know who I am. I have had eleven reasonably successful careers in my crazy mixed-up life." He was certain, he said, that he "sold substantially more than one hundred million tickets to the public" (Conrad, p. 260). After cardiovascular surgery, he developed lobar pneumonia and died at his winter home in Montego Bay, Jamaica.

• Rose's papers, scrapbooks, and other materials are in the Billy Rose Theatre Collection at the New York Public Library for the Performing Arts, Lincoln Center. A biography is Earl Conrad, *Billy Rose: Manhattan Primitive* (1968). Anthony Slide, *The Encyclopedia of Vaudeville* (1994), assesses him as a producer. An interview with Rose at the height of his producing career is S. J. Woolf, "Broadway Barnum," *New York Times Magazine*, 23 Apr. 1939. Stephen Nelson, *"Only a Paper Moon": The Theatre of Billy Rose* (1987), studies his production style. Obituaries are in the *New York Times* and the *New York Herald Tribune*, 11 Feb. 1966, and in *Variety*, 16 Feb. 1966.

WILLIAM STEPHENSON

ROSE, Ernestine (13 Jan. 1810–4 Aug. 1892), freethinker, reformer, and feminist, was born Ernestine Louise Siismondi Potowski in Piotrkow, Poland, the only child of an orthodox rabbi and his wife. Although the Jewish religion discouraged female education, Ernestine was well educated and could read Hebrew and the Scriptures; as an adolescent, however, she rejected Judaism because of its second-class treatment of women. When Ernestine was sixteen years old her mother died, leaving her a considerable inheritance. Her father used this inheritance as a dowry, promising Ernestine's hand in marriage to a much older man. Ernestine resisted and successfully argued her case before a Polish court to nullify the contract, an unprecedented move for a young Jewish woman before a Christian court. The same year her father married a sixteen-year-old woman, making Ernestine uncomfortable in the family house, and she left Poland in 1827.

For the next couple of years Ernestine moved around Europe, finally settling in England in 1831. There she created and marketed household deodorant. She also associated with a number of reformers and philanthropists, most notably utopian socialist Robert Owen. She and Owen became close friends and in 1835 founded the Association of All Classes of All Nations, an organization aimed at making the world "as happy as possible" through cultural and moral reform. At age twenty-six Ernestine married William Ella Rose, a 23-year-old jeweler, silversmith, and disciple of Owen's. They moved to New York City where Rose's husband found work as a silversmith, and she created cologne. They had no children.

Her husband was supportive of Rose's reform interests and bankrolled her activist career as she joined the movement for married women's property rights and began to lobby with Elizabeth Cady Stanton and Pauline Wright. Initially they were unsuccessful; in five months Rose received only five signatures on a petition demanding that the New York legislature reconsider the property law. By 1848, however, the legislature had agreed to partial reform of married women's legal rights, although full victory did not come until 1860.

Rose also became involved in the freethought movement, which aimed to provoke debate on social and moral issues. The freethinkers targeted religious institutions, demanding a complete separation of church and state. Rose joined this anticlerical debate, contributing to the freethought weekly *Boston Investigator* and lecturing for Benjamin Offen's Society for Moral Philanthropists. She returned to Owen's utopian socialist ideals when in Skaneateles, New York, in 1843 she helped found a utopian community, which survived only three years.

Rose's reform interests widened to include the temperance, abolition, and woman suffrage movements. As an abolitionist, she worked with Frederick Douglass and William Lloyd Garrison and was active in the Woman's Loyal National League and the American Equal Rights Association. As the Civil War erupted, many activists advocated focusing on abolition and delaying women's rights. Rose argued that both women and blacks needed freedom and later criticized Congress for enfranchising only black men. She successfully proposed that the Equal Rights Association change its name to the Woman's Suffrage Association to focus on women's rights. Elizabeth Cady Stanton was elected president while Rose and Susan B. Anthony served on its executive committee.

As Rose focused her attention on women's rights, she attacked religious institutions, which, she argued, restricted women's freedom. Challenging the idea of religion as a sphere of influence for women, Rose accused the Bible of enslaving women. She also fought for less restrictive divorce laws and greater access to education for women. She argued that divorce was necessary because restrictive laws kept women prisoners in loveless and often abusive marriages. Similarly, she contended that greater education for women would prevent them from becoming financially and intellectually dependent on their husbands, enabling true love to blossom. Rose also employed eugenics rhetoric in support of women's rights, maintaining that educated women would be stronger mothers who would create stronger children, especially sons. If women were kept weak and dependent, as the cultural ideals of the time prescribed, then these characteristics would be transmitted to sons, weakening the breed.

Throughout her adult life, Rose remained active in the suffrage movement, primarily as a traveling lecturer. She strategically appropriated the rhetoric of natural rights and American principles of freedom to promote women's rights. She became known as the "Queen of the Platform," and her close friend Susan B. Anthony came to depend on Rose's speaking skills as she herself was a weak orator. Rose's forceful presence challenged assumptions about women's intellectual inferiority. The *History of Woman Suffrage* described Rose as having "not only dealt in the abstract principles clearly, but in their application touched the deepest emotions of the human soul" (vol. 1, p. 100).

With acclaim, however, came contempt. Rose was attacked as, alternately, a Jew, a radical, an atheist, and a free lover. Journalists labeled her a "fugitive lunatic" and a "foreign propagandist." Anthony believed that Rose was too much ahead of her time to be properly understood or appreciated, but she remained a strong supporter even when many in the suffrage movement demanded that the atheist and radical Rose be removed as detrimental to the cause. Eventually the grueling traveling weakened Rose, and she took an extended break from the campaign. In 1869 she and her husband traveled throughout Europe before moving back to England. Despite being in semiretirement, Rose lectured occasionally in Europe. Her husband died in 1882, leaving her heartbroken. She died a decade later in Brighton, England.

At the Congress of Representative Women of the 1893 World's Columbian Exposition, Elizabeth Cady Stanton memorialized Rose, and Ida Husted Harper later recognized her significance as one "who [was] philosophical enough to see that the right of suffrage was the underlying principle of the whole question" (Harper, vol. 1, p. 185). She made a significant contribution to woman suffrage by eloquently spreading the ideology of women's rights and developing the philosophy of the movement. Ernestine Rose exemplified her statement that "agitation is the opposite of stagnation—the one is life, the other, death" (quoted in Eiseman, p. 47).

• Although Rose did not leave a collection of papers, many of her speeches can be found in Elizabeth Cady Stanton et al., eds., *History of Woman Suffrage*, vol. 1 (1848–1861), along with various mentions of Rose's contributions to the suffrage movement. Her suffrage activity is also discussed in Ida Husted Harper, *The Life and Work of Susan B. Anthony*, vol. 1 (1898), and Elinor Lerner, "Jewish Involvement in the New York City Woman Suffrage Movement," *American Jewish History* 70, no. 4 (1981): 442–61. Biographical accounts include Sara A. Underwood, *Heroines of Freethought* (1876); Lillian O'Connor, *Pioneer Women Orators* (1954); Alberta Eiseman, *Rebels and Reformers: Biographies of Four Jewish Americans* (1976); and Yuri Suhl, *Ernestine L. Rose and the Battle for Human Rights* (1959; rev. ed., 1990). Obituaries are in *The Times* (London), 6 Aug. 1892, and the *Woman's Journal*, 13 Aug. 1892.

ELISA MILLER

ROSE, Fred (24 Aug. 1897–1 Dec. 1954), music publisher, songwriter, and pianist, was born Knols Fred Rose in Evansville, Indiana, the son of Andrew Rose and Annie West. Little is known about either parent. His childhood in St. Louis, Missouri, was Dickensian in its poverty and insecurity; when he was as young as seven, he was singing for change in various saloons and being shuttled about to various relatives. It was little wonder that he left St. Louis when he was around fifteen, hopping a freight train to Chicago, where he established a base of operations for the following fifteen years. His first marketable skill was as a pianist, and he joined jazz great Fats Waller in cutting piano rolls for the QRS company. By the mid-1920s he had gotten enough experience singing and playing at nightclubs that he was able to win a contract with Brunswick Records. He married his first wife, Della Braico, in 1917 and soon started a family. His first son, Wesley Rose (who later took over his Nashville company), was born in 1918; his second son was born in 1920.

Rose soon found he could support his young family by providing new songs for the numerous jazz bands and dance orchestras around Chicago in the 1920s. His early hits included "Deed I Do" and "Honest and Truly" (for bandleader Isham Jones), as well as "Red Hot Mama" (for singer Sophie Tucker), "Deep Henderson" (for jazzman King Oliver), and "Flamin' Mamie" (for the Coon-Sanders radio orchestra). He wrote many songs for Paul Whiteman as well, though reports that he actually played piano for Whiteman's band have not been confirmed. About 1928 he teamed with Elmo Tanner to form a duet called the Tune Peddlers who performed on Chicago's WLS. In 1929 he and his first wife divorced, and he married Helen Holmes; this new union produced two more children. The Great Depression was making it harder and harder to survive as a songwriter, though, and in 1933 he packed his family in his car and headed south to Nashville, Tennessee, where he began to explore a different type of fare: country music.

Arriving at WSM, Rose soon began a show called "Freddie Rose's Song Shop." Though it featured pop songs, Rose met and began working (and even touring) with various members of the Grand Ole Opry, listening carefully to their music. After working with Jack Shook and his Missouri Mountaineers, Rose began to produce western songs, and by 1938 he found himself in Hollywood writing songs for the new "singing cowboy," Gene Autry. These included "Be Honest with Me" (1940) and "Tears on My Pillow" (1940). One of his prime collaborators was cowboy singer Ray Whitley.

By 1942 Rose had again returned to Nashville, working as a staff pianist for WSM and watching with fascination as Opry star Roy Acuff began attracting huge audiences with his sentimental, tear-jerking songs. He met with Acuff and formed the Acuff-Rose Publishing Company, the first Nashville publishing house devoted to country music. With Rose's contacts in Chicago, New York, and Hollywood, he was able to get the company's songs serious attention from the big-time popular music industry. Rose began to churn out country songs himself, sometimes publishing them under the name Floyd Jenkins; these included many of Acuff's biggest hits, such as "Low and Lonely," "Pins and Needles," "Fire Ball Mail," and "Blue Eyes Crying in the Rain." In 1945 Rose tried a few more records himself, recording for OKeh under the pseudonym the Rambling Rogue.

Through the late 1940s the Acuff-Rose roster grew to include most of the big names in country music: Pee Wee King, Redd Stewart, Ira and Charlie Louvin, Molly O'Day, Jenny Lou Carson, Clyde Moody, Leon Payne, and others. Their biggest discovery, however, was Alabama singer-composer Hank Williams, whom Rose discovered and recorded, and whose talent he nurtured. The incredible success of the Williams ouvre solidified the position of Acuff-Rose as the leading country music publisher and won Rose recognition as a genius at spotting talent and managing recording sessions. During the early 1950s Rose pioneered most of the publishing techniques and marketing strategies that would be used in country music for decades.

Unfortunately, Rose got to reap few of the benefits from all this. After seeing his main talent, Hank Williams, self-destruct in early 1953, Rose himself died of a heart attack in Nashville. His legacy, Acuff-Rose Publishing Company, continued as a major Nashville entity, run by his son Wesley Rose until his own death in 1990. In the late 1990s the Acuff-Rose company was part of the Gaylord Corporation's Opryland Music Group.

• An excellent account of Rose's role in the Nashville recording industry is a dissertation available from University Microfilms, John W. Rumble, "Fred Rose and the Development of the Nashville Music Industry, 1942–1954" (Ph.D. diss., Vanderbilt Univ., 1990).

CHARLES K. WOLFE

ROSE, George (19 Feb. 1920–5 May 1988), actor, was born in Bicester, a village "in a wet, marshy corner of England" near Oxford, the son of Walter John Alfred, a butcher, and Eva Sarah Rolfe. Rose said he gave his first public performance at age six. "It was 1926 and the end of a six-week general strike of rail workers and coal miners. A wealthy matron, whom my uncle drove for, put on a show. I sang 'When the Leaves Begin to Fall,' a music hall parody my father taught me. It was about how Cain and Abel came to be." His father often took him to the London music halls. Rose would mimic the performers. He began his career in Bicester with the Red Rhythmics Harmonica Band, a regional group organized by his Methodist church. He left Oxford High School at sixteen to work at Oxford University as a secretary. He served three years in World War II, then studied at London's Guild Hall School of Music.

In 1944 Rose answered a notice for singers for a Tyrone Guthrie production of *Peer Gynt*, starring Ralph Richardson and, in a lesser role, Laurence Olivier. "I wasn't a great singer, but it was war time and men were scarce," said Rose. He followed that as a spear carrier in a *Richard III* starring Olivier. "I told him I was interested in becoming an actor and asked for a letter of introduction to his alma mater, the Central School of Speech and Drama." Olivier complied, and Rose received a scholarship. "Larry came to see our play and offered me a job playing small parts at the Old Vic." Rose credited repertory for his versatility. "Once the season began, you couldn't hire actors. So they had to use who was there, which led to some miscasting. But after playing various roles for six months, you knew how to play them."

Rose came to the United States in 1946 with the Old Vic, making his debut as Peto in *Henry IV, Part 1*. He returned to England to perform Shakespeare and the classics with a sidestep into musical revues. During 1949–1950 he performed at Stratford-on-Avon with the Royal Shakespeare Company, where he first played Dogberry in *Much Ado about Nothing*. Rose's standards were set working with such luminaries as John Gielgud, a lifelong friend, Olivier, Ralph Richardson, the Lunts, Noël Coward, Peggy Ashcroft, Edith Evans, Sybil Thorndike, Paul Scofield, Richard Burton, and Katharine Hepburn. Burton once noted that his "happiest moments at Stratford were spent watching George. He had this wonderful walk, a unique way with a line, and his timing was always spot-on." Elizabeth Taylor, who was to become friends with Rose during the *Hamlet* run, related another story. In 1973, while making *Ash Wednesday* in Italy with Henry Fonda, "Richard began cutting up on the set. Henry asked, 'Who's Richard imitating?' I said, 'Oh, that's George Rose as the First Gentleman in *Henry VIII*.' Henry replied, 'George Rose. What a marvel.'"

In the 1950s he appeared on British television. He made his film debut as the coachman in *The Pickwick Papers* (1952) and went on to principal appearances "usually as a hood or a drunk." These included *The Sea Shall Not Have Them* (1955), *A Tale of Two Cities* (1958), *A Night to Remember* (1958), and *The Devil's Disciple* (1959). He became a West End regular and appeared in *The Winter's Tale*, directed by Peter Brook (1951); as Dogberry in *Much Ado about Nothing*, directed by Gielgud (1952); opposite Coward in *The Apple Cart* (1953); in *The Chalk Garden*, directed by Gielgud (1956); and with the Lunts in *The Visit* (1960).

Though he was nurturing to newcomers (singling them out at ceremonies to share an award), Rose spoke with regret of his young colleagues' lack of discipline and dedication. His learning experience came in 1956 when he and an actress giggled onstage during *The Chalk Garden*. "There had been a protest march in Trafalgar Square against tearing down theaters to put up office buildings. When the word 'marching' came out in the dialogue, we broke up. Dame Edith (Evans) sent for us. I was terrified. She admonished us, 'I won't act with people who don't take acting seriously.'"

Rose was Dogberry again in 1959 in Massachusetts at the Cambridge Drama Festival. When *Much Ado* transferred to Broadway, *New York Times* critic Brooks Atkinson wrote, "Mr. Rose's Dogberry makes it unnecessary for anyone to play the part again." Critics lauded his performances as "inimitable" and his ability to make a word give off a resonance over and above its meaning. His influences were Godfrey Teale and Gielgud, with whom he worked at the Royal Shakespeare Company. Rose attributed his successes with such Shakespearean clowns as Dogberry and Bottom to a keen eye and ear. He said, "As did Shakespeare, I based many of my characterizations on the village eccentrics I observed growing up."

In January 1961 he took over the eight-character role of the Common Man in Robert Bolt's hit *A Man for All Seasons*. When it opened on Broadway, it won six Tonys (including for play, actor, and director), but the much-acclaimed Rose was not nominated, causing outrage among his peers. Of the slight, Rose only said, "It wasn't in the cards."

Rose was vastly opinionated and took particular umbrage with the new breed of British directors and British musicals, especially those by Andrew Lloyd Webber. He said, "You get ten million dollars worth of scenery, three hundred nobodies onstage, but tweedledee and thud in the pit because the British can't sing or dance." Of American musicals, he noted, "You meet a better class of person. Dancers who can dance, singers who can sing." Then he added, "But in drama, you constantly run across actors who can't act."

After two years on Broadway and on tour, Rose settled in New York, where he devoured American blues and jazz in Harlem nightclubs. He appeared extensively on television in such productions as *Oliver Twist* (1959), *The Citadel* (1960), and *Treasure Island* (1960), for the DuMont Show of the Month; in *Captain Brassbound's Conversion* (1960) and *Cyrano de Bergerac* (1962), as Alfred Doolittle in *Pygmalion* (1963), and in *Eagle in a Cage* (1965), all for Hallmark Hall of Fame; and in *George Rose Entertains, Stage Two* (1964), a one-man music hall tribute for the CBS New York affiliate.

Rose became a constant stage fixture in a wide range of tours de force in such plans as Gielgud's *Hamlet*, *Slow Dance on Killing Ground* (1964), Peter Shaffer's *Royal Hunt of the Sun* (1965), as Hobson in *Walking Happy* (1966), in Joe Orton's *Loot* (1968), and in *Canterbury Tales* (1969). Alan Jay Lerner and André Previn's musical *Coco* (1969), starring Katharine Hepburn as designer Coco Chanel, was a turning point. Hepburn and Lerner championed Rose's talents, and he was nominated for his first Tony Award as best featured actor.

Rose was seemingly never without a lead role. Among his best known were those in *Wise Child* (1972), *My Fat Friend* with Lynn Redgrave (1974; Tony nominated, featured actor in a play), as Doolittle in *My Fair Lady* (1976 revival starring Ian Richardson; Tony Award, best actor in a musical), in the title role in *Julius Caesar* (1978), in *The Kingfisher*, which

starred Rex Harrison and Claudette Colbert (1978), as Mr. Darling/Captain Hook in *Peter Pan* (1979 revival), in *The Pirates of Penzance* (1980; Tony nominated, best actor in a musical), and in Rupert Holmes's *The Mystery of Edwin Drood*, from Dickens's unfinished novel (1985; Tony Award, best actor in a musical).

Rose's principal American films were *Hawaii* (1966) and *A New Leaf* (1971). He starred as Mr. Hacker, the butler, in the 1975 television series *Beacon Hill* and was featured in the 1978 miniseries *Holocaust*. He made countless recordings of books and plays.

Rose, who never married, was quietly homosexual but with an "old-fashioned" disdain for the gay rights movement. In 1986, reaching retirement with no family, he became obsessed with having an heir. In the Dominican Republic he adopted Domingo Antonio Rolfe Polanco, sixteen, and set him up in business near his vacation house. During a break in the 1988 *Drood* tour, witnesses reported that Rose threatened to disinherit Polanco for abandoning the business. Days later Rose was found dead in an automobile off a remote road. After questioning, the adopted son, his birth father, and an uncle confessed to the killing.

If Dogberry and Everyman were Rose's quintessential comedy/drama roles, his preening Major General in *The Pirates of Penzance* and his music hall master of ceremonies/town mayor in *Drood*'s play-within-a-play were his musical equivalents. In the latter Rose revealed his consummate artistry, hoofing like the best of dancers, impersonating doddering old men, ad-libbing rowdy jokes that reduced audiences to helpless laughter, and singing with a clarion belt. Rose was elected to the Theatre Hall of Fame in 1996. Rose was a consummate professional with boundless energy who valued craft above all else. Of his experience working with Rose as the gravedigger in John Gielgud's *Hamlet* (1964), Richard Burton observed, "Never act with kids, dogs, or George Rose."

• Much of the material above was related to the author in interviews with George Rose. Rose is mentioned briefly in Paul Ferris, *Richard Burton: An Arm's Length Biography* (1981), and Ronald Hayman, *John Gielgud* (1971). Notes on the rehearsals for *Hamlet* are in William Redfield, *Letters from an Actor* (1967). An obituary is in the *New York Times*, 6 May 1988.

ELLIS NASSOUR

ROSE, Joseph Nelson (11 Jan. 1862–4 May 1928), botanist, was born on a farm near Liberty, Indiana, the son of George W. Rose and Rebecca Jane Corrington, farmers. He attended Liberty High School and then enrolled in Wabash College in 1881, graduating with an A.B. degree in 1885. At Wabash, his principal mentor was Professor John M. Coulter, with whom Rose published *Revision of the North American Umbelliferae* (1888). Rose received an A.M. degree in 1887 and the Ph.D. in 1889, both also from Wabash College. The work on Umbelliferae was expanded into *Synopsis of*

Mexican and Central North American Umbelliferae (1900) and, later that year, the major contribution, *Monograph of the North American Umbelliferae.*

In 1888, the year of his marriage to Lou Beatrice Sims (with whom he would have five children), Rose was appointed assistant botanist in the U.S. Department of Agriculture (USDA) in Washington, D.C. At the USDA Rose worked under George Vasey and, with him, made use of the great collections of Edward Palmer on Mexican flora. This was Rose's introduction to Mexican and Central American flora, which he also studied through field trips, alone and also with Palmer, in Latin America. The result of these efforts was *Studies of Mexican and Central American Plants,* published between 1897 and 1911; essentially, these were digests and revisions of families of flowering plants, especially the genus *Agave* and the families Amaryllidaceae and Crassulaceae.

In 1896, when the National Herbarium was placed under the United States National Museum of the Smithsonian Institution, Rose was appointed assistant curator for botany. He was associate curator from 1905 to 1912. In the period from 1896 to 1912 Rose made numerous trips of botanical exploration to Mexico, collecting thousands of specimens and sending great numbers of living plants back to Washington for greenhouse cultivation. Many of the newly discovered species were described in a paper on the Crassulaceae which he coauthored with N. L. Britton in 1903. In 1905 the entire family was treated systematically in another coauthored work.

In 1912 Rose obtained unpaid leave from the Smithsonian in order to become a research associate at the Carnegie Institution of Washington, where, it was planned, he would work with Britton on preparation of a monograph on the Cactaceae of the world. Originally the plan had been to limit the study to the United States, Mexico, and the West Indies, but David MacDougal, director of the Carnegie Institution's Desert Laboratory in Tucson, Arizona, successfully urged worldwide treatment. The Carnegie board agreed and gave the project generous financing. Rose was given a salary of $3,600 per year with traveling expenses of $3,000.

For this huge project Rose traveled widely. In 1912 he visited European gardens and herbaria at Kew, Naples, Munich, Halle, Antwerp, and elsewhere in order to study types and to collect material from species in cultivation. In 1913 Rose and Britton went on an expedition to the West Indies; in 1914 Rose went to Peru, Bolivia, and Chile; in 1915, to Brazil and Argentina; in 1916, to Venezuela; and to Ecuador in 1918.

At the outset, it had been assumed that the project would require five years, but the first volume did not appear until 1919. Rose wrote to MacDougal in 1920 that the task of building up the collections was "much greater than we had supposed" and that "the classification of the cacti had to be entirely revised." He noted that a 1900 monograph on Cactaceae had listed twenty-one genera, whereas their project had already identified more than one hundred. *The Cactaceae* eventual-ly was published in four volumes (1919–1923), under the joint authorship of Britton and Rose; it was the preeminent work on that botanical family until 1958. Rose wrote of it, "Interest in the cactus family has been greatly stimulated by the publication of these volumes. In Europe the interest is so pronounced that it may almost be called a cactus craze and dealers and cactus fanciers are anxious to obtain seeds and plants."

After completion of the Cactaceae project in 1923, Rose returned to the Smithsonian as associate curator and began work, with Britton, on contributions to the *North American Flora.* The two families that they treated were the Mimosaceae and the Caesalpiniaceae; the latter was Rose's principal interest. In these studies, both Rose and Britton demonstrated their practice of expanding the number of genera—in *Cassia,* for example—by segregates, or subgeneric innovations. This approach to systematics was not always agreeable to other botanists, but it provided a thoroughness in generic analysis that had hitherto been lacking. The Mimosaceae treatment appeared in the *Flora* in 1928; the Caesalpiniaceae, in 1930. In his lifetime, Rose published nearly 200 botanical papers and books, many in collaboration with other botanists. Other contributions to *North American Flora* (34 vols., 1905–1957) were the Crassulaceae and the Burseraceae, and other works include *Plants of the Tres Marias Islands* (1899), *Notes on Useful Plants of Mexico* (1899), and *List of Plants collected by Dr. Edward Palmer in Lower California and Western Mexico* (1890).

In his lifetime, Rose was very much involved in the scientific life of Washington, serving as vice president of Botanical Science; the Washington Academy; the Washington Botanical Society; and the Washington Biological Society (president in 1918). He was noted for his generous and cooperative spirit as well as for his dedication to botany, to which he made so many significant contributions in plant systematics. A German colleague, Alwin Berger, whom Rose had befriended in Italy in 1912, recounted after Rose's death that though the Great War had interrupted all communications between Rose and himself, immediately after the war Rose began to write and to send him botanical literature and living plants. Berger, like others, saw Rose not only as a distinguished man of science but also as a man of genuine warmth and sympathy. Five plant genera are named for him: *Brittonrosea, Roseanthus, Roseocactus, Roseocereus,* and *Roseodendron.* Rose died in Washington, D.C.

• The field books, journals, reports, and correspondence of Rose can be found in the archives of the Smithsonian Institution. For biographical information, R. S. Cowan and F. A. Stafleu, "Rose and Britton: From Brittonrosea to Cassia," *Brittonia* 33, no. 3 (1981): 285–93, gives important insights into the relationship between the two men as well as the basic parts of Rose's career. A. D. Rodgers III, *John Merle Coulter: Missionary in Science* (1944), contains numerous references to Rose. Reference should also be made to Frans Stafleu, *Taxonomic Literature,* vol. 4 (1983), pp. 884–87, for biography and bibliography. Two obituaries, H. M. Wegener, "Dr. Joseph Nelson Rose," *Desert* 1 (1930): 105, and Alwin Berger, "Joseph Nelson Rose," *Zeitschrift für Sukkulentenkunde* 3, no. 13 (1928): 281–83, are important for an appreciation of Rose's character.

ROBERT F. ERICKSON

ROSE, Leonard (27 July 1918–16 Nov. 1984), cellist, was born Leonard Joseph Rose in Washington, D.C., the son of Harry Rose, a master tailor and cellist, and Jennie Frankel. Harry Rose (originally Rozofsky) played in the Washington and Baltimore orchestras and in 1922 moved his family to Miami, Florida. Leonard Rose began cello at the age of eight, studying with Walter Grossman at the Miami Conservatory of Music from age eleven. At age thirteen Rose won first prize in cello in a Florida high school music contest, and in 1933 he went to New York to study with his cousin Frank Miller, later principal cellist of the NBC Symphony. Rose entered the Curtis Institute of Music in Philadelphia in 1934, studying with Felix Salmond and serving as first cellist in the orchestra. In his third year Rose was named Salmond's assistant.

Rose graduated from Curtis in 1938. That same year he married Minnie Knopow, who died in 1964; they had two children. At the age of twenty, Rose began an impressive orchestral career. He was assistant principal cellist in the NBC Symphony in 1938 and the following year became principal cellist of the Cleveland Orchestra under Artur Rodzinski. He also taught cello at the Cleveland Institute of Music and the Oberlin Conservatory. In 1943 Rodzinski became music director of the New York Philharmonic, and Rose followed him to the orchestra as principal cellist. His solo debut with the orchestra took place in 1944. By 1949 he had played as soloist with the orchestra eighteen times in many of the major cello concertos. Rose played with some of the most famous conductors of the day, developing especially close rapport with Dimitri Mitropoulos, George Szell, and Bruno Walter. Szell once called Rose "one of the outstanding cellists of our time," and Mitropoulos said he was the finest cellist he had ever worked with. Walter was also effusive in his praise.

Rose left the New York Philharmonic and orchestral playing in 1951, embarking on a career as soloist and teacher. He began extensive tours of the United States in the early 1950s and by later in the decade had been heard in major musical centers in Europe and Latin America. A notable performance was with violinist Isaac Stern in the Brahms Double Concerto in London's Festival Hall in 1958, a work he recorded with Stern in 1957 under the baton of Bruno Walter. By the early 1970s he had played concerts in all fifty states and his touring also included the Middle East and the Orient. Rose was especially noted for his large and distinctive tone, but he also possessed a complete technical mastery of the instrument and impeccable musicianship. His performances were marked by careful and deliberate planning for maximum musical effect rather than highly emotional, spontaneous inspiration. He was especially comfortable in the major concertos of the Romantic era, recording most of them. Twentieth-century works with which he espe-

cially was associated include *Schelomo* by Ernest Bloch and *A Song of Orpheus* by William Schuman, the latter commissioned and recorded by the cellist. Rose played an exquisite cello made by Nicolo Amati in 1662.

Rose was part of an eminent trio with Stern and pianist Eugene Istomin that toured and recorded starting in the early 1960s. Although they played together irregularly, the trio became one of the most important of its type. Writing in the *New York Times*, Allen Hughes explained the trio's appeal: "They have the distinct advantage of being able to play their respective instruments better than performers who devote themselves chiefly to chamber music. . . . They can draw upon virtuoso tonal luster that gives their group playing an almost magical sheen" (16 May 1969). The trio's catalog with Columbia Records was quite large, including, for example, the complete trios of Beethoven, Schubert, and Brahms.

Rose was one of the most important cello teachers of his generation. He taught at the Juilliard School of Music from 1946 and the Curtis Institute from 1951 until 1962. His students included Lynn Harrell and Yo-Yo Ma as well as many cellists in major American orchestras. In 1977, for example, his former students were principal cellists of the Boston, Cleveland, Pittsburgh, San Francisco, St. Louis, and Toronto orchestras. In addition, many of his students went on to become teachers at major American music schools. Rose edited many cello works for the International Music Company. He died in White Plains, New York. He was survived by his second wife, Xenia Petschek, whom he had married in 1965; they had no children. As perhaps the premiere American-born and trained cellist of his generation, Rose's legacy lives on in his many fine recordings and in the work of his many students.

• In addition to articles in most music dictionaries and obituaries in major newspapers, especially useful biographical entries on Rose are found in the *Current Biography Yearbook* (1977) and David Ewen, *Musicians since 1900* (1978). A useful consideration of the Istomin-Stern-Rose trio is in Robert Jacobson, "The Intellectual, the Gambler, and the Corporate Man," *High Fidelity and Musical America* 22, no. 5 (May 1972): 53–58. Rose's approaches to cello technique and musical matters are addressed in Samuel Applebaum and Sada Applebaum, *The Way They Play, Book 1* (1972).

PAUL R. LAIRD

ROSE, Mary Davies Swartz (31 Oct. 1874–2 Feb. 1941), nutrition researcher and educator, was born in Newark, Ohio, the daughter of Hiram B. Swartz, a lawyer, judge, inventor, and mayor of Wooster, Ohio, and Martha Jane Davies, a former schoolteacher. After moving to Wooster when she was three, Mary Swartz, the first of five children, was educated in Wooster public schools and graduated first in her high school class there in 1892. Then, apparently at a loss as to what to do next, she spent nine years teaching history and botany at the Wooster high school while also studying at nearby Shepardson College, later a part of Denison University, where she received a bachelor of letters degree in 1901.

She became interested in nutrition after attending a summer Chautauqua (N.Y.) Institute in 1901, whereupon she studied the subject at the Mechanics Institute in Rochester, New York (1901–1902). From 1902 until 1905 she taught home economics at the high school in Fond du Lac, Wisconsin. She then entered Teachers College, Columbia University, where she earned a bachelor of science degree under biochemist Henry Clapp Sherman in 1906. In 1907 Teachers College awarded her a traveling fellowship for graduate work at Yale University, where in 1909 she became the first woman elected to its chapter of Sigma Xi and the first woman among the many candidates awarded doctorates in physiological chemistry trained by Yale's famed Lafayette B. Mendel. Upon completion of her doctorate, she returned to the faculty of Teachers College, where Sherman was creating a new department of nutrition and food economics in its School of Household Arts. She spent the rest of her career there, retiring in 1940.

In 1910 Mary Swartz married Anton Richard Rose, a biochemist, whom she had met while a fellow graduate student at Yale. He completed his doctorate in biochemistry at Columbia University in 1912, served on the faculty of Fordham University for a number of years, and was later chief chemist at the Prudential Insurance Company. They had one child. Although Anton once boasted that he had test-eaten all the recipes in Rose's several textbooks, his later diabetes required considerable food planning. At a time when most husbands did not want their wives to have careers, his frequent remark that "Mary's career comes first" (quoted in Eagles et al., p. 1) summarized his supportive attitude.

Always busy and well-organized, Rose conducted research in a variety of areas, especially calcium metabolism in humans and iron requirements in children and rats. She also wrote several textbooks: *Feeding the Family* (1916, 1924, 1929, and 1940), which sold 150,000 copies and was one of the first textbooks to include the amounts of calories, proteins, fats, and minerals in its menus; *Foundations of Nutrition* (1927, 1933, and 1938); and *Teaching Nutrition to Boys and Girls* (1932). According to one calculation, during her more than thirty-one years at Teachers College, Rose taught about 11,000 students, including many in the college's large summer school program. Almost all of her students were women embarking on careers in the expanding fields of nutrition, dietetics, and home economics. Among them were her successors at Teachers College (and her biographers) Grace MacLeod, Clara Mae Taylor, and Orrea Florence Pye.

During World War I Rose served as deputy director of the bureau of food conservation in the U.S. Food Administration and was known for her exhibits and children's pageants on the steps of the New York Public Library, which became a kind of community center for the duration. She was also active in professional organizations. The only woman among the eleven founders of the American Institute for Nutrition in 1928, she became its first woman president in 1937. She also served as one of three Americans on the Technical Commission on Nutrition of the Health Organization of the League of Nations (1935–1937) and was a member of the Council on Foods and Nutrition at a time when the vitamin enrichment of foods was under discussion and for which she wrote an early report on the nutritive value of quick-frozen (Birds Eye) foods (*Journal of the American Medical Organization* 114, no. 14 [16 Apr. 1940]: 1356). She died in Edgewater, New Jersey, where the Roses had moved in 1920. She was buried in Granville, Ohio.

Mary Swartz Rose was one of the few women in the early history of nutrition science, which emerged as a university subject in the early twentieth century, who was sufficiently well-trained, well-connected, and productive in research to be accepted and honored by male biochemists, though most of her career was spent in nutrition education, teaching future teachers and the public the value of correct (as they were then understood) eating habits. As a married woman and mother who had found her calling somewhat late in life, she was always in a hurry and used her strong organizational skills to accomplish a lot with little sleep.

• The archives at Teachers College, Columbia University, has some of her correspondence and research files as well as the papers of the nutrition department. Clara Mae Taylor's entry on Rose in *Notable American Women*, vol. 3, is a summary of her life and work by one of her former students. Juanita Archibald Eagles, et al., *Mary Swartz Rose, 1874–1941: Pioneer in Nutrition* (1979), contains a full bibliography of Rose's writings. Clyde B. Schuman, "Mary Swartz Rose, Scientist and Educator" (Ph.D. diss., New York Univ., 1945), contains excerpts from correspondence with many of Rose's contemporaries. See also Margaret W. Rossiter, "Mendel the Mentor: Yale Women Doctorates in Biochemistry, 1898–1937," *Journal of Chemical Education* 71, no. 3 (Mar. 1994): 215–19. Obituaries include Grace MacLeod, "Mary Swartz Rose," *Journal of Home Economics* 33, no. 4 (Apr. 1941): 221–24, and two by Henry C. Sherman, "Mary Swartz Rose—An Appreciation," *Journal of Nutrition* 21, no. 3 (Mar. 1941): 209–11, and "Mary Swartz Rose, 1874–1941," *Journal of Biological Chemistry* 140, no. 3 (Sept. 1941): 687–88.

MARGARET W. ROSSITER

ROSE, Ralph Waldo (17 Mar. 1885–16 Oct. 1913), Olympic Games weight-throwing champion, was born in Healdsville, California, the son of J. W. Rose, an attorney; his mother's name is not known. After graduating from high school in Healdsville, Rose went to the University of Michigan to study law. He was a member of the track team, and even before completing his studies, he had grown to 6′6″ and 295 pounds. For three years (1902–1904) he was Pacific Coast champion in the 16-pound shot put, the 16-pound hammer throw, and the discus toss. At the 1904 Olympic Games in St. Louis, the young giant won the shot put with a world record (48′7″) and captured silver and bronze medals in the discus and hammer, respectively. Rose continued his studies at the University of Chicago and obtained a law degree in 1908. He began practicing law in Healdsville, became a member of the San Francisco Olympic Club, and joined the United States Olympic Team in London in preparation for competition in the Games of the Fourth Olympiad (1908).

At the Opening Ceremonies Parade of Nations inside the Shepherd's Bush Stadium, Rose, now grown to over 300 pounds, joined 18 others in carrying national flags. Olympic protocol stated that in passing the royal box seat of King Edward VII, all flags should be lowered in respect to the official host and the host nation. Rose was the only one who failed to lower his flag. For weeks thereafter, the sport, political, and editorial sections of American and European newspapers were filled with articles on this "affront to the King and therefore the British people." The 24-year-old Rose claimed: "I was never told what to do." Several days later, in heavy rain, he pushed the shot 46′7½″, an Olympic record.

During these pre–World War I years, much of the sporting public was fascinated by the cult of strong men hurling objects for distance, one of these events being the 16-pound shot put for the right hand and then left hand, the combined distance determining the winner. Rose was many times national champion and world record holder in many of these throwing events, winning American titles in the shot (1907–1909), in the discus (1908–1909), and with the javelin (1909). Between 1907 and 1909, and in 1912, he established world records for the shot put (8, 12, 14, 16, and 28 pounds), with the shot put "combined," and set an unofficial world record shot put of 54′4″ on 26 June 1909.

In 1912 Rose led the American weight throwers to the Olympic Games in Stockholm. The European athletic world had never seen such American giants: Rose, Patrick J. McDonald, J. H. Duncan, and Matthew McGrath. Rose won the right hand–left hand shot put with a total 90′5⅜″ and took a silver medal in the shot put, just behind McDonald's Olympic record throw (50′4″). In a career of less than a decade, the young California lawyer had posted world class performances in the throwing events, including a prodigious 178′5″ hammer throw in 1909. He never married and died young from typhoid fever. The American Olympic Commissioner, James Edward Sullivan, called Rose's death "a severe blow to athletes, to Americans, and we will miss his presence at the next Olympic Games" (*New York Herald*, 17 Oct. 1913).

• Biographies of Rose may be found in Bill Mallon and Ian Buchanan, *Quest for Gold* (1984), and Mallon, "Ralph Rose," *The Olympian* 18 (Mar. 1992): 60–61. The infamous failure to dip the American flag is described in the *Washington Post*, 26 July 1908, and in the *Fourth Olympiad Official Report 1908* (1909), pp. 48, 90, and 97. See also David Wallechinsky, *The Complete Book of the Olympics* (1992), p. 107; Edward Lyell Fox, "Our Olympic Flyers," *Outing Magazine* July 1912, p. 397, and F. A. M. Webster, *Olympic Cavalcade* (1948), pp. 66–67. Besides the one cited in the text above, obituaries are in the *Los Angeles Times* and the *New York Times*, 17 Oct. 1913.

JOHN A. LUCAS

ROSE, William Cumming (4 Apr. 1887–25 Sept. 1985), biochemist and nutritionist, was born in Greenville, South Carolina, the son of John McAden Rose, a Presbyterian minister, and Mary Evans Santos. Rose's family moved to North Carolina in 1881, living first in Morganton, then in Laurenberg. In Laurenberg, when he was twelve, Rose was placed in the Quackenbush School, but after two years his father found his son's instruction was inadequate and decided to teach him at home. In this isolated environment, Rose's father thoroughly drilled him in Greek, Latin, and Hebrew. While Rose was receiving this classical education, he began reading Ira Remsen's textbook of chemistry that his sister had studied. This exposure instilled in Rose the desire to study chemistry.

Upon finishing his secondary education, Rose wished to attend a large university. His father, however, insisted that he attend Davidson College in Davidson, North Carolina, where the Presbyterian minister knew his son would receive a Christian education. While at Davidson Rose took a course in food analysis, and this experience made him wish to study physiological chemistry. In 1907, after four years at Davidson, Rose was awarded a B.S. degree. To pursue further chemical studies, Rose enrolled as a graduate student in the Yale Sheffield Scientific School. Soon after he arrived in New Haven, Rose was advised to consult with Russell Chittenden, the head of the Sheffield School, to plan his course in physiological chemistry. Chittenden introduced Rose to Lafayette Mendel, who assigned him a project on creatine-creatinine metabolism. Creatine is a nitrogenous organic acid found in muscle tissue that supplies energy for muscle contraction, while creatinine is a waste product created through the metabolism of creatine. This was Rose's first exposure to experimental biochemical studies, and it became the basis of his thesis. Along with Mendel, Rose isolated ten amino acids, particularly tryptophan and lysine, that were found in food. This was the first proof that the body cannot synthesize certain essential amino acids needed for growth; these have to be provided by food.

In addition to being a physiological chemist and physiologist, Chittenden was also a toxicologist; one of his projects at that time was an investigation of the toxicity of food additives. When Rose arrived at Yale, Chittenden was evaluating whether the food preservative sodium benzoate was harmful. Rose volunteered for Chittenden's study and was given a position both as a chemist and as a subject on the "Benzoate Poison Squad." The eight graduate students on the squad were given four grams of sodium benzoate to consume each day for about four months. No harmful effects were found from this benzoate consumption, and the information gained from this study resolved doubts about use of sodium benzoate as a preservative in tomato ketchup. After four years at Yale, Rose received his Ph.D. in 1911.

For postdoctoral work, Rose obtained a job as instructor in the Department of Physiological Chemistry at the University of Pennsylvania under Alonzo E. Taylor in 1911. Taylor urged Rose to continue his work on creatine-creatinine metabolism. After a few years at Penn, Rose decided he needed further training, and with Taylor's help he obtained a position in physiological chemistry at the University of Freiburg under Frantz Knoop in 1913. As a result of the assassination of Archduke Ferdinand in Serbia, Rose's visit to Germany was shortened. While in Germany, however, Rose received a telegram from the University of Texas inviting him to organize a department of biochemistry at the medical school at Galveston. At first Rose was reluctant to accept the position, for he felt he should return to Pennsylvania, but Taylor sent him a telegram encouraging him to take the job with the crusty remark, "You darned fool, I recommended you for the job." Rose remained at the University of Texas for nine years, and while there he organized the first biochemistry course for medical students.

From Texas Rose went to the University of Illinois as professor of physiological chemistry. He bore this title from 1922 until 1936, when it was changed to professor of biochemistry. In 1935 Rose announced at the annual meeting of the Federation of American Societies for Experimental Biology that he had isolated a new amino acid called threonine and was able to prepare it artificially. His discovery brought the total of known and isolated amino acids found in animal and plant protein to twenty. It was possible, reported Rose, to replace proteins in an animal's diet with a compound of these amino acids as well as other essential dietary needs, and the animal would grow. While proteins must be consumed, these amino acids could be taken directly into the bloodstream. Through this discovery, Rose became the first to successfully rear animals on a mixture of pure amino acids.

In 1942, with a better understanding of the role amino acids play in animal growth, Rose began to focus his research on humans and their amino acid requirements. In his first studies he fed graduate student volunteers a diet of starch, sucrose, butterfat, vitamins, and pure amino acids. By removing each amino acid individually and gauging its effect, Rose determined that a lack of any one of eight key amino acids resulted in a nitrogen imbalance in the subject. This imbalance caused nervousness, loss of appetite, and fatigue in the subject. Rose's research, which continued in this vein for the next ten years, would allow scientists "to evaluate the nutritive quality of any protein and its ability to meet human needs, provided the protein is known to be digestible." These nutritional studies had many practical applications in clinical medicine, particularly in surgery, making it possible to prepare amino acid mixtures for intravenous feeding of surgical patients who could not be fed by mouth.

When World War II began, Rose was called as a consultant to aid in solving the nutritional problems presented by war. His work in this period resulted in the founding of the Nutrition Foundation and the Food and Nutrition Board of the National Research Council. Rose became chairman of the Committee on Protein Foods, and in this position he played a distinct role in issuing two significant publications, *The Evaluation of Protein Nutrition and Emphasis on Amino Acid and Proportionalities* (n.d.) and *The Evaluation of Protein Nutrition* (1959).

While at the University of Illinois, Rose taught two core biochemistry courses, which were enthusiastically attended by undergraduate and graduate students. During his long career, ninety graduate students received their Ph.D.s under Rose. His monumental contributions to nutrition and nutritional chemistry were rewarded by numerous prizes, honor lectures, and membership in distinguished societies.

In 1913 Rose married Zula Franklin Hendrick; they had no children. In his spare time Rose enjoyed bird watching and motoring through the country to practice his hobby, photography. Until he reached the age of ninety-five, Rose drove each year to his alma mater, Davidson College, and gave a lecture to the chemistry class. He died in Urbana, Illinois.

• More information about Rose can be found in his own "How Did It Happen?" *Annals of the New York Academy of Science* 325 (1979): 229–34; Herbert E. Carter, "William Cumming Rose (April 4, 1887–September 25, 1985," in National Academy of Sciences, *Biographical Memoirs* 68 (1995): 253–71; and Daphne A. Roe, "William Cumming Rose, Biographical Sketch," *Journal of Nutrition* 111 (1981): 1312–20. See also *McGraw Hill Modern Men of Science* (2 vols., 1966–1968).

DAVID Y. COOPER

ROSECRANS, William Starke (6 Sept. 1819–11 Mar. 1898), soldier and congressman, was born in Delaware County, Ohio, the son of Crandall Rosecrans and Jemima Hopkins, farmers. His father died when Rosecrans was in his teens, forcing the boy to play a major role in supporting his family. Largely through his own efforts, he secured an appointment to the U.S. Military Academy, from which he graduated fifth in the 56-man class of 1842.

At West Point Rosecrans developed not only an aptitude for military engineering but a strong interest in religion that led him to convert from the Episcopal church to Catholicism. During the Civil War he enjoyed arguing theology long into the night with subordinates, staff officers, and visitors to his headquarters. Despite his zeal, Rosecrans became known for his avid taste for whiskey and his rich vocabulary of swear words. He was no drunkard, and he drew the distinction that while sometimes profane, he never blasphemed.

After graduating, Rosecrans taught at West Point before being dispatched to New England to supervise the construction of forts and the improvement of harbors. In 1843 he married Anna Elizabeth Hegeman; they had eight children. Eleven years later Rosecrans resigned his lieutenant's commission to provide for his growing family as a businessman. He superintended a coal company, was elected president of a water navigation business in western Virginia, and helped build a kerosene refinery in Cincinnati.

When the Civil War broke out in April 1861, Rosecrans quickly answered the call of his native state. Before the month's end he was a volunteer aide-de-camp on the staff of Major General George B. McClellan, and in June he was commissioned colonel of engineers and was assigned to lead a regiment of Ohio volunteers in western Virginia. As a brigadier general in the regular army, he fought under McClellan at Rich Mountain (11–12 July) and held independent command at Carnifax Ferry (10 Sept.) and Gauley Bridge (10–14 Nov.). Although his tactical expertise produced victories against able opponents, including Robert E. Lee, Rosecrans's contributions went virtually unnoticed. Following a departmental merger late in 1861, he found himself without a command.

Resentful of such treatment, Rosecrans headed east to complain to the newly appointed secretary of war, Edwin McMasters Stanton, who promised him an important command in a more active theater. Rosecrans was gratified, but he nearly squandered his good fortune by botching the first mission assigned him. Sent to the Shenandoah Valley in April 1862 to expedite the reinforcing of Major General John C. Frémont's army, Rosecrans exceeded his authority by proposing to local commanders a grandiose plan to capture Stonewall Jackson, whose Confederates were raiding valley outposts; worse, he implied that the scheme had Stanton's support. When the secretary learned of this indiscretion, he recalled Rosecrans and gave him a tongue-lashing. Stanton's visitor replied with heated invective that drove a wedge between the two men. As the general later acknowledged, "Subserviency to *men in power* is not one of my distinguishing virtues."

For a time this attitude did not harm him. Early in May Rosecrans was transferred to the Army of the Mississippi; he gained command of its 20,000 troops the following month. From the first, he enjoyed an uneasy relationship with his departmental commander, Major General Ulysses S. Grant. On 19 September the two attempted to unite against Major General Sterling Price's Confederates at Iuka, Mississippi. When Rosecrans's plan went awry and most of Price's men escaped the trap set for them, Grant seethed inwardly. The following month Rosecrans's enlarged command stood firm inside its defenses at Corinth, repulsing two days of attacks by Major General Earl Van Dorn. When the rebels retreated, however, Rosecrans staged a weak pursuit that caused Grant to vent his anger publicly. Although Corinth brought him a major generalship in the volunteers, Rosecrans made another powerful enemy by berating General in Chief Henry Halleck for not sufficiently predating his appointment to satisfy his demand for seniority.

Despite the animosities he had engendered, Rosecrans parlayed his success at Corinth into command of the 99,000-man Army of the Ohio. He joined his force at Louisville on 30 October, renamed it the Army of the Cumberland, and strove to rejuvenate it after months of debilitating service in Tennessee and Kentucky. Within a few months, Rosecrans had resupplied every arm of his command, had upgraded the officer corps, and had improved unit training. Such actions raised the army's morale as well as its readiness and won "Old Rosy" the esteem and affection of the rank and file.

Rosecrans tested his revival program in late December, when he belatedly heeded War Department orders to challenge General Braxton Bragg's army in Middle Tennessee. On the last day of the year Rosecrans moved to strike Bragg's right flank across Stones River, near Murfreesboro, only to find his own right under attack. Refusing to panic, Rosecrans recalled his assault column and shored up his embattled flank. Despite teetering on the brink of defeat throughout the day, the Army of the Cumberland held on; two days later it survived a heavy assault against its left, forcing Bragg to abandon his strategic position. The victory made Rosecrans the most celebrated commander in the Union. He received the thanks of Congress, a brevet major generalship in the regular army, and highly placed offers of support should he seek political office. Abraham Lincoln personally thanked him for salvaging a victory, when "had there been a defeat instead, the Nation could scarcely have lived over."

For all the acclaim that Stones River brought him, Rosecrans's next campaign—directed against Bragg's new position near Tullahoma, Tennessee—was a superior performance. In June 1863, after five months of preparation, the Ohioan launched simultaneous drives that threatened many sectors of the enemy line. So adroitly were these moves orchestrated that a confused and apprehensive Bragg virtually evacuated Tennessee. Rosecrans's strategic maneuvering, at minimal cost in casualties, should have solidified his reputation. Overshadowed as it was, however, by Grant's Vicksburg campaign and Lee's invasion of Pennsylvania, the Tullahoma campaign failed to gain its fair share of publicity.

In September 1863, Rosecran's troubles with the War Department increased with the arrival at his headquarters of Assistant Secretary of War Charles A. Dana, Jr., whom Rosecrans immediately sized up as Stanton's spy. Supplementing Dana's caustic criticism of Rosecrans's military and personal habits were the equally damaging comments that Rosecrans's chief of staff, Major General James A. Garfield, sent covertly to Stanton and Treasury Secretary Salmon P. Chase. When Rosecrans dallied two months before again engaging the Army of Tennessee, his standing in Washington reached its nadir.

Rosecrans should have realized that his coming showdown with Bragg would prove crucial to his career, but he failed to take precautions to ensure success. Early in September he pursued Bragg from Chattanooga into northern Georgia. With an air of overconfidence, Rosecrans marched south in loose formation, his army widely scattered. Seizing the opportunity presented him, Bragg attacked near Rossville on the nineteenth, staggering the Army of the Cumberland. Rosecrans held his ground along Chickamauga Creek until midday on the twentieth, when he made a tactical blunder that opened a gap along his right center just as Confederate reinforcements struck that sector. As the attackers poured through the hole, the Federals fell back—slowly at first, then in haste and panic. The army did not regroup until it reached Chattanooga. Bragg failed to pursue but in later weeks moved north to besiege the city, cutting its supply lines and driving Rosecrans's men to the brink of starvation.

Dispatched to rescue Chattanooga, Grant used the authority given him by Stanton to replace Rosecrans. The latter's downfall may have been hastened by the criticism of Dana and Garfield, but it had been caused by hubris, a brittle temper, a tendency to ignore War Department urgings to march and fight, and a propensity to underestimate his enemy. When Old Rosy bade a mournful farewell on 19 October, a newsman noted, "There is wailing and weeping in the Army of the Cumberland today."

Rosecrans's field service was not over. In January 1864 he accepted Lincoln's offer of a relatively minor command, the Department of Missouri. The general spent the next year trying to protect with 17,000 troops a vast region threatened by Confederate regulars and guerrillas, subversives, and hostile American Indians. He did as good a job as anyone could have in such an impossible assignment, but after Rosecrans helped curtail Price's September–October raid through the state, Grant, now general in chief of the Union armies, removed him from command without explanation. A dejected and humiliated Rosecrans was awaiting further orders when the war ended.

In postwar years Rosecrans reentered business life in Ohio then served in 1868–1869 as U.S. ambassador to Mexico—yet another post from which Grant, now president, removed him. In 1880 he moved to California, where he ranched and speculated in mining ventures. Twice elected to Congress from his adopted state as a Democrat, Rosecrans served from 1881 to 1885 and rose to chair the House Military Affairs Committee. He died near Redondo Beach, California.

• Major collections of Rosecrans's private papers repose in the libraries of the University of California at Los Angeles and Notre Dame University. The standard biography is William M. Lamers, *The Edge of Glory: A Biography of General William S. Rosecrans, U.S.A.* (1961). Other life studies include W. B. Frost, *William Starke Rosecrans: His Life and Public Services* (1880), and Gilbert C. Kniffin, *Major-General William Starke Rosecrans: Commandery of the District of Columbia, Military Order of the Loyal Legion of the United States Pamphlet 74* (1908). A latter-day assessment of Rosecrans's military career is Edward G. Longacre, "A General Vanquished in the West: The Life of General William Starke Rosecrans," *Civil War Times Illustrated* 24 (Oct. 1985): 16–19, 44–47. Rosecrans's career, especially his relationship with Grant, receives a great deal of criticism in Grant's *Personal Memoirs* (1885). Rosecrans attempted to even the score by pointing out "The Mistakes of Grant," *North American Review* 141 (1885): 580–99.

Studies of the army with which Rosecrans is most often identified include Thomas B. Van Horne, *History of the Army of the Cumberland* (1875), and John Fitch, *Annals of the Army of the Cumberland* (1864). The army leader's relations with the subordinate who eventually replaced him are recounted in Francis F. McKinney, *Education in Violence: The Life of George H. Thomas and the History of the Army of the Cumberland* (1961). Studies of Rosecrans's major campaigns include his own account of the battle of Corinth in Robert Underwood Johnson and Clarence Clough Buel, eds., *Battles and Leaders of the Civil War*, vol. 2 (1887–1888); Jacob D. Cox, "McClellan in West Virginia," in *Battles and Leaders*, vol. 1 (1887–1888); James Lee McDonough, *Stones River: Bloody Winter in Tennessee* (1980); and Peter Cozzens, *No Better Place to Die: The Battle of Stones River* (1990) and *This Terrible Sound: The Battle of Chickamauga* (1992). See also T. Harry Williams, *Lincoln and His Generals* (1952), and Kenneth P. Williams, *Lincoln Finds a General: A Military Study of the Civil War* (1949–1959). Obituaries are in the *San Francisco Bulletin*, 11 Mar. 1898, and the *New York Times*, 12 Mar. 1898.

EDWARD G. LONGACRE

ROSELIEP, Raymond (11 Aug. 1917–6 Dec. 1983), poet and Catholic priest, was born in Farley, Iowa, the son of John Albert Roseliep, a caterer, and Anna Elizabeth Anderson. When he was a child, Roseliep's family moved to Dubuque, where he developed a lifelong love for the natural world while hiking about Dubuque's hills. He also enjoyed drawing and painting. At Loras Academy his artistic interests evolved toward poetry.

Roseliep attended Loras College in Dubuque, winning prizes for his poetry and graduating in 1939. He then entered the Theological College at the Catholic University of America to study for the priesthood. Ordained in 1943, he served as assistant pastor at a parish in Gilbertville, Iowa, and later as managing editor of the Dubuque archdiocesan newspaper, *The Witness*, before joining the Loras College English department in 1946. He earned an M.A. from the Catholic University of America in 1948 and a Ph.D. from the University of Notre Dame in 1954.

Roseliep began writing poetry for publication shortly after ordination, publishing primarily in Catholic magazines. At the urging of another poet, John Logan, Roseliep moved into the secular market in the 1950s. His first published collection of poetry, *The Linen Bands*, appeared in 1961. The volume clearly reflects the author's three-part identity as poet, priest, and teacher. The title poem recalls the priest's ordination; other poems speak of students and the poet's teaching role. The poems in this first volume show great virtuosity with traditional forms (the sonnet, quatrain, terza rima) and techniques (iambics, end and internal rhyme). The poems are by a poet sensitive in both content and expression to the durability and flexibility of traditions.

The Small Rain (1963) demonstrates a shifting from iambics to syllabics in longer poems and a growing preference for concision in both line and stanza length. About this time Roseliep was discovering haiku, which would become his main poetic interest from the

1970s until his death. *Love Makes the Air Light* (1965) includes a large number of poems designated haiku, plus three-line stanzas and haiku-like poems. The haiku in this third volume follow a rigid five-seven-five syllable count, and many have an epigrammatical flavor.

Health problems led to Roseliep's retirement from teaching in 1966 and to an interruption in publication. In the same year he was appointed resident chaplain at Holy Family Hall in Dubuque, an infirmary run by the Sisters of St. Francis of the Holy Family. He held this position until his death. That he spent the last part of his life associated with Franciscans was appropriate because he shared with the saint an abiding love for the things of nature and a commitment to the peaceful union of humanity and the natural world—attitudes reflected in his poetry.

Roseliep resumed publishing in the 1970s and produced a long string of haiku collections, beginning with *Flute over Walden* in 1976. This volume of "Thoreauhaiku" written sometimes in Henry David Thoreau's voice, sometimes in the poet's, shows innovation in subject but remains committed to the five-seven-five syllabic system. Subsequent collections show Roseliep's innovations in form and minimalist tendencies that reflect his long concern with concise expression.

In *Step on the Rain* (1977) and other volumes Roseliep pushed forward the frontiers of American haiku. He deviated from his earlier syllable counting to produce haiku that often are extremely brief and sometimes combine playfulness with a serious meaning. Believing that American haiku should reflect American culture rather than slavishly imitate Japanese subjects and approaches, he often took positions contrary to the pronouncements of more traditional American haikuists, as in his willing use of figurative language, the first-person pronoun, enjambment, and occasional omission of words placing the haiku experience within a particular season. His unique approach led haiku scholar William J. Higginson to coin the term "liepku" for Roseliep's compositions. Sometimes, as in *A Day in the Life of Sobi-Shi* (1978), Roseliep wrote as Sobi-Shi, a persona that simultaneously allowed for both personal expression and emotional distancing. Among his many awards were the Harold G. Henderson Haiku Award from the Haiku Society of America (1977, 1982) and the Shugyo Takaha Award from the Yuki Teikei Haiku Society (1980). Through his widespread publishing and continuing experimentation, he helped the American haiku movement gain aesthetic maturity, increased numbers of participants, and greater critical acceptance.

In "A Poet's Belief," published in *New Catholic World* (Jan.-Feb. 1976), Roseliep writes, "Being a priest and being a poet means that you handle two callings, trying to see to it that they do not collide, hoping in fact that they blend and complement one another." He also describes the fusion of spirit and matter within these callings: "A poem is spirit made incarnate. It is matter transfigured: matter ennobled and hallowed by the act of the language" (p. 42).

Certain themes recur throughout Roseliep's poetry: love of people and nature, the psychic relationship between youth and adult, connections between spiritual and physical, and the attraction and power of light. The theme of light related directly to how he saw his two roles. As a poet, he attempted to bring order from chaos. In doing so, he projected, as he writes in "A Poet's Belief," "the dissidence at the heart of all life: the clash between darkness and light, good and evil, purposelessness and purpose, avowal and denial, the sacred and the profane, flesh and spirit, death and the thirst for immortality, Yahweh and oblivion" (p. 42). Roseliep thus rebels, he says, "against the night surrounding us . . . " (p. 41).

Before he died—in Dubuque—Roseliep purchased his cemetery monument, which he had engraved with the words "AGAINST THE NIGHT"—a phrase from a poem in *The Linen Bands*. The three words are a final definition of how he saw his life as a poet-priest.

• Roseliep's papers are in the Loras College library. He recorded selections of his poetry for the Lamont Library at Harvard University and the Fenn Series of Contemporary Authors at Fenn College in Cleveland. Among some twenty books, his most important poetry collections, besides those cited earlier, include *A Roseliep Retrospective: Poems & Other Words By & About Raymond Roseliep* (1980), *Listen to Light* (1980), and *Rabbit in the Moon* (1983). His poems have appeared in hundreds of magazines and been widely anthologized. An issue of the haiku magazine *Wind Chimes* (no. 12, 1984) was devoted to reflections on his life and poetry. An early account of the poet is by Thomas P. McDonnell, "Three Unpublished Poets," *America*, 29 Apr. 1961, pp. 213–15. Sister Mary Thomas Eulberg considers his life and poetry in "Poet of Finespun Filaments: Raymond Roseliep," *Delta Epsilon Sigma Journal* 24 (1979): 100–105, and in "Raymond Roseliep: Literary Theories on Haiku," *Delta Epsilon Sigma Journal* 28 (1983): 82–92. A survey of Roseliep's poetic career is by Donna Bauerly, "Raymond Roseliep: 'Where Are You Going? Where Have You Been?'" appears in *A Roseliep Retrospective*, pp. 29–44. The same volume includes an important essay by Bill Pauly that focuses on *The Still Point* while offering perceptive insights into Roseliep's growth as a haikuist: "A Joyous Dance in Timelessness," pp. 45–51. The *Telegraph Herald* of Dubuque printed an obituary, 7 Dec. 1983.

EDWARD J. RIELLY

ROSELLINI, Hugh J. (16 June 1909–26 Nov. 1984), Washington State Supreme Court justice, was born in Tacoma, Washington, the son of Primo Rosellini and Cesarini Marchetti. Rosellini's father had emigrated from Italy in 1898, found employment as a laborer with the Northern Pacific Railroad, and before leaving the company to settle in Tacoma had been in charge of the regional payroll department. The Rosellinis opened a grocery and supply store, which soon became the center of social and political activities for the many Italians working for the railroads and the lumber mills in the area. Growing up surrounded by working people and working himself during school vacations in local mills instilled in young Rosellini an understanding and sympathy for the struggles of the laborer. Often the subject of taunts of "Wop" and "Dago" from his classmates, Rosellini was sensitized to the special indignities vented on minorities. The importance of these earlier experiences became evident in his political and judicial career. Rosellini's sympathies always lay with the less privileged in society.

In 1922 Rosellini enrolled in St. Martin's High School in Lacey, near Olympia, Washington. In the summers he worked in an Eatonville sawmill. After high school he attended the College of Puget Sound. As was common then, Rosellini entered law school after only three years as an undergraduate, earning his law degree in 1933 from the University of Washington. In 1938 Rosellini married Yvonne Crissy, a ballet dancer and teacher, with whom he would have three children.

The deprivations of the Great Depression, and especially the antilabor reactions of business and state government, attracted the future judge to New Deal politics. Rosellini filed for the state house of representatives position in Tacoma's Twenty-eighth District. Working through Democratic clubs, ethnic groups, small social and political gatherings, door-to-door contacts, and the Grange, and with the able assistance of his wife, who proved to be a skilled campaigner, Rosellini defeated the incumbent by a few hundred votes. He quickly established himself as a supporter of liberal programs while in the state house. Both his vote and his considerable political acumen contributed to programs improving Washington State's welfare system and working conditions, regulating business concerns, and supporting public power and soldiers' benefits.

Because of the demands of his private law practice, Rosellini did not file for another term after the 1945 legislative session. However, when a vacancy on the state trial bench opened in 1948, Democratic governor Mon Walgren, with whom Rosellini worked while in the legislature, appointed the 37-year-old liberal Democrat to the vacancy, and thus Rosellini began a judicial career that spanned thirty-six years. He proved to be a competent trial judge. Although he was somewhat lenient in his sentencing of those first appearing before him, his liberalism was not extended to the repeat offender.

In 1950 Rosellini made an unsuccessful run for the state's court of last resort against a highly respected incumbent. When asked why he entered the race, he responded, "When you're young, anything seems possible." In 1954 Rosellini tried again for an open position on the supreme court, defeating a popular conservative trial judge after a hard-fought campaign. As a result of his legislative record and Democratic background, Rosellini was correctly perceived by the media and the legal profession as a jurist who would view the law from a liberal perspective.

As in the legislature and on the trial bench, Rosellini continued his strong support of individual civil rights. He generally supported labor in labor-management issues, favored the government in regulation and taxation cases, and tended to side with the underdog in housing, welfare, and workmen's compensation cases and with the plaintiff in tort cases. However, the criminal did not receive any special favors. Also, Rosellini was not altogether convinced that the Indian treaties exempted them from state fishing regulations; a view that seemed related to his love of sport fishing and hunting.

Yet despite the numerous disagreements over legal issues with the more conservative members of the bench, Rosellini provided the court with a civility that held the often divided bench together. His chambers were an informal meeting place for all the justices, where coffee was available and lively discussions focused more on baseball, fishing, and state politics than on the law. Given his years in public office, his easygoing, unpretentious manner, mellifluous voice, and polite old-world manners, Rosellini's conciliating role on the bench came to him naturally.

While serving as chief justice (1965–1967), Rosellini was instrumental in establishing a voluntary state bench-bar-press committee to reconcile the conflict between fair trials and free press, and his advocacy of a state intermediate court of appeals led to its adoption in 1968. His mediation skills brought the Alaska judiciary and the Alaska state bar association together to agree on an innovative code of ethics for the bar and bench.

Justice Rosellini loved the outdoors. Salmon and steelhead fishing, duck and pheasant hunting, and camping trips in Canada filled whatever time court recesses permitted. According to friends, he was a connoisseur of "fine dogs, fine fish, fine game, and good cooking."

Yvonne Rosellini died in September 1982. A few weeks later the justice had triple bypass heart surgery. He then announced he would retire at the end of his term. More complications with his heart required another operation, from which he never recovered. Hugh Rosellini died in Tacoma a few weeks before his planned retirement.

• Letters, interview tapes, and news items are in Charles H. Sheldon's Washington Supreme Court files at the Washington State Archives, Olympia. The record of Rosellini's judicial career is in his 800-plus opinions published in fifty-seven volumes of the *Washington Reports*. See also Sheldon, *A Century of Judging: A Political History of the Washington Supreme Court* (1988) and *The Washington High Bench: A Biographical History* (1992). The definitive biography is Orman Lee Vertrees, "Mr. Justice Hugh J. Rosellini: A Study of His Reference Groups and Washington Supreme Court Voting Record" (Ph.D. diss., Washington State Univ., 1986). An obituary is in the *Tacoma News Tribune*, 27 Nov. 1984.

CHARLES H. SHELDON

ROSEN, George (23 June 1910–27 July 1977), medical historian and public health educator, was born in Brooklyn, New York, the son of Morris Rosen, a garment worker, and Rose Handleman. Rosen's parents were immigrant Jews who spoke Yiddish at home, and it was not until he entered the New York City public schools that Rosen learned English. He graduated from Stuyvesant High School in 1926, and the College of the City of New York in 1930. A victim of the policy that restricted enrollment of Jewish students at American medical schools, Rosen then undertook medical studies at the University of Berlin where he joined several dozen young Americans (all Jews except one African American) who had been denied a high quality medical education at home. Rosen witnessed the Nazi seizure of power and lived in Nazi Germany while completing his medical education. In Berlin, Rosen met Beate Caspari, a German-Jewish medical student, whom he married in 1933; they had two children.

Rosen completed his M.D. thesis in 1935 under the direction of Paul Diepgen, professor of the history of medicine at the University of Berlin. For help in developing a topic in American medical history, Diepgen had urged Rosen to contact Henry Sigerist at the Johns Hopkins Institute of the History of Medicine. A Swiss national who had been at the University of Leipzig before moving to Baltimore in 1932, Sigerist was a liberal with increasing sympathies for the Soviet Union and was arguably the world's leading historian of medicine. He was impressed with Rosen's work and quickly fostered a mentor-protégé relationship with him. Within a few months of his return to New York in 1935, Rosen became an intern at Beth-El Hospital in Brooklyn and soon began submitting articles to Sigerist's *Bulletin of the History of Medicine*. He opened a medical practice in 1937 but was not temperamentally suited for clinical medicine, and his income suffered. He took a part-time job in the tuberculosis service of the New York City Department of Health and, with Sigerist's assistance, also found paid work as a translator and as editor of *Ciba Symposia*, a magazine published by the Swiss drug firm Ciba-Geigy.

Rosen started taking courses in the sociology department at Columbia University in 1939 and completed his Ph.D. in 1944. His dissertation, published as *The Specialization of Medicine with Particular Reference to Ophthalmology* (1944), remains a standard work on the history of medical specialization. In 1943 he took leave from his position as a full-time health officer for the New York City Department of Health to join the army. For two years he worked at the global epidemiology program in Washington, D.C., and was then transferred to medical intelligence work in London. While in the army, Rosen was invited to be founding editor of the *Journal of the History of Medicine and Allied Sciences*, a position he held from 1946 until 1952. After his discharge in April 1946, he returned to the New York City Health Department and took advantage of a fellowship-in-training that allowed him to earn an M.P.H. from the Columbia University School of Public Health in 1947. In 1949 he became director of health education for New York City, and in 1950 he left city government to head the health education efforts of the Health Insurance Plan of Greater New York (HIP). He was appointed to a professorship in health education in the public health faculty at Columbia in 1951, where he taught courses in health education, education theory, community health, the sociology of mental illness, and history of medicine; and when his position was made full time in 1957, he left HIP to concentrate on scholarship and teaching. In 1957 he also began a sixteen-year tenure as editor of the *American Journal of Public Health*, and published his most influential work, *A History of Public Health*, in the following year. Rosen achieved his career goal of a full-time position in medical history in 1969, when he became professor of the history of medicine and of public health at Yale University. He died in Oxford, while touring England on his way to an international history of science conference in Edinburgh.

Though himself a nonbeliever, indifferent to Zionism, and an aspiring cosmopolite, Rosen took pride in being identifiable as a Jewish New Yorker of proletarian origin. More significantly for both his historical and public health work, he associated himself with health issues important to the labor movement. A middle-class intellectual of the moderate left, he had an interest in Marxism as a tool for historical analysis. While a medical student in Weimar-era Berlin, he devoted himself to exploring liberal and socialist traditions in German philosophy and sociology, and he never confused the crimes of the Nazis with the general legacy of German culture, among whose positive features, he felt, was a national health insurance system with universal coverage. The importance of his work in both public health and medical historiography lay in his commitment to scholarship and pedagogy as forms of political activism, and in his ability to integrate what he learned from German sources with the functionalist sociology he encountered at Columbia. He did not share Sigerist's enthusiasm for the USSR and made a point never to join any political organization.

Rosen's program for health reform was social medicine, an approach that went beyond guaranteeing medical care and sought to create a healthy society by concentrating on the social causes of disease. Although he went into public health only because of the scarcity of academic positions in medical history, he took his work as administrator and educator seriously. At HIP he helped try to create a small-scale model of a national health system; and as editor of the *American Journal of Public Health* he forged a broad vision of public health, urging a fragmenting profession never to forget its fundamental mission of preventing the spread of disease. In his historical work, Rosen emphasized the role of the patient and the social determinants of both the knowledge base and the practices of the healing professions. With Sigerist's encouragement he was the first to explore the history of occupational disease (in *The History of Miners' Diseases: A Medical and Social Interpretation* [1943]), and his later work on the history of mental illness, *Madness in Society: Chapters in the Historical Sociology of Mental Illness* (1968), broke new ground in exploring the place of the apparently mad in a wide range of social and historical contexts. Rosen is remembered as an historian of public health, a theoretician of social medicine, and a founding practitioner of the social history of medicine.

• The George Rosen Papers, in the Yale University Archives, comprise the major manuscript source on Rosen. A nearly complete bibliography of his published work, which included nine books and over two hundred articles, appears in Charles E. Rosenberg, ed., *Healing and History: Essays for George Rosen* (1979). Useful essays on Rosen's life and work appear in *Healing and History* and in the "George Rosen Memorial Issue" of the *Journal of the History of Medicine and Allied Sciences* 33, no. 3 (July 1978). The fullest treatment to date of Rosen's life and work is Edward T. Morman, "George Rosen, Public Health and History," in the 1993 expanded edition of Rosen's *A History of Public Health*. See also Elizabeth Fee and Edward T. Morman, "Doing History, Making Revolution: The Aspirations of Henry E. Sigerist and George Rosen," in *Doctors, Politics and Society: Historical Essays*, ed. Dorothy Porter and Roy Porter (1993); and Morman, "George Rosen and the History of Mental Illness," in *Discovering the History of Psychiatry* (1994).

EDWARD T. MORMAN

ROSEN, Joseph A. (15 Feb. 1877–2 Apr. 1949), agronomist and resettlement expert, was born in Moscow, Russia, and apparently raised 100 miles south in Tula. Nothing is known of his parents and early life. He once acknowledged being held in the Boutirka prison for two months at age fifteen for reading a book that said Czar Alexander was a drunkard. He attended Moscow University in 1894 but, because of anti-czarist activities, was exiled to Siberia for five years. Within six months Rosen escaped to Germany, where he supposedly enrolled at the University of Heidelberg to study philosophy and chemistry. He supported himself by writing for Russian journals.

Rosen emigrated in 1903 to the United States, where gradually he worked his way west from New York to Michigan doing odd jobs as a day laborer and farm hand. After arriving in Lansing, Michigan, he worked on a farm for almost two years before enrolling as a special student at Michigan Agricultural College in 1905. While a student, Rosen prepared articles on American agriculture for Russian publications and worked as an assistant in the library. After he graduated with a Bachelor of Science degree in agriculture in 1908, the leaders of the province of Ekaterinoslav in the Ukraine, presumably impressed by his articles, hired him to establish and head a bureau to study American farming methods as they could be applied to Russia, whereupon he moved to Minneapolis, Minnesota, to set up the office. He referred to this position as chief of the American Agricultural Bureau of the Governmental Zemstvo of Ekaterinoslav; the sponsoring group may have been the State Agricultural Society of Kharkov. Rosen spent the first three of his six years in the position writing ten lengthy reports, then concentrated on his purchasing and sales agent responsibilities, for which he obtained large quantities of seeds and implements to be sold in Russia and sold Russian beet seeds in the United States. He introduced a strain of Russian rye into the United States; the high-yield rye seeds, presented to Michigan Agricultural College in March 1909, were named Rosen rye in his honor.

In October 1909 Rosen enrolled as a graduate student at the University of Minnesota in the College of Agriculture, Forestry, and Home Economics, but university records do not indicate if he graduated. He became a U.S. citizen in December 1909 and interrupted his studies in 1910, when called to Russia to supervise the South Russian Exhibition, an agricultural fair. He closed the Minneapolis office in 1914 and became agronomist and superintendent of the Baron de Hirsch Agricultural School in Woodbine, New Jersey, in October 1914. When the Ukrainian group resumed its activities in 1916, Rosen resigned from the school but remained a member of its Advisory Committee, and moved the bureau's office to New York City. There he became the New York representative for the Petrograd International Bank of Commerce in 1918 and served as a director of the Jewish Agricultural Society from 1919 to 1922 and in 1922–1923.

During the Russian famine of 1921–1923, American Jewish leaders Felix M. Warburg and James N. Rosenberg persuaded Rosen to become the U.S. representative of the Joint Distribution Committee (JDC) in Russia for Herbert Hoover's American Relief Administration. Hoover wrote to Rosenberg that Rosen "was during the famine period in that country a most valuable member of the staff of the American Relief Administration" (Rosenberg, pp. 301–302). Hoover later wrote to Dana Dalrymple that "I had occasion to know Rosen quite well . . . He was a fine personality, deeply devoted to our problems, and a superb administrator" (Dalrymple, p. 159). When he sailed for Russia in October 1922 to spend the $1.24 million appropriation, Rosen took with him a staff of young American agriculturalists and tractor farming specialists as traveling instructors. They successfully introduced tractors to rehabilitate the Jewish farms, and Rosen's centralized repair shops became the model for Soviet collective tractor stations.

Having found his calling, Rosen spent the rest of his life in Jewish farm relief and resettlement work. On 21 July 1924 the JDC appointed Rosen as head of their subsidiary, the American Joint Agricultural Society (called the Agro-Joint), to cooperate with the Soviet Society for Settlement of Jewish Toilers (KOMZET). Rosen believed that Russian Jews, rather than emigrating to Palestine, could integrate into the Soviet society through agricultural resettlement and training and thus gain citizenship rights previously denied them. Through his knowledge of Russian soil conditions, crop possibilities, and industrial problems, Rosen introduced modern scientific techniques of large-scale farming, promoted drought-resistant seeds, and taught crop diversification with American corn on 2.7 million acres to prevent a recurrence of the famine. Rosen compared the experiment to American frontier pioneering, with its share of troubles, disappointments, heartbreaks, and heartaches. His efforts relocated almost 300,000 Jews to more than three million acres in the Ukraine, White Russia, and the Crimea between 1924 and 1936—one of the largest Jewish colonization efforts in the world. Rosenberg praised Rosen as "a great builder, a man of creative intellect and vision, of expert knowledge and skill, [and] possessed of unflagging energy and patience" (Rosenberg, p. 314). In evaluating the outcome Rosen said in a report to Agro-Joint, "a tremendous change for the better has taken place for the Jews in the USSR and what a potent part in the improvement of the Jewish situation the work of our organization has played" (quoted in Evelyn Morrissey, *Jewish Workers and Farmers in the Crimea and Ukraine* [1937], p. 131). Rosen returned to the United States in 1937 and Agro-Joint completed its activities in September 1938 as the Soviet government halted the work under the threat of impending war with Germany. At the end of the war, any trace of these Jewish settlers—all presumably destroyed by the Nazis—had disappeared.

Seeking a haven for German Jewish refugees, Rosen conducted a resettlement study of British Guiana in 1939 as a member of a special commission appointed jointly by President Franklin D. Roosevelt's Advisory Committee on Political Refugees and the British government. He rejected the location for environmental reasons, and the American Jewish community likewise withheld support for the project. That same year for the American Friends Service Committee he surveyed Mexico as a potential resettlement location. As vice president of the JDC-sponsored Dominican Resettlement Association, Rosen subsequently directed a resettlement project for European refugees in Sosua, Dominican Republic, in 1940. Though in his sixties, he personally traveled for one month through the country on foot, by car, and on horseback to examine various tracts of land. Of 4,000 Dominican visas issued to German Jews, approximately 800 refugees settled on 40,000 acres at Sosua.

Rosen died at his New York City home, leaving his wife, Katherine N. Shoubine, and two sons.

• Rosen's personal papers are housed at Yivo Institute for Jewish Research, New York. His correspondence concerning Jewish resettlement is in the Dominican Republic Settlement Association records and the American Jewish Joint Distribution Committee countries collection in the JDC Archives, New York City. His early years in the United States and agricultural work in Russia are documented by Dana G. Dalrymple, "Joseph A. Rosen and Early Russian Studies of American Agriculture," *Agricultural History* 38 (July 1964): 157–60. The work of Rosen with the Agro-Joint project is examined in Allan L. Kagedan, "American Jews and the Soviet Experiment: The Agro-Joint Project, 1924–1937," *Jewish Social Studies* 43 (Spring 1981): 153–64. Progress reports on his projects were published in *The American Jewish Year Book Unfinished Business: James N. Rosenberg Papers*, ed. Maxwell Geismar (1967), contains Rosenberg's diary of a trip to Russia to see Rosen's work, letters to and from Rosenberg about Rosen, and a report about the Dominican Republic resettlement. An obituary is in the *New York Times*, 2 Apr. 1949.

SUSAN HAMBURGER

ROSENAU, Milton Joseph (1 Jan. 1869–9 Apr. 1946), epidemiologist and public health pioneer, was born in Philadelphia, Pennsylvania, the son of Nathan Rose-

nau, a merchant, and Matilda Blitz. After receiving his M.D. from the University of Pennsylvania in 1889, he spent a year as an intern at Philadelphia General Hospital before joining the U.S. Marine Hospital Service (later part of the U.S. Public Health Service). He spent the next two years as an assistant surgeon at the Service's hospital in Washington, D.C., then studied for a year at the Hygienic Institute of Berlin before returning to his post in Washington for another two years. In 1895 he was appointed quarantine officer for San Francisco, and for the next three years he oversaw quarantine and sanitation projects in California and the Philippine Islands. In 1898 he became the Service's quarantine officer in Cuba.

In 1899 Rosenau was appointed director of the Public Health Service's Hygienic Laboratory (later part of the National Institutes of Health) in Washington, a position he held for ten years. In 1900 he married Myra F. Frank, with whom he had three children, and studied at the Pathological Institute in Vienna and the Pasteur Institute in Paris. As director of what was initially a one-man operation, Rosenau conducted research concerning the causes and means of transmission of epidemic diseases associated with international commerce and immigration such as diphtheria, typhoid fever, yellow fever, malaria, botulism, bubonic plague, and tuberculosis. This research was greatly expanded after passage of the Biologics Control Act of 1902, which his office was tasked to administer, and by 1909 Rosenau had established separate divisions of bacteriology, chemistry, pathology, pharmacology, and zoology. He also sought to develop preventive measures against epidemic diseases and other medical conditions; this quest led him to study the usefulness of glycerin as a germicidal agent, the results of which he published in *Disinfection and Disinfectants: A Practical Guide for Sanitarians, Health and Quarantine Officers* (1902). It also led him to become one of the first researchers to study anaphylaxis, a condition that results in increased susceptibility rather than immunity to foreign protein after inoculation. This effort resulted in *A Study of the Causes of Sudden Death Following the Injection of Horse Serum* (1906), coauthored with his assistant John F. Anderson, wherein the authors showed that bacterial proteins were capable of increasing the body's sensitivity to microbes. Rosenau also studied milk sanitation, and in 1906 he showed that milk could be made safe to drink simply by heating it at 140°F for twenty minutes; when this study was published as *The Milk Question* (1912), it helped pave the way for public acceptance of the pasteurization of milk. Rosenau also taught bacteriology at the Army and Navy Medical School from 1904 to 1909 and tropical diseases at Georgetown University from 1905 to 1909.

In 1909 Rosenau became the first professor of preventive medicine and hygiene in the United States when he left public service to teach at Harvard Medical School, a position he held for twenty-six years. In 1913 he published *Preventive Medicine and Hygiene*, which went through ten editions in six languages and served for a number of years as the standard text on the subject. That same year he helped to organize the Harvard and Massachusetts Institute of Technology School for Health Officers, the first school of public health in the United States. He also served as the school's director until its disestablishment in 1922, after which he was appointed professor of epidemiology at the newly established Harvard School of Public Health. From 1914 to 1921 he was also affiliated with the Massachusetts State Board of Health as chief of the division of biologic laboratories and director of the antitoxin and vaccine laboratory.

In 1935 Rosenau married Maud Heilner Tenner, with whom he had no children (his first wife died in 1930), and retired from Harvard. The next year he joined the University of North Carolina School of Medicine as professor of epidemiology and director of the newly created division of public health. In 1940 he helped to organize this division into the School of Public Health and served as its dean until his death.

Rosenau served as president of the Society of American Bacteriologists in 1934 and the American Public Health Association (APHA) in 1944. He was awarded the Gold Medal of American Medicine for 1912–1913, the APHA's Sedgwick Memorial Medal in 1933, and the Annual Forum on Allergy's Pirquet Gold Medal in 1935. In 1963 the University of North Carolina School of Public Health named a building in his honor. He died in Chapel Hill, North Carolina.

• Rosenau's papers are located in the University of North Carolina Southern Historical Collection in Chapel Hill. Obituaries are in the *New York Times*, 10 Apr. 1946; *Transactions of the Association of American Physicians* 59 (1946): 32–33; *American Journal of Public Health* 36 (1946): 530–31; *Journal of the American Medical Association* 130 (1946): 1185; and *Journal of Bacteriology* 53 (1947): 1–3.

CHARLES W. CAREY, JR.

ROSENBACH, Abraham Simon Wolf (22 July 1876–1 July 1952), antiquarian bookseller, was born in Philadelphia, Pennsylvania, the son of Morris Rosenbach, a soft-goods merchant, and Isabella Polock. As a child, A. S. W. Rosenbach, the youngest of seven children, spent many hours in the bookshop of his uncle Moses Polock, a well-known antiquarian bookseller. There he learned to love old books and manuscripts and absorbed much about history and literature. He was the only one of his family to attend college, receiving his Ph.D. in English literature in 1901 from the University of Pennsylvania.

In 1903 A. S. W.'s brother, Philip, convinced him to enter business with him as the Rosenbach Company. Philip was president and filled the store at 1320 Walnut Street in Philadelphia with prints, objets d'art, and antique furniture. A. S. W. was secretary. Urged on by Philip, and building on his early experience in the bookshop of his uncle and on his own scholarly interest in English literature, he specialized in rare books and manuscripts.

The first few years of the Rosenbach Company were financially marginal. The company's first break came in 1905 when Rosenbach was introduced to the wealthy Widener family of Philadelphia. The youngest, Harry Widener, was beginning to collect books. He and Rosenbach became close friends, and soon the rest of the Widener family were collecting books and manuscripts as well. These purchases put the financially struggling firm on solid ground. Through the Wideners' influence, Rosenbach built up a small circle of wealthy Philadelphia customers that included William M. Elkins, A. Edward Newton, and John B. Stetson.

Gradually Rosenbach's clientele broadened, and he made sales to collectors outside Philadelphia. In 1920 the Rosenbach brothers felt confident enough about the future to open a store in New York. That same year, the bookseller George D. Smith died. Smith had dominated the American book trade. While Rosenbach had sold the occasional book to Smith's clients, he had not been able to "do business" on a large scale. After Smith's death, Rosenbach moved quickly to attach Smith's wealthiest customers. Two of these collectors were Henry E. Huntington and Henry C. Folger, both of whom collected sixteenth- and seventeenth-century English literature. Fortunately for Rosenbach, this was the area of his greatest scholarly expertise, and Folger and Huntington soon trusted Rosenbach as their agent.

With their financial backing, Rosenbach established the Rosenbach Company as the dominant force in the auction room in New York and London. American and British collectors learned that if they wanted to be sure to get a book in a sale, they should entrust the bid to Rosenbach; otherwise, he would undoubtedly be bidding against them.

The 1920s were a golden age for American book collecting and for the Rosenbach Company. Almost without exception, Rosenbach purchased every important book or manuscript to appear in the auction room and set a series of auction records. In 1925 he paid $106,000 for a copy of the Gutenberg Bible, the highest price ever paid for a printed book at auction. The following year, he paid $51,500 for a document of Button Gwinnett, signer of the Declaration of Independence, a record price for an autograph. In 1928 he paid $14,000 for a first edition of Rudyard Kipling's *The Smith Administration*, the highest sum ever given for the work of a living author; that same year he made his most famous purchase in the auction room, the original manuscript of *Alice in Wonderland*. These highly publicized purchases cemented his reputation as the greatest bookseller of his day. The *New Yorker* profiled him as the "Napoleon of Books"; the London tabloids called him the "Terror of the Auction Room"; and his friend, writer and book collector A. Edward Newton, said he was "the most astute bandit out of Wall Street."

Rosenbach's fame in the auction room made him a national figure. With the assistance of Avery Strakosch, he wrote a series of articles about book collecting for the *Saturday Evening Post* beginning in January 1927. The articles, ranging from "Old Bibles" to "Some Literary Forgeries," preached the Rosenbach philosophy that great books only increase in value and that they are a good investment. The articles were later collected and published as *Books and Bidders: The Adventures of a Bibliophile* (1927), with a second series of articles later collected as *A Book Hunter's Holiday: Adventures with Books and Manuscripts* (1936).

The auction purchases were important; the publicity they generated made Rosenbach the most famous bookseller of his day. However, the secret of the Rosenbach Company's financial success was Rosenbach's private treaty purchases. In these transactions, he would pay what the seller considered a reasonable price and then sell the books for what he thought they were worth, which was often substantially more than what he had paid for them. Rosenbach often said that great books were worth great prices, and he was not often proved wrong, so effective was his salesmanship. During the course of his career, Rosenbach bought more than seventy libraries privately as well as a host of individual books and manuscripts. His purchases included the library of Frederick Trowbridge (1925), described by the newspapers as "the largest private collection in America ever sold to a single purchaser"; the family archive of the conquistador Hernando Cortes (1928); and a group of books from York Minster Library (1930).

The stock market crash of 1929 at first had little effect on the Rosenbach Company. Rosenbach continued buying privately and at auction. Slowly, however, Rosenbach customers cut back on their buying, and the fabulously expensive sales became less frequent. Rare book prices reached their nadir after the bombing of Pearl Harbor, and then even Rosenbach was forced to lower his prices. The decline in prices was mirrored by a decline in Rosenbach's health. In the mid-1940s, as his energy waned, the Rosenbach Company survived on the sale of the residue of the great libraries purchased in the 1920s. In July 1952, just short of his seventy-sixth birthday, A. S. W. Rosenbach died in Philadelphia. Less than a year later, Philip Rosenbach died suddenly while on a trip to Los Angeles.

Because of his position at the center of the antiquarian book trade, Rosenbach was ideally placed to collect books and manuscripts as well as sell them. He collected primarily in four areas: American children's books published before 1841, a collection he presented to the Free Library of Philadelphia in 1947; American Judaica, a collection given to the American Jewish Historical Society in 1931; English literature; and Americana. As neither A. S. W. nor Philip ever married, these last two collections, along with the brothers' townhouse and Philip Rosenbach's collections of silver, furniture, portrait miniatures, and objets d'art, were inherited by the foundation established by the two brothers in 1950, now the Rosenbach Museum & Library in Philadelphia. Here are preserved many of the greatest items Rosenbach bought, the books and manuscripts he could never bring himself to sell.

A. S. W. Rosenbach's influence extends far beyond the walls of the collection he formed in Philadelphia. He passionately believed in the importance of original source material. That passion made him an effective salesman, and that belief led to the creation of some of America's greatest collections. By the time of Rosenbach's death, the United States had become the beneficiary of a vast westward flow of books from Europe, a flow that Rosenbach stimulated both through his purchases and through the cultivation of private collectors whose libraries were ultimately given to the public.

• The records of the Rosenbach Company are held by the Rosenbach Museum & Library, Philadelphia. Rosenbach's personal collections formed the basis of two bibliographies that are still standard reference works: *An American Jewish Bibliography, Being a List of Books and Pamphlets by Jews, or Relating to Them, Printed in the United States from the Establishment of the Press in the Colonies until 1850* (1926), and *Early American Children's Books* (1933). He was the author of numerous bibliographical pieces; these are listed in John Fleming, "A Bibliography of the Books, Contributions and Articles Written by A. S. W. Rosenbach," in *To Doctor R.: Essays Here Collected and Published in Honor of the Seventieth Birthday of Dr. A. S. W. Rosenbach, July 22, 1946* (1946). A. S. W. Rosenbach's only work of fiction was *The Unpublishable Memoirs* (1917).

The standard biography is *Rosenbach: A Biography* (1960), by Edwin Wolf 2nd with John F. Fleming, both of whom worked for the Rosenbach Company. Additional details of several of Rosenbach's most famous purchases and sales are given in two works by Leslie A. Morris, *Rosenbach Abroad: In Pursuit of Books in Private Collections* (1988) and *Rosenbach Redux: Further Book Adventures in England and Ireland* (1989). An obituary is in the *Pennsylvania Library Chronicle* (Winter 1952–1953).

LESLIE A. MORRIS

ROSENBERG, Anna Marie Lederer (19 June 1902–9 May 1983), labor and personnel consultant and assistant secretary of defense, was born in Budapest, Hungary, the daughter of Albert Lederer, a furniture manufacturer, and Charlotte Bacskai, a children's author and illustrator. Her father was prosperous until Emperor Franz Joseph canceled a furniture order, causing the family to go bankrupt, close down the factory, and move to the United States in 1912. Albert Lederer never forgot that experience, and, no longer at the whim of an emperor and appreciative of his newly found freedoms, he encouraged his daughter to be a patriotic American. She entered New York City's Wadleigh High School in 1914 and organized the Future Voters League to encourage woman suffrage. While in high school in 1919 she settled a strike by students protesting compulsory military training, and that same year she served as a volunteer nurse and sold Liberty Bonds financing World War I. In 1919 she married an American soldier, Julius Rosenberg; they had one son. Later that year she became a naturalized citizen.

Rosenberg became active in Democratic politics in the early 1920s. In 1922 she managed the campaign of Tammany boss Jim Hagan's son, who was elected a city alderman. By 1924 she had enough experience to open an office as a public relations, personnel, and labor consultant. Her reputation was such that Governor Franklin Delano Roosevelt sought her advice on labor matters. These connections and accomplishments made Rosenberg an important figure in the New Deal.

Rosenberg's first major appointment came in 1934 as assistant to Nathan Straus, Jr., regional director of the National Recovery Administration (NRA) for the New York area. Following Straus's resignation, Rosenberg became regional director, a post she held until the U.S. Supreme Court declared the NRA unconstitutional in 1935. Her first brush with controversy came when she accepted the position of New York regional director of the Social Security Board in 1936. Congressman Albert J. Engel considered her outside income a conflict of interest, which led to an investigation. In 1937, while still regional director of the Social Security Board, she was also chair of the Subcommittee on the Bill of Rights and General Welfare for the New York State constitutional committee. Also that year Mayor Fiorello H. La Guardia asked her to organize the New York City Industrial Relations Board. He explained that Rosenberg "knows more about labor relations and human relations than any man in the country." President Roosevelt called on Rosenberg in 1938 to study industrial relations in Great Britain and Sweden. In these offices she displayed flexibility, a keen sensitivity to people, and an ability to delegate authority. Cecilia Ager of PM said, "She has also energy, diplomacy, cajolery, common sense, decision, direction, toughness, sympathy, humor and tact."

The onset of World War II led to Rosenberg's zenith of power. In 1941 she and Mayor La Guardia formed the City Committee on Defense Recreation. She ensured visiting enlisted men had clean, comfortable, and affordable rooms, saying they deserved the same hospitality shown to guests in your own home. As a member of the New York City and State War Council, she advocated that the shortage of labor in the Upstate region be overcome by relocating workers, stressing that, in the trying times, New York City employees would have to overcome prejudices of small-town communities. She also aided small businesses in their conversion from civilian manufacturing to the production of war matériel.

In 1942 Rosenberg's job as regional director of the Social Security Board came under the scrutiny of a U.S. House Appropriations Committee, who more formally investigated the allegations of Congressman Engel. Rosenberg asserted she accepted the position when informed that she could maintain her consulting firm, whose annual earnings averaged $60,000. Critics charged this arrangement was in violation of the "dual salary" law, which stated a person could not draw a salary from two jobs totaling more than $2,000. She maintained her outside consultations did not interfere with her federal position, stating, "Any time that has been taken out has been taken out of myself, out of my social life, out of things I like to do." Convinced that Rosenberg's weekend and lunch meetings did not conflict with her Social Security duties, the committee allowed her to keep both jobs.

In 1942 Rosenberg accepted the position of director of Region Two, New York State, of the War Manpower Commission. She was the only woman to hold this post and served in that capacity until 1945. To avoid future difficulties over conflicts of interest, she resigned from the regional directorship of the Social Security Board and shelved her consultation activities for the duration of the war. She did, however, remain on the Social Security Board and the Board of the Office of Defense, Health, and Welfare Services, of which she had been named director in 1941. Rosenberg believed that her full contribution could be achieved in these three offices, and to avoid violating the dual salary law, she sacrificed any other paid activity. She also was a member of the Labor Victory Board throughout the war and authored the chapter "Social Security and the National Purpose" in The Family in a World at War in 1942.

Rosenberg's most notable achievements on the War Manpower Commission came with the recruitment of men for the Pacific Coast Kaiser shipyards and "the Buffalo Plan." The Kaiser shipyards called for the fulfillment of 20,000 jobs, which required orderly and systematic work and the relocation of as few men as possible from coast to coast. She insisted that African Americans be hired. The Buffalo Plan did with manpower what the War Productions Board did with materials. A committee prioritized labor so that men could be funneled to where they were most needed. Although both management and labor criticized the plan for infringing their authority, it was effective and was used nationwide.

In 1944 Rosenberg reluctantly accepted a job as chief assistant to Brigadier General Frank T. Hines, director of retraining and reemployment. She preferred to work in the field and agreed to take the position in Washington, D.C., only if it were of short duration. In July 1944 Roosevelt sent her to tour the European theater as his personal observer. Her mission was to find out what "the boys" wanted after the war. She discovered they wanted above all a chance to better themselves and to go to school; thus Rosenberg became a driving force in the passage of the GI Bill of Rights. The following summer President Harry S. Truman sent her on another mission to Europe, this time to evaluate the repatriation and demobilization of U.S. troops. Rosenberg then returned to her consulting firm full-time. In 1946 she served as a member of the advisory commission of the War Mobilization and Reconversion Board's subcommittee examining wage stabilization policy. She was also named to the Presidential Advisory Commission on Universal Military Training and was a member of the American Commission for the United Nations Educational, Scientific, and Cultural Organization (UNESCO) in 1946–1950, acting as alternate delegate in 1947 in Mexico City.

In 1950 the federal government again sought Rosenberg's services. Chairman of the National Security Resources Board W. Stuart Symington appointed her to the committee evaluating the mobilization policy for the Korean War. Later that year Secretary of Defense George C. Marshall offered her the post of assistant secretary of defense, responsible for the coordination of manpower problems. After her confirmation by the Senate Arms Services Committee, the appointment was revoked because of rumors that she was a former Communist and a member of the John Reed Club. Former Communist Ralph De Sola claimed she was the same Anna Rosenberg he knew to be a Communist, but a brief investigation discovered that a different Anna Rosenberg was the Communist in question. Senator Joseph McCarthy, who played a secondary role in the affair, later voted for Rosenberg's reconfirmation. Many attributed the accusations as prejudice, since she was foreign-born, Jewish, and liberal.

Once she was securely in office, Rosenberg worked on drafting the Universal Military Service and Training Act, which lowered the draft age to eighteen, thus creating a larger pool for the armed services. She can also be credited with pioneering a drive to increase the number of women in the military and ensuring that their skills were used to their full potential. In 1953 the Dwight D. Eisenhower administration replaced Rosenberg as assistant secretary of defense. Throughout the 1950s, 1960s, and 1970s, she remained active with her firm, Anna M. Rosenberg & Associates, and maintained her sobriquet "Seven Job Anna" with her participation on boards and committees. In 1962 she divorced Julius Rosenberg, and later that year she married Paul Gray Hoffman, former president of the Studebaker Corporation and director of the U.S. Economic Cooperation Administration. They had no children.

Rosenberg was the recipient of many awards. She was the first civilian to receive the Medal of Freedom (1945) and the first woman to be recognized with the Medal for Merit (1947). In 1949 she was given the Horatio Alger Award by the American Schools and Colleges Association. She was the recipient of the Department of Defense Exceptional Civilian Award (1953) and the Medallion of the City of New York (1966) for her work in beautifying the city.

Rosenberg died in Manhattan, New York. She was mourned by labor leaders, politicians, the military, and the numerous philanthropists with whom she worked. She was a pioneer of feminist views and civil rights in the 1950s. The first female assistant secretary of defense, she devoted her entire life to the service of her country.

• Rosenberg's official and personal files are at the Franklin Delano Roosevelt Library and the Harry S. Truman Library. Her oral history is at Columbia University. The most complete assessment of her government service is in *Current Biography* (1943 and 1951). See also "The Woman—What a Woman! Who Bosses the Men," *Newsweek*, 26 Feb. 1951, pp. 20–24; and Karl Detzler "Little Anna Goes to Washington," *Independent Woman*, Jan. 1951, pp. 8–10, 30. Rosenberg is also mentioned in books on McCarthyism, especially David M. Oshinsky, *A Conspiracy So Immense: The World of Joe McCarthy* (1983), and Fred J. Cook, *The Nightmare Decade: The Life and Times of Senator Joe McCarthy* (1971). Obituaries are in the *New York Times* and the *Kansas City Times*, 10 May 1983.

CHRISTY L. THURSTON

ROSENBERG, Ethel (28 Sept. 1915–19 June 1953), and **Julius Rosenberg** (12 May 1918–19 June 1953), spies, were both born in New York City. Julius was the son of Harry Rosenberg, a garment worker, and Sophie Cohen. Ethel was the daughter of Barnet Greenglass, a sewing machine repairman, and Tessie Felt. Julius and Ethel Rosenberg were both raised in poor, orthodox Jewish families in the slum-ghetto that was New York's Lower East Side during World War I. Both graduated from the Lower East Side's Seward Park High School. Julius also received religious instruction at Downtown Talmud Torah and Hebrew High School in New York. Ethel, who had musical interests, studied piano and sang as the youngest member of Hugh Ross's Schola Cantorum before her high school graduation at the age of fifteen.

Julius attended City College, was active in left-wing student circles, and studied electrical engineering, graduating with honors in February 1939. Ethel worked in a variety of clerical jobs, was active as an organizer in the trade union movement, and lived with her parents, turning her salary over to them. Julius and Ethel met in 1936 and married in 1939. They had two sons. They initially lived with Julius's mother and in furnished rooms. In 1940 Julius received a position as a junior engineer for the Army Signal Corps, and they moved to a modest three-room apartment in New York's Knickerbocker Village in the spring of 1942.

In February 1945 Julius was removed from his position in the Army Signal Corps on the grounds that he had been a Communist, which he denied. After working briefly for Emerson Radio Corporation, he started his own machine shop with Ethel's brother, David Greenglass, who during World War II as an army recruit had been assigned as a draftsman at the Los Alamos, New Mexico, atomic bomb project. Following her marriage, Ethel dedicated herself to raising their children, taking courses in child psychology at the New School for Social Research to become a better mother.

On 17 July 1950, one month after the arrest and arraignment of David Greenglass and ten months after the Soviets exploded a nuclear device, the Federal Bureau of Investigation announced Julius Rosenberg's arrest. Government officials alleged that he had been at the center of a wartime Soviet spy ring that sent crucial information on the atomic bomb to the Soviet Union. On 11 August, following her testimony before a federal grand jury investigating Soviet atomic espionage, Ethel was arrested by the FBI and made a codefendant with Julius. The Rosenbergs were indicted for participating in the conspiracy to steal the secrets of the atomic bomb. Their indictment occurred only weeks after the outbreak of the Korean War, which greatly accelerated both government and mass media campaigns against U.S. Communists.

At the trial, which began on 6 March 1951, Greenglass testified that he had made drawings of lens molds used in the development of the atomic bomb and passed them to a courier, Harry Gold, in 1945, using a torn Jello box and the password "I come from Julius" as identification. Gold then transmitted the material to the Soviets. Gold corroborated these allegations, as did Greenglass's wife, Ruth Greenglass. The Rosenbergs denied the charges and sought to discredit Greenglass, testifying he was motivated by a family conflict over their jointly owned machine shop business.

The Rosenbergs were represented by Emanuel Bloch, an undistinguished local attorney who failed to cross-examine Greenglass effectively or cross-examine Gold at all. In addition, Bloch did not present any testimony from anyone in the scientific community to challenge the allegations by the government and the media that the material was decisive to the Soviets gaining the atomic bomb in 1949. The Rosenbergs were convicted and sentenced to death by Judge Irving Kaufman on 5 April 1951.

Following the conviction, the Rosenberg case acquired a different dimension as many in the United States and throughout the world lobbied the Harry Truman and Dwight Eisenhower administrations to commute their sentences. This movement failed, given the anti-Communist hysteria generated by the stalemated Korean War and the passage of the McCarran Internal Security Act (1950) and similar legislation aimed at politically segregating Communists and other radicals from the general population. This unsuccessful movement, nonetheless, became the most significant expression of resistance to the spread of the domestic Cold War in the United States in the period.

Both the Truman and Eisenhower administrations refused to stay the executions, and on 19 June 1953 the Supreme Court vacated a temporary stay given on a technicality by Supreme Court justice William O. Douglas. The Rosenbergs were executed in the electric chair at New York's Sing Sing prison that day. Thousands of people in New York's Union Square and hundreds of thousands throughout the world demonstrated against the executions. Seeing the world movement protesting the Rosenbergs' death sentence as part of a "Communist propaganda offensive," the Eisenhower administration had privately offered them commutation if they confessed and implicated others—named names—which they refused to do.

For many radicals and anti–Cold War liberals at the time, the Rosenberg case was an American Reichstag fire case, one involving American Jews, Communists, and nuclear espionage, that would spark massive repression and perhaps a Fascist dictatorship. For conservatives and anti-Communist or Cold War liberals,

the case proved that U.S. Communists were foreign agents of the Soviet Union seeking to undermine the United States. In these circles, which were at the center of the national Cold War consensus, unquestioning belief in the Rosenbergs' guilt and Alger Hiss's guilt became a kind of loyalty oath in itself.

Although contemporary works by left-wing writers John Wexley and William Mandell had maintained the Rosenbergs' innocence during the 1950s and the Rosenbergs' prison letters were published, widely translated, and read abroad, few in the United States listened to those critics. In the midst of the later mass protest movements against the Vietnam War, Walter Schneir and Miriam Schneir's *Invitation to an Inquest* (1965) reached a significant audience with its account of the flaws and distortions in the government's case. Particularly evidential were the prior history and mental state of Gold, who had, among other things, invented a fictitious family in an earlier espionage trial at which Kaufman had been the presiding judge; the fact that the "I come from Julius" password had been fed to Gold by FBI agents; and the failure of hotel records to corroborate Gold's alleged 1945 meeting with Greenglass in Los Alamos.

Subsequent works by the Rosenbergs' sons, Michael Meeropol and Robert Meeropol, and the Meeropols' work with the National Committee to Re-Open the Rosenberg Case led to the release in the 1970s under the Freedom of Information Act of heavily censored FBI documents. While the FBI documents did not support Julius Rosenberg's innocence, they suggested that Ethel Rosenberg had been brought into the case to force her husband to confess. In the 1980s the Ronald Reagan administration campaigned to revive the political climate that prevailed at the time of the Rosenbergs' execution, and President Reagan awarded Judge Kaufman the Medal of Freedom. In 1983 former New Left historian Ronald Radosh and freelance writer Joyce Milton published *The Rosenberg File*, a work that strongly challenged the Schneirs' evidence and, based on their interpretation of the released FBI materials and interviews with the Greenglasses and others, strongly reaffirmed the Rosenbergs' guilt.

After the dismemberment of the Soviet Union in 1991, conservative writers cited declassified Soviet documents and "confessions" of KGB (Soviet secret service) operatives to argue that nuclear espionage had played a leading role in the Soviets' nuclear program. Many of these allegations, including accusations against physicists Niels Bohr and J. Robert Oppenheimer, were discredited. In July 1995 the National Security Agency released intercepted Soviet consular communiques from 1942 to 1945, decoded as part of a secret U.S. operation known as the Venona Project, that identified Julius Rosenberg as Soviet agent code named "Liberal." Thus, these transcripts have been cited as further evidence of the guilt of the Rosenbergs. In contrast to those who long affirmed the Rosenbergs' guilt and who interpreted the case, along with the Cold War, as completely closed, the National

Committee to Re-Open the Rosenberg Case and the Rosenbergs' sons challenged these documents. Others who accept the validity of the documents maintain that they do not substantiate Ethel Rosenberg's guilt.

In essence, the Rosenberg case has lived longer than the Rosenbergs, who did not see their children grow to adulthood or experience the changes in the United States and the world of the second half of the twentieth century. On a variety of important questions, from the still disputed facts of the case to its anti-Communist context and anti-Semitic subtext, the Rosenberg case has remained subject to debate and reinterpretation.

• The Verona transcripts are accessible at the National Archives, and the FBI's massive files on the Rosenberg case are accessible in the FBI Reading Room, Washington, D.C. Robert Meeropol and Michael Meeropol, *We Are Your Sons* (1986), provides the insights of the Rosenbergs' sons, who have lived with and sought to understand the case since their parents' arrests. Julius Rosenberg, *The Rosenberg Letters: A Complete Edition of the Prison Correspondence of Julius and Ethel Rosenberg*, ed. Michael Meeropol (1994), is enormously valuable in understanding the Rosenbergs as people.

NORMAN MARKOWITZ

ROSENBERG, Harold (2 Feb. 1906–11 July 1978), art critic and poet, was born in Brooklyn, New York, the son of Abraham Benjamin, a scholar and poet, and Fanny Edelman. His formal education consisted of a year at City College of New York (1923–1924) and three years at St. Lawrence University, Brooklyn, where he earned a degree in law (1927).

The year he graduated from law school Rosenberg was stricken with osteomyelitis, a life-threatening bone infection that left him permanently disabled. The crisis diverted his direction from what he called "law, love, and a predictable life" to the life of a bohemian avant-garde poet and intellectual. Rosenberg's identity as a vanguard poet and critic was established with the publication in 1930 of two surrealist-inspired stories for the Paris-based *Transition* magazine, a dramatic dialogue for Charles Henri Ford's *Blues, The Magazine of a New Rhythm*, and a poem for *Pagany*. From 1931 to 1943 he published poems, reviews, and essays in *Poetry*, the Chicago-based independent magazine. Several pieces were published by the *Symposium*, including a basic philosophical statement, "Character Change and the Drama," in 1932. That year he married May Natalie Tabak, a teacher, social worker, and writer; they had one child. In 1933 and 1934 he coedited the *New Act* with H. R. Hays.

Around 1933 Rosenberg started studying the writings of Karl Marx and published Communist-inspired poems and essays in party affiliated magazines, including the *Partisan Review* and the *New Masses*, while contributing to nonpolitical literary magazines like *Poetry*. With the inauguration of the New Deal arts projects late in 1933, the milieu of the New York School of abstract artists started to form, and Rosenberg was at its center. He was first employed by the Federal Arts Project (part of the Works Progress Administration), working in its Mural Division, and later he assisted

Willem de Kooning. Rosenberg and de Kooning became friends, and Rosenberg became educated in the meanings and metaphors of abstract painting.

Rosenberg's outlook was shaped by the politicized cultural milieu of downtown Manhattan in the 1930s. His study of Marx and revolutionary Marxists joined uneasily with his struggles within what he would call "the tensions and totalitarian temper of that extremist period." In 1936, as editor of *Art Front*, his insistence on aesthetic criteria resulted in a rally of Artist 500 Union members demanding his expulsion. Similarly in 1937 his "elitist" editing of the WPA issue, *American Stuff*, resulted in threats against him by Stalinists in the Writers' Union.

Struggles to maintain political and aesthetic independence, along with disillusionment with the anti-Fascist forces in Spain and the rising international tensions of the middle to late 1930s transformed Rosenberg into a committed anti-Communist and a radically democratic public intellectual, intent on protecting the creative independence of American artists.

From 1938 to 1942 Rosenberg worked in Washington, D.C., as the national art editor of the WPA American Guide Series. In 1942 Gotham Books printed his collection of poetry, *Trance Above the Streets*. During World War II he worked at the Office of War Information as deputy chief of the Domestic Radio Bureau in charge of the New York office. Among other wartime duties he wrote radio plays called *John Freedom*, which were aired throughout the country. In 1943 he purchased a house in East Hampton, where several French surrealists were living in exile. Within the decade the area became a famous Abstract Expressionist artists' colony. After 1945 Rosenberg's work for the War Advertising Council developed into a job as program consultant for the organization, which became known as the Advertising Council. He remained there until 1973.

Following the war Rosenberg wrote penetrating analyses of Marx and Marxism for *Les Temps Modernes* and the *Kenyon Review*. He began his incessant attacks on postwar American intellectuals for their failure to remain critical of the status quo. Alert to the dangers of authoritarianism, he translated the anti-Gaullist tract, *J'accuse de Gaulle*, by Henri de Kerillis, in 1946. He also wrestled with the issue of Jewish identity in essays appearing mostly in *Commentary* magazine.

In 1947 Rosenberg began to write about the work of artist friends and neighbors in Greenwich Village and East Hampton. These abstract expressionists were creating, Rosenberg claimed in 1957, "the most vigorous and original movement in art in the history of this nation." He and Robert Motherwell edited *possibilities 1*, formulating the anti-ideological posture of New York abstract artists in 1947–1948.

In 1952 Rosenberg's article "The American Action Painters" appeared in *Art News* magazine, bringing him instant notoriety in the art world. "Suddenly everybody wanted to be an Action Painter," critic Clement Greenberg recalled in 1992. Overnight "action painting" became the definition of abstract expressionism. Intended for the readership of *Les Temps Modernes*, "The American Action Painters" acclaimed in poetic and existential terms the creative attitude of the artists in Rosenberg's circle like de Kooning, Jackson Pollock, Hans Hofmann, Franz Kline and others. Although Pollock was offended by it, the article brought the abstract expressionists to prominence just as the United States achieved global influence.

In the 1950s Rosenberg's essays on the New York art world were published regularly in *Art News*. His commentaries on literature, politics, and society appeared in political literary reviews, including *Dissent*, *Twentieth Century*, *Les Temps Modernes*, and others. In 1956 he contributed a chapter on Marx for *Les Philosophes Célèbres*, edited by Maurice Merleau-Ponty. Rosenberg's major essays up to 1959 were collected in *The Tradition of the New* (1959). The book was widely acclaimed and subsequently published in British, French, Italian, Spanish, and Japanese editions, and earned Rosenberg his international reputation.

In 1967 Rosenberg became "The Art World" columnist for the *New Yorker*. Here he found the broad public arena where he could celebrate the vanguard artists to whom he was devoted and mock the American art establishment, especially the academic critics and curators who Rosenberg saw as conventional middle-class professionals and enemies of critical culture.

Beginning in 1966 Rosenberg taught at the University of Chicago in its Committee on Social Thought in the art department. Several collections of his essays were published: *Artworks and Packages* (1969); *Act and the Actor* (1970); *The De-Definition of Art* (1972); *Discovering the Present* (1973); *Art on the Edge* (1975). After his death *Art and Other Serious Matters* and *The Case of the Baffled Radical* appeared in 1985. Rosenberg wrote the texts for a number of artists' collections and exhibitions.

Roughly three-fifths of Rosenberg's critical production had to do with contemporary art, but his art criticism is inextricable from his writings on politics, literature, society, and the abstract expressionists. Herbert Read's 1959 appellation of Rosenberg as "the Apollinaire of Action Painting" serves as an apt summation of Rosenberg's contribution as an art critic. He gave contemporary American art serious intellectual consideration worthy of the world's attention. His long, outspoken opposition to the institutionalization of the avant-garde in America was singular.

• The Harold Rosenberg/May Tabak Papers are privately held in New York City. The Archives of American Art has two transcribed interviews by Dorothy Seckler and Paul Cummings. All the major texts on abstract expressionism address his influence. See Dore Ashton, *The New York School: A Cultural Reckoning* (1972), Irving Sandler, *The Triumph of American Painting* (1970), and Jonathan Fineberg, *Art Since 1940: Strategies of Being* (1995). For studies of the period, see Alexander Bloom, *Prodigal Sons: The New York Intellectuals and Their World* (1986); Terry Cooney, *The Rise of the New York Intellectuals: Partisan Review and Its Circle, 1934–1945* (1986); and Neil Jumonville, *Critical Crossings: The New York Intellectuals in Postwar America* (1991). See also memorial essays in *Dissent*, Fall 1978; *Critical Inquiry*, Summer 1980; and *The Village Voice Literary Supplement*, May 1986.

ELAINE O'BRIEN

ROSENBERG, Julius. *See* Rosenberg, Ethel, and Julius Rosenberg.

ROSENBERRY, Lois Carter Kimball Mathews (30 Jan. 1873–1 Sept. 1958), dean of women, was born in Cresco, Iowa, the daughter of Aaron Kimball, a banker, and Emma Wilhelmina Laird. Rosenberry's entire professional career was dedicated to education, beginning when she graduated from the State Normal School in Winona, Minnesota, at the age of seventeen. She taught elementary school in Minnesota (1890–1893) and was an assistant elementary principal in Utah (1894–1897) when she married University of Utah professor George Raynolds Mathews, who died only eighteen months later. Living in California at the time of her husband's death (1899), she again became an assistant principal. She soon decided to further her education, enrolled at Stanford, and studied history, graduating Phi Beta Kappa in 1903. She completed her master's degree at Stanford in 1904 and became a member of the Association of Collegiate Alumnae (ACA).

At the urging of Stanford professor Max Farrand and her mentor, Frederick Jackson Turner, she moved to Cambridge, Massachusetts, to pursue a Ph.D. at Radcliffe College in 1904. She spent the summer of 1905 studying with Turner in Madison, Wisconsin, and in May 1906 became the first woman to pass the Harvard examinations for the Ph.D. in the department of history, economics, and political science. Her dissertation on New England expansion between 1620 and 1865 was highly regarded, and she became an instructor of history at Vassar College. In 1910 she was appointed associate professor of history at Wellesley College. From this post, she was recruited to the University of Wisconsin.

While negotiating with Wisconsin's president, Charles Van Hise, regarding her appointment, Rosenberry demonstrated a keen awareness of the importance of title and status to achieving her goals. Van Hise offered Rosenberry the title of "advisor" to women and "instructor" in history. She insisted, however, that her title be "dean" of women and "associate" professor. Changing her title to dean caused little consternation, but no woman had ever been an associate professor at Wisconsin, and the history department was reluctant to grant her that status. She persisted, informing Van Hise, "if I were to undertake so great and serious a task as the deanship of . . . Wisconsin, it seemed to me it would be my first duty to make it in stature what it is in opportunity; and at the same time to try to make it an example to other universities in that regard." This exemplifies Rosenberry's ability to frame decisions from her personal vantage point yet with an eye to the larger implications for her profession. Turner assuaged the history department, referring to her as "a woman of exceptional power and scholarship combined with real womanliness." She prevailed and was hired in 1911 as dean and associate professor.

Once appointed, Rosenberry set about making contributions to the campus. Because of her unequivocal belief that intellectual achievement was the raison d'être of college life, she worked to ensure that women's intellectual experience was comparable to men's. She wrote, "No matter from what angle we view the college problem . . . the ultimate reason for having . . . universities is the work of the classroom." She also ardently believed that deans should be teaching members of the faculty.

Like others of her era, she acknowledged that women's education must include preparation for all aspects of life—home and work. She left the single-sex world of Vassar and Wellesley to provide women in coeducational settings the same opportunities for leadership and community that women's colleges afforded. As she told the president of the university in her first dean of women report, "there is an unrivaled opportunity in this university for development of women's resources and possibilities through education." She worked to secure for women the highest possible individual development and social responsibility.

Many of Rosenberry's duties as dean were typical—disciplining students and monitoring behavior, although she refused to chaperone dances and eventually relegated routine disciplinary matters to her staff. She was liked by students, with whom she had regular contact, especially through her weekly teas and chats known as "at homes," the cost of which came from her own salary. Former students remembered her as having a strong laugh and keen sense of humor. One member of the class of 1917 described her as "a modern woman of the time . . . elegant and proper; a stern disciplinarian, but fair. She wanted students to be proper, but she wasn't silly about it."

Rosenberry went well beyond the traditional duties, however. To provide opportunities for leadership and skill formation, she resuscitated the Women's Self-Government Association (WSGA), begun in 1897 but dormant for a decade. She encouraged Wisconsin students to organize a midwestern conference with other university women's self-government associations so that students could learn from each other.

Her second endeavor was the establishment in 1912 of the annual Vocational Conference to offer women alternatives to teaching careers. As she wrote, "College women have for at least half a century . . . gone almost without exception into teaching. . . . the enormous expansion of business has left teaching to the feminine part of the community because of the greater rewards offered men through professional life and mercantile enterprises" (*Dean of Women*, p. 109). She brought in women from various professions, including famous social workers from nearby Chicago. The vocational conferences for women lasted over thirty-five years.

Rosenberry also sought to advance the profession, giving numerous talks on the position of dean of women, publishing articles, and speaking at biannual deans' conferences. She organized a statewide conference of deans in Wisconsin and in the summer of 1915 taught the first course in women's educational administration in the Midwest. Her most lasting contribution was *The Dean of Women* (1915), probably the first book ever written on the profession that eventually became known as student affairs. The book records her views about the importance of title and scholarly achievement for deans and gives practical advice on most aspects of the job. The book became the standard for the profession for many years and sat on the bookshelf of almost every dean in the country.

She resigned as dean in 1918 when she married Marvin Rosenberry, who became the chief justice of Wisconsin's state supreme court. She continued teaching for one year, however, because many of her male colleagues were away from campus performing war-related services.

Rosenberry served as president of the ACA from 1917 to 1921 and was one of the founders of the International Federation of Women in 1919. She served as director of the local YWCA from 1923 to 1925 and was acting principal of the National Cathedral School for Girls in Washington, D.C., during the 1928–1929 school year. In 1931, ten years after the ACA became the American Association of University Women, Rosenberry coauthored, with Marion Talbot, *The History of the American Association of University Women*. During the 1930s she also published occasionally in her field of early New England history, although much of this work was based on her earlier studies.

She was an active public speaker throughout the 1930s and 1940s, giving talks for local Wisconsin women's clubs and civic organizations. Much of the remainder of her life was spent in volunteer work in Madison before ill health prevented her from activity. She was a past president of the Civics Club and the College Club. She died in Madison, following an illness of a few months. She was cremated and buried in the Kimball family plot in Cresco, Iowa, near neither of her husbands.

Lois Rosenberry's life was characterized by high scholastic achievement and a commitment to women's education. She was also a pioneer in the field of university administration and contributed to the profession of dean of women as both practitioner and scholar. The Rosenberry dormitory at the University of Wisconsin has a plaque reading " . . . Rosenberry's instruction in history meant an incisive, stimulating exploration of the New England past. For thousands of Wisconsin co-eds, the Rosenberry deanship signified new understanding and skillful, effective guidance. . . . Lois Rosenberry represented intelligent leadership and high devotion to a high cause."

• Correspondence concerning Rosenberry's appointment and duties at Wisconsin are found among the Charles Van Hise Papers at the University of Wisconsin Archives. The most valuable source regarding her work (in addition to *The Dean of Women*) is her biennial "Report of the Dean of Women," in *The University of Wisconsin, Biennial Report of the Board of Regents* beginning with the 1910–1911 and 1911–1912 report and continuing for 1912–1914, 1914–1916, and 1916–1918. See also Lois Mathews, "Raising the Standards of University Life," *Journal of the Association of Collegiate Alumnae* 9, no. 3 (1916): 69–76, and "The Deanship at Wisconsin, 1897–1918," *Journal of the National Association to Deans of Women* 11, no. 3 (1948): 130–31. Student recollections of her are found in the Oral History Project, University of Wisconsin Archives. Her accomplishments are also chronicled in the *Capitol Times*, 22 Apr. 1942.

Rosenberry's major historical works include *The Expansion of New England: The Spread of New England Settlement and Institutions to the Mississippi River, 1620–1865* (1909); "The American Frontier," *Proceedings of Nantucket Historical Association* (1910); "The Mayflower Compact and Its Descendents," *Mississippi Valley Historical Association Proceedings* (1912–1913); "Migrations from Connecticut Prior to 1800," *Tercentenary Commission of the State of Connecticut* 28 (1934); and "Migrations from Connecticut after 1800," *Tercentenary Commission of the State of Connecticut* 54 (1936).

There is no published critical biography of Lois Mathews Rosenberry to date, but useful biographical information may be obtained from Jo Ann Fley, "Student Personnel Pioneers: Those Who Developed Our Profession, Part I," *NASPA Journal* 17 (Summer 1979): 23–39.

An obituary is in the *Wisconsin State Journal* 2 Sept. 1958.

JANA NIDIFFER

ROSENBLATT, Bernard Abraham (15 June 1886–14 Oct. 1969), Zionist leader, was born in Grodok (near Bialystok), Poland, the son of Louis Rosenblatt and Mary Hachnochi, both from successful woolen factory-owning families; their home attracted Jewish nationalists, intellectuals, and artists. Spurred by the depression of 1890 to emigrate to the United States, the Rosenblatts settled in 1892 in Philadelphia. Their sizable residence was on the South Side, where an immigrant Jewish neighborhood was developing. A public school student, Bernard Rosenblatt also went to a Jewish religious school. He was to remember that at age eleven, during a Sabbath-afternoon discussion at home just prior to the first World Zionist Congress, he championed the feasibility of Zionism. Three years later, the family left Philadelphia for Pittsburgh. There, at Central High School, he formed a Zionist society; in 1903 he participated in his first American Zionist convention. The next year, the family moved to the Jewish neighborhood of Harlem in New York City, and Rosenblatt entered Columbia; by December he had established the first Zionist Society at the college. In his senior year he won the Curtis Medal with his speech "Palestine: The Future Hebrew State," in which he characterized the Zionists putting down roots in Palestine as "Jewish Puritans," pursuing a highly ethical kind of state. This appreciation of American tradition and idealistic Zionism came to characterize Rosenblatt's life work.

As a graduate student in sociology Rosenblatt received an M.A. in 1908; the year after he took his law degree at Columbia University Law School. In 1911 he attended the Federation of American Zionists' convention in Tannersville, New York, representing a

group he had been instrumental in establishing, the Collegiate Zionist League. The convention elected new leadership, from the rank and file of the movement, which was East European in origin and progressive in its leanings. As secretary of the realigned FAZ, Rosenblatt became involved in organizing a women's Zionist society. He thereby met Gertrude Goldsmith, a founder of Hadassah, the most important of the American women's Zionist organizations. In June 1914 they were married and as an example named their children David Bar-Maccabee and Jonathan Judah.

Rosenblatt's first book, *The Social Commonwealth* (1914), was dedicated to Louis D. Brandeis, "A Leader of the People in the Battle for Social Justice." According to Rosenblatt, the ideal commonwealth would strive to abolish poverty by fixing a minimum wage intended to secure a minimum standard of living. Structurally, the commonwealth would "undertake the control of those industries that are monopolies by nature and by social demand." Partial regulation of economic life, the cooperative idea, and the competition principle would be combined to derive the best benefits of a democratic and voluntary society. As a solution for major social ills and as a protection of the public interests, however, Rosenblatt advocated state ownership of land. In September 1914 he organized the American Zion Commonwealth for the purpose of buying and developing land in Palestine for its members. The company constitution accepted the principle that only agricultural land should be divided among the members and that city, town, and industrial sites (including mineral lands) must continue as the common property of all the members, under the title of "Communal Lands." Subsequently the Zionist Organization of America endorsed his enterprise and assumed the obligation to sell the Land Certificates of the American Zion Commonwealth.

Rosenblatt was briefly active in American politics in 1916 in Harlem's Twentieth Congressional District, where he ran as a Democrat against the Republican incumbent, Isaac Siegel, and a Socialist, Morris Hillquit. With a Jewish nationalist-progressive espousing President Woodrow Wilson's program, the campaign drew widespread notice.

In helping Brandeis and Horace Kallen to shape the famous program of the Pittsburgh Zionist convention (1918), which reflected social expectations of Jewish Palestine, Rosenblatt drafted articles 2 and 3, which, in order to ensure equality of opportunity, called for the establishment of "ownership and control by the whole people of the land, of all natural resources and of all public utilities"; and to lease land "on such conditions as will insure the fullest opportunity for development and continuity of possession." His progressive and humanistic vision of Palestine informs his subsequent book *Social Zionism* (1919).

During 1920–1921, a bitter conflict about the building of Palestine emerged between the more Americanized Zionists, headed by Brandeis and Julian Mack, and the less acculturated Zionists, led by Weizmann's admirers, among whom Louis Lipsky was prominent. The first faction was for clear separation between charity and commercial enterprises, and for a close cooperation with non-Zionist investors. Keren Ha-Yesod (Palestine Foundation Fund), commanded by Weizmann, epitomized for the Brandeisists the economic sloppiness and pathetic traditions of Eastern Europe. Rosenblatt—who supported Keren Ha-Yesod but largely identified with Brandeis's social-economic philosophy—constantly tried to work out a compromise between the two factions of American Zionism.

Elected to the World Zionist Executive in 1921 as the first American delegate, Rosenblatt attended a meeting of the executive in Jerusalem. On his return to the United States in 1922, he managed the sale of the first Jewish municipal bond issue, which was instrumental for developing Tel Aviv. From 1925 onward, he kept his law practice in New York City while also spending much time in Haifa, Palestine. For Rosenblatt, the development of Jewish Palestine as a viable economic entity was crucial. He played a major role in the development of the industrial region of Haifa Bay and was director of the Israel Land Development Company, the Migdal Insurance Company, and Tiberias Hot Springs. He headed the Jewish National Fund and Palestine Foundation Fund for a number of years.

Rosenblatt's Americaness was reflected in his moderate and legalistic approach to the Jewish-Arab conflict over Palestine. Following the Arab disturbances of 1929, he developed his "American solution," which was meant to reconstitute the country along the lines of the American federal pattern. By 1937 he set up a "Haifa Committee" in support of his proposal. He believed that the existence of two different nations should be fully recognized, but "instead of a physical partition of Palestine into rival and wrangling Arab and Jewish states, it should be feasible to evolve a *geographical* division of Palestine and Transjordan into two *sister states of a federated Palestine*." In this "amicable solution" the two states would be "firmly bound together in a federal union, with equal rights and equal representation in its governing council," to carry out foreign affairs, defense, tariffs, and interstate commerce and communication. "The vexatious problem of immigration would remain a state (non-federal) matter" (*Federated Palestine and the Jewish Commonwealth*, 1941).

During World War II, Rosenblatt was active in New York Democratic and Jewish politics. At war's end, he was back in Palestine and went to court, as an American citizen, to fight the British over their anti-Zionist prohibition of land sales. The partitioning of Palestine in 1947, however, rendered the matter moot. In his work "The Land Problem in the State of Israel" (1954), he called on Israel, in the name of social justice and economic efficaciousness, to own *all* lands in the state. Five years later, in *The American Bridge to the Israel Commonwealth*, he urged Israel to adopt a written constitution, safeguard civil rights, and gain a stable executive by reforming the electoral system. Im-

mediately after the 1967 Six Day War, he appealed to the Israeli leadership to adopt elements of his historic "federated Palestine" program as a decent solution for the Arab-Israeli conflict.

Rosenblatt's disappointments with Israel notwithstanding, he fully identified with the state as a national solution for Jewish homelessness. He appreciated, furthermore, Israel's distinctive social-democratic accomplishments and envisioned it as an example of an enlightened mission that would be especially meaningful for new emerging states. His return to New York followed his wife's death in 1955; he continued to maintain a keen interest in Israeli affairs until his death there.

• Aside from the works identified above, Rosenblatt published *An American Solution of the Palestine Problem* (1937) and *Two Generations of Zionism: Historical Recollections of an American Zionist* (1967). He also wrote many articles. Rosenblatt's recollections of his career until the early 1920s are in the Oral History Collection, the Institute of Contemporary Jewry, the Hebrew University of Jerusalem. The beginnings of his career are sketched in A. Friesel, *Ha-Tenu'ah ha-Tzionit be-Artzot ha-Berit ba-Shanim 1897–1914* (1970), pp. 155–57 and A. Gal, *Brandeis of Boston* (1980), pp. 164–68; his career between the two world wars is briefly discussed in M. Urofsky, *American Zionism from Herzl to the Holocaust* (1975). Obituaries are in the *New York Times*, 15 Oct. 1969, and the *Jerusalem Post*, 17 Oct. 1969.

ALLON GAL

ROSENBLATT, Josef (9 May 1882–18 June 1933), cantor and concert singer, was born in Belaya Tserkov, Ukraine, the son of Raphael Shalom Rosenblatt, a cantor, and Chayeh Sarah Pilatsky. From his earliest youth, Rosenblatt was trained to follow his father's profession. At the age of four he was already assisting in synagogue services as a member of his father's choir. By age eight Rosenblatt was traveling throughout Eastern Europe as an itinerant boy-cantor. For the Jews of Eastern Europe, cantorial performances not only enhanced their religious devotions but functioned as a major form of musical entertainment since the synagogue served as both a spiritual home and a social center. By his bar mitzvah at age thirteen Rosenblatt was a recognized star both in his home communities and on the international cantor's circuit, having also sung in congregations in Vienna and Budapest. Constantly on tour, the cantor prodigy received his general and religious education from private tutors. In August 1900 Rosenblatt married Taube Kaufman; they would have eight children.

Days after his wedding, Rosenblatt was elected cantor of the Munkacz community in Hungary, but he soon became unhappy in that post because local leaders would not provide an adequate choir to accompany him. In 1901 he accepted a post in Pressburg, Hungary, having won that position over some fifty-six other candidates. While in Pressburg, Rosenblatt published *Shirei Joseph*, a compilation of 150 liturgical compositions. While there he also made his first phonograph recording. In 1906 Rosenblatt moved to a pulpit in

Hamburg, Germany. During his six years there, he received advanced voice training and coaching in preparation for concert work that he intended to pursue after immigrating to the United States.

Harlem's Congregation Ohab Zedek tendered Rosenblatt an offer in 1912. At that point it was one of the most distinguished and affluent synagogues in this new Jewish section of New York City, which was home to upwardly mobile immigrants and their children. Having a famous cantor on staff was both a sign of status for the synagogue and a means of increasing members. Rosenblatt's original base salary of $2,400 per year then made him the best paid cantor yet employed by an Orthodox synagogue. Rosenblatt was also entitled to additional synagogue honoraria, bringing his annual income to $5,000.

While at Ohab Zedek, Rosenblatt continued his phonograph recording activities, primarily under the label of the Victor Talking Machine Company and, later, RCA Victor. He also traveled widely in the United States on concert tours. However, in 1918 he rejected an offer from the Chicago Opera Association to perform in Fromental Halévy's *La Juive* for a fee of $1,000 per appearance. His position, and that of his congregation, was that the atmosphere of the operatic stage was not in keeping with the Orthodox traditions to which he and Ohab Zedek adhered.

In 1925 Rosenblatt was forced to compromise his stance of performing only in synagogues or in the most dignified of concert stages because of personal financial problems that had grown out of his backing of a failed Jewish newspaper venture. The Yiddish-English weekly the *Light of Israel*, which often missed its deadline and frequently did not meet its payroll during its two years of existence (1923–1925), accrued debts of $191,719 from unpaid loans taken out under Rosenblatt's name. Bankrupt, the still widely popular Rosenblatt agreed to appear in touring vaudeville productions. In some cities he commanded fees in excess of $3,000 as he shared top billing with such renowned Jewish actors as Fannie Brice, Molly Picon, the Marx Brothers, and Al Jolson. The quest for increased remunerations also caused Rosenblatt to leave the Ohab Zedek pulpit, where by 1925 he was receiving an annual salary of $10,000. For the High Holiday season of 1925, Rosenblatt contracted with a Chicago group for an honorarium of $25,000, which included a choir of thirty-five voices, the net worth of which amounted to $10,000. Rosenblatt also led services at the Brilliant Palace, a facility that seated 3,000 people.

In 1927 Rosenblatt again assumed a full-time cantorial position at Congregation Anshei Sfard in Borough Park, Brooklyn. He held that post until 1930, when the synagogue's own financial problems precluded them from paying his yearly salary of $12,000. He then returned to Ohab Zedek for two years. However, in 1932 Depression-era economics, along with a shrinking membership base as Jews left Harlem for new Jewish communities, forced the congregation to sever its contract with Rosenblatt.

In 1928 Rosenblatt was offered $100,000 to star as the cantor in *The Jazz Singer*, the first talking movie. He refused the part, which ultimately went to Al Jolson, arguing once again that his performance would profane his religious calling. He did agree, however, to sing a number of nonliturgical Jewish melodies off-screen.

At the time of his death in Jerusalem, Rosenblatt had composed more than 400 synagogue liturgical compositions and had recorded more than 125 different phonograph records. In an era in which the art of the cantor was widely admired, Rosenblatt was among the most sought after performers. His enduring popularity is evidenced by the fact that some of his pieces continue to be used by cantors and that his records have been frequently reissued.

• Samuel Rosenblatt, *Yossele Rosenblatt: The Story of His Life as Told by His Son* (1954), is the major source for the life of Josef-Rosenblatt. The discography in this biography details the extent and range of Rosenblatt's phonograph recording career. Rosenblatt's career as a cantor in Harlem is put into historical context in Jeffrey S. Gurock, *When Harlem Was Jewish, 1870–1930* (1979).

JEFFREY S. GUROCK

ROSENBLOOM, Maxie (6 Sept. 1904–6 Mar. 1976), boxer, was born Max Everitt Rosenbloom in Leonard's Bridge, Connecticut, the son of Russian-Jewish immigrants (names unknown). In 1907 the impoverished family moved to New York's Lower East Side where Rosenbloom's father worked as a shoemaker; they later moved to Harlem. Rosenbloom was expelled from public school in the fifth grade for striking a teacher and was sent to the Hawthorne Reform School. He started boxing at the Union Settlement House in Harlem, influenced by an older brother who fought as Leonard Rose and perhaps encouraged by George Raft (Blady, p. 223). Rosenbloom's amateur career began inauspiciously: he lost his first six matches, in all twenty of twenty-five, until Frank Bachman became his trainer.

In 1923, after about two hundred amateur bouts, Rosenbloom turned professional as a welterweight, managed by Bachman, winning his first fight with a third-round knockout. He held various odd jobs, such as elevator operator, railroad laborer, and lifeguard, while he continued to box. Fighting often—twenty-two matches in 1924 alone—he grew into a middleweight and eventually a light heavyweight. He was originally a slugger, but after a rough fight in 1925 against Hambone Kelly he became more defense-oriented, using his long arms to ward off opponents. He won his first thirty-six professional fights and earned a draw in a nontitle match with middleweight champion Harry Greb.

Rosenbloom's first professional loss came in 1925 against Jimmy Slattery, whom he eventually fought in seven bouts, losing four times. Slattery became the champion in 1929 after Tommy Loughran relinquished the crown to move up to the heavyweight division. However, the prestigious New York State Boxing Commission recognized Slattery, not Rosenbloom, as champion. On 25 June 1930 Rosenbloom defeated Slattery in Buffalo, New York, in a fifteen-round decision to gain the New York State Boxing Commission's version of the light heavyweight crown. He secured undisputed international recognition as champion on 14 July 1932 when he decisioned Lou Scozza in fifteen rounds in Buffalo. Thereafter, he fought almost monthly, but he made no title defenses until 22 February 1933, when he won on points over Al Stillman. Rosenbloom then had two more title bouts within a month, decisioning German light heavyweight champion Adolph Heuser in fifteen rounds and, two weeks later, knocking out Bob Goodwin in four rounds. The Heuser victory was reputedly a factor in the German government's decision to ban that country's athletes from competing against Jews.

Rosenbloom did not train well, but because he fought so often, training was relatively unimportant to his preparation. That year he had twenty-nine fights, with such opponents as heavyweight contender Young Stribling, future light heavyweight champion John Henry Lewis, and—in a memorable defense—Mickey Walker, one of the great middleweights. He lost to Young Stribling in ten rounds, and to Lewis by decision. He defeated Walker in fifteen.

Rosenbloom was nicknamed "Slapsie Maxie" by New York journalist and sportswriter Damon Runyon for his unorthodox style, disliked by boxing purists, of slapping opponents with open gloves, which cut down on his punching effectiveness. This use of open blows was banned by the New York's State Athletic Commission. His lack of punching power also limited his ability to draw at the gate, some of his title defenses attracting fewer than five thousand spectators.

Rosenbloom is considered the most active champion in modern boxing history, fighting a total of 106 times while champion, although only eight of his bouts were title defenses. He did not always distinguish himself. In 1934 he lost five nontitle fights. On 16 November 1934 he lost the title to Bob Olin in a hotly disputed decision booed by his fans at New York's Madison Square Garden. The referee voted Rosenbloom fourteen rounds, but the judges saw the fight for Olin, eight rounds to seven, probably penalizing Rosenbloom for his open glove style.

Rosenbloom fought until 1938 as a heavyweight, defeating the capable Lou Nova and fighting a draw with contender Bob Pastor. His career was marked by his unusual style and remarkable antics outside the ring, which provided numerous stories for gossip columnists and sportswriters. Although he did not smoke or drink, he spent freely, gambled heavily, and was considered a playboy who chased women.

In 1937 Rosenbloom married Muriel Faider, a psychologist; they had no children and were divorced in 1945. Rosenbloom was likable and spent a great deal of time in Hollywood (where he opened a nightclub, Slapsie Maxie's, in 1943). He entered the entertainment field after his retirement from boxing, starting in

nightclubs and moving on to movies (mainly comedies). He appeared in more than a hundred films, among them *Nothing Sacred* (1937), *The Kid Comes Back* (1938), *The Amazing Dr. Clitterhouse* (1938), *Each Dawn I Die* (1939), *20,000 Men a Year* (1939), and *Irish Eyes Are Smiling* (1944), often playing a punch-drunk ex-fighter or a thug with a heavy New York accent and poor grammar. He was known for such malapropisms as fearing a "conclusion of the brain," which he often employed in his film roles. After World War II he teamed with former heavyweight champion Max Baer in a nightclub act, played Big Julie in a revival of *Guys and Dolls* (1961), and owned nightclubs in Los Angeles and San Francisco.

The 5'11" Rosenbloom weighed from 165 to 170 pounds during most of his 289 professional fights. He compiled a record of 210 wins, 35 defeats, and 23 draws, along with 21 no decisions/no contests, and he was elected to the Boxing Hall of Fame in 1972. In his 1958 autobiography, *Fifty Years at Ringside*, boxing historian Nat Fleischer ranked him the third-best defensive fighter of all time. Despite his many bouts, Rosenbloom was knocked out only twice, when he was well past his prime. However, he was a light puncher and earned just 18 knockouts. During his final years he was in ill health from Paget's Disease, which his physician believed resulted from the repeated head blows he had absorbed during his long career. He died in South Pasadena, California.

• For biographical information and contemporary views of Rosenbloom, see Francis Albertani, "Maxie Rosenbloom, Greatest Light Heavyweight Hebrew since Days of Battling Levinsky," *Ring*, Sept. 1926, pp. 28–29, 36; Nat Fleischer, "The Fighter Who Doesn't Care," *Ring*, June 1932, p. 6; Ted Carroll, "Playboy of the Ring," *Ring*, Dec. 1936, pp. 29, 45; Ted Carroll, "The Merry Madcaps," *Ring*, May 1947, pp. 28, 36; Ken Blady, *The Jewish Boxers' Hall of Fame* (1988). For a complete record of Rosenbloom's fights, see the *Ring Record Book and Boxing Encyclopedia* (1984). For an obituary, see the *New York Times*, 8 Mar. 1976. For a reminiscence, see Red Smith's article in the *New York Times*, 14 Mar. 1976.

STEVEN A. RIESS

ROSENDAHL, Charles Emery (15 May 1892–14 May 1977), aviator, was born in Chicago, Illinois, the son of Charles Oscar Rosendahl and Hannah Johnson. Rosendahl attended the U.S. Naval Academy at Annapolis, Maryland, graduating with a B.S. in engineering in 1914. He followed a fairly routine career in the navy for the next nine years, serving as a line officer on destroyers and cruisers and seeing duty in the European theater during World War I. During 1921–1923 Rosendahl served as an instructor in engineering at the Naval Academy.

When Rosendahl completed that tour of duty, his military career took an unexpected turn. He was assigned, apparently not at his suggestion, as a flight officer on the U.S.S. *Shenandoah*, the navy's first lighter-than-air vessel, a rigid airship that was intended for aerial observation and strategic bombardment. The navy was experimenting with airships because Germany had built a fearsome bombing force around Zeppelin airships and used them effectively early in the war. Although Zeppelins made huge targets and the highly flammable hydrogen that kept them aloft could be ignited with machine gun fire, until the closing months of the war their high cruising altitude ensured safety from fighter attack. The *Shenandoah*, contracted for in 1919 and delivered in the summer of 1923, would provide a similar capability for the U.S. Navy. Also, since it was inflated with helium, it would not ignite as hydrogen did. Rosendahl was aboard the *Shenandoah* when, on its 4 September 1923 maiden flight, it flew round trip between the navy's lighter-than-air facility at Lakehurst, New Jersey, and St. Louis, Missouri, in less than two days.

Rosendahl, by this time a lieutenant commander, was executive officer of the *Shenandoah* when it departed Lakehurst on 2 September 1925. En route to the Midwest the next day, the *Shenandoah* broke apart and crashed. Fourteen men died in the accident. Rosendahl's cool actions during the incident made him a hero. In part because of this, the next year he was assigned to command the navy airship U.S.S. *Los Angeles*, ZR-III. This craft had been designed and built at Friedrichshafen, Germany; Rosendahl commanded it until 1929. During his command, the *Los Angeles* was used for observation, scientific research, tests of the launching of aircraft from midair flight, and experiments with aircraft carriers. In all the *Los Angeles* made 331 flights before its retirement in 1932.

Rosendahl spent most of August 1929 as a U.S. observer aboard the around-the-world flight of the *Graf Zeppelin*, one of the most famous airships ever built. William Randolph Hearst had offered $100,000 to finance the *Graf Zeppelin*'s circumnavigation of the globe provided the flight begin at the Statue of Liberty in New York City.

For the next two years Rosendahl worked in the bureau of aeronautics with the navy, handling airship training and experimental activities. In 1931, however, with the commissioning of the new 785-foot-long airship U.S.S. *Akron*, he was again given a command. He pushed the airship through test flights and shakedown operations. In reviewing these exercises, the navy decided that it had to emphasize more fully the deployment of fighters from the airship, a change in tactics to which Rosendahl reluctantly acquiesced. He then served a normal tour of sea duty aboard the *West Virginia* and *Portland* between 1932 and 1934. After his return, in December 1934, he married Jean Wilson of Los Angeles.

Rosendahl was able to return to lighter-than-air operations in 1934 in a rather spectacular way. On 3 April 1933 the *Akron* had crashed off the New Jersey coast, killing seventy-three and sparking both a major military investigation and a congressional inquiry. Rosendahl was a key witness in both. He persuasively argued against scrapping airships entirely, citing their usefulness as observation platforms for submarines and as escorts for transport convoys. He recognized that fighters flying from airships had value as well, but

he did not view the airship as simply a flying aircraft carrier. When the congressional report came out on 14 June 1933, Senator David I. Walsh (D.-Mass.) wrote in the majority report that the airship "supplants nothing. It supplements all." Rosendahl endorsed Walsh's position. In 1934 Rosendahl took command of the navy's lighter-than-air facility at Lakehurst, where he presided over airship training and operations for the next four years. He was present at the fiery crash of the *Hindenburg* at Lakehurst on 6 May 1937. The accident spelled the end of hydrogen-filled rigid airships and of the heyday of lighter-than-air craft.

Rosendahl always disputed the accident report, which concluded that the No. 4 gas-bag had been damaged by a bracing wire, causing a hydrogen leak that was then ignited by static electricity, a residue from the thunderstorms that had recently passed through the area. Instead of accepting this verdict, Rosendahl offered a theory of sabotage. Although conclusive proof has never been offered, laboratory tests duplicating conditions at the time of the crash supported the static electricity theory. Rosendahl's belief in sabotage was probably motivated both by a sense of guilt and by a desire to keep a good reputation. As commander at Lakehurst he had given the *Hindenburg* clearance to land, implying that weather conditions were safe.

Regardless of the cause of the accident, the navy did not blame Rosendahl for the loss of the *Hindenburg*. In 1938 he was assigned to sea duty as executive officer aboard the cruiser *Milwaukee*. He served there until 1940, when he was assigned to the office of the Chief of Naval Operations. In 1943 he was appointed to head the airship training and experimentation section for the navy, where he was able to develop and implement innovative ideas about the use of lighter-than-air craft for observation, coastal patrol, submarine hunting, and convoy escort. Nondirigible airships, sometimes called blimps, were extremely effective in these operations during the war. He served in this capacity until his retirement from the navy in 1946 with the rank of rear admiral. He then took over the executive directorship of the National Air Transport Coordinating Committee in New York City, serving until the early 1960s before dying there.

Charles Rosendahl spent most of his career working in the lighter-than-air field, not only as a commander of airships and the station at Lakehurst but also as a theorist and a popularizer of the airship. He wrote extensively about its uses for such periodicals as the *U.S. Naval Institute Proceedings*, *U.S. Air Services*, the *Transactions of the American Society of Mechanical Engineers*, and *Liberty Magazine*. He also published two books publicizing the airship: *Up Ship!* (1931), about the *Shenandoah*, the *Los Angeles*, and the *Graf Zeppelin*; and *What about the Airship?* (1938), containing a long argument about the uses and safety of airships. Historian Richard K. Smith has observed that because of his crusading zeal on behalf of the airship, Rosendahl "became the most widely known personality of lighter-than-air aeronautics in the United States."

There is no formal collection of Rosendahl's papers. Material by and about him can be found in scattered collections at the Naval Historical Center, Washington Navy Yard, Washington, D.C., and at the National Air and Space Museum, Smithsonian Institution. Short sketches of his career can be found in various editions of *Who's Who in American Aviation*; Basil Collier, *The Airship: A History* (1974); Harold G. Dick with Douglas H. Robinson, *The Golden Age of the Great Passenger Airships*: Graf Zeppelin *and* Hindenburg (1985); and Richard K. Smith, *The Airships* Akron *and* Macon: *Flying Aircraft Carriers of the United States Navy* (1965). An obituary is in the *New York Times*, 15 May 1977.

ROGER D. LAUNIUS

ROSENFELD, Morris (28 Dec. 1862–22 June 1923), poet, was born Moshe Yankev Alter Rosenfeld in the village of Boksza, near Suwalki, Poland, the son of Ephraim-Leyb Rosenfeld, a military tailor, and Rachel Wilchinsky. He attended the traditional Jewish elementary school in his birthplace. When he was ten his parents moved to Warsaw, where he was tutored in German, Hebrew, and Polish. Having acquired a reading knowledge of these languages, he acquainted himself through translations with much world literature. An autodidact in poetics and prosody, Rosenfeld wrote his first poem, "Military Service," in 1878; it was not published. Two years later he married Bella Guttenberg, a cousin, from whom he was divorced after six months. In 1882 he married Rebecca Basye Jewarkowska. That same year he went to London, England, apprenticing briefly there as a tailor. To avoid conscription into the Russian army, he went to Holland, spending three months in Amsterdam (where he studied diamond cutting). He visited America and then returned to Suwalki for three years. In 1885 he, his parents, and later his wife settled in London, where their three children died. In 1886 Rosenfeld migrated with his wife to the United States, where he worked first as a tailor in clothing factories and later as a journalist. He spent the remainder of his life in the United States, much of it in bitter poverty.

Rosenfeld's first collection of Yiddish poems, *The Bell*, was published in 1888. A second collection, *A Necklace of Flowers*, appeared in 1890, and a third, *Poems and Ballads*, in 1893. A six-volume collection of his poetry and prose came out in 1910, and a three-volume edition of his collected works two years later.

A volume of Rosenfeld's poetry was discovered in 1897 by a professor of Slavic languages at Harvard University, Leo Wiener, who reviewed it enthusiastically in the *Nation* and subsequently issued a prose translation entitled *Songs from the Ghetto* (1898). Notice by a scholar of Wiener's stature launched Rosenfeld's career in the English-speaking world. The New York press hailed him as a worker-poet, and his fame spread to Europe, where he was acclaimed, translated, and published in Czech, Croatian, French, German, Polish, and Romanian. Wiener wrote, "It was left for a Russian Jew at the end of the nineteenth century to see and paint hell in colors not attempted by any one since the days of Dante."

The critic N. B. Minkoff wrote that not since the *tkhines*, moralistic penny booklets of the sixteenth and seventeenth centuries, had there been such a wide Yiddish readership as that which the proletarian poets created. Of the 150 Yiddish poets writing in America at the turn of the century, Rosenfeld was unquestionably the most read. (Because his readership comprised poorly paid proletarian workers, however, his writings did not bring him income.) *Voskhod*, an influential periodical in Russia, called him "the crown poet of the emigration." The poet laureate of the sweatshop and its "oppression, pain, and dreariness," he understood and gave eloquent expression to the struggle of the workers of his day and was widely acknowledged as the bard of the American ghetto. He did not simply chronicle this formative period in American Jewish life; he helped to shape it.

American Yiddish of the 1910s and 1920s was a rapidly changing language melding the Yiddish dialects spoken by immigrants from disparate populations of Eastern European Jews. Rosenfeld's contribution to establishing a kind of literary standard and providing models in prose and poetry was a significant advance for that time.

Although an avowed secularist, Rosenfeld lauded the Psalter and paraphrased the prophets. His esteem for the Hebrew Scriptures was profound. Acerbic in denouncing the religiously doctrinaire and the anti-Semite alike, he admired Washington, Lincoln, and Whitman. He espoused restoration of the Jewish homeland and attended the fourth Zionist Congress in London in 1900, where he met with the leading figures of the movement.

Beginning in 1901 Rosenfeld supported himself as a staff writer for the Yiddish press, where he endured a stormy relationship with editors and colleagues. The bulk of his prose writing—commentaries on the foibles and ills of the day, especially of the Lower East Side, and humorous essays of universal application—remains untranslated.

As the literary mood shifted from social protest to a more individual style more concerned with form, a younger generation, calling themselves *di Yunge* (the young ones) attacked Rosenfeld cruelly. His response was helpless, hopeless, and undignified. Arguably the best read of the labor poets, he lacked the philosophical and historical background of his more sophisticated juniors. Their negative opinion carried the day, and he was omitted from important anthologies. In 1913 he resigned from the *Forverts*, and in 1921 he was dismissed from the *Tageblatt*. A banquet was given in New York City in May 1923, celebrating Rosenfeld's sixtieth birthday. He died there the following month and is buried in the "Row of Fame" of the Workmen's Circle in Mount Carmel Cemetery, Queens, New York.

A culture hero of the workers, Rosenfeld must be counted among the first of the American Yiddish social lyricists whose work had genuine artistic quality. A protest writer and intellectual leader of the first generation of Jewish immigrants from Eastern Europe,

Rosenfeld's technical skill and thematics influenced a number of younger writers. Fusing the labor element with the Jewish national element, "Jew and worker" were his perennial focus. He was the only one of the proletarian poets of the early twentieth century to earn international renown. For the early immigrant epoch, the end of the nineteenth century and the first decade of the twentieth, he is the dominant figure in Yiddish poetry, revered but today largely unread.

• Rosenfeld's papers are at the YIVO Institute in New York City. Other works include *Songs from the Ghetto*, 2d ed., expanded, trans. Leo Wiener (1900); *Songs of Labor and Other Poems*, trans. Rose Pastor Stokes and Helena Frank (1914); *The Teardrop Millionaire and Other Poems*, trans. Aaron Kramer (1955); and *Poems of Morris Rosenfeld*, trans. Mortimer T. Cohen (1979). Biographical information is in Itche Goldberg and Max Rosenfeld, eds., *Morris Rosenfeld: Selections from His Poetry and Prose* (1964); Sol Liptzin, *A History of Yiddish Literature* (1972); and Charles Madison, *Yiddish Literature: Its Scope and Major Writers* (1971). Leon Goldenthal, *Toil and Triumph* (1960), is "a novel based on the life of Morris Rosenfeld" in which "most of the dialogue and a few of the scenes are imaginary." An obituary is in the *New York Times*, 22 June 1923, with an article in the issue of 25 June 1923.

THOMAS E. BIRD

ROSENFELD, Paul Leopold (4 May 1890–21 July 1946), music critic, essayist, and novelist, was born in the Mt. Morris section of the Bronx, in New York City, the son of Julius Rosenfeld, a successful manufacturer of textiles, and Sarah Liebmann, of the wealthy Liebmann Brewery family, a serious amateur pianist. His father was steeped in literature, music, and art. When Rosenfeld was ten years old his mother died, and his father sent him to live with his maternal grandmother, who three years later enrolled him at the Riverview Military Academy in Poughkeepsie, New York. He skipped athletics, studied music and literature, and on Saturday afternoons boarded the train for New York City to attend concerts and the theater. In 1908, just as Rosenfeld was about to enter Yale University, his father died.

At Yale Rosenfeld wrote for the Yale *"Lit"* and reviewed for a New Haven newspaper. Graduating from Yale in 1912, he enrolled at the Columbia School of Journalism, worked as reporter for the *New York Press*, and scored a scoop when, with a colleague, he hired a boat to sail out on the Hudson River to report on the Fleet. His mother and grandmother had left him an ample income, so he quit working after six months to go to Europe for a year.

Edmund Wilson, in *Paul Rosenfeld* (1948), a book of essays published after Rosenfeld's death, compared Rosenfeld (at this stage of his career) to James Huneker, the first American critic to break out of an academic mold. But unlike Huneker, who wrote quick essays to earn money for passage back to Europe, Rosenfeld believed an American art was yet to be created and rushed back to New York, living there the rest of his life writing, mainly criticism and essays. In 1915 he attended a concert by Leo Ornstein in New York and, drawn to the new atonal music, fixed on his major life's work, music criticism. He began writing an influential monthly column, "Musical Chronicles," for the *Dial*. In 1920 he published his first book, *Musical Portraits: Interpretations of Twenty Modern Composers*.

The consummate New Yorker, Rosenfeld lived all through the 1920s at 77 Irving Place, off Gramercy Park in a large wood-paneled apartment. His walls were hung with Marsden Hartley, John Marin, and Georgia O'Keeffe paintings and Alfred Stieglitz photographs, and his large living room was filled in the evening with readings by such artists and writers as Van Wyck Brooks, ee cummings, Marianne Moore, Waldo Frank, Marin, O'Keeffe, and Stieglitz. He summered in Westport, Connecticut, and the Adirondacks.

Rosenfeld's music criticism compressed the distance between listener and music. An early advocate of Charles Ives, he described Ives's music as "the essences of a practical people, abrupt and nervous and ecstatic in their movements and manifestations" (Liebowitz, p. 243). Copland, he said, "has a taste for hot colors and garish jazziness . . . his work is exciting with all sorts of percussive brazen brilliance" (Liebowitz, p. 251). Yet he was highly analytic. He dissected, for example, the significance of Stravinsky's way of changing from the "modified homophonic-harmonic principle . . . to a melodic-contrapuntal one" (Liebowitz, p. xxvi).

Rosenfeld's sentences were musical, rich, and complex, coming to a halt with surprising, apt common language, talking of masons "smearing" concrete on the purity of a skyscraper's steel structure or, in writing of the nude women Arthur B. Davies painted, "The flesh of his superhuman figures has the quality of candy . . . were one to touch these breasts with the lips they would taste sickishly of pink taffy" ("American Painting," *Dial* [Dec. 1921]: 656). Some critics found his language tangled and knotted, but a wonderful earthiness emerged from his mix of high and common language. Wilson called Rosenfeld "the music critic of the 'American Renaissance.'"

Rosenfeld had a supple, adventurous mind. Before reviewing a concert he would sit at his large grand piano and play through the entire work he was about to hear. Crushed when his romance with Florence Cane, the wife of lawyer and poet Melville Cane, abruptly ended in 1923, he found solace in the piano. "Human beings have a great way of sucking the blood out of each other," he wrote Stieglitz. "Meanwhile, there are a few oxygens still left. I race through a Beethoven symphony . . . it is a great purge and restorative" (28 June 1923). His closest ties were with Stieglitz, their symbiosis drawing Stieglitz to Rosenfeld's mind just as Rosenfeld, though losing himself but not his critical independence, found Stieglitz's personal and intellectual support crucial.

Rosenfeld ached to write beyond music, and did, on Marcel Proust, Hamlet, Jean Rimbaud, Hartley, Chaplin, Guilla Apollinaire, and others for *Seven Arts*, *Vanity Fair*, and *New Republic*.

The 1929 crash and depression wiped out many of Rosenfeld's investments. He now had to write for a living. But neither formalist nor social realist when literary and popular magazines were one or the other, he could not get the assignments he needed. Besides, his rich style, incompatible with the lean times, had gone out of favor. He felt out of touch, a failure, further depressed by the Nazis, first by their annihilation of Jews. Then he was angered by their obliterating intellectual and aesthetic standards by nationalizing Richard Wagner, making the meistersinger, the lowly hero of "Die Meistersinger," into an emboldened Nazi. Throughout his last book, *Discoveries of a Music Critic*, he discussed issues of art and national character.

Rosenfeld lived what Lewis Mumford has called an "organic morality," a private and public life devoted to building a humanly purposeful American culture. He found a patron for the young Aaron Copland before the composer's talent blossomed, and he took Sherwood Anderson and his then wife Tennessee Mitchell, a sculptor, to Europe so Anderson could infuse classic knowledge into his knowing characters. In 1946 he had begun planning, with Elliot Carter, the first critical biography of Charles Ives. However, he died of a heart attack in Greenwich Village, New York, one week after the death of his long-time friend Alfred Stieglitz.

• Rosenfeld's papers are at Beinecke Rare Book and Manuscript Library at Yale University. He wrote nine books, but he is best known for two: *Port of New York*, a collection of essays on fourteen artists and writers, and *Discoveries of a Music Critic*, his last book. With Mumford, Kreymbourg, and Brooks, he created and edited the first modern annual of American literature, *American Caravan*, which contains more than a thousand pages of poetry, essays, and fiction. First published in 1927, its final number was issued in 1936. Honoring his lifelong friend Sherwood Anderson, he selected and edited the *Sherwood Anderson Reader* (1947) after Anderson's death in 1942. He also wrote *Musical Chronicle (1917–1923)* in 1923, *Men Seen* (1925), *Modern Tendencies in Music* (1927), *By Way of Art* (1928), *Boy in the Sun* (1928), a semi-autobiographical novel, *An Hour with American Music* (1929), and with Waldo Frank, Dorothy Norman, Lewis Mumford, and Harold Rugg coedited a series of essays, *America and Alfred Stieglitz: A Collective Portrait* (1934). There are two books about Rosenfeld, Herbert Liebowitz, *Musical Impressions* (1969), with an introductory essay to a collection of his music criticism, and Jerome Mellquist and Lucie Wiese, *Paul Rosenfeld* (1948), a compilation of essays written after his death by artists and writers, which also contains complete bibliography of his published works. Sherman Paul introduced a reprint of his *Port of New York* (1961) with an analytical and an interpretive essay. More than three dozen published articles, most written in the 1920s, have appeared. An obituary is in the *New York Times*, 22 July 1946. Memorials were in the *Freeman*, the *New York Tribune*, the *New York Sun*, the *Bookman*, *Yale Review*, the *New York Herald Tribune*, *New Masses*, and *Tomorrow*—and the other magazines and newspapers for which he wrote.

JUDITH MARA GUTMAN

ROSENMAN, Samuel Irving (13 Feb. 1896–24 June 1973), jurist and presidential adviser, was born in San Antonio, Texas, the son of Russian-Jewish immigrants Sol Rosenman and Ethel Paler. His parents settled in New York City, where Rosenman attended the Manhattan public schools. He graduated from Columbia College, Phi Beta Kappa and summa cum laude, in 1915. In 1917, after completing two years at the Columbia Law School, he enlisted as a private in the U.S. Army and was discharged in August 1919 as a second lieutenant. He received his LL.B. soon after and was admitted to the New York bar in 1920.

Rosenman then turned to politics. After gaining the support of Tammany Hall district leader James J. Hines, Rosenman was elected to the state assembly in 1921 and then won annual elections through 1925. He supported such progressive causes as Robert Moses's park system, Margaret Sanger's efforts to disseminate birth control information, and rent-control legislation. These efforts brought him to the attention of the state Democratic leadership, and he obtained appointment as a legislative commissioner in 1926. In the midst of these political activities, Rosenman married Dorothy Reuben in 1924; they had two children.

After 1926 Rosenman came into closer contact with New York's governor Alfred E. Smith and intended in 1928 to work for Smith's presidential campaign, but instead Smith assigned him to the task of helping gubernatorial candidate Franklin D. Roosevelt. This was a decisive turning point in his career. Rosenman's extensive knowledge of state issues was used effectively in Roosevelt's speeches, and he emerged as one of the candidate's principal speechwriters. Rosenman became one of Roosevelt's closest aides and even lived for a time in the executive mansion. He became a key figure in Roosevelt's 1932 presidential campaign, writing speeches and serving as the principal architect of the famous "brains trust" of academic advisers that Roosevelt assembled to develop plans for economic recovery and political reform.

In spite of his contributions, however, Rosenman expressed a preference for staying in New York over obtaining an appointment in Washington. Before leaving the governorship, therefore, Roosevelt appointed Rosenman to the New York Supreme Court in 1932. When, later that year, the bosses of Tammany Hall denied Rosenman the nomination to a full judicial term in retaliation for his support of Roosevelt during Roosevelt's dispute with them, he took up a successful law practice until July 1933. Governor Herbert Lehman reappointed him to the New York Supreme Court in 1933, and he later won election to a full four-year term.

For the first several years of Roosevelt's administration Rosenman's career remained based in New York. Although "Sammy the Rose," as Roosevelt dubbed him, maintained close personal ties with Roosevelt during this period, contributed speeches, and made occasional visits to the White House, he devoted most of his time to working for Lehman's New York administration. Rosenman's relationship with Roosevelt took its definitive shape in 1936, when he became the chief presidential speechwriter during the reelection campaign and accompanied Roosevelt on two of his three major campaign trips. In 1937 he began the work for which he is chiefly remembered, the thirteen-volume *Public Papers and Addresses of Franklin D. Roosevelt* (1938–1950). In this period he also served as an adviser to Roosevelt during the ill-fated effort to reorganize the federal court system, though Rosenman does not appear to have been the source of the details of the plan.

Rosenman's importance as a presidential adviser increased during World War II. Beginning in 1939 his assignment included war mobilization and various government reorganization projects. In 1941 Roosevelt gave Rosenman wide-ranging powers to draft a reorganization plan to coordinate the war effort. His expertise resulted in the creation of the Office of Production Management, a wartime federal mobilization organization. Other projects of his included the creation of the National Housing Agency and the War Manpower Commission. He worked to streamline the Office of War Information and helped resolve disputes between the War Production Board and the Federal Power Commission over electric power priorities, and between the Secretary of War and the Justice Department over the issue of wartime antitrust prosecutions. The pressure of these varied responsibilities became so great that Rosenman moved into the White House temporarily in July 1942. His efforts, which focused on the issue of inflation, resulted in the passage of anti-inflation legislation and the creation of the Office of Economic Stabilization. Rosenman's work on housing benefited from the contributions of his wife Dorothy, who had gained a national reputation as a housing expert and who became chairman of the National Committee on Housing in 1941.

By early 1943 Rosenman's many activities had produced such severe stress that he temporarily lost sight in one eye. He lightened his workload by resigning from the New York Supreme Court but at the same time accepted appointment to the position of special counsel to the president. He was assigned responsibility for postwar planning for conversion to a peacetime economy and war-criminal trials. Economic planning, however, brought him into such severe conflict with head of the Office of Economic Stabilization James F. Byrnes that he announced his intention to leave government service as soon as the war ended. But in January 1945 Roosevelt named him to head an economic mission to Europe. In April 1945 Rosenman was in London helping prepare a report on the Yalta Conference when Roosevelt died. Rosenman stayed on with the administration of Harry S. Truman until January 1946 because he believed that he should encourage the new president to carry on in the tradition of New Deal liberalism. He was the chief promoter and drafter of Truman's pivotal twenty-one-point message of September 1945, which provided the basis for Truman's own reform program, known as the Fair Deal.

When he resigned in 1946 Rosenman returned to New York City, where he soon built a substantial law practice. He never, however, lost his zeal for politics and public service. As a member of various Jewish organizations, such as the American Jewish Committee and the Federation of Jewish Charities, he was involved in planning for the establishment of the state of Israel; he continued to serve as an adviser to the Truman administration and to Democratic governors. In 1949, for example, Truman appointed him to a investigatory board to examine the issue of pay raises for steel workers. In conjunction with this service Rosenman was the subject of a four-page interview in *U.S. News and World Report* on the value of fact-finding boards. He died in New York City.

Rosenman's contributions fall under several heads. He was one of the most significant speechwriters in recent American history, and among his many contributions in this area, he wrote the peroration to Roosevelt's acceptance speech in 1933, which added the term "New Deal" to the American political lexicon. He made a significant contribution to governmental reorganization. He was particularly effective in this area during World War II when he helped coordinate the various new agencies spawned by the emergency. He also served as a key figure in helping smooth the transition between the New Deal and the Fair Deal. Finally, Rosenman's work on the Roosevelt papers has provided a key source for scholars. Although the work has been criticized for exhibiting partisanship and selectivity, its usefulness and reliability have been generally vindicated. Rosenman's long and varied career justifies his reputation as a key presidential aide during two pivotal administrations in twentieth-century American history.

• The bulk of Rosenman's papers are housed in the Franklin D. Roosevelt Library at Hyde Park, N.Y. Approximately 100 items, which cover the period from 1926 to 1967, are in the Columbia University Library. His autobiography, *Working with Roosevelt* (1952), is invaluable. His definitive evaluation of the Roosevelt presidency is contained in *Presidential Style; Some Giants and a Pygmy in the White House* (1975), on which he was working at the time of his death. The book was completed by his wife Dorothy. A full-length biography is Samuel B. Hand, *Counsel and Advise: A Political Biography of Samuel I. Rosenman* (1979). Hand's article "Rosenman, Thucydides, and the New Deal," *Journal of American History* 55 (1968): 334–48, focuses on Rosenman's role as a historian of the Roosevelt presidency.

NELSON DAWSON

ROSENSTEIN, Nettie (26 Sept. 1893–15 Mar. 1980), fashion designer, was born in Vienna, Austria, the daughter of Joseph Rosencrans, a dry-goods merchant, and Sarah Hoffman. The family emigrated to the United States in 1899 and established a dry-goods shop in New York City at Lenox Avenue and 117th Street. Playing in the shop, Nettie began to sew her own doll clothes and fell in love with fabric while still very young. By the time she was eleven she was ambitiously making garments for people. To use her mother's sewing machine, however, she had to stand, being unable as yet to reach the foot pedal while sitting down.

Nettie never had any formal training in fashion design. Instead of sketching (a skill she never acquired), she designed by "drawing" in cloth, draping and pinning fabric on her own body, proceeding directly to cut and sew each garment. Years later, in her own shop, she continued with the same method, draping fabric on the bodies of hired models. (Curiously, the success in the 1980s of another American designer, Donna Karan, has been attributed partly to her reliance on exactly the same habit of developing her designs directly in fabric on the body.)

Nettie was still sewing only for herself, her family, and a few family friends when she married Saul Rosenstein in 1913. At about the same time, continuing the family's involvement in the clothing trade, Nettie's sister Pauline opened a millinery shop. When her customers sought advice regarding a dressmaker, Pauline sent them to the newly married Nettie; by 1916 or early 1917 Nettie had a flourishing business, operating, as many dressmakers of the era did, out of her own home. So many customers visited Nettie Rosenstein's Harlem brownstone that at one point a local policeman thought that the traffic in and out was cause for suspicion and questioned the lady of the house.

Rosenstein's clientele grew steadily, and she was employing some fifty seamstresses by 1921, when she moved her shop from the brownstone to East Fifty-sixth Street. Taking a step toward the modern, high-fashion specialty retail store, Nettie Rosenstein, Inc., started to produce chic ready-to-wear dresses rather than make clothes to order. Not long after Rosenstein had opened her new shop, one of her customers brought in a buyer from the I. Magnin chain, who was impressed by the high standards of design and materials in Rosenstein's line. He realized that her styles were, in effect, tailor-made for the new high-fashion ready-to-wear market that had emerged in the United States after 1910. In addition to I. Magnin, several other major national department stores were soon stocking Rosenstein's clothes, including Nan Duskin, Bonwit Teller, and Neiman Marcus. With prices reaching $500, Rosenstein's were among the costliest off-the-rack dresses in the country.

For reasons now unclear, Rosenstein closed up shop in 1927, but three years later she was back in the trade as a designer for Corbeau et Compagnie. In partnership with businessman Charles Gumprecht, a skilled entrepreneur who had already contributed greatly to nurturing the women's ready-to-wear market, and her sister-in-law Eva Rosencrans, Rosenstein opened a new wholesale business at Forty-seventh Street and Seventh Avenue in 1931. Freed to concentrate on design, she focused almost exclusively on evening dresses and left production largely in the hands of her partners. In the depths of the Great Depression, Rosenstein's sales reached previously unheard-of levels, surpassing $1 million in 1937.

Among Rosenstein's most enduring contributions to fashion was the introduction of the proverbial "little black dress" to American women. Rosenstein traveled regularly, seeking inspiration in the famed couture houses and on the streets of European cities, where such French designers as Vionnet and Chanel had made the simple black dress an essential for fashionable women by the 1930s. Declaring that "it's what you leave off a dress that makes it smart," Rosenstein developed her own version of the short black cocktail dress, even simpler in line and detail than the styles prevailing in Europe at the time. Over the years, she invented innumerable variations on this dress, which remained among her best-selling evening fashions for more than twenty years. Indeed, the "little black dress" became a staple of American women's clothing that remained popular through the end of the century.

In 1942 Rosenstein expanded her line to include day dresses and moved her business to 550 Seventh Avenue, in the heart of New York city's fashion district. Rosenstein also diversified, founding in 1946 the Nettie Rosenstein Accessories Company (makers of handbags and costume jewelry) and Nettie Rosenstein Perfumes, Inc., both successful ventures. Among her famous clients were actress Dinah Shore, cabaret singer Hildegarde, and actress Norma Shearer. Rosenstein created Mamie Eisenhower's inaugural ball gowns in both 1953 and 1957.

Rosenstein received the Lord and Taylor Achievement Award in 1936, the Neiman Marcus Achievement Award in 1938, the Fashion Trades Award for Best Design in 1946 for her day dresses, a Coty Award in 1947 for consistent achievement in design, and a second Coty in 1960 for accessories (making Rosenstein, along with Anne Klein, one of very few designers ever to win two Cotys). An example of Rosenstein's classic "little black dress" is in the permanent costume collection of the Smithsonian National Museum of American History in Washington, D.C., along with her two inaugural gowns.

Having established herself as one of the great classicists of American fashion design and a pioneering businesswoman, Nettie Rosenstein retired from active involvement in her clothing business in 1961 but continued to oversee the design of her accessories and perfumes for several years. She died in New York City.

• Rosenstein appears to have left no records of her career. A limited amount of information about her can be found in Eleanor Lambert, *World of Fashion: People, Places, Resources* (1976), and Josephine Ellis Watkins, *Who's Who in Fashion* (1972). The *New York Times*, 15 Mar. 1980, has an obituary.

FRED CARSTENSEN

ROSENWALD, Julius (12 Aug. 1862–6 Jan. 1932), executive and philanthropist, was born in Springfield, Illinois, the son of Samuel Rosenwald, a clothing merchant, and Augusta Hammerslough. Julius Rosenwald attended high school in Springfield for only two years. At age seventeen he left for New York to serve a clothing business apprenticeship with Hammerslough uncles. Indefatigable, Rosenwald also obtained part-time employment at other clothing establishments and managed to sample the metropolis's amusements with friends such as Henry Goldman, later a founder of the investment banking firm of Goldman, Sachs and Co.

In 1884 Rosenwald and his brother Morris opened a retail clothing and tailoring business in New York City. It failed. With financing from his uncles, Rosenwald opened the Chicago firm of Rosenwald & Weil to manufacture clothing. It survived, as did a separate clothing firm, Rosenwald & Co., enabling him to marry Augusta Nusbaum in 1891 and begin a family of five children. (He married Adelaide Rau Goodkind in 1930, after his first wife's death in 1929. He and Goodkind had no children.) But these successes did not make him wealthy. "The aim of my life," he confided to a friend, "is to have an income of $15,000 a year—$5,000 to be used for my personal expenses, $5,000 to be laid aside, and $5,000 to go to charity."

Eleven years later, fate intervened in Rosenwald's life in the person of Richard Warren Sears, who, according to Sears's sister, had sent for catalogs as soon as he learned to write. On reaching adulthood, Sears made it his objective to sell merchandise to every American via mail order, even if he had nothing to ship and the American had no rational need for the products offered. Aaron Nusbaum, Rosenwald's brother-in-law, had invested in a company that manufactured pneumatic tubes for use in department stores. He thought to sell his product to Sears, who had just formed a mail-order business with watchmaker Alvah C. Roebuck. Instead, Sears sold Nusbaum a half interest in Sears & Roebuck for $75,000. Hedging a risky investment, Nusbaum sold half of his half-interest to Rosenwald. Sears had approached Rosenwald earlier to purchase 10,000 mens' suits. Rosenwald inquired whether it might not be wiser to sell 1,000 suits, to test the market. Sears responded that he already had the orders. What he did not have were suits.

By December 1896 Rosenwald was out of the clothing business and into Sears & Roebuck, where he provided an essential stabilizing influence. Sears could not stop selling. Catalogs told prospective customers of irresistible bargains, and buyers by the tens of thousands were mailing in orders. Between 1896 and 1897 Sears & Roebuck more than doubled its annual sales.

In 1901, unable to tolerate the frenetic pace, Nusbaum sold his shares to Sears and Rosenwald for $1.25 million. Roebuck had earlier sold out to Sears for $25,000. In 1909 Sears sold his interest for $10 million, but his shares did not go to Rosenwald. They went to Goldman, Sachs and Co., and Lehman Brothers, in New York. Rosenwald, Goldman, and Philip Lehman had developed a new idea: to finance expansion of a merchandising operation with proceeds from sales of shares.

The public bought Sears & Roebuck shares with the same avidity with which it bought the company's products. Anyone who purchased 100 shares of common stock in 1906 for $5,000 and held them until November 1928 made a profit of $272,000 plus dividends of $29,775. Rosenwald, never certain exactly how many shares he owned, was estimated to be worth $150 million in 1925, when an annual income of $3,000 was considered substantial.

With two of his three early aspirations realized—and in far greater abundance than he had ever dreamed—Rosenwald turned to philanthropy. This did not mean handouts. "In the first place 'philanthropy' is a sickening word," he declared. "What I want to do is to try to cure the things that seem to be wrong."

In reality, Rosenwald's most important contribution to philanthropy was to encourage individuals to use the financial resources that he could provide to act on their own behalf. Rosenwald contributed to the construction of 5,357 public schools, shops, and teachers' homes in black areas of fifteen southern states. The total cost was $28,408,520, of which he gave $4.3 million, or 15 percent. Blacks, thought to be so poverty-stricken that they could give nothing, contributed 17 percent. Local whites contributed 4 percent. Finally, elected officials, shamed by these contributions into making some response, allocated public funds of 64 percent.

The success of the experience persuaded Rosenwald of the "unwisdom of philanthropic gifts narrowly limited." In a seminal article, "Principles of Public Giving" (*Atlantic Monthly*, May 1929), and its sequel, "The Trend Away from Perpetuities" (*Atlantic Monthly*, Dec. 1930), he defined the concept. A philanthropist's donations should be made during his lifetime and not be left to heirs for disbursal. Each generation must identify the social problems that would best be solved by that generation's resources and should not depend on the previous or the following generations for financing.

Rosenwald also made major gifts to the University of Chicago, Chicago's Museum of Science and Industry, Hebrew Union College, Jewish Theological Seminary, and the American Jewish Committee. He opposed Zionism but contributed (albeit modestly) to various Zionist enterprises. Above all, he recognized the havoc wrought in Eastern Europe during and after World War I and provided munificent sums to assist affected Jews.

At this point, anti-Semitism began to reach heights that no one could have predicted. Rosenwald emphasized that Jews, particularly in Poland, should remain where they were and not emigrate. He would help them to the extent that he could. Ironically, within thirteen years of his death in Chicago, the overwhelming majority of those people would be murdered in the Holocaust.

Rosenwald's importance stems not only from his genius for marketing and his humanitarian efforts but also from the example that he offered of applying a common-sense, practical approach to problem resolution in the public and the private sectors. Whether at Sears & Roebuck or while serving the public in Washington, he demanded a hard look "at the operation of cause and effect." Except in Eastern Europe, the approach served him and mankind well.

• The papers of Julius Rosenwald are in the Department of Special Collections, University of Chicago Library. A full-length biography is M. R. Werner, *Julius Rosenwald: The Life of a Practical Humanitarian* (1939). On Rosenwald's philanthropies, see Edwin R. Embree and Julia Waxman, *Investment in People: The Story of the Julius Rosenwald Fund* (1949). On his relationship with Sears & Roebuck, see Boris Emmet and John E. Jench, *Catalogues and Counters: A History of Sears, Roebuck and Company* (1950). An obituary is in the *New York Times*, 7 Jan. 1932.

MILTON GOLDIN

ROSENWALD, Lessing Julius (10 Feb. 1891–24 June 1978), art and book collector and philanthropist, was born in Chicago, Illinois, the son of Julius Rosenwald, a businessman, and Augusta Nusbaum. In 1908 he went to Cornell University but left in 1911 to work as a shipping clerk for Sears, Roebuck, of which his father was president. In 1913 Rosenwald married Edith Goodkind; they had five children. He served as a seaman, second class, in the U.S. Navy during World War I; after the war he returned to Sears, Roebuck. In 1920 his father sent him to Philadelphia to start that city's first Sears store.

During the 1920s Rosenwald began collecting art and rare books. By 1929 he owned 4,300 pieces of art, including works by Rembrandt, Albrecht Durer, and William Blake, and became recognized as an expert on art and rare books.

His father's death in 1932 necessitated not only that Rosenwald administer the almost $17,500,000 estate but also that he pay greater attention to business at Sears, since he succeeded his father that year as chairman of the board. Retiring in 1939, he built an elegant Georgian mansion, "Alverthorpe," in Jenkintown, Pennsylvania, a suburb of Philadelphia. One wing was designed exclusively to house his art collection. He believed that he owned his books and art as a cultural trustee for others and thus opened the Alverthorpe galleries to the public.

In 1941 Rosenwald began making donations to the National Gallery of Art and willed his collection—over 25,000 engravings, lithographs, etchings, mezzotints, dry-points, and woodcuts—to the gallery in 1943. Under the terms of the deed he was allowed to keep possession until his death. Similarly, that same year he presented his rare books (which at the time of his death numbered approximately 2,600 volumes and included the best collection of illuminated William Blake books in America) to the Library of Congress but was also allowed to keep them in his possession. During the next three decades he gradually transferred many of the works in these collections to the National Gallery and the Library of Congress. Their estimated value was $35 million at the time of his death at his estate in Jenkintown, Pennsylvania.

Rosenwald belonged to several civic organizations and boards including the Princeton Institute for Advanced Study, the American Jewish Committee, the Philadelphia Museum of Art, the Philadelphia Orchestra Association, and the Friends of the University of Pennsylvania Libraries. He played a major role in helping to start *Scientific American*. During World War II he was director of the Bureau of Industrial Conservation, an agency charged with reducing waste materials. He was also the president of the only anti-Zionist Jewish organization in America, the American Council for Judaism (ACJ), which began in 1942.

The ACJ opposed the establishment of a Jewish state in Palestine, arguing that Judaism was a religion and that Jews did not constitute a nation. During and immediately after World War II this was an extremely unpopular attitude to take among Jewish Americans. Rosenwald used the council as a base to lobby for the liberalization of American immigration laws and the admission of European displaced persons to the United States after World War II. Although he was originally motivated to seek new immigration laws because of the plight of the Jews who survived the Holocaust and who had no place to go after the war, he realized that unless new legislation included, and even focused upon, most of the other displaced persons, 80 percent of whom were Christian, there would be no possibility of getting any broadening of the immigration laws in Congress. The passage of the Displaced Persons Act of 1948, and its amended version in 1950, may be attributed directly to Rosenwald's influence. Ironically, as passed, the wording favored Germans as well as Christians exiled from Eastern Europe and discriminated against Jews.

Rosenwald's primary legacy, however, is as a bibliophile and connoisseur of fine arts. In 1984 more than half of all of the possessions in the National Gallery of Art came from the Rosenwald collection, while the illustrated books that he donated to the Library of Congress are still the jewels of the Rare Books and Special Collections Division. No library could ever have afforded to purchase the enormous number of works that Rosenwald presented as gifts. As Andrew Robinson, former curator of prints and drawings at the National Gallery of Art, said, "Lessing Rosenwald formed what is probably the most comprehensive and finest collection of prints, drawings, and illustrated books ever brought together by a single man in America" (*Washington Post*, 26 June 1978).

• Rosenwald had his own *Recollections of a Collector* privately printed in 1976. Material about his life is in *Rosenwald and Rosenbach: Two Philadelphia Bookmen* (1983); Edwin Wolf II with John F. Fleming, *Rosenbach* (1960); Ruth E. Fine, *Lessing J. Rosenwald: Tribute to a Collector* (1982); Sandra Hindman, ed., *The Early Illustrated Book: Essays in Honor of Lessing J. Rosenwald* (1982); and *The Lessing J. Rosenwald Collection: A Catalog of the Gifts of Lessing J. Rosenwald to the Library of Congress, 1943 to 1975* (1977). For his activities with the American Council of Judaism see Thomas A. Kolsky, *Jews against Zionism: The American Council for Judaism, 1942–1948* (1990); for his efforts to liberalize American immigration policy and help displaced persons after World War II see Leonard Dinnerstein, *America and the Survivors of the Holocaust* (1982). Obituaries are in the *New York Times* and the *Washington Post*, both 26 June 1978.

LEONARD DINNERSTEIN

ROSEWATER, Edward (28 Jan. 1841–30 Aug. 1906), journalist and politician, was born Edward Rosenwasser in Bukovan, Bohemia (now the Czech Republic), the son of Herman Rosenwasser and Rosalia Kohn, farmers. In 1854 the Rosenwasser family, which consisted of parents and eight children at that time, emigrated to the United States, settling in Cleveland, Ohio. Educated in Hebrew, German, and Czech in his native land, upon arriving in America Edward was sent to work peddling "notions and wares." Subsequent jobs selling tinware and stoves, and then dry-goods, were followed by a three-month term at Hollister and Felton's Commercial College in Cleveland, where he learned penmanship, bookkeeping, and accounting, and in 1859 by an apprenticeship in telegraphy. Upon attaining proficiency as a telegrapher, he took a job in Murfreesboro, Tennessee, and then moved to Stevenson, Alabama, where his responsibilities included splicing and repairing the line, maintaining batteries, and personally delivering telegrams.

After the Civil War began, Rosewater relocated to Nashville, Tennessee, and enlisted in the Union army as a telegrapher in April 1862. First stationed on the battlefield, he transmitted messages from General John Frémont and General John Pope directly to President Abraham Lincoln at the second battle of Manassas. Rosewater was transferred to Washington, D.C., in the fall of 1862 and worked in the telegraph office of the War Department.

Since there was no telegraph office in the White House, messengers would deliver Lincoln's handwritten dispatches or the president would come by to dictate them to the operator. Rosewater wrote to his fiancée, Leah Colman, in Cleveland: "The Pres't every morning about 8 o'clock comes in to read dispatches, which are copied into books. . . . Sometimes he tells an anecdote or reads a story aloud & laughs (you could hear him ½ mile)." Indeed, Lincoln stayed continuously at the telegraph office during the battle of Fredericksburg, and Rosewater noted in his diary: "When it was learned that over 13,000 men were killed, the calamity seemed to crush Lincoln. He looked pale, wan and haggard." On 1 January 1863 Rosewater telegraphed the Emancipation Proclamation to army commanders in the field, a document that he had heard the president refer to as "something of a Pope's bull against the comet."

In the fall of 1863 Rosewater relocated to Omaha, in Nebraska Territory, as chief operator of the eastern terminus of the transcontinental telegraph, which had been completed a year previously. With a population of perhaps 6,000, Omaha was a thriving business center for steamboat traffic and overland mail coaches, its streets traversed by a great variety of people. Rosewater wrote dispatches for eastern newspapers describing his experiences on the frontier. In 1864 he married Leah Colman, and the couple settled on Farnham Street in a house in which all five of their children were born.

In 1871 Rosewater was elected to the Nebraska state legislature with a campaign to develop an Omaha board of education for the growing city, which now had a population of 17,000. He printed a tabloid, the *Omaha Bee*, in support of this platform. From a single-page broadside with a circulation of 500, the *Bee* soon grew into a lively daily newspaper. In the colorful tradition of western journalism, political tensions at times spilled beyond the printed page, as when a malicious personal insult by Major Saint A. D. Balcombe, the editor of a newspaper called the *Republican*, led the diminutive Rosewater to attack Balcombe with a rawhide whip on Douglas Street; on another occasion, "that pestiferous little cus," as a rival newspaper called him, was assaulted by a 250-pound blacksmith hired by a disgruntled saloonkeeper, an event nearly leading to his demise in which he sustained severe head injuries. Undaunted, the *Bee* attacked corruption in the Post Office, the telegraph industry, and the railroads and denounced politicians' looting of the Nebraska treasury. It supported progressive issues such as compulsory public education and direct election of senators, but it opposed woman suffrage. By the late nineteenth century, the *Bee* was the leading Republican paper in the Midwest.

In 1896, at a meeting of the Republican Bi-Metallic League, Rosewater challenged 36-year-old Nebraska congressman William Jennings Bryan to a debate over the issue of free silver; in May he and Bryan spoke for hours in St. Louis before the Republican National Convention. Afterward, Bryan continued on his way to Chicago to give his celebrated "Cross of Gold" speech in favor of free silver and to receive the Democratic presidential nomination; Rosewater went back to Omaha and the *Bee*.

As a leading journalist and regional political figure, Rosewater was on speaking terms with all the presidents for half a century; he served on the Republican National Committee and was prime organizer for the Trans-Mississippi Exposition of 1898 in Omaha. Twice he ran, unsuccessfully, for the U.S. Senate. He died sitting at the back of a courtroom in the *Bee* building, having passed away of natural causes, "his Panama hat . . . resting lightly on his head."

"He was very combative and exceptionally independent, not infrequently bolting party nominations; his assaults upon politicians and 'interests' were often severe," wrote the *Springfield Republican* upon his death. He exemplified the pragmatism, public-mindedness, and pugnacious vigor of mid-nineteenth-century immigrant America.

• Rosewater's papers, more than 4,000 items (including documents related to American telegraphy, the history of the territory and state of Nebraska, and the growth of the Republican party after the Civil War, as well as letters and diaries), are in the collection of the American Jewish Archives at Hebrew Union College in Cincinnati, Ohio. His son Victor's unpublished biography, *The Life and Times of Edward Rosewater*, also housed in the American Jewish Archives, is an invaluable source of descriptive and biographical material, including letter and diary extracts quoted in the text. See also Harry Simonhoff, *Jewish Participants in the Civil War* (1963);

The Universal Jewish Encyclopedia (1943); and *Encyclopedia Judaica* (1971). An obituary is in the *Omaha Daily Bee*, 1, 2 Sept. 1906.

DAVID HELLERSTEIN

ROSOLINO, Frank (20 Aug. 1926–26 Nov. 1978), jazz musician, was born in Detroit, Michigan, the son of Vittorio Rosolino, an autoworker and amateur musician, and Rose Pino. His father taught him the mandolin and guitar and encouraged him to take up the accordion, but at age twelve he settled on the trombone. Not knowing what to do and not having a teacher, the young Rosolino practiced by imitating the exercises that he heard his older brother play on the violin. "Of course, I was stumbling all over the place," he later reflected, "but I was also developing my ears, my embouchure, and my tongue" (Underwood, p. 19). Unwittingly, he was learning to get around quickly on his horn.

As a student at Miller High School, Rosolino jammed after hours at clubs in Detroit, until his graduation in 1944, when, at the age of eighteen, he went into the service. For the next two years he played with army bands (where he finally learned to read music) in the United States and the Philippines. Back in civilian life, he was a member of the Bob Chester Band (1946–1947) and then worked successively with Glen Gray (1947), Gene Krupa (1948–1949), Tony Pastor (1949), Herbie Fields (1950), and Georgie Auld (1951). Rosolino had his own group in Detroit in 1952, until he joined the Stan Kenton Orchestra from 1952 to 1954. In the meantime, he married the singer Jeanne Smith in 1949. They had two children and divorced in 1955.

Having established himself as one of the top bebop soloists, Rosolino now based himself in the Los Angeles area, spending 1954 to 1960 with the Lighthouse All Stars, and 1962 to 1964 with Don Trenner's house band on the "Steve Allen Show," all the while becoming increasingly active as a Hollywood studio musician. In the late 1960s and early 1970s he returned to live performances, serving as a featured soloist with Supersax, touring with Benny Carter and Quincy Jones, and performing in Europe with trumpeter Conte Candoli.

"One of the finest trombone players in the history of the instrument, [Rosolino] had a superb tone, total facility, a deep Italianate lyricism, and rich invention," wrote jazz critic Gene Lees (p. 43). The validity of this opinion can be confirmed on nearly every Rosolino recording. Sheer high spirits pervade most of these, and good examples can be found in "Linda" (1954), "I'm Going to Sit Right Down" (1954), and "Frankly Speaking" (1952). Mixed note values, varied accent placement, and a wide range characterize his inventive solos in these and other pieces. On listening closely or, better yet, after transcribing one of his solos, one sees how well organized a player he is. He creates rococo complications and then resolves them neatly. On "*The Things We Did Last Summer*" and "Doxy" (both 1956) he shows great versatility; the former he plays muted

in a manner reminiscent of J. J. Johnson but with a more vocal quality, while on the latter he displays enough diversity to bring off the entire piece with the support of a rhythm section only.

Rosolino's versatility and diversity also serve him well at slower tempos and on pieces that are not usually considered bebop. His "Embraceable You" (1954) is sweet, emotional, and straightforward. "There's No You" and "Moonlight in Vermont" (both 1955) are similarly evocative and, although fast, not relentless. He makes his pyrotechnics all the more astonishing by holding them in check in numbers such as "Round Midnight" and "Who Can I Turn To?" (both 1976). Few musicians attempt Thelonious Monk's unusual pieces, but Rosolino takes up "Ruby, My Dear" (1956) and even improvises on it with memorable results.

A vocal quality is never far from Rosolino's playing, and he frequently put down his instrument to sing. Beginning with his time in the Krupa band, he was in demand almost as much for his bop vocals as for his trombone playing. In 1949 he sang an amusing scat solo on "Lemon Drop" that earned him the nickname "Lemon Drop Kid." He went on to record vocals on Stan Kenton's version of "Pennies from Heaven" (1954) and his own "Conversation" (1976). At a 1978 workshop sponsored by the International Trombone Association, his singing of "Love for Sale" got almost as enthusiastic a response as his trombone playing.

As a clinician for the Conn Corporation, Rosolino frequently appeared at workshops and clinics, where he would tell students to "be aware that technique is one thing, and how you use it is another. . . . Just as you have to learn how to walk before you can run, so you have to start out learning melodies, developing an ear, and then building from there" (Underwood, p. 44). He also advised taking every opportunity to play and to listen. Overall, though, he most frequently homilized about the means and ends of performing. "It's got to come from the soul," he would say. "It's not just sliding the horn and playing anything that comes along. It's taste. It's thought. It's feeling. It has to mean something every time you play" (Underwood, p. 44).

Rosolino's suicide in Los Angeles at the age of fifty-two took friends, family, and fans by surprise. He was at the top of his craft and, having outlasted the initial period of rock 'n' roll, was doing well financially, with plenty of work on his calendar. The coroner reported no significant amount of alcohol or drugs in his system, and detectives could find no evidence of foul play. It must have been the combination of his mercurial, impulsive nature and the proximity of a handgun.

However, Rosolino's end does not obscure his achievements as one of the outstanding brass players of the twentieth century. He entered the music world as the Swing Era gave way to the bop style, when trombone players initially had trouble keeping up with the manic tempos set by saxophonists and trumpeters. The sedate style of Tommy Dorsey, Benny Morton, Jack Teagarden, and others did not fit the energetic music of Charlie Parker and Dizzy Gillespie. Rosolino (along with Bill Harris and J. J. Johnson) developed a fluid technique that secured a place for the trombone as a solo instrument in the new musical order. As a memorial to him the International Trombone Association established the Frank Rosolino Jazz Award in 1979, and it has become one of the most prestigious prizes in the brass world.

• A critical assessment of his music and influence can be found in Gene Lees, "Why?" *International Trombone Association Journal* 13, no. 1 (1985): 43–46. Rosolino speaks briefly for himself in Ira Gitler, *Swing to Bop* (1985), pp. 140 and 215, and at length in Lee Underwood, "Frank Rosolino: Conversation with the Master," *Down Beat*, 17 Nov. 1977, pp. 18–19 and 44–46. Robert L. Machado, *Basic Discography of Frank Rosolino* (1987), is a useful guide to Rosolino's numerous recordings both as a leader and sideman. Among the best of these recordings are *The Frank Rosolino Quartet* (DeeGee 4012 [1952]), *Stan Kenton Presents the Frank Rosolino Sextet* (Capitol T6507 [1954]), *I Play Trombone* (Bethlehem 26 [1956]), *Turn Me Loose!* (Reprise 96016 [1961]), and *Thinking about You* (Sackville 2015 [1976]). Obituaries are in *Down Beat*, 25 Jan. 1979, p. 10, and *Jazz Journal International* 32, no. 2 (1979): 22.

MICHAEL MECKNA

ROSS, Alexander (2 Nov. 1782–23 Oct. 1856), fur trader, explorer, and historian, was born in the Highlands parish of Dyke, county of Nairnshire, Scotland. Neither Ross's own writings nor those of his biographers relate any details about his parents other than the fact they were farmers; even their names are unmentioned. Little is known about Ross's early years. He grew up in the Presbyterian faith and had acquired sufficient education to become a rural schoolteacher by the time he was twenty. In 1804 a family quarrel caused Ross to leave his parents' home; he emigrated to North America later that year.

Teaching school for the next five years, first in Lower and then in Upper Canada (in Glengarry County), Ross became acquainted with Scots-Canadian Alexander McKay, a veteran fur trader of the Montreal-based North West Company, which proved important to Ross's future. In 1810 McKay suggested Ross for a clerkship with American John Jacob Astor's new Pacific Fur Company venture; Ross obtained the position. In September 1810 Ross, along with a number of other Canadians hired by Astor (including McKay), sailed from New York for the mouth of the Columbia River. He spent the next fifteen years in the Far West, participating in the initial Euro-American penetration and settlement of the region. Ross devoted the last decade of his life to sharing the experiences of that time with the public, writing what became classic accounts of the fur-trade era.

The six-month voyage of the ill-starred *Tonquin* to the Columbia, marked by bitter feuding between Astor's Canadian partners and employees and the ship's obdurate Captain Jonathan Thorn, was subsequently described by Ross and other authors (foremost among them Washington Irving). Ross, whom Thorn contemptuously referred to as one of "the scribbling clerks," began his writing career during the cruise. A close observer of Hawaiian society during the ship's visit to the islands, he later composed a brief but valuable account of the native culture as it was shortly before the arrival of Protestant missionaries. Arriving in March 1811 at the mouth of the Columbia River, Ross helped build Fort Astoria, the first American settlement on the Pacific Coast. Later that summer, Ross and eight other Astorians ascended the Columbia several hundred miles to examine the unknown semiarid interior region and establish trading relations with the Indians. On a "barren and dreary" terrace overlooking the mouth of the Okanogan River, in what is now north-central Washington, Ross and his companions built a "small dwelling-house . . . constructed of driftwood." Left in charge of the isolated trading post, Ross spent the winter there alone except for his pet dog and occasional visits by local Indians. In 1813 he took an Okanogan woman named Sarah (or Sally) as his wife; they had at least twelve children who lived to adulthood. During his several years at Fort Okanogan, Ross proved himself a steady leader, a skilled negotiator, and a keen observer of native customs.

The forced sale of Astor's Pacific Fur Company enterprise to representatives of the North West Company during the War of 1812 ended the American presence in the Pacific Northwest for years. Like many fellow Astorians from Canada, Ross joined the North West Company. Promoted to second-in-command of Fort George (formerly Astoria) in 1816, Ross assumed command of Fort Kamloops (on the Thompson River, in present-day British Columbia) the next year.

In 1818 Ross assisted his friend and mentor Donald McKenzie in building Fort Nez Percés near the confluence of the Columbia and the Walla Walla rivers. Ross remained at that strategic trading post as chief trader for five years, continuing to serve in this important capacity after the 1821 merger of the North West Company with the Hudson's Bay Company (HBC).

In 1823, concerned for his health and his children's education, Ross resigned his position. He had barely begun the overland return trip to Canada when a letter from HBC governor George Simpson persuaded Ross to remain in the region for another year, as head of the Snake Country Brigade. The annual brigade's purpose was to explore and trap out the beaver streams on the southeastern periphery of the company's Columbia River territory. Ross and his party left Flathead Post (near present-day Eddy, Montana) in February 1824. This challenging expedition—bedeviled by mutinous trappers, Blackfoot raiding parties, and deep snows (which necessitated hacking an eighteen-mile passage from "Ross Hole" in the Bitterroot Valley through the ice over Gibbon Pass)—thoroughly trapped the streams of what is now central Idaho before returning to Flathead Post.

In 1825 Ross and his growing family left for the east and arrived at the HBC's Red River settlement (present-day Winnipeg, Manitoba), where he spent the rest of his life. Granted a 100-acre parcel of company land, which he dubbed "Colony Gardens," Ross assumed leadership of the settlement's fledgling schools. He rose to prominence in Red River affairs, serving for many years as the colony's first sheriff and later as governor of the jail, magistrate, and commissioner.

During his years at Red River, Ross wrote *Adventures of the First Settlers on the Oregon or Columbia River, 1810–1813* (1849) and *The Fur Hunters of the Far West* (1855), both memoirs based on his experiences in the Pacific Northwest. In them Ross included not only now-classic sketches of fur-trade life but also detailed ethnographic portraits of Chinook, Okanogan, and other Indian groups; he provided detailed descriptions of gambling games, courtship practices, religious rituals, and many other aspects of native life. Ross produced a third history, *The Red River Settlement* (1856), which traced the turbulent political and social development of what is today southern Manitoba.

An 1855 portrait of Alexander Ross shows a man of delicate features. (Ross's muttonchop whiskers may have been worn to conceal the knife scar he had received many years before on the Columbia at the hands of a drunken trapper.) A founder of the Red River colony's Presbyterian church and promoter of philanthropic causes for the displaced Indian and mixed-blood inhabitants of south-central Canada, Ross died at his home after a brief illness in 1856. His wife (known to Red River residents as "Granny Ross" and described by one contemporary as "the daughter of a great chief of the Okinackan nation"), outlived him by thirty years. Of his children, his son William, who succeeded his father as sheriff, died at the age of thirty-one. Another son, James, attended Knox College in Toronto and became an attorney; at some risk to his career, James counseled Canadian authorities against "aggressive punishment of the French" and mixed-blood insurrectionists in the aftermath of Manitoba's 1869 Riel Rebellion.

Alexander Ross participated directly in the early exploration of the Pacific Northwest. He was the first Euro-American to attempt to cross the rugged northern Cascade Range from the Columbia River to Puget Sound. However, it was as the witness to an era that Ross earned prominence. The acerbic George Simpson, in a typical fit of ill temper, once decried Ross's "empty-headed" official HBC reports as "full of bombast and marvelous nonsense"; later, a few historians criticized the "censorious Ross" for giving undue vent to prejudice and personal rancor in his historical writings. Although Ross on occasion dipped his pen in vitriol, these harsh judgments fall far wide of the mark. Historians of the Far West have come to regard Ross's work with respect. Generally objective and accurate, each of Ross's books rises well above a raconteur's simple firsthand account. Containing valuable descriptions of both native cultures and fur-trade society (colored though they are by the ethnic biases of a Victorian-era writer), Alexander Ross's lively and penetrating writings are, as he himself declared, "no armchair narrative."

• The Hudson's Bay Company Archives, in Winnipeg, hold some official Ross correspondence as well as the original copy of his 1824 Snake Country Brigade journal (an abridged version, transcribed by Agnes Laut and edited by T. C. Elliott, appeared in the 1913 volume of *Oregon Historical Quarterly*). Some of Ross's later papers are in the Alexander Ross Family Collection held by the Provincial Archives of Manitoba. Information in that collection, provided by Ross's son-in-law, documents his birthdate as 2 Nov. 1782, not 9 May 1783 as is given in most biographical accounts. However, his personal journals and letters from the period 1810–1825, which served as the basis for his first two books, evidently have not survived, but Cecil Dryden in *Up the Columbia for Furs* (1949) produced a dramatized revision of Ross's first two books that some secondary accounts mistakenly claim is based on the original journals. In addition, the papers of John Jacob Astor at the Beinecke Rare Book and Manuscript Library, Yale University, include an original manuscript of Ross's *Fur Hunters of the Far West*, ed. Kenneth A. Spaulding (1956); it is more complete than either the original 1855 edition or the 1923 edition edited by Milo Quaife. Edgar Stewart's brief biographical sketch of Ross, in LeRoy Hafen's *Mountain Men and the Fur Trade of the Far West*, vol. 6 (1968), is the most detailed available; however, Stewart echoes some of the unfair anti-Ross opinions of H. H. Bancroft and Quaife. Reprintings of *Adventures of the First Settlers* (1986) and *The Red River Settlement* (1957) also contain brief biographical introductions. James P. Ronda's *Astoria and Empire* (1990) places Ross's early career within the broader context of nineteenth-century Euro-American economic expansion and scientific inquiry.

JEFF LALANDE

ROSS, Barney (23 Dec. 1909–18 Jan. 1967), world champion boxer, was born Barnet David Rosofsky in New York City's Lower East Side, the son of Isidore Rosofsky, a Talmudic scholar from Brest Litovsk, and Sarah (maiden name unknown). The Orthodox Jewish family moved to Chicago's West Side ghetto, joining his mother's brother. In 1911 his father opened a grocery store, where he was later murdered during a hold-up just before Barney's fifteenth birthday. The family was left destitute, and his mother had a breakdown. Barney and an older brother were taken in by cousins, and their two younger brothers and sister were placed in an orphanage. Barney dropped out of Medill High School, lost interest in religion, became a street thug, and eventually became a messenger boy for Al Capone.

Even before his father's death Barney, like many slum youth, had street fights to gain acceptance and respect. He became interested in boxing in his late teens, influenced by Jackie Fields, 1924 Olympic featherweight champion. Barney trained at Kid Howard's, one of many small neighborhood gyms, determined to use boxing to reunite his family. In 1926, while working as a clerk at Sears, Roebuck, he had his first amateur bouts, fighting as Barney Ross so his mother would not know. He was a speedy, agile, and furious combatant at 5'6¾" and 118 pounds and became an instant success. He fought two or three times a week, pawning his medals for $3 apiece. By the time his mother found out, he had quit Sears and was fighting up to six nights a week. He developed a loyal following. His mother acquiesced and sewed a star of David on his trunks. In 1929 Ross won the national Golden Gloves featherweight crown and, managed by Gig Rooney, turned professional.

Ross's career improved in 1931 when the experienced team of Sam Pian and Art Winch became his new managers and trained him with Ray Arcel. Ross's first big win in early 1932 over Ray Miller gained him recognition as a lightweight contender. On 23 June 1933 Ross won the lightweight and junior welterweight titles in a 10-round decision over Tony Canzoneri, and he successfully defended his title in a 15-round rematch three months later. Ross got his siblings out of the orphanage, resumed his religious observance, and became a huge hero in the neighborhood and throughout Chicago. Ross's career coincided with the rise of Nazism in Germany, and he became a symbol within the Jewish community, demonstrating to Hitler the courage of the Jewish people. He tried to become a good role model for youth but also enjoyed his newfound wealth. He hung out with a fast crowd, bought expensive clothes, and became an easy mark for needy friends and gamblers. He once kept just $700 from the profits of two fights that earned him $70,000 because "the books got the rest." He ended up losing most of the $500,000 won during his boxing career. He married Pearl Spiegel in 1934. After five years the marriage broke up because of his long hours at the tavern, gambling, and preference for the night life.

Ross moved up into the welterweight division in 1934 and on 28 May defeated champion Jimmy McLarnin in a split 15-round decision in Long Island City. This made Ross the first man to simultaneously hold three titles, although he relinquished the lightweight crown because he couldn't make the weight. McLarnin won a fierce rematch in New York on 17 September with a hotly contested split decision. Their third championship contest occurred on 28 May 1935 at the Polo Grounds in front of 60,000 spectators. Ross won a 15-round decision despite a broken thumb. He thereafter relinquished the junior welterweight crown.

Ross successfully defended his welterweight title in 1936 against Izzy Jannazzo and in 1937, despite breaking his right thumb, defended against future champion Ceferino Garcia. However, on 31 May 1938 he was defeated by featherweight champion Henry Armstrong in 15 rounds. Armstrong cut him up badly, and Ross's handlers wanted him to give up in the twelfth, but he refused and stayed on his feet, maintaining his record of having never been knocked down. Ross immediately retired and with his $62,000 purse opened up a cocktail lounge to capitalize on his fame. He also authored a teaching manual, *Fundamentals of Boxing* (1942).

In 1942 Ross enlisted in the marines despite being overage and volunteered for combat. On Guadalcanal on 19 November his scouting patrol encountered the enemy, and the ensuing thirteen-hour battle ended with Ross the only man able to fire a weapon. He was awarded the Silver Star and a battlefield promotion.

Sergeant Ross returned home suffering from wounds and malaria. He became addicted to morphine and in four years spent $250,000 on drugs, which caused the breakup of his 1942 marriage to showgirl Catherine Howlett. In 1946 he underwent a cure at the Lexington (Ky.) Public Health Service Hospital and in 1948 remarried his wife. Ross had no children of his own in either marriage; Catherine had one daughter.

Ross's youth was the subject of John Garfield's outstanding film *Body and Soul* (1947), fictionalized once his addiction became public knowledge. Ross had to sue to collect $50,000 for the story. His escape from drug addiction was the subject of the motion picture *Monkey on My Back* (1957). After his cure Ross worked in public relations, ran a recreation program for Milton Blackstone's shipyard at Newburgh, New York, and was a speaker on drugs. He was respected for his courage and loyalty to his friends and was greatly mourned at his untimely death in Chicago from throat cancer. A member of the Boxing Hall of Fame (1956), with a career record of 74–4–3 (1 no decision) and 24 knockouts, he was rated by Nat Fleischer, founder of *Ring* magazine, as one of the best ten lightweights and welterweights of all time and by boxing historian Bert Sugar as the fourteenth best fighter ever.

• The principal source for Ross is Barney Ross and Martin Abrahamson, *No Man Stands Alone: The True Story of Barney Ross* (1957). See also Harold U. Ribalow, *The Jew in American Sport* (1955), and Ira Berkow, *Maxwell Street* (1977), which emphasizes living conditions in the old Jewish slum. To place Ross's career in the context of the Jewish-American experience, see Steven A. Riess, "A Fighting Chance: The Jewish-American Boxing Experience, 1890–1940," *American Jewish History* 74 (Mar. 1985): 223–54; and Peter Levine, *Ellis Island to Ebbets Field: Sport and the American Jewish Experience* (1992). For Ross's boxing record, see *The Ring Record Book and Boxing Encyclopedia* (1984), and Bert R. Sugar, *The 100 Greatest Boxers of All Time* (1984). For obituaries see the *New York Times*, 19 Jan. 1967, and the Chicago press, including the *Chicago Tribune*, 19 Jan. 1967, and the *Chicago Sun-Times*, 19 and 20 Jan. 1967, which gave his death major coverage.

STEVEN A. RIESS

ROSS, Betsy (1 Jan. 1752–30 Jan. 1836), legendary maker of the first American flag, was born Elizabeth Griscom in Philadelphia, Pennsylvania, the daughter of Quakers Samuel Griscom and Rebecca James. The grandson of an English carpenter who had migrated to the Delaware Valley in the 1680s, Samuel Griscom was in the building trades and may have contributed to the building of the Pennsylvania State House, now known as Independence Hall. Rebecca Griscom taught Betsy needlework, a skill that the daughter would later use in business.

Elizabeth Griscom lived in Philadelphia throughout her life and was married and widowed three times there. Her first marriage was to John Ross in 1773. Ross was an Anglican, and his wife was disowned by the Quaker meeting for marrying out of her own faith.

He was also an upholsterer. His briefly occupied shop on Arch Street is the tourist site "Betsy Ross House." John Ross died in January 1776 in a gunpowder explosion while serving militia duty. Only a year and a half later Betsy Ross married seaman Joseph Ashburn, with whom she had two children. Ashburn was taken captive by the British and died in a prison in 1782. In May 1783 his widow married one of his fellow prisoners, John Claypoole. The Claypooles had five daughters. John Claypoole died in Philadelphia in 1817.

During the American Revolution the Betsy Ross of legend is reputed to have been visited in her late husband's upholstery shop by a committee of the Continental Congress led by George Washington. At this meeting in June 1776, the committee commissioned Ross to make the first American flag. The resulting "Stars and Stripes" was partly her own design. This legend was apparently first widely circulated by the flagmaker's grandson, William Canby, in an address to the Historical Society of Pennsylvania in 1870. Attributed by Canby to his aunt's memories of stories told by her mother, Betsy Ross, the story has been perpetuated in print and illustration since the nineteenth century and is one of the most-familiar stories about the American Revolution. The flag legend is still the cornerstone of the tourist exhibit at Betsy Ross's Philadelphia home on Arch Street. The late nineteenth-century enthusiasm for historical celebration through societies, publications, and paintings commemorating the American past all but ensured that the story would endure. Thus Betsy Ross is one of the most-beloved figures of the American Revolution.

Little contemporary evidence, however, supports the story that connects her to the making of the first official American flag. George Washington was with the army in New York when his June 1776 conversation with Betsy Ross was supposed to have taken place. Rather than a specified design process as the Betsy Ross legend would suggest, flag making was still rather informal during the revolutionary war. Even in 1777, the year the Continental Congress passed a Flag Act stipulating that the naval flag have thirteen red and white stripes and thirteen white stars on a blue background, design interpretations were still left to the discretion of the makers. The first American flag used by the army is now believed to have been the so-called "Bennington Flag," first used at the battle of Bennington in August 1777 and sporting nine stripes and thirteen stars over the numbers 76.

Betsy Ross's documentable experiences during the American Revolution were interesting in their own right and perhaps more representative of the many hardships imposed by the war. Living in Philadelphia, she experienced firsthand the triumph and defeat of first the British, then the Americans as the war swept back and forth through the Delaware Valley in the late 1770s. After briefly attending the Anglican church of her first husband, she joined a group of fellow outcasts from the pacifist Quaker religion. Known as the Free Quakers or the "fighting Quakers," this group supported war against Britain. She lost two husbands to the war, one leaving her as the proprietress of a business. And she did in fact make flags for the Americans, although perhaps not any as famous as the "Stars and Stripes." In May 1777 the Pennsylvania State Navy Board paid Betsy Ross almost £15 for making "ships colors & c." Though perhaps not as memorable as a legendary meeting with George Washington and a commission and design of the future emblem of American freedom, the life of the historical Betsy Ross is compelling nonetheless for its representation of the kinds of contributions that many women made to the American revolutionary cause. She died in Philadelphia.

• Material on the Griscom, Ross, and Claypoole families can be found in Rebecca I. Graff, *Genealogy of the Claypoole Family of Philadelphia* (1893); William Wade Hinshaw, ed. *The Encyclopedia of American Quaker Genealogy*, vol. 2 (1938); and John W. Jordan, ed., *Colonial Families of Philadelphia* (1911). Additional information on Elizabeth Griscom Ross's activities during the Revolution is in Linda Grant De Pauw and Conover Hunt, *Remember the Ladies: Women in America, 1750–1815* (1976); Arthur J. Mekeel, *The Relation of the Quakers to the American Revolution* (1979); William C. Miller, "The Betsy Ross Legend," *Social Studies* 37 (Nov. 1946). The Betsy Ross legend was first widely circulated in H. K. W. Wilcox, "National Standards and Emblems," *Harper's Monthly*, July 1873, and then in such publications as Lloyd Balderson, *The Evolution of the American Flag: From Materials Collected by the Late George Canby* (1909).

KARIN A. WULF

ROSS, C. Ben (21 Dec. 1876–31 Mar. 1946), rancher, politician, and governor of Idaho, was born Charles Benjamin Ross in Parma, Idaho, the son of John M. Ross and Jeannette Hadley, ranchers. His parents were pioneers who went west from New York by way of Cape Horn. Ross's first American ancestors emigrated from Scotland in the 1740s. His great-grandfather fought in the American Revolution, and his father went to sea as a young man, eventually following the gold rush to California. After marrying in 1864, his father abandoned the uncertain life of a prospector and purchased a homestead in what is now Canyon County, Idaho. The town of Parma, which sprouted nearby when the railroad went through in 1883, became the Ross family home.

Ross worked as a cowhand, driving large herds of cattle over the sagebrush prairies of Idaho and Oregon, until he was eighteen. In those years he acquired skills as a horseman and the lifelong nickname of "Cowboy Ben." Even as a youth he nurtured a stern moralism and strong political ambition. He once boasted to fellow cowhands "that they should be proud to be riding with the future governor of the state" (Malone, p. 3). In later years he regretted his lack of a formal education. For three years after 1894 he attended business colleges in Boise, Idaho, and Portland, Oregon, and then returned to the family ranch, where for the next seventeen years he and his brother W. H. Ross managed their father's spread.

Three years after returning to the ranch, in 1900, Ross married Edna Reavis, who was a leading Democratic activist in her own right; she was known to her friends as "Governor Edna." The couple had no children but raised four foster children. The Ross family had by long tradition been Republican, but in 1896 Ross abandoned the GOP because, as he said, it had abandoned the principles of Abraham Lincoln. More likely he was lured to the Democratic fold by the Populist movement and the free silver platform of William Jennings Bryan. Ross remained a Democrat for the rest of his life.

From 1906 to 1915 Ross was vice president of the Riverside Irrigation District, and in 1915, campaigning as the "farmer's friend," he was elected chairman of the Board of County Commissioners of Canyon County, serving in that position until 1921. No longer content with local fame, he developed a driving ambition to become better known statewide, which led him to help organize the State Farm Bureau after World War I. He lectured for it in every county of the state, served as its secretary, and became its president from 1921 to 1923. In an appeal that he initiated to the Interstate Commerce Commission, he won a considerable reduction in railroad freight rates for the wheat farmers of his state. His work for the Farm Bureau gave him great political benefits at a later date.

In 1921 the family moved to a farm in Bannock County, where Ross made profitable real estate investments in nearby Pocatello. His first elective office was as mayor of that normally Republican city, then the second largest in the state. Within less than two years after arriving in Pocatello he was the undisputed leader of the progressive wing of the local Democratic party. In 1922 he was the only Democrat to be elected, and his years as mayor (1923–1930) were perhaps the most successful of his entire political career. Each time he won reelection, his majority was larger. The city's streets were paved, its water supply vastly improved, and its fire department modernized. By utilizing strict economy measures he was able to reduce the city's bonded indebtedness by more than a million dollars.

In 1928 Ross made his first bid for governor, capturing the Democratic nomination. However, 1928 was a Republican year throughout the country, and Ross was defeated by his old neighbor from Parma, H. C. Baldridge. This was only a temporary setback. In 1930, when Ross again won the nomination, almost single-handedly he defeated the well-organized and well-financed Republican state machine. Ross and his lieutenant governor, G. P. Mix, were the only successful Democratic candidates statewide that year.

In politics Ross more closely resembled the Populists of the 1890s in ideology than the New Deal philosophy of Franklin Roosevelt and the Democratic party, toward which he remained aloof in his own state. He was both individualistic and fiercely independent. He placed the farmer at the apex of the American social order and advocated monetary inflation, curbing the power of Wall Street, and an isolationist foreign policy. Great problems of government philosophy and international relations did not concern him. As one columnist put it, he was more interested in whether the water in irrigation ditch 12-A had enough gravity pressure to reach a certain farmer's potato field.

During his first term, 1931–1932, Governor Ross dismissed from state employment all married women whose husbands held regular jobs—a move aimed principally at giving employment to widows and wives of disabled veterans. He faced a preponderantly Republican and hostile legislature that greeted his announcement of a program of rigid economies during a depression with jeers and heckling. In defiance he called the legislature into special session and succeeded in ramming through a new direct primary law and new income and kilowatt tax laws to reduce the burden on property owners. His plan was to eliminate the property tax in Idaho, and he almost succeeded. Ross was a strong executive, a practical-minded progressive, an idealist, and a reformer, but he had great respect for the American political tradition and the law.

Ross was the first Democratic and native-born Idahoan to be elected to three successive terms (1931–1937) as governor. During this time the Republican party declined in popularity, and the Democrats enjoyed a period of ascendancy as liberal Republicans and independents flocked to their banner. In 1932 every major Republican candidate for office in the state went down to defeat, and Idaho voted more overwhelmingly for Ross than for Roosevelt.

Ross welcomed some New Deal programs, in particular the Agricultural Adjustment Act of 1933, the Civilian Conservation Corps, the various federal relief programs, and the mildly inflationary monetary policies of the first New Deal. Unlike many other Democrats, Ross refused to give the New Deal unreserved support. He openly criticized New Deal leaders like Harry Hopkins, Henry A. Wallace, Harold Ickes, and even Roosevelt himself. Ross's independent stance toward both the state and national Democratic organizations led to much open controversy within the ranks, yet he overcame his opposition, both Republican and Democratic, and in 1934 won an unprecedented third term. In the last year of his third term he challenged incumbent William E. Borah for the Senate seat Borah had held as a Republican since 1907 but lost in a landslide.

Ross, the "Cowboy Governor" who was a trick rider, spoke the language of the farmers. He had carried every county in the state, receiving more votes than had ever been cast for any candidate, and was a flamboyant campaigner who could speak on any subject. He often told reporters his hobbies included reading the Bible and public speaking, the former employed to enhance the latter. He had the personality of a man who could be comfortable washing dishes at Ladies' Aid Societies, and he could take credit for the fact that in six years he had reduced the state's bonded debt by many millions of dollars.

Afflicted by illness and loss of popularity, owing largely to the 2 percent sales tax he had forced through the 1935 legislative session, Ross retired to his farm, disillusioned and depressed. In 1938 he attempted a political comeback, winning the Democratic gubernatorial nomination, but in November he was defeated by a popular Republican gubernatorial candidate, C. A. Bottolfsen of Arco. After losing to his opponent by 28,000 votes, he made no other forays into politics. He died in Boise, Idaho.

• The Ross Administration Papers, 1930–1937, are in the Idaho Historical Society in Boise. A revealing profile of Ross is Michael J. Malone, "Idaho's Cowboy Governor," *Idaho Yesterdays* 10, no. 4 (Winter 1966–1967): 2–9. On the 1936 senatorial campaign, see Richard L. Neuberger, "Battle of the Idaho Titans," *New York Times Magazine*, 9 Aug. 1936, p. 20. Some material on Ross is in Merle W. Wells and Merrill D. Beal, *History of Idaho*, vol. 3 (3 vols., 1959). See also John Corlett, "Ex-Governor C. Ben Ross . . . ," (Boise) *Idaho Daily Statesman*, 1 Apr. 1946. An obituary is in the *New York Times*, 1 Apr. 1946.

MARIAN C. MCKENNA

ROSS, Charles Griffith (9 Nov. 1885–5 Dec. 1950), newspaper correspondent, editor, and presidential press secretary, was born in Independence, Missouri, the son of James Bruce Ross, a Jackson County marshal and occasional gold prospector, and Ella Thomas. Charlie's early passion for storytelling was prompted by a maternal grandmother's tall tales of the Kansas-Missouri border wars over slavery. Ross finished at the top of his high school class, which also included the future president of the United States, Harry S. Truman. Ross was a Phi Beta Kappa at the University of Missouri, graduating in 1905. He organized a writing society and reported part-time for the *Columbia* (Mo.) *Herald*, then edited by Walter Williams. He left the *Herald* to follow his father to Victor, Colorado, where the young Ross worked on the *Record*. Returning to Missouri in 1906, he reported for the *St. Louis Post-Dispatch* and headed the copy desk of the *St. Louis Republic*. The association with Williams led to Ross's appointment in 1908 as the first faculty member of the newly established School of Journalism at the University of Missouri, with Williams serving as dean. At twenty-three Ross was already a veteran reporter and editor.

Ross's decade as a university professor was the happiest of his life. In 1911 he wrote a journalism textbook, *The Writing of News*, which remained in use until after his death. In 1913 he married Florence Griffin; they had two children. Ross took a sabbatical in 1916 and worked as editor of the *Melbourne* (Australia) *Herald*. Two years later he returned to full-time newspaper work, accepting Oliver K. Bovard's offer to serve as the first Washington correspondent for the *St. Louis Post-Dispatch*.

Over the next sixteen years Ross developed a reputation as one of Washington's most thorough and thoughtful reporters. A political progressive who believed government should work to create an environment in which all persons could reach their full potential, Ross was a critical commentator on the interwar presidencies of Warren G. Harding, Calvin Coolidge,

and Herbert Hoover. His meticulous investigation of government inaction in the face of growing depression appeared in the *Post-Dispatch* on 29 November 1931 under the title "The Country's Plight—What Can Be Done about It?" and won him the Pulitzer Prize. Ross's colleagues elected him president of the Gridiron Club, an association of Washington newspeople, in 1933, and the following year Joseph Pulitzer, editor and publisher of the *Post-Dispatch*, summoned Ross to St. Louis to run the paper's editorial page.

Ross opposed Truman's candidacy for the U.S. Senate in 1934 because of his old classmate's association with the political machine of Kansas City boss Thomas J. Pendergast. Ross's increasing conservatism led him to oppose much of Franklin Roosevelt's first-term New Deal and to support Republican Alfred Landon in 1936. However, editorial writing did not particularly suit him. Ross began to weary under the constant deadline pressure, which too often sacrificed depth and context. Local politics now bored him. A past president of the Overseas Writers Club, he was alarmed at Europe's mad dash to war and longed to be back in the nation's capital. On the eve of the outbreak of World War II, Ross got his wish and returned to Washington as contributing editor for the *Post-Dispatch*.

Ross's signed column became a fixture for *Post-Dispatch* readers during the war years and included his analysis of the nation's war aims and a major series on peace and postwar problems. At fifty-nine the tall, taciturn, stoop-shouldered newspaper veteran was planning at war's end a more modest work schedule, when Truman, now president of the United States, asked him to serve as his press secretary. The job meant a $25,000 pay cut and the pressure of long hours with an increasingly aggressive White House press corps. Ross had written that the Republic "is in no great danger with the accession of Harry Truman to the presidency," but he privately admitted to his wife, "This man needs help." Ross's swearing in on 15 May 1945 was strongly endorsed by the nation's press. He was widely liked and respected. His intimacy with the president and promise of a "square deal" to White House reporters augured "the fullest possible flow of information."

Ross was a member of the president's "inner circle" of advisers and came to share Truman's animosity toward many reporters. At daily press briefings Ross refused to answer questions that seemed too trivial or irrelevant. He lectured reporters at the Big Three conference in Potsdam and argued that the president's actions "speak for themselves." When the Associated Press, in June 1946, reported cracks in the U.S.–Soviet alliance, Ross castigated the story as "a wicked piece of writing." He told assistant press secretary Eben A. Ayers that his opinion of White House correspondents "would have to be written on asbestos paper." Ross distrusted columnists, "who need to fill their columns three or four times weekly whether they have anything to say or not," and was equally annoyed by spot news reporters and their "obsession with trivia." He waged war against White House "leaks" similar to those he had cultivated as a reporter and columnist.

Members of the Washington press corps became increasingly disenchanted with Ross during his five years as press secretary. Jack Bell, the chief political writer for the Associated Press, noted that Ross "hadn't written a story in years" and did not understand the demands of news reporters to interpret the significance of breaking events. Ross's biographer notes that Ross did not see it as his job to "sell" the president or his policies. Instead, he believed his role was to be the president's protector. The effect, according to Truman watchers Robert S. Allen and William V. Shannon, made Truman even more vulnerable to his many critics in the press. Ross bridled Truman's tendency to "shoot from the lip" by coaching the president to offer no comment, but this combination of Truman's spontaneity and Ross's protectiveness often made the president appear "helpless" at his weekly press conferences.

Insiders agreed that Ross exerted an important steadying influence on Truman and that he worked assiduously to soften the blunt, occasionally harsh language that came from the president. Ross's reputation as a nonpartisan who was only interested in serving the president made him an important player in mediating staff disputes and in mounting Truman's successful election campaign of 1948. Truman's upset victory was the personal high point of Ross's service as press secretary. His work after the election was slowed by arthritis and heart problems. Members of Ross's staff urged him to cut back on his official duties, but in 1950 Ross accompanied Truman to Wake Island for his historic meeting with General Douglas MacArthur.

On the evening of 5 December 1950 Ross met with reporters at the White House to deny reports that Truman had met with British prime minister Clement Richard Attlee to consider the reinvasion of Korea. As he sat at his desk preparing to broadcast a denial of the story, Ross suddenly slumped in his chair, dead of a heart attack. A grieving president later observed that he had lost "the friend of my youth who became a tower of strength." Other friends recalled a calm and often gracious personality. Even critics noted the passing of "a public servant of highest integrity."

Few disputed Ross's intellectual powers or his singular capacity to rein in the president. His predicament with certain members of the press reflected not only his minimalist understanding of the role of press secretary but a more aggressive style of reporting that characterized the immediate postwar environment. Roosevelt's finesse and a popular war had won him a support among White House reporters that Truman never enjoyed. Ross's long estrangement from daily deadlines separated him from a growing press corps determined to uncover the details of Truman's Cold War policy making. His role as presidential confidant and occasional speech writer finally overtook his commitment to the "free flow of information" as press secretary. The consequence was an administration that frequently struggled in commanding public support for its policy initiatives.

• Ross's papers are at the Harry S. Truman Library in Independence, Mo. Also in that collection are oral history interviews with reporters who covered the Truman White House and a candid diary kept by Ross's aide Eben A. Ayers, part of which is published in Robert H. Ferrell, ed., *Truman in the White House: A Diary of Eben A. Ayers* (1991). Also see Ronald T. Farrar, *Reluctant Servant: The Story of Charles G. Ross* (1969); Harry S. Truman, *Memoirs: Years of Trial and Hope* (1956); Robert S. Allen and William V. Shannon, *The Truman Merry-Go-Round* (1950); Lester Markel, ed., *Public Opinion and Foreign Policy* (1949); Francis H. Heller, *The Truman White House: The Administration of the President, 1945–1953* (1980); Richard S. Kirkendall, *The Truman Period as a Research Field: A Reappraisal* (1974); and Bruce J. Evensen, *Truman, Palestine, and the Press: Shaping Conventional Wisdom at the Beginning of the Cold War* (1992). An obituary is in the *New York Times*, 6 Dec. 1950, and appreciations are in the *New York Times*, 7 and 10 Dec. 1950.

BRUCE J. EVENSEN

ROSS, Denman Waldo (10 Jan. 1853–12 Sept. 1935), art collector and design theorist, was born in Cincinnati, Ohio, the son of John Ludlow Ross, a merchant, and Frances Walker Waldo. Through his mother's family Ross maintained strong ties with the Boston area, and the family moved to Cambridge permanently upon Ross's entry to Harvard in 1871. Graduating with highest honors in history in 1875, he returned for further study and in 1880 earned one of the earliest doctorates awarded by the Harvard history department. Under the tutelage of Henry Adams and others, Ross was trained in "scientific history," a methodology that emphasized objectivity and universal principles; he would carry this training over into his later work in design. Ross wrote a number of articles in the early 1880s, and his dissertation was published in 1883 as *The Early History of Land-Holding among the Germans*. In 1885 he was elected a Fellow of the American Academy of Arts and Sciences.

While at Harvard Ross also attended Charles Eliot Norton's lectures and became an admirer of John Ruskin's work. In the mid-1880s Ross's attention turned from history and more directly to the arts. Real estate investments provided an independent income that allowed him to travel extensively and collect art objects throughout his life. He studied informally in Italy with the painter H. R. Newman, and in 1887 attended the Académie Julian in Paris. Back in Boston he became an active member of both the Boston Society of Architects and the Boston Architectural Club. He also began to lend and donate to various museums many of the objects he collected on his travels, believing that original works of art had to be viewed in order to increase appreciation of them: of the 16,000 objects he collected over his lifetime, he gave 11,000 to the Museum of Fine Arts, Boston (for which he became a trustee in 1895), 1,500 to the Fogg Art Museum (including the Ross Study Series—a collection of materials intended for pedagogical use that included drawings, photographs, quotations, and works of art), and a collection of textiles to Teachers College, Columbia University. He collected textiles, ironwork, ceramics, and sculpture as well as paintings; and he established significant collections of non-European art, particularly Asian, Indian, and South American. He had little interest in the historical, cultural, or chronological significance of an object, focusing instead upon its formal characteristics.

Ross's activities as a collector coincided with his interest in design theory. He became critical of much contemporary work and sought to improve it:

In the years between 1890–1900 I became interested in the idea of Design. I had been travelling in Europe and studying pictures, the pictures which were produced during the Renaissance by the great masters, the masters who were very much disregarded and forgotten by the impressionist painters. Slowly I began to lose my interest in impressionist work. It seemed to me so superficial when compared with the work of the old masters. I felt that in [the] unprecedented activity of the impressionists the craft of painting had been forgotten and with it the love of order and intelligent appreciation of beauty. (Ross papers)

To restore "order" to painting, Ross developed his "Theory of Pure Design" in which he applied to art the scientific methodology he had used as a historian. He abstracted the universal principles of harmony, balance, and rhythm and focused attention upon the elements of design: the dot, line, outline, and color. He first articulated his theory in the article "Design as a Science" (*Proceedings of the American Academy of Arts and Sciences* [1901]) and elaborated upon it in *A Theory of Pure Design* (1907). His work in color theory (addressed most fully in *The Painter's Palette* [1919]) was particularly respected by contemporaries. Although his work relied on abstraction, Ross also retained the Ruskinian notion that art should express an idea. Ross had no interest in abstract form as an end in itself and insisted that Pure Design remain a preliminary exercise to the goal of representational art. In *On Drawing and Painting* (1912) he specifically criticized the work of the postimpressionists and futurists. By grounding design in scientific methods, in investigations in the physio-psychological perception of form, and in geometry, Ross hoped to provide an objective basis for teaching design independent of stylistic preference. Further, he believed that exercises in order would improve the moral and civic life of students.

Ross began to teach in the department of architecture at Harvard in 1899; in 1909 his classes were moved to the department of fine arts, where they remained until his death. In conjunction, from 1899 to 1914 (with the exception of 1907) he also taught a summer course that was open to professionals—art educators, artists and artisans, curators, and architects—from across the continent. "The influence which he exerted indirectly as well as directly through his teaching is incalculable" (Obituary by E. Forbes, *Bulletin of the Fogg Art Museum*, Nov. 1935). Ross continued to travel, teach, and collect through the 1920s, refining his theories by keeping abreast of Hardesty Maratta and Jay Hambidge's work in dynamic symmetry. A bachelor, he died while traveling in London.

Ross's collecting and design theories contributed to the development of formalist aesthetics in the United States. He maintained a warm friendship with Bernard Berenson throughout his life; Roger Fry, deeply impressed with Ross's work, cited him in his 1909 "Essay on Aesthetics." Yet Ross's development of a pedagogical method of design—which led to friendships with art educators Arthur Dow and Henry Bailey—suggests a wider sphere of significance and influence. His emphasis on objectivity and universal principles colored not only art education in the classroom but also architecture, museum development, and art historical scholarship in the early twentieth century. His Theory of Pure Design in many ways grounded the more philosophical work of his Harvard colleagues George Santayana and Hugo Münsterberg. Despite Ross's reliance on science for objectivity and his emphasis on process in design, his commitment to transcendent ideas led John Dewey's colleague Albert C. Barnes to criticize his methods in 1925. But as Charles Hopkinson later suggested in an obituary, "his teaching was extremely valuable, for it came at a time when there was little or no idea (in this part of the world, at least) of discovering what might be described as 'terms of Art' and of formulating these terms in an orderly way so that an artist might have an instrument and a language in which to describe nature and his ideas of beauty" (*Proceedings of the American Academy of Arts and Sciences* [1937]). In many ways Ross's work provided a bridge between Ruskinian moralism and Dewey's pragmatism in American aesthetic thought.

• The bulk of Ross's papers is located in the Harvard University Art Museum Archives; a large collection of his drawings and sketches is held by the Prints and Drawings Department of the Fogg Art Museum; a collection of letters is in the Houghton Library, Harvard University. Articles by Ross include "The Arts and Crafts: A Diagnosis," *Handicraft* 1 (Jan. 1903): 229–43. Theodore Sizer (a student of Ross's) wrote the entry in the *Dictionary of American Biography*, which provides a detailed bibliography. For Ross's role in formalist aesthetics, see Mary Ann Stankiewicz, "Form, Truth, and Emotion: Transatlantic Influences on Formalist Aesthetics," *Journal of Art & Design Education* 7, no. 1 (1988): 81–95, and Marianne Martin, "Some American Contributions to Early Twentieth-Century Abstraction," *Arts Magazine*, June 1980, pp. 158–65. For Ross's contributions to the MFA see Walter M. Whitehill, *Museum of Fine Arts, Boston: A Centennial History* (2 vols., 1970), and Carol Troyen and Pamela S. Tabbaa, *The Great Boston Collectors: Paintings from the Museum of Fine Arts* (1984). For an explication of the Theory of Pure Design, see Marie A. Frank, "The Theory of Pure Design and American Architectural Education in the Early Twentieth Century" (Ph.D. diss., Univ. of Virginia, 1996).

MARIE FRANK

ROSS, Edmund Gibson (7 Dec. 1826–8 May 1907), journalist, U.S. senator, and politician, was born in Ashland, Ohio, the son of Sylvester F. Ross and Cynthia Rice, farmers. Apprenticed as a printer at the age of ten, he moved about as a journeyman printer, living at Sandusky, Ohio, Janesville, Wisconsin, and Milwaukee, where he worked as a job printer, first at the *Free Democrat* and later at the *Sentinel*. In 1848 he married Fannie Lathrop, daughter of Rodney Lathrop of New York, in Sandusky. They had seven children.

Imbued with the spirit of the Free Soilers, who opposed expansion of slavery to the territories, Ross with his family emigrated in 1856 to Kansas, an area torn between proslavery and free-state forces. Arriving at the head of ox trains formed by free-staters and bringing with him a free black man named Jonah, Ross at once took to the field to repel an armed invasion by proslavery elements. With his brother W. W. Ross, he published the Topeka *Kansas Tribune* from 1856 to 1858 and in 1859 established the *Kansas State Record*. He served in the state constitutional convention that wrote the free-state Wyandotte constitution under which Kansas was admitted into the union in 1861. He was a promoter and director of the Santa Fe Railroad, later called the Atchison, Topeka, and Santa Fe.

On 19 August 1862 Ross volunteered for a period of three years in the Army of the United States. Active in recruiting Company E, Eleventh Kansas Regiment, he became its captain. He saw action at Prairie Grove, Arkansas, took part in fifteen engagements, and on one occasion had three horses shot from under him. Commissioned a major on 24 April 1864, he served on the Kansas border until 1865. He then returned to Topeka where he edited the *Tribune* in 1865–1866.

The suicide of James H. Lane created a vacancy in the U.S. Senate to which Ross, now well known in Kansas Republican circles, was appointed in July 1866. Subsequently elected to a full term, he served until 3 March 1871. True to his Free Soil philosophy, within a short time Ross introduced in the Senate a blueprint for Radical Reconstruction. Deeply disturbed by President Andrew Johnson's clemency toward former Confederates and the southern states' rejection of the Fourteenth Amendment, Ross proposed that Congress impose "a vigorous system of government" on the recalcitrant states and require ratification of the amendment, and that it confer suffrage on black males. In a speech to the Senate he denounced as "monstrous" the exclusion of a race from what he deemed a "natural right." The southern states by treason and unconditional surrender had incapacitated themselves, he insisted, and no "legitimate local government" existed in them (*Congressional Globe*, 39th Cong., 2d sess., 20 Dec. 1866, 211–14).

As the Radical program developed, Ross voted in favor of its essentials, including the Tenure of Office Act aimed at curbing the president's power to remove officials; this was the act that tripped up President Johnson and led to his impeachment. At the time of the impeachment trial Ross essayed an ameliorative role, successfully urging Johnson to forward to the Senate the Radical constitutions of Arkansas and South Carolina. Ross also supported a motion to move the trial to a later date.

Ross vacillated over voting to convict Johnson before becoming one of the seven Republican "martyrs" who defied their party and voted acquittal. Until the fateful vote on 16 May 1868 he had given colleagues to understand he would vote for some of the eleven articles of impeachment. His vote was considered pivotal, and a crowded Senate chamber, the galleries tense, awaited anxiously until Ross clearly responded "Not guilty." It was the crucial moment in his public career and the event for which he is best known, making him, according to John F. Kennedy, "a profile in courage." He later explained that the independence of the executive was at stake.

Emotions ran high; Secretary of the Navy Gideon Welles noted, "The wrath of the conspirators . . . has, so far as Senators are concerned, turned most vindictively on Ross" (*Diary of Gideon Welles*, vol. 3 [1911], p. 359). Days before the vote he received a telegram, purportedly from 1,000 Kansans, demanding conviction. Ross replied he would vote according to his own judgment. A storm broke over him as he was assailed by his party, Kansas constituents, and a rabidly partisan press. The *New York Tribune* branded him "the greatest criminal of the age." An irate Kansan beat Ross so badly on his return home that he never fully recovered. The impeachment haunted him; nearly thirty years later he published *History of the Impeachment of Andrew Johnson* (1896), a defensive book asserting conviction would have endangered the constitutional separation of powers and perhaps would have led to making Congress "the sole, controlling force."

Ross continued to demonstrate his party independence during the remainder of his term. He voted against a Radical resolution of thanks to the Radical secretary of war, Edwin Stanton, whose dismissal had triggered impeachment; spoke in favor of repealing the Tenure of Office Act, saying it had kept corrupt and irresponsible men in office; and voted against Radical insistence on attaching conditions to the readmission of Virginia. Within weeks after the final impeachment vote he was importuning Johnson for patronage favors of "vital importance to me . . . in consequence of my action on the impeachment" (Johnson papers, 6 June 1868). Ross was at least opportunistic enough to seek a reward for his vote not to convict. But like the other Republican dissidents, he campaigned for Grant in 1868. The following year he held sufficient influence in the Senate to frustrate confirmation of a Grant appointee to a Kansas postmastership, because he was "personally obnoxious" to Ross. He spoke eloquently in favor of the Fifteenth Amendment, deploring the exclusion of blacks from suffrage, and urging extension of the "natural right" throughout all states.

Ross's declamations about racial equality drew a distinction between blacks and Native Americans. In Kansas, he told the Senate, the Indian "in his barbaric simplicity" had resisted the advance of the white man, blocking rail construction and settlement across the plains. "Our own race has claims upon us which the dictates of humanity and the instincts of self-preservation ever adjure us to regard." He called making treaties with "a few roving bands of Ishmaelites" who he believed were of inferior intelligence an absurdity. Ross urged a policy of removal "beyond the lines of civilization" and encouragement of pastoral pursuits (18 July 1867).

When his term expired, ignoring threats against him, Ross returned to Kansas, where he continued his career as a newspaperman. He supported the Liberal Republican party in 1872, joined the Democrats, and in 1882, with dim prospects for a political or business future in Kansas, moved to Albuquerque, New Mexico. Continuing to aspire to public life, he successfully solicited appointment by President Grover Cleveland as territorial governor of New Mexico. Originally a Democrat turned Free Soiler then antislavery Republican, Ross was a reformer in politics and a truth seeker as an editor.

As governor from 1885 to 1889 he strove with sparse success to combat the so-called "Santa Fe Ring" that dominated the Republican party and public land policy, in the territory where 90 percent of the land entries were fraudulent. Bluntly outspoken about his reformist purposes, belligerent, hasty, and guilty of nepotism, he failed to reconstruct the territory or gain its statehood. But he pointed in those directions, demonstrating the need for reform in finance, land policy, and education. He removed the territorial treasurer, charging speculation, instigated a federal investigation of land records, and urged establishment of a public school system.

Ross spent his last years in declining health, publishing his defense of his conduct in the impeachment trial. He died in Albuquerque, his reputation partially rehabilitated as wartime passions ebbed and reform gained strength through Populists and Progressives. His significance lies in his vote for acquittal, his support for civil rights for black Americans, and his efforts at territorial reform.

• The New Mexico State Records Center in Santa Fe has Ross's papers. Also see Edward Bumgardner, *The Life of Edmund G. Ross* (1949); John F. Kennedy, *Profiles in Courage* (1956); Ralph J. Roske, "The Seven Martyrs?" *American Historical Review* 64 (1959): 323–30; Charles A. Jellison, "The Ross Impeachment Vote: A Need for Reappraisal," *Southwestern Social Sciences Quarterly* 41 (1960): 150–55; David Miller Dewitt, *The Impeachment and Trial of Andrew Johnson* (1903); Howard R. Lamar, "Edmund G. Ross as Governor of New Mexico Territory: A Reappraisal," *New Mexico Historical Review* 36 (1961): 177–209; and the *Congressional Globe* (1866–1871). An obituary is in the *New York Times*, 9 May 1907.

JAMES A. RAWLEY

ROSS, Edward Alsworth (12 Dec. 1866–22 July 1951), sociologist and writer, was born in Virden, Illinois, the son of William Carpenter Ross, a farmer, and Rachel Alsworth, a schoolteacher. Orphaned by his mother's and father's deaths (1874 and 1876, respectively), Ross was sheltered in turn by three Iowa farm families. Of the latter, Ross regarded Mary Beach as

his foster mother. Alexander Campbell, Ross's lawyer guardian, shepherded his inheritance, thereby providing ample funds for his schooling.

Completing the A.B. at Coe College (1886), Ross studied for a year at the University of Berlin and traveled in France and England (1888–1889). In 1890 he began graduate work majoring in economics at Johns Hopkins, where his mentors included Richard T. Ely and Woodrow Wilson. With minors in philosophy and ethics, Ross earned the Ph.D. (1891). His doctoral dissertation on the public debt was published as *Sinking Funds* by the American Economic Association (1892).

Also in 1892 Ross married Rosamond Simons, niece of sociologist Lester Frank Ward. Ross looked to Ward as a mentor, observing, "to receive the outpourings of his encyclopedic mind was equivalent to a postdoctoral course." Rosamond Ross was an artist and homemaker who devoted herself to her husband and their three children.

Ross rose rapidly in academia, accepting a succession of attractive university posts: Indiana (1891–1892), Cornell (1892–1893), and Stanford (1893–1900). He was elected secretary of the American Economic Association in 1892. A demanding instructor, he assigned to his students challenging readings such as Herbert Spencer's *Principles of Sociology* and Lester Frank Ward's *Dynamic Sociology*. Beyond the classroom, Ross enjoyed giving robust public lectures and Chautauqua-style extension courses for adults. He wrote for popular magazines such as *Atlantic Monthly* and *Century*, as well as for scholarly journals, and he became known for his punchy, attention-grabbing literary style, the cream of which enlivens his *Capsules of Social Wisdom* (1948).

Ross's penchant for spirited free speaking erupted in a fin de siècle cataclysm at Stanford University. His increasingly progressive views, free silver advocacy, and general outspokenness collided with Jane Lathrop Stanford, the university's conservative benefactor and powerful guiding hand. Stanford president David Starr Jordan failed to mollify Stanford or curb Ross. Jordan initially vacillated but later capitulated to Stanford's demand that Ross be terminated and curtly dismissed him at year's end (1900). George Elliott Howard, a respected Stanford professor, was then brutally forced by Jordan to resign for having lectured Stanford students on the unfairness of firing Ross. Nearly a half-dozen Stanford faculty resignations ensued to protest the Ross and Howard dismissals, igniting national debate about freedom of expression versus the control of universities by business interests. Ross was exonerated by an investigating committee of the American Economic Association (1901). From this incident grew the organized campaign to secure tenured protection for American academics.

The collapse of sociology at Stanford was exploited by the University of Nebraska, whose populist faction obtained Ross's services as professor of sociology in 1901 and in 1904 created a professorship for Howard. The collegial efforts of Ross, Howard, and a young law professor, Roscoe Pound, briefly made Nebraska a sociological powerhouse. Directly influenced by Ross, Pound devised and promulgated "sociological jurisprudence," the assumption that law is a living body of practices rather than a fixed set of rules derived from unchanging premises, a perspective that dominated American legal thinking during much of the twentieth century.

Ross accomplished his most important intellectual work while at Nebraska. He published a revised series of articles as *Social Control* (1901), in which he identified the collective factors that promote societal stability, and he wrote a comprehensive, systematic theory of society, *Foundations of Sociology* (1905). Before leaving Nebraska, he finished the manuscript for *Social Psychology* (1908), in which he extended the ideas of French sociologist Gabriel Tarde. And, meeting informally around his desk, Ross, Howard, and Pound established the topic outline for what became Ross's *Principles of Sociology* (1920).

In 1906 Ross accepted an attractive offer from the University of Wisconsin to join its economics department under the reins of his former teacher, Richard T. Ely. He was appointed professor of sociology and, as the only sociologist, developed course offerings along his own lines. Selected to guide a separately formed Department of Sociology and Anthropology in 1929, Ross chaired the Wisconsin department from 1929 to 1937 and was further honored with election to professor emeritus in 1937.

The progressive political element in Wisconsin suited Ross well, stimulating his pen and public appearances. His popular essay on the evils of irresponsible financial greed, *Sin and Society* (1907), garnered public endorsement from President Theodore Roosevelt (1859–1919), who noted, "With almost all that you write I am in full and hearty sympathy." Ross thus proudly joined a cadre of popular reform-oriented authors, including William Allen White and Upton Sinclair.

Ross was twice elected to the presidency of the American Sociological Society (1914, 1915). As president, he sponsored ASS sessions on freedom of expression and appointed his friend Roscoe Pound, then at the Harvard Law School, to represent the ASS on an interdisciplinary committee that became the mechanism for founding the American Association of University Professors. Believing that sociology should be an active and socially responsible discipline, Ross later counseled his fellow ASS members, "There may come a time in the career of every sociologist when it is his solemn duty to raise hell."

Ross was adventuresome, a well-seasoned traveler, and a world student. He revisited Europe during his first sabbatical opportunity for independent studies at the Bibliothèque Nationale in Paris and at the British Museum in London (1898–1899). Subsequent, extended globe-trotting included China and Japan (1910), western South America (1913–1914), Russia (1917), Mexico (1922), Angola, Mozambique, and South Africa (1924), India (1924–1925), Europe and the Soviet Union (1934), a round-the-world cruise as education director of the Floating University (1928–1929), and a medically advised rest in Tahiti (1932). His travels unearthed empirical fodder for numerous articles and travel books whose royalties, in turn, funded further treks. Popular works in this genre included *The Changing Chinese* (1911), *South of Panama* (1915), *Russia in Upheaval* (1918), *The Russian Bolshevik Revolution* (1921), *The Social Revolution in Mexico* (1923), and *The Russian Soviet Republic* (1923).

Ross's Tahitian idylls ended with the unexpected news of his wife's death in the United States in 1932. A reflective Ross wrote his autobiography in 1936, eschewing earlier views about racial superiority with which he had become associated. He also revealed his gradual and complete disillusionment with religion. He married Helen Forbes, a well-known social worker, in 1940. They had no children. As capstone to his long crusade for freedom of expression, Ross served as national chair of the American Civil Liberties Union (1940–1950). He died at home in Madison, Wisconsin.

Ross was a tireless, enthusiastic advocate for professional sociology, and his work materially shaped the founding contours of that discipline at the turn of the century. His legacy today is the near-universal recognition of the right to freedom of expression by academics worldwide.

• Letters from Ross are in the Edward A. Ross Papers and the Richard T. Ely Papers in the State Historical Society of Wisconsin Library; the Edward A. Ross Papers and the George Elliott Howard Papers in the University of Nebraska, Lincoln, Library; the Roscoe Pound Papers in the Harvard University Law School Library; and the Ross Controversy Papers, the David Starr Jordan Papers, and the Jane Lathrop Stanford Papers in the Stanford University Library. See also "The Ward-Ross Correspondence, 1891–1912," *American Sociological Review* 3 (1938): 362–401; 11 (1946): 593–605, 734–48; 12 (1947): 703–20; 13 (1948): 82–94; and 14 (1949): 88–119.

His autobiography is *Seventy Years of It* (1936). Accounts of his Nebraska work are found in Bruce Keith, "The Foundations of an American Discipline: Edward A. Ross at the University of Nebraska, 1901–1906," *Mid-American Review of Sociology* 13, no. 2 (1988): 43–56, and Michael R. Hill, "Roscoe Pound and American Sociology" (Ph.D. diss., Univ. of Nebraska, Lincoln, 1989). His work in Wisconsin is discussed in Julius Weinberg, *Edward Alsworth Ross and the Sociology of Progressivism* (1972). A bibliography of his writings is found in Joyce O. Hertzler, "Edward Alsworth Ross: Sociological Pioneer and Interpreter," *American Sociological Review* 16 (1951): 597–613. For additional insights, see Committee of Economists, *Report of the Committee of Economists on the Dismissal of Professor Ross from Leland Stanford Junior University* (1901); John L. Gillin, "The Personality of Edward Alsworth Ross," *American Journal of Sociology* 42 (1937): 534–42; William L. Kolb, "The Sociological Theories of Edward Alsworth Ross," in Harry Elmer Barnes, *An Introduction to the History of Sociology* (1948); and Roscoe C. Hinkle, *Founding Theory of American Sociology 1881–1915* (1980). An obituary is in the *New York Times*, 23 July 1951.

MICHAEL R. HILL

ROSS, Erskine Mayo (30 June 1845–10 Dec. 1928), federal judge, was born at "Bel Pré," a plantation in Culpeper County, Virginia, the son of William Buckner Ross, a planter, and Elizabeth Mayo Thom. At the age of fifteen Ross enrolled at the Virginia Military Institute (VMI), but shortly thereafter, in 1861, he saw battle at Cedar Run. At his father's insistence he returned to VMI to continue his studies. Before the Civil War ended, however, Ross saw action in 1864 at the battle of Newmarket, where VMI cadets became legendary for their heroics against the Union army. He graduated from VMI in 1865.

After the war, with Virginia devastated, Ross made his way to California. His uncle, Cameron E. Thom, had set up residence in Los Angeles, a town of some 5,000 inhabitants when Ross arrived in May 1968. Ross studied law with Thom, a practicing attorney, and was admitted to the state bar in 1869. In 1874 he married Inez Bettis, who died in 1907. They had one son. After ten years in private practice, Ross was elected to the California Supreme Court in 1879 for one of the three-year terms specified under the new constitution and was reelected to a full twelve-year term in 1882. For reasons that are not entirely clear, he announced his resignation as a justice, effective 1 October 1886. A number of California lawyers petitioned Ross to reconsider because of the esteem in which his judicial decisions were held, to no effect. In 1886 he helped found the city of Glendale, California, and he became a partner of former U.S. senator Stephen M. White in private practice. Very soon thereafter, Congress established a district judgeship for the Southern District of California, to which Ross was appointed by President Grover Cleveland in 1887.

As a district judge, Ross continued to earn plaudits from the bar for his handling of cases arising out of the 1894 Pullman strike and the Chinese Exclusion Act. The latter brought him into a spat with Attorney General Richard Olney in 1894, when Ross publicly accused the Department of Justice of failing to enforce the Chinese exclusion laws.

This dispute with the attorney general in President Cleveland's cabinet did not adversely affect Ross's career, because in 1895 he was appointed to a newly created third circuit judgeship for the U.S. Court of Appeals for the Ninth Circuit, a position he held for the next thirty years. His tenure on the Ninth Circuit coincided with and his opinions as a judge played an important part in a period of enormous change and development in the West. While Ross served on the Ninth Circuit, the court had jurisdiction over many appeals from federal courts in California, Oregon, Nevada, Washington, Idaho, Montana, Arizona (as a territory and then as a state), the territories of Alaska and Hawaii, and an extraterritorial court in China. Some appeals went directly to the Supreme Court; others were heard by the court of appeals on which Ross sat, although an appeal could be taken if the Supreme Court granted discretionary review. Nonetheless, the Ninth Circuit's decision was important, because the Supreme Court on average reviewed less than 5 percent of all cases decided by the Ninth Circuit.

Even as a circuit judge, Ross continued to hear trials for nearly twenty more years and decided important cases in the mid-1890s. For example, in *Bradley v. Fallbrook Irrigation District* (1895) he struck down California's irrigation law as unconstitutional because it impaired landowners' property rights without due process of law. (The Supreme Court ultimately reversed that decision.) He rejected the U.S. government's suit against the estate of Leland Stanford to collect on bonds arising out of the building of the transcontinental railroad (*United States v. Stanford*, 1895). This decision, which was affirmed in the Ninth Circuit and in the Supreme Court, preserved the solvency of Leland Stanford Junior University, into which the Stanford estate had reposed the bulk of its assets.

Ross's principal fame deservedly rests in his service as an appellate judge. In his Ninth Circuit opinions, he displayed a suspicion of governmental power and a highly precise, lawyerly approach to judging, in which fine details in contracts and statutes were given full force even if they conflicted with the apparent intent of the drafters. His philosophy sharply diverged from that of William B. Gilbert, who served on the Ninth Circuit from 1892 to 1931. Ross and Gilbert disagreed in hundreds of cases, noteworthy because dissent was rare in the federal courts below the Supreme Court in this period. Twice Ross was prominently mentioned as a candidate for the U.S. Supreme Court, once in 1897 when Justice Stephen J. Field retired and again in 1909 when Justice Rufus Peckham stepped down. In 1909 Ross married Ida Hancock; they had no children.

During his last years on the bench, as the court wrestled with problems associated with Prohibition, Ross was in declining health and required an aide to physically carry him up to the bench for hearings. However, even in his last months on the court, he wrote lucid and powerful opinions. On 16 March 1925 he announced his resignation, effective 1 June 1925. He died less than four years later in Los Angeles. One of the finest federal judges of his generation, Ross showed great technical brilliance in analyzing the texts of statutes and contracts. Suspicious of centralized governmental power, he was fearless in guarding against unwarranted extensions of governmental influence into matters of personal interest, from the claims of miners and loggers to those of homeowners whose houses were searched during Prohibition.

• Ross's scrapbook, which contains many newspaper articles and letters as well as an autobiography, is in the Los Angeles County Law Library. The most complete modern assessment is David C. Frederick, *Rugged Justice: The Ninth Circuit Court of Appeals and the American West, 1891–1941* (1994). Other useful sources include George Cosgrave, *Early California Justice: The History of the United States District Court for the Southern District of California, 1849–1944* (1948); John C.

Sherer, *History of Glendale and Vicinity* (1922); the *Los Angeles News*, 11 Dec. 1928; and the *Los Angeles Daily Times*, 18 Mar. 1925.

DAVID C. FREDERICK

ROSS, Frank Elmore (2 Apr. 1874–21 Sept. 1960), astronomer and optical designer, was born in San Francisco, California, the son of Daniel Webster Ross, a building contractor, and Katherine Harris. He did his undergraduate work at the University of California, starting in civil engineering but switching to astronomy and geodesy, in which he earned his B.S. in 1896. He taught at a military academy for one year and then reentered Berkeley as a graduate student and fellow in mathematics in 1897. His teacher there, Armin O. Leuschner, introduced Ross to celestial mechanics and the determination of orbits. In 1898 Ross became one of the first James Lick fellows in astronomy at Lick Observatory, the University of California research institution on Mount Hamilton, California. He returned to the campus in 1899 and was briefly an assistant professor in mathematics at the University of Nevada in 1900. Ross completed his Ph.D. in mathematics at Berkeley in 1901, but his interests and entire subsequent career were in astronomy.

Ross continued working with Leuschner in Berkeley for a year on asteroid orbits and then in 1902 moved to Washington, D.C., where he began work as an assistant in the Nautical Almanac Office. In 1903 he became an assistant, then soon chief assistant, to Simon Newcomb, the retired head of the office, who was working out new, definitive orbits of all the planets, as an investigator for the Carnegie Institution of Washington. Ross was a master of manipulation of mathematical formulae, as well as of fast, practical, accurate, numerical calculations (in the days before electronic computers). After Newcomb's death in 1909, Ross completed, corrected, and improved some of his orbits, especially of the Moon and Mars. He had also calculated orbits for Jupiter VI and VII, two newly discovered outer satellites of the giant planet, whose orbits are strongly perturbed by the Sun, and of Phoebe, a similar satellite of Saturn.

From 1905 to 1915 Ross was the director (and chief observer) of the International Latitude Observatory at Gaithersburg, Maryland. While there he invented, developed, and in 1911 put into operation a photographic zenith tube, which, in comparison with the previous visual observations, greatly improved the accuracy of the measurements of the systematic variations of the declinations of stars. During much of this time Ross was also working part time for the Nautical Almanac Office, improving Newcomb's planetary orbits.

In 1915 the International Latitude Program ended, and Ross moved on to a position as a research physicist at the Eastman Kodak Laboratory in Rochester, New York. Much of his experimental work was devoted to the effects of developing, fixing, washing, and drying on photographic images of stars, and how to minimize these effects in order to measure stellar positions as accurately as possible. At Kodak Ross also began working on optical design, which required much the same mathematical skills as orbit determinations. During World War I designing a large-field, fast camera for aerial photography, Ross invented what later became known in astronomy as the Ross lens. It is a four-lens optical system, which was a great improvement over the earlier Cooke triplets used for wide-field photography.

In 1924 Ross left Rochester to join the faculty of the Yerkes Observatory of the University of Chicago, initially appointed as an associate professor, then in 1928 promoted to full professor. There he repeated, with the ten-inch Bruce photographic telescope, direct photographs of the same fields his predecessor, Edward E. Barnard, had taken years before. Comparing these pairs of photographs with a "blink microscope," which shifts the view back and forth between two photos of the same field, Ross discovered many stars with unusually large angular motion in the sky, "high proper-motion stars." Many of them turned out to be objects with intrinsically high velocities and others, nearby white dwarf or faint red dwarf stars, all of them worthy of further astrophysical study. Ross also applied his expertise to obtaining photographs of the planets, especially Venus and Mars, with the large telescopes at Lick and Mount Wilson observatories. Working as a guest observer, he took these photographs with special color filters, selected to reveal physical features in the atmosphere and on the surface of these planets.

Ross had a five-inch aperture Ross lens of his own design constructed and mounted as a wide-field photographic telescope. With it he obtained an excellent series of direct photographs of all parts of the Milky Way observable from the southern United States. He took the plates for this "Ross Atlas" at Mount Wilson, Lowell, and Lick observatories, because of their generally clear, dark skies. These photographs showed many emission nebulae and dark clouds and structures, the observable forms of matter between the stars in our galaxy, even better than the earlier Barnard Atlas had.

Soon after George Ellery Hale obtained the funds to build the 200-inch telescope in 1928, he and John A. Anderson, who was in charge of the project, brought Ross to Pasadena as their chief optical designer. His first task was to design a correcting lens system, to be used near the focus of the gigantic primary mirror, to remove (approximately) the inevitable aberration of "coma" (the natural unsharpness of the images that are not at the center of the field) that such a one-mirror telescope has. He succeeded in designing such a system, now called the "Ross corrector lens." Ross continued working half time on the 200-inch project in Pasadena for many years, usually spending some of the fall and winter months there, and the summer and some of the fall at Yerkes Observatory. He retired from his half-time University of Chicago position in 1939 and from the 200-inch project in 1942, but he kept an office in the Mount Wilson Observatory headquarters.

Ross was married three times; his first two marriages ended in divorce. He married Margaret J. Benton, of Pittsburgh, in 1904, and they had one child. In 1913 Ross married Elizabeth Bischoff, of Rockport, Missouri; they had two children. Then in 1939 he married Anna Olivia Lee, whose father, Oliver J. Lee, had been a Yerkes Observatory faculty member until 1926. Ross and his wife lived in Pasadena, where he continued to produce optical designs, mostly as a consultant for other observatories. In 1940–1941 he was a Morrison research fellow at Lick Observatory. He died in Altadena, California.

Ross was an unusually wide-ranging research scientist, who made important contributions in many quite different subfields of astronomy. He described himself as a Presbyterian and a Democrat (switching to a Republican after President Franklin D. Roosevelt's successful third-term bid in 1940), but in truth he was a maverick in any organization to which he belonged; his true allegiance was wholly to astronomical research.

• There are important collections of Ross's letters in the Mary Lea Shane Archives of the Lick Observatory in the University of California, Santa Cruz, Library; the Simon Newcomb Papers in the Library of Congress; the Yerkes Observatory Archives, Williams Bay, Wis.; and the Walter S. Adams Papers in the Mount Wilson Observatory Collection, Huntington Library, San Marino, Calif. A few of his most important writings are "Investigations on the Orbit of Phoebe," *Annals of the Astronomical Observatory of Harvard College* 53 (1905): 101–42; "Latitude Observations with the Photographic Zenith Tube at Gaithersburg, Md.," U.S. Coast and Geodetic Survey, *Special Publication No. 27* (1915): 1–127; "New Elements of Mars," *Astronomical Papers Prepared for the Use of the American Ephemeris and Nautical Almanac* 9 (1917): 251–74; "A Wide-angle Astronomical Doublet," *Journal of the Optical Society of America* 5 (1921): 123–30 (on the Ross lens); *The Physics of the Developed Photographic Image* (1924); "Photographs of Venus," *Astrophysical Journal* 68 (1928): 57–92; "Lens Systems for Correcting Coma of Mirrors," *Astrophysical Journal* 81 (1935): 156–72; and, with Mary R. Calvert and Kenneth Newman, *Atlas of the Northern Milky Way* (1934). Two published memorial biographies are by Seth B. Nicholson, "Frank Elmore Ross: 1874–1960," Astronomical Society of the Pacific, *Publications* 73 (1961): 182–84, and by W. W. Morgan, "Frank Elmore Ross," National Academy of Sciences, *Biographical Memoirs* 39 (1967): 391–402. The latter contains a complete bibliography of his published scientific papers.

DONALD E. OSTERBROCK

ROSS, George (10 May 1730–14 July 1779), lawyer and signer of the Declaration of Independence, was born in New Castle, Delaware, the son of the Reverend George Ross, a rector of Immanuel Church (Anglican), and Catherine Van Gezel. He received a classical education and studied law in Philadelphia. He moved to Lancaster, Pennsylvania, where he began his law practice in 1751, and in that same year he married Ann Lawler; they had three children.

Ross was a Lancaster burgess, the king's prosecutor from 1756 to 1768, and a provincial assemblyman from 1768 to 1775. After Britain's triumph in the French and Indian War in 1763, the Crown developed plans to reorganize colonial administration. New trade

regulations and taxes prompted colonial resistance to British authority and generated a revolutionary movement against British policies and proprietary government. Protests defending colonial rights shifted to a movement for independence. Initially, Ross held a moderate position in the controversy, but he became a more active Whig seeking independence from Britain. After the Boston Tea Party and the passage of the Coercive Acts, he presided at a Lancaster meeting held on 9 July 1774 in support of the Bostonians. He was elected to the Pennsylvania Provincial Conference on 15 July 1774 and then to the First Continental Congress. At the 1776 Fort Pitt Conference, he helped negotiate a treaty with the Indians.

In the imperial crisis, Ross advocated "wise and prudent" actions. He wrote the assembly's instructions to its delegates in the Continental Congress, urging that they obtain "a redress of . . . grievances" but "avoid every thing . . . disrespectful" to England. In 1775 Ross opposed Governor John Penn, who argued that a petition to the king was the constitutional way to obtain redress. Ross served on a committee that approved "the association of the people for the defense of their lives, liberty and property" and appointed the Pennsylvania Committee of Public Safety. He served on this committee and on the Lancaster County Committee of Observation. While on the Committee of Safety, he wrote rules of conduct for the armed forces, formed regulations for the 1776 Constitutional Convention, and prepared an ordinance defining treason and its punishment.

As vice president of the Pennsylvania Constitutional Convention, Ross helped draft the Pennsylvania Declaration of Rights of 1776. Ross eventually opposed the Pennsylvania Constitution of 1776 and supported the Republicans against the Constitutionalists. In Pennsylvania politics, the constitution of 1776 became the focal point of dispute. The plan made Pennsylvania the most democratic of any of the thirteen original states. Most governmental power was vested in a unicameral legislature composed of members elected annually by freemen. The office of governor was eliminated, and executive functions were handled by a Supreme Executive Council. The plan provided for an appointed judiciary dependent on the legislature. A Council of Censors had authority to conduct a census, direct the reapportionment of the legislature, and discover violations of the constitution and recommend amendments. Ross and other Republicans opposed the 1776 constitution because they preferred a more moderate system.

The Continental Congress conducted debates on 2–4 July 1776 to amend Thomas Jefferson's manuscript of the Declaration of Independence. Congress adopted the Declaration on 4 July, ordered copies distributed, and called for a mass public reading for 8 July. On 19 July the Congress directed that the document be engrossed on parchment and signed by every member. Elected to the Second Continental Congress on 20 July 1776, Ross signed the Declaration of Independence on 2 August, along with the other members of the Congress.

A major source of conflict in Pennsylvania politics was the various test acts, which sought evidence of loyalty to the constitution, the government, and the war effort. The Radical Constitutionalists strengthened the oath system in June 1777 in a new test act that stated that those who would not take the loyalty oath could not vote, serve on juries, sue in court, buy or sell real estate, or possess guns. Ross and other Republicans recoiled from such a system. In 1778 he continued his efforts to moderate his state's politics as vice president of the Pennsylvania Assembly.

Shortly after his appointment as judge of the Admiralty Court of Pennsylvania in March 1779, Ross presided over *Olmsted et al. v. Rittenhouse's Executors*. The case is important because it raised serious questions about the prerogatives of a state government and its courts in conflict with federal authority. Captain Thomas Houston and the crew of the Pennsylvania armed brig *Convention* seized the British sloop *Active* and brought it into the port at Philadelphia on 8 September 1778. American ex-prisoners of war, followers of Gideon Olmsted, protested that they had captured the vessel earlier, but the jury awarded them only one-fourth of the prize money. The Committee of Appeals in the Continental Congress reversed Ross's decision. Ross defied the congressional decision, claiming that a court of appeals could not reverse a judge's decree in a question of facts decided by a jury. Congress infringed "on the honor and rights of the Commonwealth." The controversy between Pennsylvania and Congress continued for approximately thirty years. In 1809 the U.S. Supreme Court set aside the Pennsylvania decision. Ross died of gout in Lancaster, Pennsylvania.

• Some of Ross's letters are in the James Hamilton Collection and the Read Family Manuscripts at the Historical Society of Pennsylvania. Some papers are in the Clymer, Meredith, and Read Collection at the New York Public Library. On Ross's part in the Revolution, see David C. Whitney, *Founders of Freedom in America: Lives of the Men Who Signed the Declaration of Independence* (1964), and Jerome H. Wood, Jr., *Conestoga Crossroads* (1979). On Ross as a jurist, see Mary E. Cunningham, "The Case of the *Active*," *Pennsylvania History* 13 (1946): 229–47. An obituary is in the *Pennsylvania Evening Post*, 16 July 1779.

RODGER C. HENDERSON

ROSS, Harold (6 Nov. 1892–6 Dec. 1951), editor, was born Harold Wallace Ross in Aspen, Colorado, the son of George Ross, a miner and later a demolition expert, and Ida Martin, a midwestern schoolteacher. In 1899 his family moved to Salt Lake City, Utah. Ross completed two years of high school before beginning a career as an itinerant journalist in Utah, California, Panama, Louisiana, and Georgia. When his ultimate goal, to work in Manhattan, faltered in New Jersey and Brooklyn, he returned west to write for the *San Francisco Call and Post*.

In 1917, soon after U.S. entrance into World War I, Ross enlisted in the U.S. Army Eighteenth Engineers Railway Regiment, which was one of the first units to land in France. He saw no combat, but he edited a regimental newspaper, the *Spiker*, at Langres, near the center of France. When Ross heard of plans to create a weekly paper for American troops in Europe, he walked, he claimed, 150 miles to Paris. The project so needed practiced journalists that the army transferred him without question. Private Ross (he never held a higher rank) contributed to and became part of the editorial core of the *Stars and Stripes* between February 1918 and April 1919. He met Alexander Woollcott, later a writer for the *New Yorker*, F. P. Adams, columnist for the *New York Tribune*, and Jane Grant, Ross's first wife and a reporter for the *New York Times*. In Paris Ross edited and published a book of jokes and stories, *Yank Talk*, culled from army newspapers, and he conceived a plan for American soldiers to donate funds for French orphans. The *Stars and Stripes* was a voice for enlisted men and not the army. When the paper was revived in World War II, it continued the editorial independence that Ross and his colleagues had established.

Ross returned to New York in May 1919 to edit the *Home Sector*, a weekly journal aimed at former servicemen who had read the *Stars and Stripes*. When the periodical foundered in the spring of 1920, *American Legion Weekly* absorbed its subscription list and its editor. Since the Legion magazine failed to revive the Paris spirit, Ross began planning a new publication. For six weeks he edited a dying humor magazine, *Judge*. In these editorial positions he evolved feature sections that later became part of the *New Yorker*. He learned also from the Algonquin Round Table, a group of writers who lunched in the hotel for conversation. Their wit appeared later in the city's newspapers, and Ross recruited his advisory editors for the *New Yorker*—Heywood Broun, Marc Connelly, Dorothy Parker, and Alexander Woollcott—from the Round Table.

Ross had but one publication, the prospectus for the *New Yorker* magazine, and he is known for a single sentence, "The *New Yorker* will be the magazine which is not edited for the old lady in Dubuque."

From the first number of the *New Yorker* (21 Feb. 1925) until his death, Ross concentrated his energies on editing. He wrote query sheets to contributors and letters to writers, but when he tried to write for publication, his words lost their flavor, character, and interest. Ross edited the opening section, "Talk of the Town," with its reports of life in the city, and an estimated nineteen editors and fact checkers read material before publication. Ross's textbooks were Mark Twain's essay "Fenimore Cooper's Literary Offenses" and H. W. Fowler's *Dictionary of Modern English Usage*. He joined the weekly art sessions to select, reject, or send back cartoons for revision or reassignment and to choose the cover art. His distinct contribution was the one-line cartoon. He vetted advertisements and, with the rise in circulation, rejected advertisements he thought were not in good taste. Ross could not articulate what he wanted for the magazine, but his taste and judgment were sure when he had material in front of him.

The *New Yorker* provided an audience for a new generation of writers and artists, such as James Thurber, E. B. White, Peter Arno, Helen Hokinson, and Gardner Rea. While the magazine published fiction by Clarence Day, John O'Hara, Sally Benson, John Cheever, Edna Ferber, Dorothy Parker, S. J. Perelman, Ring Lardner, William Maxwell, Vladimir Nabokov, and J. D. Salinger, its significant contribution to American letters may be the profiles and casuals. These essays defined the *New Yorker*'s objective tone, engaged manner, accuracy in statement, and curiosity about the culture's quirks and fancies. John Hershey's "Hiroshima," an essay of more than 30,000 words, filled a whole issue. In his prospectus Ross promised that the *New Yorker* would be "interpretive rather than stenographic," but he also promised "the whole truth without fear and without favor."

The *New Yorker*'s trained and sophisticated writers and artists pushed the bounds of convention rather than experiment with new and striking forms. In retrospect the magazine in the 1930s seems aloof from the trajectory toward World War II and the social problems of the cities. Ross believed that the world needed humor. However, during the war the magazine printed the story of John F. Kennedy on PT-109 in the South Pacific, and its reporters landed with invasion troops in Europe.

His three marriages all ended because Ross worked ten hours a day, seven days a week, on the *New Yorker*. He married Jane Grant in 1920; they were divorced in 1929, but she continued to help with the *New Yorker*. She arranged for the "pony" edition that went to the armed forces during World War II. His only child was from his second marriage in 1934 to Marie Françoise Elie. They were divorced in 1939. He had separated from his third wife, Ariane Allen, whom he married in 1940, at the time of his death.

In the summer of 1951 Ross's physicians diagnosed bronchial carcinoma (cancer of the windpipe). Radiation seemed to secure remission, but in December, Boston surgeons, finding that the cancer had metastasized, removed his right lung. Ross died of heart failure on the operating table. The death of the apparently energetic and active editor shocked his staff and contributors, but by this time Ross had so established the *New Yorker* that it continued as before under the editorship of William Shawn. Biographers and autobiographies of friends continue to try to unravel the mystery of Ross, a mystery found in his 1,399 numbers of the magazine, in his query sheets, and in his letters. Against all odds, he created an audience for American writers and artists, and his periodical records the American mind in the second quarter of the century.

• The New York Public Library has the *New Yorker*'s archives and the H. L. Mencken correspondence with Ross. The Yale University Beinecke Library has James Thurber's papers related to the *New Yorker* and Rebecca West's correspondence with Ross. The Jane Grant Papers are in the University of Oregon Library. The Katharine S. White Papers are at Bryn Mawr College's Canaday Library; Cornell University's Kroch Library has the papers of E. B. White and Frank Sullivan. Boston University's Mugar Library has the Ralph Ingersoll Collection. Correspondence from and to Ross is in the Marquis James Papers, the Elmer Holmes Davis Papers, and the Janet Flanner–Solita Solano Paper, Library of Congress, Washington, D.C., and in the Lloyd Downs Lewis Papers, Newberry Library, Chicago. Dale Kramer, *Ross and the "New Yorker"* (1951); James Thurber, *The Years with Ross* (1959); and Jane Grant, *Ross, the "New Yorker" and Me* (1968), contain biographical information, but Thomas Kunkel, *Genius in Disguise: Harold Ross of the "New Yorker"* (1995), is most complete and contains a bibliography of autobiographies and biographies of writers associated with the *New Yorker* who knew Ross. An obituary is in the *New York Times*, 7 Dec. 1951.

RICHARD C. TOBIAS

ROSS, Ishbel (15 Dec. 1895–21 Sept. 1975), journalist and biographer, was born in Sutherlandshire, Scotland, the daughter of David Ross and Grace McCrone. Ross spent her childhood in the Highlands of Scotland, living only ten miles from industrialist Andrew Carnegie's castle and near the shooting boxes of British aristocracy. Later in life she recalled her childhood in terms of watching the comings and goings of Carnegie's famous guests and reading classic literature.

After graduating from the Tain Royal Academy in 1916, Ross left Scotland and moved to Canada. In Toronto she worked for the Canadian Food Board as a publicist until landing a filing job at the *Toronto Daily News*. Ross, who would later be considered "New York's best woman reporter," needed no more than six weeks to move up the newspaper's ranks from clerical worker to reporter with a front-page headline and a byline to her credit.

Ross's rapid rise in status came when the renowned British suffragette Emmeline Pankhurst traveled to Toronto in 1917. The *Daily News*'s managing editor wanted to send a reporter to board Pankhurst's train in Buffalo and scoop the rival Toronto papers by obtaining an exclusive interview before Pankhurst set foot on Canadian soil. According to Ross, no one else was available, and she was given the plum assignment. Aboard the train, however, Pankhurst's secretary refused the young reporter's request, explaining that the suffragette leader suffered from laryngitis. Concerned about the future of her own career, Ross wrote Pankhurst a note appealing to the British woman's well-known interest in helping other women. Ross got the interview and earned herself a position as a reporter for the *Daily News*.

Ross remained at the *Daily News* until 1919 when she left Toronto for New York City and a job at the *New York Tribune* (later the *Herald Tribune*). She was one of a growing number of women working at the paper and as a general-assignment reporter had opportunities to write front-page stories and straight news in addition to stories about such subjects as dance marathons and flower shows. Among the famous stories Ross covered for the *Herald Tribune* were the lengthy and sensational divorce of Mr. and Mrs. James A. Stillman in 1923–1924, the highly publicized mystery surrounding the Hall-Mills murder in 1922, and the Lindbergh kidnapping.

Ross's professional and personal life intermingled when, while covering the Stillman divorce, she met and fell in love with Bruce Rae, who was reporting on the case for the *New York Times*. The two married in Montreal in 1922; they had one daughter. After their marriage Ross and Rae continued working for rival newspapers and frequently covered the same stories. The couple made a point of balancing high professional standards and married life. When, for example, they both covered the Hall-Mills murder, they never discussed the story at home. Rae continued working at the *New York Times* and became an assistant managing editor.

In 1932 Ross published her first novel, *Promenade Deck*. Encouraged by its success, Ross left the *Tribune* the following year to pursue a career as a novelist. Although Ross wrote four more novels, her work as a biographer ultimately overshadowed her career as a novelist. Ross first turned to biography when Stanley Walker, city editor at the *Tribune*, suggested that she write a book about famous women journalists. Her *Ladies of the Press* (1936) traced women's roles in print journalism, covering the range from stunt reporters and "sob sisters" to social crusaders, foreign correspondents, and editors in chief. She commented on the accomplishments of women as varied as Margaret Fuller, Nellie Bly, and Dorothy Dix. Ross went on to complete eighteen more works of nonfiction, most of which considered the lives of famous American women. She was particularly interested in the wives of American presidents; she wrote biographies of Mary Todd Lincoln, Julia Grant, Edith Bolling Wilson, and Grace Coolidge, among others.

Ross was also drawn to women who led unconventional lives. She wrote about women who had exciting careers, such as physician Elizabeth Blackwell; the founder of the American Red Cross, Clara Barton; and Confederate spy Rose O'Neal Greenhow. In a compilation of shorter biographies, *Charmers and Cranks: Twelve Famous American Women Who Defied Convention* (1965), Ross examined the lives of Mrs. Frank Leslie, Victoria Woodhull, Carry Nation, Nellie Bly, Isadora Duncan, and others. She also wrote more generalized nonfiction monographs, including *Journey into the Light* (1951), which covered the history of education for the blind, and *Taste in America* (1967), which examined American architecture, furnishings, fashions, and customs. Ross died in New York City soon after the publication of her final book, *Power with Grace: The Life Story of Mrs. Woodrow Wilson* (1975).

Reviewers of Ross's books frequently admired her research but criticized her style for being too "journalistic." Nonetheless most reviewers agreed that Ross's subjects—particularly the women she wrote about—were interesting and worthy of study. Before second-wave feminism entered the academy and challenged the canon of American history, Ross emphasized the importance and complexity of women's lives. By achieving success as a journalist and biographer, by balancing marriage and professional ambition, Ross herself led a life much like those she deemed worthy of study.

• A small collection of Ross's papers is in the Schlesinger Library, Cambridge, Mass. See also Bruce L. Plopper, "Ishbel Ross," in *Biographical Dictionary of American Journalism* (1989). Barbara Bannon, "Ishbel Ross," *Publishers Weekly*, 29 Sept. 1975, pp. 6–8, includes excerpts of an interview with Ross not long before her death. For a discussion and complete listing of Ross's novels see Harry R. Warfel, *American Novelists of Today* (1951). An obituary is in the *New York Times*, 23 Sept. 1975.

AMY G. RICHTER

ROSS, James (12 July 1762–27 Nov. 1847), lawyer and senator, was born near Delta in York County, Pennsylvania, the son of Joseph Ross and Jane Graham. Of Scotch-Irish descent, James received a classical education at the Slate Ridge Presbyterian Church School and then at an academy in Pequea, Pennsylvania. When Ross was eighteen, the Reverend John McMillan, an intimate friend of the Ross family, persuaded him to move to the western part of the state to teach Latin and Greek in the minister's academy near Canonsburg (now Washington and Jefferson College, Washington, Pa.). Although Ross had planned to prepare for the ministry, he followed the advice of the Pittsburgh lawyer and writer Hugh Henry Brackenridge and pursued a legal career. After studying law in Philadelphia between 1782 and 1784, he returned to Washington County to be admitted to its bar in 1784 and then to the Allegheny County bar four years later. With a specialty in land cases, Ross developed a large practice during the early 1790s. He served as the attorney for all of President George Washington's lands in western Pennsylvania and represented such Pittsburgh businesspeople and Federalists as John Neville, Presley Neville, James O'Hara, and John Wilkins. As a result of his connections with propertied men, Ross became a Federalist. In 1791 Ross married Ann Woods; they had one son.

Ross assumed an active role in Philadelphia during the Pennsylvania Constitutional Convention of 1789–1790. He was named to two significant committees: the one that drafted the new frame of government and the one that implemented it. Advancing his Federalist views during this convention, he called for a governor instead of a plural executive, a bicameral legislature, a legislative veto, and a judiciary in which judges would hold office on the principle of good behavior. He also favored an unsuccessful motion mandating the election of state senators by members of the lower house rather than by the populace. Ross, however, differed with other Federalists in supporting an unsuccessful motion that, resembling a provision in the national Bill of Rights, called for removing any religious qualifications for holding office in Pennsylvania.

When farmers in southwestern Pennsylvania remonstrated against the national government for levying an excise tax and started in 1794 the Whiskey Insurrection, Ross occupied an important place during the rebellion. On 1 August he spoke for two hours at a meeting at Braddock's Field in an attempt to discourage David Bradford and his radical supporters from deploying violence, but he failed to persuade them against marching on Pittsburgh. Washington subsequently appointed him one of the federal commissioners to deal with the insurgents. Ross attended the 14 August meeting at Parkinson's Ferry and three days later informed federal officials that radical contingents were still prevalent and well might resort to violence to protest the excise tax. Ross and the other federal commissioners continued to negotiate with the insurrectionists, and on 28 August they reached an agreement in which, for consenting to cease hostilities, the Whiskey rebels were to be granted full pardons and were not to be prosecuted. Ross thus demonstrated his leadership skills in helping to restore order in western Pennsylvania.

Albert Gallatin having failed to meet the residency requirement to serve in the U.S. Senate, on 1 April 1794 the Pennsylvania legislature elected Ross in his stead. Emerging as a major leader of the Federalist party, Ross was, in many respects, an advocate of Hamiltonian ideologies, for he was an Anglophile and favored fostering mercantile interests and westward expansion. He voted for the Jay Treaty, believing that British withdrawal from western forts would help to thwart war threats and stimulate settlement in western regions. Between March and May 1796 Ross helped draft and enact into law a bill that resembled the 1785 Land Ordinance and established ranges and townships as the basic units for western settlements.

Ross was reelected to the Pennsylvania legislature in February 1797. War threats, judicial problems, constitutional disputes, and taxes arose as major issues during his second term. He supported taking a firm stand against France during the undeclared war. In 1798 he voted for a resolution to denounce French conduct during the XYZ affair, supported bills to increase funding for the army and navy, and condemned France for its "red hot leaders of Jacobinism." His assertive leadership did not go unnoticed. In 1799 a ship in Pittsburgh was named for him, and he was elected to serve as president pro tempore of the Senate. To bolster the strength of his party in 1800, Ross worked for the passage of the Disputed Election Bill. The proposed bill provided that a grand committee, consisting of six members from each house of Congress (then controlled by the Federalists) and the chief justice of the Supreme Court, would determine the validity of electoral votes for president and vice president. This bill, after many amendments, failed to pass Congress, however. During the tied election of 1800, Ross received a letter from Alexander Hamilton (1755–1804), stating that the election of Aaron Burr (1756–1836) to the presidency would be "a fatal mistake." Ross, consequently, worked from behind the scenes for Thomas

Jefferson, evidently thinking the Virginian would not significantly alter the financial and public credit system and would act to encourage westward expansion.

In 1802 and 1803 Ross defended the Federalist-backed Judiciary Act of 1801, which, in providing for the circuit court system, allowed for the appointment of sixteen more Federalist judges. He maintained that repeal of this act would place Congress in a position of "complete tyranny" and would violate the principle of the separation of powers. He also argued that the doctrine of judicial good behavior would be voided, for "when parties change, judges must all go out" (*Annals of Congress*, 7th Cong., 1st sess., p. 166). During the Senate debate over the judicial appointments of William Marbury and other Federalists in 1803, Ross, in arguing that the executive, legislative, and judicial branches of the national government were coordinate, supported the Supreme Court's power of judicial review. He denounced the Jeffersonians for attempting to repeal Federalist internal taxes, claiming that revenues from these levies were used to pay the interest and principal of the public debt and that, if they were repealed, "no man will trust the government again" (*Annals of Congress*, 7th Cong., 1st sess., pp. 245–46). On 16 February 1803 Ross presented his Louisiana Resolutions, which, proposed after Spain withdrew the right of deposit at New Orleans, called for immediately taking the mouth of the Mississippi River, the establishment of forts on the river's banks, and parleys to secure navigational rights. These resolutions revealed the efforts of the minority Federalist party to develop an aggressive western program and to discredit the Republicans. While not adopted, the Ross resolutions did lead to positive results, demonstrating to the Jefferson administration the need to negotiate a treaty with France for the acquisition of the Louisiana territory. Acquisition was to assure use of the Mississippi River.

Ross also was involved in state and city politics. As the Federalist candidate for governor of Pennsylvania, he lost in 1799 and in 1802 to Judge Thomas McKean and in 1808 to Simon Snyder. The strength of the Pennsylvania Republicans, the rapid demise of the Federalists in the state, unsubstantiated charges that Ross was corrupt and a deist, and Ross's failure to conduct statewide campaigns contributed to his three defeats. While not actively involved either in national or in state politics after 1808, Ross did serve as president of the Pittsburgh Select Council and devoted attention to the practice of law. He was known for his erudition and his eloquent and persuasive arguments.

Ross's extensive landholdings in western Pennsylvania and eastern Ohio also occupied his attention during the first four decades of the nineteenth century. He profitably sold land parcels in the Pittsburgh vicinity and in Steubenville, Ohio, for business and manufacturing purposes. He was associated with the American Philosophical Society, the Pittsburgh Manufacturing Association, Pittsburgh Masonic Lodge Number 45, and the city's First Presbyterian Church.

Ross died in Allegheny City, which is now a part of Pittsburgh.

Ross contributed significantly to the Federalist legacy. He backed the national government during seditious times, was an effective strategist in the Senate, and promoted western business interests. He was important to the development of Pittsburgh and served as the political and legal leader of the city's prominent Federalist families.

• The most significant primary sources concerning Ross's career are in the *Annals of Congress, 1789–1824*, which contain his resolutions and speeches. Several important letters about political issues are housed in the Darlington Library of the University of Pittsburgh and in the Ross-Woods Family Papers in the Historical Society of Western Pennsylvania Archives. A fairly detailed profile of Ross is J. I. Brownson, *The Life and Times of Senator James Ross* (1910). His legal career is described in Daniel Agnew, "An Address to the Allegheny County Bar Association," *Pennsylvania Magazine of History and Biography* 13 (1889): 1–60; A. B. Reid, "Early Courts, Judges, and Lawyers of Allegheny County," *Western Pennsylvania Historical Magazine* 5 (July 1922): 185–202; and Thomas Mellon, "Reminiscences of Hon. James Ross," *Western Pennsylvania Historical Magazine* 3 (July 1920): 103–8. The central ideas Ross advanced during the 1789–1790 Pennsylvania constitutional convention are assessed in Robert L. Brunhouse, *The Counter-Revolution in Pennsylvania, 1776–1790* (1942), and Harry M. Tinkcom, *The Republicans and Federalists in Pennsylvania, 1790–1801* (1950). His role during the Whiskey Insurrection is explained in Boyd Crumrine, *History of Washington County, Pennsylvania* (1882); Leland Baldwin, *Whiskey Rebels* (1939); and Thomas Slaughter, *The Whiskey Rebellion: Frontier Epilogue to the American Revolution* (1986). Stanley Elkins and Eric McKitrick, *The Age of Federalism: The Early American Republic, 1778–1800* (1993), briefly comments on Ross's Disputed Election Bill. George Schoyer, "James Ross, Western Pennsylvania Federalist" (master's thesis, Univ. of Pittsburgh, 1947), is the most comprehensive survey of his senatorial career. See also the fine study by James Kehl, *Ill Feeling in the Era of Good Feeling: Western Pennsylvania Political Battles, 1815–1825* (1956). An obituary is in the *Pittsburgh Daily Morning Post*, 30 Nov. 1847.

WILLIAM WEISBERGER

ROSS, John (3 Oct. 1790–1 Aug. 1866), Cherokee chief, was born at Turkey Town, Cherokee Nation (near present-day Center, Alabama), the son of Daniel Ross, a trader among the Cherokees, and his mixed-blooded Cherokee wife, Mollie McDonald. John Ross's youth was a blend of his Scottish and Cherokee heritage. Only one-eighth Cherokee, he grew up in the mixed cultures of an Anglo-Indian world where he received private tutoring but played Indian games. As a child Ross may have dressed the way other Cherokee boys did, and he probably enjoyed participating in tribal ceremonies and festivals, but it is doubtful that he ever had more than a cursory knowledge of the Cherokee language—even as an adult he never learned to use its written characters. His world was more akin to that of his father and grandfather, who had come among the Cherokees as traders.

Ross's father wanted his children to adopt white ways, so about 1805 he sent Ross to an academy at Kingston, Tennessee. While there, Ross gained experience in merchandising, later becoming a clerk in a trading firm, but all the while keeping up business associations with his fellow Cherokees. By the time he reached manhood, he seemed clearly set on the path of the white world. He established Ross's Landing (present-day Chattanooga, Tennessee), and there he ran a ferry and warehousing operation. He also acquired a spacious home at Rossville, now in Georgia, as an inheritance from his grandfather. Gradually Ross turned from trading, however, to the life of a planter. He increased his slaveholdings and land improvements and eventually moved to a new home, Head of Coosa (now Rome, Georgia), where the Oostanaula and Etowah rivers merge to form the Coosa. At Coosa, Ross built a comfortable two-story home, ran a ferry on the river, and had slaves working nearly 200 acres of choice farmland nearby. By the 1830s Ross was easily one of the wealthiest men in the Cherokee Nation.

Increasing wealth meant expanding opportunities and responsibilities. Ross's move to Coosa in 1827 placed him in a more central location among his people and only a few miles from the seat of Cherokee government at New Echota. This move reflected his growing interest in the political affairs of the nation as much as it demonstrated his commitment to the planter's life. He had become increasingly involved in Cherokee political activities after 1816 as a clerk to the chiefs, as a delegate to Washington, D.C., and in 1819 as president of the National Committee, the Cherokees' legislature. During the summer of 1827 Ross served as an elected representative from Chickamauga district to the Cherokee constitutional convention and as president of the body. The constitution (first among American Indians) established a republican government and set up a system of regular elections. The following year, at the first election, Ross secured the office of principal chief, a position he would maintain through repeated elections until his death, nearly forty years later.

As principal chief during the 1830s, Ross faced the most critical period of Cherokee history. The state of Georgia pressed steadily for control and occupation of the Cherokees' lands, and the federal courts, although sympathetic to the tribe, proved ineffective. In the famous cases of *Cherokee Nation v. Georgia* and *Worcester v. Georgia* the U.S. Supreme Court ruled that the Cherokees were a "domestic, dependent nation" and that only the federal government could intercede in Cherokee affairs and deal with the tribe. State officials ignored the court's ruling since they knew they had the sympathy of the federal government under President Andrew Jackson. In fact, the president renewed efforts to gain removal agreements with the tribe. In the face of these crises Ross remained committed to retaining the tribal homeland, now much diminished from the ancestral domain. In this regard he had the support of the majority, full-blooded element of the tribe, while the dissenters, under Major Ridge and his extended family, had the following of the mixed-blooded faction. The internal dispute culminated in the minority faction signing a removal treaty in 1835 that President Jackson heartily accepted.

Ross fought the fraudulent treaty of New Echota until the very day specified for removal, but his efforts were unsuccessful. The removal to Indian Territory (now Oklahoma) was to begin in mid-1838. After attempts to remove the tribe under military direction, General Winfield Scott turned over the direction of the migration to Ross, who had finally acquiesced to the inevitable and agreed to move. Under Ross's leadership the tribe set up some thirteen detachments of about 1,000 persons each and migrated across the drought-stricken lands to Indian Territory in the winter of 1838–1839. At least one quarter of the tribe died in that passage due to the hardships of preremoval confinement, the stress of the trip, and sickness brought on by severe conditions. The Cherokees rightfully call it a "Trail of Tears." Ross's wife was a victim of the forced migration. Little is known of Elizabeth (called "Quatie") Brown Henley (c. 1791–1839). She may have been a full-blooded Cherokee, and perhaps theirs was a marriage of convenience, one that would not interfere with Ross's political ambitions. Nonetheless, she and Ross had five children who lived to adulthood.

Ross and his followers did not easily establish their government and institutions in the new land. A group of Cherokee "Old Settlers," who had migrated voluntarily many years before, vied for political power, as did the Ridge party. These two factions joined against the majority party under Ross, and a virtual civil war ensued as party rivalry deteriorated into bloodshed. Peace did not return until 1846, when a new treaty with the federal government remedied outstanding grievances and reconciled the factions. In 1844 Ross married Mary Brian Stapler, a young Quaker woman from Wilmington, Delaware. They raised two children in their splendid home at Rose Cottage, near present Tahlequah, Oklahoma, then the capital of the Cherokee Nation. The 1850s was the golden age for the Cherokees of Indian Territory. Now in his old age, Ross could look to a list of impressive accomplishments carried out under his administration: the establishment of a national press, the introduction of a free public-school program, and the existence of a stable, unified political system.

The American Civil War disrupted the Cherokees' peace and forced on Ross and his tribe an onerous decision. Although the Cherokees had sympathies with the slaveholding South, Ross felt that existing treaties necessitated loyalty to the Union. Again, the force of circumstances and a possible cleavage within the tribe placed Ross in a difficult situation. His tribesmen were divided over the question of slavery, and although Ross was a slave owner, he had the support of the non-slaveholding majority. When Confederate agents such as Albert Pike of Arkansas pressed for a decision, Ross reluctantly counseled his people to join the secession movement, and as chief he signed a treaty with the South. Ross would later declare to Union officials that he had made the decision under duress. Indeed, at the first opportunity he fled north with his family and remained in Washington, D.C., for the remainder of the war. There he tried to convince the federal officials to reoccupy Indian Territory and accept the coercive nature of the Cherokees' defection.

At the end of the war Ross again faced formidable odds and the likelihood of a Cherokee division. His wartime opponents insisted that Ross was a rebel at heart and should be divested of his office. They also wanted the tribe split along party lines based on Union loyalty or affiliation with the Confederate cause. Ross resisted the disintegration of his people and worked to obtain a treaty securing permanent land rights for the Cherokees. Even on his deathbed he actively sought to thwart dismemberment of the tribe. Just a few days before his death Ross learned that his efforts had not been in vain, for the Treaty of 1866 provided that the Cherokee Nation would remain intact.

Ross's success as a leader cannot be measured simply by the fact that he ultimately lost some great contests—the Cherokees were removed, and they were forced into the American Civil War. Ross's leadership should be analyzed with the context of his times and in comparison with the effectiveness of other tribal leaders. In negotiations with the United States the Cherokees consistently fared better than their Indian brothers in the South and in Indian Territory. Such achievements remain a monument to Ross's skill and relentless efforts. Ross was first selected as chief because the Cherokees recognized his abilities and his commitment to their ideals. He was retained in that office because of his integrity and his unending fight for the survival and unity of his people.

• Most of Ross's papers are at the Thomas Gilcrease Museum, Tulsa, Okla.; the Western History Collections, University of Oklahoma, Norman; the Oklahoma Historical Society, Oklahoma City; and the National Archives (Record Group 75), Washington, D.C. The principal manuscripts have been published in Gary E. Moulton, ed., *The Papers of Chief John Ross* (2 vols., 1985). The most recent biography is Gary E. Moulton, *John Ross, Cherokee Chief* (1978). For general works on the Cherokees (including Ross), see William G. McLoughlin, *Cherokee Renascence in the New Republic* (1986); Thurman Wilkins, *Cherokee Tragedy* (1970); and James Mooney, *Historical Sketch of the Cherokee* (1900; repr. 1975).

GARY E. MOULTON

ROSS, Martin (27 Nov. 1762–2 Feb. 1828), Baptist minister and denominational statesman, was born in Martin County, North Carolina, the son of William Ross and Mary Griffin, planters. Little is known about his life until he joined the Continental army. In 1782 he received Christian baptism from a Baptist minister, the culmination of a self-confessed personal struggle with his sinfulness and need for redemption. In 1783 he married Deborah Clayton Moore, with whom he had at least two children before her death in 1796. In 1784 he was licensed to preach, and his ordination to the Baptist ministry followed in March 1787. He immediately became pastor of a church, his profession until his death. He served the Skewarkey Church, near Williamston, from 1787 to 1796, then the Yeoppim Church, near Edenton, until 1806. Bethel Church in Perquimans County, a congregation he founded, marked his longest pastorate, from 1806 until his death. In 1806 he married Mary Harvey; they had one child, who did not live to adulthood.

Ross is best remembered, however, for his interest in religious causes more extensive than his local congregations. In 1791 he wrote a "Circular Letter" that was attached to the minutes of the eastern North Carolina judiciary to which his congregation belonged, the Kehukee Baptist Association. He appealed to the churches to provide adequate support for their ministers to free them from dependence on income from other employment. He touched a sensitive nerve. The popular, anti-institutional mood of Baptists in that time and place rejected any semblance of churches as "manmade institutions," including payment to clergymen. In fact Kehukee, which after 1805 included all the North Carolina congregations south of the Roanoke River, became identified with the antimissions and antiorganization sector of Baptists. Ross emerged as the guiding force and light of the other sector, the cooperating Baptists. Ross's spirit and outlook, while rather bold in eastern North Carolina, followed a well-worn path. In 1707 some Baptists had formed the Philadelphia Association, and in 1751 others had formed the Charleston Association. The first two efforts to organize in North Carolina were Sandy Creek in the Piedmont section in 1758 and Kehukee in 1769. When Kehukee adopted anti-institutional policies in the 1790s Ross organized the Chowan Association, which after 1805 comprised those congregations north of the Roanoke River.

A major animation of Ross's career was the worldwide missionary movement, a concern claiming several denominations' passions from the late eighteenth century. In 1801 he was appointed by the Chowan Association to correspond with the Georgia Association of Baptists, promoting cooperative missions. He was a vocal advocate of missions in the associational meeting of 1803, saying, "Is not the . . . Association, with all her numerous and respectable friends, called on in Providence, in some way, to step forward in support of that missionary effort which the great God is so wonderfully reviving amongst the different denominations of good men in various parts of the world?"

Ross's career coincided with his society's transition from a local orientation to a wider geographical sensitivity with more cosmopolitan alliances, and he contributed to the momentum toward area, state, and national organizations. In 1815 he presented the Chowan Association with thirty-one copies of a report prepared by the Board of Baptist Foreign Missions in Philadelphia and distributed by the peripatetic Luther Rice, perhaps the best known and most effective intersectional Baptist leader of that generation. This innovative report was the work of the Baptist Triennial Convention, the first national Baptist body, which comprised several agencies devoted to missionary, benevolent, and educational services. Ross's actions in spearheading cooperative, institutional, and national (intersectional) efforts presaged future North Carolina Baptist life but drew hostile fire from the Kehukee Baptists, or, as they called themselves, the "Primitive Baptists." They accused Ross and his supporters of not preaching the Gospel, of sponsoring manmade institutions, of craving "respectability in order to be like other people," of being "worldly in character," of departures from ancient orthodoxies, and of being as heretical as Methodists, Presbyterians, Episcopalians, Quakers, Campbellites, and Catholics.

From his early years as a minister, Ross yearned for improvement in the quality of ministerial leadership, seeking not only financial support by the congregations but also to lift the standards for preaching. Devoting consistent attention to a well-taught ministry, in his "Circular Letter" he insisted, "You are to feed the flock with knowledge and understanding. It is therefore necessary for you to be blessed with knowledge and understanding yourselves." His longtime friend and ministerial colleague in cooperative Baptist causes, Thomas Meredith, made Ross's vision concrete by leading the fledgling state convention to establish in 1834 Wake Forest College (now Wake Forest University) for the education of young men pursuing ministerial vocations.

Ross was an innovator, a man of liberal spirit, an organizer of cooperative Baptist activities in education and missions, and a proponent of ministerial excellence. The end of his life, in Perquimans County, came just a few years too soon to witness the founding of Wake Forest College and the 1830 formation of the Baptist State Convention of North Carolina and its statewide periodical the *Biblical Recorder* in 1835. He is justly remembered as the father of organized Baptist life in North Carolina.

• Several annual minutes of the Chowan Baptist Association offer reports and statements by Ross, including his "Circular Letter" (1809) and a resolution presented to the Kehukee Association meeting (1803). For Ross's life and career by a contemporary, see Thomas Meredith, "Memoir of Elder Martin Ross," *Chowan Baptist Association Minutes* (1828). A contemporary account of his role in the dispute between cooperative missionary Baptists and Primitive Baptists is Cushing B. Hassell, *History of the Church of God from the Creation to A.D. 1885: Including Especially the History of the Kehukee Primitive Baptist Association* (1886). Hassell relies heavily on Lemuel Burkett and Jesse Read, *A Concise History of the Kehukee Baptist Association* (1803), and Joseph Biggs, *Concise History of the Kehukee Baptist Association* (1834). The best treatments of Ross's importance are G. W. Paschal, *History of North Carolina Baptists*, vol. 1 (1930), and Paschal, "Martin Ross," *Biblical Recorder* 90 (3 Dec. 1924): 4–5.

SAMUEL S. HILL

ROSS, Nellie Tayloe (29 Nov. 1876–19 Dec. 1977), first woman governor in the United States, was born near St. Joseph, Missouri, the daughter of James Wynns

Tayloe, a merchant and farmer, and Elizabeth Blair Green. She attended public schools and was graduated from a two-year kindergarten teacher program in Omaha, Nebraska. In 1902 Tayloe married William Bradford Ross, an attorney from Tennessee who had set up his law practice in Cheyenne, Wyoming. For twenty-two years after her marriage, Ross was occupied fully as a wife and mother. The couple lived in Cheyenne, where their four sons were born. Their third son died in infancy, and another son was killed in an accident in 1928. Ross was her husband's companion and confidant as he became a political leader in Wyoming.

William Ross was elected governor of Wyoming in 1922, but he died suddenly in October 1924, three weeks before his second year in office was completed. Wyoming state law required that a special election be held in November. The Democrats nominated Nellie Tayloe Ross as their candidate for governor. She did not campaign, leaving that task for her friends and fellow Democrats. She announced, "I shall not make a campaign. My candidacy is in the hands of my friends. I shall not leave the house" (Larson, p. 457). She also announced that she would be governed by her husband's goals and principles.

Ross said later that "as long as my husband lived, it never entered my head, or his, that I would find any vocation outside our home." But she was elected governor in 1924, the only Democrat to be elected in Republican-dominated Wyoming that year. She was sworn in on 5 January 1925, the first woman governor in the United States (preceding Miriam Ferguson of Texas by several weeks). Ross's inaugural address laid the foundation for her two years in office. Her purpose was to continue the programs and policies of her husband; she later called her election "a tribute to the character and able record of my beloved husband."

As she undertook her role as governor, Ross knew she held a unique position and felt keenly the need to "vindicate the fitness of women to hold high executive office." Often in her role as governor she expressed the sentiment that if she failed, women would not be considered able to fill public office. She also felt strongly that women had a unique contribution to make in government. In a speech to the National Women's Democratic Club dinner in 1925, Ross asserted, "Now that [woman] has for the first time been admitted to a seat at the council table, it is not only vital, but highly consistent that her voice shall be the voice of humanity. In effect, she must speak a new language in politics. While loyalty to party is commendable she should never lend either her influence or ballot to unworthy principles or unworthy candidates."

Some of the political issues with which Ross had to deal in her two years as governor have continued to face Wyoming governors since. As a Democratic governor she faced attempts by the Republican legislature to divest her of power, and like other Democratic governors she dominated neither the Republican-controlled legislature nor the state boards controlled by Republican executive officials. However, many of the issues she presented to the legislature were adopted: coal mine safety regulations, a new banking code, an enlarged farm loan fund, and a child labor law. Wyoming historian T. A. Larson concluded that these legislative successes were more a reflection of the national spirit of the times than "Republican willingness to follow Democratic leadership" (p. 459), but he also asserted that "Mrs. Ross proved to be a good governor who gave the state a respectable, dignified, and economical administration" (p. 459).

Nellie Tayloe Ross was deemed by contemporaries to be intelligent, a clear thinker, a good administrator, and a fine public speaker. These were characteristics that she cultivated in order to meet the critical gaze of those skeptical of the role women might play in politics. They were also the characteristics that proved the foundation of her later successful career.

In 1926 the Wyoming Democratic party again nominated Ross as their candidate for governor, but she lost the election to state engineer Frank Emerson. The issue of the appropriateness of a woman as governor was raised during this election, but it was not a major focus of the campaign. Ross lost the election less because of her gender than because of the dominance of the Republican party in the state and concerns about the state's economic stagnation. Before she completed her term as governor, Ross was endorsed by the Wyoming Democratic convention as a vice presidential candidate for Al Smith. Although she ignored such attempts in her behalf, she received twenty-five votes, including six from Wyoming, of the nearly 1,100 votes cast on the first ballot at the Democratic National Convention of 1926.

After her defeat in the 1926 gubernatorial election, Ross continued to give public lectures around the country about her experiences as a woman governor. She became one of five vice chairmen of the Democratic National Committee in 1928, and from 1929 to 1932 she was in charge of the national Democratic party's women's activities. She campaigned for Franklin Roosevelt, and after Roosevelt's election he appointed her as director of the U.S. Mint.

Ross was one of the first women to hold such a high federal post, and she served four successive five-year terms. As director of the Mint, Ross administered eight institutions: the Bureau of the Mint in Washington; the mints in Philadelphia, Denver, and San Francisco; the Assay Offices in New York and Seattle; the Silver Bullion Depository in West Point, New York; and the U.S. Gold Depository at Fort Knox, Kentucky. She directed the Mint from the Great Depression through the Second World War and into the postwar period. She moved the operations of the Mint into the modern era by supporting technical improvements.

Ross retired from the Mint in 1952 and spent much of her time at her farms in Maryland and Virginia. Although she visited Wyoming, she continued to reside in Washington, D.C., until her death there at age 101.

Nellie Tayloe Ross will always chiefly be known as the first woman governor in the United States.

Though she served that role well, she did so for only two years, having begun a career in government only after many years as a wife and mother with no political aspirations. She was thrust by fate, through the death of her husband, into politics. But she did not just serve as a figurehead; she served as an effective governor. Her later accomplishments attested to the strength of her abilities: her success as a public speaker and her long and productive service as director of the U.S. Mint.

• A small collection of the papers of Nellie Tayloe Ross is in the Wyoming State Archives in Cheyenne, and a larger collection is in the Wyoming Heritage Center at the University of Wyoming. A useful biography of Ross is in Mabel Brown, ed., *First Ladies of Wyoming, 1869–1990* (1990), though a better analysis of her political role is given by T. A. Larson in *History of Wyoming* (1965). See also obituaries in the *New York Times* and *Washington Post*, both 21 Dec. 1977, and the *Casper Star-Tribune* and *Wyoming State Tribune*, both 20 Dec. 1977.

MAGGI MURDOCK

ROSSBY, Carl-Gustaf Arvid (28 Dec. 1898–19 Aug. 1957), meteorologist and oceanographer, was born in Stockholm, Sweden, the son of Arvid Rossby, a construction engineer, and Alma Charlotta Marelius. He was a good student in the public schools in Stockholm and as a boy became interested in music, geology, and growing orchids. He attended the University of Stockholm in 1917 and 1918 and received the degree of *Filosofie Kandidat*, with emphasis in astronomy, mathematics, and mechanics.

Rossby began graduate studies at the University of Stockholm. There he heard a lecture by Vilhelm Friman Koren Bjerknes on moving discontinuities in the atmosphere, which he later said drew his interest to meteorology. In 1919 Rossby enrolled in the Geophysical Institute in Bergen, Norway, where Bjerknes was a professor and in charge of a meteorology program. Rossby spent two years at this institute, which was carrying out significant studies on the nature of the atmosphere and its effects on weather.

Through Bjerknes a close association had formed between his institute and the Geophysical Institute of the University of Leipzig, Germany. Rossby studied at this latter institute for part of 1920 and 1921. He then returned to Sweden to continue graduate studies at the University of Stockholm. To support his college costs he worked one year for the Swedish Meteorologic-Hydrologic Service. He spent the summers of 1923 to 1925 helping in meteorology on expeditions by ship to Jan Mayen, eastern Greenland, the British Isles, and Portugal. Rossby received the degree of *Filosofie Licentiat* in mathematical physics in 1925. He did not continue for a doctor's degree.

Through a fellowship from the American-Scandinavian Foundation, Rossby traveled to the United States in 1926 to do research at the U.S. Weather Bureau. While there he published significant papers on atmospheric turbulence and convection and on the dynamics of the stratosphere. He also proposed new programs, but the administrators were not interested in them. Horace R. Byers said that, when he left Washington, "Rossby was literally *persona non grata* to the Weather Bureau and word went out to all stations to that effect" (Bolin, p. 56).

In 1927 Rossby was appointed research associate in meteorology of the Daniel Guggenheim Fund for the Promotion of Aeronautics. Enthusiasm was keen then for airplane flights, because of Richard Evelyn Byrd's flight over the North Pole in 1926, Charles Augustus Lindbergh's flight across the Atlantic Ocean in May 1927, and Byrd's intended program over the South Pole. Rossby's role was to help plan such flights. The fund also established a model airline between San Francisco and Los Angeles, California, and Rossby was assigned to develop an experimental weather service there. He set up a dense network of weather stations by early 1928 in California, which became a model for airways weather services in the United States and was turned over to the Weather Bureau to operate.

The Guggenheim Fund established the Daniel Guggenheim Aeronautical Laboratory at the Massachusetts Institute of Technology (MIT), where in 1928 Rossby became an associate professor to teach a graduate course in meteorology to navy officers. The highly successful course, which soon included civilians, incorporated methods of analysis from Norway.

In 1929 Rossby married Harriet Marshall Alexander; they had three children. He advanced to professor at MIT in 1931. With an interest also in physical oceanography and through acquaintance with Harvard professor Henry Bryant Bigelow, Rossby also became associated with the Woods Hole Oceanographic Institution (WHOI) in 1931.

While at MIT, Rossby published on the instability and overturning in a saturated atmosphere, with a graphical means of identifying specific air masses and weather fronts that is called the Rossby diagram (1932); on the mixing length and roughness at the ocean-air boundary (1932, 1935); and on friction, turbulence, and mixing in ocean currents (1936). Especially significant to meteorologists were his papers from 1937 to 1940 on large-scale circulation in the atmosphere. He developed the Rossby equation for long waves, called Rossby waves, in the upper westerly winds, summarized in "Planetary Flow Patterns in the Atmosphere" (*Quarterly Journal of Royal Meteorological Society* 66 [1940]: 68–87).

Rossby became assistant chief for research and education of the U.S. Weather Bureau in 1939, the same year that he became a citizen of the United States. With encouragement from the new chief of the bureau, Francis Wilton Reichelderfer, Rossby began intensified training programs for the staff. Separately, he persuaded the University of California to establish a department of meteorology at the University of California at Los Angeles, where Jacob Aall Bonnevie Bjerknes (the son of Vilhelm Bjerknes) was located.

In 1941 Rossby accepted an appointment as professor of meteorology at the University of Chicago to head the newly established Institute (later Department) of Meteorology. Throughout World War II Rossby and his colleagues provided an intense one-year course in meteorology to thousands of military personnel. Rossby also promoted the establishment of the Institute of Tropical Meteorology at the University of Puerto Rico, which developed models of tropical weather disturbances.

After World War II Rossby led a reorganization of the American Meteorological Society into a significant scientific organization, and he founded the *Journal of Meteorology*. He instituted climatic and meteorological investigations in Hawaii for the Pineapple Research Institute.

Rossby's significant papers during the Chicago years were on the relationships of temperature and pressure in long waves in the atmosphere (1942), on the basic concepts of the jet stream (1947), and on atmospheric vortices around the poles (1948, 1949). His work, with John von Neumann and Jule Gregory Charney, made possible the prediction of weather by computer that began in the 1950s. Because of his introduction of new techniques and his own researches, Rossby is considered by colleagues and successors as the founder of modern meteorology in the United States.

In 1950 Rossby returned to Sweden to head an international institute of meteorology at the University of Stockholm, which attracted students from many countries. There he established the first machine-forecasting center in Europe, he founded and edited the journal *Tellus*, and he established a program in atmospheric chemistry. Highly respected and at the height of his profession, Rossby died of a heart attack in Stockholm.

• Especially significant papers by Rossby are "Thermodynamics Applied to Air Mass Analysis," *MIT Papers in Physical Oceanography and Meteorology* 1, no. 3 (1932); "On the Distribution of Angular Velocity in Gaseous Envelopes under the Influence of Large-Scale Horizontal Mixing Processes," *Bulletin of American Meteorological Society* 28 (1947): 53–68; and "On the Nature of the General Circulation of Lower Atmosphere," chap. 2 in *The Atmospheres of the Earth and Planets*, ed. G. P. Kuiper (1949), pp. 16–48. Biographies of Rossby are Horace R. Byers, "Carl-Gustaf Arvid Rossby, 1898–1957," *Bulletin of American Meteorological Society* 39, no. 2 (1958): 98–100; R. C. S., "Professor C.-G. Rossby," *Quarterly Journal of Royal Meteorological Society* 84 (1958): 88–89; and Byers, "Carl-Gustaf Arvid Rossby," National Academy of Sciences, *Biographical Memoirs* 34 (1960): 249–70, which includes a bibliography. Bert Bolin, ed., *The Atmosphere and the Sea in Motion* (1959), a volume of tribute to Rossby, presents useful material on his early years, his organizational abilities, and a bibliography.

ELIZABETH NOBLE SHOR

ROSSEN, Robert (16 Mar. 1908–18 Feb. 1966), motion picture director, screenwriter, and producer, was born Robert Rosen in New York City, the son of Russian-Jewish immigrants. Little is known about his parents, except that Rossen claimed that his mother's family was of the "intelligentsia." His grandfather was a rabbi and an uncle of his was a Hebrew-language poet. Rossen grew up in a poor neighborhood in lower Manhattan, where he attended public schools. As a teenager he took up boxing, abandoning the ring after several professional bouts. He later said of his New York upbringing that life on the streets "taught him the impact of environment on character."

Rossen, who said he "always had a great feeling for literature," completed high school in the later 1920s and enrolled in classes at New York University (he did not graduate). He soon became involved with politically radical and avant-garde theater groups, primarily the Washington Square Players. In hopes of pursuing a stage career, Rossen learned every facet of theatrical production: writing, stage-managing, acting, and directing. From 1931 to 1933 he directed an antilynching drama; *Steel*, a play by John Wexley sponsored by the Communist party's newspaper, the *Daily Worker*; and *Birthright*, an anti-Nazi play around the time of Adolf Hitler's rise to power. Rossen also wrote a poolroom drama, *Corner Pocket*, which was never produced on stage but undoubtedly influenced his 1961 film *The Hustler*.

In 1934 or 1935 (sources differ) Rossen married Sue Siegal, who worked for the Literary Guild, a subscription book club in New York; they had three children. His play *The Body Beautiful*, which he also directed, opened on Broadway in 1935. The show closed after only a few performances, but the Hollywood film director and producer Mervyn LeRoy was impressed and signed Rossen to a screenwriting contract at Warner Bros.

From 1936 until 1943 Rossen was one of the studio's most prolific and skilled craftsmen. He earned sole or collaborative writing credits for ten films during that period. His concise, straightforward, often ironic dialogue perfectly suited the naturalistic, socially committed pictures that were the Warner Bros. hallmark during the 1930s and early 1940s. Rossen's scripts, which starred the studio's leading actors, included those for *Marked Woman* (1937), *They Won't Forget* (1937), *The Roaring Twenties* (1939), *The Sea Wolf* (1941), and *Edge of Darkness* (1943).

While working at Warner Bros. Rossen stayed active beyond the studio's gates. He joined the Communist party in 1937—"I wanted to be on the side of history," he said—and he took part not only in party activities but in numerous Popular Front alliances of Communists, radicals, and liberals (e.g., the Hollywood Writers Mobilization, which he headed for two years during World War II). He also became a prominent member of the Screen Writers Guild.

With his Warner Bros. contract fulfilled, Rossen independently wrote screenplays for two films in 1946: the commercially successful and, at the time, critically favored men-in-combat drama *A Walk in the Sun*; and a superior film noir, *The Strange Love of Martha Ivers*. After working as an assistant director in the filming of his own script for *Desert Fury* (1947), Rossen sold the screenplay for *Johnny O'Clock* (1947) and in the process landed his first screen directing assignment. His direction of that whodunit was unremarkable, but he did display confidence and efficiency in the primary aspects of filmmaking.

Rossen as a director next joined John Garfield and Abraham Polonsky to create a film close to their own earlier experiences on New York's streets. *Body and Soul* (1947) was a box office hit and was well liked by film reviewers. It featured strong performances by Garfield (he received an Academy Award nomination) and other cast members, an Oscar-nominated script by Polonsky, and innovative cinematography by James Wong Howe. The film remains one of the best boxing movies made in Hollywood.

For a time, however, *Body and Soul* appeared to be a last hurrah for Rossen. In October 1947 the House Committee on Un-American Activities (HUAC) opened its hearings into left-wing "subversion" of the motion picture industry. Rossen, who claimed to have left the Communist party in 1945 (he later admitted to 1947), was one of nineteen party members and former members subpoenaed to testify. When the first contingent of witnesses—soon called the Hollywood Ten—vociferously refused to cooperate with HUAC and were cited for contempt of Congress, Rossen's summons to appear was indefinitely deferred.

During that temporary respite Rossen wrote, produced, and directed one of his finest films, *All the King's Men* (1949), based on the celebrated novel by Robert Penn Warren about a southern populist demagogue's rise and fatal fall. The film was a major critical success, winning the Academy Award for best picture; Rossen himself received Oscar nominations for best direction and best screenplay.

In 1951 Rossen produced and directed *The Brave Bulls*, before again being called to appear at HUAC hearings. He refused to discuss his own acts or to name names of other party members. The tactic backfired, and he was placed among a growing number of film figures on the blacklist instituted by the major studios four years earlier. For the next two years Rossen anguished over his family's security and his shattered career. His wife later recalled that he "couldn't get a job writing, and . . . if he couldn't write he couldn't live." In May 1953 he caved in to HUAC demands, abjectly testifying and publicly identifying fifty-four of his onetime political comrades. As a result he escaped the blacklist's prohibitions, but for much of the rest of his life he was plagued with guilt and remorse for what he and others considered to be his betrayal of his friends, former allies, and basic principles.

Rather than trying to work in Hollywood, Rossen became a global nomad, cowriting and directing four films abroad during the 1950s. None of the four pictures was particularly noteworthy, and two of them—*Mambo* (1955) and *Island in the Sun* (1957)—reportedly are best forgotten. Nothing, therefore, prepared critics and audiences for his next two films.

The Hustler, starring Paul Newman, a devastating drama of poolroom hustlers, was released in 1961. The film was highlighted by brilliant acting from an ensemble cast (four of whose members were nominated for Academy Awards), a masterly directorial hand, and the stunning camerawork of Eugene Schufftan. For his direction Rossen received the New York Film Critics award and an Academy Award nomination.

Rossen's health was seriously deteriorating when he embarked on the final completed film of his life, *Lilith* (1964), a complex, moving, poetic tale of a beautiful, spell-weaving mental patient and the hospital attendant who becomes entangled in her web. In the United States the film was a commercial and critical disaster, but many French critics praised *Lilith* as an excursion for Rossen into uncharted psychological and visual depths.

By the time of Rossen's death in New York City following heart surgery, he had already signed a contract to publish his autobiography (which he had barely begun). He was also at work on a film, tentatively called "Cocoa Beach," about the U.S. manned space program.

Since the 1970s Rossen's critical stock has declined. Yet no one would deny that nine or ten of the films that he significantly shaped will be viewed and appreciated for decades to come.

• No full-scale biography of Rossen has yet been published, and no personal papers are available to the public. One book and a number of articles evaluate, with varying success, the two dozen films for which he earned screenwriting and/or directing credit. Alan Casty, *The Films of Robert Rossen* (1969), is a valuable assessment of Rossen's film career. Insightful and helpful entries can be found in Jean-Pierre Coursodon, *American Directors, Volume II*, ed. Pierre Sauvage (1983), pp. 322–25; Christopher Lyon, ed., *Directors/Filmmakers*, vol. 2 of *The International Dictionary of Films and Filmmakers* (1984), pp. 465–67; and John Wakeman, ed., *World Film Directors: 1890–1945* (1987), pp. 971–76. Two issues of *Films in Review* (June–July 1962 and Aug.–Sept. 1972) contain useful articles, and several critical pieces are available in the French film journals *Cahiers du Cinéma* (Apr. 1966), *Cahiers du Cinéma in English* (Jan. 1967), and *L'Avant-Scène du Cinéma* (Oct. 1967). The most detailed and provocative books on the blacklist years in the film industry are Larry Ceplair and Steven Englund, *The Inquisition in Hollywood: Politics in the Film Community, 1930–1960* (1983), and Victor S. Navasky, *Naming Names* (1980); both of these works glancingly discuss Rossen's encounters with HUAC and some of his political activities. An obituary is in the *New York Times*, 19 Feb. 1966.

ROBERT MIRANDON

ROSSER, Thomas Lafayette (15 Oct. 1836–29 Mar. 1910), army officer and engineer, was born in Campbell County, Virginia, the son of John Rosser, a plantation owner and sheriff, and Martha Melvina Johnson. In 1849, when he was a boy, Rosser led the family to a farm in Panola County, Texas. In 1856 Rosser was appointed to the U.S. Military Academy at West Point, then a five-year program. His roommate was John Pelham; his friends included James Dearing and George A. Custer. After the bombardment of Fort Sumter, Rosser left West Point on 22 April 1861, two weeks before his class graduated.

Rosser joined the Confederate army as a first lieutenant, serving with the Washington Artillery at the battle of First Manassas (21 July 1861). He was promoted to captain in September 1861 and was wounded in May 1862 at Mechanicsville, Virginia. He was promoted to lieutenant colonel on 10 June 1862 and became colonel of the Fifth Virginia Cavalry Regiment on 24 June 1862. Although his advancement was pushed by General "Jeb" Stuart, Rosser considered his promotion too slow and resented Stuart as a result. Rosser fought at Catlett's Station (22–23 Aug. 1862), Second Manassas (29–30 Aug. 1862), South Mountain (14 Sept. 1862), Fredericksburg (13 Dec. 1862), and Kelly's Ford (17 Mar. 1863), where he was wounded. In 1863 he married Elizabeth "Betty" Barbara Winston; they had six children.

During the Gettysburg campaign, Rosser was with Stuart. Rosser fought at Brandy Station (9 June 1863) and noted, "The Federal cavalry . . . fought better . . . than ever before" (*Addresses of Gen'l T. L. Rosser*, p. 39). At Aldie, on 17 June 1863, Rosser fought his classmate Judson Kilpatrick. After the Confederate defeat at Gettysburg, Rosser was given command of the Laurel Brigade and promoted to brigadier general on 10 October 1863 (to rank from 28 Sept.). At Buckland Mills, on 19 October 1863, he captured Custer's headquarters wagon. On 29 January 1864 he led a raid to Moorefield, West Virginia, and captured a supply train. On 11 June 1864 he was wounded at Trevilian. At Coggins' Point, on 16 September 1864, Rosser and General Wade Hampton captured 2,486 cattle.

In October 1864 Rosser was given command of General Jubal Early's cavalry in the Shenandoah Valley and, prematurely, the sobriquet "Saviour of the Valley." He was crushed by Custer at Tom's Brook on 9 October 1864. Despite being defeated again at Cedar Creek (19 Oct. 1864), Rosser was promoted to major general on 4 November 1864 (to rank from 1 Nov.). Significantly, he was still able to win with worn-out men and horses in any weather during the severe decline of the Confederate cavalry. On 28 November 1864 Rosser led a raid on New Creek, West Virginia, and captured Fort Kelley. His Beverly, West Virginia, raid (6–11 Jan. 1865) captured over 500 prisoners. In March 1865 he returned to the defenses of Richmond and Petersburg. After being shot in the arm on 31 March 1865, he was hosting a shad bake on 1 April for Generals George Pickett and Fitzhugh Lee when Federals routed Pickett's troops at Five Forks. Yet Rosser won the last large cavalry victory of the Army of Northern Virginia at High Bridge on 6 April 1865. On 9 April, at Appomattox, Rosser did not surrender with General Robert E. Lee but instead rode over the Federal cavalry blocking the Lynchburg road and escaped. Rosser was finally captured at "Courtland," his wife's estate, on 2 May 1865 and was then paroled.

After the war, Rosser tried several businesses. He lectured at New York's Cooper Institute on 2 May 1867. In 1868 he worked for the Pittsburgh and Connelsville Railroad, and in Minnesota in 1871 he was an axman for the Lake Superior and Mississippi Railroad. He switched to the Northern Pacific, becoming assistant engineer and division engineer supervising surveys and construction in Dakota and Montana. He led engineering parties to the Yellowstone in 1871 and 1873. In the latter, Rosser's surveyors were protected by the Seventh Cavalry, commanded by Custer, who said, "It seemed like the time when we were cadets together . . . discussing dreams of the future." James J. Hill hired Rosser in 1881 as chief engineer of the Canadian Pacific Railway. Rosser had become wealthy by selling town lots along railroads, but in 1882 William C. Van Horne fired him.

After returning to Virginia in 1885, Rosser bought an estate, "Rugby Hall," in Charlottesville and maintained old feuds, especially with Early and Thomas Munford. Rosser's colorful language—he called George B. McClellan's aide, the comte de Paris, "this princely 'Tramp'"—could obscure his more modern views. He believed the South should industrialize. In 1886 the Charleston, Cincinnati, and Chicago Railroad Company was formed to build a line through Appalachia with Rosser as consulting engineer. He was also president of the New South Mining and Improvement Company, created in 1887 to sell town lots. However, by 1891 his companies were failing, and in 1892 he ran for Congress in Virginia's Seventh District and lost. With debt mounting, his wife operated a dairy, and Rosser lectured on the Civil War.

In the Spanish-American War, Rosser was appointed brigadier general of U.S. volunteers by President William McKinley on 10 June 1898. At Chickamauga, Rosser trained a brigade of the Fourteenth Minnesota, First Pennsylvania, and Second Ohio Regiments until his discharge in October. Writing in 1900 to Senator John W. Daniel, Rosser mentioned commanding "the sons of Union soldiers" and the "metamorphosis of sentiment that occurred in me." In 1900 Rosser became a Republican, and in 1905 he was appointed postmaster of Charlottesville by President Theodore Roosevelt.

Rosser contributed to the unification of North America by working on two transcontinental railroads and by wearing a U.S. uniform in 1898, which made him a symbol of national reconciliation. Mrs. Rosser received a letter from Mrs. Custer noting, "how indebted our country was to the prompt act of patriotism on the part of General Rosser . . . what a wonderful cementing of the South and the North" (15 Feb. 1909, Rosser papers, Univ. of Virginia). Unable to speak after a stroke, Rosser still held his position as postmaster until his death, maintaining his motto, "THE CAVALRY Never Surrenders!" He died in Charlottesville, Virginia.

• Rosser's papers are at Alderman Library, University of Virginia, Charlottesville. Rosser's reports are in *The War of the Rebellion: A Compilation of the Official Records of the Union and Confederate Armies* (128 vols., 1880–1901). Rosser's Cooper Institute lecture, "The Last Days of the Army of Northern Virginia," is in the *New York Times*, 3 May 1867. For Rosser on Little Big Horn, see the *New York Herald*, 11 July 1876 and 22 Aug. 1876. See also *Addresses of Gen'l T. L. Ros-*

ser, at the Seventh Annual Reunion of the Association of the Maryland Line, Academy of Music, Baltimore, Md., February 22, 1889, and on Memorial Day, Staunton, Va., June 8, 1889 (1889). Elizabeth Rosser, Housekeepers' and Mothers' Manual (1895), is by his wife. See also William Naylor McDonald, A History of the Laurel Brigade (1907), and Millard K. Bushong and Dean M. Bushong, Fightin' Tom Rosser (1983). For reevaluations of Rosser as a cavalry leader, see Robert K. Krick, "Thomas Lafayette Rosser," in The Confederate General, vol. 5, ed. William C. Davis (1991), and Krick, "'The Cause of All My Disasters': Jubal A. Early and the Undisciplined Valley Cavalry," in Struggle for the Shenandoah: Essays on the 1864 Valley Campaign, ed. Gary W. Gallagher (1991). See also Mary Elizabeth Sergent, They Lie Forgotten: The United States Military Academy 1856–1861 Together with a Class Album for the Class of May, 1861 (1986), and Thomas O. Beane, "Thomas Lafayette Rosser," Magazine of Albemarle County History 16 (1957–1958): 25–46. For Rosser's work on the Canadian Pacific Railway, see Pierre Burton, The Last Spike (1971). For Rosser's views on economics and politics, see William G. Thomas III, "'UNDER INDICTMENT': Thomas Lafayette Rosser and the New South," Virginia Magazine of History and Biography 100 (Apr. 1992): 207–32. An obituary is in the New York Tribune, 30 Mar. 1910.

RALPH KIRSHNER

ROSSI, Anthony Talamo (13 Sept. 1900–24 Jan. 1993), businessman, was born Antonino Talamo-Rossi in Messina, Sicily, Italy, the son of Adolfo Talamo Rossi, a shopkeeper, and Rosaria La Via. Rossi grew up in Italy. On 28 December 1908 Messina was devastated by an earthquake; Rossi and his family moved temporarily to Syracuse, which was unaffected. In 1916 Rossi took his first job as a trolley conductor in Messina. Between 1918 and 1921 he served as a conscript in the Italian infantry. In 1921 Rossi decided to immigrate to the United States, where he found employment as a mechanic at his uncle's machine shop in the Borough of Queens, New York City. Within six months, Rossi had purchased a car and become a taxicab driver. The business proved profitable, and he purchased another taxicab and employed two drivers, while he himself also became a chauffeur during the daytime.

Rossi also developed a new sideline, the collection of eggs from the country for sale in the city. As a result, he became interested in the grocery trade and decided to sell his chauffeur and taxicab business. He used the money in 1928 to found a grocery store called Aurora Farms in Jackson Heights, Long Island. The store was a success. However, he later decided to sell it for $30,000 and became a restaurateur. The store failed under the new owners and Rossi subsequently purchased the premises and relaunched the store. During the 1930s, Rossi sold the grocery store and opened one of New York City's first large supermarkets. During his time as a grocer, Rossi married secretary Florence Stark, in 1931; they had no children, and she died in 1951. He subsequently married Sanna Morrison Barlow in 1954; they had no children.

In 1940 Rossi moved to Cape Charles, Virginia, where he cultivated tomatoes for a year. In 1941 he moved even farther south to Bradenton, Florida, where he planted tomatoes on fifty acres of leased land. During the early 1940s Rossi purchased the Floridian Cafeteria in Bradenton for $8,000. In July 1944 he purchased a second restaurant, The Terrace, in Miami Beach. This restaurant was unprofitable, and by late December Rossi had to sell it to avoid personal bankruptcy.

In December 1944 Rossi started a new business preparing and shipping citrus fruit in fancy gift boxes for major northern department stores. This venture was very profitable, and in early 1947 he returned to Bradenton from Miami, where he purchased a warehouse fully equipped with machinery for processing the citrus fruit. The warehouse was beside a railroad, and Rossi was soon shipping two carloads of gift boxes of fruit each day via Railway Express to northern states.

Rossi soon became concerned about the waste created by fruit unsuitable for the gift boxes. He decided to produce fresh-squeezed citrus fruit juice from this waste: in 1946 Rossi founded Fruit Industries, Inc., with an initial investment of $30,000. However, the Florida Citrus Commission refused to grant him an operating license to produce vacuum-packed fresh fruit sections for sale throughout the United States, because they felt his business proposition was impractical. Rossi was so confident of success that he decided to trade without a license: he transported gallons of fruit salads and orange juice to northern markets in tractor-trailers cooled to a temperature below the normal temperature of a refrigerated truck. The new business soon overtook the gift box business, which was discontinued. In 1951 Rossi acquired a significantly bigger factory, the former Florida Grapefruit Canning Plant. Here, he began the production of chilled orange juice; this was to be his most successful business venture. At the same time, Rossi renamed his company Tropicana Products, Inc., and introduced his company's famous logo, Tropic Ana, a small girl in a tropical grass skirt holding a basket of oranges on her pigtailed head.

In 1955 Rossi overcame a shortage of trucks by building a port and a $5 million cold-storage plant at Cape Canaveral and leasing an 8,000-ton ship, the SS Tropicana. In February 1957 Rossi began pumping orange juice from the plant into his ship, which then transported the juice to another plant in Whitestone, Queens, New York City. Here the juice was put into quart cartons, which were then transported by truck to dairies in New York, New England, and Pennsylvania. By the mid-1960s, Rossi had abandoned bulk shipment of his product by sea in favor of a combination of road and rail. However, this did not prove cost-effective, and in June 1970 Rossi adopted bulk shipment exclusively by rail. An especially designed and constructed mile-long Sea Board Railroad train of 150 refrigerated railroad cars was used to ship Tropicana's product between Bradenton and the company's depot in Kearney, New Jersey. Tropicana became a public company in 1969 and by the mid-1970s was one of America's leading fruit-juice processors with sales of over $120 million. Tropicana had two factories in Florida at Bradenton and Fort Pierce, its own fleet of trucks and railroad cars, and over 2,000 employees. Tropicana also exported to eighteen countries.

Rossi retired as chairman, president, and chief operating officer of Tropicana in 1978; Tropicana was sold to the Beatrice Food company for $488 million. Rossi and his two charitable foundations, the Aurora Foundation and the Bible Alliance Foundation, had together owned 20 percent of Tropicana. The two foundations promoted evangelical causes. Rossi had become a born-again Christian in 1951 and joined the Baptist church. Before his retirement, he had spent millions of dollars promoting the work of Bible schools and missionaries. After his retirement, Rossi and his Aurora Foundation built Bradenton Missionary Village, a retirement community for Christian missionaries. His Bible Alliance Foundation recorded and distributed audiotape cassettes of the Bible and sermons to visually impaired people and prison inmates.

Rossi's many and diverse business ventures before the foundation of Tropicana were not particularly successful; many ended in failure. However, the great success of his last business, Tropicana, owes much to the fact that he was a classic risk-taking entrepreneur. Rossi used his good fortune in the latter part of his life to become a major philanthropist. He died in Bradenton, Florida.

• Further information about Rossi can be found in a biography written by his wife, Sanna Barlow Rossi, *Anthony T. Rossi, Christian and Entrepreneur: The Story of the Founder of Tropicana* (1986). A feature article on Rossi is in the *New York Times*, 16 June 1974. Profiles of Rossi are in Arthur M. Louis, "The New Rich of the Seventies," *Fortune*, Sept. 1973, p. 242, and Louis, "Tony Rossi Can't Let Go," *Fortune*, 16 Jan. 1978, pp. 120–24. A profile of Tropicana is in Bob Lederer, "Profile: It's Not Just Breakfast Time Anymore: Anthony T. Rossi, Founder, President and Chairman of the Board Tropicana Products, Inc.," *Beverage World*, May 1977, pp. 20–23, 52–61. A brief obituary is in the *New York Times*, 27 Jan. 1993.

RICHARD A. HAWKINS

ROSSITER, Clinton Lawrence, III (18 Sept. 1917–10 July 1970), historian and educator, was born in Philadelphia, Pennsylvania, the son of Winton Goodrich Rossiter, an employee of the Wall Street firm James H. Oliphant & Co., and Dorothy Shaw. Clinton grew up in Bronxville, New York, and took his secondary education at Westminster School in Simsbury, Connecticut. He was an honors student and member of Phi Beta Kappa at Cornell University, where he earned his B.A. in classics in 1939. He won a Dubois Junior Fellowship and a Sanway Fellowship to study at Princeton University, from which he received his M.A. degree in politics in 1941. He continued his studies at Princeton as a Proctor fellow and was awarded a Ph.D. in constitutional law in 1942. His doctoral dissertation, "Democratic Dictatorship: The Theory and Practice of Constitutional Crisis Government," was prepared under the supervision of Edward S. Corwin. During World War II, he served as a gunnery officer in the U.S. Navy aboard the USS *Alabama* and

the USS *Los Angeles*. After eight campaigns in the Pacific, he was discharged with the rank of lieutenant. He married Mary Ellen Crane of Milwaukee, Wisconsin, in 1947. They had three children.

Following his wartime service Rossiter turned to full-time teaching. His career began as an instructor in political science at the University of Michigan in the fall term of 1946. In 1947 he returned to Cornell as an assistant professor to teach in the Department of Government. He rose through the professorial ranks, to associate professor (1949) and professor (1954), and served as chair of the department (1956–1959). At Cornell in 1959 he was named John L. Senior Professor of American Institutions, the only university professor of his era to hold appointments in two departments, history and government. His courses included U.S. constitutional and political theory, intellectual history, the presidency, and problems of democracy.

In his era Rossiter was one of the most respected scholars of the American experience. He specialized in conservative thought and represented a moderate type of conservatism associated with eighteenth-century British thinker Edmund Burke and American author Walter Lippmann. In 1956 columnist D. W. Brogan characterized Rossiter as "that very rare bird in America, a true conservative." Rossiter's publications, which exhibited a high literary quality, followed his conservative passions. In his first book, he argued that democracies in crises often turn to dictatorship. He traced the history of Anglo-American conservative thought in an important study, *Conservatism in America* (1955), and offered a "conservative program" for contemporary Americans. He was greatly enamored of the institution of the American presidency, which he felt had served the nation well, and he held that the two-party system had tended to unite the American people. His work on Alexander Hamilton expressed an indebtedness to that founding father for creating a progressive industrial society with an energetic national government and a liberating constitution. In an examination of the Constitutional Convention, he asserted that the Constitution was the logical projection of the aspirations of 1776 that saved the young republic from chaos. For the manuscript for *Conservatism in America* he was awarded the Charles A. Beard Memorial Prize in 1949, and *Seedtime of the Republic* (1953) was awarded the Bancroft Prize and the Woodrow Wilson Award of the American Political Science Association in 1953. He was a Guggenheim fellow in 1953–1954 and a Fulbright scholar in 1968.

Beyond the classroom Rossiter delivered countless lectures and served on important consultant assignments. He lectured on over fifty campuses, including Claremont Graduate School, the University of Salzburg (Austria), London University, Pomona College, Boston University, Canisius College, the University of Chicago, and Princeton University. In 1960–1961 he was Pitt Professor of American History and Institutions and fellow of Selwyn College at Cambridge University in England. In 1959 he toured Africa under the auspices of the South African Leader Exchange Program, and the U.S. Department of State sponsored him on a series of lectures in nine Asian nations in 1961–1962 and 1963. During the 1950s Robert Maynard Hutchins of the Ford Foundation asked Rossiter to head a study of the effects of communism in American life. With a team of ten scholars, he guided a series of controversial books for the Fund for the Report on Communist Influence in the United States and produced a massive bibliography on the topic. In 1956–1958 he was a consultant for the Rockefeller Foundation, and he contributed to the 1960 Presidential Commission on National Goals.

In the era of the Cold War, Rossiter openly advocated peaceful understanding between the Soviet Union and the United States. His lectureship for the Academy of Sciences of the Soviet Union gave him an enlightened view of that country, and he became an important intellectual bridge between the two nations. He cautioned against sliding into an apocalyptic view of the struggle between East and West because he believed in the eventual evolution of communism. In 1960 he commented upon national goals and values for the United States and affirmed racial equality, world peace, and cooperation. He maintained an independent political status.

Rossiter's personal values and loyalties came under serious attack at the peak of his scholarly and literary career. In 1969 and again the following year, the Cornell University campus was the scene of widespread unrest involving the African-American student community. Rossiter, a close friend of university president James Perkins, who was heavily criticized for his handling of the incidents, opposed extreme measures and took time from his personal scholarship for the work of a "Constituent Assembly" that made recommendations to the university senate. He was also shaken by President Richard Nixon's directive to bomb Cambodia in 1971 as an affront to American values in the foreign policy context.

Rossiter was found dead in the basement of his home in Ithaca, New York, an apparent suicide from a drug overdose that produced a massive heart attack. Friends speculated that the ridicule that he suffered during Cornell's "spring crisis," coupled with the disarray of international affairs, were contributing factors to his possible depression.

An Episcopalian in religious affiliation, he was active in numerous campus organizations at Cornell and civic associations in Ithaca. Remembered for his urbane sophistication, congeniality, and hearty wit, Rossiter maintained rigorous standards of discipline and unyielding integrity.

• Rossiter's personal papers have remained in the custody of his family. There is some source material in the archives at Cornell University. His publications include *Constitutional Dictatorship* (1948), *The Supreme Court and the Commander in Chief* (1951), *Seedtime of the Republic* (1953), *Conservatism in America* (1955; 2d ed., 1962), *The American Presidency* (1956; repr. 1960), *Marxism: The View from America* (1960), *Parties and Politics in America* (1960), *Alexander Hamilton and the Constitution* (1964), *1787: The Grand Convention* (1966), and

a posthumously published book, *The American Quest 1790–1860: An Emerging Nation in Search of Identity, Unity, and Modernity* (1971). His 1953 book, *Seedtime of the Republic*, was reissued in three separate volumes: *The First American Revolution* (1956), *The Political Thought of the American Revolution* (1963), and *Six Characters in Search of a Republic* (1964). In addition to scholarly articles in more than thirty journals, he also edited *Documents in American Government* (1949); with Milton R. Konvitz, *Aspects of Liberty* (1958); *The Federalist* (1961); and with James Lare, *The Essential Lippmann* (1963). There are useful biographical characterizations of Rossiter in Edward Cain, *They'd Rather Be Right* (1963), and D. W. Brogan in the *Saturday Review*, 12 May 1956. An obituary is in the *New York Times*, 12 July 1970.

WILLIAM H. BRACKNEY

ROSSITER, Thomas Pritchard (29 Sept. 1818–17 May 1871), history and figure painter, was born in New Haven, Connecticut, the son of Harry Caldwell Rossiter (profession unknown) and Charlotte Beers. Rossiter was first apprenticed to a Mr. Boyd of Winsted, Connecticut, and may have received advice from the painter and inventor Samuel F. B. Morse. In 1836, he began studying with the New Haven engraver and portrait painter Nathaniel Jocelyn.

In 1838 Rossiter opened his own studio in New Haven. Even at this early stage Rossiter seemed to obtain portrait commissions easily, since he had a fine sense of color and a knack for capturing a good likeness. Rossiter began exhibiting portraits, landscapes, and multifigure compositions at the annual exhibitions of the National Academy of Design and the Apollo Association in New York. Although Rossiter would paint landscapes throughout his career, he never considered them important. In 1840 he was elected associate member of the National Academy.

Rossiter worked briefly in Troy, New York, and in New York City before setting sail for Europe in June 1840. He desired to become a history painter, which required knowledge of composition, drawing, and the nude. Instruction on such topics was best obtained abroad. Landscape painters Frederick Kensett, his lifelong friend, as well as Asher B. Durand and John Casilear accompanied him to England. In London he had his first exposure to the great public and private art collections of Europe and visited the studios of Charles Robert Leslie and David Wilkie. He also went to medieval and Renaissance castles and other tourist spots. Rossiter and Kensett continued on to Paris, where they enrolled in a life drawing class that Kensett referred to as the École Préparation des Beaux-Arts, possibly the Académie Suisse. Rossiter began studying the Old Masters in the Louvre, preferring to copy the dramatic Baroque compositions of Rubens and works by other colorists such as the Venetians Titian and Veronese. In 1841 he traveled to Italy in the company of Thomas Cole, the leading American landscape painter, sketching scenic spots on the way.

For the next four-and-a-half years, Rossiter wintered in Rome and summered in Florence, Venice, Naples, and Germany. He quickly became immersed in the colony of American and English writers, painters, and sculptors who lived in Rome, frequenting the Café Greco and Lepri. Rossiter fell in love with the beautiful Italian landscape and the ruins from antiquity. His major Italian-period painting, *Tasso and His Friends, at the Convent of St. Onofrio, during His Last Illness*, was a large and elaborate multifigured composition probably inspired by a poem by Lord Byron.

Rossiter returned to New York in 1846 and traveled west to Cleveland and Niagara Falls in 1851 and 1852, respectively. While he supported himself by portraiture, he preferred the more elevated themes of history painting and, consequently, created his first biblical and allegorical scenes. Attitudes in the United States called for an art that would promote nationalism and morality and would appeal to the democratic public. Consequently, Rossiter turned increasingly to American history.

In 1851 Rossiter married Anna Parmly; they had three children. Two years later he toured Europe, then settled in Paris, where he would stay until 1856, when Anna died in childbirth. In France Rossiter studied the works of Florentine Renaissance artists and contemporary French academic painters, seeking to develop a painting style that would represent elevated themes in terms that were accessible to ordinary middle-class people. In 1855 he exhibited at the Paris Salon. That same year, he offered his services in decorating the U.S. Capitol, writing, "I should consider the point of my ambition attained if my long preparation in Historic Art entitled me to receive a Government Commission." Although none was forthcoming, he returned permanently to the United States, settling in New York City.

During the years leading up to the Civil War, clergymen, writers, and art critics urged the creation of a national art, and in response to their call, Rossiter turned to the theme of George Washington, creating *Washington and Lafayette at Mount Vernon* (Metropolitan Museum of Art), the first of a series of history paintings, in 1859. The image of the nation's first president called to mind a sense of unity in a country now threatened by political and social dissension. In these scenes, Rossiter presented historical events as genre scenes of everyday life, portraying America's first president as an ordinary citizen—as a farmer; entertaining guests with the help of his wife; and reading in his library. Four of the series were set at Mount Vernon. In 1854 the Mount Vernon Women's Association had been formed to save Washington's home and tomb. Rossiter and Louis Mignot (who collaborated on the landscape background of *Washington and Lafayette at Mount Vernon*) visited the estate; so concerned did Rossiter become over the destiny of the estate that he published the article "Mount Vernon Past and Present: What Shall Be Its Destiny" in *The Crayon* (1858). *Washington and Lafayette at Mount Vernon* was the largest and best known of Rossiter's series, and it toured several cities in the East.

Sometime in the late 1850s Rossiter married Mary Sterling; they had no children. Although Rossiter was well established in New York with a large, comforta-

ble home that featured a picture gallery, he and his second wife and children moved to Cold Spring on the Hudson in 1860. He maintained a New York studio for his portrait sittings, but the Civil War years were a difficult time for Rossiter, as they were for many artists. While he continued his American series, Rossiter turned increasingly to the more traditional themes of history painting: in the mid-1860s, he created a series based on Milton's *Paradise Lost* and began a series on Christ's life. In the evenings, he wrote and illustrated the poem "The Legend of Breakneck Mountain" (ms., New-York Historical Society). During his latter years, Rossiter exhibited less frequently, and what he did show was less favorably received than before. Contemporary critics suggested that his ability had appreciably diminished, but a decline in the popularity of history painting was also a factor. Rossiter planned to revisit Europe in 1868, but nothing is definitely known about his last three years. When he died at his home in Cold Spring, Rossiter ranked as one of the country's last major painters of American history.

• The Thomas P. Rossiter Collection, in the Archives of American Art, Smithsonian Institution, Washington, D.C., includes letters and Edith Bevan's typed manuscript "Thomas Pritchard Rossiter, 1818–1871 with Checklist" (1957); see also the E. Gordon Rossiter Collection of letters and scrapbook, Summit, N.J.; the John F. Kensett Papers, New York State Library, Albany; and the Kensett diary, 1840–1841, Frick Art Reference Library, New York. Contemporary assessments can be found in Henry T. Tuckerman, *Book of the Artists* (1867), and Henry W. French, *Art and Artists in Connecticut* (1879). The most thorough biography and modern assessment is Ilene Susan Fort, "High Art and the American Experience: The Career of Thomas Pritchard Rossiter" (M.A. thesis, Queens College, City Univ. of New York, 1975). See also Thomas B. Brumbaugh, "Venice Letters from Thomas P. Rossiter to John F. Kensett, 1843," *American Art Journal* 5 (May 1973): 74–78; and Margaret Broaddus, "Thomas P. Rossiter: In Pursuit of Diversity," *American Art and Antiques* 2, no. 3 (1979): 106–13.

ILENE SUSAN FORT

ROST-DENIS, Pierre Adolphe (1797–6 Sept. 1868), jurist and planter, was born in Garonne, France. His parents' names and occupations are unknown. Little is known of his early years, except that he attended the Lycée Napoléon and the École Polytechnique in Paris. He participated in the defense of Paris in 1814 and then became a member of Napoléon Bonaparte's army. After the defeat at Waterloo, Rost came to the United States in 1816, landing at Natchez, Mississippi. There he learned English and became a protégé and student in the law office of Joseph E. Davis, brother of Jefferson Davis. He served a term in the Mississippi legislature before moving to Natchitoches, Louisiana, where he practiced law. He was elected to the Louisiana legislature in 1822 and was active in the debate concerning the revision of the Louisiana *Digest of the Civil Laws Now in Force in the Territory of Orleans* (1808), which would be supplanted by the *Civil Code of Louisiana* (1825). The *Digest*, as the name suggests, was a compilation of civil law, which included

Spanish and French laws still in effect in Louisiana. This caused great confusion, and the *Civil Code* was intended to reduce all Louisiana law to a single source. Louisiana judges, however, continued to use the old laws when it suited them.

In 1830 Rost moved to St. Charles Parish, where he married a woman of a prominent Creole family, Louise Odile d'Estréhan Foucher, with whom he had five children. His wife later inherited Destréhan Plantation, where Rost resided until his death. Under his supervision, Destréhan Plantation became a leading producer in the state's sugar industry. In 1850 Rost owned 213 slaves, the largest number held by one owner in St. Charles Parish.

In 1838 Rost was appointed a judge of the Supreme Court of Louisiana (members of this court were not styled "justices" until the Louisiana Constitution of 1845 went into effect). At that time Chief Judge François-Xavier Martin's eyesight was failing, and the court's work proceeded slowly. Faced with a huge backlog of cases, Rost attempted to reform the procedures of the court in order to increase efficiency and to clear the docket. Despite his age and infirmity, Martin staunchly resisted these efforts, and Rost resigned after serving only four months on the court.

When the Supreme Court of Louisiana was reorganized under the constitution of 1845, Rost was appointed associate justice. He served the court for seven years until the constitution of 1852, which made the positions of chief justice and associate justice elective, went into effect, at which time he resigned. During his tenure on the court, Rost wrote almost all of the court's decisions concerning succession and inheritance law and was known as an expert in the field. Rost was a staunch defender of Louisiana's civil law system. In *Adams v. Routh and Dorsey* (1853), Rost ruled that William C. Adams, Jr., could not free his slave concubine, Nancy, because doing so would alienate more of Adams's estate than the state's forced heirship laws allowed: "emancipating a slave by will should . . . be considered a donation to the slave [which] must not exceed the disposable portion." One of his colleagues wrote that Rost's "mission was to widen the scope of our system of law, to teach the people of Louisiana that the civil law was founded upon the divine principle of doing unto others as we would be done by." Another praised his "clearness of diction and logical perspicacity."

During the Civil War, in 1861, Jefferson Davis appointed Rost Confederate commissioner to France. Rost's task was to attempt to persuade a reluctant French government to support the Confederate cause. Although Rost failed in this mission, in 1862 President Davis assigned him to try to win Spanish support, which proved to be impossible as well. In May 1862 Rost returned to France, where he remained for the duration of the war. He returned to Louisiana to find his wife's plantation devastated by Federal troops and occupied by Union officials. The *Daily Picayune* wrote of his death at Destréhan Plantation, "The reaper Death seems lately to have preferred to pass by ordi-

nary stalks in the great field of life to strike down the tallest among them." Although his diplomatic efforts produced no results, Rost was a success by the standards of the day as an attorney, judge, and sugar planter.

• No personal papers of Rost are known to exist. A sketch of Rost's life is in Henry Plauche Dart, "The History of the Supreme Court of Louisiana," *Louisiana Reports* 133 (1913): 6–37, and in Mark Fernandez, "From Chaos to Continuity: Early Reforms of the Supreme Court of Louisiana," *Louisiana History* 28 (1987): 19–36. His service to the Confederacy is detailed in Joseph O. Baylen, "Pierre A. Rost's Mission to Europe, 1861–1863," *Louisiana History* 2 (1961): 322–31. See also Judith Kelleher Schafer, *Slavery, the Civil Law, and the Supreme Court of Louisiana* (1994), and *Adams v. Routh and Dorsey*, no. 3009, 8 La. Ann. 121 (1853). Obituaries are in the *Daily Picayune*, 7, 8 Sept. 1868, and the *New Orleans Bee*, 8 Sept. 1868.

JUDITH SCHAFER

ROSTOVTZEFF, Michael (10 Nov. 1870–20 Oct. 1952), historian, was born Mikhail Ivanovich Rostovsev, in Zhitomir near Kiev, Ukraine, the son of Ivan Yakovlevich Rostovsev, an education official, and Maria I. Monachova. Rostovtzeff studied at the Gymnasium in Kiev, at the University of Kiev, and then, from 1890, at the University of St. Petersburg, where his teachers included Thaddeus Zielinsky and Nikodene P. Kondakov. Graduating from St. Petersburg in 1892, he taught for three years in the Gymnasium at Zarskoe-Selo, then enjoyed a traveling scholarship in Europe, the Mediterranean, and Near East. He returned to Russia in 1898 to teach Latin at St. Petersburg, where he gained a master's degree in the same year. He married Sophie M. Kulchitski in 1901. He received his doctorate in 1903 and became professor at St. Petersburg that year. He became a corresponding member of the Berlin Academy in 1914 and a member of the Russian Academy of Sciences in 1916.

The Russian Revolution brought an abrupt end to Rostovtzeff's academic prospects in his native land. He had been a founding member of the Kadets—the Constitutional Democratic party—which in November 1917 was outlawed by the Bolsheviks. In early 1918 he defected during a visit to Sweden and England. He resided in Oxford at The Queen's College for two unhappy years but contact with the American historian William L. Westermann led to the possibility of a university appointment in the United States. In August 1920 Rostovtzeff left to take up a one-year professorship at the University of Wisconsin, left vacant by Westermann's departure to Cornell. The appointment was authorized once it had been confirmed that Rostovtzeff was neither a Jew nor a Bolshevik and was made permanent in 1921. Politically, Rostovtzeff was a Russian liberal and pamphlets written by him in this period are strongly anti-Bolshevik.

The important early works that reflected his developing interests and in turn further shaped his views on the practice of history writing were his 1892 thesis on Pompeii, his 1898 master's thesis on tax-farming, and his 1903 doctoral dissertation on lead tokens (the latter two published in German). He also wrote a series of seminal articles on aspects of Roman tax collection, the imperial exchequer, and the provisioning of the army for the *Real-Encyclopädie* between 1900 and 1910. He followed these articles with *Studien zur Geschichte des römischen Kolonates* (1910).

In September 1925 Rostovtzeff moved to Yale to become Sterling Professor of Ancient History and Archaeology. He served as director of the Yale expedition at the site of Dura-Europos in Syria (1928–1938) and was president of the American Historical Association (1935–1936). He retired in June 1939 but continued as director of Archaeological Studies until 1944 when illness forced him to resign.

The main publications of his American period consist of the two-volume *A History of the Ancient World* (1926–1927), *Social and Economic History of the Roman Empire* (1926), *Social and Economic History of the Hellenistic World* (1941), and the numerous reports that he edited of the excavations at Dura. All of these works more or less reflect an interest in a synthetic approach to ancient history, the product, like Rostovtzeff himself, of nineteenth-century positivism and of optimistic notions that history as a "science" could be represented as an all-embracing organic whole. In *A History of the Ancient World*, Rostovtzeff described history as a "science" whose aim was "to define the laws under which the life of man develops," although conceding that history will always remain literary in character. This positivism was shared and advocated by Rostovtzeff's German mentor Eduard Meyer, who had encouraged him to write a single social and economic history of the ancient world as early as 1914, a project delayed by World War I and then by the Russian Revolution.

Rostovtzeff's work, especially his two great studies of economic life, was important not just for its enormous detail and meticulous documentation but also for the extensive use of archaeological data and visual material. In a 1922 work Rostovtzeff had stressed the importance of "learning how to write history with the help of archaeology" (*Iranians and Greeks in South Russia*, p. viii). He used art and archaeology not simply to provide color or illustration but to reconstruct ancient society.

Of the two books on social and economic history, the one on the Roman Empire was the most controversial: it boldly hypothesized that the prosperity of the empire rested on, indeed was defined by, a trading and manufacturing bourgeoisie under a benign autocracy; success was gradually eroded by the inherent tensions between bourgeoisie and a backward peasantry, who in the third century A.D. allied themselves with the army with catastrophic results. The interpretative flaws of the work were soon recognized; commentators have overstressed that Rostovtzeff's Roman Empire was a thinly disguised and idealized Czarist Russia. Ironically he proved to be the most Marxian of non-Marxists. He modernized the ancient economy, assuming that it differed only in quantity not quality

from the modern age; also, more serious than just the vagueness with which he transferred modern terms like "bourgeois," "factory," and "capitalism" was a fundamental misunderstanding of the notion of modern capitalism, an exaggeration of class tensions, and a failure to appreciate the full implications of the agricultural underpinning of all ancient economies. His notion of a "world commerce" in terms of an integrated Mediterranean market was overstated; and he underestimated the role of the imperial sector of the economy, which he characterized as socialistic.

His *Social and Economic History of the Hellenistic World* is a more careful study, although here too are found typical Rostovtzeffian fictions—the antagonism between town and country and the triumph of rationalism and progress. He contrasted the culturally superior Greeks with the passive Near Eastern barbarians. Present in this and other works is the contrast between Greek dynamism and "Oriental passivity" (p. 1096), which profoundly affected his interpretation of cultural history.

Despite limitations, Rostovtzeff wrote works of immense scholarship, with significant methodological implications—for instance, the seamless interweaving into the historical narrative of material such as *instrumenta domestica* (inscribed objects, such as brick- and tile-stamps, etc.) was a major contribution of Rostovtzeff. He set the agenda for future research with his treatment of such sources and by discussing topics such as industry, class groupings, and social relations between classes. He aimed to present "the social and economic features of human life not as dry abstractions, in the form of statistics and tabulations, but as living dynamic phenomena, indivisible from and closely correlated with other equally important features of that life" (p. viii).

Rostovtzeff's final major contribution to ancient studies was the excavation of Dura-Europos, a fortified city on the banks of the River Euphrates, occupied successively by the Seleucids, the Parthians, and the Romans. Begun in 1923 under Franz Cumont and the auspices of the Académie des Inscriptions et Belles Lettres, the project continued until 1938 as a fruitful partnership between Yale and the Académie, supervised jointly by Rostovtzeff and Cumont.

Rostovtzeff's dynamic personality left a deep if impermanent mark on the Yale academic environment. He singlehandedly established papyrological study at Yale and developed an impressive archaeological collection at whose heart now lay the inscriptions and artifacts from Dura. As teacher he trained a generation of scholars, including C. Bradford Welles, Rostovtzeff's immediate successor at Yale, specializing in papyrology, archaeology, and numerous aspects of Hellenistic and Roman history.

Rostovtzeff was one of the most original social and economic historians of the twentieth century. He published many scholarly articles and larger studies in German and English and had a vast network of international contacts. He was a versatile scholar who integrated social and economic issues fully into the political narrative of a period.

Rostovtzeff's intellectual development has often been explained in terms of his Russian background. If his bourgeois origin and the attitudes of his class (and its immediate reactions to Bolshevism) determined both his political stance and the way he viewed history, equally it was his travels as a youth and his exposure to archaeology and the ancillary disciplines of papyrology, epigraphy, and art history, practiced by European colleagues such as Eugen Bormann, Otto Benndorff, Bernard Grenfell, and Ulrich Wilcken, that confirmed in him a distinctive methodological approach to the study of history. His scholarly interests were indeed very broad, ultimately encompassing the ancient mystery cults and the history of Chinese art, while national pride, among other factors, led him to investigate the history and archaeology of South Russia. However it was on aspects of ancient social and economic history that he came to focus his attention.

• Rostovtzeff's papers are in the Sterling Memorial Library at Yale University, with material relating specifically to Dura-Europos in the Yale Art Gallery; at Duke University, Durham, N.C.; and the library of the University of Wisconsin. His 1898 master's thesis was published as "Geschichte der Staatspacht in der römischen Kaiserzeit bis Diokletian," *Philologus Ergänzungsband* 9 (1902): 331–512. His 1903 dissertation was published as *Römische Bleitesserae: Ein Beitrag zur Sozial-und Wirtschaftsgeschichte der römischen Kaiserzeit* (1905; repr. 1963) and as *Studien zur Geschichte des römischen Kolonates* (1910; repr. 1970). His other works include *A Large Estate in Egypt in the Third Century B.C.: A Study in Economic History* (1922; repr. 1967) and *Iranians and Greeks in South Russia* (1922; repr. 1969). His major work on the archaeology of South Russia was published in the Soviet Union after his defection as *Scythia and Bosporus* (1925) in Russian; the official version in German is *Skythien und der Bosporus. Kritische Übersicht der schriftlichen und archäologischen Quellen*, trans. E. Pridik (1931). Unpublished manuscripts formed the basis of *Skythien und der Bosporus. Band II: wiederentdekte Kapitel und Verwandtes*, trans. H. Heinen (1993). His major studies published at Yale include *A History of the Ancient World*, trans. J. D. Duff (2 vols., 1926–1927); *The Social and Economic History of the Roman Empire* (2 vols., 1926; 2d ed. rev. P. M. Fraser, 1957); and *The Social and Economic History of the Hellenistic World* (3 vols., 1941; 2d ed. rev. P. M. Fraser, 1953). Rostovtzeff also edited *Preliminary Report of the Excavations at Dura-Europos Conducted by Yale University and the French Academy of Inscriptions and Letters* (10 vols., 1929–1952) and several volumes of *Final Report of the Excavations at Dura-Europos, etc.* (1943–1949), as well as writing his own monograph *Dura-Europos and its Art* (1938).

An important study of Rostovtzeff's Russian years is Marinus Wes, *Michael Rostovtzeff, Historian in Exile: Russian Roots in an American Context* (1990), with additions and qualifications in B. D. Shaw, "Under Russian Eyes," *Journal of Roman Studies* 82 (1992): 216–28; and Wes's earlier essay, "The Russian Background of the Young Michael Rostovtzeff," *Historia* 37 (1988): 207–21. For Rostovtzeff in America see G. W. Bowersock, "Rostovtzeff in Madison," *American Scholar* 55 (1986): 391–400; and H. von Staden, "Rostovtzeff a Yale," *Quaderni di storia* (1997). For evaluations of his major works see M. Reinhold, "Historian of the Classic World: A Critique of Rostovtzeff," *Science and Society* 10 (1946):

361–91; H. W. Pleket, "Afscheid van Rostovtzeff," *Lampas* 8 (1975): 267–84; G. W. Bowersock, "*The Social and Economic History of the Roman Empire* by Michael Ivanovitch Rostovtzeff," *Daedalus* 103 (1974): 15–23; J. D'Arms, "M. I. Rostovtzeff and M. I. Finley: The Status of Traders in the Roman World," in D'Arms and J. Eadie, eds., *Ancient and Modern: Essays in Honor of Gerald F. Else* (1977): 159–79; and more generally Karl Christ, *Von Gibbon zu Rostovtzeff* (1972; 3d ed. 1989): 334–49. For earlier assessments see for instance T. Frank, *American Journal of Philology* 47 (1926): 290–92. On Dura see Clark Hopkins, *The Discovery of Dura-Europos* (1979). Among numerous tributes and necrologies see C. B. Welles, "Michael I. Rostovtzeff," in J. T. Lambie ed., *Architects and Craftsmen in History. Festschrift für Abbott Payson Usher* (1956): 55–73; Welles, *The Russian Review* 12 (1953): 128–33; Arnaldo Momigliano, *The Cambridge Journal* 7 (1954): 334–46; *Studies in Historiography* (1966): 91–104; and A. H. M. Jones, *Proceedings of the British Academy* 38 (1952): 347–61.

A. P. GREGORY

ROSZAK, Theodore (1 May 1907–2 Sept. 1981), sculptor, was born in Poznan, Poland; his parents' names are not available. Roszak's family immigrated to the United States in 1909 and settled in Chicago. Roszak attended public schools, and in his early teens, he enrolled in evening classes at the school of the Art Institute of Chicago. Roszak acknowledged the support of his family in pursuing his studies in art, particularly his mother, who had been a designer to the House of Hohenzollern in Berlin. His mother's family had been involved in the arts: a grandfather was a musician and composer; an uncle was an illustrator whose drawings appeared in Polish history texts. His father's parents had been farmers in Poland, and in Roszak's childhood his father worked in a foundry and then as a pastry chef.

Roszak began drawing seriously as a child. After graduating from high school in 1924, he became a full-time day student at the Art Institute. He won several awards for oil paintings and lithographs, but he displayed little interest in avant-garde art. In 1926 Roszak moved to New York to study with Charles Hawthorne at the National Academy of Design. Simultaneously he enrolled in philosophy courses at Columbia University. Roszak's study with Hawthorne lasted only a brief period, after which he began private instruction with George Luks. In 1927 Roszak returned to Chicago where he resumed studies at the Art Institute under John Norton, who, Roszak claimed, was one of the few Americans to understand French modernism. A traveling fellowship in 1927 enabled him to visit museums on the East Coast and to practice lithography in Woodstock, New York. On his return to Chicago that same year, he became an instructor in drawing and lithography at the Art Institute school.

Another fellowship permitted Roszak to travel abroad in 1929, and his European sojourn brought about a dramatic change in his work. He spent eighteen months in Europe, principally in Prague, and he made excursions to Paris and to cities in Italy, Austria, and Germany. Roszak was living in Prague at the time of the Exhibition of Contemporary Culture in Brno. There, Czech industrial artists demonstrated the Bauhaus concept of collaboration between artists and designers. Thus Roszak learned the ideology of the Bauhaus, which was grounded in a technological, utilitarian aesthetic, even though he never visited the famous school in Germany. He purchased Laszlo Moholy-Nagy's book *The New Vision* (1930) and returned home with an appreciation of cubism, geometric abstraction, and surrealism, and with a commitment to constructivist principles, which relied on industrial materials and geometric elements to symbolize the technological age.

Roszak won a Tiffany Foundation Fellowship in 1931, which enabled him to spend two months in Oyster Bay, Long Island. That same year he began working in a Staten Island studio and married Florence Sapir, with whom he was to have one child. As an antidote to the hardships of the depression, Roszak created visionary images of space travel. Airships, space observatories, dirigibles, and rockets appear in Roszak's drawings produced from 1932 to 1934, reflecting his interest in science fiction of the period. His images evoke a prosperous future for the country and suggest the potential of advanced technology to improve the quality of life. Inspired by the solo flight of Charles Lindbergh in 1927 and the discovery of a new planet in 1930, and stimulated by his contact with European constructivists, Roszak envisioned the future of aeronautics and space exploration.

In 1932, after completing six large plaster casts based on his futuristic drawings, Roszak became dissatisfied with plaster as a medium. He set up his own tool shop in 1934, in which he created pristine objects and reliefs that paralleled the polished metals of Bauhaus artists Moholy-Nagy, Rudolf Belling, and Oskar Schlemmer. During this period, however, Roszak was recognized primarily for his paintings, one of which was purchased by the Whitney Museum of American Art in 1935. In 1938 Roszak was appointed an instructor in two- and three-dimensional design at the Design Laboratory in New York City. Sponsored by the Fine Arts Project of the Works Progress Administration, the school was established in 1935 with the guidance of Moholy-Nagy and was dedicated to perpetuating the principles and methods of the Bauhaus.

After the United States entered World War II, when he was thirty-four, Roszak was employed at the Brewster Aeronautical Corporation in Newark, New Jersey, and later taught aircraft mechanics for both the army and navy. His alternative war service also included navigational and engineering drafting in a testing tank at the Stevens Institute of Technology in Hoboken.

When the war ended in 1945 with the annihilation caused by two atomic weapons, Roszak was disillusioned about the uses of modern technology. As a result, he put aside the Bauhaus-inspired constructions of the 1930s and began working in an expressionistic style, using welded steel for his sculpture. His drawings after 1945 parallel the abstractions created by painters of the abstract expressionist generation. Roszak's imagery suggests primordial elements in combat, predatory beasts, fantastic renderings of sacred vessels, and visions of the transformation of technology into forces of destruction. Similarly, Roszak and other artists of his generation no longer used flying birds to symbolize spirituality; instead, birds became associated with fighter bombers. Images of terrifying prehistoric creatures were employed to evoke the horror of modern weaponry. Having renounced Bauhaus principles as no longer relevant to postwar America, Roszak continued his quest for philosophical and moral values. An avid reader, he turned to the writings of Sigmund Freud, Carl Jung, and Otto Rank, and to books on Asian art and world mythology. Roszak used archetypal myths from these written sources to represent primeval forces in his works.

Roszak's welded sculpture *Spectre of Kitty Hawk* (1946–1947) signals a search for atavistic concepts in lieu of the machine imagery evoked, for example, by *Airport Structure* (1932). Related drawings of the late 1940s depict a striding beast, reminiscent of the ferocious birds painted on the sides of fighter planes during World War II. Roszak saw the rapacious pterodactyl as an archetypal symbol of man's lust for power and his predatory actions. After producing works that registered his profound reaction to the destructive capabilities of airplanes armed with nuclear weapons, Roszak began working with archetypal themes devoted to the survival of the human race, as in his sculpture *The Firebird* (1950), based on Stravinsky's ballet of the same name.

In 1952 Roszak participated in an international competition for a public sculpture entitled *Monument to the Unknown Political Prisoner*, which was to be dedicated to the memory of those who suffered political oppression. While the majority of the eleven entries from the United States were nonobjective, Roszak's maquette had a clearly figurative basis. He objected to many of the entries, which emphasized the theme of imprisonment by showing bars or cages. In contrast, Roszak's abstracted human is shown as defiant and triumphant over forces unable to incarcerate the human spirit. For his entry he was awarded £25, and the maquette was taken into the collection of the Tate Gallery in London.

Roszak returned to natural forms during the 1950s. His plant and animal forms were inspired in part by his reverence for Chinese and Japanese brush paintings, and his imagery from this period suggests his fascination with the power of cosmic forces.

In 1952 Roszak was commissioned to create the bell tower for the chapel at the Massachusetts Institute of Technology, designed by Eero Saarinen. In 1960 he made an aluminum eagle for the facade of the American embassy in London, also designed by Saarinen. At the New York World's Fair of 1964 Roszak installed his *Forms in Space* outside the Hall of Science, and in 1968 his large-scale *Sentinel* was installed in front of the Public Health Laboratory Building in New York City.

During the 1960s Roszak turned to apocalyptic visions that are virtually unparalleled in the work of other American artists of the time. His drawing style shifted to obsessively detailed images in graphite and ballpoint pen, at times combined with ink washes. In his later years Roszak returned to his youthful skill in graphics and perfected a painstaking process of rendering images through patterns of fine lines. Fully realized drawings appeared more frequently because the artist's ability to weld metals was hindered by illness. By the end of his life, Roszak seemed to reconcile his early commitment to constructivism and his later expressionistic imagery by stressing space-age technology rather than industrial design. Prodigious in his artistic production, creating not only sculptures in welded metal and constructions of various metals and plastics but also drawings in pen and ink and gouache, oil paintings, and photograms, he is among the foremost sculptors of the abstract expressionist generation.

• Roszak's papers, including unpublished interviews, catalogs, and newspaper clippings, are in the Archives of American Art, Smithsonian Institution, Washington, D.C. Roszak's most useful statement about his work is "In Pursuit of an Image," *Quadrum* 2 (Nov. 1955): 54. See also Joan Marter, *Theodore Roszak: The Drawings* (1992); Joan French Seeman, "The Sculpture of Theodore Roszak, 1932–1952" (Ph.D. diss., Stanford Univ., 1979); and Douglas Dreishpoon, "Theodore Roszak, Painting and Sculpture" (Ph.D. diss., Graduate Center, City Univ. of New York, 1993).

JOAN MARTER

ROTCH, Joseph (6 Mar. 1704–24 Nov. 1784), whaling merchant, was born in Salem, Massachusetts, the son of William Rotch and Hannah Porter. Rotch moved to Nantucket in 1725 and by 1731 had established himself as a capable ship captain interested in trading ventures. His business standing received a boost when in 1733 he married Love Macy (with whom he would have three children) and thereby entered an alliance with the prominent Macy family, one of the original English families on Nantucket. Rotch's business expanded over the next two decades as he became a major trader in Nantucket, New England, and the North Atlantic.

Rotch arrived in Nantucket when whaling had begun to boom there. From the beginning he did not limit himself to whaling, although that remained his principal focus. Trade in general merchandise with Rhode Island and colonies to the south and with Britain in whale products grew as his whaling interests expanded. Careful and calculating, Rotch rose to dominate Nantucket's business community. He was active in pressing suits for the recovery of debts, a remarkable record for even a lukewarm Friend like Rotch in Nantucket, a Quaker-dominated community where lawsuits were suspect at best and generally prohibited between members.

Rotch was not born a Friend but petitioned for and was received into membership shortly before his marriage to Love Macy. While their children were raised as Quakers, Rotch sent them to the local Congregational missionary minister, Timothy White, for formal education rather than relying on the uncertainties of the island's schools. His religious concerns seem to have been limited to family and mercantile alliances rather than active involvement as a leading Friend like his son William Rotch. The Quaker network proved useful in promoting business on and off the island. Like many eighteenth-century Quakers, Rotch found it helpful to have a religious network of trustworthy Friends who could ensure safe conduct of business in transatlantic trade, where the integrity of business correspondents was essential. While Rotch retained formal relations with Quakerism, there is some indication in Quaker records that a few Friends were uncertain about his Quaker commitments when he sought to obtain permission to move from the island to Dartmouth, Massachusetts.

Having come to dominate the Nantucket whaling trade by 1750, Rotch correctly estimated the island's limitations. Its harbor entrance could not accommodate large ships, and, by the middle of the eighteenth century, the island had become dependent on the mainland for basic supplies. In 1765, after the end of the Great War for the Empire, Rotch moved part of his business to Dartmouth, Massachusetts, leaving the rest on Nantucket under the control of his son William. As Rotch sought to expand in whaling and other trading ventures, he encountered competition from John Hancock, who used his inherited fortune as a base to challenge Rotch's whaling interests. Rotch soundly defeated Hancock, who returned to the more entertaining pursuit of resisting new British policies. Ironically, Hancock and Rotch interests clashed again when in 1773 Rotch ships carried to Boston the tea that became the focus of the Tea Party.

The War for Independence seriously affected whaling interests throughout North America as both sides impeded whaling, and Rotch interests suffered along with the rest. When Dartmouth became unsafe because of British raids early in the war, Rotch withdrew to his old home base on Nantucket, where he died. There, his son William took over the family business, which had suffered serious reverses because of the war. Nevertheless, the family would continue to lead in whaling and commerce in nineteenth-century Massachusetts.

• Limited manuscripts on Rotch are at the Nantucket Historical Association and the Old Dartmouth Historical Society, New Bedford. James Lawrence McDevitt, Jr., "The House of Rotch: Whaling Merchants of Massachusetts, 1734–1828" (Ph.D. diss., American Univ., 1978), and Edward Byers, *The Nation of Nantucket: Society and Politics in an Early American Commercial Center, 1660–1820* (1986), provide detailed accounts of Nantucket and Rotch. Also see John M. Bullard, *The Rotches* (1947).

ARTHUR J. WORRALL

ROTCH, William (4 Dec. 1734–16 May 1828), whaling merchant and New England Quaker, was born in Nantucket, Massachusetts, the son of Joseph Rotch, a whaling merchant, and Love Macy. William served his apprenticeship with his father's firm between 1748 and 1755, learning skills that included ship construction, accounting, pricing of products, and competing for new markets. He acquired an intimate knowledge of local, provincial, and international trade in these years during which his father became New England's leading whaling merchant. In 1754 Rotch married Elizabeth Barney, also of Nantucket. They had six children.

Rotch's first independent venture came in 1766 when his father moved part of the family business to Dartmouth, Massachusetts, at a site that would later be called New Bedford. Rotch was left on Nantucket to direct the rest of the family business. His success there paralleled his father's, and together they met the challenges made by John Hancock and some Rhode Island merchants to the Rotch whaling enterprises. By the time that fighting began at Lexington and Concord the Rotches dominated whaling in New England. They had made enemies in the process and now were vulnerable on two fronts: war-related measures from both sides and the difficulty of supplying Nantucket with necessities that the island could not supply for itself, ranging from wood to food.

With the outbreak of fighting, Rotch sought to reduce the likelihood of conflict on Nantucket. Appropriate to his Quaker pacifism, he destroyed weapons that might have been used in war. With other whaling merchants, he sought exceptions to wartime rules from both sides so that ships could leave on whaling voyages without threat of arrest on the high seas and so that other vessels could resupply the island. In short, Rotch and Nantucket sought noncombatant status. Rotch had limited success in this although he faced prosecution from the American side in Massachusetts and protracted negotiations with the British commanders in Newport, Rhode Island. Frequently distrusted by elements of both sides because he was a Quaker, his negotiations served to mitigate the sufferings of Nantucketers although whaling came to a virtual halt as long as the war continued. Rotch later set out these events in a memorandum composed when he was eighty.

Hardship for Nantucket and Rotch did not end with peace. While supplies were again available without hindrance from the mainland, the American whaling trade now faced the impediment of being outside the British empire. Consequently, Rotch and other American whalers were now liable for duties on whale oil landed in Britain. Rotch went to Britain in 1785. With no relief in sight after protracted negotiations with the British government, Rotch turned to France to rescue his mission and revive his family's flagging fortunes. The government of Louis XVI was eager to encourage whaling from its port of Dunkirk to assure its own supply of whale oil and gave the Rotches favorable terms to establish a base in the town. Unhappily for the Rotch interests, the French Revolution broke out just as the Nantucketers sought to establish their base at

Dunkirk. By 1793 most of the Rotches had withdrawn from France and returned to Nantucket.

On his return Rotch decided, as his father had before him, that the future of whaling and the family businesses lay in New Bedford. The sandbar at the entrance to Nantucket's harbor prevented large ships entering with cargo, and the continued shortage of local produce impeded business. He also faced considerable hostility from islanders jealous of the Rotches' success and resentful that they had already taken much of their business away from the island. In 1795 Rotch left his son-in-law Samuel Rodman to manage the remaining family business on the island and joined his son William Rotch, Jr., in New Bedford. Three years later Rodman also moved to New Bedford as Rotch interests now focused on the mainland. In 1796 Rotch retired although he continued indirectly to help manage the family firms. By the nineteenth century, management of Rotch interests had passed to the next generation, led chiefly by William Rotch, Jr., and Rodman.

For most of his life, Rotch was a prominent Quaker. First active in his Nantucket meeting, by the time of the War for Independence he was a leading Friend in New England. When Friends from outside New England in the British Isles and America sent assistance to alleviate suffering on Nantucket, Rotch distributed that aid. After the war he remained active in Quaker affairs, including during his sojourn in France, where he and his family briefly provided a Quaker and peaceful presence in that revolutionary country. The Rotches were also supportive of Job Scott, a Providence, Rhode Island, Quaker. In the 1780s and 1790s Scott advanced views, similar to theological positions of seventeenth-century Friends, that were also similar to rising unitarian views in Britain and the United States. Scott's theology may have helped inspire positions taken by the Rotches and others when schisms came to Quakers throughout North America in the 1820s. While Rotch did not formally withdraw from Quaker membership during the New Light schism in New England in the 1820s, the rest of the family did. Rotch died in New Bedford.

• The Old Dartmouth Historical Society in New Bedford holds extensive manuscript collections on the Rotches. Less numerous, although useful for background information, are the holdings at the Nantucket Historical Association and the Rhode Island Historical Society. Rotch's views are preserved in his *Memorandum Written in the Eightieth Year of His Life, 1814* (1916). James Lawrence McDevitt, Jr., "The House of Rotch: Whaling Merchants of Massachusetts, 1734–1828," (Ph.D. diss., American Univ., 1978); John M. Bullard, *The Rotches* (1947); and Edward Byers, *The Nation of Nantucket: Society and Politics in an Early American Commercial Center, 1660–1820* (1986), provide detailed information on the Rotches and their surroundings.

ARTHUR J. WORRALL

ROTCH, William, Jr. (29 Nov. 1759–17 Apr. 1850), whaling merchant and New England Quaker leader, was born in Nantucket, Massachusetts, the son of William Rotch, a whaling merchant, and Elizabeth Barney. William Rotch, Jr., belonged to the third generation of the whaling dynasty founded by his grandfather Joseph Rotch on Nantucket and continued by his father. William served his apprenticeship in his father's firm in the years of crisis leading to independence and during the war that followed. The family's whaling interests were significant when he was born and approached dominance in the New England trade in the early 1770s. During this period his grandfather sought a better base for the family's business in Dartmouth, Massachusetts, the site of the future town of New Bedford. Rotch's training in the business world went well beyond the confines of provincial Nantucket, for he had to be aware of the complexity of the whaling trade and its relationship to political reality.

Like other traders, the Rotch firms experienced major setbacks because of the War for Independence. Their survival after the war depended on adjusting to new trading conditions, outside the protective framework of the British Empire that had hitherto sheltered them. Rotch's father tried to cope with these setbacks by going first to England and then to France to open new markets. In 1785 he left his son-in-law Samuel Rodman and Rotch in charge of the family interests. They shared control until 1787, when Rotch moved his share of the firm to Dartmouth (New Bedford as of 1793), returning to the area where his grandfather had earlier sought to expand family interests. He left Rodman to manage the remaining family business on Nantucket.

Rotch's move anticipated that of the family. His father joined him in 1795 because he found so much hostility to Rotch interests on Nantucket when he returned from France, hostility that also seems to have driven Rodman from the island three years later. Thereafter, Rotch continued active in the whaling trade. He also diversified, building toll bridges and investing in banking. After twenty years in the field, he became president of the Merchants National Bank. His international business led him into politics to oppose the Jeffersonian embargoes on international trade. Remarkably for a leading New England Quaker, at a time when Friends still refrained from direct political involvement, he actively supported the Federalists and ran unsuccessfully for Congress as a Federalist candidate in 1808.

Like most leading eighteenth-century Nantucket residents, Rotch grew up a Friend and continued his father's active role in the Quaker meeting. The Rotch family was close even by Quaker standards. Rotch married the sister of his brother-in-law Samuel Rodman. Rotch and Elizabeth Rodman married in 1782 and had seven children, six of whom lived beyond childhood. Rotch, Rodman, and their wives were at the center of New England Quaker leadership with other merchants like Moses Brown of Providence, Rhode Island, who was their occasional business associate. From 1788 to 1797, in 1801, and in 1813–1819 Rotch served as clerk (chair) of the chief decision-making group, the New England Yearly Meeting. He

and his family also supported Quaker educational efforts, among them the Quaker Academy in New Bedford. Like other Quakers, he joined antislavery efforts and assisted fugitive slaves, sometimes employing them on Rotch vessels.

The family's central role in New England Quakerism made their resignation from the faith in 1823 all the more damaging. In what came to be called the New Light Schism, the Rotches and their allies anticipated the Hicksite Separation in other parts of America that developed in 1827 and 1828. Partly doctrinal in its origins, this schism reflected conflict over unitarian-like views of an eighteenth-century Rhode Islander, Job Scott, who had died in Ireland in 1793 while on a religious visit. Scott's manuscripts, which challenged the widely accepted Quaker doctrine of the Trinity, had caused much debate among Friends throughout the United States, and Rotch and Rodman were active participants in the controversy. After the schism in 1823, most Rotches and Rodmans joined the Unitarian church and so disappeared from Quaker remembrance of things past despite their previously significant role in New England Quakerism.

A year after his wife's death in 1828, Rotch married Lydia Scott, Job Scott's daughter; they had no children. Rotch died in New Bedford.

• Ample manuscript holdings on Rotch are in the Old Dartmouth Historical Society, New Bedford, Mass. For his economic activities see James Lawrence McDevitt, Jr., "The House of Rotch: Whaling Merchants of Massachusetts, 1734–1828" (Ph.D. diss., American Univ., 1978), and John M. Bullard, *The Rotches* (1947). For religious background see Arthur J. Worrall, "New England Quakerism 1656–1830" (Ph.D. diss., Indiana Univ., 1969).

ARTHUR J. WORRALL

ROTH, Ernest David (17 Jan. 1879–20 Aug. 1964), artist, was born in Stuttgart, Germany. His parents' names are unknown. When he was five his family immigrated to the United States, settling in New York. Perhaps it was employment at an art store at age thirteen that inspired Roth to become an artist. Roth subsequently worked an early morning shift in a bakery owned by his father, while pursuing his studies in the afternoon and night classes at the National Academy of Design from 1900 to 1903. Although he earned a silver medal in the men's painting class, it was his instruction in etching under James D. Smillie that determined the principal course of his artistic career.

Roth soon discovered that architecture was the most congenial subject for both his painting and etching. As did many of his contemporaries, he found the ancient cities of Italy most engaging and accordingly moved in 1905 to Florence, where he remained for three years, traveling occasionally to other European cities and producing etchings of bridges, canals, street scenes, and houses, principally in Venice and Florence. Among the best known of this early series are *Fonte Vecchio, Evening, Florence* and *A Quiet Canal, Venice*.

In 1907 Roth was introduced to Frank Jewett Mather, Jr., Marquand Professor of Art and Archaeology at

Princeton, who had established a temporary residence in Florence. Mather took an immediate liking to Roth and his etchings of Venice and Florence. In the October 1911 issue of the *Print-Collector's Quarterly* Mather described "the rigorous fidelity of his portraiture of places we loved and the patient enthusiasm with which he had enmeshed the very spirit of the two cities." Mather remarked on the carefulness of Roth's work and his obvious love of the details of the architecture he depicted, which enabled him to develop his own distinctive style in a subject treated by scores of other artists.

After another European trip, in about 1910 Roth returned to New York, which remained his principal residence for many years despite regular trips abroad. By 1911 he was a regular contributor of etchings and paintings to exhibitions at both the National and the Pennsylvania academies. While his paintings suggest speed, vigor, and spontaneity, his etchings display the full resources of a complex medium, revealing Roth as a meticulous craftsman. A 1911 list of his published plates numbered sixty-two. He was fortunate in having as his dealer Frederick Keppel, who accorded Roth his first one-man show in 1913. From then on Roth exhibited his work regularly, right up to the beginning of World War II, and he was included in most issues of the annual *Fine Prints of the Year*, published from 1923 to 1937.

In addition to his artistic work, Roth participated fully in the community of American printmakers. He was a founder of the Brooklyn Society of Etchers, a charter member of the Painter-Gravers of America, and a member of the Salmagundi Club, the American Watercolor Society, the Chicago Society of Etchers, the Print Makers Society of California, and the National Arts Club. Many of these organizations had annual exhibitions with prizes, of which Roth's work earned a goodly share, including the Samuel T. Shaw Prize for etching at the Salmagundi Club in 1911, 1912, and 1916; the bronze medal for painting and the silver medal for etching at the Panama-Pacific Exposition in 1915; first prize at the Chicago Society of Etchers exhibit of 1915; the Logan prizes of 1917 and 1918; and the Bryan Prize for the best American print at the annual exhibition of the Print Makers Society of California. He was elected an associate of the National Academy of Design in 1920 and National Academician in 1928. Recognition also came in 1929 when the Crafton Collection in New York embarked upon the publication of *American Etchers*, a series of monographs for which Roth was selected as the subject of volume one.

Following his return from a trip to Italy in 1913, Roth established a studio at 232 West Fourteenth Street in New York. He married Elizabeth Mackenzie, a painter and a member of the staff of the *Woman's Home Companion* for twenty-four years; they had no children. While maintaining a studio in Greenwich Village, which became a place of rendezvous for etchers, they bought a house in Redding, Connecticut, in 1926 for weekend and vacation use until making it

their permanent home, probably soon after the outbreak of World War II.

During the 1930s Roth took an interest in the architecture of lower Manhattan. He embarked on a series of plates, including *Coenties Slip* and *Downtown New York, Financial Towers*, showing the aging waterfront with skyscrapers in the background. Perhaps the most distinguished of this series is *Queensborough Bridge, Manhattan*. In 1938 he executed commissions for six plates each of Columbia University and the University of Pennsylvania.

Roth's contribution to American art lies in his lifelong devotion to perfection in that part he made his own. He was a consummate craftsman, printing his own plates as well as those for many of his fellow artists, including John Sloan. He also played an active role in the community of artists, serving organizations, assisting with exhibitions, and lending a hand wherever he could. He died while visiting friends in Cambridge, New York. Although his work was long neglected following World War II, after about thirty years it was again sought by those who appreciated Roth's vision, particularly of architectural subjects, and his skill in portraying it.

• The largest public collection of Roth's etchings and drawings is in the Mattatuck Museum, Waterbury, Conn., where also may be found some of his papers, correspondence, and awards. Examples of his work are in most major American art museums. The New York Public Library has a collection of exhibit brochures and newspaper clippings that has been microfilmed by the Archives of American Art. In addition to publications mentioned above, see John Taylor Arms, "Ernest D. Roth, Etcher," *Print Collector's Quarterly* 25 (1938): 33–57, and Elton W. Hall, "The Etchings of Ernest Roth and André Smith," in *Aspects of American Printmaking, 1800–1950*, ed. James O'Gorman (1988).

ELTON W. HALL

ROTH, Henry (8 Feb. 1906–13 Oct. 1995), writer, was born in Tysmenitz, located in what was then the Austro-Hungarian province of Galitzia, the son of Herman Roth, a waiter, and Leah (maiden name unknown). In 1907 the elder Roth immigrated to America first, earning money for the family's passage; Leah and eighteen-month-old Henry followed soon thereafter. After living two years in the Brownsville section of Brooklyn, the Roths moved to New York's Lower East Side in 1910, which was a predominantly Jewish enclave of recent immigrants. Henry flourished in this insular environment. When his parents decided to move to Harlem in 1914, Roth experienced great difficulty adapting. At first the family moved to a Jewish section of Harlem, but eventually they found more comfortable quarters in an Irish-dominated area. "Moving to Harlem was a disaster. . . . My identity disintegrated," Roth recalled in a 1983 unpublished interview with Margie Goldsmith. One source of escape for Roth at this difficult time was the discovery of fairy tales, from which he could create a fantasy world. After graduating from DeWitt Clinton High School in 1924, Roth attended the City College of New York.

Roth's first brush with literary success occurred at City College when his freshman English essay, "Impressions of a Plumber," was published in the college's literary magazine, the *Lavender*. Another important event at this time occurred when Roth's friend, Lester Winter, introduced Roth to his former English professor at New York University, Eda Lou Walton. Roth became intimate with Walton a short time later. She was particularly important to him as a mentor-benefactor, encouraging Roth's writing abilities and introducing him to a number of important literary and social figures. When Roth moved into Walton's Greenwich Village apartment in 1928, he further distanced himself from his family, who did not approve of his living arrangements with this much older, non-Jewish woman. Roth sought acceptance in Walton's intellectual circle, which included Margaret Mead, Hart Crane, and Louis Bogan. Whether Roth was encouraged or intimidated by this group is not exactly known.

By 1930 Roth had enough confidence to begin writing his first novel, *Call It Sleep*. With full financial support from Walton, Roth spent the next four years writing and rewriting the story of David Schearl, the six-year-old son of recently emigrated parents, whose young life closely resembled Roth's own childhood. Few publishers expressed interest in *Call It Sleep* because its moody undertones and true-to-life depictions of social and family conflicts were thought to be unmarketable to the nation's readers, who were struggling with the depression. Finally, in 1934, with Walton's persuasion, David Mandel (who later married Walton) agreed to issue the novel via the Robert O. Ballou Publishing Company, of which he was a partner. The book received many positive reviews despite a protest from leftist publications. The *New Masses*, for example, complained that "it is a pity that so many young writers drawn from the proletariat can make no better use of their working class experience than as material for introspective and febrile novels." Roth, who joined the Communist party in 1934, was surprised by the criticism of what he thought was a proletarian novel.

In 1935 Roth began a novel based on a man he met through the Communist party who was forced to sell the *Daily Worker* when he lost his right arm at a factory job. Scribners bought the rights from Ballou, which went bankrupt shortly after publishing *Call It Sleep*, and even advanced Roth some money after Maxwell Perkins responded favorably to the first seventy-five pages. The novel, however, was never completed. Only a fragment remains, titled "If We Had Bacon," which was published in 1936 in a small magazine, *Signatures: Works in Progress*.

There followed a long stretch, almost fifty years, before Roth would attempt another novel. Although he avoided the term "writer's block," Roth published only a smattering of short prose pieces after his aborted attempt at a second novel. The years that passed, though, were not wasted. Roth met his wife, Muriel Parker, a pianist and composer, at Yaddo, the artists'

colony in Saratoga Springs, New York, in 1938. They married the following year; they had two sons. Eventually the couple settled in Maine, where Roth took on a number of occupations, including teaching Latin, working as a psychiatric aide, and raising waterfowl. In 1946 Roth decided that his literary career was over and, in a symbolic purging, burned a number of manuscripts and journals. Years later he explained his action: "I felt my whole literary past no longer had any bearing on *me*. So why keep the stuff?" (Lyons, p. 173).

Roth could not have known that ten years later he would be rediscovered by critics. His road back to public recognition began with a 1956 *American Scholar* symposium, in which critics were asked to name novels that had been neglected. *Call It Sleep* was the only book mentioned by two different critics, Leslie Fiedler and Alfred Kazin. An attractive hardback edition of the novel was released in 1960 by Cooper Square Publisher, but it took an Avon Books paperback edition in 1964 for Roth to receive extensive recognition. Walter Allen, in an afterword for the 1964 Avon edition, declared that the novel was "itself enough to make any man's reputation." After Irving Howe's front-page review in the *New York Times Book Review* (1964), the novel became a national bestseller. In 1965 Roth received a grant from the National Institute of Arts and Letters. Money from the grant allowed Roth and his wife to travel extensively in Europe, Mexico, and Israel.

While in Spain, Roth became interested in the Spanish Inquisition, particularly as it pertained to the persecution of Jews. Roth later believed that his time in Spain was an attempt to find his way back "into something related to Judaism." A story he wrote out of his experiences, "The Surveyor," was published in the *New Yorker* in 1966. When the Six-Day War broke out in the Middle East, Roth found himself strongly identifying with the Israelis, despite having discarded his religious affiliation many years before. Around this time he considered moving to Israel permanently but instead decided to settle in Albuquerque, New Mexico, after spending a year as the D. H. Lawrence Fellow at the University of New Mexico. His next serious phase of writing began in 1979 with a small volume, *Nature's First Green*, which was solicited by Bill Targ, the former editor in chief of Putnam, for the limited-edition series Targ was publishing privately. Roth credits Targ with providing the encouragement he needed to continue his writing with the same dedication that resulted in *Call It Sleep*.

In 1979 Roth embarked on a massive project, a six-volume "memoir-form novel," *Mercy of a Rude Stream*, which he completed before his death in Albuquerque. Although he originally planned on publishing the work posthumously, the deaths of several people close to him, particularly his wife's in 1990, removed his fear of embarrassing anyone who might have recognized himself or herself in the portrayals. The first volume, *A Star Shines over Mt. Morris Park* (1994), is similar in theme to the story of childlike David Schearl, who struggles to find comfort and meaning in alien surroundings. Unlike *Call It Sleep*, though, the protagonist Ira Stigman appears not only as a child but as an elderly writer with rheumatoid arthritis who lives with his loving wife in a New Mexico mobile home.

The second volume of the series, *A Diving Rock on the Hudson* (1995), covers Stigman's adolescence amid the backdrop of the Roaring Twenties. *From Bondage* (1996) treats the tumultuous personal and professional relationship that Stigman maintains with an older intellectual woman, who was based on Walton. The title also suggests how imprisoned Roth felt by not completing a second novel for over fifty years and the satisfaction that he experienced once he overcame his psychological barrier. In an interview Roth spoke of his renewed ability to write: "I no longer felt that horrendous indecision immobilizing me. I found I could write, and finding I could write, I did" (Materassi, p. 257).

Roth's late work guarantees that his reputation will not be based solely on his classic *Call It Sleep*. Even so, that remarkable first novel, praised for its combination of realistic detail, psychological symbolism, and modernist techniques, marks an important transition in Jewish-American literature from the works of early immigrant writers such as Abraham Cahan and Anzia Yezierska to later modern voices such as Saul Bellow and Philip Roth.

• Roth's letters and unpublished papers are in the Mugar Memorial Library at Boston University. The most comprehensive study of Roth is Bonnie Lyons, *Henry Roth: The Man and His Work* (1977). See also Lyons, "An Interview with Henry Roth," *Shenandoah* 25 (1973): 48–71. Other useful interviews are in Mario Materassi, ed., *Shifting Landscape: A Composite, 1925–1987* (1987), a collection of essays and short stories compiled by the Italian translator of *Call It Sleep*. In addition, see Sam Girgus, *The New Covenant: Jewish Writers and the American Idea* (1984), and Gary Epstein, "Auto-Obituary: The Death of the Artist in Henry Roth's *Call It Sleep*," *Studies in American Jewish Literature* 5 (Spring 1979).

ELLYN LEM

ROTHAFEL, Roxy (9 July 1881–13 Jan. 1936), movie theater impresario and early radio host, was born Samuel Lionel Rothapfel in Stillwater, Minnesota, the son of Gustav Rothapfel, a shoemaker, and Cecelia Schwerzens. The younger Rothafel dropped the "p" from his family name at the end of World War I when names of Germanic origin were in disfavor. His family moved to Brooklyn, New York, in 1894, and his education ended with grammar school. At age fourteen, Rothafel began drifting from one temporary job to another. He joined the Marine Corps in 1902, saw action in China's Boxer Rebellion, and ended military service as a sergeant in 1905. He remained a believer in military discipline, and later uniformed ushers in his theaters drilled and saluted.

Out of the marines, Rothafel played semiprofessional baseball and gained the nickname "Roxy." He subsequently became an itinerant book salesman in the coal-mining region of Pennsylvania. His earliest experience in staging a show was a successful minstrel show he put on in Carbondale, Pennsylvania. In 1908 he became a barman at a saloon in Forest City, Pennsylvania, for a year. In 1909 he married the barkeeper's daughter, Rosa Freedman; they had two children.

Rothafel realized the saloon's back room could be used to exhibit one-reel movies for five cents, as the nickelodeons of bigger cities did. He borrowed folding chairs from the undertaker next door, hung a bed sheet as a screen, walked seven miles to Carbondale to collect the reels, and then ran the projector himself. His "Family Theater" offered piano selections and singers between the reels, and lights of changing color set a mood for his presentation.

Rothafel attempted to provide the sensual richness of sound and color missing in his flickering black-and-white movies. He even tried to appeal to smell by placing sponges soaked in rosewater in front of electric fans when he showed a reel on the Pasadena Rose Festival. According to one New York newspaper, his effects were successful: "To the coal miners and their ladies the illusion thereby created was overwhelming in its elegance" (*Herald Tribune*, 14 Jan. 1936). Local film distributors soon noticed that the little hall in Forest City was doing as much business as larger exhibitors.

In 1910 Rothafel was hired by vaudeville mogul B. F. Keith to travel the circuit of his variety houses and smarten up the presentation of short films. Soon after, Rothafel was hired to rescue a foundering legitimate theater in Milwaukee, which he converted to a movie house showing the longer "feature films" that were being made in 1911–1912. Rothafel's makeover emphasized comfort and family atmosphere.

His successful theater was noted among exhibitors, and in 1913 Rothafel was brought to New York City to rescue the Regent. Here he built an impressive stage set, including a flower-filled conservatory with a trickling fountain around the screen, and rose-tinted lights in the auditorium, as well as a ventilating system, carpet, and upholstered seats. He appealed to middle-class residents with luxurious facilities and a "cultured" film for the first program, *The Last Days of Pompeii* (1913). The *Motion Picture News* (6 Dec. 1913) called the presentation a "remarkable incident in the history of the motion picture." Rothafel had found a combination of "class" and eye-filling spectacle. He was quoted in *Green Book Magazine* (1914) as saying: "Don't 'give the people what they want'—give 'em something better."

Comfort and sensually rich spectacle prevailed in the theaters Rothafel managed from 1914 through 1919. At the Strand during 1914 and 1915 he installed four projectors to eliminate pauses in the film. Rothafel managed the Knickerbocker while its owners constructed two custom-built, elegant movie houses, the Rialto and the Rivoli, for him to manage, and in early 1916 he brought sound effects to the Knickerbocker. In both the Rialto and the Rivoli, the stage presentations related to each week's film, the cast grew, and the audience was led to its seats by drill teams of ushers. At the Rialto's opening, the feature film and short subjects were surrounded by seven stage numbers involving musicians and dancers.

In return for his ceaseless work in staging weekly presentations, Rothafel demanded a personal suite at the Rivoli, including a Japanese valet whose main duty was to grill his employer's hot dogs. Rothafel's sense of his own importance grew. His only period away from the theaters was during World War I, when he became a colonel of the Marine Corps Reserves and helped put together propaganda films to inspire patriotism.

In 1919 Rothafel quit the Rialto and the Rivoli after accountants questioned some long-distance phone calls to the Havre de Grace racetrack that he charged to the theater. He tried producing stage presentation units to tour theaters, but the venture went nowhere. At the end of the year he was hired to bring attendance and profits up at Manhattan's Capitol, where he was in charge of creating elaborate stage presentations. Rothafel's work soon put the theater in the black, and he began producing presentations that toured the forty theaters controlled by the Capitol's owners.

Rothafel let engineers use the auditorium of the Capitol to test a new public-address system in 1922. Once he found he could spare himself much shouting during rehearsals by using a microphone, he happily allowed them to set up microphones around the theater proscenium to pick up the music of the orchestra, which they relayed to their lab across town. American Telephone and Telegraph then asked to broadcast their music on their nascent radio station WEAF. Rothafel agreed and from a microphone behind the scenes narrated what was happening on stage at the time. Also on the radio station he advertised the Capitol as a good place of entertainment. Public response was so great that soon Rothafel was narrating a special program made up of Capitol performers called "Roxy's Gang." Rothafel's warm, folksy way of talking to the unseen audience, and his signature sign-off of "Good night . . . pleasant dreams . . . God bless you" made him a national radio personality. He stayed with the programs until 1925, when he left the Capitol. That same year he co-wrote *Broadcasting: Its New Day*. He also wrote the *Encyclopedia Britannica* entry on stage lighting.

Rothafel's next project was the construction of a "Cathedral of the Motion Picture" in New York: the Roxy Theater. He wanted to be its "absolute despot" and supervised every detail, down to the buttons on the ushers' uniforms. When the Roxy opened in 1927, its reported cost was $10 million, and it had a staff of hundreds. Its auditorium seated 6,200, and its music library contained 10,000 pieces and 50,000 orchestrations. Its architectural style was a dream of fantastic opulence. A 1929 cartoon in the *New Yorker* depicts a little girl in the Roxy's lobby asking, "Mama, does God live here?" Rothafel, in fact, had an apartment there.

Rothafel's grandeur declined with the arrival of talking pictures and the Great Depression. Though the movie palaces stayed in use for years to come (the Roxy was demolished in 1960), the day of spectacular staged presentations ended with silent movies.

Rothafel quit his "Cathedral" kingdom to direct the creation of a still greater movie palace, the Radio City Music Hall—and a smaller theater, intended to be called the RKO Roxy, until the courts decided Rothafel no longer owned his nickname—at Rockefeller Center. There Rothafel decided to show no movies but in a disastrous mistake presented sumptuous stage shows. His four-hour opening program tried to incorporate all he had ever done, but the public found it dull and elephantine. After the theater opening night, Rothafel had a heart attack, and when he returned months later the house offered primarily feature sound films.

Rothafel either resigned or was forced to quit, according to varying reports. In 1933 his effort to revitalize a Philadelphia movie theater failed. He died of a heart attack in a New York City hotel suite where he and his wife were living.

• Materials on the life and career of Roxy Rothafel are in the Billy Rose Theatre Collection, New York Public Library for the Performing Arts, Lincoln Center. Ben M. Hall, in *The Best Remaining Seats: The Golden Age of the Movie Palace* (1988), includes many biographical details and anecdotes about Rothafel, as well as photographs, together with numerous quotations from publications of the time. Reminiscences and anecdotes are in Terry Ramseye, "Intimate Visits to the Homes of Film Magnates," *Photoplay*, Oct. 1927, with photograph. Views of Rothafel's effect on the movies are given in Gilbert Seldes, *The Movies Come from America* (1937), and Benjamin Hampton, *The History of the Movies* (1931). Obituaries are in the *New York Times* and the *New York Herald Tribune*, both 14 Jan. 1936, and in *Variety*, 15 Jan. 1936.

WILLIAM STEPHENSON

ROTHERMEL, Peter Frederick (8 July 1812–15 Aug. 1895), painter, was born in Nescopeck, Luzerne County, Pennsylvania, the son of John Peter Rothermel and Catherine Huff Kauffman, innkeepers and farmers. At the age of twenty, Rothermel, who had worked briefly as a surveyor, moved to Philadelphia and became a sign painter. He then studied drawing under John Rubens Smith and painting with Bass Otis in the mid- to late 1830s. Initially the young artist specialized in portraiture, but in the 1840s he turned to history painting, the genre on which he built his reputation. His first success was *De Soto Discovering the Mississippi* (Saint Bonaventure University Art Collection, St. Bonaventure, N.Y.), which was exhibited at the Pennsylvania Academy of the Fine Arts in 1843 and the following year at the National Academy of Design, where it was purchased by the American Art-Union. That same year—1844—Rothermel married Caroline G. Goodhart; they had three children.

The 1840s saw Rothermel become a significant part of the Philadelphia art world. He opened a studio in "Art Row," Sansom Street, below Eighth Street.

Members of the Artists' Fund Society elected him their vice president in 1844. From 1847—the year the National Academy of Design elected him an honorary member—to 1855 Rothermel served as a director of the Pennsylvania Academy of the Fine Arts, where he played an important role in establishing a regular curriculum of instruction at the academy. During these years, illustrations by Rothermel and engraved reproductions of his paintings helped secure his artistic recognition by their appearance in such journals as *Godey's Lady's Book*, *Eclectic Magazine*, and *Sartain's Union Magazine*. The Art Union of Philadelphia commissioned him to paint *Patrick Henry in the House of Burgesses of Virginia, Delivering His Celebrated Speech against the Stamp Act* (1851, "Red Hill," Patrick Henry National Memorial Shrine, Brookneal, Va.). Art Union members received a copy of Alfred Jones's engraving of the painting and the opportunity to win the large canvas itself, as it was the union's first prize for 1852. The painting also bolstered Rothermel's national reputation, as it was exhibited in Baltimore, Washington, D.C., and Richmond. At this time a number of artists petitioned Congress to commission Rothermel to paint a large historical work for the Capitol. Nothing came of this, however.

In 1856 Rothermel traveled to Europe, visiting London, Paris, Düsseldorf, Munich, Genoa, Venice, and Florence and living for two years in Rome and nearby Genazzano. Several paintings were sold to foreign nobility, including the Grand Duchess Helena of Russia. Prior to returning home, Rothermel exhibited three works in the 1859 Paris Salon, where he received an honorable mention. Back in Philadelphia, the artist renewed his participation in various art organizations. In 1860 the Pennsylvania Academy of the Fine Arts named him a Pennsylvania Academician; in 1866 and 1867 he served as president of the academy's Council of Academicians. In 1864 he was elected president of the Artists' Fund Society and chairman of the Philadelphia artists exhibiting in the Great Central Fair of the U.S. Sanitary Commission in Logan Square. Rothermel held memberships in the Graphic Club, the Philadelphia Sketch Club, the Philadelphia Society of Artists, the Historical Society of Pennsylvania, and the American Philosophical Society and was a founding member of the Union League of Philadelphia.

In their 1884 history of Philadelphia, J. Thomas Scharf and Thompson Westcott declared, "No Philadelphia artist is more widely known than Peter F. Rothermel." While this claim was fully justified at the time, the artist's posthumous fame vanished as the type of art he practiced—history painting—fell out of favor with artists and critics attuned to modernism. History paintings depicted significant human events and actions (real and fictive) with the aim of educating, influencing, and entertaining the viewer. Modernists, wedded to an art for art's sake, abstraction, and an emphasis on the new, regarded this kind of painting as outmoded.

Longer than any other nineteenth-century American painter, Rothermel remained true to the academic tradition of grand style history painting. Stylistically, his compositions display romantically idealized figures, a theatrical sensibility, and the expressive use of heightened colors, especially orangish red. Two artists that Rothermel greatly admired, and to whom he was compared, were Peter Paul Rubens and Eugène Delacroix. Dramatic scenes of confrontation characterize a number of Rothermel's pictures, which often found their inspiration in the Bible, William Shakespeare's plays, and histories by Washington Irving and William Prescott. Among his best-known works are *The Landing of the Pilgrims* (1854, Kirby Collection, Lafayette College, Easton, Pa.); *King Lear* (1858, Schwarz Gallery, Philadelphia); *Christ among the Doctors* (1861, Reading Public Museum, Reading, Pa.); *First Reading of the Declaration of Independence* (1861, Union League of Philadelphia); *Christian Martyrs in the Coliseum* (1862, unlocated); and *State House, the Day of the Battle of Germantown* (1862, Museum of American Art, Pennsylvania Academy of the Fine Arts). Rothermel also painted portraits throughout his career (including those of Edwin Forrest, Fanny Kemble, and Hector Tyndale), but these were clearly secondary to his commitment to history painting.

Rothermel's largest and most ambitious painting was *The Battle of Gettysburg: Pickett's Charge* (State Museum of Pennsylvania). Commissioned by the commonwealth of Pennsylvania for $25,000, the huge canvas—sixteen by nearly thirty-two feet—occupied the artist from 1867 to 1870. Too big for its intended site in Harrisburg, the painting was put on tour, traveling to Boston and Chicago (where it was damaged during the Great Fire of 1871). In 1876 it appeared—conspicuously and controversially, in the eyes of New York art critics—in the art gallery of the Centennial Exhibition. Some critics found the display of the grandiose battle inappropriate during a time of reconciliation. With the completion of a building large enough to house it, the canvas was finally installed in Harrisburg in 1894.

Owing to poor health, Rothermel virtually ceased painting in the mid-1880s; his last years were spent at his country home, "Grassmere," near Linfield, Montgomery County, Pennsylvania, where he died. The Art Club of Philadelphia honored him with a large reception in 1890. Rothermel's death in 1895 signified the close of an era in the history of American art and the passing of the tradition of grand style history painting. Throughout the twentieth century, reproductions of Rothermel's history paintings appeared in a variety of texts, contributing to the shaping of the past.

• For overviews of Rothermel's art and career, see Mark Thistlethwaite, *Painting in the Grand Manner: The Art of Peter Frederick Rothermel (1812–1895)* (1995); Kent Ahrens, "Painting for Peer, Patron, and the Public," *Pennsylvania Heritage* 18 (Spring 1992): 24–31; Thistlethwaite, "Peter F. Rothermel: A Forgotten History Painter," *Antiques* 124 (Nov. 1983): 1016–22; and Thomas Dunn English, "Peter F. Rothermel," *Sartain's Union Magazine of Literature and Art* 10 (Jan. 1852): 13–16. For more specific discussions, see Donald A. Winer, "Rothermel's Battle of Gettysburg: A Victorian's View of the Civil War," *Nineteenth Century* 1 (Winter 1975): 6–10, and Edwin B. Coddington, "Rothermel's Painting of the Battle of Gettysburg," *Pennsylvania History* 27 (Jan. 1860): 1–27.

MARK THISTLETHWAITE

ROTHKO, Mark (25 Sept. 1903–25 Feb. 1970), painter, was born Marcus Rothkowitz in Dvinsk, Russia (now Daugavpils, Latvia), the son of Jacob Rothkowitz, a pharmacist, and Anna Goldin. As a child he attended Jewish religious schools. When he was about seven, religious and economic pressures caused his father to immigrate to Portland, Oregon. The family followed in 1913, and a year later his father died. Although he had spoken no English upon his arrival, he quickly caught up with his schoolmates and graduated from Lincoln High School in 1921. While in high school he helped support the family by selling newspapers and working for the tailoring business of relatives, among his other jobs. Sometime around 1940, after becoming a U.S. citizen, he began to use the name Rothko but did not settle on Mark for some time. He did not legally change his name to Mark Rothko until 1958.

Rothko was awarded a scholarship to Yale in 1921. He soon became disenchanted with university life, however, and so helped found the *Yale Saturday Evening Pest*, an underground newspaper that was critical of the school's social, rather than academic, focus. Rothko left Yale in 1923 and went to New York City, where while visiting a friend who was attending the Art Students League, he decided to study art. He had enjoyed drawing and sketching as a child but had received no formal art training. In later years he said it was the sight of art students sketching a nude model that brought him to art.

After a few months Rothko left the Art Students League and returned to Portland, where he remained for a few years, returning to New York in 1925. He initially enrolled in a class given by Arshile Gorky at the New School of Design but before long had returned to the Art Students League, where he studied with the modernist painter Max Weber. To support himself Rothko held a number of odd jobs, among them garment cutter and illustrator for an advertising agency. It was as a commercial artist that he became entangled in a legal dispute that left him deep in debt and disillusioned by the judicial system. The incident began in 1927, when Rothko met popular author Lewis Browne at the home of a mutual friend. After showing Browne samples of his work, Rothko was invited to illustrate Browne's next work, *The Graphic Bible*. Their working relationship quickly deteriorated, however, and in late 1928 Rothko sued Browne over their agreement. The case was eventually decided in Browne's favor. The many pages of Rothko's testimony provide insight into his artistic development in this period.

Also to help support himself, from 1929 to 1952 Rothko taught art to children at the Center Academy, a progressive yeshiva, or Jewish school, in Brooklyn. Around the time he began teaching at the academy,

Rothko became friends with the painter Milton Avery. Rothko and other artists, among them Adolph Gottlieb, John Graham, and Barnett Newman, were frequent visitors to Avery's studio, and Rothko remained close to Avery and his wife, Sally, until Avery's death in 1965. In the summer of 1932, while vacationing near Lake George, New York, Rothko met Edith Sachar, whom he married two months later; the couple had no children.

In 1933, while Rothko was visiting his family in Oregon, the Portland Art Museum presented a solo exhibition of his drawings and watercolors along with a selection of his students' work. That same year his first solo exhibition in New York was held at the Contemporary Arts Gallery. Two years later, in 1935, Rothko took part in a group exhibition at the Gallery Secession in New York. He and a number of other artists became dissatisfied with the gallery, however, and joined together in a loose affiliation they dubbed The Ten. The group did not draw up a manifesto but generally painted in a loose, abstract manner. Included among their number were Ben-Zion, Ilya Bolotowsky, Gottlieb, and Joseph Solman. The group often numbered less than ten and commonly were referred to as The Ten Who Are Nine. The Ten's first exhibition was held at New York's Montross Gallery in late 1935, and the group continued to exhibit until 1939.

As the economic depression worsened in the 1930s, Rothko found work through the federal government's relief projects for artists. In 1936–1937 he was a member of the Treasury Relief Art Project, and after that program ended, he joined the Works Progress Administration's Federal Art's Project, where he remained until 1939. While he was a government artist Rothko worked on murals (for which sketches exist) as well as for the easel division, and his work from this period is aptly typified by his Subway series, representational paintings that depict individuals or groups of attenuated figures. Works in this series include *Subway (Subterranean Fantasy)* (c. 1936, National Gallery of Art) and *Subway Scene* (1938, National Gallery of Art). The series is notable, in the view of art historian William Rubin, "for the pervasive loneliness that characterized his treatment of the subject" (*New York Times*, 8 Mar. 1970). Another early work, *The Rothkowitz Family* (c. 1930s, National Gallery of Art), is representative of many untitled paintings in which Rothko depicted chunky, rounded figures.

Rothko's government work, as well as his concern about the ominous events unfolding in Europe, led him to become a U.S. citizen in 1938. Two years later he became, along with Meyer Schapiro, Gottlieb, and Bolotowsky, a founding member of the Federation of Modern Painters and Sculptors. The group, which had broken off from the American Artists' Congress in protest over the Nazi-Soviet pact of late 1939, provided Rothko with an active forum for exhibiting his work. Soon after the group was formed, its First Exhibition of Paintings and Sculpture opened at the New York's World's Fair. Regular exhibitions of work by Federation members were held in New York City after

1941, and smaller exhibitions were held in many locations throughout the country.

Rothko and Sachar separated in 1943 and were divorced in 1944. The following year he married Mary Alice "Mell" Beistle, an illustrator of children's books whom he had met just months before at a party given by photographer Aaron Siskind. Rothko and Beistle had two children.

In the early 1940s Rothko became interested in Greco-Roman myths and Christian theology, and together with Gottlieb he developed a complex aesthetic based on these concepts. Among his works from this period are *The Omen of the Eagle* (1942, National Gallery of Art) and *The Syrian Bull* (1943, Collection of Mrs. Barnett Newman). The almost surreal images and biomorphic shapes of these paintings were far removed from the pictorial realism that had characterized his earlier work. Influenced by the exiled French surrealist artists, Rothko's work became more abstract, and in such paintings as *Slow Swirl at the Edge of the Sea* (1944, Museum of Modern Art) and *Birth of Cephalopods* (1944, National Gallery of Art), the biomorphic forms of later surrealism began to appear.

New York art dealer Peggy Guggenheim began to represent Rothko in late 1944, and she presented a solo exhibition of his work at her Art of This Century gallery in early 1945. In 1946 art dealer Betty Parsons signed Rothko, Jackson Pollock, Clyfford Still, and Barnett Newman—her Four Horsemen of the Apocalypse—to exhibit at the gallery she was just opening. Rothko's first solo exhibition at the Betty Parsons Gallery took place the following year, and over the proceeding four years the gallery presented five solo exhibitions of his work.

Between 1947 and 1950 Rothko made radical changes in his work, replacing the earlier biomorphic surrealist forms with his own style of abstraction. He had previously approached his art with caution, but in this period he began to experiment. By 1949, as reflected in such works as *Violet, Black, Orange, Yellow on White and Red* (1949, Guggenheim) and *Number 18* (1948–1949, Vassar College Art Gallery), he had arrived at the classic Rothko pictorial formulation. Described soon after Rothko's death by critic Harold Rosenberg, writing in the *New Yorker* (28 Mar. 1970), this formulation "consisted of the rectangle of the canvas as a one-color ground visible along the edge of—and occasionally through an opening between—three or four horizontal blocks of color with brushed surfaces and furry borders." Rothko's 1949 exhibition at the Betty Parsons Gallery was the first devoted entirely to his new style of work: abstract with simple and straightforward rather than surrealist-sounding titles. At this important time in his development, Rothko's essay "The Romantics Were Prompted" appeared in *Possibilities* (Winter 1947–1948). In this, his only extended published work on art, Rothko noted in a manner that exemplified his self-mythification: "I do not believe that there was ever a question of being abstract or representational. It is really a matter of ending this

silence and solitude, of breathing and stretching one's arms again" (quoted in Breslin, p. 245).

In early 1950 Rothko was one of eighteen painters who protested the acquisitions policy of the Metropolitan Museum of Art in New York. After the group received nationwide publicity from a profile in *Life* magazine titled "Irascible Group of Advanced Artists Led Fight against Show" (15 Jan. 1951), they came to be called "the Irascibles." In the art world the group became known both as the New York School and as abstract expressionists. An outgrowth of surrealism, abstract expressionism is characterized by large canvases, freedom from traditional motifs and traditional aesthetic values, and a de-emphasis of the figure. Although he continues to be grouped with the abstract expressionists—and is often referred to as a key figure in the group—Rothko was actually never comfortable with the label. He was active in artists' organizations and relaxed in social groups, but he disliked the extroverted egotism of some abstract expressionists, in particular, Jackson Pollock. In the split of the abstract expressionists into "uptown" and "downtown" factions, Rothko was considered part of the "uptown" group, which included Gottlieb, Robert Motherwell, and Newman, all of whom evoked a kind of mysticism in their work. Unlike the "downtown" artists—Pollock, Willem de Kooning, and Franz Kline—who exemplified the action-painting mode of abstract expressionism and met in studios and the Cedar Bar in Greenwich Village, Rothko and the "uptown" artists preferred more refined environments. Indeed, Rothko's preference was solitude.

In the spring of 1950 Rothko made his first trip to Europe, spending five months in France, Italy, and London. Soon after his return he began to teach printmaking and art theory but not painting at Brooklyn College. Other teaching posts he held included summer sessions at the California School of Fine Arts (1947 and 1948), the University of Colorado (1955), and Tulane University (1957). Rothko's work from this period was generally infused with color. Large areas of bright yellow, blue, orange, and even white dominate *Number 18* (1951, Munson-Williams Proctor Institute, Utica, N.Y.), *Ochre and Red on Red* (1954, Phillips Collection, Washington, D.C.), and *Yellow, Blue on Orange* (1955, Museum of Art, Carnegie Institute, Pittsburgh).

In 1954 Rothko became the last of Betty Parson's Four Horsemen to leave her gallery. Like Pollock and Still, he enlisted Sidney Janis as his new dealer. With Janis's help Rothko's income from painting, which had been rising steadily, dramatically increased, and in 1959 he earned more than $60,000 from the sales of his work. Financial success was not always accompanied by critical acclaim, however. In her review of his 1955 exhibition at the Sidney Janis Gallery, *New York Herald Tribune* critic Emily Genauer commented that as "Rothko's pictures get bigger and bigger" they "say less and less" (15 Apr. 1955). Rothko countered such criticism in a lecture at the Pratt Institute in 1958: "There are some artists who feel they must tell all, but

I'm not one of them," he said. As to the increasingly large scale of his work, he added, "I paint large pictures because I want to create a state of intimacy" (*New York Times*, 31 Oct. 1958). In fact, Rothko's hypnotic fields of color do not so much dominate his compositions as subsume them.

After 1957 Rothko's work began to turn darker and more somber. Examples from this period include *Light Cloud, Dark Cloud* (1957, Fort Worth Art Museum) and *Red, Brown and Black* (1958, Museum of Modern Art). Some critics, and many collectors, continued to prefer the more brilliant work from the early 1950s; others, such as Elaine de Kooning, gave more positive assessments of his newer work. In the catalog *Mark Rothko* for his 1957 exhibition at the Contemporary Arts Museum in Houston, de Kooning wrote: "His edgeless shapes loom oppressively in an incandescent void, waiting, breathing, expanding, approaching, threatening."

Along with painter Mark Tobey and sculptors David Smith and Seymour Lipton, Rothko represented the United States in the XXIX Venice Biennale in 1958. That same year he also received a commission from the Seagram company to create a series of murals for the Four Seasons restaurant, located in the company's new Park Avenue tower designed by Mies van der Rohe. While working almost exclusively on the Seagram murals, Rothko created a large suite of related works, but in 1959, after visiting the proposed location of the murals, which he claimed to have thought would be a "worker's cafeteria" rather than an upscale restaurant, he canceled the contract and returned his fee. Two years later a major retrospective of his work was held at the Museum of Modern Art in New York. Personally directing the installation, Rothko had the paintings hung close together and illuminated only with dim lights. The resulting effect made the paintings seem to glow luminously in the dark. The exhibition was well received and traveled throughout Europe.

Early in 1962 Rothko began another mural commission, this time for a dining room at Harvard University. In 1963, after the five large paintings, all on a crimson field, were exhibited at the Guggenheim Museum in New York, they were installed at Harvard. Sunlight, less-than-optimum environmental conditions, and Rothko's use of unstable paints caused the canvases to deteriorate and the panels were removed from permanent display in 1979. Also in 1962, an exhibition of pop art at the Sidney Janis Gallery led Rothko, Gottlieb, and other abstract artists to break their association with the gallery. Rothko, seeing nothing of the sublime in pop art, thought it unworthy of being called art at all. Briefly shunning the gallery system entirely, Rothko sold his paintings out of his studio, but the burden of both creating and selling his work proved to be too much, and in 1963 he signed a contract with Marlborough Galleries, which assured him of a substantial as well as steady income.

Rothko had always believed that his works would be displayed to best effect in an intimate setting in which viewers were surrounded by paintings. He got the chance in 1964 when John and Dominique de Menil of Houston commissioned him to create multiple works for an interdenominational chapel to be operated under the auspices of the city's Institute for Religious and Human Development. For the next three years Rothko worked on what eventually totaled fourteen paintings, characterized by large fields of dark, rich colors. Construction was delayed, however, and the paintings were not installed until 1971, the year the building was dedicated as the Rothko Chapel. Critics have differed on whether or not the chapel was in fact an effective setting for the display of these works.

Much of Rothko's time from 1967 to 1969 was taken up with negotiation's to present, as a gift to London's Tate Gallery, the completed final series of Seagram murals (the first series had been sold as individual works; the second, abandoned, unfinished). Rothko, characteristically attempting to control the future fate of the paintings, had the deed stipulate that the nine works were to be placed in a room by themselves and never shown with other paintings.

After Rothko suffered an aneurysm in April 1968, he had a will drawn up in which the Mark Rothko Foundation was created to care for his works and provide financial assistance to older artists after his death. Now physically incapable of working on his large-scale paintings, Rothko began to create small acrylic paintings on ragpaper. Also after his aneurysm, Rothko's second marriage began to deteriorate. In January 1969 he moved out of the couple's Manhattan townhouse and into his studio. Soon thereafter he became involved with Rita Reinhardt, the widow of Rothko's fellow "irascible" Ad Reinhardt.

Despite his receipt of numerous accolades in these years—including induction into the National Institute of Arts and Letters in 1968—Rothko became increasingly depressed, a condition that was exacerbated by the combinations of medications he was taking for his heart condition. A little over a year after separating from his wife, Rothko committed suicide in his studio by slashing his arms above the elbows. After his death, Rothko's children began a protracted legal battle against his executors and Marlborough Galleries. In late 1975 most of his remaining works were turned over to the children and the Mark Rothko Foundation. After the foundation was essentially disbanded in 1984, its archival collection and exhibition functions were transferred to the National Gallery of Art in Washington, D.C.

Although the aesthetic importance of abstract expressionism has been subjected to revaluation, the movement's impact on the course of American art cannot be underestimated. Rothko, along with Jackson Pollock and Willem de Kooning, served to define modern art in the 1950s, and their work made New York City the center of the art world. Rothko's paintings exemplified the cooler, transcendent side of the New York School, and, unlike Pollock's work, which has been overshadowed in the popular mind by his public persona, Rothko's work has stood on its own.

Rothko himself remains a central figure in the development of abstract painting in America.

• Rothko's papers, sketches, and a large photograph collection are held by the National Gallery of Art in Washington, D.C. His works are on exhibit in many settings, including the National Gallery of Art, the Tate Gallery (London), the Museum of Modern Art (New York), the Art Institute of Chicago, the Kunstsammlung Nordrhein-Westfalen (Düsseldorf), and the Phillips Collection (Washington, D.C.). James E. B. Breslin, *Mark Rothko: A Biography* (1993), is the major biographical work. Art historian Dore Ashton's *About Rothko* (1983) provides both biographical information as well as an insightful interpretation of Rothko's work. See also Diane Waldman's catalog to the posthumous exhibition (Oct. 1978–Jan. 1979) at the Guggenheim Museum, *Mark Rothko, 1903–1970: A Retrospective* (1978). Lee Seldes, *The Legacy of Mark Rothko* (1978), covers the travails involving Rothko's estate. Obituaries are in the *New York Times*, 26 Feb. 1970, and the *Washington Post*, 27 Feb. 1970.

MARTIN R. KALFATOVIC

ROTHSTEIN, Arnold (1882–6 Nov. 1928), prominent gambling entrepreneur and the suspected fixer of the 1919 World Series, was born in New York City, the son of Abraham Rothstein and Esther Kahn. The father was a successful businessman in various phases of the garment industry, and both parents were observant Jews, greatly respected within the Jewish community of the city. Unlike his siblings, Rothstein was a rebellious youth who disdained school, and he was fascinated by the excitement and gambling that he found in the street life of the city. By his mid-teens he was a pool shark and was running his own dice games. He left home at age seventeen and worked briefly as a traveling salesman, but by the time he was twenty he was building the career that would lead him to a central role as the major intermediary between the underworld and upper world of New York.

By 1902 Rothstein had become a bookmaker, taking bets on horse racing, prizefighting, and elections. By 1907 he was taking lay-off bets from other bookmakers and was increasingly respected so that big time bettors placed their bets with him. In 1904 he went to Saratoga Springs to make book during the August racing season, and in 1907 he opened a gambling house there. At the same time he operated high stakes crap games in New York City and opened a string of gambling houses. Rothstein was himself a high roller, making bets on various sporting events and becoming the owner of a stable of racing horses. As a result of his growing prominence in gambling, he made friends among the big bettors from the legitimate world and the underworld. He was or would become an associate of men like Charles Stoneham, owner of the New York Giants baseball team, newspapermen such as Bayard Swope and Damon Runyon, major figures in the underworld, and many people in theater and entertainment. Equally important, his close ties with Tim Sullivan, Charles Murphy, Jimmy Hines, and other leaders of Tammany Hall meant that by the end of World War I he was the chief coordinator between the worlds of sports, gambling, and politics.

With the famous "Black Sox" scandal of 1919, in which the favored Chicago White Sox threw the World Series to the Cincinnati Reds, Rothstein achieved an unwanted notoriety. Yet whether he directly participated in the fix remains unclear. Abe Attell, a former featherweight champion and a member of Rothstein's entourage, was in Cincinnati at the beginning of the series along with Rachel Brown, Rothstein's chief accountant. Attell bet heavily on each game and was in regular contact with the players to whom he eventually gave money. Joseph "Sport" Sullivan, a Boston sports gambler who knew Rothstein, contacted the players in Chicago. Rothstein certainly knew about the fix, as did many knowledgeable people in the gambling world, and he probably won bets on the series. For nearly a year following the World Series, Major League leaders and sportswriters carefully protected the good name of baseball rather than seek out the facts about a scandal that many knew about and many more suspected. When a Cook County, Illinois, grand jury finally undertook an investigation, Rothstein declared: "There is not a word of truth in the report that I had anything to do with the World Series of last fall" and testified voluntarily. The grand jury indicted Attell, Brown, Sullivan, and eight White Sox players. (Because the confessions of the eight players were later "lost," no one was convicted, although the players were later banned from baseball for life.) Thereafter Rothstein, although not indicted, was branded as the man who fixed the World Series, and he came to symbolize the shadowy connections between crime and power in the nation's largest city. He was the person upon whom F. Scott Fitzgerald based the character of Meyer Wolfsheim in his 1925 novel *The Great Gatsby*.

As the baseball scandal unraveled in 1920, Rothstein announced his retirement from gambling. Although he gradually dropped his gambling houses, he remained the bookmaker for big bettors, took part in high stakes poker games, bet on the races, and sought out other opportunities for profitable bets. He also used his contacts and power to expand his business interests. With the coming of Prohibition, Rothstein provided the money and political protection that helped a number of bootleggers to launch their careers. These included Jack "Legs" Diamond, "Waxy" Gordon, Bill Dwyer, and Frank Costello. For a while Rothstein took an active part in bootlegging but soon largely withdrew. Nevertheless, his involvement in bootlegging led to the smuggling of opiates into the United States, and at the time of his death he had money invested in the purchase of drugs in Europe. By the early 1920s Rothstein had also entered into various shady stock market activities, including the fencing of stolen securities and the sale of worthless stocks. He also established real estate companies for investments in Manhattan real estate, and he played an important role in the labor and business racketeering that had become an important part of the garment industry in New York City.

By the 1920s Rothstein generally worked in his office in midtown Manhattan in the afternoon. In the evenings he had a regular public place where he hung out, such as the Knickerbocker Hotel or Lindy's restaurant. There he engaged in quiet conversations with people of all walks of life who knew where to find him and who wished to talk business. Rothstein did not drink, avoided profanity, and had little of the flamboyance often associated with underworld figures. Although he often had a mistress, his chief emotional support came from his wife, Carolyn Greene Rothstein, whom he had married in August 1909; they had no children. By 1928, despite his many business investments, Rothstein seemed to face a cash shortage and became uncharacteristically lax in paying off his gambling debts. On 4 November 1928 he was shot in a room in the Park Central Hotel and was found after he stumbled down to the employees' entrance. The shooting was assumed to stem from his failure to make payment on a debt. He died in a New York City hospital.

• The standard source for Rothstein's life is Leo Katcher, *The Big Bankroll: The Life and Times of Arnold Rothstein* (1958). Another book is Donald Henderson Clarke, *In the Reign of Rothstein* (1929). After Rothstein's death his wife, Carolyn Greene Rothstein, wrote a memoir, *Now I'll Tell* (1934). Rothstein's role in the 1919 World Series fix is described in Eliot Asinof, *Eight Men Out: The Black Sox and the 1919 World Series* (1963); and in the biography of one of the players naively involved in the fix, Donald Gropman, *Say It Ain't So Joe: The Story of Shoeless Joe Jackson* (1979). The scandal is also referred to in the histories of baseball; see particularly Steven A. Riess, *Touching Base: Professional Baseball and American Culture in the Progressive Era* (1980), chap. 3; and Harold Seymour, *Baseball: The Golden Age* (1971), pp. 294–339. A number of histories of crime mention some aspects of Rothstein's career. See, for instance, relevant parts of Jenna Weissman Joselit, *Our Gang: Jewish Crime and the New York Jewish Community, 1900–1940* (1983); Albert Fried, *The Rise and Fall of the Jewish Gangster in America* (1980); and Stephen Fox, *Blood and Power: Organized Crime in Twentieth-Century America* (1989). An obituary is in the *New York Times*, 7 Nov. 1928.

MARK H. HALLER

ROTHSTEIN, Arthur (17 July 1915–11 Nov. 1985), photojournalist, was born in Harlem in New York City, the son of Isidore Rothstein, a merchant, and Nettie Perlstein. Around 1920 the family moved to Edenwald in the North Bronx, where Rothstein received his first camera, built a darkroom, and experimented with crystal radio. He qualified for Stuyvesant High School in Manhattan and then graduated in science from Columbia University in 1935. He was a Kings Crown Scholar and hoped to attend medical school. At Columbia, Rothstein was a student assistant to Roy Stryker, copying and organizing photographs for a proposed pictorial sourcebook on agriculture. He was on the *Jester* staff, served as photography editor for the yearbook, and founded the camera club.

After graduating, Rothstein was hired by Stryker to help organize the historical section of the government's Resettlement Administration (later the Farm Security Administration). The FSA's work is considered a landmark of social documentary photography, and Rothstein took several of its best-known pictures, including the controversial bleached steer skull on parched ground in South Dakota and "Dust Storm, Cimarron County (Oklahoma)," both 1936.

Equally evocative in his use of language, Rothstein described the challenge of the latter picture: "I could hardly breathe because (of) the dust. . . . It was so heavy in the air that the land and the sky seemed to merge until there was no horizon. Strong winds raced along the flat land, picking up the sandy soil and making my hands and face sting. . . . I saw the farmer and his two sons. . . . As they pressed into the wind, the smallest child walked a few steps behind, . . . covering his eyes to protect them" (O'Neal, p. 21). In 1961 Rothstein rephotographed that youngest son, surrounded by green fields. He showed the photo often, crediting the difference to the FSA and to the role of photographs in developing public support for change.

Within the FSA, Rothstein described the carefully organized images of art photographer Walker Evans as a major influence and credited artist Ben Shahn and photographer Dorothea Lange with developing his concern for social justice. Russ Lee encouraged technical skill. Although these influences remained in Rothstein's journalistic work, he brought his own sense of humor. One writer noted the occasional "Walker Evans by Arthur Rothstein" picture but with a wrinkle of whimsy by the latter (Doherty, p. 879). This wry wit later sparked the 1967 book *Look at Us*, on which Rothstein collaborated with William Saroyan; Rothstein contributed the pictures, Saroyan the words.

Beginning in 1940 Rothstein worked for *Look* magazine, edited pictures for the Office of War Information, and helped found the American Society of Magazine Photographers, which changed the structure of photojournalism by clarifying publication rights and business practices. From 1943 to 1946 he served with the Army Signal Corps, first in Astoria, New York, where he trained photographers and met Saroyan. Later he went to China, working along the Burma Road. At the end he spent six months with the United Nations' Relief and Rehabilitation Agency in Shanghai. Then he returned to *Look*, serving as its director of photography until its demise in 1971.

In 1947 Rothstein married Grace Goodman. They raised four children, who were subjects of a number of Rothstein's published photographs. The family home in New Rochelle, New York, where they moved in the early 1950s, became the setting for fashion, boating, and garden pictures; the kitchen was organized to facilitate food photography. The house remains a gallery of family moments documented by Rothstein.

Rothstein's position at *Look* made him one of the best known and most influential photojournalists of his time, and he was highly productive. He was also exceptionally innovative, both visually and technically, frequently adapting ideas from others. He developed a three-dimensional photography process called Xograph, which was first used in *Look* in 1964. He chose photographers, edited their work, and encouraged careers, notably those of John Vachon (whom he had trained at the FSA) and Douglas Kirkland. He was also a major influence in art direction and presentation.

Rothstein was also a prolific author. One of the few major photojournalists writing at the time, he produced nine books, including *Photojournalism* (1956), a textbook that went through several editions. He also wrote regularly for the *New York Times, Popular Photography,* and *U.S. Camera.* Rothstein was a generalist, proud of his versatility. In books and articles, he recommended an educational program qualifying the photojournalist to work in almost any field, and he proposed that the ideal practitioner be "intellectually mature" (*Photojournalism,* 4th ed. [1979], pp. 34–36) and able technically to "change approach to suit the subject" (*Words and Pictures,* p. 13).

In 1961 Rothstein began teaching at Columbia University. He also taught at the Universities of Miami (heading the Miami Photojournalism Conference), Missouri, Syracuse, and Maryland, as well as at Mercy College and the Parsons School of Design. He was president of the Society of Photographic Administrators, a member of the Royal Photographic Society, a life member of the National Press Photographers Association, and a Pulitzer Prize juror. He also consulted with the Environmental Protection Agency on the Documerica Project.

After *Look*'s death, Rothstein went to *Parade* magazine, where he was director of photography and then associate editor, until his death in New Rochelle, New York. He is remembered by his final editors, Jim Head and Walter Anderson, as a major influence. "He was articulate and stubborn," said Head. "He always had ideas; he would toss out creative ideas, unorthodox ideas" (interview with the author, 5 June 1995). Head also recalled that Rothstein was proud of his ethnic heritage.

Anderson, Head's successor, described Rothstein as "an extraordinary leader" and a teacher, saying, "He was graceful but firm; he didn't hesitate; he was never tentative. He was well-educated and well-read. He wrote as well as he photographed, and he challenged editors" (interview with the author, 31 May 1995). But Rothstein's greatest legacy, contends Anderson, is the "legion" of photojournalists whose careers were enhanced by his leadership.

Steve Shames, a former assistant of Rothstein's who was acclaimed for his continuing work on children of poverty, described him as "polished, gentlemanly, meticulous; always a thinker." He also recalled Rothstein reminding him to maintain his outside life in order to maintain perspective.

While Rothstein's FSA work will remain a monument, his writing and teaching as well as the work by major photographers whose careers he nurtured, ensure that he will be remembered as a seminal figure in the broader field of magazine photojournalism.

• Rothstein's personal papers are held by Grace Rothstein. Both the Farm Security Administration file and the *Look* archives are held by the Library of Congress. A major collection of his work in exhibition prints is at the International Center of Photography in New York. A widely used source is a taped interview made in 1964 by Richard K. Doud for the Archives of American Art at the Smithsonian Institution. A short essay by Rothstein concerning his style and methods, a list of exhibitions, and an evaluation by Robert J. Doherty is in *Contemporary Photographers,* 2d ed. (1988). Of Rothstein's own books, the most important are *Photojournalism* (1956, 1965, 1969, 1974, and 1979), *Words and Pictures* (1979), and *Documentary Photography* (1986), which was published posthumously. An extensive bibliography is included in Penelope Dixon, *Photographers of the Farm Security Administration: An Annotated Bibliography 1930–1980* (1983). F. Jack Hurley, *Portrait of a Decade: Roy Stryker and the Development of Documentary Photography in the Thirties* (1972; repr. 1977), provides a good analysis of both the formation of the FSA photography project and of its importance. Hank O'Neal, *A Vision Shared: A Classic Portrait of America and Its People, 1935–1943* (1976), includes excellently reproduced FSA images and interviews with each of the photographers, including Rothstein.

JOHN C. PETERSON

ROUDANEZ, Louis Charles (12 June 1823–11 Mar. 1890), physician, newspaper proprietor, and Republican party activist, was born in St. James Parish, Louisiana, the son of Louis Roudanez, a wealthy French merchant, and Aimée Potens, a free woman of color. Roudanez was raised in New Orleans as a member of the city's free black elite, but in 1844 he left to pursue a professional education in France. In 1853 the faculty of medicine at the University of Paris awarded him a degree in medicine. He graduated with a second medical degree from Dartmouth College in 1857, and soon after he returned to New Orleans to open his own office. In the same year he married Louisa Celie Seulay, and their union produced eight children.

Roudanez continued to build his medical practice during the Civil War and Reconstruction, but, like other free men of color in New Orleans, upon Federal occupation of south Louisiana in the spring of 1862 he became deeply interested in the issues of Reconstruction in his state. He was one in a group of investors who made possible the creation of the *New Orleans Union,* the wartime political voice of the city's French-speaking free black elite. The paper proved short-lived, and just weeks after its failure in July 1864 Roudanez and his brother Jean-Baptiste Roudanez founded the *New Orleans Tribune.* A bilingual publication, the *Tribune* sought to bring together former slaves and free black people in the cause of racial equality. This first black daily newspaper in the nation reported primarily on politics, and the reform program it promoted bore the ideological imprints of Roudanez and the paper's chief editor, white Belgian radical Jean-Charles Houzeau. It called for universal suffrage, office-holding rights for black men, the right of jury duty, and economic independence for former slaves through a federally sponsored division of plantations. Roudanez also used the paper to aid in the 1869 campaign to end discrimination in public accommodations in New Orleans. The *Tribune* served as the official organ of Louisiana's Republican party, although it was at times highly critical of both the state and national party. The paper rejected the 1864 state constitution because it did not extend suffrage to black men, and it was at odds with Andrew Johnson's administration over its lenient southern policy. Eventually it was Roudanez's opposition to the selection of Henry Clay Warmoth as the Republican gubernatorial candidate in 1868 and Roudanez's role in the nomination of a more radical splinter ticket that caused the party to cut its ties to the *Tribune*. His bolt from the party did much to sully his reputation among many of the black and white activists whom he previously had helped to establish the state party. His insistence on a competing ticket also prompted Houzeau to resign his post, a move which helped to undermine the already financially strapped newspaper. Consequently, it ceased publication in April 1868, although Roudanez's continuing opposition to Governor Warmoth led him to resurrect it the following year for a brief period.

Roudanez disappeared from the public spotlight until 1873, when he and other propertied New Orleanians began a political reform movement under the banner "Unification." Motivated by the perceived deleterious effect of political instability on the city's businesses, this group advocated honest government, racial cooperation in politics and government and an end to political violence, equal civil and political rights for all citizens, desegregation on public conveyances, and an equal distribution of public offices between the races. Roudanez was on the "Committee of One Hundred" that drew up the movement's platform in June of that year. Unification failed as a movement ultimately because it did not garner significant support in Louisiana's country parishes, and, ironically, because of persistent mistrust between white and black participants within the movement itself.

In addition to his activity in politics and journalism, Roudanez was involved in black community affairs. He had a well-earned reputation for philanthropy. In 1865, for example, he donated some of the funds for the building of the Providence Asylum, an institution that was operated by the Louisiana Association for the Benefit of Colored Orphans. He also strongly supported higher education, and he served for a time on the Examining Committee of Straight (now Dillard) University.

Despite his activity in the public realm, his primary professional commitment throughout his life remained in the field of medicine. In the 1870s and 1880s Roudanez ran a large and prosperous practice, reportedly treating both black and white patients. He devoted his final years to maintaining his practice. Roudanez died in New Orleans.

Roudanez's public life was brief, but it had a significant impact on the course of Reconstruction in Louisiana. His newspaper was instrumental in the formation and growth of the Republican party in the state. Its editorials undoubtedly helped to focus attention on the critical issues of Reconstruction, though its position on some matters proved too extreme for most policymakers. Roudanez himself exemplified the intense interest of black men in postbellum politics and the hopes that free men and freedmen alike invested in the Reconstruction experiment. Moreover, his conflicts with other activists highlighted the problem of disunity that plagued Reconstruction leaders in his and in other southern states and that contributed to their demise.

• There is no single collection of Roudanez papers. Valuable information on his life and career can be found in manuscript collections located at Louisiana State University, Baton Rouge; the Roman Catholic Diocese of Baton Rouge; the University of New Orleans; the Amistad Research Center; the Louisiana Collection at Tulane University; and the Louisiana Division of the New Orleans Public Library. Jean-Charles Houzeau's memoir, *My Passage at the "New Orleans Tribune"* (1984), casts light on Roudanez's roles as publisher and political activist. David Rankin's fine introductory essay directs readers to important primary source material located in European repositories. Many studies on Reconstruction in Louisiana discuss Roudanez's role in the early years, though some contain misinformation about his background. See Henry Clay Warmoth, *War, Politics and Reconstruction* (1930); Rodolphe Lucien Desdunes, *Our People and Our History* (1973); Donald E. Everett, "Demands of the New Orleans Free Colored Population for Political Equality, 1862–1865," *Louisiana Historical Quarterly* 38 (Apr. 1955): 43–65; John W. Blassingame, *Black New Orleans, 1860–1880* (1973); David C. Rankin, "The Origins of Black Leadership in New Orleans during Reconstruction," *Journal of Southern History* 40 (Aug. 1974): 417–40; Charles Vincent, *Black Legislators in Louisiana during Reconstruction* (1976). For his part in the Unification movement consult T. Harry Williams, "The Louisiana Unification Movement of 1873," *Journal of Southern History* 11 (Aug. 1945): 349–69; and the *New Orleans Times*, 28 Mar. 1873. On the history of the *Tribune*, see Laura Velina Rouzan, "A Rhetorical Analysis of Editorials in *L'Union* and the *New Orleans Tribune*" (Ph.D. diss., Florida State Univ., 1989); Finnian Patrick Leavens, "*L'Union* and the *New Orleans Tribune* and Louisiana Reconstruction" (master's thesis, Louisiana State Univ., 1966); and William P. Connor, "Reconstruction Rebels: The *New Orleans Tribune* in Post-War Louisiana," *Louisiana History* 21 (Spring 1980): 159–81. Obituaries are in the *New Orleans Picayune*, 12 Mar. 1890; the *New Orleans Abeille*, 13 Mar. 1890; and the *New Orleans Daily Crusader*, 22 Mar. 1890. The latter is reprinted in part in Charles Barthelemy Roussève, *The Negro in Louisiana* (1937).

CONNIE MEALE

ROUND, William M. F. (26 Mar. 1845–2 Jan. 1906), journalist and reformer, was born William Marshall Fitts Round in Pawtucket, Rhode Island, the son of Daniel Round, a Baptist minister, and Elizabeth Ann Fitts. After attending local schools, he enrolled in Harvard Medical School but was forced to drop out because of ill health. He then began a career as a journalist, working at various times for the *Boston Daily News*, the *Boston Golden Rule*, and the *New York Independent*. In 1873 he served as U.S. commissioner to the world's fair in Vienna. He married Ellen Miner Thomas in 1877; they had no children. During this period he began publishing novels under the pen name of Rev. Peter Pennot. These included *Achsah: A New England Life Study* (1876); *Torn and Mended, a Christmas Story* (1877); *Child Marian Abroad* (1878); *Hal, the Story of a Clodhopper* (1880); and *Rosecroft, a Story of Common Places and Common People* (1881).

Round was interested in social reform, and in 1881 he was named to the executive committee of the Prison Association of New York, an organization of private citizens interested in corrections reform. Seeking to emphasize rehabilitation rather than punishment, they called for better conditions in prison and for help to released inmates. In 1882 Round became the committee's corresponding secretary, a position that was, according to a colleague, "practically the executive officer of the association." Round served ex-officio on all committees, handled the organization's correspondence, and supervised its various departments. The Prison Association had a quasi-official role in two aspects of the state corrections system: assisting released prisoners and inspecting county jails. Round supervised the work of county committees around the state and took the major responsibility for carrying out the association's work in New York City. His annual reports provide vivid anecdotal accounts of the difficulties faced by released prisoners and his efforts to resolve those problems. They also document the grim conditions in the dirty, crowded, and ill-run county jails of the period.

In the course of his work with the association, Round allied himself with a national prison reform movement that had been gaining strength during the previous decade. In 1883 he helped reorganize the movement's principal organization, the National Prison Association (later the American Prison Association), and served for a number of years as its secretary—an unpaid position described by a fellow member as "the most exacting office of the association." Seeking to transform incarceration into rehabilitation, Round and his fellow reformers called for humane treatment of inmates, opportunities for regular work in prison, and an end to the severe physical punishment then common in many institutions. The reformers argued that treatment must be systematically adjusted to encourage reformation. If the prisoner was rebellious, the terms of his imprisonment should be made stricter; if he behaved well, he should be rewarded with more privileges and an opportunity for early release. Ideally, this principle would be embodied in "indeterminate sentencing," according to which a convict's jail term could be made as long or as short as prison administrators deemed necessary to achieve his full rehabilitation.

In 1887 Round resigned his position in the national association because of a severe illness. But within the year he accepted a new challenge in connection with his work in New York; the state Prison Association was sponsoring the establishment of a farm school for recalcitrant boys in the town of Canaan. To help launch the new institution, the association handled public information for the farm and collected most of its donations. In addition, Round was asked to serve as an adviser to the superintendent. For the next six years Round more or less directed the farm, which gave him an opportunity to try out many of the association's reform ideas. Modeling the institution on pioneering facilities in Germany and France, he arranged to house the boys in cottages rather than cells and established a "mill" system that allowed them to earn extra privileges by good behavior.

During this period Round resumed his activity with the National Association, chairing its Committee on Discharged Prisoners in 1890 and 1891, and serving on its board and executive committee from 1894 to 1900. Meanwhile, he continued to direct the affairs of the state Prison Association, including lobbying for reform legislation in Albany, working with the courts to prevent unnecessary incarceration, and doing direct casework with individual released prisoners—as "reporting office" for the state reformatory at Elmira, the association was responsible for supervising an average caseload of a hundred or more men paroled to New York City. Recognizing the crucial role that staff could play in implementing or subverting an institution's official philosophy, Round also organized the nonsectarian Order of St. Christopher as a training order for employees of public institutions. Under his direction the state association attracted continuing support from the leaders of New York society, including families like the Vanderbilts, Rhinelanders, Astors, Roosevelts, and Schermerhorns. In 1893 Round reported that over the previous decade the organization's office had expanded from one small room to an entire building, including a library, a printing service, and a large clothing department. That same year the Burnham Industrial Farm achieved full independence, dissolving its organizational ties with the Prison Association. Round's formal connection with the farm ended at the same time, though he continued to follow its progress, noting with satisfaction that under the new superintendent, "all distinctive features have been maintained."

Round's next position was at College Point, Long Island, where he ran a small orphan asylum. He also continued in the state Prison Association secretaryship until 1900, when ill health forced his resignation. He then moved to Boston, where in 1903 he collaborated with Edward Everett Hale in publishing the *Lend a Hand Record*, a journal of the Lend a Hand movement, a network of clubs that had grown up in response to Hale's writings on the need for charitable endeavor. Round died in Acushnet, Massachusetts.

The significance of Round's career lies not in the originality of his thinking but in the vigor and dedication with which he applied himself to implementing the agenda of the broader prison reform movement. Because of Round and others like him, ideas such as prison industries, probation, and parole moved from theory to reality, ultimately becoming standard features of American corrections policy. If these reforms did not achieve all that Round and his allies hoped for, they nevertheless left the American prison system a better institution than they found it.

• Round appears to have left no personal papers, but his career can be followed in the annual reports of the Prison Association of New York and the annual Proceedings of the National Prison Association. For more general context on the prison reform movement, see, for instance, Blake McKelvey, *American Prisons: A History of Good Intentions* (1977); Ronald Goldfarb and Linda R. Singer, *After Conviction* (1973); Paul W. Keve, *Corrections* (1981); and Frederick Howard Wines, *Punishment and Reformation* (1895). An obituary is in the *New York Times*, 6 Jan. 1906.

SANDRA OPDYCKE

ROUNDHEAD (?–1813), Wyandot war leader who had the Indian name Stayeghtha, was born probably in Michigan or Ohio in the 1750s. Little is known about his family, although Indian tradition credited him with being one-quarter Delaware and the older brother of the Wyandot leader Splitlog. When the Wyandots joined the Shawnees, Delawares, and Miamis in resisting U.S. expansion north of the Ohio in the 1790s, Roundhead was one of their leaders, and in August 1795 he signed the treaty of Greenville, by which the defeated Indians ceded southern and eastern Ohio. Afterward he established a village on the upper Scioto, on the Indian side of the treaty line, in present Hardin County, Ohio. The proximity of this town to growing American settlement thrust Roundhead to the forefront when difficulty between the two races required arbitration. In August 1799 he joined other leaders in defending the behavior of some of their "foolish young men" who had killed two Americans, and after the murder of Thomas Herrod in May 1803 Roundhead not only reassured settlers in councils but also circulated Governor Edwin Tiffin's appeal for the surrender of the murderers in June. One who traveled with him at that time recalled that Roundhead was "a heavy, thick-set short man." A "very sociable" companion, he enjoyed competing in a horse race. During this period Roundhead also signed a treaty with the British (Sept. 1800) ceding a tract on the Canadian side of the Detroit River to the British crown.

When the Shawnee prophet Lalawethika (later Tenskwatawa), the brother of Tecumseh, returned to Ohio from Indiana Territory in 1805 and began promoting the reform of native society, attacking alcoholism, witchcraft, and the assimilation of European-American influences, Roundhead gave him support. In 1807 he removed his following to the prophet's village at Greenville and throughout the year defended the Shawnee reformers from accusations of hostility to whites. On 24–25 June 1807 he attended a council at Springfield in which he charged Black Hoof, a Shawnee opponent of the prophet, with the murder of an American settler in May. The following September he accompanied Tecumseh and Blue Jacket to Chillicothe

to reassure the citizens of the peaceful intent of the Greenville community.

A belief that war between Britain and the United States was imminent helped unsettle the Indians at Greenville, and in 1808 the prophet withdrew to the Wabash. Roundhead remained in Ohio but later appears to have moved to the Detroit River region. Tradition places him at Brownstown, near present Gibraltar, Michigan, but at the time of the War of 1812 he was evidently living on the Canard River in Upper Canada. In any case, he remained under the influence of Tecumseh and the Shawnee prophet but was not (as popularly believed) among those who executed the Wyandot leader Leatherlips when he was charged with witchcraft in 1810.

On the outbreak of the War of 1812 Roundhead, hoping to arrest American expansion, joined Tecumseh in supporting the British. He helped bring the Michigan Wyandots across the Detroit to defend Fort Malden (Amherstburg, Ontario) in August, assisted Tecumseh to harass the communication line of the American army under Brigadier General William Hull as it attempted to invade Canada, and was present when a British-Indian force compelled Hull to surrender Detroit on 16 August. He was also commended by the British for his efforts to prevent the Wyandots from plundering settlers on the River Raisin later in the month. These successes were not easy to follow up, however, particularly after Tecumseh left to recruit warriors south of the Great Lakes. An expedition against Fort Wayne, Indiana Territory, in September, in which Roundhead was the principal Indian leader, disintegrated into a fiasco.

Roundhead's greatest moment came on 22 January 1813 when a British-Indian attack led by Colonel Henry Procter and Roundhead annihilated the army of Brigadier General James Winchester on the River Raisin, Michigan Territory. Roundhead himself captured the American general. Shortly afterward he accompanied Procter and Tecumseh to attack Fort Meigs on the Maumee River, Ohio. The fort withstood siege, but the Indians inflicted enormous losses on an American relief force on 5 May. These victories postponed but did not abort another invasion of Canada by the United States, and by the summer of 1813 Major General William Henry Harrison was ready for the attempt. To undermine the morale of Indians allied to the British, Harrison sent a delegation of the pro-American Wyandots from Sandusky to the Detroit River to speak to their kinsmen. In his last public service Roundhead rejected these overtures in a council at Brownstown on 22–23 August. Soon after, certainly before the middle of September, Roundhead died of natural causes, probably near Fort Malden. His leadership was missed during the British-Indian retreat from Fort Malden and defeat at Moraviantown on the River Thames, Upper Canada. Reflecting on it, Procter later wrote, "The Indian cause and ours experienced a serious loss in the death of Roundhead." Under a statute passed in 1823, a son and nephew of

Roundhead successfully claimed compensation for war losses from the British government.

• The military records in Record Group 8 (C ser.) of the Public Archives of Canada, Ottawa, contain scattered references to Roundhead for the years 1812–1813. Reginald Horsman, "Stayeghtha," *Dictionary of Canadian Biography*, vol. 5 (1983), lists other printed and manuscript sources. For additional comment and documentation, see Horsman, *Matthew Elliott, British Indian Agent* (1964); George C. Chalou, "The Red Pawns Go to War" (Ph.D. diss., Indiana Univ., 1971); and John Sugden, *Tecumseh's Last Stand* (1985). Traditional material in Peter Dooyentate Clarke, *Origin and Traditional History of the Wyandotts* (1870), must be used with caution. See also Wyandots to William Ward and Simon Kenton, 25 Aug. 1799, Ayer Manuscripts, Newberry Library, Chicago; the letters of Thomas Rogers to Lyman C. Draper, 2 and 17 Dec. 1862, 15 Jan. and 20 Feb. 1863, Draper Manuscripts, State Historical Society of Wisconsin, Madison, BB ser., vol. 4; and Wyandots to William Hull, 27 June 1810, registered letter received by the secretary of war, National Archives, Washington, D.C.

JOHN SUGDEN

ROUQUETTE, Adrien Emmanuel (26 Feb. 1813–15 July 1887), Catholic priest and writer, was born in New Orleans, Louisiana, the son of Dominique Rouquette, a wine merchant, and Louise Cousin. His early life was spent largely in St. Tammany Parish, north of Lake Pontchartrain, where his mother's family were landowners. Rouquette grew up speaking French, and in the pine woods around his house he developed an intimacy with the Choctaws and their lifestyle. His formal education began in 1821 at the Collège d'Orléans, but he did not prosper there. About three years later he was sent to Transylvania College in Kentucky, where he learned English, lived with Protestants, and acquired some Latin. Rouquette's father having died by suicide in 1819 and his mother having died during his years in Kentucky, his maternal relatives sent him in 1828 to a small French school in Mantua, New Jersey, outside Philadelphia, in which city his older brother Dominique was to read law. A year later he left for the Collège Royal of Nantes in Brittany, France. After some years in Brittany Rouquette passed his baccalaureate examination.

Brittany was religious and conservative, the home of François René de Chateaubriand and Felicité Robert de Lamennais, the major French writers of the postrevolutionary era, and hence a chief source of the French Catholic revival of the early nineteenth century. At Nantes, when he was twenty, Rouquette first received the Eucharist, some eight years after the customary age. Henceforward he was a devout Catholic and pursued the course that led to his ordination in July 1845 as the first native priest of American Louisiana. The ceremony was noted with scarcely veiled contempt by the New Orleans *Abeille*, a typically anti-Catholic organ, as being of possible interest to "pious souls." In the intervening years he had studied law and lived the elegant life in Paris; he also wrote verse and sent it to Louisiana French newspapers. In 1841 he published *Les Savanes*, a book of lyric poetry. He re-

turned to Louisiana in 1837 and again shortly before 1842, when he entered the struggling theological seminary at Plattenville.

From the start of his priestly life Rouquette was unhappy in the role his superiors assigned him. Bishop Antoine Blanc wanted to use this rare bird, the native priest, in his attempts to combat indifference and anticlericalism in Louisiana. Rouquette's preaching was much esteemed. He was named the bishop's secretary. His mentor, the Abbé Napoléon J. Perché, was mounting a public presence for the church that included a layman's association and a weekly newspaper, *Le Propagateur Catholique*, in both of which ventures Rouquette was to help. But Rouquette's thoughts increasingly turned to the retired ascetic life; he envisioned a new Egypt of early monastic times emerging in the pine woods of his childhood.

With the toleration of his bishop, from 1847 on Rouquette spent a great deal of time in St. Tammany among his kinsmen and the Indians, communing with God and nature. Rouquette himself implied that a serious neurosis lay behind his retreat. In a passage of his next published French work, *La Thébaïde en Amerique* (1852), he wrote, "Nervous men are like strangers in the world of men; they feel what others have never felt. . . . They are considered anomalies, and that is why . . . they flee a society that injures them and condemns them" (p. 84). Thus the bent of his piety probably had a psychological basis, and his later assignment to missionary work among the Choctaws was a practical compromise effected by his understaffed bishop, who had begun to fear that he would never get Rouquette into an urban rectory. Rouquette built four tiny dwellings, each with a chapel, along the old Florida road that skirted the north shore of Lake Pontchartrain, near modern Slidell, Lacombe, Big Branch, and Mandeville. He lived in one or another of these dwellings, especially "The Nook" in Lacombe, for the greater part of his remaining life. The Indians gave him the name "Chahta-Ima," or "Like a Choctaw," and he used this appellation to sign much of his later writing.

Rouquette's first published collection of poetry after *Les Savanes* was *Wild Flowers: Sacred Poetry* (1848). In this his English does not measure up to the standard of his French verse. His poetic efforts during the 1850s were chiefly dedicated to the completion of one large work, *L'Antoniade, ou la solitude avec Dieu* (1860). This work was published in New Orleans, first in several independently titled pamphlets (*Préludes de l'Antoniade, Poème Eremetique, Proèmes patriotiques: Suite de l'Antoniade, Le Conciliabule infernal*, and *Trois Ages, suite et fin de l'Antoniade*) followed in the same year by the collected work. The subject matter is similar to that of *Thébaïde*, namely the solitary religious life, but the poetry touches more on fads and intellectual currents of the contemporary United States. The *Conciliabule*, Miltonic in concept but satiric in content, is perhaps the portion most deserving of attention. When compared with the romantic lyricism of *Les Savanes*, *L'Antoniade* has a rather Victorian quality, full of ideas, more like the poetry of Robert Browning than that of Percy B. Shelley.

Politically, Rouquette had been a Clay Whig, but like one of his contemporaries, the historian and politician Charles Gayarré, gave for a time his adherence to the nativist American party (Know Nothings), who played down their anti-Catholic views in Louisiana. Rouquette was never an abolitionist, but as the Civil War approached he spoke out strongly for the Union. St. Tammany was a battle zone after Admiral David Farragut took New Orleans early in the war; the Choctaws lacked sufficient food and quinine to treat their malaria. Rouquette appealed to Farragut, who then allowed provisions and medical supplies to enter the area. His friendship with Farragut continued, and Rouquette's nephew later served as a midshipman on the admiral's flagship.

During his long life Rouquette knew and corresponded with several important figures. In early life he had met Chateaubriand; later he exchanged letters with poet William Cullen Bryant; Isaac Hecker, founder of the *Catholic World*; Orestes Brownson, the Transcendentalist turned Catholic; and the French writer Ernest Hello. In Rouquette's last years he and novelist and critic Lafcadio Hearn, who lived in New Orleans, were in close touch; Hearn praised *La nouvelle Atala* (1879), Rouquette's only piece of prose fiction. This rather syrupy tale of an Indian maiden alludes to Chateaubriand's *Atala*. Rouquette had earlier written an English poem about an Indian girl, "Catherine Tegahkwitha," which tells of the historical seventeenth-century Mohawk ascetic still revered by Catholics.

The most puzzling of Rouquette's works is the pamphlet *A Critical Dialogue between Aboo and Caboo* (the Abbé and novelist George Washington Cable), which carries to nearly hysterical extremes the resentment of the Louisiana French population against Cable for the picture he painted of their forebears in *Les Grandissimes* (1880). Rouquette's unpleasantly vituperative tone suggests his failing mental powers.

Before his death Rouquette wrote some autobiographic chapters and installments on American Indians for the *Propagateur Catholique* of New Orleans, but he was soon confined to the Hotel Dieu (a New Orleans hospital), where he lived for two years until his death, with moments of clarity interspersed with times when he preached to the nuns in Choctaw. In spite of his quirks, Rouquette, along with his elder brother Dominique, was one of the best poets to write in French Louisiana.

• Rouquette's manuscripts are scattered, the most important collections being in the Howard-Tilton Library at Tulane University in New Orleans, the Catholic Archdiocesan Archives in the old Ursuline convent in New Orleans, the Notre Dame Library in South Bend, Ind., the Hill Library of Louisiana State University in Baton Rouge, La., and the collection of Edward Larocque Tinker in the American Antiquarian Society's holdings in Worcester, Mass. The important James Renshaw papers, most recently used by his late daughter Dagmar Lebreton, are at present mislaid or unavailable.

For a bibliography of Rouquette's shorter and occasional writings, see Lebreton, *Chahta-Ima* (1947), the fullest and best work on Rouquette. Edward Larocque Tinker, *Les Ecrits de Langue française en Louisiane au XIXe siècle* (1932), pp. 400–414, is concerned mostly with Rouquette's life and personality but includes a substantial bibliography. Auguste Viatte, *Histoire littéraire de l'Amérique française* (1954), evaluates Rouquette with some favor. J. A. Reinecke, "Les Frères Rouquette, poètes louisianais," *Comptes rendus de l'Athénée louisianais* (Jan.–July 1920), is the first serious critical piece on Rouquette and his brother François Dominique. The short French-Choctaw dictionary in the Thompson Collection of the University of Alabama, Tuscaloosa, attributed to Rouquette, is in fact an adaptation of Cyrus Byington's *Holisso Anumpa Tosholi: An English and Choctaw Definer* (1852).

GEORGE F. REINECKE

ROUQUETTE, François Dominique (2 Jan. 1810–10 May 1890), American poet in the French language, was born on Bayou Lacombe, St. Tammany Parish, in what was soon to be the state of Louisiana, the son of Dominique Rouquette, a wine merchant from Bordeaux with a prosperous business in New Orleans, and Louise Cousin, the Louisiana-born daughter of a family of large landowners in Tammany. He too was always called Dominique. During his early years he alternated between New Orleans, where his father's handsome house on Royal Street still stands, and the homes of relatives in Bayou Lacombe and Bonfouca, where he was in frequent contact with the Choctaws. At age seven he was enrolled in the Collège d'Orléans, where he spent five ill-disciplined years. When he was nine, his father drowned himself in the Mississippi River after his business failed. Three years later, at the early age of twelve, Rouquette was sent to the Collège Royal of Nantes, in Brittany, where six years later he completed his course, just at the time when Alphonse Lamartine, then at the height of his popularity, served as a model for aspiring romantic poets. Already well established, François de Chateaubriand, a Breton himself, offered Christianity and the noble savage as appropriate topics for the young.

Rouquette returned from France to New Orleans in 1828 and soon departed for Philadelphia, where he was to read law with the noted attorney William Rawle, along with the future Louisiana historian Charles E. Gayarré. But he was unhappy as a law clerk and abandoned the notion of becoming an attorney. It was probably when he reached his majority in 1831 that he returned to Paris. Certainly he was there in 1834 and 1836 and again, after a return to New Orleans, in 1838–1839. During this period he was writing French lyric verse largely consisting of familiar epistles in the romantic style, collecting some thirty-five in 1839 in a book titled *Les Meschacébéennes*. The book's name derives from the old form of the name Mississippi, used by Chateaubriand, and the poems are accompanied by copious notes on the flora, fauna, and topography of Louisiana. The book received favorable comment from Victor Hugo, Pierre Beranger, and other French writers of the day. When the book came out, Rouquette returned to New Orleans and wrote verse fairly often for the two main French dailies, *L'Abeille* and *Le Courrier de la Louisiane*; many of these poems were later collected in his second volume, *Fleurs d'Amérique*.

In 1846 Rouquette married Marie Laure Verret, of a well-connected Louisiana family, at much the same time that he had exhausted his patrimony. The couple had two children. Shortly after, he opened a school, which soon failed; he then sought a post as a schoolmaster for the Choctaws in the Indian Territory. He did not get this appointment but moved with his wife to Fort Smith, Arkansas, the gateway to the territory, where he again opened a school. This also failed, and he started a grocery store. Here too he published his only English work, a translation of some of the eighteenth-century writer Bossu's comments on Arkansas (1850).

Forced by indigence to return to New Orleans, Rouquette once more set up as a schoolmaster, this time at Bonfouca in St. Tammany, where a number of his relatives lived. Even this did not succeed. In 1855 his wife died of tuberculosis, and he gave up any efforts to earn an American-style living. He turned his children over to his nephew Cyprien Dufour and worked at his poetry. In 1856 or 1857 he published by subscription his second volume of verse. *Fleurs d'Amérique* had more originality than his first and was well received in the press of France.

By the late 1850s Rouquette was entirely dependent on relatives, and his behavior grew more eccentric; he took to wandering about town and country wrapped Choctaw-style in an old black blanket, so that the Indians named him for it, "Shookbo-lusa." He carried a palmetto fan and smoked a strong-smelling pipe, lodging and eating in the homes of relatives and of an educated quadroon friend. This mode of life he kept up for more than thirty years. Often he stayed in one or another of the mission cabins of his priest-brother, Adrien Rouquette, north of Lake Pontchartrain.

Through these years he continued to write verse; some manuscript poems of an occasional sort still survive, as well as some clippings from the *Propagateur Catholique*, the New Orleans diocesan weekly, though others, published there, are doubtless lost with the files of that paper. In time his verse, influenced by domestic tragedy, changes in French literary style, and the pious friendship of his brother, took on a darker, more outspokenly Catholic tone. His style, however, still retained its elegance. Possessing a strong constitution, he outlived his children and Adrien, apparently dying on the street in New Orleans. He was interred in the pine-woods stronghold of his mother's family at Bonfouca. He has been esteemed by many as the best of the Louisiana-French poets.

• Manuscripts and clippings are in the Howard-Tilton Library of Tulane University; the Laroque Tinker Papers at the American Antiquarian Society, Worcester, Mass.; and the University of Texas, Austin. Tulane has Rouquette's prose manuscripts on the Choctaws, partially translated by the Works Progress Administration. He has been but little discussed by biographers and critics; Alcée Fortier wrote a short appreciation for the *Comptes Rendus de l'Athénée Louisianais*, July 1890, p. 147. J. A. Reinecke, Jr., wrote of him in "Les Frères Rouquette, Poètes Louisianais," *Comptes Rendus de l'Athénée Louisianais*, Jan., Apr., July 1920, pp. 12–84. See also Ruby van Allen Caulfield, *The French Literature of Louisiana* (1929), pp. 75–80. E. Larocque Tinker, *Les Écrits de Langue Française en Louisiane au XIXe Siècle* (1932), pp. 414–24, offers a memoir and bibliography. Auguste Viatte has an intelligent appraisal in *Histoire littéraire de l'Amérique Française* (1954). The biography of his brother by Dagmar Lebreton, *Chahta-Ima* (1947), has many important references to Rouquette. C. P. Dimitry wrote a genealogical essay on the Rouquettes in the *New Orleans Times-Democrat*, 20 Nov. 1892.

GEORGE F. REINECKE

ROURKE, Constance Mayfield (14 Nov. 1885–23 Mar. 1941), cultural historian and critic, was born in Cleveland, Ohio, the daughter of Henry Button Rourke, a hardware designer, and Constance Davis, an artist and progressive educator. When Rourke was a year old, her father entered a tuberculosis sanitarium and soon died. In 1888 her mother relocated to Grand Rapids, Michigan, where she taught metalwork and eventually became an elementary school principal. From her mother, with whom she had an unusually close relationship, Rourke acquired a lifelong commitment to creative expression.

In 1903 Rourke entered Vassar College, where she learned that educated women ought to undertake social service. Her English professors imported that premise into literary criticism, assessing writing according to whether it advanced society by broadening the reader's consciousness. Rourke derived from her college courses in "social criticism" two lasting convictions: that the art of the common people might be as "good" for humanity as recognized masterpieces, and that the critic could spur democratic reform.

After graduating in 1907, Rourke returned to Grand Rapids to teach. In 1908 she and her mother traveled in Europe, where Rourke visited experimental schools and apparently explored French folklore. She also immersed herself in the wave of modernism then breaking upon the Paris art scene. Although Rourke resumed teaching following her stay abroad—she was a tutor in 1909 and a Vassar English instructor from 1910 to 1915—the trip led her to imagine a career as a freelance writer. Her desire to live with her mother and a period of possibly psychosomatic illness (she complained of lassitude, stomach discomfort, and heart palpitations) also influenced her goals. Editing the record of Vassar's fiftieth anniversary celebration in 1916, persistent health problems, and a stint of high school teaching in 1917 disrupted her plans. In 1919, however, the *New Republic* published her first full-length freelance article, an essay on vaudeville.

During the next few years, Rourke traveled frequently to New York to secure book reviewing assignments and forge literary connections. Although she lived the rest of her life in Grand Rapids and never married, she increasingly balanced solicitude for her mother with her drive for professional success. One contact proved especially fruitful: in 1921 Van Wyck Brooks, in search of what he called a "usable past," suggested that Rourke undertake the study of nineteenth-century popular heroes that became her first book, *Trumpets of Jubilee* (1927). Brooks's ideas also figured prominently in the outlook toward American culture that Rourke had begun to articulate by the late 1920s. Nevertheless, influenced by both her Vassar training and such theorists as the eighteenth-century European writers Vico and Herder, she questioned Brooks's assumption (shared by many other prominent intellectuals) that the United States lacked a rich aesthetic heritage. Instead, Rourke argued that every culture followed its own pattern, and that, in contrast to European culture, American achievements lay in the "practical" rather than the "luxury" arts, for example, in the clean lines and functional beauty of a Shaker barn or a frontier farm implement. In particular, she identified a pervasive American propensity for fantasy and mythmaking—a trait her own mystical, introspective nature equipped her to recognize.

Her *Troupers of the Gold Coast* (1928) documented this fanciful American imagination by chronicling the California gold rush theater. Rourke further substantiated her case in her most important book, *American Humor* (1931). Her description of the tales surrounding the Yankee, minstrel, and backwoodsman, and their appropriation by writers such as Nathaniel Hawthorne and Walt Whitman, linked popular artifacts and "high" culture in a unified tradition. Her subsequent biographies—*Davy Crockett* (1934) and *Audubon* (1936)—emphasized the myths surrounding her subjects. In her friend Charles Sheeler, Rourke found a living example of an artist who perpetuated the American version of classic style. Rourke's contention in *Charles Sheeler: Artist in the American Tradition* (1938) that the form (not the content) of Sheeler's paintings resembled the unornamented handicrafts of the frontier was one of her most original insights.

In the mid-1930s Rourke began working on a multivolume history of American culture. Her role in 1934 as organizer of the National Folk Festival in St. Louis and in 1936 and 1937 as editor of the Federal Art Project's *Index of American Design* enabled her to gather research from diverse localities. Her numerous articles and reviews during this period stressed the significance of regional contributions to music, literature, and art. Rourke was convincing. In 1938 the poet William Carlos Williams hailed her as the artist's "Moses," while Brooks and Lewis Mumford, among others, acknowledged her influence on their reappraisal of the nation's traditions.

In the early 1940s Rourke applied her democratic convictions to the fight against fascism. Both that activity and her research were cut short, however, when she died in Grand Rapids of complications resulting from a fall on the ice. Fragments from her work-in-progress appeared posthumously as *The Roots of American Culture* (1942), which Brooks edited. After her death, her writings helped inspire and legitimate scholarship in the emerging field of American studies.

Rourke's vision of American culture had its limitations. Despite her insistence on discarding European standards for evaluating art, she sometimes unconsciously invoked them. Her emphasis on unity minimized class conflict; her preoccupation with myth and her use of poetic imagery tended to prettify the frontier. Nevertheless, her understanding of the interplay between "high" and popular art, her appreciation of form, and her conception of the critic's social responsibility secured her a distinguished place in the "usable past" she spent her career pursuing.

• Rourke's papers are privately held. For a full analysis of her life and work see Joan Shelley Rubin, *Constance Rourke and American Culture* (1980), and Rubin, "A Convergence of Vision: Constance Rourke, Charles Sheeler, and American Art," *American Quarterly* 42 (June 1990): 191–222. See also Stanley Edgar Hyman, *The Armed Vision: A Study in the Methods of Modern Literary Criticism* (1948); Kenneth Lynn, *Visions of America* (1973); and Charles C. Alexander, *Here the Country Lies* (1980). An obituary appears in the *New York Times*, 24 Mar. 1941.

JOAN SHELLEY RUBIN

ROUS, Francis Peyton (5 Oct. 1879–16 Feb. 1970), Nobel Prize–winning cancer researcher, was born in Baltimore, Maryland, the son of Charles Rous, a grain broker, and Frances Anderson Wood. His father's death in 1890 left the family in difficult circumstances. His mother struggled to provide educational opportunities for Rous and his two sisters. A scholarship enabled him to attend the Johns Hopkins University, where he received his bachelor's degree in 1900. The same year Rous entered the Johns Hopkins Medical School. During his medical training Rous contracted tuberculosis and spent a year working on a ranch in Texas before resuming his medical studies. After receiving his medical degree in 1905, Rous served an internship at Johns Hopkins. His disinclination for clinical medicine led him in 1906 to seek a position as an assistant in pathology in the laboratory of Aldred Scott Warthin at the University of Michigan. In 1907 he spent a year in postgraduate study in anatomy in Dresden. After his return to Michigan and after recuperating from tuberculosis in the Adirondack Mountains of New York, Rous was awarded a grant from the Rockefeller Institute for Medical Research to help fund his investigations of the cellular output of the lymph glands, bringing him to the attention of Simon Flexner, scientific director of the Rockefeller Institute. At Flexner's invitation and against the advice of friends, Rous joined the staff as a research assistant in 1909. In 1915 he married Marion Eckford de Kay. The couple had three daughters. In 1920 Rous was named a full member of the Rockefeller Institute, where he remained until his formal retirement as member emeritus in 1945. He continued his activities at the institute for another twenty-five years.

The field of cancer research was in its infancy when Rous's discovery of chicken sarcoma virus opened up new approaches to studying the disease. In 1909 Rous received a visit from a chicken fancier concerned about a Plymouth Rock hen with a large mass on its breast. Worried that disease might affect his other animals, the poultryman had approached several pathologists before reaching Rous, who recognized the bird's tumor as an unparalleled opportunity for medical research. Rous identified the growth as a spindle-cell sarcoma and in a series of experiments demonstrated that the cell-free filtrates of the tumor would transmit the disease to genetically similar birds. His first paper on chicken sarcoma virus appeared in 1911. Despite some initial enthusiasm for the discovery, cancer researchers for several decades relegated viral cancer agents to the margins of the human cancer problem. During this time Rous continued to introduce new techniques for the study of viruses, including the growth of viruses on the chorioallantoic membranes of chicken embryos. With his colleagues at the Rockefeller Institute, Rous identified two other avian tumors caused by a filterable agent. In the 1930s Rous and Richard Shope, a colleague at the Rockefeller Institute who discovered the viral cause of rabbit papilloma, demonstrated that the Shope papilloma, a benign lesion in cottontail rabbits, progressed to malignant cancer. Over the course of several decades Rous investigated the nature of chemical carcinogenesis and the role of initiating and promoting agents in tumor production. For his cancer research and the work on chicken sarcoma virus (renamed Rous sarcoma virus in spite of his resistance to the honor), Rous received the Nobel Prize for medicine or physiology in 1966, more than fifty years after his first publication on the subject. Even though recognition for his pathbreaking research was late in coming, Rous's investigations of the viral origins of cancer inspired a generation of cancer researchers in the 1950s who took up the cancer problem with renewed vigor and far-reaching effects.

In addition to his cancer research, Rous worked with associates at the Rockefeller Institute during the First World War to develop a fluid substitute for blood loss in wounded soldiers. The discovery that more than fluid replacement was necessary to revive exsanguinated animals led him to investigate methods to preserve whole blood. With his colleague at the institute Joseph R. Turner, Rous developed a citrate-sugar solution for blood preservation. Blood preserved by the Rous-Turner method was given a preliminary trial during the First World War by one of Rous's colleagues, Oswald H. Robertson. During the Second World War massive quantities of blood preserved in modified Rous-Turner solutions would be shipped overseas for use by American soldiers. In the 1920s Rous followed his studies of blood preservation with investigations of normal blood destruction and experimental hemochromatosis, a disorder of iron metabolism. He developed techniques for studying the function of the liver and the gall bladder, including methods for the permanent intubation of bile ducts as a method for studying gallstone formation, bile pigment output, and white bile.

In 1921 Rous was appointed coeditor of the *Journal of Experimental Medicine*, the leading biomedical research journal in the United States. Although he shared the editorship with Simon Flexner (and from 1922–1946 with Flexner and Herbert S. Gasser), Rous assumed major editorial responsibility for the journal for over forty years. According to one of his colleagues, Rous's leadership made the journal the *Atlantic Monthly* of medical journals. In addition to revising the prose of many of his colleagues at the Rockefeller Institute, Rous implemented several measures, including strict rules about photographic representations, to insure that articles in the journal would be less useful to critics of experimentation involving animals.

Elected to the National Academy of Science in 1927 and to the Royal Society in 1940, Rous was the recipient of many awards and honors throughout his career, in addition to the Nobel Prize and honorary degrees from twelve universities. He died of abdominal cancer in New York City.

• The Library of the American Philosophical Society holds a large collection of Rous's papers, including correspondence, lecture notes, laboratory records, and photographs, as well as extensive documentation of his editorial work for the *Journal of Experimental Medicine*. Additional materials relating to Rous's career can be found at the Rockefeller Archive Center, North Tarrytown, N.Y. Rous's classic paper is "A Sarcoma of the Fowl Transmissible by an Agent Separable from the Tumor Cells," *Journal of Experimental Medicine* 13 (1911): 397–411. His extensive bibliography, which includes his 1929 book *The Modern Dance of Death*, can be found in two significant biographical accounts: C. H. Andrewes, "Francis Peyton Rous, 1879–1970," *Biographical Memoirs of Fellows of the Royal Society* 17 (1971): 643–62, and Renato Dulbecco, "Francis Peyton Rous," National Academy of Sciences, *Biographical Memoirs* 48 (1976): 275–306. Also see O. H. Robertson, "Presentation of Kober Medal to Peyton Rous," *Transactions of the Association of American Physicians* 66 (1953): 20–26. Rous's association with the Rockefeller Institute is discussed in *A Notable Career in Finding Out* (1971), and George W. Corner, *A History of the Rockefeller Institute* (1964). An obituary is in the *New York Times*, 17 Feb. 1970.

SUSAN E. LEDERER

ROUSE, Charlie (6 Apr. 1924–30 Nov. 1988), jazz tenor saxophonist, was born Charles Rouse in Washington, D.C. His parentage is unknown. Having admired a local big band led by Bill Hester, he took up clarinet around age ten or eleven. He studied privately before joining bands and orchestras in junior high school and at Armstrong High School, where he doubled on alto saxophone. For three years he again took private lessons on clarinet, studying with a member of the Howard University faculty. For his last two years of high school he switched from alto to tenor saxophone, and during his senior year he worked in pianist John Malachi's band at the Crystal Caverns club. By this time Rouse had become friends with jazz tenor saxophonist Ben Webster, who encouraged his striving for a huge and personalized instrumental tone. Rouse also played football and after graduating from high school, apparently at age twenty, he faced a choice between college athletics and music. He had married at age eighteen. Details are unknown, but an obituary noted that he was survived by Mary Ellen Rouse and a son, presumably from this marriage.

By his own account Rouse joined Billy Eckstine's bop big band in St. Louis in June 1944. According to Malachi, who was Eckstine's pianist at the time, Rouse sat next to Charlie Parker and was so mesmerized by Parker's alto saxophone playing that he was unable to concentrate on his own parts. Soon his chair in the band was given to Gene Ammons. Rouse became a member of Dizzy Gillespie's bop big band in 1945. While participating in jam sessions at Minton's Playhouse in New York City, he first played with the pianist and composer Thelonious Monk. Performing alongside trumpeter Fats Navarro in pianist Tadd Dameron's sextet, Rouse made his first soloist recordings, "The Squirrel" and "Our Delight," in 1947.

Rouse's work in rhythm-and-blues bands included brief stays with Louis Jordan and Eddie "Cleanhead" Vinson and an extended period in a quintet that he founded with drummer Jimmy Cobb in New York. The group returned to Washington, where Duke Ellington, searching for a tenor saxophonist, heard Rouse and hired him in late 1949. He performed in the film short *Salute to Duke Ellington* (1950), but soon thereafter he was obliged to leave the band when it embarked for Europe because he had failed to locate his birth certificate and could not get a passport. Resuming freelance work, he briefly joined Count Basie's octet in May 1950.

Rouse took part in trumpeter Clifford Brown's first recordings, issued as *New Star on the Horizon* (1953). He worked with trombonist Bennie Green in 1955 and also played in bassist Oscar Pettiford's sextet, which included French horn player Julius Watkins. Subsequently Watkins and Rouse led Les Modes—soon to be renamed the Jazz Modes—a group that presented a gentle version of bop. Making its debut at Birdland in New York in 1956, it worked mainly as a quintet, with French horn added to the conventional mix of tenor saxophone, piano, string bass, and drums. For recordings and concerts Watkins and Rouse added a singer, a harpist, Latin percussionist Chino Pozo (heard on their album *The Most Happy Fella*, 1957), and—for the group's last studio session in November 1958—baritone saxophonist Sahib Shihab.

By the autumn of 1958 Rouse was rehearsing with Monk, often at the New Jersey home of Monk's patron, Baroness Pannonica de Koenigswarter. In a widely publicized incident, the two jazz musicians were traveling with the baroness when she was arrested in October for marijuana possession in Wilmington, Delaware. Later that same month or early in November Rouse substituted for Sonny Rollins in Monk's quartet for a Sunday afternoon concert at the Five Spot in New York, and he joined Monk again for a performance at Town Hall on 28 November. The Jazz Modes had no work after January 1959, by which time Rouse had formally joined Monk's quar-

tet. He stayed with Monk until 1970. Apart from his unusual tolerance of Monk's eccentricities (owing in no small part to his recognition of Monk's musical genius), the most obvious reason that Rouse's tenure lasted far longer than that of any of Monk's other sidemen was his willingness to adapt his style to Monk's work. He improvised with more deliberation than many bop instrumentalists and restated melodies often. This distinctive approach may be heard on "Shuffle Boil," from the album *It's Monk's Time* (1964), in which he reiterates the principal thematic motif, alternating with formulaic bop runs. "Many people try to interpret Thelonious' compositions their own way and it doesn't work," Rouse said. "I know how he wanted them, and when you play them like he wanted, it's very effective. Otherwise it won't go, because his composition is so personal" (Franklin, *Cadence*, p. 10).

Other recordings of note included the albums *Five by Monk by Five* (1959), *Monk's Dream* (1962), *Criss Cross* (1963), *Monk Misterioso* (1963–1965), and *Underground* (1967–1968). Rouse appeared with Monk on the BBC television series "Jazz Goes to College" (1966 or 1967), and he figured prominently in the acclaimed documentary film *Thelonious Monk: Straight, No Chaser*, which premiered posthumously in 1989. Numerous sessions apart from Monk included trumpeter Donald Byrd's album *Byrd in Hand* (1959), Rouse's own *Yeah!* and *Takin' Care of Business* (both 1960), pianist Sonny Clark's *Leapin' and Lopin'* and Benny Carter's *Further Definitions* (both 1961), and Rouse's *Bossa Nova Bacchanal* (1962).

After leaving Monk, Rouse stopped playing and studied acting. Returning to jazz, he formed a group with cellist Calo Scott, who suffered a stroke that ended the project. Rouse then worked as a freelancer, led a sextet oriented toward Latin jazz (1975), and recorded three albums as a leader, including *Moment's Notice* (1977). From 1979 until his death he belonged to the cooperative quartet Sphere, with pianist Kenny Barron, bassist Buster Williams, and drummer Ben Riley. Their first album, *Four in One*, recorded in 1982, the year Monk died, was dedicated to Monk's music. But Rouse claimed that his group's name, Sphere, was selected without realizing that it was Monk's middle name, and he argued that the connection to Monk's music was thus overemphasized in most accounts of the band. Apart from Sphere, Rouse worked regularly with his own band. In 1984 he recorded the album *Social Call*, leading a quintet that included trumpeter Red Rodney. Also during his last years Rouse and pianist Mal Waldron co-led a quartet. These groups worked frequently at the Village Vanguard in Greenwich Village.

Rouse performed in Wynton Marsalis's group at the Concord Jazz Festival (Calif.) in 1987. Early in 1988 he performed Monk's compositions with singer Carmen McRae in San Francisco; two "live" tracks are included on the ensuing disc, *Carmen Sings Monk*. (For the remaining tracks, Clifford Jordan replaced Rouse.) Throughout his career Rouse was extremely hardworking and devoted to jazz as an artistic endeavor, and he kept his problems to himself. Suffering from lung cancer, he played in a trio for a tribute to Dameron at Lincoln Center in August, and he led a tribute to Monk in San Francisco in October, seven weeks before his death in Seattle. His outstanding performance in San Francisco was recorded for broadcast and issued as *Epistrophy: The Last Concert* (1989).

• For interviews and surveys, see Dan Morgenstern, "Charlie Rouse and the Long Road to Recognition," *Metronome*, Oct. 1960, pp. 20–21; Don DeMichael, "Charlie Rouse: Artistry and Originality," *Down Beat*, 25 May 1961, pp. 17–18; Jean-Pierre Binchet, "Portrait: Monsieur passe-partout," *Jazz*, Mar. 1963, pp. 24–26; and Jean-Louis Ginibre, "La longue marche de Charlie," *Jazz*, Apr. 1964, pp. 20–24. See also Peter Danson, "Charlie Rouse," *Coda*, 1 Dec. 1982, pp. 4–8 (which incorrectly gives his birthplace as West Virginia); A. David Franklin, "Charlie Rouse," *Cadence*, June 1987, pp. 5–10; and Martin Isherwood, "Charlie Rouse," *Jazz Journal International* 41 (Feb. 1988): 16–17. Obituaries are in the *New York Times*, 2 Dec. 1988; *Down Beat*, Apr. 1989; the *Washington Post*, 4 Dec. 1988; and *San Francisco Chronicle Datebook*, 12 Feb. 1989, which includes tributes from Rouse's friends.

BARRY KERNFELD

ROUSH, Edd J. (8 May 1893–21 Mar. 1988), baseball player, was born in Oakland City, Indiana, one of twin sons of William C. Roush and Laura Herrington, farmers. The unusual spelling of his first name was never explained, and his middle initial honored two relatives, James and Joseph, variously described as his grandfathers or uncles. While in high school Roush began playing organized baseball with a local amateur or semiprofessional team, the Walk-Overs. During this time he demonstrated an ability to throw ambidextrously, giving rise to a story that he was a natural right-hander who learned how to throw left-handed after injuring his right arm. In truth, he was a left-hander who threw right-handed only until he could acquire a glove for his right hand. "I never took the trouble to deny the story," he admitted years later.

Roush turned professional in 1912 with the Class D Evansville, Indiana, team in the Kitty League. "The idea of getting paid for playing ball sounded real good to me," he recalled. After playing parts of two seasons in the minor leagues, Roush was sold to the Chicago White Sox of the American League. He appeared in nine games in 1913 with the White Sox and during the winter jumped to the Federal League, a new enterprise styling itself as a third major league. Before the 1914 season he married his hometown sweetheart, Essie Mae Swallow. They had one daughter.

In 1914 Roush hit .325 for the Indianapolis Hoosiers, the first Federal League champions. In 1915, when the Hoosiers became the Newark (N.J.) Peppers, he batted .298. In December 1915, after the Federal League ceased operations, Roush's contract was sold to the New York Giants of the National League.

The quiet, stubborn Roush clashed with John McGraw, the Giants' fiery manager. "So I was glad as I could be when he traded me to Cincinnati in the mid-

dle of the '16 season," Roush remembered. He soon became the Reds' most popular player, renowned for steady performance as a batter and outstanding defense in center field.

Roush hit only .267 in 1916, but the following spring he refused to sign a contract for $4,500, demanding $5,000 instead. Holding out became an annual Roush ritual, not only because he usually wanted more money than clubs were willing to pay him but also because he hated spring training. "Why should I go down there?" he asked. "Twist an ankle, or break a leg. I did my own spring training, hunting quail and rabbits around Oakland City."

Playing before 1920, during baseball's so-called "dead ball" era, Roush hit to all fields and did not try for home runs. He used a short, thick-handled, 48-ounce bat, reputed to be the heaviest in the game. The result was remarkably consistent hitting throughout his tenure in Cincinnati. He won National League batting championships in 1917 and 1919 and lost out in 1918 by only two percentage points. From 1921 through 1924 he hit .352, .352, .351, and .348. Twice he compiled 27-game hitting streaks. He hit only 68 home runs in 7,363 times at bat but struck out only 215 times.

Roush was also a superb outfielder. After an initial dispute with Reds rightfielder Earle "Greasy" Neale over who would handle the fly balls hit between them, Roush quickly earned a reputation for fleet defensive prowess. "Oh, what a beautiful and graceful outfielder that man was," recalled teammate Raymond "Rube" Bressler.

In 1919 Roush led the Reds to the National League pennant and to a World Series meeting with the Chicago White Sox. Cincinnati won the series, five games to three, but Roush hit only .214. "Maybe because I was the batting champion, they bore down hard on me," he explained, "and eased up on some of the other boys." Nor did Roush ever accept the contention that eight Chicago players conspired with gamblers to throw the entire series. "They didn't get their money after the first game, so they went out and tried to win," he said in 1987.

In February 1927 Roush was traded back to the Giants, but he was still not anxious to play for McGraw. Roush refused even to speak to the manager until spring training was nearly over. He then signed a three-year contract for $70,000 and extracted a promise from McGraw not to criticize him. After the 1929 season McGraw announced his intention to cut Roush's salary to $15,000. Roush responded by staging his most dramatic holdout, becoming the first major league player ever to sit out a full season in a salary dispute. "I've got 20 years of fishing to catch up on anyway," he said as he spent the summer of 1930 in Oakland City.

In 1931 Roush was released to Cincinnati and played one final season with the Reds, hitting .271 in 101 games. He ended his career with a .323 batting average and 2,376 hits. The sportswriter Frederick Lieb called him "a superlative ballplayer who did everything well—bat, throw, run, and field."

Roush served as a coach for the Reds in 1938 but spent most of his retirement in Oakland City. He invested his money wisely in real estate and blue-chip stocks and became wealthy. He also developed an interest in local politics and served on the school board and the Oakland City town board. Roush and his wife regularly spent the winter months in Bradenton, Florida. Despite his distaste for spring training during his playing career, he became a fixture at McKechnie Field in Bradenton. Until he was in his early seventies, he often greeted returning players in his uniform. After being passed over in the balloting by the Baseball Writers' Association of America, he was elected to the Hall of Fame by the Veterans Committee in 1962. He suffered a fatal heart attack while sitting in the McKechnie Field press room, shortly before the start of an exhibition game.

• Clipping files on Roush are in the National Baseball Library and Archive, Cooperstown, N.Y., and the archives of the *Sporting News*, St. Louis, Mo. For Roush's career statistics, consult John Thorn et al., eds., *Total Baseball* (1989), or *The Baseball Encyclopedia*, 10th ed. (1996). Obituaries are in the *New York Times*, 22 Mar. 1988, and *Sporting News*, 4 Apr. 1988.

STEVEN P. GIETSCHIER